# BIGELOW'S PC HARDWARE DESK REFERENCE

## ABOUT THE AUTHOR

**Stephen J. Bigelow** is the author of 15 feature-length books for TAB/McGraw-Hill, and more than 100 major articles for mainstream electronics magazines such as *Popular Electronics*, *Electronics NOW*, *Circuit Cellar INK*, and *Electronic Service & Technology*. Steve has been a contributing editor at *CNET* (the "PC Mechanic" column and feature articles) and a regular contributor with *SmartComputing*. He is an electrical engineer with a BS EE from Central New England College in Worcester, MA. You may contact him at stevebige@aol.com.

# BIGELOW'S PC HARDWARE DESK REFERENCE

**STEPHEN J. BIGELOW**

**McGraw-Hill**/Osborne

New York   Chicago   San Francisco
Lisbon   London   Madrid   Mexico City
Milan   New Delhi   San Juan
Seoul   Singapore   Sydney   Toronto

**McGraw-Hill**/Osborne
2600 Tenth Street
Berkeley, California 94710
U.S.A.

To arrange bulk purchase discounts for sales promotions, premiums, or fund-raisers, please contact **McGraw-Hill**/Osborne at the above address. For information on translations or book distributors outside the U.S.A., please see the International Contact Information page immediately following the index of this book.

### Bigelow's PC Hardware Desk Reference

Copyright © 2003 by The McGraw-Hill Companies. All rights reserved. Printed in the United States of America. Except as permitted under the Copyright Act of 1976, no part of this publication may be reproduced or distributed in any form or by any means, or stored in a database or retrieval system, without the prior written permission of publisher, with the exception that the program listings may be entered, stored, and executed in a computer system, but they may not be reproduced for publication.

1234567890 DOC DOC 0198765432

Book p/n 0-07-222526-2 and CD p/n 0-07-222527-0
parts of
ISBN 0-07-222525-4

**Publisher**
Brandon A. Nordin

**Vice President and Editor-in-Chief**
Scott Rogers

**Acquisitions Editor**
Megg Morin

**Acquisitions Coordinator**
Tana Allen

**Technical Editor**
Karen Weinstein

**Project Editor**
Madhu Prasher

**Copy Editors**
Claire Splan, Pamela Woolf, Ami Knox

**Proofreader**
Pamela Vevea

**Indexer**
Valerie Robins

**Computer Designers**
Carie Abrew, Tabitha M. Cagan

**Illustrators**
Jackie Sieben, Michael Mueller,
Melinda Lytle, Lyssa Wald

**Series Design**
Michelle Galicia, Peter F. Hancik

**Cover Series Design**
Jeff Weeks

This book was composed with Corel VENTURA™ Publisher.

Information has been obtained by **McGraw-Hill**/Osborne from sources believed to be reliable. However, because of the possibility of human or mechanical error by our sources, **McGraw-Hill**/Osborne, or others, **McGraw-Hill**/Osborne does not guarantee the accuracy, adequacy, or completeness of any information and is not responsible for any errors or omissions or the results obtained from the use of such information.

# CONTENTS AT A GLANCE

**The following chapters are on the accompanying CD in the Book PDFs folder:**

# CONTENTS

**The following chapters are on the accompanying CD in the Book PDFs Folder:**

| | |
|---|---|
| Chapter 36 | **Video Capture Devices** |
| Chapter 37 | **USB Troubleshooting** |
| Chapter 38 | **Windows 9x/Me/XP Issues** |
| Appendix B | **PC 2001 System Compliance Standards** |
| Appendix C | **PC Standards** |
| Appendix D | **Index of Filename Extensions** |
| Appendix E | **Standard ASCII Chart (0 to 127)** |
| Appendix F | **Windows 9x/Me/XP Shortcut Keys** |
| Appendix G | **PC-Related FAQs and Newsgroups** |
| Appendix H | **Preparing for A+** |
| Appendix I | **The DLS Technician's Certificate 4** |

# CST CERTIFICATION

The Computer Service Technician (CST) certification program was initiated in 1998 by the ETA-I. It has since gained popularity as the standard computer certification program for electronics technicians. The CST certification examination consists of 50 questions. The test covers nine basic areas related to personal computer maintenance, repair, upgrading and troubleshooting. The areas of competencies tested include:

- Microprocessor architecture and operational characteristics
- Video display systems
- Memory
- Bus architectures
- Hard drive installation and troubleshooting
- Printers
- I/O hardware characteristics
- Networking—basic features of LAN's and network protocols
- Network operating systems

Certified ETA-I examiners at various locations in the United States, Canada, and other countries administer the CST examinations. The fee for the exam, as well as recertification after four years, is $50. Information regarding ETA-I certifications, local test sites, exam results, and recertification may be obtained from the Electronics Technicians Association-International headquarters by calling 800-288-3824 or 765-653-4301. Or visit the ETA-I web site at www.eta-sda.com.

# INTRODUCTION

It used to be that when a PC failed, it wound up sitting on a test bench surrounded by a battalion of test equipment. An experienced technician would be hovering over the PC-logic probe or test leads in-hand. They relied on their knowledge of electronics and microprocessor operations to track the problem to a faulty chip or passive component that could then be replaced with relatively simple soldering tools. There were few add-ons or peripherals to worry about, and only a few MB of memory or so to work with. Compatibility problems and proprietary interfaces often plagued the few expansion devices that did exist.

Well, times certainly *have* changed. Today's PC is largely a collection of very inexpensive subassemblies—virtually all of which are now manufactured in the Pacific Rim and assembled in high volumes at factories around the world. The diverse array of peripherals that are now available (including tape drives, CD-RWs, graphics accelerators, DVD-ROMs, pointing devices, and so on) enjoy a remarkable level of hardware compatibility using well-established interface schemes (such as AGP, SCSI, UDMA/133, USB, PCI, and FireWire). The labor cost involved in a component-level repair today is usually more expensive than the cost of a replacement assembly. There is little doubt that the day of component-level PC repair is over.

However, PCs still fail, and they fail in ways that continue to exhaust even the most patient mind. When you realize that there are now well over 100 million PCs in operation (and growing at an astonishing rate each year), you can see that *effective* troubleshooting requires *more* than simply an arbitrary swapping of boards and drives. Now, more than ever, efficient and cost-effective troubleshooting requires an understanding of PC hardware and operating systems, along with a keen knowledge of symptoms and diagnostics. Setting up, optimizing, and upgrading a PC are three other important areas that demand the attention of today's technician.

This book is intended for the modern computer enthusiast, working technician, or PC student. It is *not* designed to explain computer theory—there are already plenty of theory books out there. Instead, this book is designed to be a hands-on desktop (or workbench) reference for PC repair, maintenance, and upgrading. This book concentrates on the symptoms and problem areas that occur in every area of the modern PC, as well as proper *diagnosis* of problems. Online resources are included for almost every chapter making the book ideal for classroom or home study. This book is meant to be a lifeline and resource to help you repair your PC, keep it running, and get the most out of it. You'll find a wealth of PC problems fully detailed and explained. There are references to hundreds more POST and diagnostic codes to help you identify even the most obscure problems.

I've taken a lot of time and effort to see that this book is the most comprehensive and understandable book on PC/peripheral repair available. If you have any questions or comments about the book, please don't hesitate to contact me through Dynamic Learning Systems at stevebige@aol.com. I'm interested in your success!

*Stephen J. Bigelow*

# DISCLAIMER AND CAUTIONS

It is IMPORTANT that you read and understand the following information. Please read it carefully!

## PERSONAL RISK AND LIMITS OF LIABILITY

The repair of personal computers and their peripherals involves some amount of personal risk. Use extreme caution when working with AC and high-voltage power sources. Every reasonable effort has been made to identify and reduce areas of personal risk. You are instructed to read this book carefully *before* attempting the procedures discussed. If you are uncomfortable following the procedures that are outlined in this book, do NOT attempt them—refer your service to qualified service personnel.

**NEITHER THE AUTHOR, THE PUBLISHER, NOR ANYONE DIRECTLY OR INDIRECTLY CONNECTED WITH THE PUBLICATION OF THIS BOOK AND ACCOMPANYING COMPUTER SOFTWARE SHALL MAKE ANY WARRANTY EITHER EXPRESSED OR IMPLIED, WITH REGARD TO THIS MATERIAL, INCLUDING, BUT NOT LIMITED TO, THE IMPLIED WARRANTIES OF QUALITY, MERCHANTABILITY, AND FITNESS FOR ANY PARTICULAR PURPOSE.** Further, neither the author, publisher, nor anyone directly or indirectly connected with the publication of this book and computer software shall be liable for errors or omissions contained herein, or for incidental or consequential damages, injuries, or financial or material losses resulting from the use, or inability to use, the material and software contained herein. This material and software is provided AS-IS, and the reader bears all responsibilities and risks connected with its use.

## VIRUS WARNING

Although the software included with this book was thoroughly checked for viruses before publication, you are *strongly* advised to inspect *all* new software, including this book's companion software, for the presence of computer viruses *before* executing the software. Antivirus software can be obtained through commercial and shareware sources. Neither the author, publisher, nor anyone directly or indirectly connected with this book assume any liability whatsoever for incidental or consequential damages, financial loss, or material loss, resulting from the occurrence of computer viruses on your system or network. You use this software at your own risk.

## VENDOR WARNING

The products, materials, equipment, manufacturers, service providers, and distributors listed and presented in this book are shown for reference and example purposes only. Their mention and use in this book shall not be construed as an endorsement of any individual or organization, nor the quality of their products or services, nor their performance or business integrity. The author, publisher, and anyone directly or indirectly associated with the production of this book expressly disclaim all liability whatsoever for any financial or material losses or incidental or consequential damages that might occur from contacting or doing business with any such organization or individual.

# SYMPTOMS AT A GLANCE

**Additional symptoms are included in the chapters on the CD in the Book PDFs folder.**

# BUILD A PC:
# A PICTORIAL GUIDE

**B**uilding your own PC can be a great learning experience, an interesting pastime or part-time job, or even a rewarding parent/child project. With the vast array of components available today (most from local computer stores), you can easily tailor a PC to meet your particular needs—all it takes is a little patience. Most PC builds can be broken down into a series of common procedures.

 To learn more about PC building, read *Bigelow's Build Your Own PC Pocket Reference* (Second Edition), a complete PDF book included on the companion CD.

**1.**
Prepare your new case by opening the outer cover (this project uses a mid-tower case). This may vary a bit between enclosures. Locate the mounting points for your motherboard, power supply, and drives.

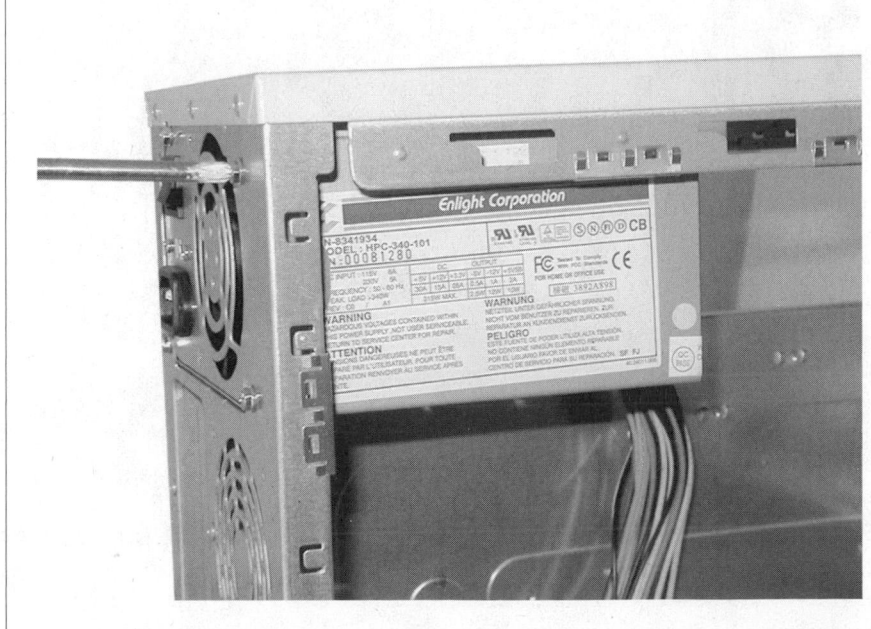

**2.**
Mount the power supply with four screws. Some cases include the power supply, so it's already installed. Make sure that the AC switch is set to 115 or 220 Vac (depending on your region of the world). Do NOT connect AC to the power supply at this time!

**3.**
Mount the CPU. For a socket-mounted CPU, insert it evenly and completely into the socket, then gently close the ZIF (zero insertion force) lever and lock it into place. Then mount the cooling unit to the top of the CPU. You can often purchase a motherboard with a CPU and cooling device already integrated for you.

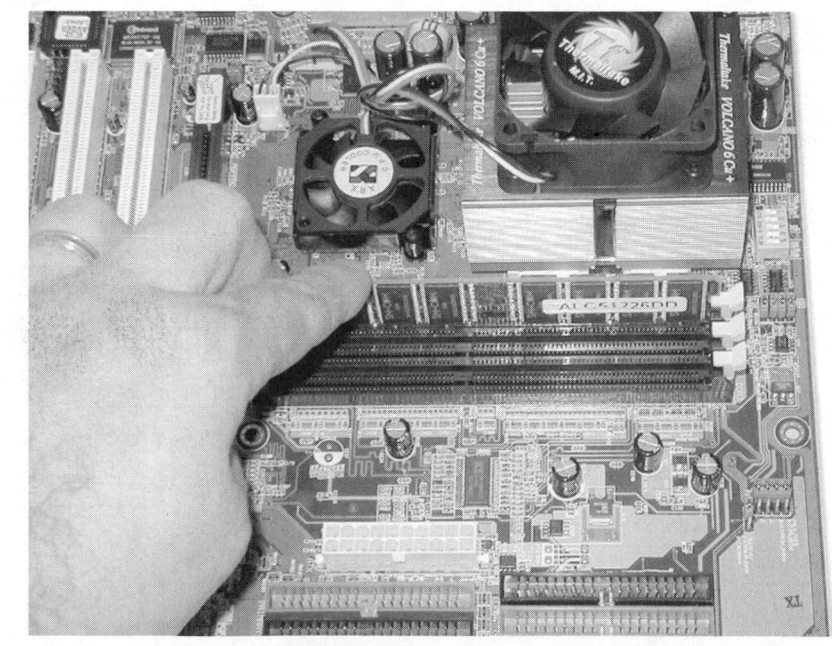

**4.**
Mount the RAM. Today, you'll usually have one or more DDR SDRAM DIMMs (or an even number of Rambus modules). A notch in the DIMM and key in the socket means the memory module can only be inserted in one way, just be sure to insert the module evenly and completely so that the white retaining clips hold the module firmly.

**5.**
Configure the jumpers. A motherboard can typically support a variety of processors and other options. You'll need to refer to the motherboard manual in order to set the bus speed, multiplier, and other options for your particular motherboard. If the CPU has already been installed for you, these jumpers should be preset, but it's always worth a second check to be sure.

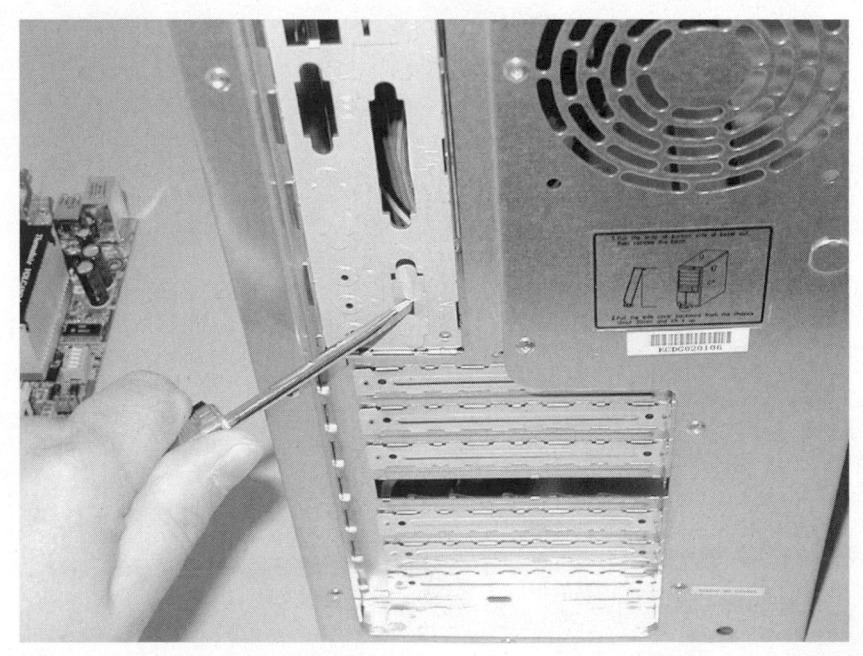

**6.**
Before installing the motherboard, make sure that your case has openings for all of the ports (e.g. serial, parallel, USB, and so on) on your particular motherboard. You may need to remove additional knockouts to allow for more ports.

**7.**
Mount the motherboard. Look at the chassis and see that there is a mounting standoff for every mounting hole on the motherboard (you may need to add or relocate standoffs to accommodate your motherboard). Now gently seat the motherboard into the chassis (making sure that each port is unobstructed) and secure it into place with screws. Be sure that the motherboard rests flat.

**8.**
Connect motherboard power. Once the motherboard is secure, locate the large 20-pin power connector from the power supply and gently connect it to the motherboard. A small plastic clip should mate and prevent the connector from slipping out.

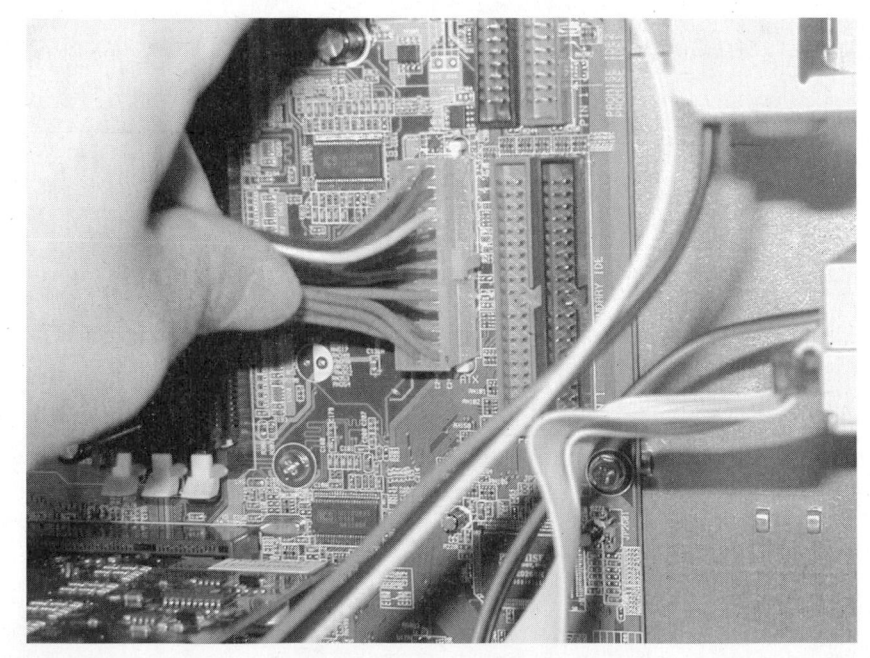

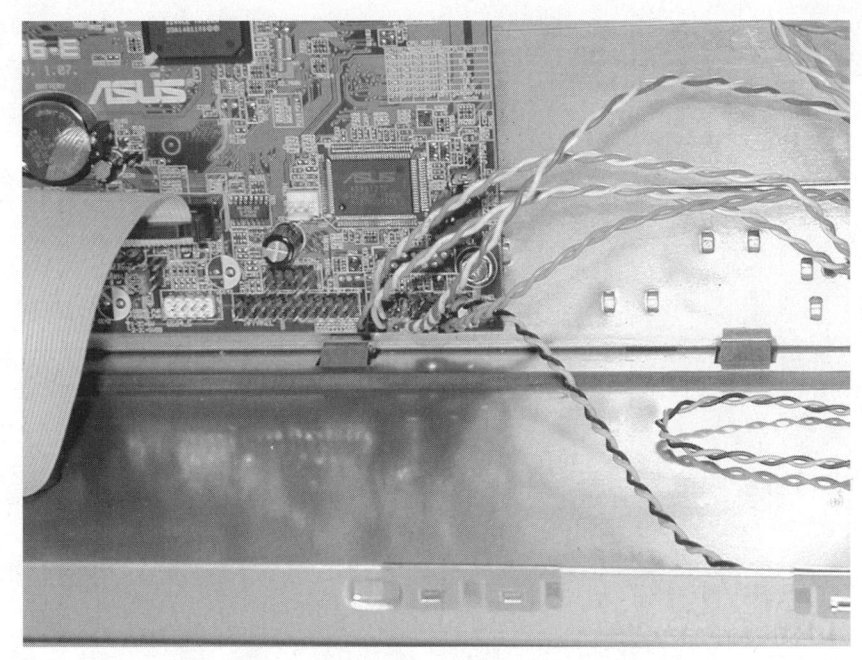

**9.**
Connect chassis cables. Your chassis will have several small cables for things like the speaker, power switch and LED, reset switch, HDD activity, and so on. Refer to the motherboard manual and connect each of these small cables to their appropriate locations on the motherboard's front panel connector.

**10.**
Install the video card. Unbox your video adapter and gently insert it into the motherboard's AGP slot (there's only one AGP slot on the motherboard). Make sure that the card is inserted evenly and completely, then secure the card's bracket to the chassis with a single screw.

**11.**
Connect the monitor.
Attach the monitor's
15-pin video cable to
the video card. If
you're using a video
card with a secondary
video port, check the
card's documentation
to locate the first
(primary) video port.
Secure the video
cable with two
thumbscrews. You
may power on the
monitor at this time
(though it is not
necessary).

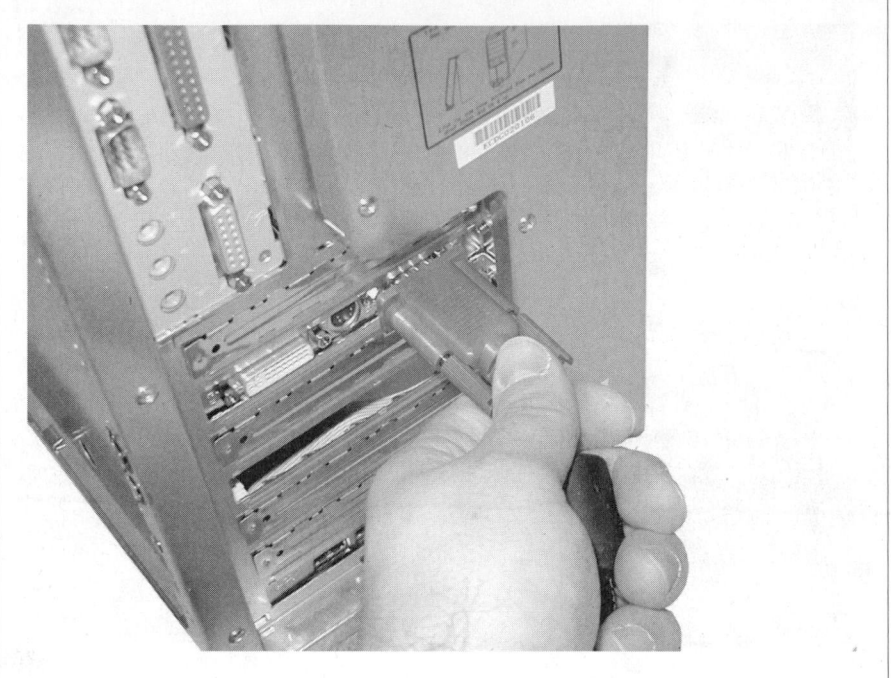

**12.**
Attach your
supplemental devices.
Connect the speaker
cable to the Line Out
audio connector (one
of your motherboard
ports in this example).
Also take a moment
to connect your
mouse and keyboard
cable(s) to their
respective ports. You
may power on the
speakers at this time
(though it is not
necessary).

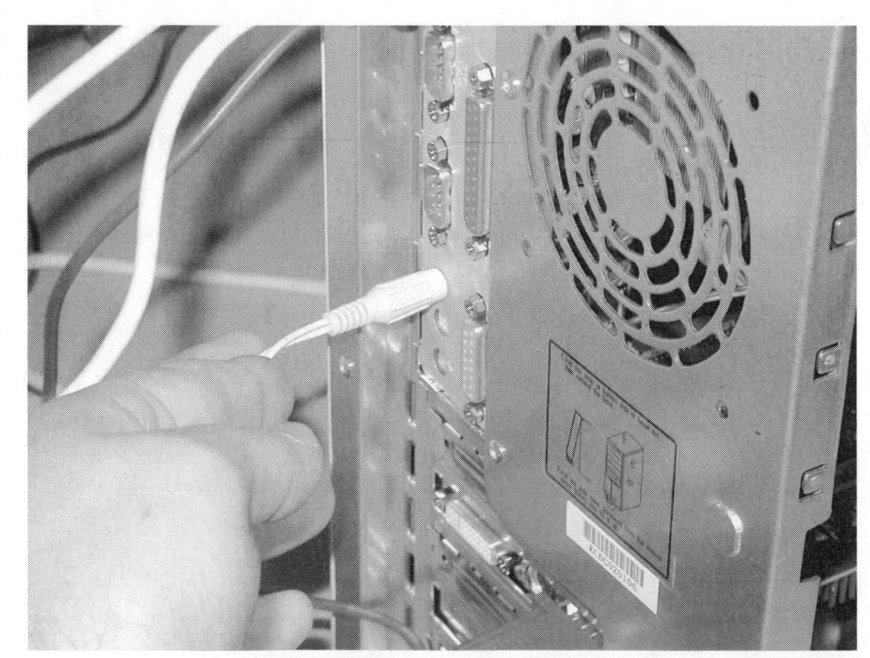

**13.**
Mount the floppy drive. Unbox your floppy drive and secure it to the chassis with four screws. In this chassis, the floppy drive mounting is part of a slide-out assembly, so you unclip and slide out the frame, screw the drive to the frame, then slide the entire frame back into the chassis until it clips into place.

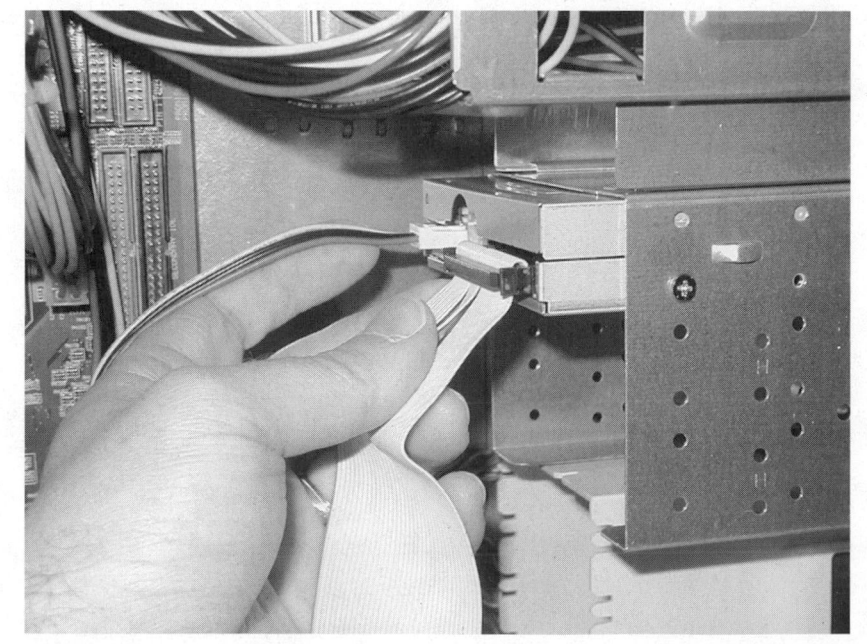

**14.**
Cable the floppy drive. Attach a 4-pin power cable from the power supply and connect it to the floppy drive. Locate the 34-pin floppy drive cable (usually included with the floppy drive or motherboard). Find the end-most connector with the "flip" in several wires and connect this end to your floppy drive. Refer to the motherboard's documentation and locate the 34-pin floppy drive controller connector, then attach the other end of the cable to that connector. The connectors themselves are often "keyed" so that you needn't worry about orientation.

**15.**
Attach the AC cable between the power supply and a nearby AC wall outlet. If the power supply has a master on/off switch, set it to the "on" position (the "1" position). Be sure to power on your monitor if you haven't already.

**16.**
Insert a bootable diskette into the floppy drive. You can make a bootable diskette on any existing Windows PC, or use a boot diskette that accompanies your new operating system (if one is included).

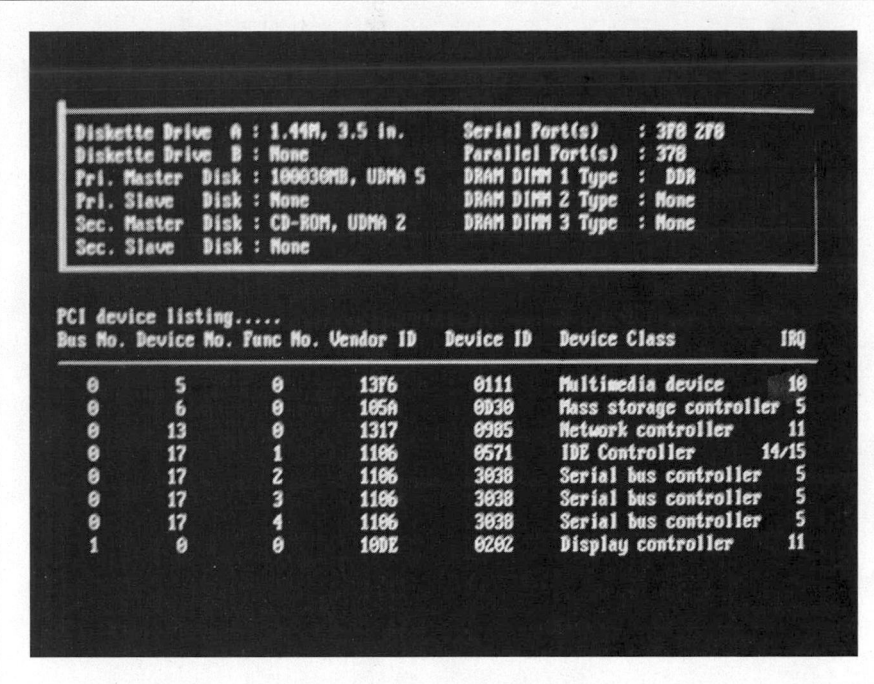

```
 Diskette Drive  A : 1.44M, 3.5 in.     Serial Port(s)   : 3F8 2F8
 Diskette Drive  B : None               Parallel Port(s) : 378
 Pri. Master   Disk : 100030MB, UDMA 5  DRAM DIMM 1 Type  :  DDR
 Pri. Slave    Disk : None              DRAM DIMM 2 Type  : None
 Sec. Master   Disk : CD-ROM, UDMA 2    DRAM DIMM 3 Type  : None
 Sec. Slave    Disk : None


 PCI device listing.....
 Bus No. Device No. Func No. Vendor ID   Device ID   Device Class          IRQ

     0        5         0       13F6        0111      Multimedia device      10
     0        6         0       105A        0D30      Mass storage controller  5
     0       13         0       1317        0985      Network controller     11
     0       17         1       1106        0571      IDE Controller        14/15
     0       17         2       1106        3038      Serial bus controller   5
     0       17         3       1106        3038      Serial bus controller   5
     0       17         4       1106        3038      Serial bus controller   5
     1        0         0       10DE        0202      Display controller     11
```

**17.**
Test boot. Press the power switch on the case. You should hear the cooling fans spin up, and see some BIOS text appear on the monitor as the POST proceeds. Finally, the boot diskette should offer a basic operating system, and you will see an A:> prompt to tell you that the startup has concluded successfully. Try a few DOS commands from the keyboard. If the system doesn't start, you can more easily troubleshoot this stripped-down system (because there's no HDD, CD drive, or other add-on devices to worry about). Power down the PC and disconnect the AC cord when you're done.

**18.**
Configure the hard drive. Unbox the hard drive and locate the jumper next to the 40-pin signal connector. You may configure the drive as a master or slave device depending on other drives that you're planning to add. Since this drive will exist by itself on the primary drive controller channel, it must be configured as the *master* device.

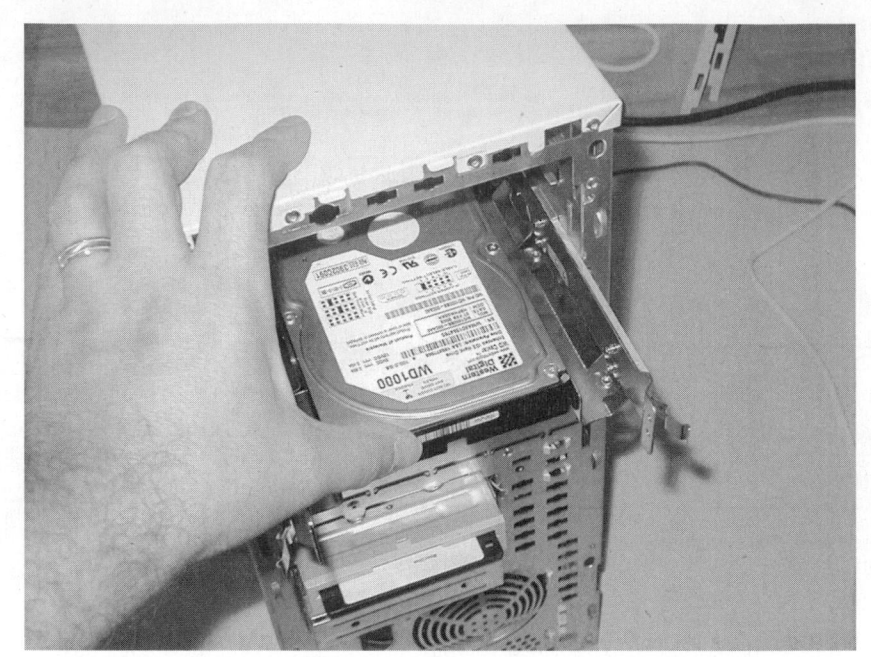

**19.**
Mount the hard drive. If the hard drive is too narrow to fill a full-sized drive bay, attach mounting rails to "widen" the drive. If your chassis uses slide-in mounting, you should also attach left and right clips. Now slide the hard drive into a bay until it clips into place.

**20.**
Cable the hard drive. Attach a 4-pin power cable from the power supply and connect it to the hard drive. Locate the 40-pin IDE drive cable (usually included with the hard drive or motherboard). Find the end-most black connector and connect this end to the 40-pin connector on the drive. Refer to the motherboard's documentation and locate the 40-pin primary IDE drive controller connector, then attach the other (blue) end of the ribbon cable to that connector. The connectors themselves are often "keyed" so that you needn't worry about orientation.

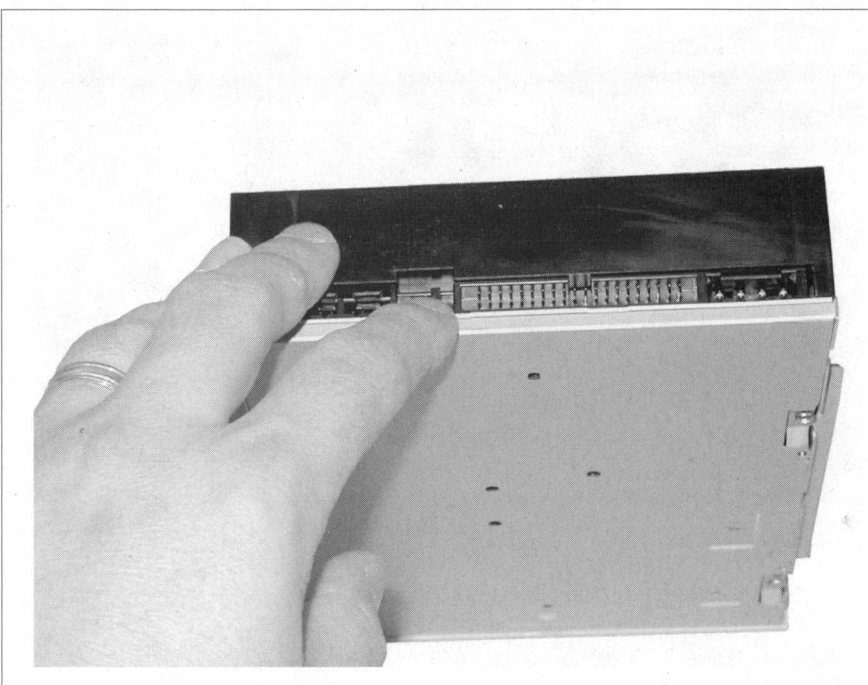

**21.**
Configure the CD-RW drive. Unbox the CD-ROM/R/RW drive and locate the jumper next to the 40-pin signal connector. Like a hard drive, you may configure the drive as a master or slave device depending on other drives that you're planning to add. Since this drive will exist by itself on the secondary drive controller channel, it must be configured as the *master* device. If you were going to attach this along side the hard drive on the same cable, you'd make the CD drive a slave device.

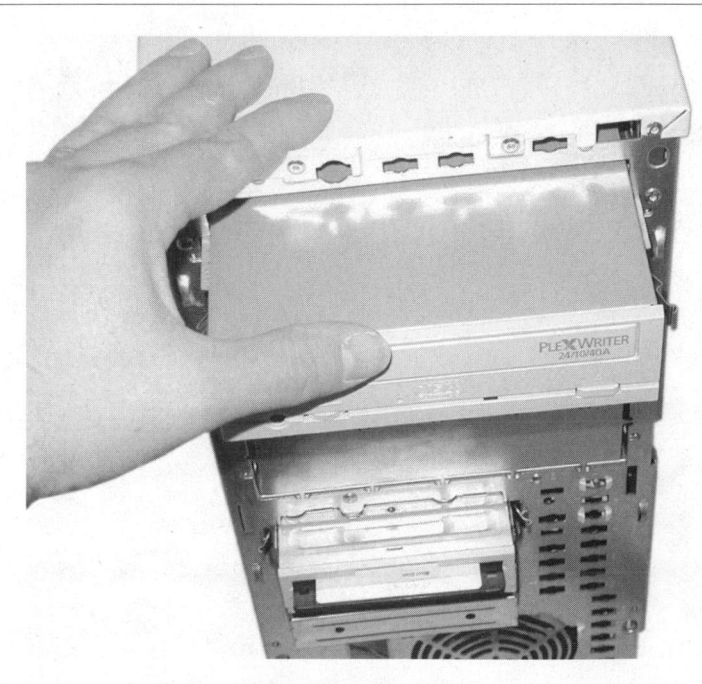

**22.**
Mount the CD-RW drive. The drive will usually be wide enough to fill a full-sized drive bay, so you won't need rails to "widen" the drive. If your chassis uses slide-in mounting, you should attach left and right clips. Now slide the CD-RW drive into a bay until it clips into place. If you're not using slide-in mounting, screw the drive into holes in the chassis.

**23.**
Cable the CD-RW drive. Attach a 4-pin power cable from the power supply and connect it to the CD-RW drive. Since we're installing this drive separately from the hard drive, locate another 40-pin IDE drive cable (usually included with the CD-RW drive or motherboard). Find the end-most black connector and connect this end to the 40-pin connector on the drive. Refer to the motherboard's documentation and locate the 40-pin secondary IDE drive controller connector, then attach the other (blue) end of the ribbon cable to that connector. The connectors themselves are often "keyed" so that you needn't worry about orientation.

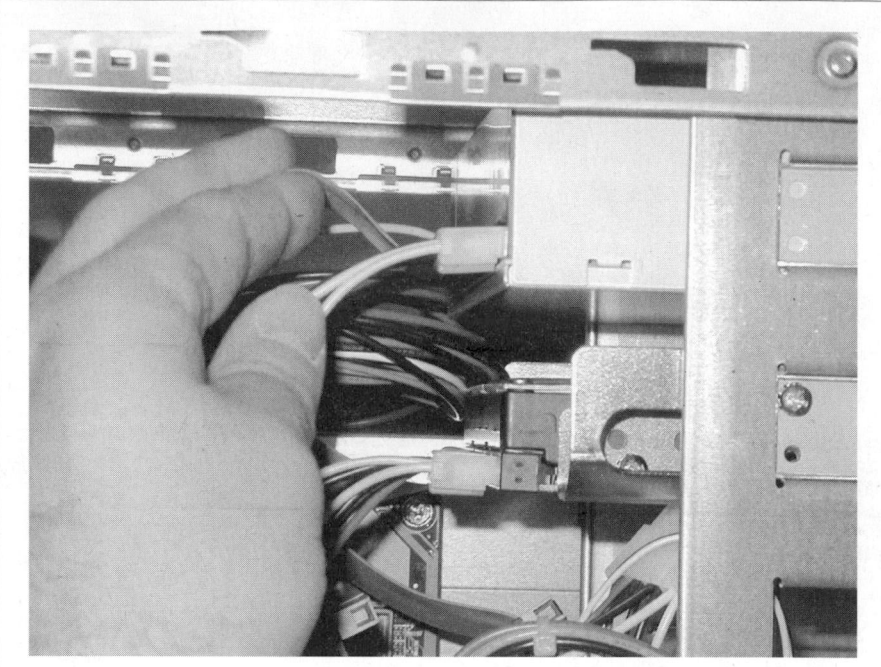

**24.**
Attach the CD audio cable. Locate the thin 4-wire CD audio cable (usually included with the CD drive) and attach it between the CD drive's audio output and your sound card's CD audio input connector. This allows you to play Red Book audio (music CDs) through your PC. In this case, our sound device is part of the motherboard, so refer to your motherboard manual to locate the correct CD audio connector.

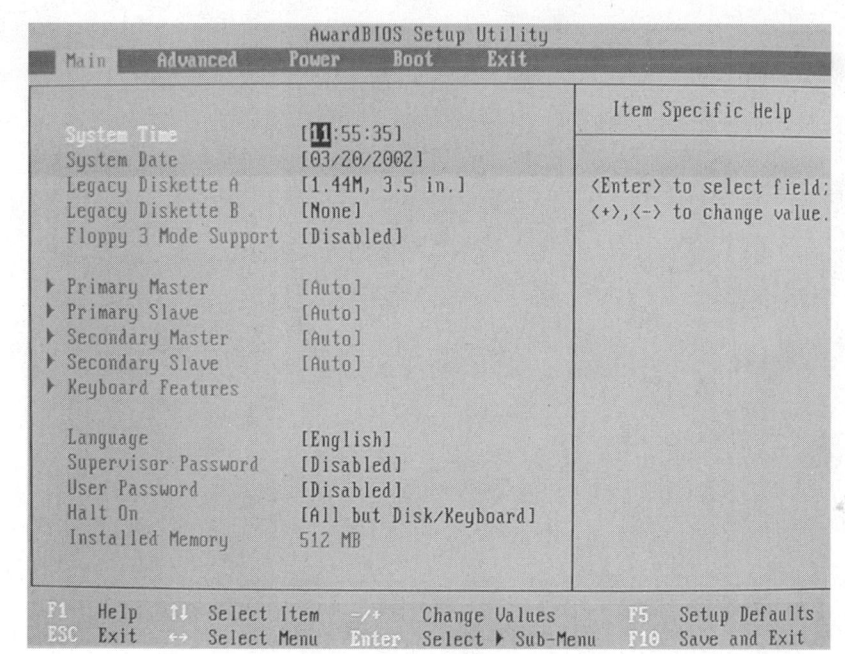

**25.**
Check the CMOS Setup. Now that you've got most of the necessary devices in the PC, reboot the system and refer to your motherboard manual to enter the CMOS Setup routine (part of the BIOS). Set the date and time, verify that your hard drive and CD drive are detected (auto-identified), and make any other needed changes to the CMOS Setup—though default values are usually fine. Remember to "exit saving changes".

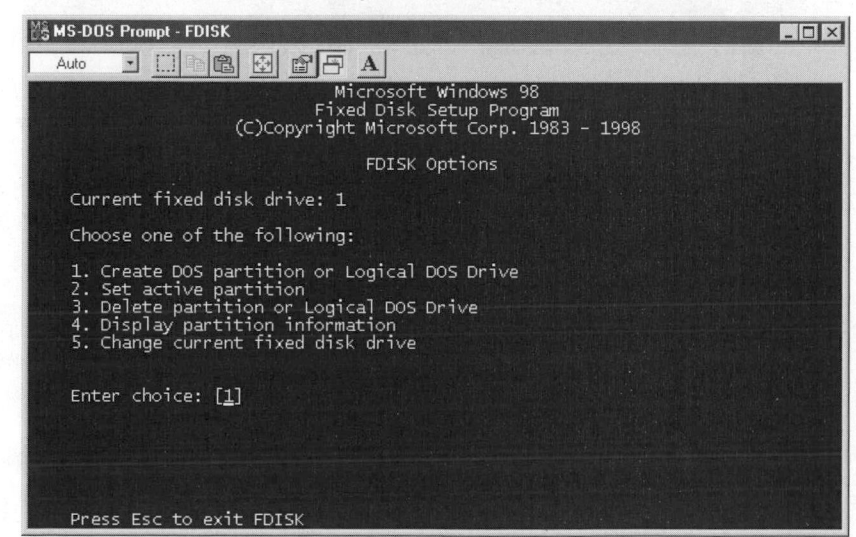

**26.**
FDISK the hard drive. Reboot the PC using your boot diskette and run FDISK from the A: command line. Use FDISK to create one or more FAT32 partitions on the hard drive that you installed. In many cases, users simply choose to create one large primary partition that takes up the drive's entire space. You can check the partition when you're done, then exit FDISK and reboot the system.

**27.**
Now it's time to install your operating system (do not install other devices until the operating system is installed). Put the full installation CD in the CD drive. If the installation CD is self-booting, you can remove the bootable diskette and reboot the system to launch the OS installation. If not, reboot from the diskette with CD-ROM support, switch to the CD drive (e.g. D:>), and start the OS setup according to the manufacturer's instructions.

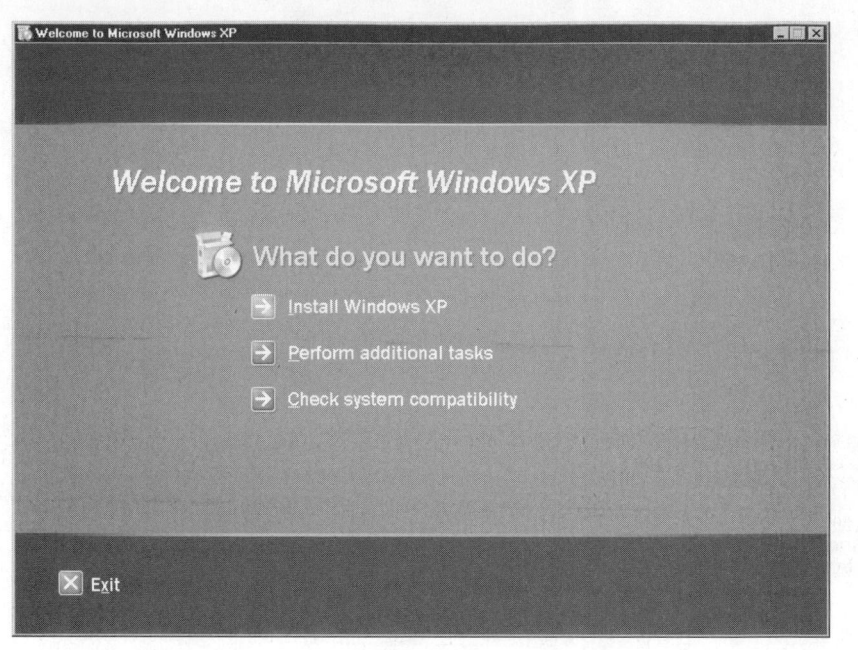

**28.**
Install motherboard drivers. Chances are that your motherboard includes a CD with additional drivers (e.g. sound port drivers). Insert the CD into your CD drive. An auto-installer will usually start and allow you to select which driver(s) you need to install. You may need to reboot the PC once the motherboard drivers are installed.

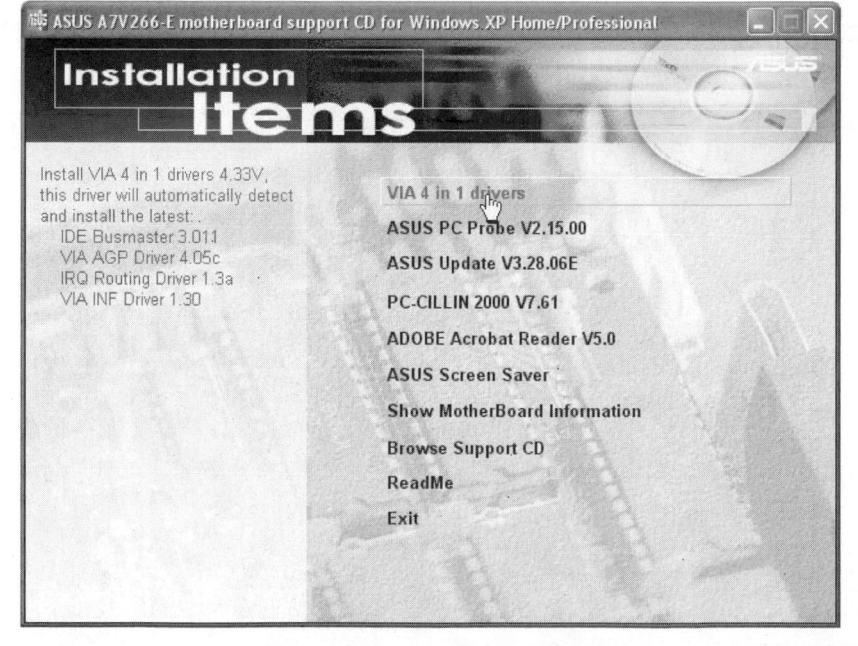

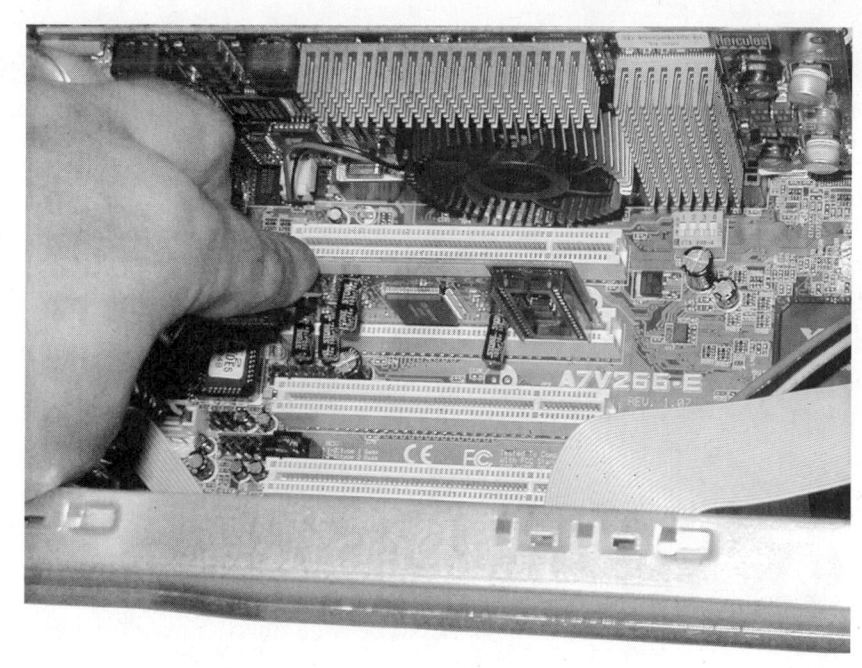

**29.**
Install other devices. Once the OS is installed, you can power down the PC, disconnect AC, and install other devices. In this case, we're installing a network adapter card into a PCI slot. Install the NIC evenly and completely, then secure the card's bracket to the chassis with a single screw.

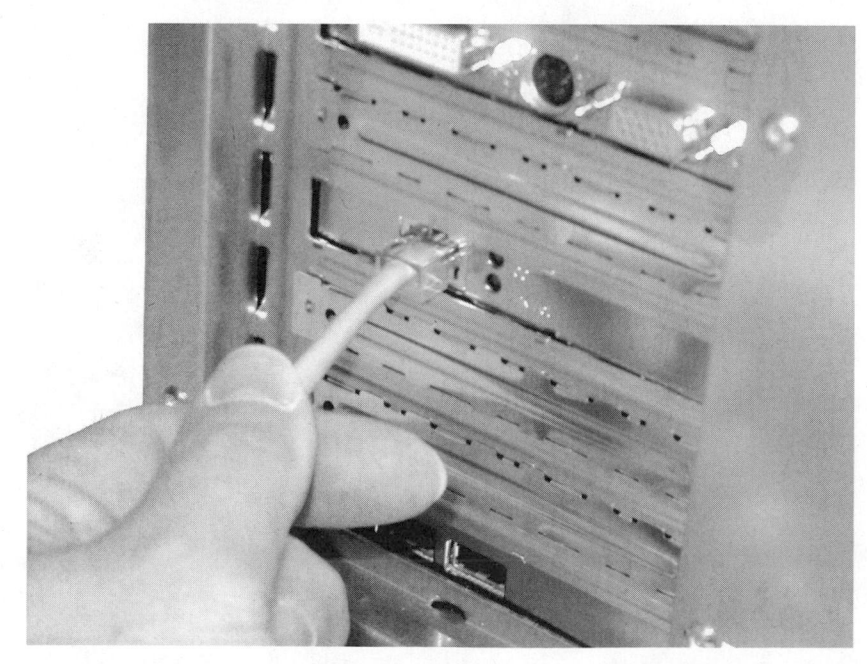

**30.**
Connect other cables. After installing other devices, attach any external cables that may be required (such as this 10/100 Ethernet cable for LAN operation). You can also attach any printers or other peripheral devices that you plan to use.

**31.**
Install other drivers. Now you can reattach power and reboot the PC. Your system should boot from the hard drive and load the operating system that you installed. If you added any other devices, the OS will probably detect those devices for you and attempt to load appropriate drivers. If not, you should install drivers yourself (such as the Hercules GeForce 3 video drivers shown here). You may need to restart the system several times as you install these drivers—that's perfectly normal.

**32.**
The final product. That should complete your basic PC assembly and OS installation. Let the PC run for a while and make sure that it starts up and shuts down without problems. If so, you can go ahead and install applications and start using your new PC—great job!

# AN INSIDE LOOK AT A CONTEMPORARY PC

In order to upgrade or troubleshoot a PC effectively, a technician must be familiar with the general mechanical and physical aspects of the PC. The technician must be able to disassemble the unit quickly (without causing damage to the case or internal assemblies in the process), and then accurately identify each subassembly, expansion board, and connector. Once a diagnosis and repair has been completed, the technician must be able to reassemble the PC and its enclosures (again without damaging assemblies or enclosures). Remember that there's no such thing as an *unimportant* part—every device serves a vital purpose, and can have an impact on the overall performance and reliability of your system. This chapter is designed to provide you with a "guided tour" of a typical PC, point out the various operating subassemblies, and offer a series of assembly guidelines.

This chapter may serve as a comprehensive introduction to PC devices for novice troubleshooters, and even experienced technicians may use this chapter as a refresher.

# The Contemporary PC

A PC doesn't just appear—it is carefully crafted into being by combining a series of key component devices and assemblies (see Figure 1-1). Before you start troubleshooting a PC, it is important that you recognize each major device on sight, and understand its role in the system. If you're new to personal computers, this part of the chapter will give you a thorough introduction to the devices that you'll typically find. Once you're comfortable tearing off a cover and poking around inside of the system, you can focus on upgrade and troubleshooting procedures.

## ENCLOSURES

The *enclosure* (also called the *case* or *chassis*) is the most obvious and least glamorous element of a PC. Yet, the enclosure serves some very important functions. First, the enclosure forms the mechanical foundation of every PC. Every other subassembly is bolted securely to this chassis. Second, the chassis is electrically grounded through the power supply. Grounding prevents the buildup or discharge of static electricity from damaging other subassemblies. Whenever you work inside of a PC, be sure to use a properly grounded anti-static wrist strap to prevent electrostatic discharge from your body from accidentally damaging circuitry inside the system. If you do not have an anti-static wrist strap handy, you can discharge yourself on the PC's metal chassis as long as the power supply is plugged in. However, since you are

**FIGURE  1-1**    The contemporary PC is a collection of highly standardized components that you can learn to quickly and accurately identify.

*strongly* urged to protect yourself by unplugging the power supply AC, do *not* rely on the chassis to discharge you. Grounding also prevents a serious shock or fire hazard if the AC should come in contact with the metal case. There are three general classifications of case: baby, desktop, and tower.

## Baby Cases

The *baby case* lives up to its name. It is a small desktop case that fits an absolute minimum of items. You're usually limited to two drives, because the 130–175W power supply is typically located right behind the drives, and there's no room left for an internally mounted hard drive. You are also limited to using a small motherboard—typically with a minimum of features or ports. Finally, the small case and motherboard will usually limit the number of expansion slots available. A baby desktop case really limits your upgrade and expandability options. The only real benefit of a baby case is when you only need a minimum system (in other words, a network terminal) and desk space is at a premium.

## Desktop Cases

*Desktop cases* come in a variety of shapes and sizes, but generally offer a lot more versatility and upgrade potential than baby cases. With regular desktop cases, you can usually count on two external drive bays and two internal drive bays—great for a floppy drive, CD or DVD drive, and one or two hard drives. If you find a desktop case with three external drive bays, you can even add a second CD drive or a tape drive. The other advantages to regular desktop cases is that they have the physical space to support larger power supplies (usually 200–250W+), they fit larger motherboards, and they support more expansion cards. A desktop case will support a low to moderate number of upgrades with few headaches.

## Tower Cases

The *tower case* is typically a large vertically mounted case, which is designed to hold the maximum number of drives. There are often four or more external drive bays, and at least four internal drive bays. The extra space also allows the largest power supplies (300W+), which are vital to support an array of different drives and other devices. Tower cases can hold the very largest of motherboards (though in practice the motherboards are rarely larger than those found in a regular desktop). Tower cases also provide the best air ventilation, and can sport two or more fans and air filters. The other advantage of good airflow is that high-end CPUs (even multiprocessor motherboards in PCs such as network servers) can be cooled most effectively. In spite of their larger size, tower cases are just slightly more expensive than desktop enclosures. Towers can also be placed on the floor (off of your desk or other work area). Tower cases are often available in mini-tower, mid-tower, and full-tower styles, so you can usually pick the tower size that meets your particular needs and esthetic preference. Figure 1-2 shows an internal view of a popular mid-tower case.

## Enclosure Issues

Most technicians do not concern themselves with PC enclosures, because they don't "break" and are almost never upgraded, and thus last the life of the PC. However, other upgrades (such as new motherboards or advanced processors) may demand the selection of another enclosure. For example, high-end processors like the AMD Athlon family have particular cooling requirements that affect chassis decisions, and you can see such chassis cooling guidelines in documents such as AMD's Thermal, Mechanical, and Chassis Cooling Design Guide at www.amd.com/us-en/assets/content_type/white_papers_and_tech_docs/23794.pdf. (You can also inspect all of AMD's system design guidelines at www1.amd.com/athlon/config.) As another example, Intel calls for a minimum of 250W (power supply) and support for an ATX 2.01 case when working with the Pentium III processor. Take a moment to understand some important enclosure issues.

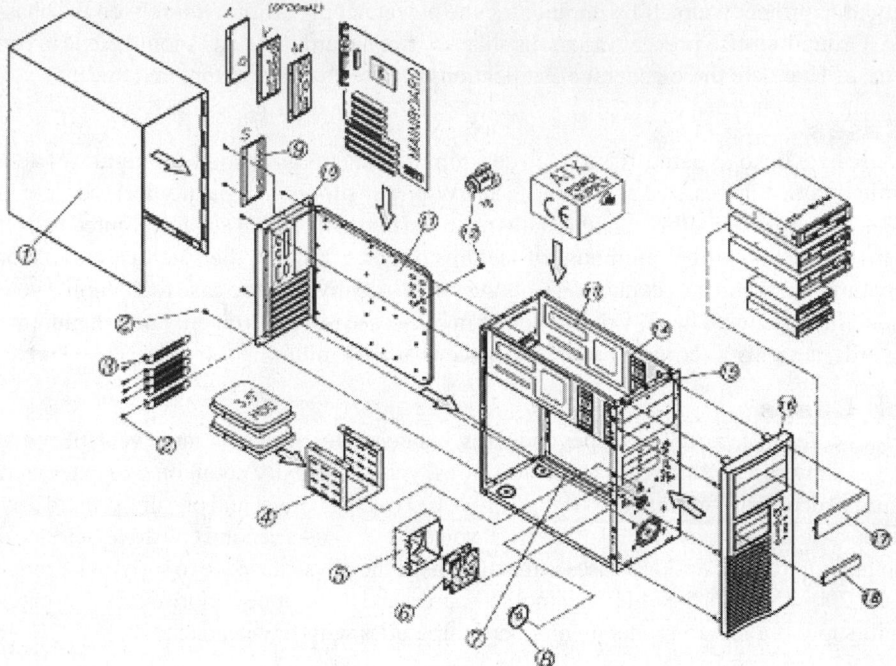

**FIGURE  1-2**    This exploded view of the Amtrade P4 mid-tower illustrates the many parts involved in constructing a quality chassis and PC (Courtesy of Amtrade).

**Available Drive Bays**    One of the most important aspects of a case is the number of drive bays it provides. There are two types of drive bays: external and internal. *External* drive bays are open to the outside of the case. Floppy drives, CD drives (which include CD-ROM, CD-R, and CD-RW), DVD drives (including DVD-ROM and DVD-RAM), and tape drives all require external drive bays. *Internal* drive bays are mounting frames located inside of the case. Typically, only hard drives use internal drive bays. As a minimum, your case should have two external drive bays (for a floppy drive and CD or DVD drive) and one internal drive bay (for the hard drive). If additional drive bays are available, you'll have room for future expansion.

**Fitting Power Supplies and Motherboards**    You also need to remember that your case will have to hold a power supply and motherboard—these things actually have to *mount* to the case, so be sure that your enclosure provides ample space and mounting points for a clean fit. There's nothing more frustrating than receiving a replacement motherboard and finding out that it won't fit in the case (or the mounting holes don't line up). Fortunately, cases are often offered with built-in power supplies, so that's one less headache to deal with. If you are upgrading to a new (typically larger) case, it may also help you to get a matched case and power supply. The new supply should offer more power capacity than your original supply, and you will probably have an easier time getting rid of or reusing the old case if it has a working power supply with it.

**System Cooling**    An important consideration in choosing a PC chassis is adequate cooling. While there are fewer heat-generating components in a modern PC, key components (e.g. the CPU and graphics processor chips) are running faster and hotter than ever. Residual heat liberated from those hot devices will have to be ventilated from the enclosure—usually with one or more chassis fans. Most chassis will provide one fan that draws cooler air into the chassis. Warmed air within the chassis is then displaced through vent openings. Some chassis designs will use a second fan to exhaust the heated air (a good policy if your PC is using numerous drives or more than one processor). Before selecting a chassis, have an idea of the airflow path(s), and determine if additional cooling fans are needed to ventilate areas of the chassis that may not be in the natural airflow path.

**Mechanical Specifications**    Given the traditional problems of matching motherboards, cases, and power supplies, the computer industry has responded by developing a series of physical specifications (called *form factors*) for the construction of motherboards, cases, and power supplies. The idea is that power supplies, motherboards, and cases all built to a certain specification will fit correctly without the problems of mixing and matching. The three most popular specifications are AT (and baby AT), ATX, and NLX. Try to obtain a case, supply, and motherboard that all use the same form factor—this should eliminate any mounting problems. See "Standardized Form Factors" at the end of this chapter for more information.

# POWER SUPPLIES

You should next familiarize yourself with the *power supply,* as shown in Figure 1-3. Whether you're replacing a failed supply, upgrading to a larger supply, or building a new system from scratch, do yourself a favor and *don't* skimp on the power supply. Buy plenty of power capacity, and go with a reputable manufacturer—marginal supplies will cause no end of trouble with erratic system operation and premature failures. Power is measured in *watts* (W). Each device in the computer demands power, so enough power must be available from the supply to run the motherboard, the drives, and all of the expansion boards in your system. Don't be afraid to "buy power"—it's okay to have more power capacity than you need—problems occur when there isn't enough power. If you go with a desktop case, plan on a 200–250W supply.

**FIGURE  1-3**    You can see a power supply box mounted in the upper-left corner of this Fong Kai FK-320 tower (Courtesy of Fong Kai).

For tower cases (with lots of drives), go with a 300–350W unit (servers or systems packed with devices may need a 400W supply).

If you really want to apply some numbers when estimating the size for a power supply, you can use the 150+12 rule. This is a baseline of 150W for the motherboard and CPU, and then 12W for every drive and expansion board you plan to add. If you want a system with a floppy drive, hard drive, CD-ROM, modem board, and video board, figure on about 210W (150+12+12+12+12+12). If you buy a 220–250W supply, you'll have plenty of power, though your upgrade options may be a bit limited.

## Power Connectors

When you look at the power supply, you'll notice two different sets of cables. One set of cables plugs into the motherboard. The other set of cables provides power to each drive. There must be enough drive power cables to run each drive in your system. Otherwise, you'll need Y cables to split power. In practice, such Y cables should be avoided, so the more drive power cables, the better off you'll be. As a rule, the more wattage offered by the power supply, the more drive cables that will be available.

There are two well-accepted sets of cables to power the motherboard: the AT/baby AT configuration, shown in Figure 1-4, and the ATX/NLX configuration, shown in Figure 1-5. The classic baby AT configuration uses two 6-pin Molex connectors (usually marked P8 and P9) that are inserted adjacent to each other. The rule here is "black wires together." A baby AT power supply provides four voltage levels (+5V, −5V, +12V, and −12V) along with a "Power Good" signal. The ATX power supply uses a significantly different 20-pin single-connector scheme, which includes a +3.3V supply along with the other conventional voltages. It is important to stress that baby AT power supply connectors will *not* mate with an ATX motherboard (and vice versa).

> An auxiliary power connector (6-pin, P4 connector) is included with some newer ATX power supplies, but not many motherboards support or use this connector. When the connector is unsupported or unused, just leave it detached.

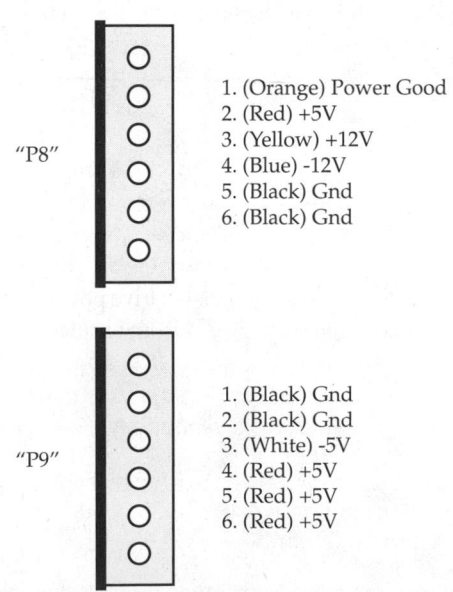

"P8"
1. (Orange) Power Good
2. (Red) +5V
3. (Yellow) +12V
4. (Blue) -12V
5. (Black) Gnd
6. (Black) Gnd

"P9"
1. (Black) Gnd
2. (Black) Gnd
3. (White) -5V
4. (Red) +5V
5. (Red) +5V
6. (Red) +5V

**FIGURE  1-4**    Baby AT-style power connectors

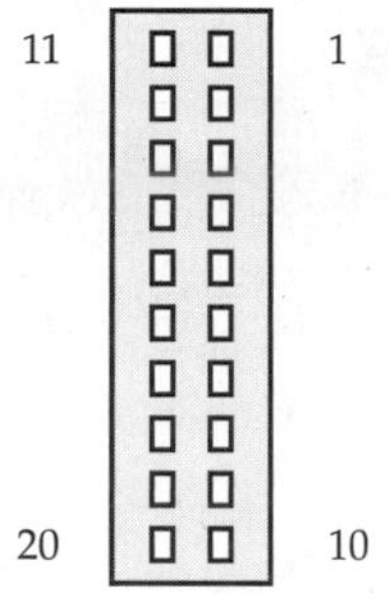

| | |
|---|---|
| 1. +3.3V | 11. +3.3V |
| 2. +3.3V | 12. -12V |
| 3. Gnd | 13. Gnd |
| 4. +5V | 14. PW_ON |
| 5. Gnd | 15. Gnd |
| 6. +5V | 16. Gnd |
| 7. Gnd | 17. Gnd |
| 8. PWRGD | 18. -5V |
|    (Power Good) | 19. +5V |
| 9. +5V SB | 20. +5Vdc |
|    (Standby for RTC) | |
| 10. +12Vdc | |

**FIGURE 1-5**    ATX-style power connectors

## Mounting Points

Of course, you actually have to mount that power supply into the case. This can get a little bit tricky with older baby AT systems, because nobody tells the case makers and the power supply makers to put their screw holes in the same places. You should make sure that the power supply will mount properly in the case. If you can find a case with a suitable power supply already mounted, that might take some of the guesswork out of your assembly. Also remember that you'll need to turn the supply on and off—this means the case has to have a hole for the power switch, as well as the AC line cord and fuse opening. Remember that ATX- and NLX-style cases and power supplies should line up without any problems at all. Today, there are relatively few mechanical compatibility problems between power supplies and cases, but keep those mounting issues in mind (especially if you're working on older systems).

Some ATX-style power supply units do *not* use an on/off switch. Instead, the ATX standard uses "soft power" signals from the case power button to the motherboard. Don't get rattled if you don't see an on/off switch on your ATX supply. If there is an on/off switch, treat it as a "master" switch, which is normally kept in the on position.

## Choosing a Supply

Power supplies are some of the most overlooked parts of a PC—probably because you never see them in operation the way you do with video boards or hard drives. Also, once a supply is operating, there is little reason to replace it. The only two reasons to replace a power supply are to exchange a defective unit, or upgrade the existing supply to support the power demands of more devices added during a PC upgrade. The supply needs to provide adequate power to the computer, fit in the physical space available, mount properly and securely, and should have an ample number of drive power cables available without having to resort to Y cables. Again, make it a point to buy supplies from reputable manufacturers! While all power supplies perform the same basic jobs, they are *not* all created equal—go with a manufacturer that uses top-quality parts in a well-designed and reliable supply that is backed with a strong warranty and friendly return policy. The best PC components in the world cannot make up for a poor power supply.

Power supply assemblies are generally regarded as extremely safe, because it is virtually impossible to come into contact with exposed high-energy circuitry. Still, exercise caution and common sense whenever working with a running power supply.

# MOTHERBOARDS AND RELATED PARTS

The *motherboard* is absolutely the heart and soul of every computer. Motherboards and the components on them (CPUs, chipsets, RAM, BIOS, and integrated controllers) largely define the capabilities and limitations of any given system. This part of the chapter covers the major elements of a motherboard, and shows you the important points to consider. Table 1-1 lists the specifications for the example motherboard shown in Figure 1-6. You can see the motherboard's review for yourself at www.motherboards.org/articlesd/motherboard-reviews/1139_1.html, or visit the Shuttle site at www.shuttleonline.com.

## Form Factor Support

The dimensions and mounting points for the motherboard are typically defined by the *form factor,* and this is often the first specification you see when evaluating the new motherboard. Your choices are generally: baby AT, ATX, or NLX (though ATX is by far the most common and popular form factor). The dimensions for a typical ATX motherboard are illustrated in Figure 1-7. The form factor is certainly not the most exciting motherboard issue when compared to processors and chipsets, but you need to understand it right up front—all the processing power in the world won't do you much good if the motherboard doesn't fit in the case.

## Expansion Slot Support

Motherboards alone rarely offer all the features that you need for your computer. Fortunately, you can easily add other devices to the motherboard by plugging them into *expansion slots* (or *bus slots*). There are

**FIGURE  1-6**    The Shuttle AV45GTR is a Socket 478 (Pentium 4) motherboard based on the VIA P4X266A and VT8233 chips (Courtesy of Shuttle).

**TABLE 1-1    BASIC SPECIFICATIONS FOR THE SHUTTLE AV45GTR PENTIUM 4 MOTHERBOARD**

| CHARACTERISTIC | DESCRIPTION |
| --- | --- |
| Form Factor | ATX |
| CPU Support | Socket 478 (Intel Pentium 4 in the 478-pin package) |
| Chipsets | (Northbridge) VIA P4X266A (supports Pentium 4 system bus) and (Southbridge) VIA VT8233 |
| Front Side Bus | 100/133 MHz (BIOS adjustable) |
| Memory | Three 184-pin DDR SDRAM sockets |
| H/W Audio | C-Media 8738 -PCI-6CH/LX |
| Expansion Slots | One AGP 2.0 compliant slot<br>Five PCI slots |
| IDE interface | Two UltraDMA/100 Bus Master IDE from VT8233<br>Two UltraDMA/133 Bus Master IDE from High Point 372<br>On board High Point 372 (optional)<br>Supports RAID 0, RAID 1, and RAID 0+1 |
| USB 2.0 Interface | On board Philip ISL1561 (optional)<br>Complies with Universal Serial Bus Specification Rev. 2.0 |
| H/W Monitoring | Built in ITE 8705F<br>Two thermal inputs from remote thermal resistor to monitor system temperature<br>One thermal input from thermal diode to monitor CPU temperature<br>Eight voltage monitor inputs<br>One chassis intrusion input<br>Monitors three fan tachometer inputs |
| Power Management | APM 1.2 compliant<br>ACPI 1.0 compliant |
| BIOS | Award PnP BIOS |

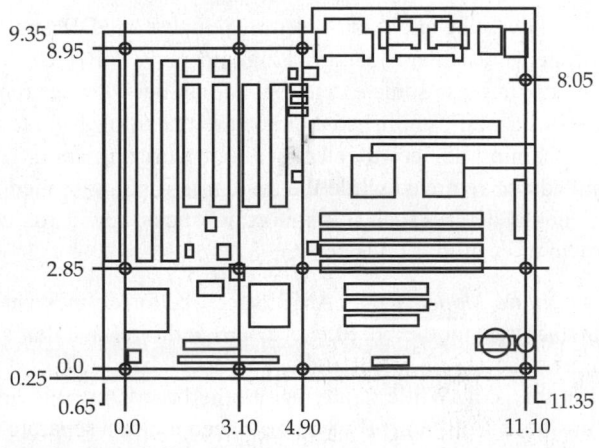

**FIGURE 1-7**    ATX motherboard dimensions

five different architectures to be familiar with: ISA, PCI, AGP, USB, and AMR. You should be familiar with each of these five bus types because virtually all new motherboards offer some (or all) of these busses, and the capabilities of your new system will largely be defined by the busses that are available on your particular motherboard. For example, you can't use an AGP video card on a motherboard that only has PCI slots. These bus types are defined next.

**ISA**    This is the classic *Industry Standard Architecture* (ISA) 16-bit, 8.3 MHz expansion bus. Although it offers limited data throughput and resources when compared to other busses, you'll still find a few 16-bit cards like modems, SCSI adapters, and sound cards. Your motherboard may have two to four ISA slots onboard—though many of the newest Pentium 4/Athlon/Duron motherboards eliminate the ISA bus completely. If you *must* use older ISA cards carried over from an existing system, make sure that your motherboard offers ISA slots. Otherwise, it's a good idea to avoid the use of ISA devices in favor of PCI and AGP devices.

**PCI**    The *Peripheral Component Interconnect* (PCI) bus originally evolved as a 32/64-bit answer to the obsolete *Video Local Bus* (dubbed the VL bus or VLB). Whereas the VLB is generally geared toward video systems, the PCI bus is designed to support general-purpose devices (though network cards, modems, and drive controllers are some of the most common). PCI is clearly a better-performing bus with superior data throughput. Its fixed 30 MHz/33 MHz clock speed makes PCI much more stable than VLB, and its bus mastering features make it ideal for high-performance devices. A modern motherboard may sport between four and six PCI slots.

**AGP**    Video continues to be a bottleneck for cutting-edge graphics applications that push video resolution, color depth, and image complexity to the limit (especially for video and real-time 3D rendering). The *Accelerated Graphics Port* (AGP) is a high-performance port using a superset of PCI architecture designed to handle huge volumes of video data. Where the 32-bit PCI bus implementation can handle 133 MB/s, the 32-bit implementation of an AGP can handle 533 MB/s—some implementations of AGP can handle 1 GB/s of video data and higher. This opens up whole new possibilities for games and visualization software. However, you will require AGP support in the motherboard's chipset, as well as the BIOS and operating system. Microsoft fully supports AGP in Windows 98 and later. The AGP also accesses main system RAM for storing graphics textures, so video RAM is not so critical. But it is still a good idea to select replacement AGP cards (or any video card) with as much onboard video memory as possible.

**USB**    Expanding a PC has always been a hassle—setting jumpers and DIP switches often leads to hardware conflicts that cause system crashes and lockups. Plug-and-play (PnP) technology has helped ease the burden of installations and upgrades to some extent, but adding new devices remains troublesome. The *Universal Serial Bus* (USB) is a well-established architecture that allows you to add devices "outside of the PC" simply by daisy-chaining devices together without worrying about resource allocation. The devices can also be installed and removed while the system is running (called *hot swapping*). USB is slanted primarily toward external devices such as monitors, joysticks, keyboards, and so on. Many modern motherboards will offer two or even four USB ports.

**AMR**    The relatively new *Audio/Modem Riser* (AMR) specification defines a hardware-scaleable OEM (original equipment manufacturer) motherboard riser board and interface that supports both audio and modem features. This allows the development and use of specialized low-cost sound/modem "combo cards" that can be used in this slot. While numerous motherboards include an AMR slot, few AMR devices are available at this time. Consequently, you may need to use a separate modem card and sound card. If your motherboard already offers a built-in sound device, you can stick with a PCI modem card.

AMR devices are often proprietary and are not widely available. For best device compatibility, you should avoid the use of AMR devices wherever possible.

## CPU Support

The *central processing unit* (called a *processor* or *CPU*) is the main processing component on your motherboard (see Figure 1-8). All program instructions and data are eventually processed through the CPU. The faster and more powerful a CPU is, the more performance your computer will offer. Keep in mind that a CPU also has to operate in conjunction with other elements of the motherboard, so a newer CPU installed into an older motherboard may not offer the same performance as a new CPU installed into a state-of-the-art motherboard. When selecting a CPU for upgrade or replacement, always verify that your motherboard will support it. In virtually all cases, the motherboard (or system) documentation will list the CPUs that are compatible with the motherboard. For example, the older Intel PD440FX motherboard will support a Pentium II CPU operating at 233 MHz or 266 MHz, and the AOpen AK72 motherboard supports AMD Athlon processors from 500 MHz to 1000 MHz, but a late-model motherboard like the Asus A7V266-E will handle AMD Socket A processors to 2 GHz. Improved CPUs are one of the most popular upgrades for a motherboard, so choose a motherboard to accommodate the CPUs that may be added in the future. Otherwise, you'll find yourself having to replace the entire motherboard.

It's a good idea to keep potential future upgrades in mind. When selecting a motherboard for upgrade or replacement, go for the *fastest* motherboard that you can afford. Later, it's a simple matter to upgrade to a faster processor once the price falls, without having to replace the entire motherboard.

**Heat Sinks and Fans**    Modern CPUs also run hot—*very* hot. If you don't want to ruin your CPU investment, you'll need to think about ways to keep the CPU cool. As a rule, use a heat sink/CPU fan that mounts directly to the CPU itself. The heat sink is simply a metal radiator that carries heat away from the CPU. A fan (built right into the heat sink) forces air through the heat sink, which makes the cooling process much more efficient. You can typically buy an appropriately sized heat sink/fan when selecting the CPU.

**FIGURE  1-8**    A front angled view of an AMD Athlon XP processor (Courtesy of AMD).

Select a "boxed" processor that is certain to include an appropriate heat sink/fan assembly. An "unboxed" or OEM processor version will offer an identical processor, but is not always certain to include the heat sink/fan.

## Main Memory (RAM) Support

All computers need memory to hold program data and instructions while the CPU is executing them, so *random access memory* (RAM) is needed on the motherboard. Older motherboards usually incorporated 1 or 2MB of RAM on the motherboard, then allowed you to add more memory in the form of Single Inline Memory Modules (SIMMs). Today, all motherboards use memory modules exclusively such as Dual Inline Memory Modules (DIMMs) or Rambus Inline Memory Modules (RIMMs). Modules make it much easier to replace defective memory without having to replace the entire motherboard. You generally choose some preinstalled amount of RAM when you select your motherboard, or purchase the RAM separately and install it yourself. Many types of RAM are available for the PC, but you should be familiar with the three most popular types, described next.

**SDRAM**    *Synchronous DRAM* is a type of enhanced memory that allows data to be transferred at any point in the system's clock cycle rather than just at certain points. This makes for dramatically faster overall memory performance. SDRAM can also "burst" large amounts of data to and from memory. SDRAM was introduced for 66 MHz motherboards (often referred to as PC66 SDRAM). A variation of SDRAM is PC100 SDRAM. With newer motherboards using a bus speed of 100 MHz, the RAM timing becomes far more critical. PC100 RAM is basically SDRAM that has been certified to run properly on 100 MHz motherboards. If you do *not* select PC100 RAM, make sure that your SDRAM is suitable for operation at 100 MHz. PC133 SDRAM is available for motherboards using a bus speed of 133 MHz. You can often use 100 MHz SDRAM on a 133 MHz motherboard, but you'll need to slow the motherboard's bus speed to 100 MHz—this will result in a terrible loss of performance for the system. You should also be able to use PC133 RAM on 100 MHz systems, but the expense of PC133 RAM makes this a bit of a waste. SDRAM is available in DIMM form.

**DDR SDRAM**    *Double data rate* (DDR) *SDRAM* is a relatively recent enhancement to SDRAM technology that can transfer data on *two* edges of the system's clock rather than on just one edge. This enhancement makes it possible to increase (ideally double) the effective performance of your SDRAM. In actual practice, DDR SDRAM does not double memory performance over ordinary SDRAM, but it does offer a real improvement. DDR SDRAM is available in DIMM form, and is supported by virtually all non-Intel motherboard chipsets (such as VIA chipsets).

**RDRAM**    *Rambus DRAM* (or *Rambus*) has dramatically grown in popularity over the last few years, and is supported in most new PCs (namely PCs using the Intel 800 series of chipsets). Rambus (www.rambus.com) uses dedicated data channels to transfer data using speeds of up to 800 MHz, and this is often dubbed PC800 RAM. PCs fitted for Rambus operation can often achieve 2-byte transfers at 800 MHz, giving the system a memory throughput of up to 1.6GB/sec. In actual practice, Rambus has not enjoyed the significant performance improvements that the technology had promised, but improvements are still being made. Intel originally did not plan on offering PC133 SDRAM support in its 800 family (810, 820, 840) of chipsets, but it was added to provide backward-compatibility with widely available and comparatively inexpensive SDRAM and DDR SDRAM. RDRAM is available in RIMM form, which are slightly bigger than DIMMs.

## BIOS Support

The *basic input/output system* (BIOS) is a form of permanent memory that holds the instructions that your motherboard hardware needs to communicate with the operating system. In short, BIOS "drives" your motherboard hardware and supports features like PnP, power conservation, and specialized busses like USB. BIOS is provided *with* the motherboard, so you don't have to select it separately, but you may choose to upgrade the BIOS later on.

Normally, BIOS should only be upgraded when there is a clear problem with the BIOS that prevents an important feature or function from working, or a BIOS upgrade would expand the capabilities of your hardware. For example, suppose you're using a motherboard video system, and you decide to upgrade the video system by adding a new video board—you'd need to disable the motherboard video system. Some poorly designed motherboards may be unable to fully disable their onboard video because of a flaw in the BIOS, and an upgrade might fix the problem. As another example, some older motherboards needed a BIOS upgrade to support the AMD K6 and K6-2, or the Cyrix MII. It would not be a surprise to see a few motherboards require a BIOS upgrade to support newer CPUs (or at least identify newer CPUs properly at start time).

## Chipset Support

In the early days of PCs, motherboards were built with hundreds of discrete logic chips (just take a look at any original IBM PC/AT). It didn't take long for designers to realize that the major PC functions could be condensed onto application-specific chips. This philosophy not only reduced the total number of chips needed to build a motherboard, but also allowed performance to improve, and reduced the power demands and costs for a motherboard. Eventually, chip design evolved to the point where *all* the major features needed for a motherboard could be provided with just a couple of related (and very complex) chips. These related chips became known as *chipsets*. Modern motherboard capabilities are largely defined by their chipset. In fact, most chipsets are specific to certain CPU families. When replacing a motherboard, be sure to select one with a chipset that supports the important features that you need (such as USB ports, advanced processors, and so on).

## Motherboard Ports

As you've seen already, motherboards rarely provide every possible feature or device needed to make a working computer—there are countless other devices that could (and should) be added to the system. Most external devices are attached to the motherboard through ports. Figure 1-9 illustrates some of the ports available for external devices.

- **Serial ports**   Get a motherboard with two serial ports. One serial port is usually for a serial mouse, and another serial port is typically for an external modem. If your motherboard does not offer serial ports, you can add serial ports by installing a multi-I/O card into an available expansion slot.

- **Parallel ports**   If you plan to use a parallel port printer (or other parallel port device such as a CD drive), at least one parallel port will be a necessity. Virtually all motherboards provide one parallel port. If your motherboard does not offer a parallel port, you can add one by installing a multi-I/O card into an available expansion slot.

- **Keyboard port**   This is really a no-brainer—there has to be a connector on the motherboard to accept the input from a keyboard. The keyboard port may be soldered directly to the motherboard itself, or there may be a cable header from the motherboard to a keyboard connector at the case. Modern motherboards include a built-in PS/2 keyboard port.

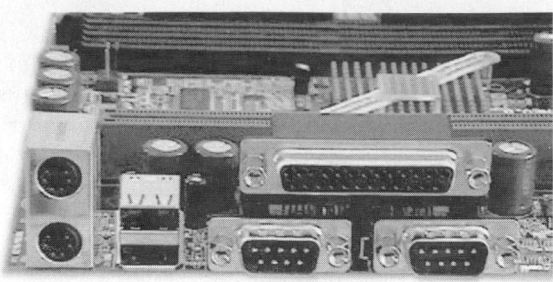

**FIGURE   1-9**    A typical selection of motherboard I/O ports

- **Mouse port**    Although you can easily install a serial mouse on an existing serial port, you may choose to get a motherboard with a built-in PS/2 mouse port. This frees up the second serial port for other uses (such as a serial printer). Keep in mind that some motherboards will require a small adapter cable to connect a PS/2 header on the motherboard to a PS/2 connector in the case.

- **USB port(s)**    While a USB port is not required, it is standard equipment on most new motherboards (www.usb.org). When used in conjunction with Windows 98 and later operating systems, the USB port offers a fast and convenient means of connecting several USB devices without even having to turn off the PC. You can even use USB keyboards, mice, and printers. Classic USB supports a port speed of 12 Mbits/s (1.5 MB/s—up to ten times faster than serial or parallel port speed), though USB 2.0 compliant ports can support much faster data transfers. It can connect up to 127 devices, provide up to 0.5 amps to external devices, and handle the *hot swapping* of devices (connecting and disconnecting devices with power on).

- **IEEE 1394 (a.k.a. FireWire)**    While classic USB is an accepted standard for lower-speed peripherals (such as keyboards, mice, game controllers, speakers, scanners, or printers), high-end digital audio/video peripherals require a high-speed port. FireWire meets this requirement with throughput speeds reaching 400 Mbits/s (50 MB/s) at this time, and is scheduled to reach 800 Mbps (100 MB/s) soon. FireWire uses a *tiered star* topology and supports peer-to-peer connections without hubs, allowing up to 63 same-speed devices to be connected to the same bus, and up to 1,023 buses to be interconnected. FireWire is also designed to be hot-swappable. Many companies involved in the development of FireWire are doing so in conjunction with a computer case standard named Device Bay. The combination of high-speed FireWire, hot-swapping, and Device Bay technologies will allow high-speed peripherals to be inserted and removed at any time (and even moved from computer to computer). Motherboards supporting FireWire are just now being introduced, but you can learn more about FireWire at www.dtvgroup.com/DigVideo/FireWire/Adaptec/1394main.html.

## Motherboard Controllers
Controllers are generally used to connect devices inside of the PC. Many of today's motherboards incorporate video and drive controllers (a few also provide a sound feature). This adds convenience to the motherboard

because it saves two expansion slots (one for the video controller, and one for the drive controller). If you choose to upgrade the motherboard's video or drive controller later, you can always disable the motherboard's controllers and install the replacement controllers in the form of expansion boards. The following are common motherboard controllers (see Figure 1-10):

■ **Floppy drive controllers (FDCs)**    You will find a 34-pin IDC header (or *ribbon cable connector*) on the motherboard for your floppy drives (usually labeled FDD). The floppy drive port will support two floppy drives (A and B) and can be disabled through a jumper on the motherboard. If you install a drive controller expansion board later, you need to disable the floppy drive port.

■ **Hard drive controllers (HDCs)**    You will probably find two 40-pin IDC headers (or *ribbon cable connectors*) on the motherboard for your hard drives (usually labeled "primary HDD" and "secondary HDD"). The primary hard drive port should support two Ultra-DMA/100/133 hard drives (C and D). The secondary hard drive port should also support two Ultra-DMA/100/133 drives, but may be limited to slightly older devices such as Ultra-DMA/66 or Ultra-DMA/33. If you install a drive controller expansion board later, you will need to disable these hard drive ports.

■ **Video controllers**    Your motherboard will probably offer a 15-pin high-density SVGA connector and 2 or 4MB of video RAM. This allows you to connect your monitor directly to the motherboard. The constant pressure to lower overall system costs has produced increased video integration. Intel 810 and 810E chipsets (and later) include built-in AGP graphics support. ALi and VIA offer chipsets that are tightly integrated with onboard AGP graphic engines from well-known video component manufacturers (ALi Aladdin TNT2 and VIA Apollo MVP4, PM601). If you need higher resolutions, color depths, more video memory, or better overall video performance, you can always disable the motherboard video system and install a video controller expansion board later on.

Hard drive connections

Floppy drive connection

**FIGURE  1-10**    You can easily see the floppy and hard drive controller connections on motherboards like this Soltek SL-75DRV5 Pentium 4 motherboard (Courtesy of Motherboards.org).

If maximum system performance and upgradeability are important, you should avoid motherboards with onboard video and select a motherboard containing a separate AGP slot. Current high-performance standards call for motherboard support for AGP 4X and video cards with at least 32MB of DDR memory.

# VIDEO SYSTEMS

All computers need a video system to display the text, graphics, and multimedia images associated with everyday computing. This is even more important for demanding video applications such as 3D rendering and visualization. A video system generally consists of two elements—the video controller and the monitor. This part of the chapter explains the issues involved with a typical video system, and shows you some important considerations in part selection.

## Video Controllers

Next to your motherboard, the video controller (see Figure 1-11) is a vitally important device. Indirectly, the video controller defines the "visualization capabilities" of your PC. With the intense interest in multimedia, video, and computer graphics, video systems are evolving at an incredible rate. The advantage of a motherboard-based video controller is convenience—you save money and need only plug a monitor into the motherboard's video connector. However, motherboard video controllers are limited in terms of memory and sophistication, and they cannot be upgraded without replacing the motherboard or installing a stand-alone video board. If you do not have a video controller already available on your motherboard (or wish to install a more powerful video system), you will have to install a stand-alone video board into a motherboard expansion slot. If your motherboard provides an AGP slot, an AGP video board will certainly offer superior performance.

**Resolutions and Color Depth**    Video boards are rated in terms of their resolution and color depth. The *resolution* is the number of pixels, which can be displayed on a monitor. Resolution is usually rated in

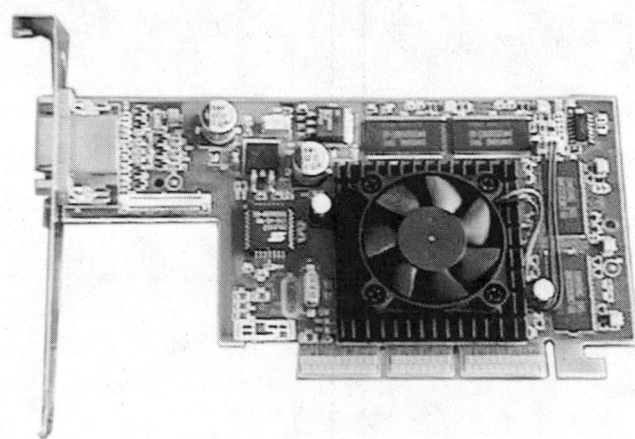

**FIGURE  1-11**    A high-performance AGP video card

terms of width × height (for example, 640 × 480). *Color depth* is the number of colors that can be displayed at a given resolution. Most current video boards can support resolutions up to 1280 × 1024 at color depths from 16 colors to 16 million colors. As a rule, Windows 98 and later will work fine with 800 × 600 resolution in 16-bit (high-color) mode. If you're considering the use of a DVD drive for MPEG-2 video, you should go for a video board that will support a minimum of 800 × 600 resolution in 24-bit or 32-bit (true color) mode.

Table 1-2 illustrates the capabilities of a typical high-end video board. For each standard resolution, you can see the various color depths that the board can handle. Note that color depths are often expressed as bits per pixel (or bits/pixel). Below each bits/pixel entry is the amount of video memory available. Note that more video memory allows higher resolutions and color depths. The relationship of bits to colors is as follows: 8 bits yields 265 colors, 16 bits supports 65 thousand colors (called *high color* mode), 24 bits provides 16 million colors (called *true color* mode), and 32 bits supplies an astounding 4 billion colors.

**Video Memory**    As you probably noticed in Table 1-2, video memory holds the data that composes your image. Higher resolutions and color depths require more video memory. The actual formula for memory is

```
total pixels x bits/pixel
```

Suppose you have an 800 × 600 image at 16 bits/pixel (65 thousand colors). That's 480,000 pixels (800 × 600). You would need 7,680,000 bits (480,000 × 16; 960,000 bytes or 960KB) of video memory to show one complete image on the screen. As a rule, select a video board with at *least* 8MB of video memory—preferably 16MB. If you're planning on a high-end 3D video board, plan on 16–32MB of video RAM.

**Video BIOS and Drivers**    All video boards running above 640 × 480 × 16 require the use of *video drivers* to support higher resolutions and color depths. While protected-mode drivers for Windows 98/Me/XP can easily support a wide range of enhanced video modes, this presents some unique problems for older DOS applications (especially games). When you select a video board, make sure that the video BIOS supports VESA 2.0 extensions or later. This eliminates the need for DOS VESA drivers. If you're using an older video board without VESA support in BIOS, try the Universal VESA display driver available from SciTech Software, Inc. at www.scitechsoft.com. Some game manufacturers also distribute the Universal VESA driver in their technical support Web site.

Given the importance of drivers, don't even think of buying a video board unless it comes with the very latest video drivers for Windows 98/Me/XP. Older Windows 3.1 video drivers will *not* work well with

**TABLE 1-2    VIDEO RESOLUTION AND COLOR DEPTH**

| RESOLUTION | BITS/PIXEL (2MB) | BITS/PIXEL (4MB) | BITS/PIXEL (8MB) |
|---|---|---|---|
| 640 × 480 | 8, 16, 24, 32 | 8, 16, 24, 32 | 8, 16, 24, 32 |
| 800 × 600 | 8, 16, 24, 32 | 8, 16, 24, 32 | 8, 16, 24, 32 |
| 1024 × 768 | 8, 16 | 8, 16, 24, 32 | 8, 16, 24, 32 |
| 1152 × 864 | 8, 16 | 8, 16, 24, 32 | 8, 16, 24, 32 |
| 1280 × 1024 | 8 | 8, 16, 24 | 8, 16, 24, 32 |
| 1600 × 1200 | 8 | 8, 16 | 8, 16, 24 |

Windows 98/Me/XP. Another issue to consider is driver age. Video drivers are some of the most frequently updated items, and you can usually find a video driver update on the video card manufacturer's technical support Web site. If you're installing a used video board that's a few years old, be sure to check for the latest drivers first.

## Monitors

The video controller drives your monitor, which actually displays the video image. In a sense, the monitor is your "window" into the PC. Choose a monitor with care—a poor-quality monitor can ruin the finest video image. In most cases, a 15- to 17-inch SVGA monitor with a dot spacing (or *pitch*) of 0.28 or less (preferably 0.26 or less) should produce a fine-looking image. If your customer works with computers extensively, you should recommend spending the extra money for a 20- or 21-inch monitor. Larger monitors support higher resolutions with great clarity (the fine detail of high resolution is not lost in the small screen), and allow you to "zoom" documents and drawings with far more clarity than you could achieve with a smaller monitor. You should also recommend monitors that are *noninterlaced*. Interlaced monitors tend to show more flicker and cause more eye fatigue. You will notice that the monitor's signal cable has a 15-pin high-density connector on the end, which will fit perfectly with the connector on your video board. You can actually use any compatible monitor to test the video output of a system. The information contained at the Hitachi Web site (www.hitachidisplays.com/how_monitors/index.htm) can take some of the mystery out of all of those monitor specifications.

Today, virtually all monitors are non-interlaced, but it's still very helpful for you to know the distinction between interlaced and non-interlaced monitors.

# SOUND SYSTEMS

Originally driven by the needs of game developers, sound boards have quickly evolved as a replacement for the obnoxious beeping and tweeting of a PC speaker. Over the last 15 years, sound has become a prominent feature of virtually all new systems. Today, good-quality sound boards (such as the SoundBlaster Audigy card in Figure 1-12) provide efficient sound-file playback, extremely precise sound synthesis, and orchestral-quality music. Whether you plan to play audio CDs, use the newest games, watch your favorite DVD movie, or make multimedia presentations, you will almost certainly need a good-quality sound device in your computer. Many traditional sound cards use an ISA slot because of its low cost and simplicity. This has generally worked well because of the relatively low bandwidth demanded by sound systems. However, in the interests of creating complete plug-and-play systems, select a newer sound card using a PCI slot, if possible.

If your motherboard already incorporates an onboard sound device, you will *not* need a separate sound board. Simply install the motherboard's sound drivers and connect your speakers to the Line Out jack (usually color-coded green) located with the rest of the motherboard's ports.

## Sound Issues

Unless you're a real audiophile, you probably won't be able to detect a significant sound difference between good-quality sound cards, so feel free to compare prices. Still, there are some issues to consider while you're recommending sound hardware for upgrades, replacements, or new builds.

**3D Sound**    If you're into computer gaming, select a sound card that supports 3D sound (for example, A3D support). This technology uses almost negligible delays and slight differences in volume to simulate "positional sound." If an enemy fires a gun or calls for help off to your left, you'll seem to hear them on

**FIGURE 1-12**    The SoundBlaster Audigy card provides excellent sound for the PC (Courtesy of Creative Labs).

your left. Positional sound is a real boon in 3D first-person "shooters," where sound can be a helpful cue. Some high-end sound cards will also include additional speaker output jacks for a true surround-sound experience—you can even hear enemies sneaking up behind you.

**MIDI/Game Port**    You'll also probably notice a 15-pin connector on the sound board. This is the MIDI port—if you have a MIDI instrument (such as a synthesizer keyboard), you can connect it to the sound board and compose your own music. If you're "musically challenged," you can switch the MIDI port to serve as a standard joystick port. You can enable or disable the game port through a jumper on the sound board. If you already have another game port (or multi-I/O card) in the system, you can leave the port disabled.

**MIDI Memory**    High-end sound boards (such as the Sound Blaster Live 5.1 or Audigy) often provide SIMM slots for additional memory. This is MIDI memory and is used when composing MIDI music, or taking sound samples. If you're not going to be composing music, don't bother buying extra memory for the sound board.

**CD Audio Connector**    When selecting a sound board, look for the CD audio connector. It's a small, 4-pin connector usually located at the top of the sound board, roughly in the middle. You'll run a thin, four-wire cable between the CD drive's audio output and the sound board—this is how you get your favorite CD to play through your sound board's speakers. Today's high-end sound boards may have two or three audio connectors to support audio from CD-ROM/CD-RW and DVD-ROM drives in the same system. A connector is also sometimes supplied for a voice modem's input/output. If there is no CD audio connector, you'll have to run a patch cable from the CD-ROM drive's headphone output to the sound card's line input, and then adjust the sound board's mixer to set the correct CD audio level.

**Speakers**    You'll also need to connect some powered speakers for the sound board. Do your customer a favor and recommend a few extra dollars for some decent powered speakers capable of a wide frequency range. Inexpensive speakers can sound "tinny" and can ruin the output of even the best sound board. If you have a choice, avoid battery-powered speakers (unless you can afford a regular stream of new batteries). Other multimedia (such as DVD movies) will also benefit from good-quality speakers. Try to avoid the speakers that are incorporated into monitors. While they are a convenience, their sound quality is often poor.

# DRIVE SYSTEMS

PCs use a wide range of drives that you should be familiar with. Drives serve two vital purposes. First, drives provide permanent storage for your programs and files (including the operating system). Second, drives allow for the convenient and economical distribution or exchange of programs and files. In most cases, you're going to use a minimum of three drives: a floppy drive, a hard drive, and a CD drive (which could be a CD-ROM, CD-R, CD-RW, or even a DVD drive), such as those shown in Figure 1-13. However, there are other drives that you should also be familiar with. This part of the chapter explores the various drives that you will commonly encounter and covers the essential points that you should be aware of.

## IDE Drive Controllers

It is quite common for a motherboard to provide two IDE-type (40-pin) drive controller ports and one floppy controller (34-pin) port as shown in Figure 1-10 earlier. If so, you do not need to use a separate drive controller card. If your motherboard does not offer an onboard drive controller, you *will* need to add one in an available expansion slot (though that is rare today). As a *minimum,* the drive controller should support up to two Ultra-DMA/100/133 hard drives on a *primary* controller port (C: and D:) and up to two more UDMA/EIDE/IDE devices on a *secondary* controller port (E: and F:). The controller should also support at least one floppy drive (usually the A: drive). If a motherboard has PCI bus slots, you should certainly recommend a PCI drive controller for best performance.

**FIGURE  1-13**    A typical PC sporting a CD-RW, hard drive, and floppy drive

If you're going to use Ultra-DMA/66 or Ultra-DMA/100/133 drives, but your motherboard does not support the corresponding Ultra-DMA drive interface, you may choose to disable the motherboard's controller and install an appropriate Ultra-DMA controller card. You can use the existing controller, but the performance of your drives will be limited to that controller.

## SCSI Controllers

Now is a good time to bring up the subject of *Small Computer System Interface* (SCSI) controllers. SCSI is a "bus-type" system that allows numerous different devices to all share a common signal bus cable. SCSI hard drives, SCSI CD-ROM drives, SCSI tape drives, SCSI scanners, SCSI Zip or Jaz drives, and numerous other SCSI devices can all coexist and share a single SCSI cable. In fact, most drives can be obtained with a SCSI interface rather than an IDE-type (40-pin) interface. While many motherboards support the UDMA interface, few support a native SCSI interface. If you plan on supporting SCSI devices in your new PC, you'll almost certainly need to add a SCSI controller board to the system.

If a motherboard provides PCI bus slots, be sure to recommend a PCI SCSI controller for optimum performance. Keep in mind that installing a SCSI controller will demand system resources (namely an IRQ and some amount of I/O space, as well as space for the SCSI BIOS). Another major issue with SCSI is *termination*—both ends of a signal cable must be properly terminated, or none of the SCSI devices may function properly. Termination is certainly not difficult, but can be tricky to master, and termination oversights are one of the most frequent causes of SCSI installation and upgrade problems.

**SCSI and UDMA**    Contrary to popular belief, SCSI and UDMA/EIDE interfaces can coexist just fine. It is certainly possible to have Ultra-DMA hard drives and a SCSI scanner and CD-ROM, or an ATAPI CD-ROM with two SCSI hard drives, or Ultra-DMA and SCSI hard drives, and so on. The trick is that your system will try to boot from UDMA/EIDE drives *first.* In other words, if you have an Ultra-DMA hard drive and a SCSI hard drive in the same system, the Ultra-DMA drive will traditionally be the boot device. However, late-model SCSI controllers are starting to offer an option that will override the UDMA/EIDE boot device and allow a SCSI drive to boot the system even if there is another drive present (this is a feature of the latest SCSI BIOS versions).

**SCSI vs. UDMA**    Even though UDMA/EIDE and SCSI devices will work together (as long as there are no hardware conflicts between the SCSI and non-SCSI controllers), the question remains as to which is "better." The line between SCSI and Ultra-DMA has grown a bit murky over the last few years. It used to be that if you needed very large drives and top performance, you stuck with SCSI. Today, SCSI and IDE-type devices share remarkably similar performance characteristics. Today, SCSI drives are typically smaller than the available Ultra-DMA models (which are exceeding 100GB) and the largest SCSI drives are generally quite expensive. Both are fine interfaces, but you need to make your choice based on the advantages and disadvantages of each interface.

SCSI only requires one controller to handle up to seven SCSI devices (like hard drives, tape drives, scanners, and so on). All of those drives can be connected to the same SCSI signal bus. As a result, the hardware and cabling requirements are simpler. When you deal with SCSI, you also need to deal with drivers—you need an ASPI driver for the SCSI controller, and all other SCSI devices in your system (except for hard drives, which are handled by the SCSI BIOS). This can be a problem if you install protected-mode drivers for Windows 98/Me/XP, and then need to use the devices under DOS. On the other hand, installing real-mode drivers for DOS can interfere with Windows operation. Finally, not all SCSI devices are equally compatible with every SCSI controller. For example, if you replace your SCSI controller with a different make and model, you'll need to install a whole new set of drivers—and probably even have to reformat your SCSI hard drives.

Mixing DOS and Windows drivers is not a problem under later Windows operating systems like XP. XP effectively does away with the real mode (DOS), so you'd need to boot from a diskette with startup files and DOS drivers on it.

By comparison, Ultra-DMA offers its own set of challenges. Some UDMA/EIDE controllers provide one fast Ultra-DMA channel, and one slower channel—both channels can only support two devices. You usually put the fast devices (e.g., your hard drives) on the Ultra-DMA channel, and put the slower devices (such as your CD drives) on the secondary channel. This complicates the installation and cabling a bit, and you may run into trouble mixing slow and fast devices (such as CD-ROM drives and hard drives) on the same channel. However, Ultra-DMA devices are readily available, and can be as much as several hundred dollars cheaper than their SCSI counterparts. UDMA/EIDE is also supported directly in BIOS, so you don't need drivers to run the drive controller (though you still need ATAPI drivers for some devices like CD-ROM drives). This makes UDMA/EIDE equally robust under DOS and Windows 98/Me/XP.

In short, Ultra-DMA is the choice when price is your top concern, and you won't need to expand your system very much. SCSI is the way to go when you need the very best multitasking performance and capacity, and you plan to add a large number of devices to the system (such as building your own Windows 2000 or XP Professional server).

**SCSI BIOS and Drivers**     SCSI BIOS is required in order to operate SCSI hard drives. If you have SCSI hard drives in your system, you'll need to have the SCSI BIOS enabled. Keep in mind that the SCSI BIOS will occupy space in the upper memory area (UMA) along with the motherboard BIOS, video BIOS, and any other BIOS in the system. If you need a SCSI controller for such things as a scanner, and there are no SCSI hard drives, you can almost always disable the SCSI BIOS.

Drivers are another important SCSI issue. The SCSI controller, and all other SCSI devices (except for hard drives), uses drivers. You'll need real-mode drivers to operate the SCSI system under DOS, and protected-mode drivers to run your SCSI devices under Windows 98/Me/XP. Drivers are always provided with the respective SCSI device, but always make it a point to keep your SCSI drivers updated. The latest SCSI drivers are typically available for download from each particular SCSI manufacturer.

## Floppy Drives

*Floppy drives* are the classical "removable media," and floppy disks remain a simple and convenient means of distributing software or moving files between PCs. Your drive controller will support at least one floppy drive, but may handle up to two (A: and B: drives). You will need a 34-pin ribbon cable to attach your floppy drive(s) to the drive controller. Today, all you really need is one 3.5-inch floppy drive, though you'll usually only need it for booting emergency DOS/rescue diskettes.

**Floppy Cables and Jumpers**     Take a look at the floppy drive cable. You'll notice that there is a single 34-pin connector at one end and two 34-pin connectors at the other. The end with the single connector attaches to the drive controller, the "middle" connector attaches to drive B:, and the endmost connector attaches to drive A:. The cable should not exceed about 2 feet (around 60 cm) in length. If the system supports only one floppy drive, the cable may not offer any middle connector.

If you look closely, you'll also notice that the floppy drive probably has several jumpers. These jumpers serve several purposes, but as a general rule, you should *not* move them. Most floppy drives are jumpered as drive B:. That's fine because the little twist you see near the drive end of your floppy cable converts the endmost drive back to A:.

## Hard Drives

The *hard drive* is really the center of your mass-storage strategy. The media is not removable, but hard drives provide huge amounts of very fast storage. An Ultra-DMA drive controller will typically support up to two fast UDMA drives and up to two UDMA/EIDE devices, so expect to find at least one Ultra-DMA hard drive (20GB or larger) on the (primary) UDMA channel. If you use an ATAPI IDE CD drive, you can place it on the secondary channel. Drive prices drop so fast that you can get very large drives for a reasonable price.

**Hard Drive Cable**    Take a look at the hard drive cable. You'll notice that there is one 40-pin connector at one end and two 40-pin connectors at the other. The end with the single connector plugs into the drive controller, and the other connectors plug into the drives. Unlike floppy drive cables, the hard drive cable has no effect on drive letter assignments. The Ultra-DMA/66, Ultra-DMA/100, or Ultra-DMA/133 cable is a 40-pin/80-conductor cable, but it is almost identical in appearance to the regular 40-pin/40-conductor IDE cable—be sure to use the correct cable for UDMA/66/100/133 drives.

It is critical that *all* the components for supporting UDMA/66/100/133 are in place before you enable it on the drive. If you place an UDMA/66/100/133 enabled drive in a system that does not fully support it, you will easily find yourself with lost or corrupt data. For example, without the proper cable, the signal will deteriorate as it passes through the cable at such high speeds. Also, there are some older BIOS versions that do not support UDMA/66/100/133. For example, these BIOS versions will detect that the drive supports Ultra-DMA/66 and instruct the drive to operate in Ultra-DMA/66 mode. The result could be corrupted data. In many cases, an improper or damaged cable will cause the BIOS to run your UDMA/66/100/133 drives in the slower UDMA/33 mode.

**Drive Jumpers**    UDMA/EIDE hard drives use jumpers to define their relationship. Drives can be set as the primary drive ("master") or the secondary drive ("slave") using jumpers as shown in Figure 1-14. A primary and secondary drive can be installed on each of the two drive channels, so the controller can support up to four drives. The first drive installed on the first (UDMA) channel should be jumpered as the primary drive (this will be C:). The second drive installed on the first (UDMA) channel should be jumpered as the secondary drive (this will be D:). The first drive installed on the second (UDMA or EIDE) channel should be jumpered as the primary drive (this will be E:), and the second drive installed on the second (UDMA or EIDE) channel should be jumpered as the secondary drive (this will be F:). As a rule, do *not* use the "cable select" (or CS) jumper option if one is available.

SCSI devices are identified in a slightly different manner using eight ID numbers (0 to 7). The SCSI controller is typically assigned ID7, and the first two SCSI hard drives are usually given ID0 (the boot drive) and ID1. Other SCSI devices use the remaining SCSI IDs. All SCSI IDs are selected through the use of jumpers.

The preceding example drive letters assume a single partition on each drive (such as FAT32). Multiple partitions will alter the actual drive letter assignments. This Microsoft article explains the procedure used by DOS/Windows to assign drive letters: support.microsoft.com/support/kb/articles/Q51/9/78.asp.

**Drive Parameters**    When installing a hard drive, you need to configure drive parameters in the system's CMOS Setup. Parameters usually include: cylinders, sectors/track, heads, landing zone, and write pre-compensation. You'll need to locate those parameters in the drive's documentation, and be sure to record them for future reference. If your BIOS and drives support *auto-detection* (as virtually all do today), you may be able to get away with auto-detecting the hard drive rather than entering specific parameters.

Drive master/slave jumper(s)

**FIGURE  1-14**    One or more jumpers are used to configure IDE-type drives as "master" or "slave" devices.

Modern motherboards and BIOS versions make installing a hard drive extremely easy—enable LBA (Logical Block Addressing) and Auto-Detect in BIOS after you attach the drive. You should see the hard drive identified and entered in the BIOS automatically. The numbers entered for Cylinders, Heads, and Sectors (if any) may not match the actual numbers for the drive (because LBA uses a mathematical formula to determine these numbers instead). Still, the size of the hard drive (in MB or GB) entered automatically by the BIOS should be correct. The auto-detection routine of the BIOS may display a list of optional results after examining your hard drive. You are then able to select between Normal, Large, and LBA modes for actually recording your drive parameters in your BIOS. LBA is almost always the best option.

If you're transferring a hard drive containing information from one system to another, you must enter the hard drive information in the new system *exactly* as it was in the original system. The auto-detection feature of modern BIOS will simplify this problem, but be sure to make a record of the original drive parameters before removing it.

## CD-ROM Drives

Virtually all major software applications are now distributed on CD (and many are even partially run from the CD). As a consequence, CD-ROM drives have emerged as an absolute necessity in the modern computer. The typical CD-ROM drive is an inexpensive and reliable device that requires almost no maintenance. More recently, CD-ROM drives have become "bootable," though you need a suitable drive, BIOS, and bootable CD media to make use of this feature. Plan on at least one CD-ROM drive for your new system, or select a fast model to replace a failed or aging drive.

Many current systems are using CD-RW drives rather than ordinary CD-ROM or CD-R drives. CD-RW drives provide the rewritability of CD-RW technology, the writability of a CD-R, and the fast disc reading of a CD-ROM drive.

CD-ROM drives are rated in terms of seek time and transfer speed. *Seek time*—the time required to locate desired information—can be as much as 100 or 200 milliseconds (ms). *Transfer speed*—the rate at which data is transferred from the drive to the interface—is a multiple of the original floppy drive transfer speed of 150 KB/sec. For example, a 2X CD transfers data at 300 KB/s, a 4X CD transfers data at 600 KB/s, and so on. Today, you can get 24X and 36X drives at very reasonable prices—48X to 56X versions are readily available. With the recent emergence of CD-R, CD-RW, and DVD technology, it is unlikely that ordinary CD-ROM drives will become much faster.

**CD-ROM Interfaces**    Older CD-ROM drives used any one of several proprietary interfaces (such as Mitsumi, Panasonic, and so forth). That worked fine with "multimedia kits," where the drive's controller was integrated into the sound board (or other proprietary card). If you didn't have a controller handy, though, you were stuck. Today, all major CD-type drives offer an ATAPI IDE interface, which is exactly the same interface as your hard drive. You can then install the CD-ROM with any IDE/EIDE/UDMA drive controller. If you have a secondary channel on your drive controller, an ATAPI IDE CD-ROM drive is a perfect fit. As a rule, never install a hard drive and CD-ROM drive together on the same channel—they certainly can operate together, but there's a possibility that the slower CD drive may impair the faster data transfers offered by the hard drive.

**CD Audio**    If you want to play CD audio through your sound board, you will need to connect the audio output of your CD-ROM drive to your sound board or motherboard (if you have built-in sound support) through a thin, four-wire audio cable. Some sound boards offer two or three input connectors to support systems with both CD-ROM/CD-RW and DVD-ROM/DVD-RAM drives. Verify that the CD-ROM drive comes with a suitable connector for CD audio.

## CD-RW Drives

The decreasing costs of CD-ROM and CD-R technology, the slow trend toward DVD recordable drive introduction, and the need to re-record a CD led to the development of CD-RW (rewriteable) drives. These drives can accomplish all the tasks of a standard CD-ROM and CD-R drive, yet you can record and erase files from a CD-RW disc with the same ease as a floppy disk. In addition, they can use both CD-R and CD-RW media for recording. The expanding number of newer CD-ROM drives with MultiRead capability also improves the likelihood of other systems being able to read a CD-R or a CD-RW disc created on a CD-RW drive.

If you don't need the capabilities of a CD-R or CD-RW drive, you should only consider purchasing MultiRead-capable CD-ROM drives so that discs recorded on other CD-RW drives will be readable on your system.

Modern CD-RW drives offer a wide variety of possibilities to meet the file management needs of the average computer owner. You can make copies of entire music and data CDs (or only copy individual files or songs). You can make your own custom CDs by recording a preselected group of files, or by creating an image file on your hard drive before using your CD-RW drive to record it. You can even tackle unattended backups of over 450MB per disc. CD-R discs created with a modern CD-RW drive can be read by just about every present-day system, which allows you to send large files through the mail on a single disc.

A major disadvantage of earlier CD-RW drives was their lack of support for drag-and-drop file copying—to copy even a single file, you had to launch the application for controlling the CD-RW drive. Modern CD-RW drives can format an entire CD-RW disc through the UDF file system. You can then leave the CD-RW disc in the drive and use it just like a big floppy drive. Any of the methods you would normally use to manipulate files on or between your floppy and hard drive can now be used with your CD-RW drive and disc. This includes drag and drop, copy and paste, right-click context menu commands, and menu bar commands.

UDF-formatted CD-RW discs can be read only by systems that have a UDF Reader utility installed. Roxio offers a free reader at its Web site (www.roxio.com).

**CD-RW Characteristics**    The two major considerations in selecting a CD-RW drive are the *interface* connection and the drive *speed*. You can choose between an ATAPI IDE or SCSI CD-RW drive. SCSI is considered a better data-transfer method (and might help to prevent buffer underrun problems), but you'll need to include SCSI support (such as installing a SCSI controller). SCSI drives are also more expensive than IDE. IDE-type drives (e.g., IDE, EIDE, or UDMA) are more popular and widely used. Almost all motherboards include two UDMA/EIDE channels supporting up to four IDE-type devices. In terms of speed, you'll see three numbers used to characterize a CD-RW drive: $record \times rewrite \times read$ (for example, $4 \times 2 \times 16$ or $4 \times 6 \times 32$). For example, a modern $10 \times 4 \times 32$ CD-RW drive offers 10X writing speed, 4X rewriting speed, and 32X reading speed (like an ordinary CD-ROM).

## DVD Drives

Today, conventional CD-ROM technology is showing its age, and a single CD no longer provides enough storage for the increasing demands of data-intensive applications and multimedia. A new generation of high-density optical storage called DVD-ROM is now becoming standard equipment on many new systems intended for entertainment. The acronym DVD stands for several different things. In the early phase of DVD development, it stood for *digital video disc.* Later on, it stood for *digital versatile disc* (because it could hold programs and data as well as video and sound). But regardless of what you call it, DVD technology can provide gigabytes of removable optical storage on your desktop PC. In addition, the DVD drive is fully backward-compatible with CD audio, CD-ROM, CD-I, and other popular CD formats, so the DVD can actually replace your existing CD-ROM drive (the DVD-ROM drive just cannot record).

**DVD Interfaces and Jumpers**    DVD drives are now available with either SCSI or ATAPI IDE interfaces, so no proprietary interface card is required. This simplifies installation and replacement quite a bit. The ATAPI IDE version can easily coexist as a secondary (or "slave" drive) with your existing hard drive on the same controller channel (unlike older CD-ROM drives, which could interfere with high-performance data transfers). You can also install the DVD drive on a secondary controller channel. Jumpers on the drive allow you to define the DVD drive as a "master," "slave," or "cable select." As a rule, avoid the use of cable select (CS). As a SCSI drive, you can place the DVD drive almost anywhere in the SCSI chain. The most critical aspect of SCSI installations is to terminate the SCSI chain properly, and jumper the DVD drive with an unused SCSI ID number (usually between ID2 and ID6).

The DVD drive does not require a stand-alone MPEG-2 decoder board for basic drive operation (such as reading files from a DVD disc), but the decoder is usually recommended for the reliable playback of DVD-video and Dolby audio.

**CD-Audio**    If you want to play audio from the DVD drive through your sound board, you will need to connect the audio output of your DVD-ROM drive to your sound board through a thin, four-wire audio cable. Make sure that the DVD-ROM drive comes with a suitable connector for CD audio. Remember, unless you buy a DVD-ROM and MPEG-2 decoder board together as a multimedia kit, you may have to buy the CD audio cable separately.

Even though a sound board is not included in a DVD kit, the CD audio cable is typically included in a DVD kit. If you already have a CD-ROM or other drive feeding CD audio to the sound card, you may wish to connect the DVD drive's audio signal there instead, or select a sound card that offers more than one CD audio connection.

**MPEG-2 Decoder Board**    One of the major advances with DVD technology is the development of high-quality video and audio playback—however, the immense volume of data required would demand several DVD discs worth of storage. To provide full-length feature movies on a single 4GB disc, the video and audio data must be highly *compressed* using the MPEG-2 standard. When the presentation is played, that compressed data must be decompressed. Decompression is a processor-intensive operation. With ever-increasing processing power, a PC can usually handle DVD decompression and playback with a software decoder and no additional hardware. However, you may find that playback may seem choppy (especially if you're running other applications in the background).

If you want to smooth out your DVD playback, consider installing a decoder card. This may be a necessity when upgrading an older PC for DVD. The DVD passes audio and video data to a PCI MPEG-2 decoder board for processing. The use of hardware decoding removes a large processing burden from the system CPU. The MPEG-2 board then passes video data directly to the monitor and audio directly to the sound board's "line input" (a pass-through is provided so that signals from your existing video board are routed through the MPEG-2 board). Keep in mind that a decoder board is not an interface for the DVD drive, but rather a supplemental part of the complete DVD package. The decoder is not used when running programs or accessing other data from a DVD disc.

# MODEMS
The Internet has become an icon of the global information age. You can access information, make purchases, read articles, solve technical problems, or even chat and exchange mail with anyone else online. If you've ever considered going online (or already have online accounts), you're going to need a modem to access the Internet, and other online resources like America Online or FTP sites. Rapid advances in modem technology have resulted in dramatic increases in connection speeds, while competition has lowered the cost of modems. Intense competition between online service providers has also lowered the costs of going online. Chances are that you'll be installing or upgrading numerous modems (see Figure 1-15) for your customers.

## Internal vs. External
You have the choice between internal and external modems. From a practical standpoint, both offer equivalent performance. The trade-off comes in considering your installation issues. *Internal* modems do not require a separate power supply, and do not take up space outside of the PC, but they do use their own built-in COM port (and IRQ). This means you may need to disable or reconfigure any corresponding COM port already in the system to avoid potential hardware conflicts. By comparison, *external* modems do need a separate power source and take up a bit of space, but you can connect it directly to any open COM port in the system—this simplifies installation a bit. Also, the external modem is mobile, and you can take it from system to system if necessary—though external modems are often a few dollars more expensive than internal models.

## Modem Speed
The rule with modems is "the faster the better," but "faster" does not always *guarantee* top-speed communication. *Both* ends of the communication link must be capable of the same top speed, or the link will be

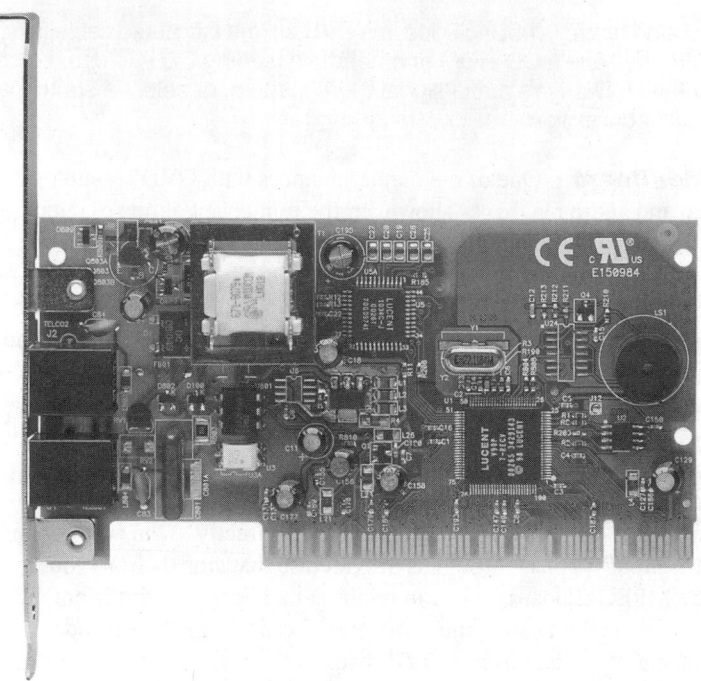

**FIGURE  1-15**   A Zoom Telephonics V.92/V.44 analog internal 56 Kbps modem provides dial-up
Internet access for individual PC users (courtesy of Zoom Telephonics).

limited by the speed of the *slowest* modem. For example, if you buy a 56 Kbps modem and call an *Internet Service Provider* (ISP) with only a 33.6 Kbps modem, the top speed you'll get is only 33.6 Kbps. Other factors such as poor telephone connections and incorrect drivers may also serve to hamper your communication performance. Opt for 56 Kbps, V.92/V.44 standard modems if your ISP will support such speeds. If you really need the highest possible speeds on your desktop, contact your local telephone or cable company to check out the costs involved with advanced technologies such as cable modem or DSL service.

> Check with your local cable provider or telephone company before selecting a cable modem or DSL modem. You must verify that the respective service is available in your area, evaluate the pricing plan(s), and set up an account. If you do opt for a high-speed service, the cable company or telephone company may even provide the appropriate modem for you as part of your service, so you might be able to save the cost of a device.

One other note—try to avoid the use of WinModems if at all possible, and opt for full-featured fax/modems wherever possible. WinModem-type products compensate for highly simplified (though inexpensive) hardware by making heavy use of Windows 98/Me/XP resources. While this may not be a problem for current Windows platforms, older systems may be bogged down by the demands of a WinModem. A WinModem will also not function under DOS.

## Modem Drivers and Software

Modems demand drivers and communication software to function. The new modem will come with drivers on disk, but you should also check the modem manufacturer's Web site to see if there are any updates or patches available (especially if you have trouble getting the modem to work). Today, you can generally forego classical communication software (like HyperTerminal or SmartCom for Windows) and simply bind TCP/IP (a.k.a. network) drivers to your modem for dial-up Internet access. Fortunately, your ISP will provide you with detailed instructions on how to do that.

# INPUT DEVICES

Of course, you also need to get commands and selections to the PC. This is accomplished through the use of *input devices*. As a minimum, you'll need a mouse and keyboard for your new system. If you play any sort of flight simulator or other interactive game, you should also plan on a joystick.

## Mouse

Select a good-quality pointing device. It can be a mouse or a trackball (depending on your personal taste). You generally have the choice between a *serial* mouse, *PS/2* mouse, and *USB* mouse. There is also a *bus* mouse, but that has fallen into disuse. Serial and PS/2 mice are basically the same thing—the port connectors are just a bit different. A USB mouse simply connects to a USB port on the PC, or USB hub. There are no real advantages of any one type of mouse.

**Two-Button or Three-Button**    The choice of two-button or three-button mice is really a matter of personal preference. Most programs only recognize two buttons (left-click or right-click). A middle button is generally used only by specialized programs (like CAD software)—otherwise, it is ignored. Unless your customer has a specific use for that third mouse button, recommend that they save a few dollars and go with a two-button unit.

**Mouse Drivers**    All mice will require a mouse driver. If you use DOS applications, you'll need a real-mode mouse driver loaded in CONFIG.SYS or AUTOEXEC.BAT. If you use Windows, you'll use a protected-mode mouse driver. The drivers will accompany your mouse on floppy disk, though Windows will auto-detect the mouse and usually load suitable drivers right from its own internal driver library. Once you install the mouse drivers, you shouldn't need to mess with them again, but if you change the mouse later, you'll want to remove the old mouse drivers before installing the new ones.

**Routine Maintenance**    A mouse requires periodic routine maintenance to clean out the dust, debris, and hair that accumulates around the mouse ball and rollers. This typically involves removing the mouse ball, and then cleaning it and the rollers. In actual practice, the process takes no longer than five minutes. Cleaning is indicated when the mouse cursor starts to "skip" or "stall" while moving the mouse. Optical mice use light to detect movement and do not need routine cleaning.

## Keyboard

Obviously, every computer needs a keyboard. There are about as many different sizes, shapes, and features for a keyboard as there are for a mouse. But there are some key points to consider. First, make sure that the keyboard connector is compatible with the keyboard connector on the motherboard. Today, most keyboards use the small PS/2-type barrel connector, and a growing number use a USB port.

**Comfort and Ergonomics**    Try the keyboard if you can, and make sure that the keys *feel* comfortable. You may also care to try an "ergonomic" keyboard, which is typically a bit easier on the hands and wrists. This may seem like a trivial matter now, but better ergonomics now can prevent persistent wrist pain and fatigue later.

**QWERTY vs. Dvorak**    You generally have two keyboard styles to choose from: QWERTY and Dvorak. The QWERTY style is the conventional typewriter key layout. This has been the standard typewriter layout for 125 years, so you will have no trouble finding QWERTY keyboards. Dvorak keyboards use a more efficient placement of keys, which results in less finger and hand movement—this reduces hand strain (and makes typing a bit faster). Dvorak keyboards are harder to find, but it is possible to convert your QWERTY keyboard to Dvorak under Windows 9*x* and later.

### Joystick

Joysticks are not required for a PC, but if your customer plans to do any serious flight simulation or other interactive 3D gaming, a good-quality joystick will be an absolute necessity. By themselves, joysticks are fairly simple devices—really little more than a couple of potentiometers, a few buttons, and a couple of springs. But when used for PC games, the joystick adds a level of control that is simply impossible to achieve with any other input device.

**Game Ports**    All joysticks require a 15-pin game port to function. Most sound boards and I/O boards incorporate a game port already, so obtaining a game port is not a problem. However, only one game port can be active in the system at any given time. If you have more than one game port in the PC, it is vital that you remember to disable all but one. Otherwise, you'll find that your joystick behaves erratically and that you have little (if any) control.

**Joystick Drivers and Calibration**    In the DOS world, joystick drivers were not required—each individual application was required to service the joystick. Under Windows 9*x*/Me/XP, joystick drivers allow a single, uniform joystick environment that any Windows game can use. Regardless of whether you use DOS or Windows, you still have to calibrate the joystick periodically, because of the way in which the game port reads the analog signals from the joystick.

**Routine Maintenance**    In general, joysticks require no routine maintenance. Still, you'll find that the exposed pivot of a joystick is a magnet for dust and debris. You should make it a point to occasionally blow out any accumulations of dust or dirt. If the joystick experiences "dead areas" (where moving the stick causes no change in the program), it could be that the X or Y potentiometers are wearing out, and you should consider replacing the joystick.

# Disassembly/Reassembly Notes

All too often, the *mechanics* of PC repair—taking the system apart and putting it back together again—are overlooked or treated as an afterthought. As you saw in the first part of this chapter, PC assemblies are not terribly complicated, but a careless or rushed approach to the repair can do more harm than good. Lost parts and collateral damage to the system are certain ways to lose a customer (and perhaps open yourself to legal recourse). This section outlines a set of considerations that can help ensure a speedy, top-quality repair effort.

## THE VALUE OF DATA

It is a fact of modern computing that the *data* contained on a customer's hard drive(s) is usually more valuable than the PC hardware itself. If your customer is an entrepreneur or corporate client, you can expect that the system contains valuable accounting, technical, reference, design, or operations information that is vital to their business. As a consequence, you should make it a priority to protect yourself from any potential liability issues connected with your customer's data. Even if the drives are *causing* the problem, a customer may hold you responsible if you are unable to restore or recover their precious information. Start a consistent regimen of written and oral precautions. Such precautions should include (but are not limited to):

- Always advise your customers to *back up* their systems regularly. Before customers bring in their system, advise them to perform a complete backup of their drives *if possible*.

- Always advise your customers to *check* (or verify) their backups—a backup is useless if it can't be restored.

- When customers deliver a system for repair, be sure that they sign a *work order.* Work orders should expressly give you authority and permission to work on the customer's system, outline such things as your hourly rate, labor minimums for evaluation and service, and show all applicable disclaimers. Your work order should include a strong disclaimer expressly relieving you of any and all liability for the contents of any magnetic media (for example, hard drives) in the system. If you attempt data recovery, the disclaimer should also disclaim any warranty or guarantee of results—that way, you're not liable if you are *unable* to recover vital files. Since liability issues vary from state to state and country to country, a local attorney can advise you on specific wording.

## OPENING THE SYSTEM

Most desktop and tower systems use a metal chassis covered by a painted metal cover or shroud that is secured with a series of screws. There are often nine screws—two on either side of the enclosure, and five at the rear of the chassis. While this pattern covers many of the desktop PCs in service, you are likely to encounter a number of variations. You may find that the screws are bolted in from the bottom rather than from the sides. There may also be more or fewer screws in the rear of the chassis. Some enclosures use snap-in covers that are bolted in the front, then covered with a plastic molding. Finally, a growing number of "screwless" enclosures allow technicians to quickly access the inside of a PC without tools (such as the Amtrade 73 mid-tower ATX screwless enclosure in Figure 1-16).

Tower cases are a bit different. The metal shroud also uses about nine screws—all secured from the rear. The bottom and front edges of the enclosure are typically bent inward to interlock with the chassis when seated properly. This approach allows the entire enclosure to fit securely along the whole chassis while using only a minimum of screws. Enclosures that do not interlock, however, may require screws along the bottom and front edges. As a general rule, PC enclosure manufacturers tend to minimize the use of visible screws in order to enhance a "seamless" appearance—this is why most screws are relegated to the back of the chassis.

There are three factors to keep in mind when removing screws and other mounting hardware. First, be extremely careful not to mark or gouge the painted metal enclosure. Customers are rightfully possessive of their PC investment, and putting a scratch or dent in an enclosure is tantamount to dinging their new car (a careless reputation is very bad for business). Be equally careful of the enclosure after removing and setting it aside. Second, store the screws in a safe, organized place. The old "egg carton" trick may seem cliché, but it really does work. Of course, you are free to use plastic bags or organizer boxes as well—the idea here is to keep screws and other hardware *off* the work surface (unless you enjoy picking them up off the floor). Third, take note of each screw as you remove it, and keep groups of screws separated. This allows you to put the right screws back into the corresponding locations. Since most enclosures use screws of equal size and length, this is rarely an issue at this phase of disassembly. But as you dismantle other subassemblies for upgrade or repair, keeping track of hardware becomes an important concern.

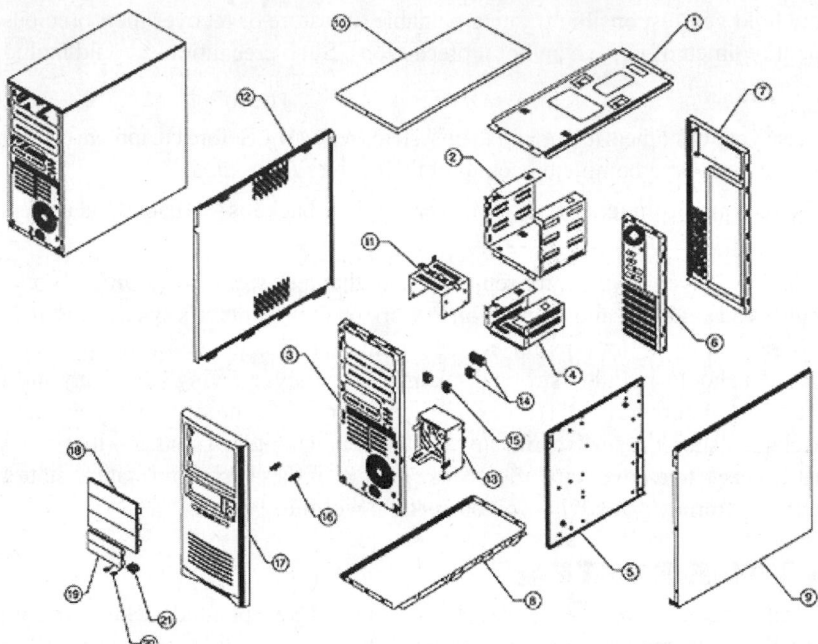

**FIGURE  1-16**    The Amtrade 73 mid-tower ATX enclosure offers screwless entry for easy system checking and upgrades (Courtesy of Amtrade).

Use care when sliding the enclosure off the chassis. Metal inserts or reinforcements welded to the cover can easily catch on ribbon cables or other wiring. This can result in damage to the cable, and damage to whatever the cable is attached to. The rule here is simple: force nothing! If you encounter any resistance at all, stop and search for the obstruction carefully—it's faster to clear an obstruction than to replace a damaged cable.

## CLOSING THE SYSTEM

After your repair or upgrade is complete, you need to close the system. Before sliding the enclosure back into place, however, make it a point to check the PC carefully. Make sure that every subassembly is installed and secured into place with the proper screws and hardware—leftover parts are *unacceptable*. A little care in organizing and sorting hardware during disassembly really pays off here. Remember to reattach power and signal cables as required. Each cable must be installed properly and completely (in its correct orientation). Take time to route each signal cable with care, and avoid jamming them into the system haphazardly. Careless cable runs stand a good chance of being caught and damaged by the enclosure during reassembly, or the next time the system needs to be disassembled. Properly routed cables also reduce the chance of signal problems (such as noise or crosstalk) that can result in unstable long-term operation. Also check the installation of any auxiliary cables, such as CD-ROM sound cables, the speaker cable, and the keylock cable.

Once the system components are reassembled securely, you can apply power to the PC and run final diagnostics to test the system. When the system checks properly, you can slide the enclosure into place (being careful not to damage any cables or wiring) and secure the enclosure with its full complement of screws.

# TIPS FOR WORKING INSIDE A DESKTOP OR TOWER PC

Whether you're troubleshooting, upgrading, or building your own PC from scratch, there's no doubt that you'll get plenty of hands-on time inside desktop and tower PCs. Unfortunately, many potential problems can be overlooked (or even caused) while working inside a PC. The following tips should help you make the most of your PC experience, and minimize the chances of collateral problems:

■ *Be extremely careful of any sharp edges along the metal cover, or inside the metal chassis itself.* Case manufacturers often save costs by omitting such production steps as burr removal and dulling sharp edges.

■ *Make sure that the chassis assembly is tight.* All chassis are *not* created equal—some stand solid as a house, while others can seem to sway freely. Take note of the chassis condition, and tighten the chassis if necessary.

■ *Watch your vents and fans for good air flow.* Make sure that the fan blades, grills, and any intake and exhaust filters are kept clean. Check to see that all fans are working.

■ *Watch for dust and debris.* When you're examining the enclosure, check for accumulations of dust or other debris. Dust is generally a thermal insulator and electrical conductor and can easily block the flow of air inside a chassis, so it is important to avoid accumulations of dust and debris wherever possible.

■ *Choose new chassis with care.* Replacing a chassis (or building a new PC from scratch) is an exciting but time-consuming effort, so plan for adequate expansion in terms of drive bays, expansion slot openings, power supply capacity, and drive power cables.

■ *Go with standardized cases, power supplies, and motherboards.* New PC systems have largely abandoned the use of AT-style cases (baby AT or full AT) in favor of ATX or NLX versions. As you'll see in the following sections, standard dimensioning ensures that cases, motherboards, and power supplies will *all* fit together.

■ *Keep drives mounted snugly.* All PC drives (whether in an internal or external drive bay) should be mounted with at least four screws. Fewer screws can allow the drive to vibrate, and this can shorten the drive's working life. Make sure that all four screws are in place and secure, but do not over-tighten the screws. Over-tightening can actually warp a drive's internal frame and cause premature failures as well.

■ *Be careful when mounting the motherboard.* Under no circumstances should you ever flex a motherboard, or install it in such a way that it is uneven. Ensure that no metal edges or standoffs touch the motherboard, and that the motherboard is not sitting flush against any part of the PC chassis.

■ *Check your cables closely.* There are myriad cables inside a PC. Make it a point to check the installation and routing of each cable. Each end of a cable should be installed evenly and completely. Cables should be run (where possible) to minimize any interruptions to air flow.

■ *Check your expansion boards.* Whenever you're working inside a PC, make sure that any expansion boards inside the system are inserted evenly and completely into their bus slots. Often, exchanging external cables can accidentally wiggle a card loose—resulting in possible system problems. Also verify that each expansion board is secured with a screw in the PC chassis.

■ *Check your memory devices.* While you're in the system, take a look at the memory devices. Make sure that each SIMM or DIMM module is clipped securely into place (especially if you're replacing or upgrading memory). If your motherboard uses COAST (cache-on-a-stick) modules for cache RAM, also verify that the COAST module is installed properly.

■ *Check the CPU heat sink/fan.* Chances are that your CPU is fitted with a heat sink/fan assembly. Check to see that the heat sink is attached securely to the CPU, and verify that the fan portion of the assembly is working once the system is powered up. The CPU itself should also be mounted securely into place.

# Standardized Form Factors

Selecting traditional PC chassis has always been somewhat of a "hit or miss" proposition. You'd choose cases, power supplies, and motherboards, and *hope* that everything would fit properly. All too often, screw holes wouldn't line up, and you'd be forced to return assemblies, or "kluge" the assemblies together—aligning as many screw holes as possible, and ignoring, clipping, or removing standoffs. Over the last few years, the PC industry has come together to develop a set of standard dimensions for key PC components (cases, motherboards, and power supplies). The three current standards are known as LPX, ATX, and NLX. This part of the chapter looks at these standards in more detail, and you can learn more at www.formfactors.org.

The use of new form factors does not have any bearing on the capabilities or performance of any new PC—only the dimensions of the motherboard, case, and power supply are affected.

## LPX FORM FACTOR

The Low-Profile Extended (or LPX) form factor proved to be the PC industry's first major step beyond AT- and baby AT-style motherboards. Developed jointly by Intel and Western Digital some years ago, the LPX specification covers the physical layout, power requirements, and electrical issues for such motherboards. A standard LPX motherboard has the same *maximum* dimensions as a baby AT board—no more than 8.5 inches wide by 13 inches long (see Figure 1-17). It also shares the same baby AT mounting hole arrangements.

The LPX approach does not support expansion cards on the motherboard. Instead, it uses a riser card inserted into a single board slot, and any cards added into the system attach to the riser card. LPX power connectors are the same as the original IBM AT power connectors: two six-pin connectors attached to the motherboard (usually labeled P8 and P9). The LPX format also provides a strict series of I/O ports arranged from left to right across the back of a board:

■ A VGA monitor connector

■ A parallel port

■ Two serial ports

■ A PS/2-style mouse port

■ A PS/2-style keyboard port

Later variations in LPX design may alter the placement of external connectors, substitute two USB interfaces in place of serial connectors, and perhaps even add local area network (LAN) and sound connectors.

In addition, an LPX motherboard typically provides two IDE drive controllers, a floppy disk controller, and 72-pin SIMM sockets. The LPX riser card slot conforms to the older EISA standard (both physically

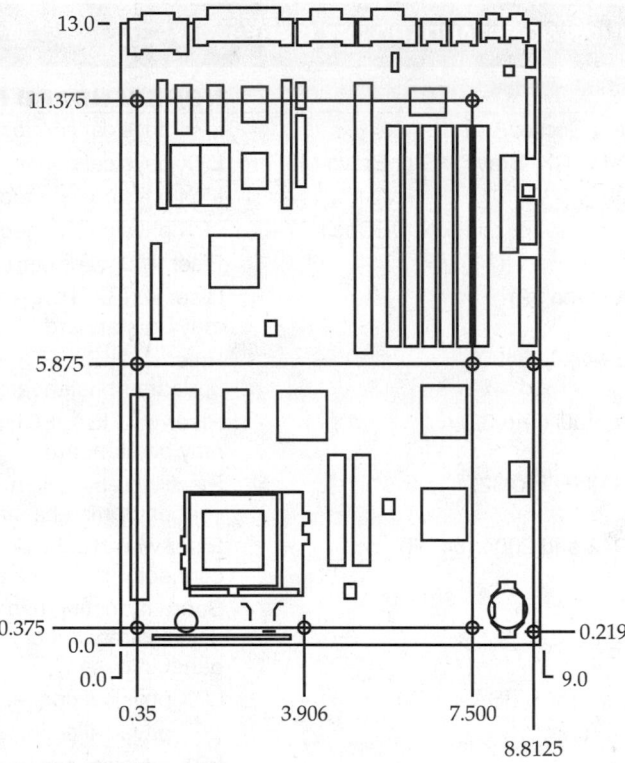

**FIGURE 1-17**    Image of an LPX motherboard

and electronically), but LPX is generally compatible with newer high-performance expansion architectures, such as PCI. As a result, it's not uncommon to find LPX riser cards offering ISA and PCI slots for expansion devices.

LPX was embraced widely by popular name-brand PC makers, such as AST, Compaq, Digital, Dell, Gateway, Hewlett-Packard, IBM, NCR, NEC, Packard-Bell, and Zenith, and LPX-type motherboards have been produced up to the introduction of Pentium II processors. The main problem with LPX was its proprietary use of riser cards. Riser cards need to meet the LPX physical and electrical connector standard—but that's the extent of LPX standardization. Otherwise, every computer manufacturer was free to choose its own riser card layout (such as the number of slots, the type of slots [ISA or PCI], the distance of the slots from the top of the LPX connector, and the size of the riser card). Table 1-3 illustrates the known compatibility issues with major LPX system manufacturers.

As a consequence of this weak standardization, riser cards were rarely interchangeable among various cases (often even for the same manufacturer), and this made it extremely difficult to replace and upgrade LPX motherboards. Eventually, the PC industry abandoned LPX in favor of the more uniform ATX and NLX form factors.

**TABLE 1-3     COMMON NONSTANDARD LPX ISSUES**

| BRAND/MODEL | NONSTANDARD FEATURE(S) |
|---|---|
| AST Advantage (before Socket 5) | LPX physical connector |
| AST Bravo LC, Bravo LC CX, Bravo MS-L, Bravo MS-T | LPX physical connector |
| Compaq DeskPro (All) | LPX physical connector |
| DEC Celebris and Venturis 4*xx* and 5*xx*, DECpc LPV+ | LPX physical connector |
| DEC Starion 200/300 | Riser w/ 5 ISA slots; connector may be ISA |
| DEC Starion 200i/300i (Trio 32) | Riser w/ ISA, PCI, shared; connector may be standard |
| DEC Starion 400/500 (C&T 63400) | Riser w/ 2 ISA, PCI, shared; connector appears nonstandard |
| DEC Starion 400i thru 900i (Trio 32) | Riser w/ 3 ISA, PCI, shared; connector may be standard |
| DEC Starion 910 thru 920 (Trio 32) | Riser w/ 8-bit, 2 ISA, PCI, shared; connector may be standard |
| DEC Starion 930 to 942 and 2001 (64-bit) | Riser w/ 8-bit, 2 ISA, PCI, shared; connector may be standard |
| Dell Optiplex 4*xx*/L | Board mounting uses two screws, oblong holes; wires that connect board to front panel of case |
| Gateway 2000 486 low-profile (ISA & PCI) | LPX physical connector |
| IBM PC350 | LPX physical connector |
| NCR 3000 series | LPX physical connector, motherboard mounting holes, power supply connector |
| Packard-Bell PB600 motherboard | Non-Intel board; connector order is VGA, keyboard, mouse (e.g. Axcel 461CDT), serial, parallel |
| Packard-Bell 386s and 486s | Connectors sometimes in different order on rear of case; some LPX riser cards have an ISA bus connector, but the card slots are placed closer to the rear of the computer case |

# ATX FORM FACTOR

The version 2.03 ATX form factor (see Figure 1-18) represents the most popular and well-established effort to standardize the major assemblies of a PC. In addition to the use of well-established mounting holes, the ATX approach makes several key improvements to the layout of a system. The CPU is relocated to a position on the motherboard that will not interfere with the use of full-length expansion boards (a common complaint of baby/full AT motherboard users). Since full-length cards can now be used in *all* the slots, it won't be necessary to shuffle expansion cards around to avoid interfering with the CPU. The CPU itself can also be upgraded without having to remove expansion cards. Connectors for memory modules are also located away from drive bays and expansion slots for easier access. The use of rear I/O ports (see Figure 1-19) and front panel connections have been standardized on the ATX motherboard, which simplifies

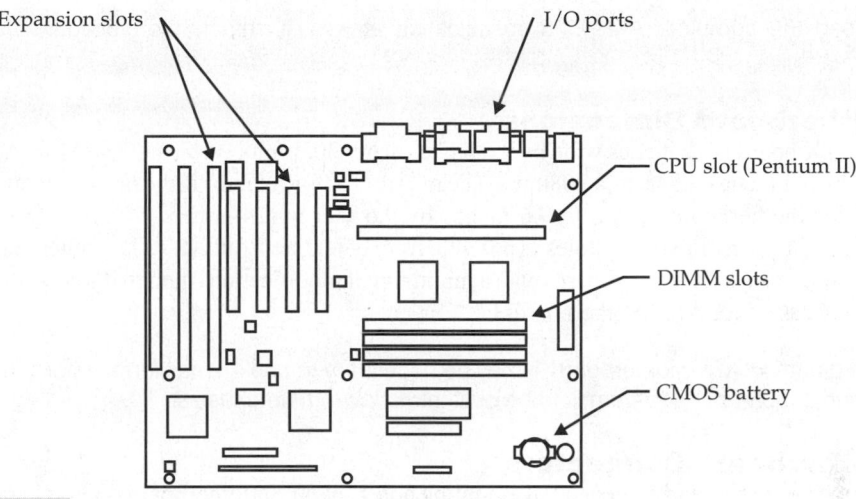

**FIGURE 1-18**    Layout of an ATX motherboard

case design and reduces the wiring on the motherboard. Integrated drive controller connections are now located closer to the drive bays to reduce drive cable lengths and reduce clutter. The ATX power supply provides power (including a native 3.3 volts) through a single 20-pin cable rather than through the two 6-pin cables used in traditional baby/full AT systems. Finally, the ATX case design is configured to be cooled by a single fan located in the ATX power supply. This not only simplifies the case and reduces power demands, but it makes the system quieter.

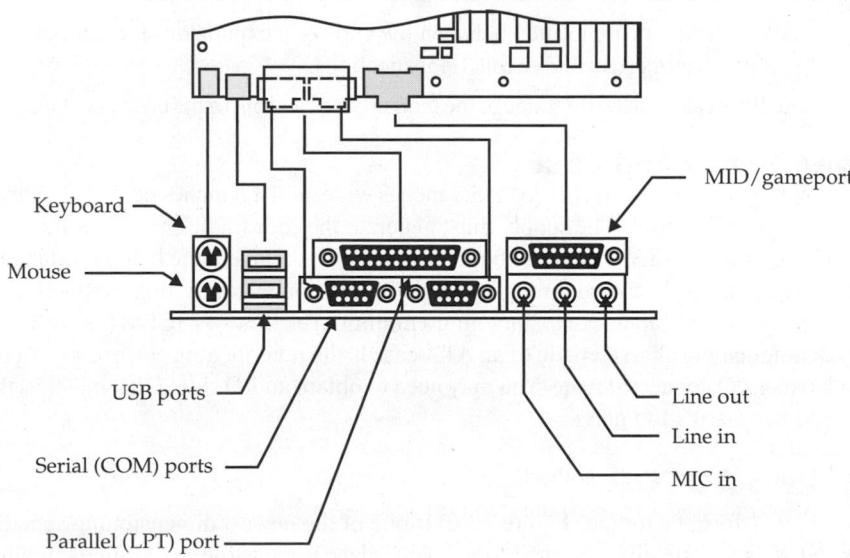

**FIGURE 1-19**    Layout of an ATX I/O port panel

You can see the complete ATX 2.03 specification at www.formfactors.org/developer/specs/atx/ atx2_03p1.pdf.

### ATX Motherboard Dimensions

A full-size ATX board is 12 inches wide by 9.6 inches deep (305mm × 244mm). The Mini-ATX board is 11.2 inches by 8.2 inches (284mm × 208mm). The microATX form factor is the newest iteration of ATX, and allows for motherboards down to 9.6 inches by 9.6 inches (244mm × 244mm). Designers have attempted to use as many mounting holes as possible from older baby/full AT-style motherboards to allow existing chassis to use ATX motherboards with a minimum of modification (though it's certainly preferable to use an ATX case with ATX motherboards).

When using a microATX motherboard, it may be necessary to use a small form factor power supply (SFX Power Supply) if the system is to be built into a low-profile chassis.

### ATX Motherboard Connectors

Aside from the board size and placement of mounting holes, an ATX motherboard is also characterized by the general placement of various connectors. The following list outlines the major connectors:

- Expansion slots (PCI/ISA) are located at the left rear of the motherboard.
- The power input connector is placed along the right edge of the board (near CPU).
- Drive signal connectors are located along the front edge of the board near the drive bays.
- Front panel I/O connectors (power switch and LED) are located along the front edge of the board—usually to the right of the expansion slots.
- Back panel I/O connectors (COM ports, parallel port, USB port, and so on) are all located on a single panel to the right rear of the motherboard. There is no single accepted layout for ATX connections, so you may find that different ATX motherboards offer unique I/O port layouts.
- Memory module connectors are located between the CPU and expansion slots, or between the CPU and drive signal connectors (usually visible on inspection).
- The CPU is usually located on the right side of the motherboard in front of the back panel I/O connectors.

### ATX Power Supply and Case

An ATX power supply is about 6.1 inches long, 5.7 inches wide, and 3.5 inches deep—roughly equivalent to a PS/2 power supply footprint. The supply must generate the four traditional PC voltage levels (+5V, −5V, +12V, −12V), as well as a 3.3V level to better support low-voltage logic being used in modern PCs. Power is provided to the motherboard through a single 20-pin connector. A single exhaust fan assembly located in the supply must be capable of maintaining a minimum airflow of 23CFM (cubic feet/minute).

The only distinguishing characteristic of an ATX case is the rear opening corresponding to the motherboard's back panel I/O connector plate. You may need to obtain an I/O shield that matches the layout of your specific motherboard's I/O ports.

## NLX FORM FACTOR

The version 1.8 NLX form factor (see Figure 1-20) is one of the newest dimensioning specifications for modern PCs. NLX is specifically designed to accommodate low-profile PC systems, while providing superior management for heat control and easy maintainability. The key to the NLX configuration is not the motherboard, but a *riser board* (similar in nature to the classic LPX form factor). The vertical riser

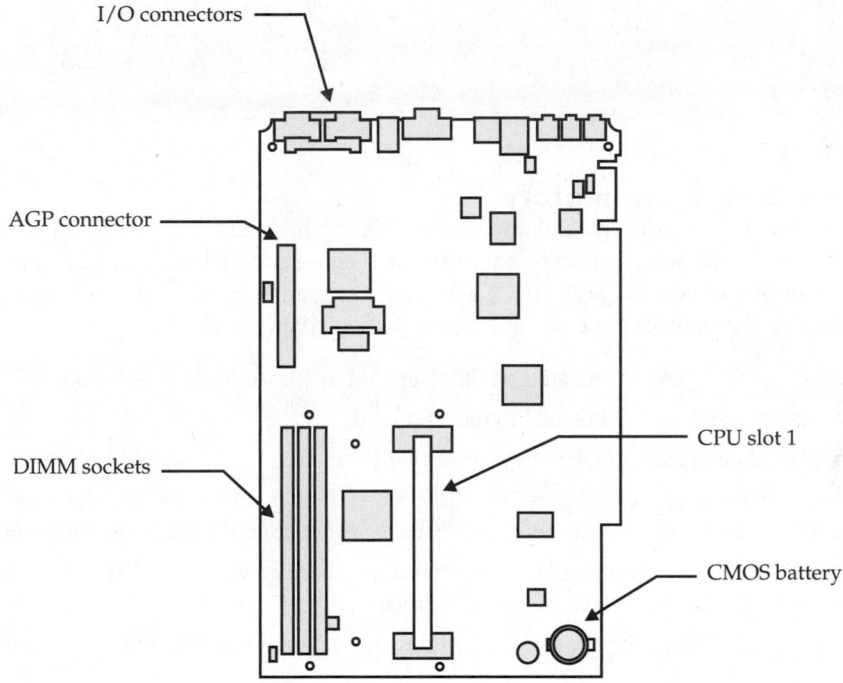

I/O connectors

AGP connector

DIMM sockets

CPU slot 1

CMOS battery

**FIGURE  1-20**    Layout of an NLX motherboard (without the riser)

board connects directly to the power supply (not the motherboard), and holds all of the expansion boards horizontally. The riser board also holds the drive cable connectors (the floppy connectors and hard drive connectors) that previously resided on the motherboard. This means that the NLX motherboard has no cables to be attached or removed when servicing the NLX system. An NLX motherboard can simply be undocked from the system's riser card, and another one can be installed in a matter of moments. A wide area for back panel I/O connectors is provided on the rear of the NLX motherboard, which allows for a large variety of high-end ports such as TV, sound, game ports, and so on. NLX motherboards were also some of the first to support the Accelerated Graphics Port (AGP) for better graphics performance on PCs. The CPU is placed toward the front of the NLX motherboard (close to the fan) to ensure better system cooling. You can get a better view of the NLX riser, motherboard, and back panel in Figure 1-21.

You can see the complete NLX 1.8 specification at http://www.formfactors.org/developer/specs/nlx/nlx1_8.pdf.

## NLX Motherboard Sizes

NLX motherboards are not as straightforward as ATX units. The NLX specification defines motherboards of 9.0 inches by 13.6 inches (maximum) and 8.0 inches by 10.0 inches (minimum). This means an NLX motherboard might run *anywhere* between these two sizes, and an NLX case must be able to support all possible sizes, though the typical NLX motherboard dimensions will be as follows (in inches):

- $10.0 \times 7.8$
- $10.0 \times 9.0$

- 11.2 × 7.8
- 11.2 × 9.0
- 13.6 × 7.8
- 13.6 × 9.0

## NLX Motherboard Connectors

Perhaps the most noticeable difference between an NLX motherboard and other motherboards is the apparent lack of expansion board connectors and drive port connectors, which have been implemented on the riser card. You'll also note the presence of a 340-pin card edge connector that interfaces to the riser card. The following list outlines the disposition of important connections:

- Expansion slots (PCI/ISA) are located on the riser card in a horizontal orientation.

- The power input connector is attached to the riser card.

- Drive signal connectors are attached to the riser card.

- Back panel I/O connectors (COM ports, parallel port, USB port, and so on) are all located on a single panel to the right rear of the motherboard. This back panel occupies the entire rear of the motherboard.

- Memory module connectors are typically located somewhere between the CPU and expansion slots, or behind the CPU toward the rear of the motherboard.

- The CPU is usually located on the left front of the motherboard in direct proximity to an NLX case intake fan.

- The AGP connector is located along the left side of the motherboard several inches from the left-rear corner of the motherboard.

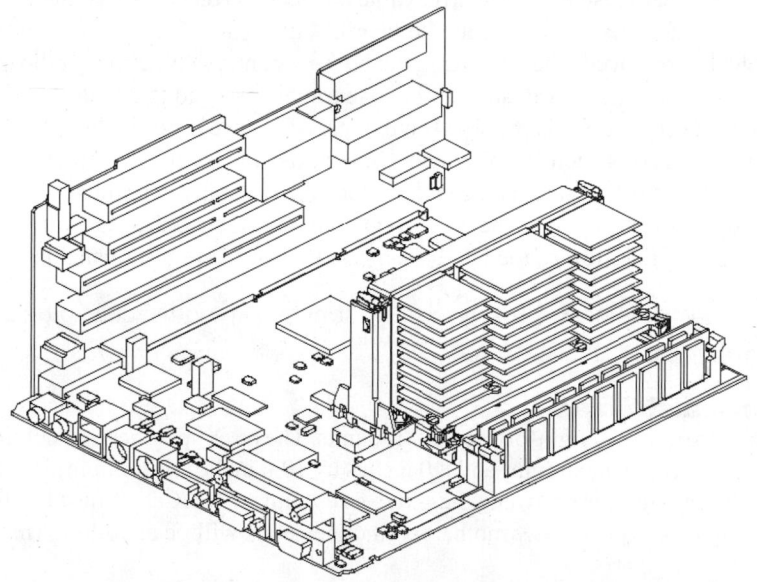

**FIGURE  1-21**    View of an NLX riser, motherboard, and I/O panel (Courtesy of Intel)

### NLX Power Supply and Case

An NLX power supply uses the same dimensions as an ATX power supply (about 6.1 inches long, 5.7 inches wide, and 3.5 inches deep). The supply must generate the four traditional PC voltage levels (+5V, −5V, +12V, −12V), as well as a 3.3V level to better support low-voltage logic being used in modern PCs. Power is provided to the riser card through a single 20-pin connector. A single exhaust fan assembly located in the supply must be capable of maintaining a minimum airflow of 23CFM.

The only distinguishing characteristic of an NLX case is the long rear opening corresponding to the motherboard's back panel I/O connector plate. There may also be hinged access or other provision to ease the installation or replacement of NLX motherboards. An additional inlet fan is located in the front-left part of the chassis to aid in cooling the CPU.

## WTX FORM FACTOR

Most recent form factors, such as ATX or microATX (and the emerging FlexATX), have focused on smaller and more highly integrated PCs. In fact, FlexATX motherboards are only a little over half the size of ATX motherboards. This trend reflects the rise of the burgeoning lower-end, sub-$1,000 PC market. Still, as PC technology continues to increase in power and performance, PCs are emerging as powerful players in the high-end professional market for high-performance workstations and network servers. Most of the current form factors are simply too small for high-end multiprocessor systems using numerous hard drives and a large amount of RAM. To address the needs of this high-end market, Intel introduced the new WTX form factor in 1998 (the *W* stands for workstation). The WTX form factor is intended to standardize the current proliferation of different large PC-based workstation and server designs (Figure 1-22).

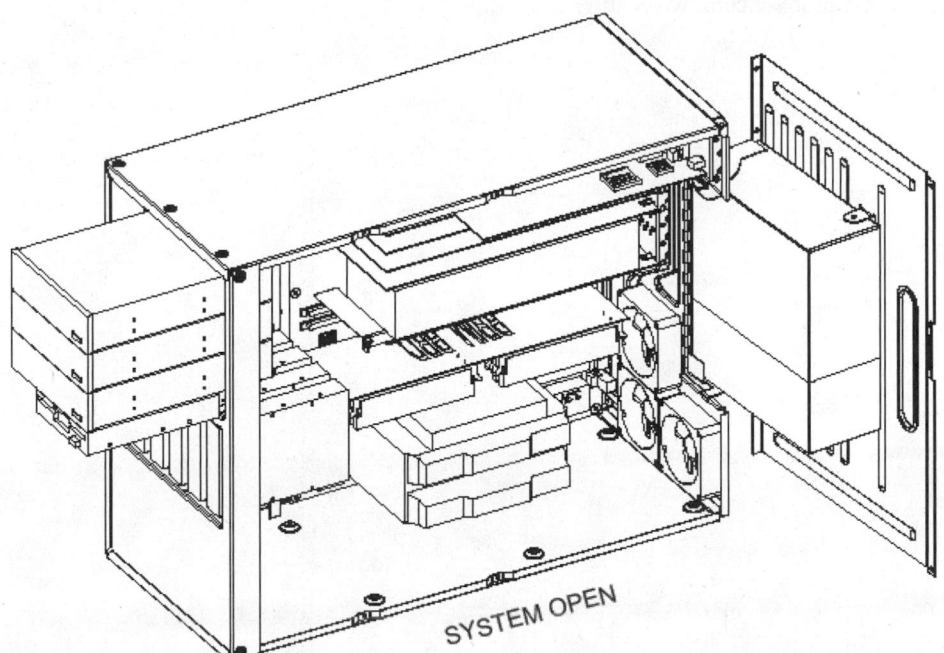

**FIGURE 1-22**    The WTX form factor is intended to support high-end workstation and server systems (Courtesy of Intel).

Maximum WTX motherboard size is a whopping 14 inches by 16.75 inches—over twice the maximum size of a regular ATX board. Since the goal of the WTX form factor is to support both current and future high-end motherboard and CPU technologies (as well as other features in demand by workstation and server users), the form factor is geared specifically toward flexibility of design. For example, exact mounting hole locations are not prescribed for the case. Rather, the motherboard is designed to mount to a metal plate that comes with it, and the plate is installed into the case. Since the WTX form factor is intended for high-end workstation and server systems, we won't discuss it any further, but you can see the complete WTX specification at www.wtx.org/WTX-Spec-11.pdf.

# Further Study

**AGP Implementers' Forum**   www.agpforum.org
**Amtrade Products**   www.amtrade.com
**Enlight**   www.enlightcorp.com
**Fong Kai Industrial**   www.fkusa.com
**Form factor information**   www.formfactors.org
**Intel AGP Web site**   developer.intel.com/technology/agp/
**Intel ATX Web site**   www.intel.com/design/motherbd/atx.htm
**Intel chipsets**   developer.intel.com/design/chipsets/
**Intel motherboards**   developer.intel.com/design/motherbd/
**InWin Development**   www.in-win.com
**Iomega**   www.iomega.com
**ProCase**   www.procase.com.tw/68.htm

# 2

# AN INSIDE LOOK AT OPERATING SYSTEMS AND THE BOOT PROCESS

**A**s a technician, it is vital for you to understand the relationship between PC hardware and software. In the early days of computers, hardware was typically the center of attention. Since early software was written for a specific computer (such as a DEC PDP system or IBM VAX), and early computers were very limited in their storage and processing capacity, software often arrived as an afterthought (we still see software development lagging behind hardware advances to this day). With the introduction of personal computers in the mid-1970s, designers realized that a wide selection of software would be needed to make PCs attractive. Instead of writing software specifically for particular machines, a uniform operating environment would be needed to manage system resources and launch applications. In this way, applications would be *portable* between systems whose hardware resources would otherwise be incompatible. This uniform applications environment became known as the *operating system* (or OS). When IBM designed the early PC, it chose to license a simple command-line-based operating system from a fledgling company called Microsoft—and the rest is history.

Although this book is dedicated to dealing with PC hardware (since it is the hardware that "breaks"), you should realize that the operating system has a profound effect on PC resources and how those resources are allocated to individual software applications. This is especially true of the more sophisticated operating systems such as Windows 98/Me/2000/XP, Linux, and so on. Every good technician is sensitive to the fact that problems with an OS (or its configuration) can result in serious problems with PC performance. This chapter explains the relationship between PC hardware and software, highlights some of the major features found in typical operating systems, and walks you through a typical PC boot process.

# The PC Hierarchy

Before we dig into the OS itself, you should understand the complex (and often frustrating) relationship between computer hardware and software. This relationship is typically expressed as a *hierarchy,* as shown in Figure 2-1. Each layer in the hierarchy serves a very specific function in PC operation. This hierarchy has four levels: the hardware, the BIOS, the OS, and the application(s).

## HARDWARE

As you might expect, *hardware* forms the core of a PC hierarchy—without the hardware, the computer doesn't exist. The hardware includes all the circuits, drives, expansion boards, power supplies, peripheral devices, and their interconnecting wiring or cables. This extends not only to the PC itself, but also to monitors, keyboards, pointing devices, printers, and so on. By sending digital information to various ports or addresses in memory, it is possible to manipulate almost anything attached to the system CPU. Any physical aspect of the PC is regarded as hardware. (Chapter 1 provides a thorough review of PC hardware.)

Unfortunately, controlling PC hardware is a difficult process that requires an intimate knowledge of a PC's electronic architecture. How is it that Microsoft can sell an OS that works on an i386-based AT, as

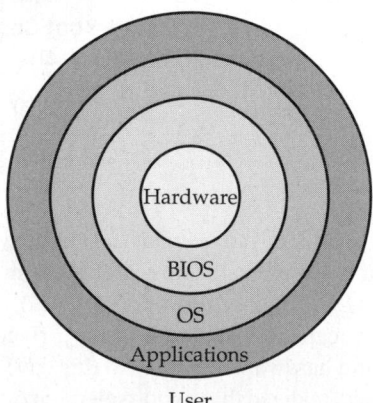

Hardware

BIOS

OS

Applications

User

**FIGURE  2-1**    A standard PC hierarchy

well as on a new Pentium 4 system? Since each PC manufacturer designs its circuitry (especially mother-board circuitry) differently, it is virtually impossible to create a universal OS without some sort of inter-face between the one standard OS and the myriad variations of hardware in the marketplace. This interface is accomplished by the *basic input/output system* (BIOS).

# BIOS

Simply stated, a BIOS is a set of small programs (or *system services*) that are designed to operate each major PC subsystem (video, disk, keyboard, and so on). Each of these system services is invoked by a set of standard calls (originally developed by IBM) that are made as needed through the OS. When the OS requests a standard BIOS service, the particular BIOS program performs the appropriate function that has been tailored to the particular hardware. Thus, each motherboard design requires its own BIOS. Using this methodology, BIOS acts as a "glue" that allows diverse (and older) hardware to operate with a single uni-form OS. In addition to system services, the BIOS executes a *power-on self-test* (POST) program each time the PC is initialized. POST checks the major subsystems before attempting to load an OS.

In practice, most BIOS code is written by a limited number of companies, such as Award or AMI. Motherboard manufacturers then license the generic BIOS code and tweak the BIOS for each partic-ular motherboard design.

Since BIOS is specific to each motherboard design, BIOS resides on the motherboard in the form of a read-only memory (ROM) chip, although newer systems employ electrically rewritable (or *flash*) ROMs that allow the BIOS to be updated without having to replace the BIOS ROM chip. You can see a typical BIOS chip in Figure 2-2. You may see BIOS referred to as *firmware* rather then software, because the BIOS instructions are permanently recorded on a chip. As you might imagine, the efficiency and elegance of BIOS code would have a profound impact on the overall operation of a PC; better BIOS routines will result in superior system performance, while clumsy, inefficient BIOS routines can easily bog down a sys-tem. *Bugs* (software errors) in BIOS can have very serious consequences for the system (including lost files and system lockups).

BIOS chip in a DIP socket for easy physical replacement/upgrade if necessary

**FIGURE  2-2**    The BIOS chip of a Transcend TS-AKR4 motherboard (Courtesy of Motherboards.org)

## OPERATING SYSTEM

The operating system serves two very important functions in the modern PC. First, an OS interacts with (and provides an extension to) the BIOS. This extension provides applications with a rich selection of high-level file handling and disk control functions. It is this large number of disk-related functions that added the term "disk" to "operating system" to give us *disk operating system,* or *DOS.* You can see how Windows XP reports disk capacity in Figure 2-3. When an application needs to perform disk access or file handling, the OS layer performs most of the work. By providing access to a library of frequently used functions through the OS, application programs can be written without the need to incorporate the code for such complex functions into each application itself. In actual operation, the OS and BIOS work closely together to give an application easy access to system resources.

Second, an OS forms an environment (or *shell*) through which applications can be executed, and provides a user interface allowing you and your customers to interact with the PC. MS-DOS uses a keyboard-driven, command-line interface signified by the command-line prompt (such as C:>_), which is now almost universally recognized. By contrast, the Windows family of operating systems provides a graphical user interface (GUI) that relies on symbols, icons, and dialog boxes that are selected with a mouse or other pointing device.

## APPLICATIONS

Ultimately, the aim of any computer is to execute applications (such as games, word processors, spreadsheets, and so on). An OS loads and allows the user to launch the desired application(s). As the application requires system resources during run time, it makes an appropriate call to the OS or BIOS, which in turn

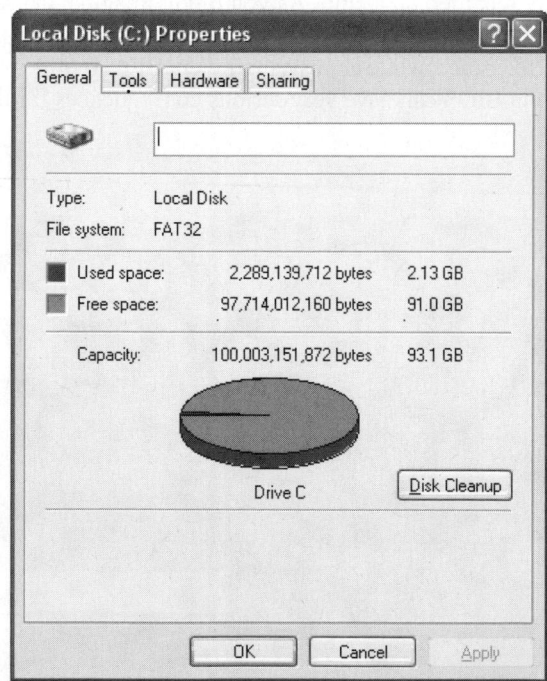

**FIGURE  2-3**    Locating disk information through a Windows XP dialog box

accesses the needed function and returns any needed information to the calling application. The actual dynamics of such an exchange are more complex than described here, but this description should give you the general idea. Now that you have an overview of the typical PC hierarchy and understand how each layer interacts with one another, it is time to take a closer look at the OS layer itself.

# Understanding Popular OS Features

Many different operating systems are written for today's computers. The range and sophistication of operating systems span the entire spectrum of features and complexity—some are large, complex, commercial giants (such as Windows 98/Me/XP, Windows 2000, and Windows NT), while others are small, freely distributed packages (like FreeBSD). Other operating systems are tailored for such features as real-time operation, true or high-performance multitasking, or networking. New, specialized operating systems are regularly being introduced to support particular systems, such as process control, manufacturing, or other mission-critical needs. Table 2-1 offers a partial listing of today's available operating systems. As a technician, you should understand the important features of today's operating systems, and why one OS might be selected over another. The following sections offer some highlights of the major commercial operating systems offered by Microsoft and IBM.

**TABLE 2-1    PARTIAL LIST OF CONTEMPORARY OPERATING SYSTEMS**

| OPERATING SYSTEM | FURTHER STUDY |
|---|---|
| 98Lite | www.98lite.net/ |
| CTOS | www.dogstar.com/Sirius/Menu/TechLibrary.NewsletterExcerpts.html |
| DR-DOS v6.0 | support.novell.com/Ftp/Updates/dsktop/drdos60/Date0.html |
| EROS | www.cis.upenn.edu/~eros/ |
| Freedows OS | www.freedows.org/ |
| GEOS | users.bergen.org/~edwdig/geos/ |
| GNU | www.delorie.com/gnu/ |
| GNU Hurd | www.gnu.ai.mit.edu/software/hurd/hurd.html |
| HP/UX | eigen.ee.ualberta.ca/ |
| JOS (Java OS) | www.jos.org/ |
| Linux, Caldera | www.caldera.com/ |
| Linux, Debian | www.debian.org/ |
| Linux, Mandrake | www.linux-mandrake.com/en/ |
| Linux, Real-Time | www.rtlinux.org/ |
| Linux, Red Hat | www.redhat.com/ |
| Linux, SuSE | www.suse.com/ |
| Linux, ZipSlack | www.slackware.com/zipslack/ |
| Mach | www.cs.cmu.edu/afs/cs.cmu.edu/project/mach/public/www/mach.html |
| MacMinix | www.pliner.com/macminix/ |
| MacOS | www.apple.com/macos/ |
| MacOS X Server | www.apple.com/macosx/server/ |
| Novell NetWare | www.novell.com/ |

**TABLE 2-1    PARTIAL LIST OF CONTEMPORARY OPERATING SYSTEMS *(CONTINUED)***

| OPERATING SYSTEM | FURTHER STUDY |
| --- | --- |
| OS/2 | www-4.ibm.com/software/os/warp/ |
| Palm | www.palm.com/software/ |
| PC-DOS v7.0 (2000) | www-4.ibm.com/software/os/dos/index.html |
| PertOS | www.trumpet.com/products.html |
| Plan9 | www.fywss.com/plan9/ |
| QNX | get.qnx.com/ |
| ReactOS | www.reactos.com/ |
| UNIX, BSD | www.bsd.org/ |
| UNIX, FreeBSD | www.freebsd.org/ |
| UNIX, KDE | www.kde.org/ |
| UNIX, Minix | www.disi.unige.it/person/DoderoG/minix/minix.htm |
| UNIX, NetBSD | www.netbsd.org/ |
| UNIX, OpenBSD | www.openbsd.org/ |
| UNIX, SCO | www.sco.com/ |
| UNIX, Solaris | www.sun.com/solaris/ |
| UNIX, Tru64 | www.tru64unix.compaq.com/ |
| UNIX, XFree86 | www.xfree86.org/ |
| V2 OS | www.v2.nl/v2_os/ |
| VMS (OpenVMS) | www.levitte.org/~ava/index.htmlx |
| Windows 95, 98, Me | www.microsoft.com/windows/default.asp |
| Windows CE | www.microsoft.com/windows/default.asp |
| Windows NT/2000 | www.microsoft.com/windows/default.asp |
| Windows XP | www.microsoft.com/windows/default.asp |
| Wine | www.winehq.com/ |
| X Window System | www.rahul.net/kenton/xsites.html |

Due to rapid consolidation in the software industry, some of the links in Table 2-1 may not be available.

## MS-DOS 6.22

MS-DOS 6.22 is the last stand-alone command-line OS designed by Microsoft for the PC, and is generally considered to be one of the most versatile and reliable DOS-type OSs ever released by Microsoft. It has numerous safety features and enhancements designed to provide the safest possible computing environment of any MS-DOS version. Table 2-2 highlights the system requirements for MS-DOS 6.22 and other popular operating systems. And the most notable features of MS-DOS 6.22 are outlined in the following list.

Today, stand-alone real-mode operating systems such as MS-DOS and PC-DOS are considered obsolete. It is increasingly difficult to locate information on these operating systems (even technical support resources are gradually disappearing). When faced with DOS, you may consider upgrading the system to a version of Windows or Linux wherever possible.

■ **Anti-Virus**  This utility can identify and remove more than 1000 different computer viruses. MS-DOS 6.22 includes a version of Anti-Virus for both DOS and Windows 3.1x.

■ **Backup**  Backup is a utility for backing up your hard disk drive. MS-DOS 6.22 includes a version of Backup for both DOS and Windows 3.1x.

■ **Defrag**  MS-DOS 6.22 includes a later version of Defrag that reorganizes files on your hard disk to minimize the time it takes your computer to access them.

■ **DriveSpace and DoubleGuard**  DriveSpace integrates disk compression into the OS and supports both hard disks and floppy disks. DriveSpace includes DoubleGuard safety checking, which protects data by verifying data integrity before writing to the disk.

■ **Interactive start**  The interactive start feature gives you the ability to bypass startup commands when you turn on your computer, by pressing F8. This allows you to choose which CONFIG.SYS and AUTOEXEC.BAT commands MS-DOS should carry out.

■ **Interlink**  This feature enables you to easily transfer files between computers. With Interlink and a cable, you can access information on another computer without using floppy disks to copy data from one computer to another.

■ **MultiConfig**  MultiConfig allows you to define more than one configuration in your CONFIG.SYS file. If your CONFIG.SYS file defines multiple configurations, MS-DOS displays a menu that enables you to choose the configuration you want to use each time you boot the computer.

■ **ScanDisk**  MS-DOS 6.22 includes a more current version of ScanDisk (limited to FAT16) that detects, diagnoses, and repairs disk errors on uncompressed drives and DriveSpace-compressed drives. ScanDisk can repair file system errors (such as cross-linked files and lost clusters) and physical disk errors.

■ **SmartDrive**  The SmartDrive program included with MS-DOS 6.22 speeds up your computer by using a disk cache that stores information being read from your hard disk or CD-ROM drive. SmartDrive can also be set to cache information being written to your hard disk.

■ **Undelete**  This feature allows you to recover deleted files. MS-DOS 6.22 includes a version of Undelete for both DOS and Windows 3.1x.

**TABLE 2-2**    **COMPARISON OF SYSTEM REQUIREMENTS FOR MAJOR OPERATING SYSTEMS**

| FEATURE | DOS | WINDOWS 98 | WINDOWS NT | WINDOWS 2000 | WINDOWS ME | WINDOWS XP |
|---|---|---|---|---|---|---|
| PC platform | Any | 486/66 MHz | 486/25 MHz, Alpha, MIPS R4X00, PowerPC | Pentium 166 MHz | Pentium 150 MHz | Pentium, Athlon, or Duron 233 MHz or faster |
| RAM | 1MB | 16MB | 16–32MB | 64MB | 32MB | 64MB (min) |
| Install drive | 1.44MB (disks) | CD-ROM | CD-ROM | CD-ROM | CD-ROM | CD-ROM |
| HDD space | 6MB | 250MB | 110MB | 250MB | 480–645MB | 1.5GB |
| Display | Mono text | VGA | VGA | VGA | VGA | SVGA |
| Mouse | Optional | Required | Required | Required | Required | Required |

# PC-DOS 7.0

PC-DOS was IBM's answer to Microsoft's MS-DOS. Early versions of PC-DOS were actually licensed to IBM from Microsoft, but the two giants eventually parted company, and IBM continued the development of PC-DOS under its own banner. Today, PC-DOS 7.0 is roughly equivalent in features and performance to MS-DOS 6.22, including disk compression, anti-virus software, and limited networking features. However, PC-DOS is not as widely distributed. System requirements are about the same, but PC-DOS 7.0 includes PCMCIA support, a DOS file update feature (to keep files synchronized between PCs), and a high-level programming language called REXX. The more important features of PC-DOS 7.0 are listed here:

- **Anti-Virus**   PC-DOS 7.0 includes IBM Anti-Virus, which checks for more than 2100 viruses.
- **File update**   A new PC DOS file update feature automatically synchronizes files between your desktop and notebook PCs so that they're always up to date.
- **Improved utilities**   There are numerous enhancements to DOS and Windows utilities, including Central Point's Backup utility, Phoenix Technology's PCMCIA support utility, and the RAMBoost Memory Optimizer.
- **REXX**   PC-DOS 7.0 includes a new integrated REXX high-level programming language.
- **Stacker**   Stacker 4.0 disk compression delivers an excellent mix of compression and performance.

# WINDOWS 95

Microsoft released Windows 95 in August 1995 as the major upgrade to Windows 3.1x. Windows 95 was designed to offer superior performance while taking advantage of emerging PC hardware and PC platform technologies such as plug-and-play, power conservation, PCI bus architecture, and so on. Windows 95 runs most Windows 3.1x and DOS programs, but also supports improved features like a built-in uninstaller, dial-up networking, multitasking, and long file names. Though aging and no longer available preinstalled on new computers, Windows 95 is still the OS used on a large number of personal computers. Its most popular features include the following:

- **Active right mouse button**   Use the right mouse button to accomplish many common tasks quickly and easily. Click almost anything in Windows 95 with your right mouse button to see a context-sensitive menu of options.
- **Dial-up networking**   This feature allows easy access to online resources (like the Internet) and supports communication between connected PCs.
- **Long file names**   Windows 95 supports long file names (up to 250 characters) to make your files and folders easier to organize and find. File names can now have sensible titles.
- **Multitasking**   Windows 95 offers improved multitasking capabilities that truly allow the system to handle multiple tasks simultaneously without system interruptions.
- **Plug-and-play**   This feature allows you to insert the card for a hardware device into your computer, and Windows automatically recognizes and sets up the hardware for you.
- **Shortcuts**   You can create links for easy access to important files, folders, drives, programs, or Web sites.

- **Taskbar**   The Taskbar acts as a home base from which you can start programs (with the Start button) and keep track of what programs have been launched. You can use the Taskbar to switch between programs, as needed, for convenient multitasking.

- **Windows Explorer**   The traditional File Manager of earlier Windows versions has been replaced by Windows Explorer for browsing through and managing your files, drives, and network connections.

## OS/2 WARP 4.*X*

OS/2 Warp has long been IBM's premier OS. Originally codeveloped with Microsoft, OS/2 development continued in-house after IBM and Microsoft ceased their cooperative ventures. OS/2 is a GUI-based operating system capable of running most Windows and DOS software, as well as native OS/2 applications in a true multitasking environment. OS/2 Warp 4.*x* focuses on network operations and connectivity— including built-in Internet applications—and offers an advantage over competing operating systems with its use of voice input controls. In spite of these advantages, OS/2 is noted for a surprising lack of hardware support. For example, it can be surprisingly difficult to find suitable OS/2 drivers for devices such as CD-ROM drives and sound boards. Today, OS/2 is rarely used and is generally considered to be obsolete. The following are its more noteworthy features:

- **Connectivity**   OS/2 is particularly noted for its strong network connectivity.

- **Reliability**   A true multitasking environment is well suited to critical applications, and OS/2 is relatively crash-proof when compared to Windows 95 and NT.

- **Software compatibility**   OS/2 runs DOS and most Windows 3.1*x* applications, along with native OS/2 and Java applications. OS/2 also supports features like TrueType, OpenGL, OpenDOC, Open32, and plug-and-play.

- **Speech recognition**   OS/2 includes VoiceType for OS/2 Warp speech recognition software.

- **Systems management**   OS/2 offers powerful system management features, including DMI (Desktop Management Interface) support.

## WINDOWS CE

Windows CE is designed to serve as an operating system for a broad range of communications, entertainment, and mobile-computing devices. It also enables new types of non-PC business and consumer devices that can communicate with each other, share information with Windows-based PCs, and connect to the Internet (for example, wallet PCs, digital information pagers, cellular smart phones, DVD players, and Internet Web phones). The first handheld PC products based on Windows CE began shipping in November 1996. It is important to note that Windows CE is released strictly as an OEM product and cannot be purchased through retail channels. Its major features are listed here:

- **Communication with Windows-based PCs**   Windows CE can seamlessly synchronize, communicate, and exchange information with Windows-based PCs.

- **Companion applications**   The Windows CE operating system supports Windows CE-based companion applications that share or synchronize information with their counterparts for Windows.

■ **Internet Explorer**   Windows CE includes a version of Internet Explorer that offers built-in Web access for many types of communications, entertainment, and mobile-computing devices.

■ **Windows development environment**   The Windows CE development environment supports a comprehensive and expandable subset of Win32 APIs, and uses familiar off-the-shelf development tools, with the goal of ensuring a strong aftermarket for Windows CE applications.

# WINDOWS NT (WORKSTATION)

Windows NT represents Microsoft's emphasis on business communication and networking. While the look and feel of Windows NT may seem quite similar to Windows 95, NT incorporates a powerful suite of networking and Internet-related features backed up by detailed security, cryptography, and system policies configurations. Windows NT also abandons DOS-mode support. Windows NT undoubtedly represents one of the most complex and versatile operating systems now in service for business and networking environments. It is surpassed only by the more recent Windows 2000 family of operating systems. The primary features of Windows NT are listed here:

■ **Client support for NDS**   Windows NT Workstation includes an improved version of Client Services for NetWare that supports Novell NetWare Directory Services (NDS). This enables users to log on to Novell NetWare 4.*x* servers running DNS to access files and print resources.

■ **Client support for PPTP**   Point-to-Point Tunneling Protocol provides a secure path to use public data networks (such as the Internet) to create virtual private networks. PPTP allows you to safely transmit confidential communications over the Internet.

■ **Cryptography APIs**   Windows NT includes a set of encryption APIs that allows developers to easily create applications that work securely over nonsecure networks (such as the Internet).

■ **Dial-up networking**   Improved dial-up networking provides the ability to easily and automatically dial up on demand.

■ **Dial-up networking multilink channel aggregation**   Dial-up networking now provides channel aggregation that enables users to combine all available dial-up lines to achieve higher transfer speeds. For example, you can combine two or more PPP ISDN B channels to achieve speeds of up to 128 Kbps.

■ **Distributed Component Object Model (DCOM)**   Windows NT provides the infrastructure that allows DCOM applications (also known as *Network OLE*) to communicate across networks without needing to redevelop applications.

■ **Hardware profiles**   Windows NT hardware profiles allow you to have different computer settings depending on the environment in which a computer is being used, and they make it easier to use computers in different configurations (such as docked and undocked laptop configurations).

■ **Internet Explorer**   Windows NT Workstation comes with Internet Explorer, which gives you full support to explore the Internet.

■ **Management and control**   Windows NT includes remote management and troubleshooting tools, and allows administrators to implement policies and standards for systemwide desktop configurations.

■ **Multimedia APIs**   Windows NT supports the multimedia APIs found in Windows 95: DirectDraw, DirectInput, DirectPlay, and DirectSound. Supporting these APIs allows developers to create games and other applications for both platforms simultaneously.

- **Peer Web Services (PWS)**   PWS enables easy publication of personal Web pages, and lets systems share that Web information over intranets. It's also ideal for developing, testing, and staging Web applications and content.

- **Setup Manager**   This Windows NT utility assists administrators in creating installation scripts and reduces the time and effort of deploying Windows NT.

- **System policies and user profiles**   System policies are used to provide a standardized, controlled desktop environment for users. User profiles contain all user-definable settings and can be stored on a Windows NT Server so that users can receive the same desktop regardless of their location.

- **Task Manager**   An integrated tool for managing applications and tasks, Task Manager maintains detailed information on each application and process running on the desktop. It also provides an effective way to terminate applications and processes that are not responding.

- **Telephony APIs**   Telephony API (TAPI) integrates telephones and PCs. Using the TAPI interface, communications applications can ask for access to a modem or telephone device, allowing them to be shared.

- **Windows messaging client**   This is a universal e-mail inbox that you can use with many different e-mail systems. It includes full Messaging API (MAPI) 1.0 support. You can send, receive, organize, and store e-mail and file system objects.

- **Windows NT Explorer**   This is the Windows NT tool for browsing and managing files, drives, and network connections. It displays your computer's contents as a hierarchy, or tree, allowing you to see the contents of each drive, folder, and network connection.

- **WINS and DNS integration**   Windows NT takes advantage of the integration between Windows Internet Name Service and Domain Name System to provide a form of dynamic DNS that makes it easier to connect to network resources.

# WINDOWS 98

With the many new hardware standards and features being developed for the PC, Windows 95 became increasingly hard-pressed to make the fullest use of system resources. Windows 98 builds on Windows 95 by adding a rich suite of refinements and improvements to a full 32-bit OS. New wizards, utilities, and resources work proactively to keep systems running more smoothly. Performance is faster for many common tasks such as application loading, system startup, and shutdown. Full integration with the Internet's World Wide Web aids online work and system versatility. After numerous delays, Windows 98 was finally released in June 1998, and an upgrade containing a year's worth of learning and improvements named "Windows 98 Second Edition" (or "Windows 98 SE") was released in September 1999. Microsoft has since released the Millennium Edition (called Windows Me), intended to focus on a broad spectrum of home users, but Windows 98/SE continues to be a popular and versatile OS for home and small office users. The most notable features and improvements of Windows 98/SE are outlined here:

- **Backup utility**   A new backup applet supports SCSI tape devices and makes backing up your data easier and more versatile.

- **Broadcast architecture**   With a TV tuner board installed, Windows 98 allows a PC to receive and display television and other data distributed over the broadcast networks, including enhanced television programs (which combine standard television with HTML information related to the programs).

- **Dial-up networking improvements**   The dial-up networking included with Windows 98 has been updated to support features like dial-up scripting and support for multilink channel aggregation, which enables users to combine all available dial-up lines to achieve higher transfer speeds.

- **Disk Defragmenter Optimization wizard**   This new wizard uses the process of disk defragmentation to increase the speed with which your most frequently used applications run.

- **Display configuration enhancements**   Display setting enhancements provide support for dynamically changing screen resolution and color depth. Adapter refresh rates can also be set with most newer display driver chipsets.

- **Distributed Component Object Model (DCOM)**   Windows 98 (and Windows NT 4.0) provides the infrastructure that allows DCOM applications (the technology formally known as *Network OLE*) to communicate across networks without needing to redevelop applications.

- **Dr. Watson**   Windows 98 includes an enhanced version of the Dr. Watson utility. When a software fault occurs (such as a general protection fault or system hang), Dr. Watson intercepts it and indicates what software failed (and why). Dr. Watson also collects detailed information about the state of your system at the time the fault occurred. A Log file is created and can be used by a technician to troubleshoot the problem. Dr. Watson does not run by default; it must be started manually or from a shortcut placed in the Startup folder.

- **Faster shutdown**   The time it takes to shut down the system has been dramatically reduced in Windows 98.

- **FAT32**   This improved version of the FAT file system allows disks over 2GB to be formatted as a single drive. FAT32 also uses smaller clusters than FAT drives, resulting in a more efficient use of space on large disks.

- **Infrared Data Association (IrDA) 3.0 support**   Windows 98 supports IrDA for wireless connectivity, which means users can easily connect to peripheral devices or other PCs without using connecting cables. Infrared-equipped laptop or desktop computers have the capability of networking, transferring files, and printing wirelessly with other IrDA-compatible infrared devices.

- **Intel MMX processor support**   Windows 98 provides support for software that uses the Pentium Multimedia Extensions (MMX and SSE) for fast audio and video support on future generations of the Pentium processor.

- **Internet connection sharing (for Windows 98 SE)**   This feature enables you to configure your home computer network to share a single connection to the Internet.

- **Multiple display support**   This feature allows you to use multiple monitors and/or multiple graphics adapters on a single PC.

- **NetWare Directory Services (NDS) support**   Windows 98 includes Client Services for NetWare that support Novell NDS. This enables Windows 98 users to log on to Novell NetWare 4.*x* servers running NDS to access files and print resources.

- **New hardware support**   Windows 98 provides support for an array of innovations that have occurred in computer hardware over the last few years. Some of the major hardware standards supported by Windows 98 include Universal Serial Bus (USB), IEEE 1394, Accelerated Graphics Port (AGP), Advanced Configuration and Power Interface (ACPI), and Digital Video Disc (DVD).

■ **PCMCIA enhancements**   There have been several enhancements to Windows 98 for PCMCIA support, including support for PC Card32 (CardBus) to implement high-bandwidth applications such as video capture and 100 Mbps networking. There is also support for PC Cards that operate at 3.3 volts, and for multifunction PC Cards (such as LAN and modem, or SCSI and sound) to operate on a single physical PC Card.

■ **PPTP support**   The Point-to-Point Tunneling Protocol provides a way to use public data networks (such as the Internet) to create virtual private networks connecting client PCs with servers. PPTP offers protocol encapsulation to support multiple protocols via TCP/IP connections and data encryption for privacy, making it safer to send information over nonsecure networks.

■ **Power management improvements**   Windows 98 includes support for the Advanced Configuration and Power Interface (ACPI), and support for the Advanced Power Management (APM) 1.2 extensions, including disk spindown, PCMCIA modem power down, and resume on ring.

■ **Remote Access Server**   Windows 98 includes all the components necessary to enable your desktop to act as a dial-up server. This allows dial-up clients to remotely connect to a Windows 98 machine for local resource access.

■ **System Configuration utility**   This utility allows for the fine-tuning of the Windows 98 startup and shutdown. Individual items in AUTOEXEC.BAT, CONFIG.SYS, SYSTEM.INI, WIN.INI, and the Startup folder can be enabled or disabled to troubleshoot conflicts or problems. It replaces and vastly improves on Windows 95 Sysedit.

■ **System File Checker**   This utility provides an easy way to verify that the Windows 98 system files (*.dll, *.com, *.vxd, *.drv, *.ocx, *.inf, *.hlp, and so on) have not been modified or corrupted. This utility also provides an easy mechanism for restoring the original versions of system files that have changed.

■ **System Information tool**   This utility provides extensive information on the system hardware and software environment. Many of the new troubleshooting, repair, and report utilities are available from the System Information utility through the Tools menu.

■ **System Troubleshooter**   This utility automates the routine troubleshooting steps used by support personnel and users when diagnosing issues with the Windows configuration. The troubleshooters are designed to address specific areas and devices. You can find the troubleshooters listed under the Help utility.

■ **Windows 98 Report tool**   Available under Tools in the System Information utility, this program allows you to submit a problem report to Microsoft. It automatically includes the information about your system that the Microsoft technicians need to have to examine the problem.

■ **Windows Media Player**   Windows 98 supports a new media-streaming architecture called ActiveMovie that delivers high-quality video playback of popular media types, including MPEG audio, WAV audio, MPEG video, AVI video, and Apple QuickTime video. The Media Player supports many popular audio, video, and combined media file formats. Updated Media Players are available for download from Microsoft.

■ **Windows System Update**   This feature helps you ensure that you're using the latest drivers and file systems available. The new Web-based service scans your system to determine what hardware and software you have installed, and then compares that information to a back-end database to determine whether newer drivers or system files are available. If there are newer drivers or system files, the service can automatically install the drivers.

# WINDOWS 2000

Released in early 2000, Windows 2000 is the successor to Windows NT and is intended for high-end business workstations and servers. Windows 2000 is a true 32-bit operating system (no DOS support) and also contains code to support 64-bit operations. Windows 2000 is divided into four versions targeted for different workplace requirements. Windows 2000 Professional is intended for desktop or workstation use and replaces Windows NT Workstation in the Microsoft product line. Windows 2000 Server Standard Edition supercedes NT Server and is intended for use in general-purpose network server environments, such as those found in small- to medium-sized businesses. Windows 2000 Advanced Server is intended for use in mission-critical environments of any medium- to large-sized business, including Internet Service Providers (ISPs). These last two versions replace Windows NT Server and Windows NT Server Enterprise Edition. A third (even more powerful) server version named Windows 2000 Datacenter Server was released in mid-2000.

Windows 2000 Professional includes all the features of Windows NT Workstation with numerous additions and improvements. The added features are meant to combine the ease of use of Windows 98 with the stability, speed, and security of Windows NT. Many of the improvements are listed here:

- **64-bit ready**   Microsoft has enabled the Windows 2000 code base to be 64-bit ready and is working toward delivering a full-featured 64-bit OS in the future (this will be fully compatible with existing 32-bit applications). The goal is to take full advantage of Intel's 64-bit "Itanium" processor when it is released.

- **Active Directory**   This is the integral directory service within Windows 2000. This service improves manageability, enables security, and extends the compatibility between Windows 2000 and other operating systems.

- **Group Policy**   Group Policy allows an administrator to define and control the state of computers and/or users in an organization. The effect of Group Policy may be adjusted using memberships in security groups.

- **Hardware wizard**   This wizard gives you a single, simple interface for dealing with many hardware issues. The options include the ability to add, configure, remove, troubleshoot and upgrade the peripherals that you use.

- **Index Server**   This utility runs in the background and creates an index of the contents of the local hard drive or files on a network (if connected). It includes the ability to select what directories and file properties to index. Index Server can operate locally or across a network to improve speed and accuracy, and search results can be ranked according to relevance.

- **Intellimirror desktop management**   This feature allows users to work at any station on a network and maintain their personal desktop settings, application data, and documents. Intellimirror gives administrators the ability to automatically distribute software (including remote OS installation). Administrators can also remotely control desktop configuration and maintenance.

- **Internet Explorer 5.x**   This Microsoft browser is fully integrated in the Windows 2000 Professional edition, though IE 6 is now available for download

- **Network Connections wizard**   A Network Connections folder in My Computer replaces the Network Settings item in the NT 4.0 Control Panel. Clicking on the Make New Connection icon opens Windows 2000's Network Connection wizard. The wizard guides you through fewer steps than were required in NT 4.0 to create a new connection. When used with Windows 2000 Server's Active Directory, the OS also adds a series of new management functions designed to simplify running a network.

- **Open/Save/Save As dialog boxes**   Windows 2000 provides an Outlook-like directory tree displayed to the left of the Open or Save dialog box, allowing for quick and easy navigation to different folders on the hard drive.

- **Personalized Start menu**   Windows 2000 tracks programs and files launched from Start | Programs. After the first six sessions, it alters the Programs menu to show just the most used items. The other entries are collapsed and available by clicking on the double arrows displayed. Windows 2000 continues to monitor file use and make adjustments to the Start menu.

- **Plug-and-play**   Windows 2000 is compatible with current plug-and-play standards, including support for the latest busses (such as USB, IEEE 1394 or "FireWire," and AGP) and other devices, such as DVD players, scanners, and digital cameras.

- **SMP support**   Symmetric Multiprocessing allows for multiple processors in the different versions of Windows 2000. The Professional and Standard Server editions support two processors, while the most advanced server edition can support up to eight processors.

- **Windows 2000 Explorer**   The Explorer in Windows 2000 includes all the individual customizable features of Windows 98 Explorer. Added improvements include enabling Thumbnail View on all files instead of on a folder-by-folder basis, customized Windows Explorer toolbars, and Folder Options in the Control Panel with a new streamlined Folder Options dialog box.

- **Windows Installer**   This utility allows for easier program installation and reduces problems caused by replacing shared DLL files with different versions during the install process. Windows Installer allows applications to examine existing DLL files in order to keep common files already installed. It also allows for adding program components at a later time and can be used to repair damaged applications. Windows Installer needs cooperative applications, so software publishers must write programs with MSI scripts that take advantage of Installer features.

## WINDOWS ME

Microsoft sought to solidify its hold on the home user PC market with its introduction of Windows Millennium Edition (Me) in September 2000. While benchmarking tests show no real performance advantages with Windows Me over Windows 98/SE, the update package does offer a wide range of enhancements, primarily focused on entertainment, multimedia, and home networking.

Major enhancements over Windows 98/SE include multimedia features such as an automated video editor with high-powered compression and simple import from video cameras, a wizard to automate scanner and still-image camera captures, and a media jukebox/recorder. New system-protection features include a wizard that restores an unstable system to an earlier, functional state, and new easy setup features simplify home networking and broadband access. In addition, support for the Universal Plug-and-Play specification will let Windows communicate with devices such as refrigerators and wearable computers (not that there are immediate applications for such features).

Two important changes are the removal of the standard Windows 9x option to restart or boot to the MS-DOS command prompt (though DOS applications are still usable in DOS windows), and an overhaul of Windows Internet services that improves performance. Windows Me uses the same desktop interface as Windows 2000 Professional, along with the new TCP/IP stack that connects to the Internet, but the new stack causes incompatibilities with some widely used Internet software. The help system has vastly improved troubleshooters and more informative error messages—the whole system is intended to be friendlier to experts and novices alike.

The System Restore feature backs up crucial system files when the computer is idle, making a snapshot of the system state every ten hours of computing time. Additional snapshots can be created at any time by running the System Restore wizard. If the system stops working, and if you can at least reboot (even if only in Safe mode), you can run the wizard and choose from among the earlier saved system states to restore. The current state of your documents and e-mail won't be overwritten, but the damaged system files will be overwritten with working copies. The System Restore component springs into action whenever you delete any potentially important files from the Windows or Program Files folder. For example, if you delete data from the Program Files folder, Windows will work in the background to restore the damage.

The System File Protection feature (based on the similar Windows File Protection in Windows 2000) silently prevents applications from overwriting crucial DLL files with older or nonstandard versions, and should drastically reduce the chance that a newly installed application will stop other programs from working. Users can also switch on the new AutoUpdate feature that downloads newer versions of system files in the background and then prompts you to restore them.

## Multimedia

Windows Movie Maker records video from an attached camera or imports existing files, and then splits the video into clips for editing that uses technology borrowed from high-end video-editing software. Existing videos can be imported from all standard formats (except RealMedia), but can be output only in Windows Media Format, not AVI or MPEG.

The Windows Image Acquisition (WIA) feature uses a wizard interface for previewing, creating, and managing images from scanners and digital still cameras. Basic features can be used with any plug-and-play scanner, but with a WIA-compatible camera, you can preview and manage pictures without downloading them. More than 60 WIA-enabled camera models (including most released in recent months) are now on the market. The wizard runs automatically when a WIA-enabled camera is plugged into a USB port or a button is pressed on a plug-and-play scanner.

The new Windows Media Player 7 works with most standard audio and video formats, with the exception of RealMedia, and includes a Web radio tuner, a jukebox, and a file-transfer utility that copies and compresses existing files or streaming media to portable MP3 players and Windows CE devices. The interface is less convoluted than most third-party media players, but Microsoft wastes a lot of screen space in an attempt to make the Media Player look cool, and the program is more crash-prone than anything else in Windows Me.

## Networking

A home networking wizard walks you through the process of setting up and customizing file, printer, and Internet sharing on a Windows Me machine connected to any peer-to-peer network. The wizard optionally creates a disk that can be used to install the Windows Me network software on other computers that you want to include on the same network, even if the other computers are running Windows 95 or 98. A new Folder Options applet in the Control Panel provides a direct route to file association and other customization features. To protect against reckless use, crucial system files cannot be viewed in Windows Explorer unless you mark a checkbox in the applet.

If you have ever installed a home network, virtual private network, or broadband software under Windows 95 or 98, you probably bumped into an error message telling you that you could use only six instances of TCP/IP. This meant that Windows 9*x* could connect to the Internet through no more than six networking components, and that no Internet connections were available for the new software you wanted to install. The new TCP/IP software built into Windows Me removes this limitation, and you can install as many networking features as you want without being forced to remove existing ones.

Internet Explorer 5.5 and Outlook Express 5.5 come with Windows Me, but the only notable enhancement over earlier versions is a new print preview feature in IE. NetMeeting 3.1 is also a part of the package, but its home-networking features are already available in downloadable versions.

# WINDOWS XP

Microsoft has traditionally provided different product families for business and home users. A prime example of this has been Windows Me for home users, and Windows 2000 for network/business applications. Over the last few years, however, Microsoft has been working to merge their personal and business operating systems into a single product family. Initially released in the latter part of 2001, Windows XP is the next version of Microsoft Windows, which brings convergence to Windows 2000 and Windows Millennium. Windows 2000 brings standards-based network security, manageability, and reliability, while Windows 98/Me provides an easy-to-use user interface, excellent hardware compatibility, and innovative support services. Windows XP is available in two basic versions: XP Home Edition for end users, and XP Professional for business users. This part of the chapter examines the most popular features common to both versions.

## User Interface

Most Windows users are familiar with navigating the many dialog boxes present in Windows 2000 and 98/Me. The user interface for Windows XP has been redesigned (see Figure 2-4). Common tasks have been consolidated and simplified, and new visual cues have been added to help you navigate the computer more easily. Windows XP has new visual styles and themes that use sharp 24-bit color icons and unique colors that can be easily related to specific tasks. For example, green represents tasks that enable you do something or go somewhere (such as the Start menu).

**Switching Users**    Under current versions of Windows, one user must save his or her work and log off the computer before a new user can log on. Windows XP employs a fast user switching technique based on

**FIGURE  2-4**    A typical Windows XP Home desktop view

terminal services to allow each user session simultaneously. Users don't need to log off and log on, and each user's data is entirely separated. For example, one user can log in and balance a checkbook. If that user walks away, another user can log in and play a game. The first user's session still runs in the background. In order to run reliable multiuser sessions on a home PC, at least 128MB of RAM is recommended. Fast user switching is also available on Windows XP Professional if you install it on a stand-alone or workgroup-connected computer. If you join a domain with a computer running Windows XP Professional, you will not be able to use fast user switching.

**Managing Files**    Windows XP uses Webview technology to help you manage files. For example, if you select a file or folder, you see a list of options allowing you to rename, move, copy, e-mail, remove, or publish it to the Web. This is similar to what you see in Windows 2000 if you right-click on a file or folder, but Windows XP takes this information and brings it into view directly on the desktop. Windows XP also provides a more manageable taskbar, grouping multiple instances of the same application. For example, instead of having nine instances of a Microsoft Word file each arranged horizontally on the taskbar, Windows XP groups them together on one taskbar button. This means you see only one taskbar button that shows the number of files that are open for the application. Clicking the button shows the vertical list of all filenames.

## Digital Media

With the explosive growth in digital media for both home and business, Windows XP includes enhanced versions of Windows Media Player and Windows Movie Maker, and improved photo support options.

**Media Player 8**    Windows Media Player 8 brings together popular digital media activities, including CD and DVD playback, jukebox management and recording, audio CD creation, Internet radio playback, and media transfer to portable devices (such as MP3 players). Windows Media Audio 8 provides nearly three times the music storage of MP3 with faster audio CD burning and intelligent media tracking for more control over digital media. The new My Music folder in Windows XP makes common music tasks easier to perform. In addition, Windows Media Player 8 includes features such as:

■ Ability to lock down Windows Media Player features in a managed network

■ Digital broadcast support

■ Accelerated video rendering

■ Video mixing and rendering

■ Expanded support for more audio cards and their features

**Movie Maker**    Windows Movie Maker 1.1 provides basic features for media capture and file creation, simple editing of video and audio, and saving/publishing Windows media files. You can record, edit, organize, and share the home video library from a PC. You could also share the home video with family and friends via e-mail or over the Web. If you want to make a video slide show, you can combine still images and publish into a Windows Media format. Although the utility produces output only in the Windows Media format, it will import all file formats and compression types supported by the DirectShow architecture. If your computer does not include video capture hardware, all other features are available and they allow for the importing and editing of media files that exist on your computer.

**Digital Photos**    Windows XP expands support for digital devices and provides many options to manipulate images, such as publishing pictures to the Web, e-mailing photos (with an option of compressing them for smaller file size), displaying pictures in an automatic slideshow, and allowing you to zoom in on images.

## Hardware Compatibility

Device and hardware support has been improved for Windows XP. Like Windows 2000, Windows XP simplifies the process of installing, configuring, and managing computer hardware. Windows XP includes plug-and-play (PnP) support for hundreds of devices not covered by Windows 2000, and enhanced support for Universal Serial Bus (USB) including USB 2.0, IEEE 1394, Peripheral Component Interconnect (PCI), and other bus architectures. Windows XP also supports 200 dpi monitors and the new Intel 64-bit Itanium processor (in some versions).

**DVD and CD Support**    Advances in storage technology have made it easier and more affordable to work with CDs and DVDs. Windows XP introduces native support for reading and writing to DVD-RAM drives, and can read the Universal Disk Format (UDF) 2.01, the common standard for DVD media, including DVD-ROM discs and DVD videos. By comparison, Windows 2000 can only read UDF 1.02- and 1.5-compatible discs.

Windows XP also allows you to master CDs in the CD-R or CD-RW formats using simple drag-and-drop features and a wizard-based process. When you save or copy a file to CD, the operating system first premasters the complete image on your hard drive, and then streams the data to your CD burner for recording. Premastering effectively minimizes the buffer underruns that generate errors in the recording process and render media useless (an all-too-frequent occurrence when recording on the fly).

## Software Compatibility and Services

Windows XP will be compatible with almost all of the top 1,000 applications that ran under Windows 9*x*, and almost every application that ran under Windows 2000. The only exceptions are antivirus programs, system utilities, and backup applications—though most manufacturers will have XP updates and patches by the time you install or upgrade to Windows XP. Application improvements in Windows XP help resolve application compatibility problems (such as those that occur when applications incorrectly detect the operating system version or when they reference memory after it has been freed). Fixes are invoked automatically by the operating system to make otherwise incompatible applications function—no user intervention is required. As new applications appear (or new fixes become available), application updates can be downloaded automatically from the Windows Update Web site using the Automatic Updates feature (similar to the feature introduced with Windows Me). There are also numerous file and print service features in Windows XP.

**WebDAV**    Web Digital Authoring & Versioning (WebDAV) technology in Windows XP enables you to publish documents on Internet servers and update them later. WebDAV is a standard Internet file access protocol that travels via HTTP over the existing Internet infrastructure (firewalls, routers, and so on). Windows XP includes a WebDAV redirector, which means you can access servers on the Internet just as you would a file share or server share at home or at work. While traditional file-sharing protocols cannot provide you with access to your data in every location, WebDAV uses Internet protocols that allow access to data repositories anywhere on the Internet. WebDAV lets you get to your data from wherever you are while using standard software applications (similar to Novell's iFolder technology for NetWare 6). In general, you can use the WebDAV redirector to publish your own Web data, or to use Internet repositories for storing data and sharing information.

**Client-Side Encryption**    Windows XP allows you to encrypt the offline files database (also known as the *Client-Side Cache,* or CSC). Encrypting the offline files database safeguards all locally cached documents from theft, while also providing additional security to your locally cached data. This is an improvement over Windows 2000, where the cached files could not be encrypted. For example, you can use offline files while keeping your sensitive data secure, and network administrators can use this feature to safeguard all local files. CSC is an excellent safeguard if your notebook computer gets stolen with confidential data saved in the offline files cache. Administrative privileges are required to configure how the offline files will be encrypted.

**FAT32 for DVD-RAM**    You can use a DVD-RAM disc with a FAT32 format and Windows XP will recognize, mount, and format your FAT32 volumes on DVD-RAM discs in superfloppy format (that is, the disk volume has no partition table). You can use a DVD-RAM disc with FAT32 formatting with any common removable media drive (such as magneto-optical and Jaz).

**NetCrawler**    NetCrawler can find, automatically install, and connect to all of the shared printers that it finds on a home or business network. The NetCrawler enables users who are unfamiliar with networking to have easy, automatically configured access to the computers and devices in a workgroup. It does this by searching the entire network folder and providing links to network resources. For example, if you configure a new computer and you want to print some documents, NetCrawler finds the available printers and displays them for you. Network shares that have not been seen by NetCrawler in 48 hours will be "aged out" of My Network Places by deleting shortcuts to those resources. NetCrawler is on by default when you install Windows XP Home, and on Windows XP Professional when the computer is in workgroup mode (not logged on to a domain). NetCrawler also checks for new resources whenever you log on to a network, and whenever you open or refresh your Printers and My Network Places folders.

**Sharing Faxes**    Fax sharing lets you send and receive faxes using your fax hardware (such as a fax-capable modem or fax board), or over a computer network offering fax-sharing services. You can send a fax using the Microsoft Outlook messaging and collaboration client (or from any other application that supports printing). The Windows XP fax-sharing feature set provides integration with the contact list in Outlook, the ability to preview a fax before it is sent, and the option to receive an e-mail confirming the fax was received. Administrators can fully control fax capabilities using the Microsoft Management Console (MMC) and the COM API. Fax sharing in Windows XP is fully interoperable with the Back Office Server (BOS)/Small Business Server (SBS) 2000 shared fax service.

## Networking and Communications

Windows XP includes Internet Explorer 6, and simplifies the setup and administration of networks by providing networks with additional features that expand the capabilities of typical network architectures.

**Device Plug-and-Play**    Ordinary plug-and-play capabilities allow administrators to set up, configure, and add peripherals to a PC. Universal Plug-and-Play extends this simplicity to include the entire network—enabling the discovery and control of devices (including networked devices and services) such as network-attached printers, Internet gateways, and consumer electronics equipment. Universal Plug-and-Play is designed to support zero-configuration, invisible networking, and automatic discovery for a range of device categories from a wide range of vendors. With Universal Plug-and-Play, a device can dynamically join a network, obtain an IP address, convey its capabilities, and learn about the presence and capabilities of other devices—all automatically. Universal Plug-and-Play uses standard TCP/IP and Internet protocols.

**Network Connections**    First introduced in Windows 98, Internet Connection Sharing (ICS) provides a convenient and economical method for more than one computer to be connected in a home using a single dial-up connection as a gateway (whether for Internet access or to a corporate network). Instead of requiring each device behind the gateway to have a globally unique IP address, it is possible to allocate private addresses to such devices.

In addition, the Home Networking Wizard automates network configuration and Internet Connection Sharing. It uses bridging to allow setup of a LAN without requiring you to know about networking protocols and physical networking requirements. In the past, a typical multisegment IP network required assigning a subnet number to each segment, configuring hosts on each subnet, and configuring packet forwarding between the subnets. Windows XP includes a media-access control (MAC) bridge component that can transparently interconnect network segments using the Spanning Tree Algorithm (STA). The MAC bridge incorporated in Windows XP allows the entire home network to operate as a single IP subnet. A *bridge* is a network device to connect two or more physical networks. It maintains a list of hardware devices on the network and checks the address of each data transmission to see if the recipient is on the network.

## Remote Desktop

With Remote Desktop, you can run applications on a remote computer running Windows XP Professional from any other client running a Microsoft Windows operating system. The applications run on the Windows XP Professional computer and only the keyboard input, mouse input, and display output data are transmitted over the network to the remote location. Remote Desktop lets you access your Windows XP computer from anywhere, over any connection, using any Windows-based client. It gives you secure access to all your applications, files, and network resources—just as if you were in front of your own workstation. Any applications that you leave running at the office are running when you connect remotely. If you're a network administrator, Remote Desktop serves as a rapid response tool. It lets you remotely access a server running Windows 2000 Server and see messages on the console, administer the computer remotely, or apply headless server control.

## System Reliability

The reliability of a PC and its resources is critically important for any network installation. Windows XP includes a range of improvements intended to enhance reliability.

**Driver Rollback**    Driver Rollback helps ensure system stability—much like the Last Known Good Configuration option first available in Windows 2000 Safe Mode and the System Restore. When you update a driver, a copy of the previous driver package is automatically saved in a special subdirectory of the system files. If the new driver does not work properly, you can restore the previous driver. Driver Rollback permits only one level of rollback (only one prior driver version can be saved at a time), and this feature is available for all device classes except printers.

**System Restore**    System Restore lets you restore your computer to a previous state in the event of a problem without losing personal data files such as documents, drawings, or e-mail. System Restore actively monitors changes to the system and some application files, and automatically creates easily identifiable restore points. Windows XP creates restore points each day by default as well as at the time of significant system events such as installing an application or driver. You can also create and name your own restore points at any time. System Restore does not monitor changes to (or recover) personal data files.

**System Recovery**    The Automated System Recovery (ASR) feature provides the ability to save and restore applications. This feature also provides the plug-and-play mechanism required by ASR to back up portions of the registry and restore that information to the registry. This is useful in a variety of disaster recovery scenarios. For example, if a hard disk fails and loses all configuration parameters and information, ASR can be applied to restore the server's data.

**Dynamic Update**    Reliability is enhanced with dynamic updates that provide application and device compatibility updates, driver updates, and emergency fixes for setup or security issues. Once the need for a Dynamic Update package has been determined, it's provided via the Windows Update Web service. If you choose the Dynamic Update option in Setup, Setup downloads the updates for devices and applications from Microsoft (instead of the original files from the CD). Organizations will also benefit because network administrators can download a complete Dynamic Update package—possibly including an applications compatibility or security fix for their users. Administrators can use the Dynamic Update package to ensure all users who install the operating system get these updated files.

**AutoUpdate**     This is an option for updating your computer without interrupting your Web experience. You don't have to visit special Web pages, interrupt Web surfing, or remember to periodically check for new updates. These downloads are configured to minimize the impact to network responsiveness, and are automatically resumed if the system is disconnected before an update is fully downloaded. Once the update has been downloaded to the PC, the user can then choose to install it.

**Windows Update**     Windows Update offers device driver support that supplements the extensive library of drivers available on the installation CD. Windows Update is an online extension of Windows XP, providing a central location for product enhancements, such as service packs, device drivers, and system security updates. For example, if you install a new device, plug-and-play will search for a driver locally and online at Windows Update. If your computer is *not* connected to the Internet and no suitable driver is found locally on the system, you will be prompted to go online and search for a driver. If an updated driver is found on Windows Update, the driver's .cab file is downloaded and the Windows Update ActiveX control selects the .INF file for installation.

## Internet Security

As with any network, security is important to ensure the safety of sensitive files, network resources, and network access. Windows XP provides a suite of enhanced security features that help to protect the network from unauthorized access.

**Internet Firewall**     Windows XP provides Internet security through a built-in feature called Internet Connection Firewall, which is suitable for home users and small businesses. It protects computers directly connected to the Internet, or connected behind an Internet Connection Sharing host computer that is running the Internet Connection Firewall. Internet Connection Firewall prevents the scanning of ports and resources (file and printer shares) from external sources. When enabled, the firewall blocks all unsolicited connections originating from the Internet using the logic of a Network Address Translator (NAT) to validate incoming requests for access to a network or the local host. If the network communication did not originate within the protected network, or no port mapping had been created, the incoming data will be dropped. Internet Connection Firewall is available for LAN, PPoE, VPN, or dial-up connections.

**Restriction Policies**     Software restriction policies in Windows XP provide a transparent way to isolate and use untrusted, potentially harmful code in a way that protects you against various viruses, Trojans, and worms that are spread through e-mail and the Internet. These policies allow you to choose how you want to manage software on your system. By executing untrusted code and scripts in a segregated area (known informally as the *sandbox*) you get the benefit of untrusted code and scripts that prove to be benign, while the tainted code is prevented from doing any damage. For example, untrusted code would be prevented from sending e-mail, accessing files, or performing other normal computing functions until verified as safe. Software restriction policies protect against infected e-mail attachments. This includes file attachments that are saved to a temporary folder as well as embedded objects and scripts.

**Wireless Security**    Secure Wireless/Ethernet LAN enhances your ability to develop secure wired and wireless local area networks (LANs). With Secure Wireless/Ethernet LAN, a computer will not usually be able to access the network until the user logs on. However, if a device has "machine authentication" enabled, then that computer can obtain access to the LAN after it has been authenticated and authorized by the IAS/RADIUS server. Secure Wireless/Ethernet LAN in Windows XP implements security for both wired and wireless LANs that are based on IEEE 802.11 specifications. This process is supported by the use of public certificates that are deployed by autoenrollment or smart cards. This enables access control for wired Ethernet and wireless IEEE 802.11 networks in public places such as malls or airports.

**Credential Management**    The Credential Management feature provides a secure store of user credentials, including passwords and X.509 RSA security certificates. This provides a consistent single sign-on experience for users (including roaming users). If you access an application within a company network, your first attempt requires authentication and you're prompted to supply a credential. After providing this credential, it will be associated with the requesting application. In future access, the saved credential will be reused without having to reenter the credential. It has three components: the Credential Manager, the Credential Collection User Interface, and the Keyring.

# The Boot Process

Computer initialization is a *process,* not an event. From the moment power is applied until the system sits idle at the command-line prompt or graphical desktop, the PC boot process is a sequence of predictable steps that verifies the system and prepares it for operation. By understanding each step in system initialization, you can develop a real appreciation for the way that hardware and software relate to one another. You also stand a much better chance of identifying and resolving problems when a system fails to boot properly. This part of the chapter provides a step-by-step review of a typical PC boot process.

## APPLYING POWER

PC initialization starts when you push the power button (or press the Reset button). When all output voltages from the power supply are valid, the supply generates a Power Good (PG) logic signal. It can take between 100ms and 500ms for the supply to generate a PG signal. When the motherboard timer chip receives the PG signal, the timer stops forcing a Reset signal to the CPU. At this point, the CPU starts processing.

## THE BOOTSTRAP

The very first operation performed by a CPU is to fetch an instruction from address FFFF:0000h. Since this address is almost at the end of available ROM space, the instruction is almost always a jump command (JMP) followed by the actual BIOS ROM starting address. By making all CPUs start at the same point, the BIOS ROM can then send program control anywhere in the particular ROM (and each ROM *is* usually different). This initial search of address FFFF:0000h and the subsequent redirection of the CPU is traditionally referred to as the *bootstrap,* because the PC "pulls itself up by its bootstraps," or gets itself going. Today, we have shortened the term to *boot* and have broadened its meaning to include the entire initialization process.

## CORE TESTS

Once the BIOS has been located, the real startup begins with a series of *core tests*. The core tests are part of the overall power-on self-test (POST) sequence, which is the most important use of a system BIOS during initialization. As you might expect, allowing the system to initialize and run with flaws in the motherboard, memory, or drive systems can have catastrophic consequences for files in memory or on disk. To ensure system integrity, a set of hardware-specific self-test routines checks and initializes the major motherboard components and identifies the presence of any other firmware in the system (e.g., drive controller BIOS, video BIOS, SCSI BIOS, and so on), which will also be loaded into memory.

BIOS starts with a test of the motherboard hardware, such as the CPU, its math coprocessor, timer chips, direct memory access (DMA) controllers, and interrupt (IRQ) controllers. If an error is detected in this early phase of testing, a series of beeps (or *beep codes*) are produced. By knowing the BIOS manufacturer and the beep code, you can determine the nature of the problem. You'll learn more about beep and error codes in later chapters. Beep codes are used because the video system has not been initialized.

Next, BIOS looks for the presence of a video ROM from memory location C000:0000h through C780:000h. In just about all systems, the search will reveal a video BIOS ROM on a video adapter board plugged into an available expansion slot. If a video BIOS is found, its contents are evaluated with a checksum test. If the test is successful, control is transferred to the video BIOS, which loads and initializes the video adapter. When initialization is complete, you see a cursor on the screen and control returns to the system BIOS. When no external video adapter BIOS is located, the system BIOS provides an initialization routine for the motherboard's video adapter and a cursor also appears. Once the video system initializes, you are likely to see a bit of text on the display identifying the system or video BIOS ROM maker and revision level. If the checksum test fails, you will see an error message such as "C000 ROM Error" or "Video ROM Error." Initialization will usually halt right there.

Now that the video system is ready, system BIOS will scan memory from C800:0000h through DF80:0000h in 2KB increments to search for any other ROMs that might be on other adapter cards in the system. If other ROMs are found, their contents are tested and run. As each supplemental ROM is executed, it will show manufacturer and revision ID information. In some cases, a supplemental (or *adapter*) ROM may alter an existing BIOS ROM routine. For example, an Ultra DMA/100 drive controller board with its own on-board ROM will replace the motherboard's older drive routines. When a ROM fails the checksum test, you will see an error message such as "XXXX ROM Error." The XXXX indicates the segment address where the faulty ROM was detected. When a faulty ROM is detected, system initialization will usually halt, and you'll need to replace the defective ROM (typically the entire adapter).

## POST

BIOS then checks the memory location at 0000:0472h. This address contains a flag that determines whether the initialization is a cold start (power first applied) or a warm start (reset button or CTRL-ALT-DEL key combination). A value of 1234h at this address indicates a warm start, in which case the POST routine is skipped. If any other value is found at that location, a cold start is assumed and the full POST routine will be executed.

The full POST checks many of the other higher-level functions on the motherboard, memory, keyboard, video adapter, floppy drive, math coprocessor, printer port, serial port, hard drive, and other subsystems. Dozens of tests are performed by the POST. This is the point when you see the memory test count up one or more times, see the list of detected drives, identify PnP device assignments, and so on. When an error is encountered, the single-byte POST code is written to I/O port 80h, where it may be read by a POST code reader card. In other cases, you may see an error message on the display (and system initialization will halt). Keep in mind that POST codes and their meanings will vary slightly between BIOS manufacturers. If the POST completes successfully, the system will respond with a single beep from the speaker. Later chapters will cover I/O port POST codes.

# FINDING THE OS

The system now needs to load an operating system (such as DOS, Windows, or Linux). The first step here is to have the BIOS search for a DOS VBS on the A: drive. If there is no disk in the drive, you will see the drive light illuminate briefly, and then BIOS will search the next drive in the boot order (usually drive C:). If there is a disk in drive A:, BIOS will load sector 1 (head 0 cylinder 0) from the disk's DOS VBS into memory starting at 0000:7C00h. There are a number of potential problems when attempting to load the VBS. Otherwise, the first program in the directory (IO.SYS) will begin to load, followed by MSDOS.SYS.

- If the first byte of the DOS VBS is less than 06h (or if the first byte is greater than or equal to 06h, and the next nine words of the sector contain the same data pattern), you will see an error message similar to "Diskette boot record error."

- If IO.SYS and MSDOS.SYS are not the first two files in the directory (or some other problem is encountered in loading), you'll see an error such as "Non-system disk or disk error."

- If the boot sector on the floppy disk is corrupt and cannot be read (DOS 3.3 or earlier), you'll probably get a "Disk boot failure" message.

If the OS cannot be loaded from any floppy drive, the system will search the first fixed drive (hard drive). Hard drives are a bit more involved than floppy drives. BIOS loads sector 1 (head 0 cylinder 0) from the hard drive's master partition boot sector (called the *master boot sector,* or *MBS*) into memory starting at 0000:7C00h, and the last two bytes of the sector are checked. If the final two bytes of the master partition boot sector are not 55h and AAh, respectively, the boot sector is invalid; you will see an error message similar to "No boot device available," and system initialization will halt. Other systems may depict the error differently. For example, classic PCs may attempt to load ROM BASIC. If the BIOS attempts to load ROM BASIC and there is no such feature in the BIOS, you'll see a "ROM BASIC error" message.

Otherwise, the disk will search for and identify any extended partitions (up to 24 total partitions). Once any extended partitions have been identified, the drive's original boot sector will search for a boot indicator byte marking a partition as active and bootable. If none of the partitions is marked as bootable (or if more than one partition is marked as bootable), a disk error message will be displayed, such as "Invalid partition table." Some older BIOS versions may attempt to load ROM BASIC, but will generate an error message in most cases anyway.

When an active bootable partition is found in the master partition boot sector, the VBS from the bootable partition is loaded into memory and tested. If the VBS cannot be read, you will see an error message similar to "Error loading operating system." When the VBS *does* load, the last two bytes are tested for a signature of 55h and AAh, respectively. If these signature bytes are missing, you will see an error message such as "Missing operating system." Under either error condition, system initialization will halt.

After the signature bytes are identified, the VBS (now in memory) is executed as if it were a program. This "program" checks the root directory to ensure that any necessary components (e.g., IO.SYS and MSDOS.SYS, or IBMBIO.COM and IBMDOS.COM under DOS) are available. In older MS-DOS versions, IO.SYS and MSDOS.SYS have to be the first two directory entries. If the DOS VBS was created with MS-DOS 3.3 or earlier, and the two startup files are not the first two files in the directory (or there is an error in loading the files), the system will produce an error code such as "Non-System disk or disk error." If the boot sector is corrupt, you may see a message like "Disk boot failure."

## LOADING DOS

If no problems are detected in the disk's DOS VBS, IO.SYS (or IBMBIO.COM) is loaded and executed. If Windows is on the system, IO.SYS may be renamed WINBOOT.SYS, which will be executed instead. IO.SYS contains extensions to BIOS that start low-level device drivers for such things as the keyboard, printer, and block devices. Remember that IO.SYS also contains initialization code that is only needed during system startup. A copy of this initialization code is placed at the top of conventional memory, which takes over initialization. The next step is to load MSDOS.SYS (or IBMDOS.COM), which is loaded such that it overlaps the part of IO.SYS containing the initialization code. MSDOS.SYS (the MS-DOS kernel) is then executed to initialize base device drivers, detect system status, reset the disk system, initialize devices such as the printer and serial port, and set up system default parameters. The MS-DOS essentials are now loaded and control returns to the IO.SYS/WINBOOT.SYS initialization code in memory.

Remember that for Windows systems, IO.SYS (or WINBOOT.SYS) combines the functions of IO.SYS and MSDOS.SYS.

## ESTABLISHING THE ENVIRONMENT

If a CONFIG.SYS file is present, it is opened and read by IO.SYS/WINBOOT.SYS. The DEVICE statements are processed first in the order they appear, and then INSTALL statements are processed in the order they appear. A SHELL statement is handled next. If no SHELL statement is present, the COMMAND.COM processor is loaded. When COMMAND.COM is loaded, it overwrites the initialization code left over from IO.SYS (which is now no longer needed). Under Windows, COMMAND.COM is loaded only if an AUTOEXEC.BAT file is present to process the AUTOEXEC.BAT statements. Finally, all other statements in CONFIG.SYS are processed, and WINBOOT.SYS also looks for the SYSTEM.DAT registry file.

When an AUTOEXEC.BAT file is present, COMMAND.COM (which now has control of the system) will load and execute the batch file. After batch file processing is complete, the familiar DOS prompt will appear. If no AUTOEXEC.BAT file is in the root directory, COMMAND.COM will request the current DATE and TIME and then show the DOS prompt. You may now launch applications or use any available OS commands. AUTOEXEC.BAT may also call a shell (such as Windows 3.1$x$) or start an application. Under Windows, IO.SYS/WINBOOT.SYS automatically loads HIMEM.SYS, IFSHLP.SYS, and SETVER.EXE, and then loads the WIN.COM kernel to officially start Windows. After the necessary Windows components load successfully, you'll see the familiar Windows desktop.

# Mastering MSDOS.SYS

In the early days of DOS, a trio of critical files was needed to boot the operating system: IO.SYS, MSDOS.SYS, and COMMAND.COM. With the advent of Windows 95 (and later, Windows 98/Me), the MSDOS.SYS file was completely implemented as a text file located in the system root folder. The file is also set with Read-Only, System, and Hidden attributes, so you normally don't see the file unless you elect to view hidden files. MSDOS.SYS contains a [Paths] section that lists the locations for other Windows files (such as the registry) and an [Options] section that you can use to personalize the boot process. If you'd like to tailor the boot process under Windows 9x/Me, you'll need to edit the MSDOS.SYS file.

Windows XP effectively eliminates the MSDOS.SYS file.

# EDITING MSDOS.SYS

In order to edit the MSDOS.SYS file, you must open the file into any basic text editor such as NotePad or WordPad using steps such as those below:

1. Click Start, highlight Find, then click Files or Folders.
2. In the Named box, type **MSDOS.SYS** (see Figure 2-5). In the Look In box, click your boot drive (usually drive C:), then click the Find Now button.
3. Right-click the MSDOS.SYS file and then click Properties.
4. Clear the read-only and hidden checkboxes to remove these attributes from the MSDOS.SYS file, and then click OK.
5. Right-click the MSDOS.SYS file and select Open With.
6. In the Choose the Program You Want to Use box, click WordPad, then click OK. The MSDOS.SYS file appears as in Figure 2-6.
7. Make the changes you want to the MSDOS.SYS file.
8. When you're finished, save the file, and quit WordPad.
9. Right-click the MSDOS.SYS file and then click Properties.
10. Click the read-only and hidden checkboxes to set the attributes for the file, then click OK.
11. Close the Find window and restart Windows so that your changes can take effect.

Make a backup copy of your MSDOS.SYS file before editing it. This way you can easily restore the original file if you have difficulty during the editing process.

One issue to remember is that some programs expect the MSDOS.SYS file to be *at least* 1,024 bytes in length. If it is not that length, those programs may not work correctly. For example, if an anti-virus program detects that the MSDOS.SYS file is less than 1,024 bytes in length, the program may assume that the

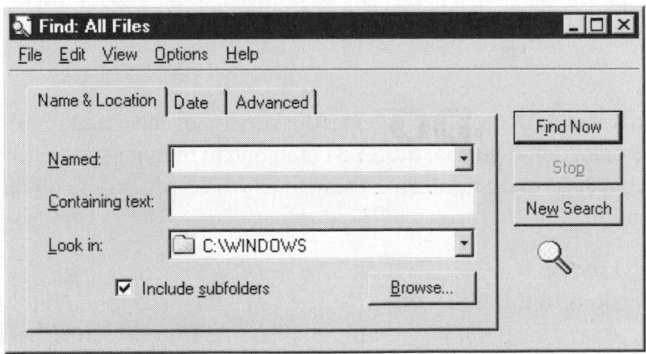

**FIGURE 2-5**   Use the Find dialog box to locate your MSDOS.SYS file.

```
[Paths]
WinDir=<Windows>
WinBootDir=<Windows>
HostWinBootDrv=C
[Options]
BootGUI=1
;
;Some programs on this system expect the MSDOS.SYS file to be at least
;1024 bytes in length; hence, the following lines create an MSDOS.SYS
;file that is greater than 1024 bytes in length. These lines are not
;needed for Windows to boot or run.
;xxxxxxxxxxxxxxxxxxxxxxxxxxxxxxxxxxxxxxxxxxxxxxxxxxxxxxxxxxxxxxxxxxxxxa
;xxxxxxxxxxxxxxxxxxxxxxxxxxxxxxxxxxxxxxxxxxxxxxxxxxxxxxxxxxxxxxxxxxxxxb
;xxxxxxxxxxxxxxxxxxxxxxxxxxxxxxxxxxxxxxxxxxxxxxxxxxxxxxxxxxxxxxxxxxxxxc
;xxxxxxxxxxxxxxxxxxxxxxxxxxxxxxxxxxxxxxxxxxxxxxxxxxxxxxxxxxxxxxxxxxxxxd
;xxxxxxxxxxxxxxxxxxxxxxxxxxxxxxxxxxxxxxxxxxxxxxxxxxxxxxxxxxxxxxxxxxxxxe
;xxxxxxxxxxxxxxxxxxxxxxxxxxxxxxxxxxxxxxxxxxxxxxxxxxxxxxxxxxxxxxxxxxxxxf
;xxxxxxxxxxxxxxxxxxxxxxxxxxxxxxxxxxxxxxxxxxxxxxxxxxxxxxxxxxxxxxxxxxxxxg
;xxxxxxxxxxxxxxxxxxxxxxxxxxxxxxxxxxxxxxxxxxxxxxxxxxxxxxxxxxxxxxxxxxxxxh
;xxxxxxxxxxxxxxxxxxxxxxxxxxxxxxxxxxxxxxxxxxxxxxxxxxxxxxxxxxxxxxxxxxxxxi
;xxxxxxxxxxxxxxxxxxxxxxxxxxxxxxxxxxxxxxxxxxxxxxxxxxxxxxxxxxxxxxxxxxxxxj
;xxxxxxxxxxxxxxxxxxxxxxxxxxxxxxxxxxxxxxxxxxxxxxxxxxxxxxxxxxxxxxxxxxxxxk
;xxxxxxxxxxxxxxxxxxxxxxxxxxxxxxxxxxxxxxxxxxxxxxxxxxxxxxxxxxxxxxxxxxxxxl
;xxxxxxxxxxxxxxxxxxxxxxxxxxxxxxxxxxxxxxxxxxxxxxxxxxxxxxxxxxxxxxxxxxxxxm
;xxxxxxxxxxxxxxxxxxxxxxxxxxxxxxxxxxxxxxxxxxxxxxxxxxxxxxxxxxxxxxxxxxxxxn
;xxxxxxxxxxxxxxxxxxxxxxxxxxxxxxxxxxxxxxxxxxxxxxxxxxxxxxxxxxxxxxxxxxxxxo
;xxxxxxxxxxxxxxxxxxxxxxxxxxxxxxxxxxxxxxxxxxxxxxxxxxxxxxxxxxxxxxxxxxxxxp
;xxxxxxxxxxxxxxxxxxxxxxxxxxxxxxxxxxxxxxxxxxxxxxxxxxxxxxxxxxxxxxxxxxxxxq
;xxxxxxxxxxxxxxxxxxxxxxxxxxxxxxxxxxxxxxxxxxxxxxxxxxxxxxxxxxxxxxxxxxxxxr
;xxxxxxxxxxxxxxxxxxxxxxxxxxxxxxxxxxxxxxxxxxxxxxxxxxxxxxxxxxxxxxxxxxxxxs
```

**FIGURE 2-6** The MSDOS.SYS text file must be at least 1,024 bytes in length and can be edited under Windows 9x/Me just like any other text document.

MSDOS.SYS file is infected with a virus. However, the version of the MSDOS.SYS file on your system may not be 1,024 bytes or longer. If you use the SYS command to transfer system files from your Windows startup disk (or other boot disk) to the hard drive, the MSDOS.SYS file that is copied to the hard disk is less than 1,024 bytes in length.

## MSDOS.SYS Options

There are two main sections to the MSDOS.SYS file: the [Paths] section defines the directory paths to major Windows file areas, and the [Options] section enables you to configure many of the available attributes used to boot a Windows 9*x*/Me system. The variables for these two sections are listed in Table 2-3.

**TABLE 2-3    TYPICAL VARIABLES USED IN THE MSDOS.SYS FILE**

| [Paths] | |
|---|---|
| HostWinBootDrv= | Indicates the location of the boot drive root directory. |
| UninstallDir= | This specifies the location of the w95undo.dat and w95undo.ini files that are necessary to uninstall Windows 95. This setting is present only if you back up your system files during Windows 95 Setup. |
| WinBootDir= | Indicates the location of the necessary startup files. The default is the directory specified during the setup process (e.g., c:\windows). |
| WinDir= | Indicates the location of the Windows 9x directory specified during setup. |
| **[Options]** | |
| AutoScan=1 | This determines whether ScanDisk is run after a bad shutdown (0 does not run ScanDisk, 1 prompts before running ScanDisk, and 2 runs ScanDisk automatically—but prompts you before fixing errors if any errors are found. This setting is used only by OSR 2 and Windows 98. |
| BootDelay=n | Sets the initial startup delay to n seconds (default is 2). A BootKeys=0 entry disables the delay. The only purpose of the delay is to give the user sufficient time to press F8 after the "Starting Windows" message appears. |
| BootSafe= | Enables Safe mode for system startup. The default is 0. |
| BootGUI= | Enables automatic graphical startup into Windows 9x. The default is 1. |
| BootKeys= | Enables the startup option keys (F5, F6, and F8). The default is 1. |
| BootMenu= | Enables automatic display of the Windows 9x Startup menu (the user must press F8 in Windows 95, or press and hold the CTRL key in Windows 98 to see the menu). The default is 0. Setting this value to 1 eliminates the need to press F8 to see the menu. |
| BootMenuDefault=# | Sets the default menu item on the Windows Startup menu; the default is 3 for a computer with no networking components, and 4 for a networked computer. |
| BootMenuDelay=# | Sets the number of seconds to display the Windows Startup menu before running the default menu item. The default is 30 seconds. |
| BootMulti= | Enables dual-boot capabilities. The default is 0. Setting this value to 1 enables the user to start MS-DOS by pressing F4, or by pressing F8 to use the Windows Startup menu. |
| BootWarn= | Enables the Safe mode startup warning. The default is 1. |
| BootWin= | Enables Windows 9x as the default OS. Setting this value to 0 disables Windows 9x as the default (useful only with MS-DOS version 5 or 6.x on the computer). The default is 1. |
| DblSpace= | Enables automatic loading of DBLSPACE.BIN. The default is 1. |
| DoubleBuffer= | Enables loading of a double-buffering driver for a SCSI controller. The default is 0. Setting this value to 1 enables double-buffering (if required by the SCSI controller). |
| DrvSpace= | Enables automatic loading of DRVSPACE.BIN. The default is 1. |
| LoadTop= | Enables the loading of COMMAND.COM or DRVSPACE.BIN at the top of 640KB memory. The default is 1. Set this value to 0 with Novell NetWare or any software that makes assumptions about what is used in specific memory areas. |
| Logo= | Enables display of the Windows 9x logo. The default is 1. Setting this value to 0 also avoids hooking a variety of interrupts that can create incompatibilities with certain memory managers from other vendors. |
| Network= | Enables Safe Mode with Networking as a menu option. The default is 1 for computers with networking installed. This value should be 0 if network software components are not installed |

If Windows 9*x* is installed in its own directory, the earlier version of MS-DOS is preserved on the hard disk. If you set BootMulti=1 in MSDOS.SYS, you can start the earlier version of MS-DOS by pressing F4 when starting Windows 9*x*.

## COMMON OS PROBLEMS

Since the operating system is an integral part of the PC, any problems with using or upgrading the OS can adversely affect system operation. Software does not fail like hardware—once software is loaded and running, it will not eventually break down from heat or physical stress. Unfortunately, software is hardly perfect. Upgrading from one OS to another can upset the system's operation (for example, older files may be carried over to the upgraded OS and affect its stability). And *bugs* in the OS can result in an unforeseen operation that might totally upset a system's reliability.

Virtually all versions of operating systems have bugs in them, especially in early releases. In most cases, such bugs are found in the transient commands that are run from the command line rather than in the three core files (IO.SYS, MSDOS.SYS, and COMMAND.COM). Even the latest stand-alone version of MD-DOS (6.22) has endured several incarnations since its initial release as 6.0. As a technician, you should be sensitive to the version of DOS, Windows 9*x*/Me/XP, Linux, or other operating systems being used by your customer. Whenever the customer complains of trouble using a particular utility (such as Backup) or of difficulties using specific software packages, one of your first steps should be to ensure that the OS version in use is appropriate. If the OS has been updated, you should try the new release or service patch. Remember that a software fault can manifest itself as a hardware problem. That is, the hardware may malfunction or refuse to respond (though this does not damage the hardware). Check with the OS maker to find its newest releases and fixes. Microsoft maintains an extensive Web site for the support of its operating systems (such as the Windows Update site for Windows XP in Figure 2-7). Check in regularly to find error reports and upgrades. If your customer is using Windows 98 or later, check the Windows Help file for a troubleshooter that deals with the error or the device that is causing the problem.

Another concern for technicians is dealing with old versions of an OS. Remember that part of the task of an OS is to manage system resources (disk space, memory, and so on). New OS versions such as Windows 98/SE and later do a much better job of hardware and resource management than Windows 3.11 and earlier. Should you recommend an upgrade to your customer? As a general rule, any Windows version older than 98 is worth upgrading to Windows XP, especially if your customer is planning to keep or upgrade the PC (and if the PC hardware supports the system requirements of the new OS). If you're already using Windows 98/SE or later, the only good reason to upgrade would be to take advantage of advanced features offered by the newer OS (such as the integrated firewall and MovieMaker in XP). Of course, if the PC hardware will not support an OS upgrade (e.g., due to insufficient processing power or disk space), you and your customer will need to evaluate the costs/benefits of PC upgrades or outright replacement.

**FIGURE 2-7**    Use the Windows Update feature to check for updates or patches that can improve the stability, performance, and security of your OS.

# Creating a Boot Diskette

The most persistent problem with PC troubleshooting is that booting a system successfully can be difficult, especially if there are hard drive problems. Thus, it is particularly important to have a bootable floppy disk on hand. There are two means of creating a boot disk: automatically through an existing Windows 9x/Me/XP platform, or manually through a DOS 6.22 platform. In either case, you need access to a running PC with an OS similar to the version you plan to install on the new PC (or that is already installed on the suspect PC).

# WINDOWS 9X/ME/XP

Windows 9x/Me/XP come with an automatic Startup Disk maker. If you have access to a Windows 9x or Me system, use the following procedure to create a DOS startup diskette:

1. Label a blank diskette and insert it into your floppy drive.

2. Click on Start | Settings | Control Panel.

3. Double-click on the Add/Remove Programs icon.

4. Select the Startup Disk tab.

5. Click on Create Disk.

6. The utility will remind you to insert a diskette, and then prepare the disk automatically. When the preparation is complete, test the disk.

 If you have a Windows XP system, the process is a bit different:

1. Insert a blank diskette into the floppy drive.

2. Open My Computer, then right-click the floppy drive.

3. Select Format in the drop-down menu.

4. Under Format options, click Create an MS-DOS Startup Disk (see Figure 2-8). You may also enter a volume label to help you identify the diskette later.

5. Click Start. The process will take place automatically.

**FIGURE  2-8**    Under Windows XP, creating a startup diskette can be accomplished as part of the diskette's formatting process.

The preparation process takes several minutes, and the Windows 95 creation process will copy the following files to your disk: ATTRIB, CHKDSK, COMMAND, DEBUG, DRVSPACE.BIN, EDIT, FDISK, FORMAT, REGEDIT, SCANDISK, SYS, and UNINSTAL. All of these files are DOS 7.-based files, so you can run them from the A: prompt. Other versions of Windows will copy different suites of files to the disk.

The startup disk made under Windows 98/Me is much more powerful and useful. The major difference between the disk made by Windows 95 and the one made by Windows 98 and later is that the Windows 98/Me diskette includes the generic drivers for your CD-ROM. If you want a Windows 95 startup disk with CD-ROM support, you have to create CONFIG.SYS and AUTOEXEC.BAT files and add the real-mode (DOS) drivers yourself. In addition, Windows 98/Me compresses a lot of utilities into a CAB file, EBD.CAB. Windows 98/Me creates a RAMdrive in memory and then expands the files in EBD.CAB to the RAMdrive. Without the compressed file, there would not be enough room on a single floppy disk to contain all the startup files, drivers, and utilities. Unfortunately, the startup diskette created by Windows XP does not provide generic real-mode support for your CD-ROM—you will simply be taken to an A: prompt. This limits the utility of an XP startup disk, so technicians may want to keep a Windows 98/Me startup disk handy.

The early Windows 95 FDISK utility reportedly has a bug that can cause problems when creating more than one partition on the same drive. Later releases of Windows 95 (such as OSR 2) claim to have corrected this issue, but if you encounter problems with FDISK, use the version with Windows 98/Me/XP.

## DOS 6.22

If you don't have access to a system with Windows 9x/Me/XP already, you need to make a boot disk manually, using DOS 6.22 utilities. Create a bootable diskette by using the SYS feature, as shown here (assuming that you buy blank diskettes that are pre-formatted):

```
C:\DOS\> SYS A:    <Enter>
```

or use the FORMAT command to make a bootable diskette, like this:

```
C:\DOS\> FORMAT A: /S    <Enter>
```

Once the disk is bootable, copy the following DOS utilities (usually from the DOS directory): FDISK, FORMAT, SYS, MEM, DEFRAG, SCANDISK, EDIT, HIMEM, EMM386, and EDIT. In addition, you will need the drivers for your CD-ROM if you want real-mode support. You may not need all of these utilities, but it can be handy to have them accessible in case you need to check a disk or memory. You'll also need to create CONFIG.SYS and AUTOEXEC.BAT files to set up any necessary DOS environment, as well as enable your CD-ROM drive.

# Multi-Boot Setup

Most PC users will employ a single operating system, but a growing number of users choose to utilize more than one OS as their PC is required to serve a larger range of roles. For example, a Web developer may need Windows 98/SE for word processing, but need Windows 2000 or XP Professional to perform development work on their Web presence. In other cases, software developers may require several different operating systems in order to verify the compatibility of their new software product. No matter what the reason may be, a technician should have a basic understanding of multi-boot concepts.

A *multi-boot* platform is simply a PC that contains two or more operating systems—the desired operating system is selected at boot time (and can be changed by rebooting the PC and selecting another OS). Any PC can support multiple operating systems so long as three key conditions are met:

- The PC's hardware meets the minimum system requirements for each desired OS.
- You have a "boot loader" utility that can be installed on your PC.
- There is adequate drive space on the PC for each OS and its related applications.

There are many different boot loaders available for the PC including TeràByte's BootIt (terabyteunlimited.com/bootitng.html), System Commander (www.v-com.com/product/sc7_ind.html), and numerous shareware boot loaders available from popular download sites like CNET.com. Normally, the master boot record points to a specific OS. When a boot loader is installed, it redirects the MBR to a small utility instead (see a screen shot of System Commander 7 in Figure 2-9) that contains a list of the operating systems you've installed. From there, you can select the desired OS, and it will boot normally.

## MIXING AND MATCHING

The trick comes when installing the various operating systems. Some tools like System Commander provide powerful wizards that can automatically prepare a PC for the operating system that you want to install. In many cases, however, getting multiple OS versions to behave properly on the same PC can sometimes be a chore. For example, suppose that you already have an operating system like Windows 98/SE, and then you install System Commander. If you wish to install Windows XP as another operating

**FIGURE  2-9**    Boot loaders like System Commander 7 allow you to select from numerous installed operating systems at start time (Courtesy of V Communications).

system, you'll need to prepare the drive for the OS, then install the OS. Let's look at the installation using System Commander's OS Wizard:

 It's helpful to check with the boot loader's Web site and look for specific instructions or known compatibility issues before you attempt a new OS installation.

1. Once System Commander is installed, reboot to the System Commander OS Selection Menu.

2. Select the OS Wizard (ALT-O). The OS Wizard appears.

3. Select the type of installation (New), the OS by name (Windows XP Home in this example), and the installation type (Isolated—XP will be on its own partition).

4. Complete the OS Wizard operation (this entire process is documented in detail in the manual). Once the drive is properly partitioned by the OS Wizard, you must complete the OS installation.

 Using a wizard to prepare the drive for your desired OS is often faster and easier than having to prepare partitions yourself.

5. It's time to install the actual OS. In this example, we're using Windows XP. Insert the Windows XP installation CD and press CTRL-ALT-DEL to boot from this media to gain access to the CD-ROM drive (you may need to configure your computer's BIOS to boot from the CD-ROM before other devices). The Windows XP installation will begin.

6. Now you're using the operating system's installation program. Remember that you're installing into the new partition (whether created manually or with the OS Wizard). This is the active partition on the C: drive. At some point, the installation will ask where you would like to install Windows XP. This screen will show you all of the partitions and free space on your drive. It is possible to direct the installation to another partition (or even another hard drive). You will also be able to convert the file system from FAT16 or FAT32 to NTFS. You should continue using FAT16 or FAT32 if you would like to be able to access your Windows XP partition from within Windows 9*x* or Me.

7. Restore System Commander's OS Selection Menu. Windows XP will typically overwrite the Master Boot Record during installation. When your OS is completely installed, you may find that at every reboot, you will boot back into the new OS (XP) rather than your boot loader (e.g., System Commander). The boot loader needs to be re-enabled in the MBR to get the OS Selection Menu back. To do this, reboot your system with System Commander's "Boot Utility disk 1." This will run the program checkmbr to automatically restore System Commander's OS Selection Menu. When you next reboot, the OS Selection Menu will appear, and the OS name (e.g., Windows XP) will appear as an OS selection. Choose this to launch Windows XP.

## Housekeeping Is Important

When multi-booting a PC, try to place each operating system into its own small partition. This keeps critical system files separate and prevents accidental overwriting from one OS to another. If your PC has a second hard drive, it's a good idea to keep your applications and data on that second drive (at least try to keep the data separate). Remember that the more you combine operating systems, applications, and data into the same partitions, the more that will be affected if you need to delete or alter those partitions. For example, if you put three operating systems, applications, and data all on the same partition, a problem with that partition will endanger everything. By comparison, if you keep each operating system on its own partition, then keep applications and data separate, a problem with one operating system will only jeopardize that particular operating system—you can always reinstall that operating system without having to restore your applications and important data.

# Further Study

**IBM**    www-4.ibm.com/software/os/warp/
**Linux Online**   www.linux.org/
**Linux Resources**   www.linuxrx.com/
**Microsoft Support**   support.microsoft.com/support/
**Microsoft Troubleshooters**   support.microsoft.com/support/tshoot/
**Novell**   www.novell.com
**V Communications (System Commander)**   www.v-com.com
**Windows Home Page**   www.microsoft.com/windows/default.asp
**Yahoo (Operating Systems)**   dir.yahoo.com/computers_and_internet/software/operating_systems/

# ARRANGING THE PRESERVICE CHECKOUT

**A**s a professional PC technician, you must understand one basic rule of business: *time is money*. Whether you're the boss or work for someone else, the ability to identify and isolate a PC or peripheral fault quickly and decisively is a critical element to your success. It requires a keen eye, some common sense, a bit of intuition, and even a little luck. It also requires an understanding of the troubleshooting process and a reliable plan of action, because even though the number of PC configurations and setups is virtually unlimited, the methodology used to approach each repair is always about the same. This chapter illustrates the concepts of basic troubleshooting and shows you how to apply a suite of cause-and-effect relationships that will help you narrow down the problem before you even take a screwdriver to the enclosure. By applying a consistent technique, you can shave precious time from every repair.

# The Universal
# Troubleshooting Process

Regardless of how complex your particular computer or peripheral device may be, a dependable trouble-shooting procedure can be broken down into four basic steps, as illustrated in Figure 3-1: define your symptoms, identify and isolate the potential source (or location) of your problem, repair or replace the suspected subassembly, and retest the unit thoroughly to be sure that you have solved the problem. If you have not solved the problem, start again from step 1. This procedure isn't limited to troubleshooting PC equipment, but rather is a universal procedure that you can apply to *any* sort of troubleshooting.

## DEFINE YOUR SYMPTOMS

When a PC breaks down, the cause may be as simple as a loose wire or connector, or as complicated as a chip or subassembly failure. Before you open your toolbox, you must have a firm understanding of all the symptoms. Think about the symptoms carefully and consider questions such as these:

■ Is the disk, CD, or tape inserted properly?

■ Are all devices installed and connected properly?

■ Is the power or activity LED lit?

■ Does this problem occur only when the computer is tapped or moved?

■ Has any user made changes (e.g., updated drivers or patched applications)?

By recognizing and understanding your PC's symptoms, tracing a problem to the appropriate assembly or component may be much easier. Take the time to write down as many symptoms as you can. This note-taking may seem tedious now, but once you have begun your repair, a written record of symptoms

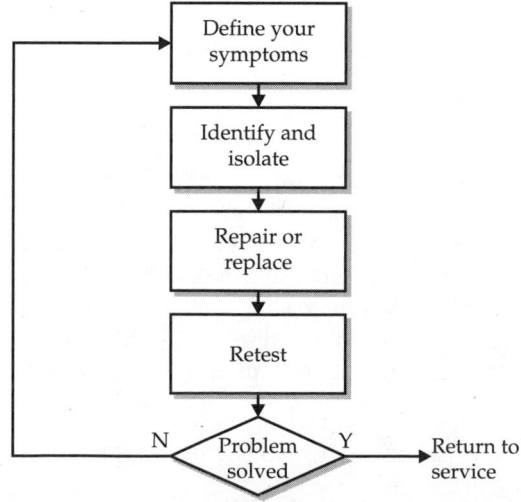

**FIGURE  3-1**    The universal troubleshooting process

and circumstances will help to keep you focused on the task at hand. This list will also help to jog your memory if you must explain the symptoms to someone else at a later date. As a professional troubleshooter, you must often log problems or otherwise document your activities anyway.

## IDENTIFY AND ISOLATE

Before you try to isolate a problem within a piece of computer hardware, you must first be sure that the equipment itself is causing the problem. In many circumstances, this will be fairly obvious, but you may encounter situations in which the cause appears ambiguous (for example, there is no power, no Windows desktop, and so on). Always remember that a PC operates because of an intimate mingling of hardware and software. A faulty or improperly configured piece of software can cause confusing system errors. Chapter 2 touched on just a few of the problems that operating systems can encounter.

When you're confident that the failure lies in your system's hardware, you can begin to identify possible problem areas. Since this book is designed to deal with subassembly troubleshooting, start your diagnostics there. The troubleshooting procedures throughout this book will guide you through the major sections of today's popular PC components and peripherals, and aid you in deciding which subassembly may be at fault. When you have identified a potential problem area, you can begin the actual repair process and swap the suspect subassembly.

## REPAIR OR REPLACE

Since computers and their peripherals are designed as collections of subassemblies, it is almost always easier to replace a subassembly than to attempt to troubleshoot the subassembly to its component level. Even if you had the necessary time, documentation, and test equipment to isolate a defective component, many complex parts are proprietary, so it is highly unlikely that you would be able to obtain replacement components without a significant hassle. The labor and frustration factor involved in such an endeavor is often more expensive than replacing the entire subassembly to begin with. On the other hand, manufacturers and their distributors often stock a selection of subassemblies and supplies. For example, it's a simple matter to replace an AGP GeForce 4 video card, but virtually impossible to replace the actual GeForce 4 graphics processor chip on the card—these are some of the difficult economic realities that technicians face every day.

During a repair, you may reach a roadblock that requires you to leave your equipment for a day or two, or maybe longer. This generally happens after an order has been placed for new parts (such as a new hard drive), and you're waiting for those parts to come in. Make it a point to reassemble your system as much as possible before leaving it. Gather any loose parts in plastic bags, seal them shut, and mark them clearly. If you are working with electronic circuitry, make sure to use good-quality anti-static boxes or bags for storage. Partial re-assembly (combined with careful notes) will help you remember how the unit goes together later on.

Another problem with the fast technological progress we enjoy is that parts rarely stay on the shelf long. That "high-performance" video card you bought last year is no longer available (if it is, it's probably in the bargain bin by now). How about that 12x CD-ROM drive you put in some time back? Today there's something newer and faster in its place. When a PC fails and you need to replace a broken device, chances are that you'll need to upgrade simply because you cannot obtain an identical replacement device. Even if a similar part is available, you can usually obtain a much newer part for just a little more money—giving the customer devices that will be supported further into the future. From this standpoint, upgrading is often a proxy of troubleshooting and repair.

# RETEST

When a repair is finally complete, the system must be reassembled carefully before testing it. All guards, housings, cables, and shields must be replaced before final testing. If symptoms persist, you will have to reevaluate the symptoms and narrow the problem to another part of the equipment. If normal operation is restored (or greatly improved), test the computer's various functions. When you can verify that your symptoms have stopped during actual operation, the equipment may be returned to service. As a general rule, it is wise to let the system run for at least 24 hours to ensure that the replacement subassembly will not fail prematurely. This is known as letting the system *burn-in*. Burn-in can usually be accomplished by leaving the system idle (and re-testing various functions periodically). However, you can use various benchmark and burn-in software utilities to stress various parts of the system before returning it to service. PassMark BurnIn Test 3.0 (Figure 3-2) is one such burn-in utility (www.passmark.com).

Don't be discouraged if the equipment still malfunctions. Perhaps you missed a jumper setting. Maybe software settings and device drivers must be updated to accommodate the replacement subassembly. If you get stuck, simply walk away, clear your head, and start again by defining your current symptoms. Never continue with a repair if you are tired or frustrated—tomorrow is another day, and even the most experienced troubleshooters get overwhelmed from time to time. You should also realize that there may be more than one bad assembly to deal with. Remember that a PC is just a collection of assemblies, and each assembly is a collection of parts. Normally, everything works together, but when one assembly fails, it may cause one or more interconnected assemblies to fail as well.

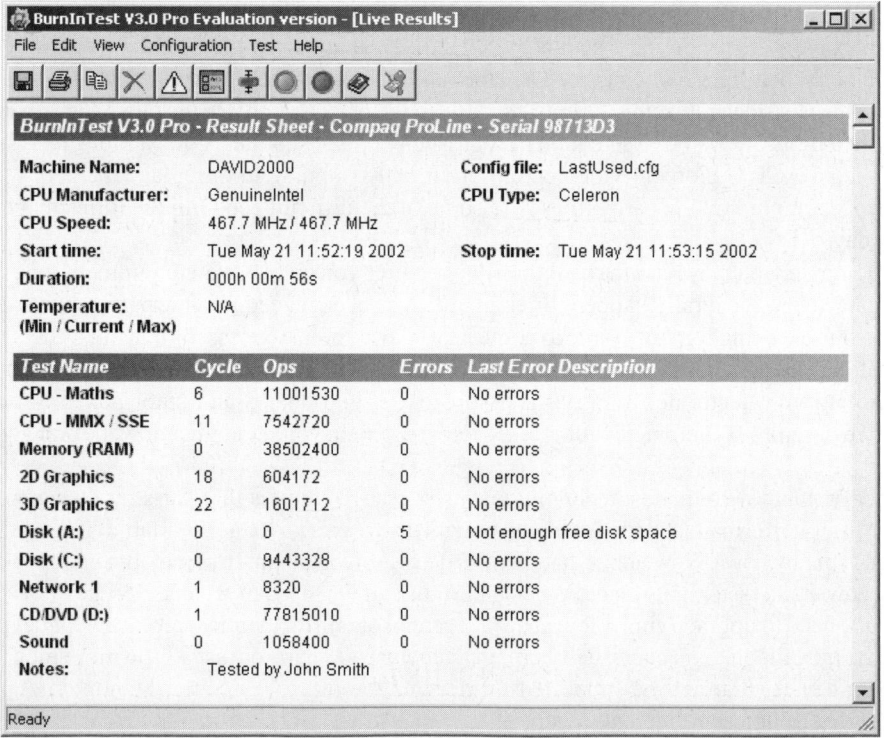

**FIGURE   3-2**   Typical PassMark BurnIn 3.0 Test results (Courtesy of PassMark)

## DOCUMENT YOUR WORK

Documentation is another important practice that is frequently overlooked. When you perform a successful repair, you should take some time to record your findings and solutions on paper. This is a habit that takes time and discipline to develop, but it's *well* worth the trouble. You can refer to your notes for future repairs, possibly saving hours of trial and error. Notes can also be an invaluable asset to other technicians faced with problems that you have already learned how to resolve.

## THE SPARE PARTS DILEMMA

Once a problem is isolated, technicians face another problem: the availability of spare parts. Novice technicians often ask what kinds and quantity of spare parts they should keep on hand. The best answer to give here is, simply, none at all. The reason for this somewhat drastic answer is best explained by the two realities of modern PC service: parts are always changing, and inventory costs money.

### Parts Are Always Changing

After more than 25 years, the PC is in its eighth generation, with processors such as the AMD Athlon/Duron and Pentium 4. As a result, a new generation matures every 18 to 24 months (and the pace is accelerating). Even standardized products such as CD-ROM/R/RW and DVD drives have proliferated in different speeds and versions (for example, CD-ROM drives can be found at speeds as high as 50x). Once production stops for a drive or board, stock rarely remains for very long. Thus, even if you know what the problem is, the chances of locating an exact replacement part are often quite slim if the part is over two years old. Note the word "exact"—this is the magic word in PC repair, and is the reason why so many repairs involve an upgrade. For example, why replace a failed EGA board with another EGA board when you can install a state-of-the-art video card (which is typically fully compatible) for the same price—or less. Choosing the right parts to stock is like hitting a moving target, so don't bother.

### Inventory Costs Money

Financial considerations also play a big role in choosing parts. For computer enthusiasts or novice technicians just tinkering in their spare time, the expense and space demands required for inventory are simply out of the question. For more serious repair businesses, the expense of inventory can burden the bottom line. And what happens if you don't actually use a part? After a while, you're stuck with an "antique." The economics of inventory are further complicated by razor-thin profit margins and the proliferation of sub-$1000 PCs that are often not worth putting additional money into.

### A Better Strategy

Unless you're in the business of selling replacement parts and upgrade components, don't waste your money and space stocking parts that are going to be obsolete in less than 24 months. Rather than worry about stocking parts yourself, work to cultivate new vendors and develop your contacts with computer parts stores and superstores that specialize in PC parts and sub-assemblies. Let them stock the parts for you. Since parts stores generally have an inside line with distributors and manufacturers, parts that they do not stock can often be ordered for you. Even many reputable mail-order firms can provide parts in under 48 hours with today's global delivery services.

# Benchmarking the PC

We all know that today's personal computers are capable of astounding performance (if you doubt that, consider any popular 3D game like HalfLife or Unreal Tournament). However, it is often important to *quantify* the performance of a system. Just saying that a PC is "faster" than another system is simply not enough. Technicians often must apply a number to that performance, against which to measure the impact of improvements offered by an upgrade or to objectively compare the performance of various systems. *Benchmarks* are used to test and report the performance of a PC by running a set of well-defined tasks on the system. A benchmark program has several different uses in the PC industry depending on what your needs are:

- **System comparisons**   Benchmarks are often used to compare a system to one or more competing machines (or to compare a newer system to older machines). Just flip through any issue of *PC Magazine* or *PC World* and you'll see a flurry of PC ads all quoting numerical performance numbers backed up by benchmarks. You may also run a benchmark to establish the overall performance of a new system before making a purchase decision.

- **Upgrade improvements**   Benchmarks are frequently used to gauge the value of an upgrade. By running the benchmark before and after the upgrade process, you can get a numerical assessment of just how much that new CPU, RAM, drive, or motherboard may have improved (or hindered) system performance. For example, if a system scores a benchmark of 1,000 before a video card upgrade, and then scores a 1,250 after the video card upgrade, you know the upgrade improved performance by 25 percent. Conversely, a post-upgrade score of 932 would mean that the upgrade actually *degraded* performance by 6.8 percent.

- **Diagnostics**   Benchmarks sometimes have a role in system diagnostics. Systems that are performing poorly can be benchmarked as key components are checked or reconfigured. This helps the technician isolate and correct performance problems far more reliably than using just simple visual observations.

## AVOIDING BENCHMARK PROBLEMS

One of the most serious problems encountered with benchmarks is the integrity of their numbers. You've probably heard that "statistics can lie," and the same thing is true of benchmarks. You must apply benchmarks objectively and consistently for them to be useful. In order for benchmarks to provide you with reliable results, you must take certain precautions:

- *Note the complete system configuration.* When you run a benchmark and achieve a result, be sure to note the entire system configuration (CPU, RAM, cache, OS version, and so on). A benchmark may yield vastly different numbers on different configurations of the same system. With two identical systems, for example, increasing the bus multiplier on one system will increase CPU speed and result in higher CPU performance numbers—even though the two systems may be exactly the same otherwise.

- *Run the same benchmark on every system.* Benchmarks are still software, and the way in which benchmark code is written can impact the way it produces results on a given computer. Often, two different versions of the same benchmark will yield two different results. When you use benchmarks for comparisons between systems, be sure to use the same program and version number.

- *Minimize hardware differences between hardware platforms.* A computer is an assembly of many interdependent subassemblies (motherboard, drive controllers, drives, CPU, and so on), but when a benchmark is run to compare a difference between systems, that difference can be masked by other elements in the system. For example, suppose you're using a benchmark to test the hard drive data transfer on two systems. Different hard drives and drive controllers will yield different results (that's expected). However, even if you're using identical drives and controllers, other differences between the systems (such as BIOS versions, TSRs, OS versions, or motherboard chipsets) can also produce different results.

■ *Run benchmarks under the same load.* The results generated by a benchmark do not guarantee that same level of performance under real-world applications. This was one of the flaws of early computer benchmarking—small, tightly written benchmark code resulted in artificially high performance, but the system still performed poorly when real applications were used. Use benchmarks that use (or simulate) actual programs, or otherwise simulate your true workload.

## OBTAINING BENCHMARKS

Benchmarks have been around since the earliest computers, and there are now a vast array of benchmark products to measure all aspects of the PC, as well as more specialized issues such as networking, real-time systems, and UNIX (or other operating system) platforms. Table 3-1 highlights a cross-section of common computer benchmarks for your reference (including a URL where you can download the complete benchmark program). The benchmarks denoted with an asterisk are described in more detail following Table 3-1. Today, Ziff Davis/PC Magazine (www.etestinglabs.com/benchmarks/) publishes a suite of freeware benchmark utilities that have become standard tools for end users and technicians alike.

**TABLE 3-1    INDEX OF MODERN PC BENCHMARKS**

| BENCHMARK | DESCRIPTION | AVAILABILITY |
| --- | --- | --- |
| 3D-Bench | PC 3D graphics benchmark | www.sysopt.com/3dbench.html www.sysopt.com/cbench.html |
| 3D WinBench 2000 (1.1)* | PC 3D graphics benchmark | www.etestinglabs.com/benchmarks/ 3dwinbench/3dwinbench.asp |
| Audio WinBench 99 (1.0.1)* | PC audio subsystem performance benchmark | www.etestinglabs.com/benchmarks/ auwinbench/auwinbench.asp |
| BatteryMon 1.1 | PassMark battery benchmark | www.passmark.com/products/ batmon.htm |
| BWS BatteryMark 2001* | Mobile PC battery benchmark | www.etestinglabs.com/benchmarks/ battmark/battmark.asp |
| Business Winstone 2001 (1.0.2)* | Windows 98/Me/2k/XP application performance benchmark | www.etestinglabs.com/benchmarks/ bwinstone/bwinstone.asp |
| CD WinBench 99 (2.0)* | CD/DVD drive performance benchmark | www.etestinglabs.com/benchmarks/ cdwinbench/cdwinbench.asp |
| Content Creation Winstone 2002* | Windows 98/Me/2k/XP performance with content applications | www.etestinglabs.com/benchmarks/ ccwinstone/ccwinstone.asp |
| i-Bench (3.0)* | Web client performance benchmark | www.etestinglabs.com/benchmarks/ i-bench/i-bench.asp |
| ModemTest (1.1) | PassMark modem benchmark | www.passmark.com/products/ modemtest.htm |
| NetBench (7.0.2)* | File server performance benchmark | www.etestinglabs.com/benchmarks/ netbench/netbench.asp |
| Oracle Applications Standard Benchmark | Oracle applications benchmark performance benchmark | www.oracle.com/apps_benchmark/ |

**TABLE 3-1   INDEX OF MODERN PC BENCHMARKS *(CONTINUED)***

| BENCHMARK | DESCRIPTION | AVAILABILITY |
|---|---|---|
| PerformanceTest (3.5) | PassMark General system benchmark | www.passmark.com/products/pt.htm |
| SciSoft SANDRA | Diagnostic and benchmarking tool | www.3bsoftware.com |
| SPEC (Standard Performance Evaluation Corp.) | General-purpose benchmarks | www.specbench.org |
| SYSmark2002 (BAPCo) | General system performance benchmark | www.bapco.com |
| SYSmarkJ (BAPCo) | Java applications benchmark | www.bapco.com www.bapco.com/SYSmarkJ.html |
| TPC (Transaction Processing Council) | POS transaction processing benchmark | www.tpc.org |
| WebBench (4.1)* | Web server performance benchmark | www.etestinglabs.com/benchmarks/webbench/webbench.asp |
| WebMark2001 (BAPCo) | Internet performance benchmark | www.bapco.com www.bapco.com/SYSmarkJ.html |
| WinBench 99 (2.0)* | General system benchmark | www.etestinglabs.com/benchmarks/winbench/winbench.asp |

## Content Creation (CC) Winstone 2002

Content Creation Winstone 2002 is a system-level, application-based benchmark that measures a PC's overall performance when running top Windows-based 32-bit "content creation" applications on Windows 98, Windows 2000, Windows Me, or Windows XP. CC Winstone 2002 uses applications such as Adobe Photoshop 6.0.1, Adobe Premiere 6.0, Macromedia Director 8.5, Macromedia Dreamweaver UltraDev 4, Microsoft Windows Media Encoder 7.01.00.3055, Netscape Navigator 6/6.01, and Sonic Foundry Sound Forge 5.0c (build 184). CC Winstone 2002 keeps multiple applications open at once and switches among those applications through a series of scripted activities to simulate real-life use, then returns a single score. Those activities focus on "hot spots" of activity that make your PC really work (e.g., the times where you're likely to see an hourglass or a progress bar).

## WebBench 4.1

WebBench 4.1 lets you measure Web server software performance by running different Web server packages on the same server hardware or by running a given Web server package on different hardware platforms. Version 4.1 of WebBench allows for more connections and other facilities that put more stress on bigger servers—more accurately modeling real-world server workloads. WebBench standard test suites produce two overall scores for the server: requests per second, and throughput (measured in bytes per second). WebBench provides both static standard test suites and dynamic standard test suites (which execute applications that actually run on the server). In addition, you can easily create your own test suites. No matter which test suites you use, your PC clients must be running either Windows 95/98 or Windows NT/2000, and the controller must be running Windows NT or Windows 2000.

## NetBench 7.0.2

NetBench 7.0.2 is a portable benchmark program that measures how well a file server handles file I/O requests from 32-bit Windows clients while those clients pepper the server with requests for network file operations. NetBench reports file throughput and client response time measurements. Version 7.0.2 of NetBench provides for greater disk coverage and more disk-testing flexibility. To run NetBench, you need a file server PC (called the controller) running Windows NT or Windows 2000 to start and monitor the tests, as well as clients that are running either Windows 95/98 or Windows NT/2000.

## Business Winstone 2001 (v.1.0.2)

Business Winstone 2001 is a system-level, application-based benchmark that measures a system's overall performance when running today's top-selling Windows-based 32-bit applications on Windows 98/SE, Windows NT 4.0 (SP6 or later), Windows 2000, or Windows Me/XP. Business Winstone actually runs real PC applications through a series of scripted activities, and uses the time a PC takes to complete those activities to produce its performance scores. (The CD-ROM that contains Business Winstone also includes all the files and application portions the benchmark needs to run.)

This benchmark generally replaces the aging Winstone 99.

## WinBench 99 (v.2.0)

Version 2.0 of WinBench 99 is a general-purpose subsystem-level benchmark that measures the performance of a PC's graphics, disk, and video subsystems in a Windows environment. WinBench 99's tests can run on Windows 95, Windows 98, Windows NT, Windows 2000, and Windows Me systems. WinBench is available for download from the Ziff Davis Web site.

## 3D WinBench 2000

3D WinBench 2000 (version 1.1) measures the performance of a computer's 3D subsystem, which includes the Direct3D software, the monitor, the graphics adapter, the graphics driver, and the bus used to carry information between the graphics adapter and the processor subsystem (the AGP bus). You can use 3D WinBench 2000 to test hardware graphics adapters, drivers, and the value of such enhancing technologies as MMX. 3D WinBench 2000 runs only on Microsoft Windows 98, Windows 98 SE, Windows 2000, and Windows Me. It won't work under Windows NT 4.0 because NT doesn't support hardware acceleration of the Windows Direct3D interface that 3D WinBench 2000 uses. 3D WinBench 2000 uses the DirectX 7.0 (and later) interface, which means you can see the benefits and performance of features such as hardware transformation and lighting effects. Version 1.1 also includes a new processor test suite and new quality tests for the latest innovations in 3D rendering.

## CD WinBench 99 (v.2.0)

CD WinBench 99 (v.2.0) measures the performance of a PC's CD-ROM or DVD-ROM drive subsystem (which includes the CD/DVD drive, controller, driver, and the system processor). This benchmark isn't available as a download, so you have to run it from the CD WinBench 99 CD-ROM while it's spinning in your system's CD drive. Version 2.0 of CD WinBench 99 includes numerous minor updates. Keep in mind that this benchmark will not test music CDs or DVD movies.

## Audio WinBench 99 (v.1.0.1)

The Audio WinBench 99 benchmark takes you deep into the heart of your PC's audio system by offering objective and subjective tests to measure CPU usage, hardware voices, 3D positioning, and more. Audio WinBench 99 measures the performance of a PC's audio subsystem, which includes the sound card and its driver, the processor, the DirectSound and DirectSound 3D software, and the speakers. Audio WinBench 99 runs on Microsoft Windows 98, Windows 98 SE, Windows NT, Windows 2000, and Windows Me. You'll need DirectX 6 or later (which includes DirectSound and DirectSound3D) to run all the Audio WinBench 99 tests. Version 1.0.1 is now available, which includes several minor updates.

### BWS BatteryMark 2001

The Business Winstone 2001 BatteryMark (BWS BatteryMark) measures battery life on notebook computers running Windows 95, Windows Me, Windows 98, Windows NT 4.0, or Windows 2000. To drain a notebook's battery, BWS BatteryMark uses the tests of other Ziff Davis benchmarks such as Business Winstone 2001. These tests involve leading Windows-based applications (including Microsoft Office 2000, Norton AntiVirus, and Netscape Communicator) in a set of scripted activities that drain a notebook's battery in a way that mimics real use. This complete redesign of BatteryMark is the most substantial change to the benchmark in several years, incorporating additions that make the test even more realistic than previous versions.

### i-Bench 3.0

i-Bench 3.0 is a comprehensive, cross-platform benchmark that tests the performance and capability of Web clients as they use the latest Web technologies and features. A *Web client* is any combination of hardware and software that you can use to retrieve content from a Web site. The benchmark provides a series of tests that measure both how well the client handles features and the degree to which network access speed affects performance. You can also use the i-Bench CD-ROM to test Web performance over a LAN.

# Viruses and Computer Service

Few developments in the personal computer field have caused more concern and alarm than the computer virus. Although viruses do not physically damage computer hardware, they can irrevocably destroy vital data, disable your PC (or shut down a network), and propagate to other systems through networks, disk swapping, and online services. Even though virus infiltration is generally regarded as rare, good PC technicians will always protect themselves (and their customers) by checking the system for viruses before and after using their diagnostic disks on the PC. A careful and systematic process of virus isolation can detect viruses on the customer's PC *before* any hardware-level work is done. Virus isolation tactics also prevent your diagnostic disks from becoming infected (and subsequently transferring the virus to other systems, for which you might be legally liable). This part of the chapter outlines a virus screening procedure for PCs.

## COMPUTER VIRUSES EXPLAINED

There have been many attempts to define a computer virus, and most definitions have a great deal of technical merit. For the purposes of this book, however, we can consider a *virus* to be some length of computer code (a program or program fragment) that performs one or more, often destructive, functions and replicates itself wherever possible to other disks and systems. Since viruses generally want to escape detection, they may also hide by copying themselves as hidden, system, or read-only files. However, this only prevents casual detection. More elaborate viruses affect the boot sector code on floppy and hard disks, or attach themselves to other executable programs. Each time the infected program is executed, the virus has a chance to wreak havoc. Still other viruses infect the partition table. Most viruses exhibit a code sequence that can be detected. Many virus scanners work by checking the contents of memory and disk files for such virus *signatures*. As viruses become more complex, however, they are using encryption techniques to escape detection. Encryption changes the virus signature each time the virus replicates itself, and for a well-designed virus, this can make detection extremely difficult.

Just as a biological virus is an unwanted (and sometimes deadly) organism in a body, "viral" code in software can lead to a slow, agonizing death for your customer's data. In actual practice, few viruses *immediately* crash a system (with notable exceptions, such as the much-publicized Michelangelo virus). Most viruses make only small changes each time they are executed, creating a pattern of chronic problems. This slow manifestation gives viruses a chance to replicate and infect backups and floppy disks, which are frequently swapped, thereby infecting other systems.

Frequent system backups are an effective protection against the damages caused by computer viruses because you can restore damaged files. Even if the backup itself is infected, the infected files can usually be cleaned once they are restored from the backup (but before they're executed and given another chance to wreck havoc).

## The Tell-Tale Signs

Viruses are especially dangerous since you're rarely made aware of their presence until it is too late and the damage is already done. However, there are a number of behaviors that might suggest the presence of a virus in your system. Once again, remember that one of the best protections against viruses (or other drive failures) is to maintain regular backups of your data. None of these symptoms alone guarantees the presence of a virus (there *are* other reasons why such symptoms can occur), but when these symptoms do surface, it is always worth running an antivirus checker just to be safe. The following symptoms are typical of virus activity:

- ■ *The hard drive is running out of disk space for no apparent reason.* Some viruses multiply by attaching copies of themselves to executable files, often multiple times. This increases the file size of infected files (sometimes dramatically) and consumes more disk space. If left unchecked, files can grow until the disk runs short of space. However, disk space can also be gobbled up by many CAD, graphics, and multimedia applications, such as video capture systems. Be aware of what kind of applications are on the disk.

- ■ *You notice that various programs have increased in size for no reason.* This is a classic indicator of a virus at work. In actual practice, few rational people make it a habit to keep track of file sizes, but dates can be a giveaway. For example, if most of the files in a subdirectory are dated six months ago when a software package was first installed, but the main EXE file is dated yesterday, it's time to run that virus checker.

- ■ *You notice substantial hard drive activity but were not expecting it.* It is hardly unusual to see the drive LED register activity as programs are being loaded or files are being saved. In disk-intensive systems such as Windows Me/XP or 2000, you should expect to see extensive drive activity due to swap file operation (especially if your PC is lean on RAM or running multiple applications). However, you should not expect to see regular or substantial disk activity when the system is idle. If you find a drive running for no apparent reason—and no background tasks have been scheduled—run the virus checker.

- ■ *System performance has slowed down noticeably.* This symptom is usually coupled with low drive space, and may very well be the result of a filled and fragmented disk, such as those found in systems that deal with CAD and multimedia applications. Run the virus checker first. If no virus is detected, try eliminating any unneeded files to free some disk space, then defragment the drive completely.

■ *Files have been lost or corrupted for no apparent reason, or there are an unusual number of access problems.* Under ordinary circumstances, files should not be lost or corrupted on a hard drive. Even though bad sectors will crop up on extremely rare occasions, you should expect the drive to run properly. Virus infiltration can easily damage and corrupt files, resulting in file errors. Such errors may occur randomly, or they may be quite consistent. You may see error messages such as "Error in .EXE file." Widespread errors may even simulate a drive failure. Try running a virus checker before running a diagnostic like ScanDisk. Keep in mind that inadequate power (e.g., an underpowered supply) can also have an effect on drive and data reliability.

■ *The system locks up frequently or without explanation.* Faulty applications and corrupted files can freeze a system or cause it to crash. While viruses rarely manifest themselves in this fashion, it is possible that random or consistent system lockups may suggest a virus (or virus damage to key files). Remember that memory and motherboard problems can also result in system lockups.

■ *There are unexplained problems with system memory or memory allocation.* It is quite common for viruses to reside in memory as background tasks—infecting other files wherever they can. Memory-resident viruses can affect the amount of free memory available to other applications. You may see error messages such as "Program too big to fit in memory," though more recent Windows platforms with lots of RAM may not suffer such problems. The best defense against memory-resident viruses is to let Windows load your virus checker at boot time and keep the virus checker running at all times. If you don't have a virus checker loading into memory (perhaps it conflicts with other software that you need), be sure to load it up and run it periodically. If the system checks clear of viruses, you can run diagnostics to check the memory.

## ANTIVIRUS SOFTWARE

In the race between good and evil, it's evil that usually has the head start. As a result, antivirus detection and elimination packages are constantly trying to keep up with new viruses and their variations (in addition to dealing with the tens of thousands of viruses that have already been identified). This leads to one important conclusion about antivirus software: they all become obsolete very quickly. Even though first-class shareware and commercial packages can be quite comprehensive, they must all be updated frequently. Some of the most notable antivirus products (see Figure 3-3) are found in Symantec's Norton AntiVirus (NAV) and VirusScan from Network Associates. DOS 6.xx users already own Microsoft AntiVirus (MSAV) as part of the DOS package.

Another important factor in antivirus programs is their inability to successfully remove all viruses from executable files. Files with a .COM extension are simply reflections of memory, but executable (e.g., .EXE) files contain header information that is easily damaged by a virus (and are subsequently unrecoverable). It is always worth trying to eliminate the virus—if the executable's header is damaged, you've lost nothing in the attempt, and you can reload the damaged program file from a backup (or even its original distribution CD if necessary). Remember that there is no better protection against viruses and other hardware faults than keeping regular backups—it's better to restore an infected backup and clean it than to forego backups entirely.

### Emergency Disks

It is possible that your infected PC may refuse to start. This may occur when the partition table or master boot record are damaged, or an infection has corrupted files needed to boot the operating system. When this happens, it may seem impossible to recover the system. After all, how do you get rid of a virus when you can't even boot the system to use the antivirus software? Most antivirus software CDs (such as Norton

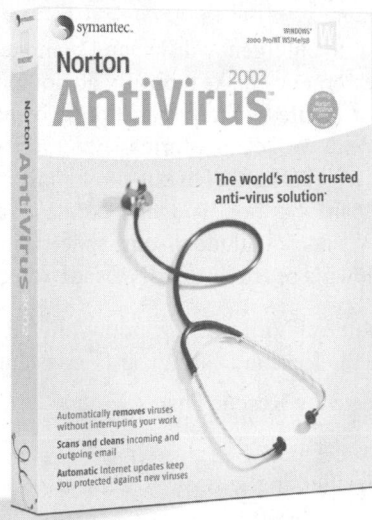

**FIGURE 3-3**    Frequently updated utilities such as Symantec's Norton AntiVirus offer users excellent protection from virus damage (Courtesy of Symantec).

AntiVirus) are bootable. That is, you can place the CD in your CD-ROM drive and use that CD to launch a DOS version of the antivirus utility. The software will then run and clean the system—attempting to recover any damaged files. If all goes well, the antivirus software can eliminate the infection and recover damaged files, allowing you to boot normally once again.

Of course, your CD-ROM and PC BIOS must support bootable CD standards (e.g., the "El Torito" standard), and virtually all hardware platforms are El Torito-compliant—allowing the PC to actually boot from a CD rather than just a floppy or hard drive. If you're working with an older PC where the BIOS (or CD drive) are not bootable, you can use the antivirus software to create a set of emergency diskettes that will allow you to boot and scan the system in the event of a boot problem. Even if you don't create emergency disks when you first install the antivirus software, it's often possible to create the disks on another PC once a virus has struck your PC. Here is an example procedure for creating emergency disks under Norton AntiVirus:

1. Insert the Norton AntiVirus CD into the CD-ROM drive.
2. Click Browse CD.
3. Double-click the support folder.
4. Double-click the edisk folder.
5. Double-click ned.exe.
6. In the Welcome window, click OK.
7. Label the first diskette and insert it into drive A:, then click Yes.
8. Insert additional diskettes as instructed.
9. When the procedure is complete, click OK.
10. Remove the final disk from drive A: and store the emergency disk set in a safe place (preferably with your system backup or OS installation CDs).

## Rescue Disks

Rescue disks are very similar to emergency disks, and many technicians use the terms interchangeably. The main difference is that emergency disks typically do not include operating system files, while rescue disks also provide system startup files and disk partition information. As a rule, rescue disks are made for DOS, Windows 9*x*, and Windows Me platforms. Emergency disks are usually made for Windows NT/2000/XP, which are able to get missing OS information from original installation media. Since rescue disks include system-specific information, you *must* create rescue disks for each system that you're protecting. Since emergency disks don't include system-specific information, you can make them on almost any suitable system. The following procedure can be used to create rescue disks with Norton AntiVirus:

1. At the top of the Norton AntiVirus main window, click Rescue. If you chose to make Rescue Disks as a post-install task, the Rescue Disk Wizard opens automatically.
2. Select drive A: to create the Rescue Disk set.
3. Click Create.
4. Label the disks as specified in the Basic Rescue Disk List window, then click OK.
5. Insert the disks as requested.

After you finish creating rescue disks, remember to test them. This means you'll need to restart your PC and verify that the disks work properly. Try the following steps under Norton AntiVirus:

1. Close all open programs.
2. Insert the disk labeled Basic Rescue Boot Floppy Disk into drive A:, and then click Restart.
3. If the Rescue Disk screen appears on your monitor, the Rescue Disk works properly. If the Rescue Disk screen does not appear, you will need to fix the disks.
4. Press ESC to exit to DOS.
5. Remove the disk from drive A:, then write-protect the diskette.
6. Restart your computer normally.

 Remember to update your rescue disks periodically—preferably whenever you make a significant hardware or software change to the system.

## Understanding "False Detections"

A *false detection* (also called a *false positive*) occurs when your antivirus software sends a virus alert message (or makes a log file entry) that identifies a virus where none actually exists. You're more likely to see false detections if you have antivirus software from more than one vendor installed on your computer, because some antivirus software stores the code signatures it uses for detection unprotected in memory. The *safest* course to take when you see an alert message or log entry is to treat it as a genuine virus threat, and to take the appropriate steps to remove the virus from your system. But if you believe that the antivirus software has generated a false detection (i.e., it flags a file as "infected" when you have used it safely for years), check for one or more of the following situations before you contact the antivirus software maker:

- *You have more than one antivirus program running*. If so, one of the scanners might detect unprotected code signatures that another program uses and report *them* as viruses. To avoid this problem, configure your PC to run only one antivirus program—this may include uninstalling unneeded antivirus software from other PCs on a LAN.

- *You have a BIOS chip with antivirus features*. Many current BIOS versions provide antivirus features (intended to prevent boot sector infection) that can trigger false detections when antivirus software runs. If a particular PC reports virus issues, you can try disabling the antivirus protection in system's BIOS through the CMOS Setup.

- *You have older PCs*. Some older PCs (from manufacturers like HP) modify the boot sectors on their hard disks each time they start up. Antivirus software might detect these modifications as viruses— when in fact they are not. To solve the problem, upgrade the offending PC(s), or use the command-line version of your antivirus software to add validation information to the startup files themselves. This method does not save information about the boot sector or the master boot record.

- *You have copy-protected software*. Depending on the type of copy protection used, your antivirus software might detect a virus in the boot sector or the master boot record on some floppy disks or other media. Check with the author of the suspect software and see if there is a patch or update (or other installation option) that will correct this problem.

If none of these conditions are true, you should contact the antivirus software maker and inform them of the false detection so that they can investigate the matter and make suitable corrections in subsequent patches and data updates.

Most modern antivirus tools load into memory each time the PC starts in order to provide full-time protection to your system. If you find that a particular situation is causing false positives (where you're confident that no actual virus activity is taking place), you can usually unload the antivirus software from memory, or temporarily disable it to stop annoying alerts. You can then re-enable the antivirus software again later, or reboot the system to allow the antivirus software to restart normally with the operating system.

## Avoiding Viruses

The problems caused by most computer viruses can be avoided by implementing a series of simple rules, and encouraging your customers to do the same:

- Make sure that your antivirus tool(s) load into memory and are active each time the PC starts.

- If you cannot keep antivirus tools running (e.g., it causes problems with other software that you use), be sure to scan removable media and downloads for viruses before you use them.

- Keep your important work files (and your entire system) backed up on a regular basis. This won't help prevent viruses, but meaningful regular backups can help you to recover if a virus should slip through and cause trouble on your system.

- Keep the signature files updated on a regular basis. Today, signature files can be downloaded directly from the antivirus software maker's Web site in a matter of minutes.

- Check in with your antivirus software maker periodically and look for any new virus alerts or warnings (especially e-mail-related viruses) that may have a particular impact on you.

- Write-protect removable media (such as floppy disks).

- Keep your rescue and emergency disks updated at all times, and store them in a place where you can access them regularly (often with recent backups or your operating system's installation CD).

- Configure the antivirus software to scan your system periodically (though this is usually set by default).

- Avoid questionable downloads. For example, fancy new utilities that promise the impossible (e.g., get AOL for free or speed up your downloads 300 percent without a faster modem) are frequent lurking places for Trojan horses and other viruses.

■  Avoid e-mail attachments from sources that you don't know. Many virus attacks are launched by e-mail as attachments sent with urgent-sounding subject lines like "here are the results of your feedback form." When you're asked to open the attached (infected) file, the virus is introduced to your system. Scan all attachments before opening them.

# Quick-Start Bench Testing

Of the many problems that can plague the PC, perhaps the most troubling problems occur during startup, when the computer fails to start at all or does not start completely. Startup problems make it almost impossible to use diagnostics or other utilities that we depend on to help isolate problems. With the advent of graphics-oriented operating systems such as Windows 9*x*/Me/XP, there are even more difficulties that can develop. This part of the chapter offers you a series of possible quick-start explanations for full and partial system failures.

## THE SYSTEM DOESN'T START AT ALL

These types of problems are easy to spot—you push the power button and nothing happens. The solution to these kinds of problems is usually quite straightforward, but the following symptoms will show you some of the wrinkles that may occur. Start with the following checklist, then see if you can match a specific symptom:

■  Check for AC from your wall outlet.

■  Reattach or replace the AC line cord.

■  Reattach the power cables between the supply and motherboard.

■  Check for improperly installed devices (e.g., expansion cards).

■  Replace the power supply.

■  Replace the motherboard.

■  Replace the CPU.

**SYMPTOM 3-1**    **There is no power indicator and you cannot hear any cooling fan**
Chances are that there is insufficient power to the computer. Use a voltmeter and confirm that there is adequate AC voltage at the wall outlet. Check the AC cord next to make sure it isn't loose or disconnected. See that the master power switch at the power supply is turned on and connected properly. Check the power supply fuse(s). The main fuse may have opened. Replace any failed fuse. If the trouble continues, try another power supply. In many cases, a poor-quality power supply will allow voltage transients to pass through and damage the motherboard (preventing any system activity)—though this rarely damages the CPU or RAM. If a new power supply doesn't correct the trouble, replace the motherboard if necessary.

**SYMPTOM 3-2**    **There is no power indicator, but you hear the cooling fan(s) running**
This usually means that there is some level of AC power reaching the system. Use a voltmeter and confirm that there is adequate AC voltage at the wall outlet. Unusually low AC voltages (such as during brownout conditions) may cause the power supply to malfunction. Verify that the power supply cables are attached properly and securely to the motherboard. Use a voltmeter (see Figure 3-4) to verify that each dc voltage output from the power supply is correct (Table 3-2 illustrates the proper dc voltage levels at each wire color). If any output is very low or absent (especially the +5 volt output), replace the power supply.

Finally, use a voltmeter and verify that the Power Good (or PwrOK) signal is +5 volts. If this signal is below 1.0 volts, it may inhibit the CPU from running by forcing a continuous Reset condition. Since the Power Good signal is generated by the power supply, try replacing the power supply. Otherwise, try another CPU.

**SYMPTOM 3-3**    **The power indicator is on, but there is no apparent system activity**
Check the power supply voltages. Use a dc voltmeter to verify that each output from the power supply is correct. Table 3-2 lists the proper voltage for each wire color. If any output is very low or absent (especially the +5 volt output), replace the power supply. Use a voltmeter and verify that the Power Good signal is +5 volts. If this signal is below 1.0 volts, it may inhibit the CPU from running by forcing a continuous Reset condition. Since the Power Good signal is generated by the power supply, try replacing the power supply.

Check that the CPU is cool, that the heat-sink/fan assembly is fitted on correctly, and that the CPU itself is inserted properly and completely into its slot or socket. Check the CPU socket. If the CPU is seated in a ZIF (Zero Insertion Force) socket, make sure that the socket's tension lever is closed and locked into place. For slot-mounted processors, verify that the processor's retention mechanism is secure. Next, check the expansion boards to make sure that they all are seated properly. Any boards that are not secured properly, or that are inserted unevenly, can short bus signals and prevent the PC from starting. Check the motherboard for shorts. Inspect the motherboard at every metal standoff and see that no metal traces are being shorted against a standoff or screw. You may want to free the motherboard and see if the system starts. If it does, use nonconductive spacers (such as a small piece of manila folder) to insulate the motherboard from each metal standoff. If the system still fails to start (and all voltages from the power supply are correct), replace the motherboard.

# THE SYSTEM STARTS BUT WON'T INITIALIZE
Now things start to get a bit more complicated. Power is clearly reaching the system, and the POST process is starting, but a serious problem somewhere very early in the system initialization process is preventing

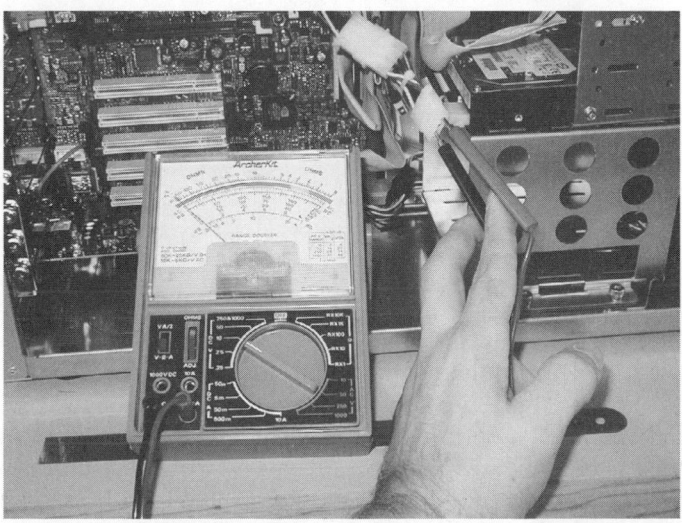

**FIGURE 3-4**    A basic dc voltmeter is indispensable when testing the outputs of your PC's power supply.

**TABLE 3-2    STANDARD POWER CONNECTOR PINOUTS**

**ATX POWER CONNECTOR**

| Color | Voltage | Pin | Color | Voltage | Pin |
|---|---|---|---|---|---|
| Orange | +3.3 Vdc | 1 | Brown | 3.3V Sense | 11 |
| Orange | +3.3 Vdc | 2 | Blue | −12 Vdc | 12 |
| Black | Ground | 3 | Black | Ground | 13 |
| Red | +5 Vdc | 4 | Green | PS-ON | 14 |
| Black | Ground | 5 | Black | Ground | 15 |
| Red | +5 Vdc | 6 | Black | Ground | 16 |
| Black | Ground | 7 | Black | Ground | 17 |
| Gray | PwrOK | 8 | White | −5 Vdc | 18 |
| Purple | +5V standby | 9 | Red | +5 Vdc | 19 |
| Yellow | +12 Vdc | 10 | Red | +5 Vdc | 20 |

**BABY AT POWER CONNECTORS**

| Color | Voltage | Pin | Color | Voltage | Pin |
|---|---|---|---|---|---|
| Orange | PwrOK | 1 (P8) | Black | Ground | 1 (P9) |
| Red | +5 Vdc | 2 (P8) | Black | Ground | 2 (P9) |
| Yellow | +12 Vdc | 3 (P8) | White | −5 Vdc | 3 (P9) |
| Blue | −12 Vdc | 4 (P8) | Red | +5 Vdc | 4 (P9) |
| Black | Ground | 5 (P8) | Red | +5 Vdc | 5 (P9) |
| Black | Ground | 6 (P8) | Red | +5 Vdc | 6 (P9) |

the system from finishing the POST or loading the operating system. In many cases, you'll find this to be a motherboard fault, or an assembly problem (for example, an expansion card is not properly seated in its expansion slot). Start with the following checklist:

■ Reattach the power cables between the power supply and motherboard.

■ Reattach the power cables to all drives.

■ Reinstall all expansion cards.

■ Check and reinstall all signal (a.k.a. ribbon) cabling.

■ Check for POST errors using a POST reader card (if available).

■ Check the CMOS Setup.

■ Replace the motherboard.

**SYMPTOM 3-4**    **The power indicator is on, but you hear two or more beeps**    There is no video. Check the video board first. Video problems can easily halt the initialization process. Turn off and unplug the PC, and then make sure that your video board is inserted completely into its expansion slot. Consider the beep code itself—any beep code means that a catastrophic fault has been detected in the power-on self-test (POST) before the video system could be initialized. BIOS makers use different numbers and patterns of beeps to indicate failures. You can determine the exact failure by finding the BIOS maker (usually marked on the motherboard BIOS chip), and then finding the error message in Chapter 17.

In the vast majority of cases, the fault will be traced to the CPU, RAM, motherboard circuitry, video controller, or drive controller—any of which can be easily checked and replaced.

**SYMPTOM 3-5**    **The power indicator is on, but the system hangs during initialization**
Video may be active (you see the raster "haze" produced by a monitor), but there may be no text in the display. The POST has detected a fault and is unable to continue with the initialization process. BIOS makers mark the completion of each POST step by writing single-byte hexadecimal completion codes to port 80h. Turn off and unplug the PC, and then insert a POST board to read the completion codes. Reboot the computer and find the last code to be written before the initialization stops—that is the likely point of failure. You can determine the meaning of that POST code by finding the BIOS maker (usually displayed in the initial moments of power-up) and then locating the corresponding error message in Chapter 17. Note that without a POST board available, identifying the problem may be extremely difficult.

**SYMPTOM 3-6**    **You see a message indicating a CMOS Setup problem**    The system parameters entered into CMOS RAM do not match the hardware configuration found during the POST, and the boot process will not continue. Enter your CMOS Setup routine and review each entry in the CMOS Setup—especially things like drive parameters and installed memory—and make sure that the CMOS entries accurately reflect the actual hardware installed on your system. If not, correct the error(s), save your changes, and reboot the system. In most current PCs, you can opt to load "BIOS Default" values.

Use a dc voltmeter to test the CMOS RAM backup battery for about 3.0 Vdc (see Figure 3-5). See if CMOS RAM will hold its contents by turning off the PC, waiting several minutes, and then rebooting the PC. If setup problems persist and you find that the values you entered have been lost, change the CMOS backup battery. A backup battery usually lasts 3–5 years, so you may see this type of trouble with older systems.

Use a dc multimeter to test the voltage of a CMOS backup battery (coin cell).

**FIGURE  3-5**    A normal coin cell battery will provide about 3.0 Vdc, which can easily be checked with a dc voltmeter (Courtesy of Motherboards.org).

**SYMPTOM 3-7**    **You see no drive light activity**    The boot drive cannot be located. The most frequent cause of drive problems is power connections. Inspect the four-pin power cable and see that it is attached properly and completely to the drive. Check the power supply voltages next. Use a voltmeter and verify that the +5 and +12 voltage levels (especially +12 volts) are correct at the four-pin connector. If either voltage is low or absent, replace the power supply. Locate the ribbon cable that connects between the motherboard (or other drive controller card) and the drive. Make sure it is attached correctly and completely at the drive and controller ends. Look for any scrapes or nicks along the cable that might cause problems. Start the CMOS Setup. If you are working on an older system (early i386 and i286 systems), you will probably need to boot the PC from a setup disk.

Review the drive parameters entered in the CMOS Setup and make sure that the CMOS entries accurately reflect the actual boot drive installed on your system. If they do not, correct the error(s), save your changes, and reboot the system. Also make sure that the drive controller board is installed properly and completely in its expansion slot, and see that any jumpers are set correctly.

Try booting the system from your boot floppy. If the system successfully boots to the A: prompt, your problem is limited to the hard drive system. Now try switching to the C: drive. If the drive responds (and you can access its information), there may be a problem with the boot sector. Try a package like Partition Magic or Norton Utilities to try to fix the boot sector. If you can't access the hard drive, try a diagnostic to check the drive controller and drive. Check for boot sector viruses (a boot sector virus can render the hard drive unbootable). If you cannot determine the problem at this point, try replacing the drive with a known-good working drive. Remember that you may have to change the CMOS Setup parameters to accommodate the new drive if your system cannot auto-detect drive types. If all else fails, try a new drive controller board or motherboard.

**SYMPTOM 3-8**    **The drive light remains on continuously**    The boot drive cannot be located. This typically happens if the signal cable is inserted backward at one end. In most cases, this type of problem happens after replacing a drive or upgrading a controller. Make sure the ribbon cable is inserted in the correct orientation at *both* the drive and controller ends. If you cannot determine the problem at this point, try replacing the drive with a known-good working drive. Remember that you may have to change the CMOS Setup parameters to accommodate the new drive if your system cannot auto-detect drive types. If all else fails, try a new drive controller board or motherboard.

**SYMPTOM 3-9**    **You see normal system activity, but there is no video**    Make sure the monitor is plugged in and turned on—the brightness adjustment should be turned up to an adequate level. This type of oversight is really more common than you might think. Make sure that the monitor works (you may want to try the monitor on a known-good system). If the monitor fails on a known-good system, replace the monitor. Next, trace the monitor cable to its connection at the video board, and verify that the connector is inserted securely. Check the video board. It is possible that the video board has failed. If the problem persists, replace the video board.

# THE SYSTEM STARTS BUT CRASHES/ REBOOTS INTERMITTENTLY

These are undoubtedly some of the most perplexing and frustrating problems that any technician can face. It's not that the solutions are particularly difficult, but there are so many possible causes that positively identifying the culprit can be difficult. Spontaneous crashes or reboots can be triggered by a wide range of problems, including resource conflicts, power anomalies, hardware faults, software conflicts, and outdated or buggy drivers (as well as many other causes).

## Isolating the Trouble

Given the many possible causes of crashes and reboots, the first step in dealing with such problems is to determine whether the trouble is related to hardware or software. This can save you countless hours of trial and error, because if the trouble is hardware-based, you can focus on the devices in your system and how they're configured, and if the trouble is software-based, you can focus on isolating and updating the offending software. The following tips can help you locate common problems.

■ *Viruses can impair stability.* It's usually best to start any diagnosis with a virus checker. Viruses can damage files that are necessary for the proper functioning of the PC. While the probability of a virus problem is rare, it's a quick and easy check, and current antivirus tools can check for thousands of viruses. Damaged files should be replaced from a backup or from original installation CDs. Then, run the system and see if stability returns. If the system checks clean, you can move on to the next point.

■ *Conflicts can impair stability.* Once the system is clear of viruses, check your Windows Device Manager (see Figure 3-6). Each device classification should appear *without* markings such as yellow exclamation marks or red Xs. If Device Manager does not report any troubles, go to the next check. If one or more devices are marked with a problem, you should resolve each problem and see if the system stabilizes. In most cases, device problems can be resolved by reconfiguring the offending device, reinstalling it, or upgrading/reinstalling the device driver(s). (See Chapter 11 for more detailed information on device conflict troubleshooting.)

■ *Buggy/damaged applications can impair stability.* Not all software works smoothly on every system, or coexists well with other software applications. If you find that the system is less stable when certain programs (or combinations of programs) are running, try shutting down those applications. Also shut down unneeded applications that may be running in the background. If the system crashes or reboots regardless of what is running, go to the next step. If you identify a suspect piece of software, try uninstalling and reinstalling it, or check for upgrades/patches from the software maker.

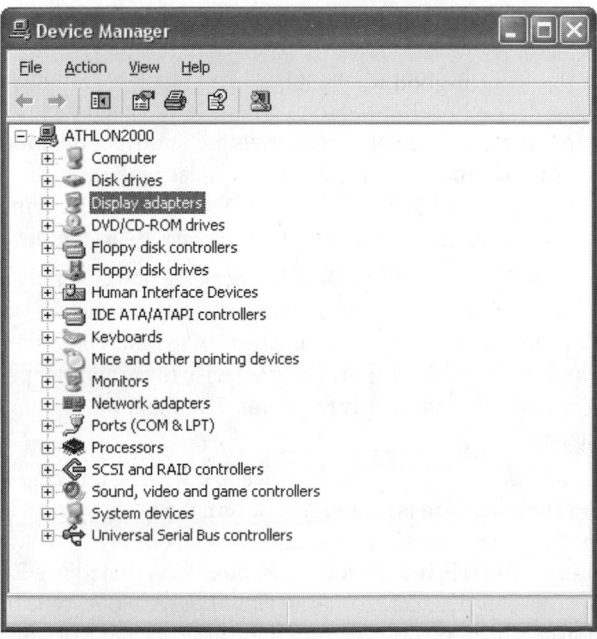

**FIGURE  3-6**    Checking the Device Manager for device problems under Windows XP

■ *Damaged/conflicting utilities can impair stability.* Start Windows in the Safe Mode. This is a diagnostic mode that loads Windows with a minimum of drivers and device support. Run the system this way for a bit and see if stability returns. If the system still crashes or reboots, go to the next step. If stability improves, chances are that software is causing the trouble. Restart the system normally, and systematically disable applications from the Startup folder and System Tray (or press CTRL-ALT-DEL and shut down tasks with the Task Manager). See if you can find a tool or utility that is causing the problem. For example, if you remove the Speaker icon from the System Tray and the system stabilizes, chances are that the problem was caused by (or is related to) that software. It is not uncommon for unique tools loaded in the System Tray or at startup (for example, a photo printer utility or antivirus software) to cause stability problems. This process of isolation takes some patience and persistence, but it's often necessary.

■ *Buggy/outdated/conflicting drivers can impair stability.* Older or buggy device drivers may compromise system stability. Check for updated device drivers for each key device on the system. Patch the operating system (e.g., use the Windows Update feature), then update DirectX drivers, video drivers, sound drivers, printer drivers, modem drivers, USB device drivers, and so on. Update one driver at a time and see if the system stabilizes. If the system continues to crash/reboot, chances are that you're faced with a hardware problem.

■ *AC problems can impair stability.* Now it's time to look at the hardware devices in your system. Try your PC on another AC outlet, preferably one that's free of high-load devices like air conditioners, coffeemakers, fans, motors, and other power-hungry electrical equipment. Install a new surge/spike suppressor (even an inexpensive UPS) on the AC outlet and see if the system stabilizes. If it does not, go to the next step.

■ *Device installation problems can impair stability.* Make sure that all expansion boards and signal cables are seated properly. Any boards that are not secured properly, or that are inserted unevenly, can short bus signals and cause spurious reboots. Inspect the motherboard at every metal standoff and make sure that no metal traces are being shorted against a standoff or screw. You may want to free the motherboard and see if the crashes or reboots go away. If so, use nonconductive spacers (such as a small piece of manila folder) to insulate the motherboard from each metal standoff. If no traces are touching but stability returns when one or more screws are removed, the motherboard may be suffering a hairline stress fracture and may need to be replaced. Also make sure that all memory modules are seated properly in their holders and locked into place. You may try removing each module, cleaning the contacts, and reinstalling the module. If problems persist, go to the next step.

■ *Power supply problems can impair stability.* Double-check the power supply connections to the motherboard and drives. Use a dc voltmeter to verify that each output from the power supply is correct as outlined in Table 3-2. If any output is low or erratic (especially the +5 volt output), replace the power supply. Even if the supply outputs seem okay, you may wish to try another power supply anyway, just to eliminate the possibility of internal supply problems. If another power supply does not stabilize the system, go to the last step.

■ *CPU heating can impair stability.* If the CPU overheats, it will stall, taking the entire system with it. Make sure that the CPU heat sink fan is running. Now turn the PC power off (wait at least 15 minutes) and check to see that the CPU heat-sink/fan assembly is fitted on correctly. Also see that the CPU itself is inserted properly and completely into its socket. If the CPU is seated in a ZIF socket, make sure that the socket's tension lever is closed and locked into place. For cartridge-type processors, verify that the slot retention mechanism is secure.

## Divide and Conquer

If you've come this far and the system is still unstable, chances are that there's an issue with one or more system devices that has escaped your detection. Now we're down to "hack and slash" troubleshooting. Remove one device at a time from the system and see if the system stabilizes. Start with unnecessary devices, such as Zip drives, and work your way to secondary hard drives, CD drives, optional cards (such as SCSI cards, sound cards, video capture cards, modems, and so on). Restart the system after removing each device and see if stability returns. If so, the *last* device you removed is probably the culprit. Once you've identified the troublesome item, you can try reinstalling it from scratch using the very latest drivers and applet software downloaded from the manufacturer's Web site. If the problem returns after reinstallation, you can try reconfiguring it (if possible). For example, if the system doesn't like your DVD-ROM drive as a slave device on a secondary controller channel, you can try making it the master device instead (and resetting the current master device as a slave device).

This is sometimes called "simplifying the system," and can be a time-consuming trial-and-error process. However, it is an option of last resort when you cannot locate stability problems in any other way.

# AFTER AN UPGRADE

Upgrades are prime places for system startup problems. In most cases, a new device is installed improperly, is incompatible with your current platform, or is conflicting with another device in the system. Fortunately, problems occurring after an upgrade are relatively simple to correct because you already know the change(s) performed on the system. The golden rule for upgrade troubleshooting is LIFO (last-in, first-out). That is, the last piece of hardware or software added to the system before the trouble occurred should be the first item that you remove to correct the trouble. For example, if you install a CD drive and now the PC won't boot, chances are that the CD drive installation caused the problem (e.g., one end of the signal cable was reversed). There are several typical symptoms that you may encounter.

**SYMPTOM 3-10**  **The system fails to boot, freezes during boot, or freezes during operation for no apparent reason**  This is the classic sign of a hardware conflict. A PC is designed with a limited number of "resources" (e.g., memory, I/O addresses, interrupt lines, DMA channels, and so on). For the PC to function properly, each device in the system must use its own unique resources. For example, no two devices can use the same IRQ, DMA, or I/O resources. When such an overlap of resources occurs, the PC can easily malfunction and freeze or crash. Unfortunately, it is virtually impossible to predict when the malfunction will occur, so a conflict can manifest itself early (any time during the boot process), or later on (after the OS has loaded), or even after an application has been running normally for quite some time.

Resolving a conflict is not difficult, but it requires patience and attention to detail. Examine the upgrade and its adapter board and check the IRQ, DMA, and I/O address settings of other boards in the system. Make sure that the upgrade hardware is set to use resources that are not in use by other devices already in the system. As one example, when adding a second hard drive, make sure that one drive is jumpered as the "master" device and the other as the "slave". If both drives are jumpered as the master device, a conflict will occur because the PC cannot distinguish between the two drives.

As another example, some motherboards offer built-in video controller circuits. Before another video adapter can be added to the system, the motherboard video adapter must be disabled—usually with a single motherboard jumper, or through the CMOS Setup. Most of today's sophisticated adapter boards (especially high-end video adapters and video capture boards) require the use of extra memory space (see Figure 3-7). If memory exclusions are needed, be sure that the appropriate entries are made in the device's

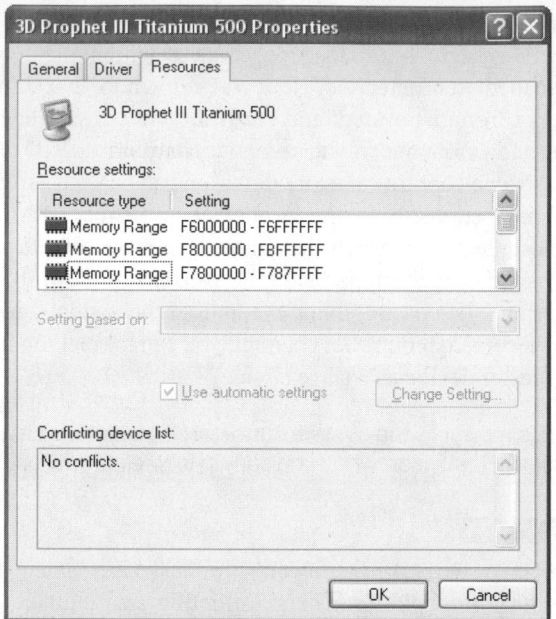

**FIGURE 3-7** The Resources tab for each device will reveal the resources assigned to it. Some resources can be changed manually in order to correct device conflicts.

Properties dialog (older DOS-based systems will require exclusions in the CONFIG.SYS and AUTOEXEC.BAT files). For example, if memory exclusions are not implemented, multiple devices may attempt to use the same memory space, which will result in a conflict. (See Chapter 11 for more detailed information on device conflict troubleshooting.)

**SYMPTOM 3-11** **The system fails to recognize the newly installed device** Even if the hardware is installed in a system correctly, the PC may not recognize the upgrade device(s) without the proper software loaded. A great example of this is the CD-ROM drive in real mode (DOS). It is a simple matter to install the drive (and a controller card if necessary), but the PC will not even recognize the drive unless the low-level CD-ROM device driver is added to CONFIG.SYS, and the MS-DOS CD-ROM extension (MSCDEX) is included in AUTOEXEC.BAT. If the PC is running in a stable fashion but does not recognize the expansion hardware, make sure that you have loaded all required software correctly. If you're having trouble with a device under Windows, recheck the device's installation procedure and see if any software needed to be loaded *before* the actual installation of the hardware. For example, some high-end drives (such as DVD drives) and USB devices may need software before attaching the device for the first time.

If you're mixing and matching existing subassemblies from new and old systems, make sure that each device is fully compatible with the PC. Incompatibilities between vintages and manufacturers can lead to operational problems. For example, adding a 3.5-inch floppy drive to an old i286 AT system can result in problems because the older BIOS cannot format 3.5-inch high-density (1.44MB) floppy disks. A DOS utility (such as DRIVER.SYS) is needed to correct this deficiency. Today, devices are much more versatile, but it still pays to verify the minimum system requirements for each device, and have its latest drivers available for your operating system.

It is also possible that the upgrade device may simply be defective or installed incorrectly. Open the system and double-check your installation. Pay particular attention to any cables, connectors, or drive jumpers.

When you confirm that the hardware and software installations are correct, suspect a hardware defect. Try the upgrade in another system if possible. If the problem persists when you attempt the upgrade on another PC, one or more elements of the upgrade hardware are probably defective. Return the upgrade hardware to the vendor for a prompt refund or replacement. If the upgrade works on another system, the original system may be incompatible with the upgrade, or you may have a hardware conflict in the original system that is preventing the new hardware from being detected.

**SYMPTOM 3-12**    **One or more applications fail to function as expected after an upgrade**    This is not uncommon among video adapter and sound board (multimedia) upgrades. Often, applications are configured to work with various sets of hardware. When that hardware is altered, the particular application(s) may no longer run properly (this is especially true under Windows 9x/Me/XP). The best way to address this problem is to check and change the hardware configuration for each affected application. Most DOS applications come with an executable setup utility. Under Windows 9x/Me/XP, you can access system configuration settings through the Device Manager.

In other cases, the drivers that were installed with the new device may have broken the link to important program relations. For example, you may have trouble playing DVD movies after installing a new video card, because the new video drivers that "took over" from the existing DVD drivers may not be compatible with the DVD drive. Reinstalling the affected device (the DVD drivers or playback software) may reestablish that "link" and restore normal playback operation.

# WINDOWS 9X/ME/XP BOOT SYMPTOMS

After the POST finishes checking hardware, BIOS looks for a master boot record and tries to initiate loading the operating system, which is some version of Windows in virtually all cases today. Even when the hardware checks out properly, there are many different problems that can plague a complicated operating system such as Windows and prevent it from loading. For our purposes, the most common issues to consider are software interference (such as old drive overlay software) and damaged Windows components (such as a damaged kernel file or other DLL). The symptoms described next are typical of Windows startup problems. If problems persist, removing and reinstalling Windows will often correct the trouble.

**SYMPTOM 3-13**    **Windows XP continually asks you to insert a disk into drive A: at startup**    Each time you start the system, you receive an error such as "Please insert a disk into drive A:". This error repeats until you insert a diskette into drive A:, or you click Cancel. This happens when you select the Restore Previous Folder Windows at Logon checkbox in Folder Options (see Figure 3-8), then shut down or restart the PC while the floppy drive is being viewed. When the system restarts, it expects to see that same floppy. You can avoid this problem by exiting Windows Explorer before restarting the PC, or disabling the Restore Previous Folder Windows at Logon option.

**SYMPTOM 3-14**    **The Windows XP computer restarts continually**    When you try to start Windows XP, a black startup screen may appear briefly, then your computer restarts repeatedly. This problem can happen if a fatal system error causes the computer to stop, and the Automatically Restart option is selected under System Failure in the Startup and Recovery dialog box in your System Properties. Try to replace the registry files from the repair directory by using the Recovery Console, and then restore the system to a current state with System Restore. This can also occur if the Windows XP paging file is smaller than the amount of RAM installed on the computer—in this event, installing more RAM may correct the trouble.

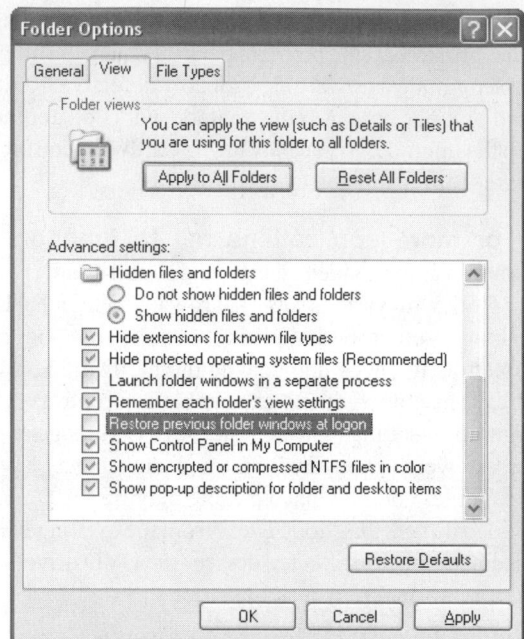

**FIGURE 3-8**   Disable the Restore Previous Folder Windows at Logon option to prevent Windows XP from repeatedly searching for a floppy diskette.

Try to restart your computer in Safe Mode. This may allow you to troubleshoot the error message.

**SYMPTOM 3-15**   **The Windows 9x/Me boot drive is no longer bootable after restoring data with the DOS Backup utility**   This happens frequently when a replacement drive is installed and you attempt to restore the Windows 9x/Me backup data. Unfortunately, the DOS version of Backup is not configured to restore system files. Start Backup and restore your root directory with System Files, Hidden Files, and Read Only Files checked. Next, boot the system from an MS-DOS 6.x upgrade setup disk 1, or a Windows 9x/Me startup disk, and then use the SYS command to make the hard drive bootable such as:

```
A:\> sys c:              <Enter>
```

You should then be able to restore the remainder of your files. When backing up a Windows 9x/Me/XP system, your best approach is to use a current Windows Backup program. Once the new drive is installed, partitioned, and formatted, install a new copy of Windows 9x/Me/XP, start the Windows Backup program, and then restore the remaining files to the drive.

**SYMPTOM 3-16**   **Windows 9x/Me will not boot, and ScanDisk reports bad clusters that it cannot repair**   This is a problem encountered with Western Digital hard drives. If your WD drive fails in this way, you can recover the drive, but you will lose all information on it. Back up as much information from the drive as possible before proceeding:

1.  Download the Western Digital service files wdatide.exe and wd_clear.exe from WD at www.wdc.com. You can also get these files from AOL by typing the keyword WDC.

2.  Copy these files to a clean boot floppy disk.

3. Boot to DOS from a clean disk (no CONFIG.SYS or AUTOEXEC.BAT files) and run wd_clear.exe. This utility clears all data on the media (and destroys all data).

4. Run the wdatide.exe utility to perform a comprehensive surface scan.

5. Repartition and reformat the drive, and then restore your data.

**SYMPTOM 3-17**    **You see a "Bad or missing <filename>" error on startup**    A file used by Windows 9x/Me/XP during startup has probably become corrupt. Locate the file mentioned in the error message. If you can find the file, erase it and try reinstalling it from the original Windows 9x/Me installation CD. If you can get Windows XP to start in the Safe Mode, you may be able to use the System Restore feature to recover the problem.

**SYMPTOM 3-18**    **Windows 9x/Me/XP reports damaged or missing files, or a "VxD error"**    During startup, Windows 9x/Me/XP depends on several key files being available. If a key file is damaged or missing, Windows will not function properly (if it loads at all). You can use System File Checker to verify the integrity of your operating system files, to restore them if they are corrupted, and to extract compressed files (such as drivers) from your installation disks. You can have System File Checker back up the existing files before restoring the original files. Under Windows 9x, you can start System File Checker by selecting Start | Programs | Accessories | System Tools | System Information. In System Information, click Tools, and then click System File Checker. Under Windows Me/XP, you can use the System Restore Wizard (see Figure 3-9) to restore the PC to an earlier working state. Otherwise, you may need to reinstall Windows from scratch.

**SYMPTOM 3-19**    **After installing Windows 98/Me, you can't boot from a different drive** The Windows setup program checks all hard disks to find just one that contains the 80h designator in the DriveNumber field of a boot sector. Windows 98/Me will typically force the first drive to be bootable, and prevent other drives from booting. However, there are two ways to correct the problem after Windows is installed:

■ Use the version of FDISK included with Windows 9x to set the primary active partition.

■ Use a disk editor utility to change a disk's DriveNumber field so that you can boot from that hard disk.

**SYMPTOM 3-20**    **Windows 9x/Me registry files are missing**    There are two registry files: USER.DAT and SYSTEM.DAT. They are also backed up automatically as USER.DA0 and SYSTEM.DA0. If a DAT file is missing, Windows will automatically load the corresponding DA0 file. If both the DAT and DA0 registry files are missing or corrupt, Windows will start in the Safe Mode, offering to restore the registry. However, this cannot be accomplished without a backup. Either restore the registry files from a tape or disk backup, or run Windows setup to create a new registry. Unfortunately, restoring an old registry or creating a new registry from scratch will reload programs and re-add hardware to restore the system to its original state, which is a long and difficult procedure. Use RegEdit to back up your registry files, or use the following DOS procedure to back up the registry files to a floppy disk:

```
attrib -r -s -h system.da?
attrib -r -s -h user.da?
copy system.da? A:\
copy user.da? A:\
attrib +r +s +h system.da?
attrib +r +s +h user.da?
```

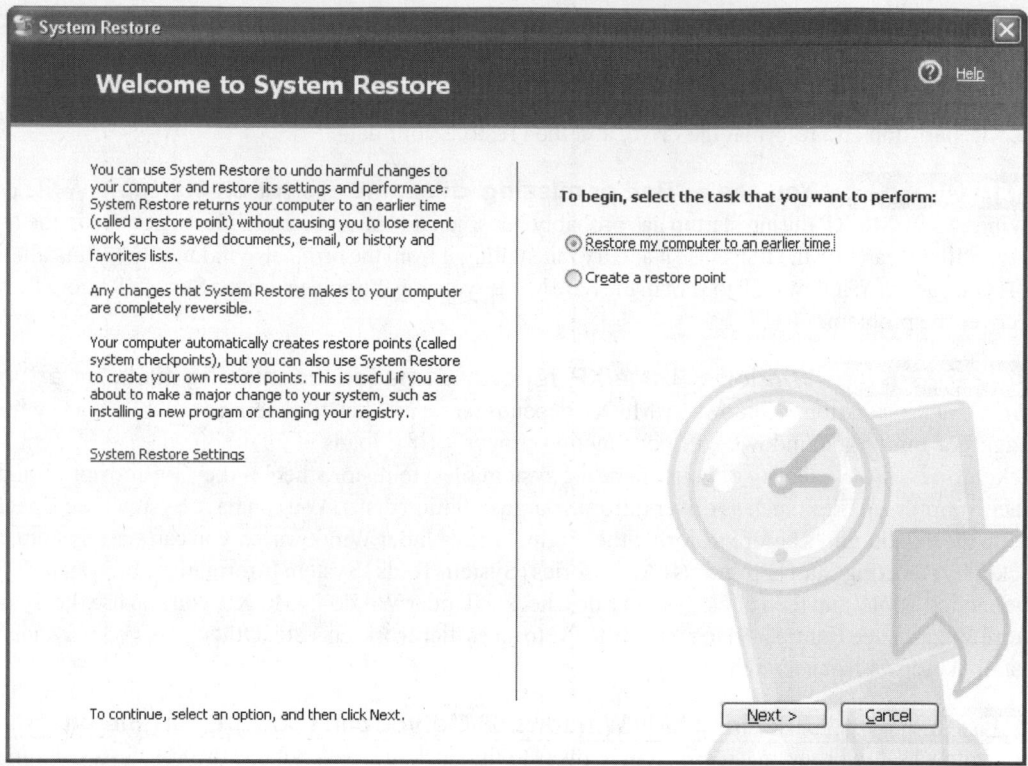

**FIGURE  3-9**    The System Restore Wizard can verify files and restore your Windows Me/XP platform to an earlier point when it was working properly.

 Under Windows Me/XP, you can generally use the System Restore Wizard to check the integrity of system files and restore the system to a previous working state.

**SYMPTOM 3-21    During the Windows 98/Me boot, you get an "Invalid System Disk" error**    This often happens during the first reboot during Windows setup, or when you boot from the startup disk. When you a see a message such as "Invalid system disk. Replace the disk, and then press any key," there may be several possible problems. First, your disk may be infected with a boot-sector virus. Run your real mode antivirus emergency or rescue disk and check closely for boot sector viruses. Windows setup may also fail if there is antivirus software running as a TSR, or your BIOS has enabled boot sector protection. Make sure that any boot sector protection is turned off before installing any version of Windows. Check for disk overlay software (Windows 98/Me may not detect older versions of overlay software such as Disk Manager, EZ-Drive, or DrivePro), and overwrite the master boot record (MBR). See the documentation that accompanies your particular management software for recovering the MBR. To reinstall the Windows 98/Me system files, follow these steps:

1. Boot the system using the Windows 98/Me emergency boot disk.
2. At the DOS command prompt, type the following lines:
```
c:
cd\windows\command
attrib c:\msdos.sys -h -s -r
```

```
ren c:\msdos.sys c:\msdos.xxx
a:
sys c:
del c:\msdos.sys
ren c:\msdos.xxx c:\msdos.sys
attrib c:\msdos.sys +r +s +h
```

**3.** Remove the emergency boot disk and reboot the system.

**SYMPTOM 3-22**    **Windows 9x/Me will not install on a compressed drive**    You are probably using an old version of the compression software that Windows does not recognize. Although Windows 9x/Me should be compatible with all versions of SuperStor, it does require version 2.0 or later of Stacker. Make sure your compression software is recent, and that enough free space exists on the host drive to support Windows 9x/Me installation. If you have a PlusPack for Windows, you should be able to install DriveSpace 3 for best Windows support. If the problem persists, it is often best to back up the compressed data, then remove all compression support (e.g., repartition and reformat the drive before installation). Given the huge size and great performance of today's hard drives, a drive upgrade is often preferable to compression.

Windows XP supports NTFS compression if you set up the drive(s) for NTFS. See Windows XP Help for additional information.

**SYMPTOM 3-23**    **Windows Me won't mount a compressed volume**    Information contained on a DriveSpace-compressed volume is not available after you upgrade to Windows Me; the compressed volume appears in My Computer as a drive labeled "Host for Drive $X$:" (where $X$ is the drive letter assigned to the compressed volume). Windows Me does not support fixed-disk compressed volumes, and will not start with the compressed volume mounted. To have the compressed volume mount after every reboot:

**1.** Right-click Start and then click Explore.

**2.** In the right Windows Explorer pane, double-click the Programs folder.

**3.** In the right Windows Explorer pane, double-click the Startup folder.

**4.** In the right Windows Explorer pane, right-click an empty area, point to New, and then click Shortcut.

**5.** In the Command Line box, type **drvspace /mount x:**, where $x$ is the drive letter of the host drive.

**6.** Click Next, and then click Finish.

**SYMPTOM 3-24**    **You receive a kernel error when starting Windows 98/Me**    When you start Windows, you see an error such as "Error Loading Kernel. You must reinstall Windows." Windows quits after you receive this message. This error can occur if the KERNEL32.DLL file is missing or damaged. You need to extract a new copy of the KERNEL32.DLL file from your original Windows CD:

**1.** Restart your computer. When you see the "Starting Windows" message, press the F8 key and choose Command Prompt Only from the Startup menu. If you're using Windows Me, start your computer with the Windows Me startup disk.

**2.** Type the following commands (press ENTER after each line):

```
cd\windows\system
ren kernel32.dll kernel32.xxx
```

3. Extract a new copy of the KERNEL32.DLL file from your original Windows CD to the Windows\System folder. If you need help extracting a file, see article Q129605 in the Microsoft Knowledge Base.

4. Restart your computer.

> Under Windows Me/XP, use the System Restore Wizard to verify system file integrity, and restore the system to an earlier working point if necessary.

**SYMPTOM 3-25**    **A drive indicates that it is in "MS-DOS compatibility mode"**    For some reason, Windows is using a real-mode (DOS) driver instead of a protected-mode (32-bit) driver. Make sure that any software related to the hard drive (especially hard disk drivers) is using the protected-mode version. Windows 98/Me should install equivalent protected-mode software, but you may need to contact the drive manufacturer and obtain the latest Windows drivers. This is not a common issue under Windows XP—partly due to XP's more robust design, and partly because the late-model PC platforms used with XP help to eliminate the hardware issues involved with drive compatibility.

If you are using Disk Manager, make sure that you're using version 6.0 or later. You can get the latest patch (DMPATCH.EXE) from the Ontrack Web site at www.ontrack.com. Finally, check your motherboard BIOS. Windows may use DOS compatibility mode on large EIDE hard disks (hard disks with more than 1024 cylinders) in some computers. This may occur because of an invalid drive geometry translation in the system ROM BIOS that prevents the protected-mode IDE device driver from being loaded. Contact your system manufacturer for information about obtaining an updated BIOS, or consider a motherboard upgrade, which will include the BIOS and drive controller support to handle the latest hard drive models.

**SYMPTOM 3-26**    **Disabling protected-mode disk driver(s) hides the partition table when FDISK is used**    As with Symptom 3-25, there are problems preventing 32-bit operation of your hard drive(s). Do not use the Disable All 32-Bit Protected-Mode Disk Drivers option. Instead, upgrade your motherboard BIOS to a later version, or upgrade the entire motherboard outright.

**SYMPTOM 3-27**    **You cannot achieve 32-bit disk access under Windows 98/Me**    If the Windows 98/Me system refuses to allow 32-bit disk access, there may be a conflict between the motherboard CMOS Setup entries for your motherboard's BIOS and the firmware on your EIDE/UDMA controller card. For example, if both BIOS have settings for Logical Block Addressing (LBA), make sure only one entry is in use.

**SYMPTOM 3-28**    **Windows 9x/Me/XP does not recognize a new device**    In some cases, Windows is unable to recognize a new device. When this happens, check to see if a hardware conflict exists between the device and other devices in the system (conflicts are represented in Device Manager with small yellow exclamation marks). Also make sure that any necessary drivers have been installed properly. If problems continue, remove the new device through your Device Manager and reinstall it through the Add Hardware Wizard (see Figure 3-10), or perform a full reboot and allow Windows to redetect the device at start time.

**SYMPTOM 3-29**    **Windows 98/Me malfunctions when installed over Disk Manager**    Late versions of Disk Manager should typically be compatible with Windows 98/Me, but there are some points to keep in mind. Check your Disk Manager version first. If you are using Disk Manager, make sure that you're using version 6.0 or later. You can get the latest patch (DMPATCH.EXE) from the Ontrack

**FIGURE 3-10**    The Add Hardware Wizard allows you to inform Windows XP about the presence of new devices that may not have been detected automatically.

Web site at www.ontrack.com. Check the slave drive with Disk Manager. Although the Windows 98/Me file system is supposed to work properly with a slave drive only using Disk Manager, problems can occur in some circumstances:

■ When an obsolete Windows 3.1*x* virtual driver replaces the Windows protected-mode driver (such as WDCDRV.386), which can happen after several OS upgrades

■ When the cylinder count in CMOS for the slave drive is greater than 1024 cylinders

■ When the motherboard CMOS settings for the slave drive are set to autodetect

As a rule, you will receive best performance by removing drive overlay software and updating the drive controller to support large EIDE/UDMA drives natively. This may require you to back up data, repartition and reformat the drive (or install a new drive), then restore your data after the operating system is installed.

**SYMPTOM 3-30**    **You have problems using a manufacturer-specific hard disk driver (such as Western Digital's FastTrack driver WDCDRV.386) for 32-bit access under Windows 9*x*/Me**    Generally speaking, Windows has 32-bit protected-mode drivers for a wide variety of EIDE devices—in practice, you should *not* need a manufacturer-specific driver. If Windows has not removed all references to the driver from SYSTEM.INI, you should edit the file and remove those references manually, and then reboot the system. Be sure to make a backup copy of SYSTEM.INI before editing it. If you're using Windows XP, there should be no manufacturer-specific disk driver on the system.

# TIPS FOR SLOW WINDOWS STARTUPS

Windows 98/Me/XP is a complex operating system, and loading the many components and drivers that are required to make it run takes time. It takes even longer when you've installed additional software and applets that must load at start time. However, there are some circumstances that can make Windows really drag. If your Windows 98/Me/XP system seems to be taking an unusually long time to start, follow the tips provided next to help streamline your platform.

**Rearrange the Disk**    The Disk Defragmenter utility under Windows Me/XP allows you to rearrange the disk contents, which can allow for faster system startup. This is a type of file defragmentation that not only makes individual files contiguous, but also reorganizes key files so that they are all together. This feature minimizes the amount of seeking that a disk needs to do, thus accelerating boot times. To use Disk Defragmenter:

1. Click Start | Settings | Control Panel | Performance and Maintenance.

2. Select Rearrange Items on Your Hard Disk to Make Programs Run Faster.

3. The Disk Defragmenter dialog opens (see Figure 3-11).

4. You may select Analyze to check the disk before defragmenting. You can use this feature to determine the extent of fragmentation.

5. Click Defragment to rearrange the disk. This may take several minutes to several hours depending on the size of your drive, the number of files, and the amount of fragmentation.

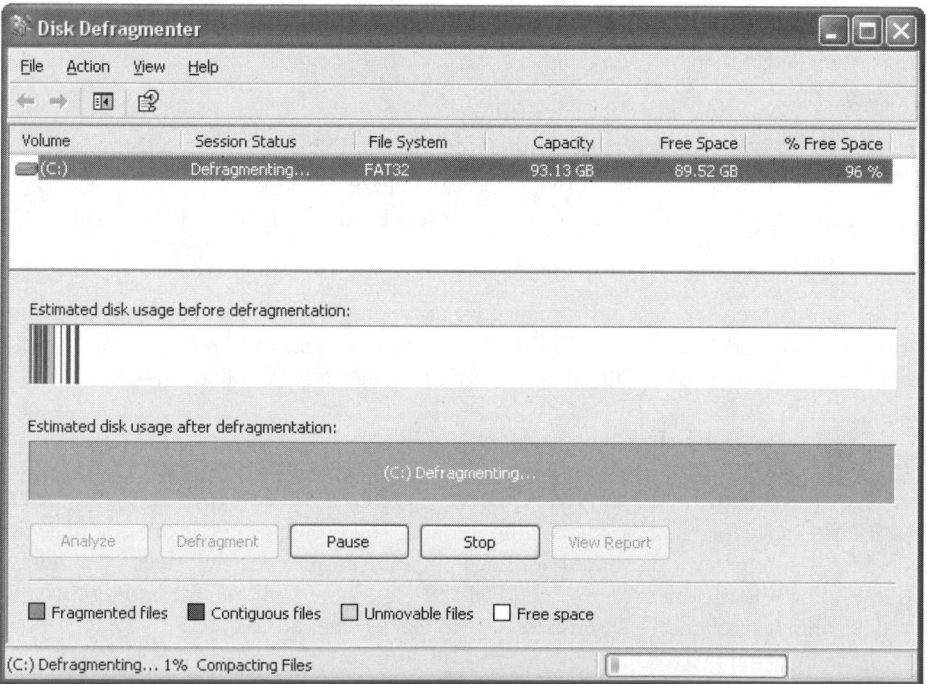

**FIGURE 3-11**    Disk Defragmenter is used to rearrange files for faster loading and minimize the amount of work that a hard drive needs to do.

**Shut Down Unneeded Programs**    The first thing to do is examine what programs you're launching at startup, and decide whether you really need them. Remember that programs can be launched from the Startup folder (under the Start menu), from the RUN= and LOAD= lines of your WIN.INI file, or from entries in the registry. Under Windows 95, you'd have to check each of these locations manually, but Windows 98/Me/XP has a convenient one-stop location to tweak them all. Just click Start, select Run, and then type **msconfig**. You can see msconfig running under Windows XP in Figure 3-12. Under the Startup tab, you'll see all the programs you are launching. By clearing the checkbox next to any item, you'll prevent it from running at startup. You can always re-enable each task later. Windows versions also let you stop programs (tasks) that are already running by pressing CTRL-ALT-DEL and using the Task Manager to highlight and exit unneeded tasks once the system has booted.

**Disable Real-Time Virus Scanning**    Virtually all of today's antivirus utilities offer real-time scanning for viruses once the system boots. Unfortunately, since the scanner loads at startup, it can seriously impact performance (because it must scan every program file as it is being loaded into memory). If you're willing to accept a bit less virus protection (e.g., periodic scans will suffice), you can accelerate your boot times by turning off real-time scanning. Instead, schedule a task to run a standard virus scan at least once a day. Not only will this shorten boot times, but it will make your system faster during any disk access.

**Don't Check the Floppy Drive**    Among its many other startup checks, Windows 98/Me checks whether you've added or changed floppy drives each time the system starts up. Chances are that you'll never reconfigure your floppy, so tell Windows to stop checking it. Click Start | Settings | Control Panel, and then double-click the System icon. Click the Performance tab, click the File System button, and then select the Floppy Disk tab. Clear the Search for New Floppy Disk Drives Each Time Your Computer Starts

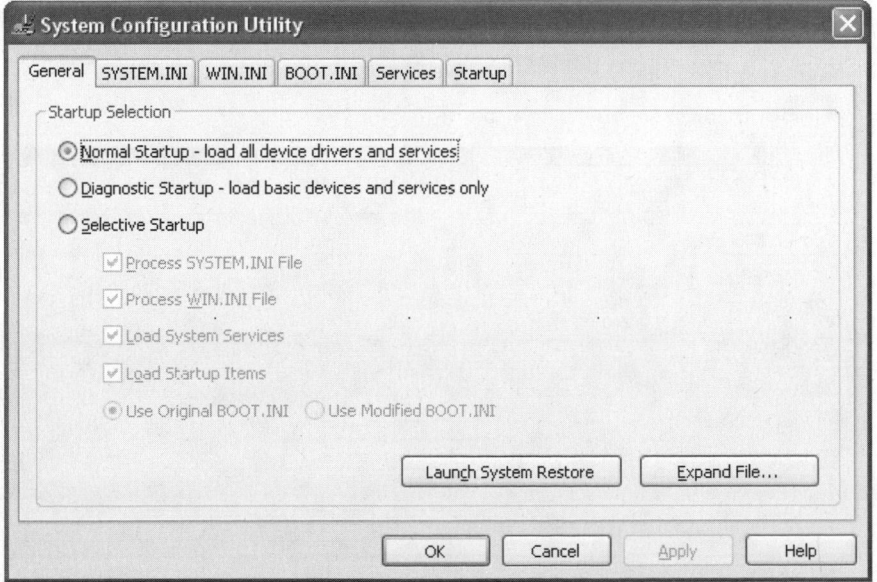

**FIGURE 3-12**    The System Configuration (msconfig) utility allows you to tailor the startup behavior of a Windows PC for diagnostic purposes.

checkbox. Apply your changes and try rebooting the computer. Windows XP does not check floppy drives, however, you can usually set the Boot Order in your CMOS Setup to skip the floppy drive as a possible boot device (saving several additional seconds on each reboot).

**Tweak Your CMOS Setup**    Check your CMOS Setup routine for options that can speed your system's boot time. Enabling options such as Quick Boot or Quick POST and shortening drive initialization delays can shave a few seconds off the system's POST process. You'll also get a faster boot sequence if the system can boot directly from the C: drive rather than first checking for a floppy, LS-120, or CD drive (this also prevents viruses from infecting your system via a boot floppy).

**Examine the Boot Log**    You may be faced with a problematic hardware component or software driver. These can be a bit difficult to diagnose, but the BOOTLOG.TXT feature can help. This allows you to generate a boot log that indicates each step in the boot process. You'll need to access the Windows startup menu, which will give you the option to generate a boot log. After the BIOS has completed its POST, hold down the CTRL key. The boot menu should appear (if the Windows 98/Me logo appears instead, you probably didn't press the CTRL key soon enough).

From the boot menu, select a "logged startup." Once Windows has finished booting up, the file BOOTLOG.TXT will be in the root of your C: drive, and you can view this file with Notepad. On a normal system, it's unusual to have any step in the boot process take more than a second or two. Large delays (10 or 20 seconds) usually indicate some sort of problem with a driver or its associated hardware.

Under Windows XP, click Start | Run, then type **msconfig**, and click the BOOT.INI tab (see Figure 3-13). Check the /BOOTLOG box, apply your changes, then click OK. When you reboot, a bootlog.txt file will be generated. You can view the bootlog.txt file with any text editor and look for problem entries which may be resulting in long boot times.

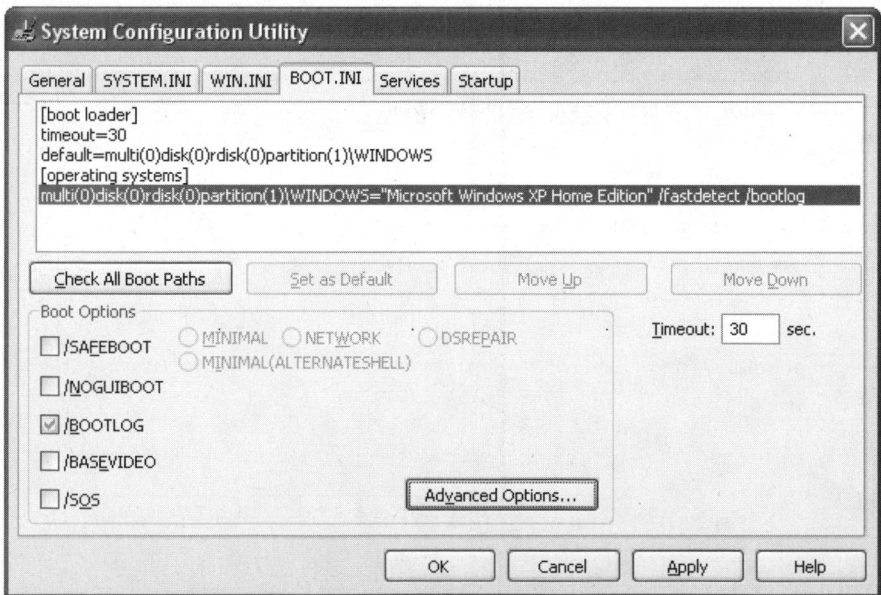

**FIGURE  3-13**    Use the System Configuration utility (msconfig) to generate a bootlog.txt file at start time. You can then review the bootlog file for problems or errors that may be extending the boot time.

# TIPS FOR WINDOWS STARTUP PROBLEMS

It's bad enough when Windows takes a long time to load, but when Windows fails to start at all, it may be difficult (or impossible) to use diagnostics and Windows tools to identify and correct the problem. This part of the chapter outlines a suite of tips that can help you track down and correct serious startup faults.

**Try the Safe Mode**    One of your first options is to try starting Windows 98/Me/XP in the Safe Mode. For Windows 98/Me, hold down the CTRL key right after the BIOS finishes its POST (but before Windows starts to load). For Windows XP, hold down the F8 key right after the BIOS finishes its POST. You should get a Startup menu of options to select from. Choose Safe Mode and allow Windows to boot. If the boot is successful, open the Device Manager and check the status of your devices. If any hardware is malfunctioning, the Device Manager tab will show it with a yellow exclamation point. (You can also use Device Manager to disable hardware manually and see if that lets you boot normally.) If you cannot boot Windows to the Safe Mode, chances are that a serious hardware problem exists in the system.

**Try a Clean Boot Under Windows Me/XP**    You can use a clean boot technique to disable common startup programs, settings, and drivers under Windows Me:

1. Click Start, click Run, type **msconfig** in the Open box, and then click OK.
2. On the General tab, click Selective Startup.
3. Click to clear all of the checkboxes under Selective Startup.
4. On the Startup tab, click to select the *StateMgr checkbox.
5. Click OK, and click Yes when you're prompted to restart your computer.

Use the following steps with Windows XP:

1. Click Start, click Run, type **msconfig** in the Open box, and then click OK.
2. On the General tab (see Figure 3-12 earlier), click Selective Startup.
3. Click to clear all of the checkboxes under Selective Startup.
4. Click Apply and OK, then restart your computer.

After the computer restarts, click Start, click Run, type **msconfig**, and then click OK again. Review the General tab and ensure that the checkboxes you cleared are still cleared. If you see a disabled or gray checkbox, your computer is not truly clean-booted. Now you can isolate the problem. If the trouble does *not* reoccur after a clean boot, select one item at a time under Selective Startup, and then restart the computer to see if the additional entry reproduces the original issue. If so, *that* is the cause of the trouble. For example, if you find that the system boots normally when you restore the system.ini file, but returns when you re-enable the win.ini file, you can suspect that the trouble is in one or more win.ini entries. You can then select the WIN.INI tab in msconfig and check individual settings to isolate the culprit. When you're done troubleshooting, you may return to a normal boot process:

1. Click Start | Run; type **msconfig** in the Open box, and then click OK.
2. On the General tab, click Normal Startup.
3. Apply your changes, click OK, and restart your computer.

**Check for Disk Errors**    If you cannot start Windows due to a disk error, it may be that the drive's power or signal cable has become loose. Check the cables and see that the drive is receiving adequate power. Try booting from a floppy disk. If you can reach a DOS prompt from a boot disk, the system hard drive may be defective.

**Use the Automatic Skip Driver Agent**    If your system crashes or hangs during the startup process, Windows 98/Me tries to avoid crashing again by skipping the operation that it "thinks" caused the problem. This is the Automatic Skip Driver (ASD) agent at work. However, the ASD may cause other problems (such as disabling some of your hardware) when a driver is skipped. To see if Windows is skipping any boot-up operations on your system, select Start, choose Run, and type **ASD**. If everything is okay, you'll receive a dialog box that says "There are no current ASD critical operation failures on this machine." If your system has had boot problems, they will be listed in this dialog box. You can put a check next to any or all of the skipped drivers to have Windows 98 retry them the next time you boot. After you boot the system again, run ASD and see if the function was disabled again; if so, you may have a problem with that hardware (or your BIOS).

Windows Me/XP allows you to verify system files and restore the system to a previous working state with the System Restore utility.

**Check for Missing Files**    If you see the message "A file needed by Windows is missing" during a boot cycle, it's often due to a poor uninstallation of an application. This can sometimes occur when you uninstall and then immediately reinstall an application without rebooting first. Take a look at the name of the missing file to see whether it yields any clue as to which application might be causing the problem, and if it does, then try to uninstall, reboot, and reinstall that application. If the offending file relates to an application that you no longer need, you can use RegEdit to find and delete the registry keys that refer to the file (be sure that you have good backups before trying this). As a last resort, you may need to reinstall Windows to fix this problem cleanly.

**Windows Protection Errors**    In some cases, earlier versions of Windows may refuse to boot, returning the message "Windows Protection Error. You need to restart your computer." At this point, you're stuck unless you boot from a floppy disk. One cause in Windows 95 is a problem between SmartDrive and a large number of installed device drivers. If you see something about "initializing IOS" in the error message, try booting from a floppy, find the file SMARTDRV.EXE (usually in the Windows directory), and rename it SMARTDRV.BAD. Now try booting the system from the hard drive again.

There is also a known problem in Windows 95 that affects AMD K6 processors that run at 350 MHz or higher speeds, and this will sometimes give a Windows Protection Error message. (You can refer to Microsoft's document Q192841 for more detailed information and a patch file.) Other solutions to Windows Protection Errors can be identified in Microsoft's document Q149962.

**Other Startup Problems**    You can refer to the Microsoft Web site and Knowledge Base to learn about numerous other startup problems:

| | |
|---|---|
| Q132571 | Cannot Start Windows or Programs in Windows |
| Q267079 | Norton AntiVirus 2000 Real Mode Virus Scanner May Not Work in Windows Me |
| Q272381 | System Configuration Utility Error Occurs at Startup |
| Q273738 | How to Troubleshoot Windows Millennium Edition Startup Problems |
| Q273746 | How to Troubleshoot Windows Me Shutdown Problems |

| Q143053 | Mouse Systems Driver May Cause Windows Protection Error |
| Q186351 | Norton AntiVirus 4.0 May Cause Windows Protection Error |
| Q186844 | "Windows Protection Error" with EZ-SCSI 4.0 and Easy-CD Pro 95 |
| Q175930 | Illegal Operations or Access Violations When Starting Windows |
| Q141898 | Windows 95/98 Boots Directly to "Shut Down" Screen |
| Q187524 | MS-DOS Based Program Starts When You Start Your Computer |

# Further Study

**IBM setup routines**    oak.oakland.edu:/SimTel/msdos/at or ftp.uu.net:/systems/msdos/simtel/at
**Innoculan AntiVirus**    www.networldwide.com/products/cheyenne.htm
**McAfee Anti-Virus**    www.mcafee.com
**Microsoft**    www.microsoft.com
**Norton AntiVirus**    www.symantec.com
**Ontrack Software**    www.ontrack.com
**PassMark BurnIn 2.2**    www.passmark.com
**SciSoft SANDRA**    www.3bsoftware.com
**Ziff Davis**    www.zdnet.com/etestinglabs/filters/benchmarks/

# 4

# BACKUP GUIDE

**F**ew events are as frightening or disturbing as losing your valuable data. It really doesn't make much difference *how* it happens—virus damage, drive failure, sabotage, user error, an improper software installation, or old age are all equally effective at disabling your computer and rendering your data inaccessible. There are countless preventative maintenance tools and data recovery tactics available, but regardless of manufacturers' claims, all of those recovery techniques have limitations (especially when the drive fails). The only *certain* means of protecting your valuable data is to back up your system—or at least the documents, spreadsheets, presentations, or other data that you need). This chapter covers some important backup considerations, offers some guidelines for preparing backups, explains the major limitations and pitfalls of backup strategies, and introduces the System Restore technology used with Windows Me/XP.

## Backup Considerations

Although it is not terribly expensive or difficult to start a backup regimen, it is hardly a trivial concern. Whether protecting a system against data loss, or archiving unused applications and data in order to clear drive space, proper backups depend on understanding the needs of the particular system being backed up.

One of the most common misconceptions about backups is that they are used solely for the purposes of protecting data. True, the threat of data loss is a major factor in any backup strategy, but there are other advantages of backups as well.

For example, backups are often used to archive older or unused files. Let's face it, even the largest hard drive will eventually run short of space. Older applications and work files can be off-loaded through a backup, then erased from the hard drive—thus freeing valuable drive space. Backups also play an important role in periodic drive maintenance. As magnetic media ages, the sector and track IDs decay slowly. In extreme cases, this identification data may become irretrievable and result in the loss of an application or its data. By maintaining timely backups, a drive can be low-level formatted (using a formatting program designed for the particular drive) to rewrite sector and track ID information, then reloaded from a most recent backup. The "refreshed" drive may then continue providing years of trouble-free service. Effective backups also demand a variety of other considerations:

■ *Consider the backup frequency.* How often should a backup be performed? This is one of the most perplexing questions surrounding tape backups—and the answer is always different depending on whom you talk to. The most common yardstick is "individual need." If you can't afford to lose what you've got, back it up. While this guideline may be effective for individual PC owners, it is not quite so simple to evaluate the backup needs of business and professional users. In such cases, need should be based on the value of data contained in the PC and how often it changes. For example, a graphic design or desktop publishing firm may need to back up every week or two. On the other hand, a busy order-entry network would probably be best served making daily backups (even several times each day).

■ *Consider the most effective type of backup.* Traditionally, there are four types of backup: full, selective, incremental, and differential. The *full* backup is just as the name implies—all files and directories on the specified drive are saved to the backup device. Full backups provide the best protection of data, and files can be restored selectively. Full backups also take the longest to complete. *Selective* backups allow you to back up only desired files or directories, and are particularly handy for saving work folders. *Incremental* backups copy only the files that were changed since the last backup. *Differential* backups copy all of the files that were changed since the last full backup (a subtle but important difference). These are the fastest but least flexible types of backup. A combination of these strategies usually provides the best level of data protection.

■ *Consider the hardware and media requirements.* There are many means of producing backups. Floppy disks, removable media disks (such as the Iomega Zip drive), all types of tape drives, and optical discs such as CD-Rs or CD-RWs are just a few of the available options. Some years ago, floppy disks were often used for backups. Today, however, it would take thousands of disks to perform a total backup of one contemporary hard drive. Floppy disks are still used for small groups of files (for example, DTP files, graphics, and data files) that are considered "work-in-progress," but they are hardly useful for serious backup work. At the other end of the range, a *redundant array of independent disks* (or RAID) provides tremendous storage capacity, but its cost and sophistication are often best suited for busy networks and high-end workstations. For the individual PC or a small network, tape drives or CD-R/RW drives generally provide the best cost/performance trade-off. A single low-end tape drive can back up 2GB on one tape—more expensive drives can hold over 8GB. In most installations, a tape drive will provide more than adequate backup capability.

■ *Get the media preformatted.* If you've ever had to format a box of floppy disks, you know what a cumbersome, time-consuming process it can be. Tapes are even more difficult to deal with. A typical mini-cartridge can take up to one hour or more to format. While this may not be a problem for individual users who back up infrequently, business users may have trouble committing hours of PC time to tape formatting. Use factory-formatted media wherever possible. Although preformatted media may cost a bit more, the savings in time are often well worth it.

■ *Consider where to store the backups.* Since backups can serve a number of practical purposes, it is important to plan where the backups will be kept and who will have access to them. Again, individuals who use their PC for casual applications can probably keep their backup tape in a desk drawer or filing cabinet without a second thought. For businesses and busy professional systems, the problem becomes a bit more complicated. One of the key reasons for backups is *disaster recovery*, so the backup should be protected from fires or floods. Often, this means securing backups in a fireproof safe or fireproof file cabinet in another room away from the original system—sometimes away from the site of business entirely. Another reason for this concern is security—you would not want confidential files falling into the wrong hands. In many companies, backup, restoration, and security are assigned to authorized individuals.

■ *Consider compression.* Data compression is an excellent means of expanding the storage capacity of a tape or CD media. For example, compression may allow a 4GB tape to hold up to 8GB of data. If your backup software supports data compression, *use it*. There may be a small penalty in reading or writing speed, but the extra capacity is usually worth it.

■ *Consider manual vs. automatic backups.* If you run your system for regular, prolonged periods, automatic backups can be configured with a scheduler feature of most backup software (or the Task Scheduler feature of Windows). This makes it possible to save desired files at regular times while remaining virtually transparent to the user. Businesses with extensive computer time can usually take advantage of automatic backups. Individuals who use PCs inconsistently are probably best served with manual backups. Keep in mind that tape drives require routine cleaning, so automatic backups should also include periods of downtime for regular scheduled cleanings.

■ *Rotate tapes periodically.* Don't rely on a single tape for reliable long-term storage. When considering a backup regimen, be sure to use multiple tapes, and alternate between them so you're certain to always have a recent backup available. The more often you must back up, the more tapes should be available in your backup rotation. For example, if you back up only once a month, use two tapes—one for odd months and the other for even months. As another example, if you back up on a weekly basis, consider four tapes—one for each week of the month.

## BACKUP LIMITATIONS

While backups are usually considered a cost-effective form of data archiving and a reliable means of data protection, backups are hardly perfect. Proper backups demand a certain amount of effort and care, and there is a whole array of common oversights that can adversely affect your backup efforts (or those of your customer). Be sure to consider the following pitfalls when planning and executing your backup regimen:

■ **Irregular or inconsistent backups**    This is probably the single most troublesome problem when implementing any backup strategy for PCs in homes and small businesses. To be effective, backups must be performed regularly. All too often, users make some initial backups on schedule, but fail to follow through with subsequent backups. Before long, the backups that *were* made fall so far out of date that they become useless. When trouble finally occurs, the investment in equipment and media just doesn't pay off. Make it a point to implement regular backups and follow through with them consistently (it can be a matter of life and death for any business).

- **Poorly labeled and stored backups**    This problem is typical of large tape rotations. Often, tapes and other backup media are left strewn around an office or department with little or no idea what is on them. Effective backup strategies demand that each tape be marked and identified clearly so that no one will accidentally discard or overwrite it. Groups of tapes should always be kept together in a drawer or on a shelf the same way you would organize volumes of books. It's hard enough to keep regular backups without having to search for the tapes and guess which ones to use. Make it a point to keep tapes (and all magnetic media) away from telephones, monitors, motors (such as air conditioners or refrigerators), power supplies, excessive heat, extreme cold, and all forms of moisture.

- **Inadequate disaster preparation**    Here's another real impediment to successful backups. Too often, businesses invest serious money in backup equipment—only to leave the tapes sitting on top of the backed-up system. If you rely on backups to store your vital files, those tapes should be stored in a secure location that is reasonably safe from disasters (for example, fire, flood, theft, or sabotage). Often, a fireproof/flood-proof safe or file cabinet will perform quite well. The same concern is true for off-site storage.

- **Inadequate testing and maintenance**    Some businesses are so preoccupied with *performing* a backup that they don't check to confirm that the backup is any good after it's made. When trouble strikes, they're horrified to find that the backup lacks vital files, is unreadable, or does not restore properly—leaving the backup completely useless. After a backup is made, it should be tested using a "compare" or "verify" function of the backup software to check the tape contents against the disk files. Although this process takes a bit longer, it's always a worthwhile step. When errors are indicated in the backup, it usually means that the drive is failing or has not been routinely cleaned as required. Try cleaning the backup drive as recommended by the manufacturer, and perform the backup again.

- **Inadequate restoration procedures**    Another common problem occurs when you need to restore the backup—nobody knows how to do it. A lot of emphasis is placed on making and checking the backup, so home and small business users may go for years without having to actually restore a backup. When trouble strikes, users are often left scrambling for the instruction manual. Businesses should consider periodic drills to restore the current backup and ensure that users and technicians understand the restoration process.

- **Inadequate attention to the media**    Like floppy disks, tapes are magnetic media. Unfortunately, magnetic media doesn't last forever. One of the big problems with frequent backups is that users mistake backup or compare errors for a problem with the drive or backup software, when it is actually the tape that has worn out. As a general rule, plan on replacing your tapes at least once a year. If you are performing frequent backups, plan on replacing your tapes even more frequently. Tape life is also dependent on tape quality. High-quality tapes typically last longer than low-quality tapes. It is often more prudent to spend a bit more for a reliable, good-quality tape, than to save a little money on a low-cost tape—only to find that the tape wears out much sooner or loses data when you need it most.

## USING BACKUP SOFTWARE

With a suitable backup drive installed, it's time to install the backup software. This part of the chapter looks at the installation and use of Seagate's BackupExec software under Windows 9*x*/Me. To install BackupExec directly from your CD-ROM, insert the CD into your CD-ROM drive. The auto-run routine starts, so just follow the instructions on your screen to install the program. Most types of backup devices are automatically detected and configured the first time you run BackupExec, and your backup device will be listed in the Where to Back Up box. When you install programs like BackupExec, the program and its folder are added to the Windows Start menu (if you have the Backup Exec icon added to your desktop during installation, you may double-click this icon to open the program). To start the software manually, follow these steps:

1.  Click the Start button on the Windows taskbar.
2.  Select Programs | BackupExec and point to the BackupExec folder.
3.  Click BackupExec.
4.  BackupExec opens (and appears on the taskbar).
5.  The BackupExec Startup window appears.

 BackupExec is shown as an example only—your own backup software should support your particular backup drive device, and may appear quite different from the software illustrated here.

## Checking the Backup System

After you install your new tape drive and software like Seagate BackupExec, you should make sure that your computer and backup software can recognize your new drive before you try to back up your data. Launch Seagate BackupExec. Look down the list of target drives in the Where to Back Up menu box. If your tape drive is listed in this drop-down list, Seagate BackupExec has recognized your new drive. This means that your tape drive and software are ready to back up data. If your drive is not listed in the drop-down list, the software cannot find the drive.

## Automatic Data Protection

Automatic Data Protection (ADP) ensures that your data is backed up on a regular basis. When you first start the backup application, you are prompted with the option of initiating Automatic Data Protection. Any backup job created with Automatic Data Protection can later be edited with BackupExec. If you configure your Advanced Power Management settings to turn off the hard disks after a set period of time, BackupExec will not be able to restart your computer in order to run a scheduled backup job. Follow these steps to use ADP:

1.  Select a day of the week for the backup job to run, or select Day or Weekday.
2.  If you choose a day of the week, the New and Changed Files option is displayed. If you choose Day or Weekday, the New and Changed Files option is not displayed, and All Selected Files backups are automatically performed.
3.  Click OK.

## One-Button Backup

The One-Button Backup feature launches a backup of all local hard disks—including the System State. To use the One-Button Backup feature with BackupExec:

1.  Double-click the One-Button Backup icon on the Desktop. Or, click the Start menu, select Programs | BackupExec, and then click One-Button Backup.
2.  The One-Button Backup dialog box appears (see Figure 4-1).
3.  Select a device in the drop-down list box (e.g., your tape drive).
4.  Click Start.

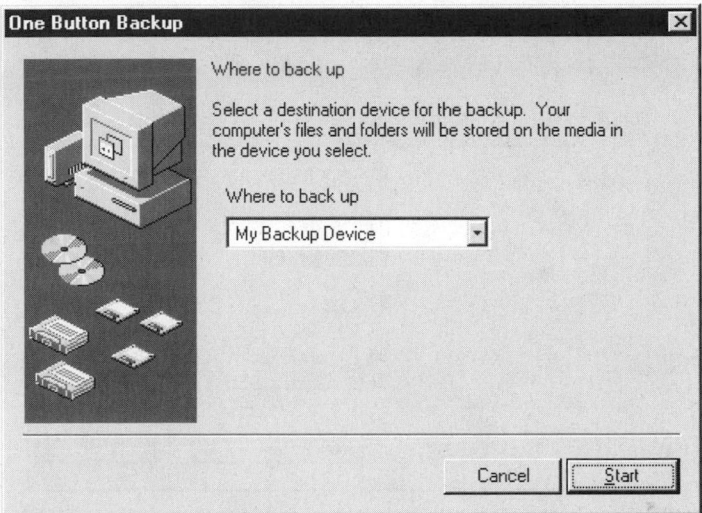

**FIGURE 4-1** One-Button Backup simplifies the backup process for busy end-users.

If your backup job exceeds the space available on a single tape, BackupExec will prompt you to insert another blank tape when the current one has been filled.

5. The backup will run as either a full or differential backup (with default settings) depending on the following criteria:

■ An All Selected Files backup is performed if ten differential backups have been performed since the last All Selected Files backup (regardless of dates), or if more than seven days have passed since the last backup.

■ A differential backup is performed if no more than seven days have passed since the last All Selected Files backup.

## One-Button Restore

The One-Button Restore feature launches a series of dialog boxes that help you perform a system restore in just a few steps. To run a One-Button Restore with BackupExec, follow these steps:

1. Click Start | Programs | BackupExec | One-Button Restore.
2. The One-Button Restore dialog box appears.
3. Select a device in the drop-down list box (e.g., your tape drive).
4. Click Next to continue.
5. Check the drives, folders, and files you want to restore (see Figure 4-2).
6. Click Start to begin restoring your files.

## Performing a Backup

BackupExec uses the notion of "backup jobs" to save and reuse file and option selections. You create a backup job by selecting desired drives and files for backup, choosing program settings and options, and

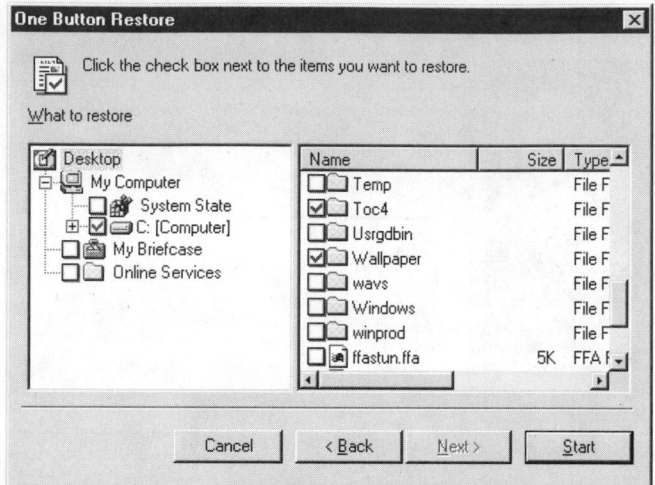

**FIGURE 4-2** With One-Button Restore, you can still select the specific drives, folders, or files that you want to be restored.

saving your selections with a new job name. A backup job includes all selections made at the time it is saved, including:

■ Drives, folders, and files to back up

■ Backup type

■ Backup device

■ Options selected or default selections

Backup jobs can be opened, saved, and deleted using the Job menu. In the Backup window, you can open a backup job with the Backup Job list. To change a backup job, simply make new file or option selections. When you run a backup, your changes are automatically saved. To save your changes under a different name, choose Save As from the Job menu and enter a new name (or type the new name in the Job Name field). If you attempt to save a new job using an existing name, the program asks you to overwrite the existing job. If you choose Overwrite, the new job replaces the existing job.

**Using the Backup Wizard**  You can use the Backup Wizard to create new backup jobs, or you can modify and rename existing job files. By saving your backup jobs, you can run them again without making your selections again. The Backup Job box lists your saved backup jobs. Type a new name in the box to save the job under a different name. Let's look at a typical backup with the BackupExec Backup Wizard:

**1.** Click Backup Wizard in the Startup window, then click OK. Alternatively, click the Backup Wizard icon on the toolbar. The What to Back Up window of the Backup Wizard appears (see Figure 4-3).

**2.** Select the drives and files you want to back up. To back up all files, folders, and drives on your computer, click Back up My Computer, then click Next to continue. The Backup Type window appears. Alternatively, to back up only some of the files, folders, or drives on your computer, click Back Up Selected Files, Folders, and Drives. The Backup Wizard Selection dialog appears.

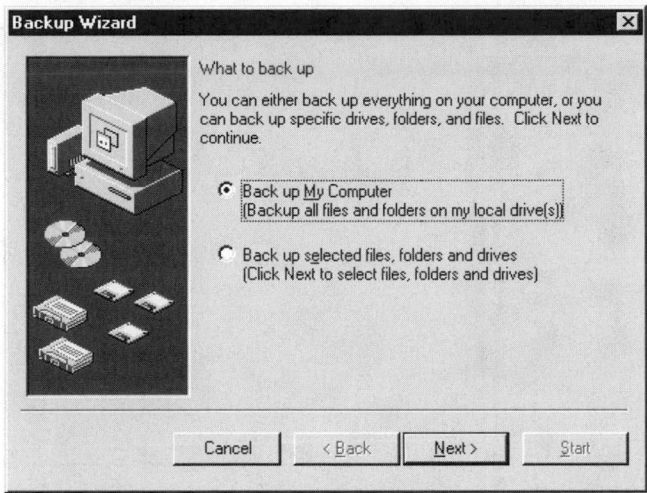

**FIGURE 4-3** Start the Backup Wizard and select complete or partial backups, depending on your particular needs.

3. Select the specific drives, folders, and files you want to back up. Click Next to continue. Select a backup type.

4. Click All Selected Files to back up all selected files (see Figure 4-4); click Next. Alternatively, click New and Changed Files to back up only files that are new or have changed since the last All Selected Files backup and click Next.

5. Select a destination for the backup (e.g., your tape drive) from the Where to Back Up list.

6. Click Next to continue. The How to Back Up window appears, as shown in Figure 4-5).

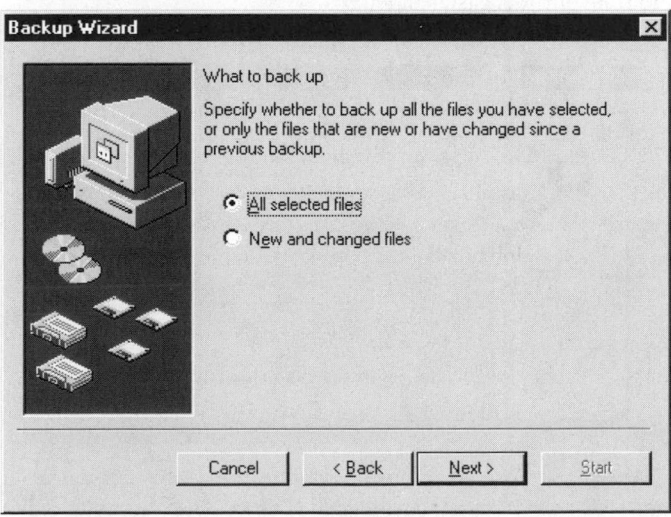

**FIGURE 4-4** You can opt to back up all files on the system, or just selected files and folders.

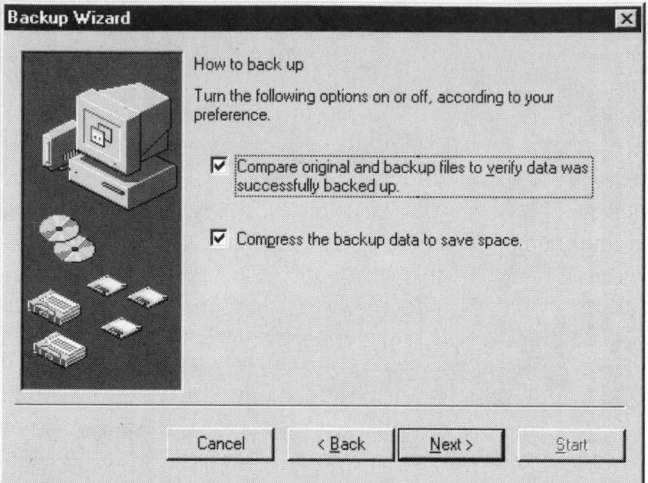

**FIGURE 4-5**    Opt to compare and compress data as required in the Backup Wizard.

7.  Select your backup options for this screen. Click Next to continue. The When to Back Up window appears.

8.  Click Now to begin this backup immediately, or click Later to schedule this backup for a later time. To back up later, specify the frequency, then set the time, date, and/or days of the week to run this backup job.

9.  Click Next to continue. The Name the Backup Job window appears (see Figure 4-6).

10.  Type a name for this backup job. Review the backup job's summary. To change an option, use the Back and Next buttons. Click Start to begin this backup job. The Backup Progress window appears. Or, click OK to run your job as scheduled.

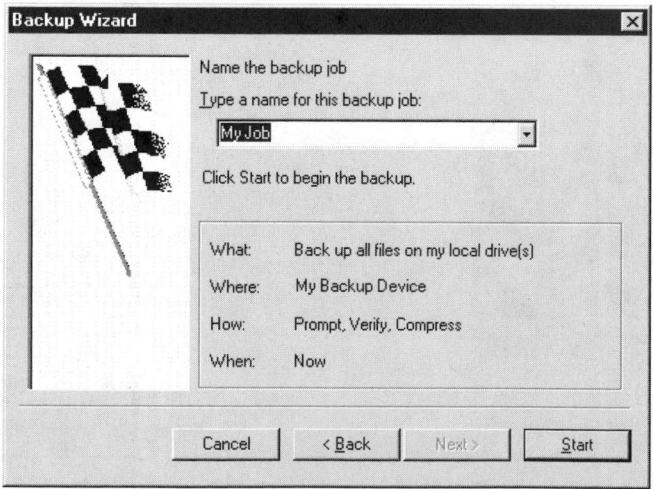

**FIGURE 4-6**    Select a name for the job, and then start the backup using the Backup Wizard.

If your backup job exceeds the space available on a single tape cartridge, BackupExec will prompt you to insert another blank tape when the current one has been filled.

## Performing a Compare

Compare is a separate function of your backup software designed to provide maximum data integrity. After you create a backup set, you use the BackupExec Compare window to verify that the information contained on the backup tape is identical to the data on the hard disk (and that the data is readable and can be restored later). At a minimum, you should perform compares after your first few backups, and after changing your system's configuration—this will confirm BackupExec is running properly on your computer. Performing a compare at any time in the future lets you see how the files in the backup set differ from the files currently on the hard disk. Selecting the Compare tab (see Figure 4-7) gives you quick access to the compare options. It consists of three main sections:

■ **Compare from**   The Compare from drop-down box lists all available backup devices to compare from. To change the drive you want to compare from, select another drive in the drop-down list box.

■ **What to compare**   This area lets you select specific files to compare by folders, media, or device.

■ **Where to compare**   You'll usually want to compare files to the same drive and directory as the one from which they were backed up. If their location has changed, however, the Where to Compare box lets you specify where the original files are now located.

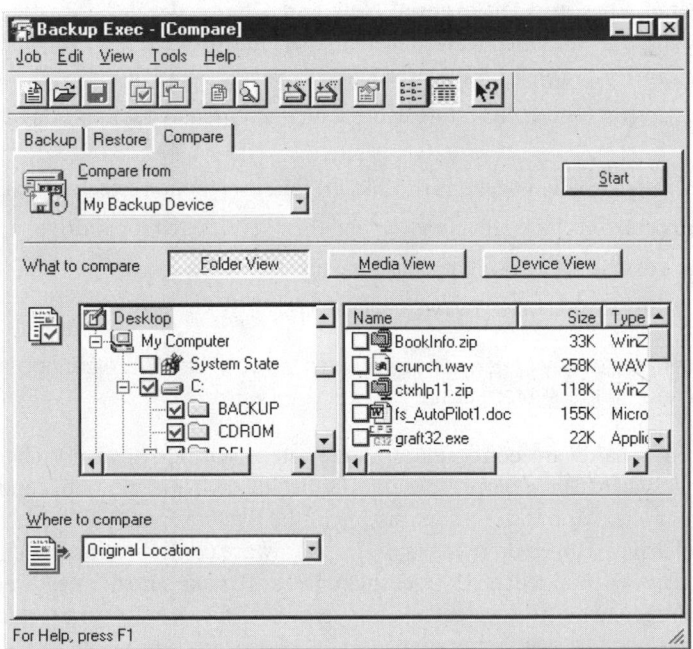

**FIGURE 4-7**   Perform a compare to verify the current backup and help to ensure reliability for future restore operations.

After making your selections, click Start to start comparing your files. When the compare process is complete, the OK and Report buttons become available. Click Report for a summary of your compare operation, or click OK to continue.

## Performing a Restore

The BackupExec Restore feature reads selected backup sets and restores those files to a specified location (usually their original location). You can restore one file, several selected files, or all files from a backup set. You can also select individual versions of a file, specify the destination for the restored files, and set options. Let's take a look at disaster recovery using the BackupExec Restore Wizard.

**Basic Disaster Recovery**   This first procedure gives you a general method to quickly and easily restore all your files in the event of a hard disk failure (this procedure can also be used to transfer all your files to a new computer). Before you can restore your files after a hard disk failure, you must prepare your hard disk (i.e., Fdisk and Format) and reinstall Windows, then follow these steps for Windows 9*x*/Me:

1.  With the hard drive working and your version of Windows reinstalled, install and configure BackupExec (or your own backup software).

2.  Collect the tapes containing your most recent All Selected Files (full) and your New and Changed Files (incremental) backups. The exact backup sets you'll need to restore depend on your backup strategy. If you performed:

    ■  **All Selected Files only**   Restore only your most recent backup set.

    ■  **All Selected Files and Differential New and Changed Files**   Restore your All Selected Files backup first, and then restore the most recent differential backup set.

    ■  **All Selected Files and Incremental New and Changed Files**   Restore your All Selected Files backup first, and then restore each of the incremental backup sets in order, starting with the oldest.

3.  Restore the All Selected Files backup set. Make the following option selections in the Restore window:

    ■  **What to restore**   Click Device view, and then select each local drive.

    ■  **Where to restore**   Choose Original Locations.

    ■  **How to restore**   Choose Always Replace.

 Restoring the system state may cause serious problems if your hardware configuration has changed since you last backed up the system state.

4.  If your system's hardware configuration and system settings have *not* changed since the last backup of the System State, place a check mark beside the System State icon in the Restore Window selection pane. All of the files consisting of the System State will be restored along with all selected local drives. However, if your system's hardware configuration *has* changed, (i.e., you've added a new drive or changed the IRQ settings on a card) make sure the Restore System State check box is *not* selected. Only files selected from your local drives will be restored.

5.  Click Start.

6.  When the restore is complete, you're prompted to reboot your computer. Click Yes to reboot the system as recommended.

7.  Now restore any New and Changed Files backup sets.

**Using the Restore Wizard**    Of course, the easiest way to restore lost or corrupted files is to use the BackupExec Restore Wizard, which simply guides you through the steps and options required to create your restore job. To create your restore job using the Restore Wizard, follow these steps:

1.  Click Restore Wizard in the Startup window and click OK, or click the Restore Wizard button on the toolbar, or select Restore Wizard from the Tools menu. The Restore From window appears (see Figure 4-8).

2.  Choose the backup device to restore from (e.g., your tape drive), and then click Next. The View Files to Restore window appears.

3.  You may select your files from the catalog stored on your hard disk or from the media in your drive. Click Next to continue. The Restore selection pane window appears.

4.  Click the checkboxes next to the items you want to restore. Click Next to continue. The Where to Restore window appears (see Figure 4-9).

5.  Choose a destination for your restored files. If you choose to restore to another location, type a path into the text box or click Browse. Files are restored in their original folder structure unless you check Restore All Files to a Single Folder. Click Next to continue. The How to Restore window appears (see Figure 4-10).

6.  Select an option and click Start.

7.  The Media Required box appears. Follow the instructions on the screen, and then click OK. The Restore Progress window appears.

> If your backup job spanned more than one tape, insert the first tape of the backup set. BackupExec will then prompt you to insert each additional tape as needed.

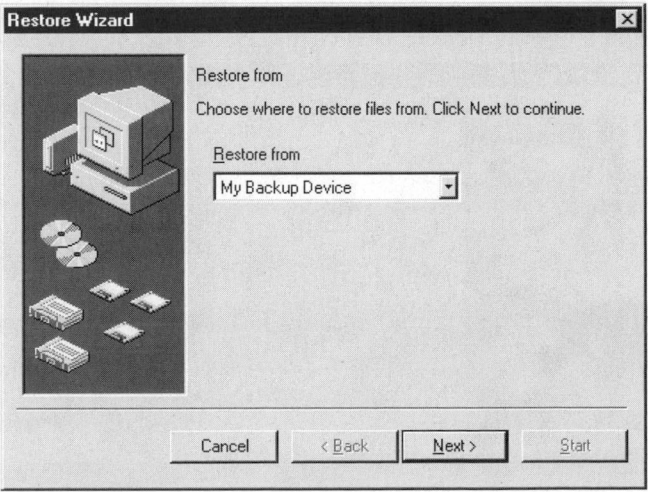

**FIGURE 4-8**    The Restore Wizard lets you choose where to restore files from.

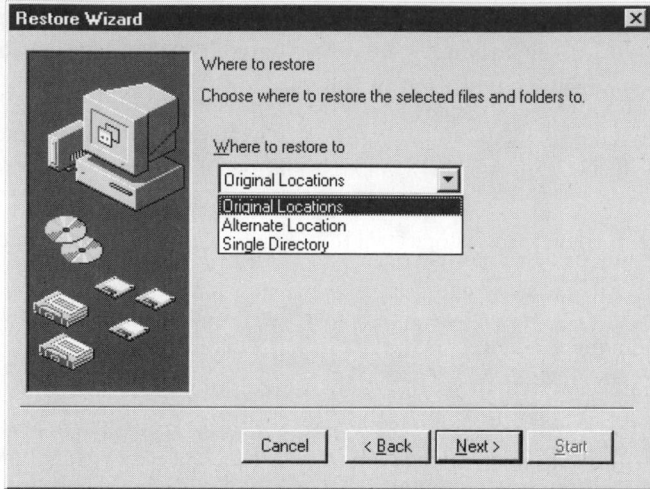

**FIGURE  4-9**    Choose the location(s) where you'd like to restore your files.

## Restoring a Disk Image

This chapter generally assumes that you'll use the traditional method of restoration, where you reinstall an OS, then reinstall the backup software, and *then* restore your backup set. While this is a tried-and-true method, it does tend to be a bit cumbersome. Some backup utilities such as NovaStor's NovaBackup software (www.no-panic.com/backup/n_backup.html) do not require you to reinstall software first. Instead, the backup software allows you to create a set of bootable diskettes that can be used to boot a PC and launch a real-mode recovery utility that can restore your *disk image* (a complete copy of your system's drives) directly from its media—usually tape or CD-R/RW. This type of approach works quite well for

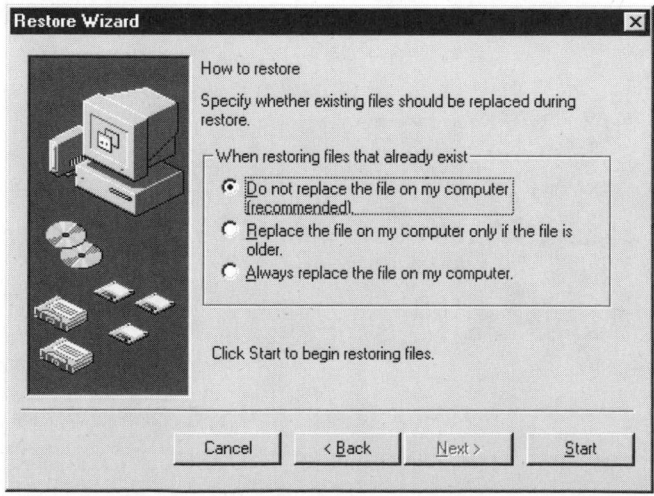

**FIGURE  4-10**    Use the How to Restore dialog box to tell the backup software how to handle files that may already be on the system you're restoring.

tasks like disk cloning where you need to make duplicate copies of your system on multiple PCs, as well as platform migration where you want to transfer your existing system to a new platform.

Remember that creating multiple copies of a system onto other PCs may violate your end-user license agreement (EULA) for the operating system and applications. Be sure that you have appropriate licensing (e.g., site licensing) for more than one copy of any software.

### Fine-Tuning

Remember that restoring a backup returns your PC to the state that it was in when the backup was created—but it's not necessarily the same state that the system was in when disaster actually struck. For example, you may have added or removed applications from the system since the backup was created, and you've almost certainly worked on new documents, spreadsheets, presentations, and so on. This means you'll need to do a little fine-tuning to check your system and return it to "exactly" where it was. Fine-tuning usually involves tweaking the OS and system devices, fixing applications, and updating your work files.

First, test your newly restored system by rebooting several times to verify that the system starts properly. If you've updated the OS (e.g., you've used the Windows Update feature) after the backup was made, you may want to repeat those updates. Now open the Device Manager and look at your system devices. Unknown devices (or devices with yellow exclamations over them) will usually need new drivers to identify them properly. Fortunately, if your OS and hardware were working properly when the backup was made, and you haven't added any new hardware or OS updates since, chances are that your OS and hardware will be working smoothly.

Look at your applications next. If you've added or removed certain applications from the system since the backup was made, you should remove or reinstall those same applications again. Applications can be reinstalled from their original installation CD(s). If you've downloaded any application patches or updates since the backup was created, you will need to download and reapply those patches as well. Launch your most important applications and verify that they're working the way you expect them to. You may need to re-tweak the configuration of certain applications. For example, you may need to reload document templates in Word, or re-create macros for Excel.

Finally, you'll need to restore any current work files (e.g., documents, spreadsheets, PowerPoint presentations, video clips, and so on). If you have recent copies of your work files on diskette or CD, you can copy them back to their appropriate locations on the recovered drive and continue working right from where you left off.

# Windows Me/XP System Restore

The whole purpose of creating a backup is to protect your system and your current work from accidental loss due to common problems like hardware (e.g., drive) faults and defective software. However, problems are not always "absolute," and many times users will find themselves with a perfectly good working system that is simply acting up—perhaps after upgrading a device, driver, or software package. Traditionally, these types of nuisance problems were difficult to correct because of the arcane way that Windows installs and registers programs. You would wind up trying to uninstall applications (and hope that there weren't traces left on the system), or uninstall and reinstall drivers, and even perhaps be forced to reinstall the operating system entirely. Nuisance problems demand a great deal of time in trial-and-error troubleshooting.

Windows Me/XP includes a System Restore feature (see Figure 4-11) that periodically saves "system states" (called *restore points*) to space reserved on your hard drive. Restore points are created daily, and during important system events (e.g., when you install a new application or device driver). You can also create your own restore points at any time. When a problem occurs, you can use System Restore to return the system to a previous state without loosing data files. System Restore under Windows XP provides several important services:

- It restores your computer to a previous state.
- It restores your computer keeping your personal files intact.
- It stores up to several weeks of past restore points.
- It manages dates associated with restore points.
- It lets you reverse all restorations.

 Windows 9*x*/Me users can get this type of functionality with third-party utilities like Roxio's GoBack 3 (www.roxio.com/en/products/datarecoverypc.jhtml).

Since all restorations are reversible, you can undo the restoration (if you don't like the state of your computer after you restore it) and select another restore point. All successful restorations are reversible,

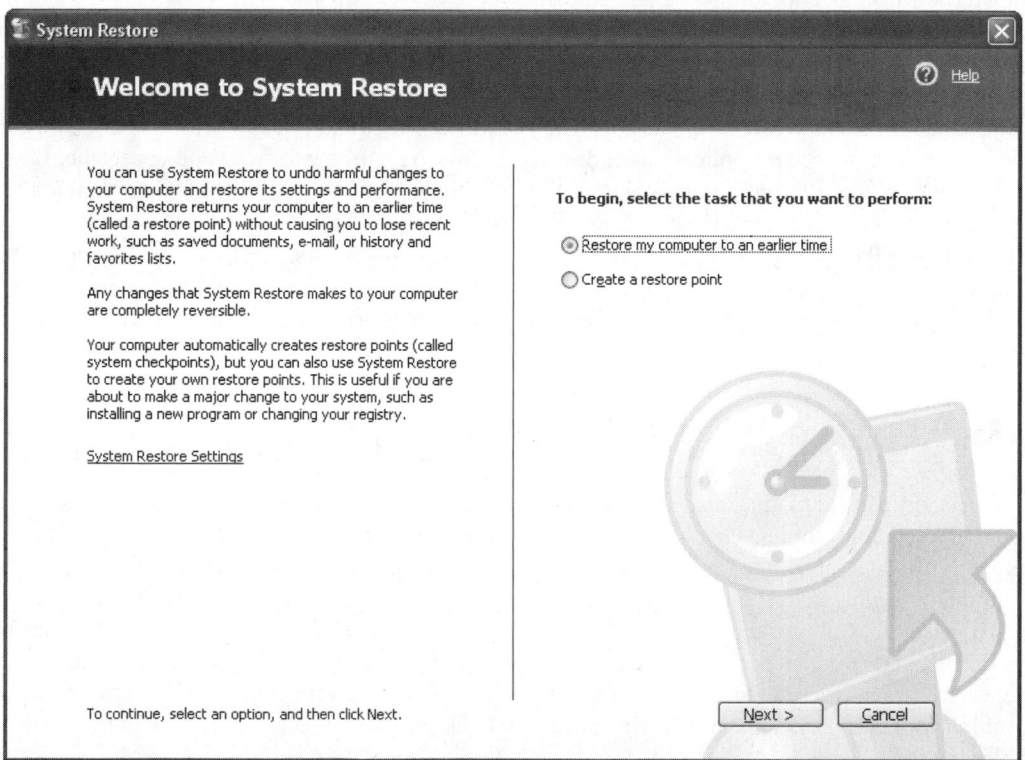

**FIGURE  4-11**    The Windows XP System Restore wizard allows you to create new restore points, or select existing restore points to return your system to a previous state.

and all failed restorations are automatically reversed by System Restore. This provides a great deal of versatility, and allows users to select the best restore point when a problem occurs.

# RESTORE POINTS

System Restore is installed as part of Windows XP, and is normally enabled. It sets aside a percentage of your hard drive space to hold restore points. The actual number of saved restore points will depend on the amount of activity on your computer, the size of your hard disk (or the partition that contains your Windows XP folder), and how much disk space has been allocated on your computer to store System Restore information. There are several types of restore points:

■ **Initial system restore point**    Initial restore points are created the first time you start your computer (after upgrading to Windows Me/XP or when you first start a new computer). This type of restore point can revert Windows Me/XP and applications to the state they were in at that time. Files with data file name extensions (such as .doc, .htm, .xls, and so on) are not restored.

■ **System restore point**    These restore points are created on a regular basis—even if you don't make any system changes. Restore points are created every 24 hours of calendar time (or every 24 hours that the system is on). When the system is off for more than 24 hours, a restore point is created the next time you start the system. Selecting one of these restore points restores Windows Me/XP and applications to the state they were in at that time. Files with data file name extensions are not restored.

■ **Program installation restore point**    When installing an application with an installer (such as InstallShield), System Restore creates a restore point. These restore points track changes to your system, and can restore a computer to the state it was in before you installed a particular application. Selecting this type of restore point removes installed files and registry settings, then restores applications and system files that were altered by the installation. Files with data file name extensions are not restored.

To undo changes made by a program that does *not* use a software installer, select the most recent restore point *before* the particular program was installed.

■ **Windows XP automatic update restore point**    When using automatic updates to receive downloaded updates to Windows XP, a restore point is created before installing the update. If items are not installed, a restore point is not created (a restore point is created only when the components start to install). These points track changes to your system, or identify updates that might conflict with other products on your computer.

■ **Manual restore point**    You can manually create your own restore points as needed. This is usually done when you like the way your computer is functioning, or before you make changes on your computer (such as installing new programs) that might affect computer operation.

■ **Restore operation points**    Each time you perform a restoration, System Restore creates restore points that track the restoration (since a restoration is in fact a change made to your computer). Select these restore operation restore points if you want to undo a restoration that you've previously selected.

■ **Unsigned device driver restore point**    Most Windows XP drivers have been signed by Windows Hardware Quality Labs (WHQL). If you try to install an "unsigned" driver, a restore point is created. If the unsigned driver causes system problems, you can select these unsigned restore points to undo the changes and restore your computer to the state before you installed the unsigned driver.

## CREATING A RESTORE POINT

Windows XP creates most restore points automatically, but you can certainly make your own restore points if you're not satisfied with the way a system is behaving. Use the following procedure to create a manual restore point:

1. Click Start | All Programs | Accessories | System Tools | System Restore.
2. The System Restore Wizard starts (see Figure 4-11 earlier). Click Create a Restore Point, and then click Next.
3. Enter a name to identify this restore point in the Restore Point Description box. System Restore automatically adds the date and time that this restore point is created.
4. Click Create to finish creating this restore point. Click Back or Cancel to cancel restore point creation.

## USING A RESTORE POINT

When you determine that it's time to restore a previous system state, start the System Restore wizard and select a suitable restore point as described in the following steps:

1. Click Start | All Programs | Accessories | System Tools | System Restore.
2. The System Restore Wizard starts (see Figure 4-11 earlier). Click Restore My Computer to an Earlier Time, and then click Next.
3. The Select a Restore Point dialog opens (see Figure 4-12). Use the calendar to see available restore points, then highlight the desired restore point and click Next.
4. Finally, the Confirm Restore Point Selection summarizes the proposed changes and lets you commit to the changes. Be sure to save any files and close any open applications before starting the restoration. Click Next to start the restore process.
5. Once the restoration is complete, the system will restart so that any changes will take effect. You'll see a Restoration Complete screen if the process was successful. If the restoration fails, the Restoration Was Unsuccessful screen is displayed (and no changes are made to the computer).

# Backup Troubleshooting

Backup software such as BackupExec offers most Windows users a simple and convenient tool for backing up important files, day-to-day work, and even their entire system. While backup software is usually compatible with a wide range of drives (both tape and removable media), it is certainly not foolproof. When you encounter problems with backup software, check the following tips before diving into the troubleshooting issues next.

## BACKGROUND TASKS

You may be receiving backup errors because too many applications are open, and Windows can't allocate the necessary system resources required. As a rule, close all background tasks before running a backup tack. To disable background tasks under Windows 9x/Me, press the CTRL-ALT-DEL keys simultaneously to bring up the Close Program window. If there are programs in this list other than Explorer and Systray, you'll need to highlight them individually and click on End Task. When finished, click Cancel and run the

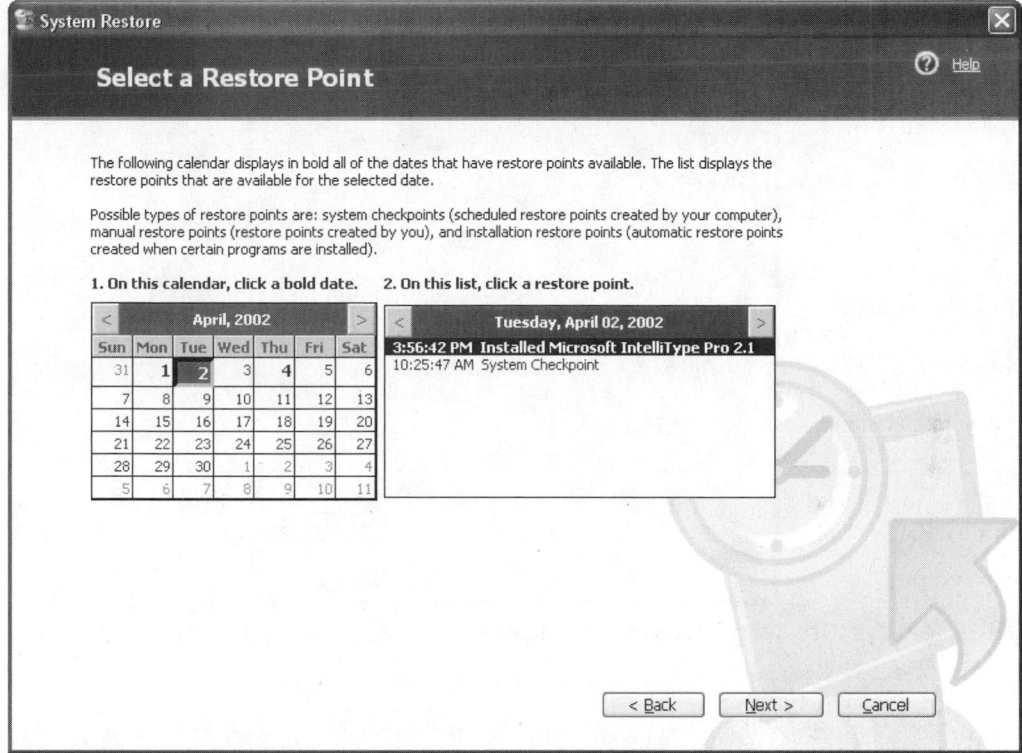

**FIGURE 4-12**   Select the day and specific restore point that you want to use.

program again. Under Windows XP, press CTRL-ALT-DEL to open the Task Manager, select the Applications tab (see Figure 4-13), then highlight and end each unnecessary application.

# TAPE DETECTION PROBLEMS

Installing a tape drive is one thing, but getting the system to recognize it is another problem entirely. There are numerous potential conflicts that can occur during drive setup. This part of the chapter covers the most common issues that cause drive detection problems.

■ *The drive is not supported.* Start with a simple sanity check and verify that your tape software supports the drive (and its adapter card if necessary). You may need to use different backup software that will support the drive (an easier solution than changing the drive hardware). New drives often come bundled with suitable backup software.

■ *There are cabling and power issues.* The signal cable(s) may not be fully connected to the tape drive or host adapter card, or the power cable may not be connected. Check all connections to verify they are tight and secure—see that the drive is getting power. The cables themselves may be a problem, and a kink could destroy a good cable. Try a different, shorter cable (sometimes length can be a problem—one foot is a good test length).

**FIGURE 4-13** Use the Windows Task Manager to stop unnecessary applications and processes.

■ *The drive is initializing or busy.* If the tape drive is busy, it may have not been able to respond to the command sent to it. Wait until the drive is idle, then try the drive again.

■ *The drive is configured incorrectly.* Most tape drives come with a *drive selector* switch or jumper set. Typically you can set drive ID as DS-0, DS-1, DS-2, DS-3, and Auto (sometimes called "Phantom"). For example, DS-0 and DS-1 are normally set for the Drive A: and Drive B:, but the best setting to have the tape drive at is Auto. This is not an intermittent problem. If this jumper is set improperly, you will not be able to see the tape drive at all.

■ *SCSI/IDE ID set incorrectly.* When using a SCSI tape drive, do not SCSI ID 0, 1, or 7 because these IDs are reserved—SCSI ID 0 and 1 are usually hard disks, and 7 is the ID of the host adapter. IDs 5 and 6 are usually safe for tape drives. Be sure to choose an ID that is *not* being used by another device. If you're using an ATAPI IDE drive, remember that the drive should be set as the master or slave device. It's usually a slave device alongside another drive like a CD-ROM.

■ *The SCSI chain terminated incorrectly.* Proper termination means that only two devices on the SCSI chain are terminated—this can be tricky. Termination involves the installation of resistor packs, external plugs, or DIP switches on SCSI devices and host adapters that eliminate bus impedance mismatches and improve data transmission reliability. Most host adapter cards are terminated with resistor packs that are inserted directly into the printed circuit card. Internal SCSI devices usually have terminating resistors installed in them when shipped. External SCSI/EIDE devices are generally shipped without terminating resistors (see the Chapter 32 for more information).

■ *Another driver is tying up the drive.* If you've changed programs (or run other programs with the tape drive), you may have a conflict between this program and others that try to use the drive. Check the SYSTEM.INI file, especially the [386 Enh] section, for conflicting drivers. Also try uninstalling any other programs that may have been used with the tape drive.

■ *The tape software is configured incorrectly.* For example, the tape software and the tape drive (its host adapter card) may be using different DMA or IRQ settings. When a QIC tape drive is auto-configured, the software must try to detect the resource settings. While this detection is usually correct, the settings should be checked against the drive's settings. Check the drive (or drive adapter) setup, then configure the tape software to match the drive's setup.

## PROBLEMS RESTORING FILES

File restoration problems are often the result of drive maintenance and system (or OS) configuration issues. Use the following tips to help troubleshoot file problems:

■ *Clean the drive.* The drive heads may be dirty. Clean the read/write heads.

■ *Check system timing issues.* Set your computer to a slower speed (for example, disable the "turbo" mode), or verify that the drive is receiving/sending data at an acceptable rate. If the rate is too fast, the drive may need to work the tape very hard to handle all of the necessary data.

■ *Use the Safe Mode.* Try to restore the files in Safe Mode. If the tape backup drive requires a protected-mode driver, it will not work in Safe Mode. For example, Colorado Trakker drives do not work in Safe Mode because the VCOMM driver doesn't load.

■ *Try a different PC.* Try to restore the files on a different computer.

■ *Check the swap file.* Verify that there is enough swap file space (a.k.a. virtual memory) on your hard drive.

## THE TAPE CANNOT BE FORMATTED

Formatting is a critical process when preparing or refurbishing tapes for backup operations. Formatting problems are usually the result of defective tapes, incompatible formats, or OS driver conflicts:

■ *Check the tape format.* See that you're using a compatible tape format. For example, you cannot format a 3010 tape in a QIC-80 drive, and you cannot format a QIC-80 Wide tape in a QIC-80 drive.

■ *Check the tape.* The tape may be bad or worn out. Try to format a different tape. Do not try to format bulk-erased tapes.

■ *Try the Safe Mode.* Try to format the tape in Windows Safe Mode. If the tape backup drive requires a protected-mode driver, it will not work in Safe Mode. For example, Colorado Trakker drives do not work in Safe Mode because the VCOMM driver doesn't load.

■ *Check for resource conflicts.* There may be a video DMA conflict (typically encountered on older PCs). Minimize the progress indicator. If formatting still fails, change the video resolution to 640 × 480 × 16 colors. If problems persist, try formatting the tape in a full-screen DOS command prompt session. (If this works, use Device Manager to look for a DMA conflict between the video card and the floppy drive controller.)

## THE TAPE DESPOOLS

If your tapes frequently despool, the end-of-tape (EOT) sensor in your tape drive may be dirty or damaged. This prevents the drive from accurately determining when the end of the tape has been reached so that it can reverse direction. Many drive manufacturers recommend cleaning the end-of-tape sensor after every eight hours of drive operation, when excessive dust or other debris accumulates on the sensor, or when a tape used in the drive becomes despooled. For specific cleaning information, refer to the documentation that came with your drive.

## TAPE COMPARISON FAILS

Tapes should always be verified (or compared) after a backup is performed. Failed comparisons almost always mean that the tape itself has failed (usually because the tape is old, or has become worn out). Try a new or known-good tape—preferably a name-brand good-quality tape.

## SOFTWARE STOPS RESPONDING

You may find that your backup software stops responding. If the backup software is unable to access the tape drive and appears to stop responding, there may be a resource conflict between IDE devices in your computer. For example, your SyQuest removable drive may be configured to use the same resources as your tape drive. Use the Device Manager to check for hardware conflicts in the system.

## PARALLEL PORT TAPE DRIVE ISSUES

If you're experiencing random backup problems with a parallel port tape drive (e.g., Colorado Trakker) on a parallel port, make sure the parallel port is *not* configured in the computer's CMOS Setup as an ECP or EPP port. If it is, reconfigure the port to a "standard" (or bi-directional) parallel port.

## DRIVE AND TAPE MAINTENANCE

Tape drives require periodic maintenance for proper operation. In general, there are two types of maintenance that you will need to handle: drive cleaning and tape maintenance. While these hardly sound like exciting procedures, they can have profound effects on your drive's overall performance, and the reliability of your backups.

 These are only general guidelines. Refer to the user's manual for your particular drive for specific cleaning recommendations and cautions listed by the manufacturer. Every drive has slightly different cleaning and preventive maintenance procedures. Some drives may also require periodic lubrication.

### Drive Cleaning

As with floppy disk drives, tape drives bring magnetic media directly into contact with magnetic R/W heads. Over time and with use, magnetic oxides from the tape rub off onto the head surface. Oxides (combined with dust particles and smoke contamination) accumulate and act as a wedge that forces the tape away from the head surface. Even if you never have cause to actually disassemble your tape drive, you should make it a point to perform routine cleaning. Regular cleaning improves the working life of your recording media and can significantly reduce the occurrence of data errors—especially during file restores where problems can keep you shut down.

The objective of drive cleaning is remarkably simple: remove any buildup of foreign material that may have accumulated on the R/W head. The most common cleaning method employs a pre-packaged cleaning cartridge. The cartridge contains a length of slightly abrasive cleaning material. When cleaning tape is run through the drive, any foreign matter on the head is rubbed away. The cleaning tape can often be used for several cleanings before being discarded. Some cleaning tapes can be run dry, while others may have to be dampened with an alcohol-based cleaning solution. The advantage to a cleaning cartridge is *simplicity*—the procedure is quick, and you never have to disassemble the drive. Since QIC and Travan-type tape moves much more slowly across a R/W head than floppy media does, you need not worry about damaging the R/W head due to friction. DAT and 8mm (helical) heads *do* move across the tape quickly, so you must be cautious about cleaning times. You will likely have better results over the long term using dry cleaning cartridges that are impregnated with a lubricating agent to reduce friction.

Cleaning cartridges are typically not rewindable—once they have been run through the drive, they are simply discarded. However, many tape drives do not detect the "end" of a cleaning tape. Be sure to inspect the cleaning cartridge regularly, and discard it after it is exhausted.

**Autoloader Cleaning**    The *autoloader* is a feature that loads and unloads helical scan DAT tapes (in much the same way that VCRs use automatic loaders and unloaders). In some DAT drives, the loader mechanism retrieves cartridges from a magazine, inserts them in the DAT drive inside the autoloader, and returns them to the magazine when the cartridges are unloaded and ejected by the internal drive. Autoloader mechanisms and guide paths should also be cleaned (and lubricated if necessary) on a regular basis—often once a month, or when an autoloader front panel error is displayed.

## Tape Maintenance

Tape cartridges are one of the more rugged items in the PC world—tape is contained in a hard plastic shell, and the R/W head aperture is usually guarded by a metal or plastic shroud. However, tapes are certainly not indestructible. They must be handled with care to ensure the integrity of their data. The following guidelines will help you get the most from your tapes:

- *Avoid fingerprints on the tape.* Do not open the tape access door of the cartridges or touch the tape itself. Fingerprints can prevent the drive from reading the tape and result in errors.

- *Set the write-protect switch.* Be sure to set the write-protect switch after backing up your data—this will reduce the possibility of accidentally overwriting critical data if you forget to label the tape.

- *Be careful of magnetic fields.* Tapes are sensitive to magnetic fields from monitors, electromechanical telephone ringers, fans, and so on. Keep the tape away from sources of magnetic fields.

- *Be careful of toner.* The toner used by laser printers and photocopiers is a microfine dust that may filter out of the device in small quantities. Keep your tapes away from printers and copiers to avoid accidental contamination by toner dust.

- *Be careful of the tape environment.* Keep the tape out of direct sunlight, keep the tape dry, and keep the tape safe from temperature extremes (sudden hot-to-cold or cold-to-hot transitions). Before using a tape, allow it to slowly assume the current room temperature.

- *Re-tension your tapes regularly.* Before using a tape that has been idle for a month or more, use your backup software to re-tension the tape first. This removes any "tight spots" that often develop on the tape.

You've probably noticed that if you play a videotape often, the picture and sound quality on the tape will begin to degrade. This is a natural effect of wear as the media passes repeatedly over the R/W heads. Tapes do not last forever, and after a period of use, they should be destroyed before their reliability deteriorates to a point where your data is not safe. Tape life is generally rated in terms of *passes*. But passes are difficult to track because a single backup or restore operation may involve many passes. Tape life also depends on how the tape is used. For example, a nightly backup to an 8mm tape may use only the first half of the tape, but leave the last half of the tape almost unused. As a rule, follow the "20-use" rule: If a tape is used daily, replace the tape every month. If a tape is used weekly, replace the tape every 6 months. If a tape is only used monthly, replace it every 18–24 months.

Regardless of how you schedule tape replacement, you should replace a tape immediately if it has been physically damaged; if it has become wet, frozen, or overheated; or if your backup application reports repeated media errors.

## Errors Due to Cleaning Neglect

Tape drives are some of the most susceptible to the buildup of contaminants. If a tape drive is not kept clean, increased dropouts will occur where the drive cannot read or write to the tape (you may lose as much as 20 percent of backup capacity and performance if the recommended head cleaning schedule is not followed). High-end tape drives typically monitor the total number of dropouts. When the number reaches a predetermined threshold (defined in the drive's firmware), an LED on the drive will slowly flash, indicating the tape drive needs cleaning. These are some of the errors that can result from failure to observe routine tape drive maintenance and cleaning:

■ **Dropouts**   A *dropout* is caused by weak signal strength from dirty read/write heads, and can result in reduced tape capacity and backup performance.

■ **Media errors**   The backup tapes can be jammed, torn, or otherwise damaged by a dirty read/write head. This may require you to replace the affected tape cartridge.

■ **Read or write errors**   Data may not be recorded on the tape during backup because of a dirty read/write head. Even if the data is on the backup tape, retrieval may not be possible if the dirty head cannot read the data.

■ **Format failures**   During backup, data is laid on the tape in a certain format for easy retrieval. A dirty write head can cause format failures, which means that data can be lost or impossible to retrieve.

■ **Bad blocks**   The tape may not accept backup data because of media damage. Also, the read/write head may be unable to retrieve data from bad blocks caused by tape failures.

## Media Problems and DAT Drives

DAT drives are particularly sensitive to contaminants and media problems. If the DAT media is marginal or defective, it will cause the drive to report an error that is either displayed on the drive's indicator(s) or passed to the backup software. There are several characteristics of a DAT tape cartridge that can cause DAT drives to fail:

■ **Head clogs**   These are the most common media problem, caused by loose media particles deposited on the read/write heads. These deposits prevent the drive from reading or writing to the tape. Head clogs are reported in several ways (depending on the firmware version in use). When a head clog occurs, clean the drive at least four times to ensure the heads are clean. Tape media problems can also result in head clogs. Keep track of when tapes fail and when they are successful for the first three uses—if a tape fails two out of three times, the tape is failing and must be replaced.

■ **High-torque cartridges**   These may be wound incorrectly during manufacturing (the tape rubs against the top and/or bottom of the inside of the tape cartridge shell). This creates enough resistance to prevent the DAT drive from moving the tape consistently. For example, autoloaders may display a message like "BAD TPE #" (where # is the slot number of the tape so you can find it in the autoloader magazine). High-torque tapes *must* be replaced.

■ **BOT/EOT prism problems**   These are caused by bad cartridges. They are not common, but when they happen, they will intermittently prevent the drive from sensing the end or beginning of tape. This causes the motors that move the tape to stop suddenly, resulting in an error message. The cartridge must be replaced.

■ **Physical tape damage**   This may be caused by the drive, or may occur during tape manufacturing. This problem always occurs on the exact same location on tape. This problem can only be verified by testing with a special debug tool that can eject the tape without rewinding so the damage is visible, and requires that the tape be captured. It is generally recommended that tapes reporting these errors be replaced.

■ **Tape hub alignment** These problems typically cause noise during high-speed tape motion such as a "rewind." When this occurs, it is recommended to replace the tape.

**Recommended Cleaning Guide for DAT Drives** To optimize the performance and reliability of DAT drives, follow these recommendations for cleaning:

■ When using new tape media for backups, DAT drives need to be cleaned after each eight hours of read/write operation until the entire data cartridge has been used five times.

■ When using data cartridges that have already been used five times or more, clean DAT drives after each 25 hours of read/write operation.

■ Clean DAT drives before performing a complete server (or major system) backup.

■ Clean only once for routine cleaning, to minimize head wear. Occasionally a single cleaning cycle will not fully clean read/write heads on a DAT drive. If the backup software reports errors, clean the drive again to eliminate the possibility that dirty heads are causing the error.

■ Clean the drive four times after a failure to ensure the heads are cleaned. A single cleaning cycle may not remove a head clog adequately.

■ When using an autoloader, keep a cleaning cartridge in the last slot. Refer to your software user manual for instructions on how to schedule and perform automatic cleaning operations using the backup software.

■ DAT cleaning cartridges typically last 30 cleaning cycles (passes). Remember to replace the cleaning cartridge after it has been exhausted.

# BACKUP SYMPTOMS

When you cannot isolate problems with the tips and guidelines provided earlier, you can refer to specific symptoms for advice and solutions. This part of the chapter examines many common issues that are known to occur with Backup under Windows.

**SYMPTOM 4-1** **The backup software indicates "Too many bad sectors" on the tape** You may also see an error such as Error Correction Failed. This type of error generally indicates that more than 5 percent of the sectors on a tape are unreadable. In many cases, this is due to dirty R/W heads. Try cleaning the R/W head assembly. If problems continue, try a new tape cartridge. If problems persist, check the drive's power and signal cables and make sure that they are installed properly and completely.

**SYMPTOM 4-2** **You experience excessive "shoe shining" during backups** In normal tape drive operations, the tape drive writes data to a single track from one end of the tape to another: It then writes data in a parallel data track back to the beginning of the tape, and so on, until the tape is full. *Shoe shining* refers to frequent back-and-forth tape motion. If you have the backup window open, minimize it. With the window open, the system has to continually update the screen, and this takes resources away from the software sending data to the tape drive. If the PC offers a "turbo mode," try disabling the turbo mode (especially when using parallel port tape drives).

**SYMPTOM 4-3** **You encounter "media errors," "bad block errors," "system errors," or "lock-ups"** These types of problems are known to occur with Travan tapes, and there are several possible problems to consider. First, try removing and reinserting the Travan data cartridge. In many cases this allows the drive mechanism to clear any errors. If problems continue, try reinitializing the data cartridge (typically handled through the backup software, such as "Tools" and "Initialize"). Note that reinitializing the cartridge will render all data on it unusable. Finally, try disabling data compression—especially if you notice a high frequency of "shoe shining," which often results in error messages.

All TR-4 data cartridges are preformatted, and these TR-4 tapes cannot be reformatted unless your tape drive mechanism is designed to format TR-4 tapes. As a consequence, do *not* "bulk erase" a TR-4 cartridge using an electromagnet or similar device.

**SYMPTOM 4-4**    **You must reactivate Windows XP after restoring a backup**    After restoring a Windows XP system from a backup, you're prompted to reactivate the operating system. This can happen if there are notable differences between the current hardware and the hardware in use when the system was backed up. Such hardware changes require product reactivation because the installation now appears to have been installed on a new (additional) computer. Windows XP may prompt you to reactivate the computer when:

■    You restore from a backup of a non-activated computer.

■    You have changed or added major hardware.

■    You restore from a backup that was made before hardware changes (but prior to activation).

To get around this problem in the future, create another backup *after* any successful hardware changes or installations. You should also create a backup *after* you reactivate the computer. However, you *will* need to reactivate Windows XP in order to verify that you have a legal copy of the OS.

**SYMPTOM 4-5**    **Backup performance appears poor under Windows**    Performing a backup operation may take (significantly) longer than you expect. This poor backup performance might also be accompanied by diminished hard drive performance while you perform other tasks in Windows. There are several important factors that can affect backup performance. First, check your available memory. A lack of available memory is typically caused by having too many programs open at the same time, or by not having enough physical RAM installed in the computer. Close all running programs before starting the backup process. If that does not improve performance, remove all programs from the Startup folder and from the "load" and "run" lines of your WIN.INI file. If performance remains poor after restarting Windows, try adding more RAM to the system.

Also check for DOS Compatibility Mode. Double-click the System icon in Control Panel, and then click the Performance tab. If the Performance tab in System properties shows that one or more of the hard drives are operating in DOS Compatibility Mode, resolve this problem as soon as possible to improve performance in Backup. Check the hard drive performance next. Even if your hard drives are not stuck in DOS Compatibility Mode, Backup performance may be affected by overall drive performance. If you're using an IDE-type hard drive, its performance may be affected by another device on the same controller channel (for example, tape drives and CD-ROMs). Move the slower device(s) to a separate IDE controller channel.

Update any compression software (or consider removing compression software before performing the backup). When using disk compression on an older (slower) computer, hard drive performance may suffer. If you're using third-party disk compression software that employs real-mode drivers to access your compressed drives, you may be able to improve performance by replacing the real-mode driver with a protected-mode driver. Also check and correct any file fragmentation. Badly fragmented hard disks can affect the performance of Backup (as well as the performance of many other tasks under Windows). Use the Disk Defragmenter utility to reorganize the files on your hard drive(s).

Finally, check the tape for defects. Backup software can usually detect and avoid unusable sectors on a tape, but the process that it uses for this type of checking can be time-consuming. If you suspect that performance problems are caused by unusable sectors on a tape, try using a new tape, or use a tape that you know does not contain bad sectors.

**SYMPTOM 4-6**     **Backup files demand more space than originally expected**     When you create a backup (e.g., using the Backup utility included with Windows Me/XP), the number of files and amount of space used by the backup are larger than estimated by the software. In other cases, you receive messages stating that files cannot be restored when you restore a backup. This problem occurs when the System Restore feature is enabled during backup. If System Restore is enabled during a backup, System Restore saves the temporary backup files. If you back up the _Restore folder, the files that System Restore saves from the temporary backup files are also backed up. To prevent temporary backup files from being saved by System Restore (and decrease the backup size), do not back up the _Restore folder. Click the plus sign (+) next to drive C in Backup, clear the checkbox next to the _Restore folder, then try the backup again.

**SYMPTOM 4-7**     **You cannot restore older backups under Windows XP**     For example, when you try to restore a backup in Windows XP that was created under Windows 9x/Me, you may receive an error message such as:

```
Unrecognized Media: The backup file contains unrecognized data and cannot be
used Backup Utility: An inconsistency was encountered on the requested media
```

This problem occurs because the Windows XP backup software (ntbackup) doesn't recognize the software compression format used by older versions of Microsoft Backup. Ntbackup only recognizes tapes that you create with Backup that do *not* use software compression. Also, since ntbackup is designed to recognize only the .BKF file format, ntbackup doesn't recognize .QIC files that you create with Backup—even if the files were created without software compression. Unfortunately, you must restore the data from the tape or file by using Microsoft Backup on a computer that is running Windows 9x/Me. In the future, you may opt for a backup application that offers better compatibility across OS platforms.

**SYMPTOM 4-8**     **Backup cannot restore a file from multiple disks**     When you try to use the Backup utility in Windows 98/Me to restore a backup set created in Windows 95 that spans multiple disks, a new folder may be created, but the file in the backup set may not be restored. This trouble occurs when your backup set contains a file that spans multiple disks. Windows 98/Me cannot restore a Windows 95 backup set that consists of a single file that spans two or more disks. To work around this problem, use the Backup utility in Windows 95 to restore your file. To correct this problem for the future, do not use the Backup tool in Windows 95 to back up a single file that spans multiple disks. Alternatively, back up more than one file from your Windows 95-based computer, and verify that the additional file is on the first disk—in its entirety.

**SYMPTOM 4-9**     **You cannot restore a Travan tape backup after upgrading to Windows Me**     For example, after you upgrade your system to Windows Me, when you attempt to restore a backup from your Travan drive (firmware revision 2.08) using the Hewlett-Packard Colorado Backup II program (version 6.0), then your computer may hang up. Your internal Travan tape drive is typically configured as the primary device on the UDMA controller. To work around this issue, configure the Travan drive as a slave device on the UDMA controller and try restoring the system again.

**SYMPTOM 4-10**   **You encounter errors with MS Backup under Windows 9x/Me/XP**
When you use Backup to create a full system backup under Windows 9x/Me or a backup that includes the \Windows folder, the status box may indicate that errors occurred during the backup process. When you click Report to view the backup report, you may see error messages such as:

```
Error: C:\WINDOWS\Cookies\index.dat - busy
Error: C:\WINDOWS\History\index.dat - busy
Error: C:\WINDOWS\Temporary Internet Files\index.dat - busy
```

This problem can occur because the INDEX.DAT files that are in each of these locations are open if Internet Explorer is running. Since IE is part of the Windows *graphical user interface* (GUI), these files are always open and therefore cannot be backed up. This behavior occurs in Windows 95 if you're running IE when you run Backup (or if IE 4.0 or 4.01 is installed on the system, and you have enabled the Windows Desktop Update component). Remember that the INDEX.DAT files are re-created each time IE starts, so it is not necessary to back up these files. All other files that you selected are successfully backed up.

**SYMPTOM 4-11**   **Backup software has trouble spanning multiple tapes when backing up to a removable media drive under Windows**   When you're using software (e.g., MS Backup) to store files to a removable disk (other than floppy disks), you note that the software doesn't prompt you to insert a second disk. If the entire backup doesn't fit on one disk, you'll receive an error such as "Errors occurred during this operation—do you want to view them now?" The incomplete backup volume on the first disk is damaged and cannot be restored.

This is a limitation of the backup software. While most software does support the use of removable disk drives (for example, Bernoulli and SyQuest drives), it may not support performing backups that span multiple disks. For example, Backup can span multiple disks only on floppy disk drives connected to the primary floppy drive controller. When you're using Backup to store files to a removable disk, perform only backups that fit on one disk. Large backups that require more than one disk should be broken up into smaller backups—each of which fits on one disk. Otherwise, you may need to patch the backup software, or use a different software package that does support multiple tapes.

**SYMPTOM 4-12**   **When starting Backup under Windows 98, you receive a driver installation error**   The error may appear similar to "Driver already installed Ref 00-02-00-00-0000." After Backup starts, you may receive another error message such as "No device found." Chances are that the backup devices in your computer will not work correctly, and running the Add New Hardware wizard will probably not correctly detect your backup device(s). In most cases, the problem is caused when Seagate Direct Tape Access (version 2.0 or 3.0) is installed on your computer. Uninstall the Seagate Direct Tape Access (version 2.0 or 3.0) software, or uninstall Microsoft Backup for Windows 98. To uninstall Backup:

1. Click Start | Settings | Control Panel and double-click Add/Remove Programs.
2. Click the Windows Setup tab, click on System Tools (not the checkbox), click Details, click the Backup check box to clear it, and then click OK.
3. Follow the instructions on the screen to finish uninstalling Backup.

**SYMPTOM 4-13**    You cannot change the destination folder in Backup under Windows 98
When you select a destination folder under Where to Back Up in Microsoft Backup and then change your backup options by clicking Options under How to Back Up, the destination folder may be changed to the default folder instead of the folder you specified. This can occur if you click the Browse button to locate the destination folder, and you change the Backup options after you specify the destination folder. To resolve this problem, manually type the path to the destination folder, or change the Backup options before you specify the destination folder.

**SYMPTOM 4-14**    You encounter an error while writing backup data    When you attempt to back up data using the Backup utility under Windows 98/SE, you may receive an error message such as:

```
An error occurred while writing the backup data. The end of the media was
approached unexpectedly. (08-22-07-01-0000)
```

This issue can occur if you compress a floppy disk or other removable media (using a tool such as DriveSpace), then try to back up more data than you have available free space on the compressed disk/media. When this happens, Backup does not prompt you to insert another blank disk or media as expected. This issue can also occur when you try to span multiple CD-RW discs. The version of Backup included with Windows 98/SE does not support CD-RW disc spanning. If compression is the problem, do not use DriveSpace if you want to back up data onto more than one blank disc or removable media. If you wish to span multiple CD-RW discs, upgrade to the full version of the Seagate backup software, or select another backup utility that offers additional versatility.

**SYMPTOM 4-15**    Backup cannot perform unattended backups that have been scheduled    When you set Task Scheduler to start an unattended backup job using Backup under Windows 98, the backup job doesn't complete if it's left unattended. This occurs even if you have configured Backup to perform an unattended backup and then added this task to Task Scheduler. Task Scheduler only starts Backup—not the backup job itself. The version of Backup that is included with Windows 98 does not support starting a backup job automatically, so you must be present to begin the backup job. To resolve this problem permanently, upgrade to a backup program that supports completely unattended backup jobs—you may be able to use the later versions of Backup included with Windows Me/XP.

**SYMPTOM 4-16**    Backup doesn't see removable media drives as backup devices
When you click the Where to Back Up box in Backup under Windows 98 to view your backup devices, removable media devices (such as floppy drives, Zip drives, Jaz drives, and so on) do not appear on the list. Unfortunately, a removable media drive is not recognized as a backup device (such as a tape drive), but instead is recognized as a regular drive with a drive letter (such as a hard disk). If you want to back up to removable media, click File in the Where to Back Up box when you make a backup.

If your PC only has a removable media drive for backup use, you receive a message stating there are no backup devices when you start Backup for the first time. When you're prompted to use Add New Hardware to find a backup device (or to continue without looking for a backup device), click No.

**SYMPTOM 4-17**    You cannot restore from multiple tapes if one or more tapes is damaged    For example, when you try to use Backup for Windows 98 to restore files from a backup that spans multiple tapes, you may receive an error message that says the backup media is damaged. If you then click OK or Cancel, the restore process stops, and you are not prompted to insert the next tape. This trouble occurs when one of the backup tapes is damaged. To circumvent this problem, manually restore whatever files you can from each tape:

1. Click Start | Programs | Accessories | System Tools | Backup.

2. Insert one of the tapes from your backup set into the tape drive, and then click Refresh on the Restore tab. Note that you cannot restore damaged files from the tape.

3. When you receive a message that says your backup spans multiple tapes, click No.

4. From the list of files on that tape, highlight the files you want to restore, and then click Start. Repeat this process with each tape in the set until you restore all the files you want, and then quit Backup.

**SYMPTOM 4-18** **Windows 98 runs poorly when backing up a large number of files**
When you're backing up a very large number of files to a tape drive (or other large-capacity device), or you're comparing an existing backup to the original files on the hard drive, Windows 98 may appear to run slowly. This problem typically occurs if you back up a large number of files (for example, 2000 to 3000+ files) while the backup software is configured to perform a comparison. A comparison will check the files on the tape versus the original files on the hard drive. This problem may also occur when you're comparing a set of files that had been backed up previously. For example, this problem is known to occur with the Onstream 30GB digital drive.

This problem is caused by a fault in the Windows 98 protected-mode disk cache (VCACHE.VXD). The error occurs when the maximum value used to track the age of blocks in the cache has been exceeded. If this occurs while the protected-mode disk cache tries to free the oldest blocks to make room for new data, it takes a long time for the operation to finish. Windows will run slowly (and continues to do so until the computer is restarted). You can download and install an updated version of VCACHE.VXD (version 4.10.2183, dated 4/7/99), or upgrade to a later version of Windows such as Me or XP.

**SYMPTOM 4-19** **The HP Colorado Backup utility doesn't detect your tape drive under Windows 98 or later** When you try to use the HP Colorado Backup for Windows 95 software under Windows 98 or later, the Colorado Backup software does not detect your tape drive—even though your tape drive is listed in the Device Manager. This might happen if Microsoft Backup is currently installed (or has been installed in the past). Backup makes subtle changes to the registry. You'll need to remove unneeded files and correct the changes to the registry. To utilize Colorado Backup software instead of Backup, uninstall Microsoft Backup first, and then reinstall Colorado Backup from scratch.

 Be sure to make a complete backup of your registry files (as well as the REGEDIT utility) to your emergency boot floppy disk. If you make a mistake editing the registry, you can install the original files from your boot floppy.

**SYMPTOM 4-20** **You see a Windows 98 error message such as "You have restored a good registry"** When you start your computer, you may receive the following error message: "You have restored a good registry. Windows found an error in your system files and restored a recent backup of the files to fix the problem." When you restart your computer, you may receive the error message again. This problem can occur if the registry backup file you're trying to restore is damaged (or if the "damage" flag in the current registry file is not being reset by the Registry Checker utility). To fix this problem, run the Registry Checker tool using the **/fix** and **/opt** switches:

1. Start your computer to the Safe Mode command prompt.

2. At the DOS prompt, type **scanreg** **/fix** and press ENTER. The **/fix** switch causes the Registry Checker tool to repair any damaged portions of the registry.

3. Press ENTER after the Registry Checker tool finishes repairing the registry.

4. At the DOS prompt, type **scanreg** **/opt** and press ENTER. The **/opt** switch causes the Registry Checker tool to optimize the registry by removing unused space.

5. Restart your computer.

6. If the problem persists, try restoring a different registry backup file using the **/restore** switch.

**SYMPTOM 4-21**    **You encounter "Out of Memory" errors when running SCANREG.EXE under Windows 98**    When you run Registry Checker (SCANREG.EXE) with the **/fix** or **/restore** switch, you may receive an "Out of Memory" error message. You may also receive this error message when SCANREG.EXE creates a backup copy of the registry (during Windows startup). This error may occur with less than 340KB of free conventional memory. When you try to launch SCANREG.EXE with the **/fix** or **/restore** switch, more than 340KB of free conventional memory may be required—depending on the size of the registry. Increase the free conventional memory to more than 340KB. The easiest way to do this is to reboot the computer to the Safe Mode command prompt, then run SCANREG.EXE with the appropriate switches.

**SYMPTOM 4-22**    **When backing up to tape under Windows, you get a media error** When you use Backup to read a backup tape, you may receive an error such as "The media is not supported by this product—please insert another media." Using a different tape generates the same error message. The error message may occur with any operation that attempts to read the tape.

The error occurs if the tape drive fails to support the Quick File Access (QFA) format—also known as *media partitioning*. Backup requires that the tape drive support QFA. The QFA format allows tapes to be divided into a large data partition and a small directory partition. The directory partition holds information about each of the backup sets on the tape and can also be used to store the exact block address of each file on the tape. This feature allows for fast file retrieval with the tape drive.

**SYMPTOM 4-23**    **You encounter problems restoring files with Backup**    No backup has value unless it can be restored, and PC users often forget to test their backup. The only thing worse than losing your work, is discovering that your backup is inaccessible. If Backup reports trouble restoring your files, there are some steps you can take to address the problem:

■ *Clean the drive.* If the drive's read/write heads are dirty, it will not be able to read the tape reliably and errors will result. This should not damage the tape or its contents, but will make restoring difficult until the heads are cleaned. Refer to the drive's particular cleaning instructions and clean the heads. (This is good routine maintenance anyway.)

■ *Use a slower tape speed.* Some parallel ports become sensitive when the PC is operating in its "turbo" mode. Often, the tape drive is forced to work much harder—pulling the tape back and forth across the heads (an undesirable behavior called *shoe shining*). If your backup or restoration process appears to be taking an unusually long time, try disabling the PC's turbo mode, or reconfiguring the parallel port to "compatibility" mode. This does not seem to be an issue with floppy interface tape drives.

- *Try the Windows Safe Mode.* Some drivers may interfere with the proper restoration of tape files. Try restarting Windows in the Safe Mode and then restoring files. Note that if the tape drive requires a protected-mode driver (such as Colorado Trakker's VCOMM file), the tape drive will not work in the Safe Mode.

- *Check your drive space.* Make sure there is enough space on your hard drive. File restoration under Windows involves the use of a swap file. Since the swap file size can change dynamically under Windows, the swap file can grow to be quite large (depending on the number of files involved). If there is very limited drive space, free some space and try again.

**SYMPTOM 4-24**    **You find that there are problems formatting your tapes**    As with any magnetic media, you must format a tape before using it to store files. Today, many common tapes are available already formatted, but if the drive does not recognize the format (or you have trouble formatting the tape yourself), here are some things to consider:

- *Check your tape standard.* Remember that you cannot format a 3010 tape in a QIC-80 drive, and you cannot format a QIC-80 Wide tape in a QIC-80 drive. Make sure you are using the right tape in the drive.

- *Try a different tape.* If you have trouble formatting or working with a particular tape (but similar tapes behave correctly), it may be worn out or otherwise defective. Throw the tape away; it is not worth trying to reuse.

Do *not* attempt to reuse the tape by degaussing it (a.k.a. "bulk erasing"). This will not restore a worn tape or repair damage to it. If data is subsequently written to bad blocks, it may render your backup unusable.

- *Try the Windows Safe Mode.* Some drivers may interfere with the proper operation of the drive. Start Windows in the Safe Mode, and then try formatting the tape. Note that if the tape drive requires a protected-mode driver, the tape drive will not work in the Safe Mode.

- *Check for hardware conflicts.* This is typical of floppy interface tape drive installations. There may be a conflict between the video board and floppy drive controller. Start the format operation and minimize the progress indicator. If problems persist, change the video mode to $640 \times 480 \times 16$. If problems continue, try formatting in a full-screen DOS session. Use the Device Manager to look for conflicts between the video board and floppy drive controller.

**SYMPTOM 4-25**    **You find that tape comparisons fail**    After a backup has been completed, Backup (and most other tape backup utilities) allows you to perform a comparison that checks the tape contents against your original files. This is how you know the data is good. When you encounter errors in comparison, it also means you will probably have trouble restoring from the tape later on. Comparison errors almost always mean that data was lost writing to the tape, or that the tape itself is defective (for example, a bad block is encountered). First, clean the tape drive read/write heads, and then check the comparison again. If the problem persists, try creating another backup now that the heads have been cleaned. If the problem still continues, the tape itself is probably worn out (or is otherwise defective) and should be replaced.

**SYMPTOM 4-26**    **Errors are reported after the backup is complete**    When you try to back up files or folders that are located on a password-protected network share under Windows, you may receive an error message such as "Backup complete—error reported." If you view the backup log, you may see errors such as:

```
Error: \\<share> - access denied
Error: \\<share> - could not be accessed
```

where <share> is the name of the network share. This trouble occurs because Backup does not prompt you for a password to access password-protected network shares. Connect to the network share and enter your password before you try to back up files or folders from this share.

**SYMPTOM 4-27    You receive an error such as "media not formatted or unreadable"**
You may need to disable the high-speed burst transfer option under your Windows 9*x*/Me system properties:

1. Right-click the My Computer icon and select Properties.
2. Click the Device Manager tab in your System Properties dialog box.
3. Click the plus (+) sign next to your "backup device type" to expand the entries, and then double-click your backup device.
4. Click the Settings tab in the Properties dialog box.
5. Uncheck the High Speed Burst Transfers option and click OK.
6. Restart your computer.

# Further Study

**@Backup**    www.atbackup.com/
**AIT Technology**    www.aittape.com
**Computer Peripherals**    www.cpuinc.com
**DLT Standards**    www.dlttape.com
**Exabyte**    www.exabyte.com
**Hewlett-Packard**    www.hp.com/tape/colorado/index.html
**LTO Standards** www.lto-technology.com
**Micro Solutions**    www.micro-solutions.com
**Microsoft (Backup)**    www.microsoft.com
**NovaStor**    www.no-panic.com/backup/n_backup.html
**PowerQuest**    www.powerquest.com
**Seagate**    www.seagate.com
**Symantec**    www.symantec.com

# 5

# BATTERIES

**O**f all the elements in a PC, few are as overlooked and ignored as the battery. Batteries play an important role in all PCs by maintaining the system's configuration data while main AC power is turned off (just imagine how inconvenient it would be to reenter the *entire* system setup in CMOS RAM before being able to use the system each time). For portable systems such as notebook and sub-notebook PCs, battery packs also provide main power for the entire system (see Figure 5-1). This chapter outlines the technologies and operating characteristics of today's battery families, and illustrates a selection of battery-related problems that can plague desktop and mobile PCs.

# A Battery Primer

The battery is perhaps the most common and dependable source of power ever developed. It is an electro-chemical device that uses two dissimilar metals (called *electrodes*) that are immersed or encapsulated in a chemical catalyst (or *electrolyte*). The chemical reaction that takes place in a battery causes a voltage differential to be developed across its electrodes. When a battery is attached to a circuit, the battery provides current. The more current required by a load, the faster a chemical reaction will occur. As the chemical

**FIGURE 5-1**   Large Li-ion battery packs can power a laptop PC for hours.

reaction continues, electrodes are consumed. This chemical consumption will cause the voltage differential to gradually drop, and the battery will eventually "go dead." It is important to realize that a *battery* and a *cell* are not necessarily the same. A *cell* is the basic element of a battery, but a *battery* may be made up of several individual cells.

For some batteries, the chemical reaction is irreversible. When the battery is dead, it must be discarded (in an environmentally responsible manner). These are known as non-rechargeable (or *primary*) batteries. Most PCs use small primary-type batteries to sustain the contents of CMOS RAM. However, some types of batteries can be recharged. By applying current to the battery from an external source (for example, a battery charger), the expended chemical reaction can be almost entirely reversed. Such rechargeable batteries are referred to as *secondary* batteries. Rechargeable batteries are used to supply main power for all mobile computers.

## BATTERY RATINGS

Batteries carry two important ratings: cell voltage and ampere-hours (Ah). *Cell voltage* refers to the cell's working voltage. Most everyday cells operate around +1.5 Vdc, but can range from +1.2 to +3.0 Vdc (or more) depending on the particular battery chemistry being used. The *ampere-hour* rating is a bit more involved, but it reflects the energy storage capacity of a battery. A high Ah rating suggests a high-capacity battery, and a low rating, a low capacity.

As an example, suppose your battery is rated for 2.0 Ah. Ideally, you should be able to draw 2 amps from the battery for one hour before it is exhausted. However, you should also be able to draw 1 amp for 2 hours, 0.5 amp for 4 hours, 0.1 amp for 20 hours, and so on. Keep in mind that the ampere-hour relationship is not precisely linear. Higher current loads may shorten battery life to less than that expected by the ampere-hour rating, while small loads may allow slightly more battery life than expected. Regardless of the ampere-hour rating, all batteries have an upper current limit—attempting to draw excess current can destroy the battery (causing its seals to rupture and leak caustic chemicals). Physically large batteries can usually supply more current (and last longer) than smaller batteries. Another way to express a battery's energy capacity is in watt-hours per kilogram (Wh/kg) or watt-hours per pound (Wh/lb). For example, a 1 kg battery rated at 60 Wh could provide 60W of power for 1 hour, 30W of power for 2 hours, 10W of power for 6 hours, and so on.

# CHARGING

In its simplest sense, *charging* is the replacement of electrical energy to batteries whose stored chemical energy has been discharged. By applying an electrical current to a discharged battery over a given period, it is possible to cause a chemical recombination at the battery's electrodes, which will restore most of the battery's spent potential. Essentially, you must "back-feed" the battery at a known, controlled rate—this recharges the battery, and most rechargable batteries can tolerate hundreds of *recharge cycles*.

Recharging only works for secondary cells such as nickel-cadmium (NiCd), nickel metal-hydride (NiMH), or lithium-ion (Li-ion) batteries. Attempting to recharge a primary battery (e.g., an alkaline battery) will quickly destroy it.

Before you dive into an overview of charging circuits and troubleshooting, you must understand the concept of C. The term *C* designates the normal current capacity of a battery (in amperes). In most circumstances, the value of C is the same as the ampere-hour current level. For example, a battery rated for 1300 mAh (1.30 Ah) would be considered to have a C value of 1.30 amps. A battery rated for 700 mAh (0.70 Ah) would have a C of 0.70 amps. Charging rates are based upon fractions or multiples of C.

To charge a battery, you must apply a reverse voltage that will cause the appropriate amount of charging current to flow back into the battery. Traditionally, a battery should be charged at a rate of 0.1C. For batteries with a C of 500 mA (0.5A), 0.1C would be 50 mA (0.05A). At 0.1C, the battery could be left connected in the charger indefinitely without damage. Low-current charge rates such as 0.1C are sometimes referred to as a *slow charge* or *trickle charge*. Slow charging produces the least physical or thermal stress within a battery and ensures the maximum possible number of charge/discharge cycles.

Many current secondary batteries can be charged well above the 0.1C rate. The *quick charge* approach uses current levels of 0.3C (three times the rate of a slow charge) to recharge the battery in four to six hours. For a battery with a C of 600 mA (0.60A), the 0.1C charging rate would be 60 mA (0.06A), but the quick charge rate would be 180 mA (0.18A). However, the quick charging process runs the risk of *overcharging* a battery. Once a battery is fully recharged, additional current at or above the quick charge rate causes temperature and pressure buildups within the cell(s). In extreme cases, a severely overcharged battery may rupture and be destroyed. When quick charging, the 0.3C charging rate should be used only long enough to restore the bulk of a battery's energy. The rate should be reduced to 0.1C (or less) for continuous operation (a.k.a. trickle charging).

Newer battery designs allow for an even faster charge of one hour. The *one-hour charge* uses a rate of 1.5C, which is 1.5 times the amount of current that the battery is intended to provide. A battery with a C of 1400 mA (1.40A) would use a one-hour charge rate of 2100 mA (2.10A). Remember that only specially designed secondary cells can be safely charged in one hour or less. With one-hour charging, current control and timing become critical issues. The battery charging current *must* be reduced as soon as the battery approaches its full charge, or catastrophic battery failure will almost certainly result. Rapid charging causes substantial temperature and pressure increases that eventually take their toll on a battery's working life. You should expect the working life of any battery to be curtailed when it is regularly operated in a one-hour charge mode.

The *constant-current charger* is designed to automatically compensate for changes in battery terminal voltage in order to maintain charging current at a constant level. Constant-current charging is very efficient, but it is not adjustable. If the charger were set to deliver substantial charging currents, the battery pack could charge quickly, but overcharging could eventually damage the pack. The charger could be set to a lower level for safe charging (perhaps 0.1C), but the low charging rate means very long charge times for a battery pack (10 hours or more). Such limitations make constant-current chargers poorly suited for use in mobile computers. Instead, constant-current chargers are typically used in stand-alone battery pack charging units.

A more effective approach for portable computers is a *variable-current* (constant-voltage) scheme. When a battery is deeply discharged and its terminal voltage is low, there will be a substantial difference between the power supply source and battery voltage level. This difference results in a sizable current flow to the battery. Charging usually starts out around the 0.5C to 0.3C rate for fast charge operation. As the battery takes on a charge, its terminal voltage increases. Higher battery voltage reduces the difference between the supply and battery—current flow into the battery decreases. When the battery pack reaches full charge, there is almost no voltage difference between the charger and battery, so only a small amount of current trickles into the battery. Current flow may reach levels as low as 0.05C.

## STORING BATTERIES

At some point, you'll probably need to store unused batteries for some time. Remember that the chemical process that makes batteries work will always continue regardless of whether the battery is installed—this means your battery will eventually go dead even if you don't use it. You can extend your battery's shelf life by reducing its temperature. Typically, this means storing your batteries in the refrigerator (in a vapor-proof container to prevent drying the battery's electrolyte due to the low humidity). The cold will slow the chemical reaction and keep the battery "fresh" much longer. Just remember to remove the battery from the refrigerator and to allow it to stabilize at room temperature for at least 24 hours before using it.

# CMOS Backup Batteries

When IBM released its PC/AT in the early 1980s, one of the many design changes over the older PC/XT was the elimination of DIP switches used to set the system configuration. Instead of discrete physical switches, PC designers chose to set system parameters using bit sequences stored in small areas of low-power static RAM (or SRAM). Since it would be necessary to maintain the contents of this RAM even when system power is off, designers choose to use RAM chips based on *complementary metal oxide semiconductor* (CMOS) fabrication. This extremely low-power memory became known as CMOS RAM. CMOS RAM can be maintained for years using only a single small battery or battery pack incorporated onto the motherboard (Figure 5-2) called a *CMOS backup battery*. All motherboards require a CMOS backup battery.

Do not confuse CMOS batteries with standby batteries. Mobile computers such as IBM's ThinkPad series often employ additional batteries to serve as a standby power source. These *standby batteries* are rechargeable battery packs frequently used to supplement the main battery in mobile computers. Traditionally, you'd need to shut down a laptop and replace a main battery pack, then reboot the system in order to keep working. If the main battery pack were to fail, you'd lose any work in progress (and perhaps corrupt important files). With a standby power source, the system can automatically enter a "suspend" mode where almost no power is used, but files and data can be kept active in memory. You can then replace the main battery and leave the suspend mode to keep working without the time and trouble to reboot and

**FIGURE  5-2**    A Rayovac Computer Clock battery (Courtesy of Rayovac Corp.)

reload your applications. If the main battery should fail, the standby batteries can keep your work intact for up to several days until you can exchange the main battery pack, or find an AC outlet for a battery eliminator.

## LITHIUM BATTERIES

Lithium/manganese-dioxide ($Li/MnO_2$ or simply, lithium) batteries are commonly employed as CMOS backup batteries. Lithium batteries use a layer of lithium as the anode, a specially formulated manganese-dioxide alloy as the cathode, and a conductive organic electrolyte. Depending on the overall size and shape of the cell, a lithium battery can supply +3.0 Vdc at up to 230 Wh/kg of energy density. Lithium cells also offer a five-year shelf life with almost no loss of power. While their energy density is quite high, lithium cells offer only low ampere-hour ratings between 76 mAh (0.076 Ah) and 500 mAh (0.500 Ah). Limited Ah ratings allow lithium cells to maintain an almost constant output voltage over a long working life.

The classical type of lithium battery is the *coin cell*. The typical coin cell is designed in two halves with a lithium anode at the top and a manganese-dioxide cathode layer on the bottom. Both halves are separated by a thin membrane containing a conductive electrolyte. The finished electrochemical assembly is then packaged into a small metal can. The lid forms the negative electrode, while the side walls and bottom of the coin form the positive electrode. The lid is physically isolated from the rest of the metal can by a thin insulating grommet—thus, the coin cell is not totally sealed. A grommet keeps moisture and contaminants out, yet will allow any pressure buildup to escape the battery.

# BACKUP BATTERY REPLACEMENT

Battery life has a limit. Eventually, all backup batteries will discharge to the point where they can no longer sustain the system. When the battery finally does fail, CMOS information is lost. The next time you attempt to turn the PC on, the system will generate an error code or message indicating that the system configuration does not match the CMOS Setup information. The loss of CMOS RAM contents suddenly leaves a system disabled until new (and correct) CMOS information is entered. This presents a serious problem for most PC users, since few users bother to back up or record their CMOS Setup. As you might imagine, it then becomes an exercise in frustration to load the setup routine and reconstruct the system setup from scratch.

Fortunately, there are two things you can do to avoid this problem. First, make it a point to routinely replace the backup battery every two years (no more than three years). If you change the backup battery for a customer, note the battery part number and replacement date on a sticker, and then place the sticker inside the PC enclosure (you might also note the next replacement date on your customer's bill). Second, back up the system CMOS entries *before* replacing the battery. You can note the entries on paper, though it's often much more convenient to simply select the BIOS Default option to reload typical entries from scratch after the battery is replaced.

The actual process of backup battery replacement is simply a matter of removing the old battery and inserting a new one. Since the battery is often located prominently on the motherboard (see Figure 5-3), it is possible to replace a backup battery with system power applied (this lets the system maintain its CMOS settings). However, working inside a "hot" system is against the safety protocols that we have established for this book, so be sure to note the CMOS settings first; then power-down and unplug the PC before opening it. Replace the battery, and then restart the PC and reload the CMOS settings (or select defaults). Replacing the backup battery in a notebook or sub-notebook PC is sometimes easier since the battery is usually accessible from a small panel on the bottom enclosure (you do not have to disassemble the notebook enclosures to replace the battery). Even with easy access, you should make it a point to remove power before replacing the battery.

If you act quickly when replacing the CMOS backup battery, there may be enough of a latent charge in CMOS RAM that the contents will remain intact for several minutes after the old battery is removed. However, each motherboard is designed differently, and there is no guarantee how long CMOS RAM contents may remain intact once the battery is removed. Always be prepared to restore CMOS settings from scratch *before* removing the CMOS backup battery.

# BACKUP BATTERY TROUBLESHOOTING

Lithium CMOS backup batteries are typically rugged and reliable devices whose greatest threat is simply old age. Since lithium cells are the primary type, they cannot be recharged, so they must be replaced periodically. Under most circumstances, only a few symptoms account for the majority of backup battery problems. In a few cases, you may find a motherboard that employs a nickel-cadmium (rechargeable) battery to maintain the CMOS RAM. In that case, the backup battery is recharged whenever the system is running. The problem with NiCd backup batteries is that NiCd has a very short "shelf life," so you must run the system periodically to keep the backup battery charged—otherwise, you may lose your CMOS data just letting the system sit idle.

## Checking the CMOS Backup Battery

It is usually a simple matter to check the CMOS backup battery. Power-down the system and expose the motherboard. Locate the CMOS backup battery. The positive (+) side of the battery is exposed, and you

Typical CMOS RAM
backup battery

**FIGURE 5-3**    The circular coin cell is normally installed with the large flat side up, as on this
Gigabyte GA-7VRXP motherboard (Courtesy Motherboards.org).

can put the negative (–) lead on any ground line (e.g., a black wire in any unused drive power cable). Touch
the battery with the positive probe lead and measure the battery voltage—you should read between 2.5 and
3.7 Vdc (see Figure 5-4). If the backup battery voltage is correct, there may be a software program or
motherboard failure. If the backup battery reads low, replace the battery. If the battery discharges again
quickly, there is a problem on the motherboard that is shorting the CMOS backup battery.

Do not remove the CMOS backup battery from the motherboard in order to check it—this will clear
your CMOS configuration and make it difficult for the system to boot until the CMOS settings are
restored. Check the battery level "in circuit," but be sure to keep the PC power *off.*

### Symptoms

The following symptoms outline some of the more common problems that you may encounter when
working with typical CMOS RAM backup batteries:

**SYMPTOM 5-1**    **You see an error such as "System hardware does not match CMOS
configuration"**    For some reason(s), the BIOS has identified different hardware than that listed in the
CMOS Setup, or the CMOS RAM contents have been lost. Start by checking your CMOS RAM contents
through the CMOS Setup routine. Make sure that the CMOS Setup is configured properly (configuration
errors can happen frequently when new drives or RAM is added to the system). Remember to save your
changes to CMOS RAM before exiting the Setup routine. If the CMOS RAM contents won't hold, check
the battery connector to see that the battery is secure. A loose or corroded battery connector may effectively "disconnect" the battery—even if the battery is working perfectly. If the CMOS RAM contents still
won't hold, you should replace the CMOS backup battery. When replacing the battery, be sure to install
the new battery in the proper orientation and to verify that it is secure in its connector.

**FIGURE 5-4**     Once the PC is powered off, check the backup battery by measuring the battery's positive side versus any ground (black) power wire.

This error often happens when RAM is added to the system—even though there is no entry for installed RAM anywhere in the CMOS Setup. Try to "exit saving changes" though you may not have actually changed any settings.

**SYMPTOM 5-2**     **You notice corrosion from the CMOS battery on the battery holder and motherboard**     This frequently occurs with older motherboards (i386 and i486 vintage motherboards) that have been stored for prolonged periods. The battery has ruptured due to old age and electrolyte has leaked onto the holder, or onto the motherboard itself. Battery chemicals are very caustic to metals, and chances are that any traces or solder connections that have come in contact with the battery leakage have been ruined. Unfortunately, this also means that the motherboard has been ruined and must be replaced.

If you're planning to remove and store a motherboard for any period, record any CMOS Setup pages before removing the motherboard, and then store the old motherboard with the battery *removed.* You may place the battery in a small, heavy-gauge plastic bag at the bottom of the motherboard's anti-static box. When resurrecting the motherboard later, you can replace the battery (or use as new battery) and restore the original CMOS settings.

**SYMPTOM 5-3**     **The system configuration is lost intermittently**     A lithium battery generally produces a very stable output voltage until the very end of its operating life. When the battery finally dies, it tends to be a permanent event. When a system loses its setup configuration without warning, but seems to hold the configuration once it is restored, a loose or intermittent connection is suggested. Turn the PC off and unplug it. Check the battery and make sure it is inserted correctly and completely in its holder. A coin cell should fit snugly. If the cell is loose, gently tighten the holder's prongs to hold the cell more securely. Make sure to remove any corrosion or debris that may be interfering with the contacts. High-quality electrical contact cleaner on a moistened swab is particularly effective at cleaning contacts.

When the battery is attached by a short cable, see that the cable is not broken or frayed, and make sure it is inserted properly into its receptacle. If problems persist, replace the CMOS backup battery.

**SYMPTOM 5-4**    **The backup battery is going dead frequently**    This is a rare and perplexing problem that is often difficult to detect because it may only manifest itself several times a year. Ideally, a lithium coin cell should last for several years (perhaps three years or more). A lithium or alkaline battery pack can last five years or more. When a system loses its setup more than once a year due to battery failures, it is very likely that an error in the motherboard design is draining the backup batteries faster than normal. Unfortunately, the only way to *really* be sure is to replace the motherboard with a different or updated version. Before suggesting this option to your customer, you may wish to contact technical support for the original motherboard manufacturer and find out if similar cases have been reported. If so, find if there is a fix or correction that will rectify the problem (it may be necessary to return the motherboard—under RMA—to the manufacturer for corrective action).

**SYMPTOM 5-5**    **You see a "161" error or message indicating that the system battery is dead**    Depending on the particular system you are working with, there may also be a message indicating that the CMOS Setup does not match the system configuration. In either case, the backup battery has probably failed and should be replaced. Remember to turn off the system before replacing the battery. Once the backup battery is replaced, restart the system. You will likely receive a message that the CMOS Setup does not match the system configuration. Restore the configuration from paper notes or a file backup. The system should now function normally.

# Mobile Batteries

Besides providing power to back up the system's configuration, notebook and sub-notebook computers rely on batteries for main power when operating away from AC. Such power is typically provided from one or more battery packs installed from the bottom or side of the computer (see Figure 5-5). Newer laptops which include active matrix screens, fast processors, CD/DVD drives and more, create increased power demands making the requirements for battery packs ever more stringent—packs have to provide as much power for as long as today's technology will allow, yet be as light and small as possible. Further, today's battery packs must be quickly rechargeable and offer a long working life through hundreds of recharging cycles. Most of the laptop computers on the market today use a Lithium-ion (Li-ion) battery. Nickel metal-hydride (NiMH) batteries are still available in some lower-end laptops, and the nickel-cadmium (NiCd) batteries have largely been phased out of mobile computers.

## NICKEL-CADMIUM

Nickel-cadmium (NiCd) battery packs have been widely used in mobile computers (primarily laptops and notebooks) as a main power source. NiCd batteries are secondary (rechargeable) devices using an anode of nickel hydroxide and a cathode consisting of a specially formulated cadmium compound. The electrolyte is made of potassium hydroxide. NiCd cells can supply up to +1.2 Vdc each with ampere-hour ratings from 500 mAh (0.50 Ah) to 2300 mAh (2.30 Ah). Energy densities in NiCd cells can approach 50 Wh/kg (23 Wh/lb). Respectable ampere-hour ratings allow NiCd cells to supply sizable amounts of current, but their inherently low energy density means that NiCds must be recharged fairly often.

**FIGURE 5-5**   Most laptop PCs can accommodate one battery, or replace the drive bay with a second battery for extended running time.

## Memory Effects

The NiCd *memory effect* is a unique battery phenomenon that is not entirely understood. In operation, a NiCd battery can develop a "memory" that serves to limit either the capacity or terminal voltage of a cell. As you might expect, either limit can result in problems with the battery. *Voltage memory* is generally caused by prolonged charging over weeks and months. High ambient temperatures and high charging currents can accelerate this condition. In effect, the battery is charged for so long, or at such a high rate or temperature, that the efficiency of the electrochemical reaction is impaired. As a result, the battery suffers from low terminal voltage. The *memory capacity* problem is probably more widely recognized and is usually expressed as the loss of a NiCd's ability to deliver its full power capacity. The generally accepted cause of capacity problems is the result of frequent partial battery discharge, followed by a full recharge. Over several such cycles, the battery "learns" that only a portion of its capacity is used. This renders the battery unable to deliver a full discharge time when needed.

Fortunately, the memory effect appears to be only a temporary condition that can usually be cleared by forcing the battery through several *full* discharge/recharge cycles. If you are in the habit of using your notebook or laptop PC until you receive low-battery warnings, you will probably not have to worry about NiCd memory problems. It is interesting to note that the newer lithium-ion (Li-ion) batteries do not seem to suffer from memory problems.

## Self-Discharge

NiCd cells also have a very limited charged life when sitting idle. While alkaline and lithium cells can hold close to their original charge for years, NiCds will lose approximately 25 percent to 35 percent of their remaining charge each month. After several months of inactivity, a NiCd battery pack will need to be recharged before use. As a general rule, you should fully recharge any new or rarely used NiCd battery or battery pack prior to use. Today, NiCd batteries have largely been phased out of mobile computer use in favor of more robust NiMH and Li-ion batteries.

# NICKEL METAL-HYDRIDE

Nickel metal-hydride (NiMH) batteries are a somewhat newer type of rechargeable battery designed to offer substantially greater energy density than NiCd cells for mobile computer applications. Since their introduction in 1990, NiMH cells have already undergone some substantial improvements and cost reductions that have clearly made NiMH the dominant type of battery for mobile computers.

NiMH batteries are remarkably similar in construction and operating principles to NiCds. A positive electrode of nickel-hydroxide remains the same as that used in NiCds, but the negative electrode replaces cadmium with a metal-hydroxide alloy. When combined with a uniquely formulated electrolyte, NiMH cells are rated to provide at least 40 percent more capacity than similarly sized NiCd cells. NiMH batteries can provide +1.2 Vdc with discharge ratings from 800 mAh (0.80 Ah) to more than 2400 mAh (2.40 Ah) at continuous discharge currents of 9A or more. Energy densities can exceed 80 Wh/kg (38.1 Wh/lb). This means a NiMH battery can power a laptop and support additional features (for example, a larger active-matrix color display) for longer times. NiMH batteries also seem to suffer the "memory effects" that plague NiCd batteries, but certainly not to the same extent. Keep in mind that NiMH has a fairly short shelf life (often a matter of days)—so you'll need to keep your NiMH batteries fully charged before traveling.

Most of the laptop batteries manufactured in the late 1990s are NiMH.

## LITHIUM-ION AND ZINC-AIR

Lithium-ion (Li-ion) batteries are the most commonly used batteries for the current generation of mobile computers. The formulation of the Li-ion battery allows 20–30 percent more running time than a similarly sized NiMH battery (at about 115 Wh/kg) and retains a charge for a long time while on the shelf. Li-ion batteries are also free of the memory effects found in NiCd and NiMH batteries and will last through 800 to 1000 recharge cycles (normally 12 to 18 months of average use). Li-ion batteries represent the newest generation of "smart" batteries, because status information on the battery's remaining charge can be communicated to the host system for an accurate determination of running time.

Typical lithium-ion battery packs hold between four to eight Li-ion cells (nine or more cells would be considered a "high capacity" battery). In actual practice, however, there is no reason to open the pack—you cannot replace individual cells. When cells start to fail, the battery's terminal voltage will not achieve full charge (or not hold a full charge for long), and the entire battery pack will need replacement. Li-ion packs also offer fast recharge times, and can fully charge in about one hour with the laptop power off and the unit connected to AC. If the laptop is running on AC, you may need from two to two and a half hours to charge the Li-ion battery pack.

Li-ion technology is also prized because it is environmentally friendly—Li-ion batteries do not contain harmful cadmium or mercury found in older battery technologies.

Zinc-air batteries are another recent development in mobile battery design, and the batteries now appearing in the field offer almost twice the energy density of Li-ion batteries (at a whopping 220 Wh/kg). In actual practice, however, zinc-air batteries have proven extremely large and heavy. They are also quite expensive. These factors have kept zinc-air batteries out of most small mobile systems. Still, the high-energy potential of zinc-air will keep development active. Over the next few years, Li-ion batteries should continue to be the major power sources for mobile systems.

## IDENTIFYING NICD AND NIMH BATTERIES

Although it is often difficult to distinguish between a NiCd and NiMH battery pack at first glance, there are some tips that might help you tell the difference. NiCd battery packs typically use three metal contacts (a slightly longer "negative" contact bridges contacts in the laptop and indicates the presence of the battery to the system). By comparison, NiMH battery packs are newer and "smarter" than NiCd packs, so the

NiMH packs will typically include a type and temperature sensing contact located near the positive terminal of the battery pack. The firmware of some laptops will not begin charging the battery pack if the battery temperature is over 104°F (or if the temperature rises above 140°F while charging).

If the battery pack is unmarked, you may be able to identify the technology of the battery pack based on the pack's output voltage. NiCd packs will be a multiple of 1.25V, lead-acid packs will be a multiple of 2.0V, and alkaline packs will be a multiple of 1.5V. For example, if you measure ~3.75 Vdc across a battery pack, you can guess that it is probably a NiCd pack.

## IDENTIFYING A RESERVE BATTERY

Many current laptop designs employ a *reserve battery,* which powers the system for a few minutes—allowing the main battery to be replaced without having to shut down the system or connect to AC power. In many cases, the internal reserve battery is a pack of four half-length AA-size, 270 mAh, NiCd batteries in an inline stack. When fully charged, this pack can power the system for about eight minutes before being fully discharged. In operation, the reserve battery is permitted to support the computer for two to three minutes at the most before forcing a system shutdown. Reserve batteries are available in countless shapes and sizes.

## RECHARGEABLE BATTERY GUIDELINES

Rechargeable batteries are reliable and robust devices, but there are a number of guidelines that need to be observed to get the most from them:

- *Plan on charging the battery before use.* For safety reasons, rechargeable batteries are typically shipped in a discharged state. You will need to prepare (or *condition*) your battery pack (according to manufacturer's instructions) prior to placing the battery pack into use.

- *Cycle the battery pack as recommended.* Rechargeable batteries generally need to be *cycled* (fully charged and discharged) as many as five times before they will perform at full load capacity. Your laptop's instruction manual should explain the exact process for breaking in the battery.

- *New batteries may fool a status indicator.* A new battery may cause the battery status indicator on your computer to indicate a dead or low battery condition. If this happens, try letting the battery charge in the system overnight so that the PC's charging circuit might synchronize with the battery pack. If you have trouble using battery packs with a certain make and model of mobile PC, the system's BIOS may be at fault (check with the system maker for a BIOS upgrade).

- *Store the battery carefully.* When the battery pack is not in use, remove it from the system and store it in a cool, dry place.

- *Never short-circuit the battery terminals.* Although some battery packs are protected by internal self-resetting fuses, short circuits can still cause considerable damage to the battery. Use extreme care when packing spare batteries with other equipment during transit or storage.

- *Handle the battery pack carefully.* Do not drop, hit, or abuse the battery pack in any way. Not only might this damage the battery's internal cells, but a break in the casing may also release electrolyte or expose cell contents—this material is corrosive and can damage circuitry in the PC.

- *Check for excessive heat.* It is perfectly normal for a battery pack to become warm to the touch when charging or discharging. However, if the battery pack gets extremely warm (that is, over 50°C or 122°F), there may be a problem with the charging circuit. If you're using a stand-alone battery charger, do not leave the battery connected to the charger—this can overcharge the battery and shorten its working life.

■ *Keep an eye on your running time.* Running time depends on the power demands of your system components and the way in which the computer is used. Changing screen types and adding accessories will often shorten actual run times. After 300 to 500 recharges, a shortened run time may indicate that the battery needs to be replaced.

## Battery Charging and Replacement Tips

Rechargeable batteries are usually reliable and forgiving devices, but they do require a certain amount of care. For best results with rechargeable batteries, try the following guidelines:

■ Remember that AC adapters are generally designed for specific laptops in order to handle the specific power requirements of the laptop and its add-on devices (for example, a Dell Token Ring Advanced Port Replicator). This means you typically cannot mix and match AC adapters. Be sure to use only the AC adapter intended for your laptop model.

■ Each time the computer is connected to AC power (or a battery is installed in a computer that is connected to AC power), the computer checks the battery's charge. The AC adapter then charges the battery (if needed) and the reserve battery (if one is present), and then maintains the battery's charge.

■ For lithium-ion battery packs with built-in charge indicators, you can check the battery's charge by pressing the Battery Test button. For a fully charged battery pack, all the indicators should light up. Otherwise, the number of indicators lit will correspond to the amount of battery power remaining. For example, if there are five LEDs, each LED would represent 20 percent of the battery's capacity. If one of the battery cells is shorted, you'll probably see a blinking indicator for that cell (the battery pack should be replaced).

■ Do not attempt to replace the main battery while running on battery power without first placing the computer in battery-swap (reserve battery) or "suspend-to-disk" mode. Otherwise, a loss of data will probably result.

■ Today, an AC adapter requires about 1.25–1.5 hours to charge a battery if the computer is off. Since additional current is needed to power a running PC, the battery charges in 2.75–3 hours if the computer is on.

■ For maximum battery performance, charge the battery only at normal room temperature.

■ The battery starts charging immediately. The corresponding battery indicator lights while the battery is being charged and turns off when the cycle is complete.

■ If a battery indicator blinks while the AC adapter is connected to the computer, the battery may be defective or installed improperly. Check the documentation for your particular laptop, and verify that you're seeing the correct charging indicator.

## Conserving Mobile Battery Power

Battery life is affected by the current drawn by a computer—higher current demands result in shorter battery life, and lower demands result in longer battery life. A large portion of battery troubleshooting is to ensure that your system setup is adequate. The following steps should help you to optimize battery life (Table 5-1 illustrates typical settings for power conservation):

■ Take advantage of special power modes like *suspend* or *hibernation*. These modes use very little power and should be selected when you'll be away from the running laptop for any period of time.

■ Remove or disable any unnecessary devices in the laptop. For example, you may not need that PCMCIA modem card or sound card during that flight cross-country, so remove the card. If you can *disable* unneeded devices (that is, shut down power to the built-in infrared communication unit), that will also save substantial power.

■ Use the lowest screen brightness that you are comfortable with by adjusting the display's brightness and contrast control(s).

■ LCD backlights gobble up substantial amounts of power, so set a short timeout interval for the backlight (one or two minutes is often a good selection).

■ A setting with light characters and images on a dark background generally consumes less power than dark characters or images on a light background. Try setting your screen mode to a "light on dark" configuration. If you're using Windows 98/Me, select a dark color scheme like the High Contrast Black setting. Under Windows XP, you may need to configure the desktop appearance manually (see Figure 5-6).

■ The hard disk drive is another major power user—not only by spinning, but during spinup as well. Select a moderate timeout interval for the hard drive (not so long that it spins forever, and not so short that it is constantly starting). Otherwise, you will waste more power constantly spinning up the drive than you save by turning it off. Also, constant starting and stopping can reduce the life expectancy of the drive.

■ RAM consumes much less power than hard drives, so try setting up a disk cache or RAM disk to reduce the number of disk accesses. This allows the hard drive to spin down faster and not require access for a relatively long time. If your system has lots of RAM, you might even opt to disable virtual memory to prevent additional disk access for the swap file.

**FIGURE 5-6**   Configuring a display appearance with light characters on a dark background may help conserve battery power.

- Processor speed can be a serious drain on battery power. If your laptop computer allows you to select processor speed (e.g., processor throttling), use the slowest speed possible for all but the most demanding applications. Most word processors and utility software runs just fine with slower processor speeds.

- Most mobile batteries have trouble retaining their full charge capacity when left unused for prolonged times. For example, IBM tests suggest that after a one-year shelf life at room temperature, a Li-ion battery retained 95 percent of its original capacity (about 90 percent for NiMH). If you purchase several batteries for a mobile computer, be sure to alternate the use of each battery.

- Since motorized drives use a fair amount of power, avoid playing music CDs or DVDs while the PC is on battery power.

## MOBILE BATTERY TROUBLESHOOTING

When discussing batteries as main power sources, not only are the batteries or battery pack involved, but a whole host of other circuitry is included as well (such as battery charging, battery protection, and power management circuits). As a result, you should understand that problems running or charging the battery may be originating *outside* of the battery compartment itself. Since batteries power notebook and sub-notebook systems, trouble may be on the motherboard (where most charging and power management functions are located).

### Recognizing Rechargeable Battery Failures

Rechargeable batteries can and do fail. The process of discharge and recharge generates physical stress in the battery that will eventually wear it out. As a rule of thumb, a NiCd battery will last from about three to five years (through 500 to 1500 complete charge cycles). NiMH and lithium-ion batteries will generally last somewhat longer. However, proper charging in a cool environment can extend battery life much further (up to as many as 10,000 complete charge cycles have been reported). Over the life of a rechargeable battery, microscopic "whiskers" of conductive compounds develop between the electrodes. Ultimately, these deposits work to short-circuit the battery from inside. Although "zapping" techniques have been developed using brief surges of current to remove these deposits, such techniques are very risky since the battery stands a good chance of exploding. Another failure mode is the premature loss of liquid electrolyte

| TABLE 5-1    RECOMMENDED POWER-SAVING SETTINGS | |
|---|---|
| **FOR THIS FEATURE...** | **CONFIGURE THE SYSTEM TO...** |
| Power button mode | Standby/Resume |
| PM Control | Battery |
| Power Savings | Maximum Battery Life |
| Sleep Timeout | 2 Minutes |
| Standby Timeout | 10 Minutes |
| Hard Disk Timeout | 2 Minutes |
| Video Timeout | 4 Minutes |
| Audio Timeout | 2 Minutes |
| Battery Low Standby | Enabled |
| Auto Dim With Battery Only | On |
| Cooling control | Silence |

during high-current or high-temperature charging. Improperly designed "quick-charge" chargers can drive a battery so hard that electrolyte starts to corrode the battery's pressure-relief vent. If the vent is damaged or frozen in the open position, electrolyte will continue to evaporate and the battery will fail.

## Check the Battery Pack

When the battery refuses to take or hold a charge, it will often be necessary for you to verify the integrity of your mobile battery. The following steps outline the procedure:

1. Power-down the laptop or notebook computer, and remove the battery pack according to the instructions for your particular system.

2. Once the battery pack is removed, measure the voltage between battery terminals. If there are more than two terminals (as in Figure 5-7 for an IBM ThinkPad battery), be sure to measure across the proper two terminals. For the example of Figure 5-7, you would measure across pins 1 and 4. If you read an extremely low voltage (e.g., 1 Vdc), the battery pack is defective and should be replaced.

The remaining pins on the battery pack are typically used for thermal sensors and other communication between the mobile PC and the battery.

3. If the voltage across the battery terminals is less than the optimum value (usually less than +11.0 Vdc), the battery pack has probably been discharged through self-discharge (being left on the shelf) or use in the PC. Recharge the battery pack. If the voltage is still less than what the fully charged voltage should be after recharging, replace the battery pack.

4. If the voltage is more than +11.0 Vdc, measure the resistance between the thermal sensor and ground terminals (pins 3 and 4 in Figure 5-7). The resistance should be about 4 to 30 k$\Omega$. If the resistance is not correct, the thermal sensor has failed. This can make it impossible to charge the battery properly, so replace the battery pack.

5. If the resistance is correct, the battery charging circuit has probably failed.

Some batteries (like the Dell 14.4 Vdc Li-ion pack in Figure 5-8) include an onboard battery meter. This is a very handy feature because you can check the battery status without a voltmeter. Just press the button and check the LED indicators.

■  If all of the indicators are lit, the battery is fully charged and ready to be used. If it's not powering the laptop, it's a laptop problem—not a battery problem.

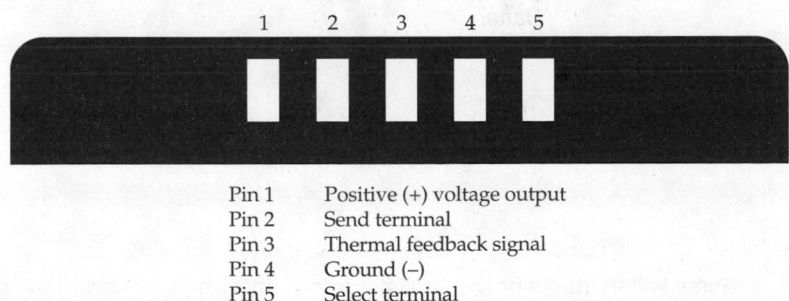

| | |
|---|---|
| Pin 1 | Positive (+) voltage output |
| Pin 2 | Send terminal |
| Pin 3 | Thermal feedback signal |
| Pin 4 | Ground (−) |
| Pin 5 | Select terminal |

**FIGURE  5-7**    Battery terminals for an IBM ThinkPad battery pack

■ If most (but not all) of the indicators are lit, the battery is not fully charged. Try charging the battery normally. If the battery doesn't charge properly (and other batteries do), the battery pack is failing and should be replaced.

■ If few (or none) of the indicators are lit, the battery is exhausted. Try charging the battery normally. If the battery doesn't charge properly (and other batteries do), the battery pack has failed and must be replaced.

### Recalibrate the Battery

Today's "smart" lithium-ion batteries are designed to communicate with your laptop system and provide the system with vital information about the amount of charge that remains in the battery pack—this feature allows your system to accurately monitor the amount of charge (or running time) left on your battery. To provide the proper information to your laptop, a battery must be *calibrated* so that it "knows" the difference between a full charge and an empty charge.

When your laptop goes into a standby mode prematurely and without warning (for example, while you're typing or watching a DVD video), it's possible that the battery has "forgotten" the difference between a full and empty charge. When this occurs, the battery may need to be *recalibrated*. The following steps outline a general procedure, but check with your laptop maker for more specific details:

1. Power-up your notebook.
2. Start the laptop's CMOS Setup routine.
3. Check the Advanced or Power Management menus and locate a Battery Calibrate or Recalibrate feature (some laptops refer to this function as "Recalibrate Gas Gauge").
4. Press ENTER. A screen opens prompting you to start the recalibration program.
5. Press ENTER to start discharging the battery. A message appears indicating the amount of time the discharge process will take.
6. When the battery has been fully discharged, the notebook will turn itself off.
7. You can now fully charge the battery, and the laptop's battery meter should display an accurate status of your battery's charge level.

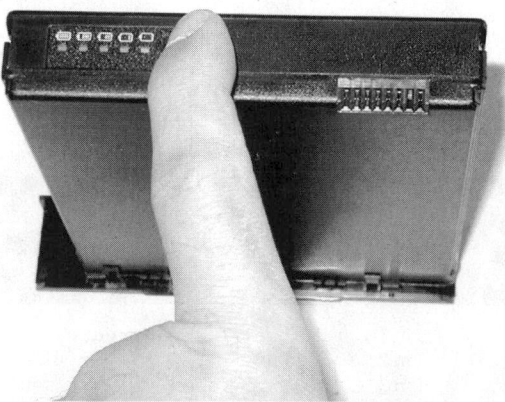

**FIGURE 5-8** Some battery packs provide an integrated battery meter that lets you check battery status without a voltmeter.

If you're connected to AC power, you'll be prompted to disconnect the AC power adapter (after you have disconnected the AC power, the discharge process should start automatically). You might need to repeat the recalibration procedure more than once.

## Symptoms

The following symptoms highlight a wide range of problems that you may encounter while working with rechargeable batteries:

**SYMPTOM 5-6** **You cannot deep discharge the main battery on your laptop**   Often, early laptop systems needed to *deep discharge* the main battery when battery life became shorter—this feature was designed to help correct the "memory" problem encountered with NiCd and some NiMH batteries. Some laptops (such as the Dell Latitude LX or Latitude M) provide a deep discharge feature. Each laptop has its own specific deep discharge procedure, but try the following guideline:

1. Reboot your system and enter the CMOS Setup. Select Power Management Control from the main menu.

2. Check for a submenu in Power Management Control, and then select the Deep Discharge option and enable it.

3. Save your changes and reboot the system again. When the system reboots, it will be in deep discharge mode—this means that it is using battery power as quickly as possible. Now allow the system to run on battery power until it powers-off.

4. Recharge the battery fully, and then repeat the process (you may need to repeat this process as many as three times). If your battery will still not hold a charge (or has a weak charge), you may need to replace the battery pack.

Use extreme caution when employing this tactic. Some batteries may not tolerate this deep discharge process very well, and battery damage may result. Check with the laptop maker to see if deep discharging is permitted (or if an alternative deep discharge process is recommended).

**SYMPTOM 5-7** **The battery pack does not charge**   In this type of situation, the computer may run fine from the AC-powered supply, and the system may very well run from a fully charged battery when the AC-powered supply is removed. However, the battery pack does not appear to charge when the AC supply is connected and running. Without a charge, the battery will eventually go dead. Remember that some computers (especially older laptops) may not recharge their battery packs while the system is on—the computer may have to be turned off with the AC supply connected in order for the battery pack to charge. Refer to the user manual for your particular system to review the correct charging protocol.

Your clue to the charging situation comes from the computer's battery status indicator. Most notebook/laptop systems incorporate a multicolor LED or an LCD status bar to show battery information. For example, the LED may be red when the small-computer is operating from its internal battery. Yellow may appear when the AC-powered supply is connected to indicate the battery is charging. The LED may turn green when the battery is fully charged. If the battery status indicator fails to show a charging color when the AC-powered supply is being used, that is often a good sign of trouble. Table 5-2 lists the status indicators for an IBM ThinkPad (check the user manual for your particular computer).

Check the battery pack with all computer power off. Make sure that the battery pack is inserted properly and completely into its compartment. Also check any cabling and connectors that attach the battery

**TABLE 5-2    STATUS INDICATORS FOR AN IBM THINKPAD COMPUTER**

| MODE | COLOR | MEANING |
|---|---|---|
| Charging | Green | Battery fully charged |
| | Orange | Battery charging |
| | Blinking orange | Battery needs charging |
| Conservation | Green | Computer is in suspend mode |
| | Blinking green | Computer is entering suspend mode or hibernation mode, or resuming normal operation |
| Status | Green | Power on |

pack to the charging circuit. Loose or corroded connectors, as well as faulty cable wiring, can prevent energy from the AC-powered supply from reaching the battery. Reseat any loose connectors and reattach any loose wiring that you may find.

After you are confident of your connections, you should trace charging voltage from the AC-powered supply to the battery terminals. If charging voltage does not reach the battery, the battery can never charge. Set your multimeter to measure DC voltage (probably in the 10 to 20 Vdc range), and measure the voltage across your battery pack. You should read some voltage below the pack's rated voltage because the battery pack is somewhat discharged. Now, connect the computer's AC-powered supply, and measure voltage across your battery pack again. If charging voltage is available to the battery, your voltage reading should climb *above* the battery pack's rated voltage (this causes charging current to flow back into the battery). If charging still does not seem to take place, try replacing the battery pack, which may be worn out or damaged. If charging voltage is not available to your battery pack, the charging circuit is probably faulty. Replace the charging circuit. Since the charging circuit is typically located on the motherboard, it may be necessary to replace the entire motherboard assembly.

**SYMPTOM 5-8**    **The system does not run on battery power, but runs properly from main (AC) power**    This symptom usually suggests that your computer runs fine whenever the AC-powered supply is being used, but the system will not run from battery power alone. The system may or may not initialize, depending on the extent of the problem. Before you disassemble the computer or attempt any sort of repair, make sure that you have a fully charged battery pack in the system. Remove the battery pack and measure the voltage across its terminals. You should read approximately the battery voltage marked on the pack (e.g., 14.4 Vdc for a Li-ion pack). A measurably lower voltage may indicate that the battery is not fully charged. Try a different battery pack, or try to let the battery pack recharge. The charging process may take several hours on older systems, but newer small-computer battery systems can charge in an hour or so. If the battery will not charge (or hold a charge), the battery may be failing.

When you have a fully charged battery, check to be sure that it is inserted completely and connected properly. Inspect any wiring and connectors that attach the battery pack to its load circuit. Faulty wiring, corroded connections, or loose connectors can cut off the battery pack entirely. At this point, it is safe to assume that battery power is not reaching the laptop circuit(s). In this event, the battery charging/protection circuit may be defective and should be replaced. If the circuit is incorporated into the motherboard, the motherboard should be replaced.

**SYMPTOM 5-9    Your laptop no longer has a Standby option on the Shutdown menu**

This is a classic symptom that sometimes appeared with APM-based laptops using older operating systems like Windows 98/SE. You notice that the plug icon always appears in the system tray while using battery power (rather than the battery icon). In virtually all cases, you'll need to reinstall the laptop's *Advanced Power Management* (APM) feature. Here is the process for Windows 98:

1. Shut down all running applications.

2. Choose Start | Settings | Control Panel, and then double-click the System icon.

3. Click the Device Manager tab, and then click the View Devices by Type radio button.

4. Click the plus (+) next to System Devices, select Advanced Power Management, select Remove, and then click OK. Restart the system when prompted to do so.

5. Once the system has rebooted, click Start | Settings | Control Panel, and then double-click the Add New Hardware icon.

6. Click Next to search for new hardware. Click Next again to search for any new plug-and-play devices. The system may find new hardware (and list the items). If Advanced Power Management Support is not listed, select Yes for Windows to search for your new hardware, and then click Next to begin the search.

7. Once device detection is finished, select Details—it should find Advanced Power Management Support.

8. Select Finish to begin the installation. The system will prompt you to insert your Windows 98 CD. After the necessary files are installed, you'll be promoted to reboot the system.

9. Once the system has rebooted, the system will find the APM Battery Slot.

After the system finishes booting, click Start, select Shut Down, and you should see Standby as one of the Shutdown options. Switch from AC power to battery power, and the plug icon should change to a battery icon. If you're using a newer operating system like Windows Me/XP, chances are that your laptop is supporting ACPI, and probably will not suffer from this type of symptom. However, if you're upgrading Windows on an older APM-based laptop, try the following steps:

1. Shut down all running applications.

2. Select Start | Control Panel | Performance and Maintenance.

3. Double-click the System icon and select the Hardware tab.

4. Click the Device Manager button.

5. Click the plus (+) next to System Devices, right-click Advanced Power Management (if it exists on your system), select Uninstall, and then click OK. Restart the system when prompted to do so.

6. Once the system has rebooted, return to the Device Manager, select Action, and choose Scan for Hardware Changes.

7. Once device detection is finished, Advanced Power Management Support should be listed, and you should be able to enable this on the laptop (you may need to insert the Windows XP installation CD for needed files).

8. After the necessary files are installed, you'll be promoted to reboot the system.

9. Once the system has rebooted, APM should be re-enabled. Check the shutdown options to see that the Standby option is available. Switch from AC power to battery power, and the plug icon should change to a battery icon.

**SYMPTOM 5-10** **The system suffers from a short battery life** Today's mobile computers are designed to squeeze up to six hours of operation (or more) from every charge. Most systems get at least two hours from a charge. Short battery life can present a perplexing problem—especially if you do a great deal of computing on the road. All other computer functions are assumed to be normal.

Begin your investigation by inspecting the battery pack itself. Check for any damaged batteries. Make sure the battery pack is inserted properly into the computer, and see that its connections and wiring are clean and intact. Try replacing the battery pack. Keep in mind that rechargeable batteries do not last forever. Typical NiCd packs are usually good for about 500 cycles, NiMH packs are often suitable for up to 800 cycles, and Li-ion packs are usually rated for 800 to 1000 cycles. Fast-charge battery packs are subject to the greatest abuse and can suffer the shortest life spans. It is possible that one or more cells in the battery pack may have failed. The battery pack may also have developed a "memory" problem. Try several cycles of completely discharging and recharging the pack. If the problem remains, replace the battery pack.

The computer's configuration itself can largely determine the amount of running time that is available from each charge. The CPU, the display (and its backlight), the hard drive, and floppy drive/CD-ROM drive access consume substantial amounts of power. Many mobile computers are designed to shut down each major power consumer after some preset period of disuse. For example, an LCD screen may shut off if there is no keyboard activity after two minutes, or the hard drive may stop spinning after three minutes if there is no hard drive access, and so on. Even reducing CPU clock speed during periods of inactivity (a.k.a. processor throttling) will reduce power consumption. The amount of time required before shutdown can usually be adjusted through setup routines in the computer or through the operating system. See the "Conserving Mobile Battery Power" section earlier in the chapter.

**SYMPTOM 5-11** **The battery pack becomes extremely hot during charging** Current must be applied to a battery from an external source in order to restore battery charge. When a battery receives significant charging current (during or after the charging process), its temperature will begin to rise. Temperature rise continues as long as current is applied. If high charging current continues unabated, battery temperature may climb high enough to actually damage the cells. Even under the best circumstances, prolonged high-temperature conditions can shorten the working life of a battery pack. Today's high-current charging circuits must be carefully controlled to ensure a full, rapid battery charge and to prevent excessive temperature rise and damage.

Battery packs or compartments are fitted with a *thermistor* (a temperature-sensitive resistor). When the battery pack is fully charged, the thermistor responds to the subsequent temperature increase and signals charging circuitry to reduce or stop its charging current. In this way, temperature is used to detect when full charge has been reached. It is normal for most battery packs to become a bit warm during the charging process—especially packs that use fast-charge currents. However, the cell(s) should not give off an obnoxious odor or become too hot to touch. Hot batteries are likely to be damaged. In many cases, the thermistor (or thermistor's signal conditioning circuitry) has failed and is no longer shutting down charge current. Try another battery pack. If the new pack also becomes very hot, the fault is in the charging circuit, which should be replaced. If the new pack remains cooler, the fault is probably in the original battery pack.

**SYMPTOM 5-12**   **After several days of disuse, your laptop may not power up properly**
This may happen regardless of whether you use the AC adapter or battery. You find that the battery shows a full charge. The system may have failed to detect (or have misdetected) the available power. With the system powered off, unplug the AC adapter from the back of the computer, and remove the battery from the case so that both power sources are removed. Then replace the battery and AC adapter cord before turning the unit on—your laptop should power up normally.

**SYMPTOM 5-13**   **Your laptop locks up if you hot- or warm-swap a CD-ROM module with a battery**   This lockup is caused from system detection problems. If a CD-ROM drive is detected by Windows at boot time, and then at some point that drive is removed, the operating system is not made aware of this (and will attempt to poll the device when My Computer is opened). At this point, the operating system will continue to wait for a response from the device until it times out. This can take anywhere from four to six minutes—during which the system appears to be locked up. Operating systems like Windows Me/XP should support such device swapping, but your laptop hardware must specifically support it also. If in doubt, place the laptop into a Suspend or Hibernate state first, "warm swap" the device, resume the system, and let Windows detect any changes.

Swapping problems are caused whenever the OS and hardware fail to cooperate. Today's PC hardware and operating systems like Windows XP are more forgiving of device swapping/docking.

**SYMPTOM 5-14**   **A "battery problem" indicator comes on and will not go out**   The system appears to work normally. This is a known problem on systems like the Gateway Solo 2300/9100 and is almost always caused by a problem with the BIOS. Generally, a BIOS upgrade will correct the problem and allow the computer to communicate properly with the "smart" battery. Once the BIOS is upgraded, be sure to charge the battery to 100 percent. If the battery indicator light still turns red, it should only last four to five seconds, and then return to orange (charging) or green (charged fully).

**SYMPTOM 5-15**   **The computer quits without producing a low-battery warning**
Computers are rarely subtle with regard to low-power warnings. Once a battery pack falls below a certain voltage threshold, the computer initiates a series of unmistakable audible (and sometimes visual) cues that tell you there are only minutes of power remaining. Such a warning affords you a last-minute opportunity to save your work and switch over to AC power if possible. If you choose to ignore a low-power warning, the system will soon reach a minimum working level and crash.

Mobile computers measure their battery voltage levels constantly. A custom chip on the motherboard is typically given the task of watching over battery voltage. When voltage falls below a preset level, the detector chip produces a logic alarm signal. The alarm, in turn, drives an interrupt to the CPU, or passes the signal to a power management chip, which then deals with the CPU or system controller. Once the alarm condition reaches the CPU, the computer typically initiates a series of tones, flashes a "power" LED, or sometimes both (see Table 5-2 earlier).

Most PCs produce at least one beep during initialization in order to test the internal speaker. If you do not hear this beep, the speaker or its driving circuit may be damaged. Try replacing the speaker; then try replacing the motherboard. When a beep is heard during initialization, there is probably a fault in the computer's battery detection or power management circuits. Try cleaning the battery contacts first, and then try replacing the laptop's motherboard.

**SYMPTOM 5-16**     **Your battery indicator displays a 0 percent charge, even though the battery has been fully charged**     After attempting to charge a laptop's battery, the battery may display a status of 0 percent (and may not accept a charge). This typically occurs only after the battery has been left completely discharged for an extended time, or after a fully charged battery has been left completely out of a computer for several months or more. This issue is often avoided by regularly charging the battery. For example, seat or reseat the battery and AC adapter as necessary, and (with the computer plugged into the adapter) allow the battery to charge up to approximately 100 percent. Here are some tips to resolve the issue:

- Verify that the latest version of the computer's BIOS is installed on the system.
- Reseat the battery and AC adapter to ensure a good connection.
- If your laptop uses battery monitoring/conditioning software, be sure to install the latest version (which can typically be downloaded directly from the laptop manufacturer).
- If the battery still shows 0 percent (or does not accept a charge), the battery may be defective and need to be replaced.

# Battery Recycling

Most types of batteries use metals and electrolyte chemicals that are harmful to the environment. As a consequence, many states and provinces have enacted legislation that prohibits the dumping or discarding of batteries (especially lead-acid, NiCd, and alkaline). NiMH and lithium batteries are somewhat less toxic, but often can also be recycled. To support a cleaner environment, many vendors who sell PC batteries are accepting returns of the old defective batteries to be recycled.

Before purchasing new batteries, verify that the vendor will accept your spent batteries—if not, contact your local town recycling center to see if they will take exhausted batteries. For example, 1-800-Batteries (a major battery vendor) accepts returns (at 408-879-1930). IBM is now offering a PC recycling program. For the relatively low cost of $29.99 (including UPS shipping), you can send your old PC along with your monitor and printer to Envirocycle, where they will recycle any manufacturer's system in an "environmentally friendly" manner, or refurbish the system and arrange for its donation to Gifts in Kind International. You can learn more about IBM's recycling offer at www.ibm.com/news/2000/11/ 142.phtml. As another alternative, contact the Rechargeable Battery Recycling Corporation at 1-800-822-8837 (or online at www.rbrc.org). They will provide you with the address of the recycling center nearest to you.

# Further Study

**Direct Power**   www.dpp.com/index.html
**Duracell**   www.duracell.com
**Energizer**   www.energizer.com
**Fedco**   www.fedcoelectronics.com
**Rayovac**   www.rayovac.com
**Rechargeable Battery Recycling Corp**   www.rbrc.org
**Tadiran**   www.tadiranbat.com
**Varta**   www.varta.com/index.html

# 6

# BIOS

**A**lthough every personal computer uses the same essential subassemblies, each subassembly is designed a bit differently. This is especially true of the processing components (that is, chipsets and controllers) contained on a motherboard. This is understandable given the tremendous speed at which PC components and technology continue to advance. Unfortunately, such dramatic variations in hardware make it difficult to use a single standard operating system. Instead of tailoring an operating system (and applications) to specific computer hardware configurations, a *basic input/output system* (BIOS or "firmware") is added on ROM chips to provide an interface between the raw PC hardware and a standardized operating system like Windows XP. BIOS (such as the replaceable chip in Figure 6-1) gives an OS access to a standard set of functions. As a result, every system uses a slightly different BIOS, but each BIOS references the same set of functions that an OS can interface to. This chapter focuses on the major players in the development of BIOS software for the PC. They are American Megatrends (AMI), Phoenix Technologies, and Award Software (acquired by Phoenix Technologies in 1998). Additionally, this chapter explains the internal workings of a typical BIOS, illustrates some means of identifying BIOS versions, and shows you the many features a modern BIOS must support.

Although most BIOS versions carry enough routines to support video and drive controller operations in addition to other motherboard features, BIOS is not limited solely to the motherboard. What happens when a new video card is developed that the system BIOS does not know how to work with, or an advanced drive controller board becomes available? A common practice in computer design is to include firmware for major subsystems such as video and drive controllers. One of the early steps of system initialization is to check for the presence of other valid firmware ROMs located in upper memory (between 640KB and 1024KB). These are usually referred to as "expansion," "option," or "adapter" ROMs. When another BIOS is located, it is also checksum-tested and used by the PC.

# Typical Motherboard BIOS

The typical BIOS ROM occupies 128KB of space in the system's *upper memory area* (UMA) from E0000h to FFFFFh (within the PC's first megabyte of memory). Contrary to popular belief, BIOS is not a single program, but an arsenal of individual routines—most quite small. In general, BIOS code supports three important tasks: the *power-on self-test* (POST), the *CMOS Setup* routine, and the *system service* routines. The particular section of BIOS code that is executed depends on the computer's state and its activities at any given moment.

Replaceable
BIOS chip

**FIGURE  6-1**    Like most motherboards, the Soyo P4I FireDragon includes firmware as a replaceable chip (Courtesy of Motherboards.org).

## POWER-ON SELF-TEST (POST)

Although many novice technicians are aware that POST checks the system, few are aware that POST actually manages the entire system startup. The power-on self-test handles virtually all of the initialization activities for a PC. POST performs a low-level diagnostic and reliability test of the main processing components—including ROM programs and system RAM. It tests the CPU, initializes the motherboard's chipset, checks the 128 bytes (or more) of CMOS for system configuration data, and sets up an index of interrupt vectors for the CPU from 0000h to 02FFh. POST then sets up a BIOS Stack Area from 0300h to 03FFh, loads the *BIOS Data Area* (BDA) in low memory 0400h to 04FFh, detects any optional equipment (adapter BIOS ROMs) in the system, and proceeds to boot the operating system from an available disk.

## CMOS SETUP ROUTINE

The hardware configuration for any given computer is maintained in a small amount of very low-power CMOS RAM, and a CMOS Setup routine is required for you to access the system's configuration. Older i286 and i386 systems provided the CMOS Setup routine as a separate utility included with the system on a floppy disk. In most cases, the setup disk was promptly misplaced or discarded. Starting with late-model i386 and later systems, the CMOS Setup routine has been integrated into the motherboard BIOS itself. At boot time, the POST gathers information about the system's hardware and compares it with the settings in CMOS RAM. If the information matches, the hardware is deemed to be operational and the boot process may continue. Otherwise, the boot process halts and a "system setup" error appears. The actual CMOS Setup program can vary tremendously between system manufacturers and motherboards, so there is no one standard for what settings can be controlled, or where those entries are located.

Many Compaq systems place the setup routine on a *diagnostic partition* on the hard drive. If the drive fails (or is repartitioned), the diagnostic partition may be lost—it may be impossible to adjust the system's configuration until the diagnostic partition is restored.

## SYSTEM SERVICE ROUTINES

The system services (also referred to as *BIOS services*) are a set of individual functions that form the normal operating layer between hardware and the operating system. It is this versatility that allows a single operating system to work with such a proliferation of motherboard designs, bus architectures, processor types, chipsets, and expansion devices. Services are called through the use of interrupts. An *interrupt* essentially causes the CPU to stop whatever it was working on and send program control to another address in memory that usually starts a subroutine designed specifically to deal with the particular interrupt. When the interrupt handling routine is complete, the CPU's original state is restored, and control is returned to where the PC left off before the interrupt occurred. There is a wide range of interrupts that can attract the attention of a CPU, and interrupts can be produced from three major sources: the CPU itself, a hardware condition, and a software condition.

Interrupts produced by the CPU itself (known as *processor interrupts*) are often the result of an unusual, unexpected, or erroneous program result. For example, if a program tries to divide a number by zero, the CPU will generate INT 00h, which causes a "Divide by zero" error message. There are five processor interrupts (00h to 04h).

The *hardware interrupts* are generated when a device needs the CPU's attention to perform a certain task, and these are the system resources that we are most familiar with. Hardware interrupts are invoked by asserting a logic level on a physical *interrupt request* (IRQ) line. The CPU suspends its activities and executes the interrupt handling routine. When the interrupt handler is finished, the CPU resumes normal operation. For example, each time a keyboard key is pressed, the keyboard buffer asserts a logic line corresponding to INT 09h (IRQ 1). This invokes a keyboard handling routine. PC/AT-compatible systems typically provide 16 hardware interrupts (IRQ 0 to IRQ 15) that correspond to INT 08h to 0Fh and 70h to 77h, respectively.

*Software interrupts* are generated when a hardware device must be checked or manipulated by the PC. The "print screen" function is a prime example of a software interrupt. When the PRINTSCREEN button is pressed on the keyboard, an INT 05h is generated. The interrupt routine dumps the contents of its video character buffer to the printer port.

# BIOS Features

PC technology is constantly advancing in CPUs, chipsets, memory, video, drives, and so on. As the hardware continues to advance, the BIOS must also advance to keep pace with the resources emerging on today's systems. As a result, it is important for you to recognize the key features that are included in a modern BIOS. You do not need to understand the details of each feature right now, but you should at least recognize a "current" BIOS by reviewing its feature set.

- **CPU support** BIOS should support a rich range of CPUs, preferably from various CPU makers like Intel, AMD, and Cyrix. Look for Pentium II/III/4 and AMD Athlon/Duron support (though one BIOS may not support *all* these CPU families).

- **Chipset support** The BIOS should support the latest chipset families (such as Intel's 840 or 850 chipset). Chipset support is critical because the chipset allows motherboard designers to implement other features like power management, USB, and advanced memory architectures such as DDR SDRAM or Rambus.

- **Memory support** The BIOS should be able to autosize and support the most modern forms of memory (for example, SDRAM, DDR SDRAM, and Rambus). Memory error checking (such as "parity" and "ECC") should also be supported. Modern BIOS can support up to 4GB of RAM (far more for servers), though the system's motherboard may not handle that much.

- **Power management support** The BIOS should fully comply with the *Advanced Configuration and Power Interface* (ACPI) specification (revision 1.0 or later), and support APM BIOS specifications through version 1.2 or later. Power management is vitally important for mobile systems and is widely used in desktop/tower systems to reduce energy waste. The BIOS should also support DPMS (*Display Power Management System*) for monitors and other display devices.

- **Drive support** The BIOS must support 32-bit disk transfers and huge Ultra-ATA hard drives (over 1024 cylinders) with very fast data transfer modes like Ultra-DMA/66, and Ultra-DMA/100/133. It is increasingly common for BIOS to support (even boot from) removable media devices such as CD-ROM/R/RW and Zip. In some cases, the BIOS may even include support for basic RAID functions such as RAID 0 (striping).

- **PC 2001 support** The BIOS should comply with the current Microsoft PC 2001 BIOS requirements (or later).

- **$I^2O$ support** The BIOS may support $I^2O$ (Intelligent I/O), which allows the dynamic assignment of ports and resources for I/O devices in the PC. This is more commonly found in server platforms.

- **Boot versatility support** The BIOS should be able to boot from a number of different drives, and include the BIOS Boot Specification for *Initial Program Load* (IPL) devices. This currently supports booting from up to four IDE-type drives (including all types of CD drives), SCSI drives, and network cards. Boot support for removable media drives (e.g., Iomega Zip or SyQuest drives) is an advantage.

■ **Plug-and-play support**    The BIOS must detect and configure PnP devices during POST. The BIOS also communicates with Windows 9*x*/Me/XP to determine system resources, and to support IRQ Steering for PCI bus devices.

■ **Parallel port support**    The BIOS should support a full range of parallel port modes including *Standard Parallel Port* (SPP or "compatibility" mode), bi-directional mode, *Enhanced Capabilities Port* (ECP), and *Enhanced Parallel Port* (EPP)—collectively part of the IEEE 1284 standard.

■ **PCI and AGP support**    The BIOS must support Intel's *Peripheral Component Interconnect* (PCI) bus specification (version 2.1 or later), including PCI-to-PCI and PCI-to-ISA bridging. The BIOS must also support the Accelerated Graphics Port (AGP) version 2.0 or later.

■ **USB support**    The BIOS should support both Universal and Open HCI standards. It should maintain full core compatibility and provide legacy support for USB hardware and multilayered USB hubs. You may also find support for USB 2.0 (high-speed USB) in current BIOS versions.

■ **Anti-virus protection**    The BIOS should offer the option of virus protection. At a minimum, the BIOS should prevent changes to the master boot record (often a classic sign of virus activity).

Table 6-1 outlines the extensive feature set for current Award BIOS.

Whether you're trying to learn the capabilities of your current BIOS or planning a BIOS upgrade, you can learn a lot about a BIOS and its features by studying the BIOS ID codes. This part of the chapter explains several means of identifying popular BIOS versions and will help you to understand the information encoded in the BIOS ID string.

---

**TABLE 6-1    SPECIFICATION LIST FOR A RECENT VERSION OF AWARD BIOS**

**TECHNOLOGY SUPPORT**

| | |
|---|---|
| ACPI/APM | Award BIOS complies with the Advanced Configuration and Power Interface (ACPI) specification, revision 1.0, and supports APM BIOS specifications through 1.2. |
| NetPC | NetPC support in Award BIOS lowers the Total Cost of Ownership of computer systems. |
| PC 2001 | Award BIOS complies with PC 2001 requirements. |
| Managed PC | Award BIOS implements software to support the Managed PC initiative. |
| I²O (Intelligent I/O) | Award BIOS supports I²O architecture—handy on server platforms. |
| System Management BIOS | The SMBIOS specification is a successor to the Desktop Management BIOS specification, and is fully supported in the Award BIOS. |
| Plug and Play | Award BIOS detects and configures PnP devices during POST and, through its PnP extensions, communicates with Windows to determine system resources. |
| PCI | Award BIOS supports Intel's Peripheral Component Interconnect (PCI) bus specification ver. 2.1, including PCI-to-PCI and PCI-to-ISA bridging. |
| USB | The Award BIOS USB module supports both Universal and Open HCI standards, maintaining full core compatibility and providing legacy support for USB HID (human input device) hardware and multilayered USB hubs. |

**TABLE 6-1    SPECIFICATION LIST FOR A RECENT VERSION OF AWARD BIOS *(CONTINUED)***

### INDUSTRY STANDARDS SUPPORTED

| |
|---|
| ACPI, SMBIOS (DMI), USB |
| BIOS Boot Specification |
| Plug-and-Play |
| PC Card |
| Legacy PC AT ISRs and DSRs |
| PC2001 |

### CPU SUPPORT

| |
|---|
| Intel, AMD, Cyrix, IBM, TI, IDT, and so on |
| Low-power SMM & SMI |

### CHIPSET SUPPORT

| |
|---|
| ACC, ALI, AMD, Intel, ITE, NSC, OPTi, SiS, UMC, VIA, and so on |

### BUS SUPPORT

| |
|---|
| PCI, ISA, EISA, VL-Bus |
| PCI-to-PCI & PCI-to-ISA bridging |

### POWER MANAGEMENT

| |
|---|
| ACPI 1.0 and APM 1.2 |

### PLUG-AND-PLAY READY

| |
|---|
| Resource allocation for PCI and PnP/legacy ISA busses |

### OPERATING SYSTEM READY

| |
|---|
| DOS/MS Windows 3.*x* |
| MS Windows NT/2000 |
| MS Windows 95/98/Me/XP |
| OS/2 Warp |
| NetWare |
| SCO UNIX |
| RTOS |

### DRIVE SUPPORT

| |
|---|
| HDD, FDD, and ATAPI CD drives |
| Selectable boot drive options, including CD-ROM, LS-120, SCSI, Iomega Zip, and network cards |
| Auto-IDE detection |
| "Fast" DMA transfer/Ultra DMA |
| PIO modes 0-4 |
| High-performance LBA transfers |
| Hard drives over 8.4 GB |
| Extensive POST |

### OPTION ROM SUPPORT

| |
|---|
| SCSI |
| Video |
| PC Card boot |
| Ethernet |

**TABLE 6-1     SPECIFICATION LIST FOR A RECENT VERSION OF AWARD BIOS (CONTINUED)**

**FLASH SUPPORT**

Boot block BIOS for fault recovery

**MEMORY MANAGEMENT**

RAM support up to 4GB

Auto-memory chipset sizing

Auto-sizing for cache mapping

System and video BIOS shadowing

Memory parity check

ECC support

**OPTIONS**

Bus-mastering support

Fast gate A20 support

PS/2-style mouse support

Combo-I/O controller support

HDD LBA mode support

Tick timer support

Watchdog timer support

CMOS backup

Award Preboot Agent for remote system management and troubleshooting

LM78 support and GUI utility

**UTILITIES**

AWDFLASH flash update

CBROM binary combiner

NVRAM archive/restore

PCI configuration manager

EISA configuration utility

**SECURITY PRODUCTS**

Boot sector virus protection

Multi-level password protection

# AMI BIOS

American Megatrends (AMI) has been a major player in the development of leading BIOS versions for the PC and has been very popular with Pacific Rim motherboard makers. (Though popularity with domestic U.S. motherboard makers is growing.) The AMI BIOS code appears in the lower portion of the POST display—usually during the memory count. The code's format will indicate the relative age of the BIOS. The following format indicates an older AMI BIOS made between 1986 and 1990:

```
DINT-1123-040990-K8
```

This older BIOS code uses an **AAAA-BBBB-DDMMYY-Kx** format where:

■ **AAAA**   *BIOS type*. This includes chipset identification codes.

■ **BBBB**   *AMI customer reference number*. This code identifies the motherboard manufacturer that AMI tailored the BIOS for (see Table 6-2 to reference the motherboard maker).

■ **DDMMYY**   *BIOS release date*. This is in day/month/year format.

■ **Kx**   *Keyboard BIOS*. This indicates the revision level of the keyboard BIOS code.

A more recent AMI BIOS (released after 1990) normally appears as shown next:

`51-0102-zz`**`5123`**`-00111111-101094-AMIS123-P`

This recent BIOS code uses an **A#-BBBB-CCCCC-DDDDDDDD-EEEEE-FFFFFFFF-G** format where:

■ **A**   *CPU type*. This code identifies the CPU vintage, where 0 = 8086 (or 8088), 2 = 80286, 3 = 80386, 4 = 80486, 5 = Pentium, and so on.

■ **#**   *BIOS size*. This code tells the size of the BIOS chip, where 0 = 64KB, and 1 = 128KB.

■ **BBBB**   *BIOS version number*. This is the main version number that you would use to identify the BIOS currently on the system.

■ **CCCCC**   *AMI customer reference number*. This code identifies the motherboard manufacturer that AMI tailored the BIOS for. (See Table 6-2 to reference the motherboard maker.)

■ **DDDDDDDD**   *AMIBCP settings*. This is a set of eight logical "flags" that define several key operating parameters of the BIOS (0 = no, 1 = yes):

1   Halt on error during POST.
2   Initialize CMOS RAM at every boot.
3   Keyboard controller output pin 23, 24 blocked.
4   Mouse support in BIOS and keyboard controller.
5   Wait for in case of POST error.
6   Display floppy error during POST.
7   Display video error during POST.
8   Display keyboard error during POST.

■ **EEEEE**   *BIOS release date*. This is in day/month/year format.

■ **FFFFFFFF**   *BIOS type*. This includes chipset identification codes.

■ **G**   *Keyboard BIOS*. This indicates the revision level of the keyboard BIOS code.

In this version, the BIOS identification number for this BIOS identification string would be zz5123. If the first of the **bold** numbers is

■ **1, 2, 8**, or a **letter**, you have a non-AMI Taiwanese-manufactured motherboard.

■ **3, 4,** or **5**, you have a true AMI motherboard.

■ **50** or **6**, you have a non-AMI U.S.-made motherboard.

■ **9**, you have an evaluation BIOS for a Taiwanese manufacturer.

The second set of numbers (BBBB or 1123 in this case) would immediately identify the BIOS as a Non-AMI foreign-made motherboard. The complete code identifies Magtron Technology Co., Ltd. (from Table 6-2) as the consumer of this BIOS version released on 09/04/90. The second set of numbers (5123) would indicate that the motherboard is a true AMI motherboard (not listed in Table 6-2).

 AMI provides a utility called AMIMBID that is designed to help technicians identify the manufacturer of a motherboard using AMI BIOS. You can obtain the utility from www.ami.com/support/mbid.html.

### TABLE 6-2    AMI OEM IDENTIFICATION CODES

| NON-U.S. MOTHERBOARD MANUFACTURERS | | NON-U.S. MOTHERBOARD MANUFACTURERS | |
| --- | --- | --- | --- |
| Code | Customer | Code | Customer |
| 1101 | Sunlogix, Inc. | 1147 | Integrated Technology Express, Inc. |
| 1102 | Soyo Technology Co., Ltd. | 1150 | Achitec Corp. Ltd. |
| 1105 | Autocomputer Co., Ltd. | 1151 | Accos Enterprise Co., Ltd. |
| 1106 | Dynasty Computer Inc. | 1152 | Top-Thunder Technology Co., Ltd. |
| 1107 | DataExpert Corp. | 1154 | San Li Technology Co., Ltd. |
| 1108 | Chaplet Systems Inc. | 1156 | Technica House Inc. |
| 1109 | Fair Friend Ent. Co., Ltd. | 1158 | Hi-Com Industrial Co., Ltd. |
| 1111 | Paoku P&C Co., Ltd. | 1159 | Twinhead International Corp. |
| 1112 | Aquarius Systems Inc. | 1161 | Monterey International Corp. |
| 1113 | Micro Leader Enterprises Corp. | 1163 | Softek Systems Co., Ltd. |
| 1114 | Iwill Corp. | 1165 | Mercury Computer Corp. |
| 1115 | Senor Science Co., Ltd. | 1169 | Micro-Star International Co., Ltd. |
| 1116 | Chicony Electronics Co., Ltd. | 1170 | Taiwan Igel Co., Ltd. |
| 1117 | A-Trend Technology Co., Ltd. | 1171 | Shing Yunn Electronics Enterprise Corp. |
| 1120 | Unicorn Computer Corp. | 1176 | Sigma Computer Corp. |
| 1121 | First International Computer, Inc. | 1178 | Clevo Co. |
| 1122 | Microstar Computer Corp. | 1188 | Quanta Computer Inc. |
| 1123 | Magtron Technology Co., Ltd. | 1195 | GNS Technologies Inc. |
| 1124 | Tekram Technology Co., Ltd. | 1196 | Universal Scientific Industrial Co. |
| 1126 | Chuntex Elex., Co., Ltd. | 1197 | Golden Way Electronic Corp. |
| 1128 | Chaintech Computer Co., Ltd. | 1199 | GigaByte Co., Ltd. |
| 1130 | Pai Jung Electronic Ind. Co., Ltd. | 1201 | New Tech International Co., Ltd. |
| 1131 | Elitegroup Computer Co., Ltd. | 1203 | Sunrex Technology Corp. |
| 1132 | Dkine Enterprise Co., Ltd. | 1204 | Bestek Computer Co., Ltd. |
| 1133 | Seritech Enterprise Co., Ltd. | 1209 | Puretek Industrial Co., Ltd. |
| 1135 | Acer Inc. | 1210 | Rise Computer Inc. |
| 1136 | Sun's Electronics Co., Ltd. | 1211 | Diamond Flower Electronic Co., Ltd. |
| 1138 | Win-Win Electronic Co., Ltd. | 1214 | Rever Computer Inc. |
| 1140 | Angine Ltd. Taiwan Branch (H.K.) | 1218 | Elite Computer Co., Ltd. |
| 1141 | Nuseed Technology Inc. | 1223 | Biostar Microtech International Corp. |
| 1142 | Firich Enterprises Co., Ltd. | 1225 | Yunglin Technology Corp. |
| 1143 | Crete Systems Inc. | 1234 | Leadman Electronic Co., Ltd. |
| 1144 | Vista Technology Co., Ltd. | 1241 | Mustek Corp. |
| 1146 | Taste Corp. | 1242 | Amptek Technology Co., Ltd. |

## TABLE 6-2    AMI OEM IDENTIFICATION CODES *(CONTINUED)*

| NON-U.S. MOTHERBOARD MANUFACTURERS | | NON-U.S. MOTHERBOARD MANUFACTURERS | |
|------|-----------------------------------|------|-----------------------------------|
| Code | Customer | Code | Customer |
| 1244 | Flytech Technology Co., Ltd. | 1440 | Great Electronics Corp. |
| 1246 | Cosmotech Computer Corp. | 1451 | Ecel Systems Corp. |
| 1247 | Abit Computer Corp. | 1452 | United Hitech Corp. |
| 1256 | Lucky Star Technology Co., Ltd. | 1453 | Kai Mei Electronic Corp. |
| 1258 | Four Star Computer Co., Ltd. | 1461 | Hedonic Computer Co., Ltd. |
| 1259 | GVC Corp. | 1462 | Arche Technologies Inc. |
| 1262 | Arima Computer Corp. | 1470 | Flexus Computer Technology |
| 1266 | Modula Tech. Co., Ltd. | 1472 | Datacom Technology Co., Ltd. |
| 1271 | Tidal Technologies Inc. | 1484 | Mitac International Corp. |
| 1273 | UFO Computer Co., Ltd. | 1490 | Great Tek Corp. |
| 1274 | Full Yes Industrial Corp. | 1491 | President Technology Inc. |
| 1276 | Jet Way Information Co., Ltd. | 1493 | Artdex Computer Corp. |
| 1277 | Tarng Bow Co., Ltd. | 1494 | Pro Team Computer Corp. |
| 1281 | EFA Corp. | 1500 | Netcon Co., Ltd. |
| 1283 | Advance Creative Computer Corp. | 1503 | Up Right Tech Co., Ltd. |
| 1284 | Lung Hwa Electronics Co., Ltd. | 1514 | Wuu Lin Electronics Co., Ltd. |
| 1291 | Taiwan Mycomp Co., Ltd. | 1519 | Epox Computer Co., Ltd. |
| 1292 | AsusTek Computer Inc. | 1526 | Eagle Computer Technology Co., Ltd. |
| 1297 | DD&TT Enterprise Inc. | 1531 | Force System Inc. |
| 1301 | Taken Corp. | 1540 | BCM Computers Co., Ltd. |
| 1304 | Dual Enterprises Corp. | 1546 | Golden Horse Computer Co., Ltd. |
| 1309 | Protronic Enterprises Corp. | 1549 | CT Continental Corp. |
| 1317 | New Comm Technology Co., Ltd. | 1564 | Random Technology Inc. |
| 1318 | Unitron Inc. | 1576 | Jetta Computer Co., Ltd. |
| 1343 | Holco Enterprise Co., Ltd. | 1585 | Gleem Industries Co., Ltd. |
| 1346 | Snobol Industrial Corp. | 1588 | Boser Technology Co., Ltd. |
| 1351 | Singdak Electronic Co., Ltd. | 1593 | Advantech Co., Ltd. |
| 1353 | J. Bond Computer Systems Corp. | 1608 | Consolidated Marketing Corp. |
| 1354 | Protech Systems Co., Ltd. | 1612 | Datavan International Corp. |
| 1367 | Coxswain Technology Co. Ltd. | 1617 | Honotron Corp. |
| 1371 | ADI Corp. | 1618 | Union Genius Computer Co., Ltd. |
| 1373 | Silicon Integrated Systems Corp. | 1621 | New Paradise Enterprise Co., Ltd. |
| 1379 | Win Technologies Co., Ltd. | 1622 | R.P.T. Intergroups International Ltd. |
| 1391 | Aten International Co., Ltd. | 1628 | Digital Equipment International Ltd. |
| 1392 | Acc Taiwan Inc. | 1630 | Iston Computer Corp. |
| 1393 | Plato Technology Co., Ltd. | 1647 | Lantic Inc. |
| 1396 | Tatung Co. | 1652 | ASE Technologies Inc. |
| 1398 | Spring Circle Computer Inc. | 1655 | Kingston Technology Inc. |
| 1404 | Alptech Logic Products Inc. | 1656 | Storage System Inc. |
| 1421 | Well Join Industry Co., Ltd. | 1658 | Macrotek International Corp. |
| 1422 | Labway Computer Co., Ltd. | 1666 | Cast Technology Inc. |
| 1437 | Hsing Tech Enterprise Co., Ltd. | 1671 | Cordial Far East Corp. |

**TABLE 6-2    AMI OEM IDENTIFICATION CODES** *(CONTINUED)*

| NON-U.S. MOTHERBOARD MANUFACTURERS | | NON-U.S. MOTHERBOARD MANUFACTURERS | |
|---|---|---|---|
| **Code** | **Customer** | **Code** | **Customer** |
| 1672 | Lapro Corp. | 1868 | Soyo Technology Co., Ltd. (H.K. office) |
| 1675 | Advanced Scientific Corp. | 1879 | Aeontech International Co., Ltd. |
| 1685 | High Ability Computer Co., Ltd. | 1881 | Manufacturing Technology Resources |
| 1691 | Gain Technology Co., Ltd. | 1888 | Seal International Corp. |
| 1707 | Chaining Computer & Communication Co. | 1889 | Rock Technology Co., Ltd. |
| 1708 | E-San Electronic Co., Ltd. | 1906 | Freedom Data Technology Co., Ltd. |
| 1719 | Taiwan Turbo Technology Co., Ltd. | 1914 | Aquarius Systems Inc. |
| 1720 | Fantas Technology Co., Ltd. | 1917 | Source of Computer Co., Ltd. |
| 1723 | NTK Computer Inc. | 1918 | Lanner Electronics Inc. |
| 1727 | Tripod Technology Corp. | 1920 | Ipex ITG International Ltd. |
| 1737 | Ay Ruey International Co., Ltd. | 1924 | Join Inc. |
| 1739 | Jetpro Infotech Co., Ltd. | 1926 | Kou Sheng Computer Co., Ltd. |
| 1743 | Mitac Inc. | 1927 | Seahill Technology Co., Ltd. |
| 1762 | Ansoon Technology Co. | 1928 | Nexcom International Co., Ltd. |
| 1770 | Acer Inc. | 1929 | CAM Enterprise Inc. |
| 1771 | Toyen Computer Co., Ltd. | 1931 | Aaeon Technology Co., Ltd. |
| 1774 | Acer Sertek Inc. | 1932 | Kuei Hao Industrial Co., Ltd. |
| 1776 | Joss Technology, Ltd. | 1933 | ASMT Corp. |
| 1780 | Acrosser Technology Co., Ltd. | 1934 | Silver Bally Inc. |
| 1783 | Efar Microsystems, Inc. | 1935 | Prodisti Co., Ltd. |
| 1788 | Systex Corp. | 1936 | Codegen Technology Co., Ltd. |
| 1792 | U-Board Computerize Ltd. | 1937 | Orientech Electronics Corp. |
| 1794 | CMT-Taiwan, Inc. | 1938 | Project Information Company Ltd. |
| 1796 | J&J Technology Co., Ltd. | 1939 | Arbor Technology Corp. |
| 1801 | Palit Microsystems Inc. | 1940 | Suntop Computer Systems Corp. |
| 1806 | Interplanetary Information Co., Ltd. | 1941 | Funtech Entertainment Corp. |
| 1807 | Expert Electronic Corp. | 1942 | Sunflower Systems Inc. |
| 1810 | Elechands International Co., Ltd. | 1943 | Needs System Development Co., Ltd. |
| 1815 | Powertech Electronic Co., Ltd. | 1945 | Norm Advanced Technology Corp. |
| 1820 | Ovis Enterprises Co., Ltd. | 1947 | Ten Yun Co., Ltd. |
| 1823 | Inlog Micro Systems Co., Ltd. | 1948 | Beneon Co., Ltd. |
| 1826 | Tercomputer Technologies Corp. | 1949 | National Advantages Computer Inc. |
| 1827 | Anpro Inc. | 1950 | MITS Technology Co. |
| 1828 | Axiom Technology Co., Ltd. | 1951 | Macromate Corp. |
| 1840 | New Union H.K. Ltd. | 1953 | Orlycon Enterprise Co., Ltd. |
| 1845 | PC Direct Technology Co., Ltd. | 1954 | Chung Yu Electronics Co., Ltd. |
| 1846 | Garnet International Corp. | 1955 | Yamashita Systems Corp. |
| 1847 | Brain Power Co. | 1957 | High Large Corp. |
| 1850 | HTR Asia Pacific Inc. | 1958 | Young Micro Systems |
| 1853 | Veridata Electronics Inc. | 1959 | Fastfame Computer Co., Ltd. |
| 1856 | Smart D&M Technology Co., Ltd. | 1960 | Acqutek Corp. |
| 1867 | LTH Rong Electronic Enterprise Co. | 1961 | Deson Trade Inc. |

**TABLE 6-2　AMI OEM IDENTIFICATION CODES** *(CONTINUED)*

| NON-U.S. MOTHERBOARD MANUFACTURERS | | NON-U.S. MOTHERBOARD MANUFACTURERS | |
|---|---|---|---|
| Code | Customer | Code | Customer |
| 1962 | Astra Communication Corp. | 1990 | Expen Tech Electronics Co., Ltd. |
| 1963 | Dimensions Electronics Co., Ltd. | 1994 | Japan Cere'Bro Computers Inc. |
| 1964 | Micron Design Technology, Ltd. | 1996 | Ikon Technologies Corp. |
| 1965 | Cantta Enterprises Co., Ltd. | 1998 | Chang Tseng Corp. |
| 1968 | Khi Way Enterprise Co., Ltd. | **U.S. MOTHERBOARD MANUFACTURERS** | |
| 1969 | Gemlight Computer Ltd. | Code | Customer |
| 1970 | Mat Technologies, Ltd. | 6105 | Dolch Computer Systems |
| 1971 | Norm Advanced Technology Corp. | 6132 | Technology Power Enterprises |
| 1973 | Fugu Tech Enterprise Co., Ltd. | 6156 | Genoa |
| 1974 | Green Taiwan Computer Co., Ltd. | 6259 | Young Micro |
| 1975 | Supertone Electronic Co., Ltd. | 6285 | Tyan |
| 1977 | AT&T Taiwan Telecommunications Co. | 6326 | Crystal |
| 1978 | Winco Electronic Co., Ltd. | 6328 | Alaris |
| 1980 | Teryang Systems Co., Ltd. | 6386 | Pacific Information, Inc. |
| 1981 | Nexcom International Co., Ltd. | 6389 | Supermicro |
| 1982 | China Semiconductor Corp. | 6423 | APC |
| 1985 | Top Union Electronics Corp. | 8003 | QDI |
| 1986 | DMP Electronics Co., Ltd. | 8045 | VTech/PCPartner |
| 1988 | Concierge Co., Ltd. | 428003 | Quantum Designs (H.K.) Ltd. |
| 1989 | Atherton Technology Co., Ltd. | 428054 | Pine |

## AWARD BIOS

Award is another popular BIOS maker with many years of BIOS development experience behind them. As with most other BIOS versions, the Award BIOS code appears in the lower portion of the POST display—usually during the memory count—and can be used to reveal the supported chipset and motherboard manufacturer. The typical Award BIOS ID format is

`2A59IZ1DC-00`

Award uses the first five characters (that is, 2A59I) to indicate the chipset used on the motherboard. The 2A59I entry indicates the Intel Triton TX chipset, and you can find many more chipset codes in Table 6-3. The sixth and seventh characters (Z1 in this case) are used to represent the motherboard manufacturer. For example, the Z1 code indicates a Tomato motherboard made by Zida. Table 6-4 provides a comprehensive listing of manufacturers.

| TABLE 6-3 | CHIPSET SUPPORT CODES FOR AWARD BIOS |
| --- | --- |

| BIOS CODE STRING | CORRESPONDING CHIPSET |
| --- | --- |
| 213V1 | SARC RC2018 |
| 21480 | HiNT SC9204 (Sierra), HMC82C206 |
| 214D1 | HiNT SC9204 (Sierra), HMC82C206 |
| 214I8 | SiS 85C471 |
| 214I9 | SiS 85C471E |
| 214L2 | VIA VT82C486A |
| 214L6 | VIA Venus VT82C486A/VT82C495/VT82C496G |
| 214W3 | VD 88C898 |
| 214X2 | UMC 491 chipset |
| 215UM | OPTi 82C546/82C597 |
| 21917 | ALD chipset |
| 219V0 | SARC RC2016 |
| 2A431 | Cyrix MediaGx Cx5510 chipset |
| 2A432 | Cyrix GXi Cx5520 chipset |
| 2A433 | Cyrix GXm Cx5520 chipset |
| 2A434 | Cyrix GXm Cx5530 chipset |
| 2A496 | Intel Saturn chipset |
| 2A498 | Intel Saturn II chipset |
| 2A499 | Intel Aries chipset |
| 2A4H2 | Contaq 82C596-9 chipset |
| 2A4IB | SiS 496/497 chipset |
| 2A4J6 | Winbond W83C491(SL82C491 Symphony Wagner) |
| 2A4KC | ALi 1439/45/31 chipset |
| 2A4KD | ALi 1487/1489 chipset |
| 2A4L4 | VIA 486A/482/505 chipset |
| 2A4L6 | VIA 496/406/505 chipset |
| 2A4O3 | EFAR EC802GL, EC100G chipset |
| 2A4UK | OPTI-802G-822 chipset |
| 2A4X5 | UMC 8881E/8886B chipset |
| 2A597 | Intel Mercury chipset |
| 2A59A | Intel Natoma (Neptune) chipset |
| 2A59B | Intel Mercury chipset |
| 2A59C | Intel Triton FX chipset (Socket 7-based motherboard) |
| 2A59F | Intel Triton II HX chipset (430HX PCIset—Socket 7-based motherboard) |
| 2A59G | Intel Triton VX chipset (Socket 7-based motherboard) |
| 2A59H | Intel Triton VX chipset (Socket 7-based motherboard) |
| 2A59I | Intel Triton TX chipset (Socket 7-based motherboard) |
| 2A5C7 | VIA VT82C570 chipset |

**TABLE 6-3   CHIPSET SUPPORT CODES FOR AWARD BIOS** *(CONTINUED)*

| BIOS CODE STRING | CORRESPONDING CHIPSET |
|---|---|
| 2A5G7 | VLSI VL82C594 chipset |
| 2A5GB | VLSI Lynx VL82C541/VL82C543 chipset |
| 2A5IA | SiS 501/02/03 chipset |
| 2A5IC | SiS 5501/02/03 chipset |
| 2A5ID | SiS 5511/12/13 chipset |
| 2A5IE | SiS 5101-5103 chipset |
| 2A5IF | SiS 5596/5597 chipset |
| 2A5IH | SiS 5571 chipset |
| 2A5II | SiS 5582/5597/5598 chipset |
| 2A5IJ | SiS 5120 mobile chipset |
| 2A5IK | SiS 5591 chipset |
| 2A5IM | SiS 530 chipset |
| 2A5KB | Ali 1449/61/51 chipset |
| 2A5KE | ALi 1511 chipset |
| 2A5KF | ALi 1521/23 chipset |
| 2A5KI | ALi IV+ M1531/M1543 Chipset (a.k.a. Super TX chipset) |
| 2A5KK | Ali Aladdin V chipset |
| 2A5L7 | VIA VT82C570 chipset |
| 2A5L9 | VIA VT82C570M chipset |
| 2A5LA | VIA Apollo VP1 chipset (VT82C580VP—a.k.a. VXPro chipset) |
| 2A5LC | VIA Apollo VP2 chipset (a.k.a. AMD640 chipset) |
| 2A5LD | VIA VPX chipset (a.k.a. VXPro+ chipset) |
| 2A5LE | VIA Apollo (M)VP3 chipset |
| 2A5LH | VIA Apollo VP4 chipset |
| 2A5R5 | Forex FRX58C613/601A chipset |
| 2A5R6 | Forex FRX58C613A/602B/601B |
| 2A5T6 | ACC Micro 2278/2188 (Auctor) chipset |
| 2A5UI | Opti 82C822/596/597 chipset or OPTi 596/546/82 |
| 2A5UL | Opti 82C822/571/572 chipset |
| 2A5UM | Opti 82C822/546/547 chipset |
| 2A5UN | Opti Viper-M 82C556/557/558 chipset or Opti Viper 82C556/557/558 |
| 2A5UP | Opti Viper Max |
| 2A5X7 | UMC 82C890 chipset |
| 2A5X8 | UMC UM8886BF/UM8891BF/UM8892BF chipset |
| 2A5XA | UMC 890C chipset |
| 2A69H | Intel 440FX chipset (Pentium II/Pentium Pro-based chipset) |
| 2A69J | Intel 440LX/EX chipset (Pentium II-based chipset) |
| 2A69K | Intel 440BX/ZX chipset (Pentium II/III-based chipset) |
| 2A69L | Intel "Camino" 820 chipset |
| 2A69M | Intel "Whitney" 810 chipset |

**TABLE 6-3    CHIPSET SUPPORT CODES FOR AWARD BIOS** *(CONTINUED)*

| BIOS CODE STRING | CORRESPONDING CHIPSET |
|---|---|
| 2A69N | Intel Banister mobile chipset with C&T 69000 video |
| 2A6IL | SiS 5600 chipset |
| 2A6IN | SiS 620 chipset |
| 2A6KL | Ali 1621/1543C chipset |
| 2A6KO | ALi M1631/M1535D |
| 2A6LF | VIA Apollo Pro (691/596) chipset |
| 2A6LG | VIA Apollo Pro Plus (692/596) chipset |
| 2A6LI | VIA MVP4 VIA 601 (Trident video on-chip)/686A (modem on-chip, sound on-chip) |
| 2A6LJ | VIA 694X/596B and VIA 694X/686A (modem on-chip, sound on-chip) |
| 2A9KG | ALi M6117/M1521/M1523 chipset |
| 2AG9H | Intel Neptune ISA chipset |
| 2B496 | Intel Saturn I EISA chipset |
| 2B597 | Intel Mercury EISA chipset |
| 2B59A | Intel Neptune EISA chipset |
| 2B59F | Intel 430HX EISA chipset |
| 2B69D | Intel Orion EISA chipset |
| 2C460 | UNIchip U4800-VLX chipset |
| 2C470 | HYF82481 chipset |
| 2C4D2 | HiNT SC8006 (Sierra), HMC82C206 |
| 2C4I7 | SiS 461 chipset |
| 2C4I8 | SiS 85C471B chipset |
| 2C4I9 | SiS 85C471B/E/G chipset |
| 2C4J6 | Winbond W83C491(SL82C491 Symphony Wagner) |
| 2C4K9 | ALi 14296 chipset |
| 2C4KC | Ali 1439/45/31 chipset |
| 2C4L2 | VIA 82C486A chipset |
| 2C4L6 | VIA VT496G chipset |
| 2C4L8 | VIA VT425MV chipset |
| 2C4O3 | EFAR EC802G-B chipset |
| 2C4S0 | AMD Elan 470 |
| 2C4T7 | ACC Micro 2048 (Auctor) |
| 2C4UK | OPTI 82C895/82C602 |
| 2C4X2 | UMC UM82C491/82C493 chipset |
| 2C4X6 | UMC UM498F/496F |
| 3A6LF | Via Apollo Pro (691/596) chipset with Award BIOS v4.60PGA |
| 6A450 | STMicroelectronics PC Client ST86 processor |
| 6A69L | Intel "Camino" i820 chipset with Award BIOS v6.00 |
| 6A69M | Intel i810(E) chipset with Award BIOS v6.00 |
| 6A69R | Intel "Solano" i815(E) chipset with Award BIOS v6.00 |

**TABLE 6-3    CHIPSET SUPPORT CODES FOR AWARD BIOS (CONTINUED)**

| BIOS CODE STRING | CORRESPONDING CHIPSET |
|---|---|
| 6A69S | Intel i850 chipset with Award BIOS v6.00 |
| 6A6IS | SiS 730 chipset with Award BIOS v6.00 |
| 6A6IU | SiS 733 chipset with Award BIOS v6.00 |
| 6A6LJ | VIA 694X/686A (Apollo Pro 133A) chipset with Award BIOS v6.00 |
| 6A6LK | VIA VT8371 (KX-133) chipset with Award BIOS v6.00 |
| 6A6LM | VIA VT8363 (KT-133) chipset with Award BIOS v6.00 |
| 6A6LN | VIA VT8365 (KM-133)/VT8364 (KL-133) chipset with Award BIOS v6.00 |
| 6A6LU | VIA Apollo Pro266 chipset with Award BIOS v6.00 |
| 6A6LV | VIA VT8366/VT8233 chipset with Award BIOS v6.00 |
| 6A6S2 | AMD 751 chipset with Award BIOS v6.00 |
| 6A6S6 | AMD 760 chipset with Award BIOS v6.00 |
| JA6LM | VIA VT8363 (KT-133) chipset |

**TABLE 6-4    MANUFACTURER CODES FOR AWARD BIOS**

| BIOS CODE STRING | CORRESPONDING MANUFACTURER |
|---|---|
| A0 | Asustek |
| A1 | Abit |
| A2 | Atrend |
| A3 | Bcom (ASI) |
| A7 | AVT (formerly Concord) |
| A8 | Adcom |
| AB | AOpen |
| AD | Anson |
| AK | Advantech |
| AM | Acme |
| AT | ASK Technology |
| AX | Achitec |
| B0 | Biostar |
| B1 | BEK-Tronic Technology |
| B2 | Boser |
| B3 | BCM |
| C0 | Matsonic |
| C1 | Clevo |
| C2 | Chicony |
| C3 | Chaintech |
| C5 | Chaplet |
| C9 | Computrend |

**TABLE 6-4** MANUFACTURER CODES FOR AWARD BIOS *(CONTINUED)*

| BIOS CODE STRING | CORRESPONDING MANUFACTURER |
| --- | --- |
| CF | Flagpoint |
| CS | Gainward or CSS Labs |
| D0 | DataExpert |
| D1 | DTK |
| D2 | Digital |
| D3 | Digicom |
| D4 | DFI (Diamond Flower) |
| D7 | Daewoo |
| DE | Dual Tech |
| DI | Domex (DTC) |
| DJ | Darter |
| DL | Delta Electronics |
| E1 | Elitegroup (ECS) |
| E3 | EFA |
| E4 | ESPCo |
| E6 | Elonex |
| E7 | Expen Tech |
| EC | ENPC |
| F0 | FIC (FICA) |
| F1 | Flytech Group |
| F2 | Flexus |
| F3 | Full Yes |
| F5 | Fugutech |
| F8 | Formosa Industrial Computing |
| F9 | Redfox |
| FG | Fastfame Technology Co., Ltd. |
| FI | FIC (FICA) |
| G0 | GigaByte |
| G1 | (unknown) |
| G3 | Gemlight |
| G5 | GVC |
| G9 | Global Circuit Technology |
| GA | Giantec |
| GE | Zaapa |
| H0 | Hsing-Tech (PCChips) |
| H2 | Shuttle (HolCo) |
| HH | HighTech Information System |
| I3 | Iwill |
| I4 | Inventa |
| I5 | Informtech |

**TABLE 6-4    MANUFACTURER CODES FOR AWARD BIOS *(CONTINUED)***

| BIOS CODE STRING | CORRESPONDING MANUFACTURER |
| --- | --- |
| I9 | ICP |
| IA | Infinity |
| IC | Inventec |
| IE | Itri |
| J1 | Jetway (a.k.a. Jetboard or Acorp) |
| J2 | Jamicon |
| J3 | J-Bond |
| J4 | Jetta |
| J6 | Joss |
| K0 | Kapok |
| K1 | Kaimei |
| KF | Kinpo |
| L1 | Lucky Star |
| L7 | Lanner Electronics, Inc. |
| L9 | Lucky Tiger |
| LB | LeadTek |
| M0 | Matra |
| M2 | Mycomp (TMC) and Megastar |
| M3 | Mitac |
| M4 | Micro-Star |
| M8 | Mustek |
| M9 | Micro Leader Enterprises (MLE) |
| MH | Macrotek |
| N0 | Nexcom |
| N5 | NEC |
| NM | New Media Communication (NMC) |
| NX | Nexar |
| O0 | Ocean (Octek) |
| P1 | PCChips |
| P4 | Asus |
| P6 | Pro-Tech |
| P8 | Proteam |
| P9 | Powertech |
| PA | Epox and 2TheMax |
| PC | Pine |
| PF | President |
| PN | Procomp |
| PS | Palmax |
| PX | Pionix |
| Q0 | Quanta |

**TABLE 6-4** MANUFACTURER CODES FOR AWARD BIOS *(CONTINUED)*

| BIOS CODE STRING | CORRESPONDING MANUFACTURER |
| --- | --- |
| Q1 | QDI |
| RA | RioWorks Solutions Inc. |
| R0 | Mtech (Rise) |
| R2 | Rectron |
| R3 | Datavan International Corp. |
| S2 | Soyo |
| S3 | Smart D&M Technology |
| S5 | Shuttle (HolCo) |
| S9 | Spring Circle |
| SA | Seanix |
| SC | Sukjung (Auhua Electronics) |
| SE | Newtech or SMT or Professional Technologies |
| SH | SYE (Shining Yuan Enterprises) |
| SJ | Sowah |
| SL | Winco |
| SM | San-Li, Hope Vision, and Superpower |
| SN | Soltek |
| SR | (unknown) |
| SW | S&D (Some A-Corp and Zaapa motherboards use this code.) |
| T0 | Twinhead |
| T1 | Taemung, Fentech, or Trang Bow |
| T4 | Taken |
| T5 | Tyan |
| T6 | Trigem |
| TB | Taeil |
| TG | Tekram |
| TJ | Totem |
| TL | Transcend Information Inc. |
| TP | Commate, Ozzo |
| U0 | U-Board |
| U1 | USI (Universal Scientific Industrial) |
| U2 | AIR (UHC) |
| U4 | Unicorn |
| U5 | Unico |
| U6 | Unitron |
| U9 | Warp Speed |
| V3 | Vtech (PC Partner) |
| V5 | Vision Top Technology |
| V6 | Vobis |
| V7 | YKM (Dayton Micro) |

| TABLE 6-4 | MANUFACTURER CODES FOR AWARD BIOS *(CONTINUED)* |
|---|---|
| **BIOS CODE STRING** | **CORRESPONDING MANUFACTURER** |
| W0 | Wintec (Edom) |
| W1 | Well Join |
| W5 | Winco |
| W7 | Win Lan |
| XA | ADLink Technology |
| X3 | A-Corp |
| X5 | Arima |
| Y2 | Yamashita |
| Z1 | Zida (Tomato motherboards) |
| Z2 | (unknown) |
| Z3 | ShenZhen Zeling Industrial |

# INTEL BIOS DESIGNATORS

Intel produces a large number of motherboards that feature their latest processors and chipsets. Many of these motherboards are not distributed to end users (e.g., PC builders), but instead are integrated into the systems of mainstream manufacturers (such as Dell or Gateway systems). Classic Intel motherboards use a very distinctive BIOS code that usually follows a format such as:

`1.00.xx.BIO`

Table 6-5 identifies the make and model associated with many classic (legacy) Intel BIOS codes. For example, a code of 1.00.xx.BYOR identifies the system as a Packard Bell LG 74CDT SUP, Legend 823CDT, or Packard Bell "Pack-Mate 6100." More recent Intel motherboards forego the distinctive 1.00.xx format and use a format such as:

`MV85010A.86A.0011.P05`

| TABLE 6-5 | MOTHERBOARD/OEM IDENTIFICATION CODES FOR CLASSIC INTEL BIOS |
|---|---|
| **BIOS CODE STRING** | **CORRESPONDING MANUFACTURER** |
| 1.00.xx AF2T | OEM version of Intel Premiere/PCI Baby-AT Board (Batman Revenge) |
| 1.00.xx.AB0 | Intel Classic E-Series |
| 1.00.xx.AC0 | Intel Classic R/R-Plus (Monsoon motherboard) |
| 1.00.xx.AF1 | Intel Premiere/PCI Expandable Desktop (Batman motherboard) |
| 1.00.xx.AF2 | Intel Premiere/PCI ED (a.k.a. Batman's Revenge) |
| 1.00.xx.AK0 | Intel Xpress Servers or Deskside Xpress LX (Cortez motherboard) |
| 1.00.xx.AM0 | Intel Xpress Servers or Xpress LM |
| 1.00.xx.AQ0 | Intel Classic/PCI Expandable Desktop (Alfredo motherboard) |
| 1.00.xx.AU0 | Intel Premiere/PCI Low Profile (Robin motherboard) |
| 1.00.xx.AU0R | Packard Bell OEM version of Intel Premiere/PCI Low Profile (PB 5000) |

**TABLE 6-5**    MOTHERBOARD/OEM IDENTIFICATION CODES FOR CLASSIC
INTEL BIOS *(CONTINUED)*

| BIOS CODE STRING | CORRESPONDING MANUFACTURER |
|---|---|
| 1.00.xx.AX1 | Intel Premiere/PCI II Exp. Desktop (Plato motherboard) |
| 1.00.xx.AX1T | Gateway 2000 OEM version of Intel's Plato MB (Premier II and P54C) |
| 1.00.xx.AX1Z | Intel Premiere/PCI II (Plato motherboard) |
| 1.00.xx.AY0 | Intel Classic/PCI ED (Ninja motherboard) |
| 1.00.xx.AZ0 | Intel Classic/PCI LP (Entrada motherboard) |
| 1.00.xx.BB0 | Intel Premiere/PCI LX Low Profile (Socrates motherboard) |
| 1.00.xx.BB0R | Packard Bell LG 401 CD |
| 1.00.xx.BC0 | Intel Premiere/PCI LC Low Profile (Robin LC motherboard) |
| 1.00.xx.BC0R | Packard Bell OEM version of Intel Premiere/PCI LC Low Profile (PB 527R w/ Cirrus Video Card on board or PB LG 200 CD) |
| 1.00.xx.BC0K | NEC OEM version of Intel Premiere/PCI LC Low Profile |
| 1.00.xx.BF0 | Intel Premiere/PCI GX Low Profile |
| 1.00.xx.BF0B | AT&T Globalyst Solutions (now NCR) model is 1006 with an Intel Premiere/PCI GX |
| 1.00.xx.BG0 | Intel XXpress Server (Extended Xpress—Medusa motherboard) |
| 1.00.xx.BI0 | Intel ALTServer/CS (Altair motherboard) |
| 1.00.xx.BL0 | Intel Premiere /ATLX (Hendrixx motherboard) |
| 1.00.xx.BP0 | Intel Mercury motherboard |
| 1.00.xx.BR0 | Intel Advanced/ZE (Zappa E or Tahiti motherboards) |
| 1.00.xx.BR0T | Gateway OEM version of Intel Alladin (Zappa ZE or Advanced/ZE) board |
| 1.00.xx.BS0 | Intel Advanced/ZP (Zappa motherboard) |
| 1.00.xx.BS0H | Vobis OEM version of Intel's Zappa ZP or ED (Advanced/ZP board) |
| 1.00.xx.BT0 | Intel Advanced/MN (Morrison motherboard) |
| 1.00.xx.BU0 | Intel Advanced/MA (Monaco motherboard) |
| 1.00.xx.BU0Q | AST OEM version of Intel Advanced/MA (Monaco motherboard) |
| 1.00.xx.BX0J | Dell XPS 100c |
| 1.00.xx.BY0R | Packard Bell LG 74CDT SUP (Intel OEM) or Legend 823CDT or Packard Bell "Pack-Mate 6100" |
| 1.00.xx.CA0 | Intel Advanced/AL (Alladin motherboard) |
| 1.00.xx.CA0U | Zenith GT P100 |
| 1.00.xx.CA2 | Intel Advanced/MN (Morrison motherboard) |
| 1.00.xx.CA2L | HP Pavilion model 7090 |
| 1.00.xx.CA3 | Intel Advanced/MN (Morrison motherboard) |
| 1.00.xx.CB0 | Intel Advanced/EV (Endeavour motherboard) |
| 1.00.xx.CB0H | Vobis OEM version of Intel's Endeavor EV or Advanced/EV |
| 1.00.xx.CG0 | Intel Performance/AU (Aurora motherboard) |
| 1.00.xx.CH0 | Advanced/MN or Advanced/MC (Talladega motherboard) |
| 1.00.xx.CJ0 | Intel Pocono motherboard |
| 1.00.xx.CL0 | Intel Advanced/AS (Atlantis motherboard) |
| 1.00.xx.CN0 | Intel Advanced/ATX (Thor motherboard) |

**TABLE 6-5** MOTHERBOARD/OEM IDENTIFICATION CODES FOR CLASSIC INTEL BIOS *(CONTINUED)*

| BIOS CODE STRING | CORRESPONDING MANUFACTURER |
|---|---|
| 1.00.xx.CNOT | Gateway OEM version of Intel Thor motherboard |
| 1.00.xx.CP0R | Packard Bell OEM motherboard |
| 1.00.xx.CS1 | Intel VS440FX (Venus motherboard) |
| 1.00.xx.CS1H | Vobis OEM version of Intel VS440FX motherboard |
| 1.00.xx.CS1T | Gateway OEM version of Intel VS440FX (Venus motherboard) |
| 1.00.xx.CT1 | Intel AP440FX (Apollo motherboard) |
| 1.00.xx.CV2 | Intel Advanced/RH (Rhinestone motherboard) |
| 1.00.xx.CW0 | Intel Advanced/RU (Ruby motherboard) |
| 1.00.xx.CY1 | Intel TE430VX (Tiger Eye motherboard) |
| 1.00.xx.CY1T | Gateway OEM version of Intel TE430VX motherboard |
| 1.00.xx.DA0 | Intel BB440FX (Server) |
| 1.00.xx.DB0 | Intel Advanced/ML (Marl motherboard) |
| 1.00.xx.DC0 | Intel Advanced/RU (Ruby motherboard) |
| 1.00.xx.DC0L | Hewlett-Packard 7275z |
| 1.00.xx.DH0 | Intel TC430HX (Tucson motherboard) |
| 1.00.xx.DI0 | Intel PR440FX (Providence motherboard) |
| 1.00.xx.DK0 | Intel CU430HX (Cumberland motherboard) |
| 1.00.xx.DL0 | Intel Advanced/RU (Ruby motherboard) |
| 1.00.xx.DL0Q | AST Advantage 7303 |
| 1.00.xx.DM0 | Intel RC440FX (Server) |
| 1.00.xx.DN0R | Packard Bell OEM version of Intel Orlando motherboard |
| 1.00.xx.DQ0 | Intel TE430VX (Tiger Eye motherboard) |
| 1.00.xx.DQ0T | Gateway 2000 P5200 |
| 1.00.xx.DT0 | Intel PD440FX (Portland motherboard) |
| 1.00.xx.R0 | Intel Xpress Servers and Desktop Xpress |
| 1.00.xx.S0 | Intel Professional Workstation |
| 1.00.xx.V0 | Intel Xpress Servers and Deskside Xpress |
| 1.00.xx.W0 | Intel Classic S-Series |
| 1.00.xx.Y3 | Intel Professional/GX |
| 1.00.xx.YM1 | Intel YM430TX |

where the first set of characters (before the first period) designates the motherboard. In this example, the MV85010A BIOS identifier would indicate an Intel Desktop Board D850MV. Table 6-6 identifies more recent Intel motherboard models.

**TABLE 6-6**    MOTHERBOARD IDENTIFICATION CODES FOR CURRENT INTEL BIOS VERSIONS

| BIOS CODE STRING | CORRESPONDING MANUFACTURER |
|---|---|
| 4A3NT0X0.86A | Intel AN430TX Motherboard |
| 4A4LL0X0.86A | Intel AL440LX Motherboard |
| 4B4IZ0XA.86A | Intel BI440ZX Motherboard |
| 4B4LZ0XA.86A | Intel BL440ZX Motherboard |
| 4C3NT0X0.86A | Intel CN430TX Motherboard |
| 4C3NT0X0.86C | Intel CN430TX Motherboard |
| 4D4KL0X0.86A | Intel DK440LX Motherboard |
| 4J4NB0X1.86A | Intel JN440BX Motherboard |
| 4K4UE0X0.86A | Intel KU440EX Motherboard |
| 4L3TT0X0.86A | Intel LT430TX Motherboard |
| 4L4ML0X0.86A | Intel LM440LX Motherboard |
| 4L4ML0X0.86C | Intel LM440LX Motherboard |
| 4M4SG0X0.86E | Intel MS440GX Workstation Board |
| 4M4UE0X1.86A | Intel MU440EX Motherboard |
| 4M4UE0X3.86A | Intel MU440EX Motherboard |
| 4N4XL0X0.86A | Intel NX440LX Motherboard |
| 4R4CB0XA.86A | Intel RC440BX Motherboard |
| 4S4EB0X1.86A | Intel SE440BX Motherboard |
| 4S4EB2X0.86A | Intel SE440BX-2 Motherboard |
| 4S4RB0XA.86A | Intel SR440BX Motherboard |
| 8C1A100A.86A | Intel CA810 Motherboard |
| ASPN0.86B | Intel AD450NX Server Platform |
| ASPN1.86B | Intel AC450NX Server Platform |
| BN81510A.86A | Intel Desktop Board D815BN |
| C440GX0.86B | Intel C440GX+ Server Board |
| CA81020A.86A | Intel CA810E Motherboard |
| CA81030A.86A | Intel Desktop Board D810E2CA3 |
| CB81010A.86A | Intel Desktop Board D810E2CB |
| CC82010A.86A | Intel CC820 Motherboard |
| EA81510A.86A | Intel Desktop Board D815EEA |
| EA81520A.86A | Intel Desktop Board D815EEA2/D815EPEA2 |
| EA81520A.86A | Intel Desktop Board D815EFV/D815EPFV |
| EA81520a.86B | Intel Server Board S815EBM1 |
| EW81510A.86A | Intel Desktop Board D815EGEW |
| GB85010A.86A | Intel Desktop Board D850GB |
| HV84510A.86A | Intel Desktop Board D845HV |

**TABLE 6-6   MOTHERBOARD IDENTIFICATION CODES FOR CURRENT INTEL BIOS VERSIONS (CONTINUED)**

| BIOS CODE STRING | CORRESPONDING MANUFACTURER |
|---|---|
| HV84510A.86A | Intel Desktop Board D845WN |
| L440GX0.86B | Intel ISP2150 Internet Server Platform |
| L440GX0.86B | Intel ISP2150G Internet Server Platform |
| L440GX0.86B | Intel LB440GX Rack Server Platform |
| L440GX0.86B | Intel L440GX+ Server Board |
| MADRO0.86B | Intel MB440LX Server Platform |
| MO81010A.86A | Intel Desktop Board D810EMO |
| MV85010A.86A | Intel Desktop Board D850MD |
| MV85010A.86A | Intel Desktop Board D850MV |
| NIGHTS0.86B | Intel N440BX Server Board |
| NIGHTS0.86B | Intel NA440BX Server Platform |
| NIGHTS0.86B | Intel NC440BX Server Platform |
| NITELT0.86B | Intel T440BX Server Board |
| OR840600.86E | Intel OR840 Workstation Board |
| PT030LEA.86B | Intel Server Platform SRMK2 |
| PT84510A.86A | Intel Desktop Board D845BG |
| PT84510A.86A | Intel Desktop Board D845PT |
| REDWD0.86B | Intel R440LX Server Board |
| REDWD0.86B | Intel RC440LX Server Platform |
| S450NX0.86B | Intel SC450NX Server Platform |
| SABR1.86B | Intel OCPRF100 Server Platform |
| SAI20.86b | Intel Server Board SAI2 |
| SBT20.86B | Intel SBT2 Server Board |
| SCB20.86B | Intel Server Board SCB2 |
| SDS21.86B | Intel Server Board SDS2 |
| SKA40.86B | Intel ISP4400 Internet Server Platform |
| SKA40.86B | Intel SPKA4 Server Platform |
| SKA40.86B | Intel SRKA4 Server Platform |
| STL20.86B | Intel STL2 Server Board |
| SU81010A.86A | Intel Desktop Board SU810 |
| TR440BXA.86B | Intel ISP1100 Internet Server Platform |
| VC82010A.86A | Intel Desktop Board D820LP |
| VC82010A.86A | Intel Desktop Board VC820 |

# MICROID RESEARCH BIOS (MR BIOS)

The MR BIOS identification string is located at the top-right corner of the Summary screen (and all or most of the Setup screens). The code directly relates to a specific motherboard model and manufacturer, as shown in Table 6-7. For example, a code of ACER309 means the MR BIOS was designed for an Acer/ALI M1209 motherboard using a Cyrix 486SLC processor.

**TABLE 6-7    IDENTIFICATION STRINGS FOR MR BIOS**

| BIOS CODE STRING | MOTHERBOARD AND/OR CHIPSET |
|---|---|
| ACER300 | Acer/ALI M1209 |
| ACER301 | Acer/ALI M1209 |
| ACER304 | Acer/ALI M1209 |
| ACER305 | Acer/ALI M1209 |
| ACER306 | Acer/ALI M1209 |
| ACER307 | Acer/ALI M1209 |
| ACER308 | Acer/ALI M1209—Cyrix 486SLC |
| ACER309 | Acer/ALI M1209—Cyrix 486SLC |
| ACER30C | Acer/ALI M1209—Cyrix 486SLC |
| ACER30D | Acer/ALI M1209—Cyrix 486SLC |
| ACER30E | Acer/ALI M1209—Cyrix 486SLC |
| ACER30F | Acer/ALI M1209—Cyrix 486SLC |
| ACER310 | Acer/ALI M1217 |
| ACER311 | Acer/ALI M1217 |
| ACER314 | Acer/ALI M1217 |
| ACER315 | Acer/ALI M1217 |
| ACER316 | Acer/ALI M1217 |
| ACER317 | Acer/ALI M1217 |
| ACER318 | Acer/ALI M1217—Cyrix 486SLC |
| ACER319 | Acer/ALI M1217—Cyrix 486SLC |
| ACER31C | Acer/ALI M1217—Cyrix 486SLC |
| ACER31D | Acer/ALI M1217—Cyrix 486SLC |
| ACER31E | Acer/ALI M1217—Cyrix 486SLC |
| ACER31F | Acer/ALI M1217—Cyrix 486SLC |
| C&T_300 | Chips & Technologies CS8230 |
| C&T_304 | Chips & Technologies CS8230 |
| C&T_305 | Chips & Technologies CS8230 |
| C&T_308 | Chips & Technologies CS8230 |
| C&T_309 | Chips & Technologies CS8230 |
| CNTQ400 | Contaq 82C591/82C592 WriteBack |
| CNTQ404 | Contaq 82C591/82C592 WriteBack |
| CNTQ405 | Contaq 82C591/82C592 WriteBack |
| CNTQ406 | Contaq 82C591/82C592 WriteBack |
| CNTQ407 | Contaq 82C591/82C592 WriteBack |
| CNTQ410 | Contaq 82C596 WriteBack |
| CNTQ411 | Contaq 82C596 WriteBack |
| CNTQ412 | Contaq 82C596 WriteBack |
| EFAR400 | Efar Microsystems 82EC495 WriteBack |
| EFAR401 | Efar Microsystems 82EC495 WriteBack—82C711 Combo I/O |
| EFAR402 | Efar Microsystems 82EC495 WriteBack—PC87310 Super I/O |

**TABLE 6-7    IDENTIFICATION STRINGS FOR MR BIOS (CONTINUED)**

| BIOS CODE STRING | MOTHERBOARD AND/OR CHIPSET |
|---|---|
| EFAR404 | Efar Microsystems 82EC495 WriteBack |
| EFAR405 | Efar Microsystems 82EC495 WriteBack |
| EFAR406 | Efar Microsystems 82EC495 WriteBack |
| EFAR407 | Efar Microsystems 82EC495 WriteBack |
| EFAR408 | Efar Microsystems 82EC495 WriteBack—82C711 Combo I/O |
| EFAR409 | Efar Microsystems 82EC495 WriteBack—82C711 Combo I/O |
| EFAR40A | Efar Microsystems 82EC495 WriteBack—82C711 Combo I/O |
| EFAR40B | Efar Microsystems 82EC495 WriteBack—82C711 Combo I/O |
| EFAR40C | Efar Microsystems 82EC495 WriteBack—PC87310 Super I/O |
| EFAR40D | Efar Microsystems 82EC495 WriteBack—PC87310 Super I/O |
| EFAR40E | Efar Microsystems 82EC495 WriteBack—PC87310 Super I/O |
| EFAR40F | Efar Microsystems 82EC495 WriteBack—PC87310 Super I/O |
| EFAR410 | Efar Microsystems 82EC798 WriteBack |
| EFAR411 | Efar Microsystems 82EC798 WriteBack—82C711 Combo I/O |
| EFAR412 | Efar Microsystems 82EC798 WriteBack—PC87310 Super I/O |
| EFAR414 | Efar Microsystems 82EC798 WriteBack |
| EFAR415 | Efar Microsystems 82EC798 WriteBack |
| EFAR416 | Efar Microsystems 82EC798 WriteBack |
| EFAR417 | Efar Microsystems 82EC798 WriteBack |
| EFAR418 | Efar Microsystems 82EC798 WriteBack—82C711 Combo I/O |
| EFAR419 | Efar Microsystems 82EC798 WriteBack—82C711 Combo I/O |
| EFAR41A | Efar Microsystems 82EC798 WriteBack—82C711 Combo I/O |
| EFAR41B | Efar Microsystems 82EC798 WriteBack—82C711 Combo I/O |
| EFAR41C | Efar Microsystems 82EC798 WriteBack—PC87310 Super I/O |
| EFAR41D | Efar Microsystems 82EC798 WriteBack—PC87310 Super I/O |
| EFAR41E | Efar Microsystems 82EC798 WriteBack—PC87310 Super I/O |
| EFAR41F | Efar Microsystems 82EC798 WriteBack—PC87310 Super I/O |
| EFAR41G | Efar Microsystems 82EC798 WriteBack—Cyrix 486DLC |
| EFAR41H | Efar Microsystems 82EC798 WriteBack—Cyrix 486DLC—82C711 Combo I/O |
| EFAR41J | Efar Microsystems 82EC798 WriteBack—Cyrix 486DLC—PC87310 Super I/O |
| EFAR41K | Efar Microsystems 82EC798 WriteBack—Cyrix 486DLC |
| EFAR41L | Efar Microsystems 82EC798 WriteBack—Cyrix 486DLC |
| EFAR41M | Efar Microsystems 82EC798 WriteBack—Cyrix 486DLC |
| EFAR41N | Efar Microsystems 82EC798 WriteBack—Cyrix 486DLC |
| EFAR41P | Efar Microsystems 82EC798 WriteBack—Cyrix 486DLC—82C711 Combo I/O |
| EFAR41Q | Efar Microsystems 82EC798 WriteBack—Cyrix 486DLC—82C711 Combo I/O |

**TABLE 6-7    IDENTIFICATION STRINGS FOR MR BIOS** *(CONTINUED)*

| BIOS CODE STRING | MOTHERBOARD AND/OR CHIPSET |
|---|---|
| EFAR41R | Efar Microsystems 82EC798 WriteBack—Cyrix 486DLC—82C711 Combo I/O |
| EFAR41S | Efar Microsystems 82EC798 WriteBack—Cyrix 486DLC—82C711 Combo I/O |
| EFAR41T | Efar Microsystems 82EC798 WriteBack—Cyrix 486DLC—PC87310 Super I/O |
| EFAR41U | Efar Microsystems 82EC798 WriteBack—Cyrix 486DLC—PC87310 Super I/O |
| EFAR41V | Efar Microsystems 82EC798 WriteBack—Cyrix 486DLC—PC87310 Super I/O |
| EFAR41W | Efar Microsystems 82EC798 WriteBack—Cyrix 486DLC—PC87310 Super I/O |
| EFAR41X | Efar Microsystems 82EC798 WriteBack—Cyrix 486DLC |
| ELIT320 | Elite Microelectronics Eagle Rev. A1 |
| ELIT324 | Elite Microelectronics Eagle Rev. A1 |
| ELIT325 | Elite Microelectronics Eagle Rev. A1 |
| ELIT420 | Elite Microelectronics Eagle Rev. A1 |
| ELIT424 | Elite Microelectronics Eagle Rev. A1 |
| ELIT425 | Elite Microelectronics Eagle Rev. A1 |
| ELIT426 | Elite Microelectronics Eagle Rev. A1 |
| ELIT427 | Elite Microelectronics Eagle Rev. A1 |
| ETEQ301 | Eteq Microsystems 82C491/82C493 Bobcat Rev. A |
| ETEQ303 | Eteq Microsystems 82C491/82C492 Cougar Rev. B, C |
| ETEQ304 | Eteq Microsystems 82C491/82C492 Cougar Rev. B, C |
| ETEQ305 | Eteq Microsystems 82C491/82C492 Cougar Rev. B, C |
| ETEQ311 | Eteq Microsystems 82C491/82C493 Bobcat Rev. A |
| ETEQ314 | Eteq Microsystems 82C491/82C493 Bobcat Rev. A |
| ETEQ315 | Eteq Microsystems 82C491/82C493 Bobcat Rev. A |
| ETEQ321 | Eteq Microsystems 82C4901/82C4902 Bengal WriteBack |
| ETEQ324 | Eteq Microsystems 82C4901/82C4902 Bengal WriteBack |
| ETEQ325 | Eteq Microsystems 82C4901/82C4902 Bengal WriteBack |
| ETEQ401 | Eteq Microsystems 82C491/82C493 Bobcat Rev. A |
| ETEQ403 | Eteq Microsystems 82C491/82C492 Cougar Rev. B, C |
| ETEQ404 | Eteq Microsystems 82C491/82C492 Cougar Rev. B, C |
| ETEQ405 | Eteq Microsystems 82C491/82C492 Cougar Rev. B, C |
| ETEQ421 | Eteq Microsystems 82C4901/82C4902 Bengal WriteBack |
| ETEQ428 | Eteq Microsystems 82C4901/82C4902 Bengal WriteBack |
| ETEQ429 | Eteq Microsystems 82C4901/82C4902 Bengal WriteBack |
| FORX300 | Forex 36C300/200 [36C300/46C402] WriteThru |
| FORX303 | Forex 36C300/200 [36C300/46C402] WriteThru |

**TABLE 6-7     IDENTIFICATION STRINGS FOR MR BIOS** *(CONTINUED)*

| BIOS CODE STRING | MOTHERBOARD AND/OR CHIPSET |
| --- | --- |
| FORX320 | Forex 36C311 Single Chip 386SX with Cache |
| FORX323 | Forex 36C311 Single Chip 386SX with Cache |
| FORX410 | Forex 46C411/402 WriteThru |
| FORX413 | Forex 46C411/402 WriteThru |
| FORX418 | Forex 46C411/402 WriteThru |
| FORX419 | Forex 46C411/402 WriteThru |
| FORX420 | Forex 46C521 WriteBack or Forex 46C421A/422 WriteBack |
| FORX421 | Forex 46C521 WriteBack or Forex 46C421A/422 WriteBack |
| FORX422 | Forex 46C521 WriteBack or Forex 46C421A/422 WriteBack |
| FORX423 | Forex 46C521 WriteBack or Forex 46C421A/422 WriteBack |
| FORX424 | Forex 46C521 WriteBack or Forex 46C421A/422 WriteBack |
| FORX425 | Forex 46C521 WriteBack or Forex 46C421A/422 WriteBack |
| FORX426 | Forex 46C521 WriteBack or Forex 46C421A/422 WriteBack |
| FORX427 | Forex 46C521 WriteBack or Forex 46C421A/422 WriteBack |
| FORX428 | Forex 46C521 WriteBack or Forex 46C421A/422 WriteBack |
| FORX429 | Forex 46C521 WriteBack or Forex 46C421A/422 WriteBack |
| FTDI400 | FTDI 82C3480 WriteBack/WriteThru |
| FTDI401 | FTDI 82C3480 WriteBack/WriteThru with 82C711 Combo I/O |
| FTDI402 | FTDI 82C3480 WriteBack/WriteThru with PC87310 Super I/O |
| FTDI408 | FTDI 82C3480 WriteBack/WriteThru |
| FTDI409 | FTDI 82C3480 WriteBack/WriteThru with 82C711 Combo I/O |
| FTDI40A | FTDI 82C3480 WriteBack/WriteThru with PC87310 Super I/O |
| HDK_200 | EverTech 286 Hedaka |
| HDK_210 | EverTech 286 Hedaka—built-in EMS |
| HKT_301 | Hong Kong Technology HK3000 (Phoenix 8242 Keyboard Controller) |
| HKT_302 | Hong Kong Technology HK3000 (MR BIOS 8042 Keyboard Controller) |
| HT12200 | Headland Technologies HT12/HT12+ |
| HT12201 | Headland Technologies HT12/HT12+ |
| HT12202 | Headland Technologies HT12/HT12+ |
| HT12210 | Headland Technologies HT12/HT12+ with built-in EMS |
| HT12211 | Headland Technologies HT12/HT12+ with built-in EMS |
| HT22300 | Headland Technologies HT22/HT18C |
| HT22302 | Headland Technologies HT22/HT18C |
| HT22303 | Headland Technologies HT22/HT18C |
| HT2230A | Headland Technologies HT22/HT18C with 82C711 Combo I/O |
| HT2230B | Headland Technologies HT22/HT18C with PC87310 Super I/O |
| HT2230C | Headland Technologies HT22/HT18C with 82C711 Combo I/O |
| HT2230D | Headland Technologies HT22/HT18C with PC87310 Super I/O |
| HT2230E | Headland Technologies HT22/HT18C with 82C711 Combo I/O |
| HT2230F | Headland Technologies HT22/HT18C with PC87310 Super I/O |

**TABLE 6-7    IDENTIFICATION STRINGS FOR MR BIOS** *(CONTINUED)*

| BIOS CODE STRING | MOTHERBOARD AND/OR CHIPSET |
|---|---|
| HT32300 | Headland Technologies HT320 Shasta |
| HT32302 | Headland Technologies HT320 Shasta |
| HT32303 | Headland Technologies HT320 Shasta |
| HT3230A | Headland Technologies HT320 Shasta with 82C711 Combo I/O |
| HT3230B | Headland Technologies HT320 Shasta with PC87310 Super I/O |
| HT3230C | Headland Technologies HT320 Shasta with 82C711 Combo I/O |
| HT3230D | Headland Technologies HT320 Shasta with PC87310 Super I/O |
| HT3230E | Headland Technologies HT320 Shasta with 82C711 Combo I/O |
| HT3230F | Headland Technologies HT320 Shasta with PC87310 Super I/O |
| HT34400 | Headland Technologies HT340 Shasta |
| HT34408 | Headland Technologies HT340 Shasta |
| HT34409 | Headland Technologies HT340 Shasta |
| HT3440A | Headland Technologies HT340 Shasta with 82C711 Combo I/O |
| HT3440B | Headland Technologies HT340 Shasta with PC87310 Super I/O |
| HT3440C | Headland Technologies HT340 Shasta with 82C711 Combo I/O |
| HT3440D | Headland Technologies HT340 Shasta with PC87310 Super I/O |
| HT3440E | Headland Technologies HT340 Shasta with 82C711 Combo I/O |
| HT3440F | Headland Technologies HT340 Shasta with PC87310 Super I/O |
| MOSL400 | Mosel MS400 Single Chip |
| MOSL403 | Mosel MS400 Single Chip |
| MOSL404 | Mosel MS400 Single Chip |
| MOSL410 | Mosel MS400 Single Chip with 82C711 Combo I/O |
| MOSL413 | Mosel MS400 Single Chip with 82C711 Combo I/O |
| MOSL415 | Mosel MS400 Single Chip with 82C711 Combo I/O |
| MXIC300 | Micronix MX83C305/306 (with built-in 8KB cache) |
| MXIC302 | Micronix MX83C305/306 (with built-in 8KB cache) |
| MXIC303 | Micronix MX83C305/306 (with built-in 8KB cache) |
| MXIC304 | Micronix MX83C305/306 (with built-in 8KB cache) |
| MXIC305 | Micronix MX83C305/306 (with built-in 8KB cache) |
| MXIC308 | Micronix MX83C305/306 (with built-in 8KB cache) |
| MXIC30A | Micronix MX83C305/306 (with built-in 8KB cache) |
| MXIC30B | Micronix MX83C305/306 (with built-in 8KB cache) |
| MXIC30C | Micronix MX83C305/306 (with built-in 8KB cache) |
| MXIC30D | Micronix MX83C305/306 (with built-in 8KB cache) |
| OPTI306 | OPTi 82C381 WriteThru |
| OPTI308 | OPTi 82C381 WriteThru |
| OPTI309 | OPTi 82C381 WriteThru |
| OPTI315 | OPTi 82C281 SxPW Single-Chip Posted-Write |
| OPTI316 | OPTi 82C281 SxPW Single-Chip Posted-Write |
| OPTI317 | OPTi 82C283 SxPI Single-Chip |

**TABLE 6-7    IDENTIFICATION STRINGS FOR MR BIOS** *(CONTINUED)*

| BIOS CODE STRING | MOTHERBOARD AND/OR CHIPSET |
|---|---|
| OPTI318 | OPTi 82C283 SxPI Single-Chip |
| OPTI319 | OPTi 82C281 SxPW Single-Chip Posted-Write with 82C711 Combo I/O |
| OPTI31A | OPTi 82C281 SxPW Single-Chip Posted-Write with PC87310 Super I/O |
| OPTI31B | OPTi 82C283 SxPI Single-Chip with 82C711 Combo I/O |
| OPTI31C | OPTi 82C283 SxPI Single-Chip with PC87310 Super I/O |
| OPTI31D | OPTi 82C283 SxPI Single-Chip |
| OPTI31E | OPTi 82C283 SxPI Single-Chip |
| OPTI31F | OPTi 82C283 SxPI Single-Chip with 82C711 Combo I/O |
| OPTI31G | OPTi 82C283 SxPI Single-Chip with 82C711 Combo I/O |
| OPTI31H | OPTi 82C283 SxPI Single-Chip with PC87310 Super I/O |
| OPTI31J | OPTi 82C283 SxPI Single-Chip with PC87310 Super I/O |
| OPTI31K | OPTi 82C281 SxPW Single-Chip Posted-Write |
| OPTI31L | OPTi 82C281 SxPW Single-Chip Posted-Write |
| OPTI31M | OPTi 82C281 SxPW Single-Chip Posted-Write with 82C711 Combo I/O |
| OPTI31N | OPTi 82C281 SxPW Single-Chip Posted-Write with 82C711 Combo I/O |
| OPTI31P | OPTi 82C281 SxPW Single-Chip Posted-Write with PC87310 Super I/O |
| OPTI31Q | OPTi 82C281 SxPW Single-Chip Posted-Write with PC87310 Super I/O |
| OPTI324 | OPTi 82C391 WriteBack Rev. A & Rev. B |
| OPTI32B | OPTi 82C391 WriteBack Rev. A & Rev. B with 82C711 Combo I/O |
| OPTI32C | OPTi 82C391 WriteBack Rev. A & Rev. B with PC87310 Super I/O |
| OPTI32E | OPTi 82C391 WriteBack Rev. A & Rev. B |
| OPTI32F | OPTi 82C391 WriteBack Rev. A & Rev. B |
| OPTI32G | OPTi 82C391 WriteBack Rev. A & Rev. B |
| OPTI32H | OPTi 82C391 WriteBack Rev. A & Rev. B |
| OPTI32J | OPTi 82C391 WriteBack Rev. A & Rev. B with 82C711 Combo I/O |
| OPTI32K | OPTi 82C391 WriteBack Rev. A & Rev. B with 82C711 Combo I/O |
| OPTI32L | OPTi 82C391 WriteBack Rev. A & Rev. B with 82C711 Combo I/O |
| OPTI32M | OPTi 82C391 WriteBack Rev. A & Rev. B with 82C711 Combo I/O |
| OPTI32P | OPTi 82C391 WriteBack Rev. A & Rev. B with PC87310 Super I/O |
| OPTI32Q | OPTi 82C391 WriteBack Rev. A & Rev. B with PC87310 Super I/O |
| OPTI32R | OPTi 82C391 WriteBack Rev. A & Rev. B with PC87310 Super I/O |
| OPTI32S | OPTi 82C391 WriteBack Rev. A & Rev. B with PC87310 Super I/O |
| OPTI330 | OPTi 82C496/497 DxPI Rev. A & Rev. B |
| OPTI331 | OPTi 82C496/497 DxPI Rev. A & Rev. B with 82C711 Combo I/O |
| OPTI332 | OPTi 82C496/497 DxPI Rev. A & Rev. B with PC87310 Super I/O |
| OPTI334 | OPTi 82C496/497 DxPI Rev. A & Rev. B |
| OPTI335 | OPTi 82C496/497 DxPI Rev. A & Rev. B |
| OPTI336 | OPTi 82C496/497 DxPI Rev. A & Rev. B |
| OPTI337 | OPTi 82C496/497 DxPI Rev. A & Rev. B |
| OPTI338 | OPTi 82C496/497 DxPI Rev. A & Rev. B with 82C711 Combo I/O |

**TABLE 6-7** IDENTIFICATION STRINGS FOR MR BIOS *(CONTINUED)*

| BIOS CODE STRING | MOTHERBOARD AND/OR CHIPSET |
|---|---|
| OPTI339 | OPTi 82C496/497 DxPI Rev. A & Rev. B with 82C711 Combo I/O |
| OPTI33A | OPTi 82C496/497 DxPI Rev. A & Rev. B with 82C711 Combo I/O |
| OPTI33B | OPTi 82C496/497 DxPI Rev. A & Rev. B with 82C711 Combo I/O |
| OPTI33C | OPTi 82C496/497 DxPI Rev. A & Rev. B with PC87310 Super I/O |
| OPTI33D | OPTi 82C496/497 DxPI Rev. A & Rev. B with PC87310 Super I/O |
| OPTI33E | OPTi 82C496/497 DxPI Rev. A & Rev. B with PC87310 Super I/O |
| OPTI33F | OPTi 82C496/497 DxPI Rev. A & Rev. B with PC87310 Super I/O |
| OPTI340 | OPTi 82C291 SxWB Single-Chip WriteBack |
| OPTI341 | OPTi 82C291 SxWB Single-Chip WriteBack with 82C711 Combo I/O |
| OPTI342 | OPTi 82C291 SxWB Single-Chip WriteBack with PC87310 Super I/O |
| OPTI344 | OPTi 82C291 SxWB Single-Chip WriteBack |
| OPTI345 | OPTi 82C291 SxWB Single-Chip WriteBack |
| OPTI346 | OPTi 82C291 SxWB Single-Chip WriteBack |
| OPTI347 | OPTi 82C291 SxWB Single-Chip WriteBack |
| OPTI348 | OPTi 82C291 SxWB Single-Chip WriteBack with 82C711 Combo I/O |
| OPTI349 | OPTi 82C291 SxWB Single-Chip WriteBack with 82C711 Combo I/O |
| OPTI34A | OPTi 82C291 SxWB Single-Chip WriteBack with 82C711 Combo I/O |
| OPTI34B | OPTi 82C291 SxWB Single-Chip WriteBack with 82C711 Combo I/O |
| OPTI34C | OPTi 82C291 SxWB Single-Chip WriteBack with PC87310 Super I/O |
| OPTI34D | OPTi 82C291 SxWB Single-Chip WriteBack with PC87310 Super I/O |
| OPTI34E | OPTi 82C291 SxWB Single-Chip WriteBack with PC87310 Super I/O |
| OPTI34F | OPTi 82C291 SxWB Single-Chip WriteBack with PC87310 Super I/O |
| OPTI406 | OPTi 82C481 WriteThru |
| OPTI408 | OPTi 82C481 WriteThru |
| OPTI409 | OPTi 82C481 WriteThru |
| OPTI424 | OPTi 82C491 WriteBack (original) |
| OPTI428 | OPTi 82C491 WriteBack Rev. A & Rev. B |
| OPTI42B | OPTi 82C491 WriteBack Rev. A & Rev. B with 82C711 Combo I/O |
| OPTI42C | OPTi 82C491 WriteBack Rev. A & Rev. B with PC87310 Super I/O |
| OPTI42E | OPTi 82C491 WriteBack Rev. A & Rev. B |
| OPTI42F | OPTi 82C491 WriteBack Rev. A & Rev. B |
| OPTI42G | OPTi 82C491 WriteBack Rev. A & Rev. B |
| OPTI42H | OPTi 82C491 WriteBack Rev. A & Rev. B |
| OPTI42J | OPTi 82C491 WriteBack Rev. A & Rev. B with 82C711 Combo I/O |
| OPTI42K | OPTi 82C491 WriteBack Rev. A & Rev. B with 82C711 Combo I/O |
| OPTI42L | OPTi 82C491 WriteBack Rev. A & Rev. B with 82C711 Combo I/O |
| OPTI42M | OPTi 82C491 WriteBack Rev. A & Rev. B with 82C711 Combo I/O |
| OPTI42P | OPTi 82C491 WriteBack Rev. A & Rev. B with PC87310 Super I/O |
| OPTI42Q | OPTi 82C491 WriteBack Rev. A & Rev. B with PC87310 Super I/O |
| OPTI42R | OPTi 82C491 WriteBack Rev. A & Rev. B with PC87310 Super I/O |

**TABLE 6-7    IDENTIFICATION STRINGS FOR MR BIOS (CONTINUED)**

| BIOS CODE STRING | MOTHERBOARD AND/OR CHIPSET |
| --- | --- |
| OPTI42S | OPTi 82C491 WriteBack Rev. A & Rev. B with PC87310 Super I/O |
| OPTI430 | OPTi 82C496/497 DxPI Rev. A & Rev. B |
| OPTI431 | OPTi 82C496/497 DxPI Rev. A & Rev. B with 82C711 Combo I/O |
| OPTI432 | OPTi 82C496/497 DxPI Rev. A & Rev. B with PC87310 Super I/O |
| OPTI434 | OPTi 82C496/497 DxPI Rev. A & Rev. B |
| OPTI435 | OPTi 82C496/497 DxPI Rev. A & Rev. B |
| OPTI436 | OPTi 82C496/497 DxPI Rev. A & Rev. B |
| OPTI437 | OPTi 82C496/497 DxPI Rev. A & Rev. B |
| OPTI438 | OPTi 82C496/497 DxPI Rev. A & Rev. B with 82C711 Combo I/O |
| OPTI439 | OPTi 82C496/497 DxPI Rev. A & Rev. B with 82C711 Combo I/O |
| OPTI43A | OPTi 82C496/497 DxPI Rev. A & Rev. B with 82C711 Combo I/O |
| OPTI43B | OPTi 82C496/497 DxPI Rev. A & Rev. B with 82C711 Combo I/O |
| OPTI43C | OPTi 82C496/497 DxPI Rev. A & Rev. B with PC87310 Super I/O |
| OPTI43D | OPTi 82C496/497 DxPI Rev. A & Rev. B with PC87310 Super I/O |
| OPTI43E | OPTi 82C496/497 DxPI Rev. A & Rev. B with PC87310 Super I/O |
| OPTI43F | OPTi 82C496/497 DxPI Rev. A & Rev. B with PC87310 Super I/O |
| OPTI450 | OPTi 82C498 DxWB WriteBack |
| OPTI451 | OPTi 82C498 DxWB WriteBack with 82C711 Combo I/O |
| OPTI452 | OPTi 82C498 DxWB WriteBack with PC87310 Super I/O |
| OPTI454 | OPTi 82C498 DxWB WriteBack |
| OPTI455 | OPTi 82C498 DxWB WriteBack |
| OPTI456 | OPTi 82C498 DxWB WriteBack |
| OPTI457 | OPTi 82C498 DxWB WriteBack |
| OPTI458 | OPTi 82C498 DxWB WriteBack with 82C711 Combo I/O |
| OPTI459 | OPTi 82C498 DxWB WriteBack with 82C711 Combo I/O |
| OPTI45A | OPTi 82C498 DxWB WriteBack with 82C711 Combo I/O |
| OPTI45B | OPTi 82C498 DxWB WriteBack with 82C711 Combo I/O |
| OPTI45C | OPTi 82C498 DxWB WriteBack with PC87310 Super I/O |
| OPTI45D | OPTi 82C498 DxWB WriteBack with PC87310 Super I/O |
| OPTI45E | OPTi 82C498 DxWB WriteBack with PC87310 Super I/O |
| OPTI45F | OPTi 82C498 DxWB WriteBack with PC87310 Super I/O |
| OPTI470 | OPTi 82C495SxLC |
| OPTI471 | OPTi 82C495SxLC with 82C711 Combo I/O |
| OPTI472 | OPTi 82C495SxLC with PC87310 Super I/O |
| OPTI474 | OPTi 82C495SxLC |
| OPTI475 | OPTi 82C495SxLC |
| OPTI476 | OPTi 82C495SxLC |
| OPTI477 | OPTi 82C495SxLC |
| OPTI478 | OPTi 82C495SxLC with 82C711 Combo I/O |
| OPTI479 | OPTi 82C495SxLC with 82C711 Combo I/O |

**TABLE 6-7    IDENTIFICATION STRINGS FOR MR BIOS** *(CONTINUED)*

| BIOS CODE STRING | MOTHERBOARD AND/OR CHIPSET |
| --- | --- |
| OPTI47A | OPTi 82C495SxLC with 82C711 Combo I/O |
| OPTI47B | OPTi 82C495SxLC with 82C711 Combo I/O |
| OPTI47C | OPTi 82C495SxLC with PC87310 Super I/O |
| OPTI47D | OPTi 82C495SxLC with PC87310 Super I/O |
| OPTI47E | OPTi 82C495SxLC with PC87310 Super I/O |
| OPTI47F | OPTi 82C495SxLC with PC87310 Super I/O |
| OPTI47G | OPTi 82C495SxLC |
| OPTI47H | OPTi 82C495SxLC with 82C711 Combo I/O |
| OPTI47J | OPTi 82C495SxLC with PC87310 Super I/O |
| OPTI47K | OPTi 82C495SxLC |
| OPTI47L | OPTi 82C495SxLC |
| OPTI47M | OPTi 82C495SxLC |
| OPTI47N | OPTi 82C495SxLC |
| OPTI47P | OPTi 82C495SxLC with 82C711 Combo I/O |
| OPTI47Q | OPTi 82C495SxLC with 82C711 Combo I/O |
| OPTI47R | OPTi 82C495SxLC with 82C711 Combo I/O |
| OPTI47S | OPTi 82C495SxLC with 82C711 Combo I/O |
| OPTI47T | OPTi 82C495SxLC with PC87310 Super I/O |
| OPTI47U | OPTi 82C495SxLC with PC87310 Super I/O |
| OPTI47V | OPTi 82C495SxLC with PC87310 Super I/O |
| OPTI47W | OPTi 82C495SxLC with PC87310 Super I/O |
| OPTI480 | OPTi 82C499 DxSC Single Chip |
| OPTI481 | OPTi 82C499 DxSC Single Chip with 82C711 Combo I/O |
| OPTI482 | OPTi 82C499 DxSC Single Chip with PC87310 Super I/O |
| OPTI484 | OPTi 82C499 DxSC Single Chip |
| OPTI485 | OPTi 82C499 DxSC Single Chip |
| OPTI486 | OPTi 82C499 DxSC Single Chip |
| OPTI487 | OPTi 82C499 DxSC Single Chip |
| OPTI488 | OPTi 82C499 DxSC Single Chip with 82C711 Combo I/O |
| OPTI489 | OPTi 82C499 DxSC Single Chip with 82C711 Combo I/O |
| OPTI48A | OPTi 82C499 DxSC Single Chip with 82C711 Combo I/O |
| OPTI48B | OPTi 82C499 DxSC Single Chip with 82C711 Combo I/O |
| OPTI48C | OPTi 82C499 DxSC Single Chip with PC87310 Super I/O |
| OPTI48D | OPTi 82C499 DxSC Single Chip with PC87310 Super I/O |
| OPTI48E | OPTi 82C499 DxSC Single Chip with PC87310 Super I/O |
| OPTI48F | OPTi 82C499 DxSC Single Chip with PC87310 Super I/O |
| OPTI48G | OPTi 82C499 DxSC Single Chip |
| OPTI48H | OPTi 82C499 DxSC Single Chip with 82C711 Combo I/O |
| OPTI48J | OPTi 82C499 DxSC Single Chip with PC87310 Super I/O |
| OPTI48K | OPTi 82C499 DxSC Single Chip |

**TABLE 6-7    IDENTIFICATION STRINGS FOR MR BIOS** *(CONTINUED)*

| BIOS CODE STRING | MOTHERBOARD AND/OR CHIPSET |
|---|---|
| OPTI48L | OPTi 82C499 DxSC Single Chip |
| OPTI48M | OPTi 82C499 DxSC Single Chip |
| OPTI48N | OPTi 82C499 DxSC Single Chip |
| OPTI48P | OPTi 82C499 DxSC Single Chip with 82C711 Combo I/O |
| OPTI48Q | OPTi 82C499 DxSC Single Chip with 82C711 Combo I/O |
| OPTI48R | OPTi 82C499 DxSC Single Chip with 82C711 Combo I/O |
| OPTI48S | OPTi 82C499 DxSC Single Chip with 82C711 Combo I/O |
| OPTI48T | OPTi 82C499 DxSC Single Chip with PC87310 Super I/O |
| OPTI48U | OPTi 82C499 DxSC Single Chip with PC87310 Super I/O |
| OPTI48V | OPTi 82C499 DxSC Single Chip with PC87310 Super I/O |
| OPTI48W | OPTi 82C499 DxSC Single Chip with PC87310 Super I/O |
| OPTI48Z | OPTi 82C499 DxSC Single Chip with PC87311/312 Super I/O |
| OPTI490 | OPTi 82C495 SLC |
| OPTI491 | OPTi 82C495 SLC with 82C711 Combo I/O |
| OPTI492 | OPTi 82C495 SLC with PC87310 Super I/O |
| OPTI493 | OPTi 82C495 SLC |
| OPTI494 | OPTi 82C495 SLC with 82C711 Combo I/O |
| OPTI495 | OPTi 82C495 SLC with PC87310 Super I/O |
| OPTI496 | OPTi 82C495 SLC |
| OPTI497 | OPTi 82C495 SLC with 82C711 Combo I/O |
| OPTI498 | OPTi 82C495 SLC with PC87310 Super I/O |
| OPTI499 | OPTi 82C495 SLC |
| OPTI49A | OPTi 82C495 SLC with 82C711 Combo I/O |
| OPTI49B | OPTi 82C495 SLC with PC87310 Super I/O |
| OPTI4A0 | OPTi 82C801 SCWB2 Single Chip WriteBack |
| OPTI4A1 | OPTi 82C801 SCWB2 Single Chip WriteBack with 82C711 Combo I/O |
| OPTI4A2 | OPTi 82C801 SCWB2 Single Chip WriteBack with PC87310 Super I/O |
| OPTI4A3 | OPTi 82C801 SCWB2 Single Chip WriteBack with PC87311 Super I/O |
| OPTI500 | OPTi 586 VHP Pentium Chipset |
| PKDM301 | Chips & Technologies CS82310 PEAKset DM Rev-0 |
| PKDM304 | Chips & Technologies CS82310 PEAKset DM Rev-0 |
| PKDM305 | Chips & Technologies CS82310 PEAKset DM Rev-0 |
| PKDM311 | Chips & Technologies CS82310 PEAKset DM Rev-0— 82C711 Combo I/O |
| PKDM314 | Chips & Technologies CS82310 PEAKset DM Rev-0— 82C711 Combo I/O |
| PKDM315 | Chips & Technologies CS82310 PEAKset DM Rev-0— 82C711 Combo I/O |
| PKDM321 | Chips & Technologies CS82310 PEAKset DM Rev-B1 |
| PKDM322 | Chips & Technologies CS82310 PEAKset DM Rev-B1 |
| PKDM323 | Chips & Technologies CS82310 PEAKset DM Rev-B1 |

**TABLE 6-7**    IDENTIFICATION STRINGS FOR MR BIOS *(CONTINUED)*

| BIOS CODE STRING | MOTHERBOARD AND/OR CHIPSET |
|---|---|
| PKDM324 | Chips & Technologies CS82310 PEAKset DM Rev-B1 |
| PKDM325 | Chips & Technologies CS82310 PEAKset DM Rev-B1 |
| PKDM331 | Chips & Technologies CS82310 PEAKset DM Rev-B1— 82C711 Combo I/O |
| PKDM332 | Chips & Technologies CS82310 PEAKset DM Rev-B1— 82C711 Combo I/O |
| PKDM333 | Chips & Technologies CS82310 PEAKset DM Rev-B1— 82C711 Combo I/O |
| PKDM334 | Chips & Technologies CS82310 PEAKset DM Rev-B1— 82C711 Combo I/O |
| PKDM335 | Chips & Technologies CS82310 PEAKset DM Rev-B1— 82C711 Combo I/O |
| PKDM420 | Chips & Technologies CS82310 PEAKset DM Rev-B1 |
| PKDM421 | Chips & Technologies CS82310 PEAKset DM Rev-B1 |
| PKDM424 | Chips & Technologies CS82310 PEAKset DM Rev-B1 |
| PKDM425 | Chips & Technologies CS82310 PEAKset DM Rev-B1 |
| PKDM428 | Chips & Technologies CS82310 PEAKset DM Rev-B1 |
| PKDM429 | Chips & Technologies CS82310 PEAKset DM Rev-B1 |
| PKDM430 | Chips & Technologies CS82310 PEAKset DM Rev-B1— 82C711 Combo I/O |
| PKDM431 | Chips & Technologies CS82310 PEAKset DM Rev-B1— 82C711 Combo I/O |
| PKDM434 | Chips & Technologies CS82310 PEAKset DM Rev-B1— 82C711 Combo I/O |
| PKDM435 | Chips & Technologies CS82310 PEAKset DM Rev-B1— 82C711 Combo I/O |
| PKDM438 | Chips & Technologies CS82310 PEAKset DM Rev-B1— 82C711 Combo I/O |
| PKDM439 | Chips & Technologies CS82310 PEAKset DM Rev-B1— 82C711 Combo I/O |
| SARC302 | SARC RC2016A Rev. A3 (standard) |
| SARC306 | SARC RC2016A Rev. A3 with built-in EMS |
| SARC30A | SARC RC2016A Rev. A3 Cyrix |
| SARC30E | SARC RC2016A Rev. A3 Cyrix, with built-in EMS |
| SCAT300 | Chips & Technologies 82C236 SCATsx |
| SCAT304 | Chips & Technologies 82C236 SCATsx |
| SCAT305 | Chips & Technologies 82C236 SCATsx |
| SIS_303 | SiS 85C310/320/330 Rabbit Rev. A, B & C |
| SIS_306 | SiS 85C310/320/330 Rabbit Rev. A, B & C |
| SIS_307 | SiS 85C310/320/330 Rabbit Rev. A, B & C |
| SIS_308 | SiS 85C310/320/330 Rabbit Rev. A, B & C |
| SIS_309 | SiS 85C310/320/330 Rabbit Rev. A, B & C |

**TABLE 6-7    IDENTIFICATION STRINGS FOR MR BIOS** *(CONTINUED)*

| BIOS CODE STRING | MOTHERBOARD AND/OR CHIPSET |
|---|---|
| SIS_400 | SiS 85C460 & 85C461V Single-Chip |
| SIS_404 | SiS 85C460 & 85C461V Single-Chip |
| SIS_405 | SiS 85C460 & 85C461V Single-Chip |
| SLGC301 | SysLogic 386 non-cache |
| SLGC302 | SysLogic 386 with cache |
| SLGC304 | SysLogic 386 non-cache |
| SLGC305 | SysLogic 386 non-cache |
| SLGC306 | SysLogic 386 with cache |
| SLGC307 | SysLogic 386 with cache |
| SLGC401 | SysLogic 486 no external cache |
| SLGC404 | SysLogic 486 no external cache |
| SLGC405 | SysLogic 486 no external cache |
| STD_202 | Generic 286 (TTL/Discrete Logic) |
| STD_203 | Generic 286 (TTL/Discrete Logic) |
| STD_286 | Generic 286 (TTL/Discrete Logic) |
| STD_302 | Generic 386 (TTL/Discrete Logic) |
| STD_303 | Generic 386 (TTL/Discrete Logic) |
| STD_386 | Generic 386 (TTL/Discrete Logic) |
| STD_408 | Generic 486 (TTL/Discrete Logic) |
| STD_409 | Generic 486 (TTL/Discrete Logic) |
| STD_486 | Generic 486 (TTL/Discrete Logic) |
| SYML401 | Symphony Labs SL82C46x Haydn Rev. 1.1 |
| SYML402 | Symphony Labs SL82C46x Haydn Rev. 1.1 with 82C711 Combo I/O |
| SYML403 | Symphony Labs SL82C46x Haydn Rev. 1.1 with PC87310 Super I/O |
| SYML404 | Symphony Labs SL82C46x Haydn Rev. 1.1 |
| SYML405 | Symphony Labs SL82C46x Haydn Rev. 1.1 |
| SYML406 | Symphony Labs SL82C46x Haydn Rev. 1.1 with 82C711 Combo I/O |
| SYML407 | Symphony Labs SL82C46x Haydn Rev. 1.1 with 82C711 Combo I/O |
| SYML408 | Symphony Labs SL82C46x Haydn Rev. 1.1 with PC87310 Super I/O |
| SYML409 | Symphony Labs SL82C46x Haydn Rev. 1.1 with PC87310 Super I/O |
| SYML411 | Symphony Labs SL82C46x Haydn Rev. 1.2 |
| SYML412 | Symphony Labs SL82C46x Haydn Rev. 1.2 with 82C711 Combo I/O |
| SYML413 | Symphony Labs SL82C46x Haydn Rev. 1.2 with PC87310 Super I/O |
| SYML414 | Symphony Labs SL82C46x Haydn Rev. 1.2 |
| SYML415 | Symphony Labs SL82C46x Haydn Rev. 1.2 |
| SYML416 | Symphony Labs SL82C46x Haydn Rev. 1.2 with 82C711 Combo I/O |
| SYML417 | Symphony Labs SL82C46x Haydn Rev. 1.2 with 82C711 Combo I/O |
| SYML418 | Symphony Labs SL82C46x Haydn Rev. 1.2 with PC87310 Super I/O |
| SYML419 | Symphony Labs SL82C46x Haydn Rev. 1.2 with PC87310 Super I/O |
| TACT300 | Texas Instruments TACT83000 Tiger non-cache |

**TABLE 6-7    IDENTIFICATION STRINGS FOR MR BIOS** *(CONTINUED)*

| BIOS CODE STRING | MOTHERBOARD AND/OR CHIPSET |
|---|---|
| TACT302 | Texas Instruments TACT83000 Tiger with Intel 82385 cache |
| TACT303 | Texas Instruments TACT83000 Tiger with Austek cache |
| TACT30A | Texas Instruments TACT83000 Tiger non-cache |
| TACT30B | Texas Instruments TACT83000 Tiger non-cache |
| TACT30C | Texas Instruments TACT83000 Tiger with Austek cache |
| TACT30D | Texas Instruments TACT83000 Tiger with Austek cache |
| TACT30E | Texas Instruments TACT83000 Tiger with Intel 82385 cache |
| TACT30F | Texas Instruments TACT83000 Tiger with Intel 82385 cache |
| TACT400 | Texas Instruments TACT83000 Tiger no external cache |
| TACT40A | Texas Instruments TACT83000 Tiger no external cache |
| TACT40B | Texas Instruments TACT83000 Tiger no external cache |
| UMC_301 | UMC 82C48x WriteBack Rev. 0 |
| UMC_302 | UMC 82C48x WriteBack Rev. A & Rev. B |
| UMC_304 | UMC 82C48x WriteBack Rev. A & Rev. B |
| UMC_310 | UMC 82C330 Twinstar |
| UMC_314 | UMC 82C330 Twinstar |
| UMC_315 | UMC 82C330 Twinstar |
| UMC_401 | UMC 82C48x WriteBack Rev. 0 |
| UMC_402 | UMC 82C48x WriteBack Rev. A & Rev. B |
| UMC_403 | UMC 82C48x WriteBack Rev. A & Rev. B |
| UMC_404 | UMC 82C48x WriteBack Rev. A & Rev. B |
| UMC_405 | UMC 82C48x WriteBack Rev. A & Rev. B |
| UMC_406 | UMC 82C48x WriteBack Rev. A & Rev. B |
| UMC_407 | UMC 82C48x WriteBack Rev. A & Rev. B |
| UMC_40A | UMC 82C48x WriteBack Rev. B |
| UMC_40B | UMC 82C48x WriteBack Rev. B |
| UMC_40C | UMC 82C48x WriteBack Rev. B |
| UMC_40D | UMC 82C48x WriteBack Rev. B |
| UMC_40E | UMC 82C48x WriteBack Rev. B |
| UMC_40F | UMC 82C48x WriteBack Rev. B |
| UMC_40G | UMC 82C48x WriteBack Rev. A & Rev. B |
| UMC_410 | UMC 82C491 Single-Chip |
| VLSI301 | VLSI Technology 386 Topcat—Intel 82340 non-cache |
| VLSI302 | VLSI Technology 386 Topcat—Intel 82340 non-cache with 82C106 IPC |
| VLSI312 | VLSI Technology 386 Topcat—Intel 82340 with 82385 cache and 82C106 IPC |
| VLSI401 | VLSI Technology 386 Topcat—Intel 82340 |
| VLSI402 | VLSI Technology 386 Topcat—Intel 82340 with 82C106 IPC |
| VLSI404 | VLSI Technology 386 Topcat—Intel 82340 with 82C106 IPC |

# IDENTIFYING YOUR BIOS CHIP

There may also be times when it becomes necessary to identify the flash BIOS chip itself in order to replace the chip or more closely identify the motherboard. The most obvious sign of a BIOS chip is the presence of a sticker carrying the name of a known BIOS maker such as AMI, Award, Phoenix, MR BIOS, and so on. When you gently peal back the sticker, you can determine the characteristics of your flash BIOS chip from the part number. Table 6-8 identifies many of the most popular flash chips.

**TABLE 6-8    IDENTIFYING BIOS CHIPS BY PHYSICAL PART NUMBER**

| PART NUMBER | IDENTIFICATION |
| --- | --- |
| 27Cxxx | With window—EPROM—read-only, requires programmer to write and UV to erase |
| 28Cxxx | EEPROM—not flash memory |
| 28EE011 | SST 5-volt flash ROM |
| 28F001BX-B | Intel 12-volt flash ROM |
| 28F001BX-T | Intel 12-volt flash ROM |
| 28F010 | Fujitsu 12-volt flash ROM (or ISSI 12-volt flash ROM) |
| 28F010 | Intel 12-volt flash ROM |
| 29EE010 | SST 5-volt flash ROM |
| 29LVxxx | 3-volt Flash memory (rare) |
| A28F010 | Intel 12-volt flash ROM |
| Am28F010 | AMD 12-volt flash ROM |
| Am28F010A | AMD 12-volt flash ROM |
| Am29F010 | AMD 5-volt flash ROM |
| AT28C010 | Atmel 5-volt flash ROM |
| AT28MC010 | Atmel 5-volt flash ROM |
| AT29C010 | Atmel 5-volt flash ROM |
| AT29LC010 | Atmel 5-volt flash ROM |
| AT29MC010 | Atmel 5-volt flash ROM |
| CAT28F010 | Catalyst 12-volt flash ROM |
| CAT28F010I | Catalyst 12-volt flash ROM |
| CAT28F010V5 | Catalyst 5-volt flash ROM |
| CAT28F010V5I | Catalyst 5-volt flash ROM |
| DQ28C010 | SEEQ 5-volt flash ROM |
| DQ47F010 | SEEQ 12-volt flash ROM |
| DQ48F010 | SEEQ 12-volt flash ROM |
| DQM28C010A | SEEQ 5-volt flash ROM |
| DYM28C010 | SEEQ 5-volt flash ROM |
| HN28F101 | Hitachi 12-volt flash ROM |
| HN29C010 | Hitachi 12-volt flash ROM |
| HN29C010B | Hitachi 12-volt flash ROM |

**TABLE 6-8** IDENTIFYING BIOS CHIPS BY PHYSICAL PART NUMBER *(CONTINUED)*

| PART NUMBER | IDENTIFICATION |
| --- | --- |
| HN58C1000 | Hitachi 5-volt flash ROM |
| HN58C1001 | Hitachi 12-volt flash ROM |
| HN58V1001 | Hitachi 12-volt flash ROM |
| KM29C010 | Samsung 5-volt flash ROM |
| M28F010 | SGS-Thomson 12-volt flash ROM |
| M28F1001 | SGS-Thomson 12-volt flash ROM |
| M5M28F101FP | Mitsubishi 12-volt flash ROM |
| M5M28F101P | Mitsubishi 12-volt flash ROM |
| M5M28F101RV | Mitsubishi 12-volt flash ROM |
| M5M28F101VP | Mitsubishi 12-volt flash ROM |
| MSM28F101 | OKI 12-volt flash ROM |
| MX28F1000 | MXIC 12-volt flash ROM |
| PH29EE010 | SST ROM Chip—Flashable |
| TMS28F010 | Texas Instruments 12-volt flash ROM |
| TMS29F010 | Texas Instruments 5-volt flash ROM |
| W27F010 | Winbond 12-volt flash ROM |
| W29EE011 | Winbond 5-volt flash ROM |
| X28C010 | XICOR 5-volt flash ROM |
| X28C010I | XICOR 5-volt flash ROM |
| XM28C010 | XICOR 5-volt flash ROM |
| XM28C010I | XICOR 5-volt flash ROM |

Anything without a quartz window that doesn't have a "28" or "29" as the preceding digits of the part number is most likely a standard ROM chip that cannot be reprogrammed.

# BIOS and Boot Sequences

The next step in understanding the BIOS is to recognize how it *boots*—the series of steps that takes a PC from power-on to the point where it's loading an operating system. While every BIOS follows a similar pattern of steps, each BIOS is written a bit differently and may have more or fewer steps than comparable BIOS versions. This part of the chapter looks at the typical boot sequences for several popular BIOS versions.

Remember that BIOS is usually tweaked for each particular motherboard, so different motherboards may demonstrate slightly different boot procedures (even though each may use the same core BIOS).

# AMERICAN MEGATRENDS

American Megatrends (AMI) is renowned for their BIOS, PC diagnostics, and motherboards. Classic AMI BIOS performs a fairly comprehensive suite of 24 steps in order to check and initialize the PC. The general AMI BIOS POST procedure follows:

1. *Disable the NMI.* BIOS disables the nonmaskable interrupt line to the CPU. A failure here suggests a problem with the CMOS RAM chip or its associated circuitry.

2. *Power-on delay.* The system resets the soft and hard reset bits. A fault here indicates a problem with the keyboard controller chip or system clock generator chip.

3. *Initialize chipsets.* BIOS initializes any particular motherboard chipsets (such as the Intel or VIA chipsets) that may be present in the system. A problem here may be caused by the BIOS, the clock generator chip, or the chipset itself.

4. *Reset determination.* The system reads the reset bits in the keyboard controller to determine whether a hard or soft reset (cold or warm boot) is required. A failure here may be caused by the BIOS or keyboard controller chip.

5. *BIOS ROM checksum.* The system performs a checksum test of ROM contents and adds a factory preset value that should make the total equal to 00h. If this total does not equal 00h, the BIOS ROM is defective.

6. *Keyboard test.* A command is sent to the 8042 (keyboard controller), which performs a test and sets a buffer space for commands. After the buffer is defined, the BIOS sends a command byte, writes data to the buffer, checks the high order bits (pin 23) of the internal keyboard controller, and issues a *No Operation* (NOP) command. A fault here is likely caused by the keyboard controller chip.

7. *CMOS shutdown check.* BIOS tests the shutdown byte in CMOS RAM, calculates the CMOS checksum, and updates the CMOS diagnostic byte. The system then initializes a small CMOS area in conventional memory and updates the date and time. A problem here is likely in the RTC/CMOS chip, or in the CMOS backup battery.

8. *Controller disable.* BIOS now disables the DMA and IRQ controller chips before proceeding. A fault at this point suggests trouble in the respective controller.

9. *Disable video.* BIOS disables the video controller chip. If this procedure fails, the trouble is probably in the video adapter board.

10. *Detect memory.* The system proceeds to check the amount of memory available. BIOS measures system memory in 64KB blocks. A problem here may be in the memory chip(s).

11. *PIT test.* BIOS tests the *programmable interrupt timer* (PIT), vital for memory refresh. A problem with the PIT test may reflect a fault in the PIT IC or in the RTC chip.

12. *Check memory refresh.* BIOS now uses the PIT to try refreshing memory. A failure indicates a problem with the PIT chip.

13. *Check low address lines.* The system checks the first 16 address lines controlling the first 64KB of RAM. A problem with this test typically means a fault in an address line.

14. *Check low 64KB RAM.* The system now checks the first 64KB of system RAM. This is vital since this area must hold information that is critical for system initialization. A problem here is usually the result of a bad RAM chip.

**15.** *Initialize support chips.* BIOS proceeds to initialize the *programmable interrupt timer* (PIT), the *programmable interrupt controller* (PIC), and the *Direct Memory Access* (DMA) chips. A fault here would be located in one of those locations.

**16.** *Load INT vector table.* BIOS loads the system's interrupt vector table into the first 2KB of system RAM.

**17.** *Check the keyboard controller (KBC).* BIOS reads the keyboard controller buffer at I/O port 60h. A problem here indicates a fault in the keyboard controller chip.

**18.** *Video tests.* The system checks for the type of video adapter in use, then tests and initializes the video memory and adapter. A problem with this test typically indicates a fault with the video memory or adapter, respectively. After a successful video test, the video system will be operational.

**19.** *Load the BDA.* The system now loads the *BIOS data area* (BDA) into conventional memory.

**20.** *Test memory.* BIOS checks all memory below 1MB. A problem here is typically the fault of one or more RAM modules, the keyboard controller chip, or a bad data line.

**21.** *Check DMA registers.* BIOS performs a register-level check of the DMA controller(s) using binary test patterns. A problem here is often due to a failure of the DMA chip(s).

**22.** *Check the keyboard.* The system performs a final check of the keyboard interface. An error at this point is usually the fault of the keyboard.

**23.** *Perform high-level tests.* This step involves a whole suite of tests that check such high-level devices as the floppy and hard disks, serial adapters, parallel adapters, mouse adapter, and so on. The number and complexity of these tests vary with the BIOS version. When an error occurs, a corresponding text message will be displayed. If the system hardware does not match the setup shown in the CMOS Setup, a corresponding error code will be displayed.

**24.** *Load the OS.* At this point, BIOS triggers INT 19h, which is the routine that loads an operating system. An error here generally results in an error message such as "Non-system disk."

## AWARD SOFTWARE

Award is another popular and well-established BIOS maker whose products can be found in a wide range of PCs spanning almost every generation. The procedure outlined next is generally found with Award BIOS v4.2 and later.

 Award Software was acquired by Phoenix Technologies in September 1998.

**1.** *Test the CPU.* The BIOS checks the error flags in the CPU, then performs a register test by writing and reading bit patterns. Failure here is normally due to the CPU or clock chip.

**2.** *Initialize support chips.* Video is disabled along with parity/DMA and NMI; then the PIT/PIC and DMA chips are initialized. Failure at this point is normally due to the PIT or DMA chips.

**3.** *Initialize the keyboard.* The keyboard and *keyboard controller* (KBC) are initialized. Problems here are due to keyboard connection faults or a failure of the KBC chip.

**4.** *ROM BIOS test.* A checksum is performed on the ROM BIOS. Failure here is normally due to the ROM BIOS chip that would normally be reprogrammed or replaced.

**5.** *CMOS RAM test.* A test of the CMOS chip is performed (which should also detect a bad battery). Trouble here is due to either the CMOS chip or the CMOS backup battery.

6. *Memory test.* The first 356KB of memory is tested with any diagnostic routines in the chipsets. A fault at this point is normally due to defective memory chips, SIMMs, or DIMMs.

7. *Cache initialization.* Any cache external to the main chipset is activated. Failure to control the cache here is normally caused by a fault in the cache controller or cache chips.

8. *Initialize the vector table.* Interrupt vectors are initialized, and the interrupt table is installed into low memory. Failure here is normally caused by the BIOS or a fault in low memory.

9. *CMOS RAM checksum.* The CMOS RAM is checksum tested (BIOS defaults are loaded if the CMOS RAM checksum is invalid). When trouble occurs here, it may be necessary to replace the CMOS RAM chip.

10. *Keyboard initialization.* The keyboard is initialized and the Num Lock is set On. Check the keyboard or *keyboard controller* (KBC) if you have problems here.

11. *Video circuit test.* The video adapter circuit is tested and initialized.

12. *Video memory test.* Memory is tested on "Mono" and "CGA" adapters (if installed). Check the adapter card if trouble occurs here.

13. *DMA controller test.* The DMA controllers and page registers are tested. Check the DMA chips when problems occur here.

14. *PIC tests.* The 8259 PIC chips are tested.

15. *EISA mode test.* A checksum is performed on the extended data area of CMOS where EISA information is stored. If the test passes, the EISA adapter is initialized.

16. *Enable EISA slots.* Slots 0–15 (for EISA adapters) are enabled if the test passes.

17. *Check memory size.* Memory addresses above 265KB are written in 64KB blocks, and any addresses found are initialized. If a bit is bad, the entire block containing it (and those above it) will not be seen. Replace any defective memory chips, SIMMs, or DIMMs.

18. *Memory test.* A read/write test is performed on memory over 256KB. A failure would be due to a bad bit in RAM, and the defective memory chip, SIMM, or DIMM should be replaced.

19. *Check EISA memory.* This checks memory on any adapters initialized previously. If there are problems here, check the memory chips/devices on those adapters.

20. *Mouse initialization.* This checks for a mouse and installs the appropriate interrupt vectors if one is found. Check the mouse adapter if there is a problem.

21. *Cache initialization.* The cache controller is initialized (if present).

22. *Shadow RAM setup.* Any shadow RAM that is present (according to the CMOS Setup) is enabled.

23. *Floppy test.* Test and initialize the floppy controller and drive.

24. *Hard drive test.* Test and initialize the hard disk controller and drive. If there is trouble here, there may be an improper setup, a bad controller, or a defective hard drive.

25. *Serial/parallel port test.* Any serial and parallel ports found at the proper addresses are initialized.

26. *Initialize math coprocessor.* The MCP is initialized if found.

27. *Boot speed.* This sets the default speed at which the computer boots.

28. *POST loop.* A reboot occurs if the "loop pin" is set. (This is used only for manufacturing purposes.)

29. *Security.* The system will ask for the password (if one has been configured). If this does not happen, check the CMOS data or the CMOS RAM chip. For example, a CMOS password may have been cleared if the CMOS backup battery was removed.

30. *Write to CMOS RAM.* The BIOS tries to write the CMOS values from setup to CMOS RAM. Failure here is normally due to an invalid CMOS configuration.

31. *Initialize adapter ROM(s).* Any adapter ROMs between C800h and EFFFh are initialized. The ROM will do an internal test before giving back control to the system ROM. Failure here is normally due to the adapter ROM or the attached hardware that should be replaced.

32. *Set up the time.* This sets the CMOS time to the value located at 40h of the *BIOS Data Area* (BDA).

33. *Boot the system.* Control is given to the INT 19 boot loader.

## PHOENIX TECHNOLOGIES

Phoenix Technologies is one of the premier BIOS manufacturers for IBM-compatible PCs, known for their extensive POST and versatility with OEMs. A typical Phoenix BIOS performs essentially the same steps as an AMI BIOS, but there are several variations, as shown next:

1. *Check the CPU.* The registers and control lines of the CPU are checked. Any problems will usually be the result of a faulty CPU or clock chip.

2. *Test CMOS RAM.* The CMOS chip is tested. A fault is usually due to a failure of the RTC/CMOS chip.

3. *BIOS ROM checksum.* A checksum is performed on the BIOS ROM. If the calculated checksum does not match the factory-set value, an error is generated. A checksum problem is typically the result of a faulty BIOS ROM. Try replacing the BIOS ROM.

4. *Test chipset(s).* The system checks any chipsets (such as the Intel or VIA chipsets) for proper operation with the BIOS. A problem here is typically due to a fault in the chipset. Replace the motherboard.

5. *Test PIT.* The *programmable interrupt timer* (PIT) is tested to ensure that all interrupt requests are handled properly. A problem here indicates that the PIT chip is defective.

6. *Test DMA.* The *Direct Memory Access* (DMA) controller is tested next. A fault at this point is typically caused by the CPU, the DMA chip, or an address line problem.

7. *Test base 64KB memory.* BIOS checks the lowest 64KB of system RAM. A problem here is due to a fault in memory or an address line problem.

8. *Check serial and parallel ports.* The system checks the presence of serial and parallel port hardware, and I/O data areas are assigned for any devices found.

9. *Test PIC.* The *programmable interrupt controller* (PIC) is tested to see that proper interrupt levels can be generated. A problem here is typically due to a fault in the PIC chip.

10. *Check keyboard controller (KBC).* The keyboard controller chip is tested for proper operation. When a problem occurs, the keyboard controller is likely defective.

11. *Verify CMOS data.* Data within the CMOS is checked for validity. If the extended area returns a failure, CMOS data has probably been set up incorrectly. However, continuous failures typically represent a faulty RTC/CMOS chip.

**12.** *Verify video system.* Video RAM is tested; then the video controller is located, tested, and initialized. A fault is usually the result of a defective video controller. If the controller is located on an expansion board, try replacing the video board.

**13.** *Test RTC.* The *real-time clock* (RTC) is tested next, and each frequency output is verified. A problem here is usually due to a fault in the RTC, PIT, or system crystal.

**14.** *Test CPU in protected mode.* The CPU is switched to protected mode and returned to POST at the point indicated in CMOS RAM offset 0Fh. When this step fails, the CPU, keyboard controller chip, CMOS chip, or address line(s) may be at fault.

**15.** *Verify PIC 2.* Counter #2 is tested on the PIC chip. If this test fails, the PIC chip is likely defective.

**16.** *Check NMI.* The NMI is checked to be sure it is active. A problem here often indicates trouble with the CMOS chip, but could also reflect problems in the BIOS ROM, PIC chip, or CPU.

**17.** *Check the keyboard.* The keyboard buffer and controller are checked.

**18.** *Check the mouse.* BIOS initializes the mouse (if present) through the keyboard controller. A fault is usually caused in the mouse adapter circuit.

**19.** *Check system RAM.* All remaining system RAM is tested in 64KB blocks. Trouble usually means a defective memory module.

**20.** *Test disk controller.* Fixed and floppy disk controllers are checked using standard BIOS calls. Problems here are usually the result of defective controllers or faulty drives. If the controllers are installed on expansion boards, you can try replacing the respective expansion board.

**21.** *Set shadow RAM areas.* The system looks at CMOS to find which ROM(s) will be shadowed into RAM. Problems here are often due to a faulty adapter ROM or problems in RAM.

**22.** *Check extended ROMs.* BIOS looks for signatures of 55AAh in memory, which indicate the presence of additional ROMs. The system then performs a checksum test on each ROM. A problem with this step generally indicates trouble with the extended ROM or related adapter circuitry.

**23.** *Test cache controller.* The external cache controller chip is tested. A problem is usually due to a fault in the cache controller chip itself or a defect in cache memory.

**24.** *Test CPU cache.* The internal cache present in the CPU is tested. A problem here is almost always due to a CPU fault.

**25.** *Check hardware adapters.* BIOS proceeds to check the high-level subsystems such as the video system, floppy disk, hard disk, I/O adapters, serial ports, and parallel ports. Problems usually reflect a fault with the respective adapter or an invalid CMOS Setup.

**26.** *Load the OS.* At this point, BIOS triggers INT 19h, which is the routine that loads an operating system. An error here generally results in an error message such as "Non-system disk."

# BIOS Shortcomings and Compatibility Issues

No matter how much time and effort are put into BIOS code development, there are still many times when BIOS can come up short (especially when trying to install the newest, state-of-the-art devices in existing systems). Before you start troubleshooting, you should have an understanding of the places where BIOS is weakest.

# DEVICE DRIVERS

As you might expect, a BIOS cannot possibly address every piece of hardware in the PC marketplace, or keep pace with the rapid advances of those devices that a BIOS does support. Therefore, PC designers have devised a way to augment BIOS through the use of *device drivers*. When the BIOS cannot identify a piece of hardware for the operating system, you must install a device driver so that the operating system is able to use that particular device.

Sound cards are a good example. There are countless sound cards in use today—each with its own unique circuitry. Today's plug-and-play (PnP) systems can detect the presence of the sound card and assign hardware resources to it (e.g., interrupts, DMA channels, and I/O ranges). But the BIOS cannot run the sound card directly, and the operating system itself may not be able to fully identify the particular sound device. In order to operate the sound device, a device driver is added under the operating system. For example, you'd want Windows XP drivers to operate a sound card under Windows XP. Video, SCSI, and network adapters all make use of device drivers at some level.

# "FLASH" LAZINESS

The broad acceptance of "flash" memory allows BIOS to be reprogrammed "in-system" using a downloadable program. There is no need to exchange BIOS chips, or even open the PC. This offers BIOS makers a great deal of versatility in the development of new BIOS, but it can also foster an attitude of laziness. Given the astounding speed at which new developments are proliferating, BIOS makers are under a great deal of pressure to create ever-more-powerful and diverse BIOS versions. With traditional BIOS, programmers needed to create solid, well-tested code—because replacing thousands of BIOS chips in the field is an expensive and cumbersome customer service task. Now that BIOS updates can be quickly downloaded directly from the Internet, BIOS programmers can sometimes take the "release it now and patch it later" attitude. As a rule, BIOS code is still quite solid, but you should be aware that the potential for BIOS problems and oversights are now much higher than in years past.

# BIOS SHADOWING

Another problem with BIOS chips is their inherently slow speed. BIOS is typically recorded onto flash ROM chips (older BIOS used conventional ROM chips or other programmable ROM chips). These read-only devices are necessary because BIOS data must be maintained even when power is removed. Unfortunately, permanent storage chips such as these have hideously slow access times (150nS to 200nS) when compared with the fast RAM used in today's PCs (with effective access times of just a few nS). When you consider that the services stored in a BIOS ROM are used almost continuously, it is easy to see that each delay is additive—the net result is an overall reduction in PC performance.

To overcome this limitation, it would be necessary to accelerate the access time of BIOS ROM. However, this is not too likely. The process of "shadowing" basically copies ROM contents from a slower BIOS chip into available RAM. In practice, the 64KB memory range F000-FFFF is reserved for the BIOS, and the BIOS chip is accessed at this address. However, the same address range exists in RAM. If shadowing is enabled, the BIOS is copied from the ROM chip into the same location in RAM during its boot-up process. Once the copy is complete, the system will work from the *copy* rather than the original. This allows BIOS routines to take advantage of faster RAM. System BIOS shadowing should normally be enabled on all PCs, but shadowing can typically be turned on or off through the CMOS Setup routine.

Not all BIOS can be successfully shadowed. Shadowing problems can cause erratic system behavior and lockups. Whenever you encounter problems configuring a system, you should always try stabilizing the system by shutting down all shadowing options. You can restore shadowing options later and observe if system problems return.

Not only system BIOS, but other BIOS can be shadowed and controlled through CMOS Setup options (e.g., video BIOS is particularly popular for shadowing). For example, the video BIOS is normally addressed at C000-C7FF. If video BIOS shadowing is enabled, the system BIOS will copy the video BIOS to RAM at C000-C7FF during its boot-up process. Video BIOS shadowing would normally be enabled on all PCs. The system BIOS may also allow for shadowing other ROMs such as on a network card. These ROMS would normally be located somewhere in the upper memory area in the range between C800 and EFFF.

## DIRECT CONTROL

In the race to wring every last clock-tick of performance from a PC, even the most elegantly written BIOS is simply too slow for high-performance applications. If the application could work with PC hardware directly, system performance (especially disk and video subsystems) could be substantially improved. Writing directly to hardware is hardly new—pre-IBM PCs relied on direct application control. IBM included the use of BIOS to ensure that variations in PC hardware would remain compatible with operating system and application software. As it turns out, today's PC hardware functions are remarkably standardized (even though the actual components can vary dramatically). With this broad base of relatively standard features, software developers are reviving the direct control approach and ignoring the use of BIOS services in favor of drivers or routines written into the application. The trouble with this approach is that direct hardware control may not work on all system configurations, and any changes to the system hardware (for example, upgrade or replacement parts) may cause the PC to malfunction when the particular application or driver is executed.

## BIOS BUGS

As with all software-based products, BIOS code is subject to accidental errors or omissions (software *bugs*). When BIOS is developed, it is replicated by the thousands and purchased by motherboard manufacturers who incorporate the BIOS into their motherboards. If a bug is present in the BIOS, the system will typically lock up or crash unexpectedly or during a certain operation. Since the same core BIOS may be used in many different motherboards, the bug may not manifest itself in all cases. As one example, some users of AMI BIOS (dated 04/09/90 or earlier) reported problems with the keyboard controller when running Windows or OS/2. As you can imagine, BIOS bugs are particularly frustrating. If an application contains a bug, you can turn the application off. Unfortunately, you cannot turn off the BIOS, so the only way to correct a bug in BIOS is to update the BIOS chip, flash the BIOS with an updated BIOS file, or replace the entire motherboard.

When investigating a customer complaint for a PC, you may wish to check with the motherboard's manufacturer (through technical support, fax-back service, or their Internet Web site). Find if there have been any problems with the BIOS when used in the particular motherboard. For example, a given Phoenix BIOS version may exhibit a peculiar symptom when used in a particular Intel motherboard. If your symptoms match other symptoms that have been reported, a quick BIOS upgrade may save the day for your customer and eliminate the need for more drastic action.

# BIOS Troubleshooting

You've got to be familiar with the myriad error messages that a system can generate. Each time you start the PC, the power-on self-test (POST) initiates a comprehensive series of tests to verify the computer's hardware. Traditionally, the POST generates two types of error messages: beep codes and POST codes. Beep codes are generated through the PC speaker before the video system has properly initialized. POST codes are single-byte hexadecimal characters written to I/O port 80h (or other I/O port) as each POST test is started. You can read the POST code using a POST reader card. By matching the beep code or POST code to your particular BIOS, you can determine the exact fault. You can find a thorough listing of beep and POST codes in Chapter 17.

The problem with beep codes and POST codes is their cryptic nature—you need a detailed code listing in order to match the code to the fault. However, current generations of BIOS and operating systems are starting to employ more user-friendly error messages. By displaying complete error messages (rather than simple codes), a great deal of guesswork is removed from the troubleshooting process. Remember that BIOS error messages are designed to enhance (rather than replace) beep and POST codes. You should also note that unlike beep codes and POST codes, many BIOS error messages are not fatal—that is, the system will continue to run after the error has been generated.

## GENERAL SYMPTOMS

The BIOS can report myriad useful error messages during the POST, and most can be traced to memory, setup, and drive problems. The following symptoms represent a range of possible errors that you may encounter across many system versions.

**SYMPTOM 6-1**    **GA20 Error**    This may also appear as "8042 Gate—A20 Error." There is a fault using gate A20 when switching to the protected mode (accessing memory over 1MB). One or more memory modules (e.g., DIMMs or RIMMs) may be loose, or the *keyboard controller* (KBC) may have failed. Check that each memory module is installed securely. Try replacing the keyboard controller (if possible), or replace the entire motherboard if necessary.

**SYMPTOM 6-2**    **Address line short**    There is a serious problem with the memory address decoding circuitry on your motherboard. In some cases, this may be a spontaneous error that can be cleared by turning the system off for a few seconds and rebooting. Check the motherboard for any loose metal pieces (such as staples or paper clips or mounting screws touching printed traces). If the problem persists, you should replace the motherboard.

**SYMPTOM 6-3**    **BIOS ROM checksum error—System halted**    The checksum of the BIOS code in the BIOS chip is incorrect—this is a *fatal* problem indicating that the BIOS code may have become corrupt. If your BIOS includes a "boot block," you may be able to boot to a floppy disk and try "reflashing" the BIOS according to the motherboard manufacturer's directions. If your system is unable to boot, you'll need to replace the motherboard BIOS chip (or replace the motherboard) before the system will initialize.

**SYMPTOM 6-4** **C: (or D:) drive error** You may also see this presented as "Pri/Sec Master/Slave—ATAPI Incompatible." The system cannot detect the designated drive(s). The hard disk "type" is probably set incorrectly in the CMOS Setup, or the disk may not be connected or formatted properly. In some cases, the BIOS may not have auto-detected or auto-typed the drive properly, and you may need to enter this information manually in the CMOS Setup. Check the CMOS Setup, recheck the drive jumpers, and reconnect the drive(s). You may need to repartition and reformat the drive.

**SYMPTOM 6-5** **C: (or D:) drive failure** The drive was detected, but it failed to respond properly within a given time frame. This is more serious than an error and generally means that the drive is defective. Double-check the drive signal cable, and replace the drive if necessary. In some cases, the drive may simply not have had enough time to initialize. You can try extending the Power On Delay (or similar) setting in the CMOS Setup.

**SYMPTOM 6-6** **Cache memory bad, do not enable cache** POST has determined that your L2 (external) cache memory is defective. Do *not* attempt to enable the cache in your system. You should replace the cache RAM at your earliest opportunity. Until then, you may notice a decline in system performance. If you're using a Pentium II/III/4 or similar CPU where the L2 cache is integrated into the CPU cartridge itself, try replacing the CPU. On older motherboards with the L2 cache on the motherboard rather than the CPU, try replacing the motherboard.

**SYMPTOM 6-7** **Check date and time settings** BIOS found the date or time out of range and reset the real-time clock (RTC). You can set a legal date (e.g., from 1991 to 2099) and time manually. If the problem persists, the RTC may have a problem that requires RTC chip (or entire motherboard) replacement.

**SYMPTOM 6-8** **CMOS battery failed** You may also see this presented as "System battery is dead." The CMOS RAM backup battery is no longer functional. You will need to replace the CMOS battery as soon as possible. If you haven't yet lost CMOS contents, take a PRINTSCREEN of each CMOS Setup page immediately to record the setup configuration, and then power-down the system and install a new battery.

**SYMPTOM 6-9** **CMOS battery state low** The CMOS RAM backup battery voltage level is getting low. Make it a point to record your CMOS settings as soon as possible, and then replace the CMOS battery promptly. If your motherboard uses a rechargeable (NiCd) backup battery, be sure to leave the system plugged in (and turned on if necessary) long enough for the NiCd battery to charge.

**SYMPTOM 6-10** **CMOS checksum error—defaults loaded** CMOS RAM contents have become corrupt, so the CMOS checksum is incorrect. The system usually loads the default equipment configuration in an effort to ensure that the system can start. A weak CMOS RAM backup battery may have caused this error. Check the CMOS backup battery and replace if necessary. If a new battery will not correct the trouble, the CMOS RAM may have failed, and you will need to replace the motherboard.

**SYMPTOM 6-11** **CMOS display type mismatch** The video type indicated in CMOS RAM is not the one detected by the BIOS. Check your CMOS Setup and make sure the correct video type is selected (usually VGA rather than EGA). Remember to save your changes before exiting and rebooting. Also verify that there is no conflict between an integrated video adapter (on the motherboard) and a video adapter card in your system. You may need to disable an onboard video adapter using a motherboard jumper, or through the CMOS Setup.

**SYMPTOM 6-12**    **CMOS memory size mismatch**    The amount of memory recorded in the CMOS Setup configuration does not match the amount of memory detected by the POST. If you have added new memory, start your CMOS Setup and make the appropriate corrections (or simply save changes and reboot even though you change nothing). If you've made no changes to the system, try rebooting the computer. If the error appears again, some of your memory may have failed. Try a systematic replacement to locate the defective memory module(s).

**SYMPTOM 6-13**    **CMOS system options not set**    You may also see this reported as "CMOS settings wrong." The values stored in CMOS RAM are either corrupt or nonexistent. Check your CMOS backup battery and replace it if necessary. Enter the CMOS Setup routine and reload any missing or corrupted entries (or select BIOS Default settings). Remember to save your changes before exiting and rebooting.

**SYMPTOM 6-14**    **CPU at "nnn"**    This displays the running speed of the CPU (where *nnn* is the speed in MHz). This is not an error, but a measurement. If the displayed speed is known to be different from the actual clock speed, you should check the motherboard's clock settings and multipliers, or suspect an error in BIOS speed detection. (You may need to update the BIOS to achieve an accurate measurement.)

**SYMPTOM 6-15**    **Data error**    The floppy disk or hard drive that you are accessing cannot read the data. One or more sectors on the disk(s) may be corrupted. If you are using DOS, run the CHKDSK or ScanDisk utility to check the file structure of the floppy disk or hard disk drive. If you find errors, rerun the utility to correct those errors. Keep in mind that it may be necessary to reload any applications or data files that were subject to file structure problems. If the problem persists, it may be necessary to discard the defective diskette, or replace the troublesome hard drive.

**SYMPTOM 6-16**    **Decreasing available memory**    An error has been detected in system memory, and the available memory is being reduced below the point at which the fault was detected. Either a memory module (e.g., a SIMM/DIMM/RIMM) has failed, or one or more memory modules may be improperly seated. Try reinstalling your memory modules, or systematically replace them.

**SYMPTOM 6-17**    **Diskette drive 0 (or 1) seek failure**    Your floppy drive was unable to seek to the desired track. A cable may be loose or the CMOS Setup information may not match your actual floppy drive hardware (e.g., the CMOS Setup is looking for a 5.25" drive when a 3.5" drive is installed). Check and correct your CMOS Setup, check your signal cable, and replace the floppy drive if necessary.

**SYMPTOM 6-18**    **Diskette read failure**    This may also be displayed as a "Diskette boot failure." The system was unable to read from a floppy disk. This is usually due to dirty read/write heads, a loose signal cable, or a defective floppy disk. Try cleaning the read/write heads, try a different floppy disk, check/replace the floppy signal cable, and replace the floppy drive if necessary.

**SYMPTOM 6-19**    **Diskette subsystem reset failed**    The PC was unable to access the floppy drive system. The disk drive controller may be faulty. If you're using a stand-alone drive controller, make sure that the drive controller is seated properly in its bus slot. Verify that all cables are attached securely. Try the drive controller in another slot, and replace the drive controller if necessary. If you're using a drive controller on the motherboard, you may need to replace the motherboard.

**SYMPTOM 6-20**    **Display switch is set incorrectly**    Some older motherboards provide a display switch that can be set to either monochrome or color. This message indicates the switch is set to a different setting than indicated in CMOS Setup. Determine which video setting is correct, and then either turn off the system and change the motherboard jumper, or enter CMOS Setup and change the video selection.

**SYMPTOM 6-21**    **DMA (or DMA #1 or DMA #2) error**    A serious fault has occurred in the DMA controller system of your motherboard. In virtually all cases, the motherboard will have to be replaced (unless you can replace the DMA controller).

**SYMPTOM 6-22**    **DMA bus time-out**    A device has driven the bus signal for more than 7.8 microseconds. This may be a random fault, but chances are that a DMA-dependent device in the PC has failed (such as your sound card or Ultra-DMA drive controller). Reboot the computer and see if the problem clears. If not, try removing expansion devices first. Otherwise, replace the motherboard.

**SYMPTOM 6-23**    **Drive not ready**    No floppy disk is in the drive. Make sure that the valid disk is secure in the drive before continuing. Try another known-good diskette, or replace the floppy drive outright.

**SYMPTOM 6-24**    **EISA CMOS checksum failure**    The checksum for your EISA CMOS RAM is bad. This means the CMOS RAM is defective or the backup battery is exhausted. Try replacing the backup battery first. If the problem persists, replace the CMOS RAM chip (or replace the entire motherboard).

**SYMPTOM 6-25**    **EISA CMOS not operational**    A read/write failure occurred in extended CMOS RAM. Either the CMOS RAM backup battery has died, or the CMOS RAM chip itself has failed. Try replacing the CMOS backup battery. If the problem persists, replace the CMOS RAM chip (or replace the entire motherboard).

**SYMPTOM 6-26**    **EISA configuration is not complete**    The slot configuration information stored in the EISA CMOS RAM is incomplete. When this error appears, the system will boot in ISA mode, which allows you to run the *EISA Configuration Utility* (ECU). Run the system's ECU (normally on a floppy disk that accompanied the system) and finish configuring the system; then save your changes and reboot.

**SYMPTOM 6-27**    **Enable/disable expansion board**    One of your EISA expansion boards suffered a *nonmaskable interrupt* (NMI). You can usually press E to enable that board, or press D to disable it—this allows the system to finish booting. Try rebooting the system and see if the problem clears. If the problem persists, try replacing the suspect expansion board.

**SYMPTOM 6-28**    **Expansion board not ready at slot "X"**    Your EISA BIOS cannot find the expansion board assigned to slot "X." Verify that the expansion board is in the correct slot and is seated properly. If the problem persists, try replacing the expansion board or moving it to (and reconfiguring it for) another available slot.

**SYMPTOM 6-29**    **Floppy disk controller failure**    This may also be reported as an "FDC Error." There is a problem with the floppy drive system—either the floppy drive or drive controller has failed. Check the floppy drive controller first, and make sure it's seated properly in its bus slot. Try a different bus slot. Check that all the drive cables are secure. Make sure that the floppy drive is receiving power. Try a new drive controller, and try a different floppy drive if necessary. If the floppy drive controller is integrated onto the motherboard, you may need to replace the motherboard outright.

**SYMPTOM 6-30** **Floppy disk(s) fail** You may also see this reported as an "A: Drive Error." The PC cannot find or initialize the floppy drive controller or the floppy drive itself. Make sure the drive controller is installed correctly. (You might try a different expansion slot.) If no floppy drives are installed, be sure the "Diskette Drive" entries in CMOS Setup are set to "none" or "not installed" or "AUTO." Otherwise, verify that the floppy drive is listed correctly in the CMOS Setup, and then replace the floppy disk drive if necessary. If the floppy drive controller is integrated onto the motherboard, you may need to replace the motherboard outright.

**SYMPTOM 6-31** **Hard disk configuration error** The system could not initialize the hard drive in the expected fashion. This is often due to an incorrect configuration in the CMOS Setup. Make sure that the correct hard drive geometry is entered for the drive (or try auto-detecting and auto-configuring the drive). If the drive was originally partitioned in another system with different parameters, you may need to duplicate those parameters in order to access the drive. If the problem persists, try repartitioning and reformatting the drive, or replace the hard drive.

**SYMPTOM 6-32** **Hard disk controller failure** This may also be reported as an "HDC Error." There is a problem with the hard drive system—either the hard drive or drive controller has failed. Check the drive controller first, and make sure it's seated properly in its bus slot. Try a different bus slot. Check that all the drive cables are secure. Make sure that the hard drive is spinning up. Try a new drive controller, and try a different hard drive if necessary. If the hard drive controller is integrated onto the motherboard (virtually all are), you may need to replace the motherboard outright.

**SYMPTOM 6-33** **Hard disk(s) diagnosis fail** Your BIOS may run specific disk diagnostic routines. This type of message appears if one or more hard disks return an error when those diagnostics are run. In most cases, the drive itself is installed improperly or is defective. Check the drive installation, and replace the drive if necessary.

**SYMPTOM 6-34** **Hard disk failure** The hard drive failed initialization, which usually suggests that the drive has failed. Make sure that the drive power and signal cables are attached properly, and see that the drive spins up. Replace the hard drive if necessary. In some cases, the drive may not have had enough time to initialize. Use the CMOS Setup to extend the "Power On Delay" (or similar) setting, or use extended memory testing to increase the amount of POST time before the drive is accessed.

**SYMPTOM 6-35** **Hard disk drive read failure** The drive cannot read from the hard drive, which usually suggests that the drive has failed. Make sure that the drive signal cable is attached properly, and see that the drive spins up. Replace the hard drive if necessary.

**SYMPTOM 6-36** **Incompatible Processor: CPU0 (or CPU1) is XX step or below** You have installed an old version of a CPU that is not supported by the BIOS. In a single-microprocessor system, CPU0 refers to the system board microprocessor; in a dual-microprocessor system, it refers to the secondary microprocessor on the add-in card. The CPU1 message appears only on a dual-microprocessor system and always refers to the system board microprocessor. Replace the microprocessor with a current version of the microprocessor.

**SYMPTOM 6-37** **Incompatible Processor: Cache sizes different** This message appears for a dual-microprocessor system if the CPUs use differing L2 cache sizes. Replace one of the microprocessors to make the L2 cache sizes match. Only a few motherboards allow you to "mix" multiple processors—most require an exact match.

**SYMPTOM 6-38**    **Insert Bootable Media**    You may also see this reported as "No boot device available." The BIOS cannot find a bootable media. Insert a bootable floppy disk or bootable CD, or switch to a known-good bootable drive.

**SYMPTOM 6-39**    **INTR #1 (or INTR #2) error**    A serious fault has occurred with your *programmable interrupt controller* (PIC) on the motherboard. In virtually all cases, the motherboard will have to be replaced entirely.

**SYMPTOM 6-40**    **Invalid Boot Diskette**    The BIOS can read the disk in floppy drive A, but cannot boot the system from it. Use another known-good boot disk, or try booting from a different drive.

**SYMPTOM 6-41**    **Invalid configuration information—please run SETUP program**
The system configuration information in your CMOS Setup does not match the hardware configuration detected by the POST. Enter the CMOS Setup program, and correct the system configuration information (or select BIOS Defaults). Remember to save your changes before exiting and rebooting.

**SYMPTOM 6-42**    **Invalid configuration information for slot "X"**    The configuration information for the EISA board in slot "X" is not correct, which usually means that the system has been reconfigured without running the *EISA Configuration Utility* (ECU). Run the ECU, being sure to configure the system properly and save your changes before exiting.

**SYMPTOM 6-43**    **I/O Card Parity Error at xxxxx**    An expansion card has failed. If the address can be determined, it is displayed as "xxxxx." If not, the message is "I/O Card Parity Error ????". In either case, you'll need to find and reconfigure the offending device, or replace the defective expansion card.

**SYMPTOM 6-44**    **Keyboard clock line failure**    The BIOS has not detected the keyboard clock signal when testing the keyboard. Often, the keyboard connector is loose or the keyboard is defective. Check the keyboard cable and try another keyboard if necessary. If the problem persists, the *keyboard controller* (KBC) may have failed. Try replacing the keyboard controller chip, or replace the entire motherboard.

**SYMPTOM 6-45**    **Keyboard controller failure**    This may also be denoted as a "Keyboard interface error." The keyboard controller on the motherboard is not responding as expected. Start by checking the keyboard connection, and try a different keyboard. If the problem persists, the *keyboard controller* (KBC) may have failed. Try replacing the KBC chip or replace the entire motherboard.

**SYMPTOM 6-46**    **Keyboard data line failure**    The BIOS has not detected the keyboard data signal when testing the keyboard. Often, the keyboard connector is loose or the keyboard is defective. Check the keyboard cable and try another keyboard if necessary. If the problem persists, the keyboard controller may have failed. Try replacing the keyboard controller (KBC) chip or replace the entire motherboard.

**SYMPTOM 6-47**    **Keyboard error or no keyboard present**    The system cannot initialize the keyboard. Make sure the keyboard is attached correctly, and see that no keys are pressed during POST. To purposely configure the system without a keyboard (for example, if you're setting up a server), you can configure the CMOS Setup to ignore the keyboard. To do this, the error halt condition must be set to HALT ON ALL, BUT KEYBOARD.

**SYMPTOM 6-48**    **Keyboard is locked out—unlock the key**    If your system comes fitted with a key lock switch, make sure that the switch is set to the "unlocked" position. If there is no key lock switch (or the switch is set properly), one or more keys may be pressed or shorted on the keyboard. Try a new keyboard.

**SYMPTOM 6-49**    **Keyboard stuck key failure**    In almost all cases, this is a keyboard problem. POST has determined that one or more keys on the keyboard are stuck. Make sure that nothing is resting on the keyboard, and see that no paper clips or staples may have fallen into the keyboard. Try a different keyboard.

**SYMPTOM 6-50**    **Memory address line failure at <address>, read <value> expecting <value>**    An error has occurred in the address decoding circuitry used in memory. In many cases, one or more memory modules (e.g., SIMM/DIMM/RIMM) may be improperly seated. Check that all memory modules are installed correctly. If the problem continues, try systematic replacement to locate a defective memory module. If you cannot find a defective memory module, there is likely a problem elsewhere on the motherboard. Replace the motherboard.

**SYMPTOM 6-51**    **Memory data line failure at <address>, read <value> expecting <value>**    An error has been encountered in memory. In virtually all cases, one or more memory modules may be faulty or improperly seated. Make sure that every SIMM, DIMM, or RIMM is seated correctly, and try a systematic replacement to locate a defective memory module.

**SYMPTOM 6-52**    **Memory double word logic failure at <address>, read <value> expecting <value>**    An error has been encountered in memory. In virtually all cases, one or more memory modules may be faulty or improperly seated. Make sure that every SIMM, DIMM, or RIMM is seated correctly, and try a systematic replacement to locate a defective memory module.

**SYMPTOM 6-53**    **Memory odd/even logic failure at <address>, read <value> expecting <value>**    An error has been encountered in memory. In virtually all cases, one or more memory modules may be faulty or improperly seated. Make sure that every SIMM, DIMM, or RIMM is seated correctly, and try a systematic replacement to locate a defective memory module.

**SYMPTOM 6-54**    **Memory parity failure at <address>, read <value> expecting <value>**    An error has been encountered in memory. In virtually all cases, one or more memory modules may be faulty or improperly seated. Make sure that every SIMM, DIMM, or RIMM is seated correctly, and try a systematic replacement to locate a defective memory module.

**SYMPTOM 6-55**    **Memory size changed**    You may also see this as "Memory size increased" or "Memory size decreased." If you have not altered the memory configuration of your system, chances are that one or more memory devices have failed. Make sure that every memory module is seated correctly, and try a systematic replacement to locate a defective memory module. If the memory checks properly, try entering the CMOS Setup and simply "exit saving changes" (even if you made no changes). This may help the system reset its detection of the available RAM.

**SYMPTOM 6-56**    **Memory write/read failure at <address>, read <value> expecting <value>**    An error has been encountered in memory. In virtually all cases, one or more memory modules may be faulty or improperly seated. Make sure that every memory module in the system is seated correctly, and try a systematic replacement to locate a defective memory module.

**SYMPTOM 6-57**    **Memory size in CMOS invalid**    The amount of memory recorded in the CMOS Setup configuration does not match the memory detected by the POST. If you have added new memory, start your CMOS Setup and make the appropriate corrections. If you've made no changes to the system, try rebooting the computer. If the error appears again, some of your memory may have failed. Try a systematic replacement to locate a defective memory module.

**SYMPTOM 6-58**    **Memory verify error at <address>**    This suggests an error verifying a value already written to memory and almost always indicates a bad memory device. Use the <address> location along with your system's memory map to locate the defective memory devices, or systematically replace your memory module(s) until the defective memory device is found.

**SYMPTOM 6-59**    **No boot device available**    The computer cannot find a viable floppy disk or hard drive—typically because the drives have not been entered properly into CMOS. Enter the CMOS Setup program and configure the proper drive information. You should also verify that your floppy disk or hard drive has been prepared as "bootable." You may need to repartition and/or reformat the hard drive.

**SYMPTOM 6-60**    **No boot sector on hard disk drive**    The PC is refusing to boot from the hard drive. This is usually because the drive is not configured properly. Check the CMOS Setup and verify that the correct drive information has been entered (or select auto-detect). Also make sure to partition the drive with an active bootable partition, and format it as a bootable device. If the problem continues, try replacing the hard drive.

**SYMPTOM 6-61**    **No timer tick interrupt**    The interrupt timer on the motherboard has failed. This is a fatal error that will probably require you to replace the motherboard.

**SYMPTOM 6-62**    **Non-system disk or disk error**    The floppy disk is in drive A: or your hard drive does not have a bootable operating system installed on it. If you're booting from a floppy drive, make the disk bootable. If you're booting from a hard drive, make sure that the drive is partitioned and formatted for bootable operation.

**SYMPTOM 6-63**    **Not a boot diskette**    There is no operating system on the floppy disk. Boot the computer with a disk that contains an operating system.

**SYMPTOM 6-64**    **Off-board parity error**    There is a parity error in memory installed in an expansion slot (for example, a memory module on the video adapter). The format is OFF BOARD PARITY ERROR ADDR (HEX) = (XXXX), where XXXX is the hex address where the error occurred. Chances are that the memory installed at the error address has failed. Try replacing the suspect memory, or replace the device in the affected expansion slot.

**SYMPTOM 6-65**    **On-board parity error**    There is a parity error in memory installed on the motherboard in one of the SIMM, DIMM, or RIMM slots. The format is ON BOARD PARITY ERROR ADDR (HEX) = (XXXX), where XXXX is the hex address where the error occurred. Chances are that the memory installed at the error address has failed. Use a systematic approach to isolate and replace the suspect memory device.

**SYMPTOM 6-66** **Override enabled—defaults loaded** If the system cannot boot using the current CMOS configuration for any reason, the BIOS can override the current configuration using a set of defaults designed for the most stable, minimal-performance system operations. The CMOS may be ignored if the CMOS RAM checksum is wrong, or if a critical piece of CMOS information is missing that would otherwise cause a fatal error. Check the CMOS RAM backup battery and replace it if necessary.

**SYMPTOM 6-67** **Parity error** A parity error has occurred in system memory at an unknown address. Chances are that a memory module has failed. Try a systematic "check and replace" approach to isolate and replace the defective memory component.

**SYMPTOM 6-68** **Plug-and-play configuration error** The system has encountered a problem in trying to configure one or more (usually PCI) expansion cards. Start the CMOS Setup routine, and check that any PnP options have been set correctly (or select BIOS Default settings). If PnP or PCI configuration utilities are included with your particular system, try running those utilities to resolve any configuration issues.

**SYMPTOM 6-69** **Press TAB to show POST screen** Some system OEMs (such as Acer, Intel, Dell, and so on) may replace the normal BIOS POST display with their own proprietary display—usually a graphic logo. When the BIOS displays this message, the operator is able to switch between the OEM display and the default POST display. This can be helpful for troubleshooting purposes.

**SYMPTOM 6-70** **Previous boot incomplete—Default configuration used** The previous POST did not complete successfully. POST will typically load default values and offer to run Setup. If the failure was caused by incorrect values (and they are not corrected), the next boot will likely fail also. Incorrect wait state (memory-related) settings can frequently cause this type of problem. Run Setup and verify that all settings (including the wait-state configuration) are correct, or select BIOS Default settings. This error should be cleared the next time the system boots.

**SYMPTOM 6-71** **Primary master hard disk fail** POST detects an error in the primary ("master") hard drive on the primary drive controller channel. Double-check the drive's installation, jumpering, and cable connections. Otherwise, replace the drive. In some cases, the drive may not have adequate time to initialize. Try extending the "Power On Delay" (or similar setting) in your CMOS Setup.

**SYMPTOM 6-72** **Primary slave hard disk fail** POST detects an error in the secondary ("slave") hard drive on the primary drive controller channel. Double-check the drive's installation, jumpering, and cable connections. Otherwise, replace the drive. In some cases, the drive may not have adequate time to initialize. Try extending the "Power On Delay" (or similar setting) in your CMOS Setup.

**SYMPTOM 6-73** **Resuming from disk** Award BIOS (and now many other BIOS versions) offers a save-to-disk feature for notebook computers (usually referred to as *hibernation*). This message may appear when the operator restarts the system after a save-to-disk shutdown. You will almost never find this type of message on a desktop or tower system.

**SYMPTOM 6-74** **Secondary master hard disk fail** POST detects an error in the primary ("master") hard drive on the secondary drive controller channel. Double-check the drive's installation, jumpering, and cable connections. Otherwise, replace the drive. In some cases, the drive may not have adequate time to initialize. Try extending the "Power On Delay" (or similar setting) in your CMOS Setup.

**SYMPTOM 6-75    Secondary slave hard disk fail**    POST detects an error in the secondary ("slave") hard drive on the secondary drive controller channel. Double-check the drive's installation, jumpering, and cable connections. Otherwise, replace the drive. In some cases, the drive may not have adequate time to initialize. Try extending the "Power On Delay" (or similar setting) in your CMOS Setup.

**SYMPTOM 6-76    Should be empty but EISA board found**    A valid EISA board ID was found in a slot that was configured as having no board installed. This is normally due to an improper system configuration, so run the *EISA Configuration Utility* (ECU) and reconfigure the system properly. Remember to save any changes and reboot the system.

**SYMPTOM 6-77    Should have EISA board but none found**    The board installed in a given EISA slot is not responding to the expected ID request. (Or no board ID has been found in the indicated slot.) This is normally due to an improper system configuration, so run the *EISA Configuration Utility* (ECU) and reconfigure the system properly. Remember to save any changes and reboot the system. If the problem persists, the board in the suspect slot may be defective.

**SYMPTOM 6-78    Shutdown failure**    There is a serious fault on the motherboard—usually associated with the CMOS RAM/RTC function. In most cases, you'll need to replace the motherboard.

**SYMPTOM 6-79    System halted—Press CTRL-ALT-DEL to reboot**    This error indicates the current boot attempt has been aborted, and the system must be rebooted. In most cases, the system files on the boot drive have been damaged or the boot drive itself has failed. Try booting from another drive (for example, a floppy disk). You may need to repartition and reformat the boot drive as a bootable device, or replace the boot drive.

**SYMPTOM 6-80    Terminator/processor card not installed**    This is an error that occurs with dual-CPU systems when neither a "terminator" card nor a secondary microprocessor card is installed in the secondary CPU slot/socket. Make sure either a terminator card or a secondary microprocessor card is installed in the second slot/socket. Install the appropriate CPU or terminator and start the system again.

**SYMPTOM 6-81    Time of day clock stopped**    The *real-time clock* (RTC) has stopped. The CMOS battery may be dead (or almost dead). Enter the CMOS Setup and correct the date and time. If the trouble continues, try replacing the CMOS backup battery.

**SYMPTOM 6-82    Time or date in CMOS is invalid**    The time or date displayed in the CMOS Setup does not match the system clock. This can happen often under Windows 98/Me/XP or other operating systems that can "desynchronize" the system clock. Enter the CMOS Setup utility and correct the date and time. If the problem reoccurs, you may be able to determine a specific application that is causing the problem.

**SYMPTOM 6-83    Timer chip counter 2 failed**    There is a serious fault on the motherboard—probably due to a failure of a *programmable interrupt timer* (PIT). In most cases, you'll need to replace the motherboard.

**SYMPTOM 6-84**     **Unexpected interrupt in protected-mode**     An interrupt has occurred unexpectedly. Loose or poorly inserted memory modules can cause such a problem, so start by checking and reinstalling the SIMMs, DIMMs, or RIMMs in the system. A faulty *keyboard controller* (KBC) can also result in interrupt problems. Try replacing the keyboard controller if possible, or replace the entire motherboard.

**SYMPTOM 6-85**     **Warning—Thermal Probes failed**     This error is usually found in Pentium Pro (and later) systems with one or two thermal probes. At system startup, the BIOS has detected that one or both of the thermal probes in the computer are not operational. You can continue to use the system, but be aware that the temperature probe(s) are disabled—a processor overheat condition will not shut down the system. You will probably have to replace the motherboard to correct this fault.

> The Pentium Pro has a built-in thermocouple that halts microprocessor operation if the CPU exceeds its rated temperature.

**SYMPTOM 6-86**     **Warning—Temperature is too high**     During system startup, the BIOS has detected that one or both microprocessors are overheated. This can happen if you try to restart the system too soon after a thermal shutdown. After displaying this message, the BIOS halts the processes and turns off the system. Let the system cool down before attempting to restart it.

**SYMPTOM 6-87**     **Wrong board in slot "X"**     This is typically an EISA system error when the board's ID does not match the ID stored in the EISA nonvolatile memory. Run the EISA Configuration Utility to reconfigure your device layout and save any system changes.

## PCI SYMPTOMS

In addition to general error detection and reporting, most modern BIOS versions can now detect and report problems associated with the PCI bus and devices. The following symptoms are generally caused by problems with PCI devices or the motherboard's PCI bus architecture. In some cases, you may need to update the motherboard's bus master drivers or enable IRQ steering to correct these issues.

**SYMPTOM 6-88**     **Bad PnP serial ID checksum**     The serial ID checksum of a plug-and-play card is invalid. Try reconfiguring or replacing the offending expansion card.

**SYMPTOM 6-89**     **Floppy disk controller resource conflict**     The floppy disk controller has requested a resource that is already in use by another device. Try reconfiguring or freeing the resources that are requested by the PnP system.

**SYMPTOM 6-90**     **NVRAM checksum error, NVRAM cleared**     The *extended system configuration data* (ESCD) was reinitialized because of an NVRAM checksum error. Try rerunning the *ISA Configuration Utility* (ICU) to configure legacy devices on the system if necessary. If the problem persists, replace the NVRAM chip or replace the motherboard entirely.

**SYMPTOM 6-91**     **NVRAM cleared by jumper**     The "Clear CMOS" jumper on the motherboard has been moved to the "Clear" position, and the system has been initialized. CMOS RAM and ESCD have been cleared and now must be reconfigured/reloaded with the necessary data. If you've cleared the CMOS RAM using that jumper, you must reset the jumper to a protected position before proceeding or re-entering CMOS data.

**SYMPTOM 6-92**   **NVRAM data invalid, NVRAM cleared**   Invalid data has been found in the ESCD (which may mean that you have changed devices in the system). When this message is displayed, the BIOS has already rewritten the ESCD with current configuration data. Try rebooting the system once again, or enter the CMOS Setup and "exit saving changes," even though you may not change anything.

**SYMPTOM 6-93**   **Parallel port resource conflict**   The parallel port requested a resource that is already in use by another device. Try reconfiguring or freeing the resources requested by the PnP system.

**SYMPTOM 6-94**   **PCI error log is full**   The maximum number of PCI conflict errors have been detected and no additional PCI errors can be logged. Deal with the PCI errors already contained in the log in order to reduce the total number of errors, and address subsequent errors as they occur.

**SYMPTOM 6-95**   **PCI I/O port conflict**   Two devices have requested the same I/O address, resulting in a conflict. Try reconfiguring or freeing the I/O resources needed to allow both devices to be configured properly.

**SYMPTOM 6-96**   **PCI IRQ conflict**   Two devices have requested the same IRQ, resulting in a conflict. Try reconfiguring or freeing the IRQs needed to allow both devices to be configured properly.

**SYMPTOM 6-97**   **PCI memory conflict**   Two devices have requested the same memory range resources, resulting in a conflict. Try reconfiguring or freeing the memory ranges needed to allow both devices to be configured properly.

**SYMPTOM 6-98**   **Primary boot device not found**   The designated primary boot device (for example, a hard disk drive, floppy disk drive, or CD-ROM drive) could not be found. Check the installation and configuration of each possible boot device. Also verify that the CMOS Setup reflects your preference of boot devices. For example, if the CMOS Setup defaults to a floppy drive as the first boot device, you may wish to change this to an available hard drive (or even the CD-ROM drive).

**SYMPTOM 6-99**   **Primary IDE controller resource conflict**   The primary IDE controller has requested a resource that is already in use by another device. Try reconfiguring or freeing the resources that are needed to allow the IDE controller to operate.

**SYMPTOM 6-100**   **Primary input device not found**   The designated primary input device such as the keyboard or mouse (or other device if input is redirected) could not be found. Check the installation and configuration of all your input devices. Make sure that the input devices are also enabled in the CMOS Setup.

**SYMPTOM 6-101**   **Secondary IDE controller resource conflict**   The secondary IDE controller has requested a resource that is already in use by another device. Try reconfiguring or freeing the resources that are needed to allow the IDE controller to operate.

**SYMPTOM 6-102**   **"Static device resource conflict" or "System board device resource conflict"**   A non–plug-and-play (a.k.a. "legacy") ISA card has requested a resource that is already in use by another device. Try reconfiguring the ISA card to use other resources, or try freeing the resources needed by the ISA card.

# BIOS Upgrades

You might wonder why it would be necessary to bother with an upgrade. Ideally, a BIOS ROM should be viable for the life of a PC. While this is true in a majority of situations, there are two compelling reasons to undertake a BIOS upgrade. First, a newer BIOS can add support for drives and devices that are not currently supported (or that now require device drivers or TSRs). For example, a possible reason to upgrade a BIOS is to add PnP support to an older motherboard. Two examples might include the addition of bootable CD-ROM drives (e.g., using the El Torito standard) and the addition of support for huge hard drives. Placing support on a BIOS ROM means that there is one less device driver demanding space in your conventional memory. This factor used to be considered most important for older systems (i386 and slower i486-based PCs), but with the addition of so many new hardware devices, even new PCs are prime candidates for BIOS upgrades.

Second (and maybe even more important), BIOS ROM is fundamentally a piece of software. Like all software, there are sometimes defects or oversights (bugs) that cause problems with system operations. This is especially true when the same core BIOS code is "OEMed" into a variety of motherboards. For example, some motherboards may require a BIOS upgrade to better support the main chipset, or to properly identify non-Intel CPUs. Bugs and compatibility problems virtually demand a BIOS upgrade.

## RECOGNIZING BIOS PROBLEMS

Unfortunately, diagnosing a BIOS bug is not a simple task. There are no diagnostics to check BIOS operations. BIOS manufacturers rarely publicize their errors, so there is no centralized index of symptoms that you can refer to that suggest a faulty BIOS or incompatibility. However, BIOS problems tend to fall into several categories that might alert you to the possibility of BIOS trouble. You can then address the symptoms with the system or motherboard manufacturer directly.

■ *The BIOS displays odd text or characters.* The BIOS normally displays some text during the POST. This text is usually clean, and contains accurate information. If the BIOS displays odd characters (e.g., ordinary spelling errors) or fails to accurately identify system devices, a BIOS upgrade will often fix such problems.

■ *The CMOS Setup does not allow (or retain) all settings.* Virtually all of the motherboard's configuration can be accomplished through the CMOS Setup. There are numerous entries available to fine-tune the system. You may find that you're unable to access certain settings (that are not properly "grayed-out" by other selections you've made) In other cases, you find that settings you've changed are not saved when you exit and reboot (even though you've saved changes). This is often a BIOS bug that can be fixed by a BIOS upgrade.

■ *The BIOS does not identify or support certain processors.* BIOS is often tweaked by motherboard makers, and may not accurately interpret the CPUID function returned by every suitable CPU. If your selected CPU is supposed to be supported by the motherboard, but is not supported (or identified improperly), a BIOS upgrade will usually allow for later processors to be used (such as the AMD Athlon XP 2000+).

■ *The BIOS does not support current hard drives.* Even with LBA, BIOS makers often cut corners and may not support hard drives over a certain size (e.g., 40GB, 75GB, or 137GB). If you find that huge, late-model hard drives are not properly auto-detected or useable to their full physical size, a BIOS upgrade (or new drive controller card) will usually improve drive support.

■ *The BIOS does not support current memory technologies.* If you find that the motherboard won't support certain late model memory technologies or implementations (even though it's supposed to), a BIOS upgrade may be needed to correct the trouble. For example, some BIOS updates may allow support for 512MB memory modules, while other updates may improve the compatibility of DDR SDRAM. Another BIOS update enables features like Fast DRAM Precharge for better performance.

■ *The BIOS reports unusual POST failures.* Problems with the POST may cause one or more devices (usually non-critical devices) to report failures—yet the device(s) seem to work properly. For example, some BIOS updates fix floppy and game port test failures during POST. A BIOS update will usually fix these types of problems.

■ *The system is not achieving optimum performance.* For example, you may find that the integrated video system is not as efficient as the manufacturer has indicated. This is often due to poor support for the integrated feature, and a BIOS update will often correct this. As an example, one particular update will set the CMOS Setup "In-Order Queue Depth" default to 4, increasing the integrated video performance. As another example, a BIOS upgrade may be needed to fully support the AGP 4X mode.

■ *The system is not properly implementing power conservation.* You usually notice that the system cannot enter (or return from) power conservation modes under certain operating systems—often after upgrading to later OS versions like Windows Me/XP. In many cases, the BIOS must be tweaked to accommodate the later OS versions. For example, one BIOS update fixes the inability of Windows Me to enter the S1 power state, and another BIOS update fixes ACPI functions under Windows XP.

■ *The BIOS does not identify or support certain devices.* Given the proliferation of devices in the PC industry, you may encounter situations when certain devices are not detected. BIOS updates will often fix these types of errors. For example, one BIOS update fixes a SCSI HDD detection problem when booting from a SCSI CD-ROM and executing FDISK. Another BIOS update enhances the compatibility of CD-ROM and DVD-ROM drives when attached to the primary IDE channel. BIOS updates are also released to improve the compatibility with chipset components, or streamline chipset performance.

■ *The system does not seem to handle all ports properly.* You may notice that your parallel, serial, or USB ports are acting up, or causing system instability under certain conditions. These types of problems are often OS-specific. For example, one BIOS update fixes an auto reset issue when connecting USB devices on USB Port 3 under Windows 98/SE.

■ *The system's date and time do not properly roll over.* This problem first appeared with the year 2000 (Y2K) issue, but has cropped up on a few occasions after the millennium. This is often a BIOS oversight, and a BIOS upgrade will easily correct this type of problem (if you cannot correct the date manually).

Of course, there are countless other motherboard and OS-specific problems that can be solved with BIOS updates. Always check with the motherboard manufacturer for BIOS updates, and skim their readme files for explanations of the various fixes. If there's a fix that addresses your particular problem, implement the BIOS upgrade.

There is no need to upgrade a BIOS indiscriminately—only attempt a BIOS upgrade to correct a specific problem, or to facilitate features that are not previously supported.

# GATHERING INFORMATION

The BIOS upgrade process is not terribly difficult, but success depends on obtaining the correct replacement or upgrade. To ensure that you order (or download) the proper BIOS, it is important to collect some information about the system. In most cases, locating the following five items should help ensure an accurate upgrade:

- PC make and model
- Motherboard manufacturer and CPU (motherboard chipset also, if possible)
- Make and version of existing BIOS (shown on the display during initialization)
- Part number of the ROM chip itself (you may have to peel back the ROM label)
- Make, model, and part numbers of main motherboard chipset(s) (if any)

When you consider how closely BIOS is related to PC hardware, you can understand why this information is necessary. Today, virtually all PC BIOS is recorded on flash chips, which can be reprogrammed in the field. If you find that you must replace the actual BIOS chip (due to a BIOS failure or corrupted flash process), upgrades can usually be purchased from a BIOS maker, or the original system manufacturer. For your protection, though, place orders only with firms that offer a reasonable return policy (in the event that the new BIOS does not work as expected).

# PERFORMING AN UPGRADE

There are several methods of incorporating a BIOS upgrade into your PC, and in all cases, the proper solution will rely on an understanding of the options available to you. For the purposes of this book, there are four upgrade solutions available to a technician: (1) using a BIOS patch, (2) replacing the BIOS chip, (3) "burning" a new EPROM, and (4) "flashing" the BIOS. The solution you choose will depend on the age of the particular machine.

## Using a BIOS Patch

As distracting and unsettling as a BIOS problem may be, few BIOS problems are fatal. Since device drivers and TSRs can serve to supplement a BIOS, they can also support shortfalls in BIOS operation. By adding a corrective file to CONFIG.SYS, AUTOEXEC.BAT, or your Windows 98/Me/XP system, many BIOS problems can at least be abated without opening the PC enclosure. As just one example, the use of drive overlay utilities (like Data Lifeguard Tools) allows a system to access hard drives that might be too large for the BIOS to handle natively. While this tactic will not repair the problem entirely, a corrective routine can at least allow the system to work until a suitable BIOS upgrade becomes available. To find patches and corrective files for a BIOS, you will need to search the online resources for your particular motherboard manufacturer. This solution is usually best for the oldest systems, for which BIOS upgrades cannot be obtained.

## Replacing the BIOS Chip

Replacing the BIOS chip(s) is the classic solution for many older PC designs. Traditional ROMs are 28- or 32-pin *dual inline package* (DIP) devices (see Figure 6-2), and IBM PC/XT (8088), PC/AT (286), 386-, and many 486-based motherboards used traditional DIP ROM chips. Late-model 486 and Pentium-based

A DIP-style
BIOS chip

**FIGURE   6-2**    The Soyo SY-K7VEM motherboard uses a DIP ROM chip for easy field replacement
if necessary (Courtesy of Soyo).

motherboards often used a socket-mounted *plastic-leaded chip carrier* (PLCC) chip for BIOS. While today's PCs and expansion products make extensive use of surface-mount chips and other components, BIOS devices are the single remaining element still implemented in DIP or PLCC sockets. You may be able to obtain updated ROM chips from the motherboard's manufacturer or from one of the BIOS vendors listed at the end of this chapter. (In a few cases, you may be able to obtain updates directly from the BIOS manufacturer.)

BIOS chip replacements are becoming ever more rare as the rapid advances in PC technology continue. If you cannot replace a physical BIOS chip, consider a motherboard upgrade.

Before proceeding with a BIOS upgrade, remove all power from the PC and disconnect the AC line cord. Remove the outer enclosure and locate the BIOS ROM(s) on the motherboard. Remember to use an antistatic wrist strap to prevent accidental static discharge from damaging the motherboard. Pay particular attention to the orientation (or *keying*) of pin 1. When more than one chip is involved, also note which ROM is "even" and which one is "odd." Remove DIP chips very carefully. You can use a DIP removal tool, or rock the chip gently from its socket using the wide edge of a regular screwdriver. Be extremely careful when removing DIP chips—you may have to put them back if things go wrong. *Gentle* is definitely better here. A specialized removal tool will be needed to remove PLCC chip devices.

You should be equally cautious when installing new DIP chips. If those 28 or 32 little pins are not inserted evenly and straight, they will bend—and break. PLCCs are a bit more forgiving since there are no leads to bend, but make sure to install the chips completely. Before restoring power, make sure the chips are inserted in their proper orientation. If the chips are installed in an orientation opposite from the one intended, you may damage the ROM. If the system fails to initialize, the chip(s) may not be inserted completely, or you may have transposed the "even" and "odd" ROMs. Double-check your work if necessary. Depending on your particular upgrade, you may also find yourself replacing the motherboard's keyboard controller chip.

## Burning New EPROMS

If you handle a large number of BIOS upgrades and have access to PC-based EPROM programming equipment, you can program (or *burn*) your own ROMs. The term EPROM stands for *erasable programmable read-only memory,* so given the proper BIOS data, you can translate the contents of a BIOS disk file to a physical chip. (You might call this the "BIOS-while-u-wait" method.) EPROM programming equipment is not terribly expensive and can be obtained from any full-service electronics catalog store, but a good model with PC compatibility can easily run over $500. As you might expect, this kind of workbench BIOS requires a bit of technical skill and is certainly *not* a worthwhile endeavor for the occasional PC hobbyist.

However, the ability to burn your own EPROMs does offer some unique advantages for an enterprising technician. Knowledgeable technicians versed in machine language can actually customize the BIOS (for example, adding new hard drive parameters to the hard drive table). You can also create backup copies of older BIOS for systems that may no longer be in production, as well as other BIOS for video or drive systems. Of course, modifying a BIOS can have unforeseen consequences for a system—mistakes and errors will disable or crash the PC. Fortunately, you are not altering the *original* BIOS ROM, so you can always restore the original chip.

It is a simple matter to back up your BIOS contents to a disk file. All you need is the DOS DEBUG utility on a simple bootable floppy disk. *Altering or duplicating BIOS code may violate the copyright of the BIOS manufacturer.* A BIOS should *only* be duplicated or modified for the benefit of your individual customers. The typical DEBUG BIOS backup procedure is illustrated next:

```
C:\> DEBUG
- N BIOSBACK.ROM          ;name the backup file
- R BX                    ;alter the CPU's BX register
BX 0000                   ;from zero
:1                        ;to one (this indicates a 64KB file)
- M F000:0 FFFF CS:0      ;move BIOS data in preparation for recording
- W 0                     ;write the file from offset 0
Writing 10000 bytes       ;10000h = 64KB
- Q                       ;quit DEBUG
```

This procedure will save the entire 64KB data segment from F000:0000h to F000:FFFFh as a disk file. If the BIOS in your particular system is 128KB (usually starting at E000:0000h), replace the starting address in the "move" command. You can also back up other ROMs to disk, but you must know the starting address and size of the ROM. For example, a ROM that starts at D400:0000h and is 16KB long can be backed up with a procedure such as:

```
C:\> DEBUG
- N TEST.ROM              ;choose a name for the file
- R CX                    ;alter the CPU's CX register (for short transfers)
CX 0000                   ;from zero
:4000                     ;to 4000h (16KB)
- M D400:0 3FFF CS:0      ;move BIOS data in preparation of recording
- W 0                     ;write the file from offset 0
Writing 04000 bytes       ;4000h = 16KB
- Q                       ;quit DEBUG
```

## Flashing the BIOS

Flash BIOS represents the current and most popular class of BIOS ROM chips, which have typically been included in PCs since the era of fast i486 systems, so your AMD Athlon/Duron or Pentium II/III/4-based PCs will almost certainly have a flash BIOS chip. A flash BIOS is essentially an *electrically erasable programmable read-only memory* (EEPROM)—that is, the chip can be erased and reprogrammed right on the motherboard. Rather than worry about warehousing and shipping new BIOS chips, a BIOS or motherboard manufacturer can provide the updated BIOS code and flash loader utility as a downloadable file.

The name of the file is typically coupled to only a particular motherboard. For example, updating the flash BIOS on an Intel VC820 Pentium II/III motherboard requires a file named **VC82010A.86A.0040.P17**. If this file name is not used, the BIOS will not be reprogrammed. The Soyo P4S Dragon Ultra Pentium 4 motherboard requires the file name **P4SX2AA3.ZIP**, and so on. When attempting a flash procedure, use the following points as a guideline. (But be sure to check the documentation for your particular system.)

1. You *must* have a flash BIOS chip in the computer (refer to Table 6-8). If the chip does not use flash technology, you won't be able to reprogram it.

2. Make a complete backup of your system hard drive(s) *first*—just in case there are drive problems with the new BIOS after the flash process is complete.

3. Make a complete record of all CMOS Setup settings *before* flashing the BIOS. Since the flash loader utility will often clear the CMOS RAM anyway, you'll need to restore or tweak the CMOS Setup again after performing the flash upgrade. Pay particular attention to the hard drive geometry settings and other drive configurations. In many cases, you can simply select BIOS Default settings rather than record individual settings manually.

4. Record the current BIOS version number and/or release date, and verify that you do not already have this version running on your system (it's pointless to try flashing your system with the same BIOS version).

5. When downloading the flash file (usually several BIOS data files, a flash loader utility, and brief documentation all compressed into a single ZIP file), be certain to only download the flash package for your *exact* PC make and model. If you're not sure, verify the proper file with the motherboard or system manufacturer.

Downloading and flashing the INCORRECT BIOS upgrade can render your computer unbootable—forcing you to restore the original BIOS or replace the physical BIOS chip.

6. Create a clean, bootable floppy disk with any version of DOS, or as a Windows 98/Me/XP startup disk.

7. Copy the downloaded ZIP file containing your flash package to the floppy disk, and decompress the ZIP file into its constituent files (usually an EXE file as the flashing utility, a BIN or ROM file as the new BIOS data file, and one or more TXT files as the documentation). In some cases, you may need to download a generic EXE flash loader, and then download the new BIN file separately.

*Never* attempt to flash a BIOS by running the flash utility from a hard drive. Proceed from the floppy drive only.

8. You may need to set the "Flash Enable" jumper on your particular motherboard. If so, turn off and open the PC, locate this jumper (refer to your system documentation), and set it to the "program" or "write enabled" position. You can see an example of this on the Gigabyte GA-8TX Pentium 4 motherboard in Figure 6-3.

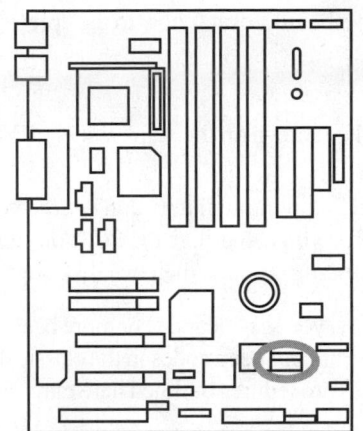

Normal
(Default)

Write
Protection

| Pin No. | Definition |
|---------|-----------|
| 1-2 close | Write Protection |
| 2-3 close | Normal (Default) |

Please note, T flash/upgrade BIOS on this MB JP 11 must be set to 2 and 3. We recommend JP 11 to be set to 1 and 2, whenever user does not need to flash/upgrade the BIOS.

**FIGURE 6-3** Your motherboard's documentation will denote the BIOS write protect/enable jumper and other important jumpers (Courtesy of Gigabyte).

**9.** Reboot the PC and start your CMOS Setup to verify that the PC will boot from the floppy drive first. This is usually indicated as a "Boot Order" or "Boot Sequence" of A:/C:.

**10.** Once the PC boots clean from the bootable floppy disk, start the flash loader utility with a command such as

```
A:\> awdflash          <Enter>
```

**11.** When the flash loader program starts, it may ask you for the name of the BIN or ROM file you wish to use as an upgrade. Type in the exact name of this file when prompted to do so. In some cases, the flash utility will automatically use the only available source file on the diskette.

**12.** Many flash loader utilities will ask you to back up your current BIOS. If you have this opportunity, *please* make a backup copy of the current BIOS to floppy disk before proceeding. Enter the file name to save, and continue. In some cases, the flash loader program will assign a backup file name automatically (for example, BACKUP.BIN). If the flash process fails, that backup BIOS file may be the only way to recover your system.

**13.** You will then be asked if you are sure you want to continue; answer Yes.

**14.** Once the flash process begins, you'll usually see a progress indicator at the bottom of the display that will keep track of the flashing process.

It is critical that you do *not* power-down or reset the PC while the flash process is proceeding. Doing so will interrupt the flash process and leave your BIOS corrupt and perhaps even unrecoverable.

**15.** When the progress indicator has stopped (or the flash process has otherwise concluded), you'll probably see a message such as "Please cycle power or reset this machine."

**16.** Turn your computer completely off. Your new BIOS is installed and is ready to use.

**17.** If you had to set a "Flash Enable" jumper on the motherboard, reset it now to the "protected" position before restoring power to the PC.

**18.** Remove the bootable floppy disk from the system.

**19.** Restart the computer now. The new BIOS version will be shown on the display screen. You're done with the BIOS upgrade.

**20.** In virtually all cases, you'll need to enter your CMOS Setup immediately and restore your CMOS Setup parameters (for example, your drive types) before you can utilize the PC. You can often just restore the BIOS Default settings to get your system running quickly, then tweak the settings later.

If there is an error at any point in the reprogramming process, you may hear one or more beeps. Table 6-9 outlines the beeps and descriptions for AMI flash BIOS. These are *not* beep codes in the classical sense, but flash BIOS procedural errors. Keep in mind that the flash BIOS procedures outlined here may vary for your particular system.

## UPGRADING MODEM FIRMWARE

As PC communication pushes the limits of classical telephone system technologies, modem makers often release modems before new standards are finalized. When new standards finally emerge, users can often make use of enhanced speeds and modem capabilities by updating the modem's firmware. For example, many K56flex or X2 (both 56Kbps modems) can be updated to the ITU V.90 or V.92 standards. You can use a technique similar to that used for your motherboard's BIOS to update your modem's firmware.

 Before you upgrade a modem, make sure that your Internet Service Provider (ISP) has upgraded its servers to V.90/V.92 before you upgrade your modem. If your ISP has not upgraded its servers to V.90/V.92, do not upgrade your modem. If you upgrade before your ISP does, you will be limited to modem speeds of 33.6Kbps and below—if this happens, reflash your modem to the previous version.

Download the complete flash update kit for your exact modem model from the manufacturer's Web site—you may need to check your modem's firmware version first. For example, you'd update a Diamond Multimedia SupraExpress 56I SP modem with the V90_208X.EXE file. Open (unzip) the flash update kit and review the specific instructions according to your operating system. In most cases, you can update the

| TABLE 6-9 | AMI FLASH PROGRAMMING BEEP MESSAGES |
|---|---|
| **BEEPS** | **MEANING** |
| None | No error—successful completion. |
| Continuous single beep | No floppy disk in drive A. |
| Five beeps | Needed ROM program not present on floppy disk. |
| Seven beeps | Floppy read error. |
| Six beeps | BIOS file size error. |
| Eight beeps | The expected flash EEPROM is not present. |
| Continuous two beeps | Problem erasing the flash EEPROM. |
| Continuous three beeps | Problem programming the flash EEPROM. |
| Continuous four beeps | BIOS is not able to reset the CPU. |

modem's BIOS through Windows 98/Me/XP without having to leave the Windows environment. You can use the following procedure to check your modem firmware through Windows 98:

1. Click Start | Programs | Accessories | HyperTerminal. If you're using Windows 98, try clicking Start | Programs | Accessories | Communications | HyperTerminal.
2. Click the HYPERTRM icon.
3. When you're asked to enter a name, type **TEST** and click OK.
4. When you're asked for a phone number, type **1234** (it doesn't matter what this number is). Make sure the correct modem is selected in the Connect Using box, and then click OK.
5. When the Connect screen appears, click Cancel.
6. Now at the terminal screen, type **ATZ** and press ENTER. You should see an "OK" response.
7. Type **ATi92** and press ENTER, and you will see an entry such as "SUPxxxx"—this would be your modem's model number.
8. Type **ATi3** and press ENTER—this should display the modem's firmware version.
9. Exit HyperTerminal (it's OK to close the connection).

Use the following steps if you're working under Windows XP:

1. Click Start | All Programs | Accessories | Communications | HyperTerminal.
2. The Connection Description dialog opens. Type **TEST** and click OK.
3. When you're asked for a phone number, type **1234** (it doesn't matter what this number is). Make sure the correct modem is selected in the Connect Using box, and then click OK.
4. Once you reach the terminal screen, type **ATZ** and press ENTER. You should see a response of "OK."
5. Type **ATi92** and press ENTER, and you will see an entry such as "SUPxxxx"—this would be your modem's model number.
6. Type **ATi3** and press ENTER—this should display the modem's firmware version.
7. Exit HyperTerminal (it's okay to close the connection).

# UPDATING VIDEO FIRMWARE

Video systems are not typically updated, but it's not uncommon to find firmware updates that correct hardware incompatibilities or firmware bugs in video and 3D accelerators with "flashable" firmware. For example, the older Diamond Multimedia Viper V550 can be updated with BIOS version 195CBIOS.EXE. You can use a technique similar to that used for your motherboard's BIOS to update your video card's firmware:

1. Make a bootable floppy.
2. Insert the blank floppy in the A: drive.
3. At the DOS command prompt, type **FORMAT A: /S**.
4. Extract all files from the 195CBIOS.EXE file to your A: drive.
5. Reboot using the floppy disk. This will start the flash loader and begin the update process.
6. When the process is complete, remove the floppy disk and reboot the system.

# UPGRADING DRIVE FIRMWARE

It's rather rare to update the firmware in a drive (for example, a CD, DVD, or hard drive), but there are times when a firmware update may be necessary to correct a firmware bug or to tweak a drive's performance or features. For example, Western Digital has developed a firmware update to reduce the mechanical noise associated with Western Digital's "wear leveling" feature. This firmware update is applicable to WD Caviar models AC11200, AC22000, AC22500, AC33200, AC34000, AC34300, and AC35100. The firmware update will only reduce the noise associated with wear leveling and will not affect the performance of the wear leveling feature.

1. Download the firmware update file (that is, download the WDOVRLY4.EXE utility for the WD update mentioned earlier).

2. Copy the firmware update file to a bootable floppy disk.

3. Restart the system with the floppy disk in the drive, and run the utility from your A: prompt.

4. Once the firmware update software starts, it will detect which drives are available—and whether they need to be updated. Allow the utility to update any drives that require service.

5. Turn off your system after the upgrade is complete. Then restart the system to allow the new firmware to take effect.

# BOOT BLOCK RECOVERY

Not every BIOS upgrade goes as well as expected. You may flash the wrong version, power may be interrupted, or you may encounter problems with other drivers or TSRs running on the system. So what happens when there's a problem? Normally, a bad BIOS upgrade will leave your system unbootable, and this would require you to replace the BIOS chip. More recently, system BIOS has been designed with a "boot block" area that is protected from being overwritten during a flash process. If the flash process is interrupted, you can use the boot block to at least start the system to restore the original BIOS file, or try reloading the BIOS upgrade. The boot block recovery procedure for an Intel Classic R motherboard is shown next.

Before recovering the boot block, you'll need a *recovery disk* for your BIOS. In most cases, a recovery disk is made before the flash process is started. If you do not have a recovery disk, you'll need to create one using an image file from the BIOS maker's Web site. For example, you can use the TIGERRD.EXE file for the Tigereye (TE430VX) motherboard from www.firmware.com/support/recovery. If there is a working BIOS present, the system can also be booted from this floppy disk to flash the BIOS on this disk into the flash chip.

1. Turn off and unplug the system.

2. Move the "boot block" jumper to the enable position. You may also need to set the flash chip's "write-protect" jumper to the "program" or "write enabled" position.

3. Insert the recovery disk. If you did not create a recovery disk when you tried flashing the BIOS, check for a recovery "image file" from the BIOS maker.

4. Turn on the system.

5. After a few seconds, the floppy drive's light will come on.

6. About 20 or 30 seconds later, the speaker will beep once to indicate that the flash process has started.

7. The disk access light will remain on, but there will be nothing on the display.

8. After another 45 to 60 seconds, the speaker will beep twice to indicate that the process has finished. The floppy disk drive light may remain on.

9. Turn the system off and remove the disk.

10. Reset the system's "boot block" jumper (and the flash chip's "write protect" jumper if necessary).

11. Turn on the system and enter the CMOS Setup to restore the system's configuration.

If you encounter more than two beeps (for example, four long low beeps), there may be no floppy disk in the drive (or the disk drive is not installed properly). If any disk besides a valid recovery disk is used, no action will be taken.

## BIOS UPGRADE TROUBLESHOOTING

Ideally, a BIOS upgrade can be accomplished quickly and easily, and upgrades are rarely plagued by problems. However, BIOS upgrade problems can and do occur—and can be quite serious under the right circumstances. This part of the chapter looks at a series of common BIOS upgrade symptoms and solutions.

**SYMPTOM 6-103**    **The flash loader utility refuses to run**    This is a known problem with BIOS flash utilities that have been customized for particular motherboards. Chances are that the flash loader was designed to run on a different motherboard. For example, the MR BIOS ZIP file includes a flash loader that was specifically customized for certain Intel motherboards. The file name of that flash loader will resemble the BIOS image file name (with the .BIO extension)—but other generic motherboards will typically use Zip files that contain either 29C010.EXE or 28F010.EXE (or both) flash loaders.

In most cases, the flash loader (whether it's custom or generic) attempts to qualify the flash ROM in your computer as a type that it's able to program. If not, an error message to that effect is displayed, and the flash loader aborts. When this happens, you should check that a "flash-protect" jumper is set correctly to permit flash operations. If your motherboard is set for flashing but the flash loader utility refuses to run, chances are that you're trying to install a BIOS upgrade that is not intended for your specific motherboard. Verify that you've downloaded the correct BIOS update and flash loader utility. Do *not* attempt to "force" a flash update by using other flash loader utilities.

**SYMPTOM 6-104**    **You receive an "erase chip failure" when trying to run a flash loader**    The flash BIOS chip must be erased *before* the new BIOS code can be programmed into the chip. The flash loader program is reporting that it cannot erase the flash chip, which may be due to several reasons.

The flash chip's voltage setting may be set to a different voltage than the chip requires. For example, most flash BIOS chips are 12 volts, but some manufacturers deliberately set the flash voltage setting on the motherboard to 5 volts. This acts like a "write protect" for the BIOS chip, which means you cannot reprogram the BIOS without first setting the voltage jumper back to 12 volts. This also protects you from certain viruses such as the CIH Virus that would try to erase the BIOS and effectively "kill" your computer. Consult your motherboard's manual for the location and settings of your "flash voltage" and "write protect" jumpers.

In other cases, the motherboard's manufacturer may have installed a flash BIOS chip that the flash loader cannot erase. Verify that you've downloaded the correct flash loader and BIOS update file for your particular motherboard. You may need to download and use a different flash loader. If there is no alternate flash loader utility for your motherboard, it will be necessary to replace the BIOS chip.

**SYMPTOM 6-105**    **You receive a "flash chip not supported" error when trying to run a flash loader**    The flash loader utility must first check the type of flash chip that is currently installed on the motherboard, then determine whether the flash loader can read and write to the flash chip safely. When you encounter this error, the flash loader is indicating that it does not recognize the type of flash chip currently installed on the motherboard. Verify that you've downloaded the correct flash loader and BIOS update file for your particular motherboard. You may need to download and use a different flash loader. If there is no alternate flash loader utility for your motherboard, it will be necessary to replace the BIOS chip.

**SYMPTOM 6-106**    **After installing a new BIOS, the system now asks for a password**    Your BIOS stores the configuration data for your system in the CMOS RAM/real-time clock chip that is installed on the motherboard. The data values for the new BIOS (and the way that data is arranged) may differ from your original BIOS data configuration since new commands and features are added to newer versions of the BIOS. The first time you turn on the computer after installing the new BIOS, your new BIOS is reading the old data configuration and mistakenly thinks that a password is set.

To correct this problem, you must clear the old configuration data from your CMOS RAM chip. Some motherboards offer a "Clear CMOS" or "Clear Password" jumper located near the CMOS RAM/RTC chip. When this jumper is set and the system is booted, you can erase the CMOS data (or just the password, depending on which jumper is available to you). Turn off the PC and reset those jumpers to their original positions; then restart the system directly to the CMOS Setup and reconfigure each of the system's setup values. (Or simply select the BIOS Defaults option to load a set of basic parameters into your CMOS Setup.)

**SYMPTOM 6-107**    **After flashing the BIOS and reloading the system setup, the system refuses to recognize your drives**    This is almost always due to unforeseen motherboard updates that the BIOS was not designed for. During the course of a production run, a motherboard manufacturer may make a design change that may be as simple as a wiring trace change, or as complex as changing the components used on the motherboard. For example, when the Super I/O chip of the motherboard has been changed, the BIOS can no longer initialize and "talk" to the IDE controllers—in effect, this "cuts off" your hard drives. In most cases, you'll need to contact the motherboard maker and determine whether a new BIOS chip is available to replace the existing BIOS chip. If you have the original BIOS file on diskette, you may be able to reflash the original BIOS back to the system.

**SYMPTOM 6-108**    **After installing a new BIOS, you cannot print under DOS or Windows**    Chances are that the new BIOS has defaulted the printer port to "standard" mode (SPP), which is inadequate for your particular printer. You'll need to enter the CMOS Setup and change the parallel port mode setting to EPP or ECP, and verify that your LPT1 port is set to address 378h. Save your changes and reboot the system.

**SYMPTOM 6-109**    **You cannot flash a MR BIOS version on a Super Micro motherboard**    Super Micro motherboards normally use a 28F001 flash chip that contains a boot block loader. The boot block loader not only functions as a boot loader for BIOS recovery, but also contains the standard jump vector used during normal boot up. To use MR BIOS on this type of motherboard, you must overwrite this boot block with MR BIOS boot code. However, the boot block portion of the flash chip is write protected and cannot be flashed. You are able to update the flash chip using the Super Micro flash loader because it only updates the non-boot block portion of the flash chip. To update the motherboard to MR BIOS, you'll need to use a flash loader from MR BIOS that is specifically designed work around this boot block issue:

1. Run the MRSUPER2 flash loader.
2. Select the Backup option to create a backup copy of the original BIOS code.
3. When your backup is complete, select the Update option and specify the correct MR BIOS flash update. Allow the update to proceed.
4. After updating, power-off the system and set jumper J37 to 2-3. This jumper should remain in this position even when updating the flash to future revisions of MR BIOS.

To restore your original Super Micro BIOS from a backup file after MR BIOS is installed:

1. Run the MRSUPER2 flash loader.
2. Select the Update option and specify the appropriate file name for the Super Micro backup BIOS file. Allow the update to proceed.
3. After updating, power-off the system and set jumper J37 to 1-2.

**SYMPTOM 6-110**    **The PC does not boot after upgrading the BIOS**    This is a classic problem that frequently haunts technicians. When you've replaced the physical BIOS chip(s), double-check the chip(s) for proper orientation and installation. Make sure that all of the pins are inserted into the socket, and that none of the DIP pins have been bent under the chip's body. If you're replacing "even and odd" BIOS chips, make sure that you have not accidentally transposed the even and odd chip locations. If the problem persists, try replacing the original BIOS chips—if the original chips work, you may have defective or improper replacement chips.

If you've flashed the BIOS, chances are that your problem is a little stickier. You've either flashed the wrong BIOS version, or the flash process failed for some reason. In either case, there's nothing you can do except replace the BIOS chip (you'll need to contact the system or motherboard manufacturer for a replacement) or restore the original BIOS from the boot block.

**SYMPTOM 6-111**    **You accidentally reset or power-down the PC during a BIOS flash, and now the PC won't start**    The great weakness of flash BIOS is that it cannot be interrupted once the flash process is under way—otherwise, the BIOS will be left partially programmed and totally corrupted. Your only course of action here is to replace the BIOS chip (you'll need to contact the system or motherboard manufacturer for a replacement) or restore the original BIOS from the boot block.

**SYMPTOM 6-112**    **The BIOS upgrade proceeded properly, but now the system behaves erratically, or other errors appear**    There are several potential causes here. Most of the time, you've either flashed the wrong BIOS version (probably for a system using an almost identical motherboard), or the BIOS became corrupted during the flash process. If you made a backup copy of the original BIOS file during the flash process, repeat the process and restore the original BIOS version. If the system works, you can verify that you downloaded the correct flash file (and repeat the upgrade if possible). If you cannot restore the original BIOS, or the problems persist, replace the BIOS chip. If the problem occurs when replacing physical chips, chances are that you've installed the BIOS for the wrong PC or motherboard, and you'll need to replace the original BIOS chip(s) until you get the proper replacements.

**SYMPTOM 6-113**   **The BIOS upgrade proceeded properly, but system performance seems poor**   This is a frequent (but little-discussed) complaint with BIOS upgrades. In many cases, a new BIOS will require you to restore or tweak your CMOS Setup for proper performance. If you recorded your original CMOS Setup contents before attempting your upgrade, you can enter the CMOS Setup and compare the current settings to the original ones. Chances are that one or more performance-oriented settings have been disabled. Here are some points for quick tweaking. (Remember that not all of these features may be available in all BIOS versions.) For fastest booting:

- Set the Boot Sequence to C:/A:.
- Set the Boot Up Floppy Drive Seek to DISABLED.
- Set the Boot Up System Speed to HIGH.
- Set the Quick Power-on Self Test to ENABLED.

For highest overall system performance:

- Enable all shadowing unless you are using an adapter that absolutely requires that shadowing be disabled for a specified address. Video shadow will increase the video speed.
- Set Auto Configuration to DISABLE.
- Reduce all the memory timings to their minimum values.
- Enable the Turbo Read Lead Off.
- Enable the Speculative Lead Off.
- Enable the Turn Around Insertion.
- Increase the ISA Speed by setting *ISA Clock* to **PCICLK/3**.
- Lower 8- and 16-bit recovery times to **1** (one) each.
- Set the System BIOS Cacheable to ENABLE.
- Set the Video BIOS Cacheable to ENABLE.
- L2 Cache Cacheable Size—If you're installing 64MB of RAM or more, set to **512MB** (64MB is the default).
- Pipeline Cache Timing—Set to FASTEST if there is only 256KB total pipeline cache (FASTER is the default).

 When tweaking BIOS settings in the CMOS Setup, be sure to change only one parameter at a time; retest the system's performance each time.

**SYMPTOM 6-114**   **You see a message such as "Update ESCD Successfully" on boot-up**   This is not really an error, but more of an informational message. The ESCD (*extended system configuration data*) is a method that the BIOS uses to store resource information for both PnP and non-PnP devices. The reason it shows this message is because the system has at least one legacy device in it, and it is running Windows 98/Me/XP. The ESCD boot-up sequence arranged by Windows 98/Me/XP is different from the ESCD boot-up sequence arranged by the BIOS. So on boot-up, the system BIOS will attempt to update the ESCD. This will in no way affect system performance.

**SYMPTOM 6-115**    **You just upgraded the BIOS and now can't boot from the A: drive**
Otherwise, the A: drive seems to be working normally. In virtually all cases, the updated BIOS defaulted the CMOS Setup to a Boot Sequence of C:/A: instead of A:/C:, so the system isn't even checking the floppy drive at startup. Start your CMOS Setup and tweak the "Boot Sequence" to A:/C:, and then save your changes and try the system again. Also verify that you actually have a working bootable floppy disk in the drive.

**SYMPTOM 6-116**    **You get a message saying: "Incompatible BIOS translation detected—unable to load disk overlay"**    This typically happens when you upgrade a BIOS to support new drive features, but the hard drive in your system is already using overlay software such as Disk Manager. Since overlay software is usually incompatible with LBA and other drive features, you'll need to either disable LBA in the CMOS Setup (to continue using the disk overlay software), or remove the overlay software from the hard drive. Since you probably upgraded the BIOS to support LBA anyway, chances are that you'll want to remove the overlay software:

1. Back up the hard drive before proceeding.
2. Boot the system from a bootable floppy disk.
3. Run FDISK and delete all partitions on the hard drive.
4. Reboot and check with FDISK to be sure that all the partitions on the drive have been removed.
5. You can repartition and reformat the drive, then restore your files from a backup.

If you cannot remove all partitions from the hard drive with FDISK, you can use the following procedure to erase the *master boot record* (MBR) on the hard drive. You'll need the DEBUG utility on your bootable floppy disk before proceeding.

```
A:\> debug
F 200 L200 0
a 100
mov ax,301
mov bx,200
mov cx,1
mov dx,0080                    ;Note: use 0081 for second fixed disk
int 13
int 3
(enter a blank line here)
G=100
q
```

The drive should now have no partitions on it. Reboot and use FDISK to partition the drive, and FORMAT to reformat each partition. You can then restore the operating system and recover files from your backup.

# Further Study

**American Megatrends**   www.ami.com
**Award**   www.award.com
**IBM SurePath BIOS page**   www.ibm.com/products/surepath/
**Micro Firmware**   www.firmware.com
**Phoenix Technologies**   www.phoenix.com/
**SystemSoft**   www.systemsoft.com
**Unicore**   www.unicore.com
**Wim's BIOS page**   www.wimsbios.com

7

# BUSSES

**W**hen it was first introduced, the IBM PC was no gem. It was a slow, clunky contraption with virtually no system resources (mcmory, interrupts, DMA channels, and so on). Yet, the IBM PC ushered in the personal computer era that we know today. Certainly, it was not speed or efficiency that brought IBM systems to the forefront of technology. Instead, it was a revolutionary (and rather risky) concept called *open architecture*. Rather than designing a computer and being the sole developer of proprietary add-on devices (as so many other computer manufacturers were at the time), IBM chose to incorporate only the essential processing elements on the motherboard. Additional functions were left to add-on devices (a.k.a. expansion boards) that could be manufactured by just about anybody and plugged into standardized bus connectors (such as the PCI and AGP slots in Figure 7-1). The use of expansion busses made the PC extraordinarily versatile, because a system could be configured according to the devices that were added. This chapter is intended to familiarize you with the major expansion bus types found in modern PCs: ISA, PCI, and AGP.

# Industry Standard Architecture (ISA)

The venerable *Industry Standard Architecture* (ISA), shown in Figure 7-2, is the first open system bus architecture used for IBM-type personal computers. Any manufacturer was welcome to use the architecture

**FIGURE  7-1**   This Soyo P4I FireDragon motherboard features PCI and AGP bus connectors supporting a wide variety of PC expansion devices (Courtesy of Motherboards.org).

for a nominal licensing fee. Since no restrictions were placed on the use of ISA busses (also referred to simply as "PC busses"), they were duplicated in every IBM-compatible clone that followed. The use of a standardized bus not only paved the way for thousands of manufacturers to produce compatible PCs and expansion devices, but also helped to support the use of standardized operating systems and applications software. Both an 8-bit and 16-bit version of the ISA bus are available, although all motherboards manufactured since the mid-1980s had abandoned the 8-bit XT version in favor of the faster, more flexible 16-bit AT version.

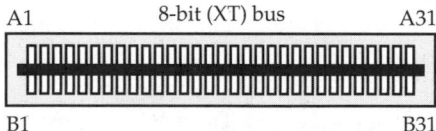

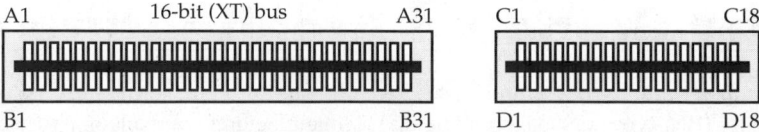

**FIGURE  7-2**   Diagram of 8-bit and 16-bit ISA bus slots

## 8-BIT ISA

Use of the 8-bit XT bus started in 1982. The 8-bit ISA bus consists of a single card edge connector with 62 contacts. The bus provides 8 data lines and 20 address lines, which allow the board to reside within the XT's 1MB of conventional memory. The bus also supports connections for six interrupts (IRQ2–IRQ7) and three DMA channels (DMA0–DMA2). The XT bus runs at the system speed of 4.77 MHz. Although the bus itself is relatively simple, IBM failed to publish specific timing relationships for data, address, and control signals. This ambiguity left early manufacturers to find the proper timing relationships by trial and error.

Although each connector on the bus is supposed to work the same way, early PCs designed with eight expansion slots required any card inserted in the eighth slot (the slot closest to the power supply) to provide a special "card selected" signal on pin B8. Timing requirements for the eighth slot are also tighter. Contrary to popular belief, the eighth slot has nothing to do with the IBM expansion chassis. The demands of slot 8 were to support a keyboard/timer adapter board for IBM's special configuration called the 3270PC. Most XT clones did not adhere to this "eighth slot" peculiarity.

### Knowing the XT Signals

Table 7-1 shows the pinout for both an XT and AT ISA bus configuration. The Oscillator pin provides the 14.3 MHz system oscillator signal to the expansion bus, while the Clock pin supplies the 4.77 MHz system

| **TABLE 7-1** | **ISA 8-BIT (XT) BUS CONNECTOR PINOUT** | | |
|---|---|---|---|
| **SIGNAL** | **PIN** | **PIN** | **SIGNAL** |
| Ground | B1 | A1 | – I/O Channel Check |
| Reset | B2 | A2 | Data Bit 7 |
| +5 Vdc | B3 | A3 | Data Bit 6 |
| IRQ 2 | B4 | A4 | Data Bit 5 |
| –5 Vdc | B5 | A5 | Data Bit 4 |
| DRQ 2 | B6 | A6 | Data Bit 3 |
| –12 Vdc | B7 | A7 | Data Bit 2 |
| – Card Selected | B8 | A8 | Data Bit 1 |
| +12 Vdc | B9 | A9 | Data Bit 0 |
| Ground | B10 | A10 | I/O Channel Ready |
| – SMEMW | B11 | A11 | AEN |
| – SMEMR | B12 | A12 | Address Bit 19 |
| – I/O W | B13 | A13 | Address Bit 18 |
| – I/O R | B14 | A14 | Address Bit 17 |
| – DACK 3 | B15 | A15 | Address Bit 16 |
| DRQ 3 | B16 | A16 | Address Bit 15 |
| – DACK 1 | B17 | A17 | Address Bit 14 |
| DRQ 1 | B18 | A18 | Address Bit 13 |
| – REFRESH | B19 | A19 | Address Bit 12 |
| Clock (4.77 MHz) | B20 | A20 | Address Bit 11 |
| IRQ 7 | B21 | A21 | Address Bit 10 |
| IRQ 6 | B22 | A22 | Address Bit 9 |
| IRQ 5 | B23 | A23 | Address Bit 8 |

**TABLE 7-1**   ISA 8-BIT (XT) BUS CONNECTOR PINOUT *(CONTINUED)*

| SIGNAL | PIN | PIN | SIGNAL |
|--------|-----|-----|--------|
| IRQ 4 | B24 | A24 | Address Bit 7 |
| IRQ 3 | B25 | A25 | Address Bit 6 |
| – DACK 2 | B26 | A26 | Address Bit 5 |
| T/C | B27 | A27 | Address Bit 4 |
| BALE | B28 | A28 | Address Bit 3 |
| +5 Vdc | B29 | A29 | Address Bit 2 |
| Oscillator (14.3 MHz) | B30 | A30 | Address Bit 1 |
| Ground | B31 | A31 | Address Bit 0 |

clock signal. When the PC needs to be reset, the RESET DRV pin drives the whole system into a reset state. The 20 address pins (0–19) connect an expansion board to the system's address bus; when address signals are valid, the Address Latch Enable (ALE) signal indicates that the address may now be decoded. The eight data lines (0–7) connect the board to the system's data bus.

Signal labels marked with a minus sign (–), such as – REFRESH, indicate what's known as *active low logic,* where the signal is true when the logic level is low.

The – I/O Channel Check (–IOCHCK) line flags the motherboard when errors occur on the expansion board. Note that the minus sign (–) preceding the signal indicates that the signal uses active low logic. The I/O Channel Ready is active when an addressed expansion board is ready. If this pin is logic 0, the CPU will extend the bus cycle by inserting wait states. Six hardware interrupts (IRQ2 to IRQ7) are used by the expansion board to demand the CPU's attention. Interrupts 0 and 1 are not available to the bus since they handle the highest priorities of the timer chip and keyboard. The – I/O Read (–I/O R) and – I/O Write (–I/O W) lines indicate that the CPU or DMA controller wants to transfer data to or from the data bus. The – Memory Read (–MEMR) and – Memory Write (–MEMW) signals tell the expansion board that the CPU or DMA controller is going to read or write data to main memory.

The XT bus supplies three DMA Requests (DRQ1 to DRQ3) so that an expansion board can transfer data to or from memory. DMA requests must be held until the corresponding –DMA Acknowledge (–DACK1 to –DACK3) signals become true. If the Address Enable (AEN) signal is true, the DMA controller is controlling the bus for a data transfer. Finally, the Terminal Count (T/C) signal provides a pulse when the DMA transfer is completed.

# 16-BIT ISA

The limitations of the 8-bit ISA bus were soon obvious. With a floppy drive and hard drive taking up two of the six available interrupts, COM 3 and COM 4 taking up another two interrupts (IRQ 3 and IRQ 4), and an LPT port taking up IRQ 7, competition for the remaining interrupt was fierce. Of the three DMA channels available, the floppy and hard drives take two, so only one DMA channel remains available. Only 1MB of address space is addressable, and 8 data bits form a serious bottleneck for data transfers. It would have been a simple matter to start from scratch and design an entirely new bus, but that would have rendered the entire installed base of XT expansion cards obsolete—a serious faux pas in the world of open bus architectures.

The next logical step in bus evolution came in 1984/85 with the introduction of Intel's 80286 processor in IBM's PC/AT. System resources were added to the bus while still allowing XT boards to function in the expanded bus. The result became what we know today as the 16-bit AT bus. Instead of a different bus connector, the original 62-pin connector was left intact, and an extra 36-pin connector was added, designated "C" and "D," as shown in Table 7-2 (the pin assignments for the 32-pin A/B connector are identical to Table 7-1). An extra 8 data bits were added to bring the total data bus to 16 bits. Five interrupts and four DMA channels were included. Four more address lines were also provided, in addition to several more control signals. Clock speed was increased on the AT bus to 8.33 MHz. It is important to note that although XT boards *theoretically* should work with an AT bus, not all older XT expansion boards will work on the AT bus.

## Knowing the AT Signals

The – System Bus High Enable (–SBHE) is active when the upper 8 data bits are being used. If the upper 8 bits are not being used (an XT board is in the AT slot), –SBHE will be inactive. If the expansion board requires 16-bit access to memory locations, it must return an active –MEM CS16 signal. If the expansion board requires 16-bit access to an I/O location, it must make the –I/O CS16 signal active. The – Memory Read (–MEMR) and – Memory Write (–MEMW) signals provided by an expansion board tell the CPU or DMA controller that memory access is needed up to 16MB. The –SMEMR and –SMEMW signals only indicate memory access for the first 1MB. The –MASTER signal can be used by expansion boards that are able to take control of the bus through use of a DMA channel. It is interesting to note that small, highly integrated AT systems are available for embedded systems and dedicated applications.

**TABLE 7-2    THE 16-BIT ISA (AT) EXTENDED BUS CONNECTOR PINOUT**

| SIGNAL | PIN | PIN | SIGNAL |
|---|---|---|---|
| – MEM CS16 | D1 | C1 | – SBHE |
| – I/O CS16 | D2 | C2 | Address Bit 23 |
| IRQ 10 | D3 | C3 | Address Bit 22 |
| IRQ 11 | D4 | C4 | Address Bit 21 |
| IRQ 12 | D5 | C5 | Address Bit 20 |
| IRQ 15 | D6 | C6 | Address Bit 19 |
| IRQ 14 | D7 | C7 | Address Bit 18 |
| – DACK 0 | D8 | C8 | Address Bit 17 |
| DRQ 0 | D9 | C9 | – MEM R |
| – DACK 5 | D10 | C10 | – MEM W |
| DRQ 5 | D11 | C11 | Data Bit 8 |
| – DACK 6 | D12 | C12 | Data Bit 9 |
| DRQ 6 | D13 | C13 | Data Bit 10 |
| – DACK 7 | D14 | C14 | Data Bit 11 |
| DRQ 7 | D15 | C15 | Data Bit 12 |
| +5 Vdc | D16 | C16 | Data Bit 13 |
| – MASTER | D17 | C17 | Data Bit 14 |
| Ground | D18 | C18 | Data Bit 15 |

## Mixing 8-Bit and 16-Bit ISA Boards

ISA 16-bit architecture was developed on the foundation of IBM's original 8-bit XT bus. By *extending* the original XT bus rather than redesigning an expansion bus from scratch, IBM was able to develop its AT PC so that it would accommodate new, more sophisticated 16-bit expansion boards while still being backward compatible with the installed base of 8-bit boards. For the most part, this strategy worked quite well—the ISA bus remained a prominent feature of PCs for many years, and has only recently been phased out. However, there is a potential problem with the ISA bus when inserting 8-bit and 16-bit adapters that both use ROM residing in the same memory region. Such a problem generally results in trouble with the 8-bit board.

To understand how this problem arises, you should be familiar with the ISA bus pinouts shown in Tables 7-1 and 7-2. There is an initial 62-pin connector (A1 through A31 and B1 through B31), followed by the extended 36-pin connector (C1 through C18 and D1 through D18). Notice that Address Bits 17, 18, and 19 are repeated on pins C8, C7, and C6. When a 16-bit board is inserted in the system, those repeated address lines indicate that a memory access is about to occur somewhere within 128KB of the address signals on A17, A18, and A19. The lower 17 address lines (A0 to A16) specify *exactly* where in that 128KB range the access will take place. If a 16-bit expansion board has memory (such as a video BIOS ROM or hard drive controller ROM) within the 128KB range about to be accessed, it uses the –MEM CS16 or –I/O CS16 line to tell the system that its memory is ready for access in 16-bit transfers. If the system receives no response from either of these lines, data is transferred in 8-bit sections.

The problem here is that 8-bit boards may also have memory within that 128KB range, but since they cannot detect the three extra address lines, the board cannot respond to the system. If a 16-bit board tells the system to proceed with a 16-bit data transfer, but there is also an 8-bit board in that same address range, the 8-bit board will be forced to receive 16-bit data transfers. As you might expect, this is quite impossible for an 8-bit board, so the 8-bit board will appear to malfunction. Since most expansion boards reserve their ROM addresses for the 128KB block between 768KB to 896KB (C0000h to DBFFFh, sometimes called the *ROM Reserve*), this is where most problems reside.

It is important for you to understand that this problem does not refer to a hardware conflict. The ROM locations of the 8-bit and 16-bit boards certainly *cannot* overlap at any point. As you might realize, however, it is possible to have several different ROMs contained within the same 128KB of system memory. If one such ROM is on a 16-bit board and one is on an 8-bit board, the 8-bit board will likely malfunction due to the way in which 16-bit boards handle ISA bus operation. Correcting such a problem is generally a matter of replacing the 8-bit board with a 16-bit version. It might also be possible to disable the 8-bit ROM using an onboard jumper, and then use the motherboard BIOS ROM instead (depending on the task your 8-bit board is performing).

## ISA Retirement

Today, the ISA bus architecture is completely obsolete in the face of more versatile expansion slots like PCI or AGP. Most current motherboard designs forego use of the ISA bus entirely (such as the Gigabyte GA-7VRXP in Figure 7-3), though a scant few motherboards continue to provide one or two ISA slots for backward compatibility with "legacy" devices. Do *not* expect ISA bus slots to be available on motherboard upgrades or new PC builds.

**FIGURE 7-3**    Current motherboards like this Gigabyte GA-7VRXP eliminate the ISA bus entirely in favor of PCI and AGP (Courtesy of Motherboards.org ).

# Peripheral Component Interconnect (PCI)

By the late 1980s, the proliferation of 32-bit CPUs and graphics-based operating systems like Windows made it painfully obvious that the 8.33 MHz ISA bus was no longer satisfactory. The PC industry began to develop alternative architectures for improved performance. Two architectures emerged: VL and PCI. While the VL (*video local*) bus seemed more straightforward, it had some serious limitations to overcome. Perhaps most important is the VL bus dependence on CPU speed. Another problem is that the VL standard is voluntary, and not all manufacturers adhere to VESA specifications completely. In mid-1992, Intel and a comprehensive consortium of manufacturers introduced the *Peripheral Component Interconnect* (PCI) bus. Whereas the VL bus was designed specifically to enhance PC video systems, the 188-pin PCI bus looked to the future of CPUs (and PCs in general) by providing a more general-purpose bus architecture that also supports peripherals such as hard drive controllers, network adapters, and so on. This part of the chapter shows you the layout and operations of the PCI bus.

## PCI BUS CONFIGURATION AND SIGNALS

PCI is a 33 MHz fixed-frequency bus architecture capable of transferring 32 bits of data at 132 MB/sec—a great improvement over the 16.6 MB/sec transfer rate of the 16 bit 8.33 MHz ISA bus. Another key advantage of the PCI bus is that it has automatic configuration capabilities for switchless/jumperless peripherals. Auto-configuration (the heart of plug-and-play architecture) takes care of all addresses, interrupt requests, and DMA assignments used by a PCI peripheral. The most current PCI bus (version 2.3) includes the following features:

- Data bursting as normal operating mode (both read and write)
- Linear burst ordering
- Concurrency support (deadlock, buffering solutions)
- Low latency guarantees for real-time devices
- Access-oriented arbitration (not time slice)
- Support for multiple loads (PCI boards) at 33 MHz
- Error detection and reporting
- Multimaster and peer-to-peer communication
- 32-bit multiplexed, processor-independent operation
- Synchronous 132 MB/sec operation
- Variable length, linear bursting (both read and write)
- Parity on address, data, and command signals
- Concurrency/pipelining support
- Initialization hooks for auto-configuration
- Arbitration support
- 64-bit extension transparently compatible with 32-bit
- Movement from 5 Vdc to 3.3 Vdc (low voltage logic) signaling

PCI SIG (Special Interest Group) members can download complete PCI 2.3 specifications from www.pcisig.com.

The PCI bus supports *linear bursts,* which is a method of transferring data that ensures the bus is continually filled with data. The peripheral devices expect to receive data from the system main memory in a linear address order. This means that large amounts of data are read from or written to a single address, which is then incremented for the next byte in the stream. The linear burst is one of the unique aspects of the PCI bus since it will perform both burst reads and burst writes. In short, it will transfer data on the bus *every* clock cycle. This doubles the PCI throughput compared to buses without linear burst capabilities.

The devices designed to support PCI have low *access latency,* reducing the time required for a peripheral to be granted control of the bus after requesting access. For example, an Ethernet controller card connected to a LAN has large data files from the network coming into its buffer. Waiting for access to the bus, the Ethernet is unable to transfer the data to the CPU quickly enough to avoid a buffer overflow—forcing it to temporarily store the file's contents in extra RAM. Since PCI-compliant devices support faster access times, the Ethernet card can promptly send data to the CPU.

The PCI bus supports *bus mastering*, which allows one of a number of intelligent peripherals to take control of the bus to accelerate a high-throughput, high-priority task. PCI architecture also supports *concurrency,* a technique that ensures the microprocessor operates simultaneously with these masters, instead of waiting for them. As one example, concurrency allows the CPU to perform floating-point calculations on a spreadsheet while an Ethernet card and the LAN have control of the bus. Finally, PCI was developed as a dual-voltage architecture. Normally, the bus is a +5 Vdc system like other busses. However, the bus can also operate in a +3.3 Vdc (low-voltage) mode.

## PCI BUS LAYOUT

The layout for a PCI bus slot is shown in Figure 7-4. Note that there are two major segments to the full 64-bit PCI connector, though most PCs only use the 32-bit portion (A1/B1 through A62/B62). A +3.3 Vdc-version connector adds a key in the 12/13 positions to prevent accidental insertion of a +5 Vdc PCI board into a +3.3 Vdc slot. Similarly, the +5 Vdc slot is keyed in the 50/51 position to prevent placing a +3.3 Vdc board into a +5 Vdc slot. The pinout for a PCI bus is shown in Table 7-3.

As you will see in Chapter 11, devices cannot use the same system resources. Otherwise, a hardware conflict will result. The PCI bus is an exception to this rule because it supports a technique called *IRQ steering* that allows IRQs to be dynamically held and reassigned as needed. To facilitate this form of IRQ sharing, the PCI bus uses its own internal interrupt system for dealing with requests from the cards on the bus. These PCI interrupts are often called #A, #B, #C, and #D, to avoid confusion with the normal system IRQs (for example, IRQ 7), though they are sometimes called #1 through #4 instead. These PCI interrupt levels are not generally seen by the user, but can be accessed in the system's CMOS Setup routine, where they can be adjusted to control how PCI cards operate. If interrupts are needed by PCI cards in the slots, the PCI interrupts are mapped to regular interrupts (normally IRQ 9 through IRQ 12). The PCI slots in most systems can be mapped to (at most) four regular IRQs. In systems that have more than four PCI slots, or that have four slots and a USB controller (which uses PCI), two or more of the PCI devices share an IRQ.

## KNOWING THE PCI SIGNALS

The PCI bus clock is usually derived from the front side bus (FSB) speed. This is the clock that drives the processor and memory, and often appears as 100 MHz/133 MHz, 200/266 MHz, or even 400 MHz in the case of Pentium 4 processors. In an *asynchronous* configuration, the speed of a PCI bus can be set independently of the FSB speed, though this is rare in all but the latest motherboards. In a *synchronous* configuration (used by most PCs), the 33 MHz PCI speed is divided from the FSB. For example, if the FSB is 66 MHz, a divisor (usually in the form of a CMOS Setup entry or motherboard jumper) divides the FSB in half to achieve 33 MHz. More recent motherboards with faster FSB speeds use additional divisors. For example, a 133 MHz FSB would use a 1:4 divisor to achieve 33 MHz. Synchronous PCI clocking can become very important in overclocking, because overclocking the FSB will cause PCI peripherals to be overclocked as well, often leading to system stability problems.

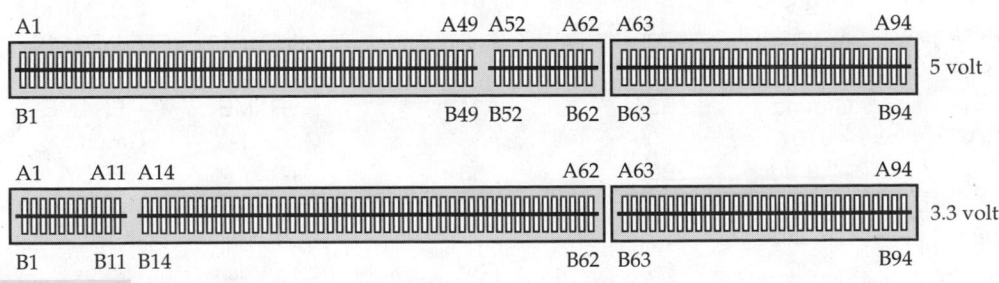

**FIGURE 7-4**   PCI expansion bus diagrams

**TABLE 7-3**    THE FULL 64-BIT PCI BUS PINOUT—5 VOLT AND 3.3 VOLT

| 5 VOLT | 3.3 VOLT | PIN | PIN | 3.3 VOLT | 5 VOLT |
|---|---|---|---|---|---|
| −12 Vdc | −12 Vdc | B1 | A1 | − TRST | − TRST |
| TCK | TCK | B2 | A2 | +12 Vdc | +12 Vdc |
| Ground | Ground | B3 | A3 | TMS | TMS |
| TDO | TDO | B4 | A4 | TDI | TDI |
| +5 Vdc | +5 Vdc | B5 | A5 | +5 Vdc | +5 Vdc |
| +5 Vdc | +5 Vdc | B6 | A6 | − INTA | − INTA |
| − INTB | − INTB | B7 | A7 | − INTC | − INTC |
| − INTD | − INTD | B8 | A8 | +5 Vdc | +5 Vdc |
| − PRSNT1 | − PRSNT1 | B9 | A9 | Reserved | Reserved |
| Reserved | Reserved | B10 | A10 | +3.3 Vdc (I/O) | +5 Vdc |
| − PRSNT2 | − PRSNT2 | B11 | A11 | Reserved | Reserved |
| Ground | Key | B12 | A12 | Key | Ground |
| Ground | Key | B13 | A13 | Key | Ground |
| Reserved | Reserved | B14 | A14 | Reserved | Reserved |
| Ground | Ground | B15 | A15 | − RST | − RST |
| Clock | Clock | B16 | A16 | +3.3 Vdc | +5 Vdc |
| Ground | Ground | B17 | A17 | − GNT | − GNT |
| − REQ | − REQ | B18 | A18 | Ground | Ground |
| +5 Vdc | +3.3 Vdc | B19 | A19 | Reserved | Reserved |
| Adr/Dat 31 | Adr/Dat 31 | B20 | A20 | Adr/Dat 30 | Adr/Dat 30 |
| Adr/Dat 29 | Adr/Dat 29 | B21 | A21 | +3.3 Vdc | +5 Vdc |
| Ground | Ground | B22 | A22 | Adr/Dat 28 | Adr/Dat 28 |
| Adr/Dat 27 | Adr/Dat 27 | B23 | A23 | Adr/Dat 26 | Adr/Dat 26 |
| Adr/Dat 25 | Adr/Dat 25 | B24 | A24 | Ground | Ground |
| +5 Vdc | +3.3 Vdc | B25 | A25 | Adr/Dat 24 | Adr/Dat 24 |
| C/ − BE3 | C/ − BE3 | B26 | A26 | IDSEL | IDSEL |
| Adr/Dat 23 | Adr/Dat 23 | B27 | A27 | +3.3 Vdc | +5 Vdc |
| Ground | Ground | B28 | A28 | Adr/Dat 22 | Adr/Dat 22 |
| Adr/Dat 21 | Adr/Dat 21 | B29 | A29 | Adr/Dat 20 | Adr/Dat 20 |
| Adr/Dat 19 | Adr/Dat 19 | B30 | A30 | Ground | Ground |
| +5 Vdc | +3.3 Vdc | B31 | A31 | Adr/Dat 18 | Adr/Dat 18 |
| Adr/Dat 17 | Adr/Dat 17 | B32 | A32 | Adr/Dat 16 | Adr/Dat 16 |
| C/ − BE2 | C/ − BE2 | B33 | A33 | +3.3 Vdc | +5 Vdc |
| Ground | Ground | B34 | A34 | − FRAME | − FRAME |
| − IRDY | − IRDY | B35 | A35 | Ground | Ground |
| +5 Vdc | +3.3 Vdc | B36 | A36 | − TRDY | − TRDY |
| − DEVSEL | − DEVSEL | B37 | A37 | Ground | Ground |
| Ground | Ground | B38 | A38 | − STOP | − STOP |
| − LOCK | − LOCK | B39 | A39 | +3.3 Vdc | +5 Vdc |
| − PERR | − PERR | B40 | A40 | SDONE | SDONE |

**TABLE 7-3    THE FULL 64-BIT PCI BUS PINOUT—5 VOLT AND 3.3 VOLT** *(CONTINUED)*

| 5 VOLT | 3.3 VOLT | PIN | PIN | 3.3 VOLT | 5 VOLT |
|--------|----------|-----|-----|----------|--------|
| +5 Vdc | +3.3 Vdc | B41 | A41 | – SBO | – SBO |
| – SERR | – SERR | B42 | A42 | Ground | Ground |
| +5 Vdc | +3.3 Vdc | B43 | A43 | PAR | PAR |
| C/ – BE1 | C/ – BE1 | B44 | A44 | Adr/Dat 15 | Adr/Dat 15 |
| Adr/Dat 14 | Adr/Dat 14 | B45 | A45 | +3.3 Vdc | +5 Vdc |
| Ground | Ground | B46 | A46 | Adr/Dat 13 | Adr/Dat 13 |
| Adr/Dat 12 | Adr/Dat 12 | B47 | A47 | Adr/Dat 11 | Adr/Dat 11 |
| Adr/Dat 10 | Adr/Dat 10 | B48 | A48 | Ground | Ground |
| Ground | Ground | B49 | A49 | Adr/Dat 9 | Adr/Dat 9 |
| Key | Ground | B50 | A50 | Ground | Key |
| Key | Ground | B51 | A51 | Ground | Key |
| Adr/Dat 8 | Adr/Dat 8 | B52 | A52 | C/ – BE0 | C/ – BE0 |
| Adr/Dat 7 | Adr/Dat 7 | B53 | A53 | +3.3 Vdc | +5 Vdc |
| +5 Vdc | +3.3 Vdc | B54 | A54 | Adr/Dat 6 | Adr/Dat 6 |
| Adr/Dat 5 | Adr/Dat 5 | B55 | A55 | Adr/Dat 4 | Adr/Dat 4 |
| Adr/Dat 3 | Adr/Dat 3 | B56 | A56 | Ground | Ground |
| Ground | Ground | B57 | A57 | Adr/Dat 2 | Adr/Dat 2 |
| Adr/Dat 1 | Adr/Dat 1 | B58 | A58 | Adr/Dat 0 | Adr/Dat 0 |
| +5 Vdc | +3.3 Vdc | B59 | A59 | +3.3 Vdc | +5 Vdc |
| – ACK64 | – ACK64 | B60 | A60 | – REQ64 | – REQ64 |
| +5 Vdc | +5 Vdc | B61 | A61 | +5 Vdc | +5 Vdc |
| +5 Vdc | +5 Vdc | B62 | A62 | +5 Vdc | +5 Vdc |
| Key | Key | Key | Key | Key | Key |
| Key | Key | Key | Key | Key | Key |
| Reserved | Reserved | B63 | A63 | Ground | Ground |
| Ground | Ground | B64 | A64 | C/ – BE7 | C/ – BE7 |
| C/ – BE6 | C/ – BE6 | B65 | A65 | C/ – BE5 | C/ – BE5 |
| C/ – BE4 | C/ – BE4 | B66 | A66 | +3.3 Vdc | +5 Vdc |
| Ground | Ground | B67 | A67 | PAR64 | PAR64 |
| Adr/Dat 63 | Adr/Dat 63 | B68 | A68 | Adr/Dat 62 | Adr/Dat 62 |
| Adr/Dat 61 | Adr/Dat 61 | B69 | A69 | Ground | Ground |
| +5 Vdc | +3.3 Vdc | B70 | A70 | Adr/Dat 60 | Adr/Dat 60 |
| Adr/Dat 59 | Adr/Dat 59 | B71 | A71 | Adr/Dat 58 | Adr/Dat 58 |
| Adr/Dat 57 | Adr/Dat 57 | B72 | A72 | Ground | Ground |
| Ground | Ground | B73 | A73 | Adr/Dat 56 | Adr/Dat 56 |
| Adr/Dat 55 | Adr/Dat 55 | B74 | A74 | Adr/Dat 54 | Adr/Dat 54 |
| Adr/Dat 53 | Adr/Dat 53 | B75 | A75 | +3.3 Vdc | +5 Vdc |
| Ground | Ground | B76 | A76 | Adr/Dat 52 | Adr/Dat 52 |
| Adr/Dat 51 | Adr/Dat 51 | B77 | A77 | Adr/Dat 50 | Adr/Dat 50 |
| Adr/Dat 49 | Adr/Dat 49 | B78 | A78 | Ground | Ground |

**TABLE 7-3 THE FULL 64-BIT PCI BUS PINOUT—5 VOLT AND 3.3 VOLT *(CONTINUED)***

| 5 VOLT | 3.3 VOLT | PIN | PIN | 3.3 VOLT | 5 VOLT |
|---|---|---|---|---|---|
| +5 Vdc | +3.3 Vdc | B79 | A79 | Adr/Dat 48 | Adr/Dat 48 |
| Adr/Dat 47 | Adr/Dat 47 | B80 | A80 | Adr/Dat 46 | Adr/Dat 46 |
| Adr/Dat 45 | Adr/Dat 45 | B81 | A81 | Ground | Ground |
| Ground | Ground | B82 | A82 | Adr/Dat 44 | Adr/Dat 44 |
| Adr/Dat 43 | Adr/Dat 43 | B83 | A83 | Adr/Dat 42 | Adr/Dat 42 |
| Adr/Dat 41 | Adr/Dat 41 | B84 | A84 | +3.3 Vdc | +5 Vdc |
| Ground | Ground | B85 | A85 | Adr/Dat 40 | Adr/Dat 40 |
| Adr/Dat 39 | Adr/Dat 39 | B86 | A86 | Adr/Dat 38 | Adr/Dat 38 |
| Adr/Dat 37 | Adr/Dat 37 | B87 | A87 | Ground | Ground |
| +5 Vdc | +3.3 Vdc | B88 | A88 | Adr/Dat 36 | Adr/Dat 36 |
| Adr/Dat 35 | Adr/Dat 35 | B89 | A89 | Adr/Dat 34 | Adr/Dat 34 |
| Adr/Dat 33 | Adr/Dat 33 | B90 | A90 | Ground | Ground |
| Ground | Ground | B91 | A91 | Adr/Dat 32 | Adr/Dat 32 |
| Reserved | Reserved | B92 | A92 | Reserved | Reserved |
| Reserved | Reserved | B93 | A93 | Ground | Ground |
| Ground | Ground | B94 | A94 | Reserved | Reserved |

To reduce the number of pins needed in the PCI bus, data and address lines are multiplexed together (Adr./Dat 0 to Adr./Dat 63). It is also interesting to note that PCI is the first bus standard designed to support a low-voltage (+3.3 Vdc) logic implementation. On inspection, you will see that +5 Vdc and +3.3 Vdc implementations of the PCI bus place their physical key slots in different places so that the two implementations are *not* interchangeable. The Clock (CLOCK) signal provides timing for the PCI bus only, and can be adjusted from DC (0 Hz) to 33 MHz. Asserting the –Reset (–RST) signal will reset all PCI devices. Since the 64-bit data path uses 8 bytes, the Command/ –Byte Enable signals (C/ –BE0 to C/ –BE7) define which bytes are transferred. Parity across the Address/Data and Byte Enable lines is represented with a Parity (PAR) or 64 Bit Parity (PAR64) signal. Bus mastering is initiated by the –Request (–REQ) line and granted after approval using the –Grant (–GNT) line.

When a valid PCI bus cycle is in progress, the –Frame (–FRAME) signal is true. If the PCI bus cycle is in its final phase, –Frame will be released. The –Target Ready (–TRDY) line is true when an addressed device is able to complete the data phase of its bus cycle. An –Initiator Ready (–IRDY) signal indicates that valid data is present on the bus (or the bus is ready to accept data). The –FRAME, –TARGET READY, and –INITIATOR READY signals are all used together. A –Stop (–STOP) signal is asserted by a target asking a master to halt the current data transfer. The ID Select (IDSEL) signal is used as a chip select signal during board configuration read and write cycles. The –Device Select (–DEVSEL) line is both an input and an output. As an input, –DEVSEL indicates whether a device has assumed control of the current bus transfer. As an output, –DEVSEL shows that a device has identified itself as the target for the current bus transfer.

There are four interrupt lines (–INTA to –INTD). When the full 64-bit data mode is being used, an expansion device will initiate a –64 Bit Bus Request (–REQ 64) and await a –64 Bit Bus Acknowledge (–ACK64) signal from the bus controller. The –Bus Lock (–LOCK) signal is an interface control used to ensure use of the bus by a selected expansion device. Error reporting is performed by –Primary Error (–PERR) and –Secondary Error (–SERR) lines. Cache memory and JTAG support are also provided on the PCI bus.

# Accelerated Graphics Port (AGP)

One of the remarkable advantages of the PC is its ability to "visualize" information. Whether you're graphing out your spreadsheet data for a corporate report or slashing your way through the latest virtual dungeon, the PC's graphics sub-system continues to improve in color depth, resolutions, and a wide range of visual effects. All of this video information requires a tremendous amount of data. This data not only requires memory, but also needs a lot of bandwidth to pass that data to the video card. The *Accelerated Graphics Port* (AGP) opens a freeway for graphics information that is especially well suited for 3D applications.

For example, the fast floating-point performance of today's CPUs can smooth the drawing of 3D meshes and animation effects and add depth to a 3D scene. The next step is to add lifelike realism. To do this, the PC must render a 3D image by adding textures, alpha-blended transparencies, texture mapping, lighting, and other effects. AGP technology accelerates graphics performance by providing a dedicated high-speed bus for the movement of large blocks of 3D texture data between the PC's graphics controller and system memory. In practice, AGP enables a hardware-accelerated graphics controller to execute texture maps directly from system RAM (instead of caching them in the relatively limited local video memory). It also helps speed the flow of decoded video from the CPU to the graphics controller. In addition, off-loading this tremendous data overhead from the PCI bus leaves PCI free to handle drive data transfers and other controllers.

High bandwidth is the key to AGP's power. The 32-bit 66 MHz AGP interface is positioned between the PC's chipset and graphics controller, as shown in Figure 7-5. This architecture significantly increases the bandwidth available to a graphics accelerator. In its basic form, AGP offers a bandwidth of 266MB/s (twice the bandwidth of PCI). This is referred to as "AGP 1X." With advanced data handling techniques, 2 bytes can be passed on every AGP clock for a bandwidth of 532MB/s (known as AGP 2X). Further refinements to AGP data handling and the introduction of new chipsets allow 4 bytes to be passed on every AGP clock for a bandwidth of more than 1GB/s (called AGP 4X). Today, the computer industry is refining the specifications for an AGP bus offering bandwidths greater than 2GB/s (dubbed AGP 3.0, or AGP 8X). You can learn more about this emerging AGP 8X standard at developer.intel.com/technology/agp/agp_draft9.htm.

## AGP SIMILARITIES TO PCI

The 32-bit AGP bus gets its roots in the PCI local bus specification, but makes some significant improvements and additions intended to optimize AGP for high-performance 3D graphics. The most notable difference is the clock speed. PCI uses a fixed 33 MHz bus, but AGP ups the clock speed to 66 MHz. Other major differences include the following:

- Deeply pipelined memory read and write operations. This hides memory access latency and effectively speeds memory performance.

- Demultiplexing of address and data on the bus, allowing almost 100 percent bus efficiency.

- AC timing for the 3.3V electrical specification that provides for one (AGP 1X) or two (AGP 2X) data transfers per 66 MHz clock cycle, allowing for real data throughput in excess of 500 MB/s.

- A new low-voltage 1.5 Vdc electrical specification allows four (AGP 4X) data transfers per 66 MHz clock cycle, providing real data throughput of over 1 GB/s.

- The bus slot defined for AGP uses a new connector body (for electrical signaling reasons) that is not compatible with the PCI connector, so PCI and AGP boards are not mechanically interchangeable.

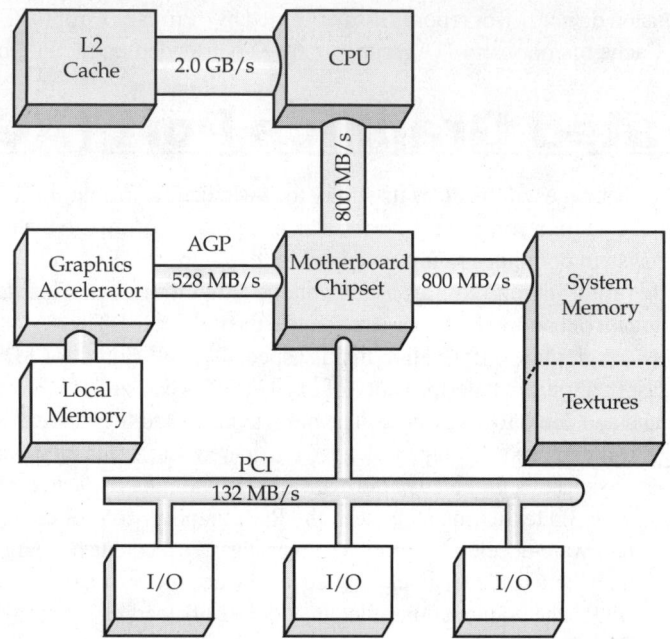

**FIGURE  7-5**    Block diagram of the AGP interface (Courtesy of Intel Corporation)

## AGP BUS LAYOUT

The AGP bus is a low-profile 132-pin connector intended to be used on ATX- and NLX-style mother-boards (though many current AT and baby AT motherboards will include an AGP bus). There are three variations of the AGP bus: 3.3V (Figure 7-6), Universal (Figure 7-7), and 1.5V (Figure 7-8). The signal

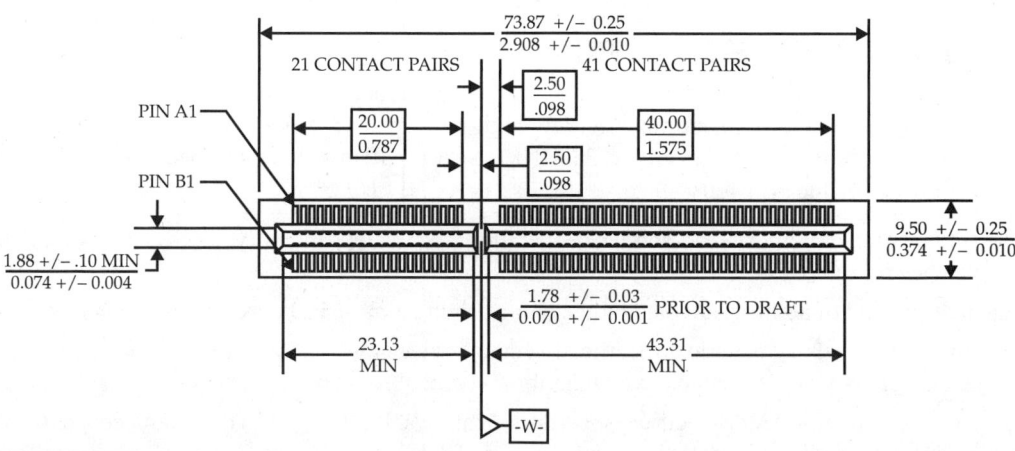

**FIGURE  7-6**    3.3V AGP bus connector

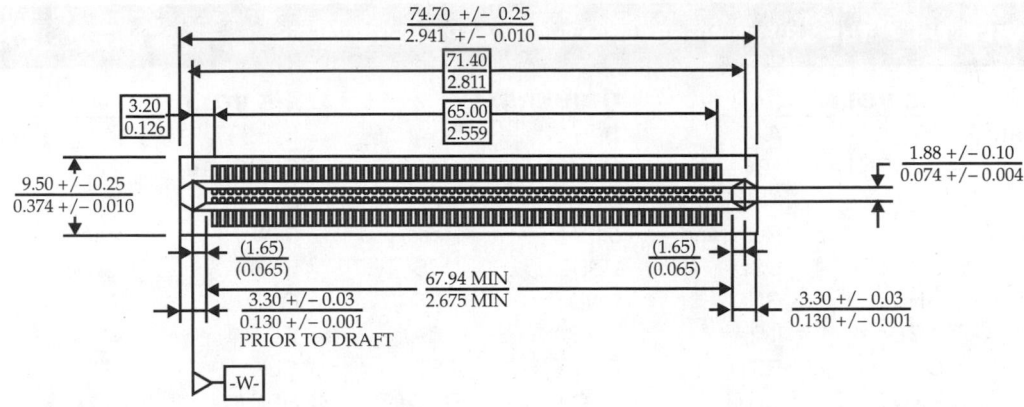

**FIGURE  7-7**    Universal AGP bus connector

layout (Table 7-4) is very similar between all three versions, but the key locations are different. As a result, 3.3V and 1.5V AGP cards are not interchangeable.

> The AGP connector is not hot-swappable. Be sure that the system and motherboard power is off. Unplugging an AGP card with power at the connector may cause irreparable damage to the card and/or system boards.

## KNOWING THE AGP SIGNALS

The PIPE# request is asserted by the current master to indicate that a full width request is to be queued by the target. The master queues one request with each rising edge of CLK while PIPE# is asserted. When PIPE# is de-asserted, no new requests are queued across the AD bus. The SideBand Address port (SBA[7 through 0]) provides an additional bus to pass requests (address and command) to the target from the master.

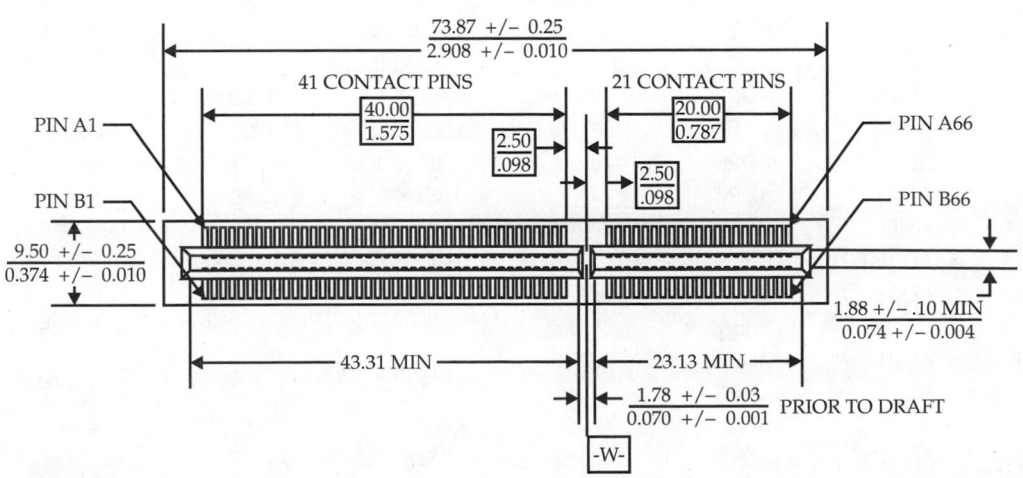

**FIGURE  7-8**    1.5V AGP bus connector

**TABLE 7-4**     THE 3.3V, UNIVERSAL, AND 1.5V AGP BUS PINOUTS

| | 3.3 VOLT | | UNIVERSAL | | 1.5 VOLT | |
|---|---|---|---|---|---|---|
| Pin | B | A | B | A | B | A |
| 1 | OVRCNT# | 12V | OVRCNT# | 12V | OVRCNT# | 12V |
| 2 | 5.0V | TYPEDET# | 5.0V | TYPEDET# | 5.0V | TYPEDET# |
| 3 | 5.0V | Reserved | 5.0V | Reserved | 5.0V | Reserved |
| 4 | USB+ | USB– | USB+ | USB– | USB+ | USB– |
| 5 | GND | GND | GND | GND | GND | GND |
| 6 | INTB# | INTA# | INTB# | INTA# | INTB# | INTA# |
| 7 | CLK | RST# | CLK | RST# | CLK | RST# |
| 8 | REQ# | GNT# | REQ# | GNT# | REQ# | GNT# |
| 9 | VCC3.3 | VCC3.3 | VCC3.3 | VCC3.3 | VCC3.3 | VCC3.3 |
| 10 | ST0 | ST1 | ST0 | ST1 | ST0 | ST1 |
| 11 | ST2 | Reserved | ST2 | Reserved | ST2 | Reserved |
| 12 | RBF# | PIPE# | RBF# | PIPE# | RBF# | PIPE# |
| 13 | GND | GND | GND | GND | GND | GND |
| 14 | Reserved | Reserved | Reserved | WBF# | Reserved | WBF# |
| 15 | SBA0 | SBA1 | SBA0 | SBA1 | SBA0 | SBA1 |
| 16 | VCC3.3 | VCC3.3 | VCC3.3 | VCC3.3 | VCC3.3 | VCC3.3 |
| 17 | SBA2 | SBA3 | SBA2 | SBA3 | SBA2 | SBA3 |
| 18 | SB_STB | Reserved | SB_STB | SB_STB# | SB_STB | SB_STB# |
| 19 | GND | GND | GND | GND | GND | GND |
| 20 | SBA4 | SBA5 | SBA4 | SBA5 | SBA4 | SBA5 |
| 21 | SBA6 | SBA7 | SBA6 | SBA7 | SBA6 | SBA7 |
| 22 | KEY | KEY | Reserved | Reserved | Reserved | Reserved |
| 23 | KEY | KEY | GND | GND | GND | GND |
| 24 | KEY | KEY | 3.3Vaux | Reserved | 3.3Vaux | Reserved |
| 25 | KEY | KEY | VCC3.3 | VCC3.3 | VCC3.3 | VCC3.3 |
| 26 | AD31 | AD30 | AD31 | AD30 | AD31 | AD30 |
| 27 | AD29 | AD28 | AD29 | AD28 | AD29 | AD28 |
| 28 | VCC3.3 | VCC3.3 | VCC3.3 | VCC3.3 | VCC3.3 | VCC3.3 |
| 29 | AD27 | AD26 | AD27 | AD26 | AD27 | AD26 |
| 30 | AD25 | AD24 | AD25 | AD24 | AD25 | AD24 |
| 31 | GND | GND | GND | GND | GND | GND |
| 32 | AD_STB1 | Reserved | AD_STB1 | AD_STB1# | AD_STB1 | AD_STB1# |
| 33 | AD23 | C/BE3# | AD23 | C/BE3# | AD23 | C/BE3# |
| 34 | Vddq3.3 | Vddq3.3 | Vddq | Vddq | Vddq1.5 | Vddq1.5 |
| 35 | AD21 | AD22 | AD21 | AD22 | AD21 | AD22 |
| 36 | AD19 | AD20 | AD19 | AD20 | AD19 | AD20 |
| 37 | GND | GND | GND | GND | GND | GND |
| 38 | AD17 | AD18 | AD17 | AD18 | AD17 | AD18 |

**TABLE 7-4    THE 3.3V, UNIVERSAL, AND 1.5V AGP BUS PINOUTS** *(CONTINUED)*

| | 3.3 VOLT | | UNIVERSAL | | 1.5 VOLT | |
|---|---|---|---|---|---|---|
| Pin | B | A | B | A | B | A |
| 39 | C/BE2# | AD16 | C/BE2# | AD16 | C/BE2# | AD16 |
| 40 | Vddq3.3 | Vddq3.3 | Vddq | Vddq | Vddq1.5 | Vddq1.5 |
| 41 | IRDY# | FRAME# | IRDY# | FRAME# | IRDY# | FRAME# |
| 42 | 3.3Vaux | Reserved | 3.3Vaux | Reserved | KEY | KEY |
| 43 | GND | GND | GND | GND | KEY | KEY |
| 44 | Reserved | Reserved | Reserved | Reserved | KEY | KEY |
| 45 | VCC3.3 | VCC3.3 | VCC3.3 | VCC3.3 | KEY | KEY |
| 46 | DEVSEL# | TRDY# | DEVSEL# | TRDY# | DEVSEL# | TRDY# |
| 47 | Vddq3.3 | STOP# | Vddq | STOP# | Vddq1.5 | STOP# |
| 48 | PERR# | PME# | PERR# | PME# | PERR# | PME# |
| 49 | GND | GND | GND | GND | GND | GND |
| 50 | SERR# | PAR | SERR# | PAR | SERR# | PAR |
| 51 | C/BE1# | AD15 | C/BE1# | AD15 | C/BE1# | AD15 |
| 52 | Vddq3.3 | Vddq3.3 | Vddq | Vddq | Vddq1.5 | Vddq1.5 |
| 53 | AD14 | AD13 | AD14 | AD13 | AD14 | AD13 |
| 54 | AD12 | AD11 | AD12 | AD11 | AD12 | AD11 |
| 55 | GND | GND | GND | GND | GND | GND |
| 56 | AD10 | AD9 | AD10 | AD9 | AD10 | AD9 |
| 57 | AD8 | C/BE0# | AD8 | C/BE0# | AD8 | C/BE0# |
| 58 | Vddq3.3 | Vddq3.3 | Vddq | Vddq | Vddq1.5 | Vddq1.5 |
| 59 | AD_STB0 | Reserved | AD_STB0 | AD_STB0# | AD_STB0 | AD_STB0# |
| 60 | AD7 | AD6 | AD7 | AD6 | AD7 | AD6 |
| 61 | GND | GND | GND | GND | GND | GND |
| 62 | AD5 | AD4 | AD5 | AD4 | AD5 | AD4 |
| 63 | AD3 | AD2 | AD3 | AD2 | AD3 | AD2 |
| 64 | Vddq3.3 | Vddq3.3 | Vddq | Vddq | Vddq1.5 | Vddq1.5 |
| 65 | AD1 | AD0 | AD1 | AD0 | AD1 | AD0 |
| 66 | Reserved | Reserved | Vrefcg | Vrefgc | Vrefcg | Vrefgc |

SBA[7 through 0] are outputs from the master, and an input to the target. This port is ignored by the target until enabled.

The Read Buffer Full signal (RBF#) indicates whether the master is ready to accept previously requested low-priority read data. When RBF# is asserted, the arbiter is not allowed to initiate the return of low-priority read data to the master. A Write Buffer Full signal (WBF#) indicates whether the master is ready to accept data from the core logic. When WBF# is asserted, the core logic arbiter is not allowed to initiate a transaction to provide data.

The Status bus (ST[2 through 0]) provides information from the arbiter to the master on what it may do. ST[2 through 0] signals only have meaning to the master when its GNT# is asserted. When GNT# is de-asserted, these signals have no meaning and must be ignored. The master may queue AGP requests by asserting PIPE# or start a PCI transaction by asserting FRAME#. ST[2 through 0] signals are always output from the core logic and input to the master.

The AD Bus Strobe 0 signal (AD_STB0) provides timing for the 2x data transfer mode on address lines AD[15 through 00]. The agent that is providing data drives this signal. The AD Bus Strobe 0 complement (AD_STB0#, along with AD_STB0) provides timing for the 4x data transfer mode on address lines AD[15 through 00]. The agent that is providing data drives this signal. The AD Bus Strobe 1 signal (AD_STB1) provides timing for the 2x data transfer mode on address lines AD[31 through 16]. The agent that is providing data drives this signal. The AD Bus Strobe 1 complement (AD_STB1#, along with AD_STB1) provides timing for the 4x data transfer mode on address lines AD[31 through 16]. The agent that is providing data drives this signal.

The SideBand Strobe signal (SB_STB) provides timing for SBA[7 through 0] (when supported) and is always driven by the AGP master. When the SideBand Strobes have been idle, a synch cycle needs to be performed before a request can be queued. The SideBand Strobe complement (SB_STB#, along with SB_STB#) provides timing for SBA[7 through 0] signals (when supported) when 4x timing is supported and is always driven by the AGP master.

Clock (CLK) provides timing for AGP and PCI control signals. The USB Positive Differential Data Line (USB+) is used to send USB data and control packets to external peripheral devices. The USB Negative Differential Data Line (USB−) is used to send USB data and control packets to external peripheral devices. The USB Overcurrent Indicator (OVRCNT#) is low when too much current has been taken from the 5-volt power supply (Vbus) line on the bus connector. Otherwise, the line is at a level between 2.4 volts and Vddq. The Power Management Event signal (PME#) is not used by the AGP protocol, but is used by the PCI target interface when being power-managed by the operating system. The Type Detect signal (TYPEDET#) indicates whether the interface is 1.5 volt or 3.3 volt.

## CONFIGURING AN AGP SYSTEM

The AGP bus requires a 66 MHz clock. This clock is developed from the motherboard's front side bus clock (noted "FSB" or the "CPU clock"). When the motherboard is operated at 66 MHz, your AGP bus can use this clock directly. When the motherboard is operated at 100 MHz or higher, it will have to be divided down 2:3 to achieve 66 MHz. If the motherboard is operated at 133 MHz, you'd use a 1:2 divisor. Normally, you can adjust this divisor (e.g., 1:1, 1:2, or 2:3) using a jumper on the motherboard, or directly through the CMOS Setup.

Be sure that you configure the system correctly depending on the clock speed. If the divisor is set to 2:3 when the system clock is 66 MHz, you will be *underclocking* the AGP bus. On the other hand, if the divisor is set to 1:1 when the system clock is 100 MHz, you will be *overclocking* the AGP bus. With today's motherboards supporting a wider range of FSB speeds, you will usually find a greater variety of clock divisors available, or the AGP bus will run asynchronously of the FSB, and you won't need to configure an AGP divisor at all. There are several additional settings that you may encounter in the Advanced | Video Configuration menu of your CMOS Setup:

■ **AGP Aperture Size**   This selects the amount of system memory assigned to a motherboard's integrated AGP video controller. The default is often set at 64MB, but you may opt for larger amounts of RAM (e.g., 256MB) if the system has a large amount of memory available.

■ **Primary Video Adapter**   This lets you select between AGP and PCI video adapters at boot time. This is almost always set to AGP, but if there's a PCI video adapter in the system, you'll need to set this option to PCI—otherwise there will be no video.

■ **Video Repost**    This setting enables or disables the video BIOS coming out of the S3 power conservation state. This option is disabled by default because a PC normally has the appropriate drivers to run the video adapter. If the drivers for the video adapter are not installed, or the PC is set to standard VGA mode, this option should be enabled.

# Communication and Networking Riser (CNR)

While the PC industry has mainly focused on a few powerful, general-purpose bus architectures (like PCI), the last few years have seen a trend toward smaller, more proprietary busses (dubbed "risers"). Intel is leading this movement with their *communication and networking riser* (or CNR). You can see a typical CNR slot in Figure 7-9. The goal of any "riser" architecture is to simplify the design and implementation of common PC peripherals by providing direct access to one or more interfaces supported by the motherboard's chipset—allowing peripheral makers to produce versatile but inexpensive devices for the PC. CNR version 1.2 provides access to the following interfaces of Intel's i850 chipset:

■ **AC '97 interface**    This allows audio and modem functions to be integrated onto a CNR board.

■ **LAN interface**    This provides one of two LAN interfaces for networking functions: an eight-pin interface for use with Platform LAN Connection (PLC-based) devices, and a 17-pin interface for Media Independent Interface (MII-based) devices.

■ **SMBus interface**    This provides plug-and-play functionality for the CNR board. It also includes power signals required for power management.

■ **USB interface**    This provides a USB interface for the CNR board.

CNR slot

**FIGURE 7-9**    The MSI KT3 Ultra-ARU sports a CNR bus slot along with PCI and an AGP slot (Courtesy of Motherboards.org).

# CNR BUS LAYOUT

The serial CNR interface uses a keyed 30-pin bus slot connector, and motherboards typically only include one CNR slot. The bus pinout is shown in Table 7-5. You can see the network data signals (marked "LAN"), the USB signals (marked "USB"), SMBus signals (marked "SMB"), and audio/modem signals (marked "AC97").

# CONFIGURING A CNR DEVICE

Most motherboards can automatically detect the presence of a CNR device, and either disable corresponding devices on the motherboard, or add the CNR device as a secondary function. However, you may need

**TABLE 7-5    THE CNR BUS PINOUT**

| SIGNAL NAME | PIN | PIN | SIGNAL NAME |
|---|---|---|---|
| Reserved | A1 | B1 | Reserved |
| Reserved | A2 | B2 | Reserved |
| Ground | A3 | B3 | Reserved |
| Reserved | A4 | B4 | Ground |
| Reserved | A5 | B5 | Reserved |
| Ground | A6 | B6 | Reserved |
| LAN_TXD2 | A7 | B7 | Ground |
| LAN_TXD0 | A8 | B8 | LAN_TXD1 |
| Ground | A9 | B9 | LAN_RSTSYNC |
| LAN_CLK | A10 | B10 | Ground |
| LAN_RXD1 | A11 | B11 | LAN_RXD2 |
| Reserved | A12 | B12 | LAN_RXD0 |
| USB+ | A13 | B13 | Ground |
| Ground | A14 | B14 | Reserved |
| USB- | A15 | B15 | +5Vdc |
| +12Vdc | A16 | B16 | USB_OC |
| Ground | A17 | B17 | Ground |
| +3.3Vdc | A18 | B18 | −12Vdc |
| +5Vdc | A19 | B19 | +3.3Vdc |
| Ground | A20 | B20 | Ground |
| EEDI | A21 | B21 | EED0 |
| EECS | A22 | B22 | EECK |
| SMB_A1 | A23 | B23 | Ground |
| SMB_A2 | A24 | B24 | SMB_A0 |
| SMB_SDA | A25 | B25 | SMB_SCL |
| AC97_RESET | A26 | B26 | CDC_DWN_ENAB |
| Reserved | A27 | B27 | Ground |
| AC97_SDATA_IN1 | A28 | B28 | AC97_SYNC |
| AC97_SDATA_IN0 | A29 | B29 | AC97_SDATA_OUT |
| Ground | A30 | B30 | AC97_BITCLK |

to enable the CNR device through Advanced | Peripheral Configuration menu of the CMOS Setup. If a CNR device with a modem or LAN function is installed, you may need to configure the following settings:

- **Audio Device**   This option enables or disables the motherboard's onboard audio and is enabled by default. For boards with no onboard audio, this option does not appear. However, this option does appear if a CNR card with an audio sub-system is installed. With a CNR audio device installed, you may need to disable the motherboard's audio system.

- **LAN Device**   This enables or disables the motherboard's onboard LAN device, and is enabled by default. For boards with no onboard LAN audio subsystem, this option will not appear unless a CNR card with a LAN subsystem is installed. With a CNR LAN device installed, you may need to disable the motherboard's LAN feature.

- **Modem Device**   This option enables or disables a modem device on a CNR card, and is enabled by default. This option appears only when a CNR card with a modem feature is installed. If a CNR modem device is installed, you may need to disable other modem devices in the system.

# Further Study

**AGP**   www.agpforum.org
**CompactPCI Home Page**   www.compactpci.com
**CNR Specification**   developer.intel.com/technology/cnr/index.htm
**Intel's AGP interface specification**   ftp://download.intel.com/technology/agp/downloads/agp20.pdf
**Intel's AGP site**   developer.intel.com/technology/agp/index.htm
**PCI Special Interest Group Home Page**   www.pcisig.com
**Small PCI**   www.pcisig.com/specifications/small_pci

# 8

# CD DRIVES

The *compact disc* (CD) first appeared in the commercial marketplace in early 1982. Sony and Philips developed the CD as a joint venture and envisioned it as a reliable, high-quality digital replacement for aging analog phonograph and cassette tape technology. With the introduction of the audio CDs, designers demonstrated that huge amounts of information could be stored simply and very inexpensively on common, non-magnetic media. Unlike previous recording media, the CD stores data in *digital* form encoded as physical "pits" and "lands" in the disc. The digital approach allowed excellent stereo sound quality that does not degrade each time the disc is played. This optical storage technology also found its way into the PC and has evolved into a complete family of reliable high-volume storage devices: the CD-ROM, CD writer (or CD-R), and CD rewriter (or CD-RW). This chapter examines the basics of these technologies, offers some handy installation guidelines, and covers a wealth of troubleshooting issues.

# The CD-ROM Drive

The CD-ROM drive that we know today (Figure 8-1) has its origins in digital audio recording, but it was quickly adapted for the PC by designers who saw CDs as a natural solution for storing all types of computer information (such as text, graphics, programs, video clips, audio files, and so on). The CD-ROM drive can only *read* data—it cannot write. However, the CD-ROM is known for its low cost, high data transfer speeds, good reliability, and broad media (disc) compatibility. In fact, the CD-ROM proved *so* popular that it quickly became standard equipment on both desktop and mobile PC systems. This part of the chapter outlines the elements of CD-ROM drives and technologies that a technician should be familiar with.

## CD MEDIA

Commercial CDs are mass-produced by stamping the pattern of pits and lands onto a molded polycarbonate disc (known as a *substrate*). It is this stamping process (much like the stamping used to produce vinyl records) that places the data on the disc. But the disc is not yet readable—there are finish steps that must be performed to transform a clear plastic disc into a viable, data-carrying medium. The clear polycarbonate disc is given a silvered (reflective) coating so that it will reflect laser light. Silvering coats all parts of the disc side (pits and lands) equally. After silvering, the disc is coated with a tough, scratch-resistant lacquer that seals the disc from the elements (especially oxygen, which will oxidize and ruin the reflective coating). Finally, a label can be silk-screened onto the finished disc before it is tested and packaged. Figure 8-2 illustrates each of these layers in a cross-sectional diagram.

The word *disc* is not a spelling error—the PC industry uses the term "disk" to refer to magnetic media (such as a floppy disk), but the term "disc" refers to optical media (such as a rewritable disc).

## CD DATA

Unlike magnetic media, such as floppy disks or hard drives, CDs are not segregated into concentric tracks and sectors. Instead, CDs are recorded as a single, continuous spiral track running from the spindle (inner) to the lead-out (outer) area. Figure 8-3 shows an example of the spiral pattern as it might be recorded on a CD. The inset illustrates the relationship between the pits and lands. Each pit is about 0.15μm (micrometers) deep and 0.5μm wide. Pits and lands may range from 0.83μm to 3.0μm in length.

**FIGURE 8-1**    CD drive mechanisms like this CD-RW drive provide fast playback and writing/rewriting versatility for all types of PC users.

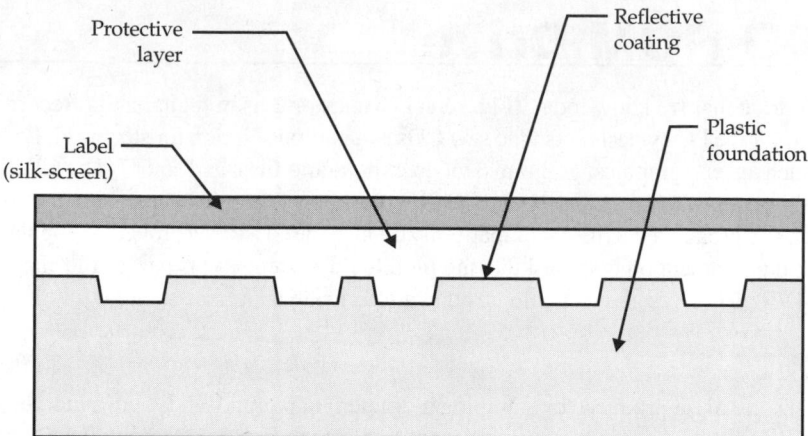

**FIGURE 8-2**    Cross-section of a common CD disc

There are approximately 1.6µm between each iteration of the spiral. Given these microscopic dimensions, a CD-ROM disc offers about 16,000 tracks per inch (tpi), compared to 96 tpi for an ordinary floppy disk. If unrolled, the line of pits and lands would stretch four miles.

During playback, CDs use a highly focused laser beam and laser detector to sense the presence or absence of pits. Figure 8-4 illustrates the reading behavior. The laser/detector pair is mounted on a carriage that follows the spiral track across the CD. A laser is directed at the underside of the CD, where it penetrates more than 1mm of clear plastic before shining on the reflective surface. When laser light strikes a land, the light is reflected toward the detector, which, in turn, produces a very strong output signal. As laser light strikes a pit, the light is slightly out of focus. As a result, most of the incoming laser energy is scattered away in all directions, so very little output signal is generated by the detector. As with floppy and hard drives, it is the *transition* from pit to land (and back again) that corresponds to binary levels, *not* the presence or absence of a pit or land. The analog light signal returned by the detector must be converted to logic levels and decoded, which is accomplished in a process described next.

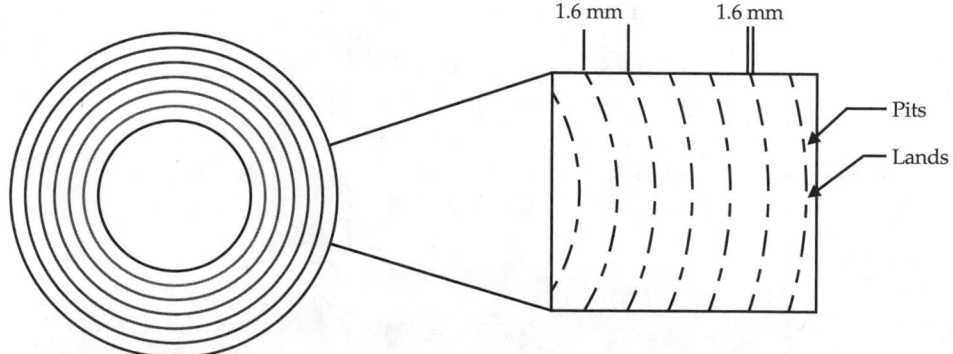

**FIGURE 8-3**    Close-up of a CD spiral track pattern

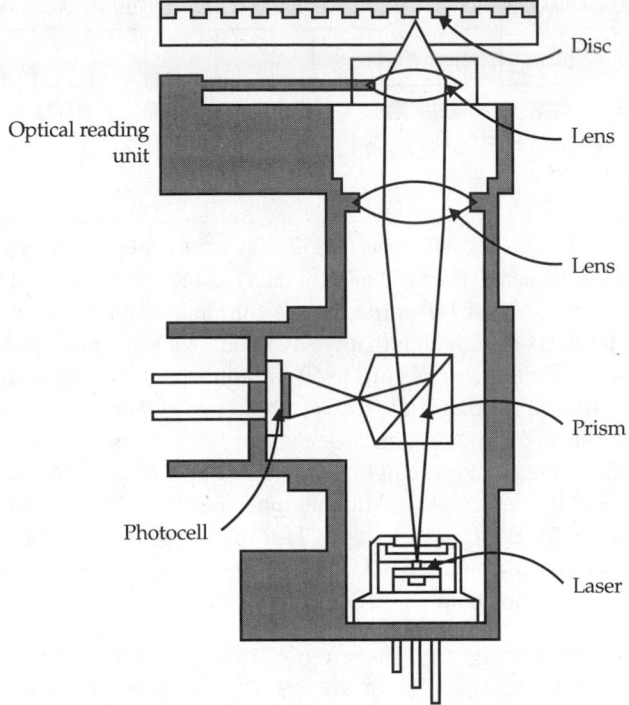

**FIGURE 8-4**    Reading a typical compact disc

## EFM Basics

A complex decoding process is necessary to convert this arcane sequence of pits and lands into meaningful binary information. The technique of *eight-to-fourteen modulation* (EFM) is used with CD-ROMs. For hard disk drives, techniques such as *2,7 RLL encoding* can be used to place a large number of bits into a limited number of flux transitions. CDs using EFM have this same ability, and user data, error correction information, address information, and synchronization patterns can all be contained in a bit stream represented by pits and lands.

Magnetic media encodes bits as flux *transitions—not* the discrete orientation of any magnetic area. The same concept holds true with CD-ROMs, where binary 1's and 0's do not correspond to pits or lands. A binary 1 is represented wherever a *transition* (pit-to-land or land-to-pit) occurs. The *length* of a pit or land represents the number of binary 0's. Figure 8-5 illustrates this concept. The eight-to-fourteen encoding technique equates each byte (eight bits) with a fourteen-bit sequence (called a *symbol*), where each binary 1 must be separated by at least two binary 0's. Table 8-1 shows part of the eight-to-fourteen conversion. Three bits are added to merge each fourteen-bit symbol together.

## Data Storage

A CD-ROM *frame* is composed of 24 synchronization bits, 14 control bits, 24 of the 14-bit data symbols you saw previously, and 8 complete 14-bit error correction (EC) symbols. Keep in mind that each symbol is separated by an additional 3 merge bits, bringing the total number of bits in the frame to 588. Thus, 24 bytes of data is represented by 588 bits on a CD-ROM, expressed as a number of pits and lands. There are 98 frames in a data

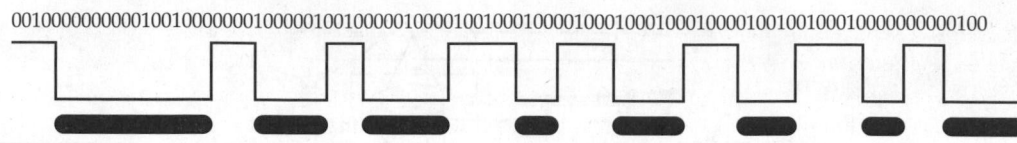

0010000000000100100000000100000100100000100001001000100001001000100010001000100100100010000000000100

**FIGURE 8-5**   An example of EFM in action

*block*, so each block carries [98 × 24] 2,048 bytes (2,352 with error correction, synchronization, and address bytes). The basic 1X CD-ROM can deliver 153.6KB of data (75 blocks) per second to its host controller.

Remember that the CD-ROM disc is recorded as one continuous spiral track running around the disk, so ordinary sector and track ID information that we associate with magnetic disks does not apply very well. Instead, information is divided in terms of 0 to 59 *minutes*, and 0 to 59 *seconds* recorded at the beginning of each block. A CD-ROM (like an audio CD) can hold up to 79 *minutes* of data. Many commercial CD-ROMs tend to limit this to 60 minutes, because the last 14 minutes of data are encoded in the outer 5mm of disc space, which is the most difficult to manufacture and keep clean in everyday use. There are 270,000 blocks of data in 60 minutes. At 2,048 data bytes per block, the 60 minute disc's capacity is 552,950,000 bytes (about 550MB). Today, average CD-R discs provide up to 74 minutes with a capacity of about 681MB (usually rounded down to 650MB), and high-capacity 80-minute discs can provide up to 737MB (usually rounded down to about 703MB).

Disc media rated for higher storage capacities (e.g., 770MB) may be using 2,352 bytes per sector rather than 2,048. Since those additional bytes are for error correction and other housekeeping tasks, the higher capacity is misleading.

## CAV and CLV

Floppy and hard drives spin the media at a constant rate under the read/write heads (regardless of where those heads are located on the media). This technique is called *constant angular velocity* (or CAV) since it takes the same amount of time for one complete turn of the disk at all times. This means CAV-based drives wind up packing data closer together on the inner tracks, but today's hard drives compensate for this with

**TABLE 8-1    A SAMPLE OF EIGHT-TO-FOURTEEN MODULATION CODES**

| NUMBER | BINARY PATTERN | EFM PATTERN |
|---|---|---|
| 0 | 00000000 | 01001000100000 |
| 1 | 00000001 | 10000100000000 |
| 2 | 00000010 | 10010000100000 |
| 3 | 00000011 | 10001000100000 |
| 4 | 00000100 | 01000100000000 |
| 5 | 00000101 | 00000100010000 |
| 6 | 00000110 | 00010000100000 |
| 7 | 00000111 | 00100100000000 |
| 8 | 00001000 | 01001001000000 |
| 9 | 00001001 | 10000001000000 |
| 10 | 00001010 | 10010001000000 |

*zoned recording*—placing more sectors on the outer tracks. CAV-based drives also have faster data transfers when reading the outer tracks because the data passes under the heads at a higher linear speed.

CD-ROMs work differently—they adjust the speed of the spindle motor dynamically so that the linear velocity of the disk is always *constant*. The disc rotates slower when the head is near the outside of the disc, and faster as the head nears the inside (usually between 200 and 500 RPM). This approach is called *constant linear velocity* (or CLV) and it ensures that the same amount of data always goes past the read head in a given period of time. CLV is a throwback to the early days of CD audio players. Early CD players couldn't deal with bits arriving at a different rate (depending on what part of the disk they were on), so the CD standard was designed around CLV to guarantee that the same data rate would be available from the disk each second regardless of where the data was located. CD-ROM drives were designed to follow this methodology.

As the years passed, designers realized that they could increase spindle speed to improve the data transfer rates of data CDs. This led to 2X, 4X, 8X, 12X, and up to the 50-58X drives that we see today. But there's a problem with CLV at such high speeds—it's extremely difficult to control spindle speed. Today's CD drives use large buffers, and use mainly data CDs, so most CD drives employ both CAV and CLV. CAV is used when reading the outside of the disc, then CLV is used to speed up the disc while reading the inner tracks. Of course, the drive reverts back to CLV for playing audio CDs at 1X speeds.

## CARING FOR CDS

Read-only, recordable, and rewriteable compact discs are a remarkably reliable long-term storage medium (conservative expectations place the life estimates of a current commercial CD around 30 years and more). However, the longevity of a CD is affected by its storage and handling—a faulty CD can cause file and data errors that you might otherwise interpret as a defect in the drive itself. Here are some tips to help protect and maintain the disc itself:

- *Don't bend the disc.* Polycarbonate is a forgiving material, but you risk cracking or snapping (and thus ruining) the disc.

- *Don't heat the disc.* Remember, the disc is plastic. Leaving it by a heater or on the dashboard of your car will cause melting.

- *Don't scratch the disc.* Laser wavelengths have a tendency to "look past" minor scratches, but a major scratch can cause problems. Be especially careful of circular scratches (ones that follows the spiral track). A circular scratch can easily wipe out entire segments of data, which would then be unrecoverable.

- *Don't use chemicals on the disc.* Chemicals containing solvents such as ammonia, benzene, acetone, carbon tetrachloride, or chlorinated cleaning solvents can easily damage the disc's plastic surface.

Eventually, a build-up of excessive dust or fingerprints can interfere with the laser beam enough to cause disc read errors. When this happens, the disc can be cleaned easily using a dry, soft, lint-free cloth. Hold the disc from its edges and wipe radially (from hub to edge). Do not wipe in a circular motion! For stubborn stains, moisten the cloth in a bit of fresh isopropyl alcohol (do not use water which can leave streaks and mineral deposits). Place the cleaned disc in a caddie or jewel case for transport and storage.

## CD STANDARDS AND CHARACTERISTICS

Like so many other PC peripheral devices, the early CD-ROM faced a serious problem of industry standardization. Just recording the data to a CD is not enough—the data must be recorded in a way that any CD-ROM drive can read. Standards for CD-ROM data formats were developed by consortiums of influential PC manufacturers and interested CD-ROM publishers. Ultimately, this kind of industry-wide cooperation made the CD-ROM one of the most uniform and standardized peripherals in the PC market. Because of the broad introduction of CD recorders and rewriters into the marketplace, it is also important for you to understand the major concepts and operations of CD recorders. This part of the chapter explains many of these key ideas and standards.

## High Sierra

In 1984 (before the general release of CD-ROM technology), the PC industry realized that there must be a standard method of reading a disc's *volume table of contents* (VTOC)—otherwise the CD-ROM market would become extremely fragmented as various (incompatible) standards vied for acceptance. PC manufacturers, prospective CD publishers, and software developers met at the High Sierra Hotel in Lake Tahoe, California, to begin developing just such a uniform standard. By 1986, the CD-ROM standard file format (dubbed the *High Sierra* format) was accepted and approved. High Sierra remained the standard for several years, but it has since been replaced by ISO 9660.

## ISO 9660

High Sierra was certainly a workable format, but it was primarily a domestic U.S. development. When placed before the *International Standards Organization* (ISO), High Sierra was tweaked and refined to meet international needs. After international review, High Sierra was absorbed (with only a few changes) into the *ISO 9660* standard. Although many technicians refer to High Sierra and ISO 9660 (a.k.a. "Yellow Book") interchangeably, you should understand that the two standards are *not* the same. For the purposes of this book, ISO 9660 is the principle file format for storing digital data (computer files) on a CD-ROM or CD-R disc. All CD-ROM, CD-R, and CD-RW drives can read ISO 9660 discs, and all CD-R/RW drives are capable of recording a CD-R disc in the ISO 9660 format (though rewritable drives use the later UDF format when working with CD-RW media).

## CD-ROM Standards ("Books")

When Philips and Sony defined the proprietary standards that became CD audio, CD-ROM, and so on, the documents were bound in different colored covers. By tradition, each color now represents a different level of standardization:

- **Red Book**    Also known as the Compact Disc Digital Audio Standard (CEI IEC 908). This defines the media, recording and mastering process, and the player design for CD audio. This is sometimes dubbed CD-DA (for CD Digital Audio), and allows for up to 74 minutes of audio per disc. When you listen to your favorite audio CD, you are enjoying the benefits of the Red Book standard. CDs conforming to Red Book standards will usually have the words "digital audio" printed below the disc logo. Today, Red Book audio may be combined with programs and other PC data on the same disc.

- **Yellow Book**    The Yellow Book standard (dubbed ISO 10149:1989) makes CD-ROM possible by defining the additional error-correction data needed on the disc and specifying detection hardware and firmware needed in the drive. When a disc conforms to Yellow Book, it will usually be marked "data storage" beneath the disc logo. *Mode 1* Yellow Book is the typical operating mode that supports computer data. *Mode 2* Yellow Book (also known as the *CD-ROM XA format*) supports compressed audio data and video/picture data. The Yellow Book standards build on the Red Book, so virtually all CD-ROM drives are capable of playing back CD audio discs.

- **Orange Book**    The Orange Book (or *Recordable Compact Disc Standard*) is the key to recordable (CD-R) and rewritable (CD-RW) drives with multisession capability, and serves to extend the basic Red and Yellow Book standards by providing specifications for recordable products such as (Part 1) *magneto-optical* (MO) drives, (Part 2) *write-once CD-R* drives, and (Part 3) *rewritable CD-RW* drives. Any time that you write files to CD-R/RW media, you're using the Orange Book standard.

■ **Green Book**    The Green Book standard defines a set of supplemental standards for data recording and provides an outline for a specific computer system that supports CD-I (compact disc-interactive). CD-I standards include real-time still video image coding, decoder and visual effects, a Compact Disc Real Time Operating System (CD-RTOS), and support for full motion MPEG video. CD-I can store 19 hours of audio, 7,500 still images, and 72 minutes of full screen/full motion MPEG video in a standard CD format. Interactive kiosks and information systems using CD-I discs have typically been based on Green Book standards, but CD-I has fallen into disuse.

■ **Blue Book**    Otherwise known as CD-Extra or CD-Plus, this is the standard for Enhanced Music CDs, which include both audio and data formats. Blue Book CDs are ISO 9660-compliant and intended to be played in ordinary home CD players, but can also be used in PCs which can play back pictures and other data.

■ **White Book**    The White Book standard (also known as *CD-I Bridge*) is a Philips/Sony specification intended to play on CD-I players (e.g., information kiosks) and other platforms such as the PC. It includes support for audio and video data, and outlines a disc format defining CD-I Bridge discs (conforming to the CD-ROM XA specification) and an ISO 9660 directory structure. A CD-I application program is mandatory and stored in the CDI directory. All MPEG-1 film titles conform to the White Book standard for Video CDs, which may be read on any White Book-compatible machine (including CD-I and suitable CD-ROM drives). The video and sound are compressed together using the MPEG-1 standard, and recorded onto a CD Bridge disc.

## Digital Audio Extraction (DAE)

With the introduction of recordable CDs, it didn't take long for audio enthusiasts to express an interest in creating their own music CDs and compilations. This process typically involved recording the CD audio in the form of WAV files to the system hard drive—those files could then be post-processed and organized for recording on a CD-R. However, this procedure presented a unique problem for CD drives. While most CD drives are capable of playing digital audio, they often prove to be a poor solution for recording that audio on the hard drive in the form of WAV files. While just about every CD-ROM/R/RW drive will *play* standard Red Book digital audio, *not* every drive will allow you to read and *record* the digital audio data directly—a process sometimes called *CD-DA extraction*, or *digital audio extraction* (DAE).

If you're looking to create your own music CDs from existing audio CDs, you will need to use a CD drive that is suitable for good quality DAE (a specification or notation usually added to the drive box or spec sheet). A drive that is not well suited for DAE will cause artifacts such as pops, clicks, or gaps in the recorded WAV file. Technicians should be aware of this problem and that the solution to poor-quality DAE is often to upgrade the CD drive that is reading the original music CD (the *source drive*).

 Keep in mind that it is *illegal* to duplicate music or other CD contents that have been copyrighted. You cannot duplicate copyrighted materials without permission from the copyright holder.

## The Multi-Speed Drive

The Red Book standard defines CD audio as a stream of data that flows from the player mechanism to the amplifier (or other audio manipulation circuit) at a rate of 150 KB/sec. This data rate was chosen to take music off the disc for truest reproduction. When the Yellow Book was developed to address CD-ROMs, this basic data rate was carried over. Designers soon learned that computer data can be transferred *much* faster than Red Book audio information, so the *multi-speed* drive was developed to work with Red Book audio at the normal 150 KB/sec rate, while running faster for Yellow Book data in order to improve the effective data throughput.

The first common multi-speed drives available were 2X drives. By running at two times the normal data transfer speed, data throughput can be doubled from 150 KB/sec to 300 KB/sec. CD-ROM drives with 4X transfer speed (600 KB/sec) can transfer data four times faster than a Red Book drive. If Red Book audio is encountered, the drive speed drops back to 150 KB/sec. Today, you can find CD-ROM drives with reading speeds higher than 50X (50 × 150 KB/s) or 7.5 MB/s. At 50X, a CD with 650MB of data can ideally be read in 86.7 seconds (650 / 7.5)—about a minute and a half! As you see, increased data transfer rates make a real difference in CD-ROM performance—especially for data-intensive applications such as audio/video clips.

> Today, the term "multi-speed" is rarely used because it is redundant—all CD drive types operate at some high multiple of the original Red Book speed (e.g., 50X to 58X). You can find CD-RW drives with 20x recording speed (CD-R), 10x rewriting speed (CD-RW), and 40x reading speed (CD-ROM).

### MMC

The problem with advanced drives like today's CD-ROM, CD-R, and CD-RW drives is that each one tends to use its own unique "command set"—a language that defines each function or feature of the drive. Traditionally, each manufacturer of CD drives used a different command set (even varied the commands with each new drive model). This practice caused a real struggle for programmers who had to write drivers and recording software that would be compatible with a growing number of drives—each with its own diverse command set. The resulting recording software packages often took a long time to develop and were huge in size.

To combat this proliferation of command sets, some CD drive developers embraced a common command set called MMC (Multi Media Command). Since MMC-compliant drives use a common command set, software developers could write a set of drivers and writing software for one MMC-compliant recorder that would be able to run other MMC-compliant drives. CD writing software can run just about any MMC-compliant drive, so you don't need to update or mix software packages when you add or replace drives. In actual practice, MMC compliance is a nice benefit, but it is not essential because virtually all CD drives ship with suitable software and drivers anyway. You should first select a drive for its speed, format compatibility, and other features. If MMC-compliance happens to be one of those features, that's great, but don't sacrifice important features for MMC compliance.

### Bootable CD-ROM (El Torito)

Traditionally, CD-ROM/R/RW drives have *not* been bootable devices. Since the CD drives need software drivers in order for the operating system to support them, the PC always had to boot *first* in order to load the drivers. This process invariably required a bootable hard drive or floppy drive. When building a new system, this required you to boot from a floppy disk with CD-ROM support, and *then* pop in your Windows Installation CD for setup. In early 1995, the El Torito standard was finalized, which provided the hardware and software specifications needed to implement a *bootable* CD-ROM. Virtually all CD drives meet El Torito requirements today, so most CD drives (even CD-R and CD-RW drives) can be installed and recognized as CD-ROM drives under Windows 9x/Me/XP. This gives you immediate CD-ROM functionality for the drive (allowing you to read discs) from BIOS—without the installation of OS-specific drivers. Of course, you'll need to install drivers and other software to take full advantage of CD-R and CD-RW drives. You need three elements to implement a bootable CD-ROM:

- A bootable CD drive mechanism (almost always fitted with an ATAPI IDE interface). Today, virtually every CD-ROM/R/RW drive supports the El Torito standard.
- A BIOS version that supports the bootable CD-ROM (now standard on virtually every mother-board)—you'll find that the CMOS Setup even provides an option for CD-ROM in the Boot Order.
- A CD with boot code and an operating system on it. If you don't already have a bootable CD (such as a "restoration CD" from your PC manufacturer), see the "Creating a Bootable CD" section later in this chapter.

Once all three elements are in place, you can insert a bootable CD in the drive, switch the PC's Boot Order in the CMOS Setup (setting the CD drive as the first boot device), then reboot the system. As the system restarts, it will read from the CD rather than the floppy or hard drive. This is particularly handy when you need to restore an operating system or return a system to its "out of the box" state. As a technician, you can also create your own bootable CD with an OS and lots of diagnostics.

### CD Compatibility Notes

Given the staggering array of CD drive types and vintages, it is sometimes difficult to determine just which disc type is compatible with what drive type. Table 8-2 compares a variety of drive types with disc compatibility. For example, a Standard (older) CD-ROM Drive can play CD-DA discs, but only some drives can handle DAE. The drive can also handle CD-ROM discs, but usually just single-session CD-R discs (ISO 9660).

## CD-ROM CONSTRUCTION

Now that you know the essentials of CD-ROM media and standards, it is time to review a typical drive in some detail. CD-ROM, CD-R, and CD-RW drives are impressive pieces of engineering. The drive must be able to accept standard-sized disks from a variety of sources (each disk may contain an assortment of unknown surface imperfections). The drive must then spin the disk at a *constant linear velocity* (CLV)—though most drives also support CAV for reading data discs at high speed. A drive must be able to follow the spiral data path on a spinning CD-ROM accurately to within less than 1μm along the disk's radius. The drive electronics must be able to detect and correct any unforeseen data errors in real time, operate reliably over a long working life, and be available for the low price that computer users have come to expect.

### CD-ROM Mechanics

You can begin to appreciate how a CD drive achieves its many features by examining the typical CD-ROM shown in Figure 8-6. At the center of the drive is a cast aluminum or rigid plastic *frame assembly*. As with other drives, the frame is the single primary structure for mounting the drive's mechanical and electronic components. The *front bezel*, *lid*, *volume control*, and *eject button* attach to the frame, providing the drive with its clean cosmetic appearance and offering a fixed reference slot for CD insertion and removal. Keep in mind that the vast majority of drives use a sliding tray (caddie-loaded drives have become almost extinct), so the front bezel will be similar for every drive.

 Although the laser type and drive electronics are somewhat different, the physical descriptions and electronic details for CD-ROM drives are also generally true for CD-R and CD-RW drives.

**TABLE 8-2**    GENERAL COMPATIBILITY GUIDELINES FOR CD DRIVE AND DISC TYPES

| TYPE OF DRIVE | CD-DA | CD-ROM | CD-ROM XA | BRIDGE CD | CD-I | VIDEO CD | PHOTO CD | CD-R | CD-RW |
|---|---|---|---|---|---|---|---|---|---|
| Audio CD Player | Play | No | No | No | No | No | No | Single Session | No |
| Standard (Older) CD-ROM Drive | Play (some DAE) | Yes | No | No | No | No | No | Single Session | No |
| (Newer) CD-ROM XA Drive | Play (some DAE) | Yes | Yes | Yes | No | Some | Some | Single Session | No |
| Multi-Session CD-ROM XA Drive | Play and DAE | Yes | Yes | Yes | No | Yes | Yes | Multi-Session | Some |
| CD-I Player | Play | No | No | Yes | Yes | Yes | Yes | Single Session | No |
| CD-R Drive | Play and DAE | Yes | Yes | Yes | Yes | Yes | Yes | Multi-Session | Some |
| CD-RW Drive | Play and DAE | Yes | Yes | Yes | Yes | Yes | Yes | Multi-Session | Yes |

You can also see the main components of the drive engine. A motorized *tray* slides out to accept the disc, then closes to position the disc properly inside the drive mechanism. As the CD sits inside the tray's circular opening, a *spindle motor* gently clamps the disc and spins it. You cannot see the motor in Figure 8-6, but you can see the white clamp retainer, which also spins. The most critical part of the CD engine is the *optical head* containing the laser diode (typically a 780nm 0.6mW gallium aluminum arsenide GaAlAs laser) and detector, along with the optical focus and tracking components. The optical device slides in and

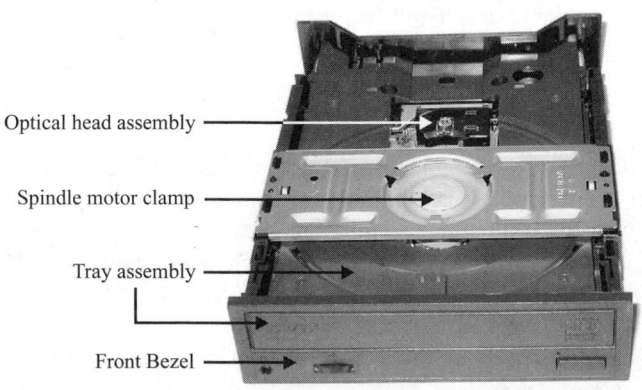

Optical head assembly

Spindle motor clamp

Tray assembly

Front Bezel

**FIGURE  8-6**    Exposed view of basic CD drive mechanics showing the spindle clamp and optical head

out along the disc's radius (mounted on two guide rails). Laser light shines through an opening in the sub-frame. This combination of device mounting and guide rails is called a *sled*.

CD-R and CD-RW drives will use lasers with different power and wavelength characteristics, though you may not be able to distinguish between a CD-ROM, CD-R, or CD-RW head at first glance.

A sled must follow the spiral data track along the disc. While floppy disks (using clearly defined concentric tracks) can easily make use of a stepping motor to position the head assembly, a CD drive ideally requires a *linear motor* to act much like the voice coil motor used to position hard drive R/W heads. By altering the signal driving a sled motor and constantly measuring and adjusting the sled's position, a sled can be made to track very smoothly along a disk—free from the sudden, jerky motion of stepping motors. The drive's main PC board is responsible for managing these operations.

This optical approach overcomes the problems often associated with magnetic media drives. The optical head remains a safe distance from the disc surface, so there is no microscopic "flying height" to threaten head crashes. Since there is no physical contact between the head and media, the CD does not wear out like floppy disks. However, the laser beam *must* be unobstructed, so the optical head and disc must be kept clean. You can see that the optical head in Figure 8-6 is pointed up—dust, cigarette smoke, and other debris can eventually accumulate on the head and cause reading problems.

## CD-ROM Electronics

The electronics package is usually located beneath the drive (see Figure 8-7), and is shielded by a thin aluminum cover. The electronics package must handle three important tasks: it manages the physical drive (e.g., the motors, optics, and so on), it processes CD audio (giving you a headphone jack, volume control, and audio output to a sound card), and it interfaces the drive to your PC (usually through an ATAPI IDE or SCSI interface). As you can see, there are only a few powerful chips needed to run the drive, and several small ribbon cables connect the drive's motors and sensors.

You can see a simplified block diagram for a basic CD-ROM drive in Figure 8-8. The block diagram can be divided into two major areas: the *controller* section and the *drive* section. The controller section is dedicated to the peripheral interface—its connection to the PC's drive controller. Much of a CD-ROM's electronic sophistication can be traced to the controller section. Notice that the controller circuitry shown in Figure 8-8 is dedicated to handling a SCSI interface, though many CD-ROM drives today use an ATAPI IDE interface, which will support a CD-ROM right along with your existing UDMA hard drive(s). This kind of standardized controller arrangement allows the unit's "intelligence" to be located right in the drive itself. You need only connect the drive to a system-level interface such as a SCSI host adapter or IDE-type drive controller (e.g., a UDMA/33/66/100/133 controller) and set the drive's device identification to establish a working system.

The *drive section* electronics will manage all of the CD-ROM's physical operations (e.g., load/unload, spin the disk, move the sled, and so on), as well as EFM data decoding and error correction. Drive circuitry converts an analog output from the laser diode into an EFM signal, which is, in turn, decoded into binary data and CIRC (Cross-Interleaved Reed-Solomon Code) information. A drive controller chip and servo processor chip are responsible for directing laser focus, tracking, sled motor control (and feedback), spindle motor control (and feedback), and loading/unloading motor control.

**FIGURE 8-7**   Exposed view of a basic CD drive electronics package

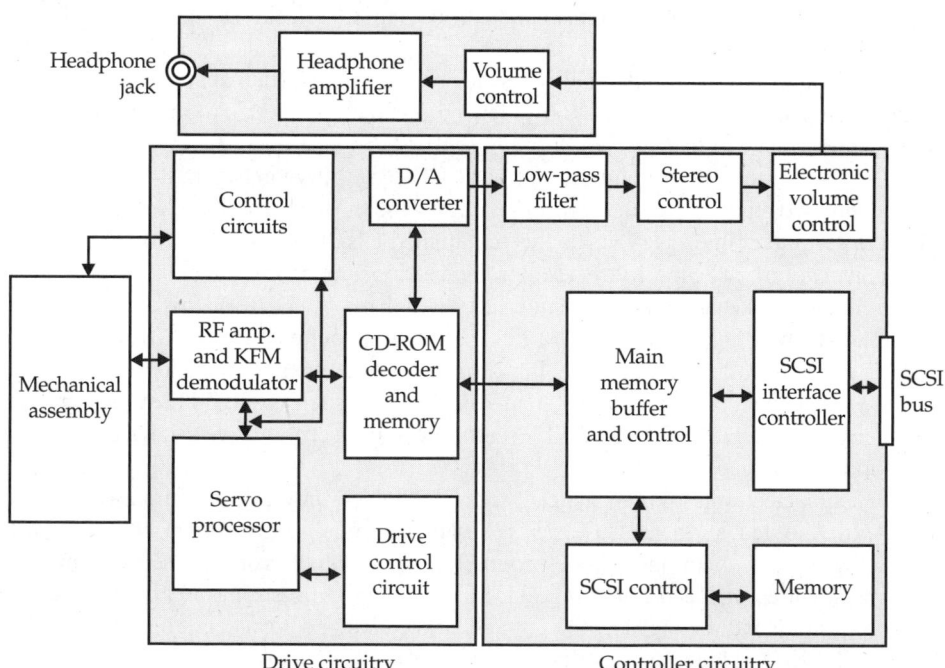

**FIGURE 8-8**   Simplified electronic block diagram for a typical SCSI CD-ROM drive

# CD-ROM SOFTWARE

CD-ROM drives require far more than El Torito support in the BIOS for proper drive operation. Driver software is needed to identify the drive, and ensure that your particular operating system can take full advantage of the drive's services. This part of the chapter looks at the software aspects of CD drives, and offers some tips for best performance.

## Windows Drivers

Today's plug-and-play (PnP) operating systems like Windows $9x$/Me/XP can usually identify the CD drive automatically and install the appropriate set of drivers needed to support that specific drive. This process usually starts when you restart the system after installing (or upgrading) the physical drive. Windows detects the new device and tries to identify it. If a suitable default driver is available, Windows will install the driver and you may start using the drive immediately. If the driver isn't available (or the drive is identified improperly), you'll need to install the correct driver yourself. For example, start by checking the Device Manager to verify the CD drive (as in the Windows XP Device Manager of Figure 8-9). If the drive is not listed (or is listed improperly), you can use the Add New Hardware wizard to specify the particular make and model, then load the appropriate drivers from the installation CD that accompanied the drive.

Always check with the drive manufacturer for the latest CD drivers.

If the Device Manager shows a secondary listing for a drive that's already been removed (e.g., the old drive that you've replaced or upgraded), highlight and remove the drive listing from Device Manager, reboot the PC, and allow Windows to re-detect and reinstall the drive automatically before resorting to the Add New Hardware wizard.

**FIGURE 8-9**    Verify that the CD drive is properly recognized in the Device Manager.

## DOS Drivers and MSCDEX

Windows does not use real-mode (DOS) drivers, but you may need to enable the CD drive for DOS operation during troubleshooting, or when ressurecting older PCs. DOS CD support includes two parts: the low-level device driver and the DOS extension. A low-level device driver allows programs to access the CD drive properly at the register (hardware) level. Since most drives are designed differently, they require similar (but often different) device drivers. If you change or upgrade the drive at any point, the device driver must be upgraded as well. A typical real-mode device driver uses a .SYS extension and is enabled by adding its command line to the PC's CONFIG.SYS file, such as:

```
DEVICE=HITACHIA.SYS /D:MSCD000 /N:1 /P:300
```

 The DEVICE command may be replaced by the DEVICEHIGH command if you have available space in the upper memory area (UMA).

A CD device driver will typically have three command line switches associated with it. These parameters are needed to ensure that the driver installs properly. For the example command line shown earlier, the **/D** switch is the "name" used by the driver when it is installed in the system's device table. This name must be unique and matched by the **/D** switch in the MSCDEX.EXE command line (covered later). The **/N** switch is the number of CD-ROM drives attached to the interface card. The default is 1 (which is typical for most general purpose systems). Finally, the **/P** switch is the I/O port address the drive's adapter card resides at. As you might expect, the port address should match the port address on the physical interface. If there is no **/P** switch, the default is 0300h.

There's an additional wrinkle when using SCSI-based CD drives. SCSI support also means that the PC must be fitted with a SCSI host adapter and configured with a real-mode ASPI driver in order to allow the SCSI adapter to interface to the drive (this is also true if you're using other SCSI drives and devices). Again, if the SCSI drive is being enabled under Windows 9*x*/Me/XP, you'll use a protected-mode driver to run the SCSI host adapter before the protected-mode CD drivers load. However, you may still need a real-mode driver for the SCSI host adapter if you're using the SCSI adapter to operate other devices under DOS. A typical real-mode ASPI driver entry might appear in CONFIG.SYS as:

```
DEVICE=C:\SCSI\ASPIPPA3.SYS /L=001
```

 If there are no SCSI hard drives in the system, the SCSI adapter's onboard BIOS ROM can usually be disabled. This saves a bit of space in the UMA.

Now it's time for the drive to be recognized under DOS. MS-DOS was developed in a time when no one anticipated that large files would be accessible to a PC, so it is severely limited in the file sizes that it can handle. With the development of CD-ROMs, Microsoft created a DOS extension that allows software publishers to access 650MB CDs in a standard fashion—the *Microsoft CD-ROM Extensions* (or MSCDEX). As with most software, MSCDEX offers some vital features (and has a few limitations), but it is required by a vast majority of CD-ROM, CD-R, or CD-RW products when you're working in DOS. Obtaining MSCDEX is not a problem—it is generally provided on the same disk or CD containing the CD drive's low-level device driver. The last (legacy) versions of MSCDEX can be obtained from the Microsoft Web site (www.microsoft.com). A typical MSCDEX command line would appear in the AUTOEXEC.BAT file such as:

```
C:\DOS\MSCDEX.EXE /D:MSCDD001 /V
```

Although the vast majority of CD drive bundles include installation routines that automate the installation process for the low-level driver and MSCDEX, you should understand the various command line switches (shown in Table 8-3) that make MSCDEX operate. Understanding these switches may help you to overcome setup problems.

# CD-ROM INSTALLATION AND REPLACEMENT

CD drives are generally easy devices to install or replace. Most are installed as *master* devices located on the secondary Ultra-DMA drive controller channel (or an EIDE controller on older PCs), though most current CD drives will coexist just fine as *slave* devices alongside a hard drive or other ATAPI IDE drive device. The most important issue to remember is that the BIOS will not fully support the CD-ROM directly (even if the BIOS identifies the CD-ROM at boot time, and even if El Torito support allows you to boot from the CD)—you'll need real-mode drivers for the CD-ROM under DOS, or protected-mode drivers for the CD-ROM under Windows 9*x*/Me/XP. This part of the chapter covers the guidelines needed to install a basic internal ATAPI IDE-type CD-ROM drive (these guidelines will also support CD-R and CD-RW drives).

## Set Jumper Configurations

Generally, any current ATAPI IDE-type CD-ROM drive may be installed as a *master* or *slave* device on any hard drive controller channel. These master/slave settings are handled through one or two jumpers

**TABLE 8-3    COMMAND LINE SWITCHES FOR MSCDEX**

| SWITCH | NAME | DEFINITION |
| --- | --- | --- |
| /D:x | Device Name | The label used by the low-level device driver when it loads. MSCDEX must match this label for the device driver and MSCDEX to work together. A typical label is MSCD000. |
| /M:x | Buffers Allocated | The number of 2KB buffers allocated to the CD-ROM drives. There are typically 8 buffers (16KB) for a single drive, and 4 buffers for each additional drive. This number can be set to 1 or 2 when conventional memory space is at a premium. |
| /L:x | Drive Letter | This is the optional drive letter for the CD-ROM. If this is not specified, the drive will be automatically assigned to the first available letter (usually D:). There must be a LASTDRIVE= entry in CONFIG.SYS to use a letter higher than the default letter. When choosing a letter for the LASTDRIVE entry, do not use Z—otherwise, network drives may not install after MSCDEX. |
| /N | Verbose Option | This switch forces MSCDEX to show memory usage statistics on the display each time the system boots. |
| /S | Share Option | This switch is used with CD-ROM installations in network systems. |
| /K | Kanji Option | Instructs MSCDEX to use Kanji (Japanese) file types on the CD if present. |
| /E | Expanded Mem. | Allows MSCDEX to use expanded memory for buffers. There must be an expanded memory driver running (EMM386.EXE) with enough available space to use it. |

located on the rear of the drive (right next to the 40-pin signal cable connector) as in Figure 8-10. One of your first decisions when planning an installation should be to decide the drive's configuration:

- If you're installing the CD-ROM as the first drive on the secondary drive controller channel, it must be jumpered as the "master" device.

- If you're installing the CD-ROM drive alongside another drive (on either the primary or secondary drive controller channel), the CD-ROM must be jumpered as the "slave" device.

> Refer to the documentation that accompanies your particular CD-ROM drive in order to determine the exact "master/slave" jumper settings. If you do not have the drive documentation handy, check the drive manufacturer's Web site for online information. The jumper locations may be printed on the drive itself.

A SCSI drive is frequently identified by setting a SCSI ID between 2 and 6. Once again, you must set the ID using a series of jumpers on the rear of the drive, and the ID must be unique for the drive (SCSI devices cannot share IDs). If your system has a SCSI controller, you can probably see the IDs being used by other devices at boot time—then it's just a matter of selecting an ID that isn't used.

### Attach Cables and Mount the Drive

After you've determined where to install the drive and configured its master/slave or SCSI ID settings properly, you'll need to attach cables and mount the drive. Follow these steps:

1. Turn off and unplug the PC, and then remove the outer cover to expose the computer's drive bays.

2. For an ATAPI IDE-type drive, attach one end of the 40-pin drive interface cable to the drive controller connector on your motherboard (or drive controller card). For a SCSI drive, attach a 50- or 68-pin SCSI cable to the SCSI host controller. Remember to align pin 1 on the cable (the side of the cable with the blue or red stripe) with pin 1 on the drive controller connector.

3. Locate an available drive bay for the CD drive. Remove the plastic housing covering the drive bay, then slide the drive inside. Locate the four screw holes needed to mount the drive. In some cases, you may need to attach mounting rails to the drive so that the drive will be wide enough to fit in the drive bay. In virtually all cases, you should mount a tray-driven CD drive horizontally (though caddy-loaded CD-ROM drives may sometimes be mounted vertically).

CD audio connector

Master/slave jumper block

40-pin ATAPI IDE connector

Drive power connector

**FIGURE   8-10**    Set the drive's "master/slave" jumper depending on how you plan to install it in the system.

4. Attach the signal cable and the four-pin power connector to the new drive, then bolt the drive securely into place (see Figure 8-11). Do not overtighten the screws since this may damage the drive. If you do not have an available four-pin power connector, you may use an appropriate Y adapter if necessary to split power from another drive (preferably the floppy drive). If your chassis uses "screwless" drive bays, just clip the drive into place.

5. Attach the small four-pin CD audio signal cable from the CD drive to the CD audio input connector on your sound card. This connection allows you to play music CDs directly through your sound card. Verify that the CD audio cable is compatible with your sound card (otherwise you may need a special cable from the sound card's manufacturer).

## Configure the CMOS Setup

Although the CD-ROM *does* require driver support, most current motherboard designs can identify the ATAPI IDE CD-ROM drive in BIOS, so if possible you should configure your computer's BIOS to accept the drive (through the CMOS Setup):

1. After the drive is installed, turn the computer on. As your computer starts up, watch for a message that describes how to run the CMOS Setup (for example, "Press F1 for Setup"). Press the appropriate key to start the CMOS Setup program.

2. Select the basic setup menu where you can specify hard drive settings and choose the drive location occupied by the CD-ROM drive (that is, primary slave, secondary slave, or secondary master—depending on how you've physically jumpered and installed the drive).

3. Select *automatic drive detection* if available—this option should automatically identify the new CD drive. If your BIOS does *not* provide automatic drive detection, select NONE or NOT INSTALLED for the CD-ROM, and rely on drivers ONLY.

4. Save the settings and exit the CMOS Setup program. Your computer will automatically reboot to the operating system.

## Install the Software

In order to complete your CD drive installation, you'll need to install the software drivers and any application software that accompanied the drive on diskette or CD. Windows 9*x*/Me/XP systems will generally

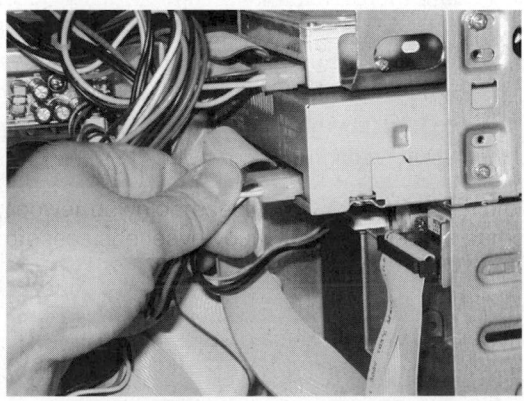

**FIGURE 8-11** Attach the power and signal cables to the CD drive, then secure it in the drive bay.

detect the presence of the new CD drive and prompt you for the protected-mode drivers (or select appropriate drivers automatically from the Windows driver library). Under DOS, you may need to run an "installer" routine to add the real-mode drivers to your system and to update your CONFIG.SYS and AUTOEXEC.BAT files to load those drivers. If there's no real-mode "installer," you'll need to update your startup files manually (see the section on "CD-ROM Software" earlier in the chapter). After you install the drivers and reboot the system, the CD-ROM should be identified, assigned a suitable drive letter, and be ready for use.

 Although current operating systems can use almost any CD-R/RW drive as a CD-ROM, you will still need to install CD authoring software (and perhaps DirectCD) to use the drive's CD-R/RW features.

### Reassemble the Computer

After you've confirmed that the new drive is installed and identified properly, shut down the PC and warp up the physical system. Double-check all of your signal and power cables to verify that they are secure, then tuck the cables gently into the computer's chassis. Check that there are no loose tools, screws, or cables inside the chassis. Now reattach the computer's outer housing(s), and your installation should be complete.

## CD-ROM RETIREMENT

While CD-ROM drives have been standard equipment on PCs for many years, their days in desktop systems may be numbered. Ordinary CD-ROM drives are fast and reliable, but they are being aggressively replaced by the current generation of CD-RW drives. For a relatively small additional cost, a CD-RW drive can read CDs, write CD-R media, and rewrite CD-RW media—providing PC users with a very versatile tool for creating audio CDs, making photo albums, performing thorough system backups, and so on. Only very low-end entry-level PCs continue to offer CD-ROM drives today.

# The CD-R Drive

While traditional CD-ROM drives brought a great deal of reliable storage potential to the PC, it was only since the late 1990s that we could *record* CDs on the desktop—prior to that time, the technology required to create audio and computer CDs had been terribly complex and expensive, and limited by PC computing power of the day. However, the interest in CD recording (or CD-R) technology increased dramatically, and recordable drives steadily became more reliable and economical. CD recorders allow huge files, databases, and multimedia presentations to be developed and distributed with ease. Virtually any Pentium PC (or later) with a SCSI or Ultra-DMA interface and 1GB or more of hard drive space can support a CD-R drive. Although now obsolete, external CD-R drives like the Teac 4X12 SCSI drive shown in Figure 8-12 offer the benefit of mobility between PCs. This part of the chapter builds on the fundamentals of CD-ROM drives and explains the issues of CD-R technology and media.

 CD-R drives are fully backward-compatible with CD-ROM drives, so, all the concepts covered for CD-ROM drives apply to CD-R drives also.

## CD-R MEDIA VARIATIONS

The appearance of recordable media is very similar to that of the "pressed" CD media illustrated in Figure 8-2, but with two important variations. First, the polycarbonate CD-R substrate is pre-formed with a track spiral into which data will be written during the recording process. This does away with the pre-formed pits and lands

**FIGURE  8-12**    External SCSI CD recorders offer mobility between multiple PCs with external
SCSI interfaces.

found in "mastered" CDs. The substrate is then coated with a greenish or bluish translucent layer and backed
with a reflective layer of gold, and finally a protective lacquer is applied over the gold layer. When laser energy
is applied to the disc during writing, the exposed areas along the pre-formed track are selectively "burned" to
change the way that laser light is reflected—this effectively mimics the presence of pits and lands on the disc. It
is important to note that CD-R media can only be written *once* and *cannot* be erased (though additional data can
be written to a CD-R disc in subsequent writing sessions). Writing errors will render the disc unusable.

## Orange Book Certified Media

The Orange Book (Part II) is the primary specification for CD-R media, and all CD-R media should certainly meet the Orange Book criteria for recordability and playback. Philips and Sony (the originators of
the Orange Book specification) provide Orange Book certification of CD-R media. If you want best media
compatibility and reliability, ensure that your CD-R media is "Orange Book certified" and produced from
a vendor that is recommended by the drive's manufacturer.

## High-Speed Media

Since a laser must deliver energy to the disc medium, it takes a finite amount of time to write information
to CD-R or CD-RW discs—the faster a drive can write, the less time it will take to complete the operation.
For example, a 16X drive can write a disc much faster than a 10X drive. The problem is that there is often
trouble with ordinary CD-R/CD-RW media writing at speeds above 4X. If you try ordinary media in faster
drives (e.g., running above 4X), you'll usually see an error such as a *media error* or *writing error*. This is
why most drive makers will suggest that you try lowering the writing speeds when you see errors. To keep
pace with today's faster writing speeds, you can use "high speed" media. CD-R discs are often rated for
their top writing speed (for example, "certified to 12X writing speeds"). CD-Rs are also generally backward-compatible, so CD-R media rated for higher speeds should work just fine in slower drives. If you
have a fast CD-R drive, be sure to use suitable high-speed media for best performance.

However, the rules are a little bit different for high-speed CD-RWs. The high-speed CD-RW media
format *prevents* older 1X to 4X CD-RW drives from writing to it. Trying to write high-speed discs in older
CD-RW drives may result in a variety of errors seemingly unrelated to the media, so you'll need a drive
with 4X or faster writing speeds in order to use high-speed CD-RW media. You can't upgrade an older
drive to be compatible with high-speed media (e.g., a drive firmware upgrade won't help), but you can
replace the drive entirely. Still, you can read high-speed CD-RW media in 1X to 4X drives (and other
Multi-Read drives). These CD-RW compatibility factors led to the introduction of a new CD-RW system,
complete with a proprietary and separately licensed logo, known as "Compact Disc Re-Writable, High
Speed." You can look for this logo to verify that your CD-RW disc is high-speed media. Similarly, you can
record only high-speed media with CD-RW drives showing the high-speed CD-RW logo.

# MULTISESSION CDS

One of the problems with recording early CDs is that once the CD was written, it could not be appended. This means if 123MB of data is written to a 650MB disc, the remaining 527MB of storage potential on the disc would be lost. CD developers sought a means of adding new data to a CD that had been previously recorded (but still has unused space available). This *multisession* capability means that a CD is written in "sessions," with subsequent sessions linked to previous sessions—allowing the CD to be systematically filled to its capacity.

A CD-R recorder that supports multisession recording can write a disc that will have multiple sessions linked together—each session containing its own lead-in, data, and lead-out areas. In effect, each session is treated as a different CD, but one session leads seamlessly into another. Any multisession-capable CD drive can access the data in any session. By comparison, a pressed CD-ROM or a CD-R written in Disc At Once mode contains only one lead-in area, program area, and lead-out area.

## Multisession Problems

Multisession technology is clearly important because it allows you to add data to a CD-R disc incrementally (a bit at a time) as needed. This makes it possible to eventually utilize the entire disc. However, there are two general problems reading multisession discs: either you can read data only in the first session, or you can read data only in the last session.

If you can read data only in the *first* session of the disc, there is probably a compatibility issue between the disc and the drive. For example, you may have recorded the disc in standard Yellow Book CD-ROM (Mode 1) format, while your multisession CD-ROM drive works only with CD-ROM XA (Mode 2) multisession discs. In other cases, the CD-ROM drive may be too old to support multisession discs at all. Try the disc on several current drives and see if another drive will read subsequent sessions. If so, you may need to upgrade your drive to ensure multisession compatibility.

If you can only read data in the *last* session of the disc, the disc may have been recorded improperly. For example, you may have forgotten to link your new data (the last session) with sessions that were previously recorded on the disc. Often, you would need to re-record this disc and verify that all sessions are linked. However, some of the later CD pre-mastering software (such as Easy CD Creator 5 Platinum: www.roxio.com/en/products/ecdc/index.html) will allow you to switch to different sessions using a "session selector" feature. When the selected session is *enabled*, it can be read from the CD drive as if it were the only session on the disc (any files linked from previous sessions on the same disc will still be readable). Check your own CD-R software to see if it supports such a feature. Otherwise, record a new disc from scratch.

# FIXATION VS. FINALIZATION

Each session written to a disc (whether multisession or single session) must be *fixed* before the session can be read. *Fixation* is the process of writing the session's lead-in and lead-out information to the disc. This process finishes a writing session and creates a table of contents. Fixation is *required* before a CD-ROM or CD audio player can play the disc. Discs that are "fixated for append" can have additional sessions recorded later (each with their own session lead-in and lead-out) creating a multisession disc. When a disc is *finalized*, the absolute lead-in and lead-out for the entire disc are written, along with information that tells the drive *not* to look for subsequent sessions. This final table of contents (TOC) conforms to the ISO 9660 file standard.

# DISK IMAGES

CD creation normally starts by selecting a list of files and folders to be copied. Once you've chosen the content, it's time to do the actual recording. When recording a CD, you can typically choose between writing on the fly or writing from a disk image. There are some important tradeoffs to be familiar with. Writing "on the fly" simply opens each file as needed, then transfers the data to the CD-R drive's recording buffer in real time. This works great on relatively new PCs with a fast drive interface (and CD-R drives with sizable recording buffers). However, any interruptions in the flow of data may allow the buffer to empty, and the resulting "buffer underrun" error will ruin the disc.

Rather then writing on the fly it's possible for the writing software to create an "image file" before writing to the disc. This is basically an image of what the complete disc would look like once the recording is complete. Image files are handy when you need to master a number of duplicate discs. Since the hard drive is then only concerned with reading the image file, it doesn't have to rush around the entire hard drive to find the component files and folders. This means the disk system doesn't have to work as hard to keep the recording buffer filled, so image files are often used with older systems with inadequate processing power to write on the fly. However, a CD can hold up to 650MB, so you may need up to 650MB of free disk space to hold the compiled image file (drive manufacturers often recommend up to 1GB of free disk space just to be safe).

## DISC-AT-ONCE

*Disc-at-Once* is a CD writing mode that requires data to be written continuously, without any interruptions, until the complete set of files is transferred to the CD-R. The complete lead-in, data, and lead-out are written in a single writing process. While the latest drives may be able to write complete discs on the fly, it's often better to create an image file of the disc on the PC's hard drive prior to recording in the Disc-at-Once mode. Recording in the Disc-at-Once mode eliminates the linking and other housekeeping overhead tasks associated with multisession and packet recording (a.k.a. DirectCD) modes (which often are interpreted as uncorrectable errors during the CD-ROM mastering process).

The Disk-at-Once mode is usually preferred for discs that are sent to a CD-ROM replication facility when CD-R is the source media.

## TRACK-AT-ONCE

The Track-at-Once writing mode is the key to multisession capability, and allows a session to be written in a number of discrete write events, called *tracks* because the written sessions contain complete "tracks" of information. The disc can be removed from the writer and read in another drive (if the drive is compatible) before the session is fixated.

Track-at-Once writing is a form of incremental write that mandates a minimum track length of 300 blocks and a maximum of 99 tracks per disc. A track written "at once" has 150 blocks of overhead for run-in, run-out, pre-gap, and linking purposes. On the other hand, *packet write* is a method where several write events are allowed *within* a track, thus reducing the demands of overhead data. Each writing "packet" is bounded by seven blocks of data: four for run-in, two for run-out, and one for linking. Packet writing is the basis for rewritable CDs.

## CARING FOR RECORDABLE CDS

As a rule, recordable CDs are as rugged and reliable as ordinary "pressed" CDs. Still, you should exercise some additional rules in the careful handling and storage of recordable media:

■ *Maintain a comfortable environment.* Don't expose recordable discs to sunlight or other strong light for long periods of time. Also, avoid high heat and humidity, which can damage the physical disc. Always keep blank or recorded media in clean jewel cases for best protection.

■ *Don't write on the disc.* Don't use alcohol-based pens to write on discs—the ink may eventually eat through the top (lacquer) surface and damage your data. Also don't use ball-point or other sharp-tipped pens because you may scratch right through the lacquer surface and damage the reflective gold layer (and ruin your data).

■ *Don't use labels on the disc.* Don't put labels on discs unless they are *expressly* designed for record-able CDs. The glue may eat through the lacquer surface just as some inks do, or the label may unbal-ance the disc and cause problems in reading it back or recording subsequent sessions. Never try to remove a label—you might tear off the lacquer and some of the reflecting surface.

■ *Watch your media quality.* Many different brands of recordable CD media are now available in the marketplace. Quality varies from brand to brand (and even from batch to batch within a given brand). If you have repeated problems that can be traced to the blank media you are using, try using a different brand or even a different batch of the same brand.

■ *Don't use Kodak Photo CDs.* Avoid the use of Kodak Photo CDs on everyday CD recorders (unless the drive is specifically listed as supporting Photo CDs). Kodak Photo CDs are designed to be used only with Kodak Photo CD professional workstations. Although the discs are inexpensive, they have a pro-tection bit that prevents them from being written on many CD recorders. When you attempt to write these discs on the recorders that recognize the protection bit, you will receive an error message.

# CREATING A BOOTABLE CD

When the hard drive fails to boot a PC, technicians have traditionally been forced to deal with boot disks. While doing this could certainly start a system to the A: prompt, there was hardly any opportunity for sophisticated diagnostics, and diagnostics with a sophisticated operating system such as Windows was out of the question. With the adoption of the El Torito standard, BIOS support made it possible to boot from the CD drive. This opened many possible applications for "bootable CDs" and allowed the creation of powerful recovery CDs that could boot and restore a crippled system to its original state—most com-mercial PCs sold today come with one or more *recovery CDs* for just this purpose. Creating a bootable CD allows you to combine operating systems with boot and diagnostic utilities to test defective systems or to standardize the process of new system setups. The problem is that placing bootable code on a CD has gen-erally been a cumbersome, time consuming, and error-prone process. Let's examine a more modern approach that will allow you to create a fully bootable CD for your system.

## Checking for Support

Of course, a bootable CD won't do much good unless the PC supports it. Start your CMOS Setup and check the Boot Order entry. In most cases, the order is set as "A: then C:," but you will probably be able to select the particular device(s) used to boot the system. If you can select a CD-ROM as a boot device, your BIOS supports bootable CDs. Most systems manufactured after 1996 will support bootable CDs. If you're dealing with an older system that does not allow the CD-ROM as a boot device, a BIOS upgrade or moth-erboard replacement may be needed to update the system.

## Rules for Boot Emulation

When a bootable CD is created, a *boot record* is put at the very beginning of the disc (just as it is with a bootable floppy or hard disk). This record specifies whether the CD is to emulate a floppy or hard disk drive and contains a pointer to the location of the actual boot image file. The El Torito specification was designed to be completely compatible with the ISO 9660 CD standard, and it adds to the ISO 9660 specification by requiring a boot record at sector 11 of the last session on the CD. The boot record contains an absolute sector number that points to the "boot catalog," but there is no restriction on the location of the boot catalog. The catalog contains a list of entries describing all the "boot images" present on the CD. Again, there is no restriction on where the boot images can be on the CD. There can be any number of them, but they fall into three different types:

- *Bootable emulation* causes the bootable disc image to be mapped to drive A: or C:—resembling (or emulating) a conventional bootable storage device.
- *Non-bootable emulation* maps the image as a conventional storage device, and allocates the last drive letter to it.
- *No emulation* is a special mode that loads the image into memory and executes it directly—extremely useful when developing copy protection or "smart" CDs designed for a variety of systems. For example, the "no emulation" mode is used in the Windows NT operating system CDs.

In addition, system vendors can create multi-image CDs where the boot image is selected dynamically by the system BIOS, but doing this requires a lot of manual assembling and editing (and is beyond the scope of this book).

A CD can be configured to boot as drive A: or C:. To boot as drive A:, the boot image must be made in the same format as a 1.2MB, 1.4MB, or 2.88MB floppy disk. The first floppy disk drive (if present) will become the B: drive. If the system has a second floppy disk drive, it will not be accessible. In effect, the bootable disc will "take the place of" the emulated drive. If the CD is set to boot as the C: drive, it replaces the normal hard disk drive C: and has no size limit other than that of the CD itself. However, the source drive image must have only one partition. This partition must be both the first entry in the partition table and a standard DOS partition.

## A Basic Bootable CD

Most current CD-R publishing packages are capable of reading a floppy disk and creating a boot image from it. With the appropriate menu choices made, the recording software will automatically "apply" the selected boot image to the CD image file. With this method, it is extremely easy to make a bootable CD. Some of the more advanced packages (like Nero) can create a bootable CD from any disk image as well as allow fine-tuning of parameters such as the emulation type and startup message. The generic process for making a bootable CD from a floppy disk is described next:

1. Create a bootable floppy disk that has all the required driver and startup software on it such as a Windows 98/Me/XP Startup Disk with generic CD-ROM support (remember that you'll need a CD driver in order to use the CD in a conventional manner once the system has finished booting). It is wise to use a generic CD driver if you plan on using the finished CD in a few different systems.

2. Make sure that any path names in the CONFIG.SYS and AUTOEXEC.BAT files do *not* specify drive letters. This is because simple bootable emulation will cause drive letters to shift. You may need to copy any necessary files to the diskette and edit your startup files accordingly.

3. Verify that your boot process does *not* attempt to write to the disk. Set the read-only flag on all files and write-protect the disk if possible. If your system tries to write to the CD on boot-up, the system will crash.

4. Test this startup diskette thoroughly in whatever PC environment(s) you plan to use it. This gives you the chance to make any last-minute changes to the diskette.

5. Once you're happy with the bootable disk, create the CD with your CD-R publishing package. Selecting the "bootable" option will usually prompt for the floppy disk. Put any other data (for example, diagnostics or an operating system) onto the CD in the *same* session.

## Recording Software Considerations

Until several years ago, bootable CDs had to be made manually with a combination of low-level tools (for instance, hex editors). Utility programs such as BOOTISO and DISKIMG were used to read bootable disks and write images to disk files. These disk images were then hex edited and manually added to the CD layout. Now that most current CD writing software is able to make bootable CDs from floppy or hard disk images, the process of bootable CD creation has become much easier.

Notable software packages include Easy CD Creator, Win-On-CD, CDRWIN, HyCD, and Nero. Generally speaking, Nero is an extremely powerful tool that offers complete control of the CD writing process and that can create bootable CDs for many platforms. It can also create *oversized* CDs that can be used to gain a small amount of copy protection. Many of these software products are available in demo, shareware, or evaluation versions, so you can try each product to see if it suits your needs *before* making a purchase.

## Using Easy CD Creator

Once you have your bootable diskette working just the way you want it, it's time to make a bootable CD. You can see how recording software has matured to support bootable CDs by examining a typical CD creation process with a product like Roxio's Easy CD Creator (www.roxio.com):

1. Make sure that your bootable diskette is in the floppy drive. Insert a blank CD-R disc and launch the CD writing software.

2. Opt to create an ordinary "data CD" project. If you're given the opportunity to create a new project, be sure to select or identify the project as a "Bootable CD."

3. Now select the type of bootable CD that you want to create. In this case, you'll need to choose Floppy Disk Emulation so that the CD will appear as a diskette at boot time.

4. For our purposes, you should leave the Emulation Options, Sector Count, Load Segment, and any other options at their default settings.

5. Click OK to start processing the boot information. Several boot files (e.g., bootcat.bin and bootimg.bin) will be added to your list of files to be recorded.

6. When you're ready to burn the actual CD, click the Record button.

7. If you must select any recording options, choose Disc-at-Once and be sure to close the disc when recording is complete.

8. When the recording is complete, mark the CD with an indelible marker that's safe for CD surfaces. Now change the boot order so that the CD-ROM drive is checked first, and reboot your system to test the CD. If you're using a SCSI CD-ROM, you may need to set the boot order so that the SCSI entry is first.

## UPGRADING CD-R/CD-RW FIRMWARE

You may be able to update the firmware used in your CD-R or CD-RW drive. Doing this may be necessary to correct bugs or fix drive compatibility problems with various media or the host PC. The following steps offer a guideline that you can refer to when upgrading CD-R/CD-RW firmware.

> The following steps are intended as an example only. You should always refer to the Web page or README file that accompanies the new firmware download. Be sure to download the correct firmware version for your drive—installing the wrong firmware can permanently disable the drive.

1. Power off your system completely.

2. Locate the CD-R/CD-RW drive. If the drive uses a "flash" jumper to protect the firmware, place the "flash" jumper in the flash upgrade position.

3. Make sure the power cable and the signal cable (SCSI or IDE) are still connected.

4. Power on your system and boot "clean" to a command-line prompt.

5. Make sure that the CD-R/CD-RW appears in "program mode." As an example, an internal Plextor SCSI CD-R will cause all four LEDs on the front panel of the drive to blink. However, your own drive may be quite different, so be sure to check the README file for detailed information.

6. After the PC boots, execute the new firmware program (firm123.exe), which you may receive or download from the manufacturer, and use the new firmware (*.bin) file.

7. When the flash application starts, specify the location of the .BIN file.

8. Click the Update button to begin the flash process.

9. When the Update button becomes highlighted again, the flash process is complete.

10. Power off the system. If the CD-R/CD-RW drive has a "flash" jumper, reset the drive's "flash" jumper to its original position.

11. Power on the system and verify that the CD-R drive is responding normally.

# The CD-RW Drive

CD recording offers a powerful tool for backing up important files or archiving completed work. Recording also makes it possible to distribute projects or multimedia presentations on simple and inexpensive media. The problem with CD recording is that it's a one-time deal—once the media is written, it cannot be erased or rewritten. Within the last several years, *rewritable* CD technology (or CD-RW) has developed a lot of interest by allowing specialized optical CD media to be written, erased, then rewritten as easily as for a floppy disk. Such capability allows CD rewriters (see Figure 8-13) to be used for large local file storage (rather than simple archiving). Almost any Pentium PC (or later) with a SCSI or Ultra-DMA interface can support a CD-RW drive. This part of the chapter outlines the important points of CD-RW technology and media.

> CD-RW drives are fully backward-compatible with CD-ROM and CD-R drives, so all the concepts covered for CD-ROM and CD-R drives apply to CD-RW drives. In effect, the CD-RW drive has made CD-R-only drives obsolete.

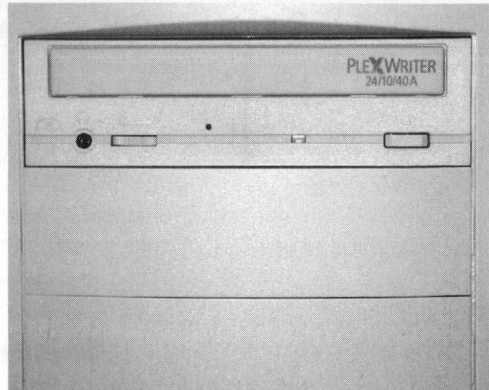

**FIGURE 8-13**    The Plextor 24/10/40A internal ATAPI IDE CD-RW drive supports rewriting, writing, and everyday reading in one drive mechanism.

## CD-RW MEDIA VARIATIONS

Recordable discs use a layer of material along a pre-fabricated spiral track. When the material is "burned" by laser light, the reflective properties of the disc can be changed—and the disc can emulate the pits and lands of a pressed CD-ROM. Unfortunately, this change is permanent, so CD-R media is not suitable for rewritable CDs. To address this concern, designers adopted a disc chemestry based on *phase changes* of the material.

As with CD-R media, a CD-RW starts with a prefabricated spiral track for the optical head to follow. However, a series of layers are applied to the disc. When one level of laser energy is applied, the exposed material changes its state (creating one level of reflectivity). To erase the disc, another level of laser energy is applied that returns the exposed material to its original reflective state. The disc is not "burned"—only altered in a way that can be reversed. However, the drive's optical head is a bit more complicated because several levels of laser light are needed: one level to read a disc, one level to change a CD-RW disc state, and a third level to "unchange" the previously altered state.

 Rewritable discs will not last forever. Repeated phase changes can eventually cause read/write problems with the disc. Make it a point to watch the manufacturer's recommendations for CD-RW disc life, and retire any media that begins to experience problems.

## BURNPROOF TECHNOLOGY

BurnProof technology is licensed from Sanyo and is employed by a growing number of CD-R/RW drive manufacturers as a means of "failsafe" disc writing. When a CD-R/RW drive performs a write operation, it demands a constant, uninterrupted flow of data to operate the writing laser. If the flow of data stops, the write operation fails, and the disc (namely the writable disc) is ruined. To prevent this kind of interruption, every CD-R/RW drive has a buffer—which is simply RAM that serves as a temporary storage area. However, the buffer can be emptied quickly (especially when you write at high speeds). It can also empty if you use other applications in the background (such as playing games or watching movies) while writing, or if your source drive cannot read data fast enough. Any of these factors can produce a "buffer underrun error."

BurnProof technology is able to turn off the writing laser if a buffer underrun occurs and to "remember" where the writing stopped on the disc. Once data is available again, the drive picks up where it left off, and the writing process continues. Using a drive with BurnProof technology (such as the Plextor 24/10/40 CD-RW) allows you greater flexibility to work on other tasks in the background without worrying about buffer underruns and ruined discs. It's a worthwhile technology that should be seriously considered when selecting a fast new CD-RW drive.

# UDF CONCEPTS

The ISO 9660 file system has long been the established standard in CD-ROM and CD recording (Mac systems use the HFS approach). In fact, ISO 9660 is one of the key elements that propelled CD-ROM drives to the status of "standard equipment" on the PC by the early 1990s. With the broad introduction of CD-RW drives, however, ISO 9660 has been replaced by the *Universal Data Format* (UDF) file system. This section of the chapter offers some essential background on UDF and explains how the use of UDF affects the compatibility of CD-RW discs with existing CD-ROM and CD-RW drives.

Let's start with some perspective on ISO 9660. As you saw earlier in the chapter, the ISO 9660 file system grew out of the original High Sierra file system of the late 1980s. All the files read on your CD-ROM or recorded on your CD-R use the ISO 9660 format. Both Windows and Mac operating systems can read ISO 9660 discs because they provide built-in ISO 9660 readers—the "reader" is totally transparent to the end user. While ISO 9660 is just fine for existing CD-ROM and CD-R drives, it is really not sufficient to support the use of CD-RW drives or the higher-capacity DVD drives. CD-RW drives require that files be added incrementally (e.g., one file at a time), *without* a waste of overhead space, and that individual files can be erased "at will" to make room on a disc. In addition, DVD drives require a file system that can support drives at least 4GB in size. These demands are well beyond the scope of ISO 9660.

UDF addresses all of these concerns by providing a format that can add and erase individual files as needed as well as support the large disc space promised by DVD. Another advantage of UDF is its "cross-platform" compatibility—a UDF disc can be read by both a Mac and Windows platform. For example, a file could be written using a Mac, then read back on a Windows PC. The UDF file format is also able to maintain Mac file attributes (for example, icons, resource forks, and file types), while ISO 9660 cannot.

The *DirectCD* technology used with CD-RW drives reads and writes to the CD-RW disc using the UDF format. If you're working on a PC with a CD-RW drive (or plan on installing one yourself), chances are that you'll be using a DirectCD applet under Windows to invoke UDF on that disc. For example, when you insert a new CD-RW disc under Windows XP, the disc is immediately identified as a CD-RW disc, and you can begin saving files right away (see Figure 8-14). If you're using DirectCD under Windows 9x/Me/XP today, chances are that you're using UDF 5.0x or later. You can learn about the history of DirectCD at www.roxio.com/en/support/dcdwin/dcdwinvhist.html.

## Disc Capacity Under UDF

An important issue to keep in mind when using DirectCD is that you never get the same data capacity from a CD-RW disc that you do from a CD-R disc under ISO 9660. Traditional CD-Rs under ISO 9660 can provide a full 650MB from a blank 74-minute disc. DirectCD formats CD-RW discs in fixed-length packets that support the random erase feature. This requires more space on disc than variable-length packets (which vary in length to fit the size of the data), so it's normal to have about 550MB left for writing after formatting.

DirectCD also uses a technique called *sparing*. If you were to erase and write to the same spot on CD-RW media over and over, that hot spot would eventually wear out (after a few thousand writes)—even if the rest of the disc was still unused. Sparing is a technique that writes data evenly over the disc, significantly extending its life. However, sparing also requires significant overhead.

**FIGURE 8-14** Windows XP detects the CD-RW media and allows you immediate access for reading and writing.

The situation is a little different for CD-R discs formatted with DirectCD. Since CD-R media does not require random erase (CD-R is write-once media and cannot be erased), fixed packet writing and sparing is not required, so CD-R discs have over 600MB of free space after being formatted for DirectCD.

## UDF and Disc Compatibility

There's only one little problem with UDF—Windows 95 (and early versions of Windows 98) does not support it natively. The DirectCD drivers installed with a CD-RW drive will allow Windows 95 to read UDF discs in a CD-RW drive, but using DirectCD (UDF) discs in other drives is a little trickier. When DirectCD begins writing data to a disc, it opens a session. Before any CD-ROM drive can read a disc, the session must be closed. When you eject a disc from a CD-RW drive using the DirectCD applet, you can choose to close the disc to ISO 9660. If you do *not* close the disc to ISO 9660 when you eject it, you cannot read it on a CD-ROM drive—you must read it on a CD-R or CD-RW drive fitted with DirectCD. This is a limitation of CD-ROM drives, not the DirectCD software. As a rule, you can expect a ISO 9660 CD-R disc to play on any CD-R or CD-RW drive. On the other hand, a CD-RW disc will usually *not* play on an older CD-R drive and might not play on a newer CD-R drive without a UDF Reader utility.

Windows 98/SE (and subsequent versions of Windows) with DVD support should fully support UDF, so a separate UDF "reader" should not be needed. But check for upgrades in the event that there are any problems.

If you close the disc to UDF, you can still read the UDF format, but you'll need a "multi-read" CD-ROM drive and a UDF Reader utility. For example, when you install Adaptec's UDF Reader in your system, you should be able to read your closed session CD-R and CD-RW discs on CD-ROM drives regardless of whether they are ISO 9660 or UDF.

## Multi-Read CD-ROM Drives

UDF reader utilities are designed to support the current generation of Multi-Read CD-ROM drives. Multi-Read is a specification developed and endorsed by the Optical Storage Technology Association (OSTA) and accepted by the industry at large. Virtually all CD-ROM drives on the market today (manufactured after mid-1997) are Multi-Read-compatible. To be Multi-Read compliant, a CD-ROM drive must be able to:

■  Read CD-RW discs

■  Read packet-written discs (both CD-R and CD-RW)

■  Support the operating system to utilize the UDF file system

There are some non-Multi-Read CD-ROM drives that can read UDF formatted CD-R media (but not CD-RW media) using an appropriate UDF Reader utility.

## UDF Readers

A UDF reader enables Multi-Read CD-ROM drives to read closed-session UDF formatted CD-R and CD-RW media under Windows 9*x*/Me/XP and the Macintosh operating system. The UDF reader for Windows is called UDF Reader Driver, and the UDF Reader for Mac OS is called UDF Volume Access. UDF readers are particularly useful if you're using DirectCD to *record* data to a CD-RW disc, because you will then be able to read the CD-RW disc in a Multi-Read CD-ROM drive. Without a UDF reader, you could read the UDF disc only in another CD-RW drive using DirectCD. Since UDF is designed to be a cross-platform file format, UDF Readers also allow you to interchange UDF-formatted discs between Mac and Windows systems.

Most companies that develop DirectCD software (such as Roxio—formerly Adaptec) already offer UDF Reader utilities free of charge. You can download the Roxio UDF Reader from the Roxio Web site at www.roxio.com or more directly from their patch/upgrade Web page at www.roxio.com/en/support/udfwin/ index.html. For more information, you could also send e-mail to Roxio at support.roxio.com/en/support/roxio_support/contact_select.html.

Remember that you might not need a separate UDF reader if you're using a compliant drive with a current version of DirectCD on an operating system like Windows Me/XP.

## UDF Reader Compliance

Since UDF is intended to provide a universal file interchange format, any UDF Reader utility *should* be able to read all UDF formatted media (media formatted with DirectCD). However, there is no independent third-party organization to test for UDF compliance, so there is no guarantee that all media claiming to be "UDF formatted" will be readable by every UDF Reader under all conditions. If you have trouble reading a UDF disc with one particular reader utility, you might wish to try another reader utility.

## UDF and Audio CDs

A popular use of CD-R and CD-RW discs has been to record music for playback on an ordinary CD player (for example, copying old vinyl LPs to CD). While this is a tried and true process for CD-R discs recorded under ISO 9660, this will *not* work with UDF discs recorded with DirectCD. Audio files recorded under UDF will *not* work when played back in a commercial CD player (unless the player specifically supports music files on CD-R/RW media). But audio files played back on a CD-R or CD-RW drive under DirectCD should work normally.

### Windows 98/Me/XP and UDF

While Windows 95 does not provide direct support for UDF, Windows 98SE/Me/XP do support UDF 1.02 for DVD-ROM and DVD Video discs. However, Windows 98 doesn't provide native support for UDF 1.5, so DirectCD software and UDF readers may still be required after Windows 98 is installed. Windows 98SE, Windows Me, and Windows XP do not require a separate UDF reader.

## CARING FOR REWRITABLE CDS

As a rule, rewritable CDs are as rugged and reliable as ordinary "pressed" CDs. Still, you should exercise some rules in the careful handling and storage of rewritable media:

- *Maintain a comfortable environment.* Don't expose rewritable discs to sunlight or other strong light for long periods of time. Also avoid high heat and humidity, which can damage the physical disc. Always keep blank or recorded media in clean jewel cases for best protection.

- *Don't write on the disc.* Don't use alcohol-based pens to write on discs—the ink may eventually eat through the top (lacquer) surface and damage your data. Also don't use ball-point or other sharp-tipped pens, because you may scratch right through the lacquer surface and damage the reflective gold layer (and ruin your data).

- *Don't use labels on the disc.* Don't put labels on discs unless they are *expressly* designed for rewritable CDs. The glue may eat through the lacquer surface just as some inks do, or the label may unbalance the disc and cause problems in reading it back or recording subsequent sessions. Never try to remove a label—you might tear off the lacquer and some of the reflecting surface.

- *Watch your media quality.* Many different brands of rewritable CD media are now available in the marketplace. Quality varies from brand to brand (and even from batch to batch within a given brand). If you have repeated problems that can be traced to the blank media you are using, try using a different brand or even a different batch of the same brand. Discs that are old should be discarded.

- *Don't use Kodak Photo CDs.* Avoid the use of Kodak Photo CDs on everyday CD rewriters (unless the drive is specifically designed to support that type of media). Kodak Photo CDs are designed to be used only with Kodak Photo CD professional workstations. Although the discs are inexpensive, they have a protection bit that prevents them from being written on many CD recorders. When you attempt to write these discs on the recorders that do not recognize the protection bit, you will receive an error message.

- *Be careful about power.* If you lose power while writing to your CD-RW (or if you exit an application or press CTRL-ALT-DEL) while writing to CD, you may be able to salvage your rewritable CD. Leave the CD in the drive—do *not* open the tray. Turn the machine off, then turn it back on. Reenter the application you were using. Once the application tries to access the CD-RW drive, the recovery operation will make it appear that the last session is there. However, only a part of the CD's directory may be there—your rewritable CD is still usable if you can read that directory. Repeat the entire copy operation to make sure that your files are copied successfully.

# Troubleshooting CD Drives

CD drives typically install and operate with a minimum of difficulty, but compatibility issues, poor media quality, outdated driver versions, conflicting software applets, and even operating system versions can cause problems with CD drives. As a technician, you should understand the common symptoms and solutions that occur most frequently. This part of the chapter focuses on the troubleshooting procedures that are common across a wide range of CD-ROM, CD-R, and CD-RW drives.

## RECORDING PARAMETERS

Although the default settings are usually adequate, Windows XP allows you to configure the recording behavior of CD-R/RW drives. Open the Device Manager, right-click your CD-R/RW drive, then select Properties. Now choose the Recording tab (see Figure 8-15). There are four entries under Desktop CD Recording that are used to tweak performance.

- **Enable CD recording**   Keep the Enable CD Recording on the Drive box checked if you want to record CD-R/RW discs on the drive. However, you may want to uncheck this box if security is an issue and you need to prevent other users from absconding with your work.

- **Image file location**   If you choose to record from an "image file" rather than on the fly, you'll need a partition that can hold at least one full CD's worth of data (at least 650MB). Select a drive letter with about 1GB of free space.

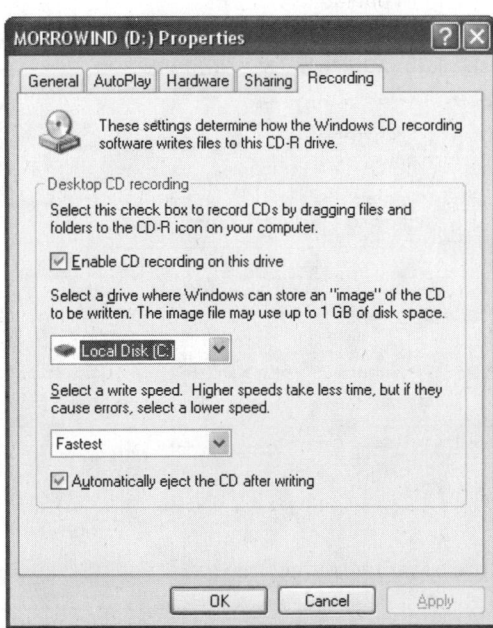

**FIGURE  8-15**     The Recording tab in the CD drive's Properties dialog lets you tailor recording performance for your own system.

- **Writing speed**   As a rule, select Fastest writing speeds for the shortest recording times. However, if you don't have media certified for high-speed recording (or you encounter errors when recording at high speeds), you can select a slower recording speed and try to improve reliability.
- **Automatic ejection**   When the Automatically Eject the CD After Writing box is checked, the disc will be ejected when the writing cycle is finished. If you want to keep the disc in the drive (perhaps to write additional files), uncheck this box.

## CD AUDIO SETTINGS

CD drives have proven themselves to be an ideal platform for playing multimedia like video and audio discs. When Windows XP users complain about CD audio problems (e.g., no volume), you should also remember that there's a "master" CD audio volume control in the drive's Properties dialog box—this needs to be checked along with the CD audio cable and system mixer settings. Follow these steps for Windows XP:

1.  Click Start | Control Panel | Performance and Maintenance | System.
2.  Select the Hardware tab and click Device Manager.
3.  Expand the DVD/CD-ROM entry and double-click the drive to open the Properties dialog.
4.  Click the Properties tab (see Figure 8-16) and check the CD Player Volume slider.
5.  Also check the Digital CD Playback checkbox. If the hardware is installed properly and volumes are set properly, try unchecking this box.
6.  Click OK to save your changes.

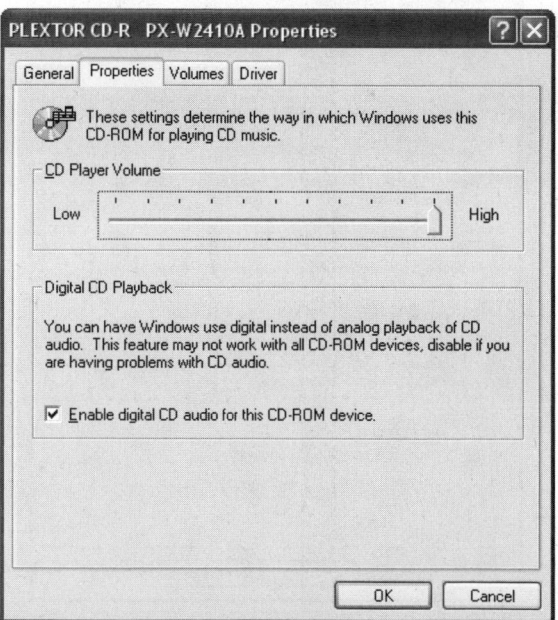

**FIGURE  8-16**    Set the CD audio volume and digital playback mode under Windows XP.

# CHANGING DRIVE LETTERS

All Windows versions will assign a drive letter to each CD drive in the system at start time. Although the initial assignment is automatic, you can adjust the drive letter if necessary. Use the following steps to change a CD drive letter under Windows XP:

You will need administrative rights to change a drive letter under Windows XP, so be sure to log onto the PC accordingly.

1. Choose Start | Control Panel | Performance and Maintenance | Administrative Tools.
2. Click Computer Management | Storage | Disk Management. This lists the drives in your PC and allows you to change any drive letter but the boot drive (see Figure 8-17).
3. Right-click the CD drive that you need to change and select Change Drive Letter and Paths.
4. Select the CD drive and click the Change button.
5. Select an available drive letter (see Figure 8-18) and click OK.

Use the following steps under Windows 9x/Me:

1. Click Start | Settings | Control Panel.
2. Double-click the System icon, then click the Device Manager tab.
3. Highlight the CD-ROM drive you want to change, and then click the Properties button.
4. Click the Settings tab (Figure 8-19).

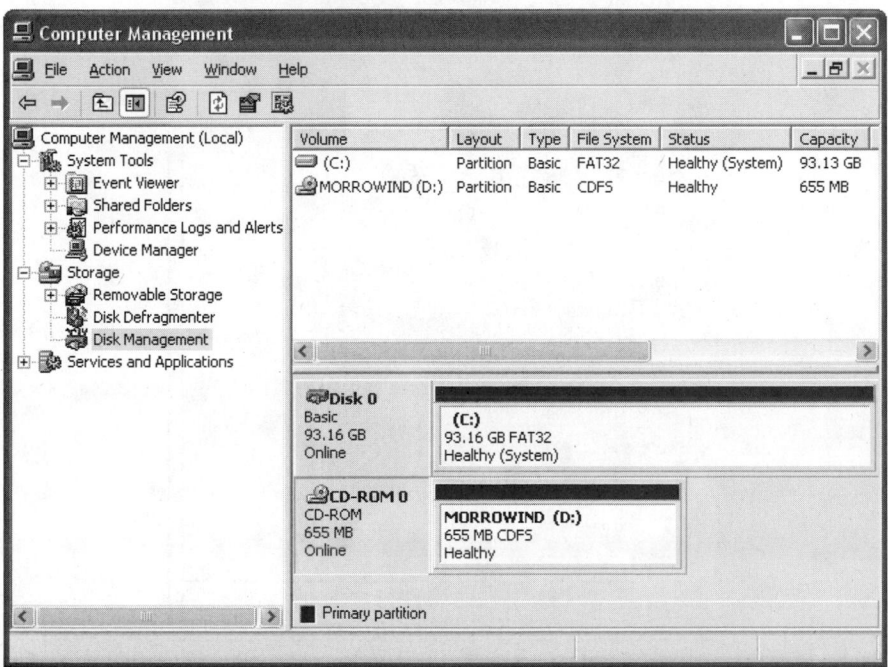

**FIGURE 8-17**    The Windows XP Computer Management dialog allows you to change drive letters.

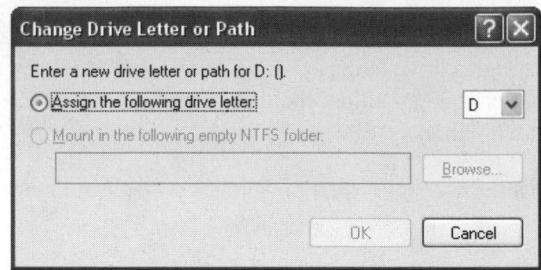

**FIGURE  8-18**    Windows XP lets you select from a list of available drive letters.

5. In the Reserved Drive Letters section, set Start Drive Letter and End Drive Letter to the drive letter you want the CD-ROM drive to use. Click OK until you return to Control Panel.

6. Restart the computer for your changes to take effect.

## AUTO INSERT NOTIFICATION

You may notice that the CD drive light blinks every few seconds. This may occur even if there is no read operation in progress and even if there is no disc in the drive. This is usually a normal side-effect of the Auto Insert Notification (AIN) feature of Windows 9*x*/Me/XP, which allows a disc to be automatically detected and launched when inserted in the drive. Normally, the AIN is a harmless feature, but there may

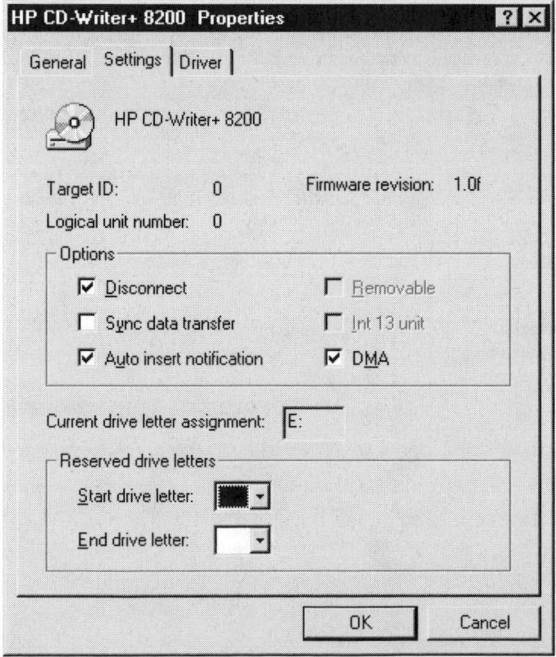

**FIGURE  8-19**    Changing the CD drive letter through the drive's Properties dialog

be some performance-sensitive programs that are affected by AIN. Follow these steps to disable AIN under Windows 9*x*/Me (you cannot disable AIN under Windows XP):

1.  Open the Control Panel and double-click the System icon.

2.  Click the Device Manager tab, double-click CD-ROM, and then double-click the desired CD drive.

3.  Click the Settings tab (as in Figure 8-19 earlier); then click the Auto Insert Notification checkbox to clear it.

4.  Click the Close button and restart your computer when prompted to do so.

Simply repeat these procedures and recheck the AIN box to enable the feature once again.

If your computer contains a SCSI host adapter, Windows polls the SCSI bus periodically to determine the status of the bus and installed devices. On some computers, the disk drive access light on the front panel illuminates when any SCSI device (or the SCSI bus itself) is accessed. If the computer contains a SCSI CD-ROM drive, the CD-ROM access light may blink in conjunction with the disk drive access light. Keep in mind that this blinking of the SCSI CD-ROM access light is independent of the AIN feature, and the steps listed previously will *not* prevent the CD-ROM light from blinking.

# CD DRIVE PERFORMANCE

When you run a program that accesses a CD drive, you may notice that the program is not performing as well as it could. For example, you notice slow data transfers in a business or reference program. You may also find that the audio and video in a multimedia program is slow (or seems to skip or stutter). This trouble can occur under Windows 9*x*/Me when the Supplemental Cache Size and Optimize Access Pattern For settings are not configured properly for your CD drive. You can optimize the CD drive settings for Windows 9*x*/Me as described here (these settings are not available under Windows XP):

1.  Click Start | Settings | Control Panel, and then double-click the System icon.

2.  On the Performance tab, click File System.

3.  Click the CD-ROM tab (as in Figure 8-20).

4.  Move the Supplemental Cache Size slider to the right to allocate more system RAM for caching data from the CD drive, or to the left to allocate less RAM for caching data.

Many multimedia programs perform better with a *smaller* cache because these programs tend not to reuse data.

5.  When reading continuous data (such as .AVI files), use a higher setting in the Optimize Access Pattern For box. When reading random data, increase the Supplemental Cache Size setting and decrease the Optimize Access Pattern For setting.

6.  Click OK and then click Close. Restart your computer when prompted to do so.

These settings are for Windows only and will have no effect when using real-mode drivers for your CD drive.

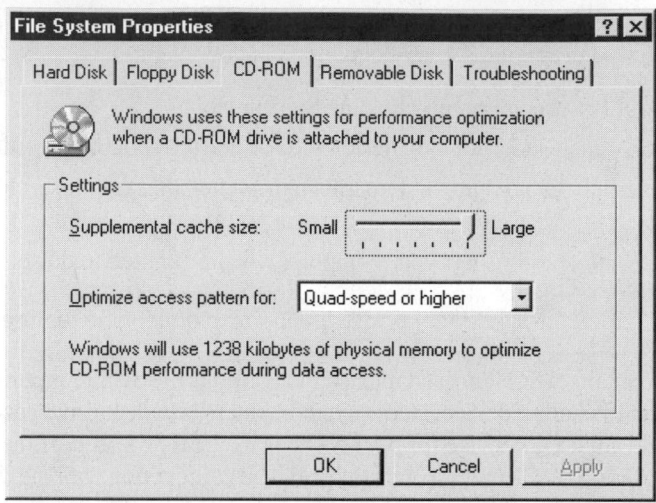

**FIGURE  8-20**     You can tweak the CD drive performance under Windows 9x/Me by adjusting the cache settings.

## OPTIMIZING DATA TRANSFERS

On older systems DMA (*direct memory access*—also referred to as *bus mastering*) is a technique that some PC devices use to transfer data directly to and from memory *without* passing through the processor. As a result, DMA-based data transfers reduce CPU overhead by providing a mechanism for data transfers that do not require direct intervention from the CPU. If your PC is configured to support bus mastering operation, you can usually enable DMA drive support to improve the data transfer performance for your CD drives. Use these steps to enable DMA under Windows 9x/Me:

 If your version of Windows (such as Windows 95) does not include DMA support, obtain and install the most current bus master motherboard driver for your computer—or install any version of Windows 98/Me/XP for more robust DMA support.

1. Click Start | Settings | Control Panel, and then double-click the System icon.

2. On the Device Manager tab, double-click the CD-ROM branch to expand it and then double-click the desired CD drive.

3. On the Settings tab (as in Figure 8-19 earlier), click the DMA checkbox to select it and then click OK.

4. Restart your computer, then test to determine if your CD drive is working properly. If your CD drive does not work properly with DMA enabled, disable DMA by clearing the DMA checkbox.

Windows XP does not provide a specific DMA checkbox. Instead, it attempts to use the best drive controller mode to achieve optimum data transfers. These settings can be accessed through the IDE ATA/ATAPI Controllers entry under your Device Manager. Open the Windows XP Device Manager, expand the IDE ATA/ATAPI controllers entry, and select either the Primary or Secondary controller (whatever channel your CD drive is using). Since many CD drives are placed on the Secondary controller channel, double-click the entry and check the Channel Properties dialog (see Figure 8-21). On this particular system, the CD-RW drive is

**FIGURE 8-21**     Windows XP sets optimum data transfer modes through the drive controller properties.

the first and only (master) device on the secondary channel. The system will attempt to use a DMA transfer mode if the system supports it. Since DMA is supported, Windows XP has selected Ultra DMA Mode 2 data transfers. If you have trouble with drive communication, you can select an alternate (lower) data transfer mode from the drop-down menu.

# TROUBLESHOOTING GUIDELINES

CD drives have come a long way in the last few years. In spite of the standardization that CD drives employ, the early ATAPI IDE drives under older versions of Windows were sometimes plagued with compatibility and performance issues. Continuing advances in drive design and Windows (such as XP) have helped to improve hardware compatibility and streamline drive performance—eliminating many of the more arcane problems covered in prior editions. However, CD drives are certainly not without their share of troubles. Before you search for specific symptoms, try the following checklist to help isolate common troubles.

- *Check the disc.* If the drive has trouble reading (or writing) a disc, make sure that the disc itself is appropriate for the drive. See that the disc is clean and undamaged, and try the disc in another PC (if possible) to confirm that it's readable. If you're writing, see that the disc media is certified to run at your desired writing speed. Otherwise, reduce the writing speed and try the disc again.

- *Check for drive error codes.* Some drives (especially late model CD-R/RW drives) employ firmware that will produce a series of flashes on the drive's LED(s) in the event of an internal problem. Refer to the manufacturer's documentation for your particular drive to determine the meaning of each specific code (if any). In most cases, any LED error code indicates a faulty drive, which should be replaced immediately.

■ *Check drive power.* CD drives are powered through a standard four-pin drive power connector. If the drive's power LED is out (or the drive isn't recognized by the system), check this power cable to see that it's securely attached. You should never power a CD drive through a "Y adapter"—this can split power from another drive, causing erratic drive behavior.

■ *Check the signal cable.* CD drives use a 40-pin IDE cable (or a 50/68-pin SCSI cable) to exchange data and commands with the host drive controller. New installations are often hampered when a cable is loose or inverted at one end. Existing installations may suffer when an end of the cable is accidentally pulled loose. Check both ends of the cable to see that they're secure. If the cable appears cut, scuffed, or otherwise damaged, it should be replaced. If you're using a SCSI interface, remember that the SCSI cable must be properly terminated, and additional settings may be required in the SCSI host adapter's BIOS (depending on the manufacturer's instructions).

■ *Check the audio cable.* The audio from music CDs is passed to the sound card along a thin four-wire cable. See that this cable is installed properly at both ends. In many cases, the audio cable is inserted into the wrong connector on the sound card (or sound circuit on the motherboard). In other cases, the cable may be wired improperly due to differing pin assignments between the CD drive and sound device, so try another audio cable. Of course, you should also check the CD audio volume settings in the drive Properties (under Windows XP as in Figure 8-16 earlier) and master mixer volume levels (see Figure 8-22).

■ *Check the drive ID jumper(s).* An ATAPI IDE CD drive must be configured as a "master" or "slave" device (see Figure 8-10 earlier), and a SCSI CD drive must use a unique SCSI ID (usually between 2 and 6). Recheck the jumper(s) on the drive to see that the ID is set properly, and that it doesn't conflict with other drive(s) on that same controller channel. For example, two drives set as "master" on the same channel will result in system problems. Avoid the use of "cable select" (or CS) assignments for ATAPI IDE drive since this demands the use of special cables that are not shipped with most drives.

■ *Check drive recognition under BIOS.* If your CD drive isn't responding, watch the BIOS startup text. Most modern drives will return a model number or other manufacturer's information to the BIOS at boot time, and you should see this text along with similar designations for your system's hard drives or other drive devices. You may start the CMOS Setup and verify that the CD drive's position is set to "auto-detect" or "auto-configure." If the corresponding drive position (e.g., first secondary drive) is set to "none" or "not installed," the BIOS may forego detection of the drive. If the drive *was* being listed by the BIOS, but is no longer detected, you may have a power or cable problem, or the drive has failed.

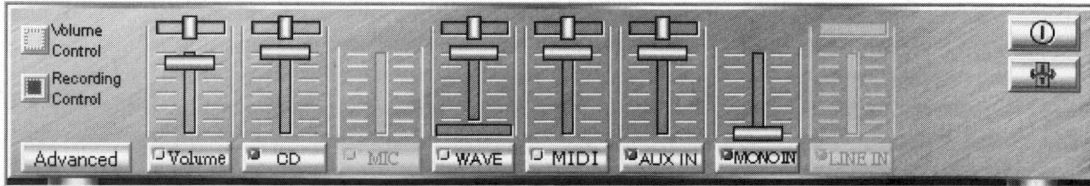

**FIGURE  8-22**     The master mixer applet allows you to mix volume levels from various sound devices into a final output.

■ *Check drive recognition under Windows.* Windows should recognize the CD drive, install the appropriate drivers for it, and list the drive correctly in the Device Manager. Check the Device Manager and see that the CD drive is listed correctly. If the drive is not listed at all, Windows cannot use the drive. Try the Add New Hardware wizard to install the drive manually. If the drive is still inaccessible, you may have a power, signal cable, or drive fault that is preventing the drive from operating. If the drive is listed incorrectly (e.g., the wrong make or model), try removing the entry from Device Manager and reboot the system so that Windows can re-detect the drive, or use the Add New Hardware wizard to install the drive manually.

■ *Check for driver updates.* Current versions of Windows (such as XP) have an extensive driver library that should accommodate many types of CD drives. However, drive problems and obscure errors should always prompt you to check with the drive manufacturer for driver updates. Once a suitable update has been downloaded, you can use the Driver tab in your CD drive Properties dialog to start an update process (see Figure 8-23).

■ *Check for firmware updates.* Firmware is the "program" that operates your CD drive, and is normally recorded onto a chip located in the drive's electronics package. There are some cases where firmware errors result in obscure drive problems—usually under odd combinations of hardware and OS versions. While you're checking for driver updates, also take a look for a firmware update that addresses your specific problem (don't bother with firmware updates unless they deal with your particular issue).

■ *Replace the drive.* If you're still unable to resolve your particular CD drive problem, it may be worth replacing the drive with a different make or model. This may help to resolve compatibility or performance problems that sometimes still occur.

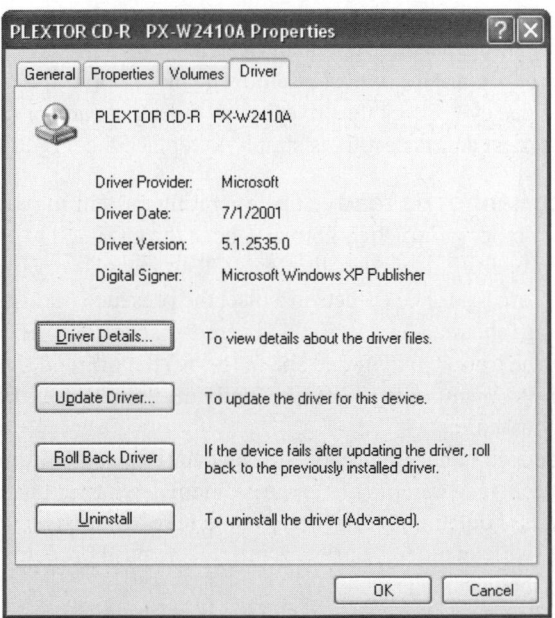

**FIGURE  8-23**    Windows XP allows you to update, roll back, and uninstall device drivers.

# CD-ROM SYMPTOMS

Let's start with a series of basic drive symptoms. Though the vast majority of CD-ROM problems are due to software or setup problems, the drives themselves are delicate and unforgiving devices. Considering that their prices have plummeted to the point where they are virtually disposable devices, there is little economic sense in attempting a lengthy repair. When a fault occurs in the drive or in its drive controller (e.g., a SCSI host adapter), your best course is typically to replace the defective device outright.

The following symptoms may denote a CD-ROM, but are also applicable to CD-R and CD-RW drives (unless otherwise noted).

**SYMPTOM 8-1** **The drive has trouble accepting or rejecting a CD** This problem is typical of motorized CD-ROM drives where the disc is accepted into a slot or placed in a motorized tray—you don't see this issue in "caddy-type" CD-ROM drives. Before performing any disassembly, power down the drive and check the assembly through the CD tray for any obvious obstructions. If there is nothing obvious, expose the mechanical assembly and check each linkage and motor drive gear very carefully. Carefully remove or free any obstruction. Be gentle when working around the load/unload assembly. Pay particular attention to any shock mounts or other vibration dampening devices. If the problem persists, there is most likely a problem in the tray motor or mechanism. Your best course is to replace the CD-ROM drive.

You can sometimes free a jammed drive tray by inserting a thin paperclip into the emergency release hole located just below the tray.

**SYMPTOM 8-2** **Optical read head does not seek (a drive "seek" error)** The operating system may report this as a "seek" or "read" error. An optical head is used to identify pits and lands along a CD-ROM and to track the spiral data pattern as the head moves across the disk. The optical head must move very slowly and smoothly to ensure accurate tracking. Head movement is accomplished using a linear stepping motor (or *linear actuator*) to shift the optical assembly in microscopic increments—head travel appears perfectly smooth to the unaided eye. Check the drive for any damaged parts or obstructions. When the optical head fails to seek, the easiest and fastest fix is simply to replace the CD-ROM mechanism.

**SYMPTOM 8-3** **Disc cannot be read** The operating system may report this as a "sector not found," "drive not ready," or other type of "read" error. Check the CD itself to ensure that it is the right format for the drive, inserted properly, and physically clean. Cleanliness is very important to a CD. While the laser will often "look past" small surface defects in a disc, the presence of dust or debris on a disc surface can produce serious tracking (and read) errors. Try a different disc to confirm the problem. If a new or different disc reads properly, the trouble may indeed be in (or *on*) the original disc itself. Not only must the disc be clean, but the head optics must also be clear. Gently dust or clean the head optics as suggested by your drive's particular manufacturer.

Examine the power connector and signal cable between the drive and its controller board. Be sure that the cable is connected correctly and completely. If the problem persists, chances are that either the drive's optical head or electronics are defective. Your best course here is to try replacing the drive outright. If problems persist on a drive with an older proprietary interface, you'll probably need to upgrade the drive to an ATAPI IDE or SCSI model.

**SYMPTOM 8-4** **The disc does not turn** You may not hear the disc "spin up" for access. The disc must turn at a *constant linear velocity* (CLV), which is directed and regulated by the spindle motor. If the disc is not spinning during access, check to be sure that the disc is seated properly and is not jammed or obstructed. Also verify that the drive is installed properly and is recognized by the PC. If the drive isn't detected, it may not be able to spin the disc. For example, the drive may appear in the list of drives detected by the BIOS at boot time, and will also be listed in the Device Manager.

Once you've confirmed the drive's installation, consider possible problems with the optical head. If your particular drive provides you with instructions for cleaning the optical head aperture, perform that cleaning operation and try the drive again—a fouled optical head can sometimes upset spindle operation. Finally, if the drive's Activity LED comes on when drive access is attempted but the disc still doesn't turn (you may also see a corresponding DOS error message), the drive spindle system is probably defective, so replace the drive.

**SYMPTOM 8-5** **The optical head cannot focus its laser beam** To compensate for the minute fluctuations in disc flatness, the optical head mounts its objective lens into a small focusing mechanism, which is little more than a miniature voice coil actuator—the lens does not have to move very much at all to maintain precise focus. If focus is out or not well maintained, the laser detector may produce erroneous signals—often resulting in "read" errors (or other drive error messages). If random but consistent DOS errors appear, check the disc to be sure that it is *optically* clean—dust and fingerprints can result in serious access problems. Try another disc. If a new disc continues to perform badly, try cleaning the optical aperture with clean (photography-grade) air. When problems persist, the optical system is probably damaged or defective. Finally, try replacing the CD-ROM drive mechanism.

**SYMPTOM 8-6** **You see an error such as "Not ready reading from drive D:"** If the drive is recognized by the BIOS and is listed properly in the Device Manager, a drive that is "not ready" may have a media issue or some other mechanical problem. Make sure that a suitable disc is inserted properly in the drive (it should not bind in the tray). Also check for drive activity and the spinup of your spindle motor. If these things do not occur, the drive may be damaged and require immediate replacement. Otherwise, a drive that is not detected by the system may have an installation problem. Recheck the power and signal cables, master/slave jumpers, and so on. You can even try moving the CD drive to its own drive controller channel if possible. If the hardware appears sound, recheck the CD driver(s). For example, you may need to use the Add New Hardware wizard to install the CD drive under Windows. When working with older versions of Windows, you may need updated drivers from the drive maker.

 If the CD drive is powered through a "Y adapter," try attaching the drive directly to a power cable—a power supply upgrade may be required.

**SYMPTOM 8-7** **You see an error indicating that the CD-ROM drive is not found** This type of problem may also appear as loading problems with the device driver(s). There are several possible reasons why the drive hardware cannot be found. Power and signal problems are likely culprits. Make sure the four-pin power connector is inserted properly and completely. If the drive is being powered by a Y adapter, try removing the Y adapter and powering the CD drive directly. Use a voltmeter and measure the +5 volt (pin 4) and +12 volt (pin 1) levels. If either voltage (especially the +12 volt supply) is unusually low or absent, replace the power supply. See that the drive's signal interface cable is connected securely at both the drive and controller. If the cable is visibly worn or damaged, try a new one.

Also verify that the master/slave drive ID settings on the drive don't conflict with another drive on the same channel (a common oversight during new installations or upgrades). If your CD-ROM uses a SCSI interface, make sure that the SCSI bus cable is properly terminated at both ends. If problems persist, replace the drive controller first, then replace the CD-ROM drive if necessary. If problems continue, replace the CD drive outright.

**SYMPTOM 8-8** **You cannot get the CD-ROM drive to run properly when mounted vertically** CD-ROM drives with motorized drive trays generally cannot be mounted vertically—disc tracking simply will not work correctly. The only CD-ROM drives that can be mounted vertically are those with caddys, but you should check with those manufacturers before proceeding with vertical mounting.

**SYMPTOM 8-9** **You see an error such as "Unable to detect ATAPI IDE CD-ROM drive, device driver not loaded"** You have a problem with the configuration of your IDE/EIDE/UDMA drive controller hardware. Check the signal cable first and make sure that the 40-pin signal cable is attached properly between the drive and controller. ATAPI IDE CD-ROM drives are typically installed on a secondary 40-pin IDE port. Make sure that there is no device in the system using the same IRQ or I/O address as your secondary IDE port (unlikely in today's PnP systems), and verify that the master/slave settings of the drive are correct. If you're using the drive under DOS, make sure that any command line switches for the low-level driver in CONFIG.SYS are set properly, or try booting from a Windows 98/Me/XP startup diskette with generic CD drive support.

**SYMPTOM 8-10** **The CD-ROM drive door will not open once the 40-pin IDE signal cable is connected** You should need power only to operate the drive door. If the door stops when the signal cable is attached, there are some possible problems to check. Power and signal cabling are likely culprits, so make sure that both +5 and +12 volts are available at the power connector. See that the power connector is attached securely to the back of the CD-ROM drive. The 40-pin signal cable is probably reversed at either the drive or controller ends. Try a different signal cable. Also make sure that the 40-pin IDE drive is plugged into a true IDE port—not a proprietary (non-IDE 40-pin) port. If problems persist, try a known-good IDE-type CD-ROM drive.

**SYMPTOM 8-11** **The tray will not open** Assuming that the drive is properly powered and recognized by the system, there are two common issues that will lock the disc tray. First, close any applications that may be locking the tray. Once you've shut down any background software, try rebooting the PC and see if the tray can be opened. If there's no software locking the tray, the CD may simply be stuck. In this case, shut down the PC and use the emergency eject hole (usually located beneath the tray) to gently free the tray and remove the disc.

**SYMPTOM 8-12** **The auto insert notification feature prevents a system's suspend mode from working** Most current computers now include power management features that place the computer in a power-down mode (suspend) after a given period of inactivity. If the Auto Insert Notification (AIN) option is enabled for IDE-type CD-ROM drives when power management is also enabled, the computer may not suspend automatically. This typically occurs because some IDE-type CD-ROM drives use certain ATA commands for polling. But a power management system will detect the action as "drive activity." Since a drive then appears to be in use, the power management system will not power-down the system (for example, this is a known issue with Windows 95 OSR2). You can work around this issue by disabling the Auto Insert Notification option for affected drives. As a more permanent fix, you may also choose to patch or update your version of Windows to Me/XP if possible.

**SYMPTOM 8-13**    You notice that the LED indicator on the CD-ROM is always on

The drive seems to be otherwise working properly. This is not necessarily a problem. Some CD-ROM drive models use the LED indicator as a READY light instead of as a BUSY light. Whenever a CD is loaded in the drive, the LED will be lit, and it will remain lit whether the drive is being accessed or not. In other cases, the LED may remain lit, but flash when the disc is accessed. This feature tells the user whether or not a CD-ROM disc is currently loaded in the drive by simply checking the LED. There may be a jumper on the CD-ROM drive that allows you to switch the indicator light from Ready mode to Busy mode. However, it should not be necessary for you to change the drive's behavior.

**SYMPTOM 8-14**    An IDE CD-ROM is not detected when slaved to an IBM hard drive

This is an unusual problem that is known to occur with Aztech IDE CD-ROM drives and IBM Dala 3450 hard drives. The problem is related to IDE signaling—the timing of one or more signals is not long enough for the CD-ROM to identify itself properly. This results in the improper detection of an Aztech IDE CD-ROM. You should make the CD-ROM drive a master device on its own IDE channel or (if possible) upgrade the CD-ROM drive's firmware to utilize more reliable timing. If the CD-ROM manufacturer has no firmware upgrades available, and you cannot reconfigure the CD-ROM on another IDE channel, you'll need to replace the CD-ROM or the hard drive.

**SYMPTOM 8-15**    The CD-ROM drive will not read or run CD Plus or Enhanced CD titles

This is a known problem with older CD-ROM drive models (e.g., Acer CD-ROM models 625A, 645A, 655A, 665A, 525E, 743E, 747E, and 767E were known to exhibit this problem). The CD Plus (or *Enhanced CD*) titles use a modified data format intended for interactive CD titles that incorporate video clips and music, and the data structures on these CDs cannot be recognized by these CD-ROM drive models. In this situation, you'll need to upgrade the CD-ROM drive to a newer model that *can* accommodate newer file types.

**SYMPTOM 8-16**    The drive vibrates or makes a great deal of noise with certain discs

This is almost always due to an unbalanced disc in high-speed (that is, 12X and faster) CD-ROM drives. A disc may become unbalanced from improper silk-screening or the application of an adhesive label. When that unbalanced disc is rotated at high speeds, the entire drive tends to vibrate (often this vibration resonates inside the case, making the sound seem even louder). Make sure that each disc used in the drive is evenly marked or labeled. If the problem seems to occur on all discs, verify that the drive itself is mounted securely to the chassis.

**SYMPTOM 8-17**    An IDE CD-ROM is not detected on an older motherboard    This is a rather unusual problem sometimes seen when using Aztech CD-ROM drives and 486 PCI motherboards with SIS 82C497 chipsets. The motherboard bus noise is far too high and results in the misinterpretation of the IDE interface handshaking signals (namely the DASP and PDIAG signals). As a consequence, the CD-ROM drive is sometimes (or always) not detected. You may be able to resolve this problem by connecting the IDE CD-ROM drive as a slave device to the hard disk—though you may need to slow the hard drive's data transfer mode (through the CMOS Setup) to accommodate the slower CD-ROM drive. Alternatively, you can opt to use a different CD-ROM drive, or upgrade the motherboard.

**SYMPTOM 8-18**    Audio is not being played by the sound card    In most cases, there is a problem with the CD audio connection or system mixer setting. Start with your disc and verify that the CD you're trying to play actually contains Red Book audio (don't try to "play" data CDs). Next, try playing the music CD with a set of headphones attached to the CD-ROM drive directly. If there is no audio from the headphone jack, adjust the volume control. If there is still no music, the drive is probably defective and should be replaced immediately.

Try playing WAV or MIDI files through the sound card (for example, try the Sounds icon in the Control Panel) and verify that the card's volume setting is adequate. If you cannot play any sounds at all, there may be a problem with the sound card or its drivers rather than with the CD-ROM drive. Open the sound card's mixer applet and verify that the CD audio channel volume is enabled and turned up to an appropriate level. Finally, verify that the CD audio cable is appropriate for your sound card and CD-ROM drive and see that it's attached securely at both ends. Try another CD audio cable.

**SYMPTOM 8-19**    **There is no audio being generated by the drive**    Normally you can listen to CD audio using the drive's headphone jack. Check your headphones on another stereo and see that the headphones are working. Also adjust the headphone volume using the small dial located on the front of the CD-ROM drive. If the problem persists and *no* audio is being generated, the headphone amplifier circuit in the CD-ROM is probably defective and the drive should be replaced outright.

**SYMPTOM 8-20**    **The drive is recognized, but no audio is produced**    Remember that a CD-ROM, CD-R, or CD-RW drive is generally a data-only device—the analog signals produced by CD audio must be routed to a sound board (or sound device on the motherboard). Make sure that the thin, four-wire audio cable is connected between the drive and the sound board. Adjust the master mixer volume control to achieve an adequate output. You could also check audio using the drive's headphone jack. Adjust the drive's headphone volume control for an adequate output. If there is sound from the headphones but none from the sound board, the sound board may be faulty, or the cable carrying the audio signal to the sound board may be disconnected or faulty.

**SYMPTOM 8-21**    **You are using an old CD-ROM and can play CD audio, but you cannot access directories or other computer data from a CD**    You may encounter this problem when resurrecting old CD-ROM drives under DOS. Older proprietary CD-ROM drives often used *two* low-level drivers (one for audio, and one for data). You probably only have one of the drivers installed. Check your low-level drivers first and see that any necessary low-level drivers are loaded in the CONFIG.SYS file. Also see that any command line switches are set properly. Some older sound boards with integrated proprietary CD-ROM drive controllers may not work properly with the drivers required for your older CD-ROM drive. You may have to alter the proprietary controller's IRQ, DMA, or I/O settings (and update the driver's command line switches) until you find a combination where the driver and controller will work together. If the problems persist, consider an upgrade to a current ATAPI IDE CD-ROM drive.

**SYMPTOM 8-22**    **Windows XP reads a data disc, but cannot play audio CDs**    In virtually all cases, Windows XP has not installed the proper audio codecs to support CD audio playback. Open the Control Panel, select Sounds, Speech, and Audio Devices, choose Sounds and Audio Devices, and click the Hardware tab (see Figure 8-24). Verify that the CD drive is listed (at the top of the list), along with an Audio Codecs entry. If these items are not in the list, you'll need to add them with the Add New Hardware Wizard.

**SYMPTOM 8-23**    **Windows XP does not show the CD drive**    You find that the CD drive is not listed in Device Manager or My Computer. You may also notice that any devices listed under the DVD/CD-ROM entry of your Device Manager are marked with question marks. This is a software problem

**FIGURE 8-24**    Windows XP must list the CD drive and Audio Codecs to play CD audio.

caused by the use of incorrect device drivers. Open the Properties dialog for the troubled drive and select the Driver tab, then click Uninstall (be sure to confirm the removal). If there is more than one device marked with a question mark, remove all affected devices. Now use the Action menu and scan for hardware changes. This will allow Windows XP to redetect any hardware and reinstall the appropriate drivers for them. If there are no native XP drivers for the CD drive, contact the drive manufacturer for suitable drivers.

**SYMPTOM 8-24**    **The computer locks up while browsing a CD-ROM**    This often occurs under Windows 9*x* (it is not known to occur in later versions of Windows), and has been cited after installing a Hewlett-Packard CD-RW drive in some Compaq Deskpro computers. In actual practice, the computer may halt when you try to use My Computer or Windows Explorer to view the CD drive. In most circumstances, this type of problem is driver-related rather than hardware-based. For example, Compaq systems use a custom device driver file named CPQDFVS.VXD. This file, located in the \Windows\System\Iosubsys folder, can lock up the computer when you try to read from the CD drive. To work around this problem for the Compaq, delete or rename the CPQDFVS.VXD file. To correct this issue on a more permanent basis, contact Compaq for a patch or update to the CPQDFVS.VXD file. Problems with other combinations of hardware may also be corrected by updating errant drivers.

**SYMPTOM 8-25**    **The CD-ROM drive disables your IDE channel under Windows 9*x*/Me**
You may see a yellow exclamation point next to an IDE port in your Device Manager. This drive-related problem frequently occurs when you have a Pioneer CD-ROM drive (for example, the DR-UA124X) installed on your computer and you cannot access the CD-ROM drive connected to that IDE port. The Pioneer DR-UA124X CD-ROM drive's *firmware* causes this issue. Contact Pioneer (or your particular drive maker) for a firmware update or exchange, or replace the drive with an alternate make and model.

**SYMPTOM 8-26**    **Your PC locks up when Windows 98 starts**    This is a known issue with certain hardware platforms (such as the Toshiba Tecra 750 PC) with CD-ROM drives and can occur if all of the following conditions exist:

■  The computer uses an ATAPI IDE CD-ROM drive.

■  The IDE controller that is operating the CD-ROM drive is using the driver shipped with Windows 98 (the problem isn't known to occur under later versions of Windows).

■  You enable direct memory access (DMA) support for the CD-ROM drive.

This problem is caused by the IDE controller chip used in the PC (e.g., Toshiba Tecra 750 computers). You may be able to correct this trouble by installing the Toshiba drivers rather than using the native Windows drivers:

1.  Turn off the computer.
2.  Physically remove the CD-ROM drive from the computer.
3.  Restart the computer.
4.  Install the manufacturer's drivers for the IDE controller (e.g., if you don't have the drivers on a floppy disk already, download them from Toshiba's Web site for the Tecra).
5.  Shut down the computer.
6.  Put the CD-ROM drive back into the computer.
7.  Restart your computer.
8.  Windows should start normally and redetect the CD-ROM drive.

**SYMPTOM 8-27**    **You receive a "no disc loaded" error with an audio CD in the drive**
This driver-related problem can occur under Windows 9$x$/Me and is typically caused when the MCI CD audio driver is not installed (this problem does not seem to occur under Windows XP). You'll need to verify that the CD audio device driver is enabled under Windows 9$x$/Me:

1.  Open the Control Panel and double-click the Multimedia icon.
2.  On the Advanced or Devices tab, double-click Media Control Devices.
3.  Double-click CD Audio Device (Media Control).
4.  Verify that the Use This Media Control Device entry is selected (Figure 8-25).

If the driver is enabled and you still receive the error message, try removing and reinstalling the device. To accomplish this, click Remove on the General tab in your CD Audio Device (Media Control) properties and then follow these steps:

1.  Open the Control Panel and double-click the Add New Hardware icon.
2.  Click Next, click No, and then click Next.
3.  In the Hardware Types box, click Sound, Video, and Game Controllers, and then click Next.
4.  In the Manufacturers box, click Microsoft MCI.
5.  In the Models box, click CD Audio Device (Media Control).
6.  Click Next, click Finish, and then restart your computer.

**FIGURE 8-25** Enabling the CD Audio device under Windows 98/SE

**SYMPTOM 8-28** **Two CD-ROM drive letters appear in My Computer under Windows**
When you use My Computer or Windows Explorer, two CD-ROM drives may be displayed (even though you have only one CD-ROM drive in your computer). When you try to access either CD-ROM drive, your computer may lock up. This trouble can occur if you have both the real-mode CD-ROM device drivers *and* the Windows 9*x*/Me CD-ROM device drivers installed. This trouble is increasingly rare today because late-model Windows platforms are aggressively abandoning real-mode support. If you should encounter this problem, use the System Configuration Editor (sysedit.exe) to disable the real-mode CD-ROM device drivers:

1. Click Start, click Run, type **sysedit** in the Open box, and then click OK.
2. Select the AUTOEXEC.BAT file, locate the line that loads the real-mode CD-ROM device drivers, and then type **rem** followed by a space at the beginning of the line. For example:

   ```
   rem c:\windows\command\mscdex.exe /d:mscd001
   ```
3. Select the CONFIG.SYS file, locate the line that loads the real-mode CD-ROM device drivers, and then type **rem** followed by a space at the beginning of the line. For example:

   ```
   rem device=c:\cdrom\cdrom.sys /d:mscd001
   ```
4. On the File menu, click Exit.
5. Click Yes when you're prompted to save the CONFIG.SYS and AUTOEXEC.BAT files.
6. Restart your computer.

**SYMPTOM 8-29** **The CD-ROM refuses to run automatically under Windows 9*x*/Me when a disc is inserted** This may occur even when the Auto Insert Notification feature is enabled. In most cases, the trouble is caused by an incorrect value in the registry. To resolve this problem, use Registry Editor to locate the following key:

HKEY_CURRENT_USER\Software\Microsoft\Windows\CurrentVersion\Policies\
Explorer\NoDriveTypeAutoRun

Then modify the value for the NoDriveTypeAutoRun key to **0000 95 00 00 00** (or **0x95** in REGEDT32.EXE). After you make this change, quit the Registry Editor and restart your computer.

**SYMPTOM 8-30**  **A CD-ROM icon appears for a hard drive under Windows 95 OSR2 or Windows 98**  This is an older issue that does not appear under Windows Me/XP. When you attempt to review your drives through My Computer, your hard disk icon may appear as a CD-ROM icon. If you double-click the CD-ROM icon in My Computer, you may receive an error message such as: "Cannot find autorun.exe." This problem can occur if the AUTORUN.INF file has been located in the root folder of your hard disk. To correct the problem, rename the AUTORUN.INF file to AUTORUN.OLD:

1. Click Start, point to Find, and then click Files or Folders.
2. In the Named box, type **autorun.inf** and then click Find Now.
3. Right-click AUTORUN.INF in the list of found files, and then click Properties.
4. Click the Read-Only checkbox to clear it, and then click OK.
5. Right-click AUTORUN.INF in the list of found files, and then click Rename.
6. Type **autorun.old** and then press ENTER.
7. Restart your computer.

**SYMPTOM 8-31**  **You see a message such as: "CD-ROM can run, but results may not be as expected"**  This simply means that Windows 9*x*/Me is using real-mode drivers—the drive is running in MS-DOS Compatibility Mode. If protected-mode drivers are available for the CD-ROM drive, you should use those instead. You may download and install protected-mode drivers from the CD-ROM manufacturer's Web site.

**SYMPTOM 8-32**  **The CD-ROM works fine in DOS or Windows 3.1*x*, but sound or video appears choppy under Windows 9*x*/Me/XP**  There are several factors that can affect CD-ROM performance under Windows. Windows performance (and stability) is severely degraded by real-mode drivers, so start by removing or disabling any real-mode drivers. Try installing the protected-mode drivers for your CD-ROM drive instead. Real-mode applications that are run under Windows 9*x*/Me/XP can cripple a system's performance. Try exiting any DOS or Windows 3.1*x* applications that may be running on the Windows 9*x*/Me/XP desktop. Also exit unneeded Windows applications since additional applications take a toll on processing power. Finally, try rebooting the system to ensure that Windows 9*x*/Me/XP has the maximum amount of resources available before running your CD-ROM application.

**SYMPTOM 8-33**  **You can't read CD-I discs in Windows 95 with an ATAPI IDE CD-ROM drive**  This problem is not present in later versions of Windows, but is sometimes encounterd with older machines. The built-in ATAPI driver in Windows 95 cannot read raw data in 32-bit disk access mode. Note that such symptoms can also happen to any ATAPI/IDE-compatible CD-ROM as long as it is using the built-in ATAPI driver in Windows 95. You should update the CD-ROM's ATAPI driver to a current manufacturer-specific version, or you should update your version of Windows. As another alternative, you can use the following procedure:

1. Disable the 32-bit disk access feature of Windows 95.
2. On the Windows 95 desktop, click Start and choose Settings | Control Panel.
3. Click the System icon and select the Performance option.
4. Choose File System and select the Troubleshooting option.
5. At the Troubleshooting dialog, click on Disable All 32-Bit Disk Access.
6. Edit AUTOEXEC.BAT and append the following line (where <path> is the path name of your Windows 95 software):

```
C:\<path>\COMMAND\MSCDEX.EXE /D:MSCD000
```

**SYMPTOM 8-34** **After upgrading to Windows 98 or later, you notice multiple CD-ROM letters** For example, you may see up to four CD-ROM drives displayed in My Computer or Windows Explorer, even though you have only *one* CD-ROM drive in the computer. This is a software problem that has been known to occur with older NEC CD-ROM drives if you've installed the NEC Single CD tool software in your previous version of Windows. To correct the problem, simply reinstall the NEC Single CD tool under Windows 98/Me/XP using the disk included with your NEC CD-ROM drive (you may need to uninstall the software first). You may also wish to download and install the latest versions of that software (and the CD-ROM drivers) from the manufacturer.

**SYMPTOM 8-35** **The PC halts when copying large amounts of data from a CD-ROM drive** This is an older problem that sometimes occurred when copying a large set of files from a CD-ROM drive to a local hard disk under Windows 9*x*/Me (this does not appear to be a problem under Windows XP), the computer may hang at some point—forcing you to reboot and regain control of the system. The trouble is often related to caching. The protected-mode Windows CD-ROM file system includes a read-ahead feature designed to provide smoother video playback with faster and more efficient data streaming. Unfortunately, the read-ahead feature can cause the CD-ROM drive controller to be driven faster than it was intended to be, and doing this can lock up the system. Try the following steps to fix the trouble:

1. Click the Start button, then click Settings | Control Panel.
2. Double-click the System icon.
3. On the Performance tab, click File System.
4. Click the CD-ROM tab (as in Figure 8-20).
5. In the Optimize Access Pattern For box, click the setting that matches the CD-ROM drive you are using. Click OK, then restart the computer when prompted.

If this doesn't solve the problem, repeat the steps, but in the Optimize Access Pattern For box, click No Read Ahead. Click OK, then restart the computer when prompted.

**SYMPTOM 8-36** **You notice that a CD-ROM drive is mis-detected as a different make or model** For example, the drive returns "Matshita" (instead of "Matsushita") as the device description when it's enumerated by Windows. This occurs under older versions of Windows such as Windows 95, Windows 95 OSR2, and early Windows 98, but is usually traced to an error in the drive's firmware. You'll need to check with the drive manufacturer for a firmware upgrade, driver fix, or other corrective options. You may also choose to replace the CD-ROM drive to a later model.

**SYMPTOM 8-37**    **The SCSI CD-ROM drive refuses to work when connected to an Adaptec SCSI interface**    Other SCSI drives are working fine in this situation. This is a common type of problem among SCSI adapters, particularly with Adaptec boards because of their great popularity. In most cases, the Adaptec drivers are the wrong version for your SCSI host adapter (or they're corrupted). Try turning off Sync Negotiations on the Adaptec SCSI interface and rebooting the system. Your SCSI drivers may also be buggy or outdated. Check with Adaptec technical support (www.adaptec.com) to determine if there are later drivers that you should use instead. You may need to uninstall the current drivers and reinstall the new host adapter drivers from scratch.

**SYMPTOM 8-38**    **The LCD on your CD-ROM displays an error code**    Even without knowing the particular meaning of *every* possible error message, you can be assured that most CD-based error messages can be traced to the following causes (in order of ease of fixes):

- **Bad caddy (or disc insertion)**    The CD caddy is damaged or inserted incorrectly. The CD may also be inserted into the caddy improperly. With a motorized tray, the CD may be inserted improperly.

- **Bad mounting**    The drive is mounted improperly, or mounting screws are shorting out the drive's electronics.

- **Bad power**    Check the +12 and +5 volts powering the CD-ROM drive. Low power may require a new or larger supply. Remove any Y-splitter that may be tapping the drive's power.

- **Bad drive**    Internal diagnostics have detected a fault in the CD-ROM drive. Try replacing the drive.

- **Bad drive controller**    Drive diagnostics have detected a fault in the drive controller. Try replacing the drive controller or SCSI adapter (whichever interface you're using).

**SYMPTOM 8-39**    **When a SCSI CD-ROM drive is connected to a SCSI adapter, the system hangs when the SCSI BIOS loads**    In most cases, the CD-ROM drive supports plug-and-play, but the SCSI controller's BIOS does not. Disable the SCSI BIOS through a jumper on the controller (or remove the SCSI BIOS chip entirely) and use a SCSI driver in CONFIG.SYS instead. You may need to download a low-level SCSI driver from the adapter manufacturer. If there are other SCSI drives on the adapter that rely on the SCSI BIOS (for example, SCSI hard drives), it may not be possible to disable the SCSI BIOS. In that case, a separate SCSI controller may be needed.

**SYMPTOM 8-40**    **The front panel controls of your SCSI CD-ROM drive do not appear to work under Windows 9x/Me**    Those same controls appear to work fine in DOS. Windows 9x/Me uses SCSI commands to poll removable media devices every two seconds in order to see if there has been a change in status. Since SCSI commands to the CD-ROM generally have higher priority than front panel controls, the front panel controls may appear to be disabled under Windows. Try pressing the front panel controls repeatedly. You may be able to correct this by disabling the CD-ROM polling under Windows. This problem does not seem to appear under Windows XP.

**SYMPTOM 8-41**    **You see the following message when attempting to list a directory: Not ready reading drive [drive letter]:**    There is a communication problem between the SCSI host controller and the CD-ROM, CD-R, or CD-RW drive caused by an undesirable SCSI ID for the drive. Your first step should be to power-down the computer and check that the drive is connected properly to the SCSI host controller. Also make sure that the CD is inserted into the drive with the right side facing up. If problems continue, change the drive's switch settings to select a new SCSI device number. Reboot the computer and try the directory listing again. If the error message persists, you might need to try several different SCSI device ID numbers. You may also upgrade the SCSI controller with a PnP adapter designed for the PCI bus.

**SYMPTOM 8-42**    **You see the following message during initialization: No SCSI host adapter(s) detected**    Your system cannot find the SCSI host controller board. This problem often occurred with older "legacy" devices, and isn't often seen on today's PnP systems. The problem may be due to faulty I/O, IRQ, or DMA settings on the host controller itself or to a memory conflict in hardware or software. Begin your investigation by powering down the computer and checking the host controller's resource settings. Use your documentation for the host controller and carefully verify each jumper or dip switch setting. A missing or improperly configured jumper can render the controller inoperative. Reset the controller board if necessary, then reboot the computer.

If the problem persists (or if you cannot find faulty controller settings), you may be encountering trouble due to memory conflicts. Possible sources of conflict exist in the use of memory shadowing or disk caching, which is enabled through your system CMOS Setup program. Access your CMOS setup and set all Disk Caching, BIOS Shadow, Shadow RAM, Video BIOS Shadow, or any Shadow options to the DISABLE condition. Reboot the computer and try the CD-ROM, CD-R, or CD-RW drive again.

Conflicts can also occur in various computer peripherals (your video card, modem card, scanner card, and so on). If your SCSI host adapter address range overlaps the address(es) of any other board, your system can encounter problems. Check the address settings of each installed peripheral, move that peripheral's address out of range of the SCSI controller, and modify the address (if necessary) in the peripheral's setup or configuration program. As a check, you may wish to simply remove the peripheral to see if the problem goes away. Once you make a change, reboot the computer and try the drive again. Finally, if the system simply refuses to acknowledge the SCSI controller, you may wish to try replacing the SCSI host controller with a PnP-compliant model.

**SYMPTOM 8-43**    **SmartDrive is not caching the CD-ROM properly in DOS**    Here's an older issue that sometimes creeps up on vintage PCs running DOS or Windows 3.1x, and the trick is usually to upgrade SmartDrive to the last available version under DOS 6.22. The version of SmartDrive supplied with DOS 6.2x provides three forms of caching, although older forms of SmartDrive (such as the ones distributed with Windows 3.1, DOS 6.0 and 6.1) will *not* adequately cache CD-ROM drives. The BUFFERS statement also does *not* help caching. So if you are looking to SmartDrive for a CD-ROM cache, you should be using the version distributed with DOS 6.2x. You should also set **BUFFERS=10,0** in the CONFIG.SYS file, and the SmartDrive command line should come *after* MSCDEX. When using SmartDrive, you can change the buffers setting in the MSCDEX command line (/**M**) to 0—this allows you to save 2KB per buffer.

SmartDrive is *not* used by Windows 9x/Me/XP, which employ their own CD caching schemes. You should remove SmartDrive when using any version of Windows other than 3.1x.

**SYMPTOM 8-44**    **After installing the CD-ROM drivers, system reports significantly less available RAM**    This is usually a very rare caching issue with CD-ROM driver software, and you may need to adjust the CD-ROM driver software accordingly. For example, this type of problem has been documented with Teac CD-ROM drives and CORELCDX.COM software (but should not occur when using standard real-mode or generic CD support drivers). Try booting with CD support from a Windows 98/Me startup diskette and see if the problem disappears—if so, you know it's a driver-related problem.

If the software offers a command line switch to change the amount of XMS allocated, reduce the number to 512 or 256. Check with tech support for your particular drive for the exact command line switch settings.

**SYMPTOM 8-45**    **The CD-ROM drivers will not install properly on a drive using compression software**    This is usually because you booted from a floppy disk and attempted to install real-mode drivers *without* loading the compression software *first*. Before doing anything else, check the loading order—allow your system to boot from the hard drive *before* installing the CD-ROM drivers. This allows the compression software to load and assign all drive letters. As an alternative, boot from a compression-aware floppy disk, which you can make. If you *must* boot the system from a floppy disk, make sure the disk is configured to be fully compatible with the compression software being used.

Compression software is virtually unused today. If you encounter an older system with compression software (e.g., DriveSpace 3), it may be worth considering a hard drive upgrade (and controller upgrade if necessary) to eliminate compression from the system.

**SYMPTOM 8-46**    **You cannot access the CD-ROM drive letter under DOS**    The drive is probably available and working normally under Windows 9*x*/Me/XP, but you may see an error message such as "Invalid drive specification" when attempting to use the drive under DOS (e.g., when booting from diskette). Obviously, the drive is working fine, so this is a problem with the real-mode CD-ROM drivers—chances are that the low-level driver or MSCDEX has not loaded. Check your CONFIG.SYS file and verify that the CD drive's low-level driver is listed properly. Then check the AUTOEXEC.BAT file for the MSCDEX command line. Be sure to check each command line switch. For example, make sure that the label used in the **/D** switch is the same for both the low-level driver and MSCDEX. If the label is not the same, MSCDEX will not load. If you are using MS-DOS 5.0, be sure the SETVER utility is loaded. You could also try updating MSCEDX to v2.30 or later.

If you're booting from diskette, simply use a Windows 98/Me/XP startup disk that provides generic real-mode CD support files—this can avoid the need to edit CONFIG.SYS and AUTOEXEC.BAT files.

**SYMPTOM 8-47**    **You see an error when trying to load the low-level CD-ROM driver**
If the drive is working properly under Linux or Windows, the hardware is fine and it's likely to be a driver problem. Check that you are using the proper low-level device driver for your CD-ROM drive. If you're swapping the drive with a new make and model, you'll almost certainly need to install a new real-mode driver. If the driver fails to load with original hardware, the drive's jumper settings may not match those in the driver's command line switches.

If the drive isn't working at all, verify the drive's hardware installation. Check power and check the signal cable running between the drive and adapter board. If the cable is crimped or scuffed, try replacing the cable. Next, try replacing the controller (e.g., try a different ATAPI IDE controller channel). If problems persist, try replacing the CD drive mechanism itself.

**SYMPTOM 8-48**    **You see a "Wrong DOS version" error message when attempting to load MSCDEX**    This is a problem that plagues older systems that are running MS-DOS 4, 5, or 6 with a version of MSCDEX that does not support it. The solution is to change to the correct version of MSCDEX. The version compatibility for MSCDEX is shown listed here:

- v1.01 14,913 bytes (No ISO9660 support—High Sierra support only)
- v2.00 18,307 bytes (High Sierra and ISO9660 support for DOS 3.1-3.3)

- v2.10 19,943 bytes (DOS 3.1-3.3 and 4.0—DOS 5.x support provided with SETVER)
- v2.20 25,413 bytes (same as above with Win 3.x support—changes in audio support)
- v2.21 25,431 bytes (DOS 3.1-5.0 support with enhanced control under Win 3.1)
- v2.22 25,377 bytes (DOS 3.1-6.0 and higher with Win 3.1 support)
- v2.23 25,361 bytes (DOS 3.1-6.2 and Win 3.1 support—supplied with MSDOS 6.2)

Upgrading the operating system to some version of Windows or Linux (if possible) should avoid the need for real-mode drivers and MSCDEX.

When using MS-DOS 5.x to 6.1, you will need to add the SETVER utility to CONFIG.SYS in order to use MSCDEX v2.10 or v2.20 properly (**device = c:\dos\setver.exe**). SETVER is used to tell programs that they are running under a different version of DOS than DOS 5.0. This is important since MSCDEX (v2.10 and v2.20) refuses to work with DOS versions higher than 4.0. SETVER is used to fool MSCDEX into working with higher versions of DOS. In some versions of DOS 5.0 (such as Compaq DOS 5.0), you will need to add an entry to SETVER for MSCDEX (that is, SETVER MSCDEX.EXE 4.00). This entry modifies SETVER without changing the file size or date.

**SYMPTOM 8-49**   **You're having trouble setting up more than one CD-ROM drive under DOS**   For example, Windows recognizes both of your ATAPI IDE drives normally, but you can't seem to get both drives running properly under DOS. Obviously, the drive hardware is fine if both drives are working under Windows, so chances are that you've got a problem with your low-level DOS drivers. Remember that you'll need a separate low-level driver for each drive (even if the drives are identical), so check the CONFIG.SYS file and make any necessary additions. Make sure that the command line switches for each driver match the hardware settings of the corresponding drive. Finally, check your copy of MSCDEX. You need only one copy of MSCDEX in AUTOEXEC.BAT, but the **/D:** switch must appear twice—once for *each* drive ID.

# CD-R SYMPTOMS

CD recorders present some special problems for the typical PC. Many high-performance CD-R units use the SCSI interface in order to handle more consistent data transfer from the system to the drive. Installing a CD-R may require the addition (and expense) of a SCSI host adapter and associated driver software. CD recording demands a substantial commitment of hard drive space—perhaps as much as 1GB—in order to create an *image file* for recording (an "image file" basically converts the data to be recorded into the "pits" and "lands" that must be encoded to the blank disc). So if you're tight on drive space, you may also need another hard drive to support the CD-R. Finally, CD-Rs require a constant and uninterrupted flow of data during the recording process. If the CD-R data buffer empties, the recording process will halt, and your blank CD will be ruined (unless the drive employs BurnProof technology). This means you'll need fast hard drives and a high-performance interface (often a minimum of UDMA/66 or faster). This part of the chapter explains some of the problems associated with using a CD-R and illustrates a series of troubleshooting symptoms and solutions.

## CD Recording Issues

Writing data to a recordable CD is a complex process that demands a great deal from your PC's hardware and software. Most of this complexity is hidden by the power of the CD authoring program, but there are a number of important factors that you should be aware of that can influence the success of CD recording.

**File Sizes**     The sheer *amount* of data being written to the CD is less important than the individual file sizes—the recorder may have trouble locating and opening small files quickly enough to send them smoothly to the CD recorder, where fewer large files would typically record without problems. If you have trouble writing lots of small files on the fly you might need to compile an image file before recording.

**System Interruptions**     Any interruption in the flow of data is fatal to CD recording, so make sure that any CONFIG.SYS and AUTOEXEC.BAT files do not load any TSR utilities that may periodically interrupt the computer's drive operations. Unneeded background applications should also be shut down. Utilities like screen savers, calendar alarms, or reminders, as well as incoming faxes are just a few "features" that can interrupt disc writing. If the PC is part of a network, you should temporarily disable network sharing (if possible) so that no one tries to access local files while you're trying to write the CD.

**The Hard Disk**     The hard drive is a critical component of the CD-R system because you must transfer data from the HDD to the CD-R at a rate adequate to keep the recorder's buffer filled. There are three major issues involving your hard drive: speed, file fragmentation, and thermal calibration.

- **Speed**     In order to write a virtual data to a compact disc, the hard disk from which you are writing must have a transfer rate fast enough to keep the CD-R drive buffer full. This usually means an average hard disk access time of 15mS or less. It would also help to use a high-performance drive interface such as Ultra-DMA/100, Ultra-DMA/133, or a relatively recent SCSI interface such as SCSI-3.

- **Fragmentation**     This issue is also related to speed. Searching all over a very fragmented hard disk for files (even a pre-processed image file can be fragmented) can impair the performance of your drive operations. In many cases, a badly fragmented hard drive cannot support CD-R operations. Be sure to defragment your hard drive before writing "on the fly" or creating an image file.

- **Thermal calibration**     All hard disks periodically perform an automatic thermal calibration to ensure proper performance. Calibration interrupts hard disk operations for as much as 1.5 seconds. Some hard disks "force" a calibration at fixed intervals (even if the disk is in use), causing interruptions that are fatal to CD writing. This problem is worse when the image file is large and the writing process takes longer. If you can select a new hard drive to support CD-R operations, choose a drive with "intelligent" thermal calibration (it postpones recalibration until the drive is idle).

**CD Recorder Speed**     Typical CD recorders are capable of writing at 24 times the standard writing/playback speed of 150KB/s (and faster). Recording speed is simply a matter of how fast the bits are inscribed by the laser on the disc surface. It has nothing to do with how fast you read them back or how much data you can fit on the disc. However, higher recording speeds can accomplish a writing process in a shorter period of time. Faster recording speeds are certainly a time saver, but they also mean that larger recording buffers are required (and those buffers empty much faster). As a consequence, faster recorders will demand a faster hard drive and interface to support data transfer. In most cases, "buffer underrun" type problems can often be corrected by slowing down the recording process rather than by upgrading the drive system.

When you write a real ISO image file from hard disk to CD, speed is rarely a problem because the image is already compiled into one gigantic file. The files and structures are already in order and divided into CD-ROM sectors, so it is necessary only to stream data off the hard drive to the CD recorder. When you write from a *virtual* image ("on the fly"), things get trickier because a virtual image is little more than a list of files. The CD authoring program must consult the virtual image database to find out where each file should go in the image and where each file actually is stored on the hard disk. The authoring software must then open the file and divide it into CD-ROM sectors—all while sending data to the CD recorder in a smooth, continuous stream. Locating and opening each file is often the more time-consuming part of the recording process (which is why "on-the-fly" writing is more difficult when you have many small files).

**CD Recorder Buffer**   All CD recorders have a small amount of on-board buffer memory. The CD recorder's buffer helps to ensure that there is always data ready to be written because extra data is stored as it arrives from the computer. The size of the buffer is critical to trouble-free writing—a slow-down or interruption in the transfer of data from the computer will not interrupt writing so long as the buffer is not completely emptied. The larger the buffer, the greater safety margin you have in case of interruptions. For example, the recent Plextor 24/10/40 CD-RW drive provides a respectable 4MB buffer. If your CD recorder has a very small buffer and your hard disk is slow, you may find it difficult (or impossible) to write virtual images on the fly to CD. When this occurs, you can make a real ISO image file on the hard disk and record to CD from that, use a faster hard disk sub-system, or upgrade your CD recorder's buffer (if possible).

## Typical Compatibility Problems
Even when CDs record perfectly, it is not always possible to read them correctly in other drives. The following notes highlight three common compatibility issues.

**Problems Reading Recordable CDs**   Recordable CDs frequently cannot be read in older CD-ROM drives (though current CD-ROM drives are completely compatible reading CD-Rs and CD-RWs). If the CD can be read when used on the CD-R but *not* on an existing CD-ROM drive, check the disc recording utility to make sure that the session containing the data you just wrote is *closed*—CD-ROM drives cannot read data from a session that is not closed. If your recorded disc is ejected, you receive an error message, or if you have any random problems accessing files from the recorded disc, the problem may be that your CD-ROM drive is not properly designed to read recorded CDs. Try the disc on another CD-ROM drive or upgrade the CD-ROM drive itself.

40X and later CD-ROM drives should be able to read CD-Rs and CD-RWs with no difficulty, though you may need to check the drive's specifications to ensure that it supports 80 minute media.

**Problems Reading Multisession CDs**   If you can see only data recorded in the first session on the CD—but not in subsequent sessions—it may be that the disc was recorded in CD-ROM (Mode 1) format, while your multisession CD-ROM drive recognizes only CD-ROM XA (Mode 2) multisession CDs. If this happens, you may need to re-record the disc in the correct mode. Of course, your CD-ROM drive must support multisession operation in the first place. If you can see only data recorded in the last session, you may have forgotten to link your new data with data previously recorded on the CD. Refer to the instructions for your CD recorder and recording software and review the suggested steps required to create a multisession CD.

**CD-ROM Drive Incompatibility with Recordable CDs**   It may happen that you can write a CD without trouble and can read it properly on your CD-R—but when you put the disc in a standard CD-ROM drive, the disc is ejected. You may also see error messages such as "No CD-ROM" or "Drive not ready," or you have random problems accessing some files or directories. You may also find that the problems disappear when reading the CD on a different CD-ROM drive. Although you may suspect the problems stem from the original CD-ROM drive, they may actually be due to incompatibility between some CD-ROM drives (especially older ones) and recorded CDs. Some CD-ROM drive lasers are not calibrated to read recordable CDs (often the surface is different from that of factory-pressed CDs). If your CD-ROM drive reads mass-produced (silver) CDs but not recordable CDs, check with the CD-ROM drive manufacturer to determine whether this is the problem. In some cases, a drive upgrade may be available that will resolve the problem.

The combination of blank disc's brand and CD recorder can also make a difference. Use blank CD media that has been recommended by the CD-R manufacturer.

## Typical Multisession CD Issues

You may encounter older CD-ROM drives that have trouble reading multisession CDs. Multisession discs are recorded according to the Orange Book (Part II) standard, which states that sessions can be written in *either* the CD-ROM or CD-ROM XA format. A fully compliant multisession CD-ROM drive should always be able to access at the last session on a disc *regardless* of its format.

Unfortunately, there have been misunderstandings and misinterpretations of the Orange Book standard, but to understand the problems, you need to know a bit of history. Multisession recording was first used by Kodak for their Photo CD initiative. Now, one roll of film does *not* fill up a Photo CD disc, so when you take your disc and a new roll of film for new Photo CD processing, the new photos are added in a "new session." This new session is linked to previous sessions so that you can see *all* the photos on the disc—no matter how many sessions they are recorded in.

Kodak chose the CD-ROM XA standard for its Photo CD disc format for reasons that had *nothing* to do with the Orange Book standard. But since Photo CD was the first reason that CD-ROM drive manufacturers had to create multisession drives, many assumed that the Kodak approach to multisession (the CD-ROM XA) was the *only* way. They accordingly wrote software drivers that assume that a multisession disc must also be XA. When one of these drivers sees a disc that is not XA, it assumes that the disc is also *not* multisession, and it tells the CD-ROM drive to read only the first session on the disc. The result is that a multisession disc is read as if it were a single-session disc, and you see only the data in the first session.

CD-ROM drive manufacturers have generally resolved this glitch in virtually all but the very oldest drives and drivers (e.g., 8X CD-ROM and later drives), but if you record a multisession disc in CD-ROM format you may find that some older drives—even if specified as a "multisession" drive—may not read beyond the first session on the disc. If you need to share multisession discs with others, you should test to see which format their CD-ROM drives can handle. To be on the safe side, write your disc in the CD-ROM XA format. A more permanent fix is to upgrade the older CD-ROM to a model that is fully multisession-compliant.

You cannot mix formats on the same disc—a multisession disc containing both CD-ROM and CD-ROM XA sessions would be unreadable on most drives.

## Buffer Underruns

CD writing is a real-time process that must run constantly at the selected recording speed *without interruptions*. Most of the time, your computer will pass data to the CD-R faster than it is needed. This keeps the CD-R's buffer constantly filled with a reserve of data waiting to be written, so small slowdowns or interruptions in the flow of data from the computer will not interrupt the writing process. The CD-R's internal buffer stores this extra data as it arrives to help maintain a steady flow of data to the writing laser.

The size of the buffer is critical to trouble-free writing. Remember that a slowdown or interruption in the transfer of data from the computer will not stop a writing cycle so long as the buffer is not *completely* emptied. The larger the buffer, the more safety margin you have in case of interruptions. A *buffer underrun* error means that for some reason the flow of data from hard disk to CD-R was interrupted long enough for the CD recorder's buffer to be emptied, and writing was halted. If this occurs during an actual write operation (rather than a pre-writing test), your recordable disc may be ruined. This checklist covers many of the typical issues that may trigger a buffer underrun:

- **"Dumb" thermal recalibration**    Disable thermal recalibration on the hard drive before writing or allow one hour or so for the system temperature to stabilize before writing.

- **Excessive file fragmentation**    Defragment the hard drive with Defrag before "burning" a CD.

- **Insufficient free space**    The CD-R will almost certainly require some amount of "temporary" workspace on the hard drive. If there is insufficient free space on the hard drive, you may need to free additional space by offloading unneeded files or upgrading the drive itself.

- **Too many small files**    When recording on the fly, many small files may present too much of a load on your data transfer system, so try making an ISO "image file" first.

- **Damaged files**    Files that are damaged or corrupted will often cause errors that will interrupt the flow of data. Run ScanDisk and Defrag to locate any possible file system problems before recording.

- **Recording files in use**    Make sure that no files to be recorded are currently in use by any application. For example, attempting to copy a saved Word document that is currently open within Word may cause writing problems.

- **Slow hard drives**    Older hard drives may not support data transfer speeds high enough to keep the CD-R buffer filled. If you use slow hard drives, make an ISO "image file" first rather than writing "on the fly." Otherwise, upgrade the drive system for better performance.

- **Burst data transfers**    Source devices that operate in *burst* data transfer modes may have difficulty keeping the CD-R buffer filled. Try disabling the "burst" mode for your hard drive through the CMOS Setup. While doing this may slow the overall data transfer, it may also "even out" the flow of data, making it easier to keep the recorder's buffer filled.

- **CD-R controller configuration**    Verify that the IDE or SCSI controller operating the CD-R is configured for optimum performance (for example, use bus master drivers for UDMA controllers).

- **Sync problems**    Certain combinations of drives and controllers may not synchronize data properly. Check that you're using the recommended hardware devices for proper CD-R operation.

- **Outdated device drivers**    Verify that you're using the latest device drivers for the CD-R, drive controller, and other related devices in the system.

- **Slow computer speed**    Systems older then 486 platforms may simply be too old to support the data transfer needs of a CD-R. Verify that your system meets the minimum system requirements for your particular CD-R model.

- **CD-R quality**    Be sure to use good quality CD-R discs that are recommended by the CD-R manufacturer. Dirty, old, or scratched discs may not function.

- **Memory-resident software issues**    CD-R systems may encounter buffer underrun problems when certain types of software are at work on your system. These include anti-virus utilities, screen savers, system agents, task schedulers, TSR (Terminate and Stay Resident) utilities, network connections, system sounds, animated icons or utilities, and any program that may activate on its own. Make sure to stop or disable any unnecessary software or services running on the PC before writing a disc.

■ **Disable Auto Insert Notification**    If you have more than 16MB of RAM, disable Auto Insert Notification for the CD drives. This stops regular drive polling and frees a bit of processor time.

■ **Change the system's role**    If you have more than 16MB of RAM, change the hard drive's Typical Role to Network Server. This alters the way Windows caches the drive system to emphasize file handling performance.

**Avoiding Buffer Underruns**    Although current PCs generally provide the speed and drive performance that are vital for CD recording, modern high-speed drives can empty a buffer in moments. This means buffer underruns continue to be a serious issue for technicians and end-users alike. The following tips may help you avoid buffer underruns:

■ Always set audio discs to write at 1X. You may select a slower writing speed for data discs (e.g., select 12X rather than 24X).

■ Whatever writing speed you choose, verify that the media is certified for your desired speed. Writing at 24X on a blank CD-R that's only rated for 10X will cause problems.

■ Change the UDMA transfer rate for the drive controller card being used (that is, select the fastest data transfer rate available for your system and drives). Windows XP handles this in the drive controller's Properties dialog (see Figure 8-21 earlier).

■ Defragment your hard drives at least once a week to prevent files from being scattered across the hard drive.

■ Disable or remove all software in the computer *except* the operating system, the recording software, and the drivers for your source devices and CD-R.

■ Copying audio requires a source CD-ROM drive that supports "digital audio extraction" (or DAE). Fortunately, most current CD-ROM/R/RW drives support DAE.

■ Do not record across a network—copy the desired files to your local hard drive first.

■ Do not try to copy empty directories, zero byte files, or files that may be in use by the system at the time.

■ For best results use SCSI-2 (or faster) source devices (preferably SCSI-3). Fast Ultra-DMA devices (such as Ultra-DMA/100/133) will also provide good results.

■ In any operating system, always use the newest drivers from your SCSI controller card's manufacturer.

■ Log out of any networks if possible (including Windows for Workgroups and/or Microsoft Network).

■ Make sure your hard drive does Smart Thermal Recalibration—it won't recalibrate if the drive is being used.

■ Make sure your SCSI controller card is *fully* ASPI-compliant.

■ More than 10,000 very small files should be written to an .ISO image first or recorded at 1X if possible in order to ease data transfer demands.

■ The temporary directory should always have space free for at least twice the size of the largest file you are recording.

■ Try a different hard disk and/or high-quality gold recordable disc.

■ If there is any trouble writing on the fly, write an .ISO image to the hard disk first (if you have enough hard drive space).

## Media Matters

CD-R drives can be very picky in their support of recordable media types, and the media must be certified for your intended recording speed. For example, you can often encounter recording problems when using "off brand" non-certified media to perform high-speed recording. Check the documentation that accompanies the CD-R drive and verify that you're using approved "high-speed" media. Today, most name-brand CD-R media (e.g., Maxell or Verbatim) should work properly, but it's still worth double-checking to make sure—especially if you're having recording problems.

## Enable BurnProof Support

As you saw earlier, BurnProof is a technology that allows writing laser power to be controlled by the drive during a write operation. If the drive's buffer empties, the drive will shut down the laser in order to prevent ruining the disc. As new data reaches the recorder's buffer, the laser will reactivate and writing will continue. If your drive and recording software support BurnProof technology, you can eliminate a lot of writing errors by enabling BurnProof support.

## Pops and Clicks

One of the most popular uses for CD-R/RW drives involves audio recording (e.g., creating a "mix" of your favorite music tracks to CD). Unfortunately, many users encounter audio problems when recording CD audio. For example, when copying audio tracks from one CD to another, the resulting audio includes clicks, pops, hisses, and so on—you may also encounter frequent buffer underrun errors, but reducing the write speed of the CD drive has little (if any) effect on the resulting audio quality. The trouble is often caused by poor audio extraction. This occurs because the source drive that is taking the audio track (e.g., a CD-ROM drive) intensifies the many insignificant audio errors that occur during normal playback. While listeners cannot hear these errors, they can become audible if you're using a source drive that is not capable of synchronizing the source and the destination devices properly. There are two ways to manage audio recording problems.

One popular workaround is to pre-record the audio tracks to the hard drive. Rather than attempting to write audio tracks on the fly, use the CD-R/RW drive (which typically have good digital audio extraction capabilities) to copy the desired tracks to WAV files on the hard drive, then use the WAV files as source files to burn the CD as a separate step. For example, Easy CD Creator lets you drag a track into your audio CD layout. After the track is added to a layout, highlight the track, click Track on the toolbar, and then choose Pre-record to WAV. Then you just name the track and choose a destination folder on your hard drive. Repeat this process for each track. Once a track is recorded, you can listen to the WAV file on your hard drive to verify that it is faithful to the original (if not, there's an issue with the drive you're extracting from). When all desired tracks have been converted to WAV, start a new CD layout. Find the drive and directory where you saved the WAV files, then drag them into the audio CD layout. When all of the tracks are in the layout, write the CD normally.

If you work with audio frequently, and the thought of pre-recording every track to the hard drive makes you shudder, it may be worth considering an upgrade to a fast source drive that's adept at digital audio extraction (e.g., a 50X or faster CD-ROM drive). Of course, if there's only room in the system for one CD drive, you're stuck with the pre-recording approach.

## General Symptoms

CD recorders are subject to a large number of potential errors during operation. Many typical recording errors are listed in the following set of symptoms. In most cases, the error is not terribly complex and can be corrected in just a few minutes once the nature of the problem is understood. Keep in mind that the actual error message is dependent on the CD recorder software in use, so your actual error messages may vary just a bit.

For more general CD drive-related issues, refer to the CD-ROM troubleshooting information earlier in this chapter.

**SYMPTOM 8-50**    **You receive an "Absorption control error <xxx>" message**    This error generally means that there is a slight problem writing to a recordable disc—perhaps caused by a smear (e.g., a fingerprint) or speck of dust. It does not *necessarily* mean that your data has not been correctly recorded. A sector address is usually given so that you can (if you wish) verify the data in and around that sector. When writing is completed, try cleaning the disc (on the non-label side) gently with a lint-free cloth. If the error occurs again, try a new disc, or try cleaning the drive mechanism.

**SYMPTOM 8-51**    **You receive an "Application code error" message**    This error typically occurs when you try to write Kodak recordable CDs (Photo CDs) on non-Kodak CD recorders. These discs have a protection bit that is recognized only by the Kodak CD-R—all other recorders will not record these discs. In this case, you'll need to use "standard" blank CDs (or use a recorder that is certified to work with Photo CDs).

**SYMPTOM 8-52**    **You receive a "Bad ASPI open" error message**    This error indicates a problem in the SCSI support for your drive. The CD-R ASPI driver is bad or missing, and the SCSI CD-R drive cannot be found. Check the installation of your CD-R drive and SCSI adapter, then check the driver installation. Try reinstalling the latest SCSI driver(s) for the drive (and the host adapter if necessary).

**SYMPTOM 8-53**    **You receive a "Buffer underrun at sector <xxx>" message**
Whether "on the fly" or from an image file, CD writing is a real-time process that must run constantly at the selected recording speed—*without interruptions*. The CD recorder's buffer is constantly filled with data from the hard drive waiting to be written. This buffering action ensures that small slowdowns or interruptions in the flow of data from the computer do not interrupt the writing process. A *buffer underrun* message indicates that the flow of data from hard disk to CD recorder was interrupted long enough for the CD recorder's buffer to be emptied, and writing was halted. If this occurs during an actual write operation rather than a test, your CD may be damaged.

To avoid buffer underruns, you should remove as much processing load as possible from the system. For example, make sure that no screen savers or other Terminate and Stay Resident (TSR) programs are active (they can momentarily interrupt operations). Close as many open windows as possible. See that your working hard disk cannot be accessed via a network. For SCSI CD-R drives, the CD recorder's position in the SCSI chain—or the cable length between the computer and CD recorder—may cause data slowdowns. Try connecting the CD recorder as the first peripheral in the SCSI chain (if not done already), and use a shorter SCSI cable (if possible) between the CD recorder and the SCSI host adapter. Verify that the SCSI bus is terminated properly. For more information, see the earlier section "Buffer Underruns."

Enable BurnProof support if your drive and recording software support it.

**SYMPTOM 8-54**    **Current disc already contains a closed audio session**    Under the Red Book standard for audio CDs, all audio tracks must be written in a *single* session (Disk-at-Once). If you add audio tracks in more than one session, playback results will be unpredictable. Most CD-ROM drives will play back all audio tracks on a CD even if they are recorded in several different sessions, but most home and car CD players can only play back the tracks in the *first* session. If you continue and record audio in a different session, you may have problems reading subsequent audio sessions.

**SYMPTOM 8-55** **Current disc contains a session that is not closed** In actual practice, CD-ROM drives can read back only one data track per session, so avoid recording another data track in an open session. Be sure to close any open session *before* writing additional data to the disc (as a new session).

**SYMPTOM 8-56** **Currently selected source CD-ROM drive or CD recorder cannot read audio in digital format** This is more of a warning than a fault. Reading audio tracks in "digital format" is *not* the same as playing the music, and few CD-ROM drives are able to read audio tracks in digital format (only Red Book format). You may need to copy the music data from the CD to the hard drive first, then post-process the digital audio data through the application used to make the new CD. In a more contemporary setting, this type of problem indicates that the source drive cannot adequately handle digital audio extraction (DAE). You may need to upgrade the drive itself in order to achieve good DAE performance.

**SYMPTOM 8-57** **You receive a "Data overrun/underrun" error message** The SCSI host adapter has reported an error that is almost always caused by improper termination or a bad SCSI cable. Recheck the installation of your SCSI adapter, cabling, and termination. You may also need to reduce the processing overhead needed by unused applications. Refer to the earlier section "Buffer Underruns" for more details.

**SYMPTOM 8-58** **An error indicates that the destination disc is smaller than the source disc** This error commonly occurs when you're trying to duplicate an existing CD to the CD-R. There is not enough room on the recordable CD to copy the source CD. Try recording to a blank CD-R. Use 74-minute media instead of 60-minute media. Some CDs cannot be copied because of the TOC (Table of Contents) overhead in CD recorders as well as the calibration zone overhead. You may need to break up the source CD between two or more different CD-Rs.

 Some software makers intentionally fit a "non-standard" amount of data on the original disc so that it cannot be copied.

**SYMPTOM 8-59** **Disc already contains tracks and/or sessions that are incompatible with the requested operation** This error appears if you're trying to add data in a format that is different from the data format already on the disc. For example, you'll see this type of error when trying to add a CD-ROM XA session to a disc that already contains a standard CD-ROM session. A disc containing multiple formats is generally *unreadable*, so you are not allowed to record the different session type. You may need to use a different blank CD to record data in another format.

**SYMPTOM 8-60** **You receive a "Disc write-protected" message** This is often more of a warning than an error. You are attempting to write to a CD-R disc that has already been closed to further writing (finalized). Do *not* try writing to discs that are closed—instead, use a fresh blank disc for writing.

**SYMPTOM 8-61** **You receive an "Error 175-xx-xx-xx" message** This error code often indicates a "buffer underrun." See the information in the earlier section "Buffer Underruns."

**SYMPTOM 8-62** **You receive an "Error 220-01-xx-xx" message** This error code often indicates that some of your software cannot communicate with a SCSI device—possibly because your SCSI bus was reset. In many cases, this is caused by conflicts between real-mode and protected-mode SCSI drivers working in a Windows system. Try REMing (remarking-out) any real-mode SCSI drivers in your CONFIG.SYS file (the protected-mode drivers provided for Windows should be sufficient on their own). You may need to download and install updated protected-mode drivers for the SCSI host adapter and CD-R drive (as well as other SCSI devices that may be installed).

**SYMPTOM 8-63**    **You receive an "Error 220-06-xx-xx" message**    This error code often indicates a SCSI Selection Time-Out error, which suggests a SCSI setup problem—usually with the SCSI host adapter. Contact your SCSI host adapter manufacturer for detailed installation and testing instructions. You may need to adjust the SCSI BIOS Setup or update the SCSI drivers in your system. In extreme cases, you may need to upgrade the SCSI host adapter card.

**SYMPTOM 8-64**    **Error reading the Table of Contents (TOC) or Program Memory Area (PMA) from the disc**    This recordable disc is defective or has been damaged (probably during a previous write operation, or the current write operation). Do *not* try to write to this disc. Unfortunately, there is very little you can do here except to discard the defective disc. Try a fresh, good quality disc that has been recommended by the drive manufacturer.

**SYMPTOM 8-65**    **You receive a "General protection fault" error**    This type of software problem has been identified with the Adaptec AHAr-152x family of SCSI host adapters and is caused by outdated driver software. You can solve this problem by upgrading to version 3.1 (or later) of Adaptec's EZ-SCSI software. If you're not using Adaptec software, check for current drivers for whatever SCSI host adapter you're using.

**SYMPTOM 8-66**    **You receive an "Invalid logical block address" error**    This error message usually means that the CD mastering software has requested a data block from the hard disk that either does not exist or is illegal—this may suggest a corrupted hard disk or damaged ISO file. Exit the CD mastering software and run ScanDisk and Defrag to check and reorganize your hard drive. You may need to rebuild an ISO file or reload damaged files from a backup.

**SYMPTOM 8-67**    **You receive a "Last two blocks stripped" error message**    This message appears when copying a track to hard disk if the track you are reading was created as multisession-compliant (following the Orange Book standard). This is because a multisession track is always followed by two run-out blocks. These are included in the count of the total size (in blocks) of the track, but they do not contain data and cannot be read back. This message appears in order to alert you just in case you notice that you have two blocks fewer than were reported for the Read Length. Don't panic—you haven't lost any data.

**SYMPTOM 8-68**    **MSCDEX errors are being encountered**    Early versions of MSCDEX (prior to v.2.23) had problems with file names containing "illegal" ASCII characters such as a hyphen. If a directory contains a file name with an "illegal" ASCII character, you can still see all the files by doing a directory (DIR) from DOS, or you can open the illegally named file. However, one or more files listed *after* the illegal one may not be accessible or may give errors. You should update MSCDEX to the latest available version. As an alternative, you may REM out the real-mode driver and MSCDEX command lines in your startup files and allow Windows to rely exclusively on protected-mode drivers (this is the preferred solution).

**SYMPTOM 8-69**    **You receive a "No write data (buffer empty)" error**    The flow of data to the CD-R drive must be extremely reliable so that its working buffer is never empty when it prepares to write a block of information to disc. This message indicates that the flow of data from the hard disk to the CD recorder has been interrupted (similar to the "Buffer Underrun" error). Ensure that there are no active screen savers, other TSR utilities, or unneeded open windows that might momentarily interrupt operations. Your working hard disk should not be accessible over a network. Next, suspect the SCSI setup. The SCSI CD recorder's position in the SCSI chain, or the length of cabling between the SCSI adapter and CD recorder, may also cause data slowdowns. Try connecting the CD recorder as the first device in the SCSI chain (you may need to re-terminate the SCSI chain) and keeping the SCSI cable as short as possible.

**SYMPTOM 8-70**    **You receive a "Read file error" message**    A file referenced by the virtual image database (when writing on the fly) cannot be located or accessed on the source drive. Make sure that the suspect file is not being used by you or by someone else on a network. The file may also be damaged or corrupt, so exit the CD-R application and run ScanDisk and Defrag to check the file system for problems. You may need to reload damaged files from a backup.

**SYMPTOM 8-71**    **Selected disc image file was not prepared for the current disc** This type of error message occurs if you prepared the disc image file for a blank CD, but are now trying to record it to a CD *already* containing data, or vice versa. In either case, you would wind up writing a CD that couldn't be read at all because the CD locations calculated for the disc image are wrong for that actual CD. If you are given the option of writing anyway, select No to abort, because it is very unlikely that the writing operation would yield a readable CD. Retry the operation with a known-blank CD-R.

**SYMPTOM 8-72**    **Selected disc track is longer than the image file**    The disc verify process fails immediately because the source ISO 9660 image file and the actual ISO 9660 track on CD are not the same size—the disc track is actually longer than the image file, possibly indicating a defective CD-R drive. Retry the operation with a good quality CD-R disc. If the problem persists, you might try replacing the CD-R drive.

**SYMPTOM 8-73**    **Selected disc track is shorter than the image file**    The disc verify process fails immediately because the source ISO 9660 image file and the actual ISO 9660 track on CD are not the same size—the disc track is actually shorter than the image file, and could indicate a defective CD-R drive. Retry the operation with a good quality CD-R disc. If the problem persists, you might try replacing the CD-R drive with a later model.

**SYMPTOM 8-74**    **The "disc in" light on the drive does not blink after you turn on the computer**    In virtually all cases, there is no power reaching the CD-R drive. For internal CD-R drives, make sure the computer's four-pin power cable is properly connected to the CD-R drive unit. For external CD-R drives, make sure the power cord is properly connected to the back of the CD-R drive unit and is plugged in to a grounded power outlet. Make sure the power switch on the back of the drive is *on*. Refer to your CD-R drive's installation guide for more detailed information.

**SYMPTOM 8-75**    **You receive a "Write emergency" message**    This error occurs if the drive is interrupted during a write action. It is commonly seen when writing Red Book audio, but it can also occur with data recordings. For example, one typical reason for a write emergency is dust particles that cause the laser to jump off track. In most cases, the CD-R is ruined and you'll need to retry the write process with a good quality disc.

**SYMPTOM 8-76**   **The CD-R is recognized by Windows 9x/Me, but it will not function as a normal CD-ROM drive**   The drive appears normally in the Windows 9x/Me Device Manager (though this is not a problem that seems to occur with Windows XP). The driver that is operating the CD-R drive may not allow the drive to function as a normal CD-ROM reader. For example, this is a known problem with the older Philips CDD2000 CD-R. Check to see if there is an updated Windows 9x/Me CD-R driver that can overcome this limitation. If not, you may need to replace the CD-R drive with an upgraded model whose drivers *do* support CD-ROM-type functionality on the CD-R drive.

**SYMPTOM 8-77**   **You cannot read CD-R (gold) discs in some ordinary CD-ROM drives**
This is actually a very complex issue because there are a number of important factors that affect the way in which a CD is read. Laser calibration may be a factor. Some older CD-ROM drive lasers are not calibrated to read recordable discs (whose recorded surface is slightly different from that of "pressed" discs). If your CD-ROM drive reads mass-produced (silver) CDs but not recordable CDs, check with the CD-ROM drive manufacturer to determine whether laser calibration is the problem. You may be able to return the CD-ROM drive for factory recalibration or replace the CD-ROM drive with a newer model that is better calibrated for reading both CD-ROM and CD-R discs.

Fast CD-ROM drive operations may be another problem. In order for some CD-ROM models to work as fast as they do, they must perform unconventional operations, such as a laser calibration in the lead-out area to determine the approximate position of several tracks. With some CD recorders, the session lead-out is not recorded correctly, causing problems with gold disc compatibility.

The CD-R authoring software can be a problem. Any authoring software can sometimes produce incorrect tracks due to bugs or recording glitches. A good way to check whether incompatibility problems lie with the originating software is to test the same gold disc on several CD-ROM drives. If one drive is capable of reading the gold disc back correctly, chances are that the problem was *not* in the recording process. If *no* drives can read the CD-R, the disc might have been damaged in the recording process.

**SYMPTOM 8-78**   **You encounter "buffer miscompare" errors when using a SCSI host adapter diagnostic utility**   In many cases, you have a DMA channel conflict with another card (or device) in the system. Check the settings of every card or device that uses an IRQ, DMA channel, or I/O port address and compare these settings to the ones used for the SCSI host adapter. If there is a DMA conflict, change the DMA channel on the SCSI card to an unused channel.

Another possibility is that you're dealing with a motherboard that doesn't support bus mastering (not all PCs support bus mastering). For example, a Gateway 2000 P5-133 has only one bus mastering slot, which is normally occupied by the video adapter. If the SCSI adapter (an Adaptec AHA-1535 card, for instance) is installed in a non-bus-mastering slot in this machine, the system may freeze when trying to access a CD from the CD-R drive. It might be necessary to upgrade the motherboard to access additional bus mastering PCI slots.

**SYMPTOM 8-79**   **You encounter a "servo tracking error" when writing a CD**   A "servo tracking error" message is reported by the CD-R drive when it is unable to record to the media (the blank disc)—this is similar to when a needle "skips" on a phonograph. There is a microscopic groove imprinted on the surface of each CD-R disc that guides the laser during writing. There are a number of reasons why a "servo tracking error" might occur.

Check for defective media first. *Defective media* can include a bad disc, a bad lot of discs, or an unsupported brand of media (not all CD-R disc media work the same on all CD-R drives). For example, the Pinnacle Micro RCD-1000/5020/5040 series drives support the following disc brands: DOT, Taiyo Yuden,

Mitsubishi, Sony, 3M, TDK, Verbatim, and Kodak Infoguard. Make sure that you're using a blank disc that's certified to work with your particular drive—try another disc (or disc brand) if necessary. There may be a dirty lens within the drive that prevents the laser from focusing on the surface of the media. Use a can of clean compressed air to blow out the inside of the drive through the front access door or tray.

Next, verify that the amount of data you are trying to record does not exceed the capacity of the disc. Your recording software will usually prevent you from making that mistake, but it has no way of adjusting for previously failed sessions or bad blocks on the media—these can cause the software to make an incorrect calculation of the remaining free space, which will differ from what is *actually* free.

Finally, a servo tracking error may occur if the ambient temperature inside the drive itself is too high. If your drive is external, remove the filter from the back of the drive and use compressed air to clean it out. Confirm that the cooling fan works when the unit is powered on—if not, the drive may need to be replaced. If your drive is internal, verify that it receives enough air circulation by removing the computer's case, letting the drive cool off for a while, and then rerunning the recording session. If the problem persists, replace the drive.

**SYMPTOM 8-80**    You notice frequent "pops" or "clicks" between CD audio tracks

This is almost always a result of your particular CD recording software. The "pops" or "clicks" heard between tracks on CD digital audio (CD-DA) discs are caused when recording *without* using the Disc-at-Once option. When you select the Disc-at-Once option in the authoring software, the laser will remain powered on between each track (and run-in/run-out blocks are written without interruption). Remember that the Disc-at-Once feature may be unavailable on a few older software packages, so check the manual of your CD authoring software to see if there is a Disc-at-Once feature—if not, you may have an outdated or "lite" version, which will require an upgrade. However, most CD recording software will offer a Disk-at-Once recording mode today.

Another possible cause for "pops" between tracks occurs when a WAV file is created improperly (or it is corrupt). Some early shareware audio editing software had problems saving WAV files properly, and bugs caused "pops" to occur between tracks (and at other various points throughout a song). These WAV files were corrupted by the editing software. The most recent problem with WAV files is the use of "extended information." Some WAV editing software packages allow the user to save the WAV file in an Extended WAV Format as well as the standard WAV format. If "extended information" is included in the WAV file (author name, date, and so on), this will cause a "pop" to occur when played back through a standard audio CD player. Make sure you can save a WAV file *without* this extra information to avoid the problem.

Today, pops and clicks *in* an audio track are often the result of poor digital audio extraction (DAE). You can try slowing the DAE rate in your recording software, or upgrading the drive to a model that is well suited for DAE use.

**SYMPTOM 8-81**    On your home stereo, the disc will not repeat play after the last track

When you set your home stereo CD player to Repeat Playback after the last track, the CD playback simply stops—it will not repeat. Some audio CD players cannot play back a "burned" audio disc properly if there are B0h and C0h pointers in the disc's Table Of Contents. B0h and C0h pointers are used to point to the next session and are created on discs written using the Track-at-Once (or multisession) option. CDs written using Disc-at-Once do not contain these pointers because there are no subsequent sessions. If you would like to have a disc that is fully compatible with "audio CD," use the Disc-at-Once option during recording.

**SYMPTOM 8-82**   **You receive an error when recording an audio track under four seconds**   If you try to record an audio track or WAV file that is less than four seconds long, you will get a message indicating that a certain track cannot be written because it is less than four seconds long. Do not use WAV files of less than four seconds. The audio standard for compact disc (Red Book) does not allow for audio files of less than four seconds. Make the audio file longer (e.g., insert "dead air" before and after the audio) and try recording it again.

**SYMPTOM 8-83**   **You get poor audio quality from the CD-R**   Changes in recording speed (such as from 24X to 12X to 1X) have little or no effect on the quality of the recording. Most current CD authoring software will allow the use of IDE-style CD-ROM devices as "source drives" for copying audio CDs (Red Book or CD-DA). The Digital Audio Extraction (or DAE) test will pass, yet the copy process results in poor audio quality. Program and data CDs usually copy without problems. In virtually all cases, the problem is the source CD-ROM drive.

Use the source CD-ROM drive to extract a troublesome audio CD track to the hard disk as a WAV file (name it CDTEST.WAV). Now use the CD-R to extract the same audio track to the hard disk as a WAV file (name it WTEST.WAV). Play the two WAV files from the hard drive and compare them. If the CDTEST.WAV file contains the same clicks/pops as you encountered during recording, yet the CD-R is producing clean WAV files, then your source drive is *not* producing good quality digital audio extraction. There are three ways around this problem:

- Use the CD-R as the source *and* destination (check the CD-R manual and CD authoring software for detailed instructions on how to do this).
- Purchase a new CD-ROM drive guaranteed to support high-speed DAE.
- Use the CD authoring software settings to slow down the DAE rate. For example, in Easy CD Creator, the DAE rate is found under Tools | Options on the Advanced tab. You can experiment by extracting tracks as WAV files after making those changes, then testing their quality by playing them from the hard drive.

## CD-RW SYMPTOMS

Although UDF, DirectCD, and CD-RW drives are now well-established industry standards, there are still a number of compatibility problems and operating issues that technicians may eventually need to address. This part of the chapter examines a selection of UDF issues and CD-RW problems.

For basic CD reading and recording issues, refer to the previous parts of this chapter for CD-ROM and CD-R troubleshooting information.

### Troubleshooting Tips

CD-RW drive problems are not terribly complicated issues to troubleshoot, but they can present some peculiar problems for technicians and do-it-yourselfers. Before you attempt to troubleshoot a CD-RW issue with your system, take a moment to work through this checklist:

- Verify that your system meets the minimum requirements for your CD-RW drive. If not, the system may fail to run properly (or not at all).
- Make sure that each device (including the CD-RW drive) has power. Connect any devices that are not receiving power. The drive should be recognized properly under BIOS and the Windows Device Manager.

- Turn off the computer's power, wait 15–20 seconds, then reboot the system. Doing this can clear some software conflicts.

- Repeat the write operation with different (known good quality) CD-RW media.

- Make sure that you're using the right type of CD for the task at hand.

- Check the README file that came with the CD-RW drive for any last-minute compatibility or performance notes that might be present with your system. Also check the CD-RW drive maker's Web site for the latest drivers and firmware upgrades.

- If the problems occur with power management, disable your PC's power management modes.

## General Symptoms

Rewritable CD drives are subject to a large number of potential errors during operation, and many typical rewriting errors are covered next. In most cases, the error is not terribly difficult to understand and can be corrected in just a few minutes, once the nature of the problem is understood. Keep in mind that the actual error message is dependent on the CD recorder software in use, so your actual error messages may vary just a bit.

**SYMPTOM 8-84**    **You cannot add more information to the CD-R/RW disc**    There are several possible issues that can prevent you from adding files to a disc that you've written to previously. First, take a moment to check that there's enough free space on the disc—you can't add a 100MB file if there's only 50MB free on the disc. Next, consider any differences between drives and software (this is especially true for CD-Rs). If you write a disc on one PC using a particular drive and writing software version (e.g., WinOnCD), you may encounter problems changing software versions, or trying to write on another PC with a different drive and software (e.g., Nero). Try writing on the original PC and see if the problem disappears.

**SYMPTOM 8-85**    **The CD-ROM drive refuses to read CD-RW discs**    This is a common problem that is related to the age of the CD-ROM drive itself. Older CD-ROM drives (manufactured prior to mid/late-1997) are probably *not* Multi-Read/UDF-compatible and *cannot* read UDF formatted discs at all. CD audio players also cannot read UDF discs. If your CD-ROM is not Multi-Read-compliant, you'll need to upgrade to a Multi-Read-compliant model, or record your discs (especially audio discs) in a conventional ISO 9660 format using the CD-RW or CD-R drive.

CD-ROM drives manufactured after mid/late-1997 will probably offer Multi-Read capability, but still may not be able to read a UDF-formatted disc without the assistance of a UDF Reader utility. In most cases, you can obtain a free UDF Reader from the company providing the DirectCD software (such as Roxio). Windows 98/SE and later generally offer native UDF support for a Multi-Read drive, so a separate reader utility may not be necessary.

**SYMPTOM 8-86**    **A backup disc will not run properly**    DirectCD is not suitable for making backup copies of game or application discs where the application must run from the CD. This is because DirectCD uses a different method of writing data to disc (*packet writing*) than any discs produced with the ISO 9660 format. Packet-written (UDF) discs cannot be read by many standard CD-ROM drives or game machines. The only real way to work around this sort of problem is to use other recording software (such as Easy CD Creator for Windows or Toast for the Mac) to make a backup copy of the disc to CD-R.

Keep in mind that some games and commercial application discs use forms of copy protection that recording software cannot work around or "break." Also remember that you cannot copy commercial software because of copyright restrictions.

**SYMPTOM 8-87**    **You cannot "see" a second session reading a CD-RW disc from a CD-ROM drive**    First, make sure that you're trying to read the disc on a newer Multi-Read-compatible CD-ROM drive (along with a UDF Reader utility, if necessary). Try ejecting the CD and reinserting it in the drive; then refresh the screen by selecting My Computer from inside Windows Explorer. Finally, try reading the disc from the CD-RW drive (or from another suitable CD-ROM drive). If another drive can read the disc, the problem is likely to be with the suspect CD-ROM drive, which may need to be upgraded. If the disc cannot be read in any drive, the problem is likely to be with the disc itself. Try re-recording the disc.

**SYMPTOM 8-88**    **You receive an error such as "CD-RW is not under Direct CD control"** You'll typically notice this problem under Windows 9*x*/Me when you attempt to erase, format, or copy data to a CD-RW (though this problem does not seem to occur with Windows XP). This type of problem is most frequently encountered when using a Ricoh CD-RW drive and Roxio (Adaptec) Direct CD software. The problem can occur when the CD-RW drive uses older firmware (for example, a Ricoh CD-RW drive with v.2.03 firmware or earlier), or if you're using Roxio (Adaptec) DirectCD 2.0 or earlier. Try updating the drive's firmware and CD authoring software.

**SYMPTOM 8-89**    **The CD-RW media cannot be used when the UDF format is interrupted** If power is lost while formatting a CD-RW disc, the disc will become unusable in any application and will fail if another format is attempted. To correct this issue, use the DirectCD Full Erase feature to wipe the disc, then try the format operation again. Otherwise, discard the damaged disc and try another one.

**SYMPTOM 8-90**    **Files recorded in a second session do not appear**    If the files that you recorded in a second session do not appear when you try to read the disc in a CD-ROM drive, try the following tips:

■  Try ejecting and reinserting the CD.

■  Refresh the file list—select the CD-RW icon in My Computer or Windows Explorer, and then press F5.

■  Check the drive. CD-RW discs can be used only in CD-RW drives or newer Multi-Read CD-ROMs.

■  Try reading the CD in other CD-ROM drives. If other drives are able to read the disc, the problem is probably with the original CD-ROM drive.

**SYMPTOM 8-91**    **Your computer loses power while writing a CD-RW disc, and now the disc is inaccessible**    If you lose power while writing to your CD (the CD-RW's drive light is on) or if you press CTRL-ALT-DELETE while writing to a CD, you'll interrupt the disc. But you may be able to salvage your disc. Leave your CD-RW disc in the drive and don't open the CD tray. Turn your computer off and cycle the power back on. Then restart the utility that you were using. Once the DirectCD utility tries to access the CD-RW drive/disc again, the recovery operation will make it appear that the last session is there, but actually only a *part* of the CD's directory may be there. Your recordable CD is still usable if you can read the directory. Just repeat the entire copy operation to make sure that your files are copied to the rewritable CD.

**SYMPTOM 8-92**    **You receive a "Buffer Underrun" error when you're writing in CD-R mode**    A CD-RW drive can also write CD-R discs. CD recordable devices require an uninterrupted data stream from the hard drive to write successfully to a CD. A "buffer underrun" message appears when the data stream is interrupted—this can occur if another program interrupts the writing process (or if the CD-RW drive's write speed is set too high for the speed at which the hard drive is running). See the "Buffer Underruns" section earlier in this chapter for more detailed information on buffer underrun errors.

**SYMPTOM 8-93**    **There is no DirectCD window after inserting a new CD-RW disc**    Windows XP does not display DirectCD windows, but Windows 98/Me do. Verify that the CD-RW drive's DirectCD software and utilities have been installed properly. If the DirectCD window doesn't appear on the screen after you insert a new disc, follow these steps:

1. Wait a moment—it can take up to 15 seconds for the DirectCD window to appear.
2. If the rewritable disc is already formatted, you can force the window by clicking Start on the taskbar, choosing Programs, and then selecting Create a CD.
3. To prepare a CD with Easy CD Creator or DirectCD, the disc must be blank (you may have inserted a disc that is already formatted). Remove the disc and insert a good quality blank one.
4. The disc may have an unreadable format. DirectCD has a ScanDisk utility that *may* be able to recover data on the disc—simply double-click the CD icon on the Windows taskbar. Start ScanDisk and allow the process to run. A message will appear when ScanDisk is finished.

**SYMPTOM 8-94**    **The CD-RW drive doesn't show up in My Computer or Windows Explorer**    In effect, the drive is "disconnected" from the rest of the system. There are many possible problems that can cause this kind of behavior. If the drive doesn't appear in Explorer, click View from the top menu, then click Refresh. You might also try rebooting the computer (from a cold start) so that the PnP BIOS can recognize the CD-RW drive.

Check the drive's cabling next. Make sure that the drive's power connector is attached securely. Test the power by opening and closing the drive tray using the Eject button. Also make sure that the drive's SCSI or IDE signal cable is oriented properly and secured between the drive and drive controller. Chances are that you installed the CD-RW as a "master" IDE device. Verify that the drive jumpers are set properly and see that any other drive on that channel has been rejumpered as a "slave" drive. If you're using a SCSI CD-RW drive, see that the SCSI ID for the CD-RW is unique, and that the SCSI chain is properly connected and terminated.

Verify that the latest CD-RW drivers and utility software are installed. If problems persist, try another CD-RW drive or reconfigure the drive so that it is alone on its controller channel (that is, disconnect the "slave" IDE drive).

**SYMPTOM 8-95**    **The device that is sharing the IDE signal cable with your CD-RW drive no longer responds**    In most cases, that other drive was accidentally disconnected or unpowered when the new CD-RW drive was installed. Turn off and unplug your computer, then make sure that the power cables are securely attached to both drives. You can verify power to the drives by observing their power LEDs or by ejecting their disk trays. Also verify that the SCSI or IDE signal cable is oriented properly and connected securely at both drives. When using a SCSI controller, verify that the SCSI chain is properly terminated. When working with an ATAPI IDE drive, the master/slave relationship of the drives may also be an issue. If you installed the CD-RW drive as a slave device, try reconfiguring the devices so that the CD-RW drive is the master. For example, when using a CD-RW drive with Sony or Goldstar CD-ROMs, try configuring the CD-RW drive as the master and setting the CD-ROM as the slave.

Try the suspect drive by itself (disconnect the CD-RW drive). If the suspect drive returns to normal, there may be a conflict between the CD-RW drive and the other device—you may need to assign the two devices to different drive controller channels. If the problem persists, try replacing the suspect device.

**SYMPTOM 8-96**    **You receive an error message when double-clicking on the CD-RW icon**    There are several possible issues, which are typically caused by the drive's inability to read the disc. Here are a few things to check:

- There is no CD in the CD-RW drive. Insert a good quality CD and try reading again.

- After inserting a CD, you need to wait a moment to let the CD-RW drive read the disc information. When the LED on the front of the drive stops flashing and stays green, click on the CD-RW drive's icon again.

- The CD may be in the tray upside-down or a little off-center. Try reinserting the CD—the disc label should be facing up.

- You may be trying to read from a blank recordable CD. Copy some information to the disc and try reading it again.

**SYMPTOM 8-97**    **You receive an "invalid media" error when trying to boot from the CD-RW**    In virtually all current PC platforms, it *is* possible to boot from a CD-RW drive rather than a floppy or hard drive. An "invalid media" error from the CD-RW drive generally means that the disc doesn't contain the bootstrap files needed to begin the boot process and load your operating system. Chances are that the disc itself isn't bootable. Use a bootable CD (such as a *system rescue* disc or an OS disc such as Windows NT).

If you need to work around this problem, simply remove the disc from the CD-RW. During boot, the BIOS will skip the CD-RW and move directly to the next drive in the Boot Order (the hard drive). If you want to prevent your system from checking the CD-RW at boot time, go into the system's CMOS Setup and change the Boot Order so that the CD-RW is not included. For example, you might change the Boot Order to "A:/C:" or "C:/A:."

**SYMPTOM 8-98**    **You cannot copy directly from a CD-ROM drive to the CD-RW drive**
This is a very common problem that is almost always caused by inadequate hardware capabilities. The *source drive* (typically a CD-ROM) must support the extremely fast data transfers found in late-model ATAPI IDE or SCSI-2/3 drives. If you're copying audio CDs, the source drive must be capable of digital audio extraction (or DAE). It may be necessary to upgrade the source drive or drive controller in order to support faster data transfers.

If you're using an IDE-type source and CD-RW drive, make sure that the *source* and *destination* drives are *not* on the same IDE controller channel. You may need to reconfigure your drives so that the source and destination drives are split on separate controller channels. Finally, some CDs have a copy-prevention feature (or other features) that do not allow a CD-to-CD copy. If that's the case, it may not be possible to copy that particular disc.

 Make sure that you copy *only* material that belongs to you or that you have written permission to copy.

**SYMPTOM 8-99**     **Audio from the CD-RW drive is poor or absent**     Whenever you have trouble with CD audio from a CD-ROM, CD-R, or CD-RW drive, try listening to the audio using a set of headphones into the headset connector on the drive's front panel. If you cannot hear the audio (and volume adjustments don't help), then the drive is probably defective and should be replaced. If you hear the audio normally, the problem is likely in the PC's sound system. Make sure that the four-wire audio cable is completely plugged into the sound card and into the CD-RW drive. If you already have a CD-ROM or other drive providing CD audio to the sound card, you cannot connect the CD-RW's audio cable unless you either remove the current CD audio cable or use a sound card with more than one CD audio port. Make sure that the CD audio channel is not muted in the mixer software and see that the CD audio level is turned up adequately. You may need to update the sound card's drivers or application software if the sound system is not currently supporting CD audio.

If the problem is with WAV file playback from the disc, try listening to the WAV files from your hard drive. If the problem persists, the problem is with poor WAV recordings (not with the CD-RW drive or sound card). If the WAV files sound correct from the hard drive (but not from the CD), the problem may be poor recording to the CD—it may be necessary to re-record the disc using updated or alternate recording software.

**SYMPTOM 8-100**     **Video playback is choppy from a CD-RW drive**     This is generally *not* a problem with the CD-RW drive, but rather with the system's capability to handle streaming audio/video data from a CD. Your best solution is typically to reduce the system's processing overhead in order to provide more processing power to the video playback software (such as Windows Media Player):

■ Shut down any background applications, TSRs, and screen savers.

■ Reduce the size of your video playback window.

■ Download and install the latest versions of DirectX, your video drivers, and your multimedia player (such as Windows Media Player).

■ Many CD-RW drives tend to be rather slow (10X, for example), resulting in interference with data transfers on some system configurations. Try playing the video from another faster drive, such as your system's CD-ROM drive.

■ If problems persist, you may need to make one or more hardware upgrades to improve your system's multimedia playback capability (such as a faster video card, more system RAM, and a faster CPU).

**SYMPTOM 8-101**     **Your CD-ROM drive cannot "see" a second (or subsequent) session recorded on discs from a CD-RW drive**     There are several possible issues that can occur when reading multisession discs created on a CD-RW drive with DirectCD software. Start by ejecting and reinserting the disc. This allows the drive to redetect the disc and to read its sessions once again. You should also try refreshing the display—select the My Computer icon in Windows Explorer, then press F5.

As a rule, CD-RW discs can be used only in CD-RW drives or newer Multi-Read CD-ROMs (compatible with the UDF file system). If you're trying to read the disc on an older CD-ROM which is *not* Multi-Read-compliant, you may need to upgrade the CD-ROM to a newer version. Finally, multisession CDs created with DirectCD cannot be read in DOS or Windows 3.*x*. Make sure that you're in Windows 9*x*/Me/XP, or some other UDF-compliant operating system.

**SYMPTOM 8-102**    **You cannot get an application to "find" a CD in the CD-RW drive**
This is almost always a problem with the application itself rather than the drive. Many programs (such as CD-based games) look for only the first logical drive letter assigned to a CD-ROM drive or CD-RW drive. For example, if a CD-ROM drive is assigned to D: and the CD-RW drive is assigned to E:, the program will probably look for the CD *only* in drive D: and will not see the CD in drive E:. If you want to use the CD-RW drive with such programs, reassign the drive letters to make the CD-RW drive precede the CD-ROM drive:

1. For Windows 9*x*/Me, click Start | Settings | click Control Panel. Double-click the System icon, select the Device Manager tab, and double-click the CD-ROM entry.

2. Double-click the CD-ROM drive, then click the Settings tab. Under Reserved drive letters, select the drive letter after the existing letter (for both *start* and *end* drive letter) and click OK.

3. Now double-click the CD-RW drive entry, then click the Settings tab. Under Reserved drive letters, select the drive letter before the current one and click OK.

You cannot alter drive letter assignments under Windows XP. In this case, you'll need to uninstall the application and reinstall it from the desired drive so that it will reference the correct drive.

**SYMPTOM 8-103**    **DirectCD and CD writing software don't co-exist**    In rare cases, some CD-R software doesn't co-exist with DirectCD on the same system. For example, WinOnCD should generally not be installed on the same system with DirectCD. Since each CD writing application loads its own driver to control the CD drive, these drivers can cause conflicts with each other that can cause your write to fail. Check with the drive and authoring software makers for patches or upgrades that will correct this software compatibility problem. To work around the trouble temporatily, uninstall the CD authoring software and stick with CD-RW media under DirectCD.

# Further Study

Adaptec   www.adaptec.com
Creative Labs   www.creaf.com
Diamond Multimedia   www.diamondmm.com
El Torito specification   www.phoenix.com/PlatSS/products/specs.html
Hewlett-Packard   www.hp.com
HiVal   www.hival.com
NEC   www.nectech.com/products/index.htm
Pinnacle Micro   www.pinnaclemicro.com
Plextor   www.plextor.com
Roxio   www.roxio.com
Teac America   www.teac.com/DSPD/DesktopCDRW.html

# 9

# CHIPSETS

In the early days of the PC, motherboards were designed and built with discrete logic gates. If you were around in the days of the PC/XT and PC/AT, you probably remember the huge motherboards packed with over 150 to 200 individual chips. Discrete chips demanded a lot of power and took up lots of room. It didn't take designers long to realize that standard functions of the PC (like floppy drive interface circuits, DMA controllers, programmable interrupt controllers, and so on) could easily be integrated into *application-specific integrated circuits* (ASICs). With the use of these custom-made chips, PCs were able to drop their chip count, reduce construction costs, improve reliability, and reduce power requirements.

But there are also performance advantages to such high levels of feature integration. Combining a PC's sophisticated logic circuitry onto a few chips dramatically shortens the signal paths and allows the circuits to operate at much higher speeds (a crucial factor in today's high-performance systems). By optimizing the signal paths within the chip itself, performance could be improved even further. Designers quickly saw that they could integrate *all* the core logic needed to facilitate a complete state-of-the-art PC in just a few highly integrated chips. Since these chips are specifically designed to serve as a *set* on the motherboard, they were dubbed the *chipset* (Figure 9-1).

# Understanding Chipsets

Today, chipsets play a critical role in the design and fabrication of modern personal computers. Where early motherboards could use hundreds of chips, you'd be hard-pressed to find more than 20 chips on a current motherboard. In fact, chipsets are *so* important that new chipsets often must be developed to support each new computer technology or processor. For example, you'll find that Intel's 820 chipset supports features such as RDRAM, AGP 4X, and Ultra-DMA/66, but the venerable 440 BX Pentium II/III chipset does not. As a result, motherboards with a 440 BX chipset would have to be replaced with a motherboard using the 820 chipset (or later) before those features would be supported. Ultimately, the overall features and capabilities of your PC are largely defined by the motherboard chipset (sometimes referred to as the computer's *core logic*).

**FIGURE  9-1**    The Intel 845MP chipset supports the mobile Pentium 4 processor (Courtesy of Intel Corporation).

# CHIP TYPES

A chipset is an efficient and inexpensive way to bring a large number of powerful features to a PC. Figure 9-2 illustrates a typical application of an Intel 850 chipset intended for the Pentium 4 processor. The i850 chipset actually consists of three devices: the 82850 Memory Controller Hub (MCH), the 82801BA I/O

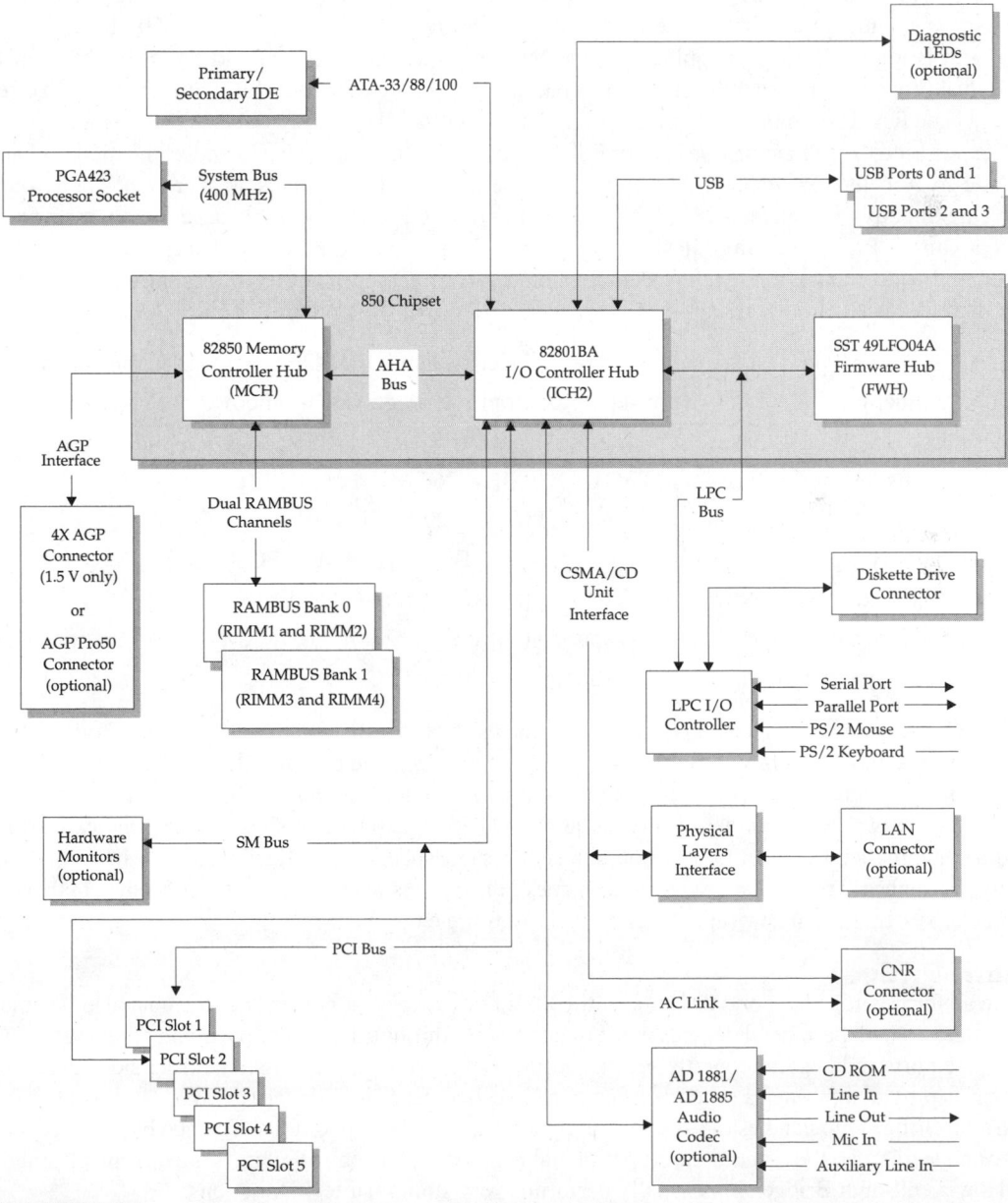

**FIGURE 9-2**    The i850 chipset on Intel's D850GB motherboard (Courtesy of Intel Corporation)

Controller Hub (ICH2), and the SST 49LF004A 4Mb Firmware Hub (FH—this is where the motherboard's BIOS is held). Obviously, other chipsets will use different numbering schemes and may employ additional chips, but the ideas here are almost identical. Let's look at the role each chip plays in the system.

## North Bridge

In a chipset, one chip is usually responsible for interfacing (a.k.a. connecting) the CPU, main memory, and the local bus (in this case, the AGP graphics bus). This principle device is often called the *North Bridge* chip (some manufacturers simply use one word, *Northbridge*). In Figure 9-2, the 82850 MCH would be the North Bridge chip. In this application, the MCH provides clock signal and timing support for the Pentium 4 processor along a 400 MHz system bus, and supports two banks of Rambus memory. In effect, the CPU and RAM communicate through the 82850. This 400 MHz pathway between the CPU and RAM is often referred to as the *front side bus* (or FSB). In addition, the 82850 MCH handles the motherboard's 1.5 Vdc 4X Accelerated Graphics Port (AGP) bus. The video card that you install in an AGP slot will communicate directly through the 82850 (this also allows the AGP card to quickly access main memory for video textures). Rather than an AGP slot, a designer could incorporate an AGP video chip and supply integrated AGP video capability right on the motherboard. A North Bridge chip typically controls the following system attributes:

- The processor types that are supported (e.g., Celeron, Pentium II/III/4, Athlon, Duron, and so on)
- The number of processors that are supported (for multiprocessing motherboards)
- The processor speeds that are supported (such as 800 MHz, 1.5 GHz, 2.0 GHz, and so on)
- The front side bus speed (e.g., 133 MHz, 200 MHz, 266 MHz, or 400 MHz)
- The FSB multiplier needed to operate the CPU (e.g., 200 MHz FSB x5 = 1 GHz CPU)
- The memory types that are supported (e.g., PC266 DDR SDRAM or PC800 RDRAM)
- The maximum amount of memory that is supported
- The memory technologies that are supported (64Mbit or 128Mbit SDRAM)
- The type of memory error correction supported (parity or ECC)

All chipsets are not created equal, so do not underestimate the importance of the North Bridge chip. It sits squarely at the center of your PC's processing components, and a poorly designed North Bridge can result in poor system performance—even when the processor and memory are very fast. You can see this in effect when two PCs with identical CPUs and RAM are benchmarked side by side. Ideally, both PCs should benchmark the same if they're operating at the same speeds, but differing chipsets may cause profound differences in performance. This is also one of the reasons why some older PCs seem to outperform the newer systems when new (and unrefined) chipsets are employed.

## South Bridge

While a North Bridge supports the bulk of the PC's raw processing power, the PC must also be able to communicate with peripheral devices in the outside world through a series of ports and other system busses. Since ports and busses generally operate at speeds that are far slower than the front side bus, system support is provided through a second chip, typically called the *South Bridge* (or *Southbridge*). As a rule, the South Bridge chip handles the system's peripheral and I/O bus operations. They go by many different names depending on the manufacturer: peripheral controller, I/O controller, integrated controller, and so on. However, South Bridge chips usually perform a very similar suite of functions.

Take another look at Figure 9-2 and you'll see the 82801BA I/O Controller Hub (ICH2). The ICH2 interfaces directly to the system's PCI expansion bus (note that the older ISA bus is not supported), along with a single CNR slot. Other South Bridge chips usually support serial ports, parallel ports, floppy controllers, faster UDMA/133 drive controllers, and will accommodate other features like integrated audio and hardware monitors. As a rule, expect a South Bridge chip to handle the following features:

■ PCI bus support (usually from four to six slots), and possibly one AMR/CNR slot

■ Four to six USB ports

■ One or more serial (RS-232) ports

■ A parallel (IEEE 1284) port

■ Hardware monitors (e.g., fan tachometers, voltage sensors, temperature sensors, and so on)

■ Two-channel UDMA/100/133 hard drive controller

■ Floppy drive controller

■ Power management features (APM or ACPI, DPMS, or SMM)

■ Keyboard controller (KBC), including support for a PS/2 mouse

## Integrated Features

On some motherboards, additional chips are included to perform some of the common functions normally found on expansion cards. In Figure 9-2, the Analog Devices AD1881/AD1885 chip provides audio features for Intel's D850GB motherboard. This has its pros and cons. In general, incorporating built-in circuitry offers lower cost, but may limit system upgradability. If you end up adding a Sound Blaster Audigy and a GeForce 4 graphics accelerator because you don't like the performance of your integrated components, you aren't really saving any money. There are four popular integrated features:

■ Video adapters

■ Sound adapters

■ Network adapter

■ SCSI adapter

## Finding Technical Information

If you're looking for detailed technical information about today's chipsets, you can usually download the complete technical manual from the chipset manufacturer's Web site (usually in Adobe Acrobat's PDF format). Table 9-1 provides the URLs for downloading many of today's chipset manuals. Table 9-2 outlines the chipsets covered in this chapter and explains their functions.

**TABLE 9-1     LOCATING TECHNICAL INFORMATION FOR MODERN PC CHIPSETS**

| CHIPSET | COVERAGE | RESOURCE |
|---------|----------|----------|
| ALi M1531 | Intel, Cyrix, AMD: Socket 7 | *No longer available* |
| ALi M1533 | South Bridge chip | *No longer available* |
| ALi M1535 | South Bridge chip | www.aliusa.com/images/documentation/1535pb01.pdf |
| ALi M1535+ | South Bridge chip | www.aliusa.com/images/documentation/1535pbp1.pdf |

**TABLE 9-1    LOCATING TECHNICAL INFORMATION FOR MODERN PC CHIPSETS**
**(CONTINUED)**

| CHIPSET | COVERAGE | RESOURCE |
|---|---|---|
| ALi M1535d | South Bridge chip | www.aliusa.com/images/documentation/1535pbd1.pdf |
| ALi M1535d+ | South Bridge chip | www.aliusa.com/images/documentation/1535pbdp1.pdf |
| ALi M1541 | Intel, Cyrix, AMD: Socket 7 | www.aliusa.com/images/documentation/1541pbc4.pdf |
| ALi M1543c | South Bridge chip | www.aliusa.com/images/documentation/1543pbcb.pdf |
| ALi M1561 | AMD K6-III: Socket 7 | www.aliusa.com/images/documentation/1561pb03.pdf |
| ALi M1621 | Pentium II | www.aliusa.com/images/documentation/1621pbc1.pdf |
| ALi M1631 | Pentium II | www.aliusa.com/images/documentation/1631pb05.pdf |
| ALi M1632m | Pentium II/III, Celeron | www.aliusa.com/images/documentation/1632pbm1.pdf |
| ALi M1641/B | Pentium II/III | www.aliusa.com/images/documentation/1641pb01.pdf |
| ALi M1644/T | Pentium II/III, Celeron | www.aliusa.com/images/documentation/m1644pb.pdf |
| ALi M1646 | AMD Athlon, Duron | www.aliusa.com/images/documentation/m1646pb.pdf |
| ALi M1647 | AMD Athlon, Duron | www.aliusa.com/images/documentation/1647pb01.pdf |
| ALi M1651 | Pentium II/III, Celeron | www.aliusa.com/images/documentation/1651pb01.pdf |
| ALi M1651T | Pentium II/III, Celeron (Tualatin Core) | www.aliusa.com/images/documentation/1651tpb1.pdf |
| ALi M1671 | Pentium 4 | www.aliusa.com/images/documentation/m1671dm.pdf |
| ALi M1672 | Pentium 4 | www.aliusa.com/images/documentation/m1672dm.pdf |
| AMD 640 | AMD K5 and K6: Socket 7 | *No longer available* |
| AMD 750 | AMD Athlon | www.amd.com/us-en/Processors/ProductInformation/ 0,,30_118_756_759^873^1185,00.html |
| AMD 760 | AMD Athlon | www.amd.com/us-en/Processors/ProductInformation/ 0,,30_118_756_759^873^1106,00.html |
| AMD 760 MP | AMD Athlon MP | www.amd.com/us-en/Processors/TechnicalResources/ 0,,30_182_873_1066,00.html |
| AMD 760 MPX | AMD Athlon MP | www.amd.com/us-en/Processors/TechnicalResources/ 0,,30_182_873_4366,00.html |
| Intel 430 FX | Pentium | support.intel.com/support/chipsets/430FX/ |
| Intel 430 HX | Pentium | developer.intel.com/design/chipsets/datashts/ 290551.htm |
| Intel 430 TX | Pentium | developer.intel.com/design/chipsets/datashts/ 290559.htm |
| Intel 430 VX | Pentium | support.intel.com/support/chipsets/430VX/ |
| Intel 430 MX | Mobile Pentium | developer.intel.com/design/chipsets/datashts/ 245052.htm |
| Intel 440 BX | Pentium II, III | developer.intel.com/design/chipsets/datashts/ 290633.htm |
| Intel 440 EX | Celeron | developer.intel.com/design/chipsets/datashts/ 290616.htm |
| Intel 440 MX | Celeron | developer.intel.com/design/chipsets/datashts/ 245052.htm |

**TABLE 9-1    LOCATING TECHNICAL INFORMATION FOR MODERN PC CHIPSETS (CONTINUED)**

| CHIPSET | COVERAGE | RESOURCE |
|---|---|---|
| Intel 440 ZX | Pentium II, III | developer.intel.com/design/chipsets/datashts/ 290650.htm |
| Intel 440 FX | Pentium Pro | developer.intel.com/design/chipsets/datashts/ 290549.htm |
| Intel 440 GX | Pentium II, III Xeon | developer.intel.com/design/chipsets/datashts/ 290638.htm |
| Intel 440 LX | Pentium Pro | developer.intel.com/design/chipsets/datashts/ 290564.htm |
| Intel 450 GX/KX | Pentium Pro | developer.intel.com/design/chipsets/datashts/ 290523.htm |
| Intel 450 NX | Pentium II, III Xeon | developer.intel.com/design/chipsets/datashts/ 243771.htm |
| Intel 810 | Celeron, Pentium III | developer.intel.com/design/chipsets/datashts/ 290656.htm |
| Intel 810E | Celeron, Pentium III | developer.intel.com/design/chipsets/datashts/ 290676.htm |
| Intel 810E2 | Celeron, Pentium III | developer.intel.com/design/chipsets/datashts/ 290676.htm |
| Intel 815 | Celeron, Pentium III | developer.intel.com/design/chipsets/datashts/ 290688.htm |
| Intel 815E | Celeron, Pentium III | developer.intel.com/design/chipsets/datashts/ 290688.htm |
| Intel 815EG | Celeron, Pentium III | developer.intel.com/design/chipsets/datashts/ 290714.htm |
| Intel 815G | Celeron, Pentium III | developer.intel.com/design/chipsets/datashts/ 290714.htm |
| Intel 815EP | Celeron, Pentium III | developer.intel.com/design/chipsets/datashts/ 290693.htm |
| Intel 815P | Celeron, Pentium III | developer.intel.com/design/chipsets/datashts/ 290693.htm |
| Intel 815EM | Celeron, Pentium III Mobile | developer.intel.com/design/chipsets/datashts/ 290689.htm |
| Intel 820 | Pentium III | developer.intel.com/design/chipsets/datashts/ 290630.htm |
| Intel 820E | Pentium III | developer.intel.com/design/chipsets/datashts/ 290630.htm |
| Intel 830 | Celeron, Pentium III Mobile | developer.intel.com/design/chipsets/datashts/ 298338.htm |
| Intel 840 | Pentium II, III Xeon | developer.intel.com/design/chipsets/datashts/ 298020.htm |
| Intel 845 | Pentium 4 | developer.intel.com/design/chipsets/datashts/ 298604.htm |

**TABLE 9-1    LOCATING TECHNICAL INFORMATION FOR MODERN PC CHIPSETS
(CONTINUED)**

| CHIPSET | COVERAGE | RESOURCE |
| --- | --- | --- |
| Intel 850 | Pentium 4 | developer.intel.com/design/chipsets/datashts/290691.htm |
| Intel 860 | Pentium Xeon | developer.intel.com/design/chipsets/datashts/290713.htm |
| OPTi | Chipset family (general) | http://www.opti.com/html/support.html |
| SiS | Chipset family (general) | www.sis.com/products/chipsets/index.htm |
| SiS 600 | Pentium II | *No longer available* |
| SiS 620 | Pentium II AGP chipset | www.sis.com/products/chipsets/integrated/socket370/620.htm |
| SiS 630 | Pentium II | www.sis.com/products/chipsets/integrated/socket370/630.htm |
| SiS 630E | Celeron, Pentium II/III | www.sis.com/products/chipsets/integrated/socket370/630e.htm |
| SiS 630S | Celeron, Pentium II/III | www.sis.com/products/chipsets/integrated/socket370/630s.htm |
| SiS 633 | Celeron, Pentium III | www.sis.com/products/chipsets/oa/socket370/633.htm |
| SiS 633T | Celeron, Pentium III Tualatin | www.sis.com/products/chipsets/oa/socket370/633t.htm |
| SiS 635 | Celeron, Pentium III Tualatin | www.sis.com/products/chipsets/oa/socket370/635.htm |
| SiS 635T | Celeron, Pentium III Tualatin | www.sis.com/products/chipsets/oa/socket370/635t.htm |
| SiS 645 | Pentium 4 DDR-SDRAM | www.sis.com/products/chipsets/oa/pentium4/645.htm |
| SiS 645DX | Pentium 4 DDR-SDRAM | www.sis.com/products/chipsets/oa/pentium4/645dx.htm |
| SiS 650 | Pentium 4 DDR-SDRAM | www.sis.com/products/chipsets/integrated/pentium4/650.htm |
| SiS 700 | AMD Athlon, Duron | www.sis.com.tw/products/slota/slota.htm |
| SiS 730S | AMD Athlon, Duron | www.sis.com/products/chipsets/integrated/socketa/730s.htm |
| SiS 733 | AMD Athlon, Duron | www.sis.com/products/chipsets/oa/socketa/733.htm |
| SiS 735 | AMD Athlon, Duron DDR-SDRAM | www.sis.com/products/chipsets/oa/socketa/735.htm |
| SiS 740 | AMD Athlon, Duron DDR-SDRAM | www.sis.com/products/chipsets/integrated/socketa/740.htm |
| SiS 745 | AMD Athlon, Athlon XP, Duron DDR-SDRAM | www.sis.com/products/chipsets/oa/socketa/745.htm |
| SiS 961 | South Bridge | www.sis.com/products/chipsets/oa/pentium4/645fea.htm |
| VIA VT82C597 | Socket 7 North Bridge (VP3) | www.viatech.com/pdf/productinfo/597.pdf |

**TABLE 9-1** LOCATING TECHNICAL INFORMATION FOR MODERN PC CHIPSETS *(CONTINUED)*

| CHIPSET | COVERAGE | RESOURCE |
|---|---|---|
| VIA VT8231 | AMD KM133 South Bridge | www.viatech.com/en/ProSavage%20Chipsets/km133.jsp |
| VIA VT8233 | Highly Integrated South Bridge: Socket 370 and Slot 1 CPUs | www.viatech.com/en/apollo/KT266.jsp |
| VIA VT82C496 | Pluto chipset | *No longer available* |
| VIA VT82C580 | Socket 7 North Bridge (VPx) | www.viatech.com/pdf/productinfo/580vpx.pdf |
| VIA VT82C580VP | Socket 7 North Bridge (VP) | www.viatech.com/pdf/productinfo/apollovp.pdf |
| VIA VT82C586B | Socket 7 South Bridge | www.viatech.com/pdf/productinfo/586b.pdf |
| VIA VT82C595 | Socket 7 North Bridge | www.viatech.com/pdf/productinfo/595.pdf |
| VIA VT82C596A | Mobile PC South Bridge | www.viatech.com/pdf/productinfo/596A.pdf |
| VIA VT82C596B | Socket 7 South Bridge (MVPx) | www.viatech.com/pdf/productinfo/596b.pdf |
| VIA VT82C598 | Socket 7 North Bridge (MVP3) | *No longer available* |
| VIA VT82C598AT | Socket 7 North Bridge (MVP3) | www.viatech.com/en/apollo/MVP3.jsp |
| VIA VT82C601 | Intel, Cyrix III North Bridge | www.viatech.com/pdf/productinfo/dspm601brief.pdf |
| VIA VT82C686A | Intel, AMD South Bridge | www.viatech.com/pdf/productinfo/686a.pdf |
| VIA VT82C691 | Pentium II North Bridge | www.viatech.com/pdf/productinfo/691.pdf |
| VIA VT82C693 | Celeron Pentium II North Bridge | www.viatech.com/pdf/productinfo/693.pdf |
| VIA VT82C693A | Intel, Cyrix 133 MHz North Bridge | www.viatech.com/en/apollo/PRO133.jsp |
| VIA VT82C694X | Intel, Cyrix III North Bridge | www.viatech.com/pdf/productinfo/694X.pdf |
| VIA VT8363 | AMD Athlon North Bridge: graphics | www.viatech.com/pdf/productinfo/kt133.pdf |
| VIA VT8365 | AMD Athlon North Bridge: graphics | www.viatech.com/pdf/productinfo/dspm605brief.pdf |
| VIA VT8366 | AMD Athlon North Bridge: DDR-SDRAM | www.viatech.com/en/apollo/KT266.jsp |
| VIA VT8371 | AMD Athlon 133 MHz North Bridge | *No longer available* |
| VIA VT8501 | Socket 7 North Bridge (MVP4) | www.viatech.com/pdf/productinfo/501brief.pdf |
| VIA VT8605 | Intel, Cyrix North Bridge: graphics | www.viatech.com/pdf/productinfo/dspm605brief.pdf |
| VIA VT8633 | Intel, Cyrix North Bridge: DDR-SDRAM | www.viatech.com/en/dm/pro266_o.pdf |

**TABLE 9-1     LOCATING TECHNICAL INFORMATION FOR MODERN PC CHIPSETS**
*(CONTINUED)*

| CHIPSET | COVERAGE | RESOURCE |
|---|---|---|
| VIA VT82C598AT | Socket 7 North Bridge (MVP3) | www.viatech.com/en/apollo/MVP3.jsp |
| VIA VT82C694T | Intel Tualatin, Cyrix North Bridge | www.viatech.com/en/apollo/PRO133T.jsp |
| VIA VT8361 | AMD Athlon North Bridge: graphics | www.viatech.com/en/apollo/KLE133.jsp |
| VIA VT8363A | AMD Athlon North Bridge: 266 MHz FSB | www.viatech.com/en/apollo/KT133A.jsp |
| VIA VT8366A | AMD Athlon North Bridge: DDR-SDRAM | www.viatech.com/en/dm/KT266A.pdf |
| VIA VT8367 | AMD Athlon North Bridge: DDR-SDRAM | www.viatech.com/en/images/kt333/wp2501002kt333rib.pdf |
| VIA VT8601 | Intel, Cyrix North Bridge: graphics | www.viatech.com/en/dm/ple133_o.pdf |
| VIA VT8602 | Intel, Cyrix North Bridge: graphics | www.viatech.com/en/dm/ple133T-O.pdf |
| VIA VT8603 | Intel, Cyrix North Bridge: graphics | www.viatech.com/en/ProSavage%20Chipsets/pn133.jsp |
| VIA VT8604 | Intel, Cyrix North Bridge: graphics | www.viatech.com/en/dm/PL133T-O.pdf |
| VIA 8613 | Intel, Cyrix North Bridge: graphics | www.viatech.com/en/ProSavage%20Chipsets/pn266_whitepaper.pdf |
| VIA VT8653 | Intel, Cyrix North Bridge: DDR-SDRAM | www.viatech.com/en/apollo/PRO266T.jsp |
| VIA VT8751 | Pentium 4 North Bridge: Graphics: DDR-SDRAM | www.viatech.com/en/dm/P4M266.pdf |
| VIA VT8754 | Pentium 4 North Bridge: DDR-SDRAM | www.viatech.com/en/apollo/p4x333_whitepaper.pdf |
| VIA VT8753 | Pentium 4 North Bridge: DDR-SDRAM | www.viatech.com/en/apollo/P4X266.jsp |
| VIA VT8753A | Pentium 4 North Bridge: DDR-SDRAM | www.viatech.com/en/apollo/p4x266a.jsp |
| VIA VT8235 | Pentium 4 South Bridge ATA-133 | www.viatech.com/en/apollo/p4x333.pdf |
| VIA VT8233A | Pentium 4 South Bridge ATA-133 | www.viatech.com/en/apollo/p4m266.jsp |
| VIA VT8233C | Pentium 4 South Bridge3Com Ethernet | www.viatech.com/en/apollo/p4x266a.jsp |
| NVIDIA nForce SPP | AMD Athlon, Duron System Platform Processor | www.nvidia.com/docs/IO/16/ATT/nForce_Platform_Processing_Architecture_Tech_Brief.pdf |
| NVIDIA nForce IGP-64 | AMD Integrated Platform Processor | www.nvidia.com/docs/IO/16/ATT/nForce_Platform_Processing_Architecture_Tech_Brief.pdf |

**TABLE 9-1** LOCATING TECHNICAL INFORMATION FOR MODERN PC CHIPSETS
*(CONTINUED)*

| CHIPSET | COVERAGE | RESOURCE |
|---------|----------|----------|
| NVIDIA nForce IGP-128 | AMD Integrated Platform Processor | www.nvidia.com/docs/IO/16/ATT/nForce_Platform_Processing_Architecture_Tech_Brief.pdf |
| NVIDIA nForce MCP | Media/Communications Processor | www.nvidia.com/docs/lo/557/SUPP/nForce_MCP_Overview.pdf |
| NVIDIA nForce MCP-D | Media/Communications Processor | www.nvidia.com/docs/lo/557/SUPP/nForce_MCP_Overview.pdf |

**TABLE 9-2** SUMMARY OF MOTHERBOARD CHIPSET COMPONENTS

| CHIPSET DESIGNATION | COMPONENT | #NEEDED | FUNCTION |
|---------------------|-----------|---------|----------|
| ALi CyberMAGiK | M1646 | 1 | System controller |
|  | M1535+ | 1 | PCI/IDE/USB controller |
| ALi MAGiK 1 | M1647 | 1 | System controller |
|  | M1535D+ | 1 | PCI/ISA/IDE/USB controller |
| ALi CyberAladdin P4 | M1672 | 1 | System controller |
|  | M1535+ | 1 | PCI/IDE/USB controller |
| ALi Aladdin P4 | M1671 | 1 | System controller |
|  | M1535D+ | 1 | PCI/ISA/IDE/USB controller |
| ALi Aladdin Pro 5T | M1651T | 1 | System controller |
|  | M1535D+ | 1 | PCI/ISA/IDE/USB controller |
| ALi Aladdin Pro 5M | M1651 | 1 | System controller |
|  | M1535+ | 1 | PCI/ISA/IDE/USB controller |
| ALi Aladdin Pro 4 | M1641 | 1 | System controller |
|  | M1535 | 1 | PCI/ISA/IDE/USB controller |
| CyberALADDiN-T | M1644T | 1 | System controller |
|  | M1535+ | 1 | PCI/ISA/IDE/USB controller |
| CyberBLADE ALADDiN i1 | M1632M | 1 | System controller |
|  | M1535+ | 1 | PCI/ISA/IDE/USB controller |
| ALi Aladdin TNT2 | M1631 | 1 | System controller |
|  | M1543C | 1 | PCI/ISA/IDE/USB controller |
| ALi Aladdin Pro 2 | M1621 | 1 | System controller |
|  | M1533 | 1 | PCI/ISA/IDE/USB controller |
| ALi Aladdin 7 | M1561 | 1 | System controller |
|  | M1535D+ | 1 | PCI/ISA/USB controller |
| ALi Aladdin-5 | M1541 | 1 | System controller |
|  | M1543C | 1 | PCI/ISA/IDE/USB controller |
| ALi Aladdin 4/4+ | M1531B | 1 | System controller |
|  | M1533 | 1 | PCI/ISA/IDE/USB controller |

**TABLE 9-2     SUMMARY OF MOTHERBOARD CHIPSET COMPONENTS *(CONTINUED)***

| CHIPSET DESIGNATION | COMPONENT | #NEEDED | FUNCTION |
|---|---|---|---|
| AMD 760 MPX | AMD 762 | 1 | System controller |
| | AMD 768 | 1 | PCI/ISA/IDE/USB controller |
| AMD 760 MP | AMD 762 | 1 | System controller |
| | AMD 766 | 1 | PCI/ISA/IDE/USB controlle |
| AMD 760 | AMD 761 | 1 | System controller |
| | AMD 766 | 1 | Peripheral bus controller |
| AMD 750 | AMD 751 | 1 | System controller |
| | AMD 756 | 1 | Peripheral bus controller |
| AMD 640 | AMD-640 | 1 | System controller |
| | AMD-645 | 1 | Peripheral bus controller |
| Intel 860 | 82860 | 1 | Memory controller hub |
| | 82801BA | 1 | Integrated controller hub |
| | 82806AA | 1 | 64-bit PCI controller (optional) |
| | 82803AA | 1 | Memory repeater hub RDRAM (optional) |
| Intel 850 | 82850 | 1 | Memory controller hub |
| | 82801BA | 1 | Integrated controller hub |
| | 82802AB | 1 | Firmware hub |
| Intel 845 | 82845 | 1 | Memory controller hub |
| | 82801BA | 1 | Integrated controller hub |
| Intel 840 | 82840 | 1 | Memory controller hub |
| | 82803 | 1 | Memory repeater hub RDRAM |
| | 82804 | 1 | Memory repeater hub SDRAM |
| | 82806 | 1 | 64-bit PCI controller |
| | 82801 | 1 | Integrated controller hub |
| | 82802 | 1 | Firmware hub |
| Intel 820E | 82820 | 1 | Memory controller hub |
| | 82820DP | 1 | Memory controller hub, dual processor |
| | 82801BA | 1 | Integrated controller hub |
| | 82802AB | 1 | Firmware hub |
| Intel 820 | 82820 | 1 | Memory controller hub |
| | 82820DP | 1 | Memory controller hub, dual processor |
| | 82801 | 1 | I/O controller hub |
| | 82802 | 1 | Firmware hub |
| | 82380AB | 1 | PCI-ISA bridge |
| 815G | 82815G | 1 | Graphics/memory hub |
| | 82801AA | 1 | I/O controller hub |
| 815EG | 82815G | 1 | Graphics/memory hub |
| | 82801BA | 1 | I/O controller hub |

**TABLE 9-2    SUMMARY OF MOTHERBOARD CHIPSET COMPONENTS *(CONTINUED)***

| CHIPSET DESIGNATION | COMPONENT | #NEEDED | FUNCTION |
|---|---|---|---|
| Intel 815EM | 82815EM | 1 | Graphics/memory hub |
| | 82801BAM | 1 | I/O controller hub |
| | 82807AA | 1 | Video controller hub |
| Intel 815P | 82815EP | 1 | Memory hub |
| | 82801AA | 1 | I/O controller hub |
| Intel 815EP | 82815EP | 1 | Memory hub |
| | 82801BA | 1 | Integrated controller hub |
| | 82802AB | 1 | Firmware hub |
| Intel 815E | 82815 | 1 | Graphics/memory hub |
| | 82801BA | 1 | Integrated controller hub |
| | 82802 | 1 | Firmware hub |
| Intel 815 | 82815 | 1 | Graphics/memory hub |
| | 82801AA | 1 | Integrated controller hub |
| | 82802 | 1 | Firmware hub |
| Intel 810E2 | 82810E | 1 | Graphics/memory hub |
| | 82801BA | 1 | Integrated controller hub |
| | 82802 | 1 | Firmware hub |
| Intel 810E | 82810E | 1 | Memory controller hub |
| | 82801 | 1 | Integrated controller hub |
| | 82802 | 1 | Firmware hub |
| Intel 810 | 82810 | 1 | Graphics/memory controller hub |
| | 82801 | 1 | Integrated controller hub |
| | 82802 | 1 | Firmware hub |
| Intel 440 GX | 82443GX | 1 | Host bridge/controller |
| | 82371EB | 1 | Peripheral bus controller (PIIX4E) |
| Intel 440 ZX | 82443ZX | 1 | System/AGP controller |
| | 82371AB & EB | 1 | PCI ISA IDE Xcelerator (PIIX4 & E) |
| Intel 440 EX | 82443EX | 1 | System AGP controller |
| | 82371AB | 1 | PCI ISA IDE Xcelerator (PIIX4) |
| Intel 440 MX | 82443MX | 1 | AGP host bridge controller PCI ISA IDE Xcelerator (PIIX4) Integrated North-South Bridge |
| Intel 440 BX | 82443BX | 1 | AGP host bridge controller |
| | 82371AB | 1 | PCI ISA IDE Xcelerator (PIIX4) |
| Intel 430 VX (Triton II*) | 82437VX | 1 | System controller |
| | 82371SB | 1 | PCI ISA IDE Xcelerator (PIIX3) |
| | 82438VX | 2 | Data path unit |
| Intel 430 TX | 82439TX | 1 | System controller |
| | 82371AB | 1 | PCI ISA IDE Xcelerator (PIIX4) |
| Intel 430 HX (Triton II*) | 82439HX | 1 | System controller |

**TABLE 9-2** SUMMARY OF MOTHERBOARD CHIPSET COMPONENTS *(CONTINUED)*

| CHIPSET DESIGNATION | COMPONENT | #NEEDED | FUNCTION |
|---|---|---|---|
| | 82371SB | 1 | PCI I/O IDE Xcelerator (PIIX3) |
| Intel 430 FX (Triton*) | 82437FX | 1 | System controller |
| | 82371FB | 1 | ISA bridge, PCI/ISA/IDE Xcelerator (PIIX) |
| | 82438FX | 2 | Data path unit |
| Intel 430 MX | 82437MX | 1 | System controller |
| | 82438MX | 2 | Data path units |
| | 82371MX | 1 | PCI I/O IDE Xcelerator (MPIIX) |
| Intel 440 FX (Natoma*) | 82441FX | 1 | PCI and memory controller |
| | 82442FX | 1 | Data bus accelerator |
| | 82371SB | 1 | PCI ISA IDE Xcelerator (PIIX3) |
| Intel 450 KX (Orion*) | 82451KX | 4 | Memory interface component |
| | 82452KX | 1 | Data path unit |
| | 82453KX | 1 | Data controller |
| | 82454KX | 1 or 2 | PCI bridge |
| Intel 450 GX (Orion*) | 82451GX | 4 | Memory interface component |
| | 82452GX | 1 | Data path unit |
| | 82453GX | 1 | Data controller |
| | 82454GX | 1 or 2 | PCI bridge |
| Intel 440 LX | 82443LX | 1 | PCI AGP system controller |
| | 82371AB | 1 | PCI ISA IDE Xcelerator (PIIX4) |
| VIA Apollo P4X333 | VT8754 | 1 | System controller |
| | VT8235 | 1 | PCI/IDE/USB controller |
| VIA Apollo P4X266A | VT8753A | 1 | System controller |
| | VT8233A | 1 | PCI/IDE/USB controller |
| VIA Apollo P4X266 | VT8753 | 1 | System controller |
| | VT8233 | 1 | PCI/IDE/USB controller |
| VIA Apollo KT333 | VT8367 | 1 | System controller |
| | VT8233 (A,C) | | PCI/IDE/USB controller |
| VIA Apollo KT266A | VT8366A | 1 | System controller |
| | VT8233 | 1 | PCI/IDE/USB controller |
| VIA Apollo KT266/AMD | VT8366 | 1 | System controller |
| | VT8233 | 1 | PCI/IDE/USB controller |
| VIA KX133 Athlon | VT8371 | 1 | System controller |
| | VT82C686A | 1 | PCI/ISA/IDE/USB controller |
| VIA Apollo KT133A | VT8363A | 1 | System controller |
| | VT82C686B | 1 | PCI/ISA/IDE/USB controller |
| VIA Apollo KT133/AMD | VT8363 | 1 | System controller |
| | VT82C686A | 1 | PCI/ISA/IDE/USB controller |
| VIA Apollo KLE133 | VT8361 | 1 | System controller |

**TABLE 9-2**    SUMMARY OF MOTHERBOARD CHIPSET COMPONENTS *(CONTINUED)*

| CHIPSET DESIGNATION | COMPONENT | #NEEDED | FUNCTION |
| --- | --- | --- | --- |
| | VT82C686B | 1 | PCI/ISA/IDE/USB controller |
| VIA ProSavageDDR PN266T | VT8613 | 1 | System controller |
| | VT8233 (C) | 1 | PCI/IDE/USB controller |
| VIA ProSavageDDR KM266 | VT8375 | 1 | System controller |
| | VT8233A | 1 | PCI/IDE/USB controller |
| VIA ProSavageDDR KN266 | VT8372 | 1 | System controller |
| | VT8233C | 1 | PCI/IDE/USB controller |
| VIA ProSavage P4M266 | VT8751 | 1 | System controller |
| | VT8233C | 1 | PCI/IDE/USB controller |
| VIA ProSavage KM133 (AMD) | VT8365 | 1 | System/graphics controller |
| | VT8231 | 1 | PCI/ISA/IDE/USB controller |
| VIA Apollo Pro 266T | VT8653 | 1 | System controller |
| | VT8233 | 1 | PCI/IDE/USB controller |
| VIA Apollo Pro 266 | VT8633 | 1 | System controller |
| | VT8233 | 1 | PCI/IDE/USB controller |
| VIA ProSavage PL133T | VT8604 | 1 | System controller |
| | VT8231 | 1 | PCI/ISA/IDE/USB controller |
| VIA ProSavage PN133T | VT8603 | 1 | System controller |
| | VT8231 | 1 | PCI/ISA/IDE/USB controller |
| VIA ProSavage PM133 | VT8605 | 1 | System/graphics controller |
| | VT82C686A | 1 | PCI/ISA/IDE/USB controller |
| VIA ProSavage KN133 | VT8363A | 1 | System controller |
| | VT82C686B | 1 | PCI/ISA/IDE/USB controller |
| VIA Apollo Pro 133T | VT82C694T | 1 | System controller |
| | VT82C596B | 1 | PCI/ISA/IDE/USB controller |
| VIA Apollo Pro 133A Dual | VT82C694X | 1 | System controller |
| | VT82C686A | 1 | PCI/ISA/IDE/USB controller |
| VIA Apollo Pro 133A | VT82C694X | 1 | System controller |
| | VT82C596B | 1 | PCI/ISA/IDE/USB controller |
| VIA Apollo PLE133T | VT8602 | 1 | System controller |
| | VT82C686B | 1 | PCI/ISA/IDE/USB controller |
| VIA Apollo PLE133 | VT8601 | 1 | System/graphics controller |
| | VT82C686A | 1 | PCI/ISA/IDE/USB controller |
| VIA Apollo PM601 | VT8601 | 1 | System/graphics controller |
| | VT8231 | 1 | PCI/ISA/IDE/USB controller |
| VIA Apollo Pro 133 | VT82C693A | 1 | System controller |
| | VT82C686A | 1 | PCI/ISA/IDE/USB controller |
| VIA Apollo Pro Plus | VT82C693 | 1 | System controller |
| | VT82C686A | 1 | PCI/ISA/IDE/USB controller |

**TABLE 9-2**   SUMMARY OF MOTHERBOARD CHIPSET COMPONENTS *(CONTINUED)*

| CHIPSET DESIGNATION | COMPONENT | #NEEDED | FUNCTION |
|---|---|---|---|
| VIA Apollo Pro | VT82C691 | 1 | System controller |
| | VT82C686A | 1 | PCI/ISA/IDE/USB controller |
| VIA MVP4 | VT8501 | 1 | AGP system controller |
| | VT82C686A | 1 | PCI/ISA/IDE/USB controller |
| VIA Apollo MVP3 | VT82C598AT | 1 | System controller |
| | VT82C686A | 1 | PCI/ISA/IDE/USB controller |
| VIA Apollo P6 | VT82C685VP | 1 | System controller |
| | VT82C586 | 1 | PCI/ISA/IDE/USB controller |
| | VT82C687 | 1 | Memory controller |
| VIA Apollo VP3 | VT82C597 | 1 | System controller |
| | VT82C586B | 1 | PCI/IDE/USB controller |
| VIA Apollo VP2/97 | VT82C595 | 1 | System controller |
| | VT82C586B | 1 | PCI/IDE/USB controller |
| VIA Apollo VPX/97 | VT82C585VPX | 1 | System controller |
| | VT82C586B | 1 | PCI/ISA/IDE/USB controller (PC97) |
| | VT82C586A | 1 | PCI/ISA/IDE/USB controller (non-97) |
| | VT82C587VP | 2 | Share frame buffers |
| VIA Apollo VP-1 | VT82C585VP | 1 | System controller |
| | VT82C586 | 1 | PCI/IDE/ISA/USB controller |
| | VT82C587VP | 2 | Share frame buffers |
| VIA Apollo Master | VT82C575M | 1 | System controller |
| | VT82C576M | 1 | PCI/ISA/IDE controller |
| | VT82C577M | 2 | Frame buffers |
| | VT82C416 | 1 | Support controller |
| SiS 745 | 745 | 1 | Integrated system controller |
| SiS 740 | 740 | 1 | System Controller |
| | 961 | 1 | Bus controller |
| SiS 735 | 735 | 1 | Integrated system controller |
| SiS 733 | 733 | 1 | Integrated system controller |
| SiS 730S | 730S | 1 | Integrated system controller |
| SiS 650 | 650 | 1 | System controller |
| | 961 | 1 | Bus controller |
| SiS 645DX | 645DX | 1 | System controller |
| | 961 | 1 | Bus controller |
| SiS 645 | 645 | 1 | System controller |
| | 961 | 1 | Bus controller |
| SiS 635T | 635T | 1 | Integrated system controller |
| SiS 635 | 635 | 1 | Integrated system controller |
| SiS 633T | 633T | 1 | Integrated system controller |

**TABLE 9-2** SUMMARY OF MOTHERBOARD CHIPSET COMPONENTS *(CONTINUED)*

| CHIPSET DESIGNATION | COMPONENT | #NEEDED | FUNCTION |
|---|---|---|---|
| SiS 633 | 633 | 1 | Integrated system controller |
| SiS 630E | 630E | 1 | Integrated system controller |
| SiS 630S | 630S | 1 | Integrated system controller |
| SiS 630 | 630 | 1 | Integrated system controller |
| SiS 620 | 620 | 1 | System controller |
| | 5595 | 1 | Bus controller |
| SiS 600 | 600 | 1 | System controller |
| | 5596 | 1 | Bus controller |
| SiS 540 | 540 | 1 | Integrated system controller |
| SiS 530 | 530 | 1 | System controller |
| | 5595 | 1 | Bus controller |
| SiS 5598 | 5598 | 1 | Integrated system controller |
| SiS 5597 (Jedi) | 5597 | 1 | Integrated system controller |
| SiS 5596 | 5596 | 1 | System controller |
| | 5513 | 1 | USB controller |
| SiS 5591 | 5591 | 1 | System controller |
| | 5595 | 1 | Bus controller |
| SiS 5582 | 5582 | 1 | Integrated system controller |
| SiS 5571 (Trinity) | 5571 | 1 | Integrated system controller |
| SiS 551X | 5511 | 1 | System controller |
| | 5512 | 1 | Bus controller |
| | 5513 | 1 | USB controller |
| SiS 85C49X (486) | 85C496 | 1 | System controller |
| | 85C497 | 1 | Bus controller |
| OPTi Discovery | 82C650 | 1 | System controller |
| | 82C651 | 1 | Bus controller |
| | 82C652 | 1 | Auxiliary PCI bus controller |
| OPTi Vendetta | 82C750 | 1 | Integrated system controller |
| OPTi Fire Star | 82C700 | 1 | Integrated system controller |
| NVIDIA nForce Enthusiast | SPP | 1 | System Platform Processor |
| | MCP-D | 1 | Media/Communication Processor |
| NVIDIA nForce Mainstream | IGP-64 | 1 | Integrated Graphics Processor |
| | MCP-D | 1 | Media/Communication Processor |
| NVIDIA nForce 420D Performance | IGP-128 | 1 | Integrated Graphics Processor |
| | MCP-D | 1 | Media/Communication Processor |
| NVIDIA nForce Value | IGP-64 | 1 | Integrated Graphics Processor |
| | MCP | 1 | Media/Communication Processor |

* Chipset names (such as Orion) are not officially used by Intel—only part numbers are actually referred to.

There is a tremendous rivalry between the major chipset manufacturers. This chapter does not advocate the use of any given chipset (or manufacturer) over another, or attempt to make any kind of product recommendation. Rather, this chapter merely familiarizes you with the key features of each chipset, and allows you to make objective assessments of system capabilities based upon the particular core logic in use.

# ALi Chipsets

At one time, Acer Laboratories, Inc. (or ALi as they now call themselves) had its very existence challenged by the introduction of the Intel TX chipset. The TX chipset represented Intel's entry into the low-cost/low-end chipset market—a market that provided the very foundation for manufacturers such as ALi and VIA. ALi has survived by providing less-than-cutting-edge, lower-cost chip solutions for entry-level motherboard and systems manufacturers' needs. ALi has attempted to reduce buyers' costs even further by including a video/3D graphics engine in some of its chipset products while still supporting modern features like USB, UDMA/66/100/133, PC100/133, and high-speed DDR-SDRAM memory.

## ALI CYBERMAGIK

Intended for mobile PCs, the CyberMAGiK chipset includes the M1646 North Bridge (see Figure 9-3) and M1535+ South Bridge. It features full support for AMD Slot/Socket A Athlon and Duron processors using FSB (Front Side Bus) speeds of 200/266 MHz, and supports up to 3GB of both PC1600/PC2100 DDR and conventional PC133 SDRAM memory. The chipset also serves to extend mobile battery life by

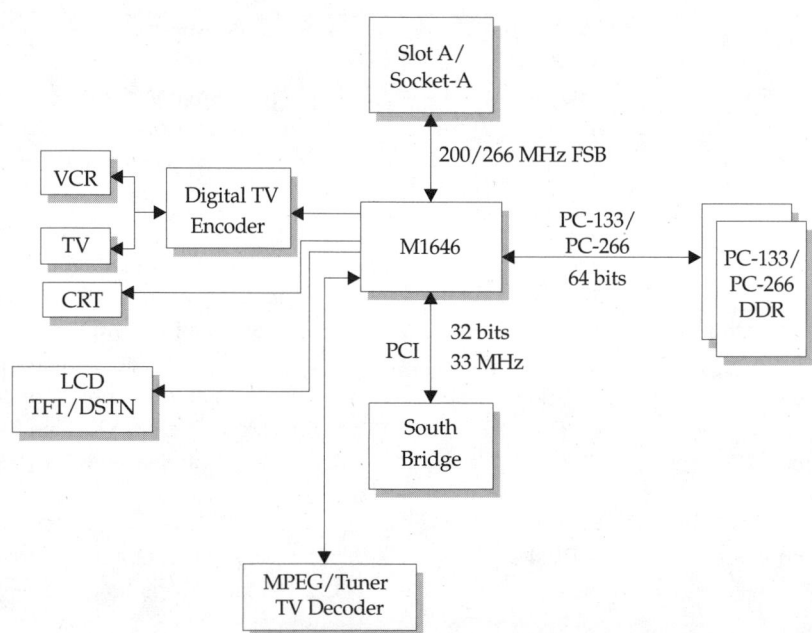

**FIGURE  9-3**   Application diagram of the ALi CyberMAGiK M1646 North Bridge (Courtesy ALi Corporation)

supporting all ACPI power management states (along with support for legacy APM power management features) and AMD's PowerNow! technology.

PC2100 DDR memory provides a peak memory bandwidth of up to 2.1 GB/s, yet requires only 2.5 Vdc (important features to mobile PC designers). The high memory bandwidth provided by PC2100 DDR SDRAM also improves performance of the integrated graphics system over regular PC133 SDRAM. The CyberMAGiK 128-bit dual pixel graphic engine is based on the Trident CyberBlade XP, and handles AGP 1X/2X/4X and advanced graphics rendering features. It includes a hardware transform-and-lighting unit, support for DirectX 7.0 (and higher), and numerous other graphics features. CyberMAGiK uses SMA (Share Memory Architecture) to eliminate the need for a local graphics frame buffer.

The M1535+ South Bridge of the CyberMAGiK chipset integrates the ALi AC-Link host controller, Host Signal Processing (HSP) software modem interface, a two-channel Ultra-DMA/33/66/100 controller, and integrated Sound Blaster Pro/16 audio features. The South Bridge supports up to six USB ports with two USB host controllers. Built in Super I/O offers a standard floppy disk controller, two serial ports, and one parallel port. Fast Infra-Red (Fast I/R) support provides for short-range wireless communications with other devices. The older M1535 South Bridge offers similar features, but is limited to Ultra-DMA/33/66 and only supports up to four USB ports. Table 9-3 compares the features for an ALi CyberMAGiK chipset.

**TABLE 9-3    COMPARISON OF CURRENT ALI CHIPSET FEATURES AT A GLANCE**

| CHIPSET | CYBERMAGIK | ALIMAGIK | ALI CYBERALADDIN P4 | ALI ALADDIN P4 | ALADDINPRO 5/T |
|---|---|---|---|---|---|
| Processor | AMD Athlon/Duron | AMD Athlon/Duron | Intel Pentium P4 | Intel Pentium P4 | Pentium II/III Celeron |
| Number of Processors | 1 | 1 | 1 | 1 | 1 |
| FSB | 200/266 MHz | 200/266 MHz | 400 MHz | 400 MHz | 66/100/133 MHz |
| Max. Memory | 3GB | 3GB | 3GB | 3GB | 3GB |
| Memory Type | PC66/100/133 SDRAM 200/266 MHz DDR SDRAM | PC66/100/133 SDRAM 200/266 MHz DDR SDRAM | PC100/133 SDRAM 200/266 MHz DDR SDRAM | PC100/133 SDRAM 200/266/333 MHz DDR SDRAM | PC66/100/133 SDRAM 200/266 MHz DDR SDRAM |
| Memory Bus | 66/100/133 MHz | 66/100/133 MHz | 100/133 MHz | 100/133 MHz | 66/100/133 MHz |
| ECC Support | N/A | N/A | N/A | N/A | N/A |
| PCI Spec. | PCI v2.2 | PCI v2.2 | PCI v2.2 | PCI v2.2 | PCI v2.2 |
| Integrated Graphics | Y | N | Y | N | N |
| AGP-Compliant | AGP 2.0 | AGP 2.0 | AGP 2.0 | AGP 2.0 | AGP 2.0 |
| SMA | 4/8/16/32MB | N/A | N/A | N/A | N/A |
| External AGP Slot | N | Y | N | Y | Y |
| USB | 6 Ports | Supported | 6 Ports | 6 Ports | 6 Ports |
| Max. IDE | UDMA/100 | UDMA/100 | UDMA/100/133 | UDMA/100/133 | UDMA/100 |
| Ethernet | N/A | N/A | N/A | N/A | N/A |
| AC97 | Y | Y | Y | Y | Y (w/ MC97) |

## ALI ALIMAGIK 1 AND MOBILEMAGIK

The ALiMAGiK 1 chipset supports AMD Athlon and Duron processors. It includes support for PC1600/PC2100 DDR SDRAM and 133 MHz SDRAM memory. Designed for desktop PCs, the ALiMAGiK 1 chipset includes the M1647 North Bridge and the M1535D+ South Bridge (see Figure 9-4). The MobileMAGiK 1 chipset is similar to the ALiMAGiK 1 (with the addition of some power conservation features) and is designed for portable systems utilizing mobile AMD processors. It includes the M1647 North Bridge and the M1535+ South Bridge. Both the ALiMAGiK and MobileMAGiK chipsets support AGP v2.0 4X/2X/1X modes through a graphics slot, and interface with AMD's 200/266 MHz front side bus. The memory controller in the M1647 supports up to 3GB of PC1600/PC2100 DDR or 66/100/133 SDRAM. PC2100 DDR enables 2.1GB/s peak bandwidth between the system memory and the North Bridge.

Power conservation is another important consideration, and both chipsets support AMD's PowerNow! technology. When used in mobile PCs, the M1647's support for AMD's PowerNow! technology allows CPU operating frequency and voltage to be changed to save power and extend battery life. The ALiMAGiK-series chipsets also provide Advanced Configuration and Power Interface (ACPI) support, Ultra-DMA/66/100 support, built-in hardware-based Sound Blaster Pro/16 compatibility, a host signal processing (HSP) software modem interface, a USB and Super-I/O controller, serial/parallel ports, and a floppy interface. Table 9-3 lists the details for ALiMAGiK chips.

## ALI CYBERALADDIN P4

The ALi CyberAladdin chipset is designed for use with Intel Pentium 4 processors, and offers integrated graphics support (see Figure 9-5). The set combines an ALi M1672 North Bridge with the ALi M1535+

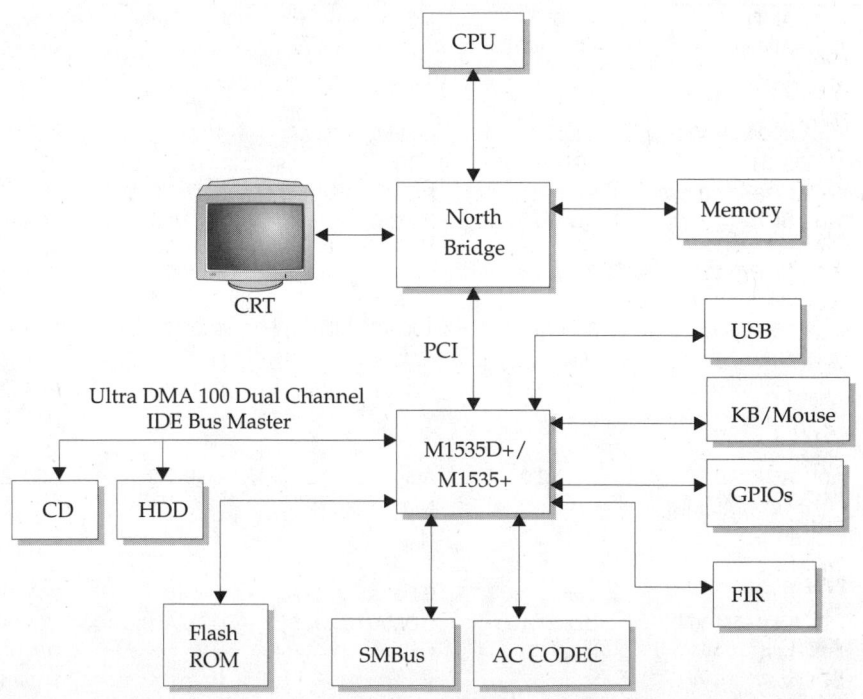

**FIGURE   9-4**     Application diagram of the ALi ALiMAGiK M1535+ South Bridge (Courtesy ALi Corporation)

**FIGURE 9-5**    The ALi CyberAladdin P4 chipset's M1672 North Bridge supports Pentium 4 processors with a 400 MHz FSB (Courtesy of ALi Corporation).

South Bridge (though other M1535 series South Bridges can also be used). The North Bridge supports 400 MHz Front Side Bus (FSB) speeds featuring up to 3.2 GB/s bandwidth between the processor and memory controller, and handles a total of 3GB of RAM. Multiple memory types and speeds are supported including 100/133 MHz SDRAM and 200/266 MHz DDR SDRAM. The M1672 integrates the Trident CyberBlade XP2 graphics core, and supports DirectX 8 along with DVD motion compensation. The interface is AGP V2.0-compliant with fast write capability.

North-to-South Bridge communication bandwidth of 133 MB/s is provided through a PCI bus. Up to seven PCI masters are supported along with full compliance for PCI Rev. 2.2 standards. The chipset's PCI bus features also include a synchronous/asynchronous clock mode with the processor bus, support for delayed transaction, and support for concurrent PCI bus burst transfers with zero wait-states.

The CyberAladdin P4 chipset usually includes the M1535+ South Bridge, providing support for modern mobile PCs, though it can also be configured with other M1535 series South Bridges for use in larger desktop systems. The South Bridge supports a keyboard, mouse, floppy disk interface, serial port, and parallel port. It also provides an Ultra-DMA/66/100/133 interface for modern high-capacity hard drives. Three USB hub controllers are possible—offering up to six USB ports. The South Bridge offers modern power management features including ACPI 1.0b and legacy APM support. Table 9-3 compares the features of the ALi CyberAladdin P4 chipset.

## ALI ALADDIN P4

Similar to the CyberAladdin P4, the ALi Aladdin Pentium 4 chipset matches the ALi M1671 North Bridge with one of the ALi M1535 series South Bridges (usually the M1535D+). The North Bridge provides a 400 MHz FSB speed with up to 3.2 GB/s of bandwidth between the processor and memory controller. Up to 3GB of 100/133 MHz SDRAM or 200/266/333 MHz DDR SDRAM is allowed (DDR333 mem—dubbed PC2—allows a peak bandwidth of 2.7 GB/sec). An AGP 4X v2.0-compliant graphics interface is provided (including fast write support).

The Aladdin P4 chipset can include any of the M1535 series South Bridges, though the M1535D+ South Bridge offers the most common match for desktop systems. Communication between bridges is provided on a 133 MB/s v2.2-compliant PCI bus. Up to seven PCI masters are supported. The chipset's PCI bus features include support for a synchronous/asynchronous clock mode with the processor bus, support for delayed transaction, and support for concurrent PCI bus burst transfers with zero wait states. South Bridge features include standard support for a keyboard, mouse, floppy disk, serial port, and parallel port controllers. It provides an Ultra-DMA/66/100/133 interface, allowing the use of very large hard drives. Three USB hub controllers will support up to six USB ports. The South Bridge offers power management features including ACPI 1.0b and legacy APM support. Table 9-3 compares features of the ALi Aladdin P4 chipset.

## ALI ALADDIN PRO 5/T

The ALi Aladdin Pro 5 includes the M1651/T North Bridge together with the M1535D+ South Bridge. It offers full support for Pentium II/III and Celeron processors, and can accommodate those processors in both Slot 1 and Socket 370 packages. The Aladdin Pro 5 allows the use of 66/100/133 MHz SDRAM, or 200/266 MHz DDR SDRAM memory. The PC266 DDR SDRAM memory provides 2.1 GB/s peak bandwidth between the system memory and North Bridge chip for best system performance. Now slightly dated, this chipset supports the PCI 2.2 specifications, offers UDMA/100 and AC97/MC97 support, and offers AGP 4X compatibility. You can see the ALi Aladdin Pro 5/T compared to other ALi chipsets in Table 9-3.

The Aladdin Pro 5T chipset supports the Tualatin series Intel Pentium III and Celeron processors when the M1651T North Bridge is used on the motherboard.

## ALI ALADDIN PRO 4

Now somewhat outdated, the ALi Aladdin Pro 4 chipset consists of the M1641 North Bridge system controller, and either the M1535 South Bridge bus controller for desktops or the M1535D controller for mobile systems. It supports Pentium II/III processors that use a 66/100 MHz FSB speed. It can also support the 66 MHz Celeron FSB setting. The Pro 4 chipset handles PC100 and PC133 SDRAM memory, and it provides support for UDMA/33/66, four USB ports, and AGP 2X. Table 9-4 highlights the ALi Aladdin Pro 4 features.

| **TABLE 9-4** | **COMPARISON OF OLDER ALI CHIPSET FEATURES AT A GLANCE** | | | | |
|---|---|---|---|---|---|
| **CHIPSET** | **ALADDIN PRO 4** | **CYBERALADDIN-T** | **CYBERBLADE ALADDIN I1** | **ALADDIN TNT2** | **ALADDIN PRO 2** |
| Processor | Pentium II/III Celeron | Pentium II/III Celeron | Pentium II/III Celeron | Pentium II/III Celeron | Pentium II |
| Number of Processors | 1 | 1 | 1 | 1 | 1-2 |
| FSB | 66/100 MHz | 66/100/133 MHz | 66/100 MHz | 66/100/133 MHz | 60/66/100 MHz |
| Max. Memory | 1.5GB | 3GB | 1.5GB | 1.5GB | 1GB |
| Memory Type | PC100/133 SDRAM | PC100/133 SDRAM 200/266 MHz DDR SDRAM | EDO SDRAM VC SDRAM | EDO SDRAM VC SDRAM | FPM EDO SDRAM |
| Memory Bus | 66/100/133 MHz | 100/133 MHz | 66/100 MHz | 66/100/133 MHz | 60/66/100 MHz |
| ECC Support | Y | N/A | N/A | Y | Y |
| PCI Spec. | PCI v2.2 | PCI v2.2 | PCI v2.2 | PCI v2.2 | PCI v2.1 |
| Integrated Graphics | N | Y | Y | Y | N |
| AGP-Compliant | AGP 2.0 | AGP 2.0 | AGP 2.0 | AGP 2.0 | AGP 1.0 |
| SMA | N | 4/8/16/32MB | 2-8MB | N | N |

**TABLE 9-4    COMPARISON OF OLDER ALI CHIPSET FEATURES AT A GLANCE (CONTINUED)**

| CHIPSET | ALADDIN PRO 4 | CYBERALADDIN-T | CYBERBLADE ALADDIN I1 | ALADDIN TNT2 | ALADDIN PRO 2 |
|---------|---------------|----------------|------------------------|--------------|---------------|
| External AGP Slot | Y | N | N | N | Y |
| USB | 4 Ports | 6 Ports | 6 Ports | 3 ports | 3 ports |
| Max. IDE | UDMA/33/66 | UDMA/66/100 | UDMA/66/100 | UDMA/66 | UDMA/33 |
| Ethernet | N/A | N/A | N/A | N/A | N/A |
| AC97 | Y | Y (w/ MC97) | N | N | N |

## ALI CYBERALADDIN-T

Designed for use primarily in mobile systems, the CyberAladdin-T supports Intel Pentium II/III and Celeron Slot 1/Socket 370 processors (including newer Tualatin core units and Intel mobile processors) operating at FSB speeds up to 133 MHz. The chipset includes an ALi M1644T North Bridge and the M1535+ South Bridge. The North Bridge contains an integrated AGP 2.0-compliant Trident CyberBlade XP graphics core supporting DirectX 7.0 (or later) and uses a 128-bit internal data path operating at 133 MHz. DVD motion compensation is also included. The CyberAladdin-T uses SMA (Shared Memory Architecture) to utilize 4, 8, 16, or 32MB of system memory for the graphics frame buffer, eliminating the need for separate graphics memory. This chipset can handle up to 3GB of standard PC100/133 SDRAM, or the newer 200/266 MHz DDR SDRAM (providing a bandwidth up to 2.1 GB/s).

The M1535+ South Bridge in the CyberAladdin-T chipset is also designed for use in mobile systems. It includes extensive power management functions such as Power On Suspend, Suspend to RAM, Suspend to Disk, and so on. The 2D/3D engines are also throttled back when idle to conserve additional power. ACPI and legacy APM standards are also supported. The M1535+ South Bridge provides for two channels of Ultra-DMA/66/100, Super I/O, and USB port support. It also offers integrated AC97 audio and MC97 modem features. Table 9-4 lists the main features of the CyberAladdin-T chipset.

## ALI CYBERBLADE ALADDIN I1

The older ALi CyberBLADE Aladdin i1 is a low-power chipset that includes an LCD controller with standard North Bridge features. The M1632M North Bridge is designed for mobile systems based on Intel Pentium II/III and Intel Celeron processors using an FSB speed of 66 MHz or 100 MHz. The M1632M supports up to 1.5GB of EDO, SDRAM, and VC-SDRAM memory. The AGP 2X graphics controller core incorporates a 2D/3D graphics engine and video accelerator that also handles DVD playback with motion compensation, video capture, and TV output features. Shared Memory Architecture (SMA) eliminates the need for an external frame buffer and independent graphics memory. The CyberBLADE Aladdin i1 North Bridge offers pipelined burst and concurrent data transfers between the graphics engine, CPU, cache, system memory, and PCI bus.

The ALi M1535+ South Bridge chip is most often used with the CyberBLADE Aladdin i1 chipset. The integrated Super I/O controller provides a serial port, parallel port, floppy disk controller, and fast I/R support. Integrated audio features full Sound Blaster compatibility, and is PC98/PC99-compliant (now an older standard). The integrated audio can replace all the functions of a wavetable-based legacy audio ISA card. In addition, it offers Ultra-DMA66/100 support, but not the faster UDMA/133. Two USB host controllers can handle up to six USB ports. It includes full support for ACPI and OS controlled power management meeting PC98/PC99 requirements. Table 9-4 lists the main features of the ALi CyberBLADE Aladdin i1 chipset.

## ALI ALADDIN TNT2

Acer Laboratories combines the M1631 AGP/PCI/3D graphics system controller with any of four ALi South Bridge (usually the M1535D or 1543C) chips to create the Aladdin TNT2 package. This older chipset supports the Pentium II/III or Celeron processor interface in either the Slot 1 or Socket 370 configuration. The TNT2 supports system bus speeds from 66 MHz to 133 MHz (along with a built-in graphics engine and numerous multimedia enhancements). The TNT2 will also support up to 1.5GB of EDO, SDRAM, or VC SDRAM main memory (including support for ECC). The TNT2 also integrates a NVidia RIVA TNT2 128-bit 3D graphics controller. The integrated graphics and host interface communicates through an AGP 2X bus.

The Aladdin TNT2 is designed to improve system performance with memory and I/O throughput. Pipelined memory design helps reduce the effects of memory latency and refresh cycles. For I/O data transfers, deep data I/O buffers reduce the PCI latency. The chipset is compliant with the PCI 2.2 specification (including flexible PCI latency control). The Aladdin TNT2 can support up to six PCI masters. The South Bridge provides UDMA/66 support, and offers up to three USB ports. Power management features of the chipset include power-on suspend, suspend to disk, and so on—achieving a very flexible power management configuration. Table 9-4 lists major characteristics for the TNT2.

ALi also offers the CyberBLADE Aladdin i1 (shown earlier) integrated graphics chipset for mobile systems. It uses the CyberBLADE graphics engine integrated into the M1632M North Bridge chip.

## ALI ALADDIN PRO 2

The older Aladdin Pro 2 was ALi's entry-level offering for the Pentium II system market, consisting of the M1621 and M1543C chips. The Aladdin Pro 2 supports the classic Pentium II-class processors. It provides parity protection over the PCI bus, along with independent EC and ECC protection in memory to improve EDO/SDRAM reliability and performance (a powerful feature for older network servers). To support the 3D graphics functions, the chipset supports both a 66 MHz graphics bus and 1X/2X AGP.

The Aladdin Pro 2 includes a data path with multiport buffers for improved data transfers, and an external I/O controller chip to support multiple Pentium II processors (another important feature for older servers). A floppy disk controller, ISA bus support, and an IEEE 1284 parallel port are included. As shown in Table 9-4, support for USB and UDMA/33 round out the Aladdin Pro 2 package of the M1621 system controller combined with either the M1533 or the M1543 peripheral bus controller. However, the support is missing for accepted standards such as IEEE 1394 FireWire, UDMA/66/100/133, and other current standards.

## ALI ALADDIN 7

Now considered obsolete, the Aladdin 7 was a low-cost transitional chipset designed to support both 66/100 MHz Socket 7-style processors like the AMD K6-3 and later-model Slot 1 Pentium II processors. The chipset supports an integrated graphics engine and up to 1GB of PC66/100 SDRAM. Combining the M1561 North Bridge system controller with the PC99-compliant M1535D+ South Bridge bus controller, the Aladdin 7 offers support for the standard Socket 7-vintage features, along with an integrated 2D/3D graphics engine and 33 MHz PCI v2.2 bus.

# AMD Chipsets

AMD (Advanced Micro Devices) certainly is no stranger to the CPU arena, but it is a relative newcomer to the chipset market. Traditionally, AMD relied on other chipset makers like ALi or VIA to support its line of CPUs (e.g., the K6, K6-2, and K6-3). However, not all chipset makers provided the optimum support for AMD's products. Consequently, AMD jumped into the chipset market and originally developed the 640 chipset for use with its K6 and K6-2 CPU. In addition, the introduction of AMD's Athlon processor required AMD to develop a supporting chipset if it wanted the widest possible acceptance of the Athlon's unique architecture. The result was the AMD 750 chipset, generally regarded as one of the most stable and best-performing chipsets for the early Athlon series. AMD continued the practice of producing at least one chipset to support its processors with the addition of the AMD 760 chipset and its later variations.

## AMD 760 MP/X

Intended for server and high-end workstations, the AMD 760 MP (Multi-Processor) and 760MPX (Multi-Processor eXtended) chipsets build on the earlier 760 chipset and feature support for dual Athlon MP class processors. The 760 MP incorporates the AMD 762 North Bridge and the AMD 766 South Bridge (see Figure 9-6). The similar 760 MPX chipset combines the AMD 762 North Bridge and the AMD 768 South Bridge. Both chipsets support popular system features like PC2100 DDR SDRAM (up to 4GB), AGP 4X slot, a USB host controller supporting up to four ports, and two UDMA/66/100 controllers. However, the 760MPX provides extended features with support for a 66 MHz 64/32-bit PCI v2.2 bus (the 760MP is limited to a 33 MHz 64/32-bit PCI bus). A peripheral bus controller provides PCI-to-PCI bridging, power management support, and AC97 audio eliminates the need for a separate sound card. Table 9-5 lists the main 760 MP/X features.

## AMD 760

The AMD 760 chipset offers enhanced performance for a single AMD Athlon processor or other 200/266 MHz AMD system processors such as the Duron. The AMD 760 chipset includes the AMD 761 North Bridge system controller, along with the AMD 766 South Bridge peripheral bus controller. The AMD 761 system controller supports the 266 MHz Athlon system bus, up to 4GB of PC2100 DDR-SDRAM system memory, an AGP 4X graphics slot, and a 33 MHz 32-bit PCI bus (with up to five PCI slots). The AMD 766 peripheral bus controller features a PCI-to-ISA bridge, four OHCI-compliant USB ports, a dual channel UDMA/33/66/100 controller, and a system management (SM) bus. The South Bridge also provides access to a serial port, parallel port, mouse port, and keyboard port. You can learn more about the standard AMD 760 chipset in Table 9-5.

## AMD 750

The aging AMD 750 is a highly integrated system chipset that offers the features and enhanced performance needed to support the AMD Athlon processor (and other Athlon-compatible processors such as the Duron). The AMD 750 chipset consists of the AMD 751 system controller and the AMD 756 peripheral bus controller.

The AMD 751 system controller supports a 200 MHz front side bus (FSB), a 32-bit PCI v2.2-compliant bus interface at 33 MHz (supporting up to six masters), and a 66 MHz AGP 2.0-compliant interface to support the AGP 2X data transfer mode. Currently, the AMD 751 system controller is designed to support up to 768MB of PC100 SDRAM DIMMs using 16Mbit, 64Mbit, and 128Mbit memory technologies.

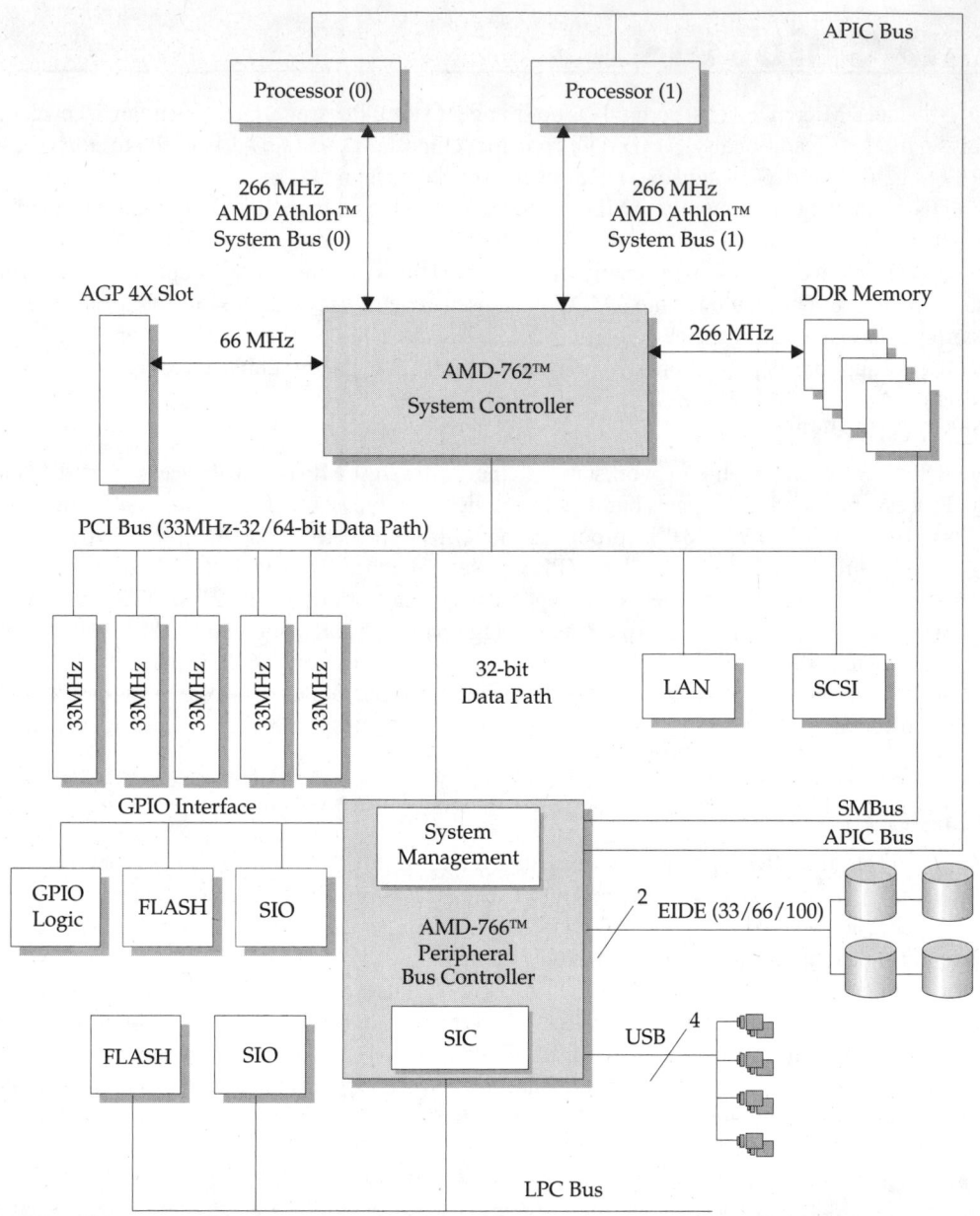

**FIGURE 9-6** The AMD 760 MP chipset supports up to two Athlon MP processors for server or workstation use (Courtesy of AMD).

The 200 MHz FSB includes synchronous clocking for high-speed data transfers (up to 1.6 GB/s at 200 MHz). The combination of the 200 MHz system bus and the AMD 750 chipset enables high data through-put between system components like CPU, memory, AGP, and PCI. This provides improved performance for 3D video and multimedia applications that require high-speed data transfers and calculations.

**TABLE 9-5**    COMPARISON OF AMD FAMILY CHIPSETS

| CHIPSET | AMD 760MP/X | AMD 760 | AMD 750 |
|---|---|---|---|
| Processor | AMD Athlon MP | AMD Athlon MP | AMD Athlon and Duron |
| Number of Processors | 2 | 1 | 1 |
| FSB | 266 MHz | 266 MHz | 200 MHz |
| Max. Memory | 4GB | 4GB | 768MB |
| Memory Type | PC2100 DDR SDRAM | PC2100 DDR SDRAM | PC100 SDRAM |
| Memory Bus | 266 MHz | 266 MHz | 200 MHz |
| ECC Support | Y | N/A | Y |
| PCI Spec. | PCI v2.2 | PCI v2.2 | PCI v2.2 |
| Integrated Graphics | N | N | N |
| AGP-Compliant | AGP 2.0 | AGP 2.0 | AGP 2.0 |
| SMA | N | N | N |
| External AGP Slot | Y | Y | Y |
| USB | 4 Ports | 4 Ports | 4 Ports |
| Max. IDE | UDMA/100 | UDMA/100 | UDMA/66 |
| Ethernet | N/A | N/A | N/A |
| AC97 | Y | Y | N |

The AMD 756 peripheral bus controller adds PCI-ISA bridge support, bus master IDE control with UDMA/33/66 and USB support (4 ports), and includes an integrated keyboard/mouse controller. Plug-and-play and power management features are supplied by the AMD 756 chip, enabling AMD 750-based systems to be Microsoft PC99-compliant. Table 9-5 compares highlights for the AMD 750 chipset.

# Intel Chipsets

Intel Corporation provided the 8086 CPU that went into the first PC and has often led the way in CPU development ever since. Though competitors like AMD have largely closed the performance gap (especially AMD with its Athlon and Duron processor families), Intel has remained competitive with the fastest high-performance CPUs like the Pentium II, III, and 4. Since Intel is normally the first to release new CPUs, it is also ideally positioned to develop the chipsets to complement those CPUs. Intel is also a frequent collaborator with Microsoft in the proposal of new industry initiatives (such as ACPI and AGP), so it often has a powerful head start in supporting those initiatives. As you'll see in this section, Intel offers a wide range of chipsets for high-end PC platforms.

## INTEL 860 (XEON)

The Intel 860 chipset supports dual Intel Xeon processors for use in high-performance workstations or server systems. The two main components are the 82860 Memory Controller Hub (MCH) and the 82801BA I/O Controller Hub (ICH2). The 82806AA 64-bit PCI Controller Hub (P64H) and the 82803AA RDRAM Memory Repeater Hub (MRH-R) may also be used optionally. The 82860 MCH is the core component used to interface the 400 MHz processor host bus, the dual RDRAM memory channels, and the AGP graphics interface. Up to 4GB of Rambus memory is supported using two 82803AA repeater hubs. The 860 chipset supports 1.5V 66 MHz AGP 2.0 (including 4X AGP data transfers and the 2X/4X fast write protocol).

The P64H PCI controller hub adds support for 64-bit PCI slots at speeds of either 33 MHz or 66 MHz. The ICH2 chip offers integrated support for the 32-bit PCI bus, and it also provides support for UltraDMA/100, two USB host controllers (4 ports), and AC97 sound compatibility. The Intel 860 chipset is also ACPI-compliant and supports Full-On, Stop Grant, Suspend to Disk, and Soft-Off power management states. By including a suitable LAN device, the 860 chipset also supports wake-on-LAN for remote administration and troubleshooting. The Intel 860 chipset architecture eliminates the ISA expansion bus (originally integrated into traditional PCIsets/AGPsets). This eliminates many conflicts that occur when installing legacy ISA hardware and drivers. Table 9-6 compares features of the 860 with other high-end Intel chipsets.

**TABLE 9-6    COMPARISON OF INTEL 860, 850/E, 845, 840, AND 440GX CHIPSET FEATURES**

| CHIPSET | INTEL 860 | INTEL 850/E | INTEL 845 | INTEL 840 | INTEL 440GX |
|---|---|---|---|---|---|
| Processor | (Pentium 4) Xeon | Pentium 4 | Pentium 4 | Pentium III (Xeon) | Pentium II/III (Xeon) |
| Number of Processors | 2 | 2 | 1 | 2 | 2 |
| FSB | 400 MHz | 400 MHz (533 MHz for 850E) | 400 MHz | 133 MHz | 100 MHz |
| Max. Memory | 4GB | 2GB | 2GB SDRAM 3GB RDRAM | 8GB | 2GB |
| Memory Type | PC600/PC800 RDRAM | PC600/PC800 RDRAM | PC133 SDRAM PC600/PC800 RDRAM | PC100 SDRAM PC600/PC800 RDRAM | PC100 SDRAM |
| Memory Bus | 400 MHz | 400 MHz | 400 MHz | 133 MHz | 100 MHz |
| ECC Support | Y | Y | Y | Y | Y |
| PCI Spec. | PCI v2.2 | PCI v2.2 | PCI v2.2 | PCI v2.2 | PCI v2.1 |
| Integrated Graphics | N | N | N | N | N |
| AGP-Compliant | AGP 2.0 | AGP 2.0 | AGP 2.0 | AGP 2.0 | AGP 1.0 |
| SMA | N | N | N | N | N |
| External AGP Slot | Y | Y | Y | Y | Y |
| USB | 4 Ports | 4 ports | 4 ports | 2 ports | 2 ports |
| Max. IDE | UDMA/100 | UDMA/100 | UDMA/100 | UDMA/33/66 | UDMA/33 |
| Ethernet | Y | Y | Y | N/A | N/A |
| AC97 | Y | Y | Y | Y | N/A |

# INTEL 850/E (PENTIUM 4)

The Intel 850 chipset was designed to support the Intel Pentium 4 processor and Intel NetBurst architecture for desktop PCs and entry-level workstations. The chipset is composed of the 82850 memory controller hub (MCH) and the 82801BA I/O controller hub (ICH2) as in Figure 9-7. It provides a "quad-pumped" 100 MHz system bus, effectively enabling a 400 MHz data bus that allows a high-bandwidth connection between the Intel Pentium 4 processor and the North Bridge. Note that the 850E supports a 533 MHz processor bus with up to 4.2 GB/s memory bandwidth.

The 82850 MCH supports dual RDRAM memory channels and the 400 MHz system bus (remember that support for SDRAM or DDR SDRAM memory is *not* available in the 850 or 860 chipsets). The 850 chipset also supports up to 2GB of PC600/PC800 (300/400 MHz) RDRAM when 256Mb RIMM technology is implemented. This allows dual RDRAM channels at 3.2 GB/s, providing far more memory bandwidth than platforms based on Intel Pentium III processors. You can see the relationship between devices in Figure 9-8. Graphics support is provided through a 1.5V AGP 4X interface. The AGP 4X interface allows graphics controllers to access main memory at over 1 GB/s (twice the performance of previous AGP platforms).

The enhanced 82801BA I/O ICH2 makes a direct connection to the MCH for faster access to system peripherals. Dual UDMA/100 controllers support fast IDE interface for large drive devices. Additional performance is achieved using Intel's Storage Driver (rather than standard IDE drivers). The ICH2 also provides a 33 MHz, v2.2-compliant PCI interface for "off the shelf" expansion devices. The ICH2 integrates a PCI arbiter that supports up to six external PCI bus masters (in addition to the internal ICH2 requests). The USB controller provides enhanced support that allows legacy software to use a USB-based keyboard and mouse. The ICH2 is USB v1.1-compliant, and the device supports two USB host controllers. Each host controller includes a root hub with two separate USB ports each, for a total of four USB ports.

AC97 audio support is also included, supplying six channels of audio for enhanced sound quality and full surround-sound capability for live broadcast and other advanced sound features. The LAN Connect Interface (LCI) provides versatile network solutions for home phone line and 10/100 Mbps Ethernet networking. Communication and Networking Riser (CNR) support allows flexibility in system configuration with a CNR slot that can be fitted with an audio card, modem card, or network card. You can compare the characteristics of Intel's 850 chipset to other high-end chipsets in Table 9-6.

**FIGURE 9-7**    The Intel 850 chipset includes the 82850 MCH and 82801BA ICH2 (Courtesy of Intel Corporation).

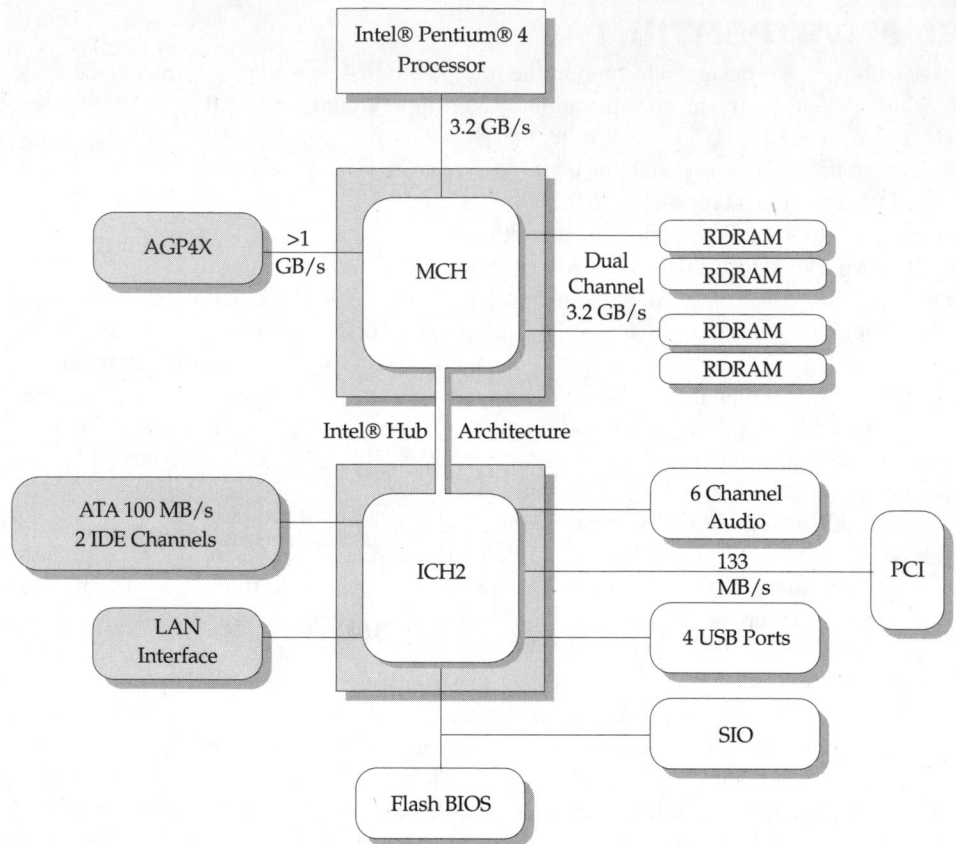

**FIGURE 9-8**    The Intel 850 chipset supports the Pentium 4, RDRAM, AGP 4X, and many other features (Courtesy of Intel Corporation).

## INTEL 845 (PENTIUM 4)

The Intel 845 chipset—though numbered earlier—was introduced *after* the 850 chipset, and the 845 continues to expand the Intel chipset line designed to support the newest Pentium 4 processors based on the 400 MHz system bus. The chipset also uses the 82801BA I/O Controller Hub (ICH2), but combines it with the 82845 Memory Controller Hub that also supports a 1.5V AGP 4X port. However, the 845 does not support dual Pentium 4 systems. The other major difference between the 845 and 850 chipset is that the 845 set supports up to 2GB of PC133 SDRAM and 200/266 MHz DDR SDRAM memory (rather than the "Rambus only" trend that Intel had started with earlier Pentium 4 sets). The other features of the 845 chipset are generally identical to those offered by the 850 chipset, and you can see the features compared in Table 9-6.

## INTEL 840 (PENTIUM III XEON)

The Intel 840 chipset is an earlier member of the 800-series chipset family intended for service in workstation systems. In addition to the basic 82801 and 82802 support chips, the 840 utilizes the 82840 MCH. This chip provides AGP 2X and 4X graphics support, dual RDRAM memory channels, and multiple PCI busses that are ideal for server and workstation applications where high-performance I/O is needed. The 840 is more versatile than its older 810E and 820 counterparts due to its ability to support three additional components that may be used with the standard core 800 components: the 82806, the 82803, and 82804.

For high-performance server and workstation platforms, the 64-bit 82806 PCI controller hub (P64H) supports 64-bit PCI slots at speeds of either 33 or 66 MHz. The P64H connects directly to the MCH using Intel's hub-based architecture, so a dedicated bus is available for high-speed data transfers. For systems requiring a large amount of RDRAM (e.g., a network server), an 82803 RDRAM memory repeater hub (MRH-R) may be added to the motherboard. The MRH-R separates each memory channel into two memory channels for expanded memory capacity. For systems that demand lots of inexpensive SDRAM instead (e.g., entry-level workstations), an 82804 SDRAM memory repeater hub (MRH-S) may be included on the motherboard. The MRH-S basically translates the native RDRAM protocol into SDRAM-based signals so a motherboard may easily employ SDRAM rather than RDRAM without major redesign.

These various chip combinations provide for SDRAM or RDRAM support, bandwidth doubling on the processor, AGP 4X, two USB ports, multiple PCI buses, and dual processor support to provide the best possible performance for a multiprocessor Pentium III/Xeon platform. This chipset supports processors using a 133 MHz system bus, and hard drives using UDMA/66 technology. BIOS code changes can easily be implemented if BIOS suppliers comply with Intel's Modular BIOS specifications. Table 9-6 compares the Intel 840 to other comparable Intel chipsets.

## INTEL 440 GX (PENTIUM II/III XEON)

Optimized for the Pentium II/III Xeon processors (in Slot1/Slot2 packages), the aging Intel 440 GX chipset is otherwise much the same as the older Intel 440 BX chipset. The chipset is a combination of the 82443GX host bridge controller (North Bridge) and the 82371EB (PIIX4E South Bridge) peripheral bus controller. It supports the full Symmetric Multiprocessor Protocol (SMP), which allows up to two processors. A 100 MHz system bus frequency is supported for the processor(s), and the integrated memory controller supports up to 2GB of ECC, registered, and unbuffered PC100 SDRAM. Up to four double-sided 16, 64, 128, or 256Mbit DIMMs (eight rows) are allowed by the Intel 440 GX chipset.

The Intel 440 GX includes support for PCI Rev. 2.1 standards on a 33 MHz 3.3V (or 5V) interface. It includes PCI-to-DRAM data streaming support and allows concurrent CPU, AGP, and PCI transactions. It also provides the suspend-to-RAM feature for power conservation. The AGP, PCI, and ISA bridges are implemented through the 82371EB (PIIX4E) component of the Intel 440 GX chipset. AGP 2X support is provided in compliance with AGP v1.0. This allows for 3.3V AGP devices of up to 133 MHz (2X). The AGP support of the Intel 440 GX chipset allows for high-priority (expedite) transactions and AGP-specific data buffering.

Additional features supported by the Intel 440 GX chipset include two USB ports, UDMA/33 IDE controller speeds, enhanced DMA, and interrupt controller and timer functions. It enables a System Management (SM) bus with support for DIMM memory Serial Presence Detect (SPD). The USB support provided by the Intel 440 GX chipset is Rev. 1.0-compliant and allows for two USB ports with serial transfer rates of 1.5 Mbit/s. It supports legacy keyboard and mouse software with two UHCI-compliant USB ports. You can compare 440 GX features in Table 9-6.

## INTEL 820/E (PENTIUM II/III)

Intel continued its development of the early 800-series chipset without integrated video, and the next member of the 800 family was the now-obsolete Intel 820/E chipset with features designed to support mainstream and performance systems. It includes the 800-series support for the "modular BIOS," which is flash-upgradeable as features are added to the chipset. Using the same two support chips as the Intel 810E chipset (the 82801 I/O controller hub and the 82802 firmware hub), the 820 adds either the 82820 or the 82820DP (dual processor) memory controller hub. Intended as a "long life" platform chipset solution in the rapidly changing PC market, the hub architecture of the 820 allows Intel to enhance and update components without forcing major system changes until the Pentium 4 (and its related chipsets) were released. The classic 820 supported SDRAM DIMMs, but the later 820E was intended for early Rambus platforms. The 820E chipset supports RDRAM technology, and provides for two memory sockets and 1GB of system memory.

When the 82801BA (ICH2) I/O controller hub was produced, it was added to the 820 family, creating the 820E chipset. The ICH2 adds support for UDMA/100 and two USB host controllers for four USB ports.

The 820E uses three integrated buses to reduce interference problems and increase data transfer rates. The Direct Rambus (memory) interface, internal hub interface, and LPC bus interface allow the doubling of bandwidth and data transfer rates. In addition, performance is improved with support for AGP v2.0 4X, UDMA/100 (the 820 only supports UDMA/66), and a 133 MHz PCI system bus. AGP 4X graphics support offers the same direct connection to the memory controller and twice the graphics bandwidth of AGP 2X (achieving transfer rates in excess of 1 GB/s). The architecture of the 820/E chipset offers a direct pipeline for audio and video data, and allows for concurrent data transfer streams over the CPU, PCI, USB, and AGP buses. Table 9-7 compares features of the 820 and 820E.

## INTEL 815P/EG/G (PENTIUM III AND CELERON)

While maintaining support for the latest Pentium III and Celeron processors, the 815G and 815EG chipsets expanded the options provided by classic Intel 815 products. Intended for value (a.k.a. "low-cost") systems, the 815G/EG offer integrated 3D video with Direct AGP support—no support for an external AGP graphics card is available. The 82815G GMCH (Graphics-Memory Controller Hub) provides the video to a flat panel or standard monitor. The 815G includes the 82801AA I/O controller while the 815EG combines with the 82801BA I/O Controller Hub. The 815P did not include integrated graphics, but the 82815EP MCH and 81801AA ICH provided good memory and controller attributes that built on older 815 chipsets. Features of these chipsets are otherwise similar to other members of the 815 chipset family. You can see the features of 815P/G/EG chipsets in Table 9-7.

## INTEL 815/E/EP (PENTIUM II/III AND CELERON)

The Intel 815-series chipsets were designed to meet the demands of users who required better AGP video performance than the older 810-series offered, and who did not want to use Rambus memory required by the 820/840 chipsets. Intel needed a chipset with support for the 133 MHz FSB that also supported AGP 4X and SDRAM memory. Attempts to add SDRAM support to the Intel 820 and 840 chipsets failed. This created a temporary situation in which Intel was not able to provide the best chipset support for its own processors. Rather than update the 440 BX chipset to support the newer IDE, AGP, PCI, and memory interfaces, Intel developed the 815-series chipsets.

The Intel 815 chipset supports the Pentium III and Celeron line of processors in the FC-PGA (Flip Chip PGA) package. It is a combination of the 82815 GMCH and the 82801AA ICH. It supports 32-bit system bus addressing and is limited to single-processor systems. AGTL+ bus voltage is supported at FSB speeds of 66 MHz, 100 MHz, and 133 MHz. The integrated SDRAM controller of the 815 chipset supports up to 512MB of PC100/133 SDRAM memory and allows for up to three double-sided DIMMs. It supports asymmetrical SDRAM addressing, but memory must be unbuffered (and not ECC). The chipset allows for suspend-to-RAM power conservation operation.

**TABLE 9-7    COMPARISON OF INTEL 820, 820E, 815P, 815EG, AND 815G CHIPSET FEATURES**

| CHIPSET | INTEL 820 | INTEL 820E | INTEL 815P | INTEL 815EG | INTEL 815G |
|---|---|---|---|---|---|
| Processor | Pentium II/III | Pentium II/III | Pentium II/III Celeron | Pentium II/III Celeron | Pentium II/III Celeron |
| Number of Processors | 1-2 | 1-2 | 1 | 1 | 1 |
| FSB | 100/133 MHz | 100/133 MHz | 66/100/133 MHz | 66/100/133 MHz | 66/100/133 MHz |
| Max. Memory | 1GB | 1GB | 512MB | 512MB | 512MB |
| Memory Type | PC100/PC133 SDRAM | PC600/PC800 RDRAM | PC100/PC133 SDRAM | PC100/PC133 SDRAM | PC100/PC133 SDRAM |
| Memory Bus | 100/133 MHz | 100/133 MHz | 66/100/133 MHz | 66/100/133 MHz | 66/100/133 MHz |
| ECC Support | Y | Y | N | N | N |
| PCI Spec. | PCI v2.2 | PCI v2.2 | PCI v2.2 | PCI v2.2 | PCI v2.2 |
| Integrated Graphics | N | N | N | Y | Y |
| AGP-Compliant | AGP 2.0 | AGP 2.0 | AGP 2.0 | Direct AGP | Direct AGP |
| SMA | N | N | N | 4MB | 4MB |
| External AGP Slot | Y | Y | Y | N | N |
| USB | 2 ports | 2 ports | 2 ports | 4 ports | 2 ports |
| Max. IDE | UDMA/66 | UDMA/100 | UDMA/66 | UDMA/100 | UDMA/66 |
| Ethernet | N/A | N/A | N/A | Y | N/A |
| AC97 | Y | Y | Y | Y | Y |

Although the Intel 815 and 815E chipsets still include integrated support for AGP video, they also support a separate AGP device (where the 815G and 815EG do not) and meet AGP 2.0 specifications. This allows for 4X AGP data transfers, dual-mode buffers, and either 3.3V or 1.5V AGP devices. The 815EP member of this chipset family does not utilize the 82815 GMCH, but instead uses the 82815EP MCH. This eliminates any possible compatibility problems the integrated graphics support might create with a separate AGP video card. The integrated graphics support of the Intel 815 and 815E chipsets (Intel 3D with Direct AGP) can also be used in conjunction with a Graphics Performance Accelerator (GPA) card. The GPA is essentially a 4MB display cache placed on a card that is inserted into the AGP slot on the motherboard. However, the integrated graphics of the 815 and 815E chipsets do not offer the performance of a current stand-alone AGP graphics card.

The 815 chipset utilizes the 82801AA ICH. The 815E and 815EP chipsets utilize the 82801BA (ICH2) hub. The 82801AA ICH of the 815 chipset makes a direct connection from the graphics and memory to the integrated AC97 controller, IDE controllers, dual USB ports, and PCI add-in cards. This delivers twice the North/South Bridge bandwidth of traditional bridge architecture through dedicated data paths. The ICH supports UDMA/66 specifications for the IDE hard drive interface. It supports a maximum of six

PCI slots and is compliant with PCI Rev. 2.2 specifications at 33 MHz. The Audio Modem Riser (AMR) slot is supported if the motherboard has one. It meets AC97 v2.1 specifications. The 815 chipset's ICH supports only one host controller and two USB ports. The system management (SM) bus offers bus master capabilities. Enhancements in the 82801BA (ICH2) hub of the 815E and 815EP chipsets include UDMA/100 support, two USB host controllers and four USB ports support, integrated LAN support, bus master and slave capabilities, and six-channel audio and telephony support. Table 9-8 compares the features of the 815/E/EP chipsets.

## INTEL 810E/E2 (PENTIUM II/III AND CELERON)

Intel began competing in the low-cost, integrated video chipset market with the introduction of their 810 chipset (dubbed the "Camino"). This is a three-chip solution including the 82810E GMCH, the 82801 ICH, and an 82802 firmware hub (the BIOS). The technology included in the 810 chipset is designed to enhance performance of the Intel Pentium II/III and Celeron processors. The chipset builds on the 440 BX AGP technology and includes additional features to provide improved graphics at a lower cost.

The 82810 chip is the core of the 810 chipset, with built-in control of memory and graphics that optimizes system memory management in a way that is similar to AGP technology. The 82810 GMCH uses "Direct AGP" to provide 2D and 3D effects and images, and integrated hardware motion compensation to improve DVD video quality without a separate MPEG decoder card. RAM memory support allows

| **TABLE 9-8** | COMPARISON OF INTEL 815, 815E, 815EP, 810E, AND 810E2 CHIPSET FEATURES | | | | |
|---|---|---|---|---|---|
| **CHIPSET** | **INTEL 815** | **INTEL 815E** | **INTEL 815EP** | **INTEL 810E** | **INTEL 810E2** |
| Processor | Pentium II/III Celeron | Pentium II/III Celeron | Pentium II/III Celeron | Pentium II/III Celeron | Pentium II/III Celeron |
| Number of Processors | 1 | 1 | 1 | 1 | 1 |
| FSB | 100/133 MHz | 100/133 MHz | 100/133 MHz | 66/100/133 MHz | 66/100/133 MHz |
| Max. Memory | 512MB | 512MB | 512MB | 512MB | 512MB |
| Memory Type | PC100/PC133 SDRAM | PC100/PC133 SDRAM | PC100/PC133 SDRAM | PC66/PC100 SDRAM | PC66/PC100 SDRAM |
| Memory Bus | 100/133 MHz | 100/133 MHz | 100/133 MHz | 66/100 MHz | 66/100 MHz |
| ECC Support | N | N | N | N | N |
| PCI Spec. | PCI v2.2 | PCI v2.2 | PCI v2.2 | PCI v2.2 | PCI v2.2 |
| Integrated Graphics | Y | Y | N | Y | Y |
| AGP-Compliant | Integrated AGP | Integrated AGP | AGP 2.0 | Integrated AGP | Integrated AGP |
| SMA | 4MB | N | N | 32-48MB | 32-48MB |
| External AGP Slot | Y | Y | Y | N | N |
| USB | 2 Ports | 4 ports | 4 ports | 2 ports | 4 ports |
| Max. IDE | UDMA/66 | UDMA/100 | UDMA/100 | UDMA/66 | UDMA/100 |
| Ethernet | N/A | Y | Y | N/A | Y |
| AC97 | Y | Y | Y | Y | Y |

use of up to 512MB of PC100 memory. Dynamic Video Memory Technology (DVMT) provides efficient memory utilization and Direct AGP (though the operating system must use Intel software drivers and support Intel's memory arbiter to implement graphics applications).

The 82801 ICH uses the Intel accelerated hub architecture to interface the graphics and memory subsystems of the North Bridge to the South Bridge features including an integrated Audio Codec 97 (AC97) controller, dual UDMA controllers, multiple USB ports, and the standard PCI expansion bus. The accelerated hub architecture provides twice the bandwidth of the PCI bus at 266 MB/s, which allows better data transfer from the I/O controller to the memory controller. True UDMA/66 and PCI v2.2 support are provided by the Intel 810 chipset. The 82802 firmware hub (FWH) is the third member of the set, which stores system BIOS and video BIOS.

By the time Intel was able to make the 810 chipset available, PC133 memory on a 133 MHz bus forced Intel to quickly make some improvements to the 810—dubbed the Intel 810E. The Intel 810E chipset includes all the features of the 810, with added support for faster speeds. Intel's design of the hub architecture chipset implementation enables it to easily integrate improvements in the I/O controller hub. The 82801BA (ICH2) hub was added to the 810 chipset family when it became available. This adds support for UDMA/100 and four USB ports to the core features of the 810 chipset, and is identified as the 810E2 chipset. You can compare the features of the 810E and 810E2 chipsets in Table 9-8.

## INTEL 440 BX (PENTIUM II/III)

Now obsolete, the Intel 440 BX was the last and most powerful X-series chipset before Intel decided the new "Camino" chipset architecture needed a new naming method. The 440 BX consists of the 82443BX AGP host bridge controller (North Bridge) and the 82371AB (PIIX4E) PCI-ISA peripheral bus controller (South Bridge). The chipset supports both 66 MHz and 100 MHz processor bus speeds, which support a wide range of Pentium II or older Pentium III processors. Dual processors are also supported with full SMP. The Intel 440 BX was the first 100 MHz chipset designed for use in Pentium II mobile systems, and the first one optimized for Pentium III performance in 3D and video applications.

Memory support is provided through an integrated DRAM controller allowing for up to four SDRAM DIMMs for a total of 1GB of memory (if registered DIMMs are used). The 440 BX enables "open page architecture" supporting multiple SDRAM pages to improve 3D performance. Additional video features include AGP 2X (using sideband signaling) and AGP-specific data buffering support. The chipset enables concurrent CPU, AGP, and PCI data transfers to main memory.

The PIIX4E controller in this chipset provides PC98 ACPI power management support that allows use of the 440 BX in mobile systems. The chip is PCI v.2.1-compliant to support PCI-to-ISA bridges in both 3.3V and 5V 33 MHz configurations. The USB host interface has support for two USB ports, and the integrated IDE controller supports up to UDMA/33. The Intel 440 BX chipset is presented as UDMA/66-compatible, but this does not mean that the chipset supports UDMA/66. It means you can use a UDMA/66 hard drive in a 440 BX-based system, but transfer speeds will be limited to the UDMA/33 standard. Table 9-9 lists the features of an Intel 440 BX chipset.

## INTEL 440 ZX (PENTIUM II/III AND CELERON)

Consisting of the 82443ZX system controller and 82371EB (PIIX4E) peripheral bus controller, the now-obsolete 440 ZX chipset was designed to be a lower-cost alternative to the 440 BX chipset (see Table 9-9). By eliminating dual processor support, cutting maximum memory support to 256MB, and dropping the support for ECC, Intel hoped this chipset would attract manufacturers producing low-cost Pentium II/III systems. Intel even included a 66 MHz version of the 440 ZX (the 440 ZX-66) for early Celeron sup-

**TABLE 9-9     COMPARISON OF INTEL 440BX AND 440ZX CHIPSET FEATURES**

| CHIPSET | INTEL 440BX | INTEL 440ZX |
|---|---|---|
| Processor | Pentium II/III Celeron | Pentium II/III Celeron |
| Number of Processors | 1–2 | 1 |
| FSB | 66/100 MHz | 66/100 MHz |
| Max. Memory | 1GB | 256MB |
| Memory Type | PC100 SDRAM | PC100 SDRAM |
| Memory Bus | 66/100 MHz | 66/100 MHz |
| ECC Support | Y | N |
| PCI Spec. | PCI v2.1 | PCI v2.1 |
| Integrated Graphics | N | N |
| AGP-Compliant | AGP 1.0 | AGP 1.0 |
| SMA | N/A | N/A |
| External AGP Slot | Y | Y |
| USB | 2 ports | 2 ports |
| Max. IDE | UDMA/33 | UDMA/33 |
| Ethernet | N/A | N/A |
| AC97 | N | N |

port. However, the ZX did not prove as popular as Intel had hoped. PC manufacturers producing a 100 MHz Pentium II/III system wanted some of the features eliminated in the 440 ZX, and instead opted for the 440 BX chipset.

The Intel 440 FX, 440LX, 450GX, 450KX, 430 VX, 430 TX, 430 HX, 430FX, and 430 MX chipsets are now completely obsolete, and have been dropped from this edition.

# VIA Chipsets

Founded in 1987, VIA Technologies, Inc. is perhaps the greatest threat to Intel's dominance of the chipset market. Its line of Apollo chipsets has provided an effective alternative for the support of Intel, AMD, and Cyrix processors. VIA chipsets are generally recognized as full-featured, high-performance solutions that are used on many motherboards. VIA also produces a selection of network and peripheral controller chips for computer applications. This part of the chapter outlines the most popular VIA motherboard chipsets available for the PC.

With the increasing acceptance and popularity of AMD Athlon and Duron processors, VIA has greatly expanded its resources supporting this line of CPUs. VIA's use of separate system and peripheral bus controllers (North Bridge and South Bridge chips) allows it to quickly update its products to support new and improved technologies such as UDMA/133 IDE data rates and high-speed DDR SDRAM memory. An improved peripheral bus controller can be substituted for an older one and combined with existing system controllers to update an entire line of chipsets at once. The same can be done with improved system controllers and existing peripheral bus controllers. This tactic allows VIA to remain competitive in a fast-changing PC marketplace.

VIA has further diversified its product line with the addition of the VIA Cyrix line of processors. VIA is now in the position of designing processors to mate with its own chipsets, with performance enhancements integrated in both while under the control of VIA Technologies. In a joint venture, VIA Technologies and S3 Graphics have developed integrated system/graphics controller chipsets. These chipsets combine VIA's system controllers with S3's Savage4, Savage8, and other graphics chip core technologies, and enable motherboards to include on-board graphics systems. This venture should continue to provide inexpensive, highly integrated chipset solutions for popular low-cost systems.

## VIA APOLLO P4X333

Designed for use with the Socket 423/478 Intel Pentium 4 processor, the VIA Apollo P4X333 chipset combines the VIA VT8754 North Bridge with the VIA VT8235 South Bridge (see Figure 9-9). This leading chipset supports current high-performance bus standards including FSB speeds of both 400 MHz and 533 MHz. The North Bridge also offers support for AGP 8X and up to 32GB of PC2700 (DDR333) DDR SDRAM memory (for a 2.7 GB/s memory bandwidth). PC1600 (DDR200) and PC2100 (DDR266) memory is also supported. The AGP 8X bus conforms to AGP 3.0 specifications, providing a graphics bandwidth of 2.1 GB/s, but it is backward compatible with AGP 2X and AGP 4X standards.

The VIA Apollo P4X333 uses VIA's double-speed V-Link technology for communications between the North Bridge and the South Bridge chips. This offers a peak communication bandwidth of 533 MB/sec—four times the bandwidth of the 132 MB/s offered by older chipsets. As Figure 9-10 illustrates, the VIA VT8235 South Bridge provides support for modern high performance bus specifications and peripherals. USB 2.0 support offers data transfer speeds of up to 480 Mb/s (40 times faster than the 12Mb/s rate with USB 1.1). Up to six high-speed USB ports allow the USB bus to handle a variety of video peripherals and interactive gaming features. The VT8235 South Bridge also features support for two Ultra-DMA/133 channels, a serial port, a parallel port, a floppy disk controller, keyboard, and mouse. Additional South Bridge features include support for five PCI slots, integrated 10/100 Ethernet, integrated modem, and integrated AC97 audio. Table 9-10 lists the features for the VIA P4X333 chipset.

**FIGURE 9-9** The VIA Apollo P4X333 chipset provides support for high-speed FSB and DDR SDRAM operation (Courtesy of VIA Technologies, Inc.)

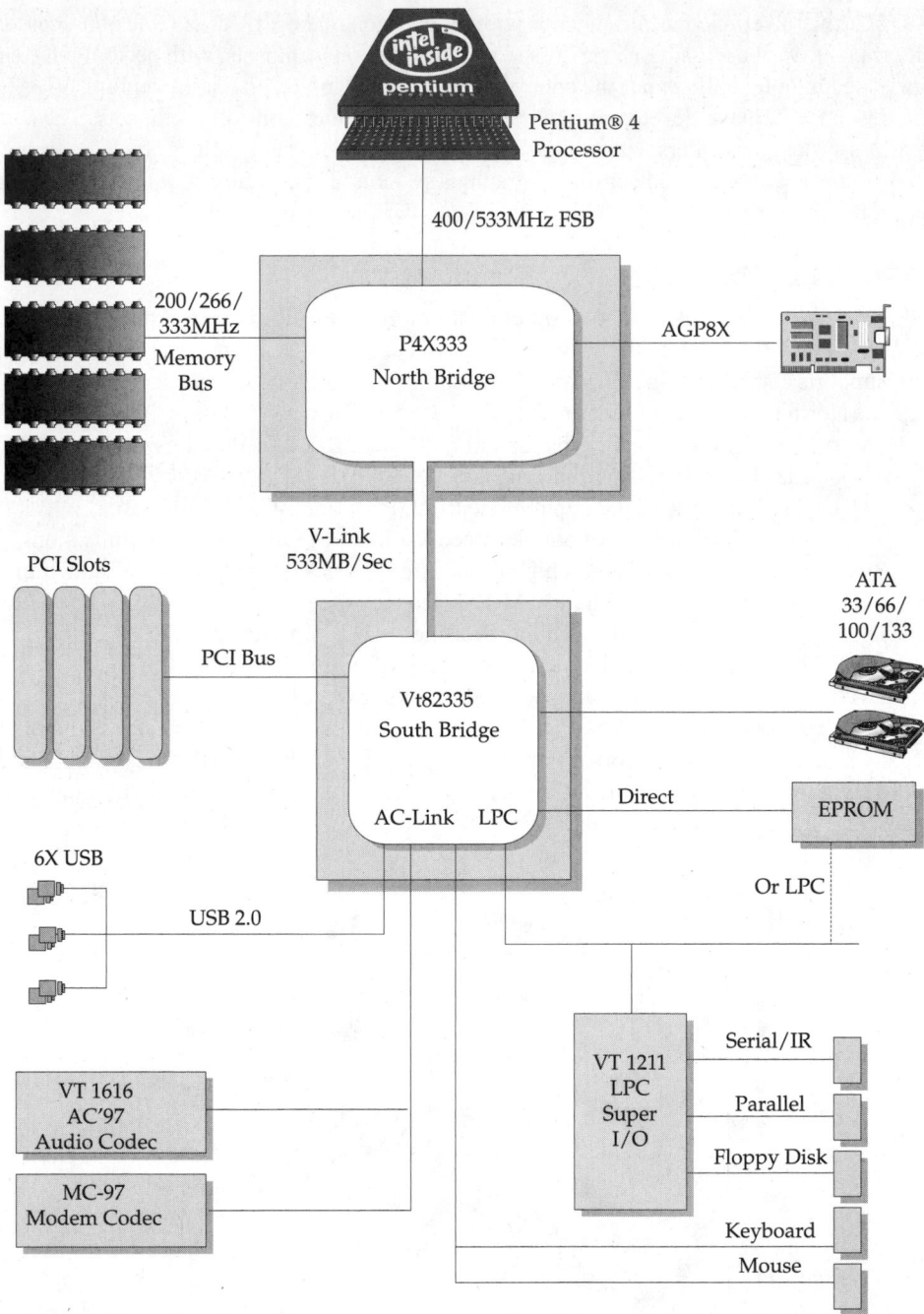

**FIGURE 9-10** Block diagram of a typical VIA Apollo P4X333 chipset implementation (Courtesy of VIA Technologies, Inc.)

| TABLE 9-10 | COMPARISON OF VIA P4X333, P4X266/A, APOLLO PRO 266, P4M266, AND PN266T CHIPSET FEATURES | | | | |
|---|---|---|---|---|---|
| **CHIPSET** | **VIA APOLLO P4X333** | **VIA APOLLO P4X266/A** | **VIA APOLLO PRO 266** | **VIA PROSAVAGE DDR P4M266** | **VIA PROSAVAGE DDR PN266T** |
| Processor | Pentium 4 | Pentium 4 | Pentium III, Celeron, VIA C3 | Pentium 4 | Pentium III, Celeron, VIA C3 |
| Number of Processors | 1 | 1 | 1 | 1 | 1 |
| FSB | 400/533 MHz | 400 MHz | 66/100/133 MHz | 400 MHz | 100/133 MHz |
| Max. Memory | 32GB | 4GB | 4GB | 4GB | 4GB |
| Memory Type | 200/266/333 MHz DDR SDRAM | 200/266 MHz DDR SDRAM PC100/PC133 SDRAM | 200/266 MHz DDR SDRAM PC100/133 SDRAM | 200/266 MHz DDR SDRAM PC100/133 SDRAM | 200/266 MHz DDR SDRAM PC100/133 SDRAM |
| Memory Bus | 200/266/333 MHz | 200/266 MHz | 200/266 MHz | 200/266 MHz | 200/266 MHz |
| ECC Support | Y | Y | Y | N/A | N/A |
| PCI Spec. | PCI v2.2 | PCI v2.2 | PCI v2.2 | PCI v2.2 | PCI v2.2 |
| Integrated Graphics | N | N | N | Y | Y |
| AGP-Compliant | AGP 3.0 | AGP 2.0 | AGP 2.0 | AGP 2.0 | Integrated |
| SMA | N | N | N | To 32MB | To 32MB |
| External AGP Slot | Y | Y | Y | Y | N |
| USB | 6 Ports (USB 2.0) | 6 ports | 6 ports | 6 ports | 6 ports |
| Max. IDE | UDMA/133 | UDMA/100 | UDMA/100 | UDMA/100/133 | UDMA/100 |
| Ethernet | Y | Y | Y | Y | Y |
| AC97 | Y (w/ MC97) | Y (w/ MC97) | Y (w/ MC97) | Y (w/ MC97) | Y (w/ MC97) |

# VIA APOLLO P4X266/A

The VIA P4X266A is a current high-performance chipset (updated from the earlier P4X266) designed to support Intel Pentium 4 processors (see Figure 9-11). The P4X266A uses the VIA VT8753A North Bridge including an improved memory controller supporting up to 4GB of 200 MHz (PC1600) or 266 MHz (PC2100) DDR SDRAM memory. The North Bridge is also backward compatible with PC100/133 SDRAM memory. The VT8753A includes support for the "quad-pumped" 400 MHz system processor bus. It supports AGP 4X standards and provides a graphics data bandwidth of up to 1 GB/sec. Support for the AGP Pro's standard higher voltage is also included.

The VT8753A North Bridge can be combined with any VIA V-Link compatible South Bridge such as the VT8233, the VT8233C, or the VT8233A chips. The VT8233 and VT8233C chips support Ultra-DMA/100,

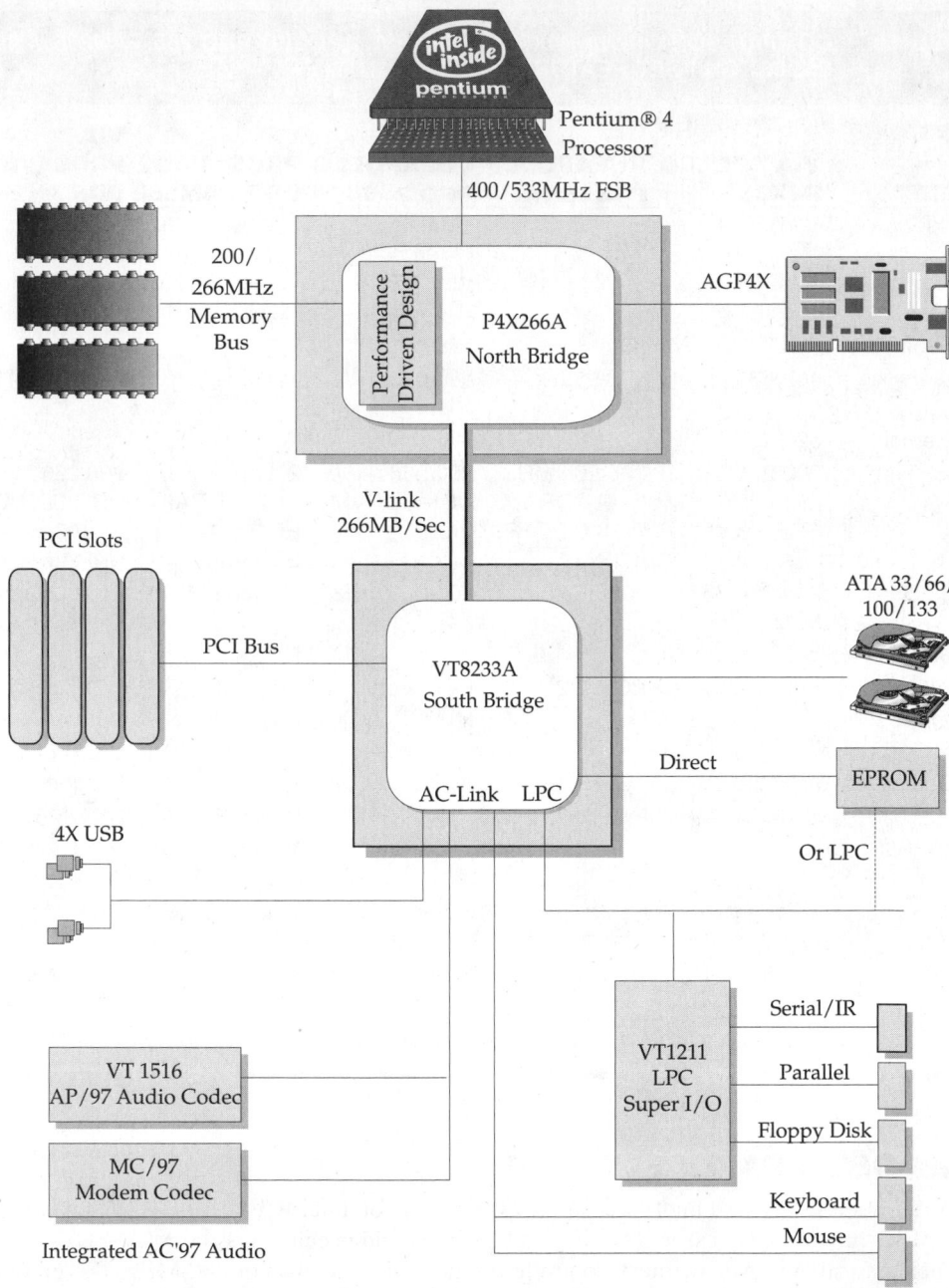

**FIGURE  9-11**    Block diagram of a typical VIA Apollo P4X266A chipset implementation (Courtesy of VIA Technologies, Inc.)

six USB ports, and six PCI slots. The VT8233A chip offers faster Ultra-DMA/133 IDE performance, but only supports four USB ports. The VT8233 offers VIA Ethernet support (the VT8233C features 3Com Ethernet support). All VIA V-Link South Bridges offer AC97 v2.2 sound capabilities and an MC97 software modem interface. V-Link technology provides a dedicated bus between the North and South Bridges with a bandwidth of 266 MB/s (twice that available from the PCI bus)—this also frees the PCI bus to deal with peripheral device communications.

VIA's V-MAP architecture allows the integration of a third high-performance chip. For example, the VT8101 VPX-64 64-bit PCI controller allows existing VIA chipsets to support high-bandwidth 64-bit PCI in both 33 MHz and 66 MHz modes (ideal for server and workstation platforms). This enables VIA Apollo chipsets to offer up to 533 MB/s of PCI bandwidth for high-end peripherals like Gigabit Ethernet, Fibre Channel, and Ultra SCSI/320. Table 9-10 compares the main features of the P4X266A chipset.

## VIA APOLLO PRO 266T

The VIA Apollo Pro 266T chipset combines the VIA VT8653 North Bridge with either the VIA VT8233 or the VT8233C South Bridge. It supports the same features as the VIA Apollo Pro 266 (below) chipset with the addition of support for the newer Socket 370 Tualatin core Intel Pentium III, Celeron processors.

## VIA APOLLO PRO 266

The VIA Apollo Pro 266 supports Intel Pentium III, Celeron, and VIA C3 processor-based platforms. It supports single or dual Socket 370 processors and features a 200/266 MHz memory bus. The VIA Apollo Pro 266 chipset uses memory controller architecture that supports up to 4.0GB of DDR 200/266 SDRAM (PC1600/2100) at a peak bandwidth of 2.1 GB/s. DDR 266 SDRAM lowers memory power consumption to 2.5 volts. The chipset also supports Virtual Channel Memory (VCM) DRAM. With its 133 MHz FSB, the VIA Apollo Pro 266 chipset supports the latest Intel Pentium III/Celeron processors as well as VIA's C3 processor. The VIA Apollo Pro 266 chipset's asynchronous bus design also supports Intel Pentium III and Intel Celeron processors running at FSB speeds of 66, 100, and 133 MHz.

The VIA Apollo Pro 266 chipset is a two-chip set consisting of the VT8633 system controller (North Bridge) and the VT8233 peripheral bus controller (South Bridge). The Apollo Pro 266 also features a high-speed low-latency "V-Link" bus that doubles the communication bandwidth between the North and South bridge to 266 MB/s (previous chipset architectures used PCI bus standards for communication that limited transfer rates to 133 MB/s). Additional features include support for six USB ports, an AC97 link for audio and modem, hardware monitoring, ACPI/OnNow power management, and integrated 10/100 Mbps Ethernet. The VIA Apollo Pro 266 chipset also includes an AGP 4X interface. The UDMA/100 interface on the VIA Apollo Pro 266 chipset provides a high-speed connection to UDMA/100 hard disk drives (delivering burst data transfer rates of 100 MB/s). Features of the VIA Apollo Pro 266 are listed in Table 9-10.

## VIA PROSAVAGEDDR P4M266

The VIA ProSavageDDR P4M266 chipset offers support for Intel Pentium 4 processors. The VIA VT8751 North Bridge will work with three possible South Bridge chips: the VT8233, the VT8233A, or the VT8233C (see Figure 9-12). The VT8751 North Bridge contains an integrated ProSavage8 2D/3D graphics engine. This 128-bit graphics core offers AGP 8X bandwidth and an internal frame buffer up to 32MB. An optional external AGP 2X/4X slot is also supported. Graphics and system performance are further improved with support for Intel's 400 MHz "quad-pumped" FSB, and up to 4GB of 200/266 MHz DDR SDRAM memory. PC100/133 SDRAM memory is also supported, but the lower bandwidth provided by this type of memory impedes graphics and overall system performance (DDR266 memory supplies an

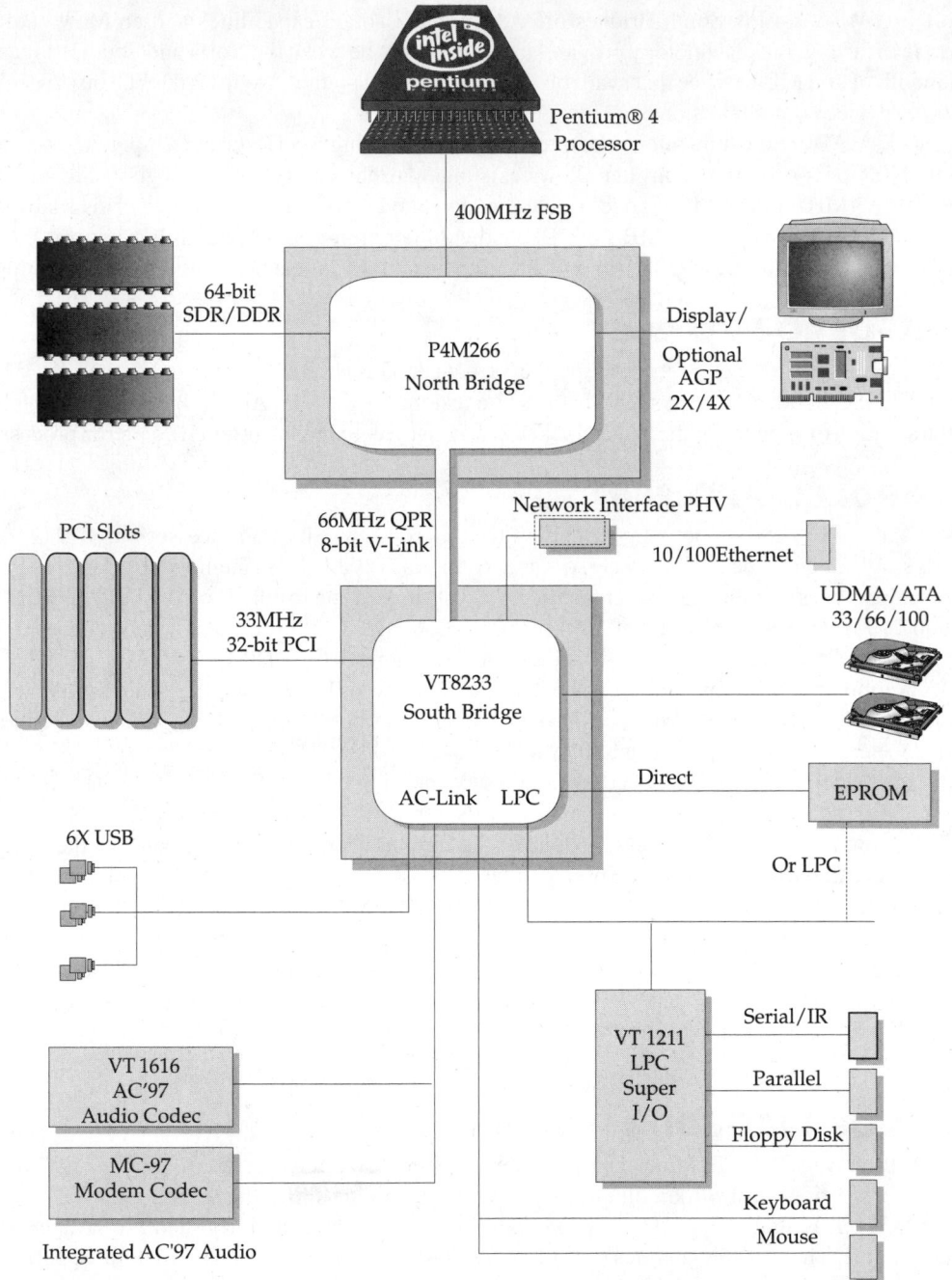

**FIGURE 9-12** Block diagram of a typical VIA ProSavageDDR P4M266 chipset implementation (Courtesy of VIA Technologies, Inc.)

AGP 8X equivalent bandwidth of 2.1 GB/s). The VIA ProSavageDDR P4M266 utilizes VIA's V-Link hub architecture to provide a dedicated 266 MB/s bus for North-South Bridge data transfers.

Members of the VIA VT8233 series can be used to provide South Bridge features. The VT8233 and VT8233C chips support two Ultra-DMA/100 controllers (the VT8233A chip offers UltraDMA/133 support), six USB ports, and six PCI slots. Super I/O features include support for a serial port, parallel port, and floppy disk controller. ACPI and APM power management support is integrated in all VT8233 series chips. The VT8233C South Bridge includes an integrated Ethernet controller for 10/100 BaseT Ethernet and HomePNA networking. These VIA South Bridge chips also offer AC97 2.2 audio and MC97 modem interface support. These features can be implemented through the supported ACR (Advanced Communication Riser) slot or integrated directly on the system board. Table 9-10 compares the main features of the ProSavageDDR P4M266 chipset.

## VIA PROSAVAGEDDR PN266T

The VIA ProSavageDDR PN266T (see Figure 9-13) is designed specifically for mobile systems based on the Intel Pentium III mobile or VIA C3 mobile processors. It combines the VIA VT8613 North Bridge with either the VIA VT8233 or VT8233C South Bridge. The North Bridge features an integrated S3 Graphics ProSavage8 AGP 8X 2D/3D graphics engine. It supports up to 4GB of 200/266 MHz DDR SDRAM memory, and standard PC100/133 SDRAM. SMA (Shared Memory Architecture) enables the chipset to utilize system memory for frame buffer and texture memory on a 128-bit internal data path—this eliminates the need for a separate frame buffer and lowers power consumption of the graphics subsystem. Intel Speedstep technology also reduces system power consumption to improve battery life. VIA V-Link hub architecture offers a dedicated 266 MB/s bus used to link the North and South Bridge chips.

South Bridge chip options for the ProSavageDDR PN266T include the VT8233 and the VT8233C chips. Both offer a full set of networking and communication features. The VT8233 provides integrated 10/100 Ethernet and HomePNA support. The VT8233C offers an integrated 3Com 10/100 Mbps Ethernet controller. Both chips also support two Ultra-DMA/100 controllers, six PCI slots, and three USB hubs (allowing up to six USB devices). ACPI and APM power management features are integrated into all VT8233 series chips. The VT8233 series also includes support for six channel AC97 v2.2 audio and

**FIGURE 9-13**    The VIA ProSavageDDR PN266T chipset provides support for mobile Pentium II or VIA C3 systems (Courtesy of VIA Technologies, Inc.)

MC97 modem interface. Super I/O provides a serial port, parallel port, and floppy disk controller. Table 9-10 lists the main features of the ProSavageDDR PN266T chipset.

# VIA PROSAVAGE PL133T

The VIA ProSavage PL133T chipset includes the VIA VT8604 North Bridge and the VIA VT8231 South Bridge. Designed specifically for the value PC market, this highly integrated chipset offers on-board video and audio support. The VT8604 North Bridge includes the Apollo Pro 133A North Bridge combined with the S3 Graphics Savage4 graphics core. The resulting chipset supports Intel Pentium III and Celeron processors (including the newer Tualatin core units) and VIA's own C3 line of processors. North Bridge features include 66/100/133 MHz FSB settings, memory support for up to 2GB of PC66/100/133 SDRAM or VC-SDRAM memory, and integrated AGP 4X capabilities. The VT8604 allows for asynchronous CPU and memory bus speed settings, so a wide variety of CPU and memory combinations can be used while maintaining optimal speed settings for both. The integrated graphics system supports CRT, LCD flat panels, and TV displays.

Features of the VT8231 South Bridge include support for a standard keyboard, mouse, floppy drive controller, a serial port, and a parallel port. Support for legacy devices and older ISA bus features is included, though legacy-free system designs can be offered through UHCI-compliant USB ports. The South Bridge provides two Ultra-DMA33/66/100 channels, and offers support for AC97 audio and MC97 modem standards. A network interface is provided through integrated 10/100 Ethernet controller. Finally, the South Bridge supports modern power management such as APM and ACPI/OnNow. Table 9-11 lists the main features of the ProSavage PL133T chipset.

| TABLE 9-11 | COMPARISON OF VIA PL133T, PN133T, PM133, PRO 133A/T, AND PLE133/T CHIPSET FEATURES | | | | |
|---|---|---|---|---|---|
| CHIPSET | VIA PROSAVAGE PL133T | VIA PROSAVAGE PN133T | VIA PROSAVAGE PM133 | VIA APOLLO PRO 133A/T | VIA APOLLO PLE133/T |
| Processor | Pentium III, Celeron, VIA C3 | Pentium III, Celeron, VIA C3 | Pentium II/III, Celeron, VIA C3 | Pentium II/III, Celeron, VIA C3 | Pentium II/III, Celeron, VIA C3 |
| Number of Processors | 1 | 1 | 1 | 1-2 | 1 |
| FSB | 66/100/133 MHz | 66/100/133 MHz | 66/100/133 MHz | 66/100/133 MHz | 66/100/133 MHz |
| Max. Memory | 1.5GB | 1.5GB | 1.5GB | 1.5GB | 1.5GB |
| Memory Type | PC100/PC133 SDRAM | PC100/PC133 SDRAM | PC100/PC133 SDRAM | PC100/PC133 SDRAM | PC100/PC133 SDRAM |
| Memory Bus | 66/100/133 MHz | 66/100/133 MHz | 66/100/133 MHz | 66/100/133 MHz | 66/100/133 MHz |
| ECC Support | N/A | N/A | N/A | N/A | N/A |
| PCI Spec. | PCI v2.2 | PCI v2.2 | PCI v2.2 | PCI v2.1 | PCI v2.2 |
| Integrated Graphics | Y | Y | Y | N | Y |
| AGP-Compliant | AGP 2.0 | Integrated | AGP 2.0 | AGP 2.0 | AGP 1.0 |

**TABLE 9-11    COMPARISON OF VIA PL133T, PN133T, PM133, PRO 133A/T, AND PLE133/T CHIPSET FEATURES (CONTINUED)**

| CHIPSET | VIA PROSAVAGE PL133T | VIA PROSAVAGE PN133T | VIA PROSAVAGE PM133 | VIA APOLLO PRO 133A/T | VIA APOLLO PLE133/T |
|---|---|---|---|---|---|
| SMA | 2-32MB | 8-32MB | 2-32MB | N | N |
| External AGP Slot | Y | N | Y | Y | N |
| USB | 4 Ports | 4 ports | 4 ports | 4 ports | 4 ports |
| Max. IDE | UDMA/100 | UDMA/66/100 | UDMA/66/100 | UDMA/66 | UDMA/66 |
| Ethernet | Y | N | Y | N | Y |
| AC97 | Y (w/ MC97) | Y (w/ MC97) | Y (w/ MC97) | Y (w/ MC97) | Y |

# VIA PROSAVAGE PN133T

Designed for mobile systems, the VIA ProSavage PN133T chipset (dubbed "Twister") supports mobile Intel Pentium III, Celeron, and VIA C3 processors with 66 MHz, 100 MHz, and 133 MHz FSB speeds. It combines the VIA VT8603 North Bridge and the VIA VT8231 South Bridge. The North Bridge includes the S3 Graphics Savage4 2D/3D graphics core providing AGP 4X performance with a graphics bandwidth of 1 GB/s. Additional graphics features include an integrated 250 MHz RAMDAC and direct support for CRT, DVI, and TV displays. SMA (Shared Memory Architecture) provides an internal graphics frame buffer between 8 and 32MB, so system memory may be used for graphics. Memory support allows the use of up to 1.5GB of PC100/133 SDRAM or VC-SDRAM.

The VIA VT8231 South Bridge offers integrated multimedia and networking capabilities that include support for two channel AC97 audio, MC97 modem, and ACR (Advanced Communication Riser) capability. Power management features include APM and ACPI/OnNow support. The South Bridge also offers Ultra-DMA33/66/100, four USB ports, and integrated hardware monitoring. Table 9-11 compares the main features of the ProSavage PN133T chipset.

# VIA PROSAVAGE PM133

The VIA ProSavage PM133 chipset is the result of a joint venture between VIA Technologies and S3 Graphics. The chipset supports 66 MHz, 100 MHz, and 133 MHz CPU front side bus (FSB) frequencies, and supports Socket 370/Slot 1 VIA C3, Intel Celeron, and Intel Pentium II/III processors. The ProSavage PM133 chipset is composed of the VT8605 integrated system/graphics controller (North Bridge) and the VT8231 peripheral bus controller (South Bridge). The VT8605 integrates VIA's VT82C694X system controller and S3's Savage4 2D/3D graphics accelerator into a single-chip package. The ProSavage PM133 supports up to 1.5GB of system memory in six banks of SDRAM and VC SDRAM using 256Mbit technology. The DRAM controller can run at either the host CPU bus frequency (66/100/133 MHz) or pseudo-synchronous to the CPU bus frequency (66/100/133 MHz).

The VT8605 system controller also supports full AGP v2.0 capability for maximum bus utilization, including 1X/2X/4X mode transfers. Windows mini-port drivers are supported for compatibility with integrated Savage4 graphics, AGP expansion card graphics, and DVD-capable multimedia accelerators. The ProSavage PM133 supports an optional AGP interface that allows for additional AGP card integration and upgrades. The chipset's integrated Savage4 graphics accelerator provides 2D, 3D, and DVD video acceleration and supports AGP 4X and S3's DX6 texture compression (S3TC).

The ProSavage PM133 is PCI 2.2-compliant. The VT8231 (South Bridge) also includes an integrated Super-I/O interface. This includes an RTC with 256-byte CMOS RAM, a two-channel UDMA/33/66/100 controller, and an integrated four-port UHCI-compliant USB interface. The chipset provides an integrated AC97 link for basic audio and MC97 modem functions, integrated hardware monitoring, and an OnNow/ACPI-compliant power management interface (including suspend-to-RAM operation). Features of the VIA ProSavage PM133 chipset are listed in Table 9-11.

Earlier versions of the VIA ProSavage PM133 chipset used the VT82C686A peripheral bus controller (South Bridge)—this combination only provided UDMA/66 IDE support.

## VIA APOLLO PRO 133A/T

The Apollo Pro 133A is a newer version of the Apollo Pro 133, the major difference being the added support for AGP 4X and for dual processors. The Apollo Pro 133A chipset combines the VT82C694X system controller chip (North Bridge) with the versatile VT82C596B bus controller chip (South Bridge). The Apollo Pro 133A chipset offers support for asynchronous FSB speeds and dual processors. This allows the chipset to be used in conjunction with a wide range of Intel and VIA processors. The Apollo Pro 133A supports the 100 MHz and 133 MHz Pentium II/III and VIA "Joshua" processors. The chipset also supports the 66 MHz speed used by older Intel Celeron processors before they were upgraded to 100 MHz. The chip combination also supports UDMA/66 IDE, USB, PCI, and ISA data busses, as well as AC97 audio and MC97 modem standards, which allows for inexpensive sound and fax/modem implementation. It maintains the standard support for current memory technologies, including PC133 SDRAM and VC133 DRAM. Total memory supported is up to 1.5GB. Table 9-11 outlines the main features of the Apollo Pro 133A chipset. The VIA Apollo Pro 133T is an improved version of the Apollo Pro 133A chipset, and the VT82C694T North Bridge adds support for Tualatin core Intel processors.

## VIA APOLLO PLE133/T

The VIA Apollo PLE133 chipset provides support for Slot1/Socket 370 Intel Pentium II/III and Celeron processors, along with support for VIA C3 CPUs. The VT8601 system/graphics controller (North Bridge) offers an integrated AGP 4X-compliant 2D/3D graphics accelerator feature. The core logic portion of the chip is based on the VIA Apollo Pro 133, and the integrated graphics accelerator is based on the Trident Blade 3D graphics engine. The VT8601 system controller is combined with either the VT82C596B or the VT82C686A PCI-to-ISA South Bridge. Both South Bridge chips are PC98/PC99-compliant with integrated UDMA/33/66, four USB ports, and a complete power management feature set. The VT82C686A also integrates hardware monitoring, Super-I/O functions (floppy disk drive interface and serial/parallel ports), and an AC97 link supporting digital audio and HSP modem functions. The VT8602 North Bridge of the updated Apollo PLE133T chipset adds support for newer Tualatin core Intel processors.

The Apollo PLE133 supports six banks of DRAMs for up to 1.5GB using synchronous FSB speeds at 66/100/133 MHz. The DRAM controller supports standard Fast Page Mode (FPM) DRAM, EDO DRAM, SDRAM, and VC SDRAM. The chipset also supports full AGP v1.0 capability with an internal 2D/3D graphics engine. With an integrated video display and a capture engine, the chipset supports dual apertures on the PCI bus. The Apollo PLE133 graphics controller is integrated with DVD video hardware for motion compensation. The graphics controller can use both the dedicated graphics memory and system memory for graphics operations. However, the VT8601 system/graphics controller does *not* allow for use of optional external AGP graphics cards. The VT82C686A includes the UHCI v1.1 USB root hub with four ports. Additional features include a keyboard controller with PS/2 mouse support, an RTC with extended CMOS, and support for the ACPI power management standard. A list of features is contained in Table 9-11.

> The Apollo PM601 chipset is similar to the Apollo PLE133 and uses the same VT8601 system controller with the same integrated graphics engine. However, the Apollo PM601 uses the VT8231 peripheral bus controller (South Bridge) and only supports 66/100 MHz FSB settings.

## VIA APOLLO KT333

The VIA Apollo KT333 chipset (see Figure 9-14) combines the VIA VT8367 North Bridge and the VIA VT8233/A/C South Bridge to provide support for the latest AMD Athlon XP and AMD Duron (Socket A) processors. The major improvement offered by the VT8367 chip over the VT8366A North Bridge of the VIA Apollo KT266A chipset is support for PC2700 (DDR333) DDR SDRAM memory to handle memory bandwidth up to 2.7 GB/s. Other major features include support for up to 4GB of memory and AGP 4X (the same for both the KT333 and the KT266A chipsets).

VIA's V-Link architecture is used for communication between the North Bridge and the South Bridge. This technology provides a bandwidth of 266 MB/s—twice the bandwidth of the 133 MB/s PCI bus used in older chipsets. The VT8233 family of South Bridge chip is suitable for use in the VIA Apollo KT333 chipset. These chips provide integrated support for AC97 audio, MC97 modem, and Ethernet. PCI and IDE bus support is included, with the VT8233A chip featuring support for Ultra-DMA/133 (the other South Bridge chips only support UltraDMA/66/100). Table 9-12 lists the features of the VIA Apollo KT333 chipset.

## VIA PROSAVAGEDDR KM266

The VIA ProSavageDDR KM266 chipset combines the VIA VT8375 North Bridge with any of the VIA VT8233/A/C series South Bridges. The chipset is designed to support AMD Athlon and AMD Duron processors, including the newer Athlon XP units. It features an integrated S3 Graphics ProSavage8 2D/3D

**FIGURE 9-14**    The VIA Apollo KT333 chipset supports late-model AMD Athlon XP and Duron processors (Courtesy of VIA Technologies, Inc.).

**TABLE 9-12**   COMPARISON OF VIA APOLLO KT333, KM266, KN266, KM133, AND KN133 CHIPSET FEATURES

| CHIPSET | VIA APOLLO KT333 | VIA PROSAVAGE DDR KM266 | VIA PROSAVAGE DDR KN266 | VIA PROSAVAGE KM133 | VIA PROSAVAGE KN133 |
|---|---|---|---|---|---|
| Processor | AMD Athlon and Duron | AMD Athlon and Duron | AMD Athlon 4 and Duron | AMD Athlon and Duron | AMD Athlon and Duron (mobile) |
| Number of Processors | 1 | 1 | 1 | 1 | 1 |
| FSB | 200/266 MHz | 200/266 MHz | 200 MHz | 200 MHz | 200/266 MHz |
| Max. Memory | 4GB | 4GB | 4GB | 1.5GB | 1.5GB |
| Memory Type | 200/266/333 MHz DDR SDRAM | 200/266 MHz DDR SDRAM | 200/266 MHz DDR SDRAM PC100/PC133 SDRAM | PC100/PC133 SDRAM | PC100/PC133 SDRAM |
| Memory Bus | 200/266/333 MHz | 200/266 MHz | 200/266 MHz | 66/100/133 MHz | 66/100/133 MHz |
| ECC Support | N/A | N/A | N/A | N/A | N/A |
| PCI Spec. | PCI v2.2 | PCI v2.2 | PCI v2.2 | PCI v2.2 | PCI v2.2 |
| Integrated Graphics | N | Y | Y | Y | Y |
| AGP-Compliant | AGP 2.0 | AGP 2.0 | Integrated | AGP 2.0 | AGP 2.0 |
| SMA | N/A | to 32MB | to 32MB | to 32MB | 8-32MB |
| External AGP Slot | Y | Y | N | Y | N |
| USB | 6 ports | 6 ports | 6 ports | 4 ports | 4 ports |
| Max. IDE | UDMA/133 | UDMA/133 | UDMA/100 | UDMA/66 | UDMA/100 |
| Ethernet | Y | Y | Y | Y | N |
| AC97 | Y (w/ MC97) | Y (w/ MC97) | Y (w/ MC97) | Y | Y (w/ MC97) |

accelerator with AGP 8X support and DVD motion compensation. The North Bridge supports up to 4GB of standard PC100/133 SDRAM or the more advanced 200/266 MHz DDR SDRAM. Use of DDR SDRAM offers memory bandwidth up to 2.1 GB/s for improved system and graphics performance. SMA (Shared Memory Architecture) uses system memory for the 32MB graphics frame buffer and texture memory, eliminating the need for separate external graphics memory. An external AGP 4X bus is also included for stand-alone AGP graphics cards. The VIA ProSavageDDR KM266 includes VIA's V-Link hub architecture. This provides a dedicated 266 MB/s communication bus between the North and South Bridge.

The VIA VT8233 family of South Bridges include the VT8233, the VT8233A, and the VT8233C. All of these South Bridge chips support integrated two-channel AC97 audio, MC97 modem, support for Ultra-DMA33/66/100, five PCI slots, and four or six USB ports. The VT8233A adds support for Ultra-DMA/133 while the VT8233C includes support for an integrated 3Com network controller. Power management features include ACPI and APM. Table 9-12 compares the features of the ProSavageDDR KM266 chipset.

# VIA PROSAVAGEDDR KN266

The VIA ProSavageDDR KN266 chipset is designed for mobile systems using the AMD Athlon 4 and AMD Duron mobile processors. It combines the VIA VT8372 North Bridge with a VIA VT8233/C series South Bridge. Intended to meet the power management needs of mobile systems, the chipset includes integrated S3 Graphics ProSavage8 graphics, support for lower voltage DDR SDRAM, integrated audio, support for ACPI, and AMD's PowerNow technology. Other features offered by the ProSavageDDR KN266 chipset are similar to those included in the ProSavageDDR KM266 chipset, but the KN series omits support for external AGP graphics cards. You can see the features of the ProSavageDDR KN266 detailed in Table 9-12.

# VIA PROSAVAGE KM133

The VIA ProSavage KM133 is a slightly older chipset that supports Socket A AMD Athlon and Duron processors with 200 MHz FSB frequencies. It supports DDR data transfers on the EV6 bus for 200 MHz or 266 MHz effective bus speeds. The ProSavage KM133 uses the VT8365 system/graphics controller (North Bridge). The system controller provides pipelined, burst, and concurrent operation between the CPU, DRAM, AGP bus, and PCI bus. It supports up to 1.5GB of SDRAM or VC SDRAM system memory. The DRAM controller can run at either the host CPU bus frequency (66/100/133 MHz) or pseudosynchronous to the CPU bus frequency (66/100/133 MHz). The ProSavage KM133 integrates S3's Savage4 graphics accelerator into a single chip for 2D, 3D, and DVD video acceleration, though the VT8365 North Bridge also supports full AGP v2.0 1X/2X/4X capability as a separate AGP bus for optional graphics cards.

The VT8365 peripheral bus controller (South Bridge) supports two 32-bit 3.3/5V system buses (one AGP and one PCI) that are synchronous/pseudosynchronous to the CPU bus. The chip also contains a built-in bus-to-bus bridge to allow simultaneous concurrent operations, an integrated RTC, a super I/O controller, and a two-channel Ultra-DMA/33/66 controller. The VT8231 provides support for the ISA/PCI/USB/IDE bus interfaces and is PC99-compliant. The chip contains an integrated LAN Fast Ethernet controller, along with an integrated AC97 audio codec and integrated hardware monitoring. An OnNow/ACPI-compliant advanced configuration and power management interface rounds out the South Bridge chip. You can see the features of the KM133 chipset in Table 9-12.

# VIA PROSAVAGE KN133

The VIA ProSavage KN133 (dubbed the TwisterK) chipset is designed for mobile PCs using the AMD mobile Athlon and mobile Duron processors operating at FSB speeds of 200/266 MHz. The chipset combines the VIA VT8363A North Bridge and the VIA VT82C686B South Bridge, and it offers a high level of integrated features including built-in graphics and audio. The North Bridge includes the S3 Graphics Savage4 graphics core offering AGP 4X performance. SMA (Shared Memory Architecture) uses system memory for the 8 to 32MB graphics frame buffer. Memory support allows the use of up to 1.5GB of PC100/133 SDRAM or VC-SDRAM. The VIA ProSavage KN133 uses a PCI bus with an available bandwidth of 133 MB/s for North-South Bridge communication.

The VIA VT82C686B South Bridge offers integrated audio and communication features with support for 2 channel AC97 audio, an MC97 modem, and an ACR (Advanced Communication Riser). The chip also includes support for Ultra-DMA33/66/100, four USB ports, and Advanced ACPI/OnNow power management standards. Table 9-12 compares the features of the ProSavage KN133 chipset.

# VIA APOLLO KT266A

Designed to support AMD Athlon/Duron processors, the VIA KT266A chipset combines the VIA VT8366A North Bridge with either the VIA VT8233 or the VIA VT8233C South Bridge. The VIA Apollo KT266A chipset is an improved version of the VIA KT266 chipset. Similar to the other VIA chipsets, it offers high-performance timing and larger queues to increase memory and system bus operations (the South Bridge chips are identical except for the type of integrated Ethernet support offered). The VT8366A North Bridge supports FSB speeds of 200 MHz and 266 MHz. The chip features support for AGP 2X/4X and AGP Pro voltage requirements. The North Bridge also provides support for up to 4GB of 200/266 MHz DDR SDRAM memory. It also allows the use of older PC100/133 SDRAM or VC-SDRAM memory. VIA V-Link hub architecture is included providing a dedicated chip communication bandwidth of 266 MB/s.

Both the VT8233 and the VT8233C South Bridge chips offer support for two UltraDMA33/66/100 drive controllers, six USB ports, and six PCI slots. Power management features include support for ACPI, APM, and AMD PowerNow! technology. Audio and communication features include integrated AC97 audio, MC97 modem, and Advanced Communications Riser (ACR) support. The integrated network controller offers support for 10/100BaseT Ethernet (while the VT8233C supports a 3Com Ethernet controller). Table 9-13 lists the features for the KT266A chipset.

| TABLE 9-13 | COMPARISON OF VIA KT266A, KT266, KLE133, KT133A, AND KT133 CHIPSET FEATURES | | | | |
|---|---|---|---|---|---|
| **CHIPSET** | **VIA APOLLO KT266A** | **VIA APOLLO KT266** | **VIA APOLLO KLE133** | **VIA APOLLO KT133A** | **VIA APOLLO KT133** |
| Processor | AMD Athlon and Duron | AMD Athlon and Duron | AMD Athlon and Duron | AMD Athlon and Duron | AMD Athlon and Duron |
| Number of Processors | 1 | 1 | 1 | 1 | 1 |
| FSB | 200/266 MHz | 200/266 MHz | 200/266 MHz | 200/266 MHz | 200 MHz |
| Max. Memory | 4GB | 4GB | 3GB | 1.5GB | 1.5GB |
| Memory Type | 200/266 MHz DDR SDRAM | 200/266 MHz DDR SDRAM PC100/PC133 SDRAM | PC100/PC133 SDRAM | PC100/PC133 SDRAM | PC100/PC133 SDRAM |
| Memory Bus | 200/266 MHz | 200/266 MHz | 66/100/133 MHz | 100/133 MHz | 100/133 MHz |
| ECC Support | N/A | Y | N/A | N/A | N/A |
| PCI Spec. | PCI v2.2 | PCI v2.2 | PCI v2.2 | PCI v2.2 | PCI v2.2 |
| Integrated Graphics | N | N | Y | N | N |
| AGP-Compliant | AGP 2.0 | AGP 2.0 | Integrated | AGP 2.0 | AGP 2.0 |
| SMA | N/A | N/A | N/A | N/A | N/A |
| External AGP Slot | Y | Y | N | Y | Y |
| USB | 6 ports | 6 ports | 4 ports | 4 ports | 4 ports |
| Max. IDE | UDMA/100 | UDMA/100 | UDMA/100 | UDMA/100 | UDMA/66 |

| **TABLE 9-13** | COMPARISON OF VIA KT266A, KT266, KLE133, KT133A, AND KT133 CHIPSET FEATURES *(CONTINUED)* | | | | |
|---|---|---|---|---|---|
| **CHIPSET** | **VIA APOLLO KT266A** | **VIA APOLLO KT266** | **VIA APOLLO KLE133** | **VIA APOLLO KT133A** | **VIA APOLLO KT133** |
| Ethernet | Y | Y | Y | N | N |
| AC97 | Y (w/ MC97) | Y (w/ MC97) | Y (w/ MC97) | Y (w/ MC97) | Y (w/ MC97) |

# VIA APOLLO KT266

The VIA Apollo KT266 chipset is a high-performance system controller for the development of AGP/PCI desktop PC systems based on 64-bit Socket A processors like the AMD Athlon and Duron. The KT266 chip set consists of the VT8366 system controller (North Bridge) and the VT8233 V-Link peripheral bus controller (South Bridge). The VT8366 system controller provides support for communication between the CPU, DRAM, AGP bus. The VT8233 V-Link client controller is a highly integrated PCI/LPC controller. The VT8233 also provides a dedicated 266 MB/s interface for efficient North/South Bridge communication. The chipset supports five PCI slots with arbitration and decoding for all integrated functions and a Low Pin Count (LPC) bus.

The VT8366 supports eight banks of SDRAM or DDR SDRAMs for up to 4GB of system RAM. The DRAM controller supports standard SDRAM and VC SDRAM in a flexible mix/match manner, or it can be configured to support DDR SDRAM mode. The DRAM controller also supports optional ECC (single-bit error correction and multibit detection) or EC (error checking) capability, and it can run either synchronous or pseudosynchronous mode with the host CPU bus frequency (66/100/133 MHz). The VIA Apollo KT266 chipset also supports full AGP v2.0 2X/4X capability.

The VT8233 South Bridge supports up to five PCI slots and is PCI v2.2-compliant. It provides an integrated networking controller with a standard interface for 10/100BaseT Ethernet. The VT8233 also includes an integrated keyboard controller with PS/2 mouse support, an integrated DS12885 style RTC, and an integrated UDMA/33/66/100 drive controller. AC97 and MC97 features will support onboard sound and modem capabilities. The chipset includes an integrated UHCI v1.1-compliant USB interface with six function ports, distributed DMA support, and an OnNow/ACPI-compliant configuration and power management interface. You can see the features of a KT266 chipset in Table 9-13.

# VIA APOLLO KLE133

Designed for value platforms, the VIA KLE133 chipset is designed to offer adequate performance and low cost. It combines the VIA VT8361 North Bridge with the VIA VT82C686B South Bridge. The North Bridge supports Socket A AMD Athlon and AMD Duron processors with FSB settings of 200 MHz or 266 MHz. Total system cost is reduced with an integrated AGP 4X graphics core. The KLE133 supports up to 3GB of low-cost PC66/100/133 SDRAM or VC-SDRAM memory.

The highly integrated VT82C686B South Bridge features support for UltraDMA33/66/100, four USB ports, Super I/O, up to eight PCI slots, and hardware monitoring. Overall system cost is further reduced with included support for a 10/100 BaseT Ethernet controller, AC97 audio, MC97 modem, and advanced power management features. You can see how the KLE133 compares to other chipsets in Table 9-13.

## VIA APOLLO KT133A

The VIA Apollo KT133A is an updated version of the venerable Apollo KT133 chipset. It adds support for newer, higher performance bus specifications—the most noticeable additions are support for UDMA/100 IDE data transfer speeds and the 266 MHz FSB speeds of Socket A AMD Athlon and Duron processors. The VIA Apollo KT133A combines the VT8363A system controller (North Bridge) with the VT82C686B peripheral bus controller (South Bridge). The VT8363A adds the support for the faster 266 MHz EV6 system bus, and the VT82C686B includes UDMA/100 IDE standards. The chipset adds these items to the comprehensive list of features already offered in the Apollo KT133 chipset (refer to Table 9-13).

## VIA APOLLO KT133

The aging KT133 chipset supports 64-bit Socket A (AMD Athlon and Duron) processors. It consists of the VT8363 system controller (North Bridge) and the VT82C686A peripheral bus controller (South Bridge). The VT8363 supports up to 1.5GB of memory, including standard SDRAM and VC SDRAM in a flexible mix/match manner, and memory speeds of 66/100/133 MHz are allowed. The VT8363 system controller also supports full AGP v2.0 capability for maximum bus utilization including 1X/2X/4X mode transfers.

  The VIA Apollo KT133 chipset is PCI 2.2-compliant and includes an integrated keyboard controller with PS/2 mouse support, along with an integrated RTC and extended 256-byte CMOS RAM. The chipset supports an Ultra-DMA/33/66 drive controller. It also provides a USB interface with a root hub and four function ports, and is OnNow/ACPI-compliant. Additional features include AC97 audio, MC97 modem support, serial ports, parallel port, floppy drive interface, and game port. For power management, the KT133 provides independent clock stop control for the CPU/SDRAM, PCI, and AGP buses. Suspend-to-RAM operation is also supported. The VIA Apollo KT133 also includes a complete hardware monitoring sub-system for monitoring and control of internal and external (motherboard and system) conditions, including voltages, temperatures, fan speeds, switch open/close states, and so on (refer to Table 9-13).

The VIA Apollo KX133, Apollo Pro Plus, Apollo Pro, Apollo MVP4, Apollo MVP3, Apollo P6, Apollo VP3, Apollo VP2, Apollo VPX/97, and Apollo VP1 chipsets are now completely obsolete, and have been dropped from this edition.

# SiS Chipsets

SiS is another major manufacturer of chipsets that support core logic (motherboards) as well as mobile PCs and multimedia applications. Figure 9-15 illustrates the SiS 645 chipset intended for Intel Pentium 4 support. Although SiS originally started out a bit behind VIA and Intel in chipset development, they gained recognition for their inclusion of video accelerator hardware into the chipset (particularly in its later products). This made SiS chipsets particularly appealing to entry-level PCs, where minimizing cost is very important. Today, all chipset makers include some form of video support, and SiS now competes very aggressively with ALi, Intel, and VIA. Since SiS products are not as widely used as other chipsets, we won't detail specific chipsets here, but Tables 9-14, 9-15, 9-16, and 9-17 compare important features of the current SiS line. You can always refer to the SiS Web site for additional features and detailed technical data.

**FIGURE 9-15**    The SiS 645 chipset supports Intel's Pentium 4 processor (Courtesy of SiS).

| TABLE 9-14 | COMPARISON OF SIS 745, 740, 735, 733, AND 730S (AMD ATHLON/DURON) CHIPSET FEATURES | | | | |
|---|---|---|---|---|---|

| CHIPSET | SIS 745 | SIS 740 | SIS 735 | SIS 733 | SIS 730S |
|---|---|---|---|---|---|
| Processor | AMD Athlon and Duron | AMD Athlon and Duron | AMD Athlon and Duron | AMD Athlon and Duron | AMD Athlon and Duron |
| Number of Processors | 1 | 1 | 1 | 1 | 1 |
| FSB | 200/266 MHz | 200/266 MHz | 200/266 MHz | 200/266 MHz | 200/266 MHz |
| Max. Memory | 3GB | 1.5GB | 1.5GB | 1.5GB | 1.5GB |
| Memory Type | 266/333 MHz DDR SDRAM | 200/266 MHz DDR SDRAM PC100/PC133 SDRAM | 200/266 MHz DDR SDRAM PC100/PC133 SDRAM | PC100/PC133 SDRAM | PC100/PC133 SDRAM |
| Memory Bus | 266/333 MHz | 100/133 MHz | 100/133 MHz | 100/133 MHz | 100/133 MHz |
| ECC Support | N/A | N/A | N/A | N/A | N/A |
| PCI Spec. | PCI v2.2 | PCI v2.2 | PCI v2.2 | PCI v2.2 | PCI v2.2 |
| Integrated Graphics | N | Y | N | N | Y |
| AGP-Compliant | AGP 2.0 | AGP 2.0 | AGP 2.0 | AGP 2.0 | AGP 2.0 |
| SMA | N/A | 8-128MB | N/A | N/A | 8-64MB |
| External AGP Slot | Y | N | Y | Y | Y |
| USB | 6 ports | 6 ports | 6 ports | 6 ports | 6 ports |
| Max. IDE | UDMA/100 | UDMA/100 | UDMA/100 | UDMA/100 | UDMA/100 |
| Ethernet | N | Y | Y | N | Y |
| AC97 | Y (w/ IEEE 1394) | Y | Y | Y | Y |

**TABLE 9-15     COMPARISON OF SIS 650, 645DX, AND 645 (PENTIUM 4) CHIPSETS**

| CHIPSET | SIS 650 | SIS 645DX | SIS 645 |
|---|---|---|---|
| Processor | Pentium 4 | Pentium 4 | Pentium 4 |
| Number of Processors | 1 | 1 | 1 |
| FSB | 400 MHz | 400 MHz | 400 MHz |
| Max. Memory | 3GB | 3GB | 3GB |
| Memory Type | 266 MHz DDR SDRAM PC133 SDRAM | 266/333 MHz DDR SDRAM PC133 SDRAM | 266/333 MHz DDR SDRAM PC133 SDRAM |
| Memory Bus | 133/266 MHz | 133/266/333 MHz | 133/266/333 MHz |
| ECC Support | N/A | N/A | N/A |
| PCI Spec. | PCI v2.2 | PCI v2.2 | PCI v2.2 |
| Integrated Graphics | Y | N | N |
| AGP-Compliant | AGP 2.0 | AGP 2.0 | AGP 2.0 |
| SMA | 8–64MB | N/A | N/A |
| External AGP Slot | Y | Y | Y |
| USB | 6 ports | 6 ports | 6 ports |
| Max. IDE | UDMA/100 | UDMA/133 | UDMA/100 |
| Ethernet | Y | Y | Y |
| AC97 | Y | Y | Y |

**TABLE 9-16     COMPARISON OF SIS 635/T AND 633/T (PENTIUM III/CELERON) CHIPSET FEATURES**

| CHIPSET | SIS 635T | SIS 635 | SIS 633T | SIS 633 |
|---|---|---|---|---|
| Processor | Pentium III, Celeron (Tualatin core) | Pentium III, Celeron | Pentium III, Celeron (Tualatin core) | Pentium III, Celeron |
| Number of Processors | 1 | 1 | 1 | 1 |
| FSB | 100/133 MHz | 100/133 MHz | 100/133 MHz | 100/133 MHz |
| Max. Memory | 1.5GB | 1.5GB | 1.5GB | 1.5GB |
| Memory Type | 200/266 MHz DDR SDRAM PC100/PC133 SDRAM | 200/266 MHz DDR SDRAM PC100/PC133 SDRAM | PC100/PC133 SDRAM | PC100/PC133 SDRAM |
| Memory Bus | 100/133 MHz | 100/133 MHz | 100/133 MHz | 100/133 MHz |
| ECC Support | N/A | N/A | N/A | N/A |
| PCI Spec. | PCI v2.2 | PCI v2.2 | PCI v2.2 | PCI v2.2 |
| Integrated Graphics | N | N | N | N |
| AGP-Compliant | AGP 2.0 | AGP 2.0 | AGP 2.0 | AGP 2.0 |
| SMA | N/A | N/A | N/A | N/A |

**TABLE 9-16**    COMPARISON OF SIS 635/T AND 633/T (PENTIUM III/CELERON) CHIPSET FEATURES *(CONTINUED)*

| CHIPSET | SIS 635T | SIS 635 | SIS 633T | SIS 633 |
|---|---|---|---|---|
| External AGP Slot | Y | Y | Y | Y |
| USB | 6 ports | 6 ports | 6 ports | 6 ports |
| Max. IDE | UDMA/100 | UDMA/100 | UDMA/100 | UDMA/100 |
| Ethernet | Y | Y | N | N |
| AC97 | Y | Y | Y | Y |

# NVIDIA Chipsets

A recent entrant in the motherboard chipset market, NVIDIA is best known for their high-performance graphics chipsets. The increasing popularity of motherboard chipsets with integrated graphics features has allowed NVIDIA to design and produce a series of chipsets based on their standard GeForce family of

**TABLE 9-17**    COMPARISON OF SIS 630 FAMILY (PENTIUM III/CELERON) CHIPSET FEATURES

| CHIPSET | SIS 630ST | SIS 630S | SIS 630ET | SIS 630E | SIS 630 |
|---|---|---|---|---|---|
| Processor | Pentium III, Celeron | Pentium III, Celeron | Pentium III, Celeron | Pentium III, Celeron | Pentium III, Celeron |
| Number of Processors | 1 | 1 | 1 | 1 | 1 |
| FSB | 66/100/133 MHz | 66/100/133 MHz | 66/100/133 MHz | 66/100/133 MHz | 66/100/133 MHz |
| Max. Memory | 3GB | 3GB | 3GB | 3GB | 3GB |
| Memory Type | PC100/PC133 SDRAM | PC100/PC133 SDRAM | PC100/PC133 SDRAM | PC100/PC133 SDRAM | PC100/PC133 SDRAM |
| Memory Bus | 66/100/133 MHz | 66/100/133 MHz | 66/100/133 MHz | 66/100/133 MHz | 66/100/133 MHz |
| ECC Support | N/A | N/A | N/A | N/A | N/A |
| PCI Spec. | PCI v2.2 | PCI v2.2 | PCI v2.2 | PCI v2.2 | PCI v2.2 |
| Integrated Graphics | Y | Y | Y | Y | Y |
| AGP-Compliant | AGP 2.0 | AGP 2.0 | AGP 2.0 | AGP 2.0 | AGP 2.0 |
| SMA | 8–64MB | 8–64MB | 8–64MB | 8–64MB | 8–64MB |
| External AGP Slot | Y | Y | N | N | N |
| USB | 6 ports | 6 ports | 5 ports | 5 ports | 5 ports |
| Max. IDE | UDMA/100 | UDMA/100 | UDMA/100 | UDMA/66 | UDMA/66 |
| Ethernet | Y | Y | Y | Y | Y |
| AC97 | Y | Y | Y | Y | Y |

graphics engines (e.g., the GeForce 2). Named nForce "Crush" the NVIDIA chipsets support AMD SocketA Athlon and Duron processors. This chipset includes the nForce SPP/IGP (System Platform Processor/Integrated Graphics Processor) North Bridge and the nForce MCP (Media-Communications Processor) South Bridge. The North Bridge is available in either 64-bit or 128-bit versions offering 2.1 GB/s or 4.2 GB/s memory bandwidth with 266 MHz DDR SDRAM memory. Support for an external 4X AGP slot is also provided. The South Bridge is also available in two versions—the MCP or the MCP-D. Both versions include support for six USB ports, Ultra-DMA/100, 10/100 Ethernet and HomePNA networking, and MC97 software modem. The MCP-D unit adds support for Dolby Digital 5.1 to the integrated AC97 audio features of both MCP units. Given NVIDIA's leadership in high-performance PC graphics, there will undoubtedly be a proliferation of powerful chipsets in the coming years.

The SPP North Bridge versions do not include integrated video, while the IGP North Bridge provides integrated GeForce 2 video.

# Further Study

**ALi**   www.aliusa.com/
**AMD**   www.amd.com
**Intel**   www.intel.com/design/chipsets/
**Micron**   www.micron.com/
**NVIDIA**   www.nvidia.com/
**OPTi**   www.opti.com
**SiS**   www.sis.com/products/chipsets/index.htm
**VIA**   www.viatech.com/en/index/index.jsp
**VLSI** (acquired by Phillips)   www.semiconductors.philips.com/

# 10

# CMOS

**W**ith the introduction of their PC/AT computer, IBM abandoned the configuration DIP switches that had been used for the PC/XT. Rather than limit the system's configuration options, IBM chose to store the system's setup parameters in a small, low-power RAM chip called the CMOS RAM, which is often combined on the same chip with the *real-time clock* (RTC). In practice, the CMOS RAM (and RTC) are now located on the South Bridge chip of most current chipsets (see Chapter 9). By using memory locations, the discrete switches of the XT were replaced with logical "switches" of each CMOS bit. (After all, a bit can be high or low, just as a switch can be on or off.) When a modern personal computer starts, the system attributes—stored in the CMOS RAM—are read by the BIOS, which then uses those attributes during normal system operation. It is vitally important that the *correct* settings be used when configuring a system. Otherwise, system problems may result. This chapter explains a broad selection of CMOS parameters in detail, then provides some guidelines for proper CMOS optimization and battery maintenance.

One important note before we continue. Many PC enthusiasts (and even experienced technicians) use the terms *BIOS* and *CMOS* interchangeably. However, BIOS and CMOS RAM are not the same thing—though the two are intimately related. *BIOS* refers to the firmware instructions located on the BIOS

ROM chip, while *CMOS* refers to the low-power RAM that holds the system's setup parameters. BIOS reads the CMOS RAM into main memory at start time, and provides the *Setup* routine, which allows you to change the contents of CMOS, but the CMOS RAM device is a totally different chip (typically integrated into the chipset's South Bridge). It's important that you understand the difference.

# The Role of CMOS

In simplest terms, CMOS RAM is nothing more than very low-power static RAM. Older CMOS RAM devices offered 64 bytes, and later implementations provide an extra 64 bytes (128 bytes total). The latest motherboards use 512 bytes or more to store the CMOS Setup along with ESCD (extended system configuration data) information needed by the PC's *plug-and-play* (PnP) system. Since RAM is naturally lost when system power is removed, a battery is added to the PC that continues to provide power to the CMOS RAM (and RTC). This "CMOS backup battery" keeps the date, time, and system parameters intact until you turn the system on again. Of course, if the battery should fail, the system will lose its date, time, and all of its setup parameters. Many a tear has been shed trying to reconstruct lost system parameters by trial and error.

Today, most CMOS Setup routines provide a "BIOS Default" selection that will automatically load a set of acceptable parameters in order to start the system quickly. This can be a real labor saver when CMOS RAM contents are lost.

# Configuring the CMOS Setup

As you might expect, CMOS data does not simply materialize out of the ether. It must be entered manually (initially by the system manufacturer, and later by you or your customers) through a Setup routine. Early AT-compatible PCs relied on a disk-based setup utility. That is, you needed to boot the computer from a floppy disk containing the CMOS Setup utility. The big problem with a setup disk is that the floppy disk may fail and leave you without a setup disk, or you may lose the setup disk as the system changes hands or falls into disuse. If you find yourself with a setup disk, be sure to make a backup copy of it as soon as possible. Late-model 386 and subsequent systems abandon the use of setup disks and incorporate the setup utility onto the BIOS chip. When the setup routine resides on the system, you can usually access the setup during system initialization by pressing one or more keys simultaneously (such as DEL or CTRL+F1, and so on). This part of the chapter is intended to familiarize you with the options found in current CMOS Setup programs and to illustrate the typical defaults.

Keep in mind that the listings of CMOS Setup features found in this chapter are assembled from a number of different sources. Your CMOS Setup may offer more or fewer options to choose from depending on your BIOS maker and the vintage of your particular PC.

### ENTERING CMOS SETUP

The first trick in configuring your CMOS Setup is to launch the setup utility in the first place. BIOS manufacturers are rarely consistent when it comes to accessing the setup utility. In most cases, you can only launch setup in the first few moments after the system boots—just after the memory test is finished, but **before** the operating system starts to load (if you see the message "Starting Windows...", you've waited too long). A note on the display will usually indicate the correct key or key combination, such as:

```
Press <F1> to enter Setup...
```

Some BIOS versions allow these setup entry messages to be turned off through the CMOS Setup, so you may **not** see a message displayed on the monitor. However, the setup routine should still be accessible.

Unfortunately, there are about as many key combinations as there are BIOS makers, and unless you have a manual for the motherboard, knowing the proper key combinations for every system can be an exercise in frustration. Table 10-1 lists the known key combinations for many popular BIOS and system types. When you're stuck and cannot enter CMOS with any of the key combinations in Table 10-1, you might be able to *force* the CMOS Setup routine by causing a configuration change (such as removing a DIMM or two). This sometimes causes a CMOS configuration error and allows you to proceed to the setup routine.

For security purposes, some new motherboard designs allow access to CMOS Setup to be disabled through a motherboard jumper. If you absolutely cannot access the setup using a proper key combination or a forced configuration change, check the motherboard to see if the setup access jumper has been disabled.

Of course, if you've got a 286 or early 386 model PC sitting on your workbench, you'll need a setup disk to load the CMOS Setup utility. If you've actually got a setup disk for the system, consider yourself lucky. They are usually the first things to be lost. If you need a setup utility, you may be able to download a suitable third-party freeware utility from ftp://ftp.uu.net/systems/. For IBM PS/2 systems, you can get a setup utility from the IBM site at www.pc.ibm.com/files.html. Finally, setup utilities for Panasonic computers are available on the web at www.panasonic.com/support/software/download.html.

## BASIC CMOS OPTIMIZATION TACTICS

As PCs continue to evolve, the ever-increasing variety of memory types, busses, PC technology initiatives, and system architectures has forced BIOS makers to provide more and more entries in the CMOS

| **TABLE 10-1** | **TYPICAL CMOS SETUP KEY SEQUENCES** |
|---|---|
| **BIOS/SYSTEM** | **KEY (OR KEY SEQUENCE)** |
| ALR PC | F2 (for PCI systems) or CTRL-ALT-ESC (for non-PCI systems) |
| AMI BIOS | DEL key during the POST |
| Award BIOS | CTRL-ALT-ESC |
| Compaq PCs | F10 |
| DTK BIOS | ESC key during the POST |
| Gateway 2000 PCs | F1 |
| HP Pavilion PCs | F1 |
| IBM PS/2 BIOS | CTRL-ALT-INS *after* CTRL-ALT-DEL |
| Intel Motherboards | F2 |
| Phoenix BIOS | CTRL-ALT-ESC or CTRL-ALT-S |
| Sony PC | F3 while the PC is starting (you see the Sony logo), then F1 |
| Unknown/Other | Try DEL, INS, ESC, F1, F2, F10, CTRL-ALT, CTRL-DEL, CTRL-INS, CTRL-ESC, ALT-ESC, CTRL-ALT-ESC, or CTRL-ALT-ENTER |

Setup. Today, there are dozens of possible setup entries in any given BIOS—each yielding hundreds of potential combinations. This variety makes it very difficult to select the optimum settings for a system. However, if you're really just interested in getting the most from your setup, the following points may come in handy:

■ *Check the basics.* Make sure that all standard CMOS settings correspond to the installed components of your system. For instance, you should verify the date, time, and available memory (if possible). Also verify any entries for hard disks, CD drives, and floppy disks. (See "Configuring the Standard CMOS Setup" later in this chapter.)

■ *Enable all processor cache.* Make sure that all your processor cache (both internal and external) is enabled. For older PCs, you must have internal (L1) and external (L2) cache memory present in the system—which is always the case for any pre-Pentium systems that may remain in service. (See "Configuring the Advanced CMOS Setup" later in this chapter.)

■ *Minimize RAM wait-states.* Make sure that the wait-state values used for your main system RAM (e.g., SDRAM, DDR SDRAM, or RDRAM) are set at the minimum possible. You must be careful here because if values are too low, your system may freeze (hang up) or crash. BIOS default values are usually adequate if the system RAM is properly identified. For more information, check out "Configuring the Advanced (Chipset) Setup" later in this chapter.

■ *Enable ROM shadowing.* At a minimum, you should shadow your video and system ROM. On older systems, this may improve performance significantly. Newer systems (with faster "flash" ROM devices) may not benefit as much from shadowing. If system performance problems develop, try disabling the ROM shadowing. (See "Configuring the Advanced CMOS Setup" later in this chapter.)

■ *Enable power management.* Make sure to employ the power management features supported by your BIOS. Proper power management will conserve electricity and can extend the working life of many of the system components. However, all of the system hardware must support the same power management scheme (e.g., ACPI), so using older "legacy" components may prevent the system from entering or returning from its power conservation mode. (See "Configuring Power Management" later in this chapter.)

■ *Optimize drive access.* Hard disk data transfer speeds are a major bottleneck for system performance. Use the fastest data transfer protocol that your hard disk system will support (for example, Ultra-DMA/100 or Ultra-DMA/133). Remember that both the drive and drive controller must support the chosen data transfer protocol. In most cases, the BIOS will select the best data transfer mode once the drives are identified, so there's usually no need to change the default setting unless the drive is improperly identified.

■ *Go with the BIOS Defaults.* With modern systems, it's often unnecessary to reenter every CMOS Setup parameter from scratch. Suitable default settings are now typically incorporated into the BIOS itself, so you can get a system running without messing with individual entries. (You just need to enter the drives properly.) You can find this as a "Select BIOS Defaults" option in your CMOS Setup main menu. BIOS defaults will generally not optimize your system's performance, but they will get you out of a tough spot when you have trouble after changing one or more settings.

# HIDDEN BIOS SETTINGS

Although today's BIOS has more options than ever, there's no guarantee that you'll be able to access every available option through the CMOS Setup. In some cases, there may be hidden settings that you cannot see in the CMOS Setup (and such hidden settings cannot be altered using the CMOS Setup routine). This can be a major impairment since many settings such as DRAM timings and cache settings can have a serious impact on PC performance. In actual practice, the settings still exist, but they are masked—often because the PC maker doesn't trust you to modify the settings. There are several tools that you can use to view and modify hidden system settings depending on the version of your BIOS.

## AMI BIOS Versions

Robert Muchsel has written a program called AMI Setup (v.2.99) that will allow you to access and change the hidden settings of your AMI BIOS. The program works with AMI's High Flex BIOS versions—as well as with AMI WinBIOS. The shareware version has excellent documentation to assist you in your optimization efforts. If you need help on what a particular setting affects, take a look at the long list of BIOS options presented in the following sections. You can download AMI Setup 2.99 from www.aco.ee/files/dosutils/amis2990.zip or www.tweakpc.com/Download_files/amis2990.zip.

## Non-AMI BIOS Versions

For systems that do not use an AMI BIOS (for example, MR BIOS, Award, Phoenix), you can use the more generic CTCHIPZ utility available from www.sysopt.com/pub/ctchip34.zip. As with AMI Setup, the CTCHIPZ utility checks and accesses "undocumented" system settings. The one wrinkle with CTCHIPZ is that you'll need to know which chipset your system uses in order to select the correct configuration (CFG) file for your particular system. Check the documentation for CTCHIPZ in order to find the correct CFG file name. The CTCHIPZ program can be a bit tricky to comprehend and use since it's in German. You can find an English translation for the documentation at www.sysopt.com/ctdocs.html.

Another popular utility often used to control "hidden" system settings is TweakBIOS (v.1.53b) by Miro Wikgren. This utility supports a variety of PC platforms including those with Intel 820/840; VIA Apollo Pro; and SiS 530, 540, 560, 600, 620 chipsets. Additional platforms should be supported in future versions of TweakBIOS. You can download this freeware from www.miro.pair.com/tweakbios/twk153b.zip.

# CONFIGURING THE STANDARD CMOS SETUP

The standard CMOS Setup (such as the Award BIOS example for an AOpen AK72 motherboard in Figure 10-1) typically recognizes and assigns resources for the hardware components in your PC. This usually comprises one screen of basic data about your system's date, time, installed processor and RAM, and attached devices (primarily floppy drives, CD drives, and hard drives). It is important for you to get this data correct because the system will refuse to boot unless it is aware of all the drives installed (especially your boot hard drive, which is usually drive C:). The following alphabetic listing highlights common entries found in the standard setup menu(s).

Menus such as Figure 1 are presented as an example only—your own CMOS Setup may appear quite different.

**Assign IRQ for VGA**   When enabled, this option causes the system to assign an IRQ for the video card in order to speed the transfer of data between the CPU and video card. This option must be enabled if your video card requires bus mastering (such as Matrox Mystique cards with 3D graphics features). By disabling this option, you'll free up an IRQ for use elsewhere in the system.

**Boot Up NumLock Status**   This field is related to the keyboard, and enables users to activate the Num Lock function when the system boots. This feature is normally on by default, but you can turn the option off.

```
          CMOS Setup Utility - Copyright (C) 1984-2000 Award Software
                           Standard CMOS Features

     Date (mm:dd:yy)           Wed, Feb 16 2000        Item Help
     Time (hh:mm:ss)           16 : 27 : 15
                                                  Menu Level   ►
   ► IDE Primary Master        Press Enter None
   ► IDE Primary Slave         Press Enter None     Change the day, month,
   ► IDE Secondary Master      Press Enter None     year and century
   ► IDE Secondary Slave       Press Enter None

     Drive A                   1.44M, 3.5 in.
     Drive B                   None

     Video                     EGA/VGA
     Halt On                   All Errors

     Base Memory                    640K
     Extended Memory              64512K
     Total Memory                 65536K


  ↑↓→←:Move  Enter:Select  +/-/PU/PD:Value  F10:Save  ESC:Exit  F1:General Help
   F3:Language F5:Previous Values F6:Setup Defaults F7:Turbo Defaults
```

**FIGURE  10-1**    Using the Standard Setup to define key hardware such as drives, processors, memory, and so on (Courtesy of AOpen)

**Date and Time**    Use these settings to change the date and time of the system clock. The date format is typically month, day, and year (mm:dd:yy or mm:dd:yyyy). The time format is usually based on 24-hour military time (hh:mm:ss).

RTC devices are notoriously inaccurate devices. Depending of the quality of the motherboard, you should expect to lose (or gain) several seconds per month. You should periodically check the date and time, and correct it as necessary.

**Daylight Savings**    When enabled, this feature allows the RTC to automatically adapt to the daylight savings scheme (removing one hour on the last Sunday of October and adding one hour on the last Sunday of April). As a rule, this can be enabled. Otherwise, you'll need to correct for daylight savings time manually.

**Error Halt**    This entry determines whether the PC will stop if an error is detected during initialization (similar to Halt On later):

■ **No errors**    The system boot will not be stopped for any error that may be detected.

■ **All errors**    Whenever the BIOS detects a nonfatal error, the system will be stopped and you will be prompted.

■ **All, but keyboard**    The system boot will not stop for a keyboard error, but it will stop for all others.

■ **All, but disk**    The system boot will not stop for a disk error, but it will stop for all others.

■ **All, but disk/keyboard**    The system boot will not stop for a keyboard or disk error, but it will stop for all others.

**Floppy Drive A**    Set this entry to reflect the type of floppy drive installed for drive A:. In most cases, the drive will be 1.44MB 3.5-inch, though a few systems may use a 2.88MB 3.5-inch floppy. Older systems may use 720KB 3.5-inch, 1.2MB 5.25-inch, or even 360KB 5.25-inch floppy drives.

**Floppy Drive B**    Set this entry to reflect the type of floppy drive installed for drive B:. The typical selections for a floppy drive are shown for "Floppy Drive A."

**Halt On**    This entry tells the BIOS which errors to skip during the POST. For example, if you want the BIOS POST to continue whether or not it gets an error on a missing keyboard, set this option to "All, but keyboard" (See "Error Halt" earlier.)

**Hard Disk C**    Sometimes referred to as *IDE Primary Master*, this number is the BIOS drive table number of your primary (master) hard drive. In virtually all cases today, this number is 47 (User Defined), which means that you must specify the drive specs according to your hard drive manual. Otherwise, you can typically autodetect the drive parameters. SCSI drives in the C: position should be set to None or Not Installed. If you cannot autodetect the drive, there are typically six parameters that define your hard drive:

- **Cyl**    The number of cylinders (or tracks) on your hard disk.
- **Heads**    The number of heads in the hard disk.
- **WPre**    This setting specifies the cylinder where Write Precompensation begins and uses additional energy to write the "compensated" cylinders. Today, WPre is essentially useless. Set it either to –1 or the maximum number of cylinders on the drive. For EIDE/IDE hard drives, it is not necessary to enter a WPre cylinder.
- **LZ**    This setting specifies the cylinder used as the landing zone for older drives without an "autoparking" feature. Today, LZ is essentially useless. Set it either to 0 or the maximum number of cylinders on the drive.
- **Sect/Trk**    This setting specifies the number of *sectors per track* (SPT). It is often 17 for MFM drives, and 26 for RLL drives. Modern types of drives use Zoned Recording, and the number of sectors per track will vary (increasing on the outer tracks). There is usually one translation number (63) provided for the drive.
- **Size**    The total drive size is automatically calculated according to the number of cylinders, heads, and sectors entered earlier. The number is given in MB according to the formula (Hds*Cyl*Sect*512)/1048.

**Hard Disk D**    Sometimes referred to as *IDE Primary Slave*, this number is the BIOS drive table number of your secondary (slave) hard drive. In virtually all cases today, this number is 47 (User Defined), which means that you must specify the drive specs according to your hard drive manual. Otherwise, you can typically autodetect the drive parameters. SCSI drives set to the D: position should be set to None or Not Installed. If you cannot autodetect the drive, the six parameters that define your hard drive are listed under "Hard Disk C" earlier.

If your drive controller supports four hard drives, you may find an additional two hard drive entries (for example, Hard Disk E: and Hard Disk F:). These would be a *secondary master* and *secondary slave* drive.

**HDD Delay**    Some hard drives require several seconds in order to be identified (initialized) correctly by the BIOS. With fast boots, there may not be enough time to identify the hard drive properly. This setting allows you to artificially delay the boot-up so that the drive may be initialized. You can select from several possible time options. To keep your boot speed as fast as possible, be sure to select the *lowest* possible delay that ensures proper drive initialization. This is sometimes referred to as *Power-On Drive Delay* or *Power-On Boot Delay*.

**Keyboard**    This sets whether a keyboard is attached. In virtually all cases, the proper entry is *installed*. If *not installed*, the BIOS will pass the keyboard test in the POST, allowing a PC to boot without a keyboard, and without the BIOS producing a keyboard error (most commonly encountered in file servers, printer servers, and so on).

**Memory**    This category allows you to select which memory element(s) are displayed at start time. The contents are determined by the BIOS POST:

■ **Base Memory**    The BIOS POST determines the amount of base (conventional) memory installed in the system.

■ **Extended Memory**    The BIOS POST determines the amount of extended memory installed in the system.

■ **Other Memory**    This is memory that can be allocated for different applications. The most common uses for this area are shadow RAM and AGP (video) buffer areas.

■ **Total Memory**    The total memory is the sum of Base, Extended, and Other memory areas.

■ **OS Select for DRAM > 64MB**    If you're using OS/2, select the OS/2 option. If you're using DOS or Windows, select Non-OS/2. Generally, Non-OS/2 is selected.

**Memory Configuration**    Errors in system memory are detected using techniques like parity, and more recently ECC. If ECC memory is installed in the system, this option will usually be set to "ECC" automatically. If non-ECC memory is detected in the system, this option must be set to "non-ECC"—otherwise, serious errors will result and the system will refuse to boot. Mission-critical platforms should use ECC to contain memory errors that may result in system crashes and lost data.

**Multi-Sector Transfers**    Modern hard drives can transfer multiple sectors in a single burst. This option automatically sets the number of sectors that can be transferred (up to the highest number supported by the drive). Typical options include Disabled, 2 Sectors, 4 Sectors, 8 Sectors, 16 Sectors, 32 Sectors, and Maximum (the default). When the drive is autodetected, this field is automatically configured (though the set value may not always be the fastest value for the drive). However, this field can be optimized manually. Remember that the **Type** field must be set to "User Defined" before making changes to this field.

**PCI/VGA Palette Snoop**    This option must be enabled if any ISA card installed in the PC requires VGA palette snooping. For example, an MPEG card can be synchronized with the PCI VGA system. However, few (if any) modern cards require palette snooping, so this option is generally left disabled.

**Primary Display**    This entry specifies the general type of display you are using. The most frequent selection for older systems is VGA/PGA/EGA, though current systems shorten this to VGA, which is adequate for virtually all current systems. If you have an older black/white display, select Mono or Hercules. If your video adapter card is text only, select MDA.

**Quick Power-On Self-Test**    If you have hard drives that initialize quickly, you may be able to speed your boot time even more by selecting the Quick POST. When enabled, the BIOS will shorten or skip some items during the POST (such as no memory count). This option is normally disabled to allow the normal POST routine, and should be kept disabled if you're including a HDD Delay (described earlier in the section "HDD Delay").

**SMART Monitoring**    Most modern hard drives allow the use of *Self-Monitoring Analysis and Reporting Technology* (SMART), which utilizes internal hard disk drive monitoring techniques to detect and report possible drive faults. This feature is normally disabled because system resources used in this feature may slightly decrease system performance, but mission-critical platforms (e.g., servers and workstations) should enable this feature.

**Swap Floppy Drives**    This option allows you to reverse the A: and B: floppy drive assignments when enabled without having to physically swap the drives. Normally, this option is disabled because few systems have more than one floppy drive.

**Translation Mode**    IDE drives below 528MB are typically set as Cylinder Head Sector (CHS) addressing, while EIDE, Fast-ATA, and Ultra-ATA drives use Logical Block Addressing (LBA) instead. Today, virtually all hard drives use LBA or Large translation modes, and the appropriate mode is usually selected automatically when the drives are autodetected.

If you alter a drive's translation mode after the drive has been partitioned and formatted, the data contained on the drive will be inaccessible. You'll need to repartition and reformat the drive.

# CONFIGURING THE ADVANCED CMOS SETUP

The advanced CMOS Setup normally relates to the features found in your particular computer. This menu contains the settings needed to tweak your boot characteristics and to optimize the performance of memory and cache. Most of the options found here are not vital to the system's basic operation, but they can help you tailor the system to your particular tastes and needs. You can see an example of Award BIOS on an AOpen AK72 motherboard in Figure 10-2.

**Above 1MB Memory Test**    Enable this feature if you want the system to check the memory above 1MB for errors. The HIMEM.SYS driver for DOS 6.2 verifies the XMS anyway, so the test would be redundant in this case. In most cases, all memory is tested by the BIOS. But for faster boot performance, leave the feature disabled.

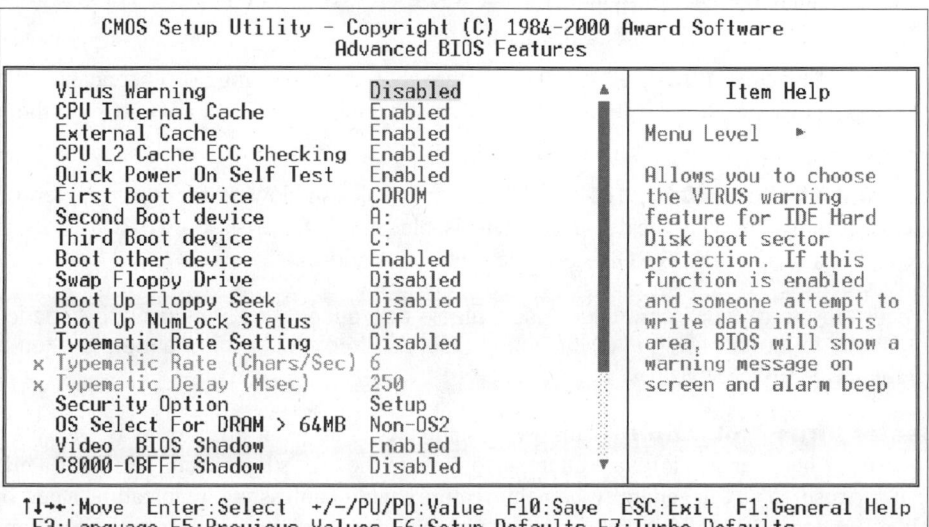

**FIGURE 10-2**    The Advanced Setup, which allows you to tweak performance-related options that are usually integrated into the motherboard chipset (Courtesy of AOpen)

**Adapter ROM Shadow C800, 16K**    This feature enables shadowing for other adapter ROMs at C800h (for example, SCSI or network controller BIOS) that may be in the system. If there are no other adapter devices in the system, keep this feature disabled.

**Adapter ROM Shadow CC00, 16K**    This feature enables shadowing for other adapter ROMs that may be in the system at CC00h. This feature is often disabled by default because some hard drive adapters use the CC00h address.

**Adapter ROM Shadow D000, 16K**    This feature enables shadowing for other adapter ROMs that may be in the system at D000h. This is the default address for most network adapters, so it should usually be disabled unless there is a network adapter in the system, or some other known device with ROM at D000h.

**Adapter ROM Shadow D400, 16K**    This feature enables shadowing for other adapter ROMs that may be in the system at D400h. Since some special controllers (for example, controllers that support four floppy drives) often use this space, the default is often set disabled.

**Adapter ROM Shadow D800, 16K**    This feature enables shadowing for other adapter ROMs that may be in the system at D800h. The default is often disabled unless there is a known ROM in the system at that address.

**Adapter ROM Shadow DC00, 16K**    This feature enables shadowing for other adapter ROMs that may be in the system at DC00h. The default is often disabled unless there is a known ROM in the system at that address.

**Adapter ROM Shadow E000, 16K**    This feature enables shadowing for other adapter ROMs that may be in the system at E000h. The default is often disabled unless there is a known ROM in the system at that address.

**Adapter ROM Shadow E400, 16K**    This feature enables shadowing for other adapter ROMs that may be in the system at E400h. The default is often disabled unless there is a known ROM in the system at that address.

**Adapter ROM Shadow E800, 16K**    This feature enables shadowing for other adapter ROMs that may be in the system at E800h. The default is often disabled unless there is a known ROM in the system at that address.

**Adapter ROM Shadow EC00, 16K**    This feature enables shadowing for other adapter ROMs that may be in the system at EC00h. The default is often disabled unless there is a known ROM in the system at that address. SCSI adapter BIOS ROMs are often set to this address.

 Some recent forms of SCSI controllers use writable addresses and should not be shadowed or cached. Check for such warnings or cautions in the SCSI controller manual before attempting to shadow the SCSI BIOS ROM.

**Boot Sector Virus Protection**    This well-established feature in all current BIOS versions provides a warning whenever any software attempts to write to the disk's boot sector, which is a main target for computer viruses. You can generally keep this feature enabled unless you're installing a new operating system (like Windows 9x/Me/XP) that needs to write to the boot sector during installation. You can disable the boot sector virus protection before installing the OS, then reenable the feature afterward.

**Boot Up Floppy Seek**   See "Floppy Drive Seek at Boot" later.

**ECC Event Logging**   High-end PCs that support ECC in memory can sometimes log ECC events (e.g., ECC errors). System administrators can then refer to those logs later to determine the specifics of a problem, and formulate the corrective action needed to resolve any trouble. When enabled (usually by default), this option will record ECC events to a log file. If you do not need to track ECC events, you can disable this option.

**Event Logging**   High-end PCs (e.g., network servers and workstations) can sometimes log events such as startup errors. System administrators or technicians can then refer to those logs later to determine the specifics of a problem, and formulate the corrective action needed to resolve any trouble. When enabled (usually by default), this option will record system-level events to a log file. If you do not need to track system-level events, you can disable this option.

**External Cache Memory**   This feature allows you to enable or disable the external (L2) cache in the system. If there is L2 cache in the system, make sure that this feature is enabled for best performance. (Virtually all 486 and Pentium-type systems use L2 cache on the motherboard, but Pentium II/III/4 CPUs include L2 cache right in the processor cartridge.) If there is no L2 cache, keep this feature disabled. Enabling the L2 cache when there is no cache in the system may cause the PC to lock up. It may also be necessary for you to disable the L2 cache if there are system stability issues. This feature may also be presented as CPU External Cache.

**Fast Gate A20 Option**   This relates to the first 64KB of extended memory (A0 to A19) known as the *high memory area* (HMA). This option controls the use of the A20 address line to access memory above 1MB. Normally, all RAM access above 1MB is handled through the A20 gate in the keyboard controller chip (8042 or 8742). In virtually all cases, this option should be enabled. Disabling this option may make it impossible to access memory over 1MB.

**Floppy Drive Seek at Boot**   This feature selects whether a floppy drive will be checked at boot time. Keep this feature disabled for faster booting and reduced damage to floppy R/W heads. Enable this feature if you want to check for a bootable floppy disk (important for "booting clean" and running diagnostic utilities).

Disabling the floppy drive, changing the system boot sequence, and setting a CMOS password are good techniques for adding some security to a PC.

**Hard Disk Type 47 RAM Area**   This selection allows you to choose the location of the Type 47 HDD data area in memory. The BIOS has to place the HD type 47 data somewhere in memory. You can choose DOS memory or the I/O address space at 0:300h. DOS memory is valuable in real mode (you only have 640KB to work with), so you should try to use the I/O space instead. However, there may be some peripheral, for example, a sound card or network card, that needs this area too. Note that this feature is redundant if BIOS is shadowed (except possibly for very old BIOS).

**Internal Cache Memory**   This feature allows you to enable or disable the internal (L1) cache in the CPU. If there is an L1 cache in the system, make sure that this feature is enabled for best performance. (All 486-, Pentium-, and Pentium II/III/4-type CPUs use L1 cache.) If there is no L1 cache (or you have reason to believe that the CPU's L1 cache is damaged), keep this feature disabled. Enabling the L1 cache when there is no cache in the CPU may cause the PC to lock up. This feature may also be presented as "CPU Internal Cache."

Some CMOS Setup utilities combine the cache control into a single entry such as Cache Memory and allow you to select Disabled, Internal Cache Only, or Both Enabled.

**Memory Parity Error Check**    This feature controls the parity checking of your system's memory. Parity checking can help improve the integrity of data in memory. When enabled, parity checking will generate an error such as "PARITY ERROR AT 0AB5:00BE SYSTEM HALTED" if an error is detected. Otherwise, errors in memory will go undetected—possibly corrupting and crashing the system. If you're using parity memory on the system, go ahead and enable parity checking. If you're using any non-parity memory on your system, parity checking must be disabled.

Besides being caused by data errors, parity errors can also be caused by insufficient wait-states or by mixing slower memory with faster memory components.

**Memory Test Tick Sound**    When enabled, this feature generates a sequence of audible tones (or "ticks") as the memory test executes. It also provides an audible confirmation of your CPU clock speed/turbo switch setting. The idea is that an experienced user can hear if something is wrong with the system just by the tick sound pattern. However, since PCs now have much more memory than before, this setting is used infrequently. If the noise is annoying, disable the test. If you cannot hear the test when it's enabled, check the speaker.

**Numeric Processor Test**    This feature will test the math coprocessor. All 486DX and later CPUs use a built-in coprocessor, and this test should be enabled. (Otherwise, the coprocessor function may not be enabled.) 486SX, 486DLC, 486SLC, and all older CPUs use a separate math coprocessor, and you should set this feature depending on whether a coprocessor is present.

**Password Checking Option**    This option controls whether a password is used to access the system, or to access the CMOS Setup, or both. When it's enabled, you'll need to set a password, then enter the appropriate password(s) as required. Always remember to note your password(s) in a safe place, and change your passwords frequently. If you forget a password, or encounter a system with a password option in place, see the section "CMOS Password Troubleshooting" at the end of this chapter.

**Shadow Memory Cacheable**    *Shadowing* is the process of copying ROM to RAM. Once the ROM contents are copied into RAM, making that RAM space cacheable can often increase performance even further. You can enable this feature to cache shadow memory, or disable it to prevent caching of shadow memory. Shadow caching is usually a good idea for DOS- and Windows-based platforms and should be enabled. But Linux and other UNIX-like operating systems will not benefit from this feature, and it can remain disabled.

**System Boot Sequence**    This feature controls the order in which system drives are checked for an operating system. The typical sequence is A:/C:, but C:/A: can be selected for faster booting. Modern BIOS also supports booting from other items such as the CD-ROM (if it meets the El Torito bootable CD-ROM specification) and SCSI drives (even while UDMA/EIDE/IDE drives are in the system).

**System Boot-Up CPU Speed**    This is commonly referred to as the *turbo mode* and allows you to specify what processor speed the system will boot to. The typical settings are High and Low. High speed is recommended for best performance, but if you encounter booting problems, you should try the Low speed. Today, this setting has been largely abandoned, and a PC will always attempt to boot to its maximum possible speed.

**System Boot-Up Num Lock**    This specifies whether you want the NUM LOCK key to be activated at boot-up. You are free to keep this feature enabled or disabled as you prefer.

**System ROM Shadow F000, 64K**    Memory hidden in the "I/O hole" of 0x0A0000h to 0x0FFFFFh may be used to shadow the system ROM, where the contents of the motherboard BIOS ROM are copied into RAM, and the faster RAM copy is used instead. It is generally recommended to enable this feature, though systems with faster "flash" motherboard BIOS may not see as much performance benefit. You should disable motherboard ROM shadowing if you need to update a motherboard's flash BIOS, or if you're using some memory-resident utility to shadow the BIOS. Note that motherboard ROM shadowing may also cause some operating systems (other than DOS or Windows) or applications to lock up.

**Turbo Switch Function**    This feature enables or disables the turbo switch. This setting is now rarely used in modern systems (and has been deleted from current BIOS versions) because PCs are always run at their top speed. (There is no need to slow down a PC artificially.) If there is a turbo switch in the system, keep this feature enabled. Otherwise, disable this feature.

**Typematic Rate**    This is how fast a depressed key will repeat (in characters per second or CPS). A typical setting is 15CPS, though you can adjust this rate as your taste dictates. This option is sometimes called *Keyboard Auto-Repeat Rate*.

**Typematic Rate Delay**    This sets the initial delay (in milliseconds or mS) before a depressed key starts repeating. (This is how long you've got to press a key *before* it starts repeating.) A setting of 500mS (0.5s) is recommended, though you can adjust this delay as your taste dictates. This option is sometimes called *Keyboard Auto-Repeat Delay*.

**Typematic Rate Programming**    This feature enables the typematic rate programming of the keyboard, which determines how a keyboard will respond if a key is held down. If enabled, a key will repeat automatically if it is held down. If disabled, the key will not repeat. This feature is often disabled.

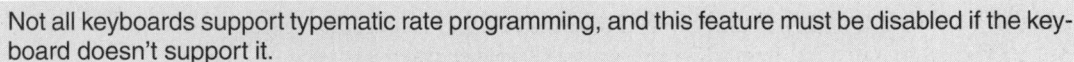
Not all keyboards support typematic rate programming, and this feature must be disabled if the keyboard doesn't support it.

**Video ROM Shadow C000, 32K**    Memory hidden in the "I/O hole" of 0x0A0000h to 0x0FFFFFh may be used to shadow video ROM, where the contents of the video ROM are copied into RAM, and the faster RAM copy is used instead. It is generally recommended to enable this feature, though systems with faster "flash" video BIOS may not see as much performance benefit. You should disable video ROM shadowing if you need to update a flash video BIOS, or if you're using a memory-resident utility to shadow the video BIOS. Note that video ROM shadowing may also cause some operating systems or applications to lock up.

**Virus Warning**    See "Boot Sector Virus Protection" earlier.

**Wait for F1 If Any Error**    If enabled, the system will halt and wait for F1 keyboard input before proceeding. If disabled, the system will simply continue after displaying an error message without waiting for any keyboard input. Disable the feature if you want the system to operate as a server (without a keyboard). Otherwise, you can enable the feature.

**Weitek Coprocessor**    This feature is normally found on older 386 motherboards from a period when Weitek coprocessors were popular. This high-performance coprocessor has two to three times the performance of the comparable Intel coprocessors. Weitek uses some RAM address space, so memory from this region must be remapped elsewhere. If you have a 386 system with a Weitek unit, enable the feature. If you do not have a Weitek unit, disable the feature. This setting is normally found on 386 motherboards, so don't worry about it on later/current systems.

# CONFIGURING THE INTEGRATED PERIPHERALS SETUP

Typical motherboards now incorporate many diverse ports, including a parallel port, serial ports, USB ports, and FDD/HDD drive controllers. More recent motherboards can also include an IR port as well as audio, modem, and LAN devices. Traditionally, this meant motherboard jumpers were needed to enable the ports, but now most motherboard designs use the CMOS Setup to control and configure each port or device such as the Award BIOS on an AOpen AK72 motherboard in Figure 10-3.

**Audio Device/Interface**    For motherboards with an integrated audio device, this option enables or disables the onboard audio system (though the option is enabled by default). This option may also appear if a CNR slot is available on the motherboard, and a compliant audio card is installed.

**FDD Controller**    Use this feature to enable or disable your motherboard's onboard floppy disk controller. You probably want this feature enabled unless you're using a separate drive controller card and do not need the integrated floppy controller. You can also disable this feature if your PC is not fitted with a floppy drive.

**IDE DMA**    Normally this is set to Auto. Enable this feature if your drives are UDMA capable (such as UDMA/33/66/100/133). Windows 98 SE/Me/XP can configure this feature for you by enabling a drive's DMA feature.

**LAN Device/Interface**    For motherboards with an integrated network interface, this option enables or disables the onboard LAN adapter (though the option is enabled by default). This option may also appear if a CNR slot is available on the motherboard, and a compliant LAN card is installed.

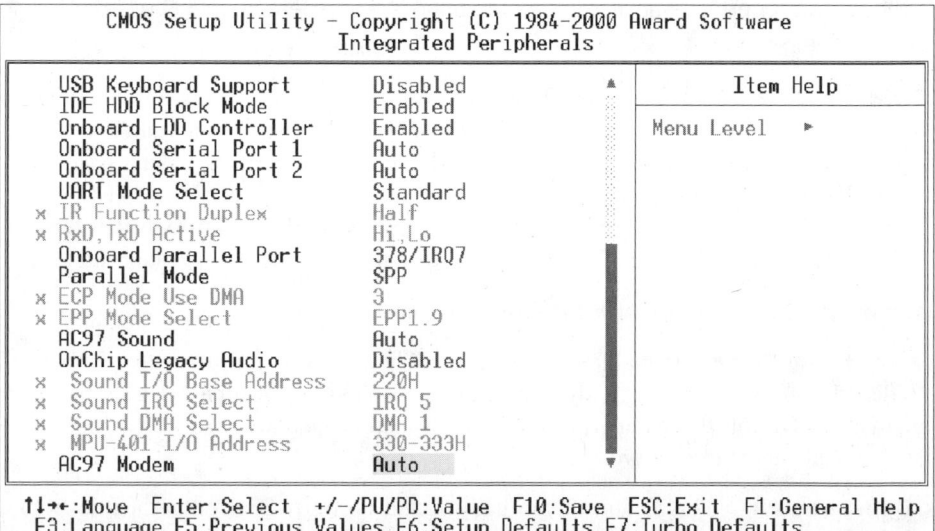

**FIGURE  10-3**    Using the Integrated Peripherals Setup to adjust the parameters of onboard devices like serial ports, parallel ports, audio devices, and so on (Courtesy of AOpen)

**Modem Device/Interface**    For motherboards with an integrated modem device, this option enables or disables the onboard modem system (though the option is enabled by default). This option may also appear if a CNR slot is available on the motherboard, and a compliant modem card is installed.

**Onboard IR Port**    This option is for motherboards with integrated IR communication ports, but is disabled by default. When enabled, this field activates the onboard standard infrared feature and sets the second serial UART to support the infrared module connector on the motherboard. If your system already has a second serial port connected to the onboard COM2 connector, it will no longer work if you enable the infrared feature.

**On-Chip PCI IDE**    This feature is used to either enable or disable your onboard IDE controllers if such controllers are integrated into your motherboard chipset. If you wish to use a stand-alone drive controller card (e.g., to upgrade aging motherboard controllers), you may need to disable this feature. Otherwise, the onboard controllers will be enabled.

**Parallel Port**    This feature is used to disable or enable a parallel port, and to change the parallel port mode (such as standard, bidirectional, ECP, or EPP) and IRQ and I/O resources assigned to the port. Use ECP mode if possible since that will support faster data transfers between the system and other parallel port devices. Disabling parallel ports can free the corresponding IRQ and I/O resources for the system, and may be necessary if you're installing hardware that might conflict with parallel port resources. For example, a sound card often uses IRQ5, which is commonly used by LPT2.

**Primary PIO**    This function allows IDE drives to transfer several sectors at a time. Several modes are possible. Mode 0 means one sector at a time. Mode 1 uses no interrupts. Mode 2 means sectors are transferred in a single burst. Mode 3 means 32-bit instructions at up to 11.1 MB/sec. Mode 4 offers data transfers to 16.6 MB/sec. Mode 5 is an unusual mode that supports up to 20 MB/sec. The standard PIO mode for most drives today is PIO mode 4. Many BIOS versions offer an automatic setting that will automatically make the best decision for your drive. Data transfer modes must be set for each drive. This setting may have no value (and may not even be used) on newer DMA-type (Ultra-DMA/33/66/100/133) drive controllers.

**Serial Port(s)**    This feature is used to control the motherboard's serial port(s). In many cases, you can specify the IRQ and I/O port address for the hardware in addition to simply enabling or disabling the ports. Normally, your serial (COM) ports are enabled, but you can disable the serial port(s) if necessary. Disabling serial ports can free the corresponding IRQ and I/O resources for the system and may be necessary if you're installing expansion hardware (such as a modem) that might conflict with serial port resources.

**SMART Support**    See "SMART Monitoring" earlier.

**USB Controller**    Most current motherboards will offer two or more USB hub ports, and these hubs can be controlled through the CMOS Setup. If your computer has one or more USB ports, use this setting to enable or disable your motherboard's onboard USB controller. Disabling the ports will typically free an IRQ for other system devices.

# CONFIGURING THE ADVANCED (CHIPSET) SETUP

The core logic (or *chipset*) is responsible for providing many of the advanced features that we take for granted in today's PCs. Consequently, there are a tremendous number of variables involved in the proper configuration of a chipset. This part of the CMOS Setup allows you to tweak the performance of your chipset (namely memory timings, memory refresh options, data bus performance, cache enhancements, AGP setup, and so on).

> The advanced chipset setup requires a more detailed understanding of chipset operation and features, and should be attempted only by experienced technicians. Incorrect chipset configurations can easily impair system performance. Remember to *always* record your original CMOS Setup settings before changing any parameters.

**16-Bit I/O Recovery Time**    This is an additional delay time inserted after every 16-bit operation and is sometimes needed to support older (slower) 16-bit devices. The delay value is added to the minimum delay inserted after every AT bus cycle. You may not find this parameter on current PCs—especially motherboards that have abandoned the use of ISA bus slots.

**16-Bit Memory, I/O Wait-State**    This entry lists the number of wait-states inserted with 16-bit memory and I/O operations. Too many wait-states will reduce bus performance, and too few wait-states can cause bus errors and system lockups. If your system uses this entry, it is normally safe to stay with the BIOS Default value. You may not find this parameter on current PCs that have abandoned the use of ISA bus slots.

**8-Bit Memory, I/O Wait-State**    This entry lists the number of wait-states inserted with 8-bit memory and I/O operations. Too many wait-states will reduce bus performance, and too few wait-states can cause bus errors and system lockups. If your system uses this entry, it is normally safe to stay with the BIOS Default value. You may not find this parameter on current PCs that have abandoned the use of ISA bus slots.

**AGP Low-Priority Timer**    This option sets the AGP low priority timer, which dictates how quickly "low-priority" AGP processes are handled. The settings are in units of AGP clocks, and include disabled, 16, 32, 48, 64, 80, 96, 112, 128, 144, 176, 192, 208, 224, and 240 clocks. As a rule, the default setting is the best choice. Lower values will handle low-priority requests faster, but may impair overall performance.

**AGP Multi-Trans Timer**    This option sets the AGP multiple transaction (multi-trans) timer, which determines how quickly multiple AGP transactions are handled. The settings are in units of AGP clocks, and include disabled, 32, 64, 96, 128, 160, 192, and 224 clocks. As a rule, the default setting is the best choice. Lower values will handle multiple transactions faster, but may impair overall performance.

**Alternate Bit in Tag RAM**    *Tag bits* are used to determine the state of the information that is stored in the L2 (external) cache. The level of error determination is set with this option. If you use the Write Back caching method, use the "7+1" setting to receive best results. Otherwise, use the "8+0" setting. You will generally not find this option in Pentium II/III/4 and other systems where L2 cache is integrated into the processor.

**AT Bus Clock Selection (or AT Bus Clock Source)**    This selects a division of the CPU clock (or system clock) so it can approximate the ISA/EISA bus clock of 8.33 MHz. The settings are in terms of CLK/$x$ (or CLKIN/$x$ and CLK2/$x$), where $x$ may have values like 2, 3, 4, or 5. CLK represents your bus processor speed. For example, 486DX33, 486DX2/66, and 486DX3/99 all use a 33 MHz bus speed and should have a divider value of 4 for an ISA speed of 8.25 MHz. For 286 and 386 processors, CLK is half the speed of the CPU. Here are some typical settings:

| | |
|---|---|
| CLK/2 | All 286 and 386 systems |
| CLK/3 | SX/DX16, DX20, DX25, DX2/50, DX4/100 |

| CLK/4 | SX/DX33, DX2/66, DX3/99 |
| CLK/5 | DX40, DX2/80 |
| CLK/6 | DX50, DX2/100 |
| CLK/7 | 60 MHz bus |
| CLK/8 | 66 MHz bus |

The bus speed doesn't have to be precisely 8.33 MHz, but that's what to shoot for. An improper setting may cause significant decrease in performance. If the divider is too high, the ISA bus speed will be too low (below 8.33 MHz), and the ISA devices will perform poorly. If the divider is too low, the ISA bus speed will be too high (above 8.33 MHz), and the ISA devices may malfunction. You may not find this option on later motherboards where the ISA bus speed is asynchronous of the system clock, or on motherboards that have abandoned use of the ISA bus entirely.

**AT Cycle Wait-State**    This entry indicates the number of wait-states inserted whenever an operation is performed with the AT bus. You may need some additional wait-states if old ISA cards are used, especially if they are used together with fast adapter cards. Too many wait-states will reduce bus performance, and too few wait-states can cause bus errors and system lockups. When this option is available, the BIOS Default value is often the best choice. You may not find this parameter on current PCs that have abandoned the use of ISA bus slots.

**Automatic Configuration**    When enabled, this feature allows the BIOS to **automatically** set the settings in the advanced chipset setup (for example, clock dividers and wait-states). If you're uncertain about configuring the advanced chipset features, keep this feature enabled. Disable this feature if you're going to make manual changes to the chipset setup. You may have to disable this feature when some highly specialized adapter cards are used in the system.

**Burst Copy-Back Option**    This caching option may be enabled or disabled. When it's enabled and a read from the memory to the processor results in a "cache miss," the chipset will try a second read (when the data transfers in burst mode). This feature is often enabled by default, but you may wish to disable this option in the event of system stability problems.

**Burst Refresh**    When enabled, this feature performs several memory refresh cycles at once, and can greatly improve memory performance by reducing refresh "overhead." This feature can normally be enabled unless your system uses an unusual memory type or configuration. The feature should be disabled if system stability problems occur.

**Burst SRAM Cycle**    This feature lets you specify the timing of the burst mode read and write cycles to and from the external cache memory (L2). Typical options include 4-1-1-1 and 3-1-1-1 timings, so choose the lowest setting that works well with your system. Choosing a setting that is too low will cause problems with the cache (or system instability). You will generally not see this entry on newer PCs in which the L2 cache is integrated into the processor.

**Burst Write**    When enabled, the processor will write to the cache in bursts and can make caching more efficient. When disabled, the CPU will not write to the cache in bursts. Burst writing is more efficient and will generally enhance system performance. You may not find this parameter on current PCs that integrate L2 cache into the processor.

**Bus Mode**    This feature selects the clock mode that is used to drive the bus. In *synchronous* mode, the CPU clock is used to drive the bus. In *asynchronous* mode, a separate clock source is used. In most cases, the synchronous mode is selected, though asynchronous mode will generally provide better compatibility for overclocked systems. For example, an overclocked system in asynchronous mode can push the processor through the front side bus, but keep the AGP and PCI busses locked at 66 MHz and 33 MHz, respectively.

**Cacheable RAM Address Range**    Older chipsets usually allow memory to be cached just up to 32MB or 64MB. This is to limit the number of memory address bits that need to be saved in the cache together with its contents. Set this entry to match as much of your installed RAM as possible. For example, if you only have 32MB of RAM, select 32MB—don't enter 64MB. This entry may not be present on newer PCs that can cache huge amounts of RAM.

**Cache Read Option**    Often called the *SRAM Read Wait-State* or *Cache Read Hit Burst*, this specifies the number of clocks needed to load four 32-bit words into a CPU internal cache (typically specified as clocks per word). A timing of 2-1-1-1 indicates five clocks to load the four words and is the theoretical minimum for most CPUs (e.g., Pentium, Pentium II/III/4, and so on). This timing determines the number of wait-states for the cache RAM in normal and burst transfers (the latter for 486 systems only). Timing of 4-1-1-1 is usually recommended, but the faster timing that a computer can support, the better.

**Cache Timing Control**    This option sets the timing parameters on older motherboards for reading/writing to cache. The typical selections are usually fast, medium, normal, and turbo. When this feature is available, select the fastest suitable option for best performance.

**Cache Wait-State**    This feature is used on older motherboards to introduce additional wait-states for cache operations. Like conventional memory, fewer wait-states will result in better cache performance (but it will demand faster cache). An entry of 0 will give the optimal performance, but 1 wait-state may be required for older PCs with bus speeds higher than 33 MHz. This feature is generally not used on current PCs because available speeds allow caching within the CPU.

**Cache Write Option**    This is the same as the Cache Read Option (see earlier), but is used to control cache write timing.

**CAS-Before-RAS**    When enabled, this option reduces refresh cycles and power consumption.

**CAS Width in Read Cycle**    This feature expresses the number of wait-states for the CPU to read DRAM. Lower figures are better for system performance.

**Concurrent Refresh**    This feature enables both the processor and the refresh hardware to have access to the memory at the same time. If this feature is disabled, the processor has to wait until the memory refresh cycle has finished, and this can slow system performance slightly. Many systems enable concurrent refresh by default.

**CPU Level 1 Cache/CPU Level 2 Cache**    These features allow a technician to enable or disable the CPU's L1 and/or L2 cache. In virtually all cases, these features should be *enabled* because this yields the very best processing performance (and this is the default). However, you can selectively disable these features to check for cache problems with the processor.

**CPU Level 2 Cache ECC Check**    Some L2 processor cache provides ECC error-checking capability to ensure data integrity on the system, but imposes a slight performance penalty. By default L2 ECC is disabled for best system performance, but mission-critical platforms (e.g., servers and workstations) should have this feature enabled. Of course, the processor(s) running on the PC must also support L2 cache with ECC for this feature to be available.

**CPU Speed**    This is an option that is commonly available on "jumperless" motherboards. The CPU speed is selected from a series of available options (depending on the range of frequencies supported by the particular motherboard). This option may sometimes be set automatically once the processor is autodetected by the BIOS POST, but you can change the setting manually—often to overclock the processor. If this option is not available, chances are that the CPU speed is set manually using a series of jumpers on the motherboard.

**CPU Vcore**    This is an option that is commonly available on "jumperless" motherboards. The CPU core voltage is displayed here. This option may sometimes be set automatically once the processor is autodetected by the BIOS POST, but you can change the setting manually—often to overclock the processor. If this option is not available, chances are that the CPU core voltage is set manually using a series of jumpers on the motherboard.

**CPU Write Back Cache**    When enabled, the system will use *write back* caching. If disabled, the system will use *write through* caching. Write back caching will generally result in better system performance, but write through caching can ease some compatibility issues.

**Decoupled Refresh Option**    When enabled, this feature allows the ISA bus and the RAM to refresh separately. Because refreshing the ISA bus is a slower process, separating the refresh cycles this way causes less strain on the CPU. This option is often enabled. You may not find this parameter on current PCs that have abandoned the use of ISA bus slots.

**DMA Clock Source**    This entry indicates the source of the DMA clock, which is used for DMA transfers. This setting will affect DMA performance for any peripheral (like floppy, tape, network, and SCSI adapters) using DMA. The maximum setting for traditional ISA-based PCs is 5 MHz. You may not find this parameter on current PCs that have abandoned the use of ISA bus slots.

**DMA Wait-States**    This entry lists the number of wait-states inserted before *direct memory access* (DMA) is attempted. Lower numbers (fewer wait-states) result in better DMA performance.

**DRAM Burst at 4 Refresh**    This is a slight variation of Burst Refresh, where the refresh is occurring in bursts of four. This feature can normally be enabled unless the RAM is not compatible with such a refresh operation.

**DRAM CAS Timing Delay**    DRAM is organized into rows and columns, and is accessed through strobe lines. The CPU activates a RAS (Row Access Strobe) line to find the row containing the required data, and then a CAS (Column Access Strobe) line specifies the column. As a result, RAS and CAS signals are used to identify a location in a DRAM chip. When using slow RAM, it may be necessary to introduce a delay into the CAS timing. The default is no CAS delay.

**DRAM Integrity Mode**    This option sets the type of system memory checking used on the platform. The settings are

- **Non-ECC**    No error checking or reporting is done.
- **EC**    Errors are detected, but no errors are corrected (e.g., parity).
- **ECC**    Errors are detected, and single-bit errors can be detected.

**DRAM Refresh Method**    This feature selects the refresh method used for RAM. The options are RAS Only and CAS-before-RAS. Most current systems use CAS-before-RAS timing by default.

**DRAM Refresh Rate**    This option specifies the interval between refresh signals to DRAM system memory. Since fewer refresh cycles will free up system overhead, larger settings will improve system performance. The settings are 15.6μs (microseconds), 31.2μs, 62.4μs, 124.8μs, and 249.6μs.

**E0000 ROM belongs to ATBUS**    This entry indicates if the E0000h area (upper memory) belongs to the motherboard DRAM or to the AT bus. For most systems, enabled (yes) is recommended. You may not find this parameter on current PCs that have abandoned the use of ISA bus slots.

**Extended DMA Registers**    With a standard AT type of computer, DMA support is only provided for the first 16MB of system RAM. With this feature enabled, DMA support will be extended for up to 4GB of RAM. In most cases, this feature can be left disabled. You may not find this parameter on current PCs that have abandoned the use of ISA bus slots.

**Extended I/O Decode**    The normal range of I/O addresses is 0–0x3FFh using only 10 address bits. With this feature enabled, the system will support a 16-bit I/O-address bus allowing a 64KB I/O space. Most classical motherboards or I/O adapters can be decoded by only 10 address bits, so this feature can usually be left disabled. You may not find this parameter on current PCs that have abandoned the use of ISA bus slots.

**Fast AT Cycle**    When enabled, this feature may speed up data transfer rates with ISA cards (and can have an important effect on ISA video boards). You may need to disable this feature for system stability. You may not find this parameter on current PCs that have abandoned the use of ISA bus slots.

**Fast Cache Read/Write**    This allows enhanced cache performance through memory interleaving techniques, so enable this feature if you have two banks of cache (64KB or 256KB). Otherwise, leave this feature disabled. You may not find this parameter on current PCs, which include cache on the processor rather than on the motherboard.

**Fast Decode Enable**    This refers to some hardware that monitors the commands sent to the keyboard controller chip. The original AT used special codes not processed by the keyboard itself to control the switching of the 286 processor back from protected mode to real mode. The 286 itself had no hardware to do this, so the CPU has to be reset to switch back. PC makers added a few logic chips to monitor the commands sent to the keyboard controller chip, and when the reset CPU code was detected, the logic chips did an immediate reset. This fast decode of the keyboard reset command allowed OS/2 and Windows to switch between real and protected modes faster and enabled much better performance. You will generally find this entry on 286 and early 386 systems, since newer processors *do* have hardware instructions for switching between modes.

If you find this entry on a current system, the "Fast Decode Enable" command is probably defined a bit differently. The design of the original AT bus made it very difficult to mix 8-bit and 16-bit RAM or ROM within the same 128KB block of high address space. An 8-bit BIOS ROM on a VGA card forced all other peripherals using the C000h–DFFFh range to also use 8 bits. By doing an "early decode" of the high address lines along with the 8/16-bit select flag, the I/O bus could then use mixed 8- and 16-bit peripherals. In both cases, you should probably have this feature enabled.

**Fast Page Mode DRAM**    When enabled, this feature speeds up memory access for FPM DRAM. When memory access occurs in the same memory "page," the overhead of RAS and CAS sequences is not necessary, and memory performance is improved. This option is only found on older systems that support FPM RAM and is not used on current systems with SDRAM, DDR SDRAM, or RDRAM.

**Graphics Aperture Size**    This option specifies the amount of system memory that can be used by the Accelerated Graphics Port (AGP) system (this kind of "shared memory" eliminates the need for separate video RAM). Typical settings include 4MB, 8MB, 16MB, 32MB, 64MB, 128MB, and 256MB. Keep in mind that your PC will need ample RAM available before allocating a large graphics aperture.

**Hidden Refresh**    This feature allows the RAM refresh memory cycles to take place in memory banks not used by your CPU at this time, instead of with the normal refresh cycles, which are executed every time the interrupt DRQ0 is called (every 15mS). There are typically three types of refresh schemes: cycle steal, cycle stretch, or hidden refresh. *Cycle steal* actually steals a clock cycle from the CPU to do the refresh. *Cycle stretch* delays a cycle from the processor to do the refresh. (Since it only occurs every 4mS or so, it's an improvement over cycle steal.) *Hidden refresh* simply refreshes idle memory banks. Most systems enable hidden refresh by default, but some memory supports hidden refresh better than others do. Try hidden refresh, but if the computer crashes or locks up, disable the hidden refresh.

**Hi-Speed Refresh**    This is also called *Fast Refresh*. When enabled, this feature causes refresh cycles to occur at higher frequencies in order to accomplish a refresh cycle in a shorter period. When combined with features like burst refresh, the overall system performance can improve. Not all types of memory can support Fast Refresh, and it uses more power than Slow Refresh.

**IDE 32-Bit Transfer**    When enabled, the read/write performance of the hard disk is faster. When disabled, only 16-bit data transfers are possible. Enable this feature if possible. It should be supported on all but the oldest systems/drives.

**IDE DMA Transfer Mode**    This defines the means by which DMA transfers are executed. The three typical settings are Disabled, Type B (for EISA), and Standard (for PCI). Standard is the fastest, but may cause problems with IDE CD-ROMs. The standard type is Type F.

**IDE Multi-Block Mode**    This feature (also referred to as *IDE Block Mode*) enables IDE drives to transfer several sectors per interrupt. Six modes are possible:

- Mode 0 (standard mode transferring a single sector at a time)
- Mode 1 (no interrupts)
- Mode 2 (sectors are transferred in a single burst)
- Mode 3 (speeds up to 11.1 MB/s—sometimes abbreviated as "32-bit mode")
- Mode 4 (up to 16.7 MB/s)
- Mode 5 (up to 20 MB/s—not used in actual drive implementations)

The important attribute for block mode is the number of sectors per interrupt. The maximum number of sectors per interrupt is often (but not always) related to the drive's buffer size. If this setting is not set properly, communication with IDE devices may not work. If the block size (sectors/interrupt) is set too large, you may experience excessive CRC errors. To fix this, decrease the block size, or disable block mode transfers altogether.

**IDE Multiple Sector Mode**   When IDE DMA Transfer Mode is enabled, this feature sets the number of sectors per burst (with a maximum of 64). Problems may occur with IDE devices if this setting is configured improperly.

**Interleave Mode**   When enabled, the system will use an interleaved approach to access system memory. If the motherboard is not designed to support interleaved memory (or uses an advanced form of high-performance memory), this option should be disabled. This option is typically not available on newer PCs.

**I/O Recovery Time**   The I/O recovery time is the number of wait-states to be inserted between two consecutive I/O operations (generally specified as a two-number pair such as 5/3). The first number is the number of wait-states to insert for an 8-bit operation. The second is the number of wait-states for a 16-bit operation. In general, this feature can be disabled. If the AT Bus Clock is running fast (over 8.33 MHz), or you're using slow peripherals, it may be necessary to enable I/O Recovery Time starting with a value like 5/3. You may not find this parameter on current PCs—especially motherboards that have abandoned the use of ISA bus slots.

A few BIOS versions specify an I/O Setup Time (or AT Bus (I/O) Command Delay). It is specified similarly to I/O Recovery Time, but is a delay before *starting* an I/O operation rather than a delay *between* I/O operations.

**ISA IRQs**   This entry informs the PCI cards of IRQs used by ISA cards so that the PCI cards will not attempt to assign those legacy resources. If you have no ISA devices in your system, make sure that no IRQs are reserved—this will free system resources for other devices.

**Keyboard Reset Control**   This feature enables the CTRL-ALT-DEL warm reboot. As a security measure, disable this feature if you want to prohibit this kind of warm reboot. Otherwise, keep this option enabled.

**Method of Memory Detection**   The BIOS will normally autodetect the amount and characteristics of system memory each time the system boots. This option selects the way that the memory will be detected. *Serial Presence Detect* (SPD) provides specific data to the motherboard. Auto lets the BIOS use its own algorithm for identifying the system RAM. As a rule, select the "Auto+SPD" option so that both techniques are available to the BIOS.

**Memory Hole At 15M-16M**   Some legacy ISA devices may require the use of memory space in the 15- to 16MB range. Since this range overlaps a portion of RAM, the memory hole option allows you to reserve that space for ISA devices. This option is normally disabled unless one or more ISA devices require it. You may not find this parameter on current PCs that have abandoned the use of ISA bus slots.

**Memory Read Wait-State**   This is also referred to as *DRAM Read Wait-States*. The CPU is often much faster than RAM, and it is necessary to introduce wait-states to allow the slower RAM to catch up to the CPU. Each wait-state effectively adds several nanoseconds (ns) of RAM speed. Fewer wait-states result in better system performance, and the ideal number of wait-states is 0 (though 1 wait-state is typically required). The traditional number of wait-states necessary is approximately $(RamSpeed[ns] + 10)*Clock[MHz]/1000 - 2$. If there are too many wait-states, system performance will suffer because precious processing time is being wasted. If there are too few wait-states, parity errors and system crashes will occur because RAM contents are not available to the processor.

**Memory Remapping**   This feature remaps the memory used by the BIOS (A0000h to FFFFFh or 384KB) above the 1MB limit. If it's enabled, you cannot shadow video and system BIOS. In many cases, you should set this feature to disabled.

**Memory Write Wait-State**   Also referred to as *DRAM Write Wait-States*, this is the same as Memory Read Wait-State, but it applies to RAM writing. Some BIOS versions combine Memory Read/Write Wait-State options as the "DRAM Wait-States." In this case, the number of read and write wait-states must be equal.

**Non-Cacheable Block-1 Base**   Enter the base address of the area you don't want to cache. It must be a multiple of the Non-Cacheable Block-1 Size selected later. When this is disabled, set this to 0KB.

**Non-Cacheable Block-2 Base**   This is the same as Non-Cacheable Block-1 Base and is usually set to 0KB.

**Non-Cacheable Block-1 Size**   The non-cacheable region is intended for a memory-mapped I/O device that isn't supposed to be cached. For example, some video cards can present all video memory at 15MB to 16MB so software doesn't have to bank-switch. If the non-cacheable region covers actual RAM memory you are using, expect a significant performance decrease for accesses to that area. If the non-cacheable region covers only nonexistent memory addresses, there should be no performance hit. If you are using devices that should not be cached, enable this feature to set aside some memory from caching. Otherwise, you can leave this entry disabled.

**Non-Cacheable Block-2 Size**   This is the same function as Non-Cacheable Block-1 Size and is normally left disabled.

**PCI 2.1 Latency Compliant**   This function has appeared on a few older PCI-based PCs, and allows you to enable or disable PCI 2.1-compliant features including passive release and delayed transaction. In virtually all cases, this option should be enabled. However, newer PCs supporting PCI 2.2 or later will generally not include this type of option.

**Port 64/60 Emulation**   Enabling this option allows a USB keyboard to act like a legacy (PS/2) keyboard under Windows NT. If this option is disabled, USB keyboard lights will not work under Windows NT. With other operating systems (such as Windows XP), a USB keyboard will work normally with this option disabled.

**PS/2 Mouse Function Control**   When set to Auto (the default), the system can detect a PS/2 mouse on startup, and assign IRQ12 for the PS/2 mouse. If a PS/2 mouse is not detected, IRQ12 will be reserved for expansion devices in the system. Enabling this option will always reserve IRQ12 (whether a PS/2 mouse is detected or not).

**RAS Active Time**   This is the amount of time a RAS signal can be kept open for multiple accesses. Higher figures will improve system performance, but RAS can only be kept active for a relatively short time.

**RAS Precharge Time**   This is the time interval during which the *Row Access Strobe* (RAS) signal to DRAM is held low for normal read and write cycles. This is the minimum interval between completing one read or write and starting another from the same (nonpage mode) DRAM. Advanced techniques such as memory interleaving or the use of page mode DRAM are often used to avoid this delay. The RAS Precharge value is typically about the same as the RAM access time. For a 33 MHz CPU, an entry of 4 is a good choice, while lower values should be selected for slower speeds. Keep in mind that this option has generally been replaced with SDRAM RAS Precharge options on SDRAM-compliant systems.

**RAS-to-CAS Delay Time**    This is the amount of time a Column Address Strobe (CAS) is performed after a Row Access Strobe (RAS). Lower figures are better for system performance, but some DRAM will not support low figures. Keep in mind that this option has generally been replaced with SDRAM RAS-to-CAS Delay options on SDRAM-compliant systems.

**Refresh RAS Active Time**    This is the amount of active time needed for RAS during refresh. Lower entries are usually better.

**Refresh Value**    The lower this value is, the better the performance.

**SDRAM Configuration**    This sets the optimal timings for SDRAM depending on the particular memory modules that you're using. The default setting uses Serial Presence Detect (SPD) by reading the SPD contents of the memory device. The small serial EEPROM on the memory module stores critical parameter information about the SDRAM module (such as memory type, size, speed, voltage interface, and so on). This SPD data is read by the BIOS at boot time. If your SDRAM does not include SPD, set the option to User Define and set the following three options based on the specifications of your SDRAM modules:

- **SDRAM CAS Latency**    This sets the latency between the SDRAM read command and the time that the data actually becomes available.
- **SDRAM RAS-to-CAS Delay**    This adjusts the latency between the SDRAM active command and the read/write command.
- **SDRAM RAS Precharge Time**    This selects the number of idle clock cycles after issuing a precharge command to the SDRAM.

**SDRAM Cycle Time**    This feature controls the number of SDRAM clocks used to set the timing for SDRAM parameters. Typical options include 6T/8T (the default) and 5T/7T. The first number specifies the minimum number of clocks required between an SDRAM active command and precharge command. The second number specifies the minimum clocks required between active command and reactive command. Faster SDRAM modules may accommodate the shorter 5T/7T timing.

**SDRAM RAS Precharge**    This option specifies the length of the RAS precharge portion of the system memory access cycle when SDRAM system memory is installed in the computer. The typical settings are Auto, 2 clocks, and 3 clocks. Auto, the preferred setting, allows the actual timing to be set based on the type of SDRAM detected at boot time. (See "SDRAM Configuration" earlier.)

**SDRAM RAS-to-CAS Delay**    This option specifies the length of the delay inserted between the RAS and CAS signals of the system memory access cycle if SDRAM is installed. The settings are Auto (this is the default), 2 clocks, and 3 clocks. (See "SDRAM Configuration" earlier.)

**Single ALE Enable**    *Address Latch Enable* (ALE) is an ISA Bus Signal (Pin B28) that indicates that a valid address is posted on the bus, and this bus is used to communicate with 8- and 16-bit peripheral cards. Some chipsets have the capability to support an enhanced mode in which multiple ALE assertions may be made during a single bus cycle. Single ALE Enable enables or disables this capability. Since this feature may slow the video bus if enabled, it is generally set as disabled (no). You may not find this parameter on current PCs that have abandoned the use of ISA bus slots.

**Slow Memory Refresh Divider**    If you can extend the refresh cycles of your system (using techniques like Slow Refresh), you can free more CPU time, and system performance improves. This feature allows you to select a divider that slows the refresh cycles. If you slow the refresh too much, you'll get parity errors and system crashes due to data loss from inadequate memory refresh.

**Slow Refresh**    This option reduces the frequency of RAM refresh. This increases system performance slightly due to the reduced contention between the CPU and refresh circuitry, but not all RAM types necessarily support these reduced refresh rates (in which case you will get parity errors and system crashes). Many systems enable the slow refresh by default.

Here's a tip for mobile PC users—refresh cycles take power, so using Slow Refresh to reduce the number of refresh cycles can save power.

**Staggered Refresh**    When enabled, refresh is performed on memory banks sequentially. This results in less power consumption and less interference between memory banks. Many systems enable Staggered Refresh by default.

**System/SDRAM/PCI (MHz)**    When the CPU's internal frequency is set to "manual," this option determines the frequency ratio between the front side bus, SDRAM, and PCI bus. Typical options include 66:100:33, 100:100:33, 133:133:33, and 133:100:33, but other options may be available depending on your particular system. Keep in mind that the memory clock frequency can be set synchronously or asynchronously with respect to the Front Side Bus frequency.

**Tag RAM Includes Dirty**    When enabled, the cache is not replaced during cycles, simply overwritten. This results in a performance increase. However, the maximum range of cacheable memory is cut in half because a bit is needed as a "dirty bit" tag. In general, you can leave this feature disabled unless you have little system RAM.

**Video BIOS Area Cacheable**    This feature can enable or disable caching the video BIOS. Caching the video BIOS can often enhance video performance, but with many of today's accelerated video cards, it may be necessary to prevent caching.

**Video Memory Cache Mode**    Some PCs can improve display speed by caching the display data. This is a relatively new cache technology called *Uncacheable Speculative Write Combining* (USWC), and is intended to support a system's video memory. If the system's graphics adapter cannot support USWC, set this option to UC (uncacheable), which is the default setting. If the graphics system does support USWC, you can try selecting the USWC mode. However, setting the mode improperly may prevent the system from booting.

# CONFIGURING PLUG-AND-PLAY/PCI

*Plug-and-play* (PnP) and the PCI (Peripheral Component Interconnect) bus are two tightly related features designed to ease the configuration burden of PC devices. They provide modern devices with a high-performance bus capable of working directly with the CPU and main memory. However, plug-and-play and PCI features must be configured properly in BIOS in order to ensure trouble-free operation. This part of the chapter explains the options used to configure PCI slots and PnP behavior, and you can see a typical PnP/PCI menu for an Award BIOS on an AOpen AK72 motherboard in Figure 10-4.

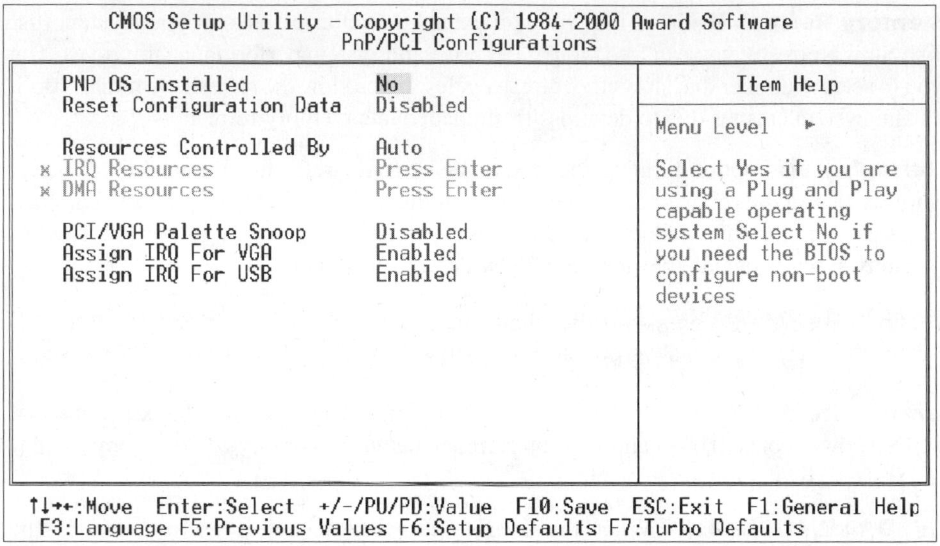

```
          CMOS Setup Utility - Copyright (C) 1984-2000 Award Software
                           PnP/PCI Configurations

     PNP OS Installed             No                    Item Help
     Reset Configuration Data     Disabled
                                                 Menu Level    ▶
     Resources Controlled By      Auto
   x IRQ Resources                Press Enter     Select Yes if you are
   x DMA Resources                Press Enter     using a Plug and Play
                                                 capable operating
     PCI/VGA Palette Snoop        Disabled        system Select No if
     Assign IRQ For VGA           Enabled         you need the BIOS to
     Assign IRQ For USB           Enabled         configure non-boot
                                                 devices




   ↑↓→←:Move  Enter:Select  +/-/PU/PD:Value  F10:Save  ESC:Exit  F1:General Help
   F3:Language F5:Previous Values F6:Setup Defaults F7:Turbo Defaults
```

**FIGURE  10-4**    The PnP/PCI Configurations menu, which allows you to adjust the operating characteristics of PnP devices, PCI slots, and related hardware (Courtesy of AOpen)

**Action When Write Buffer Full**    This feature sets the behavior of the system when the write buffer is full. By default, the system will immediately retry (rather than wait for it to be emptied).

**AT/ISA Bus Clock Frequency**    This is the AT bus speed in a PCI system. Select a divisor that will give you a bus speed closest to 8.33 MHz (depending on the speed of the PCI bus). In some systems, the ISA bus speed is set independently (asynchronously) from the bus clock. You may not find this parameter on current PCs that have abandoned the use of ISA bus slots.

**Base I/O Address**    This entry lists the base of the I/O address range from which the PCI device resource requests are handled.

**Base Memory Address**    This entry lists the start of the 32-bit memory address range from which the PCI device resource requests are handled.

**Burst Copy-Back Option**    When this feature is enabled, if a cache miss occurs, the chipset will initiate a second burst cache line fill from main memory to the cache—the goal being to maintain the status of the cache.

**Byte Merge Support**    Eight-bit or 16-bit data traveling from the CPU to the PCI bus is held in a buffer where it is accumulated, or merged, into 32-bit data, giving faster overall performance. In this case, enabling this feature means that CPU-PCI writes are buffered. You may not find this parameter on PCs with 32-bit architectures.

**Byte Merging**    This feature allows writes to sequential memory addresses to be merged into one PCI-to-memory operation, which increases performance for older applications that write to video memory in bytes rather than words. This feature is not supported well on all PCI video cards. Enable this feature unless you encounter graphics problems. You may not find this parameter on PCs with 32-bit architectures.

**Configuration Mode**   This entry sets the method by which information about legacy cards is conveyed to the system:

■ **Use ICU**   The BIOS depends on information provided by plug-and-play software (such as the Configuration Manager or ISA Configuration Utility). Only select this if you have the utilities needed.

■ **Use Setup Utility**   The BIOS depends on information provided in the CMOS Setup routine—don't use configuration utilities.

You may not find this parameter on current PCs that have abandoned the use of ISA bus slots.

**CPU Burst Write Assembly**   The Intel 450GX/KX Orion chipset maintains four posted write buffers. When this feature is enabled, the chipset can assemble long PCI bursts from the data held in them. By default, the feature is disabled.

**CPU Dynamic-Fast-Cycle**   This feature gives you faster access to the ISA bus. When the CPU issues a bus cycle, the PCI bus examines the command to determine if a PCI agent claims it. If not, then an ISA bus cycle is initiated. The Dynamic-Fast-Cycle then allows for faster access to the ISA bus by decreasing the latency (or delay) between the original CPU command and the beginning of the ISA cycle. You may not find this parameter on current PCs that have abandoned the use of ISA bus slots.

**CPU Line Read**   This feature enables or disables (default) full CPU line reads.

**CPU Line Read Multiple**   A line read means that the CPU is reading a full cache line. When a cache line is full, it holds 32 bytes (eight DWORDS) of data. Because the line is full, the system knows exactly how much data it will be reading and doesn't need to wait for an end-of-data signal, freeing it to do other things. When this feature is enabled, the system is allowed to read more than one full cache line at a time. The default is disabled.

**CPU Line Read Prefetch**   When this feature is enabled, the system is allowed to prefetch the next read instruction and to initiate the next process.

**CPU Master DEVSEL Timeout**   When the CPU initiates a master cycle using an address (target) that has not been mapped to PCI/VESA or ISA space, the system will monitor the DEVSEL (device select) pin for a period of time to see if any device claims the cycle. This entry allows you to determine how long the system will wait before timing out. Choices are 3 PCICLK, 4 PCICLK, 5 PCICLK, and 6 PCICLK (default).

**CPU Master Fast Interface**   This entry enables or disables what is known as a *fast back-to-back* interface when the CPU operates as a bus master. When enabled, consecutive reads/writes are interpreted as the CPU high-performance burst mode.

**CPU Master Post-W/R Buffer**   When the CPU operates as a bus master for either memory access or I/O, this entry controls its ability to use a high-speed posted write buffer. Choices are N/A, 1, 2, and 4 (default).

**CPU Master Post-W/R Burst Mode**   When the CPU operates as a bus master for either memory access or I/O, this entry controls its ability to use a high-speed burst mode for posted writes to a buffer.

**CPU Memory Sample Point**   This feature allows you to select the cycle checkpoint, which is where memory decoding and cache hit/miss checking takes place. Each selection indicates that the check takes place at the end of a CPU cycle, with one wait-state indicating more time for checking to take place than zero wait-states. A longer check time allows for greater stability at the expense of some performance.

**CPU/PCI Post Write Delay**    This is the delay time before the CPU writes data into the PCI bus.

**CPU/PCI Write Phase**    This feature determines the turnaround between the address and data phases of the CPU master to PCI slave writes. Choices are 1 LCLK (default) or 0 LCLK.

**CPU Pipelined Function**    This feature allows the system controller to signal the CPU for a new memory address even before all data transfers for the current cycle are complete. This results in increased data throughput. The default is usually disabled, so pipelining is off. Enabled means that address pipelining is active.

**CPU Read Multiple Prefetch**    A prefetch occurs during a process (such as reading from the PCI bus or memory) when the chipset peeks at the next instruction and actually begins the next read. The Intel 450GX/KX Orion chipset has four read lines. A multiple prefetch means the chipset can initiate more than one prefetch during a process. By default, the feature is disabled.

**CPU-to-PCI Burst Memory Write**    When enabled, back-to-back sequential CPU memory write cycles to PCI are translated to PCI burst memory write cycles. Otherwise, each single write to PCI will have an associated FRAME signal sequence. Keeping this feature enabled is best for performance, but some nonstandard PCI cards (for example, older VGA adapters) may have problems.

**CPU-to-PCI Post/Burst**    Data from the CPU to the PCI bus can be posted (buffered by the controller) and/or burst. This entry sets the methods used:

- **POST/CON.BURST**    Posting and bursting supported (default)
- **NONE/NONE**    Neither supported
- **POST/NONE**    Posting but not bursting supported

**CPU-to-PCI Post Memory Write**    This feature enables up to four double words (DW) of data to be posted to PCI. Otherwise, not only is buffering disabled, but completion of CPU writes also is limited. (The CPU write does not complete until the PCI transaction completes.) Keeping this feature enabled is best for performance.

**CPU-to-PCI Read Buffer**    This is also sometimes termed the *PCI-to-CPU Write Buffer*. When enabled, up to four double words (DW) can be read from the PCI bus without interrupting the CPU. When disabled, a write buffer is not used, and the CPU read cycle will not be completed until the PCI bus signals that it is ready to receive the data. Enabling the buffer is best for system performance.

**CPU-to-PCI Read-Burst**    When enabled (on), the PCI bus will interpret CPU read cycles as the PCI burst protocol, meaning that back-to-back sequential CPU memory read cycles addressed to the PCI will be translated into fast PCI burst memory cycles. Performance is improved, but some nonstandard PCI adapters (for example, older VGA adapters) may experience problems.

**CPU-to-PCI Read-Line**    When enabled (on), more time will be allocated for data setup with faster CPUs. This feature may only be required if you add an Intel OverDrive processor to your 486-class system. You may not find this parameter on current PCs using fast Intel or AMD processors.

**CPU-to-PCI Write Buffer**    This is the same as CPU-to-PCI Read Buffer, only for writing.

**CPU-to-PCI Write Posting**    The Intel 450GX/KX Orion chipset maintains its own internal read and write buffers that are used to help compensate for the speed differences between the CPU and the PCI bus. When this feature is enabled, writes from the CPU to the PCI bus will be buffered. When disabled (default), the writes will not be buffered, and the CPU will be forced to wait until the write is completed.

**Delay for SCSI/HDD**    Also called the *SCSI Boot Delay*, this is the length of time (in seconds) that the BIOS will wait for the SCSI hard disk to be ready for operation. If the hard drive is not ready, the PCI SCSI BIOS might not detect the hard drive correctly. The range is from 0 to 60 seconds.

**DMA Line Buffer**    This feature allows DMA data to be stored in a buffer so PCI bus operations are not interrupted. Disabled means that the line buffer for DMA is in single-transaction mode. Enabled allows it to operate in an 8-byte transaction mode for greater efficiency. This feature should be enabled for best system performance.

**DMA Line Buffer Mode**    This feature allows DMA data to be stored in a buffer so as not to interrupt the PCI bus. When the Standard mode is selected, the line buffer is in single-transaction mode. When the Enhanced mode is selected, the feature allows it to operate in 8-byte transaction mode.

**E8000 32K Accessible**    This 64KB area of upper memory is used for BIOS purposes on PS/2s, 32-bit operating systems, and plug-and-play. This setting allows the second 32KB page to be used for other purposes when not needed (in the same way that the first 32KB page of the F range is usable after boot-up has finished).

**Enable Master**    This feature enables the selected device as a PCI bus master and checks whether the device is capable of performing as a PCI master.

**Fast Back-to-Back**    When this feature is enabled, the PCI bus will interpret CPU read cycles as the PCI burst protocol, meaning that back-to-back sequential CPU memory read cycles addressed to the PCI will be translated into the fast PCI burst memory cycles. By default the feature is enabled.

**FRAMEJ Generation**    When the PCI bus bridge is acting as a PCI Master and receiving data from the CPU, a fast CPU-to-PCI buffer will be enabled if this selection is also enabled. Using the buffer allows the CPU to complete a write even though the data has not been delivered to the PCI bus. This reduces the number of CPU cycles involved and speeds overall processing:

- Normal Buffering not employed (default)
- Fast Buffer used for CPU-to-PCI writes

**HCLK PCICLK**    This entry allows you to set the host CLK/PCI CLK divider. The options are AUTO, 1-1, and 1-1.5. If this option is available on your system, select Auto for most reliable operation.

**IBC DEVSEL Decoding**    This feature allows you to set the type of decoding used by the *ISA Bridge Controller* (IBC) to determine which device to select. The longer the decoding cycle, the better chance the IBC has to correctly decode the commands. Choices are Fast, Medium, and Slow (default). You may not find this parameter on current PCs that have abandoned the use of ISA bus slots.

**IDE Buffer for DOS and Windows**    When enabled, this feature provides IDE read-ahead and posted-write buffers, so you can increase throughput to and from IDE devices by buffering reads and writes. However, this feature may actually slow older devices, so it should be disabled unless all IDE devices support the buffers.

**IDE Master (Slave) PIO Mode**    This option changes the IDE data transfer speed to Mode 0–4 or Auto. Rather than have the BIOS issue commands to effect transfers to or from the disk drive, PIO allows the BIOS to tell the controller what it wants, and then lets the controller and the CPU perform the complete task by themselves. Modes 1–4 are available for EIDE systems, but set to Auto for an automatic configuration. DMA modes (for Ultra-DMA drive systems) may also be available for later PC platforms.

**I/O Cycle Post-Write**    When this feature is enabled (default), data being written during an I/O cycle will be buffered for faster performance.

**I/O Cycle Recovery**    When enabled, the PCI bus will be allowed a recovery period for back-to-back I/O (which slows back-to-back data transfers). It's like adding wait-states to the PCI bus, so disable this feature (default) for best performance.

**I/O Recovery Period**    This feature sets the length of time for the I/O Cycle Recovery—a programmed delay that allows the PCI bus to exchange data with the slower ISA bus without data errors. The range is from 0 to 1.75 microseconds in 0.25-microsecond intervals. Typical settings include

| | |
|---|---|
| 2 BCLK | Two BCLKs (default) |
| 4 BCLK | Four BCLKs |
| 8 BCLK | Eight BCLKs |
| 12 BCLK | Twelve BCLKs |

You may not find this parameter on current PCs that have abandoned the use of ISA bus slots.

**IRQ 3–IRQ 15**    These entries are used to list what IRQs are in use (or reserved) by ISA legacy cards. If you don't use specific IRQs, set the respective entries to Available. Otherwise, set Used by ISA Card, which reserves the IRQ so that nothing else can use it. You may not find this parameter on current PCs that have abandoned the use of ISA bus slots.

**IRQ Line**    If you have installed a device requiring an IRQ service into the given PCI slot, use this entry to inform the PCI bus which IRQ it should initiate. Choices range from IRQ 3 through IRQ 15.

**ISA Linear Frame Buffer**    This feature enables a buffer if you use an ISA card that features a linear frame buffer (for example, a second video card for AutoCAD). The buffer address will be set automatically. You may not find this parameter on current PCs that have abandoned the use of ISA bus slots.

**ISA Master Line Buffer**    ISA master buffers are designed to isolate the slower ISA I/O operations from the PCI bus for better performance. Keeping this feature disabled means the buffer for ISA master transaction is in single mode. Enabling this feature means it is in 8-byte mode that increases the ISA master's performance. You may not find this parameter on current PCs that have abandoned the use of ISA bus slots.

**ISA Shared Memory Size**    This option sets a block of system memory that will not be shadowed. This feature should normally be disabled unless you have an ISA card that uses the upper memory area. If you enable this feature, you'll also need to configure the ISA Shared Memory Base Address. Enter the base address—if you choose 64K, you can only choose D000h or below. You may not find this parameter on current PCs that have abandoned the use of ISA bus slots.

**ISA VGA Frame Buffer Size**     Also called the *ISA LFB Size*, this feature allows you to use a VGA frame buffer and 16MB of RAM at the same time. The system will allow access to the graphics card through a "hole" in its own memory map. In other words, access to addresses within this hole will be directed to the ISA bus instead of main memory. This feature should be set to disabled unless you're using an ISA card with more than 64KB of memory that needs to be accessed by the CPU, *and* you are not using the plug-and-play utilities. If you have less than 8MB of memory, or use MS-DOS, this feature will be ignored. You may not find this parameter on current PCs that have abandoned the use of ISA bus slots.

**Keyboard Controller Clock**     This entry sets the speed of the keyboard controller (PCICLKI = PCI bus speed). Typical options are

| | |
|---|---|
| 7.16 MHz | (Default) |
| PCICLKI/2 | 1/2 PCICLKI |
| PCICLKI/3 | 1/3 PCICLKI |
| PCICLKI/4 | 1/4 PCICLKI |

**Latency for CPU-to-PCI Write**     This is the delay time before a CPU writes data to the PCI bus.

**Latency from ADS Status**     This feature allows you to configure how long the CPU waits for the *Address Data Status* (ADS) signal. It determines the CPU-to-PCI POST write speed. When set to 3T, this is 5T for each double word. With 2T (default), it is 4T per double word. For a quad word (Qword) PCI memory write, the rate is 7T (2T) or 8T (3T). The default should be correct, but if you add a faster CPU to your system, you may find it necessary to increase it. The choices are 3T (three CPU clocks) or 2T (two CPU clocks, the default).

**Latency Timer (PCI Clocks)**     This entry controls the length of time that a device on the PCI bus can hold the bus when another device has requested it. Since the PCI bus runs faster than the ISA bus, the PCI bus must be slowed during interactions with it. This setting allows you to define how long the PCI bus will delay for a transaction between the given PCI slot and the ISA bus. This number depends on the PCI master device in use, and ranges from 0 to 255. The default is often 66, but 40 is a good place to start. Smaller values result in faster access to the bus (with better response times), but bandwidth and data throughput become lower. Normally, you'd leave this setting alone unless you're working with latency-sensitive devices (for example, audio cards or network cards with small buffers). You may not find this parameter on current PCs that have abandoned the use of ISA bus slots.

**Latency Timer Value**     This is the maximum number of PCI bus clocks that the master may burst. A longer latency time gives the CPU more of a chance to control the bus.

**LDEV Check Point**     You will probably not see this entry on current systems. The VESA local device (LDEV#) check point is where the VL-bus device decodes the bus commands and checks for errors within the bus cycle itself:

| | |
|---|---|
| 0 | Bus cycle point T1 (default) |
| 1 | During the first T2 |
| 2 | During the second T2 |
| 3 | During the third T2 |

**LDEVJ Check Point Delay**    This feature allows you to select how much time is allocated for checking bus cycle commands. These commands must be decoded to determine whether a local bus device access signal (LDEVJ) is being sent, or an ISA device is being addressed. Increasing the delay increases stability (especially in the VESA subsystem) while very slightly degrading the performance of the ISA subsystem. Settings are in terms of the feedback clock rate (FBCLK2) used in the cache/memory control interface:

| | |
|---|---|
| 1 FBCLK2 | One clock |
| 2 FBCLK2 | Two clocks (default) |
| 3 FBCLK2 | Three clocks |

**Local Memory Check Point**    This entry allows you to select between two techniques for decoding and error checking local bus writes to DRAM during a memory cycle:

| | |
|---|---|
| Slow | Extra wait-state; better checking (default) |
| Fast | No extra wait-state used |

**M1445RDYJ to CPURDYJ**    This feature determines whether the PCI Ready signal is to be synchronized by the CPU clock's ready signal or bypassed (default).

**Master Arbitration Protocol**    This is the method by which the PCI bus determines which bus master device gains access to the bus.

**Master IOCHRDY**    When this feature is enabled, it allows the system to monitor for a VESA master request to generate an I/O channel ready (IOCHRDY) signal. You may not find this feature on current PCs that have abandoned the use of VL bus slots.

**Master Retry Timer**    This feature sets how long the CPU master will attempt a PCI cycle before the cycle is unmasked (terminated). The choices are measured in PCICLKs with the PCI timer. Values are 10 (default), 18, 34, or 66 PCICLKs.

**Max. Burstable Range**    This feature sets the size of the maximum range of contiguous memory that can be addressed by a burst from the PCI bus. Longer burst durations should improve performance.

**Memory Start Address**    This feature is for devices with their own memory that use part of the CPU's memory address space. It allows you to determine the starting point in memory where PCI device memory will be mapped.

**Multimedia Mode**    This feature enables or disables palette snooping for multimedia cards.

**Onboard PCI/SCSI BIOS**    You should enable this feature if your system motherboard had a built-in SCSI controller attached to the PCI bus, and you want to boot from it.

**Parity**    When enabled, this feature allows parity checking of PCI devices.

**PCI Arbiter Mode**    Devices gain access to the PCI bus through arbitration. There are two modes, mode 1 (default) and mode 2. The idea is to minimize the time it takes to gain control of the bus and move data. Generally, mode 1 should be sufficient, but try mode 2 if you encounter problems with PCI bus access.

**PCI Arbit. Rotate Priority**    Typically, the system manages (or arbitrates) access to the PCI bus on a first-come-first-served basis. When priority is rotated, once a device gains control of the bus, it is assigned the lowest priority, and every other device is moved up one in the priority queue. This helps to prevent any one device from monopolizing the PCI bus.

**PCI Bursting**    When this feature is enabled, consecutive writes from the CPU will be regarded as a PCI burst cycle. This feature should normally be enabled.

**PCI Bus Parking**    This is a sort of bus mastering—a device parking on the PCI bus has full control of the bus for a short time. This feature improves performance when that device is being used, but excludes others. Try enabling this feature with network cards and hard disk controllers.

**PCI CLK**    This feature determines whether the PCI clock is tightly synchronized with the CPU clock, or is asynchronous. If your CPU, motherboard, and PCI bus are running at multiple speeds of each other, choose to synchronize. Today, many PCs with very fast FSB speeds will run the PCI clock asynchronously of the CPU.

**PCI Concurrency**    When enabled, this means that more than one PCI device can be active at a time. With Intel chipsets, it allocates memory bus cycles to a PCI controller while an ISA operation (such as bus-mastered DMA) is taking place, which normally requires constant attention. This involves turning on additional read and write buffering in the chipset. The PCI bus can also obtain access cycles for small data transfers without the delays caused by renegotiating bus access for each part of the transfer, so the feature is meant to improve performance and consistency. Today, concurrency is a standard attribute of the PCI bus, so you may not see this option on current PCs.

**PCI Cycle Cache Hit**    This option defines how the cache is refreshed during PCI operation. Normal refresh will produce a cache refresh during normal PCI cycles. Fast refresh will produce a cache refresh without a PCI cycle for CAS. Fast performance is usually better.

**PCI Device, Slot 1/2/3**    This feature enables I/O and memory cycle decoding for PCI slots. There are three options: Enable (enables the device as a slave PCI device), Enable Master (enables the device as a master PCI device), and Use Default Latency Timer. If this is enabled (yes), you don't need to set the Latency Timer value.

**PCI Dynamic Decoding**    When this feature is enabled, the system can remember the PCI command that has just been requested. If subsequent commands fall within the same address space, the cycle will be automatically interpreted as a PCI command.

**PCI IDE 2nd Channel**    Disable this feature if you're not using the second channel on the PCI IDE card. This frees up IRQ 15. Otherwise, you will lose IRQ 15 for other devices in the system. Today, the IDE controller is normally integrated into the chipset's South Bridge, so this option is rarely available (IRQ15 is simply assigned to the secondary channel of the chipset's integrated controller).

**PCI (IDE) Bursting**    This is similar to PCI Bursting, but this one enables burst mode access to video memory over the PCI bus. The CPU provides the first address, and consecutive data is transferred at one word per clock. The device must support burst mode.

**PCI IDE IRQ Map To**    On older PCs, this option allows you to configure your system to the type of IDE disk controller. An ISA device is assumed. If you have a PCI IDE controller, this setting allows you to specify which slot has the controller and which PCI INT# (A, B, C, or D) is associated with the connected hard drives. Note that this refers to the hard disk rather than individual partitions. Since each IDE controller supports two drives, you can select the INT# for each. Also note that the primary channel has a lower interrupt than the secondary channel. There are four modes:

- **PCI-Auto**   If the IDE is detected by the BIOS on one of the PCI slots, then the appropriate INT# channel will be assigned to IRQ 14.
- **PCI-Slot X**   If the IDE is not detected, you can manually select the slot.
- **Primary IDE INT#, Secondary IDE INT#**   This assigns two INT# channels for primary and secondary channels (if supported).
- **ISA**   This option assigns no IRQs to PCI slots. Use this mode for PCI IDE cards that connect IRQs 14 and 15 directly from an ISA slot using a table from a legacy paddle board.

**PCI IDE Prefetch Buffers**   This feature allows you to enable or disable a set of prefetch buffers in the PCI IDE controller. You may need to disable this feature with an operating system (like Windows NT) that doesn't use the BIOS to access the hard disk and that doesn't disable interrupts when completing a programmed I/O operation. Disabling also prevents errors with faulty PCI-IDE interface chips that can corrupt data on the hard disk (as can happen with true 32-bit operating systems). You can usually leave this feature disabled.

**PCI I/O Start Address**   The I/O devices make themselves accessible by occupying an address space. This allows you to make additional room for older ISA devices by defining the I/O start address for the PCI devices. You may not find this parameter on current PCs that have abandoned the use of ISA bus slots.

**PCI IRQ Activated By**   This lists the method by which the PCI bus recognizes an IRQ request (Level or Edge). Use the default entries unless advised otherwise by your PCI device manufacturer, or if you have a PCI device that only recognizes one of these methods.

**PCI-ISA BCLK Divider**   On older systems where the ISA bus clock is divided from the PCI clock, this entry allows you to set the PCI Bus CLK/ISA Bus CLK divider. The options are AUTO, PCICLK1/3, PCICLK1/2, and PCICLK1/4.

**PCI Master Accesses Shadow RAM**   This feature enables the shadowing of a ROM on a PCI master for better performance.

**PCI Master Burst Mode**   When a PCI device operates as a bus master for either memory access or I/O, this entry controls its use of a high-speed burst mode for posted writes to a buffer.

**PCI Master DEVSEL Timeout**   When a PCI device initiates a master cycle using an address (target) that has not been mapped to PCI/VESA or ISA space, the system will monitor the DEVSEL (device select) pin for a period of time to see if any device claims the cycle. This entry allows you to determine how long the system will wait before timing out. Choices are 3 PCICLK, 4 PCICLK (default), 5 PCICLK, and 6 PCICLK.

**PCI Master Fast Interface**   This feature enables or disables what is known as a *fast back-to-back* interface when a PCI device operates as a bus master. When enabled, consecutive reads/writes are interpreted as the PCI high-performance burst mode.

**PCI Master Latency**   This option sets the time that a PCI master can control the bus. If your PCI master controls the bus for too long, there is less time for the CPU to control it. A longer latency time gives the CPU more time to control the PCI bus.

**PCI Master Post-W/R Buffer**    When a PCI device operates as a bus master for either memory access or I/O, this entry controls its use of a high-speed posted write buffer. Choices are N/A, 1, 2, and 4 (default).

**PCI Master Timing Mode**    This entry gives you the ability to choose between two timing modes: 0 (default) and 1.

**PCI Post-Write Fast**    When this feature is enabled (default), data being written during a PCI cycle will be buffered for faster performance.

**PCI Preempt Timer**    This entry sets the length of time before one PCI master preempts another when a service request has been pending. Typical entries are

| | |
|---|---|
| Disabled | No preemption (default) |
| 260 LCLKs | Preempt after 260 LCLKs |
| 132 LCLKs | Preempt after 132 LCLKs |
| 68 LCLKs | Preempt after 68 LCLKs |
| 36 LCLKs | Preempt after 36 LCLKs |
| 20 LCLKs | Preempt after 20 LCLKs |
| 12 LCLKs | Preempt after 12 LCLKs |
| 5 LCLKs | Preempt after 5 LCLKs |

**PCI Pre-Snoop**    Pre-snooping is a technique by which a PCI master can continue to burst to the local memory until a 4KB page boundary is reached, rather than just a line boundary. This feature can usually be enabled.

**PCI Slot x INTx**    Use this entry to assign PCI interrupts (INT#s) to specific PCI slots: Once an interrupt is assigned with PCI Slot x INTx, the Edge/Level Select option programs PCI IRQs to single-edge or logic-level triggering modes. Most PCI cards use level triggering, while most ISA cards use edge triggering. However, try selecting edge triggering for PCI IDE.

**PCI Streaming**    Data is typically moved to and from memory and between devices in discrete chunks of limited sizes, because the CPU is involved. On the PCI bus, data can be *streamed*—that is, much larger chunks can be moved without the CPU being used. This feature should be enabled for best performance.

**PCI-to-CPU Write Pending**    This feature sets the behavior of the system when the write buffer is full. By default, the system will immediately retry. (But you can set it to wait for the buffer to be emptied before retrying.)

**PCI-to-DRAM Buffer**    When enabled, this feature improves PCI-to-DRAM performance by allowing data to be stored if a destination is busy. Buffers are needed for this feature because the PCI bus is separate from the CPU.

**PCI-to-ISA Write Buffer**    When enabled, the system will temporarily write data to a buffer so the CPU is not interrupted. When disabled, the memory write cycle for the PCI bus will be directed to the slower ISA bus. As a result, keeping this feature enabled is best for performance. You may not find this parameter on current PCs that have abandoned the use of ISA bus slots.

**PCI/VGA Palette Snoop**    This feature alters the VGA palette setting while graphic signals pass through the feature connector of PCI VGA card and are processed by the MPEG card. VGA snooping is used by multimedia video devices (for example, video capture boards) to look ahead at the video controller (VGA device) to see what color palette is currently in use. Enable this feature if you have MPEG connections through the VGA feature connector. (This means you can adjust PCI/VGA palettes.) Otherwise, go ahead and disable the feature.

**PCI Write-Byte-Merge (or CPU-to-PCI Byte Merge)**    When enabled, this allows data sent from the CPU to the PCI bus to be held in a buffer. The chipset will then write the data in the buffer to the PCI bus when appropriate.

**Post Write CAS Active**    This is the pulse width of the Column Address Strobe (CAS) signal when the PCI master writes to system RAM.

**Preempt PCI Master Option**    When this feature is enabled, PCI bus operations can be preempted by certain system operations, such as DRAM refresh. Otherwise, they can take place concurrently.

**Primary Frame Buffer**    When this feature is enabled, the system can use unreserved memory as a primary frame buffer. Unlike the VGA frame buffer, this would reduce overall available RAM for applications. The default is usually disabled.

**Primary VGA BIOS Sequence**    This option is sometimes found on older PCs with both PCI and AGP VGA controllers. You can use this entry to select the default video controller at start time. Selecting PCI (or PCI/AGP) tells the system to use the PCI-based video device. Selecting AGP (or AGP/PCI) causes the system to use the AGP video system. Today's PCs use AGP almost exclusively, so this option is rarely available. However, this can be a handy troubleshooting option if you suspect a video failure and only have an older PCI video adapter handy.

**Residence of VGA Card**    This option lists whether the VGA card resides on a PCI or VL Bus. Today, the default is PCI, though current systems will usually not include this feature because of the influence of AGP.

**Slot 1/5, Slot 2, Slot 3, Slot 4, Slot 5 IRQ**    These entries set the assignments of IRQs for each PCI slot. The default setting for each field is Auto, which utilizes autorouting to determine IRQ use (this is the preferred approach). However, you can also select "no IRQs" (N/A) or any standard IRQ (usually between IRQ3 and IRQ15).

**Slot X Using INT#**    This entry selects an interrupt (INT#) channel for a PCI slot, and there are four (A, B, C, and D) for each one. That is, each PCI bus slot supports interrupts A, B, C, and D. INT#A is allocated automatically, and you would only use #B, #C, and #D if the PCI card needs to use more than one (PCI) interrupt service. For example, select #D if your PCI card needs four interrupts. Often, it is simplest to use the Auto mode.

**Snoop Ahead**    This feature is only applicable if the cache is enabled. When enabled, PCI bus masters can monitor the VGA palette registers for direct writes and translate them into PCI burst protocol for greater speed, which can enhance the performance of multimedia video.

**Snoop Filter (or Cache Snoop Filter)**    This feature saves the need for multiple inquiries to the same line if it was checked previously. When enabled, cache snoop filters ensure data integrity (cache coherency) while reducing the snoop frequency to a minimum.

**State Machines**    The chipset uses four state machines to manage specific CPU and/or PCI operations. Each can be thought of as a highly optimized process center designed to handle specific operations. Generally, each operation involves a master device and the bus it wishes to employ. The four state machines are CPU master to CPU bus (CC), CPU master to PCI bus (CP), PCI master to PCI bus (PP), and PCI master to CPU bus (PC). Each state machine has the following settings:

- **Address 0 WS**    This refers to the length of time the system will delay while the transaction address is decoded. When enabled, there will be no delay.
- **Data Write 0 WS**    This is the length of time the system will delay while data is being written to the target address. When enabled, there will be no delay.
- **Data Read 0 WS**    This is the length of time the system will delay while data is being read from the target address. When enabled, there will be no delay.

**Stop CPU when PCI Flush**    When this feature is enabled, the CPU will be stopped when the PCI bus is being flushed of data. Disabling this feature (default) allows the CPU to continue processing, giving better system performance.

**Stop CPU at PCI Master**    When this feature is enabled, the CPU will be stopped when the PCI bus master is operating on the bus. Disabling this feature (default) allows the CPU to continue processing, giving better system performance.

**SCSI BIOS**    If your motherboard includes an onboard SCSI controller (such as a Symbios controller), this option will allow the system to detect and initialize the SCSI controller at boot time. This option is normally set to Auto. If the SCSI controller is detected, the motherboard's SCSI BIOS will be enabled. If no SCSI controller is detected, the onboard SCSI BIOS will be disabled. You can also disable the SCSI BIOS so that the motherboard's SCSI controller will remain disabled (this may be necessary if you plan to use a PCI-based SCSI host adapter card).

**Use Default Latency Timer Value**    This option determines whether the default value for the latency timer will be loaded or the succeeding latency timer value will be used. If yes is selected (default), no further programming is needed for the latency timer value.

**VESA Master Cycle ADSJ**    This feature allows you to increase the length of time the VESA (VL) Master has in order to decode bus commands. Typical choices are Normal (default) and Long. Today's PCs have abandoned the VL bus in favor of the PCI and AGP architecture, so this option is probably not available.

**VGA 128K Range Attribute**    When this feature is enabled, it allows the chipset to apply features like CPU-to-PCI Byte Merge and CPU-to-PCI Prefetch to VGA memory range A0000H–BFFFFH. When enabled, the VGA receives CPU-to-PCI functions. When disabled, the system retains the standard VGA interface.

**VGA Performance Mode**    When this feature is enabled, the VGA memory range of A0000h–B0000h will use a special set of performance features. This feature has little or no effect using video modes beyond the standard VGA most commonly used for Windows, OS/2, UNIX, and so on, but this memory range is heavily used by games.

**VGA Type**    This entry is used when the video BIOS is being shadowed. The BIOS uses this information to determine which bus to use. Choices are Standard (default), PCI, and ISA/VESA. This option is not found on today's AGP-based systems.

**Video Palette Snoop**    This feature controls how a PCI graphics card can snoop write cycles to an ISA video card's color palette registers. Snooping essentially means interfering with a device. This is a powerful performance option, so only disable it if (1) an ISA card connects to a PCI graphics card through a VESA connector, (2) the ISA card connects to a color monitor, and (3) the ISA card uses the RAMDAC on the PCI card, and palette snooping (RAMDAC shadowing) is not operative on the PCI card. You may not find this parameter on current PCs that have abandoned the use of ISA bus slots.

**Xth Available IRQ**    This feature selects (maps) an IRQ for one of the available INT#s (A, B, C, or D). There are eleven selections (3, 4, 5, 6, 7, 9, 10, 11, 12, 14, and 15). The "1st available IRQ" means the BIOS will assign this IRQ to the first PCI slots (order is 1, 2, 3, 4), and so on. N/A means the particular IRQ has been assigned to another device in the system (usually the ISA bus on older PCs) and is therefore not available to a PCI slot.

# CONFIGURING SECURITY

Although few employees must share a PC today, companies recognize the high cost of maintaining and troubleshooting systems that are used by everyday workers. Modern BIOS versions allow a series of passwords and protective restrictions to be applied. This can prevent unauthorized users from accessing or powering-up a system, prevent changes from being made to the CMOS Setup, and so on. Security measures can often help to prevent accidental (or malicious) changes to a system that may require time-consuming and costly labor to fix. This section outlines many of the common security features that you might encounter.

**Diskette Access**    When enabled, the system requires a password to boot from or access the floppy disk. This is a handy protective measure that can prevent malicious users from booting from (or introducing a virus through) a floppy disk.

**Fixed Disk Boot Sector**    This may be normal or write protected. In the write-protected mode, no software may write to the boot sector of a hard drive, and the drive is effectively protected from boot sector viruses. You will require a password to Format or FDISK the hard disk.

**Password on Boot**    When enabled, the boot process will halt and ask for the supervisor password (which must be previously set). If the supervisor password is set and this option is disabled, the BIOS assumes a user is booting.

**Set Supervisor Password**    This allows you to enter a password of up to about seven alphanumeric characters. Pressing ENTER displays a dialog for entering the supervisor password. In most current system designs, this password gives full access to CMOS Setup menus.

**Set User Password**    This allows you to enter a password of up to about seven alphanumeric characters. Pressing ENTER displays the dialog box for entering the user password. In most current system designs, this password gives limited access to CMOS Setup menus.

**System Backup Reminder/Virus Check Reminder**    This feature displays a message during boot-up asking (Y/N) if you have backed up the system/scanned it for viruses. The typical options for this feature are Disabled, Daily, Weekly, or Monthly. Daily displays the message on the first boot of the day, Weekly on the first boot after Sunday, and Monthly on the first boot of the month.

# CONFIGURING POWER MANAGEMENT

Energy is expensive, and in a world of dwindling energy reserves and escalating energy demands, PCs are often required to work longer hours and pack in more features, yet be energy efficient. Today's PCs use far less energy than their early counterparts—largely because there are fewer components—but also because PCs employ a wide range of energy-saving techniques designed to reduce power demands as the system remains idle for a time. (These are collectively known as *green PCs*.) Most power management features are selectable through the CMOS Setup. This part of the chapter illustrates how to deal with typical power management features, and you can see an example of Award BIOS on an AOpen AK72 motherboard in Figure 10-5.

Some power management characteristics are also adjusted through the operating system, but the OS still depends on the BIOS (and CMOS Setup) to enable power management features.

**AC PWR Loss Restart**    When the PC loses power, it will crash (and you will lose unsaved work). However, you can use this option to determine how the system should respond once power returns. The "disabled" option leaves your system off. The "enabled" option will automatically reboot your system. The "previous state" option (the default) sets your system back to the state it is before the power interruption.

**Automatic Power Up**    This feature allows an unattended or automatic system power up. You may configure your system to power up at a certain time of the day by selecting "everyday," or at a certain time and day by selecting "by date." This feature will not work if the system is powered down by operating systems that have ACPI support enabled, and it is usually disabled by default.

**Doze Timer**    This feature sets the time delay before the system will reduce 80 percent of its activity. Ten to 20 minutes is usually the preferred time.

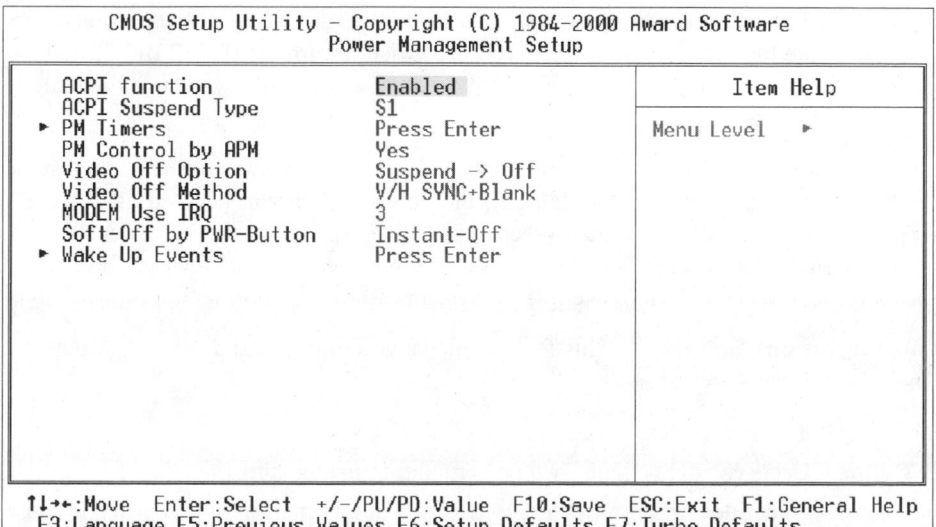

**FIGURE 10-5**    Using the Power Management Setup menu to enable power-saving modes and select important timeout parameters (Courtesy of AOpen)

**FAN OFF at Suspend**    This option allows you to set the behavior of the CPU cooling fan, and save additional power when the system enters a suspend mode. If this option is enabled, the CPU fan will turn off when the system enters the suspend mode. If disabled, the CPU fan will remain on while the system is in suspend mode. If the CPU tends to run very hot, and suspend durations are typically short, leave the CPU fan on (disable this mode). If the PC is used only intermittently and suspend durations are long, go ahead and turn the CPU fan off (enable this mode).

**Green Timer of Main Board**    This feature allows you to set the time before a CPU of an idle system will shut down. The usual options are Disabled or a time interval ranging from 1 to 15 minutes. As a rule, 5 to 10 minutes is recommended.

**HDD Standby Timer**    This feature sets the time after which the hard disk of an HDD idle system (no HDD access) will shut down (or spin down). Ten to 20 minutes is usually the preferred time. Keep in mind that this feature usually doesn't affect SCSI drives—only IDE-type drives.

**Modem Use IRQ**    Enter the IRQ assigned to the modem on your system (if any). If there is activity on the selected IRQ, the system will "awaken." This allows features such as "wake on ring."

**PM Control by APM**    If disabled, the system BIOS will ignore Advanced Power Management (APM) when managing the system power. When enabled, system BIOS will wait for an APM prompt before it enters any power management mode (for example, doze, standby, or suspend). If APM is installed and there is a task running (even if the timer has timed out), the APM will not prompt the BIOS to put the system into any power-saving mode. This feature is usually not present on current systems built to the ACPI standard (rather than the older APM standard).

**PM Wake-Up Events**    You can specify which events will wake the system and take it out of power-saving mode. When an event is disabled, the event's activity will not affect the PM timers or wake the system. When an event is enabled, the specified activity will reset the PM timers and wake the system. For example, if you have a modem on IRQ3, you can turn on IRQ3 as a wake-up event, so an interrupt from the modem can wake the system. Conversely, you may wish to turn off IRQ12 (the PS/2 mouse) as a wake-up event, so accidentally brushing the mouse does not awaken the system. By default, keyboard activity is the typical wake-up event.

**PWR Button < 4 Secs**    This option controls the way your power switch is used to turn the system off. When set to "soft-off" (usually the default), the power switch can be used as a normal system power-off button when pressed for less than 4 seconds. In the "suspend" mode, the power button has a dual function: pressing less than 4 seconds will place the system in sleep mode. However, holding the power switch for more than 4 seconds will power off the system regardless of the setting.

**Power Management Scheme**    This feature allows you to define the amount of power management taking place in the system:

- **Disabled**    Global power management will be disabled.
- **User Define**    Users can define their own power management settings.
- **Min Saving**    Predefined timer values are used such that all timers are in their maximum value.
- **Max Saving**    Predefined timer values are used such that all timers are in their minimum value.

**Power Up On PCI Card**    When your system is powered off, this option allows the system to be started remotely from another computer via a network by sending a "wake-up" signal. This normally requires that a network (LAN) card or modem be installed in the system. In most cases, your PC will also require an ATX-compliant power supply with a standby power rating of at least +5V @ 720mA. This feature is normally disabled by default, and should only be enabled if the system must be accessed remotely.

**Power Up On PS2 KB/Mouse**    When your system is powered off, this option allows the system to be started locally with a PS/2 keyboard, PS/2 mouse, or consumer IR device. This feature will require an ATX-compliant power supply with a standby power rating of at least +5V @ 300mA. This feature is normally disabled by default, and should only be used if the system is physically inaccessible (where the power switch cannot be conveniently accessed). Also, this feature will not work if the power supply is inadequate (even if the feature is enabled).

**RTC Wake-Up**    This feature lets you select a specific time for the system to power up. When enabled, you can select the specific hour and minute for the event (though these fields will not be available if the option is disabled). Keep in mind that the system must have been booted past the POST before it was last shut down. If you turn the system off before the POST, the system will not be able to wake up using this function.

**Slow Clock Ratio**    When the system enters a standby power-saving mode, the system clock can be throttled back to save additional power. This option specifies the speed at which the system clock runs in the standby mode, and is expressed as a percentage of the normal CPU clock speed. Settings typically include 0-12.5%, 12.5%-25%, 25%-37.5%, 37.5%-50%, 50%-62.5%, 62.5%-75%, and 75-87.5%.

**Standby Timer**    This feature sets the time delay before the system will reduce 92 percent of its activity. Thirty to 45 minutes is usually the preferred time, though systems that are frequently left idle can benefit from a shorter time.

**Suspend Switch**    This setting is used for enabling or disabling the "hardware suspend" switch on the motherboard. If your motherboard has a hardware suspend switch, enabling this option activates the suspend switch, and disabling this option deactivates the suspend switch.

**Suspend Timer**    This feature sets the time after which the system goes into the most inactive state possible (which is 99 percent). Once this state is entered, the system will require a warm-up period so the CPU, hard disk, and monitor may go online. Forty-five to 60 minutes is usually the preferred time, though systems that are frequently left idle can benefit from a shorter time.

**Suspend-to-RAM Capability [Disabled]**    Suspend-to-RAM (STR) is an energy-saving feature whereby all devices on the computer are turned off, except for the system RAM. The typical PC consumes less than 5 watts of power in this mode. This feature is normally disabled by default because not all hardware platforms support the STR mode, and the power supply requires a standby power rating of at least +5V @ 720ma. If any devices (e.g., expansion cards) on the motherboard do not support the STR function, you must leave this field disabled.

**System Slow Down**    This feature will slow the CPU clock dramatically after the timer has elapsed—reducing CPU heating and saving a great deal of power. A time anywhere from 30 to 60 minutes is usually acceptable. (See "Slow Clock Ratio" earlier.)

**Video Off Method**    This option defines the method used to disable video during a power-saving mode. For example, the Display Power Management System (DPMS) option allows the BIOS to control the video display card if it supports the DPMS feature. The Blank Screen option only blanks the screen, and is a good choice for monitors without power management or "green" features. The V/H SYNC+Blank option blanks the screen and turns off vertical and horizontal scanning. Configuration options include Blank Screen, V/H SYNC+Blank, DPMS Standby, DPMS Suspend, DPMS OFF (this is the default), and DPMS Reduce ON.

**Wake/Power Up On Ext. Modem**    When enabled, this feature allows the PC to be powered on when the external modem receives a call. Turning an external modem off and then back on while the computer is off will also result in an initialization string that will cause the system to power on. Keep in mind that the computer cannot receive or transmit data until the computer and applications are fully running, so connections cannot be made on the first try. This feature is normally disabled by default.

# Making Use of BIOS Autoconfiguration

Virtually all current motherboards provide a default or autoconfiguration option—taking most of BIOS setup problems out of the technician's hands. In the majority of cases, an autoconfigured BIOS will work just fine. But you must remember that autoconfiguration is not an optimization of the system's setup, but rather a set of efficient settings that should ensure a working system. You will have to disable this setting if you want to tweak the CMOS Setup yourself. (Otherwise, your settings will be ignored.) If you're stuck with CMOS settings, you should be able to get the system running by using system defaults. There are two levels of default you can work with: BIOS defaults and power-on defaults.

## BIOS DEFAULTS

BIOS defaults may not be (and usually aren't) tuned for your particular motherboard or chipset, but they give a reasonable chance of getting the system to boot without having to enter and tweak each individual setting. The BIOS default settings are also a good place to start fine-tuning your system. BIOS defaults can also recover your setup if you enter completely unacceptable values in CMOS Setup and the system refuses to boot (or if the CMOS RAM should fail due to a low backup battery). Of course, you'll have to start optimizing all over again.

## POWER-ON DEFAULTS

When powering-up the system, the BIOS puts the system into the most conservative state possible—turbo off, all caches disabled, all wait-states set to maximum, and so on. This ensures that you can always enter CMOS Setup. This mode is particularly useful if the settings returned by BIOS defaults fail. If the system still refuses to boot, then there is a serious hardware issue with the motherboard (or elsewhere in the system) that you will need to address first.

Not all systems provide a "power-on default" setting for the CMOS Setup—many BIOS versions simply provide one "BIOS Default" option.

# CMOS Maintenance and Troubleshooting

Although it is very rare for CMOS RAM/RTC devices to fail, there *are* many circumstances where CMOS contents may be lost or corrupted, and system performance may be compromised by a poorly configured CMOS Setup. Beyond the traditional beep and POST codes that suggest a CMOS problem (Chapter 17), or the more recent BIOS error messages (Chapter 6), a wide range of PC symptoms can indicate an improperly or incompletely configured CMOS. This part of the chapter identifies a series of symptoms that can suggest CMOS Setup problems and offers suggestions for corrective action.

## TYPICAL CMOS-RELATED SYMPTOMS

The following symptoms highlight many of the most common issues to strike the CMOS RAM/RTC portion of a system.

**SYMPTOM 10-1**    **Changes to CMOS are not saved after rebooting the PC**    In virtually all cases, you have exited the CMOS Setup routine incorrectly. This is a very common oversight (especially given the proliferation of different BIOS versions and CMOS Setup routines). Try making your changes again, and then be sure to select "Save Then Exit and Reboot" or "Exit Saving Changes" from the Setup utility's main menu.

**SYMPTOM 10-2**    **The system appears to be performing poorly**    The system must be stable. If it crashes frequently, or certain devices refuse to work, you may be dealing with a system conflict in hardware or software. Use a diagnostic tool such as the Device Manager (in Windows 9x/Me/XP) to help identify and correct possible points of conflict.

If the system is free of hardware or software conflicts, you can focus on performance. Performance is often a subjective evaluation and should first be verified using a benchmark test compared to other similar PCs (identical systems if possible). If you find that your particular system is performing below its optimum level, suspect a CMOS Setup problem. In some cases, the CMOS RAM may have been loaded with its "power-on" or "autoconfiguration" defaults. While defaults will almost always allow the system to function, they will rarely offer top performance. Check the advanced CMOS and chipset setup pages (particularly the memory-, cache-, and bus speed–related entries). Refer to the "Basic CMOS Optimization Tactics" section toward the beginning of this chapter.

**SYMPTOM 10-3**    **CMOS mismatch errors occur**    These errors occur when the PC hardware devices found during the POST (e.g., hard drives) do not match equipment listed in CMOS. In most cases, the CMOS backup battery has failed and should be replaced. You can then load the CMOS defaults and tweak the setup as necessary to optimize the system (an easy task if you've got a record of the CMOS settings). Otherwise, refer to the "Basic CMOS Optimization Tactics" section earlier in this chapter.

If you've cleared the CMOS Setup (using a "clear" jumper on the motherboard), be sure that you've reset the jumper so as not to continue clearing the CMOS RAM with each subsequent boot of the system.

**SYMPTOM 10-4**    **Some drives are not detected during boot**    This happens most often with hard drives or other devices in the Basic CMOS Setup page. In some cases, the device simply may not be listed or entered properly. (For example, you may have forgotten to enter your newly installed hard drive or floppy drive in the CMOS Setup.) Try to autodetect or autoconfigure any drives. In other cases, the drive may need more time to initialize at boot time. Try increasing the "boot delay" or disabling any "quick boot" feature that might be in use.

**SYMPTOM 10-5**    **The system boots from the hard drive, even though there is a bootable floppy disk in the drive**    Note that the system still boots and runs properly. The floppy disk is fully accessible. (If not, check the floppy drive, power, and signal cables.) This type of issue is usually not a problem, but due instead to an improper boot sequence. Most BIOS versions allow the PC to search through several different drives to locate an operating system and will boot from the first suitable drive where an operating system is found. Chances are that your boot sequence is set to "C: A:," where drive C: is checked first. Since drive C: is connected and functional, drive A: will simply be ignored. To boot from the drive A:, you'll need to change the boot sequence to something like "A: C:." Remember to save any changes before exiting the CMOS Setup.

**SYMPTOM 10-6**    **Power management features are not available**    First, make sure that your BIOS supports power management to begin with. Modern PC power management is typically handled by a combination of BIOS and the operating system (for example, APM under Windows 95 or ACPI under Windows 98/Me/XP). However, power management must be supported by BIOS and enabled under the CMOS Setup in order for the operating system to make use of it. If you can't use power management (or it is not available in the Windows 9x/Me/XP Control Panel), it probably isn't enabled in the CMOS Setup. Check the Power Management page of your CMOS Setup (or the Advanced Chipset Setup), and make sure that power management features are enabled. You may also want to review and adjust the various device timeouts as required. When you restart the operating system, you should then be able to configure the corresponding power management features.

**SYMPTOM 10-7**    **PnP support is not available, or PnP devices do not function properly**
First, make sure that your BIOS supports *plug-and-play* (PnP) standards. If not, you'll need to employ a DOS ISA Configuration Utility (or ICU) to support any PnP devices in the system (though this is virtually nonexistent today). Also make sure that you're using an operating system that supports PnP (for example, Windows 9x/Me/XP). If you can't get support for PnP devices, make sure that PnP support is enabled in the CMOS Setup, and verify that PnP-related settings (such as Configuration Mode or IRQ3-IRQ15) are all configured properly. If necessary, try loading the BIOS defaults for your CMOS Setup, which should give you baseline PnP support if your BIOS and OS support it. Be sure to record your original CMOS settings before attempting to load defaults.

**SYMPTOM 10-8**    **Devices in some PCI slots are not recognized or not working properly**
First, make sure that your motherboard supports PCI (Peripheral Component Interconnect) slots, and verify that there is at least one PCI adapter board in the system. All systems today will support PCI. Consequently, there is a proliferation of PCI-related configuration settings in the PnP/PCI area of a CMOS Setup, so it is extremely difficult to suggest any one probable oversight. If you cannot get PCI devices to work (or work properly), try loading the BIOS defaults for your CMOS Setup, which should give you baseline PCI support. Be sure to record your original CMOS settings before attempting to load defaults. If your motherboard was designed early during the development of PnP, you may need a BIOS upgrade to provide adequate PnP support.

**SYMPTOM 10-9**    **You cannot enter CMOS Setup even though the correct key combination is used**    Make sure that you're pressing that key combination quickly enough. Many BIOS versions only allow a few moments during POST to enter CMOS Setup. Once the operating system begins to load, you'll need to reboot. Also verify that you are in fact using the correct key or key combination. It is also possible that access to CMOS Setup has been disabled through a motherboard jumper. Refer to the documentation for your particular motherboard, and locate the "CMOS access" jumper. The jumper (if it exists) should be in the position that allows access.

Careful that you don't accidentally confuse this access jumper with the "CMOS clear" jumper—the two serve completely different purposes.

**SYMPTOM 10-10**    **The system crashes or locks up frequently**    There are many reasons for a PC to crash or lock up. Everything from a hardware fault to a bad driver to a software bug can interfere with normal system operation. Before you check the CMOS Setup, run a diagnostic to verify that the system hardware is performing properly, and check that there is no hardware conflict in the system. Then check the Device Manager and look for any signs of conflicting or inoperative devices (marked with yellow or red exclamation marks). If the system runs properly when DOS is booted clean (or Windows 9x/Me/XP is started in the Safe Mode), there may be a buggy or conflicting driver (or TSR) that is interfering with system operation.

If problems persist, there may be any of several different problems in the CMOS Setup. Typical oversights include insufficient wait-states, memory speed mismatches (for example, mixing 60ns and 70ns memory), and enabling cache (L1 or L2) when there is no such cache in the system. Review your system configuration very carefully. It is also possible that shadowing and snooping features can interfere with system operation. Try systematically disabling video ROM shadowing, motherboard ROM shadowing, and other shadowing options. Then try disabling video palette snoop, and other snooping or "pre-snoop" options.

If problems still continue, try loading the BIOS defaults into CMOS. The defaults should ensure some level of hardware stability, but you'll still need to optimize the CMOS Setup manually for best performance.

**SYMPTOM 10-11**    **COM ports don't work**    Assuming that the COM ports are installed and configured properly, operating problems can sometimes be traced to IDE Block Mode or IDE Multiple Sector Mode issues. Try disabling the Block Mode or Multiple Sector Mode, or scale back the block mode to a lower level. Of course, you should also check that the suspect COM ports are enabled and that their resource assignments do not conflict with other devices in the system.

**SYMPTOM 10-12**    **The RTC doesn't keep proper time over a month**    This is a very common problem for *real-time clock* (RTC) units. RTCs are notoriously inaccurate devices anyway—often straying by as much as several minutes per month. Some third-tier RTCs (or units burdened by heavy interrupt activity) may be off by more than several minutes (or more) per week. In practice, there is very little that can be done to correct this kind of poor timekeeping other than to replace the motherboard with one using a better-quality RTC (hardly an economical solution), or to use a "time-correcting utility" that compensates for the RTC's drift.

**SYMPTOM 10-13**    **The RTC doesn't keep time while system power is off**    Time seems maintained while system power is on, but the RTC appears to stop while the system is turned off. This is often a classic sign of impending CMOS backup battery failure. Since the RTC usually takes a bit more power than the CMOS RAM—and CMOS RAM can be maintained by a latent change—this kind of "clock stall" is often the first sign that the CMOS battery is failing. Record your CMOS Setup and replace the CMOS battery at your earliest opportunity.

**SYMPTOM 10-14**    **You see an "Invalid System Configuration Data" error**    This type of error often means that there is a problem with the extended system configuration data (ESCD). This is a storage space for the configuration data in a plug-and-play system. Once you have configured your system properly, the plug-and-play BIOS uses your ESCD to load the same configuration from one boot to the next. If this error message is displayed, take these steps:

1. Go into Setup and find a field labeled Reset Configuration Data.
2. Set this field to yes.
3. Save and exit the CMOS Setup program. The system restarts and clears the ESCD during POST.
4. Run whatever PnP configuration tool is appropriate for your system:
   - If you have Windows 9x/Me/XP (or other plug-and-play operating system), just restart your computer. Windows 9x/Me/XP will automatically configure your system and load the ESCD with the new data.
   - If you don't have Windows 9x/Me/XP, run the DOS ICU (ISA Configuration Utility) to reset the ESCD (though this should be unnecessary with today's PC platforms).

**SYMPTOM 10-15**    **You encounter "CMOS checksum" errors after updating a flash BIOS**    Flashing a BIOS chip will typically require you to clear the CMOS Setup and to reconfigure the Setup again from scratch. Most current motherboards offer a "Clear CMOS" jumper that can be used to wipe out all the CMOS settings. This is sometimes referred to as a *CMOS clear* or *CMOS NVRAM clear*. Try clearing the CMOS RAM, and then load the BIOS defaults. At that point, the errors should stop, and you may need to optimize the CMOS Setup entries in order to tweak the system. If you documented the original CMOS Setup entries with PRINTSCREEN before upgrading the BIOS, you should be able to reset key entries in a matter of minutes. Remember to save your changes when exiting.

**SYMPTOM 10-16**    **You notice that only some CMOS Setup entries are corrupted when running a particular application**    This rare kind of error sometimes happens with several games and other programs on the market that access memory locations used by CMOS RAM and the *BIOS Data Area* (BDA) that are shadowed into the *Upper Memory Area* (UMA). This can alter or corrupt at least some CMOS locations. One solution is to contact the program maker and see if there is a patch or fix that will prevent CMOS access. Alternatively, try disabling BIOS shadowing features through the CMOS Setup.

## CMOS PASSWORD TROUBLESHOOTING

Passwords are usually regarded as a necessary evil—a means of keeping out the malicious and the curious. However, passwords also cause their share of problems. As systems are passed from person to person or department to department, passwords often become lost or forgotten. This means the system won't start. The trick with all system passwords (that is, passwords that must be entered before the operating system loads) is that they are stored in CMOS RAM along with the rest of the system's settings. If you can clear the CMOS RAM, you can effectively disable the CMOS password protection. Still, simply clearing the CMOS RAM is not always an acceptable solution because the myriad CMOS settings are almost impossible to restore without a great deal of tweaking. The following tips will help you deal with unwanted CMOS passwords:

■ *Does anybody know the password?* Check with friends, colleagues, supervisors—someone just might know the password. This will save you a lot of hassle, and you can always disable the password in CMOS Setup once you're "in." If you're using an AMI BIOS and the password feature has been enabled (but no new password has been entered), try **AMI**. For Award BIOS, you can try **BIOSTAR** or **AWARD_SW**. There's no guarantee such defaults will work, but it's worth a try.

■ *Check for a "Password Clear" jumper.* Open the case and take a look at the motherboard. There's probably a jumper that will clear the password without wiping out the entire CMOS Setup. In some cases, the jumper is even marked "Clear Password" (so much for security). If you can find such a jumper, set it, and then boot the system. After the system boots, power-down again and reset the jumper. Your password should now be cleared, while leaving the CMOS settings intact.

■ *Force a configuration change.* Try removing a SIMM or DIMM and powering up the PC. In many cases, the BIOS will recognize the configuration change and generate an error such as "CMOS mismatch—Press F1 for Setup." This gets you into CMOS, where you can disable the password without clearing the CMOS RAM entirely. You'll have to save your changes and reboot. Keep in mind that when you finally replace that SIMM/DIMM, you'll probably see another CMOS error. Just go back into CMOS and do a quick correction. Remember that newer BIOS versions are getting smarter and may still require the password before the CMOS Setup routine will start, but it's worth a shot.

■ *Clear the CMOS RAM.* There's no doubt that this is your least desirable choice. There are several ways to clear the CMOS. Look for a motherboard jumper that says "CMOS Clear" or some similar marking. Set the jumper and power-up the system. When you see a message indicating that CMOS is clear, or that default settings have been loaded, power-down the PC and reset the jumper (the password should now be gone). You can then restart the PC and reconfigure your CMOS Setup from scratch. If you're using an AMI, Award, or Phoenix BIOS (and can't find the proper jumper), you can use the DOS DEBUG utility on a clean bootable floppy disk. Start DEBUG and use the following commands for an AMI BIOS. (Don't try this through a DOS window.)

```
C:\DEBUG
-O 70 17
-O 71 17
Q
```

If you're using a Phoenix BIOS, try the following DEBUG commands:

```
C:\DEBUG
-O 70 FF
-O 71 17
Q
```

As another option, you can remove the CMOS battery and wait for the CMOS RAM to clear. As a rule, you should wait for at least 30 minutes, but I've seen CMOS RAM hold a latent charge for days. To accelerate the process, you can short a 10-kOhm resistor across the empty battery terminals. Be sure to turn the system power off and unplug the PC first. If that doesn't work, you can use the same resistor to short the CMOS RAM power pins directly, as shown in Table 10-2. Again, remember that all system power should be off before you do this. Once your CMOS RAM is clear, you will need to restore the setup (probably starting with BIOS defaults). After the CMOS is restored, be sure to take a PRINTSCREEN of each setup page and keep the copies with the PC's documentation.

**TABLE 10-2** LISTING OF COMMON CMOS RAM CHIP POWER PINS

| BRAND | PART | SHORT PIN #S |
|---|---|---|
| Benchmarq | BQ3258S | 12 and 20 |
| Benchmarq | BQ3287AMT | 12 and 21 |
| Benchmarq | BQ3287MT | Cannot clear (replace the chip) |
| C&T | P82C206 | 12 and 32 |
| Dallas | DS1287 | Cannot clear (replace the chip) |
| Dallas | DS1287A | 12 and 21 |
| Dallas | DS12885S | 12 and 20 |
| Hitachi | HD146818AP | 12 and 24 |
| Motorola | MC146818AP | 12 and 24 |
| OPTi | F82C206 | 3 and 26 |
| Samsung | KS82C6818A | 12 and 24 |

# CMOS BATTERY MAINTENANCE

Ordinarily, the RTC/CMOS chip requires no maintenance. However, the backup battery will need to be replaced on a fairly regular basis (often every few years). Before replacing the battery (or battery pack), be sure that you have a valid CMOS backup—either on paper or floppy disk. Turn off system power, unplug the system, and remove the battery. This will cause the CMOS RAM chip to eventually lose its contents—it may take moments, or hours, depending on the CMOS RAM chip. Recycle the original battery and install the new one according to the system manufacturer's instructions. Secure the new battery and restart the system. When the system boots, go directly to the CMOS Setup routine and restore each setting. If you have CMOS information recorded in a file, boot the system from a floppy disk, and use the CMOS backup/restore utility to restore the file. If there are no records of the CMOS Setup, simply select BIOS Defaults or Power-On Defaults and tweak specific settings as needed. You should then be able to restart the system as if nothing had happened.

Some CMOS RAM chips can retain their contents for hours on a "latent" charge and may not have to be reprogrammed after replacing the battery. However, there is no guarantee of just how long CMOS contents will remain intact. Always be prepared to restore CMOS settings.

If you're going to be storing old (replaced) motherboards for any period of time, make it a point to remove the CMOS backup battery *first*. Batteries tend to be very safe and reliable, but there are many instances where they can and *do* leak. Since batteries use an acid-based electrolyte, battery leakage can easily damage battery contacts, or spill over onto the motherboard itself—damaging printed circuit traces and ruining the motherboard beyond repair.

# Further Study

**American Megatrends**    www.ami.com
**Award BIOS**    www.award.com
**BIOS Recovery**    www.sysopt.com/articles/recoverbios/index.html
**Dallas Semicon (Maxim)**    www.maxim-ic.com/
**MicroFirmware**    www.firmware.com/catalog2.htm
**Tom's Hardware**    www6.tomshardware.com/mainboard/97q1/970101/index.html
**Unicore (MR BIOS)**    www.unicore.com
**Wim's BIOS Page**    www.wimsbios.com/

# 11

# CONFLICT TROUBLESHOOTING

The incredible acceptance and popularity of the PC is largely due to the use of an *open architecture*. An open architecture allows any manufacturer to develop new devices (such as video cards, drive adapters, modems or LAN cards, sound cards, and so on) that will work seamlessly in conjunction with the PC. When a new expansion card is added to the PC, the device uses various system resources to obtain CPU time and transfer data across the expansion bus (for example, the PCI or AGP bus). Ultimately, each device that is added to the system requires unique resources. Traditionally, no two devices can use the same resources—otherwise, a hardware conflict will result. Low-level software programs (such as device drivers and TSRs) that use system resources can also conflict with one another during normal operation. This chapter explains the concept of *system resources* and then shows you how to detect and correct conflicts that can arise in both hardware and software.

## Understanding System Resources

The key to mastering and eliminating conflicts is to understand the importance of each system resource that is available to you. PCs provide four typical types of resources: interrupts (or IRQs), DMA channels, I/O areas, and memory, another important resource for the PC. Many controllers and network devices also utilize BIOS, which requires memory space. Do *not* underestimate the importance of these resource areas—conflicts can occur anywhere, and carry dire consequences for a system's stability.

# INTERRUPTS

An *interrupt* is probably the most well known and understood type of resource. Interrupts are logical signals used to demand attention from the CPU. This allows a device or subsystem to work in the background until a particular event occurs that requires system processing. Such an event may include receiving a character at the serial port, striking a key on the keyboard, or any number of other real-world situations. An interrupt is invoked by asserting a logic level on one of the physical *interrupt request* (or IRQ) lines accessible through any of the motherboard's expansion bus slots. PCs provide 16 IRQ lines (noted IRQ 0 to IRQ 15). Table 11-1 illustrates the common IRQ assignments for current computer systems. These signal lines run from pins on the expansion bus connector to programmable interrupt controllers (PICs) on the motherboard (today, PICs are normally integrated into the motherboard's chipset). The output signals generated by a PIC trigger the CPU interrupt. Keep in mind that Table 11-1 covers hardware interrupts only. A proliferation of processor- and software-generated interrupts also exists.

The use of IRQ 2 in an AT system deserves a bit of explanation. An AT uses IRQ 2 right on the motherboard, which means the expansion bus pin for IRQ 2 is now empty. Instead of leaving this pin unused, IRQ 9 from the AT extended slot is wired to the pin previously occupied by IRQ 2. In other words, IRQ 9 is being *redirected* to IRQ 2. Any AT expansion device set to use IRQ 2 is actually using IRQ 9. Of course, the vector interrupt table is adjusted to compensate for this sleight of hand.

After an interrupt is triggered, an interrupt handling routine saves the current CPU register states to a small area of memory (called the *stack*), and then directs the CPU to the *interrupt vector table,* a list of program

| TABLE 11-1 | IRQ ASSIGNMENTS FOR A TYPICAL PC |
|---|---|
| **IRQ** | **FUNCTION** |
| NMI | (Non-Maskable Interrupt) I/O channel check |
| 0 | (Reserved) Interval/system timer |
| 1 | (Reserved) Keyboard buffer full |
| 2 | (Reserved) Cascade interrupt from slave PIC—see IRQ9 |
| 3 | Serial port 2 (COM2: 2F8h-2FFh and COM4: 2E8h-2EFh) |
| 4 | Serial port 1 (COM1: 3F8h-3FFh and COM3: 3E8h-3EFh) |
| 5 | Parallel port 2 (LPT2: 378h or 278h): often used for integrated audio device |
| 6 | Floppy disk controller |
| 7 | Parallel Port 1 (LPT1: 378h [color] or 3BCh [mono]) |
| 8 | Real-time clock (RTC) chip |
| 9 | Unused (redirected to IRQ 2) |
| 10 | USB controller (on systems so equipped—can be disabled) |
| 11 | Available for expansion—often used for Windows sound system when so equipped (can be disabled) |
| 12 | Available for expansion—often used for motherboard mouse port (a.k.a. PS/2 mouse port) |
| 13 | (Reserved) Math coprocessor |
| 14 | Primary AT/IDE hard disk controller |
| 15 | Secondary AT/IDE hard disk controller (on systems so equipped—can be disabled) |

locations in memory that correspond to each interrupt. When an interrupt occurs, the CPU will jump to the *interrupt handler* routine at the location in memory specified in the interrupt vector table and execute the routine. In most cases, the interrupt handler is a device driver associated with the board generating the interrupt. For example, an IRQ from a network card will likely call a network device driver to operate the card. For a hard disk controller, an IRQ calls the BIOS ROM code that operates the drive. When the handling routine is finished, the CPU's original register contents are "popped" from the stack, and the CPU picks up from where it left off without interruption.

As a technician, it is not vital that you understand precisely how interrupts are initialized and enabled, but you should know the basic terminology. The term *assigned* simply means that a device is set to produce a particular IRQ signal. For example, a typical hard drive controller board is assigned to IRQ 14 (primary controller) and IRQ 15 (secondary controller). Assignments are usually made with one or more jumpers or DIP switches, or are configured automatically through the use of Plug-and-Play (PnP) and/or the CMOS Setup. Next, interrupts can be selectively enabled or disabled under software control. An *enabled* interrupt is an interrupt where the programmable interrupt controller (PIC) has been programmed to pass on an IRQ to the CPU. Just because an interrupt is enabled does not mean that there are any devices assigned to it. Finally, an *active* interrupt is a line where real IRQs are being generated. Note that "active" does not mean assigned or enabled.

Interrupts are an effective and reliable means of signaling the CPU, but the conventional ISA bus architecture—used in virtually all but the current generation of PCs—does not provide a means of determining which slot contains the board that called the interrupt. As a result, multiple devices cannot share interrupts. In other words, no two devices can be actively generating interrupt requests on the same IRQ line at the same time. If more than one device is assigned to the same interrupt line, a hardware conflict can occur. In most circumstances, a conflict may prevent the newly installed board (or other previously installed boards) from working. In some cases, a hardware conflict can hang up the entire system. As you will see later in the chapter, IRQ steering is one established means of extending the use of interrupts in PCI bus slots, but non-PCI devices cannot share interrupts.

## DMA CHANNELS

The CPU is very adept at moving data. It can transfer data between memory locations, I/O locations, or from memory to I/O and back with equal ease. However, PC designers realized that transferring large amounts of data (one word at a time) through the CPU is a hideous waste of CPU time. After all, the CPU really isn't *processing* anything during a data move—it's just shuttling data from one place to another. If there were a way to "off-load" such redundant tasks from the CPU, data could be moved more efficiently than would be possible with CPU intervention. *Direct Memory Access* (DMA) is a technique designed to move large amounts of data from memory to an I/O location, or vice versa, without the direct intervention by the CPU. In theory, the DMA controller chip acts as a stand-alone "data processor," leaving the CPU free to handle other tasks.

 Traditional DMA transfers are not very popular. This is why so few devices rely on them. However, today's IDE drive controllers use a high-speed type of DMA data transfer called Ultra-DMA. These transfers can support burst data transfers as high as 100 or 133 MB/s.

A traditional DMA transfer starts with a DMA Request (DRQ) signal generated by the requesting device (such as the floppy disk controller board). If the channel has been previously enabled through software drivers or BIOS routines, the request will reach the corresponding DMA controller chip on the motherboard. The DMA controller will then send a HOLD request to the CPU, which responds with a Hold

Acknowledge (HLDA) signal. When the DMA controller receives the HLDA signal, it instructs the bus controller to effectively disconnect the CPU from the expansion bus and allow the DMA controller chip to take control of the bus itself. The DMA controller sends a DMA Acknowledge (DACK) signal to the requesting device, and the transfer process may begin. Up to 64KB can be moved during a single DMA transfer. After the transfer is done, the DMA controller will reconnect the CPU and drop its HOLD request—the CPU then continues with whatever it was doing without interruption. This process is simply repeated for subsequent blocks of data. Table 11-2 illustrates the use of DMA channels for current computer systems.

As with interrupts, a DMA channel is selected by setting a physical jumper or DIP switch on the particular expansion board (or assigned automatically through the use of PnP). When the board is installed in an expansion slot, the channel setting establishes a connection between the board and DMA controller chip. In older real-mode operation, accompanying software drivers often used a command-line switch that points to the corresponding hardware DMA assignment. Also, DMA channels cannot be shared between two or more devices. Although DMA sharing is possible in theory, it is extremely difficult to implement in actual practice. If more than one device attempts to use the same DMA channel at the same time, a conflict will result.

## I/O ASSIGNMENTS

Computers provide space for 1,024 I/O (input/output) ports. An I/O port acts very much like a memory address, but it's not for storage. Instead, an I/O port provides the means for a PC to communicate directly with a device—allowing the PC to efficiently pass commands and data between the system and various expansion devices. Each device must be assigned to a unique address (or address range). Table 11-3 lists the typical I/O port assignments for a recent Intel D850GB Pentium 4-based motherboard.

I/O assignments are generally made manually by setting jumpers or DIP switches on the expansion device itself (or automatically through the use of PnP). As with other system resources, it is vitally important that no two devices use the same I/O port(s) at the same time. If one or more I/O addresses overlap, a hardware conflict will result. Commands or data meant for one device may be erroneously interpreted by another. Keep in mind that while many expansion devices can be set at a variety of addresses, some devices cannot, and devices that use a range of addresses should not, overlap with the addresses (or ranges) used by other devices.

| **TABLE 11-2** | **DMA ASSIGNMENTS FOR A TYPICAL PC** | |
|---|---|---|
| **DMA** | **TRADITIONAL FUNCTION** | **CURRENT FUNCTION(S)** |
| 0 | Dynamic RAM refresh | Audio system |
| 1 | Unused | Audio system or parallel port |
| 2 | Floppy disk controller | Floppy disk controller |
| 3 | Unused | ECP parallel port or audio system |
| 4 | Reserved (used internally) | (Reserved) DMA controller |
| 5 | Unused | Unused |
| 6 | Unused | Unused |
| 7 | Unused | Unused |

**TABLE 11-3**   I/O ASSIGNMENTS FOR AN INTEL D850GB PENTIUM 4 MOTHERBOARD

| ADDRESS (HEX) | SIZE | DESCRIPTION |
|---|---|---|
| 0000-000F | 16 bytes | DMA controller |
| 0020-0021 | 2 bytes | Programmable interrupt control (PIC) |
| 0040-0043 | 4 bytes | System timer |
| 0060 | 1 byte | Keyboard controller byte/reset IRQ |
| 0061 | 1 byte | System speaker |
| 0064 | 1 byte | Keyboard controller, CMD/STAT byte |
| 0070-0071 | 2 bytes | System CMOS/real-time clock (RTC) |
| 0072-0073 | 2 bytes | System CMOS |
| 0080-008F | 16 bytes | DMA controller |
| 0092 | 1 byte | Fast A20 and PIC |
| 00A0-00A1 | 2 bytes | PIC |
| 00B2-00B3 | 2 bytes | APM control |
| 00C0-00DF | 32 bytes | DMA |
| 00F0 | 1 byte | Numeric data processor |
| 0170-0177 | 8 bytes | Secondary IDE channel |
| 01F0-01F7 | 8 bytes | Primary IDE channel |
| 0220-022F or 0240-024F | 16 bytes | Audio (Sound Blaster Pro–compatible) |
| 0228-022F | 8 bytes | LPT3 |
| 0278-027F | 8 bytes | LPT2 |
| 02E8-02EF | 8 bytes | COM4 or video (8514A) |
| 02F8-02FF | 8 bytes | COM2 |
| 0376 | 1 byte | Secondary IDE channel command port |
| 0377 | 1 byte | Secondary IDE channel status port |
| 0378-037F | 8 bytes | LPT1 |
| 03B0-03BB | 12 bytes | Intel 82850 memory controller hub (MCH) |
| 03C0-03DF | 32 bytes | Intel 82850 MCH |
| 03E8-03EF | 8 bytes | COM3 |
| 03F0-03F5 | 6 bytes | Diskette channel 1 |
| 03F6 | 1 byte | Primary IDE channel command port |
| 03F8-03FF | 8 bytes | COM1 |
| 04D0-04D1 | 2 bytes | Edge/level-triggered PIC |
| LPTn + 400 | 8 bytes | ECP port, LPTn base address + 400h |
| 0CF8-0CFB | 4 bytes | PCI configuration address register |
| 0CF9 | 1 byte | Turbo and reset control register |
| 0CFC-0CFF | 4 bytes | PCI configuration data register |
| FFA0-FFA7 | 8 bytes | Primary bus master IDE registers |
| FFA8-FFAF | 8 bytes | Secondary bus master IDE registers |
| Relocatable | 96 bytes | I/O controller hub—ICH2 (ACPI + TCO) |
| Relocatable | 64 bytes | D850GB (particular motherboard) board resource |

| ADDRESS (HEX) | SIZE | DESCRIPTION |
|---|---|---|
| | | **TABLE 11-3   I/O ASSIGNMENTS FOR AN INTEL D850GB PENTIUM 4 MOTHERBOARD (CONTINUED)** |
| Relocatable | 64 bytes | Onboard audio controller |
| Relocatable | 32 bytes | I/O controller hub—ICH2 (USB controller #1) |
| Relocatable | 16 bytes | I/O controller hub—ICH2 (SMBus) |
| Relocatable | 4096 bytes | Intel 82801BA PCI bridge |
| Relocatable | 256 bytes | I/O controller hub—ICH2 Audio Mixer |
| Relocatable | 64 bytes | I/O controller hub—ICH2 Audio Bus Mixer |
| Relocatable | 256 bytes | I/O controller hub—ICH2 Modem Mixer |
| Relocatable | 32 bytes | I/O controller hub—ICH2 (USB controller #2) |
| Relocatable | 96 bytes | LPC47M102 chip |

## MEMORY ASSIGNMENTS

Memory is another vital resource for the PC. While early devices relied on the assignment of IRQ, DMA channels, and I/O ports, most current devices (such as SCSI controllers, network cards, video boards, modems, and so on) demand memory space for the support of each device's onboard BIOS ROM (their "firmware"). As with I/O space, no two ROMs can overlap in their addresses—otherwise, a conflict will occur. Table 11-4 lists a memory map for an Intel D850GB Pentium 4 motherboard.

## THE ROLE OF PLUG-AND-PLAY (PNP)

Traditional PCs used devices that required manual configuration—each IRQ, DMA, I/O port, and memory address space had to be specifically set through jumpers on the particular device. If you accidentally configured two or more devices to use the same resource, a conflict would result. This would require you to isolate the offending device(s), identify available resources, and reconfigure the offending device(s) manually. Taken together, this was often a cumbersome and time-consuming process.

| ADDRESS RANGE (DECIMAL) | ADDRESS RANGE (HEX) | SIZE | DESCRIPTION |
|---|---|---|---|
| | | | **TABLE 11-4   MEMORY ASSIGNMENTS FOR AN INTEL D850GB PENTIUM 4 MOTHERBOARD** |
| 1024KB–2,097,152KB | 100000–7FFFFFFF | 2047MB | Extended memory |
| 960KB–1024KB | F0000–FFFFF | 64KB | Runtime BIOS |
| 896KB–960KB | E0000–EFFFF | 64KB | Reserved |
| 800KB–896KB | C8000–DFFFF | 96KB | Available high-DOS memory (open to the PCI bus) |
| 640KB–800KB | A0000–C7FFF | 160KB | Video memory and BIOS |
| 639KB–640KB | 9FC00–9FFFF | 1KB | Extended BIOS data (movable by memory manager software) |
| 512KB–639KB | 80000–9FBFF | 127KB | Extended conventional memory |
| 0KB–512KB | 00000–7FFFF | 512KB | Conventional memory |

In the early 1990s, PC designers realized that it was possible to automate the process of resource allocation each time the system initializes. This way, a device need only be installed, and the system handles its configuration and assigns available resources without the assistance or intervention of the installer. This concept became known as Plug-and-Play (PnP), and has long been standard in the PC arena. PnP systems require three elements in order to function:

- PnP-compliant devices (such as video boards, modems, drive controllers, and so on)
- PnP-compliant BIOS (now used in all Pentium-class systems)
- PnP-compliant operating systems (like Windows 95/98/Me/XP)

When the PnP system works properly, a PnP device can be installed in an available expansion slot on a PnP-supported motherboard (with a PnP BIOS). When Windows 9*x*/Me/XP starts, it recognizes the new PnP device, assigns resources, and then attempts to install the proper protected-mode driver (which could be installed from a manufacturer's floppy disk or the device's installation CD). Thereafter, the system "remembers" the new device, and reconfigures it each time the system starts. Ideally, if the PnP device is ever removed, Windows will automatically clear the device from its "system" and free the resources for other devices.

However, if any of these elements are missing, devices will not be "autoconfigured." For example, PnP won't work under DOS (though there are DOS PnP drivers that can be used to initialize PnP devices). Older, jumper-configured devices (called *legacy devices*) also won't support PnP, and resources need to be reserved for legacy devices to prevent the PnP system from ignoring them entirely.

PnP "autoconfiguration" information is stored in the Extended System Configuration Data (ESCD) area, and is cleared when the CMOS RAM is cleared or lost.

## CHECKING RESOURCE ASSIGNMENTS

Whether you're fixing a system problem, or just learning how your system is configured, you may need to identify any resources assigned to each device in the PC. In the early days of computing, identifying resources meant dragging out tedious manuals and checking each jumper setting by hand. Today, Windows provides convenient system tools that allow you to check resource assignments in a matter of moments using Device Manager. To open Device Manager under Windows 9*x*/Me, click Start, highlight Settings, and then click Control Panel. When Control Panel opens, double-click the System icon, and then select the Device Manager tab in the System Properties dialog box. Under Windows XP, click Start | Control Panel | Performance and Maintenance | System, select the Hardware tab, and then click the Device Manager button. A device tree will open, as shown in Figure 11-1. Devices that are conflicting, disabled, or unidentified will be marked accordingly, so you can locate potential trouble spots quickly.

This Device Manager lists all the devices that Windows "sees" in the system, and any device problems normally appear here as well. To see a summary of the system resource assignments under Windows 9*x*/Me, select the Computer entry at the top of the device tree, and then click the Properties button. The Computer Properties dialog box will appear. Click the View Resources tab (if it's not already selected). By default, the Interrupt Request (IRQ) radio button is selected, and you can scroll down the list to see what IRQ is assigned to which device.

The Windows XP Device Manager is a bit more versatile: simply click View in the menu bar, select Resources By Type, and then expand the type of resource you want to review (I/O, DMA, IRQ, memory), as in Figure 11-2. For example, you can see that the standard IRQ 9 is assigned to an "MPU-401 Compatible MIDI Device." Note that this IRQ is marked "ISA" because it is a traditional (non-shared) IRQ—there

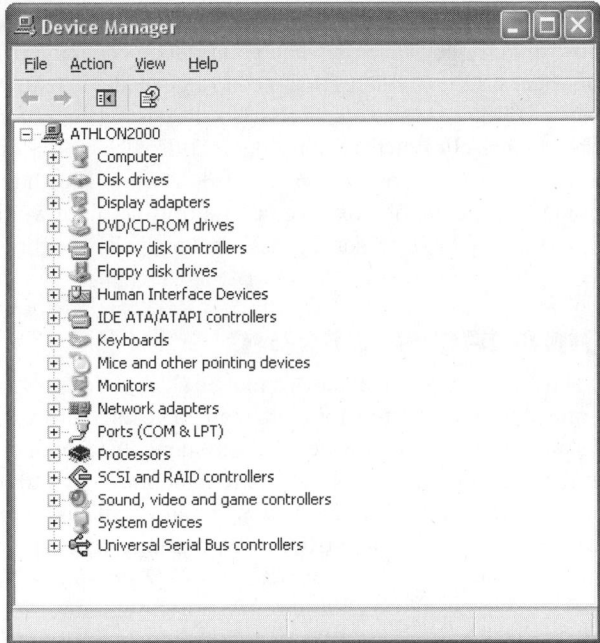

**FIGURE  11-1**    Checking installed devices through the Windows XP Device Manager

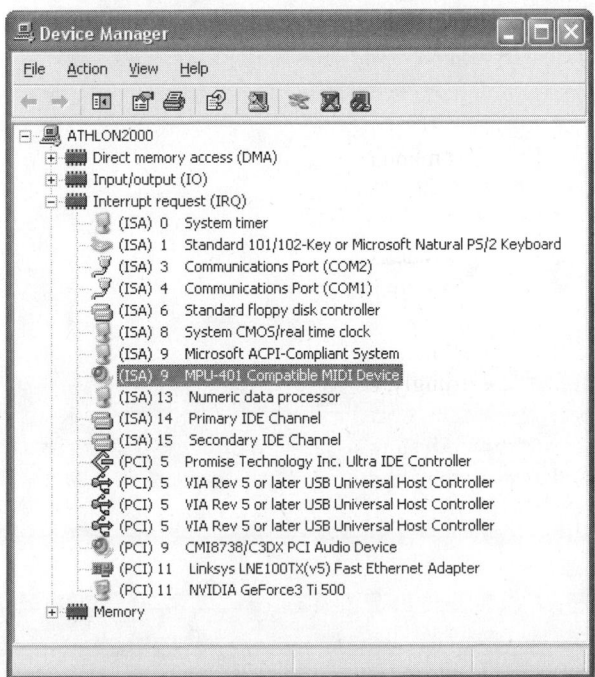

**FIGURE  11-2**    Checking Windows XP resource assignments through the Device Manager dialog box

are no ISA slots in this particular system. You can also expand the other resource types to view their detailed assignments. Close the Device Manager when you're done checking resources.

Alternatively, you can check all the resources assigned to a given device. In Device Manager, expand the device category (for example, Display Adapters), right-click the desired device, and click Properties in the drop-down menu (or simply double-click on the desired device). The Properties dialog box for that device will appear. Select the Resources tab, as shown in Figure 11-3. You will see all the resources assigned to that device listed in the middle of the dialog box—you can simply scroll down the list to see additional resources. You may also be able to alter any resources assigned to the device through this dialog box, but just click Cancel for now.

## UNDERSTANDING IRQ STEERING

The one overriding issue about resources is that they cannot be shared—otherwise, a conflict may occur. This has been a cardinal rule of troubleshooters for more than 20 years. However, modern PCs use many different devices, and this proliferation of hardware places tremendous demands on very limited system resources (most notably IRQs). If it were possible for more than one device to use the same IRQ, a PC could support a larger number of expansion devices. Although traditional bus architectures (like ISA) cannot handle IRQ sharing, the PCI bus does allow IRQs to be dynamically assigned to PCI devices. This technique of dynamic IRQ assignment is known as *PCI bus IRQ steering.* IRQ steering is supported through Windows 95 OSR2, Windows 98/SE, Windows Me, and Windows XP. Keep in mind that the retail releases of Windows 95 and Windows 95 OSR1 do *not* provide support for PCI bus IRQ steering.

**FIGURE 11-3**     Checking the Windows XP resources assigned to a specific device

## Assigning IRQs to PCI Devices

PCI bus IRQ steering gives Windows 9x/Me/XP the flexibility to dynamically reassign PCI interrupts when reconfiguring PnP PCI and ISA resources around non-PnP ISA devices. This gives Windows a very powerful tool that can automatically resolve many possible IRQ conflicts without direct intervention on the part of the user (or technician). If PCI bus IRQ steering is *disabled* in Windows, the BIOS assigns IRQs to PCI devices. But if PCI bus IRQ steering is *enabled,* Windows will assign IRQs to PCI devices (overriding any BIOS assignments).

When your Windows 9x/Me system supports PCI bus IRQ steering, you will notice numerous *IRQ holders* when you view IRQ assignments (such as "ACPI IRQ Holder for PCI IRQ Steering" shown in Figure 11-4). IRQ Holder for PCI IRQ Steering indicates that an IRQ has been programmed to PCI mode and is unavailable for ISA devices, even if no PCI devices are currently using the IRQ. However, you will note that Windows XP (as in Figure 11-2 earlier) does not list IRQ holders; it merely indicates IRQs that are being used/shared with the PCI bus.

## Managing IRQ Steering Under Windows 9x/Me

As a rule, you should expect PCI bus IRQ steering to be enabled on virtually every modern PC. While Windows XP handles PCI IRQ sharing automatically, you can usually verify that IRQ steering is enabled on Windows 9x/Me platforms by checking the IRQ assignments (as in Figure 11-4). If one or more entries are marked as IRQ Holders, chances are that IRQ steering is enabled. Still, you can verify IRQ steering support using the following steps:

1. Click Start, highlight Settings, click Control Panel, and then double-click the System icon.

2. Click the Device Manager tab.

3. Expand the System Devices entry (near the bottom of the device tree).

4. Locate and double-click the PCI Bus entry, and then click the IRQ Steering tab (see Figure 11-5). You should see either IRQ Steering Enabled or IRQ Steering Disabled in the IRQ Routing Status area.

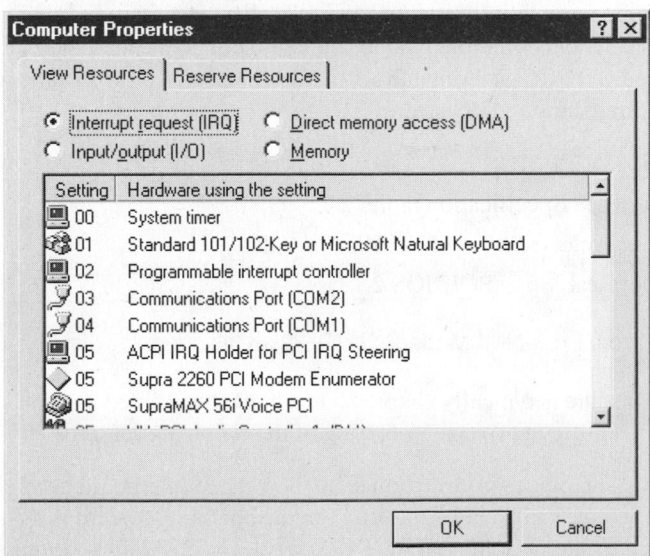

**FIGURE  11-4**    IRQ holders are used to facilitate IRQ steering on PCI-based platforms.

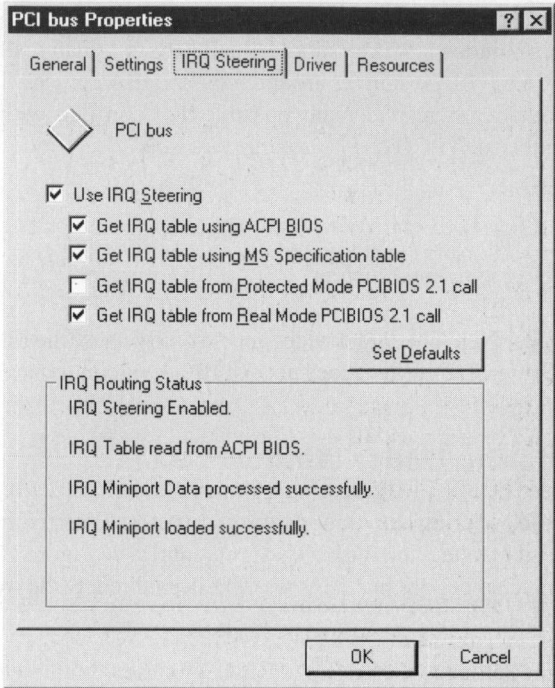

**FIGURE 11-5**    Checking the status of your system's IRQ steering support

PCI bus IRQ steering is disabled by default in Windows 95 OSR2.

Windows needs routing table information to support IRQ steering, and there are several potential sources available to the system. Only one viable source is actually needed, but you will frequently find several sources selected. The IRQ Steering tab settings (in Figure 11-5) determine which routing table(s) Windows uses when programming IRQ steering:

- Get IRQ table using ACPI BIOS
- Get IRQ table using MS Specification table
- Get IRQ table from Protected Mode PCIBIOS 2.1 call
- Get IRQ table from Real Mode PCIBIOS 2.1 call

The Get IRQ Table From Protected Mode PCIBIOS 2.1 Call check box is *not* selected by default.

The IRQ Steering feature is typically enabled (and *should* be enabled for best system performance), but may appear disabled in Device Manager for any of the following reasons:

- The IRQ routing table provides information about how the motherboard is configured for PCI IRQs, but the IRQ routing table provided by the BIOS to the operating system is missing or incorrect. Try selecting an alternate source for the routing table (see the routing table options earlier). Otherwise, a BIOS upgrade may be needed to correct the trouble.

- The Use IRQ Steering check box is not selected. Simply check the box to enable IRQ steering, and select one or more viable sources for the IRQ routing table.

- The Get IRQ Table From Protected Mode PCIBIOS 2.1 Call check box is not selected. While this option is normally deselected by default, check this box to enable the feature.

- Your computer's BIOS does not support PCI bus IRQ steering (though this usually occurs with old PCs). Check with the BIOS or system manufacturer for a suitable BIOS upgrade. If the system is old enough that no BIOS upgrade is available, it may be necessary to upgrade the motherboard outright.

You generally do not need to disable IRQ steering unless there is trouble with the PCI bus (or devices that are using the bus). Follow these steps to disable PCI bus IRQ steering under Windows 9*x*/Me if necessary. (This is not available under Windows XP.)

1. Click Start, highlight Settings, click Control Panel, and then double-click the System icon.
2. Click the Device Manager tab.
3. Expand the System Devices entry.
4. Double-click the PCI Bus entry, and then select the IRQ Steering tab.
5. Click the Use IRQ Steering check box to clear it, click OK, and then click OK again. Click Yes to restart your computer.

If you find that you need to disable IRQ steering, it may also be necessary to disable IRQ steering support in the CMOS Setup.

# Recognizing and Correcting Conflicts

Fortunately, conflicts are almost always the result of a PC upgrade gone awry. Thus, a technician can be alerted to the possibility of a system conflict by applying the *last upgrade* rule. The rule consists of three parts:

- A piece of hardware and/or software has been added to the system *very* recently.
- The trouble occurred *after* a piece of hardware and/or software was added to the system.
- The system was working fine *before* the hardware and/or software was added.

If all three of these common-sense conditions are true, chances are very good that you're faced with a hardware or software conflict (rather than a defective device) caused by the last piece of hardware or software added to the system. Unlike most other types of PC problems, which tend to be specific to the faulty subassembly, conflicts usually manifest themselves as much more general and perplexing problems. The following symptoms are typical of serious hardware or software conflicts:

- The system locks up during the POST or operating system initialization.
- The system locks up during a particular application (when a particular feature is used, or at any point in the application).
- The system locks up when a particular device (such as a TWAIN scanner) is used.
- The system locks up randomly or without warning regardless of the application or desktop state.
- The system may not crash, but the device that was added may not function (even though it seems properly configured). Devices that were in the system previously may still work correctly.

■   The system may not crash, but a device or application that was working previously no longer seems to function. The newly added device (and accompanying software) may or may not work properly.

What makes these problems so generic is that the severity and frequency of a fault (as well as the point at which the fault occurs) depend on several factors. These factors include the particular devices that are conflicting, the resource(s) that are conflicting among the devices (for example, IRQs, DMAs, or I/O addresses), and the function being performed by the PC when the conflict manifests itself. Since every PC is equipped and configured a bit differently, it is virtually impossible to predict a conflict's symptoms more precisely.

## CONFIRMING AND RESOLVING CONFLICTS

Recognizing the possibility of a conflict is one thing, but proving and correcting it is another issue entirely. However, there are some very effective tactics at your disposal. The first rule of conflict resolution is Last In First Out (or LIFO). The LIFO principle basically states that the fastest means of overcoming a conflict problem is to remove the hardware or software that resulted in the conflict. In other words, if you install board X and board Y ceases to function, board X is probably conflicting with the system, so removing board X should restore board Y to normal operation. The same concept holds true for software. If you add a new application to your system, and then find that an existing application fails to work properly, the new application is likely at fault. Unfortunately, removing the offending element is not enough. You still have to install the new device or software in such a way that it will no longer conflict in the system.

## DEALING WITH SOFTWARE CONFLICTS

There are two types of software that can cause conflicts in a typical PC: TSRs and device drivers. *TSRs* (sometimes called *popup utilities*) load into memory, usually during initialization, and wait until a system event (such as a modem ring or a keyboard "hot key" combination). There are no DOS or system rules that define how such utilities should be written. As a result, many tend to conflict with application programs (and even DOS itself). If you suspect that such a popup utility is causing the problem, find its reference in the AUTOEXEC.BAT file and disable it by placing the command REM in front of its command line, such as this:

```
REM C:\UTILS\NEWMENU.EXE /A:360 /D:3
```

The REM command turns the line into a "REMark," which can easily be removed later if you choose to restore the line. Remember to reboot the computer so that your changes will take effect.

TSRs are extremely rare today and are usually found on only the oldest systems. However, you should still take a moment to check for them, if for no other reason than to rule them out as a potential cause of problems.

Device drivers present another potential problem that is far more common. Most hardware upgrades require the addition of one or more device drivers. Such drivers are loaded with Windows, or are called from the CONFIG.SYS file during system initialization.  Real-mode drivers often use a series of command-line parameters to specify the system resources that are being used. This is often necessary to ensure that the driver operates its associated hardware properly. If the command-line options used for the device driver do not match the hardware settings (or overlap the settings of another device driver), system problems can result. If you suspect that a device driver is causing the problem, find its reference in the

CONFIG.SYS file and disable it by placing the command REM in front of its command line, such as in this example:

```
REM DEVICE = C:\DRIVERS\NEWDRIVE.SYS /A360 /I:5
```

The REM command turns the line into a "REMark," which can easily be removed later if you choose to restore the line. Remember that disabling the device driver in this fashion will prevent the associated hardware from working, but if the problem clears, you can work with the driver settings until the problem is resolved. Remember to reboot the computer so that your changes will take effect.

Device drivers under Windows are a bit more forgiving since you don't need to tweak specific command-line switches. However, such protected-mode drivers may still be buggy or defective, and this can result in device problems and system stability issues. In other cases, an incorrect driver version may fail to identify a device properly. Windows lets you check the device driver information through the Device Manager, and later Windows versions like Me/XP even allow you to update drivers on the fly, or roll back drivers to earlier versions (a handy tactic when routine driver updates go awry). To manage drivers under Windows XP, open the Device Manager, expand the device tree to locate the specific device (such as the display adapter), then right-click the device and select Properties. When the Properties dialog box opens, click the Driver tab (see Figure 11-6) to learn about the current device driver. From here, you can remove, update, or roll back the driver. Windows Me/XP also provides a System Restore feature that lets you return the system to a prior working state before the offending device was first installed. You may want to remove the offending device completely before using System Restore.

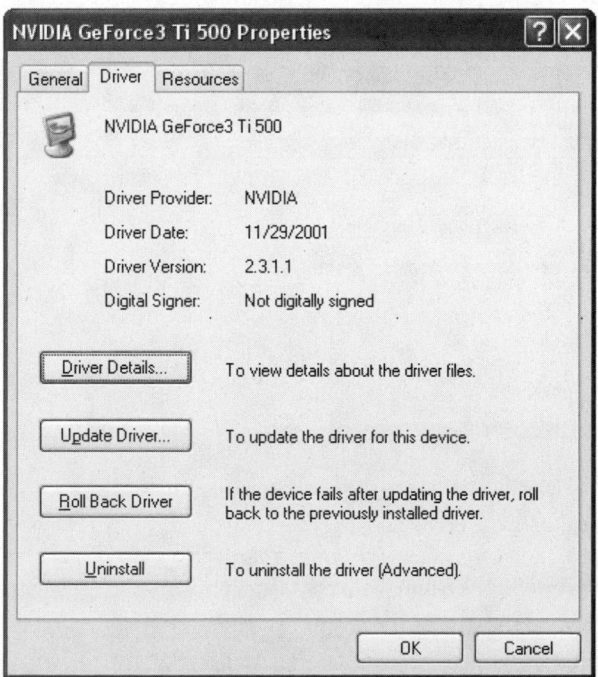

**FIGURE  11-6**    Windows XP allows you to update, remove, and roll back drivers.

Under Windows 98/SE/Me, you can use the Automatic Skip Driver (ASD) agent in your System Information utility to selectively prevent suspect drivers and other Windows components from loading at start time. (Windows XP does not provide an ASD agent.) With Windows XP, you can use the System Configuration utility (named "msconfig") to isolate potential problem software. Click Start | Run, type **msconfig**, and click OK. The msconfig dialog box will open (see Figure 11-7). You can opt to stop portions of the boot process, or use specific tabs to uncheck specific items on the system. For example, you can use the General tab and click the Selective Startup radio button, then uncheck the Process SYSTEM.INI File box. If you save those selections and reboot normally (that is, the problem seems to go away, even though certain devices may no longer work), you can return to msconfig, select the SYSTEM.INI tab, and work with specific settings until you find the culprit. Otherwise, you can recheck the Process SYSTEM.INI File on the General tab, uncheck the Process WIN.INI File box, and repeat the process of trial-and-error isolation until you find the general area of the problem.

Finally, consider the possibility that the offending software is buggy or defective. Try contacting the software manufacturer. There may be a fix or undocumented feature that you are unaware of. There may also be a patch or update that will solve the problem.

## DEALING WITH HARDWARE CONFLICTS

Consider an example of a hardware conflict: a PC user recently added a CD-ROM and adapter board to their system. The installation went flawlessly using the defaults—a ten-minute job. Several days later when attempting to back up the system, the user noticed that the parallel port tape backup did not respond (although the printer that had been connected to the parallel port was working fine). The user tried booting the system from a "clean" bootable floppy disk (no CONFIG.SYS or AUTOEXEC.BAT files to eliminate

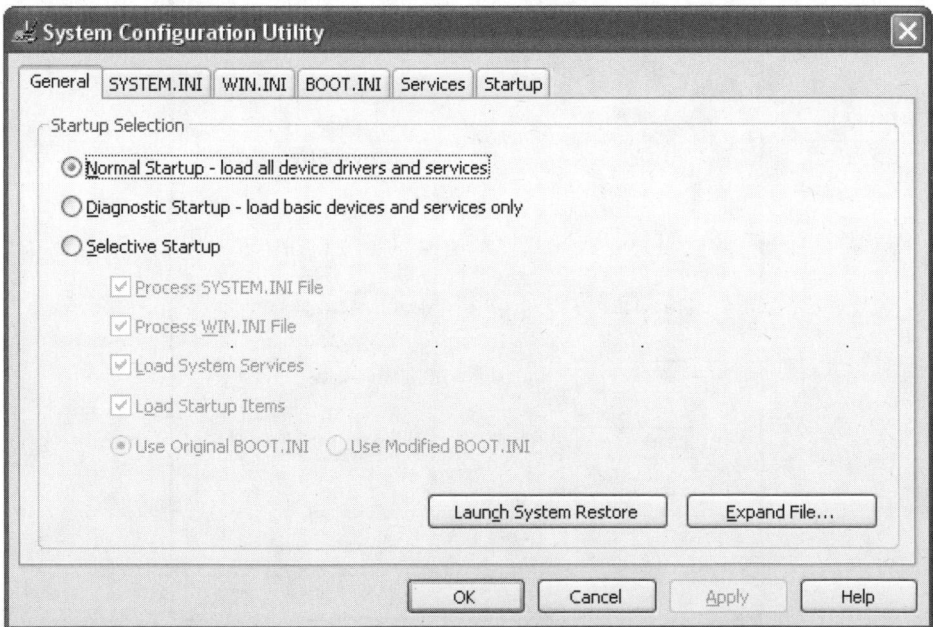

**FIGURE 11-7**    Windows XP provides you with the msconfig utility to help locate problem software at start time.

the device drivers), but the problem remained. After a bit of consideration, the user powered down the system, removed the CD-ROM adapter board, and booted the system from a "clean" bootable floppy disk. Sure enough, the parallel port tape backup started working again.

Stories such as this should remind technicians that hardware conflicts are not always the monstrous, system-smashing mistakes that they are made out to be. In many cases, conflicts have subtle, noncatastrophic consequences that may not appear for days (even weeks) after the conflict occurs. In our scenario above, since the CD-ROM was the last device to be added in the example, it was the first to be removed. It took about five minutes to realize and remove the problem. However, *removing* the problem is only part of conflict troubleshooting—reinstalling the device *without* a conflict is the real challenge.

Ideally, the way to correct a conflict would be to alter the conflicting setting. That's dynamite in theory, but another thing in practice. The trick is that you need to know what resources are in use and which ones are free. In the "old days" of DOS, you'd need to track down the user manual for every board in the system, inspect each board individually to find its settings, and then adjust the conflicting setting(s) accordingly. This approach worked, but it was cumbersome and time consuming. Today, real-mode operating systems like DOS have been abandoned in favor of protected-mode operating systems like Windows 9x/Me/XP. Since virtually all current PC hardware and OS software supports Plug-and-Play, you typically don't need to worry about setting resource assignments or resolving jumper-based problems. Windows avoids many potential conflicts for you, but you can still use the Device Manager to locate—and often correct—a wide range of device issues.

## Working with Device Manager

As you saw earlier in the chapter, determining resources is much easier under Windows 98/Me/XP using the Device Manager. When you open Device Manager under Windows 9x/Me, double-click the Computer entry at the top of the device list. The Computer Properties dialog box will open. Select the View Resources tab, and check the assignments for IRQs, DMA, I/O, or memory. Under Windows XP, simply click View in the menu bar, then select Resources By Type, and expand the type of resource you want to review (I/O, DMA, IRQ, or memory), as shown in Figure 11-2 earlier. By reviewing these entries, you can quickly determine which resources are assigned, and which (if any) are free. Device Manager is also a handy tool for identifying problem devices. Devices that are missing, disabled, conflicting, or operating in some unexpected fashion will be marked prominently in the device tree. Also, the problem device has one of the following symbols to indicate the type of problem:

 A problem code and detailed explanation of the problem is usually displayed for the offending device.

- A black exclamation point (!) on a yellow triangle indicates that the device is not behaving as expected (usually because of a conflict). Keep in mind that the suspect device may still be functioning (though other devices may be affected).

- A red *X* indicates a disabled device. A disabled device is hardware that is physically present in the computer (and has system resources assigned to it), but does not have a protected-mode driver loaded. Consequently, a disabled device will not function.

- A blue lowercase *i* on a white marker indicates that the Use Automatic Settings feature is not selected for that device, and that assigned resources were manually selected. Remember that this does not necessarily indicate a malfunctioning or disabled device.

- Under Windows Me/XP, a green question mark over a device means that a device-specific driver (a driver from the device manufacturer) for this device is not installed. Instead, a "compatible" driver is being used, and this may suggest the possibility that the device may not be fully functional (for example, a basic Hayes-compatible driver supporting a V.92 modem).

Keep in mind that some sound cards and display adapters do not report all of the resources they are using to Windows. Consequently, Device Manager may show only one device in conflict, or show no conflicts at all. You can quickly verify this issue by disabling the sound card or using the standard VGA (640 × 480 ×16) video driver to see if the "conflict" is resolved.

## Editing Device Resources

When you open the Properties dialog box for a device (such as shown previously in Figure 11-3), you'll see that the Resources tab may allow you to adjust the resource assignments that have been made for that device. If the device is conflicting with another device in the system, an error code and explanation of the problem will appear in the Conflicting Device List at the bottom of the dialog box. Note the Use Automatic Settings check box. If Windows successfully detects a device, this check box is selected, and the device should function correctly. However, if the resource settings are based on Basic Configuration $<n>$ (where $<n>$ is any number from 0 to 9), it may be necessary to change the configuration by selecting a different basic configuration from the list. If the particular configuration you want for the device is not listed as a basic configuration, it may be possible to click the Change Setting button to manually adjust the resource values. (If the Use Automatic Settings box is grayed out, you cannot change the device's resource assignments.) For example, to edit an Input/Output Range setting:

1. Click the Use Automatic Settings check box to clear it.
2. Click the Change Setting button.
3. Click the appropriate I/O range for the device.
4. Save your changes and reboot the system. Recheck the resources again to see that your changes have been accepted by the system.

To disable a device in the Windows 9x/Me Device Manager, open the Properties dialog for the device, select the General tab, and then clear the Original Configuration (Current) selection. Under Windows XP, select Do Not Use This Device (Disable) in the Device Usage drop-down menu.

## Device Manager Errors

When Windows detects a device problem, that error is typically presented in the device's Properties dialog box in the form of an error code (sometimes called a Device Manager Code). The major codes, their meanings, and suggested solutions are presented below for your reference. However, regardless of the particular code, corrective actions can usually be broken down into the following steps:

- ■ **Check device installation.** Make sure that the offending device is installed and cabled properly. If there are any jumpers on the device, verify that they are set properly.
- ■ **Update device drivers.** Download the latest drivers for the offending device and update the drivers through the Driver tab in the device's Properties dialog. In some cases, the new driver may be self-installing (which simplifies things a bit).
- ■ **Remove and reinstall.** You may need to remove the offending device through the Device Manager, then reboot the system and allow Windows to redetect and reinstall the device (using the latest drivers), or use the Add New Hardware wizard to oversee installation yourself.
- ■ **Reconfigure resources.** When conflicts persist, you may be able to reassign the conflicting resource(s) manually through the device's Resources tab.

■ *Free additional resources.* If there are no free resources, you may need to remove unneeded devices to free resources that can be reassigned to the offending device.

■ *Remove or upgrade.* If you're stuck, you may need to replace the offending device with a later version or a different make/model. Otherwise, you may simply not be able to use the offending device on your particular platform.

**Code 1**   "This device is not configured correctly. To update the drivers for this device, click Update Driver." This error code means the system has not had a chance (insufficient time) to configure the offending device, or attempts to configure the device have failed. Follow any instructions presented in the Device Status box to resolve the trouble. (Usually, updating the driver is an adequate solution, but you should also verify the device's installation.) You may also be able to resolve this problem by removing the device in Device Manager, and then run the Add New Hardware wizard to redetect and reinstall the device from scratch.

**Code 2**   You may see either of two different messages (depending on which device is failing), but this error code means that the device loader did not successfully load a device. When this device is a root device loader, the following message appears: "Windows could not load the driver for this device because the computer is reporting two <type> bus types." The <type> entry indicates a type of bus. In this case, you should check for an updated BIOS for your system's motherboard. When the device is not a root device loader, the following message appears: "The <type> device loader(s) for this device could not load the device driver." In this case, the <type> designation lists another system device. To fix this trouble, click the Update Driver button to update the offending device's driver. In addition, try removing the device from Device Manager and then running the Add New Hardware wizard to redetect the offending device from scratch.

**Code 3**   "The driver for this device may be bad, or your system may be running low on memory or other resources." It's important to verify that you have sufficient memory (RAM) and drive space for the devices and software on your particular system. To check your system's memory and system resources under Windows 9*x*/Me, right-click My Computer on your desktop, click Properties, and then click the Performance tab. Under Windows XP, use the System Information utility to check available memory and disk space. Click Start | All Programs | Accessories | System Tools | System Information (see Figure 11-8). If there are adequate resources, try clicking the Update Driver button and updating the offending device's driver(s). As an alternative, try using Device Manager to remove the device, and then run the Add New Hardware wizard to redetect and reinstall the device from scratch.

**Code 4**   "This device is not working properly because one of its drivers may be bad, or your Registry may be bad." This error code suggests that the INF file for this device may be incorrect, or the related Registry entries may be damaged. To update the drivers for this device, click the Update Driver button. If the problem persists, run **scanregw.exe** to check and fix your Registry. Under Windows XP, you may be able to correct Registry problems with System Restore. You can also use Device Manager to remove the device, and then run the Add New Hardware wizard to reinstall the device from scratch. If you still continue to receive this error, contact the hardware manufacturer for an updated INF file. If the problem cannot be resolved with a driver or INF file update, you may need a "clean" reinstall of Windows to correct the Registry.

**Code 5**   "The driver for this device requested a resource that Windows does not know how to handle." This error code indicates that there was a device failure due to the lack of an *arbitrator*—software that assigns and manages resources and use requests. If a device requests a resource without an arbitrator, you'll receive this error because resources could not be assigned to the device successfully. To fix this problem, update the device driver, or use Device Manager to remove the device, and then run the Add New Hardware wizard to redetect and reinstall the device from scratch.

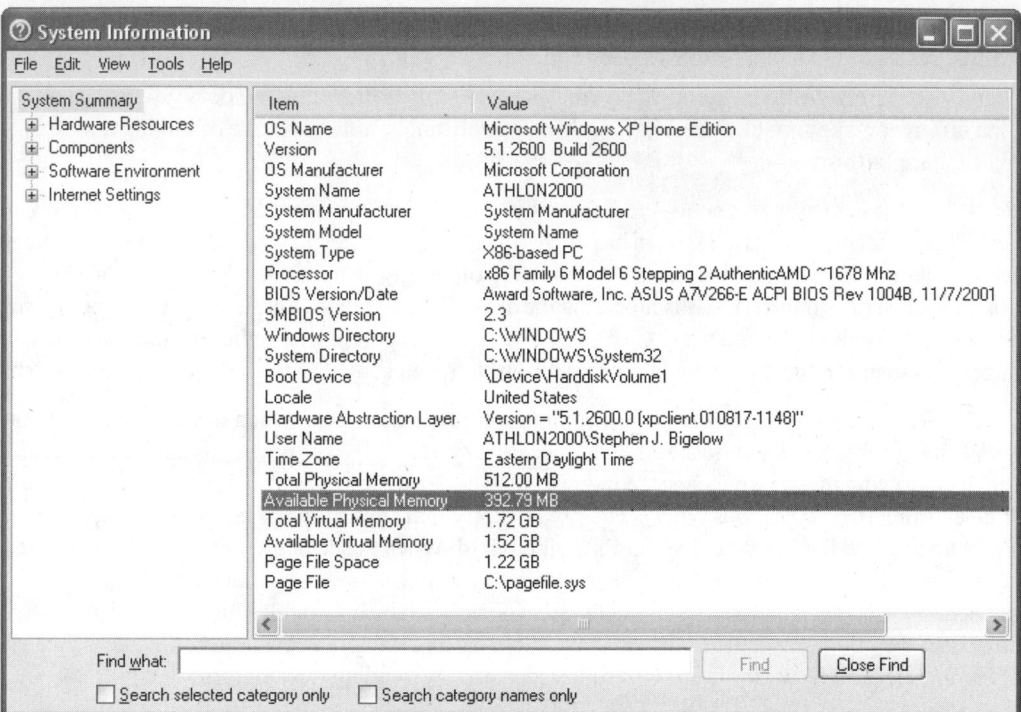

**FIGURE  11-8**    The Windows XP System Information utility can reveal a wealth of specific information about your system and its current status.

**Code 6**    "Another device is using the resources this device needs." This error code means that there's a conflict between two devices in the system. This is a straightforward conflict where two or more devices are using the same resource(s). To correct this issue, shut down your computer, and then adjust the resources for this device (if it must be adjusted manually). When you've finished, restart Device Manager and change the resource settings for the offending device accordingly. If you cannot change resources for the offending device, you may be able to adjust the resources for the device that it is conflicting with. Otherwise, remove the offending device from the system.

**Code 7**    "The drivers for this device need to be reinstalled." This error code means that the offending device cannot be configured properly, usually because the driver(s) are damaged, missing, or installed improperly. To reinstall the drivers for this device, click Reinstall Driver (or the Update Driver button under Windows XP) and install the latest versions of the device drivers downloaded from the manufacturer. If the device does not work correctly, use Device Manager to remove the device, and then run the Add New Hardware wizard to redetect and reinstall the device from scratch (see Figure 11-9). If you continue to receive this error code (and the device does not function properly), check with the hardware manufacturer for an updated driver. You may need to upgrade or replace the offending device.

**Code 8**    Several different error messages can be displayed for this error depending on the specific issue that is detected by the system. If the device loader for a device cannot be found, you should reinstall or update the driver through the Driver tab in the device's Properties dialog. Otherwise, use Device Manager to remove the device, and then run the Add New Hardware wizard to redetect and reinstall the offending

**FIGURE 11-9**    The Add New Hardware wizard allows new devices to be added to an existing PC, even when the system fails to detect the devices automatically.

device from scratch. If you continue to receive this error code, contact the hardware manufacturer for updated drivers. When the problem is specifically related to an issue in the system device loader, Windows should be reinstalled, because this issue is part of the operating system itself.

**Code 9**    The information in the Registry is incorrect or invalid for this device. If this is a BIOS- or ACPI-enumerated device, the following error appears: "This device is not working properly because the BIOS in your computer is reporting the resources for the device incorrectly." Check with the system or BIOS manufacturer to get an updated BIOS for your motherboard. If this is not a BIOS- or ACPI-enumerated device, the following error appears: "This device is not working properly because the BIOS in the device is reporting the resources for the device incorrectly." In some cases, you may be able to remove the offending device, then use the Add New Hardware wizard to reinstall the device from scratch. Otherwise, contact the device manufacturer to get an updated firmware version for your offending device. If the problem persists, you may need to remove the device from the system.

**Code 10**    "This device is either not present, not working properly, or does not have all the drivers installed." This is often a hardware installation problem; technicians frequently encounter this when upgrading a system. To resolve this problem, make sure the device is connected to the computer correctly. For example, make sure all cables are securely connected, and see that all adapter cards are properly installed. Try upgrading the driver(s) for the offending device, or remove the device and use the Add New Hardware wizard to redetect and reinstall the device from scratch.

**Code 11**    This error appears: "Windows stopped responding while attempting to start this device, and therefore will never attempt to start this device again." To work around this error under Windows 9x/Me, run the Automatic Skip Driver (ASD) utility from the System Information tool. (ASD is not available under Windows XP.) With Windows XP (or if the problem persists under Windows 9x/Me), contact the hardware manufacturer for updated drivers. It may be necessary to remove the offending device, its drivers, and any supporting applet software from the system; then reinstall the device from scratch using updated drivers and other software.

**Code 12**    "This device cannot find any free <IRQ/DMA/IO> resources to use." This error code means that one of the resource arbitrators failed, and resources cannot be assigned to a particular device. This usually occurs because the system does not have an available resource for the device (for example, all the interrupts are in use, or the device requests an interrupt that is currently used by another device). If you want to use the offending device, you must disable another device that is using the same resources. You may be able to do this by reassigning the other device's resources (through its Resources tab), or simply disable the other device outright. You can disable a device through the General tab of its Properties dialog. Remember that you won't be able to use any device(s) that are disabled, so overall system operation may be impaired.

**Code 13**    "This device is either not present, not working properly, or does not have all the drivers installed." This error code indicates that the device driver did not find its related hardware, usually due to a hardware failure. To have Windows try to detect the device again, click Detect Hardware. (Under Windows XP, simply scan for hardware changes.) Otherwise, use Device Manager to remove the device, and then run the Add New Hardware wizard to redetect and reinstall the device from scratch. If you still cannot detect the hardware, the device may be damaged or installed improperly. (Check the expansion card's installation, and verify that any cables are attached securely.)

**Code 14**    "This device cannot work properly until you restart your computer." In many cases, this error may be a temporary issue with one or more devices in the system. To resolve this error, shut down Windows, shut down your computer, wait several seconds, and then turn the system back on. If the problem persists, you may need to remove the device and allow Windows to redetect it, or use the Add New Hardware wizard to redetect and reinstall the device.

**Code 15**    "This device is causing a resource conflict." This straightforward error code means that one or more of the device's resources are conflicting with another device's resources, often caused by PnP/PCI re-enumeration. To resolve the conflict, use the conflict-resolution process outlined later in this chapter, or click Hardware Troubleshooter and follow the instructions presented in the wizard. In some cases, you may be able to remove the offending device and allow Windows to redetect and reinstall the device from scratch.

**Code 16**    "Windows could not identify all the resources this device uses." This error code means that the device was not fully detected at start time. When a device is not fully detected, all of its resources may not be reported to Windows. This may impair some (or all) of the device's features. To correct this error, use the Resources tab in the device's Properties dialog to manually enter the new resource settings. You may also be able to remove the device and allow Windows to redetect the device automatically.

**Code 17**    "The driver information file <filename> is telling this child device to use a resource that the parent device does not have or recognize." This error code occurs with a multiple-function device when the INF file for that device is not providing enough information to properly support the various "child" device(s). To fix this error, use Device Manager to remove the device, and then run the Add New Hardware wizard to redetect and reinstall the device from scratch. If this error code persists, check with the hardware's manufacturer about an updated INF file and drivers.

**Code 18**    "The drivers for this device need to be reinstalled." This error code means that an error has occurred in accessing the drivers for a device, and the device (and its drivers) needs to be reinstalled. In many cases, the drivers are damaged or installed improperly. To resolve this issue, reinstall the latest drivers for this device. If you cannot use the Update Drivers button, try removing the device from Device Manager, and then run the Add New Hardware wizard to redetect and reinstall the offending device.

**Code 19**    "Your registry may be bad." This code means that your Registry encountered a serious problem, usually because one or more entries are incorrect, or the Registry file itself is damaged. To resolve this problem, click Check Registry (which will run **scanreg.exe**). If this does not correct the issue, type **scanreg /restore** from a command prompt. Under Windows XP, you may be able to correct Registry problems with System Restore. Finally, remove the device from Device Manager, and then redetect it from scratch using the Add New Hardware wizard.

**Code 20**    "Windows could not load one of the drivers for this device." This error code means that the VxD Loader encountered a serious problem when attempting to load device drivers for a particular piece of hardware. Consequently, the device isn't operating properly (if at all). To correct this trouble, download the latest drivers from the manufacturer and click Update Driver to update the drivers for the offending device. If that doesn't work, try removing the device from Device Manager, and then run the Add New Hardware wizard to redetect and reinstall the device from scratch.

**Code 21**    "Windows is removing this device." This error code means that the device has a problem (usually with its power-on initialization process that is preventing Windows from accessing the device properly). However, this may be resolved by restarting your computer. To correct this trouble, shut down Windows and turn off your computer, wait several seconds, and then turn the system back on. If the problem persists, you may need to remove the device and allow Windows to redetect it from scratch.

**Code 22**    There are several possible errors that may be displayed depending on your particular system configuration and operating conditions. If the device is disabled because you disabled it using Device Manager, the following message appears: "This device is disabled." You may also encounter an error message such as: "This device is not started." These error codes mean that the device is either disabled or has not started. Simply click Enable Device or Start Device to reenable this device. If you cannot reenable the device, it may be damaged or installed improperly. Check the device installation, and replace the device if necessary.

If the device is disabled due to problems with a driver or program, the following message appears: "This device is disabled." However, you'll find that you can't enable this device here because it's been disabled by Windows itself. Try removing the device in Device Manager and then redetect it with the Add New Hardware wizard. If the problem persists, try booting to the Safe Mode to rule out software conflicts. Otherwise, the device may be damaged and require replacement.

**Code 23**    There are several possible error codes that may appear depending on your particular situation. If the following text appears: "This display adapter is functioning correctly. The problem is with the main display adapter", the device loader delayed the start of a device, and then did not inform Windows when it was ready to start the device. Verify the settings for the primary display adapter in Display Properties. Try removing the primary and secondary display adapters from Device Manager and then reboot to allow Windows to redetect and reinstall these devices. Also verify that the display drivers are current and installed properly.

If the offending device is not a display adapter, the error may appear such as: "The loaders for this device cannot load the required drivers." In most cases, updated device drivers will correct this type of problem. Download the latest drivers from the device manufacturer, and then click Update Driver. If that does not work, remove the device from Device Manager, and then redetect and reinstall the offending device using the Add New Hardware wizard.

**Code 24**    "This device is either not present, not working properly, or does not have all the drivers installed." The offending device was not successfully detected. Make sure the device is connected to your computer correctly. For example, verify that all cables are securely attached, or see that all expansion cards are properly seated. If the device is PnP, you may also try upgrading the drivers for this device. Otherwise, remove the device and allow Windows to redetect and reinstall the device (or use the Add New Hardware wizard).

**Code 25**    "Windows is in the process of setting up this device." This problem typically occurs only during the first and second boots after Windows Setup copies all the files to the host PC. So if this code appears, it is likely to be caused by an incomplete Windows installation. To complete the setup, click Restart Computer to reboot the system. If the reboot does not resolve the issue, you may need to reinstall Windows from scratch. If the problem persists, you should try removing or replacing the offending device and determine if the Windows Setup will finish normally. (Then try installing the device after Windows Setup has finished.)

**Code 26**    "Windows is in the process of setting up this device." This error means that a device did not load, usually due to a problem during Windows Setup. A driver may be damaged or missing, or the driver may have been improperly installed. Click Restart Computer to reboot the system, or restart the system through the Shut Down menu. Hopefully, Windows will detect the device upon restart. If this does not work, use Device Manager to remove the device, and then run the Add New Hardware wizard to redetect and reinstall the device from scratch. If problems persist, check with the hardware's manufacturer for an updated driver. If the problem persists, you may try removing or replacing the offending device and determine if the Windows Setup will finish normally. (Then try installing the device after Windows Setup has finished.)

**Code 27**    "Windows can't specify the resources for this device." This error indicates that one or more resource entries in the Registry are not valid, but the Registry itself is probably not damaged. You may be able to select an alternate configuration for the device. Select the Resources tab, and then modify the resource configuration used by the offending device. You might also use Device Manager to remove the device, and then run the Add New Hardware wizard to redetect and reinstall the device from scratch. If the device still does not work, check for updated drivers from the manufacturer.

**Code 28**    "The drivers for this device are not installed." This message means that the device was not installed completely (usually due to an error during installation). To reinstall the drivers for this device, click Reinstall Driver or Update Driver (under Windows XP). You may need to obtain updated drivers from the device manufacturer. You might also use Device Manager to remove the device, and then run the Add New Hardware wizard to redetect and reinstall the device from scratch.

**Code 29**    Windows 9x/Me may report this as: "This device is disabled because the BIOS for the device did not give it any resources." Windows XP may list this as: "This device is disabled because the firmware for the device did not give it a required resource." In either case, this error code means that the device has been disabled because it does not work properly under your version of Windows. This code may also occur if the device is disabled through the CMOS Setup (the BIOS). For example, this may occur if the CMOS backup battery fails and CMOS contents are lost. You may be able to fix this problem by enabling the device in the computer's CMOS Setup (which takes precedence over Windows). Otherwise, the offending device may be defective and need to be replaced outright.

**Code 30**    "This device is using an Interrupt Request (IRQ) resource that is in use by another device and cannot be shared. You must change the conflicting setting or remove the real-mode driver causing the conflict." This error message indicates that an assigned IRQ cannot be shared, usually due to a conflict between protected-mode and real-mode assignments. (Windows cannot change real-mode resource assignments.) For example, this error may occur when a PCI device is using an IRQ that is also referenced by a real-mode device driver in your startup files. Check for real-mode drivers (and disable any suspected real-mode drivers with the REM statement). Ideally, all real-mode drivers should be removed from your Windows 98/Me/XP platform.

**Code 31**    "This device is not working properly because <device> is not working properly." This error code occurs when one device relies upon another device for proper operation, and <device> is the dependent device that must be available in order for the offending device to work normally. Check the Properties for all offending devices, and follow all the recommended solutions offered by the error dialog box. In some cases, one of the devices may be conflicting or disabled, and it may be a simple matter to reconfigure or reenable the parent device. If the devices still do not work, remove both of the affected devices from Device Manager, and then use the Add New Hardware wizard to redetect and reinstall them. Also check with the hardware manufacturer(s) for updated device drivers.

**Code 32**    "Windows cannot install the drivers for this device because it cannot access the drive or network location that has the setup files on it." This error code indicates that the installation drive was not available to install the drivers (for example, the floppy drive, CD-ROM drive, or network connection is not available). This is usually a Windows Setup error that typically occurs during the first or second reboot after all the files are copied to the system. To correct this problem, click Restart Computer to reboot the system, or restart the system through the Shut Down menu. This should resume the Setup and allow you to correct possible problems. Otherwise, copy all the Setup files onto your hard drive, and run Setup from there. If the problem persists, you may be experiencing problems with the installation disk or CD drive, which you'll need to troubleshoot further.

**Code 33**    This code usually means that a device is not working. The exact message that is displayed for this error is specific to the particular driver or enumerator software. If the driver does *not* provide information as to why it failed, the following message appears: "This device isn't responding to its driver." If the driver provides more detailed failure information, the error message may be more specific. This error code typically is displayed when the hardware has failed (or has been installed improperly). Recheck the hardware installation, and replace the defective device if necessary.

## A Conflict Troubleshooting Process

One of the biggest problems with conflict troubleshooting is that every conflict situation is a bit different. Variations in PC equipment and available resources often reduce conflict troubleshooting to a "hit or miss" process. Fortunately, conflict troubleshooting can be accomplished quickly and easily by using the tools provided by Windows 98/Me/XP (namely, Device Manager). This part of the chapter provides a step-by-step process that you can use for conflict resolution under Windows 98/Me/XP. Keep in mind that there may be other ways of resolving the troubles listed here, but these steps are often a good starting point.

The steps described next should be read like a flowchart, and you'll find many references that will take you back and forth to various steps throughout this section.

**Step 1: Getting Started**    Begin troubleshooting by starting Device Manager. With Windows 98/Me, click Start | Settings | Control Panel. Double-click the System icon, and then click the Device Manager tab. (Make sure that the View Devices By Type option is selected.) With Windows XP, click Start | Control Panel | Performance and Maintenance | System. Select the Hardware tab and click the Device Manager button. The Device Manager dialog will appear (see Figure 11-1 earlier in the chapter). Any hardware suffering from conflicts or other problems should be shown in the device list, and marked with a yellow exclamation mark, red *X*, or other marking.

Check to see if the device was installed twice. Is the device you were installing (or that suffers from the conflict) listed twice in Device Manager?

- If the device is listed only once, go to Step 2.
- If the device is listed twice, and there's only supposed to be one such device in the system, go to Step 3.
- If the device is listed twice, but there are supposed to be two such devices in the system (two display adapters, for example), go to Step 2.

**Step 2: Device Listed Only Once**    If the offending device is listed only once, view the resource settings for that conflicting device:

1. Double-click the hardware that shows a conflict. Its Properties dialog box should open with the General tab selected.

2. Under Windows 98/Me, the Disable In This Hardware Profile box should be unchecked, and the Exists In All Hardware Profiles box may be checked. In Windows XP, see that the Use This Device (Enable) option is selected in the Device usage drop-down (see Figure 11-10).

3. Click the Resources tab.

Do you see a box with resource settings such as in Figure 11-11? Check to see if the Conflicting Device List has any entries that indicate a problem.

- If the box with resource settings appears, go to Step 4.
- If the Set Configuration Manually button appears instead (typically under Windows 9*x*/Me), go to Step 5.
- If the device doesn't have a Resources tab, go to Step 6.

**Step 3: Device Listed Twice**    The device was probably installed improperly. Remove *all* instances of the duplicated device(s), and install the device again:

1. Remove each duplicate item from the Device Manager's hardware list. Right-click the device, and then select Remove. (Select Uninstall under Windows XP.) When you are finished, no instances of the conflicting hardware should be listed.

2. Click OK.

3. Start the Add New Hardware wizard. If you see a message that you already have a wizard open, click Finish in that wizard, and then click the button in this step to start a new wizard. Under Windows XP, you can also use the Add New Hardware wizard, or you can simply select the Scan For Hardware Changes icon in the menu bar.

4. Click Next.

5. Click the option to automatically detect your hardware, and then click Next. Continue until you finish with the wizard. In some cases, you may need to select the device make/model manually.

**FIGURE  11-10**   Verify that the suspect device is enabled in the current hardware profile.

**FIGURE  11-11**   Check the Resources tab to look for resource assignments and device conflicts.

You may need to reboot the system. Did this fix the problem?

■ If the conflict no longer appears, this should correct the problem, and you should be done. Exit Control Panel and restart Windows (if necessary).

■ If the conflict still appears, go back to Step 2.

**Step 4: Resource Settings Appear**    You need to identify exactly which resources are causing the conflict. In the Conflicting Device List box on the Resources tab, identify the hardware that is using conflicting resources. Determine if more than one resource conflict is listed.

■ If more than one resource conflict is listed, go to Step 7.

■ If only one conflict is listed, go to Step 8.

■ If no conflicts are listed, or if one or more indications show System Reserved as the conflict, go to Step 9.

**Step 5: Manual Button Appears**    Determine why the resources are not displayed for the device. If the Resources tab shows a Set Configuration Manually button, then either the device has a conflict (or other problem) and is disabled or the resource settings used by this device are working properly but don't match any of the known configurations. Otherwise, you can tell which situation applies by reading the text above the button. Which text message do you see?

■ If you see a message that says "The device is conflicting, or the device is not currently enabled or has a problem," then go to Step 10.

■ If you see a message that says "The resource settings don't match any known configurations," there is no further solution to the problem. You should probably remove the conflicting device from the system. You may need to upgrade the offending device, or select an alternate make/model that will be more compatible with your particular PC platform.

**Step 6: No Resources Tab Appears**    You have probably chosen the wrong device in Device Manager. Select the correct device:

1. Click Cancel to return to the Device Manager hardware list.

2. Carefully double-click the hardware that has a conflict. The General tab should appear.

3. Under Windows 98/Me, the Disable In This Hardware Profile box should be unchecked, and the Exists In All Hardware Profiles box may be checked. In Windows XP, see that the Use This Device (Enable) option is selected in the Device usage drop-down (see Figure 11-10 earlier).

4. Click the Resources tab.

Do you see a box with resource settings now?

■ If the box with resource settings now appears, go back to Step 4.

■ If you see a Set Configuration Manually button, go back to Step 5.

■ If the resource settings still do not appear, there is no further solution to the problem. You should probably remove the conflicting device from the system. You may need to upgrade the offending device, or select an alternate make/model that will be more compatible with your particular PC platform.

**Step 7: More Than One Conflict Is Listed**    Often, only one device is listed with a conflict, but multiple devices may be listed. At this point, you should determine just how many devices are listed as being *conflicting*:

- If you only see one device causing all the conflicts, go to Step 11.
- If more than one device is causing the conflicts, go to Step 12.

**Step 8: Only One Conflict Is Listed**    Look for a resource setting that doesn't conflict:

1. In the Resource Setting box, double-click the icon next to the resource setting that is conflicting. If you see a message that says "You must clear the Use Automatic Settings box before you can change a resource setting," click OK to close the message, and then clear the Use Automatic Settings box. If the Use Automatic Settings box is grayed out, you cannot change resource settings for the device.
2. Scroll through the available resource settings.
3. For each setting, look at the Conflicting Device List box to see if the setting conflicts with any other hardware.
4. If you find a free setting, click OK to select the new resource for the device.

Did you find a setting that doesn't conflict with any other hardware?

- If you can find a setting that does not conflict, go to Step 13.
- If you cannot find a setting that does not conflict, go to Step 14.
- If you see a message stating that the resource setting cannot be modified (or the Use Automatic Settings box is grayed out), go to Step 15.

**Step 9: No Conflicts Are Listed**    If there are no conflicts listed in the Conflicting Device List box, either you are not viewing resources for the correct device or the conflict has already been resolved (you need to restart your computer to allow Windows to configure the hardware). Look at the top of the dialog box to see if you're viewing resources for the correct device. There is no further solution to this problem. If restarting Windows does not clear the problem, you may simply need to remove the conflicting device from the system. You may need to upgrade the offending device, or select an alternate make/model that will be more compatible with your particular PC platform.

**Step 10: The Device Is Conflicting**    Now you need to identify which hardware in the system is conflicting with your offending device. Click Set Configuration Manually. In Windows 98/Me/XP, clear the Use Automatic Settings box. In the Conflicting Device List box, identify the other hardware that is using the conflicting resources. Is more than one resource conflict listed?

- If more than one resource conflict is listed, go to Step 16.
- If only one resource conflict is listed, go to Step 17.
- If no conflicts are listed, go back to Step 9.

**Step 11: Only One Device Is Conflicting**    If only one device is causing the conflict(s), you may be able to disable the offending device (though you will lose its functionality). Do you want to disable the device that is causing all the conflicts?

- If you wish to disable the conflicting device, go to Step 18.
- If you must use the hardware that is causing the conflicts, go to Step 17.

**Step 12: More Than One Device Is Conflicting**    If more than one device is conflicting, check for resource settings that don't conflict. In most cases, you may only need to alter the resources of one conflicting device in order to clear the conflict:

1. In the Resource Setting box, double-click the icon next to a resource setting that is conflicting. If you see a message that says "You must clear the Use Automatic Settings box before you can change a resource setting," click OK to close the message, and then clear the Use Automatic Settings box.
2. Scroll through the available resource setting(s).
3. For each setting, look in the Conflicting Device List box to see if the setting conflicts with any other hardware.
4. When you find a free setting, click OK.
5. Repeat steps 1 through 4 for each conflicting resource.

Did you find a free setting for each conflicting resource?

- If you do find free settings for each conflicting resource, go to Step 19.
- If some (or all) resources are still conflicting, go to Step 20.
- If you see a message indicating that the resource setting cannot be modified, go to Step 15.

**Step 13: There Is a Free Setting**    When a free setting is available, you will need to change the configuration to resolve the conflict:

1. Enter the new setting value.
2. Make a note of the old and new settings for later reference. (This may be important for future reference.)
3. Click OK. If you see a message prompting you to restart your computer, click No.

Depending on the type of hardware you have, you may have to change the jumpers on your hardware card to match the new setting(s), or you may have to run a configuration utility provided by your hardware manufacturer. If the jumper settings on your card aren't set properly, your hardware will not work, even if you resolved the conflict correctly. Refer to your hardware documentation for instructions on changing jumpers.

4. Click OK.
5. You may see a message prompting you to restart your computer. Click No.
6. Click the Start button, click Shut Down, and then click OK. Under Windows XP, click Start | Turn Off Computer | Turn Off (see Figure 11-12).
7. Turn off your computer so you can configure the hardware devices that you've changed (if necessary). If you don't need to reset jumpers or make other hardware changes, you can simply restart the PC.

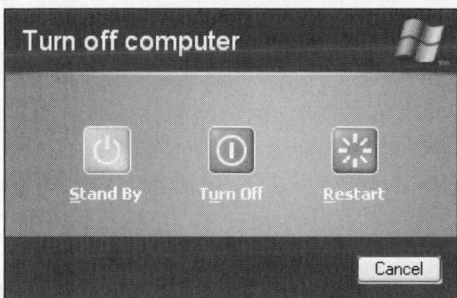

**FIGURE 11-12** Use the Turn Off button to shut down your Windows XP system, or use the Restart button to reboot.

This should correct the problem, and the hardware conflict should now be resolved once the PC is restarted.

**Step 14: All Other Settings Conflict** If multiple settings are conflicting, and you cannot resolve the conflict(s) by altering resources, you may need to remove hardware from the system in order to free resources that can be assigned to ease the conflict. Identify hardware you no longer need. Scroll through the available resource settings. When a conflict appears in the Conflicting Device List box, determine whether you still need to use the device that is causing the conflict. Can you identify a hardware device that you no longer need to use?

■ If you can disable the conflicting device, go to Step 21.

■ If you cannot disable the conflicting device, go to Step 22.

**Step 15: Resource Settings Cannot Be Modified** If you cannot modify resources for the offending device (the Use Automatic Settings box is grayed out), you may need to identify and adjust resources for the other device that is involved in the conflict. View the resources for the other device:

1. In the Conflicting Device List box, make a note of which device is using the resource that cannot be modified.

2. Click Cancel.

3. In the hardware list, find and double-click the device that is using the resource.

Does this device have a Resources tab?

■ If a Resources tab is available, go to Step 23.

■ If a Resources tab is not available, go to Step 24.

**Step 16: There Is More Than One Conflict** There are cases where multiple devices are involved in a conflict. This can complicate the reassignment of system resources. How many devices are listed as conflicting?

■ If only one device is causing the conflicts, go back to Step 11.

■ If more than one device is causing the conflicts, go back to Step 12.

**Step 17: There Is Only One Conflict**    If only one conflict is identified, you will need to reassign any conflicting resources. Look for a resource setting that doesn't conflict:

1. In the Resource Setting box, double-click the icon next to the resource setting that is conflicting. If you see a message that says "You must clear the Use Automatic Settings box before you can change a resource setting," click OK to close the message, and then clear the Use Automatic Settings box.

2. Scroll through the available resource settings.

3. For each setting, look in the Conflicting Device List box to see if the setting conflicts with any other hardware.

4. If you find a free setting, click OK.

Did you find a setting that doesn't conflict with any other hardware?

- If you manage to find a setting that does not conflict, go back to Step 13.

- If you see a message indicating that the resource setting cannot be modified, go back to Step 15.

- If all other settings conflict with other hardware, there is no further solution to the problem, and you should probably remove the conflicting device from the system. You may need to upgrade the offending device, or select an alternate make/model that will be more compatible with your particular PC platform.

**Step 18: Disable Conflicting Hardware**    In some cases, you may need to disable the conflicting device (at least temporarily) in order to resolve a conflict. Determine the best way to disable the conflicting hardware:

1. On the Device Manager hardware list, double-click the hardware that you want to disable.

2. Under Windows 98/Me, the Disable In This Hardware Profile box should be unchecked, and the Exists In All Hardware Profiles box may be checked. In Windows XP, see that the Use This Device (Enable) option is selected in the Device usage drop-down (see Figure 11-10 earlier).

3. Click the Resources tab. If there is a Set Configuration Manually button, Windows can disable and free up resources used by this hardware without your removing its card from your computer.

Do you see a Set Configuration Manually button?

- If the button exists, you can effectively disable the device, so go to Step 19.

- If the button is not available, go to Step 25.

**Step 19: Resources Now Set Without Conflicts**    Now be sure to document your changes. Print out a report for each device you changed:

1. In the Device Manager hardware list, click a device whose resource settings you changed while resolving the conflict. If you do not see the hardware list, click OK until you return to it.

2. Click Print. (In Windows XP, simply click the printer icon in the menu bar.)

3. Click the second option to print the selected class or device.

4. Click OK.

5. Repeat steps 1 through 4 for each device that you changed during this troubleshooting process.

This should correct the problem, and you should be done. Keep those printouts with the system documentation for future reference.

**Step 20: Some Resources Are Still Conflicting**     If you find that there are several conflicts across multiple devices, try setting resources to conflict with only one device:

1. Double-click a resource that is still conflicting. If you see a message that says "You must clear the Use Automatic Settings box before you can change a resource setting," click OK to close the message, and then clear the Use Automatic Settings box.

2. Scroll through the available resource settings. For each value, write down the setting and the name of the hardware it conflicts with. Then click Cancel.

3. Repeat steps 1 and 2 for each conflicting resource.

4. Looking at the list, see if you can change the resource settings so they conflict with only one device—preferably one you could disable.

Are all conflicts now with just one device?

■ If all the conflicts are with only one device, go back to Step 11.

■ If resources still conflict with more than one device, there is no further solution to the problem, and you should probably remove the conflicting device from the system. You may need to upgrade the offending device, or select an alternate make/model that will be more compatible with your particular PC platform.

**Step 21: Disable the Unneeded Device**     You may be able to free resources to resolve a conflict by disabling an unneeded device. Determine whether the hardware you want to disable is PnP:

1. Select each resource setting that conflicts with the hardware you will disable, and then click OK.

2. When the message appears saying the setting conflicts with another device, click Yes to continue.

3. Click OK until you return to the Device Manager hardware list.

4. Click the plus sign (+) next to the type of hardware that you want to disable.

5. Double-click the hardware that you want to disable.

6. Under Windows 98/Me, the Disable In This Hardware Profile box should be unchecked, and the Exists In All Hardware Profiles box may be checked. In Windows XP, see that the Use This Device (Enable) option is selected in the Device usage drop-down (see Figure 11-10 earlier).

7. Click the Resources tab.

8. If there is a Set Configuration Manually button, Windows can disable and free up resources used by this hardware without you having to remove its card from your computer.

Do you see a Set Configuration Manually button?

■ If the button exists, you can effectively disable the device, so go back to Step 19.

■ If the button is not available, go to Step 25.

**Step 22: All Devices Are In Use**     It may be possible to rearrange resources for the conflicting device(s). Start by recording a list of all devices using resources:

1. Scroll through the resource settings. On a piece of paper, write down the name of each piece of conflicting hardware and its setting.

2. Click Cancel until you return to the hardware list.

Rearrange resource settings for conflicting hardware:

1. On the Device Manager hardware list, click the plus sign (+) next to the hardware type for the first item on your written list.

2. Double-click the desired hardware entry.

3. Click the Resources tab.

4. Double-click the resource setting that you wrote down. If you see a message that says "You must clear the Use Automatic Settings box before you can change a resource setting," click OK to close the message, and then clear the Use Automatic Settings box.

5. Scroll through the available resource settings. For each setting, look in the Conflicting Device List box to see if it conflicts with any other hardware.

6. If you find a free setting other than the one you wrote down, write down the new values, and continue.

7. If you do not find a free setting, repeat steps 1 through 5 until you run out of hardware to try or you find a free setting.

Did you find a free resource setting?

■ If you found free resources, go to Step 26.

■ If you could not locate free resources, go to Step 27.

**Step 23: Resource Information Is Available**   If you're able to check the resources used by a device, check to see if the device can use a different resource:

1. Click the Resources tab.

2. In the Resource Setting box, double-click the resource setting that you need to free for the other device. If you see a message that says "You must clear the Use Automatic Settings box before you can change a resource setting," click OK to close the message, and then clear the Use Automatic Settings box.

3. Scroll through the available resource settings.

4. For each setting, look in the Conflicting Device List box to see if it conflicts with any other hardware.

5. If you find a free setting, click OK. If you see a message prompting you to restart your computer, click No.

Did you find a free resource setting?

■ If you found free resources, go to Step 28.

■ If you could not locate free resources (or the settings cannot be modified), go to Step 29.

**Step 24: Resource Information Is Not Available**   If you cannot access the device's resources, you may need to resolve the conflict by disabling one of the devices involved in the conflict. Decide which device you should disable. Because both devices need to use the same resource setting, you must decide which device you want to use. You must disable and/or remove the other device. It probably is easier to remove the device that had the original conflict. If you choose to remove the other device, you may see a message telling you that you still have a conflict after completing the procedure. Just restart the procedure and continue resolving the conflict. Which device would you like to disable?

- If you'd rather disable the original device, go to Step 30.
- If you'd rather disable the other conflicting device, go to Step 31.

**Step 25: Manual Button Not Available**     If you cannot configure the device manually, you may need to disable the conflicting hardware by removing it:

1. On the Device Manager hardware list, click the plus sign (+) next to the type of hardware that you want to disable. If you do not see the hardware list, click Cancel until you return to it.
2. Click the hardware you want to disable.
3. Click Remove.

Go back to Step 19.

**Step 26: Free Resources Found**     If you find that you can reconfigure the conflicting device to use available resources, change the resource settings to utilize the free resources:

1. Save the new setting by clicking OK and then clicking OK again.
2. If you see a message about restarting your computer, click No.
3. Double-click the hardware that first had the conflict.
4. Click the Resources tab.
5. Double-click the resource that is conflicting. If you see a message that says "You must clear the Use Automatic Settings box before you can change a resource setting," click OK to close the message, and then clear the Use Automatic Settings box.
6. Change the resource setting to the value you just freed. The Conflicting Device List box may show a conflict with the other hardware that you just changed.
7. Click OK. If you see a message, click Yes to continue.

Go back to Step 19.

**Step 27: No Free Resources Available**     If you cannot locate free resources, you must disable some hardware to relieve the conflict. Do you want to disable the hardware that caused the original conflict?

- If you want to disable the hardware that originally caused the conflict, go back to Step 18.
- If you must use *all* of the hardware in the system, there is no further solution to the problem because the conflict cannot be resolved. You should probably remove the conflicting device from the system. You may need to upgrade the offending device, or select an alternate make/model that will be more compatible with your particular PC platform.

**Step 28: Free Setting Found**     Once you've made some resource changes, determine if there are any remaining conflicts that need to be addressed:

1. Click OK to return to the Device Manager hardware list.

2.  Double-click the device that had the original conflict.

3.  Click the Resources tab.

4.  See if there are any remaining conflicts listed in the Conflicting Device List box.

 If the conflict you just resolved is listed, you can ignore it. It will no longer conflict after you restart your computer later.

Are there still conflicts listed?

■   If all the resources are now set without any conflicts, go back to Step 19.

■   If some or all of the resources are still conflicting, go back to Step 20.

**Step 29: No Free Setting Found**    You must decide which device to disable. Because both devices need to use the same resource setting, you must decide which device you want to use. You must disable and remove the other device. It probably is easier to remove the device that had the original conflict at this point. If you choose to remove the other device, you may see a message telling you that you still have a conflict after you finish and restart your computer. Just restart this procedure and continue resolving the conflict. Which device would you like to disable?

■   If you choose to disable the device with the original conflict, go to Step 30.

■   If you choose to disable the other device that it is conflicting with, go to Step 31.

**Step 30: Disable Original Conflicting Device**    Once you've identified a device to be disabled, determine whether you have to remove the device to disable the hardware:

1.  On the Device Manager hardware list, double-click the hardware that you want to disable. If you do not see the hardware list, click Cancel until you return to it.

2.  Under Windows 98/Me, the Disable In This Hardware Profile box should be unchecked, and the Exists In All Hardware Profiles box may be checked. In Windows XP, see that the Use This Device (Enable) option is selected in the Device usage drop-down (see Figure 11-10 earlier).

3.  Click the Resources tab. If there is a Set Configuration Manually button, Windows can free up resources for this hardware without you having to remove its card from your computer.

Do you see a Set Configuration Manually button?

■   If you do see that button, and there are no resource settings listed in the box, you need to restart your computer:

1.  Click OK, and then click OK again.

2.  You may be prompted to restart your computer. Click Yes.

■   If no button is available, you need to disable the physical hardware by removing it from the system:

1.  On the Device Manager hardware list, click the plus sign (+) next to the type of hardware that you want to disable. If you do not see the hardware list, click Cancel until you return to it.

2.  Click the hardware you want to disable.

3.  Click Remove, and then click OK.

4.  You may be prompted to restart your computer. You will have to remove the device from your computer, so you need to shut down instead of restarting. Click No.

5.  Click the Start button, click Shut Down, and then click OK. Under Windows XP, click Start | Turn Off Computer | Turn Off (see Figure 11-12 earlier). Turn off your computer and remove the device from your computer.

6.  Restart your PC and check if your problem has been resolved.

This should correct the conflict, and complete your troubleshooting procedure.

**Step 31: Disable Other Conflicting Device**    If you've elected to disable the other device involved in the conflict, determine whether you have to remove the device to disable that hardware:

1.  On the Device Manager hardware list, double-click the hardware that you want to disable. If you do not see the hardware list, click Cancel until you return to it.

2.  Under Windows 98/Me, the Disable In This Hardware Profile box should be unchecked, and the Exists In All Hardware Profiles box may be checked. In Windows XP, see that the Use This Device (Enable) option is selected in the Device usage drop-down (see Figure 11-10 earlier).

3.  Click the Resources tab. If there is a Set Configuration Manually button, Windows 95 can free up resources for this hardware without you having to remove its card from your computer.

    Do you see a Set Configuration Manually button?

■  If you see the button, go to Step 32.
■  If you don't see the button, go to Step 33.

**Step 32: Disable the Other Device**    Determine whether there are any remaining conflicts:

1.  Click OK to return to the Device Manager hardware list.

2.  Double-click the device that had the original conflict.

3.  Click the Resources tab.

4.  See if there are any remaining conflicts listed in the Conflicting Device List box. If the conflict you just resolved is listed, you can ignore it. It will no longer conflict after you restart your computer later.

    Are there still conflicts listed?

■  If there are no further conflicts, go back to Step 19.
■  If one or more conflicts are still listed, go to Step 34.

**Step 33: Remove the Other Device**    Disable hardware by removing it through software—you're not removing hardware from the system at this point:

1.  On the Device Manager hardware list, click the plus sign (+) next to the type of hardware that you want to disable. If you do not see the hardware list, click Cancel until you return to it.

2.  Click the hardware you want to disable.

3.  Click Remove.

Go back to Step 19.

**Step 34: There Are Still Some Conflicts**    If there are still conflicts between various devices, try setting resources to conflict with only one device:

1. Double-click a resource that is still conflicting. If you see a message that says "You must clear the Use Automatic Settings box before you can change a resource setting," click OK to close the message, and then clear the Use Automatic Settings box.

2. Scroll through the available resource settings. For each value, write down the setting and the name of the hardware it conflicts with, and then click Cancel.

3. Repeat steps 1 and 2 for each conflicting resource.

4. Looking at the list, see if you can change the resource settings so they conflict with only one device—preferably one you could disable.

   Are all conflicts now with one device?

■ When all the conflicts are with only one device, go back to Step 11.

■ If the resources still conflict with more than one device (or cannot be changed), there is no further solution to this problem, and you should probably remove the conflicting device from the system. You may need to upgrade the offending device, or select an alternate make/model that will be more compatible with your particular PC platform.

# Further Study

**Microsoft**   www.microsoft.com
**PCWiz**   www.datadepo.com/datadepo.htm
**WinDrivers.com**   www.windrivers.com
**Windsor Technologies**   www.windsortech.com/

# 12

# CPU IDENTIFICATION AND TROUBLESHOOTING

The *central processing unit* (also called a *CPU*, *microprocessor*, or simply a *processor*) has become one of the most important developments ever realized in integrated circuit technology (Figure 12-1). On the surface, a CPU is a rather boring device—in spite of its extraordinary complexity, a typical CPU performs

**FIGURE  12-1**    A 1.7 GHz Intel Celeron processor (Courtesy of Intel Corporation)

only three general functions: mathematical calculations, logical comparisons, and data manipulation. This isn't a very big repertoire for a device now carrying well over 30 million transistors. (Some versions of Intel's Pentium 4 now sport 55 million transistors.) When you look deeper, however, you realize that it is not the *number* of functions that makes a CPU so remarkable, but that each function is carried out as part of a *program* that the CPU reads and follows. By changing the *program*, the activities of a CPU could be completely rearranged without modifying the computer's physical circuitry.

Once the concept of a "generic" central processing function was born, designers realized that the same system could be used to solve an incredibly diverse array of problems (given the right set of instructions). This was the quantum leap in thinking that gave birth to the modern computer and created the two domains that we know today as "hardware" and "software." As you might have guessed, the idea of *central processing* is hardly new. The very earliest computers of the late 1940s and 1950s applied these concepts to simple programs stored on punched cards or paper tape. The mainframe and minicomputers of the 1960s and 1970s also followed the central processing concept. However, it was the integration of central processing functions onto a single silicon chip (the *microprocessor chip*) in the mid-1970s that made the first "personal" computers possible and spawned the explosive developments in CPU speed and performance that we have seen ever since.

Although a CPU can handle mathematical calculations, the CPU itself was not (until recently) designed to handle floating-point math as an internal function. Of course, floating-point math was possible through software emulation, but the performance of such an approach was unacceptable for math-intensive applications (such as CAD, scientific programs, and 3D graphic calculations). In order to deal with high-performance floating-point math in hardware, a *math co-processor* (MCP), or *numerical processing unit* (NPU), was developed to work in conjunction with the CPU. While the classical MCP was implemented as a stand-alone device (such as the Intel 8087, 80287, and 80387), newer generations of CPUs incorporate the MCP's functions right into the CPU itself. You'll find that all current processors incorporate MCP features.

The CPU is closely related to the overall speed and performance of personal computers. As a technician, you should understand the essential specifications and characteristics of CPUs. This chapter is intended to provide some insights into CPU evolution and capabilities and to illustrate some of the problems that can manifest themselves in microprocessor operation.

# CPU Essentials

A typical microprocessor (such as an AMD Athlon) can be represented by a block diagram such as the one in Figure 12-2. As you can see, there are several sets of processor signals (or *busses*) that you should be familiar with: the *data* bus, the *address* bus, and the *control* bus (usually represented as individual control

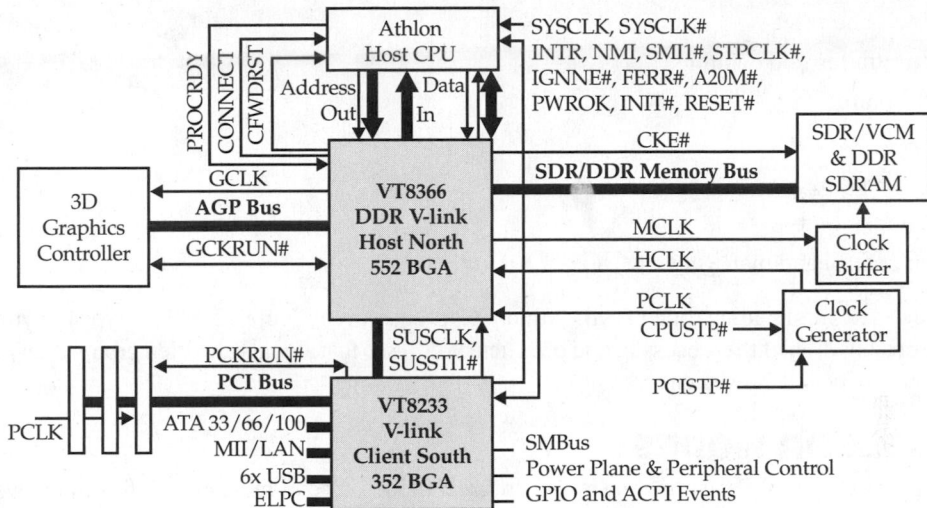

**FIGURE 12-2**    Diagram of an Athlon CPU with a VIA KT266 chipset (Courtesy of VIA Technologies, Inc.)

signals, as you see in the figure). It is these three busses that allow the CPU to communicate with the other elements of the PC (today, that's almost always the North Bridge of the motherboard's chipset) and control its operations.

 Today, many system logic diagrams present all of these busses as a single set of signals, often dubbed the *system bus*.

## THE BUSSES

The *data bus* carries information to and from the CPU, and it is perhaps the most familiar yardstick of CPU performance. The number of wires in the bus represents the number of bits (or data volume) that can be carried at any point in time. Data lines are typically labeled with a *D* prefix (D0, D1, D2, D*n*, and so on). The size of a data bus is typically 8, 16, 32, or 64 bits. As you might expect, larger data busses are preferred, since they allow more data to be transferred simultaneously. The Athlon processor shown in Figure 12-2 provides a 64-bit data bus to the VIA VT8366 North Bridge chip. These data lines would be shown as D0 to D63.

In order for the CPU to read or write data, it must be able to specify the precise I/O port or location in system memory. "Locations" are defined through the use of an *address bus*. The number of bits in the address bus represent the number of physical locations that the CPU can access. For example, a CPU with 20 address lines can address $2^{20}$ (1048576) bytes. A CPU with 25 address lines can address $2^{24}$ (16777216) bytes, and so on. Address lines are generally represented with an *A* prefix (A0, A1, A19, and so on).

Finally, *control signals* are used to synchronize and coordinate the operation of a CPU with other devices in the computer. While the number and use of each control signal varies a bit from generation to generation, most control signals fall into one of the following categories:

■ Reading or writing functions (to memory or I/O locations)

■ Interrupt channels

■  CPU test and reset

■  Bus arbitration and control

■  DMA control

■  CPU status

■  Parity checking

■  Cache operation

■  Power control and management

You can see the signaling for an AMD Athlon XP processor in Figure 12-3. This type of symbol is a logical representation of the processor, and even here you'll see that signals are often grouped together for the sake of clarity and convenience.

# PROCESSOR MODES

Processors are capable of operating in several different modes. The term "mode" refers to the way(s) in which a processor creates (and supports) an operating environment for itself. The processor mode controls how the processor sees and manages the system memory and the tasks that use it. Three different modes of operation have evolved for the PC: the real mode, the protected mode, and the virtual real mode. You should have a basic understanding of these three modes.

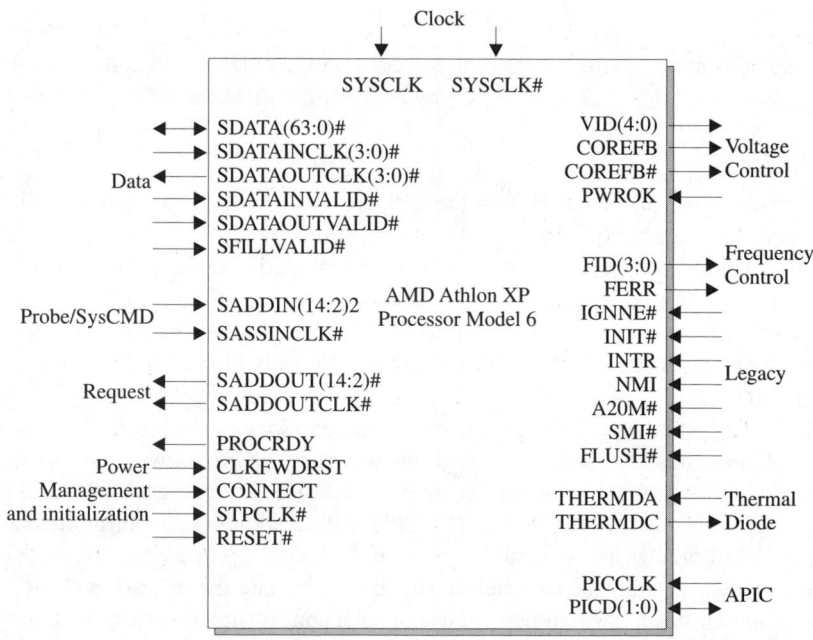

**FIGURE  12-3**    A logical diagram of the AMD Athlon XP processor shows each critical signal group (Courtesy of AMD)

## Real Mode

The original IBM PC could address only 1MB of RAM. The decisions made in those early days have carried forward, and in each new processor, the processor had to support a mode that would be compatible with the original Intel 8088 chip—this is called *real mode*. When a processor is running in real mode, it has the advantage of speed, but it otherwise accesses memory with the same restrictions of the original 8088: an addressable RAM limit of 1MB and memory access that doesn't take advantage of the 32/64-bit processing found in modern CPUs. All processors can support the real mode—in fact, the computer normally starts up in real (DOS) mode. Real mode is used by DOS and "standard" DOS applications. The processor is typically switched to the protected mode (discussed next) when Windows starts.

## Protected Mode

Starting with the IBM AT, a new processor *protected mode* was introduced. This is a much more powerful mode of operation than real mode and is used in all modern multitasking operating systems. The protected mode has numerous advantages:

- The protected mode offers full access to **all** of the system's memory (there is no 1MB limit in protected mode).

- The protected mode has the ability to multitask, meaning that the operating system can manage the execution of multiple programs simultaneously.

- The protected mode offers support for virtual memory, which allows the system to use the hard disk to emulate additional system RAM when needed.

- The protected mode offers faster (32/64-bit) access to memory and faster 32-bit drivers to handle I/O transfers.

Each running program has its own assigned memory locations, which are "protected" from conflicting with other programs. If a program tries to use a memory address that it isn't allowed to, a "protection fault" is generated. All of the major operating systems today use protected mode: including Windows 98/Me/XP, Windows NT/2000, OS/2, and Linux. Even DOS (which normally runs in real mode) can access protected-mode memory using DPMI (DOS Protected Mode Interface), which is used by many DOS games to break the 640KB DOS conventional memory barrier. The 386 (and later) processors can switch on-the-fly from real to protected mode, and vice versa. Protected mode is also sometimes called *386 Enhanced Mode*, since it became mainstream with that family of processors.

## Virtual Real Mode

The third mode of processor operation is actually an enhancement of the protected mode. Protected mode is normally used to run graphical multitasking operating systems, such as the various types of Windows. There is sometimes a need to run DOS programs under Windows, but DOS programs need to be run in real mode—not protected mode. *Virtual real mode* was created to solve this problem. It emulates the real mode from within the protected mode and allows DOS programs to run. A protected-mode operating system such as Windows can actually create multiple *virtual real-mode* machines—though numerous "virtual machines" can be created, each "virtual machine" acts as if it's the only one on the PC. Each virtual machine gets its own 1MB address space, an image of the real hardware BIOS routines, and so on. Virtual real mode is what is used when you use a DOS window or run a DOS game in Windows 98/Me. When you start a DOS application, Windows creates a virtual DOS machine for it to run under.

# Modern CPU Concepts

There is a lot more to CPU technology than just busses and addressing modes—in fact, there are entire books written on modern microprocessors. We won't get into many of those concepts in this book, but there is a wide range of concepts that you *should* understand when working with today's PCs.

## CISC VS. RISC CPUS

You may sometimes see processors referred to as "CISC" or "RISC" processors. Traditional CPUs are based on a CISC (*Complex Instruction Set Computing*) architecture. This approach allows any number of instructions to be used in the CPU, and the CPU must provide all of the internal circuitry needed to process each instruction. Since each new instruction requires many new transistors for processing, CISC offers versatility at the expense of CPU performance. CISC CPUs (such as the Intel Pentium II, III, and 4 or the AMD Athlon and Duron) are typically found in general-purpose desktop and mobile computers.

By comparison, a RISC (*Reduced Instruction Set Computing*) architecture uses a limited number of very powerful instructions. This CPU type requires fewer transistors in the CPU for processing and generally results in faster CPU performance with far lower power consumption. However, RISC processors are often less versatile than their CISC counterparts. CISC CPUs appear in dedicated peripheral devices such as laser printers. Designers are still trying to develop processors that combine CISC versatility with RISC performance, though a number of RISC-type CPUs (like the DEC Alpha or MIPS Orion 4600 devices) have appeared in high-end workstations.

## CIRCUIT SIZE AND DIE SIZE

The *circuit size* (or *feature size*) relates to the level of miniaturization in a processor. To make more powerful processors, more transistors are needed—this means the transistors must be made continually smaller. Technology advancements in integrated circuit fabrication allow circuit sizes to shrink. It was once considered impossible to shrink the circuit size below 1 micron, but most recent processors use a 0.25 micron process—0.18 micron processors are commonplace, and newer chips employ a 0.13 micron process. It is now thought that fabrication technology can eventually be shrunk to as low as 0.08 microns. The issue of *heat* is important here. Packing more transistors onto a chip causes additional heat generation, so each transistor must be made smaller. The size and layout of transistors will also have an effect on die size.

By comparison, the *die size* of the processor refers to its physical surface area—the area of the "chip"—and it is typically measured in square millimeters ($mm^2$). Smaller die sizes allow designers to get more "chips" from a single wafer, so manufacturing costs are lower (and the resulting processor tends to be less expensive). Smaller die sizes also consume less power.

## PROCESSOR SPEED

Processor speed is typically rated in gigahertz (GHz, or billions of processing cycles per second), though older processors denote their speed in megahertz (MHz). The processor's speed is a function of several critical factors. Speed is largely related to the design of the processor circuit itself—the design dictates the internal timing requirements that limit the maximum speed the processor can handle. Speed is also influenced by manufacturing factors such as the circuit size and die size. In general, smaller chips can run faster because of shorter signal runs and lower power consumption. Finally, process quality (how well the manufacturer uses their equipment to make wafers) can vary, with some chips running faster than others even though they were produced with the same process (and even with the same wafer). Processors are tested and rated for their speed during the testing phase of the manufacturing process.

# VERSIONS AND STEPS

A processor represents a very complex and intricate design. As with any hardware design, there are often bugs that are discovered (for instance, old-timers in the PC business may remember the "floating point" bug with early Pentium processors). This means that a given processor may exist in many different design revisions, where newer versions fix the problems encountered with older versions. Intel uses the term *stepping* (or *S-step*) to indicate a processor's revision, and the S-step is typically marked right on the processor. AMD uses a model number to indicate the processor's revision. For example, a late-model Intel Pentium III processor may use an S-step of "SL3WA." It is not necessary that you be able to interpret the S-step (or other manufacturer's revision markings) on sight—you can usually find a manufacturer's table that details the processor's characteristics based on its S-step number.

New features are generally not introduced with higher processor steps—only problems are corrected and performance issues resolved.

As a rule, the processor's revision number will have little if any impact on the system's performance, but it might. Problems may be encountered when using particular processor revisions with certain motherboard and BIOS combinations. When you encounter system reliability problems, check with the motherboard maker for possible issues with your processor step. Certain minimum step levels and step matching may also be important when using several processors on the motherboard.

# PROCESSOR POWER AND MANAGEMENT

Processors consume a relatively large amount of power. For example, the AMD Athlon XP processor family demands between about 54 to 64 watts (from 1500+ to 2100+ models, respectively). In order to reduce the PC's power demands and improve performance, the traditional +5 volt operating voltages of years past have given way to processors, support chips, and expansion devices that operate at far lower voltages. The first step in this evolution was to reduce the operating voltage level to +3.3 volts. This was apparent in early Pentium processors. Newer processors (such as the Pentium MMX and Pentium II/III/4) reduce voltage levels even more using a *dual voltage* (or *split rail*) design. A split rail processor uses two different voltages. The *external* (or *I/O voltage*) is usually +3.3 volts, a level that ensures compatibility with the other chips on the motherboard. The *internal* (or *core voltage*) is somewhat lower (usually +2.5 to +2.9 volts, though +1.8 to +2.4-volt operation is becoming commonplace in the latest processors). The I/O voltage lets the processor "talk" to the motherboard, while the core voltage allows the processor to run cooler internally.

Traditionally, you'd need to set the correct operating voltage for your particular processor(s) by configuring one or more voltage regulation jumpers on the motherboard. Today, processor voltages are set automatically by voltage selection pins on the processor itself—all you need to do is plug in the processor and boot the computer.

Since the power consumption of a CPU is related to its processing speed and internal activity, Intel eventually developed power management circuitry that enables processors to conserve power (and lengthen battery life in laptop systems). Power management was originally introduced with the Intel 486SL processor (an enhanced version of the 486DX processor), and power management features were soon after standardized and incorporated into all Pentium and later processors. These power management features were referred to as System Management Mode (or SMM). SMM circuitry is integrated into the physical processor chip but operates independently to control the processor's power use based on its activity level. SMM allows the system to specify time intervals after which the CPU will be powered down partially or fully (a.k.a. *throttled back*) and also enables the suspend/resume feature that supports today's system standby and hibernate modes. SMM settings are normally controlled through the CMOS Setup. Today, processor and system power conservation techniques are based on the Advanced Configuration and Power Interface (ACPI) standard. While the techniques differ from SMM, the objectives are the same.

# PROCESSOR COOLING

The millions of transistors operating inside a processor all liberate a small amount of heat each time they switch on or off. When this switching action takes place hundreds of millions (even billions) of times each second, heat management becomes a serious concern. Processors have a specified "safe" temperature range that represents their limits for normal operation. For example, the AMD Athlon XP processor family cites an absolute maximum die temperature of 90 degrees C. If the processor overheats, serious system problems will usually result. These will usually take the form of system reboots, lockups, or crashes. An overheated processor can also manifest itself through memory errors, application errors, disk problems, or a host of other things. A severely (or repeatedly) overheated processor can also be permanently damaged—though this rarely happens. These problems can be *extremely* difficult to diagnose because they often appear rooted in other parts of the system. For example, a system crash or lockup is often associated with a software bug or hardware conflict rather than an overheated CPU.

Processors are cooled by "active" heat sinks, which are composed of a small fast fan mounted to a large metal heat sink with numerous fins (see Figure 12-4). The heat sink "pulls" heat away from the processor package, and the fan in turn cools the heat sink. Air warmed by the heat sink is vented from the case (this is the warm air you feel exhausting from the back of the case). The problem with "active" heat sinks is that they rely on the fan. If the fan fails, the processor can overheat in a very short time. To protect the processor from an accidental fan failure, many motherboards integrate tachometers that check the fan's rotational speed and thermostats that measure the processor's case temperature. If the fan stops turning or the processor's temperature climbs over a preset limit, a warning will indicate the fault and allow you to address the trouble before a crash or other system problem occurs.

# SYSTEM CLOCKS

Every modern PC uses multiple system clocks. Each clock runs at a specific frequency—normally measured in MHz. A clock *tick* is the smallest unit of time in which processing takes place and is sometimes

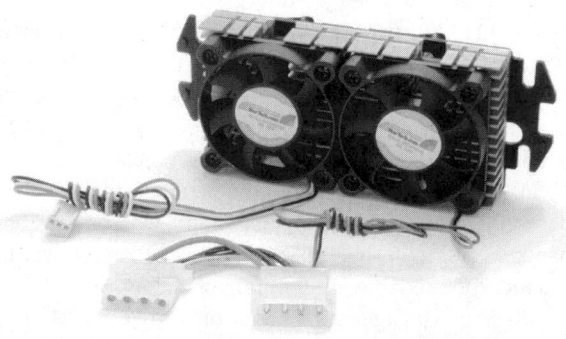

**FIGURE  12-4**    Active heat sinks play a critical role in system reliability by keeping the processor cool. (Courtesy of StarTech.com.)

called a *cycle*. Some types of processing work can be done in one cycle while other tasks require many cycles. The operation of these clocks is what drives the various circuits in the PC, and the faster they run, the more performance you can expect from your system. Original PCs had a unified system clock—a single clock drove the processor, memory, and I/O bus. A typical PC today may have as many as five different clocks. The term *system clock* generally refers to the speed of the memory bus running on the motherboard (and usually not that of the processor).

The various clocks in a modern PC are typically created using a single clock generator circuit (on the motherboard) to generate the "main" system clock, and then various clock multiplier (or divider) circuits create the other clock signals. Today, clocks can be synchronous or asynchronous to the system clock. This can be very important with special PC configurations (such as overclocking the processor). With a synchronous clock scheme, increasing the processor's clock speed would also bump up the other clock speeds (the AGP and PCI clocks), and this could lead to system problems. Keeping the clocks asynchronous allows one clock to be changed without affecting the others.

System performance is tied to the speed of the system clock—this is why increasing the system clock speed is usually more important than increasing the raw processor speed. The processor spends a great deal of time waiting for information from much slower devices (especially the system busses). While a faster processor will offer better performance, the increase in speed will not add nearly as much performance if the processor is sitting idle waiting for slower parts of the system.

## PROCESSOR PACKAGES

Raw chips (the small *dies*) are not used directly—they are far too fragile and sensitive. Instead, the die is placed in a *package* that will protect the die and help it to dissipate heat. That standardized package normally takes the form of a *slotted* or a *socketed* device. Each generation of CPU uses a different number of pins (and pin assignments), so a different physical socket or slot must be used on the motherboard to accommodate each new generation of processor. Slot-type processors are normally classified as "Slot 1," "Slot 2," or "Slot A." Socket-type processors are usually denoted as "Socket 370" or "Socket A."

Early CPUs were not readily interchangeable, and upgrading a CPU typically meant upgrading the entire motherboard. With the introduction of Intel's 486 CPUs, a type of "OverDrive" processor technology became popular—replacing an existing CPU with a pin-compatible replacement processor that operated at higher internal clock speeds to enhance system performance. Table 12-1 shows that the earliest "sockets" were

**TABLE 12-1    COMPARISON OF MAJOR PROCESSOR PACKAGES**

| SOCKET | PINS | VOLTS | CPU | COMPATIBLE OVERDRIVE PROCESSOR(S) |
|---|---|---|---|---|
| Socket 1 | 169 | 5v | 486 SX | BOXDX4ODP75, BOXDX4ODP100 |
| | | | 486 DX | BOXDX4ODPR75, BOXDX4ODPR100 |
| Socket 2 | 238 | 5v | 486 SX | BOXDX4ODP75, BOXDX4ODP100 |
| | | | 486 DX | BOXDX4ODPR75, BOXDX4ODPR100 |
| | | | 486 DX2 | BOXPODP5V63, BOXPODP5V83 |
| Socket 3 | 237 | 3v/5v | 486 SX | BOXDX4ODP75, BOXDX4ODPR75 |
| | | | 486 DX | BOXDX4ODP100, BOXDX4ODPR100 |
| | | | 486 DX2 | BOXPODP5V63, BOXPODP5V83 |
| | | | 486 DX4 | n/a |
| Socket 4 | 273 | 5v | 60/66 MHz Pentium | BOXPODP5V133 |

**TABLE 12-1**　COMPARISON OF MAJOR PROCESSOR PACKAGES *(CONTINUED)*

| SOCKET | PINS | VOLTS | CPU | COMPATIBLE OVERDRIVE PROCESSOR(S) |
|---|---|---|---|---|
| Socket 5 | 320 | 3v | 75/90/100 MHz Pentium | BOXPODP3V125, BOXPODP3V150, BOXPODP3V166 |
| Socket 6 | 235 | 3v | 486 DX4 | n/a |
| Socket 7 | 321 | 2.5/3.3v | 75/90/100 MHz Pentium | BOXPODP3V125, BOXPODP3V150, BOXPODP3V166 |
| Socket 8 | 387 | 2.5v | Pentium Pro | n/a |
| Slot 1 | 242 | n/a | Pentium II/III | n/a |
| Slot 2 | 330 | n/a | Pentium II/III Xeon | n/a |
| Socket 370 | 370 | n/a | Pentium III/Celeron | n/a |
| Socket 423 | 423 | n/a | Pentium 4 | n/a |
| Socket 478 | 478 | n/a | Pentium 4 | n/a |
| Socket 603 | 603 | n/a | Pentium 4 Xeon | n/a |
| Slot A | 242 | n/a | AMD Athlon | n/a |
| Socket A | 462 | n/a | AMD Athlon/Duron | n/a |
| PAC418 cartridge | 418 | n/a | Intel Itanium | n/a |

designated Socket 1 for early 486SX and DX processors. As CPUs advanced, socket types proliferated to support an ever-growing selection of compatible processors. Today, a motherboard can typically accommodate a wide range of processor speeds in the same slot or socket design. You can see a typical "Socket 462" (Socket A) for AMD Athlon 2000+ processor on the Soyo KT333 Dragon Ultra Platinum motherboard in Figure 12-5.

Though aging, Socket 370 remains a popular choice for low-budget systems. Socket 370 motherboards support most Pentium III/Celeron-type processors. By setting the proper clock speed and multiplier, a Socket 370 motherboard can support a wide variety of Pentium III/Celeron-class CPUs without requiring any other hardware changes. It is this kind of versatility that has made sockets so important and that has extended the working life of current PCs by providing a viable upgrade path for future CPUs. While high-performance processors from Intel and AMD use even denser slots and sockets, the Socket 370 scheme

Socket 462 (Socket A) ZIF connector for an AMD Athlon processor

**FIGURE 12-5**　The Socket 462 connector on this Soyo KT333 Dragon Ultra Platinum motherboard supports an AMD Athlon 2000+ processor. (Courtesy of Motherboards.org.)

remains popular and available because of its versatility. You can review the evolution of Intel's processor packaging (including some shots of classic CPU packages) at www.intel.com/technology/ itj/q32000.htm.

Although processor makers had temporarily shifted to a slot-type (or cartridge-type) processor package, most processors are now manufactured in a socket style (such as Socket 478 or Socket 462). Slot-type processors are quickly fading into disuse.

## P-RATING (PR) AND TRUE PERFORMANCE

CPUs are traditionally classified by their clock speed. For example, a 1.4 GHz Pentium 4 is generally regarded as a better performing CPU than a 900 MHz Pentium III. However, a unique and perplexing marketing problem for competing CPU manufacturers was presented by the fact that a non-Intel CPU at a given clock speed can perform as well as an Intel processor at another clock speed. Although Intel continues to lead CPU development, other CPU makers like AMD and Cyrix kept the pressure on by packing more performance into fewer clock cycles. In early 1996, Cyrix, IBM Microelectronics, and SGS Thomson (all Intel competitors) gathered to create the P-Rating (or PR) system for describing their CPUs. By using a "PR" designation, a CPU can be equated to an Intel Pentium. As an example, the AMD 133 MHz Am5x86 processor is marked PR75, and performs comparably to an Intel 75 MHz Pentium. When the rating includes a "+" or "++" suffix (such as PR75++), it means that the CPU is delivering *better* performance than the corresponding Intel part. P-Ratings are determined through a method of direct comparison:

1. The Winstone benchmark is run on a specifically configured PC system powered by an Intel processor of a given clock speed.

2. The Intel processor is removed from the system and replaced with a competing processor. The Winstone benchmark is run again and a second Winstone score is obtained from the same system now running the competing processor. The system configuration remains identical, and all peripherals are carefully documented.

3. The competing processor is assigned the highest P-Rating at which it delivers Winstone scores equal to or greater than a given Pentium. For example, if an AMD K5 processor delivers performance equal to or better than a 90 MHz Pentium, it receives a P-Rating of 90 (that is, PR90).

The practice of assigning a P-Rating to non-Intel processors was discontinued with AMD's K-series processors. As competing processors proliferated, the PR system became too cumbersome and confusing. AMD introduced the "True Performance Initiative" as an attempt to establish an industry policy of rating processors according to accepted *benchmarks,* not by pure speed in MHz. For example, the AMD Athlon XP processors use this scheme, which "names" each model according to the Intel Pentium 4 speeds shown to be comparable in certain benchmarks. The Athlon XP 2000+ (operating at 1667 MHz) has benchmark results comparable to the Intel Pentium 4 operating at 2000 MHz (2 GHz)—thus the name Athlon XP 2000+. (Again, the + indicates performance that exceeds the comparable processor.)

## ARCHITECTURAL PERFORMANCE FEATURES

The past several years have seen an explosion of technologies and techniques intended to wring more performance out of a processor. Designers have invested tremendous effort to develop the improvements that we take for granted each time we boot the system. This part of the chapter describes some of the performance enhancing features found in a modern microprocessor.

### Superscalar Architecture

Program instructions are processed through circuits in the processor called *execution units* or *execution engines*. The term *superscalar architecture* refers to the use of multiple execution units to allow the CPU to process more than one instruction simultaneously with every clock cycle. For example, the Pentium Pro processor uses two execution "pipes" (dubbed *U* and *V*). This is a form of multiprocessing within the CPU itself, since multiple processing chores are taking place at the same time. Most modern processors are superscalar at one level or another. By combining pipelining with the multiple execution engines of a superscalar architecture, CPUs are making extremely efficient use of every clock cycle.

## Pipelining

CPUs process instructions and generate results through a complex series of transistor switches inside the CPU die itself (just as any other logic chip). Early CPUs processed one instruction at a time—that is, an instruction was fetched and processed *completely*, then a new instruction was fetched. Processing could be accomplished in several clock cycles (the exact number of clock cycles depended on the particular instruction). Simple instructions could be processed in 2 or 3 clocks, while complex instructions might demand as much as 7 or 8 clocks.

The *pipelining* technique (also called *instruction pipelining*) allows a new instruction to start processing while a current instruction is still being processed. This way, a CPU can actually work on several instructions during the same clock cycle. In other words, for any given clock cycle, there may be several instructions "in the pipeline." Pipelining lets the CPU make use of execution resources that would otherwise sit idle while an instruction is being completed. Still, the CPU can only finish (generate results for) one instruction per clock cycle.

## Superpipelining and Hyperpipelining

As you saw previously, instructions are processed in a pipeline, with each step in the processing pipeline performing a certain amount of work on the instruction. By making the pipeline longer (with more stages), each stage performs less work, and the processor can be scaled to a higher clock frequency. This is known as *superpipelining* and is generally regarded an improvement over regular pipelining. While superpipelining may have 10 stages or so, even larger pipelines are available. Intel's Pentium 4 processor uses a 20-stage pipeline—dubbed *hyperpipelining*. With large processing pipelines, it becomes very important that program instructions are written in a way that keeps each stage of the pipeline full. If an instruction is not available, that stage will remain empty (and the clock cycles it uses will be wasted).

## Speculative Execution and Branch Prediction

Some CPUs have the ability to execute multiple instructions at once. In some cases, not all of the results of the execution will be used, because changes in the program flow may mean that the given instruction should never have been executed in the first place. This often occurs in the vicinity of program branches—where a condition is tested, and the program path is altered depending on the results (for instance, an "if/then" statement). Branches represent a real problem for pipelining, because you can't always be sure that instructions will go in a linear sequence. A less sophisticated processor may stall the pipeline until the results are known, and doing this can hurt performance. More advanced processors will *speculatively execute* the next instruction anyway. The hope is that the CPU will be able to use the results if the branch goes the way it thinks it will.

Even more advanced processors combine this with *branch prediction*, where the processor can actually predict (with fairly good accuracy) which way the branch will go based on past history. Branch prediction improves the handling of branches by making use of a special small cache called the *branch target buffer* (or BTB). Whenever the processor executes a branch, it stores information about it in this area. When the processor next encounters the same branch, it is able to make an informed "guess" about which way the branch is likely to result. This helps keep the pipeline flowing and improves performance.

## Dynamic (Out-of-Order) Execution

Even the fastest CPU executes instructions in the order in which they are written within the particular program. This means an improperly or inefficiently written program can reduce the processing efficiency of the CPU. In many cases, even well-written code can become impaired during the software assembly and linking process. The *dynamic execution* technique allows the processor to evaluate the program's flow and "choose" the best order in which to process instructions. For example, instruction 2 can be executed before instruction 1 has finished. The results of the execution are "reassembled" in the correct order to ensure that the program runs correctly. When implemented properly, this "selective reordering" of instructions allows the CPU to make even better use of its processing resources—and aids overall CPU performance.

## Register Renaming and Write Buffers

*Register renaming* is a technique used to support multiple execution paths without conflicts between different execution units trying to use the same registers. Instead of just one set of registers being used, multiple sets are put into the processor. This allows different execution units to work simultaneously without unnecessary stalls in the pipeline. *Write buffers* are used to hold the results of instruction execution until they can be written back to registers or memory locations. More write buffers allow more instructions to be executed without stalling the pipelines.

## Multiprocessing

*Multiprocessing* is the technique of running a system with more than one processor. The idea is that you can double system performance using two processors instead of one, quadruple performance with four processors instead of one, and so on. It doesn't always work that well in actual practice, but multiprocessing can certainly result in improved performance under certain conditions. In order to employ multiprocessing effectively, the host computer must have all of the following elements in place:

- ■ **Motherboard support**   A motherboard capable of handling multiple processors. This means additional sockets or slots for the extra CPUs and a chipset capable of handling the multiprocessor configuration.

- ■ **Processor support**   Processors that are suitable for use in a multiprocessing system. Not all processors are suitable, and only some versions of the same processor are suitable. For example, Intel Pentium 4 Xeon and AMD Athlon MP processors are both intended for multiprocessor platforms. Be sure to check the motherboard's documentation for appropriate processor recommendations.

- ■ **Operating system support**   An operating system that supports multiprocessing, such as Windows NT/2000/XP or UNIX. Other operating systems such as Windows 98/Me do not support multiprocessing.

Multiprocessing is most effective when used with application software designed specifically for it. Multiprocessing is managed by the operating system, which allocates different tasks to be performed by the various processors in the system. Applications designed for multiprocessing are said to be *threaded*—they are broken into smaller routines that can be run independently. This allows the operating system to let threads run on more than one processor simultaneously, and that is how multiprocessing results in improved performance. If the application isn't designed this way, it can't take advantage of multiple processors (though the operating system can still make use of the additional processors if you use more than one application at a time).

Multiprocessing can be said to be either asymmetric or symmetric. These terms indicate how the operating system divides tasks between the processors in the system. *Asymmetric* multiprocessing designates some processors to perform system tasks only, and others to run applications only. This rigid design results in poor performance during times when the computer needs to run more system tasks than user tasks, or vice versa. *Symmetric* multiprocessing (or SMP) allows *either* system or user tasks to run on any processor. It's a more flexible approach, and therefore offers better performance. SMP is what most multiprocessing PC motherboards use.

For a processor to support multiprocessing, it must support a multiprocessing protocol that dictates the way that the processors and chipset talk to each other in order to implement SMP. Intel processors typically use an SMP protocol called "APIC," and Intel chipsets that support multiprocessing are designed to work with these chips. APIC is a proprietary Intel standard, so even though AMD and Cyrix can make Intel-compatible processors, they cannot make them work in SMP configurations. AMD and Cyrix implemented their own early SMP standard called "OpenPIC," though AMD now implements other multiprocessing technologies like "Smart MP."

## Multimedia Extensions

With the growth in graphics, presentation, and other multimedia software, processor throughput often "bogged down" with the intensive calculations that were required. It became necessary to speed up certain computer-intensive processing/calculation procedures related to multimedia and communications applications. While those processes typically occupy 10 percent or less of the overall application code, they can account for up to 90 percent of the program's execution time. Intel and AMD have been locked in a bitter rivalry to provide the best "multimedia extensions" to their processors.

**MMX**    By 1996, Intel had introduced its MMX extensions into the Pentium processor family (dubbed "Pentium MMX") with 57 powerful new instructions. MMX instructions process multiple data elements in parallel using a technique called *Single Instruction Multiple Data* (SIMD). This technique allows processes to be performed on large amounts of data simultaneously, and reducing the overall processing required to handle the large amounts of video and audio information typically associated with multimedia. Subsequent Intel processors (such as the Pentium II/III/4 and Celeron) are compatible with the MMX instruction set. MMX provides most of its support for 2D images and audio.

**3DNow!**    AMD also saw the need to optimize a processor's multimedia capability. But rather than focus on 2D instructions as Intel did with MMX, AMD chose to focus 21 new instructions on 3D-related features that significantly enhance the processing of 3D graphics images (as well as MPEG decoding). AMD released its 3DNow! technology in 1998 (fully nine months ahead of Intel's SSE technology). Since 3DNow! offered enhanced 3D processing well ahead of Intel, AMD's K6, K6-2, Athlon, and Duron processor lines presented an appealing alternative for 3D games and visualization programs. Current AMD Athlon processors offer Enhanced 3DNow! with support for 24 new instructions to improve MMX integer math, and enhance data transfers for Internet streaming applications. This also includes 5 DSP extensions for soft modem, soft ADSL, Dolby Digital, and MP3 applications. You can learn more about 3DNow! at www.amd.com/products/cpg/k623d/inside3d.html.

**SSE and SSE-II**    By 1999, Intel had updated its multimedia extensions by introducing SSE (*Streaming SIMD Extensions*) for the Pentium III processor. SSE builds on MMX by adding 70 new instructions that enable advanced imaging, powerful 3D graphics (floating point) processing, streaming video and audio, speech recognition, and added Internet features. SSE features are intended for the standard end-user family of Pentium III processors. The introduction of the Pentium 4 processor added 144 new multimedia enhancement instructions, now referred to as SSE-II (or SSE2).

# The Intel CPUs

There is little doubt that Intel Corporation has been a driving force behind the personal computer revolution. Each new generation of microprocessor represents not just mediocre improvements in processing speed, but technological leaps in execution efficiency, raw speed, data throughput, and design enhancements (such as dynamic execution, hyperpipelining, and SIMD). This part of the chapter provides a historical overview of Intel microprocessors and compares their current characteristics.

## 8086/8088 (1978–1979)

The 29,000-transistor 8086 marked the first 16-bit microprocessor—that is, there are 16 data bits available from the CPU itself. This immediately offered twice the data throughput of earlier 8-bit CPUs. Each of the 24 registers in the 8086/8088 were expanded to 16 bits rather than just 8, and 20 address lines allowed direct access to 1,048,576 bytes (1MB) of external system memory. Although 1MB of RAM is considered almost negligible today, chip designers at the time never suspected that more than 1MB would ever be needed. Both the 8086 and 8088 (as well as many subsequent Intel CPUs) could address 64KB of I/O space (as opposed to RAM space). The 8086 was available for four clock speeds: 5 MHz, 6 MHz, 8 MHz, and 10 MHz. Three clock speeds allowed the 8086 to process 0.33, 0.66, and 0.75 MIPS (Millions of Instructions Per Second). The 8088 was available only in 5 MHz and 8 MHz versions (for 0.33 and 0.75 MIPS, respectively), but its rather unique multiplexing nature reduces its data bandwidth to only 2MB/s.

For all intents and purposes, the 8088 is identical to the 8086. They are exactly the same microprocessor with only one exception: the 8088 multiplexes (time-shares) 8 of the 16 address lines between the address bus and the data bus. If you look at a pinout of an 8088, you will see only 8 data lines available to the outside world (D8 to D15). During one part of a bus cycle, the lower 8 address lines serve as the lower 8 data bits (D0 to D7). During another part of the bus cycle, those 8 shared bits are used as the lower 8 bits of the address bus (A0 to A7). Both CPUs are designed to work with the 8087 math co-processor (MCP).

## 80186 (1980)

The 16-bit 80186 built on the x86 foundation to offer additional features such as an internal clock generator, system controller, interrupt controller, DMA (Direct Memory Access) controller, and timer/counter circuitry right on the CPU itself. No Intel CPU before or since has offered so much integration in a single CPU. The 80186 was also first to abandon 5 MHz clock speeds in favor of 8 MHz, 10 MHz, and 12.5 MHz. Aside from these advances, however, the 80186 remained similar to the 8086/8088 with 24 registers and 20 address lines to access up to 1MB of RAM. The 80186 processors were used as CPUs in embedded applications and never saw service in personal computers. The limitations of the early x86 architecture in the PC demanded a much faster CPU capable of accessing far more than 1MB of RAM.

## 80286 (1982)

The 24 register, 134,000-transistor 80286 CPU (first used in the IBM PC/AT and compatibles) offered some substantial advantages over older CPUs. Design advances allow the 286 to operate at 1.2 MIPS, 1.5 MIPS, and 2.66 MIPS (for 8, 10, and 12.5 MHz respectively). The 286 also breaks the 1MB RAM barrier by offering 24 address lines instead of 20 which allow it to directly address 16MB of RAM. In addition to 16MB of directly-accessible RAM, the 286 can handle up to 1GB (gigabyte) of *virtual memory*, which allows blocks of program code and data to be swapped between the 286's real memory (up to 16MB) and a secondary (or "virtual") storage location, such as a hard disk. To maintain backward compatibility with the 8086/8088 (which can address only 1MB of RAM), the 286 can operate in a real mode. One of the great failings of the 286 is that, while it can switch from real mode to protected mode, it cannot switch *back* to real mode without a warm reboot of the system. The 286 uses a stand-alone math co-processor, the 80287.

## 80386 (1985–1990)

The next major microprocessor released by Intel was the 275,000-transistor, 32 register, 80386DX CPU in 1985. With a full 32-bit data bus, data throughput is immediately double that of the 80286. The 16, 20, 25, and 33 MHz versions allow data throughput up to 50 MB/s and processing power up to 11.4 MIPS at 33 MHz. A full 32-bit address bus allows direct access to a then unprecedented 4GB of RAM in addition to a staggering 64TB (terabytes) of virtual memory capacity. The 386 was the first Intel CPU to enhance processing through the use of instruction *pipelining*, which, as described earlier, allows the CPU to start working on a new instruction while waiting for the current instruction to finish. A new operating mode (called the *virtual real mode*) enables the CPU to run several real-mode sessions simultaneously under operating systems such as Windows.

Intel took a small step backward in 1988 to produce the 80386SX CPU. The 386SX uses 24 address lines for 16MB of addressable RAM and an external data bus of 16 bits instead of the full 32 bits with the DX. Correspondingly, the processing power for the 386SX is only 3.6 MIPS at 33 MHz. In spite of these compromises, a significantly less expensive CPU helped to propagate the 386 family into desktop and portable computers. Aside from changes to the address and bus width, the 386 architecture is virtually unchanged from that of the 386DX.

By 1990, Intel integrated the 386 into an 855,000-transistor, low-power version called the 80386SL. The 386SL incorporated an ISA (Industry Standard Architecture)-compatible chipset along with power management circuitry that optimized the 386 for use in mobile computers. The 386SL resembled the 386SX version in its 24 address lines and 16-bit external data bus. Each member of the 386 family use stand-alone math co-processors (80387DX, 80387SX, and 80387SL). All versions of the 80386 can switch between real mode and protected mode as needed, so they will run the same software as, and are backwardly compatible with, the 80286 and the 8086/8088.

## 80486 (1989–1994)

The consistent push for higher speed and performance resulted in the development in 1989 of Intel's 1.2 million-transistor, 29 register, 32-bit microprocessor called the 80486DX. The 486DX provides full 32-bit addressing for access to 4GB of physical RAM and up to 64TB (terabytes) of virtual memory. The 486DX offers twice the performance of the 386DX with 26.9 MIPS at 33 MHz. Two initial versions (25 MHz, 33 MHz) were available.

As with the 386 family, the 486 series uses pipelining to improve instruction execution, but the 486 series also adds 8KB of *cache memory* right on the chip. Cache saves memory access time by predicting the next instructions that will be needed by the CPU and loading them into the cache memory *before* the CPU actually needs them. If the needed instruction is indeed in cache, the CPU can access the information from cache without wasting time waiting for memory access. Another improvement of the 486DX is the inclusion of a floating point unit (an MCP) in the CPU itself rather than requiring a separate co-processor chip. This is not true of all members of the 486 family however. A third departure for the 486DX is that it is offered in 5 volt and 3 volt versions. The 3 volt version is intended for laptop, notebook, and other low-power mobile computing applications.

Finally, the 486DX is *upgradeable*. Up to 1989/1990, personal computers were limited by their CPU—when the CPU became obsolete, so did the computer (more specifically the *motherboard*). This traditionally forced the computer user to purchase a new computer (or upgrade the motherboard) every few years in order to utilize current technology. The architecture of the 486 is intended to support CPU upgrades where a future CPU using a faster internal clock can be inserted into the existing system. Intel dubbed this "OverDrive" technology. While OverDrive performance is not as high as that of a newer PC, it is much less expensive and allows computer users to protect their computer investments for a longer period of time. It is vital to note that not all 486 versions are upgradeable, and the CPU socket on the motherboard itself must be designed specifically to accept an OverDrive CPU.

The 486DX was only the first in a long line of variations from Intel. In 1991, Intel released the 80486SX and the 80486DX/50. Both the 486SX and 486DX/50 offer 32-bit addressing, a 32-bit data path, and 8KB of on-chip cache memory. The 486SX takes a small step backward from the 486DX by removing the math co-processor and offering slower versions at 16, 20, 25, and 33 MHz. At 33 MHz, the 486SX is rated at 20.2 MIPS. Such design compromises reduced the cost and power dissipation of the 486SX, which accelerated its acceptance into desktop and portable computers. The 486SX is upgradeable with an "OverDrive" CPU (if the computer's motherboard is designed to accept an "OverDrive" CPU), is compatible with an 80487 CPU/MCP, and is available in 5 volt and 3 volt versions. The 486DX/50 operates at a clock speed of 50 MHz and performs at 41.1 MIPS. The 486DX/50 *does* integrate an onboard math co-processor, but it is not OverDrive upgradeable or available in a 3 volt version.

The first wave of OverDrive CPUs arrived in 1992 with the introduction of the 80486DX2/50 and the 80486DX2/66. The "2" along with the "DX" indicates that the chip is using an internal clock that is double the frequency of the system. The 486DX2/50 actually runs in a 25 MHz system, yet the CPU performs at 40.5 MIPS. The 486DX2/66 runs in a 33 MHz system, but it runs internally at 54.5 MIPS. Using a faster CPU with a slower motherboard speed allowed the CPU to work directly with existing PC motherboard designs. Both OverDrive CPUs offer onboard math co-processors and are themselves upgradeable to even faster OverDrive versions. The 486DX2/50 is available in 5 volt and 3 volt versions, while the 486DX2/66 is available only in the 5 volt version.

In 1992, Intel produced a highly integrated, low-power version of the 80486 called the 80486SL. Its 32-bit data bus, 32-bit address bus, 8KB of onboard cache, and integrated math co-processor make it virtually identical to other 486 CPUs, but the SL uses 1.4 million transistors. The extra circuitry provides a low-power management capability that optimize the SL for mobile computers. The 486SL is available in 25 and 33 MHz versions and 3 volt and 5 volt designs. At 33 MHz, the 486SL operates at 26.9 MIPS.

Intel rounded out its 486 family in 1993 with the introduction of three other CPU models: the 80486DX2/40, the 80486SX/SL-enhanced, and the 80486DX/SL-enhanced. The 486DX2/40 is the third OverDrive CPU intended to run in 20 MHz PCs, while the CPU's internal clock runs at 40 MHz and performs at 21.1 MIPS. The 486SX/SL (26.9 MIPS at 33 MHz) and 486DX/SL (26.9 MIPS at 33 MHz) are identical to their original SX and DX versions, but the SL enhancement provides power management capability intended to support portable computers, such as notebooks and sub-notebooks.

By 1994, Intel was finishing its 486 series with the DX4 OverDrive processors. Contrary to the DX4 designation, these 3.3V OverDrive devices are clock *triplers*—so a 486DX4/100 actually runs at a motherboard clock speed of 33 MHz. It is important to note that all versions of the 80486 will run the same software and are backward compatible with all CPUs back to the 8086/8088. Also, the 486 series, like the 386, fully supports each of the three different modes of operation.

# PENTIUM (1993–1998)

By 1992, the 486 series had become well entrenched in everyday desktop computing, and Intel was already laying the groundwork for its next generation of CPU. While most users expected Intel to continue with its traditional numbering scheme and dub its next CPU the 80586, legal conflicts regarding trademarking forced Intel to use a name that it could trademark and call its own. In 1993, the 3.21 million-transistor Pentium microprocessor (dubbed "P5" or "P54" series) was introduced to eager PC manufacturers. The Pentium retains the 32-bit address bus width of the 486 family. With 32 address bits, the Pentium can directly address 4GB of RAM and can access up to 64TB of virtual memory. The 64-bit external data bus width can handle twice the data throughput of the 486s. At 60 MHz, the Pentium performs at 100 MIPS, and 66 MHz yields 111.6 MIPS (twice the processing power of the 486DX2/66). Early releases of the Pentium contained a bug in the processor's floating point unit, but Intel was able to isolate the problem. They offered replacements for all the affected processors. Table 12-2 shows a comparison of Pentium performance ratings in versions from 60 MHz to 200 MHz. All versions of the Pentium include an onboard math co-processor and are intended to be compatible with future OverDrive designs.

**TABLE 12-2    COMPARISON OF INTEL PENTIUM FAMILY PROCESSORS**

| CHIP | MHZ | BUS SPEED | L1 CACHE | L2 CACHE | FABRICATION | TRANSISTORS | FORM FACTOR | AVAILABILITY |
|------|-----|-----------|----------|----------|-------------|-------------|-------------|--------------|
| Pentium | 60 | 60 | 16KB | --- | 0.8 | 3.1 mil | Socket 4 | Obsolete |
| | 66 | 66 | 16KB | --- | 0.8 | 3.1 mil | Socket 4 | Obsolete |
| | 75 | 50 | 16KB | --- | 0.6 | 3.3 mil | Socket 5/7 | Obsolete |
| | 90 | 60 | 16KB | --- | 0.6 | 3.3 mil | Socket 5/7 | Obsolete |
| | 100 | 66 | 16KB | --- | 0.6 | 3.3 mil | Socket 5/7 | Obsolete |
| | 120 | 60 | 16KB | --- | 0.6 | 3.3 mil | Socket 5/7 | Obsolete |
| | 133 | 66 | 16KB | --- | 0.35 | 3.3 mil | Socket 5/7 | Obsolete |
| | 150 | 60 | 16KB | --- | 0.35 | 3.3 mil | Socket 7 | Obsolete |
| | 166 | 66 | 16KB | --- | 0.35 | 3.3 mil | Socket 7 | Obsolete |
| | 200 | 66 | 16KB | --- | 0.35 | 3.3 mil | Socket 7 | Obsolete |
| Pentium MMX | 133 | 66 | 32KB | --- | 0.35 | 4.5 mil | Socket 7 | Obsolete |
| | 150 | 66 | 32KB | --- | 0.35 | 4.5 mil | Socket 7 | Obsolete |
| | 166 | 66 | 32KB | --- | 0.35 | 4.5 mil | Socket 7 | Obsolete |
| | 200 | 66 | 32KB | --- | 0.35 | 4.5 mil | Socket 7 | Obsolete |
| | 233 | 66 | 32KB | --- | 0.35 | 4.5 mil | Socket 7 | Obsolete |
| Mobile Pentium MMX (Tillamook) | 166 | 66 | 32KB | --- | 0.25 | 4.5 mil | MMO | Obsolete |
| | 200 | 66 | 32KB | --- | 0.25 | 4.5 mil | MMO | Obsolete |
| | 233 | 66 | 32KB | --- | 0.25 | 4.5 mil | MMO | Obsolete |
| | 266 | 66 | 32KB | --- | 0.25 | 4.5 mil | MMO | Obsolete |
| | 300 | 66 | 32KB | --- | 0.25 | 4.5 mil | MMO | Obsolete |
| Pentium Pro | 150 | 60 | 16KB | 256KB | 0.35 | 5.5 mil | Socket 8 | Obsolete |
| | 166 | 66 | 16KB | 256KB | 0.35 | 5.5 mil | Socket 8 | Obsolete |

**TABLE 12-2    COMPARISON OF INTEL PENTIUM FAMILY PROCESSORS (CONTINUED)**

| CHIP | MHZ | BUS SPEED | L1 CACHE | L2 CACHE | FABRICATION | TRANSISTORS | FORM FACTOR | AVAILABILITY |
|---|---|---|---|---|---|---|---|---|
| | 166 | 66 | 16KB | 512KB | 0.35 | 5.5 mil | Socket 8 | Obsolete |
| | 180 | 60 | 16KB | 256KB | 0.35 | 5.5 mil | Socket 8 | Obsolete |
| | 200 | 66 | 16KB | 256KB | 0.35 | 5.5 mil | Socket 8 | Obsolete |
| | 200 | 66 | 16KB | 512KB | 0.35 | 5.5 mil | Socket 8 | Obsolete |
| | 200 | 66 | 16KB | 1MB | 0.35 | 5.5 mil | Socket 8 | Obsolete |
| Pentium II (Klamath) | 233 | 66 | 32KB | 512KB | 0.35 | 7.5 mil | Slot 1 | Obsolete |
| | 266 | 66 | 32KB | 512KB | 0.35 | 7.5 mil | Slot 1 | Obsolete |
| | 300 | 66 | 32KB | 512KB | 0.35 | 7.5 mil | Slot 1 | Obsolete |
| Pentium II (Deschutes) | 333 | 66 | 32KB | 128KB | 0.25 | 7.5 mil | Slot 1 Socket 370 | Obsolete |
| | 333 | 66 | 32KB | 512KB | 0.25 | 7.5 mil | Slot 1 | Obsolete |
| | 350 | 100 | 32KB | 512KB | 0.25 | 7.5 mil | Slot 1 | Available |
| | 366 | 66 | 32KB | 128KB | 0.25 | 7.5 mil | Slot 1 Socket 370 | Available |
| | 400 | 66 | 32KB | 128KB | 0.25 | 7.5 mil | Slot 1 Socket 370 | Available |
| | 400 | 100 | 32KB | 128KB | --- | 7.5 mil | Socket 370 | Available |
| | 400 | 100 | 32KB | 512KB | 0.25 | 7.5 mil | Slot 1 | Available |
| | 433 | 66 | 32KB | 128KB | 0.25 | 7.5 mil | Slot 1 Socket 370 | Available |
| | 450 | 100 | 32KB | 128KB | --- | 7.5 mil | Slot 1 Socket 370 | Available |
| | 450 | 100 | 32KB | 512KB | 0.25 | 7.5 mil | Slot 1 | Available |
| | 466 | 66 | 32KB | 128KB | 0.25 | 7.5 mil | Socket 370 | Available |
| | 500 | 66 | 32KB | 128KB | 0.25 | 7.5 mil | Socket 370 | Available |
| | 500 | 100 | 32KB | 128KB | --- | 7.5 mil | Socket 370 | Available |
| | 533 | 66 | 32KB | 128KB | 0.25 | 7.5 mil | Socket 370 | Available |
| | 566 | 66 | 32KB | 128KB | --- | 7.5 mil | Socket 370 | Available |
| | 600 | 66 | 32KB | 128KB | --- | 7.5 mil | Socket 370 | Available |
| | 633 | 66 | 32KB | 128KB | --- | 7.5 mil | Socket 370 | Available |
| Pentium II (Timna) | 600 | 100 | 32KB | 128KB | 0.18 | 22 mil | Socket 370 | Obsolete |
| Mobile Pentium II (Deschutes) | 233 | 66 | 32KB | 512KB | 0.25 | 7.5 mil | MMO | Obsolete |
| | 266 | 66 | 32KB | 512KB | 0.25 | 7.5 mil | MMO | Obsolete |
| | 300 | 66 | 32KB | 512KB | 0.25 | 7.5 mil | MMO | Obsolete |
| Mobile Pentium II - PE (Dixon) | 333 | 66 | 32KB | 256KB | 0.25 | 37 mil | MMO | Obsolete |
| | 366 | 66 | 32KB | 256KB | 0.25 | 37 mil | MMO | Obsolete |
| | 400 | 66 | 32KB | 256KB | 0.18 | 37 mil | MMO | Available |

**TABLE 12-2** COMPARISON OF INTEL PENTIUM FAMILY PROCESSORS *(CONTINUED)*

| CHIP | MHZ | BUS SPEED | L1 CACHE | L2 CACHE | FABRICATION | TRANSISTORS | FORM FACTOR | AVAILABILITY |
|---|---|---|---|---|---|---|---|---|
| Pentium II Celeron (Covington) | 266 | 66 | 32KB | none | 0.25 | 7.5 mil | Slot 1 | Obsolete |
| | 300 | 66 | 32KB | none | 0.25 | 7.5 mil | Slot 1 | Obsolete |
| Pentium II Celeron (Mendocino /300A) | 300 | 66 | 32KB | 128KB | 0.25 | 7.5 mil | Slot 1 Socket 370 | Obsolete |
| | 333 | 66 | 32KB | 128KB | 0.25 | 7.5 mil | Slot 1 Socket 370 | Obsolete |
| | 366 | 66 | 32KB | 128KB | 0.25 | 7.5 mil | Slot 1 Socket 370 | Available |
| | 400 | 66 | 32KB | 128KB | 0.25 | 7.5 mil | Slot 1 Socket 370 | Available |
| | 433 | 66 | 32KB | 128KB | 0.25 | 7.5 mil | Slot 1 Socket 370 | Available |
| | 466 | 66 | 32KB | 128KB | 0.25 | 7.5 mil | Socket 370 | Available |
| | 500 | 66 | 32KB | 128KB | 0.25 | 7.5 mil | Socket 370 | Available |
| | 533 | 66 | 32KB | 128KB | 0.25 | 7.5 mil | Socket 370 | Available |
| Pentium II Xeon | 400 | 100 | 32KB | 512KB 1MB | 0.25 | 7.5 mil | Slot 2 | Available |
| | 450 | 100 | 32KB | 512KB 2MB | 0.25 | 7.5 mil | Slot 2 | Available |
| Pentium III (Katmai) | 450 | 100 | 32KB | 512KB | 0.25 | 9.5 mil | Slot 1 | Available |
| | 500 | 100 | 32KB | 512KB | 0.25 | 9.5 mil | Slot 1 | Available |
| | 533B | 133 | 32KB | 512KB | 0.18 | 9.5 mil | Slot 1 | Available |
| | 550 | 100 | 32KB | 512KB | 0.25 | 9.5 mil | Slot 1 | Available |
| | 600 | 100 | 32KB | 512KB | 0.25 | 9.5 mil | Slot 1 | Available |
| | 600B | 133 | 32KB | 512KB | 0.18 / 0.25 | 9.5 mil | Slot 1 | Available |
| Pentium III (Copper-mine) | 500E | 100 | 32KB | 256KB | 0.18 | 28 mil | Slot 1 Socket 370FC | Available |
| | 533 EB | 133 | 32KB | 256KB | 0.18 | 28 mil | Slot 1 Socket 370FC | Available |
| | 550E | 100 | 32KB | 256KB | 0.18 | 28 mil | Slot 1 Socket 370FC | Available |
| | 600E | 100 | 32KB | 256KB | 0.18 | 28 mil | Slot 1 Socket 370FC | Available |
| | 600 EB | 133 | 32KB | 256KB | 0.18 | 28 mil | Slot 1 Socket 370FC | Available |

**TABLE 12-2     COMPARISON OF INTEL PENTIUM FAMILY PROCESSORS (CONTINUED)**

| CHIP | MHZ | BUS SPEED | L1 CACHE | L2 CACHE | FABRICATION | TRANSISTORS | FORM FACTOR | AVAILABILITY |
|------|-----|-----------|----------|----------|-------------|-------------|-------------|--------------|
| | 650E | 100 | 32KB | 256KB | 0.18 | 28 mil | Slot 1 Socket 370FC | Available |
| | 667 EB | 133 | 32KB | 256KB | 0.18 | 28 mil | Slot 1 Socket 370FC | Available |
| | 700E | 100 | 32KB | 256KB | 0.18 | 28 mil | Slot 1 Socket 370FC | Available |
| | 733 EB | 133 | 32KB | 256KB | 0.18 | 28 mil | Slot 1 Socket 370FC | Available |
| | 750E | 100 | 32KB | 256KB | 0.18 | 28 mil | Slot 1 Socket 370FC | Available |
| | 800E | 100 | 32KB | 256KB | 0.18 | 28 mil | Slot 1 Socket 370FC | Available |
| | 800 EB | 133 | 32KB | 256KB | 0.18 | 28 mil | Slot 1 Socket 370FC | Available |
| | 850E | 100 | 32KB | 256KB | 0.18 | 28 mil | Slot 1 Socket 370FC | Available |
| | 866 EB | 133 | 32KB | 256KB | 0.18 | 28 mil | Slot 1 Socket 370FC | Available |
| | 900E | 100 | 32KB | 256KB | 0.18 | 28 mil | Socket 370FC | Available |
| | 933 EB | 133 | 32KB | 256KB | 0.18 | 28 mil | Slot 1 Socket 370FC | Available |
| | 1000E | 100 | 32KB | 256KB | 0.18 | 28 mil | Slot 1 Socket 370FC | Available |
| | 1000 EB | 133 | 32KB | 256KB | 0.18 | 28 mil | Slot 1 Socket 370FC | Available |
| | 1100E | 100 | 32KB | 256KB | 0.18 | 28 mil | Socket 370FC | Available |
| | 1133 EB | 133 | 32KB | 256KB | 0.18 | 28 mil | Slot 1/370FC | Available |
| (Tualatin) | 1133 | 133 | 32KB | 512KB | 0.13 | 44 mil | Socket 370FC | Available |
| | 1200 | 133 | 32KB | 256KB | 0.13 | 28 mil | Socket 370FC | Available |

**TABLE 12-2    COMPARISON OF INTEL PENTIUM FAMILY PROCESSORS *(CONTINUED)***

| CHIP | MHZ | BUS SPEED | L1 CACHE | L2 CACHE | FABRICATION | TRANSISTORS | FORM FACTOR | AVAILABILITY |
|---|---|---|---|---|---|---|---|---|
| | 1266 | 133 | 32KB | 256KB | 0.13 | 28 mil | Socket 370FC | Available |
| | 1333 | 133 | 32KB | 256KB | 0.13 | 28 mil | Socket 370FC | Available |
| | 1400 | 133 | 32KB | 512KB | 0.13 | 44 mil | Socket 370FC | Available |
| Mobile Pentium III (Coppermine) | 400 | 100 | 32KB | 256KB | 0.18 | 28 mil | --- | Available |
| | 450 | 100 | 32KB | 256KB | 0.18 | 28 mil | --- | Available |
| | 500 | 100 | 32KB | 256KB | 0.18 | 28 mil | --- | Available |
| (Low Voltage) | 500 | 100 | 32KB | 256KB | 0.18 | 28 mil | --- | Available |
| (Ultra Low Voltage) | 500/ 300 | 100 | 32KB | 256KB | 0.18 | 28 mil | --- | Available |
| (Speed-step) | 600/ 500 | 100 | 32KB | 256KB | 0.18 | 28 mil | --- | Available |
| (Ultra Low Voltage) | 600/ 300 | 100 | 32KB | 256KB | 0.18 | 28 mil | --- | Available |
| (Low Voltage) | 600/ 500 | 100 | 32KB | 256KB | 0.18 | 28 mil | --- | Available |
| (Speed-step) | 650/ 500 | 100 | 32KB | 256KB | 0.18 | 28 mil | --- | Available |
| (Speed-step) | 700/ 500 | 100 | 32KB | 256KB | 0.18 | 28 mil | --- | Available |
| | 700/ 300 | 100 | 32KB | 512KB | 0.13 | 44 mil | --- | Available |
| (Low Voltage) | 700/ 500 | 100 | 32KB | 256KB | 0.18 | 28 mil | --- | Available |
| | 700/ 550 | 100 | 32KB | 256KB | 0.18 | 28 mil | --- | Available |
| | 750/ 350 | 100 | 32KB | 512KB | 0.13 | 44 mil | --- | Available |
| | 750/ 450 | 100 | 32KB | 512KB | 0.13 | 44 mil | --- | Available |
| (Low Voltage) | 750/ 500 | 100 | 32KB | 256KB | 0.18 | 28 mil | --- | Available |
| (Speed-step) | 750/ 600 | 100 | 32KB | 256KB | 0.18 | 28 mil | --- | Available |
| | 800A/ 500 | 100 | 32KB | 512KB | 0.13 | 44 mil | --- | Available |
| | 800/ 533 | 133 | 32KB | 512KB | 0.13 | 44 mil | --- | Available |
| (Speed-step) | 800/ 650 | 100 | 32KB | 256KB | 0.18 | 28 mil | --- | Available |

**TABLE 12-2   COMPARISON OF INTEL PENTIUM FAMILY PROCESSORS *(CONTINUED)***

| CHIP | MHZ | BUS SPEED | L1 CACHE | L2 CACHE | FABRICATION | TRANSISTORS | FORM FACTOR | AVAILABILITY |
|---|---|---|---|---|---|---|---|---|
| | 850/ 500 | 100 | 32KB | 512KB | 0.13 | 44 mil | --- | Available |
| (Speed-step) | 850/ 700 | 100 | 32KB | 256KB | 0.18 | 28 mil | --- | Available |
| | 866/ 533 | 133 | 32KB | 512KB | 0.13 | 44 mil | --- | Available |
| | 866/ 667 | 133 | 32KB | 512KB | 0.13 | 44 mil | --- | Available |
| | 900/ 700 | 100 | 32KB | 256KB | 0.18 | 28 mil | --- | Available |
| | 933/ 733 | 133 | 32KB | 512KB | 0.13 | 44 mil | --- | Available |
| | 1000/ 700 | 100 | 32KB | 256KB | 0.18 | 28 mil | --- | Available |
| | 1000/ 733 | 133 | 32KB | 512KB | 0.13 | 44 mil | --- | Available |
| | 1066/ 733 | 133 | 32KB | 512KB | 0.13 | 44 mil | --- | Available |
| | 1133/ 733 | 133 | 32KB | 512KB | 0.13 | 44 mil | --- | Available |
| | 1200/ 800 | 133 | 32KB | 512KB | 0.13 | 44 mil | --- | Available |
| | 1266 | 133 | 32KB | 256KB | 0.13 | --- | --- | Available |
| Pentium III Celeron | 533 | 66 | 32KB | 128KB | 0.25 | 7.5 mil | Socket 370 | Available |
| | 566 | 66 | 32KB | 128KB | 0.18 | 7.5 mil | Socket 370 | Available |
| | 600 | 66 | 32KB | 128KB | 0.18 | 7.5 mil | Socket 370 | Available |
| | 633 | 66 | 32KB | 128KB | 0.18 | 7.5 mil | Socket 370 | Available |
| | 667 | 66 | 32KB | 128KB | 0.18 | 7.5 mil | Socket 370 | Available |
| | 700 | 66 | 32KB | 128KB | 0.18 | 7.5 mil | Socket 370 | Available |
| | 733 | 66 | 32KB | 128KB | 0.18 | 7.5 mil | Socket 370 | Available |
| | 766 | 66 | 32KB | 128KB | 0.18 | 7.5 mil | Socket 370 | Available |
| | 800 | 100 | 32KB | 128KB | 0.18 | 7.5 mil | Socket 370 | Available |
| | 850 | 100 | 32KB | 128KB | 0.18 | 7.5 mil | Socket 370 | Available |
| | 900 | 100 | 32KB | 128KB | 0.18 | 7.5 mil | Socket 370 | Available |
| | 900 | 100 | 32KB | 128KB | 0.13 | --- | FC-PGA2 | Available |
| | 950 | 100 | 32KB | 128KB | 0.18 | 7.5 mil | Socket 370 | Available |
| | 950 | 100 | 32KB | 128KB | 0.13 | --- | FC-PGA2 | Available |
| | 1000 | 100 | 32KB | 128KB | 0.18 | 7.5 mil | Socket 370 | Available |
| | 1000 | 100 | 32KB | 128KB | 0.13 | --- | FC-PGA2 | Available |
| | 1000A | 100 | 32KB | 256KB | 0.13 | --- | FC-PGA2 | Available |
| | 1100 | 100 | 32KB | 128KB | 0.18 | 7.5 mil | Socket 370 | Available |
| | 1100A | 100 | 32KB | 256KB | 0.13 | --- | FC-PGA2 | Available |
| | 1200 | 100 | 32KB | 256KB | 0.13 | --- | FC-PGA2 | Available |

**TABLE 12-2    COMPARISON OF INTEL PENTIUM FAMILY PROCESSORS** *(CONTINUED)*

| CHIP | MHZ | BUS SPEED | L1 CACHE | L2 CACHE | FABRICATION | TRANSISTORS | FORM FACTOR | AVAILABILITY |
|---|---|---|---|---|---|---|---|---|
| | 1300 | 100 | 32KB | 256KB | 0.13 | --- | FC-PGA2 | Available |
| Pentium III Xeon (Tanner) | 500 | 100 | 32KB | 512KB 2MB | 0.25 | 9.5 mil | Slot 2 | Available |
| | 550 | 100 | 32KB | 512KB 2MB | 0.25 | 9.5 mil | Slot 2 | Available |
| | 600 | 133 | 32KB | 256KB | 0.18 | 28 mil | Slot 2 | Available |
| | 700 | 100 | 32KB | 1MB 2MB | 0.18 | 28–140 mil | Slot 2 | Available |
| | 900 | 100 | 32KB | 2MB | 0.18 | 140 mil | Slot 2 | Available |
| Pentium III Xeon (Cascades) | 667 | 133 | 32KB | 256KB | 0.18 | 28 mil | Slot 2 | Available |
| | 733 | 133 | 32KB | 256KB | 0.18 | 28 mil | Slot 2 | Available |
| | 800 | 133 | 32KB | 256KB | 0.18 | 28 mil | Slot 2 | Available |
| | 866 | 133 | 32KB | 256KB | 0.18 | 28 mil | Slot 2 | Available |
| | 933 | 133 | 32KB | 256KB | 0.18 | 28 mil | Slot 2 | Available |
| | 1000 | 133 | 32KB | 256KB | 0.18 | 28 mil | Slot 2 | Available |
| Mobile Celeron III | 400 | 100 | 32KB | 128KB | 0.18 | 22 mil | --- | Available |
| | 450 | 100 | 32KB | 128KB | 0.18 | 22 mil | --- | Available |
| | 500 | 100 | 32KB | 128KB | 0.18 | 22 mil | --- | Available |
| | 550 | 100 | 32KB | 128KB | 0.18 | 22 mil | --- | Available |
| | 600 | 100 | 32KB | 128KB | 0.18 | 22 mil | --- | Available |
| | 650 | 100 | 32KB | 128KB | 0.18 | 22 mil | --- | Available |
| | 700 | 100 | 32KB | 128KB | 0.18 | 22 mil | --- | Available |
| | 733 | 133 | 32KB | 128KB | 0.13 | --- | --- | Available |
| | 750 | 100 | 32KB | 128KB | 0.18 | 22 mil | --- | Available |
| | 800 | 100 | 32KB | 128KB | 0.18 | 22 mil | --- | Available |
| | 800A | 133 | 32KB | 128KB | 0.13 | --- | --- | Available |
| | 850 | 100 | 32KB | 128KB | 0.18 | 22 mil | --- | Available |
| | 866 | 133 | 32KB | 128KB | 0.13 | --- | --- | Available |
| | 900 | 100 | 32KB | 128KB | 0.18 | 22 mil | --- | Available |
| | 933 | 133 | 32KB | 128KB | 0.13 | --- | --- | Available |
| | 1133 | 133 | 32KB | 256KB | 0.13 | --- | --- | Available |
| Pentium 4 (Willa-mette) | 1300 | 400 | 20KB | 256KB | 0.18 | 42 mil | Socket 423 | Available |
| | 1400 | 400 | 20KB | 256KB | 0.18 | 42 mil | Socket 423/478 | Available |
| | 1500 | 400 | 20KB | 256KB | 0.18 | 42 mil | Socket 423/478 | Available |
| | 1600 | 400 | 20KB | 256KB | 0.18 | 42 mil | Socket 423/478 | Available |

**TABLE 12-2    COMPARISON OF INTEL PENTIUM FAMILY PROCESSORS *(CONTINUED)***

| CHIP | MHZ | BUS SPEED | L1 CACHE | L2 CACHE | FABRICATION | TRANSISTORS | FORM FACTOR | AVAILABILITY |
|---|---|---|---|---|---|---|---|---|
| | 1700 | 400 | 20KB | 256KB | 0.18 | 42 mil | Socket 423/478 | Available |
| | 1800 | 400 | 20KB | 256KB | 0.18 | 42 mil | Socket 423/478 | Available |
| | 1900 | 400 | 20KB | 256KB | 0.18 | 42 mil | Socket 423/478 | Available |
| | 1600 | 400 | 20KB | 512KB | 0.13 | 55 mil | Socket 478 | Available |
| | 1800 | 400 | 20KB | 512KB | 0.13 | 55 mil | Socket 478 | Available |
| | 2000 | 400 | 20KB | 512KB | 0.13 | 55 mil | Socket 478 | Available |
| | 2200 | 400 | 20KB | 512KB | 0.13 | 55 mil | Socket 478 | Available |
| | 2400 | 400 | 20KB | 512KB | 0.13 | 55 mil | Socket 478 | Available |
| | 2533 | 533 | 20KB | 512KB | 0.13 | 55 mil | Socket 478 | Available |
| (Mobile P4) | 1400 | 400 | 20KB | 512KB | 0.13 | --- | --- | Discont. |
| | 1500 | 400 | 20KB | 512KB | 0.13 | --- | --- | Discont. |
| | 1600 | 400 | 20KB | 512KB | 0.13 | --- | --- | Available |
| | 1700 | 400 | 20KB | 512KB | 0.13 | --- | --- | Available |
| | 1800 | 400 | 20KB | 512KB | 0.13 | --- | --- | Available |
| | 1900 | 400 | 20KB | 512KB | 0.13 | --- | --- | Q3 2002 |
| | 2000 | 400 | 20KB | 512KB | 0.13 | --- | --- | Q4 2002 |
| (Xeon P4) | 1400 | 400 | --- | 256KB | 0.13 | --- | Socket 603 | Available |
| | 1500 | 400 | --- | 256KB | 0.13 | --- | Socket 603 | Available |
| | 1700 | 400 | --- | 256KB | 0.13 | --- | Socket 603 | Available |
| | 1800 | 400 | --- | 512KB | 0.13 | --- | Socket 603 | Available |
| | 2000 | 400 | --- | 256-512KB | 0.13 | --- | Socket 603 | Available |
| | 2200 | 400 | --- | 512KB | 0.13 | --- | Socket 603 | Available |
| (Gallatin) Multi-Processor | 1400 | 400 | --- | 256KB L2 512KB L3 | 0.13 | --- | Socket 603 | Available |
| | 1500 | 400 | --- | 256KB L2 512KB L3 | 0.13 | --- | Socket 603 | Available |
| | 1600 | 400 | --- | 256KB L2 1MB L3 | 0.13 | --- | Socket 603 | Available |
| | 2000 | 400 | --- | 1MB-2MB | 0.13 | --- | Socket 603 | Q4 2002 |

The original Pentium uses two 8KB caches—one for instructions and another for data (16KB total). A dual pipelining technique allows the Pentium to actually work on *more* than one instruction per clock cycle. Another substantial improvement in the Pentium's design was the inclusion of onboard power management features (similar to the 486SL line), allowing it to be used effectively in portable computers.

Early Pentium models started at 5 volts, but all models starting at about 100 MHz (P54C) use 3.3 volts or less. Finally, the Pentium is fully backward-compatible with all software written for the 8086/8088 and later CPUs. Intel has released various versions of the Pentium up to 200 MHz. Faster versions did not appear because of more powerful processors, such as the Pentium MMX, Pentium Pro, and of course, the Pentium II/III/4. Technicians who want the nitty-gritty details on Pentium operation can download the Pentium-family processor manuals from the Internet, as listed in Table 12-3.

The number of Pentium versions and features greatly proliferated over the years—so much so that it is *extremely* difficult to tell whether a motherboard is configured properly for a given CPU. However, you can use the Intel S-step rating (the engineering revision level) marked on each Pentium, Pentium MMX, and later processors to reveal key operating characteristics of the particular CPU. For Intel processors, you can access the Processor Spec Finder at processorfinder.intel.com/scripts/default.asp (as in Figure 12-6) to locate specific information based on the processor's S-step number. Simply enter the product order code or S-step number into the corresponding box and click Find. The Web site will return a set of specs for that processor, including details like package type, revision (engineering) step, core/bus speeds, and so on.

**TABLE 12-3    DETAILED PROCESSOR MANUALS AND TECHNICAL INFORMATION**

| PROCESSOR | MANUAL URL |
|---|---|
| Pentium Processor Manuals | developer.intel.com/design/pentium/manuals/ |
| Pentium MMX Manuals | developer.intel.com/design/mmx/manuals/ |
| PentiumPro Processor Manuals | developer.intel.com/design/pro/manuals/ |
| Pentium II Manuals | developer.intel.com/design/PentiumII/manuals/ |
| Pentium III Manuals | developer.intel.com/design/pentiumiii/manuals/ |
| Pentium 4 Manuals | developer.intel.com/design/Pentium4/manuals/ |
| Itanium Manual | developer.intel.com/design/itanium/manuals/ |
| Am486DX2 Manual | www.amd.com/products/cpg/techdocs/datasheets/19200.pdf |
| Am486DX4 Manual | www.amd.com/products/cpg/techdocs/datasheets/19160.pdf |
| 5x85 Manual | www.amd.com/products/cpg/techdocs/datasheets/19751.pdf |
| K5 Manual | www.amd.com/products/cpg/techdocs/appnotes/18524.pdf |
| K6 Manual | www.amd.com/K6/k6docs/pdf/20695.pdf |
| Athlon (K7) Manual | www.amd.com/us-en/assets/content_type/white_papers_and_tech_docs/23792.pdf |
| Athlon XP | www.amd.com/us-en/assets/content_type/white_papers_and_tech_docs/24309.pdf |
| Athlon MP | http://www.amd.com/us-en/assets/content_type/white_papers_and_tech_docs/25480.pdf |
| AMD Duron | www.amd.com/us-en/assets/content_type/white_papers_and_tech_docs/24310.pdf |
| AMD Athlon 4 | http://www.amd.com/us-en/assets/content_type/white_papers_and_tech_docs/25429B_Mobile_Athlon_4WP.pdf |
| VIA C3 | www.viatech.com/en/viac3/VIAC3_S2datasheet.pdf |
| VIA Cyrix MII | www.viatech.com/en/viac3/cyrix_MII.jsp |

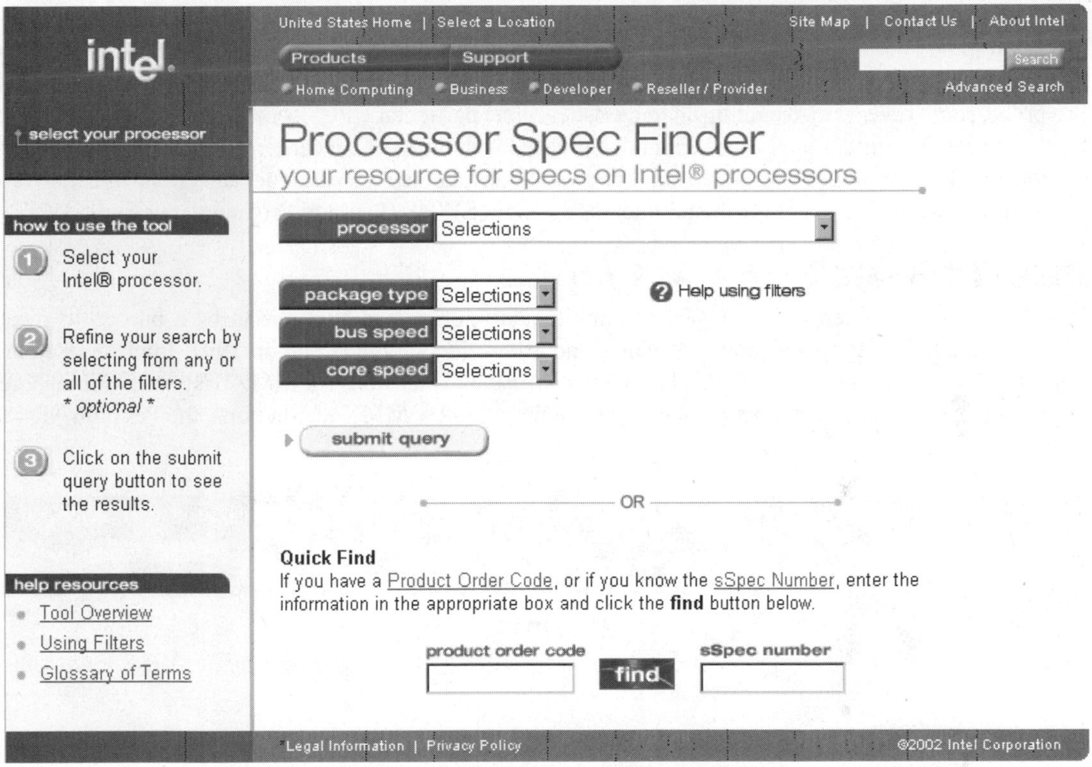

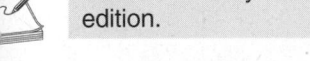

**FIGURE 12-6** Web-based tools like Intel's Processor Spec Finder let you look up processor specs with only the S-step number.

Given the ready availability of Internet access, specific S-step tables have been dropped from this edition.

## PENTIUM PRO (1995–1999)

Even though the Pentium has proven adept at handling 16-bit and 32-bit operating systems, designers continued to seek ways to optimize the Pentium for 32-bit performance—especially for operating systems like Windows NT and the then-emerging Windows 95. The Pentium Pro (dubbed "P6" or "PPro") evolved as an "optimized" Pentium intended to support "business systems," such as high-end desktop workstations and network servers of the day. The P6 processors range from 150 MHz to 200 MHz and can handle multiprocessing in systems up to four CPUs.

The Pentium Pro uses dynamic execution to improve its performance and employs two separate 8KB L1 caches—one for data, and one for instructions. Another major improvement in the Pentium Pro is its use of up to 1MB of onboard L2 cache. This maximizes the P6's performance without relying on the motherboard to supply L2 cache. You can see the use of L1 and L2 cache and Pentium Pro family performance in Table 12-2.

While not as prolific as the "classic" Pentium and Pentium MMX, there are still a number of Pentium Pro versions and features to contend with—this variety can make it difficult to determine the proper motherboard configuration for a given P6. However, you can use the "S-step" rating marked on each Pentium Pro processor to reveal key operating characteristics of the particular CPU. Access Intel's Processor Spec Finder at processorfinder.intel.com/scripts/default.asp (as in Figure 12-6 earlier) to locate specific information based on the processor's S-step number. Once you enter the S-step number and click Find, the Web site will return detailed specs for the product, such as the SY048 (Pentium Pro) shown in Figure 12-7.

## PENTIUM MMX (1997–1999)

The data processing demands imposed by multimedia applications continue to be a burden to most PCs—especially for graphics-intensive games and other video applications. In 1997, Intel released an important enhancement to the Pentium known as *multimedia extensions* (or MMX). By streamlining and improving the existing Pentium architecture and adding 57 new MMX instructions, the Pentium MMX

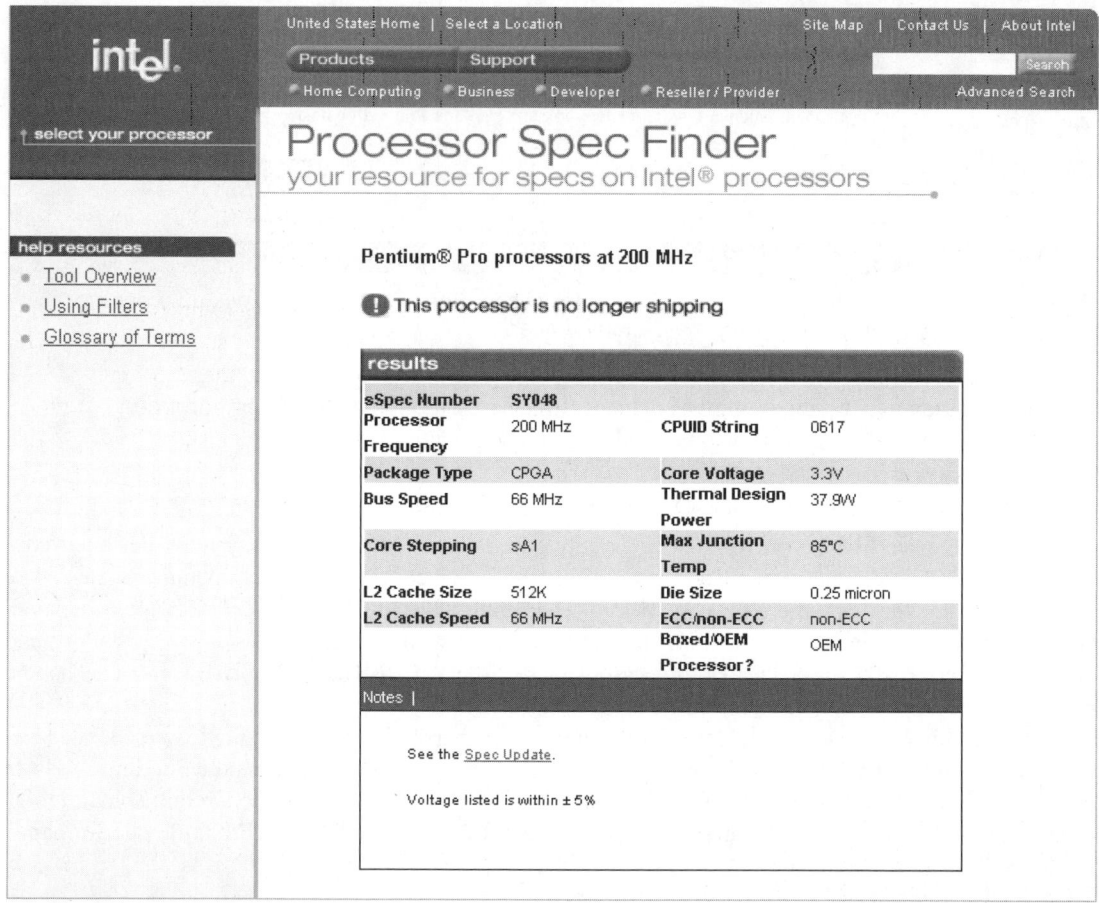

**FIGURE  12-7**    Intel's Processor Spec Finder returns a suite of product specs that can help you verify a system's configuration.

was poised as the premier mid-range CPU into the late 1990s. With speeds from 133 MHz to 233 MHz, the Pentium MMX can typically execute existing software 10–20 percent faster than "classic" Pentium processors at the same clock speed. When using software written specifically for MMX instructions, the PC can deliver higher color depths and higher resolutions while still maintaining high frame rates for rendering and video playback.

The Pentium MMX doubled the code and data caches to 16KB each. Larger and separate internal caches improve performance by reducing the average memory access time and providing fast access to recently used instructions and data. The data cache supports a write-back (or write-through on a line-by-line basis) policy for memory updates. Pentium MMX processors also employ improved dynamic branch prediction to boost performance by predicting the most likely set of instructions to be executed.

There are many other features included in the Pentium MMX line. The superscalar architecture is capable of executing two integer instructions in parallel in a single clock cycle for improved integer processing performance. A pipelined floating point unit (FPU) supporting 32-bit, 64-bit, and 80-bit formats is capable of executing two floating-point instructions in a single clock. An additional instruction pipe was added to further improve instruction processing. A pool of four write buffers is shared between the dual pipelines to improve memory write performance. There is also a multiprocessor interrupt controller on-chip that allows low-cost symmetric multiprocessing (SMP), and there are SL technology power management features for efficient power control. Use Intel's Product Spec Finder at processorfinder.intel.com/scripts/default.asp to locate specific details for each Pentium MMX processor.

## PENTIUM II (1997–2001)

With the Pentium MMX and Pentium Pro processors firmly entrenched in the PC community, Intel sought to combine the best features of both—the software performance of the Pentium Pro and the multimedia performance of the Pentium MMX. The result appeared in 1997 as the "Pentium II" (or "P II," previously dubbed the "Klamath"). As with the Pentium Pro, the Pentium II is optimized for use with 32-bit operating systems and software (such as Windows 98/Me/XP or Windows NT). Yet the P II also includes the architecture and 57 new instructions needed to handle MMX applications. At 266 MHz, the Pentium II processor can provide from 1.6 to over 2 times the performance of a 200 MHz Pentium processor.

The Pentium II also employs the dynamic execution technology used in the Pentium Pro. Dynamic execution uses multiple branch prediction to predict the flow of the program through several branches (accelerating the flow of work to the processor). A data flow analysis then creates an optimized (reordered) schedule of instructions by analyzing the relationships between instructions. And, finally, speculative execution carries out the instructions "speculatively" (assuming the execution order to be correct) on the basis of this optimized schedule. Dynamic execution keeps the processor's superscaler "execution engines" busy and boosts overall performance.

The Pentium II uses a 32KB L1 cache—this allows a 16KB cache for data, and a 16KB cache for instructions. It also provides 512KB of L2 cache right in the CPU package to maximize the processor's performance without relying on the motherboard for cache. The P II supports up to 64GB of physical RAM and allows dual processors—so motherboards can be designed for basic symmetric multiprocessing (SMP). A pipelined floating point unit (FPU) supporting 32-bit, 64-bit, and 80-bit formats is capable of executing two floating-point instructions in a single clock, and of sustaining over 300 million floating-point instructions per second at 300 MHz. Table 12-2 outlines the performance comparison for Pentium II processors from 233 MHz to 633 MHz (using the "Deschutes" core).

One of the most noticeable departures from previous CPUs was the package style. Intel abandoned the use of Socket 7 (Pentium) and Socket 8 (Pentium Pro) packages and adopted a "cartridge style" package known as the "Single Edge Contact" (or "SEC") cartridge. We generally know this as the "Slot 1" style of connector. While not quite as prolific as the "classic" Pentium, the Pentium MMX, or even the Pentium Pro, there are still a large number of Pentium II versions and features to contend with. This variety can make it difficult to determine the proper motherboard configuration for a given P II. However, you can reference the S-step rating marked on each Pentium II processor to reveal key operating characteristics of the particular CPU. Use Intel's Product Spec Finder at processorfinder.intel.com/scripts/default.asp to locate specific details for each Pentium II processor.

## PENTIUM II OVERDRIVE (1998–2001)

Two Pentium II OverDrive processors have been produced for upgrading Pentium Pro (Socket 8) processors. One OverDrive replaces the 150–180 MHz Pentium Pro (60 MHz bus speed) and provides a performance increase to 300 MHz. The other OverDrive replaces the 166–200 MHz (66 MHz bus speed) Pentium Pro processors and increases performance to 333 MHz. The integrated on-die L2 cache design of the Socket 8 package style also provides a performance increase by allowing the L2 cache to operate at full core speed. Pentium II OverDrive processors for Socket 8 systems are extremely rare today.

## PENTIUM II/III CELERON (1998–CURRENT)

Commonly known as just the "Celeron," this CPU was introduced by Intel in April of 1998. It was originally manufactured as a "stripped down" version of the Pentium II. The Intel Celeron uses the same P6 core and provides the same features as the Pentium Pro and Pentium II. It has 32KB L1 cache (16KB for data and 16KB for instructions). It includes MMX features, pipelined floating point unit, and dynamic execution architecture, and it is constructed with the same 0.25 micron process to reduce heat production. Later Celerons used the "Coppermine" Pentium III core and were manufactured using a 0.18 micron process. Current Celerons use the "Tualatin" 0.13 micron core.

Most noticeably *missing* from the first Celerons was the presence of an L2 cache. This cost-cutting move was intended to increase competition against the low cost CPUs being produced by AMD and Cyrix, while maintaining the selling power of the "Intel Inside" mystique. Additional cost reductions were achieved by eliminating the fancy Pentium II plastic cover creating the Single Edge Processor Package (SEPP or Slot 1) style Celeron, and adding a PPGA (Plastic Pin Grid Array) style case for use in Socket 370 connectors. The latest Socket 370-compatible Celeron processors are available in the popular FC-PGA2 (Flip Chip-Pin Grid Array) style package, which offers better cooling for the processor.

> Not all Socket 370 motherboards will support both PPGA and FC-PGA style processors. Be sure the selected package style is supported by the motherboard.

The lack of built-in L2 cache severely limited the performance of Intel's early Celerons. Less expensive competing processors *included* L2 cache, and they out-performed Celerons of the same or similar clock speeds. Beginning with the Celeron 300A model, Intel returned 128KB of built-in cache to the Celeron processors. For the Celeron PPGA and FC-PGA, Intel integrated the L2 cache directly on the processor die. This integration allows the L2 cache speed to scale (or "match") processor speed and improves performance even further. In fact, 128KB of integrated L2 Celeron cache running *at* the processor speed is said to match the performance of the Pentium II 512KB off-die L2 cache running at half the processor speed. The latest Celeron processors include 256KB of L2 cache.

There were other Pentium II features missing in the Celeron. For example, there is no support for dual processors or for streaming SIMD extensions (SSE), limiting the Celeron's versatility in multimedia applications. However, SSE support was added with the introduction of the PIII core Celeron. There is also a lower front side bus (FSB) speed—66 MHz compared to 100 MHz. This feature allows computer manufacturers to use lower-cost, lower-performance parts and thereby reduce overall system cost. Fortunately, the rapid cost reductions in 100 MHz-compatible components (along with severe competition from AMD) finally forced Intel to add 100 MHz FSB support to the Celeron processor line. Celeron processors (based on the Pentium III core) can reach speeds of 1.3 GHz and up and support the 100 MHz FSB.

Today, Intel has settled on the FC-PGA/2 package for the Celeron processor. This provides for lower cost, better cooling, and integrated L2 cache. Also, motherboard redesign costs are less expensive (because of the Socket 370 style attachment)—the changes needed to go from a Socket 7 to a Socket 370 are fewer and less expensive than redesigning a motherboard for a Slot 1 connector. Third parties make an adapter (referred to as a "Slot-Ket") that allows Socket 370 Celerons to be used in Slot 1 motherboards. Celerons from 266 MHz to 433 MHz are available in the Single Edge Processor Package (SEPP) style, while Celerons from 300 MHz and up are available in both the Plastic Pin Grid Array (PPGA) and the Flip Chip-Pin Grid Array (FC-PGA) style package. You can see a recent Celeron in Figure 12-1 earlier. The differences in cache and package styles make for an interesting variety of available products. For additional information, use Intel's Product Spec Finder at processorfinder.intel.com/scripts/default.asp to locate specific details for each Celeron processor based on the S-step number.

## PENTIUM III (1999–CURRENT)

First made available in February of 1999, the Intel Pentium III continues to use the same basic P6 core as the Pentium Pro and the Pentium II (so the main features of the line remain unchanged). Later Pentium III models use a 0.18 and 0.13 micron manufacturing process (compared to their prior standard 0.25 micron process), which helps lower processor operating temperatures. Processor heat is also addressed with the use of a new SECC 2 (Single Edge Contact Cartridge) package, which covers only one side of the chip—this approach decreases weight, lowers cost, and allows for a more efficient attachment of the heat sink assembly. Realizing the advantages of a "socket" connector with the Pentium III (as well as the Celeron), Intel began to produce the Pentium III in an FC-PGA (Flip Chip-Pin Grid Array) package. Intel has since discontinued development of slot-style processors. They have improved the socket-style connector with the introduction of the FC-PGA2 package. This style includes an Integrated Heat Spreader (IHS) to address problems with chips cracking when the heat sink was attached.

The overall performance of the Pentium III continues to improve with the introduction of higher processor speeds and the ability to utilize a 133 MHz front side bus (FSB). You can see the proliferation of Pentium III models in Table 12-2. Intel's Streaming SIMD Extensions (SSE) technology (introduced in the Pentium III) added new registers and instructions to the processor chip—bringing the total number of transistors in the core logic to over 9.5 million. As with MMX extensions, applications must be specifically written to take advantage of these SSE instructions and thereby produce any increase in 3D/graphics performance. Other performance features include a 32KB L1 cache, 4GB addressable memory with ECC, and dual processor support.

The earliest Pentium III processors (manufactured using a 0.25 micron process) use the "Katmai" core. These processors come in speeds from 450 MHz to 600 MHz and offer 512KB of L2 cache. The cache is located on a separate die from the processor and runs at one-half the core processor speed. The later Pentium III processors use a 0.18 micron manufacturing process. This core was named "Coppermine" and comes in speeds of 500 MHz up to 1 GHz. The improved manufacturing process allows for the inclusion of 256KB of L2 cache on the same die as the processor. This smaller L2 cache runs at the same speed as the core processor, so performance is not impaired. The latest "Tualatin" core Pentium IIIs use a 0.13 micron manufacturing process and are available in speeds from 1 GHz to 1.4 GHz.

The different versions of the Pentium III can be identified by the presence or absence of several letters in the speed part of the name. If an "E" is part of the name (such as 600E), the processor includes 256KB of L2 cache. If a "B" is part of the name (such as 600B), the processor uses a FSB speed of 133 MHz. Pentium III processors without any added letters offer 512KB of slower L2 cache and use an FSB speed of 100 MHz. So, versions may be available with no letters, with an "E," with a "B," or with "EB" added to the name. The later 0.18 micron Pentium IIIs all include the "EB" suffix, offering 256KB of high-speed, on-die L2 cache designed to run at a 133 MHz FSB speed. Processors manufactured using the 0.13 micron process have dropped the use of any suffix.

Intel introduced the integrated "processor serial number" (or "PSN") with the Pentium III. This number allows individual processors (and possibly entire systems) to be identified remotely over a network. Identification can even take place over the Internet. Seen by Intel as a security enhancement for online transactions, this feature was viewed as an invasion of privacy by a large segment of users. Public pressure first forced Intel to make it possible to disable this feature, and finally to ship Pentium IIIs with this feature *disabled* by default. End users can still enable processor serial number identification if they wish. The latest 0.13 micron Pentium IIIs do not include this serial number and do not offer support for dual processors. Intel's focus on the Pentium 4 may limit any further development or improvements in the Pentium III line of processors.

There are a large number of Pentium III versions and features to contend with, and this can make it difficult to determine the proper motherboard configuration for a given P III. However, you can use the S-step rating marked on each Pentium III processor to reveal key operating characteristics of the particular CPU. Use Intel's Product Spec Finder at processorfinder.intel.com/scripts/default.asp to locate specific details for each Pentium III processor based on the S-step number.

## PENTIUM II/III/4 XEON (1999–CURRENT)

The Xeon processor is the high-performance model of the Pentium II/III/4 family. It is intended for demanding workstation and server environments. The Pentium Xeon's expanded features include support for up to eight processors, L2 cache speed *equal* to core processor speed, and an increased choice of L2 cache size. The Xeon processor is available with L2 cache amounts of 512KB, 1MB, and 2MB. The physical size of larger cache prohibits placing the cache directly on the processor die—instead, it must be in a separate package next to the core processor. Intel has overcome the cache speed problems associated with the separate core-cache location, thus enabling the Xeon cache to run at core processor speeds. The increased physical size created by this arrangement also means the Pentium Xeon cannot use the Slot 1 motherboard connector. The Slot 2 connector was developed to accommodate the Xeon's increased size. With the introduction of the Pentium 4 Xeon processor, Intel went back to a socket-style connector for the Xeon product line. Pentium 4 Xeon processors use a Socket 603 connector and offer either 256KB or 512KB of L2 cache. Use Intel's Product Spec Finder at processorfinder.intel.com/scripts/default.asp to locate specific details for each Pentium Xeon processor based on the S-step number.

## PENTIUM 4 (2000–CURRENT)

As the Pentium II/III family pushes the 1 GHz speed range, the inherent limitations in the traditional P6 core architecture begin to limit the performance improvements that can be achieved. Intel has responded to this by introducing its newest Pentium 4 processors (see Figure 12-8) sporting a redesigned "NetBurst" micro-architecture. The NetBurst micro-architecture delivers a number of new and innovative features, including hyperpipelined technology, a 533/400 MHz System Bus, and a Rapid Execution Engine.

Other enhanced features include Advanced Dynamic Execution, an Enhanced Floating-Point and Multimedia Unit, and the next generation of Streaming SIMD Extensions (known as SSE2). At current operating speeds of 1.3 GHz to 2.2 GHz, the Pentium 4 is supported by the Intel 845 and 850 chipsets. It is streamlined to support a wide range of multimedia and communications-focused tasks. These applications include Internet audio and streaming video, image processing, video capture and editing, speech recognition, 3D, CAD, games, and multitasking environments.

The 42 million transistor Pentium 4 was originally produced in a socket-style package, currently known as PGA 423-pin socket for the Intel Pentium 4 Processor in an Olga on Interposer (OOI) package. Newer Pentium 4s are produced in a 428-pin package (requiring a new socket). This may limit the ability to upgrade current Pentium 4 systems. The first 428-pin Pentium 4 uses the Prescott core and became available in early 2001. A few of the more notable features of the Pentium 4 are outlined next.

- **Additional SIMD instructions**    The existing SSE extensions have been augmented with 144 new or improved SIMD extensions (known as SSE2). SSE2 allows the Pentium 4 to utilize 128 bits of data at once for greatly improved data handling. These additional instructions are designed to improve multimedia performance, including streaming video, speech recognition, and 3D operations.

- **Hyperpiplining and Rapid Execution**    Hyperpipelining technology doubles the pipeline depth of the older P6 architecture. For example, the Branch Prediction/Recovery pipeline in the P6 architecture is 10 stages deep, but hyperpipelining increases this to 20 stages deep. A Rapid Execution engine—actually two arithmetic logic units (or ALUs) running at two times the frequency of the core processor—is also added. This allows simple number functions (Add, Subtract, Logical And, Logical Or, and so on) to require only 1/2 clock cycle. This means the Rapid Execution Engine of the 2.2 GHz Pentium 4 effectively runs at 4.4 GHz.

- **Advanced Level 2 cache**    The Pentium 4 offers 256KB or 512KB of L2 cache. 256KB L2 cache is available with processor speeds of 1.3 GHz to 2 GHz. 512KB is available with processor speeds of 2 GHz and up. The improved L2 cache design of the Pentium 4 is a 256-bit (32-byte) interface that transfers data on each core clock cycle. The cache is located on-die and operates at the same speed as the core processor. For the 1.5 GHz Pentium 4, this means cache data transfer rates of 48 GB/s (32 bytes × 1 data transfer per clock × 1.5 GHz) compared to only 16 GB/s for a 1.0 GHz Pentium III. The 2.2 GHz Pentium 4 offers effective data transfer rates of 70 GB/s.

- **Advanced Dynamic Execution**    This feature is an expanded speculative execution engine that allows the Pentium 4 to view 126 instructions loaded in the pipeline. It also provides enhanced branch prediction abilities, reducing the number of branch misses by about 33 percent over the Pentium III and other P6 core architecture processors. This means the Pentium 4 is better at "guessing" where the next piece of needed data will be and is able to store a larger number of possible pieces of data.

- **400/533 MHz System Bus**    The Pentium 4 uses a scheme named "Quad-Pumping" that allows for a sustained effective data transfer rate of 400 MHz on a 100 MHz system bus. This delivers 3.2GB of data per second into and out of the processor, compared to 1.06 GB/s in a 133 MHz Pentium III. This 3.2 GB/s data transfer speed of the Pentium 4 also requires dual pipelined Rambus (RDRAM) memory and is supported by the 850 chipset. RDRAM provides the necessary 1.6 GB/s transfer rate per pipeline. Newer Pentium 4 systems offer a 133 MHz quad-pumped system bus (to 533 MHz). With the introduction of the Intel 845 chipset, Intel offered support for SDRAM and DDR SDRAM memory on Pentium 4 systems. PC2700 DDR SDRAM offers a memory bandwidth of 2.7 GB/s, though Rambus memory will continue to offer the best system performance.

**FIGURE  12-8**    The Intel Pentium 4 processor in a socket package (Courtesy of Intel Corporation)

Early releases of the Pentium 4 did not provide the stunning performance improvements that Intel had hoped for. Intel had to abandon or scale back certain features that have compromised the overall performance of the Pentium 4. Original plans called for 16KB of L1 cache and two fully functional floating point units (FPUs). Also missing is the proposed addition of 1MB of a new, external L3 cache. These shortfalls all contribute to numerous performance problems recorded at many popular Internet sites that review computer hardware. AMD processors running at 900 MHz and 1 GHz outperformed the 1.5 GHz Pentium 4. However, Pentium 4 performance is improving as Intel updates and refines the design. For example, the deeper 20-stage pipeline and manufacturing technology improvements have allowed for rapid increases in Pentium 4 speeds. This has allowed Intel to achieve a performance advantage over the AMD Athlon (and motivated AMD to implement their "True Performance Initiative" processor naming convention based on benchmark performance rather than actual clock speeds).

Another factor that had impaired the acceptance of the Pentium 4 was the increased cost from the required use of expensive Rambus (RDRAM) memory. Intel addressed this problem with the release of the 845 chipset that offers support for DDR SDRAM memory. Rambus RDRAM memory prices have fallen with time, so DDR SDRAM and RDRAM are currently similar in cost. Use Intel's Product Spec Finder at processorfinder.intel.com/scripts/default.asp to locate specific details for each Pentium 4 processor based on the S-step number.

## ITANIUM AND ITANIUM 2 (2001–CURRENT)

Released in May 2001, the Intel Itanium is the first 64-bit processor. Intel's IA-64 architecture combines a number of innovative features to address the performance limitations of traditional processor types. The Itanium architecture is based on "next generation" performance features, such as Explicit Parallelism, Predication, and Speculation, producing superior processing efficiency and increased instructions per cycle (IPC). This added processing power will help address future demanding requirements of Internet, high-end server, and workstation applications. In addition, the IA-64 architecture provides headroom and scalability for continued future growth. However, a user-friendly 64-bit operating system will be needed (such as the 64-bit version of Windows XP) before the Itanium—or any other 64-bit processor—becomes widely accepted for use in personal computers.

The next generation of Itanium processors, the Intel Itanium 2, is scheduled for release in mid-to-late 2002. This new Itanium 2 processor will operate at 1 GHz, versus the Itanium, which runs at 800 MHz. The Itanium 2 improves upon the use of predicting application needs, which results in substantially quicker processing times. Like the Itanium, the Itanium 2 is designed to meet the needs of demanding high-end requirements. Third- and fourth-generation Itanium processors, which are to be compatible with the Itanium 2, will be introduced in the future. Code names for these future Itanium processors are Madison and Montecito.

# The AMD CPUs

Advanced Micro Devices (AMD), once Intel's ally, has become its single biggest competitor. AMD is known for providing well-designed and highly compatible "alternative" processors to the PC industry and has been active in processor manufacturing and marketing since the days of the 386 (when one of its processors was the AMD Am386). Although AMD had tended to lag just a little behind the release of new Intel CPUs, that gap is now closed. With the release of AMD's newest processors (such as the Athlon XP and Duron), AMD is actually pushing a bit ahead in terms of processor performance and operating speeds in some benchmarks. The Pentium 4 put Intel slightly ahead in some 3D and network benchmarks (for a time at least), but the battle of the processors is a bitter one. This means that choosing the fastest processor will greatly depend on what applications you are using on your system. This part of the chapter will examine the characteristics and highlights of major AMD offerings.

## AM486DX SERIES (1994–1995)

The Am486 series was AMD's answer to Intel's 486 clock doubling and tripling OverDrive processors of the early 1990s. They incorporate write-back cache and enhanced power management features: including 3 volt operation, SMM (system management mode), and clock control (appealing for Energy Star-compliant "green" desktop systems and portable PCs). Available as Am486DX4/75, Am486DX4/100, and Am486DX4/120, the AMD 486 line saw service in many late-model, low-cost 486-compatible platforms. These processors are now totally obsolete today, and chances are that you will not see them in service unless you're retrofitting a fairly old system.

## AM5X86 (1995–1999)

This is really the processor that put AMD on the map. With the appearance of Intel's Pentium line, PC users were faced with the choice of upgrading their motherboard to accommodate a "true" Pentium CPU or of using an expensive Pentium OverDrive processor in a 486 system. AMD rose to the challenge by developing the Am5x86 (or simply the "5x86") as an alternative to Intel's Pentium OverDrive processors. The Am5x86 achieves Pentium-level performance by running "clock quadrupled" at 133 MHz (using the 33 MHz bus speed of a 486 motherboard). This native 33 MHz speed also supported the then-emerging 33 MHz PCI bus perfectly. Additional features such as a unified 16KB cache using write-back technology further improved the 5x86's performance. In actual practice, Am5x86 microprocessors provided greater performance than a Pentium 75 MHz while costing far less. The 5x86 became the *standard* CPU upgrade for 486 owners who wanted to utilize Pentium-class software without a major hardware upgrade.

The 5x86 also offered integrated power management features, including 3 volt operation, SMM, and clock control. This allowed the 5x86 to consume less power and run cooler than Pentium 75 MHz or 486DX4/100 processors. Both desktop and mobile PCs benefited from these features. The 5x86 is totally obsolete today, though you may encounter them when retrofitting old 486-based systems.

## K5 SERIES (1996–1999)

Although the Am5x86 proved to be an extremely popular processor, it was not a "true" Pentium alternative. It was not until 1996, when AMD released its *K5* series to the PC industry, that it offered a true Pentium alternative. The K5 is fully compatible with Socket 7 (Pentium) motherboards—a drop-in replacement chip. At most, the K5 might require a motherboard BIOS upgrade for proper identification and support with the motherboard's chipset. But the K5 is fully compatible with all x86 operating systems and software.

The K5 series is rated using the P-Rating (or PR) system (see the "The P-Rating (PR) System" earlier in the chapter). Rather than using iCOMP or Spec benchmarks to categorize the processor's performance, each K5 is assigned a PR number that corresponds to an Intel Pentium operating at the given clock speed. For example, a K5 PR120 performs equivalently to a true Pentium at 120 MHz. Table 12-4 lists a comparison of K5 performance figures.

**TABLE 12-4    COMPARISON OF AMD FAMILY PROCESSORS**

| CHIP | MHZ | BUS SPEED | L1 CACHE | L2 CACHE | FABRICATION | TRANSISTORS | FORM FACTOR | AVAILABILITY |
|---|---|---|---|---|---|---|---|---|
| **AMD K5.x Family** | | | | | | | | |
| K5.0 – P75 (no MMX) | 75 | 50 | 24KB | --- | 0.35 | 4.3 mil | Socket 7 | Obsolete |
| K5.0 - P90 | 90 | 60 | 24KB | --- | 0.35 | 4.3 mil | Socket 7 | Obsolete |
| K5.0 - P100 | 100 | 66 | 24KB | --- | 0.35 | 4.3 mil | Socket 7 | Obsolete |
| K5.1 - P120 | 90 | 60 | 24KB | --- | 0.35 | 4.3 mil | Socket 7 | Obsolete |
| K5.1 - P133 | 100 | 66 | 24KB | --- | 0.35 | 4.3 mil | Socket 7 | Obsolete |
| K5.2 - P166 | 116 | 66 | 24KB | --- | 0.35 | 4.3 mil | Socket 7 | Obsolete |
| **AMD K6 Family (classic with MMX)** | | | | | | | | |
| K6-166 | 166 | 66 | 64KB | --- | 0.35 | 8.8 mil | Socket 7 | Obsolete |
| K6-200 | 200 | 66 | 64KB | --- | 0.35 | 8.8 mil | Socket 7 | Obsolete |
| K6-233 | 233 | 66 | 64KB | --- | 0.35/0.25 | 8.8 mil | Socket 7 | Obsolete |
| K6-266 | 266 | 66 | 64KB | --- | 0.25 | 8.8 mil | Socket 7 | Obsolete |
| K6-300 | 300 | 66/100 | 64KB | --- | 0.25 | 8.8 mil | Super 7 | Obsolete |
| K6 Mobile-233 | 233 | 66 | 64KB | --- | 0.25 | 9.3 mil | Socket 7 | Obsolete |
| K6 Mobile-266 | 266 | 66 | 64KB | --- | 0.25 | 9.3 mil | Socket 7 | Available |
| K6 Mobile-300 | 300 | 66 | 64KB | --- | 0.25 | 9.3 mil | Socket 7 | Available |
| **AMD K6-2 Family (Chompers or "K6 3D MMX")** | | | | | | | | |
| K6-2/266 | 266 | 66 | 64KB | --- | 0.25 | 9.3 mil | Socket 7 | Obsolete |
| K6-2/300 | 300 | 66/100 | 64KB | --- | 0.25 | 9.3 mil | Socket 7 Super 7 | Obsolete |
| K6-2/333 | 333 | 95 | 64KB | --- | 0.25 | 9.3 mil | Super 7 | Obsolete |
| K6-2/350 | 350 | 100 | 64KB | --- | 0.25 | 9.3 mil | Super 7 | Obsolete |
| K6-2/366 | 366 | 66 | 64KB | --- | 0.25 | 9.3 mil | Socket 7 | Obsolete |
| K6-2/380 | 380 | 95 | 64KB | --- | 0.25 | 9.3 mil | Super 7 | Obsolete |
| K6-2/400 | 400 | 100/66 | 64KB | --- | 0.25 | 9.3 mil | Super 7 | Obsolete |
| K6-2/450 | 450 | 100 | 64KB | --- | 0.25 | 9.3 mil | Super 7 | Obsolete |
| K6-2/475 | 475 | 95 | 64KB | --- | 0.25 | 9.3 mil | Super 7 | Obsolete |
| K6-2/500 | 500 | 100 | 64KB | --- | 0.25 | 9.3 mil | Super 7 | Available |
| K6-2/533 | 533 | 133 | 64KB | --- | 0.25 | 9.3 mil | Super 7 | Available |
| K6-2/550 | 550 | 100 | 64KB | --- | 0.25 | 9.3 mil | Super 7 | Available |
| **AMD K6-2/P (Mobile K6-2 Family)** | | | | | | | | |
| K6-2P/266 | 266 | 66 | 64KB | --- | 0.25 | 9.3 mil | Socket 7 | Obsolete |

**TABLE 12-4    COMPARISON OF AMD FAMILY PROCESSORS** *(CONTINUED)*

| CHIP | MHZ | BUS SPEED | L1 CACHE | L2 CACHE | FABRICATION | TRANSISTORS | FORM FACTOR | AVAILABILITY |
|---|---|---|---|---|---|---|---|---|
| K6-2P/300 | 300 | 100 | 64KB | --- | 0.25 | 9.3 mil | Super 7 | Available |
| K6-2P/333 | 333 | 66 | 64KB | --- | 0.25 | 9.3 mil | Socket 7 | Available |
| K6-2P/350 | 350 | 100 | 64KB | --- | 0.25 | 9.3 mil | Super 7 | Available |
| K6-2P/366 | 366 | 66 | 64KB | --- | 0.25 | 9.3 mil | Super 7 | Available |
| K6-2P/380 | 380 | 95 | 64KB | --- | 0.25 | 9.3 mil | Super 7 | Available |
| K6-2P/400 | 400 | 100 | 64KB | --- | 0.25 | 9.3 mil | Super 7 | Available |
| K6-2P/433 | 433 | 66 | 64KB | --- | 0.25 | 9.3 mil | Super 7 | Available |
| K6-2P/450 | 450 | 100 | 64KB | --- | 0.25 | 9.3 mil | Super 7 | Available |
| K6-2P/475 | 475 | 95 | 64KB | --- | 0.25 | 9.3 mil | Super 7 | Available |
| **AMD K6-2+ Family** | | | | | | | | |
| K6-2+/450 | 450 | 100 | 64KB | 128KB | 0.18 | --- | Super 7 | Available |
| K6-2+/475 | 475 | 100 | 64KB | 128KB | 0.18 | --- | Super 7 | Available |
| K6-2+/500 | 500 | 100 | 64KB | 128KB | 0.18 | --- | Super 7 | Available |
| K6-2+/533 | 533 | 133 | 64KB | 128KB | 0.18 | --- | Super 7 | Available |
| K6-2+/550 | 550 | 100 | 64KB | 128KB | 0.18 | --- | Super 7 | Available |
| **AMD K6-3 Family (Sharptooth or K6+ 3D MMX)** | | | | | | | | |
| | 400 | 100/66 | 64KB | 256KB | 0.25 | 21.3 mil | Super 7 | Available |
| | 450 | 100 | 64KB | 256KB | 0.25 | 21.3 mil | Super 7 | Available |
| **AMD K6-3/P (Mobile K6-3 Family)** | | | | | | | | |
| K6-3P/350 | 350 | 100 | 64KB | 256KB | 0.25 | 21.3 mil | --- | Available |
| K6-3P/366 | 366 | 66 | 64KB | 256KB | 0.25 | 21.3 mil | --- | Available |
| K6-3P/380 | 380 | 95 | 64KB | 256KB | 0.25 | 21.3 mil | --- | Available |
| K6-3P/400 | 400 | 100 | 64KB | 256KB | 0.25 | 21.3 mil | --- | Available |
| K6-3P/433 | 433 | --- | 64KB | 256KB | 0.25 | 21.3 mil | --- | Available |
| K6-3P/450 | 450 | --- | 64KB | 256KB | 0.25 | 21.3 mil | --- | Available |
| **AMD K6-III+** | | | | | | | | |
| K6-III+/450 | 450 | 100 | 64KB | 256KB | 0.18 | --- | --- | Available |
| K6-III+/500 | 500 | 100 | 64KB | 256KB | 0.18 | --- | --- | Available |
| K6-III+/550 | 550 | 100 | 64KB | 256KB | 0.18 | --- | --- | Available |
| **AMD K7 (Standard Athlon Family)** | | | | | | | | |
| K7/500 | 500c (a) | 200 | 128KB | 512KB | 0.25 (0.18) | 22 mil | Slot A | Available |
| K7/550 | 550c (a) | 200 | 128KB | 512KB | 0.25 (0.18) | 22 mil | Slot A | Available |
| K7/600 | 600c (a) | 200 | 128KB | 512KB | 0.25 (0.18) | 22 mil | Slot A | Available |
| K7/650 | 650c (a) | 200 | 128KB | 512KB | 0.25 (0.18) | 22 mil | Slot A | Available |
| K7/700 | 700c (a) | 200 | 128KB | 512KB | 0.25 (0.18) | 22 mil | Slot A | Available |
| K7/750 | 750 | 200 | 128KB | 512KB | 0.18 | 22 mil | Slot A | Available |
| K7/800 | 800 | 200 | 128KB | 512KB | 0.18 | 22 mil | Slot A | Available |
| K7/850 | 850 | 200 | 128KB | 512KB | 0.18 | 22 mil | Slot A | Available |
| K7/900 | 900 | 200 | 128KB | 512KB | 0.18 | 22 mil | Slot A | Available |

**TABLE 12-4    COMPARISON OF AMD FAMILY PROCESSORS *(CONTINUED)***

| CHIP | MHZ | BUS SPEED | L1 CACHE | L2 CACHE | FABRICATION | TRANSISTORS | FORM FACTOR | AVAILABILITY |
|---|---|---|---|---|---|---|---|---|
| K7/950 | 950 | 200 | 128KB | 512KB | 0.18 | 22 mil | Slot A | Available |
| K7/1000 (Copper) | 1000 | 200 | 128KB | 512KB | 0.18 | 22 mil | Slot A | Available |
| **AMD K7 (Athlon "Ultra" or Thunderbird Family)** | | | | | | | | |
| | 650 | 200 | 128KB | 256KB | 0.18 | 22 mil | Slot A | Obsolete |
| | 700 | 200 | 128KB | 256KB | 0.18 | 22 mil | Slot A | Available |
| | 750 | 200 | 128KB | 256KB | 0.18 | 22 mil | Slot A Socket A | Available |
| | 800 | 200 | 128KB | 256KB | 0.18 | 22 mil | Slot A Socket A | Available |
| | 850 | 200 | 128KB | 256KB | 0.18 | 22 mil | Slot A Socket A | Available |
| | 900 | 200 | 128KB | 256KB | 0.18 | 22 mil | Slot A Socket A | Available |
| | 950 | 200 | 128KB | 256KB | 0.18 | 22 mil | Slot A Socket A | Available |
| | 1000 | 200 | 128KB | 256KB | 0.18 | 22 mil | Slot A Socket A | Available |
| | 1100 | 200 | 128KB | 256KB | 0.18 | 22 mil | Socket A | Available |
| | 1200 | 200 | 128KB | 256KB | 0.18 | 22 mil | Socket A | Available |
| | 1300 | 200 | 128KB | 256KB | 0.18 | 22 mil | Socket A | Available |
| | 1400 | 200 | 128KB | 256KB | 0.18 | 22 mil | Socket A | Available |
| AMD Athlon-C | 1000 | 266 | 128KB | 256KB | 0.18 | 22 mil | Socket A | Available |
| | 1133 | 266 | 128KB | 256KB | 0.18 | 22 mil | Socket A | Available |
| | 1200 | 266 | 128KB | 256KB | 0.18 | 22 mil | Socket A | Available |
| | 1333 | 266 | 128KB | 256KB | 0.18 | 22 mil | Socket A | Available |
| | 1400 | 266 | 128KB | 256KB | 0.18 | 22 mil | Socket A | Available |
| AMD Athlon XP & MP (Palomino) | 1000 (MP) | 266 | 128KB | 256KB | 0.18 | 37.5 mil | Socket A | Available |
| | 1200 (MP) | 266 | 128KB | 256KB | 0.18 | 37.5 mil | Socket A | Available |
| 1500+ MP & XP | 1333 | 266 | 128KB | 256KB | 0.18 | 37.5 mil | Socket A | Available |
| 1600+ MP & XP | 1400 | 266 | 128KB | 256KB | 0.18 | 37.5 mil | Socket A | Available |
| 1700+ XP | 1467 | 266 | 128KB | 256KB | 0.18 | 37.5 mil | Socket A | Available |
| 1800+ MP & XP | 1533 | 266 | 128KB | 256KB | 0.18 | 37.5 mil | Socket A | Available |
| 1900+ MP & XP | 1600 | 266 | 128KB | 256KB | 0.18 | 37.5 mil | Socket A | Available |
| 2000+ MP & XP | 1667 | 266 | 128KB | 256KB | 0.18 | 37.5 mil | Socket A | Available |

**TABLE 12-4    COMPARISON OF AMD FAMILY PROCESSORS** *(CONTINUED)*

| CHIP | MHZ | BUS SPEED | L1 CACHE | L2 CACHE | FABRICATION | TRANSISTORS | FORM FACTOR | AVAILABILITY |
|------|-----|-----------|----------|----------|-------------|-------------|-------------|--------------|
| 2100+ MP & XP | 1733 | 266 | 128KB | 256KB | 0.18 | 37.5 mil | Socket A | Q2 2002 |
| 2200+ MP & XP | 1800 | 266 | 128KB | 256KB | 0.18 | 37.5 mil | Socket A | Q3 2002 |
| Thorough-bred 2200+ XP | 1800 | 266 | 128KB | 256KB | 0.13 | --- | Socket A | Available |
| 2400+ XP | 2000 | 266 | 128KB | 256KB | 0.13 | --- | Socket A | Q2 2002 |
| 2600+ XP | 2200 | 266 | 128KB | 256KB | 0.13 | --- | Socket A | Q2 2002 |
| Barton 2xxx+ XP | 2400 | 333 | 128KB | 512KB | 0.13 SOI | --- | Socket A | Q3 2002 |
| **AMD K7 Mobile (Mobile Athlon Family)** | | | | | | | | |
| Palomino | 850 | 200 | 128KB | 256KB | 0.18 | 37.5 mil | Socket A | Available |
| | 900 | 200 | 128KB | 256KB | 0.18 | 37.5 mil | Socket A | Available |
| | 950 | 200 | 128KB | 256KB | 0.18 | 37.5 mil | Socket A | Available |
| | 1000 | 200 | 128KB | 256KB | 0.18 | 37.5 mil | Socket A | Available |
| | 1100 | 200 | 128KB | 256KB | 0.18 | 37.5 mil | Socket A | Available |
| | 1200 | 200 | 128KB | 256KB | 0.18 | 37.5 mil | Socket A | Available |
| 1500+ | 1300 | 200 | 128KB | 256KB | 0.18 | 37.5 mil | Socket A | Available |
| 1600+ | 1400 | 200 | 128KB | 256KB | 0.18 | 37.5 mil | Socket A | Available |
| Athlon 4 1800+ | 1500 | 200 | 128KB | 256KB | 0.18 | 37.5 mil | Socket A | Q2 2002 |
| Athlon 4 1900+ | 1600 | 200 | 128KB | 256KB | 0.18 | 37.5 mil | Socket A | Q3 2002 |
| **AMD Standard Duron Family** | | | | | | | | |
| Spitfire | 600 | 200 | 128KB | 64KB | 0.18 | 25 mil | Socket A | Available |
| | 650 | 200 | 128KB | 64KB | 0.18 | 25 mil | Socket A | Available |
| | 700 | 200 | 128KB | 64KB | 0.18 | 25 mil | Socket A | Available |
| | 750 | 200 | 128KB | 64KB | 0.18 | 25 mil | Socket A | Available |
| | 800 | 200 | 128KB | 64KB | 0.18 | 25 mil | Socket A | Available |
| | 850 | 200 | 128KB | 64KB | 0.18 | 25 mil | Socket A | Available |
| | 900 | 200 | 128KB | 64KB | 0.18 | 25 mil | Socket A | Available |
| | 950 | 200 | 128KB | 64KB | 0.18 | 25 mil | Socket A | Available |
| Morgan | 1000 | 200 | 128KB | 64KB | 0.18 | 25 mil | Socket A | Available |
| | 1100 | 200 | 128KB | 64KB | 0.18 | 25 mil | Socket A | Available |
| | 1200 | 200 | 128KB | 64KB | 0.18 | 25 mil | Socket A | Available |
| | 1300 | 200 | 128KB | 64KB | 0.18 | 25 mil | Socket A | Available |
| Appaloosa | 1500 | 266 | 128KB | 64KB | 0.13 | --- | Socket A | 2002 |
| **AMD Mobile Duron Family** | | | | | | | | |
| Spitfire | 600 | 200 | 128KB | 64KB | 0.18 | 25 mil | Socket A | Available |
| | 700 | 200 | 128KB | 64KB | 0.18 | 25 mil | Socket A | Available |
| Morgan | 800 | 200 | 128KB | 64KB | 0.18 | 25 mil | Socket A | Available |
| | 850 | 200 | 128KB | 64KB | 0.18 | --- | Socket A | --- |

**TABLE 12-4** COMPARISON OF AMD FAMILY PROCESSORS *(CONTINUED)*

| CHIP | MHZ | BUS SPEED | L1 CACHE | L2 CACHE | FABRICATION | TRANSISTORS | FORM FACTOR | AVAILABILITY |
|---|---|---|---|---|---|---|---|---|
| | 900 | 200 | 128KB | 64KB | 0.18 | --- | Socket A | --- |
| | 950 | 200 | 128KB | 64KB | 0.18 | --- | Socket A | Available |
| | 1000 | 200 | 128KB | 64KB | 0.18 | --- | Socket A | Available |
| | 1100 | 200 | 128KB | 64KB | 0.18 | --- | Socket A | Available |
| | 1200 | 200 | 128KB | 64KB | 0.18 | --- | Socket A | Available |

# K6 SERIES (1997–2000)

The K6 processor closed much of the "performance gap" between AMD and Intel processors. Based on AMD's RISC86 superscalar micro-architecture, the K6 was touted as being competitive with Intel's Pentium II processor in terms of performance. The K6 also incorporates a full suite of support for MMX instructions and should be fully compatible with all x86 operating systems and software (as well as software designed for MMX enhancements). Since the K6 continues to use the well-established Socket 7 architecture, it should serve as a drop-in replacement for K5 and Pentium CPUs to provide MMX capability. At most, the K6 may require an upgrade to the motherboard BIOS for proper identification and support with the motherboard chipset. Table 12-4 lists the major K6 variations.

The K6 incorporates seven parallel "execution engines" and employs two-level branch prediction. When coupled with speculative and full out-of-order execution techniques, the 166-300 MHz K6 family presented a serious challenge to Intel's Pentium MMX and early Pentium II processors. A large 64KB L1 cache provides 32KB for data and 32KB for instructions. The IEEE 754-compatible floating point unit (FPU) provides performance at least equivalent to the Pentium MMX, and full support for SMM (system management mode) ensures excellent power control. Mobile versions of the K6 have been optimized for use in laptop PC systems.

# K6-2 AND K6-3 (1998–CURRENT)

AMD introduced an improved K6 processor in 1998. The *2* in K6-2 is earned with the addition of higher clock speeds and higher bus speeds with the K6 core. Bus speeds up to 100 MHz are supported on Super 7 (Socket 7 with AGP support) motherboards. A significant addition to the K6-2 was the introduction of AMD's 3DNow! technology. 3DNow! is a set of 21 multimedia instructions increasing performance in 3D, multimedia, and floating-point–intensive applications. It is an extension to MMX using SIMD (Single Instruction Multiple Data) technology—3DNow! technology is also employed by IDT/Centaur and Cyrix in their newer processors. The use of 3DNow!, a large L1 cache, integrated "core speed" L2 cache, and Socket 7 compatibility are a few of the features that help the K6-2 to maintain its popularity and achieve its high performance. The K6-3 is merely a K6-2 with 256KB of full core speed on-die L2 cache. The K6-2 and K6-3 are AMD's answer to Intel's Pentium II/III (and competing with the Pentium name is as important as competing with Pentium performance). Table 12-4 lists the available K6-2 and K6-3 processors.

AMD's K6 processors get a boost in the competitive performance arena by being able to run as close to their upper limits as possible. Compatible motherboards must be capable of supplying the required split voltages at *very* close tolerances. A list of truly compatible and tested motherboards is kept at the AMD Web site (www.amd.com). The upper limit operation of the K6 processors requires that close attention be paid to heat dissipation. Heat sinks and fans must be securely attached, and thermal grease should generally be used. System airflow should provide for maximum CPU cooling. When working on an AMD system exhibiting erratic behavior, both these areas should be examined closely.

If you plan to upgrade your system from a K6-2 to a K6-3 processor, you may need a BIOS upgrade to fully support the K6-3.

# ATHLON (1999–CURRENT)

With the introduction of the AMD Athlon, competition in the high-performance processor market reached a new level. First produced at 500 MHz, the Athlon's current speeds are over 1.667 GHz (dubbed XP 2000+). The AMD Athlon and Intel's Pentium 4/Itanium initiatives basically eliminated any other manufacturer's ability to compete in this market, although VIA is making some progress with its low-cost C3 product line. AMD's constantly improving ability to compete head-to-head with Intel in the Socket 7 style processors is thought to be part of the reason Intel changed to a Slot style connector. Rather than developing a compatible Slot 1 processor, AMD decided it was time to implement its own ideas on how a processor should be integrated in a system. AMD accepted the slot form factor so that motherboard manufacturers would not have to completely redesign the layout of their motherboards to accept the Athlon, but shape and pin count are the only constants. AMD's slot connector is named Slot A. While both utilize a 242-pin interface, Slot A and Slot 1 processors are not interchangeable. You can see a mobile AMD Athlon XP processor in Figure 12-9.

AMD, along with Intel, quickly realized the shift to a slot type processor connection was a mistake. A socket style connector allows for simpler and less expensive manufacturing processes and better heat dissipation characteristics. Newer manufacturing techniques also allowed AMD and Intel to integrate sizable L2 cache directly on the main processor die. This allowed for smaller, less expensive L2 cache while at the same time maintaining (or even improving) processor performance. Even though AMD and Intel agree on the best style of connector for high-performance CPUs, the sockets (Socket A - 462 Pin, Socket 370, Socket 423, and so on) are not in any way compatible. It seems that AMD and Intel processors will never again be interchangeable in the same system.

In general, the Athlon is optimized for high clock frequencies featuring a super-pipelined, super-scalar micro-architecture. It contains a total of nine execution pipelines: three for address calculations, three for integer calculations, and three for executing x87 (floating point), 3DNow!, and MMX instructions. AMD specifically addressed its floating point and gaming image problem with the first fully pipelined superscalar floating-point engine and enhanced 3DNow! technology. According to some tests, the floating-point performance of the AMD Athlon is more than 35 percent higher than an equally clocked Pentium III Xeon processor.

**FIGURE 12-9** The mobile AMD Athlon XP processor is a popular choice for laptop PCs. (Courtesy of AMD, Inc.)

Enhanced 3DNow! adds 24 new instructions—there are 19 instructions to improve MMX integer math calculations and to enhance data movement for Internet streaming applications, and there are 5 DSP extensions for soft modem, soft ADSL, Dolby Digital, and MP3 applications. The Pentium III does not support this new DSP functionality of the AMD Athlon. L1 cache on the Athlon is 128KB, and the 64-bit backside L2 cache controller supports L2 cache sizes from 256KB to 8MB. The cache design utilizes the processor's high-performance system bus and minimizes bottlenecks caused by bus bandwidth limitations. The L2 cache for Slot A style Athlon processors is located off-die, is 512KB in size, and runs at only 1/2, 2/5, or 1/3 core speed. The L2 cache for Socket A style Athlons is 256KB, is on-die, and runs at full core processor speed.

AMD's claim that the Athlon is a seventh generation (7x86) processor is based on the implementation of an entirely different system bus architecture than that utilized by the Intel Pentium family of CPUs. AMD licensed the Alpha EV-6 bus technology from Digital Equipment Corporation. The Athlon system bus operates at 200 MHz or 266 MHz with a bandwidth capable of 1.6 GB/second data transfer speeds. The system bus can support multiple processors and can scale up to 3.2 GB/sec at 400 MHz. It includes such advanced technology as point-to-point topology, source-synchronous packet based transfers, and low-voltage signaling. You can compare the 500 MHz-1.66 GHz Athlon models in Table 12-4. There are numerous variations of the Athlon, so a little clarification is in order. The first Athlon processors were manufactured using a 0.25 micron process and can be identified by the letter $C$ located to the right of the part number listed on the processor's plastic shell. AMD soon produced Athlon models using a 0.18 micron process, which have the letter $A$ to the right of the part number. Eventually, manufacturing will shift to a 0.13 micron process in the second half of 2002. The first major improvement of the original Athlon core was introduced in June 2000 and was known as the "Thunderbird" core. The Thunderbird Athlon has an improved 16-set associative L2 cache, and was soon available in speeds of 1 GHz and above. This Athlon was also the first to support a 266 MHz (133 MHz x 2) FSB.

The "Palomino" core was introduced in October 2001. AMD added support for Intel SSE multimedia instructions, data prefetch to improve memory transfers, and lower power consumption. This is also when AMD began naming the Athlon according to comparable Pentium 4 benchmark results instead of actual processor speed (their "True Performance Initiative"). They also added "XP" to the name to show a close association with the Microsoft XP operating system. For example, the Athlon processor operating at 1.667 GHz is named XP 2000+. The current Athlon series includes the Athlon XP for desktop models, the Athlon MP for Dual (Multi) processor servers and workstations, and the Athlon 4 for mobile systems. The Athlon 4 will also be available for desktop and server systems.

The AMD Athlon processor bus architecture is designed to support scalable multiprocessing. The number of AMD Athlon processors in a multiprocessor system is a function of chipset implementation and not the AMD Athlon processor design. The AMD 760 MPX chipset supports multiple processors and is designed for use with Athlon MP processors. Although supporting chipsets were scarce at first, all major motherboard manufacturers are now producing models supporting the AMD Athlon, with a choice of chipsets from AMD, VIA, or ALi. AMD is currently working on a 64-bit processor line, code-named "Hammer," to compete with the Intel Itanium series.

## DURON (2000–CURRENT)

The AMD Duron processor is a scaled-down version of the Athlon designed to compete with the Intel Celeron in low-cost systems. The Duron uses the same core as the Athlon and offers most of the standard Athlon features, including the high-speed system bus, superscalar floating point unit (FPU), enhanced 3DNow! functions, and 0.18 micron manufacturing process. The main difference in the Duron series is reduced cache. The Duron contains the same 128KB L1 cache as the Athlon, but it has only 64KB of on-die L2 cache. The cache architecture on AMD processors is designed so that the same information is not duplicated in L1 and L2 cache. For the Duron, this means performance is similar to a full 192KB of cache memory. The fact that the AMD Duron is little different from the Athlon has made the processor a favorite of "overclockers." The AMD Duron is currently available in speeds from 600 MHz to 1.3 GHz (Table 12-4).

While AMD has been able to eliminate the competitive gap with Intel for the desktop market, it still has work to do to compete with Intel for the mobile system processor market. AMD processors use significantly more power than Intel's. AMD has released a version of its Duron series for the mobile market, but the 700 MHz mobile Duron and the Athlon 4 1.0 GHz use 24 watts of power—a comparable Intel Pentium III uses only 14 watts. AMD partially addressed the problem with the introduction of their PowerNow! technology. AMD's PowerNow! technology controls the mobile system's level of processor performance automatically, dynamically adjusting the operating frequency and voltage according to current processing demands. This approach can result in significantly longer battery life. Microsoft has integrated support for AMD PowerNow! technology into the Windows XP operating system. For some notebook PCs running previous Windows versions (including Windows 98/Me/2000), AMD PowerNow! drivers will need to be installed at the factory, or as an option during the initial system setup.

# The VIA Cyrix CPUs

Cyrix emerged as a major "alternative" processor manufacturer first in 1992 with the release of the Cyrix 486SLC and, later in 1993, with the 486DX4. By 1995, the Cyrix 5x86 (the M1sc) presented the only serious competition to the AMD 5x86. Based in no small part on its relationship with IBM, Cyrix established itself in the PC industry behind Intel and AMD but was unable to overcome the technology and performance gap that plagued some of its later processor offerings. In 1999, the Cyrix name, assets, and product research were purchased by VIA Technologies, the well-known chipset designer and manufacturer. A short time later, VIA also purchased Centaur Technology. Centaur was started in 1995 and had manufactured the processor known as the WinChip. These two acquisitions gave VIA important access to the processor market.

VIA continued development of a high-performance processor based on the newest Cyrix technologies, code-named "Joshua." The Cyrix III, based on the Cyrix-VIA Joshua core, was made available for review but was never put into large-scale production. VIA has also continued development of the Centaur core, and it was this design that was chosen for the actual public release of the Cyrix III (C3) processor. The performance and cost of the Joshua chip simply was not competitive in the low-cost processor market. The Centaur-based Cyrix III (C3) was developed under the code name "Samuel." This processor is discussed later in this chapter under the section "VIA C3-Samuel 1 (1999–Current)."

## 6X86 SERIES (1995–1999)

Cyrix introduced its 6x86 (dubbed the "M1"—later versions were called "M1R") in 1995 as an answer to the Intel Pentium and was optimized for both 16-bit and 32-bit software. The 6x86 Socket 7 processor achieves its performance through the use of two optimized super-pipelined integer units and an on-chip FPU. The integer and floating point units are tailored for maximum instruction throughput by using such techniques as register renaming, out-of-order completion, data dependency removal, branch prediction, and speculative execution. It includes a 16KB unified write-back cache. In most respects, the 6x86 uses many of the same techniques found in other Pentium-class processors.

The 6x86 series uses P-Rating (PR) figures instead of iCOMP or Spec numbers to indicate relative performance. For example, a Cyrix PR150+ processor will perform as well as a Pentium processor running at 150 MHz. You'll find PR120+, PR133+, PR150+, PR166+, and PR200+ versions of the 6x86 available (the "+" indicates performance *better* than the corresponding Pentium). Table 12-5 outlines the various characteristics for each version.

**TABLE 12-5    COMPARISON OF VIA CYRIX FAMILY PROCESSORS**

| CHIP | MHZ | BUS SPEED | L1 CACHE | L2 CACHE | FABRICATION | TRANSISTORS | FORM FACTOR | AVAILABILITY |
|------|-----|-----------|----------|----------|-------------|-------------|-------------|--------------|
| **Cyrix 6x86 (M1) Family** | | | | | | | | |
| 6x86-P120 | 100 | 50 | 16KB | --- | 0.6 | 3 mil | Socket 7 | Obsolete |
| 6x86-P133 | 110 | 55 | 16KB | --- | 0.6 | 3 mil | Socket 7 | Obsolete |
| 6x86-P150 | 120 | 60 | 16KB | --- | 0.6 | 3 mil | Socket 7 | Obsolete |
| 6x86-P166 | 133 | 66 | 16KB | --- | 0.6 | 3 mil | Socket 7 | Obsolete |
| 6x86-P200 | 150 | 75 | 16KB | --- | 0.6 | 3 mil | Socket 7 | Obsolete |
| **Cyrix MediaGX/MediaPC Family** | | | | | | | | |
| | 120 | 60 | 16KB | --- | 0.45 | --- | --- | Obsolete |
| | 133 | 66 | 16KB | --- | 0.45 | --- | --- | Obsolete |
| | 150 | 60 | 16KB | --- | 0.45 | --- | --- | Obsolete |
| | 166 | 66 | 16KB | --- | 0.35 | --- | --- | Obsolete |
| | 180 | 60 | 16KB | --- | 0.35 | --- | --- | Obsolete |
| | 200 | 60 | 16KB | --- | --- | --- | --- | Obsolete |
| | 233 | 66 | 16KB | --- | --- | --- | --- | Obsolete |
| | 266 | 66 | 16KB | --- | --- | --- | --- | Obsolete |
| | 300 | 66 | 16KB | --- | --- | --- | --- | Obsolete |
| **VIA/Cyrix 6x86MX (M2) Family** | | | | | | | | |
| 166-PR | 150/ 133 | 60/66 | 64KB | --- | 0.35 | --- | Socket 7 | Obsolete |
| 200-PR | 160/ 150 | 66/75 | 64KB | --- | 0.35 | --- | Socket 7 | Obsolete |
| 233-PR | 188/ 166 | 75/83 | 64KB | --- | 0.35 | --- | Socket 7 | Obsolete |
| 266-PR | 208 | 83 | 64KB | --- | 0.30 | --- | Socket 7 | Obsolete |
| 300-PR | 233 | 66 | 64KB | --- | 0.30 | --- | Socket 7 | Available |
| 333-PR | 250 | 83 | 64KB | --- | 0.30 | --- | Socket 7 | Available |
| 366-PR | 250 | 100 | 64KB | --- | 0.25 | --- | Super 7 | Available |
| 400-PR | 266 | 100 | 64KB | --- | 0.18 | --- | Super 7 | Available |
| 433-PR | 300 | 100 | 64KB | --- | 0.18 | --- | Super 7 | Available |
| 466-PR | 333 | 100 | 64KB | --- | 0.18 | --- | Super 7 | Discontinued |
| **VIA "Joshua" (a.k.a. Gobi/Jedi/MII+) Family** | | | | | | | | |
| PR400 | --- | 133 | 64KB | 256KB | 0.18 | --- | Socket 370 | Discontinued |
| PR450 | --- | 133 | 64KB | 256KB | 0.18 | --- | Socket 370 | Discontinued |
| PR500 | --- | 133 | 64KB | 256KB | 0.18 | --- | Socket 370 | Discontinued |

## TABLE 12-5    COMPARISON OF VIA CYRIX FAMILY PROCESSORS *(CONTINUED)*

| CHIP | MHZ | BUS SPEED | L1 CACHE | L2 CACHE | FABRICATION | TRANSISTORS | FORM FACTOR | AVAILABILITY |
|---|---|---|---|---|---|---|---|---|
| Cyrix Mojave (a.k.a. Jalapeno/MIII) Family | | | | | | | | |
| | 1200 | --- | --- | 256KB | 0.18 | --- | Socket 370 | Discontinued |
| Cyrix Mxi Family | | | | | | | | |
| | 466 | --- | 64KB | --- | 0.18 | --- | --- | Discontinued |
| | 500 | --- | 64KB | --- | 0.18 | --- | --- | Discontinued |
| VIA C3 Family | | | | | | | | |
| Samuel 1 | 500 | 66/100/133 | 128KB | --- | 0.18 | 11 mil | Socket 370 | Available |
| | 550 | 66/100/133 | 128KB | --- | 0.18 | 11 mil | Socket 370 | Available |
| | 600 | 66/100/133 | 128KB | --- | 0.18 | 11 mil | Socket 370 | Available |
| | 650 | 66/100/133 | 128KB | --- | 0.18 | 11 mil | Socket 370 | Available |
| | 667 | 66/100/133 | 128KB | --- | 0.18 | 11 mil | Socket 370 | Available |
| | 700 | 66/100/133 | 128KB | --- | 0.18 | 11 mil | Socket 370 | Available |
| | 733 | 66/100/133 | 128KB | --- | 0.18 | 11 mil | Socket 370 | Available |
| | 750 | 66/100/133 | 128KB | --- | 0.18 | 11 mil | Socket 370 | Available |
| | 800 | 66/100/133 | 128KB | --- | 0.18 | 11 mil | Socket 370 | Available |
| VIA Samuel II Family | | | | | | | | |
| Samuel 2 | 600 | 66/100/133 | 128KB | 64KB | 0.15 | 15 mil | Socket 370 | Discontinued |
| | 650 | 66/100/133 | 128KB | 64KB | 0.15 | 15 mil | Socket 370 | Discontinued |
| | 700 | 66/100/133 | 128KB | 64KB | 0.15 | 15 mil | Socket 370 | Available |
| | 733 | 66/100/133 | 128KB | 64KB | 0.15 | 15 mil | Socket 370 | Available |
| | 750 | 66/100/133 | 128KB | 64KB | 0.15 | 15 mil | Socket 370 | Available |
| | 800 | 66/100/133 | 128KB | 64KB | 0.15 | 15 mil | Socket 370 | Available |
| Ezra | 800 | 66/100/133 | 128KB | 64KB | 0.13 | 15 mil | Socket 370 | Available |
| | 850 | 66/10/133 | 128KB | 64KB | 0.13 | 15 mil | Socket 370 | Available |
| | 866 | 66/100/133 | 128KB | 64KB | 0.13 | 15 mil | Socket 370 | Available |
| Ezra-T | 800 | 66/100/133 | 128KB | 64KB | 0.13 | 15 mil | Socket 370 | Available |

**TABLE 12-5**   COMPARISON OF VIA CYRIX FAMILY PROCESSORS *(CONTINUED)*

| CHIP | MHZ | BUS SPEED | L1 CACHE | L2 CACHE | FABRICATION | TRANSISTORS | FORM FACTOR | AVAILABILITY |
|------|-----|-----------|----------|----------|-------------|-------------|-------------|--------------|
| | 866 | 66/100/133 | 128KB | 64KB | 0.13 | 15 mil | Socket 370 | Available |
| | 933 | 66/100/133 | 128KB | 64KB | 0.13 | 15 mil | Socket 370 | Available |
| | 950 | 66/100/133 | 128KB | 64KB | 0.13 | 15 mil | Socket 370 | Q2 2002 |
| Nehemiah | 1200 | --- | 128KB | 256KB | 0.13 | --- | Socket 370 | 2H 2002 |
| Esther | 1500 | --- | 128KB | 256KB | 0.13 | --- | Socket 370 | 2H 2002 |
| | 1700 | --- | 128KB | 256KB | 0.13 | --- | Socket 370 | 2003 |

There are two drawbacks to the common Cyrix 6x86. First, the floating point unit (FPU) does not perform as well as those of similar Intel and AMD processors. While this does not really affect most basic software and operating systems, math-intensive programs (especially 3D computer games) can suffer reduced performance. There is little that can be done with this issue in the 6x86 family, though subsequent processor versions (like the M2) do provide a better FPU. The second drawback to the 6x86 has been excessive heating. In practice, 6x86 processors produce more heat than their AMD or Intel counterparts. Cyrix has addressed this issue by releasing the 6x86L (or M1R) series in 1996. The "L" designation means "low power." More specifically, the 6x86L uses a split voltage of 3.3 volts to handle I/O operations with other chips and 2.8 volts to run the core of the CPU itself. Traditional 6x86 processors use 3.3 volts or 3.52 volts only. In order to support a 6x86L, a motherboard must provide split voltages, or a voltage regulator module must be added between the CPU socket and processor.

The split voltage operation of a 6x86L uses the same voltage levels as an MMX processor. However, the 6x86L is *not* an MMX-compatible processor. These split voltages were chosen so that the 6x86L would be compatible with split-voltage motherboards and could be later replaced with an MMX-compatible device, such as the 6x86MX (or M2).

## MEDIAGX (1996–1999)

Traditional PCs need stand-alone media-related devices, such as a video card and a sound card. These increase the overall cost of a PC and create the potential for hardware conflicts. The Cyrix MediaGX processor incorporates the features of audio and video, along with many other conventional motherboard components. This high level of integration provided the basis for low-cost entry-level systems that still offer good performance. The 3.3–3.6 volt MediaGX system actually consists of two chips: the MediaGX processor itself and the MediaGX Cx5510 companion chip.

The MediaGX processor is a 64-bit device with a proven x86-compatible processor core. The CPU directly interfaces to a PCI bus and DRAM memory. High-quality SVGA graphics are provided by an advanced graphics accelerator right on the MediaGX processor. The graphics frame buffer is stored in main memory and avoids the performance degradation associated with traditional Unified Memory Architecture (UMA) through the Display Compression Technology (DCT) approach. The processor is available from 120 to 300 MHz (Table 12-5). It includes a 16KB unified L1 cache, a floating point unit, and enhanced system management mode (SMM) features. The PCI controller handles fixed, rotating, hybrid or ping-pong bus arbitration. It supports four masters (three on PCI bus). It uses a synchronous CPU/PCI bus frequency and supports concurrent CPU and PCI operations. The video system supports up to $1280 \times 1024 \times 8$, and $1024 \times 768 \times 16$ display modes. The MediaGX also works with EDO RAM and supports up to 128MB of RAM in four banks.

The MediaGX Cx5510 companion chip represented a new generation of integrated, single-chip controllers for Cyrix's line of MediaGX-compatible processors. The Cx5510 bridges the MediaGX processor over the PCI bus to the ISA bus, performs traditional chipset functions, and supports a sound interface compatible with industry-standard sound cards, such as the Creative Labs Sound Blaster.

The key issue to keep in mind with the MediaGX series is that it is *not* Socket 7-compatible. The MediaGX and companion chip are a surface-mounted solution designed for dedicated motherboards. This means that MediaGX motherboards are *not* upgradeable to other Socket 7 processors. The MediaGX line is considered to be obsolete.

## 6X86MX (1997–1999)

The 6x86MX (referred to as the "MII") was the Cyrix response to MMX processors like the AMD K6 and Intel Pentium MMX. The 6x86MX design quadruples the original 6x86 internal cache size to 64KB and increases the operating frequency to 200 MHz and beyond. Additionally, it features the 57 new MMX instructions that speed up the processing of certain computing-intensive loops found in multimedia and communication applications. The 6x86MX processor also contains a scratch-pad RAM feature and supports performance monitoring. It delivers optimum 16-bit and 32-bit performance while running Windows 95/98, Windows NT, OS/2, DOS, UNIX, and other x86 operating systems. The 6x86MX processor features a super-pipelined architecture and advanced techniques, including register renaming, out-of-order completion, data-dependency removal, branch prediction and speculative execution.

You'll usually find 6x86MX processors available in 150 MHz (PR166), 166 MHz (PR200), 188 MHz (PR233), 225 MHz (PR266), and 250 MHz (PR300) versions. Current Cyrix MII processors are produced at speeds up to 333 MHz (PR433). As with other Cyrix processors, performance is rated using the P-Rating (PR) nomenclature. For example, a Cyrix 6x86MX at 160 MHz performs at a level equal to an Intel Pentium processor at 200 MHz (Table 12-5).

## VIA C3-SAMUEL 1 (1999–CURRENT)

The VIA C3 processor is the latest offering from VIA Technologies in the continuing development of the Centaur WinChip core (dubbed "Samuel" by VIA). Produced specifically for the low-cost segment of the computer market, the VIA C3 uses the standard Socket 370 interface. Because of licensing agreements, it is also able to utilize the P6 Intel system bus. This helps keep costs down and allows for easy integration into existing platforms.

Available in speeds from 500 MHz to 800 MHz, the VIA C3 offers 128KB of full speed L1 cache. It does not offer any L2 cache, which limits performance in demanding 3D and graphics applications. Performance is also limited by a floating point unit operating at only 1/2 core processor speed. It does support AMD's 3DNow! and Intel's MMX technology, and it operates at modern front side bus (FSB) speeds of 66 MHz, 100 MHz, or 133 MHz. Table 12-5 outlines the attributes of each version.

The VIA C3 is manufactured using a 0.18 micron process and uses only 10 watts of power at full speed. This keeps heat production low and may make the processor an attractive choice for portable systems. The release of the VIA C3 also saw the end of using the PR system to determine processor performance—the VIA C3 is designed to be a full-speed competitive processor.

## VIA C3-SAMUEL 2 (2001–CURRENT)

As the successor to the original C3-Samuel, the C3-Samuel 2 processor sports the addition of 64KB of L2 cache and a floating point unit (FPU) running at full clock speed. The L2 cache is "exclusive," so data in the L1 cache is not duplicated in the L2 cache (such as with the Intel Pentium III and Celeron L2 caches). This provides storage for 192KB of cached data. The VIA Samuel 2 L2 cache performs similarly to the Celeron L2 cache, but its performance doesn't match the 8-way associative Pentium III L2 cache, or the 16-way associative AMD Athlon/Duron L2 cache. The C3-Samuel 2 offers support for 3DNow! and MMX multimedia instructions. It is available in FSB speeds of 100 MHz and 133 MHz.

The VIA C3-Samuel 2 is manufactured using a 0.15 micron process. This allows for a very small die size, minimizes power consumption, and reduces heat dissipation. This allows the VIA C3 processors to run virtually "cold," even eliminating the need for a processor fan in some cases. The original 0.15 micron Samuel 2 is available in speeds from 700 MHz to 800 MHz. VIA soon moved to a 0.13 micron core, named Ezra. This core is currently available in speeds of 800 MHz to 933 MHz. The latest C3 Ezra-T processors are compatible with Intel Tualatin type Socket 370 connectors. VIA has released a 1 GHz processor, and hopes to reach speeds in excess of 1.2 GHz with this core (and they plan to increase L2 cache to 256KB). However, the current fastest C3 processor is less than half as fast as the currently available Intel and AMD processors. As a result, C3 processors are generally not viable options for performance-oriented desktops and workstations.

# CPU Overclocking

PC evolution is often a race for performance, and designers are constantly struggling to make the most of every last clock tick. Many factors are involved in computer performance, but CPU speed is one of the most important—faster and better CPUs have been a driving force in computer development, and older CPUs are frequently upgraded with new ones in order to wring evermore performance from current systems. While CPU replacements are common, they can also be expensive. As an alternative to CPU replacement, PC users and enthusiasts alike often turn to *overclocking* as a means of maximizing the performance of an existing CPU. This part of the chapter offers a comprehensive set of guidelines and procedures that can help you make informed overclocking decisions.

Overclocking is basically the practice of reconfiguring a PC to operate a CPU at a *higher* speed than the particular CPU has been specified for. This is usually accomplished by adjusting the bus speed and multiplier to result in a higher effective processor clock. A system can be reconfigured to overclock a CPU in a matter of minutes simply by changing one or two jumpers on the motherboard, or tweaking CMOS settings. Ideally, this higher clock speed should increase the CPU's performance *without* damaging the CPU or reducing its working life. The economics of overclocking can be compelling. In most cases, overclocking can be accomplished with most modern CPUs for less than $30 for a new cooling unit—as opposed to $200–$500 (or more) for a new CPU.

Overclocking carries inherent risks to the CPU, which include permanent damage to the CPU itself, and should *never* be undertaken without careful consideration of the consequences. CPU overclocking is *not* encouraged as a regular practice, and can be *illegal* if an overclocked system is sold without informing the buyer!

# OVERCLOCKING REQUIREMENTS

The most important factor to grasp about CPU overclocking is that it is *not a universally successful technique*. In many cases, your efforts to overclock a PC will fail. There are four critical elements of any PC that influence overclocking: the CPU, the motherboard, system RAM, and CPU cooling. Trouble in any one of those elements will result in overclocking problems.

## CPU Issues

Older CPUs manufactured by Intel (especially the Celerons) seem to be the most successful at overclocking—usually because AMD K5, K6, and VIA Cyrix CPUs are often running very close to their rated limits already in an effort to compete with their Intel counterparts. However, not all Intel CPUs are so suitable. For example, CPUs marked with the SY022 and SU073 S-step numbers are often limited to clock multipliers of more than x2. Also check for "faked" CPUs (which have been re-marked and resold at higher clock speeds already). Re-marked CPUs have been reported as a frequent practice in Europe, but it's always worth a check of the CPU first before proceeding. As a rule, if you can peel off any stickers underneath the CPU, it is re-marked, and most likely running over its originally rated speed anyway.

> The main idea to remember is that your overclocking success can vary with the processor make, model, and speed, as well as the engineering step and even the manufacturing batch. Overclocking results aren't always repeatable between similar systems.

Many current CPUs have *locked* clock multipliers. The manufacturers claim that this is both to protect the end user from re-marked CPUs and to assure the integrity of performance claims. The overclocking community thinks that locked multipliers are implemented in order to force the purchase of a new CPU to improve performance. Regardless of the reason, "locked" multipliers can complicate your overclocking effort (unless your system allows bus speeds to be adjusted in small increments).

## Motherboard Issues

Even if your CPU seems perfect for overclocking, the motherboard may not be. Signal reflections and other electrical limitations with its bus signals can cause the system to crash or hang. Overclocked CPUs are also more sensitive to unstable signals from the bus and will crash if the motherboard can't deliver "clean" signals. Brand-name motherboards such as Tyan (www.tyan com) or Supermicro (www.supermicro.com) often *tend* to support CPU overclocking better than cut-priced no-name motherboards. As a result, you may find that some PCs can be overclocked easily, while others suffer severe performance problems (or will not operate at all after overclocking). Motherboard makers Abit (www.abit-usa.com), AOpen (www.aopen.com), and Asus (www.usa.asus.com) have also become well known for the overclocking versatility of their motherboards.

Motherboard bus speeds can present another wrinkle. Most classic motherboards support bus speeds only up to 66 or 100 MHz, but more recent motherboard designs can operate at 112 MHz, 133 MHz, 143 MHz, 150 MHz, and up. These higher bus speeds will greatly affect the clock multiplier ratio when configuring your overclocking strategy, so be sure to understand the clock speed limits and multipliers for your particular motherboard. A few motherboards allow changing bus speeds in increments of 5 MHz or less.

Finally, the motherboard should also support a wide range of CPU supply voltages. For example, a STD voltage of 3.3V and a VRE voltage of 3.45V are common with Pentium-class systems. If you use an MMX-type CPU (such as the P55C, the 6x86MX, or the K6) you'll need access to "split voltage" support (2.8V and 3.3V are typical). Late model Athlon or Duron processors may operate with voltages down to 1.6V.

This may not sound so important because you're not "changing" the CPU. But in some cases, you may need to boost the CPU supply voltage just a bit to support overclocking. Today, you'll find that Slot 1/Slot A motherboards set their CPU voltages automatically when the CPU is installed, so don't panic if you have trouble locating CPU voltage jumpers (you may still be able to tweak CPU voltages through the system's CMOS Setup).

### RAM Issues

System RAM can also be a problem in overclocked systems with bus speeds that exceed 66 MHz—you'll require high-end EDO RAM or SDRAM. As a rule, EDO RAM works best with 66 MHz motherboards, while low-end SDRAM tends to be best with 75 MHz and 83 MHz motherboards. Well-established bus speeds of 100 MHz and 133 MHz require high-end SDRAM, memory certified for PC100 (100 MHz) and PC133 (133 MHz) bus speeds, respectively. Even more recent systems will rely on 200/266/333 MHz DDR SDRAM or Rambus memory. Keep this in mind when planning to tweak the FSB speed.

### Cooling Issues

Perhaps the most overlooked problem with CPU overclocking is insufficient cooling. CPUs draw current with each clock tick. The more clock cycles in a given period, the more current required—and the more heat generated. Most current CPUs run hot to begin with, but when overclocked, a CPU can easily overheat and crash (or perhaps suffer permanent damage). As a consequence, you should *never* attempt to overclock a CPU without making accommodations for better cooling. Consider a high-capacity, top-quality heat sink/fan assembly with a reliable ball-bearing fan offering a K/W (Kelvin per Watt) value of 1 K/W or **less**. You may need to go to a hobby electronics store or full-featured computer store to find a *good* heat sink/fan (such as the Slot 1 processor cooling unit in Figure 12-4 earlier). When installing the cooling unit, make sure that it fits to the CPU tightly without any air gaps, and use a thin layer of thermal grease between the CPU and heat sink. Serious overclocking enthusiasts may even employ a piezoelectric or liquid-cooled chilling unit for the CPU. For example, Ram Electronics sells a variety of cooling units at www.ramelectronics.net/html/cpu_cooling_fans.html.

## POTENTIAL PITFALLS

Before we actually get into the techniques of CPU overclocking, there are some potential hazards that you should be aware of. There are three typical failures associated with CPU overclocking: intermittent operation, shortened life span, and outright failure. All three faults are heat related.

- **Intermittent operation**   The added heat produced in the CPU can result in internal signal errors (a lost bit or shift of critical signal timing), which can easily cause the PC to crash—forcing you to power down the system until the CPU cools.

- **Shortened life span**   This is another heat-related problem. Rather than an immediate failure, excessive heat can shorten a CPU's life through a process of *electromigration*. Rather than a CPU working for ten years, it may work for only two years or five years (it's impossible to say for certain).

- **Failure**   A CPU is generally designed to operate from -25 to 80 degrees C. If the CPU is not cooled properly, the CPU die can exceed its maximum working temperature and fail. Though there are millions of transistors on a modern CPU, it only takes the failure of one or two to destroy a CPU.

## OVERCLOCKING THE SYSTEM

At this point, you're ready to try some overclocking yourself. Generally speaking, overclocking requires three basic steps: change the bus speed, change the multiplier, and change the CPU supply voltage (if necessary).

Note that you do *not* always have to change all three settings in order to successfully overclock a CPU. The general steps in overclocking a CPU are outlined next:

1. Turn off and unplug the computer. Open it up and get your motherboard manual. If you don't have a manual for the motherboard, you can usually download a copy from the motherboard maker, or from a site like Motherboards.org (www.motherboards.org/manuals.html).

2. Check the markings on the top and bottom of your CPU, write them down, and reinstall the CPU (this helps to ensure that the CPU is "real" and not re-marked).

3. Check the current clock speed and multiplier jumper settings on your motherboard, compare them with your manual, and write them down. On "jumperless" motherboards, you can usually find this information in the CMOS Setup. For example, a 600 MHz processor may use an FSB of 133 MHz and a multiplier of 4.5x, an FSB of 100 MHz and a multiplier of 6x, and so on.

4. Check the supply voltage jumper settings on your motherboard, compare them with the manual and your CPU marking, and write them down. On "jumperless" motherboards, you can usually find this information in the CMOS Setup.

5. Inspect the cooling unit on your CPU, and upgrade the cooling unit (if necessary). Remember that the system should be off and unplugged, and you should allow at least 15 minutes for the CPU heat sink to cool before working with it.

6. Change the jumper settings for clock speed and/or multiplier according to your target overclocked level. On "jumperless" motherboards, you can usually alter these settings through the CMOS Setup. For example, a PIII 933 MHz processor may use an FSB of 124 MHz and a multiplier of 7.5x, but you can up the FSB to 150 MHz and set the multiplier to 7x to achieve 1050 MHz operation. Other combinations are certainly possible.

7. Double-check that the new settings are configured as expected.

8. Start the computer and allow it to boot to the CMOS Setup.

9. Does it boot or reach the CMOS Setup? (If "yes," go to step 12; if "no," continue with step 10.)

10. Turn off and unplug the computer, and then change the CPU voltage jumper to a *slightly* higher voltage (if possible). Of course, you can leave the PC running if you must make changes through the CMOS Setup. This should usually not be increased more than 0.1 Vdc.

11. If you still can't boot or reach the CMOS Setup, return the voltage setting to its original value. You cannot overclock at this desired speed. Return the clock speed and multiplier settings to their original values and quit, or repeat step 6 with a lower bus/multiplier combination.

12. Tweak your CMOS Setup settings to optimum performance values as required (this may not be necessary). In some cases, you may need to adjust RAM or bus timings to accommodate the changes to your processor settings.

13. Does the system boot to a full working operation system? (If "no," check your cooling unit and repeat step 11; if "yes," continue with step 14.)

14. Start testing with a utility like PCMark 2002 (www.madonion.com) and allow the system to "burn-in" thoroughly. Check for any crashes or other intermittent system operation. If the system proves unstable, you cannot overclock at this level. Return the clock speed and multiplier settings to their original values and quit, or repeat step 6 with a lower bus/multiplier combination.

15. If everything works well—congratulations! Otherwise, check your cooling unit and repeat step 11.

Operating systems such as Windows 98/Me/XP are reputed to be *very* sensitive to overclocking. This means you may not be able to overclock a system with Windows 98/Me/XP, even though the system may overclock fine under DOS or another operating system—the best solution is to experiment and see what happens.

## Change the Bus Speed

The *internal* clock of a CPU runs at a different speed than the *external* clock (or "front side bus speed"). The external clock is the speed at which the cache and the main memory run—and is usually divided down to yield suitable clock signals for the AGP bus, PCI bus, and other bus architectures in the system. There are only three different "official" bus speeds used by the Pentium, Pentium Pro, and the AMD K5: 50, 60, and 66 MHz. The Cyrix/IBM 6x86 uses five bus speeds: 50, 55, 60, 66, and 75 MHz. There are also new motherboards available that support the unofficial bus speeds of 83 MHz to 148 MHz. Typical Pentium II/III motherboards run at speeds between 66 and 133 MHz. Athlon processors use 200 MHz and 266 MHz speeds. Pentium 4 motherboards use a 400/533 MHz processor bus speed.

To change the bus speed, look in your motherboard manual for something like "Clock Speed," "CPU External (BUS) Frequency Selection," or "Front Side Bus (FSB)"—these are the jumpers you will have to change. You will probably have to change several different jumpers to establish each new bus speed. If you are lucky and happen to have a motherboard with "SoftMenu" (jumperless) technology, you can change the bus speed settings in the CMOS Setup menu without even opening the case. Only increase the bus speed one step at a time (that is, go from 60 MHz to 66 MHz, not 60 MHz to 75 MHz or 66 MHz to 133 MHz). This is usually the most successful way to overclock.

## Change the Multiplier

The CPU's internal clock is controlled by an internal clock multiplier in each CPU, which is programmed via CPU pins. Intel Pentium CPUs support the following multipliers: x1.5, x2, x2.5, and x3. Intel Pentium Pro CPUs support x2.5, x3, x3.5, and x4. The 6x86 CPUs support only x2 and x3, but the M2 will support x2, x2.5, x3, and x3.5. Current Pentium II/III/4s support multipliers from x3.5 up to x14 and more. To change the multiplier setting, find a set of jumpers marked with a designation such as "Clock Multiplier" or "CPU to BUS Frequency Ratio Selection" in your motherboard manual. There are usually several jumpers used to change these settings. Again, you can do all of this in the CMOS Setup menu if you have a SoftMenu (jumperless) motherboard, such as the newer Abit motherboards (**www.abit.com.tw**). Keep in mind that this procedure will not work if the multiplier has been "locked," as is the case with late-model Intel Pentium III/4s and Celerons. AMD Athlon and Duron processors are locked, but it may be possible to "unlock" them. If you're an avid overclocker and have trouble because of locked CPUs, select a motherboard that allows FSB speeds to be changed in small increments. This gets around the locked multiplier by giving you a much wider selection of FSB speeds instead.

## Change the Supply Voltage

There are some circumstances when boosting the CPU supply voltage (from 3.3V STD to 3.45V VRE) may be necessary to make the CPU run reliably at a higher bus speed to account for the bigger voltage difference between the digital "high" and "low" conditions. The bigger difference results in "cleaner" signals for the CPU and other motherboard devices. If you can't run your CPU reliably at one particular clock speed, it's always worth considering jumping to the slightly higher supply voltage. (Don't increase the CPU voltage more than 0.1 Vdc.) However, more voltage will produce more heat, so you must be *very* careful about cooling. If you cannot stabilize an overclocked system by tweaking the voltage, be sure to return the voltage setting to its original value in order to prevent undue processor heating.

## Special Notes for Higher Bus Speeds

Many traditional Pentium-class motherboards handle clock speeds up to 66 MHz, but later model Pentium/MMX motherboards operate up to 75 MHz, and even 83 MHz. Current motherboards use 100/133 MHz clock speeds. There are some precautions to keep in mind when using some older motherboards with enhanced bus frequencies:

■ **PCI bus issues**    When set in synchronous mode, the PCI bus is taken (divided down) from the clock speed. At 60 or 66 MHz, the PCI bus speed is 30 or 33 MHz (this is the recommended speed for PCI). However, at 75 or 83 MHz, the PCI bus runs at 37.5 or 41.6 MHz, respectively. This faster speed can lead to problems with some PCI devices such as SCSI controllers, video cards, and network cards. Often, SCSI controllers and network cards refuse to work at the faster speed, and some video boards just get much hotter than usual (though some older video cards like the Diamond Stealth 64 aren't affected at all by higher bus speeds). Fast, modern motherboards at 100/133 MHz often make the expansion bus speed independent (*asynchronous*) of the FSB, so this may not be an issue on new motherboards.

■ **EIDE bus issues**    The speed of an EIDE interface is not only determined by the PIO or DMA modes, but it is also highly dependent on the PCI clock. This is one reason why an EIDE interface is always slower in systems with 60 MHz bus speeds or less. However, the EIDE interface will be faster when you are running at 75 or 83 MHz bus speeds. This sounds fine at first, but either the interface or the hard disk is often not up to the faster bus speeds. For example, I've seen HDDs work fine at 75 MHz bus speeds, but at 83 MHz, I've had to scale back to PIO mode 2. This failure to work at faster bus speeds also applies to EIDE CD-ROM drives and could very well be the culprit if you're running into strange lockups under Windows. Again, modern motherboards with Ultra-DMA drive interfaces are often immune to such speed-related issues.

■ **ISA bus issues**    In some cases, the ISA bus speed is divided directly from the PCI bus. If the PCI bus is running faster, the ISA bus may also be running faster. This condition can cause some serious problems for ISA boards (especially older ISA boards). For example, I've heard AWE32 soundboards make strange whistling sounds when being run at a fast bus speed. You can sometimes correct for ISA speed problems by introducing ISA wait states in the CMOS Setup. Of course, modern motherboards that do not employ ISA slots are not subject to this potential problem at all.

 These speed issues generally do *not* relate to today's Pentium II/III/4 or Athlon/Duron motherboards, which reach 100 to 133 MHz and higher.

As standard FSB speeds have increased, currently to 100 MHz and 133 MHz, chipsets have been developed to include dividers that maintain peripheral bus speeds at the specification's limits. PCI specifications call for 33 MHz, and the AGP bus is designed to operate at 66 MHz. Some modern chipsets (such as the Intel 440BX) offer only the 1/1 and 2/3 AGP bus settings. This is fine for 66 MHz and 100 MHz FSB speed systems but does not provide for current 133 MHz FSB speed processors.

■ **AGP bus issues**    The AGP bus is designed to operate at 66 MHz and is usually set as a fraction of the system bus speed. On a 100 MHz or 133 MHz system bus, the AGP bus speed would be set at 2/3 or 1/2, respectively, in the CMOS Setup. A 66 MHz system, the Intel Celeron for instance, would be set to 1/1. This means overclocking the system bus can also overclock the AGP bus, and this can lead to system stability problems if the AGP video card does not support the higher bus speed. Some motherboards may offer more than the 2/3 or 1/2 fraction option for the AGP bus speed. You may be able to find an option that keeps the AGP bus speed at or below 66 MHz. Remember, anything below 66 MHz will hinder graphics performance. Be sure to monitor your video card for overheating symptoms when experimenting with higher clock settings.

The latest chipsets include a wider selection of peripheral bus settings, and many high-end AGP video cards will operate at speeds higher than the standard 66 MHz.

## OVERCLOCKING THE INTEL CELERON

With the addition of L2 cache, the Intel Pentium II Celeron became an overclocker's favorite. The Pentium core, lower price, and high production quality combined to attract users looking for performance gains through overclocking. Intel sought to limit the Celeron's use in overclocking with a locked multiplier *and* a locked bus speed of 66 MHz. Some motherboard makers have not complied with the locked bus speed implementation, providing an avenue to overclock Celerons through higher bus speeds. Common motherboard bus speeds higher than 66 MHz are 75 MHz, 83 MHz, 100 MHz, and 133 MHz.

With the implementation of locked multipliers, half of the processor speed setting capability has been eliminated for overclocking. Overclockers have had to depend more on motherboard features and their own ingenuity to achieve higher speeds. Many motherboard manufacturers have responded with additional front side bus (FSB) and processor voltage settings. They have seen how product reviewers focus on the ability of a motherboard to remain stable when overclocked. The trend, then, has been for modern motherboards to include numerous FSB settings covering a wide range of possible settings. They also include an increased number of voltage settings that can be easily altered in small steps.

To make it even easier for the novice to experiment with different FSB and voltage settings, most motherboards have moved control of these settings from hardware to software. Older motherboards used jumpers on the motherboard to set clock multipliers, bus speed options, and voltage settings, but many current motherboards have these options included in the CMOS Setup routine. You do not have to disconnect everything and open the case just to increase CPU voltage or up the FSB. It is also easy to increase the number of available settings when the options are selected with a click of a mouse or press of a key, instead of having to figure out if six to eight jumpers are in the correct on/off positions.

Consider the following example for a 600 MHz Celeron processor where the clock multiplier is locked at 6x. Since the multiplier cannot be changed, the motherboard maker has provided fine control that allows you to adjust the FSB in 5 MHz increments:

- $6 \times 100$ MHz = 600 MHz (Standard)
- $6 \times 105$ MHz = 630 MHz (Overclocked)
- $6 \times 110$ MHz = 660 MHz
- $6 \times 115$ MHz = 690 MHz
- $6 \times 125$ MHz = 750 MHz
- $6 \times 133$ MHz = 798 MHz

Of course, even this is a very limited example. Modern motherboards offer FSB settings from 66 MHz to 170 MHz, often in increments of 3–5 MHz. Though specified to operate on a 66 MHz system bus, Celerons will usually operate at the standard Pentium III system bus speed of 100 MHz. This choice is made even easier by the fact that all other components (i.e. memory, AGP video, and so on), are typically designed to operate at 100 MHz. For example, a Celeron 566, which normally runs with settings of $8.5 \times 66$ MHz, usually operates at 850 MHz ($8.5 \times 100$ MHz) without any other changes. Keep in mind that higher FSB speeds can affect memory and bus timing, so you might need SDRAM memory rated for 150 MHz, along with motherboards that support compatible PCI and AGP bus speeds—even at a 150 MHz FSB.

The ability to successfully overclock a Celeron CPU may also depend on the availability of higher voltages. It sometimes takes a little more voltage to reach a faster signal speed. Modern motherboards again satisfy this requirement by offering a wide range of possible core voltage settings. Due to the fact that AMD and Intel processors are no longer interchangeable, motherboards would only have to support a limited number of voltages. The reality is that most motherboard manufacturers have enabled setting the CPU voltage higher than the standard voltage required by the CPU installed. This is also an option added to the CMOS Setup routine—though some motherboards still require that the voltage be set using jumpers located on the motherboard. If you find that your system will not boot after increasing the FSB setting, try slowly increasing the core voltage setting. Keep a very close watch on your CPU temperature when doing this. Any system instability or failure means you have gone too far. You should overclock only to a point where your system remains completely stable and reliable. Table 12-6 highlights numerous overclocking options and voltage

**TABLE 12-6**    AVERAGE CELERON OVERCLOCKING POTENTIAL

| PROCESSOR | RATED SPEED | AVERAGE OVERCLOCKED SPEED |
|---|---|---|
| Celeron 266 | 266 MHz | 455 MHz |
| Celeron 300 (cacheless) | 300 MHz | 440 MHz |
| Celeron 300 (Slot 1) | 300 MHz | 474 MHz |
| Celeron 300 (Socket 370) | 300 MHz | 501 MHz |
| Celeron 333 (Slot 1/Socket 370) | 333 MHz | 488 MHz |
| Celeron 366 (Slot 1/Socket 370) | 366 MHz | 542 MHz |
| Celeron 400A (Slot 1/Socket 370) | 400 MHz | 542 MHz |
| Celeron 433 (Slot 1/Socket 370) | 433 MHz | 569 MHz |
| Celeron 466 (Socket 370) | 466 MHz | 572 MHz |
| Celeron 500 (Socket 370) | 500 MHz | 603 MHz |
| Celeron 533 (Socket 370) | 533 MHz | 627 MHz |
| Celeron II 533A | 533 MHz | 848 MHz |
| Celeron II 566 | 566 MHz | 885 MHz |
| Celeron II 600 | 600 MHz | 928 MHz |
| Celeron II 633 | 633 MHz | 976 MHz |
| Celeron II 667 | 667 MHz | 986 MHz |
| Celeron II 700 | 700 MHz | 1018 MHz (1.0 GHz) |
| Celeron II 733 | 733 MHz | 1068 MHz (1.0 GHz) |
| Celeron II 766 | 766 MHz | 1042 MHz (1.0 GHz) |
| Celeron II 800 | 800 MHz | 1128 MHz (1.1 GHz) |
| Celeron II 850 | 850 MHz | 1122 MHz (1.1 GHz) |
| Celeron II 900 | 900 MHz | 1188 MHz (1.1 GHz) |
| Celeron II 950 | 950 MHz | 1227 MHz (1.2 GHz) |
| Celeron II 1000 | 1000 MHz (1.0 GHz) | 1264 MHz (1.2 GHz) |
| Celeron II 1100 | 1100 MHz (1.1 GHz) | 1298 MHz (1.2 GHz) |
| Celeron Tualatin 1000 | 1000 MHz (1.0 GHz) | 1400 MHz (1.4 GHz) |
| Celeron Tualatin 1100 | 1100 MHz (1.1 GHz) | 1500 MHz (1.5 GHz) |
| Celeron Tualatin 1200 | 1200 MHz (1.2 GHz) | 1567 MHz (1.5 GHz) |
| Celeron Tualatin 1300 | 1300 MHz (1.3 GHz) | 1570 MHz (1.5 GHz) |

settings for Celeron processors. You can learn more about current Celeron overclocking options from sites like SysOpt.com (www.sysopt.com/ocdatabase.html).

Keep in mind that the average overclocked speeds shown in Table 12-6 (and subsequent tables) are just that—*averages*. You may be able to attain even higher speeds if your particular system conditions support it. In other cases, you may not even be able to achieve the average.

## OVERCLOCKING THE INTEL PENTIUM II/III/4

Early Pentium II (a.k.a. "Klamath") processors were manufactured using a 0.35 micron process and were available in speeds from 233 MHz to 300 MHz using a 66 MHz front side bus (FSB). Intel then moved to a 0.25 micron process for Pentium II ("Deschutes") processors at speeds of 333 MHz to 450 MHz. The 333 MHz Pentium II still used the 66 MHz FSB, but from 350 MHz up, the FSB was increased to 100 MHz. The first Pentium III processors were manufactured using the 0.25 micron process ("Katmai") and were available in speeds from 450 MHz to 600 MHz. Intel then produced the Pentium III using a 0.18 micron process ("Coppermine"). These Pentium IIIs are available in speeds from 500 MHz and up.

Since August 1998, Intel has been locking the clock multiplier on its CPUs, so it probably will not be possible to change the multiplier when overclocking a 350 MHz, 400 MHz, 450 MHz Pentium II, or any Pentium III or Pentium 4. If you try, the CPU will either refuse to boot the machine or boot it up at 1/3 its proper speed. To get around this limitation, a Pentium II overclocker's primary option is to increase the speed of the front side bus. Increasing the speed of the FSB also increases the speed of the PCI and AGP busses, so errors might result from some older components refusing to run properly at the higher bus speeds. For instance, overclocking a 100 MHz FSB to 112 MHz results in the PCI bus being overclocked to 37 MHz (instead of 33 MHz), and the AGP bus being overclocked to 74 MHz (instead of 66 MHz). Since newer PCI and AGP cards are being designed with greater tolerances, however, such differences are becoming less of a problem. It is also helpful to select a motherboard with asynchronous PCI and AGP clocks so that those bus speeds remain constant regardless of the FSB.

Depending on the model of Pentium II/III/4 that you're attempting to overclock, you'll need to be able to adjust the clock multiplier, front side bus speed, and/or core voltage. You will also need to examine the effectiveness of your CPU cooling arrangement and improve the cooling if possible. Installing some kind of CPU temperature monitor is highly recommended. Many of the most current motherboards have a wide range of settings for multipliers, FSB speeds, and voltages—some even include integrated temperature monitors. Table 12-7 lists some popular options for Pentium II/III/4 overclocking. The one thing that you

| **TABLE 12-7** | **AVERAGE PENTIUM II/III/4 OVERCLOCKING POTENTIAL** | |
| --- | --- | --- |
| **PROCESSOR** | **RATED SPEED** | **AVERAGE OVERCLOCKED SPEED** |
| Pentium II 233 | 233 MHz | 368 MHz |
| Pentium II 266 | 266 MHz | 386 MHz |
| Pentium II 300 | 300 MHz | 463 MHz |
| Pentium II 333 | 333 MHz | 472 MHz |
| Pentium II 350 | 350 MHz | 466 MHz |
| Pentium II 400 | 400 MHz | 505 MHz |
| Pentium II 450 | 450 MHz | 582 MHz |
| Pentium III 450 | 450 MHz | 589 MHz |

**TABLE 12-7     AVERAGE PENTIUM II/III/4 OVERCLOCKING POTENTIAL *(CONTINUED)***

| PROCESSOR | RATED SPEED | AVERAGE OVERCLOCKED SPEED |
|---|---|---|
| Pentium III 500 | 500 MHz | 613 MHz |
| Pentium III 500 E | 500 MHz | 744 MHz |
| Pentium III 533 B | 533 MHz | 628 MHz |
| Pentium III 533 EB | 533 MHz | 654 MHz |
| Pentium III 550 | 550 MHz | 674 MHz |
| Pentium III 550 E | 550 MHz | 787 MHz |
| Pentium III 600 | 600 MHz | 692 MHz |
| Pentium III  600 EB | 600 MHz | 740 MHz |
| Pentium III 600 E | 600 MHz | 846 MHz |
| Pentium III 650 | 650 MHz | 885 MHz |
| Pentium III 667 | 667 MHz | 822 MHz |
| Pentium III 700 | 700 MHz | 955 MHz |
| Pentium III 733 | 733 MHz | 893 MHz |
| Pentium III 750 | 750 MHz | 953 MHz |
| Pentium III 800 | 800 MHz | 987 MHz |
| Pentium III 800 EB | 800 MHz | 991 MHz |
| Pentium III 850 | 850 MHz | 1026 MHz (1.0 GHz) |
| Pentium III 866 | 866 MHz | 1043 MHz (1.0 GHz) |
| Pentium III 900 | 900 MHz | 1044 MHz (1.0 GHz) |
| Pentium III 933 | 933 MHz | 1080 MHz (1.0 GHz) |
| Pentium III 1000 | 1000 MHz (1.0 GHz) | 1190 MHz (1.1 GHz) |
| Pentium III 1100 | 1100 MHz (1.1 GHz) | 1291 MHz (1.2 GHz) |
| Pentium III 1133 (256KB L2) | 1133 MHz (1.1 GHz) | 1305 MHz (1.3 GHz) |
| Pentium III 1133 (512KB L2) | 1133 MHz (1.1 GHz) | 1370 MHz (1.3 GHz) |
| Pentium III 1200 | 1200 MHz (1.2 GHz) | 1425 MHz (1.4 GHz) |
| Pentium III 1260 | 1260 MHz (1.2 GHz) | 1588 MHz (1.5 GHz) |
| Pentium III 1400 | 1400 MHz (1.4 GHz) | 1550 MHz (1.5 GHz) |
| Pentium 4 1.3 | 1300 MHz (1.3 GHz) | 1700 MHz (1.7 GHz) |
| Pentium 4 1.4 | 1400 MHz (1.4 GHz) | 1662 MHz (1.6 GHz) |
| Pentium 4 1.5 1500 MHz (1.5 GHz) | 1865 MHz (1.8 GHz) | 1900 MHz (1.9 GHz) |
| Pentium 4 1.6 | 1600 MHz (1.6 GHz) | 1933 MHz (1.9 GHz) |
| Pentium 4 1.6 (Northwood) | 1600 MHz (1.6 GHz) | 2411 MHz (2.4 GHz) |
| Pentium 4 1.7 | 1700 MHz (1.7 GHz) | 2075 MHz (2.0 GHz) |
| Pentium 4 1.8 | 1800 MHz (1.8 GHz) | 2089 MHz (2.0 GHz) |
| Pentium 4 1.8 (Northwood) | 1800 MHz (1.8 GHz) | 2491 MHz (2.4 GHz) |
| Pentium 4 1.9 | 1900 MHz (1.9 GHz) | 2229 MHz (2.2 GHz) |
| Pentium 4 2.0 | 2000 MHz (2.0 GHz) | 2300 MHz (2.3 GHz) |
| Pentium 4 2.0 (Northwood) | 2000 MHz (2.0 GHz) | 2621 MHz (2.6 GHz) |
| Pentium 4 2.2 (Northwood) | 2200 MHz (2.2 GHz) | 2852 MHz (2.8 GHz) |

will notice is that Pentium II/III/4 processors—especially the faster models—are not nearly as tolerant of overclocking as Celeron units. However, you can still tinker even if you don't see your particular processor in the table—just remember to test in very small increments.

To run reliably with a 100 MHz FSB, you need to have 100 MHz SDRAM (PC100 RAM) installed in your system. The same restriction applies when overclocking a standard 100 MHz system (you may need 133 MHz /PC133 SDRAM) or 133 MHz system (you may need 150 MHz /PC150 SDRAM). In many of the cases listed here, increasing the FSB speed requires you to *lower* the clock multiplier on your system.

## OVERCLOCKING THE CYRIX 6X86

Generally speaking, the older Cyrix 6x86 CPUs are much more difficult to overclock than comparable Intel CPUs. There are two reasons for this. First, Cyrix CPUs (even the later production steps) produce tremendous amounts of heat. Overclocking them would produce so much heat that it would be difficult to remove it all without huge heat sink/fans or powered Peltier coolers. Second, 6x86 CPUs support only two multiplier settings (x2 and x3), so there are far fewer overclocking options available. Try a Cyrix P120+ (100 MHz) as a P133+ (110 MHz). Try a P133+ (110 MHz) as a P150+ (120 MHz). Finally, try a P150+ (120 MHz) as a P166+ (133 MHz).

You'll generally achieve the best success with 2.7 or 3.7 stepped 6x86 CPUs—they are more stable and produce less heat.

## OVERCLOCKING THE AMD K5

AMD has put itself on the map with its 5x86/133 MHz CPU and earned a lot of respect with the K5. However, the older PR75, PR90, and PR100 versions of the K5 do not seem to tolerate overclocking very well—probably because those CPUs were running at their performance limits already. By comparison, the later K5 versions (such as the PR120, PR133, PR150, and PR166) and the newer K6 and K6-2 seem to be much more tolerant of overclocking. When selecting an overclocking level, choose the next level up. For example, if you have a K5 PR120, try configuring it as a PR133, and so on.

## OVERCLOCKING THE AMD K6-2 AND K6-3

The AMD K6-2 series processors use various core revisions, including the AFR, AFQ, AFX, AHX, and AGR revisions. These processors are already using comparatively high voltages and require good cooling even at rated speeds. The AMD K6-2 and K6-3 series processors offer only limited overclocking options, and even minor increases will require additional cooling. Table 12-8 shows some common overclocking potential that might be achieved with the K6-2 and K6-3 families.

## OVERCLOCKING THE AMD ATHLON AND DURON

AMD uses the same core for both the Athlon and Duron line of processors. The major differences are a smaller L2 cache and lower core voltage for the Duron series; this makes the Duron very attractive to overclockers. The trouble with Athlon/Duron overclocking is the FSB speed—Athlon and Duron processors use an identical standard front side bus speed of 200 MHz (100 MHz × 2) because of their use of the EV6 system bus. Current Athlons support a FSB setting of 266 MHz (133 MHz × 2). Given these very fast speeds, it is difficult to use altered FSB speeds to overclock AMD processors. The EV6 bus can be dependably raised only 10 to 15 percent over the default speed. This means a maximum FSB speed of 112 MHz to 115 MHz for the 100 MHz bus, and 145 MHz to 153 MHz for the 133 MHz bus.

**TABLE 12-8    AVERAGE AMD K6-2 AND K6-3 OVERCLOCKING POTENTIAL**

| PROCESSOR | RATED SPEED | AVERAGE OVERCLOCKED SPEED |
|---|---|---|
| AMD K6-2 266 | 266 MHz | 392 MHz |
| AMD K6-2 300 | 300 MHz | 388 MHz |
| AMD K6-2 333 | 333 MHz | 396 MHz |
| AMD K6-2 350 | 350 MHz | 423 MHz |
| AMD K6-2 366 | 366 MHz | 428 MHz |
| AMD K6-2 380 | 380 MHz | 445 MHz |
| AMD K6-2 400 | 400 MHz | 477 MHz |
| AMD K6-2 450 | 450 MHz | 517 MHz |
| AMD K6-2 475 | 475 MHz | 532 MHz |
| AMD K6-2 500 | 500 MHz | 564 MHz |
| AMD K6-2 533 | 533 MHz | 579 MHz |
| AMD K6-2 550 | 550 MHz | 597 MHz |
| AMD K6-3 400 | 400 MHz | 454 MHz |
| AMD K6-3 450 | 450 MHz | 534 MHz |
| AMD K6-3 500 | 500 MHz | 587 MHz |

Fortunately, AMD has made it fairly easy to unlock the locked multiplier. For the early cartridge-style Athlons, you had to make a device to unlock the multiplier and then remove the cartridge's outer case to install it. Obviously, this was well beyond the abilities of casual users, but prefabricated devices with installation instructions were soon available from commercial sources. These products were dubbed "GFDs" (or "Golden Finger Devices"), referring to the gold contacts on the edge connector that are used to unlock the multiplier. For the Socket A-style Athlon and Duron processors, AMD made it even easier to unlock the multiplier—all you really need is a lead (graphite) pencil. The entire operation consists of drawing a heavy line across a small gap between gold contacts on top of the processor. You can see this for the AMD processor in Figure 12-10. There are several sites on the Internet that discuss this matter in great detail, including www.motherboards.org/articlesd/how-to-guides/41_1.html, www4.tomshardware.com/cpu/00q3/000711/index.html, and www.extremeoverclocking.com/reviews/cpu/AMD_Unlock_Epoxy_1.html.

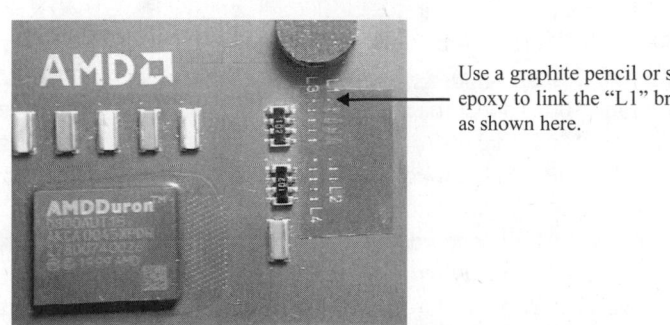

Use a graphite pencil or silver epoxy to link the "L1" bridges as shown here.

**FIGURE  12-10**    Unlocking an AMD Socket A processor's multiplier (Courtesy of ExtremeOverclocking.com)

Once the processor has been unlocked, overclocking is as simple as increasing the multiplier to a number higher than the default multiplier for that specific processor.

You will also need to increase the core voltage setting for an overclocked Athlon or Duron processor. The maximum voltage for both processors that can be chosen is 1.85V. This means the Athlon Thunderbird core can be increased only 0.15V above its default voltage of 1.7V (less than a 10 percent increase). The Duron fares a little better—you can add up to 0.35V to the 1.5V default voltage, which should be more than enough for most attainable clock speeds. Table 12-9 highlights the overclocking potential for AMD Athlon and Duron processors. Remember that it is important to have motherboard support for numerous FSB, multiplier, and voltage settings, and even a slight increase in FSB speed can provide significant performance improvements.

**TABLE 12-9**    **AVERAGE AMD ATHLON/DURON OVERCLOCKING POTENTIAL**

| PROCESSOR | RATED SPEED | AVERAGE OVERCLOCKED SPEED |
|---|---|---|
| AMD Athlon 500 | 500 MHz | 743 MHz |
| AMD Athlon 550 | 550 MHz | 751 MHz |
| AMD Athlon 600 | 600 MHz | 772 MHz |
| AMD Athlon 650 | 650 MHz | 833 MHz |
| AMD Athlon 650 (Thunderbird) | 650 MHz | 1054 MHz (1.0 GHz) |
| AMD Athlon 700 | 700 MHz | 886 MHz |
| AMD Athlon 700 (Thunderbird) | 700 MHz | 905 MHz |
| AMD Athlon 750 | 750 MHz | 948 MHz |
| AMD Athlon 750 (Thunderbird) | 750 MHz | 982 MHz |
| AMD Athlon 800 | 800 MHz | 968 MHz |
| AMD Athlon 800 (Thunderbird) | 800 MHz | 971 MHz |
| AMD Athlon 850 | 850 MHz | 1000 MHz (1.0 GHz) |
| AMD Athlon 850 (Thunderbird) | 850 MHz | 1016 MHz (1.0 GHz) |
| AMD Athlon 900 | 900 MHz | 1055 MHz (1.0 GHz) |
| AMD Athlon 900 (Thunderbird) | 900 MHz | 1070 MHz (1.0 GHz) |
| AMD Athlon 950 | 950 MHz | 1080 MHz (1.0 GHz) |
| AMD Athlon 950 (Thunderbird) | 950 MHz | 1130 MHz (1.1 GHz) |
| AMD Athlon 1000 | 1000 MHz (1.0 GHz) | 1256 MHz (1.2 GHz) |
| AMD Athlon 1000 (Thunderbird) | 1000 MHz (1.0 GHz) | 1345 MHz (1.3 GHz) |
| AMD Athlon 1000 (Thunderbird/MP) | 1000 MHz (1.0 GHz) | 1377 MHz (1.3 GHz) |
| AMD Athlon 1000 (Morgan) | 1000 MHz (1.0 GHz) | 1270 MHz (1.2 GHz) |
| AMD Athlon 1100 (Thunderbird) | 1100 MHz (1.1 GHz) | 1318 MHz (1.3 GHz) |
| AMD Athlon 1100 (Morgan) | 1100 MHz (1.1 GHz) | 1254 MHz (1.2 GHz) |
| AMD Athlon 1133 (Thunderbird) | 1133 MHz (1.1 GHz) | 1375 MHz (1.3 GHz) |
| AMD Athlon 1200 (Thunderbird) | 1200 MHz (1.2 GHz) | 1417 MHz (1.4 GHz) |
| AMD Athlon 1200 (Thunderbird/MP) | 1200 MHz (1.2 GHz) | 1566 MHz (1.5 GHz) |
| AMD Athlon 1300 (Thunderbird) | 1300 MHz (1.3 GHz) | 1515 MHz (1.5 GHz) |
| AMD Athlon 1333 (Thunderbird) | 1333 MHz (1.3 GHz) | 1537 MHz (1.5 GHz) |
| AMD Athlon 1400 (Thunderbird) | 1400 MHz (1.4 GHz) | 1608 MHz (1.6 GHz) |
| AMD Athlon XP/MP 1500 | 1330 MHz (1.3 GHz) | 1678 MHz (1.6 GHz) |

**TABLE 12-9**    *AVERAGE AMD ATHLON/DURON OVERCLOCKING POTENTIAL (CONTINUED)*

| PROCESSOR | RATED SPEED | AVERAGE OVERCLOCKED SPEED |
|---|---|---|
| AMD Athlon XP 1500 (Palamino) | 1330 MHz (1.3 GHz) | 1596 MHz (1.5 GHz) |
| AMD Athlon XP/MP 1600 | 1400 MHz (1.4 GHz) | 1606 MHz (1.6 GHz) |
| AMD Athlon XP 1600 (Palamino) | 1400 MHz (1.4 GHz) | 1635 MHz (1.6 GHz) |
| AMD Athlon XP 1700 (Palamino) | 1470 MHz (1.4 GHz) | 1683 MHz (1.6 GHz) |
| AMD Athlon XP/MP 1800 | 1533 MHz (1.5 GHz) | 1853 MHz (1.8 GHz) |
| AMD Athlon XP 1800 (Palamino) | 1533 MHz (1.5 GHz) | 1743 MHz (1.7 GHz) |
| AMD Athlon XP/MP 1900 | 1600 MHz (1.6 GHz) | 1951 MHz (1.9 GHz) |
| AMD Athlon XP 1900 (Palamino) | 1600 MHz (1.6 GHz) | 1793 MHz (1.7 GHz) |
| AMD Athlon XP/MP 2000 | 1670 MHz (1.6 GHz) | 1819 MHz (1.8 GHz) |
| AMD Athlon XP 2000 (Palamino) | 1670 MHz (1.6 GHz) | 1890 MHz (1.8 GHz) |
| AMD Athlon XP 2100 (Palamino) | 1730 MHz (1.7 GHz) | 1957 MHz (1.9 GHz) |
| AMD Duron 600 | 600 MHz | 947 MHz |
| AMD Duron 650 | 650 MHz | 915 MHz |
| AMD Duron 700 | 700 MHz | 949 MHz |
| AMD Duron 750 | 750 MHz | 962 MHz |
| AMD Duron 800 | 800 MHz | 1000 MHz (1.0 GHz) |
| AMD Duron 850 | 850 MHz | 1037 MHz (1.0 GHz) |
| AMD Duron 900 | 900 MHz | 1087 MHz (1.0 GHz) |
| AMD Duron 950 | 950 MHz | 1147 MHz (1.1 GHz) |
| AMD Duron 1000 | 1000 MHz (1.0 GHz) | 1241 MHz (1.2 GHz) |
| AMD Duron 1200 (Morgan) | 1200 MHz (1.2 GHz) | 1390 MHz (1.3 GHz) |
| AMD Duron 1300 (Morgan) | 1300 MHz (1.3 GHz) | 2076 MHz (2.0 GHz) |
| AMD Duron 1400 (Morgan) | 1400 MHz (1.4 GHz) | 1540 MHz (1.5 GHz) |

Like the Intel Celeron with respect to the Pentium II/III, the AMD Duron is often a better candidate for overclocking than is the Athlon. It provides a wider range of settings and overclocking options, mainly as a result of its lower default core voltage of 1.5V. The AMD Athlon, even with its more limited overclocking options, still outperforms the Duron at comparable speeds. The larger L2 cache of the Athlon provides this performance advantage.

 Keep in mind that overclocking immediately voids any processor warranty. Adequate preparation and precautions are an absolute requirement before attempting to overclock any processor. You should have a dependable method of monitoring processor temperature, along with additional cooling resources, installed on the system.

# Troubleshooting CPU Problems

The term *"microprocessor troubleshooting"* is not the misnomer it once was. Early CPUs such as the 8088 carried only 29,000 transistors. When one of those transistors failed, it would usually result in a complete system failure—the PC would crash or freeze entirely. Further, the system would subsequently fail to boot at all. However, CPUs have become far more complex in the last 20 years or so, and new generations such as the Pentium 4 are exceeding *40 million* transistors. With so many more transistors, the probability of an immediate *catastrophic* fault is far less. Of course, *any* CPU fault is *very* serious, but there are now many cases where a system may boot, but crash when certain *specific* CPU functions are attempted (for instance, trying to execute protected-mode instructions). These kinds of errors may give the impression that a piece of software is corrupt or that one or more expansion devices may be faulty. This part of the chapter looks at a selection of CPU failure modes and offers some tactics to help resolve the problems.

# TIPS FOR CONTROLLING HEAT

Heat remains the greatest enemy of overclocking (even normal processor operations), so managing that heat is an important priority on any system, especially today's 2 GHz and faster platforms. Try some of the following remedies to help you overcome CPU heating issues:

- Use a good-quality heat sink/fan that is more than adequately rated for your particular CPU.

- Use a thin layer of heat-sink compound to improve heat transfer between the CPU case and heat sink (available at Radio Shack; Cat. No. 276-1372).

- For extremely hot CPUs, try a Peltier cooler or similar refrigeration unit (see "Further Study" at the end of this chapter for contacts).

- Select reliable ball-bearing-type fans with extended service lifetimes.

- If your system's CMOS Setup allows you to turn off the cooling fan during power-saving modes, opt to disable this feature and leave the fan running. This will help to cool the processor faster.

- Fold and tie cables away from areas requiring free air circulation (such as the vicinity of the CPU fan). Clear away any obstructions.

- Make sure the CPU heat sink/fan is in close thermal contact with the processor surface (using heat-sink compound if needed). It should attach securely to the CPU or the CPU and socket. If it does-n't, get a new heat sink/fan.

- Use a CPU cooler with an audio alarm system that will alert you in case of either fan malfunction or excessive CPU temperature. If your system supports tachometer or thermocouple input (usually part of current "hardware monitoring" features), be sure that the hardware is properly configured and enabled in the CMOS Setup.

- If you are overclocking your CPU, compensate for the increased heat generated by using an "upsized" heat sink/fan, Peltier active cooler, or other effective chilling device.

- Clean fan blades, fan support struts, and power supply louvers of accumulated dirt at least annually. Canned compressed air and vacuum sweeper brushes work well.

- Increase air circulation in and out of your computer case by using an auxiliary chassis fan.

# GENERAL GUIDELINES

As a rule, processor problems fall into three categories: outright failure, heating failure, and compatibility issues. Chances are that you'll experience all three types of problems at one time or another. Here are some tips that can help you deal with these common troubles:

- **Outright failure**    If the CPU fails, the system fails—it's as simple as that. You'll normally see outright failures as systems that refuse to start (not even POST), and crashes that simply cannot be recovered. When you suspect an outright failure, check your power levels first (or try a different supply) before replacing the processor. This can save you a little time and money in the event that the power supply is faulty.

■ **Heating failure** Processors run hot, so you need to cool them with some sort of heat sink fan unit. If the heat sink is loose or the fan stops, the processor will usually overheat. This often results in a temporary system crash. (The system will start working again once you turn it off and give the CPU some time to cool.) You must identify and fix heating problems as soon as possible because repeated overheatings can destroy the processor.

■ **Compatibility issues** A motherboard is limited in the number and speed range of processors that it can accommodate. If a newly built or upgraded system won't boot, verify that the processor is appropriate, and see that the motherboard is configured accordingly (for example, check bus speed and multiplier settings). If the processor or its speed are identified improperly during POST, the FSB or multipliers may be set wrong, or the BIOS must be updated so that it identifies the processor correctly.

## SYMPTOMS

When you encounter trouble starting or running the PC, check for the following symptoms as possible explanations and corrective actions.

**SYMPTOM 12-1** **The system is completely dead (the system power LED lights properly)**
CPU faults are *never* subtle. When a CPU problem manifests itself, the system will invariably crash. Consequently, systems that do not boot (or freeze without warning during the boot process) stand an excellent chance of suffering from a CPU fault. The frustration with this kind of symptom is that the PC typically does not run long enough to execute its POST diagnostics, nor does the system boot to run any third-party real-mode (DOS) diagnostics. As a result, such "dead" systems require a bit of blind faith on the part of a technician.

Before considering a CPU replacement, you should use a multimeter and check the power supply outputs very carefully. Even though the power LED is lit, one or more outputs may be low or absent. Excessively low outputs can easily result in logic errors that will freeze the system. If this problem occurred *after* adding an upgrade, the supply may be overloaded—try removing the upgrade. If system operation returns, consider upgrading the power supply. If an output is low or absent and there has been no upgrade (or the problem continues after removing the upgrade), try replacing the power supply.

Next, strip the system of its peripherals and expansion boards, then try the system again. If operation returns, one of the expansion devices is interrupting system operation. Reinstall one device at a time and check the system. The last expansion device to be installed when the PC fails is the culprit. Replace the defective device. If the failure persists, try a new CPU. Remember to shut down and unplug the PC before continuing. When removing the original CPU, be *extremely* careful to avoid bending any of the pins (you may want to reinstall the CPU later). Use care when installing the new CPU as well—bent pins will almost always ruin the chip. If a new CPU fails to correct the problem, replace the motherboard.

Also make it a point to look for loose screws, paper clips, staples, or other metal parts that might be shorting out your system devices.

**SYMPTOM 12-2** **You get a beep code or I/O POST code indicating a possible CPU fault**
The system will almost always fail to boot. When the POST starts, it will test each of the key motherboard components (including the CPU). If a CPU fault is indicated during the POST (usually a single-byte hexadecimal code written to port 80h and read with a POST card), check each output from the system power supply. If one or more outputs is low or absent, there may be a problem in the supply. Try a new supply. If all supply outputs measure properly, try a new CPU. If a new CPU does not resolve the problem, replace the motherboard.

**SYMPTOM 12-3**    **The system boots with no problem, but crashes or freezes when certain applications are run**    It may seem as if the application is corrupt, but try a diagnostic such as AMIDIAG from AMI or TuffTest from Windsor Technologies (www.tufftest.com). Run repetitive tests on the CPU. While the CPU may work in real mode, diagnostics can detect errors running protected-mode instructions and perform thorough register checking. AMIDIAG stands out here because of the very specific error codes that are returned. Not only will it tell you if the CPU checks bad, but it will also tell you the specific reason *why*. When an error code is returned suggesting a CPU fault, try another CPU. If a CPU fault is not detected, expand the diagnostic to test other portions of the motherboard. If the entire system checks properly, you may indeed have a corrupt file in your application.

**SYMPTOM 12-4**    **The system boots with no problem, but crashes or freezes after several minutes of operation**    This happens regardless of the application being run. You will also probably note that no diagnostic indicates a CPU problem. If you shut the system off and wait several minutes, the system will probably boot fine and run for several more minutes before stopping again—this is typical of thermal failure. When the system halts, check the CPU for heat. *Use extreme caution when checking for heat—you can easily be burned!* Your CPU may not be fitted with a heat sink, or its cooling fan is disconnected (or has failed). As a rule, all Pentium-class and later processors (such as the Pentium MMX, Pentium II/III/4, Athlon, and Duron) require an adequately sized heat sink/fan assembly for proper cooling. Replace any defective cooling fan.

Make sure that the system cooling fan is working and that there is an unobstructed path over the CPU. If not, consider applying a heat sink with an adequate helping of thermal compound. If the CPU is already fitted with a heat sink, make sure that there is an ample layer of thermal compound between the CPU case and heat sink base. In many cases, the compound is omitted, impairing the transfer of heat and allowing the CPU to run much hotter. If you find that there is no thermal compound, allow the PC to cool, then add thermal compound between the CPU case and heat sink.

**SYMPTOM 12-5**    **The system BIOS mis-identifies the processor**    This frequently happens after a processor upgrade and is almost always due to a problem with the BIOS. Most BIOS versions will query the CPU with a CPUID instruction, then identify the CPU through a look-up table in the BIOS. If the CPU does not have an entry in the BIOS, it will not be identified (or will be identified incorrectly). The general way to correct this problem is to upgrade the motherboard BIOS to a later version or upgrade the motherboard.

**SYMPTOM 12-6**    **An older system refuses to run properly when the CPU's internal (L1) cache is enabled**    This type of symptom occurred frequently with older processors (such as the AMD Am486) and can almost always be traced to a configuration issue. The processor may fail if run at an incorrect bus speed (for instance, overclocking), so check and correct the motherboard bus speed and multiplier to accommodate the specific CPU's requirements. This symptom can also occur when running the CPU at an incorrect operating voltage. Check the voltage level and reconfigure the motherboard for the correct voltage (if necessary). Finally, the motherboard must be compatible with the L1 cache type on the CPU. For example, installing a CPU with a write-back cache on a motherboard that doesn't support write-back cache can cause problems. However, this is not an issue on current motherboards where the L1/L2 cache is located on the processor.

**SYMPTOM 12-7**    **You cannot run a 3.45V CPU in a 5V motherboard, even though an appropriate voltage regulator module is being used**    Here's another problem that frequently crops up with older motherboards. Double-check the voltage regulator module (VRM). The VRM must have adequate current handling capacity to support the CPU's power demands. Otherwise, the VRM will be overloaded and fail to provide adequate power. Check with the CPU manufacturer for its VRM recommendations. You might also try the CPU/VRM in another 5V motherboard. If the CPU/VRM fails in another 5V motherboard, chances are that the VRM is underrated or has failed. If the CPU/VRM does work on another 5V motherboard, it is possible that the original motherboard's BIOS could not support the particular requirements of the new CPU. Check with the motherboard manufacturer to see if there is an updated BIOS (either flash or ROM chip) available for the system.

**SYMPTOM 12-8** **A system malfunctions under HIMEM.SYS or DOS4GW.EXE after installing a new CPU** This type of symptom occurred frequently with older CPUs and could generally be traced to errors in the motherboard CPU voltage and type settings (opposed to the newer bus speed/multiplier configurations). Check the motherboard's CPU configuration jumpers. Also, running a 3.45V CPU at 5V or running a non-SL enhanced CPU as an SL enhanced part can cause these types of problems to occur. So make sure that the correct part is being used and see that the CPU voltage is correct (use a voltage regulator module if necessary).

**SYMPTOM 12-9** **The P4 or Athlon XP speed is reported incorrectly** In most cases, the problem occurs because the FSB is set improperly. A Pentium 4 quadruples the FSB (100 MHz becomes 400 MHz, and 133 MHz becomes 533 MHz), and the Athlon processors double the FSB (100 MHz becomes 200 MHz, and 133 MHz becomes 266 MHz). If the processor's speed is reported incorrectly, chances are that the FSB is set improperly either on motherboard jumpers or the CMOS Setup. If the FSB is set correctly, suspect a problem in the BIOS (which may need to be updated).

**SYMPTOM 12-10** **L2 cache fails after upgrading to a Pentium OverDrive processor** Installing an OverDrive-type processor can sometimes result in the secondary (L2 or "external") cache being disabled. This is usually due to a BIOS version that is not compatible with the OverDrive processor. You may need to leave the L2 cache disabled until you can upgrade the motherboard BIOS. In a few cases, a patch utility may be available for the motherboard that can be run from the CONFIG.SYS or AUTOEXEC.BAT file and that will re-enable the L2 cache as the system boots. This problem does not exist on current systems where L1/L2 cache is located on the processor.

**SYMPTOM 12-11** **Some software locks up on systems running 5x86 processors** This is a frequent problem with high-end software such as AutoDesk's 3D Studio. Often, older versions of programs like 3D Studio use software timing loops in the code. The 5x86 processor executes these loop instructions faster than previous x86 CPUs, thereby interfering with timing-dependent code inside the program. In most cases, the software manufacturer will offer a patch for the offending program. For 3D Studio, you can download the FSTCPUFX.EXE file from Kinetix (ftp://ftp.fh-merseburg.de/pub/hardware/mainboard/asus/FSTCPUFX.EXE). Run the executable patch file and follow the instructions. The patch alters the 3D Studio executable file.

Another prime example of software-related problems is with older Clipper applications. Clipper inserts software timing loops into the applications when the code is compiled, and this also interferes with timing-dependent code in the program. For Clipper, you can download the PIPELOOP.EXE file (ftp://ftp.ascod.ru/SOFT/Cyrix/pipeloop.exe) and put it in your AUTOEXEC.BAT file.

Regardless of your system's vintage, software that refuses to work on your system may indicate incompatibility. Double-check the minimum system requirements of the software, and check with the software maker for any known CPU or other compatibility issues. This can save a great deal of time troubleshooting hardware that isn't really defective.

**SYMPTOM 12-12**    **The Windows 95 Device Manager identifies the CPU incorrectly**
In many cases, the CPU is mis-identified as a 486 or other older CPU. This mistake is due to an issue with Windows 95. The algorithm used in Windows 95 to detect the CPU was likely completed before the particular CPU was released, and therefore the CPU responds to the algorithm just as a 486 does. Use a diagnostic, which *will* identify your particular CPU correctly, or check with the CPU maker for a Windows 95 patch that will support proper identification. This problem happens often with Cyrix 6x86 CPUs and can be corrected by downloading a patch such as 6XOPT074.ZIP. Later versions of Windows (such as 98/Me/XP) typically have no problems identifying a processor correctly.

**SYMPTOM 12-13**    **The heat sink/fan will not secure properly**    You cannot achieve a tight fit between the heat sink and the surface of the CPU. This can be a serious problem for the system because a loose heat sink/fan will *not* cool the processor correctly. There are three classical solutions to this issue. First, make sure that you have the heat sink/fan model that is recommended for your particular CPU (a common error when building a new PC). Second, make sure that the heat sink attaches to either the CPU chip itself or the ZIF socket that the CPU mounts in. Third, verify that the CPU has not been altered or faked. "Faked" CPUs are often ground down to remove their original markings, then new markings are placed on the CPU. The grinding process reduces the package thickness and can prevent the heat sink/fan from being secure. (Faked CPUs have been reported in Europe, though it's not as common as it used to be.)

**SYMPTOM 12-14**    **The Cyrix 6x86 system crashes or freezes after some period of operation**    This is almost always a heat-related problem caused by inadequate cooling of the 6x86. If you're not using a heat sink/fan, install one before continuing (be sure to use a thin layer of thermal grease to improve heat transfer between the CPU and heat sink). Make sure that you are using a good-quality heat sink/fan with *plenty* of capacity and see that it is securely attached to the CPU. Also see that the CPU itself is securely seated in its socket.

You might also consider installing a different 6x86 model. The Type C028 version uses 3.52 volts, and the Type C016 uses 3.3 volts, so just changing models can reduce power demands. You might also try installing a version 2.7 or later 6x86, which is better able to deal with heat. Best yet, install a 6x86L CPU (and regulator). A third possible cause of intermittent system operation is a poorly designed BIOS. Check with the motherboard maker or system manufacturer and see if there is a BIOS upgrade to better support Cyrix CPUs.

**SYMPTOM 12-15**    **The Cyrix 6x86 system crashes and refuses to restart**    This is another classic heat-related problem and may often indicate that the CPU or its associated voltage regulator has failed. Check the voltage regulator—regulators are more susceptible to failure with Cyrix 6x86 CPUs because of the higher current demands. If the voltage regulator checks out, replace the CPU itself (perhaps with a lower-power model, as mentioned in Symptom 12-14).

**SYMPTOM 12-16**    **You notice poor Cyrix 6x86 performance under Windows NT 4.0**
In virtually all cases, NT has detected the 6x86 and has elected to shut down the write-back L1 cache completely. This results in the performance hit. Fortunately, there are several ways to address this problem. First, you can download the DIRECTNT.ZIP patch from this Web site: **compunet.hypermart.net/hardware.htm**); this patch re-enables the L1 cache under NT 4.0. This fix brings performance back up, but it also can cause instability for NT. A more practical resolution is to replace the CPU with a 6x86 version 2.7 or

higher, or a 6x86L (and suitable voltage regulator), as mentioned in Symptom 12-14. Keep in mind that VIA Technologies does *not* provide any support for older, obsolete Cyrix processors. One other alternative is to upgrade the motherboard and processor entirely, eliminating the old Cyrix processor from the system.

**SYMPTOM 12-17** **Applications do not perform well** For example, you can't get your version of Quake (or other graphics-intensive program) to run nearly as well on a Cyrix 6x86 system as it does with a similar Pentium system. This is an issue involving Cyrix FPU performance. There is no real resolution for the problem at this time—later 6x86 versions do not correct the FPU. You may replace the CPU with an AMD or Intel model, or you can check the performance offered by the Cyrix 6x86MX (M2), if you could still find one available. In many cases, this type of problem is better resolved by upgrading the motherboard and processor.

**SYMPTOM 12-18** **A Cyrix 6x86 CPU won't work on your motherboard** There are several possible problems when upgrading to any non-Intel CPU. First, check the motherboard's chipset and make sure that the chipset and other attributes such as bus speed are compatible with the 6x86. As you saw earlier, some 6x86 iterations require unusual bus speeds in order to function. Motherboard settings are always important when installing a CPU. You will probably need to set a new clock speed to accommodate the 6x86. In some cases, you may also need to specify a CPU type. Finally, you'll need to set the CPU voltage (if your motherboard provides a "switchable" voltage regulator). Otherwise, you'll need to install a voltage regulator with enough power capacity to handle a 6x86 adequately. If you select an underrated regulator, the regulator can overheat and burn out. The last issue to consider is your BIOS. Often the BIOS must detect a CPU correctly and make slight variations in BIOS routines to use the new CPU most effectively. If the BIOS does not support your 6x86, you'll need to get a BIOS upgrade from the motherboard maker or system manufacturer.

If all else fails, try slowing down the clock speed to the next level. If the CPU runs properly then, there is probably an incompatibility between your motherboard and the 6x86. Check with the motherboard manufacturer (or system maker) and see if there are any compatibility issues that have been identified (and if there is a fix available).

**SYMPTOM 12-19** **You notice performance degradation when using a Cyrix 6x86 under older versions of Windows** In many cases, performance problems when using non-Intel CPUs is related to BIOS support. Often the BIOS must identify a CPU, and adjust to accommodate any particular nuances. If the BIOS is not supporting the CPU correctly, overall performance problems can result. Check with the motherboard maker or system manufacturer for any BIOS upgrades that will better support your new CPU.

Clock speed and cache are two other issues that can affect system performance. Check the motherboard jumpers and verify that the clock speed is set correctly for your Cyrix CPU. Also check for cache jumpers and see that any cache settings are correct. You may also verify that Internal (L1) and External (L2) caching are enabled in BIOS. In many cases, this problem can be resolved by upgrading the version of Windows, or upgrading the motherboard and processor.

**SYMPTOM 12-20** **The system does not boot up at all after reconfiguring the system for overclocking** This is a common problem that almost always means that you *cannot* overclock the CPU at the level you have chosen. Try bumping up the processor voltage a bit. If that fails, scale back the clock speed or the multiplier until the system starts up, or return the clock and multiplier to their original values.

**SYMPTOM 12-21**    **The system starts after overclocking, but locks up or crashes after some short period of time**    Overclocking causes substantial heating of the CPU, and cooling must be improved to compensate for this additional heat—otherwise, the overheated CPU can lock-up and crash the system. Check the heat sink/fan and see that it is attached correctly and has a thin layer of thermal grease between the CPU and heat sink. It may be necessary to "up-size" the heat sink/fan or use a Peltier cooler.

**SYMPTOM 12-22**    **You see memory errors after increasing the bus speed for overclocking**    Memory performance is tightly coupled to bus speed (or "FSB speed"). For example, most 60ns RAM types will work fine up to 66 MHz, but you may need high-end 50ns EDO RAM or 50ns SDRAM when pushing the bus speed to 75 MHz or 83 MHz. Overclocking a 100 MHz FSB may require PC133 (133 MHz) SDRAM, and overclocking a 133 MHz FSB may demand PC150 (150 MHz) SDRAM. Try some faster memory in the PC (or do not attempt to overclock the system). In more current systems, you can often adjust the FSB speed and multiplier asynchronously of the memory bus and other system busses. This makes system performance a bit more forgiving.

**SYMPTOM 12-23**    **After reconfiguring for overclocking, the system works, but you see a rash of CPU failures**    Chances are that the CPU is running far too hot and is resulting in premature CPU failures. Check the cooling unit and see that it is securely attached and that there is a thin layer of thermal grease between the CPU and heat sink. It may be necessary to "up-size" the heat sink/fan or use a Peltier cooler.

**SYMPTOM 12-24**    **After reconfiguring for overclocking, you find that some expansion board or other hardware is no longer recognized or working**    When run synchronously, AGP, PCI, and ISA bus clocks are often tied to the FSB speed. Consequently, increasing the FSB speed will also increase the AGP, PCI, and ISA clocks. This can upset the operation of some sensitive adapter boards. Check your CMOS Setup—there may be provisions to adjust divisors that will set the correct speeds. For example, when you go from an FSB of 100 MHz to 133 MHz, you may need to set the AGP divisor from 2/3 to 1/2 so that the AGP bus will stay as close to 66 MHz as possible. Similar settings may be available for the PCI bus. In some motherboard designs, the bus clocks may be independent (asynchronous) of the FSB. You may also be able to replace the suspect hardware with a more tolerant adapter, but it is often safer to return the clock speed and multiplier settings to their original values if you cannot tweak them yourself.

**SYMPTOM 12-25**    **After reconfiguring for overclocking, you notice that a number of recent files are corrupt, inaccessible, or missing**    In effect, the system is not stable. Check for excessive processor heat first. Otherwise, you should *not* overclock this particular system. Try scaling back the overclocking configuration or return the clock speed and multiplier settings to their original values.

**SYMPTOM 12-26**    **The CPU core voltage is set at 1.7V, but hardware monitoring tools report a reading of 1.74V**    This is not necessarily a problem. Voltage output fluctuations can be caused by your power supply unit, but a core voltage deviation of 0.05V is safe with AMD CPUs. For more serious deviations, you may need to tweak the voltage setting so that your measuring tools report an acceptable level. Remember that there is always a little tolerance between the ideal value represented by a setting and the actual value that occurs as the result of that setting—this is normal in the real world—however, the tolerance should be very small (just a few percent).

**SYMPTOM 12-27**    **The system will not boot when a processor at one speed is set to a lower speed (after loading the fail-safe or optimized default option)**    This is usually an issue with the processor's information in the CMOS Setup. For example, if you experience a 600 MHz Duron failing to boot when set to 500 MHz (either manually or by fail-safe/optimized default loading), clear the CMOS via the "Clear CMOS" jumper. Now manually set the CPU to the correct frequency and multiplier to achieve the correct processor speed (such as 600 MHz).

**SYMPTOM 12-28**    **A Pentium III 600B is being detected as a Pentium III 450**    Pentium III processors are "multiplier locked" to inhibit overclocking. For example, the Pentium III 600B is locked at 4.5x with the 133 MHz BUS. If your motherboard does not support the 133 MHz BUS, then it will run at 100 MHz, causing the processor to run at 450 MHz. Some motherboards state that the BUS will run at 133 MHz, but this is not supported by the manufacturer and may interfere with the AGP and PCI bus speeds causing problems. Unless your motherboard supports the 133 MHz BUS and processors from the manufacturer, your supported speed will only be 100 MHz. Reconfigure the motherboard to the proper FSB speed or replace the motherboard.

# Further Study

**AMD**   www.amd.com
**AMI**   www.ami.com/ (AMIDIAG)
**ARM**   www.arm.com
**Athlon Overclocking**   www.athlonoc.com
**CPU Central**   www.cpu-central.com
**Cyrix**   *See* VIA Technologies
**Hardware Central**   www.hardwarecentral.com/hardwarecentral/subjects/75/
**IBM PowerPC**   www-3.ibm.com/chips/products/powerpc/
**Intel**   www.intel.com
**Intel (Pentium 4 site)**   developer.intel.com/design/pentium4/
**MIPS**   www.mips.com
**Motherboard HomeWorld**   www.motherboards.org/docoverclock.html
**Overclockers Online**   www.overclockersonline.com
**Sharky Extreme**   www.sharkyextreme.com/hardware/celeron_oc/1.shtml
**Texas Instruments**   www.ti.com
**Tom's Hardware**   www.tomshardware.com
**VIA Technologies**   www.viatech.com

# 13

# DATA RECOVERY TECHNIQUES

It's almost ironic that the value of a PC's hardware is often insignificant when weighed against the data that PC contains. Recent history is replete with examples of businesses that have suffered terrible financial hardship—even gone out of business—after losing vital data files. While the consequences are not nearly as severe for home offices or casual PC users, damaged files, accidental deletions, and hard drive failures are always difficult. This chapter is intended to provide some guidance that will help to protect your drive from failure and to offer some procedures that will help you recover lost or damaged data. The one thing to keep in mind here is that the drive hardware *must* be working. If the drive should fail, you may not be able to recover anything.

If you must recover data from a damaged hard drive, there are numerous "data recovery" businesses (listed at the end of this chapter) that might be able to help. Recovering data from a damaged drive is expensive and is usually only worthwhile for large corporations and government organizations. Backups are the best protection from data loss due to hardware faults.

# Understanding Data Loss

The first step in overcoming data loss is to know its causes. Data is extremely vulnerable and may be damaged by many different factors. This part of the chapter explains the major causes of data loss and offers some suggestions to minimize the dangers.

## HARDWARE AND SYSTEM FAILURES

By far, hardware faults are the leading cause of data failure—accounting for at least 44 percent of all data loss. Hardware failures can occur from such events as an electrical failure (or shutting down the PC improperly), a disk drive head crash, or a failure of the drive circuitry or electromechanical mechanisms. You'll see hardware problems indicated by error messages (for example, an error message stating that the device is "not recognized" or "not available"). You may also notice that previously accessible data is suddenly gone. In many cases, the hard drive may not even spin, or you may hear a scraping or rattling sound coming from the hard drive.

You can usually work to prevent hardware and system failures by keeping the system in a clean, temperature- and humidity-controlled environment. Protect against power surges and other types of electrical failures by employing an *uninterruptible power supply* (UPS). For mission-critical data—such as an important network server or central workstation—use a *redundant array of independent disks* (RAID) system to mirror your main data drive(s). When properly configured, RAID will often allow you to re-create the data lost on a drive.

As a rule, *never* open a hard drive (other than inside a Class 100 or better industrial cleanroom environment). Otherwise the accumulation of dust and debris in everyday air can render the drive unusable. If you must reclaim data from a failed drive, send it to a company that has the specialized cleanroom facilities to attempt a hard drive repair (such as those listed at the end of this chapter). Do not attempt to operate a hard drive that you suspect may have hardware or system failure. The failure may continue to corrupt data on the drive and exacerbate the data loss. Finally, never use software recovery utilities (such as Norton Disk Doctor or Ontrack's EasyRecovery) to recover data in a hardware failure situation. These utilities assume that the hardware is functional, and can cause further damage to the data.

## HUMAN ERROR

Contrary to popular belief, human error ranks second (about 32 percent) as the cause of all data loss. In most cases when the system seems to work properly, but previously accessible data is suddenly gone, chances are that human error is responsible at some level. For example, letting your young nephew poke around on your system without supervision is a great way to lose important data. It may be as simple as an accidental deletion of a file, or as serious as impact damage caused by accidentally dropping a drive or tape.

Human error can be prevented by keeping regular and up-to-date data backups of your current work. Also, you should avoid attempting any installations, repairs, or system operations with which you do not have previous experience. Fortunately, files and folders that are accidentally deleted can usually be recovered from the Recycle Bin of Windows 9x/Me/XP (or with the Undelete feature included in earlier operating systems such as DOS). If you must bring in another individual to help recover your data, make sure that the individual has the experience needed to recover files successfully.

## SOFTWARE BUGS

Improper software design accounts for roughly 14 percent of all data loss. We typically refer to these as "bugs" in the software. Bugs are usually caused by improper software design and testing on the part of the software maker. Even when software is working perfectly, the software may have unforeseen effects on particular system platforms or combinations of hardware. In many cases, you'll notice software bugs as error messages stating that the data is inaccessible or corrupted. (The problem usually occurs after installing new software.) You may also see memory errors or other PC errors. You'll need to identify the software responsible for your data loss (usually the last application to be installed before the problems surfaced), and contact the software maker for the appropriate patches or upgrades.

## COMPUTER VIRUSES

While the popular media seems to focus on computer viruses as a primary cause of data loss, viruses really only account for about 7 percent of all data loss (though that percentage is growing a bit with the popularity of Internet downloads). Tens of thousands of computer viruses are currently known to exist, and that number grows daily, but viruses still have had a limited impact on data, simply because antivirus software catches most of them before the system is infected. In most cases, you'll see a virus infection broadcast with a message on the display (for example, "Your computer is now stoned"), though there may be many other strange or unpredictable behaviors that accompany the data loss.

Your best defense against computer viruses is to use a *current* antivirus tool, and to scan all incoming floppy disks, downloads, and even CDs for viruses. (This includes packaged software, software carried on-site by other users, and software downloaded from the Internet.) Also, do not accept e-mail file attachments from people you do not know, and virus-check any attachments that you do receive before opening them. Data is usually accessible after the virus has been removed, but be sure to remove the virus first. Also, avoid reformatting your hard drive or floppy disk as a means of eliminating viruses—this doesn't always work.

## THEFT AND MALICIOUS DAMAGE

Data loss can also be traced to the occurrence of theft or malicious damage. Computers are notoriously easy to transport and sell, so they are often the target of home or office break-ins. Of course, once the PC disappears, any data that was in it goes as well. Even if the system is eventually recovered, any data probably will have been wiped clean by the system's new user. This is a prime example of where off-site backups (either in a physical safe or online via the Internet) can save the day.

If you've worked in business for any length of time, you've probably seen more than one coworker terminated or laid off. Some folks vent their anger and frustration by erasing files, loading viruses, and even physically damaging their system (though there is certainly criminal liability for such actions). If you're the boss and find yourself handing out pink slips, remember to change a user's password first.

## NATURAL DISASTERS

Fire, flood, earthquake, lightning strikes—all the forces of nature account for just 3 percent of all data loss. While there is little you can do to prevent the physical destruction of your system in the face of a natural disaster (like a hurricane or tornado), your best protection is to keep a current backup of your data stored off-site in another protected water/fire-proof location.

# Protecting Drives and Data

Sooner or later, your hard drive is going to fail. It is not a question of whether, it is a question of when. While this may sound gloomy, there is absolutely no reason why a hard drive should not perform perfectly throughout its entire normal working life. Just as people can improve the quality of their life by eating right and exercising regularly, drive life can be lengthened (and your data protected) by taking some fairly common-sense precautions. The following pointers can reduce downtime and are sure ways to win a customer's loyalty.

## UNINTERRUPTIBLE POWER SUPPLY (UPS)

Often, a power loss only occurs for a few minutes, or a few seconds. But even a brief interruption in power can crash a PC, taking your valuable work with it. Consequently, a surprisingly effective way to prevent data loss is to maintain power to the system when AC fails at the wall outlet. This is the job of the uninterruptible power supply. A UPS is simply a battery-powered "generator." When AC is available from the wall outlet, it powers your PC normally, and the UPS stands by (keeping its internal batteries fully charged). When a power loss occurs, the UPS kicks in, converting the DC battery power into AC that will continue to power the PC.

In most cases, a UPS only provides enough power to operate a monitor and PC for just a few minutes, but those crucial minutes allow you to save your work and shut down the PC in an orderly manner. This can save hours in lost work, avoid potential damage to important operating system files, and even save your system from possible hardware damage. Today, a UPS is available for just about every budget and level of user, and they can easily pay for themselves with work/productivity saved in the face of a power outage. As a technician, you can't go wrong recommending a UPS to your customers.

## HANDLE CRASHES GRACEFULLY

Virtually every computer system will stop from time to time—programs cease running, and the system won't respond to commands. We usually say the system is frozen, halted, or hung up. A system can halt for many reasons (including hardware faults), but buggy software is usually the problem. The trick is correcting the problem and regaining control of the system. As a rule, never turn off the system power. Windows usually has numerous files open, and there are numerous tasks running in memory. When the system hangs, those files are left open, so try to clear the problem before taking drastic action:

■ *Close other programs and tasks.* If you can access other items on your task bar (for example, the Start button or other background programs), make sure to close any other programs or tasks that may be open. Try saving as many open files (such as current documents) as you can. When one application fails, it can often destabilize your entire PC, so minimize the potential for damage if you can. Use the Windows Shut Down dialog to reboot the system.

■ *Try to clear the failed process first by pressing CTRL-ALT-DEL.* This should open the Close Program dialog. (Windows XP calls this the Task Manager.) If the dialog opens (see Figure 13-1) and you see that one or more applications are not responding, you can highlight them and click the End Task button. In many cases, this will terminate the problem software with a minimum of fuss and allow you to regain

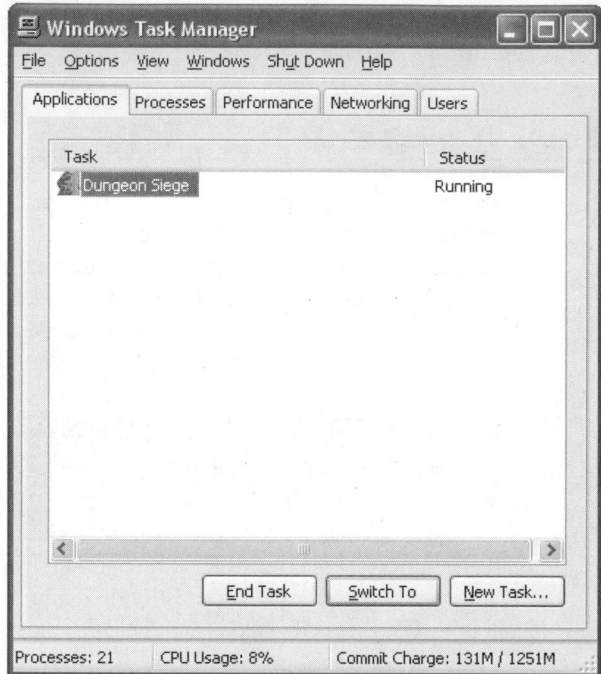

**FIGURE 13-1** Windows XP provides a powerful Task Manager that can help you to terminate misbehaving applications.

control of the system (at least enough to reboot in an orderly fashion). Once you press CTRL-ALT-DEL, it may take a few seconds for the system to respond, so don't panic if the dialog doesn't open right away.

- *Use the Shut Down button.* If you can open the Close Program or Task Manager dialog, but cannot regain control of the system, try the Shut Down button (or click Turn Off under Windows XP). This is a "back door" that allows you to turn the system off in an emergency. You may lose some unsaved data, but it can prevent serious Windows problems.

- *Warm boot the system.* If the system remains "stuck," things get a little more serious. You're now forced to reboot the PC and will certainly lose any unsaved data. Check your hard drive activity LED. If the LED is out (and you don't hear the drive working), try pressing the PC's Reset button on the front panel. Windows should reboot, though it will probably run ScanDisk automatically to check for file problems. Avoid pressing the Reset button if the drive activity LED is on or flashing (indicating that drive activity is taking place) unless it's absolutely necessary.

- *Cold boot the system.* In rare circumstances, the Reset button may fail to reboot the system. This indicates a serious problem, though not unrecoverable. In this case, you'll need to press the Power button. With most systems, you may need to hold in the Power button for several seconds (perhaps up to 5 or 6 seconds) until the power supply turns off. Wait a few seconds after the PC shuts down, and then try powering-up the system again. Windows will probably run ScanDisk automatically to check for file problems. As with the Reset button, avoid using the Power button if the drive activity LED is on or flashing (indicating that drive activity is taking place) unless absolutely necessary.

# CHILDPROOF THE SYSTEM

Children have a heartwarming sense of curiosity, but when it comes to computers, you need to take special precautions to protect your data from prying eyes and mischievous fingers. As always, backups are handy tools to prevent data loss, but there are other more useful tactics that may help reduce the threat of accidental data loss:

■ *Employ system passwords to prevent unauthorized access to the system.* This will keep curious children off the system until you're around to supervise. You can use either the BIOS password (invoked through the CMOS Setup) or the Windows logon password. If you are frequently away from your system and it is idle, use a screen-saver password to prevent a child from casually playing on the keyboard when you've got your back turned. Of course, this doesn't prevent access to files and directories once the PC is unlocked.

Children are notoriously adept at finding their way around a PC. If you allow children (especially older children) to work with your PC, be sure to set up the system for multiple users and employ passwords yourself; otherwise, you may find yourself locked out of your own system.

■ *Employ file passwords to prevent access to sensitive files.* Many applications will let you encrypt their data files with a password (see Figure 13-2). For example, most word processors allow you to do this. Of course, be careful not to lose the password, or you will lock yourself out of your own files.

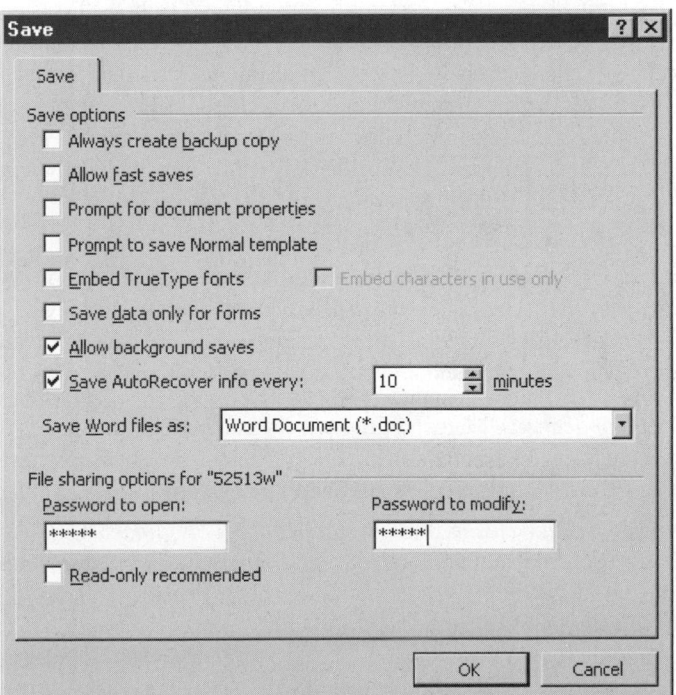

**FIGURE 13-2**    Applications like MS Word allow you to assign passwords to protect individual documents.

■ *Set file attributes to limit the access to important files or directories.* You can set the hidden and/or read-only file attributes of sensitive files or directories to make them harder to find or delete. This is a simple preventative tactic that will work in many cases to protect against accidental damage, though it certainly isn't a high-security option.

■ *Try aftermarket program shells or navigators.* Most operating systems have special programs available that are specifically designed to provide a customized environment for kids to use on the PC. When loaded, the program sits on top of the operating system as a special user environment that allows the user to access only programs and data that have been set up and authorized for use. This can in many ways be the best solution (especially for young kids) since these shells not only protect the system, but also often provide a much more kid-friendly way for young users to access their educational programs, games, and so on. Current operating systems (like Windows XP) let you create environments for multiple users (see below).

■ *Consider a dedicated PC for the kids.* With the price of PCs falling rapidly, it is not very expensive to get a slightly older PC and set it up as a machine for the kids to use. Some people do this when they upgrade—they get a new system and pass the older one down to the kids.

■ *Don't forget to educate your children about important computing issues.* Children readily learn how computers work, so teaching your children about what they can use and what they should (and should not) touch can help avoid problems. This should certainly include some serious discussions about Internet features like chat and Web browsing. Very young children should always be supervised when using the PC.

■ *Create multiple user profiles.* Operating systems like Windows XP allow the system to be configured for multiple users (see Figure 13-3). Each user can set his or her own desktop appearance and other preferences. Users can be switched simply by logging off as one user, then allowing another user to log on (though Windows XP does support multiple simultaneous logons). Programs can also be shared or separated across user profiles, so you can install firewall software to run under every user, then let your children install their favorite game under their profile only (reducing clutter in your profile).

## KEEP THE DISK(S) CLEAN

With today's huge operating systems, multi-megabyte Internet downloads, and powerful creativity programs, it's surprisingly easy to fill even a large hard drive. Just try capturing a few video clips and see how quickly the drive can fill. Cache files, temporary files, and unemptied Recycle Bins can also leave unneeded information on the drive. As a rule, you should periodically run tools to clean and maintain your disks:

■ *Uninstall unneeded applications.* Many programs today can be absolutely huge (especially games). If you're finished or bored with applications on the system, uninstall them according to the publisher's recommendations. This can save lots of disk space, and you can always reinstall them later if you want.

■ *Clean up the disk with the Disk Cleanup tool in your System Tools folder.* Disk Cleanup (see Figure 13-4) will remove Internet cache data, temporary files, and other clutter that frequently creeps up on your available disk space.

■ *Check the disk with ScanDisk.* Here's another tool in your Windows 9x/Me System Tools folder that can be an invaluable aid in verifying the integrity of your files and disk media. ScanDisk can check for cross-linked files and lost allocation units—revealing the presence of potentially damaged files. ScanDisk can also perform a test of the drive platters and can alert you to possible media issues. Windows XP does *not* offer ScanDisk as an end-user tool.

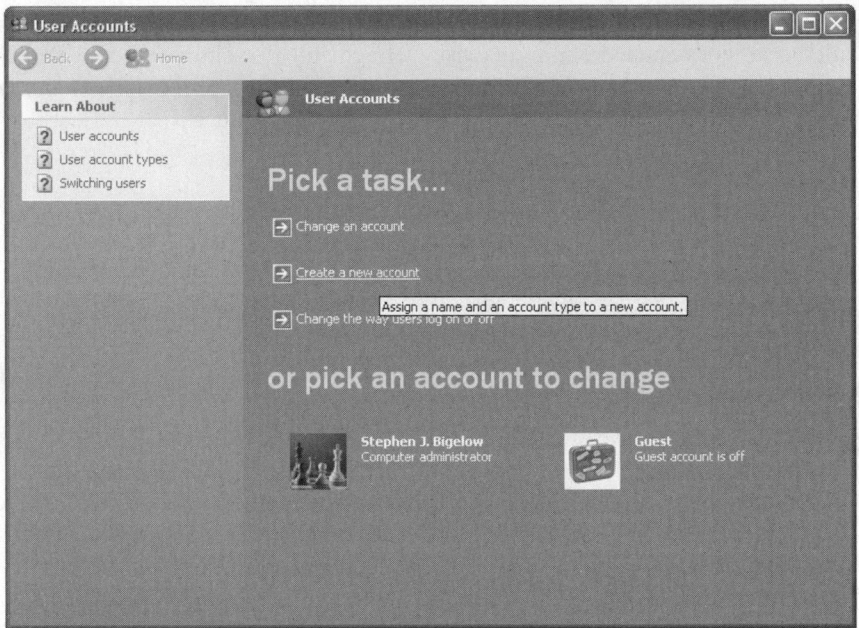

**FIGURE  13-3**      Windows XP can be configured for multiple users without having to install any
additional shell or supporting software.

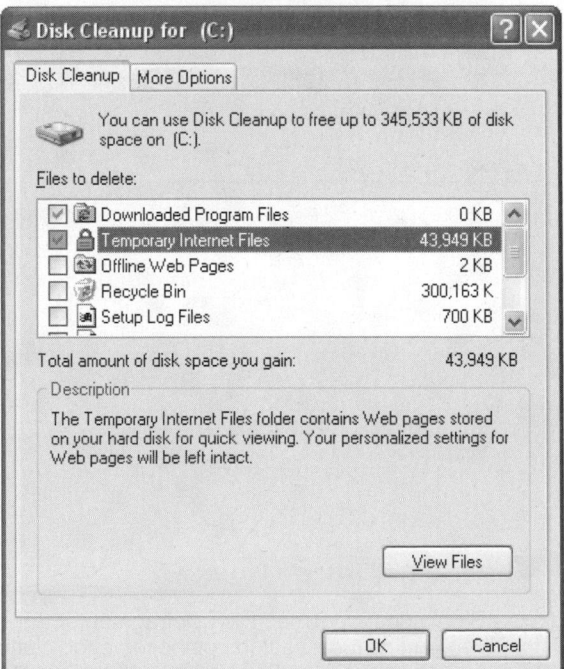

**FIGURE  13-4**      Windows XP provides a version of Disk Cleanup that will check for and remove
clutter on your hard drive(s).

■ *Defragment the disk with Disk Defragmenter.* This is the third tool in your System Tools folder that you should use after scanning your disks. Disk Defragmenter (or simply "Defrag") will reorganize your files so that the clusters of each file are contiguous. This type of reorganization should help to keep your disk running at peak efficiency (see Figure 13-5), and reduce wear and tear that could compromise its working life.

If you want to delete something but aren't sure if it's really needed by the system, try renaming it first to another name. To the software, it is the same as if you deleted the file, since any software that needs it will be unable to find it with the new name (and will cause an error if this is the case). Since you haven't actually deleted it, you can restore the original name later if necessary. If you rename it and after a few weeks no application seems to need it, you can probably delete it permanently.

## CHECK THE POWER QUALITY

Hard drives tend to be quite sensitive to variations in AC power—especially voltage spikes caused by lightning or inductive equipment (for example, motors) sharing the same AC circuit in your home or office. If there is a lot of motorized equipment or high-energy equipment in the same area as the PC, consider having a new AC line installed exclusively for the computer, or consider investing in an *uninterruptible power supply* (UPS) with ample surge and spike protection.

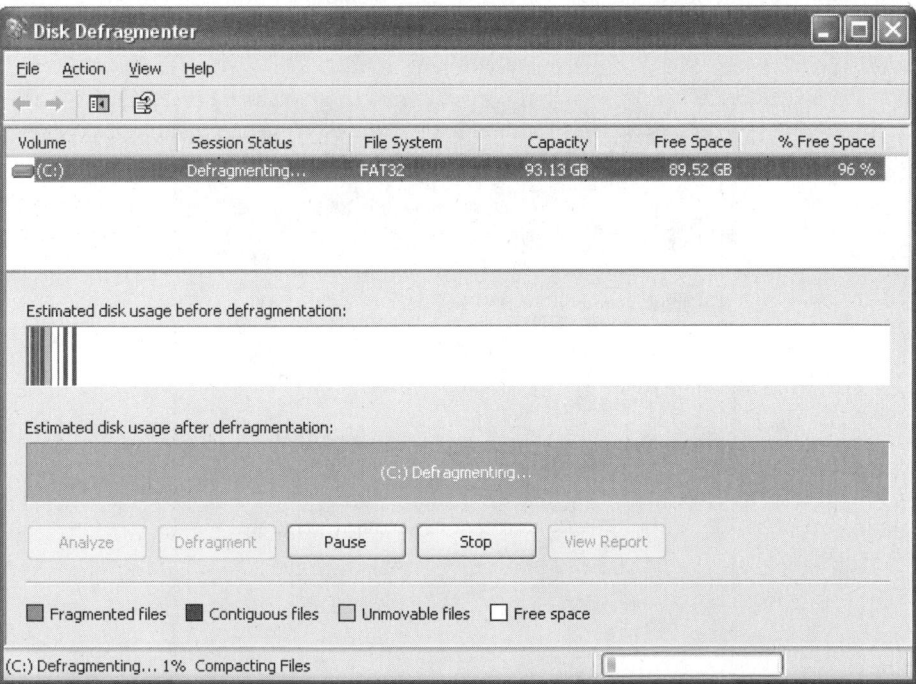

**FIGURE  13-5**    Windows XP provides a detailed Disk Defragmenter that can analyze your drive and let you reorganize the files if things become too cluttered.

# CHECK THE DRIVE ENVIRONMENT

The way hard drives are mounted and used can have a profound impact on their overall reliability. Noise, vibrations, and handling are just a few of the issues to be concerned with:

- *Noise*    Hard drives often make a little bit of whirring noise when spinning up, and subtle clicking as the heads move from track to track—this is perfectly normal. However, drives that make loud clacking or grinding noises may be close to failure. You should back up and replace such suspect drives at your earliest opportunity before they fail. If such a noisy drive cannot be accessed, it may have already failed.

- *Smoke*    Cigar and cigarette smoke can be detrimental to a hard drive. Although the air drawn into a hard drive is passed through an extremely fine filter, any smoke particles that do manage to penetrate the drive housing are much larger than the spacing between a R/W head and platter. A single smoke particle caught between the head and platter can literally be "dragged" along the disk, eventually resulting in media damage.

- *Mounting screws*    In spite of their rigid enclosure, hard drives can be warped just slightly when tightly secured by four mounting screws. In some cases, this effect is just enough to throw out a drive's alignment and cause data problems. If you encounter drive problems after moving or remounting the drive, try loosening one or more of the screws (you need not remove them). Just taking the pressure off will usually eliminate the problem. However, don't leave a drive without the proper number of mounting screws.

- *Drive handling*    If you must remove the drive for any reason (for example, during an upgrade), be very careful to handle the drive gently, and rest it on a soft, anti-static foam surface. You should avoid any impacts or hard surfaces. When re-installing the drive, be certain to use only the correct screws. Screws that are too long will warp the drive. Worse, excessive force can crack the cast enclosure, allowing dust and smoke to enter the drive freely, precipitating a rapid drive failure. Also be sure to use an anti-static wrist strap whenever working inside a PC or handling a drive outside of the system.

- *Vibration*    Hard drives are very sensitive to vibration. Shocks and impacts can cause R/W heads to mark platter surfaces. If the drive is not secured properly, a pattern of regular vibrations may set up in the mechanical assemblies. While such subtle vibrations will rarely damage the drive, they can certainly shorten the drive's working life. Be sure to mount the drive evenly with four screws—do not leave screws out.

# DRIVE FORMATTING

Since the drive works in terms of microscopic dimensions, the effects of gravity and thermal expansion play a role in the accuracy of head positioning. Make sure that the drive has reached a stable running temperature (perhaps 15 minutes or more) before starting the partitioning and formatting processes. Also see that the drive is oriented correctly (horizontally or vertically) prior to partitioning and formatting. If you've moved a drive from one place to another, be sure to let the drive adjust to its new environment (that is, temperature and humidity) for at least 24 hours before using it.

# AVOID HEAD PARKING

In the early days of hard drives, designers realized that head impact could damage the media. Drive designers allowed for a "landing zone"—an unused track where heads could be positioned before power-down. With a landing zone, it did not matter if heads contacted the platter since there was no data there to lose. A utility could "park" the heads over the landing zone. However, virtually all drives are now designed to autopark. Before the drive spins down, heads are automatically positioned over the landing zone based on CMOS Setup data. Third-party head parking programs are no longer needed and can even position the heads incorrectly before power-down (a common problem with older IDE drives that operate in translation mode). Also, most drives are dynamically loaded, so R/W heads are removed from the platters once power is removed. Avoid using parking utilities unless the utility is intended specifically for your particular older drive model.

## BACK UP, BACK UP, BACK UP

Regular, complete system backups are generally regarded as the best, most reliable protection against drive failures. No matter what happens to the drive, you can't really "lose" anything as long as you have a copy of it. In addition to applications and data files, however, you should also make it a point to back up the partition table, autoconfigure record, file allocation table, and root directory. Third-party utilities can create backup copies of these critical areas. (HP Disaster Recovery included with HP CD-R/RW drives is just one example.)  In most cases, current backup software will do an excellent job of preserving your critical system files, along with your everyday applications and work files.

## CHECK FOR VIRUSES

You should aggressively protect against possible infection of a drive by using a *current* anti-virus program. Run the virus checker regularly. Even allow the antivirus software to load into memory and run in real time. Be sure to check new software, file attachments, and file downloads before executing them. Update the virus checker's signature files regularly to ensure that you have the latest protection.

# Recovering Files and Folders

Sooner or later, you're going to delete a file (or folder) that you actually needed. While this is frustrating, it's almost always possible to recover your deleted file(s). In most cases, you can recover files and folders simply by using the Windows 9*x*/Me/XP Recycle Bin:

1. On the desktop, double-click the Recycle Bin icon.
2. The Recycle Bin dialog will open (Figure 13-6).
3. Scroll through the list of files in the Recycle Bin.
4. Highlight the file(s) or shortcut(s) to retrieve, click File, and then click Restore. Under Windows XP, simply highlight the file to restore, then click Restore This Item from the left menu.
5. If you wish to restore several files at once, hold down the CTRL key and click each desired file; then click File and Restore. Under Windows XP, select the desired files and click Restore The Selected Items from the left menu.

This should return selected files to their original location(s) on the drive. If you restore a file that was originally located in a deleted folder, the folder is re-created, and that file is restored in the folder. If you're working under DOS 6.2x, you can use the UNDELETE command (derived from the old Central Point PC Tools package) to recover your deleted file(s):

1. From a command prompt, switch to the directory that contained your deleted file(s).
2. Type **undelete** to start the Undelete utility. Table 13-1 lists the traditional command-line switches for Undelete.

**FIGURE 13-6**    Using the Windows XP Recycle Bin to recover files

| **TABLE 13-1** | **COMMAND-LINE SWITCHES FOR DOS 6.2X UNDELETE** |
|---|---|
| **SWITCH** | **MEANING** |
| /ALL | Causes Undelete to recover everything possible using the best possible recovery method. |
| /DS | Uses Undelete Sentry mode for recovery. |
| /DT | Uses Undelete Tracking mode for recovery. |
| /LIST | Lists the deleted files in the current directory, but does not recover them. |
| /LOAD | Loads Undelete into memory (making Undelete a TSR). |
| /PURGE[drive] | Cleans the contents of your Undelete Sentry directory. You can no longer recover those files, but you'll protect yourself from anyone who might try to recover your private erased file(s). |
| /S[drive] | Enables Undelete Sentry mode to protect the drive indicated. For example, **undelete /SC** enables the Undelete Sentry for drive C:. |
| /STATUS | Shows the current status of Undelete. |
| /T[drive][-entries] | Enables Undelete Tracking mode to protect the drive indicated, and defines the number of files that will be tracked (1 to 999 files). For example, to track 50 file deletions on drive C: you'd use **undelete /TC-50**. |
| /U | Unloads Undelete from memory (if it's been placed in memory). |

**3.** DOS will list the deleted file(s) that it finds and prompt you for which ones you want to recover.

**4.** When you see the file(s) you want, simply answer yes.

You must remember here that Windows 98/Me/XP uses the Recycle Bin as its Undelete function, and there is no real-mode Undelete feature under Windows 98/Me/XP. This means if you empty the Recycle Bin or delete files under DOS, you *cannot* restore those files without a third-party data recovery tool such as Ontrack's EasyRecovery. If you have access to an older DOS 6.2x system with Undelete on it (and your current system is using FAT16), you may be able to use Undelete copied onto your boot floppy disk.

The most important issue in file recovery is to restore your file(s) *as soon as possible* after deletion. Remember that "deleted" files are not wiped out—their clusters are simply marked as "free." If you go on and save new files, you may overwrite some or all of the clusters containing your deleted file(s), and this may render them unrecoverable.

# Recovering FAT and Directory Damage

Many drives eventually develop file structure problems because of viruses, age, and even normal everyday operation. DOS and Windows 98/Me/XP provide tools that allow you to check the disk's condition and (to some extent) define and repair problems with the directory structure and *File Allocation Table* (FAT). The CHKDSK utility is a basic DOS disk "fix" utility that you can use, and ScanDisk is a somewhat more powerful tool that you should be familiar with.

## UNDERSTANDING CHKDSK

Although it's rather crude compared with ScanDisk or third-party software tools, CHKDSK allows you to perform several important disk operations. First, CHKDSK processes the disk to provide a detailed disk space and available memory report. The disk report is what most users think of when they consider CHKDSK, but its real function is to inspect directories and FATs to see if any discrepancies are found. Keep in mind that CHKDSK does not actually check *individual* files. CHKDSK can also check files for contiguity. Contiguous files occupy adjacent clusters on a disk. This makes the files much faster to load and save. When files become noncontiguous (fragmented), not only does disk access take longer, but also portions of the fragmented file may become lost or disassociated. CHKDSK can identify and recover such lost clusters (also known as *allocation units*).

### Running CHKDSK

The generic DOS command line for CHKDSK is **CHKDSK** *drive:\path filename* **/F /V**. The *drive* parameter specifies which logical drive is to be analyzed. By default, the current drive will be examined, but if you boot from the A: drive, you should specify C:\ as the drive and path. If you wish to check specific files for fragmentation (in addition to the full drive analysis), you should include the appropriate entries for the *path* and *filename* parameters. The /F switch allows CHKDSK to fix any problems that it finds with directories or FATs. Keep in mind that if the /F switch is removed, CHKDSK is *prohibited* from writing to the disk. This allows you to run CHKDSK at your discretion without the danger of accidental file corruption. You are advised to always run CHKDSK in this read-only mode until you understand the nature and extent of any problems. The /V switch forces CHKDSK to display the results of its testing "verbatim," which will list all files in a disk's directories and (in some cases) provide details of any errors encountered.

The CHKDSK utility should also be available in the real mode under Windows 98/Me/XP. For Windows 98, click Start, highlight Programs, and then click MS-DOS Prompt. For Windows Me, Click Start, highlight Programs, point to Accessories, and then click MS-DOS Prompt. Type the CHKDSK command line (such as **chkdsk**), and then press ENTER. Under Windows XP, simply click Start, choose Command Prompt, then type **chkdsk** and press ENTER.

When you're finished with CHKDSK in the real mode, type **exit** at the command prompt, and then press ENTER to return to Windows.

## Interpreting a CHKDSK Report

By itself, the traditional report is pretty straightforward. The first five lines indicate the overall drive size, how much of that space is consumed by files, and how much space is left. If there were bad sectors on the disk, a sixth report line would be added to show the number of bytes in bad sectors. You can see a typical report under Windows XP in Figure 13-7. Keep in mind that a bad sector report poses no danger and does not reflect a faulty drive. Virtually all drives have some bad sectors, which are marked in the FAT so that DOS will never attempt to use those bad areas. Most IDE-type drives are able to map out such elements entirely so that the operating system does not even have to deal with such problems. You may not see a bad sector report, but even the best drives have bad sectors.

The next three lines indicate the size of each cluster (or allocation unit), the total number of clusters, and the remaining clusters. For this particular drive, you see that each cluster is 32,768 bytes (32KB). You also see that there are 3,051,854 available allocation units on the disk ( 32,768 x 3,051,854 = 100,003,151,872 bytes, or 100GB, which is roughly the total disk space shown in line 1).

If you were to add a path and filename to the traditional CHKDSK command line, one or more lines would be added to the report indicating the files' contiguity. If the file was contiguous, you would see "All specified file(s) are contiguous." If there are one or more noncontiguous file blocks, you would see a report similar to "*filename* contains *xxx* non-contiguous blocks" where the *filename* is the name of the file

```
Microsoft Windows XP [Version 5.1.2600]
(C) Copyright 1985-2001 Microsoft Corp.

C:\Documents and Settings\Stephen J. Bigelow>chkdsk
The type of the file system is FAT32.
Volume Serial Number is 3148-1405
Windows is verifying files and folders...
File and folder verification is complete.
Windows has checked the file system and found no problems.
    97,659,328 KB total disk space.
       922,816 KB in 665 hidden files.
        58,880 KB in 1,831 folders.
    10,669,536 KB in 36,221 files.
    86,008,064 KB are available.

        32,768 bytes in each allocation unit.
     3,051,854 total allocation units on disk.
     2,687,752 allocation units available on disk.

C:\Documents and Settings\Stephen J. Bigelow>_
```

**FIGURE 13-7**     A typical diagnostic report generated by CHKDSK under Windows XP

being tested, and *xxx* corresponds to the number of noncontiguous blocks found. If disk errors are detected, one or more error messages will be produced.

# USING CHKDSK

Simply stated, CHKDSK is a directory checker and patcher. CHKDSK compares the drive's directory tree with the FAT to ensure that they match. When a discrepancy is detected between the FAT and directory structure, a corresponding error message is generated. As a result of this operation, most problems that CHKDSK reports are software related rather than a drive hardware fault. Four types of errors are reported most commonly: lost allocation units, allocation errors, cross-linked files, and invalid allocation units. Of these four categories, CHKDSK will only help you resolve lost allocation units and cross-linked files.

## Recovering Lost Allocation Units

Lost allocation units are usually generated when a program stops running unexpectedly without saving or deleting temporary files. Over time, lost allocation units can accumulate and take up valuable file space. When lost allocation units are detected, CHKDSK will alert you with an error message such as:

```
10 lost allocation units found in 3 chains.
Convert lost chains to files?
```

If you answer yes, lost allocation units will be converted to files with filenames such as FILE0000.CHK. You can then delete these files to free the recovered space for reuse. It's a great idea to use CHKDSK to recover lost allocation units before running a defragmenter or compression utility such as DoubleSpace.

> It's important for you to realize that this is the only type of problem that CHKDSK can actually fix effectively. Any other errors reported by CHKDSK cannot be fixed with CHKDSK. This is why it is so important that CHKDSK be run without the /F switch until you are aware of any particular problems. Allowing CHKDSK to fix a disk indiscriminately can do more harm than good.

## Freeing Cross-Linked Files

Cross-linked files are generated when two or more files or directories are listed in the FAT as using the same disk space. (One or more allocation units are overlapping.) When cross-linked files are detected, you will see an error message similar to:

```
JOHNSON.TXT is cross linked on allocation unit 11234
```

CHKDSK cannot fix a cross-linked file. It has no way to separate the overlap in allocation units. You should erase the original file(s), run Disk Defragmenter, and then copy the file(s) specified in the error message back onto the drive (so they will use different allocation units). Keep in mind that some information in the cross-linked files may be corrupt, and you may have to restore any such damaged files from a backup.

## Traditional Limitations of CHKDSK

There are a number of instances where CHKDSK may not operate properly (if at all). CHKDSK will not process drives—or portions of drives—that have been created using SUBST, ASSIGN, or JOIN commands. CHKDSK also does not work on network drives. SUBST creates a "virtual" volume, which is little more than a subdirectory under the original volume that uses a different logical drive name. To use CHKDSK in a subdirectory created using SUBST, you must use the TRUENAME function to specify the actual path to the desired files. Note that TRUENAME is only available in DOS 4.0 and later. Suppose you used the SUBST function to create a virtual volume such as:

```
C:\> subst e: c:\tests\diagnostics
```

When you switch to the E: drive, you are actually switching to the C:\TESTS\DIAGNOSTICS subdirectory. If you do not know what the actual subdirectory is, use the TRUENAME function:

```
E:\> truename e:
```

The system would respond with:

```
C:\TESTS\DIAGNOSTICS
```

You can then use the CHKDSK function on the true directory listing:

```
E:\> chkdsk c:\tests\diagnostics\*.*
```

To use CHKDSK on an ASSIGNed drive, you must first "unassign" the drive. For example, if you assign a drive, such as ASSIGN A=B, you will have to unassign the drive, such as ASSIGN A=A. You can then run CHKDSK. After CHKDSK is complete, you can reassign the drive. There is no known way to use CHKDSK on a JOINed drive, which is basically a directory tree created by the JOIN command. JOIN adds one disk volume to another disk volume as a subdirectory. Only the portion that is JOINed is skipped—all other portions of the drive are checked. To run CHKDSK on a network drive, you must reach the desired PC with the drive to be tested, and suspend or disable any sharing of the drive while CHKDSK is executed.

In actual practice, it is unlikely that you will deal with such limitations on modern computers, but this may be handy reference information when faced with the repair or resurrection of an older PC.

# UNDERSTANDING SCANDISK

More recent versions of DOS and Windows 98/Me have basically paired the older CHKDSK utility with ScanDisk. In most respects, ScanDisk performs all of the same functions found in CHKDSK, such as checking the directory structure, locating and recovering lost allocation units, and identifying cross-linked files. However, ScanDisk not only provides additional checking and media surface scan features that can help to identify a wider array of potential problems, but also can mark out sectors on the drive that may be failing. Under Windows 9x/Me, you can use ScanDisk for all the features found in older versions of CHKDSK.

## Running ScanDisk

ScanDisk is primarily a protected-mode (Windows 98/Me) tool that you launch by clicking Start, highlighting Programs, selecting Accessories, highlighting System Tools, and then clicking ScanDisk. Remember that ScanDisk isn't available under Windows XP. The main ScanDisk dialog will appear, as in Figure 13-8. From this dialog, you can select the partition to be tested and invoke a thorough surface scan of the media. If you wish ScanDisk to fix any errors that it finds, simply select the "Automatically fix errors" check box. Clicking the Advanced button opens the ScanDisk Advanced Options dialog (Figure 13-9), where you can tailor the behavior of ScanDisk—especially the way it deals with lost file fragments and cross-linked files.

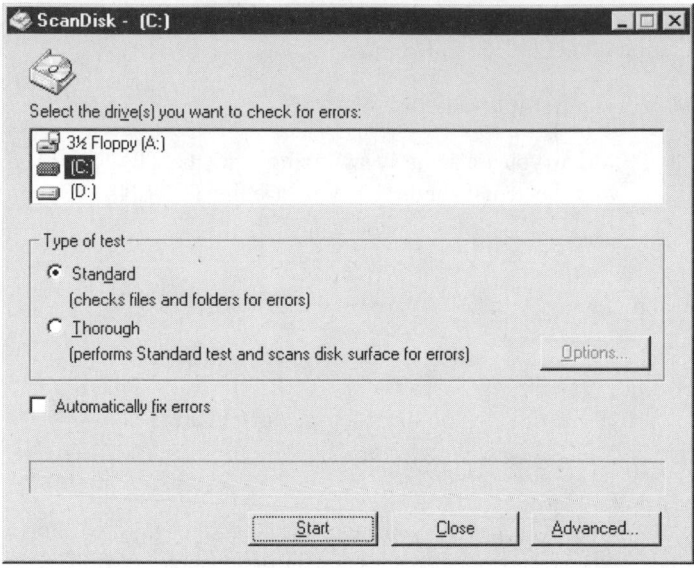

**FIGURE  13-8**    The main ScanDisk dialog

 Do not use an older version of ScanDisk (for example, FAT16) on a newer FAT32 partition. Older versions of ScanDisk can report a great deal of erroneous information, and even result in extensive file corruption if left to "fix errors" automatically.

When you allow ScanDisk to run a complete cycle, it generates a report remarkably similar to CHKDSK (Figure 13-10), including any errors that may have been detected on the disk. If ScanDisk does detect lost file fragments or cross-linked files on the disk, you may need to erase the files involved, defragment the disk, and then recopy the offending file(s) to their proper directory from your most current backup.

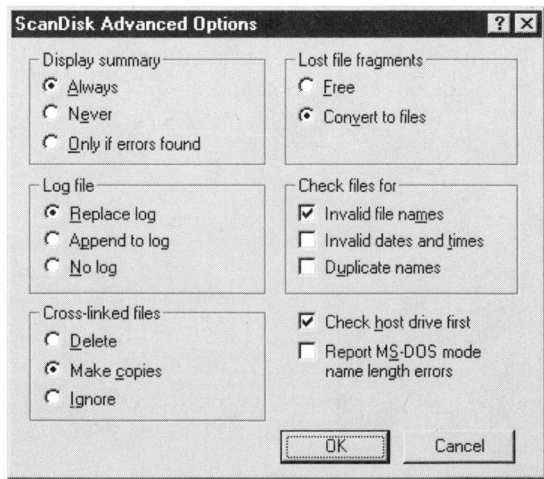

**FIGURE  13-9**    Configuring advanced settings under ScanDisk

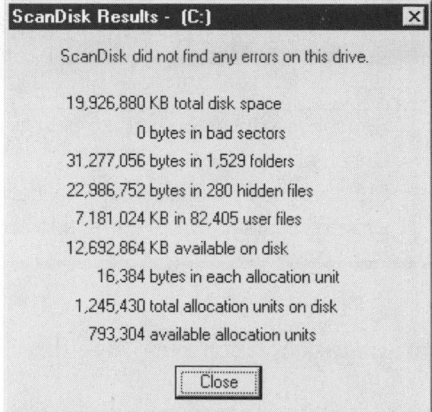

**ScanDisk Results - (C:)**

ScanDisk did not find any errors on this drive.

19,926,880 KB total disk space
0 bytes in bad sectors
31,277,056 bytes in 1,529 folders
22,986,752 bytes in 280 hidden files
7,181,024 KB in 82,405 user files
12,692,864 KB available on disk
16,384 bytes in each allocation unit
1,245,430 total allocation units on disk
793,304 available allocation units

Close

**FIGURE 13-10**    A typical report generated by ScanDisk

Performing a surface scan of the drive may take a considerable amount of time, especially for large drives partitioned and formatted under FAT32.

## Using ScanDisk at Startup

Although Windows should run ScanDisk at start time in the event of an incorrect shutdown, you may wish to place ScanDisk in a system's Startup folder so that it will run each time the system starts. This can be helpful when diagnosing persistent disk problems. To add ScanDisk to your Windows 9*x*/Me Startup folder:

1. On the task bar, right-click the Start button and click Open.
2. Highlight the Programs folder, and then click the Startup folder.
3. On the File menu, highlight New, and then click Shortcut.
4. In the "Command line" entry, type

   scandskw.exe

5. Click Next.
6. In the "Select a name for the shortcut" line, type

   ScanDisk

7. Click Finish.

You can also configure ScanDisk with certain features each time the system starts:

1. In your Startup folder, right-click ScanDisk.
2. Click Properties.
3. On the Shortcut tab, type one or more of the switches in Table 13-2 after the text that appears in Target.

For example, to check drive D: and start and quit ScanDisk automatically, type in the Target entry:

c:\windows\scandskw.exe d: /n

| TABLE 13-2    COMMAND-LINE SWITCHES FOR SCANDISK | |
|---|---|
| **TYPE...** | **TO...** |
| x: (substitute drive letter for x) | Specify the drive you want to check |
| /a | Check all your local hard disks |
| /n | Start and quit ScanDisk automatically |
| /p | Prevent ScanDisk from correcting any errors it finds |

To check all hard disks but prevent ScanDisk from correcting any errors it finds, type in the Target entry:

```
c:\windows\scandskw.exe /a /p
```

# Recovering the MBR

The partition table (the *master boot record* or MBR) is the single most important sector on your hard drive. This one sector (512 bytes) contains specifications for up to four logical partitions, but it also provides instructions for starting the operating system. Without a viable MBR, the system will not even recognize the presence of the drive—let alone boot from it. Unfortunately, when the MBR is lost, it is extremely difficult to reconstruct (without losing access to all the data on the hard drive). There are several tools available for rebuilding these critical files. You can use third-party tools (such as Norton Utilities 2002 or later) under Windows 98/Me/XP, you can use MIRROR and UNFORMAT under DOS 6.2x (and FAT16), or you can also use FDISK as a last-resort means of rebuilding a damaged MBR.

## USING MIRROR AND UNFORMAT

Prevention is always faster and easier than a cure—the same is true of data recovery. If you are using DOS 5.0 or later, you have access to two DOS utilities that will allow you to back up and restore the master boot record: MIRROR.EXE and UNFORMAT.COM. Before the hard drive fails, type

```
MIRROR /PARTN
```

MIRROR will start and prompt you for a drive. Place a bootable floppy disk in drive A: (or B:), and let MIRROR copy the partition table to the floppy drive. If you do this regularly (say, twice a year), you will have a good emergency backup in the event of drive trouble. When trouble occurs, simply boot from the floppy disk (which should contain a copy of UNFORMAT and the partition backup file), and then type

```
UNFORMAT /PARTN
```

UNFORMAT will ask for the location of the backup file (usually named PARTNSAV.FIL). Reference drive A: or B: (whichever drive contains the file) and continue. If the partition information looks appropriate, you can confirm the restoration, then reboot the system from the hard drive. Assuming a faulty MBR was the only problem, the hard drive should now work properly.

# USING FDISK /MBR

Earlier, you read that FDISK should not be used for data recovery since it made changes that would render your data inaccessible—that is not entirely true. There is an undocumented feature of FDISK that restores the startup code at the beginning of the MBR without touching the partition table itself. When the MBR cannot be rebuilt or restored by any other means, it may be possible to use FDISK /MBR and attempt to rebuild part of the MBR. When FDISK is run in this way, it is virtually automatic. You will not even see the FDISK menu—it will simply restore the startup code and return to the DOS prompt. Given the touchy nature of FDISK, you should attempt this undocumented function only as a last resort. FDISK /MBR should not render your data inaccessible, but it might, so be sure to back up as much of your drive as possible before proceeding.

When using FDISK, be sure to use the version that corresponds to your operating system. For example, if you're using Windows 98 or later, be sure to use the version of FDISK that's placed on a Windows 98/Me Startup Disk.

# RECOVERING AN ACCIDENTAL REFORMAT

A high-level format process is invoked with the FORMAT command, and this rewrites the boot sector, FAT, and root directory of your disk. Formatting also checks each cluster to map out any damaged or unreadable ones in the FAT. Normally, formatting is destructive to your data. The data itself is not overwritten, but formatting renders it inaccessible. This means that if you accidentally format the wrong partition on your drive, the data on it can be lost. Windows 98/Me/XP offers no native tools for recovering from an accidental format. Fortunately, there are third-party tools (such as Reboot, a boot and partition repair utility from Dtidata.com at www.dtidata.com) that will save a copy of that critical data and use it to reconstruct the partition lost during an accidental format. If you're working under DOS 6.2x, you can use the Unformat command (also a relative of the old Unformat tool with Central Point's PC Tools package) to recover your disk. For example:

```
unformat c:
```

The important thing to remember here is that you must Unformat *immediately* after formatting. Once the format process is finished, the FAT is cleared, so writing new files to the disk may upset the Unformat process and prevent some (or all) of your files from being recovered.

# USING EASYRECOVERY

When a hard drive physically fails, you'll need to send the disk to a professional data recovery house, and let them try to resurrect the unit just long enough to wring your data from it. If the drive hardware is still working, however, you can often use software tools such as Ontrack's EasyRecovery utility to search out and rescue inaccessible data. EasyRecovery 6.0 (www.ontrack.com/easyrecovery/) is a do-it-yourself data recovery tool that is capable of capturing lost or inaccessible data from your drive and reconstructing the file system (including partitions larger than 8.4GB). EasyRecovery does not attempt to repair corruption on the drive itself and never writes to the suspect drive. Instead, it rebuilds the file table in memory to allow safe transfer of data to another device (such as another hard drive). This part of the chapter offers some practical data recovery tips by examining some of the features and attributes of EasyRecovery.

## Obtaining EasyRecovery

EasyRecovery 6.0 is not located on the companion CD. A free demo version of the software (which will identify all recoverable files and recover up to five files) can be downloaded from Ontrack at www.ontrack.com/freesoftware/. If you find the software useful, you can purchase it online directly from Ontrack.

## About EasyRecovery

The interesting thing about EasyRecovery is that it's a nondestructive and read-only tool that does not place any data onto the suspect (crashed) drive. Instead, data that's read from the drive is placed in memory and written to another drive (for example, another hard drive, floppy disk, or your local network). EasyRecovery can recover data from drives without readable boot sectors, readable FATs, or readable directories. It can also handle drives that are no longer recognized by the operating system. This type of operation makes EasyRecovery particularly handy for disks that have been damaged by a computer virus, formatted, partitioned, crashed with a power failure, or damaged by rogue software (bugs).

EasyRecovery automatically creates a "virtual drive" in memory and offers access to the files through an ordinary-looking file manager applet. You can see the lost directories and files from your crashed drive. Files and directories can be viewed and copied to a safe medium (another drive), where the software's pattern recognition technology allows the various pieces of a recovered file to be assembled properly.

> Like virtually all software data recovery tools, EasyRecovery 6.0 is not intended to operate a defective drive unit. If you experience drive damage (for example, you hear strange grinding noises), turn off the PC immediately. You may require the services of a data recovery house.

EasyRecovery works from a DOS command line to recover files from DOS, Windows 98/Me/XP, Windows NT, or Novell. It is not recommended that EasyRecovery be used in a DOS window from within Windows 98/Me/XP. There are several different versions of EasyRecovery that can be downloaded based on your particular system requirements. The "basic" edition recovers files from DOS; Windows 3.x, 95, 98, and Me/2000/XP; IDE/ATA/EIDE hard drives; SCSI hard drives; system disks; floppy disks; and Zip and Jaz removable media. The Professional Edition recovers files from DOS; Windows 3.x, 95, 98, Me/XP, 2000, and NT; IDE/ATA/EIDE hard drives; SCSI hard drives; floppy disks; and Zip and Jaz removable media, and provides advanced data recovery options such as:

- Configure system inputs with advanced tuning options to achieve better and faster data recovery results.
- Utilize an emergency boot disk to recover data from systems that cannot boot to Windows.
- Repair Zip files as well as MS Outlook, Access, Excel, PowerPoint, and Word files.
- Use disk diagnostic features (including Ontrack Data Advisor) to quickly evaluate the condition of a hard drive.
- View the contents of any file in both ASCII and hex format to find the data you need. You can search more than 225 different file types, including MIDI music files, voice files, and digital media files.
- Specify criteria to select recovered files and/or folders for backup using advanced tagging options to pinpoint specific data.
- Generate reports to document files selected for backup for your records.

## Using EasyRecovery

In most cases, data recovery consists of booting the system with EasyRecovery 6.0 on a bootable floppy disk (or from a working hard drive), selecting the drive or file(s) to be recovered, then allowing EasyRecovery to process the selected drive (Figure 13-11). When EasyRecovery finishes its analysis, you'll see a listing of the virtual drive, and you can select and copy desired files/folders to the recovery drive. Of course, there are numerous features and options that can be selected within the EasyRecovery program, but you'll need to refer to the documentation files for complete explanations. You may start, stop, and resume the recovery (or copying) processes at any point. EasyRecovery allows you to find missing or corrupt volumes on your system using partition finder options to improve the speed and success of your recovery. You can also monitor the status of your recovery using the recovery progress option to check the remaining time, or the number and names of files recovered.

Depending on your system's speed, the size of your drive, and the number of files on the drive, EasyRecovery can take from 15 minutes to several hours to complete its task. EasyRecovery may require up to 24 hours to analyze the partition of an NTFS or Novell drive.

# Data Recovery Tips

Regardless of the particular data recovery software that you're using, data recovery is a fairly automatic process. You recover the file(s) or you don't. However, there are numerous tips that may help you get the most from your data recovery process:

■ The most important data recovery tip is to always keep a current backup of your work in progress. Even if you have to reinstall an operating system and applications from scratch, you can easily restore the backup of your work and keep going. If you have no backup, and you're unable to recover the data,

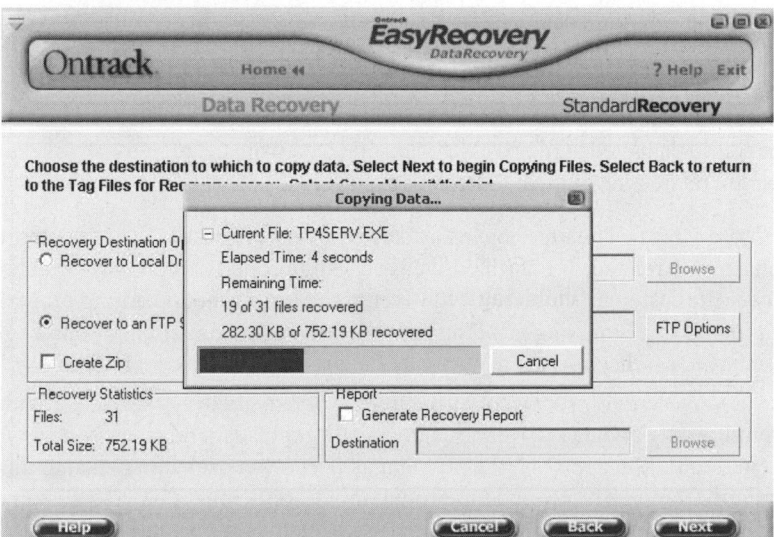

**FIGURE 13-11**    Ontrack's EasyRecovery allows technicians and end-users to analyze and recover data on their hard drive(s). (Courtesy of Ontrack Data International, Inc.)

you may need to start from scratch. Periodically, you should practice restoring your backups to verify the media and restoration process. Backups won't do any good if you don't know how to restore them.

■ Always make sure that the suspect drive is specified correctly in the CMOS Setup. Changing a drive's geometry can render the drive inaccessible (until the original drive geometry settings are restored). This happens frequently when moving hard drives from one system to another.

■ Don't mix and match data recovery tools. For example, don't use CHKDSK before running EasyRecovery. More advanced tools may misinterpret the disk recovery efforts of more basic tools like CHKDSK. Never use data recovery software if you're experiencing a physical hard drive failure.

■ Select a recovery drive in advance (such as another hard drive, network drive, CD-RW drive, or Zip drive). This is where the recovery program will place your recovered data, so make sure that there is ample space on the recovery drive, or see that you have ample Zip/Jaz media available. For example, a CD-RW drive is an excellent option to receive recovered files.

■ Select as much RAM as possible for your swap area (where recovered data is held before writing to the recovery drive). If you can create swap space on a drive, make sure that there is ample space available on that drive, and never swap to the suspect drive.

■ Data recovery routines can take quite some time to run, so be sure to allow plenty of time to run your data recovery software.

■ Before using any data recovery software, verify that it's compatible with your partition type (FAT16, FAT32, or NTFS) and partition size (for example, 100GB versus 8GB). If the software cannot handle your partition type or size, running the software will probably destroy any chance of ever recovering your lost data. In fact, the software may make things worse. Make sure that you obtain the latest updates and patches for your data recovery software before running it.

■ Use a UPS to prevent the system from crashing during data analysis and recovery.

## DATA RECOVERY SERVICES

As a technician, you have limited data recovery capability—there's only so much you can do with recovery software. When more serious issues arise (such as impact damage or virus infiltration), you may need to forward the customer's drive to a data recovery firm (like Ontrack or DriveSavers) that specializes in recovering data from damaged hard drives or other media. These services often have the cleanroom facilities to open and rebuild damaged hard drives to coax vital data from the platters. If you plan to work with a recovery service, there are a few things to keep in mind:

■ *Prevent further data loss.* The first step in any data recovery effort should be to determine whether the problem is hardware related. If not (the drive is running properly), you may be able to use software tools to recover the customer's lost data. However, if the drive is not operating properly (for example, it's not spinning up or it's making grinding noises), you should not attempt to use software recovery techniques. Shut down the system and evaluate data recovery services if necessary.

■ *Evaluate and select a recovery service.* There are lots of data recovery service providers. Just browse any search engine under "data recovery." Choosing a "good" data recovery service, however, takes a little care, and you should approach the problem as if you were selecting an auto mechanic or home repair contractor. Compare prices and turnaround time. (Remember that your customers will be waiting for their important data.) Also, look for experience and recommendations from other customers.

- *Get customer approval before sending the drive.* Data recovery services are expensive (anywhere from $200 to $400 or more to recover a drive), and there are no guarantees of success. If you're unable to recover data from a drive using software tools, you should confer with your customer and get their *written* approval to send the drive out for recovery. Such approval should include a rough estimate of the cost and a disclaimer/release for all data on the drive. Written permission is important because the drive may contain confidential or sensitive business information that the customer wouldn't want to allow outside of your care. It also makes your customer acknowledge the added costs involved.

- *Stay in touch with the recovery service.* Once you ship a drive for recovery, be sure to check in periodically with the recovery provider. Remember that your customer is waiting for his precious data, so he'll probably be calling you also. The more current information that you have from the recovery provider, the better you'll be able to satisfy your own customer. If there are any other unforeseen costs during the recovery, be sure to communicate that to your customer as soon as possible.

# Data Recovery Troubleshooting

Whether you use EasyRecovery or some other data recovery tool, you may encounter errors and problems during the process of your recovery. This part of the chapter examines a few typical troubles that often plague data recovery efforts.

**SYMPTOM 13-1**    **The system stops responding, and the data recovery software seems to have crashed**    If there is no error message, it may simply be that the data recovery process is still running. It can take many hours to fully analyze a disk. Be patient and allow up to 24 hours for a data recovery cycle to run. Data recovery software often performs analysis in conventional memory, then swaps the results out to extended memory (or a disk file). If there is severe data corruption, or a large number of small files, there may not be enough conventional or extended memory (or disk space) available. There are a few tricks that might help (depending on your software's particular options):

- Try recovering only a part of the drive at a time. This can be accomplished by selecting a range of sectors on the drive to be analyzed.

- Try lowering the threshold where a file is considered "bad" (sometimes called a "Bad File Acceptance Setting").

- Try swapping the analysis out to a disk file (on a known-good drive) rather than extended memory.

If the problem persists, you may need to try another data recovery tool, or send the drive out for professional data recovery techniques.

**SYMPTOM 13-2**    **The data recovery software reports the wrong drive size**    Check the drive size as reported by the data recovery software, and verify that it accurately reflects the size of the drive you're trying to recover. If the software takes an incorrect drive size from your system BIOS, you will not get reliable data recovery results. Check the following issues:

- Check the CMOS Setup and verify that the drive geometry is accurate for your drive. If not, enter the correct values. If you've entered exact values, try to let the BIOS auto-detect the drive. Check with the drive's manufacturer to see if there's an acceptable "translation geometry" that you can use instead.

■ If the drive has "disk overlay" software installed (for example, Disk Manager or MaxBlast), the CMOS Setup may not contain the appropriate drive values. You may need to use a boot disk that enables the DDO first before booting and launching the data recovery software.

■ Check the LBA mode. Drives bigger than 528MB should have the LBA mode enabled in the CMOS Setup.

■ Check the drive's reported values. Some huge drives report their geometry as 16,383×16×63 regardless of their actual size. This may mean you'll need a BIOS upgrade or new drive controller to adequately support the suspect drive.

**SYMPTOM 13-3**    **Your data recovery software returns invalid results because it could not recognize the correct drive structure**    If your data recovery software supports automatic drive structure recognition, you should try turning that feature off, then running the recover operation again. Without automatic identification, the software should present its interpretation of the drive structure for your approval (for example, cluster size [number of sectors in a cluster], data start cluster, and data end cluster). Since the size of your partition (in KB) is roughly defined by:

```
([data end cluster-data start cluster] * [cluster size * 512]) / 2
```

If the result is equal to the partition size that you're trying to recover, you can try proceeding with the recovery. If you're not satisfied with the results, you can search again and look for the correct structure. If you simply cannot find an appropriate structure, make sure that you're using the data recovery software that's right for your file system. (For example, using software for FAT32 may show structure errors if you're using a FAT16 drive.)

**SYMPTOM 13-4**    **The data recovery software does not recover all missing files or directories**    This may often occur if the software's recognition routine is too loose. Try tightening the recognition algorithm's parameters. The recovery process may take longer, but a stronger setting may catch more directories and files.

**SYMPTOM 13-5**    **The hard drive is making loud scraping noises, or there is clanking during disk access**    All disks make a little bit of noise as the platters spin and the disk is accessed—this is perfectly normal. But when a drive makes loud or "damaged-sounding" noises, it probably is damaged. If the drive is accessible, back up as much data as possible, and replace the drive before it fails. If the drive has already failed, do not attempt to use data recovery software. Instead, send the drive out for professional data recovery, or replace the drive and restore your most recent backup.

**SYMPTOM 13-6**    **You cannot recover a specific file**    A file that you want to repair cannot be found. Chances are that the file was deleted (or not recently saved). Search the complete partition for the desired file. If the file is still inaccessible, it may be damaged beyond the ability of your recovery software. You can try an alternative recovery software product, or send the drive out for recovery.

**SYMPTOM 13-7**    **Your recovery software repaired a file, but it doesn't open**    The recovery software indicated that a particular file was repaired, but you cannot open the file with its related application. Chances are that the particular file was damaged beyond recovery. In other cases, you may be looking at the wrong file. Many recovery tools will create more than one type of file as part of the recovery process, and some tools will create more than one destination file in an attempt to retrieve the data. Be sure to try all destination files that have been generated. Otherwise, the file may simply be unrecoverable.

**SYMPTOM 13-8** **Disk diagnostics report many bad sectors on the hard drive** It's perfectly normal for a hard drive to have a limited number of bad sectors—these are typically sparred out to prevent disk errors. However, when a diagnostic (whether part of the recovery software or not) reports a large number of bad sectors, or a growing number of bad sectors, chances are that the drive is failing. Your best course is to back up the drive and replace it as soon as possible *before* it fails.

# Further Study

**CBL Data Recovery** www.cbltech.com
**Data Recovery Group** www.datarecoverygroup.com
**Data Recovery Labs** www.actionfront.com/
**Drive Savers** www.drivesavers.com
**Easy Recovery** www.ontrack.com/easyrecovery/
**Norton Utilities** www.symantec.com/product/
**Ontrack** www.ontrack.com
**Ontrack Data Advisor** www.ontrack.com/op/op_1.asp
**Reynolds Utilities** www.data-recovery.com/reynolds/
**Symantec (Norton Ghost 2002)** www.symantec.com
**TechParts** www.recoverdata.com

# 14

# DRIVE ADAPTERS AND RAID BASICS

**D**rives are generally considered to be peripheral devices. This means they must be interfaced to the host system so that the drive and system may communicate with one another. Integrated Drive Electronics (IDE) has proven to be an extremely versatile and cost-effective interface scheme that can support hard drives, CD-ROM drives, DVD-ROM drives, and almost any other drive device. IDE has also proven its longevity by enduring numerous upgrades and improvements through the years. The latest iteration of IDE (referred to as Ultra-DMA/133) offers burst data transfer rates of up to 133 MB/s, and this helps to put IDE data transfers on par with many general-purpose SCSI implementations. In addition, redundant array of independent disks (RAID) technology is growing in popularity as desktop users seek more powerful and inexpensive ways to protect their valuable data. This chapter outlines the important issues of IDE and RAID, discusses controller installation issues, and offers a suite of controller troubleshooting procedures.

# Understanding the IDE Family

From a historical perspective, the Integrated Drive Electronics interface developed in 1988 in response to an industry push to create a standard software interface for SCSI peripherals. That industry consortium, known as the Common Access Method Committee (or CAMC), attempted to originate an AT Attachment (ATA) interface that could be incorporated into low-cost AT-compatible motherboards. The CAMC completed its specification, which was later approved by ANSI. The term "ATA interface" generally refers to the controller interface, while "IDE" refers to the drive itself. Today, IDE simply refers to an interface type and can be applied to either the drive or controller. For example, an IDE drive requires an IDE controller.

Even though there are numerous iterations of the IDE family today (such as EIDE, UDMA/33, UDMA/66, UDMA/100, and UDMA/133), the family is still commonly referred to as "IDE-type."

## IDE/ATA

IDE and ATA are basically one and the same thing—a scheme designed to integrate controlling electronics onto the drive itself instead of relying on a stand-alone controller board, as obsolete MFM and RLL drives did. This approach reduces interface costs and makes drive firmware implementations easier. IDE proved to be a low-cost, easily configured system—so much so that it created a boom in the disk drive industry. Although the terms IDE and ATA are sometimes used interchangeably, ATA is the formal standard that defines the drive and how it operates, while IDE is really the "trade name" that refers to the 40-pin interface and drive controller architecture designed to implement the ATA standard.

### Classic IDE Features and Architecture

IDE drives are typically "intelligent"—that is, almost all the functions relegated to a separate controller board in older drives are now integrated onto the drive itself. Data is transferred through a single cable attached to a relatively straightforward *adapter board* (a simple controller board that is often little more than a buffer). Older PCs added an IDE drive adapter to the system's ISA or PCI expansion bus, but virtually all systems today integrate a dual-channel IDE controller right into the South Bridge of the motherboard's chipset (so you can connect drive cables to the motherboard rather than a separate add-in card). Today, classical IDE drives are fairly slow, offering data transfer rates rarely exceeding 10 Mbits/s. "Classic" IDE is also limited to supporting drives up to 528MB. EIDE and more recent Ultra-DMA iterations of the IDE interface break the traditional 528MB barrier and can support drives larger than 100GB at this time. While IDE lacks the overall flexibility and expandability of SCSI, IDE is relatively inexpensive to implement. Thus, it is often the choice for simple, inexpensive, low-to-mid-range PCs that are not expected to expand much. More recently, the use of an IDE interface has extended beyond hard drives to include such devices as CD-ROM/R/RW drives, DVD-ROM/RAM drives, Zip drives, and tape drives through the use of the AT Attachment Packet Interface (ATAPI) interface protocol (more on ATAPI a little later in the chapter).

A great deal of discussion has concentrated on IDE intelligence. The *intelligence* of an IDE system is determined by the capabilities of the onboard controller. For the purposes of this book, intelligent IDE drives are capable of the following functions. First, intelligent IDE drives support *drive translation*—the feature that allows CMOS drive parameters to be entered in any combination of cylinders, heads, and sectors that add up to equal or less than the true number of sectors on the drive. This is particularly handy when the actual number of cylinders exceeds 1024 (as all modern IDE-type drives do). Non-intelligent IDE drives were limited to a physical mode, where CMOS parameters were entered to match physical parameters. Intelligent drives also support a number of enhanced commands that are an optional part of the original ATA specification.

Another advancement of intelligent IDE technology is *zoned recording,* which allows a variable number of sectors per track. This allows an overall increase in the number of sectors on each platter and adds to the drive's overall capacity. However, BIOS can only deal with a fixed number of sectors per track, so the zoned IDE drive must always run in translation mode. When running IDE drives in translation mode, you cannot alter interleave or sector skew factors, and you cannot change factory defect information.

A typical motherboard-based, dual-channel IDE-type controller layout is shown in Figure 14-1. The physical interface for a standard IDE device consists of a 40-pin data/control cable (old IBM implementations used either a 44-pin or 72-pin cable). This *signal cable* is responsible for carrying data and control signals between the drive and controller board. IDE-type drives also use terminating resistors to ensure reliable signal characteristics, but terminating resistors are usually fixed and cannot be removed. In most cases, two IDE-type drives can work together with terminating resistors in place. While there will be several jumpers on the drive, a set of *drive select* jumpers allows the drive to be set as the primary (master) or secondary (slave) drive.

The signal cable for an IDE-type drive is typically a 40-pin insulation displacement connector (IDC) cable, as shown in Table 14-1. Unlike the obsolete ST506/412 or ESDI interfaces, the IDE family uses both the even- and odd-numbered wires as signal-carrying lines. Also note that most of the signal labels have dashes beside their names, indicating that the particular signal is *active low*—that is, the signal is *true* in the logic 0 state instead of being true in the logic 1 state. All signal lines on the IDE interface are fully TTL compatible where a logic 0 is 0.0 to +0.8 Vdc, and a logic 1 is +2.0 to Vcc.

Data points and registers in the IDE-type drive are addressed using the Drive Address Bus lines DA0 to DA2 (pins 35, 33, and 36, respectively) in conjunction with the -Chip Select Drive inputs -CS1FX and -CS3FX (pins 37 and 38). When a true signal is sent along the *-Drive I/O Read* (-DIOR, pin 25) line, the drive executes a read cycle, while a true on the -Drive I/O Write (-DIOW, pin 23) line initiates a write cycle.

Primary and secondary UDMA/133 controller ports

**FIGURE   14-1**    Typical dual-port Ultra-DMA/133 controller connections on a Soyo KT333 Dragon Ultra Platinum motherboard (Courtesy of Motherboards.org)

**TABLE 14-1    PIN ASSIGNMENTS FOR A TYPICAL IDE-TYPE SIGNAL CABLE**

| PIN | NAME | PIN | NAME |
|-----|------|-----|------|
| 1 | Reset | 2 | Ground |
| 3 | DD7 | 4 | DD8 |
| 5 | DD6 | 6 | DD9 |
| 7 | DD5 | 8 | DD10 |
| 9 | DD4 | 10 | DD11 |
| 11 | DD3 | 12 | DD12 |
| 13 | DD2 | 14 | DD13 |
| 15 | DD1 | 16 | DD14 |
| 17 | DD0 | 18 | DD15 |
| 19 | Ground | 20 | Key (slot only) |
| 21 | DMARQ | 22 | Ground |
| 23 | -I/O Write Data (-DIOW) | 24 | Ground |
| 25 | -I/O Read Data (-DIOR) | 26 | Ground |
| 27 | -I/O Channel Ready (-IORDY) | 28 | unused |
| 29 | -DMA Acknowledge (-DMACK) | 30 | Ground |
| 31 | Interrupt Request (INTRQ) | 32 | -Host 16-bit I/O (-IOCS16) |
| 33 | DA1 | 34 | -Passed Diagnostics (-PDIAG) |
| 35 | DA0 | 36 | DA2 |
| 37 | -Host Chip Select 0 (-CS1FX) | 38 | -Host Chip Select 1 (-CS3FX) |
| 39 | -Drive Active (-DASP) | 40 | Ground |

The IDE interface provides TTL-level input and output signals. Where older interfaces were serial, the IDE interface provides 16 bi-directional data lines (DD0 to DD15, pins 3 to 18) to carry data bits into or out of the drive. Once a data transfer is completed, a -DMA Acknowledge (-DMACK, pin 29) signal is provided to the drive from the hard disk controller IC. Finally, a true signal on the drive's Reset line (pin 1) will restore the drive to its original condition at power-on. A Reset is sent when the computer is first powered on or rebooted.

An IDE-type physical interface also provides a number of outputs back to the motherboard. A Direct Memory Access Request (DMARQ, pin 21) is used to initiate the transfer of data to or from the drive. The direction of data transfer is dependent on the condition of the -DIOR and -DIOW inputs. A -DMACK signal is generated in response when the DMARQ line is asserted (made true). -IORDY (pin 27) is an -I/O Channel Ready signal that keeps a system's attention if the drive is not quite ready to respond to a data transfer request. A drive Interrupt Request (INTRQ, pin 31) is asserted by a drive when a drive interrupt is pending (the drive is about to transfer information to or from the motherboard). The -Drive Active line (DASP, pin 39) becomes logic 0 when any hard drive activity is occurring. A -Passed Diagnostic (PDIAG, pin 34) line provides the results of any diagnostic command or reset action. When PDIAG is logic 0, the system knows that the drive is ready to use. Finally, the 16 bit -I/O Control line (IOCS16, pin 32) tells the motherboard that the drive is ready to send or receive data. Notice that there are several return (ground) lines (pins 2, 19, 22, 24, 26, 30, and 40), and a key pin (20) that is removed from the male connector.

## Cabling the IDE-type Interface

The ATA IDE interface is intended to support up to two drives on the same cable (or channel) in a daisy-chain fashion. A current IDE controller cable is illustrated in Figure 14-2. Although tradition dictates that drive 0 be attached to the end connector (as the primary, or master, drive) and a second drive be attached to the middle connector (as a secondary, or slave, drive), it is important to note that IDE supports either drive in either location. For the purposes of IDE, you need only set the proper drive jumpers to select a drive as a master or slave. The 40-pin ribbon cable (IBM uses 44-pin or 72-pin cables) should not exceed 61 cm (24 inches) in length. Ideally, the IDE cable should not exceed 46 cm (18 inches) in length. Since IDE-type drives rely on distributed termination as a means of signal conditioning, it is not necessary to install or remove terminating resistors.

However, you may encounter problems when running two older IDE drives together. Older IDE drives did not fully adhere to the CAMC ATA IDE specification. When trying to run older drives together (especially drives from different manufacturers), they may not respond to their master/slave relationship properly, and conflicts will result—in many cases, such problems will disable both drives. When planning a dual-IDE installation using older drives, try to use the latest possible drives that are both from the same manufacturer. If you cannot match drives, try reversing the master/slave relationship between the drives.

> Compatibility and performance are improved dramatically with current Ultra-DMA-type drive devices.

## BIOS Support of the IDE Family

Unlike SCSI controllers, which use an expansion ROM to provide supplemental BIOS, the firmware needed to provide IDE support is written into the motherboard's BIOS. Although systems manufactured since about 1990 are fully compatible with ATA IDE drives, adding an IDE drive to an older PC often resulted in problems. After the broad introduction of IDE, it was discovered that IDE drive operations placed different timing demands on the PC, which frequently caused disk errors such as data corruption and failure to boot. BIOS makers quickly found a solution to this timing problem, and it was incorporated into BIOS that appeared after early 1990. If you encounter a PC with pre-1990 BIOS, you should consider upgrading it before adding an IDE drive, or if the current IDE drive is exhibiting problems. Today, you may also need to upgrade a motherboard's BIOS if the drive controller cannot support the full size of a given drive (32GB, 40GB, 60GB, 100GB, and so on).

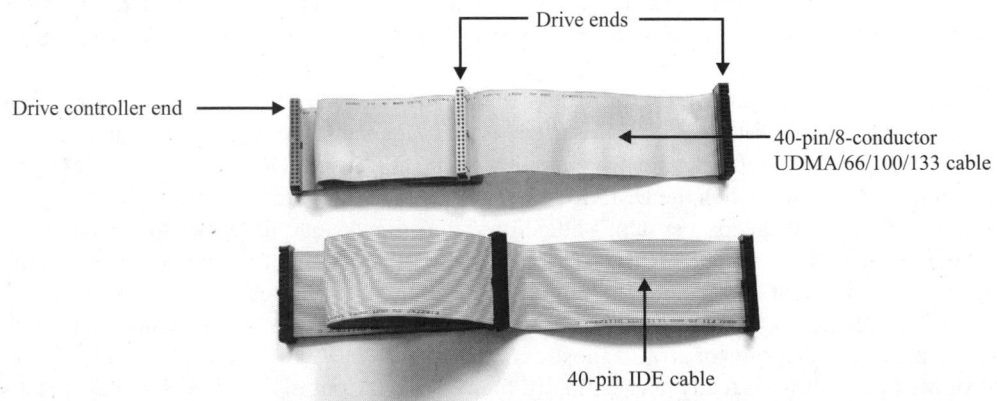

Drive ends

Drive controller end

40-pin/8-conductor
UDMA/66/100/133 cable

40-pin IDE cable

**FIGURE  14-2**    A current 40-pin/80-conductor IDE cable used with UDMA/66/100/133 drives shown against a traditional 40-pin IDE cable

If you add an IDE controller card to your existing system, that card's firmware will typically take over drive operations from the system BIOS.

## ATAPI

One of the major disadvantages of ATA is that it was designed for hard drives only. With the broad introduction of CD-ROM drives in the late 1980s, designers needed a means of attaching CD-ROMs (and other devices such as tape drives) to the existing ATA (IDE) interface—rather than employing a stand-alone (proprietary) controller card. The *ATA Packet Interface* (ATAPI) is an extension of the ATA (IDE) interface that's designed to allow devices other than hard drives to plug into an ordinary ATA (IDE) port. Whereas hard drives enjoy ATA (IDE) support through the BIOS, ATAPI devices require a device driver to support them. Booting from an ATAPI CD-ROM is only possible with an El Torito CD-ROM and more recent motherboard BIOS versions.

## ATA-2, FAST-ATA, AND EIDE

By the early 1990s, it became clear that the classic ATA architecture would soon be overwhelmed by advances in hard drive technology. The hard drive industry responded by developing the ATA-2 standard as an extension of ATA. ATA-2 is largely regarded as a significant improvement to ATA. It defines faster PIO (Programmed I/O) and DMA (Direct Memory Access) data transfer modes, adds more powerful drive commands (such as the "Identify Drive" command to support auto-identification by the BIOS), adds support for a second drive channel, handles block data transfers (Block Transfer Mode), and defines a new means of addressing sectors on the hard drive using Logical Block Addressing (LBA). LBA has proven to be a very effective vehicle for overcoming the traditional 528MB hard drive size limit. Yet ATA-2 continues to use the same 40-pin physical interface used by ATA, and the interface scheme is backward compatible with ATA (IDE) drives.

Along with ATA-2, you'll probably find two additional terms: EIDE (Enhanced IDE) and Fast-ATA. These are not "standards" per se—merely different implementations of the ATA-2 standard. EIDE represents the more popular Western Digital implementation of ATA-2 that builds upon both the ATA-2 and ATAPI standards. This has been so effective that EIDE has become the generic term. Seagate and Quantum have thrown their support behind the Fast-ATA implementation of the ATA-2 standard. However, Fast-ATA builds on ATA-2 only. For all practical purposes, there is no significant difference between ATA-2, EIDE, and Fast-ATA, and you'll probably see these three terms used interchangeably (though this is not technically correct).

### Understanding the 528MB IDE Limit

The 528MB IDE limit, probably the most important and compelling limitation to IDE architecture, is the result of a simple lack of planning between the developers of BIOS and the developers of the WD1003 drive controller architecture. To understand the limitations of drive size, you must understand how IDE drives are addressed. The classic addressing scheme is known as Cylinder Head Sector (CHS) addressing. Simply stated, you place the cylinder number, head number, and sector number you need to get to into the WD1003 controller registers and then call the Int 13 routine in BIOS, which runs the drive to the desired location for reading or writing.

This works just fine in theory, but a problem exists in practice because the limiting values for cylinders, heads, and sectors are not the same in both the BIOS and the WD1003 architecture. Table 14-2 illustrates these values, and you can see their impact on drive size. BIOS specifies a maximum of 1024 cylinders, 255 heads, and 63 sectors per track. If you multiply these together, and then multiply 512

**TABLE 14-2    CHS VALUES VS. DRIVE SIZE**

|  | BIOS | WD1003 | RESULTING LIMIT |
|---|---|---|---|
| Cylinders | 1024 | 65536 | 1024 |
| Heads | 255 | 16 | 16 |
| Sectors | 63 | 255 | 63 |
| Max. Capacity | 8.4GB | 136.9GB | 528MB |

bytes/sector, you get 8,422,686,720 bytes (or 8.4GB) of theoretical capacity. For the WD1003 controller, you should be able to have 65,536 cylinders, 16 heads, and 255 sectors per track. When this is multiplied by 512 bytes per sector, you get a whopping $1.36899_{10}{}^{11}$ bytes (or 136.9GB) of theoretical capacity.

The problem is that you can only use the *lowest* common number for each approach. Therefore, the maximum number of cylinders you can use is 1024, the maximum number of heads is 16, and the maximum number of sectors is 63. When you multiply these out, and then multiply times 512 bytes/sector, you only get 528MB. The real tragedy here is that if BIOS designers and WD1003 designers had sat down and come up with the same numbers, we could easily have had IDE drives with capacities up to 136.9GB from the start, and this early issue would have been moot. But instead, a traditional IDE hard drive can only address up to 528MB.

Today, hard drives are approaching and exceeding the "absolute limit" of 137GB using Big Drives technology spearheaded by companies like Maxtor (www.maxtor.com/products/bigdrive/default.htm).

This explains why IDE worked so well with drives up to 528MB—but not more. Of course, there are ways to work around this limitation. Since BIOS is essentially software, the easiest and most economical way to overcome the 528MB barrier is to "augment" the BIOS Int 13 routine by introducing a driver when the PC is initialized. Int 13 enhancements allow the support of drive sizes up to 64GB and more. For example, Maxtor's MaxBlast (www.maxtor.com/products/diamondmax/software/maxblast/default.htm) and Ontrack's Disk Manager are two popular drive-overlay utilities. They allow the PC to access the entire space of a large IDE drive—not just 528MB.

EIDE and UDMA modes can work with such overlay software, and Disk Manager (or one of its similar cousins) is frequently bundled with today's huge hard drives. However, there are some compelling reasons why overlay drivers are not desirable. First, drivers take memory space—typically precious space within the first 640KB of RAM. Few systems have space remaining in the upper memory area for an overlay driver. Second, older overlay drivers don't always accommodate Windows 98/Me/XP very well at all, so using large hard drives with overlay software under Windows can sometimes be a problem. Third, the overlay driver may conflict with other device drivers and TSRs that may be on your PC.

Ultimately, the preferred method of large drive support for EIDE and UDMA modes is to update the BIOS itself with a version that contains the necessary Int 13 enhancements. AMI and Micro Firmware were early entrants into the EIDE-compatible BIOS arena, but EIDE support quickly became standard in all BIOS and drive controller versions. Today, UDMA/66, UDMA/100, and UDMA/133 support is common, but this is fully backward compatible with older EIDE and IDE modes. Although upgrading a BIOS is a bit more involved than adding a driver, the rewards (such as more free memory and better OS compatibility) are almost always worth it. As an effective alternative to the trials of a motherboard BIOS upgrade, you can choose to upgrade your current drive controller with a new drive adapter containing onboard BIOS extensions for Int 13.

## Understanding LBA

Another source of great confusion in the use of EIDE and UDMA modes is the need for Logical Block Addressing. Where traditional CHS (cylinder/head/sector) addressing requires the specification of a discrete cylinder, head, and sector, an LBA address simply requires the specification of a sector (for example, "go to sector 324534"). The LBA algorithm (implemented in BIOS) will translate the sector to the appropriate CHS equivalent. FAT-based operating systems such as DOS and Windows *require* the use of LBA addressing. As a consequence, you'll need to update your motherboard BIOS or use an EIDE/UDMA controller with onboard BIOS. On the other hand, non-FAT operating systems (such as OS/2 and Novell Netware) do *not* require LBA addressing. When you actually have an EIDE controller in hand, you may note that the controller provides a jumper that allows you to enable or disable LBA addressing. If you are using DOS (or Windows), keep this jumper *enabled*.

 Current UDMA-compliant controllers will forego a physical jumper for an entry in the CMOS Setup. Locate the "LBA" entry and verify that it's enabled.

An important consideration in choosing CHS or LBA addressing is the format of your hard drive(s). If you choose to invoke LBA addressing, you'll need to repartition and reformat your hard drive(s). You must also remember that once a hard drive is formatted for LBA, the drive will be recognized *only* by PCs that support LBA. As a result, if you take an older drive formatted under CHS and install it into a PC with a drive controller channel that's configured for LBA, the drive will simply not be recognized, and you will have to repartition and reformat the drive again. In all cases, remember to perform a *complete* backup of your hard drive(s) before implementing UDMA on your system.

## Drive Support

One of the main advantages of SCSI has traditionally been its ability to support up to seven varied devices on the same bus (hard drives, CD-ROMs, tape drives, and so on). This approach went a long way toward eliminating the proliferation of proprietary controllers and system configuration problems that remain prevalent in non-SCSI systems. Although a classic IDE controller allows two drives (master and slave) to reside on the same controller port (1F0h) and interrupt (IRQ 14), it does not support any other devices. EIDE and UDMA modes seek to overcome this limitation by adding a second channel to the EIDE/UDMA controller.

Be careful when evaluating a controller with two channels. While the primary channel will normally support the fastest devices, the secondary channel may not. For example, it was common for early EIDE controllers to fully support EIDE on the primary channel, but only support ATAPI IDE on the secondary channel. You may also find that a UDMA/100 controller supports up to two UDMA/100 devices on the primary channel, but only supports UDMA/66 (or slower) devices on the secondary channel. Although this wrinkle has largely been ironed out in today's current systems, it's still a "gotcha" that is worth checking. Verify the specifications for each channel before you start attaching devices.

In theory, an older IDE drive will work on an EIDE or UDMA channel, but you may run into trouble when mixing faster and slower devices on the same controller channel. A classic example of this is on systems that use a new fast UDMA hard drive, and then add on an IDE ATAPI CD-ROM as the slave device. In many cases, the slower CD-ROM may interfere with the UDMA drive, thereby reducing the drive's maximum data transfer rates and slowing drive performance. In more pronounced cases, the CD-ROM may not even be recognized. In extreme cases, the hard drive (and perhaps the CD-ROM also) may not be recognized, and the system won't even boot. Reconfiguring the hardware to make the slower CD-ROM a master device on the other (secondary) controller channel will almost always correct this type of problem.

Today's UDMA/133, UDMA/100, and UDMA/66 drive controllers are somewhat more "intelligent" and are better able to dynamically adjust the data transfer speeds to accommodate devices of differing speeds on the same channel. For example, even though a 52x CD-ROM drive has a far lower data transfer speed than a UDMA/133 hard drive, current controllers will "see" the slower CD-ROM and adjust data transfer rates accordingly. Still, speed compatibility issues can come into play. For example, you may find that using a UDMA/100 hard drive and a non-UDMA/100 device together on the same channel may cause the maximum data transfer to fall to UDMA/66 or UDMA/33 levels.

As a rule, keep the faster devices on the primary controller channel and use the slower devices on the secondary controller channel.

## ATA-3

A more recent implementation of the ATA standard is ATA-3. It does not define any new data transfer modes, but it does improve the reliability of PIO mode 4. It also offers a simple password-based security scheme, more sophisticated power management features, and Self-Monitoring Analysis and Reporting Technology (SMART). ATA-3 is also backward compatible with ATA-2, ATAPI, and ATA devices. Since no new data transfer modes are defined by ATA-3, you may also see the generic term "EIDE" used interchangeably (though this also is not technically correct).

## ULTRA-ATA/33 (ATA-4)

The push for ever-faster data transfer rates is a never-ending one, and the Ultra-ATA standard represents an implementation of ATA/ATAPI-4 providing high-performance bus mastering at burst data rates up to 33MB/s using DMA data transfers. The implementation of Ultra-ATA is usually called Ultra-DMA/33 (or UDMA/33). You'll need an Ultra-ATA drive, controller, and BIOS to support an Ultra-ATA drive system, but it is fully backward compatible with previous ATA standards. You can use ordinary 40-pin IDE-type cables for UDMA/33 unless any of the following issues occur:

- The standard cable is low quality, damaged, or weakened by many installs/removals. In this case, simply replace the cable.

- The system suffers from excessive signal noise—for example, these systems may have multiple drives, dual power supplies, or an integrated CRT. Try changing the cable's route, or use a 40-pin/80-conductor cable.

- The system is overclocked (or otherwise configured beyond the manufacturer's supported specifications). Try returning the PC to its non-overclocked state.

## ULTRA-ATA/66 (ATA-5)

The Ultra-ATA standard for ATA/ATAPI-4 was upgraded to support an even faster high-performance bus mastering with burst data rates up to 66MB/s using DMA data transfers. This more recent implementation of Ultra-ATA is usually called Ultra-DMA/66 (ATA/ATAPI-5 or UDMA/66). You'll need an Ultra-ATA/66 drive, controller, cable, and BIOS to support an Ultra-ATA/66 drive system, but it is fully backward compatible with previous ATA standards. Unlike the Ultra-ATA/33 approach, you *cannot* use ordinary 40-pin IDE-type cables to connect drives and controllers. Instead, you'll need a specially designed 40-pin/80-conductor cable as in Figure 14-2 earlier (typically provided with UDMA/66 drives). Also keep in mind that the operating system (such as Windows 98/Me/XP) must be enabled for DMA transfers.

## Common UDMA/66 Issues

The move to Ultra-DMA/66 and faster standards like Ultra-DMA/100/133 should be fairly trouble-free, but some common troubles plague new installations or upgrades. Take a moment to familiarize yourself with the following issues:

▪ Make sure that the signal cable is Ultra-ATA/66, Ultra-ATA/100 or Ultra-ATA/133 capable. An Ultra-ATA/66/100/133-compliant cable is a 40-pin/80-conductor cable with a black connector on one end, a blue connector on the other end, and a gray connector in the middle (see Figure 14-2 earlier). In addition, pin 34 on the cable should be notched or cut (though this may be difficult to see at first glance).

▪ Make sure the system board (motherboard) controller is capable of supporting Ultra-ATA/66, Ultra-ATA/100, or Ultra-ATA/133. An Ultra-ATA/66/100/133-capable controller has a "detect circuit" that can detect whether line 34 is missing on the cable. If there is no detect circuit, the system can wrongly detect the presence of an Ultra-ATA/66/100/133 cable and try to configure the device for a higher transfer rate.

▪ Some system board (motherboard) controllers may not successfully handle Ultra-ATA/66, Ultra-ATA/100 or Ultra-ATA/133 on both the primary and secondary channels. If you have difficulty with a UDMA/66/100/133 device on the secondary controller channel, consider troubleshooting with the device in the primary master position.

▪ If you have trouble getting a UDMA/66, UDMA/100, or UDMA/133 system configured properly, contact the system board or controller card manufacturer for the latest BIOS upgrade (and any Ultra-ATA/66/100/133 device drivers or patches).

▪ Make sure the operating system is DMA capable, and verify that the DMA mode is activated. For Windows 98/Me, check the drive's Properties dialog box in the Device Manager (Figure 14-3). With Windows XP, check the DMA mode assigned to the primary and secondary drive controller channel (as in Figure 14-4), not the drives specifically.

▪ Make sure the Ultra-ATA/66, Ultra-ATA/100, or Ultra-ATA/133-capable drive has been configured to run at Ultra-ATA/66/100/133 transfer rates, respectively. Some drives ship with the UDMA/66/100/133 mode disabled by default, and require a jumper change and/or software utility in order to activate the faster UDMA/66/100/133 mode. Check the drive's installation instructions for any specific mode-enabling steps that may be needed.

# ULTRA-ATA/100/133 (ATA-6 AND ATA-7)

With the growing dependence on huge files and data-intensive multimedia streams (such as video and audio), hard drive data transfer rates are still under pressure to increase. By late 2000, the PC industry embraced the move to Ultra-ATA/100 drives (also called Ultra-DMA/100 or UDMA/100) that are capable of 100MB/s data burst rates. The continued push for ever-faster and larger hard drives ushered in Ultra-ATA/133 drives (or Ultra-DMA/133 or UDMA/133) into late 2001 and 2002. UDMA/133 drive systems support burst data transfers up to 133 MB/s. Based on the original protocols introduced with earlier Ultra-ATA interfaces, UDMA/100/133 also incorporates the same 40-pin/80-conductor cables and connectors that were used with Ultra-ATA/66. Yet UDMA/100/133 remains fully backward compatible with existing EIDE/UDMA hard drives, removable media drives, and CD-ROM/R/RW drives.

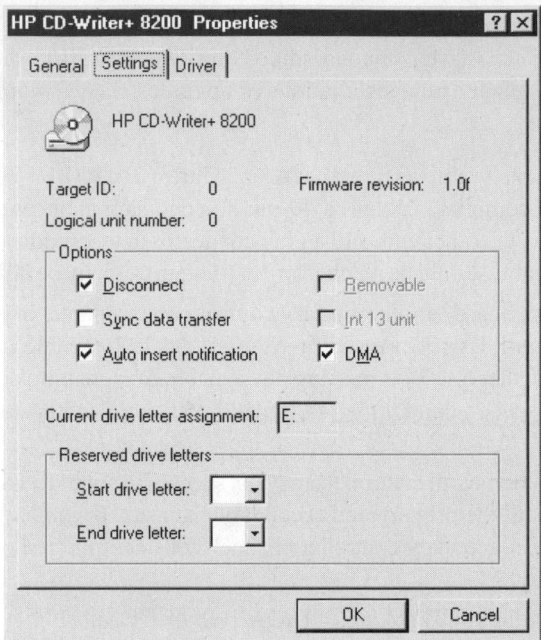

**FIGURE  14-3**    Checking the DMA mode in a drive's Properties dialog box under Windows 98/Me

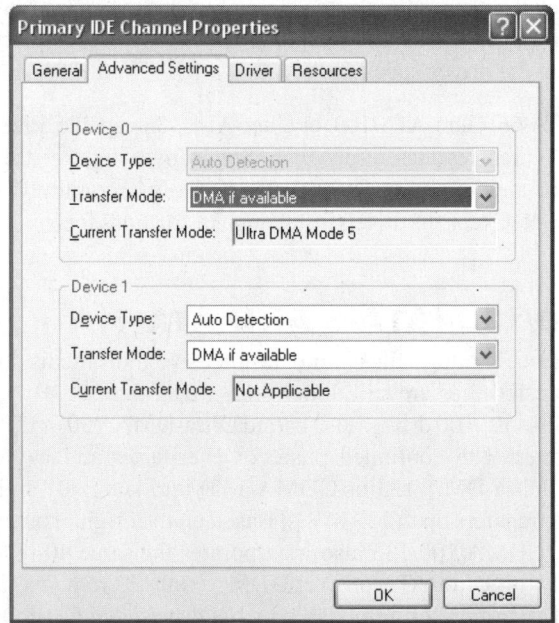

**FIGURE  14-4**    Checking DMA data transfer settings under Windows XP

Remember that each drive connected to a UDMA/100/133 controller channel should be fully UDMA/100/133 compliant. If not, that drive may impair the ability of the controller to adjust for changes in transfer speeds with slower drives, resulting in reduced channel performance for all drives.

# DATA TRANSFER RATES

Data transfer rates play a major role in drive performance. In practice, there are **two** measures of data transfer: the rate at which data is taken from the platters, and the rate at which data is passed between the drive and controller. The internal data transfer between the platters and drive buffer is typically the slower rate, often considered to be the "sustained" data transfer rate. Older drives could run around 5 MB/sec. Newer Ultra-ATA/133 drives, such as the Maxtor DiamondMax Plus D740X, can support a sustained data transfer (at the drive's inner diameter) of 24 MB/s (faster at the drive's outer diameter). The external data transfer between the drive and controller (the *interface rate*) is normally the faster rate, but often can be sustained only for short durations (or bursts). Older drives provided between 5 and 8 MB/sec, but ATA-2 (EIDE) drives can operate up to 16 MB/sec in PIO mode 4. Ultra-DMA/66 drives can burst data at 66 MB/s, Ultra-DMA/100 drives can handle burst data transfers of 100 MB/s, and Ultra-DMA/133 drives can employ burst transfers to 133 MB/s. The modern standards of IDE external data transfer are listed in Table 14-3 as PIO and DMA modes.

You may notice that the EIDE-specific modes (PIO-3 and PIO-4) use the IORDY hardware flow control line. This means that the drive can use the IORDY line to slow down the interface when necessary.

**TABLE 14-3    COMPARISON OF DATA TRANSFER SPEEDS**

| PIO MODES | CYCLE TIME (NS) | TRANSFER RATE (MB/S) | NOTES/STANDARDS |
|---|---|---|---|
| 0 | 600 | 3.3 | The old ATA (IDE) modes |
| 1 | 383 | 5.2 | |
| 2 | 240 | 8.3 | |
| 3 | 180 IORDY | 11.1 | Newer ATA-2 (EIDE) modes |
| 4 | 120 IORDY | 16.6 | |

| DMA MODES | CYCLE TIME (NS) | TRANSFER RATE (MB/S) | NOTES |
|---|---|---|---|
| Single Word 0 | 960 | 2.1 | Also in ATA |
| Single Word 1 | 480 | 4.2 | |
| Single Word 2 | 240 | 8.3 | |
| DMA Multiword Mode 0 | 480 | 4.2 | Also in ATA |
| DMA Multiword Mode 1 | 150 | 13.3 | Also in ATA-2 |
| DMA Multiword Mode 2 | 120 | 16.6 | Also in ATA-2 |
| Ultra-DMA Mode 0 | 240 | 16.6 | Also in ATA/ATAPI-4 |
| Ultra-DMA Mode 1 | 160 | 25.0 | |
| Ultra-DMA Mode 2 | 120 | 33.0 | (UDMA/33) |
| Ultra-DMA Mode 3 | 90 | 44.0 | Also in ATA/ATAPI-5 |
| Ultra-DMA Mode 4 | 60 | 66.0 | (UDMA/66) |
| Ultra-DMA Mode 5 | 40 | 100.0 | (UDMA/100) |
| Ultra-DMA Mode 6 | --- | 133.0 | (UDMA/133) |

Interfaces without proper IORDY support may cause data corruption in the fast PIO modes (so you'd be stuck with the slower modes). When choosing an EIDE drive and controller, always be sure to check that the IORDY line is being used.

By comparison, DMA data transfers mean that the data is transferred *directly* between the drive and memory without using the CPU as an intermediary (as is the case with PIO). In true multitasking operating systems like OS/2, Windows NT, or Linux, DMA transfers leave the CPU free to do something useful during disk transfers. In a DOS or Windows environment, the CPU will have to wait for the transfer to finish anyway, so in these cases, DMA transfers don't offer that much of a multitasking advantage. There are two distinct types of DMA: ordinary DMA and bus-mastering DMA. Ordinary DMA uses the DMA controller on the system's motherboard to perform the complex task of arbitration, grabbing the system bus, and transferring the data. With bus-mastering DMA, all of this is done by logic in the drive controller itself.

# Controller Installation

In many cases, you'll find that the motherboard will provide a primary and secondary drive controller channel that will suit a wide variety of drives in the market at the time the system was manufactured. Over time, new drive types, larger drive capacities, and enhanced data transfer modes may require you to upgrade the motherboard's controller feature. It may also be necessary to install a new controller in the event that an existing controller fails. This part of the chapter highlights the major points involved in controller preparation and installation.

## PREPARING FOR A NEW CONTROLLER

Although a new drive controller should work with your existing drives, there may be some circumstances where a new controller may cause problems. This happens most frequently when the old controller is not removed or disabled properly, or the new controller uses an addressing scheme that is not compliant with the drive's current setup. Before you unwrap that new controller, take some time to prepare your system:

- *Check the system requirements.* Virtually all current PCs easily meet and exceed the minimum requirements for new drive controllers (such as Maxtor's Ultra-ATA/133 PCI card). However, it's still worth a quick "sanity check" to verify that your host system has the required processor, RAM, and OS version to support the new controller.

- *Back up the drive(s).* Before performing any type of drive-related work, protect your valuable data by creating a complete backup of the drive(s) on your system to tape, CD-R/RW, Iomega Jaz, or other suitable media. Boot to the CMOS Setup and record the geometry settings for each drive (you may need to reenter them later).

- *Ready your software.* You should have your Windows 98/Me/XP installation CD handy in the event you need to reinstall the operating system or load new drivers when the controller is installed. If there are drivers with the new controller, you should also have that disc on hand (or download the newest driver versions from the controller's manufacturer).

- *Remove old drive overlay software.* One of the main reasons for upgrading a drive controller is to support larger and faster drive mechanisms without the need for "overlay software." If you've installed drive overlay software (such as Data Lifeguard Tools or MaxBlast), you may wish to remove the software before proceeding. Note that you will need to repartition and reformat the drive(s) after upgrading the controller, so be sure to back up your system first.

■ *Review your current controller.* Eventually, you'll need to remove or disable the current controller, so take a moment to review the documentation for your system and understand the required methods for disabling the current controller. If the controller is currently integrated into your motherboard, it can typically be disabled through the CMOS Setup. (Older motherboards may use a jumper instead.) Controllers that are implemented on stand-alone expansion cards can usually just be removed. In some cases, installing a new drive controller card will automatically disable the motherboard's drive controllers. Be sure that you know how the existing controller is disabled; this will avoid a hardware conflict later on.

■ *Preconfigure your new controller.* Study the documentation that comes with your new controller card. If the controller offers a number of controller features (a floppy controller, game port, COM ports, or other features), you should make it a point to disable any features that are *not* going to be used. Remember that each feature will demand system resources, so don't allow those extra features to remain enabled and conflict with similar features still operating on the motherboard.

■ *Check the firmware (BIOS) version.* It's not uncommon for firmware updates to change frequently. Check with the new controller's manufacturer to see if there's a new firmware version that should be updated after you've installed the new controller. For example, you may need a firmware update to support Windows XP.

## INSTALLING THE NEW CONTROLLER

There's certainly no magic to successfully installing a new controller card, but there are a few minor wrinkles that you should be aware of. This part of the chapter examines a typical set of steps needed to install a new drive controller card:

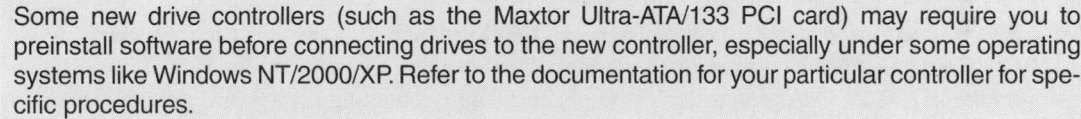
Some new drive controllers (such as the Maxtor Ultra-ATA/133 PCI card) may require you to preinstall software before connecting drives to the new controller, especially under some operating systems like Windows NT/2000/XP. Refer to the documentation for your particular controller for specific procedures.

1. Turn off and unplug the system, and then unbolt the outer housing and remove it. Set the housing and screws aside in a safe place.

2. Locate the old drive controller (either as an expansion card or connectors on the motherboard) and gently disconnect the 40-pin cables from the controller end, but leave them connected to the drive(s). You may choose to label the signal cable(s) so that you can easily locate the primary and secondary channels.

3. Remove the old controller card (if there is one), and insert the new controller card into its expansion slot. Otherwise, unbolt the bracket from another appropriate expansion slot and insert the new controller there (use the bracket to cover up the unused slot). Bolt the new controller card to the chassis. If the original controller is integrated onto the motherboard, there is nothing to remove, but you may need to disable the controller through a motherboard jumper or the system's CMOS Setup once you reboot the system again.

In many cases, you may wish to place the new drive controller card in a PCI slot nearest the processor. These slots typically use a higher interrupt priority and can help to support better drive system performance.

4. If your computer case offers a "hard drive activity" LED, you can generally connect this cable to the small "activity" header on the new controller card. However, this is generally optional, and you may leave the activity LED connected to a drive if you wish.

5. Locate the new drive controller header connectors. The primary channel may be labeled "Pri-IDE" or "IDE 0." The secondary channel may be labeled "Sec-IDE" or "IDE 1." Connect the primary and secondary drive cables to their corresponding headers on the controller.

Remember that UDMA/66, UDMA/100, and UDMA/133 drives and controllers must be connected via a 40-pin/80-conductor cable specially intended for UDMA/66/100/133 use. If you're upgrading drives along with the controller, be sure to use this cable, which should not exceed 18 inches.

## CONFIGURING THE NEW CONTROLLER

Once the new controller is secure and connected, it's time to start the computer and make any necessary configuration changes to use the new controller and avoid system conflicts. Leave the computer's housing off for the time being and follow these tips:

■ *Adjust the motherboard's CMOS Setup.* Boot the system directly to the CMOS Setup. If your old controller was integrated into the motherboard, you may need to disable the old onboard controller(s). However, since we're not changing drives in this exercise, you should verify the drive geometry settings, or reenter them if necessary. No changes are needed for CD-ROM (or other ATAPI) drives that are attached to the controller. The PnP-compliant motherboard will automatically assign the IRQ and I/O resources to the new controller. Save your changes and reboot the system. Remember that many newer systems will detect the new controller and disable the onboard drive controller ports automatically. You may not need to change anything manually.

■ *Access the new controller's BIOS.* Since virtually all drive controller cards use their own onboard BIOS (firmware) chip, chances are that you'll see a BIOS banner for the new controller's BIOS. If you press the key listed in the controller's BIOS banner while rebooting the system, you can access the controller's BIOS and configure specific attributes of the controller's operation. Refer to the controller's manual for specific options and suggested settings. Most installations work just fine with default settings, and you never need to change the controller's internal configuration.

## SOFTWARE INSTALLATION

The new controller's onboard BIOS should fully support normal system operation in the real mode (DOS). However, Windows 98/Me/XP will probably require the installation of numerous drivers to support the controller (especially the UDMA/66, UDMA/100, or UDMA/133 DMA drivers). The following steps highlight a general installation scenario under Windows 98/Me:

1. Try booting the system to DOS, and then check each drive letter. Try taking a directory of each drive. If you can access all of the drives that you could before installing the new controller, you can be confident that the hardware portion of your installation was successful. If you cannot access one or more drives, recheck the motherboard's CMOS Setup and verify that all of the drive-related settings are identical to those used for the old controller. If you cannot emulate the LBA translation characteristics of the original controller, you may need to repartition and reformat the drive(s).

2. Reboot the system and allow Windows 98/Me to boot normally. Chances are that you'll see "New Hardware Detected" as a "PCI Mass Storage Controller" (the exact hardware found will depend on your version of Windows).

3. In most cases, the Add New Hardware wizard will appear, informing you that the new device has been found. Click Next.

4. Select "Search for a better driver than the one your device is using now" then click Next.

5. Click Browse, insert the floppy or CD with the controller's device drivers, and then browse to the folder containing the drivers. Click Next.

6. When the driver location is found, click Next.

7. When the installation is complete, click Finished.

8. It is common for modern controllers to install twice—once for the primary channel and once for the secondary channel. Do *not* reboot the computer after installing the primary channel. Finish the secondary channel (generally, repeat these steps for the second "PCI Mass Storage Device") and then reboot the PC.

9. When the new controller is installed properly, you'll see the entries listed under Hard Disk Controllers or SCSI Controllers in your Device Manager.

Windows XP-based systems may require a slightly different procedure depending on how the drive controller is designed. The following steps illustrate a typical controller installation under an existing version of Windows XP:

1. Open the Windows XP Device Manager.

2. Expand the "SCSI and RAID controllers" entry.

3. Right-click the controller identified by your system and click Properties.

4. Click the Driver tab and click Update Driver.

5. The Hardware Update wizard opens (see Figure 14-5). Click Install From A List Or Specific Location, and click Next.

6. When asked to choose your search and installation options, insert the controller's CD into the drive, select Don't Search, I Will Choose The Driver To Install (see Figure 14-6), and click Next.

7. You can then browse to a list of possible drivers on the installation CD, select the appropriate driver (such as the Promise driver in Figure 14-7), and click Next to proceed with the installation.

8. Click Finish once the new driver has been installed. You can reboot and check the Device Manager again to verify that the correct driver is still being used.

9. Power-off your system and attach the hard drive(s) to the new drive adapter card.

## Confirming a Driver

Once you install the supporting software for a new drive controller, you'll want to verify that the drivers were installed properly. Open the Device Manager and expand the drive adapter entry (or the SCSI adapter entry), and look for a reference to your new controller (for example, "Maxtor Ultra-ATA/133 adapter"). If you find the appropriate entry, chances are that the controller was installed properly, and you can start using the newly installed drive system. Otherwise, recheck your installation for a missed step.

**FIGURE 14-5** Opting to update a Windows XP device driver starts the Hardware Update wizard.

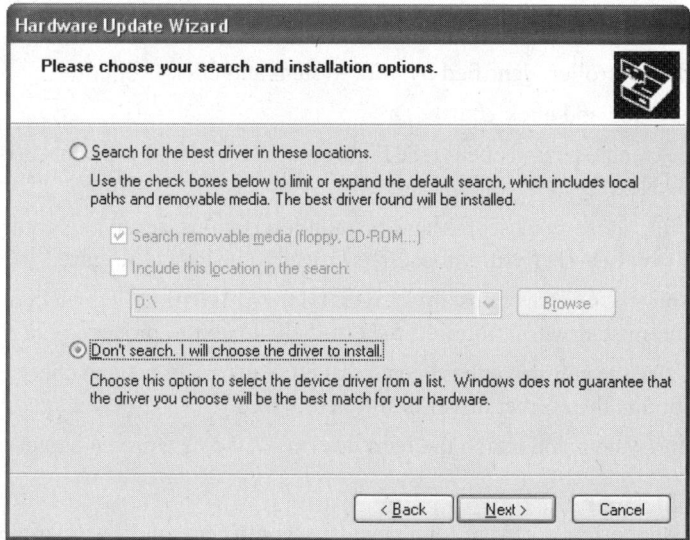

**FIGURE 14-6** If you have the disc with a suitable driver, opt to specify the location of the driver yourself.

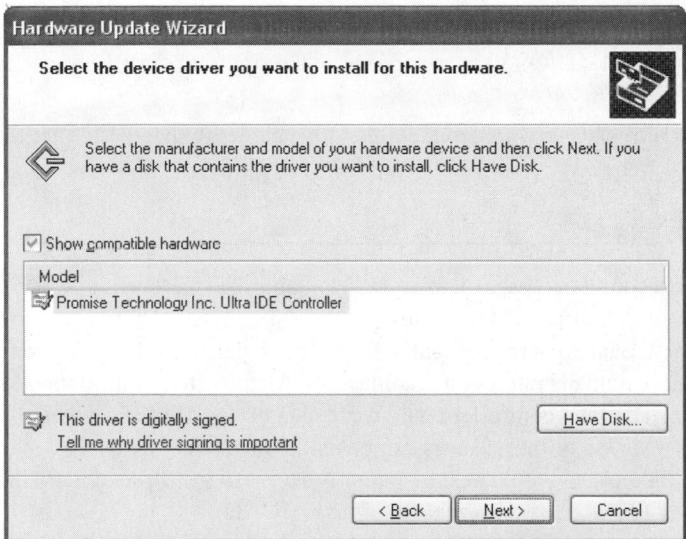

**FIGURE 14-7**    Select the proper driver from a list and finish the installation.

## UPGRADING THE CONTROLLER'S BIOS

From time to time, you may need to upgrade the drive controller's firmware in order to correct bugs, streamline features, or improve compatibility with various systems and devices. When you see that a suitable BIOS update is available, download the update and then follow these guidelines:

Before upgrading the controller's BIOS, power the system off and disconnect all hard drive signal cables from the controller. Insert the bootable disk into the A: drive and power the system on.

1. Create a bootable floppy disk, and then copy the flash utility (for example, PTIFLASH.EXE) and the new BIOS file (for example, ULBIOS.BIN) to the disk.

2. Reboot the system from the floppy disk (you'll see the A: command prompt).

3. Launch the flash loader program (for example, type **ptiflash** and press ENTER). A main menu should appear.

4. Select the option to save a backup copy of the controller's current firmware to the floppy disk. As with motherboards, saving the current firmware allows you to restore the original file if the upgrade should prove buggy or unstable.

5. Once the firmware backup is finished, select the option to update the BIOS from a file.

6. A dialog box will appear. Enter the path and name of the new BIOS file (for example, **a:\ulbios.bin**). If you see an error indicating that the file was not found, double-check your path and file name.

7. The utility will update the controller's firmware, and you will see a message when the process is complete.

8.  Remove the disk and reboot the system.

9.  When the controller's BIOS banner appears, make sure that the BIOS version is in fact the new (updated) version.

10. Power the system back down, reconnect the drive cable(s), then power-up the system normally.

# RAID Primer

Traditionally, the most common means of protecting valuable data has been to perform routine and consistent backups to tape or other media. While this has proven to be a tried-and-true method, it often is not implemented properly. Backups are frequently forgotten or performed inconsistently. Even automated backup schemes require human interaction at some level. All too often, some data is lost during a disk failure. Designers realized that if a controller could write data to *one* drive, then the data could be written to *two* drives just as easily. One or more drives can be made to "mirror" a master drive in real time—if the main drive were to fail, the data would be transparently accessed from a secondary drive. This is the basic premise behind a *redundant array of independent disks* (RAID).

The problem with RAID is that it costs money to implement. You'll need a drive controller that supports RAID (such as the Promise FastTrack TX2000 for UDMA/133 drives) and an additional drive for each drive that you need to mirror. The extra drives don't give you more storage space, they simply mimic the original drive(s), and you need additional power and drive space for the RAID drives. End-users don't often choose to spend their money on such protection, but it's common on network servers and busy workstations. This part of the chapter highlights several basic RAID concepts and explains some setup options that you may encounter.

## DISK ARRAY

A *disk array* is formed from a group of two or more disk drives that appear to the system as a single drive. The advantage of an array is to provide better performance and data fault tolerance. Better performance is accomplished by sharing the data transfer workload in parallel among multiple physical drives. Fault tolerance is achieved through data redundant operation, where if one (or more) drives should fail (or suffer a sector failure), a mirrored copy of the data can be found on another drive(s). For optimal results, select identical drives for installation in disk arrays. The drives' matched performance allows the array to function better as a single drive. The individual disk drives in an array are called *members*. Each member of a specific disk array is coded in its reserved sector with configuration information that identifies the drive as a member of the given array.

## DISK ARRAY ADAPTER (DAA)

The generic term used for the RAID controller is the *disk array adapter*—the device that supports your mirrored drive(s), which is generally termed the disk array. Most RAID controllers are implemented using the SCSI interface, but Promise Technologies offers the FastTrack TX2000 for RAID with UDMA/133 drives, and the older FastTrack100 for RAID with UDMA/100 hard drives. The controller will virtually always incorporate a BIOS that fully supports the drive operations (such as UDMA/100/133) and provide a setup feature (similar to the CMOS Setup) that will allow you to configure the RAID controller's features.

# RESERVED SECTOR

Vital information is saved in a special location on each disk member called the *reserved sector*. This area contains array configuration data about the drive and other members in the disk array. If reserved data on any member of the array becomes corrupt or lost, the redundant configuration data on the other members can be used for rebuilds. As a rule, disk array members do not have specific drive positions. This allows drives to be placed on different RAID controller connectors or cards within the system without reconfiguring or rebuilding the array.

# DISK ARRAY TYPES

A typical RAID controller supports four general operating modes: striping, mirroring, striping/mirroring, and spanning. The choice of RAID mode will affect your drive capacity, drive performance, or fault tolerance. To appreciate the versatility of RAID, you should understand a little more about each of these common RAID modes.

Remember that all disk members in a formed disk array are recognized as a single physical drive to the host system.

## Striping (RAID 0)

In striping mode, sectors of data are interleaved between multiple drives, effectively forming one large drive from two or more smaller ones. Striping is regarded as a performance enhancement rather than fault tolerance. Performance is better than a single drive because the read/write workload is duplicated between the array members, and this array type is encountered in high-performance systems. Identical drives are recommended for performance (as well as data storage efficiency). The disk array data capacity is equal to the number of drive members times the smallest member capacity. For example, one 40GB and three 60GB drives will form a 160GB (4 × 40GB) disk array—the additional space on the three 60GB drives isn't used. The weakness with RAID 0 is that it provides no redundancy—when any disk member fails, it affects the entire array because some portion of the overall "drive" is lost.

## Mirroring (RAID 1)

The mirroring approach writes duplicate data onto a pair of drives, while reads are performed in parallel (improving read performance). IDE-type RAID 1 is fault tolerant because data is duplicated, and each drive of a mirrored pair is installed on separate connectors. The RAID controller (such as FastTrack TX2000 or FastTrack100) performs reads using data handling techniques that distribute the workload in a more efficient manner than using a single drive. When a read request is made, the controller selects the drive positioned closest to the requested data, and then looks to the idle drive to perform the next read access.

If one of the mirrored drives suffers a mechanical failure (such as a spindle failure) or does not respond, the remaining drive will continue to function (this is called *fault tolerance*). If one drive has a physical sector error, the mirrored drive will also continue to function. On the next reboot, the RAID software utility will display an error in the array and recommend replacing the failed drive. Users may choose to continue using their PC; however, it's often best to replace the failed drive as soon as possible.

Due to redundancy, the drive capacity of the array is half the total drive capacity. For example, two 60GB drives that have a combined capacity of 120GB would have 60GB of usable storage. With drives of different capacities, there may be unused capacity on the larger drive.

**Spare Drive**   Under a RAID 1 configuration, an extra *hot spare* drive can be attached to the RAID controller, but cannot be assigned to the array. In this case, the spare drive is put on standby. This drive will be activated to replace a failed drive that is part of the mirrored array. In most cases, a rebuild is performed automatically in the background to mirror the good drive onto the spare. At a later time, the system can be powered off, and the failed drive can be physically removed and replaced. Spare drives must be the same or larger capacity than the smallest array member.

### Striping/Mirroring (RAID 0+1)

Striping/mirroring is a combination of the striping and mirroring array types. It can increase performance by reading and writing data in parallel while protecting data with duplication. A minimum of four drives needs to be installed. With a four-drive disk array, two pairs of drives are striped, and each pair mirrors the data on the other pair of striped drives. The data capacity is similar to a standard mirroring array with half of the total capacity dedicated for redundancy.

### Spanning (JBOD)

A spanning disk array (also aptly named "JBOD" for "just a bunch of drives") is equal to the sum of all drives when the drives used are of different capacities. Spanning stores data onto a drive until it is full, and then proceeds to store files onto the next drive in the array. There are no major performance or fault tolerance array features in this mode. When any disk member fails, the failure affects the entire array.

Spanning may be considered for performance in certain instances. With striping, array performance is affected directly by the stripe block size. Block size should be tailored to the typical I/O on the drive, whether it is generally more random or sequential. However, if there is no predictability of the type of I/O access, and both random and sequential I/O occur unpredictably, the performance of a striped array will fluctuate. In the end, this may result in no overall performance gain. With spanning, the performance factor simply reflects a single drive's performance level. This offers a more predictable transfer rate and allows the use of mismatched drives.

# Troubleshooting a Drive Adapter

A properly configured drive adapter will rarely cause problems in a PC because BIOS, IRQ, and I/O assignments are very strongly established in the PC industry (and today's PnP systems eliminate many potential installation issues). However, a variety of problems can plague drive adapter replacements and upgrades. This part of the chapter looks at troubleshooting for IDE-type drive systems.

**SYMPTOM 14-1**    **You cannot get the drive adapter software to install properly**
When installing or upgrading drive controller software, it is not uncommon to encounter problems, usually due to the many advanced features of the drive controller itself. If you cannot get new software installed, try the following steps to overcome the problem. First, start the CMOS Setup and disable the high-performance features usually related to drive controllers, such as IDE Block Mode, Multi-Sector Transfer, and 32-bit Disk Access. If there are other options for the secondary drive controller channel, try disabling them as well. You might also try moving the controller BIOS address range (for example, change the address range from C800h to CF00h).

If you still cannot get the controller software installed, there may also be trouble with "overlay software" (such as Disk Manager or MaxBlast software) used to partition and format a drive. You may need to uninstall the overlay software and update the CMOS Setup by enabling LBA support for the drive. If you can't uninstall the overlay software, you can run FDISK /MBR to overwrite the overlay software. Once the overlay software is removed, repartition and reformat the drive. If you cannot wipe the drive clean, check with the drive manufacturer for such a utility. You should now be able to install the new drive software.

This step is destructive to any data on the drive. Be sure to make a complete system backup (and have a bootable disk on hand) before removing the overlay software.

**SYMPTOM 14-2**    **The controller will not support a drive with more than 1,024 cylinders**
This often happens when building a new system or piecing together a system from used parts. To support a drive with more than 1,024 cylinders, the controller must support LBA (discussed earlier in the chapter), and the feature must be enabled. The controller's onboard firmware (BIOS) should support LBA, but you may need to install a driver for the controller in order to support LBA. (For example, a Promise Technologies controller needs the DOSEIDE.SYS driver to support LBA.) If the controller is integrated onto the motherboard, the motherboard BIOS **must** support LBA. If it is not integrated, you'll need to upgrade the motherboard BIOS or install a drive adapter with an LBA-aware BIOS. Second, the hard drive itself must support LBA. Make sure the drive is an EIDE or UDMA-type hard drive. Finally, check the CMOS Setup and verify that the drive is using the LBA mode rather than the older CHS mode. You may need to repartition and reformat the hard drive.

**SYMPTOM 14-3**    **Loading a disk driver causes the system to hang or generate a "Bad or missing COMMAND.COM" error**    This is a known problem with some older versions of the DTC DTC22XX.SYS or DOSEIDE.SYS drivers, but frequently occurs with other controllers that use disk drivers. The controller is probably transferring data *too fast* to the drive. When the disk driver loads, it obtains information from the drive, including drive speed. Sometimes the drive reports that it can support PIO mode 4 or PIO mode 3 when in actuality it cannot. In many cases, the original drivers are outdated, and the immediate solution is to slow down the data transfer rate manually. Download and install the newest drivers—until then, you may be able to add a command-line switch to the disk driver. For example, DTC recommends adding a switch to its DOSEIDE.SYS driver as in the following (where *x* is the drive designation):

```
doseide.sys /v /dx:m0 /dx:p0
```

If your problems started after loading the disk drivers "high" (into the upper memory area), adjust CONFIG.SYS to load the drivers into conventional memory. Some drive adapters have reported better success with driver software when the Hidden Refresh feature is enabled in CMOS Setup (in the Advanced CMOS Setup area). This alters the way in which the system timing refreshes RAM and may better support the disk drivers. Also try disabling advanced controller options such as IDE Block Mode, Multi-Sector Transfer, and 32-bit Disk Access. Finally, if you're using overlay software (such as Disk Manager or MaxBlast), the disk driver may not work with the overlay software. You'll then need to remove the overlay software and repartition and reformat the drive before the disk driver will work. (Remember to perform a complete system backup before removing overlay software.)

**SYMPTOM 14-4**    **Drive performance is poor—data transfer rates are slow**    This often happens when installing a replacement drive controller. First, make sure that you're not running any antivirus software. Antivirus utilities that load at boot time can degrade drive performance. If the controller uses a "speed" jumper, make sure you have properly configured the jumper settings on the card to match the speed of the IDE drive and processor (for example, this is a known issue with older DTC 2278VL and 2270 controllers). Also make sure that the highest possible data transfer rate is selected in the CMOS Setup (PIO mode 4 for older setups, or UDMA/33, UDMA/66, UDMA/100, or UDMA/133 in newer systems). If the drive adapter uses a disk driver for optimum performance, make sure that the correct disk driver software is loaded, and that any necessary command-line switches are entered. Finally, remove any third-party software (such as Disk Manager or MaxBlast) that may have shipped with the drive itself. If the problem persists, check for updated firmware for the drive controller.

**SYMPTOM 14-5** **You cannot boot from a new IDE drive controller** This may happen when you install a new IDE drive controller (such as an Ultra133 card), but the motherboard's drive controllers are still active. Many newer controllers can coexist with existing motherboard controllers without necessarily disabling them. However, you may find that the system still tries to boot from drives attached to the old motherboard controller channels rather than the drives connected to the new drive controller. There are typically two ways to correct this issue.

First, you can disconnect drives from the motherboard and attach them to the new drive controller card. The motherboard will not find a bootable device at start time, and allow the new controller (such as the Maxtor Ultra-ATA/133) to boot. You may also be able to turn the autodetection off on your motherboard and set all the hard drives in the CMOS Setup to "None" or "Not Installed," though this will render any such connected drives inaccessible. The second option is to change the Boot Sequence in your CMOS Setup to boot from SCSI *first*. Since a PC will normally see a new drive controller card as a "SCSI" device, changing the boot order will tell the motherboard to ignore its own controllers and use the card as the boot device. Keep in mind that older motherboards may not allow you to select SCSI as the first boot device (a BIOS upgrade may be needed).

**SYMPTOM 14-6** **The PC refuses to boot after a drive adapter is installed** There are many possible reasons for this kind of problem. First make sure that the drive adapter is installed properly and completely into its bus slot, and then verify that the drive signal cables are oriented and attached properly. If the drive adapter uses jumpers to match the drive and processor speeds (such as the older DTC 2278VL or 2270), make sure that the adapter is configured correctly. Verify that the drive itself is properly jumpered as a master or slave. Finally, check the CMOS Setup and confirm that the proper drive parameters are being used (and verify that any original drive controller devices have been disabled). Try disabling advanced features like IDE Block Mode and 32-bit Disk Access. If the problem still persists, try repartitioning and reformatting the drive.

**SYMPTOM 14-7** **Windows generates a "Validation Failed" error** This type of problem most frequently occurs after loading the Windows disk driver, and is almost always due to a 1,024-cylinder limit in the drive system. Make sure that the drive and drive controller are able to support more than 1,024 cylinders (both EIDE or UDMA). Check the CMOS Setup and verify that the LBA mode is selected. Once the proper hardware is configured correctly, try reinstalling the latest disk driver from the manufacturer.

**SYMPTOM 14-8** **Windows hangs or fails to load files after loading the controller's driver** In most cases, Windows hangs, or every file after the offending driver is unable to load. In some cases, you may see an error message such as: "Cannot find KRN.386". Load SYSTEM.INI into a text editor and move the controller's driver (such as WINEIDE.386) to the last line in the [386enh] section. Also make sure that the classic WDCTRL driver is commented out, such as in the following:

```
;device=*WDCTRL
```

If problems persist, the controller's driver may be old or buggy. Download and install the newest disk driver version from the controller maker. If all else fails, disable the block mode and mode speed using the driver's internal switches or setup routine. For example, the WINEIDE.386 driver provides the switch WINEIDESWITCH that you can use, as shown next:

```
device=wineide.386
wineideswitch= /dx:m0 /dx:p0
```

You can use the System Configuration utility (**msconfig**) to review and edit your system's startup files to help you isolate any possible offending drivers.

**SYMPTOM 14-9**    **The controller misidentifies the drive**    For example, a UDMA/100 controller detects the UDMA/100 (DMA mode 4) drive as UDMA/33 (DMA mode 2). Generally speaking, there are only two reasons why the drive controller's BIOS won't detect a UDMA/66/100/133-capable hard drive properly. First, some drives (such as many Western Digital or Maxtor ATA/100 drives) require you to run a utility to enable UDMA/100/133 support. These utilities can be obtained directly from the drive manufacturer. For example, Maxtor's DiamondMax60 family of 60GB hard drives (such as model 96147U8) require running the 66TO100.EXE utility in order to enable UDMA/100 operation.

Cabling is another issue. Only a certain type of IDE cable can support data transfers of up to 66/100/133 MB/s. These 80-wire/40-pin cables have twice as many ground wires as traditional IDE cables. (A suitable cable is usually included with new drives, and you can see an example in Figure 14-2 earlier.) This dramatically decreases the electrical signal noise that a 40-wire/40-pin IDE cable would otherwise produce when attempting UDMA/66/100/133 transfers. If the cable is damaged or unsuitable for UDMA/66 or faster operation, the controller will automatically "downshift" itself to UDMA/33. Enable the UDMA/66/100/133 mode, or replace the signal cable.

**SYMPTOM 14-10**    **You cannot boot to a CD after installing a new drive controller**    For example, you cannot boot to the Windows XP installation disc after installing an Ultra133 card. In many cases, the new controller may be conflicting with another PCI device, or the slot that it's installed in doesn't have enough priority to ensure proper operation. Try powering down the PC and moving the drive controller card to a higher priority slot (often closer to the processor). If the problem persists, it's possible that the ESCD did not properly save or detect the 133 ATA PCI card. You may need to clear the system's ESCD (an area of memory used to save configuration information about the hardware on the system) through the CMOS Setup routine. By resetting the ESCD, it will redetect the system hardware properly.

**SYMPTOM 14-11**    **You cannot play DVD movies with a UDMA/100/133 controller installed**    This is a known issue with Promise Technologies drive controllers like the Ultra100 or the Ultra133, and is normally related to the SMART driver. For example, some DVD playback problems have been traced to a bug in the SMART driver. The latest Promise Ultra100 driver can be downloaded from ftp://ftp.promise.com/Controllers/IDE/Ultra100/. However, SMART's function is to notify you of any hard drive problems that may occur during the drive's life, and thus is not performance related; a temporary solution is to rename the SMART driver. For example, the Ultra100 SMART driver should be located in the c:\windows\system\iosubsys directory. Rename the PU100VSD.VXD file to **PU100VSD.PTI** and reboot the system. If an updated SMART driver doesn't help (or isn't available), check for updated drive controller firmware.

**SYMPTOM 14-12**    **Drives over 65GB are not reported correctly in the controller's banner**    For example, the Promise Technologies Ultra100 does not display the correct size of hard drives with more than 65GB in the BIOS banner. In virtually all cases, this is an issue with the controller's BIOS. According to Promise Technologies, this problem is purely cosmetic and does not interfere with the operating system's use of the drive. The operating system will still use the full storage space of the disk. The display problem has been fixed in the Ultra100 v2.00 BIOS (build 12 and above). The best solution to this issue is to update the drive controller's firmware.

**SYMPTOM 14-13**    **You find that FDISK reports a very low drive capacity for partitions larger than 64GB**    This is typically a problem with FDISK rather than the drive or controller. The version of FDISK.EXE included with some older versions of Windows does not correctly report the capacity of hard drives that exceed 64GB. This is only a reporting issue, and it will not affect FDISK's ability to partition huge drives. Microsoft has an updated version of FDISK.EXE that corrects this problem.

**SYMPTOM 14-14**    **After replacing a drive adapter with a different model, the hard drive is no longer recognized**    This can happen frequently with all types of IDE drives and controllers. You will find that the new controller probably is not using the same translation geometry used when the drive was originally partitioned. Verify that the drive geometry and LBA settings are as close as possible to the settings used on the older controller. You may need to use "user-defined" settings rather than "autodetect" to ensure that the geometry settings are identical. In order for the new drive adapter card to recognize an existing drive, you may have to repartition and reformat the drive with FDISK and FORMAT. Reinstall the original controller and perform a complete system backup before continuing. After the drive is prepared, you can restore the backup and continue working.

**SYMPTOM 14-15**    **You cannot enable 32-bit Disk Access under Windows**    In most cases, you're using the wrong protected-mode (Windows) driver for the drive adapter, or the driver should be upgraded with a newer version. Download and install the latest disk drivers for your drive adapter. Before installing the new driver(s), be sure to disable advanced data transfer features such as IDE Block Mode and 32-bit Disk Access (if enabled). Load SYSTEM.INI into a text editor. Make sure that the protected-mode disk driver is installed under the [386enh] section, and verify that the WDCTRL driver is remarked out. Note that many Windows drivers will not support an IBMSLC2 processor or Ontrack's Disk Manager, and will *not* work with 32-bit disk access.

**SYMPTOM 14-16**    **The IDE-type drive adapter's secondary port refuses to work**    If the drive adapter has a secondary drive channel, that secondary channel is not working. In many cases, this type of problem occurs in real-mode systems when the drive adapter relies on a disk driver for proper operation. The secondary channel often must be enabled specifically through the disk driver's command line in CONFIG.SYS, such as:

```
device=doseide.sys /v /2
```

Make sure that the drive attached to the secondary channel is jumpered as the master drive, and verify that the signal cable between the drive and controller is oriented properly. Also remember that a secondary drive channel requires a unique interrupt (usually IRQ 15). Make sure there is no hardware conflict between the secondary port's IRQ and other devices in the system. Try disabling advanced data transfer features in the CMOS Setup like IDE Block Mode and 32-bit Disk Access. If your hard drive is an older IDE drive, it may not support Multi-Sector Transfer. Try disabling this feature in the CMOS Setup, or add the necessary command-line switch to the disk driver command line in CONFIG.SYS, such as:

```
device=doseide.sys /v /2 /d0:m0
```

**SYMPTOM 14-17**    **The drive adapter's BIOS doesn't load**    First, the drive adapter may not load its BIOS if there are no drives connected (or detected), so recheck the connections and jumper assignments for all of your attached drives. Make sure that the BIOS is enabled (usually through a jumper on the drive adapter), and see that the BIOS chip is seated correctly and completely in its socket on the drive adapter. If problems persist, try changing the BIOS address—it's probably conflicting with another BIOS in the system. Also check the IRQ and I/O port assignments for the drive adapter for possible conflicts, or try moving the drive adapter to a different PCI slot. If all else fails, try another drive controller.

**SYMPTOM 14-18**    **The drive adapter BIOS loads, but the system hangs up**    First, make sure that the drive parameters are set properly in the CMOS Setup. Inexperienced users frequently mistake the parameters for a second drive in CMOS ( a "primary slave") with a drive on the secondary channel (a "secondary master/slave"). When no drive is in the primary slave position, the second drive should be "none" or "not installed." In most cases, the BIOS will autodetect the drives adequately, but it's still worth a check. If you have an onboard drive controller, make sure to disable it; otherwise, you'll have a hardware conflict between the two drive controllers. Check the individual drives attached to the controller and verify that each drive is jumpered as a unique master or slave device (try reversing the drive order or working with only one drive). Finally, try disabling some of the advanced drive performance parameters in CMOS, such as IDE Block Mode.

**SYMPTOM 14-19**    **The ATAPI CD drive is not recognized as the slave device vs. an IDE master**    First, verify that the CD-ROM/R/RW drive is in fact ATAPI compatible and suitable for use on an IDE-type interface. Second, make sure that the proper low-level ATAPI driver for the CD-ROM drive is in use. If the driver is old, try downloading and installing the newest version of the driver. If problems persist, the trouble is probably due to a fast IDE-type device (such as the hard drive) coexisting with a slower IDE ATAPI device (such as the CD drive). Reconfigure the CD drive as the master device on the secondary drive controller channel. You may need to update the ATAPI driver command line in CONFIG.SYS if you're using real-mode support.

**SYMPTOM 14-20**    **Hard drives are not recognized on the secondary drive controller channel**    This is a problem that sometimes appeared with older drive adapter cards. Make sure that all the hard drives are jumpered correctly. If only one drive is on the secondary channel, it should be configured as the single or master drive. If two drives are on the secondary channel, verify that the drives are jumpered as master and slave. If the drive adapter uses a disk driver to support EIDE or secondary channel operation, make sure that the command line in CONFIG.SYS uses the correct switch(es) to enable the secondary drive channel. For example, the older Promise Technologies 2300 would add an /S switch to the command line such as:

```
device=c:\eide2300\eide2300.sys /S
```

Check that your system's power management features are not using IRQ 15 (and confirm that no other devices are conflicting with IRQ 15). If the drive is set to "auto-configure" in the CMOS Setup, try entering the drive's parameters specifically. The drive may be too old to understand the IDC (Identify Drive Command) needed for auto-configuration. Finally, try booting the system clean (with just disk driver software if necessary) to see if there are any other driver or TSR conflicts.

**SYMPTOM 14-21**    **The drive adapter can only support 528MB per disk**    First, make sure that the LBA mode is enabled. This is often accomplished through the CMOS Setup, but it may also be necessary to enable an LBA support jumper on some older EIDE drive adapters. If problems persist, the drive adapter's BIOS is probably too old and should be upgraded to a new version. If you cannot upgrade the drive adapter's BIOS, install a new drive adapter, such as the Maxtor Ultra-ATA/133 PCI card or Promise Ultra133 TX2.

**SYMPTOM 14-22**    **You get a "Code 10" error relative to the drive adapter**    You notice that Windows 98/Me is running in MS-DOS Compatibility Mode, and the system only boots in Safe Mode. You'll probably find one or more devices (including the drive adapter) marked with a yellow exclamation point, and the properties for the device may report an error such as "This device is either not present, not working properly, or does not have all the drivers installed (Code 10)." Disk overlay software (such as Disk Manager, EZ-Drive, or MaxBlast) will often cause problems when used in conjunction with drive adapters that use their own disk driver software. The disk overlay must be removed *before* installing the adapter's disk drivers. Remove the overlay software, or simply repartition and reformat the drive (remember to do a complete backup *before* repartitioning). Next, remove or disable any 32-bit disk drivers previously installed under Windows.

Remove the conflicting device(s) from Device Manager and let Windows redetect and install the device using the latest drivers, or use the Add New Hardware wizard to install the latest drivers from floppy disk or CD. (See Chapter 11 for detailed conflict troubleshooting information.) There may also be a DMA conflict. Some older drive adapters take advantage of DMA when the parallel port is in the ECP mode (the conflict occurs most often with the soundboard). To find out which devices use DMA, open the Device Manager and check the DMA channel assignments. You can then either switch the controller's use of DMA or disable it altogether. You may need to alter the DMA setting on the drive controller itself, and then switch the parallel port's mode to EPP.

**SYMPTOM 14-23**    **You encounter mouse problems after changing the drive adapter**
This is a known problem with Logitech pointing devices or standard pointing devices using Logitech drivers under Windows 9x. (This is not known to be an issue with Windows Me/XP.) In most cases, you can correct the problem by downloading and installing version 7.0 or later Logitech drivers, or switch to the Windows native serial mouse driver for Windows 9x:

1. Open the Control Panel and double-click on the System icon.
2. Select Device Manager and double-click on the Mouse.
3. Click once on Logitech and choose Remove.
4. Start the Add/New Hardware wizard in the Control Panel.
5. Choose No when Windows prompts to autodetect the device.
6. Select Mouse. Click on Standard Serial Mouse. Click on Finish.
7. Reboot the computer.

Another solution may be to disable the COM port's FIFO buffer under Windows 9*x*/Me/XP. Open the Device Manager. Double-click on Ports [COM & LPT]. Choose the communications port that the mouse uses (for example, COM 1) by clicking on it once, and then click on Properties. Select Port Settings and choose Advanced. Uncheck the box next to Use FIFO Buffers (see Figure 14-8), and then click OK.

**SYMPTOM 14-24**    **You cannot run Norton Antivirus with Promise drive adapters**
This appears to be an issue with the Norton Anti-Virus (NAV) software itself. According to Symantec (www.symantec.com), a patch has been released that corrects this problem. Check with Symantec and install the patch (or upgrade the antivirus software to a later version), or upgrade the drive adapter to a different make/model.

**SYMPTOM 14-25**    **The system hangs after counting through system memory**    You may also receive error messages such as "Get Configuration Failed!" or "HDD Controller Failure." First, make sure that you have at least one hard drive attached to the controller, and see that the signal cable is oriented properly at both ends. It is also possible that you may have a problem when more than one drive is connected. Make sure that the drives are jumpered in the desired master and slave relationship. Try working with only one drive or reverse the drive relationship. In all cases, verify that the CMOS Setup entries accurately reflect the drives that are connected. If your drive adapter uses onboard RAM, the RAM may be bad. Try replacing the controller's onboard RAM, or replace the drive controller outright.

**SYMPTOM 14-26**    **There are errors reading or writing to floppies after replacing/ upgrading a drive adapter**    This is almost always due to a hardware conflict between the floppy adapter on the new controller and another floppy adapter elsewhere in the system. Disable the floppy adapter port on the new drive controller card. If you're using the new floppy port, disable the floppy port already in the system.

If you cannot successfully disable a current or preexisting floppy controller, you'll need to remove the new drive controller and install a controller without a floppy port (or one that can be disabled properly).

**SYMPTOM 14-27**    **Your drive controller won't function with a 75 MHz bus speed**
This problem often appeared on older motherboards, and occurs because the odd bus speed results in a PCI speed of about 37.5 MHz (which is higher than the 33 MHz that the PCI bus is designed for). This effectively "overclocks" the PCI bus, and can often result in unstable or erratic operation for sensitive PCI devices such as the drive controller. The best solution here is to drop the bus speed to 66 MHz so that the clock can be divided down to 33 MHz for the PCI bus, or reset the PCI bus divisor speed to an appropriate level for 100 MHz or 133 MHz motherboards. This problem doesn't appear with current motherboards where the PCI/AGP speeds can run asynchronously of the FSB.

**SYMPTOM 14-28**    **You cannot use APM with hard drives operated from a new drive controller**    This is a known issue with controllers such as the Promise FastTrack66. In most cases, this symptom occurs because the system sees the new controller card as a SCSI controller. Using IDE commands for APM will not work because the card is seen as a SCSI card. SCSI commands for APM will not work because the drives are IDE. You will need to replace the controller with a model suitable for APM use, or forego the use of APM modes. In more recent drive adapters, you may be able to correct this type of issue by updating the drive adapter's firmware, or updating the driver for your operating system.

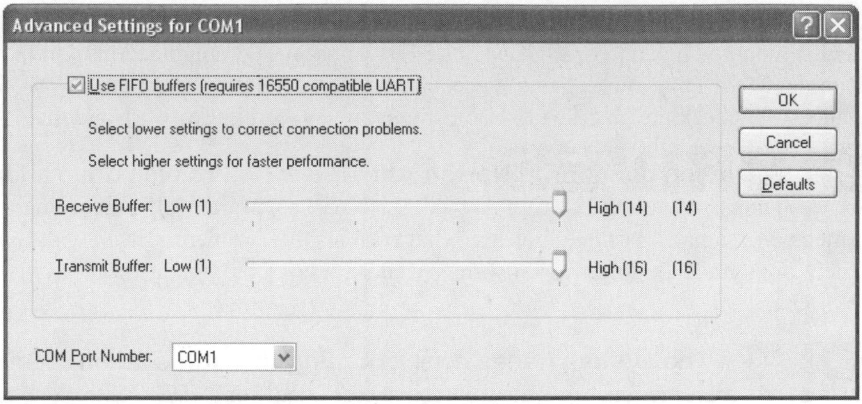

**FIGURE  14-8**    Try disabling FIFO buffers to restore mouse operation.

**SYMPTOM 14-29**    **You can't boot from a new IDE controller if you have a SCSI card in the system already**    Chances are that you'll need to tweak the setup of your new IDE controller (such as Ultra100 or Ultra133) and existing SCSI card. If you have an actual SCSI controller in the system, the computer will attempt to boot from whichever controller is recognized first. To get one controller to be recognized before another, you must get its BIOS to load first. Manipulating the BIOS address that the card is set to use normally takes care of this.

However, virtually all IDE controllers are fully PnP, which means that only the PnP BIOS on the motherboard can control which resources the card uses. Generally, the PCI slot with the highest priority will be assigned the lowest BIOS address. On most motherboards, the PCI slot with the highest priority is PCI slot 1. If you cannot assign a specific memory address or loading order to your PCI devices through the CMOS Setup, try inserting the IDE drive controller so that it's in PCI slot 1 (usually the slot closest to the processor). If the IDE or SCSI adapter (or both) are integrated into the motherboard, you may be able to select the boot order through the system's CMOS Setup.

**SYMPTOM 14-30**    **You find that your IDE controller is conflicting with the USB controller**    This is a BIOS problem with the IDE controller itself. Check to see if a new BIOS version is available for your controller. For a Promise Ultra66, a new BIOS has been released to fix the conflict. You can download that BIOS from ftp://ftp.promise.com/Controllers/IDE/Ultra66/U66_0628.zip. For other drive controllers, you must contact the specific manufacturer for their recommendations and updates.

# Further Study

**Adaptec**   www.adaptec.com
**Connect.Com**   www.connectcom.net/
**DTC**   www.datatechnology.com
**Maxtor**   www.maxtor.com/products/ultraata133/default.htm
**Promise Technologies**   www.promise.com
**RAID Advisory Board**   www.raid-advisory.com
**T13 Committee (ATA standards)**   www.t13.org

# DVD DRIVES

The *compact disc* opened up a whole new world of possibilities for the PC. These simple, mass-produced plastic discs could hold up to an hour of stereo music, or 650MB (or more) of computer programs and data. Software makers quickly found the CD-ROM to be an outstanding medium for all types of multimedia applications, large databases, and interactive games. But today, the CD-ROM (and later drives like the CD-R/RW) is showing its age, and a single CD no longer provides enough storage for the increasing demands of data-intensive applications. A new generation of high-density optical storage called *DVD* is now widely available for the desktop PC (Figure 15-1). "DVD" stands for "digital versatile disc"

**FIGURE  15-1**    A Creative Labs DVD-ROM drive kit (Courtesy of Creative Labs)

(because it can hold programs and data as well as video and sound). But whatever you call it, DVD technology promises to supply up to 17GB of removable storage on your desktop PC. This chapter covers the background and workings of a DVD package, shows you the steps for DVD installation, and offers a series of basic troubleshooting solutions.

# The Potential of DVD

The argument for DVD is a compelling one because having gigabytes of removable storage to work with opens up some exciting possibilities for entertainment and software development. As DVD continues to work its way into the marketplace, you will probably notice two distinct designations: DVD-Video and DVD-ROM. *DVD-Video* is the approach used to store movies on the disc (analogous to the way audio is placed on CDs). Eventually, DVD-Video is expected to replace videotape players in home entertainment systems. This trend will probably accelerate as DVD-RAM drives (rewritable DVDs) become common in the market. *DVD-ROM* refers to computer-based software and data recorded on the disc. Where audio CDs can be played on CD-ROM drives, DVD-Video discs will be playable on DVD-ROM drives in your PC. Understandably, there are a lot of players looking to make the most of what DVD has to offer:

■ Hollywood has been a major factor in the development of DVD-Video—placing full-length movies, sound tracks, special scenes ("director's cuts"), and even multilingual subtitling on a single disc. Since all DVD discs are read by laser, there is no physical contact between the disc and its player. The result is that the disc won't wear out like VHS videotapes.

■ Business presentations, education, and professional training will also benefit from DVD technology. Complex animations, charts, and interactive applets can be integrated with real-time video. This offers a truly immersive training experience that CD-ROM technology has only scratched the surface of.

■ Applications for archiving are limitless. Mapping programs, telephone directories, and encyclopedias—any software that now spans several CDs can be concentrated on one DVD disc and dramatically expanded to offer unprecedented detail.

■ Any data-intensive computer software (especially 3D and other interactive games) will get a real boost from the sheer storage volume offered by DVD-ROM technology.

# Specifications and Standards

The next step in exploring DVD is to understand the various specifications "on the box" and to become familiar with the specifications that make DVD work and with what a DVD will support. You don't need a lot of technical details, but you should recognize the most important points that you'll probably run across while reading documentation.

## ACCESS TIME

The *access time* is the time required for the drive to locate the required information on a disc, so smaller access times can benefit the drive's performance. Optical drives like CD and DVD drives are relatively slow and can demand up to several hundred milliseconds (mS) to access information. For example, the older Toshiba DVD drive bundled with Diamond Multimedia's Maximum DVD Kit quotes a DVD access time of only 200 mS (compared to about 100 mS for CDs). However, DVD drives have become considerably faster over the last few years, and today's DVD drives are easily on par with CD-ROM access times. For example, the recent Creative Labs Ovation 16x DVD drive lists an access time of only 120 mS.

## DATA TRANSFER RATES AND INTERFACE DATA RATES

Once data has been accessed, it must be transferred off of the disc to the system. The data transfer rate measures how fast data can be read from the disc. There are two typical means of measuring the data rate. First is the speed at which data is read into the drive's onboard buffer (the *sequential* or sustained data transfer rate). Second is the speed at which data is transferred across the interface to the drive controller (the *buffered* or burst data transfer rate, sometimes called the interface rate). You may see both rates quoted on the drive's spec sheet. For example, the MDI 16x DVD-ROM lists a sustained data transfer rate of 22.1 MB/s. The drive also lists an interface rate of 33.3 MB/s (using Ultra-DMA Mode 2) and 16.6 MB/s (at MultiWord-DMA Mode 2). By comparison, the older Creative Labs Encore 12x DVD drive offers a buffered data transfer rate of up to 16.2 MB/s (using PIO Mode 4). The main issue to remember here is that the interface rate is usually (but not always) higher than the sustained data transfer rate. It's interesting to note that the sustained data transfer rates for DVD-RAM drives are considerably lower—around 2.7 MB/s.

Interface data rates are also important for system compatibility. In order to achieve the best performance from a drive, the ATAPI IDE interface of the host system must be equal to (or better than) the drive's interface. For example, a DVD-ROM drive with a UDMA/33 interface (like the MDI drive mentioned above) would work fine on a PC with a UDMA/66/100/133 interface. It would also work on an older EIDE interface (PIO Mode 4), but the slower interface capacity will restrict the drive's maximum data rate; in some cases, this may interfere with DVD video playback.

 Some DVD-ROM drives use the SCSI interface rather than an ATAPI IDE interface.

## ASPECT RATIOS

*Aspect ratio* refers to the width-to-height ratio of a television image. Traditional television sets have always conformed to the 4:3 ratio (roughly square in appearance). Wide-screen displays with a 16:9 or 20:9 ratio (similar to theater screens) appear more rectangular. DVD technology brings more versatility to on-screen viewing by incorporating four different display capabilities. Video can be stored on a DVD disc in a standard TV 4:3 format or 16:9 wide screen. DVD players can output video in four different ways:

- Full frame 4:3 video (for 4:3 display)
- Letterbox 16:9 video (for 4:3 display)

- Pan and scan 16:9 video (for 4:3 display)
- Wide screen 16:9 video (for 16:9 display)

### Full Frame

Full frame video is generally normal television footage converted for storage on DVD disc. This would include most television shows on the market today and movies that have been converted for television viewing.

### Letterbox

When showing a movie in letterbox mode, the player adds black bars to the top and bottom of the image. The image is then filtered so that the remaining area of the screen is filled in—allowing the viewer to see the movie in the same aspect as it appeared in the theater. With NTSC titles, this results in an image consisting of 360 lines of resolution. The image still contains a third more viewable lines than VHS tape, which consists of 242 viewable lines.

### Pan and Scan

Pan and scan can either be automatic or manual sideways-panning in a movie. Automatic pan and scan will change the camera view based upon a prerecorded selection made by the producer of the DVD disc. Manual pan and scan allows viewers to choose between different camera viewpoints at their leisure. As with other features (such as language selection), the publisher of the disc must incorporate the feature for it to be available to the viewer.

Zooming (often confused with pan and scan) is a feature where the hardware will store a portion of the screen in memory and then allow a user to dynamically enlarge that portion of the screen. Usually, the zoomed image will be enhanced so that it does not appear grainy when enlarged. Zooming is *not* a feature supported by the DVD standard.

### Wide Screen

The wide-screen mode is often compared to letterbox mode when viewed on a computer monitor or television, but it's not the same thing. TVs and monitors are designed to a standard 4:3 ratio, and the displayed image will be put into a letterbox when displayed on the screen. Look carefully at the top and bottom of a wide-screen image. There will be a few extra black lines added. The black lines were added when the movie was mastered to DVD because movie film does not exactly match the 16:9 screen ration of wide screen. (Movies are slightly wider.)

Unlike letterbox images, wide-screen movies do not sacrifice vertical resolution to fill the display area. On a high-resolution computer monitor, it would be easy to see the crispness of the image compared with a letterboxed image. If the player did not letterbox the image (and the image were allowed to fill the whole screen), the characters in the movie would seem stretched to appear very tall and skinny. As wide-screen digital television becomes more available, wide-screen movies will be able to play back to their full height and width without the letterbox.

## BOOKS AND STANDARDS

As you saw in Chapter 8, CD technology is defined by a set of accepted standards. We have come to know these as *books*. Since each CD book was bound in a different color jacket, each standard is dubbed by color. For example, the standard that defines CD audio is called Red Book. Similarly, DVD technology is defined by a set of books (denoted A through E) such as those outlined in Table 15-1.

**TABLE 15-1    SUMMARY OF CONTEMPORARY DVD STANDARDS**

### DVD SPECIFICATIONS FOR READ-ONLY DISC

| | |
|---|---|
| DVD-ROM (Book A) | This read-only standard uses ISO9660 and UDF file support. It includes both physical specifications and file system specifications.<br>Part 1: Physical Specifications Ver. 1.0<br>Part 2: System Specifications Ver. 1.0 |
| DVD-Video (Book B) | This read-only standard builds on Parts 1 and 2 of DVD-ROM and adds MPEG-2 video support along with audio compression.<br>Part 3: Video Specifications Ver. 1.1<br>Jacket Picture Format Ver. 1.0<br>IEC958 (non-PCM encoded audio bitstreams) Ver. 1.0 |
| DVD-Audio (Book C) | This read-only standard builds on books A and B to support high-quality audio on DVD disc.<br>Part 4: Audio Specifications Ver. 1.2<br>Packed PCM: MLP Reference Information Ver. 1.0 |

### DVD SPECIFICATIONS FOR RECORDABLE DISC

| | |
|---|---|
| DVD-R (Book D) | This read-only standard is the foundation for "write once" DVD disc technology, though it is Version 2.0 of the following entries that allows for practical DVD writing.<br>Part 1: Physical Specifications Ver. 1.0<br>Part 2: File System Specifications Ver. 1.0 |
| DVD-R for General Use (Book D) | This standard is used with DVD-R drives as would appear in host PC systems for file archiving.<br>Part 1: Physical Specifications Ver. 2.0<br>Part 2: File System Specifications Ver. 2.0 |
| DVD-R for Authoring Use (Book D) | This standard is generally used for media creation such as DVD-Video and other multimedia.<br>Part 1: Physical Specifications Ver. 2.0<br>Part 2: File System Specifications Ver. 2.0 |

### DVD SPECIFICATIONS FOR REWRITABLE DISC

| | |
|---|---|
| 2.6GB DVD-RAM (Book E) | The following standards all support rewritable 2.6/4.7GB DVD discs for PC users.<br>Part 1: Physical Specifications Ver. 1.0<br>Part 2: File System Specifications Ver. 1.1 |
| 4.7GB DVD-RAM (Book E) | Part 1: Physical Specifications Ver. 2.1<br>Part 2: File System Specifications Ver. 2.0 |

### DVD SPECIFICATIONS FOR RE-RECORDABLE DISC

| | |
|---|---|
| DVD-RW (Book E) | Part 1: Physical Specifications Ver. 1.1<br>Part 2: File System Specifications Ver. 1.0 |

### DVD SPECIFICATIONS FOR DVD-RAM/DVD-RW/DVD-R FOR GENERAL DISCS

| | |
|---|---|
| DVD Video Recording (Book E) | Part 3: Video Recording Ver. 1.1 |
| DVD Stream Recording (Book E) | Part 5: Stream Recording Ver. 1.0 |

## DVD Disc Sizes

DVD technology allows for much higher capacities than CDs, and a single surface of a DVD can hold up to 4.7GB of data. In addition, DVD supports up to four data layers (two sides, each with two data layers), for a maximum capacity of 17.1GB. However, not all DVDs are made the same way. You should be familiar with the important read-only and rewritable DVD disc layouts as listed in Table 15-2.

 Any double-sided DVD disc must be removed and turned over in order to play the other side. This will interrupt the disc playback.

**DVD-5 (4.7GB) Single Sided/Single Layer**    DVD-5 is a single-sided disc with just one data layer, which allows a capacity of 4.7GB (about 5GB, thus the term "DVD-5"). This is the most common and inexpensive type of DVD disc available. Only one side of the disc contains data, and the other side is blank, but the two substrates are bonded together to form a disc roughly 1.2mm thick. The blank side of the disc can be printed on with any conventional method (such as silk screening), or the blank side can be molded and metalized for a 3D effect.

**DVD-9 (8.5GB) Single Sided/Dual Layer**    DVD-9 is a single-sided disc with two data layers on the same side. This gives the disc a capacity of about 8.5GB, and the disc doesn't need to be flipped over to read a second side. However, the 8.5GB capacity is slightly less than twice the single layer version, making it easier for the second layer to be read (pits on both layers are about 10 percent longer than on a DVD-5 or DVD-10 disc). Each layer is molded onto one substrate, and the two substrates are joined with an optically transparent bonding layer. The blank side of the disc can be printed on with any conventional method (such as silk screening).

**DVD-10 (9.4GB) Double Sided/Single Layer**    The DVD-10 disc provides a single data layer on both sides of the disc. Since a single data layer can hold up to 4.7GB, two data layers offer up to 9.4GB. This means you'll need to flip the disc in order to read both sides (though some DVD players offer a dual-laser configuration that can read both sides without flipping the disc). While DVD-10 discs offer great storage capacity, labeling is a serious problem because there's data on both sides of the disc. The only practical place to label the disc is in the hub area.

**DVD-18 (17.1GB) Double Sided/Dual Layer**    DVD-18 discs supply two data layers on both sides of the disc, allowing for a total data capacity of up to 17.1GB. This can support many hours of high-quality video, or a wealth of data (for example, telephone directories or multimedia encyclopedias). These are the most expensive and complex discs to manufacture because of the additional stamping machinery required. Thus, there are few DVD-18 discs available today.

**TABLE 15-2    COMPARISON OF DVD DISC SIZES/LAYOUTS**

| NAME | CAPACITY (GB) | SIDES | LAYERS | NOTES |
|---|---|---|---|---|
| DVD-5 | 4.7GB | 1 | 1 | A typical read-only one-sided disc |
| DVD-9 | 8.5GB | 1 | 2 | A read-only one-sided two-layered disc |
| DVD-10 | 9.4GB | 2 | 1 | A read-only two-sided single-layered disc |
| DVD-18 | 17.1GB | 2 | 2 | A two-sided two-layered disc |
| DVD-R | 4.7/9.4GB | 1/2 | 1 | A one- or two-sided recordable DVD disc |
| DVD-RAM | 2.6/5.2GB | 1/2 | 1 | A one- or two-sided rewritable DVD disc |
| DVD-RW | 4.7GB | 1/2 | 1 | A one- or two-sided re-recordable DVD disc |

# DATA FORMATS

All DVD discs must use a data format that describes how data is laid out. Data formats are critical because they outline data structures on the disc such as volumes, files, blocks, sectors, CRCs, paths, records, file allocation tables, partitions, character sets, time stamps, as well as methods for reading and writing. The early format used by most books was called the *UDF Bridge*. The UDF Bridge is a combination of the UDF (Universal Data Format) created by OSTA (Optical Storage Technology Association) and the established ISO-9660 format used for CDs. You may see the UDF referred to as standard ISO/IEC 13346. The UDF is a very flexible format that has been adapted to CD-RW and DVD, and has been made backward compatible to existing ISO-9660 operating system software (such as Windows 98/Me/XP). With the release of Windows 98 and later operating systems, the UDF Bridge has been abandoned in favor of full UDF support. Today, UDF is employed for DVD-ROM, DVD-R, and DVD-RW discs.

## Audio and Video Standards

Even with the huge data capacities offered by DVD, an entire movie's worth of real-time audio and video would never fit on a DVD without some form of compression. Both audio and video must be extensively compressed, and MPEG (Moving Pictures Experts Group) compression has been the scheme of choice. Video compression uses fixed data rate MPEG-1 (ISO/IEC 1117-2) at 30 frames per second with resolutions of 352 × 240, or variable data rate MPEG-2 (ISO/IEC 13818-2) at 60 frames per second with resolutions of 720 × 480. Audio compression uses MPEG-1 (ISO/IEC 1117-3) stereo, MPEG-2 (ISO/IEC 13818-3) 5.1 and 7.1 surround sound, or Dolby AC-3 5.1 surround and stereo. MPEG-2 and AC-3 audio compression allow 48,000 samples per second, where MPEG-1 allows only 44,100 samples per second. MPEG-2 compression is typically regarded as the preferred scheme for DVD.

The audio designations "5.1" and "7.1" indicate five (or seven) signal channels, plus one subwoofer channel.

## CD Compatibility

One of the most important aspects of any technology is backward compatibility—how well the new device will support your existing media. The same issue is true for DVD drives. Since DVD technology is designed as an improvement over existing CD-ROMs, the DVD was designed to replace the CD-ROM rather than coexist with it. Ideally, you'd remove your CD-ROM and replace it with a DVD-ROM drive. This means the DVD must be compatible with as many existing CD-ROM standards as possible. Older DVD-ROM drives supported only a limited number of formats such as CD-Audio, CD-ROM, CD-I, CD Extra, CD-ROM/XA, and Video CD formats. Multisession (such as Photo CD) and CD-R discs were a bit more problematic. Today's drives such as the Creative Labs Ovation 16x support a full suite of disc formats including CD-Audio, CD-I, CD Extra, CD-ROM, CD-ROM/XA, Photo CD, CD-R, CD-RW, Video CD, DVD-Video, and even DAE (digital audio extraction).

If you discover that an older DVD drive refuses to support Photo CD and CD-R discs, it may be necessary to upgrade the drive's firmware (or the entire drive mechanism) in order to handle more recent formats.

# Content Protection

One of the problems with electronic media is that it's easy to transfer and manipulate. Copyright laws prohibit the unauthorized use of electronic media, but with the ease of electronic data transfers, companies are constantly devising new ways to protect and control the distribution of their intellectual property. There are several approaches in place to manage content protection.

## REGION CODE CONTROL

Motion picture studios want to control the home release of movies in different countries because theater releases are not simultaneous. Therefore, they have required that the DVD standard include codes that can be used to prevent playback of certain discs in certain geographical regions. Each player is given a code for the region in which it's sold. The player will refuse to play discs that are not allowed in that region. This means that discs bought in one country may not play on players bought in another country. Table 15-3 lists the code numbers and the regions each number covers. Keep in mind that region codes are entirely optional, and discs without codes will play on any player in any country.

More recent DVD drives are actually sold *without* a region code assigned. The code is assigned when a disc is inserted and can typically be changed up to four or five times before being fixed by the drive's firmware.

### Region Codes and Windows

Under Windows 98/Me/XP, the initial default DVD region is chosen during setup when you select a country in the Establishing Your Location dialog. If you choose None for a country location, the default region selection is based on the country code and time zone. The first time a DVD movie is placed in the drive, Windows 98/Me/XP compares the disc's region with the region selected during setup. If the DVD disc and setup region entries are different, the Windows default is changed to match the DVD movie.

Once the selected region has been used to watch a movie, you can change it up to four more times (for a total of five possible settings). If the disc is from a region other than the default, a dialog appears to tell you that the disc is from a different region. That dialog then displays the region for the current movie disc and the current player region—along with a list of new player regions and countries you can select (if possible). If you then select a new region, a warning appears stating the number of region changes remaining before the change is written permanently. The DVD drive itself will enforce the changes. Each time the region is

| TABLE 15-3 | STANDARD DVD REGION CODES |
|---|---|
| **CODE** | **REGION** |
| 0 | Region-free/All regions |
| 1 | Canada, United States, and U.S. territories |
| 2 | Japan, Europe, South Africa, Middle East (including Egypt) |
| 3 | Southeast Asia, East Asia (including Hong Kong) |
| 4 | Australia, New Zealand, Pacific Islands, Central America, South America, Caribbean |
| 5 | Former Soviet Union, Indian Subcontinent, Africa (also North Korea, Mongolia) |
| 6 | China |

changed, the new region is written to the drive's firmware. When the region change limit is reached, the DVD firmware locks out further attempts until the drive unit is replaced or reset by the manufacturer.

## MACROVISION

Macrovision (for example, Macrovision 7) is a proprietary piracy protection scheme that utilizes the signal in the nondisplayed region of a video signal to prevent copying. Macrovision varies the signal controlling the automatic gain control (AGC) of a recording deck, thereby washing out and darkening the recording signal of a tape or DVD disc being recorded. Macrovision does not protect RGB or YUV outputs. (New methods are required and are currently being investigated.) To use this protection, Macrovision must license the content owner, and the authoring studio must enable protection in their mastering equipment.

## COPY GENERATION MANAGEMENT SYSTEM (CGMS)

DVD-Video discs may contain information that can be used to prevent copying of the disc on equipment (such as a VCR) if the VCR is equipped with a *Copy Generation Management System* (CGMS). Several video recorder manufacturers have adopted CGMS, which works by embedding a signal in the video image in an area of the screen not normally seen by viewers. CGMS does not work unless both the player and recorder allow the signal to be present during playback.

## CONTENT SCRAMBLING SYSTEM (CSS)

To protect its movie titles from being copied in perfect digital fidelity, the motion picture industry endorses a key-based data encryption system called *Content Scrambling System* (CSS). Operation involves authentication of the device, the exchange of keys, and decryption of the DVD content. Data other than audio/video (such as bonus software) is not encrypted. Some PC-DVD solutions include hardware decryption integrated within the MPEG-2 decoder board. This approach helps to ensure that only approved combinations of hardware and software are used. Keys should be unique for every disc title, and are encrypted by the CSS Licensing Authority. Security is obviously critical, so the keys used (plus the encryption algorithms that produce them) must be kept secret. Only those companies involved in designing hardware and software for CSS encoding/decoding need information on the algorithms and systems used. CSS II (a variant of CSS) is being developed for DVD-Audio discs.

## DIGITAL VIDEO EXPRESS (DIVX)

Now an obsolete scheme of copy protection and media distribution, Digital Video Express (Divx) was a proprietary encoding scheme principally sponsored by consumer electronics retailer Circuit City and the law firm of Ziffren, Brittenham, Branca, and Fischer. This scheme required users to have a Divx player for playback and a dial-up connection. Divx players were more expensive than DVD players (costing nearly $100 more than a standard DVD player) and did not reach the market until February 1998.

A Divx DVD disc—suggested retail price, $4.99—would play back for a 48-hour period starting when the disc was inserted in the drive. Once the 48 hours passed, the player would no longer play the disc. Not only would the disc be unplayable, the player automatically registered the disc online when it was inserted in the player. Disconnecting the Divx player from the phone line rendered the player unusable until it was reconnected to the Divx online service. The disc also could not be played in any other player unless the user chose to connect and buy more time (a.k.a. "pay for view"), or the user paid to completely unlock the disc.

Regular DVD players cannot access a Divx disc because the access coding method directs playback first to an embedded instruction that is not recognized by normal DVD players. The normal DVD player will display an error indicating that there are no playable files on the disc.

The Divx scheme has been abandoned today because of continuing problems involving Divx disc and player compatibility, as well as immense pressure from inexpensive DVD players and poor overall industry support.

# DVD Media

At its core, DVD technology is identical to classical CD-ROMs. Data is recorded in a spiral pattern as a series of pits and lands pressed into a plastic substrate. The actual size and dimensions of a DVD are identical to our current compact discs. However, there are some key differences that give DVD its advantages. First, data is highly concentrated on the disc. Where classical CDs use spiral tracks that are 1.6µm apart, DVD tracks are only 0.74µm apart. A typical pit on a classic CD is 0.83µm, but DVD pits are just 0.4µm. Table 15-4 compares the specifications for DVD and CD media. In short, the data on a DVD is much denser than on a regular CD. Figure 15-2 illustrates the differences between DVDs and CDs. To detect these smaller geometries, the laser used in a DVD operates at a much shorter wavelength (a short-wavelength red laser).

Second, DVD can employ multiple layers of pits and lands (each in their own reflective layer), so one physical disc can hold several layers' worth of data. The DVD drive's laser focus control can select which layer to read. Finally, a regular CD only uses one side of the disc, but both sides of the DVD can be used. Combined with this multilayer technique, the DVD can theoretically supply up to four layers of data to a DVD drive (Figure 15-3). In actual practice, DVD-ROM discs will likely only use one side of the disc—at least for a while. What all this means is that a DVD disc can offer up to 8.5GB of storage for a single-sided double-layer disc, or up to 17GB of storage for a double-sided double-layer disc. See the section "DVD Disc Sizes" earlier.

## CARING FOR A DVD DISC

As with CDs, a DVD disc is a remarkably reliable long-term storage media. (Conservative estimates of the life of a DVD disc are about 100 years.) However, the longevity of an optical disc is affected by its storage and handling. A faulty DVD can cause file and data errors that you might otherwise interpret as a defect in

| TABLE 15-4 | COMPARISON OF DVD AND CD MEDIA SPECIFICATIONS | |
|---|---|---|
| **SPECIFICATION** | **DVD** | **CD-ROM** |
| Diameter (mm) | 120 | 120 |
| Disc thickness (mm) | 1.2 | 1.2 |
| Substrate thickness (mm) | 0.6 | 1.2 |
| Track pitch (µm) | 0.74 | 1.6 |
| Minimum pit size (µm) | 0.4 | 0.83 |
| Wavelength (nm) | 635/650 | 780 |
| Single-layer capacity (GB) | 4.7 | 0.65 |

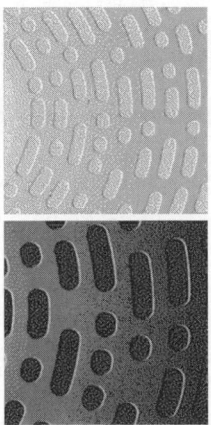

**FIGURE 15-2** Comparison of DVD and CD data density

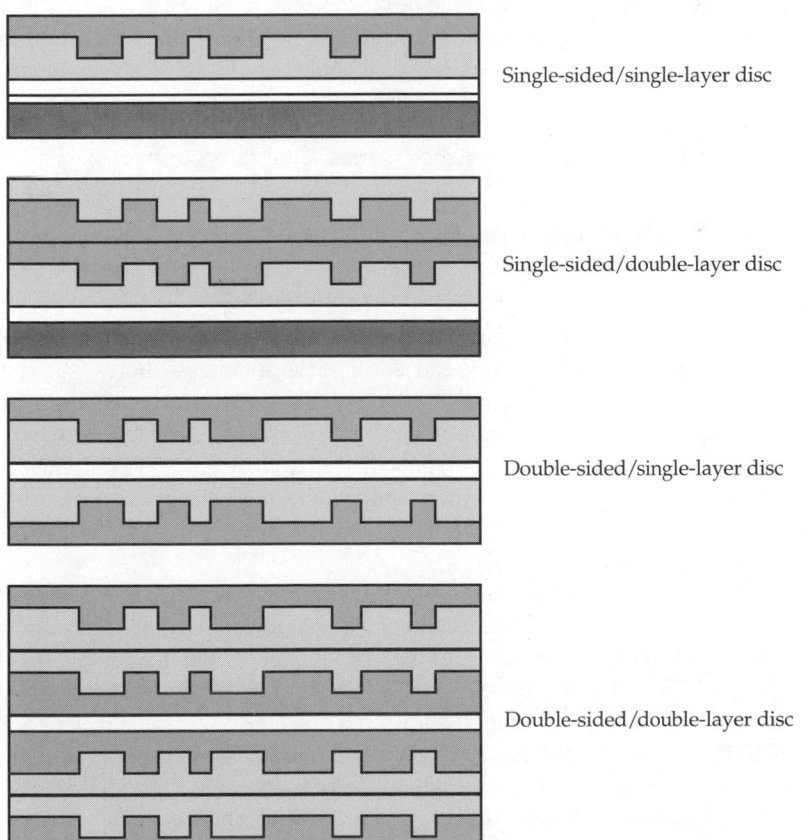

Single-sided/single-layer disc

Single-sided/double-layer disc

Double-sided/single-layer disc

Double-sided/double-layer disc

**FIGURE 15-3** Layers and sides in DVD discs

the drive itself, or cause artifacts and problems with DVD audio/video playback. You can get the most life out of your optical disc by obeying the following rules:

- *Don't bend the disc.* Polycarbonate is a forgiving material, but you risk cracking or snapping (and thus ruining) the disc.

- *Don't heat the disc.* Remember, the disc is plastic. Leaving it by a heater or on the dashboard of your car will cause melting.

- *Don't scratch the disc.* Laser wavelengths have a tendency to "look past" minor scratches, but a major scratch can cause problems. Be especially careful of circular scratches (ones that follow the spiral track). A circular scratch can easily wipe out entire segments of data that would be unrecoverable. This issue is even more important with double-sided DVDs where data is available on both sides of the disc. Like ordinary CDs, DVD discs can be protected from scratches by storing them in plastic "jewel" cases.

- *Don't use chemicals on the disc.* Chemicals containing solvents such as ammonia, benzene, acetone, carbon tetrachloride, or chlorinated cleaning solvents can easily damage the plastic surface.

Eventually, a buildup of excessive dust or fingerprints can interfere with the laser beam enough to cause disc errors. When this happens, the disc can be cleaned easily using a dry, soft, lint-free cloth. Hold the disc by its edges and wipe radially (from hub to edge). Do not wipe in a circular motion. For stubborn stains, moisten the cloth in a bit of fresh isopropyl alcohol. *Do not use water or ammonia.* Place the cleaned disc in a caddy or jewel case for transport and storage.

Contrary to popular belief, DVD discs are **not** more sensitive to scratches or dust than ordinary CDs.

# The DVD Drive and Decoder

A DVD drive looks almost identical to a CD-ROM drive in size, shape, and layout. In fact, if not for the "DVD" logo on the tray, you'll probably mistake a DVD-ROM drive for a CD-ROM, CD-R, or CD-RW drive. The front of a DVD drive (Figure 15-4) carries all of the standard features that you'd find on any CD-ROM. A motorized disc tray loads and unloads the disc. You can close or open the tray by toggling the Load/unload (or Eject) button. Most current DVD-ROM drives won't eject a disc that is "locked" by a software application (such as a running movie). You will need to close your DVD application before ejecting the locked disc. The drive activity LED (or Busy indicator) lights whenever data is being read from the drive. Since the DVD drive also supports CD audio, you can connect headphones to the headphone jack and adjust volume right from the front panel.

Much of the rear of a DVD-ROM will also probably look familiar (Figure 15-5). Power is connected through a 4-pin Molex connector, so you can use any suitable power connector from your power supply. The signal connector, which is typically either EIDE/UDMA (40-pin) or SCSI (50- or 68-pin), connects the drive directly to your existing drive adapter. Unlike early CD-ROM drives, DVD-ROM drives do not use proprietary drive controllers. A series of small jumpers allows you to set the drive's identity. For SCSI-type drives, you can set the SCSI ID (usually ID2 through ID6). For EIDE or UDMA-type drives, you will set the drive as either a primary (master) or secondary (slave) drive. If you're running an EIDE/UDMA DVD-ROM along with a hard drive, the hard drive would typically be the master device, and the DVD-ROM drive would be the slave device. If you're running the DVD-ROM drive alone, set it as the master device on the secondary drive controller channel. Finally, there are two audio output connectors: a 4-pin CD audio connector that attaches

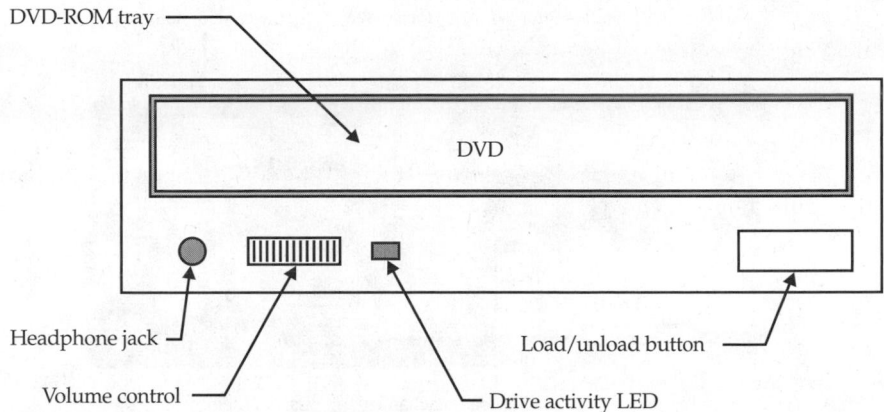

**FIGURE 15-4**    Front view of a typical DVD-ROM drive

to a sound board, and a 2-pin digital audio connector that supplies sound to a *digital audio tape* (DAT) or other digital recording system (though this output is rarely used).

Since DVD drives almost always use EIDE/UDMA interfaces rather than older IDE interfaces, they may be used along with fast EIDE/UDMA hard drives on the same controller channel with no (or negligible) degradation in hard drive performance.

# INSIDE THE DRIVE

Things get a little more interesting when you look inside a DVD-ROM drive (such as Figure 15-6). Looking in from the top of the drive, you'll see the major subassemblies needed to operate the drive. That black circular wheel near the tray is the *spindle motor* that turns the disc. You can also see the laser assembly and the *laser sled* that the laser rides back and forth on. A small motor drives a screw that runs the sled.

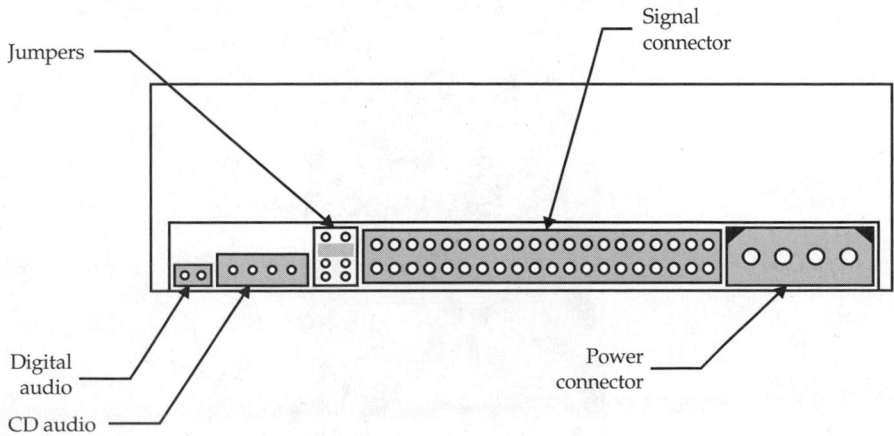

**FIGURE 15-5**    Rear view of a typical DVD-ROM drive

Spindle motor      Laser sled     Laser sled motor

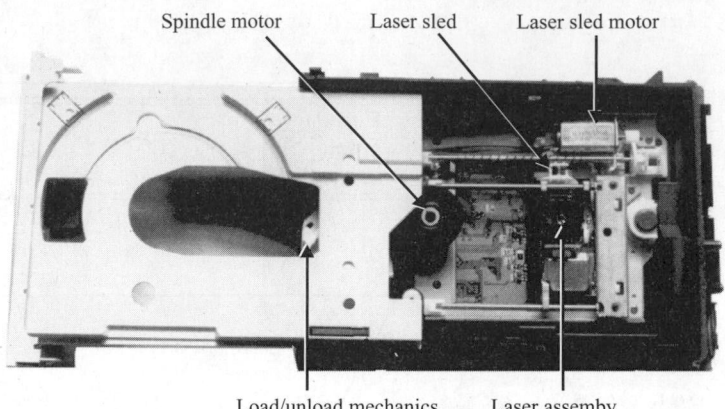

Load/unload mechanics     Laser assemby

**FIGURE  15-6**    Looking into the top of a typical DVD-ROM drive

The load/unload mechanics run the disc tray in and out (though the mechanical parts are obscured below the plastic tray). The main electronics deck is mounted on the underside of the drive (as in Figure 15-7). This is a single printed circuit board that contains all of the circuitry needed to run the drive interface, load/unload motor, audio amplifiers, spindle motor, laser, and laser sled.

## REGION CODE CONTROL

One item of particular interest in Figure 15-7 is the removable chip. This chip contains firmware for the drive, as well as the unit's region codes. As you saw earlier in the chapter, motion picture studios want to

Drive firmware and
region control chip

**FIGURE  15-7**    Looking at the bottom of a typical DVD-ROM drive

control the home release of movies in different countries because theater releases are not simultaneous. Therefore, they have required that the DVD standard include codes that can be used to prevent playback of certain discs in particular geographical regions. Each player is given a code for the region in which it's sold (or can be assigned a code based on the first few discs that are played in it). You can see an example of this region control on the DVD Region tab in Figure 15-8. Once a region code is fixed, the drive will refuse to play discs that are not allowed in that region. This means that discs bought in one country may not play on players bought in another country. Table 15-3 earlier in the chapter lists the code numbers and the regions each number covers. Keep in mind that region codes are entirely optional, and discs without codes will play on any player in any country.

Firmware isn't always on a removable chip; it may also be located on a chip permanently soldered to the drive's electronics unit.

## THE MPEG-2 DECODER

Although a DVD disc can easily provide over 4GB of storage, that is still not nearly enough space to hold the audio and video data required for an average-length Hollywood movie. Movie data must be highly compressed before being recorded on the disc. (Compression typically follows the MPEG-2 standard.) This presents some unique problems for the PC during playback. The compressed movie audio and video data is passed along the SCSI or EIDE/UDMA cable to the drive controller. However, the overhead processing needed to decode the compressed sound and picture data can easily bog down all but the fastest systems. This can result in poor playback performance, such as broken audio and dropped video frames.

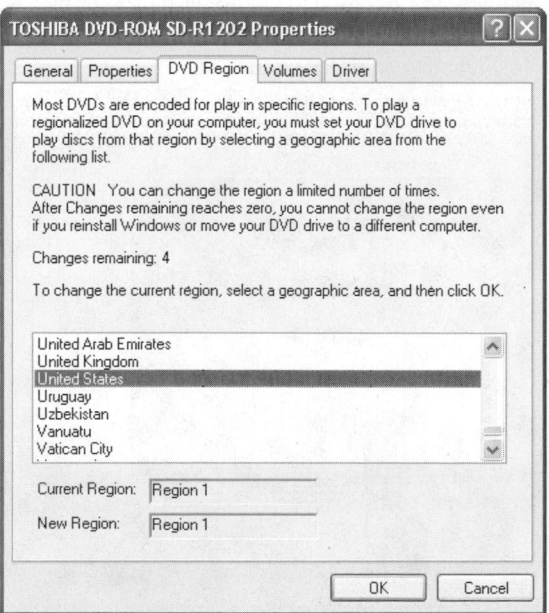

**FIGURE 15-8**    The DVD drive's Properties dialog box will show the current region and remaining region settings on the DVD Region tab.

To ensure smooth, real-time playback of the DVD movie, a hardware-based MPEG-2 decoder card (such as Sigma Designs' REALmagic Xcard in Figure 15-9) is normally added to an available PCI slot, and connected directly to the monitor. (Video output from the graphics accelerator is passed through the decoder card to the monitor.) The decoder card takes over the job of decompressing the MPEG-2 information—relieving a tremendous amount of work from the system processor. Decoded audio from the movie is also passed from the decoder card to the sound card using a CD audio connection.

There's a continuing debate over the need for separate MPEG-2 decoder cards on current PCs. In the early days of DVD, MPEG-2 decoders were a necessity because of the processing overhead imposed by MPEG-2. As PCs got faster, the later processors and system bus architectures were better able to handle the decoding process without the need for separate hardware. With faster (1 GHz+) systems, MPEG-2 decoders are generally not required. However, you may wish to include an MPEG-2 decoder when adding DVD to an older PC, or when the PC is used heavily (for example, with multiple background applications that may take precious time away from the decoding process). Keep in mind that many full-featured video adapters/graphics accelerators now include "DVD assistance," which incorporates MPEG-2 decoding right into the video card's core chipset. This means you can add hardware support for DVD simply by upgrading the video card, and eliminate the need for an additional card in the system. As a rule, you can skip the MPEG-2 decoder unless the system needs it.

## A BRIEF LOOK AT MPEG-2

When the original video source is recorded for DVD, MPEG-2 analyzes the video picture for redundant data. Over 95 percent of the digital data that represents a video signal is redundant and can be compressed without visibly harming the picture quality (also referred to as *loss-less compression*). By eliminating redundant data, MPEG-2 achieves excellent video quality at far lower bit rates.

MPEG-2 encoding for DVD is a two-stage process. The original signal is first evaluated for complexity. Then higher bit rates are assigned to complex pictures, and lower bit rates are assigned to simple pictures. This allows for an adaptive variable bit-rate process. The DVD-Video format uses compressed bit

**FIGURE  15-9**    The Xcard from Sigma Designs supports high-resolution DVD playback through the PC. (Courtesy of Sigma Designs)

rates with a range of up to 10Mbits/s. Although the average bit rate for digital video is often quoted as 3.5Mbits/s, the actual figure will vary according to movie length, picture complexity, and the number of audio channels required. With MPEG-2 compression, a single-layer, single-sided DVD disc has enough capacity to hold 2 hours and 13 minutes of video and audio on a 12cm disc. At the nominal average data rate of 3.5Mbits/s, this still leaves enough capacity for discrete 5.1 channel digital sound in three languages, plus subtitles in four additional languages.

## SOFTWARE DVD DECODERS

While a hardware decoder card is highly recommended, it is not always required. Decoding on current PCs can be accomplished using software applications. The advantage of software decoding is simplicity. DVD upgrades are easier since you don't need the hardware decoder card. However, considering the amount of processing power required for real-time MPEG-2 decoding, you will need a very fast Pentium III/4 platform in order to sustain an adequate DVD-Video frame rate. Slower PCs (or other processing overhead such as running background applications) may not be able to support software-only decoding. This may manifest itself as choppy video, lost frames, and/or distorted audio. Make certain that your PC meets the minimum system requirements (preferably the recommended system configuration) for DVD decoding software.

If your PC does not meet the minimum requirements for decoding software, you may wish to update your video card to a model that offers motion compensation, or other types of DVD playback assistance. For example, various ATI graphics chips (including the Rage 128, Rage PRO, and Rage LT PRO) contain DVD-processing hardware that can assist in decoding DVD without the need for a full hardware decoder card. Still, if you need to consider a video card upgrade, it is often more efficient to leave the video device in place and add a full hardware decoder card instead.

## NOTES ON DOLBY AC-3

Dolby AC-3 (also called Dolby Surround AC-3 or Dolby Digital) is another method of encoding DVD audio besides MPEG-2 audio. With five channels and a common subwoofer channel (known as "5.1"), you get the effects of 3D surround sound with right, left, center, left ear, right ear, and common subwoofer speakers. AC-3 runs at 384Kbits/s. In actual practice, DVD products sold in North America and Japan will include Dolby AC-3 sound on the accompanying MPEG-2 board, while DVD products sold in Europe will likely use the MPEG-2 audio standard.

## DECODER BOARD CONNECTIONS

There are several major connections on the MPEG-2 decoder board, as shown for the Creative Labs Dxr3 decoder in Figure 15-10: an analog input jack, an analog output jack, a digital output jack, a monitor connector, and a video input connector. The analog input (or audio input) is rarely (if ever) used in normal operations, but it may be handy for mixing-in an auxiliary audio signal to the decoder board. The analog output (or line output) signal provides the master audio signal that is fed to the line input of your existing sound board. The advantage of using a line input is that you don't need a volume control on the decoder board. Instead, you can set the line input volume through your sound board's mixer applet. When you play a DVD video, any audio will continue to play through your sound board and speakers. The digital output is intended to drive an external Dolby Digital device, so you will probably not be using the digital output in most basic PC setups.

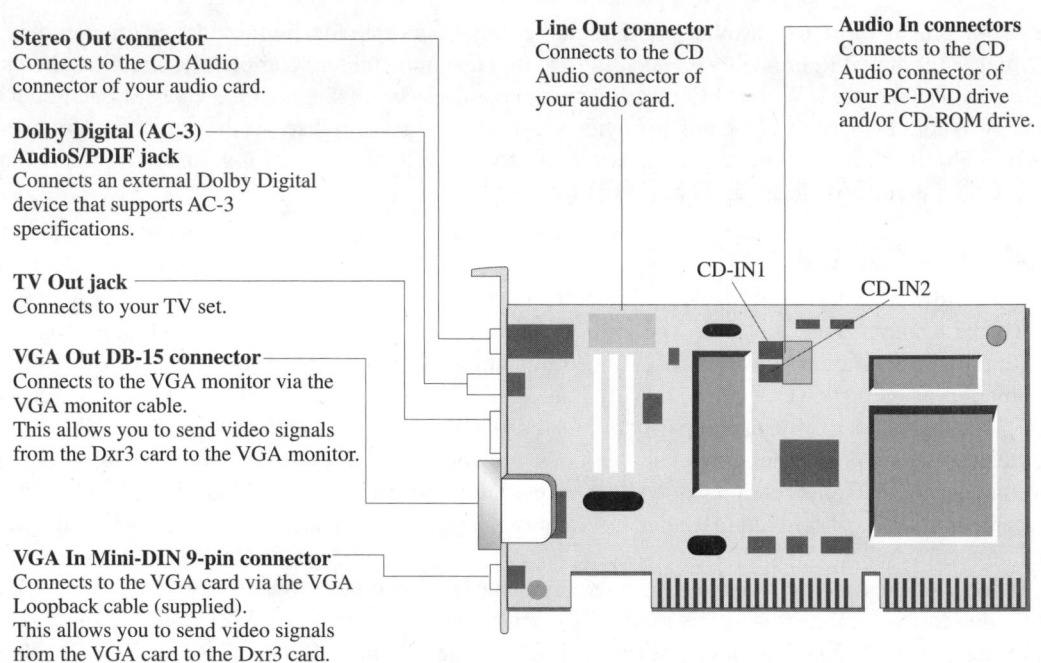

**Stereo Out connector**
Connects to the CD Audio
connector of your audio card.

**Dolby Digital (AC-3)
AudioS/PDIF jack**
Connects an external Dolby Digital
device that supports AC-3
specifications.

**TV Out jack**
Connects to your TV set.

**VGA Out DB-15 connector**
Connects to the VGA monitor via the
VGA monitor cable.
This allows you to send video signals
from the Dxr3 card to the VGA monitor.

**VGA In Mini-DIN 9-pin connector**
Connects to the VGA card via the VGA
Loopback cable (supplied).
This allows you to send video signals
from the VGA card to the Dxr3 card.

**Line Out connector**
Connects to the CD
Audio connector of
your audio card.

**Audio In connectors**
Connects to the CD
Audio connector of
your PC-DVD drive
and/or CD-ROM drive.

CD-IN1

CD-IN2

**FIGURE   15-10**    Decoder board connections for the Creative Labs Dxr3 (Courtesy of Creative Labs)

The MPEG-2 decoder board will now drive your VGA/SVGA monitor through the monitor connector. This is important because the decoded video stream is converted to RGB information and fed to the monitor directly. This avoids having to pass the video data across the PCI/AGP bus to your video card. The normal output from your video card is looped from your video board to the decoder card; so while the decoder board is idle, your normal video signal is just "passed through" the MPEG-2 board to the monitor.

# DVD Drive Installation
# and Replacement

DVD-ROM/RAM drives are generally easy devices to install or replace. Most are installed as master devices located on the secondary EIDE/UDMA drive controller channel, though many will coexist as slave devices alongside a hard drive or other drive device. In the early days of DVD drives, BIOS would not support the DVD drive or allow you to boot from the drive (as you might boot from a CD drive). However, advances in DVD drives now support the El Torito standard. This means the BIOS should initially recognize your DVD drive as an ordinary CD-ROM, and you should be able to boot from a CD in the DVD drive to restore a system or reinstall Windows. This is important if the DVD drive is the only CD-type drive in the PC. However, once the operating system starts, you'll need drivers to support the DVD drive (and MPEG-2 decoder if installed), along with a DVD player application. This part of the chapter covers the guidelines needed to install a basic internal ATAPI IDE-type DVD-ROM/RAM.

Before beginning the installation, be sure to set the Display mode to 640 × 480 × 16 (60 Hz refresh rate) or other default video mode as suggested by the DVD maker's installation instructions. Once the DVD drive is installed and running, you can readjust the video mode to an appropriate resolution, color depth, and vertical refresh rate.

## SELECT JUMPER CONFIGURATIONS

An IDE-type DVD-ROM/RAM drive may be installed as a master or slave device on any current hard drive controller channel. These master/slave settings are handled through one or two jumpers located on the rear of the drive (right next to the 40-pin signal cable connector). One of your first decisions when planning an installation should be to decide the drive's configuration:

■ If you're installing the DVD-ROM/RAM as the first drive on the secondary drive controller channel, it must be jumpered as the master device.

■ If you're installing the DVD-ROM/RAM drive alongside another drive (on either the primary or secondary drive controller channel), the DVD drive must be jumpered as the slave device.

Refer to the documentation that accompanies your particular DVD-ROM/RAM drive to determine the exact master/slave jumper settings. If you do not have the drive documentation handy, check the drive manufacturer's Web site for online information.

## ATTACH CABLES AND MOUNT THE DRIVE

Once the DVD drive is configured the way you want it, it's time to install the drive in your system. The following steps outline a general installation process:

1.  Turn off and unplug the PC, and then remove the outer cover to expose the computer's drive bays.

2.  Attach one end of the 40-pin drive interface cable to the drive controller connector on your motherboard (or drive controller card). Remember to align pin 1 on the cable (the side of the cable with the blue or red stripe) with pin 1 on the drive controller connector.

3.  Locate an available drive bay for the DVD drive. Remove the plastic housing covering the drive bay, and then slide the drive inside. Locate the four screw holes needed to mount the drive. In some cases, you may need to attach mounting rails to the drive so that the drive will be wide enough to fit in the drive bay. In virtually all cases, you should mount a tray-driven DVD-ROM/RAM drive horizontally (though rare caddy-loaded drives may be mounted vertically).

4.  Attach the 40-pin signal cable and the 4-pin power connector to the new drive, and then bolt the drive securely into place. Do not overtighten the screws since this may damage the drive. If you do not have an available 4-pin power connector, you may use an appropriate Y-adapter if necessary to "split" power from another drive (preferably the floppy drive).

5.  Attach the small 4-pin digital audio (or CD audio) signal cable from the DVD-ROM/RAM drive to the CD audio input connector on your sound card. This connection allows you to play music CDs directly from the DVD-ROM/RAM through your sound card. Verify that the CD audio cable is compatible with your sound card. (Otherwise you may need a specialized cable from the sound card's manufacturer.)

If you already have a CD-ROM drive in the system providing CD audio to the sound card, you may choose to use the DVD-ROM instead, or leave the CD-ROM's audio cable alone. If your sound card has a second CD audio connector, you may be able to wire the DVD-ROM's audio to your sound card too.

## INSTALLING THE DECODER CARD

This is an optional step and may be omitted if you're using a software-based MPEG-2 decoder or a video card with "DVD assist" features. Locate an open PCI card slot, and install the PnP MPEG-2 decoder card into the slot. In most cases, you simply need to disconnect the monitor from the video output, attach the monitor to the decoder card's monitor output port, and then use a short pass-through cable to connect the video output to the decoder card's video input connector. This ties in the decoder card with the video system.

If you'll be using a software decoder, you may not need to install a hardware decoder card, and this part of the installation may be omitted.

## CONFIGURING THE CMOS SETUP

Although the DVD-ROM/RAM drive does require driver support for playback, recent motherboard designs can identify the ATAPI IDE DVD drive in BIOS and allow the drive to boot the system or serve as a basic CD-ROM. You should configure your computer's BIOS to accept the drive if possible (through the CMOS Setup).

**1.** Turn the computer on. As your computer starts up, watch for a message that describes how to run the CMOS Setup (for example, "Press F1 for Setup"). Press the appropriate key to start the CMOS Setup program.

**2.** Select the "hard drive settings" menu, and choose the drive location occupied by the DVD-ROM drive (such as the "primary slave," "secondary slave," or "secondary master" depending on how you've physically jumpered and installed the drive).

**3.** Select "Automatic drive detection" if available. This option will automatically identify the new drive. If your BIOS does not provide automatic drive detection, select "none" or "not installed" for the DVD-ROM, and rely on drivers only.

**4.** Save the settings and exit the CMOS Setup program. Your computer will automatically reboot.

## REASSEMBLE THE COMPUTER

Double-check all of your signal and power cables to verify that they are secure, and then tuck the cables gently into the computer's chassis. Check that there are no loose tools, screws, or cables inside the chassis. Now reattach the computer's outer housing(s). You may choose to leave the outer housings off the system until you've confirmed that the DVD drive (and the rest of the system) is working properly.

## INSTALL THE SOFTWARE

To complete your DVD-ROM installation, you'll need to install the software drivers that accompanied the drive on floppy disk or CD. Windows 98/Me/XP systems will generally detect the presence of the new DVD-ROM/RAM (and hardware decoder if appropriate), and automatically prompt you for the installation CDs with protected-mode drivers. After you install the drivers and reboot the system, the DVD drive should be ready for use. Before you can play DVD movie discs, you'll also need to install the DVD player software (for example, the PowerDVD player in Figure 15-11) and other utilities from the drive's installation disc. If you're using the "DVD assist" features of your video card, you may also need to install the appropriate video codecs, or simply update the video drivers from the card's manufacturer.

Most DVD-ROM drives will not support real-mode (DOS) drivers, so they will only work under Windows 9x/Me/XP.

# UPGRADING DVD DRIVE FIRMWARE

You may be able to update the firmware used in your DVD-ROM/RAM drive. This may be necessary to correct bugs or fix drive compatibility problems with the system. The following steps offer a guideline that you can refer to when upgrading DVD-ROM/RAM firmware.

You should always refer to the Web page or README file that accompanies the new firmware download. Be sure to download the correct firmware version for your drive. Installing the wrong firmware can permanently disable the drive.

1.  Power-off your system completely.
2.  Locate the DVD drive, and place its "flash" jumper in the flash upgrade position. If there is no flash jumper, it may not be possible to upgrade the drive's firmware (but check the manufacturer's documentation for specific steps).
3.  Make sure the power cable and the signal cable (SCSI or IDE) are still connected.
4.  Power-on your system and boot clean to a command-line prompt.
5.  Make sure that the DVD-ROM/RAM appears in program mode. You'll need to refer to the documentation for your particular drive in order to identify the correct program mode.

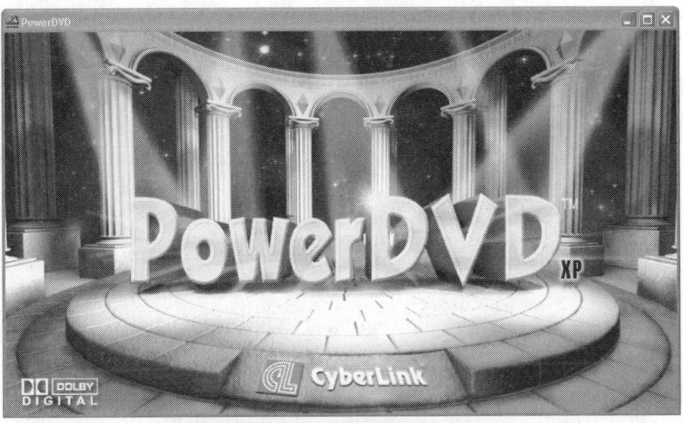

**FIGURE 15-11**  Tools like PowerDVD let you play DVD movies right on the PC using VCR-like controls.

6. When the system comes up, execute the new firmware program (such as **firm123a.bin**), which you may receive or download from the manufacturer, and use the new firmware (*.BIN) file.

7. When the EXE applications starts, specify the location of the BIN file.

8. Click the Update button to begin the flash process.

9. When the Update button becomes highlighted again, the flash process is complete.

10. Power-off the system and reset the DVD-ROM/RAM drive's flash jumper to its original position (if necessary).

11. Power-on the system normally and continue using the DVD drive.

# Troubleshooting DVD Drives

Even though a DVD-ROM/RAM package should install with an absolute minimum of muss and fuss, and run with all the reliability of a CD-ROM, there are times when things just don't go according to plan. Both software and hardware problems can interrupt your DVD-ROM/RAM system. This part of the chapter provides a series of guidelines and tips to resolve a wide range of problems and covers some of the most common troubleshooting issues.

## INITIAL SETUP AND TIPS

When installing or correcting problems on a DVD drive system, it may help to set the DVD system configuration to a default state using the criteria outlined next:

- **Minimum requirements** Virtually all current PCs should easily meet the minimum system requirements for DVD drives and MPEG-2 decoder hardware/software. Still, it's worth a brief check to ensure that there's adequate processor, RAM, drive, and OS version support.

- **Video configuration** Regardless of the amount of video RAM provided by your video adapter (or system RAM assigned to video memory), try setting the display to 640 × 480 using 16-bit color (the high-color mode). You might also try setting the monitor type to standard VGA.

- **DirectX installation** If you're using Windows 95 OSR2 (4.00.950 B) or earlier, or do not have any Windows 95 games installed, chances are that you don't have DirectX installed (or you're using a very old version). Though DirectX versions 2.0 and higher should support DVD, using the latest version may increase your system's video performance (since it also includes newer DirectDraw drivers for your video card). Check for the latest version of DirectX (for example, DirectX 8.0a or 8.1 for Windows XP) at www.microsoft.com/directx.

- **DVD drivers** Drivers are being updated regularly to provide better hardware compatibility, so you should check for the latest DVD drive and MPEG-2 decoder drivers and the latest release of DVD player software from your DVD maker. (See, for example, Axeda Systems, Inc. (formerly Quadrant International) at www.axeda.com.) Of course, driver and software updates from the DVD manufacturer may also improve performance and compatibility with other devices in the system.

- **Video drivers** Many video drivers are also updated regularly for better video performance and compatibility. Check the Web page for your video card vendor for updated video drivers. This may be especially important if you're using a video card with motion compensation or other DVD video decoding features instead of a full hardware decoder card.

■ **IDE controller compatibility**    There is also a lingering issue with the IDE controllers on some older motherboards (depending on which version of Windows you're using). If you have trouble with your IDE controllers, check the Intel Developer's Page for more details and fixes at developer.intel.com/ design/motherbd/ideinfup.htm. Late versions of Windows 95 and Windows 98/Me/XP should have **no** problems with IDE controller identification and setup.

# DVD SYMPTOMS

If the preceding tips don't help you to resolve the problem, you can check the following symptoms for specific issues and corrective action.

**SYMPTOM 15-1**    **You see a black playback window when the DVD starts**    When you try to start a DVD movie in your system, a black screen appears in the Windows Media Player window, or the DVD starts to play, and then stops. This type of problem is often caused by the authoring system that created the DVD disc, not by your drive or software. If the DVD disc doesn't include a lookup table that directs the DVD player to the location of video on the disc, an error in the DVD player results, and the video play is stopped. Other discs should play back just fine. If other discs play back properly, contact the disc maker for a suitable replacement. If other discs cause the same problem, try updating to Windows XP, or update the DVD drivers and codecs.

**SYMPTOM 15-2**    **Video performance is poor with PCMCIA DVD video adapters**  When you install a PC Card (PCMCIA) video adapter that's intended to play back DVDs on a laptop system, you find that the video is badly distorted. The PCMCIA device may also be marked in the Device Manager. This almost always occurs because of a driver problem. Chances are that the PCMCIA video device's driver isn't compatible with your version of Windows. The best way to resolve this issue is to upgrade the PCMCIA device's driver to the latest version that is certified to be compatible with your OS. Otherwise, you may need to remove the device, or replace it with another make/model with suitable drivers.

**SYMPTOM 15-3**    **The DVD drive isn't detected**    There are several possible reasons why a DVD drive may not be detected. Check the power connector attached to the drive, and make sure that the drive isn't being powered from a Y-splitter power cable. Check the signal cable next. Both SCSI and EIDE/UDMA signal cables must be attached securely to the drive. SCSI interfaces are complicated a bit by termination, so verify that any SCSI bus is properly terminated. Make sure that the drive is jumpered properly for its SCSI ID or EIDE/UDMA master or slave relationship. Finally, make sure that the DVD drivers are installed and running. Check the drivers under the Sound, Video, and Game Controllers (or CD-ROM) entry of your Device Manager.

**SYMPTOM 15-4**    **The DVD drive stops working when the PC returns from a power-saving mode**    In order for the system to remain stable after returning from a power-saving mode (such as hibernation), all of the hardware and firmware in the system must be compatible with the power conservation standards being used. If any of the system hardware or firmware isn't compatible, the system may become unstable after coming out of its power-saving state. For example, when you try to access the DVD drive after returning from hibernation, you may see an error message such as:

```
The request could not be performed because of an I/O device error
```

Chances are that either the firmware or the hardware is outdated or is experiencing some other underlying problem (such as a hardware conflict), or the system BIOS is outdated. Check for and correct any hardware conflicts. Check with the DVD drive maker for updated firmware. If that doesn't help, try updating the motherboard BIOS. In the meantime, you can prevent this problem by disabling the PC's power-saving mode. For example, use the following steps to temporarily disable the system's Hibernation mode under Windows XP. (You can restore power conservation when the problem is fixed.)

1. Click Start, and select Control Panel.
2. Click Performance and Maintenance, then click Power Options.
3. Select the Hibernation tab.
4. Click the Enable Hibernation check box to clear it (see Figure 15-12).
5. Click Apply, and then click OK.

**SYMPTOM 15-5**    **You see an error message that the drive is not fully compatible with the software**    You may also see this as a message that no DVD drive is found. This frequently occurs when installing a DVD drive in conjunction with Zip, Jaz, tape, or CD-ROM drives. The DVD drive will need to be the next available drive letter after any IDE or SCSI hard drives. Alphabetically, there should be no other drives (such as Zip, Jaz, tape, or CD-ROM drives) with drive letters *before* that of the DVD drive.

To change the drive letter assignment in your system, power-down and disconnect all the affected drives except the DVD drive, and then boot to Windows 9x/Me/XP Safe Mode and remove the drives (including the DVD drive) from Device Manager. Restart to normal mode, and the DVD drive will be

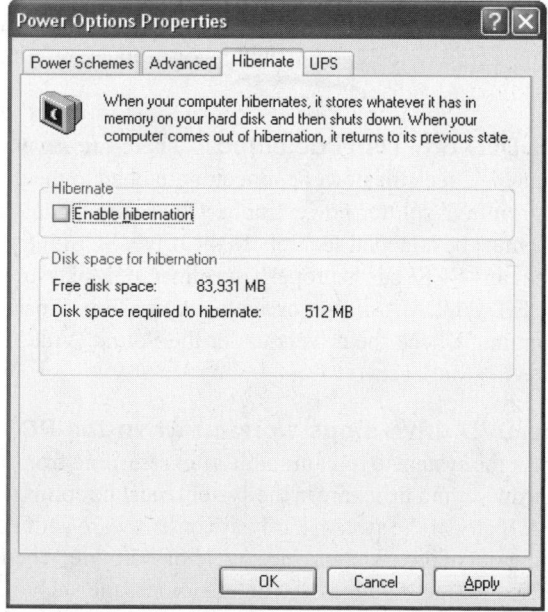

**FIGURE  15-12**    Clear the Enable Hibernation check box to prevent the PC from using that power-saving mode.

reassigned the lowest available drive letter. Next, power-down again and reconnect the other drives. Restart the system, and they will automatically be redetected and assigned drive letters higher than the DVD drive.

**SYMPTOM 15-6**    **The DVD movie stops when the PC returns from a screen saver**
For example, if a screen saver starts while a DVD movie is playing, you'll only hear audio. When you try to return from the screen saver (by moving the mouse, for example), the player may stop playing the DVD movie entirely. To recover from this problem, you may need to exit and restart the player applet (such as Windows Media Player). This is typically related to a problem with operating systems like Windows XP, and you may be able to fix the trouble by updating Windows from the Microsoft site. In the meantime, you should disable the screen saver through the Display Properties dialog box. In some cases, the movie player may have an option that will prevent a screen saver from running during DVD playback.

**SYMPTOM 15-7**    **The DVD drivers refuse to install**    This is almost always because Windows 9x/Me/XP is having a problem with one or more .INF files on your driver installation disc(s). Check with your DVD vendor to confirm whether you need to delete one or more entries in your OEM*xx*.INF file(s) (where *xx* is any suffix). For example, if you're using an older MKE DVD kit, you may also need to delete one or more entries from a MKEDVD.INF file. The INF files are typically contained in the C:\WINDOWS\INF\OTHER directory. Once you've corrected the appropriate INF file(s), you can remove and reinstall the latest DVD drivers. Use the following steps for Windows XP:

1. Click Start | Control Panel | Performance and Maintenance | System.
2. Select the Hardware tab and click Device Manager.
3. Expand the DVD/CD-ROM drives entry (see Figure 15-13), right-click the drive, and select Uninstall.
4. Exit the Device Manager and reboot the system, or use the Add New Hardware wizard to reinstall the DVD drive.

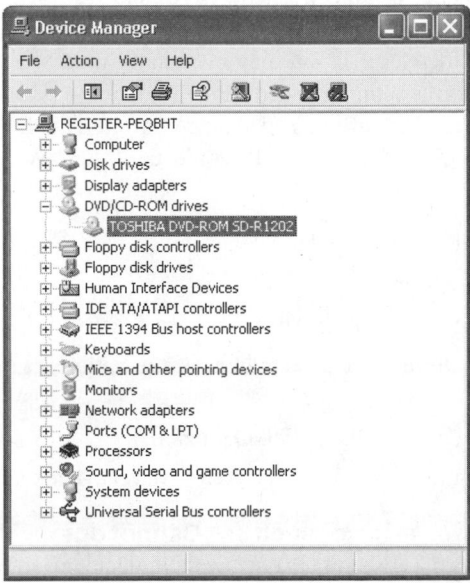

**FIGURE 15-13**    Locating the DVD entry in Windows XP Device Manager

**SYMPTOM 15-8**    **You see an error indicating the DVD device driver could not be loaded**
The DVD drive or decoder card may wind up being listed under "Other devices" in the Device Manager
(for example, it may appear as a "PCI Multimedia Device"). You'll need to check the DVD driver installation, or update the drivers manually. To do this, you will need to open the Device Manager, expand the category of Other Devices, select PCI Multimedia Device and click on Properties. In the Properties dialog,
select the Driver tab and click on Change Driver (or Update Driver under Windows XP). Browse to the
DVD Drivers Installation CD and click OK. Click OK again, select the proper device (such as your particular decoder board), and click OK again. Exit the PCI Multimedia Device Properties by clicking OK
again, and Windows will copy over the proper drivers. You may then need to restart the machine so that
your changes can take effect.

**SYMPTOM 15-9**    **You cannot play DVD movies on a multi-monitor platform**    The problem usually occurs on laptop PCs when sending a video signal simultaneously to two different locations
(such as the LCD and a TV or other external monitor). This may also occur if you try to switch between output modes during playback. If you try to play a DVD movie through an applet such as Windows Media
Player, you may see an error such as:

```
Windows Media Player is currently unable to play DVD video
```

This happens because DirectShow cannot create the video overlay needed for DVD playback on two
devices at the same time, so the playback fails. The only way to work around this problem is to use one display device at a time during DVD playback. This may require you to disconnect external monitors or close
the laptop's LCD panel so that only the external monitor is operating. (Refer to the documentation for your
particular PC.)

**SYMPTOM 15-10**    **DVD playback is choppy or absent after installing a hardware
decoder**    This type of problem can happen when you're using a software decoder, and then you install
a hardware decoder card in the system. DVD playback in Windows Media Player may then become
choppy (or there may be no video at all); you may even think there's a problem with the decoder. By
default, some DVD players (such as Windows Media Player) use the system's software decoder, so installing a hardware decoder may cause a conflict. You should configure the DVD player to use the new hardware decoder. For example, under Windows XP, you'd configure Windows Media Player with the
following steps:

1.  Start the Windows Media Player applet.
2.  Click Tools and select Options.
3.  Click the Performance tab and select Advanced (see Figure 15-14).
4.  Select Hardware in the Preferred Decoder area. (If the option is grayed out, there is no hardware
    decoder in the system.)
5.  Click OK to save your changes, then click OK again.
6.  You may wish to reboot the system and try your DVD playback again.

**SYMPTOM 15-11**    **You see an error such as "Cannot open <filename>, video and audio
glitches may occur"**    This type of error almost always indicates a fault with the driver installation, and
you should rerun the setup utility that accompanied the DVD drive product. You may also wish to check for

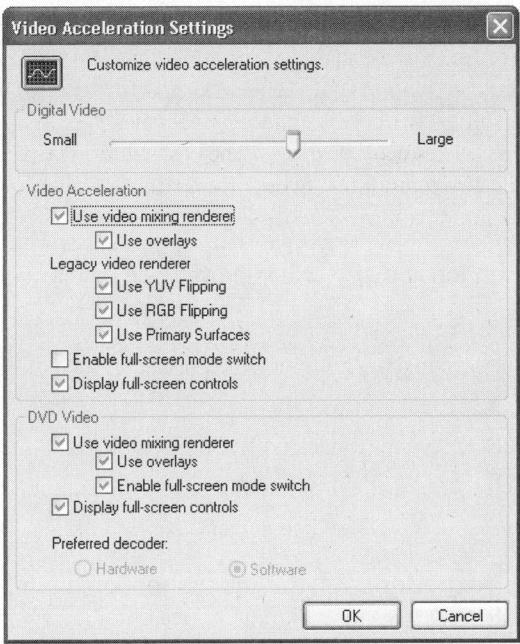

**FIGURE 15-14**    Configure the DVD player to use hardware decoding for best overall performance.

driver bug fixes or patches from the drive maker. You may need to remove the product from Device Manager, then reboot or use the Add New Hardware wizard to redetect and reinstall the device from scratch.

**SYMPTOM 15-12**    **There is no audio when playing an audio CD in the DVD drive**
This is a common problem, especially during new DVD drive installations. Chances are that you did not connect the 4-wire CD audio cable between the DVD drive and the sound board. If so, the cable may be reversed (or defective). Of course, if you're still using your original CD-ROM/R/RW drive and the CD drive is connected to the sound board, there will be no CD audio from the DVD drive. There is no way to "parallel" or "gang" the sound cable. If the DVD drive's audio cable is connected to the sound board, make sure that the CD audio input of your sound board's mixer applet is turned up to a reasonable level.

If you wish to continue using an existing CD drive as the CD audio drive, you can still use audio from the DVD drive by using a patch cable to feed the headphone output signal from the drive to the sound card's line in jack. Then adjust the sound card's line in mixer so that you can hear audio from the DVD headphone. Alternately, you can upgrade the sound card to a model that provides **two** different CD audio channel inputs.

**SYMPTOM 15-13**    **You receive an "access denied" or "copyright protection" error when trying to play a DVD**    These types of access problems usually mean that the region has not been set in the drive or decoder card. You should install and run the setup software that accompanies your DVD drive and/or MPEG-2 decoder card and be sure to set the initial region properly. Once you can configure the DVD playback system and play videos through the manufacturer's native applets, you should then be able to play videos using other player applets (such as Windows Media Player).

**SYMPTOM 15-14    DVD players may not work under Windows**    This is known to happen with older DVD hardware (for example, first-generation Creative DVD kits or MKE DVD kits) under Windows 98/Me/XP. For example, you may no longer be able to write to your DVD-RAM drive. This problem occurs because the older kits rely on the *Compact Disc File System* (CDFS), but Windows 98/Me/XP loads the UDF file system for DVD drives. The best solution is to upgrade the older DVD drive/decoder with a current product. To temporarily work around this issue, disable UDF for the DVD drives. (You cannot use these steps under Windows XP.)

 This symptom is rarely seen today due to the improved compatibility of current DVD drives and decoders.

1. Click Start, click Run, type **msconfig** in the Open box, and then click OK.
2. Click Advanced (Figure 15-15).
3. Select the Disable UDF File System check box (second entry from the bottom), and then click OK.
4. Click OK again and click Yes when prompted to restart the computer.
5. When your computer restarts, UDF is disabled and the DVD kit should work.

**SYMPTOM 15-15    You experience error messages or system lockups during DVD software installation**    Movies play, but white lines appear randomly on the screen. In virtually all cases, the problem is being caused by an IRQ or memory range conflict. Open the Device Manager and check for resource conflicts between the decoder and other system devices. For example, you may need to assign a unique IRQ to the card. This can usually be accomplished through the BIOS of your computer, or possibly by moving the decoder card to another PCI slot closer to the processor.

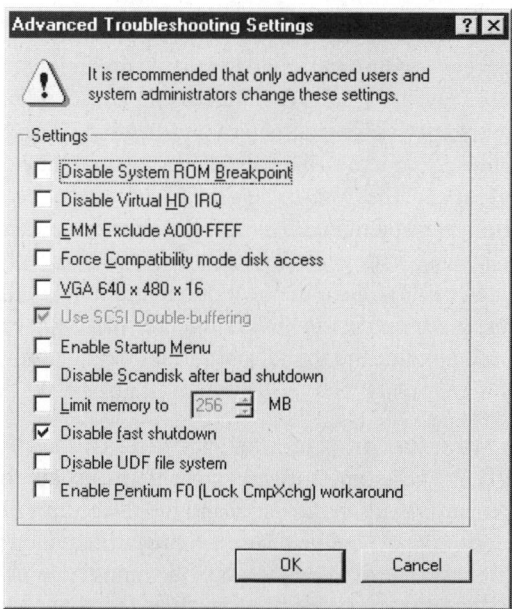

**FIGURE  15-15**    Disabling UDF support under Windows 98/SE

**SYMPTOM 15-16**   **Your DVD-ROM will not autoconfigure using the automatic configuration utility provided with the drive**   In many cases, this is a problem caused by an unusually high video refresh rate. DVD systems seem to operate best at video refresh rates of 60 Hz or so. Try lowering your video refresh rate to 75 Hz or lower through the video card's Properties dialog or Display control settings.

**SYMPTOM 15-17**   **You can play DVD-based games, but the system hangs up when inserting a DVD-Video**   When the system hangs, the video window either stays black, or the DVD logo comes up—and then the machine freezes. This is often a surprisingly simple issue. Frequently, setting the video adapter's settings to the default values will correct the problem. Although your current video settings may work wonderfully with static images (even through other player software), the unique demands of your DVD decoder board may cause too much information to be directed at your video card at once. Start with your basic video default settings, and then systematically increase resolution and color depth to an acceptable quality level.

As an alternative, you might try rearranging your drives so that the DVD drive is the first "CD-ROM" in the system. This is a particularly useful tactic when playing back CD-I and Video CD movies with software (such as Xing), but it also helps the DVD player software utilize the DVD-ROM drive.

**SYMPTOM 15-18**   **Movies appear bright (then dim) when watching a DVD-Video from the video card's TV output**   This problem only occurs when a VCR is connected between the "TV output" of the video adapter and the TV set. Video display adapters with TV output capability will enable Macrovision copy protection during DVD movie playback. The Macrovision-encoded video signal will effectively prevent a VCR from recording a watchable movie.

If you videotape a Macrovision-encoded movie and then play it back, you'll typically see occasional glimpses of the movie interspersed with 20 to 30 seconds of no picture (or possibly just a blue screen). Even if you're not actually recording, the VCR attempts to compensate for the Macrovision-encoded signal, and this generally leads to the symptom described. To resolve this symptom, simply connect the video card's TV output directly to the TV set using either the "composite" or "S-Video" connections.

Remember that sound connections are completely independent of video connections, and if you wish to hear the DVD movie through the TV set, you will also need to connect the audio output of the PC to the TV set.

**SYMPTOM 15-19**   **When playing DVD-Video, the image appears distorted**   This type of issue is often described as a "spaghetti western," and is usually associated with older Matrox Millennium or Mystique video cards, but can also occur with other types of video cards. In virtually all cases, the trouble is with your video drivers. They may be old, buggy, or incompatible with the DVD drivers and video player software at work on your system. Download and install the latest video drivers, update DirectX if necessary, and try flashing the video card's BIOS (if possible). If the problem persists, disable DirectDraw for Overlays, and resize the screen to the recommended default sizes.

**SYMPTOM 15-20**   **You cannot resize the movie display to full screen (or select any display size other than the default)**   This is particularly associated with Matrox video cards, but may occur with other video cards. These video cards probably don't support the hardware-based video scaling required for DVD. Try upgrading the video drivers, and flash the video card's BIOS (if possible). Otherwise, you have little alternative except to upgrade the video card or to continue using the smaller DVD playback window size.

**SYMPTOM 15-21**    **You receive a "display overlay not available" error message when launching the DVD player software**    This is a known issue with older DVD player software (such as ATI DVD player 1.2 software), but similar problems can occur with other players. Chances are that the DVD player software requires additional display adapter memory (beyond what is used by the current display mode). If the current display mode uses most of the display adapter's memory, there's no memory left over for the DVD player, and the error message will occur.

This message is most likely to occur when the display adapter has only 4MB of display memory, and 1152 × 864 at 32 *bits per pixel* (bpp) is selected as the display mode. This display mode consumes almost 4MB of display memory just to paint the Windows desktop. To resolve this problem, simply select a lower color depth or (lower resolution). For example, if you're running at 32bpp, try 16bpp. This will consume only half as much display memory and should leave an adequate amount for the display overlay and other DVD functions. In other cases, you might consider upgrading the video card to a model with more video memory.

If the error message persists after reducing the display resolution (and/or color depth), it may be the result of interference by other video-related processes. Check for "WebTV" or "WaveTop" background tasks. These are normally visible in the task bar. Right-click the icons for these tasks, and select Pause, Suspend, Quit, or Exit to disable them. Then try the DVD player software again.

**SYMPTOM 15-22**    **The DVD decoder card is not recognized by Windows**    When you attempt to use the Windows DVD Player, you may receive an error message such as:

```
To use the DVD player, you need to install either a software DVD decoder, or
a hardware DVD decoder.
```

For example, this problem can occur with certain decoder cards (e.g. a Sigma Designs Hollywood Plus DVD decoder or a Creative Labs Dxr3 decoder card). In virtually all cases, the current device drivers for the decoder card are not compatible with the Windows DVD Player. Verify that the MPEG-2 decoder card is installed properly and listed in Device Manager without any conflicts or other problems. Contact the manufacturer of your decoder card for any Windows device driver updates. You may need to remove the decoder card and reinstall it from scratch with the latest drivers.

**SYMPTOM 15-23**    **You cannot restart or resume a DVD movie**    When using Microsoft DVD Player under Windows 98/Me/XP, you cannot resume the movie once it's playing. Some DVD movies require that you use the movie's menu rather than the DVD Player program's menu. Try using the movie's menu displayed in the viewing window while you're playing the DVD movie. You can also try updating the DVD Player software.

**SYMPTOM 15-24**    **You cannot change display resolutions with DVD software**    For example, when you play a DVD using the Mediamatics/Compaq DVDExpress DVD player, and you attempt to change the display resolution, you may receive an error message such as:

```
Cdvdplay has caused an error in QDVD.DLL. Cdvdplay will now close.
```

In virtually all cases, the problem is with the DVDExpress software and can generally be corrected by updating the software through the software maker's Web site. You can easily work around this problem by not changing resolutions while the DVDExpress software is running.

**SYMPTOM 15-25** **You get "blue screen" errors when ejecting a DVD** The error occurs when manually ejecting a DVD under DVD Player software, and you'll normally see an error message such as:

```
Error Reading CD-ROM in drive X:
```

Not all drives exhibit this behavior, but it is known to occur on some DVD drives due to the way that the DVD movie is stopped. Avoid ejecting the disc manually while the DVD player is running. Quit the DVD Player software before manually ejecting the DVD movie, or click Eject in the program to eject the DVD.

**SYMPTOM 15-26** **A hardware DVD decoder doesn't handle zoom functions** For example, this is a known issue when using older decoders such as a Creative Dxr2 decoder card. If you have the Creative WDM drivers installed for the Creative Dxr2 DVD decoder card, you cannot use the Zoom In/Out command while playing a DVD title using Microsoft's DVD Player. This is almost always an issue with the Creative Dxr2 DVD decoder, so check the Creative Labs Web site (www.creaf.com) for driver updates. If the problem persists, you may wish to upgrade the decoder card, or remove the decoder card and use a software decoder instead.

**SYMPTOM 15-27** **The DVD motorized tray won't open or close** The most common issue here is the DVD application itself. Some DVD applications (such as DVD-Video player applications) will lock the disc tray closed while a video DVD disc is playing. Try closing all open applications. If the tray still won't open, try restarting the PC. This should clear any software lock. If the tray still refuses to open or close, the drive itself may be defective. You can force the tray open using a straightened paper clip in the emergency-eject hole in the front of the drive.

**SYMPTOM 15-28** **There is no DVD audio while playing a movie or other multimedia presentation** Here's another common oversight during new DVD installations. Check the external audio cable attached between the MPEG-2 decoder board and the line in connector of your sound board. The cable may be reversed, plugged into the wrong jack(s), or the cable may simply be defective. Also check the sound board's mixer applet, and see that the line in volume control setting is turned up to an acceptable level. If you're connecting the DVD drive's CD audio cable to the sound card, verify that the cable is attached securely, and see that the cable is compatible with the drive and the sound card.

**SYMPTOM 15-29** **Video quality appears poor** MPEG-2 compression is well respected for its ability to reproduce high-quality images. The problem of poor image quality is almost always because of your video configuration. Your color depth or resolution is probably too low. DVD-Video playback is best at resolutions of $800 \times 600$ or higher, and color depths of 16-bits (High Color) or higher (for example, 24-bit True Color). In most cases, 256 colors will result in a dithered image.

**SYMPTOM 15-30** **The video image is distorted when trying to play an MPEG file** Other video operations probably seem fine. A full or partially distorted MPEG image can be the result of two problems. First, the video connections on the back of the card could be loose. Verify that all connections to the MPEG-2 decoder card are secure. Another common cause of distorted playbacks is that the refresh rate on your video card is set too high. It is recommended that the video refresh rate be kept *below* 85 Hz when running MPEG files. Try adjusting the vertical refresh rate to 72 Hz, or even 60 Hz.

**SYMPTOM 15-31**    **The picture is beginning to occasionally pixelize or "break apart"**
The audio may also seem periodically distorted. It is highly likely that the DVD disc needs to be cleaned. Clean the DVD disc properly and try it again, or try another disc. Also try closing any unused applications running in the background. If the problem persists with another DVD disc as well (and both discs are in good condition), try reinitializing the drive by powering down and rebooting the system. If the problem still persists, the internal optics of the DVD-ROM drive may need to be cleaned with a bit of photography-grade compressed air. Otherwise, try replacing the DVD-ROM drive.

**SYMPTOM 15-32**    **You notice the DVD-ROM light flashing regularly without a disc inserted**    System performance may be reduced. This is often because the DVD-ROM drive's properties are set for "Auto insert notification" under Windows 9x/Me. (You cannot adjust AIN under Windows XP.) Start the Device Manager, highlight the DVD-ROM drive, and click the Properties button. You'll see the DVD-ROM Properties dialog. In the Options area of the Properties dialog, locate the "Auto insert notification" check box and uncheck it. Save your changes. (You might need to reboot the system.) This should stop the drive's constant checking for a disc.

**SYMPTOM 15-33**    **The DVD drive's "busy" indicator flashes slowly once a disc is inserted**    The drive is not recognizing the disc. In most cases, the disc is simply dirty. Try cleaning the disc in a radial motion (from the hub to the edge, like the spokes of a wheel). Try another disc. If the drive cannot recognize other discs, the drive's optical reader may be dirty. Try using a can of photography-grade compressed air to clean any accumulations of dust from the drive. If the drive's "busy" indicator is on all the time (and doesn't recognize any discs), the drive may be defective.

**SYMPTOM 15-34**    **You see an error message that says "Disk playback unauthorized"**
The region code on the DVD disc does not match the code embedded into the drive. There isn't much that can be done when this error occurs. Some drives allow you to change the region setting several times before locking the drive (as in Figure 15-8 earlier), but once the limit has been reached, you'll need to replace the drive or have it reset by the manufacturer. Note that region code limitations are only applied to DVD-Video movie releases. Programs and data discs are generally not marked with region codes.

**SYMPTOM 15-35**    **The display turns magenta (red) when attempting to adjust the DVD video overlay feature**    When adjusting the video overlay, you may have some trouble finding the video window. It often helps to change your background to magenta so you can see where the video window is. To do this, right-click on your background, and select Properties. Select the Background tab and select "none" as both the Pattern and the Wallpaper. Then select the Appearance tab, and select Magenta as the color of the desktop. Click OK to finish changing your background color to magenta. It should now be easier to locate the video window while adjusting the overlay.

**SYMPTOM 15-36**    **The DVD drive cannot read CD-R or Photo CD discs**    This is not an error—most first-generation DVD drives will not read CD recordable or Photo CD (Kodak) discs. In some cases, it is even possible to damage CD recordable discs due to the laser wavelength and energy used in the DVD drive. Do not attempt to read CD-R or Photo CD discs in the DVD unless the drive specifications specifically state that the drive is compatible with those types of discs. Chances are that you'll need to update the older DVD drive's firmware (or replace the DVD drive completely) to correct the problem.

**SYMPTOM 15-37** **You experience difficulties with a particular DVD movie title even though others play normally** If most movies play normally, chances are that the problem movie is an older edition (version). Some older DVD-ROM movie releases contained mastering problems that cause playback errors. Try exchanging the movie for a later edition. If the problem persists (or you cannot play most movies properly), you may need updated DVD-ROM drivers. Download the latest drivers from the DVD manufacturer's Web site and install them. You can try upgrading the drivers through the drive's Properties dialog box, or remove the drive through Device Manager and reboot, or use the Add New Hardware wizard to reinstall the device from scratch.

**SYMPTOM 15-38** **You experience difficulties with the DVD software's Parental Control feature** The Parental Control is not working properly or is causing user problems. This is often because the Parental Control feature is not working properly in the DVD software, and you'll need to uninstall and reinstall the DVD software to disable Parental Control.

First, uninstall the DVD software. To do this, open the Add/Remove Programs applet. Highlight the particular DVD software (such as Creative Labs' Encore or Ovation software) and click on Add/Remove. After the uninstall is complete, reinstall the software choosing the option for a custom install. Make sure there is not a check mark next to "Parental Control" in the select list. This will reinstall the software without the Parental Control feature. A later release of the DVD software (or a patch) may address this problem and allow you to resume using the Parental Control feature.

**SYMPTOM 15-39** **Your screen saver turns on while playing a DVD title** Since a screen saver is activated after some period of inactivity, leaving the keyboard/mouse untouched while watching a DVD movie can allow the screen saver to activate. Screen savers do not check for the presence of DVD activity, so you'll need to disable the screen saver (through the Display icon in the Control Panel) before using the DVD-ROM drive to watch movies. In other cases, the DVD player software may offer an option that lets you disable the screen saver while a DVD is playing.

**SYMPTOM 15-40** **You notice a reddish tint when playing movies with the DVD-ROM drive** This is typically an end-user issue that can easily be corrected by reducing contrast or by adjusting the tint setting through the DVD player application software.

**SYMPTOM 15-41** **You find that MPEG-1 files play back fine on your DVD player software, but there is no sound** However, you find that MPEG-2 files and DVD-Video (movies) play back correctly with sound. You may not even notice this problem if you don't play MPEG-1 files. This is generally a problem with the DVD player software that may require a patch or upgrade. (Check with the player software's manufacturer.) As a temporary work-around, use a generic MPEG file player (such as Windows Media Player) to run MPEG-1 files until the DVD player can be upgraded or replaced.

**SYMPTOM 15-42** **You cannot play a DVD or CD in the DVD drive, or certain types of discs cannot be read in the drive** There are many possible (often simple) issues that can prevent a disc from playing in an optical drive. First, the disc may be placed upside-down in the disc tray, or the disc may be dirty. Recheck the disc orientation, and clean the disc if necessary. If the disc is warped or seriously damaged, it may need to be replaced.

The drive's optical reader may be dirty. This can happen on older drives, or drives that are operated in dusty/dirty environments. Use a can of photography-grade compressed air to gently blow dust out of the drive. Finally, DVD movie discs are released with a region code that must correspond to the code contained in the drive. If the codes are different, the DVD disc will not play. You may need to obtain a disc with the correct region code.

**SYMPTOM 15-43**    **When attempting to play a disc, you receive a message such as "Disc does not contain DVD-Video data"**    DVD player software cannot find the title track and/or information files on the disc. If you're trying to use a DVD movie disc, the disc may be scratched or damaged. Clean the disc if possible, or replace the damaged disc. If you're simply trying to play MPEG video from an ordinary CD, click OK to close the error dialog. The disc may still play.

**SYMPTOM 15-44**    **You receive an error message such as "Unable to locate DVD-ROM drive"**    The DVD drive may not have been properly configured by Windows 9x/Me/XP or may be disconnected. Verify that the DVD drive is jumpered properly, and see that its power and signal cables are oriented and secured. Try another signal cable if necessary, or try the DVD drive as the only device on the drive controller. Reboot the PC from a cold start, and see if Windows will redetect the DVD drive. If not, run the Windows 9x/Me/XP Add New Hardware wizard to "force" Windows to detect the hardware. If the Add New Hardware wizard fails to detect the DVD drive, you may need to specify the drive make and model manually. In all cases, be sure to have the latest DVD drivers on hand.

**SYMPTOM 15-45**    **During the DVD video configuration process, you receive an error such as "Auto Alignment failed"**    This error almost always suggests that the hardware MPEG-2 decoder card cable may not be properly connected. Check the cable connection on the hardware decoder card (particularly "VGA In" and "VGA Out"), and see that the cable is secure. Try another cable if possible. Start the DVD player software, press the Settings button, and select Video Configuration. Press the Auto button to have the video automatically configured. Otherwise, refer to the documentation for the software and try to align the video manually (if possible).

**SYMPTOM 15-46**    **After connecting an MPEG-2 decoder card, the video image seems blue (or contains a blue tint)**    This is generally due to the improper connection or setup of the MPEG-2 card. The VGA loopback cable between the video card and the MPEG-2 decoder card is not connected correctly. Check the loopback cable, and try reseating the connector if possible. DVD video alignment may not be set correctly. Open the Video Configuration utility and set the video alignment. Try using the Auto feature to automatically configure the video. If automatic configuration does not work, try making minor adjustments manually.

Your color key value may not be set correctly. Change the color scheme of your Windows 9x/Me/XP desktop. Right-click on the Windows 9x/Me/XP desktop and click Properties. In the Display Properties dialog, click the Appearance tab. Then select Desktop in the Item list, and select a different color scheme from the list. (Under Windows XP, just select a different color scheme.) Click OK to accept the changes.

**SYMPTOM 15-47**    **The DVD-ROM drive cannot play a DVD disc, or certain other types of disc media (such as CD-plus)**    There are several possible issues that might cause this type of problem. First, make sure that the entire suite of drivers has been installed for your drive. Check for the latest drivers and download any available patches or updates. You also may not have the correct player software for your drive, so make sure to download and install the latest version of your player software. Also verify that the DVD disc is the correct format for the type of system that you're using. For example, a PC should use an ISO9660-compatible format, rather than an Apple/Mac HFS disc or UNIX disc format. Finally, your DVD drivers/software may have been corrupted by a virus. Run a virus scan program, and then remove/reinstall any damaged software.

**SYMPTOM 15-48    After upgrading the video card, DVD movies will not play**
Chances are that your new video card is neither defective nor incompatible. Instead, the problem is that the link(s) between your video and DVD drivers have been broken. When new video cards are installed, they change entries in the Registry that associate MPEG playback with video card drivers. The new video card's MPEG drivers are probably not DVD compliant, but since they took precedence over the MPEG drivers of the older DVD system, this is likely to be the problem. Try reinstalling the video card from scratch, and then reinstall the DVD drivers and software. This should reinstall the proper DVD MPEG-ready drivers and correct the problem.

**SYMPTOM 15-49    Windows 98/Me/XP halts or reboots when running a software DVD player designed for Windows 95**    This is an older issue most frequently associated with the Zoran SoftDVD player, but may occur with other software products. In most cases, the system halts immediately after the Play button is clicked, but this may also occur at other points within the player software. In some instances, the system may reboot or report an "Unrecoverable Application Error." Generally, the SoftDVD player may successfully play a single DVD movie or file, and then report an error (such as "your computer is not configured to start DVD") when attempting to play a second movie. Chances are that the subtle design changes between Windows 95 and Windows 98/Me/XP are causing a problem with the player software (tailored for Windows 95). Try the following:

- Remove and reinstall the DVD player application.
- Check to see if a patch or update is available for your DVD player.
- Experiment with different video resolutions, color depths, and refresh rates.
- Try an alternate or updated video driver.

**SYMPTOM 15-50    Even when a DVD system is properly configured under Windows 95, you get no sound from the speakers**    This is almost always due to an old (original) release of Windows 95. The use of old Windows 95 drivers was corrected in Windows 95 OSR2 and is not an issue with Windows 98/Me/XP. If you cannot upgrade your operating system to Windows 95 OSR2 or Windows 98/Me/XP, check with the DVD package manufacturer for updated drivers and patches that might correct the problem. Keep in mind that the DVD drive will still read data DVD discs and other CDs properly.

**SYMPTOM 15-51    You receive a "media error" when using Windows Explorer to eject a DVD movie**    For example, this issue has been reported with Toshiba DVD players. When you use Windows Explorer to eject a DVD movie that is currently being played by a Toshiba DVD player, you receive the following "blue screen" error message:

```
Re-insert the media and press any key to continue.
```

When you insert the DVD movie back into the player and press a key, you may receive the same error message (and the movie may be automatically ejected). This problem may occur if you press a key before the DVD movie is fully spun up. To resolve the problem, insert the DVD movie into the player, but wait to press a key until the light on the Toshiba DVD player is turned off. This indicates that the DVD movie is fully spun up.

**SYMPTOM 15-52**    **The screen appears clipped when playing a DVD movie**    This is a known issue when using older drivers (such as Cinemaster 1.2 drivers) under Windows 98/Me (though this is not known to occur with current drivers on Windows XP systems). Both sides of the screen may appear "clipped." This is caused by an aspect ratio bug in the DVD player software. You'll need to contact Microsoft or the maker of your DVD player software to obtain the correct patch or software update for your DVD player. For example, Microsoft offers an update for the DVDPLAY.EXE file (09/29/98, 9:43a, 125,440 bytes or later), which should correct this aspect ratio problem. Keep in mind that you may also need to update your DirectX components (for example, DirectX 8.0a or later) before updating the DVD player software.

# Further Study

**Creative Labs**   www.creaf.com
**Diamond Multimedia**   www.diamondmm.com
**DVD Forum**   www.dvdforum.org
**Hitachi**   www.hitachi.com
**Matsushita**   www.panasonic.com/office/storage/stor.html
**Panasonic**   www.panasonic.com
**Sigma Designs**   www.sigmadesigns.com/products/xcard.htm#
**Toshiba**   www.toshiba.com/taecdpd/

# 16

# ENHANCING SYSTEM PERFORMANCE

$\mathbf{P}$C users receive the best return on their system investment when it's operating at peak efficiency. However, new hardware isn't always the answer. Even with state-of-the-art hardware, there are many important operating system and setup factors that will affect the performance of a system. Swap file problems, inadequate memory, and poor system settings are just a few of the issues that can reduce the system's effectiveness.

This chapter is intended to help you identify the key performance areas of a typical Windows 98/Me/XP PC and offers a set of handy guidelines that will help you get the most from an existing system.

# Checking System Performance

1.  The first step in improving your system's performance is to investigate the current performance level of your system. If you're using Windows 98/Me/XP, you can get an overview of the system's performance through the System Properties dialog. This will give you a broad overview of the system's key resources and the way in which Windows perceives them. You can access this dialog through the System icon under Windows 9x/Me: Click Start | Settings | Control Panel.

2.  Once the Control Panel opens, double-click the System icon.

3.  Click the Performance tab (Figure 16-1).

 Under Windows XP, the General tab under the System Properties dialog box does not provide as much useful information, so we will use the System Information utility later in this chapter.

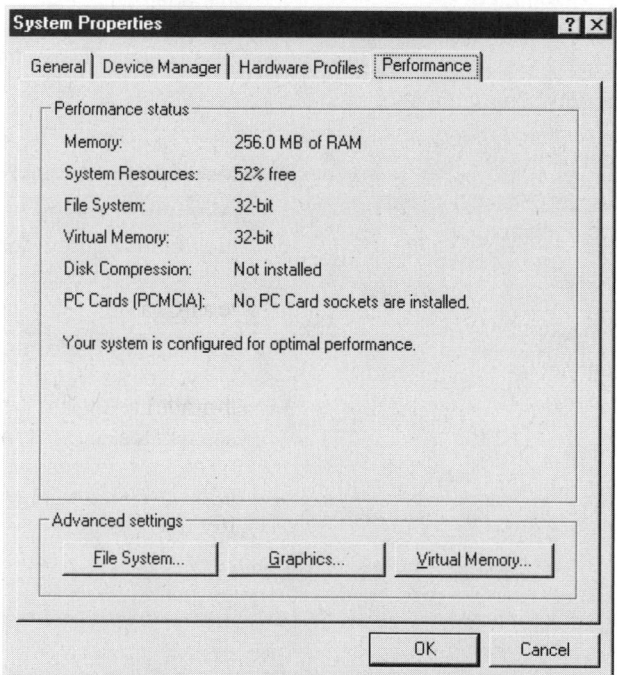

**FIGURE 16-1**    Getting an overview of the Windows 98/Me system through the System Properties dialog

# UNDERSTANDING THE RESOURCES

The Windows 9x/Me Performance tab will list six major parameters that will affect your system performance. You should understand how to interpret each of these settings:

■ **Memory**    This specifies the amount of physical memory (RAM) in your computer that's recognized by Windows. If this value is less than the amount reported by BIOS during the POST memory count, you may have a problem with the way Windows recognizes or handles your RAM. This is also a quick way to tell how much RAM is in your customer's system. At a minimum, there should be enough RAM to properly support the operating system installed.

■ **System Resources**    This indicates the percentage of free system resources (generally taken to mean "free RAM"). If this number is too low, your computer may perform slowly due to excessive use of virtual memory. You can correct this by closing unused background applications, or by adding more RAM to the system. A system that has too little RAM may perform poorly due to extensive disk swapping.

■ **File System**    This entry specifies the type of file system that you're using (for example, MS-DOS or 32-bit), and this will affect the efficiency with which files are read from or written to your system drives. Your disk's performance will be slower if you're using the DOS Compatibility Mode, and this may mean that there's one or more drives in the system that are using the incorrect drivers, or are configured improperly. Windows will perform best using the 32-bit file system.

■ **Virtual Memory**    Virtual memory is hard disk space that is used as extra RAM. This entry indicates whether virtual memory is enabled (using 32-bit or DOS Compatibility Mode) or disabled. If virtual memory is enabled in the DOS Compatibility Mode, the disk being used for virtual memory is also using that mode. The same is true for the 32-bit virtual memory mode. A disk using DOS Compatibility Mode is slower than a disk using 32-bit mode, and system performance will suffer accordingly.

■ **Disk Compression**    This specifies whether you've installed any disk compression software on your computer (for example, DriveSpace 3). If not, the entry will state "Not installed." If you do use compression software, the 32-bit version will yield optimal performance. Real-mode (DOS Compatibility Mode) compression software will run more slowly and impair overall system performance.

■ **PC Cards (PCMCIA)**    This entry indicates if you have a PC (a.k.a. PCMCIA) card slot enabled and is most commonly used with laptop systems. If there are no socket services installed, the entry will note "No PC Card sockets are installed." Otherwise, the entry will list either 32-bit software (for optimum performance) or DOS Compatibility Mode (real-mode) software. With 32-bit Windows PC Card support, you can insert and remove PC Cards while your computer is running.

Ideally, your system should offer ample memory and utilize 32-bit protected-mode drivers for all of the features installed on your system. This will generally offer the best overall performance, and the system will typically display a message such as "Your system is configured for optimal performance" below the PC Cards entry (such as in Figure 16-1 earlier). If you're missing a protected-mode driver, or there's a device installed in the system that Windows doesn't recognize, it will almost always "fall back" to suitable real-mode (DOS Compatibility Mode) drivers instead. If your computer's performance status is not optimal, a description of the performance problem(s) will appear below the PC Cards line. For more information on a given problem, click an item, and then click Details.

# SYSTEM INFORMATION

Windows 9*x*/Me/XP provides a System Information utility that reveals a great deal of hardware, software, and configuration information about the system. To start the utility, click Start | Run, type **msinfo32**, and press ENTER. The System Information utility will scan the system and report its essential details (see Figure 16-2). Immediately, you can see details such as the processor type and speed, BIOS information, physical memory (RAM), virtual memory, and OS details. From here, you can closely examine the system's hardware, components, software, and Internet settings by expanding the left pane.

To review hardware resources on the system, expand the Hardware Resources entry in the left pane, then opt to see conflicts (a particularly handy feature when troubleshooting), DMA assignments, forced (legacy) hardware, I/O assignments, IRQ assignments, or memory ranges assigned to various system devices. The Components category breaks down hardware by classification, so you can check on multimedia, CD, sound, display, storage, and other major types of devices on the system. The Problem Devices entry is also useful for identifying devices that may not be operating properly. When you select the Software Environment category, System Information will report information about your system configuration, including drivers, environment variables, current print jobs, and so on. For example, you can check for potential driver problems by looking for certified (signed) drivers as in Figure 16-3.

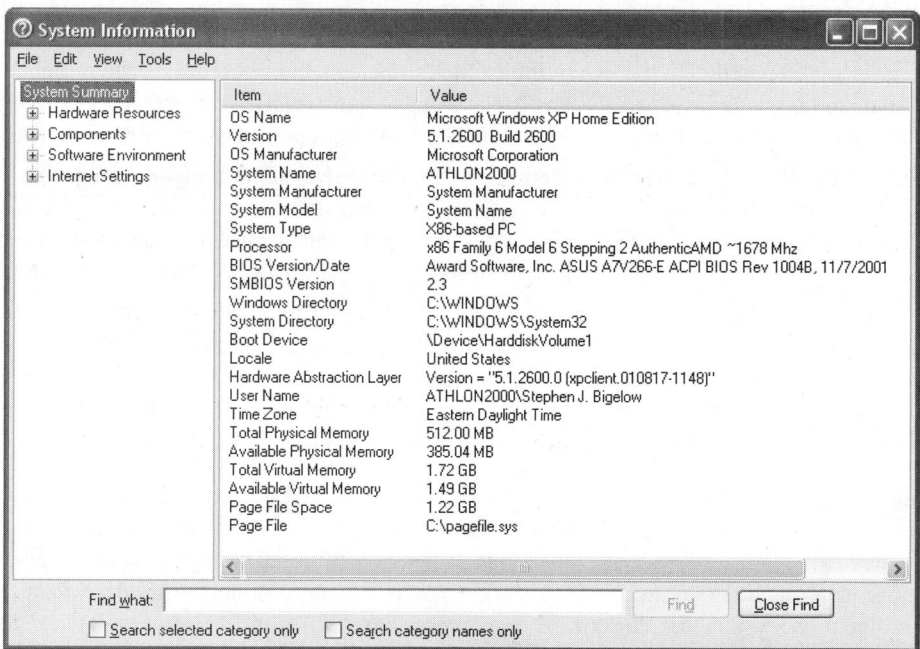

**FIGURE 16-2** Windows XP provides the System Information utility that allows technicians to access detailed hardware and software information.

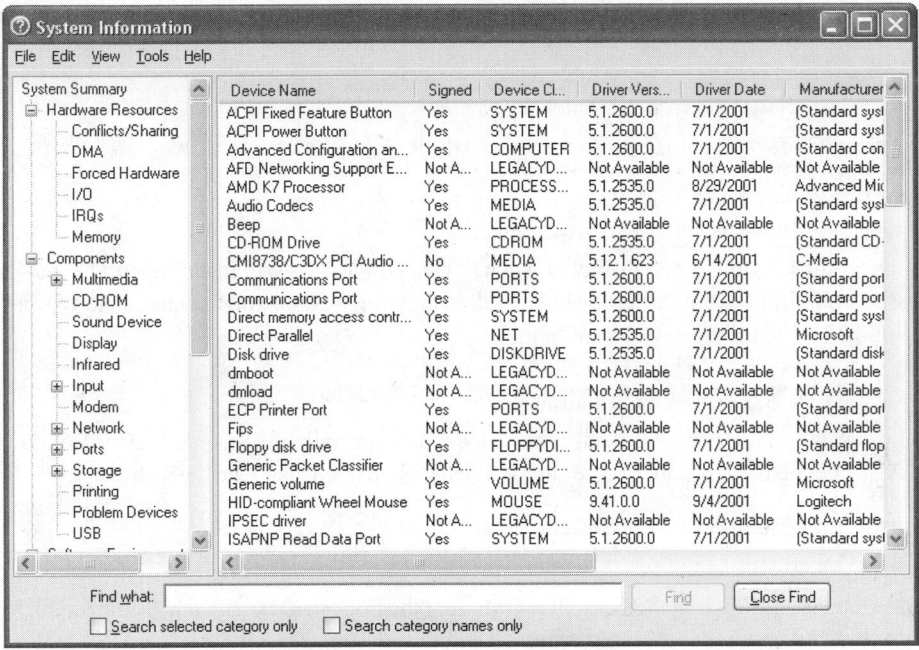

**FIGURE 16-3**   Outdated or noncompliant drivers can be found by checking for certified (signed) drivers with the System Information utility.

# System Monitor and Performance

System Monitor is a Windows 9x/Me/XP tool that measures the performance of hardware, software services, and applications. (The versions included with Windows 98/Me/XP will also log performance over time.) When you make changes to the system configuration, System Monitor shows the effect of your changes on overall system performance. This offers you a powerful tool that can help determine the effect of system upgrades, or help find the cause of problems on a local or remote computer. For example, logging memory allocation while using a specific application could be helpful in detecting programs with memory leaks or unexpected processing overhead. As another example, you could measure system performance before making a configuration change, and changes in performance may help you identify performance bottlenecks. This part of the chapter briefly covers the installation and use of System Monitor.

 The Windows XP version of System Monitor is displayed in a dialog box marked Performance, and this can cause a bit of confusion.

## INSTALLING SYSTEM MONITOR

If you're using Windows XP, the System Monitor utility is already installed on the system; you only need to launch and configure it. If System Monitor is not currently installed on your Windows

9*x*/Me system, you may easily install System Monitor using the Add/Remove Programs wizard, as shown next:

1. Click Start | Settings | Control Panel.
2. Once the Control Panel is open, select the Add/Remove Programs icon.
3. Click the Windows Setup tab.
4. Select System Tools, and then click Details.
5. Click System Monitor, and then click OK (Figure 16-4). This will install System Monitor on your system. If Windows CAB files are not installed on your system, you may need the Windows installation CD to install System Monitor.

## USING SYSTEM MONITOR

System Monitor is considered to be a diagnostic tool and is normally not installed under Windows 98/Me. Fortunately, it's very easy to install. Before attempting to install it, check to see if it's already on your system:

1. Click Start | Programs | Accessories.
2. Select System Tools.
3. If System Monitor is installed, it will appear near the bottom of the System Tools menu. If it's present, you can start System Monitor simply by clicking on the menu entry.
4. By default, the System Monitor display appears as shown in Figure 16-5, and the charting will start automatically.

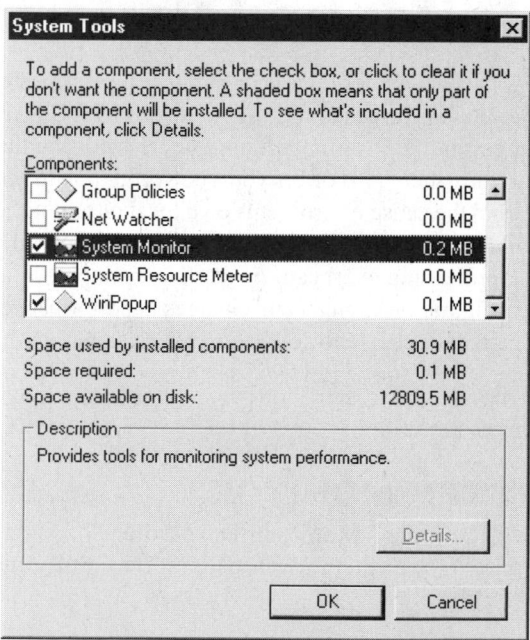

**FIGURE 16-4**   Installing System Monitor under Windows 9*x*/Me

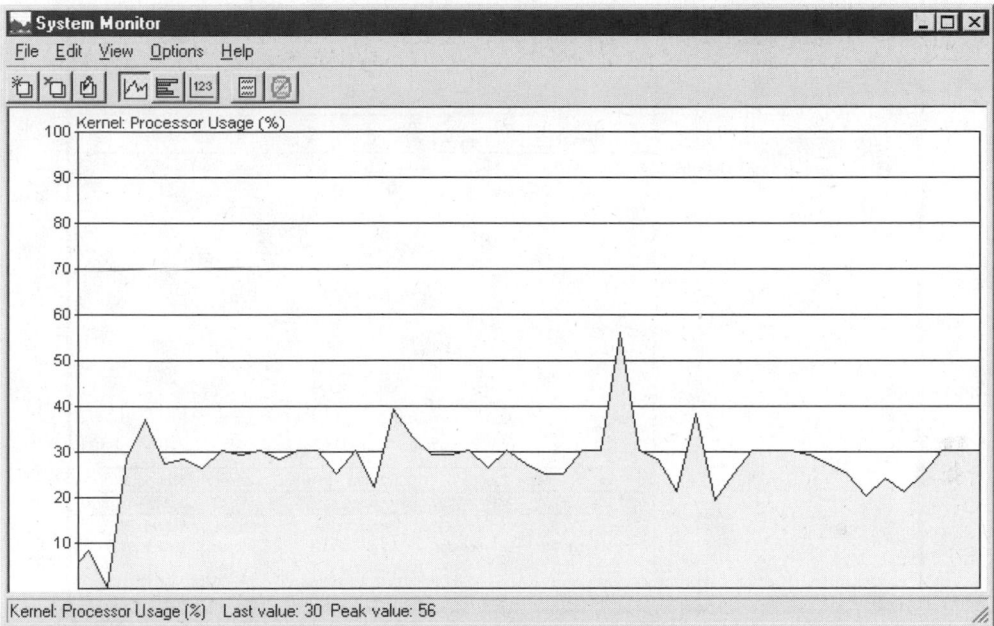

**FIGURE 16-5**    Starting System Monitor in its default mode under Windows 9*x*/Me

You can use the following steps to launch System Monitor under Windows XP:

1. Click Start | Control Panel | Performance and Maintenance.
2. Click Administrative Tools and double-click the Performance shortcut.
3. The Performance dialog box will open (see Figure 16-6) and begin charting with default values.
4. Once charting starts, you can proceed to add other variables or modify the charting behavior.

## Adjusting the Chart Format
By default, System Monitor uses a "strip-chart" format (as in Figure 16-6), but it also offers bar charts or numeric charts, depending on how you'd prefer to view the information. Once System Monitor is running, you can click View, then select the desired chart format. There are also shortcut buttons below the main menu. In most cases, you'll leave the utility in its "chart" format.

## Adjusting the Chart Appearance
You can control the color and update frequency under System Monitor. To adjust a color, click Edit, and then select Edit Item. Choose the item you want to adjust, and the Chart Options dialog will appear. For example, you can change the color and scale of Kernel Processor Usage in Figure 16-7. If you need to adjust the update frequency, click the Options menu, click Chart, and adjust the update slider accordingly.

The System Monitor utility in Windows XP provides a number of additional features that let you tailor the graph to your own individual tastes. Open the Properties dialog box by right-clicking in the counter area and selecting Properties. The General tab lets you configure the general appearance and update

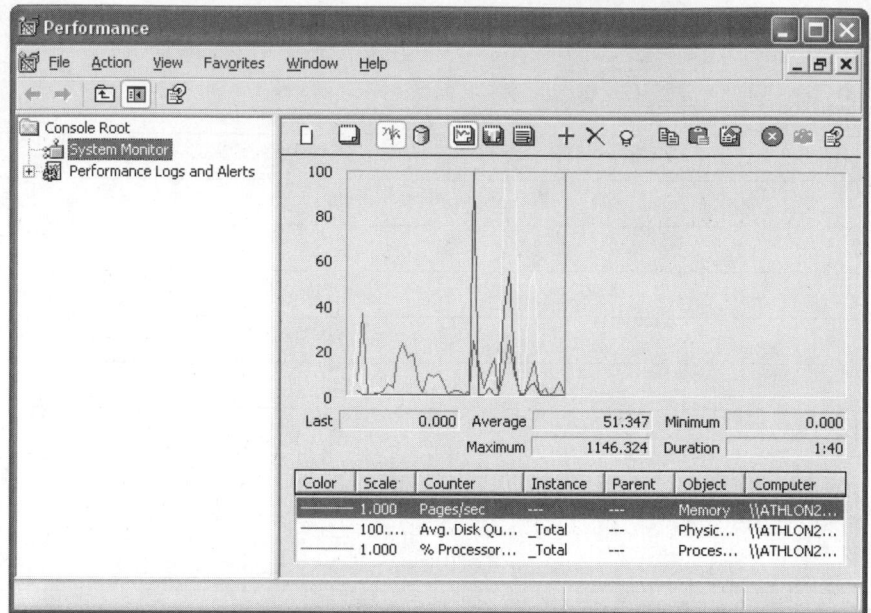

**FIGURE  16-6**    The System Monitor (a.k.a. Performance) utility allows critical system parameters to be tracked in real time under Windows XP.

frequency of the display. The Data tab (see Figure 16-8) lets you add and delete *counters* (variables to measure), and tailor their colors and line appearance. A complex graph that tracks a large number of variables may take several minutes to configure properly. You can see in Figure 16-8 that our default Performance display is tracking three common performance-oriented variables:

- **Memory\Pages/s**   How quickly the memory subsystem is responding
- **Physical Disk (Total)\Avg. Disk Queue Length**   How fast the disk sub-system is working
- **Processor (Total)\%Processor Time**   How much stress the processor is under

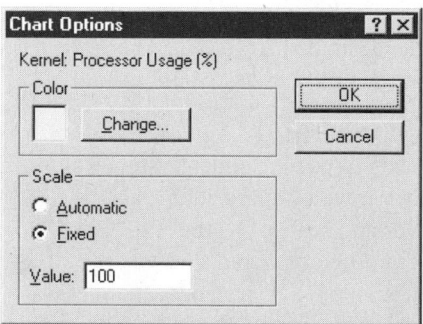

**FIGURE  16-7**    Adjusting chart characteristics under Windows 9*x*/Me

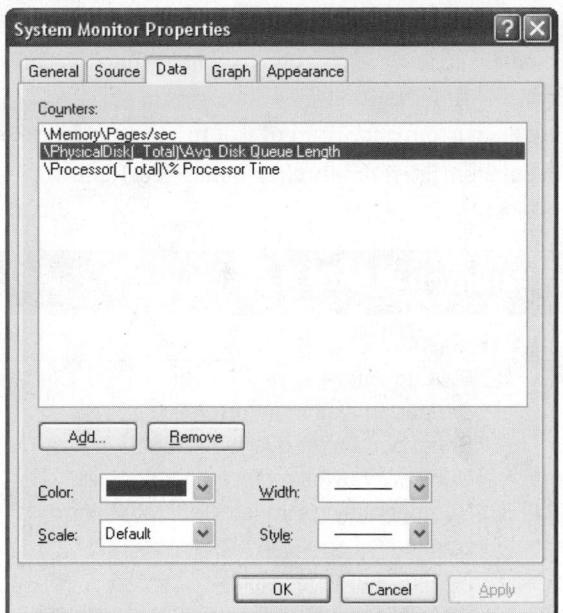

**FIGURE 16-8**    The Data tab lets you add or delete counters and tailor each counter's appearance.

## Logging System Performance

System Monitor offers the capability to log any of the parameters that it's measuring. You can then use the log information to analyze performance issues later on. To begin a logging session with System Monitor under Windows 9*x*/Me:

1. Start System Monitor (if it's not already running).
2. Click File, and then select Start Logging.
3. Enter a file name for the log file, and then click Save.
4. On the File menu, click Stop Logging to halt the log process.

Things are a little easier with System Monitor under Windows XP. Simply right-click in the graph window and select Save Data As. A Save Data As dialog will open, and you can name the file and elect to save the data as an HTML file or a TSV report format. Logging will start when you elect to save the file.

## Configuring System Monitor

System Monitor uses the dynamic data information in the Windows registry to report on the state of many different processes. You can select exactly which of those processes must be displayed in System Monitor:

1. With System Monitor running, click the Edit menu, and then click Add Item.
2. In the Category list, click the resource that you want to monitor. System Monitor will work with seven major categories, which are outlined in Table 16-1.

3. In the Item list, select one or more resources that you want to monitor.

4. When you've selected an item, you may click Explain for more information about a selected resource.

5. Click OK. You'll see the performance chart of that resource added to System Monitor.

6. If you wish to remove an item later, simply click Edit, select Remove Item, highlight the item to be removed, and then click OK.

---

**TABLE 16-1    SYSTEM MONITOR PARAMETERS (COUNTERS)**

**DIAL-UP ADAPTER SETTINGS**

| Setting | Measurement |
|---|---|
| Alignment errors | Serial port alignment errors. |
| Buffer overruns | Serial port buffer overrun errors. |
| Bytes received/second | Number of bytes received per second. |
| Bytes transmitted/second | Number of bytes transmitted per second. |
| Connection speed | Connection speed in bits per second. |
| CRC errors | Number of frames with CRC errors. |
| Frames received/second | Number of good frames received per second. |
| Frames transmitted/second | Number of frames transmitted per second. |
| Framing errors | Serial port framing errors. |
| Incomplete frames | Number of incomplete frames received. |
| Overrun errors | Serial port overrun errors. |
| Timeout errors | Serial port timeout errors. |
| Total bytes received | Total number of bytes received. |
| Total bytes transmitted | Total number of bytes transmitted. |

**DISK CACHE SETTINGS**

| Setting | Measurement |
|---|---|
| Cache buffers | Number of active buffers in a cache, including any and all compressed buffers. |
| Cache hits | Number of times data found in the cache, resulting in I/O requests. |
| Cache misses | Number of times data not found in the cache, resulting in I/O requests. |
| Cache pages | Current number of disk cache pages. |
| Failed cache recycles | Number of times a recycling request (either least recently used [LRU] or random) has failed. This can happen in low memory situations or when all cache buffers are currently in use. |
| LRU cache recycles | Number of times the cache is sequentially searched for a buffer to recycle, beginning with the oldest data. This happens when new data needs to be added to the cache, or when memory manager needs to borrow memory from the cache. |
| Maximum cache pages | Maximum number of disk cache pages. |
| Minimum cache pages | Minimum number of disk cache pages. |
| Random cache recycles | Number of times the cache is randomly searched for a buffer to recycle. This can happen whenever the cache becomes filled with data not used lately. |

**TABLE 16-1** **SYSTEM MONITOR PARAMETERS (COUNTERS)** *(CONTINUED)*

**FILE SYSTEM SETTINGS**

| Setting | Measurement |
|---|---|
| Bytes read/second | The number of bytes read from the file system each second. |
| Bytes written/second | The number of bytes written by the file system each second. |
| Dirty data | The number of bytes waiting to be written to the disk. Dirty data is stored in cache blocks, so the number reported might be larger than the actual number of bytes waiting. |
| Reads/second | The number of read operations delivered to the file system each second. |
| Writes/second | The number of write operations delivered to the file system each second. |

**KERNEL SETTINGS**

| Setting | Measurement |
|---|---|
| Processor usage (%) | The approximate percentage of time the processor is busy. |
| Threads | The current number of threads present in the system. |
| Virtual machines | The current number of virtual machines present in the system. |

**MEMORY MANAGER VMM32 SETTINGS**

| Setting | Measurement |
|---|---|
| Allocated memory | The total amount in bytes of other memory and swappable memory. If this value is changing when there is no activity on the computer, it indicates that the disk cache is resizing itself. |
| Discards | The number of pages discarded from memory each second. (The pages are not swapped to the disk because the information is already on the disk.) |
| Disk cache size | The current size, in bytes, of the disk cache. |
| Instance faults | The number of instance faults each second. |
| Locked memory | The amount of allocated memory that is locked. |
| Locked non-cache pages | Number of non-cache locked pages. |
| Maximum disk cache size | The largest size possible for a disk cache. This is a fixed value loaded at system startup. |
| Mid-disk cache size | The mid-disk cache size. This is a fixed value loaded at system startup. |
| Minimum disk cache size | The smallest size possible for a disk cache. This is a fixed value loaded at system startup. |
| Other memory | The amount of allocated memory not stored in the swap file, for example, code from Win32 *dynamic link libraries* (DLLs) and executable files, memory mapped files, nonpageable memory, and disk cache pages. |
| Page faults | The number of page faults each second. |
| Page-ins | The number of pages swapped into memory each second, including pages loaded from a Win32-based executable file or memory-mapped files. This value does not necessarily indicate low memory. |
| Page-outs | The number of pages swapped out of memory and written to disk each second. |

| TABLE 16-1    SYSTEM MONITOR PARAMETERS (COUNTERS) *(CONTINUED)* | |
|---|---|
| **MEMORY MANAGER VMM32 SETTINGS** | |
| Pages mapped from cache | Used to monitor MapCache/WinAlign changes. The swap file size in use at the same time as this setting should be monitored for differences after running the WinAlign tool. |
| Swap file defective | The number of bytes in the swap file that are found to be physically defective on the swap medium. Because swap file frames are allocated in 4096-byte blocks, a single damaged sector causes the whole block to be marked as defective. |
| Swap file in use | The number of bytes being used in the current swap file. |
| Swap file size | The size, in bytes, of the current swap file. |
| Swappable memory | The number of bytes allocated from the swap file. Locked pages still count for the purpose of this value. This includes code from 16-bit applications and DLLs, but not code from Win32 DLLs and executable files. |
| Unused physical memory | Amount of physical memory (RAM) not currently in use. |
| **MICROSOFT NETWORK CLIENT SETTINGS** | |
| **Setting** | **Measurement** |
| Bytes read/second | The number of bytes read from the redirector each second. |
| Bytes written/second | The number of bytes written to the redirector each second. |
| Number of nets | Number of networks currently running. |
| Open files | Number of open files on the network. |
| Resources | Number of resources. |
| Sessions | Number of sessions. |
| Transactions/second | The number of server message block (SMB) transactions managed by the redirector each second. |
| **MICROSOFT NETWORK SERVER/NETWARE SETTINGS** | |
| **Setting** | **Measurement** |
| Buffers | The number of buffers used by the server. |
| Bytes read/sec | The total number of bytes read from a disk. |
| Bytes written/sec | The total number of bytes written to a disk. |
| Bytes/sec | The total number of bytes read from and written to a disk. |
| Memory | The total memory used by the server. |
| NBs | Server network buffers. |
| Server threads | The current number of threads used by the server. |

To select more than one item, press CTRL while clicking the items that you want to select. To select several items in a row, click the first item, and then hold down SHIFT while clicking the last item.

With System Monitor under Windows XP, simply right-click the counters area, select Properties, and choose the Data tab (as in Figure 16-8 earlier). Use the Add button to configure the counter(s) that must be measured. Old or unneeded counters can be highlighted and deleted with the Delete button. Given the many counters available under Windows XP, I won't include a table here, but you can click the counter of interest and click Explain (as in Figure 16-9), and the utility will provide you with a detailed explanation of the particular counter.

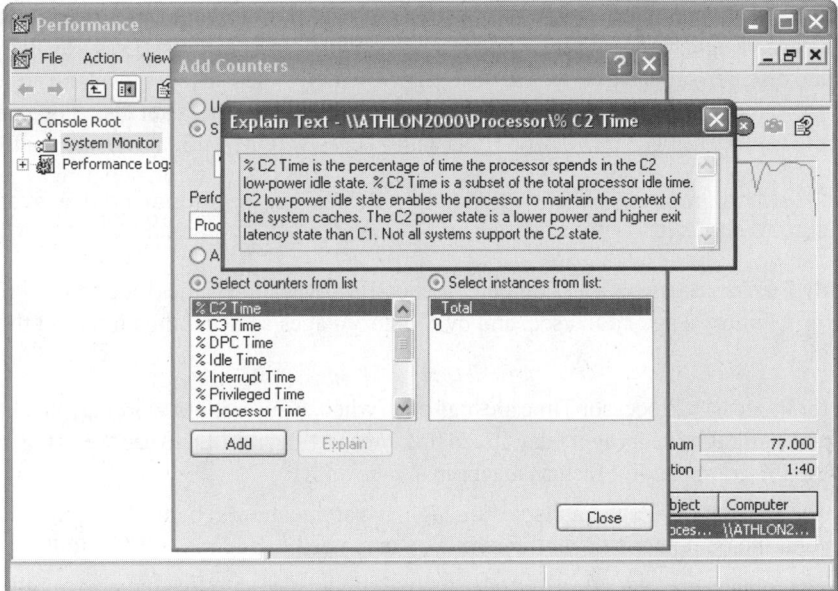

**FIGURE 16-9**    Use the Explain button to learn more about particular counters before selecting them under Windows XP.

## Troubleshooting with System Monitor

System Monitor is a versatile program that can measure a wide variety of important system parameters, but you'll need to have some idea of just what you're looking for in order to interpret the data that's displayed. This section offers some guidelines for basic performance troubleshooting under Windows XP.

**Processor Stress**    When system performance appears slow, check the processor counters to determine the total processor time (and idle time) available to the system. If the total processor time (Processor\%Processor Time) is consistently high (over 50 percent), and idle processor time (Processor\%Idle Time) is low, it may be time to consider a processor upgrade. In other cases, you may find that certain applications are demanding unusually large amounts of processor time. Also check the system's interrupt activity (Processor\Interrupts/sec). A large number of interrupts can keep the processor working on "real world" events, leaving less time to process applications. You may need to disable or reconfigure system devices causing excessive interrupt rates.

**Memory Leaks**    If you suspect that an application might not be freeing memory when you've finished using it (sometimes called *memory leaks*), you should monitor the value of Process\Thread Count over time. This will indicate whether the application is starting threads and not reclaiming them later. Windows 98/Me/XP should automatically remove such threads when the application closes, but if you identify a leak while the application is running, you may decide to restart the application periodically. (You can also check for patches or updates for the application that may fix the memory leak.)

**Insufficient Memory**    For example, if the values for Memory\Available MBytes and Memory\Pages/sec indicate a great deal of activity, performance problems might be related to system memory "stress" (often referred to as a "memory bottleneck"). These values might indicate a need for more physical memory (RAM) in the system.

**Disk Stress**    Poor performance in the disk sub-system can also impair system performance. Check for free disk space (Logical Disk\%Free Space), disk activity (PhysicalDisk\Disk Reads/sec and Disk Writes/sec), and disk performance (PhysicalDisk\%Disk Time). When space is low (and activity and disk time are high), you may need to upgrade the disk sub-system with a larger, faster disk. For example, it may be worthwhile to replace a 20GB UDMA/66 HDD with a 100GB UDMA/133 HDD and controller card.

> Low system RAM can result in excessive paging to virtual memory, impairing disk system performance. Be sure to check for memory stress before making disk upgrades.

**Poor Overall Performance**    If a computer seems slow, check the values reported by Process\%Processor Time, by Memory\Page Faults/sec, and by Memory\Pages/sec, and then interpret them using the following guide:

- If values for Process\%Processor Time are high even when the user is not working, check to see which application(s) might be keeping it busy. To do this, press CTRL-ALT-DEL to see the list of tasks running in the Close Program dialog (Task Manager in Windows XP).

- If the values for Memory\Page Faults/sec are high, the application(s) being used might have memory needs beyond the computer's capabilities, so you may need to add more RAM to the system.

- If the Memory\Pages/sec statistics are consistently high, inadequate free memory might be affecting performance because of excessive disk paging (using virtual memory). Also, you might be running an application that locks memory unnecessarily. Check your application(s) first to verify they're not locking memory, and then try adding more RAM to the system.

# Graphics Performance

Graphics adapter technology is advancing in leaps and bounds, especially in the area of graphics "acceleration." Powerful 2D and 3D chipsets (such as the GeForce 4 Ti 4600) speed the opening of screens and dialog boxes, or vastly increase the frame rate in your favorite 3D "shooter" or other visualization software. Unfortunately, graphics acceleration techniques are not always standard, and Windows 98/Me/XP may sometimes assume that a particular accelerator feature is present when it is not. You might see such problems ranging anywhere from small display irregularities to random system crashes. Windows 98/Me/XP allows control over your graphics accelerator in order to isolate possible accelerator-related problems. This allows you to continue using Windows until the driver can be updated (or the adapter can be replaced).

## ADJUSTING GRAPHICS ACCELERATION

You can manage the level of graphics acceleration used on your system through the Advanced Display Properties dialog and slider in Windows XP:

1. Right-click anywhere in the desktop and click Properties. The Display Properties dialog box opens.
2. Select the Settings tab and click the Advanced button. The Advanced Display Properties dialog box opens.

**3.** Select the Troubleshoot tab (see Figure 16-10). You'll see the hardware acceleration slider and write combining checkbox.

**4.** Windows XP provides six settings in the hardware acceleration slider (from Full to None). Ideally, you'd want to set the slider to Full. If you suspect trouble with the system's graphics acceleration, use this slider to systematically decrease the level of acceleration:

■ **Full**   All acceleration features are enabled (this is the optimum setting).

■ **4/5**   This disables the cursor and bitmap acceleration features.

■ **3/5**   This disables the cursor and all advanced drawing acceleration features.

■ **2/5**   This disables all DirectDraw and Direct3D acceleration features.

■ **1/5**   This shuts down all but basic hardware acceleration features.

■ **None**   All graphics acceleration features are disabled.

**5.** Select Apply and OK to save your changes. You may need to reboot the system so that your changes can take effect. In many cases, upgrading DirectX, the graphics card's drivers (or firmware), or upgrading the graphics card outright can correct any acceleration problems.

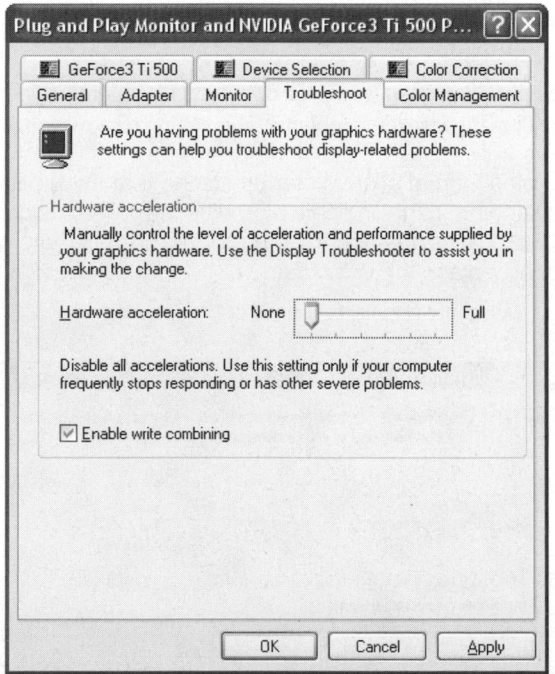

**FIGURE  16-10**    You can adjust graphics hardware acceleration under Windows XP to improve performance or help isolate possible problems.

Windows XP also provides the Enable Write Combining checkbox. This box is usually checked by default, and helps video performance by increasing the rate at which information is sent to the monitor. However, this type of acceleration can cause problems (such as video corruption) in some hardware setups. Try unchecking the Enable Write Combining checkbox if video corruption occurs.

1. A similar hardware acceleration slider is also available under Windows 9*x*/Me:Click Start | Settings | Control Panel.

2. When the Control Panel opens, click the Performance tab.

3. Click the Graphics button in the Advanced Settings area.

4. The Advanced Graphics Settings dialog will appear (Figure 16-11).

Note the slider's current position in case you want to return the slider to this starting point later. You can alter the level of hardware acceleration by moving the slider left or right:

■ The default setting is Full. This turns on all graphics hardware acceleration features available in the display driver. (This is the optimum setting.)

■ The first notch from the right (75%) can often be set to correct mouse pointer display problems.

■ The second notch from the right (50%) can be set to correct certain display errors. This setting prevents some bit block transfers from being performed on the display card and disables memory-mapped I/O for some display drivers.

■ The last notch from the right (None) can be selected to correct problems if your computer frequently stops responding to input or suffers other severe problems. This setting removes all driver acceleration support.

As an example, an error message at system startup stating that an application caused "an invalid page fault in module <unknown>" might indicate a problem between the display driver and the Windows 98 DIB engine. In such cases, the None setting should correct the problem until you're able to update the display driver or replace the video card.

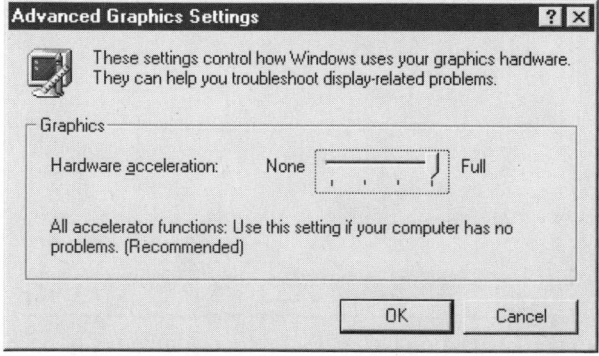

**FIGURE  16-11**    Adjusting the graphics hardware acceleration level under Windows 9*x*/Me

# CHECKING AND ADJUSTING DISPLAY SETTINGS

Video performance will also be affected by the Display settings of your video system. Often, reducing resolutions or selecting a smaller color palette can improve display frame rates (at least until the video driver
or adapter card can be upgraded). To check the current Display configuration under Windows XP:

1. Right-click on the desktop and select Properties.
2. The Display Properties dialog box opens.
3. Select the Settings tab (see Figure 16-12).
4. Note the Display description (for example, "Plug and Play Monitor on NVIDIA GeForce3 Ti 500").
5. The color depth is listed in the Color Quality drop-down list, while the resolution is shown by the
   Screen Resolution slider. You can adjust the color depth and resolution as needed, then apply those
   changes to your display system.

To check the current display setting under Windows 9*x*/Me:

1. Click Start | Settings | Control Panel.
2. When the Control Panel opens, click the Display tab.
3. Select the Settings tab.

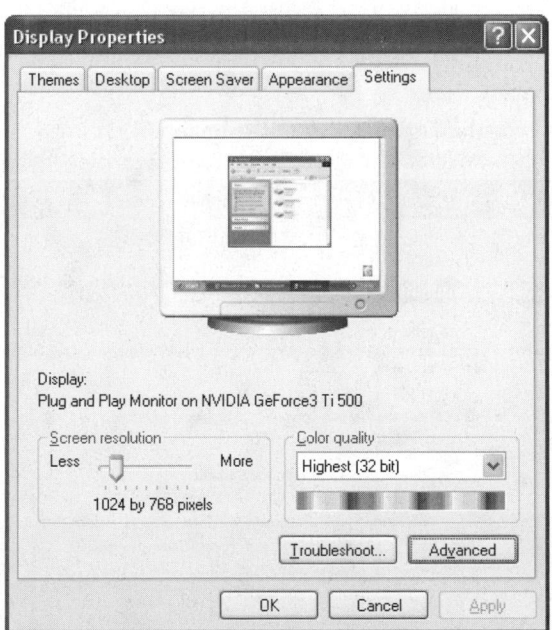

**FIGURE 16-12**    Check and adjust the Windows XP display using the Settings tab in your Display
Properties dialog box.

4. Note the Display description (for example, "Plug and Play Monitor on Voodoo 3 AGP").

5. The color depth is listed in the Colors drop-down list, while the resolution is shown by the Screen Area slider. You can adjust the color depth and resolution as needed, then apply those changes to your display system.

Your monitor must be capable of displaying the resolution that you select. Make sure that you do not increase the resolution above the monitor's capability. Otherwise, the screen image will be terribly distorted, and you may damage the monitor.

## Limited Resolution and Color Depth

If you notice that you cannot select resolutions higher than 640 × 480 or cannot select color depths higher than 16 colors, chances are that the display driver for your video card has not been installed (or is installed incorrectly). This happens frequently after reinstalling Windows or replacing the video adapter. You can almost always correct this problem by upgrading the display driver. As an alternative, you can remove the video adapter entry in the Device Manager, reboot the computer, and then allow Windows 98/Me/XP to redetect the adapter so that you may install the correct drivers at that time.

## Checking DirectX

Modern Windows platforms rely on the use of Microsoft's DirectX APIs to provide the complex suite of video, sound, and input device support that is required for many current games and multimedia software packages. If you're playing games or just viewing an occasional video clip, it's important that you install the latest version of DirectX on your system. You can download DirectX from Microsoft's Web site at www.microsoft.com/directx. (DirectX 8.1 is the latest version available for the PC.) Before installing or upgrading DirectX for Windows 9x/Me/XP, you should check the version (if any) currently installed on your system:

1. Click Start and then click Run.

2. In the Open dialog, type **dxdiag** and click OK (Figure 16-13).

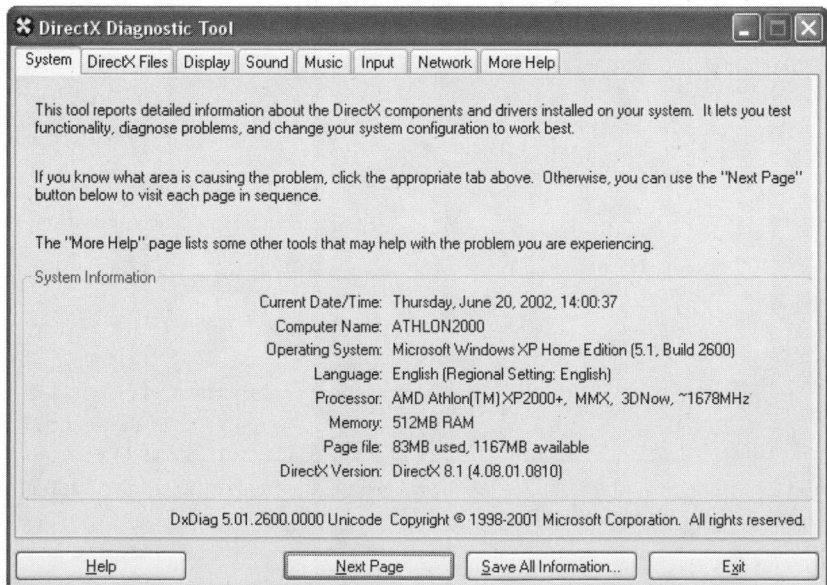

**FIGURE  16-13**   The DXDIAG diagnostic dialog for DirectX under Windows XP

3. Select the System tab (if it's not already selected), and look at the System Information area. The DXDIAG utility reveals several pieces of information about your system and lists the installed DirectX version at the bottom, such as "DirectX 8.1 (4.08.01.0810)." You can also check on other system hardware such as the processor, memory, and page file.

4. Click Exit when you're done checking the version.

In many cases, you can update DirectX using the Windows Update feature.

# Memory Performance

Memory interacts very closely with the CPU, and memory performance can have a profound impact on overall system performance. You must install an adequate amount of memory with the right characteristics, then configure the system to utilize that memory in the best possible way. You should also be concerned with system cache, and verify that it's properly enabled. The following points highlight the memory issues that you should be aware of.

■ **Memory amount**   You should install enough physical memory to adequately support your operating system and the application(s) that you intend to run. Generally, 32MB is considered to be the minimum amount of memory for Windows 95/98 and most general applications, but most systems with Windows 98/Me are fitted with 128MB of RAM. Today's PCs with Windows XP often sport 256MB, 512MB, or more. More memory is helpful for graphics, multimedia, and other memory-intensive applications (such as 3D computer action games). If there is not enough memory to support your system, you'll see a great deal of hard drive activity as data is passed back and forth to the swap file, and overall system performance will suffer. (You can see these performance hits with tools like System Monitor.) Check the amount of installed RAM during the POST, or use a utility like System Information (as in Figure 16-2 earlier) to determine the available RAM.

Older motherboards could only cache a limited amount of RAM, and memory accessed outside the cacheable memory range could impair performance. Today's motherboards do not suffer from this limitation, and can cache a huge amount of physical RAM. But when working with older systems, be sure to check the Maximum Cacheable RAM specification for the motherboard.

■ **Memory characteristics**   When selecting RAM for your system, choose RAM with the optimum characteristics for your particular motherboard. Consider the memory type first. Ordinary SDRAM is generally considered to be an adequate memory type and is supported by many Pentium II/III/4 motherboards. Use PC133 (133 MHz) SDRAM wherever possible. More recent Pentium III/4 systems employ Double Data Rate (DDR) SDRAM for even better memory performance, and this is preferred wherever possible. An alternative to SDRAM is Rambus DRAM (RDRAM), which uses dedicated high-speed channels to exchange data between the CPU and memory. PC800 and PC1066 RDRAM is typical today and is widely supported on many motherboards using Intel's 800 series chipsets. (PC2100 and even faster Rambus modules are appearing.) Also consider the memory speed, since faster memory will respond better than slower memory. For example, SDRAM uses 12ns, 10ns, or 8ns "Cycle Time." The 8ns SDRAM will be faster. Also select SDRAM with a "CAS Latency" of 2 rather than 3 (if possible). When comparing standardized modules, larger numbers are faster (for example, PC266 DDR SDRAM is faster than PC133 SDRAM).

Error checking features such as parity or ECC generally do not affect memory performance, but cost a bit more, so you can select RAM with or without such features.

■ **AGP video memory**    When an AGP video system is integrated onto your motherboard, some amount of system RAM is typically assigned to serve as a frame buffer, store textures, and so on. Video memory is directly subtracted from the available RAM in the system. For example, a PC with 128MB of RAM and a 32MB AGP frame buffer will only have 96MB available for the operating system, applications, and data. You can normally adjust the AGP buffer size through the system's CMOS Setup (see Chapter 10). If you must assign a large AGP buffer, you may consider adding RAM to the system.

■ **Avoiding "SIMM/DIMM Stackers"**    As DIMM slots became commonplace on motherboards, some manufacturers developed adapters that allowed you to "stack" several smaller SIMMs/DIMMs into a single device that would fit in a DIMM slot. This technology worked fine, but upsets the RAM timing because of the added distance between the RAM and the motherboard (introduced by the SIMM adapter). This can degrade the RAM's performance. You may need to add a wait state in the system's CMOS Setup in order to compensate for this added delay. As a rule, forgo memory adapters, and use suitable RAM devices that are appropriate for your system's speed.

SIMM/DIMM stackers are very rarely used today, so you may not encounter them, but it's important to recognize their impact on memory performance.

■ **Optimizing the CMOS Setup**    You can often wring a bit more performance from your memory by manually optimizing the memory settings in your CMOS Setup (usually under the Advanced Chipset Setup menu). The trick is to keep wait states and latencies as low as possible, while keeping memory access techniques at a level that is appropriate for the memory type that you're using. Pushing the RAM too far will cause errors and may prevent the system from even booting. You should refer to the manual that accompanies your motherboard for detailed information regarding your CMOS Setup (or refer to Chapter 10).

# Drive Performance

To improve the performance of a hard drive, you must first understand the factors that influence drive performance. The two most important factors are time-related: the amount of time it takes to locate a file, and the rate at which data can be passed back and forth between the drive and system. Every other concern is intimately related to those two issues.

## SEEK TIME AND LATENCY

Since read/write heads are mechanical devices, it takes a finite amount of time to move them across a disk platter. The time required to accomplish this move depends on the size of the drive and the type of mechanism moving the heads. Newer drives are typically quite small, so the distances that must be traversed are short. Smooth and efficient voice-coil actuators are the head drive mechanism of choice, so movement is also enhanced. The combination of these factors has drastically reduced seek time over the last 20 years, but seek time is still a major part of overall drive delays.

Unfortunately, *seek time* is a rather generic term—different manufacturers each measure seek time as a slightly different parameter. The best-case seek time is referred to as *track-to-track seek time,* where the R/W heads only need to step in or out to the next adjacent track (or cylinder). This time is typically only a few hundred microseconds. If the best case seek time is the time required to step between two adjacent tracks, the worst-case seek time is the time needed to step from the outermost track to the innermost track (or vice versa). Few manufacturers actually use this time since it seems so large. Instead, most drive manufacturers use an *average seek time,* which is the time needed to step halfway across the disk surface. Today, most drives offer average seek times between 6ms and 12ms. There is no way to accelerate seek times other than to simply upgrade the drive to a newer model with a smaller seek time specification.

Another part of drive performance is *latency.* Latency refers to the time it takes for the drive platters to rotate under the read/write heads once they've stepped into position. As with seek time, there are several different ways of measuring latency. *Maximum latency* is the time it takes for the platters to make one full turn, while *average latency* (more commonly used) is the time for one half turn. Average latency seems to run about 4ms for today's 7200 rpm drives. Once again, there is no way to reduce latency without upgrading to a faster physical drive.

## DATA TRANSFER RATES

Once the drive's R/W heads and platters have moved into position, data can flow to or from the drive. The rate at which data can flow is known as the *data transfer rate.* Data transfer is generally given in Mbits/s. If you divide this figure by 8, you will get MB/s. A more practical measure of data transfer is the data rate between the hard drive and the drive controller (across the interface). EIDE hard drives can support burst data transfer rates up to 16 MB/s, though Ultra-ATA hard drives can reach bursts of 133 MB/s (100 MB/s for Ultra-DMA/100, 66 MB/s for Ultra-DMA/66, or 33 MB/s for Ultra-DMA/33). This is comparable with fast SCSI-2 drive configurations, as shown in Table 16-2. In virtually all cases, you can speed the performance of your hard drive system by upgrading the drive and controller to newer models (for example, an Ultra-DMA/133 drive and compatible PCI-based controller card if necessary).

Data transfer rates are a key part of drive delay. Most of the hesitation and pauses you see in the everyday operation of DOS or Windows 98/Me/XP are largely because the operating system is waiting for the drive to catch up. That is, the operating system typically must wait for a file to be loaded or saved before any other operations can continue. The faster a file's data can be transferred to or from the drive, the shorter those delays would be. Today, "apparent" drive performance is enhanced through the aggressive use of caching, where drive data is cached to RAM so the system may continue, then written to the drive as time allows.

## FILE FRAGMENTATION

The interaction of operating systems also affects drive performance. When a drive is high-level formatted with an operating system, the drive's space is segregated into sets of adjacent sectors (called *clusters*). The size of a cluster depends on the size of the drive, but today's large, multi-gigabyte drives usually use 32KB to 64KB clusters under FAT16, or 4KB to 8KB clusters under FAT32. The cluster approach was designed to simplify file "housekeeping"—easing file storage tracking requirements while keeping wasted space minimal. Although the system is less than ideal, it works, and has been in use since the earliest versions of DOS were able to support hard drives. The problem with cluster-based file storage is that files are stored wherever clusters are available. Ideally, all of the clusters that compose a file should be contiguous (adjacent to one another), but that is a rare occurrence in actual practice. As a drive fills, old files are erased, and new files are added, clusters are filled and reclaimed throughout the drive.

As a result, changing files gradually become scattered across the drive as DOS searches for any available clusters. This scattering behavior is called *file fragmentation,* and it is a natural side effect of "cluster-based" file systems. The problem with file fragmentation is that each time the continuity of a file is broken, the drive's R/W heads have to be repositioned before another cluster can be read (also incurring

**TABLE 16-2**   COMPARISON OF HARD DRIVE DATA TRANSFER RATES

| DATA TRANSFER MODE | BURST DATA RATE (MB/S) | NOTES |
|---|---|---|
| Single Word DMA 0 | 2.1 | Old ATA (IDE) drives |
| PIO Mode 0 | 3.3 | IDE drives |
| Single Word DMA 1 | 4.2 | IDE drives |
| Multi Word DMA 0 | 4.2 | IDE drives |
| SCSI-1 | 5.0 | 8-bit SCSI |
| PIO Mode 1 | 5.2 | IDE drives |
| PIO Mode 2 | 8.3 | IDE drives |
| Single Word DMA 2 | 8.3 | IDE drives |
| Fast SCSI-2 | 10.0 | 16-bit SCSI |
| Wide SCSI-2 | 10.0 | 16-bit SCSI |
| PIO Mode 3 | 11.1 | Newer ATA-2 (EIDE) drives |
| Multi Word DMA 1 | 13.3 | EIDE drives |
| PIO Mode 4 | 16.6 | EIDE drives |
| Multi Word DMA 2 | 16.6 | EIDE drives |
| Fast/Wide SCSI-2 | 20.0 | 16-bit SCSI |
| Fast-20 SCSI-3 | 20.0 | 8-bit SCSI |
| Multi Word DMA 3 | 33.0 | Ultra-ATA (Ultra-DMA/33) drives |
| Wide/Fast-20 SCSI-3 | 40.0 | 16-bit SCSI |
| Fast-40 SCSI-3 | 40.0 | 8-bit SCSI |
| Multi Word DMA 4 | 66.0 | Ultra-ATA (Ultra-DMA/66) drives |
| Wide/Fast-40 SCSI-3 | 80.0 | 16-bit SCSI |
| Multi Word DMA 5 | 100 | Ultra-ATA (Ultra-DMA/100) drives |
| Multi Word DMA 6 | 133 | Ultra-ATA (Ultra-DMA/133) drives |

additional latency). If a file uses four clusters, and each cluster is several tracks apart, the heads will have to be repositioned four times to read or write that file. These additional seek times and latencies prolong the loading or saving of a file. In addition to these delays, the extra mechanical demands of R/W head positioning can eventually lead to premature drive failure.

## Managing File Fragmentation

DOS and Windows 98/Me/XP offer the Disk Defragmenter tool (often called Defrag), which should be used periodically to reorganize the disk clusters so that all clusters related to a particular file are made contiguous. Once your related clusters are relocated together, the drive doesn't have to work as hard to load or save files. This often makes your drive access seem faster. You can find Defrag in your Windows 9x/Me/XP System Tools menu:

1. Click Start | Programs (All Programs under Windows XP) | Accessories | System Tools.
2. Click on Disk Defragmenter. The Defrag window will open. (The Windows XP Disk Defragmenter is shown in Figure 16-14.)

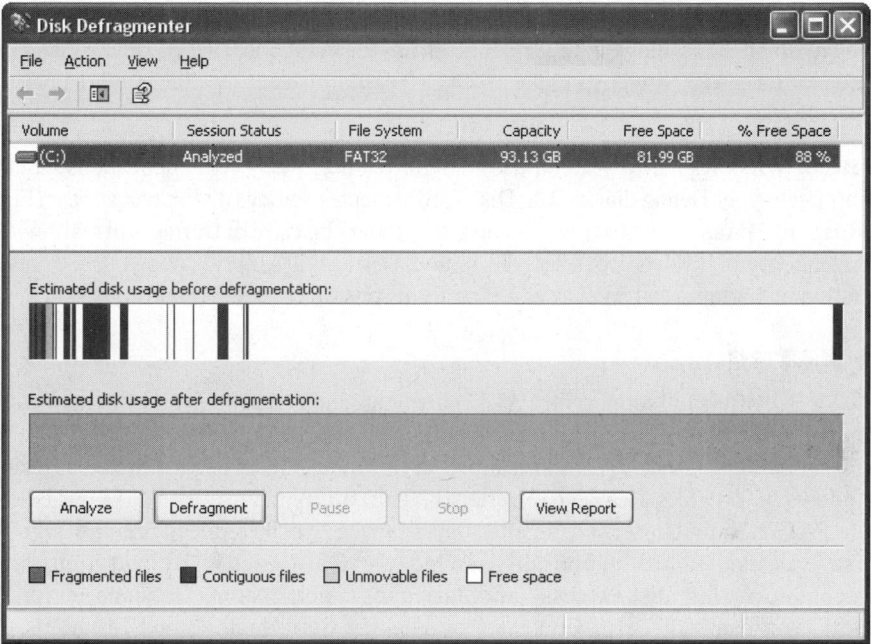

**FIGURE  16-14**     Defragmenting the selected hard drive under Windows XP

3.  You can select the drive(s) to be defragmented, and then start the process by clicking OK. Windows XP allows you to analyze the drive first to estimate the effectiveness of a defrag process. You can view the results of a defrag analysis as in Figure 16-15.

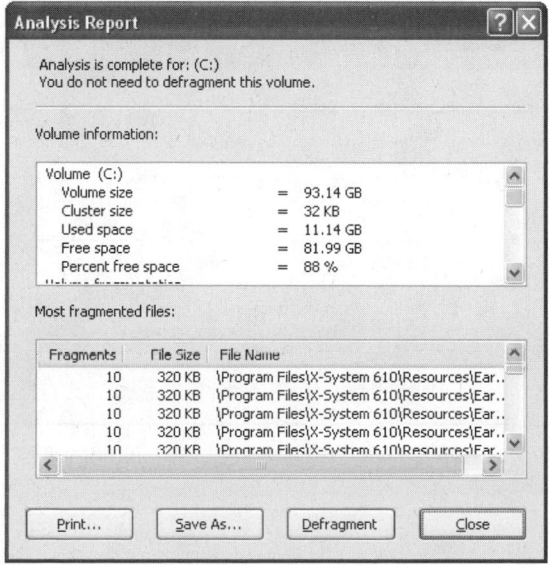

**FIGURE  16-15**     Windows XP provides a detailed analysis of drive fragmentation.

**4.** If it's recommended that you defrag the drive, go ahead and start the process. It may take a while for Defrag to finish, depending on the size of the drive, the number of files it contains, and the extent of fragmentation. FAT32 drives can take much longer to finish because there are many more clusters for Defrag to work with.

If you're using Windows 98/Me, you can also configure Defrag to help your applications start faster. Select the Settings option in your Defrag dialog. The Disk Defragmenter Settings dialog will appear (Figure 16-16). Check the "Rearrange program files so my programs start faster" box so that Defrag will rearrange your applications for faster boot-up. If you do not select this option, Defrag will simply group your file clusters without any consideration of startup speed. Windows XP performs this function automatically.

## USING FAT32

Windows 98/Me/XP offers full support for FAT32 partitions, and FAT32 is clearly the standard file system on all current PCs. (Network servers and workstations may use NTFS under Windows NT/2000/XP.) FAT32 uses smaller clusters than FAT16 and allows drives over 2GB to be partitioned as a single logical volume. Windows 98 provides a Drive Converter (FAT32) utility that can convert your existing FAT16 partition(s) to FAT32. Since clusters are smaller, "slack space" can be reduced dramatically—freeing up as much as several hundred MB on your drive. Windows 98 also uses FAT32 partitions far more efficiently, which allows fast disk access (and fast application loading in conjunction with Disk Defragmenter). You can start Drive Converter by clicking Start, highlighting Programs, pointing to Accessories, selecting System Tools, and then clicking Drive Converter. The converter will start and allow you to convert your selected drive(s).

Windows XP uses FAT32 or NTFS only. You can convert a FAT16 drive to FAT32 during Windows XP Setup. In some cases, it's easier to repartition and reformat the drive as FAT32 before installing the operating system.

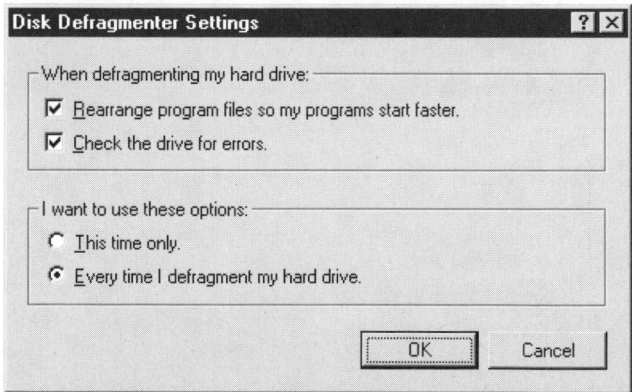

**FIGURE 16-16** Improving application startup speed with Defrag under Windows 9*x*/Me

There are some important tips to remember before you use the converter under Windows 98:

■ Once you convert a partition to FAT32 format using Drive Converter, you cannot return to the FAT16 format unless you repartition and reformat the FAT32 drive. If you converted the drive on which Windows 98 is installed, then you must reinstall Windows 98 after repartitioning the drive as FAT16.

■ Older disk compression software (including DriveSpace 3) is not compatible with FAT32. If your drive is already compressed, you may not be able to convert to FAT32. You may need to uncompress the drive (perhaps upgrade the drive system) before converting to FAT32.

■ If you convert a removable disk to FAT32, and use that disk with an operating system that is not FAT32-compatible, you cannot access the disk when running the other operating system. For example, an OS under FAT16 cannot access a Jaz disk using FAT32.

■ If your computer has a "hibernate" feature, the conversion process may turn this feature off. You may need to reenable this feature manually.

■ Some disk utilities that depend on FAT16 may not work with FAT32 drives. You will be prompted if you're running one of these utilities. Contact your disk utility manufacturer to see if there is an updated version that is compatible with FAT32.

■ Converting your hard drive to FAT32 using Drive Converter may affect your ability to dual boot the system.

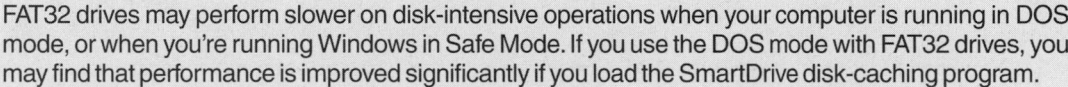
FAT32 drives may perform slower on disk-intensive operations when your computer is running in DOS mode, or when you're running Windows in Safe Mode. If you use the DOS mode with FAT32 drives, you may find that performance is improved significantly if you load the SmartDrive disk-caching program.

## CHECKING FOR DISK ERRORS

With Windows 9x/Me, you can use the ScanDisk utility to check the disk for file problems such as lost allocation units and cross-linked files. Such file problems are quite common with FAT-based operating systems, and file damage can corrupt an application, driver, or data file. You should run ScanDisk periodically and allow it to correct any problems that it finds. If you detect damaged file(s), be sure to defragment the drive, then reinstall the damaged file(s) from a backup or the original installation disks. You can run ScanDisk from DOS by simply exiting Windows to DOS, switching to the drive that you need to test, then typing

```
C:> SCANDISK              <Enter>
```

1. You can then follow the on-screen directions to correct any error that's encountered. For a deeper test, select Yes to perform a surface test on the drive. (This may take anywhere from several minutes to several hours.) Finally, select View Log to review any actions and results taken by ScanDisk. If you're having trouble starting Windows, use the DOS version of ScanDisk. Otherwise, use ScanDisk through Windows 9x/Me: Click Start | Programs | Accessories | System Tools.

2. Click ScanDisk. The ScanDisk dialog will open (Figure 16-17).

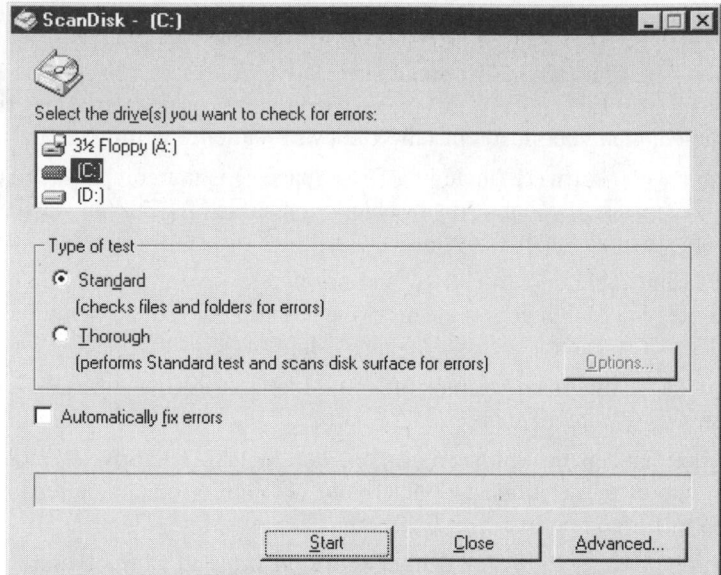

**FIGURE 16-17**   Checking and correcting disk problems with ScanDisk under Windows 9*x*/Me

3. You can select the drive to be tested, along with a surface scan or other advanced options.

4. In most cases, you should run ScanDisk to test for errors first, but do not allow ScanDisk to fix errors automatically until you've identified the errors.

Be very careful with ScanDisk versions. If you're using a FAT32 partition, be sure to use the Windows 98/Me version of ScanDisk. Using an older version of ScanDisk on a FAT32 partition may cause file damage.

Windows XP does not provide a "formal" ScanDisk utility per se, but you can use Windows XP to check the disk and correct errors. Click Start and select My Computer. Right-click a hard drive and select Properties, then choose the Tools tab (see Figure 16-18). Click Check Now to start the test. You can opt to automatically fix file system errors, and recover bad sectors on the drive during the test. Windows XP will report any problems that were found (and corrected).

You can also launch Disk Defragmenter from this point.

# 32-BIT DRIVERS WITH WINDOWS 9X/ME

Ideally, Windows 98/Me will apply a 32-bit protected-mode driver to every drive in the system—this ensures optimum performance. You can verify the use of 32-bit drivers by reviewing the File System entry in your Performance tab under the System icon. By default, 32-bit disk access is always enabled unless Windows 98/Me detects a real-mode disk driver that does not have a protected-mode replacement. This could be an older Stacker driver, a hard-disk security or encryption driver, or other legacy driver for a hard drive. To prevent the performance loss that occurs when Windows 98/Me is forced to use a real-mode disk driver, upgrade to a protected-mode replacement for the offending driver. It may

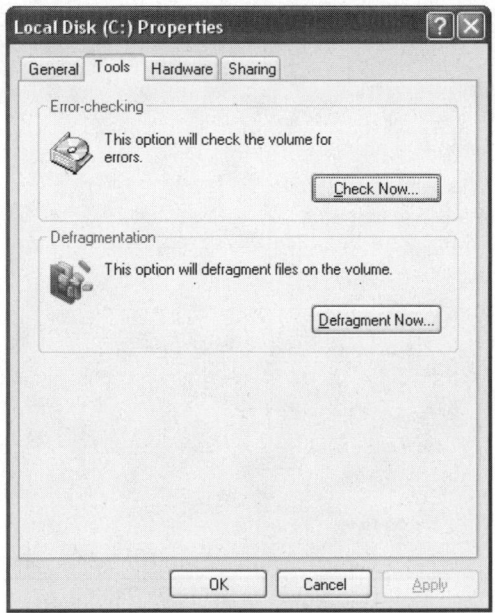

**FIGURE 16-18** Windows XP provides an error checking utility for your hard drives.

also be necessary to systematically delete or REMark out any real-mode device entries in **config.sys** or **autoexec.bat** files.

 If you need to determine why a real-mode disk driver was installed under Windows, check the IOS.LOG file.

## BUS MASTERING

Traditionally, a *bus* is simply a means of allowing devices access to system resources, and this was almost always accomplished under the direction of a master device—the system CPU. This meant that most data transfers between the drive controller and host system were accomplished through *Programmed I/O* (PIO) modes (see Table 16-2). With the introduction of "intelligent" bus architectures such as PCI, individual devices on the bus could assume control and initiate data transfers without the direct intervention of the CPU. This technique is generally called *Direct Memory Access* (DMA). There's nothing really new about DMA, and PCs have offered DMA channels since the early IBM PCs. The difference is that today's busses allow high-performance DMA transfers by devices that temporarily assume control of that bus. Such *bus mastering* requires the use of bus master drivers.

If your system has bus mastering drivers installed (and devices that support DMA data transfers), you'll see a DMA checkbox in the Options area of the Properties dialog for that device, such as in Figure 16-19. By default, the DMA checkbox is usually unselected under Windows 9*x*/Me. If you select the DMA checkbox, the drive will attempt to use DMA data transfers. Be extremely careful when enabling DMA data transfers. If your system hardware does not fully support bus mastering (or the bus master drivers are old or corrupt), you may find that drive performance actually decreases—or the system may even become unstable. Try installing the latest bus master drivers for your motherboard/chipset before enabling DMA data transfers.

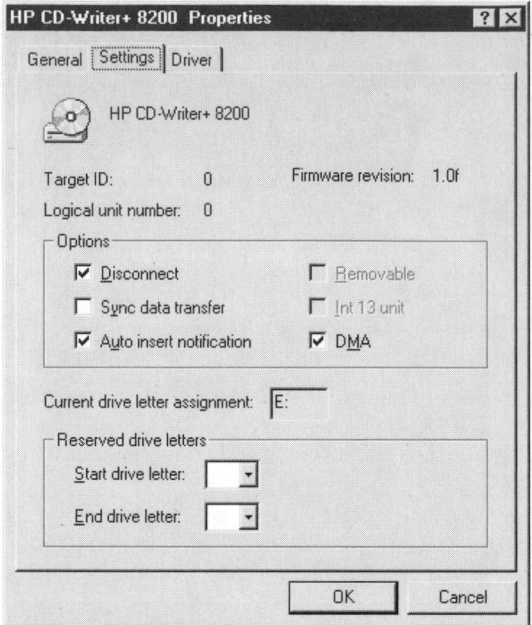

**FIGURE  16-19**    Enabling DMA data transfers through the Windows 9*x*/Me device's Properties dialog

Under Windows XP, DMA transfer modes are handled through the drive controller's Properties dialog box, not through the individual drive's Properties. The primary and secondary IDE drive controllers can be accessed through the Device Manager.

## OPTIMIZING VIRTUAL MEMORY

Windows 98/Me/XP uses a special file on your hard disk called a *virtual memory swap file* (also called a *paging file*). When using virtual memory under Windows 98/Me/XP, some of your program code and data are kept in memory (system RAM), while other information is swapped temporarily to "virtual memory" on the hard drive. When that information is required again, Windows 98/Me/XP pulls it back into RAM (and swaps other information to virtual memory if necessary). This activity is transparent to the end user, though you might notice that your hard disk is working. Virtual memory allows you to run more programs at one time than the computer's existing RAM would normally allow. The Windows 98/Me/XP swap file is dynamic, so it can shrink or grow as needed based on the tasks at hand and available disk space. It can also occupy a fragmented region of the hard disk with no substantial performance penalty.

The best way to ensure good swap file performance is to ensure that the drive containing your swap file has ample free space. This way, the swap file size can shrink and grow as needed.

Although your system's default settings usually provide good overall swap file performance, you can manually adjust the parameters used to define the swap file. For example, to optimize swap file performance on a computer with multiple hard drives, you can override the default location of the Windows swap file. As a rule, the swap file should be placed on the drive with the **fastest** performance. If you've placed the swap file on a drive that's extremely busy, performance might be boosted by relocating the swap file to another one of the drives that's not as busy. To adjust your virtual memory swap file size under Windows XP:

1. Click Start | Control Panel | Performance and Maintenance | System.

2. Select the Advanced tab. Click the Settings button in the Performance area.

3. The Performance Options dialog box opens. Select the Advanced tab (see Figure 16-20).

4. The "Total paging file size for all drives" is listed for you. In this case, the size has been set at 768MB (for this system's 100GB hard drive).

5. If you need to adjust the paging file size, click the Change button. The Virtual Memory dialog opens (see Figure 16-21).

6. You can set a custom size (within a range), allow Windows XP to set the paging file size automatically, or turn off the paging entirely (though that's only advisable if there is *a lot* of RAM in the system).

7. Click the Set button to accept any changes, then click OK.

To adjust the swap file size under Windows 9*x*/Me:

1. Open the Control Panel, double-click the System icon, click the Performance tab, and then click Virtual Memory. The Virtual Memory dialog appears, as in Figure 16-22.

2. By default, the "Let Windows manage my virtual memory settings" option is selected.

3. To specify a different hard disk, click the "Let me specify my own virtual memory settings" option, and then specify the new disk in the Hard disk box. As an alternative, type values (in KB) in the Minimum or Maximum box, and then click OK.

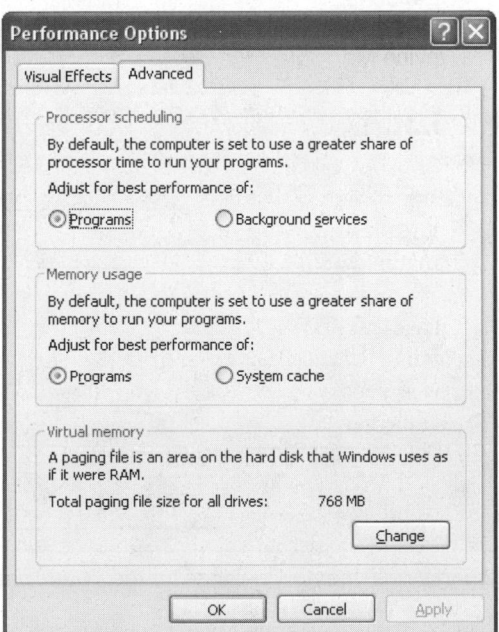

**FIGURE  16-20**    The Performance Options dialog will list the current paging file size and allow you to make changes if necessary.

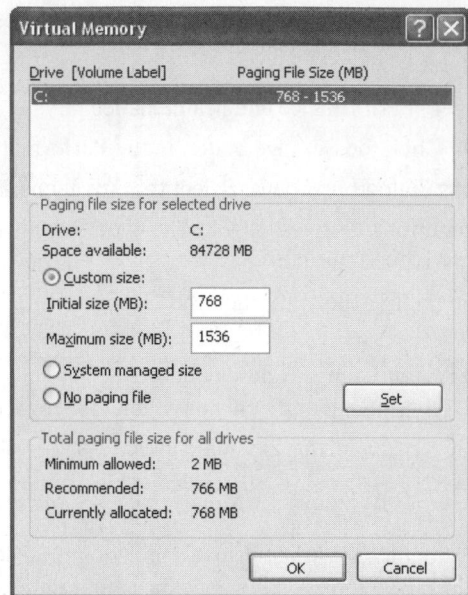

**FIGURE 16-21**    Set the paging file size manually, let Windows XP manage it for you, or turn off the paging file.

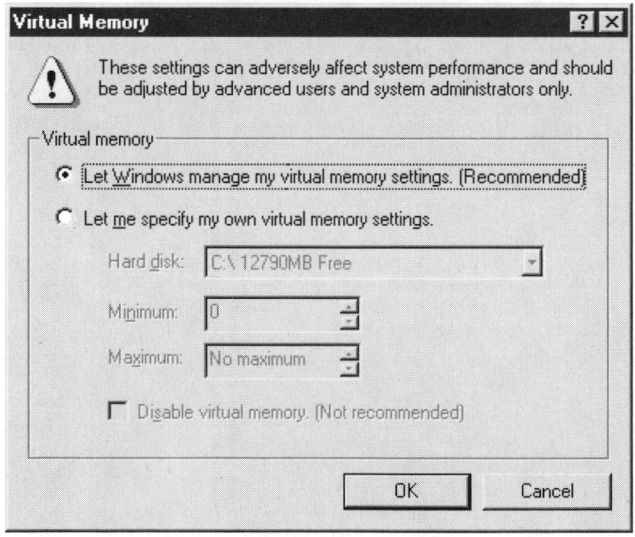

**FIGURE 16-22**    Configuring virtual memory settings for the Windows 9x/Me PC

If you set the maximum swap file size in the Virtual Memory dialog to use the amount of free space currently on a drive, Windows 98/Me assumes that it can increase the swap file beyond that size if more free disk space becomes available. If you want to impose a fixed limit on the swap file size, make sure that the limit you choose is less than the current maximum drive space.

# OPTIMIZING THE HARD DRIVE FILE SYSTEM

In Windows XP, hard drive caching is controlled automatically. However, you can check the hard drive and ensure that write caching is enabled for best performance. Open the Device Manager, expand the Disk Drives entry, double-click the hard drive that you're interested in, and select the Policies tab (see Figure 16-23). Make sure that the Enable Write Caching On The Disk box is checked. Write caching saves data to a small area of RAM until disk time is available to place the cached data on the drive. Obviously, if power fails or the system crashes before the cached data can be written to the disk, that data will be lost. In most cases, it's best to have this feature enabled.

In Windows 98/Me, file system and drive performance can be controlled based on how the computer is used in most situations. The option for configuring file system performance is controlled only by the user. None of these settings is affected by other configuration changes that might be made in Windows 98/Me (such as installing file and printer sharing services). To optimize file system performance under Windows 9x/Me, open the Control Panel, double-click the System icon, click the Performance tab, click File System, and then select the Hard Disk tab (Figure 16-24). You can adjust cache optimizations by moving the

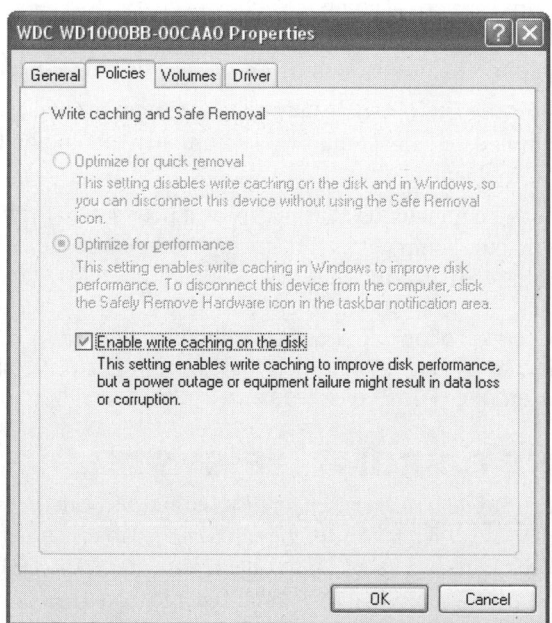

**FIGURE 16-23**     Be sure to enable write caching to the disk under Windows XP.

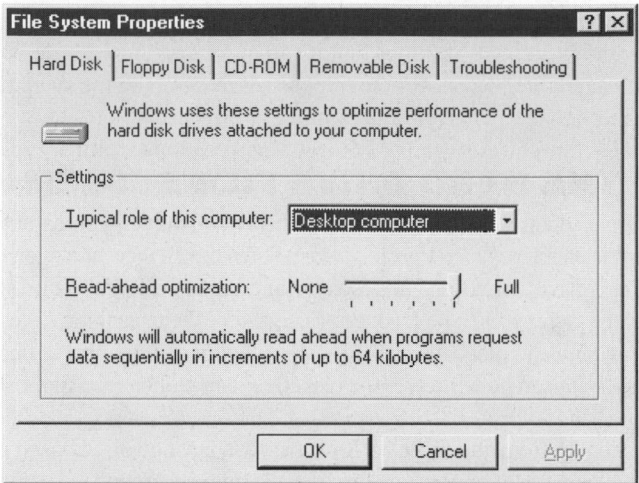

**FIGURE 16-24**    Setting system file properties for the hard drive(s)

Read-Ahead Optimization slider. In the "Typical role of this computer" entry, select the most common role for this computer, and then click OK. Each role is outlined next:

■ **Desktop computer**    This is a normal computer acting primarily as a network client, or an individual computer with no networking. This configuration assumes that there is more than the minimum required RAM and that the computer is running on AC power (rather than a battery).

■ **Mobile or docking system**    This is usually any computer with limited memory. This configuration assumes that RAM is limited, and the computer is commonly running on battery power, so the disk cache should be flushed frequently.

■ **Network server**    This is a computer used primarily as a peer server for file or printer sharing. This configuration assumes that the computer has adequate RAM and frequent disk activity, so the system is optimized for a large amount of disk access.

 The time to launch an application often depends on cluster size (therefore, the particular file system). Smaller cluster sizes allow applications to launch faster—a 4KB cluster size (FAT32) is best, but larger cluster sizes (for example, FAT16) give less of a performance boost.

## OPTIMIZING THE CD-ROM FILE SYSTEM

The CD-ROM cache is separate from the cache used for disk file and network access because the performance characteristics of the CD-ROM are different. The cache can be paged to disk (the file and network cache cannot). This reduces the work for Windows 98/Me, but still allows better CD-ROM performance. When Windows 98/Me is retrieving data from a compact disc, it's still faster to read a record from the cache—even if it's been paged to disk—since the disk-access time is much faster than the CD-ROM access time.

 A small CD-ROM cache makes a big difference in streaming performance, but a much larger cache does not pay off as significantly unless the cache is large enough to contain entire multimedia streams.

To set the supplemental cache size for your Windows 98 CD file system:

1. Open the Control Panel, double-click the System icon, click the Performance tab, and then click File System.

2. Click the CD-ROM tab and then drag the slider to set the Supplemental Cache Size (Figure 16-25).

3. Move the Supplemental Cache Size slider to the right to allocate more RAM for caching data from the CD-ROM drive, or to the left to allocate less RAM for caching data. Note that many multimedia programs perform better with a smaller cache because they tend not to reuse data.

4. In the "Optimize access pattern for" box, select a setting based on your computer's CD-ROM drive speed.

5. Click OK; then shut down and restart the computer.

You cannot adjust CD drive caching under Windows XP.

# OPTIMIZING REMOVABLE DISK PERFORMANCE

Windows 98/Me gives you the option to use write-behind caching to improve the performance of removable disk drives, such as the Zip or Jaz drive. To set write-behind caching for removable disk drives under Windows 98/Me:

1. Open the Control Panel, double-click the System icon, click the Performance tab, click File System, and then click the Removable Disk tab.

2. Select the "Enable write-behind caching on all removable disk drives" checkbox, and then click OK.

3. If this causes a problem with disk operations, repeat the first step, then clear the "Enable write-behind caching on all removable disk drives" checkbox, and click OK.

You cannot adjust CD drive caching under Windows XP.

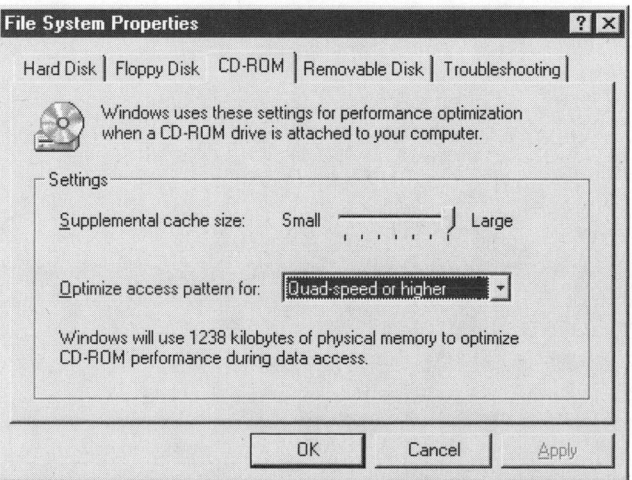

**FIGURE 16-25**    Setting Windows 9*x* system file properties for the CD-ROM drive(s)

# FILE SYSTEM TROUBLESHOOTING TIPS

The System option in Control Panel presents a set of options for changing file system performance under Windows 9*x*/Me. You can use these options when you experience rare hardware or software compatibility problems. To display the file system troubleshooting options with Windows 9*x*/Me:

**1.** Open the Control Panel, double-click the System icon, and then click the Performance tab.

**2.** Click File System and then click the Troubleshooting tab (see Figure 16-26).

Enabling any of these file system troubleshooting options will seriously degrade system performance. Enable these options only if necessary, and disable them when your troubleshooting is completed.

You can then select one or more troubleshooting options. Each option is highlighted next:

- *Disable new file sharing and locking semantics.* This option changes the internal rules for file sharing and locking hard disks. This option should be selected if a DOS-based application has problems sharing files under Windows.

- *Disable long name preservation for old programs.* This option disables the preservation of long file names when files are opened and saved by programs that do not recognize long file names. This option should be checked when an important legacy program is not compatible with long file names.

- *Disable protected-mode hard disk interrupt handling.* This option prevents Windows from bypassing the BIOS routine that handles interrupts from the hard disk controller. Some hard disk drives might need this option to be checked for interrupts to be processed correctly. If this option is checked, the BIOS routine handles the interrupts, slowing system performance.

- *Disable synchronous buffer commits.* The "file commit" function guarantees integrity of data being written to the drive. Applications use this feature so that critical data is written to the disk before returning to the OS. Choosing this option disables this feature. Data is still written to disk, but it is written to disk in the background—at the convenience of the operating system.

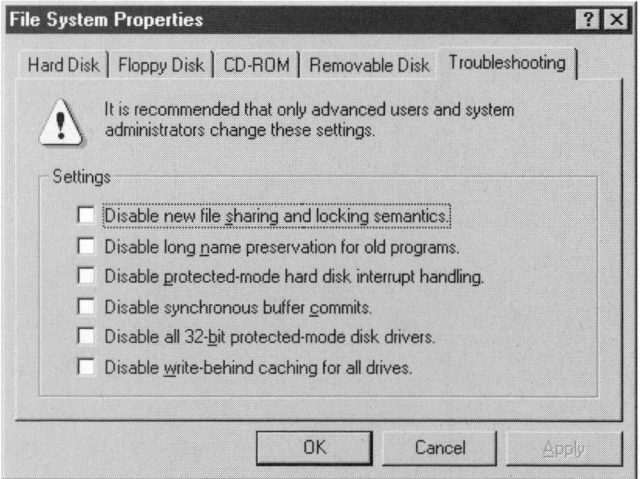

**FIGURE  16-26**    Windows 9*x*/Me provides a Troubleshooting tab in the File System Properties dialog that can help you to systematically isolate problems.

■ *Disable all 32-bit protected-mode disk drivers.* This option ensures that no 32-bit disk drivers are loaded in the system (except the floppy driver). Typically, you'd check this option if the computer does not start because of disk peripheral I/O problems. If this option is enabled, all I/O will go through real-mode drivers or the BIOS.

■ *Disable write-behind caching for all drives.* This option ensures that all data is passed immediately to the hard disk – this removes any performance benefits gained from disk caching. This option should be checked if you're performing sensitive operations and must prevent data loss.

These troubleshooting options are not available under Windows XP.

# RECOVERING LOST DISK SPACE

Your hard drive serves as a repository for many types of information. Some of this information is essential (for example, work files and important applications), but a great deal of information may be nonessential. Internet files (Web pages that have been cached to your PC), downloaded program files, items lingering in the Recycle Bin, and other temporary files can eventually take up a substantial amount of disk space. You can recover this lost disk space by using the Disk Cleanup tool under Windows 98/Me/XP. Click Start | Programs (All Programs under Windows XP) | Accessories | System Tools | Disk Cleanup. Select the drive you'd like to clean, and a dialog will appear with an analysis of the space that may be recovered (Figure 16-27). You can select any items to be kept or simply select OK to recover this wasted disk space.

Disk Cleanup also offers several options that can help recover even more space. Click the More Options tab (see Figure 16-28) and opt to delete unneeded Windows components or remove installed programs that you don't use anymore. Windows 9*x*/Me lets you use the FAT32 file converter (if your disk partition is currently FAT16), but Windows XP also lets you launch the System Restore wizard from this dialog box.

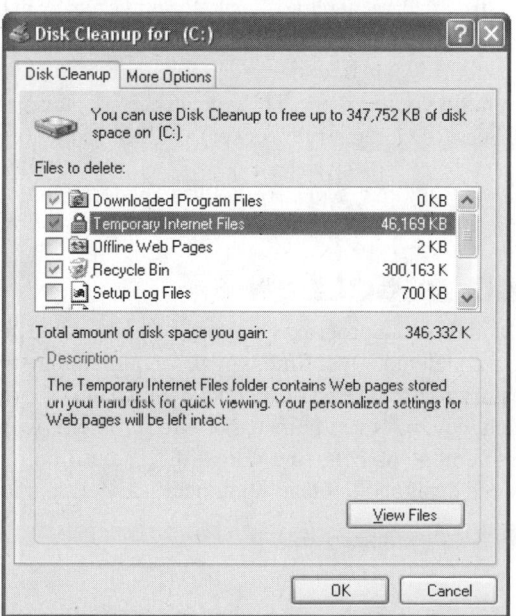

**FIGURE 16-27**    Recovering wasted disk space with the Disk Cleanup wizard under Windows XP

**FIGURE 16-28**    Windows XP Disk Cleanup lets you remove Windows components or unneeded applications, or start the System Restore wizard.

# Managing the Registry

The Windows 98/Me/XP registry is a critical part of your Windows platform that maintains a great deal of information about your system hardware and software. When problems occur with the registry, your system may become unstable or fail to start in extreme circumstances. Windows offers several tools that allow you to manage and maintain your registry. This part of the chapter offers a series of handy tips for RegClean (Registry Clean), ScanReg (Registry Checker), and RegEdit (Registry Editor).

If you cannot correct registry problems, you can use the System Restore wizard under Windows Me/XP to restore your system (including the registry) to a previous working state.

## UNDERSTANDING REGCLEAN

When you install, uninstall, and reinstall programs on your computer, you'll find that registry entries (or *keys*) are created, modified, and deleted. Over time, your computer's registry may begin to contain corrupted, unused, and unnecessary registry keys—especially if unneeded keys are not removed when you uninstall a program. As a result, you may eventually experience problems when using important Windows features (for example, OLE to embed objects, or automation to control other programs). The RegClean utility under Windows 9*x*/Me is designed to clean up unnecessary entries in your registry.

RegClean is not available under Windows XP.

## Running RegClean

If you do not have RegClean installed on your Windows 9*x*/Me system, you may need to install that component from your original Windows installation disc. Double-click the RegClean icon to start the utility. RegClean displays a progress dialog. While the progress dialog box is displayed, RegClean loads a copy of the parts of the registry that it's going to check and then performs the actual scanning. Depending on how much information is in your registry (and the speed of your CPU), the scanning process takes from about 30 seconds to as much as 30 minutes. Once these progress meters have disappeared, you will be prompted for the next action.

If you have many entries in your registry, RegClean might sometimes appear to have stopped working. RegClean might appear completely halted whenever it is checking remote or removable drives. Don't worry about this; simply allow RegClean to finish its cycle.

You can do two things at this point. If RegClean did not find any errors in your registry (or if you don't want RegClean to fix the errors that it may have found), click Cancel to exit the utility. Otherwise, click Fix Errors to prompt RegClean to remove any entries containing errors that may have been found in the registry. A progress meter is displayed while RegClean does this. When the progress meter disappears, RegClean is done. Click Exit to close RegClean. Clicking Fix Errors also creates an UNDO.REG file in the folder where you ran RegClean. The file will have the following title:

```
UNDO <computer> yyyymmddhhmmss.REG
```

where <computer> is the name of your computer, yyyymmdd is the date, and hhmmss is the time. If you'd like to undo or replace what RegClean removed from your registry at any point, double-click the UNDO.REG file.

RegClean does not fix every known problem with the registry. It does not fix a "corrupt" registry. It is limited to fixing problems with normal registry entries located in HKEY_CLASSES_ROOT.

# UNDERSTANDING SCANREG

When Windows 9x/Me starts successfully, the Registry Checker (**scanreg.exe**) automatically creates a backup of system files and registry configuration information (including user account information, protocol bindings, software program settings, and user preferences) once daily. Files that the Registry Checker backs up include SYSTEM.DAT, USER.DAT, SYSTEM.INI, and WIN.INI. ScanReg automatically scans the system registry for invalid entries and empty data blocks each time it's started. If invalid registry entries are detected, it will restore the previous day's backup. If no backups are available, ScanReg tries to make repairs to the registry. If the registry contains more than 500KB of empty data blocks, ScanReg automatically optimizes it. Finally, Windows Setup runs ScanReg to verify the integrity of the existing registry before it performs an upgrade. (If it detects registry damage, ScanReg tries to fix the damage automatically.)

ScanReg is not available under Windows XP.

## Using ScanReg

You can start ScanReg through the Windows 9*x*/Me System Information utility. Simply click Start, highlight Programs, point to Accessories, select System Tools, and then click System Information. On the

Tools menu, click Registry Checker. You can also start ScanReg from the Windows Run command line. Simply click Start, click Run, type **scanregw.exe** (or **scanreg.exe** for the real-mode version) in the Open box, and then click OK. To restore individual registry files, follow these steps:

1.  Click Start | Find | Files or Folders.

2.  In the Named box, type **rb0\*.cab**, and then click Find Now.

3.  Double-click on the "cabinet file" that has the correct registry file to be restored.

4.  Right-click the file you want to restore, click Extract, and then choose the folder where the new file is to be placed.

## UNDERSTANDING REGEDIT

In addition to scanning and cleaning the registry, Windows provides a registry editor (regedit.exe) that allows you to load, edit, and save the system registry under Windows 9*x*/Me/XP. Windows and its applications/wizards routinely make automatic changes to the registry, but editing the registry manually is generally discouraged. This is because the registry is a critical part of Windows, and any inappropriate edits may prevent the system from starting. In extreme cases, you may need to reinstall Windows to rebuild a working registry. As a rule, do not edit the registry unless it's absolutely necessary to do so, and be sure to make a backup copy of the registry to the hard drive or bootable floppy disk before making any edits. This way, you can always restore a known-good registry in the event of a problem.

 Incorrectly editing a registry file can prevent the system from booting, and perhaps require a reinstallation of Windows. Do not use RegEdit unless absolutely necessary.

### Using RegEdit

The RegEdit utility can be started from within Windows. To launch RegEdit under Windows 9*x*/Me/XP, simply click Start | Run | type **regedit**, and click OK. The editor dialog box will open (see Figure 16-29). Navigating the registry is just a matter of expanding and scrolling through the keys (folders) in the left pane until you've found the key of interest. To change the value of a key, highlight the desired entry, click Edit in the top menu, then click Modify. An appropriate dialog will appear, allowing you to enter a new value. You can also add new keys and new values as necessary, though it should not be necessary in all but the most serious circumstances.

Although Windows makes backup copies of the registry each time the system boots successfully, you can also export copies of the registry elsewhere on the disk, or to a floppy disk. Simply click File in the top menu, then choose to Export the registry. Follow the prompts to select a location and file name. You can reverse this process to Import (restore) a registry from elsewhere on the disk or backup floppy.

### Restoring a Working Registry

Windows XP provides a convenient means of restoring the last working registry *without* the need to manually edit or restore a registry file:

1.  Click Start | Turn Off | Restart.

2.  As the PC reboots, press F8 just before the operating system starts.

3.  A real-mode troubleshooting menu appears. Use the up/down arrows to highlight the "Last Known Good Configuration" option, then press ENTER.

4.  Select the appropriate operating system (if there's more than one on your system) and press ENTER.

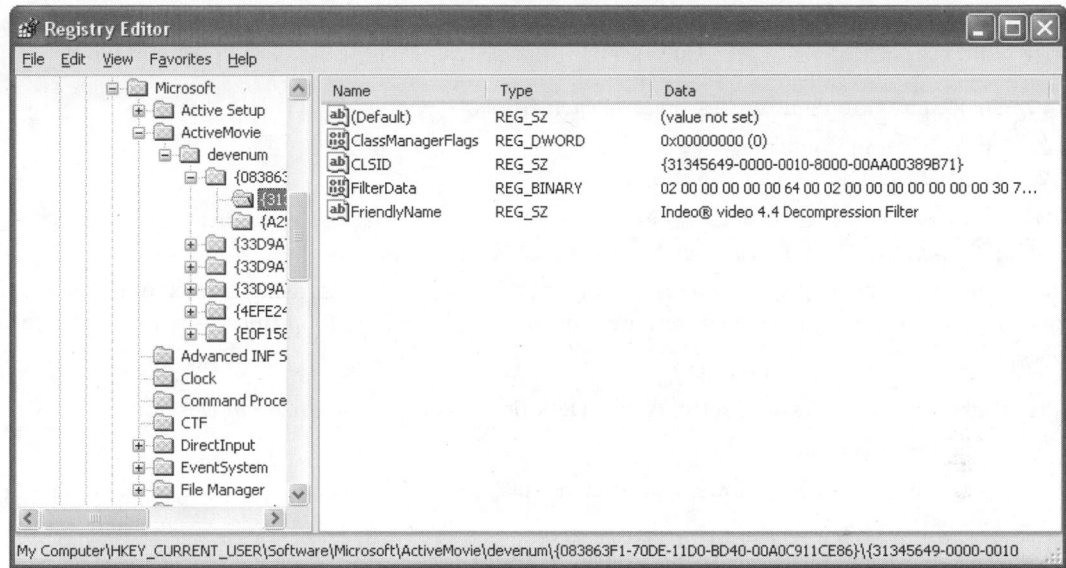

**FIGURE 16-29** The registry editor lets you load, change, and save the contents of your registry files, but should be used with extreme caution.

Keep in mind that this will not fix a damaged or missing registry file; it will only help to recover the last good registry in the event that you installed a faulty driver or made an improper system change.

# More Windows Performance Tips

Of course, there are numerous other tactics that you can use to improve the performance of your Windows platform. Just a few of the more common recommendations are covered next.

## USE WINDOWS UPDATE

It's hard to know when you need to update important Windows files on your computer. Windows 98/Me/XP provides a resource site on the Web (called "Windows Update") that you can use to identify new updates and patches that might help your computer run better. Windows Update can automatically review the system software on your computer, and then recommend when you need to install updates specific to your computer. To use Windows Update while you're online, click Start, and then click Windows Update. Under Windows XP, click Start | All Programs | Windows Update. This will open a Web browser and take you directly to Microsoft's update site.

## CHECK YOUR REGISTRY

Since the registry often loads drivers and other programs at start time, you should periodically run ScanReg or RegClean to inspect the registry for unused or "faulty" entries that can waste time and valuable

RAM loading unneeded elements on your Windows platform. Use these steps to launch Registry Checker under Windows 9*x*/Me:

1. Click Start | Programs| Accessories | System Tools.
2. Click System Information.
3. Click Tools from the menu bar and then click Registry Checker.

## DISABLE DESKTOP ANIMATIONS

Animations may seem pretty and interesting, but they can demand a surprising amount of memory and processing power. You can free these resources by turning off your desktop animations under Windows 9*x*/Me:

1. Right-click your desktop, select Active Desktop, and click Customize My Desktop.
2. Click the Effects tab.
3. Clear the "Animate windows, menus, and lists" and "Show window contents while dragging" options.
4. Save your changes and reboot the system if necessary.

Windows XP provides a large number of desktop features that can impact the performance of "underpowered" PCs. You can gain some desktop performance by disabling some of these unneeded features (or let Windows XP choose the optimum settings for your system):

1. Click Start | Control Panel | Performance and Maintenance | System.
2. Select the Advanced tab.
3. In the Performance area, click the Settings button.
4. The Visual Effects tab appears (see Figure 16-30) listing a wide range of Windows XP desktop visual effects.
5. By default, Windows XP selects the optimum settings for you, but you can opt to set the visual effects for best appearance, best performance, or customize the settings to your own tastes.
6. Click Apply and OK to accept your changes.

## TWEAK POWER CONSERVATION

Power-saving techniques often spin down the hard drive and power-off the monitor during periods of inactivity. Make sure that your idle periods are suitable for the way in which you use the system. If your idle periods are too short, you may find yourself waiting for the display to reappear, or the drive to spin up for disk access. If you cannot determine more suitable idle time settings, disable your power saving modes.

## REMOVE DISK COMPRESSION

Disk compression utilities (such as DriveSpace 3) slow the drive performance a bit due to their use of on-the-fly compression. You can reconfigure DriveSpace to compress files only if drive space drops below some preset amount, or disable/remove the compression utility entirely. This will reduce your free drive space, but speed the drive's performance. Today, disk compression is rarely used since huge hard drives are readily available, and compression does impose a performance penalty. But this is still a handy tip for older systems.

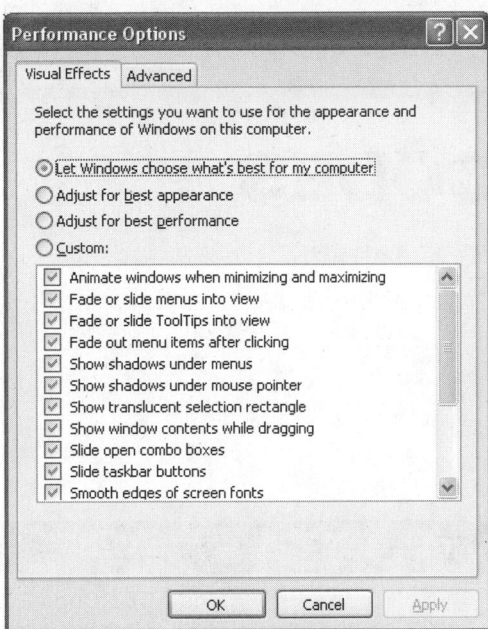

**FIGURE 16-30**    Set the visual effects to pick up additional desktop performance.

# Further Study

**Maxtor**    www.maxtor.com
**Microsoft**    www.microsoft.com
**Quantum**    www.quantum.com
**Seagate**    www.seagate.com
**Western Digital**    www.wdc.com

# 17

# ERROR CODES

**M**ost computers are remarkably adept at testing their own hardware and reporting serious errors during start time. They do this through the Power-On Self-Test (POST) routine written into BIOS. Since BIOS is written expressly for a particular processor, chipset, and other motherboard hardware, the BIOS is an ideal choice for basic startup diagnostics. However, startup diagnostics pose a unique problem—it's hard to report an error to the user when the system isn't fully functional. BIOS reports POST errors through the use of audible signals (called *beep codes*) as well as through hexadecimal codes (called *POST codes*) that are written to established I/O addresses. This chapter presents the most popular beep and POST codes used on today's PCs.

## Beep Codes

When a fault is detected *before* the video system is initialized, errors are indicated with a series of beeps (the beep codes) through the system's speaker. Since each BIOS is a bit different, the accuracy, precision, and quality of error detection and reporting varies from BIOS to BIOS. While most POST routines today follow a remarkably similar pattern, the reporting style can vary greatly. Some routines (such as AMI) generate a continuous string of beeps, while other routines (such as Phoenix) create short beep sequences. This part of the chapter is intended to help you understand and interpret the beep codes produced by major BIOS makers:

If your BIOS isn't listed below, assume that beep codes are related to video, RAM, or power issues—in that order.

| | |
|---|---|
| AMI (American Megatrends) | Table 17-1 |
| AMI BIOS 8 | Table 17-2 |
| Dell (PowerEdge) | Table 17-3 |
| Compaq (AlphaServer) | Table 17-4 |
| IBM desktop (Aptiva) | Table 17-5 |
| Phoenix Technologies | Table 17-6 |

It's important to remember that a system must have a speaker connected to the motherboard in order to hear beep codes. If no speaker is installed (or it's not properly connected to the motherboard), you'll lose the beep codes.

**TABLE 17-1** TRADITIONAL AMI BIOS BEEP CODES

| BEEPS | ERROR MESSAGE |
|---|---|
| 1s | System RAM Refresh Failure. The programmable interrupt timer (PIT) or programmable interrupt controller (PIC) has probably failed. Replace the motherboard. |
| 2s | Memory Parity Error. A parity error has been detected in the first 64KB of RAM. The RAM is probably defective. Replace the memory or motherboard. |
| 3s | Base 64KB Memory Failure. A memory failure has been detected in the first 64KB of RAM. The RAM is probably defective. Replace the memory or motherboard. |
| 4s | System Timer Failure. The system clock/timer chip has failed. |
| 5s | CPU Failure. The system CPU has failed. Try replacing the CPU or motherboard. |
| 6s | Gate A20 Failure. The keyboard controller chip has failed, so Gate A20 is no longer available to switch the CPU into protected mode. Replace the keyboard controller or motherboard. |
| 7s | Exception Error. The CPU has generated an exception error due to a fault in the CPU or some combination of motherboard conditions. Replace the motherboard. |
| 8s | Video Memory Read/Write Error. The system video adapter is missing or defective. Try replacing the video adapter. |
| 9s | ROM Checksum Error. The contents of the system BIOS ROM do not match the expected checksum value. The BIOS ROM is probably defective and should be replaced. |
| 10s | CMOS Shutdown Register Read/Write Error. The shutdown register for the CMOS memory has failed. Try replacing the RTC/CMOS chip. |
| 11s | Cache Error/L2 Cache Bad. The L2 cache is faulty. Replace the L2 cache or integrated L2 cache hardware device. |
| 1l-3s | Memory Test Failure. A fault has been detected in memory over 64KB. Replace the memory or the motherboard. |
| 1l-8s | Display Test Failure. The display adapter is missing or defective. Replace the video adapter board. If the video adapter is on the motherboard, try replacing the motherboard. |

**TABLE 17-2**     AMI BIOS 8 BEEP CODES

| BEEPS | ERROR MESSAGE |
|---|---|
| 1 | Memory refresh timer error. RAM refresh circuitry on the motherboard has probably failed, and the motherboard should be replaced. |
| 2 | Parity error. A location in system RAM has failed. Systematically replace the RAM. |
| 3 | Main memory read/write test error. A location in system RAM has failed. Systematically replace the RAM. |
| 4 | Motherboard timer not operational. The motherboard has failed and should be replaced. |
| 5 | Processor error. The processor has failed. Check the processor's installation and replace if necessary. |
| 6 | Keyboard controller (KBC) test error. Replace the motherboard. |
| 7 | General exception error. Test the system RAM and replace any defective modules, or replace the motherboard. |
| 8 | Display memory error. Replace defective system RAM (if used as the display buffer), or replace the display adapter. |
| 9 | ROM checksum error. Replace the motherboard's BIOS chip, or replace the motherboard outright. |
| 10 | CMOS shutdown register read/write error. Replace the defective motherboard. |
| 11 | Cache memory bad. Replace motherboard cache, or replace the processor (when cache is on the processor). |

**TABLE 17-3**     DELL BEEP CODES (POWEREDGE FAMILY)

| BEEPS | ERROR MESSAGE |
|---|---|
| 1-1-3 | NVRAM write/read failure. The CMOS RAM has probably failed. Replace the main board. |
| 1-1-4 | BIOS checksum failure. The BIOS chip has probably failed. Replace the main board. |
| 1-2-1 | Programmable interval-timer failure. Replace the main board. |
| 1-2-2 | DMA initialization failure. Replace the main board. |
| 1-2-3 | DMA page register write/read failure. Replace the main board. |
| 1-3-1 | Main-memory refresh verification failure. Remove and reseat the DIMMs. If the problem persists, replace the memory module(s). |
| 1-3-2 | No memory installed. Remove and reseat the DIMMs and reboot the system. If the problem persists, replace the memory module(s). |
| 1-3-3 | Chip or data line failure in the first 64 KB of main memory. Remove and reseat the DIMMs and reboot the system. If the problem persists, replace the memory module(s). |
| 1-3-4 | Odd/even logic failure in the first 64 KB of main memory. Remove and reseat the DIMMs and reboot the system. If the problem persists, replace the memory module(s). |
| 1-4-1 | Address line failure in the first 64 KB of main memory. Remove and reseat the DIMMs and reboot the system. If the problem persists, replace the memory module(s). |
| 1-4-2 | Parity failure in the first 64 KB of main memory. Remove and reseat the DIMMs and reboot the system. If the problem persists, replace the memory module(s). |
| 2-1-1 to 2-4-4 | Bit failure in the first 64 KB of main memory. Remove and reseat the DIMMs and reboot the system. If the problem persists, replace the memory module(s). |

| TABLE 17-3 | DELL BEEP CODES (POWEREDGE FAMILY) *(CONTINUED)* |
|---|---|

| BEEPS | ERROR MESSAGE |
|---|---|
| 3-1-1 | Slave DMA-register failure. Replace the main board. |
| 3-1-2 | Master DMA-register failure. Replace the main board. |
| 3-1-3 | Master interrupt-mask register failure. Replace the main board. |
| 3-1-4 | Slave interrupt-mask register failure. Replace the main board. |
| 3-2-4 | Keyboard-controller test failure. Check the keyboard cable and connector for proper connection. If the problem persists, replace the main board. |
| 3-3-1 | CMOS RAM failure. Replace CMOS/RTC chip or the main board. |
| 3-3-2 | System configuration check failure. Replace the main board. |
| 3-3-3 | Keyboard controller not detected. |
| 3-3-4 | Screen initialization failure. Verify that the monitor cable is correctly connected. If the problem persists, replace the main board. |
| 3-4-1 | Screen-retrace test failure. Ensure that the monitor cable is correctly connected. If the problem persists, replace the main board. |
| 3-4-2 | Video ROM detection failure. Replace the main board or install another video card. |
| 4-2-1 | No timer tick. Replace the main board. |
| 4-2-2 | Shutdown failure. Replace the main board. |
| 4-2-3 | Gate A20 failure. Replace the main board. |
| 4-2-4 | Unexpected interrupt in protected mode. Verify that all expansion cards are properly seated, and then reboot the system. |
| 4-3-1 | Improperly seated or faulty DIMM, DIMMs not installed in sets, or a faulty or improperly seated memory module. Be sure that the DIMMs are installed in sets, if necessary, and in the proper sockets for each memory bank in use. If this does not resolve the problem, remove and reseat the DIMMs. If the problem persists, replace the DIMMs or the memory module(s). |
| 4-3-3 | Defective system board. Replace the main board. |
| 4-3-4 | Time-of-day clock stopped. Replace the battery. If the problem persists, replace the main board. |
| 4-4-1 | Faulty I/O chip or Super I/O controller failure. The system board is defective, so replace the system board. |
| 4-4-2 | Parallel-port test failure. The system board is defective, so replace the system board. |
| 4-4-3 | Math co-processor failure. This means a defective microprocessor, so replace the microprocessor. |
| 4-4-4 | Cache test failure. This means a defective microprocessor, so replace the microprocessor. |

| TABLE 17-4 | COMPAQ BEEP CODES (ALPHASERVER FAMILY) |
|---|---|

| BEEPS | ERROR MESSAGE |
|---|---|
| 1 | No error. |
| 1-3 | VGA monitor not plugged in. Graphics option card different from the one shipped with the system. |

**TABLE 17-4    COMPAQ BEEP CODES (ALPHASERVER FAMILY)** *(CONTINUED)*

| BEEPS | ERROR MESSAGE |
|-------|---------------|
| 1-1-2 | A ROM data path error was detected while loading SRM/AlphaBIOS console code. |
| 1-1-4 | The SROM code is unable to load the console code, or an FROM header area or checksum error detected. |
| 1-1-7 | No boot block on floppy device. |
| 1-2-1 | TOY NVRAM failure. |
| 1-2-4 | B-cache error. |
| 1-3-3 | No usable memory detected. |
| 3-3-1 | Generic system failure. |
| 3-3-3 | Failure of onboard SCSI controller. |

**TABLE 17-5    IBM BEEP CODES (APTIVA 2173 SERIES)**

| BEEPS | ERROR MESSAGE |
|-------|---------------|
| 1-1-3 | CMOS read/write error. The system may be configured improperly. Run the system setup routine. |
| 1-1-4 | ROM BIOS checksum error. Replace the main board. |
| 1-2-X | DMA controller error. Replace the main board. |
| 1-3-X | Memory module error. Check, reinstall, or replace the memory module(s) or replace the main board. |
| 1-4-4 | Keyboard error. Check the keyboard and its installation. Replace the keyboard, or replace the main board. |
| 1-4-X | Error detected in first 64 KB of RAM. One or more memory modules may have failed. Try reseating the memory module(s), replace the memory module(s), and then replace the main board. |
| 2-1-1 | System board fault. Run the system setup routine or replace the main board. |
| 2-1-2 | System board fault. Run the system setup routine or replace the main board. |
| 2-1-X | Error detected in first 64 KB of RAM. One or more memory modules may have failed. Try reseating the memory module(s), replace the memory module(s), and then replace the main board. |
| 2-2-2 | Video adapter fault. The onboard video system has failed. Install a stand-alone video card or replace the main board. |
| 2-2-X | Error detected in first 64 KB of RAM. One or more memory modules may have failed. Try reseating the memory module(s), replacing the memory module(s), and then replacing the main board. |
| 2-3-X | Memory module error. Check, reinstall, or replace the memory module(s) or replace the main board. |
| 2-4-X | Memory module error. Check, reinstall, or replace the memory module(s) or replace the main board. |
| 3-1-X | DMA register failed. Replace the main board. |
| 3-2-4 | Keyboard controller chip failed. Replace the main board. |

## TABLE 17-5    IBM BEEP CODES (APTIVA 2173 SERIES) *(CONTINUED)*

| BEEPS | ERROR MESSAGE |
| --- | --- |
| 3-3-4 | Screen initialization failed. The video system has failed. Replace the video adapter, or replace the main board if the video system is integrated into the main board. |
| 3-4-1 | Screen retrace test error. The video system has failed. Replace the video adapter, or replace the main board if the video system is integrated into the main board. |
| 3-4-2 | Cannot locate video ROM. The video system has failed. Replace the video adapter or replace the main board if the video system is integrated into the main board. |
| 4 | Video adapter fault. The onboard video system has failed. Install a stand-alone video card or replace the main board. |
| 1l-1s | Base 640 KB memory error or shadow RAM error. Replace the defective memory module(s) or replace the motherboard. |
| 1l-2s | Video adapter fault. The onboard video system has failed. Install a stand-alone video card or replace the main board. |
| 1l-3s | Video adapter fault. The onboard video system has failed. Install a stand-alone video card or replace the main board. |
| 3s | Memory failure. Check, reinstall, or replace the memory module(s) or replace the main board. |
| Continuous | System board failure. Replace the motherboard. |
| Repeating | Stuck key on the keyboard, keyboard cable detached or damaged, or main board failure. Clean or replace the keyboard, or replace the motherboard. |

## TABLE 17-6    PHOENIX BIOS BEEP CODES

| BEEPS | ERROR MESSAGE |
| --- | --- |
| 1-1-2 | CPU Register Test Failure. The CPU has likely failed. Replace the CPU. |
| Low 1-1-2 | System Board Select Failure. The motherboard is suffering from an undetermined fault. Try replacing the motherboard. |
| 1-1-3 | CMOS Read/Write Failure. The RTC/CMOS IC has probably failed. Try replacing the RTC/CMOS chip. |
| Low 1-1-3 | Extended CMOS RAM Failure. The extended portion of the RTC/CMOS IC has failed. Try replacing the RTC/CMOS chip. |
| 1-1-4 | BIOS ROM Checksum Error. The BIOS ROM has probably failed. |
| 1-2-1 | Programmable Interval Timer (PIT) Failure. The PIT has probably failed. |
| 1-2-2 | DMA Initialization Failure. The DMA controller has probably failed. |
| 1-2-3 | DMA Page Register Read/Write Failure. The DMA controller has probably failed. |
| 1-3-1 | RAM Refresh Failure. The refresh controller has failed. |
| 1-3-2 | 64KB RAM Test Disabled. The test of the first 64KB of system RAM could not begin. Try replacing the motherboard. |
| 1-3-3 | First 64KB RAM or Data Line Failure. The first RAM chip/module has failed. |
| 1-3-4 | First 64KB Odd/Even Logic Failure. The first RAM control logic has failed. |
| 1-4-1 | Address Line Failure 64KB of RAM. |
| 1-4-2 | Parity Failure First 64KB of RAM. The first RAM chip/module has failed. |

**TABLE 17-6** PHOENIX BIOS BEEP CODES *(CONTINUED)*

| BEEPS | ERROR MESSAGE |
| --- | --- |
| 1-4-3 | EISA Failsafe Timer Test Fault. Replace the motherboard. |
| 1-4-4 | EISA NMI Port 462 Test Failure. Replace the motherboard. |
| 2-1-1 | Bit 0 First 64KB RAM Failure. This data bit in the first RAM chip has failed. |
| 2-1-2 | Bit 1 First 64KB RAM Failure. |
| 2-1-3 | Bit 2 First 64KB RAM Failure. |
| 2-1-4 | Bit 3 First 64KB RAM Failure. |
| 2-2-1 | Bit 4 First 64KB RAM Failure. |
| 2-2-2 | Bit 5 First 64KB RAM Failure. |
| 2-2-3 | Bit 6 First 64KB RAM Failure. |
| 2-2-4 | Bit 7 First 64KB RAM Failure. |
| 2-3-1 | Bit 8 First 64KB RAM Failure. |
| 2-3-2 | Bit 9 First 64KB RAM Failure. |
| 2-3-3 | Bit 10 First 64KB RAM Failure. |
| 2-3-4 | Bit 11 First 64KB RAM Failure. |
| 2-4-1 | Bit 12 First 64KB RAM Failure. |
| 2-4-2 | Bit 13 First 64KB RAM Failure. |
| 2-4-3 | Bit 14 First 64KB RAM Failure. |
| 2-4-4 | Bit 15 First 64KB RAM Failure. |
| 3-1-1 | Slave DMA Register Failure. The DMA controller has probably failed. |
| 3-1-2 | Master DMA Register Failure. The DMA controller has probably failed. |
| 3-1-3 | Master Interrupt Mask Register Failure. The interrupt controller has probably failed. |
| 3-1-4 | Slave Interrupt Mask Register Failure. The interrupt controller has probably failed. |
| 3-2-2 | Interrupt Vector Loading Error. BIOS is unable to load the interrupt vectors into low RAM. Replace the motherboard. |
| 3-2-3 | Reserved. |
| 3-2-4 | Keyboard Controller Test Failure. The keyboard controller has failed. |
| 3-3-1 | CMOS RAM Power Bad. Try replacing the CMOS backup battery. Try replacing the RTC/CMOS chip. Replace the motherboard. |
| 3-3-2 | CMOS Configuration Error. The CMOS configuration has failed. Restore the configuration. Replace the CMOS backup battery. Replace the RTC/CMOS chip. Replace the motherboard. |
| 3-3-3 | Reserved. |
| 3-3-4 | Video Memory Test Failed. There is a problem with the video memory. Replace video memory or replace the video adapter board. |
| 3-4-1 | Video Initialization Test Failure. There is a problem with the video system. Replace the video adapter. |
| 4-2-1 | Timer Tick Failure. The system timer chip has failed. |
| 4-2-2 | Shutdown Test Failure. The CMOS chip has failed. |
| 4-2-3 | Gate A20 Failure. The keyboard controller has probably failed. |
| 4-2-4 | Unexpected Interrupt in Protected Mode. There is a problem with the CPU. |
| 4-3-1 | RAM Test Address Failure. System RAM addressing circuitry has failed. |

| TABLE 17-6 | PHOENIX BIOS BEEP CODES *(CONTINUED)* |
|---|---|
| **BEEPS** | **ERROR MESSAGE** |
| 4-3-3 | Interval Timer Channel 2 Failure. The system timer chip has probably failed. |
| 4-3-4 | Time of Day Clock Failure. The RTC/CMOS chip has failed. |
| 4-4-1 | Serial Port Test Failure. A fault has developed in the serial port circuit. |
| 4-4-2 | Parallel Port Test Failure. A fault has developed in the parallel port circuit. |
| 4-4-3 | Math Co-processor Failure. Try replacing the math co-processor. |

# POST Codes

During initialization, the POST performs a self-diagnostic routine designed to check key areas of the motherboard (and common peripherals) for major faults. When an error is detected early in the test cycle, you'll probably hear a series of one or more beep codes, as described above. BIOS makers came to realize that most beep code sequences are not terribly specific, and a beep code can often represent any one of a number of possible failures. In order to make more specific information available to technicians, POST procedures are designed to output a single hexadecimal byte to I/O port 80h (or other suitable I/O address) as each step in the initialization is started or completed. These codes are displayed by a POST code reader card (such as the PocketPOST card in Figure 17-1). If the PC should fail at any point during startup, the code at port 80h represents the *last* step to be successfully completed. By knowing the full sequence of I/O POST codes generated by a BIOS, a technician can quickly determine the test step that failed and thus pinpoint the fault with reasonable confidence. This part of the chapter presents the POST sequences for popular PC BIOS versions.

**FIGURE 17-1** The PocketPOST card from PCWiz fits in an ISA slot and displays the hexadecimal byte at port 80h. (Courtesy of PCWiz, Inc.)

# INTERPRETING POST CODES

When working with POST codes, it is important to understand that not all codes are the direct result of a test. Many codes simply indicate that a CPU is attempting to initialize various areas of the PC. These types of codes are known as *checkpoints*—they simply show that certain initialization steps are being completed. Just because you see a hexadecimal code does not *necessarily* mean that anything has failed.

Also remember that few listings of BIOS codes are actually complete. With the exception of publicly available code lists (for the IBM PC, XT, and AT), most BIOS manufacturers are generally unwilling to release the full context of their POST codes. As a result, POST code indexes such as those in this book are often compilations of data extracted from a number of different sources. If you encounter a POST code that is not covered in this book, your best course is usually to contact the BIOS manufacturer directly for specific details.

Another area of confusion can arise (particularly for the novice technician) over when the POST process starts and ends. When a system is first started with a POST board installed, the POST display is typically blank—this is *normal* for the initial moments after PC power is applied. After that, codes should begin flashing across the seven-segment LEDs. If the LEDs remain blank, you can assume that no data is reaching the card. In that event, make sure that your system produces POST codes (a few systems do *not*), and see that the POST board's I/O address is set properly (some systems use I/O ports other than 80h). After the POST is complete, a system will attempt to boot an operating system. Ordinarily, the last code on the display is 00h or FFh, so don't worry if either of these codes remain on the seven-segment display. In some cases—depending on the particular BIOS—some *other* code may be left in the display. If the system appears to boot normally, you rarely need to worry about this. Also keep in mind that not all tests are performed in numerical order. You will find that the POST code sequences in many of the following tables are a bit mixed, so look over each table carefully:

All of the POST codes presented in the following tables are "hexadecimal" (or "h") numbers. For example, a POST code of 13 would be "13h" (or "hex").

| | | | |
|---|---|---|---|
| Acer | Table 17-7 | Award PnP BIOS (4–5.x) | Table 17-24 |
| AMI (prior to 04/1990) | Table 17-8 | Award non-PnP BIOS (4.5x) | Table 17-25 |
| AMI (04/1990–02/1991) | Table 17-9 | AwardBIOS Version 6.00 | Table 17-26 |
| AMI (02/1991–12/1991) | Table 17-10 | Compaq BIOS (general) | Table 17-27 |
| AMI (06/1992–08/1993) | Table 17-11 | Dell BIOS | Table 17-28 |
| AMI WinBIOS (12/1993+) | Table 17-12 | Hewlett-Packard Vectra | Table 17-29 |
| AMI version 2.2x | Table 17-13 | IBM PC/AT BIOS | Table 17-30 |
| AMI Plus BIOS | Table 17-14 | IBM PS/2 BIOS | Table 17-31 |
| AMI Color BIOS | Table 17-15 | Microid Research 1.0A BIOS | Table 17-32 |
| AMI EZ-Flex BIOS | Table 17-16 | Microid Research (modern) | Table 17-33 |
| AMIBIOS 8 BIOS | Table 17-17 | Microid Research 3.4x BIOS | Table 17-34 |
| Award AT BIOS v.3.0 | Table 17-18 | Phoenix ISA/EISA/MCA BIOS | Table 17-35 |
| Award AT BIOS v.3.0-3.03 | Table 17-19 | Phoenix BIOS Plus (v.1.0) | Table 17-36 |
| Award AT BIOS v.3.1 | Table 17-20 | Phoenix UMC chipset BIOS | Table 17-37 |
| Award AT BIOS 3.3 | Table 17-21 | Phoenix PCI BIOS | Table 17-38 |
| Award AT ISA/EISA BIOS 4.0 | Table 17-22 | Phoenix BIOS 4.0 BIOS | Table 17-39 |
| Award EISA BIOS | Table 17-23 | Phoenix BIOS 4.0 (Rev.6.0) BIOS | Table 17-40 |

**TABLE 17-7** ACER BIOS POST CODES

| CODE | DESCRIPTION |
| --- | --- |
| 04 | POST Start |
| 08 | Shutdown Condition 0 |
| 0C | Testing the BIOS ROM checksum |
| 10 | Testing the CMOS RAM shutdown byte |
| 14 | Testing the DMA controller |
| 18 | Initializing the system timer |
| 1C | Testing the memory refresh system |
| 1E | Determining the memory type |
| 20 | Testing the low 128KB of memory |
| 24 | Testing the 8042 keyboard controller IC |
| 28 | Testing the CPU descriptor instruction |
| 2C | Testing the 8259 interrupt controller IC |
| 30 | Setting up a temporary interrupt |
| 34 | Configure the BIOS interrupt vectors and routines |
| 38 | Testing the CMOS RAM |
| 3C | Determining the memory size |
| 40 | Shutdown Condition 1 |
| 44 | Initializing the video BIOS ROM |
| 45 | Setting up and testing RAM |
| 46 | Testing cache memory and controller |
| 48 | Testing memory |
| 4C | Shutdown Condition 3 |
| 50 | Shutdown Condition 2 |
| 54 | Shutdown Condition 7 |
| 58 | Shutdown Condition 6 |
| 5C | Testing the keyboard and auxiliary I/O |
| 60 | Setting up BIOS interrupt routines |
| 64 | Testing the real-time clock |
| 68 | Testing the floppy disk drive |
| 6C | Testing the hard drive |
| 70 | Testing the parallel port |
| 74 | Testing the serial port |
| 78 | Setting the time of day |
| 7C | Detect and invoke any optional ROMs |
| 80 | Checking for the math co-processor |
| 84 | Initializing the keyboard |
| 88 | Initializing the system (step 1) |
| 8C | Initializing the system (step 2) |
| 90 | Boot the operating system |
| 94 | Shutdown Condition 5 |

**TABLE 17-7    ACER BIOS POST CODES (CONTINUED)**

| CODE | DESCRIPTION |
| --- | --- |
| 98 | Shutdown Condition A |
| 9C | Shutdown Condition B |

**TABLE 17-8    AMI BIOS POST CODES (PRIOR TO APRIL 1990)**

| CODE | DESCRIPTION |
| --- | --- |
| 01 | NMI is disabled and the i286 register test is about to start |
| 02 | i286 register test has passed |
| 03 | ROM BIOS checksum test (32KB from F8000h) passed OK |
| 04 | 8259 PIC has initialized OK |
| 05 | CMOS interrupt disabled |
| 06 | Video system disabled and the system timer checks OK |
| 07 | 8253/4 programmable interval timer test OK |
| 08 | Delta counter channel 2 OK |
| 09 | Delta counter channel 1 OK |
| 0A | Delta counter channel 0 OK |
| 0B | Parity status cleared |
| 0C | The refresh and system timer check OK |
| 0D | Refresh check OK |
| 0E | Refresh period checks OK |
| 10 | Ready to start 64KB base memory test |
| 11 | Address line test OK |
| 12 | 64KB base memory test OK |
| 13 | System interrupt vectors initialized |
| 14 | 8042 keyboard controller checks OK |
| 15 | CMOS read/write test OK |
| 16 | CMOS checksum and battery OK |
| 17 | Monochrome video mode OK |
| 18 | CGA color mode configured properly |
| 19 | Attempting to pass control to video ROM at C0000h |
| 1A | Returned from video ROM |
| 1B | Display memory R/W test OK |
| 1C | Display memory R/W alternative test OK |
| 1D | Video retrace test OK |
| 1E | Global equipment byte set for proper video operation |
| 1F | Ready to initialize video system |
| 20 | Video test OK |
| 21 | Video display OK |

**TABLE 17-8    AMI BIOS POST CODES (PRIOR TO APRIL 1990)** *(CONTINUED)*

| CODE | DESCRIPTION |
| --- | --- |
| 22 | The power-on message is displayed |
| 30 | Ready to start the virtual mode memory test |
| 31 | Virtual memory mode test started |
| 32 | CPU has switched to virtual mode |
| 33 | Testing the memory address lines |
| 34 | Testing the memory address lines |
| 35 | Lower 1MB of RAM found |
| 36 | Memory size computation checks OK |
| 37 | Memory test in progress |
| 38 | Memory below 1MB is initialized |
| 39 | Memory above 1MB is initialized |
| 3A | Memory size is displayed |
| 3B | Ready to test the lower 1MB of RAM |
| 3C | Memory test of lower 1MB OK |
| 3D | Memory test above 1MB OK |
| 3E | Ready to shutdown for real-mode testing |
| 3F | Shutdown OK—now in real mode |
| 40 | Ready to disable gate A20 |
| 41 | A20 line disabled successfully |
| 42 | Ready to start DMA controller test |
| 4E | Address line test OK |
| 4F | System still in real mode |
| 50 | DMA page register test OK |
| 51 | Starting DMA controller 1 register test |
| 52 | DMA controller 1 test passed, starting DMA controller 2 register test |
| 53 | DMA controller 2 test passed |
| 54 | Ready to test latch on DMA controller 1 and 2 |
| 55 | DMA controller 1 and 2 latch test OK |
| 56 | DMA controller 1 and 2 configured OK |
| 57 | 8259 PIC initialized OK |
| 58 | 8259 PIC mask register check OK |
| 59 | Master 8259 PIC mask register OK |
| 5A | Ready to check timer interrupts |
| 5B | Timer interrupt check OK |
| 5C | Ready to test keyboard interrupt |
| 5D | ERROR detected in timer or keyboard interrupt |
| 5E | 8259 PIC controller error |
| 5F | 8259 PIC controller OK |
| 70 | Start of keyboard test |
| 71 | Keyboard controller OK |

## TABLE 17-8 AMI BIOS POST CODES (PRIOR TO APRIL 1990) *(CONTINUED)*

| CODE | DESCRIPTION |
|------|-------------|
| 72 | Keyboard test OK |
| 73 | Keyboard global initialization OK |
| 74 | Floppy setup ready to start |
| 75 | Floppy controller setup OK |
| 76 | Hard disk setup ready to start |
| 77 | Hard disk controller setup OK |
| 79 | Ready to initialize timer data |
| 7A | Verifying CMOS battery power |
| 7B | CMOS battery verified OK |
| 7D | Analyzing CMOS RAM size |
| 7E | CMOS memory size updated |
| 7F | Send control to adapter ROM |
| 80 | Enable the SETUP Routine if DELETE is pressed |
| 81 | Return from adapter ROM |
| 82 | Printer data initialization is OK |
| 83 | RS-232 data initialization is OK |
| 84 | 80x87 check and test OK |
| 85 | Display any soft-error message |
| 86 | Give control to ROM at E0000h |
| 87 | Return from system ROM |
| 00 | Call the INT 19 boot loader |

## TABLE 17-9 AMI BIOS POST CODES (APRIL 1990 TO FEBRUARY 1991)

| CODE | DESCRIPTION |
|------|-------------|
| 01 | NMI disabled and 286 register test about to start |
| 02 | 286 register test passed |
| 03 | ROM BIOS checksum (32K at F800:0) passed |
| 04 | Keyboard controller test with and without mouse passed |
| 05 | Chipset initialization over; DMA and Interrupt controller disabled |
| 06 | Video disabled and system timer test begins |
| 07 | CH-2 of 8254 initialization half way |
| 08 | CH-2 of timer initialization over |
| 09 | CH-1 of timer initialization over |
| 0A | CH-0 of timer initialization over |
| 0B | Refresh started |
| 0C | System timer started |
| 0D | Refresh link toggling passed |
| 10 | Refresh on and about to start 64K base memory test |
| 11 | Address line test passed |

**TABLE 17-9** AMI BIOS POST CODES (APRIL 1990 TO FEBRUARY 1991) *(CONTINUED)*

| CODE | DESCRIPTION |
| --- | --- |
| 12 | 64K base memory test passed |
| 15 | Interrupt vectors initialized |
| 17 | Monochrome mode configured |
| 18 | Color mode configured |
| 19 | About to look for optional video ROM at C000 and give control to ROM if present |
| 1A | Return from optional video ROM |
| 1B | Shadow RAM enable/disable completed |
| 1C | Display memory read/write test for display type as set in the CMOS setup program |
| 1D | Display memory read/write test for alternate display type complete if main display memory read/write test returns error |
| 1E | Global equipment byte set for proper display type |
| 1F | Video mode configured, call for mono/color begins |
| 20 | Video mode configuration completed |
| 21 | ROM type 27256 verified |
| 23 | Power-on message displayed |
| 30 | Virtual mode memory test about to begin |
| 31 | Virtual mode memory test started |
| 32 | Processor executing in virtual mode |
| 33 | Memory address line test in progress |
| 34 | Memory address line test in progress |
| 35 | Memory below 1MB calculated |
| 36 | Memory above 1MB calculated |
| 37 | Memory test about to start |
| 38 | Memory below 1MB initialized |
| 39 | Memory above 1MB initialized |
| 3A | Memory size display initiated. Will be updated when BIOS goes through memory test |
| 3B | About to start below 1MB memory test |
| 3C | Memory test below 1MB completed; about to start above 1MB test |
| 3D | Memory test above 1MB completed |
| 3E | About to go to real mode (shutdown) |
| 3F | Shutdown successful and processor in real mode |
| 40 | Cache memory on and about to disable A20 address line |
| 41 | A20 address line disable successful |
| 42 | 486 internal cache turned on |
| 43 | About to start DMA controller test |
| 50 | DMA page register test complete |
| 51 | DMA unit-1 base register test about to start |
| 52 | DMA unit-1 base register test complete |
| 53 | DMA unit-2 base register test complete |
| 54 | About to check F/F latch for unit-1 and unit-2 |

**TABLE 17-9     AMI BIOS POST CODES (APRIL 1990 TO FEBRUARY 1991)** *(CONTINUED)*

| CODE | DESCRIPTION |
|------|-------------|
| 55 | F/F latch for both units checked |
| 56 | DMA unit 1 and 2 programming over; about to initialize 8259 interrupt controller |
| 57 | 8259 initialization over |
| 70 | About to start keyboard test |
| 71 | Keyboard controller BAT test over |
| 72 | Keyboard interface test over; mouse interface test started |
| 73 | Global data initialization for keyboard/mouse over |
| 74 | Display SETUP prompt and about to start floppy setup |
| 75 | Floppy setup over |
| 76 | Hard disk setup about to start |
| 77 | Hard disk setup over |
| 79 | About to initialize timer data area |
| 7A | Timer data initialized and about to verify CMOS battery power |
| 7B | CMOS battery verification over |
| 7D | About to analyze POST results |
| 7E | CMOS memory size updated |
| 7F | Look for DEL key and get into CMOS setup if found |
| 80 | About to give control to optional ROM in segment C800 to DE00 |
| 81 | Optional ROM control over |
| 82 | Check for printer ports and put the addresses in global data area |
| 83 | Check for RS232 ports and put the addresses in global data area |
| 84 | Co-processor detection over |
| 85 | About to display soft error messages |
| 86 | About to give control to system ROM at segment E000 |
| 00 | System ROM control at E000 over. Now give control to INT 19h boot loader |

**TABLE 17-10     AMI BIOS POST CODES (FEBRUARY 1991 TO DECEMBER 1991)**

| CODE | DESCRIPTION |
|------|-------------|
| 01 | Processor register test about to start and NMI to be disabled |
| 02 | NMI is disabled—power-on delay starting |
| 03 | Power-on delay complete. Any initialization before keyboard BAT is in progress |
| 04 | Initialization before keyboard BAT complete. Reading keyboard SYS bit to check soft reset/power-on |
| 05 | Soft reset/ power-on determined. Going to enable ROM (that is, disable shadow RAM/cache) |
| 06 | ROM enabled, calculating ROM BIOS checksum, waiting for KB controller input buffer to be free |
| 07 | ROM BIOS checksum passed (KB controller I/B free) going to issue BAT command to keyboard controller |

**TABLE 17-10    AMI BIOS POST CODES (FEBRUARY 1991 TO DECEMBER 1991)**
**(CONTINUED)**

| CODE | DESCRIPTION |
|------|-------------|
| 08 | BAT command to keyboard controller issued. Going to verify BAT command |
| 09 | Keyboard controller BAT result verified. Keyboard command byte to be written next |
| 0A | Keyboard command byte code issued. Going to write command byte data |
| 0B | Keyboard controller command byte written. Going to issue Pin 23 & 24 blocking/unblocking command |
| 0C | Pin 23 & 24 of keyboard controller is blocked/unblocked. NOP command of keyboard controller to be issued next |
| 0D | NOP command processing done. CMOS shutdown register test to be done next |
| 0E | CMOS shutdown register R/W test passed. Going to calculate CMOS checksum and update DIAG byte |
| 0F | CMOS checksum calculation is done. DIAG byte written. CMOS initialization to begin (If "INIT CMOS IN EVERY BOOT" is set) |
| 10 | CMOS initialization done (if any). CMOS status register about to initialize for Date and Time |
| 11 | CMOS Status register initialized. Going to disable DMA and Interrupt controllers |
| 12 | DMA Controller #1 & #2, interrupt controller #1 & #2 disabled. About to disable video display and initialize port-B |
| 13 | Video display disabled and port-B initialized. Chipset initialization/auto memory detection about to begin |
| 14 | Chipset initialization/auto memory detection over, 8254 timer test about to start |
| 15 | CH-2 timer test halfway, 8254 CH-2 timer test to be complete |
| 16 | Ch-2 timer test over, 8254 CH-1 timer test to be complete |
| 17 | CH-1 timer test over, 8254 CH-0 timer test to be complete |
| 18 | CH-0 timer test over. About to start memory refresh |
| 19 | Memory Refresh started. Memory refresh test to be done next |
| 1A | Memory Refresh line is toggling. Going to check 15 microsecond ON/OFF time |
| 1B | Memory refresh period 30 microsecond test complete. Base 64KB memory test about to start |
| 20 | Base 64KB memory test started. Address line test to be done next |
| 21 | Address line test passed. Going to do toggle parity |
| 22 | Toggle parity over. Going for sequential data R/W test |
| 23 | Base 64KB sequential data R/W test passed. Setup before Interrupt vector initialization about to start |
| 24 | Setup before vector initialization complete. Interrupt vector initialization about to begin |
| 25 | Interrupt vector initialization done. Going to read I/O port of 8042 for turbo switch (if any) |
| 26 | I/O port of 8042 is read. Going to initialize global data for turbo switch |
| 27 | Global data initialization is over. Any initialization after interrupt vector to be done next |
| 28 | Initialization after interrupt vector is complete. Going for monochrome mode setting |
| 29 | Monochrome mode setting is done. Going for Color mode setting |
| 2A | Color mode setting is done. About to go for toggle parity before optional ROM test |
| 2B | Toggle parity over. About to give control for any setup before optional video ROM check |

**TABLE 17-10    AMI BIOS POST CODES (FEBRUARY 1991 TO DECEMBER 1991)
(CONTINUED)**

| CODE | DESCRIPTION |
|------|-------------|
| 2C | Processing before video ROM control is done. About to look for optional video ROM and give control |
| 2D | Optional video ROM control done. About to give control to do any processing after video ROM returns control |
| 2E | Return from processing after the video ROM control. If EGA/VGA not found, then do display memory R/W test |
| 2F | EGA/VGA not found. Display memory R/W test about to begin |
| 30 | Display memory R/W test passed. About to look for retrace checking |
| 31 | Display memory R/W test/retrace check failed. About to do alternate display memory R/W test |
| 32 | Alternate display memory R/W test passed. About to look for alternate display retrace checking |
| 33 | Video display checking over. Verification of display with switch setting and card to begin |
| 34 | Verification of display adapter done. Display mode to be set next |
| 35 | Display mode configuration complete. BIOS ROM data area about to be checked |
| 36 | BIOS ROM data area check over. Going to set cursor for power-on message |
| 37 | Cursor setting for power-on message ID complete. Going to display the power-on message |
| 38 | Power-on message display complete. Going to read new cursor position |
| 39 | New cursor position read and saved. Going to display the reference string |
| 3A | Reference string display is over. Going to display the "Hit ESC" message |
| 3B | "Hit ESC" message displayed. Virtual mode memory test about to start |
| 40 | Preparation for virtual mode test started. Going to verify from video memory |
| 41 | Returned after verifying from display memory. Going to prepare the descriptor tables |
| 42 | Descriptor tables prepared. Going to enter in virtual mode for memory test |
| 43 | Entered in the virtual mode. Going to enable interrupts for diagnostics mode |
| 44 | Interrupts enabled (if diagnostics switch is on). Going to initialize data to check memory wrap around at 0:0 |
| 45 | Data initialized. Going to check for memory wrap around at 0:0 and finding the total system memory size |
| 46 | Memory wrap around test done (memory size calculation over). About to go for writing patterns to test memory |
| 47 | Pattern to be tested written in extended memory. Going to write patterns in base 640KB |
| 48 | Patterns written in base memory. Going to determine amount of memory below 1MB |
| 49 | Amount of memory below 1MB found and verified. Going to determine amount of memory above 1MB |
| 4A | Amount of memory above 1MB found and verified. Going for BIOS ROM data area check |
| 4B | BIOS ROM data area check over. Going to check ESC and clear memory below 1MB for soft reset |
| 4C | Memory below 1MB cleared (soft reset). Going to clear memory above 1MB |
| 4D | Memory above 1MB cleared (soft reset). Going to save the memory size |

**TABLE 17-10** AMI BIOS POST CODES (FEBRUARY 1991 TO DECEMBER 1991)
*(CONTINUED)*

| CODE | DESCRIPTION |
|------|-------------|
| 4E | Memory test started (no soft reset). About to display the first 64KB memory test |
| 4F | Memory size display started (this will be updated during memory test). Going for sequential and random memory test |
| 50 | Memory test below 1MB complete. Going to adjust memory size for relocation/shadow |
| 51 | Memory size adjusted for relocation/shadow. Memory test above 1MB to follow |
| 52 | Memory test above 1MB complete. Preparing to go back to real mode |
| 53 | CPU registers are saved including memory size. Going to enter real mode |
| 54 | Shutdown successful (CPU in real mode). Going to restore registers saved during preparation for shutdown |
| 55 | Registers restored. Going to disable gate A20 address line |
| 56 | A20 address line disable successful. BIOS ROM data area about to be checked |
| 57 | BIOS ROM data area check halfway. BIOS ROM data area check to be complete |
| 58 | BIOS ROM data area check over. Going to clear "Hit ESC" message |
| 59 | "Hit ESC" message cleared and "WAIT" message displayed. About to start DMA and interrupt controller test |
| 60 | DMA page register test passed. About to verify from display memory |
| 61 | Display memory verification over. About to go for DMA #1 base register test |
| 62 | DMA #1 base register test passed. About to go for DMA #2 base register test |
| 63 | DMA #2 base register test passed. About to go for BIOS ROM data area check |
| 64 | BIOS ROM data area check halfway. BIOS ROM data area check to be completed |
| 65 | BIOS ROM data area check over. About to program DMA unit 1 and 2 |
| 66 | DMA unit 1 and 2 programming over. About to initialize 8259 interrupt controller |
| 67 | 8259 initialization over. About to start keyboard test |
| 80 | Keyboard test started (clearing output buffer, checking for stuck key). About to issue keyboard reset |
| 81 | Keyboard reset error/stuck key found. About to issue keyboard controller interface test command |
| 82 | Keyboard controller interface test over. About to write command byte and initialize circular buffer |
| 83 | Command byte written. Global data initialization done. About to check for lock-key |
| 84 | Lock-key checking over. About to check for memory size mismatch with CMOS |
| 85 | Memory size check done. About to display soft error; check for password or bypass setup |
| 86 | Password checked. About to do programming before setup |
| 87 | Programming before setup complete. Going to CMOS setup program |
| 88 | Returned from CMOS setup and screen cleared. About to do programming after setup |
| 89 | Programming after setup is complete. Going to display power-on screen message |
| 8A | First screen message displayed. About to display "WAIT" message |
| 8B | "WAIT" message displayed. About to perform main and video BIOS shadow |
| 8C | Main/Video BIOS shadow successful. Setup options programming after CMOS setup about to start |

**TABLE 17-10    AMI BIOS POST CODES (FEBRUARY 1991 TO DECEMBER 1991)**
**(CONTINUED)**

| CODE | DESCRIPTION |
|------|-------------|
| 8D | Setup options are programmed, mouse check and initialization to be done next |
| 8E | Mouse check and initialization complete. Going for hard disk floppy reset |
| 8F | Floppy check returns that floppy is to be initialized. Floppy setup to follow |
| 90 | Floppy setup is over. Test for hard disk presence |
| 91 | Hard disk presence test over. Hard disk setup to follow |
| 92 | Hard disk setup complete. About to go for BIOS ROM data area check |
| 93 | BIOS ROM data area check halfway. BIOS ROM data area check to be completed |
| 94 | BIOS ROM data area check over. Going to set base and extended memory size |
| 95 | Memory size adjusted due to mouse support hdisk type 47. Going to verify from display memory |
| 96 | Returned after verifying from display memory. Going to do any initialization before C800 option ROM control |
| 97 | Any initialization before C800 option ROM control is over. Option ROM check and control next |
| 98 | Option ROM control is done. About to give control to do any required processing after option ROM returns control |
| 99 | Any initialization required after option ROM test over. Going to set up timer data area and printer base address |
| 9A | Return after setting timer and printer base address. Going to set the RS-232 base address |
| 9B | Returned after RS-232 base address. Going to do any initialization before co-processor test |
| 9C | Required initialization before co-processor is over. Going to initialize the co-processor next |
| 9D | Co-processor initialized. Going to do any initialization after co-processor test |
| 9E | Initialization after co-processor test complete. Going to check extended keyboard and ID and Num Lock |
| 9F | Extended keyboard check done and ID flag set. Num Lock on/off. Keyboard ID command to be issued |
| A0 | Keyboard ID command issued. Keyboard ID flag to be reset |
| A1 | Keyboard ID flag reset. Cache memory test to follow |
| A2 | Cache memory test over. Going to display any soft errors |
| A3 | Soft error display complete. Going to set the keyboard typematic rate |
| A4 | Keyboard typematic rate set. Going to program memory wait states |
| A5 | Memory wait states programming over. Screen to be cleared next |
| A6 | Screen cleared. Going to enable parity and NMI |
| A7 | NMI and parity enabled. Going to do any initialization required before giving control to optional ROM at E000 |
| A8 | Initialization before E000 ROM control over. E000 ROM to get control next |
| A9 | Returned from E000 ROM control. Going to do any initialization required after E000 optional ROM control |

**TABLE 17-10**   AMI BIOS POST CODES (FEBRUARY 1991 TO DECEMBER 1991) *(CONTINUED)*

| CODE | DESCRIPTION |
|------|-------------|
| AA | Initialization after E000 optional ROM control is over. Going to display system configuration |
| 00 | System configuration is displayed. Giving control to INT 19h boot loader |

**TABLE 17-11**   AMI BIOS POST CODES (JUNE 1992 TO AUGUST 1993)

| CODE | DESCRIPTION |
|------|-------------|
| 01 | Processor register test about to start and NMI to be disabled |
| 02 | NMI is disabled. Power-on delay starting |
| 03 | Power-on delay complete. Any initialization before keyboard BAT is in progress next |
| 04 | Any initialization before keyboard BAT is complete. Reading keyboard SYS bit, to check soft reset/power-on |
| 05 | Soft reset/power-on determined. Going to enable ROM (disable shadow RAM/cache) if any |
| 06 | ROM is enabled. Calculating ROM BIOS checksum and waiting for 8042 keyboard controller input buffer to be free |
| 07 | ROM BIOS checksum passed. KB controller input buffer free. Going to issue BAT command to the keyboard controller |
| 08 | BAT command to keyboard controller is issued. Going to verify the BAT command |
| 09 | Keyboard controller BAT result verified. Keyboard command byte to be written next |
| 0A | Keyboard command byte code is issued. Going to write command byte data |
| 0B | Keyboard controller command byte is written. Going to issue Pin 23 & 24 blocking/unblocking command |
| 0C | Pin 23 & 24 of keyboard controller is blocked/unblocked. NOP command of keyboard controller to be issued next |
| 0D | NOP command processing is done. CMOS shutdown register test to be done next |
| 0E | CMOS shutdown register R/W test passed. Going to calculate CMOS checksum and update DIAG byte |
| 0F | CMOS checksum calculation is done and DIAG byte written. CMOS initialization to begin (if "INIT CMOS IN EVERY BOOT" is set) |
| 10 | CMOS initialization done (if any). CMOS status register about to initialize for Date and Time |
| 11 | CMOS Status register initialized. Going to disable DMA and interrupt controllers |
| 12 | DMA controller #1 & #2, interrupt controller #1 & #2 disabled. About to disable video display and initialize port-B |
| 13 | Disable video display and initialize port B. Chipset initialize/auto memory detection about to begin |
| 14 | Chipset initialization/auto memory detection complete. 8254 timer test about to start |
| 15 | CH-2 timer test halfway. 8254 CH-2 timer test to be completed |
| 16 | CH-2 timer test over. 8254 CH-1 timer test to be completed |
| 17 | CH-1 timer test over. 8254 CH-0 timer test to be completed |
| 18 | CH-0 timer test over. About to start memory refresh |

| **TABLE 17-11** | **AMI BIOS POST CODES (JUNE 1992 TO AUGUST 1993)** *(CONTINUED)* |
|---|---|

| CODE | DESCRIPTION |
|---|---|
| 19 | Memory refresh started. Memory refresh test to be done next |
| 1A | Memory refresh line is toggling. Going to check 15 microsecond ON/OFF time |
| 1B | Memory refresh period 30 microsecond test complete. Base 64KB memory test about to start |
| 20 | Base 64KB memory test started. Address line test to be done next |
| 21 | Address line test passed. Going to do toggle parity |
| 22 | Toggle parity over. Going for sequential data R/W test |
| 23 | Base 64KB sequential data R/W test passed. Any setup before interrupt vector initialization about to start |
| 24 | Setup required before vector initialization complete. Interrupt vector initialization about to begin |
| 25 | Interrupt vector initialization done. Going to read I/O port of 8042 for turbo switch (if any) |
| 26 | I/O port of 8042 is read. Going to initialize global data for turbo switch |
| 27 | Global data initialization is over. Any initialization after interrupt vector to be done next |
| 28 | Initialization after interrupt vector is complete. Going for monochrome mode setting |
| 29 | Monochrome mode setting is done. Going for Color mode setting |
| 2A | Color mode setting is done. About to try toggle parity before option ROM test |
| 2B | Toggle parity over. About to give control for any setup required before option video ROM check |
| 2C | Processing before video ROM control is done. About to look for optional video ROM and give control |
| 2D | Option video ROM control done. About to give control for processing after video ROM returns control |
| 2E | Return from processing after video ROM control. If EGA/VGA not found, do display memory R/W test |
| 2F | EGA/VGA not found. Display memory R/W test about to begin |
| 30 | Display memory R/W test passed. About to look for the retrace checking |
| 31 | Display memory R/W test or retrace checking failed. About to do alternate display memory R/W test |
| 32 | Alternate display memory R/W test passed. About to look for the alternate display retrace checking |
| 33 | Video display checking over. Verification of display type with switch setting and actual card to begin |
| 34 | Verification of display adapter done. Display mode to be set next |
| 35 | Display mode setup complete. BIOS ROM data area about to be checked |
| 36 | BIOS ROM data area check over. Going to set cursor for power-on message |
| 37 | Cursor setting for power-on message complete. Going to display power-on message |
| 38 | Power-on message display complete. Going to read new cursor position |
| 39 | New cursor position read and saved. Going to display the reference string |
| 3A | Reference string display over. Going to display the "Hit ESC" message |
| 3B | "Hit ESC" message displayed. Virtual mode memory test about to start |
| 40 | Preparation for virtual mode test started. Going to verify from video memory |

**TABLE 17-11** AMI BIOS POST CODES (JUNE 1992 TO AUGUST 1993) *(CONTINUED)*

| CODE | DESCRIPTION |
|------|-------------|
| 41 | Returned after verifying from display memory. Going to prepare descriptor tables |
| 42 | Descriptor tables prepared. Going to enter in virtual mode for memory test |
| 43 | Entered in virtual mode. Going to enable interrupts for diagnostics mode |
| 44 | Interrupts enabled (if "diags" switch on). Going to initialize data to check memory wrap around at 0:0 |
| 45 | Data initialized. Going to check for memory wrap around at 0:0 and find total memory size |
| 46 | Memory wrap around test done (size calculation finished). About to go for writing patterns to test memory |
| 47 | Pattern to be tested written in extended memory. Going to write patterns in base 640KB memory |
| 48 | Patterns written in base memory. Going to find out amount of memory below 1MB |
| 49 | Amount of memory below 1MB found and verified. Going to find amount of memory above 1MB |
| 4A | Amount of memory above 1MB found and verified. Going for BIOS ROM data area check |
| 4B | BIOS ROM data area check over. Going to check ESC and clear memory below 1MB for soft reset |
| 4C | Memory below 1MB cleared (soft reset). Going to clear memory above 1MB |
| 4D | Memory above 1MB cleared (soft reset). Going to save memory size |
| 4E | Memory test started (no soft reset). About to display first 64KB memory test |
| 4F | Memory size display started (this will be updated during memory test). Going for sequential and random memory test |
| 50 | Memory test below 1MB complete. Going to adjust memory size for relocation/shadow |
| 51 | Memory size adjusted for relocation/shadow. Memory test above 1MB to follow |
| 52 | Memory test above 1MB complete. Preparing to go back to real mode |
| 53 | CPU registers saved including memory size. Going to enter real mode |
| 54 | Shutdown successful (CPU in real mode). Going to restore registers saved during prep for shutdown |
| 55 | Registers restored. Going to disable gate A20 address line |
| 56 | A20 address line disable successful. BIOS ROM data area about to be checked |
| 57 | BIOS ROM data area check halfway. BIOS ROM data area check to be completed |
| 58 | BIOS ROM data area check over. Going to clear "Hit ESC" message |
| 59 | "Hit ESC" message cleared and "WAIT" message displayed. About to start DMA and PIC test |
| 60 | DMA page register test passed. About to verify from display memory |
| 61 | Display memory verification over. About to go for DMA #1 base register test |
| 62 | DMA #1 base register test passed. About to go for DMA #2 base register test |
| 63 | DMA #2 base register test passed. About to go for BIOS ROM data area check |
| 64 | BIOS ROM data area check halfway. BIOS ROM data area check to be completed |
| 65 | BIOS ROM data area check over. About to program DMA unit 1 and 2 |
| 66 | DMA unit 1 and 2 programming over. About to initialize 8259 interrupt controller |
| 67 | 8259 initialization over. About to start keyboard test |

**TABLE 17-11     AMI BIOS POST CODES (JUNE 1992 TO AUGUST 1993)** *(CONTINUED)*

| CODE | DESCRIPTION |
|------|-------------|
| 80 | Keyboard test started (clearing output buffer, and checking for stuck key). About to issue keyboard reset |
| 81 | Keyboard reset error/stuck key found. About to issue keyboard controller interface command |
| 82 | Keyboard controller interface test over. About to write command byte and initialize circular buffer |
| 83 | Command byte written and global data initialization done. About to check for lock-key |
| 84 | Lock-key checking over. About to check for memory size mismatch with CMOS |
| 85 | Memory size check done. About to display soft error and check for password or bypass setup |
| 86 | Password checked. About to do programming before setup |
| 87 | Programming before setup complete. Going to CMOS setup program |
| 88 | Returned from CMOS setup program, screen is cleared. About to do programming after setup |
| 89 | Programming after setup complete. Going to display power-on screen message |
| 8A | First screen message displayed. About to display "WAIT" message |
| 8B | "WAIT" message displayed. About to do main and video BIOS shadow |
| 8C | Main/video BIOS shadow successful. Setup options programming after CMOS setup about to start |
| 8D | Setup options programmed. Mouse check and initialization to be performed next |
| 8E | Mouse check and initialization complete. Going for hard disk and floppy reset |
| 8F | Floppy check indicates that floppy is to be initialized. Floppy setup to follow |
| 90 | Floppy setup is over. Test for hard disk presence to be performed |
| 91 | Hard disk presence test over. Hard disk setup to follow |
| 92 | Hard disk setup complete. About to go for BIOS ROM data area check |
| 93 | BIOS ROM data area check halfway. BIOS ROM data area check to be completed |
| 94 | BIOS ROM data area check over. Going to set base and extended memory size |
| 95 | Memory size adjusted due to mouse support and hard disk type 47. Going to verify from display memory |
| 96 | Returned after verifying from display memory. Going to do any initialization before C800 option ROM control |
| 97 | Any initialization before C800 option ROM control is over. Option ROM check and control will be done next |
| 98 | Option ROM control is done. About to give control to do any required processing after option ROM returns control |
| 99 | Any initialization required after option ROM test is over. Going to set up timer data area and printer base address |
| 9A | Return after setting timer and printer base address. Going to set the RS-232 base address |
| 9B | Returned after RS-232 base address. Going to do any initialization before co-processor test |
| 9C | Required initialization before co-processor is over. Going to initialize the co-processor next |
| 9D | Co-processor initialized. Going to do any initialization after co-processor test |
| 9E | Initialization after co-processor test is complete. Going to check extended keyboard and keyboard ID and NUMLOCK |
| 9F | Extended keyboard check is done, ID flag set, NUMLOCK on/off. Keyboard ID command to be issued |

## TABLE 17-11    AMI BIOS POST CODES (JUNE 1992 TO AUGUST 1993) *(CONTINUED)*

| CODE | DESCRIPTION |
| --- | --- |
| A0 | Keyboard ID command issued. Keyboard ID flag to be reset |
| A1 | Keyboard ID flag reset. Cache memory test to follow |
| A2 | Cache memory test over. Going to display soft errors |
| A3 | Soft error display complete. Going to set keyboard typematic rate |
| A4 | Keyboard typematic rate set. Going to program memory wait states |
| A5 | Memory wait states programming over. Screen to be cleared next |
| A6 | Screen cleared. Going to enable parity and NMI |
| A7 | NMI and parity enabled. Going to do any initialization before giving control to option ROM at E000 |
| A8 | Initialization before E000 ROM control over. E000 ROM to get control next |
| A9 | Returned from E000 ROM control. Going to do any initialization after E000 option ROM control |
| AA | Initialization after E000 option ROM control is over. Going to display the system configuration |
| 00 | System configuration is displayed. Giving control to INT 19h boot loader |

## TABLE 17-12    AMI WINBIOS POST CODES (DECEMBER 1993 AND LATER)

| CODE | DESCRIPTION |
| --- | --- |
| 01 | Processor register test about to start. Disable NMI next |
| 02 | NMI is disabled. Power-on delay starting |
| 03 | Power-on delay complete (to check soft reset/power-on) |
| 05 | Soft reset/power-on determined. Going to enable ROM (disable shadow RAM cache if any) |
| 06 | ROM is enabled. Calculating ROM BIOS checksum |
| 07 | ROM BIOS checksum passed. CMOS shutdown register test to be done next |
| 08 | CMOS shutdown register test done. CMOS checksum calculation next |
| 09 | CMOS checksum calculation done. CMOS diagnostic byte written, and CMOS initialization to begin |
| 0A | CMOS initialization done (if needed). CMOS status register to initialize Date and Time |
| 0B | CMOS status register initialization done. Initialization before keyboard BAT to be done next |
| 0C | KB controller I/B free. Going to issue the BAT command to keyboard controller |
| 0D | BAT command to keyboard controller is issued. Going to verify the BAT command |
| 0E | Keyboard controller BAT result verified. Any initialization after KB controller BAT next |
| 0F | Initialization after KB controller BAT done. Keyboard command byte to be written next |
| 10 | Keyboard controller command byte is written. Going to issue Pin 23 & 24 blocking/unblocking command |
| 11 | Keyboard controller Pin 23 & 24 blocked/unblocked. Check for INS key during power-on |
| 12 | Checking for INS key during power-on finished. Going to disable DMA/IRQ controllers |
| 13 | DMA controller #1 and #2 and IRQ controller #1 and #2 disabled. Video display disabled, and port B initialized—chipset initialization/auto memory detection next |

**TABLE 17-12** AMI WINBIOS POST CODES (DECEMBER 1993 AND LATER) *(CONTINUED)*

| CODE | DESCRIPTION |
|------|-------------|
| 14 | Chipset initialization/auto memory detection over. Uncompress the POST code if using a compressed BIOS |
| 15 | POST code is uncompressed. 8254 timer test about to start |
| 19 | 8254 timer test over. About to start memory refresh test |
| 1A | Memory refresh line is toggling. Going to check 15 microsecond ON/OFF time |
| 20 | Memory refresh 30 microsecond test complete. Base 64KB memory/address line test about to start |
| 21 | Address line test passed. Going to try toggle parity |
| 22 | Toggle parity finished. Going for sequential data R/W test on base 64KB memory |
| 23 | Base 64KB sequential data R/W test passed. Going to set BIOS stack and do any setup before Interrupt |
| 24 | Setup required before vector initialization complete. Interrupt vector initialization about to begin |
| 25 | Interrupt vector initialization done. Going to read input port of 9042 for turbo switch (if any) and clear password if POST diagnostic switch is ON |
| 26 | Input port of 8042 is read. Going to initialize global data for turbo switch |
| 27 | Global data initialization for turbo switch is over. Any initialization before setting video mode to be done next |
| 28 | Initialization before setting video mode is complete. Testing mono mode and color mode setting |
| 2A | Monochrome and color mode settings done. About to toggle parity before option ROM test |
| 2B | Toggle parity is finished. About to give control for any setup required before option video ROM check |
| 2C | Processing before video ROM control is finished. About to look for option video ROM and give system control |
| 2D | Option video ROM control is finished. About to give control for any processing after video ROM returns control |
| 2E | Return from processing after video ROM control. If EGA/VGA not found, do display memory R/W test |
| 2F | EGA/VGA not found. Display memory R/W test about to begin |
| 30 | Display memory R/W test passed. About to look for the retrace checking |
| 31 | Display memory R/W test or retrace checking failed. About to do alternate display memory R/W test |
| 32 | Alternate display memory R/W test passed. About to look for the alternate display retrace checking |
| 34 | Video display checking over. Display mode to be set next |
| 37 | Display mode setup. Going to display the power-on message |
| 39 | New cursor position read and saved. Going to display the "Hit DEL" message |
| 3B | "Hit DEL" message displayed. Virtual mode memory test about to start |
| 40 | Going to prepare the descriptor tables |
| 42 | Descriptor tables prepared. Going to enter in virtual mode for memory test |
| 43 | Entered in virtual mode. Going to enable interrupts for diagnostics mode |

**TABLE 17-12    AMI WINBIOS POST CODES (DECEMBER 1993 AND LATER) *(CONTINUED)***

| CODE | DESCRIPTION |
| --- | --- |
| 44 | Interrupts enabled (if diagnostic switch is on). Going to initialize data to check memory wrap around at 0:0 |
| 45 | Data initialized. Going to check for memory wrap around at 0:0 and find total system memory size |
| 46 | Memory wrap around test done (memory size calculation over). About to go for writing patterns to test memory |
| 47 | Pattern to be tested written to extended memory. Going to write patterns in base 640KB memory |
| 48 | Patterns written to base memory. Going to find amount of memory below 1MB |
| 49 | Amount of memory below 1MB found and verified. Going to find out amount of memory above 1MB |
| 4B | Amount of memory above 1MB found and verified. Check for soft reset. Going to clear memory below 1MB for soft reset next (if power-on, go to POST step 4Eh) |
| 4C | Memory below 1MB cleared (soft reset) |
| 4D | Memory above 1MB cleared (soft reset). Save memory size next (go to POST step 52h) |
| 4E | Memory test started (not soft reset). Display first 64KB memory size next |
| 4F | Memory size display started (this will be updated during memory test). Sequential and random memory test next |
| 50 | Memory testing/initialization below 1MB complete. Going to adjust displayed memory size for relocation/shadow |
| 51 | Memory size display adjusted for relocation/shadow. Memory test above 1MB to follow |
| 52 | Memory testing/initialization above 1MB complete. Going to save memory size information |
| 53 | Memory size information is saved, and CPU registers are saved. Going to enter real mode |
| 54 | Shutdown successful (CPU in real mode). Disable gate A20 line next |
| 57 | A20 address line disable successful. Going to adjust memory size depending on relocation/shadow |
| 58 | Memory size adjusted for relocation/shadow. Going to clear "Hit DEL" message |
| 59 | "Hit DEL" message cleared, and "WAIT" message displayed. About to start DMA and interrupt controller test |
| 60 | DMA page register test passed. About to go for DMA #1 base register test |
| 62 | DMA #1 base register test passed. About to go for DMA #2 base register test |
| 65 | DMA #2 base register test passed. About to program DMA unit 1 and 2 |
| 66 | DMA unit 1 and 2 programming over. About to initialize 8259 interrupt controller |
| 67 | 8259 initialization finished. About to start keyboard test |
| 80 | Keyboard test started. Clear output buffer, check for stuck key, and issue reset keyboard command next |
| 81 | Keyboard reset error/stuck key found. About to issue keyboard controller interface test command |
| 82 | Keyboard controller interface test over. About to write command byte and initialize circular buffer |
| 83 | Command byte written and global data initialization done. Check for lock-key next |

**TABLE 17-12    AMI WINBIOS POST CODES (DECEMBER 1993 AND LATER)** *(CONTINUED)*

| CODE | DESCRIPTION |
|------|-------------|
| 84 | Lock-key checking finished. About to check for memory size mismatch with CMOS |
| 85 | Memory size check done. About to display soft error and check for password or bypass setup |
| 86 | Password checked. About to do programming before setup |
| 87 | Programming before setup complete. Uncompress SETUP code and execute CMOS setup |
| 88 | Returned from CMOS setup and screen is cleared. About to do programming after setup |
| 89 | Programming after setup complete. Going to display power-on screen message |
| 8B | First screen message displayed, and "WAIT" message displayed. About to do main/video BIOS shadow |
| 8C | Main and video BIOS shadow successful. Setup options programming after CMOS setup about to start |
| 8D | Setup options are programmed. Mouse check and initialization next |
| 8E | Mouse check and initialization complete. Going for hard disk controller reset |
| 8F | Hard disk controller reset done. Floppy setup to be done next |
| 91 | Floppy setup is complete. Hard disk setup to be done next |
| 94 | Hard disk setup is complete. Going to set base and extended memory sizes |
| 96 | Memory size adjusted due to mouse support and hard disk type 47. Any initialization before C800 done. Option ROM control next |
| 97 | Initialization before C800 option ROM control is finished. Option ROM check and control next |
| 98 | Option ROM control finished. About to give control for any required processing after option ROM returns control next |
| 99 | Any initialization required after option ROM test over. Going to set up timer data area and printer base address |
| 9A | Return after setting timer and printer base address. Going to set the RS-232 base address |
| 9B | Returned after RS-232 base address. Going to do any initialization before co-processor test |
| 9C | Required initialization before co-processor is finished. Going to initialize the co-processor next |
| 9D | Co-processor initialized. Going to do any initialization after co-processor test |
| 9E | Initialization after co-processor test complete. Going to check extended keyboard and test keyboard ID and NUMLOCK |
| 9F | Extended keyboard check is done and ID flag is set. NUMLOCK on/off. Issue keyboard ID command next |
| A0 | Keyboard ID command issued. Keyboard ID flag to be reset |
| A1 | Keyboard ID flag reset. Cache memory test to follow |
| A2 | Cache memory test over. Going to display any soft errors |
| A3 | Soft error display complete. Going to set the keyboard typematic rate |
| A4 | Keyboard typematic rate set. Going to program memory wait states |
| A5 | Memory wait state programming over. Going to clear the screen and enable parity/NMI |
| A7 | NMI and parity enabled. Going to do any initialization required before giving control to option ROM at E000 |
| A8 | Initialization before E000 ROM control over. E000 ROM to get control next |
| A9 | Returned from E000 ROM control. Going to do required initialization |

**TABLE 17-12    AMI WINBIOS POST CODES (DECEMBER 1993 AND LATER)** *(CONTINUED)*

| CODE | DESCRIPTION |
|------|-------------|
| AA | Initialization after E000 option ROM control is finished. Going to display the system configuration |
| B0 | System configuration is displayed. Going to uncompress SETUP code for hot-key setup |
| B1 | Uncompressing of SETUP code is complete. Going to copy any code to specific area |
| 00 | Copying of code to specific area done. Giving control to INT 19h boot loader |
| F0 | Initialization of I/O cards in slots is in progress (EISA) |
| F1 | Extended NMI sources enabling is in progress (EISA) |
| F2 | Extended NMI test is in progress (EISA) |
| F3 | Display any slot initialization messages |
| F4 | Extended NMI sources enabling in progress |

**TABLE 17-13    AMI BIOS POST CODES (VERSION 2.2X)**

| CODE | DESCRIPTION |
|------|-------------|
| 00 | Flag test (the CPU is being tested) |
| 03 | Register test |
| 06 | System hardware initialization |
| 09 | Test BIOS ROM checksum |
| 0C | Page register test |
| 0F | 8254 timer test |
| 12 | Memory refresh initialization |
| 15 | 8237 DMA controller test |
| 18 | 8237 DMA controller initialization |
| 1B | 8259 PIC initialization |
| 1E | 8259 PIC test |
| 21 | Memory refresh test |
| 24 | Base 64KB address test |
| 27 | Base 64KB memory test |
| 2A | 8742 keyboard test |
| 2D | MC146818 CMOS IC test |
| 30 | Start the protected-mode test |
| 33 | Start the memory sizing test |
| 36 | First protected-mode test passed |
| 39 | First protected-mode test failed |
| 3C | CPU speed calculation |
| 3F | Reading the 8742 hardware switches |
| 42 | Initializing the interrupt vector area |
| 45 | Verifying the CMOS configuration |

**TABLE 17-13    AMI BIOS POST CODES (VERSION 2.2X) *(CONTINUED)***

| CODE | DESCRIPTION |
| --- | --- |
| 48 | Testing and initializing the video system |
| 4B | Testing unexpected interrupts |
| 4E | Starting second protected-mode test |
| 51 | Verifying the LDT instruction |
| 54 | Verifying the TR instruction |
| 57 | Verifying the LSL instruction |
| 5A | Verifying the LAR instruction |
| 5D | Verifying the VERR instruction |
| 60 | Address line A20 test |
| 63 | Testing unexpected exceptions |
| 66 | Starting the third protected-mode test |
| 69 | Address line test |
| 6A | Scan DDNIL bits for null pattern |
| 6C | System memory test |
| 6F | Shadow memory test |
| 72 | Extended memory test |
| 75 | Verify the memory configuration |
| 78 | Display configuration error messages |
| 7B | Copy system BIOS to shadow memory |
| 7E | 8254 clock test |
| 81 | MC46818 real-time clock test |
| 84 | Keyboard test |
| 87 | Determining the keyboard type |
| 8A | Stuck key test |
| 8D | Initializing hardware interrupt vectors |
| 90 | Testing the math co-processor |
| 93 | Finding available COM ports |
| 96 | Finding available LPT ports |
| 99 | Initializing the BIOS data area |
| 9C | Fixed/Floppy disk controller test |
| 9F | Floppy disk test |
| A2 | Fixed disk test |
| A5 | Check for external ROMs |
| A8 | System key lock test |
| AE | F1 error message test |
| AF | System boot initialization |
| B1 | Call INT 19 boot loader |

**TABLE 17-14**     AMI BIOS POST CODES (AMI PLUS FAMILY)

| CODE | DESCRIPTION |
| --- | --- |
| 01 | NMI disabled |
| 02 | CPU register test complete |
| 03 | ROM checksum tests OK |
| 04 | 8259 PIC initialization OK |
| 05 | CMOS interrupt disabled |
| 06 | System timer (PIT) OK |
| 07 | PIC channel 0 test OK |
| 08 | Delta count channel (DMA) 2 test OK |
| 09 | Delta count channel (DMA) 1 test OK |
| 0A | Delta count channel (DMA) 0 test OK |
| 0B | Parity status cleared (DMA/PIT) |
| 0C | Refresh and system time check OK (DMA/PIT) |
| 0D | Refresh link toggling OK (DMA/PIT) |
| 0E | Refresh period on/off 50% OK (RAM or address line) |
| 10 | Ready to start 64KB base memory test |
| 11 | Address line test OK |
| 12 | 64KB base memory test OK |
| 13 | Interrupt vectors initialized |
| 14 | 8042 keyboard controller test |
| 15 | CMOS read/write test OK |
| 16 | CMOS checksum and battery test |
| 17 | Monochrome mode setup OK (6845 chip) |
| 18 | CGA mode setup OK (6845 chip) |
| 19 | Checking video ROM |
| 1A | Optional video ROM checks OK |
| 1B | Display memory R/W test OK |
| 1C | Alternate display memory checks OK |
| 1D | Video retrace check OK |
| 1E | Global byte setting for video OK (video adapter) |
| 1F | Mode setting for mono/color OK (video adapter) |
| 20 | Video test OK |
| 21 | Video display OK |
| 22 | Power-on message display OK |
| 30 | Ready for virtual mode memory test |
| 31 | Starting virtual mode memory test |
| 32 | CPU now in virtual mode |
| 33 | Memory address line test |
| 34 | Memory address line test |
| 35 | Memory below 1MB calculated |
| 36 | Memory size computation OK |

**TABLE 17-14    AMI BIOS POST CODES (AMI PLUS FAMILY)** *(CONTINUED)*

| CODE | DESCRIPTION |
|------|-------------|
| 37 | Memory test in progress |
| 38 | Memory initialization below 1MB complete |
| 39 | Memory initialization above 1MB complete |
| 3A | Display memory size |
| 3B | Ready to start memory below 1MB |
| 3C | Memory test below 1MB OK |
| 3D | Memory test above 1MB OK |
| 3E | Ready to switch to real mode |
| 3F | Shutdown successful |
| 40 | Ready to disable A20 gate (8042 chip) |
| 41 | A20 gate disabled (8042 chip) |
| 42 | Ready to test DMA controller (8237 DMA chip) |
| 4E | Address line test OK |
| 4F | CPU now in real mode |
| 50 | DMA page register test OK |
| 51 | DMA unit 1 base register OK |
| 52 | DMA unit 1 channel OK |
| 53 | DMA unit 2 base register OK |
| 54 | DMA unit 2 channel OK |
| 55 | Latch test for both DMA units OK |
| 56 | DMA units 1 and 2 initialized OK |
| 57 | 8259 PIC initialization complete |
| 58 | 8259 PIC mask register OK |
| 59 | Master 8259 PIC mask register OK |
| 5A | Check timer and keyboard interrupt |
| 5B | PIT timer interrupt OK |
| 5C | Ready to test keyboard interrupt |
| 5D | ERROR...timer/keyboard interrupt |
| 5E | 8259 PIC error |
| 5F | 8259 PIC test OK |
| 70 | Start the keyboard test |
| 71 | Keyboard test OK |
| 72 | Keyboard test OK |
| 73 | Keyboard global data initialized (8042 chip) |
| 74 | Ready to start floppy controller setup |
| 75 | Floppy controller setup OK |
| 76 | Ready to start hard drive controller setup |
| 77 | Hard drive controller setup OK |
| 79 | Ready to initialize timer data |
| 7A | Verifying CMOS battery power |

**TABLE 17-14    AMI BIOS POST CODES (AMI PLUS FAMILY)** *(CONTINUED)*

| CODE | DESCRIPTION |
|------|-------------|
| 7B | CMOS battery verification complete |
| 7D | Analyze test results for memory |
| 7E | CMOS memory size update OK |
| 7F | Check for optional ROM at C0000h |
| 80 | Keyboard checked for SETUP keystroke |
| 81 | Optional ROM control OK |
| 82 | Printer ports initialized OK |
| 83 | Serial ports initialized OK |
| 84 | 80 x 87 test OK |
| 85 | Ready to display any soft errors |
| 86 | Send control to system ROM E0000h |
| 87 | System ROM E0000h check complete |
| 00 | Call INT 19 boot loader |

**TABLE 17-15    AMI BIOS POST CODES (AMI COLOR FAMILY)**

| CODE | DESCRIPTION |
|------|-------------|
| 01 | CPU flag test |
| 02 | Power-on delay |
| 03 | Chipset initialization |
| 04 | Hard/soft reset |
| 05 | ROM enabled |
| 06 | ROM BIOS checksum |
| 07 | 8042 KBC test |
| 08 | 8042 KBC test |
| 09 | 8042 KBC test |
| 0A | 8042 KBC test |
| 0B | 8042 protected-mode test |
| 0C | 8042 KBC test |
| 0D | 8042 KBC test |
| 0E | CMOS checksum test |
| 0F | CMOS initialization |
| 10 | CMOS/RTC status OK |
| 11 | DMA/PIC disable |
| 12 | DMA/PIC initialization |
| 13 | Chipset and memory initialization |
| 14 | 8254 PIT test |
| 15 | PIT channel 2 test |
| 16 | PIT channel 1 test |

**TABLE 17-15    AMI BIOS POST CODES (AMI COLOR FAMILY)** *(CONTINUED)*

| CODE | DESCRIPTION |
|------|-------------|
| 17 | PIT channel 0 test |
| 18 | Memory refresh test (PIT chip) |
| 19 | Memory refresh test (PIT chip) |
| 1A | Check 15µS refresh (PIT chip) |
| 1B | Check 30µS refresh (PIT chip) |
| 20 | Base 64KB memory test |
| 21 | Base 64KB memory parity test |
| 22 | Memory read/write test |
| 23 | BIOS vector table initialization |
| 24 | BIOS vector table initialization |
| 25 | Check of 8042 KBC |
| 26 | Global data for KBC configured |
| 27 | Video-mode test |
| 28 | Monochrome-mode test |
| 29 | CGA-mode test |
| 2A | Parity enable test |
| 2B | Check for optional ROMs in the system |
| 2C | Check video ROM |
| 2D | Reinitialize the main chipset |
| 2E | Test video memory |
| 2F | Test video memory |
| 30 | Test video adapter |
| 31 | Test alternate video memory |
| 32 | Test alternate video adapter |
| 33 | Video-mode test |
| 34 | Video mode setup |
| 35 | Initialize the BIOS ROM data area |
| 36 | Power-on message display |
| 37 | Power-on message display |
| 38 | Read cursor position |
| 39 | Display cursor reference |
| 3A | Display SETUP start message |
| 40 | Start protected-mode test |
| 41 | Build descriptor tables |
| 42 | CPU enters protected mode |
| 43 | Protected-mode interrupt enabled |
| 44 | Check descriptor tables |
| 45 | Check memory size |
| 46 | Memory read/write test |

**TABLE 17-15    AMI BIOS POST CODES (AMI COLOR FAMILY)** *(CONTINUED)*

| CODE | DESCRIPTION |
|------|-------------|
| 47 | Base 640KB memory test |
| 48 | Check 640KB memory size |
| 49 | Check extended memory size |
| 4A | Verify CMOS extended memory |
| 4B | Check for soft/hard reset |
| 4C | Clear extended memory locations |
| 4D | Update CMOS memory size |
| 4E | Display base RAM size |
| 4F | Perform memory test on base 640KB |
| 50 | Update CMOS RAM size |
| 51 | Perform extended memory test |
| 52 | Resize extended memory |
| 53 | Return CPU to real mode |
| 54 | Restore CPU registers for real mode |
| 55 | Disable the A20 gate |
| 56 | Recheck the BIOS vectors |
| 57 | BIOS vector check complete |
| 58 | Display the SETUP start message |
| 59 | Perform DMA and PIT test |
| 60 | Perform DMA page register test |
| 61 | Perform DMA #1 test |
| 62 | Perform DMA #2 test |
| 63 | Check BIOS data area |
| 64 | BIOS data area checked |
| 65 | Initialize DMA chips |
| 66 | Perform 8259 PIC initialization |
| 67 | Perform keyboard test |
| 80 | Keyboard reset |
| 81 | Perform stuck key and batch test (keyboard) |
| 82 | Run 8042 KBC test |
| 83 | Perform lock key check |
| 84 | Compare memory size with CMOS |
| 85 | Perform password/soft-error check |
| 86 | Run CMOS equipment check |
| 87 | CMOS setup test |
| 88 | Reinitialize the main chipset |
| 89 | Display the power-on message |
| 8A | Display the wait and mouse check |
| 8B | Attempt to shadow any option ROMs |

**TABLE 17-15    AMI BIOS POST CODES (AMI COLOR FAMILY)** *(CONTINUED)*

| CODE | DESCRIPTION |
|------|-------------|
| 8C | Initialize XCMOS settings |
| 8D | Rest hard/floppy disks |
| 8E | Compare floppy setup to CMOS |
| 8F | Initialize the floppy disk controller |
| 90 | Compare hard disk setup to CMOS |
| 91 | Initialize the hard disk controller |
| 92 | Check the BIOS data table |
| 93 | BIOS data table check complete |
| 94 | Set memory size |
| 95 | Verify the display memory |
| 96 | Clear all interrupts |
| 97 | Check any optional ROMs |
| 98 | Clear all interrupts |
| 99 | Setup timer data |
| 9A | Locate and check serial ports |
| 9B | Clear all interrupts |
| 9C | Perform the math co-processor test |
| 9D | Clear all interrupts |
| 9E | Perform an extended keyboard check |
| 9F | Set the NUMLOCK on the keyboard |
| A0 | Keyboard reset |
| A1 | Cache memory test |
| A2 | Display any soft errors |
| A3 | Set typematic rate |
| A4 | Set memory wait states |
| A5 | Clear the display |
| A6 | Enable parity and NMI |
| A7 | Clear all interrupts |
| A8 | Turn over system control to the ROM at E0000 |
| A9 | Clear all interrupts |
| AA | Display configuration |
| 00 | Call INT 19 boot loader |

**TABLE 17-16    AMI BIOS POST CODES (AMI EZ-FLEX FAMILY)**

| CODE | DESCRIPTION |
|------|-------------|
| 01 | NMI disabled...starting CPU flag test |
| 02 | Power-on delay |
| 03 | Chipset initialization |
| 04 | Check keyboard for hard/soft reset |

## TABLE 17-16    AMI BIOS POST CODES (AMI EZ-FLEX FAMILY) *(CONTINUED)*

| CODE | DESCRIPTION |
| --- | --- |
| 05 | ROM enable |
| 06 | ROM BIOS checksum |
| 07 | 8042 KBC test |
| 08 | 8042 KBC test |
| 09 | 8042 KBC test |
| 0A | 8042 KBC test |
| 0B | 8042 protected-mode test |
| 0C | 8042 KBC test |
| 0D | Test CMOS RAM shutdown register |
| 0E | CMOS checksum test |
| 0F | CMOS initialization |
| 10 | CMOS/RTC status OK |
| 11 | DMA/PIC disable |
| 12 | Disable video display |
| 13 | Chipset and memory initialization |
| 14 | 8254 PIT test |
| 15 | PIT channel 2 test |
| 16 | PIT channel 1 test |
| 17 | PIT channel 0 test |
| 18 | Memory refresh test (PIT chip) |
| 19 | Memory refresh test (PIT chip) |
| 1A | Check 15µS refresh (PIT chip) |
| 1B | Test 64KB base memory |
| 20 | Test address lines |
| 21 | Base 64KB memory parity test |
| 22 | Memory read/write test |
| 23 | Perform any setups needed prior to vector table initialization |
| 24 | BIOS vector table initialization in lower 1KB of system RAM |
| 25 | Check of 8042 KBC |
| 26 | Global data for KBC setup |
| 27 | Perform any setups needed after vector table initialization |
| 28 | Monochrome-mode test |
| 29 | CGA-mode test |
| 2A | Parity enable test |
| 2B | Check for optional ROMs in the system |
| 2C | Check video ROM |
| 2D | Determine if EGA/VGA is installed |
| 2E | Test video memory (EGA/VGA not installed) |
| 2F | Test video memory |
| 30 | Test video adapter |

**TABLE 17-16** AMI BIOS POST CODES (AMI EZ-FLEX FAMILY) *(CONTINUED)*

| CODE | DESCRIPTION |
|------|-------------|
| 31 | Test alternate video memory |
| 32 | Test alternate video adapter |
| 33 | Video-mode test |
| 34 | Video mode setup |
| 35 | Initialize the BIOS ROM data area |
| 36 | Set cursor for power-on message display |
| 37 | Display power-on message |
| 38 | Read cursor position |
| 39 | Display cursor reference |
| 3A | Display SETUP start message |
| 40 | Start protected-mode test |
| 41 | Build descriptor tables |
| 42 | CPU enters protected mode |
| 43 | Protected-mode interrupt enable |
| 44 | Check descriptor tables |
| 45 | Check memory size |
| 46 | Memory read/write test |
| 47 | Base 640KB memory test |
| 48 | Find amount of memory below 1MB |
| 49 | Find amount of memory above 1MB |
| 4A | Check ROM BIOS data area |
| 4B | Clear memory below 1MB for soft reset |
| 4C | Clear memory above 1MB for soft reset |
| 4D | Update CMOS memory size |
| 4E | Display base 64KB memory test |
| 4F | Perform memory test on base 640KB |
| 50 | Update RAM size for shadow operation |
| 51 | Perform extended memory test |
| 52 | Ready to return to real mode |
| 53 | Return CPU to real mode |
| 54 | Restore CPU registers for real mode |
| 55 | Disable the A20 gate |
| 56 | Recheck the BIOS data area |
| 57 | BIOS data area check complete |
| 58 | Display the SETUP start message |
| 59 | Perform DMA page register test |
| 60 | Verify display memory |
| 61 | Perform DMA #1 test |
| 62 | Perform DMA #2 test |
| 63 | Check BIOS data area |

**TABLE 17-16** AMI BIOS POST CODES (AMI EZ-FLEX FAMILY) *(CONTINUED)*

| CODE | DESCRIPTION |
| --- | --- |
| 64 | BIOS data area checked |
| 65 | Initialize DMA chips |
| 66 | Perform 8259 PIC initialization |
| 67 | Perform keyboard test |
| 80 | Keyboard reset |
| 81 | Perform stuck key and batch test (keyboard) |
| 82 | Run 8042 KBC test |
| 83 | Perform lock key check |
| 84 | Compare memory size with CMOS |
| 85 | Perform password/soft-error check |
| 86 | Run CMOS equipment check |
| 87 | Run CMOS setup if selected |
| 88 | Reinitialize the main chipset after setup |
| 89 | Display the power-on message |
| 8A | Display the wait and mouse check |
| 8B | Attempt to shadow any option ROMs |
| 8C | Initialize system per CMOS settings |
| 8D | Rest hard/floppy disks |
| 8E | Compare floppy setup to CMOS |
| 8F | Initialize the floppy disk controller |
| 90 | Compare hard disk setup to CMOS |
| 91 | Initialize the hard disk controller |
| 92 | Check the BIOS data table |
| 93 | BIOS data table check complete |
| 94 | Set memory size |
| 95 | Verify the display memory |
| 96 | Clear all interrupts |
| 97 | Check any optional ROMs |
| 98 | Clear all interrupts |
| 99 | Setup timer data |
| 9A | Locate and check serial ports |
| 9B | Clear all interrupts |
| 9C | Perform the math co-processor test |
| 9D | Clear all interrupts |
| 9E | Perform an extended keyboard check |
| 9F | Set the NUMLOCK on the keyboard |
| A0 | Keyboard reset |
| A1 | Cache memory test |
| A2 | Display any soft errors |
| A3 | Set typematic rate |

**TABLE 17-16**    AMI BIOS POST CODES (AMI EZ-FLEX FAMILY) *(CONTINUED)*

| CODE | DESCRIPTION |
|------|-------------|
| A4 | Set memory wait states |
| A5 | Clear the display |
| A6 | Enable parity and NMI |
| A7 | Clear all interrupts |
| A8 | Turn over system control to the ROM at E0000 |
| A9 | Clear all interrupts |
| AA | Display configuration |
| 00 | Call INT 19 boot loader |

**TABLE 17-17**    AMI BIOS VERSION 8 POST CODES

| CODE | DESCRIPTION |
|------|-------------|
| 03 | Disable NMI, parity, video for EGA, and DMA controllers. Initialize BIOS, POST, and run-time data area |
| 04 | Check CMOS diagnostic byte to determine if battery power is OK and CMOS checksum is OK. Initialize the 8259 compatible PICs in the system |
| 05 | Initialize the interrupt controller hardware (generally PIC) and interrupt vector table |
| 06 | R/W test on count register. Initialize system timer. Enable IRQ 0 in PIC for system timer interrupt |
| 08 | Initialize the CPU and test the keyboard controller. Program the keyboard controller command byte after detecting the keyboard |
| 0A | Initialize the 8042 compatible keyboard controller (KBC) |
| 0B | Detect the presence of PS/2 mouse |
| 0C | Detect the presence of a keyboard in KBC port |
| 0E | Test and initialize input devices. Uncompress all available language, BIOS logo, and silent logo modules |
| 13 | Early POST initialization of chipset registers |
| 24 | Uncompress and initialize any platform- (motherboard) specific BIOS modules |
| 30 | Initialize system management interrupt |
| 2A | Disable all PCI devices and PnP ISA cards and assign PCI bus numbers. Initialize all static devices, including manually configured peripherals and noncompliant PCI devices. Search for and initialize any PnP, PCI, or AGP video devices |
| 2C | Detect and initialize the video adapter installed in the system that has optional ROMs |
| 2E | Initialize all output devices |
| 31 | Allocate memory for ADM module and uncompress it. Initialize and activate ADM module |
| 33 | Initialize silent boot module |
| 37 | Display sign-on message, CPU information, setup key message, and any OEM-specific information |
| 38 | Search for and configure PCI input devices, and detect standard keyboard controller. Search for and configure all PnP and PCI boot devices. Configure all onboard peripherals set to an automatic configuration, and configure all remaining PnP and PCI devices |

**TABLE 17-17**    AMI BIOS VERSION 8 POST CODES *(CONTINUED)*

| CODE | DESCRIPTION |
|------|-------------|
| 39 | Initialize DMA Controllers 1 and 2 |
| 3A | Initialize the RTC date/time |
| 3B | Test for total memory installed in the system. Check for DEL or ESC keys to limit memory test. Display total memory in the system |
| 3C | Mid-POST initialization of chipset registers |
| 40 | Detect different devices (such as parallel ports, serial ports, or CPU coprocessor) successfully installed in the system and update the BDA, ESCD, and so on |
| 50 | Implement any adjustment to memory size (for example, program the ISA memory hole) if needed |
| 52 | Update CMOS memory size entry from memory found in memory test. Allocate memory for ESCD from base memory |
| 60 | Initialize NUM LOCK status and program the KBD typematic rate |
| 75 | Initialize INT 13 and prepare for IPL detection |
| 78 | Initialize IPL devices controlled by BIOS and option ROMs |
| 7A | Initialize remaining option ROMs |
| 7C | Generate and write contents of ESCD in NVRAM |
| 84 | Log any errors encountered during POST |
| 85 | Display errors to the user and get user response if necessary |
| 87 | Execute CMOS Setup routine if needed or requested |
| 8C | Late POST initialization of chipset registers |
| 8E | Program any peripheral parameters and enable/disable the NMI as selected |
| 90 | Late POST initialization of system management interrupt |
| A0 | Check boot password if installed |
| A1 | Perform cleanup work needed before booting to OS |
| A2 | Take care of run-time image preparation for different BIOS modules. Initialize the Microsoft IRQ Routing Table. Prepare the run-time language module |
| A4 | Initialize run-time language module |
| A7 | Display the system configuration screen (if enabled). Initialize the CPU before boot |
| A8 | Prepare CPU for OS boot |
| A9 | Wait for user input if needed |
| AA | Uninstall POST INT 1Ch and INT 09h vectors, then remove the ADM module |
| AB | Prepare BBS for INT 19 boot |
| AC | End of POST initialization of chipset registers |
| B1 | Save system context for ACPI |
| 00 | Pass control to OS Loader (typically INT 19h) |

**TABLE 17-18** AWARD BIOS POST CODES (AT BIOS VERSION 3.0)

| CODE | DESCRIPTION |
|------|-------------|
| 01 | Test CPU flag registers |
| 02 | Power-up check...initialize motherboard chipset |
| 03 | Clear the 8042 KBC |
| 04 | Reset the 8042 KBC |
| 05 | Test the keyboard |
| 06 | Disable video system, parity, and DMA controller |
| 07 | Test CPU registers |
| 08 | Initialize CMOS/RTC IC |
| 09 | Perform BIOS ROM checksum |
| 0A | Initialize the video interface |
| 0B | Test the 8254 timer channel 0 |
| 0C | Test the 8254 timer channel 1 |
| 0D | Test the 8254 timer channel 2 |
| 0E | Test CMOS RAM shutdown byte |
| 0F | Test extended CMOS RAM (if present) |
| 10 | Test the 8237 DMA controller channel 0 |
| 11 | Test the 8237 DMA controller channel 1 |
| 12 | Test the 8237 DMA controller page registers |
| 13 | Test the 8741 KBC interface |
| 14 | Test the memory refresh and toggle circuits |
| 15 | Test the first 64KB of system memory |
| 16 | Set up the interrupt vector tables in low memory |
| 17 | Set up video I/O operations |
| 18 | Test MDA/CGA video memory unless an EGA/VGA adapter is found |
| 19 | Test the 8259 PIC mask bits channel 1 |
| 1A | Test the 8259 PIC mask bits channel 2 |
| 1B | Test the CMOS RAM battery level |
| 1C | Test the CMOS RAM checksum |
| 1D | Set system memory size from CMOS information |
| 1E | Check base memory size 64KB at a time |
| 1F | Test base memory from 64KB to 640KB |
| 20 | Test stuck interrupt lines |
| 21 | Test for stuck NMI |
| 22 | Test the 8259 PIC |
| 23 | Test the protected mode and A20 gate |
| 24 | Check the size of extended memory above 1MB |
| 25 | Test all base and extended memory found up to 16MB |
| 26 | Test protected-mode exceptions |
| 27 | Initialize shadow RAM and move system BIOS (and video BIOS) into shadow RAM |
| 28 | Detect and initialize 8242 or 8248 chip |

**TABLE 17-18    AWARD BIOS POST CODES (AT BIOS VERSION 3.0)** *(CONTINUED)*

| CODE | DESCRIPTION |
| --- | --- |
| 2A | Initialize the keyboard |
| 2B | Detect and initialize the floppy drive |
| 2C | Detect and initialize serial ports |
| 2D | Detect and initialize parallel ports |
| 2E | Detect and initialize the hard drive |
| 2F | Detect and initialize the math co-processor |
| 31 | Detect and initialize any adapter ROMs |
| BD | Initialize the cache controller if present |
| CA | Initialize cache memory |
| CC | Shutdown the NMI handler |
| EE | Test for unexpected processor exception |
| FF | Call the INT 19 boot loader |

**TABLE 17-19    AWARD BIOS POST CODES (VERSION 3.0 TO 3.03 C.1987)**

| CODE | DESCRIPTION |
| --- | --- |
| 01 | Processor test part 1: processor status verification—tests following CPU status flags: set/clear carry zero sign and overflow (fatal)—infinite loop if failed or continue test if OK |
| 02 | Determine type of POST test—fails if keyboard interface buffer filled with data—infinite loop if failed or continue test if OK |
| 03 | Clear 8042 keyboard interface—send verify TEST_KBRD command (AAh)—continue test if OK |
| 04 | Reset 8042 keyboard controller—verify AAh return from 03 |
| 05 | Get 8042 keyboard controller manufacturing status—read input port via keyboard controller to determine manufacturing or normal mode operation |
| 06 | Initialization chips on board LSI chips—disable color/mono video, parity, and DMA (8237A)—reset co-processor, initialize (8254) timer 1, clear DMA page registers and CMOS shutdown byte |
| 07 | Processor test #2: read/write verify SS/SP/BP registers with FFh and 00h data pattern |
| 08 | Initialize CMOS chip |
| 09 | EPROM checksum for 32 KB |
| 0A | Initialize video interface |
| 0B | Test 8254 channel 0 |
| 0C | Test 8254 channel 1 |
| 0D | Test 8254 channel 2 |
| 0E | Test CMOS date and timer |
| 0F | Test CMOS shutdown byte |
| 10 | Test DMA channel 0 |
| 11 | Test DMA channel 1 |
| 12 | Test DMA page registers |

**TABLE 17-19** AWARD BIOS POST CODES (VERSION 3.0 TO 3.03 C.1987) *(CONTINUED)*

| CODE | DESCRIPTION |
|------|-------------|
| 13 | Test 8741 keyboard controller |
| 14 | Test memory refresh toggle circuits |
| 15 | Test 1st 64KB of system memory |
| 16 | Set up interrupt vector table |
| 17 | Set up video I/O operations |
| 18 | Test video memory |
| 19 | Test 8259 channel 1 mask bits |
| 1A | Test 8259 channel 2 mask bits |
| 1B | Test CMOS battery level |
| 1C | Test CMOS checksum |
| 1D | Set up configuration byte from CMOS |
| 1E | Sizing system memory & compare w/CMOS |
| 1F | Test found system memory |
| 20 | Test stuck 8259 interrupt bits |
| 21 | Test stuck NMI (parity or I/O check) bits |
| 22 | Test 8259 interrupt functionality |
| 23 | Test protected mode and A20 gate |
| 24 | Sizing extended memory above 1MB |
| 25 | Test found system/extended memory |
| 26 | Test exceptions in protected mode |
| 27 | Reserved |
| 2A | POST_KEYBOARD present during reset. Keyboard before boot has no relationship to POST 19 |
| 2B | POST_FLOPPY present during initialization of floppy controller and drive(s) |
| 2C | POST_COMM present during initialization of serial cards |
| 2D | POST_PRN present during initialization of parallel cards |
| 2E | POST_DISK present during initialization of hard disk controller and drive(s) |
| 2F | POST_MATH present during initialization of math co-processor—result remains after DOS boot; left on the port 80 display |
| 30 | POST_EXCEPTION present during protected-mode access or when processor exceptions occur—a failure indicates that protected-mode return was not possible |
| CC | POST_NMI present when selecting the F2 system halt option |

**TABLE 17-20** AWARD BIOS POST CODES (AT BIOS VERSION 3.1)

| CODE | DESCRIPTION |
|------|-------------|
| 01 | Test CPU flag registers |
| 02 | Power-up check...initialize motherboard chipset |
| 03 | Clear the 8042 KBC |
| 04 | Reset the 8042 KBC |

| | |
|---|---|
| **TABLE 17-20** | **AWARD BIOS POST CODES (AT BIOS VERSION 3.1)** *(CONTINUED)* |

| CODE | DESCRIPTION |
|---|---|
| 05 | Test the keyboard |
| 06 | Disable video system, parity, and DMA controller |
| 07 | Test CPU registers |
| 08 | Initialize CMOS/RTC chip |
| 09 | Perform BIOS ROM checksum |
| 0A | Initialize the video interface |
| 0B | Test the 8254 timer channel 0 |
| 0C | Test the 8254 timer channel 1 |
| 0D | Test the 8254 timer channel 2 |
| 0E | Test CMOS RAM shutdown byte |
| 0F | Test extended CMOS RAM (if present) |
| 10 | Test the 8237 DMA controller channel 0 |
| 11 | Test the 8237 DMA controller channel 1 |
| 12 | Test the 8237 DMA controller page registers |
| 13 | Test the 8741 KBC interface |
| 14 | Test the memory refresh and toggle circuits |
| 15 | Test the first 64KB of system memory |
| 16 | Set up the interrupt vector tables in low memory |
| 17 | Set up video I/O operations |
| 18 | Test MDA/CGA video memory unless an EGA/VGA adapter is found |
| 19 | Test the 8259 PIC mask bits channel 1 |
| 1A | Test the 8259 PIC mask bits channel 2 |
| 1B | Test the CMOS RAM battery level |
| 1C | Test the CMOS RAM checksum |
| 1D | Set system memory size from CMOS information |
| 1E | Check base memory size 64KB at a time |
| 1F | Test base memory |
| 20 | Test stuck interrupt lines |
| 21 | Test for stuck NMI |
| 22 | Test the 8259 PIC |
| 23 | Test the protected mode and A20 gate |
| 24 | Check the size of extended memory above 1MB |
| 25 | Test all base and extended memory found up to 16MB |
| 26 | Test protected-mode exceptions |
| 27 | Initialize shadow RAM and move system BIOS (and video BIOS) into shadow RAM |
| 28 | Detect and initialize 8242 or 8248 chip |
| 2A | Initialize the keyboard |
| 2B | Detect and initialize the floppy drive |
| 2C | Detect and initialize serial ports |
| 2D | Detect and initialize parallel ports |

**TABLE 17-20**   AWARD BIOS POST CODES (AT BIOS VERSION 3.1) *(CONTINUED)*

| CODE | DESCRIPTION |
|------|-------------|
| 2E | Detect and initialize the hard drive |
| 2F | Detect and initialize the math co-processor |
| 31 | Detect and initialize any adapter ROMs at C8000h to EFFFFh (and F0000h to F7FFFh) |
| 39 | Initialize the cache controller if present |
| 3B | Initialize cache memory |
| CA | Detect and initialize alternate cache controller |
| CC | Shutdown the NMI handler |
| EE | Test for unexpected processor exception |
| FF | Call the INT 19 boot loader |

**TABLE 17-21**   AWARD BIOS POST CODES (AT BIOS VERSION 3.3)

| CODE | DESCRIPTION |
|------|-------------|
| 01 | Test 8042 KBC |
| 02 | Test 8042 KBC |
| 03 | Test 8042 KBC |
| 04 | Test 8042 KBC |
| 05 | Test 8042 KBC |
| 06 | Initialize any system chipsets |
| 07 | Test the CPU flags |
| 08 | Calculate the CMOS checksum |
| 09 | Initialize the 8254 PIT |
| 0A | Test the 8254 PIT |
| 0B | Test the DMA controller |
| 0C | Initialize the 8259 PIC |
| 0D | Test the 8259 PIC |
| 0E | Test ROM BIOS checksum |
| 0F | Test extended CMOS |
| 10 | Test the 8259 PIT chip |
| 11 | Test the 8259 PIT chip |
| 12 | Test the 8259 PIT chip |
| 13 | Test the 8259 PIT chip |
| 14 | Test the 8259 PIT chip |
| 15 | Test the first 64KB of RAM |
| 16 | Initialize the BIOS interrupt vector tables |
| 17 | Initialize the video system |
| 18 | Check video memory |
| 19 | Test 8259 PIC 1 mask |
| 1A | Test 8259 PIC 2 mask |

**TABLE 17-21    AWARD BIOS POST CODES (AT BIOS VERSION 3.3)** *(CONTINUED)*

| CODE | DESCRIPTION |
| --- | --- |
| 1B | Check CMOS battery level |
| 1C | Verify the CMOS checksum |
| 1D | Verify the CMOS/RTC chip |
| 1E | Check memory size |
| 1F | Verify memory in the system |
| 20 | Initialize DMA |
| 21 | Initialize PIC |
| 22 | Initialize PIT |
| 24 | Check extended memory size |
| 25 | Test all extended memory detected |
| 26 | Enter the protected mode |
| 27 | Initialize the shadow RAM and cache controller |
| 28 | Test the shadow RAM and cache controller |
| 2A | Initialize the keyboard |
| 2B | Initialize the floppy drive controller |
| 2C | Check and initialize serial ports |
| 2D | Check and initialize parallel ports |
| 2E | Initialize the hard drive controller |
| 2F | Initialize the math co-processor |
| 31 | Check for any option ROMs in the system |
| FF | Call the INT 19 boot loader |

**TABLE 17-22    AWARD BIOS POST CODES (AT BIOS VERSION 4.0)**

| CODE | DESCRIPTION |
| --- | --- |
| 01 | Processor test 1: Verify CPU status flags—set, test, clear, and test the carry, zero, sign, overflow flags (fatal) |
| 02 | Processor test 2: Write/read/verify all CPU registers, except SS, SP, and BP with data patterns FF and 00 |
| 03 | Calculate BIOS EPROM and sign-on message checksum—fail if not 0 |
| 04 | Test CMOS RAM interface and verify battery power is available |
| 05 | Initialize chips: Disable NMI, PIE, AIE, UEI, SQWV; disable video, parity checking, and DMA; reset math co-processor, clear all page registers and CMOS RAM shutdown byte. Initialize timers 0, 1 and 2, and set EISA timer to a known state; initialize DMA controllers 0 and 1; initialize interrupt controllers 0 and 1; initialize EISA registers |
| 06 | Test memory refresh toggle to ensure memory chips can retain data |
| 07 | Set up low memory—initialize chipset early—test presence of memory—run OEM chipset initialization routines, clear lower 256KB of memory—enable parity checking and test parity in lower 256KB, then test lower 256KB of memory |

**TABLE 17-22** AWARD BIOS POST CODES (AT BIOS VERSION 4.0) *(CONTINUED)*

| CODE | DESCRIPTION |
|------|-------------|
| 08 | Set up interrupt vector table and initialize first 120 interrupt vectors with SPURIOUS_INT_HDLR and initialize INT 00-1F according to INT_TBL |
| 09 | Test CMOS RAM checksum and load default if checksum is bad |
| 0A | Initialize keyboard—detect type of keyboard controller (optional) and set NUMLOCK status |
| 0B | Initialize video interface—read CMOS RAM location 14 to find out type of video in use; detect and initialize the video adapter |
| 0C | Test video memory and write sign-on message to screen |
| 0D | OEM specific |
| 0E | Reserved |
| 0F | Test DMA controller 0 with AA, 55, FF, 00 pattern |
| 10 | Test DMA controller 1 with AA, 55, FF, 00 pattern |
| 11 | DMA page registers—use I/O ports to test address circuits |
| 12-13 | Reserved |
| 14 | Test 3254 timer 0 counter 2 |
| 15 | Verify 8259 interrupt controller channel 1 by toggling interrupt lines off/on |
| 16 | Verify 8259 interrupt controller channel 2 by toggling interrupt lines off/on |
| 17 | Test stuck 8259 interrupt bits—turn interrupt bits off and verify no interrupt mask register is on |
| 18 | Test 8259 functionality—force an interrupt and verify the interrupt occurred |
| 19 | Test stuck NMI bits (parity I/O check)—verify NMI can be cleared |
| 1A-1E | Reserved |
| 1F | Set EISA mode—if EISA non-volatile memory checksum is good, execute EISA initialization—if not, execute ISA tests and clear EISA mode. Test EISA configuration, memory checksum, and communication ability |
| 20 | Initialize and enable EISA slot 0 (system board) |
| 21-2F | Initialize and enable EISA slots 1-15 |
| 30 | Size base memory from 256-640KB and test with various patterns |
| 31 | Test extended memory above 1MB using various patterns—press ESC to skip |
| 32 | If EISA mode flag set, test EISA memory found during slot initialization—press ESC to skip |
| 33-3B | Reserved |
| 3C | Verify CPU can switch in/out of protected, virtual 86, and 8086 page modes |
| 3D | Detect if mouse is present, initialize it, and install interrupt vectors |
| 3E | Initialize cache controller according to CMOS RAM setup |
| 3F | Enable shadow RAM according to CMOS RAM setup or if MEM TYPE is SYS in the EISA configuration information |
| 40 | Reserved |
| 41 | Initialize floppy disk drive controller and any drives |
| 42 | Initialize hard disk drive controller and any drives |
| 43 | Detect and initialize serial ports |
| 44 | Detect and initialize parallel ports |

**TABLE 17-22    AWARD BIOS POST CODES (AT BIOS VERSION 4.0)** *(CONTINUED)*

| CODE | DESCRIPTION |
| --- | --- |
| 45 | Detect and initialize math co-processor |
| 46 | Print Setup message ("press CTRL-ALT-ESC to enter Setup") at bottom of the screen and enable setup |
| 47 | Set speed for boot |
| 48-4D | Reserved |
| 4E | Reboot if manufacturing POST loop pin is set—otherwise, display any messages for non-fatal POST errors—enter setup if user pressed CTRL-ALT-ESC |
| 4F | Security check (optional)—ask for password |
| 50 | Write all CMOS RAM values back to CMOS RAM, and clear the screen |
| 51 | Pre-boot enable—enable parity, NMI, cache before boot |
| 52 | Initialize ROMs between C80000-EFFFF—when FSCAN enabled, initialize from C80000 to F7FFF |
| 53 | Initialize time value at address 40 of BIOS RAM area |
| 55 | Initialize DDNIL counter to NULLs |
| 63 | Boot attempt—set low stack and boot by calling INT 19 |
| B0 | Spurious interrupt occurred in protected mode |
| B1 | Unclaimed NMI—if unmasked NMI occurs, display "Press F1 to disable NMI, F2 to boot" |
| BF | Program chipset—called by POST 7 to program chipset from CT table |
| C0 | OEM specific—turn on/off cache |
| C1 | OEM specific—test for memory presence and size on-board memory |
| C2 | OEM specific—initialize board and turn on shadow and cache for fast boot |
| C3 | OEM specific—turn on extended memory DRAM select and initialize RAM |
| C4 | OEM specific—handle display/video switch to prevent display switch errors |
| C5 | OEM specific—fast gate A20 handling |
| C6 | OEM specific—cache routine for setting regions that are cacheable |
| C7 | OEM specific—shadow video/system BIOS after memory proven good |
| C8 | OEM specific—handle special speed switching |
| C9 | OEM specific—handle normal shadow RAM operations |
| D0-DF | Debug—available POST codes for use during development |
| E0 | Reserved |
| E1-EF | Set up pages: E1 = page 1, E2 = page 2, and so on |
| FF | If no error flags such as memory size are set, boot via INT 19—load system from drive A: or C: and display error message if boot device not found |

 EISA codes may be sent to I/O port 300h. Be sure to set your POST reader card to the address that's appropriate for your system.

**TABLE 17-23    AWARD BIOS POST CODES (EISA BIOS FAMILY)**

| CODE | DESCRIPTION |
|---|---|
| 01 | Test the CPU flags |
| 02 | Test the CPU registers |
| 03 | Initialize the DMA controller, PIC, and PIT |
| 04 | Initialize memory refresh |
| 05 | Initialize the keyboard |
| 06 | Test BIOS ROM checksum |
| 07 | Check CMOS battery level |
| 08 | Test lower 256KB of RAM |
| 09 | Test cache memory |
| 0A | Configure the BIOS interrupt table |
| 0B | Test the CMOS RAM checksum |
| 0C | Initialize the keyboard |
| 0D | Initialize the video adapter |
| 0E | Test video memory |
| 0F | Test DMA controller 0 |
| 10 | Test DMA controller 1 |
| 11 | Test page registers |
| 14 | Test the 8254 PIT chip |
| 15 | Verify 8259 PIC channel 1 |
| 16 | Verify 8259 PIC channel 2 |
| 17 | Test for stuck interrupts |
| 18 | Test 8259 functions |
| 19 | Test for stuck NMI |
| 1F | Check extended CMOS RAM (if available) |
| 20 | Initialize and enable EISA slot 0 |
| 21-2F | Initialize and enable EISA slots 1 to 15 |
| 30 | Check memory size below 256KB |
| 31 | Check memory size above 256KB |
| 32 | Test any EISA memory found during slot initialization |
| 3C | Enter protected mode |
| 3D | Detect and initialize mouse |
| 3E | Initialize the cache controller |
| 3F | Enable and test shadow RAM |
| 41 | Initialize floppy disk drive controller |
| 42 | Initialize hard disk drive controller |
| 43 | Detect and initialize serial ports |
| 45 | Detect and initialize math co-processor |
| 47 | Set speed for boot |
| 4E | Display any soft errors |
| 4F | Ask for password (if feature is enabled) |

**TABLE 17-23    AWARD BIOS POST CODES (EISA BIOS FAMILY)** *(CONTINUED)*

| CODE | DESCRIPTION |
|------|-------------|
| 50 | Check all CMOS RAM values and clear the display |
| 51 | Enable parity, NMI, and cache memory |
| 52 | Initialize any option ROMs present from C8000h to EFFFFh or F7FFFh |
| 53 | Initialize time value at address 40 of BIOS RAM area |
| 63 | Call INT 19 for boot loader |
| B0 | NMI still in protected mode (protected mode failed) |
| B1 | Disable NMI |
| BF | Initialize any system-specific chipsets |
| C0 | Cache memory on/off |
| C1 | Check memory size |
| C2 | Test base 256KB RAM |
| C3 | Test DRAM Page Select |
| C4 | Check video modes |
| C5 | Test shadow RAM |
| C6 | Configure cache memory |
| C8 | Check system speed switch |
| C9 | Test shadow RAM |
| CA | Initialize OEM chipset |
| FF | Call INT 19 boot loader |

**TABLE 17-24    AWARD BIOS POST CODES (PNP BIOS VERSION 4-5.X)**

| CODE | DESCRIPTION |
|------|-------------|
| C0 | Turn off OEM specific cache, shadow RAM. Initialize all the standard devices with default values |
| C1 | Auto detection of onboard DRAM & cache |
| C3 | Test the first 256K DRAM. Expand the compressed codes into temporary DRAM area, including the compressed system BIOS & Option ROMs |
| C5 | Copy the BIOS from ROM into E000-FFFF shadow RAM so that POST will go faster |
| 01-02 | Reserved |
| 03 | Initialize EISA registers (EISA BIOS only) |
| 04 | Reserved |
| 05 | Keyboard Controller Self-Test. Enable Keyboard Interface |
| 06 | Reserved |
| 07 | Verifies CMOS's basic R/W functionality |
| BE | Program defaults values into chipset |
| 09 | Program the configuration register of Cyrix CPU. OEM specific cache initialization |
| 0A | Initialize the first 32 interrupt vectors. Initialize INTs 33 to 120. Issue CPUID instruction to identify CPU type. Early Power Management initialization |

**TABLE 17-24    AWARD BIOS POST CODES (PNP BIOS VERSION 4-5.X)** *(CONTINUED)*

| CODE | DESCRIPTION |
|------|-------------|
| 0B | Verify the RTC time is valid. Detect bad battery. Read CMOS data into BIOS stack area. Perform PnP initializations (PnP BIOS only). Assign IO & Memory for PCI devices (PCI BIOS only) |
| 0C | Initialization of the BIOS data area (40:00-40:FF) |
| 0D | Program some of the chipset's value. Measure CPU speed for display. Video initialization including MDA, CGA, EGA/VGA |
| 0E | Initialize the APIC (Multi-Processor BIOS only). Test video RAM (if monochrome display device found). Show startup screen message |
| 0F | DMA channel 0 test |
| 10 | DMA channel 1 test |
| 11 | DMA page registers test |
| 12-13 | Reserved |
| 14 | Test 8254 timer 0 counter 2 |
| 15 | Test 8259 interrupt mask bits for channel 1 |
| 16 | Test 8259 interrupt mask bits for channel 2 |
| 17 | Reserved |
| 19 | Test 8259 functionality |
| 1A-1D | Reserved |
| 1E | If EISA NVM checksum is good, execute EISA initialization (EISA BIOS only) |
| 1F-29 | Reserved |
| 30 | Get base memory & extended memory size |
| 31 | Test base memory from 256K to 640K. Test extended memory from 1M to the top of memory |
| 32 | Display the Award Plug & Play BIOS extension message (PnP BIOS only). Program all onboard super I/O chips (if any) including COM ports, LPT ports, FDD port, and so on |
| 33-3B | Reserved |
| 3C | Set flag to allow users to enter CMOS setup utility |
| 3D | Initialize keyboard. Install PS/2 mouse |
| 3E | Try to turn on level 2 cache |
| 3F-40 | Reserved |
| BF | Program the rest of the chipset |
| 41 | Initialize floppy disk drive controller |
| 42 | Initialize hard drive controller |
| 43 | If it is a PnP BIOS, initialize serial & parallel ports |
| 44 | Reserved |
| 45 | Initialize math co-processor |
| 46-4D | Reserved |
| 4E | If there is any error, show all the error messages on the screen & wait for user to press F1 |
| 4F | If password is needed, ask for password. Clear the Energy Star logo (Green BIOS only) |
| 50 | Write all the CMOS values currently in the BIOS stack areas back into the CMOS |

**TABLE 17-24**    AWARD BIOS POST CODES (PNP BIOS VERSION 4-5.X) *(CONTINUED)*

| CODE | DESCRIPTION |
|------|-------------|
| 51 | Reserved |
| 52 | Initialize all ISA ROMs. Later PCI initializations (PCI BIOS only). PnP initializations (PnP BIOS only). Program shadow RAM according to setup settings. Program parity according to setup setting. Power Management initialization |
| 53 | If it is not a PnP BIOS, initialize serial & parallel ports. Initialize time in BIOS data area |
| 54-5F | Reserved |
| 60 | Set up virus (boot sector) protection |
| 61 | Try to turn on level 2 cache. Set the boot up speed according to setup setting. Last chance for chipset initialization. Last chance for Power Management initialization. Show the system configuration table |
| 62 | Set up daylight savings according to setup values. Program the NUMLOCK, type rate & type speed according to setup setting |
| 63 | If there are any changes in the hardware configuration, update the ESCD information (PnP BIOS only). Clear memory areas that have been used. Boot system via INT 19h |
| FF | System booting. This means that the BIOS already passed control to the operating system |

**TABLE 17-25**    AWARD BIOS POST CODES (NON-PNP BIOS VERSION 4-5.X)

| CODE | DESCRIPTION |
|------|-------------|
| C0 | Turn Off Chipset. OEM Specific Cache control |
| 01 | Processor Test 1. Processor Status (1FLAGS) Verification |
| 02 | Processor Test 2. Read/Write/Verify all CPU registers |
| 03 | Initialize Chipset. Disable NMI, PIE, AIE, UEI, SQWV. Disable video, parity checking, DMA. Reset math co-processor. Clear all page registers and CMOS shutdown byte. Initialize DMA controllers 0 and 1. Initialize interrupt controllers 0 and 1 |
| 04 | Test Memory Refresh Toggle. RAM must be periodically refreshed to keep the memory from decaying. This function ensures that the memory refresh function is working properly |
| 05 | Blank video and initialize keyboard. Keyboard controller initialization |
| 06 | Reserved |
| 07 | Test CMOS Interface and Verify Battery Status. CMOS is working correctly, detects bad battery |
| BE | Chipset Default Initialization. Program chipset registers with power-on BIOS defaults |
| C1 | Memory Presence Test. OEM Specific-Test to size on-board memory |
| C5 | Early Shadow. OEM Specific-Early Shadow enable for fast boot |
| C6 | Cache Presence. External cache size detection test |
| 08 | Set up Low Memory. Early chipset initialization. Memory presence test. OEM chipset routines. Clear low 64K of memory. Test first 64K memory |
| 09 | Early Cache Initialization. Cyrix CPU initialization and cache initialization |

**TABLE 17-25** AWARD BIOS POST CODES (NON-PNP BIOS VERSION 4-5.X) *(CONTINUED)*

| CODE | DESCRIPTION |
|------|-------------|
| 0A | Set up Interrupt Vector Table. Initialize first 120 interrupt vectors |
| 0B | Test CMOS RAM Checksum. Test checksum—if bad, or INSERT key pressed, load defaults |
| 0C | Initialize Keyboard. Detect type of keyboard controller |
| 0D | Initialize Video Interface. Detect CPU clock. Read CMOS location 14h to find the type of video in use. Detect and initialize video adapter |
| 0E | Test Video Memory. Write sign-on message to screen. Set up shadow RAM |
| 0F | Test DMA Controller 0. BIOS checksum test. Keyboard detect and initialization |
| 10 | Test DMA Controller 1 |
| 11 | Test DMA Page Registers |
| 12-13 | Reserved |
| 14 | Test Timer Counter 2 |
| 15 | Test 8259-1 Mask |
| 16 | Test 8259-2 Mask |
| 17 | Test Stuck Keys |
| 18 | Test 8259 Interrupt Functionality |
| 19 | Test Stuck NMI Bits |
| 1A | Display CPU clock |
| 1B-1E | Reserved |
| 1F | Set EISA Mode. If EISA non-volatile memory checksum is good, execute EISA initialization. If not, execute ISA tests and clear EISA mode flag |
| 20 | Enable Slot 0. Initialize slot 0 (System Board) |
| 21-2F | Enable Slots 1-15. Initialize slots 1 through 15 |
| 30 | Size Base and Extended Memory. Size base memory from 256K to 640K and extended memory above 1MB |
| 31 | Test Base and Extended Memory. Test base memory from 256K to 640K and extended memory above 1MB using various bit patterns |
| 32 | Test EISA Extended Memory. If EISA flag is set, then test EISA memory found in slots |
| 33-3B | Reserved |
| 3C | Set up Enabled |
| 3D | Initialize and Install Mouse. Detect if mouse is present; initialize and install interrupt vectors |
| 3E | Set up Cache Controller |
| 3F | Reserved |
| BF | Chipset Initialization. Program chipset registers with Setup values |
| 40 | Display "Virus Protect" Disable or Enable |
| 41 | Initialize Floppy Drive and Controller |
| 42 | Initialize Hard Drive and Controller |
| 43 | Detect and Initialize Serial/Parallel Ports |
| 44 | Reserved |
| 45 | Detect and Initialize Math Co-processor |
| 46 | Reserved |

**TABLE 17-25**   AWARD BIOS POST CODES (NON-PNP BIOS VERSION 4-5.X) *(CONTINUED)*

| CODE | DESCRIPTION |
|------|-------------|
| 47 | Reserved |
| 48-4D | Reserved |
| 4E | Manufacturing POST Loop or Display Messages |
| 4F | Security Password |
| 50 | Write CMOS. Write all CMOS values back to RAM and clear screen |
| 51 | Pre-boot Enable. Enable parity checker. Enable NMI. Enable cache before boot |
| 52 | Initialize Option ROMs. Initialize any option ROMs present from C8000h to EFFFFh. |
| 53 | Initialize Time Value |
| 60 | Set up Virus Protect |
| 61 | Set Boot Speed |
| 62 | Set up NUMLOCK |
| 63 | Boot Attempt |
| B0 | Check for interrupts in protected mode |
| B1 | Unclaimed NMI. If unmasked NMI occurs, display "Press F1 to disable NMI, F2 reboot" |
| E1-EF | Set up Pages |
| FF | Call Boot Loader |

**TABLE 17-26**   AWARD BIOS VERSION 6.0 POST CODES

| CODE | DESCRIPTION |
|------|-------------|
| C0 | Turn off chipset and test the CPU |
| C1 | Check the amount of available RAM and start testing |
| C2 | Initialize the system RAM |
| C3 | Extend the memory select process |
| C4 | Special display handling |
| C5 | Set up early ROM shadowing |
| C6 | Cache presence test |
| CF | Check the CMOS |
| B0 | Check for interrupts in protected mode |
| B1 | Check for unclaimed NMI |
| BF | Program the motherboard chipset |
| 1 | Load default settings to the chipset |
| 2 | Reserved |
| 3 | Initialize the Super I/O chip early |
| 4 | Reserved |
| 5 | Blank the video display |
| 6 | Reserved |
| 7 | Initialize the keyboard controller (KBC) |
| 8 | Test the keyboard |
| 9 | Reserved |

**TABLE 17-26    AWARD BIOS VERSION 6.0 POST CODES** *(CONTINUED)*

| CODE | DESCRIPTION |
| --- | --- |
| A | Initialize the mouse |
| B | Initialize onboard audio (if present) |
| C | Reserved |
| D | Reserved |
| E | Check the integrity of the ROM BIOS |
| F | Reserved |
| 10 | Autodetect the BIOS EEPROM chip |
| 11 | Reserved |
| 12 | Check the CMOS |
| 13 | Reserved |
| 14 | Load chipset defaults |
| 15 | Reserved |
| 16 | Initialize the system clock |
| 17 | Reserved |
| 18 | Identify the CPU |
| 19 | Reserved |
| 1A | Reserved |
| 1B | Set up the interrupt vector table |
| 1C | Reserved |
| 1D | Early processor mode initialization |
| 1E | Reserved |
| 1F | Reinitialize the keyboard |
| 20 | Reserved |
| 21 | Initialize HPM |
| 22 | Reserved |
| 23 | Test CMOS interface and battery status |
| 24 | Reserved |
| 25 | Reserved |
| 26 | Reserved |
| 27 | Final initialization of the KBC |
| 28 | Reserved |
| 29 | Initialize the video interface |
| 2A | Reserved |
| 2B | Reserved |
| 2C | Reserved |
| 2D | Test video memory |
| 2E | Reserved |
| 2F | Reserved |
| 30 | Reserved |

| CODE | DESCRIPTION |
|------|-------------|
| **TABLE 17-26** | **AWARD BIOS VERSION 6.0 POST CODES** *(CONTINUED)* |
| 31 | Reserved |
| 32 | Reserved |
| 33 | Set up the PS/2 mouse |
| 34 | Reserved |
| 35 | Test DMA controller 0 |
| 36 | Reserved |
| 37 | Test DMA controller 1 |
| 38 | Reserved |
| 39 | Test DMA page registers |
| 3A | Reserved |
| 3B | Reserved |
| 3C | Test Timer Counter 2 |
| 3D | Reserved |
| 3E | Test 8259-1 mask bits |
| 3F | Reserved |
| 40 | Test 8259-2 mask bits |
| 41 | Reserved |
| 42 | Reserved |
| 43 | Test stuck 8259 interrupt bits, and test 8259 interrupt functionality |
| 44 | Reserved |
| 45 | Reserved |
| 46 | Reserved |
| 47 | Set EISA mode (if necessary) |
| 48 | Reserved |
| 49 | Size the base and extended memory |
| 4A | Reserved |
| 4B | Reserved |
| 4C | Reserved |
| 4D | Reserved |
| 4E | Test the base and extended memory |
| 4F | Reserved |
| 50 | Initialize the system USB controller |
| 51 | Reserved |
| 52 | Memory test |
| 53 | Reserved |
| 54 | Reserved |
| 55 | Display CPU type/speed |
| 56 | Reserved |
| 57 | Initialize the PnP system |
| 58 | Reserved |
| 59 | Set up BIOS virus protection |

**TABLE 17-26** AWARD BIOS VERSION 6.0 POST CODES *(CONTINUED)*

| CODE | DESCRIPTION |
| --- | --- |
| 5A | Reserved |
| 5B | Load flash routine |
| 5C | Reserved |
| 5D | Initialize onboard I/O |
| 5E | Reserved |
| 5F | Reserved |
| 60 | Enable CMOS Setup |
| 61 | Reserved |
| 62 | Reserved |
| 63 | Initialize and install the mouse |
| 64 | Reserved |
| 65 | Set up special PS/2 mouse features |
| 66 | Reserved |
| 67 | Initialize ACPI |
| 68 | Reserved |
| 69 | Set up cache controller |
| 6A | Reserved |
| 6B | Entering CMOS Setup |
| 6C | Reserved |
| 6D | Initialize floppy drive and controller |
| 6E | Reserved |
| 6F | Install/enable FDD |
| 70 | Reserved |
| 71 | Reserved |
| 72 | Reserved |
| 73 | Initialize hard drive and controller |
| 74 | Reserved |
| 75 | Install/enable HDD |
| 76 | Reserved |
| 77 | Detect and initialize serial/parallel ports |
| 78 | Reserved |
| 79 | Reserved |
| 7A | Detect and initialize math coprocessor |
| 7B | Reserved |
| 7C | HDD check for write protection |
| 7D | Reserved |
| 7E | Reserved |
| 7F | POST error check |
| 80 | Reserved |
| 81 | Reserved |
| 82 | Security check |

**TABLE 17-26     AWARD BIOS VERSION 6.0 POST CODES** *(CONTINUED)*

| CODE | DESCRIPTION |
|------|-------------|
| 83 | Write CMOS data as necessary |
| 84 | Pre-boot enable |
| 85 | Initialize option ROMs |
| 86 | Reserved |
| 87 | Reserved |
| 88 | Reserved |
| 89 | Reserved |
| 8A | Reserved |
| 8B | Reserved |
| 8C | Reserved |
| 8D | Reserved |
| 8E | Reserved |
| 8F | Reserved |
| 90 | Reserved |
| 91 | Reserved |
| 92 | Reserved |
| 93 | Boot media detection |
| 94 | Final initialization |
| 95 | Special KBC patch |
| 96 | Prepare to boot |
| FF | Transfer control to boot loader |

**TABLE 17-27     COMPAQ BIOS POST CODES (GENERAL)**

| CODE | DESCRIPTION |
|------|-------------|
| 00 | Initialize flags |
| 01 | Read manufacturing jumper |
| 02 | 8042 Received Read command |
| 03 | No response from 8042 |
| 04 | Look for ROM at E000 |
| 05 | Look for ROM at C800 |
| 06 | Normal CMOS reset code |
| 08 | Initialize 8259 |
| 09 | Reset code in CMOS byte |
| 0A | Vector via 40:67 reset function |
| 0B | Vector via 40:67 with E01 function |
| 0C | Boot reset function |
| 0D | Test #2 8254 Counter 0 |
| 0E | Test #2 8254 Counter 2 |

**TABLE 17-27    COMPAQ BIOS POST CODES (GENERAL)** *(CONTINUED)*

| CODE | DESCRIPTION |
|------|-------------|
| 0F | Warm boot |
| 10 | PPI disabled |
| 11 | Initialize VDU controller |
| 12 | Clear Screen; turn on video |
| 13 | Test time 0 |
| 14 | Disable RTC interrupts |
| 15 | Check battery power |
| 16 | Battery has lost power |
| 17 | Clear CMOS diagnostics |
| 18 | Test base memory (first 128KB) |
| 19 | Initialize base memory |
| 1A | Initialize VDU adapters |
| 1B | The system ROM |
| 1C | CMOS checksum |
| 1D | DMA controller/page registers |
| 1E | Test keyboard controller |
| 1F | Test 286 protected mode |
| 20 | Test real and extended memory |
| 21 | Initialize time-of-day |
| 22 | Initialize 287 co-processor |
| 23 | Test the keyboard and 8042 |
| 24 | Reset A20 |
| 25 | Test floppy disk subsystem |
| 26 | Test fixed disk subsystem |
| 27 | Initialize parallel printer |
| 28 | Perform search for optional ROMs |
| 29 | Test valid system configuration |
| 2A | Clear screen |
| 2B | Check for invalid time and date |
| 2C | Optional ROM search |
| 2D | Test timer 2 |
| 2F | Write to diagnostic byte |
| 30 | Clear first 128KB bytes of RAM |
| 31 | Load interrupt vectors 70-77 |
| 32 | Load interrupt vectors 00-1F |
| 33 | Initialize MEMSIZE and RESETWD |
| 34 | Verify CMOS checksum |
| 35 | CMOS checksum not valid |
| 36 | Check battery power |
| 37 | Check for game adapters |

## TABLE 17-27    COMPAQ BIOS POST CODES (GENERAL) *(CONTINUED)*

| CODE | DESCRIPTION |
|------|-------------|
| 38 | Check for serial ports |
| 39 | Check for parallel printer ports |
| 3A | Initialize port and communication timeouts |
| 3B | Flush keyboard buffer |
| 40 | Save RESETWD value |
| 41 | Check RAM refresh |
| 42 | Start write of 128KB RAM test |
| 43 | Rest parity checks |
| 44 | Start verify of 128KB RAM test |
| 45 | Check for parity errors |
| 46 | No RAM errors |
| 47 | RAM error detected |
| 50 | Check for dual frequency in CMOS |
| 51 | Check CMOS VDU configuration |
| 52 | Start VDU ROM search |
| 53 | Vector to VDU option ROMs |
| 54 | Initialize first display adapter |
| 55 | Initialize second display adapter |
| 56 | No display adapters installed |
| 57 | Initialize primary VDU mode |
| 58 | Start of VDU test (each adapter) |
| 59 | Check existence of adapter |
| 5A | Check VDU registers |
| 5B | Start screen memory test |
| 5C | End test of adapter |
| 5D | Error detected on an adapter |
| 5E | Test the next adapter |
| 5F | All adapters successfully tested |
| 60 | Start of memory tests |
| 61 | Enter protected mode |
| 62 | Start memory sizing |
| 63 | Get CMOS size |
| 64 | Start test of real memory |
| 65 | Start test of extended memory |
| 66 | Save size memory (base) |
| 67 | 128KB option installed CMOS bit |
| 68 | Prepare to return to real mode |
| 69 | Back in real mode attempt successful |
| 6A | Protected-mode error during test |
| 6B | Display error message |

**TABLE 17-27      COMPAQ BIOS POST CODES (GENERAL)** *(CONTINUED)*

| CODE | DESCRIPTION |
|------|-------------|
| 6C | End of memory test |
| 6D | Initialize KB "OK" string |
| 6E | Determine size to test |
| 6F | Start MEMTEST |
| 70 | Display XXXXXKB "OK" |
| 71 | Test each RAM segment |
| 72 | High order address test |
| 73 | Exit MEMTEST |
| 74 | Parity error on bus |
| 75 | Start protected mode test |
| 76 | Prepare to enter protected mode |
| 77 | Test software exceptions |
| 78 | Prepare to return to real mode |
| 79 | Back in real mode successful |
| 7A | Back in real mode not successful |
| 7B | Exit protected test |
| 7C | High order address test failure |
| 7D | Entered cache controller test |
| 7E | Programming memory cache |
| 7F | Copy system ROM to high RAM |
| 80 | Start of 8042 test |
| 81 | Do 8042 self-test |
| 82 | Check result received |
| 83 | Error result |
| 84 | OK 8042 |
| 86 | Start test |
| 87 | Got acknowledge |
| 88 | Got result |
| 89 | Test for stuck keys |
| 8A | Key seems to be stuck |
| 8B | Test keyboard interface |
| 8C | Got result |
| 8D | End of test |
| 90 | Start of CMOS test |
| 91 | CMOS seems to be OK |
| 92 | Error on CMOS read/write test |
| 93 | Start of DMA controller test |
| 94 | Page registers seem OK |
| 95 | DMA controller is OK |
| 96 | 8237 initialization is complete |

**TABLE 17-27** COMPAQ BIOS POST CODES (GENERAL) *(CONTINUED)*

| CODE | DESCRIPTION |
|------|-------------|
| 97 | Start of NCA RAM test |
| A0 | Start of floppy disk tests |
| A1 | FDC reset active (3F2h bit 2) |
| A2 | FDC reset inactive (3F2h bit 2) |
| A3 | FDC motor on |
| A4 | FDC timeout error |
| A5 | FDC failed reset |
| A6 | FDC passed reset |
| A8 | Start to determine drive type |
| A9 | Seek operation initiated |
| AA | Waiting for FDC seek status |
| AF | Floppy disk tests completed |
| B0 | Start of fixed disk drive tests |
| B1 | Combo board not found—exit |
| B2 | Combo controller failed—exit |
| B3 | Testing drive 1 |
| B4 | Testing drive 2 |
| B5 | Drive error (error condition) |
| B6 | Drive failed (failed to respond) |
| B7 | No fixed drives—exit |
| B8 | Fixed drive tests complete |
| B9 | Attempt to boot from floppy disk |
| BA | Attempt to boot fixed drive |
| BB | Boot attempt failed FD/HD |
| BC | Boot record read, jump to boot record |
| BD | Drive error, retry booting |
| BE | Weitek co-processor test (386, 386/xxe, 386 & 486/33L, P486c) |
| C0 | Disable NMI |
| C1 | Turn off hard disk subsystem |
| C2 | Turn off video subsystem |
| C3 | Turn off floppy disk subsystem |
| C4 | Turn off hard disk/modem subsystems |
| C5 | Go to standby |
| C6 | Update BIOS time of day |
| C7 | Turn on hard disk/modem subsystems |
| C8 | Turn on floppy disk subsystem |
| C9 | Turn on video subsystem |
| CB | Flush keyboard input buffer |
| CC | Re-enable MNI |
| D0 | Entry to clear memory routine |

**TABLE 17-27     COMPAQ BIOS POST CODES (GENERAL)** *(CONTINUED)*

| CODE | DESCRIPTION |
|------|-------------|
| D1 | Ready to go to protected mode |
| D2 | Ready to clear extended memory |
| D3 | Ready to reset back to real mode |
| D4 | Back in real mode, ready to clear |
| D5 | Clear base memory, CLIM register initialization failure (SLT/286) |
| D7 | Scan and clear DDNIL bits |
| D9 | 4-way cache detect |
| DD | Built-in self-test failed |
| E0 | Ready to replace E000h ROM |
| E1 | Completed E000h ROM replacement |
| E2 | Ready to replace EGA ROM |
| E3 | Completed EGA ROM replacement |
| E8 | Looking for serial external boot ID (Deskpro 2/386N, 386s/20) |
| E9 | Receiving for serial external boot sector (2/386N, 386s/20) |
| EA | Looking for parallel external boot ID (2/386N, 386s/20) |
| EB | Receiving parallel external boot sector (2/386N, 386s/20) |
| EC | Boot record read, jump to boot record (2/386N, 386s/20) |

**TABLE 17-28     DELL BIOS POST CODES (GENERAL)**

| CODE | DESCRIPTION |
|------|-------------|
| 01 | CPU register test in progress |
| 02 | CMOS R/W test failed |
| 03 | BIOS ROM checksum bad |
| 04 | 8254 PIT test failed |
| 05 | DMA controller initialization failed |
| 06 | DMA page register test failed |
| 08 | RAM refresh verification failed |
| 09 | Starting first 64KB RAM test |
| 0A | First 64KB RAM or data line bad |
| 0B | First 64KB RAM odd/even logic bad |
| 0C | First 64KB address line bad |
| 0D | First 64KB parity error |
| 10 | Bit 0 bad in first 64KB |
| 11 | Bit 1 bad in first 64KB |
| 12 | Bit 2 bad in first 64KB |
| 13 | Bit 3 bad in first 64KB |
| 14 | Bit 4 bad in first 64KB |
| 15 | Bit 5 bad in first 64KB |
| 16 | Bit 6 bad in first 64KB |

**TABLE 17-28    DELL BIOS POST CODES (GENERAL) (CONTINUED)**

| CODE | DESCRIPTION |
| --- | --- |
| 17 | Bit 7 bad in first 64KB |
| 18 | Bit 8 bad in first 64KB |
| 19 | Bit 9 bad in first 64KB |
| 1A | Bit 10 bad in first 64KB |
| 1B | Bit 11 bad in first 64KB |
| 1C | Bit 12 bad in first 64KB |
| 1D | Bit 13 bad in first 64KB |
| 1E | Bit 14 bad in first 64KB |
| 1F | Bit 15 bad in first 64KB |
| 20 | Slave DMA register bad |
| 21 | Master DMA register bad |
| 22 | Master interrupt mask register bad |
| 23 | Slave interrupt mask register bad |
| 25 | Loading interrupt vectors |
| 27 | Keyboard controller test failed |
| 28 | CMOS RAM battery bad |
| 29 | CMOS configuration validation in progress |
| 2B | Video memory test failed |
| 2C | Video initialization failed |
| 2D | Video retrace failure |
| 2E | Searching for a video ROM |
| 30 | Switching to video ROM |
| 31 | Monochrome operation OK |
| 32 | Color (CGA) operation OK |
| 33 | Color operation OK |
| 34 | Timer tick interrupt in progress (or bad) |
| 35 | CMOS shutdown test in progress (or bad) |
| 36 | Gate A20 bad |
| 37 | Unexpected interrupt in protected mode |
| 38 | RAM test in progress or high address line is bad |
| 3A | Interval timer channel 2 bad |
| 3B | Time of day test bad |
| 3C | Serial port test bad |
| 3D | Parallel port test bad |
| 3E | Math co-processor test bad |
| 3F | Cache memory test bad |

**TABLE 17-29    HP BIOS POST CODES (VECTRA FAMILY)**

| CODE | DESCRIPTION |
|------|-------------|
| 01 | LED test |
| 02 | Processor test |
| 03 | System (BIOS) ROM test |
| 04 | RAM refresh timer test |
| 05 | Interrupt RAM test |
| 06 | Shadow the system ROM BIOS |
| 07 | CMOS RAM test |
| 08 | Internal cache memory test |
| 09 | Initialize the video card |
| 10 | Test external cache |
| 11 | Shadow option ROMs |
| 12 | Memory subsystem test |
| 13 | Initialize EISA/ISA hardware |
| 14 | 8042 self-test |
| 15 | Timer 0/Timer 2 test |
| 16 | DMA Subsystem test |
| 17 | Interrupt controller test |
| 18 | RAM address line independence test |
| 19 | Size the extended memory |
| 20 | Real-mode memory test (first 640KB) |
| 21 | Shadow RAM test |
| 22 | Protect-mode RAM test (extended RAM) |
| 23 | Real time clock (RTC) test |
| 24 | Keyboard test |
| 25 | Mouse test |
| 26 | Hard disk test |
| 27 | LAN test |
| 28 | Flexible disk controller subsystem test |
| 29 | Internal numeric co-processor test |
| 30 | Weitek co-processor test |
| 31 | Clock speed switching test |
| 32 | Serial port test |
| 33 | Parallel port test |

**TABLE 17-30    IBM BIOS POST CODES (AT-TYPE)**

| CODE | DESCRIPTION |
|------|-------------|
| 01 | CPU flag and register test |
| 02 | BIOS ROM checksum test |

**TABLE 17-30    IBM BIOS POST CODES (AT-TYPE) (CONTINUED)**

| CODE | DESCRIPTION |
|------|-------------|
| 03 | CMOS shutdown byte test |
| 04 | 8254 PIT test—bits on |
| 05 | 8254 PIT test—bits on |
| 06 | 8237 DMA initialize registers test 0 |
| 07 | 8237 DMA initialize registers test 1 |
| 08 | DMA page register test |
| 09 | Memory refresh test |
| 0A | Soft reset test |
| 0B | Reset 8042 KBC |
| 0C | KBC reset OK |
| 0D | Initialize the 8042 KBC |
| 0E | Test memory |
| 0F | Get I/P buffer switch settings |
| DD | RAM error |
| 11 | Initialize protected mode |
| 12 | Test protected-mode registers |
| 13 | Initialize 8259 PIC #2 |
| 14 | Setup temporary interrupt vectors |
| 15 | Establish BIOS interrupt vectors |
| 16 | Verify CMOS checksum and battery OK |
| 17 | Set the defective CMOS battery flag |
| 18 | Ensure CMOS set |
| 19 | Set return address byte in CMOS |
| 1A | Set temporary stack |
| 1B | Test segment address 01-0000 (second 64KB) |
| 1C | Decide if 512KB or 640KB installed |
| 1D | Test segment address 10-0000 (over 640KB) |
| 1E | Set expansion memory as contained in CMOS |
| 1F | Test address lines 19-23 |
| 20 | Ready to return from protected mode |
| 21 | Successful return from protected mode |
| 22 | Test video controller |
| 23 | Check for EGA/VGA BIOS |
| 24 | Test 8259 PIC R/W mask register |
| 25 | Test interrupt mask registers |
| 26 | Check for hot (unexpected) interrupts |
| 05 | Display 101 error (system board error) |
| 27 | Check the POST logic (system board error) |
| 28 | Check unexpected NMI interrupts (system board error) |
| 29 | Test timer 2 (system board error) |

**TABLE 17-30     IBM BIOS POST CODES (AT-TYPE)** *(CONTINUED)*

| CODE | DESCRIPTION |
| --- | --- |
| 2A | Test 8254 timer |
| 2B | System board error |
| 2C | System board error |
| 2D | Check 8042 KBC for last command |
| 2F | Go to next area during a warm boot |
| 30 | Set shutdown return 2 |
| 31 | Switch to protected mode |
| 33 | Test next block of 64KB |
| 34 | Switch back to real mode |
| F0 | Set data segment |
| F1 | Test interrupts |
| F2 | Test exception interrupts |
| F3 | Verify protected-mode instructions |
| F4 | Verify protected-mode instructions |
| F5 | Verify protected-mode instructions |
| F6 | Verify protected-mode instructions |
| F7 | Verify protected-mode instructions |
| F8 | Verify protected-mode instructions |
| F9 | Verify protected-mode instructions |
| FA | Verify protected-mode instructions |
| 34 | Test keyboard |
| 35 | Test keyboard type |
| 36 | Check for "AA" scan code |
| 38 | Check for stuck key |
| 39 | 8042 KBC error |
| 3A | Initialize the 8042 |
| 3B | Check for expansion ROM in 2KB blocks |
| 40 | Enable hardware interrupts |
| 41 | Check system code at segment E0000h |
| 42 | Exit to system code |
| 43 | Call boot loader |
| 3C | Check for initial program load |
| 3D | Initialize floppy for drive type |
| 3E | Initialize hard drive |
| 81 | Build descriptor table |
| 82 | Switch to virtual mode |
| 90-B6 | Memory and bootstrap tests |
| 32 | Test address lines 0-15 |
| 44 | Attempt to boot from fixed disk |
| 45 | Unable to boot...go to BASIC |

| TABLE 17-31 | IBM BIOS POST CODES (PS/2-TYPE) |
|---|---|

| CODE | DESCRIPTION |
|---|---|
| 00 | CPU flag test |
| 01 | 32-bit CPU register test |
| 02 | Test BIOS ROM checksum |
| 03 | Test system enabled |
| 04 | Test system POS register |
| 05 | Test adapter setup port |
| 06 | Test RTC/CMOS RAM shutdown byte |
| 07 | Test extended CMOS RAM |
| 08 | Test DMA and page register channels |
| 09 | Initialize DMA command and mode registers |
| 0A | Test memory refresh toggle |
| 0B | Test keyboard controller buffers |
| 0C | Keyboard controller self-test |
| 0D | Continue keyboard controller self-test |
| 0E | Keyboard self-test error |
| 0F | Set-up system memory configuration |
| 10 | Test first 512KB RAM |
| 11 | Halt system if memory test occurs |
| 12 | Test protested-mode instructions |
| 13 | Initialize interrupt controller 1 |
| 14 | Initialize interrupt controller 2 |
| 15 | Initialize 120 interrupt vectors |
| 16 | Initialize 16 interrupt vectors |
| 17 | Check CMOS/RTC battery |
| 18 | Check CMOS/RTC checksum |
| 19 | CMOS/RTC battery bad |
| 1A | Skip memory test in protected mode |
| 1B | Prepare for CMOS shutdown |
| 1C | Set up stack pointer to end of first 64KB |
| 1D | Calculate low memory size in protected mode |
| 1E | Save the memory size detected |
| 1F | Set up system memory split address |
| 20 | Check for extended memory beyond 64MB |
| 21 | Test memory address bus lines |
| 22 | Clear parity error and channel lock |
| 23 | Initialize interrupt 0 |
| 24 | Check CMOS RAM validity |
| 25 | Write keyboard controller command byte |
| 40 | Check valid CMOS RAM and video system |

**TABLE 17-31** IBM BIOS POST CODES (PS/2-TYPE) *(CONTINUED)*

| CODE | DESCRIPTION |
|------|-------------|
| 41 | Display error code 160 |
| 42 | Test registers in both interrupt controllers |
| 43 | Test interrupt controller registers |
| 44 | Test interrupt mask registers |
| 45 | Test NMI |
| 46 | NMI error has been detected |
| 47 | Test system timer 0 |
| 48 | Check stuck speaker clock |
| 49 | Test system timer 0 count |
| 4A | Test system timer 2 count |
| 4B | Check if timer interrupt occurred |
| 4C | Test timer 0 for improper operation (too fast or too slow) |
| 4D | Verify timer interrupt 0 |
| 4E | Check 8042 keyboard controller |
| 4F | Check for soft reset |
| 50 | Prepare for shutdown |
| 51 | Start protected-mode test |
| 52 | Test memory in 64KB increments |
| 53 | Check if memory test done |
| 54 | Return to real mode |
| 55 | Test for regular or manufacturing mode |
| 56 | Disable the keyboard |
| 57 | Check for keyboard self-test |
| 58 | Keyboard test passed |
| 59 | Test the keyboard controller |
| 5A | Configure the mouse |
| 5B | Disable the mouse |
| 5C | Initialize interrupt vectors |
| 5D | Initialize interrupt vectors |
| 5E | Initialize interrupt vectors |
| 60 | Save DDNIL status |
| 61 | Reset floppy drive |
| 62 | Test floppy drive |
| 63 | Turn floppy drive motor off |
| 64 | Set up serial ports |
| 65 | Enable real-time clock interrupt |
| 66 | Configure floppy drives |
| 67 | Configure hard drives |
| 68 | Enable system CPU arbitration |
| 69 | Scan for adapter ROMs |

**TABLE 17-31** IBM BIOS POST CODES (PS/2-TYPE) *(CONTINUED)*

| CODE | DESCRIPTION |
|------|-------------|
| 6A | Verify serial and parallel ports |
| 6B | Set up equipment byte |
| 6C | Set up configuration |
| 6D | Set keyboard typematic rate |
| 6E | Call INT 19 boot loader |

**TABLE 17-32** MR BIOS POST CODES (MICROID RESEARCH VERSION 1.0A)

| CODE | DESCRIPTION |
|------|-------------|
| 01 | Chipset problem |
| 02 | Disable NMI and DMA |
| 03 | Check BIOS ROM checksum |
| 04 | Test DMA page register |
| 05 | Keyboard controller test |
| 06 | Initialize the RTC, 8237, 8254, and 8259 |
| 07 | Check memory refresh |
| 08 | DMA master test |
| 09 | OEM-specific test |
| 0A | Test memory bank 0 |
| 0B | Test PIC units |
| 0C | Test PIC controllers |
| 0D | Initialize PIT channel 0 |
| 0E | Initialize PIT channel 2 |
| 0F | Test CMOS RAM battery |
| 10 | Check video ROM |
| 11 | Test RTC |
| 12 | Test keyboard controller |
| 13 | OEM-specific test |
| 14 | Run memory test |
| 15 | Keyboard controller |
| 16 | OEM-specific test |
| 17 | Test keyboard controller |
| 18 | Run memory test |
| 19 | Execute OEM memory test |
| 1A | Update RTC contents |
| 1B | Initialize serial ports |
| 1C | Initialize parallel ports |
| 1D | Test math co-processor |
| 1E | Test floppy disk |

**TABLE 17-32    MR BIOS POST CODES (MICROID RESEARCH VERSION 1.0A)** *(CONTINUED)*

| CODE | DESCRIPTION |
|------|-------------|
| 1F | Test hard disk |
| 20 | Validate CMOS contents |
| 21 | Check keyboard lock |
| 22 | Set number lock on keyboard |
| 23 | OEM-specific test |
| 29 | Test adapter ROMs |
| 2F | Call INT 19 boot loader |

**TABLE 17-33    CONTEMPORARY MR BIOS BEEP AND POST CODES (MICROID RESEARCH)**

| BEEP | CODE | DESCRIPTION |
|------|------|-------------|
| LH-LLL | 03 | ROM-BIOS checksum failure |
| LH-HLL | 04 | DMA page register failure |
| LH-LHL | 05 | Keyboard controller self test failure |
| LH-HHL | 08 | Memory refresh circuitry failure |
| LH-LLH | 09 | Master (16 bit) DMA controller failure |
| LH-HLH | 09 | Slave (8 bit) DMA controller failure |
| LH-LLLL | 0A | Base 64K pattern test failure |
| LH-HLLL | 0A | Base 64K parity circuitry failure |
| LH-LHLL | 0A | Base 64K parity error |
| LH-HHLL | 0A | Base 64K data bus failure |
| LH-LLHL | 0A | Base 64K address bus failure |
| LH-HLHL | 0A | Base 64K block access read failure |
| LH-LHHL | 0A | Base 64K block access write failure |
| LH-HHHL | 0B | Master 8259 failure |
| LH-LLLH | 0B | Slave 8259 failure |
| LH-HLLH | 0C | Master 8259 interrupt address failure |
| LH-LHLH | 0C | Slave 8259 interrupt address failure |
| LH-HHLH | 0C | 8259 interrupt address error |
| LH-LLHH | 0C | Master 8259 stuck interrupt error |
| LH-HLHH | 0C | Slave 8259 stuck interrupt error |
| LH-LHHH | 0C | System timer 8254 CH0/IRQ0 failure |
| LH-HHHH | 0D | 8254 channel 0 (system timer) failure |
| LH-LLLLH | 0E | 8254 channel 2 (speaker) failure |
| LH-HLLLH | 0E | 8254 OUT2 (speaker detect) failure |
| LH-LHLLH | 0F | CMOS RAM read/write test failure |
| LH-HHLLH | 0F | RTC periodic interrupt / IRQ8 failure |
| LH-LLHLH | 10 | Video ROM checksum failure |

**TABLE 17-33** CONTEMPORARY MR BIOS BEEP AND POST CODES (MICROID RESEARCH) *(CONTINUED)*

| BEEP | CODE | DESCRIPTION |
|------|------|-------------|
| None | 11 | RTC battery discharged or CMOS contents corrupt |
| LH-HLHLH | 12 | Keyboard controller failure |
| None | 12 | Keyboard error—stuck key |
| LH-LHHLH | 14 | Memory parity error |
| LH-HHHLH | 14 | I/O channel error |
| None | 14 | RAM pattern test failed |
| None | 15 | Keyboard failure or no keyboard present |
| LH-LLLHH | 17 | A20 test failure due to 8042 timeout |
| LH-HLLHH | 17 | A20 gate stuck in disabled state |
| None | 17 | A20 gate stuck in asserted state |
| None | 18 | Parity circuit failure |
| None | 19 | Data bus test failed, or address line test failed, or block access read failure, or block access read/write failure, or banks decode to same location |
| LH-LHLHH | 1A | Real time clock (RTC) is not updating |
| None | 1A | RTC settings are invalid |
| None | 1E | Diskette CMOS configuration invalid, or diskette controller failure, or diskette drive A: failure, or diskette drive B: failure |
| None | 1F | FDD CMOS configuration invalid, or fixed disk C: failure, or fixed disk D: failure |
| None | 20 | Fixed disk configuration change, or diskette configuration change, or serial port configuration change, or parallel port configuration change, or video configuration change, or Memory configuration change, or co-processor configuration change |
| None | 21 | System key is in locked position |
| None | 29 | Adapter ROM checksum failure |

In Table 17-33, L=low tone and H=high tone.

**TABLE 17-34** MR BIOS POST CODES (MICROID RESEARCH VERSION 3.4X)

| CODE | DESCRIPTION |
|------|-------------|
| 00 | Cold Start, output EDX register to I/O ports 85h, 86h, 8Dh, 8Eh for later use |
| 01 | Initialize any Custom KBD controller, disable CPU cache, cold initialize onboard I/O chipset, size & test RAM, size cache |
| 02 | Disable critical IO (monitor, DMA, FDC, I/O ports, speaker, NMI) |
| 03 | Checksum the BIOS ROM |
| 04 | Test page registers |
| 05 | Enable A20 Gate, issue 8042 Self-test |

**TABLE 17-34    MR BIOS POST CODES (MICROID RESEARCH VERSION 3.4X)** *(CONTINUED)*

| CODE | DESCRIPTION |
|------|-------------|
| 06 | Initialize ISA I/O |
| 07 | Warm initialize custom KBD controller, warm initialize onboard I/O chipset |
| 08 | Refresh toggle test |
| 09 | Test DMA Master registers, test DMA Slave registers |
| 0A | Test 1st 64K of base memory |
| 0B | Test Master 8259 mask, test Slave 8259 mask |
| 0C | Test 8259 Slave, test 8259 slave's interrupt range, initialize interrupt vectors 00–77h, initialize KBD buffer variables |
| 0D | Test Timer 0, 8254 channel 0 |
| 0E | Test 8254 Ch2, speaker channel |
| 0F | Test RTC, CMOS RAM read/write test |
| 10 | Turn on monitor, show any possible error messages |
| 11 | Read and checksum the CMOS |
| 12 | Call video ROM initialization routines, show Display sign-on message, show ESC Delay message |
| 13 | Set 8MHz AT bus |
| 14 | Size and test the base memory, stuck NMI check |
| 15 | No KB and PowerOn: Retry KB initialization |
| 16 | Size and test CPU cache |
| 17 | Test A20 OFF and ON states |
| 18 | Size and test external memory, stuck NMI check |
| 19 | Size and test system memory, stuck NMI check |
| 1A | Test RTC time |
| 1B | Determine Serial ports |
| 1C | Determine parallel ports |
| 1D | Initialize numeric co-processor |
| 1E | Determine floppy disk controllers |
| 1F | Determine IDE controllers |
| 20 | Display CMOS configuration changes |
| 21 | Clear screens |
| 22 | Set/reset NUMLOCK LED, perform security functions |
| 23 | Final determination of on-board serial/parallel ports |
| 24 | Set KB typematic rate |
| 25 | Initialize floppy controller |
| 26 | Initialize ATA disks |
| 27 | Set the video mode for primary adapter |
| 28 | Cyrix WB-CPU support, Green PC: purge 8259 slave, relieve any trapped IRQs before enabling PwrMgmt, set 8042 pins, CTRL-ALT-DEL possible now, Enable CPU features |
| 29 | Reset A20 to OFF, install Adapter ROMs |
| 2A | Clear Primary Screen, convert RTC to system ticks, set final DOS timer variables |

**TABLE 17-34**   MR BIOS POST CODES (MICROID RESEARCH VERSION 3.4X) *(CONTINUED)*

| CODE | DESCRIPTION |
| --- | --- |
| 2B | Enable NMI and latch |
| 2C | Reserved |
| 2D | Reserved |
| 2E | Fast A20: Fix A20 |
| 2F | Purge 8259 slave; relieve any trapped IRQs before enabling Green-PC. Pass control to INT 19 boot |
| 32 | Test CPU Burst |
| 33 | Reserved |
| 34 | Determine 8042, set 8042 warm-boot flag STS.2 |
| 35 | Test HMA Wrap, verify A20 enabled via F000:10 HMA |
| 36 | Reserved |
| 37 | Validate CPU: CPU Step NZ, CPUID Check. Disable CPU features |
| 38 | Set 8042 pins (Hi-Speed, Cache-off) |
| 39 | PCI Bus: Load PCI; Processor Vector initialized, BIOS Vector initialized, OEM Vector initialized |
| 3A | Scan PCI bus |
| 3B | Initialize PCI bus with intermediate defaults |
| 3C | Initialize PCI OEM with intermediate defaults, OEM bridge |
| 3D | PCI bus or Plug and Play: Initialize AT Slotmap from AT bus CDE usage |
| 3E | Find phantom CDE ROM PCI-cards |
| 3F | PCI bus: final Fast Back-to-Back state |
| 40 | OEM POST Initialization, Hook Audio |
| 41 | Allocate I/O on PCI bus, logs-in PCI-IDE |
| 42 | Hook PCI-ATA chips |
| 43 | Allocate IRQs on the PCI bus |
| 44 | Allocate/enable PCI memory/ROM space |
| 45 | Determine PS/2 mouse |
| 46 | Map IRQs to PCI bus per user CMOS, enable ATA IRQs |
| 47 | PCI-ROM install, note user CMOS |
| 48 | If Setup conditions: execute Setup utility |
| 49 | Test F000 Shadow integrity, transfer EPROM to Shadow-RAM |
| 4A | Hook VL ATA Chip |
| 4B | Identify and spin-up all drives |
| 4C | Detect Secondary IRQ, if VL/AT-Bus IDE exists but IRQ not known yet, then auto-detect it |
| 4D | Detect/log 32-bit I/O ATA devices |
| 4E | ATAPI drive M/S bitmap to Shadow-RAM, Set INT 13 Vector |
| 4F | Finalize Shadow-RAM variables |
| 50 | Chain INT 13 |
| 51 | Load PnP, Processor Vector initialized, BIOS Vector initialized, OEM Vector initialized |
| 52 | Scan Plug and Play, update PnP Device Count |

**TABLE 17-34    MR BIOS POST CODES (MICROID RESEARCH VERSION 3.4X)** *(CONTINUED)*

| CODE | DESCRIPTION |
|------|-------------|
| 53 | Supplement IRQ usage—AT IRQs |
| 54 | Conditionally assign everything PnP wants |
| 58 | Perform OEM Custom boot sequence just prior to INT 19 boot |
| 59 | Return from OEM custom boot sequence. Pass control to 1NT 19 boot |
| 5A | Display MR BIOS logo |
| 88 | Dead motherboard and/or CPU and/or BIOS ROM |
| FF | BIOS POST finished |

**TABLE 17-35    PHOENIX BIOS POST CODES (ISA/EISA/MCA BIOS)**

| CODE | DESCRIPTION |
|------|-------------|
| 01 | CPU register test |
| 02 | CMOS R/W test |
| 03 | Testing BIOS ROM checksum |
| 04 | Testing 8253 PIT chip |
| 05 | Initializing the 8237 DMA controller |
| 06 | Testing the 8237 DMA page register |
| 08 | RAM refresh circuit test |
| 09 | Test first 64KB of RAM |
| 0A | Test first 64KB RAM data lines |
| 0B | Test first 64KB RAM parity |
| 0C | Test first 64KB RAM address lines |
| 0D | Parity failure detected for first 64KB RAM |
| 10-1F | Data bit (0-15) bad in first 64KB RAM |
| 20 | Slave DMA register faulty |
| 21 | Master DMA register faulty |
| 22 | Master PIC register faulty |
| 23 | Slave PIC register faulty |
| 25 | Initializing interrupt vectors |
| 27 | Keyboard controller test |
| 28 | Testing CMOS checksum and battery power |
| 29 | Validate CMOS contents |
| 2B | Video initialization faulty |
| 2C | Video retrace test failed |
| 2D | Search for video ROM |
| 2E | Test video ROM |
| 30 | Video system checks OK |
| 31 | Monochrome video mode detected |

**TABLE 17-35** PHOENIX BIOS POST CODES (ISA/EISA/MCA BIOS) *(CONTINUED)*

| CODE | DESCRIPTION |
|------|-------------|
| 32 | Color (40 column) mode detected |
| 33 | Color (80 column) mode detected |
| 34 | Timer tick interrupt test |
| 35 | CMOS shutdown byte test |
| 36 | Gate A20 failure (8042 KBC) |
| 37 | Unexpected interrupt |
| 38 | Extended RAM test |
| 3A | Interval timer channel 2 |
| 3B | Test time-of-day clock |
| 3C | Locate and test serial ports |
| 3D | Locate and test parallel ports |
| 3E | Locate and test math co-processor |
| 41 | System board select bad |
| 42 | Extended CMOS RAM bad |

**TABLE 17-36** PHOENIX BIOS BEEP AND POST CODES (PLUS VERSION 1.0)

| BEEP | CODE | DESCRIPTION |
|------|------|-------------|
| none | 01 | CPU register test in progress |
| 1-1-3 | 02 | CMOS write/read failure |
| 1-1-4 | 03 | ROM BIOS checksum failure |
| 1-2-1 | 04 | Programmable interval timer failure |
| 1-2-2 | 05 | DMA initialization failure |
| 1-2-3 | 06 | DMA page register write/read failure |
| 1-3-1 | 08 | RAM refresh verification failure |
| none | 09 | 1st 64KB RAM test in progress |
| 1-3-3 | 0A | 1st 64KB RAM chip or data line failure multi-bit |
| 1-3-4 | 0B | 1st RAM odd/even logic failure |
| 1-4-1 | 0C | Address line failure 1st 64K RAM |
| 1-4-2 | 0D | Parity failure 1st 64K RAM |
| 2-1-1 | 10 | Bit 0 1st 64KB RAM failure |
| 2-1-2 | 11 | Bit 1 1st 64KB RAM failure |
| 2-1-3 | 12 | Bit 2 1st 64KB RAM failure |
| 2-1-4 | 13 | Bit 3 1st 64KB RAM failure |
| 2-2-1 | 14 | Bit 4 1st 64KB RAM failure |
| 2-2-2 | 15 | Bit 5 1st 64KB RAM failure |
| 2-2-3 | 16 | Bit 6 1st 64KB RAM failure |

**TABLE 17-36** PHOENIX BIOS BEEP AND POST CODES (PLUS VERSION 1.0) *(CONTINUED)*

| BEEP | CODE | DESCRIPTION |
| --- | --- | --- |
| 2-2-4 | 17 | Bit 7 1st 64KB RAM failure |
| 2-3-1 | 18 | Bit 8 1st 64KB RAM failure |
| 2-3-2 | 19 | Bit 9 1st 64KB RAM failure |
| 2-3-3 | 1A | Bit A(10) 1st 64KB RAM failure |
| 2-3-2 | 1B | Bit B(11) 1st 64KB RAM failure |
| 2-4-2 | 1C | Bit C(12) 1st 64KB RAM failure |
| 2-4-2 | 1D | Bit D(13) 1st 64KB RAM failure |
| 2-4-3 | 1E | Bit E(14) 1st 64KB RAM failure |
| 2-4-4 | 1F | Bit F(15) 1st 64KB RAM failure |
| 3-1-1 | 20 | Slave DMA register failure |
| 3-1-2 | 21 | Master DMA register failure |
| 3-1-3 | 22 | Master interrupt mask register failure |
| 3-1-4 | 23 | Slave interrupt mask register failure |
| none | 25 | Interrupt vector loading in progress |
| 3-2-4 | 27 | 8042 keyboard controller test failure |
| none | 28 | CMOS power failure/checksum calculation in progress |
| none | 29 | CMOS configuration validation in progress |
| 3-3-4 | 2B | Screen memory test failure |
| 3-4-1 | 2C | Screen initialization failure |
| 3-4-2 | 2D | Screen retrace test failure |
| none | 2E | Search for video ROM in progress |
| none | 30 | Screen believed running with video ROM |
| none | 31 | Mono monitor believed operable |
| none | 32 | Color monitor (40 column) believed operable |
| none | 33 | Color monitor (80 column) believed operable |
| 4-2-1 | 34 | Timer tick interrupt test in progress or failed (non-fatal) |
| 4-2-2 | 35 | Shutdown failure (non-fatal) |
| 4-2-3 | 36 | Gate A20 failure (non-fatal) |
| 4-2-4 | 37 | Unexpected interrupt in protected mode (non-fatal) |
| 4-3-1 | 38 | Memory high address line fail at 01000-0A000 (non-fatal) |
| 4-3-2 | 39 | Memory high address line fail at 100000-FFFFFF (non-fatal) |
| 4-3-3 | 3A | Timer chip counter 2 failed (non-fatal) |
| 4-3-4 | 3B | Time-of-day clock stopped |
| 4-4-1 | 3C | Serial port test |
| 4-4-2 | 3D | Parallel port test |
| 4-4-3 | 3E | Math co-processor test |
| low 1-1-2 | 41 | System board select bad |
| low 1-1-3 | 42 | Extended CMOS RAM bad |

## TABLE 17-37    PHOENIX BIOS POST CODES (UMC CHIPSET/PCI BUS)

| CODE | DESCRIPTION |
|------|-------------|
| 02 | Verify real mode |
| 04 | Get CPU type |
| 06 | Initialize system hardware |
| 08 | Initialize chipset registers with initial POST values |
| 09 | Set in-POST flag |
| 0A | Initialize CPU registers |
| 0C | Initialize cache to initial POST values |
| 0E | Initialize I/O |
| 10 | Initialize power management |
| 11 | Load alternate registers with initial POST values |
| 12 | Jump to User Patch 0 |
| 14 | Initialize keyboard controller |
| 16 | BIOS ROM checksum |
| 18 | 8254 timer initialization |
| 1A | 8237 DMA controller initialization |
| 1C | Reset PIC |
| 20 | Test DRAM refresh |
| 22 | Test 8742 keyboard controller |
| 24 | Set ES segment register to 4GB |
| 26 | Enable Address Line A20 |
| 28 | Autosize DRAM |
| 2A | Clear 512KB base RAM |
| 2C | Test 512KB base address lines |
| 2E | Test 512KB base memory |
| 30 | Test base address memory |
| 32 | Test CPU bus clock frequency |
| 34 | Test CMOS RAM |
| 35 | Test chipset register initialized |
| 36 | Test check resume |
| 37 | Reinitialize the chipset |
| 38 | Shadow system BIOS ROM |
| 39 | Reinitialize the cache |
| 3A | Autosize the cache |
| 3C | Configure advanced chipset registers |
| 3D | Load alternate registers with CMOS values |
| 3E | Read hardware configuration from keyboard controller |
| 40 | Set initial CPU speed |
| 42 | Initialize interrupt vectors |
| 44 | Initialize BIOS interrupts |
| 46 | Check ROM copyright notice |

**TABLE 17-37** PHOENIX BIOS POST CODES (UMC CHIPSET/PCI BUS) *(CONTINUED)*

| CODE | DESCRIPTION |
|------|-------------|
| 47 | Initialize manager for PCI option ROMs |
| 48 | Check video configuration against CMOS |
| 49 | Initialize PCI bus and devices |
| 4A | Initialize all video adapters |
| 4C | Shadow video BIOS ROM |
| 4E | Display copyright notice |
| 50 | Display CPU type and speed |
| 52 | Test keyboard |
| 54 | Set key click if enabled |
| 56 | Enable keyboard |
| 58 | Test for unexpected interrupts |
| 5A | Display prompt "Press F2 to Enter Setup" |
| 5C | Test RAM between 512KB and 640KB |
| 5E | Test base memory |
| 60 | Test expanded memory |
| 62 | Test extended memory address lines |
| 64 | Jump to User Patch 1 |
| 66 | Configure advanced cache registers |
| 68 | Enable external and CPU caches |
| 69 | Set up power management |
| 6A | Display external cache size |
| 6C | Display shadow message |
| 6E | Display non-disposable segments |
| 70 | Display error messages |
| 72 | Check for configuration errors |
| 74 | Test RTC |
| 76 | Check for keyboard errors |
| 7A | Enable keylock |
| 7C | Set up hardware interrupt vectors |
| 7E | Test co-processor if present |
| 80 | Disable onboard I/O ports |
| 82 | Detect and install external RS232 ports |
| 84 | Detect and install external parallel ports |
| 86 | Reinitialize onboard I/O ports |
| 88 | Initialize BIOS data area |
| 8A | Initialize extended BIOS data area |
| 8C | Initialize floppy controller |
| 8E | Hard disk "auto-type" configuration |
| 90 | Initialize hard disk controller |
| 91 | Initialize local bus hard disk controller |

**TABLE 17-37    PHOENIX BIOS POST CODES (UMC CHIPSET/PCI BUS)** *(CONTINUED)*

| CODE | DESCRIPTION |
| --- | --- |
| 92 | Jump to User Patch 2 |
| 94 | Disable A20 address line |
| 96 | Clear huge ES segment register |
| 98 | Search for option ROMs |
| 9A | Shadow option ROMs |
| 9C | Set up power management |
| 9E | Enable hardware interrupts |
| A0 | Set time of day |
| A2 | Check key lock |
| A4 | Initialize typematic rate |
| A8 | Erase F2 prompt |
| AA | Scan for F2 key stroke |
| AC | Enter Setup |
| AE | Clear in-POST flag |
| B0 | Check for errors |
| B2 | POST done |
| B4 | One beep |
| B6 | Check password (optional) |
| B8 | Clear global descriptor table |
| BC | Clear parity checkers |
| BE | Clear screen (optional) |
| BF | Check virus and backup reminders |
| C0 | Try to boot with INT 19 |
| D0 | Interrupt handler error |
| D2 | Unknown interrupt error |
| D4 | Pending interrupt error |
| D6 | Initialize option ROM error |
| D8 | Shutdown error |
| DA | Extended Block Move |
| DC | Shutdown 10 error |
| E2 | Initialize the chipset |
| E3 | Check for Forced Flash |
| E5 | Check HW status of ROM |
| E6 | BIOS ROM is OK |
| E7 | Do a complete RAM test |
| E8 | Do OEM initialization |
| E9 | Initialize interrupt controller |
| EA | Read in the bootstrap code |
| EB | Initialize all vectors |
| EC | Boot the flash program |

**TABLE 17-37**  PHOENIX BIOS POST CODES (UMC CHIPSET/PCI BUS) *(CONTINUED)*

| CODE | DESCRIPTION |
|------|-------------|
| ED | Initialize the boot device |
| EE | Boot code was read OK |

**TABLE 17-38**  PHOENIX BIOS POST CODES (PCI BUS)

| CODE | DESCRIPTION |
|------|-------------|
| 02 | If the CPU is in protected mode, turn on A20 and pulse the reset line, forcing a shutdown |
| 04 | On a cold boot, save the CPU type-information value in the CMOS |
| 06 | Reset DMA controllers, disable videos, clear pending interrupts from RTC, and set up port B register |
| 08 | Initialize chipset control registers to power-on defaults |
| 0A | Set a bit in the CMOS that indicates POST—used to determine if the current configuration causes the BIOS to hang |
| 0C | Initialize I/O module control registers |
| 0E | External CPU caches are initialized and cache registers are set to default |
| 10/12/14 | Verify response of 8742 |
| 16 | Verify BIOS ROM checksums to zero |
| 18 | Initialize all three of 8254 timers |
| 1A | Initialize DMA command register and initialize 8 DMA channels |
| 1C | Initialize 8259 interrupt controller and cascade and edge-triggered mode |
| 20 | Test DRAM refresh by polling refresh bit in port B |
| 22 | Test 8742 keyboard controller and send self-test command to 8742—also read the switch inputs from the 8742 and write the keyboard controller command byte |
| 24 | Set ES segment register to 4GB |
| 26 | Enable Address Line A20 |
| 28 | Autosize DRAM |
| 2A | Clear first 64KB of RAM |
| 2C | Test RAM address lines |
| 2E | Test first 64KB bank of memory consisting of a chip address line test and a RAM test |
| 30/32 | Find true MHz value |
| 34 | Clear CMOS diagnostic byte, check RTC, and verify battery has not lost power—checksum the CMOS and verify it has not been corrupted |
| 36/38/3A | External cache is autosized and its configuration saved for enabling later in POST |
| 3C | Configure advanced cache features and configure external cache's configurable parameters |
| 3E | Read hardware configuration from keyboard controller |
| 40 | Set system power-on speed to the rate determined by the CMOS—if the CMOS is invalid use a conservative speed |
| 42 | Initialize interrupt vectors 0-77h to the BIOS general interrupt handler |

| TABLE 17-38 | PHOENIX BIOS POST CODES (PCI BUS) *(CONTINUED)* |
|---|---|

| CODE | DESCRIPTION |
|---|---|
| 44 | Initialize interrupt vectors 0-20h to proper values from the BIOS interrupt table |
| 46 | Check copyright message checksum |
| 48 | Check video configuration |
| 4A | Initialize both monochrome and color graphics video adapters |
| 4C/4E | Display copyright message |
| 50 | Display CPU type and speed |
| 52 | Test for the self-test code if a cold start—when powered by the keyboard, performs a self-test and sends an AA if successful |
| 54 | Initialize keystroke clicker during POST |
| 56 | Enable keyboard |
| 58 | Test for unexpected interrupts |
| 5A | Display prompt "Press F2 to Enter Setup" |
| 5C | Determine and test the amount of memory available |
| 5E | Perform address test on base memory |
| 60 | Determine and test the amount of extended memory available |
| 62 | Perform an address line test on A0 to the amount of memory available |
| 68 | External and CPU caches are enabled (if present) and non-cacheable regions are configured if necessary |
| 6A | Display cache size onscreen if non-zero |
| 6C | Display BIOS shadow status |
| 6E | Display the starting offset of the non-disposable section of the BIOS |
| 70 | Check flags in CMOS and in the BIOS data area to see if any errors have been detected during POST—if so, display error messages onscreen |
| 72 | Check status bits for configuration errors—if so, display error messages onscreen |
| 74 | Test RTC if the battery has not lost power |
| 76 | Check status bits for keyboard errors—if so display error messages onscreen |
| 78 | Check for stuck keys on the keyboard—if so display error messages onscreen |
| 7A | Enable keylock |
| 7C | Set up hardware interrupt vectors |
| 7E | Test co-processor if present |
| 80-82 | Detect and install RS232 ports |
| 84 | Detect and install parallel ports |
| 86-88 | Initialize timeouts/key buffer/soft reset flag |
| 8A | Initialize extended BIOS data area and initialize the mouse |
| 8C | Initialize both floppy disks and display an error message if failure was detected |
| 8E | Hard disk autotype configuration |
| 90 | If the CMOS RAM is valid and intact and fixed disks are defined, call the fixed disk routine to initialize the fixed disk system and take over the appropriate interrupt vectors |
| 92-94 | Disable A20 address line |
| 96-98 | Scan for ROM BIOS extensions |
| 9E | Enable hardware interrupts |

**TABLE 17-38** PHOENIX BIOS POST CODES (PCI BUS) *(CONTINUED)*

| CODE | DESCRIPTION |
|---|---|
| A0 | Set time of day |
| A2 | Set up NUMLOCK indicator and display a message if key switch is locked |
| A4 | Initialize typematic rate |
| A6 | Initialize hard disk autoparking |
| A8 | Erase F2 prompt |
| AA | Scan for F2 key strokes |
| AC | Check to see if SETUP should be executed |
| AE | Clear ConfigFailedBit and InPostBit in CMOS |
| B0 | Check for POST errors |
| B2 | Set/clear status bits to reflect POST complete |
| B4 | One beep |
| B6 | Check for password before boot |
| B8 | Clear global descriptor table (GDT) |
| BA | Initialize the screen saver |
| BC | Clear parity error latch |
| BE | Clear screen |
| C0 | Try to boot with INT 19 |
| D0-D2 | If an interrupt occurs before interrupt vectors have been initialized, this interrupt handler will try to see if the interrupt caused was an 8259 interrupt |
| D4 | Clear pending timer and keyboard interrupts and transfer control to the double word address located at RomCheck |
| D6-D8-DA | Return from extended block move |

**TABLE 17-39** PHOENIX BIOS POST CODES (VERSION 4.0)

| BEEP | CODE | DESCRIPTION |
|---|---|---|
| 1-1-1-3 | 02 | Verify real-mode operation |
| 1-1-2-1 | 04 | Get the CPU type |
| 1-1-2-3 | 06 | Initialize system hardware |
| 1-1-3-1 | 08 | Initialize chipset registers with POST values |
| 1-1-3-2 | 09 | Set POST flag |
| 1-1-3-3 | 0A | Initialize CPU registers |
| 1-1-4-1 | 0C | Initialize cache to initial POST values |
| 1-1-4-3 | 0E | Initialize I/O |
| 1-2-1-1 | 10 | Initialize Power Management |
| 1-2-1-2 | 11 | Load alternate registers with POST values |
| 1-2-1-3 | 12 | Jump to UserPatch0 |
| 1-2-2-1 | 14 | Initialize keyboard controller |

**TABLE 17-39    PHOENIX BIOS POST CODES (VERSION 4.0)** *(CONTINUED)*

| BEEP | CODE | DESCRIPTION |
|------|------|-------------|
| 1-2-2-3 | 16 | BIOS ROM checksum |
| 1-2-3-1 | 18 | 8254 timer initialization |
| 1-2-3-3 | 1A | 8237 DMA controller initialization |
| 1-2-4-1 | 1C | Reset Programmable Interrupt Controller |
| 1-3-1-1 | 20 | Test DRAM refresh |
| 1-3-1-3 | 22 | Test 8742 Keyboard Controller |
| 1-3-2-1 | 24 | Set ES segment to register to 4 GB |
| 1-3-3-1 | 28 | Auto-size DRAM |
| 1-3-3-3 | 2A | Clear 512K base RAM |
| 1-3-4-1 | 2C | Test 512 base address lines |
| 1-3-4-3 | 2E | Test 512K base memory |
| 1-4-1-3 | 32 | Test CPU bus-clock frequency |
| 1-4-2-4 | 37 | Reinitialize the motherboard chipset |
| 1-4-3-1 | 38 | Shadow system BIOS ROM |
| 1-4-3-2 | 39 | Reinitialize the cache |
| 1-4-3-3 | 3A | Autosize cache |
| 1-4-4-1 | 3C | Configure advanced chipset registers |
| 1-4-4-2 | 3D | Load alternate registers with CMOS values |
| 2-1-1-1 | 40 | Set initial CPU speed |
| 2-1-1-3 | 42 | Initialize interrupt vectors |
| 2-1-2-1 | 44 | Initialize BIOS interrupts |
| 2-1-2-3 | 46 | Check ROM copyright notice |
| 2-1-2-4 | 47 | Initialize manager for PCI Options ROMs |
| 2-1-3-1 | 48 | Check video configuration against CMOS |
| 2-1-3-2 | 49 | Initialize PCI bus and devices |
| 2-1-3-3 | 4A | Initialize all video adapters in system |
| 2-1-4-1 | 4C | Shadow video BIOS ROM |
| 2-1-4-3 | 4E | Display copyright notice |
| 2-2-1-1 | 50 | Display CPU type and speed |
| 2-2-1-3 | 52 | Test keyboard |
| 2-2-2-1 | 54 | Set key click if enabled |
| 2-2-2-3 | 56 | Enable keyboard |
| 2-2-3-1 | 58 | Test for unexpected interrupts |
| 2-2-3-3 | 5A | Display prompt "Press F2 to enter SETUP" |
| 2-2-4-1 | 5C | Test RAM between 512 and 640k |
| 2-3-1-1 | 60 | Test expanded memory |
| 2-3-1-3 | 62 | Test extended memory address lines |
| 2-3-2-1 | 64 | Jump to UserPatch1 |
| 2-3-2-3 | 66 | Configure advanced cache registers |

**TABLE 17-39     PHOENIX BIOS POST CODES (VERSION 4.0)** *(CONTINUED)*

| BEEP | CODE | DESCRIPTION |
|------|------|-------------|
| 2-3-3-1 | 68 | Enable external and CPU caches |
| 2-3-3-3 | 6A | Display external cache size |
| 2-3-4-1 | 6C | Display shadow message |
| 2-3-4-3 | 6E | Display non-disposable segments |
| 2-4-1-1 | 70 | Display error messages |
| 2-4-1-3 | 72 | Check for configuration errors |
| 2-4-2-1 | 74 | Test real-time clock |
| 2-4-2-3 | 76 | Check for keyboard errors |
| 2-4-4-1 | 7C | Set up hardware interrupts vectors |
| 2-4-4-3 | 7E | Test co-processor if present |
| 3-1-1-1 | 80 | Disable onboard I/O ports |
| 3-1-1-3 | 82 | Detect and install external RS232 ports |
| 3-1-2-1 | 84 | Detect and install external parallel ports |
| 3-1-2-3 | 86 | Re-initialize onboard I/O ports |
| 3-1-3-1 | 88 | Initialize BIOS data area |
| 3-1-3-3 | 8A | Initialize extended BIOS data area |
| 3-1-4-1 | 8C | Initialize floppy controller |
| 3-2-1-1 | 90 | Initialize hard-disk controller |
| 3-2-1-2 | 91 | Initialize local-bus hard-disk controller |
| 3-2-1-3 | 92 | Jump to UserPatch2 |
| 3-2-2-1 | 94 | Disable A20 address line |
| 3-2-2-3 | 96 | Clear huge ES segment register |
| 3-2-3-1 | 98 | Search for option ROMs |
| 3-2-3-3 | 9A | Shadow option ROMs |
| 3-2-4-1 | 9C | Set up Power Management |
| 3-2-4-3 | 9E | Enable hardware interrupts |
| 3-3-1-1 | A0 | Set time of day |
| 3-3-1-3 | A2 | Check key lock |
| 3-3-3-1 | A8 | Erase F2 prompt |
| 3-3-3-3 | AA | Scan for F2 key stroke |
| 3-3-4-1 | AC | Enter SETUP |
| 3-3-4-3 | AE | Clear in-POST flag |
| 3-4-1-1 | B0 | Check for errors |
| 3-4-1-3 | B2 | POST done—prepare to boot operating system |
| 3-4-2-1 | B4 | One beep |
| 3-4-2-3 | B6 | Check password (optional) |
| 3-4-3-1 | B8 | Clear global descriptor table |
| 3-4-4-1 | BC | Clear parity checkers |
| 3-4-4-3 | BE | Clear screen (optional) |
| 3-4-4-4 | BF | Check virus and backup reminders |

**TABLE 17-39     PHOENIX BIOS POST CODES (VERSION 4.0)** *(CONTINUED)*

| BEEP | CODE | DESCRIPTION |
|------|------|-------------|
| 4-1-1-1 | C0 | Try to boot with INT 19 |
| 4-2-1-1 | D0 | Interrupt handler error |
| 4-2-1-3 | D2 | Unknown interrupt error |
| 4-2-2-1 | D4 | Pending interrupt error |
| 4-2-2-3 | D6 | Initialize option ROM error |
| 4-2-3-1 | D8 | Shutdown error |
| 4-2-3-3 | DA | Extended Block Move |
| 4-2-4-1 | DC | Shutdown 10 error |
| 4-3-1-3 | E2 | Initialize the motherboard chipset |
| 4-3-1-4 | E3 | Initialize refresh counter |
| 4-3-2-1 | E4 | Check for forced Flash |
| 4-3-2-2 | E5 | Check HW status of ROM |
| 4-3-2-3 | E6 | BIOS ROM is OK |
| 4-3-2-4 | E7 | Do a complete RAM test |
| 4-3-3-1 | E8 | Do OEM initialization |
| 4-3-3-2 | E9 | Initialize interrupt controller |
| 4-3-3-3 | EA | Read in bootstrap code |
| 4-3-3-4 | EB | Initialize all vectors |
| 4-3-4-1 | EC | Boot the Flash program |
| 4-3-4-2 | ED | Initialize the boot device |
| 4-3-4-3 | EE | Boot code was read OK |

**TABLE 17-40     PHOENIX BIOS 4.0 (REV.6.0) POST/BEEP CODES**

| BEEP | CODE | DESCRIPTION |
|------|------|-------------|
|  | 02 | Verify real mode for the processor |
|  | 03 | Disable nonmaskable interrupt (NMI) |
|  | 04 | Get CPU type (CPUID) |
|  | 06 | Detect and initialize system hardware |
|  | 07 | Disable ROM shadow and execute code from the ROM |
|  | 08 | Initialize chipset with starting POST values |
|  | 09 | Set IN POST flag |
|  | 0A | Initialize CPU registers |
|  | 0B | Enable CPU cache |
|  | 0C | Initialize caches to starting POST values |
|  | 0E | Initialize I/O components |
|  | 0F | Initialize the local bus IDE |
|  | 10 | Initialize power management features |
|  | 11 | Load alternate registers with initial POST values |

**TABLE 17-40    PHOENIX BIOS 4.0 (REV.6.0) POST/BEEP CODES** *(CONTINUED)*

| BEEP | CODE | DESCRIPTION |
|------|------|-------------|
| | 12 | Restore CPU control during warm boot |
| | 13 | Initialize PCI bus mastering devices |
| | 14 | Initialize keyboard controller (KBC) |
| 1-2-2-3 | 16 | BIOS ROM checksum |
| | 17 | Initialize cache before memory autosize |
| | 18 | 8254 timer initialization |
| | 1A | 8237 DMA controller initialization |
| | 1C | Reset programmable interrupt controller (PIC) |
| 1-3-1-1 | 20 | Test DRAM refresh |
| 1-3-1-3 | 22 | Test 8742 keyboard controller |
| | 24 | Set ES segment register to 4GB |
| | 28 | Autosize DRAM |
| | 29 | Initialize POST memory manager |
| | 2A | Clear 512KB base RAM |
| 1-3-4-1 | 2C | RAM failure on address line *xxxx* |
| 1-3-4-3 | 2E | RAM failure on data bits *xxxx* of low byte of memory address |
| | 2F | Enable cache before system BIOS shadow |
| | 32 | Test CPU bus-clock frequency |
| | 33 | Initialize Phoenix Dispatch Manager feature |
| | 36 | Warm start shutdown |
| | 38 | Shadow system BIOS ROM |
| | 3A | Autosize cache |
| | 3C | Advanced configuration of chipset registers |
| | 3D | Load alternate registers with CMOS values |
| | 41 | Initialize extended memory for RomPilot |
| | 42 | Initialize interrupt vectors |
| | 45 | POST device initialization |
| 2-1-2-3 | 46 | Check ROM copyright notice |
| | 47 | Initialize $I^2O$ support |
| | 48 | Check video configuration against CMOS RAM |
| | 49 | Initialize PCI bus and devices |
| | 4A | Initialize all video adapters in system |
| | 4B | QuietBoot start (optional) |
| | 4C | Shadow video BIOS ROM |
| | 4E | Display BIOS copyright notice |
| | 4F | Initialize MultiBoot feature |
| | 50 | Display CPU type and speed |
| | 51 | Initialize EISA board |
| | 52 | Test keyboard |
| | 54 | Set key click (if enabled) |

**TABLE 17-40    PHOENIX BIOS 4.0 (REV.6.0) POST/BEEP CODES** *(CONTINUED)*

| BEEP | CODE | DESCRIPTION |
|---|---|---|
| | 55 | Enable USB devices |
| 2-2-3-1 | 58 | Test for unexpected interrupts |
| | 59 | Initialize POST display service |
| | 5A | Display Setup prompt (for example, "Press F2 to enter SETUP") |
| | 5B | Disable CPU cache |
| | 5C | Test RAM between 512 and 640KB |
| | 60 | Test extended memory |
| | 62 | Test extended memory address lines |
| | 64 | Jump to UserPatch1 |
| | 66 | Configure advanced cache registers |
| | 67 | Initialize Multi Processor APIC |
| | 68 | Enable external and CPU caches |
| | 69 | Set up System Management Mode (SMM) area |
| | 6A | Display external L2 cache size |
| | 6B | Load custom defaults (optional) |
| | 6C | Display shadow-area message |
| | 6E | Display possible high address for UMB recovery |
| | 70 | Display error messages |
| | 72 | Check for configuration errors |
| | 76 | Check for keyboard errors |
| | 7C | Set up hardware interrupt vectors |
| | 7D | Initialize intelligent system monitoring |
| | 7E | Initialize coprocessor if present |
| | 80 | Disable onboard Super I/O ports and IRQs |
| | 81 | Late POST device initialization |
| | 82 | Detect and install external RS-232 ports |
| | 83 | Configure non-MCD IDE controllers |
| | 84 | Detect and install external parallel ports |
| | 85 | Initialize PC-compatible PnP ISA devices |
| | 86 | Reinitialize onboard I/O ports |
| | 87 | Configure motherboard configurable devices (optional) |
| | 88 | Initialize BIOS Data Area |
| | 89 | Enable nonmaskable interrupts (NMIs) |
| | 8A | Initialize Extended BIOS Data Area (EBDA) |
| | 8B | Test and initialize PS/2 mouse |
| | 8C | Initialize floppy controller |
| | 8F | Determine number of ATA drives (optional) |
| | 90 | Initialize hard-disk controllers |
| | 91 | Initialize local-bus hard-disk controllers |
| | 92 | Jump to UserPatch2 |

**TABLE 17-40    PHOENIX BIOS 4.0 (REV.6.0) POST/BEEP CODES** *(CONTINUED)*

| BEEP | CODE | DESCRIPTION |
|------|------|-------------|
|      | 93   | Build MPTABLE for multi-processor motherboards |
|      | 95   | Install CD-ROM for boot (if enabled) |
|      | 96   | Clear huge ES segment register |
|      | 97   | Fix up multi-processor table |
| 1-2  | 98   | Search for option ROMs. One long, two short beeps on checksum failure. |
|      | 99   | Check for SMART drive (optional) |
|      | 9A   | Shadow option ROMs |
|      | 9C   | Set up power management feature |
|      | 9D   | Initialize security engine (optional) |
|      | 9E   | Enable hardware interrupts |
|      | 9F   | Determine number of ATA and SCSI drives |
|      | A0   | Set time of day |
|      | A2   | Check key lock |
|      | A4   | Initialize typematic rate |
|      | A8   | Erase F2 prompt |
|      | AA   | Scan for F2 key stroke |
|      | AC   | Enter CMOS Setup |
|      | AE   | Clear boot flag |
|      | B0   | Check for errors |
|      | B1   | Inform RomPilot about the end of POST |
|      | B2   | POST done—prepare to boot operating system |
| 1    | B4   | One short beep before boot |
|      | B5   | Terminate QuietBoot feature (optional) |
|      | B6   | Check password (optional) |
|      | B7   | Initialize ACPI BIOS |
|      | B9   | Prepare boot |
|      | BA   | Initialize SMBIOS |
|      | BB   | Initialize PnP Option ROMs |
|      | BC   | Clear parity checkers |
|      | BD   | Display MultiBoot menu |
|      | BE   | Clear screen (optional) |
|      | BF   | Check virus and backup reminders |
|      | C0   | Try to boot with INT 19 |
|      | C1   | Initialize POST Error Manager (PEM) |
|      | C2   | Initialize error logging |
|      | C3   | Initialize error display function |
|      | C4   | Initialize system error handler |
|      | C5   | PnP dual CMOS (optional) |
|      | C6   | Initialize note dock (optional) |
|      | C7   | Initialize note dock late |

**TABLE 17-40    PHOENIX BIOS 4.0 (REV.6.0) POST/BEEP CODES** *(CONTINUED)*

| BEEP | CODE | DESCRIPTION |
|------|------|-------------|
|  | C8 | Force check (optional) |
|  | C9 | Extended checksum (optional) |
|  | CA | Redirect INT 15h to enable remote keyboard |
|  | CB | Redirect INT 13h to memory technologies |
|  | CC | Redirect INT 10h to enable remote serial video |
|  | CD | Remap I/O and memory for PCMCIA |
|  | CE | Initialize digitizer and display message |
|  | D2 | Unknown interrupt |
|  | E0 | Initialize the chipset |
|  | E1 | Initialize the bridge |
|  | E2 | Initialize the CPU |
|  | E3 | Initialize system timer |
|  | E4 | Initialize system I/O |
|  | E5 | Check force recovery boot |
|  | E6 | Checksum BIOS ROM |
|  | E7 | Go to BIOS |
|  | E8 | Set huge memory segment |
|  | E9 | Initialize multi-processor system |
|  | EA | Initialize OEM special code |
|  | EB | Initialize PIC and DMA controllers |
|  | EC | Initialize memory type |
|  | ED | Initialize memory size |
|  | EE | Shadow boot block from ROM |
|  | EF | System memory test |
|  | F0 | Initialize interrupt vectors |
|  | F1 | Initialize run-time clock |
|  | F2 | Initialize video |
|  | F3 | Initialize system management system |
| 1 | F4 | Output one beep |
|  | F5 | Clear huge memory segment |
|  | F6 | Boot to "Mini DOS" |
|  | F7 | Boot to "Full DOS" |

# The POST Code Reader Card

Although virtually all current PC BIOS versions make use of port 80h, the port itself is merely a repository for that information. In order for you to read the contents of port 80h, you will need a POST board (such as the PCWiz PocketPOST card shown in Figure 17-1 earlier), which should be installed in an open slot prior to troubleshooting and then removed once troubleshooting is completed. *Remember to turn the PC off before installing or removing a POST card.* Essentially, the design of a POST board is quite simple. It reads the byte at the POST I/O port, and displays the hexadecimal code in the two seven-segment displays. However, many POST boards today provide a technician with a much more powerful troubleshooting tool. As an example, the PocketPOST card supplies a series of LEDs that check for main voltages (+12Vdc, −12Vdc, +5Vdc, and −5Vdc). Some cards provide additional LEDs that report the presence of key signals on the expansion bus (address latch, I/O read, I/O write, memory read, memory write, system clock, and so on). Even an onboard logic probe attachment may be provided.

## I/O PORTS

While most traditional ISA-based PCs make use of port 80h, not all PCs follow this rule. The Compaq PC outputs codes to port 84h, and PS/2 models 25 and 30 send codes to port 90h. PS/2 model 20-286 sends codes to port 190h. Even most EISA-based PCs use port 80h, but Compaq PCs continue to use port 84h. EISA machines with Award BIOS use port 300h. Systems with a micro channel bus architecture (MCA) use port 680h. Take note that some PS/2 models, Olivetti, early AT&T, some NCR, and a few AT clones will send POST codes to a printer port at 3BCh, 278h, or 378h. The current generation of POST boards typically provides a DIP switch or jumper array for selecting the active port location. Before choosing a POST board, make sure that it can read the *proper* port address for your system.

With the widespread abandonment of the ISA bus, leading POST reader manufacturers are releasing PCI versions of their POST reader products. If you do not have access to a PCI POST reader now, it may be time to consider updating your toolbox.

Another issue to keep in mind is that *not all* PCs produce POST codes. The original IBM PC, the AMI XT, and some systems using HP, DTK, and ERSO BIOS do not send out POST codes during initialization. If you are testing such a system, you will be unable to see hexadecimal codes using the POST card (but power and signal indicators should still work).

## INTERPRETING THE LEDS

Before working with the various POST codes in detail, you should have an understanding of the many discrete signal LEDs that accompany current POST boards. These individual signals can be a great asset when interpreted in conjunction with the POST code. Keep in mind that each POST card will offer a different selection of LEDs, so your own POST card *may not* have all of the indicators shown here. The traditional indicators are explained below:

- ■ *Power LEDs*    The PC will not work correctly (if at all) if any power supply voltage is low or absent. Typical POST cards provide four LEDs that light when +5Vdc, +12Vdc, −5Vdc, and −12Vdc are available. If any of those LEDs are dim or out, there may be a problem with the power supply or its connection to the motherboard. If problems occur after upgrading the system, the power supply may be overloaded. In any case, power LEDs help you to identify power problems quickly and effectively.

- ■ *ALE*    The *Address Latch Enable* signal is generated by the CPU and is used by virtually all devices in the PC that must capture address signals (such as BIOS). When this LED is on, address generation by the CPU is probably working fine. If this LED is out, there is a problem manipulating addresses in the system. You should then suspect the CPU, DMA controller, Bus Buffer/Controller, or Clock Generator/System Controller chip. This alert can be very helpful for technicians who choose to troubleshoot to the component level.

- *I/OW*   An *I/O Write* LED will generally light whenever BIOS attempts to write data to an I/O device such as a floppy disk. The BIOS will then attempt to read what was written to confirm that that portion of the system is working as expected. If the I/OW LED stays out, you should suspect a fault in either the BIOS or the system's DMA controller chip.

- *I/OR*   An *I/O Read* LED will generally light whenever BIOS attempts to read data back from an I/O device after data has been written. If this LED remains out, you should suspect a fault in either the BIOS or the system's DMA controller chip.

- *MR/W*   During POST, the BIOS will attempt to write various data patterns into memory, then read those patterns back to verify memory integrity. The *Memory R/W* LED will light during both the read and write operations (it will flicker a bit). If the MW/R LED does not light, there is likely to be a problem with the BIOS, DMA Controller, Memory Controller, or System Controller chip.

- *Reset*   When the system is first turned on, the reset line will be asserted. This keeps the CPU neutralized until the *Power Good* signal is received from the power supply. At this point, the reset line should be released, and the *Reset* LED should go out—the initialization process will begin. The reset line should not light again unless the PC's Reset button is pressed. If the Reset LED stays lit, it could indicate a problem with the Power Good signal at the supply or motherboard. The reset line may also be shorted—in which case you may have to replace the motherboard.

- *CLK*   The *clock* LED(s) light to indicate the presence of synchronizing signals generated by the PC's clock generator chip. If these signals are not being generated, the CPU simply will not function. If the clock indicator(s) do not light, you should suspect a fault in the system time base crystal or the clock generator chip. Keep in mind that micro channel systems do not supply clock signals to the bus.

- *OSC*   The *oscillator* LEDs indicate the presence of a 14.138 MHz signal. XT systems used this signal for all internal timing, but AT systems use the oscillator only as a color burst signal for the video adapter. If the oscillator indicator(s) do not light, you should suspect a fault in the color burst crystal or the clock generating circuitry. This indicator (if present) will usually not work on current motherboards with very fast bus signals.

# Further Study

**American Megatrends (AMI)**   www.ami.com
**Data Depot**   www.datadepo.com
**Micro2000**   www.micro2000.com
**Phoenix Technologies**   www.phoenix.com/en/home/
**TriniTech Omni Analyzer**   www.pcanalyzer.com/Eng_omni.htm
**Ultra X Post Cards**   www.uxd.com/products.html

# 18

# FANS AND COOLING DEVICES

**W**hen electrical power is applied to a circuit, the circuit uses that power to perform work. In the case of a PC, *work* would be the myriad processing operations that go on throughout the computer every moment. For computers (as with all machines), the conversion of power into work is not a perfect one—a portion of power is dissipated in the form of *heat*. Over time, an excessive buildup of heat will cause a chip (and thus the PC) to fail prematurely. As a result, it is very important that a computer system be properly outfitted to deal with heat. This chapter is intended to illustrate the various methods used to cool a PC, explain the effects that inhibit cooling, and show you how to deal with cooling problems.

## The Importance of Heat Management

You might wonder why heat is taken so seriously—after all, the vast majority of chips and passive components found in a PC dissipate very little heat at all. Unfortunately, it is the few components that *do* produce heat that cause most problems: drive motors, power supply regulating circuits, the CPU(s), and graphics processors. Heat affects the reliability of all electronic devices, and manufacturers of processors and other computer components specify a maximum operating temperature for their products. Most devices are not certified to function properly beyond 50°C–80°C (122°F–176°F). However, in a loaded PC with only standard cooling, operating temperatures can easily exceed the limits. The result can be memory errors, hard disk read-write errors, faulty video, and other problems not commonly recognized as heat related.

If we look at this in more mathematical terms, the life of an electronic device is directly related to its operating temperature. Each $10^\circ$C ($18^\circ$F) temperature rise reduces component life by 50 percent. Engineers and scientists may recognize that this is based on the Arrhenius equation, which states that time to failure is a function of $e^{-Ea/kT}$, where Ea is activation energy of the failure mechanism being accelerated, k is Boltzmann's constant, and T is absolute temperature. Fortunately, we don't need to actually work this equation—we just need to appreciate that heat *kills* electronic devices. Conversely, each $10^\circ$C ($18^\circ$F) temperature reduction increases component life by 100 percent. In actual practice, it is recommended that computer components be kept as cool as possible (within an acceptable noise level) for maximum reliability, longevity, and return on investment. As a technician, you must take the steps that are necessary to cool critical PC devices, and manage the overall operating temperature of the system.

# COOLING METHODOLOGIES

To understand how various cooling devices work, you must understand some basic principles about heat transfer. First, heat tends to travel from places of *more* heat to places of *less* heat. If you don't believe this, apply a hot soldering iron to one end of a wire and see how long it takes the other end to get warm. While this is a tremendous oversimplification, you get the basic idea. There are three general modes of heat transfer: convection, conduction, and radiation.

*Convection* is the transfer of heat through air currents. A heat source warms nearby air, which rises. The warmer rising air is replaced (or displaced) by cooler air, which is then heated. Eventually, a circulating airflow develops. This is the basic principle behind the radiators that heat your home in the winter. It is also an essential element of PC cooling. You might ask how heating and cooling can be the same thing. Well, as heat is transferred to the air, the device providing the heat is cooled. When a CPU heats up, it tends to heat the surrounding air. Unfortunately, such *static convection* has a very limited effect in a PC. Static convection does not remove enough heat to cool a very hot device (such as a CPU). Static convection also relies on a circulating flow of air, which is difficult to establish in the close quarters of a highly obstructed PC. A way to multiply the effect of convection is to *force* an airflow across the heated device. Fans are used to force air through the PC. This *forced convection* provides much more effective cooling and can be directed to specific areas around the PC. Most of the cooling methods covered in this chapter rely on forced convection.

*Conduction* is the transfer of heat through physical contact. The radiator system in your car works this way. By circulating cooler liquid around a warmer surface, the cooler liquid picks up the surface heat, thus cooling the surface. The liquid, now warmed, is circulated to a chilling assembly, which is intended to take away any heat picked up by the liquid so that the liquid is kept cooled. In a car, this is the front radiator, which is cooled by the forced air of a large fan. Although conduction is a much more effective means of cooling than convection, conduction can only cool the areas of contact, whereas convection can cool large areas. Some CPU cooling devices use circulating liquid, but these *chillers* are relatively rare and expensive. As a consequence, you will rarely find conductive cooling techniques in PCs.

Finally, *radiation* is the transfer of heat through infrared emission. For example, the warmth you feel from sunlight or a sun lamp is due to the effects of infrared radiation. Since there are no significant infrared emission sources in a PC, radiation will not be discussed further. At this point, you can see how these heat transfer principles are employed in a PC environment.

## Natural Convection

Natural (or static) convection is the cooling technique employed in most computer monitors. Take a look at the rear enclosure on your monitor and notice the open slots along the top and bottom of the enclosure. The openings beneath the monitor are for air intake, and the upper slots allow air to escape. These slots provide a free flow of air through the monitor. Yet, this process works without the benefit of a fan. You can easily see how this process works. Let the monitor run for a while, and place your hand over the upper slots—you can feel hot air rising. The warm circuitry inside the running monitor heats the surrounding air, which rises up and out. As warm air is displaced, new cooler air is drawn in from the bottom slots. Although monitor circuits will heat up (especially the power supply), none of the components becomes hot enough to require forced convection.

As you might expect, the success of this method depends on an unobstructed air path. If "Fluffy" the cat curls up on top of the monitor, the exhaust vents will be blocked. This interrupts the flow of air, and temperatures inside the monitor will increase. Eventually, you may notice the display rolling or shifting position—an initial warning that the monitor circuits are overheating. If the blockage continues for an extended period, the monitor may fail prematurely. Besides monitors, dot matrix and ink-jet printers typically rely on convection to cool their circuits.

## Heat Sinks

Another rule of heat transfer is that the effectiveness with which heat is transferred depends on the amount of surface area that is exposed. Check out the radiator in your car—each of those tiny fins adds a small amount of surface area to the overall radiating surface. This is the principle behind *heat sinks*. By adding a heat sink to a heated component, you increase the effective surface area of the component's case that is open to the air. Since more air can flow over a larger surface (through natural or forced convection), more heat is carried away and the component stays cooler. For components that become inordinately hot during normal operation (such as voltage regulator chips, graphics processors, or CPUs), a heat sink is a very simple and inexpensive way to enhance cooling (see Figure 18-1). Of course, heat sinks are not just for chips. Take a look at the print head of a dot matrix printer. You'll find a set of cast aluminum fins set right into the head assembly. Many different production methods are used to create heat sinks for processors and other chips. A few of the more popular production methods are described here:

- **Extrusion**    The most popular production method for heat sinks, it is inexpensive and can result in very fine structures (for example, see Figure 18-1 earlier). In most cases, liquid aluminum is pressed through a form so that a long stick with the shape of the heat sink is created. After this extruded stick has cooled down, it is cut into pieces as needed. However, not all heat sink types can be made with extrusion.

- **Folded fin**    Produces heat sinks that are made of a thin metal plate, which is folded and bonded onto a base plate. The radiator in your car uses this design. The advantage is that the fins are hollow, so they have a bigger surface and allow better airflow (and thus better cooling). Folded fin heat sinks are light, compact, and very efficient. However, heat sinks with folded fins are more expensive to produce, and only a few manufacturers offer coolers using this design.

- **Bonded fin**    Produces heat sinks that are very similar to the folded fin design, but instead of folding a long continuous piece of metal, this method bonds many smaller metal plates onto the base plate. The advantages and disadvantages are the same as for the folded fin method.

**FIGURE 18-1**   Attaching a heat sink to a typical cartridge-style processor
(Courtesy of Intel Corporation)

■ **Die casting**   A production method that gives the designer a lot of freedom, and allows for certain heat sink shapes that cannot be produced using extrusion. Die casting also allows for highly integrated cooling. For example, the heat sinks used on dot matrix print heads are almost always extruded. However, the fins of a die cast heat sink cannot be very fine, and this may limit the amount of surface area handled by the casting.

■ **Cold forging**   A relatively exotic and expensive production method for heat sinks. However, it is used for heat sinks with many small pin fins, and high-end coolers such as the Alpha PFH6035MUC are produced using this approach.

■ **Milling**   Also a very unusual and expensive production method for heat sinks. Milling is used when it's necessary to create relatively large and very complex cooling units such as the heat sinks by HP PolarLogic. The heat sinks used for chillers are often milled.

**Heat Sink Compound**   The surface of a chip or a heat sink is never entirely flat. If you place a heat sink directly on a CPU or other chip, tiny (although microscopic) gaps will exist between the two surfaces. Since air conducts heat poorly, these gaps will slightly impair the heat transfer from the chip to the heat sink. Therefore, an *interface material* with a high thermal conductivity is needed to fill these gaps, and thus improve heat conductivity.

The most commonly used interface material in electronics cooling is *thermal grease* (also called *heat sink compound*). This is a white, sticky, acrid-smelling paste applied directly on the heat sink or CPU. A good-quality thermal grease will provide the best possible cooling performance. However, thermal grease is quite messy to handle. For this reason, most heat sink manufacturers ship their heat sinks with a *thermal pad,* which is supposed to replace thermal compound. Cheap heat sinks usually come with silver/gray graphite pads. Graphite pads are inexpensive, but provide poor performance unless a high pressure is applied to the pad, and this is not the case when a CPU and heat sink are installed in a typical way. A graphite pad is better than no interface material at all, though. Today, far more advanced thermal pads are available, made by companies such as Power Devices, Bergquist, and Chomerics, to name a few. You can see a thermal pad and a tube of thermal compound in the CPU cooler of Figure 18-2. These pads come very close to thermal compound in terms of performance.

If you have a heat sink with a thermal pad and you would like to use thermal compound, you should scratch off the thermal pad. Under no circumstances should you use both together.

**FIGURE  18-2**    A properly designed thermal pad between a heat sink and CPU surface
(Courtesy of Cooler Master Ltd.)

When using thermal grease, you should apply a very thin (paper thin) layer on the heat sink with your finger before installing it. Don't use too much—thinner layers are better. Then, secure the heat sink firmly to the CPU. Thermal grease does not get hard, so you could even reuse it when you buy a new CPU. Standard silicone-based thermal compound can be purchased at almost any electronics store including Radio Shack (Cat. No.: 276-1372) for about $2. High-end thermal compounds with even better thermal performance are available from specialized heat sink retailers.

You may notice that the heat sink gets a bit hotter after using thermal grease. This does **not** mean that the CPU is getting hotter. It means that more heat is being removed from the CPU, which is therefore a bit cooler—this is a good thing.

## Fans

There are limits to what convection can do, and the heat liberated by devices in a PC will usually build up within the system. Fans are commonly used to produce strong local airflow. When attached to a heat sink (such as the Pentium 4 cooling unit in Figure 18-3), a fan can force air across the many fins and keep the processor or graphics chip significantly cooler than can a heat sink alone. Of course, the heated air removed from a heat sink can be evacuated from a chassis through the use of one or more large fans.

Two kinds of fans are being used on CPU heat sinks: ball bearing and sleeve bearing fans. *Sleeve bearing* fans are usually less expensive and often quieter, but are often unreliable over the long term. Poor-quality sleeve bearing fans are known to fail in six months or less. The cheapest kind of sleeve bearing fan simply consists of a ring made of a porous material that has been dipped in a lubricant. The fan motor's shaft rotates inside this ring and is lubricated by the lubricant stored inside the porous material. *Ball bearing* fans use a rotating shaft that is surrounded by tiny balls, which allow smooth rotation with hardly any wear and tear. These fans are a bit more expensive (and sometimes a little louder), but they are generally far more reliable. Keep in mind that a few fans use Teflon sleeve bearings, which can be just as reliable as ball bearing fans, and the Teflon sleeves may be quieter.

**FIGURE 18-3** A TMD Socket 478 CPU cooling unit for Pentium 4 processors (Courtesy of Pham Computer)

If a sticker on the fan says "Ball Bearing," you're typically getting a fan that uses both ball bearings and sleeve bearings. A fan needs two bearings, and the popular 50 × 10mm "ball bearing" fans that come with many heat sinks are usually fans with one ball bearing and one sleeve bearing. Larger fans (60 × 25mm and up) sometimes have two ball bearings, and these are often referred to as *two ball bearing* or *dual ball bearing* fans.

High airflow always creates noise, a reality that cannot be avoided. For this reason, even a very high-quality fan can be quite loud. With a good fan, however, most of the noise that is created comes from air turbulence, *not* from the fan motor itself. In fact, fan vibrations are a sign of poor quality. If you hold the fan in your hand, you should not feel any significant vibrations. In actual practice, a larger fan that spins at a lower speed will be less noisy than a smaller fan spinning at a high speed, even if the two provide the same amount of airflow. So bigger fans are usually better.

The most common unit for specifying airflow is cubic feet per minute (or CFM). The metric equivalent is cubic meters per minute (or $m^3$/min). Table 18-1 shows the conversions between typical units. For example, 1 CFM equals 0.47 liters/sec. Common 50 × 10mm CPU fans usually move up to 10 CFM. High-speed 50 × 10mm fans with 6000 rpm can move even more air. Many 60 × 25mm fans can move

**TABLE 18-1** CONVERTING BETWEEN AIR HANDLING UNITS

| CONVERT FROM | | CFM | M³/MIN | M³/HOUR | L/S | L/MIN |
|---|---|---|---|---|---|---|
| Cubic feet/minute | 1 CFM = | 1 | 0.028 | 1.7 | 0.47 | 28.3 |
| Cubic meter/minute | 1 m³/min = | 35.28 | 1 | 60 | 16.67 | 1000 |
| Cubic meter/hour | 1 m³/h = | 0.588 | 0.017 | 1 | 0.28 | 16.67 |
| Liter/second | 1 l/s = | 2.12 | 0.06 | 3.6 | 1 | 60 |
| Liter/min | 1 l/m = | 0.035 | 0.001 | 0.06 | 0.017 | 1 |

between about 20 and 30 CFM, $80 \times 25$mm fans handle around 30 to 40 CFM, and 120mm fans can pass over 100 CFM of air. For example, the TMD Socket 478 cooler in Figure 18-3 earlier is specified for 29.6 CFM. When buying a fan, remember that you'll always have to choose between high performance and low noise. The goal is to find a good compromise for your system.

To convert Fahrenheit to Celsius, use the following: $°C = (5/9) * (°F-32)$. To convert Celsius to Fahrenheit, use the following: $°F = (°C * (9/5)) + 32$.

**Chassis Fans**    Natural convection is fine for cooling monitors and printers, but PCs are too cramped and obstructed to establish a consistent airflow. As a result, heated air must be evacuated from the enclosure. This is usually accomplished with one or more axial or radial fans positioned in the system (such as the Adda UltraSpeed 120mm fan in Figure 18-4). By positioning the fans blowing out of the enclosure, cooler air can be vacuumed into the system through strategically located intake slots in the housing. Some systems use a second fan blowing into the enclosure from the front chassis. This kind of push-pull cooling develops a very strong airflow.

According to the ATX form factor specification, a power supply fan should blow air **into** the case, through the power supply, and toward the motherboard. Since the CPU is located on an ATX motherboard just beyond the power supply fan, the idea is that the CPU benefits from this more direct airflow. However, as the power supply gets hot, the fan would blow warm air toward the CPU (which usually isn't a good idea). So, many case manufacturers are ignoring the ATX specifications and shipping their cases with a power supply fan that blows air out of the system.

If your power supply fan blows air in, it might sometimes be beneficial to reverse the fan. Remember that you must reverse the entire fan unit. Reversing polarity won't work, and might even damage your fan.

The rule of thumb is that when more than one fan is used, the fans should be blowing in the *same* direction. For example, if the power supply fan (which may be located in the top rear of a tower chassis) is evacuating air out of the unit, a second fan (usually located in the lower front of a tower chassis) should be blowing air into the system. Having fans compete with each other (both directing air into or out of the system) can actually decrease the effective airflow and impair effective cooling. Another issue to consider is vent holes. If there are ventilation holes in your case right next to the secondary fan, or other openings such as an open card slot or I/O panel opening, it can sometimes be helpful to close these holes to ensure proper airflow.

**FIGURE  18-4**    The Adda 120mm 12 Vdc chassis fan, which handles air at 98.6 CFM (Courtesy of Pham Computer)

Finally, consider the connectors on your chassis fans. If there is a free fan connector on your motherboard, then you'll probably want a fan with a three-pin connector. This allows the motherboard to regulate the fan and measure rpm (so the system's hardware monitoring feature is able to report stalled fans). Otherwise, you'll need to use fans with standard Molex-type drive power connectors, and the fans will run at full duty while the system is on.

**Fan Duct**  Traditionally, the CPU was just about the only major heat source inside a computer case. Today, times have changed, and graphics chips, chipsets, and memory chips run hot as well. These additional devices often require special heat sinks or even fans. In the future, you might end up with three to five fans inside your system, which would be extremely noisy, and also expensive for system integrators. Intel has introduced a new cooling methodology called *fan duct* (Figure 18-5). The fan duct system will distribute air from a single fan to all parts of the system that require cooling. This way, all components will get fresh, cool air from outside the case (even without their own fan).

The fan duct approach provides cooler air in the system chassis and provides air directly to the core components that need it most. This is accomplished by mounting a fan directly over these key components, including the processor, memory, and chipset configurations. The fan duct also supplies cooling to an AGP expansion card (even though the fan is not mounted over the card). In addition, the fan duct solution employs a tube that draws in fresh air from the outside and spreads it around the entire core of the system, instead of merely cooling the processor. As an open specification, Fan Duct 1.0 provides a universal solution across the industry that enables OEMs of all sizes to provide cost-effective system cooling. You can learn more about Fan Duct 1.0 at www.intel.com/update/archive/issue12/stories/top5.htm.

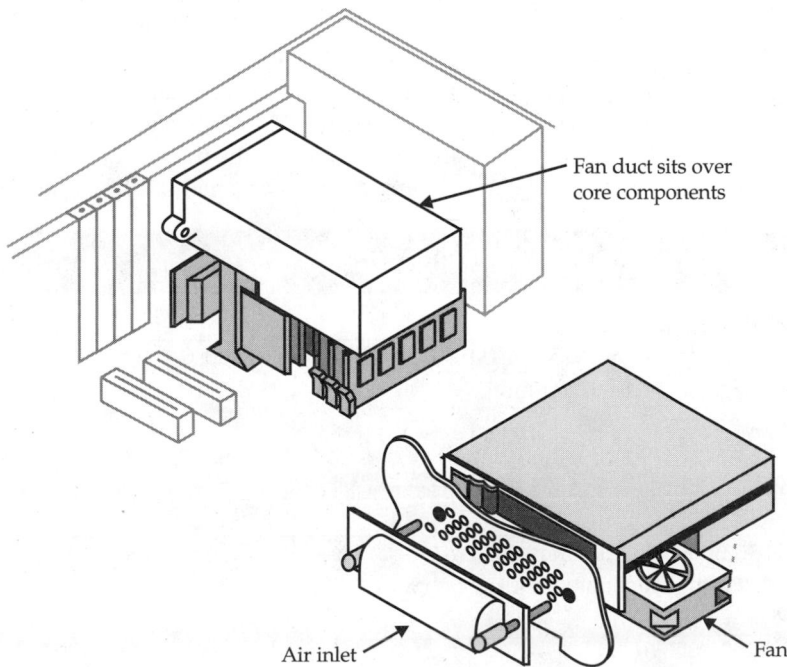

**FIGURE 18-5**  Example of a fan duct system (Courtesy of Intel Corporation)

**Fan Cards**    Even with good-quality chassis-mounted fans, some high-performance systems require an extra measure of cooling, especially in the CPU area. An ongoing trend in PC cooling is the use of a *fan card*—a standard-sized ISA or PCI expansion board with one or two +12 Vdc fans mounted to it. This allows you to place the fan card in the immediate vicinity of a CPU or drive to improve the local airflow. However, there are some limitations to fan cards that you should be aware of. First, many expansion boards are full-sized boards, so the chances are very good that at least one side of the fan card will be somewhat obstructed by another full-slot expansion board. As long as the fan card is blowing *away* from the adjacent expansion board, this should not present a problem. If the fan card is blowing *toward* the adjacent expansion board, a region of turbulent air will be produced, which reduces the fan card's overall effectiveness.

Another concern is EMI produced by the fan motors. As inductive devices, fans are notorious for producing unwanted electromagnetic interference. If the fan card is placed in close proximity of a sensitive device such as a drive controller or video capture board, the electrical noise produced by the fans can degrade the other device's performance or cause operating errors. There is also the possibility that electrical noise from the fans may travel back along the +12 Vdc voltage line and interfere with other devices in the system that are using +12 Vdc. It is always wise to approach fan cards with a certain amount of suspicion, especially if you have problems with a device after the fan card is installed.

> The vibrations produced by fan cards are also notorious for rocking the fan card right out of its slot, so be sure to bolt the fan card into its slot using the expansion card bracket.

**CPU Fans**    CPUs have always run hot, and the reason is readily understandable—a single microscopic transistor dissipates virtually no heat, but the combined heat from over 40 million+ transistors crammed into a wafer the size of a fingernail becomes *extreme*. The surface temperature of a Pentium processor can easily exceed 70°C (Pentium II/III/4 processors can run even higher). With such a strong concentration of heat, even forced air through a heat sink can leave a CPU running hot. As you've seen earlier in this chapter, a CPU heat sink/fan must be employed to manage heat in the latest Athlon and Pentium III/4 processors. Basically, a CPU fan mounts a small, high-speed fan that blows down into a heat sink assembly (see the TMD cooler in Figure 18-3 earlier). The in-rushing air cools the heat sink (and thus the CPU) very effectively. Table 18-2 lists the typical operating temperatures for popular CPUs. The idea here is that a

**TABLE 18-2    TYPICAL CPU CASE TEMPERATURES**

| **AMD ATHLON AND DURON** | |
| --- | --- |
| Socket A CPUs (Athlon, Duron), up to 1 GHz | 90°C |
| Socket A CPUs (Athlon), 1.1 GHz or more | 95°C |
| Socket A CPUs (Athlon XP 1700+ to 2100+) | 90°C |
| Socket A CPUs (Athlon XP 2200+ and higher) | 85°C |
| All Slot A CPUs (Athlon classic, Athlon Thunderbird) | 70°C |
| **AMD K6 SERIES** | |
| All K6 CPUs (166-300 MHz) and most K6-2/K6-III CPUs | 70°C |
| K6-2/K6-III CPUs with model name ending with X (K6-2-450AFX) | 65°C |
| K6-2-400AFQ (uncommon) | 60°C |
| K6-2+, K6-III+, and most mobile K6/K6-2 CPUs | 85°C |
| Mobile K6/K6-2 models ending with K (mobile K6-2-P-400AFK) | 80°C |

| TABLE 18-2 | TYPICAL CPU CASE TEMPERATURES *(CONTINUED)* |
| --- | --- |
| **INTEL ITANIUM** | |
| Itanium 733 and 800 MHz | 66°C |
| **INTEL PENTIUM 4** | |
| Pentium 4, 1.3 GHz | 69°C |
| Pentium 4, 1.4 GHz | 70°C |
| Pentium 4, 1.5 GHz | 72°C |
| Pentium 4, 2.0-2.5 GHz | 68-71°C |
| **INTEL PENTIUM III** | |
| Pentium III Socket 370, 500-866 MHz | 80-85°C |
| Pentium III Slot 1 (first generation, OLGA), 550-600 MHz | 80-85°C |
| Pentium III Slot 1 (Coppermine), 500-866 MHz | 80-85°C |
| Pentium III Socket 370 and Slot 1, 933 MHz | 75°C |
| Pentium III Slot 1, 933 MHz | 60°C |
| Pentium III Slot 1 1 GHz | 60-70°C |
| Pentium III Slot 1, 1.13 GHz (first version) | 62°C |
| **INTEL CELERON** | |
| Celeron 266-433 MHz | 85°C |
| Celeron 466-533 MHz (0.25µ) | 70°C |
| Celeron 533-600 MHz (Coppermine) | 90°C |
| Celeron 633 and 667 MHz | 82°C |
| Celeron 700 MHz and higher | 80°C |
| **INTEL PENTIUM II** | |
| Pentium II (1st generation and Klamath) | 72-75°C |
| Pentium II (2nd generation, 2.0V core), 266-333 MHz | 65°C |
| Pentium II (350-400 MHz) | 75°C |
| Pentium II (450 MHz) | 70°C |
| **INTEL PENTIUM PRO** | |
| Pentium Pro, 256 or 512K L2 cache | 85° |
| Pentium Pro, 1MB L2 cache | 80°C |

CPU case can reach anywhere from 60°C to 90°C depending on the make and model of the processor—cooling is absolutely essential for proper operation and long-term reliability.

Unfortunately, there are some disadvantages to the CPU fan. First, the added height of a heat sink/fan combination can obstruct full-length expansion boards. This is typical of poorly designed AT-style motherboards (though ATX and NLX motherboards position the CPU well away from expansion slots). Similarly, if your particular motherboard places the CPU under a low-hanging drive or other chassis obstruction, a CPU fan may not fit. Before using a CPU fan, make sure that you have several cubic inches of available space *over* the CPU.

The CPU fan also requires power. Check that you have a power connector available from the power supply, or make sure that the CPU fan assembly comes with a built-in Y-connector. Today, the power management and cooling features provided by most motherboards allow you to plug the fan(s) directly into connectors on the motherboard. This allows the motherboard to regulate fan speed and measure rpm to detect failing or stalled fans.

Another possible problem involves vibration. Since the fan is now physically coupled to the CPU, there is a bit of debate over what (if any) long-term damage is done to the CPU by fan vibrations. The best defense against vibration and premature failure is to use a good-quality ball bearing fan unit. There are three attributes to consider when selecting a processor cooling unit:

- Large heat sink area for extra heat dissipation area to ensure that the CPU temperature stays below its maximum level (see Table 18-2 earlier)
- Long-life and low-noise ball bearing fan (or Teflon sleeve)
- Convenient and well-designed clips to ease installation at the CPU, yet maintain a snug fit

> If you must use a Y-splitter cable to power a CPU heat sink/fan, *never* split power from a hard drive or other critical drive. Split power from a floppy drive instead or upgrade the power supply to a model with additional drive power connectors.

## Liquid-Cooled Cases

With the growth in overclocked, multiprocessor, and other high-performance PCs, some manufacturers are including water cooling systems in their cases. You can see a Koolance PC2-C water-cooled case in Figure 18-6. Water cooling uses principles similar to the radiator in your car. Water is circulated through plastic tubes and passed through metal heat sinks attached to the processor, graphics coprocessor, chipset components, drive coolers, and so on. The water absorbs heat from each device as it circulates. Eventually, the water passes through a "radiator" assembly where powerful fans drive off the heat, cooling the water—which is then recirculated. Since water cools by conduction, the process is typically very efficient.

**FIGURE  18-6**   The Koolance PC2-C case, which uses a circulating water/radiator system to cool each device in the PC (Courtesy of Koolance, Inc.)

Of course, there are two drawbacks to this type of cooling. First, a water-cooled case is more expensive than an ordinary ATX PC enclosure. The Koolance PC2-C in Figure 18-6 retails for about $189. The second potential problem is the water itself. Since water is conductive (and usually corrosive because of natural minerals), any leak in the water loop can cause short circuits that will damage components. Consequently, water cooling systems demand more care and attention in the PC's assembly than do regular cases.

## Liquid Cooling (the "Heat Pipe")

CPU cooling can also be accomplished through conductive devices generally known as heat pipes. A small number of liquid-cooling devices are available for CPUs, most of which are used in Pentium II/III notebook systems that do not have the space for heat sinks or CPU fans (though there are heat pipe-based coolers with heat sink and fan components for desktop/tower use). The drawback to a liquid-cooled system is clear enough—a breach in the cooling loop can deposit liquid onto the motherboard and result in real damage. Extra expense is another consideration.

The basic principles behind the heat pipe are well known among refrigeration professionals, but are not all that intuitive to computer technicians. Basically, a vacuum-tight tube is filled with a low boiling point fluid. The tube is run through a small heat sink fitted over the CPU. The advantage here is that since heat does not have to dissipate to the air, the heat sink can be quite thin.

This CPU heat sink is known as the *evaporator*, since the fluid running through it is evaporated ("flashed" to vapor) by the CPU's heat. Since the process of evaporation is a cooling process, heat is transferred from the CPU to the evaporated fluid, which then travels back up through the tube where it runs through a somewhat larger metal plate (sometimes a heat sink) known as the *condenser*. In a mobile PC, the condenser is usually located under the notebook's keyboard assembly where there is enough empty space for the heat to dissipate and allow the fluid to return to its liquid state. Once the liquid returns to its liquid state, it is free to recirculate back to the heat sink. Two of the most interesting elements of the heat pipe are that it requires absolutely no electricity and has no moving parts. So long as the evaporator remains in good contact with the CPU, the heat pump should continue operating indefinitely. Circulation is driven by the natural phase changes of the liquid.

Although the heat pipe is a relatively simple and reliable mechanism, it poses some unique problems for small computer assemblies. If you upgrade or repair mobile computers at all (or use a desktop/tower CPU cooler with an integrated heat pipe), you will need to know the important issues for heat pipe assembly and installation:

■ *Be careful of liquid.* Remember that you are basically dealing with a delicate liquid vessel mounted in the bowels of your computer. As a result, you must be extremely careful during disassembly and reassembly procedures. Crimping the tube at any point will reduce the pipe's effectiveness. Breaking the heat pipe can result in chemicals being spilled into the main board.

■ *Be careful of dust and debris.* As you saw, the evaporated liquid sheds its heat in the condenser (the heat sink), which is located under the keyboard in mobile PCs. But just like convection heating in the home, heat will have trouble leaving the condenser if it is "insulated"—covered with dust and debris accumulated from long periods of use. If you find yourself working on a PC using a heat pipe, be sure that the condenser is clean and free of dust. You may choose to blow away any dust and debris with compressed air.

■ *Be careful of contact.* As far as the CPU is concerned, the heat pipe's evaporator is just another heat sink. Like any heat sink, there must be good physical contact between the CPU and the evaporator in order for proper cooling to occur. If the evaporator is left loose (or otherwise mounted incorrectly), the heat pipe will be ineffective.

## Piezoelectric Coolers

Piezoelectric devices (called *Peltier coolers*) mount a layer of piezoelectric material over the CPU. As the crystal layer vibrates, a temperature differential develops through it, which actually results in a cooler surface (applied against the CPU). This means the elements actually have a "hot" side and a "cold" side. To accomplish this, the Peltier element uses power (a lot of power). So, in addition to *pumping* heat, a Peltier element will actually *produce* heat. Overall, the system will run hotter, but the Peltier element will cool the CPU where it is needed. You can see a complete Peltier kit available from FrozenCPU.com at www.frozencpu.com/cgi-bin/frozencpu/pek-01.html. The problem with piezoelectric chillers is their expense, as well as the yet-unclear potential for CPU damage from long-term exposure to vibration. Though a Peltier cooler can be a perfect thermal solution, poorly designed or improperly installed fans can be dangerous. Here are a few Peltier-related dangers:

Good Peltier coolers cool significantly better than conventional heat sinks, making them suitable for overclocking. It is important to note that the heat sink of a Peltier cooler will get hotter than the heat sink of a conventional cooler, because of the heat the Peltier element produces.

- **Overheating**   Peltier coolers come with a heat sink and fan. If the fan dies, the additional heat of the Peltier element may damage your CPU. Also, you must ensure proper airflow through the system. A Peltier cooler will add heat to the system, so other heat-sensitive devices like hard disks must be properly ventilated or cooled. Make sure that there are no cables that disturb the airflow or even cover the fan. As with all other heat sink units, you should use thermal grease.

- **Excessive power demands**   The Peltier will draw a lot of power, possibly more than your power supply can cope with (the Peltier unit shown at www.frozencpu.com/cgi-bin/frozencpu/pek-01.html uses 85 watts). This is especially a problem at boot-up—while your hard disk(s) is spinning up, it uses more power. If the Peltier starts drawing its power immediately, it may overload the supply. Good Peltier coolers solve this problem by turning on the Peltier element only after a certain time (when the CPU gets warm). Peltier wiring can be another problem. If the gauge of the wiring is too small (a common issue on some cheap Peltiers), the wiring may overheat due to the current. As a rule, the Peltier cooler should have a dedicated power connector from the power supply—don't let your Peltier share a line with a hard disk or floppy drive.

- **Water condensation**   This is a particular problem when you use your computer in a damp location. When your CPU runs very cool (in the time just after turning on your computer), it might become chilled *below* room temperature, and this can cause condensation on the CPU, the socket, and under the socket. The hotter and the more humid the air inside your computer case is, the more likely you are to experience condensation problems. Good Peltier coolers solve this problem by turning on the Peltier element only *after* the CPU has reached a preset temperature. In actual practice, short circuits due to condensation are very unlikely.

- **Peltier sizing**   The Peltier element must have the right size. If the Peltier element is bigger than the part of the CPU it covers (sometimes a problem with CPUs that have a smaller metal plate in the middle), then condensation might occur. On the other hand, if the Peltier element is too small (a problem with the AMD K6, which has a big metal plate on the top), then cooling might be inadequate.

## Advanced Configuration and Power Interface (ACPI)

Today's PCs are extremely power-conscious in order to comply with the growing trends of global power conservation. ACPI is a power conservation feature supported by the system BIOS and operating system.

ACPI systems can power-down to several different levels, eventually using as little as 5W of power in a "hibernation" mode. ACPI enables a PC to measure temperatures of critical components within its system. Temperature-sensing circuits can then be read by the BIOS and operating system, and critical temperature triggers can be programmed to cause alarm events. Alarms then initiate systematic power-saving modes that will cool corresponding elements of the system.

A system is generally divided into thermal zones (processor, memory, and chipset), so different power management regimes may be applied to the various zones independently. Cooling policies may be either passive or active. In a *passive* policy, device performance is limited to reduce heat generation. In an *active* policy, fan speed and on/off controls are used to limit temperature as heat increases. Cooling policies may be mixed and can be used in any order. For example, suppose that the processor's temperature starts to rise. The operating system senses a critical temperature and downshifts the processor's clock speed to limit power dissipation. If temperature continues to rise, a cooling fan is switched on (slow speed). Further increases in temperature cause the operating system to increase the fan speed. If the fan speed maximum is reached and the temperature continues to rise, the system shuts down entirely to prevent damage to the processor.

Ultimately, you want to be sure to use power conservation modes to save power and keep the PC cooler during idle periods.

# Cooling Problems

Cooling is often one of the most overlooked and neglected features of a PC. In many basic off-the-shelf systems, cooling is sufficient—but just barely. But over time, constant use, environmental factors, and upgrades, the cooling plan may need to be reviewed or revised. As with so many other elements of PC service, successful troubleshooting means knowing where to look. This part of the chapter shows you the factors to consider when evaluating PC cooling and cooling problems.

## FAN WEAR

Fans don't last forever. They are electromechanical devices, and eventually the motor or rotating shaft will wear out and fail. Normally, PC cooling fans are very quiet devices—they have to be, since loud operation in a home or office environment would quickly become maddening for the user. The first sign of fan failure is excessive *noise*. A persistent buzz or grinding sound immediately points to a fan problem. The fan motor may also be unusually hot. In extreme cases, the fan will hang up and stop altogether (it may start again if you nudge it gently). The best way to deal with a cranky fan is to replace it. A new fan must have the same three major characteristics of the original fan: (1) physical mounting dimensions, (2) operating voltage—usually +12 Vdc, and (3) airflow rate.

If your PC supports hardware monitoring features, the system may actually warn you if the fan rpm should fall below a preset level or CPU temperature becomes excessive.

## BAD HEAT SINK CONTACT

In order for a heat sink to be effective, it must have a strong physical connection to the host chip that it's cooling. This ensures that the maximum amount of heat is transferred from the chip to the heat sink/fan. The better that contact is (that is, the lower the "thermal resistance"), the more efficiently that heat is transferred into the heat sink—and the cooler the chip runs. There are a variety of ways to secure a heat sink/fan, but clipping the chip and heat sink together has been easiest and most popular. However, not all heat sink clips are tight, and even a tight clip does not guarantee good contact. Check to see that the heat sink is attached securely, and be sure to add a layer of thermal grease between the chip and heat sink. Thermal grease fills in any air space between the chip and heat sink, so heat transfer is enhanced. Suspect heat sink problems when the system locks up randomly for no apparent reason or the CPU suffers chronic failures.

> Thermal grease is toxic and can stain clothing. When using thermal grease, be sure to work carefully, and avoid getting it on hands and clothing.

One of the more recent trends in heat sink marketing is the use of stick-on heat sinks—just peel off an adhesive backing and stick the heat sink in place. It sounds terrific in principle, but adhesive is often more of a thermal insulator than a thermal conductor. As a general rule, go with the clip-on heat sinks wherever possible.

## CPU VIBRATION FAILURE

CPU heat sink/fans are generally regarded as one of the most effective CPU cooling devices available, but there is a certain amount of debate over the effect of long-term fan vibration on the CPU. Some manufacturers argue that since the fan is physically attached to the heat sink (and CPU), the fan's vibrations will be carried directly into the CPU die, which will shorten the chip's working life. However, there are no studies available to prove or disprove that possibility. As a result, you should rely on your own experience when checking or recommending CPU heat sinks. Normally, it is reasonable to expect that the cooler CPU should run longer and more reliably. So if you find that the CPU fails frequently when fitted with a CPU fan, try a large heat sink or high-quality heat sink/fan instead.

## SUNLIGHT

Anyone who has ever been in the sunlight understands how warming it can be. This natural warming can be magnified through glass, so sunlight indoors can feel even warmer. When a PC sits exposed to sunlight for prolonged periods, the metal enclosures tend to pick up much of that heat (and heat the air inside). Although sunlight alone rarely provides enough heating to endanger the system, it can intensify the cooling demands while the system is operating. As a general rule, do not expose the PC and its peripherals to direct sunlight for extended periods of time.

## THERMAL CYCLING

Turn it off or leave it on? This is the perennial PC question and one that continues to be a hotbed of debate among technicians. The best way to answer this question is to approach it both theoretically and practically. Theoretically, each time material heats up, it expands. When the material cools down again, it contracts. Thus, every time a PC is turned on, the chips, solder joints, and wiring tend to expand until the system reaches a stable operating temperature. When the PC is turned off, it gradually cools down and its components contract until the PC returns to room temperature. Over time, this "accordion effect" of expansion and contraction (referred to as *thermal cycling*) is known to cause material to fatigue and fracture—a chip breaks down, or a solder joint becomes intermittent—you get the idea. As a consequence of this effect, long-time PC veterans argue that the PC should be left on constantly. This allows the system to achieve a stable temperature, so thermal cycling is eliminated.

From a practical standpoint, however, the view is a bit different. First, the damaging effect of thermal cycling is dependent on the *amount of temperature difference*. Frankly, today's PCs just don't get that hot (although CPUs and graphics processors can fail if not properly cooled). Cooler PCs are affected less by thermal damage. Drive wear is also another nonissue, with current, cool-running designs exhibiting

MTBFs of over 300,000 hours. The other consideration is the rising cost of power, which is wasted by simply leaving the PC on overnight or over weekends. On the other hand, there is no reason to power down the PC each time you get up for a coffee. Ultimately, the current thinking is to go ahead and turn the PC off overnight, or whenever you must leave the system for more than a few hours. If your system offers power conservation support (such as "standby" and "hibernation" modes), you should employ those techniques to lower the system's total power demands during idle periods.

## EXCESSIVE DEVICES

Many PCs are eventually upgraded with more RAM, more drives, new CPUs, and so on. Each new device added to the system contributes to its overall heat production. For heavily expanded systems, it may be necessary to augment cooling with a supplemental exhaust fan or inlet fan at the chassis. The general yardstick for judging the need for extra cooling is to feel the air exhausting from the system. If the air feels comfortable or somewhat warm, chances are that cooling is adequate. If the air feels hot, it's time to add a new fan. True, this is a rather subjective means of measurement, but it is accurate enough for most situations.

## DUST

Perhaps the most significant problem of reliable, long-term PC cooling is *dust*, which is always present in everyday air. For the purposes of this book, "dust" includes other contaminants too, such as pet hair and cigarette smoke. Dust has two effects on the PC. First, dust collects on the fan blades and intake vents or filters. This interrupts and limits airflow into and out of the system. Second, dust can collect on a printed circuit board where airflow is limited. The dust acts as a *thermal blanket* that prevents normal convective cooling. When upgrading or servicing a PC, make it a point to vacuum or blow out any accumulations of dust in or around the system.

 If you blow out dust with compressed air, be sure to do so outside or in clear open space—otherwise, you're likely to get a cloud of dust in the face.

## AC POWER PROBLEMS

Power supplies can be serious sources of heat, especially in the regulator portion of the supply, which is designed to maintain a stable voltage output as AC input levels and load demands change. If AC climbs over its nominal value, the regulator must work harder to maintain a constant output. This results in excessive power supply heating. Lagging AC levels result in larger amounts of current being drawn to keep the power output steady, which also causes extra heating. Persistent power supply failures or unusually hot operation may suggest problems with AC (or an overloaded system power supply).

 PCs in regions with chronic power distribution problems may benefit from the use of uninterruptible power supply (UPS) systems between the AC outlet and system.

## BLOCKED VENTS

Air needs a clear path into and out of the system, which is usually accommodated through vent slots strategically located around the enclosure. If the vent slots are obstructed or blocked, airflow may be interrupted. (This is especially detrimental to devices relying on natural convection for cooling, like monitors.) You can see the importance of proper ventilation by reviewing the installation guidelines for almost any piece of consumer electronics. Most guidelines recommend that you leave several inches of free space on each side of the enclosure. Make sure that vent slots are unobstructed and clear of dust or debris. Keep in

**FIGURE  18-7**     Checking CPU voltages with the Processor Protector (Courtesy of Autotime)

mind that more openings are not necessarily better. Unexpected openings in the chassis (open expansion slots or missing I/O panel covers, for example) may allow air to enter or leave the chassis unexpectedly, and this may "short circuit" the proper airflow and cooling through the system.

## EXCESSIVE CPU VOLTAGE

Not all CPUs use the same voltage. Intel, AMD, and Cyrix CPUs use slightly different voltage levels for proper operation (usually between +2.4 Vdc and +3.6 Vdc). If the CPU voltage is tweaked a bit too high for the particular CPU, it will generate excessive heat. This happens frequently when a processor is overclocked. Another typical oversight comes with the use of Pentium MMX (and later) processors that use dual voltages (approximately +2.8 Vdc and +3.3 Vdc) for reduced power and lower heating. Again, if the CPU voltage is set too high, excessive heating will result, which can shorten the CPU's working life. Devices like Autotime's Processor Protector (Figure 18-7) are tools that you can use to quickly and efficiently verify the CPU voltage(s). A Slot 1 type tester, the Processor Protector II, is also available.

# Troubleshooting Cooling Problems

Cooling problems manifest themselves in a variety of ways—usually through intermittent system operation and frequent failures. This part of the chapter is intended to illustrate some of the more perplexing cooling problems that you should be aware of.

## HEAT DETECTORS

To deal with system heat problems, you should know when excessive heating occurs. Today, the power management and cooling systems of most motherboards incorporate hardware monitoring that will report cooling fan speeds and (if properly equipped) indicate the CPU temperature. You can then set alarm points that will alert you if a cooling fan stops or CPU temperature exceeds your preset value. If you're working with older systems (or systems that do not incorporate such hardware monitoring features), you can use after-market heat detectors (such as the 110 Alert unit from PC Power & Cooling at www.pcpowerandcooling.com/products/alarmandaccesories/alert/index.htm) to alert you to excess heat.

Devices like the 110 Alert monitor interior case temperature and processor cooler fan rotation inside any computer. At 110°F (40°C), a loud audible alarm will sound. The 110 Alert also monitors electrical current to the processor's cooling fan, so the audible alarm will sound when the cooling fan slows by 30 percent or more. To install a device such as the 110 Alert, connect a spare power lead to the connector labeled "110 Alert," and then connect the opposite end directly to the processor's cooling fan power connector. (Power for the processor cooling fan must be supplied by the 110 Alert; otherwise, the alarm may sound continuously.) Remove the protective backing from the mounting tape, and mount the unit on a smooth, clean surface in a convenient location within the top third of the computer.

Do not locate the heat detector near the CPU or other high heat source, because this may result in a nuisance alarm. Also, do not connect a Y-splitter between a 110 Alert and the processor cooling fan. You cannot split the power to the processor cooling fan and another device such as a hard disk drive. This will cause intermittent nuisance alarms because the 110 Alert is sensing the current of both devices.

## GENERAL SYMPTOMS

The following set of symptoms may help you to resolve specific issues that frequently occur on modern PCs.

**SYMPTOM 18-1**    **The fan is producing an unusual amount of noise, but it seems to be working properly**    This can often happen after replacing a fan and is typically the result of fan vibrations being introduced to the PC chassis. While this is rarely harmful to the system, it can become quite annoying. Check the way in which the new fan is mounted. See that the fan is mounted securely, and be sure that any damping material is in place. Otherwise, you may try adding small standoffs of foam around each mounting screw to damp vibration. Of course, if the fan is original equipment, it may be wearing out and need to be replaced. Try a new fan.

**SYMPTOM 18-2**    **The fan has stopped turning**    You may see this problem reported as an alert (if the system supports hardware monitoring features). First, check to see if the fan is the type that works intermittently by means of a small internal thermostat. If so, the fan may simply have stopped normally. You should see it start and stop as required. However, most fans turn continuously, so if the fan has stopped, it may have become disconnected or it may have failed. Check the fan's power connection. If the problem persists, try a new fan.

**SYMPTOM 18-3**    **The CPU freezes intermittently**    This is a classic sign of CPU overheating. While overheating will not necessarily destroy a CPU immediately, prolonged or repeated overheating can precipitate a permanent failure. Check the heat sink or CPU fan attached to the CPU. Remount or upsize the CPU cooling unit if necessary.

Be sure to let the system cool **before** touching the heat sink. If the cooling device is loose, reattach it securely (be sure to use thermal compound). If the heat sink is secure, but overheating continues, try a more aggressive device such as a CPU fan or heat pipe-based cooling unit.

**SYMPTOM 18-4**    **You are experiencing frequent CPU failures**    Chronic CPU failures are rare occurrences and can often be traced to insufficient cooling—especially after the system has been overclocked. If the CPU does not have a heat sink, try adding one. If a heat sink is already attached, try a larger heat sink or CPU fan. However, if a CPU fan is already in use, there may be a vibration problem, which shortens the CPU's working life. Try "downgrading" to a regular heat sink, or use an alternative cooling device such as a Peltier cooler.

**SYMPTOM 18-5**    **You are experiencing frequent drive failures**    This is typical of the hard drive in an overloaded system. When replacing the hard drive, take careful note of the exhaust heat and the overall number of devices in the system. If the exhaust is unusually warm, or there are many adjacent drives in the system, try mounting the replacement drive by itself away from other drives—maybe in a rear drive bay. If possible, try mounting the drive vertically. If it is impossible to relocate the offending drive, try adding a supplemental fan, or a fan card, to improve airflow over the drive. You may also try a specialty drive-cooling unit available from some electronics/computer retailers. For example, the Koolance hard drive cooler (see Figure 18-8) is an aluminum chilling block that mounts within it up to two hard drives. Water is circulated through the block to keep the drives cool. Other devices use fans to pass air over the drives.

**SYMPTOM 18-6**    **You note condensation in the system**    This type of problem, which may not be immediately apparent, occurs when Peltier coolers are oversized for the CPU (or the PC is used in damp environments). You should first disassemble the CPU and cooling unit and dry any residual condendation. Select a new cooling unit that is properly sized for the particular CPU make and model. You may need to consult a retailer for additional sizing and selection information. If condensation has corroded any printed circuitry in the system, it may be necessary for you to replace the affected device(s) to prevent future reliability problems.

**SYMPTOM 18-7**    **The system doesn't alert you to CPU temperature or fan speed problems**    Recent PCs typically employ hardware monitoring features that monitor factors such as CPU temperature and fan speeds (such as the CPU fan and chassis fan speeds), then provide alerts if hardware problems arise. In order for a system to use those features, they must be supported in the BIOS and operating system, and you must have suitable hardware in place. For example, you'll need to use a fan with a tachometer output—a simple four-pin fan that plugs into an ordinary drive power connector won't report anything to the system. Check the system documentation to determine just what features are supported, and how those features should be enabled.

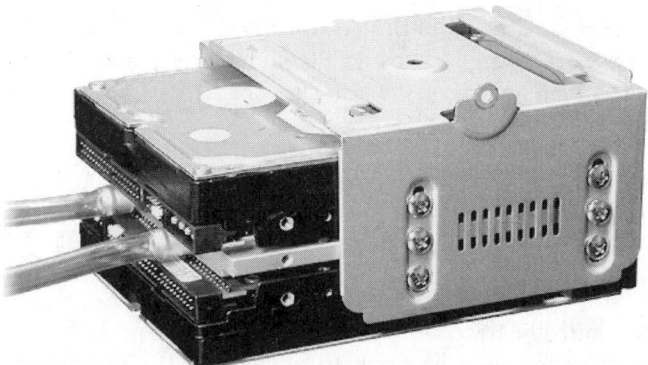

**FIGURE  18-8**    The Koolance hard drive cooler, which can be used with water-cooled systems to chill up to two hard drives (Courtesy of Koolance, Inc.)

# Further Study

**Autotime**   www.autotime.com
**CoolerGuys**   www.coolerguys.com
**Cooler Master**   www.coolermaster.com
**Intel (Fan Duct)**   www.intel.com/update/archive/issue12/stories/top5.htm
**Koolance**   www.koolance.com
**PC Power & Cooling**   www.pcpowercooling.com
**Pham Computer**   www.phamcomputer.com

# 19

# FLOPPY DRIVES

The ability to interchange programs and data between various compatible computers is a fundamental requirement of almost every computer system. It is just this kind of file exchange compatibility that helped rocket IBM PC/XTs into everyday use and spur the personal computer industry into the early 1980s. A standardized operating system, file structure, and recording media also breathed life into the fledgling software industry. With the floppy disk, early software developers could finally distribute programs and data to a mass market of compatible computer users. The mechanism that allowed this quantum leap in compatibility is the *floppy disk drive* (or FDD, shown in Figure 19-1). Although floppy drives are quite inexpensive and reliable, they are also very limited in their storage space—allowing only up to 1.44MB on a traditional disk, and 2.88MB on rare super high-density media. This chapter examines the operating concepts, installation guidelines, and troubleshooting issues for conventional 3.5" floppy drives.

# The Floppy Drive

A venerable floppy disk drive (FDD) is one of the least expensive and most reliable forms of mass storage ever used in computer systems. Virtually every one of the millions of desktop personal computers sold each year continues to incorporate at least one floppy drive. Most notebook and laptop computers also offer a single floppy drive. Not only are floppy drives useful for transferring small files and limited amounts of data between various systems, but the advantage of removable media—the floppy disk

**FIGURE 19-1**     NEC FD1138H floppy drive (Courtesy of NEC Technologies, Inc.)

itself—makes floppy drives an almost intuitive backup for your important data files (e.g., Microsoft Money backups). Although floppy drives have evolved through a number of iterations—from 8 inches to 5.25 inches to 3.5 inches—their basic components and operating principles have changed very little.

# MAGNETIC STORAGE CONCEPTS

Magnetic storage media has been attractive to mainframe and minicomputer designers for many years—long before the personal computer had established itself in homes and offices. This popularity is primarily due to the fact that magnetic media is *nonvolatile*. Unlike system RAM, no electrical energy is needed to maintain the information once it is stored on magnetic media. Although electrical energy is used to read and write magnetic data, magnetic fields do not change on their own, so data remains intact until other forces (such as another floppy drive) act upon it. It is this smooth, straightforward translation from electricity to magnetism and back again that has made magnetic storage such a natural choice. To understand how a floppy drive works and why it fails, you should have an understanding of magnetic storage. This part of the chapter describes the basic storage concepts used for floppy drives.

## Magnetic Media

For the purposes of this book, *media* is the physical material that actually holds recorded information. In a floppy disk, the media is a small Mylar disk coated on both sides with a precisely formulated magnetic material often referred to as the *oxide* layer. Every disk manufacturer uses their own particular formula for magnetic coatings, but most coatings are based on a naturally magnetic element (such as iron, nickel, or cobalt) that has been alloyed with nonmagnetic materials or rare earth. This magnetic material is then compounded with plastic, bonding chemicals, and lubricant to form the actual disk media coating.

The fascinating aspect of these magnetic layers is that each and every particle of the media acts as a microscopic magnet. Each magnetic particle can be aligned in one orientation or another under the influence of an external magnetic field. If you have ever magnetized a screwdriver's steel shaft by running a permanent magnet along its length, you have already seen this magnetizing process in action. For a floppy disk, microscopic points along the disk's surfaces are magnetized in one alignment or another by the precise forces applied by read/write (or R/W) heads. The shifting of alignment polarities would indicate a logic 1, while no change in polarity would indicate a logic 0. (You will see more about data recording and organization later in this chapter.)

In analog recording (such as audio tapes), the magnetic field generated by read/write heads varies in direct proportion to the signal being recorded. Such linear variations in field strength cause varying amounts of magnetic particles to align as the media moves. On the other hand, digital recordings such as floppy disks save binary data by applying an overwhelming amount of field strength. Very strong magnetic fields *saturate* the media—that is, *so much* field strength is applied that any further increase in field strength will not cause a better alignment of magnetic particles at that point on the media. The advantage to operating in saturation is that the digital information is remarkably resistant to the degrading effects of noise that eventually appear in analog magnetic recordings.

Although the orientation of magnetic particles on a disk's media can be reversed by using an external magnetic field, particles tend to resist the reversal of polarity. *Coercitivity* is the strength with which magnetic particles resist change. Higher coercitivity material has a greater resistance to change, so a stronger external field will be needed to cause changes. High coercitivity is generally considered to be desirable (up to a point) because signals stand out much better against background noise, and signals will resist natural degradation caused by age, temperature, and random magnetic influences. As you might expect, a highly coercive media requires a more powerful field to record new information.

Another advantage of increased coercitivity is greater "information density" for media. The greater strength of each media particle allows more bits to be packed into less area. The move from 5.25-inch to 3.5-inch floppy disks was possible due largely to a superior (more coercive) magnetic layer. This coercitivity principle also holds true for hard drives. To pack more information onto ever-smaller platters, the media must be more coercive. Coercitivity is a common magnetic measurement with units in *oersteds* (pronounced "or-steds"). The coercitivity of a typical floppy disk can range anywhere from 300 to 750 oersteds. For example, Maxell disks specify 730 oersteds (www.maxell-data.com/pdfs/1.pdf). By comparison, hard drive and magneto-optical (MO) drive media usually offer coercitivities of 6000 oersteds or higher.

The main premise of magnetic storage is that it is *static* (once recorded, information is retained without any electrical energy). Such stored information is presumed to last forever, but in actual practice, magnetic information begins to degrade as soon as it is recorded. A good magnetic media will reliably "remember" (or retain) the alignment of its particles over a long period of time (five years and longer). The ability of a media to retain its magnetic information is known as *retentivity*. Even the finest, best-formulated floppy disks degrade eventually (although it could take many years before an actual data error materializes).

Ultimately, the ideal answer to media degradation is to refresh (or write over) the data and sector ID information. Data is rewritten normally each time a file is saved, but sector IDs are only written once when the disk is formatted. If a sector ID should fail, you will see the dreaded "Sector Not Found" disk error, and any data stored in the sector cannot be accessed. This failure mode also occurs in hard drives. There is little that can be done to ensure the integrity of floppy disks other than maintaining one or more backups on freshly formatted disks. However, some commercial software is available for restoring disk data (especially hard drives).

## Magnetic Recording Principles

The first step in understanding digital recording is to see how binary data is stored on a disk. Contrary to popular belief, binary 1's and 0's are *not* represented by discrete polarities of magnetic field orientations as you may have thought. Instead, binary digits are represented by the presence or absence of flux *transitions,* as illustrated in Figure 19-2. By detecting the *change* from one polarity to another instead of simply detecting a discrete polarity itself, maximum sensitivity can be achieved with very simple circuitry.

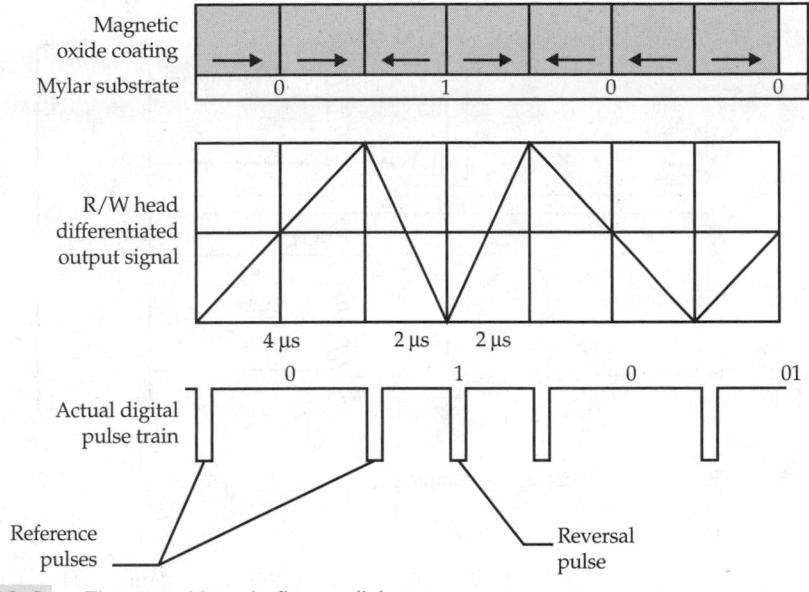

**FIGURE 19-2**    Flux transitions in floppy disks

In its simplest form, a logic 1 is indicated by the presence of a flux reversal within a fixed time frame, while a logic 0 is indicated by the absence of a flux reversal. Most floppy drive systems insert artificial flux reversals between consecutive 0's to prevent reversals from occurring at great intervals. You can see some example magnetic states recorded on the media of Figure 19-2. Notice that the direction of reversal does not matter at all—it is the reversal **event** that defines a 1 or 0. For example, the first 0 uses left-to-right orientation, while the second 0 uses a right-to-left orientation, but both can represent 0's. The second trace in Figure 19-2 represents an amplified output signal from a typical read/write head. Notice that the analog signal peaks wherever there is a flux transition—long slopes indicate a 0, and short slopes indicate a 1. When such peaks are encountered, peak detection circuits in the floppy drive cause marking pulses in the ultimate data signal. Each bit is usually encoded in about 4 µs.

Often, the most confusing aspect of flux transitions is the artificial reversals. Why reverse the polarities for consecutive 0's? Artificial reversals are added to guarantee synchronization in the floppy disk circuitry. Remember that data read or written to a floppy disk is serial, and without any clock signal, such serial data is *asynchronous* of the drive's circuitry. Regular flux reversals (even if added artificially) create reference pulses that help to synchronize the drive and data without use of clocks or other timing signals. This approach is loosely referred to as the *modified frequency modulation* (MFM) recording technique. Early hard drives (such as ST506/412 drives) also employed MFM recording.

The ability of floppy disks to store information depends upon being able to write new magnetic field polarities on top of old or existing orientations. A drive must also be able to sense the existing polarities on a disk during read operations. The mechanism responsible for translating electrical signals into magnetic signals (and vice versa) is the R/W head. In principle, a *head* is little more than a coil of very fine wire wrapped around a soft, highly permeable core material, as illustrated in Figure 19-3.

When the head is energized with current flow from a driver chip, a path of magnetic flux is established in the head core. The direction (or orientation) of flux depends on the direction of energizing current.

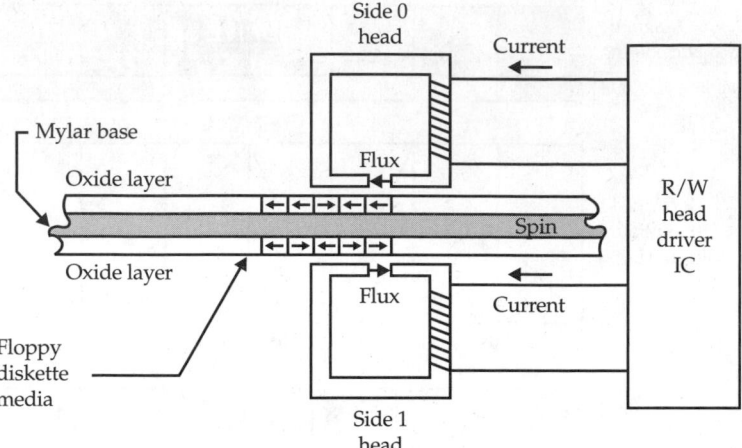

**FIGURE  19-3**    Floppy drive recording principles

To reverse a head's magnetic orientation, the direction of energizing current must be reversed. The small head size and low current levels needed to energize a head allow very high frequency flux reversals. As magnetic flux is generated in a head, the resulting, tightly focused magnetic field aligns the floppy disk's particles at that point. In general practice, the current signal magnetizes an almost microscopic area on the media. R/W heads actually contact the media while a disk is inserted into a drive.

During a read operation, the heads are left unenergized while the disk spins. Just as varying current produces magnetism in a head, the reverse is also true—varying magnetic influences (from data on the disk) cause currents to be developed in the head(s). As the spinning media moves across a R/W head, a current is produced in the head coil. The direction of induced current depends on the polarity of each flux orientation. Induced current is proportional to the flux density (how closely each flux transition is placed) and the velocity of the media across each head. In other words, signal strength depends on the rate of change of flux versus time.

## Data and Disk Organization

Another important aspect of drive troubleshooting is to understand how data is arranged on the disk. You cannot place data just *anywhere*. The drive would have no idea where to look for the data later on, and wouldn't even be able to determine whether the data is valid. For a disk to be of use, information must be sorted and organized into known, standard locations. Standardized organization ensures that a disk written by one drive will be readable by another drive in a different machine. Table 19-1 compares the major specifications of different drive types.

It is important to note that a floppy disk is a two-dimensional entity possessing both height and width (depth is irrelevant here). This two-dimensional characteristic allows disk information to be recorded in concentric circles, which creates a random-access type of media. *Random access* means that it is possible to move around the disk almost instantly to obtain a desired piece of information. This is a much faster and more convenient approach than a sequential recording medium such as magnetic tape.

Floppy disk organization is not terribly complicated, but there are several important concepts that you must be familiar with. The disk itself is rotated in one direction (usually clockwise) under read/write heads that are perpendicular (at right angles) to the disk's plane. The path of the disk beneath a head describes a circle.

| | TABLE 19-1 COMPARISON OF GENERAL FLOPPY DRIVE SPECIFICATIONS | | | | |
|---|---|---|---|---|---|
| **SPECIFICATION** | **5.25 INCH (360KB)** | **5.25 INCH (1.2MB)** | **3.5 INCH (720KB)** | **3.5 INCH (1.44MB)** | **3.5 INCH (2.88MB)** |
| Bytes per sector | 512 | 512 | 512 | 512 | 512 |
| Sectors per track | 9 | 15 | 9 | 18 | 36 |
| Tracks per side | 40 | 80 | 80 | 80 | 80 |
| Sectors per cluster | 2 | 1 | 2 | 1 | 2 |
| FAT length (sectors) | 2 | 7 | 3 | 9 | 9 |
| Number of FATs | 2 | 2 | 2 | 2 | 2 |
| Root directory length | 7 sectors | 14 sectors | 7 sectors | 14 sectors | 15 sectors |
| Max. root entries | 112 | 224 | 112 | 224 | 240 |
| Total sectors on disk | 708 | 2371 | 1426 | 2847 | 5726 |
| Media base | Ferrite | Ferrite | Cobalt | Cobalt | Cobalt |
| Coercitivity (oersteds) | 300 | 300 | 600 | 600 | 720 |
| Media descriptor byte | FDh | F9h | F9h | F0h | F0h |
| Encoding format | MFM or FM | MFM or FM | MFM | MFM | MFM |
| Data rate (KB/sec) | 250 or 125 | 500 or 250 | 500 | 500 | 500 |

As a head steps in and out along a disk's radius, each step describes a circle with a different circumference—rather like lanes on a roadway. Each of these concentric "lanes" is known as a *track*. A typical 3.5-inch disk offers 160 tracks—80 tracks on each side of the media. Tracks have a finite width that is defined largely by the drive size, head size, and media. When a R/W head jumps from track to track, it must jump precisely the correct distance to position itself in the middle of another track. If positioning is not correct, the head may encounter data signals from two adjacent tracks. Faulty positioning almost invariably results in disk errors. Also notice that the circumference of each track drops as the head moves toward the disk's center. With less space and a constant rate of spin, data is densest on the innermost tracks (79 or 159 depending on the disk side) and least dense on the outermost tracks (0 or 80). A track is also known as a *cylinder*.

Every cylinder is divided into smaller units called *sectors*. There are 18 sectors on every track of an 3.5-inch disk. Sectors serve two purposes. First, a sector stores 512 bytes of data. With 18 sectors per track and 160 tracks per disk, an 8.89cm disk holds 2,880 sectors [18 × 160]. At 512 bytes per sector, a formatted disk can handle about (2,880 × 512) 1,474,560 bytes of data. In actual practice, this amount is often slightly less, to allow for boot sector and file allocation information. Sectors are referenced in groups called *clusters* or *allocation units*. While hard drives can group 16 or more sectors into a cluster, floppy drives only use 1 or 2 sectors in a cluster.

Second, and perhaps more important, a sector provides housekeeping data that identifies the sector, the track, and error-checking results from cyclical redundancy check (CRC) calculations. The location of each sector and housekeeping information is set down during the format process. Once formatted, only the sector data and CRC results are updated when a disk is written. Sector ID and synchronization data is never rewritten unless the disk is reformatted. This extra information means that each sector actually holds more than 512 bytes, but you only have access to the 512 data bytes in a sector during normal disk read/write operations. If sector ID data is accidentally overwritten or corrupted, the user data in the afflicted sector becomes unreadable.

The format process also writes a bit of other important information to the disk. The boot record is the first sector on a disk (sector 0). It contains several key parameters that describe the characteristics of the disk. If the disk is bootable, the boot sector will also run the files (e.g., IO.SYS and MSDOS.SYS) that load DOS. In addition to the boot record, a File Allocation Table (FAT) is placed on track 00. The FAT acts as a table of contents for the disk. As files are added and erased, the FAT is updated to reflect the contents of each cluster. As you might imagine, a working FAT is critical to the proper operation of a disk. If the FAT is accidentally overwritten or corrupted, the entire disk can become useless. Without a viable FAT, the computer has no other way to determine what files are available or where they are spread throughout the disk. The very first byte in a FAT is the *media descriptor* byte, which allows the drive to recognize the type of disk that is inserted.

## Media Problems

Magnetic media has come a long way since the early days of the PC. Today's high-quality magnetic materials, combined with the benefits of precise, high-volume production equipment, produce disks that are exceptionally reliable over normal long-term use in a floppy disk drive. However, floppy disks are removable items. The care they receive in physical handling and the storage environment where they are kept will greatly impact a disk's life span.

The most troubling and insidious problem plaguing floppy disk media is the accidental influence of magnetic fields. Any magnetized item in close proximity to a floppy disk poses a potential threat. Permanent magnets such as refrigerator magnets or magnetic paper clips are prime sources of stray fields. Electromagnetic sources like telephone ringers, monitor or TV degaussing coils, and all types of motors will corrupt data if the media is close enough. The best policy is to keep all floppy disks in a dedicated container placed well away from stray magnetic fields.

Disks and magnetic media are also subject to a wide variety of physical damage. Substrates and media are manufactured to very tight tolerances, so anything at all that alters the precise surface features of a floppy disk can cause problems. The introduction of hair, dirt, or dust through the disk's head access aperture, wild temperature variations, fingerprints on the media, or any substantial impact or flexing of the media can cause temporary loss of contact between media and head. When loss of contact occurs, data is lost and a number of disk errors can occur. Head wear and the accumulation of worn oxides also affect head contact. Once again, storing disks in a dedicated container located well out of harm's way is often the best means of protection.

# DRIVE CONSTRUCTION

At the core of a floppy drive (see Figure 19-4) is a frame assembly (number 15 in the figure). It is the single main structure for mounting the drive's mechanisms and electronics. Frames are typically made from die-cast aluminum to provide a strong, rigid foundation for the drive. The front bezel (number 18) attaches to the frame to provide a clean, cosmetic appearance, and to offer a fixed slot for disk insertion or removal. For 3.5-inch drives, bezels often include a small colored lens, a disk ejection button hole, and a flap to cover the disk slot when the drive is empty. A spindle motor assembly (number 17) uses an outer-rotor DC motor fabricated onto a small PC board. The motor's shaft is inserted into that large hole in the frame. A disk's metal drive hub automatically interlocks to the spindle. For 5.25-inch disks, the center hole is clamped between two halves of a spindle assembly. The halves clamp the disk when the drive lever is locked down. The disk activity LED (number 20) illuminates through the bezel's colored lens whenever spindle motor activity is in progress. Figure 19-5 shows the spindle motor assembly from the underside of the drive.

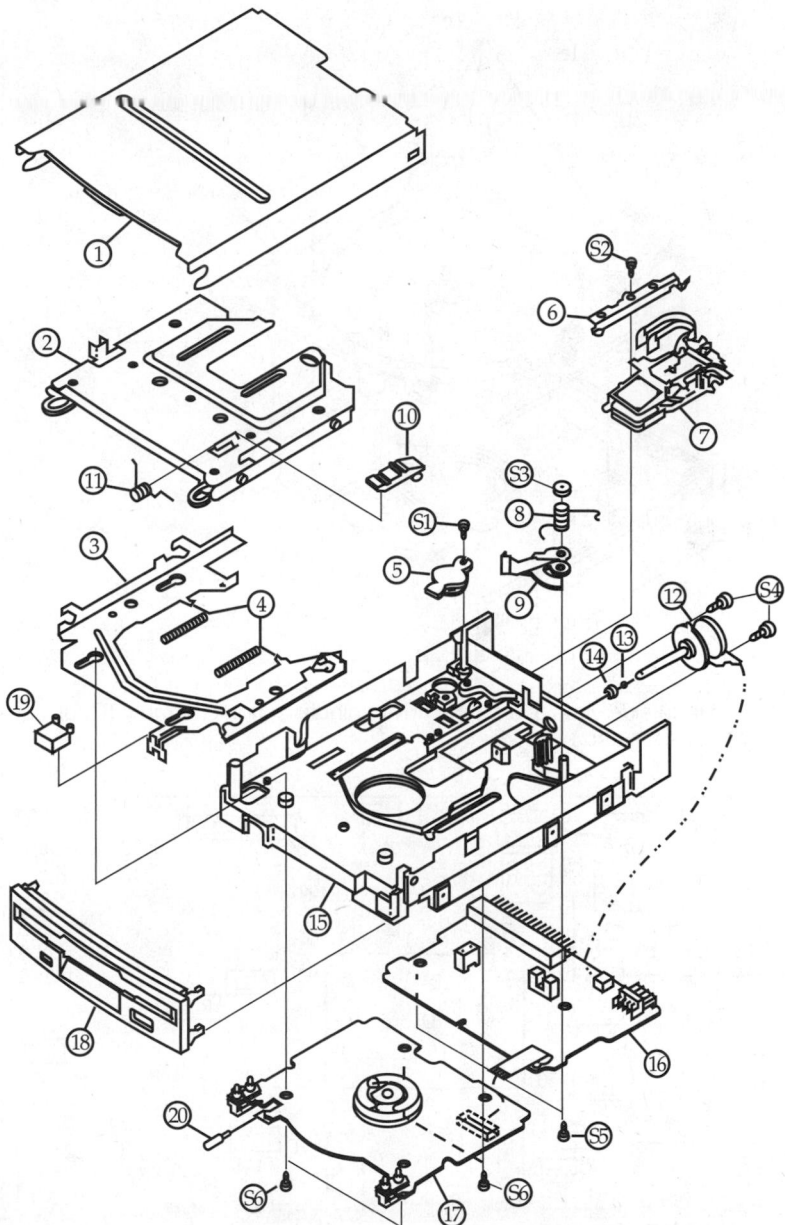

**FIGURE 19-4** Exploded diagram of a floppy disk drive assembly (Courtesy of Teac America, Inc.)

Just behind the spindle motor is the drive's control electronics (number 16 in Figure 19-4). It contains the circuitry needed to operate the drive's motors, R/W heads, and sensors. A standardized interface is used to connect the drive to a floppy drive controller. Figure 19-6 shows a close-up of a drive's control board (note the optoisolator just below the chip marked "U1"). The read/write head assembly (number 7

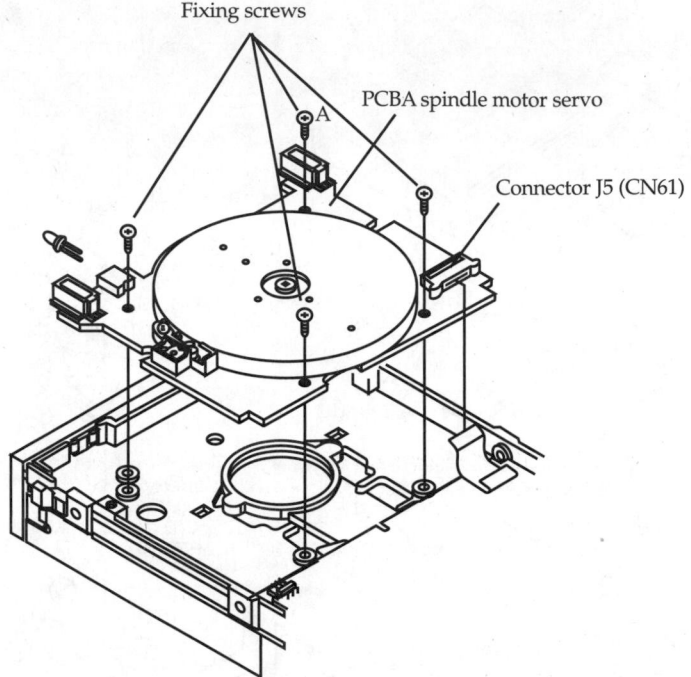

**FIGURE 19-5**    Underside view of a floppy drive spindle motor assembly (Courtesy of Teac America, Inc.)

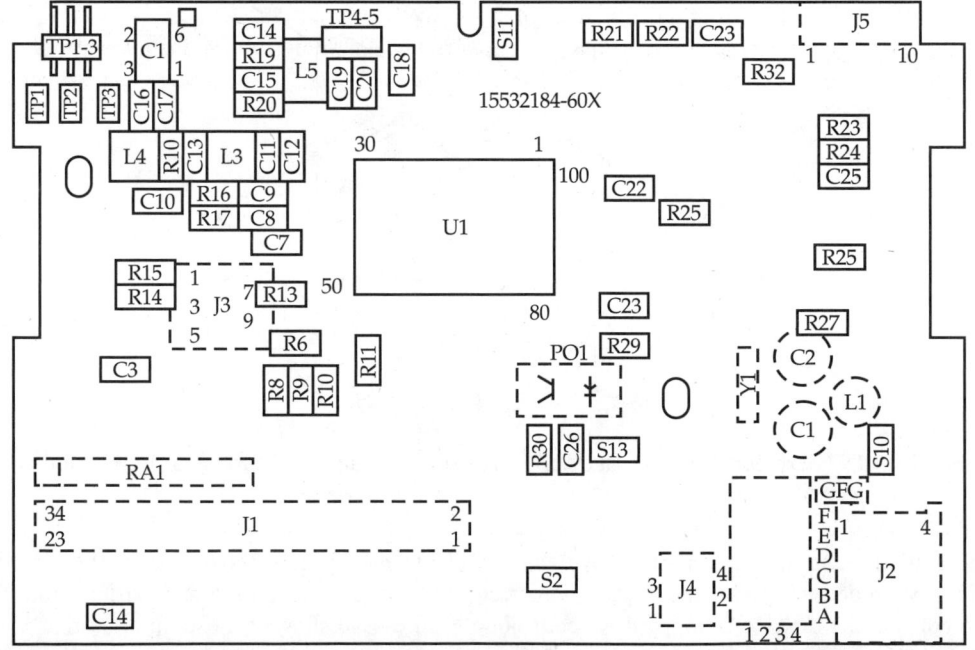

**FIGURE 19-6**    Typical floppy drive main logic/interface board (Courtesy of Teac America, Inc.)

on Figure 19-4), also sometimes called a head carriage assembly, holds a set of two R/W heads. Head 0 is the lower head (underside of the disk), and head 1 is on top. A head stepping motor (number 12) is added to ensure even and consistent movement between tracks. A threaded rod at the motor end is what actually moves the heads. A mechanical damper (number 5) helps to smooth the disk's travel into or out of the drive. Figure 19-7 shows a close-up of the R/W heads and stepping motor.

When a disk is inserted through the bezel, the disk is restrained by a disk clamp assembly (number 2 in Figure 19-4). To eject the disk, you would press the ejector button (number 19), which pushes a slider mechanism (number 3). When the ejector button is fully depressed, the disk will disengage from the spindle and pop out of the drive. For 5.25-inch drives, the disk is released whenever the drive door is opened. Your particular drive may contain other miscellaneous components. Finally, the entire upper portion of a drive can be covered by a metal shield (number 1).

## Drive Electronics

Proper drive operation depends on the intimate cooperation between magnetic media, electromechanical devices, and dedicated electronics. Floppy drive electronics is responsible for two major tasks: controlling the drive's physical operations and managing the flow of data into or out of the drive. These tasks are not nearly as simple as they sound, but the sleek, low-profile drives in today's computer systems are a far cry from the clunky, full-height drives found in early systems. Older drives needed a large number of chips spanning several boards that had to be fitted to the chassis. However, the floppy drive in your computer right now is probably implemented with only a few highly integrated chips that are neatly surface mounted on two small, opposing PC boards. This part of the chapter discusses the drive's operating circuits. A complete block diagram for a Teac 3.5-inch floppy drive is illustrated in Figure 19-8 (shown with a floppy disk *inserted*).

Write-protect sensors are used to detect the position of a disk's file-protect tab. For 3.5-inch disks, the write-protect notch must be covered to allow both read and write operations. If the notch is open, the disk can only be read. Optoisolators are commonly used as write-protect sensors, because an open notch will easily allow light through, while a closed notch will cut off the light path.

Before the drive is allowed to operate at all, a disk must be inserted properly and interlocked with the spindle. A disk-in-place sensor detects the presence or absence of a disk. Like the write-protect sensor,

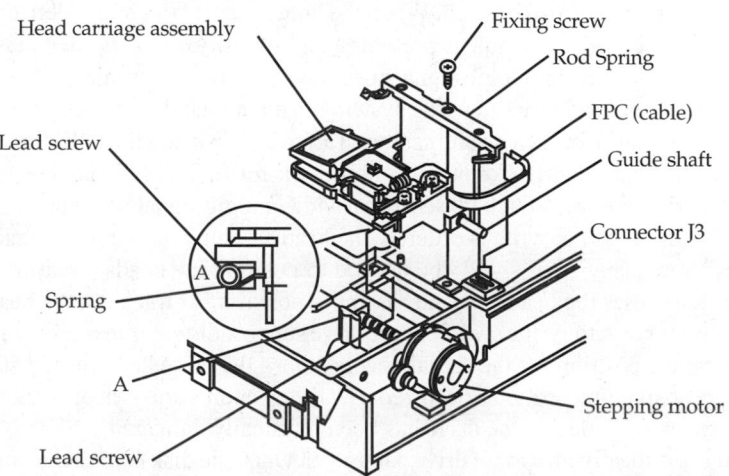

**FIGURE  19-7**    Detailed view of a R/W head and stepping motor (Courtesy of Teac America, Inc.)

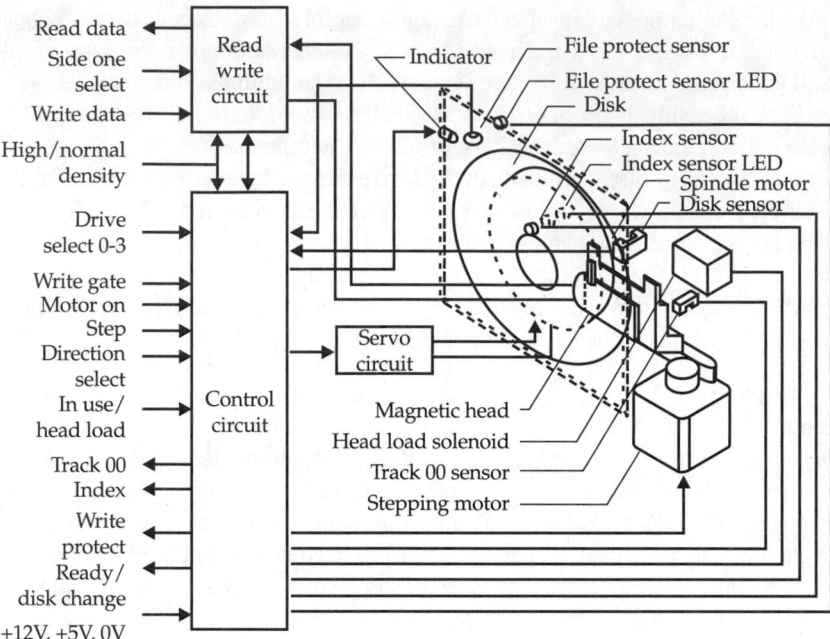

**FIGURE 19-8** Block diagram of a floppy drive (Courtesy of Teac America, Inc.)

disk sensors are often mechanical switches that are activated by disk contact. If drive access is attempted without a disk in place, the sensor causes the drive's logic to induce a DOS "Disk Not Ready" error code. It is not unusual to find an optoisolator acting as a disk-in-place sensor.

The electronics of a 3.5-inch drive must be able to differentiate whether the disk contains normal (double) density or high-density media. A high-density sensor looks for the hole that is found near the top of all high-density disk bodies. A mechanical switch is typically used to detect the high-density hole, but a separate LED/detector pair may also be used. When the hole is absent (a double-density disk), the switch is activated upon disk insertion. If the hole is present (a high-density disk), the switch is not actuated. All switch conditions are translated into logic signals used by the drive electronics.

Before disk data can be read or written, the system must read the disk's boot sector information and FAT. Programs and data can be broken up and scattered all over a disk, but the FAT must always be located at a known location so that the drive knows where to look for it. The FAT is always located on track 00—the first track of disk side 0. A track 00 sensor provides a logic signal when the heads are positioned over track 00. Each time a read or write is ordered, the head assembly is stepped to track 00. Although a drive "remembers" how many steps should be needed to position the heads precisely over track 00, an optoisolator or switch senses the head carriage assembly position. At track 00, the head carriage should interrupt the optoisolator or actuate the switch. If the drive supposedly steps to track 00 and there is no sensor signal to confirm the position (or the signal occurs *before* the drive has finished stepping), the drive assumes that a head-positioning error has occurred. Head step counts and sensor outputs virtually always agree unless the sensor has failed or the drive has been physically damaged.

Spindle speed is a critically important drive parameter. Once the disk has reached its running velocity (usually 300 or 360 rpm), the drive must maintain that velocity for the duration of the disk access process.

Unfortunately, simply telling the spindle motor to move is no guarantee that the motor is turning—a sensor is required to measure the motor's speed. This is the *index sensor*. Signals from an index sensor are fed back to the drive electronics, and spindle speed is adjusted to maintain a constant rotation. Most drives use optoisolators as index sensors. They work by detecting the motion of small slots cut in a template or the spindle rotor itself. When a disk is spinning, the output from an index sensor is a fast logic pulse sent along to the drive electronics. Keep in mind that some index sensors are magnetic. A magnetic sensor typically operates by detecting the proximity of small slots in a template or the spindle rotor, but the pulse output is essentially identical to that of the optoisolator.

## Floppy Drive Interface

The drive must receive control and data signals from the computer and deliver status and data signals back to the computer as required. The series of connections between a floppy disk PC board and the floppy disk controller circuit is known as the *physical interface*. The advantage to using a standard interface is that various drives made by different manufacturers can be mixed and matched by computer designers. A floppy drive working in one computer will operate properly in another computer regardless of the manufacturer as long as the same physical interface scheme is being used.

Floppy drives use a physical interface that includes two cables: a power cable and a signal cable. Both cable connections are illustrated in Figure 19-9, and Table 19-2 lists the pin assignments. The classical power connector is a 4-pin Molex connector, although many low-profile drives used in current computer models employ a low-profile 4-pin connector. Floppy drives require two voltage levels: +5.0 Vdc for logic and +12.0 Vdc for motors. The return (ground) for each supply is also provided at the connector. The signal connector is typically a 34-pin *insulation displacement connector* (IDC or "ribbon") cable. Notice that all odd-numbered pins are ground lines, while the even-numbered pins carry active signals. Logic signals are all TTL-level signals.

In Table 19-2, the small dash (-) before certain signal names indicates an "active low" logic state. For example, pin 2 is the Normal/-High-Density signal. When the signal is "logic 1", the drive is in Normal mode. When the signal is "logic 0", the drive is in High Density mode.

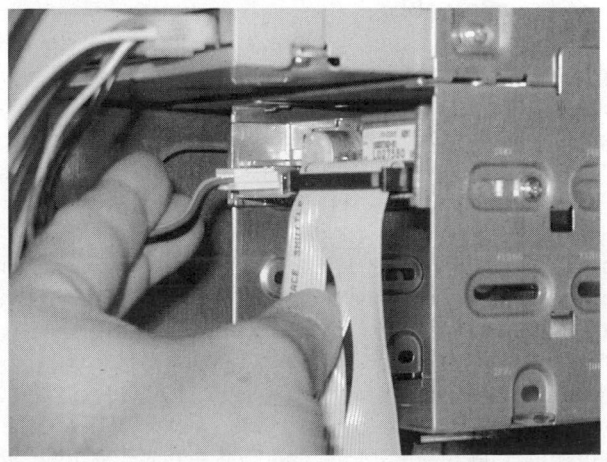

**FIGURE 19-9** Cable connections for a standard 34-pin floppy drive interface

**TABLE 19-2     PIN ASSIGNMENTS FOR THE STANDARD 34-PIN FDD INTERFACE**

| DESCRIPTION | PIN | PIN | DESCRIPTION |
| --- | --- | --- | --- |
| Normal/-High-Density | 2 | 1 | Ground |
| In Use/-Head Load | 4 | 3 | Ground |
| -Drive Select 3 | 6 | 5 | Ground |
| -Index | 8 | 7 | Ground |
| -Drive Select 0 | 10 | 9 | Ground |
| -Drive Select 1 | 12 | 11 | Ground |
| -Drive Select 2 | 14 | 13 | Ground |
| -Motor On | 16 | 15 | Ground |
| -Direction | 18 | 17 | Ground |
| -Step | 20 | 19 | Ground |
| Write Data | 22 | 21 | Ground |
| -Write Gate | 24 | 23 | Ground |
| -Track 00 | 26 | 25 | Ground |
| -Write Protect | 28 | 27 | Ground |
| Read Data | 30 | 29 | Ground |
| -Side Select | 32 | 31 | Ground |
| Disk Change/-Ready | 34 | 33 | Ground |

In a system with more than one floppy drive, the particular destination drive must be selected before any read or write is attempted. A drive is selected using the appropriate "drive select" line (drive select 0 to 3) on pins 10, 12, 14, and 6 respectively. For notebook or sub-notebook systems where only one floppy drive is used, only drive select 0 is used. The remaining select inputs may simply be disconnected. The spindle motor servo circuit is controlled through the "motor on" signal (pin 16). When pin 16 is logic 0, the spindle motor should *spin up* (approach a stable operating speed). The media must be spinning at the proper rate before reading or writing can take place.

To move the R/W heads, the host computer must specify the number of steps a head carriage assembly must move, and the direction in which steps must occur. A "direction select" signal (pin 18) tells the coil driver circuit whether the heads should be moved inward (toward the spindle) or outward (away from the spindle). The "step" signal (pin 20) provides the pulse sequence that actually steps the head motor in the desired direction. The combination of step and direction select controls can position the R/W heads over the disk very precisely. The "side select" control pin (pin 32) determines whether head 0 or head 1 is active for reading or writing—only one side of the disk can be manipulated at a time.

Two signals are needed to write data to a disk. The "write gate" signal (pin 24) is logic 0 when writing is to occur, and logic 1 when writing is inhibited (or reading). After the write gate is asserted, data can be written to the disk over the "write data" line (pin 22). When reading, the data that is extracted from the disk is delivered from the "read data" line (pin 30).

Each of the drive's sensor conditions are sent over the physical interface. The "track 00" signal (pin 26) is logic 0 whenever the head carriage assembly is positioned over track 00. The "write protect" line (pin 28) is logic 0 whenever the disk's write-protect notch is in place. Writing is inhibited whenever the write protect signal is asserted. The "index" signal (pin 8) supplies a chain of pulses from the index sensor.

Media type is indicated by the "normal/high-density" sensor (pin 2). The status of the disk-in-place sensor is indicated over the "disk change ready" line (pin 34).

# FLOPPY DRIVE INSTALLATION AND REPLACEMENT

Unlike many of the various peripherals and drives that are now available for a PC, floppy drives are almost universal in their design and features, meaning you usually have very little to consider because the drives are all the same. However, you must concern yourself with the following three issues. After you've selected the drive, installation should be very straightforward.

## Drive Bay Space

The trend toward smaller, low-profile enclosures has put a lot of pressure on available drive space. Given that many systems are already fitted with a floppy drive, hard drive, and CD-ROM/R/RW drive, rarely is a fourth bay available for even a second hard drive. One of the first problems when planning for a new floppy drive is to locate a 3.5-inch external drive bay. If you do not have an external drive bay available, you may be able to move a hard drive to an internal drive bay. This relocates the hard drive and frees an external drive bay for another floppy drive. If you cannot free a drive bay for another floppy drive, you may need to consider a larger case (such as a tower case with more external drive bays), use an external "USB" floppy drive (such as the Teac FD05PUB at www.teac.com/DSPD/USBFloppy.htm ), or remove another unneeded drive to make space for the floppy.

> Today, some systems (e.g. "diskless workstations") are eliminating floppy drives in favor of bootable CD-RW drives, but the vast majority of systems sold continue to offer a single 3.5-inch FDD.

## BIOS Compatibility

One problem with old PC/AT (i286) and early i386 systems was that their BIOS often did not support the high-density 3.5-inch drive format. The drive could be read from and written to properly, but the BIOS would only allow disks to be formatted to 720KB (instead of 1.44MB). The solution to this incompatibility has been either to upgrade the BIOS (to a version later than 11/85) or to use the DRIVER.SYS utility in DOS to explicitly specify the physical drive as a high-density device. If you suspect that DRIVER.SYS is needed to support a 3.5-inch high-density floppy drive on an older PC, open your CONFIG.SYS file and try a command line such as:

```
device=c:\dos\driver.sys /D:1 /F:7
```

This command line creates a new "logical" floppy drive that is actually the same physical floppy drive specified by the /D switch (0=A:, 1=B:). The /F switch determines the type of drive to be created. In this case, a value of 7 indicates a 3.5-inch 1.44MB drive. Check your DOS manual for additional parameters. This problem has been completely eliminated in virtually all subsequent BIOS releases after late 1985 and early 1986, but it can cause some confusion when dealing with very old PCs.

You may also encounter BIOS problems on older systems when using a 2.88MB "super high-density" (or SHD) floppy drive. Verify that the BIOS can support a 2.88MB floppy drive, and remember to update the CMOS Setup to reflect the 2.88MB unit. If you do not have an option for a 2.88MB FDD available in the CMOS Setup, this may be a tipoff that the system doesn't support it—a BIOS upgrade may be necessary to correct the problem.

## Power Connections

A power supply only offers a limited number of drive power connectors. Small systems may not have a free drive power connector for another floppy drive. When this occurs, you may use a Y-splitter cable to add another power connector. However, place the Y cable in with the existing floppy drive (never split power from critical drives such as the hard drive). If you're simply replacing a defective floppy, just reuse the existing power connector. Also check for the low-profile 4-pin floppy power connector—you can't use this connector with any other drives.

## Typical Installation

In most cases, installing a second floppy drive is a three-step process: configure the drive jumper(s), mount and cable the drive, and configure the new drive in CMOS. Although a floppy drive installation is often a quick and painless procedure—even for a novice—there are a few nuances that you should be aware of. When followed carefully, this process can typically be completed in under 30 minutes. If you're simply replacing an old or defective floppy drive, remove the old drive first, and then follow the procedures outlined next.

 It's normally a good idea to perform a complete system backup of your hard drives before attempting any kind of drive work. Although floppy drive installation should **not** affect your hard drives in any way, backups will protect your data and system configuration from accidental data loss.

**Prepare the System**   Turn the system off and unplug it from the AC receptacle before proceeding. Remove the screws holding the outer cover and place them aside in a safe place. Gently remove the PC's outer cover and set it aside (out of the path of normal floor traffic). You should now be able to look into the PC and observe the open drive bay, the motherboard, and any expansion boards and drives that are installed.

 Remember to use an anti-static wrist strap whenever working inside a PC. This will prevent accidental static discharge, which can damage the computer's delicate electronics.

**Prepare the Drive Bay**   Now that the outer cover is removed, you should open the desired drive bay. In many cases, this is as simple as just removing the plastic bezel that covers an empty bay (the bezel will usually pop right out). If you must relocate an existing drive, things get a bit more complicated. First, decide where the drive (almost always a hard drive) will be relocated—often to an internal bay in the rear of the PC. You can then remove the mounting screws, disconnect the power and signal cables from the hard drive, and slide the hard drive out of the bay. Remount the hard drive in the internal bay, and gently secure each screw into place. (Be careful not to overtighten the screws.) Reattach the power and signal cables to the hard drive. Pay particular attention when connecting the signal cable. If the cable is installed backward, the hard drive will not function. The red or blue stripe along one side of the ribbon cable always marks pin 1.

The procedure is a bit different when replacing an existing floppy drive. Unbolt the existing drive, disconnect the power and signal cables, and slide the old drive out of the bay and set it aside carefully. If you have a good-quality antistatic bag available, seal the old drive in the antistatic bag. At this point, you should have an open drive bay. Take a quick inventory and make sure that you have a floppy signal cable and power connector available. You may need a Y-splitter connector to tap power from another drive.

 When using a Y-splitter to tap power from another drive, never split power from a hard drive. This can cause erratic drive (and system) operation.

**Set the Floppy Jumpers**    Before installing the new drive, remove it from any protective packaging and locate any jumpers or DIP switches on the drive. A manual will be important here. It will be necessary to set at least four conditions: the drive select jumper, the disk change jumper, the media sensor jumper, and the terminating resistors.

The drive select (or DS) jumper allows the drive to be set as drive 0, 1, 2, or 3. Although most XT and AT controllers support four floppy drives, each cable supports only two. As a general rule, you will set both the drives as B: (you'll see why below). However, interpreting the jumper selections is not always intuitive, because different manufacturers mark the jumpers differently. For example, instead of 0, 1, 2, and 3, a drive may be labeled 1, 2, 3, and 4. Other variations include DS0 and DS1, or DS1 and DS2. As a rule of thumb, the lowest designation is generally considered to be drive A:, the next highest digit is considered drive B:, and so on. Since just about all floppy drive cables use a twist between the two floppy drive connectors, both floppy drives can be set to the second jumper position (drive B:). As a consequence, the twist will automatically swap the endmost drive to A:. If in doubt, and there's a twist in the cable, set the drive select jumpers to B:. Now, if there is no twist in the floppy cable (a very rare occurrence), be sure to set the endmost drive to A:, and set the middle drive to B:. (Since this is a daisy-chain configuration, you could actually reverse this order, but it is not traditional.)

Terminating resistors add another wrinkle to the drive setup. As with many other daisy-chain cable applications, terminating resistors are used at both ends of the signal cable to establish ideal signal characteristics. Normally, floppy drives come equipped with terminating resistors installed. Since most systems use a single drive installed at the end of the cable (as drive A:), this is generally a good default. When installing a single drive, be sure that the drive has terminating resistors installed. When installing a second floppy drive as drive A:, be sure it has terminating resistors in place, and check that the second drive (in the middle cable position) has no terminating resistors. When installing a second floppy drive as drive B:, be sure that the terminating resistors are removed.

 Although the "middle" (B:) floppy drive should have its terminating resistors removed or disabled, this is not always necessary because of the low-frequency signals on the floppy drive cable. In most cases, you could leave the middle (B:) floppy drive with its terminating resistors in place.

The disk change jumper is a vital part of almost all contemporary drives. This signal tells the PC when a disk is removed so that when a new disk is inserted and read, the directory information will be cached in the system. The disk change signal should be enabled on all drives except for old 5.25-inch 360KB drives. Finally the media sensor (on 1.44MB and 2.88MB drives) jumper should be enabled wherever possible. The sensor allows the drive to detect whether a 760KB, 1.44MB, or 2.88MB disk is installed.

**Mount the New Floppy Drive**    Now that the floppy drive is configured, slide it gently into the open drive bay. Line up the four mounting holes and screw the drive in carefully. Be sure not to tighten the mounting screws excessively, which can warp the drive's frame and cause R/W problems or premature drive failure. Make it a point to use screws of the proper size and length to do the job.

**Connect Power and Signal Cables**    Once the drive is installed and mounted securely, connect the power and signal cables as required. The 4-pin power cable is relatively foolproof because of its keyed shape. For the signal cable, however, take care to install the card edge or IDC-type connector in the correct orientation. If the signal cable is installed backward, the drive will not work (the system may not even boot). The red or blue stripe along one side of the ribbon cable always represents pin 1.

**Update CMOS Settings**    If the steps are performed correctly, the new floppy drive should now be fully installed. Before you can actually use the drive, you must update the system's CMOS Setup entries to accommodate the new drive. Make sure that any tools or extra hardware are removed from the system, reattach the AC cord to the power supply, and then reboot the computer. As the system boots, start the CMOS Setup routine and adjust the configuration as needed for your new floppy drive. You'll need to specify whether a 5.25-inch 360KB, 5.25-inch 1.2MB, 3.5-inch 720KB, 3.5-inch 1.44MB, or 3.5-inch 2.88MB floppy drive is installed. If you have updated or replaced an old drive, make sure that the drive parameters reflect the new device. If you've added a second drive, enter the appropriate parameters for that new drive. When the settings are correct, save the system CMOS and reboot the system so that your changes can take effect.

**Test the Drive**    Insert a known-good disk in the drive. If the installation is correct, you should see the new drive designator under DOS, as an available option under the Windows Explorer, or as a new drive entry when double-clicking on My Computer on the Windows 9x/Me/XP desktop (see Figure 19-10). Try writing and reading a few files from the drive. You might also try formatting a blank disk in the new drive. If these tests are successful, you can be confident that the new drive is working properly. Be sure to remove

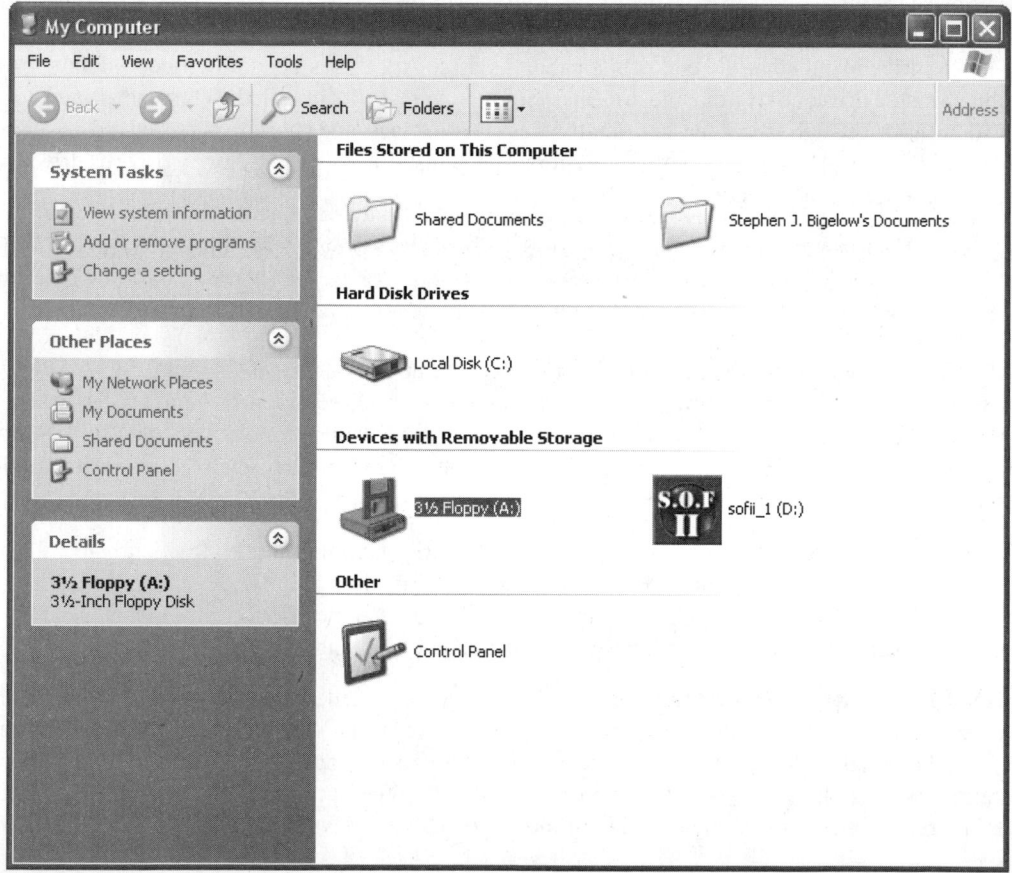

**FIGURE  19-10**    Checking for the presence of a floppy drive in My Computer

any tools or hardware from the system, and then reinstall the system's outer housings. Do not use excessive pressure to tighten the screws. Try the drive one more time, and return the system to service.

## Reversing Floppy Drive Assignments

Reversing the letter assignments of your floppy drives is sometimes necessary. This often happens when you wish to boot from a floppy drive that is not in a boot order supported by the BIOS. For example, you may want to change the boot order if you have a 3.5-inch 2.88MB drive as A: and a 3.5-inch 1.44MB drive as B:, and the boot order doesn't support booting from the 2.88MB A: drive. Fortunately, you can easily reverse the drive order by reversing the drives physically and logically. Remember to power-down and unplug the computer before beginning.

**Leave the Drive Jumpers in Place**   Remember that for most PCs, both floppy drives are jumpered as B:. (It is the "flip" in the floppy drive cable that turns the end-most drive to A:.) If your floppy drive cable does indeed have a flip, you can leave the floppy drives jumpered the way they are. The only time you'll need to reverse the drive's ID jumpers is when there is no flip in the cable, and each drive must be jumpered with a unique ID.

**Exchange the Floppy Cable Connections**   Reconnect the floppy drive cable by placing the middle drive at the end, and the endmost drive at the middle. Depending on the way each drive is arranged in your system's case (and the amount of slack in the floppy cable), it may be necessary to actually exchange the floppy drives in the drive bays also. If this is the case, you should disconnect the power cables from the floppy drives, unbolt each drive, reinstall each drive in the opposite drive bay, and then reattach the power and signal cables. Now is also a good time to check all connections of the floppy signal cable. If the cable is loose or appears damaged, it should be replaced.

If the middle drive had terminating resistors disabled, you may need to enable those terminating resistors when you place that drive at the end of the cable (A:), and disable the terminating resistors on the drive that you swapped to the middle of the cable (B:).

**Reverse the Drive Assignments in CMOS**   When you first reapply power to the PC, you will probably receive an error message indicating that the equipment detected does not match the equipment specified in the CMOS Setup. This error occurs because the physical drives are now reversed, but the CMOS still "expects" to find the floppy drives in their original positions. You'll need to start the CMOS Setup and reverse the floppy drive assignments. For example, if you had a 3.5-inch 2.88MB floppy as A: and a 3.5-inch 1.44MB floppy as B:, you'll need to assign a 3.5-inch 1.44MB floppy as A: and a 3.5-inch 2.88MB floppy as B: after you make the physical drive swap. Save your changes and reboot the computer so that your changes can take effect. Test both drives to verify that each is working.

# Floppy Troubleshooting

In most cases, floppy drives (and their media) should provide long and reliable service. However, there are circumstances when a drive installation or replacement doesn't go as planned, or you're faced with a faulty drive on a customer's system. This part of the chapter examines some troubleshooting guidelines for floppy drives, and offers some solutions for a range of specific symptoms.

## CARING FOR A FLOPPY DISK

As a rule, floppy disks are rugged and reliable media that we often take for granted. Still, you do need to exercise some good judgement and common sense when handling and storing disks. The following tips may help:

■ *Be careful of magnetic fields.* Remember that disks are magnetic media, so the influence of any stray magnetic fields (e.g., a monitor's degaussing coil or a bulk take eraser) can damage the data and require you to reformat the disk. Store disks in a location well away from magnets and magnetic fields.

■ *Be careful of extreme environments.* Heat and cold can damage the disk media. For example, leaving a disk in a car where it can freeze in the winter or bake in the summer will undoubtedly damage the disk. You should allow the disk to stabilize for 30 minutes or so when taking it in from heat/cold.

■ *Don't touch the media.* That metal shroud covering the media is there to prevent dust, fingerprints, and other debris from fouling the disk. Unlike CD-ROMs, you cannot clean the disk media if it gets dirty.

## CREATING A WINDOWS STARTUP DISK

When troubleshooting a PC, it is often necessary to boot a system from the floppy drive in order to run real-mode diagnostics. This is particularly important when a hard drive fails and there are no other bootable devices in the system. If you don't already have a boot disk, you can make one through Windows 9*x*/Me/XP. Use the following steps to create a boot disk under Windows 9*x*/Me:

1. Click Start | Settings | Control Panel.
2. Double-click the Add/Remove Programs icon and select the Startup Disk tab.
3. Put a blank floppy disk in the drive and click the Create Disk button.
4. Windows will format the disk and place the necessary startup files on it (including real-mode support for your CD-ROM drive).

Creating a bootable disk under Windows XP is similar:

1. Insert a formatted disk in the floppy drive.
2. Click Start | My Computer.
3. Right-click the floppy disk icon and select Format.
4. In the Format dialog box (see Figure 19-11), check the "Create an MS-DOS startup disk" box.
5. Click Start. The formatting process will proceed automatically.

Once the disk is created, take a moment to test the disk by booting from it. However, you should remember that Windows XP does not add real-mode support files—it simply formats the disk. This means the Windows 9*x*/Me startup disk is more useful than one created under Windows XP.

Windows XP does **not** allow formatting 720KB disks (though it will read/write them properly); only 1.44MB formatting is supported in Windows XP.

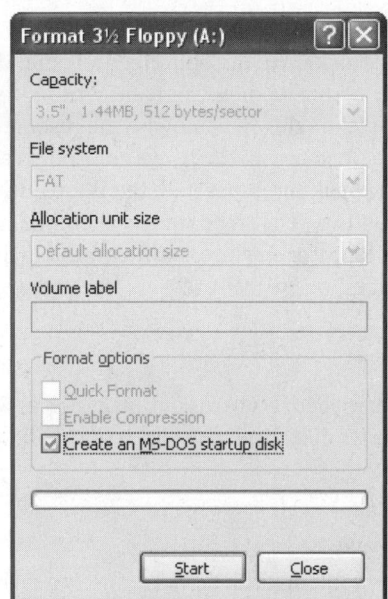

**FIGURE 19-11**    Opting to create a bootable disk when formatting a disk under Windows XP

# FLOPPY TROUBLESHOOTING GUIDELINES UNDER WINDOWS

Today, a great deal of everyday work takes place under Windows 9$x$/Me/XP. As a result, floppy drive problems are often first noticed under Windows. When Windows reports trouble reading a floppy drive, try the steps below to identify and resolve the issue through Windows.

## Clean the Floppy Drive

Remember that the heads of a floppy drive actually contact the surface of disk media. Over time, dust, debris, and residual oxides from the disks coat the read/write heads. This eventually leads to simple read/write errors as the heads become "wedged" away from the disk surfaces. You can suspect a problem with the heads when disks read fine in other drives, but produce read/write errors in the suspect drive. Fortunately, head cleaning is a very effective means of correcting common read/write problems.

Traditionally, cleaning was performed manually using a little fresh isopropyl alcohol on a thin swab. The technician would then gently rub any accumulations of debris from the heads (a process that might be repeated several times), and allow ample time for residual alcohol to dry before testing the drive again. Today, technicians often rely on disk cleaning "kits" that use a specially designed floppy with a porous fiber disk inside. The technician can apply a few drops of cleaning solution to the fiber, insert the disk, and run several read cycles (e.g., by trying to open the disk in Windows Explorer). If cleaning does not help, the FDD should be replaced.

A cleaning disk only has a limited number of uses. Be sure to mark the disk each time it is used, and discard the disk after it's reached the maximum number of uses.

## Check for Device Conflicts

Device conflicts between the floppy disk drive or controller and other devices in the system (reported by the Device Manager) can cause problems reading from and writing to floppy disks. You can generally resolve device conflict problems by changing or removing the resources from Device Manager that are causing the conflict. Typical conflicts occur with hard drive controller cards, video cards, and COM ports.

Open the Device Manager and check for issues with the floppy drive or controller. Correct any conflicts or other device issues that you may find, reboot the system, then try the floppy drive again. If the problems persist, try removing the floppy drive and controller through the Device Manager, then reboot to allow Windows to redetect the devices, or use the Add New Hardware wizard to redetect and reinstall the devices from scratch.

## Suspect Your Disk(s)

One or more of your disks may be damaged. Use a disk utility (such as ScanDisk) to test the disk for damage, or try a known-good, high-quality disk. You may also try the following command from a DOS command prompt:

```
C:\> copy a:\*.* nul          <Enter>
```

For example, if you are having problems with drive A:, insert a disk you are having problems with in drive A: and type the command as shown. This command copies the files on the disk to a null device. If there is a problem copying the files, error messages appear on the screen, and that disk is probably defective. You can confirm this by trying the disk in other systems.

> Never use a disk utility that is not compliant with your version of Windows. Non-compliant disk utilities can damage DMF (compressed) disks. The Windows ScanDisk tool recognizes DMF disks and does not damage them.

## Suspect Your Tape Backup

Floppy problems are known to occur under Windows when using an Irwin tape backup unit under Windows 9*x* (this is not known to happen with later versions of Windows). Windows 9*x* setup should remove the following statement from the [386Enh] section of the SYSTEM.INI file:

```
device=<path>\VIRWT.386
```

If you reinstall the Irwin tape backup software after you install Windows 9*x*, this statement is placed in the SYSTEM.INI file again, and can cause conflicts with floppy disk access in Windows. When this occurs, you must comment-out that line in SYSTEM.INI.

## Check the CMOS Setup

Reboot your computer and verify that the floppy drive entries in your CMOS Setup are correct. If not, Windows will not be able to recognize your floppy drive hardware. If you must make changes to your CMOS Setup, remember to save your changes as you exit.

# FLOPPY SYMPTOMS

Floppy drives will usually give you years of reliable service, but there are some cases when the drive, controller, media (and even the system's configuration) can cause problems. When trouble occurs, you can refer to the symptoms below to help you isolate and correct the problem.

**SYMPTOM 19-1**    **The floppy drive is completely dead**    The system boots, but the disk does not even initialize when inserted. This behavior can be caused by a number of important problems, so consider each possibility carefully before acting.

■ *Check the floppy disk.* Make sure the disk is properly inserted into the floppy drive assembly. If the disk does not enter and seat just right within the drive, disk access will be impossible. Try several different disks to ensure that the test disk is not defective. It may be necessary to partially disassemble the computer to access the drive and see the overall assembly. Free or adjust any jammed assemblies or linkages to correct disk insertion. If you cannot get disks to insert properly, replace the floppy drive.

■ *Check the drive power.* Loose connectors or faulty cable wiring can easily disable a floppy drive. Use your multimeter to measure DC voltages at the power connector. Place your meter's ground lead on pin 2 and measure +12 Vdc at pin 1. Ground your meter on pin 3 and measure +5 Vdc at pin 4. If either or both of these voltages is low or missing, troubleshoot your computer power supply or replace the supply.

■ *Check the signal cable.* Verify that the drive's 34-pin ribbon cable is attached securely at the drive(s) and at the drive controller. Reattach the signal cable if it's loose, and try another signal cable if necessary.

■ *Replace the floppy drive.* If the problem persists, chances are that the floppy drive is defective (perhaps the disk-in-place sensor has failed). Try replacing the floppy drive with a known-good drive from another system.

■ *Replace the floppy drive controller.* If a new floppy drive still does not resolve the problem, you may have a defective floppy drive controller circuit. If so, you may also receive a floppy drive or controller error from the system BIOS at boot time. Try disabling the existing floppy controller (usually located on the system motherboard) and install an expansion card controller (with only the floppy controller portion enabled).

**SYMPTOM 19-2**    **The floppy drive rotates a disk, but will not seek to the desired track**
This type of symptom generally suggests that the head-positioning stepping motor is jammed or defective, but all other floppy drive functions are working properly.

■ *Check the drive for obstructions.* Carefully inspect the head-positioning assembly to be certain that there are no broken parts or obstructions that could jam the read/write heads. You may wish to examine the mechanical system with a disk inserted to be certain that the trouble is not a disk alignment problem that may be interfering with head movement. Gently remove any obstructions that you may find. Be careful not to accidentally misalign any linkages or mechanical components in the process of clearing an obstruction.

■ *Check the drive power.* Remove any disk from the drive and reconnect the drive's signal and power cables. Apply power to the computer and measure drive voltages with your multimeter. Ground your multimeter on pin 2 of the power connector and measure +12 Vdc at pin 1. Move the meter ground to pin 3 and measure +5 Vdc on pin 4. If either voltage is low or absent, troubleshoot your computer power supply or replace the supply.

■ *Check the signal cable.* Verify that the drive's 34-pin ribbon cable is attached securely at the drive(s) and at the drive controller. Reattach the signal cable if it's loose, and try another signal cable if necessary.

■ *Replace the floppy drive.* If the problem persists, chances are that the floppy drive is defective (perhaps the head-positioning system has failed). Try replacing the floppy drive with a known-good drive from another system.

■ *Replace the floppy drive controller.* If a new floppy drive still does not resolve the problem, you may have a defective floppy drive controller circuit. If so, you may also receive a floppy drive or controller error from the system BIOS at boot time. Try disabling the existing floppy controller and install an expansion card controller (with only the floppy controller portion enabled).

**SYMPTOM 19-3**    **The floppy drive heads seek properly, but the spindle does not turn**
This symptom suggests that the spindle motor is jammed or defective, but all other floppy drive functions are working properly.

■ *Check the drive for obstructions.* Power-down the computer and remove the floppy drive. Carefully inspect the spindle motor, drive belt (if used), and spindle assembly. Make certain that there are no broken parts or obstructions that could jam the spindle. If there is a belt between the motor and spindle, make sure the belt is reasonably tight—it should not slip. You should also examine the floppy drive with a disk inserted to be certain that the disk's insertion or alignment is not causing the problem. Double-check your observations using several different disks. Gently remove any obstruction(s) that you may find. Be careful not to cause any accidental damage in the process of clearing an obstruction. Do not add any lubricating agents to the assembly, but gently vacuum or wipe away any significant accumulations of dust or dirt.

■ *Check the drive power.* Remove any disk from the drive and reconnect the drive's signal and power cables. Apply power to the computer and measure drive voltages with your multimeter. Ground your multimeter on pin 2 of the power connector and measure +12 Vdc at pin 1. Move the meter ground to pin 3 and measure +5 Vdc on pin 4. If either voltage is low or absent, troubleshoot your computer power supply or replace the supply.

■ *Check the signal cable.* Verify that the drive's 34-pin ribbon cable is attached securely at the drive(s) and at the drive controller. Reattach the signal cable if it's loose, and try another signal cable if necessary.

■ *Replace the floppy drive.* If the problem persists, chances are that the floppy drive is defective (perhaps the spindle motor control system has failed). Try replacing the floppy drive with a known-good drive from another system.

■ *Replace the floppy drive controller.* If a new floppy drive still does not resolve the problem, you may have a defective floppy drive controller circuit. If so, you may also receive a floppy drive or controller error from the system BIOS at boot time. Try disabling the existing floppy controller and install an expansion card controller (with only the floppy controller portion enabled).

**SYMPTOM 19-4**    **The floppy drive will not read from/write to the disk**    All other operations appear normal. This type of problem can manifest itself in several ways, but your computer's operating system will usually inform you when a disk read or write error has occurred.

■ *Check the disk.* Begin by trying a known-good, properly formatted disk in your suspect drive. A faulty disk can generate some very perplexing read/write problems.

■ *Clean the floppy drive.* If a known-good disk does not resolve the problem, try cleaning the read/write heads thoroughly. Do not run the drive with a head-cleaning disk inserted for more than 30 seconds at a time, or you risk damaging the heads with excessive friction.

■ *Check the signal cable.* Verify that the drive's 34-pin ribbon cable is attached securely at the drive(s) and at the drive controller. Reattach the signal cable if it's loose, and try another signal cable if necessary.

■ *Replace the floppy drive.* If the problem persists, chances are that the floppy drive is defective (perhaps the head read/write system has failed). Try replacing the floppy drive with a known-good drive from another system.

■ *Replace the floppy drive controller.* If a new floppy drive still does not resolve the problem, you may have a defective floppy drive controller circuit. If so, you may also receive a floppy drive or controller error from the system BIOS at boot time. Try disabling the existing floppy controller and install an expansion card controller (with only the floppy controller portion enabled).

**SYMPTOM 19-5**    **The drive is able to write to a write-protected disk**    When this kind of problem occurs, it is almost always the drive itself that is defective. In many cases, the write-protect sensor has failed.

■ *Check the disk.* Remove and examine the disk itself to verify that it is actually write protected. If the disk is **not** write protected, write-protect it appropriately, and try the disk again. You might also try a different disk.

■ *Clean the floppy drive.* Try cleaning the drive by blowing clean compressed air into the drive (pay particular attention to cleaning off the write-protect sensor).

■ *Replace the floppy drive.* If the problem persists, chances are that the floppy drive is defective—perhaps the write-protect sensor or onboard drive electronics has failed. Try replacing the floppy drive with a known-good drive from another system.

**SYMPTOM 19-6**    **The drive can only recognize either high- or double-density media, but not both**    This type of problem usually appears in 3.5-inch drives during the disk format process when the drive must check the media type.

■ *Check the disk.* Verify that you're using the correct disk type. (This is actually a common oversight, because many generic disks are unmarked or marked obscurely.)

■ *Clean the floppy drive.* Try cleaning the drive by blowing clean compressed air into the drive (pay particular attention to cleaning off the "media type" sensor).

■ *Check the signal cable.* Verify that the drive's 34-pin ribbon cable is attached securely at the drive(s) and at the drive controller. Reattach the signal cable if it's loose, and try another signal cable if necessary.

■ *Replace the floppy drive.* If the problem persists, chances are that the floppy drive is defective—perhaps the media-type sensor or onboard drive electronics has failed. Try replacing the floppy drive with a known-good drive from another system.

**SYMPTOM 19-7**    **When a new disk is inserted in the drive, a directory from a previous disk appears**    You may have to reset/reboot the system in order to get the new disk to be recognized. This is the classic "phantom directory" problem and is usually due to a drive or cable fault.

■ *Check the signal cable.* Verify that the drive's 34-pin ribbon cable is attached securely at the drive(s) and at the drive controller. Reattach the signal cable if it's loose, and try another signal cable if necessary.

■ *Check the driver's jumpers.* If this is a new drive installation, check the floppy drive's jumpers. Some floppy drives allow the Disk Change signal to be enabled or disabled. Check the manufacturer's documentation for your particular drive, and make sure that the Disk Change signal is enabled.

■ *Replace the floppy drive.* If the problem persists, chances are that the floppy drive is defective—perhaps the disk change logic has failed in the drive's electronics. Try replacing the floppy drive with a known-good drive from another system.

If you suspect a phantom directory problem, do not initiate any writing to the disk. Its FAT table and directories could be overwritten, rendering the disk's contents inaccessible without careful data recovery procedures.

**SYMPTOM 19-8    Double-density (720KB) 3.5-inch disks are not working properly when formatted as high-density (1.44MB) disks**   This is a common problem when double-density disks are pressed into service as high-density disks. In practice, double-density disks use a lower-grade media than high-density disks, which makes double-density disks unreliable when used in high-density mode. Some good-quality disks will tolerate this misuse better than other lower-quality disks. As a general rule, do **not** use double-density disks as high-density disks.

**SYMPTOM 19-9    Your 3.5-inch high-density floppy disk cannot format high-density disks**   You can read and write to them just fine. This is a problem that plagues older computers (i286 and i386 systems) with after-market high-density drives added. The problem is a lack of BIOS support for high-density formatting—the system is just too old. In such a case, you have a choice. First, you can upgrade your motherboard BIOS to a version that directly supports 3.5-inch high-density disks. You could also use the DRIVER.SYS utility—a DOS driver that allows an existing 3.5-inch drive to be "redefined" as a new logical drive providing high-density support. A typical DRIVER.SYS command line would appear in CONFIG.SYS similar to this:

```
device = c:\dos\driver.sys /D:1
```

If you encounter this trouble on a newer system, the drive itself has probably failed (it may be unable to identify the media type) and should be replaced.

**SYMPTOM 19-10    The A: drive appears in My Computer even though no drive is installed**   When you double-click My Computer on a Windows 9*x*/Me system with no floppy disk drive installed, a removable disk (A:) appears (this is not known to occur under Windows XP). When you view the drives in Device Manager, no floppy disk drive is listed because none exists on the computer. This occurs because DOS always creates drive A: on a computer. When Windows starts, this information is sent to the real-mode manager (RMM). Unfortunately, this issue occurs by design, and no workaround is available.

**SYMPTOM 19-11    The floppy drive runs randomly while using the system**   This problem usually arises when a folder that includes a .PIF file that references a program file on a floppy disk drive is opened. For example, if you have a .PIF file with a command line such as **a:\edit.com** in the \Windows\Temp folder, your floppy disk drive may be active when you start the PC. Change the command-line reference in the Properties of the shortcut, or delete the shortcut in Windows 9*x*/Me:

1. Click Start, point to Find (or Search in Windows Me), and then click For Files Or Folders.
2. In the Named box (or "Search For Files Or Folders Named" in Windows Me), type **\*.lnk**, click the location you want to search in the Look In box, and then click Find Now.
3. Right-click a shortcut on the list of found files, click Properties, and then click the Program tab.

4. Delete any reference to drive A: or drive B: on the Command box or Working section, and then click OK. For example, if the command line reads **a:\edit.com**, simply change the line to read **edit.com**.

5. Repeat the last two steps until you have corrected all the shortcuts, and then quit the Find tool.

Windows XP provides you with another powerful search tool that can help locate potential problem shortcuts:

1. Click Start | Search.

2. The Search Results dialog box opens. Click "All files and folders".

3. In the "All or part of the filename" box, type **\*.lnk** and click Search.

4. Windows XP will search the drive and return each shortcut.

5. Right-click a shortcut on the list of found files, click Properties, and then click the Shortcut tab (see Figure 19-12).

6. Delete any reference to drive A: or drive B: in the Target or Start in box, and then click OK. For example, if the command line reads **a:\edit.com**, simply change the line to read **edit.com**.

7. Repeat the last two steps until you have corrected all the shortcuts to the A: or B: drives, and then quit the Find tool

This problem can also occur on other removable media besides floppy disks, such as Zip disks.

**SYMPTOM 19-12**  **You can't access the hard drive after booting from a disk**   After you start your Windows 9x/Me/XP computer from a floppy disk for troubleshooting purposes (or to install an operating system), you may see an "Invalid Drive Specification" error message when changing to the hard disk—even though the hard disk is correctly partitioned and formatted. This error usually means that you have a drive overlay program installed, and you did not follow the proper procedures to boot from an "overlay aware" floppy disk. When a drive overlay program is loaded, you cannot boot directly from a floppy disk if you want to be able to access the hard disk. You must first load the drive overlay program and then boot from the floppy disk. Check the documentation included with your drive overlay software for information about how to boot from a floppy disk and access the hard disk.

**SYMPTOM 19-13**  **The floppy controller prevents system hibernation or standby**
When your Windows Me system has been idle long enough to enter standby mode (or if you try to use standby mode manually), your computer refuses to enter standby mode or returns from standby mode immediately. You may also receive an error message such as this:

```
Your computer cannot hibernate or standby because the standard floppy disk
controller cannot enter into low-power state.
```

This is typically traced to a software issue, and is known to occur when Iomega Ditto Tools are installed on your computer. Ditto Tools installs drivers that prevent you from using suspend mode. To correct this problem, contact Iomega (www.iomega.com) to inquire about software updates and patches. To work around this issue temporarily, disable all power management features when you are using Ditto Tools (or uninstall the Ditto Tools software—though you will lose the features of your Ditto drive).

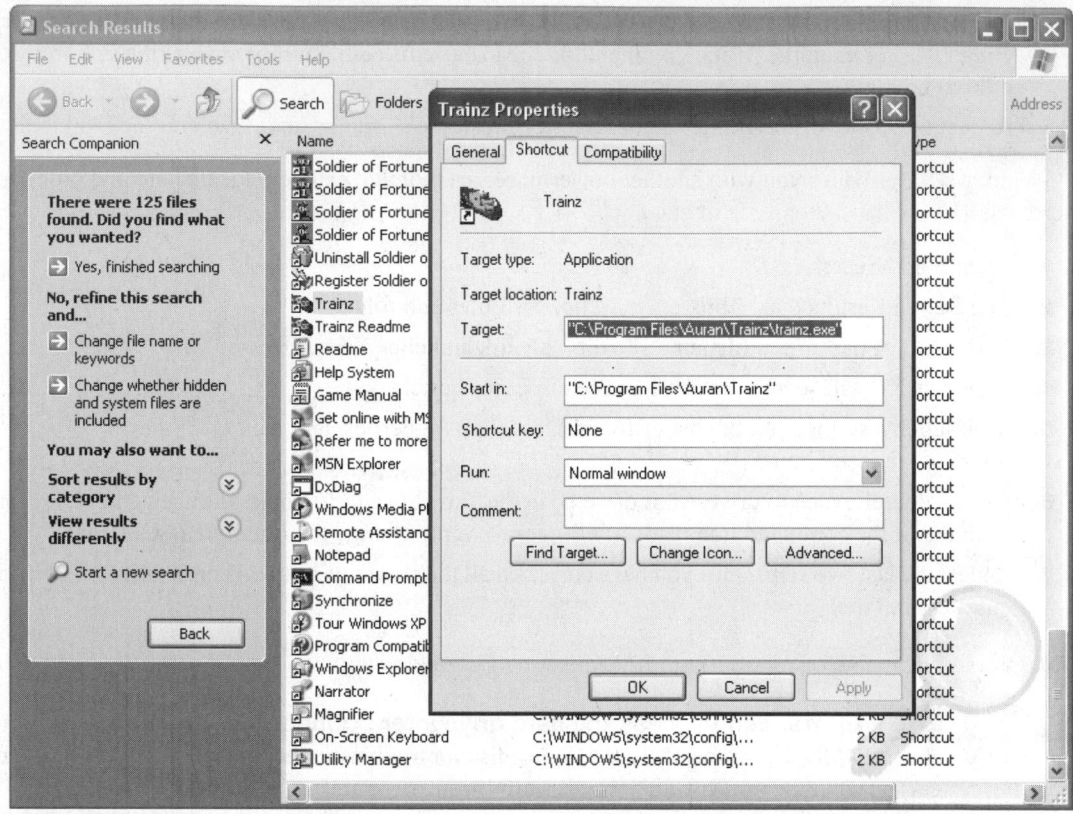

**FIGURE  19-12**    Using the Windows XP search tool to locate and correct shortcuts that link to a floppy drive

**SYMPTOM 19-14**    **There are no jumpers available on the floppy disk, so it is impossible to change settings**    This is not a problem as much as it is an inconvenience. Typically, you can expect "unjumpered" floppy disks to be set to the following specifications:

| Drive select | 1 (B: drive) |
|---|---|
| Disk change (pin 34) | Enabled |
| Frame ground | Enabled |

This configuration supports traditional single and dual (1.44MB) floppy drive systems using twisted floppy cables.

**SYMPTOM 19-15**    **When using a combination floppy drive (called a "combo drive"), one of the drives does not work, but the other works fine**    This problem is often caused by a drive fault. First, check the power connector. Make sure that both +5 volts and +12 volts are adequately provided to the drive through the 4-pin "mate-n-lock" connector. If the drive is receiving the proper power, the drive itself has almost certainly failed—try a new drive.

**SYMPTOM 19-16**    **DOS reports an error such as "Cannot read from drive A:"**    A disk is fully inserted in the drive, and the drive LED indicates that access is being attempted.

■ *Check the disk.* Begin by trying a known-good, properly formatted disk in your suspect drive. A faulty disk can generate some very perplexing read/write problems.

■ *Clean the floppy drive.* If a known-good disk does not resolve the problem, try cleaning the read/write heads thoroughly. Do not run the drive with a head-cleaning disk inserted for more than 30 seconds at a time, or you risk damaging the heads with excessive friction.

■ *Check the drive for obstructions.* Carefully inspect the spindle motor, drive belt (if used), and read/write head assembly. Make certain that there are no broken parts or obstructions that could jam the heads. You should also examine the floppy drive with a disk inserted to be certain that the disk's insertion or alignment is not causing the problem. Double-check your observations using several different disks. Gently remove any obstruction(s) that you may find. Be careful not to cause any accidental damage in the process of clearing an obstruction.

■ *Check the signal cable.* Verify that the drive's 34-pin ribbon cable is attached securely at the drive(s) and at the drive controller. Reattach the signal cable if it's loose, and try another signal cable if necessary.

■ *Replace the floppy drive.* If the problem persists, chances are that the floppy drive is defective (perhaps the head read/write system has failed). Try replacing the floppy drive with a known-good drive from another system.

■ *Replace the floppy drive controller.* If a new floppy drive still does not resolve the problem, you may have a defective floppy drive controller circuit. If so, you may also receive a floppy drive or controller error from the system BIOS at boot time. Try disabling the existing floppy controller and install an expansion card controller (with only the floppy controller portion enabled).

**SYMPTOM 19-17**    **Windows searches the floppy drive randomly when an application is launched**    You may see this problem when using Windows Explorer, and rebooting the system doesn't correct the trouble. In some cases, this occurs because the system is checking drive A:—often because an application is running that checks the drive. There are several common things that you can do to correct the trouble:

■ Try clearing the Documents menu.

■ Delete unwanted entries from the Run command (under the Start menu).

■ Check for viruses on the system.

■ Search for and edit/delete any .PIF files that point to programs on the floppy drive.

■ Open the Device Manager and delete the Generic Floppy Disk entry. When Windows restarts, it will redetect the drive, and the problem should go away.

Certain applications are known to cause this problem:

■ **Norton Navigator**    Try clearing Norton Navigator's run history (or disable the run history) and download any available bug fixes from Symantec.

■ **McAfee Antivirus**    Try disabling the Access and Shutdown options (in the Scan Disks On area of the Detection tab in the VShield Configuration Manager), or remove the program entirely.

■ **FirstAid**    Try removing this program or disabling its drive checking features.

- **Long Filenames for Windows**   Try downloading and installing any patches for the application.
- **HiJack for Windows**   Turn off the "Enable HiJack shell extensions" feature in the HiJack Control Panel.
- **Konica Picture Show**   Try removing this application outright.
- **Norton Antivirus 2000**   Turn off the options that scan the floppy drive during startup and shutdown.

**SYMPTOM 19-18**    **The floppy drive activity LED stays on as soon as the computer is powered up**    This is a classic signaling problem that occurs after changing or upgrading a drive system. In virtually all cases, one end of the drive cable has been inserted backward. Make sure that pin 1 on the 34-pin cable is aligned properly with the connector on both the drive and controller. If problems remain, the drive controller may have failed. This is rare, but try a new drive controller.

**SYMPTOM 19-19**    **You are unable to swap floppy drives so that A: becomes B:, and B: becomes A:**    This often happens on older systems when users want to make their 3.5-inch after-market B: drive into their A: drive, and relegate their aging 5.25-inch drive to B: instead.

- *Check the signal cable.* For floppy cables with a wire twist, the endmost connector is A:, and the connector prior to the twist is B:. Reverse the connectors at each floppy drive to reverse their identities.
- *Check the drive jumpers.* If the cable has no twist (this is rare), reset the jumper ID on each drive so that your desired A: drive is set to DS0 (Drive Select 0), and your desired B: drive is jumpered to DS1. If you accomplish this exchange, but one drive is not recognized, try a new floppy signal cable.
- *Check the CMOS settings.* You'll need to reverse the floppy drive entries for your A: and B: drives, and then reboot the system.

**SYMPTOM 19-20**    **The new drive does not work, or the system does not recognize the new drive**    This classic problem of the system not recognizing the newly installed drive is typically the result of incorrect or overlooked CMOS settings.

- *Check the CMOS settings.* Reboot the system and start the CMOS Setup routine. Verify the floppy drive parameters against the actual physical drives in the system, and then make sure that the correct data is entered in CMOS. You may have forgotten to save the data initially. Save the new data correctly and try the system again.
- *Check the signal cables.* Inspect the power and signal cables at the drive. Loose or incorrectly attached cables can effectively disable the drive. Install each cable carefully and try the system again.
- *Replace the floppy drive.* If the problem persists, chances are that the new floppy drive is defective. Try replacing the floppy drive with a known-good drive from another system.

**SYMPTOM 19-21**    **You cannot boot the system from the new floppy drive**    If the drive is recognized properly and operates as expected, the failure to boot actually may not be a failure—rather, the boot order established in your CMOS Setup may not be set to include the new drive. Often, the boot order is A: then C:, or C: then A:. If you installed a new floppy as B:, the system will not attempt to boot because it is not included in the boot order. Restart the CMOS Setup routine and adjust the boot order to address your new floppy drive first (for example, B:/C:, or A:/B:/C:).

**SYMPTOM 19-22**    **After the second floppy is installed, there are a lot of signal problems, such as read or write errors**    Chances are that you left the terminating resistors in place on the second (middle) floppy drive, resulting in signal errors. You should have a terminating resistor pack on the drive at the *end* of the daisy-chain cable. Check that the terminating resistors are in place on drive A:, and remove the terminating resistors from the middle drive (B:). Also check that the signal cables are installed securely on both drives. Loose or damaged cables can cause signal problems.

**SYMPTOM 19-23**    **The floppy drive light comes on even when there is no disk in the drive**    This may happen at any time, or particularly during shutdown or reboot of the system. When floppy drive access seems to occur during shutdown or reboot, it may be that you have anti-virus software (such as McAfee's VirusScan or Norton AntiVirus AutoProtect) set to check the floppy drive automatically. You'll need to disable autochecking of the floppy drive. For McAfee's VirusScan, right-click its icon from the task bar and select Properties. Under the Scan Floppies On entry in the Detection tab, uncheck the Shutdown box. Remember to save your changes. For Norton AntiVirus AutoProtect, right-click its icon from the task bar and select Options. Click the Advance button and, under the Check Floppies entry, uncheck the Check Floppies When Reboot Computer box. Remember to save your changes.

**SYMPTOM 19-24**    **You cannot create a Windows startup disk**    There are many possible problems that may prevent Windows from properly creating a startup disk, but the following points outline the most common issues.

- *Check the disk.* The disk itself may have ten or more bad sectors, or the first sector may be damaged. Try a known-good disk (preferably a high-quality or premium-grade disk). Also, Windows 9*x*/Me/XP generally requires a high-density (1.44MB) floppy disk to create a startup disk.

- *Check your antivirus software.* Many antivirus tools can interfere with floppy disk operations. Disable or uninstall your antivirus software according to the manufacturer's instructions.

- *Check the CMOS settings.* Reboot the system and start the CMOS Setup routine. Verify the floppy drive parameters against the actual physical drives in the system, and then make sure that the correct data is entered in CMOS. You may have forgotten to save the data initially. Save the new data correctly and try the system again.

- *Disable/remove floppy tape devices.* Some older tape backup devices utilizing the floppy controller may prevent you from gaining access to the floppy drive. To work around this behavior, disconnect the tape backup device from the floppy controller before you attempt to create a Windows startup disk, or disable the tape backup driver(s).

- *Replace the floppy drive.* If the problem persists, chances are that the new floppy drive is defective. Try replacing the floppy drive with a known-good drive from another system.

# Further Study

**Imation**    www.imation.com
**Mitsumi**    www.mitsumi.com
**Maxell**    www.maxell.com
**Sony**    www.storagebysony.com/categories/categorymain.asp?id=1#
**Teac**    www.teac.com/DSPD/floppy.html

# 20

# HARD DRIVES

The *hard disk drive* (or HDD) evolved to answer the incessant demands for permanent, high-volume, high-speed file and data storage in the PC (Figure 20-1). Early floppy disks provided simple and inexpensive storage, but they are slow, and programs quickly became far too large to store adequately on them. Switching between multiple floppy disks also proved to be a cumbersome proposition. By the early 1980s, hard drives had become an important part of PC architecture and helped to fuel further OS and applications development—today, the hard drive is an absolutely indispensable element of the modern PC. The hard drive holds the operating system that boots the system, stores the multi-megabyte applications and files we rely on, and even provides "virtual memory" for systems lean on RAM. Hard drive performance also has a profound effect on overall system performance. As you might imagine, hard drive problems can easily cripple a system. This chapter presents some essential principles of hard disk drives and file systems and provides you with some guidelines for drive testing and troubleshooting.

# Basic Drive Concepts

The first step in understanding hard drives is to learn the basic concepts involved. Many of the essential ideas discussed with floppy drives (see Chapter 19) also apply to hard drives, but the additional performance requirements and operating demands placed on hard drives have resulted in an array of important new concepts. In principle, a hard disk drive is very similar to a floppy drive—a magnetic recording media is applied to a substrate material that is then spun at a high rate of speed. Magnetic read/write heads in close proximity to the media can step rapidly across the spinning media to detect or create flux transitions as required. When you look closely, however, you can see that there are some major physical differences between floppy and hard drives.

## PLATTERS AND MEDIA

While floppy disks use magnetic material applied over a thin, flexible substrate of mylar (or some other plastic), hard drives use rugged, solid substrates called *platters*. You can clearly view the platters of a hard drive in Figure 20-2. A platter was traditionally made of aluminum because aluminum is a light material, it is easy to machine to desired tolerances, and holds its shape under the high centrifugal forces that occur at high rotation rates. But today, most platters are made from ceramic composite materials—these light,

**FIGURE 20-1**    A contemporary hard drive unit (Courtesy of NEC Technologies, Inc)

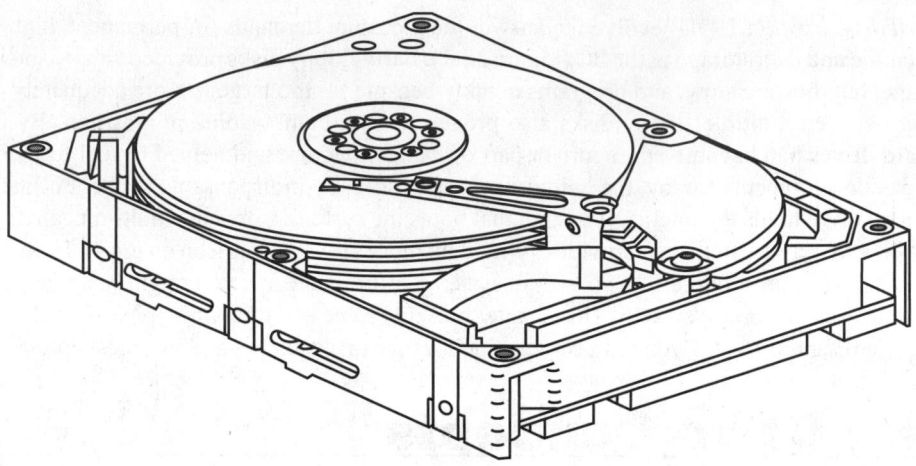

**FIGURE  20-2**     Maxtor hard drive (Courtesy of Maxtor Corporation)

strong materials have a *very* low thermal expansion (so there are fewer media problems) and can withstand higher centrifugal forces than can aluminum. A major advantage of a hard drive is speed, and ceramic platters are rotated at about 7,200 rpm to as much as 15,000 rpm (compared to older hard drives that ran at 3,600 to 5,400 rpm). A hard drive generally uses two or more platters, though extremely small drive assemblies may use only one platter.

Hard drives must be capable of tremendous recording densities—well over 10,000 bits per inch (BPI). To achieve such substantial recording densities, platter *media* is far superior to the oxide media used for floppy disks. First, the media must have high coercivity, so that each flux transition is well defined and easily distinguishable from every other flux transition. Coercivity of hard drive media typically exceeds 6,000 oersteds. Second, the media must be *extremely* flat across the entire platter surface to within microscopic tolerances. Hard drive R/W heads do not actually contact the media, as floppy drives do, but ride within a microscopic flow of air over the platter surfaces. A miniscule surface defect or foreign matter (such as a dust particle) can collide with a head and scratch the media. Such a *head crash* is often a catastrophic defect that requires hard drive replacement. You'll see more about head flight and surface defects later in this chapter.

Media today is a thin film that has long since replaced magnetic oxides. Thin-film media is a microscopic layer of pure metal (or a metal compound) that is bonded to the substrate surface through an interim layer. The media is then coated with a protective layer to help in surviving head crashes. Thin-film media also tends to be very flat, so R/W heads *can* be run at microscopic distances from the platter surfaces.

## AIRFLOW AND HEAD FLIGHT

Read/write heads in a hard disk drive must travel extremely close to the surface of each platter, but they can *never* actually contact the media while the drive is running. The heads could be mechanically fixed, but fixed-altitude flight does not allow for shock or natural vibration that is always present in a drive assembly. Instead, R/W heads are made to float above a platter surface by suspending the heads on a layer of moving air. Figure 20-3 illustrates the typical airflow in a hard drive. Disk (platter) rotation creates a slight cushion that elevates the heads. You may also notice that some air is channeled through a fine filter that helps to remove any particles from the drive's enclosure.

Air flow path

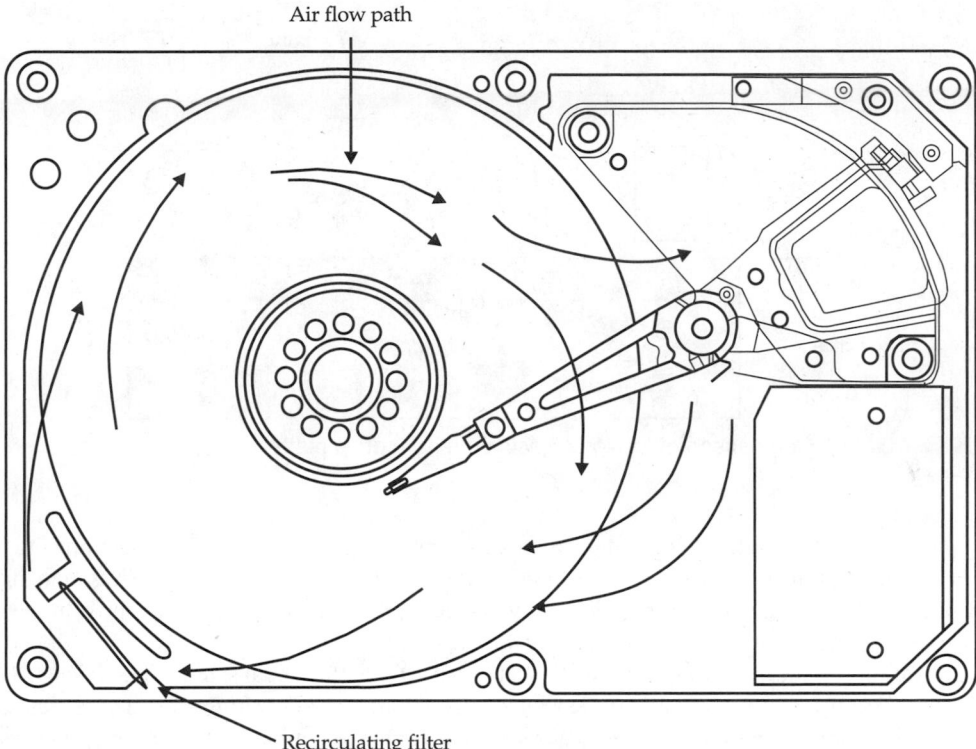

Recirculating filter

**FIGURE 20-3**    Airflow patterns in a hard drive (Courtesy of Maxtor Corporation)

It is important to note that *all* hard drives seal their platter assemblies into an airtight chamber. The reason for such a seal is to prevent contamination from dust, dirt, spills, or strands of hair. Contamination that lands on a platter's surface can easily result in a *head crash*. A head crash can damage the head, the media, or both—and any physical damage can result in an unusable drive. Consider the comparison shown in Figure 20-4. During normal operation, a hard drive's R/W head flies above the media at microscopic distances. Many technical professionals relate this to a jumbo jet flying 30 feet above the ground at 600 miles per hour. It follows then that any variation in surface flatness due to platter defects or contaminants can have catastrophic effects on head height. Even an average particle of smoke is ten times *wider* than this flying height. With such proportions, you can understand why it's critically important that the platter compartment remain sealed at all times. The platter compartment can be opened only in a *cleanroom* environment (a small, enclosed room where the air is filtered to remove any contaminants larger than 3 microns). Hard drive assemblers wear gloves and cleanroom suits that cover all but their faces—masks cover their mouth and nose to prevent breath vapor from contaminating the platters.

# DATA DENSITY CHARACTERISTICS

It is desirable to pack as much information as possible in the media of hard drive platters. The *areal density* of a media describes this maximum amount of capacity in terms of megabytes per square inch (sometimes noted as "MBSI" or "MB/in$^2$") or gigabytes per square inch (denoted as "GBSI" or "GB/in$^2$").

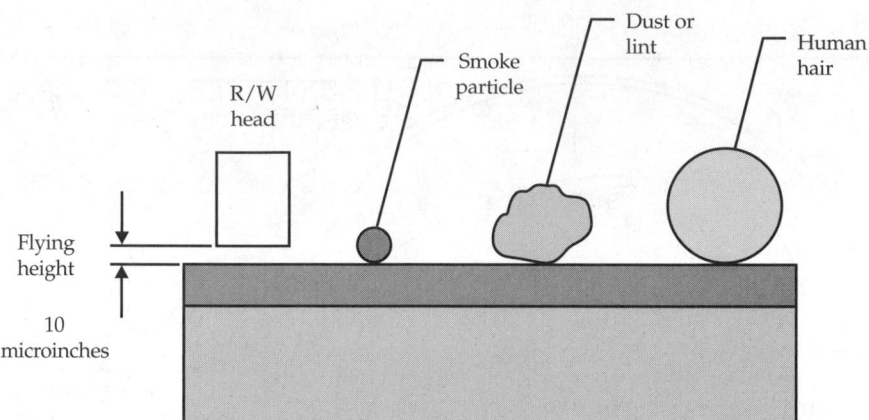

**FIGURE  20-4**    Comparison of foreign objects on a hard drive platter

Today's hard drives used in most computers use media supporting over 10GB/in$^2$. For example, the MDI 40GB HDD specifies an areal density of 15.3GB/in$^2$ (with early PC hard drives, this figure was more like 400 to 800MB/in$^2$). As you might imagine, physically smaller platters must hold media with a higher areal density to offer storage capacities similar to larger drives.

There are several major factors that affect a real density. First, the actual size of magnetic particles in the media places an upper barrier on areal density—smaller particles allow higher areal densities. Larger coercitivity of the media and smaller R/W heads with tighter magnetization fields allow higher areal densities. Finally, head height (the "altitude" of a R/W head over the platter surface) affects density. The closer a R/W head passes to its media, the higher areal densities can be. As heads fly further away, magnetic fields spread out, resulting in lower densities. Surface smoothness is then another major limiting factor in areal density, since smoother surfaces allow R/W heads to fly closer to the media.

There are other factors that define the way in which data can be packed onto a drive, most of which are related to areal density. *Track density* indicates the number of tracks per inch (TPI). The track density is also influenced by the precision of the R/W head positioning system—finer precision allows more tracks to be defined. *Flux density* indicates the number of individual magnetic flux transitions per linear inch of track space and is rated as flux changes per inch—termed *FCI* or *KFCI* (for "thousands of FCI"). Finally, you'll probably see references to *recording density*, which is basically the number of bits per linear inch of track space and is specified as bits per inch—termed *BPI* or *KBPI* (for "thousands of BPI"). For the MDI 40GB HDD in our earlier example, the drive sports a track density of 34,000 TPI, and a recording density of 449,000 BPI. By comparison, late-model Maxtor 80GB HDDs (such as the DiamondMax Plus D740X-6L) specify 60,000 TPI and 568,451 TPI. These figures are larger for 100 and 137GB (and larger) hard drives.

## LATENCY AND SEEK

As fast as a hard drive is, it cannot work instantaneously. There is a finite period of delay between the moment that a read or write command is initiated over the drive's physical interface and the moment that desired information is available (or placed). This delay is known as *latency*. More specifically, latency refers to the time it takes for needed bytes to pass under a R/W head. If the head has not quite reached the desired location, latency can be quite short. If the head has just missed the desired location, the head must wait almost a full rotation before the needed bits are available again, so latency can be rather long. In general, a disk drive is specified with *average latency* that (statistically) is time for the spindle to make half of a full rotation. For a disk rotating at 5,400 rpm (or 60 rotations per second), a full rotation is completed in 11.1ms [1/60]. Average latency would then be 5.6ms [11.1/2]. Disks spinning at 7,200 rpm offer an average latency of 4.2ms, and so on. As a rule, the faster a disk spins, the lower its latency will be. Ultimately, disk speed is limited by centrifugal forces acting on the platters.

The time it takes to step the R/W heads between tracks adds yet another delay to hard drive performance, and this is known as *seek time*. There are numerous ways of listing seek time. *Track-to-Track Seek* is the time needed to step between two adjacent tracks on the platter and is usually very short (only 0.8ms for a Maxtor D740X-6L drive). *Full Stroke Seek* is the time needed to step from the innermost to the outermost tracks, and is relatively long (about 20ms). The *Average Seek* is usually taken as half of the Full Stroke Seek (10ms for this example).

Seek and latency work together when loading and saving files. For example, when loading a file, it takes a certain amount of seek time to locate the track containing the start of your file. There is also some latency while the platter rotates around to the necessary sector. The disk may read several sectors in rapid succession but then need to jump to another track to continue reading—this imparts more seek time and additional latency while the disk looks for that next desired sector. And so it goes until the file is completely read.

File fragmentation can influence this performance. Heavily fragmented files may force the drive to seek multiple tracks—each time incurring some latency. Keeping file clusters contiguous helps to minimize this "jumping around" the drive.

You can imagine that if the head tries to step directly from the end of one track to the beginning of another, the head will arrive too late to catch the new track (because the disk has spun too much by the time the heads arrive). This means the drive will have to wait almost an entire rotation to pick up the start of that track. By offsetting the start points of each successive track, as in Figure 20-5, head travel time can be compensated for. This *cylinder skewing* technique is intended to improve hard drive performance by reducing the disk time lost during normal head steps. A head should be able to identify and read the desired information from a track within one disk rotation.

## TRACKS, CYLINDERS, AND SECTORS

As with floppy drives, you cannot simply place data anywhere on a hard drive platter—the drive would have no idea where to look for data or whether the data is even valid. The information on each platter must

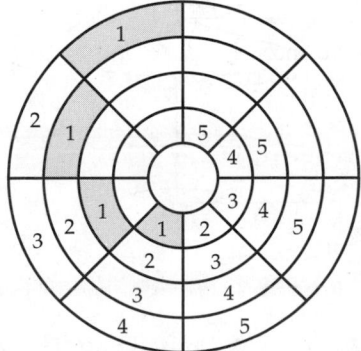

**FIGURE   20-5**    An example of cylinder skewing

be sorted and organized into a series of known, standard locations. Each platter side can be considered as a two-dimensional field possessing length and width. With this sort of geometry, data is recorded in sets of concentric circles running from the disk spindle to the platter edge. A drive can move its R/W heads over the spinning media to locate needed data or programs in a matter of milliseconds. Every concentric circle on a platter is known as a *track*.

While each surface of a platter is a two-dimensional area, the number of platter surfaces involved in a hard drive (four, six, eight, or more) brings a third dimension (height) into play. Since each track is located directly over the same tracks on subsequent platters, each track in a platter assembly can be visualized as a *cylinder* that passes through every platter. The number of cylinders is equal to the number of tracks on one side of a platter. Thus, the terms "track" and "cylinder" are used interchangeably. Figure 20-6 shows data organization on a simple platter assembly. Note that only one side of the three platters is shown.

A typical platter physically contains many thousands of tracks—for example, the Maxtor DiamondMax 80GB drive provides 158,816 physical tracks (though you would enter only 16,383 *logical* tracks in the CMOS Setup, because Logical Block Addressing [LBA] drive translation handles the conversion in the BIOS). Consider what happens with the 80GB Maxtor drive when you enter 16,383 cylinders, 16 heads, and 63 sectors per track (at 512 bytes per sector)—the result is only 8,455,200,768 bytes (8.4GB), which is the CHS (cylinder/head/sector) limit for BIOS. Obviously, this cannot be right, even though that's what you enter in the CMOS Setup. If you substitute the actual number of cylinders for the drive, you get 81,964,302,336 bytes (81.96GB) which *is* exactly what Maxtor specifies for the drive's capacity. Later drive models easily support over 200,000 tracks (cylinders).

In most cases, you do *not* need to know the actual number of drive cylinders because the BIOS will use LBA to translate the common 16,383 × 16 × 63 entry into the correct geometry without your direct intervention.

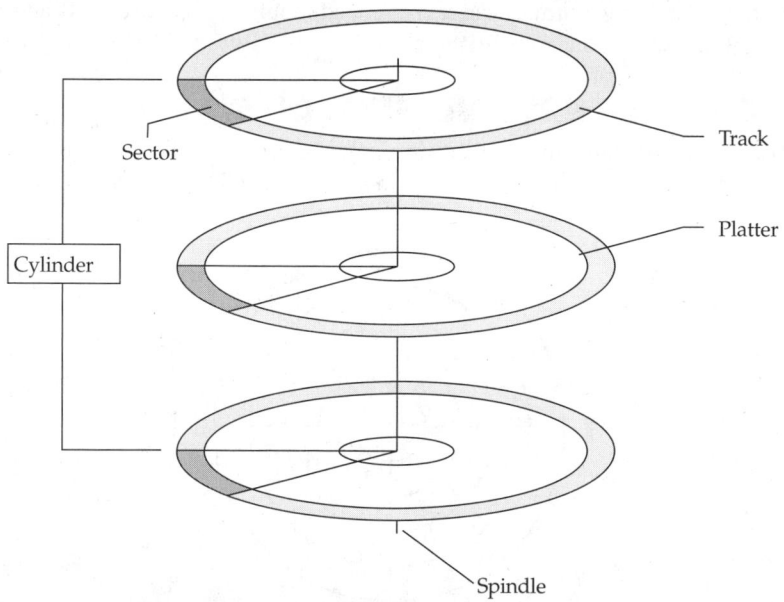

**FIGURE  20-6**    Data organization on a hard drive

Tracks are broken down even further into small segments called *sectors*. As with DOS floppy disks, a sector holds 512 bytes of data, along with error-checking and housekeeping data that identifies the sector, track, and results calculated by cyclical redundancy checking (CRC). The location and ID information for each sector is developed when the drive is low-level formatted at the factory. After formatting, only sector data and CRC bytes are updated during writing. If sector ID information is accidentally overwritten or corrupted, the data recorded in the afflicted sector becomes unreadable.

Figure 20-7 shows the layout for a typical sector on a Maxtor SCSI drive. As you can see, there is *much* more than just 512 bytes of data. The start of every sector is marked with a pulse. The pulse signaling the first sector of a track is called the *index pulse*. There are two portions to every sector: an address area and data area. The *address area* is used to identify the sector. This is critically important because the drive must be able to identify precisely which cylinder, head, and sector location is about to be read from or written to. This location information is recorded in the *address field* and is followed by two bytes of cyclical redundancy check (CRC) data. When a drive identifies a location, it generates a CRC code that it compares to the CRC code recorded on the disk. If the two CRC codes match, the address is assumed to be valid, and disk operation can continue. Otherwise, an error has occurred and the entire sector is considered invalid. This failure usually precipitates a catastrophic DOS error message.

After a number of bytes are encountered for drive timing and synchronization, up to 512 bytes can be read from or written to the *data field*. The data is processed to derive eleven bytes of ECC error-checking code using Reed Solomon encoding. If data is being read, the derived ECC is compared to the recorded ECC. When the codes match, data is assumed to be valid and drive operation continues. Otherwise, a data read error is assumed. During writing, the old ECC data is replaced with the new ECC data derived for the current data. It is interesting to note that only the data and ECC fields of a sector are written after formatting. All other sector data remains untouched until the drive is reformatted. If a retentivity problem eventually causes one or more bits to become corrupt in the address area, the sector will fail.

## ZONED RECORDING

In the early days of hard drives, every track had the same 63 sectors (unusually numbered 1 through 63). This worked well, but designers realized that for a constant angular velocity (CAV) drive, the data was recorded

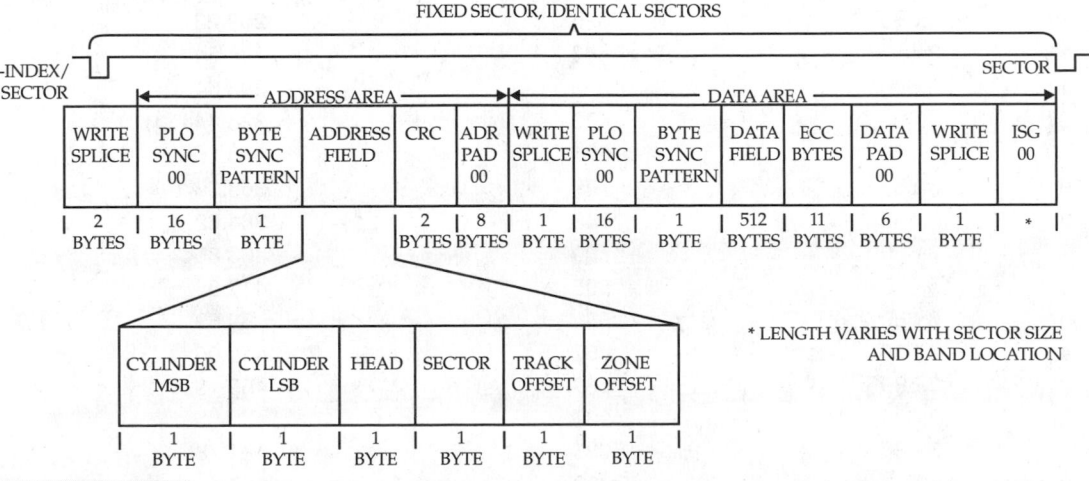

**FIGURE 20-7**    A typical hard drive sector layout (Courtesy of Maxtor Corporation)

more densely on the inner tracks where the circumference is smaller than on the outer tracks where the circumference is larger. A feature known as *zoned recording* was added to the drive, which allows a *variable* number of sectors per track. The total number of tracks is divided up into several areas, or *zones* (usually 16 zones) across the platter. All of the tracks within a given zone use the same number of sectors, but inner zones use fewer sectors, while outer zones use more sectors. For example, the Maxtor D740X-6L 80GB HDD uses 16 zones (0 to 15) with 481 sectors per track at the inside, and 882 sectors per track at the outside. Zoned recording lets hard drives make the most efficient use of their storage space. Zoned recording is managed by the drive itself, so you still enter a fixed number in the "Sectors per Track" entry under the CMOS Setup (usually 63). Typical hard drives can run from 195 to 312 physical sectors per track. Table 20-1 shows the cylinder composition for a Maxtor D540X hard drive (keep in mind that zone 15 is the innermost zone).

63 sectors per track is still used in CMOS Setup even though the actual number may vary across the platter—LBA will again translate the geometry for the drive.

## SECTOR SPARING

Not all sectors on a hard drive are useable. When a drive is formatted, bad sectors must be removed from normal use. The *sparing* process is a form of defect management and works to ensure that each track has access to the appropriate number of working sectors. When sparing is performed *in-line* (as a drive is being formatted), faulty sectors cause all subsequent sectors to be shifted up one sector. In-line sparing is not widely used. *Field defect* sparing (after the format process is complete) assigns (or remaps) faulty sectors to other working sectors located in spare disk tracks that are reserved for that purpose. For example, EIDE/UDMA hard drives use field defect sparing. It reserves a full 16 tracks for spare sectors (often referred to as the *defect management zone*). Faulty sectors are typically marked for reallocation when the disk is formatted.

| **TABLE 20-1** | **THE EFFECT OF ZONED RECORDING ON SECTORS PER TRACK AND EFFECTIVE DATA RATES** | | |
|---|---|---|---|
| **ZONE** | **NUMBER OF TRACKS** | **SECTORS PER TRACK** | **DATA RATE (MB/S)** |
| 15 | 3,562 | 487 | 251.01 |
| 14 | 3,680 | 525 | 269.23 |
| 13 | 3,680 | 560 | 286.54 |
| 12 | 3,680 | 600 | 298.64 |
| 11 | 3,680 | 633 | 325.44 |
| 10 | 3,680 | 671 | 346.15 |
| 9 | 3,680 | 709 | 365.38 |
| 8 | 3,680 | 742 | 384.62 |
| 7 | 3,680 | 800 | 403.85 |
| 6 | 3,680 | 805 | 417.58 |
| 5 | 3,680 | 836 | 432.69 |
| 4 | 3,680 | 857 | 445.05 |
| 3 | 3,680 | 883 | 459.13 |
| 2 | 3,680 | 907 | 472.85 |
| 1 | 3,680 | 925 | 481.78 |
| 0 | 60 | 400 | 197.44 |

The only place where faulty sectors are *absolutely* not permitted is on track 00. Track 00 is used to hold a hard drive's partition and FAT information. If a drive cannot read or write to track 00, the entire drive is rendered unusable. If a sector in track 00 fails during operation, reformatting the drive to lockout the bad sector will not necessarily recover the drive's operation. Track 00 failures usually necessitate reformatting the drive from scratch or replacing it entirely.

## LANDING ZONE

The R/W heads of a hard drive fly at only a microscopic distance from their respective platter surfaces—held aloft with faint air currents produced by the spinning platters. When the drive is turned off, however, the platters slow to a halt. During this *spindown* period, airflow falls rapidly and heads can literally crash into the platter surfaces. Whenever a head touches a platter surface, data can be irretrievably destroyed. Even during normal operation, a sudden shock or bump can cause one or more heads to skid across their surfaces. Although a drive can usually be reformatted after a head crash, data and programs would have to be reloaded from scratch.

In order to avoid a head crash during normal startup or spindown cycles, a cylinder is reserved (either the innermost or outermost cylinder) as a *landing zone* (LZ). No data is stored on the landing zone, so any surface problems caused by head landings are harmless. All hard drives today will automatically move the head assembly over the landing zone before spindown (known as *parking the head*), then gently lock the heads into place until power is restored. Locking helps to ensure that random shocks and vibrations do not shake the heads onto adjacent data-carrying tracks and cause damage while power is off. Older hard drives required a specific "landing zone" entry in the CMOS Setup. But today, the process is automatic, so you can usually just enter "0" for the LZ or allow the system to autodetect the LZ with the rest of the drive geometry.

## INTERLEAVE

The *interleave* of a hard drive refers to the order in which sectors are numbered on a platter. Interleave was a critical factor in older desktop computer systems where the core logic (CPU and memory) was relatively slow compared to drive performance. It was necessary to create artificial delays in the drive to allow core logic to catch up. Delays were accomplished by physically separating the sectors (numbering contiguous sectors out of order). This ordering forced the drive to read a sector, then skip one or more sectors to reach the next subsequent sector. The "interleaved" drive would have to make several rotations before all sectors on a track could be read.

The ratio of a sector's length on the platter to the distance between two sequential sectors is known as the *interleave factor*. For example, if a drive reads a sector and skips a sector to reach the next sequential sector, the interleave factor would be 1:3, and so on. The greater the interleave, the more rotations that would be needed to read all the sectors on a track, and the slower the drive would be. To achieve highest disk performance, interleave should be eliminated. Since drive and interface logic today is so much faster than even the fastest hard drive, the issue of interleave is largely irrelevant now. Drives no longer interleave their sectors, so all sectors are in sequential order around the track, and the interleave factor is 1:1—all data on a track can ideally be read in one disk rotation. An interleave factor of 1:1 yields optimal drive performance.

 As a rule, *never* allow any drive utility to adjust or "optimize" the drive interleave. Changing the interleave not only destroys existing data, but it can also seriously impair drive performance.

## WRITE PRECOMPENSATION

As you have already seen, a hard drive spins its platter(s) at a constant rate (such as 7,200 rpm)—its constant angular velocity (CAV). While constant rotation requires only a very simple motor circuit, extra demands are placed on the media. Tracks closer to the spindle are physically shorter than tracks toward the platter's outer edge. Shorter tracks result in shorter sectors. For inner sectors to hold the same amount of data as outer sectors, data must be packed more densely on the inner sectors—each magnetic flux reversal is actually closer together. Unfortunately, smaller flux reversals produce weaker magnetic fields in the R/W heads during reading.

If the inner sectors are written with a stronger magnetic field, flux transitions stored in the media will be stronger. When the inner sectors are then read, a clearer, better-defined signal will result. The use of increased writing current to compensate for diminished disk media response is known as *write precompensation* (WP). The track where write precompensation is expected to begin is specified in the drive's parameter table in CMOS Setup. Write precompensation filled an important role in early drives that used oxide-based media. Today's thin-film media and very small drive geometries (combined with Zoned Recording techniques) result in low signal differences across the platter area, so write precompensation (although still specified in the drive geometry) is rarely meaningful anymore. In most cases, you can enter "0" for WP, or allow the system to autodetect the WP.

## START TIME

Booting a computer can take about 30 seconds—often more. Some of this time is an artificial delay needed to initialize the hard drive(s) from a cold start. From the moment power is applied to the hard drive, it can take anywhere from 7 to 10 seconds for the drive's onboard control circuitry to start and initialize the drive so that it can be recognized by the system POST. This period is known as the drive's *start time*. Boot problems with a new hard drive are frequently caused by an insufficient start time. The BIOS attempts to check for the presence of a hard drive that has not yet had time to initialize. When you find that drives are not recognized at boot time, but are readable once the system boots, adding several seconds to the drive's start time (or power-on boot delay) in the CMOS Setup may correct the problem.

## DRIVE POWER MODES

Modern hard drives are not simply "on" or "off." They operate in any one of several modes, and each mode makes different power demands on the host system. This characteristic is particularly important because today's PCs are becoming ever more power conscious, so the ability to control drive power is an integral part of PC power conservation systems. Typical hard drives operate in any of five different power modes that are controlled by the operating system (such as Windows 9x/Me/XP):

- **Spin-up**   The drive is spinning up following initial application of power and has not yet reached full speed. This demands about 14W and is particularly demanding of the power supply (if the supply is marginal or overloaded, the hard drive may not spin-up properly).

- **Seek**   This is a random access operation by the disk drive as it tries to locate the required track for reading or writing. This demands about 8.5–9.0W.

- **Read/Write**   A seek has been completed, and data is being read from or written to the drive. This uses about 5.0W.

■ **Idle**    This is a basic power conservation mode where the drive is spinning and all other circuitry is powered on, but the head actuator is parked and powered off. This drops power demands to about 4W, yet the drive is capable of responding to read commands within 40ms.

■ **Standby**    The spindle motor is not running (the drive "spins down"). This is the main power conservation mode that requires just about 1W. It may take up to several seconds for the drive to leave this mode (or spin-up) upon receipt of a command that requires disk access.

## SERVO TECHNIQUES

Modern hard drives use voice coil actuators to position the R/W heads over the desired track. However, drives need to verify that the heads are positioned correctly *before* reading or writing can take place. The drive needs feedback to tell it where the heads actually are (versus where the drive thinks the heads are). If the heads are positioned incorrectly, the drive can make the necessary adjustments. Think of driving a car in a 50 mph zone. You step on the accelerator to make the car move, but you need to check the speedometer to see what the actual speed is. If the speed is still too slow, you can give the car more gas. If the speed is too fast, you can apply less gas (or the brake if needed). This constant feedback is called a *servo loop*.

For the hard disk, feedback information is provided from the platters themselves, using special codes (called *servo codes*) written on the disk that let the drive know where the heads are as the actuator moves. Servo codes are read by the heads and fed back to the actuator control logic. By putting different codes on each track of the disk, the actuator can always figure out which track the heads are on. There are three different ways to implement a hard disk servo mechanism:

■ **Wedge Servo**    Servo information is recorded in a wedge of each platter (like a slice out of a pie). The remainder of the platter contains data. The problem is that the servo information is in only one location on the hard disk. To position the heads, a lot of waiting must be done for the servo wedge to rotate around to where the heads are (a.k.a. *latency*), and these delays make the positioning performance of such drives painfully slow. This technique is used in older drives and is now considered obsolete.

■ **Dedicated Servo**    This approach was found on many drives through the 1990s. An entire surface of one disk platter is dedicated for servo information, and no servo information is recorded on the other surfaces. One head is constantly reading servo information—this allows very fast servo feedback and eliminates the delays associated with wedge servo designs. Unfortunately, an entire surface of the disk is wasted because it can contain no user data. There are other problems; for example, the heads where data is recorded may not always line up exactly with the head that is reading the servo information, so adjustments must be made to compensate. Also, since the servo platter may be warmer or cooler than the data platters, these drives are notorious for needing frequent thermal recalibration. Dedicated servo drives usually have an odd number of heads.

■ **Embedded Servo**    The newest servo technique intersperses servo information with data across the entire surface of all of the hard disk platter surfaces. This means servo information and data are read by the same heads, and the heads never have to wait for the disk to rotate the servo information into place (as with wedge servo). This method doesn't provide the constant positioning information available with a dedicated servo, but it also doesn't cause an entire surface to be wasted on servo overhead. The need for constant thermal recalibration is also greatly reduced, since the servo information and data are the same distance from the center of the disk and will expand or contract together. All modern hard disks now use embedded servo.

In all cases, the servo codes are written to the disk surfaces at the time the hard disk is manufactured. This process requires special, complex, and expensive equipment, and servo codes are intended to last the life of the drive. Servo codes cannot be rewritten without returning the drive to the factory. Remember that the disk heads themselves are locked out at the hardware level (by the drive's electronics) from writing to any areas where servo information is written. The creation of this precise servo information is part of the *low-level formatting* of a modern drive—which is now always a factory process. Modern IDE-type hard drives do *not* need low-level formatting, and traditional BIOS routines to invoke low-level formatting are largely ignored by the drive.

Do *not* attempt to low-level format any type of IDE drive—doing this can damage the drive's servo information and render the drive unusable.

## THERMAL RECALIBRATION

When hard drives operate, heat naturally produced by the electronics, spindle motor, and voice coil actuator causes the drive media to expand. This gradually changes the location of each track, and the drive must periodically adjust for such changes. As designers continued to pack more tracks on a platter (and the number of tracks per inch increases), it became more important than ever to allow for thermal expansion—especially with *dedicated servo* drives. For servo information and data on different platters, adjustments were necessary to ensure that servo and user data did not become misaligned. Such adjustments are known as *thermal recalibration*.

To address this problem, most drives manufactured in the mid-1990s include a thermal recalibration feature. Every few minutes (or as needed), the heads are moved and the distance between tracks measured. This information is recorded in the drive's memory, and is used to help position the heads for reading or writing. When the recalibration occurs, you can hear the disk operate as if you were accessing it (even if you're not). The problem with thermal recalibration is that disk access is delayed until the recalibration process is complete. This process doesn't cause data to be lost, but it can affect operations that depend on real-time drive access (such as video captures, CD-R creation, or digital audio extraction). Drive makers responded to thermal recalibration problems by allowing the recalibration to be put off until the drive was idle. Such drives were frequently advertised as "audio/visual" (A/V) drives in the late 1990s. Today, thermal recalibration is still required, but its need has been greatly reduced with embedded servo drives. Embedded servo drives almost eliminate the interruptions to "real-time" disk access, and thermal recalibration can even be disabled on some newer embedded servo drive models.

# IDE Drive Standards and Features

IDE hard drive technology has come a long way since its introduction in the late 1980s. In fact, IDE technology has come *so* far that it's difficult to keep all of the terminology straight. Let's start this part of the chapter by examining the important concepts and evolution of IDE technology.

## BINARY MEGABYTES VS. DECIMAL MEGABYTES

Most folks know that hard drive sizes are measured in megabytes (MB) and gigabytes (GB)—however, beginners and experienced technicians alike are often confused by the difference between *binary megabytes* and *decimal megabytes* (as well as gigabytes). For example, you'll notice that when you install a new 4GB hard drive, utilities like the CMOS Setup, FDISK, and Windows Explorer will report only about 3.72GB, but other utilities like CHKDSK report about 4GB. This difference is often confusing, but it's due to the way in which manufacturers and software makers calculate drive capacity. Technically, hard drive capacity is calculated by multiplying the number of cylinders, sectors, and heads times 512, such as this:

```
Capacity = Cylinders x Heads x Sectors x 512 (bytes per sector)
```

So, if you're using a Maxtor 4G120J6 120GB drive with 238,216 cylinders, 16 heads, and 63 sectors, you'd wind up with:

```
238,216 x 16 x 63 x 512 = 122,942,324,736 bytes (120GB)
```

By comparison, an older AC34000 drive with 7752 cylinders, 16 heads, and 63 sectors would yield:

```
7752 x 16 x 63 x 512 = 4,000,776,192 bytes
```

The problem is that hard drive manufacturers use the notion of *decimal megabytes* (or decimal gigabytes) to determine the size of their hard drives. To calculate drive sizes in decimal megabytes, just divide the drive size by 1,000,000 (or 1,000,000,000 for GB). For the 4G120J6, you'd get

```
122,942,324,736 / 1,000,000,000 = 122.9GB
```

For the older AC34000, you'd get

```
4,000,776,192 / 1,000,000,000 = 4.0GB
```

Makes sense, right? Unfortunately, many software makers will use *binary megabytes* (or binary gigabytes) to calculate drive sizes. A binary megabyte is 1,048,576 bytes, and a binary gigabyte is 1,073,741,824 bytes, so here's how a lot of software will report the 4G120J6:

```
122,942,324,736 bytes / 1,073,741,824 = 114.5GB
```

And here's the calculation for the older AC34000:

```
4,000,776,192 bytes / 1,073,741,824 = 3.72GB
```

These are simply two slightly different ways of representing the same drives, so *both* methods are *correct*. The important issue here is to recognize the difference and to *not* mistake that difference as being a problem with the drive.

## IDE/ATA

IDE (*Integrated Drive Electronics*) and ATA (*AT Attachment*) are basically one and the same thing—a disk drive scheme designed to integrate the controller onto the drive mechanism itself, instead of relying on a stand-alone controller board as older MFM and RLL drives did. This approach reduces interface costs and makes drive firmware implementations easier. IDE proved to be a low-cost, easily configured system—so much so that it created a boom in the disk drive industry. Although the terms "IDE" and "ATA" are sometimes used interchangeably, ATA is the formal standard that defines the drive and how it operates, while IDE is really the "trade name" that refers to the 40-pin interface and drive controller architecture designed to implement the ATA standard.

The AT Attachment interface was submitted to the American National Standards Institute (ANSI) for approval in 1990, and it was finally published in 1994 as ANSI standard X3.221-1994, titled *AT Attachment Interface for Disk Drives*. This standard is sometimes called *ATA-1* to distinguish it from its successors. The original IDE/ATA standard defines the following features and transfer modes:

- The specification calls for a single channel in a PC, shared by two devices that are configured as master and slave.
- ATA includes support for PIO modes 0, 1, and 2.
- ATA includes support for single-word DMA modes 0, 1, and 2 and multiword DMA mode 0.

ATA does not include support for enhancements such as ATAPI support for non-hard-disk IDE/ATA devices, block mode transfers, logical block addressing, Ultra-DMA modes, or other advanced features. The ATA-1 standard is now completely obsolete, and drives developed to meet this standard are no longer made. At the recommendation of the T13 Technical Committee, ATA-1 was withdrawn as an official ANSI standard in 1999.

## ATAPI

Originally, the IDE/ATA interface was designed to work only with hard drives. Other devices such as CD-ROMs and tape drives used proprietary interfaces (often implemented on sound cards), the floppy disk interface (which is slow and cumbersome), or SCSI. In the early 1990s, designers realized that there would be enormous advantages to using the standard IDE/ATA interface to support devices other than hard drives. The intention was not to replace SCSI, but rather to eliminate proprietary interfaces and the slow floppy interface for tape drives.

Unfortunately, given the ATA command structure, it wasn't possible to put non–hard drive devices on the IDE channel and expect them to work. A special protocol was developed called the *AT Attachment Packet Interface*, or *ATAPI*. The ATAPI standard is used for devices like CD-ROM, tape, and removable media drives. It enables them to use the standard IDE cable used by IDE/ATA hard drives and to be configured as master or slave, just like a hard drive. When you see a CD-ROM or other non-HDD peripheral denoted as an "IDE device," it is really using the ATAPI protocol. Internally, the ATAPI protocol is not at all similar to the standard ATA command set used by hard drives. The name "packet interface" suggests that commands to ATAPI devices are sent in groups called *packets*. In some ways, ATAPI resembles SCSI more than IDE in terms of its command set and operation. The first ATAPI standard document was called *SFF-8020* (later renamed *INF-8020*), which is now quite old and obsolete. In the late 1990s, the T13 Technical Committee took over control of the ATAPI command set and protocol, combining it with ATA into the ATA/ATAPI-4 standard.

A special ATAPI driver is used to communicate with ATAPI devices—this driver must be loaded into memory before the device can be accessed (though most newer operating systems such as Windows support ATAPI internally and load their own drivers for the interface). The actual data transfers use regular PIO or DMA modes—just like hard disks—though support for the various modes differs widely by device. For the most part, ATAPI devices will coexist with IDE/ATA devices. From the user's perspective, ATAPI devices behave as if they are regular IDE/ATA disks on the channel. Newer BIOS versions will even allow the system to boot from ATAPI CD-ROM drives.

# ATA-2, FAST-ATA, AND EIDE

By the early 1990s, it became clear that ATA architecture would soon be overwhelmed by advances in hard drive technology. The ATA interface committee responded by developing the ATA-2 standard, which essentially combined the features and attributes defined by marketing programs created at Seagate, Quantum, and Western Digital. This standard was published in 1996 as ANSI standard X3.279-1996, called the *AT Attachment Interface with Extensions*. ATA-2 is largely regarded as a significant improvement to ATA-1. It defines faster PIO (Programmed I/O) and DMA (Direct Memory Access) data transfer modes, adds more powerful drive commands (such as the "Identify Drive" command to support auto-identification in CMOS), adds support for a second drive channel, handles block data transfers (Block Transfer Mode), and defines a new means of addressing sectors on the hard drive using Logical Block Addressing (LBA). LBA has proven to be a very effective vehicle for overcoming the traditional 528MB hard drive size limit. Yet ATA-2 continues to use the same 40-pin physical interface used by ATA-1, and it is backward compatible with ATA (IDE) drives.

Along with ATA-2, you'll probably find two additional terms: EIDE (*Enhanced IDE*) and *Fast-ATA*. These are not standards—merely different implementations of the ATA-2 standard. EIDE represents the Western Digital implementation of ATA-2, which builds upon both the ATA-2 and ATAPI standards. This has been *so* effective that *EIDE* has become the "generic" term. Seagate and Quantum have thrown their support behind the Fast-ATA implementation of the ATA-2 standard. However, Fast-ATA builds on ATA-2 only. For all practical purposes, there is no significant difference between ATA-2, EIDE, and Fast-ATA, and you'll probably see these three terms used interchangeably (though this is not *technically* correct).

# ATA-3

A more recent implementation of the ATA standard is ATA-3, which was published in 1997 as ANSI standard X3.298-1997 called *AT Attachment 3 Interface*. It does not define any new data transfer modes, but it does improve the reliability of PIO Mode 4. It also offers a simple password-based security scheme, more sophisticated power management features, and Self-Monitoring Analysis and Reporting Technology (SMART). ATA-3 is also backward compatible with ATA-2, ATAPI, and ATA devices. Since no new data transfer modes are defined by ATA-3, you may also see the generic term "EIDE" used interchangeably (though this is also not technically correct).

You may see a "PIO Mode 5" described in some places with the claim that it was introduced in ATA-3. This mode was suggested by some controller manufacturers but never approved and never implemented. It is not defined in any of the ATA standards and exists only in some BIOS versions.

ATA-3 does *not* define any of the Ultra-DMA modes—these were first defined with the ATA/ATAPI-4 standard. ATA-3 is also not the same as ATA-33 (ATA-33 is often used as a slang term for Ultra-DMA/33).

# ATA/ATAPI-4 (ULTRA-ATA/33)

The next significant enhancement to the ATA standard saw the ATA Packet Interface (ATAPI) feature set merged with the conventional ATA command set and protocols to create ATA/ATAPI-4. This standard was published by ANSI in 1998 as NCITS 317-1998, *AT Attachment with Packet Interface Extensions*. Aside from combining ATA and ATAPI, this standard defined several other significant enhancements and changes:

■  High-speed Ultra-DMA modes 0, 1, and 2 were created, defining transfer rates of 16.7, 25, and 33.3 MB/s.

■  A 40-pin/80 conductor IDE cable was first defined in this standard. It was thought that the higher-speed Ultra-DMA modes would require the use of this cable in order to eliminate signal problems caused by the higher speed. The use of this cable was left optional for this standard, though it became mandatory under the faster UDMA modes defined in ATA/ATAPI-5.

■  Cyclical Redundancy Checking (CRC) was added to ensure the integrity of data sent using the faster Ultra-DMA modes.

■  The command set was cleaned up, several older and obsolete commands were removed, and special command queuing and overlapping protocols were defined.

Obviously, the Ultra-DMA (UDMA) modes were the most exciting part of this new standard. Ultra-DMA modes 0 and 1 were never really implemented by hard disk manufacturers, but UDMA mode 2 made a real impression since it doubled the throughput of the fastest transfer mode then available to 33.3 MB/s. Ultra-DMA mode 2 was quickly dubbed *Ultra-DMA/33,* and drives conforming to ATA/ ATAPI-4 are often called *Ultra-ATA/33* drives (which is technically inaccurate).

In actual practice, you'll need an Ultra-ATA drive, controller, and BIOS to support an Ultra-ATA drive system, but it is fully backward compatible with previous ATA standards. You can use ordinary 40-pin IDE-type cables for UDMA/33 *unless* any of the following issues occur:

■  The standard 40-pin drive controller cable is of low quality, damaged, or weakened by many installations.

■  The system suffers from excessive signal noise—these systems may have multiple drives, dual power supplies, multiple video cards, and so on.

■  The system is overclocked (or otherwise configured beyond the manufacturer's supported specifications). This often results in excessive signal noise.

## ATA/ATAPI-5 (ULTRA-ATA/66)

With the rapid adoption of ATA/ATAPI-4, the T13 committee immediately began work on its next generation of interface standard dubbed ATA/ATAPI-5. This standard was published by ANSI in 2000 as NCITS 340-2000, the *AT Attachment with Packet Interface-5.* The changes defined in ATA/ATAPI-5 include

■  More high-speed Ultra-DMA modes 3 and 4, defining transfer rates of 44.4 and 66.6 MB/s, respectively.

■  The 40-pin/80-conductor IDE cable that was optional in ATA/ATAPI-4 is made mandatory for UDMA modes 3 and 4. ATA/ATAPI-5 also defines a method by which a host system can detect if an 80-conductor cable is in use, so it can determine whether or not to enable the higher-speed transfer modes.

■  Numerous interface commands were changed, and some old ones were deleted.

As with ATA-3, not that many changes were made in ATA/ATAPI-5. However, the main change was certainly important—another doubling of the throughput of the interface to 66.6 MB/s. Many companies quickly labeled ATA/ATAPI-5 drives running Ultra-DMA mode 4 as "Ultra-ATA/66." During late 1999 and early 2000, new IDE/ATA drives conforming to this standard began appearing on the market.

You'll need an Ultra-ATA/66 drive, controller, and BIOS to support an Ultra-ATA/66 drive system, but it is fully backward compatible with previous ATA standards. Unlike the Ultra-ATA/33 approach, you'll need a specially designed 40-pin/80-conductor cable (typically provided with new [boxed]

UDMA/66 drives). Also keep in mind that the operating system must also be enabled for DMA transfers. Keep the following issues in mind when implementing a UDMA/66 system:

- Make sure that the signal cable is Ultra-ATA/66-capable. An Ultra-ATA/66-compliant cable is a 40-pin, 80-conductor cable with a black connector on one end, a blue connector on the other end, and a gray connector in the middle. In addition, pin 34 on the cable should be notched or cut (though this may be difficult to see with the human eye).

- Make sure the system board (motherboard) controller is capable of supporting Ultra-ATA/66. An Ultra-ATA/66 capable controller has a detect circuit that can detect missing line 34 on the cable. If there is no detect circuit, the system can wrongly detect the presence of an Ultra-ATA/66 cable and try to configure the device for a higher transfer rate.

- Some system board (motherboard) controllers may not successfully handle Ultra-ATA/66 on both the primary and secondary channels. If you have difficulty with a UDMA/66 device on the secondary controller channel, consider troubleshooting with the device in the primary master position.

- If you have trouble getting a UDMA/66 system configured properly, contact the system board (motherboard) or controller card manufacturer for the latest BIOS upgrade (and any Ultra-ATA/66 device drivers or patches).

- Make sure the operating system is "DMA-capable," and verify that the DMA mode is activated. For Windows 9x/Me, check the drive's Properties dialog box in the Device Manager. For Windows XP, check the Drive Controller Properties in Device Manager.

- Make sure the Ultra-ATA/66-capable drive has been configured to run at Ultra-ATA/66 transfer rates. Some drives ship with the UDMA/66 mode disabled by default and require a jumper change and/or software utility in order to activate the UDMA/66 mode.

## ATA/ATAPI-6 AND 7 (ULTRA-ATA/100/133)

By 2001, the T13 Technical Committee (www.t13.org) had completed and released the next ATA/ATAPI-6 standard for *Ultra-ATA/100 drives* (also called *Ultra-DMA/100* or *UDMA/100*), which are capable of 100 MB/s data burst rates. In addition to faster burst transfer speeds, UDMA/100 also supports hard drive noise reduction (acoustic management) that allows the mechanics of the drive to be modified under software control—allowing the user to choose between higher performance or quieter operation. Additional ATA commands have been added to support audio and video streaming (or other multimedia operations).

The T13 Technical Committee is currently working on the ATA/ATAPI-7 standard supporting 133 MB/s burst data transfers, along with other features including "Big Drives" support (drives larger than the BIOS Int13 limit of 137GB). Although this standard is currently under development, UDMA/133 drives are readily available, and the 48-bit LBA addressing scheme proposed by Maxtor (their "Big Drives" technology) can address $2^{48}$ (281,474,976,710,656) sectors. At 512 bytes per sector, drives can be up to 144,115,188,075,855,872 bytes (144 petabytes, or PB) in size. In terms of current hard drives, that's an astonishing 144,115,188GB. Additional addressing commands and features have also been included in ATA/ATAPI-7.

You'll need an Ultra-ATA/100/133 drive, controller, and BIOS to support an Ultra-ATA/100/133 drive system, but both are fully backward compatible with previous ATA standards. As with Ultra-ATA/66 systems, you'll need a specially designed 40-pin/80-conductor cable (typically provided with new, "boxed" UDMA/100/133 drives). Also keep in mind that the operating system must be enabled for DMA transfers (virtually a requirement under Windows XP). Keep the following issues in mind when implementing a UDMA/100/133 system:

■ Make sure that the signal cable is Ultra-ATA/100/133 capable. An Ultra-ATA/100/133-compliant cable is a 40-pin/80-conductor cable with a black connector on one end, a blue connector on the other end, and a gray connector in the middle. In addition, pin 34 on the cable should be notched or cut (though this may be difficult to see with the human eye).

■ Make sure the system board (motherboard) controller is capable of supporting Ultra-ATA/100/133. An Ultra-ATA/100/133-capable controller has a detect circuit that can detect whether line 34 is missing on the cable. If there is no detect circuit, the system can wrongly detect the presence of an Ultra-ATA/100/133 cable and try to configure the device for a higher transfer rate.

■ Some system board (motherboard) controllers may not successfully handle Ultra-ATA/100/133 on both the primary and secondary channels (though this is extremely rare today). If you have difficulty with a UDMA/100/133 device on the secondary controller channel, consider troubleshooting with the device in the "primary master" position.

■ If you have trouble getting a UDMA/66 system configured properly, contact the system board (motherboard) or controller card manufacturer for the latest BIOS upgrade (and any Ultra-ATA/100/133 device drivers or patches). In some cases, you may need to upgrade the drive controller by installing a Maxtor Ultra-ATA/133 card or Promise Ultra133 TX2 card.

■ Make sure the operating system is "DMA capable," and verify that the DMA mode is activated. For Windows 9x/Me, check the drive's Properties dialog box in the Device Manager. For Windows XP, check the Drive Controller Properties in Device Manager.

■ UDMA/100/133 remains fully backward compatible with existing EIDE/UDMA hard drives, removable media drives, and CD-ROM/R/RW drives—though you'll be limited to the maximum data transfer rate of the interface.

Remember that each drive connected to a UDMA/100/133 controller channel should be fully UDMA/100/133 compliant. If a particular drive is not, that drive may impair the ability of the controller to adjust for changes in transfer speeds with slower drives—resulting in reduced channel performance for all drives.

# SERIAL ATA

Virtually all hard drive interfaces have employed a parallel data bus to transfer data between a drive and host PC. However, leading drive makers such as Maxtor have been working to develop a serial interface capable of burst data transfers up to 150 MB/s (eventually slated to reach 300 MB/s)—while still using the same command set as other traditional ATA/ATAPI-type drives. Serial ATA controllers can coexist with current parallel ATA/ATAPI controllers, allowing both serial and parallel drives in the same system. With a few serial ATA drives in the market (such as Seagate's 120GB Barracuda Serial ATA V drive) and plenty of headroom for additional data transfer performance, chances are you'll see much more about serial ATA drives in coming years.

# DATA TRANSFER MODES

Data transfer rates play a major role in drive performance. In practice, there are two measures of data transfer: the rate at which data is taken from the platters and the rate at which data is passed between the drive and controller. The *internal* data transfer between the platters and drive buffer is typically the slower rate. Older Ultra-ATA drives like the Maxtor DiamondMax 2160 run at 14 MB/s, but their newer DiamondMax D540X (UDMA/133) drives can move information between the buffer and media at up to 43.4 MB/s. The *external* data transfer between the drive and controller (the "interface rate") is often the *faster* rate. Older ATA-2 (EIDE) drives can operate up to 16 MB/s using PIO mode 4. Ultra-DMA/66 drives can burst data from the buffer to the interface at 66 MB/s, Ultra-DMA/100 drives can handle burst data transfers of 100 MB/s, and Ultra-DMA/133 drives can handle bursts up to 133 MB/s.

The modern standards of external data transfer are listed as PIO (or *Programmed I/O*) and DMA (*Direct Memory Access*) modes. PIO modes are managed by the system processor. The PIO mode specifies how fast data is transferred to and from the drive, as shown in Table 20-2.

You may notice that the EIDE-specific modes (PIO-3 and PIO-4) use the IORDY hardware flow control line. This means that the drive can use the IORDY line to slow down the interface when necessary. Interfaces without proper IORDY support may cause data corruption in the fast PIO modes (so you'd be stuck with the slower modes). When choosing an EIDE drive and controller, always be sure to check that the IORDY line is being used.

By comparison, DMA data transfers mean that the data is transferred *directly* between the drive and memory without using the CPU as an intermediary (as is the case with PIO). In true multitasking operating systems like OS/2, Windows NT, or Linux, DMA transfers leave the CPU free to do something useful during disk transfers. In a DOS or Windows 98/Me/XP environment, the CPU will have to wait for the transfer to finish anyway, so in these cases DMA transfers don't offer that much of a multitasking advantage. There are two distinct types of direct memory access: ordinary DMA and bus-mastering DMA. *Ordinary DMA* uses the DMA controller on the system's motherboard to perform the complex task of arbitration, grabbing the system bus, and transferring the data. With *bus-mastering DMA*, all this is done by logic in the drive controller itself. DMA transfer modes are listed in Table 20-3.

# BLOCK MODE TRANSFERS

Traditionally, an interrupt (IRQ) is generated each time a read or write command is passed to the drive. This causes a certain amount of overhead work for the host system and CPU. If it were possible to transfer *multiple* sectors of data between the drive and host without generating an IRQ, data transfer could be accomplished much more efficiently. *Block mode* transfers allow up to 128 sectors of data to be transferred

**TABLE 20-2    DATA TRANSFER SPEED FOR PIO MODES**

| PIO MODE | CYCLE TIME (NS) | TRANSFER RATE (MB/S) | NOTES |
|---|---|---|---|
| 0 | 600 | 3.3 | These are the old ATA (IDE) modes. |
| 1 | 383 | 5.2 | |
| 2 | 240 | 8.3 | |
| 3 | 180 IORDY | 11.1 | These are the newer ATA-2 (EIDE) modes. |
| 4 | 120 IORDY | 16.6 | |

**TABLE 20-3   DATA TRANSFER SPEED FOR DMA MODES**

| DMA MODE | CYCLE TIME (NS) | TRANSFER RATE (MB/S) | NOTES |
| --- | --- | --- | --- |
| Single Word 0 | 960 | 2.1 | Also in ATA |
| 1 | 480 | 4.2 | |
| 2 | 240 | 8.3 | |
| Multi Word 0 | 480 | 4.2 | Also in ATA |
| 1 | 150 | 13.3 | |
| 2 | 120 | 16.6 | |
| Ultra-DMA Mode 0 | 240 | 16.6 | Also in ATA/ATAPI-4 |
| Ultra-DMA Mode 1 | 160 | 25.0 | |
| Ultra-DMA Mode 2 | 120 | 33.0 | Ultra-DMA/33 |
| Ultra-DMA Mode 3 | 90 | 44.0 | Also in ATA/ATAPI-5 |
| Ultra-DMA Mode 4 | 60 | 66.0 | Ultra-DMA/66 |
| Ultra-DMA Mode 5 | 40 | 100.0 | Ultra-DMA/100 |
| Ultra-DMA Mode 6 | --- | 133.0 | Ultra-DMA/133 |

at a single time and can improve transfers as much as 30 percent. However, block mode transfers are not terribly effective on single-tasking operating systems like DOS—any improvement over a few percent usually indicates bad buffer cache management on the part of the drive. Finally, the block size that is optimal for drive throughput isn't always the best for system performance. For example, the DOS FAT file system tends to favor a block size equal to the cluster size.

## BUS MASTERING DMA

Conventional DMA is called *third-party DMA*, which means that the DMA controllers on the motherboard coordinate the DMA transfers (the third party is the DMA controller itself). Unfortunately, these DMA controllers are old and very slow—basically unchanged since the earliest days of the PC. They are also tied to the old ISA bus, which has been all but abandoned for performance reasons. When multiword DMA modes 1 and 2 became popular, so did the use of the high-speed PCI bus for IDE/ATA controller cards. At that point, the old method of DMA transfers had to change.

Modern IDE/ATA hard disks use first-party DMA transfers. The term *first-party* means that the peripheral device itself does the work of transferring data to and from memory, with no external DMA controller involved—this is also called *bus mastering* because the transferring device becomes the "master of the bus." Bus mastering IDE (or BM IDE) allows the hard disk and memory to work without relying on the old DMA controller built into the system or needing any support from the CPU. It requires the use of the PCI bus and achieves the efficient transfer of data to and from the hard disk and system memory. Bus mastering DMA keeps CPU utilization *low*.

While there are obvious advantages to bus mastering DMA, the use of bus-mastering multiword DMA mode 2 never really caught on—primarily due to the poor state of support for the technology for the first couple of years. PIO modes required no work and were very simple, but DMA was not even supported by the first version of Windows 95 (special drivers had to be used). Problems with implementing bus mastering DMA on systems between 1996 to 1998 included buggy drivers, software the didn't work properly, CD-ROM drives that wouldn't work with the drivers, and so on. Thus, DMA didn't offer much incentive to make the switch.

Bus mastering DMA finally took off when the industry moved to Ultra-DMA. Once Ultra-DMA/33 doubled the interface transfer rate, DMA had an obvious speed advantage over PIO (in addition to its other efficiency improvements). Support for DMA was also cleaned up and made native in Windows 9x/Me/XP, and most of the problems with the old drivers were eliminated. Today, the use of Ultra-DMA data transfers are standard in the industry, and you rarely (if ever) encounter IDE-type hard drives using PIO data transfers (unless you're resurrecting a very old hard drive). To make the most of bus master performance, your system must have *all* of the following elements:

- The motherboard (drive controller) must be bus master IDE (BM IDE)-compliant.
- The motherboard BIOS must support bus mastering.
- You need a bus master-compliant operating system (OS) such as Windows 9x/Me/XP.
- A bus mastering device driver is needed for the operating system.
- And you need a bus mastering-compatible IDE device (disk drive, CD-ROM) that supports "DMA multi-word" modes.

You *can* use bus master IDE and non-bus master IDE devices in the same system, but the non-bus master IDE devices may reduce the overall performance of the bus mastering devices. Still, bus mastering IDE is not a cure-all for system performance problems. In fact, bus mastering will probably not benefit the system significantly if you run DOS applications, work with only single applications at a time, or use multiple applications that are not disk-intensive.

## Windows Bus Master IDE Drivers

As mentioned previously, you'll need a bus master driver to support your operating system (namely Windows 9x/Me/XP). The initial release of Windows 95 offered only a generic solution (ESDI_506.PDR), and the version released with OSR2 is still quite basic. The bus master drivers shipped with Windows 98 and later will generally offer better performance. For top performance, you should use the bus master driver that accompanies your motherboard (or other bus master-compliant drive controller). You can check Drivers Headquarters at www.drivershq.com for current bus master drivers. Windows XP provides excellent native bus mastering support, and you generally don't need to install third-party drivers unless Windows XP doesn't support the motherboard or chipset hardware properly. For example, Ultra-DMA data transfer modes can be selected through the drive controller's Properties dialog box in the Device Manager (see Figure 20-8).

## Bus Master Driver Issues

While bus mastering can clearly enhance the drive performance of a busy multitasking system, it is not without its problems. As it turns out, bus master driver issues are the most prevalent problems. The two most common issues are

- The CD-ROM or IDE-type HDD on the secondary drive channel disappears after installing the bus master driver.
- Windows 9x/Me takes a long time to boot after bus master drivers are installed (Windows XP generally doesn't suffer from BM driver problems).

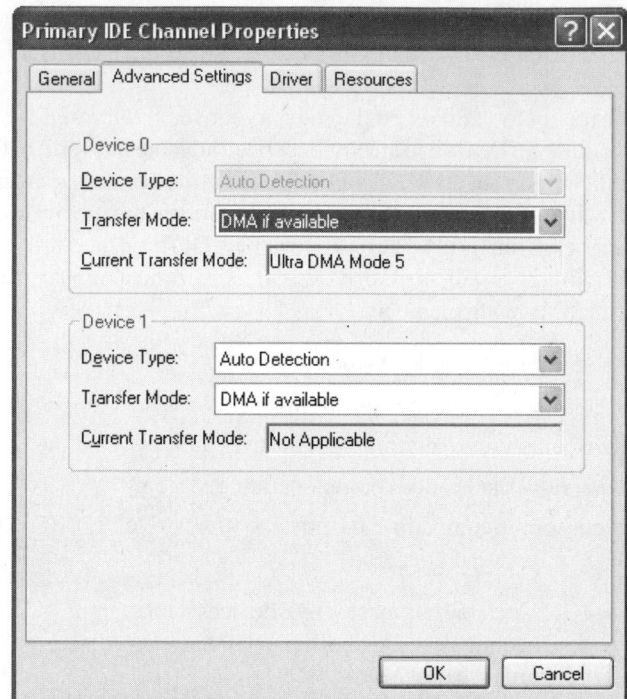

**FIGURE 20-8**  Tweaking the data transfer modes through the drive controller Properties dialog box

In both cases, you'll notice that the secondary controller channel (IDE) no longer appears in the Device Manager. This is because bus master drivers do not support ATA (IDE) controllers correctly. You'll need to install the bus master driver for the primary (EIDE) drive channel and leave the PIO driver in place to support the secondary (IDE) drive channel. Install the bus master driver, then alter the Windows 98/Me Registry to manually redirect the secondary IDE drive channel to use a standard IDE driver again (you should not need this process under Windows XP):

 Altering the Windows Registry can have a profound effect on your system and even prevent the system from booting. Always make a backup copy of the original Registry files (SYSTEM.DAT and USER.DAT) before attempting to edit them.

1. Start REGEDIT, load the Registry file, and find the entry

   `HKEY_LOCAL_MACHINE/System/CurrentControlSet/control/Services/Class/hdc`

2. There should be four sub-directories: 0000-0003

3. Find the one where DriverDesc reads something like "Primary Bus Master IDE controller" or "Secondary Bus Master IDE controller," according to the port you want to change (should be 0002 or 0003). You'd most likely want to change the secondary entry.

4. In this subdirectory, change PortDriver from "ESDI_506.PDR" (or whatever bus master driver you're using) to "IDEATAPI.MPD."

5. You can also change the DriverDesc to something like "Standard IDE/ESDI controller"—this will produce a more familiar entry when viewed in the Device Manager.

6. Save your changes and reboot the computer.

Your secondary (IDE) drive controller channel should now be using a standard IDE driver, and the IDE devices on that channel (such as the CD-ROM) should now appear normally. Here's another trick that may shorten the startup time—start Windows 9x/Me in Safe Mode and delete all drives in Device Manager. Then reboot the PC and allow Windows to re-detect all the drives automatically.

Some technicians have suggested that configuring an ATAPI CD-ROM as the "slave" device when it's the only device on the secondary (IDE) drive channel might work when using bus master drivers. Normally, the only IDE device would be jumpered as the master. Please note that this suggestion won't damage the CD-ROM or drive controller, but it has *not* been tested to verify whether it actually works. Given the proliferation of bus master hardware and software, there may circumstances where this suggestion may or may not work. Consider it a last resort.

# UNDERSTANDING SMART TECHNOLOGY

Self-Monitoring Analysis and Reporting Technology (SMART) is a *self-diagnostic* system that enables the PC to predict the impending failures of devices such as disk drives. With a given failure prediction, the user or system manager can back up key data, replace a suspect device *prior* to data loss, and avoid undesired downtime. SMART is a key for improving data integrity and data availability of the PC.

SMART goes by a variety of names in the computer industry. The term *Predictive Failure Analysis (PFA)* was given to SMART technology by its inventor, IBM. PFA is implemented in all of IBM's mainframe computer systems. Compaq was one of the first companies to implement SMART in its hard drives, and the feature was dubbed *Drive Failure Prediction (DFP)*. The initial Compaq Computer SMART specification was modified and submitted for general industry consideration by the Small Form Factor Committee. SMART is now a standard part of ANSI ATA-4 (ANSI X3T13 ATA\ATAPI-4) and later specifications.

To implement SMART, the host computer must have BIOS or device driver support that is capable of sending SMART commands to and from the ATA interface registers. SMART technology is growing in popularity, and all current Maxtor, Western Digital, and Seagate drives are SMART-ready. You can learn more about SMART from Maxtor at www.maxtor.com/products/DiamondMax/techsupport/misc/smart.html.

# DRIVE CACHING

All modern hard disks contain an integrated cache, also called a *buffer.* The purpose of this cache is similar to other caches in the PC, though it's not normally considered part of the PC cache hierarchy. Cache acts as a buffer between a fast device and a slow one. For hard drives, the cache holds the results of recent disk reads and fetches information that is likely to be requested (for example, the sector or sectors immediately after the one just requested). Cache improves the performance of any hard drives by reducing the number of physical accesses to the disk, and allows data to stream uninterrupted from the disk when the bus is busy. Most modern IDE hard drives have between 512KB and 8MB of internal cache (such as the Western Digital Caviar 80GB HDD at store.westerndigital.com/product.asp?sku=1903921), though some high-performance SCSI drives have as much as 16MB.

## Cache Operation

Hard drive cache helps to correct for the speed difference between the drive and the interface. Finding a piece of data on the hard drive involves random positioning and incurs a penalty of *milliseconds* as the head actuator is moved and the disk rotates on the spindle. On a typical IDE/ATA hard disk, transferring a 4KB block of data from the disk's internal cache is over 100 times *faster* than actually finding it and reading it from the platters.

The basic principle behind cache operation is relatively simple. Reading data from the drive is generally done in blocks of various sizes (not just one 512-byte sector at a time). The cache is broken into segments, each of which can contain one block of data. When a request is made for data from the drive, the cache is first queried to see if the data is present in any cache segments. If it is, the cache data is passed to the interface without accessing the drive. If the data is not in the cache, it's read from the drive, passed to the interface, and then placed into the cache in the event that it's asked for again. Since cache is limited in size, there is only a limited amount of data that can be held before the segments must be recycled. Typically the oldest piece of data is replaced with the newest one. This is called *circular, first-in/first-out* (FIFO), or *wrap-around* caching. To improve performance, most drive manufacturers today have implemented enhancements to their cache management circuitry, such as:

- **Adaptive Segmentation**   Conventional cache is chopped into a number of equal-sized segments. Since requests can be made for data blocks of different sizes, this can cause some of the cache data to be left over—and thus wasted. Many newer drives dynamically resize their cache segments based on the space required for each access. It can also change the number of segments. This is more complex to handle than fixed-size segments and can result in waste if the space isn't managed properly.

- **Pre-Fetch**   Sometimes called *read-ahead caching*, the drive's cache logic (based on analyzing access and usage patterns of the drive) attempts to load cache data that has not been requested yet, but that it *anticipates* will be requested soon. This usually means loading additional data beyond that which was just read. When done correctly, this will improve performance a bit.

- **User Control**   High-end drives have implemented a set of commands that allow detailed control of the drive's cache operation—this includes letting the user enable or disable caching, set the size of segments, control adaptive segmentation and pre-fetch, and so on.

Cache helps very little if you're doing a lot of random data access in different parts of the disk. If the disk has not loaded a piece of data recently, it won't be in the cache. The cache is also poor help if you're reading a large amount of data from the disk (normally it's pretty small). For example, when copying a 10MB file on a typical disk with a 512KB buffer, 5 percent of the file could be in the buffer at most—the rest must be read from the disk itself. This means cache doesn't have as much impact on overall system performance as you might think. Figure 20-9 illustrates the caching algorithm used by Quantum Corporation for some of their older ProDrive hard drives.

## Write Caching

With no write caching, every write to the hard drive involves a performance hit while the system waits for the hard disk to access the correct location on the drive and write data. This takes at least 10ms on most drives and really slows down performance as the system waits for the hard drive. This mode of operation is called *write-through caching*—the data written is actually put into the cache in case it needs to be read again later, but the write occurs at the same time. When write caching is enabled, the system writes to the drive, but the drive holds the data in its cache and immediately sends an acknowledgement to the operating system. The rest of the system can then continue without having to wait for the actuator to position and the disk to spin. This is called *write-back caching* because the data is stored in the cache and written back to the platters only later on. Write-back caching improves performance, but it puts data at risk because power failures or other system problems that occur before the cached data is actually written can cause data corruption. Due to this risk, write caching is not used at all in some situations—especially for applications where high data integrity is critical (e.g., network servers and important workstations).

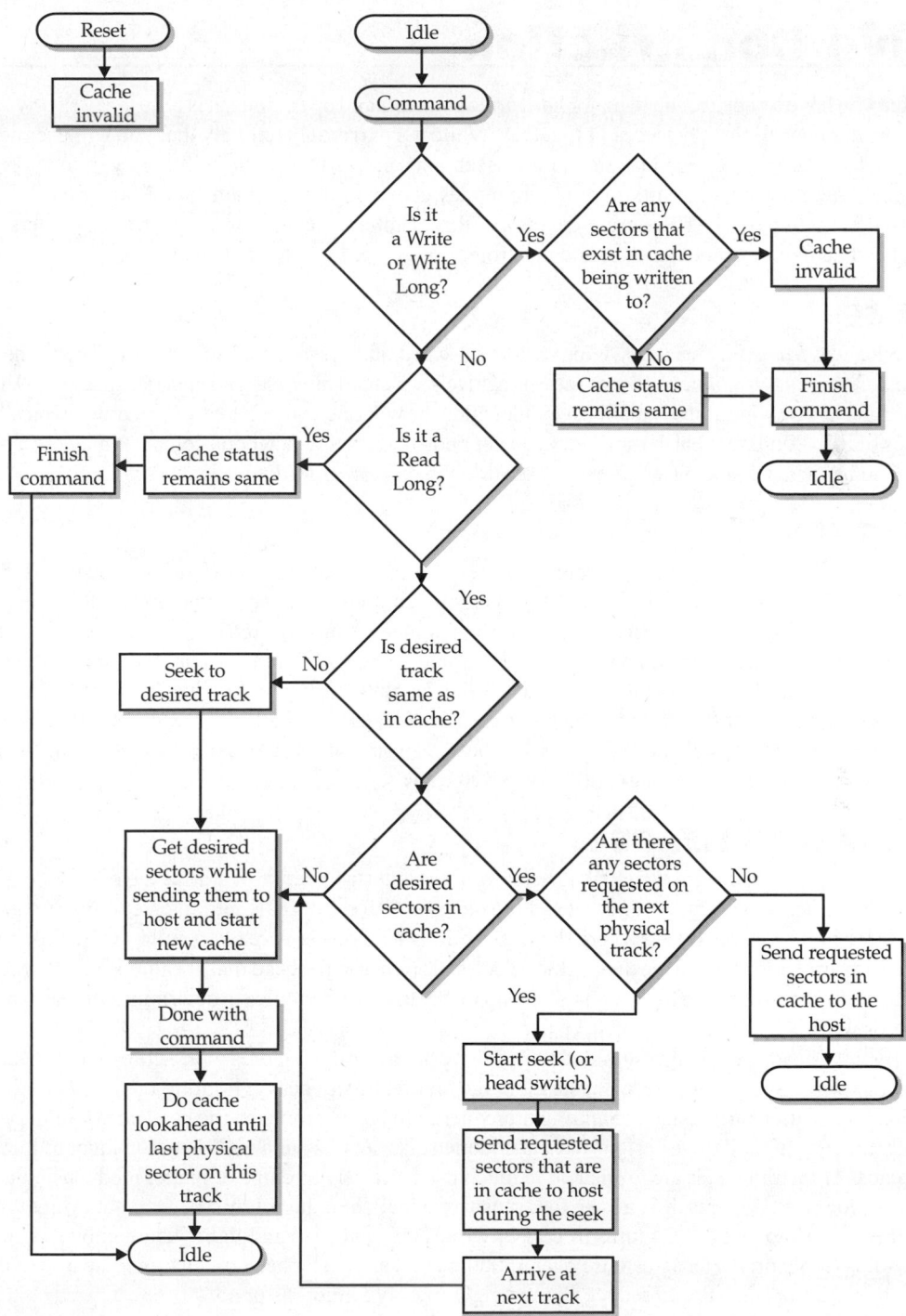

**FIGURE  20-9**     A cache control algorithm (Courtesy of Maxtor Corporation)

# Drive Construction

Now that you have a background in major hard drive concepts and operations, it is time to take a drive apart and show you how all the key pieces fit together. While it's **extremely** unlikely that you will ever need to disassemble a hard drive, the understanding of each part and its placement will help you to appreciate drive testing and the various hard drive failure modes. An exploded diagram for a Maxtor hard drive is illustrated in Figure 20-10. There are six areas that this chapter concentrates on: the frame, platters, R/W heads, head actuators, spindle motor, and electronics package. Let's look at each area.

## FRAME

The mechanical *frame* is remarkably important to the successful operation of a hard drive. The frame (also called a *base casting assembly* or *chassis*) affects a drive's structural, thermal, and electrical integrity. A frame must be rigid and provide a steady platform for mounting the working components. Larger drives typically use a chassis of cast aluminum, but the small drive in your notebook or sub-notebook computer may use a plastic frame. The particular frame material really depends on the *form factor* (dimensions) of your drive.

## PLATTERS

As you probably read earlier in this chapter, *platters* (sometimes called a *disk stack assembly*) are relatively heavy duty disks of aluminum, glass, or ceramic composite material. Platters are then coated on both sides with a layer of magnetic material (the actual media) and covered with a protective layer. Finished and polished platters are then stacked and coupled to the *DC spindle motor*. Note that some drives may only use one platter. Before the platter stack is fixed to the chassis, the *R/W head assembly* (part of the *rotary positioner assembly*) is fitted in between each disk. There is usually one head per platter side, so a drive with two platters should have three or four heads. During drive operation, the platter stack spins at 5,400 rpm, 7,200 rpm, or even higher (up to 15,000 rpm).

## READ/WRITE HEADS

As with floppy drives, read/write (R/W) heads form the interface between a drive's electronic circuitry and magnetic media. During writing, a head translates electronic signals into magnetic flux transitions that saturate points on the media where those transitions take place. A read operation works roughly in reverse. Flux transitions along the disk induce electrical signals in the head that are amplified, filtered, and translated into corresponding logic signals. It is up to the drive's electronics to determine whether a head is reading or writing.

Early R/W heads generally resembled floppy drive heads: soft iron cores with a core of 8 to 34 turns of fine copper wire. Such heads were physically large and relatively heavy, limiting the number of tracks available on a platter surface and presenting more inertia to be overcome by the head positioning system. Virtually all current hard drive designs have abandoned classical "wound coil" heads in favor of thin-film R/W heads. Thin-film heads are fabricated in much the same way as chips or platter media using photochemical processes. The result is a very flat, sensitive, small, and durable R/W head, but even thin-film heads use an air gap and 8 to 34 turns of copper wire. The small size and light weight allow for smaller track widths (large drives today can use over 16000 tracks) and faster head travel time. The inherent flatness of thin-film heads helps to reduce flying height to only 5 microns or so.

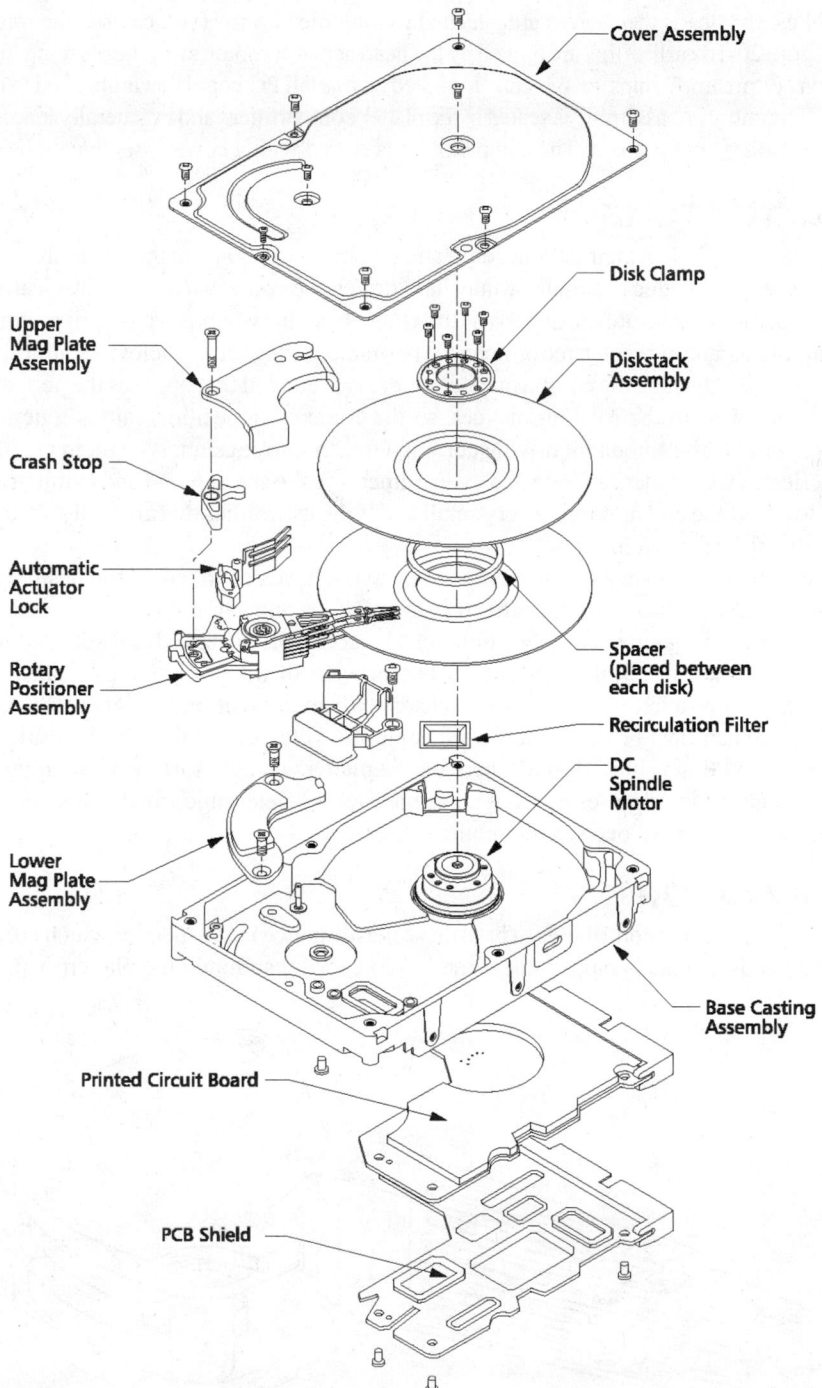

Cover Assembly

Disk Clamp

Upper
Mag Plate
Assembly

Diskstack
Assembly

Crash Stop

Automatic
Actuator
Lock

Rotary
Positioner
Assembly

Spacer
(placed between
each disk)

Recirculation Filter

DC
Spindle
Motor

Lower
Mag Plate
Assembly

Base Casting
Assembly

Printed Circuit Board

PCB Shield

**FIGURE  20-10**    An exploded diagram of a Maxtor D540X 80GB IDE hard drive (Courtesy of
Maxtor Corporation)

In assemblies, the heads themselves are attached to long metal arms (you can see the rotary positioner assembly in Figure 20-10 earlier) that are moved by the head actuator motor(s), as the close-up in Figure 20-11 shows. Read/write "preamp" chips are typically mounted on a small PC board that is attached to the head/actuator assembly. The entire subassembly is sealed in the platter compartment and is generally inaccessible unless opened in a cleanroom environment. The compartment is sealed with a *cover assembly.*

## HEAD ACTUATORS

Unlike floppy motors that step their R/W heads in and out, hard drives *swing* the heads along a slight arc to achieve radial travel from edge to spindle. Many hard drives use *voice coil motors* (also called *rotary coil motors*, rotary positioner assemblies, or *servos*) to actuate head movement. Voice coil motors work using the same principle as analog meter movements: a permanent magnet is enclosed within two opposing coils. As current flows through the coils, a magnetic field is produced that opposes the permanent magnet. Head arms are attached to the rotating magnet, so the force of opposition causes a deflection that is directly proportional to the amount of driving current. Greater current signals result in greater opposition and greater deflection. Cylinders are selected by incrementing the servo signal and maintaining the signal at the desired level. Voice coil motors are very small and light assemblies that are well suited to fast access times and small hard drive assemblies.

The greatest challenge to head movement is to keep the heads centered on the desired track. Otherwise, aerodynamic disturbances, thermal effects in the platters, and variations in voice coil driver signals can cause head-positioning error. Head position must be constantly checked and adjusted in real time to ensure that desired tracks are followed exactly. The process of track-following is called *servoing* the heads. Information is required to compare the heads' expected position to their actual position—any resulting difference can then be corrected by adjusting the voice coil signal. As you saw earlier in the chapter, servo information is placed somewhere on the platters using a variety of techniques. The servo system uses the phase shift of pulses between adjacent tracks to determine whether heads are centered on the desired track or drifting to one side or another.

## SPINDLE MOTOR

One of the major factors that contributes to hard drive performance is the speed at which the media passes under the R/W heads. Media is passed under the R/W heads by spinning the platter(s) at a high rate of

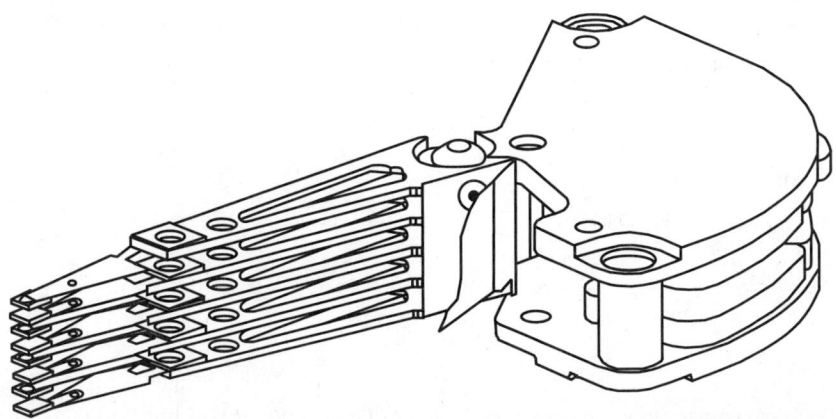

**FIGURE 20-11**    Close-up of a head actuator assembly (Courtesy of Maxtor Corporation)

speed (at least 3,600 rpm and to as high as 15,000 rpm). The *DC spindle motor* is responsible for spinning the platter(s). A spindle motor is typically a brushless, low-profile DC motor (similar in principle to the spindle motors used in floppy disk drives). An *index sensor* provides a feedback pulse signal that detects the spindle as it rotates. The drive's *printed circuit board* uses the index signal to regulate spindle speed as precisely as possible. Today's drives typically use magnetic sensors that detect iron tabs on the spindle shaft, or optoisolators that monitor holes or tabs rotating along the spindle. The spindle motor and index sensor are also sealed in the platter compartment.

Older hard drives used a rubber or cork pad to slow the spindle to a stop after drive power is removed, but virtually all IDE drives use a technique called *dynamic braking*. When power is applied to a spindle motor, a magnetic field is developed in the motor coils. When power is removed, the magnetic energy stored in the coils is released as a reverse voltage pulse. Dynamic braking channels the energy of that reverse voltage to stop the drive faster and more reliably (and with less wear and tear) than physical braking.

## DRIVE ELECTRONICS AND FIRMWARE

Hard drives are controlled by a suite of remarkably sophisticated circuitry (see the block diagram for a Maxtor D540X hard drive in Figure 20-12). The drive electronics board mounted below the chassis contains all of the circuitry necessary to communicate control and data signals with the particular physical interface, maneuver the R/W heads, read or write as required, and spin the platter(s). Each of these functions must be accomplished to high levels of precision. In spite of the demands and complexity involved in drive electronics,

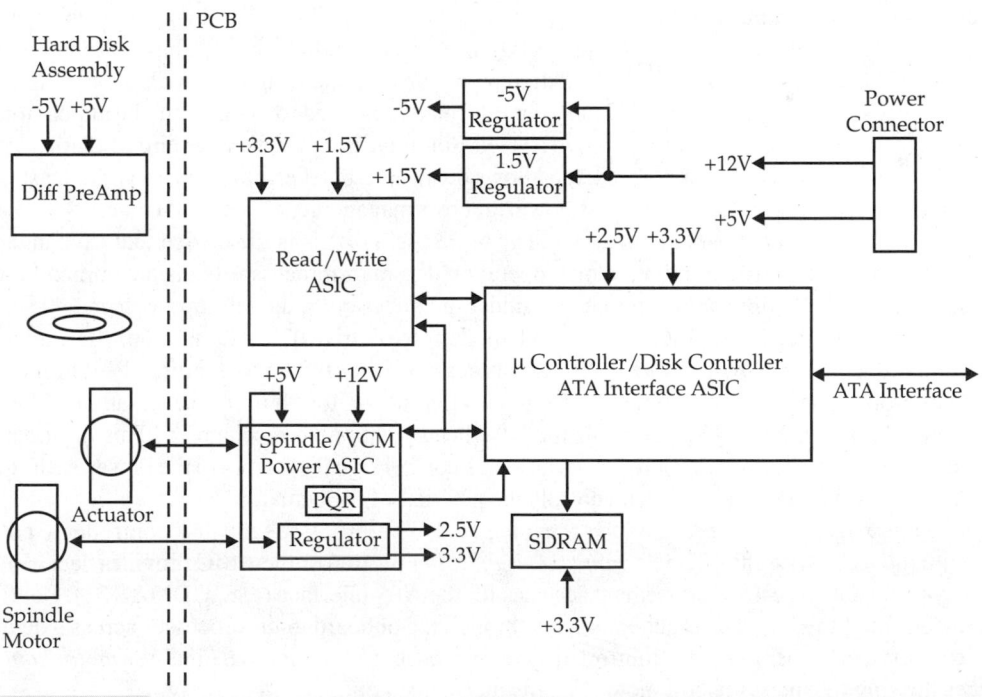

**FIGURE 20-12** Block diagram of a Maxtor D540X drive electronics system (Courtesy of Maxtor Corporation)

the entire circuit (except for the PreAmplifier and Write Driver chip mounted on the flex circuit inside of the sealed HDA) can be fabricated on a single PC board responsible for the following functions:

- Controlling the spindle motor and ensuring that the spindle runs at the correct speed
- Controlling the head actuator's positioning to various tracks (and handling servoing)
- Managing all read/write operations
- Implementing power management features
- Handling the geometry translation from *logical* (entered in the CMOS Setup) to *physical* (on the drive platters)
- Managing the internal cache and optimization features (such as pre-fetch)
- Coordinating other functions such as the flow of data over the interface, optimizing multiple requests, converting data to and from the read/write heads, and so on
- Implementing all advanced performance and reliability features (such as SMART)

You should understand the purpose of each functional module including the onboard microprocessor, digital synchronous spoke (DSS), error correction code (ECC) control, formatter, buffer controller, servo controller, serial (R/W) interface, ATA interface controller, and motor controller.

## Core Circuitry

As you can see in Figure 20-12 earlier, the *microprocessor* chip provides local processor services to the drive electronics under control of the onboard firmware. The microprocessor manages the disk controller and ATA interface, along with the read/write ASIC (chip), and the spindle driver. The *digital synchronous spoke* (or DSS) decodes servo information written on the drive at the factory to track the position of the read/write heads. It processes timing and position information needed to manage the head position. The *error correction code* (ECC) feature employs a Reed-Solomon encoder/decoder circuit that is used for disk read/write operations. Its redundant setup allows quadruple-burst error correction of at least 96 bits (and as many as 128 bits) per error—this is powerful error management for a hard drive.

The *formatter* controls the read/write channels of the ASIC. This is the device that exchanges data with the drive's R/W heads. To initiate a disk operation, the microprocessor loads a command into the ASIC's registers. The *buffer controller* operates under the direction of the microprocessor, and supports an onboard RAM buffer (often 2MB or more for modern hard drives) providing a 60 MB/s maximum buffer bandwidth. This bandwidth allows the microprocessor to access the buffer directly—eliminating a separate microprocessor RAM chip. The buffer controller allows for "buffer segmentation." The *servo processor* in the Read/Write ASIC controls the R/W head positioning mechanism. This information is processed in the controller ASIC/microprocessor, and a control signal is output to the Power ASIC to control current in the actuator coil—which controls the position of the actuator.

The *serial (read/write) interface* allows the integrated microprocessor and disk controller to communicate with the read/write chip. The *ATA interface controller* portion of the ASIC provides data handling, bus control, and data transfer management services for the ATA interface (e.g., UDMA/133). Configuration and control of the interface is accomplished through the onboard microprocessor across a dedicated bus, and data transfer operations are controlled by the buffer controller module. Finally, a *motor controller* manages the spindle and voice coil motor (VCM) mechanism on the drive.

## Read/Write ASIC

The Read/Write ASIC integrates an advanced *partial response maximum likelihood* (PRML) processor, a selectable code rate encoder-decoder (ENDEC), and a servo processor with data rates up to 270 MHz. R/W ASIC programming is accomplished through an 8-bit 40 MHz serial interface. The Read/Write ASIC is a low-power (3.3 Vdc) single supply chip with selective power management capabilities, and the chip includes 12 main features:

- Precompensator
- Variable Gain Amplifier (VGA)
- Butterworth Filter
- FIR Filter
- Flash A/D Converter
- Viterbi Detector
- ENDEC
- Servo Processor
- Clock Synthesizer
- PLL
- Serial Interface
- TA Detection and Correction

It is not vital that you understand the detailed operation of each feature, but you should recognize that the R/W ASIC manages the "low level" tasks and timings needed to exchange data with the media.

## Drive Firmware

Since all current hard drives employ an onboard microprocessor, they also require a "program" to operate the drive. Just as a motherboard's BIOS code is kept in nonvolatile memory, a drive uses firmware located in the microcontroller (or on a separate flash ROM chip) on the drive's main printed circuit board. The firmware controls four vital aspects of drive operation: disk caching, head and cylinder skewing, error detection and correction, and defect management.

**Disk Caching**    Hard drives include a disk cache to enhance drive performance (the Maxtor D540X drives incorporate a minimum 2MB disk cache, often called a *data or cache buffer*). Read and write caching can be enabled or disabled by using the Set Configuration command (more about the drive's command set later). *Adaptive caching* (sometimes called *adaptive segmentation*) allows the drive's buffer space to be dynamically allocated for read and write operations. The cache can be divided (as needed) into several segments—each segment contains one cache entry consisting of the requested read data and its corresponding pre-fetch data.

During a read cycle, the cache algorithm anticipates host-system requests for data and stores that data in the cache for faster access. When the host requests a particular segment of data, the caching feature uses a pre-fetch scheme to "look ahead" and automatically store the subsequent data from the disk into cache; if the host requests this subsequent data, the RAM is accessed rather than the disk. At least half of all disk requests are sequential, so there is a good chance that subsequent data requests will be in the cache. Since cached data can be accessed in microseconds rather than milliseconds, read caching can provide substantial performance improvements.

When a write command is executed with write caching enabled, a drive stores the data to be written in the cache buffer, and immediately sends a "Good Status" message back to the host *before* the data is actually written to the disk. The host is then free to move on to other tasks without having to wait for the drive to seek to the appropriate track, or rotate to the particular sector. While the disk is idle, it immediately writes the cached data to the disk—usually completing the write operation in less than 20ms after issuing the "Good Status" message. Write caching allows data to be transferred in a continuous flow to the drive, rather than as individual blocks of data separated by disk access delays.

**Head and Cylinder Skewing**    Head and cylinder skewing are two firmware-directed techniques used to minimize latency time, and thus increase the drive's effective data throughput. *Head skewing* reduces the latency time incurred when the drive must switch read/write heads to access sequential data (e.g., switching heads from one platter to another). A head skew allows the next logical sector of data to be accessed under the read/write head once the head switch is made and the data is ready to be accessed. In other words, when sequential data is on the same cylinder but on a different disk surface, only a head switch is needed (not a seek, thereby saving considerable time). *Cylinder skewing* is used to minimize the latency time incurred with single-cylinder seeks. The next logical sector of data that crosses a cylinder boundary is positioned on the drive so that after a single-cylinder seek is performed (and when the drive is ready to continue accessing data), the sector to be accessed is positioned directly under the read/write head (see Figure 20-5 earlier). This eliminates the need for the platters to rotate around again so that the disk access can continue.

**Error Detection and Correction**    Even with the sophisticated circuitry used by a hard drive, errors can and do occur. Hard drives must have extremely low error rates to ensure reliability. Drives use a complex application of ECC to detect and correct data errors. Firmware directs the drive's error handling process. For example, Maxtor's D540X hard drive series employs 288-bit quadruple-burst Reed-Solomon error correction techniques to reduce the uncorrectable read block error rate to less than 1 bit in $1 \times 10^{14}$ bits read. When errors occur, an automatic retry, a double-burst, and a more rigorous quadruple-burst correction algorithm enable the correction of any sector with 4 bursts of 4 incorrect bytes each (or up to 16 multiple random 1-byte burst errors). In addition to these error correction capabilities, the drive uses an additional cross-checking code and algorithm to double-check the main ECC correction—this greatly reduces the probability of an improper correction.

**Defect Management**    Hard drives are certainly not perfect devices, and some sectors on the drive are defective. The drive must identify and "disable" defective sectors, and this defect management is directed by the firmware. The Maxtor D540X drives use two techniques for replacing (or *sparing*) defective sectors: inline replacement and offline replacement. If a sector on a cylinder is found defective during the manufacturing process, the address of the sector is added to the drive's internal defect list. The defective sector is "skipped," and is replaced by the next subsequent sector to maintain a sequential block order. This *inline sparing* technique prevents slow data transfers that would occur if the drive needed to seek another cylinder to access a replacement sector. Defects that occur in the field are known as *grown defects*. If a defective sector is found in the field (e.g., during normal drive operation), *offline sparing* reallocates the defective sector to a spare sector from the nearest available pool of spares, and the corrected data is stored in the newly allocated sector. The defect list supports a maximum of 500 grown defects.

## Drive Command Set

A modern hard drive is basically a high-performance "computer" dedicated to the tasks of reading and writing your valuable data. Consequently, the drive exchanges much more with the host PC than just data—it also employs a rich suite of commands (or a *command interface*) used to initialize, configure, and operate the drive. Table 20-4 lists the commands used by the Maxtor D540X hard drive series. It's not important for you to understand the inner workings of each command, just be aware of the many commands involved in everyday drive operation.

**TABLE 20-4    THE COMMAND SET FOR MAXTOR'S D540X HARD DRIVE LINE**

| GENERAL COMMANDS | SECURITY COMMANDS |
|---|---|
| Download Microcode | Security Set Password |
| Execute Device Diagnostic | Security Unlock |
| Flush Cache | Security Erase Prepare |
| Identify Device | Security Erase Unit |
| Initialize Device Parameters | Security Freeze Lock |
| NOP | Security Disable Password |
| Read Buffer | **SMART COMMANDS** |
| Read Multiple | SMART Disable Operations |
| Read Sector(s) | SMART Enable/Disable Autosave |
| Read Verify Sector(s) | SMART Enable Operations |
| Seek | SMART Return Status |
| Set Features | SMART Execute Off-Line Immediate |
| Set Multiple Mode | SMART Read Data |
| Write Buffer | SMART Read Log Sector |
| Write Multiple | SMART Write Log Sector |
| Write Sector(s) | **HOST PROTECTED AREA (HPA) COMMANDS** |
| **ULTRA-DMA COMMANDS** | Read Native Max Address |
| Read DMA | Set Max Address |
| Write DMA | Set Max Set Password |
| **POWER MANAGEMENT COMMANDS** | Set Max Lock |
| Check Power Mode | Set Max Freeze Lock |
| Idle | Set Max Unlock |
| Idle Immediate | |
| Sleep | |
| Standby | |
| Standby Immediate | |

# Drive Preparation Concepts

You can imagine a disk drive as being a big file cabinet. When the drive is first installed, the "file cabinet" is completely empty—there are no dividers or folders or labels of any kind to organize information. In order to make the drive useful, it must be prepared for use. There are two steps needed to prepare a drive: partitioning and formatting. *Partitioning* divides the physical drive into one or more logical volumes (which receive a drive letter), and *formatting* allows the drive to store files that are suitable to the operating system. As you might imagine, these steps are critically important for the proper operation of a drive. This part of the chapter outlines the essentials of drive preparation and file systems.

## PARTITIONING

Partitioning the drive is the process of dividing the physical drive space into pieces (called *partitions* or *logical volumes*). This is one of the first things done when setting up a new hard drive, because partitions are one of the major disk structures that define how the disk is laid out. In fact, you *must* partition a drive even if you're only putting all of the space into a single volume. Partitioning is important because partition size and type will have an important impact on both performance and disk space efficiency.

There are several file systems in service today, but operating systems like DOS and Windows 9x/Me/XP continue to use the File Allocation Table (FAT) system. The main criticism of the FAT is that sectors are grouped and assigned as *clusters*—and this can be a wasteful use of drive space (especially for large drives where up to 64 sectors—32KB—may be in a single cluster). One of the newly created partitions will be assigned as the boot partition, and a *master boot record* (MBR) containing special boot code and a partition table will be written to the first sector. The MBR is often referred to as the *master boot sector* (MBS). FDISK is the DOS/Windows utility used for drive partitioning. Different operating systems carry their own partitioning limitations:

- Versions of MS-DOS and PC-DOS after 3.30 (but before 4.0) have a 32MB per partition limit.
- All versions of DOS have a 1,024 cylinder limitation. To access more cylinders, you'll need a device driver or a controller card that offers a "translate mode" (for example, LBA).
- DOS and Windows 95 (FAT16 operating systems) are limited to 2.1GB per partition.
- Versions of Windows NT 4.0 and earlier are limited to a 4.2GB boot partition.
- Windows 9x/Me/XP use FAT32 partitions that can support up to 2TB partitions.

There are a few third-party partitioning tools such as Partition Magic by PowerQuest. You may prefer a third-party tool if you need to create more than four partitions on a drive, or resize partitions without losing data—two features lacking in FDISK.

### Understanding the "Master Boot Record"

As you've seen, the master boot record (or MBR) is information that is normally stored in the first sector of the hard drive. This information is simply a small data structure that identifies where an operating system (OS) is located on the drive so that the OS can be loaded into the system's memory (RAM) at boot time. The MBR contains two elements; executable code (a "program") and a *partition table*, which identifies each partition residing on the hard drive. The MBR executable code begins the boot process by looking up the partition table to determine what partition holds the operating system. It then loads the boot sector of the partition containing the OS into RAM, and transfers execution of the "program" to the partition boot sector. The partition boot sector then finishes loading the operating system files into RAM.

**Creating/Restoring the MBR**    In actual practice, the MBR is created during the partition process (using FDISK). If the MBR is corrupted or damaged, you can often restore the MBR using FDISK with the /MBR switch, such as

```
C:\> FDISK /MBR                <Enter>
```

Remember to back up as much of the drive *before* attempting this command. It should not corrupt the drive partitions or its data, but it *could*—any changes to the boot information can render the data on your drive inaccessible.

**The MBR and "Drive Overlays"**    When a system BIOS or drive controller will not support the full size of a drive, you typically have the option of upgrading the BIOS (and/or drive controller) or using "drive overlay" software, such as MaxBlast (EZ-BIOS), Data Lifeguard Tools, or other products. The use of "overlay" software will effect the way an MBR is configured. When drive overlay software controls a hard drive (we'll use EZ-BIOS in this discussion), the MBR is stored on the *second* sector of the hard drive—the first sector contains EZ-BIOS code. Sectors 3 through 17 also contain EZ-BIOS code that is referred to as the *INT13 Handler* (INT13 deals with hard disk services). When the system is powered on, it looks at the first sector of the hard drive for boot instructions. In this case, the boot sequence is as follows:

- ■ EZ-BIOS code loads from sector 1 on the drive.
- ■ EZ-BIOS loads the INT13 Handler located in sectors 3 through 17, and uses this information to set up the hard drive for proper access at its full capacity.
- ■ EZ-BIOS loads the regular Master Boot Record found on sector 2, which in turn loads the operating system.

**Viruses and the MBR**    A common type of virus is one that replaces the MBR with its own code. Each time a computer is started, the code in the MBR is loaded into memory. If the MBR contains a virus, the virus code is loaded into memory every time a system starts up, making this type of virus *very* dangerous. Some MBR viruses do little more than display a message on your screen, while others can destroy your data. An MBR virus usually enters a system through a floppy disk that the system accessed either at startup or while the system was on. If your BIOS supports an "MBR protection" feature (often referred to as *boot sector virus protection*), this prevents new information from being written to the MBR, so make sure that this feature is *enabled* in the CMOS Setup.

 When partitioning and formatting a new hard drive, or when installing an operating system, you may need to disable boot sector virus protection in the CMOS Setup. You can easily reenable the protection once you've finished preparing the drive(s).

## FORMATTING

Even after partitioning, an operating system cannot store files on a drive. A series of data structures must be written to the drive. A *volume boot sector* (VBS), two copies of the *File Allocation Table* (FAT), and a *root directory* are written to each logical partition. High-level formatting also checks and locks out bad sectors so that they will not be used during normal operation. FORMAT is the DOS utility used for high-level formatting. It is interesting to note that the FORMAT utility will perform both low-level and high-level formatting for a floppy disk, but *not* for a hard drive. If you're installing a recent operating system such as Windows Me/XP, you need only partition the drive before launching the OS Setup routine—Setup will format the drive for you before installing the operating system.

# FAT BASICS

Microsoft DOS and Windows 9x/Me/XP use a FAT approach to organize files on the drive. Individual sectors are organized into groups called *clusters*, and each cluster is assigned a number. Floppy drives and some early hard drives used a 12-bit number known as *FAT12*, but older hard drives typically used a 16-bit number (called *FAT16*). The newest releases of Windows 95 (OSR2) and Windows 98/Me/XP assign a 32-bit number to each cluster (called FAT32). By assigning each cluster its own number, it is possible to store files in any available (unused) clusters throughout the drive without worrying about the file's size. As files are erased, those clusters become available for reuse. Overall, the FAT system has proven to be a versatile and reliable file management system.

The problem with the FAT system is that you can have only as many clusters as can be specified by the number of bits available. For a 12-bit FAT, you can only have 4,096 ($2^{12}$) clusters. For a 16-bit FAT, you can have 65,536 ($2^{16}$) clusters. If the drive is 120MB, each cluster must then be about 1.8KB (120MB/65,536)—2KB in actual practice. If the drive were 500MB, each cluster must be about 7.6KB (540MB/65,536)—8KB in actual practice. Since only *one* file can be assigned to any given cluster, the entire space for that cluster is assigned (even if the file is very small). So if you were to store a 2KB file in an 8KB cluster, you'd waste 6KB (8–2KB)! This wasted space is known as *slack space*. Of course, the FAT12 system was abandoned while hard drives were still about 32MB, but you get the idea that very large drives can waste a serious amount of space when using a FAT system.

Another frequent complaint about FAT file systems is the phenomenon of *file fragmentation*. Since clusters are all independent and clusters are assigned wherever they can be found, a file requiring more than one cluster can be scattered anywhere on the disk. For example, suppose you're editing a large image (it can take several MBs). The file may use the 20 available clusters on track 345, two more available clusters on track 1,012, 50 available clusters on track 2,011, and so on all across the disk. In theory, fragmentation is simply a harmless side effect of the FAT system. But in practice, badly fragmented files can force the hard drive to work unusually hard chasing down the various clusters associated with the file. Not only does this slow the drive's effective performance (due to the additional positioning and latency times), but the extra work required of the drive may ultimately shorten its working life. The best way to correct this issue is to periodically *defragment* the disk with a utility like *Disk Defragmenter*. Defragmenting the disk will rearrange all the clusters so that all of the clusters for any given file will be contiguous.

# FAT16

DOS (including the DOS under Windows 9x/Me—Windows XP only supports NTFS or FAT32) uses the FAT16 file system to store data. The FAT16 system uses 16-bit-cluster address numbers, which allow up to 65,536 clusters. Under FAT16, a cluster can be as big as 32KB, which translates into a maximum partition size of 2,147,483,648 bytes (2.1GB—65,536 × 32,768). While a 16-bit cluster number is much more efficient than a 12-bit cluster number, every file *must* take up at least one cluster—even if the file size is much smaller than the cluster. For the very large drives we have today, the correspondingly large clusters can result in a significant amount of slack space. If the physical drive is larger than 2.1GB, you must create subsequent logical partitions to utilize the additional space. For example, if you have a 3.1GB drive, you can create one 2.1GB partition, then create a second 1.0GB partition. One way to reduce *slack space* is to create a larger number of smaller logical partitions—doing this results in smaller clusters and creates more drive letters (one for each partition on the drive).

## Partitioning Large Hard Drives

Chances are that you're already familiar with the DOS FDISK partitioning utility and have used it at one time or another to partition older hard drives. However, large hard drives (over 2GB) present an unusual wrinkle for technicians—DOS and Windows 95 support partitions only up to 2GB. When you install a hard drive that's larger than 2GB, you need to create multiple partitions on the drive. Otherwise, you won't be able to take advantage of the full drive capacity. The procedure described next offers a step-by-step guide for partitioning large drives.

**Partitioning Large Drives with FAT16 FDISK**    If you're working with large hard drives under DOS or an early version of Windows, follow this procedure to partition hard drives using the FAT16 version of FDISK:

1. At the FDISK Options menu, select "4. Display partition information" and press ENTER. If the partition information display indicates that there are existing partition(s) on the drive, these partitions must be deleted *before* proceeding (select "3. Delete partition information" on the FDISK Options menu to remove any existing partitions).

2. At the FDISK Options menu, select "1. Create DOS partition or Logical DOS drive" and press ENTER. The "Create DOS partition or Logical DOS Drive" menu is displayed. Select "1. Create Primary DOS partition" and press ENTER.

3. The message "Do you wish to use the maximum available size for a Primary DOS Partition and make the Partition active (Y/N)" is displayed. Press N and press ENTER.

When this message is displayed, you *must* respond with N. If you reply Y, a primary partition of 2.048GB will be created, and the system will not be able to access the remainder of the drive's capacity unless the partition is deleted.

4. Type in the size of the Primary Partition (in MB). This value can be anywhere from 1MB to 2,048MB (default). Then press the ENTER key. The message "Primary DOS Partition created" is displayed. Press ESC to continue.

5. At the FDISK Options menu, select "1. Create DOS partition or Logical DOS drive" and press ENTER. The "Create DOS partition or Logical DOS Drive" menu is displayed. Select "2. Create Extended DOS partition" and press ENTER.

6. The "Create Extended DOS Partition" screen is displayed. Press ENTER to place the remaining available space on the drive into the Extended DOS partition.

If all of the remaining drive space is not placed into the Extended DOS partition, the total capacity of the hard drive will not be available to the system.

7. Press ESC to continue when the FDISK message "Extended DOS Partition created" appears on the monitor. FDISK will now prompt you to create logical drives for the Extended DOS partition. The message "Enter logical drive size in megabytes or percent of disk space (%)..." is displayed.

8. Type the value desired for the capacity value of the logical drive size (up to 2,048MB) and press ENTER. If you choose a value less than the displayed total size, you must continue entering drive sizes until all of the available space has been assigned logical drive letters.

Remember that each logical DOS drive created represents a drive letter to the operating system (such as C:, D:, E:, or F:).

9. Press ESC to continue when the FDISK message "All available space in the Extended DOS Partition is assigned to logical drives" appears.

10. If the drive is going to be the primary boot drive, select "2. Set active partition" and press ENTER at the FDISK Options menu. The "Set Active Partition" screen is displayed and the message "Enter the number of the partition you want to make active" is displayed. Press 1, then press ENTER. The message "Partition 1 made active" is displayed. Press ESC.

11. Press ESC to exit FDISK. Exiting FDISK under DOS will cause the system to reboot. Under Windows 95, the system may return to the **c:\windows\command>** prompt, and the user will have to reboot the system manually.

12. After the system reboots, each drive letter assigned to the partitioned hard drive must be formatted with FORMAT. You should now be able to use the drive.

There have been a number of problems reported with the Windows 95 version of FDISK. As a rule, use the DOS 6.22 version of FDISK or the 16-bit version of FDISK included with OSR2.

## FAT32

Obviously, the limitations of FAT16 present a serious issue with hard drives over 8GB. Since FDISK can create only four partitions of 2GB each, any space above 8GB may be inaccessible (not to mention the large number of drive letters). Microsoft responded by developing a 32-bit FAT system implemented in a service release of Windows 95 (called *OSR2*) and now standard in Windows 98/Me/XP. The upper four bits are reserved, so the system will actually access 268,435,456 ($2^{28}$) clusters (over 256 million clusters). This allows single partitions of 8GB with clusters only 4KB in size—the maximum theoretical size of any given partition is 2TB (yes, *terrabytes*—thousands of gigabytes). FAT32 also eliminates the fixed size for a root directory, so you can have as many files and directories in the root as you want.

On the surface, this probably sounds like a great deal, but there are some issues that you'll need to consider before updating to FAT32. First, DOS applications (without being rewritten) can access only files up to 2GB, and Win32 applications can work with files up to 4GB. By itself, that's not so bad, but FAT32 partitions are accessible only through FAT32-aware operating system versions, such as the OSR2-enhanced Windows 95 and Windows 98/Me/XP and their corresponding versions of DOS 7.X—no other operating system can read the partitions (including Windows NT). Also, any disk utilities written for FAT16 won't work for FAT32 (and using them can seriously damage your data).

Even though the OSR2 release ships with FAT32 versions of FDISK, FORMAT, SCANDISK, and DEFRAG, the version of DriveSpace 3 will *not* support FAT32. So, if you're using drive compression, you may need to remove the compression support before moving to FAT32. Further, there are older APIs (application programming interfaces) in service that simply won't support FAT32, so some programs may refuse to work until the software is recompiled with FAT32-compliant APIs. DOS device drivers (such as those needed to support SCSI devices) will also have to be updated for FAT32. In other words, you may lose some SCSI device functionality until suitable drivers become available. Finally, the OSR2 version of Windows 95 appears to *decrease* FAT32 drive performance (though that's not really an issue under Windows 98/Me/XP).

Today, the broad acceptance of FAT32 has largely overcome the compatibility issues discussed previously. But you should still be aware of the potential for trouble when working with older systems or OS versions.

## Partitioning and Formatting for FAT32

Before you make the decision to use FAT32, you'll need to become familiar with the issues involved in partitioning and formatting. The basic steps in drive preparation are the same as for FAT16, but FAT32 introduces a few wrinkles that you should be aware of. This part of the chapter describes the general process used to partition and format the drive under FAT32. First, a FAT32 partition can be created (with Windows 95 OSR2 or Windows 98/Me/XP) only under the following circumstances:

- The hard drive *must* be greater than 528MB in *total* capacity.

- The partition size must be greater than 528MB.

- You need an OSR2 Setup Disk or OSR2 Startup Disk made from another OSR2-configured PC (or a suitable Windows 98/Me Startup Disk, which is preferable to a Windows XP Startup Disk).

- When the FDISK prompts "Do you wish to enable large disk support? Y or N," you'll need to answer Y. If you answer N, a FAT16 partition will be created.

**Partitioning Large Hard Drives with FAT32 FDISK**    If you're working with large hard drives under a later version of Windows (or its corresponding DOS version), follow this procedure to partition hard drives using the FAT32 version of FDISK:

1. Boot the PC with the Windows 95 OSR2 (or Windows 98/Me) Startup Disk.

2. At the "Welcome to Setup" screen, press the F3 key twice—doing this will terminate the execution of the Setup program and take you to the A: prompt.

If you have a Startup Disk from another PC, you can boot from that disk instead and avoid the hassle of exiting the OSR2 "Setup" routine.

3. Type **FDISK** and press ENTER. You'll be prompted with "Do you wish to enable large disk support? Y or N."

4. Press Y to create a FAT32 partition and press ENTER. At this point, the FDISK Options menu will appear on the screen. If there is more than one hard drive in the system, use option "5. Change current fixed drive" to select the desired drive to partition. Be careful—partitioning the wrong drive will render any existing data on that drive inaccessible.

5. Select option "4. Display Partition Information" and press ENTER. For a brand new hard drive, FDISK should respond: "No Partitions Defined." Any preexisting partitions (FAT16 partitions) must be *deleted* before continuing. Remember, this will delete *all* existing data on the hard drive.

6. Press the ESC key to return to the FDISK Options menu, then select option "1. Create DOS partition or Logical DOS drive" and press ENTER. Next, select option "1. Create Primary DOS Partition" and press ENTER.

7. After FDISK verifies the drive integrity, it will prompt you with "Do you wish to use the maximum available size for a Primary DOS Partition and make the Partition active (Y/N)?" Press Y and press ENTER.

8. Exit FDISK by pressing the ESC key until you see the message "You must restart the system for changes to take effect." Press the ESC key to exit FDISK and remove the floppy disk in drive A:. Reboot the computer using CTRL-ALT-DEL if necessary.

**Formatting Large Hard Drives with FAT32 FORMAT**    If you're working with large hard drives under a later version of Windows (or its corresponding DOS version), follow this procedure to format hard drive partitions using the FAT32 version of FORMAT:

1. Boot the PC with the Windows 95 OSR2 (or Windows 98/Me) Startup Disk.

2. At the "Welcome to Setup" screen, press the F3 key twice—doing this will terminate the execution of the Setup program and take you to the A: prompt.

If you have an OSR2 Startup Disk from another PC, you can boot from that disk instead and avoid the hassle of exiting the OSR2 "Setup" routine.

3. Type **FORMAT** *<drive letter >*: and press ENTER to start formatting (such as **FORMAT D:**). After FORMAT starts, you'll see the message: "WARNING all data on non removable disk drive <letter:> will be lost proceed with format? Y/N."

4. Press Y and press ENTER. The FORMAT utility will then prepare the selected hard drive partition for use with FAT32. Keep in mind that large drives may take a long time to format as a FAT32 partition.

## Using the FAT32 "Drive Converter"

Windows 98 provides a "drive converter" that allows you to convert FAT16 partitions to FAT32 format. After you convert your hard disk to FAT32, you *cannot* convert back to the original FAT system. Before you convert to the FAT32 file system, uninstall any utilities or tools that protect or encrypt the MBR or partition table (for example, uninstall Bootlock included with Symantec Norton Your Eyes Only). The simplest method is to just type **cvt** *<drive>***: /cvt32** and then press ENTER. Remember that *<drive>* is the drive that you want to convert to the FAT32 file system. Another step-by-step approach is listed here:

1. Click Start, select Programs, highlight Accessories, choose System Tools, click Drive Converter (FAT32), and then click Next.

2. In the Drives box, click the drive that you want to convert to the FAT32 file system.

3. Click Next, then click OK.

4. Click Next, click Next, and then click Next again.

5. Allow the conversion process to complete.

6. When the conversion is complete, click Finish and reboot the PC if necessary.

The FAT32 converter may fail if your hard drive is less than 512MB or has bad sectors (often resulting in data corruption).

# Drive Capacity Limits

Capacity limitations are encountered whenever a computer system BIOS (and operating system) is unable to identify (or *address*) physical locations on a hard drive. This is *not* a problem with the design or structure of the hard drive itself, but rather a limitation of the system's BIOS or operating system. For the BIOS, it is not capable of translating the addresses of the sectors beyond a certain number of cylinders—thus limiting the capacity of the hard drive to less that its full amount. For the operating system, the file structure—the File Allocation Table—is limited in the number of physical locations (or addresses) that can be entered in the FAT. Drive manufacturers first encountered BIOS limitations in 1994 with the release of 540MB (ATA-2/EIDE) hard drives. Operating system limitations were discovered with the release of hard drives larger than 2.1GB. Your exact limitations vary depending on your BIOS version and the operating system. Today, you'll probably encounter BIOS with limitations at 2.1GB, 4.2GB, 8.4GB, 32GB, and 137GB levels. FAT16 operating systems like DOS and Windows 95 have a 2.1GB partition size limitation. Windows NT has a 4.2GB partition size limit. Windows 95 OSR2 and Windows 98/Me/XP can access much larger drives using the FAT32 file system. This part of the chapter is intended to help you understand and correct these drive size limitations.

## TYPICAL CAPACITY LIMITS

One of the most common problems with hard drives (especially when trying to add a new disk to an older system) is finding that not all of the drive is actually accessible. This is almost always due to BIOS and operating system issues that result from the shortsighted planning of the designers who invented hard disk structures, access routines, and operating systems many years ago. In some cases, they are due to actual hardware or software bugs that are not detected until hard drives grow beyond a certain size. Fortunately, there are now solutions to most of these problems. This section examines many of these issues so you can understand and get beyond these limitations.

### 1024 Cylinders (528MB)

The 528MB limitation for standard IDE/ATA hard disks started showing up in systems starting around 1994. This limitation caused a hard disk with a size *over* 528MB to appear as having only 528MB under some circumstances. This problem resulted from the geometry-specification limitations of the IDE/ATA standard and the BIOS Int 13h standard. Since only the lowest common denominator of both standards can be used, the maximum drive size that the BIOS can "see" is 1,024 cylinders × 16 heads × 63 sectors × 512 bytes/sector, which equals 528,482,304 bytes (528MB). The best way to correct this problem is to upgrade the BIOS to a version that supports translation—logical block addressing (LBA)—or to install "overlay software" such as MaxBlast or Data Lifeguard Tools.

This limit is referred to as the 504MB or the 528MB barrier—depending on whether you're looking at binary or decimal MB.

### 4,096 Cylinders (2.1GB)

As you saw previously, the basic problem with BIOS-related capacity limits is that the normal BIOS on older PCs is not designed to handle hard drives with over 1,024 cylinders. Every hard disk made today uses far more than 1,024 cylinders, causing a drastic reduction in available capacity. Systems with enhanced BIOS (using INT 13h extensions) can employ LBA translation to get around the 1,024-cylinder limitation and support larger drives. Some BIOS versions (even supporting translation) from around 1996 fail with more than 4,095 cylinders. This essentially causes the same problems at the 528MB barrier to occur all over again at the 2.1GB level.

It takes 12 bits to represent up to 4,096 cylinders, but due to poor BIOS code writing on some systems, only 12 bits of the cylinder number are available. Since it takes a 13th bit to handle numbers above 4,096 and only 12 bits are available, the BIOS is unable to "see" more than 2.1GB on the disk. On some BIOS, 4,097 cylinders may show up as only 1 cylinder if the 13th bit is just ignored and the lower-order 12 bits are used by themselves. The best way to correct this problem is to upgrade the BIOS to a version that supports more than 4,096 cylinders or to install "overlay software."

Don't confuse this problem with the FAT16 limitation of 2.1GB shown next—they are separate issues.

## FAT16 Partition Limit (2.1GB)

This 2.1GB capacity barrier is a file system problem that has nothing to do with the BIOS and is a limitation on disk volumes in the FAT16 file system. Given the way that disks use clusters, it is not possible to have more than 2.1GB in a single partition under the DOS or Windows 3.x/95A operating systems. Under Windows NT, the limit is 4GB rather then 2.1GB with FAT partitions (NTFS partitions do not have this limitation). If you install a drive over 2GB into a machine using regular FAT16, you may use the entire disk (assuming that you aren't limited by one of the other BIOS-related barriers). However, to access the full capacity of the disk, you must partition it into sections. Since this limitation is a function of the operating system, it affects IDE/ATA and SCSI hard disks equally.

This limitation does *not* apply to disks formatted using FAT32 introduced in Windows 95 OSR2. It is also not a problem in Windows 98, Windows Me, Windows XP, and Windows 2000. There is also the NTFS file system, supported by Windows NT and Windows 2000, which uses a completely different set of structures and can have enormous partitions. The best solution to this issue is to repartition and reformat the drive using FAT32 utilities, then install a FAT32-aware operating system such as Windows Me/XP.

## 6,322 Cylinders (3.26GB)

This is one of the most obscure size limitations that you may encounter—affecting only a small percentage of systems. It appears that the BIOS cannot handle drive geometry with more than 6,322 cylinders. Attempting to set a higher cylinder value than 6,322 may cause the PC to hang. This typically limits the capacity on such systems to about 3.26GB (6,322 cylinders × 16 heads × 63 sectors × 512 bytes/sector). The best way to correct this problem is to upgrade the BIOS to a version that supports more than 6,322 cylinders or install overlay software.

The significance of 6,322 cylinders is unclear, so there is no apparent reason why this limitation exists.

## Phoenix BIOS 4.0x Limit (3.28GB)

This is another obscure size limitation due specifically to a programming error in a few types of systems made in the mid-to-late 1990s. Some systems that use Phoenix BIOS (notably versions 4.03 or 4.04) have a problem with the BIOS routine that calculates the size of hard disk drives. This problem is also odd because the barrier actually isn't a single consistent level—it seems to vary with the geometry parameters, and behavior can be different based on the values entered.

Assuming standard IDE head and sector values of 16 and 63, respectively, the cylinder field can have a maximum value of 6,349 without any problems, resulting in a maximum capacity of 3.28GB. If a cylinder value of 6,350 to 8,322 is used, the CMOS Setup program may lock up. Cylinder values of 8,323 to 14,671 apparently work, but the displayed drive size is incorrect. Subsequent versions of this Phoenix BIOS code have corrected this bug, which occurred several years ago. If you still have a system exhibiting this problem, you may be able to get a BIOS upgrade to correct the problem.

> BIOS code is initially written by the BIOS maker and is subsequently tailored by specific system or motherboard manufacturers. This means that some implementations of these BIOS versions may not have this bug while others will.

### 8,192 Cylinders (4.22GB)

The normal way of circumventing cylinder limitations is to use BIOS geometry translation. Basically, translation works by dividing the hard disk's number of cylinders by a binary number, such as 2, 4, 8, or 16, and then multiplying the number of heads by the same number. This lets the number of cylinders that the BIOS "sees" remain below the INT 13h limit of 1,024. However, this translation causes a problem in some systems when using a hard disk over about 4GB in size.

When the number of cylinders on the drive is between 8,192 and 16,383, the number typically used for translation is 16. This *should* actually work because it overcomes the BIOS issues and results in geometry that falls within acceptable limits. But a problem was discovered when drives first exceeded 8,192 cylinders around 1997—DOS and early versions of Windows failed when presented with a drive that had (due to translation) 256 heads. This is actually a barrier caused by both the operating system and the system BIOS. The operating system should have been able to handle 256 heads, but the BIOS was creating the problem due to its translation.

When this problem surfaced, the easiest way to deal with it was to change the way the BIOS did translation so that BIOS stopped creating translated geometries that used 256 heads. One common way that this was done was to use 15 as the translation factor instead of 16. To help avoid some of these problems, many hard disk manufacturers also changed their geometries to use only 15 heads instead of 16. So instead of a drive being specified with 12,496 cylinders, 16 heads, and 63 sectors, it might use 13,329 cylinders, 15 heads, and 63 sectors. If you have a BIOS that suffers from this 256 head problem, you will need to upgrade the BIOS or install drive overlay software.

### 240 Head Limit (7.93GB)

The BIOS INT 13h interface normally restricts some drives to 8.46GB, given the translated limits of 1,024 cylinders, 256 heads, and 63 sectors. In some systems, however, the INT 13h interface restriction results in a smaller limit of 7.93GB. As with the 8,192 cylinder limit, DOS and some Windows versions cannot handle translated geometry that specifies 256 heads. To get around this, some BIOS versions have changed their translation method so that only 240 heads are presented to the operating system. This fixes the 256 head problem, but shaves some capacity off the INT1 3h limit. The 1,024 cylinder and 63 sector restrictions remain, but with only 240 heads the maximum drive capacity becomes 1,024 cylinders $\times$ 240 heads $\times$ 63 sectors $\times$ 512 bytes/sector = 7,927,234,560 bytes. If you find that you're not getting full capacity from an 8GB drive, a BIOS upgrade is probably in order.

### The INT 13 Limit (8.46GB)

Often just called the *8GB Barrier*, this limit is one of the most important for hard drives. Now that disk capacities have exceeded 80–100GB, this gets the attention that the old 528MB limit got in the mid-to-late 1990s. Many people run into this particular barrier as they attempt to upgrade systems originally purchased in the late 1990s with hard disks originally between 1GB and 8GB in size. This issue is also based on a BIOS limitation, but with this particular barrier, we are actually faced with the traditional limits of how hard disks are used in the PC.

The INT 13h interface standard used by the BIOS allocates 10 bits for the cylinder number (thus a maximum of 1,024 cylinders), 8 bits for the head number (maximum of 256 heads), and 6 bits for the sector number (maximum of 63 sectors, since the number 0 is not used). Multiplying these together with 512 bytes per sector, you get a maximum of 8,455,716,864 bytes (8.45GB). This is the *largest* hard disk size that can be addressed using the *standard* INT 13h interface. Unlike the old 528MB limit, there is *no* translation that can work around this because it isn't caused by a *combination* of limitations like the 528MB barrier is. To overcome this limit, there must be a change in the *way* hard disks are accessed. This means leaving INT 13h behind and using INT 13h extensions.

INT 13h extensions require support from *both* the BIOS and the operating system. Some older operating systems do not support INT 13h extensions. For example, all versions of non-Windows DOS (6.22 and earlier) and Windows NT version 3.5 will not support INT 13h extensions and cannot use hard disks over 8.4 GB in size. Windows 98/Me/XP have no trouble at all supporting INT 13h extensions with a suitable BIOS version.

### The Windows 95 Limit (32GB)

Microsoft officially announced in 1999 that Windows 95 does not support hard disks over 32GB in size. While the cause for this limitation is unclear (Microsoft does not seem to document the underlying cause), upgrading the operating system to Windows 98/Me/XP should correct the trouble.

### 65,536 Cylinders (33.8GB)

Dubbed the *32GB Barrier*, this is a relatively recent hard drive limit (it showed up in early 1999) and is yet another in a long series of limits caused by the inability of a BIOS version to handle a particular number of cylinders (much like previous smaller barriers). In this case, some versions of Award BIOS cannot handle drives that have more than 65,535 cylinders. Since hard disk parameters usually use 16 heads and 63 sectors, this works out to a capacity of about 33.8GB before trouble occurs. As of about June 1999, this problem had been corrected, so it is most likely to show up on systems purchased before that time. As a BIOS issue, the best corrective action is usually to upgrade the BIOS from the system or motherboard manufacturer.

### The ATA Limit (137GB)

To circumvent past hard disk barriers, most modern hard disks are addressed using logical block addressing and a sector number. Rather than specifying a particular cylinder, head, and sector, LBA uses a 28-bit address to define $2^{28}$ (268,435,456) unique sectors. The drive itself translates the sector into an appropriate physical location. Since each sector can hold 512 bytes, LBA addressing can support drives up to 137,438,953,472 bytes (137GB) in size—that's the absolute maximum drive size supported with 28-bit LBA addressing.

With current hard drives now exceeding 100–120GB, the industry needs an addressing scheme that will support huge drives into the foreseeable future. Rather than creating an entirely new scheme for the ATA/ATAPI-6 standard, the T13 Committee (www.t13.org) embraced Maxtor's "Big Drives" initiative, which employs 48-bit (6-byte) addressing. It also increases the number of sectors that can be transferred with a single command from 256 to 65,536—further increasing data transfer performance. With 48-bits, the drive can address $2^{48}$ (281,474,976,710,656) sectors. At 512 bytes per sector, drives can be up to 144,115,188,075,855,872 bytes (144 petabytes or PB) in size. In terms of current hard drives, that's an astonishing 144,115,188GB—144 million gigabytes! Even with the rapid growth in drive sizes, 48-bit "Big Drives" addressing is expected to support new hard drives for the next 20 years.

### The 32-bit OS Limit (2.2TB)

There is yet another potential drive size limit looming on the horizon, caused by the very nature of 32-bit operating systems such as Windows 98/Me/XP. Even though ATA/ATAPI-6 and later drives should support 48-bit addressing for drives up to 144PB at the hardware level, our operating systems continue to use 32-bit addressing schemes. If the OS is limited to 32 bits, the maximum partition size would be $2^{32}$ (4,294,967,296) × 512 bytes per sector, or 2,199,023,255,552 bytes (2.2TB). Given the fast advances being made in hard drive technology, PC users may face this limitation in just a couple of years. However, OS patches and updates will likely be available to work around this problem.

## HOW BIOS HANDLES LIMITS

When you install a hard drive into a system where the BIOS is unable to handle its size, the system can react in a number of different ways. The exact response will depend on the system, the age of the BIOS, and the integrity of the BIOS routines. But in just about all cases, the problems are normally caused by more cylinders than the BIOS supports. There are four typical ways in which a BIOS can fail to support the cylinder count:

- **Truncation**   When presented with a logical geometry containing more cylinders than it can handle, the BIOS may simply *truncate* the total to the maximum it supports. This is usually seen in older BIOS versions that does not support more than 1,024 or 4,096 cylinders and is also common in systems that do not support INT 13h extensions. Generally, truncation wastes some space on the drive but is still preferable to the other possible responses.

- **Wrap around**   Some old BIOS versions assume that the number of cylinders will always be 1,024 or below and look only at the bottom 10 bits of the cylinder number coming from the hard disk. As a result, the BIOS counts up to 1,024 and then wraps around to zero again and starts over. So if you tried to use a drive with 3,500 cylinders, the BIOS would "see" only 428 cylinders, because it would count up 1,024 three times (to yield 3,072), wrap around three times, and then end up with 428 cylinders (3,500 minus 3,072). The same thing can happen to a BIOS that supports only 4,096 cylinders—it may look only at the bottom 12 bits. This means that in some cases you can put a 2.5GB drive into your system and end up with only about 400MB of usable space showing up.

- **Incorrect reporting**   Some BIOS report the true number of logical cylinders that the drive has, suggesting that your system supports the full size of the hard disk. However, the BIOS has no real perception of the number. When you try to partition and format the hard disk, you will be stuck with the 1,024 or 4,096 limit. This is a BIOS issue that has confused and frustrated even the best technicians.

- **System failure**   Some BIOS versions will totally lock up if you try to use them with a disk larger than they can support. While this behavior is relatively rare, it is seen more frequently with larger and more obscure drive limits. If the system locks up when you try to autodetect or enter drive geometry, it's time for a BIOS upgrade.

## OVERCOMING CAPACITY LIMITS

As hard drive capacity has reached and exceeded each size limit, various hardware and software techniques have evolved to support these larger disks. Some of these solutions are simpler and more elegant than others—some are based on *fixing* the BIOS problem, while others are oriented more towards *working around* it. In general, the simpler solutions have met with the best results. More complex solutions (especially with software drivers) tend to suffer more incompatibilities and other issues. There are typically four solutions to overcome capacity limits:

- **BIOS upgrades**   These are usually the most reliable and elegant solutions, and with the advent of flash BIOS, the upgrade can usually be downloaded and installed for free (often without ever opening the system). BIOS upgrades are considered to be the most effective long-term solutions for most capacity problems.

- **BIOS expansion cards**   Basically these are just BIOS chips on an expansion card that installs in a motherboard slot to supplement (replace) the motherboard's BIOS for the IDE/ATA controllers. The new BIOS code takes over for the hard disk controller code, and lets you get around most size barriers—you continue to use the IDE/ATA connectors on your existing motherboard or controller card.

- **Controller upgrades**   Rather than just install a BIOS card, the entire drive controller can be replaced as an expansion card (along with its own onboard BIOS code). You'd then move your drives to the new controller and disable the motherboard's drive controller in the CMOS Setup. Controller upgrades are very popular because they also allow for the newest drive technologies. For example, a UDMA/133 drive controller card like the Maxtor Ultra-ATA/133 card or Promise Ultra133 TX2 card can replace an obsolete controller and allow for much larger drives (both the Maxtor and Promise cards support 48-bit addressing).

- **Overlay software**   Also called *dynamic drive overlays* (DDOs), this software overrides some of the BIOS code in your motherboard or hard disk controller, allowing access to the full size of a new hard disk on an older system. The software must be loaded immediately when the machine is booted to ensure that the driver is in place before any other piece of software tries to access the disk. Otherwise, the disk will not work properly. While such software is usually distributed free with new drives, there are often compatibility and interoperability issues that can result in problems. Overlay software should generally be used as a last resort when no BIOS upgrades are available and it's not possible (or economically feasible) to upgrade the controller hardware.

# Drive Installation/ Replacement Guidelines

Hard drives must be installed when building new PCs, adding supplemental drives to an existing system, or replacing outdated or failed drives. The installation process is not terribly complicated, but it can be a bit confusing to the novice. This part of the chapter offers some basic guidelines for IDE-type drive installation.

## SELECT JUMPER CONFIGURATIONS

An IDE-type drive may be installed as a master or slave device on any hard drive controller channel. These master/slave settings are handled through one or two jumpers located on the rear of the drive (right next to the 40-pin signal cable connector). The jumper selections for a Maxtor D540X hard drive are shown in

Figure 20-13. One of your first decisions when planning an installation should be to decide the drive's configuration:

■ If you're installing only one hard drive in the system, it must be jumpered as the master device. Note that the master drive on the primary drive controller channel will be the boot drive (that is, the drive C:).

■ If you're installing a second hard drive alongside the first, that second drive must be jumpered as the slave device.

■ If you're installing a second hard drive on the second drive controller channel, it should be jumpered as the master device (any other device should be reconfigured as a slave device).

Refer to the documentation that accompanies your particular hard drive in order to determine the exact master/slave jumper settings. If you do not have the drive documentation handy, check the drive manufacturer's Web site for online information.

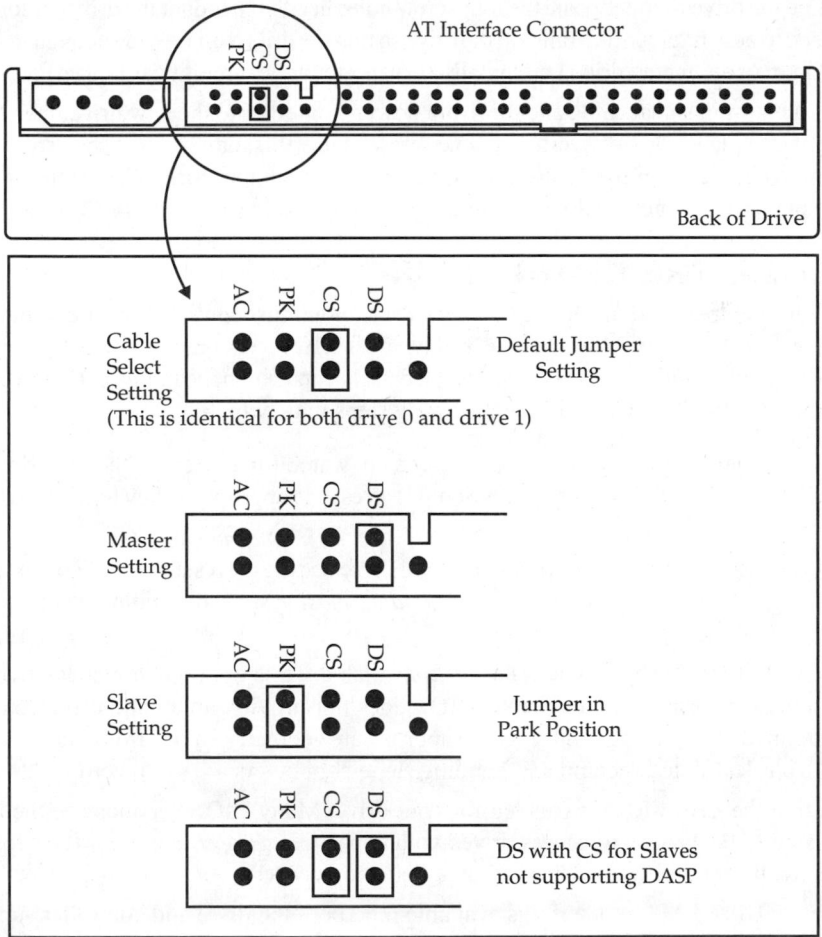

**FIGURE  20-13**    Jumper settings, which allow the drive to serve as a master or slave device on the IDE channel (Courtesy of Maxtor Corporation)

# ATTACH CABLES AND MOUNT THE DRIVE

The next phase of installation is to slide the drive into a bay, connect the power and signal cables, then secure the drive in place:

1. Turn off and unplug the PC, then remove the outer cover to expose the computer's drive bays.

2. Attach one end of the 40-pin drive interface cable to the drive controller connector on your mother-board (or drive controller card). Remember to align pin 1 on the cable (the side of the cable with the blue or red stripe) with pin 1 on the drive controller connector.

A 40-pin/80-conductor cable is *required* to run in Ultra-DMA/66/100/133 mode. Attach the blue end of the connector to the drive controller end, the black connector to the master (or single) drive, and the gray connector (if there is one) to the slave drive.

3. Locate an available drive bay for the hard drive. Remove the plastic housing covering the drive bay, then slide the drive inside. Locate the four screw holes needed to mount the drive. In some cases, you may need to attach "mounting rails" to the drive so that the drive will be wide enough to fit in the drive bay. You may mount the drive horizontally (usually with the circuit board down) or vertically.

4. Attach the 40-pin signal cable and the 4-pin power connector to the new drive, then bolt the drive securely into place. Do not overtighten the screws since this may damage the drive. If you do not have an available 4-pin power connector, you may use an appropriate Y-adapter if necessary to "split" power from another drive (preferably the floppy drive).

# CONFIGURE THE CMOS SETUP

Before you attempt to partition or format your new drive, you must configure your computer's BIOS to accept the drive (through the CMOS Setup). Today, most BIOS versions will detect and configure the drive automatically, and you'll see the new drive listed in startup text on the monitor. However, if you need to configure the CMOS Setup yourself, the following steps may help:

1. Turn the computer on. As your computer starts up, watch for a message that describes how to run the CMOS Setup (such as "Press F1 for Setup"). Press the appropriate key to start the CMOS Setup program.

2. Select the basic configuration menu with hard drive settings. To set the drive parameters, choose the *primary master* or *primary slave* (or *secondary master/slave* depending on how you've physically installed the drive).

3. Select Automatic Drive Detection (Auto) if available—this option automatically configures the computer for your new drive. If your BIOS does not provide automatic drive detection, select User-Defined drive settings and enter the appropriate geometry values from the drive documentation. As a rule, Write Precomp and Landing Zone parameters are set to zero.

4. Verify that the LBA Mode is enabled for your drive. Many BIOS versions use the logical block addressing (LBA) mode to access drives with capacities greater than 528MB. Most BIOS will automatically set this mode during the autodetection process.

5. Enable the Ultra-DMA mode if it is available (and both the drive and controller support it).

6. Save the settings and exit the CMOS Setup program. Your computer will automatically reboot.

# FINISH THE DRIVE PREPARATION

Boot the system with a Windows 9x/Me Startup Disk containing FDISK and FORMAT, which will be used to partition and format the drive, respectively (avoid the Windows XP Startup Disk if possible). Partition the disk with FDISK. If you use a FAT16 version of FDISK, you cannot create partitions greater than 2.1GB—this is *not* recommended today. If you use the FAT32 version of FDISK, you can create extremely large partitions. Now use FORMAT to prepare each partition on the drive for your operating system. Again, use the version of the FORMAT utility appropriate to the FAT system you plan on using. (You can find detailed instructions in the "Partitioning and Formatting for FAT32" section earlier.) After partitioning and formatting, you should be able to access the new drive's letter and to read and write files to it.

# REASSEMBLE THE COMPUTER

Double-check all of your signal and power cables to verify that they are secure, then tuck the cables gently into the computer's chassis. Check that there are no loose tools, screws, or cables inside the chassis. Now reattach the computer's outer housing(s).

# Drive Testing and Troubleshooting

Fortunately, not all hard drive problems are necessarily fatal. True, you may lose some programs and data (back up your hard drive frequently), but many drive problems are recoverable without resorting to drive replacement. Instead of focusing on repairing a hard drive's electronics or mechanics, today's repair tactics focus on repairing a drive's *data*. By reconstructing or relocating faulty drive information, it is often possible to recover from a wide variety of drive problems—if doing so fails to correct problems, the drive (and/or its controller) must be replaced. Before you begin any sort of drive troubleshooting, you should take the following steps:

- Gather a DOS boot disk or Windows 9x/Me Startup Disk (avoid using Windows XP Startup Disks if possible). If you don't have a boot disk on hand, you should make one now *before* continuing.

- Gather your DOS installation disk(s) or Windows 9x/Me/XP Installation CD-ROM—if you need to reinstall the operating system or any of its components at some point, these will be invaluable.

- Gather any hard drive/controller diagnostics that you'll need.

- Back up as much as you can from your hard drive(s) before attempting any sort of drive service.

# GENERAL TROUBLESHOOTING GUIDELINES

Although most drive installations and replacements will proceed flawlessly, there are many times when problems will crop up. If you've installed a hard drive and it does not function properly, perform the following basic checks before examining specific symptoms:

- *Be careful for power and static discharge.* Always turn off and unplug the computer before changing jumpers or unplugging cables and cards. Wear an anti-static wrist strap (or use other anti-static precautions) while working on your computer or handling a drive.

- *Verify compatibility.* Verify that the drive controller and drive are appropriately matched to each other (and to your computer). For example, an Ultra-DMA/133 drive will not run at top speed on an Ultra-DMA/100 controller.

- *Check all cards.* Verify that all expansion cards (including the drive controller card if installed) are seated in their slots on the motherboard, and are secured with mounting screws. Often one or more cards may be displaced when a PC is transported or opened for service.

- *Check all connectors and cables.* Make sure that all ribbon and power cables are securely connected. Ribbon cables are easily damaged (especially at the connectors). Try a new cable that you know is good. Make sure no connector pins are bent. Verify that pin 1 on the interface cable is aligned with pin 1 on the drive and the controller.

- *Verify drive jumper settings.* Review the instructions in your drive's manual (and in your host adapter installation guide) and see that all appropriate jumpers are installed—or removed—as necessary. Incorrect or duplicated jumper settings (such as two master drives on the same channel) can easily interfere with drive operation.

- *Check your power supply capacity.* Each time you add a new device to your computer, make sure your computer's power supply can support the total power demand. Install a larger (higher wattage) power supply if necessary.

- *Verify the drive settings in your CMOS Setup.* The drive settings in the CMOS Setup must not exceed the physical specifications of your drive. Also, the settings must not exceed the limitations set by the operating system and BIOS. Try the CMOS Setup's autodetect feature to identify the drive, or consider upgrading the BIOS and/or drive controller.

- *Check for viruses.* Before you use an unknown disk in your system for the first time, scan it for viruses. Also scan the system for viruses periodically.

## DRIVE DIAGNOSTICS

Most drive manufacturers provide a diagnostic utility that's specially designed to check the operation of their drive, and return error codes when a problem is detected. For example, Maxtor provides the PowerMax 3.04 utility (www.maxtor.com/products/DiamondMax/techsupport/TechnicalProcedures/20014.htm), which will perform diagnostic read/write verifications on Maxtor/Quantum hard drives. These tests will determine hard drive integrity, and any error codes returned by the utility will help to justify return authorization for warranty replacement if necessary. When the PowerMax utility encounters a failure condition during testing, it will display a six- or three-digit alphanumeric diagnostic code.

- If you receive a six digit error code with an **S57** at the end (e.g., xxxS57), try running the Write Disk Pack (Low-Level Format) option from the PowerMax utility. Remember that the write disk pack option will erase all data on the drive, so please back up all your data before using this option.

- If you receive a six-digit error code with an **MX1** at the end (e.g., xxxMX1), either the drive is not supported by PowerMax (that is, it's a non-Maxtor drive in this case), or you should try testing the drive on another IDE/ATA bus.

- All other six-digit error codes indicate that the drive has failed and should be replaced. The PowerMax diagnostic will typically provide a short description regarding the test that failed.

The PowerMax utility also generates a series of three-digit errors that refer to issues other than the drive. For example:

- **004**   Cabling/jumper configuration problems
- **005**   BIOS doesn't support capacity and/or LBA not enabled in BIOS

■  **006**   No partition detected (run FDISK)

■  **008**   Cannot identify the drive (e.g., non-Maxtor/Quantum drive)

## POTENTIAL PROBLEMS WITH Y-ADAPTERS

On rare instances, you may find that a drive will not function—or is damaged—when using a Y power adapter (Y-adapter). This can happen because a number of Y-adapters on the market are incorrectly wired. Y-adapters consist of a clear plastic plug with four metal prongs on an end that attaches to an existing power connector from the power supply. There are also two sets of wires leading to two plugs with female connections on the other ends, which are attached to internal devices such as hard drives, CD-ROM drives, and so on. The problem with some of these newer connectors is that the wires are attached incorrectly on one of the female connectors.

Examine both female connectors—make certain that both of the female connectors are lined up with the two rounded corners facing up and that both of the squared corners are facing down. The four wires attached to the female connectors should now be in the following order (from left to right):

**Yellow** (+12Vdc), **Black** (ground), **Black** (ground), and **Red** (+5Vdc)

If this order is reversed on one of the connectors, then your Y-adapter is faulty and should *not* be used. As a rule, you should never split power from the hard drive under any circumstances.

## RESOLVING "DOS COMPATIBILITY MODE" PROBLEMS

One of the great advantages enjoyed by Windows 9x/Me/XP is that it operates in the *protected-mode*—drivers and software can be executed beyond the traditional real-mode RAM limit of 1MB. By comparison, DOS is a real-mode environment. DOS programs and drivers can be executed only within the first 640KB of RAM (the conventional memory area). Although Windows XP will always use protected mode drivers, Windows 9x/Me will fall back on real-mode driver support if it cannot establish protected-mode operation for a drive—this is known as *DOS Compatibility Mode.* Unfortunately, real-mode support often impairs system performance. If you notice that one or more of the hard drives in a system is using DOS compatibility mode—there may be an error message such as "Compatibility Mode Paging reduces overall system performance"—you'll need to track down and correct the cause. In general, Windows 9x/Me may invoke the DOS compatibility mode for any of the following reasons:

Windows XP is designed to avoid "DOS Compatibility Mode", so the following steps are intended for Windows 9x/Me platforms.

■  The Windows 9x/Me protected-mode driver is damaged or deleted.

■  The Windows 9x/Me protected-mode driver is incompatible (or cannot otherwise support) the hardware.

■  A questionable device driver or computer virus has hooked the INT 21h or INT 13h chain before Windows 9x/Me loaded.

■  The hard disk controller in your computer was not detected by Windows 9x/Me. The controller may be disabled, or it may have failed outright.

■  The hard disk controller was disabled/removed from the current configuration in Device Manager.

■  There is a resource conflict between the hard disk controller and another hardware device.

## Identify the Drive

The first step is to find the offending drive, and the reason it's misbehaving. Open the Control Panel, double-click the System icon, then choose the Performance tab in the System Properties dialog box. You can identify which drive is using DOS Compatibility Mode—an explanation is often included.

## Viruses and DDO Software

If the driver name listed as causing the DOS Compatibility Mode is **mbrint13.sys**, your computer may be infected with a boot-sector virus. Otherwise, you're running real-mode disk "overlay software" (DDO software) that is *not* compatible with Windows 9x/Me protected-mode disk drivers. Run a current antivirus program to detect and remove boot sector viruses (such as Norton AntiVirus or McAfee VirusScan). You may need to rewrite your boot sector using a DOS command such as **FDISK /MBR**.

If you cannot detect any virus activity, check any drive overlay software and verify that you're using the latest version of that software for your operating system. Load SYSTEM.INI into a text editor and check to see if the **MH32BIT.386** driver is being loaded (check for a line that reads **device=mh32bit.386**). This older driver is installed by MicroHouse EZ-Drive "overlay software" and is *not* compatible with the Windows 9x/Me protected-mode disk drivers. Unfortunately, this driver is not removed by Windows 9x/Me Setup, so you'll need to disable the line manually, save your changes, and reboot the PC.

## Update Drivers in CONFIG.SYS

If the driver filename listed in the Performance tab is *also* in the CONFIG.SYS file, contact the driver's manufacturer to determine whether there is a more recent version of the driver that allows protected-mode operation in Windows 9x/Me. You may be able to download and install the latest driver version from the driver manufacturer's Web site. As a rule, you should avoid the use of real-mode drivers in CONFIG.SYS when using Windows 9x/Me.

## Reinstall the Drive Controller

If *no* driver name is listed on the Performance tab, check to make sure that the hard drive controller is listed in the Device Manager. If it's not, install it through the Add New Hardware wizard. If the wizard fails to detect the controller automatically, run the wizard again, but select the controller specifically from the hardware list (do not let it try to detect the hardware in your computer). If your particular controller is not listed, contact the manufacturer of the disk controller to obtain a Windows 9x/Me protected-mode disk driver, or upgrade the controller outright.

 If the hard disk controller *is* listed in Device Manager but has a red *X* over it, it has been removed (a.k.a. "disabled") from the current hardware profile. Click Properties for the controller in Device Manager and then click the checkbox corresponding to the current hardware profile under Device Usage.

## Resource Conflicts and Damaged Drivers

If the hard disk controller *is* listed in the Device Manager, but has a yellow "!" over it, there is a resource conflict (IRQ, I/O, DMA, or BIOS address range) with another device. In other cases, the protected-mode driver is missing or damaged, or the "Disable all 32-bit protected-mode disk drivers" checkbox has been selected in File System properties.

First, double-click the System icon in the Control Panel, click the Performance tab, and then click File System. Select the Troubleshooting tab and see that the "Disable all 32-bit protected-mode disk drivers" checkbox has **not** been selected (see Figure 20-14).

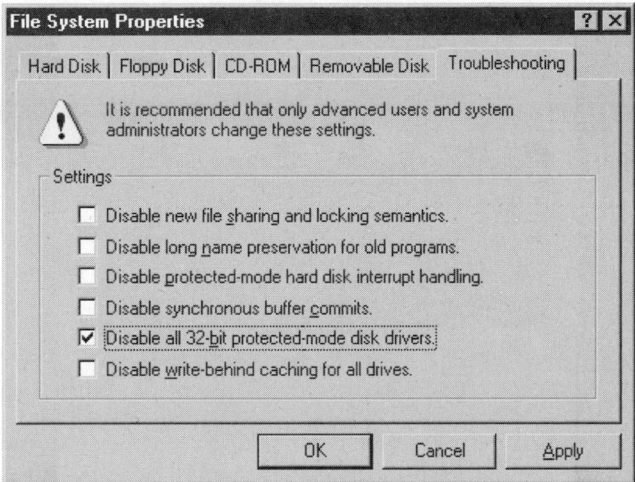

**FIGURE 20-14**    Be sure to uncheck the "Disable all 32-bit protected-mode disk drivers" box

If there are one or more resource conflicts in the system, take the time to resolve any resource conflicts with other devices in the system. In some cases, you may need to remove the conflicting device(s) and allow Windows to redetect/reinstall the device(s) from scratch (see Chapter 11 for detailed conflict troubleshooting information).

Finally, make sure that the protected-mode driver is in the **\windows\system\iosubsys** directory and is loading properly. To find which driver is providing 32-bit disk access, click Properties for the disk controller in Device Manager and click the Driver tab to see which driver files are associated with the controller. For most IDE, EIDE, and ESDI disk controllers, 32-bit disk access is provided by the **ESDI_506.PDR** driver (see Figure 20-15). For SCSI controllers, Windows often uses **SCSIPORT.PDR** and a "mini port" (or .MPD) driver. Restart Windows 9x/Me, press F8 when the "Starting Windows" message appears, then select a Logged (BOOTLOG.TXT) start. If the 32-bit driver is listed as loading properly, you're all set. Otherwise, the driver may be missing or damaged—try reinstalling the 32-bit drivers.

### Disable Advanced Features

If all else fails, you may be able to achieve protected-mode support from the disk controller by disabling any of the controller's advanced features (such as caching or fast or "turbo" modes) and reducing data transfer rates. You may also try systematically disabling advanced IDE controller features in the CMOS Setup. If problems persist, you may have to remove and reinstall the drive controller, or replace/upgrade the drive controller with a model that better supports protected-mode operation.

## OVERLAY SOFTWARE

As you've seen earlier in this chapter, a system may refuse to recognize the full capacity of a hard drive if the BIOS is not adequate. Although a BIOS upgrade or new drive controller card are certainly the preferred means of overcoming drive size limits, they can be difficult to implement. Also, there may be no BIOS updates for older PCs, and it may not be worth the added expense to upgrade the controller. Overlay software (called a *dynamic drive overlay* or *DDO*) is a software utility that is normally shipped free with new hard

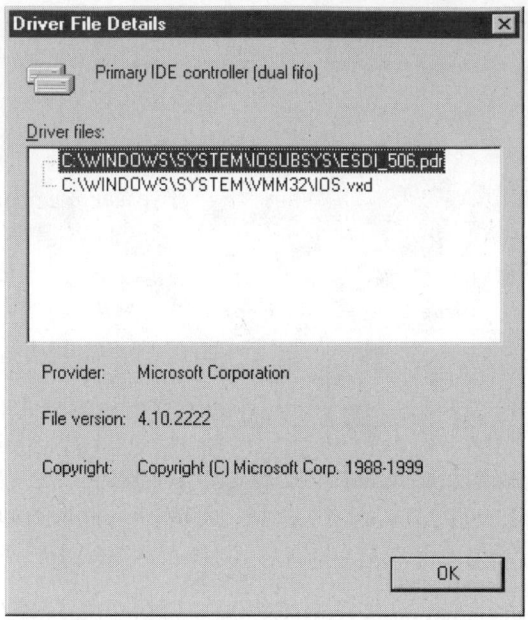

**FIGURE  20-15**    The Driver File Details dialog box, which lists the driver names related to your controller

drives. DDO software installs before the MBR and provides the additional instructions needed to access the entire drive size. This part of the chapter briefly covers the installation and removal of DDO software.

The use of DDO software is discouraged, but may be necessary in some situations.

## DDO Installation

In most cases, installing a DDO utility is simply a matter of booting from the DDO installation disk and following the installation instructions shown on the display. However, there are often a few wrinkles you need to consider depending on the operating system that you plan to use. Let's look at DDO installation under Windows 9x/Me and Windows 2000/XP.

Before installing DDO software, verify that the hard drive is correctly installed in the PC and properly configured in the CMOS Setup. You should also set the Boot Order to A:/CD-ROM/C: (at least temporarily).

The following is a typical procedure used to install Maxtor's MaxBlast Plus II DDO software to a new (blank) hard drive prior to the installation of Windows 9x/Me/2000/XP. As a rule, always download the latest version of the drive maker's DDO software before installation:

1.  Insert the DDO installation disk (e.g., the MaxBlast Plus II disk) into the floppy drive and boot the system.

2.  The system boots from the DDO disk and reports that a new unformatted hard drive has been detected. Opt to format the new drive now.

3.  A list of all devices connected to the IDE cables will illustrate the new hard disk. Select Next to continue.

4.  Follow the on-screen instructions. The overlay software (e.g., MaxBlast Plus II) asks for your system boot disk. Insert the boot disk to drive A:. The software identifies the operating system found on your disk. Verify this information and choose OK to continue.

5.  Allow the DDO software to partition and format the drive using standard options (such as the Standard Partitions option under MaxBlast Plus II). This automatically partitions the drive to its full capacity and assigns one drive letter.

6.  When the DDO utility finishes formatting the hard drive, remove the floppy from drive A: and reboot the system. When the system boots to the C: prompt, insert your operating system startup disk into A: and press CTRL-ALT-DEL to restart the system.

7.  When a message appears asking you to "Hold the CTRL key down for status screen or to boot from floppy", press the CTRL key. This opens the status screen. Choose the option to boot from drive A:.

8.  Insert your Windows boot disk (if not already in the drive) and press any key. Opt to start the computer with CD-ROM support (you'll need CD-ROM support to install the operating system).

9.  After the boot disk finishes loading, it should stop at the A:\ prompt. Insert your operating system installation CD-ROM in the CD-ROM drive.

10. Switch to the CD-ROM drive letter (e.g., drive D:), type **setup**, then press ENTER. Follow the on-screen prompts to install the operating system from CD-ROM.

## Detecting a DDO

A DDO is used to support access to a large hard drive when the system BIOS or drive controller is unable to do so. Since the DDO can sometimes cause problems with drive access and system performance, it must be detected before removal. You can use the telltale signs that follow to identify the presence of a DDO on a Windows 9x/Me system:

■ **DDO startup message**   When you boot your computer, a message may be displayed on the screen that shows the DDO manufacturer's name (or prompts you to press a key to boot to a floppy disk). Current versions of drive overlay software may not display this message by default.

■ **BIOS revision date**   Computers made before 1994 generally do not support LBA. If your BIOS shows an early revision date, it will probably need a DDO in order to support hard drives over 528MB.

■ **FDISK "/status" switch**   Boot your computer with a Windows 9x/Me Startup Disk and type **fdisk /status** from the command prompt. Verify that the sum of the existing partitions is *larger* than the total hard disk space. If so, a DDO is at work.

■ **Windows Startup Disk**   Reboot your computer with the Windows 9x/Me Startup Disk (this will prevent the DDO program from loading), and then boot to a command prompt. Check to see if files on drive C: are accessible. If not, the drive is inaccessible because a DDO has not been loaded for the hard drive.

■ **Verify file names**   Some drive overlay files use an .OVL or a .BIN extension. At the command prompt, type **dir /a *.bin** or **dir /a *.ovl** to check for the existence of files other than DRVSPACE.BIN and DBLSPACE.BIN. If there are other such files, a DDO is probably installed.

■ **Check CONFIG.SYS**   Drive overlay software may be loaded from the CONFIG.SYS file in order to access drives *other* than the active boot partition of the master drive on the primary IDE controller. If there is DDO software called in CONFIG.SYS, disable it there if necessary.

## Restoring a DDO MBR

As you've seen earlier in this chapter, a master boot record (MBR) can be corrupted due to computer viruses, power surges, program bugs, and other issues. A corrupt MBR will prevent the system from booting, and you must restore the MBR. The **FDISK /MBR** feature will restore the MBR on normal drives (without a DDO). But drives with overlay software present a special problem. DDO software shifts the location of the MBR, so using FDISK to restore the MBR can actually damage the DDO—you'll need to use the DDO utility itself to re-create an appropriate MBR. Let's look at restoring an MBR using Maxtor's MaxBlast Plus II software:

As a rule, always be sure to use the very latest version of your DDO software from the manufacturer.

1.  Insert the DDO installation disk (e.g., the MaxBlast Plus II disk) in drive A: and boot the system. Close the "New Hard Drive Installation" window (if it appears).

2.  Select Advanced Options | Backup/Restore Track 0.

3.  Select the drive that needs to be fixed, then click Restore.

4.  Click Done when finished, remove the disk, then reboot the system.

## DDO Removal

At times it may be necessary to remove a DDO from the system. For example, a BIOS or drive controller hardware upgrade may support the drive's full capacity and eliminate the need for a DDO. In other cases, a software conflict or incompatibility may only be corrected by removing the DDO. Removing a DDO is generally a matter of booting from the DDO installation disk/CD-ROM, selecting the "uninstall" option, then following the on-screen instructions. You'll need to stop the DDO software from controlling your drive first, then remove the DDO software from the drive. Let's look at removing Maxtor's MaxBlast Plus II DDO software under Windows 9x/Me/XP:

Removing a DDO may cause data loss. Be sure to back up your system before proceeding.

1.  Insert the DDO installation disk (e.g., the MaxBlast Plus II disk) into the floppy drive and boot the system. Close the "New Hard Drive Installation" window (if it appears).

2.  Select Advanced Options | Software Setup.

3.  Select the drive with the DDO and click Uninstall. You may see numerous warnings or prompts. Continue only if you're sure that the current PC BIOS/hardware will properly support the drives.

4.  Click Done when finished.

**Translation Mismatches**    When removing a DDO, you're allowing the system's hardware to take over for the DDO software. The biggest problem with DDO removal is data loss caused by differences between DDO and hardware LBA translation. Remember that the LBA translation provided by overlay software is *not* always compatible with the LBA translation decisions made by the system's hardware. Consequently, a new BIOS or drive controller may handle the hard drive perfectly. However, since the hard drive was formatted using the DDO software, slight differences in the hardware LBA mode may stop you from reading the drive. A simple test can tell you if the LBA used by a DDO is compatible with the LBA used by the BIOS/drive controller:

1.  Boot the system to a Windows 9x/Me Startup Disk. It is not necessary to select real-mode CD-ROM support. This boots the system without the DDO in memory.

2. At the A: prompt, start ScanDisk and initiate a surface scan of the drive where your DDO is located, as demonstrated here:

```
A:\> scandisk c: /surface
```

3. Press ENTER to start the ScanDisk test. ScanDisk will perform some basic tests on the selected partition and then perform a surface scan.

4. If ScanDisk returns an error, the hardware translation is *not* compatible with the DDO's translation. You should reenable the DDO until you've backed up the system—then remove the DDO and restore the backup. If ScanDisk proceeds normally and does not return an error, the LBA translations should be identical, and you can proceed to remove the DDO permanently.

Do *not* attempt to fix errors produced by ScanDisk here! Trying to fix an error using a different LBA translation will corrupt the drive.

# DRIVE NOT RECOGNIZED BY OPERATING SYSTEM

There are some circumstances when a hard drive is recognized correctly by the BIOS (for example, the drive is properly autodetected and appears in the BIOS banner information at start time), but it is not properly identified by the operating system. In virtually all cases, the problem can be traced to installation issues or drive software. Check the essential installation points first:

- Check the parameters in the CMOS Setup and verify that the drive parameters *and* translation mode (such as LBA) are set correctly.

- Contact the system or motherboard manufacturer to verify potential BIOS capacity limitations. For example, you may need a BIOS upgrade to accommodate the drive sizes that you're using.

- Ensure that newly installed drive controller cards do not conflict with the existing system BIOS. You may need to disable the motherboard's existing drive controller channel(s) through the CMOS Setup before the new controller card will be recognized by the OS.

- Systematically step down the enhanced features of your BIOS (for example, systematically disable block mode, multisector transfers, 32-bit transfers, PIO mode settings, and so on) to their minimum values, or disable the features entirely. You may also try the BIOS Default settings in your CMOS Setup.

- If you are overclocking the system, check to see if you're also overclocking any of the system busses. Try returning the clock speed to its normal value, or change the bus multipliers in the CMOS Setup to achieve proper bus speeds.

- Increase the boot process time in your CMOS Setup—you can enable Floppy Seek At Boot, Test Memory Above 1MB, and/or set the Boot Order to "A: then C:." This will allow several more seconds for the hard drive to initialize during a cold boot.

- Set Boot Speed to its slowest value in the CMOS Setup, and/or set the Boot Delay entry (if present) to its highest value.

- Double-check your partitions using FDISK. If the drive was not previously partitioned, create a Primary DOS partition on the drive. Use option 2 to set the partition "active." Exit FDISK and reboot. Format the new partition and install the system files. If the drive was previously partitioned, make sure the first partition is PRI DOS and its Status is "A." Compare the sum of all partition sizes to the Total Disk Space—they should be the same to within about 1MB. If the total is different, correct the drive parameters or translation mode in CMOS Setup and repartition the drive.

> If the drive was previously partitioned, but no partitions are currently seen in FDISK, do *not* attempt to create new partitions if data on the drive is to be saved.

- Double-check the master/slave jumpers on all drives using the primary controller.
- Install (set) the jumper for I/O Channel Ready on the drive (if that option is present).
- If you're using a SCSI drive, verify that the Parity jumper is installed. Also verify that the SCSI chain is terminated properly, and the SCSI ID is unique.
- Check all of your cable connections and try a shorter replacement cable (or connect the drive to the middle cable connector).
- Replace/upgrade the drive controller card.
- Remove the slave drive (if present) to determine the presence of any master/slave drive compatibility issues.
- You may also need to check for data corruption or errors on the drive using ScanDisk or other third-party utilities.
- Clean-boot the system with a boot disk and execute **FDISK /MBR** and **SYS C:**. Make sure the DOS version on the floppy disk is the *same* version as on the hard drive before using the SYS command.
- Bypass CONFIG.SYS and AUTOEXEC.BAT to check for problems in your startup files. If this works, use the "step-by-step" boot mode in the Windows Startup Menu to walk through each step of these files until the problem is found, then edit both the CONFIG.SYS and AUTOEXEC.BAT files and "comment out" the statement(s) causing the problem.
- Check for drive compression and try removing the compression drivers if there is no important data on the drive.
- Delete the partition using FDISK, then repartition and reformat the drive from scratch.
- Replace the hard drive.

## CHECKING FOR FAT16 AND FAT32

It may be necessary for you to identify the presence of a FAT16 or FAT32 partition *before* using disk utilities, backup software, or other applications. Doing this will prevent accidental loss of data from using an incompatible software version (such as using a FAT16 version of ScanDisk on a FAT32 partition).

- Under Windows 98/Me, double-click the My Computer icon on your desktop, then right-click the drive you're interested in. Click Properties from the drop-down menu. Look at the General tab on the line marked "File system." A FAT16 partition will simply say "FAT," while a FAT32 partition will specify "FAT32." Windows XP uses FAT32 or NTFS.
- Try the **ver** (version) command from a DOS prompt, such as:
  ```
  Windows 95A. [Version 4.00.950]
  Windows 95B. [Version 4.00.1111]
  Windows 98. [Version 4.10.1998]
  ```
- If you need a FAT32 version of FDISK, check to see that FDISK asks, "Do you wish to enable large disk support (Y/N)." If it does *not* ask this question, it's probably a FAT16 version.
- You can also check the partition type using a FAT32 version of FDISK. Select option 4 to display the partition information. The System field will read "FAT32" if the partition is FAT32 or "FAT16" if the partition is FAT16. If the partition has not been formatted, the System field will read "Unknown."

# DEALING WITH DRIVE NOISE

All hard drives make a certain amount of noise during normal operation, and the noise level will vary depending on whether the drive is spinning or accessing. However, a drive making substantial or abnormal noises may indicate an impending failure. The trick here is to tell the "normal" noises from the "abnormal" noises. A drive makes three basic sounds:

■ A "whining" noise during the drive spin-up (and a mild "whir" while the system is on).

■ Regular clicking or tapping sounds during drive access (the R/W heads stepping across the platters).

■ Hard clicks when the drive heads park before power off.

You should develop a keen ear for abnormal drive sounds such as:

■ A high-pitched whining sound (such as a screech or squeal) can be an indication of problems.

■ Noises (vibrations) caused by mounting issues. These noises are due to either a high-frequency vibration in the mounting hardware or a potential drive failure.

■ Repeated and regular tapping, grinding, or beeping. When the hard drive is suspect, it is always important to make an immediate backup of your data.

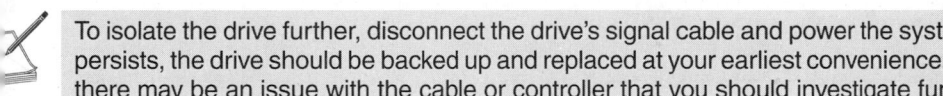

To isolate the drive further, disconnect the drive's signal cable and power the system up. If the noise persists, the drive should be backed up and replaced at your earliest convenience. If the noise stops, there may be an issue with the cable or controller that you should investigate further.

# DEALING WITH SPIN PROBLEMS

All hard drives must spin their platters at a constant rate of speed, so any spin problems can render the drive inaccessible. Spin problems can usually be broken down into three types:

■ *Drive does not spin at all.* When a system is turned on, the characteristic hard drive wind-up sounds are not present. This can also occur if the hard drive spins down (without cause) after working for a period of time.

■ *Drive spins up and spins down again.* This normally occurs during the initial power up. The hard drive will start spinning and then slow down (or it cycles up to a point and ceases to spin).

■ *Drive spins down following period of inactivity.* The hard drive fails to spin up when access is attempted.

The first things to check for are installation errors:

■ Check the jumper settings on all hard drives attached to the same interface cable. For example, check the master/slave jumpers on each drive, then check for "energy management" or "deferred spinup" jumpers. Most SCSI (and a few IDE) hard drives contain one or both jumper options.

■ Check all of the power supply cable connections. If trouble starts after adding more drives or otherwise upgrading the system, there may be inadequate power to operate the drives, and you may need to upgrade the power supply.

■ Check the interface (ribbon) cable connections. Replace any cables that are loose, scuffed, or otherwise damaged.

■ Check system software for power management and disable or uninstall that software if necessary.

Next, check for "green" or "power management" features that might be set improperly:

- Disable your drive-related power management features in the CMOS Setup.
- Disable the power management jumper on your hard drive (if present).
- Some overlay software has the ability to set power management features. For example, you can disable power management under Maxtor's MaxBlast software (versions 7.04–7.12) by removing the **/E** switch. Clean-boot the system if other power management software is the suspected culprit.
- Windows 9x/Me/XP can enable power management. This feature will need to be disabled through the operating system's Power Management icon in the Control Panel.

Finally, check for hardware failures with the drive and/or its controller:

- Try installing the drive in another system—doing this will verify the problem is with the drive, *not* the system.
- Use a different power supply plug.
- Use a different interface (ribbon) cable.
- Use a different drive controller (for example, try a PCI drive controller card).
- Disconnect the ribbon cable from the drive.
- Replace the drive.

## HARDWARE SYMPTOMS

Now that you've seen some general troubleshooting guidelines, it's time to review some specific problems and solutions. The important notion here is that a hard drive *problem* does not necessarily mean a hard drive *failure*. The failure of a sector or track does not automatically indicate physical head or platter damage—this is why software tools have been so successful at restoring operation (and even recovering data). Remember, though, that drive troubleshooting has the potential of destroying any data on the drive(s). Before attempting to troubleshoot hard drive problems, be sure to back up as much of the drive as possible. If there is no backup available, do not repartition or reformat the drive unless *absolutely* necessary and all other possible alternatives have been exhausted.

> The term "*IDE-type drive*" is taken to mean any drive using a 40-pin IDE-style interface. This includes IDE, EIDE, ATAPI IDE, Ultra-DMA/33, Ultra-DMA/66, Ultra-DMA/100, and Ultra-DMA/133 (using the 40-pin/80-conductor cable). Specific drive types or exceptions will be noted in the section on symptoms.

**SYMPTOM 20-1**    **The hard drive is completely dead**    The drive does not spin up, the drive light does not illuminate during power-up, or you see an error message indicating that the drive is not found or ready. Make sure the 4-pin power connector is inserted properly and completely. If the drive is being powered by a Y-adapter, make sure any interim connections are secure. Use a voltmeter and measure the +5 volt (pin 4) and +12 volt (pin 1) levels. If either voltage (especially the +12 volt supply) is unusually low or absent, replace the power supply. Also check your signal cable. See that the drive's signal interface cable is connected securely at both the drive and controller ends. For IDE-type drives, this is the 40-pin ribbon cable. If the cable is visibly worn or damaged, try a new cable.

The PC cannot use a hard drive that it doesn't recognize, so enter the CMOS Setup routine and see that all of the parameters entered for the drive are correct. Heads, cylinders, sectors per track, landing zone, and write precompensation must all be correct—otherwise, POST will not recognize the drive.

If you have an autodetect option available, try that also. Remember to save your changes in CMOS and reboot the system.

If problems continue, the hard drive itself may be defective. Try a known-good hard drive. If a known-good drive works as expected, your original drive is probably defective and should be replaced. If a known-good hard drive fails to operate, replace the drive controller with a new expansion board.

**SYMPTOM 20-2**   **You see drive activity, but the computer will not boot from the hard drive**   In most cases, this is due to drive failure, boot sector failure, or DOS/Windows file corruption. Make sure that the drive's signal cable is connected securely at both the drive and controller. If the cable is visibly worn or damaged, try a new one. Check the CMOS Setup and verify that all of the parameters entered for the drive are correct. Heads, cylinders, sectors per track, landing zone, and write precompensation must all correct—otherwise, POST will not recognize the drive. If the BIOS provides an option to autodetect the drive, try that as well.

Boot from a floppy disk and try accessing the hard drive. If the hard drive is accessible, chances are that the boot files are missing or corrupt. Try running **FDISK /MBR**, which will rebuild the drive's master boot record (*the FDISK /MBR command may render the files on your drive inaccessible*). If the drive has a DDO, use the DDO installation disk options to rebuild Track 0.

You may have a problem with your drive system hardware. If you cannot access the hard drive, run a diagnostic such as Windsor Technologies' *TuffTest Pro* (www.tufftest.com). Test the drive and drive controller. If the controller responds but the drive does not, try repartitioning and reformatting the hard drive. If the drive still doesn't respond, replace the hard drive. If the controller doesn't respond, replace the hard drive controller.

**SYMPTOM 20-3**   **There are errors during drive reads or writes**   Magnetic information does not last forever, and sector ID information can gradually degrade to a point where you encounter file errors. Start by checking for any file structure problems on the drive. Use a utility such as ScanDisk to examine the drive and search for bad sectors. If a failed sector involves part of an .EXE or .COM file, that file would be corrupt and should be restored from a backup. If there are no problems detected with the file structure, replace the drive signal cable (try a UDMA/66/100/133 cable). Otherwise, replace the suspect drive.

**SYMPTOM 20-4**   **Hard drive performance appears to be slowing down over time**   In virtually all cases, diminishing drive performance can be caused by file fragmentation. To a far lesser extent, you may be faced with a computer virus. Start the PC with a "clean" boot disk and make sure there are no TSRs or drivers being loaded. After a clean boot, run your anti-virus checker and make sure that there are no memory-resident or file-based viruses. If the system checks clean for computer viruses, you should check for file fragmentation next. Start your defragmentation utility (such as Disk Defragmenter) and check to see the percentage of file fragmentation. If there is more than 10 percent fragmentation, you should consider running the defragmentation utility under Windows 9x/Me/XP. This process could take from several minutes to several hours, depending on the size of your drive. Once defragmentation is complete, reboot the system normally.

To gauge the effectiveness of file fragmentation on disk performance, benchmark the disk system *before* running Defrag, then run the benchmark again afterwards. Compare the benchmark numbers.

**SYMPTOM 20-5**   **You can access the hard drive correctly, but the drive light stays on continuously**   A continuous LED indication is not *necessarily* a problem as long as the drive seems to be operating properly. Check the drive and drive controller for drive LED jumpers—examine the drive itself for any jumper that might select *latched* mode instead of *activity* mode. If there are no such jumpers on the drive, check the drive controller or motherboard. Set the jumper to *activity* mode to see the drive light during access only. Next, consider the possibility of drive light *error messages*. Some drive types (especially SCSI drives) use the drive activity light to signal drive and controller errors. Check the drive and controller documents to determine if there is any error indicated by the light remaining on.

**SYMPTOM 20-6** **You cannot access the hard drive, and the drive light stays on continuously** This usually indicates a reversed signal cable, and is most common when upgrading or replacing a drive system. In virtually all cases, one end of the IDE signal cable is reversed. Make sure that *both* ends of the cable are installed properly (remember that the red or blue stripe on one side of the cable represents pin 1). If problems persist, replace the drive controller. It is rare for a fault in the drive controller to cause this type of problem, but if trouble persists, try a known-good drive controller board.

**SYMPTOM 20-7** **You see a "No Fixed Disk Present" error message on the monitor** This kind of problem can occur during installation or at any point in the PC's working life. Make sure the 4-pin power connector is inserted properly and completely. If the drive is being powered by a Y-adapter, make sure any interim connections are secure. Use a voltmeter and measure the +5 volt (pin 4) and +12 volt (pin 1) levels. If either voltage (especially the +12 volt supply) is unusually low or absent, replace the power supply. Make sure the drive's signal cable is connected securely at *both* the drive and controller. If the cable is visibly worn or damaged, try a new one.

Enter the CMOS Setup and see that all of the parameters entered for the drive are correct. Heads, cylinders, sectors per track, landing zone, and write precompensation must all be correct—otherwise, POST will not recognize the drive. You might also try autodetecting the drive. Also verify that there are no other expansion devices in the system using the same IRQs or I/O addresses used by your drive controller. If there are, change the resources used by the conflicting device. If your drive system uses a SCSI interface, make sure that the SCSI cable is terminated properly, and verify that the drive's SCSI ID is unique. If problems continue, try a known-good hard drive. If a known-good drive works as expected, your original drive is probably defective. If problems persist with a known-good hard drive, replace the drive controller board.

**SYMPTOM 20-8** **Your drive spins up, but the system fails to recognize the drive** Your computer may flag this as a *"hard-disk error"* or *"hard-disk controller failure"* during system initialization. Make sure that the interface signal cable is inserted properly and completely at the drive and controller. Try a new signal cable. See that a first drive is configured as *master*, and a second drive is configured as *slave*. For SCSI drives, see that each drive has a unique ID setting and check that the SCSI bus is terminated properly.

Enter the CMOS Setup routine and see that all of the parameters entered for the drive are correct. Heads, cylinders, sectors per track, landing zone, and write precompensation must all be correct—otherwise, POST will not recognize the drive. Try using the autodetect feature if it is available. If the CMOS is configured properly, you should suspect a problem with the partition. Boot from a floppy disk and run FDISK to check the partitions on your hard drive. Make sure that there is at least one DOS partition. If the drive is to be your boot drive, the primary partition must be active and bootable. Repartition and reformat the drive if necessary.

Try another hard drive or controller. If a known-good drive works as expected, your original drive is probably defective. If a known-good hard drive fails to work as expected, replace the drive controller. If problems persist with a known-good floppy drive, replace the drive controller board.

**SYMPTOM 20-9**    **When a drive has multiple partitions, the last partition "disappears"**
This type of problem often surfaces if you try to implement more than one primary DOS partition on the
drive. Check the partitions with FDISK and repartition the drive so that there is only one primary DOS partition. If you must create multiple partitions on the drive, try the following steps:

1. Create a primary DOS partition with the desired size, and then reboot the system.

2. Create an extended DOS partition using 99 percent of the remaining available space (instead of 100
   percent), and then reboot the system.

3. Create as many logical DOS drives as required, but reboot the system after creating each logical drive.

**SYMPTOM 20-10**    **The drive keeps spinning down**    You notice that the drive spins up (at
least partially), then spins down again after a period of time. The trick here is to determine if the spindle
motor is failing, or if power management features are causing the spindown. The easiest way to test the
drive is to disconnect the signal (IDE) cable and power up the drive. Without a connection to the host system, the drive should not receive any power management instructions, so it should not spin down. If the
disconnected drive does spin down, the DC spindle motor may be failing, and the drive must be replaced.
If the drive runs normally, chances are that power management features in the CMOS Setup and under
Windows are causing the spindown. Tweak the power management features to find a more convenient
spindown period, or disable the drive spindown.

**SYMPTOM 20-11**    **Your IDE drive spins up when power is applied, then rapidly spins
down again**    The drive is defective, or it is not communicating properly with its host system. Make
sure the 4-pin power connector is inserted properly and completely into the drive. Also see that the interface signal cable is inserted properly and completely at the drive and controller. Try a new signal cable.
The first drive should be configured as *master*, and a second drive should be configured as *slave*. For SCSI
drives, see that each drive has a unique ID setting and check that the SCSI bus is terminated properly. If
problems persist, try a known-good hard drive. If a known-good drive works as expected, your original
drive is probably defective.

**SYMPTOM 20-12**    **During the POST, you hear a drive begin to spin-up and produce a
sharp noise**    This problem can be encountered with some combinations of drives, motherboards, and
motherboard BIOS versions. It can easily result in data loss (and media damage). Check the motherboard
BIOS version first; then contact the PC system manufacturer and see if a BIOS upgrade is necessary. Try
an upgrade if necessary; otherwise, replace the drive controller. Often a new drive controller may resolve
the problem if the motherboard BIOS cannot be replaced. If you cannot correct this issue through BIOS, the
drive itself may be defective and require replacement.

Some drive models (especially high rpm models) produce more noise than others. Check with the
drive maker and discuss the noise levels. Some drive makers provide acoustic management utilities
that can quiet typical drive operation.

**SYMPTOM 20-13**    **You see a "Drive 80 (81, 82, or 83) failure" message on the system**
This type of error appears during the boot process. Hard drive 80 is the physical drive C:, 81 is the physical drive D:, 82 is the physical drive E:, and 83 is the physical drive F:. Chances are that the drive's signal
cable is disconnected. Otherwise, the drive is probably defective and should be replaced. Start by checking the cabling:

- Make sure the power cable is connected securely to the drive.
- Make sure the data cable is connected securely to both the drive and to the controller.
- Make sure the data cable is connected to both the drive and the system with the correct orientation.
- Test the data cable by trying a different cable or trying the cable on a known working drive.
- Verify the drive's jumper settings are set correctly.
- If you're using a separate ATA controller card, test it by trying either a known working card or a known working disk drive.
- Verify that the geometry settings for the hard drive (in the CMOS Setup) are set correctly.
- Reconfigure the drive as the only hard drive device in the system and retest. Try the drive in a different system if possible.

**SYMPTOM 20-14**    **You see a "1780 or 1781 ERROR" on the system**    The classical 1780 error code indicates a *Hard Disk 0 Failure,* while the 1781 error code marks a *Hard Disk 1 Failure.* Start the PC with a clean boot disk and make sure there are no TSRs or drivers being loaded. If you haven't done so already, run your antivirus checker and make sure that there are no memory-resident or file-based viruses. If you can access the hard drive once your system is booted, chances are that the boot files are missing or corrupt. Try a utility such as Ontrack's EasyRecovery to recover the boot files, or recopy the boot files with SYS and re-create the master boot record with **FDISK /MBR**. Otherwise, you will need to repartition and reformat the disk, then restore disk files from a backup.

If you cannot access the hard drive, run a diagnostic such as Windsor Technologies' TuffTest Pro. Test the drive and drive controller. If the controller responds but the drive does not, try repartitioning and reformatting the hard drive. If the drive still doesn't respond, replace the hard drive. If the controller doesn't respond, replace the hard drive controller.

**SYMPTOM 20-15**    **You see a "1790 or 1791 ERROR" on the system**    The classical 1790 error code indicates a *Hard Disk 0 Error,* while the 1791 error code marks a *Hard Disk 1 Error.* Make sure that the interface signal cable is inserted properly and completely at the drive and controller. Try a new signal cable. Next, boot from a floppy disk and run FDISK to check the partitions on your hard drive. Make sure that there is at least one DOS partition. If the drive is to be your boot drive, the primary partition must be active and bootable. Repartition and reformat the drive if necessary. Finally, replace the hard drive or controller. If a known-good drive works as expected, your original drive is probably defective. If problems persist with a known-good floppy drive, replace the drive controller board.

**SYMPTOM 20-16**    **You see a "1701 ERROR" on the system**    The 1701 error code indicates a hard drive POST error—the drive did not pass its POST test. Make sure the 4-pin power connector is inserted properly and completely. If the drive is being powered by a Y-adapter, make sure any interim connections are secure. Use a voltmeter and measure the +5 volt (pin 4) and +12 volt (pin 1) levels. If either voltage (especially the +12 volt supply) is unusually low or absent, replace the power supply. Enter the CMOS Setup routine and see that all of the parameters entered for the drive are correct. Heads, cylinders, sectors per track, landing zone, and write precompensation must all be correct—otherwise, POST will not recognize the drive. Try autodetecting the drive. Otherwise, the drive may be defective and should be replaced.

**SYMPTOM 20-17**    **You see a "Sector not found" error message**    This problem usually occurs after the drive has been in operation for quite some time and is typically the result of a media failure. Fortunately, a bad sector will affect only one file. Use a utility such as EasyRecovery from Ontrack (www.ontrack.com/easyrecovery/), or another data recovery utility, and attempt to recover the damaged file. Be aware that you may be unsuccessful and have to restore the file from a backup later. Next, use a disk utility (such as ScanDisk) to evaluate the drive, then locate and map out any bad sectors that are located on the drive. If ScanDisk maps out bad sectors, you may need to restore any affected files from a backup.

**SYMPTOM 20-18**    **The system reports random data, seek, or format errors**    Random errors rarely indicate a permanent problem, but identifying the problem's source can be a time-consuming task. Make sure the 4-pin power connector is inserted properly and completely. If the drive is being powered by a Y-adapter, make sure any interim connections are secure (or remove the Y-adapter and power the drive directly). Use a voltmeter and measure the +5 volt (pin 4) and +12 volt (pin 1) levels. If either voltage (especially the +12 volt supply) is unusually low, replace the power supply. Make sure that the interface signal cable is inserted properly and completely at the drive and controller. Try a new signal cable. Also try re-routing the signal cable away from the power supply or "noisy" expansion devices.

If problems occur after remounting the drive in a different orientation, you may need to repartition and reformat the drive or return it to its original orientation. Try relocating the drive controller away from cables and "noisy" expansion devices. If you're overclocking the system, bus timing may be affected, so try resetting the system to its "native" clock settings. If the problem disappears, try a new drive controller. The disk media may also be defective. Use a utility such as ScanDisk to check for and map out any bad sectors. Once bad sectors are mapped out, you may need to restore some files from your backup.

Try the hard drive and controller in another system. If the drive and controller work in another system, there is probably excessive noise or grounding problems in the original system. Reinstall the drive and controller in the original system and remove all extra expansion boards. If the problem goes away, replace one board at a time and retest the system until the problem returns. The last board you inserted when the problem returned is probably the culprit. If the problem persists, there may be a ground problem on the motherboard. Try replacing the motherboard as an absolute last effort.

**SYMPTOM 20-19**    **You see an "Error reading drive C:" error message**    Read errors in a hard drive typically indicate problems with the disk media, but may also indicate viruses or signaling problems. Start with the signal cable and make sure that the interface signal cable is inserted properly and completely at the drive and controller. Try a new signal cable. Start the PC with a clean boot disk and make sure there are no TSRs or drivers being loaded. If you haven't done so already, run your antivirus checker and make sure that there are no memory-resident or file-based viruses.

If problems occur after remounting the drive in a different orientation, you may need to repartition and reformat the drive, or return it to its original orientation. Use a utility such as ScanDisk to check for and map out any bad sectors. Once bad sectors are mapped out, you may need to restore some files from your backup. Try another hard drive. If a known-good drive works as expected, your original drive is probably defective and should be replaced.

**SYMPTOM 20-20**    **You see a "Track 0 not found" error message**    A fault on track 00 can disable the entire drive, since track 00 contains the drive's File Allocation Table (FAT) and master boot record (MBR). This can be a serious problem that may require you to replace the drive. Examine the drive signal connector and verify that the interface signal cable is inserted properly and completely at the drive and controller. Try a new signal cable. Boot from a floppy disk and run FDISK to check the partitions on your hard drive. Make sure there is at least one DOS partition. If the drive is to be your boot drive, the primary partition must be active and bootable. Repartition and reformat the drive if necessary. Finally, try a known-good hard drive. If a known-good drive works as expected, your original drive is probably defective.

**SYMPTOM 20-21**    **You see a "Hard Disk Controller Failure" or a large number of defects in the last logical partition**    This is typically a CMOS Setup or drive controller problem. Enter the CMOS Setup routine and see that all of the parameters entered for the drive are correct. If the geometry specifies a larger drive, the system will attempt to format areas of the drive that don't exist—resulting in a large number of errors. If CMOS is configured correctly, there may be a problem with the hard drive controller. Try a new hard drive controller. If a new drive controller does not correct the problem, the drive itself is probably defective and should be replaced.

**SYMPTOM 20-22**    **You see "Disk Boot Failure," "non system disk," or "No ROM Basic—SYSTEM HALTED" error message**    There are several possible reasons for these errors. Check the signal connector first and make sure that the interface signal cables are inserted properly and completely at the drive and controller. Try some new signal cables. Next, start the PC with a clean boot disk and make sure there are no TSRs or drivers being loaded that might interfere with drive operation. If you haven't done so already, run your antivirus checker and make sure that there are no memory-resident or file-based viruses.

Enter the CMOS Setup routine and see that all of the parameters entered for the drive are correct. Heads, cylinders, sectors per track, landing zone, and write precompensation must all be entered accurately. Now boot from a floppy disk and run FDISK to check the partitions on your hard drive. Make sure that there is at least one DOS partition. If the drive is to be your boot drive, the primary partition must be active and bootable. Finally, it is possible that the hard drive itself is defective. Try a known-good hard drive. If a known-good drive works as expected, your original drive is probably defective. If problems persist with a known-good floppy drive, replace the drive controller.

**SYMPTOM 20-23**    **An IDE drive under 528MB does not partition or format to full capacity**    When relatively small hard drives do not realize their full capacity, the CMOS Setup is usually at fault. The drive parameters entered into CMOS must specify the *full* capacity of the drive, using a geometry setup that is acceptable for both the BIOS and the drive. If you use parameters that specify a smaller drive, any extra capacity will be ignored. If there are over 1,024 cylinders, you must use an alternative "translation geometry" to realize the drive's full potential. The drive's maker can provide you with the right translation geometry. Also check your DOS version—older versions of DOS use a partition limit of 32MB. Upgrade your older version of DOS to 6.22 (or upgrade to Windows 9x/Me/XP as appropriate for your system hardware).

**SYMPTOM 20-24**    **An IDE-type drive over 528MB does not partition or format to full capacity**    This type of problem may also be due to a CMOS Setup error, but it is almost always due to poor system configuration. Check the CMOS Setup first—the drive parameters entered into CMOS must specify the *full* capacity of the drive. If you use parameters that specify a smaller drive, any extra capacity will be ignored. If there are over 1,024 cylinders, you must use an alternative "translation geometry" to realize the drive's full potential. The drive's maker can provide you with the right translation geometry. Also check the CMOS Setup for LBA. EIDE drives need Logical Block Addressing to access over 528MB. Make sure that there is an entry such as "LBA Mode" in CMOS, and see that it's enabled. Otherwise, you may need to upgrade your motherboard BIOS to have full drive capacity.

If the CMOS Setup fails to "see" the entire drive capacity, the BIOS may be at fault. If you cannot upgrade an older motherboard BIOS, install an upgraded drive controller with its own controller BIOS (such as the Maxtor Ultra-ATA/133 or Promise Ultra133 TX2 PCI cards)—doing this will supplement the motherboard BIOS. An alternative is to upgrade the motherboard outright. If neither your motherboard nor controller BIOS will support LBA mode, and you don't wish to invest in a hardware upgrade, you will need to install drive overlay software (such as MaxBlast Plus II software).

**SYMPTOM 20-25**    **The BIOS or DDO can only recognize 32GB of the drive, but the drive is larger than 32GB**    If the operating system, BIOS, or DDO software (e.g., MaxBlast) can only recognize 32GB of the drive, the trouble may be caused by jumper problems, BIOS problems, or operating system problems. Start by checking the drive jumpers. On drives larger than 32GB, there may be a *capacity limitation* (CL) jumper or *alternate capacity* (AC) jumper setting. When enabled, these jumpers will artificially limit the capacity of the drive to 32GB, and should only be used when the BIOS hangs when trying to autodetect the drive—make sure that this jumper is *not* enabled otherwise.

BIOS limitations are another common problem. On older systems (e.g., pre-November 1998), the BIOS may not support drives that are larger than 32GB. Set the drive type to autodetect in the CMOS Setup. If the BIOS detects full capacity of the drive, then the BIOS will support the capacity of the drive. If not, check with the system or motherboard manufacturer for any BIOS upgrades. If a BIOS update is not available, you may need to upgrade the system's drive controller to a model that will support larger and faster drives (e.g., 48-bit LBA addressing with Ultra-DMA/133 speeds). A final option is to install DDO software (such as MaxBlast Plus II software). Be sure that you're using the very latest DDO version from the drive maker.

**SYMPTOM 20-26**    **The BIOS can only recognize 137GB of the drive, but the drive is larger than 137GB**    As you've seen earlier in this chapter, the traditional 28-bit LBA addressing scheme used with INT 13 extensions has a maximum limit of 137GB. If you install a drive larger than 137GB on a system that is not upgraded to support the newer 48-bit LBA addressing scheme under ATA/ATAPI-6 and later, you're limited to using only up to 137GB on the drive. Your actual course of action will depend on the hardware support that's already present in the system.

For example, if your motherboard has an Intel chipset (e.g., 810, 810E, 810E2, 815, 815, 815E, 815EP, 815P, 820, 820E, 830M, 830MP, 830MG, 840, 845, 850, or 860), visit www.intel.com/support/chipsets/iaa/ and download the Intel Application Accelerator. Intel's Application Accelerator software supports the full capacity of drives larger than 137GB. If you do not have an Intel chipset available, check with the chipset or motherboard maker to see if there's a suitable motherboard driver to support 137GB+ drive addressing. If not, you can either upgrade the existing drive controller to a Maxtor Ultra-ATA/133 or Promise Ultra133 TX2 PCI card—both support 48-bit LBA. Another option is to upgrade the motherboard to later model with a chipset that does support 48-bit LBA natively.

You cannot "tweak" the CMOS Setup to recognize the drive past 137GB. If your ATA controller, chipset drivers, and/or system BIOS do not *all* properly support 48-bit Logical Block Addressing, data loss will certainly occur when storing data on the drive beyond the 137GB point.

**SYMPTOM 20-27**    **The hard drive in a PC is suffering frequent breakdowns (every 6 to 12 months)**    When drives tend to fail within a few months, there are some factors to consider. Power may be an issue. If the AC power supplying your PC is "dirty" (that is, lots of spikes and surges), power anomalies can often make it through the power supply and damage other components. Remove any high-load devices such as air conditioners, motors, or coffee makers from the same AC circuit used by the PC, or try the PC on a known-good AC circuit. You might also consider a good UPS to power your PC.

Excessive drive use may be another factor. If the drive is being worked hard by applications and swap files, consider upgrading RAM, adding cache, or disabling virtual memory to reduce dependency on the drive. Periodically run a utility like Disk Defragmenter to reorganize the files. Doing this reduces the amount of "drive thrashing" that occurs when loading and saving files. Finally, consider the environment. Constant low-level vibrations, such as those in an industrial environment, can kill a hard drive. Smoke (even cigarette smoke), high humidity, very low humidity, and caustic vapors can ruin drives. Make sure the system is used in a stable office-type environment.

**SYMPTOM 20-28**   **A hard drive controller is replaced, but during initialization the system displays error messages such as "Hard Disk Failure" or "Not a recognized drive type"**   The PC may also lock-up. Some drive controllers may be incompatible in some system configurations. Verify the minimum system requirements for your new drive controller (e.g., you may need a more recent operating system). Check with the controller manufacturer and see if there have been any reports of incompatibilities with your PC. If so, try a different drive controller board.

**SYMPTOM 20-29**   **A new hard drive is installed, but it will not boot, or a message appears such as "HDD controller failure"**   The new drive has probably not been installed or prepared properly. Make sure the 4-pin power connector is inserted properly and completely. If the drive is being powered by a Y-adapter, make sure any interim connections are secure. Use a voltmeter and measure the +5 volt (pin 4) and +12 volt (pin 1) levels. If either voltage (especially the +12 volt supply) is unusually low or absent, replace the power supply. Also make sure the drive's signal interface cable is connected securely at both the drive and controller. If the cable is visibly worn or damaged, try a new one.

Enter the CMOS Setup routine and see that all of the parameters entered for the drive are correct. Heads, cylinders, sectors per track, landing zone, and write precompensation must all be correct—otherwise, POST will not recognize the drive. The drive also might not be prepared properly. Run FDISK from a bootable disk to partition the drive, then run FORMAT to initialize the drive. Then run SYS C: to make the drive bootable. With later Windows versions, CMOS Setup will format the drive for you after partitioning.

**SYMPTOM 20-30**   **The drive will work as a primary drive, but not as a secondary (or vice versa)**   In most cases, the drive is simply jumpered incorrectly, but there may also be timing problems. Check the drive jumpers first. Make sure that the drive is jumpered properly as a primary (single drive), primary (dual drive), or secondary drive. The drive signal timing may also be off. Some IDE-type drives (especially older models) may not work as primary or secondary drives with certain other drives in the system. For example, older drive controllers may not be able to "shift" the data transfer speeds between a fast and slow drive—causing the channel to run at the slower rate. Reverse the primary/secondary relationship. If the problem persists, try the drives separately. If the drives work individually, there is probably a timing problem, so try a different drive as the primary or secondary.

**SYMPTOM 20-31**   **You install a Y-adapter that fails to work**   Some Y-adapters that are incorrectly wired can cause severe damage to any device attached to them. Examine the power connector first. Make certain that both of the female connectors are lined up with the two chamfered (rounded) corners facing up and both of the squared corners facing down. The four wires attached to the female connectors should now be in the following order from left to right: **Yellow** (+12Vdc), **Black** (ground), **Black** (ground), **Red** (+5Vdc). If this order is reversed on one of the connectors, then your Y power adapter is faulty and should *not* be used.

**SYMPTOM 20-32** **After installing a large HDD (unpartitioned), you cannot access the floppy drive** This will effectively hang the system and prevent you from completing the hard drive's installation. In most cases, this is due to an issue with the drive size. Some BIOS versions cannot perform the proper translation on an 8.4GB (or larger) drive and will hang the system as a result. Try setting the drive up using the following parameters:

- Cylinders: 1,023
- Heads: 16
- Sectors: 63

Of course, this setting represents a small IDE drive, and the system will tell you that this is a 504MB or 528MB drive. If you are then able to boot to a floppy disk, then you may either upgrade the BIOS or drive controller to support the large hard drive natively or install drive overlay software such as Disk Manager, Data Lifeguard Tools, or MaxBlast. Be sure to restore the drive's proper CMOS Setup parameters after upgrading the BIOS (or installing drive overlay software)—or simply allow the CMOS Setup to autodetect the drive's correct parameters.

**SYMPTOM 20-33** **After configuring a drive with the correct parameters (such as 16383 × 16 × 63), the system still indicates that the drive is only 504MB or 528MB** Keep in mind that 528MB (or 504MB) is the limitation of the original Cylinder/Head/Sector (CHS) translation method used on IDE drives. This problem was resolved with the LBA translation technique. Make sure that the CMOS Setup is configured to use Logical Block Addressing (LBA) if it is available. If it is not, you may need to upgrade the BIOS (or drive controller) or install drive overlay software such as Disk Manager, Data Lifeguard Tools, or MaxBlast.

**SYMPTOM 20-34** **ScanDisk marks valid clusters as "bad"** This virtually always happens when the drive is configured with incorrect geometry in the CMOS Setup. When you perform a surface scan with ScanDisk, the incorrect CMOS settings cause valid, usable clusters after a certain point on the drive to be designated as bad (unusable). For example, if you have a 160GB hard disk and the CMOS is set for a 120GB hard disk, ScanDisk may scan the first 120GB correctly, but the remaining 40GB are marked as bad. This may initially suggest that the drive is defective. To correct your cluster entries

1. Back up your files on the drive, then correct your CMOS settings.
2. Repartition the drive with FDISK.
3. Install the operating system (allow CMOS Setup to format the drive for you prior to installation).
4. Reinstall any backup software, then restore your data.

**SYMPTOM 20-35** **ScanDisk reports some bad sectors, but cannot map them out during a surface analysis** You may need a surface analysis utility for your particular drive that is provided by the drive maker. For example, Western Digital provides the WDATIDE.EXE utility for its Caviar series of drives. It will mark all "grown" defects and compensate for lost capacity by utilizing spare tracks.

 These types of surface analysis utilities are typically destructive. Make sure to have a complete backup of the drive before proceeding. Also, the utility may take a very long time to run if your drive's capacity is large.

**SYMPTOM 20-36**    **ScanDisk reports an "Out of Memory" error after copying data from a smaller drive to a larger one**    The data seems to copy successfully, but when you run ScanDisk you get an "Out of Memory" error (or you have a problem using Defrag). Chances are that you've copied data from a smaller drive to a larger drive that uses FAT32 (you're running Windows 95 OSR2 or Windows 98/Me/XP) with a utility that can copy the contents of one hard drive to another. The utility may have created an image of the drive that was copied to the other, or it copied data sector by sector from one drive to the other.

If you used an older utility (or version of EZ-Drive) to copy the data, the clusters were probably not correctly resized for the new FAT32 partition. When a partition becomes formatted, it is divided into clusters—or small blocks. These clusters are used to store data, and the size of a cluster is determined by the size of the partition. Older copy utilities often do not support FAT32 properly and will incorrectly size the cluster on the new FAT32 partition when they transfer data from the old drive to the new one.

**SYMPTOM 20-37**    **You cannot enable the DMA checkbox in the Windows 9x/Me Device Manager**    The DMA checkbox on the General tab of drive's Properties dialog box may be grayed out, or may not stay checked once the system reboots. In extreme cases, the hard drive may be forced to run in DOS Compatibility Mode until UDMA is disabled in the system BIOS. This is typically a problem with UDMA support provided by the BIOS. For example, Award BIOS versions prior to 10/28/98 may prevent Windows 9x/Me and Windows NT from handling UDMA transfers with a UDMA/66/100/133-compliant hard drive installed. This issue has been observed to only affect systems if the following conditions exist:

- The system contains an Award BIOS dated prior to 10/28/98.
- The system contains a core logic chipset that only supports Ultra-DMA/33 (such as the Intel 430TX, 440LX, or 440BX; the VIA 586A, 586B, 596, or 686; the SiS 5598, 5591, 5600, 530, or 620; and the ALi 1543C, 1533A-J, or 1543A1-F).
- The system has a hard drive that supports Ultra-DMA/66/100/133.

The best solution for this problem is to contact your system or motherboard manufacturer and obtain a BIOS update that corrects this issue. If a BIOS update is not available or is not convenient, then it may be necessary to upgrade the drive controller, or disable the Ultra ATA/66/100/133 capability of your hard drive (if possible) until a BIOS update is available.

**SYMPTOM 20-38**    **You see a "Verifying DMI pool data" message, then the system halts**    The Desktop Management Interface (DMI) is a relatively new method of managing computers in a network. The main component of DMI is the Management Information Format Database (or MIFD—the DMI pool data). This database contains all the information about the computing system and its components. Under some circumstances, a PC may halt or crash after partitioning and formatting a new hard drive, and the error may persist after the drive is removed. Try the following steps to work around the problem:

1. Boot the computer and start the CMOS Setup.
2. Set the drive type to "None" or "Not Installed". You can also try loading BIOS Defaults for the CMOS Setup.
3. Save the changes and reboot the PC with a Windows 9x/Me boot disk.
4. Shut down the PC immediately after the memory count is displayed.
5. Reconnect the power and interface cables to the hard drive.
6. Reboot the PC and start the CMOS Setup again.

7. Autodetect the hard drive and verify that the LBA mode option is enabled.

8. Save the changes and reboot the PC with a Windows 9x/Me boot disk.

9. Partition and format the hard drive using FDISK and FORMAT.

10. Reboot the system. On bootup, the display should read

    ```
    Verifying DMI Pool Data: Update Successful
    ```

11. The system should continue booting normally.

**SYMPTOM 20-39**    **You have poor write performance with the hard drive**    Although there are numerous issues that can cause poor drive performance, poor write performance may be traced to the drive's "write verify" feature. "Write verify" performs a read of the data just written to the hard drive, and validates the data with a cyclic redundancy check (CRC). This offers assurance that the data written to the hard drive was written correctly. When this feature is enabled, the write performance of the drive is reduced because a read occurs for each write.

High-end hard drives (such as Maxtor drives) are normally shipped with the "write verify" feature enabled, and this provides protection against any early drive issues (e.g., those caused by mishandling). This feature is enabled only for the first 10 power cycles, then the feature will be disabled. You can control the "write verify" feature with a utility from the drive manufacturer. For Maxtor drives, you'd use the WVSET utility. Otherwise, simply cycle the PC power several times until the feature disables itself automatically, and write performance should improve.

**SYMPTOM 20-40**    **When replacing or repartitioning certain Compaq systems, you can no longer access the system's setup**    This occurs because you removed the "diagnostic partition." Some Compaq computers store the system BIOS information in a non-DOS, or "diagnostic," partition on the hard drive, instead of storing it on a chip on the motherboard as most other systems do. If you have such a Compaq model and you install the new drive as a master, you will need to copy or reinstall the diagnostic partition onto the new drive. If you don't, you will not be able to access your CMOS Setup upon boot up. If you install the new drive as a slave or non-boot drive, you do not need to reinstall this partition. In addition, if you're planning to install the drive with an older version of Western Digital's EZ-Drive, you must use version 9.06w or later (though it's much better to use Data Lifeguard Tools or other more recent DDO products).

If you install the new drive as a master, you can use drive overlay software to copy the diagnostic partition and your data from the old drive to the new one. If you're concerned only about the diagnostic partition, you can use the drive overlay software to transfer the data, then reformat the drive. As long as you do this under the DDO's control, it will not affect the diagnostic partition. Just boot to C:, insert the startup disk, then start formatting. If you have more than one partition, make sure you format the correct drive letters corresponding to the other partitions.

When trying to access the "diagnostic partition," you may encounter an error message that refers to a memory conflict. This is a known issue and you will need to contact Compaq directly for detailed instructions should this occur.

**SYMPTOM 20-41**    **You detect hard drive errors caused by damaged data or physical damage**    In most cases, you may receive one of the following error messages when you are starting or using your computer:

```
Serious Disk Error Writing Drive <X>
Data Error Reading Drive <X>
Error Reading Drive <X>
I/O Error
Seek Error - Sector not found
```

These error messages indicate either damaged data or physical damage on the hard disk. Run ScanDisk to examine the hard drive. Running ScanDisk with the "Thorough" option selected examines the drive for physical damage—if damaged data is detected, ScanDisk allows you to save the damaged data to a file (or discard the data). Keep in mind that ScanDisk's "surface scan" may take a considerable amount of time on large hard disks (and even longer under FAT32 partitions). If ScanDisk is unable to repair damaged data (or indicates that the drive suffers from physical damage), you'll need to replace the drive.

**SYMPTOM 20-42    One or more subdirectories appear lost or damaged**    Both the root directory of a drive and its FAT contain references to subdirectories. If data in either the root directory or File Allocation Table is corrupt, one or more subdirectories may be inaccessible by the drive. Try repairing the drive's directory structure. Use ScanDisk (preferably a FAT32 version with a later version of Windows, or from a Windows 98/Me Startup Disk) to check the disk's directory structure for problems, then correct any problems that are reported.

**SYMPTOM 20-43    The hard drive is infected by a bootblock virus**    You may detect the presence of a bootblock virus (a virus that infects the MBR) by running an antivirus utility or receiving a warning from the BIOS bootblock protection feature. In every case, you should attempt to use the antivirus utility to eradicate the virus. You may also remove a bootblock virus by using **FDISK /MBR** (though doing so could render the contents of your disk inaccessible). If you're using drive overlay software such as Disk Manager or MaxBlast, you can usually restore the MBR through the setup or maintenance menu within the DDO utility itself.

 Always back up the drive before attempting any partition/format procedures.

**SYMPTOM 20-44    You see a "File Allocation Table Bad" error**    The operating system has encountered a problem with the FAT. Normally, there are two copies of the FAT on a drive—chances are that one of the copies has become damaged. It may also be possible that there is no partition on the drive to begin with. Run ScanDisk—doing this may be able to correct the problem by allowing you to select which copy of the FAT you wish to use. If the problem continues, you'll need to back up as many files as possible and reformat the drive.

**SYMPTOM 20-45    Software diagnostics indicate an average access time that is longer than specified for the drive**    The average access time is the average amount of time needed for a drive to reach the track and sector where a needed file begins. Review your drive specifications and verify the timing specifications for your particular drive—its timing may be correct. Before you replace a drive, try testing several similar drives for comparison. If only the suspect drive measures incorrectly, you may not *need* to replace the drive itself just yet, but you should at least maintain frequent backups in case the drive is near failure.

Also keep in mind that different software packages measure access time differently. Make sure that the diagnostic subtracts system overhead processing from the access time calculation. Try one or two other diagnostics to confirm the measurement. Start your defragmentation utility (such as Disk Defragmenter) and check to see the percentage of file fragmentation. If there is more than 10 percent fragmentation, you should consider running the defragmentation utility.

**SYMPTOM 20-46** **Software diagnostics indicate a slower data transfer rate than specified** This is often due to less-than-ideal data transfer rates rather than an actual hardware failure. Review your drive specifications and verify the timing specifications for your particular drive—its timing may be correct. Also keep in mind that different software packages measure access time differently. Make sure that the diagnostic subtracts system overhead processing from the access time calculation. Try one or two other diagnostics to confirm the measurement.

Next, enter the CMOS Setup routine and verify that any enhanced data transfer modes are enabled (such as DMA mode 4, 5, or 6). Doing that can increase data transfer rate substantially. Start your defragmentation utility (such as Disk Defragmenter), and check to see the percentage of file fragmentation. If there is more than 10 percent fragmentation, you should consider running the defragmentation utility. Finally, if the drive is a SCSI type, make sure the SCSI bus is terminated properly—poor termination can cause data errors and result in re-transmissions that degrade overall data transfer rates.

**SYMPTOM 20-47** **Drive diagnostics reveal a great deal of wasted space on the drive** You probably have a large drive partitioned as one or more FAT16 logical volumes. If you deal with large numbers of small files, it may be more efficient to create multiple smaller partitions utilizing smaller clusters. As an alternative, you may choose to repartition the drive using FAT32, which supports much larger partitions (while allowing for smaller clusters).

**SYMPTOM 20-48** **The FDISK procedure hangs up or fails to create or save partition records for the drive(s)** You may also see an error message such as "Runtime error." This type of problem often indicates a problem with track 00 on the drive. Make sure that the interface signal cables are inserted properly and completely at the drive and controller. Try some new signal cables if necessary. Next, enter the CMOS Setup routine and see that all of the parameters entered for the drive are correct. Heads, cylinders, sectors per track, landing zone, and write precompensation must all be appropriate. Check with the drive maker and see if there is an alternative "translation geometry" that you can enter instead. If the BIOS supports autodetection, try autodetecting the drive.

Check your version of FDISK. The version of FDISK you are using should be compliant with the OS version on your boot disk—older versions may not work. Now run FDISK and see if there are any partitions already on the drive. If so, you may need to erase any existing partitions, then create your new partition from scratch. *Remember that erasing a partition will destroy any data already on the drive.*

If partitions are not the problem, use a utility such as ScanDisk to check the media for physical defects—especially at track 00. If there is physical damage in the boot sector, you should replace the drive. Check for software from the manufacturer. Some drive makers provide low-level preparation utilities that can rewrite track 00. For example, Western Digital provides the WD_CLEAR.EXE utility. If problems still persist, replace the defective hard drive.

**SYMPTOM 20-49** **After using FDISK to partition a large hard drive, the system hangs when booting from a floppy disk** This is almost always an issue with a system BIOS (or drive controller) that cannot properly support a large (8.4GB+) drive. Some BIOS versions are confused when they encounter an 8.4GB or larger hard drive, and they assign it 0 heads by mistake. Under these conditions, you'll be able to partition the drive with FDISK, but the partition table that it creates will contain invalid information. When you boot to a floppy disk, the operating system on that floppy disk attempts to access the partition table on the hard drive. The invalid information created by FDISK causes the OS to hang. The solution is to upgrade the system BIOS (or the drive controller) to support the large drive natively or to install drive overlay software such as Disk Manager or MaxBlast.

**SYMPTOM 20-50**    **FDISK reports an error such as "no space to create partition" or "disk is write protected"**    There are several possible issues that may cause this type of behavior. Check the CMOS Setup first. Chances are that your BIOS has enabled virus protection for the master boot record (sometimes referred to as *Boot Sector Write Protect*). You must go into the system's CMOS Setup and disable that feature before partitioning a drive (or installing/upgrading an operating system). Now check the drive jumpers. Some hard drives also require the use of two jumpers rather than just one. Verify that your drive is jumpered properly for its place in your particular drive configuration (such as single master, master with slave, or slave). If the problem persists, the BIOS may not be able to support your drive properly. Check for a BIOS upgrade (or upgrade the drive controller) or install drive overlay software such as Disk Manager or MaxBlast.

**SYMPTOM 20-51**    **FDISK refuses to partition the drive and hangs the system or returns a "runtime error"**    In many cases, track 00 on the drive has been corrupted. If you can perform a low-level format of the drive, try using the disk manufacturer's LL formatting (or "drive preparation") utility to reconstruct track 00. For example, Western Digital's "Data Lifeguard Tools" utility (www.support.wdc.com) can be used to perform a "pseudo" LL format on Western Digital drives. From the main menu, choose Diagnostics, select the correct drive, and choose "Write Zeros." After the operation completes, run FDISK again. Your particular drive manufacturer may offer other similar utilities. If this does not resolve the problem, the drive itself may need to be replaced.

**SYMPTOM 20-52**    **When running CHKDSK.EXE from a command prompt, you receive an "F parameter not specified" error**    This issue may occur under Windows 9x/Me, and the entire error message usually appears as such:

```
Errors found, F parameter not specified. Corrections will not be written
to disk. CHKDSK cannot check the validity of this drive because the
following path is too long:
```

This problem typically occurs when the command line you type contains more than 67 characters. To get around this issue, use ScanDisk instead of CHKDSK to check your hard disk for errors.

**SYMPTOM 20-53**    **While using APC PowerChute, Defrag locks up the system after selecting a disk to defragment**    This problem occurs when you're using APC PowerChute Plus 5.0 or 5.0.1 under Windows 98—these older versions of PowerChute Plus are designed for Windows 95 only. To work around this problem, quit PowerChute Plus before using Defrag:

1. Press CTRL-ALT-DEL to open the Close Program dialog box.
2. Click PowerChute Plus, and then click End Task.
3. Do the same thing for Iconclnt.
4. Now run Defrag normally.

To restart PowerChute Plus after Defrag is completed, simply reboot the computer. For a more permanent fix to this problem, obtain updated software from APC (www.apcc.com/tools/download).

**SYMPTOM 20-54**    **Defrag causes a GPF in USER.EXE under Windows 9x/Me**    When you try to run Defrag from System Agent or Task Scheduler, you may receive a General Protection Fault (or GPF) in USER.EXE. This may occur if the task information for Defrag has become damaged. Delete the Defrag task from System Agent or Task Scheduler, and then create a new task.

**SYMPTOM 20-55**    **You find that a PC using an Ultra-DMA controller/drive may lock up when running Windows 95 (OSR2)**    The lockup occurs when the drive is being accessed. This problem occurs when there's a hardware error while data is being read from the hard drive. When the error happens during an Ultra-DMA data transfer, the Windows device driver does not successfully recover from the error and retry the operation—so the system halts. This is a known issue with Windows 95 OSR2, and an update file (REMIDEUP.EXE) is available for download from the Microsoft Web site. The updated file ESDI_506.PDR version 4.00.1116 (dated 8/25/97 or later) should fix the problem under Windows 95 OSR2. You may also upgrade the operating system to Windows 98/Me/XP, which should offer far better native UDMA support.

**SYMPTOM 20-56**    **You encounter errors accessing a hard drive with its "spin-down" feature enabled**    This frequently occurs under Windows 95 (and OSR2), and you may find that incorrect data is read from or written to the drive, or you may encounter GPFs. This type of problem is known to occur under Windows 95 (and OSR2) if the drive requires more than 7.5 seconds to "spin-up"—an error is then generated in the Windows 95 driver, resulting in incorrect data being read from the drive (which can result in GPFs). You can work around this problem by disabling hard disk spin-down on the Disk Drives tab using the Power tool in the Control Panel. An update file (REMIDEUP.EXE) is available for download from the Microsoft Web site. The updated file ESDI_506.PDR version 4.00.1113 (dated 12/6/96 or later) should fix the problem under Windows 95 (and OSR2). For Windows 95, the VOLTRACK.VXD version 4.00.954 (dated 3/6/96 or later) file is also installed. You may also correct this problem by upgrading the operating system to Windows 98/Me/XP.

**SYMPTOM 20-57**    **You see an "Incorrect DOS version" error**    This rare error can still occur today if you attempt to execute an external DOS command (such as FORMAT) using a version of the utility that is *not* from the same DOS version as the COMMAND.COM file currently running. Reboot with a corresponding version of COMMAND.COM or get a version of the utility that matches the current version of COMMAND.COM. Try booting from a Windows 98/Me Startup Disk for a relatively recent DOS version.

**SYMPTOM 20-58**    **You cannot empty the Recycle Bin under Windows 9x/Me**    There are several possible issues. When you right-click the Recycle Bin, the "Empty Recycle Bin" command may be unavailable (or the Properties command may be unavailable). You may also find that files you delete may be permanently deleted—rather than simply "moved" to the Recycle Bin. In virtually all cases, this problem is caused when your fixed hard disk is marked as a removable drive. You'll have to "unmark" the hard drive:

1. Click Start | Settings | Control Panel.
2. Double-click the System icon.
3. Click the Device Manager tab.

4. Double-click the Disk Drives branch to expand it.

5. Click your hard disk, then click Properties.

6. On the Settings tab, click the Removable checkbox to clear it (see Figure 20-16).

7. Click OK, then click OK again.

8. Restart your computer.

You cannot use this procedure on a *true* removable drive. If the drive is removable, the Removable option is reset when you restart the computer.

**SYMPTOM 20-59**    **After installing a new hard drive, Windows 98/Me detects the drive only if it's noted as "removable" in the Device Manager**    Chances are that you missed one or two steps and neglected to partition and format the drive. All hard disk drives must be partitioned before they can be formatted—even if the drive is only going to have a single partition. Windows 98/Me incorrectly allows you to format an unpartitioned drive *if* you designate the drive as "removable." Using a drive this way will almost certainly result in data loss. The solution is to back up any data on the drive, then remove the checkmark from the "Removable" box in the Windows 98 Device Manager (see Figure 20-16 earlier). Next, use FDISK to create at least one primary and active partition. Reboot the system, then format the partition(s) with FORMAT. This process will destroy any data on the drive, but should correct the recognition issue.

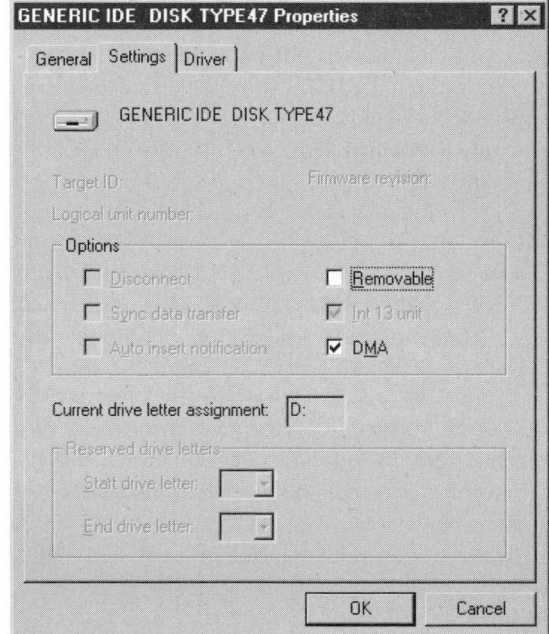

**FIGURE  20-16**    Be sure that your hard drives are *not* marked as "Removable"

**SYMPTOM 20-60**    **You cannot place a FAT32 partition on a drive**    The trick to establishing a FAT32 partition on a drive is to partition the drive correctly. Try the following steps to partition a drive:

1. In the Windows 9x/Me Device Manager, select the drive and click on Properties.
2. Click Settings, then click the INT 13 Unit checkbox to select it (see Figure 20-16 earlier).
3. Quit the Device Manager and restart Windows.
4. Once Windows is restarted, open an MS-DOS session and use the FDISK command to partition the drive (be careful not to partition an existing drive accidentally).
5. Restart Windows again. You should be able to format the drive and use the FAT32 file system.

**SYMPTOM 20-61**    **After moving a FAT32 SCSI hard drive from one controller to another, you cannot read or write reliably to the SCSI drive**    This is because SCSI drives are highly controller-dependent to begin with, and you should be prepared to repartition and reformat SCSI drives *whenever* changing the SCSI host controller. This behavior is particularly evident when you partition and format a hard disk using a SCSI controller that fully supports INT 13 extensions, and you then move the hard disk to a controller that does *not* fully support INT 13 extensions. To move a drive using the FAT32 file system to a different controller, you must verify that *both* controllers fully support INT 13 extensions in the same manner—if they do not, data loss will most likely occur.

**SYMPTOM 20-62**    **When booting from a floppy disk, you cannot access your FAT32 hard drive partition(s)**    The system boots fine from the hard drive. This is an issue with the boot disk. Boot disks made with older versions of DOS or Windows are not "FAT32-aware" and cannot support access to your FAT32 hard drive partition(s). For example, you cannot access your Windows 98 FAT32 drive when booting from a Windows 95a Startup Disk. Create a Windows 98/Me Startup Disk in order to boot your FAT32 system.

**SYMPTOM 20-63**    **The system may hang up when certain drive software is used under FAT32**    After installing the drive software (such as PC Tools Pro 9.0), the computer will probably hang up during startup after you see the following message:

```
Analyzing drive C:
Reading system areas
```

In virtually all cases, this occurs because your drive software is *not* compatible with the FAT32 file system in Windows 95 OSR2 (or Windows 98/Me/XP). You can contact the software maker (such as Symantec for PC Tools Pro 9.0 at www.symantec.com) for a FAT32-aware version of the software. As a work-around, you can use a text editor (such as EDIT or Notepad) to edit the AUTOEXEC.BAT file and disable the command line that starts the software. For PC Tools Pro 9.0, you'd REM-out its line such as:

```
REM call pctools.bat
```

**SYMPTOM 20-64**    **You encounter errors using IBM antivirus utilities on a FAT32 file system**    In actual practice, you'll probably encounter either of the following symptoms:

■   When you're installing IBM Anti-Virus, the Setup program offers to scan for viruses. If you choose to scan, you may receive an error message stating that the master boot record could not be read.

■   When you're scanning for viruses on a drive using the FAT32 file system, IBM Anti-Virus may report that errors occurred while it was checking for viruses. The error log may contain information such as: "Errors during virus checking: unexpected error code 18."

Older versions of IBM Anti-Virus are *not* written to work with the FAT32 file system included with OSR2 and Windows 98/Me/XP. There is no work-around for this, and you'll need to obtain an updated version of IBM software or use a different antivirus tool that is FAT32-aware.

**SYMPTOM 20-65**   **When using Defrag on a FAT32 system, you encounter an error message such as "DEFRAG0026 Make sure disk is formatted"**   You may also see an error such as:

```
Windows cannot defragment this drive. Make sure the disk is formatted
and free of errors. Then try defragmenting the drive again.
```

This error can be caused when running an earlier version of DEFRAG.EXE than the version included with Windows 95 OSR2 (or Windows 98/Me/XP). To resolve this problem, extract a new copy of the DEFRAG.EXE file from your original Windows 95 OSR2 (or Windows 98/Me/XP) CD-ROM.

**SYMPTOM 20-66**   **You see an "Invalid Media" error message when formatting a FAT32 partition**   When you try to format a FAT32 file system partition larger than 8,025MB (8GB) from within Windows 9x/Me, you may receive the following error message:

```
Verifying <xxx.xx>M
Invalid media or track 0 bad-disk unusable
Format terminated
```

where <*xxx.xx*> is the size of the partition. This error occurs if there is a non-DOS partition preceding the extended DOS partition *and* the primary DOS partition has been formatted using the real-mode FORMAT.EXE command. To correct this problem, you'll need to reformat the volume using the following steps:

**1.**   Click Start | Shut Down | "Restart The Computer In MS-DOS Mode" | Yes.

**2.**   Type the following command and then press ENTER:

```
format <drive>:
```

where <*drive*> is the drive letter for the partition you want to format.

**3.**   When the partition is formatted, type **exit** to restart Windows.

**SYMPTOM 20-67**   **After you install Windows 98/Me (or convert a partition to FAT32), Windows 98/Me reports "DOS Compatibility Mode"**   This can occur when the drive controller has not been detected properly under Windows 98/Me. Try rebooting the PC and see if Windows will redetect the drive controller (you may need to remove the drive controller entry from the Device Manager before rebooting the system). For specific details about resolving Compatibility Mode problems, refer to the DOS Compatibility Mode troubleshooting guide at the start of this section.

**SYMPTOM 20-68**    **After converting a drive to FAT32, you notice that tools like ScanDisk and Defrag take much longer to run**    This is an undesired side effect of the FAT32 file system. It takes Defrag and ScanDisk the same amount of time to examine a single cluster, regardless of the cluster's size. Since FAT32 uses smaller clusters, there are many times more clusters, and such utilities take considerably longer than they had before conversion. Microsoft compensates for this by including tools such as the Tune Up wizard, which allows you to schedule such tasks to take place when you're away from the computer.

**SYMPTOM 20-69**    **The FAT32 conversion utility crashed after reporting that it found bad sectors**    This is a side effect of ScanDisk. If ScanDisk has marked any sectors bad, the FAT32 converter will refuse to run, even if the sectors are fixed by third-party disk utilities (such as Data Lifeguard Tools). ScanDisk uses the FAT table to keep track of bad sectors. But even if third-party utilities remap bad sectors at the hardware level, ScanDisk is not aware of those changes. One solution is to wipe the hard drive clean and start over (in which case you'd just partition the drive using FAT32 to begin with). Here's an easier workaround when there are only a few bad sectors:

1. Before using the FAT32 conversion utility, perform a complete backup of your hard drive.
2. Run your third-party disk utility software (such as Data Lifeguard Tools or MaxBlast) to make sure that any bad sectors have been re-mapped.
3. Open a DOS window and type:

   ```
   cvt x: /cvt32
   ```

   where *x* is the drive letter you wish to convert.
4. The converter will then run, disregarding any sectors that have previously been marked bad by ScanDisk.

**SYMPTOM 20-70**    **You install Disk Manager to a hard drive, then install DOS, but DOS formats the drive back to 528MB**    After Disk Manager is installed, you must create a rescue disk to use in conjunction with your DOS installation. There are two means of accomplishing this. First, you can do the following:

1. Create a "clean" DOS-bootable disk.
2. Copy two files from the original Disk Manager disk to your bootable disk: XBIOS.OVL and DMDRVR.BIN.
3. Create a CONFIG.SYS file on this bootable disk with these three lines:

   ```
   DEVICE=DMDRVR.BIN
   FILES=35
   BUFFERS=35
   ```
4. Remove the bootable disk and reboot the system.
5. When you see "Press space bar to boot from diskette," do so—the system will halt.
6. Insert the rescue disk in drive A:, then press any key to resume the boot process.

**7.** At the A: prompt, remove your rescue disk, insert the DOS installation disk, then type **setup**.

**8.** You will now install DOS files without overwriting the Disk Manager files.

Or you may use an alternative approach:

**1.** Create a "clean" DOS-bootable disk.

**2.** Insert the original Disk Manager disk in the A: drive and type:

```
DMCFIG/D=A:
```

**3.** You will be prompted to inert a bootable floppy in drive A:.

**4.** You will need to remove and insert the bootable disk a few times as Drive Manager files are copied.

**5.** Remove the floppy and reboot the system.

**6.** When you see "Press space bar to boot from diskette," do so—the system will halt.

**7.** Insert the rescue disk in drive A:, then press any key to resume the boot process.

**8.** At the A: prompt, remove your rescue disk, insert the DOS installation disk, then type **setup**.

**9.** You will now install DOS files without overwriting the Disk Manager files.

**SYMPTOM 20-71**    **DDO software is hanging at start time**    You find that the DDO software (e.g., MaxBlast) causes the PC to freeze or crash during the boot process. In most cases, the trouble is caused by a software bug or incompatibility between the DDO software and other software or hardware on the system. For example, the ATI Radeon video cards are known to be incompatible with MaxBlast Plus II DDO software—the system will freeze when detecting one of these cards. The best solution to this problem is to contact the DDO maker for known incompatibilities, and (if any) download and install the latest version of the DDO software.

**SYMPTOM 20-72**    **You find that your FAT32 system works in "Compatibility Mode" when using Ontrack Disk Manager**    After you install FAT32 on a drive that uses Ontrack Disk Manager (version 6.03 or 7.04), all drives use MS-DOS compatibility mode, or the computer seems to take an unusually long time to boot. This happens because the Dynamic Drive Overlay (or DDO) is unable to find files in the root folder that it needs to start correctly. A Dynamic Drive Overlay makes calculations for the starting root folder cluster based on FAT12 and FAT16 volumes and returns a value of zero for FAT32 volumes (it does this because of changes made in the root directory structure). The overlay software searches all possible clusters in the root folder for its overlay files. You'll need to configure Disk Manager to avoid searching the root folder for overlay files.

 Configuring Disk Manager software to avoid searching the root folder causes Disk Manager not to hook the DOS interrupt chain—forcing Disk Manager to load low in conventional memory.

**SYMPTOM 20-73**    **You no longer see the DDO initialization message at start time**
For example, DDO software typically displays a startup message such as "EZ-BIOS Initializing". If this message no longer appears, and the drive appears inaccessible, chances are that the drive was formatted, or some other utility changed the master boot record (e.g., you executed FDISK /MBR). Use your DDO utility to restore Track 0 to a previously backed up version (usually the most recent backup). This should restore the DDO software and reenable the drive.

**SYMPTOM 20-74** **You encounter a "Drive 80 I/O Timeout" error** This type of error is usually caused by a bug or incompatibility between the drive, the DDO software, and the drive controller/BIOS. Start by downloading and installing the latest version of your DDO software from the drive manufacturer. If the problem persists, your best solution is to upgrade the drive controller to a PCI card (such as the Maxtor Ultra-ATA/133 or Promise Ultra133 TX2 cards).

**SYMPTOM 20-75** **You receive an "Unknown partition type on drive 1" error** This type of error may occur on systems that use a diagnostic partition on the primary master drive (such as some Compaq models). The installation of DDO software on the master drive (when the BIOS doesn't support the full drive capacity) can conflict with the diagnostic partition. There are two solutions for this issue. First, you can opt to remove the DDO software and upgrade the BIOS or drive controller hardware so that DDO software is not needed. Second, you can download and install the latest version of your DDO software that is compatible with diagnostic partitions.

**SYMPTOM 20-76** **You encounter an "Unable to find IDE drive for INT 13h drive 80h/81h" error** This type of problem is typically reported by the DDO software during initial installation, and is usually caused when trying to add an IDE hard drive to a system that already has a SCSI controller card in it. To use DDO software (such as MaxBlast), you will need to temporarily remove the SCSI controller from your system. An integrated SCSI controller (which cannot be physically removed) should be disabled within the system BIOS. After completing the DDO installation, you can reattach or reenable the SCSI controller and devices.

# Further Study

**Maxtor** www.maxtor.com
**Phoenix Technologies** www.phoenix.com/en/home
**PowerQuest** www.powerquest.com
**Seagate** www.seagate.com
**SerialATA** www.serialata.org
**Symantec** www.symantec.com
**Western Digital** www.wdc.com

# 21

# JOYSTICKS, CONTROLLERS, AND GAME PORTS

**F**ew peripheral devices have come to represent PC entertainment like the *joystick* (Figure 21-1). Although it is one of the simplest peripherals available for a PC, the joystick allows a user to bring an element of hand-eye coordination to interactive programs (for example, flight simulators and 3D "walk-through" games) that would simply be impossible with a keyboard or mouse. The joystick interfaces to the host PC through a basic connection called the *game port adapter* (or simply the *game port*). This chapter discusses the joystick and game port, then covers a selection of troubleshooting issues.

**FIGURE 21-1**    The EagleMax joystick from Act Labs: versatile and programmable control for popular flight simulators (Courtesy of Act Labs)

# Understanding the Game Port System

The typical game port uses a relatively simple interface to the PC. Only the lower 8 data bits are used (which explains why so many older game ports used the older 8-bit XT card style rather than switching to a 16-bit AT ISA card type). Also, only the lower 10 address bits are needed. Since the game port is an I/O device, the card uses I/OR and I/OW control signals. On virtually all PCs, port 201h is reserved for the game port. Figure 21-2 illustrates a typical game port system.

The USB port has had a profound impact on gaming devices. Many modern gaming devices (from joysticks to flight yokes to steering systems) are available with a USB interface—making the gaming device "digital" rather than "analog." Digital gaming devices often provide more features than analog devices, and can be switched/swapped quickly without having to power down and reboot the system. As you will see later in this chapter, digital gaming devices are also less prone to drift because the controller (the USB port) does not rely on analog circuitry to divine the joystick's position.

Today, a large number of joystick products use the USB interface rather than traditional 15-pin game ports.

Keep in mind that this discussion of joysticks extends to other game controllers such as "flight yokes," driving wheels, pedals, and so on. While these devices may look radically different on the surface, their internal design is very similar. For example, a driving wheel is basically a joystick with only an X (left/right) axis.

## ANALOG JOYSTICK BASICS

A traditional analog joystick is assembled with two separate potentiometers (these are adjustable resistors, which are typically 100 kOhms) arranged perpendicularly to one another. One potentiometer represents the X axis, while the other potentiometer represents the Y axis. Both potentiometers are linked together mechanically

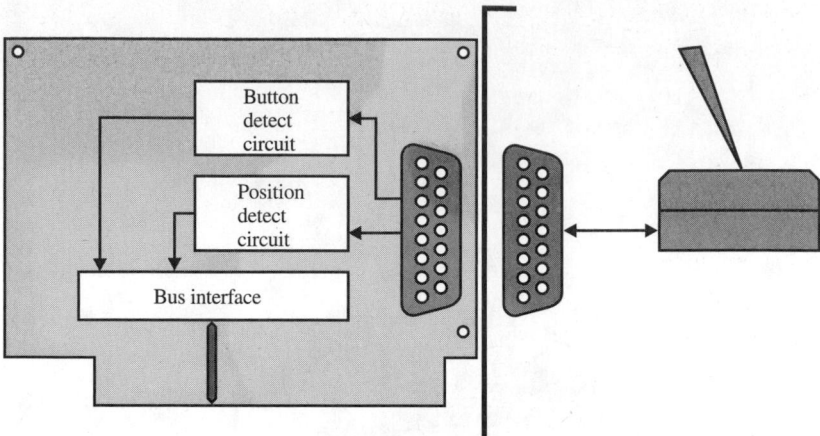

**FIGURE 21-2** Simplified diagram of a game port system

and attached to a movable stick. As the stick is moved left or right, one potentiometer is moved. As the stick moves up or down, the other potentiometer is moved. Of course, the stick can be moved in both the X and Y axes simultaneously, with the proportions of resistance reflecting the stick's position. The stick itself is normally tensioned with a series of springs so that it will return to the center position when released. You can see the wiring scheme for a standard 15-pin dual joystick port in Figure 21-3. Standard game ports use a DB-15 (15-pin) female connector, and the pinout for a standard joystick port is listed in Table 21-1.

 Don't be fooled by the fancy plastic molding, contoured grips, and "techno" appearance of today's joysticks. They may look fancy, but virtually all analog joysticks are internally identical. The same is true for digital joystick and controller devices.

Detecting the stick's X and Y position is not an intuitively obvious process. Ultimately, the analog value of each potentiometer must be converted to a digital value that is read by the game application software. This is an important wrinkle—since the game port does not generate an interrupt, it is up to the

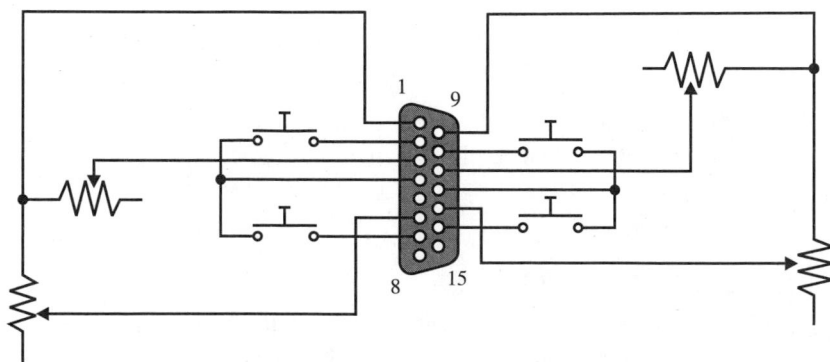

**FIGURE 21-3** Wiring diagram for a conventional dual joystick port

| TABLE 21-1 | PIN ASSIGNMENTS FOR A STANDARD 15-PIN JOYSTICK PORT |
|---|---|
| **PIN** | **JOYSTICK** |
| 1 | XY1 (Joystick 1 +5V supply) |
| 2 | Switch 1 |
| 3 | Potentiometer X1 signal |
| 4 | Ground (for switch 1 & 2) |
| 5 | Ground (for switch 2) |
| 6 | Potentiometer Y1 signal |
| 7 | Switch 2 |
| 8 | N.C. (or +5V) |
| 9 | XY2 (Joystick 2 +5V supply) |
| 10 | Switch 3 |
| 11 | Potentiometer X2 signal |
| 12 | Ground (for switch 3 & 4) |
| 13 | Potentiometer Y2 signal |
| 14 | Switch 4 |
| 15 | N.C. (or +5V) |

particular *application* to interrogate the joystick port regularly. You might imagine that such a conversion would use an *analog-to-digital converter* (ADC). However, an ADC provides much greater resolution than is needed, and its conversions require a relatively long time. Current game port conversion circuits use a "multivibrator" element.

Ultimately, the resistance of each potentiometer is determined indirectly by measuring the amount of time required for a charged capacitor to discharge through the particular potentiometer. If a certain axis is at 0 ohms, the multivibrator's internal capacitor will discharge in about 24.2µS, while at 100 kOhms, the multivibrator's capacitor will discharge in about 1124µS. Since this is a relatively linear relationship, the discharge time can easily be equated to potentiometer position. (An actual routine to accomplish this requires only about 16 lines of assembler code.) The multivibrator technique also simplifies the circuitry needed on the game port adapter. It is really the application (the game itself) that is doing the work.

A typical joystick also has one or two buttons. As you see from Figure 21-3, the buttons are typically open, and their closed state can be detected by reading the byte at I/O port 201h. Since the game port is capable of supporting two joysticks simultaneously (each with two buttons), the upper 4 bits of I/O port 201h indicate the on/off status of all four buttons.

Windows 98/Me/XP supports a joystick as a game controller through an icon in the Control Panel. You can access, add, delete, and modify your joysticks through that properties dialog box. Under Windows XP, click Start | Control Panel | Printers and Other Hardware | Game Controllers. The Game Controllers dialog box opens (see Figure 21-4). Unlike DOS applications, Windows provides joystick support to all applications, so you need only identify and calibrate the joystick once.

## ADAPTING A SECOND JOYSTICK

While the typical game port can support two joysticks, most joystick products only connect a single joystick. This means only half the game port is being utilized. You can purchase a joystick Y-adapter from

**FIGURE  21-4**    Identifying a joystick through the Windows XP Game Controllers properties dialog box

any computer store, or construct a Y-adapter using the pinout in Table 21-2. You'll need a DB-15 (15-pin) male connector to attach to the game port and two DB-15 female connectors to attach to each of the two joysticks.

**TABLE 21-2    PIN ASSIGNMENTS FOR A JOYSTICK Y-ADAPTER**

| GAME PORT (DB-15 MALE) | | JOYSTICK 1 (DB-15 FEMALE) | JOYSTICK 2 (DB-15 FEMALE) |
|---|---|---|---|
| Pin | Definition | Pin | Pin |
| 1 | XY1 (Joystick 1 +5V supply) | 1 | |
| 2 | Switch 1 | 2 | |
| 3 | Potentiometer X1 signal | 3 | |
| 4 | Ground (for switch 1 & 2) | 4 | |
| 5 | Ground (for switch 2) | 5 | |
| 6 | Potentiometer Y1 signal | 6 | |
| 7 | Switch 2 | 7 | |
| 8 | N.C. (or +5V) | 8 | |
| 9 | XY2 (Joystick 2 +5V supply) | | 1 |
| 10 | Switch 3 | | 2 |
| 11 | Potentiometer X2 signal | | 3 |
| 12 | Ground (for switch 3 & 4) | | 4 and 5 |
| 13 | Potentiometer Y2 signal | | 6 |
| 14 | Switch 4 | | 7 |
| 15 | N.C. (or +5V) | | 8 |

Some types of game port boards provide a separate 15-pin connector for each joystick. Some cut-price game port boards only provide one connector and the circuitry for one joystick. Verify the capabilities of your game port before using or replacing a joystick Y-adapter.

## JOYSTICK CALIBRATION

Unfortunately, the values of time versus resistance that you saw earlier are not the same for every system. Variations in joystick potentiometers, game port adapter circuits, and computer speed will all affect the relationship of time versus resistance. Even variations in component temperature as the PC warms up can cause changes in resistance interpretation. This is why each application program that uses a joystick (or the Windows Game Controllers icon) comes with a *calibration* routine. Calibration allows a given application to measure values for center and corner positions. With this data as a base, the application can extrapolate all other joystick positions.

Take it slowly when calibrating. This is most important when you're setting up the controller in a game. The game will ask you to supply it with specific information about your controller. If you do not provide the correct information, or do not follow the calibration process, it cannot correctly interpret the controller signals during game play. There are several types of calibration that you should be familiar with: *corner-to-corner* calibration, *low and high axis value* calibration, *full circle* calibration, and *invisible* calibration.

### Corner-to-Corner Calibration

This type of software calibration teaches the software what values your controller uses for these three requested locations. The software can then make calculations based on these positions to determine where the joystick is at any time. The main difficulty with this type of calibration is that many joysticks don't have "corners" that a game player can feel (for example, many joysticks use circular openings rather than square ones). To position the joystick in a corner, you'd need to know where the electrical corners are located, or make your best guess. Some games ask you to move your controller like this:

- Move the controller to the upper-left corner and press a button.
- Move the controller to the lower-right corner and press a button.
- Center the controller and press a button.

Make sure that you hold the joystick handle in position until after you have pressed the button. If you release the handle before you press the button, it will self-center and the game will read the wrong values.

### Low and High Axis Value Calibration

This type of software calibration teaches the software the extreme positions of each axis for your joystick. The software can then make calculations based on these positions to determine where the joystick is at any time. This is often a more comprehensive and reliable means of calibration. You can usually test and calibrate the joystick through the game controller dialog box shown in Figure 21-5. You may be asked to perform controller movements like these:

- Move the controller to the left and press a button.
- Move the controller to the right and press a button.
- Move the controller forward and press a button.
- Move the controller back and press a button.
- Center the controller and press a button.

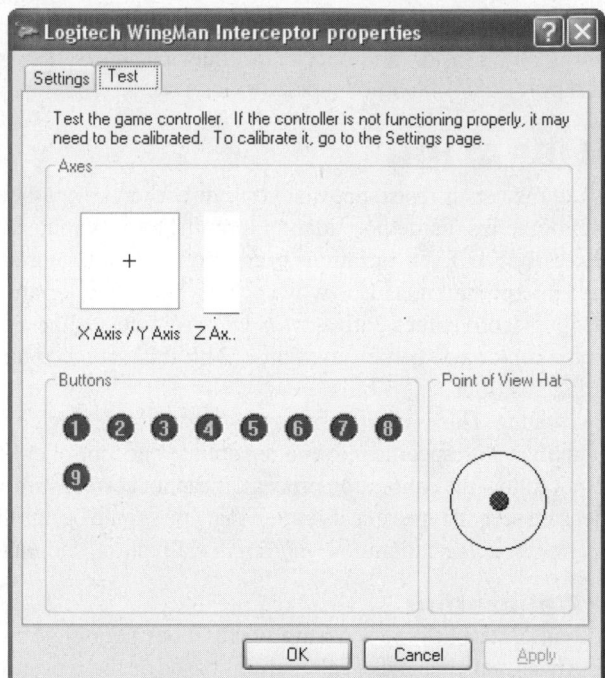

**FIGURE  21-5**    Checking the behavior of your joystick or other gaming device via the Test tab

## Full-Circle Calibration

Other calibration programs ask you to move the controller around in a full circle. After you have completed the requested movements, a button press or keystroke allows the software to determine the minimum and maximum values for the horizontal and vertical axes of the controller. Software calibration programs like this sometimes display a graph of the controller axes. This is a particularly useful approach when you're using a joystick with a circular housing opening.

## Invisible Calibration

There could be several reasons why you may not notice any kind of calibration program when you begin some games. Some games "remember" the calibration from a previous session, so if you're having problems controlling a craft or character, look at the manual (or the game's online help) for a keystroke that will allow you to recalibrate the joystick. Some games assume that the readings from a controller at game startup represent the joystick's center position. If your controller was not centered at game startup, you may experience problems. Once again, it may be necessary to recalibrate the joystick manually.

Another reason why you may not see any prompt to calibrate a joystick at the beginning of a game is because the game is defaulting to the mouse or keyboard. You will need to locate an option in the game that will let you select the correct input device. Look for a "configure" menu, or an installation or setup program. Choosing "joystick or game pad" as an input device should activate the calibration program.

# JOYSTICK DRIFT

The term *drift* (rolling) is used to indicate a loss of control by the joystick. There are several possible reasons for this. As a technician, you should understand why drift occurs and how to correct such problems.

First, drift may be the result of a system conflict. Since the game port does not generate an interrupt, conflicts rarely result in system crashes or lockups, but another device feeding data to port 201h can easily upset joystick operation. If you have sound boards or multiport I/O boards in your system equipped with game ports, be sure to disable any unused ports. (Check with the user instructions for individual boards to disable extra game ports.)

Another possible cause of drift is heat. Once PCs are started up, it is natural for the power used by most components to be dissipated as heat. Unfortunately, heating tends to change the value of components. For logic circuits, this is typically not a problem, but for analog circuits, the consequences can be much more pronounced. As heat changes the values of a multivibrator circuit, timing (and thus positional values) will shift. As the circuit warms up, an error creeps into the joystick. Well-designed game port adapters will use high-quality, low-drift components that minimize the effects of heat-related drift. It is interesting to note that the joystick itself is rarely the cause of drift. If you can't compensate for drift by periodically recalibrating the joystick, try a better-quality game port adapter board.

Finally, the quality of calibration is only as good as the calibration routine itself. A poor or inaccurate routine will tend to calibrate the joystick incorrectly. Try another application. If another application can calibrate and use the joystick properly, you should suspect a bug in the particular application. Try contacting the application manufacturer to find if there is a patch or fix available.

Digital (USB) joysticks are less prone to drift because of temperature issues, but regular calibration is still required.

## CLEANING JOYSTICKS

Ordinarily, the typical joystick should not require routine cleaning or maintenance. Most joysticks use reasonably reliable potentiometers that should last for the life of the joystick. The two major enemies of a joystick are wear and dust. Wear occurs during normal use as potentiometer sliders move across the resistive surface—it can't be avoided. Over time, wear will affect the contact resistance values of both potentiometers. Uneven wear will result in uneven performance. When this becomes noticeable, it is time to buy a new joystick. Joysticks endure violent movements during game play, and this can also shorten their working life.

Dust presents another problem. The open aperture at the top of a joystick is an invitation for dust and other debris. Since dust is conductive, it can adversely affect potentiometer values and interfere with slider contacts. If the joystick seems to produce a jumpy or nonlinear response to the application, it might be worth trying to clean the joystick rather than scrapping it. Turn off the computer and disconnect the joystick. Open the joystick, which is usually held together by two screws in the bottom housing. Remove the bottom housing and locate the two potentiometers. Most potentiometers have small openings somewhere around their circumference. Dust out the joystick area with compressed air, and spray a small quantity of good-quality electrical contact cleaner into each potentiometer. Move the potentiometer through its complete range of motion a few times, and allow several minutes for the cleaner to dry. Reassemble the housing and try the joystick again. If problems persist, replace the joystick.

Avoid the use of petrolium-based lubricants like WD-40. Although such products may appear to clean contacts, their residual oils can actually attract more dust and debris—turning the dust into a sticky glue as the lubricant evaporates.

# JOYSTICKS AND WINDOWS

Games had traditionally been a domain of DOS, so there was little support for joysticks under older Windows versions. However, now that games are universally using Windows 98/Me/XP (taking advantage of features like OpenGL, DirectX, and Direct3D), you can install and calibrate a variety of joysticks and other game control devices under Windows. Under Windows 9x/Me, open your Control Panel and look for the Game Controllers joystick icon. If a joystick icon appears in your Control Panel, joystick support is already installed, and you can skip to the Game Controller setup. If you have not yet added your PC game port as New Hardware in the Windows 9x/Me Control Panel, you should do this first:

1. Click Start | Settings | Control Panel.

2. In the Control Panel, look for a joystick icon. If it's there, skip to the Game Controller setup. If not, double-click the Add New Hardware icon to start the Add New Hardware wizard.

3. When prompted to have Windows search for new hardware, select No. Click Next to continue.

4. Select Sound, Video and Game Controllers and then click Next.

5. Select the manufacturer and game port joystick (or other appropriate model). This will add the game port as a device. Click Next.

6. If resource settings are given as 0201-0201, click Next. Windows will look for the required files. If it can't find these files, it will ask you to insert your Windows installation CD-ROM.

7. When the files have been installed, click Finished.

8. Shut down your computer, and restart Windows 98/Me to enable your game port support.

Under Windows XP, you can check for game port support by opening the Device Manager and expanding the "Sound, video and game controllers" entry (see Figure 21-6). Look for the Standard Game Port entry. If the entry is present, your game port should be enabled. Otherwise, use the Hardware Update Wizard to scan for and install a game port on the system. Today, virtually all sound cards and motherboards include a conventional 15-pin MIDI/game port connection. Once your game port driver has been added, a joystick icon appears in your Control Panel. Follow these steps to set up and calibrate your joystick:

1. Under Windows 9x/Me, double-click the Gaming Options icon in the Control Panel. Under Windows XP, open the Control Panel and click Printers and Other Hardware | Game Controllers. The Game Controllers dialog box opens (see Figure 21-4 earlier).

2. In the Game Controllers dialog box, choose the appropriate joystick (or other game controller device) from the list of installed devices, and then click Properties.

3. The Game Controller properties dialog box will appear and provide you with a basic calibration dialog box (Windows XP provides a Calibration Wizard to walk you through the process). For advanced joysticks with their own management utilities (like the Logitech WingMan Interceptor), you may see an actual representation of the device (as in Figure 21-7). In either case, test the joystick's range of motion and buttons, and then save your calibration.

4. You should now be able to use the joystick under any Windows 98/Me/XP game or other joystick-aware application. You can repeat the calibration procedure at any time—especially if the joystick or other game controller starts to drift or behave erratically.

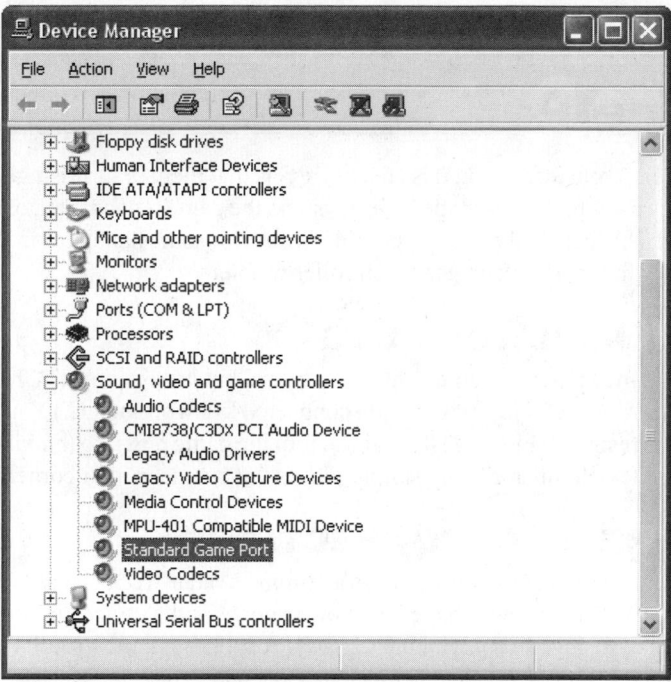

**FIGURE  21-6**    Checking the Device Manager for your game port

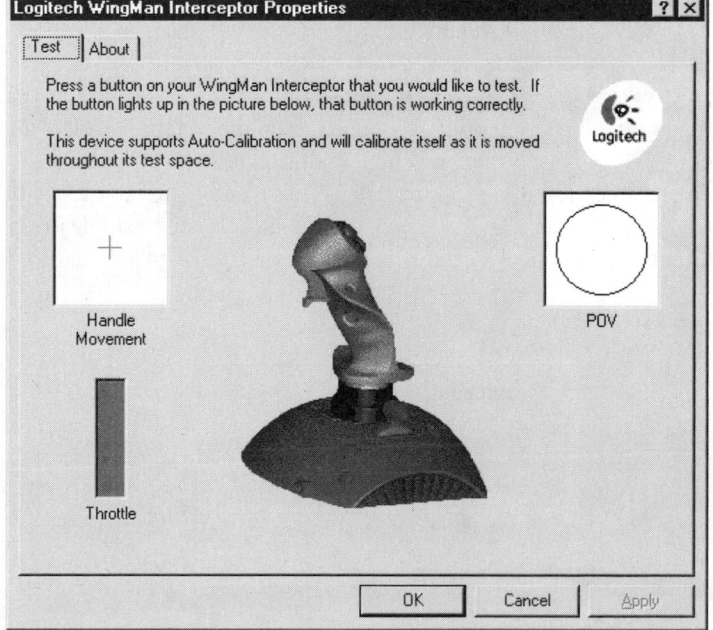

**FIGURE  21-7**    Using manufacturer's utilities to test and calibrate advanced joysticks like the
WingMan Interceptor

# Troubleshooting Joysticks and Game Ports

The unique advantage to troubleshooting this area of a PC is that there is surprisingly little to actually go wrong. In virtually all cases, problems reside in the joystick, the game port adapter, or the application software—that's about it. This part of the chapter provides you with some handy troubleshooting issues and examines some perplexing joystick and game controller problems.

## JOYSTICK ELIMINATOR PLUG

From time to time, you may find yourself testing a game port, but have no joystick handy. (Or it might be too much of a hassle to "borrow" a joystick already connected to a working PC.) You can construct a very simple circuit with two resistors (Figure 21-8) that can fool the game port into thinking that a real joystick is attached. This "joystick eliminator" plug simply places the cursor in a far corner of the display.

## ADAPTING "HEADER" CONNECTIONS

Some multi-I/O boards implement the game port as a 16-pin "header" (ribbon cable) connector—assuming that you'll use a DB-15 connector "plate" in another open card slot and simply connect the DB-15 plate to the multi-I/O card using a 16-pin ribbon cable. The pin assignments are all identical (pin 16 of the IDC connector is just left unused), but remember that the pin *order* is different between header and DB-style connectors. For example, the top row of a DB-15 connector runs pins 9 through 15, but the top row of a ribbon cable uses pins 2, 4, 5, 6, 10, 12, 14, and 16. Headers are rather rare today because of the proliferation of 15-pin game port connectors on sound devices and motherboards, but you should recognize them if they appear on older systems.

## SOUND CARDS AND Y-ADAPTER PROBLEMS

You will probably encounter difficulties when connecting commercial joystick Y-adapters to the game port on a sound board. This is because many sound card manufacturers (such as Creative Labs) have replaced pin 12 (normally the ground for joystick 2 switches 3 and 4) and pin 15 (typically N.C. or +5V) with specialized MIDI interface pins. The problem doesn't surface using a single joystick because pins 12 and 15 are normally unused. But when a second joystick is added through a Y-adapter, the second joystick

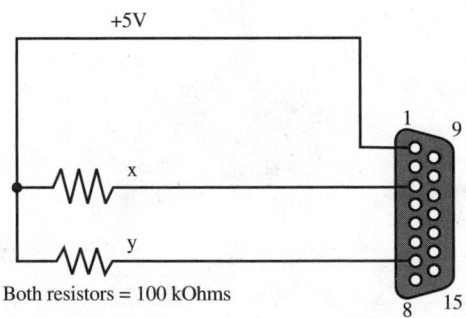

**FIGURE  21-8**   A simple "joystick eliminator" plug for game port testing

will probably fail to function. Table 21-3 illustrates a simple correction to enable a commercial Y-adapter. Essentially, you must disconnect pins 12 and 15 at the game port (sound board) end, then cross-wire pin 12 to pin 5 (ground), and cross-wire pin 15 to pin 9 (+5V). If you want to make your own sound board–compatible Y-adapter, follow the pinout in Table 21-4.

Do *not* attempt to connect a MIDI device to the sound card while this modified Y-adapter is in place. Doing so can easily damage the MIDI device or the sound card's MIDI/game port.

# BASIC JOYSTICK REPAIRS

Joysticks and other game control devices must endure a great deal of wear and tear. Fighter enthusiasts maneuver violently to avoid that incoming fire, and drivers veer hard and slam on the pedals. This quickly takes its toll on your gaming equipment. Many manufacturers sell aftermarket repair kits to replace worn potentiometers, springs, bungee cords, and other internal components prone to failure. This part of the chapter looks at a few basic repair processes.

Before attempting an internal repair of a joystick or other game controller device, consider the economic tradeoff of repairing versus replacing the device outright. It may not make sense to replace a $10 set of potentiometers in a $20-to-$30 joystick unless price is the absolute highest priority.

### Replacing Potentiometers

As you read earlier, potentiometers are "adjustable resistors" that form the X/Y axis of most gaming devices. Potentiometers eventually wear out, but can be replaced. For example, Thrustmaster (www.thrustmaster.com)

| TABLE 21-3 | PIN ASSIGNMENTS FOR A SOUND BOARD JOYSTICK CABLE ADAPTER |
|---|---|
| **DB-15 MALE (TO GAME PORT)** | **DB-15 FEMALE (TO JOYSTICK Y-ADAPTER)** |
| Wire Pin... | To Pin(s)... |
| 1 | 1 |
| 2 | 2 |
| 3 | 3 |
| 4 | 4 |
| 5 | 5 and 12 |
| 6 | 6 |
| 7 | 7 |
| 8 | 8 |
| 9 | 9 and 15 |
| 10 | 10 |
| 11 | 11 |
| 12 unused | To pin 5 |
| 13 | 13 |
| 14 | 14 |
| 15 unused | To pin 9 |

**TABLE 21-4    PIN ASSIGNMENTS FOR A SOUND BOARD–COMPATIBLE JOYSTICK Y-ADAPTER**

| GAME PORT (DB-15 MALE) Wire Pin... | JOYSTICK 1 (DB-15 FEMALE) To Pin... | JOYSTICK 2 (DB-15 FEMALE) And to Pin... |
|---|---|---|
| 1—XY1 (Joystick 1 +5V supply) | 1 | 1 |
| 2—Switch 1 | 2 | — |
| 3—Potentiometer X1 signal | 3 | — |
| 4—Ground (for switch 1 & 2) | 4 | 4 |
| 5—Ground (for switch 2) | 5 | 5 |
| 6—Potentiometer Y1 signal | 6 | — |
| 7—Switch 2 | 7 | — |
| 8—N.C. (or +5V) | 8 | — |
| 9—XY2 (Joystick 2 +5V supply) | — | 8 |
| 10—Switch 3 | — | 2 |
| 11—Potentiometer X2 signal | — | 3 |
| 12—MIDI | — | Unused |
| 13—Potentiometer Y2 signal | — | 6 |
| 14—Switch 4 | — | 7 |
| 15—MIDI | — | Unused |

sells replacement potentiometer kits for several of its joystick products. You'll need a Philips screwdriver and a soldering iron to handle this fix:

1. Remove the screws holding the base of the joystick. These may be covered by rubber feet.

2. Remove the base of the unit.

3. With the base removed, you can usually locate and remove the potentiometers from their brackets. In some cases, you may need to move or push the stick to clear the potentiometers.

4. Desolder and remove a potentiometer, then solder a new potentiometer into place (pay careful attention to the order of the three wires). Repeat for the other potentiometer.

5. Reseat the potentiometers and ensure that any alignment tabs or other hardware mate with the potentiometers properly (e.g., the potentiometers must be centered when the stick is centered, then follow the stick movement).

6. Reseat the stick/potentiometer assembly into the joystick case and reattach the base (don't forget those rubber feet).

This process is a bit different for racing kits. A steering wheel normally uses one potentiometer (for the left/right "X" axis), and pedals each use a potentiometer. The idea is to expose and remove the potentiometer assembly, exchange the worn potentiometer(s) without mixing up the wire order, then remount the potentiometer assembly in the proper alignment.

## Replacing Bungee Cords

If you've ever used a steering wheel, you've probably felt some physical resistance going into each turn. This adds a bit of realism to the driving experience, and helps to prevent you from "oversteering." Resistance is provided by a simple bungee cord strapped inside the steering wheel assembly. Over time, the cord can wear out or break. A typical process to replace a bungee cord includes several steps:

1. Remove all the screws in the steering base. A bit of care is needed here because there are often many screws, and the screws usually vary in length. Keep track of which screw goes into which hole. Remove the bottom cover and locate the bungee cord.

2. Use wire cutters to cut one of the zip ties from the end of the bungee cord (don't cut the bungee retainer that the cord wraps around on each end). Pull the bungee cord from the assembly.

3. With the old bungee cord removed, cut the other zip tie to release the other bungee retainer.

4. Take the new bungee cord and fold over one 1/4 of an inch around one of the bungee retainers. Fasten one of the zip ties around it. Trim any excess plastic off the zip tie.

5. Thread the new cord through the assembly the same way the old cord was. Pull the free end through the hole in the other side of the "U-shaped" potentiometer bracket (try not to fray the end of the cord).

6. Connect the zip tie together, but do *not* pull it closed yet.

7. Slide the tie down the bungee towards the hole you just pulled the bungee through. Pull the free end of the bungee and then fold it over the bungee retainer (the more tension you create, the "tighter" the feel of the steering wheel).

8. Now pull the loose end of the bungee through the open loop of the zip tie. While maintaining tension on the bungee, firmly pull the zip tie closed.

9. Be sure to clear all wires from pinch points and screw paths, then reattach the base cover. Screw the cover down.

## Replacing Torsion Springs

Whether you're using a rudder to tweak a landing approach, or hitting the accelerator for speed in a straightaway, pedals have become an integral part of gaming realism. Pedals use torsion springs to provide physical resistance and return the pedal to its top position. Over time, these springs can eventually fatigue and fail. The following steps outline a typical torsion spring replacement process:

1. Remove the screws holding the pedals to the pedal arms.

2. Remove the pedals. These should detach easily when the pedal screws are removed.

3. Remove all screws from the pedal base.

4. Take off the base cover. Remember that wires are often attached, so be careful.

5. Remove the retaining screw on the side that has the broken spring, and remove the plastic washer that the screw goes through.

6. Remove the spring.

7. Put the new spring into place. It may help to push the spring in with the spring arm outside of the plastic shield, and then lift the spring arm up and over the plastic shield.

8. Replace the plastic washer and retaining screw.

9. Replace the base cover and reattach the screws. Reattach the pedals to complete the process.

# BASIC JOYSTICK/CONTROLLER TROUBLESHOOTING GUIDELINES

There may be instances where your new game port or joystick is not detected or fails to respond. When this happens, try the following guidelines before attempting to research specific symptoms. The guidelines can help you isolate problems with analog, USB, and serial device detection.

It is important to discern if the issue is a *detection* issue or a *game setup* issue. Under Windows 9x/Me, click Start, highlight Settings, click Control Panel, and then click the Game Controllers icon. Under Windows XP, click Start | Control Panel | Printers and Other Hardware | Game Controllers. If the manufacturer's gaming device is listed under Game Controllers, and its status is listed as OK, you'll know that the hardware is being detected properly by the system, and the device *should* work in the Control Panel if you try to calibrate it. (Go ahead and test this.) If it *does* work properly, the issue lies within the setup of the game, and not in your hardware. However, if the gaming device is not listed under Game Controllers (or shows that the status is Not Connected), you should follow the troubleshooting steps next.

## Dealing with Analog Devices

Chances are that you're using a traditional analog-type joystick, wheel, or other controller. If you're using an analog game controller device, try the guidelines suggested here.

**Check Hardware Connections**    Examine the connectors on both the joystick cable and ports on the computer, and look for bent pins or other damage. Ensure that the connector on the joystick's cable is completely seated in the game port on the computer. If the device is attached through a switch box or Y-adapter, try connecting *directly* to the computer.

 Also verify that you've connected the 15-pin connector to a game port rather than a MIDI port. If your 15-pin port can serve as either a game port or MIDI port, see that the port is configured as a game port.

**Check Game Port**    Verify that the game port is enabled and that it is the only game port enabled on the system. Two active ports can cause an address conflict. In some cases, a game port is integrated into the motherboard of the computer, and when a game card is installed into the system, it conflicts with the pre-existing port. Disable or remove any conflicting game port hardware.

**Check the Joystick**    Open the Game Controllers dialog box, highlight the attached joystick or other gaming device, then click Properties. Test the joystick by moving it around and seeing whether the buttons work (see Figure 21-5 earlier). If the joystick responds, try to calibrate the unit. Chances are that the trouble is software related rather than hardware based. If the joystick doesn't respond, remove and reinstall the joystick according to the manufacturer's instructions, or try another gaming device.

**Check Game Port Address**    Verify that the game port is using the correct resources and that they do not conflict with other devices in the system. Try the following steps under Windows 9x/Me/XP:

1.  Open the Device Manager.
2.  Expand the "Sound, video and game controllers" entry.
3.  Double-click on the Standard Game Port entry to bring up its properties dialog box.
4.  Click the Resources tab (see Figure 21-9), and uncheck the Use Automatic Settings box.

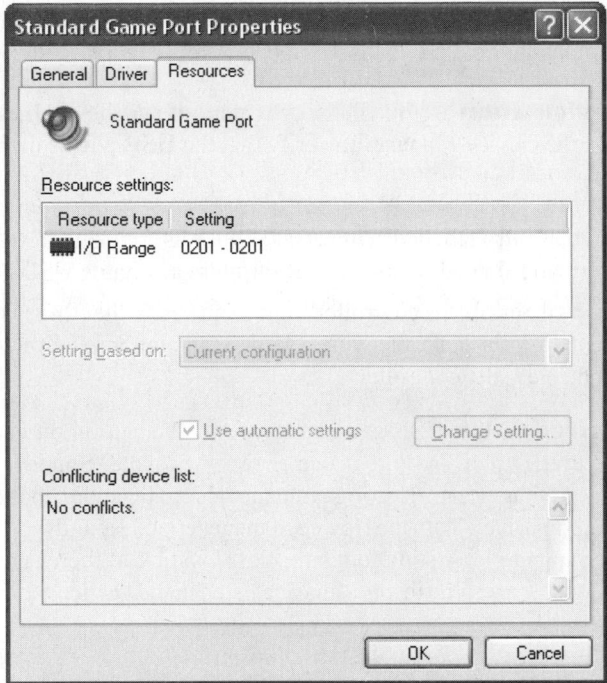

**FIGURE 21-9**     Verifying that the game port is configured for the correct I/O address

5. Select Input/Output Range under Resource Type, click on Change Setting (if the game port allows you to), and select either 0200-0207 or 0201-0201. If the game port is already configured to use I/O 201h, you don't need to change anything.

6. Click OK until the system asks to restart the computer, and answer Yes or OK.

 If the problem persists, skip ahead to the "Check for Software Problems" section.

## Dealing with Digital (USB) Devices

USB game controllers have been growing in popularity over the last few years due to the appeal of their advanced features and their ease of connection/disconnection. If you're using a digital (USB) game controller device, try the guidelines suggested here.

**Check Hardware Connections**     Connect the gaming device directly to the computer's USB port. If a USB port hub is being used, try connecting the device directly to the USB port on the computer. If the device works correctly when directly connected to the computer, contact the manufacturer of the USB hub for assistance or replacement. For some advanced joysticks (especially force feedback devices), make sure that the power adapter is plugged in and connected to the gaming device. Many early USB systems (with motherboards using the PIX 3 chip) shipped with the USB ports disabled. These systems must have their USB ports enabled through the CMOS Setup before a USB device will be detected and function properly.

Do not connect a gaming device to the serial and USB ports at the same time. Connecting a gaming device to both ports simultaneously can cause detection problems or erratic joystick behavior.

**Check USB Port Configuration**    Your PC's USB port should be enabled and supported under Windows 98/Me/XP. Use the Device Manager to verify that the USB port is correctly configured:

1. Open the Device Manager under Windows 9x/Me/XP.
2. Verify that you have an entry labelled "Universal Serial Bus controllers" (see Figure 21-10). If this entry does not exist, you'll need to install and configure a suitable USB controller.
3. Expand the "Universal Serial Bus controller" entry and verify that there is at least one USB Root Hub entry. If the entry is missing (or has an exclamation point or red *X* on it), you'll need to install and configure a suitable USB controller.

**Check Game Port Driver**    Most USB gaming devices will function on computers without game ports or sound cards. However, DirectX requires a game port entry in the "Sound, video and game controllers" section of the Device Manager in order for gaming devices to be added in the Control Panel. Check for the presence of a game port driver. With the Device Manager open, expand the "Sound, video and game controllers" entry and verify there is a listing for Game Port Joystick. If there is no listing, you'll need to add a game port driver. In some cases, the joystick may be listed in the Device Manager under the "Human Interface Devices" entry.

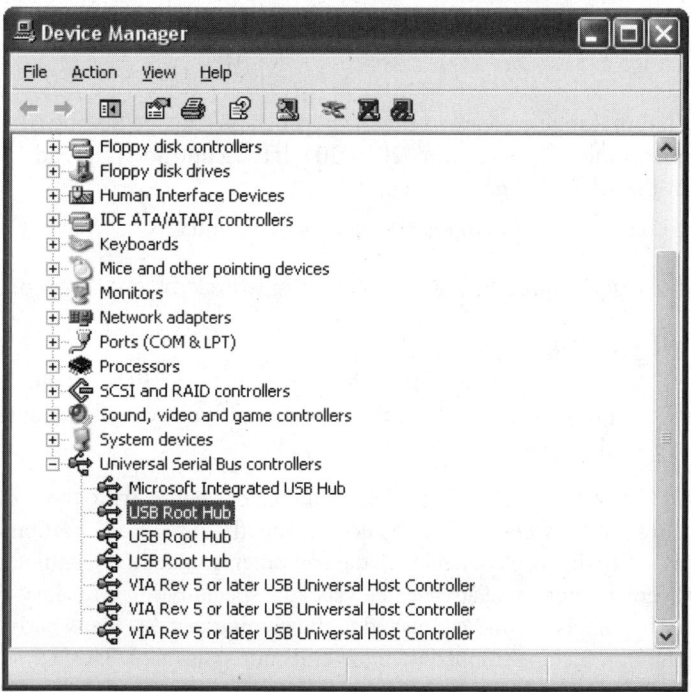

**FIGURE  21-10**    Checking the system hardware for suitable USB support

If the problem persists, skip ahead to the "Check for Software Problems" section.

## Dealing with Serial Devices

Some game controller devices use serial ports rather than game or USB ports. In some cases, advanced joystick or wheel controllers may use a game port *and* a serial port. If your game controller device uses a serial port, follow the guidelines given here.

**Check Hardware Connections**    Examine the connectors on both the joystick cable and serial ports on the computer, and look for bent pins or other damage. Ensure that the connector on the joystick is completely seated in the serial port on the computer. If the gaming device came with a power supply (such as a Logitech WingMan Force), see that the AC adapter is connected to the gaming device. If the device is attached to the serial port through a switch box or Y-adapter, try connecting it *directly* to the computer.

**Check Game Port Driver**    Most serial gaming devices will function on computers without game ports or sound cards. However, DirectX requires a game port entry in the "Sound, video and game controllers" section of the Device Manager in order for gaming devices to be added in the Control Panel. Check for the presence of a game port driver. With the Device Manager open, expand the "Sound, video and game controllers" entry and verify there is a listing for Game Port Joystick. If there is no listing, you'll need to add a game port driver. In some cases, the joystick may be listed in the Device Manager under the "Human Interface Devices" entry.

If the problem persists, skip ahead to the "Check for Software Problems" section.

**Check Serial Port Configuration**    Ensure that the serial port is correctly configured. Most serial gaming devices do not have a preset address or IRQ. They will assume the settings of the port they are connected to, such as:

- COM1: IRQ4 Address 03F8h
- COM2: IRQ3 Address 02F8h
- COM3: IRQ4 Address 03E8h
- COM4: IRQ3 Address 02E8h

For example, if you attach the joystick to COM 3 and another device in the system is using COM 1, an IRQ conflict will arise between these two devices. To correct this, connect the joystick to another serial port (if available). Also, verify that Windows 98/Me/XP has the correct settings for the serial ports:

1. Open the Device Manager under Windows 9x/Me/XP.
2. In the device list, double-click on the "Ports (COM & LPT)" entry.
3. Select the COM port where the gaming device is attached, and then click the Properties button.
4. Click on the Resources tab, and verify the I/O Address and IRQ entries are set to the proper settings (see Figure 21-11).
5. Disable Use Automatic Settings (if necessary to change settings).
6. Check the conflicting device list for possible conflicts if everything appears to be OK.

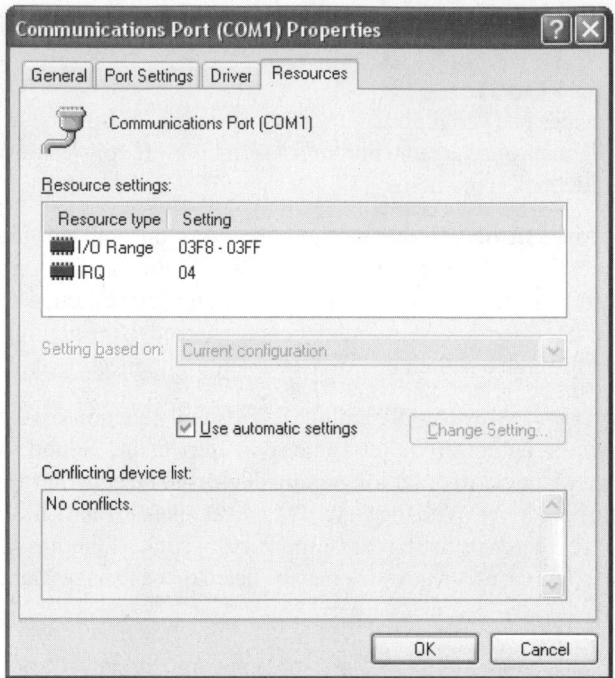

**FIGURE  21-11**    Verifying that the resource assignments are correct and not conflicting with other devices when using a serial port

If the serial ports appear to be configured correctly, it's possible that a modem or other internal card in the system may be interfering with the serial port the joystick is attached to. Try removing these cards to see if the conflict is eliminated.

## Check for Software Problems

Software conflicts can interfere with the communications between the computer and the gaming device. If the hardware seems to be working properly, try temporarily eliminating any programs running in the background and retesting the gaming device.

The following procedures are intended for Windows 9x/Me platforms. With Windows XP platforms, software configurations can be managed with the System Configuration utility (**msconfig**) launched with the Run dialog box.

**Clear the Startup Folder**    Programs in the Startup folder load and stay in memory and may interfere with the detection of the gaming device. To determine if there is a conflicting application in the Startup group, remove the icons from the Startup folder and restart Windows. To do this under Windows 9x/Me, click on Start, Settings, and then Taskbar. Click the Start Menu Programs button, and then click on Advanced. Click the plus (+) sign next to Programs, and then click on the Startup folder. Drag all the program icons onto the desktop area. This will prevent them from loading automatically when the computer boots. Restart the system and see if the issue has been resolved. If so, drag the program icons back into the Startup group, one by one, and see where the problem returns.

**Clear the Registry Run Folder**    The Run folder of your Windows 9x/Me registry is another place where programs are automatically executed when the system is started. Programs starting from this area may also interfere with the detection of your gaming device. Launch the Registry Editor by clicking Start, and then select Run. In the Open line, type **C:\WINDOWS\REGEDIT.EXE** and click the OK button. The Run folder is located in the following key:

```
HKEY_LOCAL_MACHINE\Software\Microsoft\Windows\CurrentVersion\Run
```

Once Run is highlighted, click on Registry and choose Export. Give the file a name, and save it to the desktop. This procedure makes a backup of the Run folder that can be restored by double-clicking on the REG file you saved to the desktop. When Run is highlighted, the contents of the Run folder will be displayed. Check this folder to see what else may be launched during the boot process. Only Explorer and Systray are necessary to the system. Start removing other programs, one by one, rebooting between each removal. If the problem goes away, the last program removed from the Run folder may be the conflicting software.

> Editing the registry incorrectly may stop Windows from booting. Be sure to make complete backups of the registry to your Startup Disk before proceeding.

**Clear the WIN.INI File**    Software programs may also be loaded from the "Load=" and "Run=" lines of your WIN.INI file and may also interfere with the detection of your gaming device. To check for these programs, click Start and select Run. In the Open line, type **WIN.INI**, and then click the OK button. The WIN.INI file should be opened in Notepad. Place a semicolon (;) in front of the following two lines (if present), as shown here:

```
[Windows]
;Load=
;Run=
```

Putting a semicolon at the beginning of these lines will prevent any programs listed in these lines from being loaded. Save the changes and restart Windows. If this resolves the conflict, then remove the semicolons, one by one, from the "Run=" and "Load=" lines, and restart Windows each time to see if the symptom is corrected.

**Reinstall/Update DirectX**    Most Windows 98/Me/XP software today requires the latest version of DirectX in order for pointing and gaming devices to operate properly. If an earlier version of DirectX is installed (or if the installed version is damaged), the gaming device properties will show the device as Not Connected under the Game Controllers icon in your Control Panel. Try reinstalling DirectX, or download and install the latest version (e.g., DirectX 8.1b) from Microsoft at www.microsoft.com/directx.

**Install New Game Controller Driver**    In some cases, installing an HID-compliant game controller driver will resolve some detection issues under Windows 9x/Me (Windows XP typically has a "Human Interface Device" entry):

1. Click Start | Settings | Control Panel.
2. Double-click the Gaming Options icon.

3. Click Add and then click Add Other.

4. On the left side of the window, select Standard Game Device.

5. On the right side of the window, select HID-Compliant Game Controller.

6. Click Next and then click Finish.

7. Close the Game Controllers properties dialog box and restart the system.

# "FORCE FEEDBACK" TROUBLESHOOTING GUIDELINES

The idea of *force feedback* adds yet another level of realism to computer gaming. Imaging feeling the "rat-tat-tat" of a virtual submachine gun, or the tremor when your fighter takes a direct hit. Computer games written to take advantage of the force feedback protocols in DirectX will be able to transfer such real-world signals to your force feedback–compliant joystick, such as Microsoft's SideWinder Force Feedback 2. The SideWinder Force Feedback 2 (and other force-compliant joysticks) uses MIDI signals to transmit force feedback effects. If the MIDI features of your sound card are not functioning properly, the force feedback effects will not be felt. If your game supports force feedback, but you do not feel those effects through the joystick, you can use this guide to help you isolate the problem.

## Test the Force Feedback System

If you have a force feedback game controller device installed, you can use the Windows Control Panel to check the force feedback operation of your joystick and to determine if it and the MIDI port on your sound card are operating correctly under Windows 9x/Me/XP:

1. Open the Gaming Options dialog box (such as Figure 21-4 earlier).

2. In the list of game devices, select your joystick (for example, SideWinder Force Feedback 2) and click Properties.

3. If your joystick is *not* listed in the Controller column, click Add, select the joystick, and then click OK.

4. Click the Test Forces tab or button (gaming devices without force feedback will not have this tab/button).

5. Grasp the joystick handle and press several buttons on the joystick that correspond to the types of forces you want to feel.

   If the forces work correctly in this test mode, chances are that it's the game configuration that's not set properly, so see the "Check the Game Configuration" section next. If the test mode does not work, see the "Check the Force Feedback LED" section.

## Check the Game Configuration

If force feedback effects are working in test mode, then the joystick and MIDI/game port are working. Since your joystick and software are working correctly, the lack of force feedback effects in your game is most likely caused by one (or both) of the following:

■ Your game is not force feedback enabled.

■ An incorrect setting or option was chosen in your force feedback game (for example, forces were disabled).

To resolve these problems, review the manual that came with your game, and note any special instructions that refer to enabling force feedback. Also, you may need to reinstall your game (paying particular attention to any selections that have to do with the type of sound card in your computer).

## Check the Force Feedback LED

The LED on the front of the joystick must remain lit. If it's blinking, it indicates that the joystick is not properly connected to its AC adapter (there's no power for forces), and no force feedback effects will be felt. Connect the AC adapter. The LED should be lit and not blinking. Also make sure that the joystick is connected directly to the game port on the computer (rather than to a Y-adapter or switch box) before you continue.

If the LED is now on continuously, test the forces again. If the LED was on and it's still not responding to force signals, you should remove the device from your Device Manager, download the latest version of the joystick force feedback drivers from the manufacturer, and then reinstall the joystick drivers from scratch.

## Check the MIDI Port

Make sure that the MIDI port is enabled on the sound card or motherboard, and verify that it's using a valid MIDI address. The MIDI port supplied on your sound card must be enabled in order for force feedback to work with your joystick. Check the port under Windows 9x/Me:

1. Click Start | Settings | Control Panel.
2. Double-click the Multimedia icon, and then click the Advanced tab.
3. In the Multimedia Devices area, double-click MIDI Devices and Instruments to display the list of MIDI ports installed on your computer.
4. Click the entry in the list that identifies your MIDI port (such as MIDI for External MIDI Port, MIDI for MPU-401, MIDI for Sound Blaster, or MPU-401 Compatible).
5. Click Properties and click the General tab. Make sure that the Use MIDI Features On This Device option is selected.

If you're using Windows XP, follow these steps:

1. Click Start | Control Panel | Sounds, Speech, and Audio Devices | Sounds and Audio Devices.
2. Click the Hardware tab.
3. In the Properties dialog box (see Figure 21-12), locate the MIDI device(s) installed on the computer (e.g., "MPU-401 Compatible MIDI Device"). If no MIDI devices are listed, you'll need to install a suitable MIDI device and drivers.

If the forces on your joystick still seem sluggish or intermittent, try selecting the MIDI for FM Synthesis option. If you have two external MIDI ports listed (for example, you have both MIDI for External MIDI Port and MIDI for MPU-401), then your computer has two external MIDI ports. If you enable one of the external MIDI ports and your joystick doesn't provide force feedback, enable the other external MIDI port and try the joystick again.

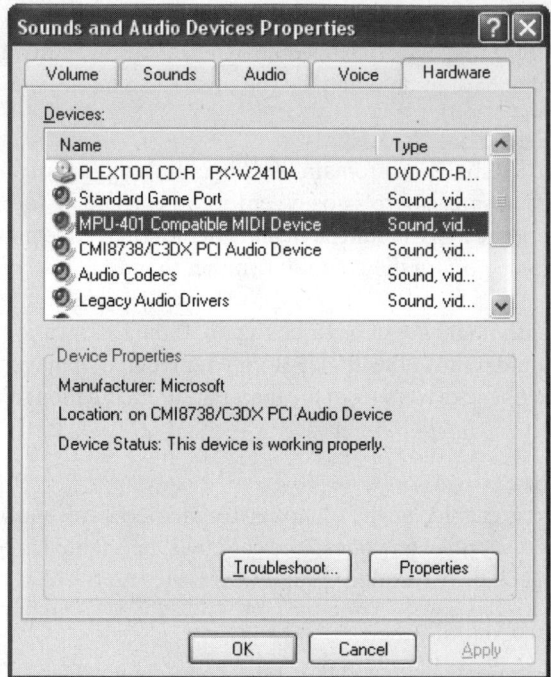

**FIGURE  21-12**    Windows XP listing of all sound and audio devices

**No MIDI Port Available**    If there is no MIDI port listed, your MIDI port is not enabled. There are two possible reasons for this:

■  Your sound card driver is installed but the MIDI port is not configured properly. (Use the Windows Device Manager to check the configuration of your external MIDI port.)

■  The incorrect driver is installed (or not set up properly) for your external MIDI port. (Install the correct driver for your sound card, and then test the forces again.)

You can usually install the correct driver by either reinstalling the sound card software from your original CD-ROM or floppy disks, or by downloading the latest driver from your sound card manufacturer's Web site. After reinstalling the sound card software (or installing new sound card drivers), check the sound card manual (or any instructions that accompanied the new drivers) to learn how to enable the external MIDI/game port.

**Configure the MIDI Port**    If no MIDI port is available, you'll need to configure your computer's external MIDI port before using force feedback devices under Windows 9x/Me/XP:

1.  Open the Device Manager.

2.  Scroll down the device list and double-click "Sound, video and game controllers."

3. Right-click the MIDI entry in the list that corresponds to your exact sound card.

4. Click Properties, and then click the Resources tab (see Figure 21-13).

5. Scroll down the Resource Settings list until you see a listing for Input/Output Range. There may be more than one entry. For the external MIDI port to operate, there must be one Resource Type entry in the list with one of the following Setting values:

```
0300 - 0301
0310 - 0311
0320 - 0321
0330 - 0331
```

**Enable Your MIDI Port**    Find a configuration from the preceding listing that enables the MIDI port. If the Use Automatic Settings box (see Figure 21-13) is not checked, select it and then click OK. Windows will attempt to configure your sound card for all available resources. It may be necessary to restart Windows to complete the process. Check new configuration settings as shown in the previous section.

**Try a "Basic Configuration"**    If you still have trouble getting the MIDI port to respond, try a new "basic configuration" for the sound card:

1. Clear the Use Automatic Settings checkbox (see Figure 21-13 earlier).

2. Select Basic Configuration 0000 from the Setting Based On list box.

3. Check the Resource Settings list again to see if the necessary Resource Type and Setting are listed. Look for one of the following four values:

```
0300 - 0301
0310 - 0311
0320 - 0321
0330 - 0331
```

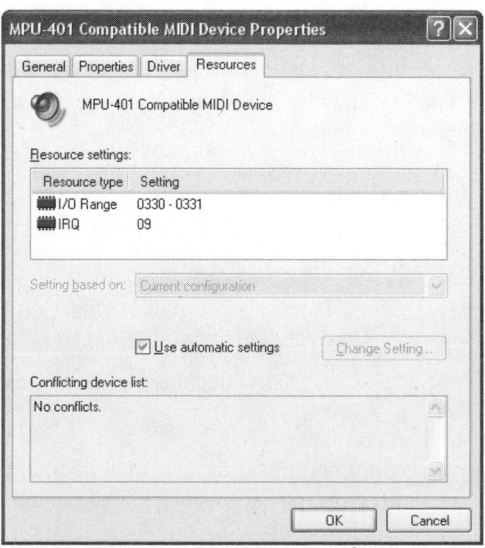

**FIGURE 21-13**    Checking the MIDI port to see that it's properly configured

4. If none of the values matches, select the next configuration setting in the Setting Based On list (that is, Basic Configuration 1, Basic Configuration 2, and so on). Repeat this process until you find a Resource Type and Setting that contains one of the four required values.

5. If you find the proper Resource Type and Setting, but a device conflict message appears in the Conflicting Device list, resolve the problem with the Windows Hardware Conflict Troubleshooter.

If none of the basic configurations have the necessary Resource Type and Setting, your sound card is not set up properly (its external MIDI port is not installed). In this case you should run the installation/setup procedure that came with your sound card again. If your computer came with the sound card already installed, look for the installation floppy disk or CD-ROM for the sound card that came with your computer. It's also possible that you do not have an external MIDI port that is compatible with the joystick. In this case, you'll need to purchase a compatible sound card, equipped with an MPU-401 compatible port, before you can use the joystick.

## Checking for "Unknown Devices"
Check for your sound card in the Unknown Devices section of Device Manager. If your sound or MIDI device is listed here, it may not operate properly. If your sound card is listed here, you may need to remove it and reinstall it following the directions provided by the sound card's manufacturer. You may also need to obtain an updated sound card driver from the manufacturer.

## Checking for Multiple Ports and Connections
Check your computer for more than one game port. Examine the back of your computer for an adapter that has 15-pin game ports mounted on it. If you have an adapter that contains two 15-pin game ports, you'll probably need to remove this adapter from your computer for the game port on your sound card to work properly. Also see that the joystick is connected *directly* to the sound card's MIDI port. Verify that there is no extension cable or Y-adapter connected to the joystick—this is very important. Some extension cables do not transmit MIDI, and some are too long to support the MIDI signal. For best joystick communications, you should have the joystick directly connected to the computer.

## Checking for "Single Mode DMA"
If the joystick seems sluggish or intermittent (or even stops responding) while playing your game—especially when music is playing—you may have a sound card that requires single mode DMA under Windows 9x/Me:

1. Click Start | Settings | Control Panel.

2. Double-click the Multimedia icon, and then click the Advanced tab.

3. In the Multimedia Devices area, double-click Audio Devices.

4. Select the listed audio device, click Properties, and then click Settings.

5. If the Settings button is unavailable (shaded), there is no Use Single-Mode DMA option on your computer. If there is a Use Single-Mode DMA checkbox, select it and reboot the system if necessary.

## Close Background Software
If problems persist, other software running on the computer may be interfering with the force feedback system. Try closing other programs that might be running in the background. Use the Task Manager (CTRL-ALT-DEL) to systematically shut down everything but essential parts of the operating system.

# SYMPTOMS

If you've followed the preceding basic troubleshooting guidelines but find that your joystick or game port is still not responding, use the following symptoms to isolate the specific problem.

**SYMPTOM 21-1    The joystick does not respond**    Make sure that the joystick is plugged into the game/USB port correctly (try connecting USB devices directly to a PC port rather than through a USB hub). When the game port has more than one connector, be sure that the joystick is plugged into the correct connector (joystick 1 or joystick 2). If the game port is running through a sound board, make sure that the sound board is configured to use the port as a game port instead of a MIDI port, and see that any joystick Y-adapter is wired properly. Refer to the application and see that it is configured to run from the joystick. (If mouse or keyboard control is selected, the joystick will not function.) Now that many new joysticks are appearing with supplemental functions (for example, hat switches, throttle controls, and so on), make sure that the application is written to take advantage of the particular joystick. If problems persist, make sure that the game port is set for the proper I/O address. (Most are fixed at 210h, but check the user documentation to be sure.) Try a known-good joystick with the game port. If a known-good joystick works, the original joystick is defective and should be replaced. If another joystick is not the problem, try a different game port board.

**SYMPTOM 21-2    Joystick performance is erratic or choppy**    Start by checking the joystick to be sure that it is connected properly. Try another joystick. When a new joystick works properly, the original joystick is probably dirty (or it's damaged and should be replaced). If a new joystick fails to solve the problem, the game port board may be too slow for the system. Remember that some game ports still use XT board types. An older board design may not be able to process joystick signals fast enough to provide adequate signaling to the system. Not only should you try another game port adapter (preferably a PCI card), but you also should use a speed-adjusting game port.

**SYMPTOM 21-3    The joystick is sending incorrect information to the system—the joystick appears to be drifting**    First, check the application to be sure that the joystick is calibrated correctly. If you cannot calibrate the joystick, the application may not support the joystick properly—try another application. Make sure that there are no other active devices in the system (such as other game ports) using I/O port 201h. If this happens, data produced on those other boards will adversely affect the game port you are using. If all unused game ports are disabled, check the active game port. Poor-quality game ports can drift. Try a newer, low-drift or speed-adjusting game port board.

**SYMPTOM 21-4    The basic X/Y, two-button features of the joystick work, but the hat switch, throttle controls, and supplemental buttons do not seem to respond**    In virtually all cases, the multifunction joystick is configured wrong. Check the game configuration or joystick management application first. Many new applications provide numerous joystick options and allow you to define the particular use of each feature from within the application itself.

Check the joystick definition files next. Your joystick probably requires a supplemental driver or definition file (for example, an FCS file) in order to use all of the joystick's particular features. Finally, check the game port type. You may need a dual-port game port adapter rather than an inexpensive single-port game port adapter. Some enhanced joysticks use both joystick positions. (For example, the XY axis and fire buttons make up one joystick, while the throttle and other buttons take up the other position.) You may need to install a dual-port game port card.

**SYMPTOM 21-5**    **You see an error such as "Joystick not connected" under Windows 98/Me/XP**    Windows doesn't recognize the game port hardware. Check the game port driver first. Use the Device Manager under Windows 98/Me/XP to examine the resources assigned to the game port driver. Typically, the resource range should be set to 201h through 201h (only one address location). If the game port entry has a yellow icon next to it, there is a hardware conflict in the system, and other hardware is also trying to use the same I/O location.

Next, check the game port hardware for proper configuration. The game port card should be installed properly in its bus slot. Make sure that the game port is enabled. (Game ports integrated onto sound cards or multi-I/O cards may need to be enabled using a jumper.) If a sound card enables you to switch a 15-pin port between MIDI and joystick, see that the jumper is set to the "joystick" position. Make sure the joystick cable is not cut or damaged anywhere, and see that it is attached securely to the game port. Finally, test a known-good joystick on the system. If a new joystick works as expected, the original joystick is probably suffering from internal wiring damage.

**SYMPTOM 21-6**    **The joystick drifts frequently and requires recalibration**    This type of symptom is usually the result of problems with the game port adapter. Try a different game port adapter, and see if the problem persists. If problems disappear, you simply need a better-quality or speed-adjusting game port. Otherwise, test a known-good joystick on the system. If a new joystick works as expected, the original joystick is probably suffering from internal wiring damage and should be replaced. You might also consider replacing an existing analog joystick with a digital USB joystick device.

**SYMPTOM 21-7**    **The joystick handle has lost tension—it no longer "snaps" back to the center**    This problem may be accompanied by a rattling sound within the joystick. In most cases, a spring has popped out of place inside the joystick. Check the joystick for internal damage. Open the joystick and see if any springs or clips have slipped out of place. Replace any springs or clips (if possible). Some joysticks also employ mechanical latches that can enable or disable the spring action of the X and Y axis. Check to see that any such latches are enabled. If you cannot locate or correct the problem, simply replace the joystick.

**SYMPTOM 21-8**    **The joystick responds, but refuses to accept a calibration**    In virtually all cases, the problem is with your game port adapter. Check the hardware setup. Make sure that there are no other devices in the system using the I/O address assigned to your game port (for example, 201h). If more than one adapter in your system has game port capability, see that only one game port is enabled. Replace the game port, or enable a different game port in the system. If drift issues continue with different applications, you may need to replace the game port adapter with a low-drift or speed-adjusting model. In some cases, you can replace an analog joystick with a digital USB joystick.

**SYMPTOM 21-9**    **The hat switch and buttons on a joystick work only intermittently (if at all)**    This problem also applies to stand-alone pedals. In most cases, erratic behavior of a joystick's enhanced features is a symptom of game port speed problems. Check the joystick first. Try a known-good joystick. If the problems disappear, the original joystick may be defective. If the problems persist, you have a game port problem. Make sure that there are no other devices in the system using the I/O address assigned to your game port (201h). If more than one adapter in your system has game port capability, see that only one game port is enabled. If drift issues continue with different applications, you may need to replace the game port adapter with a low-drift or speed-adjusting model, or replace the analog joystick with a digital USB model.

**SYMPTOM 21-10**    **When downloading FCS (or "calibration") files to a joystick, the line saying "put switch into calibrate" doesn't change when the download switch is moved**
This is a typical problem with advanced joysticks. In most cases, the joystick needs to be cleared. To clear the joystick, rock the download switch back to "analog," then to "calibrate." This should clear the joystick for a new calibration download. Try downloading the FCS file again. Under Windows 98/Me/XP, you may simply need to update the driver file(s) for your joystick, wheel, or other controller. If problems persist, the actual switch may be defective. Try a known-good joystick instead.

**SYMPTOM 21-11**    **You need to fiddle with the download switch**    To download a calibration file, you need to rock the red switch back and forth a number of times (or press the ENTER key a number of times) to get it to 100%. This is virtually always the result of a keyboard controller (keyboard BIOS) compatibility problem. Upgrade the keyboard controller (keyboard BIOS). Some advanced joystick products do not interact well with the host computer's keyboard controller. For example, Thrustmaster's Mark II experiences known microcode problems with a few of the keyboard controller chips on the market. These include AMI versions (D, B, 8, 0), Acer, and Phoenix. You may need to replace the keyboard controller or update the system BIOS with a later version. In some cases, you may not be able to use the particular joystick model on your system.

**SYMPTOM 21-12**    **You cannot use a joystick on a PC using a sound card with an older audio chipset**    The joystick may stop responding while using an application, or report a "not connected" status in the Game Controllers area of the Control Panel. This is a known problem with the ESS and OPTi sound chipsets. You'll need to set Single Mode DMA to use the joystick under Windows 9x/Me (under Windows XP, you may need to upgrade the audio device):

**1.** Click Start, select Settings, and then click Control Panel.

**2.** Double-click the Multimedia icon.

**3.** On the Advanced tab, double-click the Audio Devices entry to expand it.

**4.** Click the "Audio for..." entry that corresponds to your particular sound card, and then click Properties.

**5.** Click Settings.

**6.** Select the Use Single Mode DMA checkbox.

**7.** Click OK until you return to Windows, and then restart the PC.

**SYMPTOM 21-13**    **The game port is not removed when the sound card is removed**
The entry for your game port will still be visible in the Windows 98/Me/XP Device Manager. This is not really a problem. Windows does not recognize the game port as being part of the sound card, so removing the sound card doesn't automatically disable the game port. Also, the virtual joystick device driver (VJOYD.VXD) cannot detect whether the game port or joystick is installed, so the driver is always active. You'll need to manually remove the game port in Device Manager:

**1.** Open the Device Manager under Windows 9x/Me/XP.

**2.** Double-click the "Sound, video and game controllers" entry to expand it.

**3.** Click the joystick port, and then click Remove.

**4.** Reboot Windows to redetect and reinstall the correct hardware.

**SYMPTOM 21-14**    **You receive an error after adding a new game port to the system**
For example, after installing a device (e.g., a sound card) with a game port onboard, you receive an error such as "Maximum number of supported controllers installed." This generally happens under Windows when there's already a game port working in the system—one of the controllers will have to be disabled. If you'd prefer to use the existing game port (commonly incorporated into the audio feature of a motherboard), just disable the game port on the new device. If you'd prefer to use the new game port, disable the old game port (usually through the CMOS Setup).

**SYMPTOM 21-15**    **Your joystick doesn't work with a Sound Blaster Live card**    This is an issue with the Sound Blaster Live card. It's an excellent sound card, but the game port on the card is reported to be very slow. This means any fast analog device that is used with the Sound Blaster Live card will have trouble being "seen" by Windows. In this instance, your best solution is to disable the sound card's game port and install a fast game port card instead, or opt for a USB gaming device.

**SYMPTOM 21-16**    **The cross-hair on your axis is off center**    This is a frequent issue with digital joysticks such as the Gravis Blackhawk Digital. Chances are that you're dealing with an incorrect, outdated, or buggy driver (or multiple copies of the driver):

1. Restart your system in the Safe Mode.
2. Open the Device Manager.
3. Click the "Sound, video and game controllers" entry to expand the list. You can only have one driver that contains "game port" or "joystick" in its name.
4. Make sure you have the Windows 9x/Me/XP installation CD-ROM (or other disc containing your game port driver), and then remove all listings that refer to your game port or joystick.
5. When you restart the computer, it should detect new hardware, and may ask for the installation CD-ROM. If it tells you that it is recommended to keep your newer driver, select No and install the drivers from your disc(s).
6. Save the changes and reboot the system if necessary. Your joystick should now be on center.

**SYMPTOM 21-17**    **You get a "fatal exception" error when you open the Gaming Devices wizard in the Control Panel**    For example, you may see an error such as:

```
A Fatal Exception Error 0E occurred at 0028:58C10F3F
```

This error can occur if the game port is conflicting with another device. Use the Device Manager to see whether another device is conflicting with the game port. If Device Manager reports that there's a problem with the configuration of the game port, reconfigure the game port so that it uses resources that are not already in use by another device. If the game port is a PnP device and is conflicting with another device, you must disable the device before attempting to change the resource settings.

**SYMPTOM 21-18**    **The joystick's throttle or slider control does not work in certain games**    For example, when you use the SideWinder 3D Pro joystick, the throttle or slider control may not work in one or more of your games. This is because the throttle works only while the joystick is emulating a more basic model. For the SideWinder 3D Pro, the mode switch should be in position one. This position causes the SideWinder 3D Pro to emulate a CH Flightstick Pro. Make sure that the switch is set in this position, and calibrate the SideWinder as a CH Flightstick Pro joystick. This should correct the problem.

You may also be able to correct the problem by patching or upgrading your offending game(s) to a version that supports your specific joystick type directly.

**SYMPTOM 21-19**    **The Game Controllers tool switches between "OK" and "Not Connected"**    When you use the Game Controllers tool in Control Panel to check the status of a USB game controller, the game controller status may toggle between OK and Not Connected. In addition, you may see random buttons light up on the screen when you use the Game Controllers tool to test a USB game controller. This problem occurs when the USB game controller is connected to the game port on your computer, and the game port on your computer is not working correctly. To correct this problem, connect the USB game controller to the USB port on your computer, or install a working game port in your computer. If there is no USB port on your computer, you may be able to resolve this problem by contacting the manufacturer of your sound (or game port) card to obtain updated drivers. This may correct problems or incompatibilities with the sound card's game port controller and allow the joystick to function properly.

# Further Study

**Act Labs**    www.act-labs.com
**Advanced Gravis**    www.gravis.com
**CH Products**    www.chproducts.com
**Logitech**    www.logitech.com
**Thrustmaster**    www.thrustmaster.com

# 22

# KEYBOARDS

**K**eyboards are the classical input device for computers (Figure 22-1). By manipulating a matrix of individual electrical switches, commands and instructions can be entered into the computer one character at a time. If you've used computers or typewriters to any extent, you already have an excellent grasp of keyboard handling. However, keyboards certainly present their share of drawbacks and limitations. Although today's keyboard switches are not mechanically complex, they have a number of important moving parts. When you multiply this number of moving parts times the 80 to 100+ keys on a typical keyboard, you are faced with a substantial number of moving parts. A jam or failure in any one of these many mechanical parts results in a keyboard problem. Most keyboard failures are hardly catastrophic, but they can certainly be inconvenient. This chapter gives you the information needed to understand and repair computer keyboards.

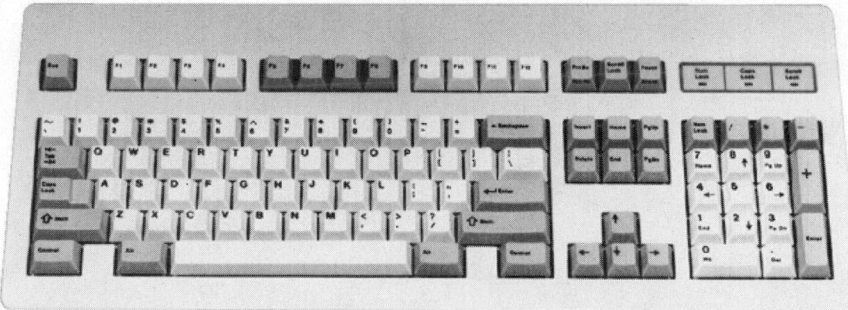

**FIGURE 22-1**    A Cherry G83-3000 keyboard (Cherry Electrical Products)

# Keyboard Basics

To understand a keyboard, you must first understand the kinds of switches that are used. In general, there are two types of switches that you should be concerned with: mechanical switches and membrane switches. Both switches are used extensively throughout the computer industry, but any single keyboard will use only one type of switch.

A *mechanical key switch* is shown in Figure 22-2. Two tempered bronze contacts are separated by a plastic actuator bar. The bar is pushed up by a spring in the switch base. When the key cap is depressed, the actuator bar slides down. This action compresses the spring and allows the gold-plated contacts to touch. Since gold is a soft metal and an excellent conductor, a good, low-resistance electrical contact is developed. When the key cap is released, the compressed spring expands and drives the plastic actuator bar between the contacts again. The entire stroke of travel on a mechanical switch is little more than 3.56mm (0.140 inch), but an electrical contact (a *make* condition) can be established in as little as 1.78mm (0.070 inch). Mechanical switches are typically quite rugged—many are rated for 100 million cycles or more.

A *membrane key switch* is illustrated in Figure 22-3. A plastic actuator rests on top of a soft rubber boot. Inside, the rubber boot is coated with a conductive silver-carbon compound. Beneath the rubber boot

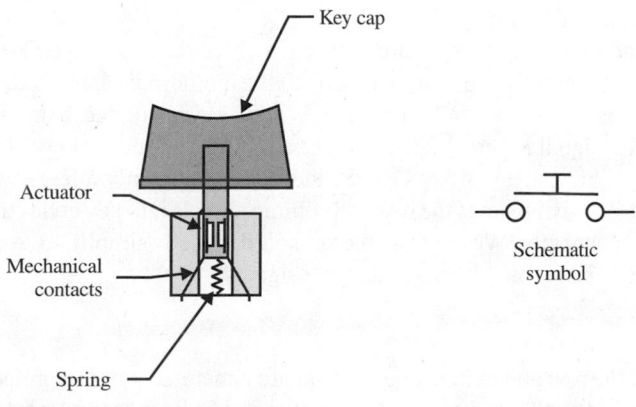

**FIGURE 22-2**    Mechanical switch assembly

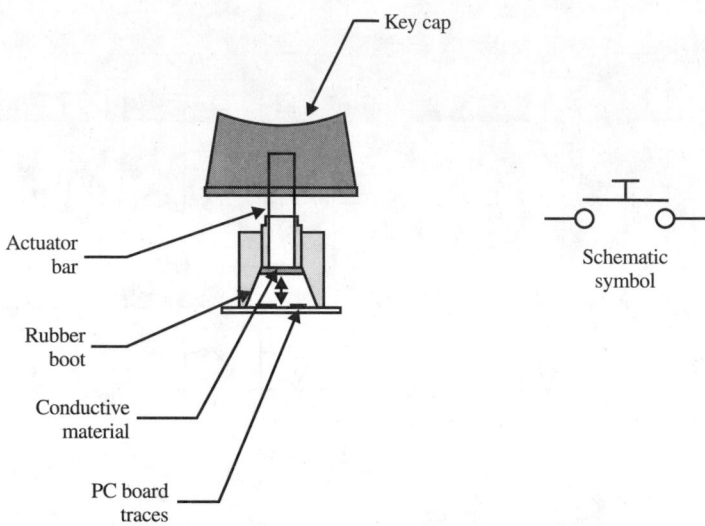

**FIGURE  22-3**   Membrane switch assembly

are two open PC board contacts. When the key cap is depressed, the plastic actuator collapses the rubber boot. Collapse forces the conductive material across both PC board contacts to complete the switch. When the key cap is released, the compressed rubber boot breaks its contact on the PC board and returns to its original shape. The full travel stroke of a membrane key switch is about 3.56mm (0.140 inch)—roughly the same as a mechanical switch. An electrical contact is established in about 2.29mm (0.090 inch). Membrane switches are not quite as durable as mechanical switches. Most switches are rated for 20 million cycles or less.

Mechanical and membrane switches offer a number of unique advantages and disadvantages. Mechanical switches tend to be highly reliable and provide a good tactile feedback when typing (that clicking noise usually associated with offices). On the other hand, mechanical keyboards are more expensive to manufacture and can be extremely sensitive to spills and foreign matter. Membrane switches are not quite as reliable, and tend to offer a softer, "mushier" feel when typing (some people prefer this feel). Due to the membrane cover used in the keyboard, membrane switches seem to withstand spills and foreign matter better than mechanical switches.

The next step in understanding a keyboard is to learn about the *key matrix*. Keys are not interpreted individually—that is, each switch is not wired directly to the motherboard. Instead, keys are arranged in a matrix of rows and columns, as shown in Figure 22-4. When a key is pressed, a unique row (top to bottom) and column (left to right) signal is generated to represent the corresponding key. The great advantage of a matrix approach is that a huge array of keys can be identified using only a few row and column signals. Circuitry within the keyboard translates the row and column signals into key codes that are passed to a host PC across the keyboard connector. Wiring from the keyboard is vastly simplified. An 84-key keyboard can be identified using only 12 column signals and 8 row signals.

## KEY CODES

When a key is pressed, the row and column signals that are generated are interpreted by a *keyboard interface* chip (typically located on the keyboard assembly itself). The keyboard interface converts the row and

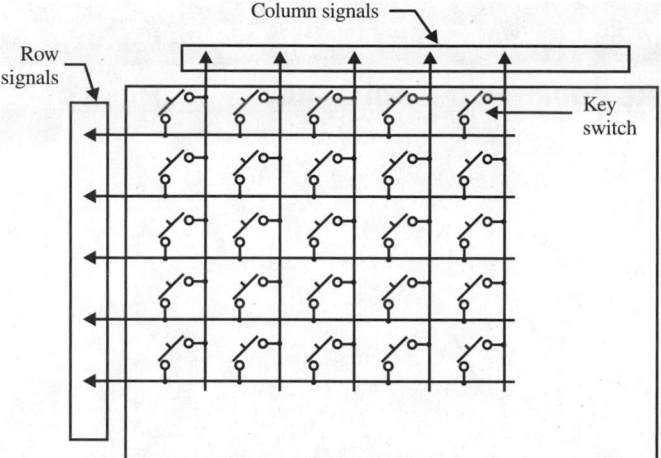

**FIGURE 22-4**    Simplified diagram of a keyboard matrix

column signals into a single-byte code (called a *key code* or *scan code*). Two unique scan codes are produced during a keystroke cycle. When the key is depressed, a *make code* byte is sent along to the system. When the key is released, a *break code* byte is generated. Both codes are transmitted to the host computer in a serial fashion. For example, a make code of 1Eh is sent when the "A" key is pressed. A 9Eh code is sent when the "A" key is subsequently released. By using two individual codes, the computer can determine when a key is held down, or when keys are held down in combinations. Just about every key on a keyboard is *typematic*—that is, it repeats automatically if it is held down for more than 500mS or so. Typematic settings can usually be adjusted in the CMOS advanced settings for your system.

The *h* in these scan codes (such as 9Eh) indicates that the code is hexadecimal.

Most computers today are prepared for multinational operation. To accommodate the special characters and punctuation used in various different countries, keyboard controllers (KBCs) can be configured to provide scan codes for different languages. Table 22-1 illustrates the make and break codes for conventional keyboards used in the domestic United States.

**TABLE 22-1    STANDARD SCAN CODES FOR U.S. KEYBOARDS**

| KEY | MAKE CODE | BREAK CODE | KEY | MAKE CODE | BREAK CODE |
|-----|-----------|------------|-----|-----------|------------|
| A | 1E | 9E | B | 30 | B0 |
| C | 2E | AE | D | 20 | A0 |
| E | 12 | 92 | F | 21 | A1 |
| G | 22 | A2 | H | 23 | A3 |
| I | 17 | 97 | J | 24 | A4 |
| K | 25 | A5 | L | 26 | A6 |
| M | 32 | B2 | N | 31 | B1 |
| O | 18 | 98 | P | 19 | 99 |

**TABLE 22-1    STANDARD SCAN CODES FOR U.S. KEYBOARDS** *(CONTINUED)*

| KEY | MAKE CODE | BREAK CODE | KEY | MAKE CODE | BREAK CODE |
|---|---|---|---|---|---|
| Q | 10 | 90 | R | 13 | 93 |
| S | 1F | 9F | T | 14 | 94 |
| U | 16 | 96 | V | 2F | AF |
| W | 11 | 91 | X | 2D | AD |
| Y | 15 | 95 | Z | 2C | AC |
| 0/) | 0B | 8B | 1/! | 02 | 82 |
| 2/@ | 03 | 83 | 3/# | 04 | 84 |
| 4/$ | 05 | 85 | 5/% | 06 | 86 |
| 6/^ | 07 | 87 | 7/& | 08 | 88 |
| 8/* | 09 | 89 | 9/( | 0A | 8A |
| ./> | 29 | A9 | -/_ | 0C | 8C |
| =/+ | 0D | 8D | [ | 1A | 9A |
| ] | 1B | 9B | ;/: | 27 | A7 |
| '/" | 28 | A8 | ,/< | 33 | B3 |
| //? | 35 | B5 | LEFT SHIFT | 2A | AA |
| LEFT CTRL | 1D | 9D | LEFT ALT | 38 | B8 |
| RIGHT SHIFT | 36 | B6 | RIGHT ALT | E0 38 | E0 B8 |
| RIGHT CTRL | E0 1D | E0 9D | CAPS LOCK | 3A | BA |
| BACKSPACE | 0E | 8E | TAB | 0F | 8F |
| SPACEBAR | 39 | B9 | ENTER | 1C | 9C |
| ESC | 01 | 81 | F1 | 3B | BB |
| F2 | 3C | BC | F3 | 3D | BD |
| F4 | 3E | BE | F5 | 3F | BF |
| F6 | 40 | C0 | F7 | 41 | C1 |
| F8 | 42 | C2 | F9 | 43 | C3 |
| F10 | 44 | C4 | F11 | 57 | D7 |
| F12 | 58 | D8 | UP ARROW | E0 48 | E0 C8 |
| DOWN ARROW | E0 50 | E0 D0 | LEFT ARROW | E0 4B | E0 CB |
| RIGHT ARROW | E0 4D | E0 CD | INSERT | E0 52 | E0 D2 |
| HOME | E0 47 | E0 C7 | PAGE UP | E0 49 | E0 C9 |
| DELETE | E0 53 | E0 D3 | END | E0 4F | E0 CF |
| PAGE DOWN | E0 51 | E0 D1 | SCROLL LOCK | 46 | C6 |

**Note:** All make and break codes are given in hexadecimal (hex) values.
Alphabetic characters represent both upper- and lowercase.

# KEYBOARD INTERFACES

Once a key is pressed and the keyboard interface converts the key matrix signals into a suitable scan code, that code must be transmitted to the KBC on the host computer's motherboard. Once key data reaches the

KBC, the KBC converts it to parallel data, which in turn generates an interrupt that forces the system to handle the key. The actual transfer of scan codes between the keyboard and PC is accomplished *serially* using one of the interfaces shown in Figure 22-5.

Today, a growing number of input devices such as keyboards and mice are using the USB port rather than a traditional keyboard/mouse port.

Note that there are really three important signals in a keyboard interface: the keyboard clock (KBCLOCK), the keyboard data (KBDATA), and the signal ground. Unlike most serial communication, which is asynchronous, the transfer of data from keyboard to controller is accomplished *synchronously*—data bits are returned in sync with separate clock signals. As you might expect, the signal ground provides a common reference for the keyboard and system. The keyboard is powered by +5 Vdc, which is provided through the keyboard interface. It is also important to note that most XT-style systems are designed with a unidirectional data path (from keyboard to system). AT-style keyboard interfaces are bidirectional. This feature allows AT keyboards to be controlled and programmed from the PC.

### Wireless Keyboards

A growing number of keyboards are using *wireless* serial connections. Rather than a cord between the keyboard and system, some keyboards use a short-range infrared link between the keyboard and a "base unit" that attaches to one of the PC's existing ports. Wireless keyboards reduce the clutter of cables, and allow users to have a certain level of comfort (e.g., resting the keyboard on their laps rather than tethered to a desktop). Wireless keyboards are typically powered by batteries, and the infrared link requires a direct line of sight with the "base unit"—these are the first things you should check whenever wireless problems arise.

## DVORAK KEYBOARDS

Virtually all technicians are familiar with QWERTY-style keyboards, the standard format for typewriters that was adopted in the late 1800s. A popular alternative to the QWERTY keyboard is the *Dvorak keyboard*. Mechanically and electronically, the Dvorak keyboard is identical to conventional keyboards. Only the key order is different. All of the vowels are located on the left side of the home row (the middle row of letters) in the pattern AOEUIDHTNS.

IBM PC/XT/AT configuration

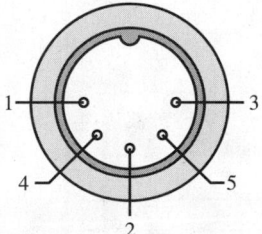

6 pin mini-DIN connector

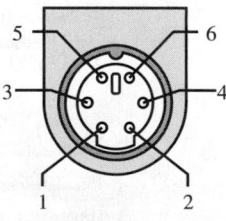

| 1 | KBCLOCK |
| 2 | KBDATA |
| 3 | nc |
| 4 | Ground |
| 5 | +5 Vdc (pr +3.0 or +3.3 Vdc) |

| 1 | KBDATA |
| 2 | nc |
| 3 | Ground |
| 4 | +5 Vdc (pr +3.0 or +3.3 Vdc) |
| 5 | KBCLOCK |
| 6 | nc |

**FIGURE  22-5**    Keyboard interface connectors

Dvorak keyboards claim several advantages over QWERTY models. Most letters typed (roughly 70 percent) are on the home row, so finger (and wrist strain) is reduced. With less reach to deal with, typing can be accomplished faster and with fewer errors. On a Dvorak keyboard, the majority of words require both hands for typing, whereas thousands of words demand one-handed typing for QWERTY keyboards. The Dvorak keyboard spreads out the strain on your hands more evenly.

## Converting to Dvorak Keyboards

There are two classical methods of implementing Dvorak keyboards: dedicated keyboards and keyboard conversions. Dedicated keyboards, just as the name implies, are ready-made Dvorak keyboards that you buy and plug in. Although the keys are located in different places, the key codes are the same, so your PC doesn't know the difference. As a result, you can interchange QWERTY and Dvorak keyboards at will without any changes to the PC or operating system. Follow these steps to convert your QWERTY keyboard to Dvorak under Windows XP:

1. Click Start | Control Panel | Regional and Language Options. The Regional and Language Options dialog box opens.

2. Select the Languages tab. Click Details in the "Text services and input languages" area. The Text Services and Input Languages dialog box opens (see Figure 22-6).

3. Click the Add button in the Installed Services area.

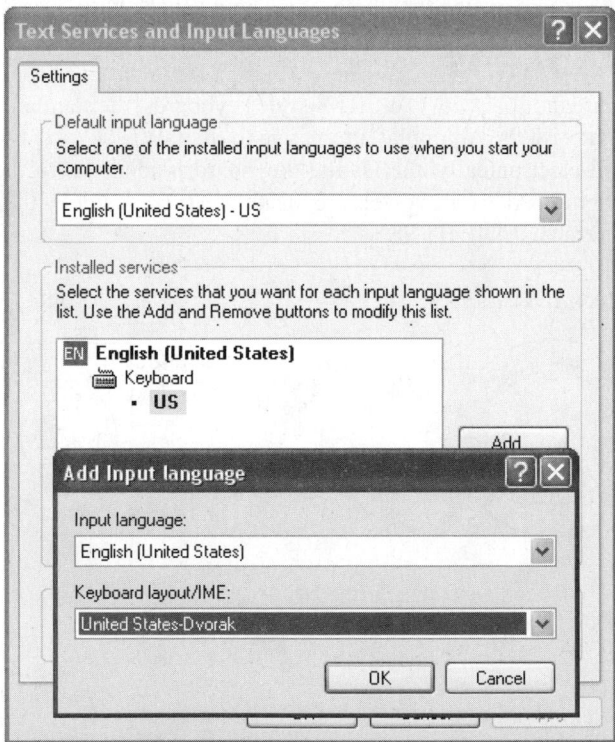

**FIGURE  22-6**    Adding and selecting system languages under Windows XP

**4.** Click the language for the keyboard layout or Input Method Editor (IME) to be added from the "Input language" list.

**5.** Select the "Keyboard layout/IME" service in the list if necessary.

**6.** Apply your changes. You may need the Windows XP CD for certain installation files.

With more than one language available, you can configure Windows XP to allow switching between languages through the task bar.

You can also convert your existing QWERTY keyboard to Dvorak under Windows 98/Me:

**1.** Open the Control Panel and double-click the Keyboard icon.

**2.** Select the Language page and double-click the English (United States) entry (or your own default entry for a different country).

**3.** Select United States–Dvorak from the list that appears.

**4.** Save your changes. You may need to install a floppy disk with the proper drivers to support Dvorak operation.

**5.** It may be necessary to reboot the system.

Once the software conversion is made, you need to exchange the keys on your QWERTY keyboard. Figure 22-7 illustrates the comparison between a QWERTY key layout and a Dvorak key layout. You can use a key-pulling tool to physically exchange the key caps, or use key stickers or overlays from Hooleon Corporation at www.hooleon.com/. You can also obtain more detailed information directly from Dvorak International at (802) 287-2434 or from the FAQ at www.cse.ogi.edu/~dylan/dvorak/DvorakIntl.html.

## ERGONOMIC ESSENTIALS

Any athlete will tell you that enough stress placed on the body will have a detrimental effect over a long period of time. For example, baseball pitchers eventually burn out their shoulders, runners ultimately have trouble with their feet and knees, and so on. Although PC use is typically a "low-impact" activity—hardly considered to be an "athletic" pursuit—users can experience repetitive stress over time. The problem is that most traditional keyboards are placed at unusual heights, forcing users to place their hands at odd, unnatural angles. A growing body of medical evidence suggests that improper long-term keyboard use may result in repetitive stress injury (RSI) to nerves and joints in the hands and wrists. Fortunately, RSI can be greatly abated with the proper selection and placement of a keyboard.

```
QWERTY
Q   W   E   R   T   Y   U   I   O   P
A   S   D   F   G   H   J   K   L   ;   '
Z   X   C   V   B   N   M   ,   .   /

Dvorak
"   ,   .   P   Y   F   G   C   R   L   /
A   O   E   U   I   D   H   T   N   S   -
;   Q   J   K   X   B   M   W   V   Z
```

**FIGURE  22-7**    QWERTY vs. Dvorak keyboard layouts

A medical professional can provide you with detailed information on repetitive stress injury (RSI).

## Proper Placement

One way to reduce the potential for RSI is to position the keyboard properly. Improper placement of the keyboard results in twisting, awkward postures, and uneven loading on the body. A keyboard too high or low contributes to poor posture of the shoulders, arms, and hands, and should be avoided for frequent or long-term keyboard use. As a rule, keyboards should be located to allow a comfortable, neutral posture during use. This usually means placing your keyboard directly in front of you, at elbow height while you're seated. Proper keyboard placement also helps to maintain a neutral keyboarding posture, which generally requires that your shoulders be back and relaxed. The upper arms should also rest down to the side of your body, elbows should make an approximate 90-degree bend. Your forearms should be horizontal (parallel to the floor), and the wrists should be in line with the forearms—with minimal bending up or down, left or right.

Since people come in all shapes and sizes, proper keyboard positioning is different for everyone. Feel free to adjust table and chair heights and alter the keyboard location until you achieve proper keyboard positioning for your particular frame.

## Regular Breaks

Regular breaks are important for PC users, especially users who spend prolonged periods at the PC each working day. This allows the user to relax their hands and ease any tensions or strains that may be occurring. In addition, a medical professional can recommend several exercises that may help to strengthen the hands and wrists, and relieve the strains of regular keyboard use. Progressive employers understand and encourage such brief breaks throughout the day.

## Ergonomic Keyboards

In addition to proper placement, keyboard designs are improving to streamline the positions of each hand, and minimize the movement and reach of fingers—thus helping to combat RSI:

The use of keyboard wrist pads is also reported to help reduce the potential for RSI. In many cases, simply rolling up a small towel and placing it in front of the keyboard may work.

- ■ **Split keyboards**   Most of the research and design efforts involve reshaping the standard keyboard (or making it more adjustable) while maintaining its basic shape and standardized QWERTY key arrangement. Typists then find it easier to switch to new keyboard designs that can improve hand and arm postures, without learning a whole new typing skill. Split keyboards can be more specifically described as fixed-split keyboards, adjustable-split keyboards, and contoured keyboards.

- ■ **Vertical keyboards**   These types of keyboards take the standard keyboard's key sections and place them upright. This allows a "handshake" position for the user that is considered the neutral posture for the forearms and hands. Some of the adjustable-split keyboards can also assume vertical positions. However, such vertical positioning may require a bit of adjustment on the part of the typist.

- ■ **Chording keyboards**   These are another alternative to the standard keyboard. Chording keyboards are smaller and have fewer keys (typically one for each finger, and possibly the thumbs). However, instead of the usual individual key presses, "chording" requires simultaneous key presses for each character typed. You might find this similar to playing a musical chord on a piano. Thus, chording requires a measurable amount of relearning on the part of a typist.

■ **Dvorak layouts**    Switching from QWERTY to Dvorak layouts can more evenly distribute typing among the fingers of both hands. While this type of layout has not yet received widespread use, it is accepted by the American National Standards Institute (ANSI), and it remains a useful ergonomic feature available to keyboarders. By relocating the letters and punctuation, Dvorak typists are able to maintain the same output with reduced finger movement—reducing strain on the hands, wrists, and arms.

# Keyboard Maintenance and Troubleshooting

Keyboards are perhaps the most abused part of any computer, yet they are often ignored until serious problems develop. With some regular cleaning and maintenance, however, a keyboard can easily last for the lifetime of a computer. This part of the chapter shows you some practical techniques for keyboard service.

## CORRECTING PROBLEM KEYBOARDS

Virtually all computer keyboards are open to the air. Over time, everyday dust, pet hair, air vapor, cigar/cigarette smoke, and debris from hands and ordinary use settles into the keyboard. Eventually, accumulations of this foreign matter cause keys to stick or prevent keys from making proper contact (for example, a key may not work every time it is pressed). In either case, keyboard problems will develop. Fortunately, correcting a finicky keyboard is a relatively straightforward process. First, remove the key caps of the offending keys. Be sure to note where each key is placed before starting your disassembly—especially if the keyboard is a Dvorak-type or unusual ergonomic design. To remove a key cap, bend an ordinary paper clip into the shape of a narrow U, and bend in small tabs at the tip of the U shape. Slip the small tabs under the key cap and pull up gently. Do not struggle with the key cap. If a cap will not come off, remove one or more adjacent caps. If there is a substantial accumulation of foreign matter in the keyboard, you should consider removing all of the key caps for a thorough cleaning, but this requires more time.

Avoid removing the SPACEBAR and ENTER keys unless it is absolutely necessary, since these keys are often much more difficult to replace than ordinary keys.

Flip the keyboard upside down and rap gently on the case. This will loosen and dislodge any larger, heavier foreign matter and allow it to fall out of the keyboard. A soft-bristled brush will help loosen the debris. Return the keyboard to an upright position. Use a can of compressed air (available from almost any electronics or photography store) to blow out the remainder of foreign matter. Since this tends to blow dust and debris in all directions, you may wish to use the compressed air outside or in an area away from your workbench. A medium- or firm-bristled brush will help loosen any stubborn debris.

Now that the keyboard is cleaned out, squirt a small amount of good-quality electronics-grade contact cleaner (also available from almost any electronics store) into each key contact, and work the key to distribute the cleaner evenly. Allow a few minutes for the contact cleaner to dry completely, and test the keyboard again before reinstalling the key caps. If the problems persist, the keyboard may be damaged, or the individual key(s) may simply be worn out beyond recovery. In such an event, replace the keyboard.

## VACUUM CLEANERS AND KEYBOARDS

There is an ongoing debate as to the safety of vacuum cleaners with computer equipment. The problem is static discharge. Many vacuum cleaners, especially small, inexpensive models, use cheap plastic and synthetic fabrics in their construction. When a fast air flow passes over those materials, a static charge is developed (just like combing your hair with a plastic comb). If the charged vacuum touches the keyboard, a static discharge may have enough potential to damage the keyboard controller (KBC) chip or even travel back into the motherboard for more serious damage.

If you do choose to use a vacuum for keyboard cleaning, take these three steps to prevent damage. First, make sure that the computer is powered down and disconnect the keyboard from the computer before starting service. If a static discharge does occur, the most that would be damaged is the keyboard itself. Second, use a vacuum cleaner that is made for electronics work and certified as "static-safe." Third, try working on an antistatic mat (such as the mat shown in Figure 22-8) that is properly grounded. This will tend to "bleed off" static charges before they can enter the keyboard or PC.

## REPLACING THE SPACEBAR

Of all the keys on the keyboard, replacing the SPACEBAR is probably the most difficult. The SPACEBAR is kept even by a metal wire that is inserted into slots on each leg of the plastic bar key. However, you have to get the wire into the slots *without depressing the wire*. If you push the wire down, you compress the wire and installation becomes impossible. As a general rule, do not remove the SPACEBAR unless absolutely necessary. If you must remove the SPACEBAR, remove several surrounding key caps also. This will let you get some tools under the SPACEBAR wire later on. Once the SPACEBAR is reinserted, you can easily replace any of the other key caps.

This type of problem is often identical for the ENTER/RETURN key.

## PREVENTING PROBLEMS

Keyboard problems do not happen suddenly (unless the keyboard is dropped or physically abused). The accumulation of dust and debris is a slow process that can take months (sometimes years) to produce serious, repetitive keyboard problems. By following a regimen of regular cleaning, you can stop problems before they manifest themselves in your keyboard. In normal office environments, keyboards should be cleaned once every four months. Keyboards in home environments should be cleaned every two months. Keyboards in harsh or industrial environments should be cleaned even more frequently.

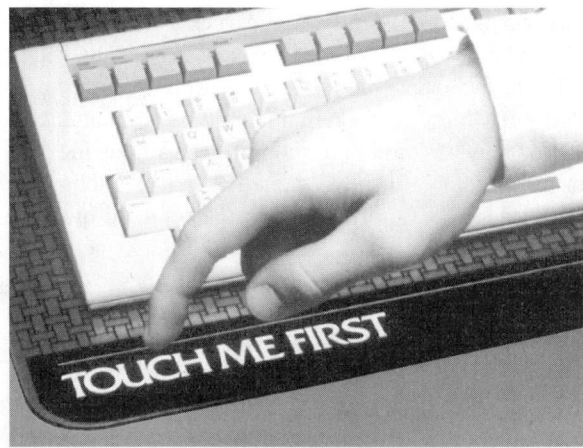

**FIGURE   22-8**    A Curtis antistatic keyboard mat (Curtis, a division of Rolodex, Secaucus, NJ)

Turn your keyboard upside down and use a soft-bristled brush to clean between the keys. This prevents debris that may already be on the keys from entering the keyboard. Next, run the long, thin nozzle of your compressed air can between the key spaces to blow out any accumulations of dust. Since compressed air tends to blow dust in all directions, you may consider doing this outside or in an area away from your workbench. Instead of compressed air, you may use a static-safe vacuum cleaner to remove dust and debris.

# DEALING WITH LARGE OBJECTS

Staples and paper clips pose a clear and present danger to keyboards. Although the odds of a staple or paper clip finding its way into a keyboard are generally slight, foreign objects can jam the key, or short it out. If the keyboard is moved, the object can wind up in the keyboard's circuitry where serious damage can occur. When a foreign object falls into the keyboard, *do not* move the keyboard. Power-down the PC, locate the object, and find the nearest key. Use a paper clip bent in a U shape with the ends of the U angled inward to remove the nearest key cap. Use a pair of nonconductive tweezers or needle-nose pliers to remove the object. Gently replace the key cap.

# DEALING WITH SPILLS

Accidental spills are probably the most serious and dangerous keyboard problem. Coffee, soda, and even tap water is highly conductive (even corrosive). Your keyboard will almost certainly short circuit. Immediately shut down your computer (you may be able to exit your application using a mouse) and disconnect the keyboard. The popular tactic is simply to let the liquid dry. The problem with this tactic is that most liquids contain minerals and materials that are corrosive to metals. Your keyboard will never be the same unless the offending liquid is *removed* before it dries. Also, liquids tend to turn any dust and smoke film into a sticky glue that will just jam the keys when dry (not even considering the sticky sugar in most sodas).

Disassemble the keyboard's main housings and remove the keyboard printed circuit assembly. As quickly as you can after the incident, rinse the assembly thoroughly in clean, room-temperature, demineralized water (available from any pharmacy for contact lens maintenance). You can clean the plastic housings separately. *Do not use tap water.* Let the assembly drip dry in air. Do not attempt to accelerate the drying process with a hair dryer or other such heat source. The demineralized water should dry clean without mineral deposits or any sticky, conductive residue. Once the assembly is dry, you may wish to squirt a small amount of good-quality, electronics-grade contact cleaner into each key switch to ensure no residue remains on the contacts. Assuming that the keyboard's circuitry was not damaged by the initial spill, you should be able to reassemble the keyboard and continue using it without problems. If the keyboard behaves erratically (or not at all), replace the keyboard.

If spills are a potential problem, try a "keyboard skin" that fits right over your particular keyboard model, and allows you to type while preventing spills and debris from entering the keyboard. Check your keyboard supplier for an appropriate "skin."

# DISABLING A KEYBOARD

Keyboards are an essential peripheral for all computers except servers. There are many cases where network administrators would prefer to restrict direct access to the server, and prevent potential tampering. Traditional PCs did not allow you to disable the keyboard, but newer systems do offer a CMOS Setup entry that can enable or disable the keyboard. When the keyboard is disabled through CMOS, the PC will boot without suffering "Keyboard not found" errors. Before starting service on a server, it may be necessary to reattach and reenable the keyboard.

## KEYBOARD SYMPTOMS

Although their appearance may seem daunting at first glance, keyboard systems are not terribly difficult to troubleshoot, primarily because of their modularity—if all else fails, replacing a keyboard is a simple matter. The keyboard's great weakness, however, is its vulnerability to the elements. Spills, dust, and any other foreign matter that finds its way between the key caps can easily ruin a keyboard. The keyboard's PC board is also a likely candidate to be damaged by impacts or other physical abuse. The following procedures address many of the most troublesome keyboard problems.

 Remember that USB keyboards can be connected/disconnected with power on, but the PC *must* be powered down when detaching/reattaching conventional AT or PS/2 keyboards.

**SYMPTOM 22-1    During initialization, you see an error message indicating that no keyboard is connected**    Check your keyboard cable and see that it is inserted properly and completely into the PC connector. Remember that you have to reboot your system to clear this error message. Try another compatible keyboard. If a new keyboard assembly works properly, there is probably a wiring fault in the original keyboard. Given the very low price of new keyboards, it is usually most economical simply to replace a defective keyboard. If you're working on a file or network server, see that the CMOS Setup has enabled the keyboard.

If a known-good keyboard fails to function, try the original keyboard on a known-good PC to verify that the keyboard itself is indeed operational. If it is, your trouble lies in the PC. Check the wiring between the PC keyboard connector and the motherboard. Check the connector pins to make sure that none of them has been bent or pushed in (resulting in a bad connection). You might also want to check the soldering connections where the keyboard connector attaches to the motherboard. Repeated removals and insertions of the keyboard may have fatigued the solder joints. Reheat any defective solder joints. If the keyboard connector is intact, the keyboard controller (KBC) chip likely has failed. Try booting the PC with a POST board installed. A KBC failure usually is indicated by the system stopping on the appropriate POST code. You can attempt to replace the KBC (typically the South Bridge of the chipset), or replace the motherboard. If a POST board indicates a fault other than a KBC (such as the programmable interrupt controller that manages the KBC's interrupt), you can attempt to replace that component, or simply exchange the motherboard anyway.

**SYMPTOM 22-2    During initialization, you see an error message indicating that the keyboard lock is on**    In many cases, the detection of a "locked" keyboard will halt system initialization. Make sure that the keyboard lock switch is set completely to the "unlocked" position. If the switch is unlocked, but the system detects it as locked, the switch may be defective. Turn off and unplug the system, then use a multimeter to measure continuity across the lock switch. (You may need to disconnect the lock switch cable from the motherboard.) In one position, the switch should measure as an open circuit. In the opposing position, the switch should measure as a short circuit. If this is not the case, the lock switch is probably bad and should be replaced. If the switch measures properly, there is probably a logic fault on the motherboard (perhaps the KBC). Your best course is to try another motherboard.

**SYMPTOM 22-3    The keyboard is completely dead—no keys appear to function at all**    All other computer operations are normal. This symptom assumes that your computer initializes and boots to its DOS prompt or other operating system as expected, but the keyboard does not respond when touched. Keyboard status LEDs may or may not be working properly. Your first step in such a situation is to try a known-good keyboard in the system. *Note that you should reboot the system when a keyboard is* *replaced*. If a known-good keyboard works, the fault is probably on the keyboard interface chip. You can attempt to replace this chip if you wish, but it is often most economical to simply replace the keyboard.

If another keyboard fails to correct the problem, use a multimeter and check the +5V supply at the keyboard connector (refer to Figure 22-5). If the +5V signal is missing, the female keyboard connector may be broken. Check the connector's soldering junctions on the motherboard. Reheat any connectors that appear fatigued or intermittent. Many motherboards also use a "pico-fuse" to protect the +5V supply feeding the keyboard connector. If your +5V is lost, locate and check the keyboard connector fuse. If problems continue, replace the motherboard.

**SYMPTOM 22-4**    **The keyboard is acting erratically. One or more keys appear to work intermittently, or are inoperative**    The computer operates normally and most keys work just fine, but one or more keys do not respond when pressed. Extra force or repeated strikes may be needed to operate the key. This type of problem can usually range from a minor nuisance to a major headache. Chances are that your key contacts are dirty. Sooner or later, dust and debris works into all key switches. Electrical contacts eventually become coated and fail to make contact reliably. This symptom is typical of older keyboards, or keyboards that have been in service for prolonged periods of time. In many cases, you need only vacuum the keyboard and clean the suspect contacts with a good-quality electronics-grade contact cleaner.

Begin by disconnecting the keyboard. Use a static-safe, fine-tipped vacuum to remove any accumulations of dust or debris that may have accumulated on the keyboard's PC board. You may wish to vacuum your keyboard regularly as preventive maintenance. Once the keyboard is clean, gently remove the plastic key cap from the offending key(s). The use of a key cap removal tool is highly recommended, but you may also use a modified set of blunt-ended tweezers with their flat ends (just the tips) bent inward. Grasp the key cap and pull up evenly. You can expect the cap to slide off with little resistance. Do not *rip* the key cap off—you stand a good chance of marring the cap and causing permanent key switch damage.

Use a can of good-quality electronics-grade contact cleaner and spray a little bit of cleaner into the switch assembly. When spraying, attach the long narrow tube to the spray nozzle—this directs cleaner into the switch. Work the switch in and out to distribute the cleaner. Repeat once or twice to clean the switch thoroughly. Allow residual cleaner to dry thoroughly before retesting the keyboard. *Never use harsh cleaners or solvents*. Industrial-strength chemicals can easily ruin plastic components and housings. Reapply power and retest the system. If the suspect key(s) responds normally again, install the removed key cap and return the system to service. As a preventive measure, you might wish to go through the process of cleaning every key.

Membrane keys must be cleaned somewhat differently from mechanical keys. You need to remove the rubber or plastic boot to clean the PC board contacts. Depending on the design of your particular membrane switch, this may not be an easy task. If you are able to see the contact boot, use a pick or tweezers to gently lift the boot. Spray a bit of cleaner under the boot, and then work the key to distribute the cleaner. If the boot is confined within the individual key, you may have to remove the suspect key before applying cleaner.

If cleaning does not work, your next step should be to disassemble the keyboard and replace the defective key switch(es). Observe the board closely for cracks or fractures. Many key switch designs still utilize through-hole soldering technology, but you should exercise extreme care when desoldering and resoldering. Extra care helps prevent accidental damage to the PC keyboard. You also have the more economical option of replacing the entire keyboard assembly.

**SYMPTOM 22-5**    **The keyboard is acting erratically. One or more keys may be stuck or repeating**    Suspect a shorted or jammed key. Short circuits can be caused by conductive foreign objects (such as staples and paper clips) falling into the keyboard and landing across PC board contacts.

Remove all power and disassemble the keyboard housing assembly. Once the keyboard is exposed, shake out the foreign object or remove it with a pair of needle-nose pliers or sharp tweezers.

Accumulations of dirt or debris can work into the key actuator shaft and restrict its movement. Apply good-quality electronics-grade contact cleaner to the key, and work the key in and out to distribute the cleaner evenly. If the key returns to normal, you may reassemble the computer and return it to service. Keys that remain jammed should be replaced. If you cannot clear the jammed key, simply replace the entire keyboard assembly. If you elect to replace the keyboard assembly, retain the old assembly for parts. Key caps, good switches, and cable assemblies can be scavenged for use in future repairs.

**SYMPTOM 22-6** **You see "KBC Error" (or a similar message) displayed during system startup** When your computer initializes (either from a warm or cold start), it executes a comprehensive self-test routine that checks the key chips in the system (the CPU, memory, drive controllers, and so on). As part of this power-on self-test (POST) routine, the computer looks for the KBCLK signal, along with a series of test scan codes generated by the keyboard controller (KBC) chip. You can see the keyboard LEDs flash as the controller sequences through its codes. If either the keyboard clock or keyboard data signals are missing, the POST knows that either the keyboard is disconnected or the KBC has failed. If you are using a POST board, it will probably display a code corresponding to a KBC error. Unless you have the tools and inclination to replace a KBC controller chip, your best course is simply to replace the motherboard.

**SYMPTOM 22-7** **The mouse and keyboard do not respond** For example, this is known to occur under Windows XP if the system starts in the Safe Mode after removing mouse keyboard drivers, and is typically caused by a corrupted Windows registry. To correct this problem, replace the current registry with the backup copy available in the repair directory using the Windows XP Recovery Console. Alternatively, you may use the System Restore feature to try recovering the system.

**SYMPTOM 22-8** **A Logitech keyboard malfunctions under Windows XP** This is typically a software-based problem that is known to occur with multifunction keyboards such as Logitech's Internet Navigator keyboard, and you may see an error such as

```
Internet Navigator has encountered a problem and needs to close.
```

The trouble can usually be traced to the itouch.exe (rev 1.82.0.0) utility for the keyboard, and results because the utility is incompatible with Windows XP. Check with Logitech for updated Windows XP drivers, or remove the offending utility and use the keyboard as a standard keyboard until a fix is available.

**SYMPTOM 22-9** **Windows XP uses an original keyboard layout** For example, the previous default keyboard layout may be used after you install and configure a new Input Method Editor (IME) as the default keyboard layout. This problem occurs when a user without administrator permissions is logged on to Windows, or when the default keyboard entry in the registry does not match the default keyboard layout. In virtually all cases, the msctf.dll file doesn't have the correct permissions to configure the new keyboard layout from the registry. This is a problem with Windows XP, so check with Microsoft for a patch or service pack that will correct the issue.

**SYMPTOM 22-10** **You cannot clear macros from a programmable keyboard** In most cases, you need to use the correct key combination to clear the macros. If the keyboard has a REMAP key, press that first (a Program light or other LED will start blinking). Press the CTRL key twice to map the key to itself. Press ALT twice to map the key to itself. Press the SUSPEND MACRO key (the Program light should stop blinking). Press the CTRL and ALT keys while pressing SUSPEND MACRO. This will clear all of the keyboard's programming. The key sequence used for your keyboard may be different, so be sure to check the procedure for your own keyboard. If problems persist, replace the keyboard.

**SYMPTOM 22-11** **The keyboard keys are not functioning as expected** Pressing a key causes unexpected results or a series of operations that ordinarily would not be attributed to that key. Chances are that the keyboard has been programmed with macros, and you'll need to clear those macros to restore normal keyboard operation. If the keyboard has a REMAP key, press that first (a Program light or other LED will start blinking). Press the CTRL key twice to map the key to itself. Press ALT twice to map the key to itself. Press the SUSPEND MACRO key (the Program light should stop blinking). Press the CTRL and ALT keys while pressing SUSPEND MACRO. This will clear all of the keyboard's programming. The key sequence used for your keyboard may be different, so be sure to check the procedure for your own keyboard. If problems persist, replace the keyboard.

**SYMPTOM 22-12** **The PC freezes when you press "volume" hot keys on the keyboard** This type of trouble is known to happen with multifunction keyboards (e.g., Microsoft IntelliType, Natural, and Internet keyboards), and can usually be traced to the use of RealPlayer software. For example, Microsoft keyboards can suffer this trouble if the IntelliType Pro software is installed while RealPlayer is running on the computer, or if you're running a version of RealPlayer that is earlier than RealPlayer G2 version 6. You may be able to resolve this problem by removing RealPlayer, clean-booting your computer, and then reinstalling the IntelliType Pro software. Now clean-boot the computer and reinstall the latest keyboard applet software (e.g., Microsoft's IntelliType Pro software), and then download and install the latest version of RealPlayer software from www.realplayer.com. Finally, reboot the system normally and test the keyboard's operation.

**SYMPTOM 22-13** **Some keys on a programmable keyboard will not remap to their default state** This can happen with some older Gateway 2000 (AnyKey) keyboards—as well as other programmable keyboards—and you may have to "force clear" the keyboard at boot time. Power-down the system. While holding down the SUSPEND MACRO key, turn the system power back on. Continue booting with the SUSPEND MACRO key depressed until the Program light (or similar LED) quits flashing. This light will stay lit until you depress and release it.

For older Gateway 2000 AnyKey keyboards, if there is an "AnykeyXX T" line in the AUTOEXEC.BAT file, this will terminate any programming function of the keyboard. If there is an "AnykeyXX A" line in the AUTOEXEC.BAT file, this will activate the programming function.

**SYMPTOM 22-14** **A wireless keyboard types random characters** The keyboard has fallen out of synchronization with the base unit, and you'll need to reset both ends of the wireless system. First, take a look at the DIP switch settings controlling the RF channel for the wireless transmitter and receiver (usually under the battery cover at the keyboard). Make sure that the transmitter and receiver are both set for the same channel. Find the "reset" button on both the transmitter and receiver. Press the RF receiver reset button first, and then press the RF transmitter button immediately after (usually within 15 seconds of one another). If the problem persists, reboot the system and try the reset process again.

**SYMPTOM 22-15** **The wireless keyboard beeps while typing** In virtually all cases, the batteries in the wireless keyboard are running low. Replace the batteries and try the wireless keyboard again—the beeping should stop and the keyboard should behave normally.

**SYMPTOM 22-16**    **The wireless keyboard isn't responding**    You notice that the infrared light on the module isn't on, and the problem persists even after replacing the batteries. It may be that the keyboard's ID codes have gotten out of synch. You will need to reset the keyboard to correct this problem. For example, position the keyboard about 1.5 feet away from the IR module and make sure that the keyboard is in low power mode (the middle power switch setting). While the keyboard is pointing directly at the IR module, press and hold down the F10 and F12 keys simultaneously with the 1 key on the top row. If the IR light stays on, then it's in sync. If the LED doesn't stay on, release the keys, wait a few seconds, and repeat the F10-F12 sequence with the 2 key. If this still doesn't work, repeat this process with the 3 through 6 keys (there are six ID codes, 1 through 6). Review the instructions for your particular keyboard for specific reset/synchronization instructions. If you cannot reset the keyboard, it may be defective and need to be replaced.

**SYMPTOM 22-17**    **Typed characters do not appear, but the cursor moves**    This issue is a result of the color scheme being used. Some of the applications reported as suffering this problem are Microsoft Works 4.0, CashGraf, Microsoft Bob (address book and letter writer), and Microsoft Publisher. Check the color scheme selected by right-clicking on the desktop. Click on Properties and then the Appearance tab. Set the scheme to Windows Standard. Click on OK to return to the desktop. The text should now appear normal. This solution can generally be attempted with any application.

**SYMPTOM 22-18**    **Some function keys and Windows keys may not work on some PC configurations**    For example, this is a known problem with Toshiba 8500 desktop systems and the Microsoft Natural Keyboard. In virtually all cases (including the Toshiba 8500), the PC keyboard controller BIOS recognizes the keyboard during the POST, but it does not recognize some of the keys—including certain function keys and Windows-specific keys. You'll need to try a generic keyboard, or upgrade the system's BIOS.

**SYMPTOM 22-19**    **One or more Windows-specific keys don't work**    This is almost always a limitation of the system BIOS. For example, a Jetkey BIOS (v.3.0) will not recognize the right Windows key on a Microsoft Natural Keyboard. You'll need to try a generic keyboard, or upgrade the system's BIOS.

**SYMPTOM 22-20**    **The PC freezes when you press the "sleep" hot key on the keyboard**    This is a known issue with certain high-end multifunction keyboards (e.g., the Microsoft IntelliType, Natural, and Internet keyboards), and is almost always due to a system configuration problem that prevents the PC from entering a power-saving mode (not a keyboard problem specifically). To correct this trouble, you should use the Device Manager to troubleshoot possible device conflicts or disabled devices on the system.

**SYMPTOM 22-21**    **Remote control programs don't work after installing keyboard drivers**    Many PC "remote control" programs (such as PC Anywhere, ReachOut, and Carbon Copy) use keyboard and mouse drivers that simply are not compatible with the keyboard's native drivers. For example, some remote control programs will not work when IntelliType software is installed for the Microsoft Natural Keyboard (this may also occur with other multifunction keyboards). You'll need to disable the remote control software, install patches for the remote control software that will properly support the keyboard, or replace the keyboard with a more generic model.

**SYMPTOM 22-22**    **Function keys do not respond, and the keyboard is incorrectly identified as an 84-key keyboard**    This is a known issue with high-end multifunction keyboards (e.g., the Microsoft Natural Keyboard Elite), and is usually due to interference by software utilities such as

Attachmate software. To resolve this issue, add the OverrideKeyboardType DWORD value to the following registry key:

```
HKEY_LOCAL_MACHINE\SYSTEM\CurrentControlSet\Services\i8042prt\Parameters
```

and then change the value data of this entry from 0 to 4. Be sure to make a complete backup of your registry to a bootable floppy disk before attempting any changes to your registry. Alternately, you can switch to a different type of keyboard.

**SYMPTOM 22-23** **On an IBM PS/2 system, you encounter keyboard errors, even though the keyboard driver loads successfully** Often, you'll see an error like "Keyboard error: keyboard not found," and you cannot access the keyboard. This type of problem is known to occur on PS/2 systems when the IBM ROM BIOS patch file (DASDDRVR.SYS) is loaded *after* the keyboard driver in CONFIG.SYS. Rearrange the CONFIG.SYS file to load the DASDDRVR.SYS file before the keyboard driver. Make sure you are loading the patch driver (DASDDRVR.SYS) that is designed for your *specific* computer (for example, you cannot use the DASDDRVR.SYS file that ships with an IBM PS/2 Model 80 on a PS/2 Model 70 computer). This device driver can normally be found on the setup disk that you received with your IBM PS/2. Otherwise, you can obtain it from IBM (www.ibm.com).

**SYMPTOM 22-24** **Assigned key sounds do not work** When you assign sounds to keystrokes (under the Options tab in the Keyboard tool in your Windows 9x Control Panel), the sounds may not play when you press the assigned keys. This problem is known to occur with some programmable keyboards when an older HiJaak Pro or HiJaak 95 Graphics Suite is installed on your computer. These products may load a device driver named "Runner" that disables programmable keyboard sounds. You may be able to work around the problem by closing the "Runner" task:

- Press CTRL-ALT-DEL to open the Close Program dialog box (the Task Manager under Windows XP).
- If "Runner" is listed, click Runner, and then click End Task.

Other utilities may also cause such problems. Systematically remove other utilities to check for software conflicts.

**SYMPTOM 22-25** **You cannot use Windows-specific keys to start task-switching software** You *can* start the desired task-switching software using CTRL-ESC or by double-clicking the desktop. Chances are that your Windows-specific key will not start any other task-switching utility if TASKSW16.EXE can be found on the path. You'll need to update the task-switching program reference in SYSTEM.INI. Load SYSTEM.INI into any text editor, and modify the line that reads:

```
TASKMAN=TASKSW16.EXE
```

to read

```
TASKMAN=<task manager>
```

where <task manager> is the name of the executable file you want to start when you press the Windows key. Rename the TASKSW16.EXE file (for example, to TASKSW16.OLD), or move it to a directory that is not in the path. Save and close the SYSTEM.INI file, and then restart the computer.

**SYMPTOM 22-26** **The NUMLOCK feature may not activate when the NUM LOCK key is pressed** This can happen with some programmable keyboards when pen software is installed on the Windows 9x/Me system (this is not known to occur under Windows XP). You should be able to correct the problem by disabling the pen device under Windows 9x/Me:

1. Click Start | Settings | Control Panel.
2. Double-click the System icon and select the Device Manager tab.
3. Double-click the Ports entry to expand it.
4. Double-click the port to which the pen (or touch-screen) device is connected.
5. In the Device Usage area on the General tab, click the Original Configuration (Current) check box to clear it. (If you're using OSR2, click the Disable In This Hardware Profile check box to select it.)
6. Click OK, and then restart the system when prompted.

 To reenable your pen device, repeat the steps above, but reselect (or re-clear) the check box in step 5. You may be able to correct this trouble by updating the pen software driver(s).

**SYMPTOM 22-27** **The "Language" section of the Keyboard tool is disabled under Windows 98/Me** When you're using the Keyboard tool in Control Panel, you may encounter the following symptom(s): a message may say "Old-Style Keyboard detected, pane disabled," or the language list may be blank (and you may not be able to change any language settings). This problem can occur if the keyboard registry key is damaged or missing:

`HKEY_LOCAL_MACHINE\System\CurrentControlSet\control\keyboard layouts`

To resolve this problem, reinstall Windows 98/Me into the same folder as the original installation.

**SYMPTOM 22-28** **You encounter keyboard problems when using IE 4.0x/5 and an Adobe Acrobat (.PDF) file under Windows 98** If you have a PDF file open in Internet Explorer, you may lose some keyboard functionality. Keys that may not work include the PAGE UP, PAGE DOWN, and arrow keys. To work around this problem, minimize and restore the IE window, use the Zoom buttons on the Adobe Acrobat toolbar, or use the mouse to scroll through the file.

**SYMPTOM 22-29** **You have problems using a real-mode keyboard driver with an international code page** If an international code page is installed in conjunction with a real-mode keyboard driver (such as KEYBOARD.SYS), you may find that console programs cannot detect extended character keystrokes (such as INSERT, DELETE, HOME, and so on). Console programs that don't work directly with the console API may not recognize extended keystrokes. When a real-mode keyboard driver is installed, the current character in the keyboard buffer is sent to the console program. With an international code page loaded, the data returned through the console API is slightly different than that in Windows 98/Me. This problem has been corrected in Windows 98 SE and later, but for older versions of Windows, you can download the patch (a new version of CONAGENT.EXE) from www.microsoft.com/support/supportnet/overview/overview.asp.

**SYMPTOM 22-30** **You find two keyboards listed in the Windows Device Manager** When you restart your computer after installing a USB keyboard, both the USB keyboard device and another keyboard (e.g., a Standard 101/102-Key or Microsoft Natural Keyboard) device are listed in the Keyboard branch of your Device Manager. This occurs because USB keyboards may still require the Standard 101/102-Key or "native" (e.g., Natural Keyboard) driver to work properly if your BIOS does not fully support USB in the real mode. This may seem awkward, but it's perfectly normal. If you disable the Standard 101/102-Key or Microsoft Natural Keyboard device in Device Manager and restart your computer, the USB keyboard will not work—Windows 98/Me automatically installs the device again. You might try a system BIOS upgrade to better support the USB ports on your motherboard, or upgrade the motherboard entirely.

**SYMPTOM 22-31** **The new USB keyboard does not operate properly under Windows 98 after installation** You know that your system should fully support USB devices. This problem can occur when you install a new USB keyboard while your system is off, and your computer is set up to have you log on when you start it. USB keyboards are not enumerated until *after* you log on to your computer. To correct this problem, click Cancel when you're prompted to log on, click Start, click Log Off <user name>, click Yes, and *then* log on to your computer.

**SYMPTOM 22-32** **You notice that the keyboard language unexpectedly changes to a "default" language** When you start a program under Windows 98/Me (or when a program is launched using OLE), your keyboard may revert to the "default" language—regardless of the language you're currently using. For example, when you start a program, you'll see the Language icon on the taskbar change to indicate that the default language is being used (but when a program is launched using OLE, the language icon may not change). To work around this problem, simply change the keyboard driver to the desired language after you start the program. Click the Language icon on the taskbar, and then click the language that you want. Now press the appropriate shortcut key combination for switching keyboard layouts (by default, this is LEFT ARROW-ALT-SHIFT).

**SYMPTOM 22-33** **The "automatic repeat" feature doesn't work for USB keyboards** For example, the keyboard won't repeat after returning from the suspend mode under Windows 98/SE. This is a known problem with Windows 98 SE, but a patch is available from Microsoft at www.microsoft.com/support/supportnet/overview/overview.asp. The English version of this patch should have the following file attributes (or later):

```
KBDHID.VXD    10/04/99    05:32p            4.10.2223          16,666KB
```

Alternately, you can opt to upgrade the operating system to Windows XP, which should provide better compatibility for a variety of input devices.

**SYMPTOM 22-34** **After installing Windows 98, your custom keyboard layout may be lost** This problem occurs when user profiles are enabled in Windows 95 and a custom keyboard layout option is selected in a user profile (rather than the default profile). Since Windows 98 setup only parses the settings for a default user during the upgrade to Windows 98, the keyboard setting changes to the default user profile during the upgrade. To correct this problem, log on to the computer using a user profile *other* than the default, and then modify the keyboard layout in Windows 98:

1. Click Start | Settings | Control Panel.
2. Click Keyboard, click Language, click Properties, and then click the layout you want to use in the Keyboard Layout box.
3. Click OK, click OK again, and then restart the computer.

**SYMPTOM 22-35** **Your laptop does not detect a PS/2 keyboard** This is a known problem with configurations such as the IBM ThinkPad and Natural Keyboard Elite. For example, when you connect the Natural Keyboard Elite to the PS/2 port on an IBM ThinkPad laptop, the keyboard may not be detected. This problem generally occurs because the PS/2 port on the IBM ThinkPad does not detect any PS/2 keyboard without the correct adapter cable or docking station. To correct this problem, you must connect the keyboard to an appropriate docking station.

**SYMPTOM 22-36** **Your particular keyboard doesn't work with a Compaq DeskPro 4000 system** For example, the Natural Keyboard Elite is known to have trouble with the Compaq DeskPro 4000. When you connect the keyboard to your computer, the keyboard may be detected the first time you start the system, but the keyboard may not be detected during subsequent starts. In virtually all cases, the keyboard device you're using will not operate on systems using the VIA UHCI chipset. Try a different (basic model) keyboard with the PC.

**SYMPTOM 22-37** **You find that you cannot use a USB keyboard in the DOS mode** For example, when you start the computer (or restart your computer) in DOS mode, the multifunction keyboard (e.g., Natural Keyboard Elite) may not function properly. You may also receive either of the following error messages:

```
Keyboard Error
```

or

```
Keyboard Not Present
```

This problem can occur if you connect the multifunction keyboard to your computer using a USB adapter, but your computer's BIOS doesn't fully support USB keyboards. Your system BIOS must support USB devices in order for any type of USB keyboard to work in DOS. You should upgrade the system BIOS with a version that supports USB devices (or upgrade the motherboard outright). To work around this issue temporarily, shut down Windows and turn off the computer. Disconnect the keyboard from the USB port, and then remove the USB adapter. Connect another keyboard to a PS/2 port on the computer, and then restart the system normally.

**SYMPTOM 22-38** **Keyboard lights do not illuminate in the DOS mode** This is a known problem when using the Natural Keyboard Elite with a Compaq Presario system under DOS. The LED lights on the keyboard may remain unlit in DOS, but may work properly under Windows. This is an issue with the Compaq system (rather than the keyboard), but no features are lost in the DOS mode.

**SYMPTOM 22-39** **Your keyboard does not work properly on an IBM Aptiva system** For example, when you connect a multifunction keyboard (e.g., Natural Keyboard or Natural Keyboard Elite) to an IBM Aptiva computer, the keyboard may not work properly. This problem may occur if you have IBM Rapid Access Keyboard software running on the Aptiva system. To correct this issue, use the Add/Remove Programs wizard to remove the IBM Rapid Access Keyboard software (this software is not needed if you use another keyboard, such as the Natural Keyboard family).

The EZ-Button program is a component of the IBM Rapid Access Keyboard software, so this program is also removed when you remove the IBM Rapid Access Keyboard software.

**SYMPTOM 22-40**  **Your keyboard does not work properly on certain Toshiba laptops**
For example, when you use a multifunction keyboard (e.g., Natural Keyboard Elite) on the PS/2 port of a Toshiba Satellite 110C, Satellite Pro 400C, Tecra 720CDT, or Tecra 500CDT laptop, the keyboard may not function properly. This problem can occur because plug-and-play hardware detection on the PS/2 port times out *before* the computer enumerates the keyboard. This is typically a problem with the keyboard. To get around this issue, use the USB adapter included with the keyboard to connect the keyboard to the USB port on the laptop (if one is available). If a USB port is not available on your computer, you'll need to return the keyboard for an updated model that operates properly on the Toshiba family of laptops.

# Further Study

**Cherry**  www.cherrycorp.com/english/
**Chicony**  www.chicony.com
**IBM Healthy Computing**  www.pc.ibm.com/us/healthycomputing/vdt8.html
**Keytronic**  www.keytronic.com
**Microsoft**  www.microsoft.com/catalog/navigation.asp?subid=22&nv=9
**Mitsumi**  www.mitsumi.com
**NMB Technologies**  www.nmbtech.com

# 23

# MEMORY TROUBLESHOOTING

**M**emory holds the program code and data that is processed by the CPU, and it is this intimate relationship between memory and the CPU that forms the basis of computer performance. Larger and faster CPUs are constantly being introduced, and more complex software is regularly developed to take advantage of the processing power. In turn, the more complex software demands larger amounts of faster memory. With the explosive growth of Windows (and most recently Windows XP), the demands made on memory performance are more acute than ever. These demands have resulted in a proliferation of memory types that go far beyond the simple, traditional DRAM. Pipeline-burst cache, fast double data rate synchronous DRAM (DDR SDRAM), flash BIOS, and Rambus now compete for the attention of PC technicians and users alike. These new forms of memory also present some new problems. This chapter will provide an understanding of memory types, configurations, installation concerns, and troubleshooting solutions.

# Essential Memory Concepts

The first step in any discussion of memory is to understand how solid-state memory works, what the important technologies are, and how memory is organized in the PC. If you already have a good grasp of memory basics, feel free to skip this part of the chapter. Otherwise, you may find the following information to be a good overview of memory basics.

## MEMORY ORGANIZATION

All memory is basically an *array* of individual storage elements organized into rows and columns, as shown in Figure 23-1. Each row is known as an *address*—there may be 1 million, 2 million, 4 million (often more) addresses on a single memory chip. The columns represent *data bits*—an older memory chip may only have one column of bits, but more recent high-density memory chips may have two or four columns of bits.

As you can see in Figure 23-1, the intersection of each column and row is an individual memory bit (known as a *cell*). This is important because the number of components that make up a cell—and the way those components are fabricated onto the memory chip—will have a profound impact on memory performance. For example, a classic *dynamic RAM* (DRAM) cell is a single MOS (metal oxide semiconductor) transistor, while *static RAM* (SRAM) cells often pack several transistors and other components onto the chip's die for every bit. Although you certainly don't have to be an expert on integrated circuit design, you should realize that the internal fabrication of a memory chip has more to do with its performance than just the way it is soldered into your computer.

## MEMORY SIGNALS

Our array of memory bits communicates with the "outside world" through three sets of signals: address lines, data lines, and control lines. Figure 23-2 illustrates these signal types. *Address lines* define which row of the memory array will be active. In actual practice, the address is specified as a binary number, and conversion circuitry inside the memory chip translates the binary number into a specific row signal. *Data lines* carry the data bits back and forth to the storage cells (columns) at the defined address. *Control lines* are used to operate the memory chip. For example, a Read/-Write (R/-W) line defines whether data is

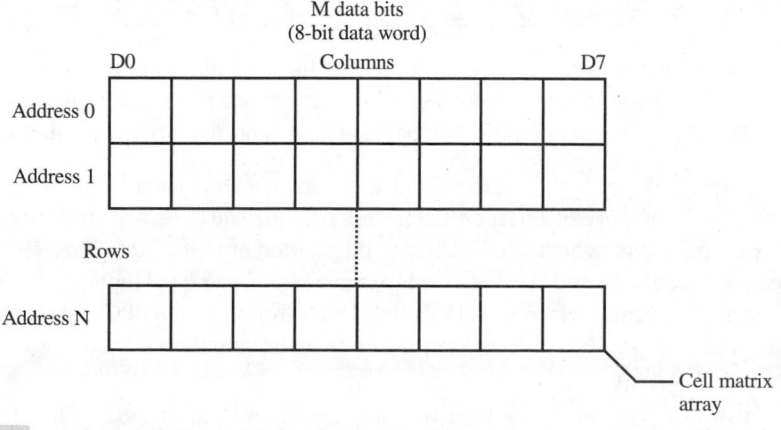

**FIGURE 23-1**    Simplified diagram of a memory array

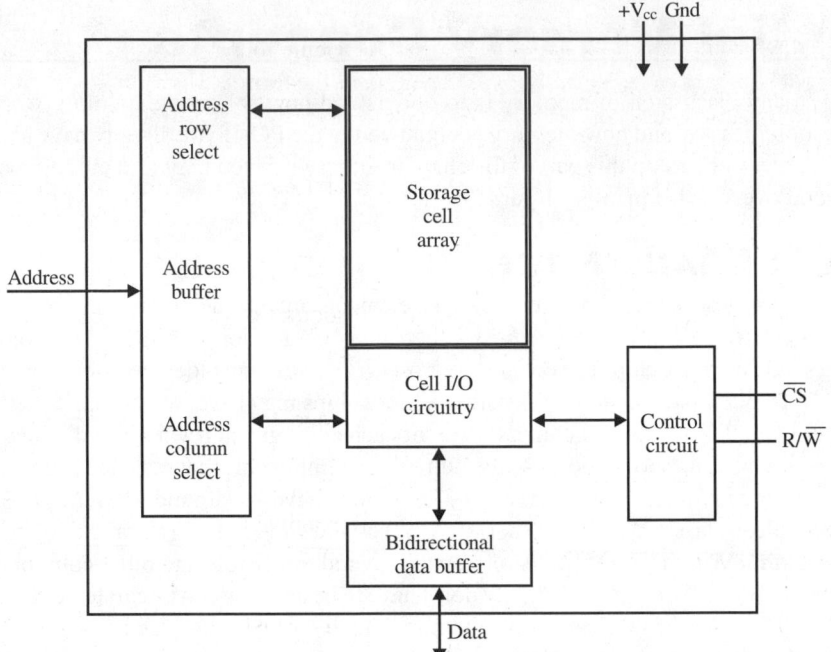

**FIGURE  23-2**   Simplified diagram of a basic memory chip

being read from the specified address, or written to it. A -Chip Select (-CS) signal makes a memory chip active or inactive. (This ability to "disconnect" from a circuit is what allows a myriad of memory chips to share common address and data signals in the computer.) Some memory types require additional signals such as row address-select (RAS) and column address-select (CAS) for refresh operations. More exotic memory types may require additional control signals, but you get the general idea.

# Memory Packages and Structures

Ultimately, the memory die is mounted in a package just like any other chip. The completed memory packages can then be soldered to your motherboard, or attached to plug-in structures such as SIMMs, DIMMs, and RIMMs. There are really only five package styles normally used for memory devices:

■  **DIP (Dual Inline Package)**   This is the classical "chip" package used for through-hole mounting (prior to the broad acceptance of surface-mount technology). The advantage of DIP packages is their compatibility with sockets, which allows chips to be inserted or removed as required. Unfortunately, the long metal pins can bend and break if the chip is inserted or removed incorrectly. Also, the overall size of the package demands extra space. DIP chips can be found in older PCs (such as 286 and earlier systems) and older VGA/SVGA video boards. DIPs are still sometimes used on motherboards to hold cache RAM or BIOS chips.

■  **SIP (Single Inline Package)**   This type of package is rarely used today—there are simply not enough pins. However, they did make a short appearance with memory devices in late-model 286 and early 386 systems that flirted with proprietary memory expansions. Long-time technicians may remember NEC using such devices in a 2MB add-on module for their 386SX/20, and you needed to add that module *before* you added even more memory in the form of proprietary SIMMs. SIPs can be troublesome because they are difficult to find replacements for, so expect replacement memory modules that use them to cost a premium.

■ **SOJ (Small-Outline "J" Lead)**   This is the contemporary package style for surface-mount circuits. The leads protrude from the package like a DIP, but are bent around just under the package in the form of a "j". There are sockets for SOJ packages, which are often employed for replaceable memory chips like the BIOS ROM, but most SOJ RAM devices are soldered directly to the motherboard as system memory (or a video board as video RAM). Memory modules often use SOJ-type memory components.

■ **TSOP (Thin, Small-Outline Package)**   Like the SOJ, a TSOP is also a surface-mount package style. However, rather than bending pins under the package, the pins extend away (almost horizontally). Its small, thin body makes TSOP memory ideal for narrow spaces. Expect to find such devices serving as memory in notebook/sub-notebook systems, or PCMCIA cards (a.k.a. PC Cards).

■ **CSP (Chip Scale Package)**   Unlike other forms of packaging, CSP doesn't use pins to connect the chip to its circuit. Instead, the package uses a series of surface-mount contact pads on the underside of the chip (similar to a ball grid array or BGA package style). At first glance, the chips may not even look soldered to the memory module or other device. Rambus memory chips typically utilize this kind of packaging to create Rambus modules (RIMMs).

# MEMORY MODULES

In the early days of PC design, memory chips were soldered to the motherboard. This gave the PC a fixed amount of RAM, but also made it terribly inconvenient to add more RAM. To expand the amount of RAM on a system, designers began to incorporate memory chips onto specialized *memory modules* that could be added later if needed. This way, an inexpensive system could be sold with a minimum amount of "base memory" on the motherboard, and then the memory could be upgraded later using one or more modules. Today, standard memory modules are used exclusively. This greatly simplifies the process of memory troubleshooting because all RAM modules can be removed and replaced if necessary. You will generally encounter three types of memory modules: SIMMs, DIMMs, and RIMMs.

## Proprietary Add-On Modules

Once Intel's 286 processor opened the door for more than 1MB of memory, PC makers scrambled to fill the void. However, the rush to more memory resulted in a proliferation of nonstandard (and incompatible) memory modules. Each new motherboard came with a new add-on memory scheme, which invariably led to a great deal of confusion among PC users and makers alike. You will likely find proprietary memory modules in 286 and early 386 systems, though no current desktop system uses proprietary memory modules.

## SIMM

By the time 386 systems took hold in the PC industry, proprietary memory modules had been largely abandoned in favor of the 30-pin *Single In-line Memory Module* (SIMM). A SIMM is light, small, and can hold anywhere between 1MB and 16MB of RAM (depending on the module's vintage). Later SIMM versions were physically larger, with 72 pins, and able to hold as much as 32MB of RAM (see Figure 23-3).

SIMMs are placed into special slots on the motherboard. The slots are specifically designed to ensure that once inserted, the SIMM will be held in place tightly. SIMMs are secured in their sockets by inserting

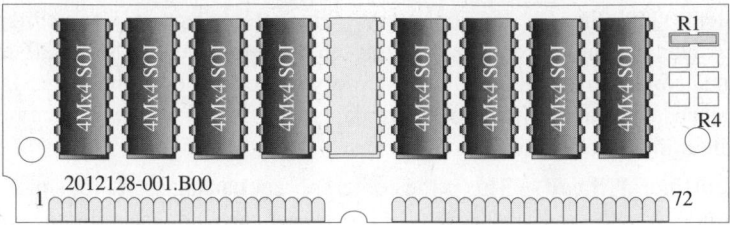

**FIGURE 23-3** A typical 72-pin ValueRAM SIMM (Courtesy of Kingston Technologies)

them at an angle (usually about 60 degrees from the motherboard) into the base of the socket, and then tilting them upward until they are perpendicular to the motherboard. Special metal clips on either side of the socket snap in place when the SIMM is inserted correctly. The SIMM is also keyed with a notch on one side, so it cannot be installed backwards.

Perhaps the greatest advantage of a SIMM is *standardization*: using a standard pin layout, a SIMM from one PC can be installed into almost any other compatible PC. The 30-pin SIMM (Table 23-1) provides 8 data bits and generally holds up to 4MB of RAM. The 30-pin SIMM proved its worth in 386 and early 486 systems, but fell short when providing more memory to later-model PCs. The 72-pin SIMM (Table 23-2) replaced the 30-pin SIMM version by providing 32 data bits, and may hold up to 32MB (or more). Table 23-3 outlines a variation of the standard 72-pin SIMM, highlighting the use of Error Correction Code (ECC) instead of parity.

Today, SIMMs are largely considered to be obsolete, and virtually all current memory types (mainly DDR SDRAM) are integrated onto larger and more versatile memory modules called *DIMMs* (see the section "DIMM" later in this chapter).

**TABLE 23-1    PIN ASSIGNMENTS FOR A STANDARD 30-PIN SIMM**

| PIN | NAME | DESCRIPTION |
|-----|------|-------------|
| 1 | VCC | +5 Vdc |
| 2 | -CAS | -Column Address Strobe |
| 3 | DQ0 | Data 0 |
| 4 | A0 | Address 0 |
| 5 | A1 | Address 1 |
| 6 | DQ1 | Data 1 |
| 7 | A2 | Address 2 |
| 8 | A3 | Address 3 |
| 9 | GND | Ground |
| 10 | DQ2 | Data 2 |
| 11 | A4 | Address 4 |
| 12 | A5 | Address 5 |
| 13 | DQ3 | Data 3 |
| 14 | A6 | Address 6 |

**TABLE 23-1    PIN ASSIGNMENTS FOR A STANDARD 30-PIN SIMM** *(CONTINUED)*

| PIN | NAME | DESCRIPTION |
|-----|------|-------------|
| 15 | A7 | Address 7 |
| 16 | DQ4 | Data 4 |
| 17 | A8 | Address 8 |
| 18 | A9 | Address 9 |
| 19 | A10 | Address 10 |
| 20 | DQ5 | Data 5 |
| 21 | -WE | -Write Enable |
| 22 | GND | Ground |
| 23 | DQ6 | Data 6 |
| 24 | n/c | Not connected |
| 25 | DQ7 | Data 7 |
| 26 | QP | Data Parity Out |
| 27 | -RAS | -Row Address Strobe |
| 28 | -CASP | -Parity Control |
| 29 | DP | Data Parity In |
| 30 | VCC | +5 Vdc |

**TABLE 23-2    PIN ASSIGNMENTS FOR A STANDARD 72-PIN SIMM**

| PIN | NON-PARITY | PARITY | DESCRIPTION |
|-----|-----------|--------|-------------|
| 1 | VSS | VSS | Ground |
| 2 | DQ0 | DQ0 | Data 0 |
| 3 | DQ18 | DQ18 | Data 18 |
| 4 | DQ1 | DQ1 | Data 1 |
| 5 | DQ19 | DQ19 | Data 19 |
| 6 | DQ2 | DQ2 | Data 2 |
| 7 | DQ20 | DQ20 | Data 20 |
| 8 | DQ3 | DQ3 | Data 3 |
| 9 | DQ21 | DQ21 | Data 21 |
| 10 | VCC | VCC | +5 Vdc |
| 11 | n/c | n/c | Not connected |
| 12 | A0 | A0 | Address 0 |
| 13 | A1 | A1 | Address 1 |
| 14 | A2 | A2 | Address 2 |
| 15 | A3 | A3 | Address 3 |
| 16 | A4 | A4 | Address 4 |
| 17 | A5 | A5 | Address 5 |
| 18 | A6 | A6 | Address 6 |

**TABLE 23-2    PIN ASSIGNMENTS FOR A STANDARD 72-PIN SIMM** *(CONTINUED)*

| PIN | NON-PARITY | PARITY | DESCRIPTION |
|-----|-----------|--------|-------------|
| 19 | A10 | A10 | Address 10 |
| 20 | DQ4 | DQ4 | Data 4 |
| 21 | DQ22 | DQ22 | Data 22 |
| 22 | DQ5 | DQ5 | Data 5 |
| 23 | DQ23 | DQ23 | Data 23 |
| 24 | DQ6 | DQ6 | Data 6 |
| 25 | DQ24 | DQ24 | Data 24 |
| 26 | DQ7 | DQ7 | Data 7 |
| 27 | DQ25 | DQ25 | Data 25 |
| 28 | A7 | A7 | Address 7 |
| 29 | A11 | A11 | Address 11 |
| 30 | VCC | VCC | +5 Vdc |
| 31 | A8 | A8 | Address 8 |
| 32 | A9 | A9 | Address 9 |
| 33 | -RAS3 | -RAS3 | -Row Address Strobe 3 |
| 34 | -RAS2 | -RAS2 | -Row Address Strobe 2 |
| 35 | n/c | PQ26 | Parity 26 (3rd) |
| 36 | n/c | PQ8 | Parity 8 (1st) |
| 37 | n/c | PQ17 | Parity 26 (3rd) |
| 38 | n/c | PQ35 | Parity 35 (4th) |
| 39 | VSS | VSS | Ground |
| 40 | -CAS0 | -CAS0 | -Column Address Strobe 0 |
| 41 | -CAS2 | -CAS2 | -Column Address Strobe 2 |
| 42 | -CAS3 | -CAS3 | -Column Address Strobe 3 |
| 43 | -CAS1 | -CAS1 | -Column Address Strobe 1 |
| 44 | -RAS0 | -RAS0 | -Row Address Strobe 0 |
| 45 | -RAS1 | -RAS1 | -Row Address Strobe 1 |
| 46 | n/c | n/c | Not connected |
| 47 | -WE | -WE | Read/-Write |
| 48 | n/c | n/c | Not connected |
| 49 | DQ9 | DQ9 | Data 9 |
| 50 | DQ27 | DQ27 | Data 27 |
| 51 | DQ10 | DQ10 | Data 10 |
| 52 | DQ28 | DQ28 | Data 28 |
| 53 | DQ11 | DQ11 | Data 11 |
| 54 | DQ29 | DQ29 | Data 29 |
| 55 | DQ12 | DQ12 | Data 12 |
| 56 | DQ30 | DQ30 | Data 30 |
| 57 | DQ13 | DQ13 | Data 13 |
| 58 | DQ31 | DQ31 | Data 31 |

**TABLE 23-2    PIN ASSIGNMENTS FOR A STANDARD 72-PIN SIMM** *(CONTINUED)*

| PIN | NON-PARITY | PARITY | DESCRIPTION |
|-----|------------|--------|-------------|
| 59 | VCC | VCC | +5 Vdc |
| 60 | DQ32 | DQ32 | Data 32 |
| 61 | DQ14 | DQ14 | Data 14 |
| 62 | DQ33 | DQ33 | Data 33 |
| 63 | DQ15 | DQ15 | Data 15 |
| 64 | DQ34 | DQ34 | Data 34 |
| 65 | DQ16 | DQ16 | Data 16 |
| 66 | n/c | n/c | Not connected |
| 67 | PD1 | PD1 | Presence Detect 1 |
| 68 | PD2 | PD2 | Presence Detect 2 |
| 69 | PD3 | PD3 | Presence Detect 3 |
| 70 | PD4 | PD4 | Presence Detect 4 |
| 71 | n/c | n/c | Not connected |
| 72 | VSS | VSS | Ground |
| **Size: (presence detect lines)** | | | |
| PD2 | PD1 | Size | |
| GND | GND | 4 or 64MB | |
| GND | NC | 2 or 32MB | |
| NC | GND | 1 or 16MB | |
| NC | NC | 8MB | |
| **Access Time: (presence detect lines)** | | | |
| PD4 | PD3 | Access time | |
| GND | GND | 50ns, 100ns | |
| GND | NC | 80ns | |
| NC | GND | 70ns | |
| NC | NC | 60ns | |

**TABLE 23-3    PIN ASSIGNMENTS FOR A 72-PIN ECC SIMM**

| PIN | ECC | OPTIMIZED | DESCRIPTION |
|-----|-----|-----------|-------------|
| 1 | VSS | VSS | Ground |
| 2 | DQ0 | DQ0 | Data 0 |
| 3 | DQ1 | DQ1 | Data 1 |
| 4 | DQ2 | DQ2 | Data 2 |
| 5 | DQ3 | DQ3 | Data 3 |
| 6 | DQ4 | DQ4 | Data 4 |
| 7 | DQ5 | DQ5 | Data 5 |
| 8 | DQ6 | DQ6 | Data 6 |

**TABLE 23-3** PIN ASSIGNMENTS FOR A 72-PIN ECC SIMM *(CONTINUED)*

| PIN | ECC | OPTIMIZED | DESCRIPTION |
|---|---|---|---|
| 9 | DQ7 | DQ7 | Data 7 |
| 10 | VCC | VCC | +5 Vdc |
| 11 | PD5 | PD5 | Presence Detect 5 |
| 12 | A0 | A0 | Address 0 |
| 13 | A1 | A1 | Address 1 |
| 14 | A2 | A2 | Address 2 |
| 15 | A3 | A3 | Address 3 |
| 16 | A4 | A4 | Address 4 |
| 17 | A5 | A5 | Address 5 |
| 18 | A6 | A6 | Address 6 |
| 19 | n/c | n/c | Not connected |
| 20 | DQ8 | DQ8 | Data 8 |
| 21 | DQ9 | DQ9 | Data 9 |
| 22 | DQ10 | DQ10 | Data 10 |
| 23 | DQ11 | DQ11 | Data 11 |
| 24 | DQ12 | DQ12 | Data 12 |
| 25 | DQ13 | DQ13 | Data 13 |
| 26 | DQ14 | DQ14 | Data 14 |
| 27 | DQ15 | DQ15 | Data 15 |
| 28 | A7 | A7 | Address 7 |
| 29 | DQ16 | DQ16 | Data 16 |
| 30 | VCC | VCC | +5 Vdc |
| 31 | A8 | A8 | Address 8 |
| 32 | A9 | A9 | Address 9 |
| 33 | n/c | n/c | Not connected |
| 34 | -RAS1 | -RAS1 | -Row Address Strobe 1 |
| 35 | DQ17 | DQ17 | Data 17 |
| 36 | DQ18 | DQ18 | Data 18 |
| 37 | DQ19 | DQ19 | Data 19 |
| 38 | DQ20 | DQ20 | Data 20 |
| 39 | VSS | VSS | Ground |
| 40 | -CAS0 | -CAS0 | -Column Address Strobe 0 |
| 41 | A10 | A10 | Address 10 |
| 42 | A11 | A11 | Address 11 |
| 43 | -CAS1 | -CAS1 | -Column Address Strobe 1 |
| 44 | -RAS0 | -RAS0 | -Row Address Strobe 0 |
| 45 | -RAS1 | -RAS1 | -Row Address Strobe 1 |
| 46 | DQ21 | DQ21 | Data 21 |
| 47 | -WE | -WE | Read/-Write |
| 48 | -ECC | -ECC | -Error Correction Control |

**TABLE 23-3    PIN ASSIGNMENTS FOR A 72-PIN ECC SIMM** *(CONTINUED)*

| PIN | ECC | OPTIMIZED | DESCRIPTION |
|-----|-----|-----------|-------------|
| 49 | DQ22 | DQ22 | Data 22 |
| 50 | DQ23 | DQ23 | Data 23 |
| 51 | DQ24 | DQ24 | Data 24 |
| 52 | DQ25 | DQ25 | Data 25 |
| 53 | DQ26 | DQ26 | Data 26 |
| 54 | DQ27 | DQ27 | Data 27 |
| 55 | DQ28 | DQ28 | Data 28 |
| 56 | DQ29 | DQ29 | Data 29 |
| 57 | DQ30 | DQ30 | Data 30 |
| 58 | DQ31 | DQ31 | Data 31 |
| 59 | VCC | VCC | +5 Vdc |
| 60 | DQ32 | DQ32 | Data 32 |
| 61 | DQ33 | DQ33 | Data 33 |
| 62 | DQ34 | DQ34 | Data 34 |
| 63 | DQ35 | DQ35 | Data 35 |
| 64 | n/c | DQ36 | Data 36 |
| 65 | n/c | DQ37 | Data 37 |
| 66 | n/c | DQ38 | Data 38 |
| 67 | PD1 | PD1 | Presence Detect 1 |
| 68 | PD2 | PD2 | Presence Detect 2 |
| 69 | PD3 | PD3 | Presence Detect 3 |
| 70 | PD4 | PD4 | Presence Detect 4 |
| 71 | n/c | DQ39 | Data 39 |
| 72 | VSS | VSS | Ground |

SIMMs are generally available as *single-sided* or *double-sided*—referring to whether DRAM chips are found on only one side or both sides of the SIMM. The 30-pin SIMMs are almost always single-sided; 72-pin SIMMs are either single-sided or double-sided. Some double-sided SIMMs are also constructed as *composite SIMMs*. Internally, composite SIMMs are wired as if they were actually two single-sided SIMMs back to back. This doesn't affect the characteristics or capacity of the module, but some motherboards cannot handle composite SIMMs because they are slightly different electrically. For example, 72-pin SIMMs that are 1MB, 4MB, and 16MB in size are normally single-sided, while 2MB, 8MB, and 32MB SIMMs are generally double-sided. This is why there are so many older motherboards that will *only* work with 1MB, 4MB, and 16MB (single-sided) SIMMs. You should always check your motherboard to see what SIMM sizes are required. Composite SIMMs will *not* work in a motherboard that doesn't support them.

## DIMM

The *Dual In-line Memory Module* (DIMM) closely resembles SIMMs, as shown in Figure 23-4, but are physically larger. The 168-pin module accommodates a 64-bit data bus width. Where a SIMM ties each pin together between the front and back, a DIMM keeps all electrical signals separate. This provides for

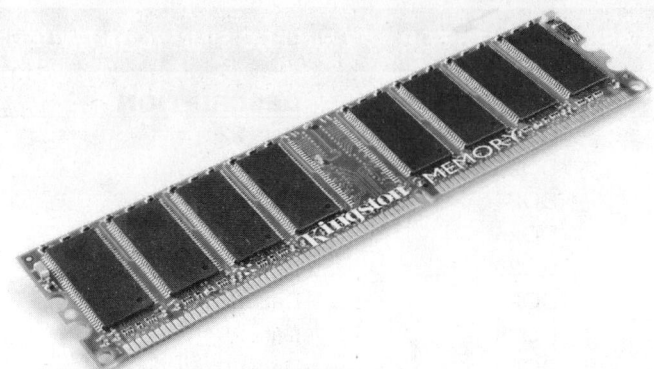

**FIGURE  23-4**    A 333 MHz DDR SDRAM DIMM (Courtesy of Kingston Technologies)

many more pins without making the module much larger. The added size and pin count of the modern DIMM easily supports 64MB, 128MB, and 256MB of RAM—allowing a substantial amount of RAM with only one or two modules. Table 23-4 lists the pinout for an unbuffered DRAM DIMM, and Table 23-5 presents the pinout for an unbuffered SDRAM DIMM.

| TABLE 23-4 | | PIN ASSIGNMENTS FOR A STANDARD 168-PIN UNBUFFERED DRAM DIMM | | | |
|---|---|---|---|---|---|
| **PIN** | **NON-PARITY** | **PARITY** | **72 ECC** | **80 ECC** | **DESCRIPTION** |
| 1 | VSS | VSS | VSS | VSS | Ground |
| 2 | DQ0 | DQ0 | DQ0 | DQ0 | Data 0 |
| 3 | DQ1 | DQ1 | DQ1 | DQ1 | Data 1 |
| 4 | DQ2 | DQ2 | DQ2 | DQ2 | Data 2 |
| 5 | DQ3 | DQ3 | DQ3 | DQ3 | Data 3 |
| 6 | VCC | VCC | VCC | VCC | +5 Vdc or +3.3 Vdc |
| 7 | DQ4 | DQ4 | DQ4 | DQ4 | Data 4 |
| 8 | DQ5 | DQ5 | DQ5 | DQ5 | Data 5 |
| 9 | DQ6 | DQ6 | DQ6 | DQ6 | Data 6 |
| 10 | DQ7 | DQ7 | DQ7 | DQ7 | Data 7 |
| 11 | DQ8 | DQ8 | DQ8 | DQ8 | Data 8 |
| 12 | VSS | VSS | VSS | VSS | Ground |
| 13 | DQ9 | DQ9 | DQ9 | DQ9 | Data 9 |
| 14 | DQ10 | DQ10 | DQ10 | DQ10 | Data 10 |
| 15 | DQ11 | DQ11 | DQ11 | DQ11 | Data 11 |
| 16 | DQ12 | DQ12 | DQ12 | DQ12 | Data 12 |
| 17 | DQ13 | DQ13 | DQ13 | DQ13 | Data 13 |
| 18 | VCC | VCC | VCC | VCC | +5 Vdc or +3.3 Vdc |
| 19 | DQ14 | DQ14 | DQ14 | DQ14 | Data 14 |
| 20 | DQ15 | DQ15 | DQ15 | DQ15 | Data 15 |
| 21 | n/c | CB0 | CB0 | CB0 | Parity/Check Bit Input/Output 0 |

**TABLE 23-4    PIN ASSIGNMENTS FOR A STANDARD 168-PIN UNBUFFERED DRAM DIMM *(CONTINUED)***

| PIN | NON-PARITY | PARITY | 72 ECC | 80 ECC | DESCRIPTION |
|-----|-----------|--------|--------|--------|-------------|
| 22 | n/c | CB1 | CB1 | CB1 | Parity/Check Bit Input/Output 1 |
| 23 | VSS | VSS | VSS | VSS | Ground |
| 24 | n/c | n/c | n/c | CB8 | Parity/Check Bit Input/Output 8 |
| 25 | n/c | n/c | n/c | CB9 | Parity/Check Bit Input/Output 9 |
| 26 | VCC | VCC | VCC | VCC | +5 Vdc or +3.3 Vdc |
| 27 | -WE0 | -WE0 | -WE0 | -WE0 | Read/-Write Input |
| 28 | -CAS0 | -CAS0 | -CAS0 | -CAS0 | -Column Address Strobe 0 |
| 29 | -CAS1 | -CAS1 | -CAS1 | -CAS1 | -Column Address Strobe 1 |
| 30 | -RAS0 | -RAS0 | -RAS0 | -RAS0 | -Row Address Strobe 0 |
| 31 | -OE0 | -OE0 | -OE0 | -OE0 | -Output Enable |
| 32 | VSS | VSS | VSS | VSS | Ground |
| 33 | A0 | A0 | A0 | A0 | Address 0 |
| 34 | A2 | A2 | A2 | A2 | Address 2 |
| 35 | A4 | A4 | A4 | A4 | Address 4 |
| 36 | A6 | A6 | A6 | A6 | Address 6 |
| 37 | A8 | A8 | A8 | A8 | Address 8 |
| 38 | A10 | A10 | A10 | A10 | Address 10 |
| 39 | A12 | A12 | A12 | A12 | Address 12 |
| 40 | VCC | VCC | VCC | VCC | +5 Vdc or +3.3 Vdc |
| 41 | VCC | VCC | VCC | VCC | +5 Vdc or +3.3 Vdc |
| 42 | DU | DU | DU | DU | Don't Use |
| 43 | VSS | VSS | VSS | VSS | Ground |
| 44 | -OE2 | -OE2 | -OE2 | -OE2 | -Output Enable 2 |
| 45 | -RAS2 | -RAS2 | -RAS2 | -RAS2 | -Row Address Strobe 2 |
| 46 | -CAS2 | -CAS2 | -CAS2 | -CAS2 | -Column Address Strobe 2 |
| 47 | -CAS3 | -CAS3 | -CAS3 | -CAS3 | -Column Address Strobe 3 |
| 48 | -WE2 | -WE2 | -WE2 | -WE2 | Read/-Write Input 2 |
| 49 | VCC | VCC | VCC | VCC | +5 Vdc or +3.3 Vdc |
| 50 | n/c | n/c | n/c | CB10 | Parity/Check Bit Input/Output 10 |
| 51 | n/c | n/c | n/c | CB11 | Parity/Check Bit Input/Output 11 |
| 52 | n/c | CB2 | CB2 | CB2 | Parity/Check Bit Input/Output 2 |

| PIN | NON-PARITY | PARITY | 72 ECC | 80 ECC | DESCRIPTION |
|---|---|---|---|---|---|
| **TABLE 23-4** | PIN ASSIGNMENTS FOR A STANDARD 168-PIN UNBUFFERED DRAM DIMM *(CONTINUED)* | | | | |
| 53 | n/c | CB3 | CB3 | CB3 | Parity/Check Bit Input/Output 3 |
| 54 | VSS | VSS | VSS | VSS | Ground |
| 55 | DQ16 | DQ16 | DQ16 | DQ16 | Data 16 |
| 56 | DQ17 | DQ17 | DQ17 | DQ17 | Data 17 |
| 57 | DQ18 | DQ18 | DQ18 | DQ18 | Data 18 |
| 58 | DQ19 | DQ19 | DQ19 | DQ19 | Data 19 |
| 59 | VCC | VCC | VCC | VCC | +5 Vdc or +3.3 Vdc |
| 60 | DQ20 | DQ20 | DQ20 | DQ20 | Data 20 |
| 61 | n/c | n/c | n/c | n/c | Not connected |
| 62 | DU | DU | DU | DU | Don't Use |
| 63 | n/c | n/c | n/c | n/c | Not connected |
| 64 | VSS | VSS | VSS | VSS | Ground |
| 65 | DQ21 | DQ21 | DQ21 | DQ21 | Data 21 |
| 66 | DQ22 | DQ22 | DQ22 | DQ22 | Data 22 |
| 67 | DQ23 | DQ23 | DQ23 | DQ23 | Data 23 |
| 68 | VSS | VSS | VSS | VSS | Ground |
| 69 | DQ24 | DQ24 | DQ24 | DQ24 | Data 24 |
| 70 | DQ25 | DQ25 | DQ25 | DQ25 | Data 25 |
| 71 | DQ26 | DQ26 | DQ26 | DQ26 | Data 26 |
| 72 | DQ27 | DQ27 | DQ27 | DQ27 | Data 27 |
| 73 | VCC | VCC | VCC | VCC | +5 Vdc or +3.3 Vdc |
| 74 | DQ28 | DQ28 | DQ28 | DQ28 | Data 28 |
| 75 | DQ29 | DQ29 | DQ29 | DQ29 | Data 29 |
| 76 | DQ30 | DQ30 | DQ30 | DQ30 | Data 30 |
| 77 | DQ31 | DQ31 | DQ31 | DQ31 | Data 31 |
| 78 | VSS | VSS | VSS | VSS | Ground |
| 79 | n/c | n/c | n/c | n/c | Not connected |
| 80 | n/c | n/c | n/c | n/c | Not connected |
| 81 | n/c | n/c | n/c | n/c | Not connected |
| 82 | SDA | SDA | SDA | SDA | Serial Data |
| 83 | SCL | SCL | SCL | SCL | Serial Clock |
| 84 | VCC | VCC | VCC | VCC | +5 Vdc or +3.3 Vdc |
| 85 | VSS | VSS | VSS | VSS | Ground |
| 86 | DQ32 | DQ32 | DQ32 | DQ32 | Data 32 |
| 87 | DQ33 | DQ33 | DQ33 | DQ33 | Data 33 |
| 88 | DQ34 | DQ34 | DQ34 | DQ34 | Data 34 |
| 89 | DQ35 | DQ35 | DQ35 | DQ35 | Data 35 |
| 90 | VCC | VCC | VCC | VCC | +5 Vdc or +3.3 Vdc |
| 91 | DQ36 | DQ36 | DQ36 | DQ36 | Data 36 |

**TABLE 23-4    PIN ASSIGNMENTS FOR A STANDARD 168-PIN UNBUFFERED DRAM DIMM (CONTINUED)**

| PIN | NON-PARITY | PARITY | 72 ECC | 80 ECC | DESCRIPTION |
|-----|-----------|--------|--------|--------|-------------|
| 92 | DQ37 | DQ37 | DQ37 | DQ37 | Data 37 |
| 93 | DQ38 | DQ38 | DQ38 | DQ38 | Data 38 |
| 94 | DQ39 | DQ39 | DQ39 | DQ39 | Data 39 |
| 95 | DQ40 | DQ40 | DQ40 | DQ40 | Data 40 |
| 96 | VSS | VSS | VSS | VSS | Ground |
| 97 | DQ41 | DQ41 | DQ41 | DQ41 | Data 41 |
| 98 | DQ42 | DQ42 | DQ42 | DQ42 | Data 42 |
| 99 | DQ43 | DQ43 | DQ43 | DQ43 | Data 43 |
| 100 | DQ44 | DQ44 | DQ44 | DQ44 | Data 44 |
| 101 | DQ45 | DQ45 | DQ45 | DQ45 | Data 45 |
| 102 | VCC | VCC | VCC | VCC | +5 Vdc or +3.3 Vdc |
| 103 | DQ46 | DQ46 | DQ46 | DQ46 | Data 46 |
| 104 | DQ47 | DQ47 | DQ47 | DQ47 | Data 47 |
| 105 | n/c | CB4 | CB4 | CB4 | Parity/Check Bit Input/Output 4 |
| 106 | n/c | CB5 | CB5 | CB5 | Parity/Check Bit Input/Output 5 |
| 107 | VSS | VSS | VSS | VSS | Ground |
| 108 | n/c | n/c | n/c | CB12 | Parity/Check Bit Input/Output 12 |
| 109 | n/c | n/c | n/c | CB13 | Parity/Check Bit Input/Output 13 |
| 110 | VCC | VCC | VCC | VCC | +5 Vdc or +3.3 Vdc |
| 111 | DU | DU | DU | DU | Don't Use |
| 112 | -CAS4 | -CAS4 | -CAS4 | -CAS4 | -Column Address Strobe 4 |
| 113 | -CAS5 | -CAS5 | -CAS5 | -CAS5 | -Column Address Strobe 5 |
| 114 | -RAS1 | -RAS1 | -RAS1 | -RAS1 | -Row Address Strobe 1 |
| 115 | DU | DU | DU | DU | Don't Use |
| 116 | VSS | VSS | VSS | VSS | Ground |
| 117 | A1 | A1 | A1 | A1 | Address 1 |
| 118 | A3 | A3 | A3 | A3 | Address 3 |
| 119 | A5 | A5 | A5 | A5 | Address 5 |
| 120 | A7 | A7 | A7 | A7 | Address 7 |
| 121 | A9 | A9 | A9 | A9 | Address 9 |
| 122 | A11 | A11 | A11 | A11 | Address 11 |
| 123 | A13 | A13 | A13 | A13 | Address 13 |
| 124 | VCC | VCC | VCC | VCC | +5 Vdc or +3.3 Vdc |
| 125 | DU | DU | DU | DU | Don't Use |
| 126 | DU | DU | DU | DU | Don't Use |

**TABLE 23-4     PIN ASSIGNMENTS FOR A STANDARD 168-PIN UNBUFFERED DRAM DIMM *(CONTINUED)***

| PIN | NON-PARITY | PARITY | 72 ECC | 80 ECC | DESCRIPTION |
| --- | --- | --- | --- | --- | --- |
| 127 | VSS | VSS | VSS | VSS | Ground |
| 128 | DU | DU | DU | DU | Don't Use |
| 129 | -RAS3 | -RAS3 | -RAS3 | -RAS3 | -Column Address Strobe 3 |
| 130 | -CAS6 | -CAS6 | -CAS6 | -CAS6 | -Column Address Strobe 6 |
| 131 | -CAS7 | -CAS7 | -CAS7 | -CAS7 | -Column Address Strobe 7 |
| 132 | DU | DU | DU | DU | Don't Use |
| 133 | VCC | VCC | VCC | VCC | +5 Vdc or +3.3 Vdc |
| 134 | n/c | n/c | n/c | CB14 | Parity/Check Bit Input/Output 14 |
| 135 | n/c | n/c | n/c | CB15 | Parity/Check Bit Input/Output 15 |
| 136 | n/c | CB6 | CB6 | CB6 | Parity/Check Bit Input/Output 6 |
| 137 | n/c | CB7 | CB7 | CB7 | Parity/Check Bit Input/Output 7 |
| 138 | VSS | VSS | VSS | VSS | Ground |
| 139 | DQ48 | DQ48 | DQ48 | DQ48 | Data 48 |
| 140 | DQ49 | DQ49 | DQ49 | DQ49 | Data 49 |
| 141 | DQ50 | DQ50 | DQ50 | DQ50 | Data 50 |
| 142 | DQ51 | DQ51 | DQ51 | DQ51 | Data 51 |
| 143 | VCC | VCC | VCC | VCC | +5 Vdc or +3.3 Vdc |
| 144 | DQ52 | DQ52 | DQ52 | DQ52 | Data 52 |
| 145 | n/c | n/c | n/c | n/c | Not connected |
| 146 | DU | DU | DU | DU | Don't Use |
| 147 | n/c | n/c | n/c | n/c | Not connected |
| 148 | VSS | VSS | VSS | VSS | Ground |
| 149 | DQ53 | DQ53 | DQ53 | DQ53 | Data 53 |
| 150 | DQ54 | DQ54 | DQ54 | DQ54 | Data 54 |
| 151 | DQ55 | DQ55 | DQ55 | DQ55 | Data 55 |
| 152 | VSS | VSS | VSS | VSS | Ground |
| 153 | DQ56 | DQ56 | DQ56 | DQ56 | Data 56 |
| 154 | DQ57 | DQ57 | DQ57 | DQ57 | Data 57 |
| 155 | DQ58 | DQ58 | DQ58 | DQ58 | Data 58 |
| 156 | DQ59 | DQ59 | DQ59 | DQ59 | Data 59 |
| 157 | VCC | VCC | VCC | VCC | +5 Vdc or +3.3 Vdc |
| 158 | DQ60 | DQ60 | DQ60 | DQ60 | Data 60 |
| 159 | DQ61 | DQ61 | DQ61 | DQ61 | Data 61 |
| 160 | DQ62 | DQ62 | DQ62 | DQ62 | Data 62 |

**TABLE 23-4     PIN ASSIGNMENTS FOR A STANDARD 168-PIN UNBUFFERED DRAM DIMM** *(CONTINUED)*

| PIN | NON-PARITY | PARITY | 72 ECC | 80 ECC | DESCRIPTION |
|-----|-----------|--------|--------|--------|-------------|
| 161 | DQ63 | DQ63 | DQ63 | DQ63 | Data 63 |
| 162 | VSS | VSS | VSS | VSS | Ground |
| 163 | CK3 | CK3 | CK3 | CK3 | Clock |
| 164 | n/c | n/c | n/c | n/c | Not connected |
| 165 | SA0 | SA0 | SA0 | SA0 | Serial Address 0 |
| 166 | SA1 | SA1 | SA1 | SA1 | Serial Address 1 |
| 167 | SA2 | SA2 | SA2 | SA2 | Serial Address 2 |
| 168 | VCC | VCC | VCC | VCC | +5 Vdc or +3.3 Vdc |

**TABLE 23-5     PIN ASSIGNMENTS FOR A 168-PIN UNBUFFERED SDRAM DIMM**

| PIN | NON-PARITY | 72 ECC | 80 ECC | DESCRIPTION |
|-----|-----------|--------|--------|-------------|
| 1 | VSS | VSS | VSS | Ground |
| 2 | DQ0 | DQ0 | DQ0 | Data 0 |
| 3 | DQ1 | DQ1 | DQ1 | Data 1 |
| 4 | DQ2 | DQ2 | DQ2 | Data 2 |
| 5 | DQ3 | DQ3 | DQ3 | Data 3 |
| 6 | VDD | VDD | VDD | +5 Vdc or +3.3 Vdc |
| 7 | DQ4 | DQ4 | DQ4 | Data 4 |
| 8 | DQ5 | DQ5 | DQ5 | Data 5 |
| 9 | DQ6 | DQ6 | DQ6 | Data 6 |
| 10 | DQ7 | DQ7 | DQ7 | Data 7 |
| 11 | DQ8 | DQ8 | DQ8 | Data 8 |
| 12 | VSS | VSS | VSS | Ground |
| 13 | DQ9 | DQ9 | DQ9 | Data 9 |
| 14 | DQ10 | DQ10 | DQ10 | Data 10 |
| 15 | DQ11 | DQ11 | DQ11 | Data 11 |
| 16 | DQ12 | DQ12 | DQ12 | Data 12 |
| 17 | DQ13 | DQ13 | DQ13 | Data 13 |
| 18 | VDD | VDD | VDD | +5 Vdc or +3.3 Vdc |
| 19 | DQ14 | DQ14 | DQ14 | Data 14 |
| 20 | DQ15 | DQ15 | DQ15 | Data 15 |
| 21 | n/c | CB0 | CB0 | Parity/Check Bit Input/Output 0 |
| 22 | n/c | CB1 | CB1 | Parity/Check Bit Input/Output 1 |
| 23 | VSS | VSS | VSS | Ground |
| 24 | n/c | n/c | CB8 | Parity/Check Bit Input/Output 8 |
| 25 | n/c | n/c | CB9 | Parity/Check Bit Input/Output 9 |
| 26 | VDD | VDD | VDD | +5 Vdc or +3.3 Vdc |
| 27 | -WE | -WE | -WE | Read/-Write |

**TABLE 23-5** PIN ASSIGNMENTS FOR A 168-PIN UNBUFFERED SDRAM DIMM *(CONTINUED)*

| PIN | NON-PARITY | 72 ECC | 80 ECC | DESCRIPTION |
|-----|-----------|--------|--------|-------------|
| 28 | DQMB0 | DQMB0 | DQMB0 | Byte Mask signal 0 |
| 29 | DQMB1 | DQMB1 | DQMB1 | Byte Mask signal 1 |
| 30 | -S0 | -S0 | -S0 | -Chip Select 0 |
| 31 | DU | DU | DU | Don't Use |
| 32 | VSS | VSS | VSS | Ground |
| 33 | A0 | A0 | A0 | Address 0 |
| 34 | A2 | A2 | A2 | Address 2 |
| 35 | A4 | A4 | A4 | Address 4 |
| 36 | A6 | A6 | A6 | Address 6 |
| 37 | A8 | A8 | A8 | Address 8 |
| 38 | A10/AP | A10/AP | A10/AP | Address 10 |
| 39 | BA1 | BA1 | BA1 | Bank Address 1 |
| 40 | VDD | VDD | VDD | +5 Vdc or +3.3 Vdc |
| 41 | VDD | VDD | VDD | +5 Vdc or +3.3 Vdc |
| 42 | CK0 | CK0 | CK0 | Clock signal 0 |
| 43 | VSS | VSS | VSS | Ground |
| 44 | DU | DU | DU | Don't Use |
| 45 | -S2 | -S2 | -S2 | -Chip Select 2 |
| 46 | DQMB2 | DQMB2 | DQMB2 | Byte Mask signal 2 |
| 47 | DQMB3 | DQMB3 | DQMB3 | Byte Mask signal 3 |
| 48 | DU | DU | DU | Don't Use |
| 49 | VDD | VDD | VDD | +5 Vdc or +3.3 Vdc |
| 50 | n/c | n/c | CB10 | Parity/Check Bit Input/Output 10 |
| 51 | n/c | n/c | CB11 | Parity/Check Bit Input/Output 11 |
| 52 | n/c | CB2 | CB2 | Parity/Check Bit Input/Output 2 |
| 53 | n/c | CB3 | CB3 | Parity/Check Bit Input/Output 3 |
| 54 | VSS | VSS | VSS | Ground |
| 55 | DQ16 | DQ16 | DQ16 | Data 16 |
| 56 | DQ17 | DQ17 | DQ17 | Data 17 |
| 57 | DQ18 | DQ18 | DQ18 | Data 18 |
| 58 | DQ19 | DQ19 | DQ19 | Data 19 |
| 59 | VDD | VDD | VDD | +5 Vdc or +3.3 Vdc |
| 60 | DQ20 | DQ20 | DQ20 | Data 20 |
| 61 | n/c | n/c | n/c | Not connected |
| 62 | Vref,NC | Vref,NC | Vref,NC | Reference Voltage |
| 63 | CKE1 | CKE1 | CKE1 | Clock Enable Signal 1 |
| 64 | VSS | VSS | VSS | Ground |
| 65 | DQ21 | DQ21 | DQ21 | Data 21 |
| 66 | DQ22 | DQ22 | DQ22 | Data 22 |
| 67 | DQ23 | DQ23 | DQ23 | Data 23 |

**TABLE 23-5** PIN ASSIGNMENTS FOR A 168-PIN UNBUFFERED SDRAM DIMM *(CONTINUED)*

| PIN | NON-PARITY | 72 ECC | 80 ECC | DESCRIPTION |
|-----|-----------|--------|--------|-------------|
| 68 | VSS | VSS | VSS | Ground |
| 69 | DQ24 | DQ24 | DQ24 | Data 24 |
| 70 | DQ25 | DQ25 | DQ25 | Data 25 |
| 71 | DQ26 | DQ26 | DQ26 | Data 26 |
| 72 | DQ27 | DQ27 | DQ27 | Data 27 |
| 73 | VDD | VDD | VDD | +5 Vdc or +3.3 Vdc |
| 74 | DQ28 | DQ28 | DQ28 | Data 28 |
| 75 | DQ29 | DQ29 | DQ29 | Data 29 |
| 76 | DQ30 | DQ30 | DQ30 | Data 30 |
| 77 | DQ31 | DQ31 | DQ31 | Data 31 |
| 78 | VSS | VSS | VSS | Ground |
| 79 | CK2 | CK2 | CK2 | Clock signal 2 |
| 80 | n/c | n/c | n/c | Not connected |
| 81 | n/c | n/c | n/c | Not connected |
| 82 | DAS | DAS | DAS | Serial Data |
| 83 | CLS | CLS | CLS | Serial Clock |
| 84 | VDD | VDD | VDD | +5 Vdc or +3.3 Vdc |
| 85 | VSS | VSS | VSS | Ground |
| 86 | DQ32 | DQ32 | DQ32 | Data 32 |
| 87 | DQ33 | DQ33 | DQ33 | Data 33 |
| 88 | DQ34 | DQ34 | DQ34 | Data 34 |
| 89 | DQ35 | DQ35 | DQ35 | Data 35 |
| 90 | VDD | VDD | VDD | +5 Vdc or +3.3 Vdc |
| 91 | DQ36 | DQ36 | DQ36 | Data 36 |
| 92 | DQ37 | DQ37 | DQ37 | Data 37 |
| 93 | DQ38 | DQ38 | DQ38 | Data 38 |
| 94 | DQ39 | DQ39 | DQ39 | Data 39 |
| 95 | DQ40 | DQ40 | DQ40 | Data 40 |
| 96 | VSS | VSS | VSS | Ground |
| 97 | DQ41 | DQ41 | DQ41 | Data 41 |
| 98 | DQ42 | DQ42 | DQ42 | Data 42 |
| 99 | DQ43 | DQ43 | DQ43 | Data 43 |
| 100 | DQ44 | DQ44 | DQ44 | Data 44 |
| 101 | DQ45 | DQ45 | DQ45 | Data 45 |
| 102 | VDD | VDD | VDD | +5 Vdc or +3.3 Vdc |
| 103 | DQ46 | DQ46 | DQ46 | Data 46 |
| 104 | DQ47 | DQ47 | DQ47 | Data 47 |
| 105 | n/c | CB4 | CB4 | Parity/Check Bit Input/Output 4 |
| 106 | n/c | CB5 | CB5 | Parity/Check Bit Input/Output 5 |
| 107 | VSS | VSS | VSS | Ground |

**TABLE 23-5    PIN ASSIGNMENTS FOR A 168-PIN UNBUFFERED SDRAM DIMM** *(CONTINUED)*

| PIN | NON-PARITY | 72 ECC | 80 ECC | DESCRIPTION |
|-----|-----------|--------|--------|-------------|
| 108 | n/c | n/c | CB12 | Parity/Check Bit Input/Output 12 |
| 109 | n/c | n/c | CB13 | Parity/Check Bit Input/Output 13 |
| 110 | VDD | VDD | VDD | +5 Vdc or +3.3 Vdc |
| 111 | -CAS | -CAS | -CAS | -Column Address Strobe |
| 112 | DQMB4 | DQMB4 | DQMB4 | Byte Mask signal 4 |
| 113 | DQMB5 | DQMB5 | DQMB5 | Byte Mask signal 5 |
| 114 | -S1 | -S1 | -S1 | -Chip Select 1 |
| 115 | -RAS | -RAS | -RAS | -Row Address Strobe |
| 116 | VSS | VSS | VSS | Ground |
| 117 | A1 | A1 | A1 | Address 1 |
| 118 | A3 | A3 | A3 | Address 3 |
| 119 | A5 | A5 | A5 | Address 5 |
| 120 | A7 | A7 | A7 | Address 7 |
| 121 | A9 | A9 | A9 | Address 9 |
| 122 | BA0 | BA0 | BA0 | Bank Address 0 |
| 123 | A11 | A11 | A11 | Address 11 |
| 124 | VDD | VDD | VDD | +5 Vdc or +3.3 Vdc |
| 125 | CK1 | CK1 | CK1 | Clock signal 1 |
| 126 | A12 | A12 | A12 | Address 12 |
| 127 | VSS | VSS | VSS | Ground |
| 128 | CKE0 | CKE0 | CKE0 | Clock Enable Signal 0 |
| 129 | -S3 | -S3 | -S3 | -Chip Select 3 |
| 130 | DQMB6 | DQMB6 | DQMB6 | Byte Mask signal 6 |
| 131 | DQMB7 | DQMB7 | DQMB7 | Byte Mask signal 7 |
| 132 | A13 | A13 | A13 | Address 13 |
| 133 | VDD | VDD | VDD | +5 Vdc or +3.3 Vdc |
| 134 | n/c | n/c | CB14 | Parity/Check Bit Input/Output 14 |
| 135 | n/c | n/c | CB15 | Parity/Check Bit Input/Output 15 |
| 136 | n/c | CB6 | CB6 | Parity/Check Bit Input/Output 6 |
| 137 | n/c | CB7 | CB7 | Parity/Check Bit Input/Output 7 |
| 138 | VSS | VSS | VSS | Ground |
| 139 | DQ48 | DQ48 | DQ48 | Data 48 |
| 140 | DQ49 | DQ49 | DQ49 | Data 49 |
| 141 | DQ50 | DQ50 | DQ50 | Data 50 |
| 142 | DQ51 | DQ51 | DQ51 | Data 51 |
| 143 | VDD | VDD | VDD | +5 Vdc or +3.3 Vdc |
| 144 | DQ52 | DQ52 | DQ52 | Data 52 |
| 145 | n/c | n/c | n/c | Not connected |
| 146 | Vref,NC | Vref,NC | Vref,NC | Reference Voltage |
| 147 | n/c | n/c | n/c | Not connected |

**TABLE 23-5**    PIN ASSIGNMENTS FOR A 168-PIN UNBUFFERED SDRAM DIMM *(CONTINUED)*

| PIN | NON-PARITY | 72 ECC | 80 ECC | DESCRIPTION |
|-----|-----------|--------|--------|-------------|
| 148 | VSS | VSS | VSS | Ground |
| 149 | DQ53 | DQ53 | DQ53 | Data 53 |
| 150 | DQ54 | DQ54 | DQ54 | Data 54 |
| 151 | DQ55 | DQ55 | DQ55 | Data 55 |
| 152 | VSS | VSS | VSS | Ground |
| 153 | DQ56 | DQ56 | DQ56 | Data 56 |
| 154 | DQ57 | DQ57 | DQ57 | Data 57 |
| 155 | DQ58 | DQ58 | DQ58 | Data 58 |
| 156 | DQ59 | DQ59 | DQ59 | Data 59 |
| 157 | VDD | VDD | VDD | +5 Vdc or +3.3 Vdc |
| 158 | DQ60 | DQ60 | DQ60 | Data 60 |
| 159 | DQ61 | DQ61 | DQ61 | Data 61 |
| 160 | DQ62 | DQ62 | DQ62 | Data 62 |
| 161 | DQ63 | DQ63 | DQ63 | Data 63 |
| 162 | VSS | VSS | VSS | Ground |
| 163 | CK3 | CK3 | CK3 | Clock signal 3 |
| 164 | n/c | n/c | n/c | Not connected |
| 165 | SA0 | SA0 | SA0 | Serial address 0 |
| 166 | SA1 | SA1 | SA1 | Serial address 1 |
| 167 | SA2 | SA2 | SA2 | Serial address 2 |
| 168 | VDD | VDD | VDD | +5 Vdc or +3.3 Vdc |

Today, DIMMs are the standard module type and are used to support high-performance SDRAM and DDR SDRAM memory.

DIMMs are also placed into special slots on the motherboard that will hold the modules tightly in place. Unlike SIMMs, a DIMM is inserted vertically and locked into place in the vertical position. Special plastic clips on either end of the socket snap in place when the DIMM is inserted correctly. The DIMM is also keyed with a series of notches (depending on type and operating voltage), so it cannot be installed backwards. Although DIMMs have largely standardized the installation of RAM in a computer, there are several other factors to consider such as voltage, buffering, and module technology.

■ **Voltage** The voltage levels used on memory modules keep decreasing in order to increase performance and manage heat. Classical computer systems used to operate at a standard of +5 volts, but most modern PCs use +3.3 volt and +2.5 volt logic circuitry. DIMMs are available in +5, +3.3, and +2.5 volt models to serve a variety of PC vintages.

■ **Registers and Buffers**   Registers and buffers improve memory operation by "re-driving" signals in the memory chips. They can be external to the memory module, or they can be located on the module itself. Having registers and buffers placed directly on the memory module enables a system to support a greater quantity of modules. *Buffering* is normally used with older FPM and EDO RAM where buffers simply re-drive the signals. Buffering allows more DIMMs to be installed on the motherboard. Most DIMMs are unbuffered because a tremendous amount of RAM can still be installed using unbuffered RAM. When installing or upgrading memory, unbuffered and buffered (or registered) modules cannot be mixed. *Registering* is used with more recent SDRAM. Registering is similar to buffering, but the data is clocked in and out of the register by the system clock. Registered modules are slightly slower than nonregistered modules, because the registering process takes one clock cycle. You will normally find registered DIMMs in network servers or other high-end PCs that demand a lot of RAM.

In actual practice, the term buffer is used with all types of RAM, though this is technically incorrect. For example, you'll see "unbuffered SDRAM," even though it should technically be "unregistered SDRAM."

■ **Composite vs. Noncomposite**   *Composite* and *noncomposite* are terms first used by Apple Computer to explain the difference between modules of the same capacity that use a different number of chips. For example, you can have a memory module with 8 of the new high-density chips, or 32 of the old density chips (even though both modules may offer the same capacity). The module using the latest technology and fewer chips is referred to as *noncomposite*, and the module using earlier technology and additional chips is called *composite*. Most PC users are better served to buy the more recent noncomposite modules.

■ **Small-Outline (SO) DIMMs/RIMMs**   Given the large number of laptop and notebook computers in use today, you may encounter small-outline (or SO) DIMMs and RIMMs. Simply, SO DIMMs and RIMMs are much smaller physically than their full-sized DIMM/RIMM counterparts. For example, a typical 168-pin DIMM is about 5.25" long, but an SO DIMM is just 2.66" (for a 144-pin SO DIMM). RIMMs and SO RIMMs use similar dimensions. The space limitations presented with small-outline devices often limit the module's capacity, but SO devices can still provide significant amounts of memory for mobile PCs.

## RIMM

The *Rambus In-line Memory Module* (RIMM) looks almost identical to DIMMs, but is slightly bigger (with several keys between the metal contact fingers). Also called the *Direct Rambus Memory Module,* these advanced memory devices transfer data in 16-bit chunks along dedicated memory channels. Early RIMM implementations used 168 pins, but the 600 MHz (PC600), 711 MHz, and 800 MHz (PC800) RIMMs available today use 184 pins. Table 23-6 lists the pin assignments for a current +2.5 volt 512MB RIMM. Rambus modules also include a long heat sink (or *heat spreader*) used to manage the elevated operating temperatures encountered with RDRAM chips (see Figure 23-5). You'll see more about Rambus DRAM later in the chapter.

**TABLE 23-6     PIN ASSIGNMENTS FOR A 184-PIN RAMBUS RIMM**

| PIN | NAME | PIN | NAME | PIN | NAME | PIN | NAME |
|-----|------|-----|------|-----|------|-----|------|
| A1 | Ground | B1 | Ground | A47 | n/c | B47 | n/c |
| A2 | LDQA8 | B2 | LDQA7 | A48 | n/c | B48 | n/c |
| A3 | Ground | B3 | Ground | A49 | n/c | B49 | n/c |
| A4 | LDQA6 | B4 | LDQA5 | A50 | n/c | B50 | n/c |
| A5 | Ground | B5 | Ground | A51 | Vref | B51 | Vref |
| A6 | LDQA4 | B6 | LDQA3 | A52 | Ground | B52 | Ground |
| A7 | Ground | B7 | Ground | A53 | SCL | B53 | SA0 |
| A8 | LDQA2 | B8 | LDQA1 | A54 | Vdd | B54 | Vdd |
| A9 | Ground | B9 | Ground | A55 | SDA | B55 | SA1 |
| A10 | LDQA0 | B10 | LCFM | A56 | SVdd | B56 | SVdd |
| A11 | Ground | B11 | Ground | A57 | SWP | B57 | SA2 |
| A12 | LCTMN | B12 | LCFMN | A58 | Vdd | B58 | Vdd |
| A13 | Ground | B13 | Ground | A59 | RSCK | B59 | RCMD |
| A14 | LCTM | B14 | n/c | A60 | Ground | B60 | Ground |
| A15 | Ground | B15 | Ground | A61 | RDQB7 | B61 | RDQB8 |
| A16 | n/c | B16 | LROW2 | A62 | Ground | B62 | Ground |
| A17 | Ground | B17 | Ground | A63 | RDQB5 | B63 | RDQB8 |
| A18 | LROW1 | B18 | LROW0 | A64 | Ground | B64 | Ground |
| A19 | Ground | B19 | Ground | A65 | RDQB3 | B65 | RDQB4 |
| A20 | LCOL4 | B20 | LCOL3 | A66 | Ground | B66 | Ground |
| A21 | Ground | B21 | Ground | A67 | RDQB1 | B67 | RDQB2 |
| A22 | LCOL2 | B22 | LCOL1 | A68 | Ground | B68 | Ground |
| A23 | Ground | B23 | Ground | A69 | RCOL0 | B69 | RDQB0 |
| A24 | LCOL0 | B24 | LDQB0 | A70 | Ground | B70 | Ground |
| A25 | Ground | B25 | Ground | A71 | RCOL2 | B71 | RCOL1 |
| A26 | LDQB1 | B26 | LDQB2 | A72 | Ground | B72 | Ground |
| A27 | Ground | B27 | Ground | A73 | RCOL4 | B73 | RCOL3 |
| A28 | LDQB3 | B28 | LDQB4 | A74 | Ground | B74 | Ground |
| A29 | Ground | B29 | Ground | A75 | RROW1 | B75 | RROW0 |
| A30 | LDQB5 | B30 | LDQB6 | A76 | Ground | B76 | Ground |
| A31 | Ground | B31 | Ground | A77 | n/c | B77 | RROW2 |
| A32 | LDQB7 | B32 | LDQB8 | A78 | Ground | B78 | Ground |
| A33 | Ground | B33 | Ground | A79 | RCTM | B79 | n/c |
| A34 | LSCK | B34 | LCMD | A80 | Ground | B80 | Ground |
| A35 | Vcmos | B35 | Vcmos | A81 | RCTMN | B81 | RCFMN |
| A36 | SOUT | B36 | SIN | A82 | Ground | B82 | Ground |
| A37 | Vcmos | B37 | Vcmos | A83 | RDQA0 | B83 | RCFM |
| A38 | n/c | B38 | n/c | A84 | Ground | B84 | Ground |
| A39 | Ground | B39 | Ground | A85 | RDQA2 | B85 | RDQA1 |
| A40 | n/c | B40 | n/c | A86 | Ground | B86 | Ground |
| A41 | Vdd | B41 | Vdd | A87 | RDQA4 | B87 | RDQA3 |
| A42 | Vdd | B42 | Vdd | A88 | Ground | B88 | Ground |
| A43 | n/c | B43 | n/c | A89 | RDQA6 | B89 | RDQA5 |
| A44 | n/c | B44 | n/c | A90 | Ground | B90 | Ground |
| A45 | n/c | B45 | n/c | A91 | RDQA8 | B91 | RDQA7 |
| A46 | n/c | B46 | n/c | A92 | Ground | B92 | Ground |

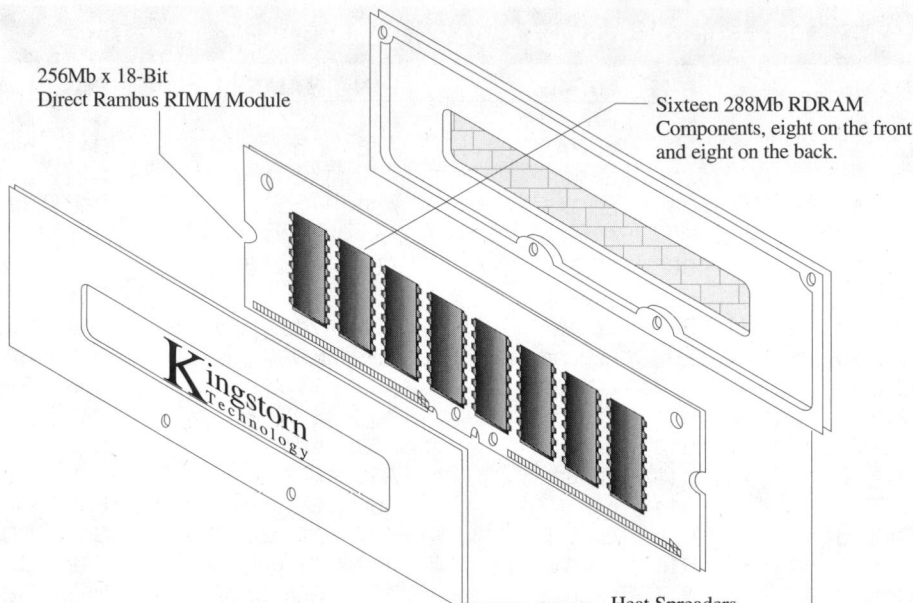

256Mb x 18-Bit
Direct Rambus RIMM Module

Sixteen 288Mb RDRAM
Components, eight on the front
and eight on the back.

Heat Spreaders

**FIGURE  23-5**    RIMMs employ a heat spreader to manage heat from the individual Rambus chips
(Courtesy of Kingston Technologies)

# Logical Memory Organization

The way a computer's memory is organized and used represents the result of evolution over several computer generations. Memory access and timing support is taken care of by your system's microprocessor and chipset. So as CPUs and chipsets improve, memory-handling capabilities have improved as well. Today's microprocessors (such as the Intel Pentium II, Pentium III, and Pentium 4) are capable of addressing more than 4GB of system memory—well beyond the levels of contemporary software applications. Unfortunately, the early PCs were not nearly so powerful. Older PCs could only address 1MB of memory due to limitations of the early 8088 microprocessor.

Since backward compatibility is so important to computer users, the drawbacks and limitations of older systems had to be carried *forward* into newer computers instead of being eliminated. Newer systems overcome their inherent limitations by using memory in different ways, along with the hardware and software needed to access the memory. This part of the chapter describes the typical classifications of computer memory use: conventional, extended, and expanded memory. This chapter also describes high memory concepts. Note that these memory types have nothing to do with the actual memory chips in your system, but the way in which the operating system and application software *use* the physical memory.

Today, the discussion of logical memory is largely academic. Windows 9x/Me/XP easily handles all of the memory space in a PC for you. However, it is important to realize that there is a distinction in the way memory is used.

# CONVENTIONAL MEMORY

*Conventional memory* is the traditional 640KB assigned to the DOS Memory Area (10000h to 9FFFFh, as shown in Figure 23-6). The original PCs used microprocessors that could only address 1MB of memory (called *real-mode memory* or *base memory*). Out of that 1MB, portions of the memory must be set aside for basic system functions. BIOS code, video memory, interrupt vectors, and BIOS data are only some of the areas that required reserved memory. The remaining 640KB became available to load and run your application, which can be any combination of executable code and data. The original PC only provided 512KB for the DOS program area, but computer designers quickly learned that another 128KB could be added to the DOS area while retaining enough memory for overhead functions; so 512KB became 640KB.

Every IBM-compatible PC still provides a 640KB "base memory" range, and most DOS application programs continue to fit within that limit to ensure backward compatibility with older systems. However, the drawbacks to the 8088 CPU were soon apparent. More memory had to be added to the computer for its evolution to continue. Yet, memory had to be added in a way that did not interfere with the conventional memory area.

# EXTENDED MEMORY (XMS)

The 80286 processor introduced in IBM's PC/AT was envisioned to overcome the 640KB barrier by incorporating a *protected mode* of addressing. The 80286 can address up to 16MB of memory in protected mode, while its successors (the 80386 and later) can handle 4GB of protected-mode memory. Today, virtually all computer systems provide hundreds of megabytes of *extended memory* (called *XMS*). Besides an advanced microprocessor, another key element for extended memory is software. Memory management software must be loaded in advance for the computer to access its extended memory. Microsoft's later

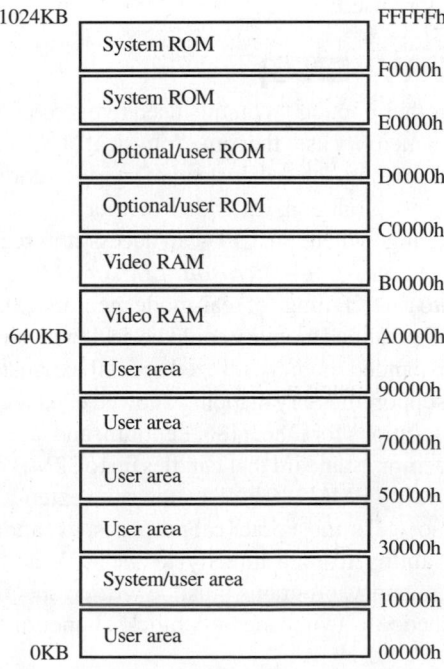

**FIGURE   23-6**    Conventional and upper memory in a typical PC

DOS versions (up to MS-DOS 6.22) provide an extended memory manager utility (HIMEM.SYS), but there are other off-the-shelf utilities as well—Windows 98/Me/XP/NT/2000 supplies its own memory manager tools, so you don't even know they're in place.

Unfortunately, DOS itself cannot make use of extended memory. You may fill the extended memory area with data, but the executable code that constitutes the program remains limited to the original 640KB of base memory. Some programs written with DOS extenders can overcome the 640KB limit, but the additional code needed for such "DOS extenders" can make such programs a bit clunky. A *DOS extender* is basically a software module containing its own memory management code that is compiled into the final application program.

The DOS extender loads a program in real-mode memory. After the program is loaded, it switches program control to the protected-mode memory. When the program in protected mode needs to execute a DOS (real-mode) function, the DOS extender converts protected-mode addresses into real-mode addresses, copies any necessary program data from protected- to real-mode locations, switches the CPU to real-mode addressing, and carries out the function. The DOS extender then copies any results (if necessary) back to protected-mode addresses, switches the system to protected-mode once again, and the program continues to run. This back-and-forth conversion overhead results in less than optimum performance compared to strictly real-mode programs, or true "protected-mode" programs.

With multiple megabytes of extended memory typically available, it is possible (but unlikely) that any one program will utilize all of the extended memory. Multiple programs that use extended memory must *not* attempt to utilize the same memory locations. If conflicts occur, a catastrophic system crash is almost inevitable. To prevent conflicts in extended memory, memory manager software can make use of three major industry standards: the *Extended Memory Specification* (XMS), the *Virtual Control Program Interface* (VCPI), or the *DOS Protected-Mode Interface* (DPMI). This chapter will not detail these standards, but you should know where they're used.

## EXPANDED MEMORY (EMS)

*Expanded memory* (EMS) is another popular technique used to overcome the traditional 640KB limit of real-mode addressing. Expanded memory uses the same "physical" RAM chips, but differs from extended memory in the way that physical memory is used. Instead of trying to address physical memory locations outside of the conventional memory range as extended memory does, expanded memory blocks are switched into the base memory range where the CPU can access it in real mode. The original expanded memory specification (called the *Lotus-Intel-Microsoft: LIM*, or *EMS* specification) used 16KB blocks of memory that were mapped into a 64KB range of real-mode memory existing just above the video memory range. Thus, four "blocks" of expanded memory could be dealt with simultaneously in the real mode.

Early implementations of expanded memory utilized special expansion boards that switched blocks of memory, but later CPUs that support memory mapping allowed expanded memory managers (EMMs or LIMs) to supply software-only solutions for i386, i486, Pentium, and later machines. EMS/LIM 4.0 is the latest version of the expanded memory standard that handles up to 32MB of memory. An expanded memory manager (such as the DOS utility EMM386.EXE) allows the extended memory sitting in your computer to emulate expanded memory. For most practical purposes, expanded memory is more useful than extended memory because its ability to map directly to the real mode allows support for program multitasking. To use expanded memory, programs must be written specifically to take advantage of the function calls and subroutines needed to switch memory blocks. Functions are completely specified in the LIM/EMS 4.0 standard.

# UPPER MEMORY AREA (UMA)

The upper 384KB of real-mode memory is not available to DOS because it is dedicated to handling memory requirements of the physical computer system. This is called the *High DOS Memory Range* or *upper memory area* (UMA). However, even the most advanced PCs do not use the *entire* 384KB, so there is often a substantial amount of unused memory existing in your system's real-mode range. Late model CPUs like the i386 and i486 can remap extended memory into the range unused by your system. Since this "found" memory space is not contiguous with your 640KB DOS space, DOS application programs cannot use the space, but small independent drivers and TSRs *can* be loaded and run from this UMA. The advantage of using this high DOS memory is that more of the 640KB DOS range remains available for your application program. Memory management programs (such as the utilities found with DOS 5.0 and higher) are needed to locate and remap these memory "blocks."

# HIGH MEMORY

There is a peculiar anomaly that occurs with CPUs supporting extended memory—they can access one *segment* (about 64KB) of extended memory beyond the real-mode area. This capability arises because of the address line layout on late model CPUs. As a result, the real-mode operation can access roughly 64KB *above* the 1MB limit. Like high DOS memory, this "found" 64KB is not contiguous with the normal 640KB DOS memory range, so DOS cannot use this high memory to load a DOS application, but device drivers and TSRs can be placed in high memory. DOS 5.0 and later is intentionally designed so that its 40–50KB of code can be easily moved into this high memory area. With DOS loaded into high memory, an extra 40–50KB or so will be available within the 640KB DOS range.

# Memory Considerations

Memory has become far more important than just a place to store bits for the microprocessor. It has proliferated and specialized to the point where it is difficult to keep track of all the memory options and architectures that are available. This part of the chapter reviews established memory types, then explains some of the current memory architectures and the major issues surrounding them.

## MEMORY SPEED AND WAIT STATES

The PC industry is constantly struggling with the balance between price and performance. Higher prices usually bring higher performance, but low cost makes the PC appealing to more people. In terms of memory, cost cutting typically involves using cheaper (slower) memory devices. Unfortunately, when slower memory is used, the CPU must be made to wait until memory can catch up.

### Access Time and Cycle Time

All memory is rated in terms of speed—specifically access time. *Access time* is the delay between the time that data in memory is successfully addressed, to the point at which the data has been successfully delivered to the data bus. For PC memory, access time is measured in nanoseconds (ns), and traditional memory offers access times of 50–60ns, whereas 70ns memory is extremely common in older i486 systems. SDRAM is an exception to this rule, and is typically rated in terms of cycle time rather than access time. *Cycle time* is the minimum amount of time needed between accesses. Cycle time for SDRAM averages around 12ns, with 10ns, 8ns (and faster) SDRAM devices available. For example, the Kingston

KVR266X72RC25 512MB 266 MHz DDR SDRAM DIMM is rated for a minimum cycle time of 7.5ns and a maximum cycle time of 12ns (www.valueram.com/datasheets/kvr266x72rc25_512.pdf).

Today's high-performance memory is rated in terms of system speed (megahertz) rather than access or cycle times. For example, PC133 SDRAM is used in systems with a 133 MHz front side bus (FSB). As another example, PC800 RDRAM transfers data on both sides of a 400 MHz Rambus channel clock.

It is almost always possible to use *faster* memory than the manufacturer recommends. The system should continue to operate normally, but there's rarely ever a performance benefit. As you'll see in the following sections, memory and architectures are typically tailored for specific performance. Using memory that is faster should not hurt the memory, or impair system performance, but it costs more, and will not produce a noticeable performance improvement—simply because the system is not equipped to employ the faster memory to its best advantage. The only time such a tactic would be advised is when your current system is almost obsolete, and you would want the new memory to be usable on a new, faster motherboard if you choose to upgrade the motherboard later.

## CAS Latency

Another important measure of SDRAM and DDR SDRAM performance is Column Address Strobe (CAS) latency—often designated as CL. Latency is normally a delay. With SDRAM and DDR SDRAM, CAS latency refers to the number of clock cycles it takes before a column can be addressed on the memory chip. SDRAM with a latency of CL2 indicates a two-clock cycle delay. SDRAM with a latency of CL3 indicates a three-clock cycle delay. Smaller numbers result in better memory performance. When SDRAM chips first came out, it was difficult to produce chips with a CAS latency as low as CL2. Although some specifications called for CL2, many modules worked fine at a CAS latency of CL3. Today, virtually all SDRAM uses a CAS latency of CL2 for best performance.

## Wait States

A *wait state* orders the CPU to pause for one or more clock cycles in order to give memory additional time to operate. Typical PCs use one wait state, though very old systems may require two or three. The latest PC designs with high-end memory or aggressive caching may be able to operate with no (zero) wait states—especially when data is transferred in a burst. As you might imagine, a wait state is basically a waste of time, so more wait states result in lower system performance. Zero wait states allow optimum system performance. Wait states let the system support old, slow memory (but the resulting system performance would be so poor that there would be little point in using the system in the first place).

There are three classical means of selecting wait states. First, the number of wait states may be fixed (common in old XT systems). Wait states may be selected with one or more jumpers on the motherboard (typical of i286 and early i386 systems). Midrange and later systems (such as i486, Pentium, and Pentium II/III/4 computers) place the "wait state" or "memory speed" control in the CMOS Setup routine—or it is selected automatically when the memory identifies itself to the system during POST. You may have to look in an "advanced settings" area to find the appropriate entry. When optimizing a computer, you should be sure to set the minimum number of wait states.

Setting too few wait states can cause the PC to behave erratically, or even prevent the system from starting.

# MEMORY REFRESH

The electrical signals placed in each DRAM storage cell must be replenished (or *refreshed*) periodically every few milliseconds. Without refresh, DRAM data will be lost. In principle, refresh requires that each storage cell be read and rewritten to the memory array. This is typically accomplished by reading and rewriting an entire row of the array at one time. Each row of bits is sequentially read into a sense/refresh amplifier (part of the DRAM chip), which basically recharges the appropriate storage capacitors, then rewrites each row bit to the array. In actual operation, a row of bits is automatically refreshed whenever an array row is selected. The entire memory array can be refreshed by reading each row in the array every few milliseconds.

The key to refresh is in the way DRAM is addressed. Unlike other memory chips that supply all address signals to the chip simultaneously, a DRAM is addressed in a two-step sequence. The overall address is separated into a row (low) address and a column (high) address. Row address bits are placed on the DRAM address bus first, and the -Row Address Select (-RAS) line is pulsed to logic 0 to multiplex the bits into the chip's address decoding circuitry. The low portion of the address activates an entire array row and causes each bit in the row to be sensed and refreshed. Logic 0's remain logic 0's, and logic 1's are recharged to their full value.

Column address bits are then placed on the DRAM address bus, and the -Column Address Select (-CAS) is pulsed to logic 0. The column portion of the address selects the appropriate bits within the chosen row. If a read operation is taking place, the selected bits pass through the data buffer to the data bus. During a write operation, the read/write line must be logic 0, and valid data must be available to the chip before -CAS is strobed. New data bits are then placed in their corresponding locations in the memory array.

Even if the chip is not being accessed for reading or writing, the memory must still be refreshed to ensure data integrity. Fortunately, refresh can be accomplished by interrupting the microprocessor to run a refresh routine, which simply steps through every row address in sequence (column addresses need not be selected for simple refresh). This row-only (or -RAS only) refresh technique speeds the refresh process. Although refreshing DRAM every few milliseconds may seem like a constant aggravation, the computer can execute quite a few instructions before being interrupted for refresh. Refresh operations are generally handled by the chipset on your motherboard. Often, memory problems (especially "parity errors") that cannot be resolved by replacing a memory module can be traced to a refresh fault on the motherboard.

Today, many memory designs include provisions for "self-refresh" operation. The refresh circuitry is included on the memory module itself, and RAM is refreshed automatically without the direct intervention of the CPU. This also reduces power consumption—especially when the PC enters power-saving modes.

# DETERMINING MEMORY SPEED

During troubleshooting, or when selecting replacement parts, it's often necessary to check memory modules for proper memory speed (that is, "access time" or "cycle time" for SDRAM). Unfortunately, it can be very difficult to determine memory speed accurately based on part markings. Speeds are normally marked cryptically by adding a number to the end of the part number. For example, a traditional part number ending in -6 often means 60ns, a -7 is usually 70ns, and a -8 can be 80ns. SDRAM often uses markings such as -12 for 12ns cycle time, or -10 for 10ns cycle time. Still, the only means of being absolutely certain of the memory speed is to cross-reference the memory part number with a manufacturer's catalog, and read the speed from the catalog's description. For example, the Kingston KVR266X72RC25 512MB Registered DDR SDRAM DIMM is specified at 64Mx72. That's 64Mx 9 bytes, or 576MB in total. Since the DIMM supports ECC, that's 8 bytes (512MB) for data, with the ninth byte used for ECC (error correction code).

## MEGABYTES AND MEMORY LAYOUT

Now is a good time to explain the idea of bytes versus megabytes. Very simply, a *byte* is 8 bits (binary 1's and 0's), and a *megabyte* is one million of those bytes (1,048,576 bytes to be exact—but manufacturers often round down to the nearest million or so). The idea of megabytes (MB) is important when measuring memory in your PC. For example, if a SIMM is laid out as 1M by 8 bits, it has 1MB. If the SIMM is laid out as 4M by 8 bits, it has 4MB. Unfortunately, memory has not been laid out as 8 bits since the IBM XT.

More practical memory layouts involve 32-bit memory (for 486 and OverDrive processors) or 64-bit memory (for Pentium II/III/4 processors). When memory is "wider" than 1 byte, it is still measured in MB. For example, a 1Mx32-bit (4 bytes) SIMM would be 4MB. That is, the *capacity* of the device is 4MB. A 4Mx32-bit SIMM would be 16MB. So when you go shopping for an 8MB 72-pin SIMM, chances are you're getting a 2Mx32-bit memory module. As a current example, the Kingston KVR333X64C25 333 MHz DDR SDRAM DIMM (www.valueram.com/datasheets/kvr333x64c25_512.pdf) uses a 64Mx64-bit layout for 512MB (no additional bits are provided for parity or ECC). Table 23-7 lists a standard set of ValueRAM products and their descriptions from Kingston Technologies.

| TABLE 23-7 | AN ABBREVIATED LIST AND DESCRIPTIONS OF KINGSTON VALUERAM MEMORY MODULES | |
|---|---|---|
| **600/700/800 MHz Rambus, 184-Pin RIMMs, 2.5v, Gold** | | |
| **64MB** | KVR800X18/64 | 800 MHz ECC 4-Device |
| | KVR800X16/64 | 800 MHz Non-ECC 4-Device |
| | KVR800X18-4/64-IS | 800 MHz ECC 4-Device |
| **128MB** | KVR800X18/128 | 800 MHz ECC 8-Device |
| | KVR800X16/128 | 800 MHz Non-ECC 8-Device |
| | KVR800X16-8/128-IS | 800 MHz Non-ECC 8-Device |
| | KVR800X18-8/128-IS | 800 MHz ECC 8-Device |
| **256MB** | KVR800X18/256 | 800 MHz ECC 16-Device |
| | KVR800X16/256 | 800 MHz Non-ECC 16-Device |
| | KVR800X16-16/256-IS | 800 MHz Non-ECC 16-Device |
| | KVR800X18-16/256-IS | 800 MHz ECC 16-Device |
| **512MB** | KVR800X18-16/512 | 800 MHz ECC 16-Device |
| | KVR800X16-16/512 | 800 MHz Non-ECC 16-Device |
| | KVR-CRIMM | Rambus Continuity RIMM |
| **266 MHz DDR SDRAM, 184-Pin DIMMs, 7.5ns, 2.5v, Gold** | | |
| **128MB** | KVR266X64C25/128 | 16Mx64 266 MHz CL2.5 |
| | KVR266X72C25/128 | 16Mx72 266 MHz ECC CL2.5 |
| | KVR266X72RC25/128 | 16Mx72 266 MHz Registered ECC CL2.5 |
| | KVR266X64C25/128I | 16Mx64 266 MHz CL2.5 |
| **256MB** | KVR266X64C25/256 | 32Mx64 266 MHz CL2.5 |
| | KVR266X72C25/256 | 32Mx72 266 MHz ECC CL2.5 |
| | KVR266X72RC25/256 | 32Mx72 266 MHz Registered ECC CL2.5 |
| | KVR266X64C25/256I | 32Mx64 266 MHz CL2.5 |

**TABLE 23-7    AN ABBREVIATED LIST AND DESCRIPTIONS OF KINGSTON VALUERAM MEMORY MODULES (CONTINUED)**

| | | |
|---|---|---|
| **512MB** | KVR266X64C25/512 | 64Mx64 266 MHz CL2.5 |
| | KVR266X72C25/512 | 64Mx72 266 MHz ECC CL2.5 |
| | KVR266X72RC25/512 | 64Mx72 266 MHz Registered ECC CL2.5 |
| | KVR266X64C25/512I | 64Mx64 266 MHz CL2.5 |
| **1GB** | KVR266X72RC25/1024 | 128Mx72 266 MHz Registered ECC CL2.5 |
| **133 MHz SDRAM, 168-Pin DIMMs, 7.5ns, 3.3v, Gold** | | |
| **64MB** | KVR133X64C3/64 | 8Mx64 133 MHz CL3 |
| | KVR133X64C3L/64 | 8Mx64 133 MHz CL3, Low Profile |
| | KVR133X72C3/64 | 8Mx72 133 MHz ECC CL3 |
| | KVR133X72RC3/64 | 8Mx72 133 MHz Registered ECC CL3 |
| **128MB** | KVR133X64C2/128 | 16Mx64 133 MHz CL2 |
| | KVR133X64C3/128 | 16Mx64 133 MHz CL3 |
| | KVR133X64C3SS/128 | 16Mx64 133 MHz CL3, Single Sided |
| | KVR133X64C3L/128 | 16Mx64 133 MHz CL3, Low Profile |
| | KVR133X72C2/128 | 16Mx72 133 MHz ECC CL2 |
| | KVR133X72C3/128 | 16Mx72 133 MHz ECC CL3 |
| | KVR133X72RC3/128 | 16Mx72 133 MHz Registered ECC CL3 |
| | KVR133X72RC3L/128 | 16Mx72 133 MHz Registered ECC CL3, Low Profile |
| | KVR133X72RC3L/128-IS | 16Mx72 133 MHz Registered ECC CL3, Low Profile |
| **256MB** | KVR133X64C2/256 | 32Mx64 133 MHz CL2 |
| | KVR133X64C3/256 | 32Mx64 133 MHz CL3 |
| | KVR133X64C3SS/256 | 32Mx64 133 MHz CL3, Single Sided |
| | KVR133X64C3L/256 | 32Mx64 133 MHz CL3, Low Profile |
| | KVR133X72C2/256 | 32Mx72 133 MHz ECC CL2 |
| | KVR133X72C3/256 | 32Mx72 133 MHz ECC CL3 |
| | KVR133X72C3L/256 | 32Mx72 133 MHz ECC CL3, Low Profile |
| | KVR133X72RC3/256 | 32Mx72 133 MHz Registered ECC CL3 |
| | KVR133X72RC3L/256 | 32Mx72 133 MHz Registered ECC CL3, Low Profile |
| | KVR133X72RC3/256-IS | 32Mx72 133 MHz Registered ECC CL3 |
| | KVR133X72RC3L/256-IS | 32Mx72 133 MHz Registered ECC CL3, Low Profile |
| **512MB** | KVR133X64C2/512 | 64Mx64 133 MHz CL2 |
| | KVR133X64C3/512 | 64Mx64 133 MHz CL3 |
| | KVR133X64C3L/512 | 64Mx64 133 MHz CL3, Low Profile |
| | KVR133X72C2/512 | 64Mx72 133 MHz ECC CL2 |
| | KVR133X72C3/512 | 64Mx72 133 MHz ECC CL3 |
| | KVR133X72C3L/512 | 64Mx72 133 MHz ECC CL3, Low Profile |
| | KVR133X72RC3/512 | 64Mx72 133 MHz Registered ECC CL3 |
| | KVR133X72RC3L/512 | 64Mx72 133 MHz Registered ECC CL3, Low Profile |
| | KVR133X72RC3/512-IS | 64Mx72 133 MHz Registered ECC CL3 |
| | KVR133X72RC3L/512-IS | 64Mx72 133 MHz Registered ECC CL3, Low Profile |

| TABLE 23-7 | AN ABBREVIATED LIST AND DESCRIPTIONS OF KINGSTON VALUERAM MEMORY MODULES *(CONTINUED)* | |
|---|---|---|
| **1GB** | KVR133X72RC3/1024 | 128Mx72 133 MHz Registered ECC CL3 |
| | KVR133X72RC3/1024A | 128Mx72 133 MHz Registered ECC CL3 (Single Board) |
| | KVR133X72RC3L/1024 | 128Mx72 133 MHz Registered ECC CL3, Low Profile |
| | KVR133X72RC3/1024I | 128Mx72 133 MHz Registered ECC CL3 |
| | KVR133X72RC3L/1024I | 128Mx72 133 MHz Registered ECC CL3, Low Profile |
| **100 MHz SDRAM, 168-Pin DIMMs, 8ns, 3.3v, Gold** | | |
| **64MB** | KVR100X64C2/64 | 8Mx64 100 MHz CL2 |
| | KVR100X64C3/64 | 8Mx64 100 MHz CL3 |
| | KVR100X72C2/64 | 8Mx72 100 MHz ECC CL2 |
| **128MB** | KVR100X64C2/128 | 16Mx64 100 MHz CL2 |
| | KVR100X64C3/128 | 16Mx64 100 MHz CL3 |
| | KVR100X64C2L/128 | 16Mx64 100 MHz CL2, Low Profile |
| | KVR100X72C2/128 | 16Mx72 100 MHz ECC CL2 |
| | KVR100X72C3/128 | 16Mx72 100 MHz ECC CL3 |
| | KVR100X72C2L/128 | 16Mx72 100 MHz ECC CL2, Low Profile |
| | KVR100X72RC2/128 | 16Mx72 100 MHz Registered ECC CL2 |
| | KVR100X72RC3/128 | 16Mx72 100 MHz Registered ECC CL3 |
| | KVR100X72C2/128-IS | 16Mx72 100 MHz ECC CL2 |
| **256MB** | KVR100X64C2/256 | 32Mx64 100 MHz CL2 |
| | KVR100X64C2L/256 | 32Mx64 100 MHz CL2, Low Profile |
| | KVR100X64C3/256 | 32Mx64 100 MHz CL3 |
| | KVR100X72C2/256 | 32Mx72 100 MHz ECC CL2 |
| | KVR100X72C2L/256 | 32Mx72 100 MHz ECC CL2, Low Profile |
| | KVR100X72C3/256 | 32Mx72 100 MHz ECC CL3 |
| | KVR100X72RC2/256 | 32Mx72 100 MHz Registered ECC CL2 |
| | KVR100X72RC2L/256 | 32Mx72 100 MHz Registered ECC CL2, Low Profile |
| | KVR100X72RC3/256 | 32Mx72 100 MHz Registered ECC CL3 |
| | KVR100X72RC2/256-IS | 32Mx72 100 MHz Registered ECC CL2 |
| **512MB** | KVR100X64C2/512 | 64Mx64 100 MHz CL2 |
| | KVR100X64C3/512 | 64Mx64 100 MHz CL3 |
| | KVR100X72C2/512 | 64Mx72 100 MHz ECC CL2 |
| | KVR100X72C3/512 | 64Mx72 100 MHz ECC CL3 |
| | KVR100X72RC2/512 | 64Mx72 100 MHz Registered ECC CL2 |
| | KVR100X72RC2L/512 | 64Mx72 100 MHz Registered ECC CL2, Low Profile |
| | KVR100X72RC3/512 | 64Mx72 100 MHz Registered ECC CL3 |
| | KVR100X72C3/512-IS | 64Mx72 100 MHz ECC CL3 |
| | KVR100X72RC3/512-IS | 64Mx72 100 MHz Registered ECC CL3 |

| TABLE 23-7 | AN ABBREVIATED LIST AND DESCRIPTIONS OF KINGSTON VALUERAM MEMORY MODULES *(CONTINUED)* | |
|---|---|---|
| **1GB** | KVR100X72RC2/1024 | 128Mx72 100 MHz Registered ECC CL2 |
| | KVR100X72RC2/1024A | 128Mx72 100 MHz Registered ECC CL2 (Single Board) |
| | KVR100X72RC3/1024 | 128Mx72 100 MHz Registered ECC CL3 |
| **66 MHz SDRAM, 168-Pin DIMMs, 10ns, 3.3v, Gold** | | |
| **64MB** | KVR66X64/64 | 8Mx64 66 MHz |
| | KVR66X72/64 | 8Mx72 66 MHz ECC |
| **128MB** | KVR66X64/128 | 16Mx64 66 MHz |
| | KVR66X72/128 | 16Mx72 66 MHz ECC |
| **66/100/133 MHz SDRAM,144-Pin SODIMMs, 3.3v, Gold** | | |
| **64MB** | KVR66X64SO/64 | 8Mx64 66 MHz CL2, 10ns |
| | KVR100X64SC2/64 | 8Mx64 100 MHz CL2, 8ns |
| | KVR100X64SC3/64 | 8Mx64 100 MHz CL3, 8ns |
| **128MB** | KVR66X64SO/128 | 16Mx64 66 MHz CL2, 10ns |
| | KVR100X64SC2/128 | 16Mx64 100 MHz CL2, 8ns |
| | KVR100X64SC2L/128 | 16Mx64 100 MHz CL2, 8ns, Low Profile |
| | KVR100X64SC3/128 | 16Mx64 100 MHz CL3, 8ns |
| | KVR133X64SC3/128 | 16Mx64 133 MHz CL3, 7.5n |
| | KVR133X64SC3L/128 | 16Mx64 133 MHz CL3, 7.5ns, Low Profile |
| **256MB** | KVR100X64SC2/256 | 32Mx64 100 MHz CL2, 8ns |
| | KVR100X64SC2L/256 | 32Mx64 100 MHz CL2, 8ns, Low Profile |
| | KVR133X64SC3/256 | 32Mx64 133 MHz CL3, 7.5ns |
| | KVR133X64SC3L/256 | 32Mx64 133 MHz CL3, 7.5ns, Low Profile |
| **512MB** | KVR100X64SC3/512 | 64Mx64 100 MHz CL3, 8ns |
| | KVR133X64SC3L/512 | 64Mx64 133 MHz CL3, 7.5ns, Low Profile |

# PRESENCE DETECT (PD)

Another feature of modern memory devices is a series of physical signals known as the *presence detect* lines. By setting the appropriate conditions of the PD signals, it is possible for a computer to immediately recognize the characteristics of the installed memory devices, and configure itself accordingly. Presence Detect lines typically specify two operating characteristics of memory: size (device layout) and speed. Table 23-8 highlights many of the most commonly used signal combinations.

The most recent memory devices forego discrete presence detect signals in favor of a *Serial Presence Detect* (or SPD) technique. With SPD, a serial nonvolatile chip on the memory module holds all of the memory attributes. The host PC reads the SPD chip during the POST, then configures the host hardware accordingly (e.g., wait states, burst timing, and other memory-related options). Using a serial chip offers more versatility and "intelligence" than discrete logic signals, and virtually all modern SDRAM, DDR SDRAM, and Rambus memory devices will include SPD.

| TABLE 23-8 | BASIC INDEX OF PRESENCE DETECT (PD) SIGNALS | | | | | |
|---|---|---|---|---|---|---|
| **72-PIN SIMM** | | **PIN 67 (PD1)** | **PIN 68 (PD2)** | **PIN 69 (PD3)** | **PIN 70 (PD4)** | **PIN 71 (PD5)** |
| Size (parity) | 256Kx32/36 | GND | N/C | -- | -- | -- |
| | 512Kx32/36 | N/C | GND | -- | -- | -- |
| | 1Mx32/36 | GND | GND | -- | -- | -- |
| | 2Mx32/36 | N/C | N/C | -- | -- | -- |
| | 4Mx32/36 | GND | N/C | -- | -- | N/C |
| | 8Mx32/36 | N/C | GND | -- | -- | N/C |
| Size (ECC) | 256Kx32/36 | GND | N/C | -- | -- | N/C |
| | 512Kx32/36 | N/C | GND | -- | -- | N/C |
| | 1Mx32/36 | GND | GND | -- | -- | N/C |
| | 2Mx32/36 | N/C | N/C | -- | -- | N/C |
| | 4Mx32/36 | GND | N/C | -- | -- | GND |
| | 8Mx32/36 | N/C | GND | -- | -- | GND |
| Speed (parity/ECC) | 60ns | -- | -- | N/C | N/C | -- |
| | 70ns | -- | -- | GND | N/C | -- |
| | 80ns | -- | -- | N/C | GND | -- |
| | 100ns | -- | -- | GND | GND | -- |
| | 120ns | -- | -- | N/C | N/C | -- |

# CLOCK LINES

SDRAM memory requires either two or four clock signal lines between the system clock and the memory module. Modules with two clock lines (called *two-clock* or *2CLK SDRAM*) are usually found with older SDRAM modules. For example, the first Intel designs were two-clock because there were only eight chips on the module. Modules with four clock lines (called *four-clock* or *4CLK SDRAM*) are generally employed on newer SDRAM modules. The four-clock designs allow for fewer chips per clock line, which decreases the signal load on each line and enables a quicker data interface.

# BURSTING AND PIPELINING

PC designers try to make the most of every memory access. Traditionally, only one piece of data is handled with every memory access cycle. Burst access (or *bursting*) is a performance improvement that lets the processor retrieve a block of information from consecutive memory addresses (rather than a single piece of information from one address). This provides the CPU with additional data from memory based on the likelihood that it will be needed. The CPU gets the instructions it needs without having to send an individual request for each one. In actual practice, bursting can work with many different types of memory and can function when reading or writing data.

*Pipelining* is a processing technique in which a task is divided into a series of stages, with some of the work completed at each stage. By dividing a larger task into smaller, overlapping tasks, pipelining is used to significantly improve system performance. Once the flow through a pipeline is started, the execution rate of instructions is high regardless of the number of stages through which they progress. Memory uses pipelining to stack up access requests, so subsequent requests can arrive before previous requests have been finished—multiple accesses can be "in the pipeline" at any given time.

Bursting and pipelining techniques first became popular at about the time that EDO memory technology became available. EDO chips that featured these functions were called *Burst EDO* or *Pipeline Burst EDO* chips.

## Burst Timing

As you saw earlier, it takes a certain amount of time to tell the RAM where to "look" for a given piece of data. This time is simply overhead that reduces your overall memory performance. Since bursting allows consecutive pieces of data to be read/written without the trouble of relocating each piece of data from scratch, that pesky overhead can be reduced. For example, a typical access may take anywhere from 5 to 7 clock cycles, but subsequent burst accesses may take place in 1 to 3 clock cycles (1 clock cycle per access is ideal). Memory devices with burst capability are often denoted with a series of timing numbers such as "x-y-y-y," where "x" is the initial number of clock cycles for a 64-bit read/write, and "y" is the number of clock cycles needed to perform subsequent 64-bit read/write operations.

Consider an example with a memory device using 5-2-2-2 timing (for a four-access burst). The initial R/W takes 5 clock cycles, but each subsequent R/W takes only 2 clock cycles—the entire burst takes only 11 clock cycles. Without bursting, each access would take 5 clock cycles (e.g., 5-5-5-5), and the entire four accesses would need 20 clock cycles. You can see that burst capability is a powerful performance advantage for memory devices. More recent SDRAM and later devices use such timing as 5-1-1-1. Proper timing is critical for best system performance and system stability. The SPD chip on a memory module will typically provide the correct timing parameters to a host system, though you can usually see and adjust the timing through the CMOS Setup.

You may see later memory devices using longer timing sequences. These devices simply sustain larger bursts, but the previously discussed ideas still hold true.

## UNBUFFERED, BUFFERED, AND REGISTERED

Memory modules may be "unbuffered," "buffered," or "registered." This distinction is defined by the way in which electrical signals are handled by the memory module, and your choice of module will affect the maximum amount of RAM that can be installed on the motherboard. An *unbuffered* memory module contains only memory devices—data passed between the memory chips is *not* boosted (or "amplified") by buffers on the module itself. Unbuffered modules are fast because there is no buffering circuitry to slow the signals, and their slightly lower cost makes them ideal for use in everyday systems. Unfortunately, unbuffered electrical signals are prone to attenuation, so only a few unbuffered modules (usually one or two) can be used at a time.

By adding *buffers* or *registers* to the memory module, the electrical signals entering and leaving the memory module are strengthened. This slows the module's performance by a few nanoseconds, but allows the use of additional memory modules—thus the motherboard can support much more memory. (This is particularly important for memory-hungry systems such as network servers.) For EDO and FPM memory modules, the process of re-driving memory signals is called *buffering*. For SDRAM and later memory modules, the process of re-driving memory signals is called *registering*. Registering is similar to buffering, but registering clocks data into and out of the module using the system's clock. The motherboard's memory controller chip determines the type of memory modules required, so you cannot use unbuffered and buffered (or registered) modules together on the same system. (They're also keyed differently so that you cannot use them on an incompatible motherboard.)

# MEMORY TYPES

In order for a computer to work, the CPU must take program instructions and exchange data directly with memory. As a consequence, memory must keep pace with the CPU (or make the CPU wait for it to catch up). Now that processors are so incredibly fast—and getting faster every few months—traditional memory architectures are being replaced by specialized memory devices that have been tailored to serve specific functions in the PC. As you upgrade and repair various systems, you will undoubtedly encounter some of the memory designations explained next (listed roughly in order of vintage).

## SRAM (Static Random Access Memory)

The SRAM is a classical memory design that is even older than DRAM. SRAM does not require regular refresh operations, and can be made to operate at access speeds that are much faster than DRAM. However, traditional SRAM cells use six transistors or more to hold a single bit. This reduces the density of SRAM and increases its power demands (which is why SRAM was never adopted for general PC use in the first place). Still, the high speed of SRAM has earned it a place as the PC's L2 (or external) cache. You'll probably encounter three types of SRAM cache schemes: Asynchronous, Synchronous Burst, and Pipeline Burst.

*Asynchronous Static RAM* (Async SRAM or ASRAM) is the "traditional" form of L2 cache introduced with i386 systems. There's really nothing too special about ASRAM except that its contents can be accessed much faster (20ns, 15ns, or 12ns) than DRAM. ASRAM does not have enough performance to be accessed synchronously and has long since been replaced by better types of cache. *Synchronous Burst Static RAM* (Sync SRAM or SBSRAM) is largely regarded as the best type of L2 cache for intermediate speed motherboards (~60–66 MHz). With access times of 8.5ns and 12ns, the SBSRAM can provide synchronous bursts of cache information in 2-1-1-1 cycles (two clock cycles for the first access, then one cycle per access—in time with the CPU clock). However, as motherboards pass 66 MHz (such as 75 MHz, 83 MHz, and later designs), SBSRAM loses its advantage to Pipelined Burst SRAM. *Pipelined Burst Static RAM* (PB SRAM) is the fastest form of high-performance cache now available for 75 MHz+ motherboards (with speeds of about 4.5ns to 8ns). PBSRAM requires an extra clock cycle for "lead off," but then can sync with the motherboard clock (with timing such as 3-1-1-1) across a wide range of motherboard frequencies.

## Classic DRAM (Dynamic Random Access Memory)

DRAM was first utilized in early personal computers. It achieves a good mix of speed and density, while being relatively simple and inexpensive to produce—only a single transistor and capacitor is needed to hold a bit. Unfortunately, DRAM contents must be refreshed every few milliseconds, or the contents of each bit location will decay. DRAM performance is also limited because of relatively long access times. Today, "vanilla" DRAM is completely obsolete, and no PC devices are known to incorporate DRAM components. Still, DRAM remains the most recognized and common form of computer memory, and we often use the term "DRAM" as a generic reference to other types of PC RAM (though that's technically inaccurate).

A typical DRAM memory access would occur as follows: The row address bits are placed onto the address pins. After a period of time, the RAS signal falls, which activates sense amps and causes the row address to be latched into the row address buffer. When the RAS signal stabilizes, the selected row is transferred onto the sense amps. Next, the column address bits are set up and then latched into the column address buffer when CAS falls. At that point, the output buffer is also turned on. When CAS stabilizes, the selected sense amp feeds its data to the output buffer.

### FPM DRAM (Fast-Page Mode DRAM)

This is a popular twist on conventional DRAM. Typical DRAM access is accomplished in a way that is similar to reading a book—a memory "page" is accessed first, and then the contents of that "page" can be located. The problem is that every access requires the DRAM to relocate the "page." The *fast-page mode* overcomes this delay by allowing the CPU to access multiple pieces of data on the same "page" without having to relocate the "page" every time. As long as the subsequent read or write cycle is on the previously located "page," the FPDRAM can access the specific location on that "page" directly.

During the early 1990s, FPM became the most widely used access method for DRAMs, and may still be encountered on old systems. The general benefit of FPM memory is reduced power consumption (because sense and restore current is not necessary during page-mode access). Though FPM was a major innovation, there are still some drawbacks. The most significant limitation is that the output buffers turn off when CAS goes high. Also, the minimum cycle time is 5ns before the output buffers turn off, which essentially adds at least 5ns to the cycle time.

Today, FPM memory is one of the least desirable forms of memory. You should only consider using FPM if your system does not support any of the later memory types (such as a 486-based system). Typical timings are 6-3-3-3 (initial latency of three clocks, with a three-clock page access). Due to the limited demand, you may find that FPM is actually more expensive than most of the faster memory technologies now available.

### EDRAM (Enhanced DRAM)

This is another, lesser-known variation of the classic DRAM developed by Ramtron International and United Memories. First demonstrated in August 1994, the EDRAM eliminates an external cache by placing a small amount of static RAM (cache) into each EDRAM device itself. In essence, the cache is distributed *within* the system RAM, and as more memory is added to the PC, more cache is effectively added as well. The internal construction of an EDRAM allows it to act like page-mode memory—if a subsequent read requests data that is in the EDRAM's cache (known as a *hit*), the data is made available in about 15ns—roughly equal to the speed of a fair external cache. If the subsequent read requests data that is not in the cache (called a *miss*), the data is accessed from the DRAM portion of memory in about 35ns, which is still much faster than ordinary DRAM. EDRAM never enjoyed much support from the PC industry, and is obsolete today.

### CDRAM (Cached DRAM)

As with EDRAM, the CDRAM from Mitsubishi incorporates cache and DRAM on the same memory chips. This eliminates the need for an external (or L2) cache, and has the extra benefit of adding cache whenever RAM is added to the system. The difference is that CDRAM used a "set-associative" cache approach that can be 15–20 percent more efficient than the EDRAM cache scheme. On the other hand, EDRAM appeared to offer better overall performance. As with EDRAM, CDRAM never received much attention from the PC industry and is now considered obsolete.

### VRAM (Video Random Access Memory)

DRAM has been the traditional choice for video memory, but the ever-increasing demand for fast video information (as in high-resolution SVGA displays) requires a more efficient means of transferring data to and from video memory. Originally developed by Samsung Electronics, video RAM achieves speed improvements by using a "dual data bus" scheme. Ordinary RAM uses a single data bus—data enters or leaves the RAM through a single set of signals. Video RAM provides an "input" data bus and an "output" data bus. This allows data to be read from video RAM at the same time new information is being written to it. You should understand that the advantages of VRAM will only be realized on high-end video systems such as 1024 x 768 x 256 (or higher), where you can get up to 40 percent more performance than a DRAM video adapter. Below that, you will see no perceivable improvement with a VRAM video adapter. Today, high-performance video adapters use SDRAM or DDR SDRAM.

### EDO RAM (Extended Data Out RAM)

Introduced in 1995, EDO RAM is a well-established variation of DRAM that extends the time in which output data is valid—thus the data's presence on the data bus is "extended." This is accomplished by modifying the DRAM's output buffer, which prolongs the time in which *read data* is valid. The data will remain valid until a motherboard signal is received to release it. This eases timing constraints on the memory and allows a 15–30 percent improvement in memory performance (using timings such as 5-2-2-2 at 66 MHz) with little real increase in cost. Because a new external signal is needed to operate EDO RAM, the motherboard must use a chipset designed to accommodate EDO. Intel's Triton chipset was one of the first to support EDO, though most chipsets of that vintage were quickly updated to support EDO. You should realize that EDO RAM can be used in non-EDO motherboards, but there will be no performance improvement. Today, EDO RAM is completely obsolete when compared to more recent SDRAM, DDR SDRAM, and Rambus DRAM memory technologies.

### BEDO (Burst Extended Data Output RAM)

This powerful variation of EDO RAM reads data in a burst, which means that after a valid address has been provided, subsequent data addresses can be read in only one clock cycle each. The CPU can read BEDO data in a 5-1-1-1 pattern (five clock cycles for the first address, then one clock cycle for subsequent addresses. While BEDO offers an advantage over EDO, it is only supported currently by the VIA chipsets: 580VP, 590VP, 680VP. Also, BEDO seems to have difficulty supporting motherboards over 66 MHz. All forms of EDO RAM are considered obsolete today in favor of later memory technologies such as SDRAM, DDR SDRAM, and Rambus.

### WRAM (Windows RAM)

Samsung Electronics has introduced WRAM as a new video-specific memory device. WRAM uses multiple bit arrays connected with an extensive internal bus and high-speed registers that can transfer data almost continuously. Other specialized registers support attributes such as foreground color, background color, write-block control bits, and true-byte masking. Samsung claims data transfer rates of up to 640MB/s—about 50 percent faster than VRAM—yet WRAM devices are cheaper than their VRAM counterparts. While WRAM has received some serious consideration in the last few years, it has been largely ignored in favor of SDRAM for video systems.

### SDRAM (Synchronous or Synchronized DRAM)

Typical memory can only transfer data during certain portions of a clock cycle. Introduced in late 1996, the SDRAM modifies memory operation so that outputs can be valid at *any* point in the clock cycle. By itself, this is not really significant, but SDRAM also provides a "pipeline burst" mode that allows a second access to begin before the current access is complete. This "continuous" memory access offers effective access speeds as fast as 10ns, and can transfer data at up to 100 MB/s and higher. SDRAM has been quite popular on recent motherboard designs, and is supported by the Intel VX (and later) chipsets, as well as VIA 580VP, 590VP, and 680VP (and later) chipsets. Like the earlier BEDO, SDRAM can transfer data in a 5-1-1-1 pattern, but it can support motherboard speeds up to 100 MHz and 133 MHz that are so vital for Pentium II/III/4 systems.

Although SDRAM is still available for older PCs, conventional SDRAM is being replaced by DDR SDRAM and Rambus technologies.

**Speed Rated SDRAM (PC100/PC133)**    Since SDRAM is synchronized with the system clock, it's possible to achieve very fast data transfers with zero wait states. However, synchronous operation "chains" the memory to the clock, so the SDRAM absolutely *must* be fast enough for the system clock. This became a problem with early SDRAM because technicians and users simply took the reciprocal of the module's nanosecond rating. For example, they assumed that a 10ns module would run at 100 MHz (the reciprocal of 10ns)—that's true in theory, but allows no deviation. The module should actually be a little faster in order to ensure it's compliance at the intended bus speed.

In order to support then-emerging 100 MHz bus speeds, Intel introduced the **PC100** specification as a guideline to manufacturers for building modules that would function properly on their 100 MHz chipsets (such as the 440BX and later). With the PC100 specification, Intel laid out a number of guidelines for trace lengths, trace widths and spacing, the number of printed circuit layers, EEPROM programming specs, and so on. PC100 SDRAM on a 100 MHz (or faster) system bus will provide a performance boost for Socket 7 systems of between 10 and 15 percent since the L2 cache is running at system bus speed. Pentium II/III systems will not see as big a boost because the L2 cache is running at half the processor speed (with the exception of the cacheless Celeron chips, of course).

With the introduction and broad acceptance of 133 MHz bus speeds, a more capable standard was needed to ensure faster operation, and the **PC133** standard was applied to SDRAM certified for 133 MHz bus speeds (roughly 7ns and faster). Pentium 4 and AMD Athlon/Duron processors require the faster PC133 SDRAM for a 133 MHz motherboard (or the more current 200/266 MHz DDR SDRAM).

Generally speaking, PC100/133 SDRAM is not technologically different from "ordinary" SDRAM—it's just certified to operate reliably at the respective speed.

## SGRAM (Synchronous Graphics RAM)
SGRAM is a video-specific extension of SDRAM technology that includes graphics-optimized read/write features. SGRAM also allows video data to be retrieved and modified in blocks instead of individually—this reduces the number of reads and writes that memory must perform, and increases the performance of the graphics controller by making the read/write process more efficient.

## DDR SDRAM
While PC133 SDRAM provided excellent performance for PC platforms, it also found limitations when used with fast processors. Not only is there a theoretical upper limit to the clock frequency, but SDRAM only transfers data once during a clock cycle. As designers sought ways to improve memory performance even further, the notion of transferring data on both edges of the clock (rising and falling) allowed for double the potential data transfer speeds. First introduced in 2000, *double data rate SDRAM* (DDR SDRAM) allows output operations to occur on *both* the rising and falling edge of the system clock. The DDR SDRAM design can double the effective speed up to at least 200 MHz or 266 MHz (dubbed PC200/PC266 DDR SDRAM, respectively). Current DDR SDRAM will operate on a 166 MHz system bus for PC333 (333 MHz) compliance. Support for DDR SDRAM is now standard on many VIA and ALi chipsets, and even Intel is embracing DDR SDRAM in its latest Pentium 4 chipsets.

DDR SDRAM is otherwise similar to ordinary SDRAM.

## SLDRAM (Synchronous Link DRAM)

The continued push for faster PC platforms resulted in a number of other creative performance improvements such as *synchronous link DRAM* (called *SyncLink* or *SLDRAM*). This technology was developed by a group of about 20 major computer industry manufacturers (the SLDRAM Consortium) working to establish SDRAM as the next standard for high-speed PC memory. SLDRAM sought to improve the performance of the memory subsystem over SDRAM, without a completely new architecture. Initial SLDRAM specifications called for a 64-bit bus running at a 200 MHz clock speed. As with DDR SDRAM, transfers occur twice on each clock cycle for an effective speed of 400 MHz. This yielded a net theoretical bandwidth of about 3.2 GB/s. Unfortunately, SLDRAM never reached acceptance in the PC marketplace. It was overtaken by Rambus technologies, which promised higher speeds and scalability into the future.

## RDRAM (Rambus DRAM)

Most of the memory alternatives so far have been variations of the same basic DRAM architecture. Rambus, Inc. (joint developers of EDRAM) has developed a relatively new memory architecture called the *Rambus Channel* (also called *Direct Rambus*). A CPU or specialized controller chip is used as the "master" device, and the RDRAMs are used as "slave" devices. Blocks of data are then sent back and forth across the Rambus channel. With a 400 MHz clock, the Rambus Channel can transfer data on both edges of the clock. This results in 16-bit data transfer rates approaching an effective 800 MHz (called *PC800 RDRAM*), and offers 1.6 GB/s of data bandwidth (2 bytes, twice per clock at 400 MHz; $2 \times 2 \times 400$). Earlier implementations of RDRAM used a 300 MHz clock, resulting in PC600 RDRAM. By late 2000, Intel had embraced Rambus completely, and the current generation of 850 chipset (for the Pentium 4 processor) supports Rambus exclusively (though later Intel chipsets provide support for more widely available and less expensive DDR SDRAM components). RDRAM components fall into several common classifications:

- **PC600 RDRAM**   300 MHz bus
- **PC700 RDRAM**   350 MHz bus
- **PC800 RDRAM**   400 MHz bus
- **PC1066 RDRAM**   533 MHz bus

There's one other wrinkle to consider when choosing Rambus memory—every Rambus slot on the motherboard *must* be filled in order to maintain the proper transmission characteristics across the entire Rambus channel. Unused Rambus slots will need to be populated with *continuity modules* (or C-RIMMs). A C-RIMM is little more than a connector that continues the transmission path across the channel (it does not contain any memory devices).

A common difficulty with Rambus memory problems is the absence of a C-RIMM. This upsets the memory channel and causes memory errors in the system.

# MEMORY TECHNIQUES

Rather than incur the added expense of specialized memory devices, PC makers often use inexpensive, well-established memory types arranged in unique architectures designed to make the most of existing memory technologies. There are four popular architectures that you will probably encounter in almost all systems: paged memory, interleaved memory, memory cache, and shadow memory.

## Paged Memory

The paged memory approach basically divides system RAM into small groups (or "pages") from 512 bytes to several KB long. Memory management circuitry on the motherboard allows subsequent memory accesses on the same "page" to be accomplished with zero wait states. If the subsequent access takes place outside of the current "page," one or more wait states may be added while the new "page" is found. This is identical in principle to fast-page mode DRAM explained earlier. You will find page-mode architectures implemented on high-end i286, PS/2 (model 70 and 80), and many i386 systems—though they are not used on current systems.

## Interleaved Memory

Simply put, *interleaved* memory combines two banks of memory into one. This technique provides better performance than paged memory. The first portion is "even," while the second portion is "odd"—so memory contents are alternated between these two areas. This allows a memory access in the second portion to begin before the memory access in the first portion has finished. In effect, interleaving can substantially improve memory performance. The traditional problem with interleaving is that you must provide memory as matched pairs. For example, you'd need to install two SIMMs, and one SIMM would be accessing while the second is being read. Today, memory such as SDRAM can be logically divided into cell banks on the DIMM itself, and employ interleaving as an integral part of its operation.

## Memory Cache

Perhaps the most recognized form of memory enhancement technique is memory cache (Figure 23-7 illustrates a classical cache configuration). *Cache* is a small amount (anywhere from 8KB to 1MB) of very fast memory such as SRAM that forms an interface between the CPU and ordinary DRAM. The SRAM typically operates on the order of 5ns to 15ns, which is fast enough to keep pace with a CPU using zero wait states. A *cache controller* chip on the motherboard keeps track of frequently accessed memory locations (as well as predicted memory locations) and copies those contents into cache. When a CPU reads from memory, it checks the cache first. If the needed contents are present in the cache (called a *cache hit*), the data is read at zero wait states. If the needed contents are not present in the cache (known as a *cache miss*), the data must be read directly from DRAM at a penalty of one or more wait states. A small quantity of very fast cache (called *Tag RAM*) acts as an index, recording the various locations of data stored in cache. A well-designed caching system can achieve a hit ratio of 95 percent or more—in other words, memory can run *without* wait states 95 percent of the time.

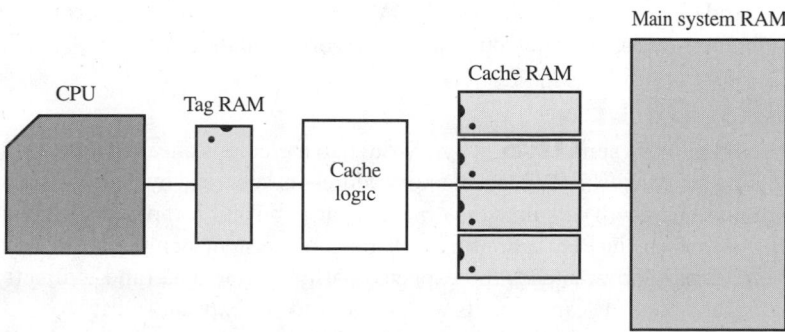

**FIGURE 23-7**    Traditional cache system components

There are two levels of cache in the contemporary PC. CPUs from the i486 onward have a small "internal cache"—known as *L1 cache*—while "external cache" (SRAM installed as DIPs or COAST modules on the motherboard) is referred to as *L2 cache*. The i386 CPUs have no internal cache (though IBM's 386SLC offers 8KB of L1 cache). Most i486 CPUs provide an 8KB internal cache. Early Pentium processors are fitted with two 8KB internal caches—one for data and one for instructions. Today's Pentium II/III/4 processors incorporate 256–512KB of L2 cache into the processor cartridge itself (so there is no L2 cache on those motherboards). Integrating all of the cache into the processor helps improve cache performance.

### Shadow Memory

ROM devices (whether the BIOS ROM on your motherboard or a ROM chip on an expansion board) are frustratingly slow, with access times often exceeding several hundred nanoseconds. ROM access then requires a large number of wait states, which slow down the system's performance. This problem is compounded because the routines stored in BIOS (especially the video BIOS ROM on the video board) are some of the most frequently accessed memory locations in your computer.

Beginning with the i386-class computers, some designs employed a memory technique called *shadowing*. ROM contents are loaded into an area of fast RAM during system initialization, and then the computer maps the fast RAM into memory locations used by the ROM devices. Whenever ROM routines must be accessed during run time, information is taken from the faster "shadowed ROM" instead of the actual ROM chip. The ROM performance can be improved by at least 300 percent.

Shadow memory is also useful for ROM devices that do not use the full available data bus width. For example, a 16-bit computer system may hold an expansion board containing an 8-bit ROM chip. The system would have to access the ROM not once but twice to extract a single 16-bit word. If the computer is a 32-bit machine, that 8-bit ROM would have to be addressed four times to make a complete 32-bit word. You may imagine the hideous system delays that can be encountered. Loading the ROM to shadow memory in advance virtually eliminates such delays. Shadowing can usually be turned on or off through the system's CMOS Setup routine.

# Parity and ECC

As you might imagine, it is vital that data and program instructions remain error free. Even one incorrect bit due to electrical noise or a component failure can crash the PC, corrupt drive information, cause video problems, or result in a myriad of other faults. PC designers traditionally approached the issue of memory integrity by employing a technique known as *parity* (the same technique used to check serial data integrity for your modem). Today, high-end DIMM and RIMM devices can include *error checking code* (ECC), which can provide more robust error detection and even correct single-bit errors.

## PARITY PRINCIPLES

The basic idea behind parity is simple—each byte written to memory is checked, and a 9th bit is added to the byte as a checking (or *parity*) bit. When a memory address is later read by the CPU, memory checking circuitry on the motherboard will calculate the *expected* parity bit and compare it to the bit actually *read* from memory. In this fashion, the PC can continuously diagnose system memory by checking the integrity of its data. If the read parity bit matches the expected parity bit, the data (and indirectly the RAM) is assumed to be valid, and the CPU can go on its way. If the read and expected parity bits do not match, the system registers an error and halts. Every byte is given a parity bit, so for a 32-bit PC, there will be 4 parity bits for every address. For a 64-bit PC, there are 8 parity bits, and so on.

## Even vs. Odd

There are two types of parity—even and odd. With *even parity*, the parity bit is set to 0 if there are an even number of 1's already in the corresponding byte (keeping the number of 1's even). If there is not an even number of 1's in the byte, the even parity bit will be 1 (making the number of 1's even). With *odd parity*, the parity bit is set to 0 if there is an odd number of 1's already in the corresponding byte (keeping the number of 1's odd). If there is not an odd number of 1's in the byte, the odd parity bit will be 1 (making the number of 1's odd).

Although even and odd parity work opposite to one another, both schemes serve exactly the same purpose, and have the same probability of catching a bad bit. The memory device itself does not care at all about what type of parity is being used—it just needs to have the parity bits available. The use of parity (and the choice of even or odd) is left up to the motherboard's memory control circuit.

If you opt to use non-parity RAM in the system, parity checking *must* be disabled—otherwise, the system will register parity errors.

## Parity Problems

While parity has proven to be a simple and cost-effective means of continuously checking memory, there are two significant limitations. First, though parity can detect an error, it cannot correct the error because there is no way to tell *which* bit has gone bad. This is why a system simply halts when a parity error is detected. Second, parity is unable to detect multi-bit errors. For example, if a 1 accidentally becomes a 0 and a 0 accidentally becomes a 1 within the same byte, parity conditions will still be satisfied. Fortunately, the probability of a multi-bit error in the same byte is extremely remote.

## Circumventing Parity

Over the last few years, parity has come under fire from PC makers and memory manufacturers alike. Opponents claim that the rate of parity errors due to hardware (RAM) faults is very small, and that the expense of providing parity bits in a memory-hungry marketplace just isn't justified anymore. There is some truth to this argument, considering that the parity technique is over 20 years old and has serious limitations.

As a consequence, many motherboard makers have removed parity support from their low-end motherboards, and others are providing motherboards that will function with or without parity (usually set in CMOS or with a motherboard jumper). Similarly, some memory makers now provide non-parity and "fake" parity memory as cheaper alternatives to conventional parity memory. *Non-parity* memory simply forgoes the 9th bit. For example, a non-parity DIMM would be designated x32 or x64 (for example, 4Mx32 or 4Mx64). If the DIMM supports parity, it will be designated x36 or x72 (for example, 4Mx36 or 4Mx72). *Fake parity* is more devious—the 9th bit is replaced by a simple (and dirt cheap) parity generator chip that "looks" like a normal DRAM chip. When a read cycle occurs, the parity chip on the memory module provides the proper parity bit to the motherboard all the time. In effect, your memory is "lying" to the motherboard.

While there's a cost savings with non-parity (or "fake parity") techniques, your memory is left with no means of error checking at all. It's a little like driving a car without a speedometer—you could go for miles without a problem, but sooner or later you'll cross a speed trap. In actual practice, you can go indefinitely without parity, but when an error *does* occur, having parity in place can save you immeasurable frustration. Unless the "lowest cost" is your absolute highest priority, it is recommended that you spend the extra few dollars for parity RAM.

Most motherboards can be operated with non-parity RAM. It is also usually possible to mix parity and non-parity memory in the same system. But in either case, you will need to disable all parity checking features for the RAM.

**Abuse and Detection of Fake Parity**   Another potential problem with "fake" parity memory is fraud. There have been numerous instances where memory was purchased as "parity" at full price—only to find that the parity memory chips were actually parity generator chips. This was determined by dissecting the chip packages and finding that the chip die in the parity position did not match the chip dies in the other bit positions. The buyer doesn't know because parity generators are packaged to look just like memory chips, and there's no other obvious way to tell just by looking at the memory module or other memory device. System diagnostic software also cannot detect the presence of parity memory versus fake memory.

There are really only two ways to protect yourself from fake memory fraud. First, industry experts indicate that many fake parity chips (the parity generators) are marked with designations such as "BP," "VT," "GSM," or "MPEC." If you find that one out of every nine chips on your memory module carries such a designation (or any other designation not matching the first eight), you may have a fraud situation. Of course, the first step in all justice is a "benefit of the doubt;" so contact the organization you purchased the memory from—they may simply have sent the wrong modules.

Second, you can check the chip dies themselves. Unfortunately, this requires you to carefully dissect several chip packages on the memory module and compare the chip dies under a microscope—resulting in the destruction of the memory device(s). If the ninth die looks radically different (usually much simpler) than the other eight, you've likely got fake parity. A nondestructive way to check the module is to use a SIMM/DIMM checker (if you have access to one) with a testing routine specially written to test parity memory. If the module works but the parity chip test fails (the tester cannot *write* to the parity memory), chances are you've got fake parity.

If you determine that you have been sold fake parity memory in place of real parity memory, and you cannot get any satisfaction from the seller, you are encouraged to inform the Attorney General in the seller's state. After all, if you're being defrauded, chances are that a lot of other people are too—and they probably don't know it.

## ECC AND EOS BASICS

Although this book supports the use of parity, it also recognizes its old age. In the world of personal computing, parity is an *ancient* technique. Frankly, it could easily be replaced by more sophisticated techniques such as Error Correction Code (ECC) or ECC-on-SIMM (EOS). ECC (which is already being employed in high-end PCs and file servers) uses a mathematical process in conjunction with the motherboard's memory controller, and appends a number of ECC bits to the data bits. When data is read back from memory, the ECC memory controller checks the ECC data read back as well. If the stored and calculated ECC values match, the data is assumed to be valid, and the system continues normally. If the values do not match, a single-bit error can actually be corrected "on the fly" without any user intervention. If a multi-bit error is detected, an error message appears and the system halts.

ECC has two important advantages over parity. It can actually *correct* single-bit errors "on-the-fly," without the user ever knowing there's been a problem. In addition, ECC can successfully detect 2-bit, 3-bit, and 4-bit errors, which makes it an incredibly powerful error detection tool. If a rare multi-bit error is detected, ECC is unable to correct it, but it will be reported and the system will halt—improving data integrity over simple parity checking. Like parity, ECC takes 1 bit for every byte, and memory makers typically add 8 bits to their 64-bit DIMM for ECC support. This means an ordinary 64-bit DIMM would become a 72-bit ECC DIMM (you can see examples of ECC and non-ECC modules in Table 23-7). For example, a 32Mx72 ECC DIMM would provide 256MB of memory plus ECC, while a 32Mx64 non-ECC DIMM would not provide any error checking. Rambus memory also demands 1 bit for every byte, but since Rambus only uses a 16-bit data bus (2 bytes), only 2 additional bits are needed. You'll see this as "16" for non-ECC or "18" for ECC Rambus modules.

EOS is a relatively new (and rather expensive) technology that places ECC functions on the memory module itself, but provides ECC results as parity—so while the memory module runs ECC, the motherboard continues to "see" parity. This is an interesting experiment, but it is unlikely that EOS will gain significant market share. Systems that use parity can be fitted with parity memory much more cheaply than with EOS memory.

# Selecting and Installing Memory

Installing memory is not nearly as easy as it used to be. Certainly, today's memory modules just plug right in, but deciding which memory to buy, how much (or how little) to buy, and how to use existing memory in new systems presents technicians with a bewildering variety of choices. This part of the chapter illustrates the important ideas behind choosing and using memory.

## GETTING THE RIGHT AMOUNT

"How much memory do I need?" This is an age-old question that has plagued the PC industry ever since Intel's 80286 CPU broke the 1MB memory barrier. With more memory, additional programs and data can be run by the CPU at any given time, which indirectly helps to improve the productivity of the particular PC. The problem is cost. Today's DDR SDRAM is running around $0.50/MB, compared with about $1.86/GB ($0.00186/MB) for hard drive space. Consequently, memory is far more expensive than hard drive space; so the goal of good system configuration is to install *enough* memory to support the PC's routine tasks. Installing *too much* memory means that you've spent money for PC resources that just remain idle. Installing *too little* memory results in programs that will not run, or suffer diminished system performance because of extensive swap file use (typical under Windows).

So how much memory *is* enough? The fact of the matter is that "enough" is an ever-changing figure. DOS systems of the early 1980s (8088/8086) worked just fine with 1MB. By the mid-1980s (80286), DOS systems with 2MB were adequate. Into the late 1980s (80386), Windows 3.0 and 3.1 needed 4MB. As the 1990s got under way (80486), Windows systems with 8MB were common (even DOS applications were using 4–6MB of EMS). Today, with Pentium II/III/4 systems and Windows XP, 64MB is considered to be an absolute minimum requirement, and 64–128MB systems are readily available. For today, 64MB is the minimum benchmark that you should use for general-purpose home and office systems, but 128MB systems are readily available. And this is not to say that 128MB systems are the pinnacle of performance. Today's file servers and industrial-strength design packages are employing 256–512MB of RAM, and motherboard chipsets can often support up to 1GB of RAM or more. Ultimately, sizing memory for a system should depend on the OS in use, the applications that are needed, and any data involved. For example, a system intended for high-quality desktop imaging should have considerably more RAM than a system that mainly surfs the Internet.

## FILLING BANKS

Another point of confusion is the idea of a "memory bank." Traditional memory devices are installed in sets (or *banks*). The amount of memory in the bank can vary depending on how much you wish to add, but there must always be enough data bits in the bank to fill each bit position. Table 23-9 illustrates a relationship between data bits and banks for the range of typical CPUs. For example, the 8086 is a 16-bit microprocessor (2 bytes). This means that 2 extra bits are required for parity, giving a total of 18 bits. Thus, one bank is 18 bits wide. You may fill the bank by adding eighteen 1-bit DIPs, or two 30-pin SIMMs.

**TABLE 23-9**  CPU VS. MEMORY "BANK" SIZE

| CPU | DATA WIDTH (W/PARITY) | XMB BY 1 DIPS | 30-PIN SIMMS | 72-PIN SIMMS | 168-PIN DIMMS |
|---|---|---|---|---|---|
| 8088 | 9 bits | 9 | 1 | - | - |
| 8086 | 18 bits | 18 | 2 | - | - |
| 80286 | 18 bits | - | 2 | 1 (2 banks) | - |
| 80386SX, SL, SLC | 18 bits | - | 2 | 1 (2 banks) | - |
| 80386DX | 36 bits | - | 4 | 1 | - |
| 80486SLC, SLC2 | 18 bits | - | 2 | 1 (2 banks) | - |
| 80486DX, SX, DX2, DX4 | 36 bits | - | 4 | 1 | - |
| Pentium (Socket 7) | 64 bits | - | 8 | 2 | 1 |
| Pentium II/III/4 | 64 bits | - | - | - | 1 |

As another example, an 80486DX is a 32-bit CPU, so 36 bits are needed to fill a bank (32 bits plus 4 parity bits). If you use 30-pin SIMMs, you will need four to fill a bank. If you use 72-pin SIMMs, only one is needed. For a newer Pentium III/4 CPU, you can fill a "bank" with only one 168-pin DIMM. Note that the size of the memory in MB does not really matter, so long as the *entire* bank is filled. Keep in mind that Rambus modules are often installed in pairs, and unused RIMM slots will require C-RIMMs.

## Classical Bank Requirements

There is more to filling a memory bank than just installing the right number of bits. Memory amount, memory matching, and bank order are three additional considerations. First, you must use the proper *memory amount* that will bring you to the expected volume of total memory. Suppose a Pentium system has 8MB already installed in Bank 0, and you need to put another 8MB into the system in Bank 1. Table 23-9 shows that two 72-pin SIMMs are needed to fill a bank, but each SIMM need only be 1M. Remember from the discussion of megabytes that a 1Mx36-bit (w/parity) device is 4MB. Since two such SIMMs are needed to fill a bank, the total would be 8MB. When added to the 8MB already in the system, the total would be 16MB.

How about another example? Suppose the same 8MB is already installed in your Pentium system, and you want to add 16MB to Bank 1 rather than 8MB (bringing the total system memory to 24MB). In that case, you could use two 2M 72-pin SIMMs where 2Mx36 is 8MB (w/parity) per SIMM. Two 8MB SIMMs yield 16MB, bringing the system total to (16MB + 8MB) or 24MB.

Now for a curve. Suppose you want to outfit that Pentium as a network server with 128MB of RAM. Remember that there's already 8MB in Bank 0, which means there's only Bank 1 available. Since the largest commercially available SIMMs are 8Mx36 (32MB w/parity), you can only add up to 64MB to Bank 1 (for a system total of 72MB). To get around this, you should *remove* the existing 1Mx36 SIMMs in Bank 0 and fill both Bank 0 and Bank 1 with 8Mx36 SIMMs, which would put 64MB in Bank 0 and 64MB in Bank 1—yielding 128MB in total. You can review many of the recommended SIMM/DIMM combinations for a basic Pentium motherboard in Table 23-10. The important thing to remember is that there are often several different ways to implement the amount of RAM that you need.

**TABLE 23-10    MEMORY MODULE COMBINATIONS FOR A TYPICAL PENTIUM MOTHERBOARD**

| MEMORY SIZE | SIMM 1 | SIMM 2 | SIMM 3 | SIMM 4 | SIMM 5 | SIMM 6 | DIMM 1 | DIMM 2 |
|---|---|---|---|---|---|---|---|---|
| 8MB | 1Mx32 | 1Mx32 | - | - | - | - | - | - |
| 8MB | - | - | - | - | - | - | 1Mx64 | - |
| 16MB | 2Mx32 | 2Mx32 | - | - | - | - | - | - |
| 16MB | 1Mx32 | 1Mx32 | 1Mx32 | 1Mx32 | - | - | - | - |
| 16MB | - | - | - | - | - | - | 2Mx64 | - |
| 16MB | - | - | - | - | - | - | 1Mx64 | 1Mx64 |
| 24MB | 1Mx32 | 1Mx32 | 2Mx32 | 2Mx32 | - | - | - | - |
| 24MB | 1Mx32 | 1Mx32 | 1Mx32 | 1Mx32 | 1Mx32 | 1Mx32 | - | - |
| 24MB | - | - | - | - | - | - | 1Mx64 | 2Mx64 |
| 32MB | 4Mx32 | 4Mx32 | - | - | - | - | - | - |
| 32MB | 2Mx32 | 2Mx32 | 2Mx32 | 2Mx32 | - | - | - | - |
| 32MB | 1Mx32 | 1Mx32 | 1Mx32 | 1Mx32 | 2Mx32 | 2Mx32 | - | - |
| 32MB | - | - | - | - | - | - | 4Mx64 | - |
| 32MB | - | - | - | - | - | - | 2Mx64 | 2Mx64 |
| 40MB | 1Mx32 | 1Mx32 | 4Mx32 | 4Mx32 | - | - | - | - |
| 40MB | - | - | - | - | - | - | 1Mx64 | 4Mx64 |
| 48MB | 2Mx32 | 2Mx32 | 4Mx32 | 4Mx32 | - | - | - | - |
| 48MB | 1Mx32 | 1Mx32 | 1Mx32 | 1Mx32 | 4Mx32 | 4Mx32 | - | - |
| 48MB | 2Mx32 | 2Mx32 | 2Mx32 | 2Mx32 | 2Mx32 | 2Mx32 | - | - |
| 48MB | - | - | - | - | - | - | 2Mx64 | 4Mx64 |
| 64MB | 8Mx32 | 8Mx32 | - | - | - | - | - | - |
| 64MB | 4Mx32 | 4Mx32 | 4Mx32 | 4Mx32 | - | - | - | - |
| 64MB | 2Mx32 | 2Mx32 | 2Mx32 | 2Mx32 | 4Mx32 | 4Mx32 | - | - |
| 64MB | - | - | - | - | - | - | 8Mx64 | - |
| 64MB | - | - | - | - | - | - | 4Mx64 | 4Mx64 |
| 72MB | 1Mx32 | 1Mx32 | 8Mx32 | 8Mx32 | - | - | - | - |
| 72MB | - | - | - | - | - | - | 1Mx64 | 8Mx64 |
| 80MB | 2Mx32 | 2Mx32 | 8Mx32 | 8Mx32 | - | - | - | - |
| 80MB | 1Mx32 | 1Mx32 | 1Mx32 | 1Mx32 | 8Mx32 | 8Mx32 | - | - |
| 80MB | - | - | - | - | - | - | 2Mx64 | 8Mx64 |
| 96MB | 4Mx32 | 4Mx32 | 8Mx32 | 8Mx32 | - | - | - | - |
| 96MB | 2Mx32 | 2Mx32 | 2Mx32 | 2Mx32 | 8Mx32 | 8Mx32 | - | - |
| 96MB | 4Mx32 | 4Mx32 | 4Mx32 | 4Mx32 | 4Mx32 | 4Mx32 | - | - |
| 96MB | - | - | - | - | - | - | 4Mx64 | 8Mx64 |
| 128MB | 16Mx32 | 16Mx32 | - | - | - | - | - | - |
| 128MB | 8Mx32 | 8Mx32 | 8Mx32 | 8Mx32 | - | - | - | - |
| 128MB | 4Mx32 | 4Mx32 | 4Mx32 | 4Mx32 | 8Mx32 | 8Mx32 | - | - |
| 128MB | - | - | - | - | - | - | 8Mx64 | 8Mx64 |
| 136MB | 1Mx32 | 1Mx32 | 16Mx32 | 16Mx32 | - | - | - | - |

**TABLE 23-10    MEMORY MODULE COMBINATIONS FOR A TYPICAL PENTIUM MOTHERBOARD** *(CONTINUED)*

| MEMORY SIZE | SIMM 1 | SIMM 2 | SIMM 3 | SIMM 4 | SIMM 5 | SIMM 6 | DIMM 1 | DIMM 2 |
|---|---|---|---|---|---|---|---|---|
| 144MB | 2Mx32 | 2Mx32 | 16Mx32 | 16Mx32 | - | - | - | - |
| 144MB | 1Mx32 | 1Mx32 | 1Mx32 | 1Mx32 | 16Mx32 | 16Mx32 | - | - |
| 160MB | 4Mx32 | 4Mx32 | 16Mx32 | 16Mx32 | - | - | - | - |
| 160MB | 2Mx32 | 2Mx32 | 2Mx32 | 2Mx32 | 16Mx32 | 16Mx32 | - | - |
| 192MB | 8Mx32 | 8Mx32 | 16Mx32 | 16Mx32 | - | - | - | - |
| 192MB | 4Mx32 | 4Mx32 | 4Mx32 | 4Mx32 | 16Mx32 | 16Mx32 | - | - |
| 192MB | 8Mx32 | 8Mx32 | 8Mx32 | 8Mx32 | 8Mx32 | 8Mx32 | - | - |
| 256MB | 32Mx32 | 32Mx32 | - | - | - | - | - | - |
| 256MB | 16Mx32 | 16Mx32 | 16Mx32 | 16Mx32 | - | - | - | - |
| 256MB | 8Mx32 | 8Mx32 | 8Mx32 | 8Mx32 | 16Mx32 | 16Mx32 | - | - |
| 256MB | - | - | - | - | - | - | 16Mx64 | 16Mx64 |

## Modern Bank Requirements

Although the idea of "banks" (and the many combinations of Table 23-10) may seem confusing, current systems make the chore much easier. Today's SDRAM and DDR SDRAM systems typically need just one DIMM to fill a "bank," and the motherboard often supports a wide range of module sizes (e.g., 32MB to 512MB and larger). Since virtually all motherboards provide several DIMM slots (see Figure 23-8), adding memory is simply a matter of installing another DIMM of the proper type, adequate speed, and acceptable size into another available DIMM slot. For example, a motherboard intended for an AMD Athlon XP

**FIGURE    23-8**    The MSI 845G Max-L motherboard, which provides three DIMM slots for up to 1.5GB of 200/266 MHz DDR SDRAM modules (Courtesy of Motherboards.org)

processor may accept one 128MB DDR SDRAM DIMM in one slot, then take a second 128MB or larger DIMM when you're ready to expand the system. RIMMs are also usually as forgiving, but pay attention to the installation of C-RIMMs to maintain the signal characteristics of the Rambus channel. Table 23-11 lists the DIMM modules suited for an Intel D845GBV motherboard.

## Memory Matching

Another bank requirement demands *memory matching*—using modules of the same size and speed within a bank. For example, when adding multiple SIMMs to a bank, each SIMM must be rated for the same access speed and share the same memory configuration (for example, 2Mx36). This issue is not quite so critical with DIMMs, where only one device is needed to constitute a "bank." Still, most DIMM-based systems have their own special requirements:

■ DIMMs must meet the required guidelines for your motherboard (such as 266 MHz DDR SDRAM in 128MB, 256MB, or 512MB modules using 64Mbit or 128Mbit technology). If the DIMM does not use the correct speed, memory type, memory size, or RAM chip technology, the system may act erratically or fail to recognize the DIMM. For example, if the system needs 333 MHz DDR SDRAM, and you install 266 MHz SDRAM, the system will not function properly (if it even recognizes the incorrect module). RIMMs should also meet the requirements for your particular motherboard.

■ DIMMs can be registered or unregistered, but motherboards may not support both (and usually not in a mix). For example, Intel's D845GBV motherboard does not support registered DIMMs, so you'll need to use unregistered memory modules.

■ Most DIMMs incorporate Serial Presence Detect (SPD), and the motherboard should support that feature for automatic memory detection and configuration for optimum performance. If you must use DIMMs without SPD, you may need to configure memory timings in the CMOS Setup manually.

■ If you have two identical DIMMs—that is, DIMMs of the same speed, type, size, chip technology, and both are single sided (or both double sided)—then you may install them in either Bank 0 or Bank 1. RIMMs are often installed in sets of two modules.

| TABLE 23-11 | ACCEPTABLE DIMM TYPES FOR AN INTEL D845GBV PENTIUM 4 MOTHERBOARD | | | |
|---|---|---|---|---|
| **DIMM CAPACITY** | **CONFIGURATION** | **DDR SDRAM DENSITY** | **DDR SDRAM ORGANIZATION (FRONT/BACK)** | **NUMBER OF DDR SDRAM DEVICES** |
| 32MB | Single Sided | 64Mbit | $4M \times 16$/empty | 4 |
| 64MB | Single Sided | 64Mbit | $8M \times 8$/empty | 8 |
| 64MB | Single Sided | 128Mbit | $8M \times 16$/empty | 4 |
| 128MB | Double Sided | 64Mbit | $8M \times 8/8M \times 8$ | 16 |
| 128MB | Single Sided | 128Mbit | $16M \times 8$/empty | 8 |
| 128MB | Single Sided | 256Mbit | $16M \times 16$/empty | 4 |
| 256MB | Double Sided | 128Mbit | $16M \times 8/16M \times 8$ | 16 |
| 256MB | Single Sided | 256Mbit | $32M \times 8$/empty | 8 |
| 512MB | Double Sided | 256Mbit | $32M \times 8/32M \times 8$ | 16 |

- If you have two DIMMs of the same size, and one is single sided and one is double sided, install the single-sided DIMM in Bank 0 and the double-sided DIMM in Bank 1.

- If you have two DIMMs of different sizes (a 64MB and 128MB DIMM, for example), install the larger DIMM in Bank 0 and the smaller DIMM in Bank 1. However, motherboards are often not as picky about bank installation preferences today—the best resource for memory information is the motherboard manual itself.

Finally, you should generally follow the *bank order*. The rule is that you'd fill Bank 0 first, then Bank 1, then Bank 2, and so on. Otherwise, memory will not be contiguous within the PC, and CMOS will not recognize the additional RAM. Keep in mind that most current motherboards will support DIMMs in almost any bank (following the guidelines set forth by the motherboard maker). This means you may not need to fill DIMM banks in a given order, but that's usually the safe way to go if you don't have documentation handy.

# Memory Troubleshooting

Unfortunately, even the best memory devices fail from time to time. An accidental static discharge during installation, incorrect installation, a poor system configuration, operating system problems, and even outright failures due to old age or poor manufacture can cause memory problems. This part of the chapter looks at some of the troubles that plague memory systems and offers advice on how to deal with them.

Memory modules are *extremely* sensitive to damage from electrostatic discharge (ESD). When removing, handling, or inserting any SIMM/DIMM/RIMM device, be sure to use an antistatic wrist strap, and keep the module in its antistatic packaging until needed.

## MEMORY TEST EQUIPMENT

If you're working in a repair-shop environment, or plan to be testing a substantial number of memory devices, you should consider acquiring some specialized test equipment. A memory tester, such as the RAMCHECK from Innoventions, Inc. (www.innoventions.com), is a modular microprocessor-based system (see Figure 23-9) that can perform a thorough, comprehensive test of various memory modules

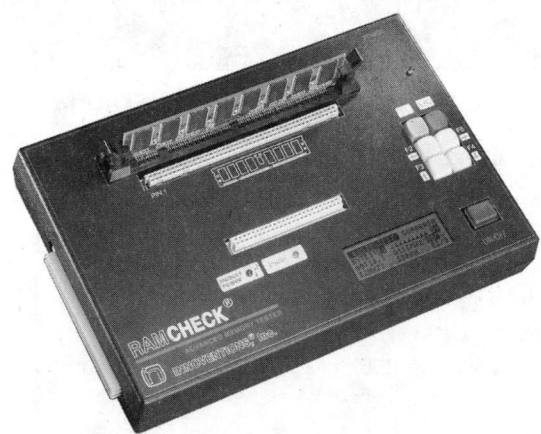

**FIGURE  23-9**   The RAMCHECK main unit, which tests a wide range of contemporary memory devices (Courtesy of Innoventions, Inc.)

and indicate the specific chip that has failed (if any). RAMCHECK will test all DDR SDRAM, SDRAM, EDO, and FPM memory modules as DIMMs or older SIMMs. The system can be configured to work with specific modules by installing an appropriate adapter module like the DDR SDRAM adapter shown in Figure 23-10. Intelligent testers work automatically and show the progress and results of their examinations on a multi-line LCD. Guesswork is totally eliminated from memory testing.

Other memory modules such as SIMMs can be tested using other plug-in modules. For example, the SIMM adapter illustrated in Figure 23-11 is another test bed for checking SIMM components from older PCs. The RAMCHECK system and plug-in modules work together to provide a full-featured test system. As you might expect, specialized tools can be an added expense, but no more so than an oscilloscope or other piece of useful test equipment. The return on your investment is less time wasted in the repair and fewer parts to replace.

## Using a Memory Tester

While most memory testers provide comprehensive options and features that you should be familiar with, the general test process can usually be broken down into a series of basic steps. The typical procedure for testing a 168-pin DIMM with the RAMCHECK is as follows:

1.  Connect the power supply to the RAMCHECK.

2.  Turn the RAMCHECK on. (Press F3 to see the demo and learn more about the unit's basic functions.)

3.  Insert a memory module (only when the Module Power LED is off). Take note of pin 1 on the module.

4.  Press F1 to start the test cycle. (Press ESC at any point to stop the testing.)

5.  **Basic Testing** determines module size, mode type, SDRAM frequency rate (or speed/cycle time for EDO/FPM), and check for basic wiring, addressing, and defective bit problems. Results are reported on the unit's LCD (see Figure 23-12). Basic testing lasts a few seconds (depending on module size), and is sufficient for most testing needs. If an error is detected, the defective bit(s) are identified and you can use various error menus to examine the details.

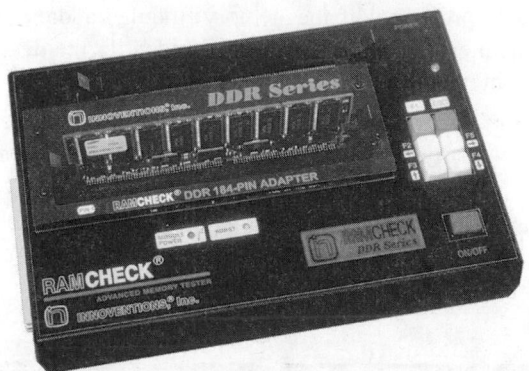

**FIGURE  23-10**    The RAMCHACK unit with a DDR SDRAM test module installed (Courtesy of Innoventions, Inc.)

**FIGURE 23-11**    The RAMCHECK SIMM adapter—one plug-in module that allows testing across many different module types (Courtesy of Innoventions, Inc.)

6. **Extensive Testing** subjects the memory module to a variety of rigorous tests (including voltage bounce, data march, and voltage cycling, along with SDRAM burst testing and chip heating in the displays of Figure 23-13). This testing verifies proper module operation under varying voltage conditions, detects intermittent problems (either temperature dependent or resulting from adjacent cell interference), and further tests the module with additional data patterns.

7. **Auto-Loop Testing** continuously runs the module, subjecting it to varying test patterns and conditions (see Figure 23-14). The loop will continue until an error occurs, or until you terminate the test. A typical auto-loop cycle should take about 20 minutes. This kind of continuous stress makes this test ideal for memory burn-in testing.

8. Use ESC to terminate the test and return to Standby Mode during any test phase (and insert a new module for testing).

## Typical Errors

Memory testers such as RAMCHECK provide detailed information about any errors revealed during testing. In most cases, you can scroll down the LCD to see specific details about problem locations, timings, and so on. However, test errors can generally be broken down into several categories:

■ **Address Error**    There is a problem with the memory module's address signals—usually an open or shorted address line. The memory tester will typically identify the details involved in the error—including the location(s) in memory where the error occurred.

■ **Connector Wiring Error**    The memory module has a wiring problem (e.g., a short or open circuit). The memory tester will typically identify the details involved in the error.

■ **Control Lines Stuck**    One or more control signals needed to operate the memory module have failed at a constant logic level (usually 0). The memory tester will typically identify the defective signal, its location, and its defect state. In many cases, the error is fatal and testing cannot continue because there's no way to control the memory module.

```
BASIC TEST  CCCCCCCC     BASIC TEST  55555555
BYTES:B1 ▲▲▲▲▲▲▲▲ B8     BYTES:B1 ▲▲▲▲▲▲▲▲ B9
00:01.2   133MHz  UBF     00:03.9   63/150nS
32Mx64    SDRAM   B1/0    16Mx72    FPM     B2/1
```

**FIGURE 23-12**    Basic testing determines essential operating information for the module (Courtesy of Innoventions, Inc.)

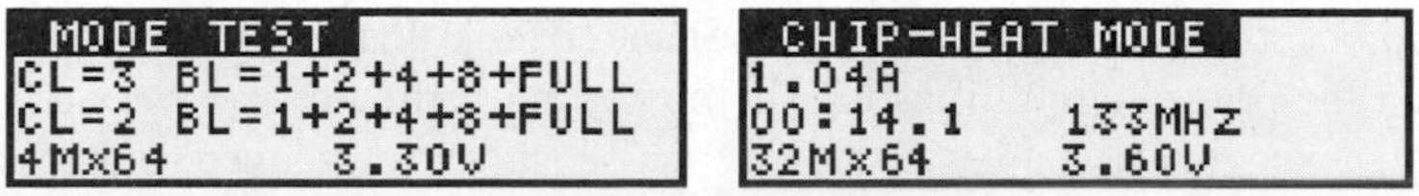

```
MODE TEST            CHIP-HEAT MODE
CL=3 BL=1+2+4+8+FULL 1.04A
CL=2 BL=1+2+4+8+FULL 00:14.1    133MHz
4Mx64      3.30V     32Mx64     3.60V
```

**FIGURE 23-13**   Extensive tests make detailed determinations of the module under varying conditions (Courtesy of Innoventions, Inc.)

■ **Data Bit Error**   A data bit at one or more addresses has failed—usually because the bit read back at that particular address did not match the bit written to that address. The memory tester will typically identify all of the details involved in the error (including the signal line, the address, the function performed during the error, and the states of other key signals).

■ **Device Type Error**   The installed memory module is not what the test unit was expecting. You may need to perform some setup operations to prepare the tester appropriately. For example, a DRAM card was set up for testing, but a regular 72-pin or 30-pin SIMM was detected.

■ **No Memory**   No memory device/module was detected by RAMCHECK. There is a major problem with the memory module's control signals, or the memory device is not supported by the testing unit.

■ **Short Circuit on Main Vdd**   The memory module's voltage (Vdd) has experienced a short circuit.

■ **Size Error**   The installed memory module showed a different physical layout than what the test unit was expecting. You may need to perform some setup operations to prepare the tester appropriately. For example, you inserted a 16Mx32 DIMM, but the tester was configured for 8Mx32.

■ **Size Measurement Error**   Some portion of the memory module has failed, and the test unit could not find all of the reported memory. Check the tester's setup, but also suspect a massive failure of a portion of the memory module.

■ **Speed Error**   The installed memory module tested slower than what the test unit was expecting. You may need to perform some setup operations to prepare the tester appropriately.

■ **Unequal Size Error**   Different banks, or groups of data bits in the memory device exhibit different sizes. There may be a possible size/address problem on one or more banks of the module. The memory tester will usually report the detected versus expected sizes for each bank or group.

## REPAIRING SIMM/DIMM/RIMM SOCKETS

If there is one weak link in the architecture of a SIMM, DIMM, or RIMM, it is the slot that connects it to the motherboard. Ideally, the memory module should sit comfortably in the slot, then gently snap in—held in place by two clips on either side of the slot (such as in Figure 23-8 earlier). In actual practice, you really have to push that module to get it into place. Taking it out again is just as tricky. As a result, it is not uncommon for a socket to break from excessive force and render your extra memory unusable.

The best (that is, the *textbook*) solution is to remove the damaged socket and install a new one. Clearly there are some problems with this tactic. First, removing the old socket will require you to remove the motherboard, desolder the broken socket, and then solder in a new socket (which you can buy from a

```
AUTO-LOOP TEST       AUTO-LOOP    33CC33CC
LOOP#241             LOOP#3980         B2/0
00:08:20.9  42/100mS 19:30:46.3   100MHZ
16Mx32    4.75V  FPM 16Mx72    3.15V  SDRAM
```

**FIGURE 23-14**   Auto testing places the module under considerable stress to locate intermittent or long-term problems (Courtesy of Innoventions, Inc.)

full-service electronics store such as DigiKey). In the hands of a skilled technician with the right tools, this is not so hard. But the printed circuit runs of a computer motherboard are *extremely* delicate, and the slightest amount of excess heat can easily destroy the sensitive, multilayer connections—ruining the motherboard entirely.

Fortunately, there are some tricks that might help you. If either of the socket's clips have been bent or broken, you can usually make use of a medium-weight rubber band that is about one inch shorter than the socket. Wrap the rubber band around the module and socket, and the rubber band should do a fair job holding the memory module in place. If any part of the socket should crack or break, it can be repaired (or at least reinforced) with a good-quality epoxy. If you choose to use epoxy, be sure to work in a ventilated area, and allow plenty of time for the epoxy to dry. This does not "fix" the problem, but it may contain the damage and allow the motherboard to serve a long and reliable working life. Otherwise, it's often best to simply replace the motherboard outright.

## CONTACT CORROSION

Corrosion can occur on a memory module's contacts if the module's contact metal is not the same as the socket's contact metal. This will eventually cause contact (and memory) problems. As a rule, check that the metal on the socket contact is the same as the module's contacts (usually tin or gold). You may be able to get around the problem in the short term by cleaning corrosion off the contacts manually using a cotton swab and good electronics-grade contact cleaner. In the meantime, if you discover that your memory and connectors have dissimilar metals, you may be able to get the memory seller to exchange your memory modules.

## PARITY/ECC ERRORS

Parity/ECC errors constitute many of the memory faults that you will see as a technician. As you saw earlier in this chapter, parity and ECC are important parts of a computer's self-checking capability. Errors in memory will cause the system to halt rather than continue blindly along with a potentially catastrophic error. But it is not just faulty memory that causes parity or ECC errors. Parity and ECC can also be influenced by your system's configuration. Here are the major causes of parity/ECC problems:

- One or more memory bits are intermittent or have failed entirely.
- Poor connections between the memory module and its socket (e.g., a loose connection or contact corrosion).
- Too few wait states or incorrect timing entered in the CMOS Setup (memory is too slow for the CPU).
- An intermittent failure or other fault in the power supply.
- A bug, computer virus, or other rogue software.
- A fault in the memory controller chip or BIOS.
- A loose or missing RIMM heat spreader, resulting in an overheated Rambus chip.

When you're faced with a parity/ECC error after a memory upgrade, you should suspect a problem with wait states/burst timings or memory type settings in the CMOS Setup routine, so check them first. If the wait states or other memory settings are correct, systematically remove each module, clean the contacts, and reseat each module properly. If the errors continue, try removing one bank of memory modules at a time. (Chances are that the memory is bad.) You may have to relocate memory so that Bank 0 remains filled. When the error disappears, the memory you removed is likely to be defective.

Some full-service PC shops may have a memory tester unit available. If so, they may be persuaded to test your suspect memory module(s) for a nominal cost (perhaps even for free).

When parity/ECC errors occur spontaneously (with no apparent cause), you should clean and reinstall each memory module *first* to eliminate the possibility of bad contacts. Next, check the power supply outputs—low or electrically "noisy" outputs may allow random bit errors. You may have to upgrade the supply if it is overloaded. Try booting the system "clean" from a write-protected floppy disk to eliminate the possibility of buggy software or computer viruses. If the problem persists, suspect a memory defect in the memory module.

# CONTEMPORARY MEMORY SYMPTOMS

With the rapid advances in computer technology, specific numerical (or "bank and bit") error codes (often seen with XT and AT vintage systems) have long-since been rendered impractical in newer systems where tens of megabytes can be stored in just a few chips. The i486, Pentium, Pentium II, and today's Pentium III/4 computers use a series of generic error codes. The *address* of a fault is always presented, but there is no attempt made to correlate the fault's address to a physical chip. Fortunately, today's memory systems are so small and modular that trial-and-error isolation can often be performed rapidly on just a few memory modules. The following symptoms below highlight many of the most common memory problems encountered in "contemporary" systems. As a rule, memory problems with new hardware installations can be traced to three potential causes:

- **Improper configuration**   You selected the wrong memory module for your computer, or neglected configuration rules. For example, you may have installed an SDRAM module when a DDR SDRAM module was needed, or you installed a double-sided DIMM when only single-sided DIMMs are supported.

- **Improper installation**   The memory may not be seated correctly, a slot is bad, or the slot (and contacts on the memory module) may need cleaning.

- **Defective hardware**   The memory module itself is defective, or the corresponding slot is damaged.

**SYMPTOM 23-1**    **The number "164" appears on the monitor**    You may also see this displayed as a "Memory Size Error"—the amount of memory found during the POST does not match the amount of memory listed in the system's CMOS Setup. Run the CMOS Setup routine and make sure that the listed memory amount matches the actual memory amount. If memory has been added or removed from the system, you will have to adjust the figure in the CMOS Setup to reflect that configuration change. If CMOS Setup parameters do not remain in the system after power is removed, try replacing the CMOS backup battery or CMOS/RTC chip.

The latest CMOS Setup routines do not actually list the amount of RAM—it is detected automatically. However, you may simply have to enter the CMOS Setup, then immediately "save changes and exit" to reset the amount of detected RAM in your system.

**SYMPTOM 23-2**    **New memory is installed, but the system refuses to recognize it**
New memory installation has always presented some unique problems since different generations of PCs deal with new memory differently. The oldest PCs require you to set jumpers or DIP switches in order to recognize new blocks of memory. The vintage i286 and i386 systems (such as a PS/2) use a setup disk to tell CMOS about the PC's configuration (including new memory). More recent i386 and i486 systems incorporate an "installed memory" setting into a CMOS Setup utility in BIOS that must be updated after the memory is installed or removed. Late-model i486, Pentium, and Pentium II/III/4 systems actually "autodetect" installed memory each time the system is booted (so it need not be entered in the CMOS

Setup, though Setup may need to "autodetect" the new RAM amount on first boot). Make sure that your memory is identified according to the vintage of your particular system.

Also check that a correct bank has been filled properly. The PC may not recognize any additional memory unless an entire bank has been filled and the bank is next in order (Bank 0, then Bank 1, and so on). You may wish to check the PC's user manual for any unique rules or limitations in the particular motherboard. Keep in mind that many late-model Pentium II/III/4 motherboards do *not* need banks filled in order, though that's usually the safest policy to follow when upgrading or troubleshooting any PC. Also remember that RIMMs may need to be installed in sets of two, and C-RIMMs are needed in any unused RIMM slots on the motherboard. If the problem persists, try other memory modules.

**SYMPTOM 23-3**    **New memory has been installed or replaced, and the system refuses to boot**    The system may also produce a beep code (see Chapter 17). Memory installations often proceed flawlessly, but when boot problems occur, you can usually narrow the problem down to several key areas. Always start by checking AC power, the system power switch, and power connections to the motherboard. Check that none of the system cabling was dislodged during the memory installation. Also see that all expansion boards and cables are inserted evenly and completely. Flexing the motherboard during memory installation may have pried one or more boards slightly out of their slots.

Your memory modules may not be inserted correctly. Take the modules out and seat them again—making sure the locking arms are holding the module securely in place. If the problem continues, you probably do not have the right memory module for that particular computer. Make sure the memory module is the correct part that is compatible with your PC. Finally, check for any particular "device order" that may be required by the motherboard. Certain systems require that memory be installed in pairs or in descending order by size. Refer to the system or motherboard manual for specific details on your exact system. If all else fails, replace the memory module(s).

**SYMPTOM 23-4**    **After adding RAM, the monitor remains blank**    This is a common oversight during memory upgrades, and is almost always caused by disconnecting the monitor or dislodging the video adapter. Power down the system and recheck the video card and monitor connection, then try booting the system again. Double-check that you have the memory modules for the computer. For example, if you have non-parity or non-ECC memory in a computer that requires error-checking memory, or DDR SDRAM memory in a computer that supports only SDRAM, the screen may remain blank. If there is simply no system activity, see Symptom 23-3 earlier for additional details.

**SYMPTOM 23-5**    **The system only recognizes half of the newly installed memory at start time**    The memory count takes place at POST, but not all of the new memory (perhaps half) is recognized by the POST. In virtually all cases, the full capacity of the memory module is not properly read (from the SPD) because the BIOS may not address the module's chip density properly. You can exchange the new memory modules for devices with an acceptable chip density (e.g., 128Mbit chips rather than 256Mbit chips). You may also be able to correct this trouble by updating the BIOS so that the module's SPD will be utilized properly.

**SYMPTOM 23-6**    **You see a general RAM error with fault addresses listed**    In actual practice, the error message may appear as any of the examples here depending on the specific fault, where the fault was detected, and the BIOS version reporting the error.

```
Memory address line failure at <XXXX>, read <YYYY>, expecting <ZZZZ>
Memory data line failure at <XXXX>, read <YYYY>, expecting <ZZZZ>
```

```
Memory high address failure at <XXXX>, read <YYYY>, expecting <ZZZZ>
Memory logic failure at <XXXX>, read <YYYY>, expecting <ZZZZ>
Memory odd/even logic failure at <XXXX>, read <YYYY>, expecting <ZZZZ>
Memory parity failure at <XXXX>, read <YYYY>, expecting <ZZZZ>
Memory read/write failure at <XXXX>, read <YYYY>, expecting <ZZZZ>
```

Each of the errors shown is a general RAM error message indicating a problem in RAM addressing, data, or error checking. The code "XXXX" is the failure segment address—an offset address may be included. The word "YYYY" is what was read back from the address, and "ZZZZ" is the word that was expected. The difference between these read and expected words is what precipitated the error.

In general, these errors indicate that at least one memory module has failed. A trial-and-error approach is usually the least expensive route in finding the problem. First, reseat each memory module and retest the system to be sure that each module is inserted and secured properly. Rotate a known-good memory module through each occupied SIMM/DIMM/RIMM socket in sequence. If the error disappears when the known-good module is in a slot, the old device that had been displaced is probably the faulty one. You can go on to use specialized module troubleshooting equipment to identify the defective chip, but such equipment is rather expensive unless you intend to repair a large volume of modules to the chip level.

If the problem remains unchanged, even though every module has been checked, the error is probably in the motherboard's memory controller (usually the North Bridge of the motherboard chipset). Run a thorough system diagnostic if possible, and check for failures in other areas of the motherboard that affect memory (such as the interrupt controller, cache controller, DMA controller, or memory management chips). If the problem prohibits a software diagnostic, use a POST board and try identifying any hexadecimal error code. If a support chip is identified, you can replace the defective chip, or replace the motherboard and retest the system.

**SYMPTOM 23-7    You see a "Decreasing Available Memory" error message**    This is basically a confirmation message that indicates a failure has been detected in memory, and that all memory *after* the failure has been disabled to allow the system to continue operating (although at a substantially reduced level). Your first step should be to reseat each memory module and ensure that they are properly inserted and secured. Next, take a known-good memory module and step through each occupied slot until the problem disappears—the device that had been removed is probably the faulty one. Keep in mind that you may have to alter the system's CMOS Setup parameters as you change memory sizes or move memory around the machine. (An incorrect setup can cause problems during system initialization.)

**SYMPTOM 23-8    You find that you cannot use 256MB DIMMs that contain 64Mbit RAM components**    This type of problem may also occur with other memory types and sizes, and is typically caused by a compatibility problem between the motherboard and memory technology. You should double-check the manufacturer's recommendations for your motherboard and verify the type of DIMM sizes and technologies best suited to the particular motherboard. Some motherboard models (such as Intel's JN440BX motherboard) cannot use such sophisticated RAM components on a DIMM of that capacity. This can cause the motherboard to produce invalid timing signals and cause unpredictable system behavior. Try smaller DIMM(s), or use DIMM(s) with less dense memory components on board.

**SYMPTOM 23-9    The system intermittently reports errors, crashes, or reboots spontaneously**    Certainly many potential problems can result in errors, crashes, and reboots, but memory issues are very common causes. Possible memory problems include electrostatic discharge

(ESD), memory overheating (often caused by inadequate ventilation), contact corrosion, and a faulty power supply. Memory devices damaged through ESD should be replaced. ESD can typically be prevented through proper grounding of the power supply and the AC electrical receptacle, and the use of anti-static precautions when handling memory components. Contact corrosion can be corrected by cleaning the memory contacts and the slots as explained earlier. If you suspect the power supply, replace the supply with a good quality model with enough power to allow for future expansion of the system.

**SYMPTOM 23-10**    **Memory devices from various vendors refuse to work together**
The system experiences a "memory failure" during the memory count at start time. The problem often occurs when the memory modules appear identical "on paper," but subtle timing differences exist that cause system performance/stability problems when modules are paired from different vendors. This tends to be a very "machine-specific" problem, though it can occur on any PC under the right circumstances. For example, Gateway Solo PCs can suffer this problem when customers use the same size memory modules (4MB, 8MB, or 16MB) made by *different* vendors. Try matching the memory modules from the same manufacturer (including part number and speed).

**SYMPTOM 23-11**    **After installing a Rambus kit, you get a "Use 40ns memory" error.**
For example, after installing a Rambus memory kit into a new P4 system, you get an error message such as "Memory is not fast enough for system. Use 40ns memory". In virtually all cases, the Rambus memory is too slow (e.g., PC600 Rambus rather than PC800 Rambus), and the motherboard requires 800 MHz 40ns Rambus modules or faster. Motherboards running at 533 MHz FSB (e.g., 2.36 GHz, 2.40 GHz, and 2.5 GHz CPUs) may require 1066 MHz RDRAM memory modules. Simply replace the memory modules with models of the required speed.

**SYMPTOM 23-12**    **The system isn't booting with 1066 MHz Rambus modules**    For example, this is a known problem with Asus P4T533-C Pentium 4 motherboards, and is caused because the BIOS settings are incorrect for 1066 MHz memory—the BIOS does not correctly identify the Rambus memory module(s) at start time. You may be able to upgrade the motherboard BIOS to correct the trouble, or enter the CMOS Setup manually and correct the memory timing options (in Advanced Options) such as

- **CPU/PCI Frequency**    [133/33] (This is for a CPU w/ 533 MHz FSB.)
- **RDRAM/FSB FREQ Ratio**    [4X] (This is for 1066 MHz Rambus—do not use autodetection.)

**SYMPTOM 23-13**    **You see a "ROM Error" message displayed on the monitor**    This may also appear as a "207" error on some systems. To guarantee the integrity of system ROM, a checksum error test is performed as part of the POST. If this error occurs, one or more ROM locations may be faulty. Your only alternative here is to replace the system BIOS ROM(s) and retest the system. (You cannot flash older AT-class ROMs.)

**SYMPTOM 23-14**    **You see an "XXXX Optional ROM Bad, Checksum = YYYY" error message**    Part of the POST sequence checks for the presence of any other ROMs in the system. When another ROM is located, a checksum test is performed to check its integrity. This error message indicates that an external BIOS ROM (such as a SCSI adapter BIOS or video card BIOS) has checked "bad," or its address conflicts with another device in the system. In either case, system initialization cannot continue.

Check the ROM address setting first. If you have just installed a new peripheral device when this error occurs (such as a SCSI controller board), try changing the new device's ROM address jumpers to resolve the conflict. Next, check the new device itself. Remove the peripheral board, and the fault should disappear.

Try the board on another PC. If the problem continues on another PC, the adapter (or its ROM) may be defective. If this error has occurred spontaneously, remove one peripheral board at a time and retest the system until you isolate the faulty board; then replace the faulty board (or just replace its ROM if possible).

**SYMPTOM 23-15**   **You see a "Cache Memory Failure—Disabling Cache" error**   The cache system has failed—usually on an older motherboard. The tag RAM, cache logic (motherboard chipset), or cache memory on your motherboard is defective. Your best course is to replace the cache RAM chip(s) or COAST (Cache-on-a-Stick) module. If the problem persists, try replacing the cache logic or tag RAM (or replace the entire motherboard). You will probably need a schematic diagram or a detailed block diagram of your system in order to locate the cache memory chip(s), so refer to the system or motherboard manual for detailed information.

**SYMPTOM 23-16**   **Windows Protection Errors occur after adding memory modules**
You may find that Windows halts with Windows Protection Errors during boot, or randomly crashes with "Fatal Exception Errors" when opening applications. For example, this is a known problem with the older Intel Thor motherboard using the 1.00.01.CNOT BIOS after installing 32MB of RAM. This issue is usually due to certain third-party SIMMs operating at speeds faster or slower than 60ns. The motherboard probably has tight memory specifications, and SIMMs that operate at the correct speed are required (not faster or slower, even though the SIMMs are "marked" properly). Some SIMM manufacturers mark the SIMMs at 60ns, but the SIMMs actually run at 45ns. Try some SIMMs from a different manufacturer. It is also possible that a BIOS upgrade may loosen timing enough to make the SIMMs usable. Even with later systems, "protection errors" that appear after adding memory can usually be traced to issues with the memory modules. Check the modules specifications against the motherboard's requirements, and exchange the modules for more appropriate versions if necessary.

**SYMPTOM 23-17**   **Windows returns a "General Protection Fault" (or GPF)**   There are several possible causes behind general protection faults under Windows. An x86-type CPU (from 80286 to Pentium III/4 processors) can detect when a program encounters a problem. The most common problems include stack faults, invalid instructions (such as software bugs), divide errors (divide by zero or "math" errors), and general protection faults. These generally indicate nonstandard code in a Windows application, in Windows itself, or in a Windows device driver.

- **Stack Fault (a.k.a. Interrupt 12)**   There are several possible reasons for a "stack fault." An instruction may try to access memory beyond the limits of the current Stack segment, or load the "SS" register with invalid information (though that shouldn't happen under Windows 95/98). Stack faults are always fatal to the current application in Windows, but Windows may not crash completely.

- **Invalid Instruction (a.k.a. Interrupt 6)**   The CPU detects most invalid instructions and generates a software interrupt to report them. Invalid instructions are always fatal to the application. This should never happen, but is usually caused by coding errors that accidentally execute data instead of code.

- **Divide Error (a.k.a. Interrupt 0)**   This error is caused when the CPU's intended destination register cannot hold the result of a divide operation—it could be divide by zero, or divide overflow. In either case, the problem is almost always due to a problem with the program.

- **General Protection Fault (a.k.a. Interrupt 13)**   Windows "protects" the memory used by programs, so that no other programs may use that space. Any protection violations that do not cause another exception cause a "general" protection exception because one of the following conditions is true:

- Exceeding a segment limit when using the certain memory segments. This is a very common bug in programs—usually caused by miscalculating how much memory is required in an allocation.

- Transferring program execution to a segment of memory that is not executable (for example, jumping to a location that contains garbage).

- Writing to a read-only or a code segment of memory.

- Loading a bad value into a segment register.

- Using a null pointer. A value of 0 is defined as a null pointer. In protected mode, it is always invalid to use a segment register that contains 0.

In virtually all cases, the solution to a "protection fault" is to try reloading the suspect program, driver, or Windows module. (Run ScanDisk to check the disk file system for errors.) If the suspect program or driver is buggy, it may be necessary to download and install a patch file to correct potential programming errors.

**SYMPTOM 23-18**    **The PC halts or crashes when entering a CPU power-down state under Windows 98**    If your system's power management settings are configured to allow the processor to enter a "C3" power state on a computer supporting the "Advanced Configuration and Power Interface" (ACPI) standard, you may encounter symptoms such as corrupted memory after several minutes of inactivity. In other cases, the computer may stop responding after several minutes of inactivity.

This problem is due to an issue with the Intel 440BX chipset under Windows 98 (caused by Windows 98 itself), that may allow memory contents to be corrupted when a CPU enters or leaves its power-down state. If that motherboard uses the Intel PIIX4-E IDE controller chipset, the computer might hang (known to occur if a bus mastering operation occurs while in the power-down state). A service patch will generally correct this trouble (or you can upgrade the operating system to Windows XP), but you can work around this issue by preventing the CPU from entering the C3 power state. To accomplish this, exit Windows and reboot the computer. Enter your CMOS Setup and set the "lvl3_latency" entry to a value greater than 0x3E8h (1000 decimal). If "lvl3_latency" is greater than 0x3E8h, the Windows 98 ACPI driver does not enter the C3 state. You'll need to save your changes and reboot the PC for those changes to take effect.

Your own PC may provide different options for disabling ACPI support in the BIOS.

**SYMPTOM 23-19**    **Windows appears unstable after disabling virtual memory**    There is not enough RAM in the system. This can occur if you disable virtual memory with inadequate RAM in the system. Later versions of Windows have higher memory requirements than earlier versions, so while there may be a "theoretical" minimum for Windows, additional RAM usually results in better system performance and stability. To resolve this problem, install more RAM in your computer, enable virtual memory, or both. To enable virtual memory under Windows 9x/Me:

1.  Restart your computer and hold down the CTRL key until the Windows 98 Startup menu appears.

2.  Choose Safe Mode from the Startup menu.

3.  Click Start | Settings | Control Panel.

4.  Double-click System, click the Performance tab, and then click Virtual Memory.

5.  Click the option labeled "Let Windows manage my virtual memory settings."

6.  Click OK, click Close, and then click Yes when you are prompted to restart your computer.

Use the following steps to enable virtual memory under Windows XP:

1. Click Start | Control Panel | Performance and Maintenance | System.
2. Click the Advanced tab and select the Settings button in the Performance area.
3. Click the Advanced tab and select the Change button in the Virtual Memory area.
4. Click the "System managed size" radio button, click Set, and click OK.
5. Reboot the system if necessary.

**SYMPTOM 23-20    You notice that Windows system resources remain lower after quitting a program**    This is often referred to as *memory leakage*, when memory is not freed by a program after it quits. Restart the PC—rebooting the PC from scratch should return any "leaked" memory. You can use this trick as a temporary workaround. Memory leakage can also occur if you start a program, and then quit before it has completely started. Do not quit a program before it has completely started. Memory leakage is often caused by poorly coded or buggy software rather than Windows itself. If you notice "leakage" with a particular program, check with the software maker's Web site to see if there is a downloadable patch or update that will correct the memory leakage.

**SYMPTOM 23-21    You see an error message such as "Insufficient memory to initialize Windows," even though there is plenty of RAM**    The problem may be "too much" RAM. When attempting to install or start Windows 9x/Me with over 768MB of RAM (perhaps 1GB or more), the system may return an erroneous "insufficient memory" message. This is generally regarded as a problem with Windows 9x/Me (and is not seen under Windows XP, which should be able to manage up to 4GB of physical RAM), but you can work around the problem by limiting the amount of RAM that Windows can use to 768MB.

1. Use Notepad to edit the SYSTEM.INI file.
2. Add the following line in the [386Enh] section of the SYSTEM.INI file:

   ```
   MaxPhysPage=30000
   ```

3. Save the SYSTEM.INI file, and then restart your computer.

If this problem occurs during Windows Setup, start the system to the command prompt (a.k.a. DOS) mode and use the DOS-based EDIT utility to modify the SYSTEM.INI file. When you save the edited SYSTEM.INI file and reboot the PC, the Windows Setup should continue.

**SYMPTOM 23-22    When trying to format a hard drive under Windows 98, you see an error message such as "Insufficient memory to load system files"**    The format process will terminate. This error occurs if you attempt to format your hard disk using the **format c: /q /u /s /v** command at a command prompt, but there is not enough free conventional memory to use the /s switch. This error may also occur if you start your computer using the Windows 98 startup disk, and then attempt to format your hard disk. This is a problem with Windows 98, but there are ways to work around the problem. First, do not use the /s switch with the **format** command—after the format process is finished, transfer the system files to the hard disk using the **SYS C:** command. If you're restarting your computer using the Windows 98 startup disk, choose "Start Computer With CD-ROM Support" on the Windows 98 Startup menu, and then use the **format** command to format your hard disk.

**SYMPTOM 23-23    Your Windows 9x/Me system returns an "internal stack overflow" error**    "*Stacks*" are small sections of reserved memory that programs use for processing hardware events (such as interrupts). A "stack overflow" occurs when there is not enough space in memory to run the hardware interrupt routines. When Windows shows an "internal stack overflow" error, there is not enough space in memory (either set aside, or available to handle the calls being made to the system hardware).

Check for resource conflicts—there may be an incompatible hardware configuration causing excessive interrupt operation. Check the port and IRQ settings of any network card, sound card, and/or modem. Make sure that there are no COM2/COM4 or COM1/COM3 conflicts, and that no devices are sharing IRQs. Disable or remove conflicting devices. Finally, the computer may need a BIOS upgrade. Check the BIOS version and contact the manufacturer of your computer for information about a BIOS upgrade.

The CONFIG.SYS file may not be properly configured for the Windows installation. Try the following values: STACKS=64,512 (this is the maximum allowed), FILES=60, and BUFFERS=40. Also check for old memory managers. Examine the CONFIG.SYS file to determine whether files such as HIMEM.SYS or EMM386.EXE are being loaded from a folder other than the Windows folder. If so, boot Windows using the Safe Mode Command Prompt Only (DOS) option. Rename the CONFIG.SYS file to CONFIG.DOS, and the AUTOEXEC.BAT file to AUTOEXEC.DOS, and then restart the computer. Ideally, you should try to minimize the real-mode settings in startup files wherever possible. Otherwise, try repartitioning and reformatting the drive and installing Windows from scratch.

**SYMPTOM 23-24    You encounter random "fatal exception" errors under Windows**
The most common cause for these error messages is faulty physical memory (RAM) on the computer. Try starting the system in Safe Mode. If the "fatal exception" errors disappear, the problem may be with one or more buggy or corrupted drivers loading in the normal mode. You may then need to systematically disable background software and drivers in order to isolate the offending software.

Check the CMOS Setup next. In some circumstances it may be possible to adjust the CMOS settings (such as changing memory wait states, burst timings, or disabling the motherboard's L2 cache) to stabilize Windows 9x/Me successfully. Finally, check/replace the RAM. To resolve "fatal exception" errors, it is often necessary to isolate and replace the defective RAM. In rare cases, the problem may be on the motherboard.

**SYMPTOM 23-25    An error indicates that there is not enough memory to start Windows (or an application)**    This problem can occur if there is not enough real and virtual memory to start the Windows shell (or the particular program). Start your computer to the DOS prompt and free some space on the hard disk containing your swap file (virtual memory). Once you free some space on your hard disk, restart Windows normally and try to run the program again. If the problem persists (or you cannot free more space on the drive), try adding RAM to the system.

**SYMPTOM 23-26    You are encountering a memory error with HIMEM.SYS under DOS**
In many cases, this is a compatibility problem with system memory. For example, the Intel Advanced/AS motherboard is incompatible with two specific Texas Instruments EDO SIMMs (part numbers TM124FBK32S-60 and TM248GBK32S-60). Other EDO SIMMs from TI and other vendors will not cause this error. Try a memory module from a different manufacturer. Also make sure that you're using the latest version of HIMEM.SYS.

**SYMPTOM 23-27**    **Windows returns a fault in the MS-DOS extender**    This kind of error can occur in Windows 9x/Me, and usually happens in either of two formats: "Bad fault in MS-DOS extender" or "Fault outside of MS-DOS extender." You may also see a "stack dump" with a format such as

```
Raw fault frame:
EC=0344 CS=031F IP=85E2 AX=001D BX=0005 CX=1800 DX=155F
SI=0178 DI=0178 BP=016E DS=027F ES=027F SS=027F SP=0166
```

An error such as "Bad fault in MS-DOS extender" generally occurs when the fault handler in DOSX.EXE (the DOS extender) generates another cascaded fault while trying to handle a protected-mode exception. This error is usually caused by one of the following factors:

- HIMEM.SYS is unable to control the A20 line (which may indicate a motherboard problem).
- DOS=HIGH is not functioning properly (perhaps HIMEM.SYS is not loaded or corrupt).
- Your RAM may be defective. You might try a RAM diagnostic to isolate any memory problems.
- You are not running MS-DOS (your system is running DR DOS, for example).
- The third-party memory manager (such as 386MAX) is not configured correctly.
- A "EMM386.EXE NOEMS x=A000-EFFF" command line is missing from the CONFIG.SYS file.
- You have an old, out-of-date BIOS ROM that isn't supporting the DOS extender properly.
- Your memory-related CMOS Setup configuration is incorrect.
- Your Windows files are old or corrupted. Run ScanDisk to test for file problems, and then reinstall Windows if necessary.
- Your system is infected with a computer virus (for example, Form, Forms, Noint, or Yankee Doodle are known to cause this type of problem). Check the system with a current anti-virus utility.

If you see an error such as "Standard mode fault outside MS-DOS extender," the Windows kernel may be generating a processor exception during initialization (before it has installed its own exception handlers), or when the kernel determines that it cannot handle an exception. The underlying causes are almost always the same as just outlined.

**SYMPTOM 23-28**    **You see a memory error such as "Unable to control A20 line"**    This error is almost always related to the HIMEM.SYS driver. The A20 line controls access to the first 64KB of extended memory (known as the *high memory area*, or "HMA"). The HIMEM.SYS device driver must control the A20 line in order to manage extended memory. The error message is reported by HIMEM.SYS if it incorrectly identifies the extended memory handling mechanism of the computer, or if the handling method in your PC's BIOS is unknown. There are two workarounds for this problem. First, you can set the "machine" switch. Add the "/M:x" (the "machine type") switch to the HIMEM.SYS command line in your CONFIG.SYS file (where "x" is the "machine number" between 1 and 14 or 16). Shut down and then restart your computer. For example:

```
DEVICE=C:\DOS\HIMEM.SYS /M:1
```

If HIMEM.SYS isn't being used on the system, check the BIOS version next. It may be necessary to upgrade your machine's BIOS, or contact your system vendor for assistance in modifying your CMOS settings—you may need to disable a FastGate (or similar) option.

An incorrect A20 machine handler may hang the system at boot-up. You should have an MS-DOS (or Windows 9x/Me) bootable floppy disk available to boot from before you experiment with different machine switches.

**SYMPTOM 23-29**   **You see a memory error such as "Cannot setup EMS buffer" or "Unable to set page frame base address"**   This is a known problem with many Dell Inspiron 7000 computers under Windows 98, and appears when starting a DOS-based program that requires Expanded Memory (EMS) page frames. EMS page frames normally require 64KB of upper memory, but Dell Inspiron 7000-series computers can only provide 54K of upper memory. This is an issue with the Dell system design, and generally cannot be corrected unless you turn off the program's use of EMS page frames (or run the program on another system).

**SYMPTOM 23-30**   **EMM386 refuses to load after installing Windows 98**   This issue can occur if you load EMM386.EXE using the /Highscan switch. The /Highscan switch can interfere with hardware detection during setup, so it is disabled by Windows 98 Setup. You can reenable EMM386 using the following steps:

1. Use Notepad to open the CONFIG.SYS file.
2. Locate the line that loads EMM386.EXE, and remove the following text from the beginning of the line:
   `rem -- by Windows 98 setup -`
3. Save and close the CONFIG.SYS file.
4. Restart the computer.

**SYMPTOM 23-31**   **You install a memory module, but Windows reports that it is "Out of Memory"**   This is typically due to an incorrect virtual memory (vcache) entry in the SYSTEM.INI file. To resolve this problem, modify the SYSTEM.INI file as outlined here:

1. Click Start | Run.
2. In the Run dialog box, type **sysedit** and click OK.
3. Click the SYSTEM.INI tab to display the file.
4. Choose the Search menu and click Find.
5. Type **vcache** and click Next. When you find the [vcache] section, add the MinFileCache= and MaxFileCache= lines to it as follows. This will limit the size of the disk cache file to between 5MB and 8MB.

   ```
   [vcache]
   MinFileCache=51200
   MaxFileCache=56320
   ```

6. Click File | Save, then close the System Configuration Editor and restart the computer.

# Further Study

**Autotime**   www.autotime.com
**CST, Inc.**   www.simmtester.com
**Innoventions**   www.innoventions.com
**Kingston**   www.kingston.com
**PNY**   www.pny.com

# 24

# MICE AND TRACKBALLS

**A**s operating systems and applications evolved beyond simple menus and began to make use of the powerful graphics systems coming into popular use during the mid-1980s (EGA and VGA graphics), ever-larger amounts of information were presented in the user interface. Simple, multilayered text menus were aggressively replaced with striking *graphical user interfaces* (GUIs). System options and selections were soon represented with symbols (graphic "buttons" or "icons") instead of plain text. Using a keyboard to maneuver through such visual software soon became a cumbersome (if not impossible) chore.

 Peripheral designers responded to this situation by developing a family of *pointing devices* (see Figure 24-1). Pointing devices use a combination of hardware and software to produce and control a graphical screen *cursor*. A software device driver generates the cursor and reports its position. As the pointing device is moved around, hardware signals from the pointing device are interpreted by the device driver, which moves the cursor in a like manner. By positioning the cursor over a graphic symbol and activating one, two, or three of the buttons on the pointing device, it is now possible to select (click or double-click) and manipulate (a.k.a. drag) options in the application program instead of using a keyboard.

 There are three factors needed to make a pointing device work: the physical signal-generating hardware itself, a software driver (the device driver), and the application program, which must be written to make use of the device driver. Today, Windows 9x/Me/XP provides the broader "environment" for the

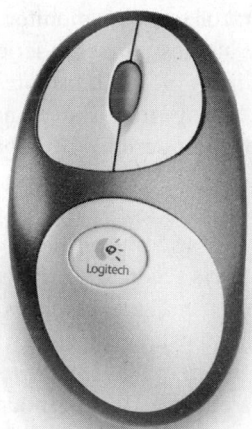

**FIGURE 24-1**    A Logitech cordless optical MouseMan provides precise positioning with wireless convenience (Courtesy of Logitech, Inc.)

mouse; all other applications work through the common OS mouse interface. If any of these three items is missing, the pointing device will not work. This chapter looks at the technology, maintenance, and troubleshooting of two popular pointing devices: the mouse and the trackball.

# The Mouse

Although the development of computer pointing devices has been ongoing since the early 1970s, the first commercial pointing device for IBM-compatible systems was widely introduced in the early 1980s. The device was small enough to be held under your palm, and your fingertips rested on its button(s). A small, thin cord connected the device to the host computer (initially the serial port was used). The device's small size, long tail-like cord, and quick scurrying movements around the desk immediately earned it the label of "mouse."

Every mouse needs at least one button. By pressing the button, you indicate that a selection is being made at the current cursor location. Many mouse-compatible software packages only make use of a single mouse button even to this day. A two-button mouse is more popular (reflecting the endurance of the mouse design) because a second button can add more flexibility to the mouse. For example, one button can work to select an item, while the second button can be used to deselect that item again, or to activate other menus and options. Windows 98/Me/XP uses the right-click to bring up a context-sensitive menu for icons, files, and folders. A few mouse designs use three buttons, but the third button is rarely supported by application programs other than CAD or high-end art applications.

## MOUSE GESTURES

While everyday PC users use the mouse as if it were second-nature, new PC users often struggle with the mouse—it's one of the first hurdles that new users must overcome. The mouse is certainly not difficult to use, but it requires a bit of hand-eye coordination that takes getting used to. The notion of moving the mouse around on a horizontal surface, and then watching the little cursor (which can be difficult to see at high resolutions; especially for older users) on a vertical monitor can be disorienting. Once you've got the movements down, it's time to master the buttons through a series of gestures.

The first mouse gesture is called *clicking,* which is little more than a single momentary press of the left mouse button (on a two-button mouse). Clicking is the primary means of making a selection in the particular application program. The second common gesture is *double-clicking,* which is simply two single clicks in immediate succession. A double-click also represents selection, but its exact use depends upon the application program—under Windows 98/Me/XP, a double-click will launch a selected application or open a desired data file. The third type of mouse gesture is the *drag,* where a graphical item can be moved around the display. Dragging is almost always accomplished by pressing and holding the left mouse button while the cursor is over the desired item, then (without releasing the button) moving the item to its new location. When the item has moved to its new position, releasing the left mouse button will "drop" the item in that location. Consequently, dragging is often called *drag and drop.*

The mouse movements and gestures are acquired by the mouse driver software and passed to the operating system (e.g., Windows) where they are interpreted and carried out. Every Windows application can access mouse information through that single uniform interface. In the early days of DOS, a real-mode mouse driver would be needed in the AUTOEXEC.BAT file, and each application would need its own built-in mouse routines.

## MOUSE CONSTRUCTION

A mouse is a relatively straightforward device consisting of four major parts: the plastic housing, the mouse ball, the electronics PC board, and the signal cable. Figure 24-2 illustrates a classical mouse assembly.

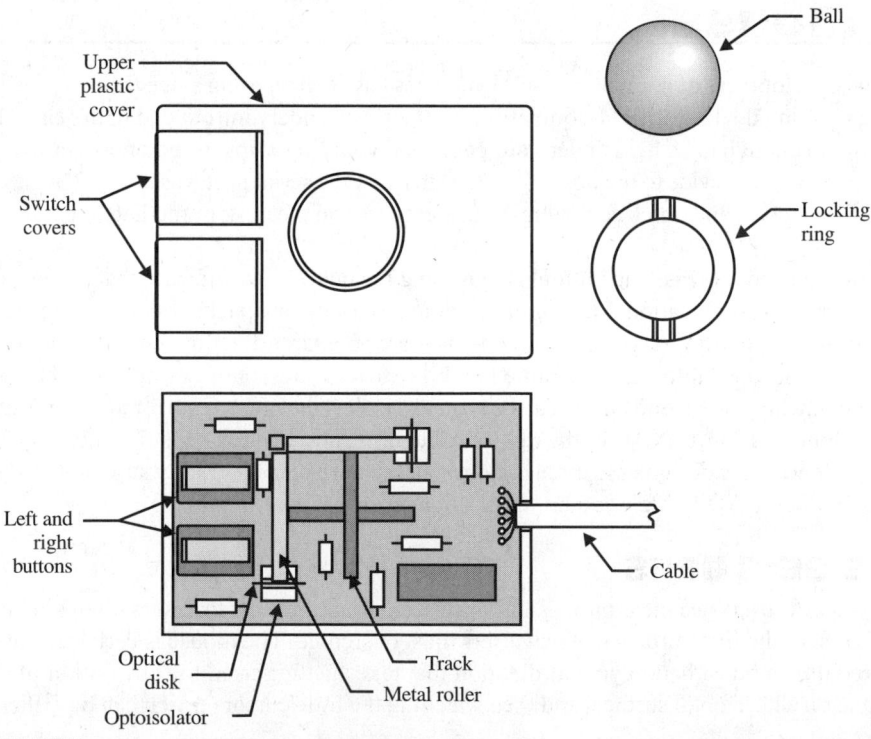

**FIGURE 24-2**    Internal construction of a basic mouse

The outer housings can vary greatly depending on the manufacturer and vintage of your particular mouse (just walk through a computer store and look at the bewildering variety of mouse styles available on the shelf), but the overall scheme is almost always identical. The mouse ball is a hard rubber ball situated up inside the mouse body just below a small PC board. When the mouse is positioned on a desktop, the ball contacts two actuators that register the mouse ball's movement in the X (left-to-right) and Y (up-to-down) directions. Both sensors generate a series of pulses that represent movement in both axes. Pulses equate to mouse movement—more pulses mean more movement. The pulses from both axes are amplified by the mouse circuit board and sent back to the computer along with information on the condition of each mouse button. Figure 24-3 shows a PointPerfect mouse.

The mouse device driver must be loaded before the mouse will work. Under DOS, the real-mode driver is loaded in CONFIG.SYS or AUTOEXEC.BAT. Under Windows 98/Me/XP, the protected-mode mouse driver is loaded as Windows boots. Once the driver is loaded, it interprets the pulses generated by the mouse and translates them into X and Y screen locations where the visible mouse cursor is positioned. As the mouse moves left and right or up and down, pulses are added or subtracted from the cursor's X and Y screen coordinates by the device driver. The application program can then call for the X and Y coordinates, as well as button states and advanced options like wheel states for a "wheel mouse". The key to a working mouse is its sensor devices. Sensors (or actuators) must be responsive enough to detect minute shifts in mouse position and generate pulses accordingly, yet be reliable enough to withstand wear, abuse, and environmental effects. There are three general types of sensors: mechanical, optomechanical, and optical.

## Mechanical Sensors

The greatest challenge in mouse design (and the largest cause of failures) is the reliable and repeatable conversion of mouse movement into serial electrical pulses. Early mouse versions used purely mechanical sensors to encode the mouse ball's movements. As the mouse ball turned against a roller (or shaft), copper contacts on the shaft would sweep across contacts on the mouse PC board—much like commutating rings and brushes on a DC motor. Each time a roller contact touches a corresponding contact in the mouse, an electrical pulse is generated. Since a mouse must typically generate hundreds of pulses for every linear inch of mouse movement, there are several sets of contacts for each axis.

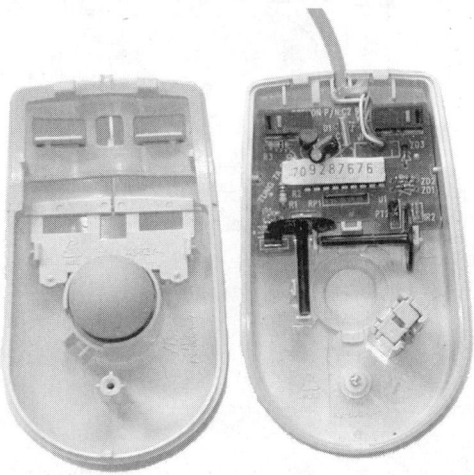

**FIGURE 24-3**    Internal view of a PointPerfect PS/2 mouse

It is important to note that mouse pulses can be positive or negative depending on the relative direction of the mouse in an axis. For example, moving the mouse right may produce positive pulses, while moving the mouse left may produce negative pulses. Similarly, moving the mouse down along its Y axis may produce positive pulses, while moving the mouse up may produce negative pulses. All pulses are then interpreted and tracked by the host computer.

Although mechanical sensors are simple, straightforward, and very inexpensive to produce, there are some significant problems that can plague the mechanical mouse. Mechanical mouse designs are not terribly reliable. The metal-on-metal contact sets used to generate pulses are prone to wear and breakage. Dust, dirt, hair, and any other foreign matter carried into the mouse by the ball can also interfere with contacts. Any contact interference prevents pulses from being generated. This condition results in a frustratingly intermittent "skip" or "stall" of the cursor while you move the mouse. It is often a simple matter to disassemble and clean the contacts. Still, mechaincal sensors have been obsolete for some time now, and chances are that you will not encounter a mouse with mechanical sensors.

### Optomechanical Sensors

The next generation of mouse designs replaced the mechanical contacts with an *optoisolator* arrangement, as illustrated in Figure 24-4. A hard rubber mouse ball still rests against two perpendicularly opposed metal or plastic actuator rollers, but instead of each roller driving an array of contacts, the rollers rotate slotted wheels that are inserted into optoisolators. An optoisolator shines LED light across an air gap where it is detected by a photodiode or phototransistor. When a roller (and slotted wheel) spins, the light path between LED and detector is alternated or "chopped." This causes the detector's output signal to oscillate—thus, pulses are generated. The pulse frequency is dependent on mouse speed. As with the mechanical mouse, the optomechanical mouse produces both positive and negative serial pulses, depending on the direction of mouse movement.

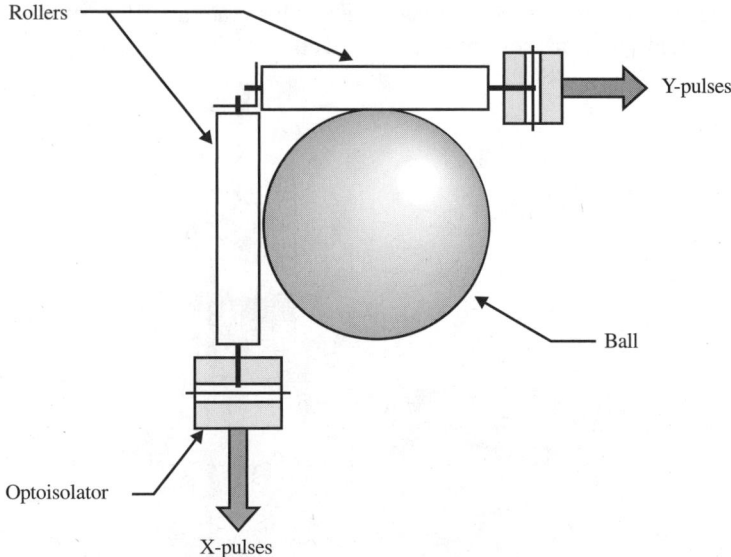

**FIGURE  24-4**    Sensor layout for an optomechanical mouse or trackball

The optomechanical mouse is a great improvement over the plain mechanical approach. By eliminating mechanical contacts, wear and tear on the mouse is significantly reduced, resulting in much longer life and higher reliability. However, the mouse is still subject to the interference of dust and other foreign matter that invariably finds its way into the mouse housing. Regular cleaning and internal dusting can prevent or correct instances of cursor skip or stall. Most mouse models in production today use optomechanical sensors.

## Optical Sensors

The one recurring problem with traditional mice is their dependence on a ball and rollers to translate physical movement into electrical signals. Over time, wear, dust, and other debris on the mousepad transfer to the ball and into the mouse. This eventually causes the mouse to stall and skip. By replacing the ball and optomechanical assembly with a completely optical sensor, it's possible to seal the mouse and avoid long-term reliability problems. Optical sensors work using an LED transmitter/receiver pair (see Figure 24-5). The LED sends out light to the tracking surface, and the light is bounced back to the receiver. As the mouse is passed back and forth across a surface, textures in the surface break up the light into pulses, and those pulses are translated into cursor movement. In addition, optical sensors are often more sensitive and can support faster tracking over a wide variety of surfaces. For example, Microsoft's IntelliEye optical sensors can track 6,000 pulses per second for travel up to 30 inches per second.

# The Trackball

The *trackball* is basically an inverted mouse. Instead of using your hand to move a mouse body around on a desk surface, you move a trackball in a stationary housing. Your hand or fingertips move the ball itself, which is mounted through the top of the device. The advantage to a trackball is that it does not move. As a result, trackballs can be incorporated into desktop keyboards or added to your work area with a minimum of required space. Such characteristics have made trackballs extremely popular with laptop and notebook computers. Today, most notebook computers incorporate pointing devices directly.

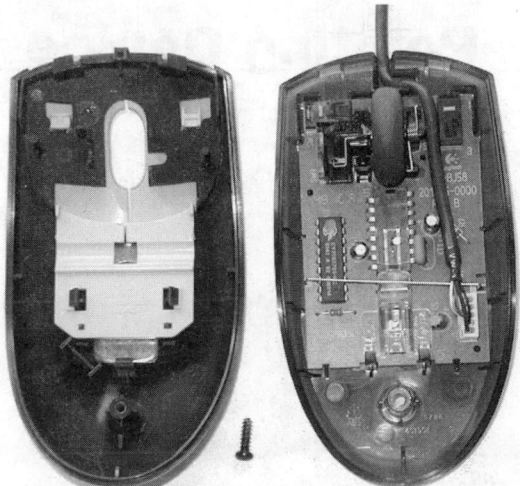

**FIGURE 24-5**   The Logitech WheelMouse uses an optical sensor to track movement across a variety of surfaces.

In spite of its advantages, however, a trackball is not quite as easy to use as a mouse. The successful use of a mouse is largely a matter of hand-eye coordination—a flick of the wrist and a click or two can maneuver you through a program at an impressive rate. Since you can move the mouse and manipulate its buttons simultaneously, dragging is a very intuitive gesture. Trackballs are usually turned with only your thumb. This positions the rest of your hand such that you can only reach one trackball button. That is a fine arrangement as long as you're only clicking a single button, but you often have to move your hand around completely to get to the second button (or you must at least let go of the ball). Dragging is also typically a cumbersome effort. Even a clumsy trackball is better than none at all, so you should be as familiar with trackballs as with a mouse.

## TRACKBALL CONSTRUCTION

Virtually all trackballs use the same optomechanical sensor technology that is used with mice (see Figure 24-6). Instead of the mouse PC board resting over the ball, a trackball sits on top of a PC board. The hard rubber ball sits at the intersection of a set of small plastic rails (or *tracks*)—thus, the term "trackball." The rails position the ball between two perpendicularly oriented metal or plastic rollers. Each roller drives a slotted wheel, which, in turn, runs between the LED and detector of an optoisolator. As the ball and rollers are made to turn, the slotted wheels cause the respective optoisolator's light path to alternate and generate signal pulses. Pulse frequency is dependent on the relative movements of each roller. Pulses are read and interpreted just as they are with a mouse.

During initialization, your computer must load a device driver designed to read the proper port, interpret any signals generated by the trackball, and make switch and roller information available to whatever program calls for it. Given the similarities of mice and trackballs, many mouse-compatible applications are capable of accessing trackball data and responding just like a mouse. Even the trackball device driver is virtually identical to a mouse driver. (Trackball drivers are usually "adopted" mouse drivers that simply compensate for the inversion of the ball.) Since the technologies and construction techniques of mice and trackballs are essentially the same, the remainder of this chapter will treat a mouse and trackball as interchangeable devices.

# Cleaning a Pointing Device

Pointing devices are perhaps the simplest peripheral available for your computer. While they are reasonably forgiving to wear and tear, trackballs and mice can easily be fouled by dust, debris, and foreign matter

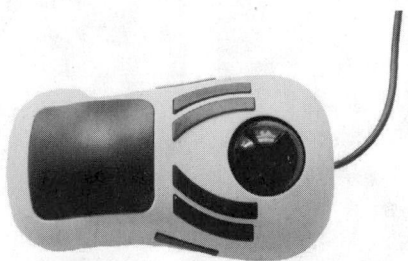

**FIGURE  24-6**    The ITAC Evolution trackball provides ergonomic hand positioning and a USB interface.

introduced from the ball. Contamination of this sort is almost never damaging, but it can cause some maddening problems when using the pointing device. A regimen of routine cleaning will help to prevent contamination problems. You can use prefabricated mouse cleaning kits (Figure 24-7) to speed the cleaning process. Turn your computer off and disconnect the mouse from the system before performing any cleaning procedures.

Optical mice can be cleaned by gently dusting the optical sensor on the bottom of the unit.

1. *Remove the ball.* A ball is held in place by a retaining ring. For a mouse, the retaining ring is on the bottom. For a trackball, the ring is in the top. Rotate the ring (usually counterclockwise) and remove it gently—the ball will fall out. Place the retaining ring in a safe place.

2. *Clean the ball.* Wash the ball in warm, soapy water, and then dry it thoroughly with a clean, lint-free towel. Place the ball in a safe place with the retaining ring.

3. *Blow out the dust.* Use a can of photography-grade compressed air to blow out any dust or debris that has accumulated inside the pointing device. You may want to do this in an open or outdoor area.

4. *Clean the rollers.* Notice that there are three rollers in the mouse/trackball: an X roller, a Y roller, and a small pressure roller that keeps the ball pressed against the X and Y rollers. Use a cotton swab dipped in isopropyl alcohol to clean off any layer of gunk that may have accumulated on the rollers. If any gunk falls off the rollers, you'll need to remove it.

5. *Reassemble and test.* Allow everything to dry completely. Then replace the ball and secure the retaining ring (usually by turning it clockwise again). You should then reconnect and test the pointing device to be sure that it is performing as expected.

Do not use harsh solvents, wood alcohol, or chemicals inside the pointing device or on the ball. Chemicals can easily melt the plastic and result in permanent damage to the pointing device.

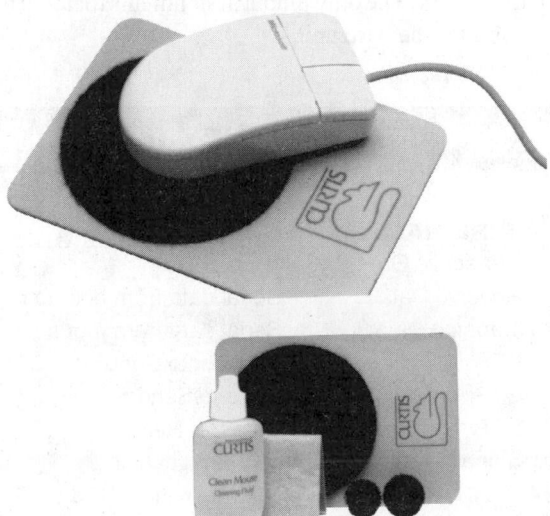

**FIGURE 24-7**   A Curtis mouse cleaning kit (Curtis, a division of Rolodex, Secaucus, NJ)

# Troubleshooting a Pointing Device

The weakest link in a pointing system is the peripheral pointing device itself. Few peripheral devices are subjected to the wear and general abuse of trackballs or mice. They are dropped, yanked, and moved constantly from place to place. Damage to the device's circuit board, cabling, and connector is extremely common due to abuse. Accumulations of dust and debris can easily work into the housing and create havoc with the rubber ball, tracks, and rollers. Even optical mouse sensors need to be dusted periodically. Hardware conflicts and driver configuration issues can also result in frequent problems. This part of the chapter guides you through some simple troubleshooting techniques for your trackball and mouse.

## MOUSE/TRACKBALL INTERFACES

From time to time, you may need to check the physical interface on a mouse or trackball. At its core, the mouse is a simple serial device—that is, it can pass serial data back and forth with the host computer using communication protocols managed by the mouse driver. There are four types of mouse interfaces commonly found in the field: serial mice, wireless mice, PS/2 mice, and USB mice. Bus mice are sometimes encountered on older PCs, so their information is also presented as a reference. This part of the chapter highlights the pinouts for each interface type.

### Serial Mice

A serial mouse connects to an existing RS-232 serial port at the PC (usually COM1 or COM2) using a standard DB-9F (9-pin female) or DB-25F (25-pin female) connector. Table 24-1 lists the pinout for a Logitech Type M, V, or W serial mouse connector.

### Wireless Mice

A growing number of mice and other pointing devices are employing radio technology to support cordless operation. A wireless mouse uses a battery powered radio transceiver to exchange data with a small base station connected to a PS/2 or USB port. Unlike infrared techniques, radio allows the mouse to work without a direct line of sight to the base unit. The only pinout assignments that you need to worry about here are the PS/2 or USB interfaces used for the base unit.

**TABLE 24-1    PIN ASSIGNMENTS FOR A SERIAL PORT MOUSE (LOGITECH)**

| DB-9F 9 PIN | DB-25F 25 PIN | WIRE NAME | COMMENTS |
|---|---|---|---|
| shell | 1 | Protective Ground | |
| 3 | 2 | Receive Data | Serial data from host to mouse |
| 2 | 3 | Transmit Data | Serial data from mouse to host (for power only) |
| 7 | 4 | RTS | Request to Send |
| 8 | 5 | CTS | Clear to Send |
| 6 | 6 | DSR | Data Set Ready |
| 5 | 7 | Signal Ground | |
| 4 | 20 | DTR | Data Terminal Ready |

## Bus Mice

There are many circumstances when it is not possible to use a serial mouse on an open COM port, and the older PC is not fitted with a PS/2 port. In this case, it may be necessary to use a bus mouse, which basically involves using a stand-alone mouse controller board (a bus mouse controller) and mouse fitted with a bus mouse connector. This is usually a male subminiature D-type connector or a miniature male DIN (circular) connector. Be careful not to mistake the 9-pin DIN connector of a bus mouse for the 6-pin circular connector of a PS/2 mouse. Table 24-2 lists the pinout for a Logitech bus mouse. Keep in mind that a bus mouse controller also requires an expansion slot—this may be a real problem on older PCs where slot space is at a premium. If you find yourself upgrading an older motherboard, you may also benefit from upgrading the mouse (to a PS/2 or USB model) and retiring the bus mouse and controller.

Today, the bus mouse is largely considered to be obsolete, but you should be able to recognize a bus mouse setup.

## PS/2 Mice

Most current computers are fitted with one or two PS/2 ports. (These are sometimes referred to as PIX ports because the older motherboard's PIX controller(s) can manage the ports directly.) PS/2 ports are basic serial interfaces that are ideal for keyboards and mice. PS/2 mice use a 6-pin DIN (barrel) connector, as shown in Table 24-3. Bi-directional data transmission is controlled by the CLK and DATA lines. Both are fed by an "open collector" device that lets either the host or mouse control the lines. During nontransmission, CLK is at logic "1," and DATA is at logic "0" or "1." The PC can inhibit mouse transmission by forcing CLK to logic "0."

## USB Mice

Most current computers are fitted with two or four Universal Serial Bus (USB) connections and can accommodate a USB mouse/trackball. The advantage of USB ports is their convenience. You can connect and disconnect USB devices with the system running, and the device will automatically be identified and enumerated under Windows 98/Me/XP. USB also allows you to "mix and match" many different types of USB devices on the same port, so you can connect a USB mouse directly to the computer's main USB

| TABLE 24-2 | PIN ASSIGNMENTS FOR A BUS MOUSE PORT (LOGITECH) | | |
|---|---|---|---|
| **WIRE COLOR** | **MINI-DIN PIN** | **LOGITECH P-SERIES SIGNAL** | **MICROSOFT INPORT SIGNAL** |
| Black | 1 | +5V | +5V |
| Brown | 2 | X2 | XA |
| Red | 3 | X1 | XB |
| Orange | 4 | Y1 | YA |
| Yellow | 5 | Y2 | YB |
| Green | 6 | Left | SW1 |
| Violet | 7 | Middle | SW2 |
| Gray | 8 | Right | SW3 |
| White | 9 | GND | Logic GND |
| SHIELD | Shell | Chassis | Chassis |

**TABLE 24-3    PIN ASSIGNMENTS FOR A PS/2 MOUSE PORT (LOGITECH)**

| PIN | WIRE NAME |
|---|---|
| 1 | DATA |
| 2 | Reserved |
| 3 | Ground |
| 4 | +5V Supply |
| 5 | CLK |
| 6 | Reserved |
| Shield | Chassis |

port, or to a connector on any USB hub attached to the system. The simple 4-pin USB connection follows this layout:

- Pin 1: Power
- Pin 2: Data −
- Pin 3: Data +
- Pin 4: Ground

## MOUSE DRIVER SOFTWARE ISSUES

Device drivers are often underrated when it comes to mouse/trackball troubleshooting. The driver plays a vital role in mouse performance, and any driver bugs or incompatibilities will have direct consequences on mouse operation. Mouse drivers are also surprisingly versatile programs, and real-mode drivers can be extensively configured through the use of command-line switches. For example, Table 24-4 lists the command-line switches for Microsoft's real-mode Mouse driver 9.0x. When dealing with any kind of mouse issue, always start by checking that the correct driver is installed, that the driver is the latest version, and that it is using any necessary command-line switches to adapt itself to the particular PC. (Default settings are not always adequate.)

**TABLE 24-4    COMMAND-LINE SWITCHES FOR THE REAL-MODE MICROSOFT MOUSE DRIVER 9.0X**

| SWITCH | EXPLANATION |
|---|---|
| ON | Enable mouse |
| OFF | Disable mouse |
| /B | Bus mouse type |
| /C<n> | Serial mouse on COM1 or COM2 |
| /E | Load mouse in low memory |
| /F | Find pointing device |
| /H<n> | Horizontal sensitivity (5–100) |
| /I<n> | InPort mouse type (1 or 2) |

| **TABLE 24-4** | **COMMAND-LINE SWITCHES FOR THE REAL-MODE MICROSOFT MOUSE DRIVER 9.0X** *(CONTINUED)* |
|---|---|

| SWITCH | EXPLANATION |
|---|---|
| /KP<n> | Small button selection (P = Primary, S = Secondary) |
| /K<n> | ClickLock (/KC = ON, /K = OFF) |
| /M<n> | Enable default cursor (/M1 = ON, /M = OFF) |
| /N<n> | Cursor delay (0–10) |
| /O<n> | Rotation angle (0–359) |
| /P<n> | Active acceleration profile |
| /Q | Load mouse quietly (no startup messages; only in 9.01) |
| /R<n> | Interrupt rate |
| /S<n> | Horizontal and vertical sensitivity (5–100) |
| /V<n> | Vertical sensitivity (5–100) |
| /Y | Disable hardware cursor |
| /Z | PS/2 mouse type |

There is much less to configure when working under Windows 9x/Me/XP. Windows will automatically detect the mouse or trackball, and then attempt to install proper drivers for it. If the manufacturer provides specific drivers on CD (or diskette), you can typically update drivers from that media (which may be necessary to correct bugs or compatibility issues with specialized pointing devices such as "wheel mice"). To check the mouse driver, open the Device Manager, expand the Mouse entry, right-click the mouse device, and click Properties. Driver information is listed on the Driver tab (see Figure 24-8). Click the Driver Details button for specific driver file names and other information.

# USING MOUSEKEYS

Windows 98/Me/XP traditionally relies on a mouse for clicking and dragging, but there is a little-known feature of Windows 98/Me/XP called *MouseKeys* that allows you to use the numeric keypad to move the mouse around the screen, click, double-click, and drag. MouseKeys can be helpful if you're caught without a mouse (or troubleshooting a defective mouse system), and you need to navigate the Windows 98/Me/XP environments.

 The MouseKeys feature is also handy if you're setting up a PC for any user that is physically impaired or otherwise unable to use a conventional mouse.

The MouseKeys feature is activated through the Accessibility properties under the Control Panel. With Windows 9x/Me, click Start | Settings | Control Panel. Double-click the Accessibility icon and select the Mouse tab. Under Windows XP, click Start | Control Panel | Accessibility Options. Click Accessibility Options again and select the Mouse tab (Figure 24-9). You can enable or disable MouseKeys by checking or

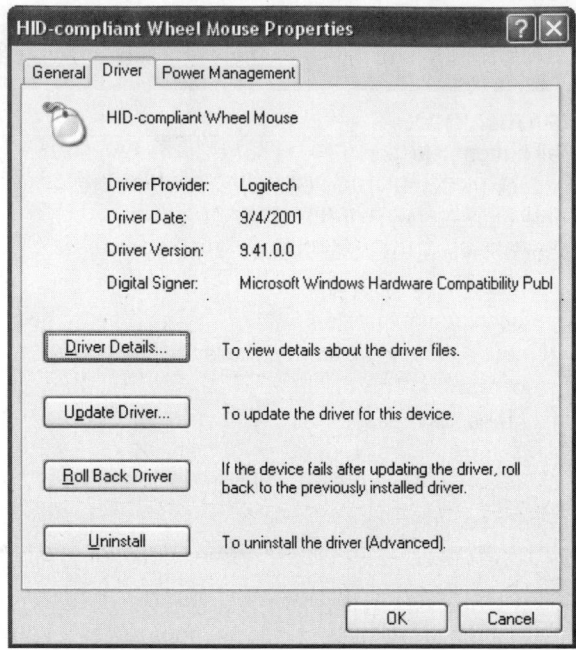

**FIGURE  24-8**    Checking the mouse driver version, date, and other details is easy under operating systems like Windows XP.

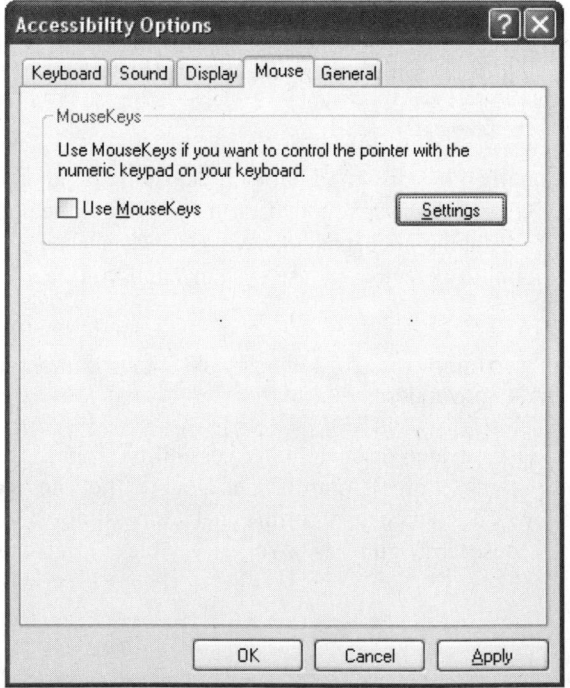

**FIGURE  24-9**    Controlling the Windows MouseKeys feature under Windows XP

clearing the check box. Once MouseKeys is enabled, you can further optimize its settings (Figure 24-10) by clicking the Settings button. If you check the Use shortcut box, you can turn MouseKeys on and off by toggling LEFT ALT-LEFT SHIFT-NUM LOCK.

Once the MouseKeys feature is turned on, move the cursor by pressing the arrow keys on the numeric keypad. Use the HOME, END, PAGE UP, and PAGE DOWN keys to move the mouse cursor diagonally. You can left-click by pressing the 5 key on the numeric keypad. To left-double-click, press the + key on the numeric keypad. To right-click, press the – button on the numeric keypad first, and then press 5 to click or + to double-click. To click as if you were using both mouse buttons at once, press the "*" key on your numeric keypad, and then press 5 to click or + to double-click. If you want to switch back to standard clicking, press / on your numeric keypad.

You'll also need to be able to drag using MouseKeys. Make sure that the MouseKeys feature is turned on, and then move the mouse pointer over the desired object. Press INS on the numeric keypad to hold down the mouse button and grab the object. Move the mouse pointer over the new desired area, and then press DEL on the numeric keypad to drop the object.

# ADJUSTING MOUSE PROPERTIES

To use a mouse comfortably and successfully, the mouse must be adjusted for your personal preferences. You'd be surprised at how many people get frustrated because they can't double-click, only to find that the "Double-click speed" property for the mouse is set too high. You can tailor the mouse to your own tastes through the Mouse Properties dialog . Under Windows 9x/Me, click Start | Settings | Control Panel. When the Control Panel is open, double-click the Mouse icon. With Windows XP, click Start | Control Panel | Printers and Other Hardware | Mouse. The Mouse Properties dialog appears (see Figure 24-11). You can

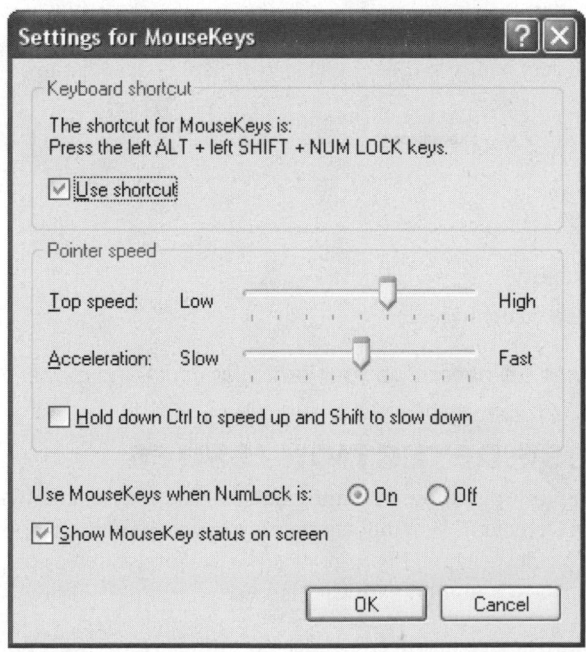

**FIGURE  24-10**    Adjusting MouseKeys for best performance under Windows XP

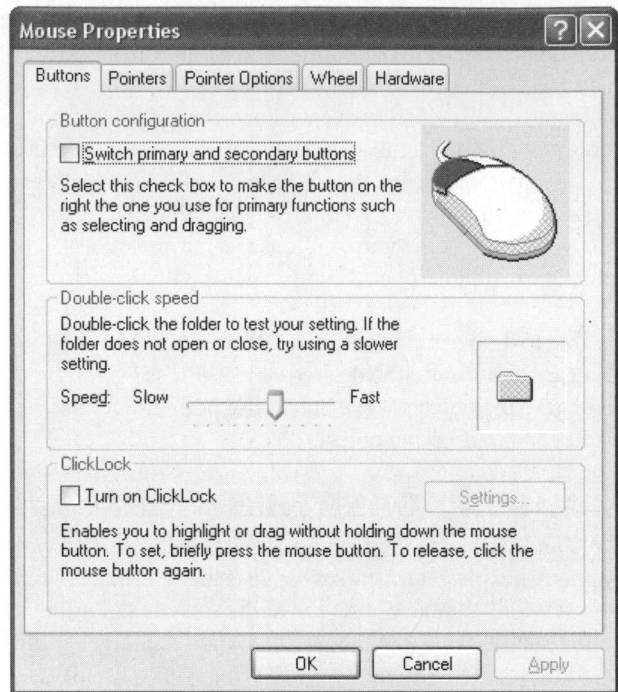

**FIGURE  24-11**    The Mouse Properties dialog under Windows XP

select the "handedness" of the mouse, its double-click speed (sensitivity), its pointer format, movement sensitivity, cursor "trails" (very handy in older LCD laptop displays), and many other attributes supported by the mouse such as:

- Left and right button uses
- Double-click sensitivity
- Pointer appearance
- Pointer speed and visibility
- Wheel sensitivity (for a wheel mouse)

The exact suite of features will depend on your particular make and model of pointing device.

## COMMON MOUSE DETECTION ISSUES

When installing, replacing, or upgrading a pointing device, you may encounter a Windows 98/Me/XP error such as "Mouse Not Detected." If Windows starts, you will be forced to use keyboard shortcuts to navigate around and exit Windows again. If you're faced with a mouse detection problem, use the following checklist to isolate the most common hardware issues:

- A port-specific pointing device has been connected to the wrong port. For example, a serial-only mouse has been connected to a PS/2 mouse port using an improperly wired adapter.

■ The port being used by the mouse/trackball is disabled, defective, or incorrectly configured. For example, a serial mouse is connected to COM1, but that COM port is also in use by an internal modem.

■ You're using an incompatible bus mouse adapter card. For example, when using a Logitech bus mouse, Logitech bus adapters must bc uscd. Verify that any third-party bus mouse adapters (and their drivers) have been removed from the system.

■ The port being used by the mouse/trackball is experiencing a hardware conflict with another device in the system. For example, a USB mouse doesn't respond because IRQ12 (typically assigned to USB support) is being used by another device, or USB has been disabled in the CMOS Setup.

■ You're inserting an extension cable or switch box between the pointing device and the system. Most pointing devices do not support the use of extension cables or switch boxes. If a switch box or extension cable is being used, remove it and connect the pointing device *directly* to the system—if normal operation returns, you know that the switch box or extension cable was to blame.

■ The pointing device is defective. Verify this by trying the device on another system. Replace the defective pointing device if necessary.

■ The pointing device is incompatible with your system. Verify this by trying another pointing device connected to the same system and port. If another pointing device fails on the same port, the problem may be with that system or port. Otherwise, try a different pointing device.

## MOUSE ISSUES WITH VIDEO DRIVERS

While driver compatibility issues are increasingly rare today, installing some third-party video drivers can cause the Windows 98/Me/XP mouse pointer to behave erratically (or not move at all). It may also cause odd types of "video corruption." (For example, the mouse pointer destroys screen elements.) Since the mouse driver uses video driver information to generate the screen cursor, some video drivers may not operate properly with your particular mouse driver. Try changing the video mode to a lower resolution or color depth (such as the "standard VGA" mode), and see if the problem disappears. If it does, you should try updating the video driver and/or the mouse driver. Otherwise, you may need to update the video card's firmware, or use a different pointing device.

## USB MOUSE TROUBLESHOOTING TIPS

USB ports offer a surprising amount of versatility when connecting external devices to the system. While USB ports should be well supported under Windows 98/Me/XP, there are numerous issues that may impair USB operation and mouse performance:

■ *Check the OS versions.* Generally speaking, USB mice require Windows 98/Me/XP. Windows 95 and OSR2.x with the USB supplement are not supported.

■ *Check the driver versions.* Connecting a USB pointing device to a USB port on your system should result in the device being detected by the system (and the default USB drivers being installed). This may require the Windows 98/Me/XP CD, so insert the CD when prompted by Windows. You may use the default USB drivers that ship with Windows 98/Me/XP. But to utilize the enhanced features of your mouse, the very latest mouse driver versions for your mouse are needed. In most cases, you can obtain the latest mouse drivers directly from the manufacturer's Web site. Uninstall any older version(s) of the pointing device software from your system before installing the version that shipped with your current device, or use the Update Drivers feature located on the Driver tab of your pointing device's Properties dialog.

■ *Check the product version.* Verify that your USB mouse/trackball is using the latest firmware. Initial product releases or prerelease (evaluation) units may not function reliably under all hardware configurations.

■ *Enable the USB controller.* Many early USB (PIX3) systems shipped with the USB ports disabled. These systems must have their USB ports enabled before the mouse will be detected and function properly. These USB ports are generally enabled through the CMOS Setup. If a USB add-on card is being used, please be sure that it is a *retail* version. Prerelease versions of USB cards may not function correctly with current USB hardware. Check with the USB card's manufacturer for new drivers or firmware updates. Check the CMOS Setup and verify that the PC's USB port(s) are enabled, and make sure a suitable IRQ is assigned.

■ *Check the USB host controller.* For a USB pointing device to function properly on the USB port, the USB Host Controller must be identified correctly by Windows 98/Me/XP. Open the Device Manager. Verify that there is an entry called Universal Serial Bus Controllers, and see that there is at least one "root hub" and "host controller" below the entry (as in Figure 24-12). If this entry is missing, the controller may not be enabled or detected properly.

■ *Check the mouse entry in Device Manager.* Open the Device Manager, and then expand the Mice and Other Pointing Devices entry. Verify that there is a mouse entry that reads "HID-compliant mouse" and another entry that states the name of your USB device (refer to Figure 24-12). You may also see a Mouse entry under the Human Interface Devices entry as in Figure 24-12. If there are any errors reported on these icons (by exclamation points or red *X*s), highlight these icons and click the Remove

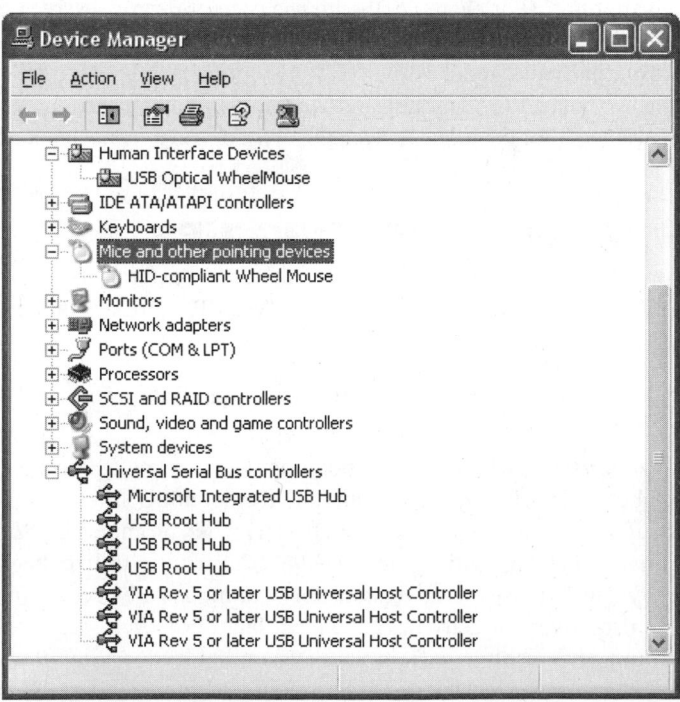

**FIGURE 24-12**    Verify USB support on the PC by checking the USB hardware in Device Manager

button. Once these icons have been removed, click the Refresh button and allow Windows to redetect the pointing device. Open the Device Manager again, and verify that there are no errors reported. Power-down the computer and restart Windows, and then test the USB device to see if it's working.

■ ***Check your external hubs.*** If two external hubs are daisy-chained together, at least one must be powered (connected to AC). If you're using two or more unpowered hubs, there may not be enough current in the second hub to properly power the USB devices connected to it. If this occurs, connect the pointing device to the first hub and test it. (Or try connecting the mouse directly to the USB port instead of a hub.) External hubs are increasingly rare today because many PCs provide four or more USB ports.

■ ***Check your USB hardware detection.*** If the USB pointing device is not detected by Windows 98/Me/XP after plugging in the device and installing the drivers, try the following:

1. Shut down the system, allow it to power-off, and then restart it.

2. Try connecting the pointing device to a second USB port (if your system has one—most do today).

3. Try connecting the mouse to a second system with a working USB port to verify the USB mouse hardware is working. Any Windows 98/Me/XP system equipped with a USB port should detect the mouse. You need not install the drivers, just see that Windows detects the mouse—if not, the device may indeed be defective.

4. Try connecting another USB device into the same USB port. If the second device is detected correctly, the mouse may be defective. If the second device is also not detected correctly, the USB port may be disabled or malfunctioning.

5. If you're using a USB hub to connect the mouse, try connecting the mouse directly to the USB port on your system.

■ ***Check for software issues.*** Windows 98/Me/XP includes a system configuration utility that can boot your system without resident programs loading from the Windows registry, the StartUp folder, and system files. Use this tool to isolate possible software conflicts:

1. Click Start and select Run. In the Open command line, type **msconfig** and click OK. The system configuration utility should appear.

2. On the General tab, click Selective Startup. Click on the WIN.INI tab (see Figure 24-13), and then click on the plus (+) sign next to each section. Check for the presence of the "LOAD=" and "RUN=" lines. If there are programs loading from either of these lines, remove the check marks from those entries. This will prevent anything in those lines from loading upon startup.

3. Click on the Startup tab, and remove the check mark from every box except the entry for essential system utilities. This will prevent memory resident programs from loading from the Run folder and other startup folders of the registry.

4. Click the OK button, and Windows should prompt you to reboot. After rebooting, test the device to see if the problem has disappeared. If it has, one of the programs loading at startup is causing the issue. Re-add each item systematically (one at time, rebooting between each addition). When you find the problem application, contact that program's manufacturer for more information or a possible work-around.

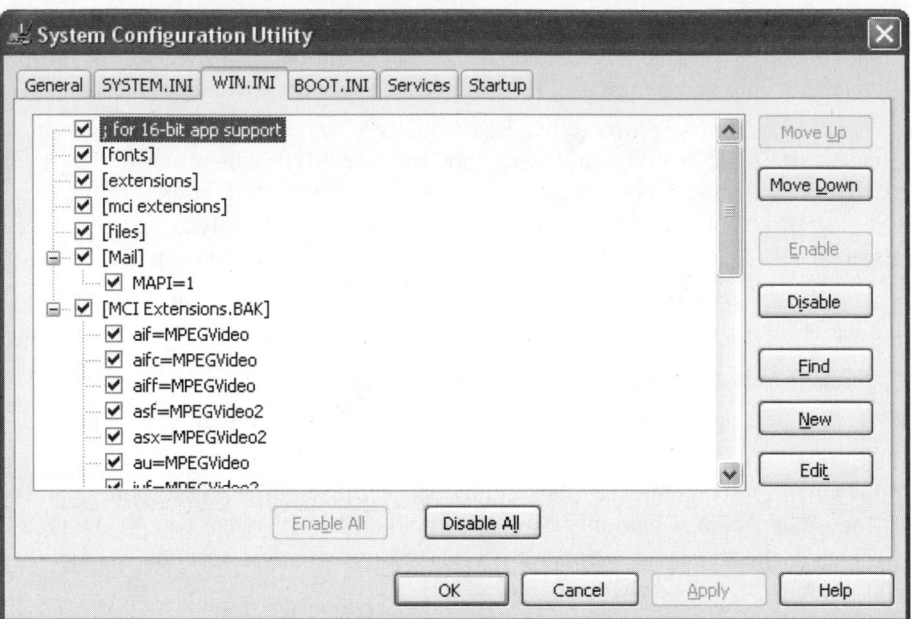

**FIGURE  24-13**    Use msconfig to help you isolate potential software conflicts with pointing devices.

## SYMPTOMS

If you cannot correct mouse problems with the preceding general guidelines, it's time to look for specific symptoms. This part of the chapter highlights a wide selection of symptoms that normally occur.

**SYMPTOM 24-1    The mouse cursor appears but it only moves erratically as the ball moves (if at all)**    This symptom may occur in either the horizontal or vertical axis. This symptom suggests that there is an intermittent condition occurring somewhere in the pointing device. You should not have to disassemble your computer at all during this procedure. Start your investigation by powering down the computer. Check the device's cable connector at the computer. Make sure the connector is tight and inserted properly. If you are in the habit of continually plugging and unplugging the mouse/trackball, excessive wear can develop in the connector pins. If the connector does not seem to fit tightly in the computer, try a new pointing device.

A more likely problem is that the device's rollers are not turning, or turning only intermittently. In most cases, roller stall is due to a dirty or damaged ball, or an accumulation of dirt blocking one or both sensors. Clean the ball and blow out any dust or debris that may have settled into the mouse/trackball housing. Refer to the preceding section on cleaning, and try to clean the device thoroughly. *Never use harsh solvents or chemicals to clean the housings or ball.*

If you have the mouse connected to a standard serial communication port (a COM port), you should check that there are no other devices using the same interrupt (IRQ). For example, COM1 and COM3 use the same IRQ, while COM2 and COM4 share another IRQ. If you have a mouse on COM1 and a modem on COM3, there will almost invariably be a hardware conflict. If possible, switch the mouse (or conflicting device) to another port and try the system again.

If there is no hardware conflict, and cleaning does not correct an intermittent condition, remove the device's upper housing to expose the PC board, and use your multimeter to check continuity across each wire in the connecting cable. Since you probably will not know which connector pins correspond to which wires at the sensor PC board, place one meter probe on a device's wire and "ring-out" each connector pin until you find continuity. Make a wiring chart as you go. Each time you find a wire path, wiggle the cable to stimulate any possible intermittent wiring. Repair any intermittent wiring if possible. If you cannot find continuity or repair faulty wiring, simply replace the pointing device.

**SYMPTOM 24-2** **One or both buttons function erratically (if at all)** Buttons are prone to problems from dust accumulation and general contact corrosion. Your first step should be to power-down your computer and disconnect the pointing device. Remove the ball and upper housing to expose the PC board and switches. Spray a small amount of electronics-grade contact cleaner into each switch, and then work each switch to circulate the cleaner.

If cleaning does not improve intermittent switch contacts, you may wish to check continuity across the connecting cable. With the ball and housing cover removed, use your multimeter to check continuity across each wire in the connecting cable. Since you probably do not know which connector pins correspond to which wires at the device, place one meter lead on a device wire and "ring-out" each connector pin until you find continuity. Once you find continuity, wiggle the cable to stimulate any possible intermittent wiring. Repair any intermittent wiring if you can, or simply replace the pointing device.

**SYMPTOM 24-3** **The screen cursor appears on the display, but it does not move** If the cursor appears, the device driver has loaded correctly. Your first step should be to suspect the serial, PS/2, or USB connection. If there is no connection, there will be no pulses to modify the cursor's position. If you find a bad connection, power-down your computer before reattaching the device's serial, PS/2, or USB connector, and then restore power and allow the system to reinitialize normally.

If the device is attached correctly to its proper serial, PS/2, or USB port, the problem probably exists in the pointing device's wiring. Remove the ball and upper housing to expose the PC board, and then use your multimeter to check continuity across each wire in the connecting cable. Since you probably do not know which connector pins correspond to which wires in the device, place one meter lead on a device wire and "ring-out" each connector pin until you find continuity. Once you find continuity, wiggle the cable to stimulate any possible intermittent wiring. Repair any intermittent or open wiring if you can, or simply replace the pointing device.

**SYMPTOM 24-4** **The mouse/trackball device driver fails to load** The *device driver* is a short program that allows an operating system to access information from a pointing device and pass that information to an application. Most computer users prefer to load their real-mode device drivers during system initialization by invoking the drivers in the CONFIG.SYS or AUTOEXEC.BAT files, though, Windows 9x/Me/XP users forego real-mode drivers in favor of protected-mode Windows drivers. Most drivers are written to check for the presence of their respective device first. If the expected device does not respond, the driver will not be loaded into memory. Other drivers load blindly regardless of whether the expected device is present.

If the device driver fails to load during initialization, your pointing device may not have been detected. Power-down your computer and check the connection of your pointing device. Ensure the device is securely plugged into the proper serial, PS/2, or USB port. If the device is missing or incorrectly inserted, install or resecure the pointing device and allow the system to reinitialize normally. If you see a "File Not

Found" error message displayed at the point your device driver was supposed to load, the driver may have been accidentally erased, may be corrupted, or may be located in another subdirectory. Try reinstalling a valid copy of your mouse device driver, and ensure that the driver is located where your calling batch file can access it. Reboot your system. Under Windows 9x/Me/XP, remove the pointing device(s) from the Device Manager and allow Windows to reboot—this should redetect and reinstall the pointing device(s) from scratch.

**SYMPTOM 24-5**   **You see a "General Protection Fault" after installing a new mouse and driver under Windows**   First, this is probably not a hardware fault. (Although it would be helpful for real-mode users to check any mouse driver command-line switches in CONFIG.SYS or AUTOEXEC.BAT.) It is more likely that the new mouse driver is conflicting with one or more drivers or is not fully compatible with your version of Windows. Check with the mouse manufacturer to see if there are any other reported problems, and find if any driver patches or updates are available. If you have an older version of the mouse driver available, try replacing that one. An older driver may not work as well as a newer one, but it may not suffer from this kind of compatibility problem. If there are no older drivers available, and no patches that you can use, you may be forced to change the mouse and mouse driver to something completely different in order to eliminate the problem.

**SYMPTOM 24-6**   **You see the error "This pointer device requires a newer version"**   In virtually all cases, you have the wrong driver installed on the system for your driver. Check the driver and make sure that the driver you are using is appropriate for the particular mouse. For example, a Logitech or Genius mouse selected in Windows setup can cause this kind of problem if you have a Microsoft mouse on the system. Change the mouse type under Windows. Under Windows 98/Me/XP, you'll need to remove the old mouse reference from the Device Manager, and then use the Add New Hardware Wizard to install the new mouse manually. Also check with the mouse manufacturer for driver updates.

**SYMPTOM 24-7**   **You see the error "Mouse port disabled or mouse not present"**   This is almost always a connection problem or a setup problem. Check the signal connector first. Make sure the mouse cable is not cut or damaged anywhere, and see that it is attached securely to the serial or PS/2 port. Many newer system BIOS versions now provide an option in the CMOS Setup for a mouse port. Check the CMOS Setup, and see that any entries for your mouse are enabled properly.

**SYMPTOM 24-8**   **The mouse works for a few minutes, then stops**   When the computer is rebooted, the mouse starts working again. This is a problem that often plagues "bargain" pointing devices, and is almost always due to buildups of static in the mouse. The static charges are interfering with the mouse circuitry and causing the mouse to stop responding (though charges are not enough to actually damage the mouse). There are generally three ways to resolve the problem: (1) spray the surrounding carpet and upholstery with very dilute fabric softener to dissipate static buildup; (2) hire an electrician to ensure that the computer and house wiring are grounded properly; or (3) replace the mouse with a more static-resistant model.

**SYMPTOM 24-9**   **You attempt a double-click but get quadruple-click, or you attempt a single-click and get a double-click**   This is a phenomenon called "button bounce" and is the result of a hardware defect (broken or poorly buffered mouse buttons). You may be able to clean the mouse buttons by spraying in some good-quality electronic-grade contact cleaner. Otherwise, you'll need to replace the mouse.

**SYMPTOM 24-10** **A single mouse click works, but double-click doesn't** When this problem occurs, it is almost always because the "double-click speed" is set too high in the Windows 98/Me/XP Mouse Propeties dialog (see Figure 24-11 earlier). Try lowering the double-click speed. Under Windows 9x/Me, click Start | Settings | Control Panel. Double-click the Mouse icon, and adjust the Double-click Speed slider under the Buttons tab. With Windows XP, click Start | Control Panel | Printers and Other Hardware | Mouse.

**SYMPTOM 24-11** **A PS/2 mouse is not detected by a notebook PC under Windows** This is typically a matter of incorrect detection or a conflict with other (older) pointing device drivers. For example, there is a known problem with PS/2 mouse detection on a Toshiba portable computer under Windows 95. You can usually correct the problem by taking the following steps:

1. Shut down the computer entirely, and physically disconnect the PS/2 mouse from the PS/2 port.
2. Restart Windows (reboot the PC if necessary).
3. Click Start | Settings | Control Panel, and double-click the System icon.
4. Select the Device Manager tab, and double-click the Mouse entry.
5. Select the mouse entry that is not being detected (for example, Toshiba AccuPoint), and click Remove.
6. Select and remove any other mouse entries.
7. Shut down the computer and reconnect the mouse, and then turn the PC back on.
8. When the system reboots, it should detect the mouse and attempt to reinstall the appropriate drivers.

If this doesn't fix the problem, a hardware issue could exist. Try a different PS/2 mouse (preferably from a manufacturer other than the current one). If a different make and model PS/2 mouse does not work, the PS/2 port may require service.

**SYMPTOM 24-12** **Mouse pointer options are not saved** This is generally a real-mode software problem, and is known to occur when you use the "extra points" features in the Mouse Manager program included with the Microsoft Mouse driver. The pointer options are not saved or written to the MOUSE.INI file when you are running a virus-protection program such as Microsoft Anti-Virus (MSAV) or Norton AntiVirus (NAV). To correct this problem, remove the CHKLIST.MS or CHKLIST.CPS file in the directory that contains the mouse files. To determine the location of that directory, type **set** at the MS-DOS command prompt. It will return a list of locations of various files and memory strings. Look for the "MOUSE=" line, and then go to that directory and delete the CHKLIST.MS or CHKLIST.CPS file. Reboot the system and try saving options again.

**SYMPTOM 24-13** **Clicking the right mouse button doesn't start the default context menus of Windows** If the mouse manager software you're running is using an assignment set for the right button, this assignment will override the Windows default setting of "context menus." Open the mouse management software utility, and change the assignment for the right button to "Unassigned." Save your changes. The right mouse button will now access the default context menus. Alternatively, you can try removing any mouse management software and allow Windows to use the pointing device natively.

**SYMPTOM 24-14** **The wheel mouse cursor jumps erratically around a laptop display** For example, when you connect a PC/2 wheel mouse to a laptop, the PS/2 mouse appears to jump around the display even though the laptop's internal touchpad may work properly. Chances are that the wheel mouse is incompatible with your laptop. For example, the wheel mouse sends data in 4-byte sets, but an internal touch pad sends in 3-byte sets. This causes the operating system to interpret the mouse movement incorrectly and cause erratic cursor movement and clicks. One way to work around this problem is to replace the wheel mouse with an ordinary PS/2 mouse. Alternatively, you can create a hardware profile where the mouse is enabled and the touchpad is disabled.

**SYMPTOM 24-15**    **The mouse resumes Windows XP from Standby mode even though that feature is disabled**    Windows XP allows you to configure the mouse so that it will not wake the computer from its Standby mode. You can set this through the Power Management tab of your Mouse Properties dialog box (see Figure 24-14). Normally, the Allow this Device to Bring the Computer Out of Standby check box is selected. However, you may find that the mouse still can bring the PC out of standby even when this feature is unchecked. This is almost always a BIOS problem rather than a mouse or Windows problem, so contact the PC or motherboard manufacturer for an updated BIOS that is compatible with Windows XP.

**SYMPTOM 24-16**    **The mouse pointer does not move after installing a mouse on the system**    Windows will generally not indicate any problems with mouse detection. There is a known compatibility problem with some older computers and mouse combinations. For example, Logitech's

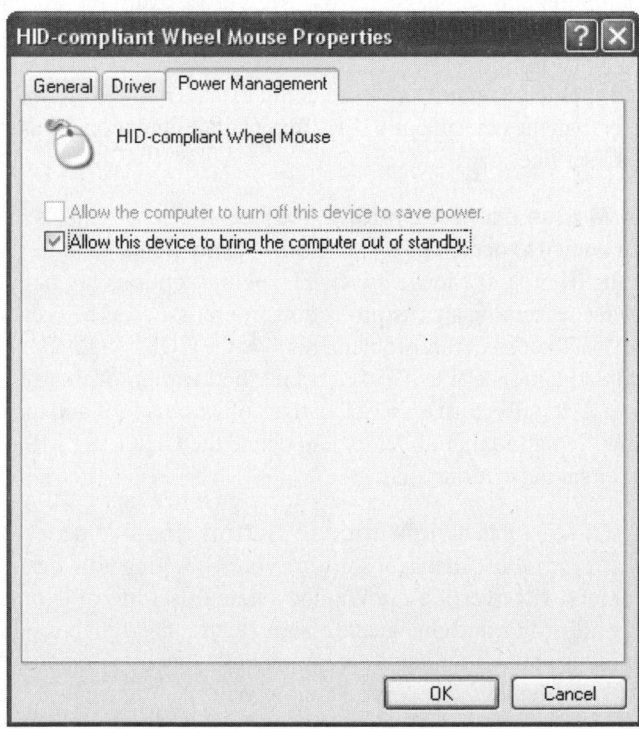

**FIGURE  24-14**    Windows XP lets you allow or prevent the mouse from bringing the PC out of standby mode.

two-button First Mouse (e.g., version M/N:M34) is reported to suffer from this type of trouble on some Packard Bell systems. You can use the keyboard to invoke a basic work-around under Windows 9x/Me:

1. Press CTRL-ESC to open the Start menu.

2. Use the arrow keys to highlight Settings, then Control Panel, and press ENTER.

3. Move the arrow key over to the Mouse icon and press ENTER. This will open the Mouse Properties dialog box.

4. Using the TAB key, tab over to the Quick Setup tab, and then use the RIGHT ARROW key to open the Devices tab.

5. On the Devices tab, tab over to the Add Mouse button and press ENTER.

The pointing device applet should now detect the two-button serial mouse, and the pointer should move properly. However, you'll need to perform this procedure each time you restart the system. If you're not using a Packard Bell system, you can remove the mouse in the Device Manager and use the Add New Hardware Wizard to reinstall the specific mouse. If your system has a dedicated PS/2 mouse port, another option is to contact the pointing device maker to see if you can exchange the serial version for a PS/2 version, or upgrade to a USB version of the pointing device.

**SYMPTOM 24-17**   **After installing a three-button mouse, you receive an error such as "pointing device on unknown port"**   You may also find that the device is only shown as a two-button mouse. In most cases, there are older mouse traces in the registry that must be removed before the new pointing device can be properly detected:

Do not attempt to edit your registry without first creating a complete registry backup on your boot floppy disk. Incorrectly editing the registry may prevent the system from booting.

1. Click Start | Run.

2. On the Open line, type **c:\windows\regedit.exe** and press ENTER.

3. Open the following key:

   Hkey_Local_Machine\System\CurrentControlSet\Services\Class\Mouse\xxxx

   where xxxx is an incremental 4-digit number starting at 0000.

4. Click each folder under the Mouse folder, and delete them until there are no 000X folders remaining.

5. Save your changes and exit the registry editor.

6. Open the properties dialog or applet for your pointing device to verify the correct detection.

If this procedure cannot correct the trouble, you might need to reinstall Windows from scratch so that only one pointing device is detected and installed.

**SYMPTOM 24-18**   **When installing a three- or four-button PS/2 pointing device on a laptop with its own pointing device, the new device only shows up as a two-button mouse**
There are several possible solutions to this issue depending on what laptop and pointing device you're using. Try disabling the internal pointing device; you may need to set up an alternate hardware configuration through the Device Manager. Some systems may require that you disable the internal pointing device first (usually through the laptop's CMOS Setup) in order to detect a new pointing device on the external

mouse port. You may also want to contact the system manufacturer to see if there is a BIOS update available, or any further information about using external pointing devices on the system.

**SYMPTOM 24-19**    **You receive a "KBC error" when connecting a pointing device to certain laptop PS/2 ports**    This is virtually always a compatibility issue, and is a known compatibility issue between the Toshiba 400 series notebook and Logitech PS/2 "combo" pointing devices. These Toshiba systems have a single PS/2 connector on the back that may accept either a mouse or keyboard, and the problem is caused by a BIOS oversight. Toshiba has a BIOS upgrade that resolves this issue. (Version v.5.40 or later can be obtained by contacting Toshiba America.) If a BIOS upgrade is not available, you may connect the Logitech "combo" pointing device to the serial port instead (use only Logitech adapters), or use an alternate pointing device.

**SYMPTOM 24-20**    **After installing the applets for your pointing device, you receive an "0E Exception" error on a blue screen**    This is almost always a software error caused by a buggy or incompatible pointing device driver or applet. When such an error occurs, you may also find that you can press ENTER and still use Windows normally, but this annoying error appears on each boot. For example, this problem is often encountered on IBM systems, and IBM has found a problem with version 1.10 of their "TrackPoint" drivers. This error produces a blue screen on boot-up if the mouse drivers are changed. The work-around for this trouble is to uninstall the IBM TrackPoint software through the Add/Remove Programs icon in the Windows Control Panel. You may then need to reinstall the latest drivers or applet software for your new pointing device.

**SYMPTOM 24-21**    **The pointing device (or system) freezes when the system wakes from its suspend mode**    Many current mouse drivers have the capability to perform a search for mice when a system wakes from its suspend mode. (For Windows, this is defined by a key in the Windows registry.) This registry setting defines the action that the driver will perform upon power management suspend/resume commands. If the mouse stops working after a resume, this parameter should be set to Off, as described next:

Do not attempt to edit your registry without first creating a complete registry backup on your boot floppy disk. Incorrectly editing the registry may prevent the system from booting.

1. Click Start | Run.
2. On the Open line, type **regedit.exe** and press ENTER.
3. Click the plus (+) sign next to HKEY_LOCAL_MACHINE.
4. Click the plus (+) sign next to SOFTWARE.
5. Click the plus (+) sign next to your pointing device maker (for example, Logitech).
6. Click the plus (+) sign next to the software name (for example, MouseWare).
7. Click the plus (+) sign next to CurrentVersion.
8. Single-click on the Technical folder, and information should be displayed on the right side of the registry editor screen.
9. Under the Name column, double-click on the APMMode entry; an Edit String dialog should appear.

**10.** Modify the Value Data line to read **Off**, and click the OK button. The full line should now read

```
HKEY_LOCAL_MACHINE\SOFTWARE\Logitech\MouseWare\CurrentVersion\Technical\APMMode="Off"
```

**11.** Exit the Registry Editor and restart your system. Then test the computer again to see if it resumes without freezing.

If you still experience APM issues, try uninstalling the mouse applet(s) using the Add/Remove Programs icon in the Control Panel. This will restore the system to the native drivers supplied by Windows. Now test your system again to see if it resumes correctly. If it still fails, try another mouse in the same port.

**SYMPTOM 24-22** **When running a DOS program from Windows 98/Me, the mouse cursor moves very slowly compared to native Windows applications** There are several possible issues to consider here. If the problem only occurs under one DOS application (and not in others), the problem may be with the particular application. You may need a patch or update for that application, or you may want to try installing the very latest mouse driver. Also try shutting down to DOS and running the program from the native DOS mode (rather than through a DOS window). If you're using Windows Me/XP with no "native" DOS mode, you may need to boot from a DOS boot diskette.

**SYMPTOM 24-23** **The modem won't start after installing new mouse management software** For example, this is a known problem when installing Logitech's MouseWare 6.60 or later under Windows 95 (though this isn't known to occur under later versions of Windows). Sometimes the mouse drivers may detect the modem as a second mouse and try to initialize it. This can cause the modem to go into a busy state. You can try uninstalling the mouse management software (and use an alternate pointing device if necessary). You may also choose to upgrade Windows to a later version. However, you can prevent the mouse drivers from searching the serial port that the modem is using:

 Do not attempt to edit your registry without first creating a complete registry backup on your boot floppy disk. Incorrectly editing the registry may prevent the system from booting.

**1.** Download the latest mouse driver for Windows 95.

**2.** Edit the Windows 95 registry by clicking Start | Run.

**3.** Type **c:\windows\regedit.exe** on the Open line.

**4.** Click OK. The registry editor will start.

**5.** Double-click the HKEY_LOCAL_MACHINE folder.

**6.** Double-click the SOFTWARE folder.

**7.** Double-click the manufacturer's folder (that is, Logitech).

**8.** Double-click the manufacturer's driver folder (that is, MouseWare).

**9.** Double-click the CurrentVersion folder.

**10.** Click the Global folder.

**11.** Let's assume the mouse is on COM1 and the modem is on COM2. On the right side of the screen, there will be a list of value data strings. Double-click the PortSearchOrder string. An Edit String dialog will appear. The Value Data line will read

```
COM1, COM2
```

**12.** Remove the space, the comma, and "COM2" so the line reads

```
COM1
```

**13.** If you only plan to use one mouse on the system, change the MaximumDevices Value Data line to **1** using the same steps as earlier. This will tell the driver to stop searching for additional mice after the primary mouse has been found.

> If you are not using a serial mouse, remove "Serial" from the "SearchOrder" Value Data line so that no serial devices are searched for at all. In general, remove any reference to the port the modem is using.

**14.** Click OK, and the values under the data value section on the right side of the screen should change. Exit the registry editor (saving is automatic). Shut down the computer and reboot from a cold start so that your changes can take effect.

**SYMPTOM 24-24**    **The mouse pointer moves only vertically**    The mouse is connected to a PS/2 port under Windows 95 (this is not known to occur under later versions of Windows). If the mouse works along one axis but not the other, it's usually due to a hardware problem—the mouse either needs cleaning or repair. However, in some cases a software configuration problem can occur when the mouse driver (for example, Mouse Power v9.5) is installed on a system with plug-and-play BIOS running Windows 95, and the mouse is connected to the PS/2-style mouse port. As soon as you touch the mouse, the pointer darts over the right edge of the screen, and then will move only up and down. You can try uninstalling the mouse software (and use an alternate pointing device if necessary). You may also choose to upgrade Windows to a later version. Otherwise, you may be able to correct the trouble by editing the registry.

> Do not attempt to edit your registry without first creating a complete registry backup on your boot floppy disk. Incorrectly editing the registry may prevent the system from booting.

**1.** To regain control over your computer, reboot in Safe mode.

**2.** Click Start | Run, then type **regedit**, and press ENTER.

**3.** Open the HKEY_LOCAL_MACHINE\Enum folder and see if "BIOS" is listed under Enum. If it is, then you know the software configuration problem is causing the issue.

**4.** Open HKEY_LOCAL_MACHINE\Enum\BIOS\*PNP0F13, and look for a key (usually "05" or "07") under "*PNP0F13." Click this key to highlight it. The key under "*PNP0F13" should now be highlighted, and the corresponding values should be displayed on the right side of the window. Note that there are "string values" with an "ab" icon next to them, and "binary values" with a "011" icon next to them.

**5.** Compare your values to those shown next. Edit your entries until all your values shown onscreen match the values shown here:

```
ab  Class      "Mouse"
011 ConfigFlags 00 00 00 00
ab  DeviceDesc  "Mouse Systems v2.18"
ab  Driver      "Mouse\0000"
ab  HardwareID  "*PNP0F0C"
ab  Mfg         "Mouse Systems"
```

6. Open HKEY_LOCAL_MACHINE\System\CurrentControlSet\Services\Class\Mouse. There should be multiple keys under Mouse (such as "0000" and "0001"). All but one are to be deleted. Carefully determine which one pertains to your current mouse (by looking at the values associated with each key), and delete all keys under Mouse except the related one.

7. Make sure the one remaining key under Mouse is labeled "0000" (rename it if necessary).

8. Click the X box in the far upper-right corner of the registry editor to close it.

9. Reboot the computer from a cold start. The computer should reboot in normal mode, and the problem with the mouse and keyboard should be gone.

**SYMPTOM 24-25**    **The new serial mouse is not detected by Windows**    For example, Windows may not detect your serial PnP mouse, EasyBall, or IntelliMouse, and using the Add New Hardware Wizard cannot correct the trouble. In virtually all cases, this occurs because the registry entries for your previous pointing device were not properly removed from the registry. This problem is known to occur with Microsoft, Microsoft-compatible, or Logitech mouse models. Try the following steps to work around the problem:

 Do not attempt to edit your registry without first creating a complete registry backup on your boot floppy disk. Incorrectly editing the registry may prevent the system from booting.

1. Click Start | Run, and then type **regedit**, and press ENTER.

2. Locate and remove the following registry key:

   HKEY_LOCAL_MACHINE\System\CurrentControlSet\Services\Class\Mouse\<nnnn>

   where <nnnn> is an incremental four-digit number starting at 0000.

3. Locate and remove the following registry keys (if they exist) such as:

   HKEY_LOCAL_MACHINE\Enum\Root\Mouse\<nnnn>

   where <nnnn> in an incremental four-digit number starting at 0000.

4. Locate and remove all registry keys under the following registry key (if they exist) such as:

   HKEY_LOCAL_MACHINE\Enum\Serenum

5. Locate and remove the following registry key (if it exists) such as:

   HKEY_LOCAL_MACHINE\Software\Logitech\Mouseware

6. Right-click My Computer, and then click Properties.

7. On the Device Manager tab, click each serial pointing device, and then click Remove.

8. Click OK and restart Windows.

9. When you restart Windows, the attached pointing device is detected, and the appropriate drivers should be installed.

**SYMPTOM 24-26**    **USB pointing devices do not work in Safe Mode**    After you try to start your computer in Safe mode, your computer may not respond to any keyboard commands, or you may receive an error message such as "Windows did not detect a mouse attached to a computer. You can safely attach a serial mouse now." The problem occurs if you're using a USB keyboard or mouse, but your system BIOS does not support USB devices in the real mode. Windows does not support the use of a USB keyboard or mouse in Safe Mode or in real mode unless the computer's BIOS supports these devices. To work around this problem, use a standard keyboard or mouse instead of a USB keyboard or mouse. To correct the trouble permanently, upgrade the motherboard's BIOS to a version that provides real-mode USB support.

**SYMPTOM 24-27**   **The serial mouse is not listed in the Device Manager under Windows Me**   After installing Windows Me (or exchanging the pointing device), the mouse is not listed in Device Manager—though it works correctly. Even clicking Refresh in the Device Manager will not update the device listing for the mouse. In most cases, you can upgrade Windows, switch to a different pointing device (e.g., PS/2 or USB), or you will need to force legacy hardware detection under Windows 9x/Me:

1. Click Start | Settings | Control Panel.
2. Double-click the Add New Hardware Wizard.
3. In the first wizard window that opens, click Next.
4. Click Next again to search for plug-and-play (PnP)–compatible devices.
5. After the PnP search is finished, click Yes, and then click Next. Windows then detects hardware that is not PnP compatible.
6. After the hardware detection is complete, click Finish to quit the Add New Hardware Wizard.
7. Reboot the system if necessary, and recheck the Device Manager to see that the pointing device is listed.

**SYMPTOM 24-28**   **A Logitech MouseMan is misidentified under Windows Me**   For example, when you install a pointing device such as a Logitech MouseMan (Wheelmouse) under Windows Me, it is identified as a Microsoft IntelliMouse. This occurs because the PnP identification reported by the Logitech mouse is identical to the information provided by the IntelliMouse. You can work around this problem by installing Logitech MouseWare 8.3 and setting up the mouse as a Wheelmouse2 (PS/2) in Device Manager. However, if the mouse is removed and redetected, Windows Me automatically defaults to the Microsoft IntelliMouse drivers. To correct this problem permanently, check with Logitech to obtain a new .INF file for the mouse. If Logitech obtains its own vendor ID information and incorporates that into an updated .INF, the mouse can be uniquely identified and installed with the correct drivers.

**SYMPTOM 24-29**   **The USB mouse causes the web browser's "Back" button to go back two pages**   This is known to occur under Windows 98/Me (Windows XP does not appear to suffer this trouble). When you click the left button on a USB mouse once to use the Back button of Internet Explorer, IE goes back two web pages when it should go back just one page. In virtually all cases, the trouble is caused by an older version of the mouse software (or selecting the incorrect mouse when installing the mouse drivers). For example, you can see this problem when installing or using an older version of Microsoft IntelliPoint software, or by selecting the incorrect mouse when first installing the Microsoft IntelliPoint software. You will need to remove the older software and reinstall the newer software under Windows 9x/Me:

1. Click Start | Settings | Control Panel.
2. In Control Panel, double-click the Add/Remove Programs Wizard.
3. Click the Install/Uninstall tab, click the mouse software (such as Microsoft IntelliPoint), and then click the Add/Remove button.

4. When prompted, restart the computer.

5. Reinstall the mouse software (for example, IntelliPoint), and choose the correct mouse.

**SYMPTOM 24-30** **The mouse pointer moves erratically when pointer speed is set high**
This is a known issue with Windows Me (though it can possibly occur with other versions of Windows) when the mouse pointer speed is set above 2/3 (to the right) and the mouse is moved rapidly. The best way to correct this trouble is to open the Mouse Properties dialog, select the Pointers Options tab, and adjust the pointer movement to mid-range or lower.

# Further Study

**Genius**   www.genius-kye.com/
**Logitech**   www.logitech.com
**Microsoft**   www.microsoft.com
**Mitsumi**   www.mitsumi.com
**Mouse Trak**   www.mousetrak.com/
**No Hands Mouse**   www.footmouse.com/

# 25

# MODEMS

Long before computers ever became *personal*, the mainframe and minicomputers of the 1960s and 1970s needed to communicate over large geographic distances—sometimes across town, sometimes around the world. Designers faced the problem of wiring the computers together—stringing a cable across even a few miles represents a serious logistical challenge (and a real financial burden). Instead of installing a network of *new* cabling, computer designers realized that they already had a sophisticated, worldwide wiring system in place: the *public switched telephone network* (PSTN). By enabling one computer to "call" another and exchange data, computers could communicate over telephone lines anywhere a telephone jack is available (or even using cellular facilities).

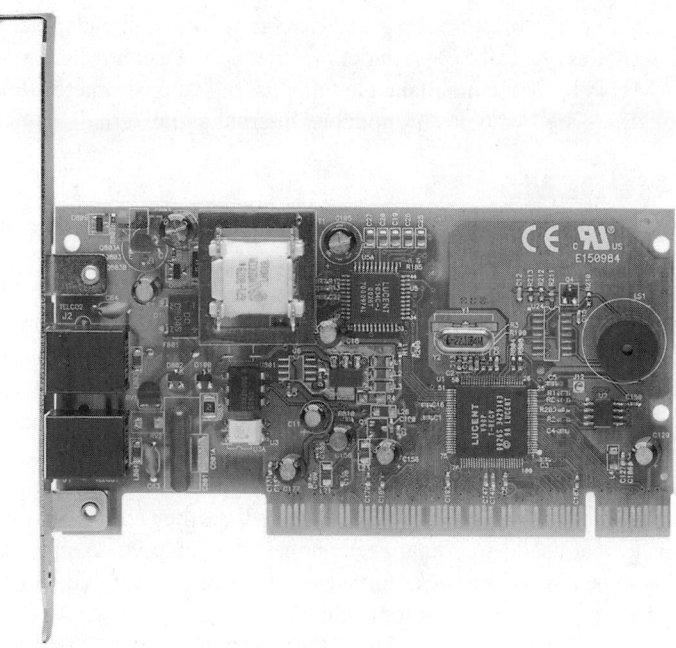

**FIGURE    25-1**    The Zoom V.92 Win-Only data/fax/voice modem is based on a Lucent chipset and provides support for 56Kbps data transfers over dial-up connections (Courtesy of Zoom Telephonics)

Of course, computers cannot work *directly* on your telephone line. The digital information processed by computers must be translated (or *modulated*) into audible sounds that are carried across telephone lines to a remote location. The sound signals coming from the telephone lines must be converted back into digital information (or *demodulated*) for the computer. A device called a MOdulator/DEModulator (MODEM, or commonly *modem*) performs this continuous process of modulation and demodulation between a computer and telephone line. A Zoom V.92 56 Kbps modem is shown in Figure 25-1. As the number of personal computers has grown into the millions, the demand for faster and more reliable modem communication has resulted in impressive speed and performance. Today's modems have also enabled high-end features such as facsimile and voice-over-data capabilities. In addition, high-speed Internet services are becoming available through existing telephone networks, as well as cable service providers. This chapter explains the operations, standards, connections, and troubles of today's conventional dial-up modems and cable/DSL interfaces.

# Dial-up Modem Construction and Operation

In order to know how a modem works (and what to do when things go wrong), you should be familiar with the typical sections of a modem circuit. Most modems today can be fabricated with only a few specialized chips and discrete parts, and virtually all computer communication systems contain the same essential parts. First, data must be translated from parallel into serial form and back again. Serial data being transmitted must be converted into an audio signal, and then placed on an ordinary telephone circuit. Audio signals received from the telephone line must be separated from transmitted signals, then converted back into serial data. All these activities must take place under the direction of a controller circuit. Finally, a modem uses non-volatile RAM (NVRAM) to maintain a lengthy list of setup parameters (or *S registers*). For the purposes of this book, there are two types of modems: internal and external.

## INTERNAL MODEMS

The *internal* modem is fabricated as a stand-alone expansion board that plugs directly into an ISA or PCI expansion bus. You can see each major modem function detailed in the block diagram of Figure 25-2. The internal modem contains its own *universal asynchronous receiver/transmitter* (UART)—it is the UART that is responsible for manipulating data into and out of serial form. A UART forms the foundation of a serial port, and its improper setting in installation of the modem can cause a serious hardware conflict for your PC. When installing an internal modem, be sure that the IRQ line and I/O address chosen for the UART "serial port" do not conflict with other serial ports (a.k.a. COM ports) already in the system. It may be necessary to disable conflicting ports.

Before being transmitted over telephone lines, serial data must be converted into audio signals. A *modulator* circuit carries out this process. The modulated audio is then coupled to the telephone line using a circuit very similar to that used by ordinary telephones to couple voice signals. Audio signals pass through a single RJ11-type (*telephone jack*) connector at the rear of the modem to the telephone line. (Many modems provide a second RJ11 jack for a telephone—this allows you to check the line and make calls while the modem is idle.) Signals received from the telephone line must be translated back into serial data. The *telephone interface* separates received signals and passes them to the *demodulator*. After demodulation, the resulting serial data is passed to the UART, which in turn converts the serial bits into parallel words that are placed on the system's data bus.

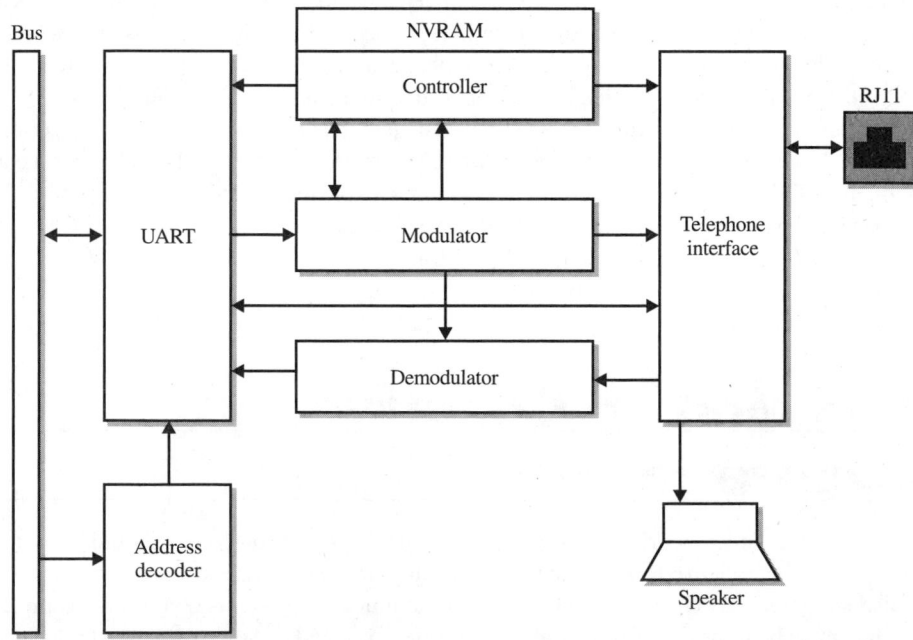

**FIGURE  25-2**     Basic block diagram of an internal modem

Besides combining and separating modulated audio data, the telephone interface generates the dual-tone multi-frequency (DTMF) dialing signals needed to reach a remote modem—in much the same way as a touch-tone telephone works. When a remote modem dials in, the telephone interface detects the incoming ring and alerts the UART to begin negotiating a connection. Finally, the telephone interface drives a small speaker. During the first stages of modem operation, the speaker is often used to hear a dial tone, dialing signals, and audio negotiation between the two modems (that high-pitched squeal that we normally associate with fax or modem connections). Once a connection is established, the speaker is usually disabled.

A *controller* circuit manages the overall operation of the modem, but, in a more general sense, it switches the modem between its *control* and *data* operating modes. The controller accepts commands from the modulator that allow modem characteristics and operating parameters to be changed. In the event of power loss or reset conditions, default modem parameters can be loaded from NVRAM. Permanent changes to modem parameters are stored in NVRAM.

## EXTERNAL MODEMS

For all intents and purposes, the *external* modem provides virtually all the essential functions offered by an internal modem. As you can see by the block diagram of Figure 25-3, many of the external functions are identical to those of an internal modem. The major difference between modems is that the external modem does *not* include a built-in UART to provide the serial port. Instead, the external modem relies on an existing serial port (or COM port) already configured in the PC. A 9-pin or 25-pin serial cable connects the PC serial port to the modem. This often makes external modem setup faster and easier than internal modems, since you need not worry about interrupt lines and I/O address settings—hardware conflicts are rare with external modems.

The other practical difference in an external modem is the way it is powered. Where internal modems are powered directly from the expansion bus, external modems must be powered from a small AC adapter (or

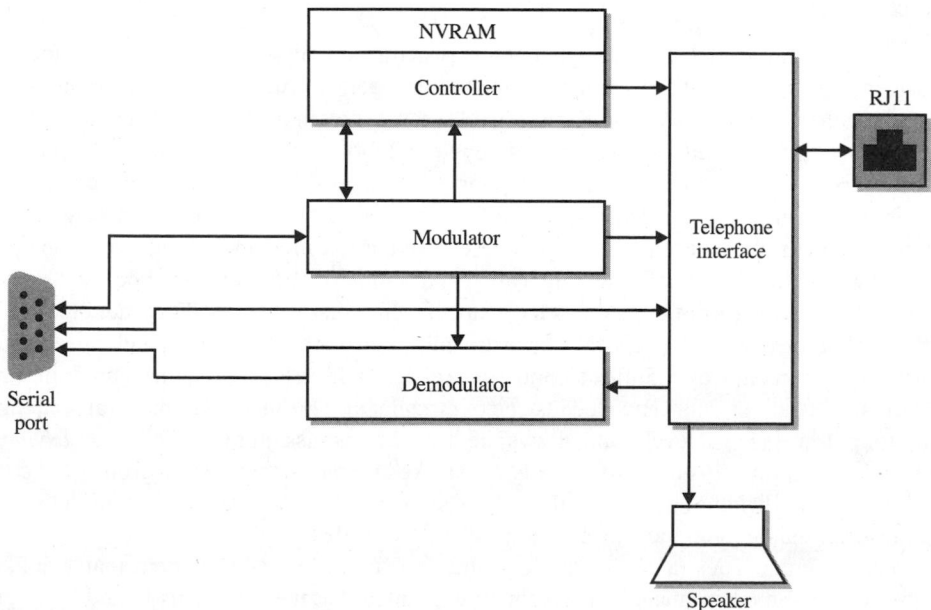

**FIGURE  25-3**    Basic block diagram of an external modem

batteries). In locations where AC outlets are scarce, this may be a problem. On the plus side, external modems provide a series of signal status LEDs. The LEDs allow you to easily check the state of serial communications. The situation is a bit different with the broad use of external USB modems. USB offers plug-and-play compatibility, and the operating system will typically recognize and install the USB modem in a matter of moments. In many cases, USB modems are also powered from the USB port (though some USB models might need the additional current provided by an external USB hub or separate AC adapter.

# NOTABLE MODEM FEATURES

Today's modems do far more than just exchange data between computers. There are myriad advanced features built into current modems that you should be aware of—a few of the more notable advancements are listed next. Keep in mind that some of the following features are dated, but you should still understand the purpose of each feature in the event that you encounter such devices in the field.

## x2 Modem Technology

Although the term "x2" is trademarked by US Robotics (now part of 3Com), x2 is often used generically to refer to high-speed modem technology employed for early 56 Kbps modems. The x2 technology was a relatively early protocol developed for 56 Kbps downloads from the Internet, corporate networks, and online services over regular phone lines. While x2 doesn't support 56 Kbps uploads or 56 Kbps transfers between modems, it did offer a powerful enhancement for PC users seeking to move beyond older 33.6 Kbps modems for the Internet or other online services. You need three elements to support x2 at 56 Kbps downloads: an ISP or other remote "x2 compatible" modem at the server, an analog loop between your home/office and the local central office, and an x2 modem (such as a US Robotics Sportster). However, x2 technology is very sensitive to telephone line issues, and it must have close to ideal conditions to achieve top-speed downloads. When uploading or communicating with other modems, an x2 modem typically runs at 28.8 Kbps. Today, x2 and K56flex features have both been replaced with V.92 modem technology.

## K56flex Modem Technology

Lucent Technologies and Rockwell Semiconductor Systems co-authored the K56flex protocol, which allowed Lucent's and Rockwell's modem chip sets to interoperate. Lucent Technologies and Rockwell had to introduce their own version of 56 Kbps-capable technology in order to remain competitive. Their version was named *K56flex* and was *not* compatible with x2 modems at speeds over 33.6 Kbps. Internet Service Providers wanting to provide 56 Kbps support had to choose between these two competing technologies. Users desiring high-speed access had to first check with their ISP to determine which version was implemented at the provider's end, then purchase a compatible modem. All this was happening even while the ITU was in the process of finalizing a universal standard for 56 Kbps (dubbed V.90—formerly called V.pcm). As with x2, K56flex features have since been replaced with V.92 modem technology.

K56flex technology used a pure digital "downstream" connection to achieve its high-speed data transfer to your computer. In this way, K56flex technology is different from other modem technologies because the "downstream" data is digitally encoded instead of modulated. This method of data transfer eliminates one analog loop, lowers noise levels, and allows the higher transmission rates. This is an *asymmetrical* technique, so "upstream" transmissions (mostly keystroke and mouse commands from your computer, which require less bandwidth) continue to flow at the slower V.34 rate. The upstream direction remains slower because an analog to digital conversion must still be made at the client end.

In order to maintain sales (and alleviate customer's fears of buying a modem that would shortly become obsolete), all modem manufacturers try to guarantee that their modems would be upgradable through a software patch (a "firmware" upgrade) to meet almost any universal standard. If it turned out that the modem could *not* be upgraded through software, the modem would have to be replaced. Both the firmware and replacement options are provided at no cost to the consumer.

## V.90 Modems

The finalized ITU standard for 56 Kbps modem transmission speeds was introduced in February of 1998. The working name of this standard was *V.pcm* (pulse code modulation) with a final release name of *V.90*. This standard continues to enable high-speed downstream data transfers by digitally encoding all downstream data. Upstream transmissions continue to run at the conventional rates of up to 33.6 Kbps (that is, upstream data—data sent from your modem—is sent as an analog signal that mirrors the V.34 standard).

Since the existing telephone network infrastructure cannot support data speeds faster than 56 Kbps, V.90 and V.92 (which added a few tweaks) will almost certainly be the *final* analog modem speed standards. Analysts predict that modem sales will grow to about 75 million modems sold per year, and almost all these will be V.90 and the later V.92. In order to support higher data transfer speeds, computer users will need to move to more performance-oriented communication technologies such as *cable modem* and *digital subscriber line* (DSL) services.

## V.92 and V.44 Modems

Although V.90 modems unified the technologies needed for faster downloads, limitations remained with slow uploads and connections that were frequently interrupted with incoming calls (call waiting service). In early 2001, the International Telecommunications Union (ITU) approved V.92 and V.44 modem standards intended to enhance the operation of dial-up modems. V.92 offers some important advantages for Internet users. Under the previous V.90 standard, modems used pulse code modulation (PCM) to support downstream rates of about 52 Kbps; they never really reached 56 Kbps. However, upstream data rates (from your PC to the ISP) rarely exceeded 33 Kbps because of the slower quadrature amplitude modulation (QAM) used for upstream communication. Under V.92, PCM is used in both directions to achieve upstream data rates approaching 48 Kbps—a real help when uploading files to an FTP site, sending e-mail with file attachments, and so on.

> The V.92/V.44 modem standards (these are typically found together on the same device) are currently the latest modem standards for data transfer and compression.

Long connect times are also a hassle for V.90 and earlier dial-up modems. V.92 modems also speed up the typical 25–30 second connection times by saving the known characteristics of the telephone line (the "analog channel") in non-volatile RAM. With subsequent calls to another V.92 modem, the answer tone is checked to verify that the line conditions are the same as previously recorded—if so, a connection can be established in 12–15 seconds. This means dial-up users can access the Internet faster.

Virtually all V.90 and earlier modems will interpret a call waiting interruption as a disconnect that knocks you offline—usually right in the middle of an important download—forcing you to dial in again, reestablish your connection, and start from scratch. Dial-up users can disable call waiting (using a dialing prefix such as *70) when making a call. V.92 modems incorporate a *modem-on-hold* feature that allows one modem to put another "on hold" for several minutes (this can be set with your ISP). This lets you drop the connection in order to take the incoming call, and then reestablish the connection and pick up where you left off.

**V.44 Compression**    Faster connect speeds are important for all modems, but data compression is also an important feature of dial-up modems. Compression searches your data for sequences that repeat, and then replaces those sequences with short "symbols". This allows you to exchange more data with fewer characters, and effectively increases your data throughput. The popular V.42bis standard was created in 1989, and wasn't very effective at compressing Web page data. However, the V.44 compression standard is optimized for Web pages and can improve your surfing experience.

**Using V.92/V.44 Modems**   Newer modems typically work well with older modems, but you're limited to the "lowest common denominator." For example, if your 56 Kbps modem connects to a 33.6 Kbps modem, your modem must negotiate to the lower 33.6 Kbps level. If you have a system with a V.92 modem now, you can connect to any dial-up ISP, but the features offered by V.92/V.44 are only available when both you and your ISP use V.92/V.44 modems. If you're planning an upgrade to V.92, it's worth checking with your ISP first to verify their compatibility (or even if they plan to upgrade). There's no sense spending money to upgrade your modem if the ISP isn't going to support V.92. Of course, you can always opt for another ISP that does support V.92.

V.92 modems are available as internal PCI, external serial, or external USB devices, so you'll need to check for a suitable slot or port on your PC. Also check that you're using an appropriate operating system such as Windows, MacOS, or Linux—most modems come bundled with the necessary drivers and utilities (like fax software) on CD.

If you're installing a new V.92 modem, installation involves powering down the PC, connecting the modem, rebooting the computer, and then allowing the operating system to detect the new modem. When the new modem is detected, you can insert the CD and load the drivers and utility software. Another reboot might be necessary for your system changes to take effect, and then you can start using the modem. If you're upgrading an existing modem, take the time to uninstall any modem utilities and remove the modem entry from your Device Manager (under Windows) before powering down the system. This can help to prevent accidental misidentification of the new modem.

## WinModems

Over the last few years, the PC industry has seen a trend away from conventional hardware fax/modem devices and toward simpler, less expensive software modems (dubbed *Windows Modems* or *WinModems*). A hardware-based modem (such as a fax/modem) contains a *controller*, *data pump*, and *phone network circuit*—all integrated into the hardware of the modem device itself. The host computer simply sends data to the modem, and the modem does the rest. By comparison, a "software modem" eliminates both the controller and data pump portions of a modem and relies on the host computer's CPU to handle those functions instead. As a result, WinModems are the simplest and least expensive modem type (generally found in low-end PCs), but they make the greatest demands on system processing power.

It is important for you to realize that most modern WinModem designs are quite reliable, but they will work *only* under Windows 9x/Me/XP and other operating systems supported by the WinModem drivers. If you use DOS programs that require modem access, you'll need to replace the WinModem with a conventional fax/modem device.

## DSVD

In addition to simply sending and receiving data, some modern modems incorporate a feature called *dual simultaneous voice and data* (or DSVD). The modem can carry your analog voice as well as computer data. In effect, the modem becomes a "speakerphone" able to transfer real-time voice and data at the same time (though the bandwidth needed to transfer voice information reduces the available bandwidth for data transfers). Note that the DSVD feature can be used only between two DSVD modems. To use DSVD, you need a soundboard with a microphone (to digitize your voice) as well as a set of speakers (to play the voice from the other end). DSVD has found a small but powerful niche among online computer gamers who want to communicate in real-time as they play.

## Voice Mail

Some modern modems are providing advanced voice mail features that essentially allow the modem (and PC) to serve as an intelligent answering machine or digital information system. When installed and configured properly, voice mail allows you to create mailboxes, record voice greetings/announcements for each mailbox, record messages to each mailbox, access each mailbox remotely, and even support "fax-on-demand." Voice mail features are particularly popular with small businesses or small-office home-office (SOHO) environments looking to automate messaging and information distribution.

## Autodetection/Auto-Switching

Virtually all current modems can detect the difference between a voice call, a modem call, and an incoming fax. The modem can then inform the system of the call and automatically employ the proper software tools to record the voice message (used with voice mail systems), start BBS or other electronic messaging software to communicate with the calling modem (ideal for remote access software), or record the fax image to the hard drive.

## Distinctive Ring

Many local phone service areas now support the *distinctive ring* feature that allows several phone numbers to be assigned to the same *physical* telephone line—each assigned number rings with a different ringing pattern (called a *cadence*). Modems that are compatible with distinctive ring can be placed on the same physical phone line with other devices, but will answer only when a certain ringing pattern is detected.

## Caller ID

Modern modems are also able to detect the caller's originating telephone number, which is transmitted to the receiving end of the communications link. In its simplest form, *caller ID* simply provides an onscreen display of the caller's telephone number (used most often when you're receiving calls with the modem in "speakerphone" mode). In its most enhanced form, database software can trap the caller ID number, then automatically pull up contact information, notes of past phone conversations, or a wide range of other caller-related information. This is an ideal feature for sales or help desk services.

# HIGH-SPEED TECHNOLOGIES

While typical dial-up modems are normally limited to ideal speeds of 56 Kbps, other connection technologies exist that use dedicated telephone, CATV, and sometimes even satellite connections to achieve high-speed connectivity with ISPs. The following technologies are now enjoying wide acceptance in urban and suburban areas.

## ISDN Modems

*Integrated Services Digital Network* (or ISDN) technology is a system of digital phone connection that has been available for almost two decades. The ISDN system allows data to be transmitted in purely *digital* form. Since ISDN is completely digital, data transfers can be extremely fast—up to 128 Kbps. There are two basic types of ISDN service: the *Basic Rate Interface* (BRI), and the *Primary Rate Interface* (PRI). BRI consists of two 64 Kbps "B" channels and one 16 Kbps "D" channel for a total of 144 Kbps. This basic service is intended to meet the needs of most individual users.

For a Basic Rate Interface ISDN line equipped with two B channels, one (or both) of the 64 Kbps B channels are connected in a virtual permanent circuit. Home and business users who install ISDN adapters in place of their modems can see complex graphic Web pages arriving very quickly (up to 128 Kbps). ISDN requires adapters at *both* ends of the transmission, so your ISP also needs an ISDN adapter. To access BRI service, it's necessary to subscribe to an ISDN phone line. The customer must also be within 18,000 feet (about 3.4 miles or

5.5 km) of the telephone company's central office for BRI service—beyond that, expensive repeater devices are required, or ISDN service may not be available at all. Customers will also need special equipment to communicate with the phone company switch and with other ISDN devices. These devices include ISDN Terminal Adapters (sometimes called "ISDN Modems," though that is technically incorrect) and ISDN Routers. ISDN is generally available from your phone company in most urban areas in the United States and Europe.

While ISDN remains a viable alternative for high-speed data communication, it is rapidly falling into disuse because of competition from other high-speed technologies such as cable and DSL.

## DSL Modems

The *Digital Subscriber Line* (called DSL, ADSL, or xDSL) is a relatively new PC communication technology that allows for the transmission of voice, video, and data over existing copper telephone lines at very high speeds. DSL provides dedicated bandwidth that can be up to 143 times faster than a 56 Kbps modem, and 62 times faster than ISDN. DSL uses your ordinary phone line, but doesn't tie it up—you can access the Internet while you're using the same phone line for a conversation (or faxing) in addition to the permanent Internet connection.

The copper telephone lines are often referred to as the *local loop*—that last mile from the telephone company's central office (CO) to the end-user's home or business.

There are several variations of DSL technologies, but the best known of these technologies are *Asymmetric Digital Subscriber Line* (ADSL) and *ADSL Lite* (dubbed "Splitterless ADSL," "Universal ADSL," or "G.lite"). Standard ADSL service is often referred to as "Full Rate ADSL" or "G.dmt," and is now also known by the ITU standard *G.992.1*. This supports up to 8 Mbps bandwidth downstream and up to 1 Mbps upstream. The asymmetrical aspect of ADSL technology makes it ideal for Internet/Intranet surfing, video-on-demand, and remote local area network (LAN) access, since these users typically download more information than they send. ADSL requires a voice/data splitter—commonly called a *POTS Splitter* (for "Plain Old Telephone Service")—to be installed at the consumer's home or business location. This device separates voice from data transmissions. For simultaneous use of the telephone and data access, additional phone wires may need to be installed at the location. Full Rate ADSL supports service up to a maximum range of 18,000 feet (about 3.4 miles or 5.5 km) from the telephone company's central office to the end-user.

*ADSL Lite* technology does *not* require a POTS splitter to be installed at the consumer's home or business, but its performance is slower. ADSL Lite provides a downstream bandwidth up to 1.5 Mbps and an upstream bandwidth up to 512 Kbps. It also supports service up to a maximum range of 18,000 feet (about 3.4 miles or 5.5 km) from the central office. ADSL Lite has also been approved as a separate standard by the ITU.

With DSL, telephone companies are competing with cable companies and their cable modem services, and it is thought that quite a few telephone companies will replace their ISDN services with DSL in most areas. Consequently, ADSL services (and other forms of DSL) are expected to become more widely available in 2002 and beyond.

## Cable Modems

While dial-up and DSL services employ the existing telephone system, regional cable service providers are also providing high-speed Internet access through cable modems—leveraging their existing cable television infrastructure to connect individual PCs to the cable network. Early cable modems simply downloaded data from the cable ISP's servers, and uploads employed a conventional 56 Kbps dial-up modem. Today's cable ISP's use a single CATV coaxial connection for high-speed uploads and downloads. Although cable and DSL technologies are different, they both provide the same "class" of high-speed Internet access to individual and SOHO users. You'll learn more about installing and configuring cable and DSL modems later in this chapter.

In areas where DSL and cable services are not available, some satellite service providers may offer Internet access through satellite dish systems.

## MODEM COMMANDS

Modems used to be "dumb" devices. It was almost impossible for them to do things like answer the ringing telephone line, dial a number, set speaker volume, and so on. In the early days of computing, Hayes Microcomputer Products developed a product called a *Smartmodem* that accepted high-level commands in the form of ASCII text strings. This was dubbed the *Hayes AT command set* (now simply called the *AT command set*), and it has been the de-facto standard for modem commands since its inception. As a consequence, virtually every modem that is *Hayes-compatible* is capable of using the AT command set. Ultimately, the AT commands go a long way to simplifying the interface between a modem and communication software. Table 25-1 provides an extensive index of the AT commands—this resource can be particularly helpful when trying to interpret command strings.

It's important to note that Hayes is no longer in business and has long-since been acquired by Zoom Telephonics (www.zoom.com). However, many modem manufacturers make reference to "Hayes compatibility" with some AT commands. While the reference may be dated, it's still used to this day, so it's helpful for you to recognize where it came from.

Settings with an underline (such as F0) are the default settings for an entry. Also note that not every modem supports every command, so always refer to the user manual for specific features and command sets.

**TABLE 25-1    GENERAL INDEX OF THE AT COMMAND SET**

### BASIC AT COMMANDS

| | |
|---|---|
| **(A/)** | Repeat Last Command |
| **(A)** | Answer |
| **(Bx)** | CCITT or Bell Modulation |
| **B0** | CCITT operation at 300 or 1200 bps |
| **B1** | BELL operation at 300 or 1200 bps |
| **B2** | V.23 originate mode: receive 1200 bps, transmit 75 bps; answer mode: receive 75 bps, transmit 1200 bps |
| **B3** | V.23 originate mode: receive 75 bps, transmit 1200 bps; answer mode: receive 1200 bps, transmit 75 bps |
| **B15** | Selects V.21 when the modem is at 300 bits/s |
| **B16** | Selects Bell 103J when the modem is at 300 bits/s (default) |
| **(Cx)** | Carrier Control. The modem will accept the C1 command without error in order to assure backward compatibility with communications software that issues the C1 command. The C0 command may instruct some modems not to send carrier (that is, it puts them in a receive-only mode). |
| **C0** | Transmit carrier always off |
| **C1** | Normal transmit carrier switching |

## TABLE 25-1    GENERAL INDEX OF THE AT COMMAND SET *(CONTINUED)*

### BASIC AT COMMANDS

**(Dx)**    Dial. The valid dial string parameters are described next. Punctuation characters may be used for clarity, with parentheses, hyphen, and spaces being ignored:

**0-9**    DTMF digits. The numbers 0 to 9

**\***    The "star" digit (tone dialing only)

**#**    The "pound" digit (tone dialing only)

**!**    Flash. The modem will go on-hook for a time defined by the value of S29

**,**    Dial pause. The modem will pause for a time specified by S8 before dialing the digits following ","

**;**    Return to command state. Added to the end of a dial string, this causes the modem to return to the command state after it processes the portion of the dial string preceding the ";". This allows the user to issue additional AT commands while remaining off-hook. The additional AT commands may be placed in the original command line following the ";" or may be entered on subsequent command lines. The modem will enter call progress only after an additional dial command is issued without the ";" terminator. Use "H" to abort the dial in progress and go back on-hook.

**^**    Enable calling tone. Applicable to current dial attempt only. The calling tone is a 1800 Hz tone every three to four seconds that alerts recipient of automatic calling equipment (as defined in CCITT V.25).

**>**    Ground pulse. If enabled by country specific parameter, the modem will generate a grounding pulse on the EARTH relay output.

**@**    Wait for silence. The modem will wait for at least five seconds of silence in the call progress frequency band before continuing with the next dial string parameter. If the modem does not detect these five seconds of silence before the expiration of the call abort timer (S7), the modem will terminate the call attempt with a NO ANSWER message. If busy detection is enabled, the modem may terminate the call with the BUSY result code. If answer tone arrives during execution of this parameter, the modem handshakes.

**$**    List. Displays a list of dial commands or "Bong Tone" detection.

**A-D**    DTMF letters A, B, C, and D

**J**    Fastest speed. Perform MNP 10 link negotiation at the highest supported speed for this call only.

**K**    Power adjustment. Enable power level adjustment during MNP 10 link negotiation for this call only.

**L**    Re-dial last number. The modem will re-dial the last valid telephone number. This command must be used immediately after the "D" with all the following characters ignored.

**P**    Select pulse dialing. Pulse dial the numbers that follow until a "T" is encountered. Affects current and subsequent dialing.

**R**    Delay. This command will cause the modem to wait 10 seconds after dialing then go into answer mode. This command must be placed at the end of the dial string.

**T**    Select tone dialing. Tone dial the numbers that follow until a "P" is encountered. Affects current and subsequent dialing.

**W**    Wait for dial tone. The modem will wait for a dial tone before dialing the digits following "W". If no dial tone is detected within the time specified by S6, the modem will abort the rest of the sequence, return on-hook, and generate an error message.

**TABLE 25-1    GENERAL INDEX OF THE AT COMMAND SET** *(CONTINUED)*

### BASIC AT COMMANDS

| | |
|---|---|
| **(Ex)** | Command Echo |
| **E0** | Disables command echo |
| **E1** | Enables command echo |
| **(Fx)** | Select Line Modulation |
| **F0** | Selects autodetect mode—all connect speeds are possible |
| **F1** | Selects V.21 or Bell 103 according to the "B" setting |
| **F2** | Not supported (some modems use this setting for 600 bps) |
| **F3** | Originator is at 75 bps and answerer is at 1200 bps |
| **F4** | Selects V.22 1200 bps or Bell 212A according to the "B" setting |
| **F5** | Selects V.22bis as the only acceptable line modulation |
| **F6** | Select V.32bis 4800 bps or V.32 4800 bps as the only acceptable line modulation |
| **F7** | Selects V.32bis 7200 bps as the only acceptable line modulation |
| **F8** | Selects V.32bis 9600 bps or V.32 9600 bps as the only acceptable line modulation |
| **F9** | Selects V.32bis 12,000 bps as the only acceptable line modulation |
| **F10** | Selects V.32bis 14,400 bps as the only acceptable line modulation |
| **(Hx)** | Disconnect [Hangup] |
| **H0** | The modem will release the line if the modem is currently online and will terminate any test (AT&T) that is in progress. |
| **H1** | If on-hook, the modem will go off-hook and enter command mode. The modem will return on-hook after a period of time determined by S7. |
| **(Ix)** | Identification |
| **I0** | Reports product code |
| **I1** | Reports pre-computed checksum from ROM |
| **I2** | Modem will respond OK |
| **I3** | Reports firmware revision |
| **I4** | Reports modem identifier string |
| **I5** | Reports Country Code parameter (for example, "022") |
| **I6** | Reports modem data pump model and internal code revision |
| **I7** | Report data pump model and internal code revision |
| **I8** | Modem will respond OK |
| **I9** | Reports country (e.g., USA) |
| **(Lx)** | Speaker Volume |
| **L0** | Low speaker volume |
| **L1** | Low speaker volume |
| **L2** | Medium speaker volume |
| **L3** | High speaker volume |

**TABLE 25-1    GENERAL INDEX OF THE AT COMMAND SET** *(CONTINUED)*

## BASIC AT COMMANDS

**(Mx)**   Speaker Control

**M0**   Speaker is always off.

**M1**   Speaker is on during call establishment, but off when receiving carrier.

**M2**   Speaker is always on.

**M3**   Speaker is off when receiving carrier and during dialing, but on during answering.

**(Nx)**   Automode Enable

**N0**   Automode detection is disabled

**N1**   Automode detection is enabled

**(Ox)**   Return to OnLine Data Mode

**O0**   Enters online data mode without a retrain

**O1**   Enters online data mode with a retrain before returning to online data mode

**O3-14**   Forces the modem to a new rate that is user defined (defined in S62)

**(P)**   Set Pulse Dial Default

**(Qx)**   Quiet Results Codes

**Q0**   Enables result codes to the DTE

**Q1**   Disables result codes to the DTE

**(Sn)**   Read/Write S-Registers

**n=v**   Sets S-register "n" to the value "v"

**n?**   Reports the value of S-register "n"

**(T)**   Set Tone Dial Default

**(Vx)**   Result Code Form

**V0**   Enables short-form (terse) result codes

**V1**   Enables long-form (verbose) result codes

**(Wx)**   Error Correction Message Control

**W0**   Upon connection, the modem reports only the DTE speed.

**W1**   Upon connection, the modem reports the line speed, the error correction protocol, and the DTE speed respectively.

**W2**   Upon connection, the modem reports the DCE speed.

**(Xx)**   Extended Result Codes

**X0**   Sends only OK, CONNECT, RING, NO CARRIER, ERROR, and NO ANSWER result codes

**X1**   Sends only OK, CONNECT, RING, NO CARRIER, ERROR, NO ANSWER, and CONNECT XXXX

**X2**   Sends only OK, CONNECT, RING, NO CARRIER, ERROR, NO DIAL TONE, NO ANSWER, and CONNECT XXXX

**X3**   Sends only OK, CONNECT, RING, NO CARRIER, ERROR, NO ANSWER, CONNECT XXXX, and BUSY

**X4**   Enables monitoring of busy tones; sends all messages

**TABLE 25-1    GENERAL INDEX OF THE AT COMMAND SET** *(CONTINUED)*

## BASIC AT COMMANDS

**(Yx)**    Long Space Disconnect

**Y0**    Disables long space disconnect

**Y1**    Enables long space disconnect

**(Zx)**    Soft Reset and Restore Profile

**Z0**    Soft reset and restore stored profile 0

**Z1**    Soft reset and restore stored profile 1

## AT "&" COMMANDS

**(&Bx)**    Autoretrain

**&B0**    Hang up on a poor received signal

**&B1**    Retrain on a poor received signal; hang up if the condition persists

**&B2**    Do not hang up; do not retrain (that is, tolerate any line)

**(&Cx)**    RLSD (DCD) Option

**&C0**    RLSD remains ON at all times

**&C1**    RLSD follows the state of the carrier

**(&Dx)**    DTR Option

**&D0**    DTR drop is interpreted according to the current &Q setting as follows:

(&Q0, 5, 6)    DTR is ignored (assumed ON). Allows operation with DTEs that don't provide DTR.

(&Q1, 4)    DTR drop causes the modem to hang up; auto-answer is not affected.

(&Q2, 3)    DTR drop causes the modem to hang up; auto-answer is inhibited.

**&D1**    DTR drop is interpreted according to the current &Q setting as follows:

(&Q0, 1, 4, 5, 6)    DTR drop is interpreted by the modem as if the asynchronous escape sequence had been entered. The modem returns to asynchronous command state without disconnecting.

(&Q2, 3)    DTR drop causes the modem to hang up; auto-answer is inhibited.

**&D2**    DTR drop is interpreted according to the current &Q setting as follows:

(&Q0-6)    DTR drop causes the modem to hang up; auto-answer is inhibited.

**&D3**    DTR drop is interpreted according to the current &Q setting as follows:

(&Q0, 1, 4, 5, 6)    DTR drop causes the modem to perform a soft reset as if the "Z" command were received. The &Y setting determines which profile is loaded.

(&Q2, 3)    DTR drop causes the modem to hang up; auto-answer is inhibited.

**(&Fx)**    Restore Factory Configuration

**&F0**    Restore factory configuration 0

**&F1**    Restore factory configuration 1

**TABLE 25-1    GENERAL INDEX OF THE AT COMMAND SET** *(CONTINUED)*

### AT "&" COMMANDS

| | |
|---|---|
| **(&Gx)** | Select Guard Tone |
| **&G0** | Disables Guard Tone |
| **&G1** | Disables Guard Tone |
| **&G2** | Selects 1800 Hz guard tone |
| **(&Hn)** | Sets Transmit Data (TD) flow control (see also &Rn) |
| **&H0** | Flow control disabled |
| **&H1** | Hardware flow control; Clear to Send (CTS) (default) |
| **&H2** | Software flow control, XON/XOFF |
| **&H3** | Hardware and software flow control |
| **(&In)** | Sets Receive Data (RD) software flow control (see also &Rn) |
| **&I0** | Software flow control disabled (default) |
| **&I1** | XON/XOFF signals to your modem and remote system |
| **&I2** | XON/XOFF signals to your modem only |
| **(&Jx)** | Telephone Jack Type |
| **&J0** | RJ11 telephone jack |
| **&J1** | RJ12 or RJ13 telephone jack |
| **(&Kx)** | Flow Control |
| **&K0** | Disables flow control |
| **&K3** | Enables RTS/CTS flow control |
| **&K4** | Enables XON/XOFF flow control |
| **&K5** | Enables transparent XON/XOFF flow control |
| **&K6** | Enables both RTS/CTS and XON/XOFF flow control |
| **(&Lx)** | Dial Up/Lease Line Option |
| **&L0** | Dial line |
| **&L1** | Leased line |
| **(&Mx)** | Asynchronous/Synchronous Mode Selection |
| **&M0** | Selects direct asynchronous operation |
| **&M1** | Selects synchronous connect mode with asynchronous offline command mode |
| **&M2** | Selects synchronous connect mode with asynchronous offline command mode |
| **&M3** | Selects synchronous connect mode |
| **&M4** | Hayes AutoSync mode |

**TABLE 25-1    GENERAL INDEX OF THE AT COMMAND SET** *(CONTINUED)*

## AT "&" COMMANDS

| | |
|---|---|
| **(&Nn)** | Sets connect speed |
| **&N0** | Variable rate (default) |
| **&N1** | 300 bps |
| **&N2** | 1200 bps |
| **&N3** | 2400 bps |
| **&N4** | 4800 bps |
| **&N5** | 7200 bps |
| **&N6** | 9600 bps |
| **&N7** | 12,000 bps |
| **&N8** | 14,400 bps |
| **&N9** | 16,800 bps |
| **&N10** | 19,200 bps |
| **&N11** | 21,600 bps |
| **&N12** | 24,000 bps |
| **&N13** | 26,400 bps |
| **&N14** | 28,800 bps |
| **&N15** | 31,200 bps |
| **&N16** | 33,600 bps |
| **&N17** | 33,333 bps |
| **&N18** | 37,333 bps |
| **&N19** | 41,333 bps |
| **&N20** | 42,666 bps |
| **&N21** | 44,000 bps |
| **&N22** | 45,333 bps |
| **&N23** | 46,666 bps |
| **&N24** | 48,000 bps |
| **&N25** | 49,333 bps |
| **&N26** | 50,666 bps |
| **&N27** | 52,000 bps |
| **&N28** | 53,333 bps |
| **&N29** | 54,666 bps |
| **&N30** | 56,000 bps |
| **&N31** | 57,333 bps |

**TABLE 25-1     GENERAL INDEX OF THE AT COMMAND SET** *(CONTINUED)*

**AT "&" COMMANDS**

**(&P***x)*   Dial Pulse Ratio

**&P0**   Make=39%, break=61% (at 10 pps for the US)

**&P1**   Make=33%, break=67% (at 10 pps for Europe)

**&P2**   Make=33%, break=67% (at 20 pps for Japan)

**(&Q***x)*   Sync/Async Mode

**&Q0**   Selects direct asynchronous operation

**&Q1**   Selects synchronous connect mode with async offline command mode

**&Q2**   Selects synchronous connect mode with async offline command mode

**&Q3**   Selects synchronous connect mode

**&Q4**   Selects AutoSync operation

**&Q5**   Modem will try to negotiate an error-corrected link

**&Q6**   Selects asynchronous operation in normal mode (speed buffering)

**&Q8**   MNP error control mode. If an MNP error control protocol is not established, the modem will fallback according to the current user setting in S36.

**&Q9**   V.42 or MNP error control mode. If neither error control protocol is established, the modem will fallback according to the current user setting in S36.

**Starting AutoSync**   Set registers S19, S20, and S25 to the desired values before selecting AutoSync operation with &Q4. After the CONNECT message is issued, the modem waits the period of time specified by S25 before examining DTR. If DTR is on, the modem enters the synchronous operating state; if DTR is off, the modem terminates the line connection and returns to the asynchronous command state.

**Stopping AutoSync**   AutoSync operation is stopped upon loss of carrier or the ON-to-OFF transition of DTR. Loss of carrier will cause the modem to return to the asynchronous command state. An ON-to-OFF transition of DTR will cause the modem to return to the asynchronous command state and either not terminate the line connection (&D1 active) or terminate the line connection (any other &Dn command active).

**(&R***x)*   RTS/CTS Option

**&R0**   In Sync mode, CTS tracks the state of RTS; the RTS-to-CTS delay is defined by S26. In Async mode, CTS acts according to V.25bis handshake.

**&R1**   In Sync mode, CTS is always ON (RTS transitions are ignored). In Async, CTS will drop only if required by flow control.

**&R2**   Received data to computer only on RTS

**(&S***x)*   DSR Override

**&S0**   DSR will remain ON at all times.

**&S1**   DSR will become active after answer tone has been detected and inactive after the carrier has been lost.

**TABLE 25-1    GENERAL INDEX OF THE AT COMMAND SET** *(CONTINUED)*

**AT "&" COMMANDS**

| | |
|---|---|
| **(&Tx)** | Test and Diagnostics |
| **&T0** | Terminates the test in progress; clears S16 |
| **&T1** | Initiates local analog loopback, V.54 Loop 3 |
| **&T2** | Returns an ERROR message |
| **&T3** | Initiates local digital loopback, V.54 Loop 2 |
| **&T4** | Enables digital loopback acknowledgment for remote request |
| **&T5** | Disables digital loopback acknowledgment for remote request |
| **&T6** | Initiates remote digital loopback |
| **&T7** | Remote digital with self-test and error detector |
| **&T8** | Initiates local analog loopback, V.54 Loop 3, with self-test |
| **(&Un)** | Sets floor connect speed |
| **&U0** | Disabled (the default) |
| **&U1** | 300 bps |
| **&U2** | 1200 bps |
| **&U3** | 2400 bps |
| **&U4** | 4800 bps |
| **&U5** | 7200 bps |
| **&U6** | 9600 bps |
| **&U7** | 12,000 bps |
| **&U8** | 14,400 bps |
| **&U9** | 16,800 bps |
| **&U10** | 19,200 bps |
| **&U11** | 21,600 bps |
| **&U12** | 24,000 bps |
| **&U13** | 26,400 bps |
| **&U14** | 28,800 bps |
| **&U15** | 31,200 bps |
| **&U16** | 33,600 bps |
| **&U17** | 33,333 bps |
| **&U18** | 37,333 bps |
| **&U19** | 41,333 bps |
| **&U20** | 42,666 bps |
| **&U21** | 44,000 bps |
| **&U22** | 45,333 bps |
| **&U23** | 46,666 bps |
| **&U24** | 48,000 bps |

## TABLE 25-1    GENERAL INDEX OF THE AT COMMAND SET *(CONTINUED)*

### AT "&" COMMANDS

| | |
|---|---|
| **&U25** | 49,333 bps |
| **&U26** | 50,666 bps |
| **&U27** | 52,000 bps |
| **&U28** | 53,333 bps |
| **&U29** | 54,666 bps |
| **&U30** | 56,000 bps |
| **&U31** | 57,333 bps |
| **(&Vx)** | Display Current Configuration and Stored Profiles |
| **&V0** | View active file, stored profile 0, and stored phone numbers |
| **&V1** | View active file, stored profile 1, and stored phone numbers |
| **(&Wx)** | Store Current Configuration |
| **&W0** | Store the current configuration as profile 0 |
| **&W1** | Store the current configuration as profile 1 |
| **(&Xx)** | Sync Transmit Clock Source Option |
| **&X0** | The modem generates the transmit clock. |
| **&X1** | The DTE generates the transmit clock. |
| **&X2** | The modem derives the transmit clock. |
| **(&Yx)** | Designate a Default Reset Profile |
| **&Y0** | The modem will use profile 0. |
| **&Y1** | The modem will use profile 1. |
| **(&ZL?)** | Displays the last executed dial string |
| **(&Zn?)** | Displays the phone number stored at position "n" (n = 0-3) |
| **(&Zn=x)** | Store Telephone Number |
| **&Zn=x** | (n = 0 to 3, and x = dial string) |

### AT "%" COMMANDS

| | |
|---|---|
| **(%BAUD)** | Bit Rate Multiplier |
| **(%Cx)** | Enable/Disable Data Compression |
| **%C0** | Disables data compression; resets S46 bit 1 |
| **%C1** | Enables MNP 5 data compression negotiation; resets S46 bit 1 |
| **%C2** | Enables V.42bis data compression; sets S46 bit 1 |
| **%C3** | Enables both V.42bis and MNP 5 data compression; sets S46 bit 1 |
| **(%CCID)** | Enable Caller ID |
| **(%CD)** | Carrier Detect Lamp |
| **(%CDIA)** | Display last DIAG |
| **(%CIDS)** | Store ID Numbers |
| **(%CRID)** | Repeat Last ID |
| **(%CSIG)** | Store SIG Numbers |

**TABLE 25-1    GENERAL INDEX OF THE AT COMMAND SET** *(CONTINUED)*

**AT "%" COMMANDS**

| | |
|---|---|
| **(%CXID)** | XID Enable |
| **(%Dx)** | V.42bis Dictionary Size |
| **%D0** | Dictionary set to 512 |
| **%D1** | Dictionary set to 1024 |
| **%D2** | Dictionary set to 2048 |
| **%D3** | Dictionary set to 4096 |
| **(%Ex)** | Enable/Disable Line Quality Monitor and Auto-Retrain Fallback/Fall Forward |
| **%E0** | Disable line quality monitor and auto-retrain |
| **%E1** | Enable line quality monitor and auto-retrain |
| **%E2** | Enable line quality monitor and fallback/fall forward |
| **%E3** | Enable line quality monitor and auto-retrain, but hang-up when EQM reaches threshold |
| **(%Gx)** | Auto Fall Forward/Fallback Enable |
| **%G0** | Disabled |
| **%G1** | Enabled |
| **(%L)** | Line Signal Level |
| **(%Mx)** | Compression Type |
| **%M0** | Compression disabled |
| **%M1** | Transmit compression only |
| **%M2** | Receive compression only |
| **%M3** | Two-way compression |
| **(%P)** | Clear Encoder Dictionary |
| **(%Q)** | Line Signal Quality |
| **(%Sx)** | Set Maximum String Length in V.42bis |
| **(%SCBR)** | Call Back Reference Outgoing Calls |
| **(%SKEY)** | Store Authentication Key Outgoing Call |
| **(%SPRT)** | Security Mode—Outgoing Calls |
| **(%SPNP)** | Serial Plug and Play Control |
| **(%SPWD)** | Password Outgoing Calls |
| **(%SSPW)** | Supervisor Password Outgoing Calls |
| **(%SUID)** | User ID Outgoing Calls |
| **(%TTx)** | PTT Testing Utilities |
| **%TT00-%TT09** | DTMF tone dial digits 0 to 9 |
| **%TT0A** | DTMF digit * |
| **%TT0B** | DTMF digit A |
| **%TT0C** | DTMF digit B |
| **%TT0D** | DTMF digit C |
| **%TT0E** | DTMF digit # |

**TABLE 25-1** **GENERAL INDEX OF THE AT COMMAND SET** *(CONTINUED)*

**AT "%" COMMANDS**

| | |
|---|---|
| **%TT0F** | DTMF digit D |
| **%TT10** | V.21 channel no. 1 mark (originate) symbol |
| **%TT11** | V.21 channel no. 2 mark symbol |
| **%TT12** | V.23 backward channel mark symbol |
| **%TT13** | V.23 forward channel mark symbol |
| **%TT14** | V.22 originate (call mark) signaling at 600 bps (not supported) |
| **%TT15** | V.22 originate (call mark) signaling at 1200 bps |
| **%TT16** | V.22bis originate (call mark) signaling at 2400 bps |
| **%TT17** | V.22 answer signaling (guard tone if PTT required) |
| **%TT18** | V.22bis answer signaling (guard tone if required) |
| **%TT19** | V.21 channel no. 1 space symbol |
| **%TT20** | V.32 9600 bps |
| **%TT21** | V.32bis 14,400 bps |
| **%TT1A** | V.21 channel no. 2 space symbol |
| **%TT1B** | V.23 backward channel space symbol |
| **%TT1C** | V.23 forward channel space symbol |
| **%TT30** | Silence (online), that is, go off-hook |
| **%TT31** | V.25 answer tone |
| **%TT32** | 1800 Hz guard tone |
| **%TT33** | V.25 calling tone (1300 Hz) |
| **%TT34** | Fax calling tone (1100 Hz) |
| **%TT40** | V.21 channel 2 |
| **%TT41** | V.27ter 2400 bps |
| **%TT42** | V.27ter 4800 bps |
| **%TT43** | V.29 7200 bps |
| **%TT44** | V.29 9600 bps |
| **%TT45** | V.17 7200 bps long train |
| **%TT46** | V.17 7200 bps short train |
| **%TT47** | V.17 9600 bps long train |
| **%TT48** | V.17 9600 bps short train |
| **%TT49** | V.17 12,000 bps long train |
| **%TT4A** | V.17 12,000 bps short train |
| **%TT4B** | V.17 14,400 bps long train |
| **%TT4C** | V.17 14,400 bps short train |

**TABLE 25-1**    GENERAL INDEX OF THE AT COMMAND SET *(CONTINUED)*

### AT "\" COMMANDS

**(\Ax)**    Select Maximum MNP Block Size

**\A0**    64 characters

**\A1**    128 characters

**\A2**    192 characters

**\A3**    256 characters

**\A4**    Max 32 characters (for ETC-enhanced throughput cellular)

**(\Bx)**    Transmit Break to Remote

**\B1-\B9**    Break length in 100 mS units (default = 3—non-error–corrected mode only)

**(\Cx)**    Set Autoreliable Buffer

**\C0**    Does not buffer data

**\C1**    Buffers data on the answering modem for four seconds

**\C2**    Does not buffer data on the answering modem

**(\Ex)**    Optimize Local Echo

**(\Gx)**    Modem-to-Modem Flow Control (XON/XOFF)

**\G0**    Disables modem-to-modem XON/XOFF flow control

**\G1**    Enables modem-to-modem XON/XOFF flow control

**(\Jx)**    Constant DTE Speed Option

**\J0**    DCE and DTE rates are independent.

**\J1**    DTE rate adjusts to DCE connection rate after online.

**(\Kx)**    Break Control. If the modem receives a break from the DTE when the modem is operating in data transfer mode:

**\K0**    Enter online command mode, no break sent to the remote modem

**\K1**    Clear data buffers and send break to remote modem

**\K2**    Same as **\K0**

**\K3**    Send break to remote modem immediately

**\K4**    Same as **\K0**

**\K5**    Send break to remote modem in sequence with transmitted data

If the modem is in the online command state (waiting for AT commands) during a data connection, and the **\B** command is received in order to send a break to the remote modem:

**\K0**    Clear data buffers and send break to remote modem

**\K1**    Clear data buffers and send break to remote modem (same as **\K0**)

**\K2**    Send break to remote modem immediately

**\K3**    Send break to remote modem immediately (same as **\K2**)

**\K4**    Send break to remote modem in sequence with data

**\K5**    Send break to remote modem in sequence with data (same as **\K4**)

If there is a break received from a remote modem during a non-error–corrected connection:

**TABLE 25-1 GENERAL INDEX OF THE AT COMMAND SET** *(CONTINUED)*

**AT "\" COMMANDS**

**\K0** Clears data buffers and sends break to the DTE

**\K1** Clears data buffers and sends break to the DTE (same as **\K0**)

**\K2** Send a break immediately to DTE

**\K3** Send a break immediately to DTE (same as **\K2**)

**\K4** Send a break in sequence with received data to DTE

**\K5** Send a break in sequence with received data to DTE (same as **\K4**)

**(\Lx)** MNP Block/Stream Mode Select

**\L0** Use stream mode for MNP connection

**\L1** Use interactive block mode for MNP connection

**(\Nx)** Operating Mode

**\N0** Selects normal speed buffered mode

**\N1** Selects direct mode

**\N2** Selects reliable (error correction) mode

**\N3** Selects auto reliable mode

**\N4** Selects LAPM error correction mode

**\N5** Selects MNP error correction mode

**(\O)** Originate Reliable Link Control

**(\Qx)** DTE Flow Control Options

**\Q0** Disables flow control

**\Q1** XON/XOFF software flow control

**\Q2** CTS flow control to the DTE

**\Q3** RTS/CTS hardware flow control

**(\S)** Report Active Configuration

**(\Tx)** Set Inactivity Timer

**n=0** Disable the inactivity timer

**n=1-90** Length in minutes

**(\U)** Accept Reliable Link Control

**(\Vx)** Protocol Result Code

**\V0** Disable protocol result code (CONNECT 9600)

**\V1** Enable protocol result code (CONNECT 9600/LAPM)

**(\Xx)** Set XON/XOFF Pass-through Option

**\X0** If XON/XOFF flow control enabled, do not pass XON/XOFF to remote modem or local DTE.

**\X1** Always pass XON/XOFF to the remote modem or local DTE.

**(\Y)** Switch to Reliable Operation

**(\Z)** Switch to Normal Operation

**TABLE 25-1    GENERAL INDEX OF THE AT COMMAND SET *(CONTINUED)***

## AT "-" COMMANDS

**(-Jx)**   Set V.42 Detection Phase

**-J0**   Disables the V.42 detection phase

**-J1**   Enables the V.42 detection phase

**(-Kx)**   MNP Extended Services

**-K0**   Disables V.42 LAPM to MNP 10 conversion

**-K1**   Enables V.42 LAPM to MNP 10 conversion

**-K2**   Enables V.42 LAPM to MNP 10 conversion; inhibits MNP Extended Services

**(-Qx)**   Enable Fallback to V.22 bis/V.22

**-Q0**   Disables fallback to 2400 bps (V.22bis) and 1200 bps (V.22); fallback only to 4800 bps

**-Q1**   Enables fallback to 2400 bps (V.22bis) and 1200 bps (V.22)

**(-SDR=n)**   Distinctive Ring Reporting

**-SDR=1**   Type 1 Distinctive Ring Detect

**-SDR=2**   Type 2 Distinctive Ring Detect

**-SDR=3**   Type 1 and Type 2 Distinctive Ring Detect

**-SDR=4**   Type 3 Distinctive Ring Detect

**-SDR=5**   Type 1 and Type 3 Distinctive Ring Detect

**-SDR=6**   Type 2 and Type 3 Distinctive Ring Detect

**-SDR=7**   Types 1, 2, and 3 Distinctive Ring Detect

*Distinctive Ring Types:*

| Type | On | Off | On | Off | On | Off | Sound |
|------|-----|-----|-----|-----|-----|-----|-------|
| 1 | 2.0 | 4.0 | | | | | Rinnnnnnnnnng |
| 2 | 0.8 | 0.4 | 0.8 | 4.0 | | | Ring Ring |
| 3 | 0.4 | 0.2 | 0.4 | 0.2 | 0.8 | 4.0 | Ring Ring Rinnng |

**(-SEC=n)**   LAPM and MNP Link Control

**-SEC=0**   Disable LAPM or MNP10; EC transmit level set in register S91

**-SEC=1, 0-30**   Enable LAPM or MNP10; EC transmit level set to value after comma (0 to 30)

**(-SKEY)**   Program Key

**(-SPRT)**   Remote Security Mode

**(-SPWD)**   Program Password

**(-SSE)**   Simultaneous Voice Data

**(-SSG)**   Set DSVD Receive Gain

**(-SSKY)**   Program Supervisor Key

**(-SSP)**   Select DVSD Port

**(-SSPW)**   Supervisor Password

**(-SUID)**   Program User ID

**(-V)**   Display Root Firmware Version Number

**TABLE 25-1    GENERAL INDEX OF THE AT COMMAND SET** *(CONTINUED)*

### AT " COMMANDS

| | |
|---|---|
| **("Hx)** | V.42bis Compression Control |
| **"H0** | Disable V.42bis |
| **"H1** | Enable V.42bis only when transmitting data |
| **"H2** | Enable V.42bis only when receiving data |
| **"H3** | Enable V.42bis for both directions |
| **("Nx)** | V.42bis Dictionary Size |
| **"N0** | 512 bytes |
| **"N1** | 1024 bytes |
| **"N2** | 1536 bytes |
| **("Ox)** | Select V.42bis Maximum String Length |
| **n=6–64** | |
| **n=32** | |

### AT "~" COMMANDS

| | |
|---|---|
| **(~Dx)** | Factory Configured Operating Profile |
| **~D0** | Disable (No Error Correction, No Data Compression) |
| **~D1** | MNP4 |
| **~D2** | MNP5 |
| **~D3** | V.42 |
| **~D4** | V.42bis |

### AT "~~" COMMANDS

| | |
|---|---|
| **(~~Lx)** | Digital Line Current Sensing On/Off |
| **~~L0** | Turn off digital line current sensing |
| **~~L1** | Turn on digital line current sensing |
| **(~~S=m)** | Digital Line Over-Current Sense Time Set |
| **m=0 through 9** | |
| **m=4** | |
| **(~~S?)** | Display Line Over-Current Sense Time Display |

### AT "+" FAX COMMANDS

Some modems support fax commands conforming to EIA standard 578. These commands are given here with short descriptions—they also typically support error correction and V.17terbo at 19.2KB and later standards.

| | |
|---|---|
| **(+DR)** | Set the modem's data compression reporting |
| **(+DS)** | Set the modem's data compression setting (e.g., +DS: 3,0,2048,32) |
| **(+DS44)** | Set the modem for V.44 data compression |
| **(+EB)** | Break handling in error control operation (e.g., +EB: 0,0,0) |
| **(+EFCS)** | Configure the 32-bit frame check sequence (e.g., +EFCS: 0) |

**TABLE 25-1     GENERAL INDEX OF THE AT COMMAND SET** *(CONTINUED)*

## AT "+" FAX COMMANDS

| | |
|---|---|
| **(+ER)** | Set the modem's error control reporting |
| **(+ES)** | Error control and synchronous mode selection (e.g., +ES=6) |
| **(+ESR)** | Enable selective repeat |
| **(+ETBM)** | Call termination buffer management (e.g., +ETBM: 0,0,0) |
| **(+FAA)** | Auto Answer Mode Parameter |
| **(+FAXERR=x)** | Fax Error Value Parameter |
| **(+FBOR=x)** | Phase C Data Bit Order Parameter |
| **(+FBUF?)** | Read the Buffer Size |
| **(+FCLASS?)** | Service Class Indication |
| **+FCLASS?** | 000 if in data mode; 001 if in fax class 1 |
| **(+FCLASS=x)** | Service Class Capabilities |
| **+FCLASS=?** | 0—modem is set up for data mode<br>0,1—modem is capable of data and fax class I services |
| **(+FCLASS=n)** | Service Class Selection |
| **+FCLASS=0** | Select data mode |
| **+FCLASS=1** | Select fax class 1 |
| **+FCLASS=8** | Select voice mode |
| **(+FCR)** | Capability to Receive |
| **(+FDCC=x)** | Modem Capabilities Parameter |
| **(+FDCS=x)** | Current Session Results |
| **(+FDIS=x)** | Current Session Negotiation Parameters |
| **(+FDR)** | Begin or Continue Phase C Receive Data |
| **(+FDT=x)** | Data Transmission |
| **(+FET=x)** | Transmit Page Punctuation |
| **(+FK)** | Terminate Session |
| **(+FLID=x)** | Local ID String Parameter |
| **(+FMDL?)** | Request Modem Model |
| **(+FMFR?)** | Request Modem IC Manufacturer |
| **(+FPHCTO)** | Phase C Time Out |
| **(+FPTS=x)** | Page Transfer Status |
| **(+FREV?)** | Request Modem Revision |
| **(+FRH=?)** | FAX SDLC Receive Capabilities |
| **(+FRH=n)** | Modem Accept Training (SDLC) |
| **(+FRM=?)** | FAX Normal Mode Receive Capabilities |
| **(+FRM=n)** | Modem Accept Training |
| **(+FRS=?)** | FRS Range Capabilities |
| **(+FRS=n)** | Receive Silence |
| **+FRS=4** | That is, wait 40 mS for silence |
| **(+FTH=?)** | FAX SDLC Mode Transmit Capabilities |

**TABLE 25-1** GENERAL INDEX OF THE AT COMMAND SET *(CONTINUED)*

**AT "+" FAX COMMANDS**

| | |
|---|---|
| **(+FTH=n)** | Modem Initiate Training (SDLC) |
| **(+FTM=?)** | FAX Normal Mode Transmit Capabilities |
| **(+FTM=n)** | Modem Initiate Training |
| **(+FTS=?)** | FTS Range Capabilities |
| **(+FTS=n)** | Transmission Silence |
| **+FTS=5** | That is, fax transmission silence for 50 ms |
| **(+GCAP)** | Request a complete list of capabilities from the modem |
| **(+GCI)** | Request the modem's country of installation |
| **(+GMI)** | Request modem manufacturer identification |
| **(+GMM)** | Request modem model identification |
| **(+GMR)** | Request modem revision identification |
| **(+GOI)** | Request global object identification |
| **(+GSN)** | Request modem serial number |
| **(+IFC: x,y)** | Set the modem's local flow control |
| **(+IPR)** | Fix the DTE rate at a given level (e.g., +IPR 57600) |
| **(+ILRR: x)** | Set the modem's local rate reporting |
| **+ILRR: 0** | Disable local rate reporting |
| **+ILRR: 1** | Enable local rate reporting |
| **(+MCR)** | Modem modulation report syntax |
| **(+MR)** | Set the modem's modulation selection (e.g., +MS: K56, 1,75,33600,75,56000) |
| **(+MR)** | Set the modem's modulation reporting control |
| **+MR: 0** | Disable modulation reporting |
| **+MR: 1** | Enable modulation reporting (+MCR and +MRR) |
| **+MR: 2** | Enable modulation reporting (+MCR) |
| **(+PCW)** | Call Waiting control |
| **+PCW: 0** | Request modem-on-hold |
| **+PCW: 1** | Hang up |
| **+PCW: 2** | Ignore call waiting |
| **(+PIG)** | Enable/disable the PCM upstream negotiation |
| **(+PMH)** | Modem-on-hold control |
| **+PMH: 0** | Enable modem-on-hold in V.92 mode |
| **+PMH: 1** | Disable modem-on-hold |
| **(+PMHF)** | Modem-on-hold flash |
| **(+PMHR: x)** | Initiate modem-on-hold |
| **(+PMHT: x)** | Set the modem-on-hold timer |
| **(+PQC)** | Set the V.92 phase control |
| **+PQC: 0** | Enable short phase 1 and phase 2 |
| **+PQC: 1** | Enable short phase 1 only |

**TABLE 25-1    GENERAL INDEX OF THE AT COMMAND SET** *(CONTINUED)*

### AT "+" FAX COMMANDS

| | |
|---|---|
| **+PQC: 2** | Not supported |
| **+PQC: 3** | Disable short phases |
| **(+PSS)** | Set the short sequence selection |
| **+PSS: 0** | Let the modem choose the sequences automatically |
| **+PSS: 1** | Reserved |
| **+PSS: 2** | Force full startup sequences |
| **(+QCPC)** | Force the full startup procedure |
| **(+QCPS)** | Save the quick-connect profile |
| **(+VCID)** | Caller ID Service |
| **+VCID=0** | Disable Caller ID reporting |
| **+VCID=1** | Enable Caller ID (formatted) |
| **+VCID=2** | Enable Caller ID (unformatted) |
| **(+VRID)** | Report Retrieved Caller ID |
| **+VRID=0** | Report Caller ID (formatted) |
| **+VRID=1** | Report Caller ID (unformatted) |

### OTHER AT COMMANDS

| | |
|---|---|
| **(_+BRC+_)** | Remote Escape into BRC State (from Host Online Data Mode) |
| **($BRC)** | Enable/Disable Host |
| **(#CID)** | Enable Caller ID Detection |
| **(:E)** | Compromise Equalizer Enable |
| **:E0** | Disables the equalizer |
| **:E1** | Enables the equalizer |
| **($GIVEBRC)** | Enter BRC State (from Target Online Command State) |
| ***B** | Display blacklisted phone numbers |
| ***D** | Display delayed phone numbers |
| **(*Hx)** | Link Negotiation Speed |
| ***H0** | Link negotiation occurs at the highest supported speed |
| ***H1** | Link negotiation occurs at 1200 bps |
| ***H2** | Link negotiation occurs at 4800 bps |
| **()Mx)** | Enable Cellular Power Level Adjustment |
| **)M0** | Disables power level adjustment during MNP 10 link negotiation |
| **)M1** | Enables power level adjustment during MNP 10 link negotiation |
| **(@Mx)** | Initial Cellular Power Level Setting |
| **@M0** | -26 dBm |
| **@M1** | -30 dBm |
| **@M2** | -10 dBm |
| **@M26** | -26 dBm |

## Interpreting Commands

Virtually all AT command strings start with the prefix "AT" (attention). For example, the command string **ATZE1Q0V1** contains five separate commands: attention (**AT**), reset the modem to its power-up defaults (**Z**), enable the command echo to send command characters back to the sender (**E1**), send command result codes back to the PC (**Q0**), and select text result codes, which causes words to be used as result codes (**V1**). While this may seem like a mouthful, a typical modem can accept command strings up to 40 characters long. The term *result codes* refers to the messages that the modem generates when a command string is processed. Table 25-2 outlines a series of typical result codes for a Zoom Telephonics V.92 modem. Either numbers (default) or words (using the **V1** command) can be returned. When a command is processed correctly, a result code OK is produced, or CONNECT when a successful connection is established.

| TABLE 25-2 | LIST OF TYPICAL MODEM RESULT CODES FOR A ZOOM TELEPHONICS V.92 MODEM | |
|---|---|---|
| **CODE** | **MESSAGE** | **DEFINITION** |
| +F4 | | High-speed fax data (V.27, V.29, V.33, or V.17) is expected but a V.21 signal is received. |
| 0 | OK | A command line has been executed. |
| 1 | CONNECT | The modem has connected to the line at 300 bps. |
| 2 | RING | An incoming ring signal is detected on the line. When cellular interface is selected, RING indicates that the cellular phone is receiving an incoming call. |
| 3 | NO CARRIER | Sent when unsuccessfully attempting to establish a call. |
| 4 | ERROR | Sent when unsuccessfully attempting to execute a command line (e.g., the command does not exist or is not supported by the modem). |
| 5 | CONNECT 1200 | The modem has connected to the line at 1200 bps. |
| 6 | NO DIALTONE | The modem has been instructed to wait for a dial tone during dialing but none is received. When cellular phone interface is selected, indicates that cellular service is not currently available. |
| 7 | BUSY | The busy signal is detected on the line when the modem is attempting to originate a call. |
| 8 | NO ANSWER | The modem is attempting to originate a call if a continuous ringback signal is detected on the line. |
| 9 | CONNECT 600 | The modem has connected to the line at 600 bps. |
| 10 | CONNECT 2400 | The modem has connected to the line at 2400 bps. |
| 11 | CONNECT 4800 | The modem has connected to the line at 4800 bps. |
| 12 | CONNECT 7200 | The modem has connected to the line at 7200 bps. |
| 13 | CONNECT 9600 | The modem has connected to the line at 9600 bps. |
| 14 | CONNECT 12000 | The modem has connected to the line at 12000 bps. |
| 15 | CONNECT 14400 | The modem has connected to the line at 14400 bps. |
| 16 | CONNECT 19200 | The modem has connected to the line at 19200 bps. |
| 17 | CONNECT 38400 | The modem has connected to the line at 38400 bps. |
| 18 | CONNECT 57600 | The modem has connected to the line at 57600 bps. |
| 19 | CONNECT 115200 | The modem has connected to the line at 115200 bps. |

**TABLE 25-2** LIST OF TYPICAL MODEM RESULT CODES FOR A ZOOM TELEPHONICS V.92 MODEM *(CONTINUED)*

| CODE | MESSAGE | DEFINITION |
|---|---|---|
| 22 | CONNECT 75TX/1200RX | The modem has established a V.23 originate connection. |
| 23 | CONNECT 1200TX/75RX | The modem has established a V.23 answer connection. |
| 24 | DELAYED | A call failed to connect and the number dialed is considered "delayed" because of country blacklisting requirements. |
| 32 | BLACKLISTED | A call failed to connect and the number dialed is considered "blacklisted." |
| 33 | FAX | A fax modem connection is established in a facsimile mode. |
| 35 | DATA | A data modem connection is established in a facsimile mode. |
| 40 | +MRR: 300 | The modem has connected to the line at 300 bps. |
| 44 | +MRR: 1200/75 | The V.23 backward channel carrier is detected. |
| 45 | +MRR: 75/1200 | The V.23 forward channel carrier is detected. |
| 46 | +MRR: 1200 | The modem has connected to the line at 1200 bps. |
| 47 | +MRR: 2400 | The modem has connected to the line at 2400 bps. |
| 48 | +MRR: 4800 | The modem has connected to the line at 4800 bps. |
| 49 | +MRR: 7200 | The modem has connected to the line at 7200 bps. |
| 50 | +MRR: 9600 | The modem has connected to the line at 9600 bps. |
| 51 | +MRR: 12000 | The modem has connected to the line at 12000 bps. |
| 52 | +MRR: 14400 | The modem has connected to the line at 14400 bps. |
| 53 | +MRR: 16800 | The modem has connected to the line at 16800 bps. |
| 54 | +MRR: 19200 | The modem has connected to the line at 19200 bps. |
| 55 | +MRR: 21600 | The modem has connected to the line at 21600 bps. |
| 56 | +MRR: 24000 | The modem has connected to the line at 24000 bps. |
| 57 | +MRR: 26400 | The modem has connected to the line at 26400 bps. |
| 58 | +MRR: 28800 | The modem has connected to the line at 28800 bps. |
| 59 | CONNECT 16800 | The modem has connected to the line, and the DTE speed is 16800 bps. |
| 61 | CONNECT 21600 | The modem has connected to the line, and the DTE speed is 21600 bps. |
| 62 | CONNECT 24000 | The modem has connected to the line, and the DTE speed is 24000 bps. |
| 63 | CONNECT 26400 | The modem has connected to the line, and the DTE speed is 26400 bps. |
| 64 | CONNECT 28800 | The modem has connected to the line at 28800 bps. |
| 66 | +DR: ALT | The modem has connected to the line in MNP Class 5 compression. |
| 67 | +DR: V.42B | The modem has connected to the line in V.42bis compression. |
| 69 | +DR: NONE | The modem has connected to the line without data compression. |
| 70 | +ER: NONE | The modem has connected to the line without any form of error correction. |

**TABLE 25-2    LIST OF TYPICAL MODEM RESULT CODES FOR A ZOOM TELEPHONICS V.92 MODEM** *(CONTINUED)*

| CODE | MESSAGE | DEFINITION |
|---|---|---|
| 77 | +ER: LAPM | The modem has connected to the line in V.42 LAPM error correction mode. |
| 78 | +MRR: 31200 | The modem has connected to the line at 31200 bps. |
| 79 | +MRR: 33600 | The modem has connected to the line at 33600 bps. |
| 80 | +ER: ALT | The modem has connected in the MNP error correction mode. |
| 83 | LINE IN USE | The modem attempted to go off-hook when an extension was already using the line. |
| 84 | CONNECT 33600 | The modem has connected to the line at 33600 bps. |
| 91 | CONNECT 31200 | The modem has connected to the line at 31200 bps. |
| 134 | +MCR: B103 | The modem has connected to the line with Bell 103 modulation. |
| 135 | +MCR: B212 | The modem has connected to the line with Bell 212 modulation. |
| 136 | +MCR: V21 | The modem has connected to the line with ITU-T V.21 modulation. |
| 137 | +MCR: V22 | The modem has connected to the line with ITU-T V.22 modulation. |
| 138 | +MCR: V22B | The modem has connected to the line with ITU-T V.22 bis modulation. |
| 139 | +MCR: V23 | The modem has connected to the line with ITU-T V.23 modulation. |
| 140 | +MCR: V32 | The modem has connected to the line with ITU-T V.32 modulation. |
| 141 | +MCR: V32B | The modem has connected to the line with ITU-T V.32 bis modulation. |
| 142 | +MCR: V34 | The modem has connected to the line with ITU-T V.34 modulation. |
| 144 | +MCR: K56 | The modem has connected to the line with K56flex modulation. |
| 145 | +MCR: V90 | The modem has connected to the line with ITU-T V.90 modulation. |
| 150 | +MRR: 32000 | The modem has connected to the line at 32000 bps. |
| 151 | +MRR: 34000 | The modem has connected to the line at 34000 bps. |
| 152 | +MRR: 36000 | The modem has connected to the line at 36000 bps. |
| 153 | +MRR: 38000 | The modem has connected to the line at 38000 bps. |
| 154 | +MRR: 40000 | The modem has connected to the line at 40000 bps. |
| 155 | +MRR: 42000 | The modem has connected to the line at 42000 bps. |
| 156 | +MRR: 44000 | The modem has connected to the line at 44000 bps. |
| 157 | +MRR: 46000 | The modem has connected to the line at 46000 bps. |
| 158 | +MRR: 48000 | The modem has connected to the line at 48000 bps. |
| 159 | +MRR: 50000 | The modem has connected to the line at 50000 bps. |
| 160 | +MRR: 52000 | The modem has connected to the line at 52000 bps. |
| 161 | +MRR: 54000 | The modem has connected to the line at 54000 bps. |
| 162 | +MRR: 56000 | The modem has connected to the line at 56000 bps. |
| 165 | CONNECT 32000 | The modem has connected to the line at 32000 bps. |
| 166 | CONNECT 34000 | The modem has connected to the line at 34000 bps. |
| 167 | CONNECT 36000 | The modem has connected to the line at 36000 bps. |
| 168 | CONNECT 38000 | The modem has connected to the line at 38000 bps. |
| 169 | CONNECT 40000 | The modem has connected to the line at 40000 bps. |
| 170 | CONNECT 42000 | The modem has connected to the line at 42000 bps. |

**TABLE 25-2    LIST OF TYPICAL MODEM RESULT CODES FOR A ZOOM TELEPHONICS V.92 MODEM** *(CONTINUED)*

| CODE | MESSAGE | DEFINITION |
|------|---------|------------|
| 171 | CONNECT 44000 | The modem has connected to the line at 44000 bps. |
| 172 | CONNECT 46000 | The modem has connected to the line at 46000 bps. |
| 173 | CONNECT 48000 | The modem has connected to the line at 48000 bps. |
| 174 | CONNECT 50000 | The modem has connected to the line at 50000 bps. |
| 175 | CONNECT 52000 | The modem has connected to the line at 52000 bps. |
| 176 | CONNECT 54000 | The modem has connected to the line at 54000 bps. |
| 177 | CONNECT 56000 | The modem has connected to the line at 56000 bps. |
| 178 | CONNECT 230400 | The modem has connected to the line at 230400 bps. |
| 180 | CONNECT 28000 | The modem has connected to the line at 28000 bps. |
| 181 | CONNECT 29333 | The modem has connected to the line at 29333 bps. |
| 182 | CONNECT 30667 | The modem has connected to the line at 30667 bps. |
| 183 | CONNECT 33333 | The modem has connected to the line at 33333 bps. |
| 184 | CONNECT 34667 | The modem has connected to the line at 34667 bps. |
| 185 | CONNECT 37333 | The modem has connected to the line at 37333 bps. |
| 186 | CONNECT 38667 | The modem has connected to the line at 38667 bps. |
| 187 | CONNECT 41333 | The modem has connected to the line at 41333 bps. |
| 188 | CONNECT 42667 | The modem has connected to the line at 42667 bps. |
| 189 | CONNECT 45333 | The modem has connected to the line at 45333 bps. |
| 190 | CONNECT 46667 | The modem has connected to the line at 46667 bps. |
| 191 | CONNECT 49333 | The modem has connected to the line at 49333 bps. |
| 192 | CONNECT 50667 | The modem has connected to the line at 50667 bps. |
| 193 | CONNECT 53333 | The modem has connected to the line at 53333 bps. |
| 194 | CONNECT 54667 | The modem has connected to the line at 54667 bps. |
| 195 | +MRR: 28000 | The modem has connected to the line at 28000 bps. |
| 196 | +MRR: 29333 | The modem has connected to the line at 29333 bps. |
| 197 | +MRR: 30667 | The modem has connected to the line at 30667 bps. |
| 198 | +MRR: 33333 | The modem has connected to the line at 33333 bps. |
| 199 | +MRR: 34667 | The modem has connected to the line at 34667 bps. |
| 200 | +MRR: 37333 | The modem has connected to the line at 37333 bps. |
| 201 | +MRR: 38667 | The modem has connected to the line at 38667 bps. |
| 202 | +MRR: 41333 | The modem has connected to the line at 41333 bps. |
| 203 | +MRR: 42667 | The modem has connected to the line at 42667 bps. |
| 204 | +MRR: 45333 | The modem has connected to the line at 45333 bps. |
| 205 | +MRR: 46667 | The modem has connected to the line at 46667 bps. |
| 206 | +MRR: 49333 | The modem has connected to the line at 49333 bps. |
| 207 | +MRR: 50667 | The modem has connected to the line at 50667 bps. |
| 208 | +MRR: 53333 | The modem has connected to the line at 53333 bps. |
| 209 | +MRR: 54667 | The modem has connected to the line at 54667 bps. |

## Controlling Attributes

Many attributes of the Hayes-compatible modem are programmable. To accommodate this feature, each parameter must be held in a series of memory locations (called *S-registers*). Each S-register is described in Table 25-3. For example, the default escape sequence for the AT command set is a series of three plusses: "+++". You could change this character by writing an new ASCII character to register S2. Default S-register values are fine for most work, but you can often optimize the modem's operation by experimenting with the register values. Since S-register contents must be maintained after power is removed from the modem, the registers are stored in nonvolatile RAM (NVRAM).

**TABLE 25-3    INDEX OF S-REGISTER ASSIGNMENTS**

| REGISTER | FUNCTION | RANGE | UNITS | DEFAULT |
|---|---|---|---|---|
| S0 | Rings to Auto-Answer | 0–255 | Rings | 0 |
| S1 | Ring Counter | 0–255 | Rings | 0 |
| S2 | Escape Character | 0–255 | ASCII | 43 |
| S3 | Carriage Return Character | 0–127 | ASCII | 13 |
| S4 | Line Feed Character | 0–127 | ASCII | 10 |
| S5 | Backspace Character | 0–255 | ASCII | 8 |
| S6 | Wait Time for Dial Tone | 2–255 | seconds | 4 |
| S7 | Wait for Carrier | 1–255 | seconds | 50 |
| S8 | Pause Time for (,) Comma | 0–255 | seconds | 2 |
| S9 | Carrier Detect Response Time | 1–255 | 1/10 sec | 6 |
| S10 | Carrier Loss Disconnect Time | 1–255 | 1/10 sec | 14 |
| S11 | Touch Tone (DTMF) Duration | 50–255 | 1/1000 sec | 95 |
| S12 | Escape Code Guard Time | 0–255 | 2/100 sec | 50 |
| S13 | *Reserved* | --- | --- | --- |
| S14 | General Bit Mapped Options | --- | --- | 138 (8Ah) |
| S15 | *Reserved* | --- | --- | --- |
| S16 | Test Mode Bit Map Options (&T) | --- | --- | 0 |
| S17 | *Reserved* | --- | --- | --- |
| S18 | Test Timer | 0–255 | seconds | 0 |
| S19 | Auto-Sync Bit Map Register | --- | --- | 0 |
| S20 | AutoSync HDLC Address or BSC Sync Character | 0–255 | --- | 0 |
| S21 | V.24/General Bit Map Options | --- | --- | 4 (04h) |
| S22 | Speaker/Results Bit Map Options | --- | --- | 118 (76h) |
| S23 | General Bit Map Options | --- | --- | 55 (37h) |
| S24 | Sleep Inactivity Timer | 0–255 | seconds | 1 |
| S25 | Delay to DTR Off | 0–255 | 1/100 sec | 5 |
| S26 | RTS-to-CTS Delay | 0–255 | 1/100 sec | 1 |
| S27 | General Bit Map Options | --- | --- | 73 (49h) with ECC 74 (4Ah) without ECC |

**TABLE 25-3    INDEX OF S-REGISTER ASSIGNMENTS *(CONTINUED)***

| REGISTER | FUNCTION | RANGE | UNITS | DEFAULT |
|----------|----------|-------|-------|---------|
| S28 | General Bit Map Options | --- | --- | 0 |
| S29 | Flash Dial Modifier Time | 0–255 | 10 ms | 70 |
| S30 | Disconnect Activity Timer | 0–255 | 10 sec | 0 |
| S31 | General Bit Map Options | --- | --- | 194 (C2h) |
| S32 | XON Character | 0–255 | ASCII | 17 (11h) |
| S33 | XOFF Character | 0–255 | ASCII | 19 (13h) |
| S34 | *Reserved* | --- | --- | --- |
| S35 | *Reserved* | --- | --- | --- |
| S36 | LAPM Failure Control | --- | --- | 7 |
| S37 | Line Connection Speed | --- | --- | 0 |
| S38 | Delay Before Forced Hangup | 0–255 | seconds | 20 |
| S39 | Flow Control | --- | --- | 3 |
| S40 | General Bit Map Options | --- | --- | 105 (69h) No MNP 10<br>107 (6Bh) MNP 10 |
| S41 | General Bit Mapped Options | --- | --- | 131 (83h) |
| S43 | Auto Fallback Character for MNP Negotiation | 0–255 | --- | 13 |
| S44 | Data Framing | --- | --- | --- |
| S46 | Data Compression Control | --- | --- | 136 (no compression)<br>138 (with compression) |
| S46* | Automatic Sleep Timer | 0–255 | 100 mS | 100 |
| S47 | Forced Sleep Timer with Power-down Mode in PCMCIA | 0–255 | 100 mS | 10 |
| S48 | V.42 Negotiation Control | --- | --- | 7 |
| S49 | Buffer Low Limit | --- | --- | --- |
| S50 | Buffer High Limit | --- | --- | --- |
| S50* | FAX/Data Mode Selection | --- | --- | 0 (data mode)<br>1 (fax mode) |
| S53 | Global PAD Configuration | --- | --- | --- |
| S55 | AutoStream Protocol Request | --- | --- | --- |
| S56 | AutoStream Protocol Status | --- | --- | --- |
| S57 | Network Options Register | --- | --- | --- |
| S58 | BTLZ String Length | 6–64 | bytes | 32 |
| S59 | Leased Line Failure Alarm | --- | --- | --- |
| S60 | Leased Line Failure Action | --- | --- | --- |
| S61 | Leased Line Retry Number | --- | --- | --- |
| S62 | Leased Line Options | --- | --- | --- |
| S62* | DTE Rate Status | 0–17 | --- | 16 (57600 bps) |
| S63 | Leased Line Transmit Level | --- | --- | --- |
| S64 | Leased Line Receive Level | --- | --- | --- |
| S69 | Link Layer k Protocol | --- | --- | --- |

**TABLE 25-3    INDEX OF S-REGISTER ASSIGNMENTS** *(CONTINUED)*

| REGISTER | FUNCTION | RANGE | UNITS | DEFAULT |
|---|---|---|---|---|
| S70 | Max Number of Retransmissions | --- | --- | --- |
| S71 | Link Layer Timeout | --- | --- | --- |
| S72 | Loss of Flag Idle Timeout | --- | --- | --- |
| S72* | DTE Speed Select | 0–18 | --- | 0 (last autobaud) |
| S73 | No Activity Timeout | --- | --- | --- |
| S74 | Minimum Incoming LCN | --- | --- | --- |
| S75 | Minimum Incoming LCN | --- | --- | --- |
| S76 | Maximum Incoming LCN | --- | --- | --- |
| S77 | Maximum Incoming LCN | --- | --- | --- |
| S78 | Outgoing LCN | --- | --- | --- |
| S79 | Outgoing LCN | --- | --- | --- |
| S80 | X.25 Packet Level N20 Parameter | --- | --- | --- |
| S80* | Soft Switch Functions | --- | --- | 1 |
| S81 | X.25 Packet Level T20 Parameter | --- | --- | --- |
| S82 | LAPM Break Control | --- | --- | 128 (40h) |
| S84 | ASU Negotiation | --- | --- | --- |
| S85 | ASU Negotiation Status | --- | --- | --- |
| S86 | Call Failure Reason Code | 0–255 | --- | --- |
| S87 | Fixed Speed DTE Interface | --- | --- | --- |
| S91 | PSTN Xmit Attenuation Level | 0–15 | -dBm | 10 |
| S92 | Fax Xmit Attenuation Level | 0–15 | -dBm | 10 |
| S92* | MI/MIC Options | --- | --- | --- |
| S93 | V.25bis Async Interface Speed | --- | --- | --- |
| S94 | V.25bis Mode Control | --- | --- | --- |
| S95 | Result Code Messages Control | --- | --- | 0 |
| S97 | V.32 Late Connecting Handshake Timing | --- | --- | --- |
| S99 | Leased Line Transmit Level | 0–15 | -dBm | 10 |
| S101 | Distinctive Ring Reporting | 0–63 | --- | 0 |
| S105 | Frame Size | --- | --- | --- |
| S108 | Signal Quality Selector | --- | --- | --- |
| S109 | Carrier Speed Selector | --- | --- | --- |
| S110 | V.32/V.32bis Selector | --- | --- | --- |
| S113 | Calling Tone Control | --- | --- | --- |
| S116 | Connection Timeout | --- | --- | --- |
| S121 | Use of DTR | --- | --- | --- |
| S122 | V.13 Selection | --- | --- | --- |
| S141 | Detection Phase Timer | --- | --- | --- |
| S142 | Online Character Format | --- | --- | --- |
| S143 | KDS Handshake Mode | --- | --- | --- |

| TABLE 25-3 | INDEX OF S-REGISTER ASSIGNMENTS *(CONTINUED)* | | | |
|---|---|---|---|---|
| **REGISTER** | **FUNCTION** | **RANGE** | **UNITS** | **DEFAULT** |
| S144 | Autobaud Group Selection | --- | --- | --- |
| S150 | V.42 Options | --- | --- | --- |
| S151 | Simultaneous Voice Data Control | --- | --- | --- |
| S154 | Force Port Speed | --- | --- | --- |
| S157 | Timeout Result Code | --- | --- | --- |
| S201 | Cellular Transmit Level (MNP 10) | 10–63 | --- | 58 (3Ah) |
| S202 | Remote Access Escape Character | 0–255 | ASCII | 170 |

**\*Note:** The register may be used for different purposes by some modems.

# MODEM INITIALIZATION STRINGS

One of the most difficult steps in configuring a new modem (or new modem software) involves the proper use of initialization strings. *Initialization strings* (or *init strings* as they are sometimes called) are vital to setting up the modem properly before each use—if the setup is not done correctly, the modem will not behave as expected (if it works at all). Years ago, you'd need to configure a modem with a specific initialization string yourself. Today, Windows 9x/Me/XP drivers provide all of the modem support, so you don't need to worry about the initialization string (just use the latest driver). However, you may still need to enter a string to optimize modem operation, enable or tweak a specific feature, or configure DOS modem software (if you're still working in the real-mode). Keep in mind that initialization strings are not absolute—except for the "AT" at the start of each line, you can modify each string as required for your own system and telephone line.

You may notice that many AT command strings are so long that they seem to "run over" onto a second line. When you enter strings into communication software, you should be sure to enter all of the commands *without* spaces or carriage returns—initialization strings are always one continuous line.

At first glance, an initialization string may seem quite daunting. But if you take a moment to examine the string in detail (and refer to the AT Command Set listed in Table 25-1), you should be able to decode even the longest command strings in just a few moments. Let's try a few basic examples. The command string

```
ATS0=0&B1&H1&W
```

tells the modem to not answer an incoming call (S0=0), use CTS flow control (&B1), use a fixed DTE rate (&H1), and store this adjusted configuration in the modem's internal memory called NVRAM (&W). Similarly, the command string

```
ATS0=0&K3&W
```

tells the modem to *not* answer an incoming call (S0=0), use hardware flow control (&K3), and store this adjusted configuration in the modem's internal memory (&W). As you can see, an initialization string is merely a list of individual commands that enable, disable, or adjust specific operating parameters for a given modem. Most modem manufacturers attempt to use basic default values so that the modem will still operate without any alteration through the initialization string, but some amount of tailoring is usually required for optimum performance. If you cannot find the appropriate initialization string for your particular modem, you should check with the modem's manufacturer.

## Initialization Strings and Windows

Modem initialization strings in Windows 9x/Me/XP and Windows Dial-Up Networking can be adjusted in the system Registry or through the Modem icon in the Control Panel. When a modem is installed on a Windows 9x/Me system, the default initialization string is written to the Registry by the modem's .INF driver file. The key containing the default string is

```
HKEY_LOCAL_MACHINE\System\CurrentControlSet\Services\Class\Modem\0000\Init
```

(Systems with multiple modems may have modem IDs of 0000, 0001, 0002 and so on.) You can use this entry in the Registry to adjust the modem's initialization string manually with the Registry Editor (regedit.exe). However, most users are uncomfortable with editing the Registry, since errors to the Registry can cause serious problems and prevent Windows 9x/Me/XP from booting. The safer and faster method of adjusting the modem's initialization string is through the Modem Properties dialog.

Use the following steps under Windows 9x/Me:

**1.** Open your Control Panel and double-click the Modem icon.

**2.** Highlight your modem and click the Properties button.

**3.** Select the Connection tab and then click the Advanced button.

**4.** The Advanced Connection Settings dialog appears (Figure 25-4).

**5.** Enter your new command string in the Extra settings box. When using this box, you do *not* need to preface your new command string with "AT."

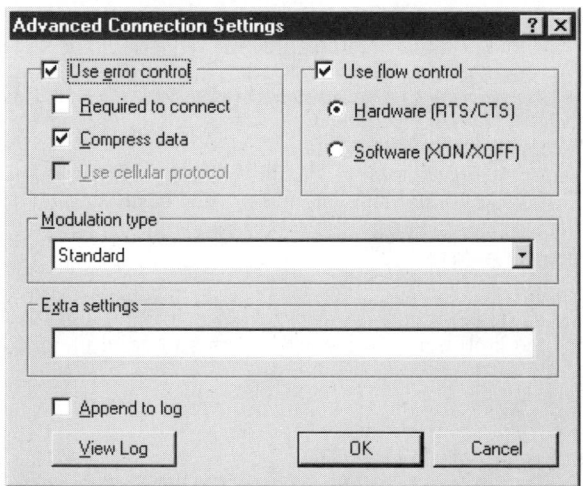

**FIGURE  25-4**    The Advanced Connection Settings dialog under Windows 98/SE

Use the following steps under Windows XP:

1. Open the Control Panel and click Printers and Other Hardware.
2. Click Phone and Modem Options and select the Modems tab.
3. Highlight the modem and click the Advanced button.
4. Enter the new command string in the Advanced Connection Settings dialog.

In most cases, the appropriate modem driver should provide all the support needed for the modem, and you should *not* need to tweak the initialization strings.

You can try this yourself. Enter **S11=40** in the Extra settings box. Click the OK button to save your changes and exit the Modem icon, and then try connecting to the Internet. Register S11 determines the amount of time (in milliseconds) between the tones of a phone number. The default setting is usually 70 ms. By entering **40** (milliseconds), you should hear a definite decrease in the time it takes to dial a number.

Just below the Extra settings text box is the Append to Log check box. If you select this option, Windows will keep a running log of the commands sent and received during a modem session. You can confirm that the correct commands are being sent. The combination of the Sent and Received commands may help you determine if a problem is caused by the system's software or hardware—or even by the Service Provider.

Be sure to check for an updated modem driver if you're experiencing modem problems or when you check for driver updates for other system components. The new modem driver may contain a different (and better) default initialization string.

## MODEM MODES

The modem is always in one of *two* primary modes: the command mode or the data mode. When first switched on (or reset), the modem starts up in *command mode*. In this mode, the controller circuit (sometimes called a *command processor*) is constantly checking to see if you have typed a valid AT command. When the modem receives a valid command, it executes that command for you. While your modem is in the command mode, you can instruct it to answer the telephone, change an S-Register value, hang up or dial the telephone, and perform any number of other command functions.

You'll be using the command mode to test the modem later in this chapter.

The other mode is the *data mode*. In the data mode, your modem is transmitting all of the data it receives from your computer or terminal along the telephone line to the remote modem. Your modem is constantly checking the state of the *Data Carrier Detect* (DCD) and *Data Terminal Ready* (DTR) signals (depending on the system configuration). It is also watching the local data stream for a command mode escape sequence. The default escape sequence the AT command set is "+++". When the proper escape sequence (or a change in the state of the DCD or DTR signal) occurs, the modem returns to a command mode where it waits for the next AT command.

## MODEM NEGOTIATION

Now that you have seen the essential elements of a modem and learned about modem signaling, you can use that background to form a picture of how the modem works in actual practice. You see, modem communication is not an event—it is a *process* whose success depends not only on your modem, but also on the modem and PC you are trying to communicate with. This part of the chapter is intended to familiarize you with an operating session for a typical external serial modem.

Communication begins when you instruct the communication software to establish a connection. For an external serial modem, control signals sent to the selected serial port cause the UART to assert the Data Terminal Ready (DTR) signal. This tells the attached modem that the PC is turned on and ready to transmit. The modem responds by asserting the Data Set Ready (DSR) line. The serial port receives this signal and tells the software that the modem is ready—both DTR and DSR *must* be present for communication to take place.

The communication software then sends an AT initialization string to the COM port (which forwards the string to the modem). In the command mode, the controller circuit interprets the initialization string that tells the modem to go off hook (get dial tone), then dial the telephone number of the destination modem. Dialing may take place in pulse (rotary) or tone (DTMF) mode, depending on the initialization string. The modem transmits an acknowledgment back to the COM port—this is often displayed right on the communication software window. The line at the destination end begins to ring. If configured properly and running communication software of its own, the remote modem will pick up the ringing line, and a complete wiring path will be established between the two modems.

When the destination modem picks up the line, your local modem sends out a standard tone (a *carrier* tone). The carrier lets the remote modem know it's being called by another modem. If the remote modem recognizes the carrier, it sends out an even higher pitched tone. You can often hear these squealing tones when your modem is equipped with a speaker. Once your modem recognizes the remote modem, it sends a Carrier Detect (CD) signal to the serial port. These mutual carriers will be modulated to exchange data.

Okay, both modems know they are talking to another modem, but now there has to be a mutual agreement on *how* they'll exchange data. They must agree on transmission speed, the proper size of a data packet, the signaling bits on each end of the data packet, whether or not parity will be used, and whether the modems will operate in half-duplex or full-duplex mode. Both modems must settle on these parameters or the data exchanged between them will make no sense. This process is known as *negotiation*. Assuming that the negotiation process is successful, both modems can now exchange data.

When the communication software attempts to send data, it tells the serial port to assert the Request to Send (RTS) signal. This checks to see if your modem is free to receive data. If the PC is busy doing something else (such as disk access), it will disable the RTS signal until it is ready to resume sending. When the modem is ready for data, it will return a Clear to Send (CTS) signal to the serial port. The PC can then begin sending data to the modem and receiving data returned from the remote end. If the modem gets backed up with work, it will drop the CTS line until it is ready to resume communication. Since a standard system of tones is used, both modems can exchange data simultaneously.

When the time comes to terminate the connection, the communication software will send another AT command string to the serial port that causes it to break the connection. If the connection is broken by the remote modem, the local modem will drop the Carrier Detect line. The communication software will interpret this as a *Dropped Carrier* condition. Those are basically all the phases involved in modem communication.

## READING THE LIGHTS

One of the appealing attributes of external modems is the series of lights that typically adorn the front face. By observing each light and the sequence in which they light, you can often follow the progress of a communication—or quickly discern the cause of a communication failure. The following markings are typical of many modems, but keep in mind that your particular modem may use fewer indicators (or be marked differently):

- **56K**   Lights when communicating in V.90 or V.92 mode.
- **AA (Auto-Answer)**   Lights when Auto-Answer is activated, and blinks when detecting an incoming ring.
- **CD (Carrier Detect)**   Lights when the Data Carrier Detect (DCD) signal from the modem to the computer is on.
- **CS (Clear to Send)**   Lights when the fax/modem can accept data from the computer.
- **DC (Data Compression)**   Lights when using V.44, V.42bis, or MNP 5 data compression.
- **EC (Error Correction)**   Lights when sending data using V.42 or MNP 4 error correction.
- **FAX**   Lights when fax connection has been made to a remote fax/modem.
- **HOLD (Modem On Hold)**   Lights when a call is detected. If you accept the call, the light stays on for the duration of the call; if you refuse the call, the light goes off.
- **HS (High-Speed)**   Lights when communicating at 48000 bps or faster.
- **MR (Modem Ready)**   Lights when the modem is turned on. Flashes when the modem is in self-test mode.
- **MSG**   Used by some software products. May light when faxes or voicemail messages are waiting.
- **OH (Off Hook)**   Lights when the modem is off hook (e.g., dialing or transferring data).
- **PWR (Power)**   Lights when the modem is turned on. Flashes when the modem is in self-test mode.
- **RD (Receive Data)**   Flashes when data is sent from the modem to your computer or other serial device. At high speeds light may appear continuously on.
- **RI (Ring Indicate)**   Blinks when detecting incoming ring.
- **SD (Send Data)**   Flashes whenever data or commands are transmitted from the serial port of your computer or other device to the modem.
- **TD (Transmit Data)**   Flashes whenever data or commands are transmitted from the serial port of your computer or other device to the modem.
- **TR (Terminal Ready)**   Lights when the computer is ready to send or receive data. Indicates the status of the DTR signal from the terminal or computer.
- **V.34**   Lights when operating in V.34 mode.
- **V.92**   Lights when operating in V.92 mode.

# Understanding Signal Modulation

Once the modem accepts a bipolar signal from an RS-232 port (or digital data across a USB port), the carrier signal being generated on the telephone line must be modulated to reflect the logic levels being transmitted. Several different means of signal modulation have been developed through the years to improve the efficiency of data transfers. This part of the chapter gives you a brief explanation of each scheme. As you would expect, modems on both ends of the connection must be capable of the same modulation scheme.

# BPS VS. BAUD RATE

In the early days of modem communication, each audio signal *transition* represented a single bit. Each audio signal is known as a *baud*, and the *baud rate* naturally equaled the transmission rate in bps (or bits per second). Unlike those early modems, newer modem schemes can encode 2, 3, or 4 or more bits into every audio signal transition (or baud). This means that modem throughput (in bits per second) now equals 2x, 3x, or 4x the baud rate (and higher) being carried across the telephone line.

For example, a modem operating at 2400 baud (2400 audio signal transitions per second) can carry 4800 bps if 2 bits are encoded onto every baud. The same 2400 baud modem could also carry 9600 bps if 4 bits are encoded onto every baud. Today, the modem's baud rate *rarely* matches the modem's throughput in bps unless a very old signaling standard is being used. If the modem were operating at 4800 baud and used 3-bit encoding, the modem would be handling 14,400 bps (14.4 Kbps). The concept of *encoding* is different from *data compression*, since encoding transfers *all* original data bits from system to system, while data compression replaces repeating sequences of bits with much shorter bit sequences (known as *symbols* or *tokens*). You will see much more about encoding schemes and data compression later in this section. Today's V.92 modems use pulse code modulation (PCM) to encode bits supporting data rates ideally up to 56 Kbps. The addition of V.44 data compression adds compression of up to 6:1, yielding effective data transfer rates across the modem that can approach 300 Kbps.

# MODULATION SCHEMES

To discuss modulation, you must first understand a *sinusoidal* waveform. There are basically three physical characteristics to any waveform: amplitude, frequency, and phase. Each of these characteristics can be adjusted to represent a bit. *Amplitude* is simply the magnitude of the wave (usually measured in volts peak-to-peak or volts RMS). Amplitude represents how far above and below the zero axis that waveform travels. *Frequency* indicates the number of times that a single wave will repeat over any period of time—measured as cycles-per-second: (Hertz, or Hz). An 1800 Hz signal repeats 1800 times per second. The signal also has a time reference known as *phase*. Phase is measured in degrees where 90 degrees is the time to travel 25 percent of a wave, 180 degrees is the time to travel 50 percent of the wave, 270 degrees is the time to travel 75 percent of a wave, and so on. Since phase can take on any one of four states (degrees), phase shifts can be made to represent 2 bits simultaneously. Data between modems is commonly modulated by altering the amplitude, frequency, and phase of a carrier signal.

*Frequency Shift Keying* (FSK) is very similar to frequency modulation (FM), where only the frequency of a carrier is changed, and is one of the oldest modulation schemes. FSK sends a logic 1 as one particular frequency (usually 1750 Hz), and a logic 0 is sent as another discrete frequency (often 1080 Hz). Frequencies are typically sent at 300 baud, and each baud can carry 1 bit, so FSK can send 300 bps. This early technique resulted in the classical "baud = bps" confusion that is still prevalent today.

*Phase Shift Keying* (PSK) is a close cousin of FSK, but the phase timing of a carrier wave is altered while the carrier's frequency stays the same. By altering the carrier's phase, a logic 1 or 0 is represented. Since phase can be shifted in several precise increments (that is, 0, 90, 180, or 270 degrees), PSK can encode 1, 2, or 3 or more bits bit per baud. For example, a 1200 baud modem using PSK can transmit 2400 bps over an 1800 Hz carrier. PSK can also be used in conjunction with FSK to encode even more bits per baud.

*Quadrature Amplitude Modulation* (QAM) uses both phase and amplitude modulation to encode up to 6 bits onto every baud, although 4 bits are usually reserved for data. Not only can four phase states represent 2 bits, but also four levels of amplitude can represent another 2 bits. Most QAM modems use a 1700 Hz or 1800 Hz carrier and a base rate of 2400 baud, so they carry up to 9600 bps.

*Trellis Coded Quadrature Amplitude Modulation* (TCQAM or TCM) also uses an 1800 Hz carrier at a 2400 baud base rate, but uses the full 6-bit encoding capability of QAM to handle 14,400 bps. Most modems using TCM offer high speed and excellent echo cancellation circuitry. TCM has been a popular modulation scheme for mid-performance modems because data can be checked on the fly with much better reliability than by using a parity bit.

*Pulse Code Modulation* (PCM) is a sampling technique for digitizing analog signals, especially audio signals. PCM samples the signal 8000 times a second: each sample is represented by 8 bits for a total of 64 Kbps. There are two standards for coding the sample level: Mu-Law and A-Law. The Mu-Law standard is used in North America and Japan, while the A-Law standard is used in most other countries. PCM was originally used with high-performance T-1 and T-3 carrier systems. These carrier systems combine the PCM signals from many lines and transmit them over a single cable or other medium. Today, however, PCM is the basis for our V.90 and V.92 56 Kbs analog modem standards.

# Signaling Standards

Now that you have covered serial concepts and modulation techniques, you can see how modulation is used in conjunction with the many communications standards (or *protocols*) that have appeared. This part of the chapter highlights each of the major standards for modems, data compression, and error correction that are now in force today. Most data sent between modems contains some amount of repetitive or redundant information. If the redundant information is located and replaced by a small "token" during transmission—the data is *compressed*. A token can be passed much faster than the redundant data, and the receiving modem can accurately recreate the original data based on the token. *Data compression* has become an indispensable technique that allows modems to increase their data throughput without increasing the baud rate or bps. Data compression can occur only when the two communicating modems support the same compression protocol (such as V.44). If modems support more than one type of compression, the communicating modems will try to use the most powerful technique common to both.

Modem *error correction* is the ability of some modems to detect data errors that may have occurred in transit between modems, then automatically resend the faulty data until a correct copy is received. As with modulation standards, both modems must be using the same error correction standard in order to operate together. However, there are few error correction standards, and most modem manufacturers adhere closely to the few that are available.

## BELL STANDARDS

The old "Bell System" largely dictated North American telecommunications standards before the company was broken up into AT&T and seven regional operating companies in 1984. Before that time, two major standards (now obsolete) were developed that set the stage for future modem development:

- **BELL103** was the first widely accepted modem standard using simple FSK modulation at 300 baud. This is the *only* standard where the data rate matches the baud rate. It is interesting to note that some modems today *still* support BELL103 as a lowest common denominator when all other modulation techniques fail.

- **BELL212A** represents a second widely accepted modem standard in North America using PSK modulation at 600 baud to transmit 1200 bps. Many European countries ignored BELL212A in favor of the similar (but not entirely identical) European standard called V.22.

# ITU (CCITT) STANDARDS

After the Bell System breakup, AT&T no longer wielded enough clout to dictate standards in North America—and certainly not to the international community, which had developed serious computing interest. It was at this time that the ITU (*International Telecommunications Union*, formally the CCITT) gained prominence and acceptance in the U.S., leading to the conformance of all U.S. modems to ITU standards. ITU specifications are characterized by the letter "V" (as in V.17). The "V" simply means *standard* (rather like the "RS" in RS-232). The number following simply denotes the particular standard. Some standards also add the term "bis," which means the *second version* of a particular standard. You may also see the term "ter" or "terbo," which indicates the *third version* of a standard. The following list provides a basic outline of ITU standards. Only the standards that appear in **boldface** relate to modems in particular, but *all* are related to communications. This index may aid you in understanding the broad specifications that are required to fully characterize the computer communications environment:

- V.1 is a very early standard that defines binary 0/1 bits as space/mark line conditions and voltage levels.

- V.2 limits the power levels (in decibels or dB) of modems used on phone lines.

- V.4 describes the sequence of bits within a character as transmitted (the data frame).

- V.5 describes the standard synchronous signaling rates for dial-up lines.

- V.6 describes the standard synchronous signaling rates for leased lines.

- V.7 provides a list of modem terms in English, Spanish, and French.

- V.8 describes the initial handshaking (negotiation) process between modems and forms the basis for call "autodetection" or "auto-switching" (voice/fax/modem).

- V.10 describes unbalanced high-speed electrical interface characteristics (RS-423).

- V.11 describes balanced high-speed electrical characteristics (RS-422).

- V.13 explains simulated carrier control (with a full-duplex modem used as a half-duplex modem).

- V.14 explains the procedure for asynchronous to synchronous conversion.

- V.15 describes the requirements and designs for telephone acoustic couplers. This is largely unused today since most telephone equipment is modular and can be plugged into telephone adapters directly rather than loosely attached to the telephone handset.

- **V.17** describes an application-specific modulation scheme for Group 3 fax, which provides two-wire half-duplex trellis-coded transmission at 7200, 9600, 12000, and 14400 bps. In spite of the low number, this is a fairly recent standard.

- V.19 describes early DTMF modems using low-speed parallel transmission. This standard is largely obsolete.

- V.20 explains modems with parallel data transmission. This standard is largely obsolete.

- **V.21** provides the specifications for 300 bps FSK serial modems (based upon BELL103).

- **V.22** provides the specifications for 1200 bps (600 baud) PSK modems (similar to BELL212A).

- **V.22bis** describes 2400 bps modems operating at 600 baud using QAM.

- V.23 describes the operation of a rather unusual type of FM modem working at 1200/75 bps. That is, the host transmits at 1200 bps and receives at 75 bps. The remote modem transmits at 75 bps and receives at 1200 bps. V.23 is used in Europe to support some videotext applications.

- V.24 this is known as EIA RS-232 in the United States. V.24 defines *only* the functions of the serial port circuits. EIA-232-E (the current version of the standard) also defines electrical characteristics and connectors.

- V.25 defines automatic answering equipment and parallel automatic dialing. It also defines the answer tone that modems send.

- V.25bis defines serial automatic calling and answering, which is the ITU (CCITT) equivalent of AT commands. This is the current ITU standard for modem control by computers via serial interface. The Hayes AT command set is used primarily in the U.S.

- **V.26** defines a 2400 bps PSK full-duplex modem operating at 1200 baud.

- **V.26bis** defines a 2400 bps PSK half-duplex modem operating at 1200 baud.

- **V.26terbo** defines a 2400/1200 bps switchable PSK full-duplex modem operating at 1200 baud.

- **V.27** defines a 4800 bps PSK modem operating at 1600 baud.

- **V.27bis** defines a more advanced 4800/2400 bps switchable PSK modem operating at 1600/1200 baud.

- **V.27terbo** defines a 4800/2400 bps switchable PSK modem commonly used in half-duplex mode at 1600/1200 baud to handle Group 3 fax rather than computer modems.

- V.28 defines the electrical characteristics and connections for V.24 (RS-232). Where the RS-232 specification defines all necessary parameters, the ITU (CCITT) breaks the specifications down into two separate documents.

- **V.29** defines a 9600/7200/4800 bps switchable PSK/QAM modem operating at 2400 baud. This type of modem is often used to implement Group 3 fax rather than computer modems.

- **V.32** defines the first of the truly modern modems as a 9600/4800 bps switchable QAM full-duplex modem operating at 2400 baud. This standard also incorporates trellis coding and echo cancellation to produce a stable, reliable, high-speed modem.

- **V.32bis** extends the V.32 specification to define a 4800/7200/9600/12,000/14,400 bps switchable TCQAM full-duplex modem operating at 2400 baud. Trellis coding, automatic transfer rate negotiation, and echo cancellation made this type of modem one of the most popular and least expensive for everyday PC communication.

- **V.32terbo** continues to extend the V.32 specification by using advanced techniques to implement a 14,400/16,800/19,200 bps switchable TCQAM full-duplex modem operating at 2400 baud. Unlike V.32bis, V.32terbo is not widely used because of the rather high cost of components.

- **V.32fast** is the informal name to a standard that the ITU has used for older high-speed modems. A V.32fast modem generally replaces V.32bis with speeds up to 28,800 bps. It is anticipated that this will be the last *analog* protocol—eventually giving way to all-digital protocols as local telephone services become entirely digital. V.32fast will probably be renamed V.34 on completion and acceptance.

- **V.33** defines a specialized 14,400 bps TCQAM full-duplex modem operating at 2400 baud.

- **V.34** defines the standard for modem communication at 2400 through 28,800 bps.

- **V.34+** is an update to V.34 outlining the enhancements needed for modem communication at 33,600 bps.

- **V.36** defines a specialized 48,000 bps *group* modem that is rarely (if ever) used commercially. This type of modem uses several conventional telephone lines.

- **V.37** defines a specialized 72,000 bps *group* modem that combines several telephone channels.

■ **V.42** is the only ITU error correcting procedure for modems using V.22, V.22bis, V.26ter, V.32, and V.32bis protocols. The standard is also defined as a *Link Access Procedure for Modems* (LAPM) protocol. ITU V.42 is considered very efficient and is about 20 percent faster than MNP4. If a V.42 connection cannot be established between modems, V.42 automatically provides fallback to the MNP4 error correction standard.

■ **V.42bis** uses a Lempel-Ziv–based data compression scheme for use in conjunction with V.42 LAPM (error correction). V.42bis is a data compression standard for high-speed modems that can compress data by as much as 4:1 (depending on the type of file you send). Thus, a 9600 baud modem can transmit data at up to 38,400 bps using V.42bis. A 14.4 Kbps modem can transmit up to a startling 57,600 bps.

■ **V.44** is a relatively recent data compression scheme optimized to handle the coding found in Web pages—effectively improving the Web browsing performance of 56 Kbps dial-up modems. V.44 is typically employed with V.92 56 Kbps modems.

■ V.50 sets standard telephony limits for modem transmission quality.

■ V.51 outlines required maintenance of international data circuits.

■ V.52 describes apparatus for measuring data transmission distortion and error rates.

■ V.53 outlines impairment limits for data circuits.

■ V.54 describes loop test devices for modem testing.

■ V.55 describes impulse noise measuring equipment for line testing.

■ **V.56** outlines the comparative testing of modems.

■ V.57 describes comprehensive test equipment for high-speed data transmission.

■ **V.90** is a standard for 56 Kbps modems approved by the International Telecommunication Union (ITU) in February 1998.

■ **V.92** is an update of the 56 Kbps standard that uses PCM to improve the upstream data transfer rates up to 48 Kbps. V.92 also offers features like reduced handshake time and modem-on-hold.

■ V.100 describes the interconnection techniques between PDNs (Public Data Networks) and PSTNs (Public Switched Telephone Networks).

# MNP STANDARDS

The *Microcom Networking Protocol* (MNP) is a complete hierarchy of standards developed during the mid-1980s that are designed to work with other modem technologies for error correction and data compression. While most ITU standards refer to modem data transfer, MNP standards concentrate on providing error correction and data compression when your modem is communicating with another modem that supports MNP. For example, MNP class 4 is specified by ITU V.42 as a backup error control scheme for LAPM in the event that V.24 cannot be invoked. Out of nine recognized MNP levels, your modem probably supports the first five. Each MNP class has all the features of the previous class plus its own:

■ **MNP class 1 (block mode)**    This is an old data transfer mode that sends data in only one direction at a time—about 70 percent as fast as data transmissions using no error correction. This level is now virtually obsolete.

■ **MNP class 2 (stream mode)**    This is an older data transfer mode that sends data in both directions at the same time—about 84 percent as fast as data transmissions using no error correction.

■ **MNP class 3**    The sending modem strips start and stop bits from a data block before sending it, while the receiving modem adds start and stop bits before passing the data to the receiving computer. About 8 percent faster than data transmissions using no error correction. The increased throughput is realized only if modems on both ends of the connection are operating in a *split speed* (or *locked COM port*) fashion—that is, the rate of data transfer from computer to modem is *higher* than the data transfer rate from modem to modem. Also, data is being transferred in big blocks (such as 1 KB) or continuously (by using the Zmodem file transfer protocol, for example).

■ **MNP class 4**    This is a protocol (with limited data compression) that checks telephone connection quality and uses a transfer technique called *Adaptive Packet Assembly*—on a noise-free line, the modem sends larger blocks of data. If the line is noisy, the modem sends smaller blocks of data (less data will have to be resent). This means more successful transmissions on the first try. About 20 percent faster than data transmissions using no error correction at all, so most current modems are MNP4 compatible.

■ **MNP class 5**    This is classical MNP data compression. MNP5 provides data compression by detecting redundant data and recoding it to fewer bits, thus increasing effective data throughput. A receiving modem decompresses the data before passing it to the receiving computer. MNP5 can speed data transmissions up to 2x over using no data compression or error correction (with the kind of data being a determinant factor in level of increased speed). In effect, MNP5 gives a 2400 bps modem an effective data throughput of as much as 4800 bps and a 9600 bps system as much as 19,200 bps.

■ **MNP class 6**    This standard uses *Universal Link Negotiation* to let modems get maximum performance out of a line. Modems start at low speeds, then move to higher speeds until the best speed is found. MNP6 also provides *Statistical Duplexing* to help half-duplex modems simulate full-duplex modems.

■ **MNP class 7**    This standard offers a much more powerful data compression process (Huffman encoding) than does MNP5. MNP7 modems can increase the data throughput by as much as 3x in some cases. Although MNP7 is more efficient than MNP5, not all modems are designed to handle the MNP7 protocol. Also, although MNP7 is faster than MNP5, MNP7 is still generally considered slower than the ITU's V.42bis.

■ **MNP class 9**    This standard reduces the data overhead (the housekeeping bits) encountered with each data packet. MNP9 also improves error correction performance because only the data that was in error has to be re-sent instead of resending the entire data packet.

■ **MNP class 10**    This standard uses a set of protocols known as *Adverse Channel Enhancements* to help modems overcome poor telephone connections by adjusting data packet size and transmission speed until the most reliable transmission is established. This is a more powerful version of MNP4. NMP class 10EC adds error correction capabilities to other class 10 features.

# FILE TRANSFER PROTOCOLS

Even with powerful data transfer, compression, and correction protocols, the way in which data is packaged and exchanged is still largely undefined by ITU and MNP standards. You see, a typical modem has no way of knowing the difference between a keyboard stroke or data being downloaded from a hard drive—the modem does not understand a file. Instead, it only works with bytes, bits, timing, and tones. As a consequence, the modem relies on communications software to manage file characteristics such as filename, file size, and content. The software routines that bundle and organize data between modems are called *file transfer protocols*. Errors that occur during file transfer are automatically detected and corrected by file transfer protocols. If a block of data is received incorrectly, the receiving system sends a message to the sending system and requests the retransmission. This process is automatic and essentially transparent to the computer users (except perhaps for a display in the communication software's file transfer status window). The following are some of the more traditional transfer protocols:

> The transfer protocols outlined next were used mainly with dial-up modem connections to BBS facilities. Modern file transfers over the Internet generally use more sophisticated networking protocols, such as File Transfer Protocol (FTP), or e-mail protocols, such as Mime.

- **ASCII**    This protocol is designed to work with ASCII text files only. Be aware that you do *not* have to use this protocol when transferring text files. The ASCII protocol is useful for uploading a text file when you are composing e-mail online.

- **Xmodem**    This is one of the most widely used file transfer protocols. Introduced in 1977 by Ward Christensen, this protocol is slow, but reliable. The original Xmodem protocol used 128-byte packets and a simple *checksum* method of error detection. A later enhancement, Xmodem-CRC, uses a more secure *Cyclic Redundancy Check* (CRC) method for error detection. Xmodem protocols always attempt to use CRC first. If the sender does not acknowledge the requests for CRC, the receiver shifts to the checksum mode and continues its request for transmission. Mismatching the two variants of Xmodem during file transfers is usually the reason for transfer problems, although many communication systems can now detect the differences automatically.

- **Xmodem-1K**    The Xmodem-1K protocol is essentially Xmodem CRC with 1KB (1,024 bytes) packets. On some systems and bulletin boards, it may also be referred to as Ymodem. Some communication software programs (most notably Procomm Plus 1.x) also list Xmodem-1K as Ymodem. Procomm Plus 2.0 no longer refers to Xmodem-1K as Ymodem.

- **Ymodem**    A Ymodem protocol is little more than a version of Xmodem-1K that allows multiple-file batch transfer (sending/receiving several files one after another unattended). On some systems it is listed as Ymodem Batch (and is sometimes called *true Ymodem*). Ymodem offers a faster transmission rate than Xmodem and better data security through a refined CRC checksum method.

- **Ymodem-g**    The Ymodem-g protocol is a variant of basic Ymodem designed for use with modems that support error correction. This protocol does not provide software error correction or recovery itself, but expects the *modem* to provide the service. It is a streaming protocol that sends and receives 1K packets in a continuous stream until instructed to stop. It does not wait for positive acknowledgment after each block is sent, but rather sends blocks in rapid succession. If any block is unsuccessfully transferred, the entire transfer is canceled.

- **Zmodem**    This is generally the best protocol to use if the electronic service you are calling supports it. Zmodem has two significant features: it is extremely efficient, and it provides automatic *crash* recovery. Like Ymodem-g, Zmodem does not wait for positive acknowledgment after each block is sent, but rather sends blocks in rapid succession. If a Zmodem transfer *crashes* (is canceled or interrupted for any reason), the transfer can be resurrected later and the previously transferred information need *not* be re-sent. Zmodem can detect excessive line noise and automatically drop to a shorter, more reliable data packet size when necessary. Data integrity and accuracy is assured by the use of reliable 16-bit CRC (cyclic redundancy check) methods rather than less reliable CRC checking of Ymodem and Xmodem.

- **Kermit**    The Kermit protocol was developed at Columbia University. It was designed to facilitate the exchange of data among very different types of computers (mainly minicomputers and mainframes). You probably will not need to use Kermit unless you are calling a minicomputer or mainframe at an educational institution.

- **Sealink**    The Sealink protocol is a variant of Xmodem. It was developed to overcome the transmission delays caused by satellite relays or packet-switching networks. However, Sealink is rarely used today.

# Installing an Analog Modem

Both internal and external analog modem devices are typically PnP devices that are designed for automatic detection and resource assignments. Still, most modem (especially WinModem) problems *start* when the card is first installed in the system—problems that are usually due to inadequate or incorrect installation of the hardware and software. This part of the chapter offers an overview of the installation process so that you can check for missing steps. When replacing the modem, remember that the initialization and operating strings often vary slightly between modem manufacturers. Consequently, be sure to use the very latest Windows modem driver. If you're working in the real-mode, be sure to alter any AT command strings in the communication software to accommodate the new modem or remove the old modem and its application software *before* exchanging the modem.

 Always use proper static precautions (such as an anti-static wrist strap) when working inside a system with sensitive devices—such as the modem card.

## SOFTWARE PREINSTALLATION

The traditional method of device installation is to install the new hardware first; then install any necessary drivers and software after the operating system recognizes the device. Today, major modem manufacturers reverse this process a bit and often allow you to preinstall the modem's drivers and application software before the modem is actually connected. This way, Windows will be able to detect, identify, and install the appropriate manufacturer's drivers once the hardware is in place. If your modem recommends or allows preinstallation, the steps are often similar to these listed here:

1. Power on the computer if it's not already running. Close any background applications that might be running.

2. Insert the CD-ROM that came with your fax/modem into your CD-ROM drive. The CD-ROM should automatically start and display an Installation dialog box.

3. When the Installation dialog box appears, click the Install Drivers button and then the PCI Drivers button. (If you're installing an external serial or USB modem, select the corresponding drivers.)

4. The installation program will run and automatically copy driver files to your hard drive. Click Finish if you are prompted to do so.

## INTERNAL HARDWARE INSTALLATION

Installing an internal modem requires a bit of care because you'll need to open the system and work inside of it. The following steps outline the general process, but be sure to reference the manufacturer's instructions for particular precautions.

 Some modem manufacturers (such as Zoom Telephonics) streamline the installation process by installing software before the hardware. Always check the recommended installation procedure before following any of the steps here.

1. Shut down Windows 9x/Me/XP, and then turn off and unplug the computer.

2. Unbolt the outer case; then remove the housing and set it (and the screws) aside in a safe place.

3. If you're replacing an existing modem with a newer, faster model, you'll need to remove the old modem first. Disconnect the telephone line cord (and other telephone cords) from the modem. Unbolt the old modem card bracket from the chassis and remove the old modem from its expansion slot. Be sure to set the old modem aside on a static-safe surface or in an anti-static bag.

If your motherboard includes an integrated modem, you will need to disable the motherboard's modem (either through a motherboard jumper or CMOS Setup) before installing the new modem card.

4. Locate a slot for the new modem card. Current modem cards (V.90/V.92 56 Kbps and later) will need a PCI slot. Find an available slot. Remove the cover for the slot you intend to use (if it's not already removed) and save the screw for the mounting bracket.

5. Insert the modem card. Push the card in firmly and evenly until it's fully seated in the slot. Replace the screw to secure the bracket of your modem card to the computer's chassis.

6. Reconnect the modem to the telephone wall jack using the modem's LINE or TELCO jack.

The phone jack you use *must* be for an *analog* phone line (the type found in most homes). Many office buildings have digital phone lines (a.k.a. PBX lines). Be sure you know which type of line you have. The modem may be damaged if you use a digital phone line.

7. If you want to use a phone on the same line that the modem is using (when the modem is not in use), plug your phone's line cord into the modem's PHONE jack.

8. If your modem model supports "simultaneous voice and data," you may need a microphone to support that feature. If so, plug the microphone into the MIC jack on the modem or soundcard, depending on the design of your modem.

9. If your modem offers full-duplex speakerphone capabilities, plug a set of powered external speakers (not included) into the SPEAKER jack on the modem. Some modem designs may simply play back sound through the soundcard's speakers, so additional speakers may not be required.

## EXTERNAL HARDWARE INSTALLATION

If you'd prefer to use a USB or serial (RS-232) modem, the installation process is a bit simpler because you need not open the system. With a USB modem, you can simply connect the modem to an available USB port and attach the telephone line. Windows will recognize the modem and use the preinstalled software to configure the new modem device (or you can install/update drivers as described next). If you're using a serial modem, follow the steps listed here.

If you're adding an external modem to replace an existing internal modem, you may still need to open the system to remove the old internal modem before connecting the new external device.

1. Make sure that the computer is shut down.

2. Connect the serial cable between the fax/modem and host computer's COM port. Tighten the screws at both ends. Make a note of the COM port that you connect the modem to.

3. Connect the telephone cord to the fax/modem and plug the other end into the wall jack.

4. Connect your telephone (optional).

5.  Connect the AC power adapter to the modem. Use only the AC adapter that came with your fax/modem.

6.  Turn the fax/modem on. The unit will perform a brief self-test and then the MR or PWR light (depending on the model) will go on. The fax/modem is ready for use.

## SOFTWARE INSTALLATION

Now that the physical hardware for your new modem card has been installed, it's time to install the modem drivers and application software that you'll need to identify the device under Windows 9x/Me/XP and use advanced features (such as a voice mail system). Leave the computer's housing off for now, but reconnect the AC cord to the computer and prepare to start the system again.

 Always refer to the README file on the modem card's driver disc to obtain the very latest feature descriptions and software installation guidelines for your particular card.

If you've preinstalled any modem drivers or other software prior to hardware installation, you may find that the new modem is recognized and configured automatically without the following steps. As Windows boots, it will detect your new fax/modem. Since your preinstallation has already provided your computer with the required files, Windows reports on its progress but does not require any action on your part. You simply need to complete the installation by checking the modem status. If you have not preinstalled any software, you might need to do so after the hardware installation. The following steps outline a typical software installation for an internal PCI fax/modem card:

1.  When Windows restarts, it should detect the modem automatically. If the modem is not PnP-compliant (or you're using an old version of Windows), you may need to use the Add New Hardware Wizard to run the modem installation process.

2.  Click Driver from Disk Provided by Hardware Manufacturer. Then click OK.

3.  Insert the driver CD into the CD-ROM, and then select the CD-ROM drive letter.

4.  Click OK. Windows will load the modem's drivers. You may need to reboot the computer.

5.  Once Windows finishes loading the information from the driver CD, you should verify that the modem installation was a success. Under Windows 9x/Me, click Start, | Settings, | Control Panel, and then double-click the Modems icon. Under Windows XP, open the Control Panel, click Printers and Other Hardware, and then click Modems.

6.  In the Modems Properties dialog, you should see a suitable description for your modem (a Windows 9x/Me dialog is shown in Figure 25-5). If so, your modem installed properly.

7.  Now you should test your modem. Click the Diagnostics tab. Select the modem (or the COM port that your modem is on), and then click the More Info button.

8.  After a few moments, you should see the More Info dialog (a Windows 9x/Me dialog is shown in Figure 25-6), which lists the modem's Port Information as well as a series of standard modem commands.

9.  If the modem responds to each of the commands, the modem should be working, and you're ready to try the modem online. You can reattach the computer's outer housing and return the system to normal service. If the modem does *not* respond or an error is generated, you should double-check the modem's installation and verify that the modem has been properly identified.

10. Once the modem is working, you can install any other applications or support software (such as voice mail or fax software) that accompanies your modem.

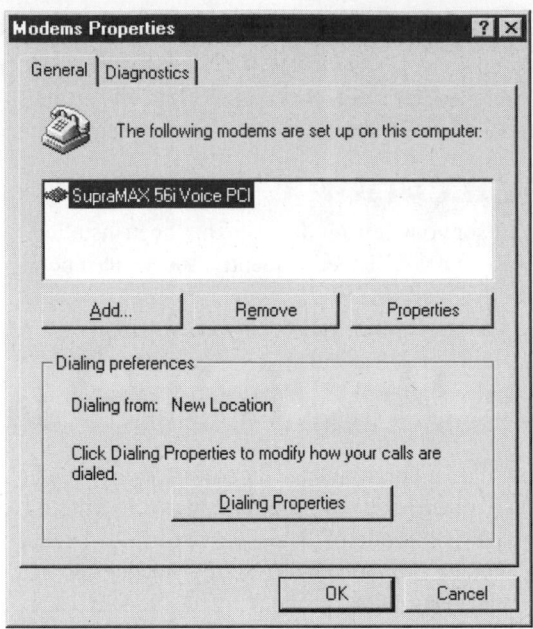

**FIGURE  25-5**    Checking your modem in the Modem Properties dialog under Windows 98/SE

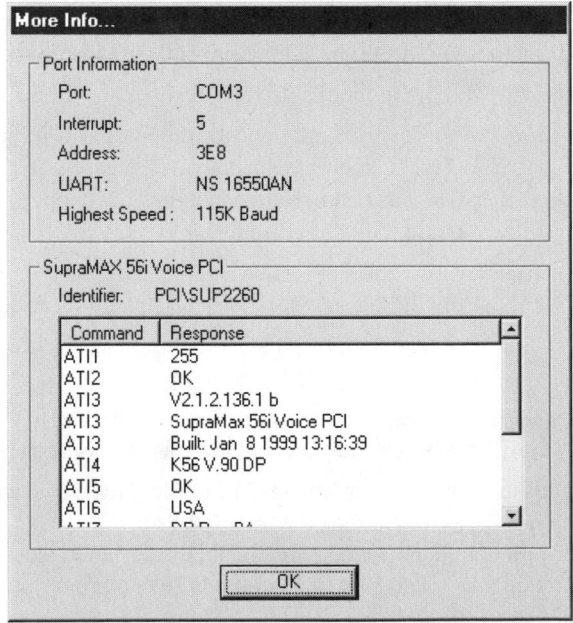

**FIGURE  25-6**    Verifying the modem's operation under Windows 98/SE

# Installing a Cable/DSL Modem

Over the last few years, the Internet has exploded with content. Not only can you view text and images, but you can now access real-time audio and video broadcasting, Java applets, ShockWave multimedia presentations, and so much more. The intense growth in Internet use and the increasing complexity of Internet media have placed a strain on the bandwidth offered by ISPs. There are simply too many users trying to access gobs of data-intensive information. Most Internet connections are dial-up, and while conventional modems have continued to improve in order to pass more data across the existing global telephone network, that is no longer enough. Regional telephone companies are implementing DSL service, allowing high-speed "always-on" connections through an existing telephone line. Cable television providers are also addressing high-speed Internet access using the existing cable network. This part of the chapter examines the steps needed to install a DSL/cable modem and configure the PC for Internet access.

## UNDERSTANDING THE CABLE/DSL MODEM

In many urban and suburban areas, your local television cable company provides cable modem service (also known as *cable data service* or *broadband Internet*). When a cable modem is used, the cable that supplies television service to your home or office is connected to the cable modem in the same way that it is connected to your television set or cable box. You then get the benefit of high-speed access to the Internet through the local cable company's service. The cable connection to the Internet does not interfere with your regular television signal,because the cable modem service is provided on different channels than cable television programming. Similarly, an *Asynchronous Digital Subscriber Line*, (ADSL or often shortened to DSL) modem uses the same telephone wiring already in place in your home or office. However, before you can use any type of DSL modem, you must make arrangements with a DSL service provider (such as AT&T). A DSL service technician may visit you to physically test the wiring for DSL compatibility. Sometimes, special filtering equipment will need to be installed in your home or office.

Early cable modems were "one way" devices, so they supplemented a conventional analog modem with a high-speed "cable modem." Internet data in those systems was requested "upstream" via your phone line (using an existing modem in much the way that you do now), and that data was sent "downstream" from the Internet via the CATV network to a computer's "cable modem" at burst rates of up to 38 Mbps. Current cable modems are fully bidirectional devices that can operate independently of analog modems, network cards, or other devices.

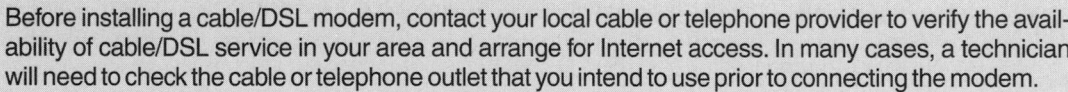

Before installing a cable/DSL modem, contact your local cable or telephone provider to verify the availability of cable/DSL service in your area and arrange for Internet access. In many cases, a technician will need to check the cable or telephone outlet that you intend to use prior to connecting the modem.

Today's cable or DSL modems may exist as an external device that attaches to a USB port, an external device that connects to an Ethernet LAN card in the PC, or an internal PCI card. Often, external cable/DSL modems are more convenient because their LED indicators can help you quickly determine the unit's status and discern any communication problems between your PC and the provider's network. A typical cable/DSL modem kit will usually contain the following items:

- Internal or external cable/DSL modem device
- Cable modem power adapter (or ac cord) for external devices
- Instruction guide(s)

- Driver/applet software CD

- Universal Serial Bus (USB) cable and/or Ethernet cable (depending on how you're connecting the modem to a USB or Ethernet port on the PC)

  As a rule, your PC must meet the following requirements:

- Pentium processor or equivalent (Pentium 166 or higher recommended). Adequate processing power is certainly not a problem for today's PCs.

- An active two-way cable line installed by your cable service provider or a suitable DSL-capable jack installed by your DSL provider.

- A length of coaxial cable (which may be provided by your cable service) or a telephone (RJ-11) cord.

- Your original Windows 9x/Me/XP installation CD.

- If you plan to connect the external cable/DSL modem through the PC's USB port, you'll need a PC running Windows 98/Me/XP or Windows 2000, along with an active USB port on your computer.

- If you plan to connect the external cable modem to an existing Ethernet port on your PC's network card, you'll need a PC running Windows 9x/Me/XP/NT4/2000. You'll also need to have the TCP/IP protocol and active Ethernet port or network interface card (NIC) installed in your computer.

Remember that cable/DSL connections are "always on". That is, your PC is connected to the Internet for as long as the system is on. You should be sure to protect the security of your system with a firewall utility such as Norton Internet Security, BlackICE Defender, or McAfee Firewall. A firewall prevents data from entering or leaving your PC without permission, and prevents unauthorized access (or hacking) of your PC—and the private information it contains.

## SOFTWARE PREINSTALLATION

As with ordinary dial-up modems, the traditional method of device installation is to install the new hardware and then install any necessary drivers and software after the operating system recognizes the device. Today, manufacturers often allow you to preinstall the modem's drivers and application software before the modem is actually connected. This way, Windows will be capable of detecting, identifying, and installing the appropriate manufacturer's drivers once the hardware is in place. If your cable/DSL modem recommends or allows preinstallation, the steps are often similar to those listed here:

1. Power on the computer if it's not already running. Close any background applications that are running.

2. Insert the CD-ROM that came with your fax/modem into your CD-ROM drive. The CD-ROM should automatically start and display an Installation dialog.

3. When the Installation dialog appears, click the Install Drivers button. A Setup Wizard will lead you through the process of installing the drivers.

4. The installation program will run and automatically copy driver files to your hard drive. When the Setup Wizard is finished, you are ready to install the PCI cable/DSL modem hardware.

## PCI HARDWARE INSTALLATION

While cable/DSL modems have generally been available as external (USB or Ethernet) devices, a growing number of these high-speed communication devices have been appearing as internal PCI expansion cards (a Zoom cable modem is shown in Figure 25-7). Before you install a cable/DSL modem, contact your ser-

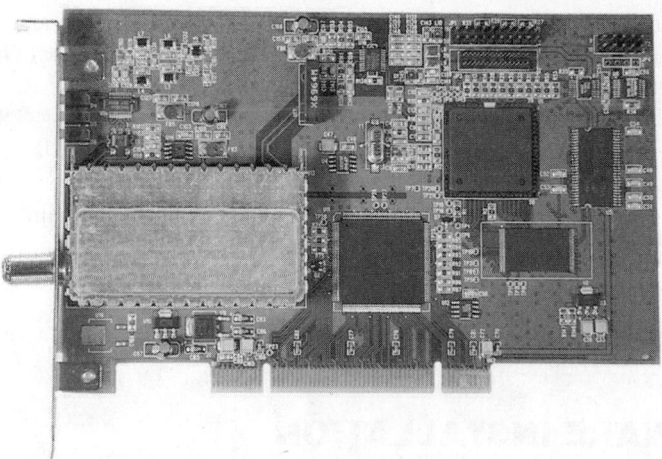

**FIGURE  25-7**    The Zoom PCI cable modem provides integrated cable Internet access through a PCI slot (Courtesy of Zoom Telephonics)

vice provider to establish a suitable account. Some cable companies will ask for the *Media Access Control* (MAC) address—the address labeled Cable Modem MAC Address or C-MAC—of your cable modem, so be sure to have that handy.

When using a cable modem, verify that your cable company provides *Data Over Cable Service Interface Specifications* (DOCSIS) compatible service. The DOCSIS standard is supported by leading cable service providers to ensure system compatibility and ease of use. Such modems are not designed to work on EuroDOCSIS or DVD/DAVIC cable systems.

Follow these steps for the actual hardware installation:

1. Shut down Windows 9x/Me/XP, and then turn off and unplug the computer.

2. Unbolt the outer case; then remove the housing and set it (and the screws) aside in a safe place.

3. You may opt to remove or disable other network interface cards (NICs) in your system before you install your PCI cable/DSL modem. This can help to prevent potential hardware conflicts between the modem and other NIC hardware in the system.

4. Locate a PCI slot for the new cable/DSL modem card. Remove the cover for the slot you intend to use (if it's not already removed) and save the screw for the mounting bracket.

5. Insert the cable/DSL modem card. Push the card in firmly and evenly until it's fully seated in the slot. Replace the screw to secure the bracket of your modem card to the computer's chassis.

6. Connect the coaxial cable or DSL line to the modem.

7. As Windows starts, it will detect your cable/DSL modem. Since the installation program has already put the needed drivers on your computer, Windows will recognize and setup your modem. Windows will report on its progress, but it will not require any action on your part.

If you're working under an older operating system like Windows 98, you may be prompted to insert the Windows installation CD to install certain Microsoft Networking files.

At this point, your cable/DSL service provider will communicate with the modem and computer to complete the installation. You can verify that the modem is synchronizing with the service by looking at the indicator lights on the modem itself (even an internal PCI modem will have several LEDs on the bracket). For example, the STS (Status) LED will blink. When synchronization is complete, the STS light will remain on. This should complete the modem's installation, and you should be ready to use the Internet.

Keep in mind that specific installations will vary between service providers, so follow the directions from your cable/DSL company. In some cases, the service provider will automatically query the modem, in other cases, you'll need to give the provider your information over the telephone (e.g., they may ask you for the MAC address).

You may need to adjust the connection used by your Internet browser. For example, your browser should be configured to connect via a LAN.

## USB HARDWARE INSTALLATION

If you do not have a network card available (or don't want the hassle of an NIC installation first), use the following steps to connect the USB cable/DSL modem to a USB port on your system (a Zoom DSL USB modem is shown in Figure 25-8). Follow the steps below:

1. Power on the computer.

2. Connect the coaxial or DSL cable (usually just an ordinary RJ-11 cable) to the modem's cable/DSL connector and to the wall cable outlet.

3. Connect the USB cable to the modem and to the computer's USB port.

4. Plug the cable modem's power supply into a surge protector or an electrical outlet.

5. Within a few minutes, the computer detects the cable modem.

You may be asked for your computer's Windows installation CD. If so, insert it into the CD-ROM drive and click OK.

6. Restart your computer if prompted to do so.

**FIGURE  25-8**    The Zoom  DSL USB modem provides convenient Internet access through a USB port (Courtesy of Zoom Telephonics)

After you restart your computer, the modem's front panel PWR indicator will be lit, indicating that the modem is on. (If not, push the switch on the front panel of the modem.) The DATA LED will blink while the modem is establishing a connection. It will remain "steady on" once a connection has been established. This should complete the modem's installation, and you should be ready to use the Internet.

# CONFIGURING TCP/IP AND BROWSER

Using a high-speed cable/DSL modem to access the Internet basically "networks" your computer with the ISP. Consequently, your PC will need to have network support in place—this means the PC will need TCP/IP (Internet) protocols installed under Windows. If you have trouble accessing the Internet once the cable/DSL modem is installed, it's always worthwhile to check TCP/IP.

## TCP/IP Under Windows

If you're working under Windows XP, use the following steps to check for TCP/IP, and install TCP/IP support if necessary:

1.  Choose Start | My Network Places | View network settings. Right-click the Local Area Connection entry and click Properties to open the Local Area Connection Properties dialog (see Figure 25-9).

2.  You will see a list of installed network components. If you see a line that includes TCP/IP, skip to step 5, If not, continue with step 3.

3.  If you don't see an entry for TCP/IP, click the Install button. The Select Network Protocol dialog box will appear.

4.  Click to highlight Internet Protocol (TCP/IP) and click OK.

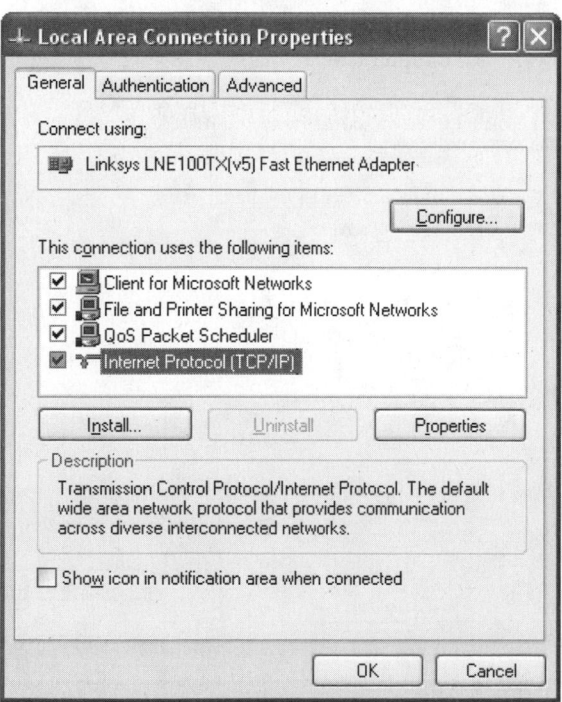

**FIGURE  25-9**   Check for TCP/IP support on the Windows XP system

5. Click to check Internet Protocol (TCP/IP), and then click Properties. The Internet Protocol (TCP/IP) Properties dialog box will appear (see Figure 25-10).

6. Click Obtain an IP address Automatically, and click Obtain DNS Server Address Automatically. Click OK to enable your settings.

7. Click OK again. Insert the Windows installation CD and click OK if prompted to do so.

8. Reboot the computer if necessary.

If you're using Windows 9x/Me as the operating system, follow these steps to enable and configure TCP/IP:

1. Click Start | Settings | Control Panel, and then double-click the Network icon. The Network dialog box will appear.

2. Click the Configuration tab. You will see a list of installed network components. If you see an entry indicating TCP/IP bound to a network device (e.g., TCP/IP -> Zoom PCI Cable Modem), skip to step 6.

3. If you don't see the TCP/IP entry, click the Add button to access the Select Network Component Type dialog box.

4. Click to highlight Protocol and click Add.

5. The Select Network Protocol dialog box will appear. Click to highlight Microsoft | TCP/IP, then click OK. There should now be a bound entry for TCP/IP (e.g., TCP/IP -> Zoom PCI Cable Modem). Click No if you are asked to restart your computer.

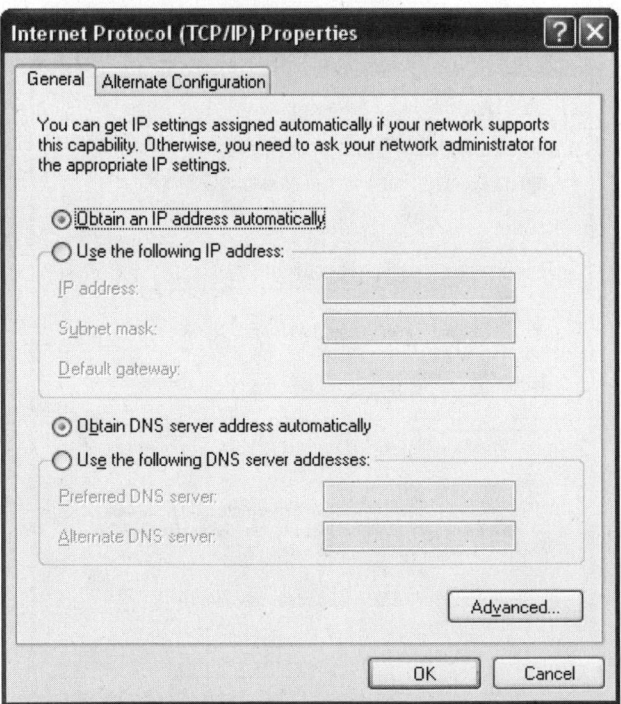

**FIGURE  25-10**    Set the desired properties for your computer's TCP/IP connection under Windows XP

6. Click to highlight the bound entry (e.g., TCP/IP -> Zoom PCI Cable Modem) and click Properties. The TCP/IP Properties dialog box will appear.

7. Click the Obtain an IP Address Automatically button.

8. Click the WINS Configuration tab, select Use DHCP for WINS Resolution, and click OK.

9. Click OK to enable your settings. Insert the Windows 98 CD and click OK if necessary.

10. Reboot the computer if prompted to do so.

## Configuring the Browser

The Web browser can be configured to connect to the Internet via phone lines or a local area network (LAN). When using a dial-up modem, the browser should be configured to use phone lines. When using a cable/DSL modem, your browser should be set to connect to the Internet via a LAN. Here are some basic guidelines for configuring the major browsers:

■ **Internet Explorer 4.0**     Start Internet Explorer and click View | Internet Options. The Internet Properties dialog box appears. Click the Connections tab and you will see options for setting or changing the connection. Click Connect to the Internet Using Local Area Network, and then click OK to enable the settings.

■ **Internet Explorer 5.0/6.0**     Start Internet Explorer and click Tools | Internet Options. The Internet Options dialog box appears. Click the Connections tab and you will see options for setting or changing the connection (see Figure 25-11). Click Setup, and the Connection Wizard will guide you

**FIGURE  25-11**     Use the IE 5/6 Connections tab to reconfigure the browser's connection scheme

through setup (or you can click LAN Settings to configure your connection manually). If you click LAN Settings, check the Automatically Detect Settings box, and then click OK.

- **Netscape Navigator**   Start Netscape Navigator and choose Edit | Preferences. You will see the Preferences dialog box. Click the Advanced option, and then click Proxies. For cable/DSL modems, select the option that allows you to connect to the Internet directly.

# Dial-up/Cable/DSL Modem Troubleshooting

Okay, the modem is installed (or replaced), the drivers are installed, the communication software (if any) is loaded, the telephone/cable/DSL line is connected—and nothing happens. This is an all-too-common theme for today's technicians and computer enthusiasts. Although the actual failure rate among modems is quite small, it turns out that modems (especially when configuring them for Internet access) are some of the more difficult and time-consuming devices to set up and configure. As a consequence, proper setup from the start can simplify troubleshooting significantly. When a modem fails to work properly, there are a number of conditions to explore:

In terms of troubleshooting, we'll use the term "modem" to mean a dial-up, cable, or DSL modem (unless otherwise specified).

- **Incorrect hardware resources**   An internal modem must be set with a unique IRQ line and I/O port. If the assigned resources are also used by another device in the system (such as a mouse), the modem or the conflicting device (or perhaps both) will not function properly. Under Windows 9x/Me/XP, you can use the Device Manager to investigate devices and examine their configurations. Reconfigure the internal modem to clear the conflict or use the CMOS Setup to disable any conflicting resources. External modems make use of existing COM ports or USB ports, so resource issues are usually not a problem unless the particular port is damaged or disabled.

- **Defective telecommunication resources**   All modems need access to an appropriate communications line in order to establish connections with other modems or networks. For example, if the telephone jack is defective or hooked up improperly, the dial-up modem may work fine, but no connection is possible. Remove the telephone line cord from the modem and try the line cord on an ordinary telephone. When you lift the receiver, you should draw dial tone. Try dialing a local number—if the line rings, chances are good that the telephone line is working. Check the RJ11 jack on the modem. One or more bent connector pins can break the line even though the line cord is inserted properly. Similar issues may exist for cable and DSL lines, so make sure to check the cabling and connections carefully.

- **Improper cabling**   An external modem must be connected to the PC port (e.g., serial or USB) with a cable. Traditional serial cables were 25-pin assemblies. Later, 9-pin serial connectors and cables became common—out of those 9 wires, only three are really vital. As a result, quite a few cable assemblies may be incorrect or otherwise specialized. Make sure that the serial cable between the PC and modem is a "straight-through" type cable (rather than a *null modem* cable). Also check that both ends of the cable are intact (installed evenly, no bent pins, and so on). Try a new cable if necessary. USB cables are a bit easier to work with because they are standard, so verify that both ends of the USB cable are secure. If you're using an Ethernet NIC to connect an external cable/DSL modem to a PC, see that you're using an RJ-45 patch cable (rather than a crossover cable), and verify that both ends of the Ethernet cable are secure.

- **Improper power**   External modems must receive power from batteries or from an AC eliminator (a few external cable/DSL modems may incorporate a power supply, and simply need an AC line cord). Make sure that any batteries are fresh and installed completely. If an AC adapter is used, see that it is connected to the modem properly. Verify that you're using the AC adapter that accompanied the modem.

- **Incorrect software settings**   Both internal and external dial-up modems must be initialized with an AT ASCII command string before a connection is established. If these settings are absent or incorrect, the modem will not respond as expected (if at all). Check the communication software and make sure that the AT command strings are appropriate for the modem being used—different modems often require slightly different command strings. Remember that modems connecting to a network environment will need to have TCP/IP support installed and configured under Windows. In all cases, be sure that you're using the latest driver and firmware versions designed specifically for your dial-up, cable, or DSL modem model.

- **Suspect the modem itself**   Modems are typically quite reliable in everyday use. If there are jumpers or DIP switches on the modem, check that each setting is placed correctly. Perhaps their most vulnerable point is the communication interface (that RJ-11 or coaxial cable from the modem to the wall jack), which is particularly susceptible to high-voltage spikes that might enter through the line. If all else fails, try another modem.

Don't be afraid to contact the cable/DSL service provider for additional support—they can be excellent resources to help resolve complex modem setup and operational issues.

# CHECK THE COMMAND PROCESSOR

The *command processor* is the controller that manages the dial-up modem's operation in the command mode, and it is the command processor that interprets AT command strings. When the dial-up modem installation fails to behave as it should, you should first check the modem command processor using the following procedure. Before going too far with this, make sure you have the modem's user guide on hand (if possible). When the command processor checks out, but the dial-up modem refuses to work under normal communication software operations, the software may be refusing to save settings such as COM port selection, speed, and character format:

1. Make sure the dial-up modem is installed properly and connected to the desired PC serial or USB port. Of course, if the modem is internal, you will need to worry only about IRQ and I/O port settings. Check the Device Manager to see that the internal modem's COM port settings (or other resource assignments) are not conflicting with an existing COM port on the PC.

2. Start the communication software and select a "direct connection" to establish a path from your keyboard to the modem (this is sometimes referred to as "terminal mode"). You will probably see a dialog box appear with a blinking cursor. If the modem is working and installed properly, you should now be able to send commands directly to the modem.

For example, under Windows 9x/Me, you can use the HyperTerminal applet under Start | Programs | Accessories | HyperTerminal. Under Windows XP, click Start | All Programs | Accessories | Communications | HyperTerminal. Once the HyperTerminal folder opens, double-click the Hypertrm icon, and type **Test1** in the Connection Description dialog. Click OK. When you're asked to enter a phone number, enter your own number and click OK. When the Connect dialog asks to dial the number, just click Cancel. A text window appears, as in Figure 25-12. Type **AT** (you may not see the letters as you type them) and press ENTER. You should see an "OK" response.

3. Type the command **AT** and then press ENTER. The modem should return an "OK" result code. When an "OK" is returned, chances are that the modem is working correctly. If you see double characters being displayed, try the command **ATE0** to disable the command mode echo. If you do not see an "OK," try issuing an **ATE1** command to enable the command mode echo. If there is still no response, commands are not reaching the modem or the modem is defective. Check the connections between the modem and serial port. If the modem is internal, check that it is installed correctly and that all jumpers are placed properly.

4. Try resetting the modem with the **ATZ** command and then pressing ENTER. Doing this should reset the modem. If the modem now responds with "OK," you may have to adjust the initialization command string in the communication software, the Registry, or the Extra settings line in your modem's properties.

5. Try factory default settings by typing the command **AT&F**, then pressing ENTER. Doing this should restore the factory default values for each S-register. You may also try the command **AT&Q0** and ENTER to deliberately place the modem into asynchronous mode. You should see "OK" responses to each attempt, indicating the modem is responding as expected—it may be necessary to update the modem's initialization command string. If the modem still does not respond, the communication software may be incompatible or the modem may be defective.

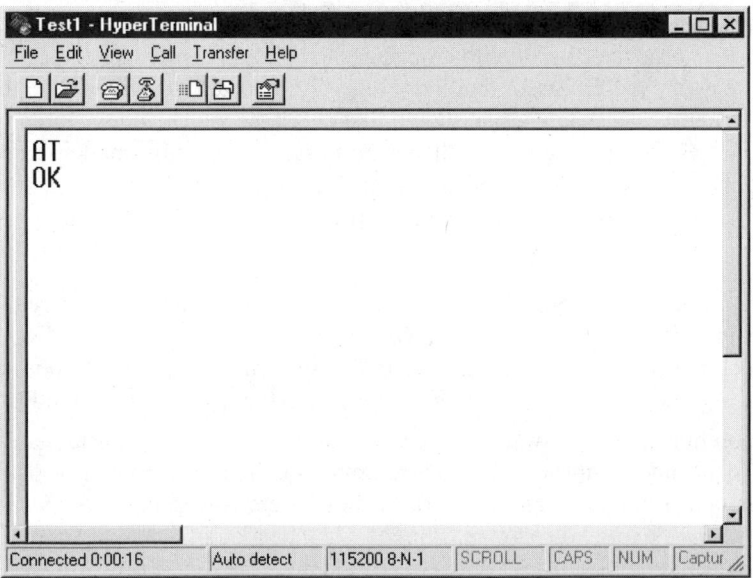

**FIGURE 25-12** Testing the modem's command processor with HyperTerminal

# CHECK THE DIALER AND TELEPHONE LINE

After you've demonstrated that the modem's command processor is responding properly, you can also check the telephone interface by attempting a call—doing this also can verify an active telephone line. When the telephone interface checks out but the modem refuses to work under normal communication software operations, the software may be refusing to save settings such as COM port selection, speed, and character format:

1.  Make sure the modem is installed properly and connected to the desired PC serial or USB port. Of course, if the modem is internal, you will need to worry only about IRQ and I/O port settings. Check that there is no conflict between the modem's COM port and the system's COM port(s), or other resource assignments.

2.  Start the communication software and select a "direct connection" to establish a path from your keyboard to the modem (this is sometimes referred to as "terminal mode"). You will probably see a dialog box appear with a blinking cursor. If the modem is working and installed properly, you should now be able to send commands directly to the modem. See the previous HyperTerminal example.

3.  Dial a number by using the **DT** (dial using tones) command followed by the full number being called—for example, **ATDT15085551212** followed by pressing ENTER . If your local telephone line supports only rotary dialing, use the modifier **R** after the **D**. If calling from a PBX, be sure to dial 9 or other outside-access codes. Listen for a dial tone, followed by the tone dialing beeps. You should also hear the destination phone ringing. When these occur, they ensure that your telephone interface dials correctly and that the local phone line is responding properly.

4.  If there is no dial tone, check the phone line by dialing with an ordinary phone. Note that some PBX systems must be modified to produce at least 48 volts DC for the modem to work. If there is no dial tone but the modem attempts to dial, the telephone interface is not grabbing the telephone line correctly (the dialer is working). If the modem draws dial tone but no digits are generated, the dialer may be defective. In either case, try another modem.

# TYPICAL DIAL-UP PROBLEMS

Even when the dial-up modem hardware is working perfectly, the serial communication process is *anything* but flawless. Problems ranging from accidental loss of carrier to a catastrophic loss of data regularly plague computer communication. To make your online time as foolproof as possible, this section of the chapter shows you how to deal with some of the most pernicious dial-up communication problems.

■ **Modem settings**   Modem settings are critically important to inter-modem communication. The number of data bits, use of parity, number of stop bits, and data transfer speed must be set *precisely* the same way on both modems. Otherwise, the valid data leaving one modem will be interpreted as complete "junk" at the receiving end. Normally, this should not happen when modems are set to auto-answer—negotiation should allow both modems to settle at the same parameters. The time that incompatible settings really become a factor is when negotiation is unsuccessful or when communication is being established manually. A typical example is an off-site technician with communication software set to 8 data bits, no parity bit, and 1 stop bit trying to dial into a remote system which runs at 7 data bits, even parity, and 2 stop bits. The aspect that stands out with incompatible settings is that virtually *nothing* is intelligible—and the connection is typically lost.

■ **Modems and UART types**    The UART is clearly the heart of a dialup modem system. It is the modem that converts bus data into serial data (and vice versa), but the UART must be able to keep pace with the modem's data transfer rate. As modem speeds have increased, UARTs have become faster also. When installing a new external modem on an older PC, an older PC's serial port may simply not be fast enough to deal with the modem. The result is often limited modem performance (if the modem works at all). Today, the 16550A UART is the device of choice. Table 25-4 compares the major UART types. When faced with an older UART, it may be possible to replace the UART chip—otherwise, it is a simple matter to *disable* the existing serial port and install a newer serial adapter card incorporating a new UART.

■ **Line noise**    While faulty settings can load a transmission with trash, even a properly established connection can lose integrity periodically. Remember that dial-up communication is made possible by a global network of switched telephone wiring. Each time you dial the same number, you typically get a different set of "wiring." Faulty wiring at any point along the network, electrical storms, wet or snowy weather, and other natural or man-made disasters can interrupt the network momentarily or cut communication entirely. Most of the time, brief interruptions can result in small patches of garbled text or damaged file transfers. This type of behavior is most prominent in real-time online sessions (such as typing in a chat message). When uploading or downloading files, file transfer protocols can usually catch such anomalies and correct errors or request new data packets to overcome the errors. When you have trouble moving files or notice a high level of "junk" online, try calling back—when a new telephone line is established, the connection quality might be better.

**TABLE 25-4    COMPARISON OF POPULAR UART TYPES**

| UART | DESCRIPTION |
|---|---|
| 8250 | This is the original PC/XT serial port UART. There are several minor bugs in the UART, but the original PC/XT BIOS corrected for them. The 8250 was replaced by the 8250B. |
| 8250A | This slightly updated UART fixed many of the issues in the 8250, but it would not work in PC/XT systems because the BIOS was written to circumvent the 8250's problems. In either case, the 8250A will not work adequately over 9600 bps. |
| 8250B | The last of the 8250 series reinserted the bugs that existed in the original 8250 so that PC/XT BIOS would function properly. The 8250B also does not run above 9600 bps. |
| 16450 | This higher-speed UART was the desired choice for AT (i286) systems. Stable at 9600 bps, the 16450 laid the groundwork for the first "high-speed" modems. However, the 16450 will not work in PC/XT systems. This chip should be replaced by the 16550A. |
| 16550 | The 16550 was faster than the 16450, allowing operation above 9600 bps, but its performance was still limited by internal design problems. This chip should be replaced by the 16550A. |
| 16550A | The fastest of the UARTs, a 16550A eliminates many of the serial port problems encountered when using a fast modem. |

■ **Transmit and receive levels** Other factors that affect both leased and dial-up telephone lines are the transmit and receive levels. These settings determine the signal levels used by the modem in each direction. Some Hayes-compatible modems permit these levels to be adjusted. The range and availability of these adjustments is in large part controlled by the local telephone system. For example, the recommended settings and ranges are different for modems sold in the UK than for those sold in the United States. See the documentation accompanying the modem to determine whether this capability is supported.

■ **System processor limitations** Some multitasking operating systems can occasionally lose small amounts of data if the computer is heavily loaded and cannot allocate processing time to the communications task frequently enough. In this case, the host computer itself corrupts data. This could also cause incomplete data transmission to the remote system. The modem will provide exact transmission of the data it receives, but if the host PC cannot "keep up" with the modem because of other tasks or speed restrictions, precautions should be taken when writing software or when adding modems with extra high speed capabilities.

One way to avoid the problem of data loss caused by the host PC is the use of an upgraded serial port such as you might find on a new PCI multi-I/O card, or a newer internal modem with a 16550A UART. Such advanced modems are powerful enough to take some of the load off of the PC processor. When processor time is stretched to the limit, try shutting down any unnecessary applications to reduce load on the system. Processor loading can become a notable issue with today's WinModem (or Win-Only) devices.

■ **Call waiting** The *call-waiting* feature now available on most dial-up lines momentarily interrupts a call. This interruption causes a click that informs voice call users that another call is coming through. While this technique is dynamite for voice communication, it is also quite effective at interrupting a modem's carrier signal—and may cause some modems to drop the connection. V.92 modems support "modem-on-hold" feature that should prevent the modem from dropping the line. Older V.90 modems (and earlier) may be able to work around this problem by setting the S-register S10 to a higher value so the modem tolerates a fairly long loss of carrier signal. Data loss may still occur, but the connection will not drop. Of course, the remote modem must be similarly configured. When originating the call, a special prefix (usually *70) can be issued as part of the dialing string to disable call waiting for the duration of the call. The exact procedure varies from area to area, so contact your local telephone system for details.

■ **Automatic timeout** Some Hayes-compatible modems offer an automatic *timeout* feature. Automatic timeout prevents an inactive connection from being maintained. This "watchdog" feature prevents undesired long-distance charges for a connection that was maintained for too long. This inactivity delay can be set or disabled with S-register S30.

■ **System lock up** There are situations where host systems *do* lock up, but in many cases it is simply that one or the other of the computers has been *flowed off*—that is, the character that stops data transfer has been inadvertently sent. This can happen during error-control connections if the wrong kind of local flow control has been selected. In addition, the problem could be the result of incompatible EIA 232-D/ITU V.24 signaling. When systems seem to cease transmitting or receiving without warning but do not disconnect, perform a thorough examination of flow control (e.g., XON/XOFF or CTS/RTS) and try a different flow control method if possible.

■ **Modem initialization strings** As you saw earlier in this chapter, modems rely on initialization strings for proper configuration at start time or when new communication software is initialized. The initialization string *must* be correct for your particular modem in order to utilize all of the modem's features and achieve optimum performance. You may be able to use "generic" initialization strings but not get full functionality from the modem (for example, you may be able to use a Hayes-compatible initialization string, but Caller ID may not work). Check the modem's initialization string, try a new driver, or enter the preferred string in the *Extra settings* line of the modem's properties dialog. In many cases, simply updating the modem's driver can improve the modem's stability and performance.

# MODEM TROUBLESHOOTING IN WINDOWS

Even with the versatility and support provided by Plug-and-Play, many modem setups are still plagued by installation, configuration, and performance problems—especially when used under a Windows platform such as Windows 98/Me/XP. This part of the chapter is intended to offer a basic troubleshooting guide for when your modem fails to dial-out under Windows 98/Me/XP.

## Verify Your Modem

Begin by checking the modem's status in your Windows system. It should be identified correctly and installed with the proper device drivers. To verify your modem under Windows 98/SE/Me, click Start | Settings | Control Panel. Double-click the Modems icon. Select the General tab, and then verify that the modem listed in that entry is correct (see Figure 25-13). Under Windows XP, choose Start | Control Panel | Printers and Other Hardware | Phone and Modem Options. Select the Modems tab, and then verify that the modem listed in that entry is correct.

If there is *no* modem listed or an incorrect modem is listed (even though Windows reported that a modem was detected), you should download the very latest driver for your modem, *remove* the current modem reference(s), then update the modem drivers. Open your Device Manager, expand the Modem entry, double-click the entry for your particular modem (or right-click the modem and select Properties). If no modems are listed, check the Other Devices entry and double-click the modem device. Select the Driver tab, and then click the Update Driver button.

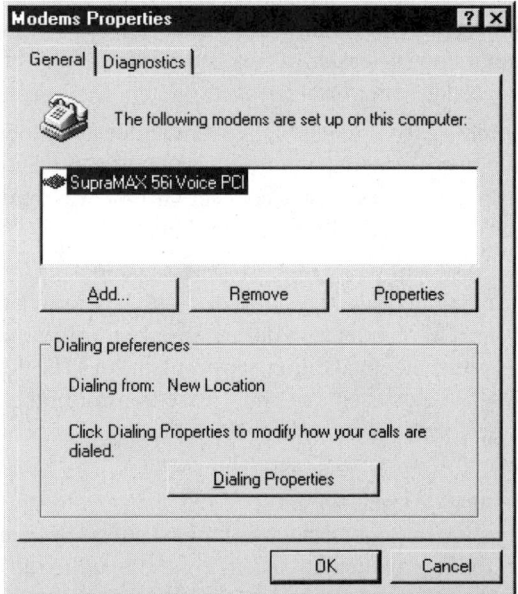

**FIGURE  25-13**    Verifying the modem entry in your system under Windows 98/SE/Me

Your Windows 98/Me Update Device Driver wizard (or the Hardware Update Wizard under Windows XP) will then search for the best driver (or display a list from which you can select the appropriate driver). If you let the wizard search for a driver, you can also specify a location for the driver. Drivers for some additional modems are included on the Windows installation CD, but if you've downloaded a new set of modem drivers from the manufacturer's web site, you may need to look for the new drivers in your \Temp or \Download directories. After the modem drivers are updated, reboot the system and verify that the correct drivers are listed, then try using your modem again. If the correct driver appears in your Device Manager, but the modem still refuses to operate properly, you may need to troubleshoot further. Follow the appropriate steps given next for your *WinModem* or *standard modem*.

## WinModem Issues

A *WinModem* (also called a *Windows-only modem* or *software modem*) depends on drivers that are specific to the operating system in order to function. This means that your modem *must* be recognized by the operating system *before* any troubleshooting can be performed. Windows 98/Me/XP should normally detect the presence of a WinModem and add it to the Device Manager properly. If a WinModem is *not* detected, you should expect one of three possible causes:

■ The WinModem has previously been detected (even though the correct drivers may not have been installed for it). In this case, the WinModem should be listed in your Device Manager, and the driver can be updated using the procedure in the previous "Verify Your Modem" section.

■ The WinModem drivers were installed and then removed, but some Registry entries remain. The Registry entries need to be removed before the WinModem can be detected again. For example, 3Com/US Robotics modems use the WMREGDEL.EXE tool included on your Windows installation CD to clear all WinModem-related Registry entries and then restart your computer. The WMREGDEL.EXE tool is located in the \Drivers\Modem\3com-usr\Winmodem folder. If Windows 98/Me/XP still does not detect your WinModem, the WMREGDEL.EXE tool may not have removed all the necessary Registry entries. If this occurs, you may need to contact the particular modem maker in order to obtain a specific fix or workaround instructions (for example, there may be a specific Registry entry that needs to be deleted manually).

■ The last option is to consider an actual WinModem defect—something may be wrong with the actual WinModem device. Try another WinModem (perhaps one from a different manufacturer) or check with your WinModem maker for specific testing instructions.

## WinModem Driver Notes

If there are no default Windows 98/Me/XP drivers for your WinModem, Windows prompts you to search for drivers. Suitable drivers may exist in the \Drivers\Modem folder on your Windows installation CD. If no drivers are located for your particular WinModem, Windows adds the device under the Other Devices branch of your Device Manager. You can then use the Device Manager to update the existing drivers with new drivers provided by your WinModem manufacturer. If your WinModem still does not work after installing and/or updating the drivers, there may be a resource conflict or an issue specific to your particular WinModem. Use the following sections of this discussion to troubleshoot further.

Given the dependence of a WinModem on operating system drivers, you *cannot* perform any troubleshooting outside of the operating system. For example, you *cannot* test a Windows 98/Me/XP WinModem at a command prompt in the DOS mode.

## Standard Modem Issues

A standard fax/modem does not offload important tasks to the host system or rely on the operating system for direct support. This means you may test the modem in DOS—even if it isn't detected by Windows. One of the easiest means of modem testing is to check direct communications with the modem port (COM port). Open a DOS window under Windows 98/Me/XP, type the following command, then press ENTER:

```
echo ATM1L3X0DT12345 > COM1
```

or replace "COM1" with the serial port number to which the modem is connected (such as COM2 or COM3). The first command, **AT** (attention), signals that the modem is about to receive information. **M1** is a universal command to turn the modem's speaker on (if it is off by default). **L3** is a universal command to raise the modem's speaker volume to the maximum level (if it is at the lowest by default). **X0** signals the modem to run the command without waiting for a dial tone—this is useful if modem and voice calls use the same phone line. Finally, the **DT12345** command instructs the modem to dial the digits **12345**. To hang up the modem again, simply type

```
echo ATH0 > COM1
```

then press ENTER. If your modem is on a port other than COM1, replace "COM1" with the serial port number to which the modem is connected (such as COM2 or COM3).

If the modem does *not* respond with a dial tone or communication signal in DOS mode, there may be something physically wrong with either the modem or the COM port. Verify that the modem's COM port is configured as expected or reconfigure the modem manually. If there is a resource conflict between the COM port and another device in the system, you may need to resolve the conflict in order to enable the modem. Otherwise, try a new modem. If the modem does *not* respond with a dial tone or communication signal in Windows 98/Me/XP but *does* respond in DOS mode, Windows 98/Me/XP itself may not be communicating correctly with your COM port. This trouble can occur for several reasons:

- The COM port has not been detected. Under Windows 9x/Me, click Start | Settings | Control Panel. Double-click Add New Hardware, and then follow the instructions on your screen to detect and install the COM port. Under Windows XP, open the Device Manager, right-click any entry, and click Scan for Hardware Changes.

- The serial port device drivers are corrupt. Use the System File Checker (or SFC) tool under Windows 9x/Me to verify the integrity of the SERIAL.VXD, VCOMM.VXD, and SERIALUI.DLL serial port drivers. To access the System File Checker, click Start, highlight Programs, highlight Accessories, point to System Tools, then choose the System Information utility. Once the System Information utility starts, click Tools on the main menu, then select the System File Checker. You may need to reinstall or update any damaged files. Under Windows XP, use System Restore to return the system to a working point, or reinstall Windows XP from scratch.

- Finally, there is a resource conflict between your COM port and another device in the system. You'll need to identify and resolve the conflict using the Device Manager, as shown in Chapter 11.

# CHECKING MODEM FIRMWARE

Today, it is common for modems to sport a "flash" BIOS (firmware) that can be updated as new firmware versions are made available. For example, many late-model 33.6 Kbps and x2 and K56flex 56 Kbps modems offered such upgradeable firmware in preparation for the V.90 standard. Today, virtually all dial-up, cable, and DSL modems provide upgradeable firmware. If you're considering a modem firmware upgrade, you'll need to check the current firmware version on your modem. You can use HyperTerminal to determine the firmware version of your dial-up modem:

For cable and DSL modems, check with the manufacturer for firmware updates and procedures.

1. Under Windows 9x/Me, click Start | Programs | Accessories | HyperTerminal. Double-click the Hyperterm icon. Under Windows XP, click Start | All Programs | Accessories | Communications | HyperTerminal.

2. When the program starts, type **TEST** for a name, and proceed.

3. When you're asked for a telephone number, just type **1234** and make sure that the correct modem device is selected from the Connect Using drop down menu. Click OK to proceed.

4. Now click Cancel (don't actually try connecting)—this will bring you to the terminal window.

5. Type **ATE1** (even if you don't see it appear on the screen) and press ENTER. The modem should respond with "OK."

6. Now you can type any AT commands you wish. Try typing **ATi3** or **ATi92**—these two AT commands will tell you the exact firmware version and type of modem that you're using. For example, a 33.6 Kbps modem may respond:

```
U.S. Robotics Sportster 33600 Fax V4.3.185
```

Once you find the firmware version, you can compare it with the new version available for download, and upgrade your firmware if the online version is newer. To determine if your modem supports the V.90 or V.92 standards, follow these steps:

1. Open the Modem Properties dialog.

2. On the Diagnostics tab, click the correct modem and then click More Info.

3. After a few moments, a series of AT commands and responses will appear in the information box.

4. Locate the line that begins with "ATI7." If your modem supports the V.90 standard, "V.90" should be listed beside that command. If the modem supports V.92, "V.92" should be listed. Otherwise, you can check with the modem's manufacturer.

5. Click OK.

## SYMPTOMS

Many of the problems that you will encounter with modems are related to their physical and software configuration. The host PC also plays an important role in the modem's overall performance and reliability. Modems themselves are rarely at fault—although they are hardly invulnerable. This part of the chapter presents you with an index of potential problems and troubleshooting solutions. When you determine that the modem itself is at fault, you should replace the modem. When replacing the dial-up modem, remember that the initialization and operating strings often vary slightly between modem manufacturers—be sure to alter any AT command strings in the communication software (if necessary) to accommodate the new modem or remove the old modem and its application software before exchanging the modem. With any modem, be sure to use the latest drivers.

In some cases, PCI modem detection problems may be corrected by moving the modem to a PCI slot with a higher priority (usually a slot closer to the processor).

**SYMPTOM 25-1**   **The PC (or communication software) refuses to recognize the modem**
First, verify that the modem is turned on (external modems only)—for internal modems, see that the modem is installed correctly and completely in its expansion slot. Check your CMOS settings and verify that the COM port for your external modem is enabled. There may be a COM port (IRQ) conflict in the system. External USB modems will need the USB port enabled and a free IRQ available (usually IRQ 12). Check the configuration of your internal modem (try the Windows Device Manager) and verify that there are no hardware conflicts. If you have trouble running the dialup modem in "terminal mode" (the dial-up modem doesn't respond to AT commands), make sure that you're entering everything in either uppercase (AT) or lowercase (at) format—mixing cases can sometimes confuse a modem. For cable and DSL modems, there may be a diagnostic or other software that can test the device. Try removing and reinstalling the modem using the latest drivers from the manufacturer (let Windows redetect the unit, or use the Add New Hardware Wizard), or try another modem.

**SYMPTOM 25-2**   **Your 33.6 Kbps dial-up modem is detected as a 28.8 Kbps modem**
This can happen if your version of Windows 9x/Me/XP doesn't supply hardware information about the faster modem that you're trying to use. In virtually every case, you'll need to supply a suitable Windows 9x/Me/XP driver for the modem in the form of an .INF file that accompanied the modem device or is available for download from the modem manufacturer's Web site. Try updating the driver, or remove and reinstall the incorrectly identified dial-up modem from scratch.

**SYMPTOM 25-3**   **The dial-up modem appears to be functioning properly, but you can't see what you're typing**   There are two types of duplex, *full* and *half*. Half-duplex systems simply transmit to and receive from each other. Full-duplex systems do that also, plus they "receive" what they transmit—echoing the data back to the sender. Since half-duplex systems do not echo, what is being sent is typically not shown on the screen. Most terminal programs (such as HyperTerminal) have an option to enable LOCAL ECHO so that what is transmitted is also displayed. You can often enable the dial-up modem's local echo by typing the **ATE1** command during a direct connection or adding the **E1** entry to the modem's initialization string. When local echo is not an option, switching to full-duplex mode will often do the same thing. Customer complaints that they can't see what they are typing are solved by turning on local echo or switching to full-duplex.

**SYMPTOM 25-4**   **The dial-up modem appears to be functioning properly, but you see double characters print while typing**   By their nature, full-duplex dial-up modem connections produce an echo. If local echo is enabled in addition, you'll see not only what you are transmitting but also that characters are being echoed, creating a double display—for example, when you hit **ABC**, you'll see "AABBCC". This can be annoying, but is otherwise totally harmless. Customer complaints of double letters are solved by turning off local echo by entering the **ATE0** command during direct connection or adding the **E0** command to the modem's initialization string.

**SYMPTOM 25-5    You encounter an "Error 630" when dialing out with your modem**

When you attempt to dial out under Windows 98/Me/XP, you may receive an error message such as:

```
Error 630: The computer is not receiving a response from the modem. Check
that the modem is plugged in, and if necessary, turn the modem off, and
then turn it back on.
```

You may also see an error indicating that the communication port is invalid or busy. This fault can occur if you have the Support SerialKey Devices Accessibility option configured to use the same COM port where your modem is connected. You'll need to disable or reconfigure the Support SerialKey Devices option:

1. Click Start | Settings | Control Panel, then double-click Accessibility Options. Under Windows XP, click Start | Control Panel | Accessibility Options | Accessibility Options.

2. On the General tab, either click to clear the Support SerialKey Devices check box or click Settings (see Figure 25-14), click a different COM port in the Serial port box, then click OK.

3. Click OK.

**SYMPTOM 25-6    Your dial-up modem encounters a "633" error under Windows 9x/Me**

Even though you have a dial-up modem installed under Windows 9x/Me, a 32-bit TAPI program may not be able to access the modem. The TAPI program may even start the Install New Modem Wizard. For

**FIGURE  25-14**    Disable the use of SerialKeys to free potential serial port conflicts

example, the Install New Modem Wizard may start when you launch the Make New Connection Wizard in Dial-Up Networking—even though a modem is already installed. The following error message may appear after you attempt to dial a connection:

```
Error 633: The modem is not installed or configured for Dial-Up Networking.
To check your modem configuration, double-click on the Modems icon in the
Control Panel.
```

In virtually all cases, this fault will occur if the Unimodem TAPI Service Provider file (UNIMDM.TSP) is missing or damaged. To correct the fault, extract a new copy of the UNIMDM.TSP file from your original Windows disks or CD to the \Windows\System folder. For Windows 95, the UNIMDM.TSP file is located in the WIN95_03.CAB cabinet file. For Windows 98, the UNIMDM.TSP file is located in the WIN98_63.CAB cabinet file. For Windows 98 Second Edition, the UNIMDM.TSP file is located in the WIN98_69.CAB cabinet file.

**SYMPTOM 25-7** **When creating a connection, your dial-up modem is missing from the Select a Device box** If you try to use an existing connection under Windows 98/Me (this is not an issue under Windows XP), you may receive an error such as:

```
Error 633: The modem is not installed or configured for Dial-Up Networking.
To check your modem configuration, double-click on the Modems icon in the
Control Panel.
```

If you test your dial-up modem by clicking More Info on the Diagnostics tab under the Modems icon in your Control Panel, your modem may respond normally—and appear to be working correctly. This problem can occur if the "TAPI service provider" entry in your Registry is missing (or corrupted) or if the TELEPHON.INI file is missing or damaged. Access the system Registry and use REGEDIT to view the following key:

```
HKEY_LOCAL_MACHINE\Software\Microsoft\Windows\Current Version\
Telephony\Providers
```

Set the value of the ProviderFilename0 to **TSP3216L.TSP**. Save the changes, quit the Registry Editor, then restart your computer. If the TELEPHON.INI file is missing or damaged, you'll need to recreate it:

1. Click Start | Find | Files O Folders.
2. In the Named box, type **telephon.ini**, then click Find Now.
3. If you do *not* find the TELEPHON.INI file, skip the next step. If you *do* find the TELEPHON.INI file, right-click the file, click Rename, type **telephon.old**, then press ENTER.
4. Quit the Find tool, click Start, click Run, type **tapiini.exe**, then press ENTER.
5. Restart your computer.

**SYMPTOM 25-8**    The modem refuses to respond or dial out under Windows 98/SE
The modem may refuse to dial out. It may also hang up and crash the communication software with an error such as:

```
The modem failed to respond. Make sure it is properly connected and turned
on. If it is an internal modem or is connected, verify that the interrupt
for the port is properly set.
```

For example, this is a known issue with the PhoebeMicro 56 Kbps modem. In virtually every case, the problem is due to faulty or outdated modem drivers accompanying the device. Contact the modem manufacturer to obtain the very latest drivers, or try default drivers on the Windows 98/SE CD.

**SYMPTOM 25-9**    Your dial-up modem properties are not available through the Modems icon in your Control Panel    When you modify your modem's properties under Windows 9x/Me, the Configure button may be unavailable in HyperTerminal or Dial-Up Networking. Also, when you click your modem and then click Properties in the Modems tool under the Control Panel, you may receive an error message such as:

```
The modem properties cannot be displayed because the modem information
is corrupt. Remove this modem by clicking Remove and add it again.
```

However, you find that removing and reinstalling the modem does *not* correct the problem. In a few cases, this problem can occur if an incorrect version of the UMDM16.DLL file is installed in the \Windows\System folder. If this occurs, rename the UMDM16.DLL file and extract a new copy of the file from your original Windows CD. In the vast majority of cases, this problem will occur if the MODEMUI.DLL file is damaged. To correct this problem, use Windows Explorer or My Computer to rename the MODEMUI.DLL file in the \Windows\System folder to MODEMUI.OLD, then extract a new copy of the MODEMUI.DLL file from your Windows CD to your \Windows\System folder.

**SYMPTOM 25-10**    Your modem refuses to dial out when using a TAPI program
When you use a TAPI program under Windows 9x/Me (such as Dial-Up Networking, Phone Dialer, or HyperTerminal), you may receive an error message such as:

```
There is no dialtone. Make sure your modem is connected to the phone line.
```

In most cases, this error occurs when you're trying to dial using a calling card and you have enabled the Wait for Dial Tone Before Dialing option. You must disable the Wait for Dial Tone Before Dialing option:

1. Click Start | Settings | Control Panel.
2. Double-click the Modems icon.
3. Select your modem, then click Properties.
4. On the Connection tab, click the Wait for Dial Tone Before Dialing check box to clear it (see Figure 25-15).
5. Click OK; then click OK again.
6. It may be necessary to restart the computer.

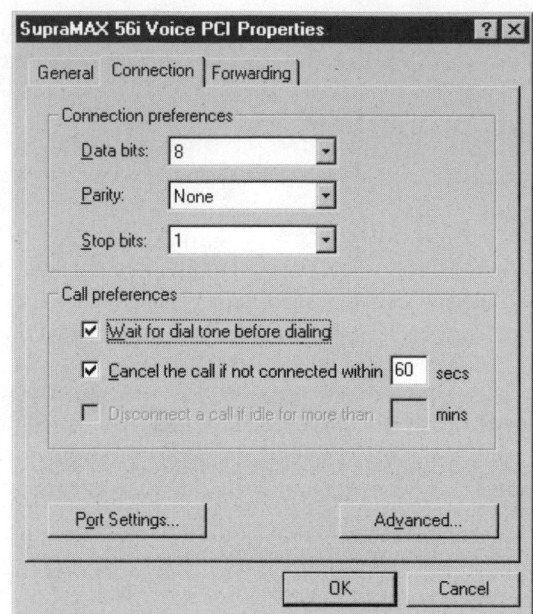

**FIGURE  25-15**    Clear the dial tone check box and try the modem again

**SYMPTOM 25-11**    **The dial-up modem is detected on the wrong COM port on your PC**
The dialup modem may not respond or work correctly and may appear to be using COM3 even if you've configured your modem to use COM1. This is a known issue with systems such as the Acer Aspire and is caused by an issue with the system's BIOS. For example, this problem can occur if COM1 is disabled in your computer's BIOS, but the system incorrectly reports the disabled status of COM1—Windows 9x/Me/XP still detects COM1, and may assign your modem to COM3 to avoid resource conflicts. The proper long-term fix is to upgrade the system BIOS. But you may work around the issue by disabling COM1 in the Device Manager:

1.  Open the Device Manager.

2.  Double-click the Ports (COM & LPT) branch to expand it, click Communications Port (COM1), and then click Properties.

3.  Under Windows 9x/Me, click to select the Disable in this Hardware Profile check box, and then click OK. Under Windows XP, select Do Not Use this Device from the Device Usage drop-down.

4.  Double-click the Modems branch to expand it, click your modem, click Remove, click OK, and then restart your computer.

5.  When your computer restarts, follow the instructions on the screen to reinstall your modem.

**SYMPTOM 25-12**    **Windows cannot find the dial-up modem on subsequent bootups**
For example, the dial-up modem appears to install properly under Windows 9x/Me/XP, but once you reboot the system, Windows cannot find the device. This normally happens when the motherboard pro-

vides an integrated modem. You typically need to disable the integrated modem through the CMOS Setup. In a few cases, you might need to reset a motherboard jumper to disable integrated modem features. If the integrated modem is provided on a dedicated expansion card (e.g., an AMR or CNR card), you may be able to remove the card.

**SYMPTOM 25-13**     **The dial-up modem will not answer at the customer's site, but it works fine in the shop**     Since deregulation of the original Bell Telephone Company, customers have been allowed to attach devices to phone lines with the proviso that they notify the phone company of each device's FCC registration and ringer equivalence number (REN). While few customers make it a point of informing their local telephone company how many phones and gadgets are connected to the telephone line, there is a good reason for doing so—you see, the amount of *ringing voltage* supplied to a site is fixed. If you load down the line beyond its maximum rating, not enough voltage will be available to ring all of the bells. The *ringer equivalence* is the amount of load that the device will place on the line. Modems have to be able to detect a ring signal before they know to pick up. If the ringing signal is too weak, the modem will not detect it properly and initiate an answer sequence.

Have the customer remove some other equipment from the phone lines and see if the problem disappears. With today's fax machines, modems, multiple extension phones, and answering machines all plugged into the same line, it would be easy to overload the ringing voltage. The customer should also take a listing of the registration numbers and ringer equivalence numbers on *all* devices connected to phone lines and notify the local phone company of them. The phone company can then boost the ringer voltage to compensate for the added loads.

As a precaution, make sure that your customer is starting the communication software properly before attempting to receive a modem call—the modem will not pick up a ringing line unless the proper software is running and the modem is in an "auto-answer" mode.

**SYMPTOM 25-14**     **Your RS-232 dial-up modem is receiving or transmitting garbage, or is having great difficulty displaying anything at all**     Serial communication is totally dependent on the data frame settings and transfer rate of the receiver and the transmitter being an exact match. The baud rate, word bits, stop bits, and parity must all match exactly or errors will show up. These errors can show as either *no* data or as *incorrect* data (garbage) on screen. You'll see this one crop up a lot when customers switch from calling a local BBS to a commercial service like CompuServe. Local BBS's are usually set for 8-bit words, no parity, and one stop bit. CompuServe, on the other hand, uses 7-bit words, even parity, and 2 stop bits. The terminal software must be reconfigured to match the settings of each service being called. Most programs allow for these differences by letting you specify a configuration for each entry in the dialing directory. Also check the method of flow control being used (such as XOFF/XON, DTR/DSR, or CTS/RTS) and make sure that it is set properly. To adjust the COM port's performance, highlight your desired COM port in Device Manager and click Properties. Select the Port Settings tab in the COM Port Properties dialog (see Figure 25-16) and make any necessary changes to the configuration.

Baud rate mismatches most often result in what looks like a dead modem—often, nothing is displayed on either end. Modems will automatically negotiate a common baud rate to connect at without regard to the terminal settings. The modems will normally connect at the highest baud rate available to the slowest modem, so if a 56 Kbps modem connects to a 33.6 Kbps modem, both will set themselves to 33.6 Kbps. If the software on the higher speed modem is still set for (forcing) the higher speed, you'll typically get large amounts of garbage or nothing at all.

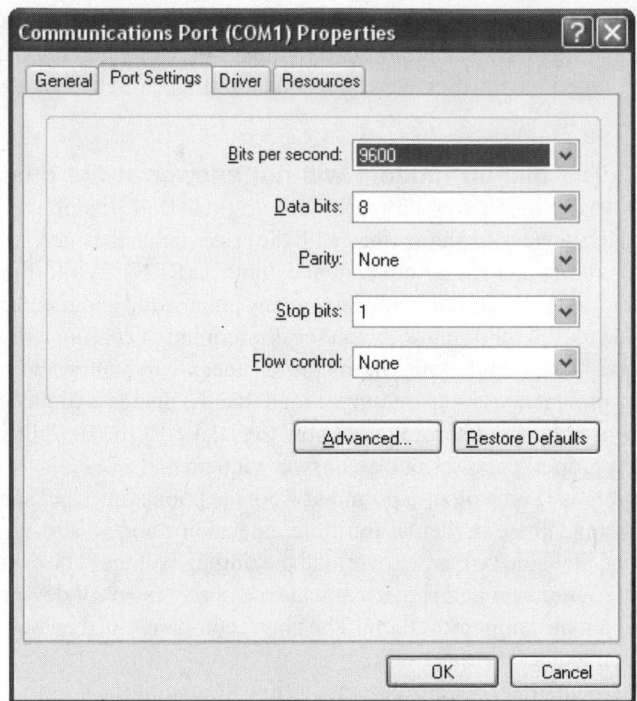

**FIGURE 25-16**    Reconfigure the COM port as needed to streamline serial communication

**SYMPTOM 25-15**    **The dial-up modem is connected and turned on, but there is no response from the modem**    The communication software's configuration must match the port settings of the modem. Check to make sure that any modem parameters are entered and saved properly. Establish a direct connection with the modem (e.g., using HyperTerminal) and enter the **ATZ** command. Doing this will reset the modem. The modem should respond "OK" or "0" (the numerical equivalent of OK). If that doesn't work, change to COM2 and try again, then COM3 and COM4. If none of the combinations work, check the DIP switches or jumpers on the modem for the correct configuration. Finally, try the modem on another PC or replace the suspect modem.

**SYMPTOM 25-16**    **The modem will not pick up the phone line**    The modem is not able to initiate a call or answer an incoming call. Most modems today come with two RJ11 telephone line connectors for the phone lines: one labeled "LINE" (where the outside line enters the modem) and the other labeled "PHONE" (where an extension telephone can be plugged in). Check that the outgoing telephone line is plugged into the LINE jack. Leave the PHONE connector disconnected while the modem is in use.

Test the modem manually by establishing a direct connection (e.g., using HyperTerminal) and typing a dial command such as **ATDT15083667683**. When you enter this command string, the modem should go off hook, draw dial tone, and dial the numbers. If this happens as expected, you can be reasonably sure that the modem is working properly—and the communication software is at fault. Check the modem initialization strings or try a new communication package. If the modem does not respond during a direct connection, check that the modem is installed and configured properly. You may need to try a new modem.

**SYMPTOM 25-17**    **The modem appears to work fine, but prints garbage whenever it's supposed to show IBM text graphics, such as boxes, or ANSI graphics**    This trouble generally doesn't occur with Internet access under Windows, but may occur when dialing into other modems using BBS or other direct access type software. Your terminal emulation mode is wrong. The communication software is probably set for 7-bit words. The IBM text graphic character set starts at ASCII 128 and has to have the eighth bit. Adjust the communication software or COM port configuration to handle 8-bit words (refer to Figure 25-16). You may also be using an unusual ASCII character set during the connection—try setting the character set emulation to ANSI BBS or TTY.

**SYMPTOM 25-18**    **You frequently see strange character groups like "[0m" appearing in the text**    This trouble generally doesn't occur with Internet access under Windows, but may occur when dialing into other modems using BBS or other direct access type software. These are ANSI control codes attempting to control your display. Popular among BBS software, ANSI codes can be used to set colors, draw ASCII boxes, clear the screen, move the cursor, and so on. DOS provides an ANSI screen driver called ANSI.SYS that can be loaded into the CONFIG.SYS when the computer is rebooted. Most of today's terminal software will offer a setting for this as well. If you are able to select character set emulation in your communication software, try setting to ANSI BBS.

**SYMPTOM 25-19**    **The modem makes audible "clicking" noises when hooked to phone line**    There is probably a short circuit somewhere in the phone line. The "clicking" is the noise of the modem trying to pick up when it sees the short and hang up when the short clears. Try replacing the line cord going from the modem to the telephone wall jack—line cords don't last very long under constant use and abuse. If problems continue, try using a different telephone line—the physical wiring may be defective between the wall jack and telephone pole. Contact your local telephone company if you suspect this to be the case. Next, try establishing a direct connection to the modem (e.g., using HyperTerminal) and enter an **AT&F** command, which will restore the modem's factory default settings. If that clears the problem, the modem's initialized state may not be fully compatible with the current telephone line characteristics. Check each modem setting carefully and adjust parameters to try and settle its operation down. If factory default settings do not help and the telephone line seems reliable, there may be a problem with the modem's telephone interface circuit—try replacing the modem.

**SYMPTOM 25-20**    **The modem is having difficulty connecting to another modem**
The modem is powered and connected properly. It dials the desired number and you can hear the modems negotiating, but they never quite seem to make a connection. This is a classic software configuration problem. You may often see a "NO CARRIER" message associated with this problem. Check each parameter in your communication software—especially the modem's AT initialization string. Make sure that each entry in the string is appropriate for your modem. If the string looks correct, try disabling the modem's MNP5 protocol. You will have to refer to the modem's manual to find the exact command, but many modems use **AT\N0**. If your modem is using MNP5 and the destination modem does not support it, the negotiation can hang up. If problems persist, try lowering the modem's data transfer rate. While most modems can set the proper transfer rate automatically, some modems that do not support it may also cause the negotiation to freeze.

Another problem may be that your modem is not configured to wait long enough for carrier from the remote modem. You can adjust this delay by entering a larger number for S-register S7. Start the communication software, establish a direct connection (terminal mode), type **ATS7?**, and press ENTER. Doing this will return the current value of register S7. You can then use the command **ATS7=10** to enter a larger delay (in this case, 10 seconds). That should give the destination modem more time to respond. If all else fails, try a modem from a different manufacturer.

**SYMPTOM 25-21**　　**The modem starts dialing before it draws a dial tone**　As a result, one or more of the numbers are lost during dialing, making it difficult to establish a connection. Chances are that the modem is working just fine, but the modem does not wait long enough for dial tone to be present once it goes off hook. The solution is to increase the time delay *before* the modem starts dialing. This can be done by changing the value in S-register S6. To find the current value, start the communication software and establish a direct connection (terminal mode), and then type **ATS6?** followed by pressing ENTER. Doing this queries the S-register. You can then enter a new value such as **ATS6=10** (which would provide a 10-second delay).

**SYMPTOM 25-22**　　**The modem has trouble sending or receiving when the system's power saving features are turned on**　This type of problem is most prevalent with PCMCIA modems running on a notebook PC. The power conservation features found on many notebook systems often interferes with the modem's operation—proper modem operation typically relies on full processing speed, which is often scaled back when power conservation is turned on. Ultimately, the most effective resolution to this problem is simply to turn the power conservation features off while you use the modem (you can reset the power features later). However, it may be possible to correct these types of problems using a BIOS upgrade for the mobile PC or an updated modem driver.

**SYMPTOM 25-23**　　**You see an error such as "Already on line" or "Carrier already established"**　These types of errors often arise when you start a communications software package while the modem is already online. You might also find this problem when the Carrier Detect (CD) signal is set *always on* (using a command string such as **AT&C0**). To make sure that the CD signal is on only when the modem makes a connection, use a command string such as **AT&C1&D2&W**. The **&W** suffix loads the settings into nonvolatile RAM. If this problem arises when you hang up the connection without signing off the modem, you will have to reboot the system to clear the CD signal—**AT&F** and **ATZ** will *not* clear the signal.

**SYMPTOM 25-24**　　**The modem refuses to answer the incoming line**　First, make sure to set the communication software to answer the calling modem—or set the modem to auto-answer mode (set S-register S0 to **1** or more). On external modems, you will see the "AA" LED lit when the auto-answer mode is active. Problems can also occur if your external modem does not recognize the DTR signal generated by the host PC. The command **AT&D** controls how the modem responds to the computer's DTR signal. An external modem turns on the TR light when it is set to see the DTR signal. If the TR light is out, the modem will not answer (regardless of whether the auto-answer mode is enabled or not). Use the **AT&D0** command if your serial port does not support the DTR signal or if your modem cable does not connect to it. Otherwise, you should use the **AT&D2** command.

**SYMPTOM 25-25**　　**The dial-up modem switches into the command mode intermittently** When this problem develops, you may have to tweak the DTR arrangement. To correct this fault, try changing the modem's DTR setting using the command **AT&D2&W**.

**SYMPTOM 25-26**　　**You notice cyclic redundancy check (CRC) errors and low characters per second (CPS) transfers**　This may simply be a matter of a poor phone connection established through the telephone network (or a busy Internet connection). Try making the call again—chances are that the call will be routed differently, resulting in a more reliable connection. Next, check the flow control scheme (XOFF/XON, CTS/RTS, and so on) to verify that it is optimum, or type **AT&F1** from the terminal mode to load the optimum flow control setting. The serial port rate in your communications software may be set too high for your modem's UART or your area's phone lines. Try lowering the serial port rate (refer to Figure 25-16) in your communications software to 38,400 bps or 19,200 bps (or lower for slower modems). The remote site you are dialing into may have trouble with the file transfer protocol you've selected. Finally, there may be a TSR program running in the background and interfering with data communications. Disable any TSR programs running in the background and try the communication again.

**SYMPTOM 25-27**  **During installation, the dial-up modem setup program cannot find the internal modem**  In virtually all cases, you have a hardware conflict between the dial-up modem and another device in the system. Check the hardware installation first. For internal modems, make sure the IRQ and I/O address are set correctly and see that there are no other devices using the same IRQ or I/O space (or other resources) as your modem. Under Windows 9x/Me/XP, the Device Manager can usually display any conflicting devices with yellow icons (exclamation marks). Next, make sure that the modem is inserted properly into its bus slot. If any of the card's gold "fingers" appear corroded or soiled, clean the fingers gently with a pencil eraser. Try the modem in another bus slot—perhaps a higher priority PCI slot (closer to the processor). Finally, check the modem switches (if any). Most external modems use a series of DIP switches to configure their various features. Refer to the modem's documentation and see that any modem switches are set properly.

**SYMPTOM 25-28**  **After installing a new internal dial-up modem, the system mouse driver no longer loads, or the mouse behaves erratically**  In virtually all cases, there is a hardware conflict between the new dialup modem and the existing mouse port. Check the hardware installation. If the mouse is connected to a COM port, make sure that your internal modem is set to use a different COM port. Remember that COM1 and COM3 use the same IRQ (and COM2 and COM4 use the same IRQ). For example, you might need to disable COM2 on the motherboard or I/O controller and set up the modem as COM2. Under Windows 9x/Me/XP, the Device Manager can usually display any conflicting devices with a yellow icon (exclamation mark).

**SYMPTOM 25-29**  **After installing modem driver software, Windows locks up or crashes**  This is almost always the result of a defective or outdated modem driver. Check the software installation. Make sure that the modem driver software you have installed is the proper version for the particular modem *and* your version of Windows (e.g., 95, 98, Me, NT, 2000, or XP). You can usually check the driver version on the modem manufacturer's Web site. If you do find that the modem driver is incorrect, run any "uninstall" utility that accompanied the software in order to remove the driver cleanly—otherwise, you'll have to remove the modem driver references from SYSTEM.INI manually. Under Windows 9x/Me/XP, you can often remove a device from the Device Manager, then allow Windows to re-detect the modem during the next boot (and reinstall the new drivers at that point).

**SYMPTOM 25-30**  **DOS communication software works fine, but Windows communication software will not**  You may also see Windows error messages suggesting that certain files are missing. In most cases, the modem drivers (and any required parameters) have not been loaded properly. Check the software installation and make sure that the modem driver software you have installed is the proper version for the particular modem *and* your version of Windows (e.g., 95, 98, Me, NT, 2000, or XP). Try uninstalling the modem drivers (if possible), then reload the drivers from scratch—making sure that they are set up properly for your system configuration. Next, check the manufacturer's Web site for any adjustments or workarounds that may be required for your particular modem and drivers. You may need to make manual adjustments to SYSTEM.INI and WIN.INI files as well as the Windows 9x/Me/XP Registry files as suggested by the modem manufacturer.

**SYMPTOM 25-31** **The dial-up modem will not provide synchronous communication**
Dialup modems are typically asynchronous devices, but most can be configured for synchronous communication with host systems such as mainframe computers. If your modem will not work in synchronous mode, chances are that the modem is not configured properly. You must configure *both* the originating modem and the answering modem. The originating modem will be configured for synchronous originate mode and will dial a stored number when a connection is attempted. You will need a dumb terminal or terminal emulation software to configure the serial dial-up modem:

1. Attach the modem to a serial port on a PC or dumb terminal using a standard RS-232 cable.

2. Configure the *port speed* setting in the dumb terminal or the terminal emulation software to match the speed that will be used on the synchronous port.

3. Configure the software for *direct connect* or *terminal mode* (e.g., using HyperTerminal) and open the connection to the port.

4. Type **AT&F&W** and press ENTER. The modem should respond with "OK". If double characters appear, type **ATE0** and press ENTER to disable local character echo.

5. Type **AT&Q2&S2&W** and press ENTER. The modem should respond with "OK."

6. Type **AT&Z0=T[phone number to store]** and press ENTER. The modem should respond with "OK."

7. Type **AT&D2&W** and press ENTER. The modem should respond with "OK."

8. Type **AT&C1E0Q1&W** and press ENTER. The modem should *not* respond with "OK" because character echo and result-code reporting have been disabled.

Next, configure the answering modem. The answering modem must be configured for synchronous answer mode. Although the answering modem is usually attached to the mainframe host system, you will first need to connect it to a dumb terminal for configuration. To configure the answering modem:

1. Attach the modem to a serial port on a PC or dumb terminal using a standard RS-232 cable.

2. Configure the *port speed* setting in the dumb terminal or the terminal emulation software to match the speed that will be used on the synchronous port.

3. Type **AT** and press ENTER. The modem should respond with "OK." If double characters appear, type **ATE0** and press ENTER to disable local character echo.

4. Type **AT&F&W** and press ENTER. The modem should respond with "OK."

5. Type **AT&Q1&S2&W** and press ENTER. The modem should respond with "OK."

6. Type **ATS0=1** (or the number of rings you want the modem to answer on) and press ENTER. The modem should respond with "OK."

7. Type **AT&D2&W** and press ENTER. The modem should respond with "OK."

8. Type **AT&C1E0Q1&W** and press ENTER. The modem should *not* respond with "OK" because character echo and result-code reporting have been disabled.

Now, disable command recognition. After each modem has been configured properly, the command recognition should be disabled as follows:

1. Turn the modems off.
2. Locate the DIP switches that define modem operations.
3. Move the proper DIP switch to turn *command recognition* off. If the modem is internal, move the appropriate jumper. The particular DIP switch or jumper will depend on your specific modem, so check the modem's documentation.
4. Turn the modems on.

Finally, establish a synchronous connection. Attach the originating modem to the SDLC or synchronous port and turn the power on. When a connection is attempted, the modem will automatically dial the stored number and attempt to connect to the other modem. Attach the answering modem to the synchronous port on the host system. The modem will answer incoming calls in **&Q1** synchronous mode.

**SYMPTOM 25-32**    **The dial-up modem appears to be set up and configured properly, but it is experiencing data loss**    Such symptoms may appear as excessive file transfer errors, missing text or characters, and jumbled ASCII text. Though modern modems are capable of data rates up to 230400 bps, data rates over 19200 bps can cause problems for older PCs because of inadequate serial port hardware. Check the UART first—your serial ports should be using 16550A UARTs for optimum performance. If the UART is older, data throughput will be limited. If you cannot upgrade the UART chip directly, you can often disable the existing serial port and install an upgraded I/O board. Any diagnostic program (such as TuffTest) can identify the UARTs in your system. Check your modem drivers and make sure that the modem driver software is up to date and optimized for your particular version of Windows (e.g., 95, 98, Me, NT4, 2000, and XP). Finally, reduce your data rates. If you cannot resolve the problem through a driver or new UART, try reducing the modem's data rate in your communication software.

**SYMPTOM 25-33**    **The dial-up modem appears to be set up and configured properly, but it regularly connects at slower speeds than it is capable of**    There are several different factors that can account for such a problem. First, dial-up modems can connect only at the maximum speed of the *slowest* modem. If the remote modem is slower than yours, your connection speed will be limited. Try connecting to a faster ISP or other online connection. Check the modem initialization string next—there may be one or more important commands missing from the command string. Look for the recommended initialization string in the modem's documentation. Also see that the correct modem is selected in any communication software (check the modem's entry in the Device Manager as well).

Check the modem's firmware version. Use the **ATI3** command to check the modem's ID information (including the firmware revision). If the firmware is old, it may need to be updated. If the firmware is very new, it may contain a bug that the manufacturer should be made aware of. Finally, try a different phone line. Faulty or noisy telephone connections can reduce effective communication speed. Also, try the call at an "off time."

**SYMPTOM 25-34**    **You are having trouble configuring the dial-up modem for hardware and software flow control**    This is usually due to invalid command strings. Try some generic command strings. The following two AT command strings can configure most Hayes-compatible modems for hardware or software flow control. Keep in mind that you may need to add additional commands in order to configure the modem completely.

- Software flow control (XON/XOFF)   **AT&F1&C1&D2\**
- Hardware flow control (CTS/RTS)   **AT&F1&C1&D2\Q3\**

Under Windows 9x/Me/XP, you can also set error correction and flow control options through the modem's Advanced Connection Settings dialog as in Figure 25-4, or through the COM port properties as in Figure 25-16.

**SYMPTOM 25-35**   **The modem's flash ROM update will not install because it cannot recognize the modem's current firmware version**   This is invariably a problem with the flash ROM update software itself. Check the software source. Contact the manufacturer to see if there is a corrected update available or see if there is a workaround to the problem. There may be one or more command line switches that can override the update's firmware autodetection.

**SYMPTOM 25-36**   **The dial-up modem establishes connections properly, but it frequently drops connections**   Both hardware and software issues can cause this kind of trouble. Problems with the telephone connection itself can cause connection problems. Try connecting to various different places. If problems seem to occur more frequently in one connection over another, the remote location may be suffering from communications problems (e.g., faulty wiring). Also try using a different local telephone line. Next, check the modem's initialization string and make sure that the modem is set up properly for data compression and error correction. Finally, check the Windows driver and ensure that you're using the latest manufacturer's driver.

**SYMPTOM 25-37**   **It seems to take the dial-up modem an unusually long time to hang up** The carrier delay time is probably set too long. Check the carrier delay time. Modems can be set to wait (often as long as 25 seconds) after a carrier is lost to see whether it comes back—if you frequently encounter poor signal quality, this feature can be quite convenient. After a legitimate hang-up, however, the modem may continue to wait. In this case, you may want to set the value of the S10 register to a low number—10 or less.

**SYMPTOM 25-38**   **The modem is configured as COM4 (IRQ3) under Windows , but the modem refuses to work**   There may be a hardware acceleration issue. Go into the Windows 9x/Me Control Panel, double-click the System icon, select Performance, and then click Graphics. If this occurs under Windows XP, open the Display Properties dialog, select the Settings tab, click the Advanced button, and select the Troubleshoot tab. Set Hardware Acceleration to None and try the modem again. Some advanced modem manufacturers have found an addressing conflict with certain graphics accelerator cards. If you configure your Windows graphics driver to basic VGA and find the modem works at that setting, then the problem is probably an addressing conflict with your graphics card. You might need to update the modem driver, update the video driver, or replace the modem with a USB model in order to resolve the COM port issue.

**SYMPTOM 25-39**   **A WinModem installed correctly and responds to AT commands fine, but whenever you call out, the modem makes a 9600 V.34 connection**   This is typically due to a problem with the current communications driver. Adding the following line:

```
ForceBridgeOrRouter=TRUE
```

to the SYSTEM.INI file may correct this problem by bypassing the current communications driver and going directly to the WinModem driver. You should also make sure that your Port Rate is set to 19,200 in your Control Panel (Port Settings) in Windows 3.1x and to 38,400 or higher in Windows 9x/Me/XP.

**SYMPTOM 25-40** **Windows 9x/Me/XP doesn't detect the serial WinModem** First, make sure that the system has a free COM port or IRQ to use. If the WinModem was previously installed on the system with Windows 3.1x running, you'll need to search the SYSTEM.INI and WIN.INI files and remove all WinModem settings so that Windows 9x/Me/XP can detect the WinModem properly. Under Windows 9x/Me/XP, make sure that the modem is not listed in the Device Manager under Other Devices. If it is, delete the reference and reinstall (you may need to use the Add New Hardware Wizard). Next, make sure the WinModem's key (such as "USR1001" for the USR WinModem) is not in the Registry—if it is, remove the reference(s) from the Registry.

**SYMPTOM 25-41** **You have difficulty using a WinModem after upgrading your Windows version** If you double-click the WinModem icon in Control Panel, you may receive the following error message:

```
Error: There is no WinModem found in your computer, but some corrupted
files were found and they have been cleaned.
```

If you view your modem in the Device Manager, you may also notice *more* than one WinModem entry. This problem generally occurs because your WinModem is *not* using the most current .INF file or device driver. To correct this problem, uninstall the WinModem drivers, remove the multiple WinModem entries in Device Manager (along with any supporting software applets), then reinstall the most current WinModem drivers from scratch.

**SYMPTOM 25-42** **The WinModem is repeatedly detected when you start Windows** For example, after you uninstall a WinModem and restart your computer, Windows may try to install the modem and prompt you to restart your computer. After you restart your computer, Windows may prompt you to restart your computer again, and this behavior may continue indefinitely. This problem can occur if you uninstall the WinModem by using Device Manager (or the Modems tool in your Control Panel) instead of using the WinModem utility provided by the modem's manufacturer. To fix this problem, use the WinModem utility to uninstall your WinModem *instead* of using the Device Manager or the Modems tool. The following example is for Windows 98/Me:

1. Restart your computer and start Windows in the Safe mode.
2. Click Start | Settings | Control Panel.
3. Use the WinModem utility to uninstall your WinModem. For detailed information about how to use the WinModem utility to uninstall your WinModem, review the documentation included with your particular modem.
4. Restart your computer normally.
5. If you're prompted to install your WinModem again, use the software included with your modem to do so.

**SYMPTOM 25-43** **The dial-up modem's speaker volume is too low or too high** Virtually all dial-up modem models have a small speaker on board that provides audible feedback of dial tones and remote connection signals (the "handshaking"). If the communication software (or modem properties items under Windows) allows you to control the volume, make sure the speaker is enabled and set to a comfortable volume. If the software does not have speaker settings, add one of these AT commands to the initialization string:

- **L1** for low volume
- **L2** for medium volume
- **L3** for highest volume
- **M0** to turn the speaker off entirely

For example, if you want the volume low and the software uses the initialization string AT&F, change it to **AT&FL1**.

**SYMPTOM 25-44**    **The dial-up modem can connect to some modems, but not others**
Chances are that the remote modem is not responding because of the extended negotiation process used to establish the common connection between the two ends. You may have to disable part or all of the negotiation process. To force different communication speeds try these AT commands and press ENTER:

- Dualmode (V.90 or V.92)—56000 bps: **AT+MS=V92,1**
- V92 only (disable V.90)—56000 bps: **AT+MS=V92,0**
- V.90 only (disable V.92)—56000 bps: **AT+MS=V90,0**
- Disable both 56K and autorate on V.34—33600 bps: **AT+MS=V34,1**
- V.34—33600 bps: **AT+MS=V34,0**
- V.32bis—14400 bps: **AT+MS=V32B,0**
- V.32—9600 bps: **AT+MS=V32,0**
- 2400 bps: **AT+MS=V22B,0**
- 1200 bps: **AT+MS=V22,0**

There are other configurations that can be forced as well. If you need to select a particular configuration, use the AT command strings shown here (you can always return to the modem's default configuration by typing **AT&F** and pressing ENTER):

- MNP 5/MNP 4 operation: **AT\N5**
- LAPM only (V.42): **AT\N4**
- MNP 4 only: **AT\N5%C0**
- V.42bis data compression: **AT+DCS=1,0**
- V.44 data compression only: **AT+DCS=0,1**
- Auto-answer: **ATS0=1**

**SYMPTOM 25-45**    **The V.92 dial-up modem doesn't connect reliably at V.92 speeds**
Several possible issues can affect modem connection reliability, but firmware is often the culprit. Verify that you have the latest modem firmware downloaded from the manufacturer's Web site. Also make sure that your ISP offers V.92 service at the access number you're calling.

**SYMPTOM 25-46    Errors are constantly occurring in your V.17 fax transmissions**
As a rule, sending fax transmissions over a modem should present no special problems for a PC, but there are some issues to keep in mind. First, your modem initialization string could be insufficient or incomplete for fax transmissions. Enter the correct initialization string (determined by your particular dialup modem) for fax support, such as **AT&H3&I2&R2S7=90**. You could also have a disruptive TSR program running in the background. Disable any TSR programs and try the communication again. There could be an outdated communications driver on your system. Load the communications driver that came with your fax software, or update the driver from the manufacturer (this may require you to reinstall your internal modem). Finally your baud rate may be set too high. Try a lower baud rate of 9600 bps.

**SYMPTOM 25-47    Your faxes are garbled when using a class 2 fax/modem**    When you open the fax in a Windows 9x/Me/XP application, the output may resemble a bar code or contain blank pages. This is almost always a problem with the fax/modem, since some class 2 fax/modems reverse the bit order of incoming faxes. To correct this problem, switch the "bit order" of incoming faxes for each of your affected fax/modems by editing the Registry:

1. Exit your fax/modem software, then launch your Registry Editor (REGEDIT).

2. Locate the following Registry key:

   ```
   Hkey_Local_Machine\Software\Microsoft\At Work Fax\Local Modems
   \TAPI0001<xxxx>
   ```

   where *<xxxx>* is a unique TAPI identifier for the fax/modem; then add the string value **CL2SWBOR** to that Registry key.

3. Set the string value for CL2SWBOR to **1**.

4. Save your changes and quit the Registry Editor, then restart your computer.

**SYMPTOM 25-48    You cannot dial phone numbers more than 32 characters long**
When you try to dial a long phone number (over 32 characters) under Windows, your dial-up modem may not respond or dial out. This is typically a driver issue and is usually caused when using a controller-less modem with a "standard" (or "generic") modem driver instead of the driver that is specifically designed for your particular modem. To resolve this issue, you should obtain and install the most current modem driver for your particular modem.

**SYMPTOM 25-49    You cannot get the modem's "distinctive ring" feature to work**
Most new dial-up modems support the "distinctive ring" service provided by many telephone companies. This allows the modem to reside on the same physical telephone line as other devices, but only answer when the proper ringing pattern is received. Improper modem configuration is the most common problem. Try calling the distinctive ring numbers associated to your telephone line and see that each number rings with the required pattern. Note that the "distinctive ring" service is not available from all telephone companies and service areas. Next, check the initialization string for **S101.** Modems supporting "distinctive ring" usually control the feature through register **S101**. A typical AT command string may appear such as "**AT&FS101=60**". A typical setting list is shown here:

| S101=0 | Detect all ringing cadences and report them with RING result code |
| S101=1 | Enables the RING result codes; all ringing types will be reported |
| S101=30 | Report only unidentified ring types |
| S101=46 | Report only ring type D |
| S101=54 | Report only ring type C |
| S101=58 | Report only ring type B |
| S101=60 | Report only ring type A |
| S101=62 | Disables *all* ringing detection—the modem will not answer any ring |

To specify a particular ring type, you must *disable* the other ring types with this register.

Next, check the initialization string for **-SDR**. Rather than using S-register 101, some modems use the **-SDR** command to configure "distinctive ring" operation. A typical AT command string may appear such as **AT&F-SDR=1**. A setting list is shown here:

| -SDR=0 | Disables the distinctive ring function |
| -SDR=1 | Enables distinctive ring type 1 |
| -SDR=2 | Enables distinctive ring type 2 |
| -SDR=3 | Enables distinctive ring type 1 and 2 |
| -SDR=4 | Enables distinctive ring type 3 |
| -SDR=5 | Enables distinctive ring type 1 and 3 |
| -SDR=6 | Enables distinctive ring type 2 and 3 |
| -SDR=7 | Enables distinctive ring type 1,2, and 3 |

**SYMPTOM 25-50**     **You cannot get the modem's Caller ID feature to work**   Many new dial-up modems support the Caller ID service provided by many telephone companies. This allows the modem to identify the telephone number and caller to the computer's communication software when the ringing line is answered. Improper modem configuration is the most common problem. Before you do anything else, check the Caller ID service. Connect any Caller ID-compatible telephone or phone box to the telephone line and make sure that the ID service is working properly. Note that the Caller ID service is not available from all telephone companies and service areas. Also, remove other Caller ID devices. It is possible that other caller ID compatible telephones of phone boxes may be interfering with the modem. Try removing any other devices from the phone line. Check the initialization string for %CCID. Modems supporting Caller ID usually control the feature through a %CCID command. A typical AT command string may appear such as **AT&F%CCID=1**. A setting list is shown here:

| %CCID=0 | Turns Caller ID off |
| %CCID=1 | Gives Caller ID data using a formatted output |
| %CCID=2 | Gives Caller ID data using an unformatted output |

Finally, check the initialization string for **#CID**. Rather than using the **%CCID** command, some modems support Caller ID using the **#CID** command. A typical command string may appear such as **AT&F#CID=1**. A setting list is shown here:

| | |
|---|---|
| AT#CID=0 | Turns Caller ID off |
| AT#CID=1 | Gives Caller ID data using a formatted output |
| AT#CID=2 | Gives Caller ID data using an unformatted output |

There are two special messages that may be sent instead of Caller ID information. "O" means that the caller is *Out* of the Caller ID service area—usually a long distance call. "P" is for *Private* and will be displayed for callers who have made arrangements with their phone company to have their numbers blocked.

**SYMPTOM 25-51**   **You cannot recall previous Caller ID data**   This assumes that normal Caller ID features are proven to be working correctly. In most cases, your communication software is not sending the correct AT command to your modem. Check the Caller ID feature and make sure that Caller ID is enabled using the **%CCID** or **#CID** commands as in the previous symptom. Caller ID *must* be enabled first before data can be recalled. Check the initialization string for **%CRID**. Caller ID data can typically be recalled using the **%CRID** command such as **AT%CRID=0** (recall formatted data) or "**AT%CRID=1**" (recall unformatted data).

**SYMPTOM 25-52**   **The modem will not establish a connection through a cellular telephone**   In most cases, the modem is not configured properly. Check the SCM setting first—make sure that the *Station Class Mark* (SCM) level is set correctly. Try resetting the modem with an **AT&F1** command. Check the phone type. Make sure that the telephone is set to *analog* mode—the digital mode may interfere with modem operation.

**SYMPTOM 25-53**   **The modem will not fax properly through a cellular telephone**   In most cases, the modem is not configured properly. Check the modem's initialization string first and make sure that the initialization string is set correctly. A basic command string may be **AT&F1E1V1&C1&D2\Q3S7=90S10=60** (though this may not work on all modems). Check the *data rate* next. For faxing, see that the data rate is set to 4800. You may use the command **AT%B4800**.

**SYMPTOM 25-54**   **You cannot connect the DSL system to the Internet**   For example, you installed the software and connected the DSL modem to a suitable phone line, but you cannot connect to the Internet. You may also find that the connection lights don't appear in the modem's Configuration and Monitoring Application dialog box. There are several common issues to check. First make sure you've securely connected the RJ-11 phone cable from the wall jack to the DSL modem connector on the back of your computer. Also double-check that you've connected the RJ-11 phone cable to a DSL line, not a standard telephone line—you *cannot* use a standard telephone line for DSL service *unless* that phone line has been identified for DSL service. Next, see that there isn't a filter installed on the phone line connected to your DSL modem. Filters should only be installed on the phone lines *not* wired for DSL service. Now review all the information given to you by your service provider (pay particular attention to the VPI and VCI numbers) and see that the information is correctly entered for the modem.

It's always worth a quick check with the service provider to verify that the service is up and available.

**SYMPTOM 25-55**    **The cable modem is installed, but it doesn't work**    Your cable modem may have been installed with an IRQ conflict. Open the Device Manager and check for a yellow exclamation point over the cable modem's entry (for example, "3Com U.S. Robotics Cable Modem") in the Network Adapters section. If the modem has a yellow exclamation point, it suffers from a resource conflict (a red "X" means the device is disabled). Uninstall the modem by highlighting it and then clicking the Remove button. You will be asked if you wish to uninstall the device. Click OK. Next, you need to free an IRQ for the modem. (See Chapter 11 for more information on conflict resolution.) Restart your computer and try reinstalling the cable modem again. Some versions of Windows will not support *both* the cable modem and a network interface card (such as an Ethernet card) at the same time. You may need to uninstall or disable any existing network interface cards in your computer before installing the cable modem card.

**SYMPTOM 25-56**    **The cable modem scans for an active channel, pauses on an active channel, but instead of locking on to it, continues to scan for active channels**    Your internal cable modem may be assigned to IRQ 12—this is often a problem (although Windows 9x/Me/XP will typically not report it as a problem). IRQ 12 is normally reserved as the interrupt for a system's PS/2 (mouse) port. Open the Device Manager and then click Network Adapters. Double-click the entry for your cable modem (for example, "3Com Cable Modem") and then click Resources. Look for "Interrupt Request" in the Resource Type column. If the number listed to the right is "12," you may need to move the cable modem to a different IRQ (or simply move the PCI modem card to another slot closer to the processor).

**SYMPTOM 25-57**    **The cable modem scans for an active channel, but never locks on to one**    Check the cable and connections between your cable modem and the CATV jack at the wall—make sure the connections are reasonably tight. Try rebooting the PC and see if the cable modem will re-scan and achieve a good channel lock. If the problem persists, the signal from your cable company's equipment may be too weak. Call your cable company to determine whether or not this may be the problem.

**SYMPTOM 25-58**    **During modem registration, you receive a "DHCP offer receive" error**    This type of error generally means that the cable modem is encountering difficulties obtaining an IP address. Click on the "Register again" button—registration may proceed in spite of this error. Start by checking the network adapter. Under Windows 9x/Me, click Start | Settings | Control Panel. Double-click the Network icon. Under Windows XP, click Start | My Network Places | View network settings. Right-click the Local Area Connection entry and click Properties to open the Local Area Connection Properties dialog (refer to Figure 25-9). In the list of installed network components that appears, highlight the TCP/IP -> Dial-Up Adapter entry and then click Properties. In the TCP/IP Properties dialog that appears, click the IP Address tab. Make sure the Obtain an IP Address Automatically option is checked. Click OK and close all open windows. Reboot the PC and try the cable modem again.

**SYMPTOM 25-59**    **During modem registration, you receive a "TFTP Error code =4 (timeout)"**    This type of error generally means that the cable modem is having troubles with the system's TCP/IP stack. Click on the "Register again" button—registration may proceed in spite of this error. Check the TCP/IP stack next. Under Windows 9x/Me, click Start | Settings | Control Panel. Double-click the Network icon. Under Windows XP, click Start | My Network Places | View network settings. Right-click the Local Area Connection entry and click Properties to open the Local Area Connection Properties dialog (such as Figure 25-9 earlier). In the list of installed network components, highlight the TCP/IP -> Dial-Up Adapter entry and then click Properties. In the TCP/IP Properties dialog that appears, click the IP Address tab. Make sure the "Obtain an IP address automatically" option is checked. Click OK and close all open windows. Reboot your computer and try again. If registration fails again after rebooting the system, contact your cable company for additional support or suggestions.

# Further Study

**Agere Systems**   www.agere.com/index.html
**Boca Research**   www.bocaresearch.com
**Sonic Blue (Diamond Multimedia)**   www.diamondmm.com
**ITU**   www.itu.int
**ModemHelp**   www.modemhelp.com/index3.html
**Motorola**   www.mot.com
**US Robotics**   www.3com.com/56k/index.html
**WinDrivers**   www.windrivers.com
**Zoom Telephonics**   www.zoomtel.com

# 26

# MOTHERBOARD TROUBLESHOOTING

The *motherboard* is the heart of any personal computer (Figure 26-1). It is the motherboard that provides system resources (such as IRQ lines, DMA channels, I/O locations), supports the core components such as the CPU, chipset(s), and *real-time clock* (RTC), and handles all system memory—including DDR SDRAM or RDRAM, BIOS ROM, and CMOS RAM. Many current motherboards also incorporate additional cost-saving features such as USB ports, integrated video, onboard sound, and even an Ethernet port for network access. Indeed, virtually all of a PC's capabilities are defined by motherboard components. This chapter provides a guided tour of contemporary motherboards and shows you how to translate error information and symptoms into motherboard repairs.

## Active, Passive, and Modular

Before going any further, you should understand the difference between a motherboard and a backplane. For the purposes of this book, a *motherboard* is a printed circuit board containing most of the processing components required by the computer (such as the typical motherboard in Figure 26-1). This is certainly the most common form of motherboard that you will encounter as a technician. PC purists often refer to a

**FIGURE 26-1**   The Gigabyte GA-8IEXP Pentium 4 motherboard provides integrated sound and LAN support, along with USB 2.0 ports (Courtesy of Motherboards.org)

motherboard as an *active backplane*. The term "active" is used because there are sophisticated chips running on the board. The advantage of a motherboard is its comprehensive nature—the motherboard virtually *is* the PC. Unfortunately, the motherboard has disadvantages. Namely, it is difficult to upgrade because everything else in the system connects to it. Aside from plugging in an upgraded CPU or adding RAM, the only real way to upgrade a motherboard is to replace it with a newer one. For example, the only way to add PCI bus slots to an all-ISA motherboard is to replace the motherboard with one containing PCI slots. Obviously, this can be a time-consuming and error-prone process for the novice.

On the other hand, a backplane (also referred to as a *passive backplane*) is little more than a board containing interconnecting slots. There are no major chips on the backplane (except perhaps some power supply regulating circuitry). The CPU, system RAM, BIOS ROM, and other central processing components are fabricated onto a board that simply plugs into one of the backplane slots. Other expansion devices (such as a video board, drive controller, sound board, and so on) just plug into adjacent slots. The PS/2 was one of the first PCs to use a backplane design. Backplane systems are typically somewhat easier to troubleshoot. Unlike traditional motherboards that require the entire system to be disassembled, a processor board can be removed and replaced as easily as any other expansion board, so it is also a simple matter to upgrade the PC by installing a new processor board. The great limitation to backplane-based systems is the bus. Where traditional motherboards can optimize a system with different busses, the backplane is limited to a single bus style that interconnects the various cards (usually ISA or MCA). High-performance bus architectures like PCI or AGP are not always available.

In an effort to provide a motherboard that is more upgradable and serviceable, manufacturers often experiment with *modular* motherboards. The modular motherboard places the CPU, math coprocessor, and key support chips on a replaceable card, which plugs into a motherboard that in turn holds the BIOS ROM, CMOS RAM, system RAM, other more traditional system controllers, and bus interfaces. The modular approach allows a motherboard to be upgraded far more than a traditional motherboard without having to replace it. The replacement processing card is much cheaper than a new motherboard. However, today's PC architectures can usually support a variety of CPU versions and an extensive amount of RAM on the original motherboard, so "modular" motherboards have never become a very popular approach.

Contrary to popular belief, expansion bus connectors are not needed to make a motherboard. You can see this in any laptop or notebook computer motherboard. The devices that traditionally demanded expansion slots (such as video and drive controllers) are easily fabricated directly onto the motherboard. Even the motherboards used in most desktop and tower PCs over the last few years frequently integrate video, sound, and drive controller circuits. If upgrades are needed in the future, the motherboard-based circuits can be disabled with jumpers (or through the CMOS Setup), and replacement subsystems are plugged into expansion slots.

# Understanding Active Motherboards

Before you can troubleshoot a motherboard effectively, it's important that you know your way around and be able to identify most of the common components. Although each motherboard is designed differently, this process of identification is not nearly as difficult as it might sound. This part of the chapter will familiarize you with the essential functions and components that you'll find on a modern motherboard.

## SOCKETS AND SLOTS

Every motherboard will require at least one processor, and a processor must be inserted into an appropriate slot or socket (see Figure 26-2). When examining a motherboard, you'll probably find it described with a slot or socket designation. Typical designations include Socket 7, Socket 8, Slot 1, Socket 370, Slot 2, or Slot A, Socket A, Socket 423, Socket 478, and more. Since processors are not interchangeable with different types of slots or sockets, it's important that you understand the role each connection scheme plays:

- **Socket 7**    These older motherboards are generally designed for Pentium and Pentium MMX CPUs, as well as AMD K6-2, K6-3, or Cyrix MIII processors. You may also see these motherboards designated as "Super 7" when there is an AGP slot available.

- **Socket 8**    These older motherboards are made for Pentium Pro CPUs. You won't find many Socket 8 motherboards still in use, and those that you do encounter will mainly be in older network servers or workstations.

- **Slot 1**    These motherboards use a Single Edge Cartridge (SEC) processor box rather than a pin grid array chip (a conventional "chip") and are intended for Pentium II and Pentium III systems. These are occasionally dubbed "Slot 242" because of the 242 contacts on the slot connector.

- **Socket 370**    These motherboards are intended for later model Pentium III and most Celeron versions of the Pentium processor. These socket-mounted processors are often easier to cool and have fewer issues with installation and retention.

- **Slot 2**    These motherboards are also intended for SEC processors, but these accommodate the slightly advanced Pentium II/III Xeon processors. In virtually all cases, Slot 2 motherboards are used

**FIGURE 26-2**    The Tyan Trinity 510 motherboard supports a single Pentium 4 processor in a Socket 478 connector (Courtesy of Tyan Computer Corp.)

in high-end network server and workstation systems, so you'll rarely (if ever) find Slot 2 motherboards in the hands of home or small-business users. These are sometimes referred to as "Slot 330" because of the 330 contacts on the slot connector.

■ **Slot A**    These motherboards are intended for the AMD Athlon processor—AMD's answer to the Intel Pentium III/4. While a Slot 1 and Slot A connector may appear identical at first glance (both use a 242-pin slot connector), they are incompatible, so you must use a Slot A motherboard when building or working on an Athlon-based system.

■ **Socket A**    These socket-based motherboards (often called "Socket 462") are designed for later model AMD Athlon and most AMD Duron processors. As with other socket-based designs, there are fewer installation, cooling, and retention issues. However, Socket A is not compatible with other socket types.

■ **Socket 423/478**    These motherboards (such as Intel's D850GB) are intended for socket versions of the Pentium 4 processor. The older Socket 423 is not compatible with other socket types. Later Pentium 4 processors employ the 478-pin socket, so opt for Socket 478 motherboards wherever possible.

■ **Socket 603**    These motherboards are intended to support the larger and more complex Intel Pentium 4/Xeon processor and are usually found with high-end workstation and network server systems. Don't be surprised to find two or four sockets for Xeon-based motherboards.

■ **PAC418**    The PAC418 is a cartridge-type slot intended for Intel's Itanium family of high-end processors. These processors are also intended for high-end workstation and network server environments; motherboards supporting the PAC418 may offer two, four, or more connectors for multiprocessing applications.

The important thing to remember here is that motherboard sockets/slots have distinct limitations. A given socket or slot type is not only limited in the type of processors that it can accept, but it is also limited in the processor speeds that can be used. For example, a DFI P2XBL (440BX chipset-based) motherboard can support Slot 1 (Pentium II) processors from 233 MHz to 500 MHz. By comparison, the later model Intel VC820 (i820 chipset-based) motherboard can support Slot 1 (Pentium III) processors from 450 MHz to 733 MHz. Both motherboards use the Slot 1 processor connector, but a different range of processors. Just because a motherboard offers a particular slot or socket, don't just assume that a corresponding processor type will work—it may not. Always check the system or motherboard documentation to verify the compatible processors for a given motherboard model.

## THE POWER OF CHIPSETS

The next thing you'll notice about most modern motherboards is the general absence of chips. There are perhaps two or three large chips on the whole motherboard (some of the most powerful support chips are cooled with their own heat sink/fan unit). That's because virtually all of the motherboard's many functions are handled by a suite of powerful interrelated chips (known as the *chipset,* detailed in Chapter 9). The chipset forms the "glue" that connects your processor and memory with your drive controllers (the FDD and HDD controllers), expansion busses (e.g., PCI, AGP, and AMR/CNR slots), I/O ports (serial, parallel, PS/2, USB), and sometimes even a video controller and sound controller. Figure 26-3 illustrates the importance of chipsets on the Intel D850GB Pentium 4 motherboard.

This block diagram places the 850 chipset squarely at the center of the motherboard's functionality. The *82850 Memory Controller Hub* (MCH) is responsible for interfacing to the processor, system memory, and AGP bus. (This is not a mistake since AGP makes use of system RAM, so a direct connection is needed through the chipset.) The *82801BA I/O Controller Hub* (ICH2) manages the UDMA/33/66/100 drive controllers, USB ports, hardware monitor, PCI bus, and a sound subsystem (eliminating the need for a separate sound card). There is also an *SST49LF004A Firmware Hub* (FWH), which basically manages the system firmware (the BIOS) and CMOS RAM/RTC functions. A powerful *LPC I/O Controller* chip provides the floppy drive interface and all of your I/O ports. Other than a few other buffer and voltage regulator chips, that's it—that's your computer.

The block diagram of Figure 26-3 serves as a recent example for the purposes of this discussion. Your own motherboard may use a very different selection of chips and features.

## EXPANSION SLOTS

Of course, our motherboard is rather incomplete by itself. There are numerous other features and functions (such as a video adapter, SCSI host controller, network card, and many other devices) that may be added to the system depending on your particular needs. These *expansion* devices are added through the use of expansion slots on the motherboard. There are three general types of expansion slots (detailed in Chapter 7): ISA, PCI, and AGP.

■  **ISA**  The *Industry Standard Architecture* bus is the "granddaddy" of expansion slots, and is rapidly falling into disuse. (You'll note that there are none on the D850GB motherboard, or the Trinity 510 shown earlier in Figure 26-2.) Older motherboard models might use an ISA slot to accommodate a low-bandwidth device such as a legacy modem or sound card, but most contemporary data-intensive devices are better served by the newer expansion slots such as PCI.

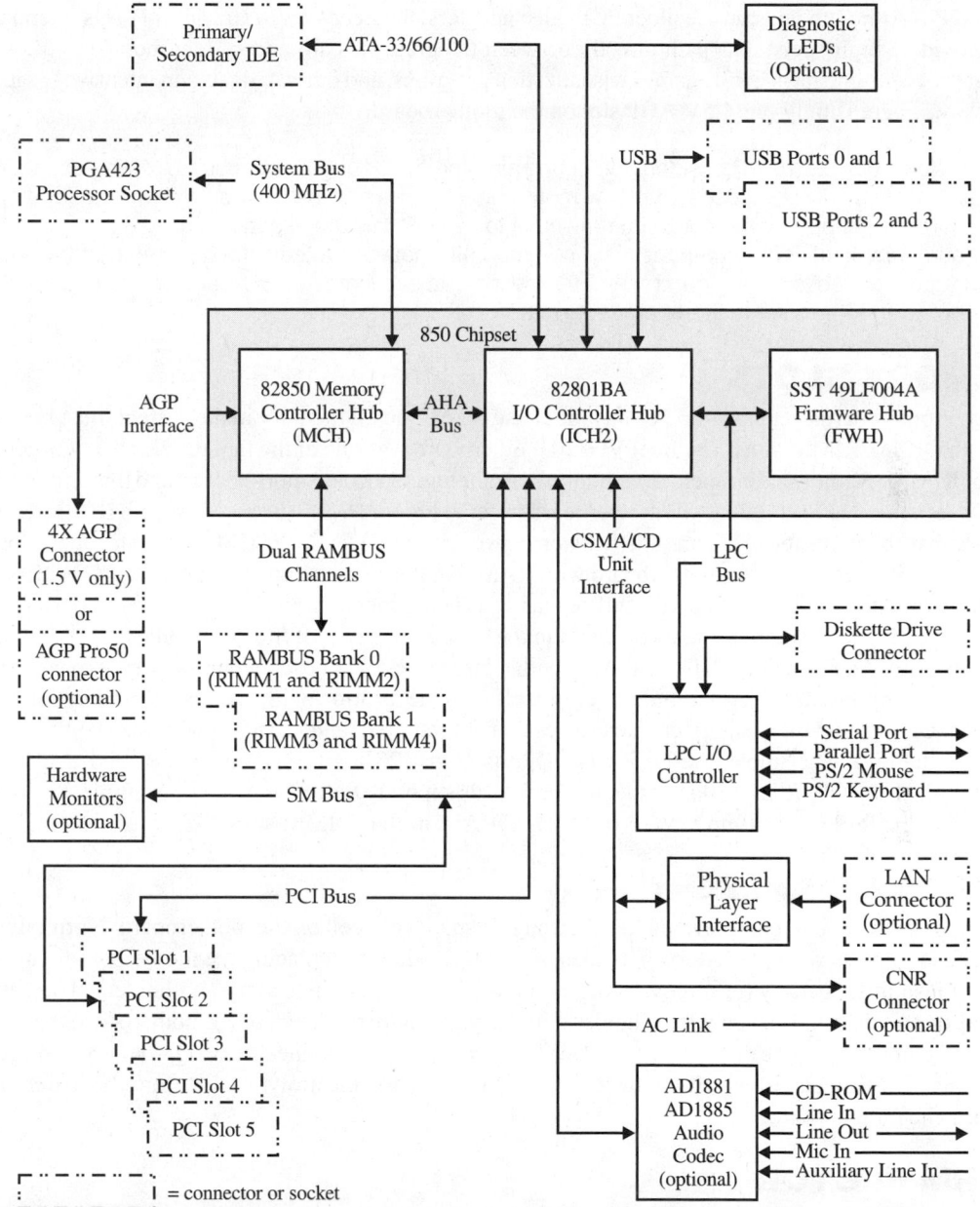

**FIGURE 26-3**    A block diagram of the Intel D850GB Pentium 4 motherboard (Courtesy of Intel Corporation)

■ **PCI**   The *Peripheral Component Interconnect* scheme is a versatile, high-speed, "intelligent" bus. It is the preferred bus architecture for today's demanding devices such as SCSI host adapters, video capture cards, and network interface cards. The D850GB offers five PCI slots that are all handled by the ICH2 (the South Bridge) component of the chipset.

■ **AGP**    Although you can use older PCI video adapters, the *Accelerated Graphics Port* is intended to provide a high-speed data path directly between the graphics card and system memory—allowing improved frame rates for 3D games, visualization programs, and other "calculation intensive" graphics work. There is only one 1.5V AGP slot on the motherboard.

Expansion slots are a vital consideration during a motherboard upgrade because existing expansion cards must typically be added to the new motherboard. If the new motherboard doesn't offer a suitable number of appropriate slots, you may have to select alternate expansion devices—raising the cost and complexity of the upgrade. One common alternative is to select a new motherboard with integrated features (such as sound or an Ethernet port) to eliminate aging expansion devices that you may not want to transfer to the upgraded system.

## MEMORY SLOTS

Today, motherboards generally do not include "base RAM," so all memory in the system must be added through DIMM/RIMM slots. The Intel VC820 motherboard was one of the first to offer the new generation of RIMM (Rambus inline memory module) slots for high-speed memory access, and this emphasis on RIMM is continued on the D850GB motherboard (refer to Figure 26-3). The problem with DIMM/RIMM slots is that there are few of them—perhaps only two or three. DIMM/RIMM units can supply lots of memory, so it's easy to stuff a motherboard with RAM, but it's harder to upgrade your RAM. With only a few memory slots, you may find yourself replacing existing memory modules with larger ones (rather then just adding more modules like you could in the "good old days" of SIMM modules). With memory prices on the rise, replacing a DIMM/RIMM with a larger model may add an unforeseen expense to the system. It's important for you to familiarize yourself with the location of the memory slots on your motherboard. Understand the memory characteristics that are required, and learn just what size combinations are acceptable. For example, the D850GB supports from 128MB to 2GB of fast PC800 and PC600 Rambus memory (RDRAM). Many other motherboards support DDR SDRAM. For example, the Trinity 510 in Figure 26-2 supports up to 2GB of DDR SDRAM in four DIMM slots.

## THE CMOS BATTERY

Your CMOS RAM contents are maintained through a small coin cell on the motherboard. Normally you don't need to mess with the battery, but when you're upgrading or replacing the motherboard, you may need to install the battery (or remove protective material between the battery and holder). The battery should sit properly and securely in its holder. Similarly, if you're taking an older motherboard out of service, remember to remove the battery and place it in a safe plastic container. Leaving a battery in place for a prolonged period can eventually allow the battery to leak, and electrolyte acids from the battery may damage the motherboard.

## FORM FACTOR

Another important classification that you must be familiar with is the motherboard's form factor. In simplest terms, the *form factor* is little more than the dimensions of the board and its mounting hole positions, as well as the general layout and placement of key components such as the CPU, memory modules, expansion slots, and I/O ports. Today, there are three major form factors to consider: AT, ATX, and NLX (though ATX is by far the most prevalent). It is important for you to understand that form factors do not directly influence performance. A "baby AT" motherboard and an NLX motherboard can offer exactly the same performance characteristics. Form factor is most important in system assembly and access for service or upgrading.

## AT-Style Motherboards

The AT-style motherboards really represent the classic approach to component placement, as shown in the obsolete Tyan S1590 Trinity 100 AT motherboard of Figure 26-4. AT-style motherboards are typically available in two variations: the baby AT and the full AT. Both variations simply affect the overall dimensions of the motherboard. (Full AT motherboards are larger.) You can usually identify an AT-style motherboard based upon

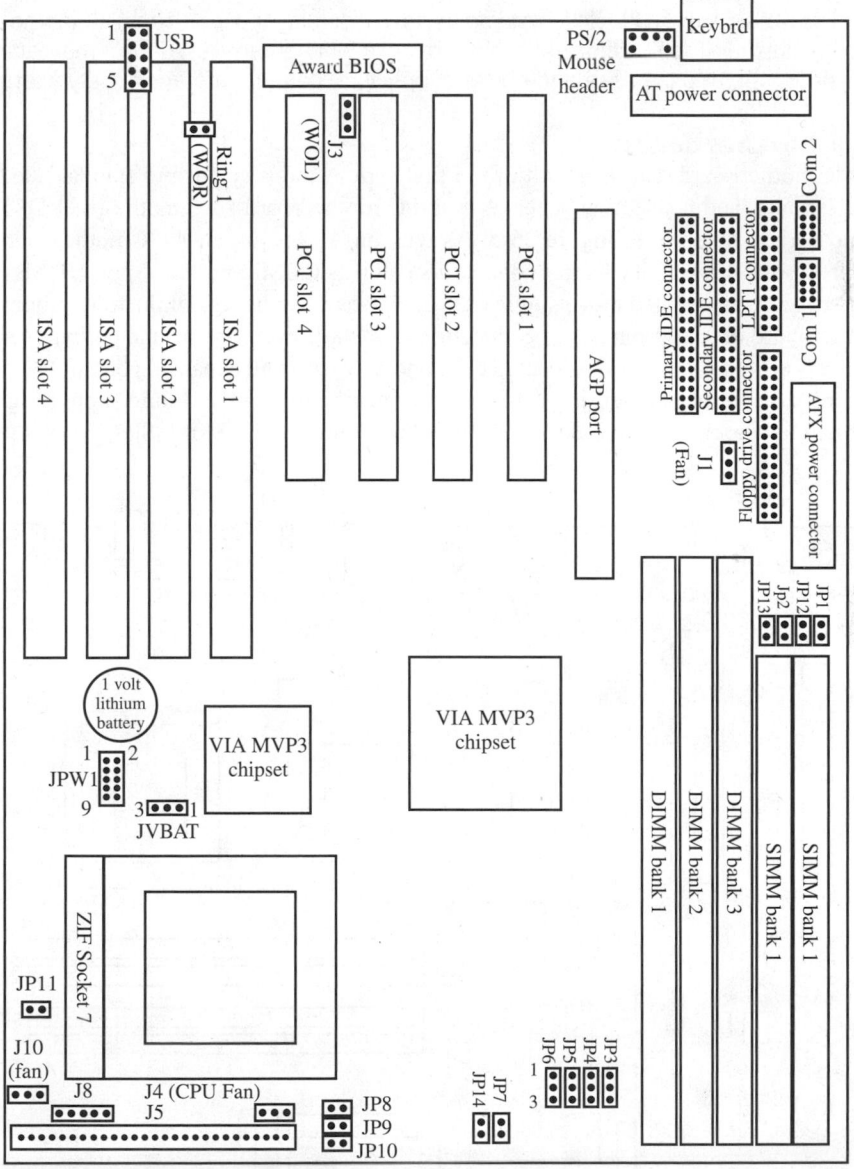

The tiny number "1"s next to jumpers of 3 pins or more indicate the position of pin 1 for that jumper.

**FIGURE  26-4**    The Tyan S1590 Trinity 100 AT-style motherboard layout (Courtesy of Tyan Computer Corporation)

three distinctions. First, look at the power connectors where the power supply attaches. An AT-style motherboard uses two sets of 6-pin inline connectors usually designated "P8" and "P9." Second, the CPU is usually positioned in line with one or more of the ISA bus slots (almost always obstructing full-length ISA cards). Third, the I/O ports of an AT motherboard (such as COM ports, LPT ports, PS/2 ports, USB ports, and so on) are often spread out along the back panel of the chassis. This often led to placement problems since case openings were not always standardized with port placement on the AT motherboard.

It is important to note that the AT style form factor is now obsolete, and few (if any) major motherboard manufacturers use the AT form factor. If you need to replace or upgrade an AT style motherboard, you may also need to upgrade the case and power supply to accommodate an ATX style form factor.

## ATX-Style Motherboards

The ATX-style motherboards are the result of the first serious industry push to standardize the dimensions, device layouts, and connection schemes of a PC motherboard such as the Intel D850GB ATX Pentium 4 motherboard shown in Figure 26-5. As with an AT layout, an ATX motherboard is distinguished by three points. First, all I/O port connectors (such as COM ports, LPT ports, USB ports, PS/2 ports, and so on) are concentrated into a single I/O panel located at the rear of the motherboard. Second, the ATX motherboard uses a 20-pin power connection from the power supply (and perhaps a supplemental 8-pin connection). Third, the CPU is located clear and away from all expansion bus slots—eliminating any interference with full-slot expansion cards. ATX motherboards can be found supporting all current CPU types (including Socket/Super 7, Socket 370, Socket A, Socket 432, Slot 1, Slot 2, Slot A, and so on).

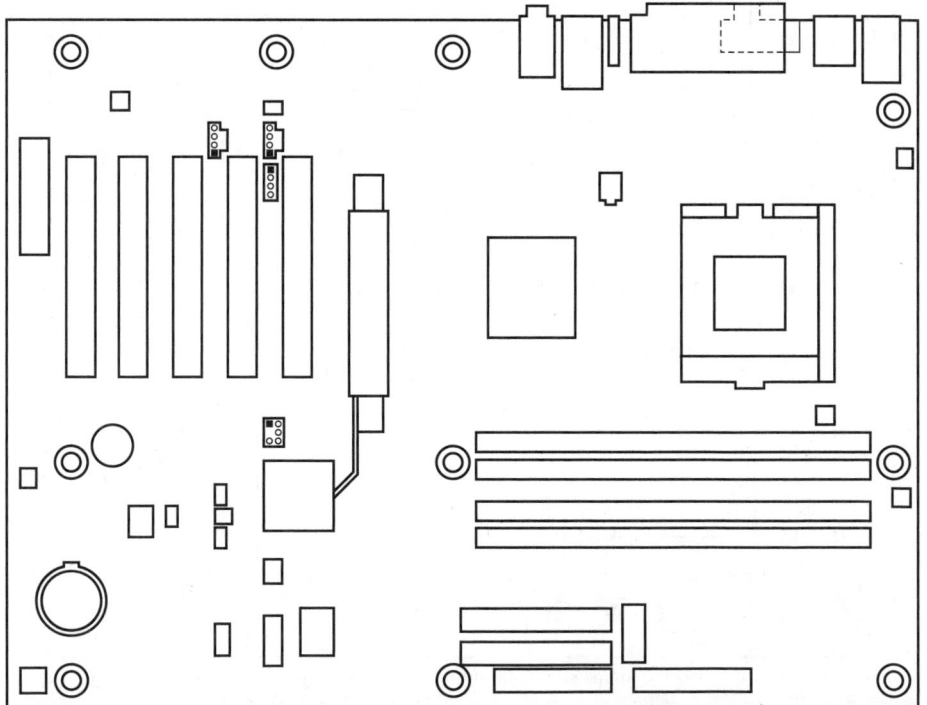

**FIGURE  26-5**    The Intel D850GB ATX-style motherboard layout (Courtesy of Intel Corporation)

## NLX-Style Motherboards

While ATX motherboards represented a good effort at standardization, they still retain all the assembly problems of AT-style motherboards—namely that the motherboard is cumbersome to install and time-consuming to upgrade or replace. The NLX-style motherboards (such as the Intel JN440BX NLX motherboard of Figure 26-6) overcome this disadvantage by making the motherboard a replaceable (also

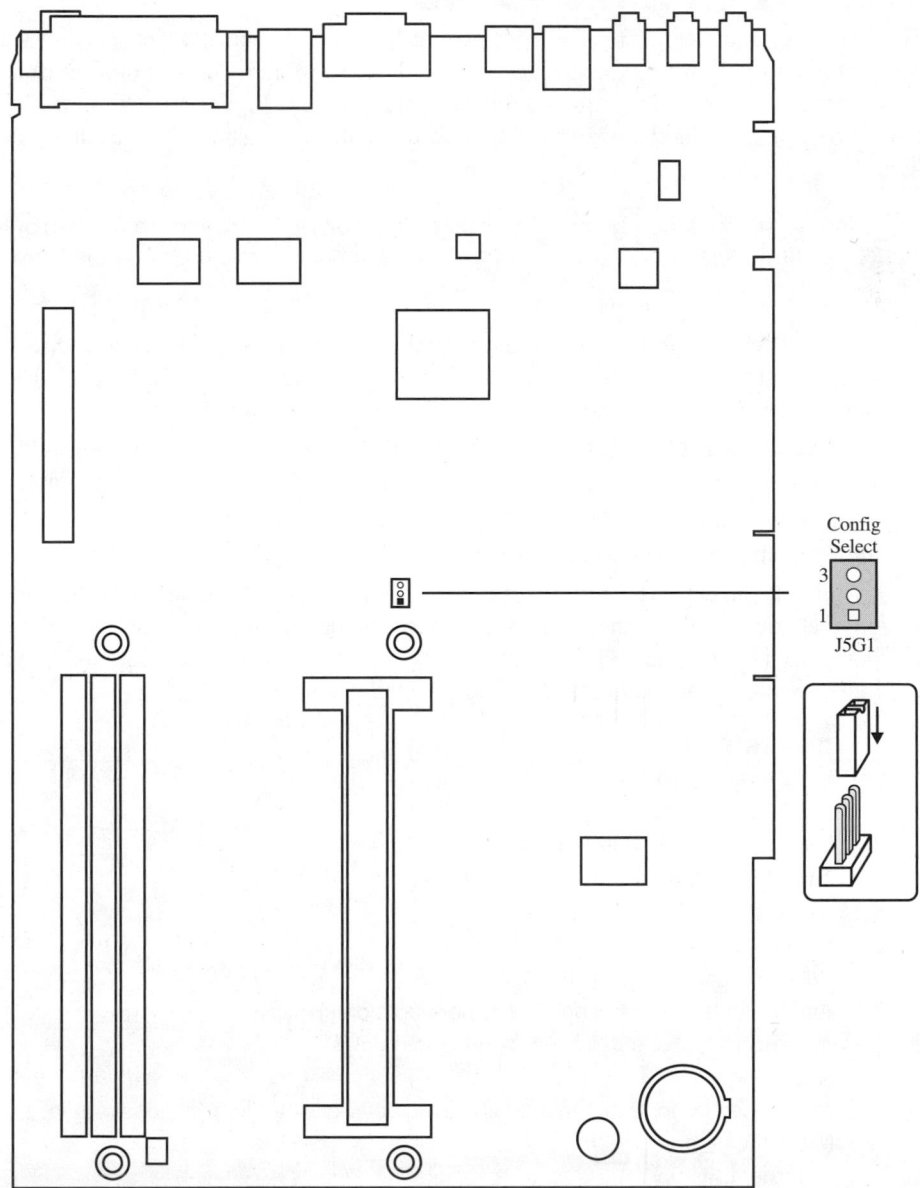

**FIGURE  26-6**     Simplified view of the Intel JN440BX NLX-style motherboard layout (Courtesy of Intel Corporation)

referred to as a *dockable*) device. All expansion slots and connection headers (such as speaker connector, power switch connector, and so on) are then moved to a *riser card*. The NLX motherboard itself then plugs into the riser card. Note the long card edge connector along the right side of the board that interfaces with the riser. In this fashion, the motherboard can quickly and easily be removed from the system to change jumpers, add memory, or install a replacement motherboard.

## LEARNING YOUR WAY AROUND

Now that you've seen some essential motherboard attributes, it's time to actually look up close at a current motherboard and identify the critical parts that you should expect to find. For the purposes of this book, we'll use the Intel D845EBT ATX Pentium 4 motherboard shown in Figure 26-7, along with the Intel D850GB motherboard. Other motherboards and form factors will appear a bit different, but the basic parts are the same.

The chipset and other components discussed next are presented for example purposes only. Your motherboard will undoubtedly use different chips (and chipsets)—each offering their own set of characteristics.

**A.    AD1980/1981A audio codec**    This optional chip can support audio features directly on the motherboard—eliminating the need to install a separate sound board. Speaker, line, and microphone connections are available on the motherboard's I/O panel.

**B.    Intel 82562ET network interface device**    The Intel 82562ET component provides a basic 10/100 Ethernet LAN interface to the back panel RJ-45 connector with integrated LEDs.

**C.    AGP bus connector**    This is the 1.5V AGP bus slot for the connection of your high-performance video adapter/accelerator.

**D.    I/O panel connections**    These are the serial, parallel, USB, Ethernet, and PS/2 ports (and so on) that you'll use to connect peripheral devices to the system. Figure 26-8 illustrates the I/O port layout for a D845EBT. The number of ports and their relative location may vary from model to model, but this figure is a good overall example.

| ITEM | DESCRIPTION |
|------|-------------|
| A | PS/2 mouse port |
| B | PS/2 keyboard port |
| C | IEEE 1394a-2000 (FireWire) port |
| D | Two USB ports |
| E | Serial port A |
| F | Parallel port |
| G | S/PDIF (optional) |
| H | Audio rear left/right out (for 6-channel audio only) |
| I | Audio center/LFE out (for 6-channel audio only) |
| J | Audio line in |
| K | Audio line out (for 2-channel audio); Front left/right out (for 6-channel audio) |
| L | Microphone in |
| M | Ethernet LAN port |
| N | Two USB ports |

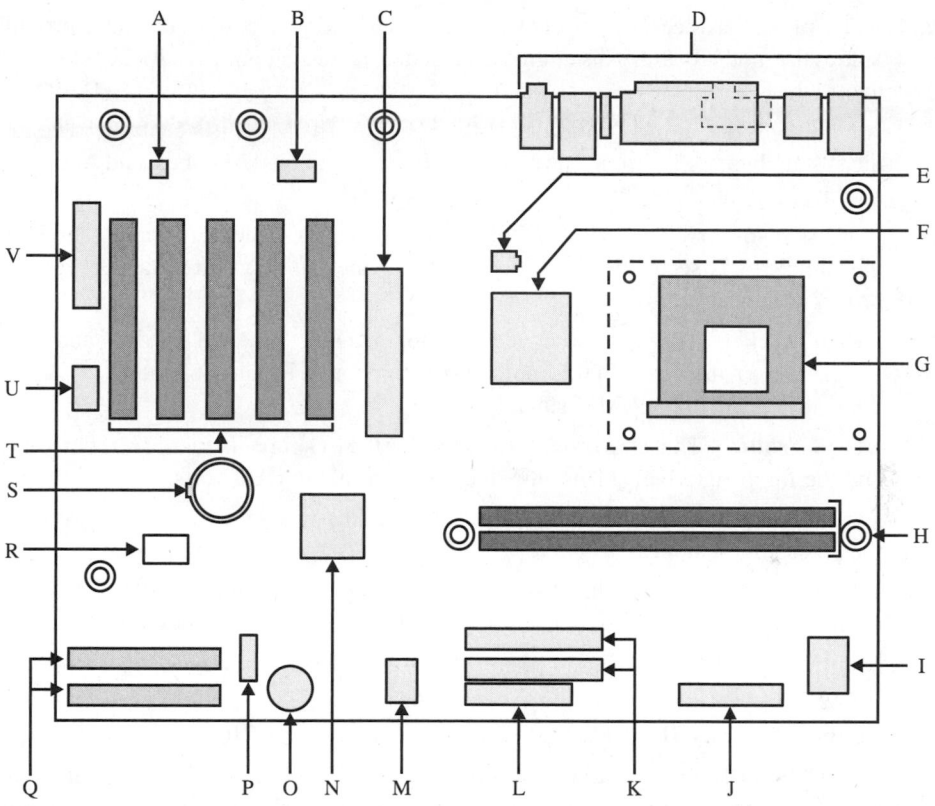

**FIGURE 26-7**    Identifying the major elements of an Intel D845EBT Pentium 4 motherboard (Courtesy of Intel Corporation)

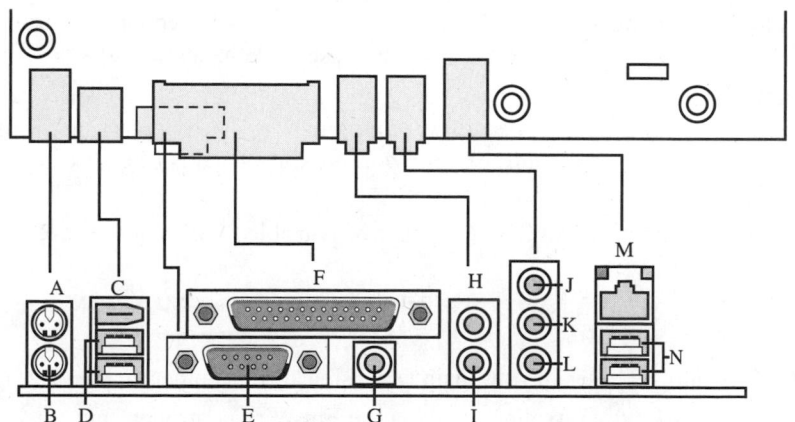

**FIGURE 26-8**    I/O connector layout for the D845EBT motherboard (Courtesy of Intel Corporation)

**E.**  **+12V power connector (ATX12V)**   This is an auxiliary power connector providing +12 Vdc to the motherboard. This might be needed to handle telephony, LAN, or other features of the motherboard.

**F.**  **Intel 82845E Memory Controller Hub (MCH)**   The MCH is a centralized controller for the system bus (a.k.a. "front side bus" or FSB), memory bus, AGP bus, and Accelerated Hub Architecture interface.

**G.**  **Processor socket**   This is the 478-pin connector for your Pentium 4 processor. Be sure that the processor is secure in the socket and that the cooling unit attaches properly to the processor housing.

**H.**  **DIMM sockets**   These two connectors support DDR SDRAM DIMMs and allow up to 2GB on the motherboard. If this motherboard supported Rambus memory (as the DB850GB does), these would be RIMM slots.

**I.**  **I/O controller**   This chip provides support for the I/O ports including serial, parallel, PS/2, and the floppy interface. (This chip does not control the USB ports.)

**J.**  **Power connector**   Connector J is the standard 20-pin ATX power connector provided by the ATX power supply.

**K.**  **IDE connectors**   These 40-pin ports handle the primary and secondary UDMA/100 IDE channels for your hard drives, CD drives, and other ATAPI/IDE devices.

**L.**  **Floppy drive connector**   This 34-pin port provides the interface for your conventional floppy drive.

**M.**  **4 Mbit Firmware Hub (FWH)**   This chip contains your BIOS and CMOS RAM.

**N.**  **Intel 82801DB I/O Controller Hub (ICH4)**   This ICH4 chip is a highly integrated controller that supports your HDD controller channels (including RAID support if it's available on your motherboard), USB ports, PCI bus, and audio subsystem chip(s).

**O.**  **Speaker**   This motherboard includes an onboard speaker device to supply beep codes at start time.

**P.**  **Front panel connector**   This header provides the pins that connect to the case wires (such as the power LED, power switch, key lock, reset switch, and so on).

**Q.**  **RAID connectors**   These 40-pin IDE connectors support additional hard drives in a RAID (redundant array of independent disks) configuration. This is a powerful feature that is used to provide redundant backups of your working drives and is often used on workstation or light-duty servers.

**R.**  **RAID controller**   This PD20267 chip is responsible for managing the RAID functions on the motherboard.

**S.**  **CMOS battery**   This is the coin cell that maintains your CMOS RAM contents. Be sure to replace the battery with an identical type.

**T.**  **PCI bus slots**   These are your main expansion slots for other PCI devices in the system.

**U.**  **IEEE 1394a-2000 controller**   This is the FireWire controller chip used to manage the FireWire port (refer to Figure 26-8).

**V.**  **CNR connector**   This connector supports the relatively new Intel CNR standard for dedicated, low-cost modem/networking devices.

## Audio Connectors

There are also numerous smaller audio connectors on the motherboard that you should be familiar with, and you can see several of them illustrated on the D850GB in Figure 26-9. Your particular motherboard may offer more or different connectors, but the D850GB supplies the following:

**A.   Auxiliary line input**   This is a sound channel that allows you to mix in an auxiliary audio signal. The pinout is listed here:

| PIN | SIGNAL NAME |
| --- | --- |
| Pin 1 | Left auxiliary signal |
| Pin 2 | Ground |
| Pin 3 | Ground |
| Pin 4 | Right auxiliary signal |

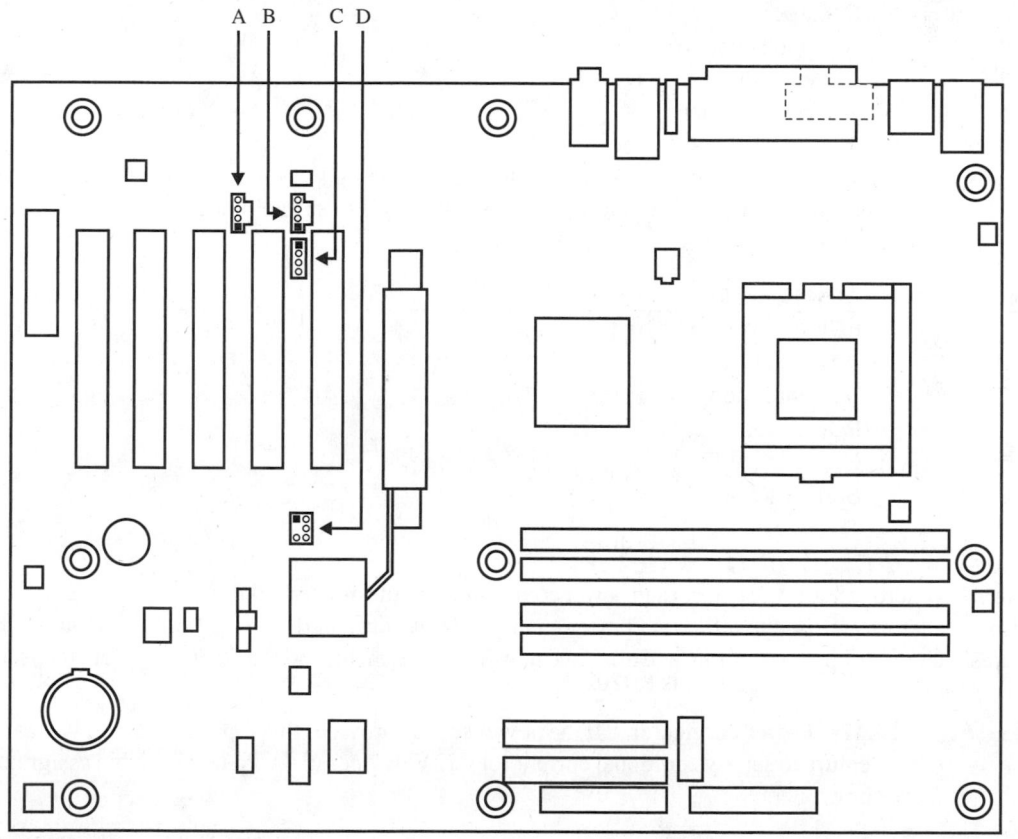

**FIGURE  26-9**   Identifying audio-based connectors on an Intel D850GB (Courtesy of Intel Corporation)

**B.  ATAPI CD audio connector**   This is a slightly different CD audio connector scheme using differential signaling. The presence of this second connector also lets you mix audio from a second compliant CD-ROM drive. The pinout is as follows:

| PIN | SIGNAL NAME |
| --- | --- |
| Pin 1 | Left audio signal |
| Pin 2 | Differential ground |
| Pin 3 | Differential ground |
| Pin 4 | Right audio signal |

**C.  "Legacy" CD audio connector**   This serves as the conventional audio connector found on most sound cards. Since the D850GB offers onboard sound support, you can feed the audio from a CD to this connector. The legacy pinout is as follows:

| PIN | SIGNAL NAME |
| --- | --- |
| Pin 1 | CD ground |
| Pin 2 | Audio left channel |
| Pin 3 | CD ground |
| Pin 4 | Audio right channel |

**D.  PC/PCI connector**   This is a serial interface to the PCI bus that can be used with several PCI-based devices that do not necessarily use a PCI bus. The pinout for this connector is listed here:

| PIN | SIGNAL NAME |
| --- | --- |
| Pin 1 | PCI data in |
| Pin 2 | Ground |
| Pin 3 | No connection |
| Pin 4 | PCI request out |
| Pin 5 | Ground |
| Pin 6 | Serial IRQ out |

## Power and Control Connectors

There are numerous hardware control and power connections on the motherboard, as shown in Figure 26-10. These connectors are used to attach the power supply, operate fans, and manage "wake" devices. These features are vital for proper cooling and effective power management, and the D850GB offers the following connections:

**A.  ATX12V Power connector**   If the power supply provides this 4-pin connector, you can use this feature to supply additional current for +12V devices in the system. The pin assignments are shown here:

| PIN | SIGNAL NAME |
| --- | --- |
| Pin 1 | Ground |
| Pin 2 | Ground |
| Pin 3 | +12V |
| Pin 4 | +12V |

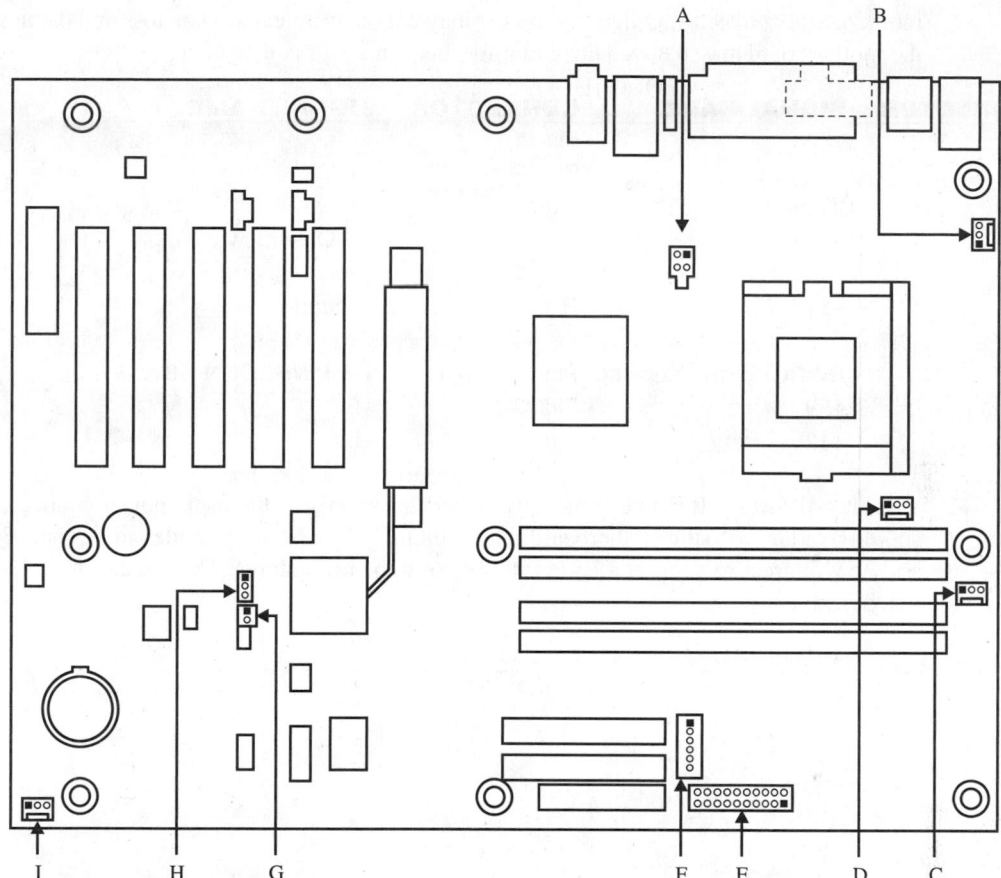

**FIGURE  26-10**    Identifying power and control connections on an Intel D850GB (Courtesy of Intel Corporation)

**B.**  **Processor Voltage Regulator Fan connector (FAN4)**    This is a 3-wire fan cable that provides power to the +12 Vdc processor voltage regulator fan. The third wire is grounded, so there is no tachometer control over the fan.

**C.**  **RIMM Fan connector (FAN2)**    This is a 3-wire fan cable that provides power to the +12 Vdc RIMM cooling fan used to cool the Rambus modules. The third wire provides a tachometer signal to the motherboard that the motherboard can use to monitor the fan's performance. Obviously, this type of cooling connection is not needed on motherboards that support SDRAM or DDR SDRAM modules.

**D.**  **Processor Fan connector (FAN3)**    This is a 3-wire fan cable that provides power to the +12 Vdc processor cooling fan. The third wire provides a tachometer signal to the motherboard that the motherboard can use to monitor the fan's performance.

**E.**  **Main Power connector**    The ATX power supply attaches to the motherboard at this 20-pin connection (item J in Figure 26-7). It is vital that this cable be securely attached to the motherboard connector. Otherwise, power may cut out erratically. Data loss and damage to the motherboard may result. The pinout for this connector is listed here:

| CONNECTOR | SIGNAL NAME | CONNECTOR | SIGNAL NAME |
|---|---|---|---|
| Pin 1 | +3.3V | Pin 11 | +3.3V |
| Pin 2 | +3.3V | Pin 12 | −12V |
| Pin 3 | Ground | Pin 13 | Ground |
| Pin 4 | +5V | Pin 14 | PS-ON# (power supply remote on/off) |
| Pin 5 | Ground | Pin 15 | Ground |
| Pin 6 | +5V | Pin 16 | Ground |
| Pin 7 | Ground | Pin 17 | Ground |
| Pin 8 | PWRGD (Power Good) | Pin 18 | TP_PWRCONN_18 |
| Pin 9 | +5V (Standby) | Pin 19 | +5V |
| Pin 10 | +12V | Pin 20 | +5V |

**F.   Auxiliary Power**   If the power supply provides a supplemental 6-pin power connector, it should be attached to the motherboard at this point. This connector provides additional +3.3V and +5V sources to support a larger number of onboard features. The pin assignments are listed next:

| PIN | SIGNAL NAME |
|---|---|
| Pin 1 | Ground |
| Pin 2 | Ground |
| Pin 3 | Ground |
| Pin 4 | +3.3V |
| Pin 5 | +3.3V |
| Pin 6 | +5V |

**G.   Wake On Ring connector**   This two-pin connector allows you to attach a device that will "wake" the system from a modem when an incoming ring is detected. The two signals are Ground and Ring.

**H.   Wake On LAN connector**   This connector allows you to attach a device that will "wake" the system from a LAN when a system is in the power-down state. The three pins are listed here:

| PIN | SIGNAL NAME |
|---|---|
| Pin 1 | +5 Vdc (standby) |
| Pin 2 | Ground |
| Pin 3 | Wake On LAN signal |

**I.   Chassis Fan connector (FAN1)**   This is a 3-wire fan cable that provides power to the +12 Vdc chassis cooling fan. The third wire provides a tachometer signal to the motherboard that the motherboard can use to monitor the fan's performance.

**Hardware Monitoring**   A growing number of motherboard makers are providing convenient tools to measure and report the thermal and power levels of a system. This type of *hardware monitoring* helps alert technicians to problems and can even flag events for investigation before serious hardware faults occur.

In many cases, the data available from voltage, fan, and temperature monitoring can be presented on demand through a Windows applet (such as the AOpen Smartguardian applet shown in Figure 26-11). In other cases, the data is accessible through the system's CMOS Setup or displayed in the BIOS banner at start time.

> You will generally need to install software to enable hardware monitoring and alerting features under Windows. This is usually available as an applet included with the motherboard's software CD.

## Front Panel Connector

Ultimately, you'll need to connect front panel cables to the motherboard to control power, reset, and so on. Figure 26-7 (shown earlier) illustrates the front panel connector for the Intel D845EBT motherboard as item "P". The pin assignments for the front panel connector are listed here:

| PIN SIGNAL | DESCRIPTION | PIN SIGNAL | DESCRIPTION |
|---|---|---|---|
| *Hard Drive Activity LED* | | Power LED | |
| 1; HD_PWR | Hard disk LED pull-up (330 ohms) to +5 V | 2; HDR_BLNK_GRN | Front panel green LED |
| 3; HAD# | Hard disk active LED | 4; HDR_BLNK_YEL | Front panel yellow LED |
| *Reset Switch* | | *On/Off Switch* | |
| 5; | Ground | 6; FPBUT_IN | Power switch |
| 7; FP_RESET# | Reset switch | 8; | Ground |
| *Power* | | *Not Connected* | |
| 9; +5 V | Power | 10; N/C | Not connected |

# MAKING SOME COMPARISONS

If you'd like to see how easily motherboards could vary from model to model, take another look at that Tyan motherboard shown earlier in Figure 26-4. There are some striking similarities, but here are a few of the differences that should stand out against a motherboard like the D845EBT or D850GB:

- ■ ***The CPU connector is different.*** The Tyan "Super 7" motherboard accommodates a Socket 7 processor rather than a Socket 423 processor for the D850GB (or a Socket 478 processor for the D845EBT). This means you'd need to stick with an AMD or Cyrix Socket 7 processor rather than a Pentium 4 socket-based processor. If the D850GB used a Slot 1 connector, you'd need to use a Pentium II/III processor.

- ■ ***The expansion slots and their layout are different.*** The Tyan sports four ISA slots, four PCI slots, and an AGP slot. This should not pose a problem unless you have no ISA cards and need more than four PCI slots. However, modern motherboards such as the D845EBT or D850GB have moved to a "legacy free" design which abandons the use of ISA slots entirely. Today, the presence of any ISA slots suggests that you're dealing with an older motherboard model. Also note how full-length ISA cards can easily interfere with the CPU, but an ATX motherboard like the D845EBT or D850GB locate the processor so that there are no obstructions.

- ■ ***The chipset is different.*** The Tyan uses a VIA MVP3 chipset rather than Intel's i850 or i845 chipset. Obviously, the choice of chipset has a profound impact on the capabilities and features of a motherboard. (See Chapter 9 for details on motherboard chipsets.)

- ■ ***I/O ports are almost nonexistent.*** Look closely at Figure 26-4, and you'll find connections for USB, PS/2 mouse, COM ports, and printer (LPT) ports. The problem is that these are "headers" rather than actual connectors. This means you'll need to purchase the port connectors on expansion card brackets

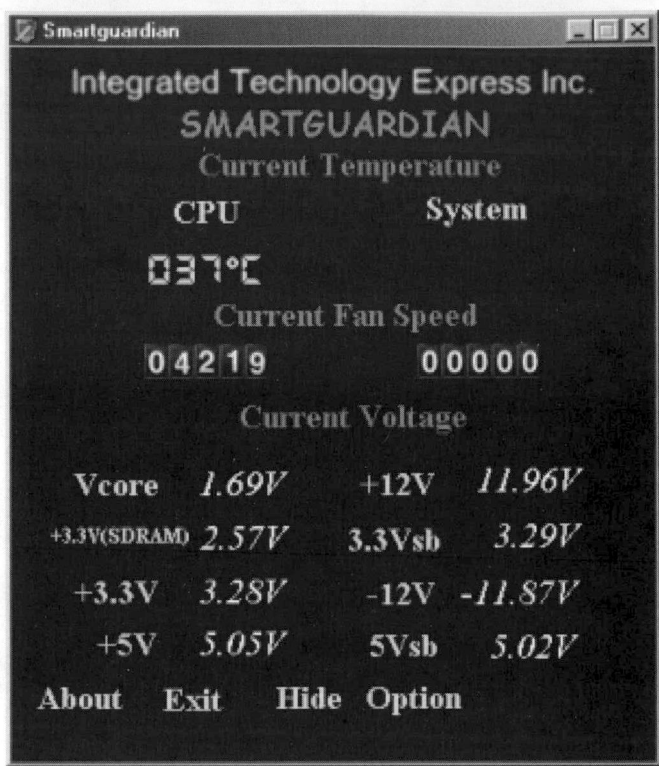

**FIGURE 26-11**    Utilities such as Smartguardian use hardware monitoring to let you track the system's voltages, fan speeds, and temperatures (Courtesy of AOpen, Inc.)

using small ribbon cables that plug into those headers—an inconvenient and error-prone approach, especially when you're shuffling expansion cards around. ATX style motherboards like the D845EBT and D850GB include a cluster of I/O ports that fit prefabricated openings in the rear panel.

■ **The memory configuration is different.** Where the D850GB uses new Rambus memory, the Tyan motherboard offers both 72-pin SIMM and 168-pin DIMM slots for memory modules. Immediately, this means the memory used for the D850GB is not compatible with the Tyan motherboard. The D845EBT supports DDR SDRAM DIMMs, but those are also not compatible with older motherboards (though that may not be apparent at first glance).

■ **Power connections are incompatible.** Remember that the AT-style motherboard uses two 6-pin connectors, while ATX and NLX motherboards use a 20-pin connector. This means the power supply connections are different. Upgrading a motherboard from AT to ATX/NLX usually means that the case and power supply must also be upgraded.

# Upgrading a Motherboard

As a PC ages, it is the motherboard that limits the system's upgradability. True, you can add RAM and upgrade a CPU, and while these tactics can prolong the working life of older systems, they have a limited impact on the overall performance of a motherboard (especially older motherboards where additional memory and suitable upgrade processors may be discontinued items). As PC technology surges ahead and the price of advanced motherboards continues to drop, replacing an outdated motherboard is becoming an increasingly cost-effective upgrade option. This part of the chapter illustrates the most important concerns when planning a motherboard upgrade, walks you through an upgrade process, and shows you how to deal with typical upgrade problems.

# CONSIDERING THE UPGRADE

Upgrading a motherboard is not particularly difficult, but it *is* a time-consuming, detail-oriented process. As a result, advance planning can be a substantial benefit. The following tips cover some important points to keep in mind when planning a motherboard upgrade. As with any upgrade, make it a point to call around and find the best price and delivery terms. Given the added expense of a motherboard, you should find a vendor with a liberal return policy just in case you accidentally obtain an incorrect or defective ("dead-on-arrival" or "DOA") replacement.

## Compare Features

All motherboards are not created equal, so check the specifications closely before making a choice. BIOS plays a vital role in such advanced features as plug-and-play, APM, Ultra-ATA/133 support, USB support, boot sector virus protection, and so much more. The move toward PC power conservation (referred to as "green" PCs) is resulting in features like ACPI. The number and type of I/O slots define system expandability. Most modern motherboards provide onboard features like drive controllers, video adapters, sound devices, and COM/LPT ports. If your major interest is enhanced video/multimedia performance, a Pentium 4 or AMD Athlon/Duron motherboard with a single AGP bus slot will probably do the trick.

## Check Dimensions and Mounting

You cannot overlook the nuts and bolts involved in a motherboard upgrade. Unfortunately, this is often the most difficult (and neglected) consideration. First, the physical dimensions of the motherboard must fit within the space currently available in your PC. A smaller motherboard is generally not a problem, but a larger (or oddly shaped) motherboard will invariably encounter interference from the chassis, the drives, and even the power supply. For example, a full-sized ATX motherboard may not fit properly within a low-profile or mini ATX case. The other issue is mounting holes. Chances are very good that mounting holes on the new motherboard will not match the original mounting holes.

The use of ATX and NLX motherboards and cases goes a long way to easing the problems of dimensioning. Since ATX and NLX form-factor motherboards, cases, and power supplies are all designed to be interchangeable, moving to these form factors can greatly ease the upgrade problems associated with physical motherboard mounting.

If you elect to replace a full AT or baby AT motherboard with an ATX or NLX motherboard, you *must* also upgrade the case and power supply as well.

## Check CPU and Slot Locations

Check the sales literature or online product documentation for the new motherboard, and find the location of the new CPU relative to the expansion slots. Since it is assumed that you will be upgrading your system to a Pentium III/4 or AMD Athlon/Duron-compatible motherboard, the use of a CPU heat sink/fan unit will be mandatory. As a result, the CPU/heat sink combination could easily interfere with the installation of one or more expansion boards (though this type of obstruction is not an issue with ATX/NLX motherboards). This could be a real problem if your current system is heavily loaded. (You can see how the CPU socket would interfere with full-length ISA cards in Figure 26-4.) Try to pick a motherboard that places the CPU out of the way of expansion boards. For ATX and NLX motherboards, the CPU's placement normally does not interfere with the expansion slots.

## Consider Collateral Upgrades

Before finally committing to a new motherboard, take a moment to evaluate the other subassemblies found in the PC, and anticipate any other immediate upgrade needs. Will your old UDMA/33 hard drive really take advantage of the new motherboard's Ultra-DMA/133 drive controller? Do you need a new memory type (such as DDR SDRAM DIMMs rather than EDO SIMMs)? Will your old PCI video accelerator be retired in favor of a high-performance AGP 3D graphics card, or will you use the video sub-system integrated into the new motherboard? If there are no ISA slots on the new motherboard, will you need a new PCI Ethernet card to replace the ISA version that you can no longer use. Or, will you select a motherboard with an integrated Ethernet port? Each of these extras will boost the ultimate cost of the upgrade that much higher, so it is always worthwhile to compare this adjusted cost against the purchase price of a similar PC available off the shelf. In some cases, it may be in your customer's best interest to simply buy or build a new PC.

## Check the Costs

Choose your new motherboard carefully, using a balance between price and cutting-edge features. New motherboards are not terribly expensive, but you can usually find a great deal if you look 6 to 12 months back. For example, a new Pentium 4 motherboard (with the Pentium 4 installed) can easily run over $600, while a recent Pentium III or off-peak motherboard (plus a CPU already integrated) can be had for well under $300. The idea is that you can save a bundle of money if you can make do with upgrades that are just slightly off the cutting edge.

Perhaps even more important, make sure you are aware of any hidden costs with the motherboard. For example, make sure that you know whether the new motherboard comes with current BIOS, a CPU, and CMOS backup battery. If you plan to be running software that demands MMX or SSE/II capability, see that the CPU is suitable. Also find out how much RAM is on the motherboard, and see if your current RAM is compatible. You might find yourself buying 64MB to 128MB (or more) of new DDR SDRAM DIMMs or RIMMs because you can't transfer the EDO SIMMs from the old motherboard to the new one. This will bump up the cost of the upgrade.

## Pros and Cons of Traditional Upgrades

Motherboard upgrades provide a much more sweeping and comprehensive improvement in system performance than changing any one element on the original motherboard itself. A new motherboard not only supports better and faster processors, but it also provides better caching, support for larger and faster hard drives, and support for larger amounts of faster RAM (such as DDR SDRAM or Rambus DRAM). You'll also find advanced bus slots for added system performance, superior data handling with current BIOS, and streamlined, highly integrated chipsets. Such upgrades can also consume a fair amount of time (easily an hour or more) depending on the amount of mechanical disassembly that is required. The other disadvantage is that of physical incompatibility. If the mounting holes on a new motherboard do not align with the original mounting standoffs, new mounting holes will have to be created (or the case will have to be replaced).

## Pros and Cons of Daughtercard Upgrades

The two great drawbacks to motherboard replacement are price and time. Some companies like Compaq addressed these disadvantages by designing a *modular motherboard*—a unit that mounts the CPU, cache, and often the system RAM on a readily accessible module referred to as a *daughtercard*. The daughtercard can be replaced in only a few minutes, with no real disassembly required. Since the daughtercard is specifically designed to carry the core processing components, an upgrade can easily yield a 100 percent to 600 percent performance improvement. These are compelling advantages, especially when many systems need to be upgraded. The problem with daughtercards is that they are proprietary devices that must be designed to mate with a specific motherboard. As a result, a daughtercard is generally quite expensive—sometimes more than a conventional motherboard. Daughtercard upgrades also prevent new bus architectures from being introduced to the system.

### NLX Motherboard Upgrades

As you've seen earlier in this chapter, NLX motherboards (such as the Intel JN440BX NLX motherboard shown in Figure 26-6) make the motherboard a replaceable (or *dockable*) device. All expansion slots and connection headers (such as speaker connector, power switch connector, and so on) have been moved to a *riser card*. The NLX motherboard itself (with all its core processing components) then plugs into the riser card that's permanently fixed in the chassis. NLX offers speed and convenience because it can be removed and upgraded quickly and with a minimum of tools. If you're planning on regular maintenance and upgrades, opt for NLX motherboards and chassis configurations to lower the time and effort needed for future work on the unit—sometimes called *lowering the total cost of ownership* (TCO).

## PERFORMING THE UPGRADE

Unlike CPU or expansion card upgrades, replacing an entire motherboard is a rather involved process that requires a substantial amount of care to be accomplished successfully. This part of the chapter covers the essential steps and precautions that you will need to remember during the upgrade. Before starting the upgrade, it is a good idea to run a benchmarking program (such as PCMark) and note the *current* system performance benchmark figure before you get started. This gives you something to measure the system against once the upgrade is finished. You are also strongly urged to perform a complete system backup before proceeding. *Collateral system damage during an upgrade is a serious possibility.*

### Static Precautions

Virtually all of the chips used in today's computers are fabricated with technologies that make them *extremely* sensitive to *electrostatic discharge* (ESD). To ensure the safe handling of motherboards and other system components during the upgrade, make it a point to take the following precautions. First, invest in an anti-static mat that is large enough to cover a majority of your work area. See that the anti-static mat is properly cabled and attached to a reliable earth ground. *Under no circumstances* should you allow a motherboard to rest on a synthetic or static-prone surface. Second, use an anti-static wrist strap whenever handling components or tools inside the PC. Cable the wrist strap to the anti-static mat or to another reliable earth ground. Third, always try to handle printed circuit boards by their edges. Avoid touching the individual chip pins or printed wiring. Fourth, have a supply of good-quality anti-static bags on hand to hold the system's expansion boards as they are temporarily removed. Finally, excessively dry environments tend to allow substantial buildups of static charges in objects, clothing, and bodies. If it is possible, try to work in an environment with at least 40 percent humidity.

It is always a sound policy to perform a complete system backup before starting any major PC upgrade or repair such as motherboard replacement.

## Save Your CMOS

Before starting your upgrade, make it a point to obtain a current record of your CMOS settings. You can do this by taking PRINTSCREEN shots of each CMOS setup page. You should be particularly interested in the hard drive setup information. You may need to load that data into the new motherboard's CMOS Setup before the system will recognize your boot drive and other devices (especially if the new BIOS doesn't autodetect the drives the same way, or uses a slightly different translation geometry to access the drives). Once you have the CMOS information, set it aside in a safe place.

> Most current BIOS versions allow you to enter "BIOS Defaults" in the CMOS Setup, which should establish a working system baseline with a minimum of fuss, but you may still need to identify your hard drives manually.

## Prepare the System

At this point, you can prepare the system for its upgrade. A word of caution is in order here: *be especially careful of screwdriver blades when working inside the PC.* If you should slip, the blade can easily gouge the motherboard and result in broken traces. It pays to be careful and gentle when upgrading a motherboard. *Before opening the PC cover, turn the system off, and unplug it from the AC receptacle.* This helps to ensure your safety by preventing the PC from being powered accidentally while you are working on it.

Remove the screws holding down the outer cover, and place those screws aside in a safe place. Gently remove the PC's outer cover and set it aside (out of the path of normal floor traffic). You should now be able to look into the PC and see the motherboard, along with any expansion boards and drives that are installed. Now that you are looking at the complete PC, this is the time for you to *label* things. Clearly marked labels will help you remember the purpose of each cable (such as power, drives, key lock, speaker, drive light, and so on) and show you where each item went on the original motherboard or on various expansion boards. *Don't be afraid to label things.* Labels need not be fancy—a roll of masking tape and an indelible marker are all that's required. Remember that you'll have to take this all apart, so anything that will help you remember where things go will be a help.

## Remove the Original Motherboard

At this point, you should begin clearing the obstructions to the motherboard. Start by removing each expansion board. Place each board into an anti-static bag, and set each bag aside on the anti-static mat. Next, remove any cables that are attached to the motherboard (such as the key lock or speaker cables). If there are floppy drive and hard drive cables connected to the motherboard, remove them as well. Finally, disconnect the power cable(s). For AT-style motherboards, you'll find two 6-pin power connectors from the power supply. For ATX/NLX motherboards, you'll find a single 20-pin power connector. If there are any drives or chassis assemblies interfering with the motherboard, remove them now, and set them aside carefully.

> NLX motherboards do not carry any of the burden found in AT-style or ATX motherboards. All of that peripheral equipment is attached to the NLX riser card. You need only detach and unplug the NLX motherboard from its riser card.

You should now have an unobstructed view of the motherboard. Locate and remove each of the screws holding the motherboard in place. In many cases, there may be at least six (sometimes eight or more). Once each of the screws has been removed, gently lift out the motherboard and lay it aside onto the anti-static mat—preferably in its own anti-static bag. (The whole board should fit on the mat.) The motherboard should lift out without difficulty. If the motherboard does not budge or lift out easily, you may have overlooked a screw, nylon standoff, or cable. *Do not force the motherboard!* Often, there may be one or more white nylon standoffs that are still clipping the motherboard in place. Patiently locate the obstruction(s), and carefully clear each one.

After you remove the original motherboard, you should also remove the CMOS backup battery and place it into a heavy-gauge plastic bag before storing the original motherboard. This will prevent an aging CMOS backup battery from rupturing and damaging the original motherboard with leaking electrolyte.

## Install the New Motherboard

You can now place the new motherboard into the chassis and see that each I/O port and mounting hole line up properly. Be sure that the new motherboard is seated evenly and completely into each standoff, and then secure it into place (see Figure 26-12). Do not use excessive force when tightening the screws. Excessive force can cause the motherboard to warp, and result in failure. When securing the board, check that there are no metal brackets or standoffs that might touch the new motherboard and cause a short circuit. It is usually recommended for you to use a thin, nonconductive washer between each standoff and the motherboard. Once the new motherboard is installed mechanically, you can start reassembling the other devices that you stripped from the system.

Refer to the user's guide that accompanies the new motherboard, and check each jumper or DIP switch. This is a particularly important step because many contemporary motherboards provide services right onboard that have traditionally been assigned to expansion boards (such as video adapters and drive controllers). For example, if you used an Ethernet LAN board with your original motherboard, but your new motherboard provides an integrated Ethernet port, you won't need the original LAN board. If you need to use that board, you will have to set motherboard jumpers to disable the onboard port(s).

The same thing is true of video adapters. If a video port is available on the new motherboard, but you have a 3D graphics accelerator board on hand, you will have to disable the onboard video port to prevent a hardware conflict. If the new motherboard provides a floppy and IDE controller (virtually all do), you can

**FIGURE  26-12**    Once the new motherboard is in place, secure it to the chassis using the appropriate number of screws.

abandon that drive controller board and plug the drives right into the appropriate connectors on the motherboard. In that case, check the drive controller jumpers to be sure they are enabled. Be sure to review each available jumper carefully. Also, verify that the motherboard's bus speed, clock multiplier, and CPU voltage settings are all configured properly for the CPU.

## Reassemble the System

Once the motherboard jumpers are set, you can install the CPU, system RAM, and power/case cables. CPU installation should go easily, but be aware that a socket-based CPU must be oriented properly in the socket relative to pin 1. Slot-based processors will generally only insert in one orientation. Chances are that the CPU will require a heat sink/fan, so be sure to install it securely if needed (along with thermal compound to improve heat transfer between the CPU and heat sink/fan assembly). If you need to install the BIOS chip(s), you may do that next. Be careful to orient each BIOS ROM properly relative to pin 1. If there is more than one BIOS ROM, be sure to install the chips in their proper places. Reversing the BIOS ROM locations should not damage them, but the system will probably not boot. The new motherboard will need a backup battery to support the CMOS/RTC chip. If there is not a battery already on the new motherboard, install a new battery (or reconnect the original battery pack).

Make sure that each DIMM or RIMM snaps gently into place. If they do not, they may be inserted improperly. When inserting cables, note that the red strip on each ribbon cable is pin 1. Make sure that pin 1 on the cable is matched to pin 1 on the corresponding connector. Inserting a ribbon cable backward is rarely damaging, but it may prevent the system from booting. Reconnect the power cables. Finally, install the expansion boards that you will need in the system. Remember that you may not need all the adapter boards you started with if the motherboard will be taking over particular functions. If you had disassembled any drives or chassis subassemblies before removing the original motherboard, be sure to reassemble those items now, and check that their power and signal cabling are secure. Reconnect any ancillary devices such as the mouse, keyboard, and monitor.

## Testing the System

At last, you will face the moment of truth. If things have gone well, this procedure should have taken no more than an hour or so. Once the components and cabling are all secure, it will be time to reconnect the AC line cord and to try applying power to the system. Make sure that your hands and any tools (or other hardware) are clear of the PC. Turn on the monitor, double-check your power cable installation one more time, and then go ahead and press the power switch.

After a moment or two, you should see a BIOS message appear on the monitor. This is a good sign. When the POST displays its message asking to start the setup procedure (usually by pressing F1), go ahead and start it. Review each screen in the setup routine, and restore as many CMOS settings as possible (especially the memory amount, floppy drive types, and hard drive configuration). Chances are that there will be several setup variables that were not in the original system. Just leave these in their default states for now. You can always optimize them later. Save the CMOS Setup and reboot the computer. Your upgraded system should now complete its POST successfully and boot to the operating system.

When booting to Windows 9x/Me/XP, the Windows platform will automatically identify the new device(s) and try installing the appropriate drivers for them. You may need to have your Windows installation CD handy. Once Windows has reconfigured itself for the new hardware, install any patches from the motherboard's installation CD (if needed). Finally, check the Device Manager for any hardware problems or conflicts. Congratulations, you have completed your motherboard upgrade.

If you cannot adequately reconfigure the CMOS Setup, select the BIOS Defaults option, which should apply the variables necessary to get the PC working. You can then tweak the CMOS values later to improve system performance.

When the system boots as expected, the last step should be to power-down the computer and reassemble the outer housing. You can then run your benchmarking program *again* to determine the new benchmarks for your PC. You can see the relative improvement in performance over that of the original system configuration.

# Troubleshooting a Motherboard

Since motherboards contain the majority of system processing components, it is likely that you will encounter a faulty motherboard sooner or later. The BIOS POST is written to test each subsection of the motherboard each time the PC is powered-up, so most problems are detected well before you ever see the DOS prompt. Errors are reported in myriad ways. Beep codes and POST codes (Chapter 17) provide indications of fatal errors that occur before the video system is initialized. Still, there are plenty of symptoms that can elude the initial testing at start time. This part of the chapter digs in and presents a lengthy selection of motherboard symptoms for you to reference.

## REPAIR VS. REPLACE

This is the perennial troubleshooting dilemma. The problem with motherboard repair is not so much the availability of replacement parts (although that *can* be a challenge) as it is the use of *surface-mount soldering* (SMT). A surface-mounted chip cannot be desoldered with conventional tools—at least, not quickly and easily. To successfully desolder a surface-mounted chip, you need to heat each of the chip's pins (often in excess of 200) simultaneously, then lift the chip off the board. It's then a simple matter to clean up any residual solder. Unfortunately, specialized surface-mount soldering equipment is required to do this. The equipment is readily available commercially, so it's easy to buy. But you can invest $1000 to $2000 to equip your workbench properly.

As you can imagine, the "repair vs. replace" decision is an economic one. It makes little sense for the part-time PC enthusiast to make such a substantial investment to exchange a defective chip (which usually cost under $20). It is generally better to replace the motherboard, which is only a fraction of the cost of such SMT equipment. On the other hand, professionals who intend to pursue PC repair as a living may be well served with surface-mount equipment. The customer's cost for labor, part(s), and markup is typically much less than that for purchasing a new motherboard (especially the high-end boards such as Pentium 4 motherboards).

## START WITH THE BASICS

Since motherboard troubleshooting does represent a significant expense, you should be sure to start any motherboard repair by inspecting the following points in the PC. *Remember to turn all power off before performing these inspections.*

- *Check all connectors.* Connector problems can happen easily when the PC is serviced or upgraded, and you accidentally forget to replace every cable (or the cable is installed incorrectly). Start with the power connectors, and inspect each cable and connector attached to the motherboard. Frayed cables should be replaced. Loose or detached cables should be reattached properly. Always be sure that ribbon cables are attached in their proper orientation.

- ■ ***Check all socket-mounted chips.*** Some chips in the computer (especially the CPU) get hot during normal operation. It is not unheard of for the repetitive expansion and contraction encountered with everyday use to eventually "rock" a chip out of its socket. The CPU, BIOS ROM, and often the CMOS/RTC module are socket mounted, so check them carefully.

- ■ ***Check power levels.*** Low or erratic AC power levels can cause problems in the PC. Use a multimeter to check AC at the wall outlet. Be very careful whenever dealing with AC. Take all precautions to protect yourself from injury. If the AC is low or is heavily loaded by motors, coffeemakers, or other highly inductive loads, try the PC in another outlet running from a different circuit. If AC checks properly, use your multimeter (or a measurement tool such as PC Power Check from Data Depot at www.datadepo.com) to check the power supply outputs. If one or more outputs are low or absent, you should repair or replace the supply. Verify that the power connections are secure at the motherboard.

- ■ ***Check the motherboard for foreign objects.*** A screw, paper clip, or free strand of wire can cause a short circuit that may disable the motherboard. Examine the motherboard carefully, and use ample lighting.

- ■ ***Check that all motherboard DIP switches and jumpers are correct.*** For example, if the motherboard provides a video port, and you have a video board plugged into the expansion bus, the motherboard's video circuit will have to be disabled through a switch or jumper. Otherwise, a hardware conflict can result that may interfere with motherboard operation. You will need the user manual for the PC in order to identify and check each jumper or switch. Today, virtually all motherboard configuration issues (including clock speeds and multipliers) are handled through the system's CMOS Setup, so jumper settings are no longer as critical as they used to be—but it always pays to double-check.

- ■ ***Check for intermittent connections and accidental grounding.*** Inspect each of the motherboard's mounting screws, and see that they are not touching nearby printed traces. Also check the space under the motherboard, and see that there is nothing that might be grounding the motherboard and chassis. As an experiment, you may try loosening the motherboard mounting screws (even lift the motherboard off the metal standoffs just a bit). If the fault goes away, the motherboard may be suffering from an intermittent connection—when all screws are tight, the board is bent just enough to let the intermittent appear. Unfortunately, intermittent connections are almost impossible to find, and you may need to replace the motherboard once again.

## SYMPTOMS

The general guidelines just covered should help you to identify and correct many of the more common problems that you may encounter. If you're stuck with a particular issue, refer to the following symptoms for specific solutions.

**SYMPTOM 26-1** **The Slot 1 retention mechanism is not holding the Slot 1 processor securely in place** You find that there is "play," which allows the processor to move (and possibly fall out of its slot). In virtually all cases, this means the retention mechanism is not mounted securely on the motherboard. It's probably sitting too high, and allowing the CPU to "float." You'll need to check the installation of that retention mechanism. Support the motherboard so that it will not bend while the retention mechanism is being pressed into the mounting holes. (But do not place the motherboard on a hard surface to install the retention mechanism.) If the retention mechanism push pins are not secured properly, the retention mechanism can become loose, causing the processor to disconnect, and even fall out of the motherboard. To install a retention mechanism with captive brass fasteners, simply use a medium Phillips screwdriver to screw the fasteners into the preinstalled brass Pemstuds. To install the retention mechanism with plastic fasteners:

1. Leave space below each mounting hole so that the fastener can protrude through the hole.
2. Find the slot 1 connector on the motherboard.
3. Position the retention mechanism on the motherboard next to the slot 1 connector.
4. Push down on the retention bracket until the black plastic fasteners are correctly seated and the retention mechanism fits *snugly* against the board.
5. Push each white retainer pin into its respective black fastener until the head of each pin is seated onto the head of each fastener. This should keep the retention mechanism securely in place.

Socket-type processors rely on a *zero insertion force* (ZIF) socket to hold the processor pins firmly in place. Make sure that the ZIF socket's lever is locked in the closed position when replacing or transferring the processor.

**SYMPTOM 26-2** **After removing a hard drive or other IDE device, the system seems to boot slowly, but seems fine otherwise** This is usually an oversight with the CMOS Setup. Chances are that the BIOS still expects an IDE device to respond, and it is waiting for the device that you removed. This is what causes the delay. If you remove a secondary drive on the primary channel, or any drive on the secondary channel, you should check the CMOS Setup and set that corresponding drive position to "none" or "not installed." Save your changes and reboot the system. You should see that the BIOS is no longer waiting for devices that you marked out in the CMOS Setup, and there should be no delay during that part of the startup process.

**SYMPTOM 26-3** **You notice that your system automatically powers back on after a power failure** This is probably the result of a CMOS Setup configuration rather than a hardware fault. This type of feature first started appearing on standard Intel-manufactured motherboard products with a Phoenix BIOS and a 430TX or 440LX chipset—though many other systems now offer this feature. You'll probably find a feature in the BIOS setup utility (usually under Boot Menu) that controls the action of the computer following a power failure. These options include Stay Off, Last State (to restore the previous power state—either on or off—before AC power was lost), or Power On (so the system will always power back on). If you check this setting in the CMOS Setup, you'll probably notice that it's set to Power On or Last State. If you'd prefer the system to remain off after a power failure, set this entry to Stay Off.

When a computer offers this feature, the computer will always power-up for 300mS when AC power is restored, reads the current setup boot values, and goes to the appropriate state (on or off).

**SYMPTOM 26-4** **You receive a "static device resource conflict" error message** A "static device resource conflict" warning message while booting Windows 9x/Me/XP may be generated from numerous (and often unrelated) situations. The majority of technicians reporting this problem have a Pro Audio Spectrum 16 card installed. The Windows 9x/Me/XP registration for this card includes both 10-bit I/O addresses (201H and 388H) and 16-bit aliases to these addresses (A201H and F388H). The BIOS detects that the 10-bit address will also overlap with the 16-bit address and flags this as a resource conflict. Because it is a single card requesting both these resources, the warning can be ignored if that is the case, though it may be better to replace or disable older devices to alleviate the trouble. There are also reports of other configurations causing "static resource conflict" warnings. Some of these instances appear to be corrected by clearing the ESCD area in NVRAM. This can be accomplished by performing a CMOS clear:

1.  Note your current settings.
2.  Turn power off.
3.  Set the CMOS Clear jumper or switch to the Clear position (see the product documentation).
4.  Turn power on.
5.  After approximately 30 seconds, turn the power off.
6.  Set the CMOS Clear jumper or switch to the Off or Normal position.
7.  Turn your system on, and enter the CMOS Setup to change settings as you require (hard drive, etc.).

**SYMPTOM 26-5**    **You cannot operate or boot from an LS-120 "floptical" drive**    In virtually all cases, this is a limitation of the motherboard's BIOS. For example, Intel motherboards that have a Phoenix BIOS and use either the Intel 430TX, 440LX, 440BX, or 440EX and later chipsets support booting from an LS-120 floppy drive. This means most other motherboards with a Pentium MMX–compliant (or later) chipset will support LS-120 drives. If you have trouble recognizing or booting from the LS-120, check with the motherboard or system maker for a BIOS upgrade. If the BIOS cannot be upgraded to support booting, you may need to upgrade the motherboard or avoid booting from an LS-120 drive (for example, opt for a bootable CD drive instead).

**SYMPTOM 26-6**    **When upgrading the motherboard, the system won't boot when using an older CPU, but it boots fine with a newer CPU**    You find that the older CPU runs fine on another system (so you know that the processor is functional). This generally means that the newer motherboard contains a "lockout" that prevents 66-MHz bus speeds. This forces the motherboard to use 100 MHz or 133 MHz bus speeds. If a 66-MHz front side bus processor is installed, the motherboard will simply not boot. If this is the case, there is no way around the problem except to use an appropriate processor model.

**SYMPTOM 26-7**    **The system displays PC100 memory even though PC133 memory is installed**    First, check the memory and see that it is actually PC133; then verify that your system bus is actually set to 133 MHz. If the bus is set to 100 MHz, the memory speed may be reported incorrectly. This error may also sometimes occur when the DRAM Clock entry in your CMOS Setup is set incorrectly. Try setting the DRAM Clock to Host CLK in the Chipset features section of your CMOS Setup. In a few cases, you may need to upgrade the motherboard BIOS so that faster memory devices are reported properly.

**SYMPTOM 26-8**    **The motherboard's COM port(s)—or other port—won't work**    This type of trouble occurs frequently when the motherboard supplies no external I/O ports—only headers that require you to connect short cables from the motherboard to ports on separate brackets. In almost every case, an inability to use a COM port (or other ports like serial, parallel, and so on) is a result of *not* using the supplied header cables, or the respective ports are disabled in the CMOS Setup. To ensure that the motherboard is recognizing and initializing the ports correctly, boot the system and check the CMOS Setup. Locate the settings that control your COM ports (or other affected ports). Verify that the ports are enabled. You should also see that the IRQs and I/O addresses are configured properly for each port. Now examine your port header cables closely. See that the header is fit over every pin and is oriented properly (look for "pin 1").

Since many motherboard makers use different pin assignments for COM port header cables, make sure that you're using the header cable that's specifically intended for your particular motherboard model.

One other point—if your system has internal modems or other serial devices (such as a multi-I/O card with one or more COM ports), see that those other serial devices are *not* conflicting with the motherboard's COM port(s). You may need to reconfigure or remove the conflicting device(s).

**SYMPTOM 26-9**    **The system halts during boot and displays an "Incompatible ATAPI Device" error**    This may occur after installing a new ATAPI device (such as a CD drive) or upgrading the motherboard while reusing an existing ATAPI device(s). For example, this is a known issue with the Pioneer 32X CD-ROM and an AMI BIOS, and can also occur with other incompatible BIOS versions and ATAPI devices. In almost every case, the solution is to upgrade the motherboard's BIOS to a newer version. Of course, you could try a different ATAPI device instead.

**SYMPTOM 26-10**    **The system will not turn off when you press the power button**    This is not really a problem, but is often an issue with the motherboard's power management settings. In many cases, the power button is designed to turn off the system *only* when you press and hold the power button for more than 5 seconds. You may be able to reconfigure the power button for "instant off" through the CMOS Setup. If you cannot reconfigure the power button for instant off, you may need a BIOS upgrade.

**SYMPTOM 26-11**    **You discover the "Wake On LAN" device has damaged your power supply**    This is probably because your power supply did not provide adequate standby current to the enabling device (e.g., the LAN card). You need to use an ATX power supply with 800 mA provided through the +5 Vsb (standby) power line. This is required by most "Wake On LAN" network cards, which require +5V@750 mA in sleep mode. Try an ATX power supply with minimum 800 mA at the +5 Vsb output to avoid over-current damage to the power supply. This may require a power supply upgrade.

**SYMPTOM 26-12**    **You encounter a "Serial Presence Detect" error at boot time**    This problem occurs when the system RAM is not identified (or identified improperly) by the system BIOS. Memory modules typically use *serial presence detect* (SPD) to identify themselves to the system at start time. If "non-SPD" memory is detected during the POST, or the BIOS cannot determine that the memory installed meets system requirements, the BIOS will display this error message:

```
SERIAL PRESENCE DETECT (SPD) device data missing or inconclusive
Properly programmed SPD device data is required for reliable operation
Do you wish to continue?
Y/N Type [Y] to continue, [N] to shut down
```

While "non-SPD" memory remains present on the system, subsequent boots will display the following message:

```
SERIAL PRESENCE DETECT (SPD) device data missing or inconclusive
100MHz memory assumed
```

If SPD memory at the proper speed cannot be confirmed during POST, the BIOS will provide this information to the user and offer the option to run the system with memory that may not meet the full operating requirements (e.g., PC100 or PC133). If the system will be used in a mission-critical application where data integrity is vital, the system should be shut down, and SPD-compliant memory should be installed before operation.

**SYMPTOM 26-13**    **After installing one or more RIMM modules in the system, you get a repeating beep code and no video**    This is often a problem with the way you installed your new Rambus DRAM. Chances are that the beep code indicates a problem during detection of the RIMM modules. If a RIMM socket is not populated with memory, ensure it is populated with a *Continuity RIMM* (C-RIMM). Also check to ensure that system memory is securely installed, and that any RIMMs in use have been specifically recommended by the motherboard manufacturer. For example, do not use PC600 RIMMs when PC800 RIMMs are required. Memory-related beep codes can also occur with other forms of memory such as SDRAM or DDR SDRAM. In either case, verify that the memory module(s) are appropriate for your system and are installed properly.

**SYMPTOM 26-14**    **You find that IRQ9 is not available to assign an ISA device**    Chances are that this is an issue related to your particular motherboard's power management system. For example, IRQ9 is not available to ISA devices on the Intel JN440BX motherboard because it is dedicated to the power management function on the motherboard's PIIX4 controller. This is also true for other motherboards that utilize the PIIX4 controller chip. You may free the IRQ by disabling the motherboard's power management features, or select another available IRQ for the device.

**SYMPTOM 26-15**    **Windows 98/Me reports insufficient memory with 32MB installed**    This is a known issue on motherboards that use the VIA MVP4 chipset (such as the AOpen MX59 Pro motherboard). The MVP4 chipset supports shared memory between system RAM and the video system; 8MB of system RAM is assigned to the onboard graphics controller by default. If this is the case, you may actually only have 24MB of RAM for Windows 98/Me, and this may not be enough. You can add more RAM to the system. You may also enter the CMOS Setup and reduce the Frame Buffer Size value from 8MB to 2MB in order to keep more of the 32MB available for Windows 98/Me. If you *do* reduce the Frame Buffer Size, be sure to also reduce the color depth and resolution under Windows 98/Me. Since Windows XP typically has higher memory requirements than Windows 9x/Me, the system will probably not even boot with just 32MB installed.

**SYMPTOM 26-16**    **The system runs fine with Setup defaults, but is unstable with Turbo defaults**    This is because the Turbo (a.k.a. high-speed) defaults generally use more aggressive settings that wring more performance out of the motherboard. In some cases, certain hardware combinations may not respond well to Turbo settings and result in system instability. Check your hardware list against the requirements for the Turbo default settings. If you identify an item that is not appropriate (such as slow RAM), you can upgrade that hardware. Otherwise, you may simply need to select the Setup defaults and stick with an acceptable level of system performance.

**SYMPTOM 26-17**    **A motherboard failure is reported, but goes away when the PC's outer cover is removed**    There is likely to be an intermittent connection on the motherboard. When the housing is secured, the PC chassis warps just slightly. This may be enough to precipitate an intermittent contact. When the housing is removed, the chassis relaxes and hides the intermittent connection. Replace the outer cover and gently retighten each screw with the system running. Chances are that you will find one screw that triggers the problem. You can leave that screw out, but it is advisable to replace the motherboard as a long-term fix.

**SYMPTOM 26-18**    **The POST (or your software diagnostic) reports a CPU fault**    This is a fatal error, and chances are that system initialization has halted. CPU problems are generally reported when one or more CPU registers do not respond as expected or have trouble switching to the protected mode. In either case, the CPU is probably at fault. Fortunately, the CPU is socket/slot mounted and should be very straightforward to replace. Be sure to remove all power to the PC, and make careful use of static controls when replacing a CPU. Mark the questionable CPU with indelible ink before replacing it.

*Zero-insertion force* (ZIF) sockets are easiest, since the processor will be released simply by lifting the metal lever at the socket's side. Slide out the original CPU, and insert a new one. Secure the metal lever, and try the PC again. However, many CPUs are mounted in *pin grid array* (PGA) sockets, and a specialized PGA removal tool is strongly suggested for proper removal. You should also be able to use a small, regular screwdriver to gently pry up each of the four sides of the CPU. But be *very* careful to avoid cracking the chip, the socket, or the motherboard—never use excessive force. When the processor is free, install the new CPU with close attention to pin alignment, and then gently press the new CPU into place. If you're working with slot-based processors (such as Slot 1 or Slot A), you'll need to release the processor's retention mechanism before removing the processor from its slot. When replacing a slot-based CPU, ensure that the retention mechanism holds the processor securely.

A word about heat sink/fans—most Pentium MMX and later CPUs are equipped with a metal heat sink (or heat sink/fan) assembly. It is vital to the proper operation of your system that the heat sink be reinstalled correctly. Otherwise, the new CPU will eventually overheat and lock up or fail. Be sure to use good-quality thermal compound to ensure proper heat transfer to the heat sink. (Remember that a sound mechanical connection does not always guarantee a good thermal connection.)

**SYMPTOM 26-19**     **The POST (or your software diagnostic) reports a problem with the floating point unit**     Math coprocessor (also called the *floating point unit* or FPU) problems are generally reported when one or more MCP registers do not respond as expected. Fortunately, MCP faults are not always fatal. It is often possible to remove the MCP or disable the MCP availability through the CMOS Setup. Of course, programs that depend on the MCP will no longer run, but at least the system can be used until a new one is installed. On older systems that use separate MCP chips, the device is socket mounted and should be very straightforward to replace. Be sure to remove all power to the PC, and make careful use of static controls when replacing an MPC. Mark the questionable MPC with indelible ink before replacing it. When the MCP function is integrated into the CPU (as is the case with all current processors), the process is a bit more expensive. You'll need to replace the entire CPU, but the replacement process is no more difficult. (Remember to remount any heat sink/fan assembly properly.)

**SYMPTOM 26-20**     **The POST (or your software diagnostic) reports a BIOS ROM checksum error**     The integrity of your system BIOS ROM is verified after the CPU is tested. This is necessary to ensure that there are no unwanted instructions or data that might easily crash the system during POST or normal operation. A checksum is performed on the ROM contents, and that value is compared with the value stored in the ROM itself. If the two values are equal, the ROM is considered good and initialization continues. Otherwise, the BIOS is considered defective and should be replaced.

Traditionally, BIOS ROM is implemented as one or two chips that are plugged into DIP or PLCC sockets. They can be removed easily with the blade of a regular screwdriver, as long as you pry the chip up slowly and gently. (Be sure to pry the chip evenly from both ends.) When installing new DIP chips, you may have to straighten their pins against the surface of a table or use a DIP pin-straightening tool. Ultimately, the DIP pins will fit nicely into each receptacle in the DIP socket. You can then ease the chip evenly down into the socket. Alignment is critical to ensure that all pins are inserted. If not, one or more pins may be bent under the chip and ruin the new ROM. Also, be sure to insert the new chip(s) in the proper orientation. If they are accidentally installed backward, they may be damaged.

Current BIOS chips use flash ROM technology, which allows the device to be erased and reprogrammed in the field without having to replace the entire BIOS ROM chip. When a flash BIOS fails its checksum test, it also has probably failed. Since flash BIOS devices are often fabricated as PLCC chips, it is a bit easier to replace them, but you will need a PLCC removal tool to take the original chip out of its socket. There simply is not enough room for a screwdriver.

In some cases, you might try reflashing the existing BIOS chip and see if that fixes the problem. If the trouble remains (or returns), you'll need to replace the BIOS chip after all.

**SYMPTOM 26-21** **The POST (or software diagnostic) reports a timer (PIT) failure, an RTC update problem, or a refresh failure** The *programmable interrupt timer* (PIT) is often an 8254 or compatible device. Ultimately, one or more of its three channels may have failed, and the PIT should be replaced. It is important to realize that all modern motherboards incorporate the PIT functions into a system controller or other chipset device. (Refer to Chapter 9 for a listing of chipsets and functions.) Since the PIT is typically surface mounted, you can attempt to replace the device or replace the motherboard entirely.

**SYMPTOM 26-22** **The POST (or software diagnostic) reports an interrupt controller (PIC) failure** The *programmable interrupt controller* (PIC) is often an 8259 or compatible device, and there are two PICs on the typical AT motherboard. (PIC 1 handles IRQ0 through IRQ7, and PIC 2 handles IRQ8 through IRQ15.) Of the two, PIC 1 is more important since the lower interrupts have a higher priority, and the lowest channels handle critical low-level functions such as the system timer and keyboard interface. Generally, a diagnostic will reveal which of the two PICs has failed. Make sure that there are no interrupt conflicts between two or more system devices. You can then replace the defective PIC. In all current systems, both PICs are integrated into a system controller chip or chipset device. You can replace the defective chip if you have the appropriate surface-mount equipment available, or replace the motherboard entirely.

**SYMPTOM 26-23** **The POST (or software diagnostic) reports a DMA controller (DMAC) failure** The *dynamic memory access controller* (DMAC) is often an 8237 or compatible device, and there are two DMACs on the typical motherboard. (DMAC 1 handles channel 0 through channel 3, and DMAC 2 handles channel 4 through channel 7.) Of the two, DMAC 1 is more important since channel 2 runs the floppy disk controller. Generally, a diagnostic will reveal which of the two DMACs has failed. Make sure that there are no DMA conflicts between two or more system devices. You can then replace the defective DMAC. In many current systems, both DMACs are integrated into a system controller chip or chipset device. You can replace the defective chip if you have the appropriate surface-mount equipment available, or replace the motherboard entirely.

**SYMPTOM 26-24** **The POST (or software diagnostic) reports a KBC fault** The *keyboard controller* (KBC) is often either an 8042 or an 8742. Since the KBC is a microcontroller in its own right, diagnostics can usually detect a KBC fault with great accuracy. The KBC may be either a socket-mounted PLCC device or (in rare cases) a surface-mounted chip—today, the KBC is integrated into the motherboard's I/O controller chip that handles the PS/2 keyboard port. Remember to remove all power and mark the old KBC before you remove it from the PC. You'll probably need a PLCC-removal tool to take out the old KBC. If you cannot exchange a defective KBC, you'll need to replace the motherboard.

**SYMPTOM 26-25** A keyboard error is reported, but a new keyboard has no effect
Remember that traditional keyboards are powered through the PS/2 port, and the +5 Vdc supply is protected by a fuse on the motherboard. (USB keyboards are powered by the USB port, which are relatively immune from such overloads.) The keyboard fuse on the motherboard may have failed. Many motherboard designs incorporate a small fuse (called a *pico-fuse*) in the +5 Vdc line that drives the keyboard. If this fuse fails, the keyboard will be dead. Use your multimeter and measure the +5 Vdc line at the keyboard connector. If this reads 0 Vdc, locate the keyboard fuse on the motherboard and replace it. (You may have to trace the line back to the fuse that looks almost exactly like a resistor.) Otherwise, you'll need to replace the entire motherboard.

**SYMPTOM 26-26** The POST (or software diagnostic) reports a CMOS or RTC fault
With either error, it is the same device that is usually at fault. The CMOS RAM and RTC are generally fabricated onto the same device—though some motherboards (such as Intel's D845EBT or D850GB) integrate these features into the Firmware Hub chipset device. RTC problems indicate that the real-time clock portion of the chip has failed or is not being updated. CMOS RAM failure can be due to a dead backup battery or a failure of the chip itself. When dealing with a CMOS or setup problem, first try a new backup battery and reload the CMOS Setup variables (usually selecting the BIOS Default values will get the system working). If a new battery does not resolve the problem, the CMOS/RTC chip should be replaced. Often, the CMOS/RTC chip is surface mounted and will have to be replaced (or the motherboard will have to be replaced). However, some manufacturers use a socket-mounted chip including the battery in a single replaceable module (such as the Dallas Semiconductor-type devices). Modules are typically replaceable DIP devices.

**SYMPTOM 26-27** The POST (or software diagnostic) reports a fault in the first 64KB of
**RAM** The first RAM page is important since it holds the *BIOS data area* (BDA) and interrupt vectors. The system will not work without it. When a RAM error is indicated, your only real recourse is to replace the motherboard RAM. On older motherboards, if the diagnostic indicates which bit has failed and you can correlate the bit to a specific memory chip, you can sometimes replace the defective chip (typically surface mounted). Otherwise, you'll need to systematically locate and replace all of the motherboard RAM, or replace the motherboard entirely. Virtually all current motherboards utilize DIMMs (and sometimes RIMMs) for *all* system memory, so it should be a relatively simple matter to cycle through each memory module with a known-good unit to isolate the defective memory module.

**SYMPTOM 26-28** The MCP does not work properly when installed on a motherboard
when external (L2) caching is enabled This is an issue that you might encounter when resurrecting older motherboards. Some non-Intel math coprocessors (a.k.a. floating point units) work in areas that must be non-cached. For example, a Cyrix EMC87 MCP with an AMI Mark IV i386 motherboard has been known to cause this type of problem. When MCP problems arise (especially during upgrades), try disabling the external (L2) cache through CMOS Setup. As another alternative, try a different math coprocessor. This rarely ever happens when the coprocessor and L2 cache are integrated into the modern processor—if a similar symptom does occur, chances are that the processor is failing and should be replaced.

**SYMPTOM 26-29** A "jumperless motherboard" receives incorrect CPU Soft Menu
settings and now refuses to boot This may occur on a motherboard such as the Abit IT5V and is usually due to accidental settings during system configuration. Fortunately, this type of problem can be corrected by removing power from the motherboard. Try turning off the system and unplugging it for several

minutes. When you restore power to the system, the CPU Soft Menu will automatically reset the CPU frequency for the lowest setting and allow the motherboard to boot. You can then go back into the CPU Soft Menu and correct any speed setting errors. If the motherboard doesn't reset automatically, you may need to reset the CMOS Setup manually (usually through a reset jumper)—check the documentation for your particular motherboard. If this were a jumpered motherboard, you would need to find the CPU speed jumper and set it correctly.

**SYMPTOM 26-30**    **Less memory is detected than the amount you installed**    This tends to be a chipset-related problem where the chipset doesn't support the memory configuration that's installed. For example, when installing two 64MB SIMMs on an older system, only 32MB of RAM are displayed when the computer powers-up. This is known to occur on motherboards with a 430VX (or similar) chipset, which—though supporting 128MB of RAM—will not support 64MB memory devices. In actual practice, the 430VX only supports the following memory devices:

- 512K×32-bit (2MB)
- 1M×32-bit (4MB)
- 2M×32-bit (8MB)
- 4M×32-bit (16MB)

The layout for a 64MB SIMM is 16M×32-bit, which isn't in the list just shown. When you install two 64MB SIMMs, the system will use the 4M×32-bit specification to calculate the memory, thus displaying 32MB. This type of problem can also occur on later systems if you attempt to install memory layouts that are incompatible with the PC. Unfortunately, this is a limitation of the motherboard and cannot be corrected without upgrading the motherboard (or using smaller memory modules).

Before installing any memory, always verify that the memory module's size, type, speed, and other characteristics are compatible with the host PC.

**SYMPTOM 26-31**    **A PnP expansion card refuses to work on one motherboard, but works on others**    For example, you find that a Creative Labs PnP sound board refuses to work on one motherboard, but the board works just fine on another motherboard (though this can also occur with other types of PnP cards). This verifies that the expansion card is working properly, and is generally an issue where the PnP BIOS is usually at fault. Check with the motherboard manufacturer to see if there is a BIOS update to correct PnP problems. If not, you may need to disable the sound card's PnP compatibility and configure the card manually (as a legacy device). If that's not possible, you may need to select another expansion card for the system.

**SYMPTOM 26-32**    **The system CD-ROM drive refuses to work once an IDE bus master driver is installed**    This is almost always caused by a driver that is not interacting properly with the IDE/EIDE/UDMA bus controller on the motherboard. In almost all cases, you should contact the motherboard or system manufacturer and update the IDE bus master driver(s), or disable bus mastering completely. Motherboards often require a set of drivers to be installed under your operating system (e.g., VIA uses "4-in-1" drivers). You may have better results repartitioning the hard drive, reinstalling Windows, and then installing the latest set of motherboard drivers from scratch before reinstalling applications and other files (though this is often a time-consuming process).

**SYMPTOM 26-33** **You cannot get an AMD 5x86 133-MHz CPU to run on your motherboard** This is a symptom found when upgrading older 486-vintage motherboards. Check your voltage first. The AMD 5x86 runs on 3.3V, so you may need a voltage regulator in the CPU socket. (The AMD CPU may already be damaged.) Also check your BIOS version. You may need an updated BIOS to support the AMD CPU properly. Check your jumper settings next. The speed or CPU type selection is almost always set wrong. If you cannot jumper the motherboard correctly (such as 33-MHz bus speed), then the motherboard itself is limited. It cannot enable the 4x internal CPU clock for the AMD 5x86. In this case, you will need to use a different CPU or replace the motherboard.

**SYMPTOM 26-34** **You cannot get a Cyrix 5x86 CPU to run on your motherboard** This is a symptom found when upgrading older 486-vintage motherboards. Check your voltage first. The Cyrix 5x86 uses 3.3V, so you may need a voltage regulator in the CPU socket (the Cyrix CPU may already be damaged). Also check your BIOS version. You may need an updated BIOS to support the Cyrix CPU properly. Check your jumper settings next. The speed (33 MHz) or CPU type selection is almost always set wrong. If problems persist, you may need a different CPU or motherboard.

**SYMPTOM 26-35** **You see the error message "System Resource Conflict" on the AMI BIOS POST display** This is an error generated by AMI PnP BIOS (though other PnP BIOS may produce similar errors) and is generated when the BIOS detects a resource conflict during initialization. You may try to force the BIOS to reconfigure the conflicting resource by pressing INSERT during POST. If problems continue, you may need a BIOS update, which may be able to resolve assignment conflicts more intelligently. Otherwise, you may need to reconfigure the conflicting resource manually (disabling its PnP support) or remove the offending device(s) entirely.

You can also try clearing the ESCD RAM (as in Symptom 26-4) and allowing the system to redetect and reassign resources—hopefully clearing the problem.

**SYMPTOM 26-36** **The system hangs after using MEMMAKER under DOS** This is most prevalent with AMI's WinBIOS that cannot support the "highscan" option used with EMM386.EXE. Make sure to disable the *highscan* option from EMM386 before running MEMMAKER. You may also choose to upgrade the system BIOS to a more recent version that may be more robust when testing memory. As a better alternative, discontinue the use of DOS in favor of Windows 98/Me/XP, and avoid the use of MEMMAKER.

**SYMPTOM 26-37** **You cannot control power management through Windows** For example, your Power Management icon does not appear in the Windows Control Panel. This occurs even though the APM parameter under the BIOS Power Management Setup is enabled. This problem occurs if you do not enable the APM function before you install Windows 9x/Me. If you have already installed Windows 9x/Me, you should reinstall it. Before doing so, however, make sure that the APM function is enabled. Under operating systems like Windows XP, see that ACPI support (and legacy APM support if available) is enabled in the CMOS Setup—preferably before installing the operating system. If Windows does not enable power management functions after enabling ACPI/APM features in the BIOS, reinstall the operating system from scratch.

**SYMPTOM 26-38** **Systems with a large HDD do not recognize the drive, and cannot boot** This is a typical problem with large hard drives that often need additional time to start up after powering the system. (You may find that a warm reboot will allow the system to boot normally.) Check the Advanced

Setup menu of your CMOS Setup and increase the Power-on Delay time, or enable extended memory or other low-level tests that will extend the POST time—even for just a few seconds. This should correct the problem. This problem may reoccur if CMOS default values are reloaded or CMOS contents are lost.

**SYMPTOM 26-39**    **After installing Windows 95, the system can no longer find the CD-ROM drive on the secondary IDE channel**    You may also find that the IDE drives are running in DOS compatibility mode. This problem occurs often with older motherboards using the Intel 430HX chipset. For example, Windows 95 doesn't recognize the Intel 82371SB drive controller on the motherboard, and this causes BIOS to disable the secondary IDE channel. Devices on the secondary channel are not being detected after the system is rebooted. In most cases, you can upgrade the BIOS to correct this problem or move the IDE devices to a separate IDE controller. You may also be able to download a patch to update the MSHDC.INF file, which will force Windows 95 to recognize the 82371SB controller. As an alternative, you can upgrade to Windows 98/Me/XP, which should overcome this trouble.

**SYMPTOM 26-40**    **The system hangs up or crashes when the chipset-specific PCI-IDE DOS driver is loaded**    This is a known problem with Micro-Star motherboards using a VIA VP1 chipset and Award BIOS 4.50PG. The problem is with the BIOS version and its interaction with the PCI controller portion of the VIA chipset. Upgrading the BIOS version should resolve the problem. Otherwise, it may be necessary to upgrade the motherboard.

**SYMPTOM 26-41**    **You notice that your motherboard is unusually picky about which memory modules it will accept**    This occurs even though the modules are all within the proper type and rating. There are several possible problems to consider. First, most chipsets are very discriminating when it comes to memory speed, so make sure that the memory speed is well within the required range (e.g., PC133). Second, try changing the burst timing in the CMOS Setup to a lower speed (such as 5-4-4-4). If your system works under this low speed, then increase the speed (such as 5-3-3-3, 5-2-2-2, 5-1-1-1, and so on), and keep trying till the best number has been reached. Finally, the memory itself may be of questionable quality. Try good-quality memory bought from a reputable vendor. Make sure the vendor offers a liberal return policy so that you can return questionable memory easily. If the problem persists with even recommended memory modules, try selecting BIOS Defaults for the CMOS Setup, and upgrade/replace the motherboard if necessary.

**SYMPTOM 26-42**    **You experience a problem with pipeline burst cache**    This is a recognized problem with UMC pipeline burst cache (especially on an older Amptron motherboard). The problem can usually be solved by adjusting the cache control to 4-4-4-4. (The default in CMOS is typically 2-3-3-3.) This will reduce performance, but should stabilize cache operations. The best long-term fix for this type of problem is to upgrade the motherboard (and the CPU and RAM if necessary).

**SYMPTOM 26-43**    **You get no display, or the system refuses to boot because of the keyboard controller**    Note that the video adapter proves out fine in another system. This is a problem with the VIA 82C41 24-pin keyboard controller (especially on the Amptron PM-7600 motherboard)—though KBC problems can occur on many different motherboards. A fault with the KBC may cause a "no display" or "fail to boot" condition. The VIA 82C41 is extremely sensitive to damage from power supply surges/spikes and ESD damage. Replace the KBC, or replace the motherboard with a more robust model.

**SYMPTOM 26-44**    **Your customers forget their BIOS password**    The PC password is stored in the CMOS RAM located in either the motherboard chipset or the *real-time clock* (RTC) chip. If it is stored in the chipset, the CMOS memory is backed up by a coin-shaped lithium battery (or other battery). If it is stored in the RTC chip, it has an internal battery to back up the CMOS RAM. For the external battery, first make a complete backup of the CMOS settings. Turn off the system, and then remove the battery for at least two hours. This should clear the CMOS setting and erase the password. For the RTC battery, determine which RTC chip you have. There are five classical kinds of real-time clock CMOS chips:

- Dallas DS 12887 Real Time
- Benchmarc
- Dallas DS 12B887
- Dallas DS 12887A
- BQ3287A

For the Dallas DS 12887 and Benchmarc RTC chips, if you can boot to the A: prompt, flash the BIOS chip with the same boot block record but different BIOS revision. For example, if you have a P/I P55TP4XE motherboard with BIOS revision 0202, flash the BIOS chip to BIOS revision 0115. A BIOS checksum error will be generated. Enter the CMOS Setup screen, reload setup defaults, and then save and exit. At this point, the password has been cleared. You can flash the BIOS back to the original revision. If you can't boot to the A: prompt, turn off the system, remove the BIOS chip, and insert another with the same boot block record but different BIOS revision. Power-on the system. A BIOS checksum error will be generated. Turn off the system. Reinstall the original BIOS. Power-on the system again, and press DEL to enter the BIOS setup screen. Reload the setup defaults, and then save and exit.

For the Dallas DS 12887A, there is a jumper on the motherboard that clears the CMOS. Please check your manual for the location of this jumper, which will vary among motherboards. Shorting this jumper should erase the system configuration information (including password) stored in the CMOS. To clear the CMOS, make sure the system is off. Short the jumper for a moment and then remove it. *Do not leave this jumper shorted.* After clearing the CMOS, the password should be erased. For the BQ3287A and Dallas DS12B887 RTC chips, short the same jumper as in the previous section, but make sure to power the system on and off *before* removing the jumper.

Many of the latest motherboards provide a jumper to clear the BIOS password (without clearing the CMOS RAM). Check the motherboard maker's documentation to locate the jumper.

**SYMPTOM 26-45** **You encounter problems with small Western Digital hard drives (the drives work on other systems)** This type of problem has been identified with ASUS motherboards using Award BIOS with older Western Digital (~1.6GB) drives. Note that problems do not appear in newer Western Digital drives. There are several means of addressing the problems. First, disable the Quick Power-on Self Test in your CMOS Setup, and enable the Floppy Seek option. This will increase the time that the drive gets to spin up. If your CMOS offers a Power-on Delay Time instead, try increasing that time. Also avoid using Disk Defragmenter, or the disk surface scan feature of ScanDisk with these older Western Digital drives. Both have been reported to increase the number of bad blocks on the disk.

Next, consider a BIOS upgrade (especially if you're using a motherboard with the Intel 430FX chipset). Some BIOS versions use a "park head" command that can cause problems with Western Digital hard drives. Finally, check the Western Digital Web site (www.wdc.com) for any drive firmware patches that might be currently available. If all else fails, you might replace the drive or upgrade the drive controller. Otherwise, upgrade the motherboard.

**SYMPTOM 26-46** **You encounter memory parity/ECC errors at boot-up** If you're using non-parity memory devices (such as a 64-bit device instead of a 72-bit device), you will need to disable ECC or parity checking through the CMOS Chipset Features settings. This problem can occur if you reload default CMOS settings, which restores parity/ECC (by default) on a system with non-parity memory. Also keep in mind that a few chipsets (such as the older Intel "Triton" chipset) do not support parity, so even if you use parity RAM, you should try disabling parity checking. If the system is configured properly, you may actually have a memory failure, and you'll need to isolate the memory fault.

**SYMPTOM 26-47** **You flash a BIOS, but now you get no video** When you flash a BIOS, the old CMOS settings are usually left useless. This means you'll have to restore the proper CMOS settings before the system may run properly. Clear your CMOS RAM and reload the proper settings (or choose the BIOS Defaults for a good system baseline). The BIOS chip itself may also be troublesome. There are some problems when flashing an older Intel flash ROM chip. Make sure that there are no warnings or cautions in the system documentation or from the manufacturer's Web site before flashing a particular BIOS chip. Try restoring the original BIOS if possible, or contact the manufacturer for a replacement BIOS chip. If the problem persists, you may need to replace the entire motherboard.

**SYMPTOM 26-48** **You are trying to use a PnP sound card and PnP modem together on the same system, but you get hardware conflicts** This is an all-too-common problem with PnP systems. In general, the modem should take COM2 (2F8h and IRQ3), and the sound card should take 220h, IRQ5, and DMA 1. Try adding the cards one at a time. For example, install the sound card first, and let Windows 9x/Me/XP detect it. Add the modem next. If problems persist, configure one or both cards manually (that is, disable their PnP support) if possible, or try alternative cards. In a few cases, try clearing the ESCD RAM (as in Symptom 26-4), and allow the cards to be redetected by the PnP BIOS.

**SYMPTOM 26-49** **After the memory speed is set in the Advanced Chipset Setup, the system crashes or refuses to boot** With newer memory devices, check the Burst Timing in the CMOS Setup, and try selecting the default value (or slower). For older memory, chances are that you have the incorrect number of wait-states set for your memory configuration; for example, 70nS RAM typically requires at least one wait-state. Disable any Auto Configure DRAM Timing feature, and then set the number of wait-states to 1. That should clear up the problem.

**SYMPTOM 26-50** **There is 32MB (or more) of memory, and the BIOS counts it all during POST, but you only see 16MB in the CMOS Setup screen** This is a problem that has been identified with some older Award BIOS versions. To correct the problem, make sure that the "memory hole" option in the Advanced Chipset Setup area is disabled. The memory hole option assumes a maximum of 16MB of physical RAM in the system. You may also try disabling the system's shadow RAM or BIOS shadow option. Otherwise, a BIOS upgrade may correct the trouble.

**SYMPTOM 26-51** **You move a working IDE drive from an older 386/486 system to your current system, but the system no longer works** In most cases, the data transfer mode is set improperly for the old IDE hard drive (for example, using LBA mode when the IDE drive requires CHS mode). Find the Peripheral Setup screen in your CMOS Setup, and make sure to change all the PIO mode settings to Mode 0. (Chances are the settings are currently at Automatic and are configuring the data transfer incorrectly.) The idea is to ensure that the drive is configured exactly the same way as it was on its original system—including the drive geometry, translation scheme, and data transfer speeds. If you cannot duplicate the original BIOS configuration, get the settings as close as you can, and then repartition and reformat the drive in order to use it on a different (older) controller.

**SYMPTOM 26-52** **Windows locks up when you install a video card and LAN card together** For example, this is known to occur when a Diamond Stealth Video 3200 board and an Intel EtherExpress Pro 10/100 network card are used together. However, you verify that both cards work fine on other systems. Problems begin when you load the Intel network driver. This is a problem that has been identified with older Premio motherboards and is due to a problem in the system BIOS. Upgrade the Premio BIOS to the latest version, or upgrade the entire motherboard.

**SYMPTOM 26-53** **You install a processor and set the jumpers for the correct speed, but the system reports an incorrect speed** For example, you install a 1.3GHz processor using a 133MHz FSB and a multiplier of 10x, but the system reports 1GHz. In virtually all cases, you have set the speed jumper(s) incorrectly. Take another look at the documentation for your motherboard, and see that the speed is indeed set correctly (e.g., 133MHz with 8x is 1GHz, rather than 133MHz with 10x for 1.3GHz). Double-check possible documentation errors with the motherboard manufacturer. If problems persist, the BIOS may not recognize the higher CPU speed correctly, so try upgrading the motherboard BIOS. As an additional check, verify that the CPU is not fake or mismarked.

**SYMPTOM 26-54** **The system frequently locks up or crashes after installing a Cyrix 6x86 CPU** This type of trouble frequently plagued older motherboards. In most cases, the Cyrix 6x86 is not being cooled properly and is overheating. Make sure that you have a heat sink/fan assembly attached properly to the Cyrix, and see that the fan is running. Also, the Cyrix 6x86 P166+ is a 3.52V CPU. Check your voltage regulator and see that it is set to provide 3.45 to 3.6 volts.

**SYMPTOM 26-55** **After installing a new motherboard, you get registry corruption or "out of memory" errors from Windows** This happens most often with older Pentium mother-boards (~100–120 MHz), though it can occur with many later system configurations. This is almost always a BIOS version problem, which causes the motherboard to misbehave under Windows. You will need to update the BIOS version for your particular motherboard or to upgrade the motherboard entirely.

**SYMPTOM 26-56** **The motherboard fails to autodetect the hard drive parameters** This is a known problem on older Data Expert EXP8551S motherboards, and is due to a problem with Windows 95 in recognizing the PCI/ISA/I/O controller portion of the chipset. You can use the following procedure to force Windows 95 to recognize the chipset properly:

1. Boot up the Windows 95 system normally.
2. Change the directory to /WINDOWS/INF.
3. Edit the hidden file MSHDC.INF.
4. Search for all lines with the "1230" device ID. Copy the lines and replace "1230" with **7010** (the correct device ID).
5. Save the file MSHDC.INF.
6. Remove the Standard IDE/ESDI Hard Disk Controller entry from the Device Manager.
7. Restart the computer, and then choose the Windows default driver following the instructions shown onscreen.

You should make a backup copy of the MSHDC.INF file before editing the file. That way, you can easily restore the original file if necessary.

If the problem persists, try entering the specific hard drive parameters for your particular drive into the CMOS Setup. As an alternative, you may be able to upgrade the motherboard's BIOS or operating system, or upgrade the motherboard entirely.

**SYMPTOM 26-57**    **The motherboard refuses to detect the SCSI controller during boot-up**    This problem has been identified with the older Data Expert EXP8551 motherboard, but may occur on many different types of PCI motherboards. In most cases, you will have to change the configuration of your PCI slots on the motherboard. For example, if the SCSI controller is installed on Slot 2, you will need to configure the PCI Slot 2 in CMOS Setup. You can also try moving the card to a different PCI slot, or upgrade the motherboard outright.

**SYMPTOM 26-58**    **You find that you cannot run a Cyrix 6x86 CPU on a particular motherboard**    However, you find that the CPU works properly on other motherboard makes or models. This is a classic problem that has been identified on older Eurone/Matsonic motherboards and is usually the result of an incompatible motherboard clock generator. Some clock generators support the Cyrix 120-, 133-, and 166-MHz models, but exempt the 200-MHz model. Other clock generators support the 120-, 150-, 166-, and 200-MHz models, but exempt the 133-MHz model. So if you're using a 133-MHz or 200-MHz Cyrix CPU, you may be using the wrong clock generator. You will have to replace the CPU with a speed suitable to the particular clock generator, or change the motherboard to one that will accommodate the particular CPU speed.

As a general rule, always verify that the motherboard can support a given processor speed.

**SYMPTOM 26-59**    **The system can count up to and recognize only 8MB of RAM though the system can accommodate even more**    This classic problem is often a problem identified with older Freetech 586F61x motherboards using Award BIOS version D or earlier. You can duplicate the problem by initiating a software reset with CTRL-ALT-DEL, then pressing the hardware reset. BIOS will only count memory up to 8MB. You will need to update the Award BIOS to version E or later. Freetech provides the BIOS patch on their Web site. Otherwise, you can upgrade the motherboard entirely.

As a general rule, always verify the compatibility of memory installed in a system.

**SYMPTOM 26-60**    **When four 8MB SIMMs are installed in the system (32MB), the system only counts up to 24MB**    This is a known problem with older Gigabyte motherboards (typically the GA-586ATE, ATM, and AP ver 1.x). The motherboard does not support double-sided SIMMs (such as 2MB, 8MB, 32MB, or 128MB) in the center bank. Install the SIMMs in bank 0 and bank 2—leaving bank 1 empty.

Some motherboards require the banks to be filled in sequential order or allow you to change the bank order with jumpers. Also be sure to verify the compatibility of memory installed in a system.

**SYMPTOM 26-61**    **Gold-plated modules do not work properly in tin-plated sockets**
As a general rule, you should avoid mixing metal types when choosing memory modules. The metal in the SIMM/DIMM/RIMM socket *must* be the same as the metal on the module itself. Otherwise, tin debris will

transfer to the gold surface and oxidize. This will eventually result in memory failures that suggest faulty memory modules (even though the modules may be fine).

**SYMPTOM 26-62** **Even though all peripherals in the system are SCSI, Windows 95 will continue to detect the PCI IDE controller** You notice that this problem occurs even though the controller was disabled in the CMOS Setup. This is a known problem with the older Iwill P54TS motherboard. Normally, Windows 95 will try to recognize and enable I/O devices, but should not enable devices that are deliberately disabled in CMOS. This is typically a BIOS problem. (The onboard IDE controllers were not properly disabled.) Try upgrading your BIOS to the latest version, or upgrade the motherboard.

**SYMPTOM 26-63** **You get an "EISA CMOS Configuration Error" when the system starts up** For older EISA systems, you must run the *EISA configuration utility* (ECU) in order to properly set up the system. Without this step, the system will not be able to detect any possible resource conflicts. This type of problem is most common when installing a new EISA motherboard, when CMOS contents are lost, or when devices (such as memory) are added or removed.

**SYMPTOM 26-64** **The SMP (dual processor) mode refuses to run in Windows NT** The most common problem is an incompatibility with the SMP HAL shipped with Windows NT (versions prior to 3.51) and the motherboard's chipset. If you are upgrading from an older version of NT (prior to 3.51), first install NT as a standard PC (single processor kernel), and then install NT with the default multiprocessor kernel it provides. (NT will not recognize your dual CPUs if you upgrade straight to a multiprocessor configuration.) This problem should not occur under Windows NT 4.0 or 2000.

**SYMPTOM 26-65** **When attempting to upgrade your flash BIOS, you encounter an "insufficient memory" error** In most cases, you simply don't have enough conventional memory available to execute the flash program. Most flash programs require about 560KB of conventional RAM. Try booting clean with a DOS floppy disk (without any CONFIG.SYS or AUTOEXEC.BAT files), and then run the flash upgrade utility.

**SYMPTOM 26-66** **You see a prolonged system message saying "Updating ESCD" each time the system boots** The *extended system configuration data* (ESCD) area is part of a PnP system, and those contents are stored in an area of the CMOS RAM. One or more PnP devices are attempting to update your BIOS settings. To stop this from occurring, set the BIOS to program mode. This message is perfectly normal when the system's hardware configuration changes, but should not occur repeatedly.

**SYMPTOM 26-67** **You notice a yellow exclamation over your USB port in the Device Manager** Windows indicates that it has detected an unknown PCI device (though this problem is far more common with older versions of Windows without full USB support). In virtually all cases, the proper driver for the USB on your system has not been installed, and Windows cannot recognize the USB hardware. You can usually correct this problem by updating your system BIOS to a newer version that supports the USB hardware better under Windows. In some cases, you may also need to upgrade Windows to a more robust version such as Windows Me/XP.

**SYMPTOM 26-68** **The Device Manager under Windows 95 indicates four COM ports (at unusual IRQs and I/O addresses), but there are only two physical ports on the motherboard** For example, this problem has been identified with the Ocean Rhino motherboard while running a very old Award BIOS. The Award BIOS has since been upgraded to provide full support for Windows 9x/Me/XP, so download the newest BIOS version from the motherboard manufacturer, or upgrade the motherboard outright.

**SYMPTOM 26-69** **The performance of a motherboard with an AMD K5 CPU seems extremely poor** This is almost always because of the old or obsolete motherboard BIOS. Chances are the BIOS was released before the AMD K5 was widely introduced, so there may be problems providing proper AMD support. Make sure that you are using the very latest BIOS, which supplies adequate AMD support, or upgrade the motherboard.

As a general rule, always verify that you're using a BIOS version that provides adequate support for the particular processor that you want to use.

**SYMPTOM 26-70** **The system hangs after installing a Cyrix 6x86 CPU** This is a classic symptom related to the processor's interaction with the motherboard. There is probably a problem with the utilization of system cache, which is causing the system to hang. Try disabling the internal (L1) and external (L2) cache through the CMOS Setup. Upgrade the BIOS to provide better 6x86 support, or upgrade the motherboard.

**SYMPTOM 26-71** **When attempting to upgrade the BIOS version, you cannot use a key sequence such as CTRL-HOME to reboot the PC in order to start the flash process** The current BIOS version does not support such key sequences. To flash the BIOS, start the flash program manually from the DOS prompt according to the manufacturer's recommendations. For example,

```
A:\> AMIFL PAIV17.ROM    <Enter>
```

**SYMPTOM 26-72** **You find that a particular video board refuses to work on a particular motherboard** However, the video board proves out fine on other systems. In most cases, this is a compatibility problem between the video chipset and the motherboard. There may be a BIOS upgrade for the motherboard or video board that can overcome the problem. You may simply have to use a different video board, or upgrade the motherboard outright.

**SYMPTOM 26-73** **When the onboard printer port is set to 3BCh (and EPP/SPP mode) and another parallel port add-on card is set to 378h or 278h, the BIOS only recognizes the add-on card** Port 3BCh seems to disappear. This may be a configuration problem with the older Winbond chipset, which specifies that LPT1 on the motherboard should be set at 378h (EPP or SPP), while add-on parallel ports should be set at 278h or 3BCh. The Winbond chip was designed this way for Windows 95. Check with the motherboard manufacturer for any available BIOS upgrades that can correct this issue, or upgrade the motherboard outright.

**SYMPTOM 26-74** **With 32MB of RAM on the motherboard, Checkit 3.0 causes the system to reboot when performing DRAM tests** This is because the older Checkit 3.0 software will not perform memory testing over 16MB. This is an issue with Checkit—not the motherboard. Upgrade to a later version of Checkit, or switch to an alternate system diagnostic utility.

**SYMPTOM 26-75** **External devices do not wake the system** Chances are that you have a power supply issue. You don't need a special power supply to support an "Instantly Available PC", but the power supply must provide enough standby current to support the needs of all wake-capable devices in the system. The more wake-capable devices in the system (e.g., a LAN card), the greater the standby current required from the power supply. Intel recommends starting with a power supply capable of providing a minimum of 1.5 Amps (2.0 Amps recommended) of +5V standby current. To be sure, total the amount of standby current required by the various components that can wake the system from the standby state. Make sure the power supply provides at least that amount of standby current. In some cases, you may need to upgrade the power supply.

**SYMPTOM 26-76**    **You cannot get parallel port devices to work on your motherboard** In most cases, you must set the proper parallel port mode (such as SPP/ECP/EPP) for the particular device you plan to use. Often, setting the port to Compatibility Mode will work for many common peripherals, but not for more advanced printers or interactive devices. Parallel port modes are selected through the CMOS Setup—usually under Integrated Peripherals or some similar heading.

**SYMPTOM 26-77**    **You notice that some configurations of memory provide less performance than others** This type of problem is most noted on older motherboards (e.g., this symptom has been reported with 440FX chipsets) and is usually the result of a BIOS problem. Try updating your BIOS to the latest available version, or upgrade the motherboard entirely.

**SYMPTOM 26-78**    **You see no performance improvement when enabling PCI/IDE bus mastering** The problem often is that you are using an older (or buggy) driver. Make sure that you have installed the most recent bus mastering driver file for your particular motherboard. If the problem persists, upgrade the motherboard to a later version. (Be sure that the motherboard comes with a CD containing the appropriate bus master drivers for your operating system.)

**SYMPTOM 26-79**    **The BIOS banner displayed on power-on is showing the wrong motherboard model** In virtually all cases, this is a problem with the BIOS version where it cannot identify the correct hardware platform. Get the latest update for your motherboard BIOS.

**SYMPTOM 26-80**    **The motherboard is installed, but the system won't boot** This is a classic sign of installation problems (especially after an upgrade). Start with the basics. Check all of the cables and connectors—especially the power connectors. Also make sure that there are no metal standoffs or brackets shorting the motherboard from underneath. Next, check for any wiring or cables that may be installed backward. While this will rarely keep a PC from booting, it is possible. Be sure that pin 1 on each cable aligns with pin 1 of each connector. Finally, double-check the socket-mounted chip such as the CPU, BIOS ROM(s), and memory modules. They should all be aligned properly and inserted evenly and completely. If you locate an incorrectly installed chip, it may or may not be damaged. Remove it from the motherboard, check it for bent or broken pins, reinsert it correctly, and try the motherboard again. If the chip is damaged, it should be replaced.

**SYMPTOM 26-81**    **The motherboard starts, but it will not boot from the hard drive or recognize the correct amount of RAM in the system** You may see an error message such as "CMOS Error; press F1 to run SETUP." This error generally indicates that the motherboard is working, but the system CMOS contains incorrect information. Either you forgot to enter the new CMOS variables, you forgot to save the settings when you updated them, or the backup battery is not installed and CMOS contents were lost after the system was powered-down. Check the backup battery first. If the battery is a coin cell, see that it is inserted properly and completely into its holder. If the battery is a "pack type," check to see that it is plugged into the proper motherboard connector in the right polarity. If the battery is installed correctly, try a new one. Run the CMOS Setup utility, and check each drive and memory setting. If you entered a drive parameter or RAM amount improperly, correct the settings and save CMOS again. Reboot the PC. If new CMOS settings are lost after the PC is powered-down, the backup battery has failed—try a new battery.

**SYMPTOM 26-82**    **The system boots and runs, but it locks up unpredictably**    This is another issue that crops up frequently after a motherboard upgrade or replacement. Make sure that the CPU and all system RAM are installed correctly and securely. Try reseating the RAM. Check the system CPU for excessive heat. An overheated CPU can lock up without warning. If the CPU is fitted with a heat sink, make sure that the heat sink is securely attached and that you have used ample amounts of thermal compound to aid heat transfer. If the CPU runs hot and there is no heat sink, try adding one.

Also consider the possibility of controller conflicts. For example, if there is a video port on the new motherboard, but you also have a video board installed in an expansion slot, you may have to set jumpers (or use the CMOS Setup) to disable the motherboard's video port. The same thing is true for drive controller conflicts, as well as serial or parallel port conflicts. Take another close look at the expansion boards in your system, and make sure that the board functions do not conflict with the functions provided on the motherboard.

**SYMPTOM 26-83**    **You cannot get SSE2 features to work with the Pentium 4 processor**    This is almost always because you're using an older version of DirectX. While DirectX 7.0a will work fine with the Pentium 4, it does not support SSE2. Upgrade to DirectX 8.0a or later from Microsoft (www.microsoft.com/directx).

**SYMPTOM 26-84**    **The system won't power-on**    If you find that your system cannot power-on on its own—requiring you to unplug and replug the power each time—clear the CMOS jumper to remove any garbage CMOS data, and reset the BIOS settings to their defaults. First, turn off the system. Then move the CMOS jumper from its default location to the Clear position for several seconds before moving it back. (Or power-on the system briefly before powering-down and moving the jumper back.) Turn on the system and press DEL to enter the CMOS Setup screen. Set the correct CPU speed, and then save and exit the setup screen.

# Further Study

**Abit Computer Corp.**   www.abit.com.tw
**Acer America Corp.**   www.acer.com
**American Megatrends (AMI)**   www.ami.com
**ASUS**   www.asus.com
**Biostar Microtech Intl.**   www.biostar.net
**CompuTrend Systems, Inc. (Premio)**   www.premiopc.com
**Data Expert Corp.**   www.dataexpert.com
**Diamond Flower, Inc. (DFI)**   www.dfiusa.com
**Elitegroup Computers, Ltd. (ECS)**   www.ecs.com.tw
**Famous Technology Co., Ltd.**   www1.magic-pro.com.hk/famous/index.html
**First International Computer, Inc. (FIC)**   www.fica.com
**Fong Kai Industrial Co. (FKI)**   www.fkusa.com

**Gemlight Computer Ltd.**   www.gemlight.com.hk
**Genoa Systems Corp.**   www.genoasys.com
**Giga-Byte Technology Co., Ltd.**   www.giga-byte.com
**Intel Corp.**   www.intel.com
**Iwill Computer**   www.iwill.com.tw
**Jbond**   www.jbond.com
**J-Mark Computer Corp.**   www.j-mark.com
**Micronics Computers, Inc.**   www.micronics.com
**Microway**   www.microway.com
**Micro Star International Co., Ltd. (MSI)**   www.msi.com.tw
**Motherboards.org**   www.motherboards.org
**PC Chips Manufacturing Ltd.**   www.pcchips.com
**Pine Technology Ltd.**   www.pinegroup.com
**Shuttle Computer International**   www.shuttlegroup.com
**Soyo Computer Inc.**   www.soyo.com.tw
**Supermicro Computer Inc.**   www.supermicro.com
**Tekram Technology**   www.tekram.com
**Tyan Computer**   www.tyan.com

# 27

# PARALLEL PORT TROUBLESHOOTING

**E**ven after more than two decades of intense computer development, the *parallel port* (also called the *LPT port*, *Centronics port*, or *printer port*) remains one of the most versatile and reliable printer connection techniques in the computer industry. By sending an entire byte of data from computer to printer port simultaneously, and managing the flow of data with discrete handshaking signals, the circuitry required to bundle and decode data and control signals (such as that needed by serial ports) is virtually eliminated. You can see a parallel port integrated into a standard ATX I/O panel in Figure 27-1. The longevity of parallel ports has been due largely to their simplicity and good overall performance, but today's parallel ports are vulnerable to failure. Cable problems, static discharge damage, and spontaneous hardware faults can easily disable printer communication. Additional parallel port problems can arise from the new generation of high-performance printers and other parallel port devices, and from port sharing. This chapter explains the pin assignment and operation of conventional parallel ports, explains the advances that have taken place, and presents a series of troubleshooting procedures intended to help you isolate and correct port problems.

While parallel ports are still a common sight on most motherboards, the universal appeal of USB (and broad availability of USB printers and other peripherals) is putting pressure on this venerable interface. Some of the latest "legacy-free" systems even forego a parallel port in favor of a "USB-only" design.

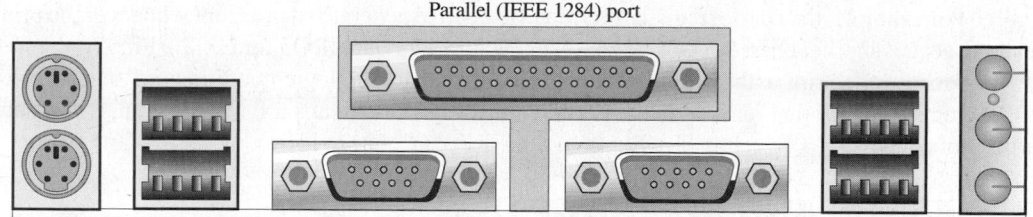

**FIGURE 27-1**    The IEEE 1284 parallel port remains a standard fixture on even the latest motherboards such as this Asus P4B533 (Courtesy of Asus Computer, Inc.)

# Understanding the Parallel Port

The parallel port interface is one of the simplest and most straightforward circuits that you will encounter in a PC. Figure 27-2 illustrates a typical bidirectional port. A parallel port is composed of three separate registers: the data register, the status register, and the control register. Address bits A0 to A9 are decoded to determine which of the three registers is active. The use of -I/OR (-I/O Read) and -I/OW (-I/O Write) lines determine whether signals on the data bus (D0 to D7) are being read from or written to the respective register. When the port is ready to accept another character, handshaking line conditions will trigger an interrupt to request a new character.

The heart of a parallel port is the *data register*. In older PCs, the data register could only be written to (which renders the port unidirectional). But virtually all PCs since the release of 386 systems provide data registers that can be read and written (which makes the port bidirectional). To access a printer, the system CPU simply loads the port data register with the value to be passed. The bidirectional *control register* manages the behavior of the port and sets the conditions under which new characters are requested from

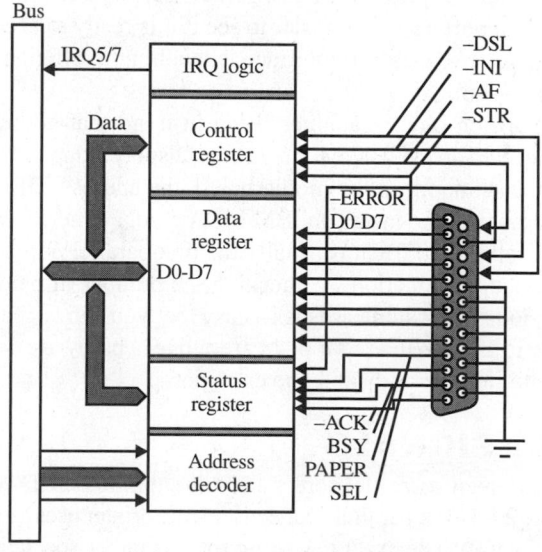

**FIGURE 27-2**    Block diagram of a basic bidirectional parallel port

the CPU. For example, the control register is typically set up to generate an interrupt whenever the printer is ready to accept another character (for example, IRQ7 for LPT1, and IRQ5 for LPT2). Finally, the *status register* is read to determine the printer's status (extracted from the logic conditions of several printer handshaking lines). All that remains is the port connector itself, which is a female 25-pin subminiature D-type connector.

## ADDRESSES AND INTERRUPTS

As previously mentioned, the conventional parallel port in a PC is implemented through a series of three registers. One register simply buffers the 8 data bits, while the other two registers handle the port's handshaking lines. Whereas older BIOS versions supported only two or three parallel ports, today's PCs use BIOS written to support up to four complete parallel ports designated LPT1, LPT2, LPT3, and LPT4. The base addresses allocated for each port are 0378h (LPT1), 0278h (LPT2), 03BCh (LPT3), and 02BCh (LPT4). The base address of each port corresponds to the data register. The status register of a respective port is accessed from the base address with an offset of 01h (that is, 0379h, 0279h, 03BDh, and 02BDh), and the control register is accessed with an offset of 02h (that is, 037Ah, 027Ah, 03BEh, and 02BEh).

> Although a typical PC can theoretically support four LPT ports, it is extremely rare for a PC to offer more than two ports. Even then, the IRQ for LPT2 (IRQ5) often conflicts with the IRQ assigned to sound functions.

During initialization, ports are checked in the following order: 03BCh, 0378h, 0278h, and 02BCh. LPT designations are assigned depending on what ports are found, so keep in mind that LPT addresses may be exchanged in a manner depending on your particular system. The specific I/O addresses for each port are kept in the BIOS data area of RAM starting at 0408h. As you might expect, only one LPT port can be assigned to a base address. If more than one parallel port is assigned to the same address, system problems will almost certainly occur.

The use of interrupts gets a bit complicated. There are basically two modes of requesting new characters for the printer: polling and interrupt-driven. *Polling,* the most popular method, occurs when the BIOS polls (or checks) the respective port's status register to see if it is ready to accept another character—no interrupts are generated. An *interrupt-driven* interface is much more efficient, but can bog down other important operations during printing.

For technicians who work on older machines, keep in mind that address 03BCh was originally reserved for a parallel port located on the IBM Monochrome Display Adapter (MDA). If you are servicing an older system with *no* video support on the motherboard, the address 03BCh may be reserved in the event that you, for some reason, want to install an IBM MDA card. For newer systems with video support located on the motherboard, address 03BCh is usually the first parallel port address.

Always begin your service examination by checking the number of parallel ports in your system. Adding parallel ports to various expansion cards is so easy that you can exceed the limit of four parallel ports without even knowing it. If more than four ports are active, a hardware conflict can result and crash the system—you will have to remove or disable the extra ports.

## PARALLEL PORT SIGNALS

IBM and compatible PCs implement a parallel port as a 25-pin subminiature D-type female connector similar to the one shown in Figure 27-3. The parallel connection at the printer uses a 36-pin Centronics-type connector (Amphenol type 57-30360). The exact reasoning for this rather specialized connector is not clear,

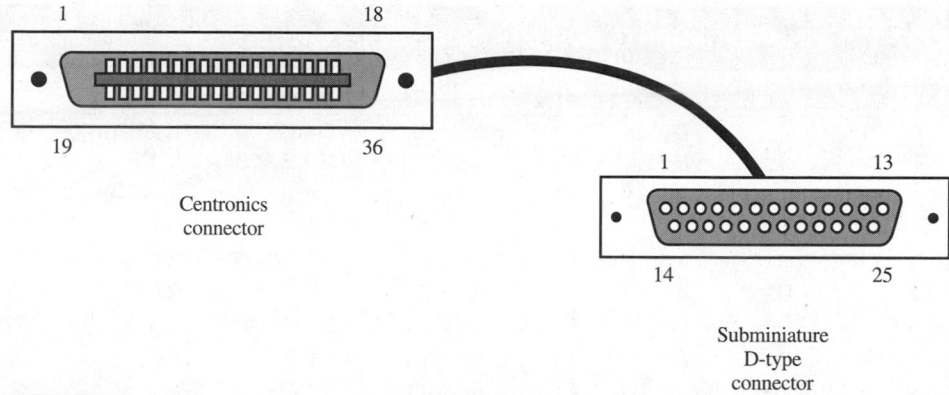

**FIGURE 27-3**   A typical parallel (printer) port cable assembly

since 11 pins of the Centronics connector will remain unused. There are three types of signals to be concerned with in parallel connections: data lines, control (or *handshaking*) lines, and ground lines. Table 27-1 identifies the name and description of each pin. The following section describes each signal. The pin numbers at both the PC and printer ends are listed for your reference. Also remember that all signals on the parallel port are compatible with conventional TTL (5-volt logic) signal levels.

## Data lines

The *data lines* are the actual data-carrying conductors that carry information from the parallel port to or from the printer or other peripheral. There are eight data lines (D0 to D7), located on pins 2 through 9. To reduce the effects of signal noise on parallel cables, each data line is given a corresponding *data ground* line (pins 20 to 27). Ground lines also provide a common electrical reference between the computer and peripheral. The remainder of a parallel port is devoted to status and handshaking signals.

## Initialize and Select

To ensure that the printer starts in a known initialized state, an -Initialize signal (-INI or -C2 on pin 16) sent from the computer is used to reset a printer to the state it powered up in. Initializing the peripheral has the same effect as turning it off and then turning it on again. The -Initialize line is active-low, so the printer must apply a logic 0 to trigger an initialization. The Select line (SEL or S4 on pin 13) tells the waiting computer that the peripheral is online and ready to receive data. Select is an active-high logic signal, so a logic 1 indicates that a device is online and ready, while a logic 0 indicates that the printer is not ready to receive data. The computer will not send data when the select line is logic 0. You can usually determine the Select line's general condition from the printer's front panel "online" light.

## Strobe, Busy, and Acknowledge

Once a computer has placed 8 valid bits on the parallel data lines, the peripheral must be told that the data is ready. A -Strobe signal (-STR or -C0 on pin 1) is applied to the peripheral from the computer just after data is valid. The brief -Strobe signal causes the peripheral to accept the byte and store it in the printer's internal buffer for processing.

Under ideal circumstances, parallel printer ports can achieve data rates of up to 500,000 characters per second. With such a tremendous throughput, the printer needs some method of coordinating data transfer—the computer must wait between characters until the printer is ready to resume accepting new characters. Printers

**TABLE 27-1** PIN ASSIGNMENTS FOR A PARALLEL PORT INTERFACE

| SIGNAL NAME | LABEL | SIGNAL PIN | | | GROUND PIN | | |
|---|---|---|---|---|---|---|---|
| | | D-sub IEEE 1284A | Centronics IEEE 1284B | IEEE 1284C | D-sub IEEE 1284A | Centronics IEEE 1284B | IEEE 1284C |
| Data bit 0 | D0 | 2 | 2 | 6 | 19 | 20 | 24 |
| Data bit 1 | D1 | 3 | 3 | 7 | 19 | 21 | 25 |
| Data bit 2 | D2 | 4 | 4 | 8 | 20 | 22 | 26 |
| Data bit 3 | D3 | 5 | 5 | 9 | 20 | 23 | 27 |
| Data bit 4 | D4 | 6 | 6 | 10 | 21 | 24 | 28 |
| Data bit 5 | D5 | 7 | 7 | 11 | 21 | 25 | 29 |
| Data bit 6 | D6 | 8 | 8 | 12 | 22 | 26 | 30 |
| Data bit 7 | D7 | 9 | 9 | 13 | 22 | 27 | 31 |
| Error (Fault) | -S3 | 15 | 32 | 4 | 23 | 29 | 22 |
| Select | S4 | 13 | 13 | 2 | 24 | 28 | 20 |
| PaperEnd | S5 | 12 | 12 | 5 | 24 | 28 | 23 |
| -Acknowledge | -S6 | 10 | 10 | 3 | 24 | 28 | 21 |
| Busy | S7 | 11 | 11 | 1 | 23 | 29 | 19 |
| -Strobe | -C0 | 1 | 1 | 15 | 18 | 19 | 33 |
| -AutoLF | -C1 | 14 | 14 | 17 | 25 | 30 | 35 |
| -Init | -C2 | 16 | 31 | 14 | 25 | 30 | 32 |
| -SelectIn | -C3 | 17 | 36 | 16 | 25 | 30 | 34 |
| HostLogic High | | | | 18 | | | 18 |
| PeriphLogic High | | | | 36 | | | 36 |

use the Busy signal (BSY or S7 on pin 11) to delay the computer until the printer is ready. Peripherals drive the Busy line to logic 1 any time a -Strobe signal is received. The Busy signal remains logic 1 for as long as it takes the peripheral to prepare for the next byte. It is important to note that a Busy signal can delay the computer indefinitely if a serious peripheral error has occurred (for example, paper exhausted or ribbon jammed).

When the peripheral has received a byte and dealt with it, the peripheral must then request another character from the waiting computer. The printer drops the Busy line and initiates a brief -Acknowledge pulse (-ACK or -S6 on pin 10). -Acknowledge signals are always active-low logic signals, and a typical acknowledge pulse lasts about 8µS. It is this interaction of data, -Strobe, Busy, and -Acknowledge signals, that handles the bulk of data transfer in a parallel port.

 This interaction of Strobe, Busy, and Acknowledge signals limit the effective data transfer rates for a conventional parallel port to about 150KB/s, though later IEEE 1284 implementations allow much higher data rates.

## Auto Feed

Some printers make the assumption that a carriage return signal (or CR) will automatically advance the paper to the next line, while other printers simply return the carriage to the beginning of the existing line without advancing the paper. Many printers make this feature selectable through the use of a DIP switch in the printer, but an -Auto Feed signal (-AF or -C1 on pin 14) from the computer can control that feature. A TTL logic 0 from the computer causes the printer to feed one line of paper automatically when a carriage return command is detected. A TTL logic 1 from the computer allows only a carriage return (paper would have to be fed manually). Most computer parallel ports keep this line at logic 0.

## Device Select

The -Device Select line (-DSL or -C3 on pin 17) allows the computer to bring the peripheral online and offline remotely. Many parallel ports leave this signal as a logic 0 so that peripherals will automatically accept data. A logic 1 on this line would inhibit printer operation.

## Error

The -Error signal (-ERROR or -S3 on pin 15) generated by a printer (or other peripheral) tells the computer that trouble has occurred, but is not specific about the exact problem. A variety of problems can cause an error—it depends on your particular peripheral and what it is capable of detecting. The error line uses active-low logic, so it is normally logic 1 until an error has occurred. An -Error signal can typically indicate an "Out of Paper," "Printer Offline," or "General Printer Fault" error condition.

# PORT OPERATION

This part of the chapter describes a standard sequence of events in a basic parallel port. The parallel data transfer begins by placing the printer online. -Strobe and -Acknowledge must be TTL logic 1, while Busy must be logic 0. In this state, the peripheral can now accept a byte of data. When printing is attempted, the CPU polls the desired LPT port and checks its status register. If the post is ready, a byte is written to the data register and passed to the peripheral.

Data must be valid for at least 0.5µS *before* the computer initiates a logic 0 -Strobe. The printer responds by returning a logic 1 Busy signal, which changes the port's status. Subsequent polling of the status register will indicate that the port is unavailable. The -Strobe pulse must last at least 1.0µS. Data must be held valid at least 0.5µS *after* the -Strobe pulse passes. This timing ensures that the peripheral has enough time to receive the data. Since Busy is now logic 1, communication stops until the data byte has been processed. Processing can take 1mS if the printer's buffer is not full. If the printer's buffer is full, communication may be halted for a second or more. After the data byte has been processed, Busy is dropped to logic 0 and the printer sends a 5.0µS logic 0 -Acknowledge pulse to request another data byte from the waiting computer. Once the -Acknowledge line returns to a TTL logic 1 condition, the interface is ready to begin a new transfer. The status register then indicates the port is ready, and when the port is next polled, a new byte can be written. Figure 27-4 illustrates this relationship—one complete cycle can take a bit over 1mS.

# ADVANCED PARALLEL PORTS

The appeal of a parallel port is easy to understand—it is *simple*. While serial devices struggle with baud rates, stop bits, and parity (problems that continue to this day), parallel devices just plug into the 25-pin D-type connector, and away you go. The parallel port offered "plug-and-play" convenience long before

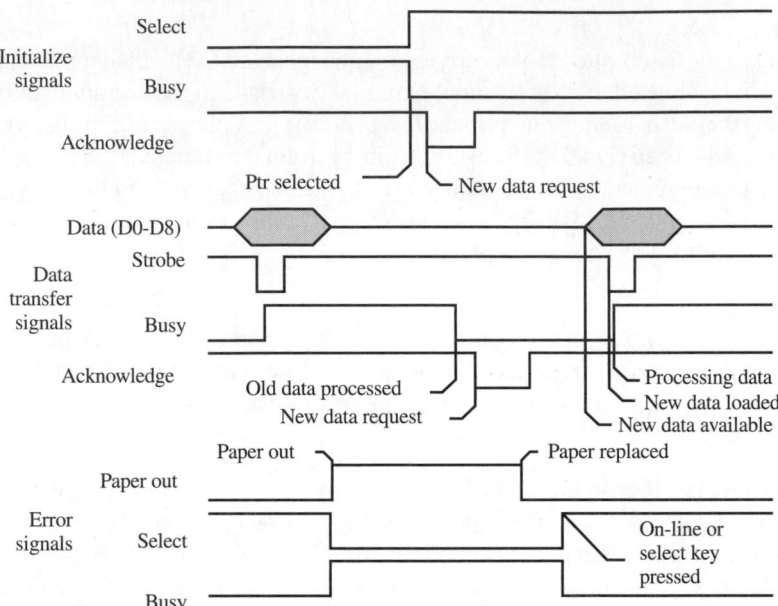

**FIGURE  27-4**   Typical parallel port timing diagram

the term ever came in vogue. Although the parallel port has been a staple of PC communication, it certainly has not gone unchanged over the last 15 years. If you've been shopping for new computers or I/O boards over the last year or two, you've probably noticed the terms Enhanced Parallel Port (EPP) and Enhanced Capabilities Port (ECP) associated with the parallel port. With the IEEE 1284 parallel port standard developed by the Institute of Electrical and Electronic Engineers (IEEE), the PC industry has finally moved past the "classical" parallel port architecture and embraced a truly improved parallel port. This part of the chapter compares the various parallel port modes.

## Unidirectional Ports

The original PC utilized a unidirectional parallel port. That is, the port sent data only one way (from the PC to the peripheral device, which was almost always a printer). For the time, unidirectional communication was adequate for general-purpose PCs, and the parallel port became synonymous with "printer port." Unidirectional ports reigned in the PC market until 1987 (around the time of the 386).

## "Type 1" Bidirectional Ports

By 1987, IBM had launched its PS/2 line. Among the other technological advances in the PS/2, IBM incorporated a bidirectional parallel port. Bidirectional ports were hardly a breakthrough (older hobby-type PCs had used similar ports), but IBM was really the first to use a bidirectional port in a commercial PC. The bidirectional port was really not any faster or better than a unidirectional port, but the ability to send data back to the PC opened up the parallel port to other devices besides printers (for example, parallel port tape drives and so on). Clone PC manufacturers jumped on the improvement, and bidirectional ports became common in almost all subsequent clones.

### "Type 3" Bidirectional Ports

One of the problems with bidirectional parallel ports is that they are CPU-intensive, requiring relatively large amounts of CPU attention in order to manage the transfer of data. Later models of the PS/2 (the 57, 90, and 95) made an attempt to increase the throughput of a parallel port by using Direct Memory Access (DMA) techniques. The DMA approach allows the CPU to define a block of memory (for example, printer ASCII characters) to be sent. A DMA controller takes over control from the CPU and transfers the data without CPU intervention—generally resulting in faster data transfer. This approach also worked when receiving data. In practice, Type 3 bidirectional ports are rarely used because today's high-performance CPUs can transfer data much faster than a DMA process.

## IEEE 1284 MODES

By the end of the 1980s, it was becoming clear that conventional bidirectional parallel ports were simply not adequate to handle the new generations of faster peripherals that were appearing for the parallel port (such as CD-ROMs, tape drives, and high-volume laser printers). The 150 KB/s parallel transfer rates that were once considered speedy were now severely limiting the performance of new peripherals. In 1991, a group of major PC manufacturers—including IBM, Lexmark, and Texas Instruments—formed the Network Printing Alliance (NPA) in an attempt to develop a new parallel port architecture. In 1994, the IEEE (in conjunction with the NPA) released the "Standard Signaling Method for a Bidirectional Parallel Peripheral Interface", also known as IEEE standard 1284.

The IEEE 1284 does not define a single parallel approach, but instead outlines *five* different operational modes for the parallel port: compatibility mode, nibble mode, byte mode, ECP mode, and EPP mode. All five modes offer some amount of bidirectional capability (known under IEEE 1284 as *back channel communication*). When the 1284-compliant parallel port is initialized, it checks to see which operating mode is most appropriate. In most cases, the port can be manually configured to use a particular operating mode through the CMOS Setup.

Currently, the operating systems that have built-in support for IEEE 1284 are Windows 95/98/Me/XP/2000, Solaris, and some versions of Linux. They have support for IEEE 1284 negotiation (a.k.a. "parallel port plug-and-play") and fast printing in ECP mode. To take advantage of this capability, you must have a printer and a parallel port with ECP capability. In addition, the parallel port must be configured in the Windows Device Manager as an "ECP Printer Port" with an IRQ and DMA channel configured. You can determine your parallel port's configuration in the Device Manager (as shown in Figure 27-5). If you don't have these settings configured (but *do* have an ECP-capable printer), the driver will "fall back" to Fast Centronics mode. If neither of these conditions is met, the driver stays in the old "slow" (or "compatibility") mode.

### Compatibility Mode

This mode defines the basic protocol used by most PCs to transfer data to a simple printer. It's commonly called Centronics mode, and is the method commonly associated with the standard parallel port. In this mode, data is placed on the port's data lines, the printer status is checked for errors and busy conditions, and then a data strobe is generated by the software that clocks the data to the printer. To output one byte of data, this port requires four I/O instructions (and at least as many additional instructions). This type of operation limits the bandwidth capabilities at the port to about 150 KB/s. This bandwidth is sufficient for communicating with dot-matrix, ink-jet, and many older laser printers, but it's a serious limitation when communicating with later parallel port devices like LAN adapters, removable disk drives, and the newest generation of laser printers.

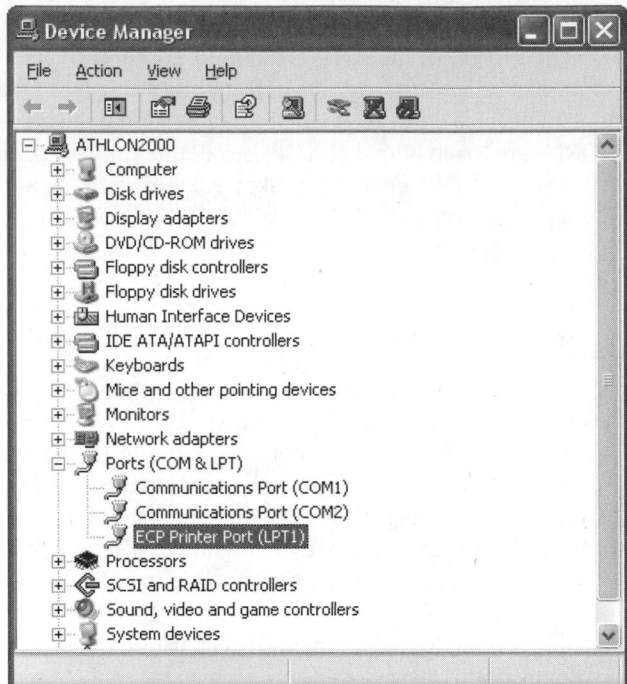

**FIGURE 27-5** Checking the parallel port mode in Device Manager under Windows XP

Many of the integrated IEEE 1284 I/O controller chips have implemented a mode that uses a FIFO (First In/First Out) buffer to transfer data with the compatibility mode protocol—this mode is referred to as Fast Centronics (or Parallel Port FIFO) mode. When this mode is enabled, data written to the FIFO port will be transferred to the printer using hardware generated strobes for the handshaking. Since there is very little latency between transfers, and the software does not have to do any of the strobing or handshake checking, data rates over 500 KB/s are achievable with some systems. Remember that this mode is *not* an IEEE 1284–defined mode.

Whenever problems are encountered with the operation of parallel port devices, try setting the parallel port to "compatibility mode" in the system's CMOS Setup. You may loose data transfer speed, but you should gain compatibility with older devices.

## Nibble Mode

Nibble mode is the most common way to get "reverse" channel data back from a printer or other peripheral. This mode is usually combined with compatibility mode (or a proprietary forward channel mode) to create a complete bidirectional data channel. All standard parallel ports provide five lines from the peripheral to the PC that can be used for external status indications. Using these lines, a peripheral can send a byte of data (8 bits) by sending 2 "nibbles" (4 bits per "nibble") of information to the PC in two data transfer cycles.

Nibble mode (like compatibility mode) requires that the software drive the protocol by setting and reading lines on the parallel port. Nibble mode is the most software-intensive mode for reverse channel data communication. For this reason, a *severe* bandwidth limitation of approximately 50 KB/s applies for this type of data transfer. The major advantage of this approach is the ability to operate on all PCs that have a parallel port. The performance limitations don't have much effect on low-bandwidth peripherals such as printers, but can be intolerable when used with other bidirectional devices.

## Byte Mode

With later implementations of the parallel port interface, some manufacturers (led by IBM on its PS/2 parallel port) added the capability to disable the drivers used for driving the data lines and allowed the data port to become an "input" data port. This enables a peripheral to send an entire byte of data to the PC in one data transfer cycle by using the eight data lines (rather than the two cycles required using nibble mode). This approach enables the byte mode for reverse channel data transfer that can be used to provide data rates *into* the PC approaching that of compatibility mode (which sends data *from* the PC). This type of port is sometimes referred to as an enhanced bidirectional port, and is often mistaken for an Enhanced Parallel Port (EPP)—the two port types are not the same thing.

## ECP Mode

The *extended capability port* (ECP) protocol was proposed by Hewlett-Packard and Microsoft, in 1992, as an advanced mode for communication with printer and scanner-type peripherals. Like the EPP protocol described next, ECP provides a high-performance bidirectional communication path between the host system and the peripheral. When the ECP protocol was proposed, a standard register implementation was also proposed (this can be found in the document "The IEEE 1284 Extended Capabilities Port Protocol and ISA Interface Standard," available from Microsoft).

The many features of ECP include Run Length Encoding (RLE) data compression for the host system's LPT port, FIFO buffers for both the forward and reverse channels, DMA channel use, and programmed I/O (PIO). The RLE feature enables real-time data compression that can achieve compression ratios up to 64:1, which is particularly useful for printers and scanners that are transferring huge amounts of data that have large strings of repetitive information. In order for the RLE mode to be enabled, both the host *and* the peripheral must support it.

*Channel addressing* is a scheme used to address multiple logical devices within a single physical device. For example, in a multifunction device such as a fax/printer/modem, a single parallel port is attached to a printer, fax, and modem. Using ECP channel addressing to access each of these devices, you could receive data from the modem device while the printer data channel is busy processing a print image. With the compatibility mode protocol, if the printer gets too busy, no more communication can occur until the printer data channel is free. With ECP, the software driver simply addresses another channel, and communication proceeds normally.

With the EPP scheme described next, a software driver may intermix read and write operations without any overhead or protocol handshaking. With the ECP protocol, however, changes in the data direction must be negotiated. The host must request a "reverse channel transfer" by asserting a request, and then wait for the peripheral to acknowledge the request by asserting an acknowledge signal. Only then can a reverse channel data transfer take place. Since the previous transfer may have been DMA-driven, the host software must either wait for the DMA transfer to complete or interrupt the DMA, backflush the FIFO (to determine the exact transferred byte count), and then request the reverse channel.

## EPP Mode

The *enhanced parallel port* (EPP) protocol was originally developed by Intel, Xircom, and Zenith Data Systems as a means of providing a high-performance parallel port link that would still be compatible with the standard parallel port. This protocol was originally implemented by Intel in its 386SL chipset (the 82360 I/O chip). This was prior to the establishment of the IEEE 1284 committee and the associated standards work. The EPP protocol offered many advantages to parallel port peripheral manufactures, and it was quickly adopted by many manufacturers as an optional data transfer method. A loose association of around 80 interested manufacturers was formed to develop and promote the EPP protocol. This association became the EPP Committee, which was instrumental in helping to get this protocol adopted as an IEEE 1284 advanced mode. Since EPP-capable parallel ports were available *prior* to the release of the IEEE 1284 standard, there is a small difference between the pre-1284 EPP ports and established 1284 EPP protocol.

One of the most important features to note here is that the entire data transfer occurs within one ISA I/O cycle. By using the EPP protocol for data transfer, a system can achieve transfer rates between 500 KB/s and 2 MB/s. This means that parallel port peripherals can operate at *close* to the same performance levels as an equivalent ISA plug-in card (the performance level from a parallel port device is one of the major features of the EPP protocol). Data transfer will take place at the speed of the slowest part of the interface (the host adapter or the peripheral device), but this speed-adaptive property is transparent to both the host and peripheral. The EPP controller will generate the necessary handshake signals and strobes to transfer the data using an EPP Data Write cycle, and will run exactly like a standard parallel port.

The ability to transfer data to or from the PC by the use of a single instruction is what enables EPP mode parallel ports to transfer data at ISA-type bus speeds. Rather than having the software implement an I/O-intensive software loop, a block of data can be transferred with a single instruction. Depending upon the host adapter port implementation and the capability of the peripheral, an EPP port can transfer data from 500 KB/s to nearly 2 MB/s. This data transfer rate is more than enough to enable data-intensive devices such as network adapters, CD-ROM drives, tape backups, and other peripherals. The EPP protocol provides a high degree of coupling between the peripheral driver and the peripheral, meaning that the software driver is always able to determine and control the state of communication to the peripheral at any given time. Mixing the read and write operations (as well as block transfers) can be accomplished easily.

## ECP/EPP CABLE QUALITY

Conventional parallel ports are limited to cable lengths of about 10 feet (about 3 meters). Beyond that, crosstalk in the parallel cable can result in data errors. Ideally, high-quality, well-shielded cable assemblies can extend that range even more, but the cheap, mass-produced cable assemblies that you often find in stores are rarely suited to support communication over more than 6 feet (about 2 meters). To support the high-speed communication promised by IEEE 1284, a new cable specification also had to be devised. This is hardly a trivial concern, especially considering that IEEE 1284 seeks to extend parallel port operation to as much as 30 feet (about 10 meters). Be sure to use an appropriate high-quality cable approved for IEEE 1284 when configuring a parallel port in ECP or EPP modes.

## IEEE 1284 ISSUES

Unfortunately, while the potential and promise of IEEE 1284 offers a lot of appeal, some serious considerations are involved in configuring an enhanced port arrangement. Specifically, you will require an IEEE 1284–compliant parallel port, cable, and peripheral (printer, tape drive, hard drive, and so on) to take full advantage of enhanced capabilities.

Installing an IEEE 1284 parallel port is certainly not a problem. Virtually all current multi-I/O boards and motherboards now provide IEEE 1284–compliant ports. The trouble is that using a $5 printer cable with your old Panasonic KX-P1124 dot-matrix printer won't provide any advantages. To start benefiting from an IEEE 1284 port, you need at least an IEEE 1284 cable and a device with significant memory capacity (such as a laser printer). At that point, you may start to see some speed improvements, but the additional speed will still fall far short of the projected figures. Ultimately, you need to install IEEE 1284–compliant peripherals that will provide ID information to the port and allow optimum performance.

# Troubleshooting the Parallel Port

While the typical parallel port is a rather simple I/O device, it presents some special challenges for the technician. Older PCs provided their parallel ports in the form of 8-bit expansion boards. When a port failed, it was a simple matter to replace the board. Today, however, virtually all PCs provide at least one parallel port directly on the motherboard—a feature usually supported by an I/O controller component of the motherboard's main chipset. When a problem is detected with a motherboard parallel port, a technician often has three choices:

Today's broad acceptance of USB has taken a considerable amount of pressure off the parallel port. In many cases, printers and other external peripherals are readily available with a USB interface, and can easily work together without the traditional compatibility problems that often plague parallel port installations.

■ Replace the South Bridge chip that supports the parallel port(s). Doing this requires access to surface-mount soldering tools and replacement chips, and can be quite economical in volume. But this is a totally impractical solution for end-user troubleshooting.

■ Set the motherboard jumpers (if possible) to *disable* the defective parallel port, and install an expansion multi-I/O board to take the place of the defective port. This assumes there is an available expansion slot. This solution uses an expansion slot, but offers a cheap, fast fix for a defective parallel port. Remember to disable all other unused ports of the multi-I/O board.

■ Replace the motherboard. This is a simple tactic that requires little overhead equipment, but can be rather expensive—a general solution of last resort if you confirm that the parallel port is defective.

If a diagnostic cannot identify the presence of a physical parallel port (a loopback plug may need to be attached), you can usually consider the port to be defective.

## PREVENTING PARALLEL PORT TROUBLE

Parallel ports are generally not complex devices, but some common issues show up regularly. Before you check out the symptoms later in this chapter, consider the following points:

■ **Cable**   You'd be surprised how many parallel port problems are caused by loose, cheap, or damaged printer cables. Make sure the cable is 6 feet or less in length and that it is secure at *both* ends. Try a different cable, or try the suspect cable in place of a known-good one. In many cases, using a good-quality IEEE 1284–approved cable will resolve many difficulties.

■ **Port mode**   Remember that modern parallel ports can operate in several different modes such as compatibility, ECP, or EPP. Not all parallel port devices work properly with ECP or EPP modes. If you have trouble with a printer or other parallel port device, try setting the parallel port to compatibility mode or standard mode in the system's CMOS Setup. In other cases, you may need to configure the port as ECP or EPP to get full functionality from a high-end printer or multipurpose parallel port device.

■ **Hardware conflicts**    LPT ports use IRQ7 and IRQ5. For systems with a second LPT port (LPT2), it is common for IRQ5 to have a conflict, because it is almost always used by sound boards (or integrated sound devices). If you must use two or more LPT ports on your system, it may be necessary to reconfigure the sound board to use another IRQ or to remove the sound board entirely.

■ **Printer driver conflicts**    This is a problem that often arises with parallel port devices such as Iomega Zip drives or SyQuest SyJet drives. The drive software sends special reserved, nonprintable characters to the parallel port; this signals the drive that the next data being placed on the parallel port cable is for that drive (not the printer). Color printers and multiple-font printers may also be using some of these special characters for their printer setups. This situation can cause conflicts between the two drivers and make each unit (the printer and the parallel port drive) look defective to the system. Many printer companies, such as Hewlett-Packard, are in the process of rewriting printer drivers to stay clear of these reserved nonprintable characters, but some drivers still use these characters and will cause conflicts that cannot be resolved. The only way to correct this problem is to use one LPT port for the parallel port drive and another LPT port for the printer. Alternatively, you can use a switch box to isolate the devices, or replace some devices with USB-compliant versions and avoid the parallel port entirely. You should contact the printer manufacture to see if it has updated drivers that will not interfere with the parallel port device.

■ **Printer monitoring software**    Another form of driver conflicts happens with printer monitoring software. Some companies, such as HP, have status drivers that monitor the printer's status. If you have these printers connected to the pass-through port of a parallel port drive, these printer monitoring drivers should be disabled. These drivers can also cause data corruption and system problems. Disabling status communications does not affect the printing.

# WINDOWS CONFIGURATION TROUBLESHOOTING

Windows has long displaced DOS as the predominant PC operating system, so the vast majority of troubles with printers and other parallel port devices will show up under Windows. This part of the chapter highlights the most common issues when configuring a parallel port device under Windows 98/Me/XP. Configuration problems usually fall into one of the following categories:

■ **Cabling problems**    Make sure that you're using a suitable cable between the PC's parallel port and the device. If there is a switch box or other pass-through-type device between the port and device, try connecting the device directly to the port. If you have another parallel port device besides the printer, consider setting up an additional parallel port on your computer to accommodate both devices. It's worth mentioning here that some parallel port devices (such as LPT scanners) provide pass-through ports that allow you to daisy-chain another parallel port device without adding a second port. However, pass-through ports are common problem areas, so try any troublesome devices directly at the PC's parallel port.

■ **Port disabled or IRQs reserved**    Reboot the PC to the CMOS Setup and check the status of the parallel port(s). Make sure that the LPT port is actually enabled (most can be disabled through the CMOS Setup). Also verify that an appropriate IRQ is assigned to the port (for example, IRQ 7 for LPT1, or IRQ 5 for LPT2)—some PnP BIOS versions may automatically reserve those IRQs.

■ **Port configured improperly**    While you're in the CMOS Setup, also check the parallel port mode. In most cases, compatibility mode or standard mode is fine for basic printers, but high-end printers and other parallel port devices may need ECP or EPP mode to operate properly. Some systems may also provide nonstandard or custom port modes that are incompatible with the device being attached.

- **Disable any status monitors**    Printer monitoring software and other printer-related TSRs are notorious for interfering with parallel port devices. Try disabling or uninstalling any kind of status monitoring software on the system. Check the Windows Startup folder and Automatic Skip Driver Agent in the System Information utility to see just what's starting at boot time. DOS TSRs and other real-mode software can be disabled by REMarking out the offending command line in CONFIG.SYS or AUTOEXEC.BAT.

- **Parallel port device set to the wrong mode**    Make sure that the printer or other parallel port device (for example, a SyQuest drive) is not set to plug-and-play mode. Check the documentation that accompanies your device to see whether any alternate modes (for example, a legacy mode) may be used instead.

- **Check and correct any IRQ conflicts**    Check the Device Manager and verify that no other devices are using the IRQ(s) allocated to your parallel port(s). This is usually not a problem with IRQ 7, but may be a problem with sound boards and IRQ 5. Reconfigure or remove the conflicting device(s). For example, consider a SyQuest drive. If you have no SCSI controllers listed (or a SyQuest Parallel Port Drive is listed under SCSI Controllers but is marked with a yellow exclamation point), that usually indicates that an IRQ conflict is preventing the SyQuest Windows driver from loading.

- **Check and remove any similar device drivers**    If you've upgraded or switched to a different parallel port device, the old drivers may still be on your system, and this may cause interference with the new device driver(s). For example, if your system has another removable media device (such as a tape backup) running a device driver in Windows, these devices may compete with SyQuest Windows drivers and prevent the SyQuest drive from installing properly under Windows. Take a moment to remove or uninstall any drivers and applet software related to the old parallel port device(s), and then reinstall the new device's drivers if necessary.

## SYMPTOMS

**SYMPTOM 27-1**    **You hear a beep code or see a POST error indicating a parallel port error**    The system initialization may or may not halt depending on how the BIOS is written. Low-level initialization problems generally indicate trouble in the computer's hardware. If the computer's beep code sequence is indistinct, you could try rebooting the computer with a POST analyzer card installed. (See Chapter 17 for detailed error codes.) The BIOS POST code displayed on the card can be matched to a specific error explanation in the POST card's documentation. Once you have clearly identified the error as a parallel port fault, you can proceed with troubleshooting.

Start with the system as a whole and remove any expansion boards that have parallel ports available. Retest the computer after removing each board. If the error disappears after removing a particular card, then that card is likely at fault. You can simply replace the card with a new one or attempt to repair the card to the component level. If there is only one parallel port in the system, it is most likely built into the motherboard.

For older systems, the fault is probably in one or more of the discrete I/O chips or latches directing the port's operation. You need to refer to the schematic(s) for your particular system motherboard to determine exact signal flows and component locations. Newer system motherboards enjoy a far lower component count, so all parallel port circuitry is usually integrated onto the motherboard's chipset (usually the South Bridge chip). A schematic would still be valuable to determine signal paths, but you could probably trace the parallel port connector directly to its controlling chip. Replace any defective components or replace the motherboard.

**SYMPTOM 27-2**    **You see a 9xx parallel adapter displayed on your system**    This type of numerical error is typically found with older PCs dating back to the IBM XT/AT, but may also be found on other systems. BIOS has not located any parallel circuit defects on initialization, but has been unable to map LPT labels to the appropriate hardware-level ports. As in Symptom 27-1 earlier, the 9xx series error codes usually indicate a hardware fault in the computer. Follow the procedures in Symptom 27-1 to isolate and resolve the problem, or replace the motherboard.

**SYMPTOM 27-3**    **The computer initializes properly, but the peripheral (printer) does not work**    Your applications software may indicate a "printer timeout" or "general printer" error. Before you even open your toolkit, you must determine whether the trouble lies in your computer or your peripheral. When your printer stops working, run a self-test to ensure the device is at least operational. Check all cables and connectors (perhaps try a different cable). If the peripheral offers multiple interfaces, such as serial and parallel, make sure the parallel interface is activated in the peripheral. Also be sure to check the software package being used (word processor, painting package, system diagnostic, and so on) to operate the printer. Ensure that the software is configured properly to use the appropriate LPT port, and that any necessary printer driver is selected. If no software is available, you can try printing from the DOS command line using the SHIFT and PRINTSCREEN keys. This key sequence will dump the screen contents to a printer.

Disconnect the printer at the computer and install a parallel loopback plug. Run a diagnostic to inspect each available parallel port. Take note of any port that registers as defective. Locate the corresponding parallel port. If the port is installed as an expansion board, replace the defective expansion board. If the port is on the motherboard, you can replace the defective port controller chip, install an alternate expansion board to take the place of the defective port, or replace the motherboard.

**SYMPTOM 27-4**    **The peripheral (printer) will not go online**    Before data can be transferred across a parallel port, proper handshaking conditions must exist: the Busy (pin 11) and Paper Out (pin 12) lines must be TTL logic 0, and the Select (pin 13) and -Error (pin 15) lines must be TTL logic 1. All four signals are outputs from the peripheral. You can examine these levels with an ordinary logic probe. If any of these signals is incorrect, the peripheral will not be online. First, try a new communication cable. An old or worn cable may have developed a fault in one or more connections. Next, try the computer with a different peripheral. If a new peripheral *does* come online, the error exists in the original peripheral's parallel port circuitry.

If a different peripheral does not operate properly, there is a problem with the computer's parallel port. Examine and alter the computer configuration to ensure that there is no conflict between multiple parallel ports. Disconnect the printer at the computer and install a parallel loopback plug. Run a diagnostic to inspect each available parallel port. Take note of any port(s) that registers as defective. Locate the corresponding parallel port. If the port is installed as an expansion board, replace the defective expansion board. If the port is on the motherboard, you can replace the defective port controller chip, install an alternate expansion board, or replace the motherboard.

**SYMPTOM 27-5**    **Data is randomly lost or garbled**    Your first step should be to check the communication cable. Make sure the cable is intact and properly secured at both ends. The cable should also be less than 2 meters (about 6 feet) long. Very long cables can allow crosstalk to generate erroneous signals. If the cable checks properly, either the port or peripheral is at fault. Start by suspecting the parallel port. Disconnect the printer at the computer and install a parallel loopback plug. Run a diagnostic to inspect each available parallel port. Take note of any port that registers as defective. Locate the corresponding parallel port. If the port is installed as an expansion board, replace the defective expansion board. If the port is on the motherboard, you can replace the defective port controller chip, install an alternate expansion board, or replace the motherboard.

If you cannot test the computer's parallel port directly, test the port indirectly by trying the peripheral on another known-good computer. If the peripheral works properly on another computer, the trouble is probably in the original computer's parallel port circuitry. Replace any defective circuitry or replace the motherboard. If the peripheral remains defective on another computer, the peripheral itself is probably faulty.

**SYMPTOM 27-6**    **You see a continuous "paper out" error even though paper is available and the printer's paper sensor works properly**    Try another printer. If another printer works, the problem is in your original printer and not in the parallel port. Use a logic probe and check the Paper Out signal at the computer. Try removing and reinserting paper while the printer is running. You should see the Paper Out signal vary between a TTL logic 0 (paper available) and a TTL logic 1 (paper missing). If the signal remains TTL logic 1 regardless of paper availability, the printer's sensor or communication circuits are probably defective. If the Paper Out signal correctly follows the paper availability, the trouble is probably in your computer's communication circuitry.

When you suspect that the problem is in the parallel port, disconnect the printer at the computer and install a parallel loopback plug. Run a diagnostic to inspect each available parallel port. Take note of any port that registers as defective. Locate the corresponding parallel port. If the port is installed as an expansion board, replace the defective expansion board. If the port is on the motherboard, you can replace the defective port controller chip, install an alternate expansion board, or replace the motherboard.

# Further Study

**ECP Technical Document**   www.fapo.com/files/ecp_reg.pdf
**Hewlett-Packard**   www.hp.com
**IEEE 1284**   www.fapo.com/ieee1284.htm
**IEEE Standards**   www.fapo.com/dotstnds.htm
**LPT Ports and Parallel Drives**   syquest.com/support/papers.html
**Printer Working Group**   4www.pwg.org

# 28

# PLUG-AND-PLAY CONFIGURATION AND TROUBLESHOOTING

One of the key appeals of the IBM-type personal computer architecture is its functional modularity—its capability to accept a variety of expansion devices such as modems, video controllers, drive adapters, video capture/TV boards, and so on. Each device that is added to a system needs to be configured in order to utilize unique IRQ, DMA, and I/O resources. Traditionally, devices were configured manually using a series of jumpers on the device. While this proved to be a straightforward approach, it also opened the way for many configuration conflicts (that is, devices accidentally configured to use overlapping resources). Reporting utilities are also imprecise, making conflict resolution somewhat of a tedious, hit-and-miss process. Current operating systems typically provide better tools for conflict resolution (see Chapter 11), but resolving conflicts still demands a certain amount of patience and expertise.

Designers have long sought to automate the device configuration process and remove the error-prone task of device configuration from the hands of end users and busy technicians. The result of this automatic configuration technology has become known as *plug-and-play* (PnP). First introduced with late-model

486 systems, PnP has long since been a standard technology implemented in all current PCs. Although PnP simplifies much of the configuration problems with new systems, there are still many situations where PnP doesn't work perfectly (especially when running devices under DOS, or using pre-PnP devices in a PnP system). This chapter describes the requirements for PnP, outlines the special requirements for implementing PnP under DOS, and provides a wide selection of troubleshooting issues.

# Understanding PnP Under Windows

The first step in troubleshooting PnP is to understand the issues involved in making it run. PnP is not one particular technology, but rather it is a combination of features brought together into a single approach. There are three components involved in a PnP system: PnP devices, PnP BIOS, and a PnP-compliant operating system—each part must be fully PnP compatible, and problems in any part can prevent PnP from working properly.

## PNP DEVICES

A PnP system requires one or more devices—the modems, video adapters, chipsets, drive adapters, and myriad other hardware elements in the PC. Ideally, every device in the PC will be PnP compatible, and today's systems do contain virtually all PnP devices. PnP devices are capable of identifying themselves and their resource requirements to the rest of the system. The only wrinkles occur when non-PnP (*legacy*) devices are mixed into the system hardware.

Today's Pentium 4-class computers have gone a long way toward eliminating legacy hardware support, creating "legacy-free" systems that depend entirely on PnP and ACPI technologies for proper device recognition and configuration.

## PNP BIOS

A PnP system requires a PnP BIOS—especially at boot time. Since PnP devices initialize in the inactive state by default, the PnP BIOS is needed to initialize the core PnP devices (such as the video adapter and boot drive) in order to complete the POST and launch the operating system. Also note that the original version of PnP BIOS (version 1.0) was finalized in May 1994. By October 1994 (version 1.0a), additional clarifications were added. As a consequence, older PnP systems are not fully compliant with the current specification. PnP support problems on older systems can usually be corrected with a BIOS upgrade. System PnP support can typically be enabled or disabled through the CMOS Setup routine—though there is rarely any reason to disable PnP support today. In addition, modern PnP systems employ the *automatic configuration and power interface* (ACPI) standard for device identification and configuration.

## PNP OPERATING SYSTEM

The PnP OS takes over where the PnP BIOS leaves off by identifying and configuring the remaining PnP devices in the system, then loading the appropriate drivers needed to initialize and operate each respective device. The OS also must keep resources aside for non-PnP (legacy) devices and report any changes to the hardware complement in the system. Windows 98/Me/XP are generally regarded as the premier PnP operating systems for end users and general-purpose PCs, while Windows NT and Windows 2000 provide PnP support for networked and business systems. Modern PnP OS versions (namely Windows XP/2000) make extensive use of the ACPI standard for PnP support. Many of the latest BIOS versions provide an ACPI OS option (see the AMI BIOS entry in Figure 28-1).

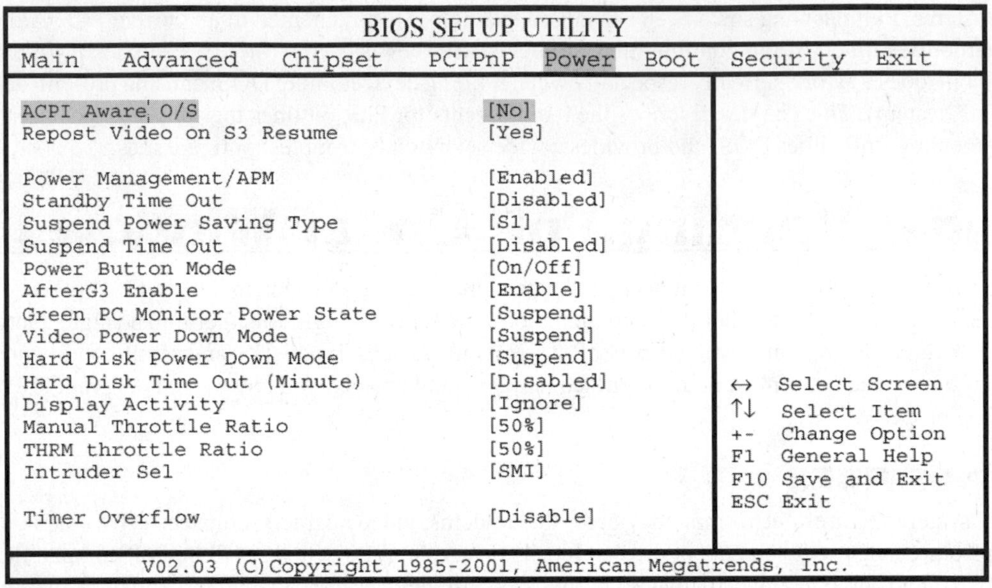

```
                        BIOS SETUP UTILITY
    Main   Advanced   Chipset   PCIPnP   Power   Boot   Security   Exit

    ACPI Aware O/S                    [No]
    Repost Video on S3 Resume        [Yes]

    Power Management/APM             [Enabled]
    Standby Time Out                 [Disabled]
    Suspend Power Saving Type        [S1]
    Suspend Time Out                 [Disabled]
    Power Button Mode                [On/Off]
    AfterG3 Enable                   [Enable]
    Green PC Monitor Power State     [Suspend]
    Video Power Down Mode            [Suspend]
    Hard Disk Power Down Mode        [Suspend]
    Hard Disk Time Out (Minute)      [Disabled]    ↔  Select Screen
    Display Activity                 [Ignore]      ↑↓ Select Item
    Manual Throttle Ratio            [50%]         +- Change Option
    THRM throttle Ratio              [50%]         F1  General Help
    Intruder Sel                     [SMI]         F10 Save and Exit
                                                   ESC Exit
    Timer Overflow                   [Disable]

    V02.03  (C)Copyright 1985-2001, American Megatrends, Inc.
```

**FIGURE  28-1**    Current AMI BIOS versions allow you to enable or disable ACPI support for the OS
(Courtesy of American Megatrends, Inc.)

# AN OVERVIEW OF PNP BEHAVIOR

Now that you've seen the essential elements of PnP, it's time to look at how it all works. A PnP system must be robust enough to handle several important functions. The major functions that must be handled by these three PnP components can be summarized as follows:

- **Identification of installed devices**    The PnP system must be able to identify each installed device. This requires each PnP device to have a certain amount of onboard intelligence.

- **Determination of device resource requirements**    Based on the device identification, the PnP system must be able to determine the kinds of resources (IRQ, DMA, I/O addresses, and BIOS or other memory space) required to support the device.

- **Creation of a complete system configuration, eliminating all resource conflicts**    After all devices have been identified, and their resource needs evaluated, the PnP system must allocate the required resources to each device every time the system initializes (without causing a resource conflict).

- **Loading of device drivers**    After the operating system starts, it must load the appropriate device drivers needed to support every device in the system.

- **Notification of configuration changes**    Each time a PnP device is added or removed from the PC, the PnP system reports the configuration change. When a device is added, the PnP system attempts to identify it and install the appropriate device drivers. When a device is removed, the PnP system attempts to remove all traces of the device and its drivers.

The PnP system starts with the BIOS at boot time. A certain amount of configuration must first be performed by the system BIOS during system initialization. For the system to boot, the PnP BIOS must configure a display device, input device, and initial boot device (such as video adapter, keyboard, and floppy/hard drives). Then, the PnP BIOS must pass the information about each of these devices to the operating system (e.g., Windows 98/Me/XP) for additional configuration of the remaining system devices.

The operating system continues the configuration process by identifying every device in the system and gathering their respective resource requirements. Each non-boot device (such as modems and video capture devices) must be inactive upon power-up so that the operating system can identify any conflicts between the resource requirements of different devices before configuring them. When different devices require the same resources, the devices must be able to provide information to the operating system about alternative resource requirements. The operating system then uses initial or alternative requirements to assemble a working system configuration. Once any resource conflicts have been resolved, the operating system automatically programs each hardware device with its working configuration and then stores all configuration information in the central database contained in *extended system configuration data* (ESCD) memory, which is part of the CMOS RAM space. Finally, the operating system loads the device drivers for each device and notifies these drivers of each resource assignment.

If a change occurs to the system configuration during operation (for example, a device is installed or removed), the hardware must be able to notify the operating system of the event so that the operating system can configure the new device. Additionally, applications must be able to respond to configuration changes to take advantage of new devices and to cease calling devices that have been removed. Such dynamic configuration events might include the insertion of a PC Card, the addition or removal of a peripheral such as a mouse, CD-ROM drive, or printer, or a docking/undocking event for a notebook computer.

In most cases, major configuration changes (such as the installation of a new expansion card or drive) are made before boot time while system power is off. Only PC Card and USB technologies support "hot" insertion and removal.

## Device Types and Identification

The PnP system is designed to support a wide variety of devices across a number of different bus architectures. In general, there are nine classifications of modern PnP devices:

- IEEE 1394 (FireWire) devices
- PCI bus cards of any type (such as video capture or drive controller cards)
- PC Card/CardBus devices (usually used with mobile PCs)
- USB devices of any type (e.g., printers, joysticks, mice, keyboards, speakers, and so on)
- SCSI devices of any type
- ATA (IDE) devices of any type
- ISA bus cards of any type
- LPT (parallel port) devices
- COM (serial port) devices

For the PC to recognize and configure a PnP device, each device must be able to identify itself and its resource requirements to the system. Even motherboard busses and devices must be able to identify themselves. Identification is accomplished through a unique manufacturer-specific code. Traditionally, each manufacturer is assigned a three-character prefix, the following character identifies the device type, and the remaining three characters identify the particular device. For example, the PnP code "PNP0907" identifies a "Western Digital VGA" device adapter. Microsoft reserves the code "PNP" for itself, but other manufacturers are assigned their own codes (for example, Creative Labs uses the "CTL" prefix). The advantage of Microsoft's prefixes is that they are "generic," and you can usually identify a device adequately by utilizing the Microsoft generic equivalent. For example, Microsoft uses these traditional classifications:

- **PNP0xxx**    System devices (e.g., timers and controllers)
- **PNP8xxx**    Network (LAN) adapters
- **PNPAxxx**    SCSI and proprietary CD adapters
- **PNPBxxx**    Sound, video capture, and other multimedia devices
- **PNPCxxx to Dxxx**    Modems and communication devices

As an example, a device ID of PNP0000 would be a generic AT timer, while a device ID of PNP0401 would be a generic ECP printer port. The actual listing of codes is quite lengthy.

Today, the increasing proliferation of hardware under Windows XP/2000 has made the assignment of unique IDs a bit more complicated. For example, Windows uses combinations of up to six values (assigned to each hardware manufacturer and device) to create an ID that is unique to any given PCI device. These values include

- Vendor ID (VID); 2 bytes
- Device ID (DID); 2 bytes
- Subsystem ID (SID); 2 bytes
- Subsystem Vendor ID (SVID); 2 bytes
- Revision ID (REV); 1 byte
- Class Code (CC); 3 bytes

The actual ID assignment may use from one to six of those values depending on the device, so a full ID code may be up to 12 bytes long. At start time, the operating system will use these IDs to install appropriate drivers, identify unresponsive devices, detect the presence of a new device, or remove a device that is no longer present. The operating system follows this process to find and use PCI IDs:

1. The system checks for PCI buses, devices, and functions.
2. IDs are created for all identified PCI elements.
3. Any exceptions (including enabling or disabling features) and workarounds are applied.
4. The PCI device driver is installed and loaded.
5. The device driver applies any exceptions needed to the device.
6. The system notifies the device driver to initialize the PCI device.

## Detection vs. Enumeration

*Detection* is the process that Windows 98/Me/XP uses during its search for legacy (or non–PnP), devices on a computer. Detection is used during Windows setup and any time that you use the Add New Hardware wizard to search for new hardware installed in your computer. Detection does not take place each time you start Windows 98/Me/XP. During the detection process, Windows creates a file called DETLOG.TXT in the root directory of the boot drive. You can use this file as a basic troubleshooting tool in order to determine which devices were detected or if any errors are encountered.

By comparison, *enumeration* is the process that Windows 98/Me/XP uses to identify the PnP devices in your computer—including those devices on PnP busses such as ISAPNP, PCI, and PCMCIA (PC Card) devices. Enumeration occurs each time Windows 98/Me/XP starts and whenever Windows 98/Me/XP receives notification that a change has occurred in the computer's hardware configuration (such as when you remove a PCMCIA card or connect a USB device).

## Extended System Configuration Data (ESCD)

While the BIOS is certainly able to assign resources to each PnP device in the system, it usually does not. After all, most people only change their system hardware on rare occasions. This saves precious time during each boot, but it also prevents the BIOS from making different assignment decisions each time the system starts. When BIOS alone assigns resources, you might find resource settings changing even when the hardware remains unchanged. To ensure that PnP resources remain consistent each time the system boots, assignments are retained in the extended system configuration data (ESCD) area. The ESCD is a small amount of *nonvolatile RAM* (NVRAM)—similar to the CMOS RAM—that holds configuration information for the PnP hardware in your system. At boot time, the BIOS checks this area of memory. If no changes have occurred since the last boot, nothing needs to be reconfigured, and the POST can skip that portion of the boot process.

The CMOS Setup typically lets you enable or disable the BIOS assignment of resources. When a PnP OS is used, select PnP OS. If the OS isn't PnP-compliant, select non-PnP OS to let the BIOS make resource assignments. AMI BIOS makes reference to ACPI for PnP support in Figure 28-1 (shown earlier).

The ESCD also serves as a link between the BIOS and the operating system. Both use the ESCD area to read the current status of PnP hardware devices and to record changes. Windows 98/Me/XP reads the ESCD to see if hardware has been changed and reacts accordingly (for example, by reporting the detection of a new device and launching the Add New Hardware wizard). Windows also allows users to override PnP resource assignments by manually changing resources in the Device Manager. This information is recorded in the ESCD area so the BIOS knows about the changes during subsequent boots and doesn't try to change the assignment back again.

**Problems Updating the ESCD**    Normally, you'll see the message "Updating ESCD" only once after hardware has been changed. However, there are relatively rare cases where you'll see the message each time the system boots (even though the hardware has not changed). This is often caused by an incompatibility between how Windows 98/Me/XP and the BIOS use the ESCD. There are several ways to address this message:

■ If the system displays "Updating ESCD...Success" after adding or removing hardware on the next boot-up only, then this is normal for most BIOS versions. No action is required on your part – simply allow the system to boot normally. Windows will likely identify the new device, and take you through the proper process for installing the necessary drivers.

■ If the system displays "Updating ESCD...Success" every time the PC boots, then there may be a conflict between the BIOS and the operating system. The ESCD information is managed by both the BIOS and by Windows 98/Me/XP to allow for PnP resource allocation. However, some BIOS versions record hardware configuration information in a way that is subtly different from Windows. When this happens, Windows will change the ESCD area back to the way it "expects" it to be on each boot. When you then reboot the system, the BIOS will see this change made by Windows and change the data back again. This tug-of-war will continue to happen each time the system is booted. Generally speaking, this does not damage the system, but a BIOS upgrade may be necessary to correct the problem. In other cases, simply clear the ESCD and reboot the system.

■ If the system displays a message like "Updating ESCD…" but the boot process stalls (either with or without displaying the word "Success"), there is a problem updating the ESCD. This can usually be traced to a problem with an expansion card or other device—usually the one you just added to the machine. It could also be a problem with the motherboard itself. Try clearing the ESCD and CMOS RAM and allow the system to reconfigure itself automatically. Otherwise, try removing the new device. If the trouble disappears, you may need to select a different device, which is more compatible with the system.

## Legacy Devices

Another issue to consider when working with PnP systems is the support of non-PnP devices (a.k.a. "legacy" devices). These are the traditional "jumpered" devices that need to be configured manually. Under DOS, legacy devices run just fine and require no special support, but they can cause a problem under Windows 98/Me/XP. Remember that a PnP system relies on the ability to automatically identify every device in the system. Since legacy devices are not designed to communicate their configuration to the BIOS or operating system, there is no way for Windows 98/Me/XP to detect the device—much less assign resources for it. This means Windows 98/Me/XP might assign resources that are already in use by a legacy device to a PnP device (resulting in resource conflicts). Windows circumvents this problem by requiring you to "register" legacy devices using the Add New Hardware wizard. Once a legacy device is installed and the system is rebooted, use the Add New Hardware wizard to "tell" Windows 98/Me/XP about the new device and install the proper drivers for it.

# Enabling PnP Under DOS

Now that PnP devices and operations have become standard, a new problem has developed for technicians—PnP support under DOS. While Windows 98/Me/XP is a natural platform for PnP devices, real-mode operating systems like DOS cannot automatically identify and configure PnP devices without additional real-mode software drivers. This makes it difficult to use many PnP devices under DOS. In other cases, older hardware platforms may lack the support to fully implement a PnP system (such as older BIOS). This part of the chapter examines the techniques used to implement PnP support under DOS.

Real-mode platforms are quite rare today, but this may help you understand why certain devices cannot be made to operate properly in the real mode, and show you the general steps that may be needed to enable PnP devices.

If you do not have access to a PnP operating system, you'll need to install a PnP configuration driver in CONFIG.SYS that will perform resource allocation and configuration for a PnP device. A PnP *configuration driver* determines the resource settings of all your system devices and legacy cards, configures PnP cards, and provides relevant configuration information to other drivers or applications that access your PnP cards. By contrast, a PnP *configuration utility* allows you to view, enter, or change the resource settings of the PnP and legacy cards in your system. The new or changed settings are then used by the PnP configuration driver to configure new PnP cards. For example, the PnP driver for an Ensonique SoundScape board is DWCFGMG.SYS entered into a CONFIG.SYS command line. The corresponding PnP utility for that Ensonique board is SSINIT.EXE, which is entered into an AUTOEXEC.BAT command line.

The following discussions are provided as examples only—your own real-mode devices may require different configuration drivers and utilities.

## THE PNP CONFIGURATION DRIVER

A PnP driver is loaded in the CONFIG.SYS file. For example, the Creative Labs PnP Configuration Manager (for Creative Labs PnP devices) would load the driver CTCM.EXE in a command line such as

```
device=c:\ctcmdir\ctcm.exe
```

where *c:\ctcmdir* is the directory where you have installed CTCM. This CTCM statement will be placed before all the statements that load other low-level device drivers (such as CTSB16.SYS and SBIDE.SYS) so that your Creative PnP cards will be configured before these device drivers try to use them. For an Ensonique SoundScape sound board, the PnP driver would be installed such as

```
device=c:\plugplay\drivers\dos\dwcfgmg.sys
```

In most cases, an automated installation routine will copy the PnP files to your hard drive and make any necessary changes to your CONFIG.SYS file. But if you have to install the software manually, make sure to place the driver command lines for each PnP device *after* the PnP configuration manager.

## THE PNP CONFIGURATION UTILITY

A PnP utility is loaded in the AUTOEXEC.BAT file. It is this utility that actually configures and initializes the PnP device. For Creative Labs PnP devices, the utility CTCU is entered in an AUTOEXEC.BAT command line(s) such as

```
set CTCM=C:\ctcmdir
C:\ctcmdir\CTCU /S /W=C:\windows
```

where *c:\ctcmdir* and *c:\windows* are the directories where your CTCM, CTCU, and Windows 3.x files are respectively installed. For an Ensonique SoundScape sound board, a typical entry would appear similar to

```
set sndscape=c:\sndscape
lh c:\sndscape\ssinit /I
```

Once again, most PnP products will come with an automated installation routine on floppy disk. But when you are troubleshooting a defective installation or performing a manual installation, the format just shown can help you avoid problems.

## BLASTER VARIABLES

When configuring a PnP sound board, you will usually have to deal with a BLASTER variable in the AUTOEXEC.BAT file. For legacy sound cards like Creative Labs Sound Blaster devices, the BLASTER variable includes fixed settings for address, interrupt, and DMA information such as:

```
set BLASTER=A220 I5 D1 T1
```

With a PnP installation, however, the BLASTER variable is redefined to "X out" the interrupt and DMA entries, as illustrated here:

```
set BLASTER=A220 IXX DX T1
```

The actual values for interrupt and DMA will be entered automatically when the PnP configuration utility runs.

## PROBLEMS WITH GENERIC PNP CONFIGURATION SOFTWARE

There are a number of generic PnP driver/utility sets designed to support a wide range of PnP devices under DOS or other non-PnP operating systems. One of the most popular sets is the *Intel Configuration Manager* (ICM) and *ISA Configuration Utility* (ICU)—both developed by Intel Corporation. In fact, this software may already be installed on your PC (or bundled with PnP cards). While the idea of generic PnP software is an appealing one, such generic software is not necessarily compatible with all types of PnP boards. When the software and hardware are incompatible, you will see one of the following error messages:

- Failed NVS write
- Failure to detect PnP BIOS machine
- Failure to assign new configuration to PnP card
- ICM may not be able to configure your PnP card properly

As a general rule, you should use the manufacturer-specific software that accompanies a PnP device rather than generic PnP software.

## PROBLEMS WITH MANUFACTURER'S PNP SOFTWARE

While manufacturer-specific PnP software will generally provide excellent service, there are some potential limitations to keep in mind. When you use a non-PnP operating system like DOS (and you do not have a PnP BIOS), your PnP card works like a software-configurable card. In such a situation, the PnP driver needs to know which resources have been reserved by each legacy card, PnP card, and system device in your system before it can allocate conflict-free resources to your new PnP card. Normally, the PnP driver can "see" all the resource settings, but you may need to use the PnP utility to enter the resource settings of all the legacy cards in your PC.

You may still encounter hardware conflicts if the resource settings specified through a PnP utility are incomplete or wrong. If this happens, use the configuration utility to select a different group of resources for the PnP card that caused the conflict. You may need to try a few combinations until you find one that works. This can be tedious, but it is easier than the traditional method of changing DIP switches or jumpers.

## HANDLING PNP CONFIGURATION ISSUES UNDER DOS

DOS PnP software allows you to use PnP devices in the DOS environment. In many cases, DOS support for PnP works adequately, but there are several issues that can arise when you do the following:

- **Choose between the PnP BIOS, PnP software, or PnP OS.** There are a number of PC setups that allow you to configure a PnP device based on the PnP BIOS, the PnP driver/utility software, or the PnP operating system. When you are faced with such a choice, it is often better to use the PnP software or operating system (e.g., Windows XP) rather than the BIOS. Set the BIOS so that it will **not** configure PnP devices. The reason is that a BIOS does not have any way of knowing how legacy devices are configured, so allowing the BIOS to configure a mixed system (with legacy and PnP devices) introduces an excellent chance for hardware conflicts.

For "pure" system configurations (containing all PnP devices) you can choose to let the PnP BIOS configure PnP devices.

■ **Upgrade a PnP system to Windows 98/Me/XP.** You may have a system with PnP devices that is running with PnP driver and utility software under DOS or other non–PnP OS. When Windows 98/Me/XP is installed, it should recognize the PnP device(s) during the hardware detection phase of the installation, then install the proper software for dealing with the device(s) under Windows 98/Me/XP. At the same time, Windows should REMark out the real-mode driver and utility software entries under CONFIG.SYS and AUTOEXEC.BAT. This loss of real-mode drivers can cause a problem when returning to the DOS mode later. You may need to re-enable any remarked-out drivers, or create a bootable diskette to configure the system environment for real-mode use.

■ **Replace generic PnP software with manufacturer-specific software.** If there is already generic software used to initialize and run your PnP device(s), that software should be disabled before installing manufacturer-specific software. You can do this by placing the REM statement before the generic software's command lines in CONFIG.SYS and AUTOEXEC.BAT. It is not necessary to remove generic real-mode PnP software files from the system.

■ **The system hangs or reboots whenever the driver software loads.** The upper memory area of your PnP BIOS machine is probably mapped by EMM386 using the HIGHSCAN option (and thus can get corrupted easily). When it does, CTCM (or other DOS PnP software) will not work properly. Your system may then hang or reboot whenever you load CTCM. To resolve this problem, remove the HIGHSCAN option in the EMM386 statement in the CONFIG.SYS file. For example, change the statement:

```
device=c:\dir\emm386.exe highscan
```

to

```
device=c:\dir\emm386.exe
```

where *c:\dir* is the directory in which your EMM386 utility is installed.

# Managing and Troubleshooting PnP Devices

Plug-and-play technology (including the later ACPI standard) provides technicians and end users with a powerful configuration tool that takes much of the guesswork and trial-and-error out of hardware installations and upgrades. Still, PnP platforms are far from perfect, and managing the mix of PnP and legacy devices in many systems takes a bit of care. This part of the chapter provides some tips for working with PnP and legacy devices under Windows 98/Me/XP, and then examines a series of PnP troubleshooting procedures.

## INSTALLING PNP DEVICES

Ideally, you simply need to install the physical device in the system. When Windows 98/Me/XP starts, it should recognize the new device automatically and install the appropriate drivers for it. If Windows cannot locate an appropriate driver already on board, it will prompt you to provide a floppy disk, CD, or other path containing the correct driver. In many cases, the manufacturer's installation CD will have the proper driver for your device, though you may be able to download a later driver for your operating system from the manufacturer's Web site.

# INSTALLING LEGACY DEVICES

Remember that legacy devices are configured manually and cannot report their configuration to Windows 98/Me/XP automatically. When installing new legacy hardware in the system, you must run the Add New Hardware wizard to register the device with Windows and add the appropriate driver. With Windows XP, you can simply open the Device Manager, right-click any device type, and click Scan for Hardware Changes. Alternatively, you can use the Add Hardware wizard under Windows XP:

1. Open the Control Panel and click Printers and Other Hardware.

2. Select Add Hardware in the upper-left pane. The Add Hardware wizard opens (see Figure 28-2).

3. Click Next and let the wizard search for new hardware; then follow the instructions to identify the device and install the proper driver.

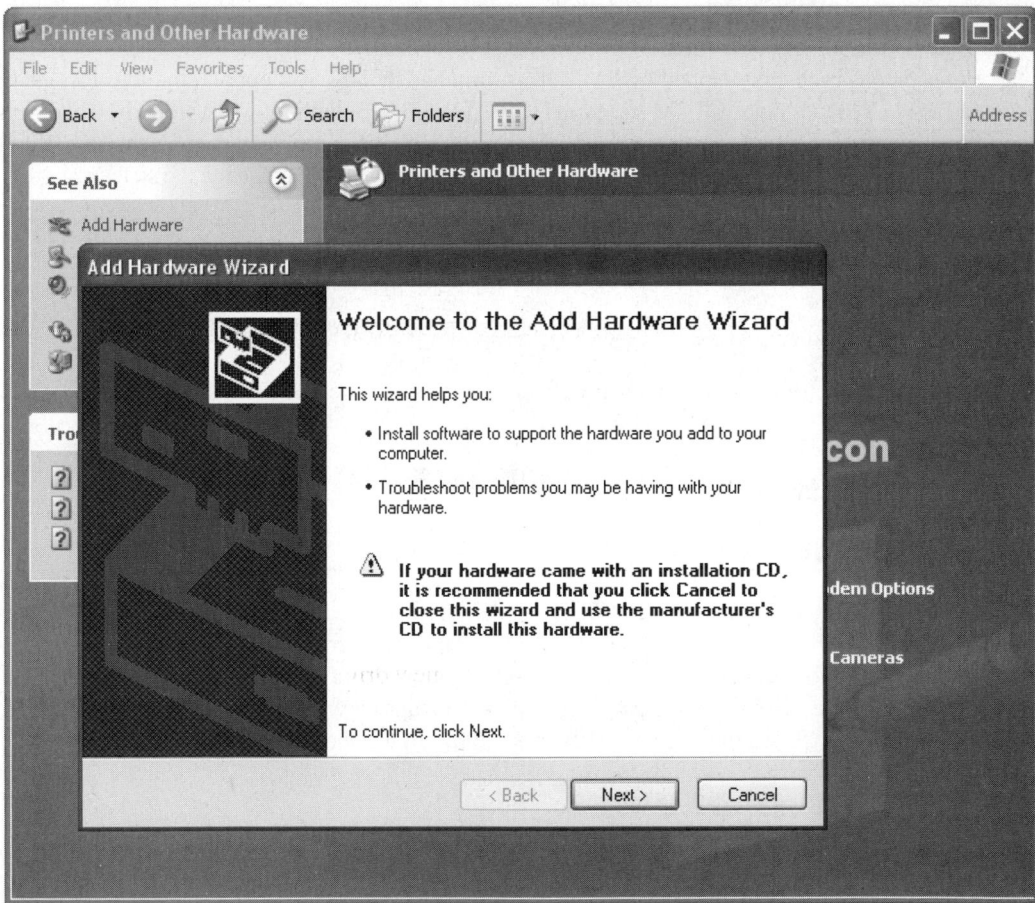

**FIGURE 28-2**    Launch the Add Hardware wizard to identify and install legacy devices or prepare PnP devices that Windows may not recognize

Keep in mind that Windows 9x/Me/XP will automatically detect the presence of PnP hardware, and may only launch the hardware wizard to help you install the correct driver. You might need to launch the Hardware wizard manually if you're adding non–PnP hardware.

Use the following steps under Windows 9x/Me:

1. Open the Control Panel, and then double-click the Add New Hardware icon.
2. In the Add New Hardware wizard, click Next, and then select Yes (Recommended) to have Windows search for hardware.
3. Allow Windows 9x/Me to detect the new device, and then follow the instructions to configure the driver.

There are some cases where the Add New Hardware wizard cannot detect the new device. You'll need to specify the new device type, manufacturer, and model, and then install the driver.

## UPDATING DEVICE DRIVERS

All devices installed under Windows 98/Me/XP (both PnP and legacy) are heavily dependent on drivers. Over time, drivers often need to be updated to resolve bugs with the driver, streamline the performance of the particular device, or overcome incompatibilities with other devices or drivers. An important part of device management under Windows 98/Me/XP involves driver updates. In days gone by, new drivers were provided on a "maintenance disk" sent by the manufacturer. Today, the new driver can quickly be downloaded from the manufacturer's tech support Web site. But in either case, all drivers must be properly installed—usually through a Windows wizard. Under Windows XP, use the Hardware Update wizard to update your device drivers:

1. Open the Device Manager and expand the device class that you're interested in.
2. Right-click the specific device and select Update Driver. (You could also select the Update Driver button on the Driver tab of the device Properties dialog.)
3. The Hardware Update wizard starts (see Figure 28-3).
4. If the proper drivers already exist under Windows, select Install the Software Automatically. Otherwise, select Install from a List or Specific Location and click Next.
5. Follow the wizard to install the driver from an appropriate CD, diskette, or a file that may have been downloaded from the Internet—you will need to specify the correct location(s).
6. When the installation is finished, you might want to reboot the PC and return to the Device Manager to verify that the device has indeed been updated properly.

The following steps outline the process for installing a new driver under Windows 9x/Me:

1. Open the Control Panel, double-click the Add New Hardware icon.
2. Click Next, click Next again, and then click No (I want to select the hardware from a list).
3. Click the type of hardware for which you are installing the driver, and then click Next.
4. Click Have Disk.
5. Type the path for the driver you are installing and click OK, or click Browse and locate the driver manually. You must type the path for or locate the OEMSETUP.INF file from the manufacturer.
6. In the dialog box listing the INF file, click OK. Click OK to continue.

**FIGURE 28-3**   The Hardware Update wizard allows you to install new drivers for specific pieces of hardware in the system.

**7.** Click the correct driver and then click OK.

**8.** Click Finish.

You should also remember that Windows 98/Me/XP systems allow you to update drivers simply by clicking the Update Driver button on the Driver tab in the device's Properties dialog (see Figure 28-4). This will also start the wizard that will walk you through the driver update process. You should note the current driver version before updating, and then compare the new driver version to see that the update has completed successfully.

## INSTALLING MODEMS MANUALLY

With the popularity of online resources such as AOL and the Internet, most current PCs are equipped with a modem. While modem installation is very similar to other device installations, modems offer some peculiar wrinkles that often demand a slightly different installation approach. (They are also not always detected with 100 percent reliability.) These steps outline a modem installation under Windows XP:

**1.** Open the Control Panel and click Printers and Other Hardware.

**2.** Click Phone and Modem Options and select the Modems tab.

**3.** Click Add. The Add Hardware wizard starts to install a new modem (see Figure 28-5).

**4.** If you want Windows XP to auto-detect your modem, click Next. If not, click the Don't Detect My Modem… check box to select it, and then click Next.

**5.** Follow the wizard to identify and install the correct modem on the corresponding port.

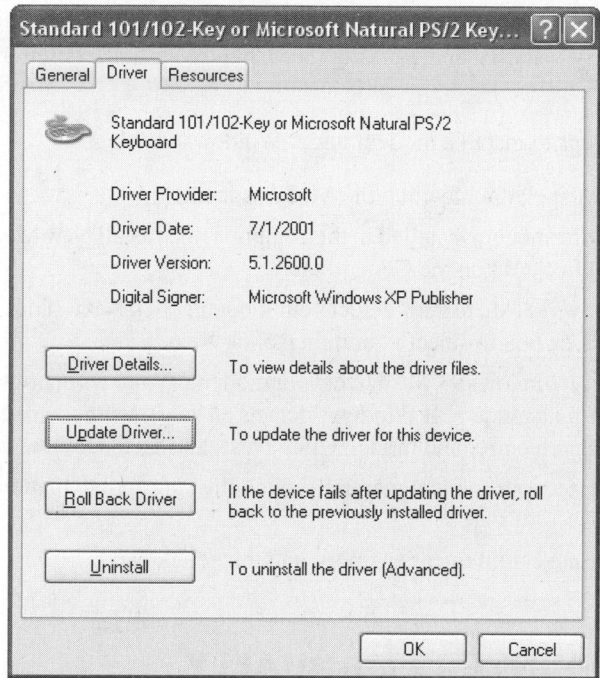

**FIGURE 28-4**     Use the Update Driver button to launch the driver update wizard for your version of Windows.

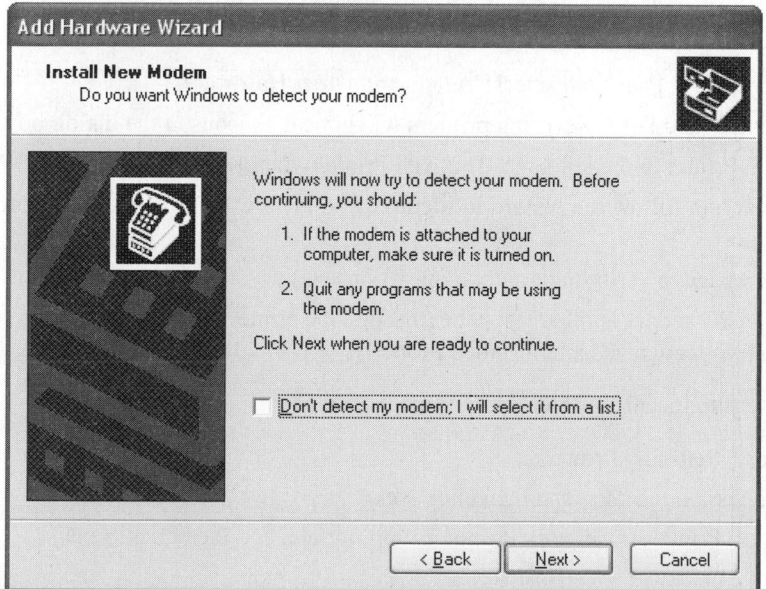

**FIGURE 28-5**     Use the Add Hardware wizard to identify and install your new modem.

6. Finish the installation and reboot the PC if necessary. Recheck the Modems tab to verify that the modem is properly installed and working (see Chapter 25 for detailed modem installation and troubleshooting).

Use the following steps to install a modem under Windows 9x/Me:

1. Open the Control Panel, double-click the Modems icon.

2. If this is to be the first modem installed in the computer, the Install New Modem wizard starts automatically. If not, click Add on the General tab.

3. If you want Windows 98/Me to auto-detect your modem, click Next. If not, click the "Don't detect my modem…" check box to select it, and then click Next.

4. If you chose to have Windows 98/Me detect your modem, Windows queries the serial ports on your computer looking for a modem. If Windows detects an incorrect modem, click Change, and select the appropriate manufacturer and model. Click Next, and then continue with Step 7.

5. If you chose to select your modem manually, click the appropriate manufacturer and model, and then click Next.

6. Click the appropriate communications port, and then click Next.

7. Click Finish.

# INSTALLING PRINTERS MANUALLY

Although the newest generation of printers are PnP compatible and can be identified automatically, most traditional printers must be specified under Windows 98/Me/XP manually. This is accomplished through the Printers icon as specified next for Windows XP:

 FireWire and USB printers are detected automatically once they're connected, so you should not need to add a printer manually with those ports.

1. Open the Control Panel and select Printers and Other Hardware.

2. Click Printers and Faxes. Existing printers will appear as icons in the dialog box.

3. Click Add Printer in the left pane. The Add Printer wizard starts (see Figure 28-6).

4. Click Next and follow the wizard to identify and install the printer to an appropriate local or network port.

5. Print a test page to verify the printer's operation.

6. Reboot the PC and try another test page (through the printer's Properties dialog) to verify that the printer is still recognized and installed properly.

Use these steps to install a printer under Windows 9x/Me:

1. Click Start | Settings | Printers.

2. Double-click Add Printer, and then click Next.

3. Click Local Printer or Network Printer as appropriate, and then click Next.

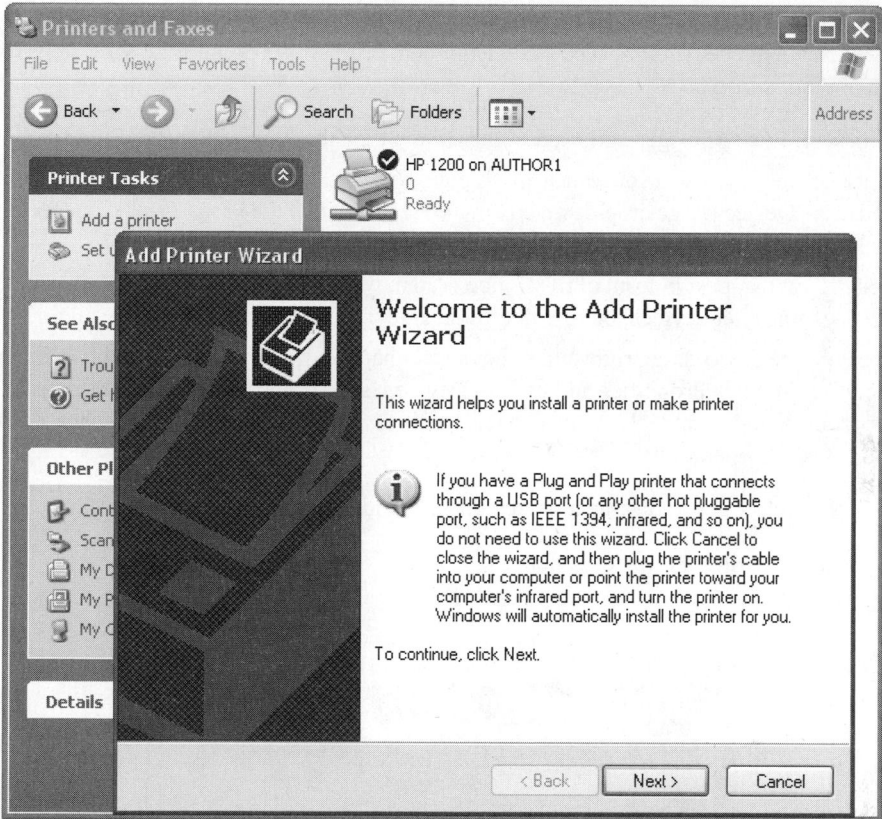

**FIGURE  28-6**    Use the Add Printer wizard to identify and install your new parallel port or
network printer.

If you click Network Printer, you are prompted for the network path for the printer. If you do not know
the correct path, click Browse, or check with your network administrator. Click either Yes or No as
appropriate in the "Do you print from MS-DOS-based programs?" area, and then click Next.

  **4.** Click the appropriate manufacturer and model for your printer, and then click Next.

  **5.** If you chose to install a local printer, click the correct port, and then click Next.

  **6.** Type a name for the printer (or accept the default name), and then click either Yes or No in the "Do
you want your Windows-based programs to use this printer as the default printer?" area. Click Next.

  **7.** To print a test page, click Yes, and then click Finish.

# DISABLING A DEVICE

Ordinarily, Windows 98/Me/XP identifies devices, assigns resources, and loads drivers for all the devices
it finds. From time to time (especially during troubleshooting), it may be necessary to disable a device. In
effect, "disabling" a device prevents Windows 98/Me/XP from loading drivers or allocating resources

associated with the device, but does not physically remove the device from the system. This is a particularly handy trick when checking for resource assignment problems. Try the following steps to remove a device under Windows XP:

1. Open the Device Manager and expand the device type that you're looking for.

2. Right-click the device that you want to disable and click Disable. Alternatively, you can click Properties and use the Device Usage drop-down box in the General tab of the Properties dialog (see Figure 28-7) to select Do Not Use this Device (Disable).

3. A red "X" will appear in front of the device. You may need to reboot the system in order to free the resources for other devices, but the neutralized device should no longer be available.

4. To restore the device later, right-click the device that you want to enable and click Enable. Otherwise, you can click Properties and use the Device Usage drop-down box in the General tab of the Properties dialog to select Use this Device (Enable). The red "X" should disappear and the device should resume operation.

Use the following steps to disable a device under Windows 9x/Me:

1. Click Start | Settings | Control Panel.

2. Double-click the System icon.

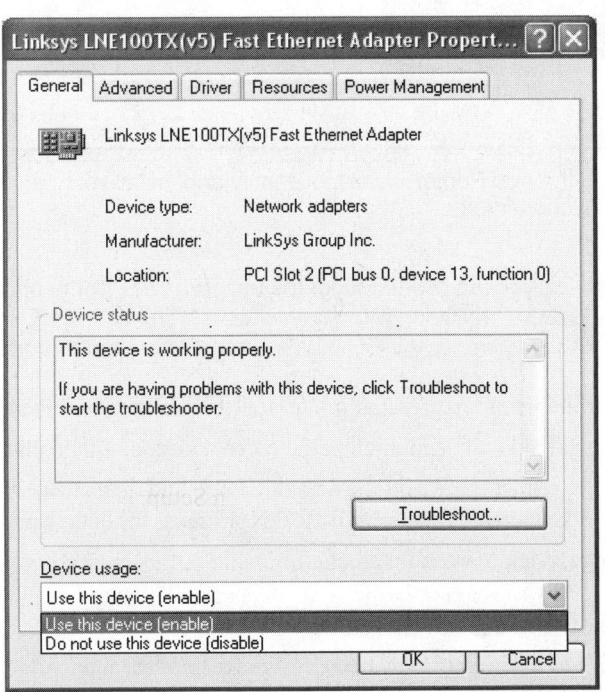

**FIGURE  28-7**    Use the device Properties box to disable the desired device.

3. On the Device Manager tab, click the device you want, and then click Properties.

4. On the General tab, click the Original Configuration (Current) check box to clear it, and then click OK. Under Windows 98/Me, you should check the box marked Disable In this Hardware Profile, and then click OK.

5. You may need to reboot the system in order to free the resources, but the neutralized device should no longer be available.

# REMOVING A DEVICE

There will be times (especially during troubleshooting) where it may be necessary to remove (a.k.a. "uninstall") a device entirely from the Windows 98/Me/XP platform in order to free resources otherwise assigned to the device. Normally, Windows should free the resources of a PnP device simply by disabling it (see "Disabling a Device" earlier), or when the device is physically removed. But legacy cards or other non–PnP devices may need to be removed manually before their assigned resources can be freed. To free resource settings used by disabled hardware under Windows 9x/Me/XP:

1. Open the Device Manager.

2. In the hardware list, click the plus sign (+) next to the type of hardware, and then click the device that is disabled (or now needs to be removed).

3. Under Windows 9x/Me, click Remove, and then click OK. With Windows XP, right-click the device and select Uninstall (see Figure 28-8).

4. Close the Device Manager and shut down the PC. Turn off and unplug your computer, and then remove the physical hardware device from inside the computer.

PnP device resources are freed automatically when you disable or remove a device. To see if resources are free after the device is disabled but before removing the device, double-click the device in the hardware list in Device Manager, and then click the Resources tab.

# SYMPTOMS

As a rule, a computer's PnP system runs in the background, and you will rarely need to work with it directly (other than to tweak a conflicting resource or disable an uncooperative device). However, when problems do arise, you can usually correct trouble by referring to the following symptoms.

**SYMPTOM 28-1** **Windows Setup crashes on first boot after configuring PnP devices**
This problem can occur if *all* the following conditions exist: (1) your computer has a PCI bus with PCI adapters, (2) there is an ISA adapter (such as a sound card) in your computer, (3) the ISA adapter was not configured (or was not running in real mode) before you ran Setup, and (4) you have not changed any of your computer's CMOS settings. If all of these conditions are true, chances are that one hardware device in the computer may be conflicting with another. When this occurs, Windows may hang up or crash.

For example, if you have a PCI-based computer with a PCI video card, PCI SCSI adapter, and ISA sound card, Setup runs its hardware detection and finds the ISA device. When Setup is finished, your computer is restarted, and the sound card driver is loaded. When Windows enumerates the PCI bus and its adapters, it finds that the BIOS has set the IRQ for one of the PCI devices to the same IRQ as the sound card—causing the conflict.

There are several possible techniques to correct this problem. First, try reserving the IRQ for your ISA devices in the CMOS Setup—this prevents the BIOS from assigning the IRQ to another device such as the

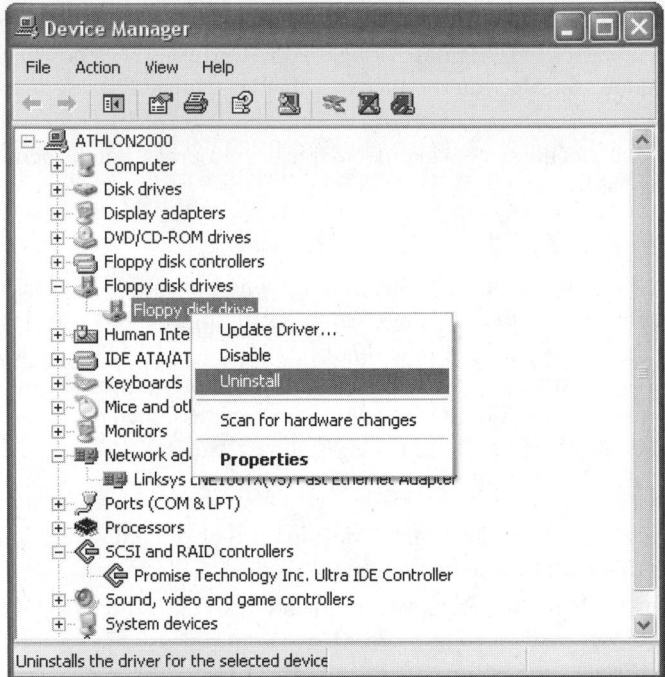

**FIGURE  28-8**    Be sure to uninstall a device before shutting down the PC and physically removing the device from the system.

PCI system. You can try removing the ISA device(s) until the computer is completely configured to run Windows 98/Me/XP, and then reinstall the device(s). After you reinstall each ISA adapter, run the Add New Hardware wizard to configure the device. Third, if the ISA device is software configurable, you may be able to assign non-conflicting resources using your Device Manager:

1. Reboot your computer. When you see the "Starting Windows" message, press F8, and then choose Safe Mode from the Startup menu.

2. Open the Device Manager.

3. Highlight the offending ISA device, and then click Properties.

4. Click the "Original configuration (current)" check box to clear it, and then click OK. Under Windows 98, select the "Disable in this hardware profile" check box. With Windows XP, select Do Not Use this Device (Disable)" in the Device Usage drop-down box. Now restart Windows.

5. If Windows starts and finishes the setup configuration, restart the Device Manager.

6. Click the offending ISA device, and then click Properties.

7. Click the Resources tab. On the Resources tab, select a non-conflicting resource for the ISA device (if one is available). If you do not have a suitable resource available, you may need to reconfigure another device to free up the appropriate resources (or remove the offending ISA device).

8. Restart the system again if necessary.

**SYMPTOM 28-2**    **Selecting a None of the Above hardware profile under Windows may reset your device configurations**    This problem was known to occur under Windows 95 and earlier versions of Windows 98. When you have multiple hardware profiles configured on your system, an option labeled None of the Above is included in the list of available hardware profiles when you start the computer. If you select None of the Above, plug-and-play enumeration occurs, and *some* devices may be reset to configurations that the drivers cannot support. When this occurs, you may have to manually reload the original device drivers. You can generally correct this problem by installing the latest service patch for your version of Windows.

**SYMPTOM 28-3**    **The Energy Star check box is not available for your monitor**    When you check the Monitor tab in the Display Properties dialog box under Windows 98, the Monitor is Energy Star Compliant check box may not be available. This trouble can occur if Windows 98 is configured to automatically detect plug-and-play monitors. You must disable the automatic detection of any plug-and-play monitor(s):

1. Click Start | Settings | Control Panel, and then double-click Display.
2. Click the Settings tab, and then click Advanced.
3. Click the Monitor tab, clear the Automatically Detect Plug & Play Monitors check box (see Figure 28-9), click OK, and then click OK again.
4. Restart the computer.

**SYMPTOM 28-4**    **After upgrading Windows, the sound device is disabled**    For example, when you check the sound device (e.g., ES1869 Plug-and-Play AudioDrive sound card) in Device Manager, you'll notice a yellow exclamation point and a status of "Code 10" for the sound card. This problem occurs after you upgrade your Windows 95/98 system to Windows 98 Second Edition (SE) or higher. To fix this problem, you'll need to remove and reinstall the sound device. For the ES1869 Plug-and-Play sound card example, follow these steps:

1. Click Start | Settings | Control Panel, and then double-click the System icon.
2. Click the Device Manager tab, click the ES1869 Plug and Play AudioDrive sound card, click Remove, click OK, and then click OK again.
3. Click Yes when you're prompted to restart your computer.
4. After your computer restarts, the ES1869 Plug-and-Play AudioDrive sound card should be detected and installed properly.

The following steps may be helpful for correcting other devices lost after upgrading the operating system.

**SYMPTOM 28-5**    **The system crashes when you run the Add New Hardware wizard under Windows 98/Me**    This issue may be caused by the incorrect interpretation of data stored in the computer's CMOS RAM (set up by the BIOS). On certain motherboards, Windows 98/Me may not be able to successfully complete the plug-and-play detection process. You can probably resolve this issue by

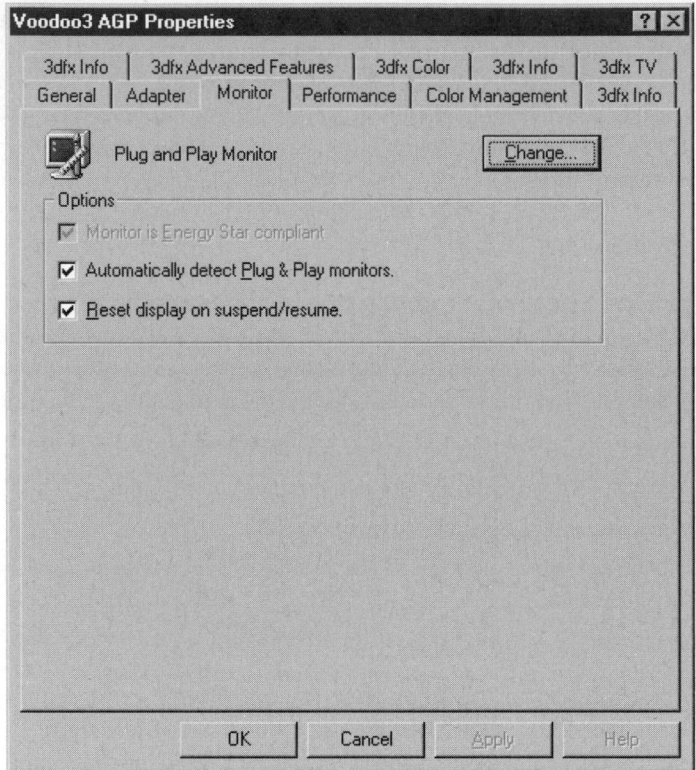

**FIGURE 28-9** Stop the Windows 98 system from detecting PnP monitors.

upgrading the system BIOS. In some cases, you can try clearing the CMOS RAM and ESCD RAM first and see if the system is capable of reconfiguring itself.

**SYMPTOM 28-6** **You encounter an error when updating a PnP device under Windows 98**
For example, after you update the Crystal Plug and Play Audio Codec driver in your Device Manager, you may receive an error message such as

```
Crystal PnP Audio CODEC
Setup cannot upgrade the existing driver for this device. Press OK to
continue.
```

This problem can occur if Windows 98 cannot safely upgrade the driver that's already installed. The problem might also occur if such an upgrade might disable a feature that the current driver provides, or if the information (.INF) file for the driver is missing. Verify that you're trying to update the latest driver for the operating system, and obtain a current .INF file if possible.

**SYMPTOM 28-7**    **You find that a joystick port is not removed when you remove the sound card**    When you remove a sound card from your computer, and remove the sound card in the Windows 98/Me Device Manager, the joystick (game port) on the sound card continues to appear in Device Manager. This trouble occurs because there is no parent-child relationship between the sound card and the joystick port. The virtual joystick device driver (VJOYD.VXD) is unable to detect whether the joystick port has been removed (or the joystick port is present but has no joystick attached), so the driver is always active. When you remove the sound card in Device Manager, the joystick port is not automatically removed. You'll need to remove the game port device manually:

1. Right-click the My Computer icon on your desktop, and then click Properties.
2. Click the Device Manager tab.
3. Click the plus sign (+) next to "Sound, video, and game controllers" to expand the branch.
4. Click the Gameport Joystick device to highlight it (see Figure 28-10), and then click Remove.

**SYMPTOM 28-8**    **You notice more than one instance of the same port in the Windows 98/Me Add New Hardware wizard**    When you're manually installing new hardware (such as a modem) using the Add New Hardware wizard, multiple instances of COM or LPT ports may appear as options in the port selection dialog. This trouble can occur when there are duplicate entries for a COM or LPT port in the registry. Duplicate entries can occur if the computer does not contain a plug-and-play BIOS. You may be able to fix this problem by removing all instances of the particular port through the

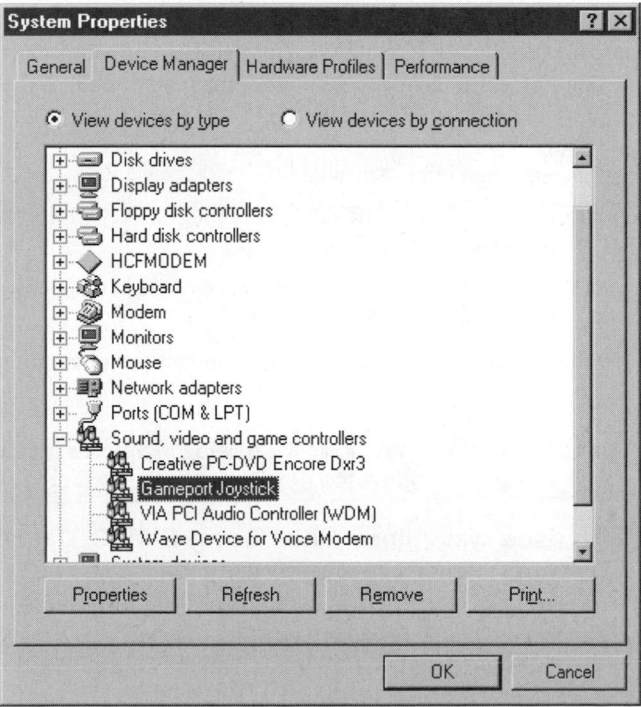

**FIGURE  28-10**    You may need to remove the joystick separately after removing a device containing a game port (such as a sound card).

Device Manager; then reboot the system and allow Windows to redetect the port(s) properly. Otherwise, you can generally correct this problem by editing the redundant registry entries manually:

Editing the registry incorrectly may prevent the system from booting. Before you edit the registry, you should first make a backup copy of the registry files (SYSTEM.DAT and USER.DAT) to your boot disk. Both are hidden files in the \Windows folder.

1. In the Registry Editor (REGEDIT), export the appropriate registry keys (for backup purposes):

   HKEY_LOCAL_Machine\Enum\Bios\*PNP0400 (or *PNP0401) for duplicate LPT ports
   HKEY_LOCAL_Machine\Enum\Bios\*PNP0500 (or *PNP0501) for duplicate COM ports

2. Now delete the appropriate registry keys:

   HKEY_LOCAL_Machine\Enum\Bios\*PNP0400 (or *PNP0401) for duplicate LPT ports
   HKEY_LOCAL_Machine\Enum\Bios\*PNP0500 (or *PNP0501) for duplicate COM ports

3. Quit the Registry Editor, and then shut down and restart your computer normally.

4. Click Start | Settings | Control Panel, and then double-click Add New Hardware.

5. Click Next, click Yes, and then click Next again. Windows automatically locates the installed ports and re-creates the correct entries in the registry without duplicates.

**SYMPTOM 28-9**    **You cannot select a higher display resolution in the Windows 98/Me Display Properties dialog**    When you try to increase the screen resolution in the Display Properties dialog, you may be unable to choose a higher resolution than the video system is capable of. For example, your monitor may support a maximum resolution of $1600 \times 1200$ pixels, but this setting may be missing from the Screen Area box. In virtually all cases, the system's ESCD contains incorrect information about your particular monitor. You'll need to install your monitor manually under Windows 9x/Me:

1. Click Start | Settings | Control Panel, and then double-click Display.

2. Click the Settings tab, and then click Advanced.

3. Click the Monitor tab, click the Automatically Detect Plug & Play Monitors check box to clear it (refer to Figure 28-9), and then click Apply.

4. Click Change, click Next, click Display a List of All the Drivers in a Specific Location, so You Can Select the Driver You Want, and then click Next.

5. Click Show All Hardware, and then follow the onscreen instructionsto finish installing your specific monitor.

If this type of problem should occur under Windows XP, delete the monitor from the Device Manager and allow the system to redetect it, or update the monitor through the Display Properties dialog.

**SYMPTOM 28-10**    **You see wavy lines when using a MAG DX-1795 monitor under Windows 98/Me**    For example, this problem is known to occur with the MAG DX-1795 monitor, and may be caused if your video adapter is configured for $1600 \times 1200$ resolution, and the Automatically detect Plug & Play Monitors check box is selected on the Monitor tab in the Display Properties dialog. To correct this problem, you'll need to reinstall your monitor manually under Windows 9x/Me:

1. Click Start | Settings | Control Panel, and then double-click Display.

2. Click the Settings tab, and then click Advanced.

**3.** On the Monitor tab, click the Automatically detect Plug & Play Monitors check box to clear it (refer to Figure 28-9), and then click Change.

**4.** Click Next, click Display a List of All the Drivers in a Specific Location, so You Can Select the Driver You Want, and then click Next.

**5.** Click Show All Hardware.

**6.** In the Manufacturers box, click MAG Technology Co., Ltd., and then click MAG DX-1795 in the Models box.

**7.** Click Next, and then follow the instructions on your screen to finish installing the monitor.

If this type of problem should occur under Windows XP, delete the monitor from the Device Manager and allow the system to redetect it, or update the monitor through the Display Properties dialog.

**SYMPTOM 28-11**    **The PC powers-down when you shut down Windows 98/Me/XP**
When you use the Shut Down command on the Start menu to shut down Windows, your computer may automatically power-down after displaying the message "Please wait while your computer shuts down." This behavior is a normal *Advanced Power Management* (APM) and *advanced configuration and power interface* (ACPI) feature. There is no way to change this action—the hardware powers-down in response to a software request. However, this occurs only on computers with a PnP BIOS that supports APM/ACPI features.

**SYMPTOM 28-12**    **You have trouble restarting the PC when a device uses IRQ 12**
When you try to restart your computer under Windows 98/Me using the Restart option in your Shut Down dialog box, your computer may hang up. This is often a problem on computers with a BIOS that "expects" IRQ 12 to be used by a PS/2-style mouse port—but instead it is used by a software-configurable hardware device such as a PnP expansion card, or some other device like a USB controller. To work around this problem, reserve IRQ 12 in Device Manager (or change the IRQ for the software-configurable device in Device Manager). You may also consider upgrading the BIOS in your computer to a later version. To reserve an IRQ with Device Manager under Windows 9x/Me:

**1.** Open the Control Panel, and then double-click the System icon.

**2.** On the Device Manager tab, double-click the Computer entry.

**3.** Click the Reserve Resources tab, click the Interrupt Request (IRQ) option, and then click Add.

**4.** In the Value box, click the IRQ you want to reserve (IRQ 12).

**5.** Click OK until you return to the Control Panel.

**6.** Reboot the PC if necessary.

If you cannot reserve an interrupt with your version of an operating system, you may be able to reserve IRQs through the PCI/PnP submenu of the CMOS Setup.

**SYMPTOM 28-13**    **The "volume control" tool may not be installed with some sound cards under Windows 98/Me**    Tools such as Volume Control are installed based on the hardware detected during the installation of Windows. If the computer contains an ISA PnP device that is not enabled by the BIOS, the device is not detected until after Windows is installed. There are two ways around this. If you're just installing Windows 98/Me now, use the Custom Setup option. When you're prompted to select the components you want, select Volume Control in the Multimedia section. If Windows is already installed, follow these steps to install Volume Control under Windows 9x/Me:

1. Open the Control Panel, and then double-click the Add/Remove Programs icon.

2. Click the Windows Setup tab, click Multimedia, and then click Details.

3. Select the Volume Control check box.

4. Click OK, and then click OK again.

5. Reboot the PC if necessary.

If Windows XP does not provide a volume control or other audio mixing applet, try controlling the speaker volume through the Audio Options dialog:

1. Open the Control Panel and select Sounds, Speech, and Audio Devices.

2. Select Sounds and Audio Devices.

3. Select the Volume tab (see Figure 28-11) and adjust the sound device volume adequately.

4. If the Place Volume Icon in the Taskbar box is available, you can check that box to place the volume control in the taskbar.

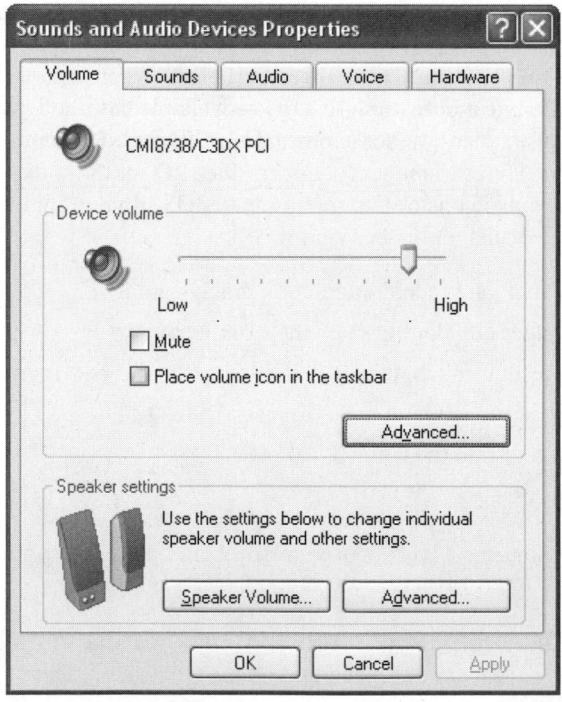

**FIGURE  28-11**    Use the master volume control to set the overall volume for the system audio device under Windows XP.

5. Check the Advanced button to open the default audio mixer panel, and see that each input is set to an adequate level (see Figure 28-12).

6. Click the Speaker Volume button to adjust the left/right speaker volume settings.

7. Apply any changes and click OK to close the dialog.

**SYMPTOM 28-14**    **The sound device is not detected when it's installed under Windows 98**    For example, this may occur with older sound devices like the ES1788 or ES688. This happens because the device is not fully PnP compliant. You'll need to install the device manually using the Add New Hardware wizard under Windows 98/Me. For the ESS example, follow these steps:

1. Click Start | Settings | Control Panel.

2. Double-click the Add New Hardware icon, click Next, and then click Next again.

3. Click No, I Want to Select the Hardware from a List, and then click Next.

4. In the Manufacturers box, click ESS Technology, Inc.

5. In the Models box, click ESS AudioDrive, click Next, and then click Next again.

6. Restart Windows when you're prompted to do so.

If a device is not detected under Windows XP, use the Add Hardware wizard as described earlier in "Installing Legacy Devices."

**SYMPTOM 28-15**    **After reinstalling Windows 98 on a multi-monitor system, you have to reconfigure some monitors after setup is completed**    This is a known problem with some older ATI video adapters. Windows 98 disables PnP functionality for older ATI video adapters because they do not handle plug-and-play correctly. To work around this problem, manually configure each monitor connected to an ATI video adapter:

1. Click Start | Settings | Control Panel.

2. Double-click the Display icon, and then click the Settings tab.

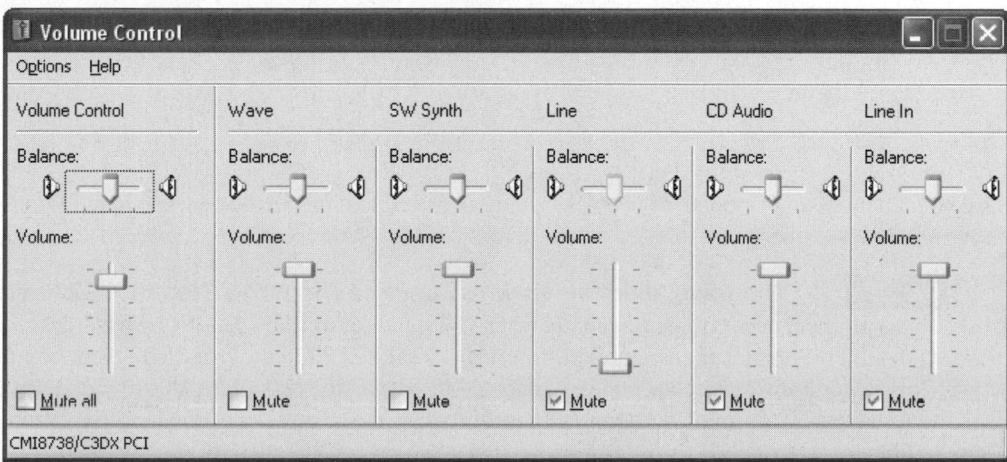

**FIGURE 28-12**    Use the master mixer to set the relative (mixed) volume for each audio input.

3. In the Display box, click the adapter you want, and then click Advanced.

4. On the Monitor tab, click Change.

5. Click Next, click Display a List of All the Drivers in a Specific Location, so You Can Select the Driver You Want, and then click Next.

6. Click Show All Hardware.

7. Click the appropriate manufacturer and model of your monitor, click Next, and then click Finish.

8. Click Close, click OK, and then reboot the system if necessary.

**SYMPTOM 28-16** **After upgrading Windows, the Display Adapters entry is missing in the Device Manager** This problem is known to occur when your video adapter uses the Nvidia Riva 128 chipset and is unable to secure an IRQ during the PnP detection portion of Windows 98 setup (this is not known to occur under Windows Me/XP). One solution is to assign an IRQ to the video system using the "Assign IRQ to VGA" option in your CMOS Setup (if available). Another option is to disable PCI bus IRQ steering in the Device Manager.

**SYMPTOM 28-17** **You see an error such as "CTSOUND1008: Invalid /BLASTER= A:xxxx argument"** When you upgrade a real-mode operating system (such as DOS or Windows 3.x) to Windows 98/Me/XP on a computer with a Creative Labs Sound Blaster 16 sound card installed, you may receive the following error when your computer restarts:

```
Error CTSOUND1008: Invalid "/BLASTER=A:xxx" argument
```

or

```
Error: DIGN8002 The BLASTER environment settings are invalid
```

This problem will generally occur if the PnP configuration drivers for your Sound Blaster 16 sound card are being loaded from the AUTOEXEC.BAT and CONFIG.SYS files. To correct this problem, you'll need to open your start-up files in a text editor and REMark out the command lines related to your sound card. For example, in AUTOEXEC.BAT:

```
REM c:\vibra16\diagnose /s /w=c:\windows
```

and under CONFIG.SYS:

```
REM device=c:\vibra16\drv\vibra16.sys /unit=0 /blaster=a:220 i:10 d:3 h:7
```

Save your changes and reboot the system. You may also need to reinstall the new version of Windows, or remove and redetect the sound device.

**SYMPTOM 28-18** **Windows 98 locks up when using a Diamond Stealth II S220 video adapter** This problem occurs most frequently when you start the Add New Hardware wizard while the Windows 98 default drivers for the Diamond Multimedia Stealth II S220 are installed—your computer may crash (this is not known to occur under Windows Me/XP). If the "standard VGA" video driver is installed, the Add New Hardware wizard runs successfully. This is almost always due to a driver problem, so be sure to obtain and install the most current version of driver for this display adapter.

**SYMPTOM 28-19** **You find a "Code 8" is shown for a PnP BIOS device after upgrading to Windows 98/Me/XP** After upgrading, a yellow exclamation point may be displayed next to the "Plug-and-Play BIOS" device in Device Manager. If you view the Properties for the Plug-and-Play BIOS device, the following message may appear:

```
This device is not working properly because the file (BIOS.VXD) that
loads the drivers for this device is bad (Code 8). To fix this problem,
click Update Driver to update the driver for this device.
```

If you then click the Update Driver button and attempt to search for a better driver, you may receive a message saying that the best driver is already installed. In virtually all cases, the Windows 95 version of the BIOS.VXD file has remained in the \Windows folder after the upgrade, and you'll need to correct this:

1. Click Start, select Find, and then click Files Or Folders.
2. In the Named box, type **bios.vxd**, and then click Find Now.
3. In the Look in box, click the drive on which the \Windows folder is located.
4. In the list of found files, right-click the BIOS.VXD file located in the \Windows folder, click Delete, and then click Yes.
5. Quit the Find tool, and restart your computer.

You may also repartition and reformat the drive, and reinstall the new version of Windows from scratch.

**SYMPTOM 28-20** **Windows fails to recognize the computer as plug-and-play** This type of problem often occurs with older Intel OEM motherboards. Windows does not recognize the computer as a plug-and-play platform—even though you receive a message during start up such as "Intel PnP BIOS Extensions Installed." Intel has developed some OEM motherboards that are equipped with a PnP BIOS that does not contain the run-time services necessary to configure motherboard devices. An example of such a motherboard is the Intel P5/90. Gateway 2000 (and possibly other OEMs) ship computers with the P5/90 motherboard. You'll need to upgrade the system BIOS to comply with the plug-and-play BIOS version 1.0a specification or later. If a BIOS upgrade is not available, it may be necessary to upgrade the entire motherboard. In other cases, upgrading the Windows version may also help.

**SYMPTOM 28-21** **You notice IRQ conflicts with PCI display adapters** When you install an older PCI video adapter that is configured to use a particular interrupt (IRQ), Windows may configure it to use another IRQ that is already in use by another device. While PCI devices can share PCI IRQs, Windows does not support sharing PCI IRQs with other non-PCI devices (such as an IDE controller). Use the Device Manager to resolve the conflict by assigning a different IRQ to one of the conflicting devices (usually the new PCI video adapter).

This kind of behavior does not occur with AGP display adapters.

**SYMPTOM 28-22** **The resources for disabled devices are not freed** Even though you disable a device in your computer's CMOS Setup, Windows 98/Me/XP re-enables the device and allocates its resources. Windows may also reinstall a device that is removed from Device Manager. This happens because Windows 98/Me/XP detects PnP devices regardless of the CMOS Setup. To prevent Windows from reactivating disabled hardware, you must disable the hardware in the computer's CMOS Setup and remove it from the current configuration in Windows 98/Me/XP. This frees the device's resources for other devices to use. Under Windows XP, follow these steps:

1. Open the Device Manager, expand the device tree, and double-click the specific device that you need to disable.

2. Click the General tab. In the Device usage drop-down box, click Do Not Use this Device (Disable).

3. Save your changes and restart directly to the CMOS Setup to disable the conflicting device in the CMOS Setup (if possible).

4. Reboot the system and let Windows start normally—this should free resources to be reassigned.

Under Windows 9x/Me, follow these steps:

1. Click Start | Settings | Control Panel.

2. Double-click the System icon.

3. Click the Device Manager tab, and then double-click the device you want to disable.

4. Click the General tab, and then click the Original Configuration (Current) check box to clear it. Under Windows 98, check the box marked Disable In This Hardware Profile.

5. Click the OK button.

6. Restart Windows when prompted.

7. Immediately start the CMOS Setup routine, and disable the device in the CMOS Setup.

8. Save the changes to CMOS, and allow the system to boot normally.

When you disable a device in Device Manager, you must restart your computer before you can reassign the device's resources to another device.

**SYMPTOM 28-23**    **An AST PnP BIOS is not registered as PnP**    The older AST plug-and-play BIOS is not registered as plug-and-play capable under Windows 9x/Me/XP. This is usually because the AST PnP BIOS contains incorrect information in its 16-bit protected-mode entry point. When Windows detects this incorrect code in the AST BIOS, it will not recognize the BIOS as plug-and-play capable. You'll need to contact AST for a BIOS upgrade, or upgrade the entire motherboard if necessary. In other cases, upgrading the Windows version may also help.

**SYMPTOM 28-24**    **A PnP ISA adapter is not recognized automatically**    If you insert a PnP ISA adapter in an older computer whose motherboard does not contain PCI slots, Windows 98/Me may not recognize the new ISA adapter automatically. (You typically do not see this problem on Windows XP platforms because hardware platforms capable of running Windows XP will include full PCI support.) The Device Manager may also display a "PCI bus" entry with an exclamation point in a yellow circle, with the status "No Plug and Play ISA bus was found. (Code 29)." This problem is typically caused by a PnP BIOS that is not supported by Windows on computers that have a PCI BIOS, but not a PCI bus. On PCI computers, it is usually the PCI driver that starts the PnP ISA driver. If the PCI driver fails, the ISA driver is not loaded, and therefore PnP ISA adapters are not automatically recognized or configured. To add a PnP adapter so that Windows 98/Me automatically recognizes it, enable the ISA PnP bus manually:

1. In Control Panel, double-click the Add New Hardware icon, and then click Next.
2. Click No, and then click Next.
3. Click System Devices, and then click Next.
4. Click ISA Plug And Play Bus, and then click Next.
5. Click Finish.
6. Restart your computer when you are prompted to do so.

You may also want to contact your computer manufacturer to see about obtaining an updated PnP BIOS that is better supported by Windows 98/Me. Otherwise, consider a motherboard upgrade.

**SYMPTOM 28-25**    **The computer no longer operates properly after docking or undocking**    As an example, the keyboard or mouse may stop working. *Hot docking* and *hot undocking* refer to inserting the computer in a docking station or removing it from the docking station while the computer is running at full power. By contrast, *warm docking* refers to docking or undocking the computer while it is in suspend mode. Laptop or portable computers with a PnP BIOS can be hot or warm docked or undocked. In virtually all cases, the computer does not have a suitable PnP BIOS. (This is mandatory for hot or warm docking and undocking.) To correct this problem on a permanent basis, you'll need to upgrade the laptop's BIOS to a version that better supports PnP. In the meantime, you can work around this problem by turning the computer off before you dock or undock it.

**SYMPTOM 28-26**    **Serial PnP devices are not recognized when an adapter is used to connect them**    For example, when you use a 9-pin to 25-pin serial adapter with a serial PnP device, the device may not be enumerated by the configuration manager at start up. This is caused by the adapter. Some 9-pin to 25-pin serial adapters do not connect the lines that pass the PnP initialization string (including adapters made by Microsoft before the release of Windows 95). Try another (more current) serial adapter. If the problem persists, add the device manually using the Add New Hardware wizard in the Control Panel.

**SYMPTOM 28-27**    **Windows 98/Me Setup hangs up when detecting SCSI controllers** This often happens with older Adaptec SCSI controllers on the first reboot while PnP devices are being detected. It is known to happen when a SCSI hard disk is supported by an Adaptec AHA 2940, Adaptec 2940AU, or Adaptec 2940W controller. You might need to update the SCSI controller, but may be able to work around this problem by disabling the SCSI controller and allowing Windows 9x/Me Setup to finish the PnP device detection:

1. Enable PnP SCAM support in the Adaptec SCSI controller BIOS Setup.
2. Disable BIOS Support For Int13 Extension in the Adaptec SCSI controller BIOS Setup.
3. Restart Windows 98/Me, press F8 when you see the Starting Windows message, and then choose Safe Mode from the Startup menu.
4. In Control Panel, double-click the System icon, click the Performance tab, click File System, and then click the Troubleshooting tab.
5. Enable the following two options: Disable Protect-mode Hard Disk Interrupt Handling and Disable All 32 bit Protect-Mode Disk Drivers.

6. Click OK, and then click OK again.

7. When you are prompted to restart your computer, click Yes to continue with Setup.

8. After Windows is installed, disable the options you enabled in step 5.

 You typically do not see this type of problem occur under Windows XP.

**SYMPTOM 28-28**    **After installing a printer, you encounter a "Fatal Exception Error" each time you run the Add New Hardware wizard**    For example, this problem is known to occur with the HP OfficeJet 300 (as well as other printer models). You'll typically see exception errors (e.g., 06, 0E, 0C, or 0D). This is because the HP OfficeJet Series 300 Device Manager software utility contends with Windows for control of the PnP system. The HP installation process sets up a shortcut in the Startup folder that runs HPOJDMAN.EXE /AUTOPROMPT. This causes HPOJDMAN.EXE to run in the background. Start the Close Program (or Task Manager under Windows XP) dialog box by pressing CTRL-ALT-DEL. Click HPOJDMAN in the list of tasks, and then click End Task. Check with HP (www.hp.com) for updated printer software utilities, or disable the utility entirely.

**SYMPTOM 28-29**    **The PS/2 mouse is disabled after installing an ISA PnP device**    For example, installing a Sound Blaster 16 "value" sound card disables the PS/2 mouse. This problem can occur on computers where the PnP BIOS (rather than Windows) assigns resources to ISA PnP devices. The PnP BIOS may assign IRQ 12 to the IDE drive and disable the mouse port. To correct this problem, disable the BIOS PnP support in the computer's CMOS Setup to allow Windows 98/Me/XP to configure the hardware instead.

**SYMPTOM 28-30**    **The Add New Hardware wizard doesn't detect a device that has been removed in Device Manager on a multiple-profile system**    This is because removing a PnP device from one profile and leaving it in another causes a flag to be set in the registry to prevent the device from being enumerated on the next start up. This may also cause the Add New Hardware wizard to bypass the device. The flag exists only in the profile in which the device was removed. To prevent this type of problem from occurring, *disable* the device in Device Manager instead of removing it. To disable a device, click the Disable In This Hardware Profile check box for the device in Device Manager (or simply right-click the device and select Disable under Windows XP). To restore (or redetect) the device, remove it from all profiles, and then run the Add New Hardware wizard.

**SYMPTOM 28-31**    **An extra serial port is displayed in the Device Manager**    When you are using Windows 95 OSR 2 or 2.1, you may see an extra communications port in Device Manager. There is an exclamation point in a yellow circle next to the port. If you remove the port, it is redetected again the next time you restart your computer. The computer's PnP BIOS is probably reporting (incorrectly) that the COM ports are not using resources—though they were detected during setup. This is a problem with Windows 95, but you do not see this type of problem under later versions of Windows. Check with Microsoft (www.microsoft.com) for any available upgrades or patches, or upgrade to a later version of Windows.

**SYMPTOM 28-32**    **You cannot set up Windows with a PnP program active**    When you try to install Windows 98/Me/XP, you may receive the following error message:

```
A fatal exception OE has occurred at 0028:xxxxxxxx in VxD VMM(06) + xxxxxxxx
```

Or, you may receive a Vwin32 error message displayed on a blue screen, a registry error message, or a *general protection* (GP) fault error message. This problem can occur if you have a PnP program active in memory when you try to install/upgrade Windows. To work around this issue, install Windows from a command prompt. Restart the computer. When you see the "Starting Windows" message, press F8, and then choose Command Prompt Only from the Startup menu. At the command prompt, type:

```
<drive>:\setup.exe
```

where *<drive>* is the drive containing your original Windows installation CD.

**SYMPTOM 28-33**    **An IBM ThinkPad doesn't support PnP under Windows 95/98**
Chances are that the older ThinkPad required a BIOS update. The following IBM ThinkPad models are known to need specific BIOS versions:

- **ThinkPad 750 family**    750/360/755 System Program Service Diskette version 1.20 or later
- **ThinkPad 755C/Cs and 360/355 family**    750/360/755 System Program Service Diskette version 1.20 or later
- **ThinkPad 755CE/CD, ThinkPad 755CX/CV, ThinkPad 755CDV**    755 System Program Service Diskette version 1.30 or later
- **ThinkPad 701C**    701C System Program Service Diskette version 3H or later
- **ThinkPad 340CSE and 370C**    340 System Program Service Diskette version 1.10 or later

The following ThinkPad models require APM BIOS 1.1 or later and PnP BIOS 1.0a or later in order for these features to work correctly with Windows 95/98:

- ThinkPad 755C/Cs
- ThinkPad 360/355 family
- ThinkPad 755CE/CD/CX/CV/CDV
- ThinkPad 340CSE
- ThinkPad 370C
- ThinkPad 701C
- ThinkPad 530CS

The following ThinkPad models require APM BIOS version 1.0 to work correctly with Windows 95/98. There is no PnP BIOS support for these models:

- ThinkPad 750 family
- ThinkPad 340 monochrome display system
- ThinkPad 230Cs

To obtain an updated BIOS or System Program Service Diskette for an IBM ThinkPad computer, please contact IBM (www.ibm.com).

**SYMPTOM 28-34**    **A PnP pointing device is not detected**    When you connect a PnP pointing device (such as Microsoft PnP serial mouse, Microsoft EasyBall, or Microsoft IntelliMouse), the new device may not be detected by Windows 98/Me/XP. Running the Add New Hardware wizard does not correct the problem. This is almost always because the registry entries for your previous pointing device were not properly removed from the registry. This problem is known to occur when your previous pointing device was a Microsoft, Microsoft-compatible, or Logitech mouse. To work around this problem, use the Registry Editor (REGEDIT) to remove the registry entries for your previous pointing device. Remove the following registry keys:

```
Hkey_Local_Machine\System\CurrentControlSet\Services\Class\Mouse\<nnnn>
```

where *<nnnn>* is an incremental 4-digit number starting at 0000. Also remove the following registry keys (if they exist):

```
Hkey_Local_Machine\Enum\Root\Mouse\<nnnn>
```

where *<nnnn>* in an incremental 4-digit number starting at 0000. Remove all registry keys under the following registry keys (if they exist):

```
Hkey_Local_Machine\Enum\Serenum
```

Remove the following registry key (if it exists):

```
Hkey_Local_Machine\Software\Logitech\Mouseware
```

Open the Windows 9x/Me/XP Device Manager, highlight each serial pointing device, and then click Remove. Click OK, and then restart Windows. When you restart Windows, the attached pointing device will be detected, and the appropriate drivers will be installed.

> Editing the registry incorrectly may prevent the system from booting. Before you edit the registry, you should first make a backup copy of the registry files (SYSTEM.DAT and USER.DAT) to your boot disk. Both are hidden files in the \Windows folder.

**SYMPTOM 28-35**   **The PnP printer is redetected every time Windows 95/98 starts**
This occurs even when the printer is already installed. When you start Windows 95/98, the following message may be displayed:

```
New Hardware Found
<device>
Windows has found new hardware and is installing the software for it
```

This problem is known to occur with Hewlett-Packard 4L and Hewlett-Packard DeskJet 660C PnP printers (though it can occur with other printers) and is usually caused by damage to the following registry key:

```
Hkey_Local_Machine\Enum\Lptenum
```

Remove the registry key and then restart your computer. When Windows restarts, it will detect the printer and install support for it. Once the printer is installed, it will no longer be detected each time you start Windows 95/98.

Editing the registry incorrectly may prevent the system from booting. Before you edit the registry, you should first make a backup copy of the registry files (SYSTEM.DAT and USER.DAT). Both are hidden files in the \Windows folder.

**SYMPTOM 28-36** **After installing Windows 95/98, none of the APM features were installed** You may also note that there is no "battery meter" for laptops. Some computers and BIOS revisions have known incompatibilities with the APM 1.1 specification. You are probably running Windows 95/98 on such a computer. As a result, the hardware "suspend" functions of your computer should still function correctly, but you cannot use the Windows 95/98 APM features. In most cases, the best solution in this kind of problem is to first verify that power management features are enabled. If that doesn't help, upgrade the motherboard BIOS to the latest version, or upgrade the motherboard outright. For example, Windows 95 turns off APM support completely on the following computers:

- AMIBIOS 07/08/1994
- AMIBIOS 07/08/94
- Any Gateway ColorBook >1.0 w/SystemSoft BIOS
- Any Gateway ColorBook with APM 1.0
- AST Ascentia 900N
- Canon Innova 150C
- DECpc LPv+ 1.00
- DECpc LPv+ 1.01
- DECpc LPv+ 1.02
- NCR/AT&T 3150
- Ultra laptop 486sx33
- Wyse Forte GSV 486/66
- Zenon P5/90

Windows 95 turns off power status polling (so you do not see a battery meter) on the following computers:

- IBM ThinkPad 500
- LexBook
- WinBook

Windows 95 uses APM 1.0 mode on NEC Versa and AT&T Globalyst systems with APM 1.1 BIOS and no plug-and-play BIOS. The following IBM ThinkPad computers support APM 1.1:

- ThinkPad 755C
- ThinkPad 360/355 Family
- ThinkPad 755CE/CD/CX/CV/CDV
- ThinkPad 340CSE
- ThinkPad 370C
- ThinkPad 701C
- ThinkPad 530CS

The following IBM ThinkPad computers work with Windows 95, but only APM BIOS 1.0 is supported:

- ThinkPad 750 family
- ThinkPad 340 (monochrome)
- ThinkPad 230Cs

The ASUS PCI/I P55SP4 motherboard with a SiS 5511/5512/5513 chipset and an Award BIOS has been known to exhibit similar problems. (The battery meter may appear on the task bar when it should not.) This problem should be fixed with PnP BIOS version 0110 (11/21/95) for revision 1.2 and 1.3 motherboards. Revision 1.4 motherboards have this fix using PnP BIOS version 0303 (11/21/95).

**SYMPTOM 28-37**    **The Device Manager reports a "PCI-to-ISA Bridge Conflict"**    The Device Manager displays a PCI-to-ISA bridge entry with an exclamation point in a yellow circle—indicating that there is a resource conflict. This problem is typically caused by a PnP BIOS that reports both a PCI and an ISA bus, but only an ISA bus is present, so there is no actual conflict. You'll need to update the PnP BIOS to a version with better detection and reporting capability.

**SYMPTOM 28-38**    **The PnP BIOS is disabled on a laptop or notebook computer**
When you install Windows 98/Me/XP on a dockable notebook computer with a PnP BIOS, you see no "Eject PC" command on the Start menu when the notebook computer is docked in a docking station. Also, no PnP BIOS node is displayed in System Devices under the Device Manager. This problem was known to occur on older IBM ThinkPad (360/750/755 series) dockable notebook computers with a PnP BIOS and occurs because early versions of dockable notebook computers with PnP BIOS are not fully compatible with Windows. When a PnP BIOS is disabled in Windows 98/Me/XP, certain features (such as warm docking) no longer work. To make your dockable notebook computer compatible with Windows, contact the manufacturer of your notebook computer and obtain the most recent PnP BIOS.

In general, a PnP BIOS dated after 7/1/95 is compatible with Windows 9x and later.

**SYMPTOM 28-39**    **The sound device on a DEC HiNote Ultra isn't working**    When you install Windows 98/Me/XP over an existing Windows installation on a DEC HiNote Ultra computer with a PnP BIOS, the sound device no longer works properly. Also, the wrong sound device is installed in Windows. This is a PnP BIOS problem—early versions of the DEC HiNote Ultra shipped with a PnP BIOS are not compatible with Windows 98/Me/XP. Contact DEC and obtain the most recent PnP BIOS for the DEC HiNote Ultra.

**SYMPTOM 28-40**    **Device resources are not updated in a "forced" configuration**
You'll notice that an exclamation point appears over a resource icon in Computer properties in the Windows 9x/Me Device Manager, or that changes you make to the resources assigned to a PnP device in the computer's CMOS Setup are not reflected in the Settings column in Computer properties under Device Manager. This is because the device is using a forced configuration instead of an automatic configuration. To remove a forced configuration and allow the PnP device to be fully configurable by the computer's BIOS and Windows, set the device to use automatic settings under Windows 9x/Me/XP, following these steps:

1. Open the Device Manager.
2. Double-click the offending device, and then click the Resources tab.

3. Click the Use Automatic Settings check box to select it.

4. Click OK.

A "forced" configuration overrides any BIOS or ROM settings (even if Windows knows the device is currently consuming a different set of resources). If you move a device to a different set of resources, you must update the forced configuration manually. When you are diagnosing hardware problems, it is a good idea to look for forced configurations and remove them.

**SYMPTOM 28-41**    **Restarting the computer causes the PC to hang**    This often happens when you try to restart your computer using the Restart the Computer option in the Shut Down Windows dialog. This problem can occur on computers with a BIOS that expects IRQ 12 to be used by a PS/2-style mouse port, but instead have a software-configurable hardware device (such as a PnP adapter or USB controller) using IRQ 12. To work around this problem, reserve IRQ 12 in Device Manager, or change the IRQ for the software-configurable device in Device Manager. You may also want to consider upgrading the BIOS in the computer to a later version. To reserve an IRQ with Device Manager under Windows 9x/Me:

1. In the Control Panel, double-click the System icon.

2. On the Device Manager tab, double-click Computer.

3. On the Reserve Resources tab, click the Interrupt Request (IRQ) option, and then click Add.

4. In the Value box, click the IRQ you want to reserve.

5. Click OK until you return to Control Panel.

If you cannot reserve an interrupt with your version of an operating system, you may be able to reserve IRQs through the PCI/PnP submenu of the CMOS Setup.

**SYMPTOM 28-42**    **Adding a PCI device causes the system to hang in Windows**    For example, this problem is known to occur with some older Dell Dimension systems (though it can occur on other systems). The BIOS in the Dell computer has probably configured the new PCI device to use IRQ 10, but another legacy device installed in the system is already configured to use IRQ 10. Although Windows is designed to recognize resource conflicts such as this, this particular conflict causes the computer to hang before the Windows Configuration Manager recognizes that the conflict exists. The PCI bus is normally a PnP-compatible bus, but the BIOS in Dell Dimension computers statically allocates IRQ 10 to a new PCI device. There is no way to disable this behavior. To work around this problem, configure the existing legacy device to use an IRQ other than IRQ 10. Alternatively, you can reserve IRQ 10 in the CMOS Setup and allow Windows to reallocate another IRQ to the new device.

**SYMPTOM 28-43**    **You cannot configure disabled devices in the Device Manager**
When you're using a PnP BIOS, you may not be able to configure (through Device Manager) a device that has been disabled in the BIOS—even though the BIOS supports configuring devices for the next time the computer starts. When you click the device in Device Manager and then click Properties, you see a message such as:

```
The device has been disabled in the hardware. In order to use this device,
 you must re-enable the hardware. See your hardware documentation for
details (Code 29).
```

This is a problem with Windows. You'll need to enable the device in the BIOS *before* you try to configure it in Device Manager.

**SYMPTOM 28-44**    **A laptop doesn't switch from LCD to external monitor**    For example, if you place a Toshiba T4900 computer into its docking station while Windows is running (a "warm dock" operation), the display may not switch from the LCD screen to the external monitor. Toshiba's PnP BIOS does not switch the display properly between the LCD screen and an external monitor. For a short-term work around, press F5 to manually toggle the display between the LCD screen and the external monitor. In the meantime, contact the laptop manufacturer for a PnP BIOS upgrade.

**SYMPTOM 28-45**    **A third port is detected with a PCI dual-port IDE controller**    For example, when using a CMD PCI Dual Port IDE controller (with at least *one* device on both the primary and secondary port), the Device Manager displays a third port. This "false" third port is displayed with an exclamation point inside a yellow circle. This happens because the PnP BIOS in your computer is erroneously reporting that a third port is present. Windows does not allocate any resources to the third port, and the existence of the third port in Device Manager should not cause any problems. A BIOS upgrade should correct the trouble (or using a different IDE controller). However, if you want to disable the third port, follow these steps:

1. Open the Device Manager and locate the third "phantom" port (it should be clearly marked with a yellow exclamation mark).

2. Right-click the port and select Properties. A Properties dialog should appear.

3. Disable the device. Click the Original Configuration (Current) check box to clear it, and then click OK. With Windows 98, click the Disable In This Hardware Profile box to select it, and then click OK. With Windows XP, click Do Not Use This Device (Disable) in the Device usage area.

4. Save your changes and reboot the PC if necessary. Return to the Device Manager and verify that the unwanted port is still disabled.

# Further Study

ACPI specifications    www.acpi.info
**Legacy PnP Guidelines**    www.pcdesguide.org/download/pnp_legacy.pdf
**PnP specifications**    www.microsoft.com/hwdev/tech/pnp/default.asp
**PnP ISA specifications**    www.microsoft.com/hwdev/resources/specs/pnpisa.asp

# 29

# POWER PROTECTION

**P**ower is one of those issues that's often taken for granted (or at least treated as an afterthought). Surges, spikes, and other power anomalies that occur in commercial power systems every day can damage the PC's power supply, and they often can affect the drives and motherboard circuitry as well. Even when no serious damage occurs to the system, power failures can result in wasted time and lost data for any office or organization. This chapter is intended to explain the concepts of power protection and show you the four major types of power protection devices that are available. As a PC technician, you can use this information to help your customers develop adequate and reliable power protection plans that will suit their needs and budgets. Proper power protection improves system reliability and reduces downtime.

# Understanding Power Problems

Generally speaking, we have all come to take power for granted. In most cases, we simply tend to plug a device in the nearest available outlet and turn it on, *assuming* that an appropriate amount of voltage and current is available. If the device fails to function as expected, the natural assumption is that the *device* is at fault. In truth, this is not always the case. Computers and peripherals need certain minimum amounts of current and voltage at the AC line. If either value is too high or too low (or unexpected interruptions occur), the computer may behave erratically—or not work at all.

Commercial power is generated as a sinusoidal (called *alternating current,* or AC) wave similar to the one shown in Figure 29-1. The amplitude of the wave represents *voltage*, and the rate at which the wave repeats represents *frequency*. Voltage and frequency characteristics vary in different regions of the world. Regardless of region, however, the AC signal should be perfectly smooth and regular. In practice, AC can suffer from a variety of ills: blackouts, brownouts, surges, and spikes.

## BLACKOUTS

A *blackout* is a complete loss of electrical power where voltage and current drop to a very low value (typically zero). Blackouts are usually caused by a physical interruption in the local power network due to accidental damage by a person or act of nature. Interruptions may also be a necessary side-effect of normal maintenance and repair of the local power grid. The interruption may affect an area as small as a street or as large as an entire region, depending on the point in the power distribution network where damage occurs.

Unless backup power is available, the loss of AC will invariably shut down the computer in a matter of milliseconds. In most cases, simply loosing power does not damage a PC—memory is lost (along with any unsaved information). This is often just an inconvenience for casual home users. For business users, however, loosing power can mean the loss of valuable data, representing hours of lost productivity. In extremely rare cases, a sudden and complete power loss can corrupt a hard drive's file structure and possibly damage files. The best and least expensive means of protection against a rare blackout is to save work

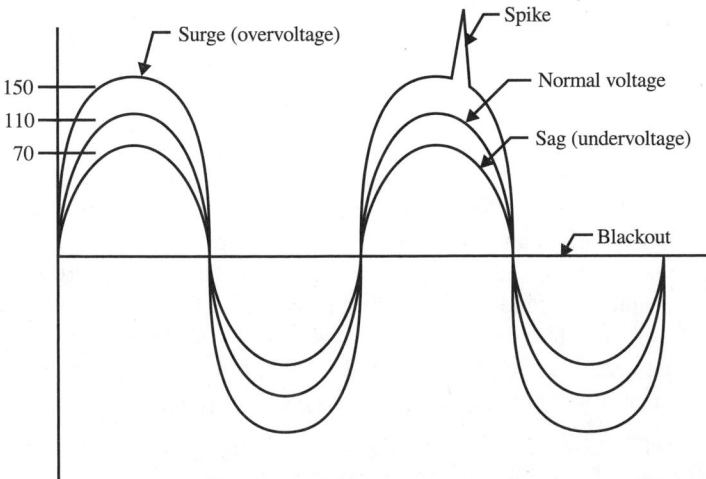

**FIGURE  29-1**    Comparison of AC sine waves during typical power problems

regularly—every 30 minutes to an hour. By taking this precaution, no more than an hour of work could be lost if power fails. For remote areas or regions that are subject to frequent power outages, a fast-switching backup power supply (BPS) or a reliable uninterruptible power supply (UPS) is highly recommended (you'll see more about power protection devices later in this chapter).

## BROWNOUTS

Perhaps more dangerous than a sudden, complete power loss is the *brownout* (or *sag*), an undervoltage condition caused by questionable electrical wiring or excessive electrical load on an AC circuit. High-load items (like air conditioners, coffee pots, fan motors, overhead projectors, photocopiers, and so on) draw so much current that the AC voltage level drops. PC supplies are *regulated,* which means the DC output provided to the computer circuitry will be constant over a range of AC input conditions. However, when AC conditions fall outside of that tolerable range, the supply will fall out of regulation, resulting in intermittent system operation (the system mysteriously freezes or reboots, random memory errors occur, files may be lost or corrupted on the hard drive, and so on).

Undervoltage conditions can also damage the power supply. Since the PC's power supply responds to low AC voltages by drawing excessive current, serious undervoltage conditions can cause unusual heating that will eventually damage a PC power supply. If your customers complain of unusual system problems such as those just described, ask them to try their system on another AC circuit. Although one circuit may be loaded down, other circuits are probably not. If your customer cannot find a lightly used circuit (or does not have access to one), ask your customer to try disconnecting high-load devices in their area, such as air conditioners, fans, and heaters. If the problems disappear, advise your customer to have a new AC circuit installed from the circuit breaker (make it very clear that the new AC circuit should be from another line phase). Urban areas suffer from summer brownouts that affect entire areas. Such regional brownouts are usually due to the massive air conditioner load that is common in the summer season.

It is difficult to overcome brownout conditions, since most BPSs do not engage until voltage levels drop below brownout levels (usually 85 to 95 Vac). However, a UPS will prevent unpleasant surprises since the computer runs from the UPS normally anyway. Brownouts and blackouts do not interrupt UPS operation.

## SURGES AND SPIKES

Basically, spikes and surges are the same villain—they just take different forms. *Surges* are small overvoltage conditions (140 Vac or more) that take place over relatively long periods (usually more than 1 second). To regulate power to a desired level, excess energy must be switched (in switching power supplies) or thrown away (in linear power supplies). In either case, excessive voltage creates overheating in the supply, and will eventually destroy it. Some power supplies are designed to shut down in the event of voltage or thermal overloads, but you cannot always count on this feature in today's proliferation of inexpensive clone PCs.

A *spike* is a large overvoltage condition (perhaps as much as 2,500 volts) that occurs in the space of milliseconds. Lightning strikes and high-energy switching can cause spikes on the AC line. Heavy equipment like drill presses, welders, grinders, and other highly motorized devices can produce tremendous power spikes during normal operation or when switched on and off. If your PC is on the same AC circuit as that heavy equipment, the spikes can damage the power supply. While some supplies are designed with surge suppression components (transformers, capacitors, gas discharge tubes, and metal oxide varistors, or MOVs), spikes that pass through surge suppression can damage the supply regulator or pass through the supply to damage many portions of the motherboard. Also bear in mind that spikes (e.g., from lightning strikes) can also pass along the telephone line and damage your modem.

## SYMPTOMS OF POWER PROBLEMS

Before you run out and invest hard-earned money in power protection equipment, you first should have some indication of power problems. Power problems are often difficult to measure because the power "event" occurs too quickly to measure without very specialized power monitoring equipment. Still, there are some situations that may suggest chronic power problems:

■  The room lights tend to flicker or periodically vary in intensity.

■  There are frequent or regular errors in data transmission between network nodes.

■  The PC stalls, crashes, or reboots for no apparent reason—sometimes even when it's sitting idle (you may see such reboots occur in concert with flickering room lights).

■  You suffer chronic or frequent component failures (for example, modems don't seem to last long, or you've had to replace the power supply more than once in the last six months).

■  You suffer chronic or frequent hard drive failures or file access problems.

■  The CMOS RAM or modem NVRAM periodically looses its contents or becomes corrupted.

■  The PC behaves erratically when other high-energy devices are turned on (e.g., your nearby air conditioner).

■  The modem regularly looses its connection, or fails data transfers.

■  The monitor display flickers or waves (often in concert with flickering room lights).

■  You encounter frequent or chronic write errors to disks.

These symptoms do not guarantee the existence of a power problem, but they should alert you to their possibility.

# Protection Devices

A well-designed power supply is built to withstand many of the ills found in urban and suburban AC power distribution. Unfortunately, the never-ending push to reduce component count and cost in systems has meant that compromises have been made in the PC power supply. You cannot always count on the presence of effective spike or overvoltage protection in original or replacement supplies. Therefore, you should understand the various options that are available to you and your customer.

## SURGE AND SPIKE SUPPRESSORS

*Surge suppressors,* such as the APC PER3T family shown in Figure 29-2, are simple and relatively inexpensive devices ($20 to $200) that are designed to absorb high-voltage transients produced by lightning and other high-energy equipment. Protection is accomplished by clamping (or shunting) voltages above a certain level (usually above 200 volts). MOVs are often included that can respond quickly and clamp voltages as high as 6000 volts. However, powerful surges such as direct lightning strikes can blow right through an MOV. Also, MOVs degrade with each spike. Once they have passed a number of surges, they are destroyed and must be replaced. There is no way to know whether or not the MOV is working, so there is no way to really tell if a surge suppressor is actually protecting the system.

Many protectors show a neon lamp or LED that goes out when the MOV has blown or when the protector is no longer active. Good suppressors also incorporate a circuit breaker rather than a fuse. This feature is a

**FIGURE 29-2**  The PER3T product line from APC (Courtesy of APCC)

great convenience, because a circuit breaker can be reset, whereas many fused units must be disassembled to replace the fuse (or the unit must be replaced). If possible, select a surge suppressor approved under UL1449 (or an international equivalent), which clearly defines the safety and "fail-safe" performance of surge suppressor devices. (You can learn more about UL 1449 at www.elec-saver.com/ul1449.htm.) Of course, you should always consider the energy-absorbing capacity of your surge suppressor. The energy of a spike or surge is measured in Joules (J). Suppressors with a higher Joule rating will provide more protection, but will cost more. For example, a $20 surge suppressor may absorb up to 650J, whereas a $50 suppressor may handle up to 2,950J. Finally, select a suppressor with an adequate number of outlets. Remember that, as a rule, surge/spike protectors are the simplest and least expensive power protection devices—they are also the most limited.

Modems and fax boards are also susceptible to damage from spikes present on everyday telephone lines. When recommending protection schemes, do not forget to include telephone line spike protection as well. Several of the APC PER3T devices shown in Figure 29-2 also provide data line protection along with AC line protection.

## LINE POWER CONDITIONERS

*Line conditioners* perform all the functions that a surge suppressor does, but they also provide some additional power protection. Whereas surge suppressors are passive devices (functioning only when a surge is present), line conditioners (such as the APC Line-R 1250 line conditioner shown in Figure 29-3) use transformers and capacitors for power isolation and high-frequency RF noise filtering. This results in a larger and more expensive—but more effective—power protection scheme. Another advantage of line conditioners is their tolerance to brief brownout conditions. Since transformers and capacitors are energy storage components, those components will continue to provide energy to the power supply during short brownouts (on the order of several milliseconds).

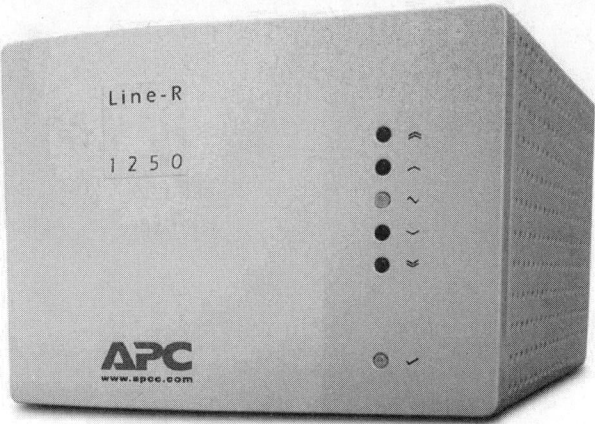

**FIGURE 29-3** The APC Line-R 1250 line voltage regulator (Courtesy of APCC)

# BACKUP POWER

Surge suppressors and line conditioners will take your customers only so far. Those devices can protect a computer from brief power anomalies and keep their systems off your workbench until it is time to upgrade. Sooner or later, though, power *will* fail. When your customer cannot afford to be in the dark (literally), you should recommend a supplemental power system. A *backup power supply* (BPS) is an offline power system that provides power to your computer *only* when main AC power fails. Power is supplied from a series of batteries that are kept charged while AC power is available. When AC fails, the DC battery power is modulated into AC and switched inline to provide power to the system. Any decent BPS (like the APC Back-UPS backup family shown in Figure 29-4) can provide power for 15 to 60 minutes, depending on the amount of load attached to it—plenty of time to save any work in progress and shut down in an orderly fashion.

**FIGURE 29-4** The APC Back-UPS family of battery backup units (Courtesy of APCC)

Although manufacturers designate their battery backups as "UPS" devices, they are not "true" UPS systems because the battery power must be switched into the circuit in the event of an AC power failure—this does present a small amount of interruption time, so the unit is not "uninterruptable."

The problem with some bargain-priced BPS units is their *switching time*. It many take several milliseconds to detect the loss of AC power and actually initiate the switch-over to battery power. In that few milliseconds, a PC may brownout or reboot anyway and defeat the point of having backup power in the first place. If a customer is having problems with power switch-over, ask them to lighten the load on the BPS. Instead of trying to back up four machines with a BPS, try one or two and experiment a bit. A lighter load may allow the BPS to switch faster and preserve the PC's operation. If operation is acceptable with a lighter load, the prescription might be more BPS installations. If problems persist, find a better BPS for your customer. A BPS that offers a *ferroresonant transformer* (FRT) is often a good bet, since an FRT can provide energy for several milliseconds to smooth the transfer to battery power.

Another problem to remember is that a BPS may not offer any significant level of power protection (e.g., surge and spike protection). Since battery power is free of AC anomalies, inexpensive BPS designs may omit surge suppression or line conditioning features for the direct AC circuit. If power protection devices are already available, the problem is moot. However, if your customer is not yet using power protection devices, recommend a BPS (such as the APC Back-UPS line) that incorporates surge/spike protection.

## UNINTERRUPTIBLE POWER SUPPLIES

The *uninterruptible power supply* (UPS) is probably the best all-around form of power protection available. It is also the most expensive. Whereas a BPS provides modulated power only when AC fails, a "true" UPS unit is designed to provide modulated DC continuously—the PC runs from battery power *all the time*. AC keeps the batteries charged, but line AC does not power the PC directly. As a result, the PC is isolated from even the worse line power anomalies. Like a BPS, a UPS provides power only for a limited time after AC fails (depending on the attached load), allowing the user to save data and shut down. However, there are no switching problems to contend with. High-end UPS systems, such as the Powerware 5125 (www.powerware.com/Products/5125/product.asp), provide an excellent combination of uninterruptible power, brownout correction, and surge and spike protection.

Today's full-featured UPS/BPS systems include a communications port that allows the UPS to automatically initiate a system save and shutdown in the event of a power failure.

One thing to consider when recommending a UPS is the type of modulation provided by the modulator. Inexpensive UPS devices modulate DC battery power into an AC square wave. This is "technically" AC, but remember that some PCs and peripherals do not work well with square waves. It is preferable to recommend a UPS with a power *inverter* circuit. The inverter produces a precise sine wave (rather than a square wave), which is compatible with all PCs and peripherals.

## SIZING A BPS/UPS

As you might expect, the batteries in a UPS cannot power a load forever. This means a UPS can only power certain pieces of equipment for a limited amount of time. The exact amount of time depends on the *load* (the amount of equipment) that you've attached to the UPS and the size (or capacity) of the UPS itself. For a UPS of any given capacity, a higher load will result in shorter running time. Lightening the load (or using a larger-capacity UPS) will increase the running time. The real trick is to determine your running time by checking the load that you're planning to attach.

All UPS systems are rated in terms of *volt amperes* (VA), which is a more technical indication of power (usually measured in watts, or W). The power requirements of your equipment should be less than or equal to the VA capacity of the UPS. For example, an IBM OfficePro 700 UPS provides 700VA capacity. A VA capacity will generally operate a load at that level for about 8–10 minutes. That means the 700VA UPS should power 700VA worth of PC equipment for about 10 minutes. If you're using half the load (350VA), the UPS should operate for twice as long (16–20 minutes). If you're using a quarter of the load (175VA), the UPS should operate for four times as long (35–40 minutes), and so on. In practice, the actual amount of running time will be a bit longer if the load is measurably lower than the UPS capacity (in other words, the UPS is overrated for the load).

The real trick is to calculate the load that you're attaching. All PC equipment makers list a load rating for their devices. This rating is usually listed on the nameplate or label near the line cord on the rear of the device. The rating may be in VA, in watts (W), or in amps (A). Ideally, all loads should be denoted in VA so that the loads can simply be added together. If a load is in watts, convert to VA by multiplying W × 1.4. If a load is in amps, convert to VA by multiplying A × 120 (for a 120V device) or A × 230 (for a 230V device). Suppose you want to use a UPS to run a monitor, PC, and tape drive. A typical example may be as follows:

| Computer VA | = | 120V×2A | = | 240VA |
|---|---|---|---|---|
| Monitor VA | = | 100W×1.4 | = | 140VA |
| Tape drive VA | = | 120V×1A | = | 120VA |
| **Total** | | | **=** | **500VA** |

In this example, a 500VA UPS will run this load for about 8–10 minutes, or a 1000VA UPS will run this equipment for about 20 minutes. Table 29-1 compares basic load and runtimes for several common UPS capacities.

**TABLE 29-1    TYPICAL COMPARISON OF UPS RUNTIME VS. LOAD**

| LOAD | 250VA | 400VA | 450VA | 600VA | 900VA | 1250VA |
|---|---|---|---|---|---|---|
| 50VA | 37min | 100min | 120min | 145min | 220min | 270min |
| 75VA | 29min | 72min | 88min | 105min | 155min | 210min |
| 100VA | 23min | 47min | 65min | 79min | 110min | 160min |
| 150VA | 14min | 30min | 41min | 54min | 83min | 115min |
| 200VA | 8min | 19min | 32min | 41min | 65min | 92min |
| 250VA | 5min | 13min | 24min | 31min | 47min | 75min |
| 300VA | — | 9min | 18min | 22min | 40min | 64min |
| 350VA | — | 7min | 14min | 17min | 35min | 54min |
| 400VA | — | 5min | 11min | 13min | 29min | 46min |
| 450VA | — | — | 8min | 10min | 24min | 40min |
| 500VA | — | — | — | 7min | 20min | 34min |
| 550VA | — | — | — | 6min | 17min | 29min |
| 600VA | — | — | — | 5min | 15min | 25min |
| 700VA | — | — | — | — | 13min | 22min |
| 800VA | — | — | — | — | 11min | 17min |
| 900VA | — | — | — | — | 10min | 13min |

| TABLE 29-1 | TYPICAL COMPARISON OF UPS RUNTIME VS. LOAD *(CONTINUED)* | | | | | |
|---|---|---|---|---|---|---|
| LOAD | 250VA | 400VA | 450VA | 600VA | 900VA | 1250VA |
| 1000VA | — | — | — | — | — | 10min |
| 1250VA | — | — | — | — | — | 9min |

Do not connect laser printers to a UPS! The power requirements of a typical laser printer are much larger than the requirements of other computer peripherals, and may trip the UPS system's protective circuit breaker. Plug laser printers into a quality surge suppressor. Print jobs can always be requeued when the power is restored.

## Selecting a UPS

Given the many makes, models, and capacities of current UPS systems, selecting the right backup power device for your PC can be a bit perplexing. The problem is even more complicated if you're trying to backup a network server or provide some additional running time to a series of peripheral devices. The following questions will help the technician determine which UPS system best fits the needs of the customer:

■  Will the UPS meet the basic power requirements of this system? (e.g., Will it provide adequate run time for an orderly shutdown?)

■  Will the UPS meet future (projected) needs of the system? (e.g., Can it support additional peripheral devices that might reasonably be added later?)

■  How many components can the UPS support (such as the number of outlets)?

■  Does the UPS communicate with the PC (e.g., through a serial port) to notify it when a power failure has occurred and the PC is running on batteries?

■  Can the UPS shut down the PC automatically during a power outtage and restart the PC again automatically once power is restored?

■  Does the UPS include surge protection to guard against power spikes and surges?

■  What is the life span of the UPS battery?

■  How long can a UPS be inactive before its batteries start to degrade?

■  Will the UPS warn the user that it is running out of power?

## UPS Installation Basics

Installing a UPS is certainly not a difficult or time-consuming process, but there are some common steps that can help you streamline the installation. Your UPS manual should provide detailed instructions, but the general guidelines are listed here:

1.  **Connect the battery connector**. In many cases, a UPS is shipped with the actual battery pack disconnected (often done for safety during shipping). Connect the battery pack before proceeding.

2.  **Connect the equipment and power to the UPS**. Connect equipment to the UPS outlets. Plug the UPS into a two-pole, three-wire, grounding receptacle only. Avoid using extension cords and adapter plugs (if possible).

3. **Charge the UPS**. Make sure the battery is connected before turning on the UPS. Press the power button on the front panel to power up your UPS—this will power up connected equipment (connected equipment should be switched *on*). The UPS charges its battery pack when it is connected to utility power. The batteries charge fully during the first few hours of normal operation, so you probably won't get full runtime during this initial charge period.

4. **Check the UPS**. The unit performs a self-test automatically when turned on and every two weeks thereafter (by default). Check the site wiring fault indicator located on the UPS. It lights up if the UPS is plugged into an improperly wired AC power outlet. Wiring faults include missing ground, hot-neutral polarity reversal, and overloaded neutral circuit. If a fault is indicated, contact a qualified electrician to fix the trouble.

5. **Install optional software and accessories**. You can connect the serial cable between the UPS and PC (if so equipped), along with power utilities needed for proper PC management in the event of a power fault.

Always refer to your manual for specific installation instructions and cautions.

## Understanding the LEDs

Most UPS systems provide an array of LEDs used to indicate power status, remaining charge, critical errors, and so on (see Figure 29-5). Any UPS installation should include an understanding of the available LEDs.

Not all UPS units offer the same suite of indicators. Be sure to check the documentation for your own UPS for specific details.

**Load**    The five-LED display on the left of the front panel shows the percentage of available power used by the connected equipment (the *load*). For example, if three LEDs are lit, the connected load is drawing between

**FIGURE 29-5**    UPS units like the APC Smart UPS use LEDs to report line voltage, remaining charge, alert conditions, and so on.

50 and 67 percent of the UPS capacity. If all five LEDs are lit, the connected load is drawing between 85 and 100 percent of capacity. Thoroughly test your entire system to make sure that the UPS will not become overloaded. The UPS maintains battery charge when it is plugged in (and utility voltage is present).

**Self-Test**    The UPS performs a self-test automatically when powered on and periodically thereafter (e.g., every two weeks)—you can change the default interval. Automatic self-test eases maintenance requirements by eliminating the need for periodic manual self-tests. During the self-test, the UPS briefly operates the connected equipment on battery. If the UPS passes the self-test, it returns to online operation. If the UPS fails the self-test, the UPS lights the Replace Battery LED and immediately returns to online operation. The connected equipment is not affected by a failed test. Recharge the battery for 24 hours and perform another self-test. If it fails, the battery must be replaced.

**Utility Power**    During normal operation, the UPS monitors the utility power and delivers power to the connected equipment. If your system is experiencing excessive periods of high or low voltage, have a certified electrician check your installation for electrical problems. If the problem continues, you may need to use an alternative source of commercial power.

**Online**    The online indicator illuminates when the UPS is supplying utility power to the connected equipment. If the indicator is not lit, the UPS is supplying battery power and the UPS sounds an alarm—four beeps every 30 seconds.

**Utility Voltage (120/230Vac)**    The UPS has a diagnostic feature that displays the utility voltage. Plug the UPS into the normal utility power. Press and hold the button to view the utility voltage bar graph display. After a few seconds, the five-LED display on the right of the front panel shows the utility input voltage. Refer to the figure on the left (screen) for the voltage reading (values are not listed on the UPS). The UPS starts a self-test as part of this procedure. The self-test does not affect the voltage display. The display indicates the voltage is between the displayed value on the list and the next higher value. For example, with three LEDs lit, the input voltage is between 114 and 124 VAC. If no LEDs are lit and the UPS is plugged into a working AC power outlet, the line voltage is extremely low. If all five LEDs are lit, the line voltage is extremely high and should be checked by an electrician.

**AVR Trim/Boost**    The AVR Trim LED indicates that the UPS is compensating for a *high* utility voltage. The AVR Boost LED indicates that the UPS is compensating for a *low* utility voltage. These conditions may suggest an overloaded or improperly powered AC circuit, and a certified electrician may be able to help correct the trouble.

**On Battery**    If the utility power fails, the UPS can provide power to the connected equipment from its internal battery for a finite period. The UPS sounds an alarm (four beeps every 30 seconds) while operating on battery power. The alarm stops when the UPS returns to online operation. When the *On Battery* power indicator is lit, the UPS is supplying battery power to the connected equipment.

**Battery Charge**    The five-LED display on the right of the front panel shows the present charge of the UPS battery as a percentage of the battery capacity. When all five LEDs are lit, the battery is fully charged. The LEDs extinguish (from top to bottom) as the battery capacity diminishes. As a low battery warning, any illuminated LEDs flash, and the UPS beeps. The low battery warning default setting can be changed from the rear panel (or through the optional power software).

**Overload**    The UPS emits a sustained alarm tone and the LED illuminates when an overload condition occurs (that is, when the connected equipment exceeds the specified "maximum load"). The alarm remains on until the overload is removed. The UPS continues to supply power as long as it is online and the breaker does not trip, but the UPS will not provide power from batteries in the event of a utility voltage interruption. Disconnect nonessential equipment from the UPS to eliminate the overload. If a continuous overload occurs while the UPS is on battery, the unit turns off output in order to protect the UPS from possible damage.

**Replace Battery**    Failure of a battery self-test causes the UPS to emit short beeps for one minute and the Replace Battery LED lights up. LED flashes indicate the battery is disconnected. The UPS repeats the alarm every five hours. Perform the self-test procedure after the battery has charged for 24 hours to confirm the replace battery condition. The alarm stops if the battery passes the self-test. Otherwise, replace the battery pack.

## Testing the UPS

After the UPS has had adequate time to charge its batteries, turn on the UPS system's power control and switch on your computer equipment. The UPS indicator should be illuminated and your equipment should operate normally. To test the operation of a UPS, simply unplug its input cord (or press and hold the Test/Alarm Disable switch on units so equipped) to simulate a utility blackout. The UPS will immediately transfer your equipment to power from the UPS internal battery. During this time, the UPS will emit a beep once every few seconds to remind you that your equipment is operating from a source of power that is limited in duration. Restore power to the UPS by plugging in the line cord (or releasing the Test control switch). Observe that your equipment operates normally during the transfer from and to AC power. Repeat this test four or five times to ensure proper operation. If the PC reboots or acts eratically after switching back and forth, the swiching time of the UPS may be inadequate, or the UPS may be heavily loaded.

If the total power requirement of your attached equipment is much greater than the capacity of the UPS, the rear circuit breaker on the UPS may trip—this is an overload situation. Once the circuit breaker trips, the UPS will attempt to operate the load using its internal batteries, but this may result in an unexpectedly short runtime. If the overload is severe, the UPS will immediately shut down and cease to power the load. In this case, the UPS will emit a loud tone to alert you of the overload. If this occurs during your test, turn off the UPS and disconnect any nonessential equipment from the UPS. The circuit breaker may be reset when the overload is removed.

## UPS Support and Windows XP

UPS systems are particularly important in PC environments where the sudden loss of power can result in interrupted work and unexpected data loss. A UPS is normally a key part of PC availability, and some UPS systems (such as an APC Back-UPS Office UPS) can communicate with the PC through a serial cable and corresponding UPS management software (i.e., APC's PowerChute for Windows). This connection allows automated, orderly shutdown of the system when power is lost. Once the UPS is properly installed, you'll need to attach the serial port on the UPS to an available serial port on the PC using the cable supplied with the UPS. You'll then need to configure management options under Windows through the Power Options icon. With Windows XP, open the Control Panel, click Performance and Maintenance, and select Power Options. Under Windows 9x/Me, open the Control Panel and double-click the Power Management icon. Look for two tabs: Hibernate and UPS.

**Hibernate**    The Hibernate tab (see Figure 29-6) is optional—it's not available on all PCs. If your PC contains the proper hardware to use a "hibernation" power state (saving the system's state to disk rather than shutting down power completely) and a minimum of 128MB, you can select Enable Hibernate Support and click Apply. This will enable the UPS to hibernate your system in the event of an extended power

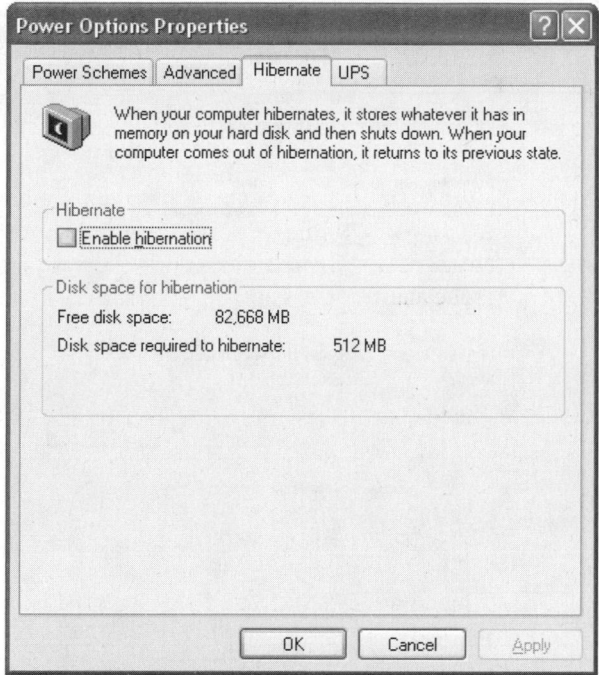

**FIGURE 29-6**    The Hibernate tab is available on PCs that fully comply with advanced power management requirements.

failure. In this condition, the hibernating PC will last much longer on battery power than the normal or "suspend" power modes.

**UPS**    The UPS tab (see Figure 29-7) provides the main options needed to configure the UPS for your PC. First, be sure to connect the UPS to the PC according to the manufacturer's instructions. Click Select, choose the manufacturer (i.e., American Power Conversion), select the model (i.e., Smart-UPS), and choose the COM port attached to the UPS (i.e., COM1). Click Finish to complete the configuration and return to the UPS tab. (You may need to click Apply or OK so that the new UPS will be enabled.) If you've enabled hibernation support, click Configure, select Hibernate (rather than Shutdown) for the Next, Instruct the Computer To setting. Now click Finish, and click Apply so that any changes can take effect.

# Backup, Backup, Backup

A strange fact of today's society is that the *information* contained in a computer is often more valuable than the computer system itself. Serious power interruptions can damage a computer, but even more important is the loss of vital data from memory or the hard drive. Power protection devices are intended to protect the PC from damage and keep the system operating in the face of poor or absent AC—at least until the system can be shut down safely. However, power protection devices are not foolproof. Regular back-ups of memory and disk files are vital to any protection plan.

Advise your customers to save their work religiously. Saving every 30–60 minutes is usually prudent (more often in a busy office environment)—it is also *free*. If your customers do not have a tape backup to

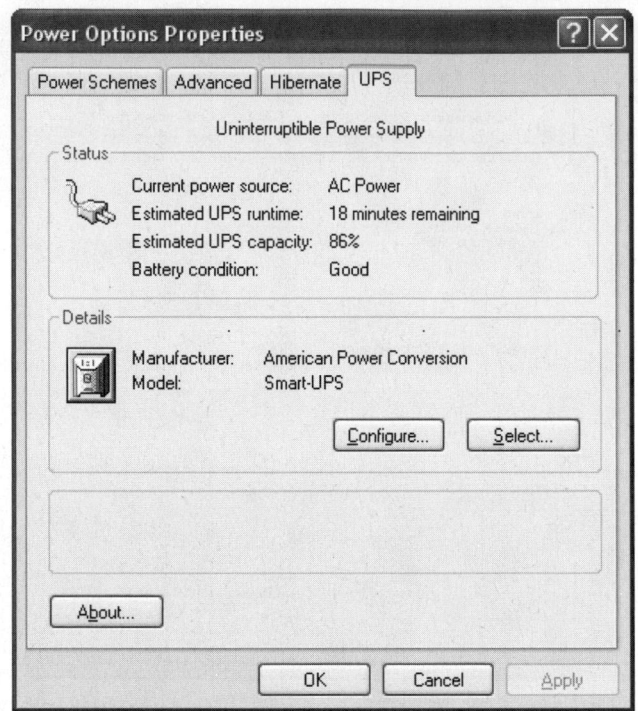

**FIGURE  29-7**     The UPS tab lets you configure the PC to work with your particular UPS make and model.

support their hard drive files, strongly recommend a tape drive or other backup medium such as a CD-RW drive. System backups once a day (even once a week) can preserve vital data in the rare event that a hard drive is damaged by a spike or brownout.

# Troubleshooting Power Protection Devices

Power protection devices (especially BPS and UPS systems) are often ignored once they are installed. In fact, power systems require a certain level of regular attention and are themselves subject to a wide array of problems that can affect the reliability of your PC or network. This part of the chapter examines many of the common problems that can affect BPS/UPS systems and offers some suggestions for corrective action.

## VERIFYING ELECTRICAL SAFETY

Before we discuss troubleshooting specifically, it would be wise to review the overall electrical power and interconnection scheme used by the PC. Electrical power "events" can be conducted by any long cable connected to your computer, LAN, or modem. The following tips can help you protect your equipment from potential damage:

- Use a UPS or surge suppressor to protect all AC operated PC equipment—especially the main system (desktop, workstation, or server) and monitor.

- Verify that your AC power receptacles are properly wired (you may need the services of a licensed electrician for this). Even though PC equipment may appear to operate properly under normal conditions, operating computer equipment from improperly wired outlets can pose a shock hazard, and power protection devices like surge and spike suppressors may fail to work.

- Plug in all power protection and/or PC equipment line cords to the same AC circuit wherever possible. This basically means that power to all the PC equipment is controlled by the same building fuse or circuit breaker.

- RS-232 serial interface ports on computers, terminals, printers, plotters, and modems are especially sensitive to damage from electrical transients because they use the computer chassis ground as a single common ground. Protect both ends of an RS-232 serial interface cable longer than 5 feet (1.5 meters) with good-quality serial port protection devices specifically designed for that purpose. Do not attempt to run RS-232 links between equipment in separate buildings—use good-quality short-haul modems instead.

- Use good-quality network protection devices to protect your Ethernet network interface cards (NICs) and other LAN equipment at each end of a network's 10Base-T UTP or coaxial Thinnet cable. Thinnet (10Base2) networks are especially susceptible to intersystem ground noise when the cable shields are inadvertently grounded at more than one location. Verify your system's true single ground point and check to be sure that T-connectors or any exposed connector barrels are not touching the metal chassis of your computer.

- Use good-quality network protection devices to protect your 4 and 16 Mbps Token Ring NICs and other LAN equipment at each end of a network's UTP cable.

- Protect the telephone port of your telecommunications equipment (modem, fax, telex, answering machine, and so on) from damage due to nearby lightning activity with a good-quality lightning or surge arrestor designed specifically for telecommunications equipment.

## TESTING BPS/UPS BATTERIES

Batteries are electrochemical devices, meaning they all will fail eventually. BPS/UPS backup batteries are certainly no exception. If there is trouble with your BPS/UPS system (or as part of regular maintenance on the power system), you should be able to test the batteries in a BPS or UPS for integrity. The following steps outline testing for +12 Vdc batteries:

1. Make sure that your BPS or UPS is connected correctly, and has at least 50 percent of its total load devices plugged in (desktop unit, monitor, scanner, and so on).

2. Turn on the system and its attached peripherals, and allow the PC to boot normally.

3. Simulate a power outage by disconnecting the BPS or UPS line cord.

4. Use a standard digital voltmeter and measure each individual battery voltage.

5. Each +12 Vdc battery should read between +11.5 Vdc and +12.5 Vdc. Any battery measuring outside of that range should be considered defective and should be replaced.

6. All batteries should measure about the same. Any battery that differs more than 0.4 volt from the rest of the batteries should be considered bad and replaced.

**7.** Wait about 5 minutes and repeat the test (looking for one weak battery to discharge faster than the others). If any battery appears to be discharging faster than the others, it should be considered bad and replaced.

You should also check that the runtime data provided by the UPS tab (as in Figure 29-7) is accurate. This is important because the PC will use that runtime data to calculate when to shutdown the system.

# UPS BATTERY REPLACEMENT

Another result of batteries being electrochemical devices is that after an ample number of charge and discharge cycles, they'll eventually wear out and need to be replaced. As a rule of thumb, you can expect to change your BPS/UPS batteries every three to five years under normal use. Other circumstances such as bad commercial power sources, elevated temperatures where the batteries are stored, and improper maintenance procedures can all reduce the working life of a battery. You should suspect battery problems when they cannot hold a charge (short run times and "low battery" alarms even after ample charging time).

If you find that battery replacement is required, you can use the following guidelines to replace the UPS batteries. Remember that you *must* replace batteries with the exact same make and model as the original batteries or use a suitable substitute recommended by the particular UPS manufacturer. If you must substitute batteries, it may be necessary to replace *all* of the batteries in that UPS (even if only one is weak). Be sure to consult with the UPS manufacturer for its recommendations. As a rule, UPS systems allow for cold (UPS off) and warm (UPS on) battery substitution.

If "warm" substitution is not specifically discussed by the UPS maker, always plan on "cold" substitution for best safety.

### Preparing for Cold Substitution

The safest way to replace UPS batteries is through *cold* substitution—powering down the UPS and all load devices, and then replacing the batteries. Use the following steps as a basis for cold substitution:

**1.** Shut down all load devices (the system, monitor, printer, and so on).

**2.** Take the UPS out of its operate mode (e.g., press the Standby button on the UPS). The ON LED goes out, and power to the load receptacles stops.

**3.** Disconnect the UPS from utility (AC) power.

**4.** Wait at least 60 seconds for the UPS internal circuitry to discharge.

### Preparing for Warm Substitution

In general, UPS batteries may be replaced without powering off the UPS (*hot-swapped*) if the UPS is *not* currently charging the batteries and is not supplying battery power to load devices—that is, normal AC power is available. To determine whether warm substitution is safe, be sure to check the UPS indicators to verify that the batteries are fully charged and that the UPS is supplying utility power rather than battery power.

Older batteries may register as fully charged but still be incapable of providing adequate backup for load devices. This means the battery charge LEDs may indicate the batteries are fully charged, while the UPS diagnostics have determined that the batteries need to be replaced.

## Removing the Battery Pack

Use the following steps as a general guideline to remove the old battery pack from the UPS (your own UPS may be different, so check with the manufacturer for its specific recommendations):

1. Open the UPS cabinet to access the battery pack. The exact procedure may vary between UPS models, so be sure to review the procedures for your own UPS system. In many cases, you must remove several screws holding a faceplate, and then detach the faceplate to reveal the LED display cable.

2. Disconnect the LED display cable from the faceplate, and then set the faceplate aside. Take care to avoid damaging the printed circuit board behind the LED display.

3. Remove the screws that are retaining the battery pack.

4. Slide the battery pack partially out of the UPS chassis to access the battery terminals.

5. Disconnect the negative (black) battery pack terminal connections.

6. Disconnect the positive (red) battery pack terminal connections.

7. Slide the battery pack out to access the battery cable retainer bracket. Remove the screw and battery cable retainer bracket.

8. Carefully slide the battery pack out until the plastic handle(s) is accessible.

9. Remove the battery pack and set it aside for proper disposal.

 Remember that UPS battery packs are generally quite heavy and can often exceed 60 pounds. Get some help when transporting the battery pack, and be sure that there is a safe location to set the pack once it's removed.

## Installing the New Battery Pack

With the old battery pack removed, use the following steps as a guideline to install the new batteries in a UPS (your own UPS may be different, so check with the manufacturer for its recommendations):

1. Slide the new battery pack into the chassis, leaving room to replace the battery cable retainer bracket.

2. When installing the bracket, position the cables to lie flat and to run under the plastic handling strap(s).

3. Reconnect the positive (red) battery pack terminal connections.

4. Reconnect the negative (black) battery pack terminal connections.

5. Reinstall the screw(s) holding the battery pack to the UPS chassis.

6. Reinstall the display faceplate, if necessary. Attach the LED display cable to the LED display.

7. Replace the screw(s) holding the faceplate to the chassis.

## Testing the Battery Pack

After the new battery pack is installed, run a UPS self test or diagnostic (press the Test/Alarm Reset button). Refer to the documentation that accompanied your specific UPS for self test or diagnostic instructions. Remember that most UPS systems will not invoke a self test until the new batteries are 90 percent charged or more, so you may need to wait a little while until the new battery pack is charged. If there are problems with the new installation, one or more battery warning displays (battery service indicators) will light. You may need to go back and check your terminal connections.

### Disposing of Old Batteries

Due to the dangerous and caustic chemicals used in batteries, it is virtually impossible to discard used batteries with ordinary trash because it's illegal in most parts of the US (and the world). When you replace UPS batteries, most vendors will also provide instructions and suitable packaging for you to ship the batteries to an appropriate disposal facility. If the vendor does not provide adequate disposal options, check your local yellow pages for a recycling center that meets all local environmental protection standards.

## UPS LOCATION TIPS

While the physical location of a UPS may not be critical, there are some tips that may help prevent backup power problems:

- Install the UPS as close as possible to the equipment that it will protect. If this distance is more than 25 feet (7.6 meters), transient noise can appear in the electrical distribution system. Fortunately, this is usually not a problem with smaller UPS systems protecting individual PCs.

- If the UPS batteries are in a separate cabinet (this is often the case with larger server-oriented installations), the battery cabinet should be as close to the UPS as possible. If the batteries will be farther away from the unit than the standard cables allow, you may need to replace the battery cables with a larger gauge wire to reduce voltage losses across the line.

- The UPS should be in a flat location in a controlled, indoor environment. Do not install the UPS next to open windows.

- Keep the UPS away from heat sources, direct sunshine, moisture, or corrosive gas.

- Do not place any objects on top of the UPS and do not install it in any type of enclosure. Do not operate the UPS or batteries in a sealed room or container.

## UNDERSTANDING LINE LOAD INDICATORS

During normal operation, a "true" UPS rectifies the AC input, and then uses it to charge the batteries and feed the inverter circuit to power your connected equipment. (A battery backup unit may only report load once AC power is lost.) If your UPS provides a Line Load indicator, this will show the amount (percentage) of UPS power that your system is actually using. Remember that a UPS can provide only a limited amount of power, so you should verify that the line load power being provided to your PC equipment is *less than* 100 percent of the total UPS capacity—otherwise, you'll overload the UPS. A Line Load indicator that's approaching 100 percent means that the UPS is in danger of overloading, and you'll need to reduce the number of devices demanding power from the UPS (or replace the UPS with a larger model).

If the Line Load indicator flashes and the UPS cuts out the AC source power, chances are that the AC feeding the UPS is too high or too low. You'll need a licensed electrician to "buck" or "boost" the AC power within a range that's appropriate for the UPS.

## UNDERSTANDING BATTERY POWER INDICATORS

When the UPS runs on battery backup power (the *inverter*), the Battery and Inverter indicators are typically illuminated—this commonly happens during a power outage or when AC input power is not acceptable to the UPS (too high or too low). If your UPS provides a Battery Charge indicator, this will show the amount of battery charge that's left in the UPS. As the UPS runs on battery power, the amount of charge (and the amount of time the UPS can continue running on battery) will decrease, and the display will generally show this decrease in operating time. It's important that main AC power be restored (or the system be shut down) before the battery charge drops out. If the Battery indicator starts flashing, the battery voltage is low and shutdown of the UPS is imminent. If your UPS is communicating with the PC, the UPS tab in the Power Properties dialog (refer to Figure 29-7) will also report the remaining (expected) runtime.

## UNDERSTANDING THE BYPASS INDICATOR

Ideally, the "true" UPS is providing power through its inverter, so AC is never *directly* connected to the system—this is not the case for ordinary battery backup units. However, if your UPS is equipped with a Bypass button and indicator, you can sometimes bypass the UPS and run the system from AC power. This happens if there is a UPS overload, if the UPS cannot run on battery power (for example, because of an inverter failure), or if you press the Bypass button. If the cause of the bypass is an overload, the UPS can automatically transfer back to normal operation after the overload has been removed.

## UNDERSTANDING THE ALARM INDICATOR

When the UPS detects a problem, you'll generally see a flashing Alarm indicator or a seven-segment error number display (often in conjunction with an alarm beep or tone). You can typically silence the audible alarm by pressing an Alarm button, but the flashing indicator (or message display) will still display a problem until it's corrected. If you don't see a solution listed in the following sections, refer to the UPS manual or contact the manufacturer's technical support.

## UPS QUICK CHECKLIST

Many of the common problems that occur with UPS systems usually fall into one of the following general categories:

- **The UPS is on but is not supplying power to the equipment** The output circuit breaker on the back of the UPS may have been tripped (possibly because of excessive load). Reset the breaker.

- **No UPS indicators are on, and no alarm is sounding** The UPS is not operating. Input power might not be available to the UPS (for example, an extended power outage may have occurred) or the input circuit breaker on the back of the UPS may have been tripped. Check the AC input power supply, and then reset the breaker and restart the UPS.

- **The Line indicator is not on even though AC line input seems to be available, and the UPS beeps every few seconds** Input power might not be available to the UPS. The output circuit breaker on the back of the UPS may have been tripped. Check the AC input power supply, and then reset the breaker and restart the UPS.

- **The amount of UPS battery run time is less than the rating** The battery may not be fully charged or may be bad, or the charger may have failed. Recharge the battery for at least ten hours by connecting the UPS to a source of AC line input, and then retest the battery backup time. If the problem persists, the batteries may need to be replaced, or the charger may need to be repaired or replaced.

- **The Battery indicator is flashing** The battery voltage is low. Recharge the battery for at least ten hours by connecting the UPS to a source of AC line input. If the problem persists, the batteries may need to be replaced, or the charger may need to be repaired or replaced.

## DEALING WITH COMMON ALARM CONDITIONS

Many of the current generation of BPS and UPS systems incorporate a certain amount of "intelligence" that oversees features such as battery charging and self-diagnostics. When important conditions are not met or errors are detected, the BPS/UPS will produce an alarm. Although the actual means used to present the alarm (for example, beeps, seven-segment codes, or alphanumeric LCD readouts) can vary quite a bit between makes and models, you should understand the essential alarm meanings and know how to respond quickly.

- **Batteries Disconnected**    The BPS/UPS batteries are not properly connected. Verify the connection of all batteries in the BPS/UPS. The UPS will not protect your system until this fault is corrected. Check any battery connections or inline fuses that may have failed.

- **Batteries Undercharged**    The PC is receiving power, but the batteries have an insufficient charge and will not protect your system for long. See that the batteries are allowed ample time to charge. If this is a persistent problem, you might want to inspect each of the batteries, replace weak batteries, or have the charging system serviced.

- **Check Battery**    The BPS/UPS has detected a possible problem with one or more of its batteries. Verify that all of your batteries are properly connected in the BPS/UPS. You should test and replace any defective batteries.

- **Check Fan**    The cooling fan inside the BPS/UPS (if any) is not functioning properly. The fan may need to be reconnected or replaced, or the BPS/UPS may require factory service or outright replacement.

- **Check Fuse Board**    The BPS/UPS has detected a possible problem with an internal fuse board. It may be possible to check/replace the fuse board, but this usually means that the BPS/UPS has failed and is in need of factory service or replacement.

- **Check Inverter**    The BPS/UPS has detected a possible problem with its inverter circuit (the circuit that actually turns battery DC back into AC for the computer). This usually means that the BPS/UPS has failed and is in need of factory service or replacement. You may need to bypass the inverter or remove the UPS from service until the problem is corrected.

- **Check MOVs**    The BPS/UPS has detected a problem with a MOV (surge/spike suppression system) inside the unit. This usually means that the BPS/UPS has failed and is in need of factory service or replacement.

- **Check Power Supply**    The unit has detected a possible problem with the unit's internal power supply (which powers the BPS/UPS microprocessor controls). This type of problem usually means that the BPS/UPS has failed and is in need of factory service or replacement.

- **Circuit Breaker Warning/Shutdown**    There is high output current being provided by the BPS/UPS. This usually occurs because excessive PC equipment is overloading the BPS/UPS. Shut down all of the PC equipment and reset the BPS/UPS. Then disconnect the extra PC equipment that is overloading the BPS/UPS.

- **High AC Out/Shutdown**    The BPS/UPS is generating an unusually high AC output voltage, and will shut down to prevent damaging the PC equipment. This usually means that the BPS/UPS has failed and is in need of factory service or replacement.

- **High Ambient Temperature**    The temperature inside the BPS/UPS is too high. Make sure that the BPS/UPS is placed where room temperature is within the system's recommended range (high-temperature industrial environments are typically bad). Also, check that any internal fans or other cooling devices are working, and make sure that nothing is blocking the cooling vents in the BPS/UPS.

■ **High Battery**    The battery voltage in the BPS/UPS is high. There may be a problem with the battery charger settings, the charging circuit itself, or one or more batteries. This condition usually means that the BPS/UPS has failed and is in need of factory service or replacement.

■ **Low AC Out/Shutdown**    The BPS/UPS is generating an unusually low AC output voltage, and will shut down to prevent damaging the PC equipment. This condition usually means that the BPS/UPS has failed and is in need of factory service or replacement.

■ **Low Battery**    Battery voltage is too low for the BPS/UPS to operate on battery power, and the unit will subsequently shut down. In most cases, you should see a "Low Runtime" error first. If the batteries are too low even while the BPS/UPS is operating from AC, there may be a problem with the charging circuit or batteries in the unit.

■ **Low Runtime**    The PC is running on battery power, and the amount of battery time remaining is low (usually two minutes or less). Do an orderly shutdown of your PC equipment immediately. In most cases, you do not need to shut off the BPS/UPS (when AC power returns, the BPS/UPS can automatically restart and begin to recharge its batteries).

■ **Memory Error**    On startup, the BPS/UPS unit has failed its automatic memory validity test (usually in "intelligent" microprocessor-based BPS/UPS units). This usually means that the BPS/UPS has failed and is in need of factory service or replacement.

■ **Output Short Circuit**    This problem is usually signaled by a continuous error tone, and typically indicates an overload condition when the UPS unit is turned on. Check the wiring and verify that you're not loading down the UPS with excessive equipment. (Similar to "Overload," described next).

■ **Overload**    The PC equipment is drawing more power than the BPS/UPS is designed to provide. This condition can seriously reduce battery runtime. You'll need to shut down extra PC equipment (scanners, printers, and so on) until the error stops.

■ **Replace Batteries**    This error is typically generated as one or more beep patterns from the UPS and suggests that one or more batteries in the unit will not hold a proper charge. You should check each battery in the UPS and replace any questionable batteries at your earliest opportunity.

■ **UPS Fault**    A serious error has occurred in the UPS. The UPS will probably not protect your system during this error condition until the fault is cleared or the UPS is replaced.

## SYMPTOMS AND SOLUTIONS

If you have trouble with a power protection device that is not addressed in the preceding general guidelines, refer to the following symptoms for specific solutions to a few common problems. For these symptoms, the term "UPS" includes a true UPS, as well as a switched battery backup (BPS) unless otherwise noted.

**SYMPTOM 29-1**    **The UPS will not turn on**    This is usually indicated when the power light doesn't come on or the unit doesn't beep. There are a variety of simple problems that may be responsible for this kind of symptom, so use a systematic approach to identify the issue:

■ **The unit is not on**    Press the On button once to power the UPS and the connected equipment.

■ **Check the source power**    The UPS may not be connected to an AC commercial power source. Check that the power cable from the UPS to the utility power supply is securely connected at both ends.

- **Check the circuit breaker** Chances are that the UPS input circuit breaker tripped. Reduce the load on the UPS by unplugging equipment and resetting the circuit breaker (on the back of UPS) by pressing the plunger in.

- **Very low (or no) utility voltage** Check the AC power supply to the UPS by plugging in a table lamp. If the light is very dim, have the utility voltage checked.

- **Battery is not connected properly** Check that the battery connectors are fully engaged.

**SYMPTOM 29-2** **The UPS will not turn off (disengage)** In virtually all cases, this is an internal problem with the UPS itself which will require repair or replacement. Do not attempt to use the UPS. Unplug the UPS, remove it from service, and have it serviced by the manufacturer immediately.

**SYMPTOM 29-3** **UPS is on battery, but normal AC exists** Normal AC is present at the wall outlet, but the UPS is running from battery power. Check the AC input circuit breaker. A surge or excessive load may have tripped the breaker—cutting off AC to the UPS. If the breaker trips repeatedly, reduce the load on the UPS by unplugging equipment and resetting the circuit breaker (on the back of UPS). Another common problem is distorted (i.e., high or low) AC line voltage, which can often happen when problems strike commercial power distribution centers. A common example is a brownout condition in the summer when the power grid is loaded by air conditioning systems (inexpensive fuel powered generators can also distort the voltage). Move the UPS to an outlet on a different circuit. Test the input voltage with the utility voltage display. If the voltage level is acceptable to the connected equipment, reduce the UPS sensitivity.

**SYMPTOM 29-4** **The UPS does not provide the expected backup time** Remember that runtime is a function of battery capacity and load—higher loads shorten the runtime. Check to see that there are no unexpected load devices (e.g., another PC or peripheral device) connected to the UPS. In other cases, this is a battery issue. The UPS battery pack may be weak because of a recent outage (it has not yet fully recharged), or the battery pack is near the end of its service life. Charge the battery pack. Batteries require recharging after extended outages. They wear faster when put into service often or when operated at elevated temperatures. If the battery is near the end of its service life, consider replacing the battery (even if the Replace Battery LED is not yet lit).

**SYMPTOM 29-5** **All UPS indicators are lit, and the unit beeps constantly** In some cases, the UPS is overloaded. Check the UPS load display, unplug unnecessary equipment (such as printers), and reset the UPS if necessary. If the trouble persists, chances are that there is a serious internal fault with the UPS itself. Do not attempt to use the UPS. Turn the UPS off, remove it from service, and have it repaired immediately.

**SYMPTOM 29-6** **UPS panel indicators are flashing sequentially** This is usually not an error condition. Instead, the UPS has been shut down remotely through software (or an optional accessory card). The UPS will restart automatically when utility power returns. If the UPS does not restart, check its connections or restart the UPS manually once normal AC returns.

**SYMPTOM 29-7** **All indicators are off, but the UPS is plugged in** The UPS is shut down because the battery has discharged from an extended outage. There is little to be done in a case like this except to restore normal AC. The UPS will return to normal operation when the power is restored and the battery has regained a sufficient charge.

**SYMPTOM 29-8**   **The Replace Battery LED is lit**   The battery pack is discharged or failing. Allow the battery to recharge for at least four hours, and then perform a UPS self-test. If the problem persists after recharging, replace the battery pack. In a few cases, you may find that the battery pack is not connected properly—check that the battery connectors are fully engaged.

**SYMPTOM 29-9**   **The UPS indicates a site wiring fault**   In most cases, the UPS has detected improper wiring at the AC receptacle. For example, the AC receptacle is ungrounded (or there's no ground wire in the UPS power cord). You may also find that the line and neutral wires have been reversed in the AC receptacle (or in the UPS power cord). In either case, contact a qualified electrician to correct the condition.

**SYMPTOM 29-10**   **A High Voltage Warning LED appears on the UPS**   This usually means that the AC voltage is too high (outside of the UPS operating range). When this occurs, the UPS typically switches to battery power in order to protect the computer equipment. If this happens repeatedly, contact a qualified electrician to check and correct any AC voltage level problems. Once the AC level returns to normal, you may need to reset the alarm condition.

**SYMPTOM 29-11**   **An Low Voltage Warning LED appears on the UPS**   This usually means that the AC voltage is too low (outside of the UPS operating range). When this occurs, the UPS typically switches to battery power in order to protect the computer equipment. If this happens repeatedly, contact a qualified electrician to check and correct any AC voltage level problems. Once the AC level returns to normal, you may need to reset the alarm condition.

**SYMPTOM 29-12**   **The UPS frequently switches between utility and battery power** In most cases, the UPS is performing normally by protecting the computer equipment from high/low AC voltage levels. First, check for loose connections at the wall outlet, and see that the AC level is in an acceptable range for the UPS. If not, contact a qualified electrician (or your utility company) to correct the problem. If AC is acceptable, but the UPS still switches frequently, you may need to adjust the UPS switching sensitivity (to make the unit less sensitive to AC changes). If the problem persists, there may be trouble with the UPS itself.

**SYMPTOM 29-13**   **A Load Warning LED appears on the UPS**   In addition to an LED indicator, you may also find that the output circuit breaker trips. This usually means that there is excessive load (too many devices) on the UPS. Make sure that the total load (in volt-amperes or VA) does not exceed the UPS capacity. If so, disconnect unnecessary devices, or upgrade the UPS to a larger model. If the load is within acceptable limits, the UPS may be damaged.

**SYMPTOM 29-14**   **The UPS tab is not available in the Power Options dialog**   When trying to configure the UPS, you may notice that the UPS tab isn't available in the Windows XP Power Options dialog, or details are not displayed. In virtually all cases, the UPS has not properly identified itself to the PC. UPS support has been integrated into Windows XP, and most UPS devices have either a serial or USB connection to a computer.

A UPS that is connected using a USB cable is represented as a battery in Windows XP, and is configured through the Power Options dialog. On laptops and desktops with a USB-connected UPS, there is no UPS tab in Power Options. In this case the UPS presents itself as a Human Input Device (HID) compliant device, and Windows automatically installs the necessary drivers. Make sure that the proper USB support is installed in the PC, and recheck the USB cable between the UPS and the system.

A UPS that is connected using a serial cable is configured using the UPS tab in the Power Options dialog. Windows XP may or may not recognize a serial PnP UPS. By default, Windows XP contains serial support for several popular American Power Conversion UPS devices. However, you can also click Generic in the Manufacturer box, and then click Custom in the Model box to manually configure the UPS signal polarity. Check your UPS documentation for information about how to configure the UPS service for your UPS. It is important to remember that UPS devices offering a serial connection may use a variety of proprietary cables (with different cables providing different levels of functionality). If you have problems configuring your UPS, it may help to contact the UPS manufacturer for information about your specific UPS cable requirements.

**SYMPTOM 29-15**   **The computer reboots when the UPS kicks in**   This condition occurs because the PC equipment does not have enough "ride-through time" until the BPS/UPS can react, and voltage levels fall enough to allow the PC to reboot. In most cases, there is an excessive load on the BPS/UPS. Remove excessive PC equipment from the BPS/UPS and try the system again. If the problem persists, you may need to replace the BPS/UPS with one offering a faster switch-over time.

**SYMPTOM 29-16**   **There is trouble with the UPS serial connection**   You may note that the UPS tab in your Windows Power Options dialog reports that UPS communication has been lost. Before you attempt to reconfigure the UPS, check that you're using the cable that accompanied the UPS (rather than a standard serial cable). Also check the UPS tab and verify that the correct UPS make and model was selected. Next, open the Device Manager and expand the COM Ports listing. Double-click the COM port used for UPS communication. In the Port Properties dialog, verify that the required port settings are configured (check the UPS manual for specific settings). As a rule, the following settings are adequate:

- **Data Rate (bps)**   2,400
- **Data**   8-bit
- **Parity**   None
- **Stop**   1
- **Flow Control**   None

# Further Study

**APC**   www.apcc.com
**Best Power (Powerware/Invensys)**   www.powerware.com
**TrippLite**   www.tripplite.com

# 30

# POWER SUPPLIES AND POWER MANAGEMENT

**P**ower supplies play a vital role in the operation of PCs and their peripherals. A *power supply* converts commercial AC into one or more levels of DC that can be used by electronic and electromechanical devices inside the computer. This may not sound very glamorous, but a faulty or low-quality supply can cause serious system problems, stability issues, data loss, and (in extreme cases) can damage your motherboard or drives. Every technician should understand the operation of a *switching power supply* and know the important characteristics to consider when replacing or upgrading a supply.

But over the last few years, "power" has become more important than just plugging in a little silver box. Global concerns about limited natural resources, spiraling costs of electricity, and "greenhouse" gasses have focused attention on the tens of millions of PCs that consume power around the world. Not only must a power supply operate correctly, but modern computers must also employ aggressive power management techniques to significantly reduce the system's power consumption during idle periods. This chapter will explain the operation of a typical switching power supply, offer reliable guidelines for selecting and upgrading a supply, and cover solutions for the most common power supply problems. You'll also review the major power management schemes for desktop and mobile PCs, see how to use those schemes, and learn how to troubleshoot many of the more troublesome power management problems.

# Understanding Switching Supplies

The great disadvantage to ordinary *linear* power supplies is their tremendous waste. At least half of all power provided to a linear supply is thrown away as heat. Most of this waste occurs in the regulator portion of the supply. Ideally, if there was "just enough" energy supplied to the regulator to achieve and maintain a stable output voltage, regulator waste could be reduced almost entirely, and supply efficiency would be vastly improved. This is the concept behind a switching power supply.

## CONCEPTS OF SWITCHING REGULATION

Instead of throwing away extra input energy, a switching power supply creates a feedback loop. A feedback circuit senses the output voltage provided to a load, then switches the AC primary (or secondary) voltage on or off as needed to maintain steady levels at the output. In effect, a switching power supply is constantly turning on and off in order to keep the output voltage(s) steady. A block diagram of a typical switching power supply is shown in Figure 30-1. There are various possible configurations, but this figure illustrates one classical design approach.

Raw AC line voltage entering the supply is immediately converted to pulsating DC, and then filtered to provide a *primary DC* voltage. Notice that unlike a linear supply, AC is not transformed before rectification, so primary DC can easily reach levels exceeding 170 volts. Remember that AC is 120 volts RMS. Since capacitors charge to the peak voltage (peak = RMS × 1.414), DC levels can be higher than your AC voltmeter readings.

 Keep in mind that high-voltage pulsating DC can be as dangerous as AC line voltage and should be treated with *extreme* caution.

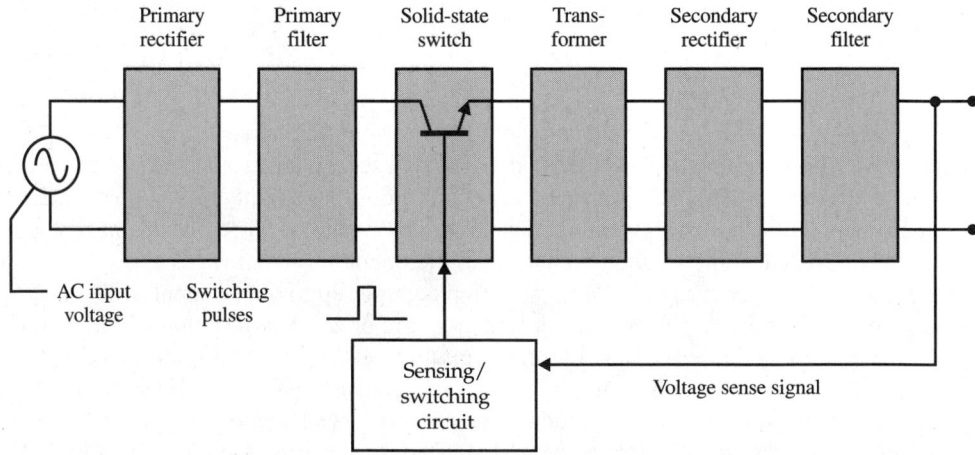

**FIGURE  30-1**    Block diagram of a switching power supply

On start up, the switching transistor is turned on and off at a high frequency (usually 20 kHz to 40 kHz) and a long duty cycle. The switching transistor acts as a *chopper,* which breaks up this primary DC to form *chopped DC* that can now be used as the primary signal for a step-down transformer. The duty cycle of chopped DC will affect the AC voltage level generated on the transformer's secondary winding (output). A long duty cycle means a larger output voltage (for heavy loads), and a short duty cycle means lower output voltage (for light loads). *Duty cycle* itself refers to the amount of time that a signal is "on" compared to its overall cycle. The duty cycle is continuously adjusted by the sensing/switching circuit. You can use an oscilloscope to view switching and chopped DC signals. Figure 30-2 illustrates a more practical representation for a switching supply.

AC voltage produced on the transformer's secondary winding (typically a step-down transformer) is *not* a pure sine wave, but it alternates regularly enough to be treated as AC by the remainder of the supply. Secondary voltage is re-rectified and refiltered to form a *secondary DC* voltage that is actually applied to the load. Output voltage is sensed by the sensing/switching circuit, which constantly adjusts the chopped DC duty cycle. As load increases on the secondary circuit (e.g., more current is drawn by the load), output voltage tends to drop. This is perfectly normal, and the same thing happens in every unregulated supply. However, a sensing circuit detects this voltage drop and increases the switching duty cycle. In turn, the duty cycle for chopped DC increases, which increases the voltage produced by the secondary winding. Output voltage climbs back up again to its desired value—output voltage is regulated.

The reverse will happen as load decreases on the secondary circuit (e.g., less current is drawn by the load). A smaller load will tend to make output voltage climb. Again, the same actions happen in an unregulated supply. The sensing/switching circuit detects this increase in voltage and reduces the switching duty cycle. As a result, the duty cycle for chopped DC decreases, and transformer secondary voltage decreases. Output voltage drops back to its desired value. Output voltage remains regulated.

Consider the advantages of a switching power circuit. Current is only drawn in the primary circuit when its switching transistor is *on,* so very little power is wasted in the primary circuit. The secondary circuit will supply just enough power to keep load voltage constant (regulated), but very little power is wasted by the secondary rectifier, filter, or switching circuit. Switching power supplies can reach efficiencies higher than 85 percent (35 percent more efficient than most comparable linear supplies). More efficiency means less heat is generated by the supply, so components can be smaller and packaged more tightly, or the supply can handle larger loads while still maintaining an established form factor.

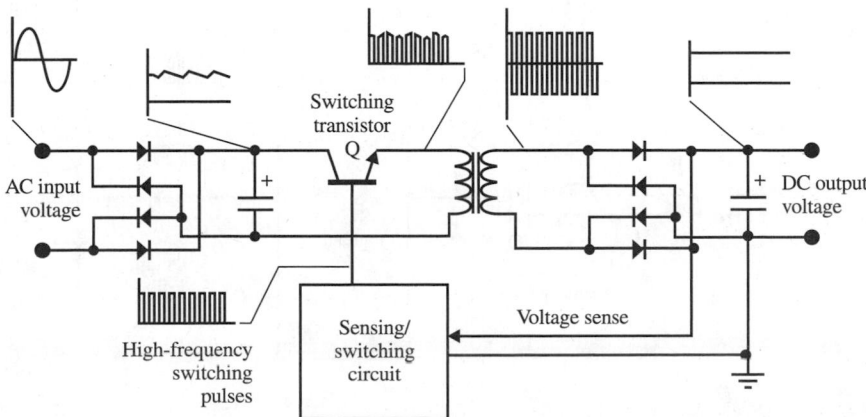

**FIGURE 30-2**    Simplified diagram of a switching power supply

Unfortunately, there are several disadvantages to switching supplies that you must be aware of. First, switching supplies tend to act as radio transmitters. Their 20-kHz to 40-kHz operating frequencies can wreak havoc on radio and television reception, not to mention the circuitry within the PC or peripheral itself. This is why you will see most switching supplies somehow covered or shielded in a metal casing. It is critically important that you replace any shielding removed during your repair. Strong *electromagnetic interference* (EMI) can easily disturb the operation of a logic circuit. Second, the output voltage will always contain some amount of high-frequency ripple. In many applications, this is not enough noise to interfere with a load. In fact, most of the noise is filtered out in a carefully designed supply. Finally, a switching supply often contains more components and is more difficult to troubleshoot than a linear supply. This is often outweighed by the smaller, lighter packaging of switching supplies. In virtually all cases today, a defective power supply unit is simply replaced.

In actual practice, sensing and switching functions can be fabricated right onto an integrated circuit. Chip-based switching circuits allow simple, inexpensive circuits to be built as shown in Figure 30-3. AC line voltage is transformed (usually stepped down), and then it is rectified and filtered before reaching a switch-regulating chip. The chip chops DC voltage at a duty cycle that will provide adequate power to the load. Chopped DC from the switching regulator is filtered by the combination of choke and output filter capacitor to reform a steady DC signal at the output. The output voltage is sampled back at the switching chip, which constantly adjusts the chopped DC duty cycle.

# CONNECTING A POWER SUPPLY

PC power supplies operate the motherboard directly, as well as a number of internal drives. This part of the chapter presents the typical connection schemes for AT, ATX, and NLX power supplies and highlights the major signals that you should be familiar with.

## AT-Style Power Connections

Although now obsolete, the AT-style power supply was largely considered to be the classic connection scheme for IBM-compatible PCs. An AT-style supply provides four voltages to the motherboard (+5 Vdc, –5 Vdc, +12 Vdc, and –12 Vdc) through a series of two heavy 6-pin connectors, as shown in Figure 30-4. You may notice that there are several wires for Ground and other voltage signals such as +5 Vdc. There is

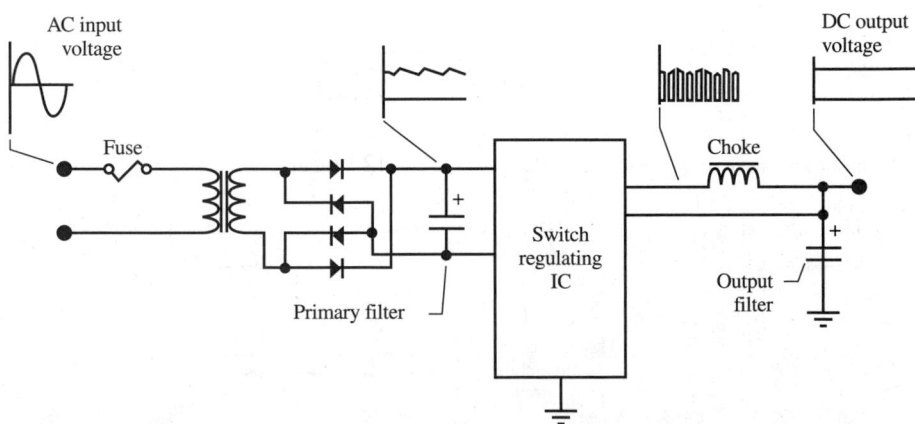

**FIGURE  30-3**    Simplified schematic of a chip-based switching power supply

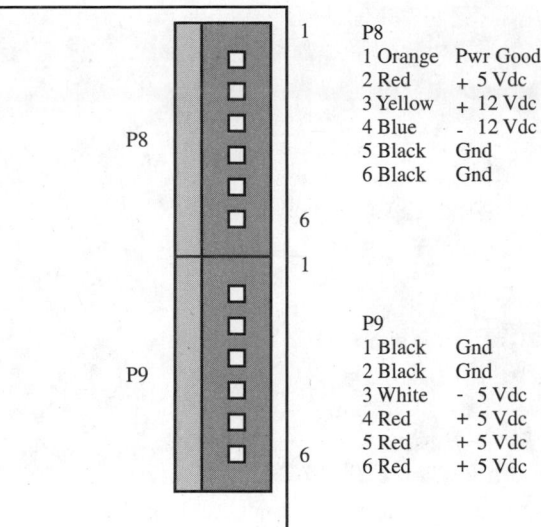

| P8 | |
|---|---|
| 1 Orange | Pwr Good |
| 2 Red | + 5 Vdc |
| 3 Yellow | + 12 Vdc |
| 4 Blue | - 12 Vdc |
| 5 Black | Gnd |
| 6 Black | Gnd |

| P9 | |
|---|---|
| 1 Black | Gnd |
| 2 Black | Gnd |
| 3 White | - 5 Vdc |
| 4 Red | + 5 Vdc |
| 5 Red | + 5 Vdc |
| 6 Red | + 5 Vdc |

**FIGURE 30-4**   AT-style motherboard power connections

no difference between these like-colored wires. The extra wires are provided simply because the additional wire is needed to help carry the required current.

If you can't remember the orientation of P8 and P9 connectors, just remember that the black ends of each connector go together.

The only discrete signal in the AT-style power connector is the Power Good (PwrGood or PG) signal. This signal is typically tied to the CPU's Reset pin. When the PC is first powered-up, this signal is logic 0, and the CPU is forced into a continuous Reset mode. After the power supply outputs are stable (usually about 0.5 second from the time you flip the power switch), this signal rises to a logic 1. This releases the Reset signal, and the CPU can begin processing—starting the POST and boot process.

## Drive Power Connections

The internal drives of a PC (such as floppy drives, hard drives, CD-ROM drives, and so on) must also be powered. Since drives are electromechanical devices that typically demand a substantial amount of current, they are powered directly from the power supply rather than from their respective interfaces. Drives traditionally use a heavy-duty 4-wire connector to provide +12 Vdc and +5 Vdc to each drive, though most current floppy drives use "low-profile" versions of the connector. You can see both connectors in Figure 30-5. The +12 Vdc signal powers the drive's motor(s), while the +5 Vdc signal operates the drive's logic circuits. The wire colors are identified as follows:

| Yellow | +12 Vdc |
|---|---|
| Black | Ground |
| Black | Ground |
| Red | +5 Vdc |

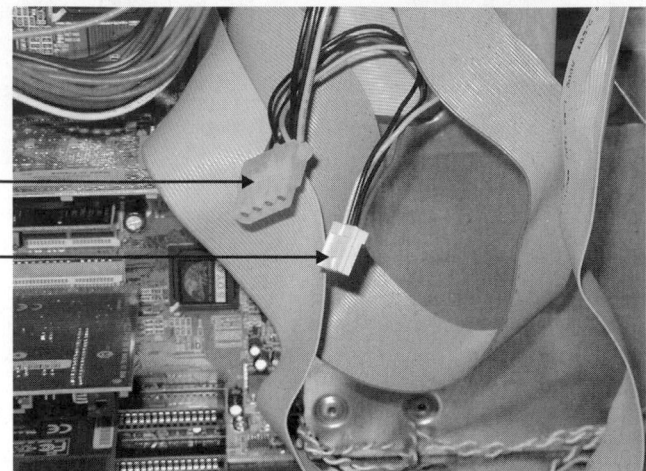

Standard 4-pin drive
power connector

Miniature 4-pin drive
power connector

**FIGURE 30-5**    Drives require a 4-pin power connector to provide +5 and +12 volts.

As a rule, there should be one drive power connector for each drive in the system. Higher-capacity power supplies typically offer more drive power connectors. If you do not have enough drive power connectors to power all of the drives in your system, you may be able to use a Y-adapter cable to transform one power connector into two. However, you should be *extremely* judicious in the use of Y-adapters. Inadequate power connectors may suggest that you're pushing the power supply beyond its capacity, and erratic system behavior can result (if the system boots at all). Also, *never* split the power connector operating a hard drive. The power diverted from a hard drive may result in erratic HDD performance and data corruption.

## ATX/NLX-Style Power Connections

While ATX and NLX form-factor systems now constitute virtually all new systems entering service today, their power requirements are remarkably similar. The ATX/NLX power supply provides five voltages to the motherboard (+5 Vdc, −5 Vdc, +12 Vdc, −12 Vdc, and +3.3 Vdc) through a 20-pin connector, as shown in Figure 30-6. The +3.3 Vdc supply is added to support the broad use of low-voltage logic that is now standard in the PC. Older AT-style motherboards could also incorporate low-voltage logic, but required an onboard voltage regulator to supply the +3.3 Vdc rather than the power supply. The ATX/NLX signals can be identified by their unique wire colors:

| | |
|---|---|
| Black | Ground |
| Blue | −12 Vdc |
| Brown | 3.3V sense |
| Gray | Power OK |
| Green | PS-ON (the "soft power" control signal) |
| Orange | +3.3 Vdc |
| Purple | 5VSB ("standby" voltage for power-managed devices) |
| Red | +5 Vdc |
| White | −5 Vdc |
| Yellow | +12 Vdc |

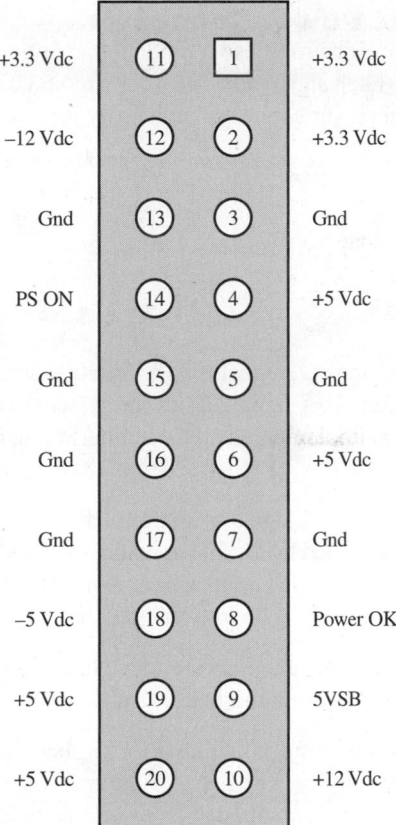

| | |
|---|---|
| +3.3 Vdc — (11) | [1] — +3.3 Vdc |
| –12 Vdc — (12) | (2) — +3.3 Vdc |
| Gnd — (13) | (3) — Gnd |
| PS ON — (14) | (4) — +5 Vdc |
| Gnd — (15) | (5) — Gnd |
| Gnd — (16) | (6) — +5 Vdc |
| Gnd — (17) | (7) — Gnd |
| –5 Vdc — (18) | (8) — Power OK |
| +5 Vdc — (19) | (9) — 5VSB |
| +5 Vdc — (20) | (10) — +12 Vdc |

**FIGURE  30-6**     ATX/NLX-style motherboard power connector

In addition to the actual DC voltages feeding the motherboard, there are also several important logic signals used to control the power system:

**PS-ON**     PS-ON is an active-low signal received from the motherboard that turns on all of the main power outputs (+3.3 Vdc, +5 Vdc, –5 Vdc, +12 Vdc, and –12 Vdc). When this signal is held high (logic 1) or left open-circuited, the power supply outputs should be *off*. In effect, this is the signal that allows "soft control" of the system power (such as automatic power-down when shutting down Windows 98/Me/XP).

**5VSB**     5VSB is a standby voltage source that may be used to "tickle" power-managed devices that require power input during the powered-down state. For example, if your PC is configured to "wake" if there's activity on the LAN card (a.k.a., "wake-on-LAN"), the LAN card will typically require an adequate standby voltage and current from the power supply. The 5VSB pin should deliver 5 Vdc (+/– 5 percent) at a minimum of 10mA for devices to operate, though most supplies can deliver several hundred mA for wake-capable devices.

**PW-OK**     PW-OK (Power OK) is a Power Good signal and should be set at logic 1 by the power supply to indicate that the +5 Vdc and +3.3 Vdc outputs are above the undervoltage thresholds of the power supply. Once this signal is received from the supply, the motherboard can begin its POST and boot process.

## Optional ATX/NLX-Style Power Connector

The ATX and NLX form-factor specifications also provide for an optional 6-pin power connector such as the one illustrated in Figure 30-7. Each signal adds a certain amount of versatility to the ATX/NLX system. You can identify the optional power connector signals by their wire colors:

| | |
|---|---|
| White | FanM |
| White/Blue stripe | FanC |
| White/Brown stripe | 3.3V sense |
| White/Red stripe | 1394V |
| White/Black stripe | 1394R |

**FanM Signal**    The FanM (Fan Monitor) signal is an open-collector, 2-pulse-per-revolution tachometer signal from the power supply fan. This signal allows the system to monitor the power supply for fan speed or failures. If this signal is not implemented on the motherboard, it should not affect the power supply function.

**FanC Signal**    The FanC (Fan Control) signal is an optional fan speed and shutdown control signal. The fan speed and shutdown are controlled by a variable voltage on this pin. This signal allows the system to request control of the power supply fan from full speed to off. The control circuit on the motherboard should supply voltage to this pin from +12 Vdc to 0 Vdc for the fan control request.

**3.3V Sense Line**    A remote 3.3V sense line can be added to the optional connector to allow for accurate control of the 3.3 Vdc line directly at motherboard loads.

**1394V Pin**    This pin on the optional connector allows for implementation of a segregated voltage supply rail for use with unpowered IEEE-1394 (FireWire) solutions. The power derived from this pin should be used to power *only* 1394 connectors (unregulated anywhere from 8 to 40 volts).

**1394R Pin**    The 1394R pin provides an isolated ground path for unpowered IEEE-1394 (FireWire) implementations. This ground should be used *only* for 1394 connections and should be fully isolated from other ground planes in the system.

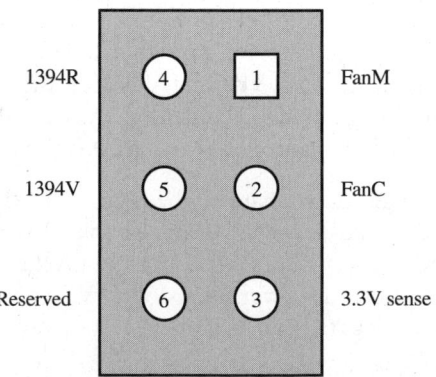

**FIGURE  30-7**    Optional ATX/NLX-style motherboard power connector

## Voltage Tolerances

If you pursue power supply testing or troubleshooting at any level, you're going to need to test the output voltages. One important aspect of voltage measurement that is often overlooked by novice technicians is the idea of *voltage tolerance.* Voltage outputs are rarely exact and may vary from their rated value by as much as 5 percent (often 3–4 percent for the +3.3 Vdc output). For example, a +5 Vdc output may actually read from +4.75 Vdc to +5.25 Vdc, while a +12 Vdc output may read from +11.4 Vdc to +12.6 Vdc. As long as the measured voltage is within a reasonable tolerance, the output should be considered good, and the PC's circuitry should have no operational problems. If the measured voltage strays outside of this reasonable tolerance (usually to the low side), chances are that excessive devices are overloading the output. If the output measures extremely low (or is absent), chances are that the output (and the power supply) is defective. You can then choose to repair or replace the power supply as you see fit.

# Upgrading a Power Supply

Power is the lifeblood of every PC. Each element of a PC—from hard drives and memory, to video boards, motherboards, and modems—demands energy from the power supply. With the constant pressure to decrease costs, many of today's PCs cut costs by using power supplies that provide just enough power to run the basic system, but not much else. When you upgrade or refit such a PC, you can often run into system problems such as random lockups, error messages, and a variety of other strange behaviors. This part of the chapter shows you how to recognize potential power problems and upgrade the supply if needed. *Use extreme caution whenever working with power systems.* AC at the wall outlet (and inside the power supply itself) can be very dangerous in the hands of untrained personnel. If you're uncomfortable dealing with the hazards of AC, refer the actual testing and upgrade procedures shown here to more experienced individuals.

## RECOGNIZING POTENTIAL POWER PROBLEMS

As with most PC problems, the key to recognizing power problems is proper diagnosis. Diagnosing a failed power supply is a relatively simple process. First, a supply malfunction will typically prevent a PC from booting—a fairly obvious symptom. A low or absent power output registered on a multimeter or POST board (equipped with voltage indicators) offers a direct indication of the problem. After you identify a failed supply, it becomes a matter of troubleshooting the supply or replacing it. Unfortunately, many power problems are intermittent. The power supply has not necessarily failed, but it is not able to supply enough power to keep the system running properly. The following chronic problems can often help you navigate this gray area:

■ **The computer freezes intermittently**    Just because your system locks up does not necessarily mean that you should call the power company. Most computers are prone to freeze due to software application and configuration errors (which are never due to power problems), especially after you install a new application. The time you should suspect power problems is when your system (that has been working fine for some time) suddenly starts freezing for no reason at all (and regardless of the operating system or applications being used). Not just once, but several times a day, and maybe even several times an hour. If the system tends to freeze when it is moved to a new location (running on a different power circuit), power problems may also be to blame.

■ **There are random memory errors**    As with system lockups, an occasional memory error message does not necessarily indicate a power problem, especially if you have just added a new application or device driver. If you suddenly see a rash of memory errors (or have just finished upgrading the system), it's always a good idea to check your power levels along with the individual memory devices. When memory errors occur after moving the PC to another location, power problems are likely at fault.

■ **Data is lost or corrupted on the hard drive**   Hard drive problems can be the result of several factors—everything from a loose data cable to operator error. Check the drive carefully to be sure that it is connected securely. If the drive seems to be having difficulty reading or writing the disk, check power first before attempting to back up the disk or run any disk-based diagnostics. If you attempt to defragment or test the disk with power problems present, subsequent problems can do even more damage. This symptom also suggests that the supply may be overloaded. This may be the case if problems developed after you installed another drive or a power-hungry expansion board into your system. If power checks correctly, you can proceed with disk-specific diagnostics.

■ **There is trouble communicating with modems or peripherals**   You may see a rash of communication errors when trying to use a modem, mouse, or other peripheral device. (You may see other communication driver error messages.) Make sure that the peripherals connected to your system are installed and configured properly. Established systems that suddenly have trouble staying online or interacting with the printer may be suffering from a power problem. In some cases, the loss of –5V from the power supply can disable the modem (and cause odd connection sounds) without causing any other system problems.

■ **The system suffers from chronic hardware failures**   Such a problem is characterized by a fault that seems to reoccur after a few days or a week. For example, you see a memory error, replace the memory, and the fault goes away, but the same fault returns a few days later. This type of problem suggests that power spikes (brief, high-voltage surges of electricity) are entering the system from the AC line. Many economy power supplies omit even the most rudimentary spike and surge suppression circuitry, so power anomalies often pass through the supply to the motherboard and drives with little (if any) protection at all. In most cases, a power anomaly will crash the system, but does not result in any real damage. In extreme cases, a strong power anomaly can actually damage one or more chips on the motherboard, expansion board(s), or drive(s). Try adding protective devices to the AC outlet, and opt for a high-quality power supply if necessary.

# DEALING WITH POWER PROBLEMS

Now that you have an idea how power problems tend to manifest themselves in the PC, you can take some decisive steps to isolate and rectify the problem. Regardless of what symptoms your particular system may be exhibiting, you should not automatically assume that your system (or power supply) is at fault. Before you even think about opening the PC, you should check the AC line voltage.

## Checking the AC

Even the most forgiving power supply needs a stable source of AC in order to function correctly. Industrial devices such as motors and heaters can draw so much power that there is insufficient AC voltage remaining to power the computer. Commercial and domestic appliances such as air conditioners, stoves, coffee makers, and refrigerators can also result in low or unsteady AC levels. Appliances are also notorious for their introduction of voltage spikes that can easily result in circuit damage.

For the most part, it is rather pointless to look for power problems with ordinary test instruments. Multimeters are good for testing overall AC levels, but they are usually too slow to catch rapidly changing power levels such as spikes. Even most surges will go undetected. Oscilloscopes are too expensive for casual 50/60-Hz measurements, and they rarely save any anomalies that are detected. Once the problem is displayed, it is gone. As a result, you are forced to sit and watch the oscilloscope until a problem occurs. Serious power observations require a dedicated power test instrument with data logging or long-term chart recording capabilities. Such equipment is available, but is far too expensive for ordinary users (though technicians may consider the PC Power Check board from Data Depot at www.datadepo.com/pcpck.htm). Fortunately, there are some trial-and-error steps that can be taken to test the problem.

First, you need to make sure that your AC outlet is providing the right amount of voltage. Use a multimeter to measure the output at your wall outlet (see Figure 30-8). Domestic U.S. voltage levels should be between 110 and 130 Vac. If voltage is too low (or too high), the objective is to find out if there is anything on the circuit that might be causing the voltage problem. Check to see if there are any high-energy devices on the same circuit (such as coffee makers or air conditioners). If so, try turning those devices off. If the AC at your computer's outlet returns to a normal value, try your system now. That may have been the problem. Eventually, you will need to turn your air conditioner or coffee maker back on, so be sure to shut down your system until you can have a new line installed or find another line for the computer.

If there are no other devices on the line (or the line voltage fails to return to a normal level), your next step should immediately be to find an outlet with the proper voltage level. If an outlet with a proper voltage cannot be found, an electrician should be consulted to install a proper AC line. An electrician should also be able to ensure that the AC line is properly grounded. When the AC line voltage seems correct, suspect the computer supply itself.

## Suspect the Supply

When the AC input seems correct, you should suspect the computer supply. If the system is suffering from chronic hardware problems, try putting a good-quality surge protector between the AC wall outlet and computer AC cord. It also would be acceptable to try the system on another AC line that may be free of surges or spikes. Open the computer and use a multimeter to check the voltage level at each supply (see Figure 30-9) output against the pin assignments shown in Table 30-1. The +12 Vdc and +5 Vdc levels should be correct. The power LEDs on a PC Power Check (or suitably equipped POST board) will also give you an approximation of supply output levels.

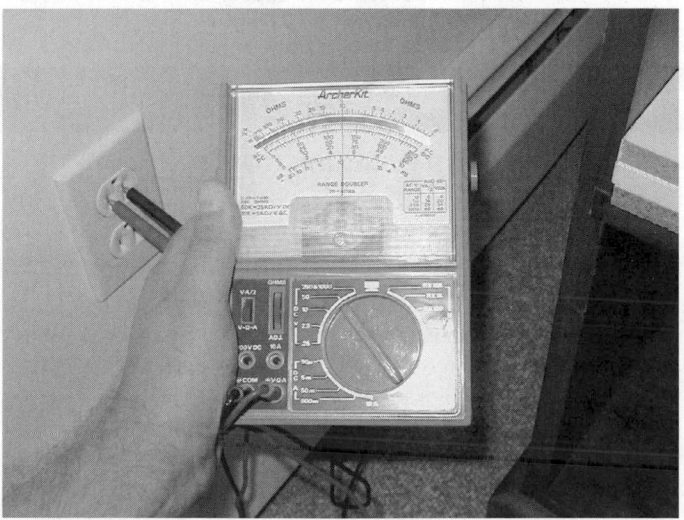

**FIGURE 30-8**    The first step in isolating power problems is to check for an appropriate level of AC at the wall outlet.

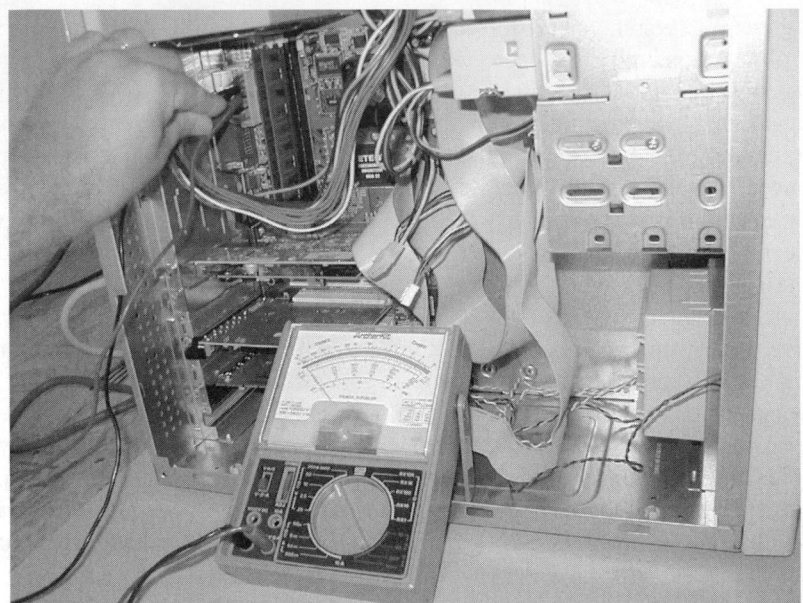

**FIGURE  30-9**    If AC levels are correct, verify each DC output from the power supply.

If *any* supply output level is low (e.g., 5 percent or more *below* the rated voltage), the supply may be overloaded by too many devices in the system. If you have just upgraded the system with a new drive or expansion board, try removing or disabling the upgrade, and see if DC voltages climb to their normal levels. If they do, the supply is overloaded and should be upgraded as shown next. If levels do not return to normal (or either or both of the voltages are high), the supply may be defective. If you determine the supply to be defective, you may troubleshoot or replace the supply at your discretion.

**TABLE 30-1    INDEX OF TYPICAL POWER SUPPLY WIRE ASSIGNMENTS**

| WIRE COLOR | VOLTAGE OR DESIGNATION |
| --- | --- |
| Black | Ground |
| Blue | −12 Vdc |
| Brown | +3.3V Sense (ATX and NLX supplies) |
| Gray | Power OK (~ +5 Vdc in ATX and NLX supplies) |
| Green | Power Supply ON ("soft control signal" for ATX and NLX supplies) |
| Orange | +3.3 Vdc (ATX and NLX supplies) |
| Orange | Power Good (~ +5 Vdc in AT-style supplies) |
| Purple | +5 Vdc Standby (ATX and NLX supplies) |
| Red | +5 Vdc |
| White | −5 Vdc |
| Yellow | +12 Vdc |

# UPGRADING THE POWER SUPPLY

It is not uncommon for power supplies to become overloaded by upgrades and peripherals, or fail after prolonged use or repeated voltage spikes. When most consumers buy a PC, the power supply capacity is often the last specification on their minds. It is the more exciting specifications such as CPU speed and hard drive capacity that get all the attention. Few people worry about upgrading a brand-new system. As a technical professional, the best advice you can give consumers is very simple: *Don't skimp on power.* If you buy a new system, get one with a supply capacity that will be big enough to support a few typical upgrades like a video capture board, an additional hard drive, a CD-R/RW drive, an internal modem, more memory, and so on. You need not invest in the biggest and best supply (unless you're building a network server, or you have a lot of expansion devices from a previous system), but don't trap yourself by getting the smallest (cheapest) one either.

## Choosing a Supply

When you determine that your supply has failed (or needs to be upgraded), there are two important factors that you need to consider: the power capacity of the new supply, and its physical dimensions. The *capacity* of a power supply is measured in *watts* (W). This is the maximum amount of power that can be supplied to a load (the computer) safely. Today's PC power supplies range from about 50W to 300W or more. Choosing the proper power rating for an upgraded supply is often a matter of approximation. You can usually calculate a safe upgrade by adding 50W to the original supply rating. For example, if the PC uses a 200W supply now, select an upgrade supply that's at least 250W.

Before you finally choose a replacement supply, you will need to consider its physical dimensions and form factor. The new supply must be able to fit within the space allotted inside the PC. The new supply must be bolted into place, so its mounting holes should align properly with the holes in the original supply. This problem is largely taken care of with the current generation of ATX and NLX form-factor power supplies that are specifically designed to be readily interchangeable with ATX/NLX cases and motherboards. When you select a standard form factor, you can also be sure that the motherboard's power connector(s) will be fully compatible.

## Making the Swap

Power supply replacement is typically quite straightforward. You'll first need to power down and unplug the PC; then open the outer housing to expose the supply—the silver box located in the corner of the chassis. Carefully disconnect the 4-pin drive power cables from each drive, and then disconnect the main power cable from the motherboard. Remove the four screws that bolt the power supply into place (be careful that the supply doesn't fall and damage the motherboard or other components); then remove the old supply and set it aside. Test fit the new power supply and see that all openings and bolt holes line up properly with the chassis. If the new supply fits properly, bolt it into place securely (see Figure 30-10). Reconnect the motherboard power cable, and reattach the drive power cables. When the new power supply is in place and connected properly, check the line voltage selector switch (110/220 Vac) on the back of the supply and verify that it is set appropriately for your region of the world.

## Test the Upgrade

Finally, reattach the AC line cord to the power supply and boot the system. The PC should boot normally and run in a stable fashion. You should open and check your most important applications. If the system checks out properly, burn-in the power supply for at least 24 hours before returning the system to service.

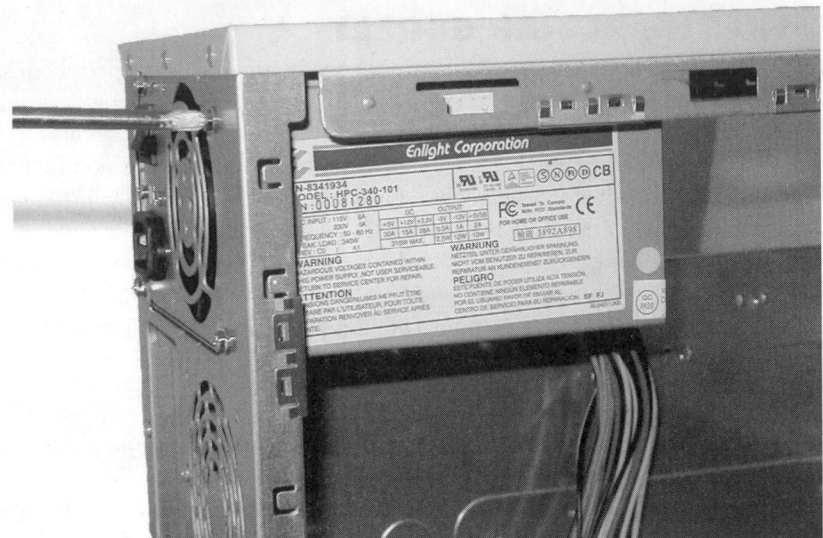

**FIGURE 30-10**    Be sure to bolt the new power supply to the PC chassis securely.

# Troubleshooting Switching Power Supplies

Troubleshooting a switching power supply can be a complex and time-consuming task. Although the operation of rectifier and filter sections is reasonably straightforward, sensing/switching circuits can be complex oscillators that are difficult to follow without a schematic. Consequently, subassembly replacement of DC switching supplies is quite common, so don't feel the need to get in there with a soldering iron.

## POWER SUPPLY SERVICE TIPS

Power and power supply problems can manifest themselves in a stunning variety of ways, but the following tips should help you to stay out of trouble:

- Power supply cooling is important. Keep the vent openings and cooling fan blades clean.

- Make sure that the *line voltage switch* (120/220 Vac) is set correctly for your region.

- Verify that the power supply connectors are attached to the motherboard and drives securely. Loose connectors can cause erratic system operation and reboots.

- Remember that for older AT-style power connections, *the black wires go together.*

- Do not use a Y-adapter to split power from an HDD. (Avoid Y-adapters entirely if possible.)

- Some Y-adapters are wired improperly. If you have trouble with a device after installing a Y-adapter, check the splitter, or try powering the device directly.

- Voltage tolerances are usually +/– 5 percent (+/– 3 percent for 3.3 Vdc), so be sure each output is within tolerance.

■ Erratic system behavior after adding a new device can be the result of an overload. Try removing the newly installed device. If the system stabilizes, consider a power supply upgrade.

# AN EXAMPLE POWER SUPPLY

For the purposes of this troubleshooting discussion, consider the chip-based switching supply of Figure 30-11. The STK7554 is a switching regulator chip manufactured as a 16-pin SIP (single in-line package). It offers a dual output of 24 Vdc and 5 Vdc. Notice that *both* output waveforms from the STK7554 are 38-volt square waves, but it is the *duty cycle* of those square waves that sets the desired output levels. The square wave's amplitude simply provides energy to the filter circuits. Filters made from coils (or "chokes") and high-value polarized capacitors smooth the square wave input (actually a form of pulsating DC) into a steady source of DC. There will be some small amount of high-frequency ripple on each DC output. Smaller, nonpolarized capacitors on each output act to filter out high-frequency components of the DC output. Finally, note the resistor-capacitor-diode combinations on each output. These form a surge and flyback protector that prevents energy stored in the choke from reentering the chip and damaging it.

# SYMPTOMS

Let's start off by troubleshooting "hard" faults with your power supply itself. The following two symptoms highlight some of the most common problems associated with power and power supply failures. (Refer to Figure 30-11 for the following symptoms.)

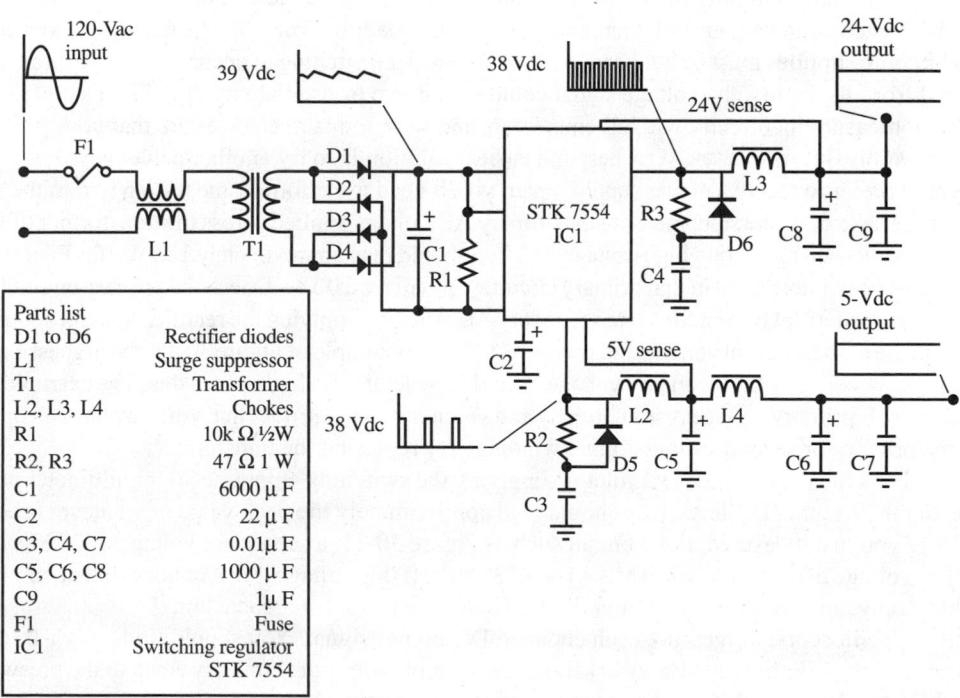

**FIGURE  30-11**    A complete chip-based switching power supply

**SYMPTOM 30-1**    The PC or peripheral is completely dead—no power indicators are lit

Check the AC line voltage entering the PC before beginning any major repair work. Use your multimeter to measure the AC line voltage available at the wall outlet powering your computer or peripheral. *Use extreme caution whenever measuring AC line voltage levels.* Normally, you should read between 105 and 130 Vac to ensure proper supply operation. If you find either very high or low AC voltage, try the device in an outlet that provides the correct amount of AC voltage. Unusual line voltage levels may damage your power supply, so proceed cautiously.

If AC line voltage is normal, suspect the main power fuse in the supply. Most power fuses are accessible from the rear of the computer near the AC line cord, but some fuses may only be accessible by disassembling the device and opening the supply. Unplug the system and remove the fuse from its holder. You should find the fusible link intact, but use your multimeter to measure continuity across the fuse. A good fuse should measure as a short circuit (0 ohms), while a failed fuse will measure as an open circuit (infinity). Replace any failed fuse and retest the PC. If the fuse continually fails, there is a serious defect elsewhere within the power supply or other computer/peripheral circuits. If your supply has an AC selector switch that sets the supply for 120 Vac or 240 Vac operation, be sure that switch is in the proper position for your region of the world. (An improperly set AC switch can disable the entire system.)

Unplug the computer and disassemble it enough to expose the power supply clearly. Restore power to the PC, and measure each DC output with your multimeter or oscilloscope. (You can find the main power connector at the motherboard or riser board.) Make sure that any power cables are securely attached. If each output measures correctly, then your trouble lies outside of the supply. A key circuit has failed elsewhere in the device (e.g., the CPU or the motherboard itself). You can try a POST board or diagnostic to trace the specific problem further. A low or absent output voltage suggests a problem within the supply itself. Check each connector and all interconnecting wiring leading to or from the supply. Remember that many switching supplies must be attached to a load for proper switching to occur. If the load circuit is disconnected from its supply, the voltage signal could shut down or oscillate wildly. When supply outputs continue to measure incorrectly with all connectors and wiring intact, chances are that your problem is inside the supply. In most cases, your best and easiest solution is to try another power supply.

If you'd prefer to tackle a power supply repair, you'll need to perform some testing within the supply itself. For the sake of discussion, measure the primary AC voltage applied across the transformer (T1). Use *extreme caution* when measuring high-voltage AC. You should read approximately 120 Vac for Figure 30-11. If voltage has been interrupted in that primary circuit, you will read 0 Vac. Check the primary circuit for any fault that might interrupt power. Measure secondary AC voltage supplying the rectifier stage. It should read higher than the highest output voltage that you expect. For the example of Figure 30-11, the highest expected DC output is 24 volts, so AC secondary voltage should be several volts higher than this. The example shows this as 28 Vac. If primary voltage reads correctly and secondary voltage does not, you may have an open circuit in the primary or secondary transformer winding. Try replacing the transformer.

Next, check the preswitched DC voltage supplying the switching chip. Use your multimeter or oscilloscope to measure this DC level. You should read approximately the peak value of whatever secondary AC voltage you just measured. For a circuit such as Figure 30-11, a secondary voltage of 28 Vac should yield a DC voltage of about [28 Vac RMS × 1.414] 39 Vdc. If this voltage is low or nonexistent, unplug AC from the supply, and check each rectifier diode. Then inspect the filter capacitor.

Use an oscilloscope to measure each chopped DC output signal. You should find a high-frequency square wave at each output (20 kHz to 40 kHz) with an amplitude approximately equal to the preswitched DC level (38 to 39 volts in this case). Set your oscilloscope to a time base of 5 or 10 μS/DIV, and start your VOLTS/DIV setting at 10 VOLTS/DIV. Once you have established a clear trace, adjust the time base and vertical sensitivity to optimize the display.

If you do not read a chopped DC output from the switching chip, either the chip is defective, or one (or more) of the polarized output filter capacitors may be shorted. Unplug the PC and inspect each questionable filter capacitor. Replace any capacitors that appear shorted. As a general rule, filter capacitors tend to fail more readily in switching supplies than in linear supplies because of high-frequency electrical stress and the smaller size of most switching supply components. If all filter capacitors check out correctly, replace the switching chip. Use care when desoldering the old regulator. Install a socket for the chip (if possible) to prevent repeat soldering work; then just plug in the new chip.

If you do not have the tools or experience to perform the work just outlined (or the problem persists), replace the power supply entirely.

**SYMPTOM 30-2**    **Supply operation is intermittent—device operation cuts in and out with the supply**    Begin by inspecting the AC line voltage into your printer. Be sure that the AC line cord is secured properly at the wall outlet and printer. Make sure that the power fuse is installed securely. If the PC/peripheral comes on at all, the fuse has to be intact. Unplug the system and expose your power supply. Inspect every connector or interconnecting wire leading into or out of the supply. A loose or improperly installed connector can play havoc with the system's operation. Pay particular attention to any output connections. In almost all cases, a switching power supply must be connected to its load circuits (e.g., the motherboard and drives) in order to operate. Without a load, the supply may cut out or oscillate wildly.

In many cases, intermittent operation may be the result of a PC board problem. PC board problems are often the result of physical abuse or impact, but they can also be caused by accidental damage during a repair. *Lead pull-through* occurs when a wire or component lead is pulled away from its solder joint, usually through its hole in the PC board. This type of defect can easily be repaired by reinserting the pulled lead and properly resoldering the defective joint. *Trace breaks* are hairline fractures between a solder pad and its printed trace. Such breaks can usually render a circuit inoperative, and they are almost impossible to spot without a careful visual inspection. *Board cracks* can sever any number of printed traces, but they are often very easy to spot. The best method for repairing trace breaks and board cracks is to solder jumper wires across the damage between two adjacent solder pads. You may also simply replace the power supply.

Some forms of intermittent failures are time or temperature related. If your system works just fine when first turned on, but fails only after a period of use, then spontaneously returns to operation later on (or after it has been off for a while), you may be faced with a "thermally intermittent" component. That is, a component may work when cool, but fail later on after reaching or exceeding its working temperature. After a system quits under such circumstances, check for any unusually hot components. *Never touch an operating circuit with your fingers—injury is almost certain.* Instead, smell around the circuit for any trace of burning semiconductor or unusually heated air. If you detect an overheated component, spray it with a liquid refrigerant (available from most electronic hardware stores). Spray in short bursts for the best cooling. If normal operation returns, then you have isolated the defective component. Replace any components that behave intermittently. If operation does not return, test any other unusually warm components. If problems persist, replace the entire power supply.

# Understanding Power Management

As millions of new PCs enter service each year, power conservation has become a matter of increasing global importance. By designing PCs that use less power and employ comprehensive power-saving techniques during periods of nonuse, a computer can actually be left on all the time, yet use only about 5W of power in its deepest power-saving state (less than most nightlights). This also reduces global pollution, lowers electric bills, and lowers the cost of running your PC(s). Power conservation is also important for mobile PCs (laptops and notebooks) in order to get the longest possible working time from each battery charge. For the purposes of this book, *power management* is achieved when a system's BIOS, chipset, operating system, and devices all cooperate to reduce the power demands of an idle computer. This part of the chapter explains the basic concepts of popular power management techniques and covers a suite of power management problems for desktop and mobile systems.

## POWER MANAGEMENT AND WINDOWS 98/ME/XP

Several important elements are required to support power management: the BIOS, chipset, devices, and operating system. The operating system provides the controls and dialogs needed for selecting your power management strategy, and it runs the various drivers needed to control each piece of power-managed hardware. Windows 98/Me/XP are largely considered the premier operating systems for power management, and you can configure just about any power-managed part of the PC through Windows' Power Properties dialog. Under Windows 9x/Me, Power Management can be accessed by clicking Start | Settings | Control Panel, and double-clicking the Power Management icon. With Windows XP, open the Control Panel, click Performance and Maintenance, and select Power Options to open the Power Options Properties dialog (see Figure 30-12).

Power management under Windows begins by selecting a *power scheme.* This basic categorization uses predefined settings that control the power-down timing of your hardware devices. However, you can also tailor the settings of a given scheme to suit your tastes. Although operating systems like Windows XP

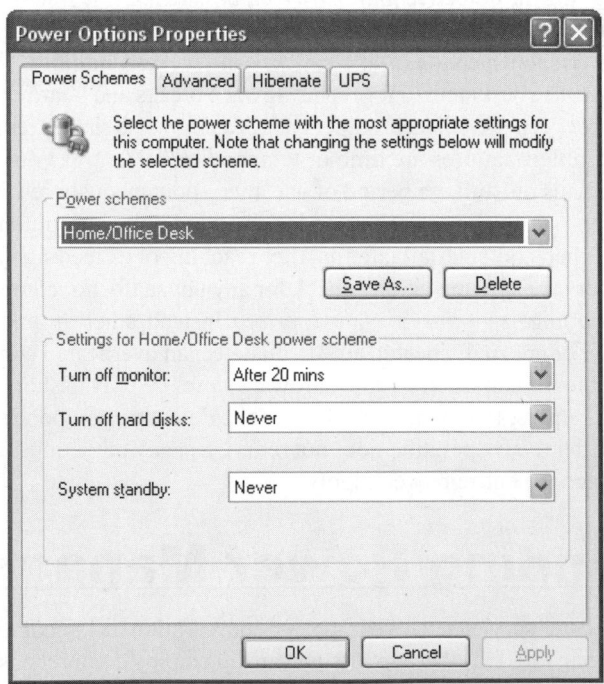

**FIGURE  30-12**    The Power Options Properties dialog under Windows XP

provide numerous prefabricated power schemes, there are three classic power-saving approaches that you should be familiar with:

- **Basic conservation**    You can turn off your monitor (or LCD backlight) and hard drive(s) automatically after a given period of inactivity (conserving a great deal of power while the rest of the system may be running normally). The various power schemes provided by the operating system typically tweak the monitor, drive, standby, and hibernation power down periods for the best advantage of each scheme.

- **Standby**    You can put the computer into a standby mode when it's idle. While in standby mode, your monitor and hard drive(s) turn off, and some computer devices are powered-down. When you want to use the computer again, it comes out of standby mode quickly, and your desktop (along with your important work) is restored exactly as you left it. Standby is particularly handy for saving battery power in laptop computers and casually reducing the idle power demands of desktop and workstation systems.

- **Hibernation**    You can put your computer into hibernation mode after longer periods of inactivity (such as you leave your office for the day). Power management's hibernate feature turns off your monitor and hard drive(s) first. (That is, it enters the standby mode first.) If idle time continues, the system will save everything in memory on disk, then turn off your computer. When you restart your computer, your computer's last state is restored to memory from the disk, and your desktop is restored exactly as you left it. It takes longer to restore the system from a hibernate mode, but power demands are drastically reduced.

The following sections outline a number of techniques that you can use to control power management under Windows 98/Me/XP.

**Selecting a Power Scheme**    To enable the system's standby mode and take advantage of your computer's power management features, you first need to select a power scheme. Under Windows 98/Me, open the Control Panel and double-click the Power Management icon (Windows Me calls this the Power Options icon). With Windows XP, open the Control Panel, click Performance and Maintenance, and then select Power Options (refer to Figure 30-12). Click the Power schemes drop-down menu, and select from the available choices that loosely define how the PC is used under Windows 98/Me:

- Always On
- Home/Office Desk
- Portable/Laptop

  Windows XP includes three additional options:

- Presentation
- Minimal Power Management
- Max Battery

When you select a scheme, you'll notice that the settings for that power scheme (System Standby, Turn Off Monitor, and Turn Off Hard Disks) will be updated to their default values. If you wish to tweak the default timer values (for example, you want to add more time before the system drops into standby mode), you can simply click the respective timer and select the desired time value from the drop-down list. Using these timer entries, you can configure the monitor, hard drive, and standby delays according to your own preferences. Be sure to Apply your changes before clicking OK.

If you're using a laptop computer, you can specify a standby delay for battery power and a different setting for AC power.

**Saving/Deleting a Power Scheme**    If you've made changes to your power scheme's timer value(s), you can save all of those settings as a unique power scheme. Once you have your timer settings the way you want them, simply click Save As, and then enter the name for your new scheme. The new scheme is added to the Power schemes drop-down list. If you no longer wish to save a particular power scheme on your system, simply select the scheme from the Power schemes drop-down list and click Delete.

**Manually Invoking the Standby Mode**    The easiest way to place your PC in the standby mode is to use the Shut Down Windows dialog (Windows XP uses the Turn off computer dialog as in Figure 30-13). You can also configure the system to let you use the standby mode whenever you press the Power button on your system (or whenever you close the lid on your laptop). Under Windows XP, open the Power Options dialog as shown earlier and click the Advanced tab (see Figure 30-14). With Windows 98/Me, open the Power Management dialog (Windows Me calls this Power Options), and click the Advanced tab. Locate the entry When I Press the Power Button on My Computer, and then click Stand By. If you're using a laptop, locate the entry When I Close the Lid of My Portable Computer, and then click Stand By. Click Apply (or OK), and then turn off the power or close the laptop's lid.

It's a good idea to save your work before putting a computer into standby mode. While the computer is in standby, information in RAM is not saved to your hard drive. If there's an interruption in power (or if the system cannot properly return from the standby mode), the information in memory can easily be lost.

**Manually Invoking the Hibernation Mode**    When you put your computer in hibernation, everything in the computer's memory is saved on your hard disk. When you turn the computer back on, all programs and documents that were open when you put the PC into hibernation are restored on the desktop. Under Windows XP, open the Power Options dialog and click the Hibernate tab (see Figure 30-15). To enable hibernation, click the Enable Hibernation check box and apply your changes. With Windows 98/Me, open the Power Management dialog (or Power Options under Windows Me), and click the Hibernate tab. To enable hibernation, click the Enable Hibernate Support check box and apply your changes. Go back to the Advanced tab (refer to Figure 30-14). Locate the entry When I Press the Power Button on My Computer, and then click Hibernate. If you're using a laptop, locate the entry When I Close the Lid of My Portable Computer, and then click Hibernate. Click Apply (or OK), and then turn off the power or close the laptop's lid.

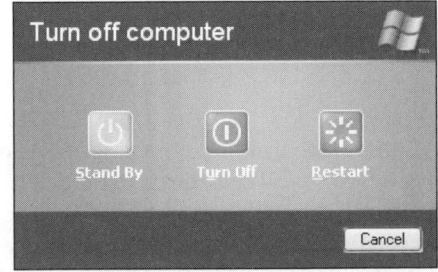

**FIGURE  30-13**    Using the "Stand by" feature of the Turn off computer dialog

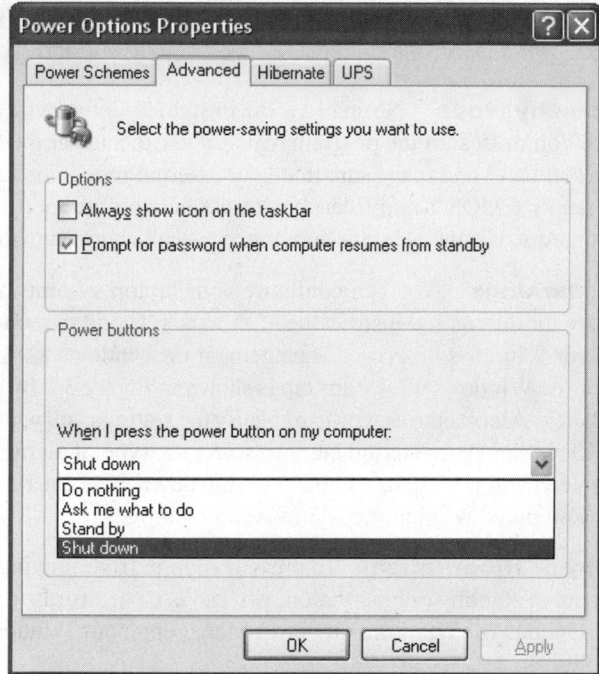

**FIGURE 30-14**    The Power Options Properties dialog under Windows XP

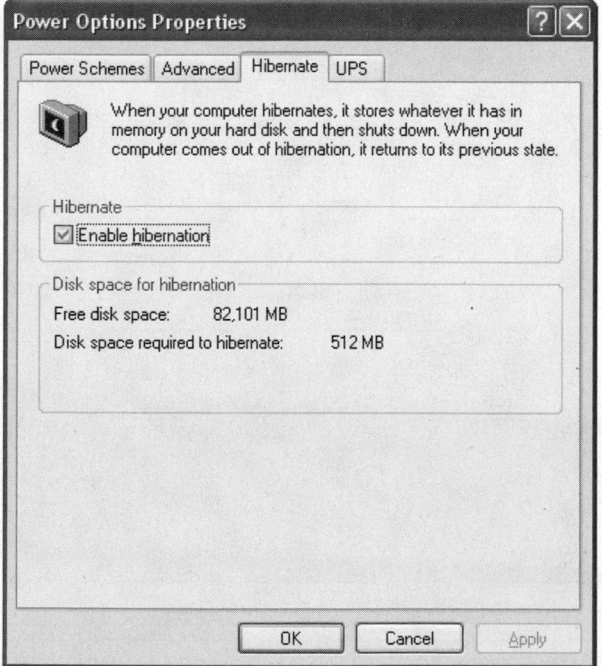

**FIGURE 30-15**    Enabling the Hibernate power saving mode under Windows XP

If the Hibernate tab is not displayed, your computer does not support this feature—usually because the system BIOS or one (or more) pieces of hardware do not fully support hibernation.

**Incoming Calls in Standby Mode**    Normally, a PC in standby mode will wake when the modem answers an incoming call. You must start the program that you use to answer the telephone (that is, your modem's communication software) and make sure that your external modem is turned on. You may also need to configure the system's CMOS Setup to enable "wake on ring" support. After the PC enters its standby mode, it should come out of standby for the duration of the call, then return to standby automatically.

**Configuring Battery Warnings**    You can configure your laptop system to produce warnings for "low" and "critical" battery conditions and instruct the PC how to respond to such alarms. Open the Windows XP Power Options (or Windows 98 Power Management or Windows Me Power Options) dialog, and click the Alarms tab. (The Windows 98 Alarms tab is shown in Figure 30-16.) For both the Low Battery Alarm and Critical Battery Alarm entries, you can specify the settings you want by dragging the slider to the appropriate level. Click the Alarm Action entry to select the type of alarm notification and power level you want. For example, if you want your computer to shut down when an alarm occurs, click "When the Alarm Goes Off, the Computer Will" in the Alarm Action dialog.

**Passwords in Standby or Hibernation**    To prevent anyone from moving a mouse or pressing a key to bring your system out of standby or hibernation, you can use passwords to protect your system on waking. Open the Power Options (or Windows 98 Power Management or Windows Me Power Options)

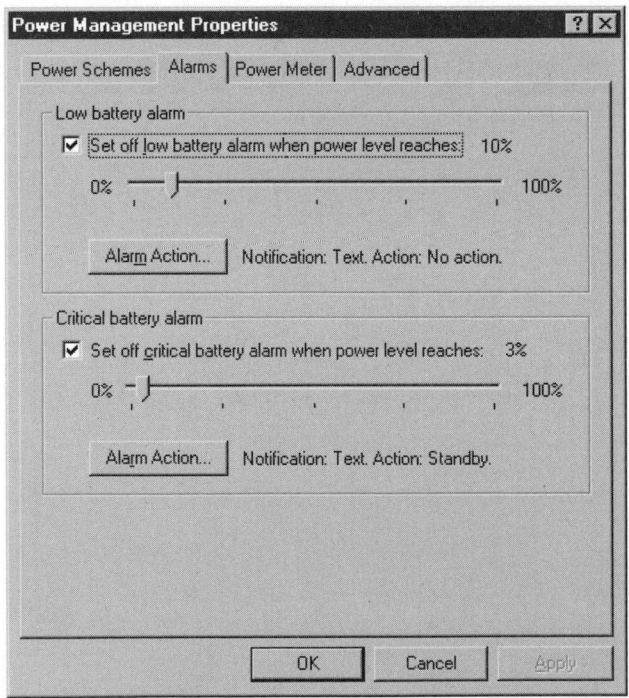

**FIGURE 30-16**    The Alarms tab is available on mobile PCs and allows you to configure alarm levels and protective actions for the system.

dialog and select the Advanced tab. To enable passwords, click Prompt for Password When Computer Goes Off Standby (Windows XP says Prompt for Password When Computer Resumes from Standby). You use your Windows password for both standby and hibernation. Remember that you are *not* required to use a password, but it does afford a certain amount of security since your system will be running while you're away from it.

## ADVANCED POWER MANAGEMENT (APM)

Although APM has been replaced by the later ACPI standards, APM represented the first major industry effort to establish a standardized power conservation method on the PC. APM concepts were in place with later versions of DOS and Windows 3.1x, but APM was really first embraced as a "system-wide" standard with the introduction of Windows 95. Today, APM support is implemented in virtually every BIOS, chipset, and device in production and is carried through into Windows 98/Me/XP. APM provides you with a mechanism for shutting down major power-consuming devices such as the monitor (or laptop's LCD backlight), spinning down the system hard drive(s), and "throttling back" the CPU during idle periods. APM can also query the battery to obtain its current charge information and report remaining battery life with great accuracy.

Current PCs will typically employ the later ACPI standard (discussed later in this chapter), but an operating system like Windows 98/Me/XP will support APM on older hardware platforms that will not fully support ACPI.

You can check for the presence of APM support by opening your Device Manager and double-clicking the System devices entry. Look for the Advanced Power Management Support line, as in Figure 30-17. If your older system has not installed APM, you may install it manually using the Add New Hardware wizard. Once APM is installed, verify that APM support has been enabled. Remember that if you do not see references to APM, but you do see references to ACPI (explained in the next section), your system is likely

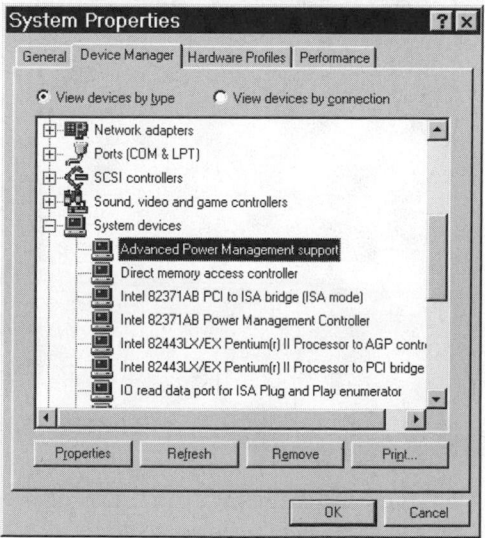

**FIGURE  30-17**     Checking the Windows 98 Device Manager for APM support

using the current ACPI standard instead of the older APM scheme. This is fine, and you do not need to install APM. Simply skip to the following section on ACPI.

There are several different versions of APM, but version 1.2 is one of the most recent. Some computers conform to the APM specification 1.0; others use APM 1.1 or 1.2. Although Windows 98/Me/XP works with all of these specifications, there are advantages to using APM 1.2. Version 1.1 is designed to give the operating system more control over power management than APM 1.0 permitted. For example, if a computer is using APM 1.2, the operating system can force the BIOS to wait until it has prepared the running programs and drivers for suspend mode. Also, a computer using APM 1.2 allows the operating system to reject the request for suspend mode. However, there may be instances where your system does not fully support APM 1.1 or 1.2, and you may need to "force" older versions of Windows to use the initial APM 1.0 system. You can do this by double-clicking the "Advanced Power Management support" entry in your Windows 98/Me Device Manager, and then clicking the Settings tab (Figure 30-18). Simply click the Force APM 1.0 Mode check box (you cannot force APM settings under Windows XP). If the system stabilizes, you'll know that one or more devices (or drivers) are having trouble with APM 1.1 or 1.2 on your system, and you can isolate and update the offending device(s) accordingly.

## ADVANCED CONFIGURATION AND POWER INTERFACE (ACPI)

ACPI has largely been introduced under Windows 98/SE and builds on the basics of APM by allowing much more comprehensive control of each device in the power-managed state. For example, an ACPI system can turn off (or "throttle back") a wider range of devices such as CD-ROMs, DVD-ROMs, modems, network devices, and so on. ACPI also allows the system to "wake" and perform predetermined tasks based upon real-world events. For example, an ACPI system may wake when the modem receives a call, connect and exchange data, and then return to a standby or hibernate state after the call is completed. Current PCs use ACPI 2.0 introduced in July 2000.

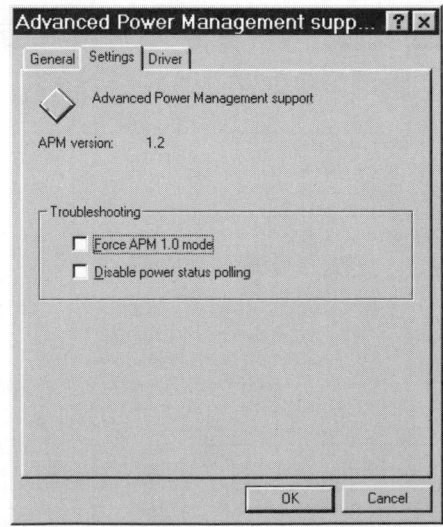

**FIGURE 30-18**    Forcing the APM 1.0 mode through the Windows 98 APM Settings tab

In addition to enabling OS-controlled power management, ACPI provides a generic system event mechanism for plug-and-play and an OS-independent interface for device configuration control. This means your ACPI system can actually manage device configuration as well as power. In effect, ACPI is a marriage of PnP and APM that offers much more precise and versatile control over a system's devices.

Hibernate modes are known to have trouble on some older FAT32 systems. If you use the hibernate mode, you may need to use FAT16 partitions. However, virtually all current systems overcome this issue.

ACPI support installs automatically with current versions of Windows such as Windows Me/XP. If you do not have ACPI support already in place when you install Windows 98, you can add ACPI support by reinstalling Windows 98 with the **/p j** command-line switches. This adds the **ACPIOption** string value with a value data of 1 to the registry. To run Windows 98 Setup using the **/p j** switches, click Start | Run, type the following command in the Open box, and then click OK:

```
setup /p j
```

Reinstalling Windows 98 is the best way to ensure that all devices are configured correctly.

To enable ACPI support in Windows 98 or later, you must first have an ACPI-compatible motherboard and an ACPI 1.0–compliant BIOS or later.

You can check the support for ACPI under Windows XP by opening the Device Manager and expanding the Computer entry (see Figure 30-19). If the ACPI entry is present and free of any problem indicators, you can be confident that ACPI is working on the system. (You may also need to enable ACPI in the CMOS Setup.)

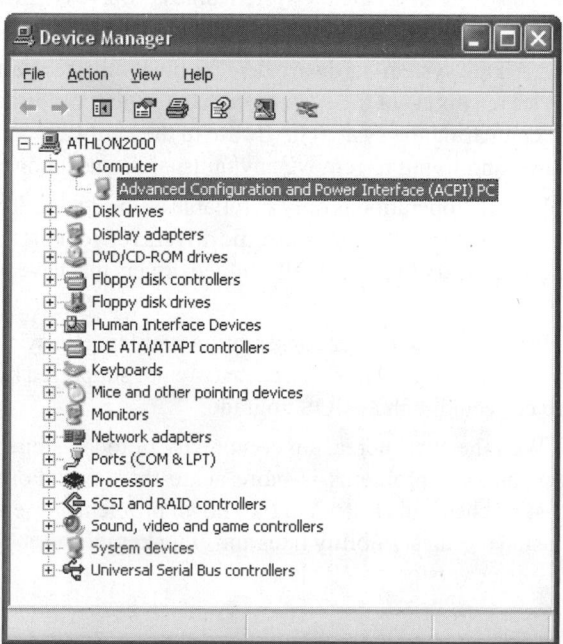

**FIGURE 30-19**   Checking the Windows XP Device Manager for ACPI support

# Troubleshooting Power Management

Power management offers some compelling advantages for the PC. Systems can be extremely responsive, yet use very little power in the idle state. Ideally, the BIOS, chipset, devices, and operating system must work together seamlessly to avoid system crashes and data corruption. Unfortunately, this doesn't always happen (especially with older systems). BIOS incompatibilities, buggy drivers, and non-compliant hardware devices are just some of the issues that can result in power management problems. This part of the chapter explores a range of power management symptoms and solutions.

## BASIC GUIDELINES

The trick with ACPI (and older APM) is that the hardware, BIOS, drivers, and operating system must all cooperate. Otherwise, you may find that the system won't invoke its power-saving modes properly, or it won't resume when you need it. Even worse, the system may become unstable (usually after resuming), and this can be extremely difficult to troubleshoot. As a rule, check the following points when experiencing any power management issues:

- **Check the CMOS Setup**    The CMOS Setup is where power conservation features are enabled and disabled at the hardware/BIOS level, so you should always make it a point to verify that any settings and selections are appropriate for your particular system. While ACPI can often override the low-level setup entries, it's a good place to start.

- **Check the Windows configuration**    Open the Device Manager and look for ACPI (or APM) entries that are marked to indicate problems such as hardware conflicts or missing drivers. You may need to correct conflicts or update drivers to calm troubled devices. You'll also need to enable services that you need. For example, you can't hibernate the system unless you've enabled hibernation under Windows (refer to Figure 30-15).

- **Check the hardware**    All the system hardware devices must fully support ACPI (or APM). Otherwise, the offending device may prevent the system from entering (or returning from) a power-saving mode. It may be worth comparing the system hardware to the hardware compatibility list (HCL) for your version of Windows, and trying to remove any unusual or unsupported hardware devices.

- **Check the drivers**    Hardware operation is only as reliable as the device drivers, so make sure that all your hardware is using the latest manufacturer-specific drivers for your particular OS. With later operating systems like Windows XP, try to use digitally signed drivers that have passed Windows compatibility tests.

- **Upgrade the BIOS**    In many cases, power conservation problems (or system stability issues related to power conservation) are often traced to features that are not supported by the system BIOS. Problems can frequently be corrected with a BIOS upgrade.

- **Upgrade Windows**    With the ever-increasing complexity of today's operating systems, the possibility of bugs and compatibility problems is more acute than ever. Fortunately, OS makers like Microsoft regularly post patches and updates to fix known problems. Use the Windows Update feature to download and install the latest stability fixes and other kernel corrections. In other cases, it may be beneficial to install a later version of Windows.

# ACPI SYMPTOMS

The *Advanced Configuration and Power Interface* (ACPI) is now the standard power management technology employed by current PCs. While ACPI offers more comprehensive and versatile control over the many devices in a system, there is also far more latitude for problems to occur. The following symptoms offer a cross-section of common ACPI issues that you should be familiar with.

**SYMPTOM 30-3**    **Windows XP reenables disabled COM ports on reboot**    This type of problem occurs when a COM port is disabled through the Device Manager under Windows XP running ACPI. If the Add Hardware wizard then scans for new hardware, the disabled COM port is detected as new hardware. Since Windows has to enumerate COM ports in several different ways (to ensure hardware compatibility), it must also recheck the COM port devices in order to avoid conflicts with other devices. When you disable the ACPI-driven COM port in Device Manager, the COM port is treated as new hardware when you run the Add Hardware wizard. As a work around, do not allow the Add Hardware wizard to reinstall the COM port when it is detected, otherwise, an additional incorrect COM port is added in Device Manager.

**SYMPTOM 30-4**    **You receive an "Illegal I/O port address" error under Windows XP**    For example, you may see an error such as "ACPI BIOS Is Attempting to Write to Illegal I/O Port Address" (more specific details about the error may be present in the Event Viewer). This problem occurs if the BIOS tries writing to a port in the ACPI Machine Language (AML), which in turn prevents Windows XP from accessing that port. In most cases, this is a BIOS issue that can often be corrected by upgrading the motherboard BIOS.

**SYMPTOM 30-5**    **You receive an ACPI embedded controller error**    This normally occurs on certain PCs (usually laptop systems) after installing Windows XP. The Device Manager will typically report an "Unknown Device" error for a Microsoft ACPI-Compliant Embedded Controller—no drivers are installed for the device, and the ACPI controller doesn't function properly. This will occur if Windows XP has no ACPI driver for the embedded ACPI controller that's in the PC. In most cases, you can correct this problem by installing a manufacturer-specific driver for the particular ACPI controller.

**SYMPTOM 30-6**    **An interrupt storm causes the Windows XP system to crash**    Under some circumstances, the system may be subjected to an "interrupt storm." This normally causes the system to lockup or crash—though you may see a specific error message informing you of the event. There are numerous circumstances that can cause an interrupt storm such as:

■  A hardware device does not release its interrupt signal after being directed to do so by the driver.

■  A driver ignores the hardware's interrupt signal (and does not instruct the hardware to release the signal).

■  A driver processes the interrupt—although the signal came from other hardware.

■  Edge/Level interrupt controls are set improperly.

In virtually all cases, the trouble can be traced back to problems with a device driver and its corresponding hardware device. Check the device driver first, and update/reinstall the device driver as necessary. If the problem persists, the hardware is probably defective and should be replaced.

**SYMPTOM 30-7**    **You see a "System Halted" error**    For example, when you try to shut down Windows Me, you may receive an error such as:

```
Your computer failed to reboot. You need to power off the computer, wait
a few seconds and power it back on.
```

This problem almost always occurs because the system's power-management driver is not compliant with the ACPI specification for rebooting a legacy-free computer. Use the Windows Update feature to patch Windows Me, or upgrade your version of Windows. To work around this problem, use the Reset or Power button on the computer to restart the computer.

**SYMPTOM 30-8**    **Your ECP parallel port prevents hibernation**    When you try to place your computer in hibernation mode, the computer may not enter hibernation mode—or it may return from hibernation mode right away. If you check the error log (e.g., SUSFAIL.TXT file), you'll see a message such as this:

```
ECP printer port (lpt1) (bios\*pnp0401\00) denied the suspend.
```

In most cases, this problem can occur if a multipurpose device (such as a printer/fax device) is attached to an ECP port and is active. (For example, the device is monitoring the port for an incoming fax.) As a work around, disable the active fax or multipurpose device before placing the computer in hibernation mode. You may also try changing the parallel port mode, though this may impair the performance of your multifunction device.

**SYMPTOM 30-9**    **The PC hangs instead of entering standby mode**    This is a known issue with systems like the Dell XPS B533R under Windows Me. The trouble usually occurs because the computer (originally shipped in ACPI mode) has been changed to APM mode. On the Dell XPS, this issue is known to occur with an A01 BIOS dated 1-06-2000. To get around this issue, access the CMOS Setup and put the computer in ACPI mode—this is the configuration that supports standby or suspend mode.

**SYMPTOM 30-10**    **You cannot get the system to hibernate when disk space is low**    When your ACPI-enabled computer attempts to hibernate under Windows Me, hibernation may not work, and you may not receive any error messages to indicate that there is a problem. You may also see reports of low disk space. This problem occurs because there is not enough free hard disk space available on your computer for the hibernate file. When you enable hibernation on a computer that is compliant with ACPI, space for the hibernate file is not allocated immediately, but rather created when the hibernate command is issued. You can see the expected disk space noted on the Hibernate tab (refer to Figure 30-15). Since this is a problem with Windows Me, use the Update Windows feature to patch Windows, or update your version of Windows entirely.

In the meantime, there are several ways to work around this problem. First, you can create additional free space on the hard drive that contains the Windows folder. (The easiest way to do this is with the Disk Cleanup utility.) Second, if your computer has multiple hard disks, partitions, or removable media, you may be able to move data and programs to drives that contain more free space—freeing space on the drive with your Windows folder.

**SYMPTOM 30-11**    **A Windows system with an ACPI BIOS and UDMA device(s) crashes when resuming from the suspend mode**    This is normally a problem that occurs when the BIOS does not support the Get Task File (_GTF) method needed by many ATAPI storage devices. Windows 98

(Second Edition) supports the optional ACPI _GTF technique for IDE hard disks *only*, and ATAPI devices are not well supported. The best solution to this problem is to update your BIOS to a version that supports the _GTF technique for ATAPI IDE devices. Until then, try changing the ACPI Sleep state to S1 instead of S3 (if your computer's BIOS allows you to do so). Otherwise, you can work around this problem by disabling the DMA support (disable the UDMA mode) on your ATAPI device(s). This will reduce the performance of the device(s), but allow for smoother power management operation until you can update the BIOS.

**SYMPTOM 30-12**     **You see ACPI errors against a red screen when starting Windows**
ACPI error messages on a red screen are generated by the computer's BIOS, so this problem occurs most frequently when your computer has a hardware or BIOS problem. To correct this issue, contact your system or BIOS manufacturer to download a BIOS upgrade that may fix this problem. If a hardware device is mentioned in the error, check for updated drivers or firmware for the suspect hardware device. You can usually determine the precise error using these guidelines:

- **1xxx**   An error during the initialization phase of the ACPI driver, and usually means the driver cannot read one or more of the ACPI devices.
- **2xxx**   An ACPI machine language (AML) interpreter error.
- **3xxx**   An error within the ACPI driver event handler—usually when the event handler is running as the result of a general-purpose event (GPE).
- **4xxx**   An ACPI thermal management error.
- **5xxx**   An error with a particular piece of ACPI-compliant hardware.

**SYMPTOM 30-13**     **The laptop's low battery alarm does not play the alarm sound or display the low battery message**     If you've set up a low (or critical) battery alarm to play a sound and display a warning message (refer to Figure 30-16), you may find that the message is displayed, but the sound is not played. Instead, the sound may be played when you click OK to close the message window, or when the window closes automatically after a five-minute delay. In other cases, you might set up the battery alarm to perform an action (such as enter the standby mode), and you may notice that the standby/shutdown action is performed, but the sound may not be played and the warning message may not be displayed.

This fault usually occurs if any action is configured for the battery alarm *in addition to* notification through a sound. This is a known problem with Windows 98 and a patch or update may be available at the Microsoft Update Windows site (you can also upgrade your version of Windows). To receive audible notification for a low or critical battery alarm in the mean time, simply do not configure any other type of notification or action in addition to the sound alarm.

**SYMPTOM 30-14**     **When a standby mode is invoked under Windows 98, the ACPI computer enters the hibernate mode instead**     If you select the standby action for the Power button on the Advanced tab of the Power Management tool in your Control Panel, and you press the Power button, the computer may hibernate instead of entering the standby mode. Second, if you select the standby mode when the laptop computer lid is closed, the computer may also hibernate instead of standing by when the lid is closed. Finally, if you click Start, select Shut down, and then click Stand by, the computer may hibernate instead of standing by.

This problem is common on ACPI systems when the "Enable hibernate support" option is enabled on the Hibernate tab in your Power Management Properties dialog. With this setup, Windows 98 causes the computer to hibernate instead of entering standby mode. This is a problem with Windows 98 (corrected in Windows 98/SE and later), and Microsoft has developed a patch that should correct the issue. Use the Windows Update feature to patch Windows 98.

The Hibernate tab appears in Power Management Properties only if the computer is configured to support hibernation.

**SYMPTOM 30-15**    **When resuming from suspend or standby mode and running a Windows 98 DirectX6 program, the PC may crash**    This is a known problem with Windows 98 (reported to be fixed in Windows 98/SE and later Windows versions) and is particularly known to occur on Compaq Presario 5720 systems. This problem can occur if your computer uses ACPI for power management, your computer contains an AGP-based video adapter, and you run a program that uses DirectX6 (or later) after you resume your computer. Microsoft has developed a patch that should correct the issue, so use the Windows Update feature to patch Windows 98.

**SYMPTOM 30-16**    **One or more ACPI devices report problems under Device Manager in Windows 98**    After you start Windows 98 on an ACPI-compliant computer, one or more hardware devices may not function properly (if at all). They may appear to have the following problems in Device Manager:

■ This device is not working properly because the BIOS in your computer is reporting the resources for the device incorrectly (Code 9).

■ This device is not present, not working properly, or does not have all the drivers installed (Code 10).

■ The drivers for this device are not installed (Code 28).

■ This device is causing a resource conflict (Code 15).

In virtually all cases, the Windows 98 ACPI driver (ACPI.SYS) is not functioning properly. This is a problem with older releases of Windows 98 that do not support the full range of ACPI features. You can download and install a new version of ACPI.SYS from Microsoft, or use the Windows Update feature to patch Windows 98. (You can also upgrade your version of Windows.)

**SYMPTOM 30-17**    **You find the Sleep button disabled after waking an ACPI computer under Windows 98**    This often happens when you press the Sleep button while the system is waking. This is a known problem with Windows 98, and there's a patch available from Microsoft. Use the Windows Update feature to patch Windows 98. (You can also upgrade your version of Windows.)

**SYMPTOM 30-18**    **An older system restarts continuously under Windows 98/SE**    After you enable ACPI support on an older system (e.g., a Packard Bell Multimedia 4350 computer), the system may restart continuously. This fault can occur if you have an incompatible sound device (e.g., a Yamaha DS-XG sound card) installed in your computer, and both the sound card and the ACPI system attempt to use interrupt IRQ9. Adjust the IRQ used for your sound card:

**1.** Start your system in the Safe mode.

**2.** Click Start | Settings | Control Panel.

**3.** Double-click the System icon, and then click the Device Manager tab.

**4.** Double-click the entry for Sound, Video and Game Controllers, and then double-click the Legacy Sound Controller.

5. On the Resources tab, clear the Use Automatic Settings check box, and click Interrupt Request.

6. In the Resource Type column, click Change Setting.

7. In the Value box, click or type a number of an available IRQ that does not conflict with any other device in your computer, and then click OK until you return to the Control Panel.

8. Close the Control Panel and reboot the computer if prompted to do so.

**SYMPTOM 30-19    You cannot use ACPI properly under Windows 98 with certain motherboards**    For example, after you install Windows 98/SE on a computer with an Asus P2B-type motherboard, the computer may not wake up after it has been suspended. This is a known problem with motherboards like the P2B-series using BIOS version 1008. This BIOS version may not function properly with ACPI. You'll need to use a BIOS version that corrects the problem. You can fall back to an older version (e.g., 1007) or try upgrading the BIOS to a later version. Otherwise, you may upgrade the motherboard entirely.

**SYMPTOM 30-20    Your system prompts you twice for a hardware profile when ACPI is enabled under Windows 98/SE**    This is a known issue with certain laptop models. When you start a system that uses ACPI power management, you may be prompted for a hardware profile twice. If you create more than one hardware profile and restart your computer, you may receive a message such as "Windows cannot determine what configuration your computer is in." This problem occurs when the computer's BIOS supports both ACPI and plug-and-play. The real-mode boot process detects the PnP BIOS and prompts for the profile, and then the protected-mode boot process detects ACPI support, but a "blue screen" error requests the profile again. This is a problem with Windows, and can be corrected using the Windows Update feature to download the appropriate patch(es).

**SYMPTOM 30-21    A system entering the ACPI S4 mode locks up when a USB device is attached**    This is a problem with Windows 98/SE. When the computer tries to enter the ACPI S4 (suspend to disk) mode, the USB Host controller is removed. When in the S4 mode, Windows is unable to cancel requests previously made to the USB devices. Use the Windows Update feature to patch Windows 98/SE (or update to a later version of Windows).

**SYMPTOM 30-22    You notice that some legacy devices may not respond after resuming from a power-saving state under Windows 98/SE**    This can happen when you resume an ACPI system, and legacy (non-PnP) devices stop functioning. The trouble can normally be traced to Windows 98/SE—usually because the virtual communications device (VCOMM) puts the LPT port into the D3 power state (powered-off) when you suspend your computer, but does not return it to the D0 (normal) state after you resume your computer. You can use the Windows Update feature to patch Windows 98/SE, or consider upgrading your version of Windows.

PnP printers that do not turn on before the computer starts may also stop working. This problem affects any device that's connected to a parallel (LPT) port on a computer running Windows 98/SE.

**SYMPTOM 30-23    Windows 98 does not support the passive cooling mode in ACPI** The ACPI specification defines two categories of cooling: active and passive. Active cooling methods may include running one or more fans to provide increased airflow and improve the dissipation of heat from active components. Passive cooling methods may include slowing down (a.k.a., throttling down) the computer's CPU so that it generates less heat. The problem is that Windows 98 only supports the active cooling mode. Windows 98 configures the computer to operate only in active cooling mode and does not provide an interface for changing the active and passive cooling set points to operate in passive cooling mode. You can try patching Windows 98 with the Windows Update feature, or upgrade your version of Windows.

**SYMPTOM 30-24**    **The Windows 98 system may hang up when you connect and disconnect a laptop's AC power cord**    For example, if you connect and then disconnect the power cord on a battery-powered ACPI-compliant computer, either the computer will hang up, or you'll receive a Fatal Exception 0E error. This is a problem with Windows 98 and has been reported with IBM ThinkPad 600 systems. Your computer may seem to retain some amount of functionality (including the ability to shut down or restart the system), but certain ACPI functions (such as thermal management) may be disabled. To get around this problem, restart your computer normally. If you're unable to shut down Windows properly, you may have to turn your computer off and then back on. To prevent this problem from occurring again, do not connect and disconnect the power cord repeatedly in rapid succession.

The loss of thermal management features may result in the computer's internal temperature reaching dangerously high levels without Windows 98 activating the appropriate cooling methods to reduce the temperature.

**SYMPTOM 30-25**    **The system is slow to resume from the hibernate mode on certain systems**    This is a known problem on systems such as the Toshiba Tecra 8000 or Protege 7020—though similar problems can occur on other laptops—and generally results as a slow boot when the system resumes. This problem typically occurs when the Battery Mode setting in the computer's CMOS Setup is set to Full Power. This is incorrect in the BIOS. This setting actually enables the PCI Clock Run power-saving feature, which causes all PCI peripherals not to run at full capacity until an ACPI-aware operating system is booted. When the computer resumes from its hibernate mode, the slow boot takes place because the boot loader is not ACPI aware. If you cannot update the BIOS to correct this misrepresentation, you can generally work around it by setting the following CMOS Setup options:

- Set the Battery Mode or BIOS Power Management option to User Setting instead of Full Power.
- Change the CPU Sleep Mode option to Disable.
- Change the Processing Speed option to High.
- Change the Cooling Method option to Performance.

The CPU speed may still be slower than expected, even if you change all of the settings just listed. For example, some units have a built-in power-saving feature that slows down the CPU when the remaining battery power is less than 50 percent (until an ACPI-aware operating system overrides the setting).

## APM SYMPTOMS

Before the introduction of ACPI, *Advanced Power Management* (APM) was the standard for PC power management. While APM is falling into disuse, many older systems continue to employ APM, and even newer systems will "fall back" to APM when trouble arises with ACPI. The following symptoms offer a selection of common APM problems that you should be familiar with.

**SYMPTOM 30-26**    **Your computer hangs while you try to shut it down under Windows 98/Me**    After you click the Shut Down the Computer option in the Shut Down Windows dialog, the computer may freeze (or display a black screen) after you see the "Please wait while your computer shuts down" message. In many cases, this problem is caused by an incompatibility between the Windows APM system and the APM BIOS in your computer. If the BIOS in your computer instructs the system to suspend (rather than shut down), Windows cannot shut down correctly. As a temporary fix, disable your APM support by double-clicking the Power icon in your Control Panel, and then setting the Power Management option to Off. To correct the problem more permanently, you'll probably need to upgrade the system BIOS.

**SYMPTOM 30-27**   **You find that a laptop PC in a docking station may not offer APM support under Windows 95**   When you use Windows 95 on a mobile computer with APM, you see that the suspend command does not appear on the Start menu. (And the APM icon does not appear in Control Panel.) You may also find that the Windows 95 Setup program does not correctly detect APM support on an APM-capable computer. Some systems will disable APM when in a docking station, and this will prevent access to the APM features in Windows 95. This is simply part of the individual system's design, and APM support on these computers is not available while they're docked. You may be able to upgrade the system's BIOS to correct this issue, but in the meantime, you'll simply need to add APM support back into Windows 95 after you remove the machine from its docking station.

**SYMPTOM 30-28**   **You cannot use APM 1.1 on certain systems under Windows 95/98** For example, this is a known problem with the old AST Ascentia 900N laptop (though it may also occur with other older systems). You cannot use APM features with this system. In virtually all cases, this is a BIOS problem. For example, the Ascentia 900N computer supports APM version 1.1, but the BIOS installed in this system returns an unexpected value when Windows 95/98 makes function calls. Therefore, the Windows protected-mode APM driver (VPOWERD.VXD) is unable to load, and APM support is not provided. A BIOS upgrade should correct the problem. In the meantime, you may be able to use APM 1.0 instead of 1.1:

1. Open the Device Manager.
2. Expand the System Devices branch of the hardware tree, click Advanced Power Management Support, and then click Properties.
3. Click the Settings tab.
4. Click the Force APM 1.0 Mode check box to select it (refer to Figure 30-18 earlier).
5. Click OK, and reboot the system if necessary.

**SYMPTOM 30-29**   **Your system reboots shortly after resuming to Windows 95/98** This is a known problem with certain older laptops. If you shut down Windows in suspend mode (or close the lid), Windows appears to shut down successfully. But when you resume Windows, the computer reboots after a short time. This occurs because those systems (e.g., the Toshiba 4500) require an additional driver file to successfully implement APM features. The APM features do not function correctly without that driver. For the Toshiba 4500, that driver is WRESUME.386. You'll need to obtain that additional driver file, then add it to the SYSTEM.INI file according to the manufacturer's instructions.

**SYMPTOM 30-30**   **The Suspend option appears on the Windows 95/98 Start menu, but it doesn't work** When you're using Windows 95/98 on a computer that supports APM, you may find that nothing happens when you click the Suspend option on the Start menu. This trouble is known to occur on numerous older systems including the Compaq Summit 60 system. In virtually all cases, the system simply doesn't support the suspend feature (though it does support APM). Windows cannot detect whether a particular computer supports the suspend feature, so the Suspend command is always on the

Start menu when APM is enabled. To correct this problem, you should consider a BIOS upgrade to a newer version that will properly support the suspend function under APM.

**SYMPTOM 30-31    You find that your system is constantly suspending and resuming**
If you click Suspend on the Start menu, and then press the Suspend button on your system before it goes completely to sleep, the computer continually suspends and resumes. You need to reboot the PC to stop the loop. This is a known issue on older systems such as the Compaq Elite under Windows 95. This occurs because the APM BIOS in the Compaq Elite computer has trouble processing a software suspend request and a hardware suspend request at the same time. You may be able to correct this issue by upgrading the system's BIOS.

**SYMPTOM 30-32    Your system does not shut down after periods of inactivity**    Even though you've configured the APM features properly, the system fails to shut down after adequate idle periods. This is a known problem on older Compaq systems under Windows 95. The computer's hard disk may stop spinning to save power during periods of inactivity and then start spinning again a few seconds later. In virtually all cases, this is a problem with the system's BIOS when running under Windows, and it can be corrected by updating the system's BIOS.

**SYMPTOM 30-33    Your laptop may not suspend automatically under Windows 95/98**
This problem often occurs on certain older Toshiba laptops under Windows. The computer may not automatically go into its low-power suspend mode. This happens because some older laptop computers monitor the system IRQ lines to determine if the system is busy. Any hardware interrupt (other than IRQ0) resets the auto-suspend timer. Windows generates interrupts that prevent these computers from going into their low-power suspended mode. A BIOS upgrade may correct this problem. In the meantime, you can suspend the computer manually by clicking Start and then clicking Suspend, or by using the hardware Suspend switch.

**SYMPTOM 30-34    Your display (monitor) does not wake after an Energy Star shutdown under Windows 95**    When you try to wake your computer after APM has shut down the display, the monitor may remain in its sleep mode. To reactivate the monitor, you must turn the computer off and back on. This problem is known to occur with several older Compaq computers (and other systems) using the Cirrus Logic 54xxx video chipset. There is a conflict between the Windows APM and the computer's BIOS. There are generally four options for dealing with this type of problem:

- Do not enable APM in the computer's CMOS Setup.
- Do not inform Windows 95/98 that the monitor is Energy Star compliant.
- Disable APM in the Device Manager under Windows 95/98.
- Obtain an APM-compliant BIOS upgrade for the system (perhaps the best solution if possible).

**SYMPTOM 30-35    You cannot install APM on a system under Windows 95/98**    When you install Windows 95/98 on an older system, the APM features are not installed, and you cannot add Windows 95/98 APM support using the Add/Remove Programs wizard. In virtually all cases, the Windows 95/98 APM drivers do not work correctly with the BIOS in that particular system, so APM support cannot be installed. To use APM features in Windows 95/98, you must install the OEM-version APM drivers that came with the particular computer. If you don't have such drivers handy, check with the system manufacturer for driver patches or updates. In other cases, you may be able to upgrade the system's BIOS to support APM properly.

**SYMPTOM 30-36**  **You encounter a system error when trying to suspend a computer under Windows 95**  Some systems will produce a system error message on a blue screen when you select the Suspend command on the Start menu under Windows 95. This is almost always a BIOS problem. Chances are that the APM BIOS in the older computer is defective and does not support the suspend process correctly. The best solution is to upgrade the system BIOS to a version that provides better APM support. In the meantime, do not use the Suspend command.

**SYMPTOM 30-37**  **Your Windows 98 system does not wake to run the task you asked it to**  When you use the Wake the Computer to Run This Task option for a given task in the Task Scheduler, your computer may not resume from its suspend state to run the scheduled task at the required time. This problem can occur if your computer's BIOS does not support APM version 1.2 or later. Unfortunately, the Wake the Computer to Run This Task check box is available on any computer—even though this feature only works on computers that support APM 1.2 or later. To fix this problem, upgrade your computer's BIOS to a version that supports APM version 1.2 (or later).

**SYMPTOM 30-38**  **You find that the APM device in the Windows 98 Device Manager shows a Code 10**  When you view the Advanced Power Management support device in your Device Manager, you see a yellow exclamation point displayed on the device, along with the following status message:

```
This device is not present, not working properly, or does not have all the
drivers installed (Code 10).
```

This problem can occur if APM support is disabled in the computer's BIOS (or if your computer does not support Microsoft's implementation of APM). Enable APM support in the computer's CMOS Setup. If APM is enabled, but the status remains unchanged, it may be necessary to upgrade the system's BIOS to a later version that offers better APM support. In extreme cases, you may need to upgrade the system's motherboard.

**SYMPTOM 30-39**  **You encounter a write data error when using a CD-RW under Windows 98**  When you try to format a blank disc with a CD-RW drive, you may receive the following error message:

```
Error: Write Data
Illegal Start Block Address (0x4000004b)
```

You will not be able to read or write to the disc. In virtually all cases, this problem can occur if APM is enabled on your computer. You can try disabling the APM temporarily:

1. Click Start | Settings | Control Panel, and then double-click the Power Management icon.
2. In the System Standby box, click Never, click Never in the Turn Off Monitor box, and then click Never in the Turn Off Hard Drive box.
3. Click Apply, click OK, and then restart your computer.

Try the CD drive normally. To restore power management later, return to the Power Management dialog and re-enable the power-down features.

**SYMPTOM 30-40**    **The monitor turns off while your DVD movie is playing under Windows 98/SE**    This problem can crop up if you're using APM, and the DVD player program you're using is not designed to work with APM. To resolve this problem, contact the manufacturer to see if there's an APM-aware version of your DVD player program, or disable APM for your monitor. If there is no player update, you should try disabling APM:

1. Click Start | Settings | Control Panel, and then double-click the Power Management icon.
2. On the Power Schemes tab, click Never in the Turn Off Monitor box.
3. Click OK and reboot the PC if necessary.

You can return to the Power Management dialog and re-enable the power down features later on.

**SYMPTOM 30-41**    **You notice that the laptop's battery drains faster when a USB device is attached**    This may happen under Windows 95/98/SE. Battery-powered computers that use APM or ACPI may experience increased power consumption leading to an increased drain of battery power when a USB device is attached. This happens because the USB bus activity prevents the CPU from switching to a C3 (Clock-Stopped) power state—preventing optimum power savings. Try to conserve battery power; disconnect all USB devices if you're not using them. As an alternative, use the Power Management tool in the Control Panel to adjust the power scheme settings. This allows you to use shorter timeout values for turning off the monitor and hard drives and for placing the computer in a system standby state.

# Further Study

**ACPI**    www.acpi.info/index.html
**Amtrade**    www.amtrade.com
**Astec**    www.astecpower.com
**Data Depot (PC Wiz)**    www.datadepo.com/index.htm
**Intel's Instantly Available PC site**    developer.intel.com/technology/iapc/
**PC Power and Cooling**    www.pcpowercooling.com
**TUV (German Standards)**    www.tuv.com/
**UL (Underwriter's Laboratories)**    www.ul.com/

# 31

# REMOVABLE MEDIA DRIVES

P erhaps the single most important complaint about hard drives has been that they are not portable—you can't just slide out one drive and pop in a new one. Hard drives are traditionally permanent installations. When that drive fills up, you must physically add another hard drive or replace the existing hard drive with a larger model. Both options require an invasive and time-consuming upgrade procedure (and then the drive must be partitioned and formatted before use). High-capacity *removable media drives* overcome this limitation—the drive hardware remains in the PC, but the media (or the disks) can be inserted and removed as needed. With a removable media drive (such as the Iomega Zip), you can finally achieve *limitless* storage simply by exchanging data cartridges. If you need to use files on another PC, you can just pop out a cartridge and take it with you to another PC with a compatible drive.

However, taking the media to another system doesn't do much good if there's no suitable drive on the other PC. With the universal implementation of the USB interface, drive makers like Iomega have also developed *portable* drives—if you can't take the media to another system, take the entire drive and just connect it to another USB port. Although removable media and portable drives are not quite as fast as traditional hard drives, they are certainly solid performers, and you can usually start programs (or sometimes even boot the PC) right from that drive. This chapter highlights a series of troubleshooting procedures for the traditional Iomega Zip and Jaz drive families.

Traditional removable media drives are under a tremendous amount of pressure from today's versatile CD-R and CD-RW drives and their very inexpensive media. Consequently, older Iomega and SyQuest type removable media drives have become obsolete.

# Iomega Zip Drives

In order for removable media to be popular, it must follow four basic guidelines: it must record quickly, it must hold a lot of data on a single cartridge (or other media), it must be reasonably inexpensive, and it must be portable between similar drives. Floppy drives are very portable, but they hold only a little data. Tapes hold a lot of data, but they are slow and not very portable between drives. Hard drives are quite fast and hold a great deal of data, but traditional hard drives are simply are not portable (though external USB HDD and CD-RW models are portable). The search for reusable, high-capacity media that is transportable between inexpensive, readily available drives has led Iomega to produce its Zip drive.

The Zip drive has become perhaps the single most popular "nonstandard" drive in production today. In fact, Zip drives are so popular that some PC makers include them as standard equipment in new systems. 250 MB Zip drives offer relatively fast seek times at 29mS, and can sustain data rates of 0.8 MB/s across the parallel port, 2.4 MB/s through a SCSI interface, and 1.4 MB/s across an ATAPI IDE or USB port.. Each cartridge can hold up to 250 MB (only 100MB in older drive versions). Iomega has also released a 750 MB Zip drive, which is large enough to hold huge illustrations, CAD layouts, and even small multimedia presentations. When used with a SCSI interface and a properly configured Adaptec SCSI controller, you may even boot your system from the Zip drive. Zip drives are available in internal ATAPI and SCSI versions, as well as external parallel port, FireWire, and USB versions. This part of the chapter offers some installation guidelines for Zip drives, provides some tips for using them most effectively, and covers a collection of troubleshooting procedures.

## ZIP DRIVE INSTALLATION AND REPLACEMENT

Zip drives generally are not too difficult to install, but there are some important guidelines that might help smooth possible problems. This part of the chapter highlights the installation sequence for parallel port, USB port, SCSI, and ATAPI IDE drives.

The following procedures are intended as examples only. Always refer to the manufacturer's installation instructions for specific procedures or cautions.

### Parallel Port

A parallel port Zip drive typically requires the preinstallation of Iomega's IomegaWare software prior to connecting the drive. Once you've installed the software, follow these steps to set up and install an external Iomega Zip drive on a conventional PC parallel port:

1. Unpack the Zip drive and verify that all the software and accessories are in the box.
2. Turn off the computer and all of its peripherals.
3. Connect the cable between the Zip drive and the computer's parallel port. Secure the cable but do not overtighten it. If there is a printer connected to the parallel port, disconnect it now.
4. Connect the drive's power supply.

You can use a Universal Power Supply—the supply included with your Zip drive can be used world-wide. It works at any voltage from 100 to 240 volts. All you need is the appropriate plug adapter.

**5.** Power-up the Zip drive.

When you want to power-down your Zip drive, first eject any disk from the drive, and then push the power button to power-down the drive.

**6.** Boot the PC and allow Windows to fully load. If you've already preinstalled the drive's software, you should see the drive listed in My Computer or Windows Explorer, and you can access the Zip disk immediately.

**7.** If you have not preinstalled the drive's software, follow the manufacturer's instructions to complete the software's installation. You'll need to restart the PC (and the setup utility) to finish the installation.

This completes the general installation of a parallel port Zip drive. If you have a printer, you can try connecting it to the Zip drive's pass-through port using a standard printer cable. In some cases, you may not be able to run the printer through a pass-through port, and may need to install a second parallel port to support the printer.

## USB Port

A USB port Zip drive typically requires the preinstallation of Iomega's IomegaWare software prior to connecting the drive. Once you've installed the software, follow these steps to set up and install an external Iomega Zip drive on a standard PC Universal Serial Bus (USB) port:

**1.** Unpack the Zip drive and verify that all of the software and accessories are in the box.

**2.** Boot the PC and allow Windows 98/Me/XP to fully load. You must be using Windows 98/Me/XP for proper USB support.

**3.** Connect the USB cable between the Zip drive and the computer's USB port. Do not use USB extension cables with the Zip drive—data loss may result.

**4.** Connect the drive's power supply. Although USB is supposed to supply power to many devices, high-power devices such as drives require the use of a supplemental power supply. The drive's power LED will come on.

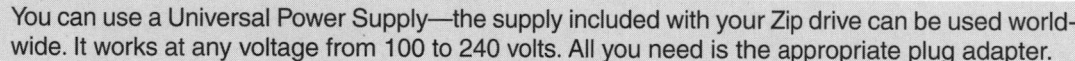

You can use a Universal Power Supply—the supply included with your Zip drive can be used world-wide. It works at any voltage from 100 to 240 volts. All you need is the appropriate plug adapter.

**5.** If you've already preinstalled the drive's software, you should see the drive listed in My Computer or Windows Explorer, and you can access the Zip disk immediately.

**6.** If you have not preinstalled the drive's software, follow the manufacturer's instructions to complete the software's installation. You may need to restart the PC (and the setup utility) to finish the installation and access the Zip disk.

This completes the general installation of a USB port Zip drive. If the drive is not detected, check the power supply, the USB connection, and the software installation. You can easily transport the USB drive between PCs.

## SCSI Port

Zip drives can be sensitive to your choice of SCSI host adapter in the PC. It is often worthwhile to check with Iomega and verify the compatibility of your SCSI adapter before attempting to install the SCSI version of a Zip drive. SCSI host adapters require the installation of drivers under your particular operating system before proceeding. Once a suitable SCSI host adapter is installed, a SCSI Zip drive typically requires the preinstallation of Iomega's IomegaWare software prior to connecting the drive. Once you've installed the software, follow these steps to set up and install an Iomega Zip drive on a SCSI port:

**1.** Unpack the Zip drive and verify that all of the software and accessories are in the box.

**2.** Check the SCSI IDs and termination settings of existing SCSI devices (make a note of each SCSI ID and the location of terminating resistors). By default, SCSI ID 5 should be available for the SCSI Zip drive.

**3.** Shut down your PC, turn off all connected devices, and disconnect the AC line cord.

**4.** Connect the SCSI Zip drive (internal or external) at the end of the SCSI chain, and verify that the drive is terminated properly. Devices that were at the end of the SCSI chain should be unterminated. If there are both internal and external SCSI devices in the system, the SCSI host adapter should be unterminated.

**5.** Connect the external drive's power supply and turn on the drive's power switch. Check that the green activity light on the Zip drive flashes briefly. When the light goes out, the drive is ready.

**6.** Restart your computer and allow Windows to boot normally.

**7.** Insert a Zip disk—you should see the Zip drive icon listed in My Computer or Windows Explorer.

## ATAPI IDE Port

An ATAPI IDE Zip drive typically requires the preinstallation of Iomega's IomegaWare software prior to connecting the drive. Once you've installed the software, follow these steps to set up and install an internal Iomega Zip drive on a system using an ATAPI IDE-type controller channel:

**1.** Evaluate your system requirements. You need an empty 3.5-inch or 5.25-inch drive bay and an open position on your primary or secondary hard drive controller (preferably EIDE or Ultra-DMA) to support an internal ATAPI IDE Zip drive.

A Zip drive meets the latest ATAPI specifications. However, some computers with early ATAPI support may not meet these specifications and may not work correctly with removable ATAPI drives like the Zip. If the computer locks up or fails to boot correctly after the Zip drive is installed, you may need to update your system BIOS and/or drive controller to a later model.

**2.** Unpack the Zip drive and verify that all of the software and accessories are in the box.

**3.** Turn off and unplug the computer, and then remove the outer cover. On some computers (especially tower models), you may need to remove a plastic face plate as well to access an available drive bay.

**4.** Identify your drive configuration. Examine the drive(s) currently connected to your primary and secondary hard drive controller ports. Based on the current configuration, you can decide on the best way to install and configure the new Zip drive.

■ If your hard drive and CD-ROM are connected to different controller channels, try installing the Zip drive as the slave drive on the secondary drive controller port.

■ If your hard drive and CD-ROM are connected to the same controller channel, try installing the Zip drive as the master drive on the secondary drive controller port.

Iomega generally recommends that you do not install the Zip drive on your primary IDE channel, so it should be a master or slave device on the secondary channel.

5. Locate your secondary IDE connector. For example, find the wide, flat ribbon cable on the back of the CD-ROM drive and follow it. If the cable also connects to a hard drive, follow the cable back to the motherboard's connector (usually marked "pri IDE"), and then locate the secondary drive controller (often marked "sec IDE"). If the cable does not also connect to the hard drive, follow the cable back to the motherboard's connector (which is often the secondary controller).

To install the Zip drive as a slave device on the secondary IDE channel:

1. Check the jumpers. The Zip drive is configured as the slave device by default. This makes it the second device on the secondary drive controller channel. Double-check to verify that the drive is jumpered as "slave." Also verify that the jumper on the first (master) device is in fact set to "master."

2. Locate an available drive bay. Select a 5.25-inch or 3.5-inch drive bay to install the Zip drive. If you select a 3.5-inch bay, you may need to remove the Zip drive's mounting rails. Since there is a limited amount of cable length between the first (master) drive and the Zip drive, try selecting a drive bay as close as possible to the master device (such as the CD-ROM drive).

3. Insert the drive into a drive bay. Be sure that the drive is level and oriented properly.

4. Remove the original IDE cable. Locate the wide ribbon cable attached between the first (master) device and the drive controller. Note the orientation of pin 1 (the red or blue stripe in the cable), and then disconnect the cable from the drive and controller, and set the cable aside.

5. Connect the new IDE cable. Connect the "long end" (the end furthest from the middle connector on the cable) to the secondary IDE port on the motherboard. Connect the middle connector to the first drive (such as the CD-ROM), and then connect the other end of the cable to the Zip drive. Be sure to verify the orientation of the cable.

6. Connect power to the Zip drive. Locate an available drive power connector from the power supply, and connect it securely to the Zip drive.

7. Bolt down the Zip drive. Use the original mounting screws and bolt the Zip drive into place. Do not overtighten the screws.

8. Recheck the cables to be sure that nothing has been accidentally loosened, and then reattach the computer's outer cover.

9. Reconnect the AC power cord, turn the PC on, and allow Windows to load. Insert a Zip disk into the drive. Since you've preinstalled the software for the ATAPI IDE Zip drive, the drive should appear in My Computer or Windows Explorer, and you should be able to access the disk immediately.

To install the Zip drive as a master device on the secondary IDE channel:

1. Check the jumpers. The Zip drive is configured as the slave device by default. This normally makes it the second device on the secondary drive controller channel. Set the jumper so that the Zip drive is configured as the master device. If there was previously a master device on the secondary IDE channel, reconfigure the device as a slave.

2. Locate an available drive bay. Select a 5.25-inch or 3.5-inch drive bay to install the Zip drive. If you select a 3.5-inch bay, you may need to remove the Zip drive's mounting rails. Since there is a limited amount of cable length between the controller and the Zip drive, try selecting a drive bay as close as possible to the drive controller.

3. Insert the drive into a drive bay. Be sure that the drive is level and oriented properly.

4. Connect the new IDE cable. Connect the "long end" (the end furthest from the middle connector on the cable) to the secondary IDE port on the motherboard. If there was previously a drive on the secondary IDE channel, connect it to the middle IDE connector. Connect the other end of the connector to the Zip drive. Be sure to verify the orientation of the cable so that pin 1 (the blue or red stripe) is aligned with pin 1 on the drive and controller.

5. Connect power to the Zip drive. Locate an available drive power connector from the power supply, and connect it securely to the Zip drive.

6. Bolt down the Zip drive. Use the original mounting screws and bolt the Zip drive into place. Do not overtighten the screws.

7. Recheck the cables to be sure that nothing has been accidentally loosened, and then reattach the computer's outer cover.

8. Reconnect the AC power cord, turn the PC on, and allow Windows to load. Insert a Zip disk into the drive. Since you've preinstalled the software for the ATAPI IDE Zip drive, the drive should appear in My Computer or Windows Explorer, and you should be able to access the disk immediately.

# USING THE ZIP DRIVE

The Zip drive is generally simple and straightforward to use, but if you're new to the Zip drive family, this part of the chapter covers some important nuances that you should be familiar with to achieve the best operation from the drive.

### Accessing a Zip Drive

To use the Zip drive, insert a Zip disk, and then select the drive letter assigned to the Zip drive in My Computer (Windows 9x/Me/XP or Windows NT 4.0) or File Manager (Windows NT 3.51 or Windows 3.1). You can now read, write, or copy files to and from the Zip drive using the same techniques used with other drives on your system.

The green power/eject button will flash when the Zip drive is transferring data, or when a Zip disk is inserted or ejected.

### Inserting a Zip Disk

Push the disk gently into the drive slot—similar to inserting a floppy disk. The green activity light will flash momentarily, and then glow continuously. If the activity light continues to blink slowly, push the eject button to eject the Zip disk, and then reinsert it carefully. Remember that drive power should be connected *before* inserting a Zip disk.

### Ejecting a Zip Disk
There are two general means of ejecting a Zip disk: use the eject button, or use the Iomega software "eject" command. Remember that you should remove a Zip disk when the drive is not in use, and remove a disk *before* disconnecting power or moving the Zip drive. Always disconnect the power supply from the drive first, then insert a paper clip into the emergency disk eject hole on the drive. The disk mechanism should release the disk.

### Powering the Zip Drive
The Zip drive generally requires that power be available to it *before* your operating system starts to load—otherwise, Windows may not detect the drive at start time. Iomega usually suggests that you connect your PC, Zip drive, and printer (or other parallel port device) to a power strip so that all three devices are powered simultaneously. Fortunately, this is not a problem with ATAPI IDE or SCSI drives because the PC itself powers those internal devices. USB drives are more forgiving, and can be connected at any time—identifying themselves to the operating system.

### Powering Down the Zip Drive
The power/eject button on the 250MB Zip drive allows you to power-down the drive when it is not in use. In power-down mode, the parallel port version of the drive uses a very small amount of power that is needed to support data pass-through (when a printer or scanner is connected to the Zip drive).

The Zip drive also has an automatic sleep mode that spins down a Zip disk after 15 minutes of inactivity. This feature minimizes power consumption when the Zip drive is not being accessed. During a "drive sleep," the green power light remains on, and the Zip disk automatically spins up again when it needs to be accessed. You can use the Iomega software to change the drive sleep setting.

## ZIP DISK GUIDELINES
Iomega Zip disks are rather delicate and sensitive, and must be treated with care to avoid damage to the disk or drive, or loss of your important data. Here are some practical guidelines that can help you get a longer working life from your disks:

- The power supply must always be connected to the drive prior to inserting a Zip disk. Otherwise, the drive may be damaged.

- A Zip disk should never be forced into or out of the drive. If the eject button doesn't work, power-down the drive and try the emergency eject feature.

- Do not use ordinary floppy drive cleaning disks on the Zip drive. Such media is not compatible with the heads on a Zip drive and will probably damage the drive.

- Avoid moving the drive when a Zip disk is inserted and in use.

- Remove the media before transporting the drive, even if it's just across the room. This is the rule for all external drives including parallel port, USB, and FireWire versions.

- Return the Zip disk to its protective case when it's not in the drive. This will keep dust and spills off the disk.

- Keep the Zip disk in a clean, dry "office environment." Otherwise, you may eventually experience data loss or drive damage.

# ZIP DRIVE SOFTWARE CONSIDERATIONS AND TESTING

Getting the most from a Zip drive requires that you keep drivers and applications software up to date, and install/uninstall those drivers manually if necessary. You'll also need to know how to adjust the Zip drive letter and how to format and write-protect your Zip media. This part of the chapter offers a series of essential Zip drive procedures.

## Obtaining Updated Zip Software

New drivers and applications software can help overcome performance problems and compatibility issues. The latest drivers for your Zip drive may be downloaded from Iomega's FTP site at www.iomega.com/software/index.html. Once you locate the proper page, choose the operating system you're using (such as Windows 9x/Me/XP, Windows NT/2000, Windows 3.1x/DOS, and so on). A listing describing each file available for download will guide you through the process. You may also order the latest Iomega software by calling 1-800-MY-STUFF (though there's a nominal charge when you order the software by phone).

## Uninstalling Zip Software

If you need to remove the Zip software (such as Iomega Tools) from your Windows 9x/Me platform, use the Add/Remove Programs wizard in your Control Panel to remove the Iomega Tools for Windows 9x entry:

1. Click Start, highlight Settings, and select Control Panel.
2. In the Control Panel, double-click the Add/Remove Programs icon.
3. Select Iomega Tools for Windows 9x in the Installed Program list box, and click Add/Remove.
4. Follow the program removal screens that appear.
5. Click OK to close the Add/Remove Programs window.
6. Restart Windows 9x.

Under Windows XP, click Start | Control Panel | Add or Remove Programs. Highlight the Iomega software and select the Change/Remove button, then follow the program removal screens that appear. You may then reboot the PC to unload the software from memory.

## Changing the Zip Drive Letter

It may be necessary for you to change the drive letter assignment of your Zip drive if you encounter drive problems or issues with other software-driven drives like CD-ROMs. Use the following steps to adjust the drive letter under Windows XP:

1. Click Start, right-click My Computer, then select Manage.
2. Expand the Storage entry and select Disk Management.
3. Click the Iomega drive's letter.
4. Click Change Drive Letter and Path.
5. Click Change.
6. Click Assign the following drive letter and pick a new drive letter for the Iomega drive.
7. Accept your changes.

Use the following steps to adjust the drive letter under Windows 98/Me:

1. Right-click the My Computer icon on your desktop, and then choose Properties.

2. Select the Device Manager tab.

3. Click on the + next to the CD-ROM or Disk Drives icon, and choose the Settings tab.

4. Choose Start Drive Letter and assign the drive letter you need from the drop-down menu.

5. Choose the same letter for End Drive Letter.

6. Click OK and allow your system to reboot for changes to take effect.

7. Repeat the preceding steps by clicking the + next to Disk Drives, and assign a different drive letter to your Iomega drive.

## Formatting Zip Disks with Iomega Software

The Iomega software that's installed with the Zip disk offers the facility for reformatting Zip disks if the need arises. Before you format a disk, remember that all the information on it will become inaccessible, so use caution to avoid accidental data loss:

1. Right-click the Zip drive icon on your Windows desktop, or from within My Computer or Windows Explorer.

2. Choose the Short Format or Long Format options.

You cannot use the Long Format option with 100MB Zip disks in a 250MB or 750MB Zip drive.

3. Click Start to format the disk.

## Formatting Zip Disks with Windows 9x/Me/XP

You can also use the conventional FORMAT utility under Windows 9x/Me/XP to format a Zip disk:

1. Under Windows 9x/Me, double-click the My Computer icon on your desktop. Under Windows XP, click Start and then select My Computer.

2. Right-click the Iomega drive icon where you'd like to format your Zip disk.

3. Select Format, and specify the format type.

4. Click Start to proceed with the format.

# Zip Drive Troubleshooting

Even though your Zip drive may be installed and configured properly, numerous problems can plague a drive. If you cannot correct drive problems with the previous guidelines, review the following symptoms for detailed corrective action.

**SYMPTOM 31-1**     **Zip drive operation seems erratic, or you experience data transfer problems**     In virtually all cases, this is a problem with the Zip drive's cabling. Always start by checking the drive's power supply connections. For external drives, check that the parallel port cable, FireWire cable, or USB cable is attached securely. See that any screws or clips are holding the cables in place. For internal drives, verify that the 40-pin IDE cable or 50/68-pin SCSI signal cable is attached securely. (SCSI cable chains must also be terminated properly.) If problems persist, there may be a problem with the controller operating your drive (the parallel port, FireWire port, USB port, IDE controller card, or SCSI adapter). Double-check the controller's configuration and see that each drive is jumpered (identified) properly.

**SYMPTOM 31-2** **A Zip disk is automatically ejected after you insert it into the drive**
The problem here is almost always the disk itself. For example, you may be using a 250MB Zip disk in a 100MB Zip drive, or using a non-Zip disk in the drive. Check the disk and verify that you're using the proper Zip media for your drive. If the problem persists and the disk operates in other Zip drives, the drive itself may be at fault.

**SYMPTOM 31-3** **The Zip drive refuses to work with software "dongles" or other pass-through devices** This is a common problem because some parallel port devices (such as multi-I/O adapters, scanners, printers, software dongles, and so on) are not fully compatible with a Zip drive. Fortunately, there are two typical options to get around the problem:

- *Remove the devices.* The easiest way to check compatibility is to remove the dongle or other parallel port device. If the Zip drive works when connected directly to the parallel port, you know the other device (the "dongle") is at fault, and it may be necessary to update the dongle or other device.

- *Add a parallel port.* If you cannot replace, remove, or tweak your existing parallel port devices, it may be necessary to add another parallel port to the system to support the Zip drive (or swap the drive type to a FireWire, USB, or an internal ATAPI/SCSI model).

**SYMPTOM 31-4** **There is no drive letter for the SCSI Zip drive under Windows 9x/Me/XP**
The drive does not appear to respond. In virtually all cases, the SCSI driver has not loaded properly.

- *Check the device driver(s).* Open the Device Manager, expand the SCSI Controllers entry, and then check the Iomega Adapter line beneath it. If there is a yellow symbol with an exclamation mark on it, the Windows 9x/Me/XP driver did not load. Check the controller next by highlighting that Iomega Adapter line and selecting Properties. Click the Resources page, and then verify that your I/O Range and IRQ options are set correctly. They must match the jumper settings (if any) on your adapter board. If you must update the resource settings manually, make sure the Automatic Settings box is not checked (and remember to save any changes). If you allocated new resources, you may have to shut off the PC and change jumper settings on the controller board itself to match the resources allocated in the Device Manager. Restart the computer. Once the system reboots, the Windows 9x/Me/XP driver should load normally.

- *Check the cables and termination.* If problems persist, check the signal connector (especially for SCSI adapters). Make sure the SCSI cable is intact and connected to the drive properly. If problems continue, your SCSI adapter is probably installed correctly, but the bus may be terminated improperly. Make sure that you terminate both ends of the SCSI bus properly.

**SYMPTOM 31-5** **There is no drive letter for the parallel port Zip drive under Windows 9x/Me/XP** Parallel port drive problems can almost always be traced to faulty connections, port configuration issues, or driver problems.

- *Check the cables.* Check the external power connector first. Parallel port drives are powered externally. Make sure that the power pack is working, and see that the power cable is connected properly to the drive. If the drive does not appear to power-up, try a different power pack or drive. Check the signal cable next, and make sure that you are using a good-quality, known-good parallel port cable that is attached securely at the PC and drive. The Zip drive is very sensitive to devices such as copy protection modules (or *dongles*), and other pass-through devices. Try connecting the drive directly to the parallel port. Also disconnect any printers on the parallel port.

- *Check the parallel port.* The parallel port setup may be incorrect. Reboot the PC and enter CMOS Setup. Check to see that the parallel port is configured in EPP or bi-directional mode. If the problem continues in EPP mode, try configuring the parallel port for compatibility mode.

- *Check your driver(s).* Open the Device Manager and find the SCSI Controllers entry (even though it is a parallel port device). If there is no such entry, the driver is not installed. If you expand the SCSI Controllers section, there should be an entry for the Iomega Parallel Port Zip Interface. If there is not, the driver is not installed. Check for hardware conflicts. If the Device Manager entry for the Iomega Parallel Port Zip Interface has a yellow circle with an exclamation mark on it, the interface is configured improperly and is conflicting with other devices. Also check for device properties. Highlight the Iomega Parallel Port Zip Interface entry, click Properties, and then select the Settings page. Find the box marked Adapter Settings, and then type:

```
/mode:nibble /speed:1
```

Save your changes and reboot the system. If that fails, try reinstalling the drivers. Highlight the Iomega Parallel Port Zip Interface and select Remove. Then reinstall the drivers from scratch.

- *Check the drive.* If the Zip drive still does not receive a drive letter, the parallel port may be faulty or incompatible with the drive. Try the drive on another system. If this tactic works on another system, the problem is definitely related to your original PC hardware. If the problem follows the drive, the fault is likely in the drive. Try another drive.

**SYMPTOM 31-6**    **An Iomega Zip drive displays a floppy disk icon under Windows 9x/Me**    However, the drive appears to operate properly. This is almost always due to the use of a real-mode DOS driver to support the Iomega drive and adapter (so this is not a problem with Windows XP). You need to update the real-mode driver to an appropriate protected-mode driver for Windows 9x/Me. For SCSI adapters, you need to find the protected-mode SCSI driver for your particular SCSI adapter and install it through the Add New Hardware wizard in the Control Panel. After the protected-mode driver is installed, you can remove the obsolete real-mode driver from CONFIG.SYS. For native Iomega SCSI adapters, get the protected-mode drivers directly from Iomega. For parallel port Zip drives, uninstall the old drive software and install the new Windows 9x/Me driver software.

**SYMPTOM 31-7**    **The Zip drive takes over the CD-ROM drive letter in Windows 9x/Me/XP**    You may simply need to switch drive letters between the Zip drive and CD-ROM drive. Use the following steps under Windows XP:

1. Insert a disk into the Iomega drive.
2. Click Start, right-click My Computer, then select Manage.
3. Under the Storage category, click Disk Management.
4. In the upper half of the window, right-click the drive letter assigned to the Iomega drive.
5. Click the Change Drive Letter and Path option.

**6.** Click Change.

**7.** Click the Assign the following drive letter drop-down menu, and choose a desired drive letter for the Iomega drive.

**8.** Click OK and then click Yes.

**9.** Repeat the process for the CD drive.

Use the following steps under Windows 9x/Me:

**1.** Open Device Manager and double-click the Disk Drives entry.

**2.** Highlight the Iomega Zip drive entry and click Properties.

**3.** Click the Settings page.

**4.** In the Reserved Drive Letters section, you will see a Start Drive Letter and an End Drive Letter setting. Enter the desired drive letter for the Zip drive in both start and end drive entries. (Be sure to use the same drive letter for both start and end.) Click on OK.

**5.** Double-click the CD-ROM entry.

**6.** Highlight your CD-ROM Drive entry and click Properties.

**7.** Click the Settings page.

**8.** In the Reserved Drive Letters section, you will see a Start Drive Letter and an End Drive Letter setting. Enter the desired drive letter for the CD-ROM drive in both start and end entries. (Be sure to use the same drive letter for both start and end.) Click OK.

**9.** Click OK to close Device Manager, and then restart the computer.

**SYMPTOM 31-8**   **You encounter Zip drive letter problems under DOS**   The drive letters following C: may change unexpectedly when Iomega drivers are installed to support a new device. This can interfere with applications that look at specific drives or with access to network resources. You need to relocate the drives before installing Iomega software. Since the GUEST.EXE utility loads at the end of AUTOEXEC.BAT, the Iomega drive will be assigned the last drive letter. DOS assigns letters to network drives alphabetically after assigning letters to any internal or external drives connected to the computer. When a new drive is added, the network drive may be "pushed down" one letter (for example, from E: to F:). Applications that reference specific drive letters may then fail to work correctly unless they are reinstalled or adjusted for the drive letter change. If you use a batch file to connect to a network, it will need to be updated to the new drive letter. A network login script may also need to be revised.

Use the DOS LASTDRIVE= command to relocate your first network drive letter farther down the alphabet. This insulates your network drive letter assignment from future changes if you add other drives to your system. For example, you can make your network drive N: by adding the following line to the end of CONFIG.SYS. This would allow you to add ten drives (D: through M:) to a system without pushing down your network drive letter.

```
LASTDRIVE=M
```

Do not set your last drive to Z:, or you will be unable to access any network drive. If you use multiple network drives, do not set your last drive to a letter late in the alphabet (such as X: or Y:) since that will limit the number of network drives you can use simultaneously.

Check your CD-ROM drive letters. CD-ROM drives have a specific drive letter determined by the /L option of MSCDEX in AUTOEXEC.BAT (for example, /L:E assigns the CD-ROM as drive E:). When a new drive is installed, DOS may assign the CD-ROM drive letter to the new drive, and the CD-ROM drive may seem to disappear. Change the drive letter for the CD-ROM to a letter not assigned to another drive. You may want to relocate your CD-ROM drive several letters down the alphabet so that you do not have to relocate it each time you add a new drive to your system. You must have a LASTDRIVE statement in CONFIG.SYS that sets the last drive equal to or later than the CD-ROM letter. Finally, check the overall system configuration. When DOS *does* reassign drive letters, be sure to check each of the following points:

- Edit the PATH statement in AUTOEXEC.BAT to correctly reference new drive letters.
- Edit any batch files (including AUTOEXEC.BAT) to correctly reference new drive letters.
- Edit all Windows INI files and Windows groups to correctly reference new drive letters.
- Check other application setup files and rerun the application's setup if drive letters cannot be edited.
- For networks, check your user login script for references to specific network drive letters.
- Reboot the computer and check major applications. Those that do not work with the new drive letter may need to be reinstalled.

**SYMPTOM 31-9** **You encounter duplicate Zip drive letters under DOS** You notice that the Zip drive (or another drive) has been assigned a duplicate drive letter under DOS. In most cases, the problem can usually be traced to a third-party SCSI adapter and drivers that conflict with Iomega SCSI drivers. *Do not use any drive before correcting this problem.* Open your CONFIG.SYS file and examine each driver that scans the SCSI bus to assign drive letters. Chances are very good that you have a third-party driver that is assigning a letter to the Zip drive, as well as an Iomega-specific driver assigning another letter to the Zip drive. Use a command-line switch with the third-party SCSI driver to limit the number of IDs that will be assigned.

**SYMPTOM 31-10** **The DOS GUEST utility cannot find an available drive letter** If all drive letters are in use, the DOS GUEST utility will not be able to assign a drive letter to the Zip drive. Change the last drive designation. Use the DOS LASTDRIVE command in the end of CONFIG.SYS to increase the number of available drive letters. Do not use a letter near the end of the alphabet.

**SYMPTOM 31-11** **The system hangs when installing parallel port drivers for Windows 9x/Me/XP** System hang-ups during installation are usually the result of hardware conflicts or problems. Check the signal cable first, and make sure that you are using a good-quality, known-good cable that is attached securely at the PC and drive. Open the Device Manager and find the SCSI Controllers entry. If there is no such entry, the driver is not installed. If you expand the SCSI Controllers section, there should be an entry for the Iomega Parallel Port Zip Interface. If there is not, the driver is not installed.

Check for hardware conflicts. If the Device Manager entry for the Iomega Parallel Port Zip Interface has a yellow circle with an exclamation mark on it, the interface is configured improperly and is conflicting with other devices. Highlight the Iomega Parallel Port Zip Interface entry, click Properties, and then select the Settings page. Find the box marked Adapter Settings, and then type

```
/mode:nibble /speed:1
```

Save your changes and reboot the system. If the Zip drive still does not receive a drive letter, the parallel port may be faulty or incompatible with the drive. Try the drive on another system. If this tactic works on another system, the problem is definitely related to your original PC hardware. If the problem follows the drive, the fault is likely in the drive. Try another drive.

**SYMPTOM 31-12**    **After installing a Zip drive, you find the other drives in the system are using the DOS compatibility mode**    This is almost always the result of the GUEST.EXE program. The real-mode GUEST.EXE program supplied by Iomega is designed to allow you to access the Zip drive in DOS and Windows 9x/Me (this isn't an issue under Windows XP), and this causes the other drives in your system to use the DOS compatibility mode. (You may also notice a decline in drive or system performance.) Try installing the protected-mode drivers for the Iomega drive:

1. In the Control Panel, double-click the Add New Hardware icon.
2. Click Next, click the No button, and then click Next.
3. Click Other Devices, and then click Next.
4. In the Manufacturers box, click Iomega, and then click Have Disk.
5. Install the files from the Windows 9x/Me CD by inserting the CD in the drive, typing the following line in the Copy Manufacturer's Files From box, and then clicking Next:

   <drive>:\drivers\storage\iomega

   Replace <drive> with the drive letter of the CD-ROM drive.
6. After the files are copied, click Finish.
7. Restart the computer when prompted to do so.

**SYMPTOM 31-13**    **A Zip guest locks up or cannot locate the drive or adapter**    Chances are that an ASPI manager referenced in the GUEST.INI file is conflicting with hardware in the PC. This often happens in systems with two SCSI adapters (and parallel ports). Try editing the GUEST.INI file. Open the GUEST.INI file on your Iomega install disk and specify which ASPI manager needs to load in order to access the Zip drive. Remember to make a backup copy of the GUEST.INI file before editing it. As an alternative, choose the Iomega SCSI adapter driver. If you are using a native Iomega SCSI adapter, choose the ASPI manager that applies to the adapter, as shown in Table 31-1. Once you've identified the proper ASPI manager for your adapter, REMark out all the other ASPI lines in GUEST.INI except for the one that you need.

**TABLE 31-1    NATIVE IOMEGA ASPI DRIVERS**

| IOMEGA ADAPTER | ASPI MANAGER |
|---|---|
| Zip Zoom SCSI Accelerator | ASPIPC16.SYS |
| Jaz Jet SCSI Accelerator | ASPI2930.SYS |
| Parallel Port Zip Drive | ASPIPPA3.SYS or ASPIPPM1.SYS |
| PPA-3 Adapter | ASPIPPA3.SYS |
| PC1616 | ASPIPC16.SYS |
| PC800 | ASPIPC8.SYS |
| PC2 | ASPIPC2.SYS |
| PC4 | ASPIPC4.SYS |

If you're using a non-Iomega SCSI adapter, you will need to add the complete path and file name for the driver to GUEST.INI, and REMark out all the other ASPI drivers. Once the GUEST.INI file is updated, save your changes and reboot the system; then run GUEST from the drive and directory containing the updated GUEST.INI file. If problems persist, try the drive on another system, or try a new drive on the suspect system.

**SYMPTOM 31-14**     **System recovery fails after the Zip Tools setup process is complete**
If the Zip Tools software for your Zip drive fails to install properly (or if the system hangs or was powered down), the Windows Startup group will have a Zip setup icon that will attempt to run each time Windows is started. Delete the Zip icon in your Startup group, and then reinstall the Zip software.

**SYMPTOM 31-15**     **The Zip drive setup could not find a Zip Tools disk for Zip parallel port drives**     This is usually an issue with the GUEST.INI file, which needs to be edited for proper operation. Start the system from a clean floppy disk, insert the Iomega installation disk, and then try running the GUEST utility. If a drive letter is assigned, there may be a driver in CONFIG.SYS or AUTOEXEC.BAT that is conflicting with the Zip drive. If GUEST fails to assign a Zip drive letter from a clean boot, open the GUEST.INI file in a text editor, locate the ASPI=ASPIPPA3.SYS line, and then add the switches; /MODE=1 /SPEED=1. This makes the complete command line appear as follows:

```
ASPI=ASPIPPA3.SYS SCAN /INFO SL360=NO SMC=NO /MODE=1 /SPEED=1
```

Reboot the PC and run the GUEST utility again. If GUEST does run but you still cannot read the Zip Tools disk, make sure that the signal cables are secure between the drive and system. If problems persist, try the Zip drive on another PC. If GUEST works on another PC, the original PC is using an incompatible parallel port. If the drive still refuses to work, try another Zip drive.

**SYMPTOM 31-16**     **You see error messages such as "Can't Find Zip Tools Disk" or "No Drive Letters Added" when using Zip parallel port drives**     In most cases, you will have to manually assign the proper ASPI driver by editing your GUEST.INI file. Open the GUEST.INI file on your Iomega install disk. Highlight the ASPI driver line that reads ASPIPPA3.SYS, and then add the following commands: /MODE=1 /SPEED=1. Remember to make a backup copy of the GUEST.INI file before editing it. The final command line should look like this:

```
ASPI=ASPIPPA3.SYS SCAN /INFO SL360=NO SMC=NO /MODE=1 /SPEED=1
```

Save your changes to GUEST.INI, and then run GUEST from the drive and directory that contains your edited GUEST.INI file. GUEST should now assign a drive letter to the Zip drive. Reboot the PC, start Windows, and then run the Iomega setup routine from the drive and directory that contains your edited GUEST.INI file. The Windows installation should now proceed normally.

Next, check the signal connector, and make sure that the parallel port or SCSI cable is connected properly between the drive and system. Try a known-good working signal cable. If problems persist, boot the system from a clean disk and try running GUEST. If a drive letter is assigned properly, then a driver loading in CONFIG.SYS or AUTOEXEC.BAT conflicts with the Zip drive. You have to systematically locate the offending driver. Finally, try the Zip drive on another PC. If GUEST works on another PC, the original PC is using an incompatible parallel port. If the drive still refuses to work, try another Zip drive.

**SYMPTOM 31-17**     **Windows allows the network drive letter to conflict with the Zip drive letter**     You may see this as a "No Zip Tools Disk Detected" message. The drive may also no longer be accessible from the Windows Explorer, My Computer, or the DOS prompt. The problem is that

Windows allows GUEST to assign a drive letter that is already used by a network drive. Remap the shared volume. Since GUEST is typically run first, you need to alter the network drive letter under Windows.

**SYMPTOM 31-18**    **You cannot print while using a Zip drive**    The Iomega parallel port Zip drive works as a pass-through device, and the software allows the drive to share a parallel port with printers. However, some printers require two-way communication between the printer and parallel port (e.g., to support printer monitoring software), and this conflicts with the Zip software. This can cause data corruption and system lockups. In many cases, disabling the bi-directional communication features of the printer will clear the problem. Otherwise, install a second parallel port (or opt for a USB or FireWire drive).

**SYMPTOM 31-19**    **You encounter problems installing a Zip SCSI drive**    In virtually all cases, SCSI problems can be traced to hardware problems or driver issues. Make sure that power is provided to the drive (see that the drive power light comes on). See that the SCSI signal cable is intact and connected securely between the drive and SCSI adapter. Try a new signal cable. Both ends of the SCSI bus must be terminated properly. Make sure that terminators are installed in the correct places. Ensure that the Zip SCSI drive is assigned to a SCSI ID that is not in use by any other SCSI device. Finally, check the drivers. The drivers for your SCSI adapter and drive must be correct, must use the right command-line switches, and must be the very latest versions. Also check for conflicts between SCSI drivers or other drivers in the system.

**SYMPTOM 31-20**    **The drive letter is lost each time the PC is turned off**    In many cases, the GUEST utility does not load properly because it is at the end of AUTOEXEC.BAT. Relocate the GUEST command line by opening the AUTOEXEC.BAT file and moving the GUEST command line to a point earlier in the file. Ideally, the GUEST command line should be the entry immediately following the MSCDEX command line. Save your changes and reboot the computer. The GUEST utility should now load each time the system is rebooted.

**SYMPTOM 31-21**    **When installing IomegaWare software for your Zip drive, a virus checker reports a virus**    For example, the typical report may indicate a "Romeo & Juliet" virus. This is often an error made by the virus checker when its virus definitions mistake the IomegaWare as a virus. Disable the antivirus software before attempting to install the software. If the IomegaWare software installs without error, you may reenable the antivirus program after the installation is complete. If not, you may need to obtain an updated version of the antivirus software.

**SYMPTOM 31-22**    **You see an error message such as "Drive X does not exist"**    There are several different reasons for this kind of problem. Check the disk first. You must use a PC-formatted disk—a Mac-formatted disk will not work in a PC. Try several different disks. If the error message occurs on only one disk, try reformatting that disk. (Remember that formatting the disk will remove all data from the disk.) If you're receiving the error while using more than one disk (or the disk will not format), the drive may be defective and should be replaced. This type of problem can also occur with older versions of the IomegaWare software. Try downloading the latest software from Iomega (www.iomega.com/software/). Unload the old software first, then install the new software from scratch.

**SYMPTOM 31-23**    **Your Windows 98 system locks up when using a USB Zip drive**
The most common problems occur when you connect or use the USB Zip drive in the wrong way. Verify that you're following the proper guidelines:

1. Power-up your USB Zip drive at the same time you turn on your computer (or immediately after), or be sure that the drive is powered up before connecting it to the USB port.

2. Wait at least 30 seconds before reconnecting your USB Zip drive to your computer (if you remove your USB Zip drive while your computer is on).

3. Confirm that your computer meets the USB 1.1 specification (or later). If it does not, do not combine your USB Zip drive with other low-speed devices (such as a USB keyboard or mouse).

4. Use only USB hubs that have an independent power supply. If you connect the USB Zip drive to a non-powered hub, your computer may lock up. The USB Zip drive may not transfer data correctly or may not be recognized by your computer. This should not be an issue when the drive is powered externally.

**SYMPTOM 31-24**     **When installing a USB Zip drive under Windows 9x/Me, you see an error such as "No Iomega drives found"**     This error occurs when the Iomega Tools software fails to assign a drive letter to your Zip drive. The problem is with your software. Iomega Tools is an older version of software that shipped with Zip and Jaz drives. IomegaWare is the latest version of the software. Iomega recommends that you obtain the most current version of the IomegaWare software from www.iomega.com/software/.

Download the IomegaWare package onto your system, and then double-click the icon to begin the installation process. Once you've downloaded and installed the software, you should no longer receive the error message. If you now have a drive letter, the updated software resolved your problem, and you can now use your drive.

**SYMPTOM 31-25**     **You notice that USB Zip drive performance is poor**     Other USB devices running at the same time as the USB Zip drive can affect performance. Digital cameras, page scanners, and other USB devices that process large amounts of data may affect performance. Here are some tips to tweak performance:

- Disconnect all USB devices from your computer, and then reconnect the USB Zip drive. Try the USB Zip alone and test performance again.

- Make sure that you are using the cable that came with your USB Zip drive.

- Close all open applications through the Task Manager.

**SYMPTOM 31-26**     **The system locks up when connecting other USB devices to your existing USB Zip drive**     Computers that are not compliant with USB hub specification 1.1 may lock up when a device (such as a USB keyboard, mouse, or joystick) is plugged in while the USB Zip drive is connected. Contact your computer manufacturer to verify that your USB hub is version 1.1 compliant (virtually all PCs now support USB 1.1 compatibility). If it is not, you will continue to experience lockups. To correct the problem, you may want to consider upgrading your USB hub. If the hub is compliant, you may need to update the USB drivers, your Windows version, or stick with the USB Zip drive only.

**SYMPTOM 31-27**     **You see an error such as "Disk in drive X not formatted"**     There are several different reasons for this kind of error. Check the disk first. You must use a PC-formatted disk—a Mac-formatted disk will not work in a PC. Try several different disks. If the error message occurs on only one disk, try reformatting that disk. (Remember that formatting the disk will remove all data from the disk.) If you're receiving the error using more than one disk (or the disk will not format), the drive may be defective and should be replaced. If the problem occurs on a parallel port Zip drive, try changing the parallel port mode through the CMOS Setup (EPP is the ideal setting).

**SYMPTOM 31-28** **When formatting a Zip disk, the Iomega format software returns a fatal exception error** This type of formatting error is almost always because of problems with outdated or corrupted Zip drivers. Such an error may appear as follows:

```
"A fatal exception 0E has occurred at 0028:C3C64C51 in VXD IOMEGA (01) + 00000CB5.
```

You'll need to update the Zip driver(s). Check the Iomega Web site at www.iomega.com and obtain a new IOMEGA.VXD file. Click Start, highlight Find, and then click Files or Folders. Find the old IOMEGA.VXD file and replace it with the newer version. Otherwise, simply remove the drive references from the Device Manager and uninstall the IomegaWare software, then reinstall the latest drivers and application software downloaded from Iomega.

**SYMPTOM 31-29** **The Zip drive's green power light does not illuminate** The green light on a Zip drive indicates that the drive is plugged in and receiving power. If the light is not on, then the drive is either turned off or not plugged in, or there is a physical problem with the drive.

■ *Check the power button.* If no disk is in the drive, press the eject button once. The eject button doubles as a power button, so pressing it will turn the drive on and off. Inserting a disk will also turn the drive on automatically. If there is already a disk in the drive, the button functions as an eject button, and the disk should be removed before turning off the power.

■ *Unplug the drive.* Disconnect the drive from power and the computer. Take the drive to another outlet and plug the power cable in. If the light comes on, there may be a problem with the first power outlet. If the light does not come on, the drive and/or power supply needs to be replaced.

**SYMPTOM 31-30** **You see an error such as "Cannot create or replace, make sure the disk is not full or write protected"** There are several different reasons for this kind of error. Check the disk first. You must use a PC-formatted disk—a Mac-formatted disk will not work in a PC. Try several different disks. If the error message occurs on only one disk, try reformatting that disk. (Remember that formatting the disk will remove all data from the disk.) If you're receiving the error using more than one disk (or the disk will not format), the drive may be defective and should be replaced. If the problem occurs on a parallel port Zip drive, try changing the parallel port mode through the CMOS Setup (EPP is the ideal setting).

**SYMPTOM 31-31** **You encounter a fatal exception error when using the Iomega Copy Machine software** This kind of problem is typically due to an issue with the Zip drive's automatic spin-down/eject feature used when doing a multiple disk copy. It may be necessary for you to disable the auto spin-down/eject function. For example, start the Copy Machine software by choosing its icon within the Iomega software folder. Next, select Options and then Runtime. Deselect the Auto Spin-Down/Eject option by removing the check from the box. Finally, choose OK to accept the changes, and reboot the PC if necessary. When performing subsequent multiple disk copies, you'll be prompted to eject each disk by pressing the eject button on the front of your Zip drive.

**SYMPTOM 31-32** **You encounter an error such as "General failure reading drive X"** There are several different reasons for this kind of error. Check the disk first. You must use a PC-formatted disk—a Mac-formatted disk will not work in a PC. Try several different disks. If the error message occurs on only one disk, try reformatting that disk. (Remember that formatting the disk will remove all data from the disk.) If you're receiving the error using more than one disk (or the disk will not format), the drive may be defective and should be replaced. If the problem occurs on a parallel port Zip drive, try changing the parallel port mode through the CMOS Setup (EPP is the ideal setting).

**SYMPTOM 31-33**    **You encounter an error such as "Insufficient disk space"**    You may also see this error as "Disk is full" or "Destination is full." This error message may be caused by several possible problems—the disk is full, is exceeding the operating system's file limit, or is bad.

■ *Check the disk space.* Use a tool like Windows Explorer to verify that enough free space exists on the Zip disk to contain the file(s) you need. If there is not enough, try copying fewer files, or use a fresh Zip disk.

■ *Check the number of files.* Make sure that you have not exceeded the file limit of your operating system. Remember that DOS will not allow you to have more than 511 files in the root directory. Use Windows Explorer (or the DOS DIR command) to list the files on your Zip disk. The number of files on the root directory should be less than 511. If the number of files is 511, you'll have to move some files into other directories to reduce the number of files on the root directory.

■ *Cycle power to the system.* If the error persists, try shutting down the computer and Zip drive, and then re-power the system in the correct order.

■ *Try several different disks.* If the error occurs on only one disk, try reformatting that disk. (Remember that formatting the disk will remove all data from the disk.) If you're receiving the error while using more than one disk (or the disk will not format), the drive may be defective and should be replaced.

**SYMPTOM 31-34**    **When using Zip drive software, you see an error such as "Program performed an illegal operation"**    In virtually all cases, there is a conflict between the Zip software and another program running on your system. You'll need to reboot the system and isolate the offending software.

■ *Reboot the system.* This will clear the error from memory and allow you to check other software. When you reboot the system, make sure to turn off the power to the drive and then turn it back on again.

■ *Close all open programs.* Open the Close Program dialog box (or Task Manager in Windows XP) by pressing CTRL-ALT-DEL at the same time. Close open programs by highlighting a program and then clicking the End Task button (do not close Explorer). As you close one application at a time, try your Zip drive again. Once the problem is resolved, the last application that was closed is the one causing the conflict. Once you have determined which application is causing the conflict, either discontinue use of that application when using your Zip drive, or obtain an updated version from the software maker (if possible).

■ *Reinstall the Zip software.* If the problem persists, uninstall and then reinstall the latest version of IomegaWare software.

**SYMPTOM 31-35**    **You receive an error message when using 1-Step Backup**    For example, when using the 1-Step Backup software to back up files to the Zip drive, you encounter an error such as

```
Backup cannot be completed due to an internal error in module MSVCRT.DLL
```

Use the following steps to clear the problem:

**1.** Open Windows Explorer.

**2.** Open the C: drive and locate the IomegaWare folder containing your 1-Step Backup software.

3. Double-click Backup.

4. Double-click ~Backupdata

5. Delete all of the files within the ~Backupdata window.

6. Close all open windows and applications.

7. Restart your computer and try the 1-Step Backup software again.

**SYMPTOM 31-36** **When using Iomega Tools software under Windows 9x/Me/XP, you see an error message such as "No Iomega drives found"** This occurs when the Iomega Tools software fails to assign a drive letter to your Zip drive, and is often a fault of old software. Iomega Tools is an older version of software that shipped with Zip drives. IomegaWare is the latest version of the software and should be updated in every possible case before troubleshooting. You can download the various components of IomegaWare from the Iomega site at www.iomega.com/software/. Start by downloading the Core IomegaWare Tools package onto your desktop, and then double-click the icon to begin the installation process. Once you have downloaded and installed the Core IomegaWare Tools software, you should no longer receive the error message.

**SYMPTOM 31-37** **You receive an error message such as "Disk is not in drive"** This type of error occurs when the Zip is using read/write protection, or the disk is inserted improperly. First see that the disk is seated completely in the drive. You may need to eject the disk from the drive, then carefully reinsert it so that the drive recognizes the disk. If the problem persists, use the following steps to remove read/write protection:

1. Open My Computer and right-click the Zip drive.

2. Select Properties and click the Iomega tab (if it's not already selected).

3. Select the Change button (Figure 31-1).

4. Enter the password.

Without a valid password, you must long format the disk to remove the password.

**SYMPTOM 31-38** **When using a Zip drive, you see an error such as "X:\ is not accessible. The device is not ready"** When the drive refuses to respond, there are several points to check.

■ *Check the Zip disk.* Verify that a properly formatted Zip disk is in the drive. If a disk is not in the drive (or if the disk is ejected after restarting your computer), Windows will display the error message. Place a disk into your Zip drive, wait a few seconds, and click the Retry button.

■ *Check/disable read/write protection.* Read/write protection is a security feature that requires a password, and it should be reserved for highly sensitive data. If your Zip disk is read/write-protected, you'll get the error message when trying to access a protected disk. The following steps should remove read/write protection:

1. Open My Computer.

2. Right-click the Zip drive, and choose the Protect option.

3. The Present Disk Status dialog box will indicate whether your disk is read/write-protected.

4. If your disk is write-protected, you must remove the read/write protection by selecting the Remove Protection button before accessing the disk.

**FIGURE 31-1**    The Iomega Zip drive properties dialog box (Courtesy of Iomega)

You'll need to enter the correct password in order to remove read/write protection. If you do not have the correct password, you won't be able to remove that protection from the disk.

■ *Check the cables.* Shut down the drive and computer, disconnect the data cable from the Zip drive, and carefully examine both ends of the cable for bent or broken pins. If the cable is damaged, it should be replaced. If it is not, reconnect it securely. Restart your computer to Windows, place a Zip disk in the drive, and try accessing the disk again.

■ *Try the drive on another PC.* Install your Zip drive on a different computer and see if you can read the disk on that system. If you can, there may be a problem with the original computer's interface. If the problem persists, the drive may be defective and require replacement.

**SYMPTOM 31-39**    **When using a Zip drive under Windows 9x/Me/XP, you see an error such as "The disk in drive X: is not formatted"**    This kind of behavior is almost always caused by incompatible formatting or software conflicts.

■ *Check the disk format.* You must use a PC-formatted Zip disk—a disk formatted for a Macintosh computer will not work. Zip disks come preformatted for either Macintosh or PC. A disk that is formatted for a Mac will have a small dot located on the lower-left corner of the disk label. If you have a Mac-formatted disk and you wish to reformat it for use on your PC (remember that formatting will permanently remove all data from that disk), follow these steps:

1. Insert the Zip disk into the drive.

2. If you receive a message such as "The disk in drive X: is not formatted. Do you want to format it now?" choose No.

3. Open My Computer and then right-click the Zip drive's icon.

4. Select Format.

5. Select Long Format.

6. Click Start and allow the process to complete.

■ *Try the disk in a "clean" environment.* Boot to DOS and see if you can access the disk. If you can, there may be a software conflict. If you cannot, the trouble may be with the disk itself.

1. Restart your computer with a blank bootable disk in drive A:.

2. When you get a "non-system disk" error message, eject the floppy disk from the A: drive and press the F8 key twice.

3. From the Windows Startup Menu, choose Safe Mode Command Prompt Only.

4. At the DOS prompt type **progra~1\iomega\tools\guest** to obtain a drive letter for your Zip drive.

5. Insert the Zip disk into the Zip drive.

6. At the DOS prompt, type **dir *x*:** (where *x* is the drive letter assigned to your Zip drive) and read the directory of files on your Zip disk.

■ *Try another Zip disk.* If the error occurs on only one disk, try reformatting that disk. If you're receiving the error message with more than one disk (or the disk will not format), the drive is probably defective and should be replaced.

■ *Try another parallel port setting.* If problems persist on a parallel port drive, try setting another parallel port mode such as bi-directional, standard, ECP, or EPP. In many cases, "downgrading" the parallel port mode will correct hardware issues, but it will reduce drive performance.

**SYMPTOM 31-40**    **You receive an "Invalid Page Fault" in module MFC42.DLL**    T h i s normally happens when a component of the 1-Step Backup software is damaged or corrupted. To fix this problem, you'll need to check for errors, then uninstall and reinstall the IomegaWare software suite. ScanDisk will check your drive for errors, and can correct most errors. To run ScanDisk under Windows 9x/Me, use the following steps:

1. Click Start | Programs | Accessories | System Tools, and then select ScanDisk.

2. Follow the screen prompts.

3. Try the backup job again.

Under Windows XP, open My Computer, right-click the drive and select Properties. Select the Tools tab and use the error checking feature.

If the problem persists, you should download the latest version of IomegaWare software from www.iomega.com/software/, then use the Add/Remove Programs tool to uninstall the old IomegaWare software. After you reboot the PC, install the updated software suite from scratch.

**SYMPTOM 31-41**    **You see an error message such as "No drives are supported by Iomega Tools"**    The trouble is with your version of the Zip drive's software. Iomega Tools is an older version of IomegaWare software. To correct this error, you should download and install the latest version of IomegaWare software from Iomega's Web site at www.iomega.com/software/. Install the IomegaWare software by double-clicking the file you have downloaded to your computer. This will begin the installation process.

**SYMPTOM 31-42**    **The Zip drive is clicking continuously**    A click is perfectly normal when inserting or removing a disk, but *continuous* clicking indicates a serious problem. This problem is often referred to as the "click of death" and is often a problem related to a fault in the Zip drive (especially older versions of the Zip drive). Check the disk first. Try another Zip disk in the drive. (Make sure that the disk is blank, to prevent damaging good disks.) If the problem persists, the drive is almost certainly defective and should be replaced. Iomega recommends the following precautions for Zip disks:

■ Eject disks prior to transporting any Zip drive. This forces the drive heads (which read and write to the disks) to park safely.

■ Avoid dropping your drive. It will almost certainly damage internal structures.

■ Make it a point to transport and store Zip disks in approved disk cases.

Iomega also offers a utility that tests the integrity of the drive heads and Zip media. If you're uncertain about the reliability of your Zip drive or disks, running the diagnostics could help isolate the problem. (Use a blank formatted disk while running these tests.)

**1.** Right-click the Zip drive in My Computer or Windows Explorer.

**2.** Choose Properties from the menu.

**3.** Click the Diagnostics tab.

**4.** Click the Diagnose Now button to start the test.

The diagnostic will report "Passed" or "Failed." If the diagnostic reports "Failed," you should contact Iomega to repair or replace the drive.

**SYMPTOM 31-43**    **The Zip drive's LED flashes continuously**    This almost always indicates a problem with the drive. When you insert or eject a disk (or copy files to or from your Zip drive), the light on the Zip drive will normally blink several times. If the light flashes continuously, there is a problem.

■ *Check the disk.* Try ejecting and reinstalling the Zip disk. (Be sure to use a blank disk to avoid accidental data loss.) You may also wish to try a different disk. If a new disk corrects the problem, the original disk is defective and should be replaced or discarded.

■ *Cycle the drive.* Power-down the computer and Zip drive, and then restart the system properly. After restarting the system, try the Zip disk(s) again. If the problem persists, the drive is probably defective and should be replaced. Otherwise, the drive simply needed to be cycled.

 If the Zip drive is an external model, unplug the power cord from the drive, wait at least five seconds, and plug the power cord back into the drive.

**SYMPTOM 31-44**    **You cannot eject a Zip disk from a drive**    This is a frequent problem reported with parallel port Zip drives, though it can certainly occur with other types of Zip drives. If the

Zip disk won't eject from the drive (either when pushing the eject button or using the software "eject" feature), there may be a hardware failure or an incorrect software setting.

- *Close your open applications.* Press CTRL-ALT-DEL to open the Close Program (or Task Manager) dialog box. Close all open applications one at a time (except Explorer and Systray) by highlighting an application and choosing the End Task button. Once all applications are closed (except Explorer and Systray), try to eject the disk from the Zip drive using the eject button on the front of the drive. If the disk ejects, there is a software application problem.

- *Cycle the drive.* Power-down the computer and Zip drive, and then restart the system properly. After restarting the system, try ejecting the Zip disk(s) again. If the problem persists, the drive is probably defective and should be replaced. Otherwise, the drive simply needed to be cycled.

- *Try another disk.* Insert a different blank formatted Zip disk into the drive (without connecting the data cable to the computer). If the disk ejects, the original disk is defective. If the disk still does not eject, the drive is probably defective and should be replaced.

- *Try the emergency eject button.* Remove the power cord from your Zip drive. Straighten out a paper clip and insert it into the emergency eject hole located on the back of the drive (above the right-hand cable connector). If the disk still refuses to eject, the drive is probably defective and should be replaced.

**SYMPTOM 31-45**    **You receive an error such as "Unsafe removal of device"**    This error often occurs with FireWire drives that are not stopped or removed properly from the system. Follow this procedure when removing a FireWire Zip drive:

1. Right-click the Unplug or eject hardware icon in the System Tray of your Taskbar.

2. Left-click the Unplug or eject hardware text box to display the Unplug or Eject Hardware dialog box (Figure 31-2).

3. Select the device to be disconnected (e.g., the Zip drive) and then click the Stop button to display the Stop a Hardware device dialog box.

4. Select the device to be stopped and click OK to display the Safe To Remove Hardware confirmation box.

5. You may now disconnect the FireWire drive from your PC.

**SYMPTOM 31-46**    **The Zip drive refuses to spin up**    There are a variety of possible problems that might contribute to this symptom.

- *Try another disk.* Insert a different blank formatted Zip disk into the drive. If the new disk works properly, the original disk is defective. If the problem persists, the trouble is with conflicting software or Zip drive problems.

- *Check the power.* All external drives must be powered by an AC adapter. If the adapter is disconnected or defective, the drive will not spin up.

- *Check the parallel port.* If you're using a parallel port Zip drive, change the mode of your parallel port to SPP, EPP, standard, or bi-directional.

- *Replace the drive.* If problems persist, the drive is probably defective and should be replaced.

**SYMPTOM 31-47**    **You notice poor performance with a parallel port 250MB Zip drive**
Parallel port Zip drive performance depends on the performance of your LPT port. Optimum performance requires a parallel port running in EPP mode—a parallel port in ECP or unidirectional mode may cause

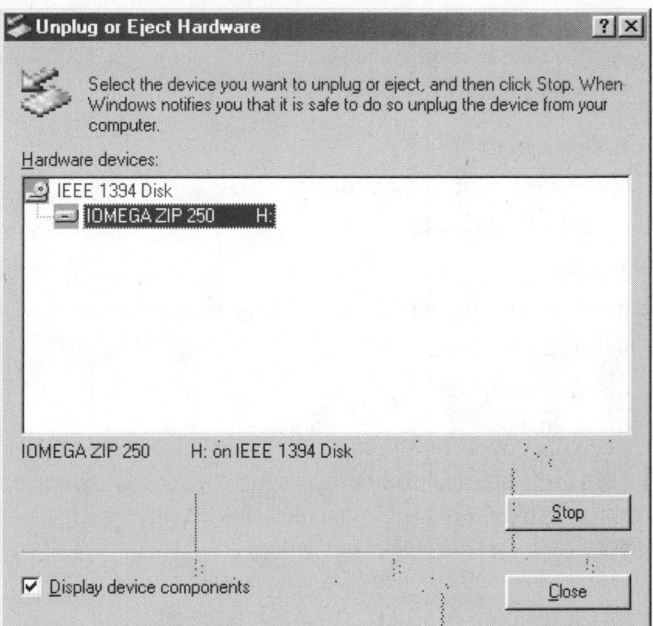

**FIGURE 31-2**    FireWire drives should be stopped properly before disconnecting them from the system (Courtesy of Iomega)

erratic performance. Access your system's CMOS Setup to reconfigure the parallel port. Once you have located the parallel port settings, choose either EPP, bi-directional, SPP, standard, AT, PS/2, or fast mode. Save your changes and reboot the system.

 Your BIOS may not allow you to change the parallel port mode (especially older systems). In this case, you may be able to change the parallel port mode through a jumper setting on the motherboard.

If you're using a SCSI Zip drive, check your cable length and optimize the chain. The combined SCSI chain length (the total of all cables in the SCSI chain) should not exceed 6 meters (about 19.6 feet), though it should ideally be much shorter. This includes both internal and external SCSI devices. The fastest device should be the last (or farthest) from the computer.

**SYMPTOM 31-48**    **You receive an error message such as "Chipset error 0x8"**    This problem is known to occur with SCSI Zip drives when the Jaz Jet PCI card is not installed properly or securely. Shut down and unplug the PC and make sure the SCSI adapter card is seated properly. You may need to remove and reinstall the Jet card. Try the system again. If the problem persists, you may need to replace the Jet card, or try another SCSI adapter.

**SYMPTOM 31-49**    **The computer locks up after running the parallel port accelerator utility**    In some cases, a system lockup may occur after installing the parallel port driver and then running the Iomega Parallel Port Accelerator. Sometimes, running the Parallel Port Accelerator utility under Windows 9x/Me will cause the drive to stop running (or even cause the system to lock up during boot).

This is not known to occur under Windows XP. Disconnect the Zip drive and reboot the computer. Remove the modifications made by the Parallel Port Accelerator:

1. Right-click the My Computer icon and select Properties.
2. Click the Device Manager tab.
3. Click the plus sign (+) next to SCSI Controllers.
4. Double-click Iomega Parallel Port Interface.
5. Click the Settings tab.
6. Remove all the information from the Adapter settings box.
7. Click OK and then click OK again.
8. Click Yes to restart your computer.
9. Reconnect the Zip parallel port drive and try it again.

**SYMPTOM 31-50** **The computer locks up when running an open application and trying to eject a Zip disk** If a file or application that resides on your Zip disk is open or in use, and you try to eject that disk, the computer may lock up. Before you eject your Zip disk, make certain that you close any files or applications that may be open (or in use).

**SYMPTOM 31-51** **There is a Zip disk read failure on the Zip drive under Windows 9x/Me/XP** In virtually all cases, the problem is a defective Zip disk. Using an improperly formatted Zip disk in the drive may also cause a problem.

■ *Check the disk.* Use a different Zip disk and see if another disk resolves the problem (or try the original disk on another Zip drive). Make sure to use a blank Zip disk so that you won't loose any critical data.

■ *Try reformatting the disk.* If a different disk works, and the original disk seems to have a problem, try reformatting the original Zip disk:

1. Open My Computer.
2. Right-click the Zip drive icon and select Format.
3. Select Long Format.
4. Click Start, and click Start again.
5. When the disk has finished formatting successfully, click OK.

If you cannot format the Zip disk successfully, the disk is almost certainly defective and should be replaced.

■ *Try the drive on another system.* If the disk can be read after moving the Zip drive to another PC, there may be a problem with the PC or with the way the drive was connected to that system. Recheck your connections at the original system.

■ *Suspect the drive.* If no disks can be read on the Zip drive, double-check the drive's installation and setup. If the problem persists, then the drive itself may be defective and should be replaced.

**SYMPTOM 31-52** **You see a "fatal exception error" when using an ATAPI IDE Zip drive** This is a known issue under Windows 95 (and OEM2), but was fixed under Windows 98. This problem occurs when you're using an Intel motherboard and AMI (or Intel) BIOS. The Zip drive may also be installed on the secondary IDE channel. The error may also occur when you start the computer without a disk in the drive, or you eject the disk from the Zip drive. This is a problem with Windows 95, but can be corrected by obtaining the latest update files for Windows, or updating to a later version of Windows.

**SYMPTOM 31-53**     **You encounter "Windows Protection" errors at startup (the Windows logo screen) when using an HP printer and parallel port Zip drive**     This issue can occur if you have an HP 4000 or 8000 series printer attached to a Zip drive, and the Zip drive is attached to the parallel port. To work around this problem, disable bi-directional support in your computer's CMOS Setup (or in the properties of your printer). To disable bi-directional support through the printer properties dialog box under Windows 9x/Me:

1. Click Start, highlight Settings, and click Printers.
2. Right-click your printer (such as HP 4000 or HP 8000), and then click Properties.
3. Click the Details tab, click Spool Settings, click Disable Bidirectional Support For This Printer, click OK, and then click OK again.

  Use the following steps under Windows XP:

1. Click Start | Control Panel | Printers and Other Hardware
2. Click Printers and Faxes.
3. Right-click the desired printer and select Properties.
4. Click the Ports tab (see Figure 31-3).

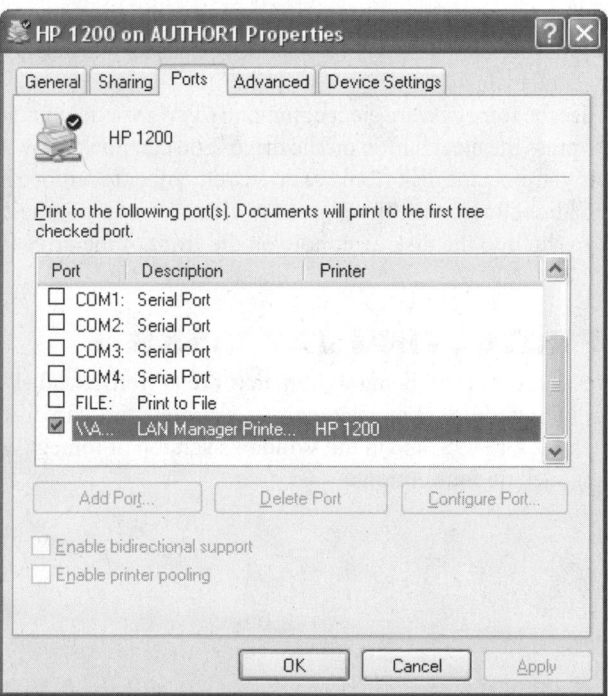

**FIGURE 31-3**     Unchecking the Enable bidirectional support checkbox to disable bidirectional support for the printer

5. Uncheck the Enable bidirectional support checkbox.

6. Click Apply and OK.

# Iomega Jaz Drives

While Iomega's Zip drive filled a need for removable storage, the 100MB and 250MB disk sizes of the day still faced limitations with large images, CAD drawings, and other data-intensive files. Iomega sought to leverage their experience with Bernoulli disk technology to create a high-capacity storage system that would support huge files such as video clips, animations, large backups, and so on. The Jaz drive was initially released with a capacity of 1GB, and later updated to 2GB. Unlike the older Bernoulli technology, which used a flexible platter forced to flex beneath a fixed read/write head, the Jaz family uses more conventional "rigid disks" that suspend the read/write heads under a thin layer of air (the same approach used in hard drives). This part of the chapter examines the typical operating and troubleshooting aspects of the Jaz drive family.

Today, the Jaz drive is generally considered to be obsolete in the face of high-capacity rewritable drives such as CD-RW and DVD-RAM drives.

## INSERTING AND EJECTING JAZ DISKS

To access a Jaz drive, simply insert a Jaz disk first. The drive's status light flashes as the disk spins up (or when the drive is busy), and glows steadily while it acquires the disk. When the light goes out, the drive is ready to use. Just open Windows Explorer or My Computer and select the Jaz drive. If you can't read or write to the Jaz disk, or it fails to mount properly on your desktop after it is inserted, eject it from the drive and insert it again (or try another Jaz disk).

To eject the Jaz disk, use the IomegaWare eject command (by right-clicking the drive in My Computer or Windows Explorer), or press the eject button on the drive. You can power down the Jaz drive and leave the Jaz disk inserted, but if you eject the disk from the drive, remember to remove it and store the disk in its protective case to prevent a buildup of dust. If you need to eject a Jaz disk in the event of a power failure, insert a straightened paper clip into the disk eject hole on the front of the drive (similar to the disk eject hole on CD drives).

## READ/WRITE-PROTECTING JAZ DISKS

Read/write protection prevents data from being written to (or read from) the disk. Jaz disks are protected electronically rather than by a traditional mechanical write-protect tab. Jaz disk protection is available from Iomega SCSI utilities 2.2 for DOS, and in the Windows version of IomegaWare (previously Iomega Tools). Protection features include four options:

- Write protection
- Read/write protection
- "Unprotect" until ejection
- Remove protection

Note that password protection is optional for write protection, but is required for read/write protection. When set, this password must be used to access the disk (or change protection options). Keep in mind that no one can recover data from a read/write-protected disk—should you forget the password. If the password is forgotten, you'll have to reformat the Jaz disk. Reformatting the disk will destroy all the data on it. You cannot use DOS FORMAT (or any other type of disk management software) to remove the password protection. To protect or unprotect a Jaz disk, you must run the Iomega SCSI utilities (or use the IomegaWare software):

1. Open My Computer.
2. Read/write-protect the Iomega disk by right-clicking the Jaz disk icon and choosing the Protect option. (If a disk is not inserted in the drive, the Protect option will not be available.)
3. Use the same processes to remove the read/write protection.

## MAINTAINING JAZ DISKS

Jaz disks are manufactured in protective housings that are specially designed to keep dust and other contaminants from the rigid disk media inside. However, Jaz disks are certainly not impervious to damage, and care is needed to ensure a long and reliable working life for the media. The following points will help you to maintain Jaz disks:

■ *Keep dust from the disk.* The Jaz disk housing should keep dust out, but don't open the door on a Jaz disk—that would let in dust, pet hair, and other debris that could cause data loss. Also be sure to clean the outside of a Jaz disk to wipe away any dust or other contaminants before inserting the disk into the Jaz drive.

■ *Handle the disk carefully.* Do not drop or crush the Jaz disk. This will physically damage the disk and cause read/write problems. Be sure to keep the Jaz disk in its protective case whenever the disk is not in use. Never force a Jaz disk into or out of a drive, and never force a 2GB Jaz disk into a 1GB Jaz drive. Forcing a disk will damage the disk (and often damage the drive as well).

■ *Label the disk with care.* Use caution when placing labels on the Jaz disk. Never stack labels—this can cause interference and trouble inserting or removing the disk. Also avoid the use of pencils and opt for ink pens instead.

■ *Check for heat and environmental problems.* It's normal for a Jaz disk to become warm during normal use. However, hot disks may indicate a serious problem with the Jaz drive. Jaz disks are also sensitive to direct sunlight, extreme heat and cold, moisture, and the presence of magnetic fields—so be extremely careful how and where you store Jaz disks.

■ *Power the Jaz drive properly.* Always power up the Jaz drive before (or at the same time as) the host PC before inserting a Jaz disk in the drive. Otherwise, mounting problems may occur.

■ *Support optimum data transfers.* For best performance, the Jaz drive should be connected to an UltraSCSI controller (such as a Jaz Jet PCI Ultra SCSI card).

## GENERAL DRIVE INSTALLATION AND REPLACEMENT

Removable media (or RM) drives are generally easy devices to install or replace. Most are installed as master devices located on the secondary IDE drive controller channel, though a growing number will coexist as slave devices alongside a hard drive or other drive device. The most important issue to remember is that the BIOS will not support an RM drive directly (even if the BIOS identifies the RM drive at boot time). You'll need real-mode drivers for the RM drive under DOS, or protected-mode drivers for the RM drive under Windows. In most cases, you'll also install a set of software utilities for features like disk cartridge partitioning, formatting, R/W protection, and so on. This part of the chapter covers the guidelines to follow to install a basic internal IDE-type RM drive.

## Select Jumper Configurations

An IDE-type RM drive may be installed as a master or slave device on any hard drive controller channel. These master/slave settings are handled through one or two jumpers located on the rear of the drive (right next to the 40-pin signal cable connector). One of your first decisions when planning an installation should be to decide the drive's configuration:

- If you're installing the RM drive as the first drive on the secondary drive controller channel, it must be jumpered as the master device.

- If you're installing the RM drive alongside another drive (on either the primary or secondary drive controller channel), the RM drive must be jumpered as the slave device.

Refer to the documentation that accompanies your particular RM drive to determine the exact master/slave jumper settings. If you do not have the drive documentation handy, check the drive manufacturer's Web site for online information.

If you're installing a SCSI-type RM drive (such as the Iomega Jaz drive), verify that a SCSI host adapter is installed, and be sure to check the SCSI IDs currently in use on the system. Set the new drive so that it uses a unique SCSI ID.

## Preinstall Any Software

Some RM drive designs require that you preinstall one or more software utilities prior to installing the physical drive. This ensures that Windows will "find" the drive after installation (especially true for exotic USB or FireWire devices). If your particular RM drive suggests that you insert a software CD and install software prior to the drive's physical installation, you should handle that software installation now. For example, Iomega recommends that you install the IomegaWare software before installing the physical Jaz drive. After the required software is installed, you can power-down the PC and begin the actual drive installation.

## Attach Cables and Mount the Drive

At this point, you'll need to connect the physical drive and secure it to the chassis, as explained for an internal ATAPI IDE-type drive here:

1. Turn off and unplug the PC, and then remove the outer cover to expose the computer's drive bays.

2. Attach one end of the 40-pin drive interface cable to the drive controller connector on your motherboard (or drive controller card). Remember to align pin 1 on the cable (the side of the cable with the blue or red stripe) with pin 1 on the drive controller connector. Keep in mind that SCSI installations will use a 50/68-pin cable, and SCSI cable chains must be properly terminated.

3. Locate an available drive bay for the RM drive. Remove the plastic housing covering the drive bay, and then slide the drive inside. Locate the four screw holes needed to mount the drive. In some cases, you may need to attach "mounting rails" to the drive so that the drive will be wide enough to fit in the drive bay. In virtually all cases, you should mount an RM drive horizontally (though some RM drive models may be mounted vertically).

4. Attach the 40-pin signal cable and the 4-pin power connector to the new drive, and then bolt the drive securely into place. Do not overtighten the screws, because doing so may damage the drive. If

you do not have an available 4-pin power connector, you may use an appropriate Y-splitter if necessary to split power from another drive (preferably the floppy drive).

## Configure the CMOS Setup

Although virtually all RM drives require real- or protected-mode driver support, recent motherboard designs can identify the ATAPI IDE RM drive in BIOS, so you should configure your computer's BIOS to accept the drive if possible (through the CMOS Setup):

1. Turn on the computer. As your computer starts, watch for a message that describes how to run the CMOS Setup (such as "Press F1 for Setup"). Press the appropriate key to start the CMOS Setup program.

2. Select the basic configuration menu, and choose the drive location occupied by the RM drive (for example, primary slave, secondary slave, or secondary master, depending on how you've physically jumpered and installed the drive).

3. Select Automatic Drive Detection, if available. This option will automatically identify the new drive. If your BIOS does not provide automatic drive detection, select none or not installed for the RM drive, and rely on drivers only.

4. Save the settings and exit the CMOS Setup program. Your computer will automatically reboot.

## Reassemble the Computer

Double-check all of your signal and power cables to verify that they are secure, and then tuck the cables gently into the computer's chassis. Check that no loose tools, screws, or cables are inside the chassis. Now reattach the computer's outer housing(s).

Since the operating system will assign a drive letter only to a partitioned and formatted disk cartridge, you should be sure to insert an appropriate disk cartridge into the drive before rebooting the system. If you do not insert a disk cartridge, the drive may not receive a drive letter at boot time.

## Install the Software

To complete your RM drive installation, you need to install the software drivers and utilities that accompanied the drive on floppy disk or CD. If you've preinstalled any software prior to installing the drive, you'll likely need to complete the software installation now. Windows 9x/Me/XP systems generally will detect the presence of the new RM drive and prompt you for the protected-mode drivers automatically. After you install the drivers and reboot the system, the RM drive should be ready for use.

# Jaz Drive Troubleshooting

Even though your Jaz drive may be installed and configured properly, there are numerous problems that can plague a drive (and adapter). If you cannot correct drive problems with the preceding guidelines, review the following symptoms for detailed corrective action.

**SYMPTOM 31-54**     **You cannot format a 1GB Jaz disk in a 2GB Jaz drive**     For example, you notice that the short format option will work correctly, but the long format option fails. The trouble here is usually due to a difference in read/write heads between the 1GB and 2GB Jaz drive models. Unfortunately, there is little that can be done to overcome this type of problem. If your 1GB Jaz disk needs a long format, you'll need to use a 1GB Jaz drive. Otherwise, you'll need to live with the short format option. If the long format fails on a 1GB Jaz drive, the 1GB disk may have failed, and should be replaced.

**SYMPTOM 31-55**   **You encounter an error such as "No Iomega adapters found"**
This error frequently occurs under Windows 9x/Me (not under Windows XP) when the IomegaWare software cannot assign a drive letter to the Jaz drive. In most cases, you'll need to download the latest version of the IomegaWare software from Iomega at www.iomega.com/software/. Now uninstall the current version of your IomegaWare software under Windows 9x/Me:

1. Click Start | Settings | Control Panel.
2. Double-click the Add/Remove Programs icon.
3. Highlight IomegaWare.
4. Click the Add/Remove button.
5. Restart your computer when prompted to do so.

Now reinstall the new version of your IomegaWare software:

1. Click Start | Run | Browse.
2. Click the Look in drop-down box.
3. Find your CD drive (or the location where you saved the updated IomegaWare software).
4. Highlight the setup.exe file, click the Open button, and click OK.
5. Follow all the prompts to complete the installation of your IomegaWare software.

**SYMPTOM 31-56**   **The external SCSI Jaz drive doesn't receive a drive letter**   As with any SCSI device, an external SCSI Jaz drive may not receive a drive letter for several different reasons. These reasons include a poor SCSI connection, a SCSI ID conflict, trouble with the SCSI drivers, or improper SCSI signal termination. Recheck the hardware and software installation for any SCSI-related oversights.

Start your investigation by checking the power and signal connections to the Jaz drive. Now reboot the PC and check for an appropriate drive letter under Windows Explorer or My Computer. If the connections are secure, verify your Jaz drive is using a unique SCSI ID number (the Jaz SCSI ID is set to ID 4 by default). Also verify that the external Jaz drive has its termination enabled—check the termination of any internal SCSI chain. If the problem persists, you may need to check the installation of your SCSI host adapter card (such as the Jaz Jet PCI SCSI adapter), and perhaps move the controller to another slot.

If the drive and controller all appear to be installed properly, you may need to download the latest IomegaWare software, uninstall the current version of IomegaWare on your system, then reinstall the latest version of the software from scratch.

**SYMPTOM 31-57**   **You receive an error such as "The directory or file cannot be created"**   This error message can occur when too many files are located under the root directory of your Jaz disk. Placing the files into a folder or folders can usually eliminate this error message. For example, first create a new folder on your hard drive. Move two or more files off your Iomega Jaz disk into the new folder. Now move the new folder with the files back onto your Iomega disk.

**SYMPTOM 31-58**   **You receive an error such as "Cannot create file or folder; disk may be full or write protected"**   This error indicates that you cannot create anything on the Jaz disk. In many cases, the Jaz disk is simply write-protected. Open My Computer and right-click the Jaz drive icon. If the term "Unprotect" appears in the context menu, the disk media is write-protected. Unprotect the disk (you may need a password) and try your operation again. If the Jaz disk is not write-protected, you may have exceeded the maximum number of files supported by the operating system. If you suspect this to be the case, see Symptom 31-57 for corrective suggestions.

**SYMPTOM 31-59** **You have problems when running Iomega Jaz Tools under Windows 9x/Me/XP** When Iomega Tools for Windows is installed on your computer, the system may crash (or you may receive an error message referencing the IOMEGA.VXD file) when you attempt to use the Iomega Jaz Tools. This occurs most frequently under FAT32 partitions of OSR 2 or later. Chances are that you're using an older version of Jaz Tools for Windows 95 (earlier than version 5.0). Earlier versions of Jaz Tools are not compatible with FAT32. You'll need to uninstall the Jaz Tools package, and then install version 5.0 or later, which is FAT32-aware. Today, IomegaWare 3.1.1 (or later) will support numerous Iomega drive models—including the Jaz drive.

**SYMPTOM 31-60** **The system runs in "DOS Compatibility Mode" when booting from a removable media drive** When your PC is configured to boot from a removable media drive, the Performance tab in System Properties may show that the computer is using DOS Compatibility Mode for virtual memory. This is known to be a frequent problem under Windows 95 and OSR 1, and is known to occur with Zip drives, Jaz drives, and SyQuest EZ drives (and may also occur with other IDE or SCSI removable media drives). This problem does not occur with Windows 95 OSR 2 and later. To avoid this problem, upgrade Windows or configure Windows 95 so that the Windows swap file is located on a non-removable disk:

1. Open Control Panel and double-click the System icon.
2. Click the Performance tab, and then click Virtual Memory.
3. Click "Let me specify my own virtual memory settings," click a nonremovable disk in the Hard Disk box, click OK, and then click OK again.

**SYMPTOM 31-61** **The Jaz drive isn't detected when connecting it through a Jaz Traveler** In many cases, this is a software problem. Boot clean (from a bootable floppy disk), and then run your GUEST software from the Jaz installation disk by typing

```
a:\guest
```

If the drive is detected using the GUEST utility under DOS, the problem is software related. Try removing the Jaz drivers and software utilities, and then reinstall the latest software version from scratch. If the problem is not resolved, the trouble is hardware related. The Jaz drive must be connected directly to the parallel port. The Jaz drive will not work properly if connected through a switch box, dongle, or software key. Also verify that no other device is using IRQ 7. Check all power connections to the Jaz drive. If the Jaz drive doesn't respond and the power connections are secure, the drive is probably defective and should be replaced.

Try the Jaz drive on a different computer. If the drive is detected properly on a different computer, there may be a problem with the first computer's configuration. If the Jaz drive is not detected on another computer, the Jaz drive may be defective.

**SYMPTOM 31-62** **The PC locks up (or does not finish booting) when connected to a SCSI Jaz drive** Make sure that you're powering on the Jaz drive and your computer at the same time. Try connecting both the computer and the Jaz drive to a power strip, and power the system from the power strip. Otherwise, power up the Jaz drive first before booting the PC.

If the computer still won't boot, there may be a problem with your system's configuration. Try the Jaz drive on a different computer. If the system boots after removing the Jaz drive, the drive may be defective.

If the Jaz drive works properly on another computer, you may need to reconfigure the system (or the SCSI adapter card). If the computer locks up, boot clean and run the GUEST utility from the Jaz installation disk by typing

```
a:\guest
```

If the drive is detected using the GUEST utility under DOS, the problem is software related. Try removing the Jaz drivers and software utilities, and then reinstall the latest software version (e.g., IomegaWare) from scratch. Try isolating any conflicting software. Open the Close Program (or Task Manager) dialog box by pressing CTRL-ALT-DEL. Close open programs by highlighting a program and then clicking the End Task button (do not close Explorer or Systray). Remember to close one application at a time, and then try your Jaz drive again. Repeat this process until the problem is resolved. Once the problem is resolved, the last application that was closed is the one causing the conflict.

If the problem is not resolved, the trouble is hardware related. Verify that no other devices are using the same IRQ as your SCSI adapter. Also make sure that your Jaz drive is correctly terminated and is not using the same SCSI ID as another SCSI device. Check all power connections to the Jaz drive. If the Jaz drive doesn't respond and the power connections are secure, the drive is probably defective and should be replaced.

Try the Jaz drive on a different computer. If the drive is detected properly on a different computer, there may be a problem with the first computer's configuration. If the Jaz drive is not detected on another computer, the Jaz drive may be defective.

**SYMPTOM 31-63**    **An incorrect icon appears for a Jaz drive**    Ideally, the icon should be a green Jaz drive, so the actual problem depends on the icon that is shown in Windows Explorer.

First, the Jaz icon may look like a floppy or hard disk drive icon. Chances are that a real-mode TSR or driver is interfering with the Jaz drive. Restart your computer. When you see the message "Starting Windows," press F8. From the Startup menu, choose Step-by-Step Confirmation. As each step is processed, answer yes to every entry except "Process your startup device drivers (CONFIG.SYS)" and "Process your startup command file (AUTOEXEC.BAT)." This will prevent real-mode drivers from loading at startup. If the incorrect Jaz icon is now replaced with the correct green Jaz icon, there is a driver conflict in either your AUTOEXEC.BAT or CONFIG.SYS file. You'll need to systematically disable each real-mode command line until you identify the offending command line. If the Jaz icon is not the correct green Jaz icon, then a Windows driver is causing the problem. You may need to remove the Jaz drivers and other software and update/reinstall that software (e.g., IomegaWare) from scratch.

If the Jaz icon takes any other form, there may be a problem with other software on the system. Open the Close Program (Task Manager) dialog box by pressing CTRL-ALT-DEL. Highlight each unknown or non-essential entry and then click the End Task button. If the problem persists, reboot your computer and run ScanDisk. Correct any file system problems indicated by ScanDisk. If the problem still continues, delete and then reinstall the Iomega Tools (or IomegaWare) software.

**SYMPTOM 31-64**    **The system locks up while installing Jaz Tools software**    In most cases, you'll notice lockups when launching the Iomega setup software. This is usually caused by a conflict with another driver that is loading during Windows 9x/Me/XP startup. To determine which file is causing this conflict, close all open programs:

1. Open the Close Program (or Task Manager) dialog box by pressing CTRL-ALT-DEL.
2. Close open programs by highlighting a program and then clicking the End Task button (do not close Explorer).

**3.** Close one application at a time, and then try your Jaz drive again.

**4.** Repeat this process until the problem is resolved. Once the problem is resolved, the last application that was closed is the one causing the conflict.

**5.** Once you have determined which application is causing the conflict, you should discontinue the use of that application when using your Jaz drive, or obtain an updated version of that software.

 Also verify that you're using the very latest version of software available for your Jaz drive (such as IomegaWare).

**SYMPTOM 31-65**    **You receive an "insufficient disk space" message writing to the Jaz disk under DOS**    This error message may be caused if the disk is full, exceeds the file limit imposed by your operating system, or is defective.

▨ *Check the disk space.* Verify that the disk has enough space available to hold the files you wish to copy.

▨ *Check the operating system.* Make sure that you do not exceed the file limit of your operating system. DOS will not allow you to include more than 511 files in the root directory. Switch to the drive letter of your Jaz drive. From the drive prompt, type **dir** and press ENTER. The number of files in the root directory should be less than 511. Otherwise, you'll have to move individual files into other directories to reduce the number of files on the root directory.

▨ *Try cycling power.* If the error persists, try shutting down the computer (and Jaz drive). Then restart the system from a "cold" start.

▨ *Try several different disks.* If the error message occurs on only one disk, try reformatting that disk (formatting the disk will remove all data from the disk). If reformatting the disk doesn't help, discard the disk and use a fresh one. If you're receiving the error message with more than one disk, the drive may be defective and should be replaced.

**SYMPTOM 31-66**    **No drives on your system are supported by Iomega Tools in DOS**
Boot the system clean, and then run GUEST from the Jaz installation disk by typing **a:\guest**. If the drive is detected using the GUEST utility under DOS, the problem is software related. Try removing the Jaz drivers and software utilities, and then reinstall the latest software version from scratch. Try isolating any conflicting software. Open the Close Program dialog box by pressing CTRL-ALT-DEL. Close open programs by highlighting a program and then clicking the End Task button (do not close Explorer or Systray). Remember to close one application at a time. Then try your Jaz drive again. Repeat this process until the problem is resolved. Once the problem is resolved, the last application that was closed is the one causing the conflict.

If the problem is not resolved, the trouble is hardware related. Verify that no other devices are using the same IRQ as your SCSI adapter. Also make sure that your Jaz drive is correctly terminated and is not using the same SCSI ID as another SCSI device. Check all power connections to the Jaz drive. If the Jaz drive doesn't respond and the power connections are secure, the drive is probably defective and should be replaced.

Try the Jaz drive on a different computer. If the drive is detected properly on a different computer, there may be a problem with the first computer's configuration. If the Jaz drive is not detected on another computer, the Jaz drive may be defective.

**SYMPTOM 31-67**    **The GUEST utility cannot locate the Jaz Tools disk**    Verify that the Jaz Tools disk is in your Jaz drive. If the Jaz Tools disk is already inserted into your Jaz drive, eject and then reinsert the Jaz Tools disk. You may also wish to try another Jaz Tools disk. Next, verify that your Jaz drive is assigned a drive letter. Double-click the My Computer icon. There should be an icon representing the Jaz drive. If your Jaz drive is not assigned a drive letter, you'll need to connect the drive properly.

Close all open programs. Open the Close Program (or Task Manager) dialog box by pressing CTRL-ALT-DEL. Close open programs by highlighting a program and then clicking the End Task button (do not close Explorer or Systray). Close one application at a time, and then try your Jaz drive again. Repeat this process until the problem is resolved. The last application that was closed is the one causing the conflict. Once you've determined which application is causing the conflict, discontinue the use of that application while using your Jaz drive (or obtain an updated version of the software).

**SYMPTOM 31-68**    **You see an error indicating that the Jaz disk in your drive is not formatted**    First verify that you're using a PC-formatted disk (a Mac-formatted Jaz disk will not work in a PC). Try several different Jaz disks. If the error message occurs on only one disk, try reformatting that disk. (Remember that formatting the Jaz disk will remove all data from that disk.) If you cannot format the suspect Jaz disk, it may be defective and require replacement. If you're receiving the error message with any Jaz disk (or the disk will not format on your drive), the drive may be defective and need to be replaced.

**SYMPTOM 31-69**    **You encounter a "general failure reading drive" message in DOS** In many cases, this is a disk problem. First check your connections and confirm that the Jaz drive's signal and power cables are attached properly. Verify that you're using a PC-formatted disk (a Mac-formatted Jaz disk will not work in a PC), and compare results with several different Jaz disks. If the error message occurs on only one disk, try reformatting that disk. (Remember that formatting the Jaz disk will remove all data from that disk.) If you cannot format the suspect Jaz disk, it may be defective and require replacement. If you're receiving the error message with any Jaz disk (or the disk will not format on your drive), the drive may be defective and need to be replaced.

**SYMPTOM 31-70**    **When backing up, you receive an error indicating that "disk linking is not supported under Windows 9x/Me"**    This is a problem with Microsoft Backup. It does not support disk linking over multiple Jaz disks. Instead, you should remove Backup and install Iomega's 1-Step Backup for Zip and Jaz software (part of the Iomega Tools and later IomegaWare software bundles) according to the manufacturer's instructions.

**SYMPTOM 31-71**    **You encounter a "fatal exception" error when using the Copy Machine software for your Jaz drive**    In virtually all cases, the problem is caused by the Auto Spin-Down/Eject feature in the Iomega Copy Machine software. You'll need to disable the feature under Windows 9x/Me. Start the Iomega Copy Machine software by clicking its icon in the Iomega Tools folder. Select Options, and then choose Runtime. Deselect the Auto Spin-Down/Eject option by clearing the checkbox. Finally, choose OK to accept the changes. Alternatively, update the Iomega software to a current version of IomegaWare.

**SYMPTOM 31-72**    **You see an error such as "program performed an illegal operation"** Try rebooting the system first (make sure to cycle power to the drive also). Close all open programs to clear possible conflicting software. Open the Close Program (or Task Manager) dialog box by pressing CTRL-ALT-DEL. Close any open programs by highlighting a program and then clicking the End Task button (do not close Explorer). Close one application at a time. Then try your Jaz drive again. Repeat this process until the problem is resolved. Once the problem is resolved, the last application that was closed is the one causing the conflict. You may be able to patch or update the offending program. As an alternative, you may be able to uninstall and reinstall the Iomega Tools software or the current version of IomegaWare software.

**SYMPTOM 31-73**    **You receive an error such as "ASPI for Win32 not installed" when working with a SCSI Jaz drive**    This error message is known to occur while trying to install the IomegaWare software under Windows 9x/Me, and is caused by a conflict with the MSWHEEL application (which is part of Microsoft IntelliMouse Pro). The MSWHEEL software controls the functionality of the wheel on the mouse. Start by closing the MSWHEEL application:

1. Open the Close Program dialog box by pressing CTRL-ALT-DEL.
2. Highlight the MSWHEEL application by clicking Mswheel.
3. Click the End Task button to close the application.

Now manually install the Iomega SCSI driver in Windows 9x/Me:

1. Insert the IomegaWare CD into your CD-ROM drive. If the installation begins automatically, cancel the installation process.
2. Click Start | Settings | Control Panel.
3. Double-click Add New Hardware from the Control Panel.
4. Click the Next button to start the installation process.
5. If you're prompted to have Windows search for new hardware, choose No.
6. Choose SCSI Controllers from the Hardware Types list, and then click Next.
7. Choose Have Disk from the next screen.
8. From the "Install from disk" prompt, click the Browse button.
9. From the Drives drop-down list, choose the drive letter of your CD-ROM drive.
10. From the Folders list, double-click the w9xstuff folder and select OK twice.
11. In the Models list, choose the driver for the Zip or Jaz drive you are installing.
12. After highlighting the driver, select Next and click Finish.
13. Restart your computer.

Finally, install the IomegaWare software manually:

1. Click Start, and then Run.
2. Click Browse. In the Browse dialog box, highlight your CD-ROM drive by clicking it in the Look In drop-down box.
3. Highlight the file setup.exe and click the Open button.
4. In the Open box (after the path and file name), type a space and then /N. This will prevent GUEST from running during the installation.
5. Follow the prompts to complete the installation of your IomegaWare software.

**SYMPTOM 31-74**    **You receive an "INST30" error with your Jaz disk under Windows 9x/Me**    When you attempt to install IomegaWare software, you may receive the following error message: "INST30—this application performed an illegal operation and will be shut down." In virtually all cases, the problem is due to a software conflict or corruption. Start by closing any background software.

Open the Close Program dialog box by pressing CTRL-ALT-DEL. Close each application (one at a time) by highlighting an application and clicking the End Task button. Remember not to close Explorer or Systray. If the error disappears, the last program to be closed was responsible for the error. You may need to stop using that software while installing the Iomega software (or the Jaz drive). In some cases, you may be able to patch or update the offending software. If the problem persists, you may need to remove and/or reinstall the IomegaWare software from its installation CD, or download and install the latest version of IomegaWare from the Iomega Web site.

**SYMPTOM 31-75**    **You get an error such as "Disk not in the drive" when using IomegaWare 2.0 under Windows 9x/Me**    This type of trouble seems to occur under Windows 9x/Me—it doesn't appear to occur under Windows XP. If you receive the error message "Disk not in the drive" when a disk is actually inserted in the drive, it may be that the disk has been read/write-protected. Double-check your Jaz drive to be sure a Jaz disk is inserted. Eject the disk and reinsert it to ensure that it is positioned properly. Also try several different disks. If no disks are detected, the drive may be defective. If only one disk is causing the problem (and the following steps don't help), the disk itself may be defective.

If the problem persists, check the read/write protection status on the Jaz disk. If the disk is protected, it may not respond until it is unprotected. Make sure that the Jaz disk is inserted properly in the drive. Locate and click the Iomega drive icon where the disk is inserted. If you don't have an IomegaWare shortcut on your desktop, click Start | Programs | Iomega, and then double-click the IomegaWare icon. From the pop-up menu, choose Properties, located at the bottom of the list. In the dialog area labeled Disk is a padlock symbol, which will indicate whether the disk has been protected or locked. If the padlock is displayed as closed (or locked), the disk has been protected using the read/write protection tool.

If you have forgotten the password, you will be given the option to perform a "long format" on the disk. Performing a long format on the Jaz disk will erase all information.

If the Jaz disk IS protected, you'll need to unlock the read/write-protected disk now. Locate and click the Iomega drive icon where the disk is inserted. If you don't have an IomegaWare shortcut on your desktop, click Start | Programs | Iomega, and then double-click the IomegaWare icon. From the pop-up menu, select Properties. Click the Change button in the Disk section. In the Unprotect window, type the password for the disk and click OK.

An option within the Unprotect window allows you to remove the read/write protection *temporarily*. Checking this option will allow you to access the disk in that session, but once the disk is ejected, it will be read/write-protected again.

**SYMPTOM 31-76**    **The Jaz drive fails to spin up**    This is a surprisingly common problem that can be caused by three issues. First check the drive's power connections. If the drive is not receiving adequate power, it will not spin up a Jaz disk. If the drive is external, you may need to replace the Jaz drive's power adapter. The disk itself may also be at fault. Make sure that the disk is inserted properly and securely (you may need to eject and reinsert the disk). Also try a new disk. If a new disk works, the original disk may be damaged or defective. Finally, boot the system clean from a floppy disk and try the drive/disk again from the GUEST utility under DOS. If the problem clears, there may be some DOS (or Windows) utility software that is conflicting with the disk. If a clean boot fails to clear the problem, the Jaz drive itself may be defective.

**SYMPTOM 31-77** **The Jaz drive will not format a disk** In many cases, this occurs when the Jaz disk is read/write-protected, so you'll need to verify that the disk is not protected. Open My Computer, right-click the Jaz drive, and select Protect. In the Disk Protect Options dialog box, choose Remove Protection. If the disk is password-protected you must supply the password used to initially write-protect the disk before removing the protection.

If the disk is not protected, you should try several different disks. If other unprotected Jaz disks format normally, the original disk is probably defective. If the problem continues with more than one disk, try a clean DOS boot and enable the drive using the GUEST utility. If problems disappear with other disks, you're probably getting software interference from one or more TSRs or drivers on the system. If the problem persists on any disk (even after booting the system clean), the Jaz drive may be defective.

**SYMPTOM 31-78** **The computer locks up after running parallel port accelerator software** This problem may occur after installing the parallel port driver and then running the Parallel Port Accelerator utility. Running the Parallel Port Accelerator utility will sometimes cause the drive not to work (or even cause the system to lock up during boot). Turn off the PC, disconnect the drive, and try rebooting the computer with the drive's signal cable disconnected. The system will almost certainly boot normally. Now remove the system changes made by your Parallel Port Accelerator software:

1. Open the Device Manager.
2. Click the plus (+) sign next to SCSI controllers.
3. Double-click Iomega Parallel Port Interface.
4. Click the Settings tab.
5. Remove all the information from the Adapter Settings box.
6. Click OK, and then click OK again.
7. Click Yes when prompted to restart your computer.

**SYMPTOM 31-79** **You cannot "long format" a 1GB Jaz disk in a 2GB Jaz drive** The internal read/write heads on a 2GB Jaz drive are different from those on a 1GB Jaz drive. A short format will work correctly on the 1GB Jaz disk, but a long format will fail. Use only a 1GB Jaz drive to perform a long format on a 1GB Jaz disk.

**SYMPTOM 31-80** **The Jaz drive makes a grinding noise when reading or writing to a disk** This is a very serious symptom that may indicate a mechanical problem with the drive. Carefully eject and reinsert the Jaz disk. Do not try another disk in the drive. If the drive is defective, it may cause damage to other Jaz disks. Immediately eject the disk if the grinding noise begins again. If the noise returns, try the disk on another Jaz drive. If the disk is readable on another Jaz drive (and there is no grinding nose), chances are that the original Jaz drive is defective and should be replaced.

# Further Study

**Exabyte** www.exabyte.com
**Fuji (for Zip media)** www.fujifilm.com
**Imation (for disk media)** www.imation.com
**Iomega** www.iomega.com
**SyQuest** www.syquest.com

# 32

# SCSI SYSTEMS AND TROUBLESHOOTING

**P**C designers have always sought ways to connect more devices to fewer cables, and achieve faster data transfer between the system and its peripheral devices. In the early 1980s, it became clear that a more versatile and intelligent interface would be needed to overcome the myriad proprietary interfaces appearing at the time. By 1986, PC designers responded with the introduction of the *Small Computer System Interface* (SCSI, pronounced "scuzzy"). SCSI proved to be a revolution for PC power users, because a single adapter could operate a number of unique devices simultaneously, all daisy-chained to the same signal cable. Whereas "low-end" PCs needed one adapter for hard drives, one adapter for the CD-ROM, another adapter for a tape drive, and so on, a system fitted with a SCSI adapter (such as the Adaptec card shown in Figure 32-1) could handle all of these devices (and more) and achieve data throughputs that other interfaces of the day couldn't begin to approach.

**FIGURE  32-1**   An Adaptec 39160 dual-channel Ultra160 SCSI adapter (Courtesy of Adaptec)

Today's PC industry has changed. Proprietary interfaces have been essentially abandoned in favor of the standardized interfaces (such as UDMA/100 and UDMA/133 for internal devices, as well as USB 1.1, 2.0, and FireWire for external devices), and these standard interface schemes now support a variety of devices while offering low cost and performance levels rivaling traditional SCSI. Yet, SCSI has endured and evolved, and it remains the interface of choice for multitasking, servers, and other high-end computer systems. This chapter will provide an overview of the SCSI interface, cover the essential installation and setup of a SCSI host adapter, and show you how to deal with the most important troubleshooting problems.

# Understanding SCSI Concepts

Ideally, peripheral devices should be *independent* of the microprocessor's operation. The computer should only have to send commands and data to the peripheral and then wait for the peripheral to respond. Printers work this way. The parallel and serial ports are actually *device-level* interfaces. The computer is unconcerned with *which* device is attached to the port. In other words, you can take a printer built 12 years ago and connect it to a new AMD Athlon-based system, and the printer will work just fine because only data and commands are being sent across the interface. This is a simple example of the concept behind SCSI. Computers and peripherals can be designed, developed, and integrated without worrying about hardware compatibility—such compatibility is established entirely by the SCSI interface.

## DEVICE INDEPENDENCE

From a practical standpoint, SCSI is both a *bus,* an organization of physical wires and terminations, where each wire has its own name and purpose, and a *command set,* a limited set of instructions that allows the computer and peripherals to communicate over that physical bus. The SCSI bus is used in systems that want to achieve device independence. For example, all hard disk drives look alike to the SCSI interface (except for their total capacity), all optical drives look alike, all printers look alike, and so on. For any particular type of SCSI device, you should be able to replace an existing device with another device without any system modifications, and new SCSI devices can often be added to the bus with little more than a driver upgrade. Since the intelligence of SCSI resides in the peripheral device itself and *not* in the computer, the computer is able to employ a small set of standard commands to accomplish data transfer back and forth to the peripheral.

# SCSI VARIATIONS

At this point, let's take a look at the evolution of the SCSI interface and examine the ways in which it has evolved and proliferated. SCSI began life in 1979 when Shugart Associates (PC "old timers" might remember it as one of the first PC hard drive makers) released its Shugart Associates Systems Interface (SASI) standard. The X3T9.2 committee was formed by ANSI in 1982 to develop the SASI standard, which was renamed SCSI. SCSI drives and interfaces that were developed under the evolving X3T9.2 SCSI standard were known as SCSI-1, though the actual SCSI-1 standard (ANSI X3.131-1986) didn't become official until 1986. SCSI-1 provided a system-level 8-bit bus (referred to as *narrow*) that could operate up to eight devices and transfer data at up to 5 MB/s. However, the delay in standardization led to a lot of configuration and compatibility problems with SCSI-1 setups. Table 32-1 compares the specifications of each SCSI standard.

 Although SCSI-1 was supposed to support all SCSI devices, manufacturers took liberties with the evolving standard. This frequently led to installation and compatibility problems between SCSI-1 devices that, theoretically, should have worked together perfectly. Today, all obsolete SCSI-1 adapters should be upgraded to SCSI-3 installations.

Earlier in 1986 (even before the SCSI-1 standard was ratified), work started on the SCSI-2 standard, which was intended to overcome many of the speed and compatibility problems encountered with SCSI-1. By 1994, ANSI approved the SCSI-2 standard (X3.131-1994). SCSI-2 was designed to be backward compatible with SCSI-1, but SCSI-2 also provided for several variations. Fast SCSI-2 (or Fast SCSI) doubles the SCSI bus clock speed and allows 10 MB/s data transfers across the 8-bit SCSI data bus. Wide SCSI-2 (or Wide SCSI), which also doubles the original data transfer rate to 10 MB/s, uses a 16-bit data bus instead of the original 8-bit data bus (the SCSI clock is left unchanged). To support the larger data bus, Wide SCSI uses a 68-pin cable instead of the traditional 50-pin cable. Wide SCSI can also support up to 16 SCSI devices. Designers then combined the attributes of fast and wide operation to create Fast Wide

**TABLE 32-1    COMPARISON OF SCSI CONVENTIONS**

| TERMS | NAME | MHZ | BUS WIDTH | MB/S | MBIT/S |
|---|---|---|---|---|---|
| SCSI-1 | SCSI-1 | 5 | 8 | 5 | 40 |
| Fast SCSI | SCSI-2 | 10 | 8 | 10 | 80 |
| Fast-Wide SCSI | SCSI-2/ SCSI-3 | 10 | 16 | 20 | 160 |
| Ultra SCSI | SCSI-3 | 20 | 8 | 20 | 160 |
| Ultra-Wide SCSI | SCSI-3 | 20 | 16 | 40 | 320 |
| Ultra2 SCSI | SCSI-4 | 40 | 8 | 40 | 320 |
| Ultra2-Wide SCSI | SCSI-4 | 40 | 16 | 80 | 640 |
| Ultra3 SCSI | Ultra 160 | 40*2[1] | 8 | 80 | 640 |
| Ultra3-Wide SCSI | Ultra 160 | 40*2[1] | 16 | 160 | 1280 |
| Ultra4 SCSI | Ultra 320 | 80*2 | 8 | 160 | 1280 |
| Ultra4-Wide SCSI | Ultra 320 | 80*2 | 16 | 320 | 2560 |

[1] Ultra3 features the same base frequency as Ultra2 (40 MHz), but transmits 2 bytes per data clock, thus doubling the total throughput.

SCSI-2 (or Fast Wide SCSI), which supports 20 MB/s data transfers across a 16-bit data bus. Whenever you see references to Fast SCSI, Wide SCSI, or Fast Wide SCSI, you're *always* dealing with a SCSI-2 implementation.

But SCSI advancement didn't stop at SCSI-2. ANSI began development of the SCSI-3 standard in 1993 (even before SCSI-2 was adopted). SCSI-3 is intended to be backward compatible with SCSI-2 and SCSI-1 devices, and many SCSI devices and controllers are using the advances offered by SCSI-3 development. These typical SCSI-3 devices are generally known as Fast-20 SCSI (or Ultra SCSI-3, also termed Ultra SCSI). Ultra SCSI uses a 20 MHz SCSI bus clock with an 8-bit data bus to achieve 20 MB/s data transfers. By using a 16-bit data bus, SCSI-3 offers Wide Fast-20 SCSI (or Ultra Wide SCSI-3, also termed Ultra Wide SCSI), which handles 40 MB/s data transfers.

SCSI development continued with the SCSI-4 implementations. The SCSI-4 standard covers Fast-40 SCSI (called Ultra2 SCSI-4 and Ultra2 SCSI) using a 40 MHz bus clock to provide 40 MB/s data transfers with an 8-bit data bus. The 16-bit data bus version is known as Wide Fast-40 SCSI (also called Ultra2 Wide SCSI-4 or Ultra2 Wide SCSI), which is supposed to support 80 MB/s data transfers. Whenever you see references to Ultra2 or Fast-40, you're almost certain to be faced with a SCSI-4 setup.

SCSI advances have continued. The Ultra3 SCSI standard (a.k.a. Ultra160) employs a 40 MHz bus clock that is "double-transitioned." This feature allows twice the effective data transfer on the same 40 MHz clock, yielding data transfers up to 80 MB/s. The Ultra3 Wide SCSI standard offers 16 data bits rather than 8. On the same double-transitioned 40 MHz clock, Ultra3 Wide SCSI can achieve data transfers up to 160 MB/s. While Ultra360 (Ultra4) SCSI standards are still in their infancy, you can be sure that even faster SCSI implementations are on the horizon.

Also keep in mind that SCSI has traditionally been a *parallel* bus—that is, 8 or 16 bits of data are transferred at a time across parallel data lines. SCSI-3 is proposing three new *serial* connection schemes. You'll see these referred to as Serial Storage Architecture (SSA), FibreChannel, and IEEE 1394 (a.k.a. FireWire or i.LINK). FireWire has been embraced as a high-speed external connection scheme for the PC, and FireWire ports can easily be added through the addition of a PCI expansion card (if there are no FireWire ports already integrated into the motherboard). These serial schemes will offer faster data transfers than their parallel bus cousins offer, but they are not backward compatible with SCSI-2 or SCSI-1.

# SINGLE-ENDED AND DIFFERENTIAL

The signal wiring used in a SCSI bus has a definite impact on bus performance. Two wiring techniques are generally used for SCSI: single-ended and differential. Both wiring schemes have advantages and disadvantages.

The *single-ended* (SE) wiring technique is just as the name implies—a single wire carries the particular signal from initiator to target. Each signal requires only one wire. Terminating resistors at each end of the cable help to maintain acceptable signal levels. A common ground (return) provides the reference for all single-ended signals. Unfortunately, single-ended circuitry is not very noise resistant, so single-ended cabling is generally limited to about 6 meters at data transfer speeds of 5MHz or less. At higher data transfer speeds, cable length can be as short as 1.5 meters. In spite of the disadvantages, single-ended operation is simple and popular because of its simplicity.

Many SCSI implementations on the PC will employ single-ended (SE) SCSI interfaces.

The *differential* (DIF) wiring approach uses *two* wires for each signal (instead of one wire referenced to a common ground). A differential signal offers excellent noise resistance because it does not rely on a common ground. This allows much longer cables (up to 25 meters) and higher-speed operation (10 MHz).

An array of pull-up resistors at each end of the cable help to ensure signal integrity. The problem with differential wiring is that it is more complicated than single-ended interfaces.

Low-voltage differential (or LVD) SCSI is an emerging standard defined in the SPI-2 document of SCSI-3 that runs on 3.3Vdc rather than 5Vdc. The goal of LVD is to allow higher data rates while combining the benefits of single-ended and differential SCSI bus schemes. LVD is less sensitive to electromagnetic noise and allows high data rates at greater cable lengths than a single-ended bus. LVD is the interface specified for use with Ultra-2 SCSI and Ultra160/m specifications. Although LVD is not directly compatible with single-ended wiring, the devices will use multimode driver circuits that automatically detect the type of bus used and switch to the appropriate mode of operation. This allows you to use an LVD/SE device on a single-ended bus without having to set any switches or jumpers. Therefore, LVD has been introduced gradually without the upgrade or replacing single-ended devices. Still, the advantages of LVD are lost when an LVD/SE device is used in a single-ended bus—as soon as one single-ended device is connected to LVD/SE bus, the whole bus switches to single-ended mode (with all its limitations).

## BUS LENGTH

As you're already aware, SCSI devices are daisy-chained together with a 50-pin or 68-pin cable. The total length of this cable makes up the overall SCSI bus. When there are only *internal* SCSI devices, the bus length is measured from the SCSI host adapter to the last internal SCSI device on the chain (the terminated device). When there are only *external* SCSI devices, the bus length is measured from the SCSI host adapter to the last external SCSI device on the chain (it should also be terminated). When there are *both* internal and external SCSI devices, the bus length is measured from the last external device to the last internal device. There are finite limits on the length of your SCSI bus. As SCSI implementations have become faster over the years, that effective bus length has shortened. Table 32-2 illustrates the maximum SCSI bus lengths for single-ended, differential, and low-voltage differential (LVD) signaling approaches.

**TABLE 32-2    MAXIMUM SCSI BUS LENGTHS**

| TERMS | SINGLE-ENDED | DIFFERENTIAL | LVD |
|---|---|---|---|
| SCSI-1 | 6m | 25m | 12m[2] |
| Fast SCSI | 3m | 25m | 12m[2] |
| Fast Wide SCSI | 3m | 25m | 12m[2] |
| Ultra SCSI | 1.5m–3m | Up to 25m | Up to 12m |
| Wide Ultra SCSI | Up to 3m | Up to 25m | Up to 12m |
| Ultra2 SCSI | [1] | 25m | 12m |
| Wide Ultra2 SCSI | [1] | 25m | 12m |
| Ultra3 SCSI | [1] | 25m | 12m |
| Wide Ultra3 SCSI | [1] | 25m | 12m |
| Ultra4 SCSI | [1] | 25m | 12m |
| Wide Ultra4 SCSI | [1] | 25m | 12m |

[1] Single-ended and high-powered differential are not defined at Ultra2 and Ultra3 speeds.

[2] Only if all devices on the bus support LVD.

# INITIATORS AND TARGETS

There are basically two types of devices on the SCSI bus: initiators and targets. An *initiator* starts communication when something has to be done, and a *target* responds to the initiator's commands. The important thing for you to understand here is that this master/slave relationship is not a one-way arrangement. An initiator may become a target at some point in the data transfer cycle, and the target may become the initiator at other points. A SCSI bus can support up to eight devices simultaneously, but there *must* be at least one initiator and one target in the system. A SCSI *host adapter* card is typically the initiator, and all other devices (such as hard drives or CD-ROMs) are usually targets, but that is not necessarily the only possible scenario.

# SYNCHRONOUS AND ASYNCHRONOUS

As a system-level interface, SCSI requires an operating *handshaking protocol* that organizes the transfer of data from a sending point to a requesting point. There are typically three handshaking protocols for SCSI: asynchronous, synchronous, and fast synchronous. The *asynchronous* protocol works rather like a parallel port. Each byte must be requested and acknowledged before the next byte can be sent. Asynchronous operation generally results in very reliable (but slow) performance. *Synchronous* and *fast synchronous* operations both ignore the request/acknowledge handshake for data transfer only. This allows slightly faster operation than an asynchronous protocol, but a certain fixed amount of time delay (sometimes called an *offset*) must be allowed for request and acknowledge timing. The fast synchronous protocol uses slightly shorter signals, resulting in even faster speed. An important point to remember is that SCSI systems can typically use any of these three protocols as desired. The actual protocol that is used must be mutually agreed to by the initiator and the target through their communications. SCSI systems normally initialize in an asynchronous protocol.

# DISCONNECT AND RECONNECT

Allowing a target to operate offline while the initiator is occupied elsewhere would be desirable in several situations, such as at tape rewind time. An important feature of SCSI is the ability to logically *disconnect* two communicating devices, and then *reconnect* them again later. Disconnect and reconnect operations allow several different operations to occur simultaneously in the system, and are the main reasons why SCSI architecture is so desirable in a multitasking environment. It is up to the initiator to grant a disconnect privilege to a target.

# TERMINATORS

When high-frequency signals are transmitted over adjacent wires, signals tend to degrade and interfere with one another over the length of the cable. This is a very normal and relatively well understood electrical phenomenon. In the PC, SCSI signal integrity is enhanced by using powered resistors at each end of the data cable to "pull up" active signals. Most high-frequency signal cables in the PC are already terminated by built-in pull-up resistors at drives and controller cards. The small resistor array is known as a *terminator*. Since there is a distinct limit to the number of devices that can be added to a floppy drive or IDE cable, designers have never made a big deal about termination—they just added the resistors, and that was it. With SCSI, however, up to eight devices can be added to the bus cable. The SCSI cable also must be terminated, but the location of terminating resistors depends on which devices are added to the bus, and *where* they are placed. As a result, termination is a much more vital element of SCSI setup and troubleshooting. Poor or incorrect termination can cause intermittent signal problems. Here are some general guidelines for termination.

SCSI cabling and termination is discussed in the section "Cabling and Termination" later in the chapter.

■ The last device in a SCSI chain (cable) must be terminated. For an internal installation, the SCSI host adapter and last (end-most) internal device must be terminated, and other devices must be unterminated. For an external installation, the SCSI host adapter and last (end-most) external device must be terminated. For an internal/external installation, the SCSI host adapter is normally unterminated, and the end-most internal and external SCSI devices are terminated.

■ Internal Ultra160 and Ultra2 SCSI devices (such as drives) come from the factory with termination **disabled** and cannot be changed. The built-in terminator at the end of the 68-pin internal LVD SCSI cable provides proper termination for these internal devices.

■ Termination on Wide SCSI, Narrow SCSI, and Ultra SCSI devices usually is controlled by manually setting a jumper or a switch on the device, or by physically removing or installing one or more resistor modules on the device—this is the "traditional" means of selecting terminators.

■ Termination on most external SCSI devices is controlled by installing or removing a SCSI terminator block on the last device's passthrough port. However, termination on some external SCSI devices is enabled or disabled by setting a switch on the back of the SCSI device.

■ By default, termination on the Adaptec SCSI host adapter card is set to Automatic (the preferred method). This means the card will be terminated or unterminated as it deems necessary. Most SCSI host adapter manufacturers recommend that you do not change this default setting.

Termination is typically either active or passive. Basically, *passive* termination consists of simply plugging a resistor pack into a SCSI device. Passive resistors are powered by the TERMPWR line. Passive termination is simple and effective over short distances (up to about 1 meter) and usually works just fine for the cable lengths inside a PC, but can be a drawback over longer distances. *Active* terminators provide their own regulated power sources, which makes them most effective for longer cables (such as those found in external SCSI devices like page scanners) or Wide SCSI systems. Most SCSI-2 and later implementations use active terminators. A variation on active termination is *forced perfect termination* (FPT), which includes diode clamps that prevent signal overshoot and undershoot. This makes FPT effective for long SCSI cable lengths.

## SCSI IDS AND LUNS

A typical SCSI bus will support up to eight devices, called *logical units*, and these devices are each identified using an ID. This means each device on the bus must have its own unique ID number (0–7). If two devices use the same ID, there will be a conflict. IDs are typically set on the SCSI adapter and each SCSI device using jumpers or DIP switches (see Figure 32-2). Typically, the SCSI adapter is set for ID7, the primary SCSI hard drive is set to ID0, and a second SCSI hard drive is ID1. Other devices can usually be placed anywhere from ID2 to ID6. Wide (16-bit) SCSI bus implementations can support up to 16 devices with IDs from 0 to 15. The Adaptec 39160 provides two 16-bit channels, so it can support up to 30 SCSI devices—

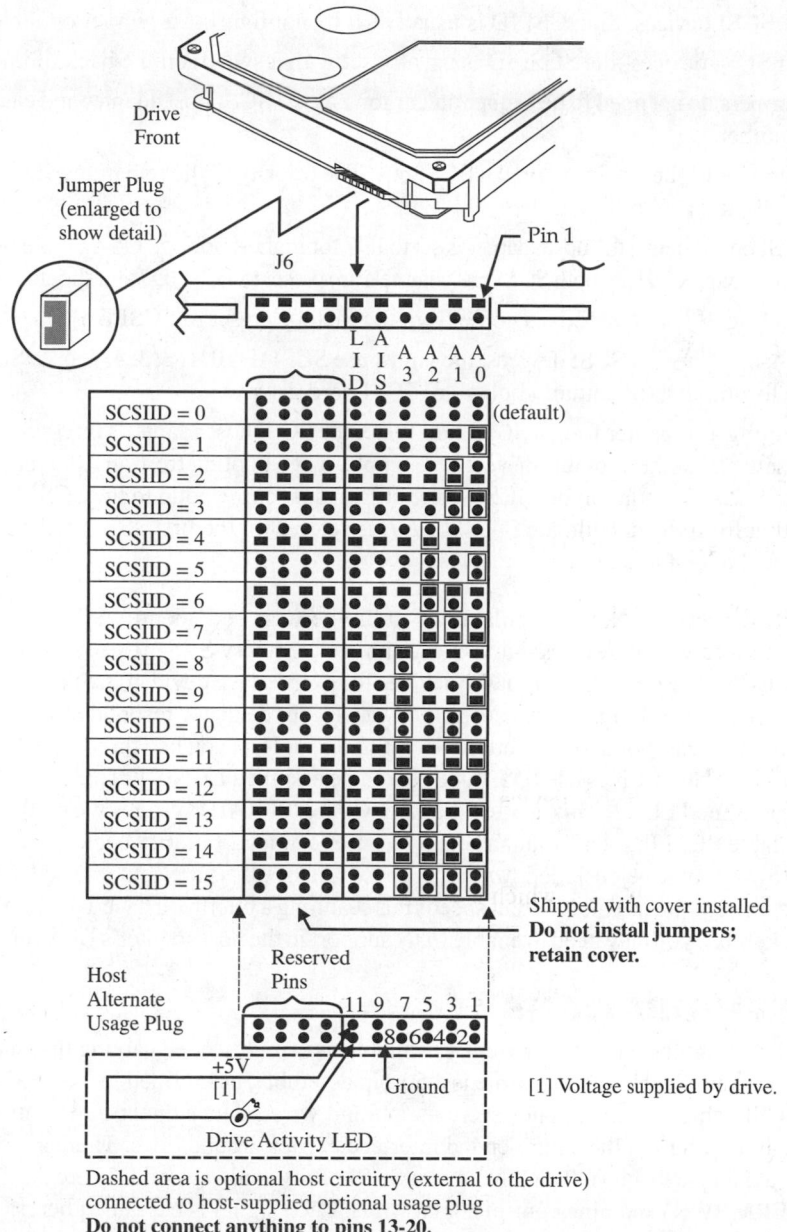

**FIGURE  32-2**     Setting a SCSI ID jumper (Courtesy of Seagate)

two 16-bit channels offer 32 IDs, minus one ID for the controller of each channel, leaving 30 available IDs. Here are some general guidelines for SCSI IDs.

- For internal SCSI devices, the SCSI ID is usually set by configuring a jumper on the device.

- For external SCSI devices, the SCSI ID is usually set with a switch on the back of the device.

- SCSI ID numbers do not need to be sequential, as long as the SCSI host adapter and each device use a **different** number.

- SCSI ID 7 has the **highest** priority on the SCSI bus. The priority of the remaining IDs (in descending order) is 6 to 0, then 15 to 8.

- On most SCSI bus systems, the host adapter is set to ID7 for highest priority. On multiple SCSI bus adapters such as the Adaptec 39160, both SCSI bus channels are preset to SCSI ID7 and should not be changed.

- Most internal SCSI hard disk drives come from the factory preset to SCSI ID0.

- If you have 8-bit (Narrow) SCSI devices, they must use SCSI IDs 0, 1, 2, 3, 4, 5, or 6. SCSI ID0 is recommended for the first (potentially bootable) SCSI hard drive.

- If you're booting a computer from a SCSI hard drive, the SCSI host adapter's internal setup must usually list the same ID as the bootable drive. For example, when booting from an Adaptec 39160 controller, the *Boot SCSI ID* setting in the SCSISelect utility must correspond to the SCSI ID of the device you're booting from. By default, the *Boot SCSI ID* is set to 0 for the first SCSI hard drive. You generally need not change this setting.

Logical unit numbers (LUNs) are similar to SCSI IDs because both identify SCSI devices. However, LUNs indicate devices within devices—divisions within IDs. Every SCSI ID from 0–7 can have up to eight LUNs (64 LUNs in SCSI-3), or eight subdevices for every given device ID. Suppose you needed to use more than eight devices on a SCSI bus. You could cause your device to respond to a SCSI ID, and have each device using the ID respond to a different LUN. For example, if you had three hard drives E:, F:, and G:, you could have all three drives use ID2, but E: could be assigned LUN0, F: could be assigned LUN1, and G: could be assigned LUN2. This is often the case with SCSI RAID systems where there are far more drives than available SCSI IDs. Unfortunately, a SCSI user cannot arbitrarily decide to use LUN assignments—the hardware must be designed for that purpose. Also, LUNs are seldom used, and many SCSI adapters don't check for them. This shortcut speeds bus scanning a bit. If you have a device that uses LUNs (such as a CD jukebox), you may need to enable LUN support in the host adapter's BIOS or device driver.

## BUS CONFIGURATIONS

Most common SCSI implementations currently available use single-ended cabling that supports an 8-bit data bus (known as an A-cable). An A-cable is a 50-pin assembly, as outlined in Table 32-3. The 50-pin single-ended SCSI cable has three major sections: ground wires, data signals, and control signals. You will notice that at least half of the single-ended interface carries ground lines. There are eight data lines (D0 to D7) and a data parity bit (DPAR). Note that SCSI parity is always odd. There are four terminator power lines (TERMPWR) and nine control signal wires. Each signal is explained here:

- **-C/D (Control/Data; driven by target)**   Allows the target device to select whether it will be returning a command or data to the initiator.

- **-I/O (Input/Output; driven by target)**   Allows the target device to determine whether it will be receiving or sending information along the data bus.

- **-MSG (Message; driven by target)**   Allows the target device to send coded status or error messages back to the initiator during the message portion of the SCSI bus cycle.

■ **-REQ (Request; driven by target)** A data strobe signal that allows a potential target device to obtain data on the bus.

■ **-ACK (Acknowledge; driven by initiator)** A data strobe signal sent in response to the target's REQ signal that informs the target device that it has gained use of the bus.

■ **-BSY (Busy; driven by initiator or target)** Allows a device to inform the bus that the device is currently busy.

■ **-SEL (Select; driven by initiator or target)** A signal used by an initiator to select a target device.

■ **-ATN (Attention; driven by initiator)** A signal produced by the initiator that informs the target that the initiator has a message ready. The target should switch to the message phase.

■ **-RST (Reset; driven by initiator or target)** A strobe signal that triggers a bus-wide reset of all devices. Usually, only one device produces a reset signal.

**TABLE 32-3** PINOUT OF A STANDARD SINGLE-ENDED A-CABLE

| SIGNAL | PIN | PIN | SIGNAL |
|--------|-----|-----|--------|
| Ground | 1 | 2 | Data 0 |
| Ground | 3 | 4 | Data 1 |
| Ground | 5 | 6 | Data 2 |
| Ground | 7 | 8 | Data 3 |
| Ground | 9 | 10 | Data 4 |
| Ground | 11 | 12 | Data 5 |
| Ground | 13 | 14 | Data 6 |
| Ground | 15 | 16 | Data 7 |
| Ground | 17 | 18 | Data Parity |
| Ground | 19 | 20 | Ground |
| Ground | 21 | 22 | Ground |
| Reserved | 23 | 24 | Reserved |
| Open | 25 | 26 | TERMPWR |
| Reserved | 27 | 28 | Reserved |
| Ground | 29 | 30 | Ground |
| Ground | 31 | 32 | -ATN |
| Ground | 33 | 34 | Ground |
| Ground | 35 | 36 | -BSY |
| Ground | 37 | 38 | -ACK |
| Ground | 39 | 40 | -RST |
| Ground | 41 | 42 | -MSG |
| Ground | 43 | 44 | -SEL |
| Ground | 45 | 46 | -C/D |
| Ground | 47 | 48 | -REQ |
| Ground | 49 | 50 | -I/O |

The differential SCSI interface replaces most of the ground wires with + signal leads. For example, pin 2 represents +D0, while pin 27 is -D0. These + and - signal pairs are the differential signals. Note that there are still a few ground wires, but the grounds are not related to differential signals as they are to single-ended signals. Just about all of the data and control signals in the differential interface serve an identical purpose in the single-ended interface, but you will notice that the signal locations have been rearranged, as shown in Table 32-4. There is one additional differential signal: the DIFFSENS (Differential Sense) line, which provides an active high-enable for differential drivers. Keep in mind that plugging a differential cable into a single-ended interface (or vice versa) can damage the device, the SCSI adapter, or both.

As you might imagine, Wide (16-bit) SCSI implementations will not work with A-cables. A 16-bit cable is needed. Early implementations of Wide SCSI used a second cable to provide the extra signal lines, but this approach was quickly abandoned in favor of a single cable assembly (called a P-cable). The single-ended P-cable is shown in Table 32-5 (see Figure 32-3). While many of the signals may look familiar,

**TABLE 32-4     PINOUT OF A STANDARD DIFFERENTIAL A-CABLE**

| SIGNAL | PIN | PIN | SIGNAL |
|---|---|---|---|
| Ground | 1 | 2 | Ground |
| +Data 0 | 3 | 4 | -Data 0 |
| +Data 1 | 5 | 6 | -Data 1 |
| +Data 2 | 7 | 8 | -Data 2 |
| +Data 3 | 9 | 10 | -Data 3 |
| +Data 4 | 11 | 12 | -Data 4 |
| +Data 5 | 13 | 14 | -Data 5 |
| +Data 6 | 15 | 16 | -Data 6 |
| +Data 7 | 17 | 18 | -Data 7 |
| +Data Parity | 19 | 20 | -Data Parity |
| DIFFSENS | 21 | 22 | Ground |
| Reserved | 23 | 24 | Reserved |
| TERMPWR | 25 | 26 | TERMPWR |
| Reserved | 27 | 28 | Reserved |
| +ATN | 29 | 30 | -ATN |
| Ground | 31 | 32 | Ground |
| +BSY | 33 | 34 | -BSY |
| +ACK | 35 | 36 | -ACK |
| +RST | 37 | 38 | -RST |
| +MSG | 39 | 40 | -MSG |
| +SEL | 41 | 42 | -SEL |
| +C/D | 43 | 44 | -C/D |
| +REQ | 45 | 46 | -REQ |
| +I/O | 47 | 48 | -I/O |
| Ground | 49 | 50 | Ground |

## TABLE 32-5 PINOUT OF A STANDARD SINGLE-ENDED P-CABLE

| SIGNAL | PIN | PIN | SIGNAL |
|--------|-----|-----|--------|
| Ground | 1 | 35 | Data 12 |
| Ground | 2 | 36 | Data 13 |
| Ground | 3 | 37 | Data 14 |
| Ground | 4 | 38 | Data 15 |
| Ground | 5 | 39 | Data Parity 1 |
| Ground | 6 | 40 | Data 0 |
| Ground | 7 | 41 | Data 1 |
| Ground | 8 | 42 | Data 2 |
| Ground | 9 | 43 | Data 3 |
| Ground | 10 | 44 | Data 4 |
| Ground | 11 | 45 | Data 5 |
| Ground | 12 | 46 | Data 6 |
| Ground | 13 | 47 | Data 7 |
| Ground | 14 | 48 | Data Parity 0 |
| Ground | 15 | 49 | Ground |
| Ground | 16 | 50 | Ground |
| TERMPWR | 17 | 51 | TERMPWR |
| TERMPWR | 18 | 52 | TERMPWR |
| Reserved | 19 | 53 | Reserved |
| Ground | 20 | 54 | Ground |
| Ground | 21 | 55 | -ATN |
| Ground | 22 | 56 | Ground |
| Ground | 23 | 57 | -BSY |
| Ground | 24 | 58 | -ACK |
| Ground | 25 | 59 | -RST |
| Ground | 26 | 60 | -MSG |
| Ground | 27 | 61 | -SEL |
| Ground | 28 | 62 | -C/D |
| Ground | 29 | 63 | -REQ |
| Ground | 30 | 64 | -I/O |
| Ground | 31 | 65 | Data 8 |
| Ground | 32 | 66 | Data 9 |
| Ground | 33 | 67 | Data 10 |
| Ground | 34 | 68 | Data 11 |

notice that there are 68 pins instead of 50—primarily to support the eight additional data lines (D8 to D15). Control lines are identical to those in the A-cable.

Table 32-6 shows the pinout for a differential 68-pin P-cable. The 80-pin implementation for a SCSI cable (called SCA-2) is listed in Table 32-7.

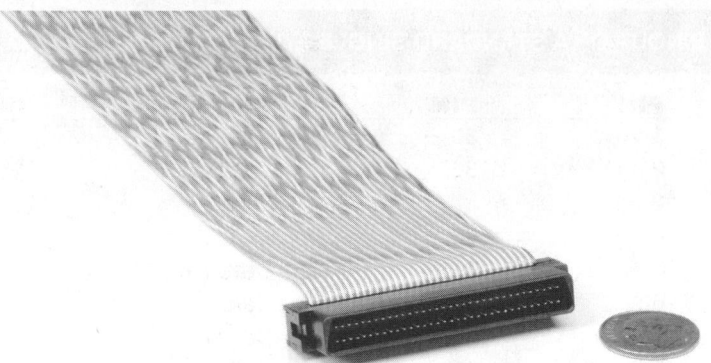

**FIGURE  32-3**   A typical internal 68-pin SCSI ribbon cable (Courtesy of Adaptec)

**TABLE 32-6    PINOUT OF A STANDARD DIFFERENTIAL P-CABLE**

| SIGNAL | PIN | PIN | SIGNAL |
|---|---|---|---|
| +Data 12 | 1 | 35 | -Data 12 |
| +Data 13 | 2 | 36 | -Data 13 |
| +Data 14 | 3 | 37 | -Data 14 |
| +Data 15 | 4 | 38 | -Data 15 |
| +Data Parity 1 | 5 | 39 | -Data Parity 1 |
| Ground | 6 | 40 | Ground |
| +Data 0 | 7 | 41 | -Data 0 |
| +Data 1 | 8 | 42 | -Data 1 |
| +Data 2 | 9 | 43 | -Data 2 |
| +Data 3 | 10 | 44 | -Data 3 |
| +Data 4 | 11 | 45 | -Data 4 |
| +Data 5 | 12 | 46 | -Data 5 |
| +Data 6 | 13 | 47 | -Data 6 |
| +Data 7 | 14 | 48 | -Data 7 |
| +Data Parity 0 | 15 | 49 | -Data Parity 0 |
| DIFFSENS | 16 | 50 | Ground |
| TERMPWR | 17 | 51 | TERMPWR |
| TERMPWR | 18 | 52 | TERMPWR |
| Reserved | 19 | 53 | Reserved |
| +ATN | 20 | 54 | -ATN |
| Ground | 21 | 55 | Ground |
| +BSY | 22 | 56 | -BSY |
| +ACK | 23 | 27 | -ACK |
| +RST | 24 | 58 | -RST |
| +MSG | 25 | 59 | -MSG |

**TABLE 32-6** PINOUT OF A STANDARD DIFFERENTIAL P-CABLE *(CONTINUED)*

| SIGNAL | PIN | PIN | SIGNAL |
|--------|-----|-----|--------|
| +SEL | 26 | 60 | -SEL |
| +C/D | 27 | 61 | -C/D |
| +REQ | 28 | 62 | -REQ |
| +I/O | 29 | 63 | -I/O |
| Ground | 30 | 64 | Ground |
| +Data | 31 | 65 | -Data |
| +Data | 32 | 66 | -Data |
| +Data | 33 | 67 | -Data |
| +Data | 34 | 68 | -Data |

**TABLE 32-7** 80-PIN SINGLE-ENDED SCSI CABLE PINOUT

| SIGNAL | PIN | PIN | SIGNAL |
|--------|-----|-----|--------|
| +12 Volt | 1 | 41 | 12-Volt GROUND |
| 12 Volt | 2 | 42 | 12-Volt GROUND |
| 12 Volt | 3 | 43 | 12-Volt GROUND |
| 12 Volt | 4 | 44 | 12-Volt GROUND |
| Reserved/NC | 5 | 45 | Reserved/NC |
| Reserved/NC | 6 | 46 | Reserved/NC |
| DB (11) | 7 | 47 | GROUND |
| DB (10) | 8 | 48 | GROUND |
| DB (9) | 9 | 49 | GROUND |
| DB (8) | 10 | 50 | GROUND |
| I/O | 11 | 51 | GROUND |
| REQ | 12 | 52 | GROUND |
| C/D | 13 | 53 | GROUND |
| SEL | 14 | 54 | GROUND |
| MSG | 15 | 55 | GROUND |
| RST | 16 | 56 | GROUND |
| ACK | 17 | 57 | GROUND |
| BSY | 18 | 58 | GROUND |
| ATN | 19 | 59 | GROUND |
| DB (P0) | 20 | 60 | GROUND |
| DB (7) | 21 | 61 | GROUND |
| DB (6) | 22 | 62 | GROUND |
| DB (5) | 23 | 63 | GROUND |
| DB (4) | 24 | 64 | GROUND |
| DB (3) | 25 | 65 | GROUND |
| DB (2) | 26 | 66 | GROUND |

| TABLE 32-7 | 80-PIN SINGLE-ENDED SCSI CABLE PINOUT *(CONTINUED)* | | |
| --- | --- | --- | --- |
| **SIGNAL** | **PIN** | **PIN** | **SIGNAL** |
| DB (1) | 27 | 67 | GROUND |
| DB (0) | 28 | 68 | GROUND |
| DB (P1) | 29 | 69 | GROUND |
| DB (15) | 30 | 70 | GROUND |
| DB (14) | 31 | 71 | GROUND |
| DB (13) | 32 | 72 | GROUND |
| DB (12) | 33 | 73 | GROUND |
| 5 Volt | 34 | 74 | 5-Volt GROUND |
| 5 Volt | 35 | 75 | 5-Volt GROUND |
| 5 Volt | 36 | 76 | 5-Volt GROUND |
| SYNC | 37 | 77 | ACTIVE LED OUT |
| RMT START | 38 | 78 | DLYD START |
| SCSI ID (0) | 39 | 79 | SCSI ID (1) |
| SCSI ID (2) | 40 | 80 | SCSI ID (3) |

# UNDERSTANDING SCSI BUS OPERATION

Now that you have learned about SCSI bus concepts and structure, you can see how the interface behaves during normal operation. Since bus wires are common to every device attached to the bus, a device must obtain permission from all other devices before it can take control of the bus. This attempt to access the bus is called the *arbitration phase*. Once a device (such as the SCSI controller) has won the bus arbitration, it must then make contact with the device to be communicated with. This device selection is known as the *selection phase*. When this contact is established, data transfer can take place. This part of the chapter will detail negotiation and information transfer over the SCSI bus.

## Negotiation

Devices must negotiate to access and use a SCSI bus. Negotiation begins when the bus is free (BSY and SEL lines are idle). A device begins arbitration by activating the BSY line and its own data ID line (data bit D0 to D7, depending on the device). If more than one device tries to control the bus simultaneously, the device with the higher ID line wins. The winning device (an initiator) attempts to acquire a target device by asserting the SEL line and the data ID line (data bit D0 to D7) of the desired device. The BSY line is then released by the initiator, and the desired target device asserts the BSY line to confirm it has been selected. The initiator then releases the SEL and data bus lines. Information transfer can now take place.

## Information

The selected target controls the data being transferred and the direction of transfer. Information transfer lasts until the target device releases the BSY line, thus returning the bus to the idle state. If a piece of information will take a long time to prepare for, the target can end the connection by issuing a *disconnect* message. It will try to reestablish the connection later with a new arbitration and selection procedure.

During information transfer, the initiator tells its target how to act on a command and establishes the mode of data transfer during the *message-out phase*. A specific SCSI command follows the message during the *command phase*. After a command is sent, data transfer takes place during the *data-in* and/or *data-out* phases. The target relinquishes control to the initiator during the command phase. For example, the command itself may ask that more information be transferred. The target then tells the initiator whether the command was successfully completed or not by returning status information during a *status phase*. Finally, the command is finished when the target sends a progress report to the initiator during the *message-in* phase. Consider this simple SCSI communication example:

1. *Bus free phase.* The system is idle.
2. *Arbitration phase.* A device takes control of the bus.
3. *Select phase.* The desired device is selected.
4. *Message-out phase.* The target sets up data transfer.
5. *Command phase.* Commands are exchanged between the target and initiator.
6. *Data-in phase.* Data is exchanged between the target and initiator.
7. *Status phase.* Results of the exchange are reported.
8. *Message-in phase.* Devices report that the exchange is complete.
9. *Bus free phase.* The system is idle.

# Installing a SCSI System

Today, virtually all SCSI host adapters are PnP devices that are designed for automatic detection and resource assignment in a motherboard's PCI slot. Still, most SCSI host adapter problems *start* when the card is first installed in the system; problems are usually due to inadequate or incorrect installation of the hardware and software. This part of the chapter offers an overview of the SCSI adapter installation process and SCSI BIOS setup so that you can check your own installation for missing steps.

 If your motherboard incorporates a SCSI host adapter, you can generally skip the installation steps and focus on the SCSI setup and configuration issues.

## INTERNAL HARDWARE INSTALLATION

Implementing SCSI on your server or workstation requires that you install a SCSI host adapter and at lease one SCSI device. The following steps outline the installation of a typical SCSI host adapter:

1. Shut down your system, and then turn off and unplug the computer.
2. Unbolt the outer case, and then remove the housing and set it (and the screws) aside in a safe place.
3. If you're replacing an existing SCSI host adapter with a newer, faster model, you'll need to remove the old SCSI adapter first. Disconnect the internal and external SCSI cable(s) from the SCSI adapter. Unbolt the old SCSI card bracket from the chassis and remove the old SCSI adapter from its expansion slot. Be sure to set the old SCSI adapter aside on a static-safe surface or in an anti-static bag.
4. Locate a slot for the new SCSI host adapter card. Most current SCSI host adapter devices will require a PCI slot, though some older SCSI cards will use an ISA slot. Find an available bus-mastering PCI slot that's appropriate for your SCSI adapter card. Remove the cover for the slot you intend to use (if it's not already removed) and save the screw for the mounting bracket.

5. Insert the SCSI host adapter card. Push the card in firmly and evenly until it's fully seated in the slot. Do NOT use excessive force—otherwise, you can break the card, and perhaps even damage the motherboard. Replace the screw to secure the bracket of your SCSI card to the computer's chassis.

6. If you're connecting any internal SCSI devices, plug the 50-pin or 68-pin SCSI connector on the end of the internal SCSI ribbon cable into the SCSI card's header. Make sure to align pin 1 on both connectors.

7. Connect your computer's drive activity LED cable to the appropriate connector on the SCSI card (if desired). This connection is designed to operate the front-panel LED found on most PC cabinets to indicate activity on the SCSI bus.

8. Make any external SCSI bus connections that may be required (for example, from your SCSI scanner or external SCSI drives).

The SCSI bus requires proper termination, and no duplicate SCSI IDs. Before you attempt to reboot the computer, verify the SCSI IDs for each SCSI device, and double-check the SCSI termination at the end(s) of your SCSI chain.

If your motherboard provides an onboard SCSI host adapter, remember that the onboard adapter may be terminated by default. If you cannot disable the onboard adapter's termination, you may be limited to using only internal or external SCSI devices, but not both. See your motherboard's documentation for specific limitations.

## SCSI Connection Notes

Although the SCSI interface is designed to accommodate a wide range of devices, their installation often presents some wrinkles you need to be aware of. As a rule, you need to check three things before connecting a SCSI device to the host adapter: the SCSI IDs, the termination, and the connect power cables. Following are some guidelines for setting SCSI IDs and termination on your various devices.

Since setup procedures can vary from device to device, always refer to each device's documentation for specific instructions.

**Check the SCSI IDs**    The SCSI host adapter and each SCSI device must have a unique ID. For example, each of the Adaptec 39160 SCSI card's channels are set to ID7, and each device you connect to a given channel must have a SCSI ID number ranging from 0 to 15. No two devices on the same SCSI channel can have the same SCSI ID. If you boot from a SCSI hard drive, make sure the drive ID is set to 0. (Most SCSI hard drives are preset to SCSI ID 0 at the factory.) The SCSI IDs for internal devices are usually set with jumpers, and the SCSI IDs for external devices are usually set with a switch on the back of the device.

**Terminate the Cable**    To ensure reliable communication on the SCSI bus, the device at the end of each cable (or the end of the cable itself) must have a *terminator* installed (or must have its internal termination enabled). Terminators must be removed (or termination must be disabled) on devices between the ends of each cable. When connecting Ultra160 or Ultra2 SCSI devices, the SCSI bus must be terminated either on the end of the cable (with a permanent terminator) or with a separate terminating connector. Ultra SCSI and earlier single-ended devices can terminate the bus directly from the device. If you use an Ultra SCSI terminator on an LVD Ultra160 and Ultra2 SCSI bus, you will force the bus to single-ended mode, limiting the speed and cable distance. For this reason, be sure that you have the necessary Ultra160 or Ultra2 cable or terminator before installing Ultra160 SCSI devices.

**Connecting Internal Ultra160 and Ultra2 Devices**    A special 68-pin internal low-voltage differential (LVD) cable is needed to connect internal Ultra160 or Ultra2 SCSI devices. If your cables are not marked, you can identify most LVD cables by the twisted pairs of flat ribbon cable between device connectors. Some cables are laminated so that they lie flat. Internal LVD cables usually have a terminator built into the end of the cable. SCSI host adapters such as the Adaptec 39160 have two separate Ultra160 SCSI channels, and each channel has an internal LVD/SE connector where you can connect internal SCSI devices. Follow these steps to connect your internal Ultra160 and Ultra2 devices:

1. Locate a 68-pin internal LVD SCSI cable (which may have either twisted wires or flat wires). As a rule, keep your Ultra160 and Ultra2 SCSI devices on a separate SCSI channel from your older Ultra SCSI devices. This allows the newer Ultra160 and Ultra2 SCSI devices to transfer data at their maximum speed.

2. Connect the non-terminated end of the cable(s) to the internal LVD/SE connector(s) at the SCSI adapter.

3. Plug the internal Ultra160 and Ultra2 SCSI devices to the other cable connectors, starting with the connector at the terminated end of the cable.

4. Connect a power cable from your computer's internal power supply to each internal SCSI device.

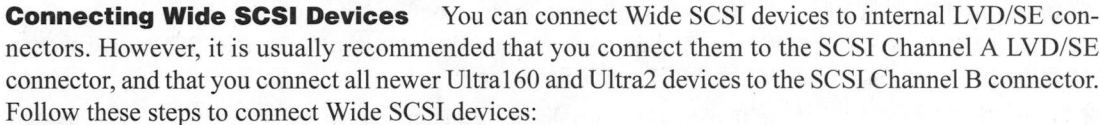
Internal Ultra 160 and Ultra2 SCSI devices come from the factory with termination disabled and often cannot be changed. Proper termination is provided by the terminator at the end of the LVD SCSI cable.

**Connecting Wide SCSI Devices**    You can connect Wide SCSI devices to internal LVD/SE connectors. However, it is usually recommended that you connect them to the SCSI Channel A LVD/SE connector, and that you connect all newer Ultra160 and Ultra2 devices to the SCSI Channel B connector. Follow these steps to connect Wide SCSI devices:

1. Locate a 68-pin internal Wide SCSI cable.

2. Connect one end of the cable to the Channel A internal 68-pin connector on the SCSI host adapter.

3. Connect the other end of the cable to a *terminated* Ultra/Fast Wide SCSI device.

4. If you have other Ultra/Fast Wide SCSI devices, attach them to the connectors between the two ends of the cable. Be sure these other devices are *unterminated*.

5. Connect a power cable from your computer's internal power supply to each internal device.

**Connecting Internal Ultra/Fast Narrow SCSI Devices**    If you have internal Ultra/Fast Narrow SCSI devices with standard 50-pin connectors, you can connect them to the 50-pin internal SE Narrow SCSI connector. Follow these steps to connect the devices:

1. Locate a 50-pin internal Ultra Narrow SCSI cable.

2. Connect one end of the cable to the 50-pin internal SE Narrow SCSI connector on the SCSI host adapter.

3. Connect the other end of the cable to a terminated Ultra/Fast Narrow SCSI device.

4. If you have other Ultra/Fast Narrow SCSI devices, attach them to the connectors between the two ends of the cable. Be sure these other devices are *unterminated*.

5. Connect a power cable from your computer's internal power supply to each internal device.

**Connecting External SCSI Devices**    You can connect external Ultra160 and Ultra2 SCSI devices to 68-pin external LVD/SE SCSI connectors. Each external device will require a 68-pin VHDCI external LVD SCSI cable. Follow these steps to connect your external SCSI devices:

1. Connect one end of an external SCSI cable to one of the external Ultra160 connectors on the SCSI host adapter (such as the Adaptec 39160 SCSI card). Connect *only* Ultra160 and Ultra2 SCSI devices to the external SCSI connectors in order to achieve the maximum data transfer rate. Also, do not combine older SCSI devices with the newer Ultra160 and Ultra2 SCSI devices on the same SCSI channel of the host adapter card.

2. Connect the other end of the cable to a SCSI connector on the back of an external device. If you are installing only one external device, terminate the device and skip to Step 4.

3. Connect the other external SCSI devices by linking each device to the previous one (in a "daisy chain" fashion). Terminate only the device at the end of the chain.

4. Connect power cables to all external device(s) and to the computer.

## SCSI Drive Notes

While connecting and terminating SCSI drives is a relatively straightforward process, you need to keep certain nuances in mind as you configure each device. The following tips should help you to make the most of your new and existing SCSI drives:

■ If you connect a SCSI hard drive to a new SCSI host adapter that was previously connected to a different SCSI card, you must repartition and reformat the drive before you can use it. Back up the data on the drive before you move it! In some cases, you may need to low-level format the SCSI drive using a utility integrated into the SCSI host adapter's firmware.

■ Every SCSI hard drive must be physically low-level formatted, partitioned, and logically formatted before it can be used to store data. Most SCSI drives are pre-formatted at the factory. If your SCSI hard disk drive has not been pre-formatted (and if your computer is running under DOS or Windows), you can format the disk with the DOS Fdisk and Format commands.

■ When using a dual-channel SCSI host adapter, connect your LVD (Ultra160 and Ultra2) SCSI devices to SCSI Channel B and your non-LVD SCSI devices (if any) to SCSI Channel A. This allows the LVD SCSI devices to run at their maximum performance levels of 160 MB/s or 80 MB/s respectively. Or you can connect LVD SCSI devices to both SCSI channels. If you combine LVD and non-LVD SCSI devices on the same SCSI channel, the data transfer rate of the LVD SCSI devices will drop down to non-LVD SCSI performance levels of up to 40 MB/s.

## Combining SCSI and Non-SCSI Devices

You can install the SCSI host adapter in a computer that already has a non-SCSI controller (such as an UltraDMA/133 controller). However, you cannot mix devices on the same interface—SCSI devices must be connected to the SCSI host adapter, EIDE/UDMA devices must be connected to their controller, and so on. When you install the SCSI host adapter and SCSI disk drives in a computer that boots from a non-SCSI disk drive, the computer will continue to boot from the non-SCSI disk drive unless you change the computer's CMOS configuration. You do not need to change the configuration if you just want to use the SCSI drives for additional file storage space. If your computer's motherboard BIOS supports the BIOS Boot Specification (or BBS) feature, you can select a different boot device without much difficulty. Table 32-8 outlines what to do in order to use different kinds of disk drives in the same computer.

| TABLE 32-8 | USE CARE WHEN ADJUSTING THE COMPUTER'S BOOT ORDER | |
|---|---|---|
| **DOES COMPUTER BIOS SUPPORT BBS?** | **WANT COMPUTER TO BOOT FROM SCSI DRIVE?** | **THEN DO THIS:** |
| No | No | No action required. SCSI drives and non-SCSI drives can be used together. |
| No | Yes | Run CMOS Setup program. Change primary hard disk setting to **None** or **Not Installed** (see computer documentation). You will not be able to use the non-SCSI drive(s) at all when you boot from the SCSI drive. |
| Yes | No | No action required. SCSI drives and non-SCSI drives can be used together. |
| Yes | Yes | Run CMOS Setup program and select SCSI drive as boot device. SCSI drives and non-SCSI drives can be used together. |

## SOFTWARE INSTALLATION

Now that the physical hardware for your new SCSI host adapter card has been installed, it's time to install the SCSI adapter drivers and application software that you'll need to identify the device under the operating system. The following steps illustrate a typical procedure for Windows 98/Me/XP, so check the adapter's recommendations for other operating systems. Leave the computer's housing off for now, but reconnect the AC cord to the computer and prepare to start the system again.

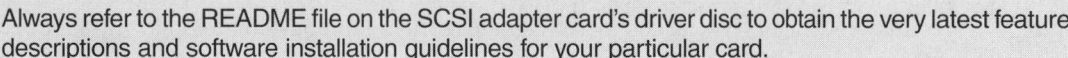

Always refer to the README file on the SCSI adapter card's driver disc to obtain the very latest feature descriptions and software installation guidelines for your particular card.

1. When Windows restarts, it should detect the SCSI host adapter automatically.
2. Click Driver From Disk Provided By Hardware Manufacturer. Then click OK. Windows XP will launch a New Hardware wizard so that you may identify the device and install appropriate drivers.
3. Insert the driver CD into the CD-ROM, and then select the CD-ROM drive letter.
4. Click OK. Windows will load the SCSI adapter's drivers.
5. Once Windows finishes loading the information from the driver CD, reboot the system if necessary.
6. Now take a moment to check the installation. Open the Device Manager.
7. Double-click the SCSI Controllers branch to expand it.
8. See that your new SCSI host adapter is listed (Figure 32-4 shows a typical Device Manager display under Windows 98). If it is, your new SCSI host adapter is probably installed properly. You can exit the Device Manager and begin using your SCSI adapter. If it is not listed, you'll need to check the installation.

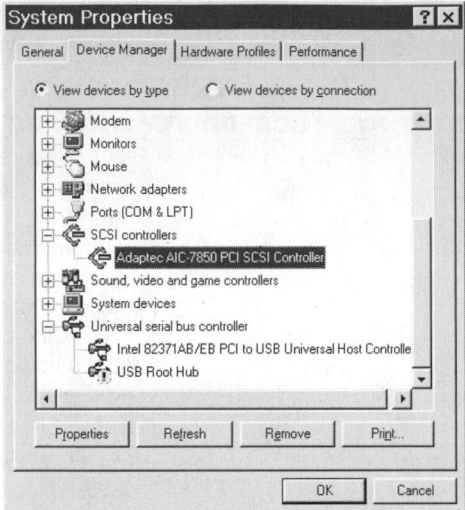

**FIGURE  32-4**   Checking the SCSI adapter after installation

# CONFIGURING THE SCSI BIOS

Whether added as an expansion device or integrated into your server's motherboard, the vast majority of SCSI host adapters employ a BIOS (or *firmware*) to configure the adapter's various operations. In most cases, the default settings of your SCSI BIOS are adequate, and you should not need to change the default configuration of the host adapter. However, you may decide to alter these default values if there is a conflict between device settings, or if you need to optimize the system's performance. This part of the chapter outlines the default settings of a common Adaptec SCSI host adapter and explains many of the SCSI BIOS settings that you may encounter. Typical default settings are listed in Table 32-9. The global settings affect your host adapter and all SCSI devices that are connected to it, but the device settings affect only individual SCSI devices.

## Using the SCSI BIOS

The SCSI host adapter's firmware can be accessed in the moments following the POST—just after the PC lets you enter the CMOS Setup. As the initialization process continues, you'll see a message such as:

```
Press <Ctrl><A> for SCSISelect Utility
```

Press the specified keys to start the SCSI Setup utility (i.e., SCSISelect). If there is more than one available channel, you can specify the channel (such as channel A or channel B) to work on. On the setup menu that appears, use the arrow keys to navigate through the various options, and press <ENTER> to make selections. When you're done reviewing or changing SCSI options, press <ESC> until you're prompted to exit and save changes. Select Yes and the PC will reboot.

**TABLE 32-9** COMMON SCSI BIOS SETTINGS USED TO CONFIGURE A SCSI HOST ADAPTER

| SCSI SELECT OPTIONS | AVAILABLE SETTINGS | DEFAULT SETTING |
|---|---|---|
| *SCSI Bus Interface Definitions:* | | |
| Host Adapter SCSI ID | 0-15 | 7 |
| SCSI Parity Checking | Enabled, Disabled | Enabled |
| Host Adapter SCSI Termination | Ch. A: | Automatic |
| | Automatic, Low On/High On, Low Off/High Off, Low Off/High On | |
| | Ch. B: | Automatic |
| | Automatic, Enabled, Disabled | |
| *Boot Device Options:* | | |
| Boot Channel | A First, B First | A First |
| Boot SCSI ID | 0-15 | 0 |
| Boot LUN Number | 0-7 | 0 |
| *SCSI Device Configuration:* | | |
| Sync Transfer Rate (MB/s) | 160, 80.0, 53.4, 40.0, 32.0, 26.8, 20.0, 16.0, 13.4, 10.0, ASYN | 160 |
| Initiate Wide Negotiation | Yes, No | Yes (Enabled) |
| Enable Disconnection | Yes, No | Yes (Enabled) |
| Send Start Unit Command | Yes, No | Yes (Enabled) |
| Enable Write Back Cache | Yes, No, N/C (No Change) | N/C (No Change) |
| BIOS Multiple LUN Support | Yes, No | No (Disabled) |
| Include in BIOS Scan | Yes, No | Yes (Enabled) |
| *Advanced Configuration Options:* | | |
| Reset SCSI Bus at IC Initialization | Enabled, Disabled | Enabled |
| Display <CTRL> <A> Messages during BIOS Initialization | Enabled, Disabled | Enabled |
| Extended BIOS Translation for DOS Drives > 1 GB | Enabled, Disabled | Enabled |
| Verbose/Silent Mode | Verbose, Silent | Verbose |
| Host Adapter BIOS | Enabled, Disabled: Scan Bus, Disabled: Not Scan | Enabled |
| Domain Validation | Enabled, Disabled | Enabled |
| Support Removable Disks Under BIOS as Fixed Disks | Disabled, Boot Only, All Disks | Disabled |
| BIOS Support for Bootable CD-ROM | Enabled, Disabled | Enabled |
| BIOS Support for Int 13 Extensions | Enabled, Disabled | Enabled |

The instructions and options shown here are provided as an example, and may vary greatly between SCSI adapters. Instructions for navigating the menus, and specific options available to your particular SCSI host adapter can be found in the adapter's user manual.

**SCSI BIOS Settings**    Once the SCSI BIOS Setup utility is running, you'll be able to adjust a large number of settings and operating parameters such as the ones listed next (default settings are listed in parentheses):

- **Host Adapter SCSI ID (7)**    This sets the SCSI ID for the SCSI card. Most SCSI cards (such as the Adaptec 39160) are set at 7, which give them the highest priority on the SCSI bus. As a rule, you should not change this setting.

- **SCSI Parity Checking (Enabled)**    When set to Enabled, this feature verifies the accuracy of data transfers on the SCSI bus. Leave this setting enabled unless any SCSI device connected to the SCSI host adapter does **not** support SCSI parity.

- **Host Adapter SCSI Termination (Automatic)**    This determines the termination setting for the SCSI card. The default setting, Automatic, allows the SCSI card to adjust the termination as needed. As a rule, you should not change this setting.

- **Boot Channel (A First)**    This specifies which of the two SCSI channels the boot device is connected to (if the computer boots from a SCSI device). If you change this setting, the change automatically applies to both SCSI channels. This type of option will not be available on SCSI host adapters with only one channel.

- **Boot SCSI ID (0)**    This specifies the SCSI ID of your boot device. As a rule, you should not change the default setting. If you change this setting, the change automatically applies to both SCSI channels.

- **Boot LUN Number (0)**    This specifies which Logical Unit Number (LUN) to boot from on your boot device. This setting is not valid unless the Multiple LUN Support feature is enabled. If you alter this setting, the change automatically applies to both SCSI channels.

- **Sync Transfer Rate (160)**    This determines the maximum synchronous data transfer rate that the SCSI card supports. As a rule, you should leave the maximum (default) value of 160 MB/s.

- **Initiate Wide Negotiation (Yes)**    When set to Yes, the SCSI card attempts 16-bit data transfer (wide negotiation). When set to No, the SCSI card uses 8-bit data transfer unless the SCSI device specifically requests wide negotiation. Set Initiate Wide Negotiation to No if you're using an 8-bit SCSI device that hangs or exhibits other performance problems with 16-bit data transfer rate enabled.

- **Enable Disconnection (Yes)**    When set to Yes, this allows the SCSI device to disconnect from the SCSI bus. Leave the setting at Yes if two or more SCSI devices are connected to the SCSI card. If only one SCSI device is connected, change the setting to No for slightly better performance.

- **Send Start Unit Command (Yes)**    When set to Yes, this sends the Start Unit Command to the SCSI device at bootup. The following three options have no effect if the SCSI Card BIOS is disabled (the SCSI Card BIOS is normally enabled by default).

- **Enable Write Back Cache (N/C)**    This option can be used to enable or disable the write-back cache on SCSI disk drives connected to the host adapter. Leave this option set to its default setting, which usually allows for optimum drive performance.

- **BIOS Multiple LUN Support (No)**    Leave this setting at No if the device does not have multiple Logical Unit Numbers (LUNs). When set to Yes, the SCSI BIOS provides boot support for a SCSI device with multiple LUNs (i.e., a CD jukebox in which multiple CDs can be accessed simultaneously).

- **Include in BIOS Scan (Yes)**    When set to Yes, the SCSI BIOS includes the device as part of its BIOS scan at bootup.

- **Reset SCSI Bus at Initialization (Enabled)**    When set to enabled, the SCSI card generates a SCSI bus reset during its power-on initialization and after a hard reset.

- **Display Messages during BIOS Initialization (Enabled)**    When set to enabled, the SCSI BIOS displays the logon message (i.e., "Press <CTRL> <A> for SCSISelect Utility") during system bootup. If this setting is disabled, you can still invoke the SCSI BIOS utility by pressing the required keys after the SCSI BIOS banner appears. If you change this setting, the change automatically applies to both SCSI channels.

- **Extended BIOS Translation for DOS Drives > 1 GB (Enabled)**    When enabled, this provides an extended translation scheme for SCSI hard disks with capacities greater than 1GB. This setting is necessary only for DOS 5.0 and later, and is not required for other operating systems like NetWare or UNIX.

Changing the translation scheme destroys all data on the drive. Be sure to back up your disk drives before changing the translation scheme.

- **Verbose/Silent Mode (Verbose)**    When set to Verbose, the SCSI card BIOS displays the host adapter model on the screen during system buildup. When set to Silent, the message will not be displayed during bootup. If you change this setting, the change automatically applies to both SCSI channels.

- **Host Adapter BIOS (Enabled)**    This feature enables or disables the SCSI card BIOS. If you change this setting, the change automatically applies to both SCSI channels. Leave this setting enabled to let the SCSI BIOS scan and initialize all SCSI devices. Set to Disabled: Not Scan if the devices on the SCSI bus (i.e., CD-ROM drives) are controlled by software drivers and do not need the BIOS, and you do not want the BIOS to scan the SCSI bus. Set to Disabled: Scan Bus if you do not need the BIOS, but you want it to scan the SCSI devices on the bus and you need to spin up the device. The following four options have no effect if the SCSI BIOS is disabled.

- **Domain Validation (Enabled)**    This determines the optimum transfer rate for each device on the SCSI bus and sets transfer rates accordingly. This also displays the resulting data transfer rate. If you change this setting, the change automatically applies to both SCSI channels.

- **Support Removable Disks Under BIOS as Fixed Disks (Disabled)**    This determines which removable-media drives are supported by the SCSI card BIOS. When disabled, no removable-media drives are treated as hard drives. Software drivers are required because the drives are not controlled by the BIOS. In Boot Only mode, only the removable-media drive designated as the boot device is treated as a hard disk drive. In All Disks mode, all removable-media drives supported by the BIOS are treated as hard disk drives.

- **BIOS Support for Bootable CD-ROM (Enabled)**    When set to enabled, the SCSI BIOS allows the computer to boot from a CD-ROM drive.

- **BIOS Support for Int 13 Extensions (Enabled)**    When set to enabled, the SCSI card BIOS supports Int 13h extensions. The setting can be either enabled or disabled (if your system is not plug-and-play).

# SCSI Considerations

Whether you're considering adding SCSI support to your own computer or planning an upgrade for a customer, there are four essential elements that you must consider: the SCSI peripheral(s), the SCSI host adapter, the SCSI cable assembly, and the SCSI software driver(s). If any one of these four elements is missing or ill-planned, your installation is going to run into problems.

# SCSI PERIPHERALS

The first items to be considered are the SCSI peripherals themselves. You first need to know what types of devices are needed (such as a SCSI hard drive or CD-ROM). The peripheral should be compatible with the architecture of your controller (for instance, SCSI-3 or SCSI-4). You may also find a growing base of Ultra160 (and more recently Ultra 320) compliant adapters and peripherals. Each SCSI peripheral device should also have a wide range of available SCSI ID settings. SCSI typically handles eight IDs (0 to 7), and the peripheral should have the flexibility to run on virtually any ID. If only a few IDs are available, you may be limited when it comes time to add other SCSI devices. Peripherals should support SCSI parity.

> Ideally, a SCSI-4 host adapter should support SCSI-3 and SCSI-2 devices. If you have any intention of employing SCSI-4 devices, be sure to use a SCSI-4 adapter.

SCSI devices are available in both internal and external versions. If you consider an internal peripheral, make sure that there is adequate drive space in the PC to accommodate the new peripheral. (Either a drive bay is available, or an existing device may be removed to make room.) If the peripheral is to be an external device (such as a printer or scanner), there should be two SCSI connectors on the device, to allow for daisy-chaining additional devices later. All SCSI peripherals other than hard drives will require device drivers. Make sure that the device driver is compatible with the same standard protocol used by the adapter (such as ASPI, CAM, or LADDR). Compatibility is a serious consideration since peripherals using incompatible device driver standards will not work properly. Finally, try to choose SCSI peripherals that offer built-in cable termination.

# SCSI HOST ADAPTER

The next item to be considered is the SCSI host adapter (often just called a host or HA), which fits in the PC expansion bus. Make sure to choose an adapter that is compatible with the PC bus in use (almost always PCI today). Bus-mastering 32/64-bit PCI SCSI adapters will provide superior performance if your system will support them. Like the peripheral itself, the adapter should also be designed to support the SCSI-3 standard (or SCSI-4 if possible). Although most adapters are assigned a SCSI ID of 7, the adapter should be flexible enough to work with any ID from 0 to 7. The host adapter will also require a device driver for using devices other than hard drives. Make sure that the host device driver uses the same standard as the peripheral(s) (ASPI, CAM, or LADDR). It is important to note here that the driver standard has nothing to do with the choice of SCSI-2, SCSI-3, or SCSI-4. It is only important that the peripherals and the adapter use the *same* driver standard.

# SCSI CABLES AND TERMINATORS

Check that you select the proper cabling for the SCSI level you are using. Although SCSI cabling is now highly standardized, some older cables may use slight modifications for particular peripherals (typical with SCSI-1 devices, though very few SCSI-1 installations remain in service). Be certain that you know of any specialized cabling requirements when choosing peripherals. Try to avoid specialized cabling if at all possible, but if you *must* use specialized cabling, you should determine what impact the cabling will have on any other SCSI peripherals that may be installed (or may be installed later). Use good-quality SCSI cables specifically intended for the SCSI level you are using (probably SCSI-3/4), and keep the cables short to minimize signal degradation.

SCSI cables must be terminated at the beginning (host adapter) and end (after the last device) of the SCSI chain. Try to choose internal peripherals that have built-in terminators. Also try to select a host adapter and peripherals that use the same type of terminator resistor network. SCSI-2 and later systems use active terminator networks. You will see much more about cabling and termination a bit later in this chapter.

Remember that SCSI host adapters integrated onto motherboards may have fixed termination enabled, and you may not be able to run both internal and external devices from that controller.

## SCSI DRIVERS

Device drivers provide the instructions that allow the SCSI host adapter to communicate with the PC, as well as with the peripherals in the SCSI chain (or the SCSI *bus*). The host adapter itself will require a device driver, as will every peripheral that is added. For example, a SCSI system with one CD-ROM will need a driver for the host adapter and a driver for the CD-ROM. Make sure that driver standards (ASPI, CAM, or LADDR) are the *same* for the host adapter and peripherals. The only exception to the device driver requirement (at this time) is the SCSI hard drive, which may be supported by the SCSI adapter's BIOS ROM.

Real-mode (a.k.a. DOS) device drivers are added by including them in your PC's CONFIG.SYS and AUTOEXEC.BAT files. One issue to keep in mind when adding device drivers is that drivers use *conventional* memory (unless you successfully load the drivers into high memory). The more drivers that are added, the more memory that will be consumed. It is possible that a large number of device drivers may prevent certain memory-demanding DOS applications from running. To keep as much conventional memory (the first 640KB in RAM) as free as possible, use the DOS devicehigh and loadhigh features to load the drivers into upper memory (from 640KB to 1MB in RAM). Windows 9x/Me/XP avoids this problem by using protected-mode drivers for the host adapter and devices.

## CABLING AND TERMINATION

Once the host adapter and peripheral are configured and installed, you must connect them with a cable. Internal devices are typically connected with a 68-pin IDC (insulation displacement connector) ribbon cable (a P-cable). By placing multiple connectors along the length of cable, daisy-chaining can be achieved with a single connector on each internal device. External devices typically connect to an external 68-pin connector on the rear of the SCSI adapter, and each device offers two connectors to allow daisy-chaining to additional devices. Most commercial adapter and drive kits are packed with an appropriate cable.

The cable(s) must be terminated. There are internal and external SCSI cable terminators, along with SCSI devices that have terminating resistor networks already built in. The concept of termination is reasonably simple: achieve the desired signal cable characteristics by *loading* each end of the SCSI chain with resistors. If the chain is not terminated properly, signals will not be carried reliably (which invariably results in system errors). For technicians and end users alike, the trouble usually arises in determining where the ends are. A number of examples will help to clarify how to determine the chain ends.

For a single SCSI drive and adapter, as shown in Figure 32-5, the ends are easy to see. One end should be terminated at the host adapter (which usually has terminating resistors built in). The other end should be terminated at the SCSI hard drive (which also usually has terminating resistors built in). In this type of situation, you need only connect the cable between both devices and verify that the terminators are in place.

When a second SCSI peripheral is added, as shown in Figure 32-6, termination becomes a bit more complex. Suppose a CD-ROM is added with a SCSI ID of 6. The terminator on the existing SCSI hard drive is no longer appropriate—it should be removed, and the termination should be made on the CD-ROM, which is now the *last device* in the SCSI chain. In most cases, a terminator network can be deactivated by flipping a DIP switch or changing a jumper on the peripheral itself. If the terminator cannot be shut off, it can almost always be removed by gently easing the resistor network out of its holder using

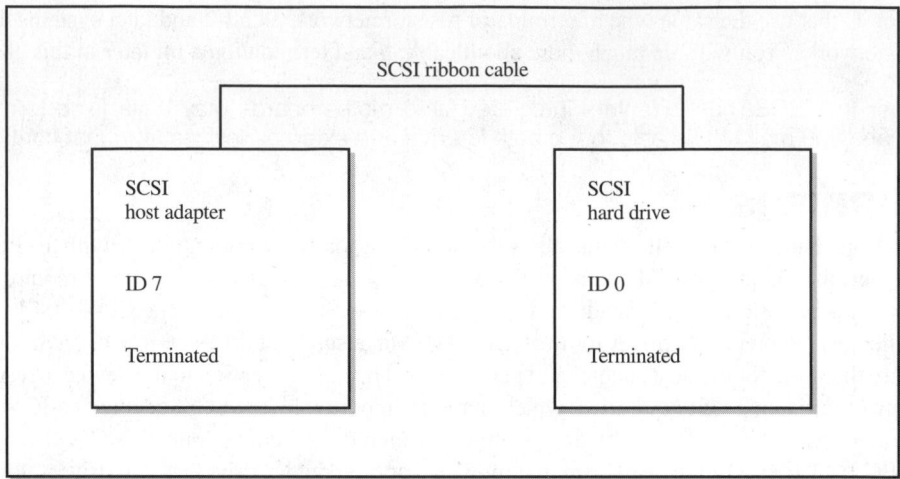

**FIGURE  32-5**    Terminating an internal SCSI adapter and hard drive

needle-nose pliers. If you remove a terminator, place it in an envelope and tape it to the inside of the PC enclosure. If it is simply impossible to remove the existing terminator on the hard drive, place the CD-ROM between the adapter and hard drive and remove the CD-ROM's terminator (rearrange the chain). The SCSI host adapter must remain terminated.

So what happens if an *external* device is used (such as a scanner), as in Figure 32-7? An external cable connects the adapter to the scanner. Since the scanner (ID 6) and adapter (ID 7) are the only two points in the chain, both are terminated. Most external devices designed for SCSI-2 compatibility allow the active terminator built into the peripheral to be switched off if necessary.

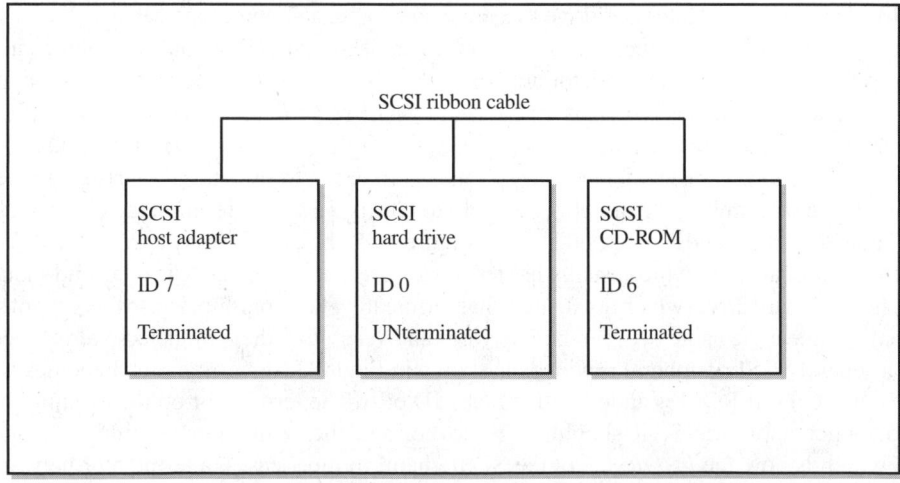

**FIGURE  32-6**    Terminating an internal SCSI adapter, HDD, and CD-ROM

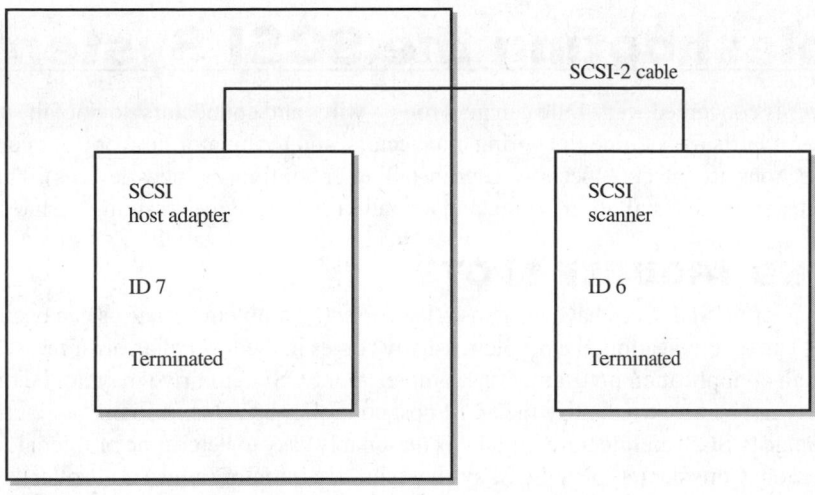

**FIGURE  32-7**     Terminating an external SCSI device

Suppose both an internal *and* an external SCSI device are being used, as shown in Figure 32-8. The SCSI host adapter (ID 7) is no longer at an end of the chain, so its terminator should be switched off or removed. It is the internal hard drive (ID 0) and external scanner (ID 6) that now form the ends, so both devices should be terminated. Since both peripherals should ideally support internal termination, nothing needs to be done except to confirm that the terminators are in place and switched on.

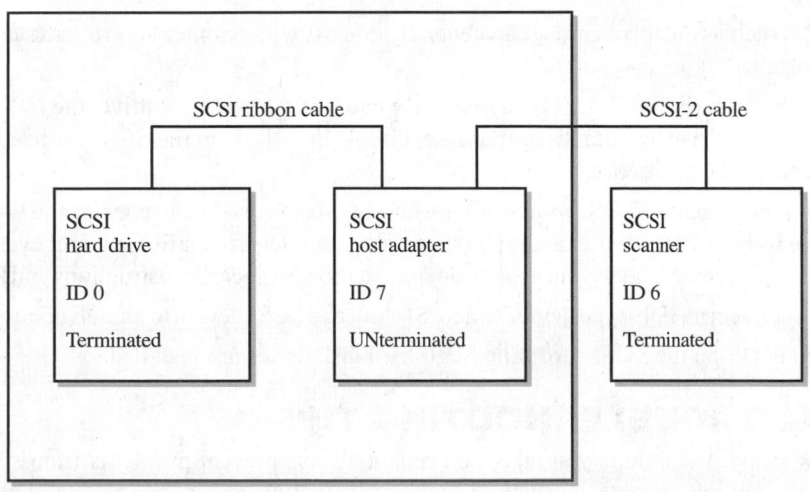

**FIGURE  32-8**     Terminating mixed internal and external SCSI devices

# Troubleshooting the SCSI System

As far as the *bus* is concerned, very little can go wrong—wires and connectors do not fail spontaneously. However, it never hurts to examine the wiring, connectors, and terminator network(s) to ensure that the physical connections are intact (especially after installing or configuring new devices). The most likely areas of trouble are in the installation, setup, and operation of the devices residing on the bus.

## ISOLATING TROUBLE SPOTS

Assuming that your SCSI devices have been installed correctly, problem scenarios can occur during normal operation. The first indication of a problem usually comes in the form of an error message from your operating system or application program. For example, your SCSI hard drive may not be responding, or the host PC may not be able to identify the SCSI host controller board, and so on.

The advantage to SCSI architecture is that it is reasonably easy to determine problem locations using intuitive deduction. Consider a typical SCSI system with one initiator (a host controller) and one target (such as a hard drive). If the hard drive fails to function, the trouble is either in the host controller or the drive itself. When you see drive access being attempted, but an error is generated, the trouble is probably in the drive. If no drive access is attempted before an error is generated, the error is likely in the host controller. As another example, consider a setup with one initiator and two or more targets (a hard drive and CD-ROM). If *both* the hard drive and CD-ROM become inoperative, the problem is likely in the host controller card, since the host adapter controls both targets. If only *one* of the devices becomes inoperative (and the other device works just fine), the trouble is likely in the particular device itself.

## USING SCSI AND IDE DEVICES

Most experienced technicians can recall trouble when mixing SCSI and IDE-type drives on the same system, resulting in boot problems and BIOS conflicts. Today, those issues have largely been resolved, so follow these points when mixing SCSI and IDE (EIDE/UDMA) support on the same PC:

- SCSI cards (such as Adaptec cards) can generally coexist with another controller (such as EIDE or UDMA) installed in the computer.
- If you have both an EIDE/UDMA hard disk drive and a SCSI hard disk drive, the IDE-type drive is typically the boot drive by default. In this case, disable the BIOS on the SCSI card according to the SCSI host adapter's instructions.
- If your computer supports BBS, *both* SCSI and non-SCSI disk drives can coexist and you can specify which drive to boot from. For example, you can elect to boot from a SCSI drive, even if IDE-type drives are in the system. Check your system documentation for specific instructions and limitations.
- You cannot connect an IDE-type device to a SCSI card, or a SCSI device to an IDE controller card.
- Disable the BIOS on the SCSI card if no SCSI hard disk drives are installed.

## GENERAL TROUBLESHOOTING TIPS

No matter how many precautions you take, you cannot always prevent problems from striking during SCSI installations or replacements. Fortunately, if you are installing devices one by one, as suggested, you will have far fewer problem areas to check. Your first diagnostic for a SCSI installation should be the host adapter's SCSI BIOS initialization message. If you see no initialization message when the system powers up, any problem is likely to be with the host adapter itself. Either it is not installed properly or it is defective. Make sure that the adapter is set to the desired ID (usually 7). Try a new or alternate SCSI adapter. If the adapter provides its initialization message as expected, the problem is probably related to driver installation. Check the installation and any command-line switches for each device driver. When installing a SCSI hard drive instead of IDE hard drives, you must ensure that any previous hard drive references are mapped out of the CMOS Setup by selecting "none" or "not installed." If preexisting drive references are not removed, the system will try to boot from IDE drives that aren't there.

Be aware that faulty SCSI ID settings can result in system problems such as "ghost" disks—disks that the system says are there but that cannot be read from or written to. Some peripherals may also not work properly with the ID that has been assigned. If you have problems interacting with an installed device, try the device with a different ID, and make sure that no two devices are using the *same* ID. Don't be surprised to find that certain types of cables don't work properly with SCSI installations. Make sure that everything is terminated correctly. Also be sure that any external SCSI devices are powered up (if possible) before the PC is initialized. If problems persist, try different cables. The following is a quick-reference checklist:

- Check the power to all SCSI devices (make sure that the power supply has enough capacity to handle all of your attached SCSI devices).

- Check the 50/68-pin signal cable to all SCSI devices. It should be a good-quality cable that is attached securely to each device.

- Check the orientation of each connector on the SCSI cable. Pin 1 must always be in the proper orientation.

- Check the SCSI ID of each device. Duplicate IDs are *not* allowed unless you're using LUN designations, which can occur when using a large number of SCSI devices, such as a RAID system.

- Check that both ends of the SCSI cable are properly terminated and that the terminators are active.

- Check the SCSI controller's configuration (IRQ, I/O, BIOS addresses, and so on). Verify that the SCSI controller is not conflicting with other devices in the system.

- Check the SCSI host adapter BIOS. If you're not booting from SCSI hard drives, you can often leave the SCSI BIOS disabled. This will also simplify the device configuration. You may be able to upgrade the host adapter's BIOS to resolve performance problems or compatibility issues.

- Check the CMOS Setup for drive configurations. When SCSI drives are in the system and IDE/EIDE drives are not, be sure that the drive entries under CMOS are set to "none" or "not installed."

- Check the PCI bus configuration in the CMOS Setup. See that the PCI slot containing the SCSI host adapter is active and is using a unique IRQ (usually named IRQ A). PCI bus mastering should also be enabled.

- Check for the real-mode drivers under DOS. If you're working under DOS, see that any needed drivers for the host adapter and non-HDD devices are installed in the CONFIG.SYS and AUTOEXEC.BAT files.

- Check for the protected-mode drivers under Windows 98/Me/XP. If you're working under Windows, see that any needed protected-mode drivers for the host adapter and SCSI devices are installed. The SCSI host adapter should be properly identified in the SCSI Adapters wizard.

- Try REMarking out real-mode drivers if problems occur only under Windows 98/Me/XP. Real-mode SCSI drivers can sometimes interfere with protected-mode SCSI drivers. If the SCSI system works fine in DOS, but not in Windows, try temporarily disabling the DOS drivers in your startup files.

# SCSI SYMPTOMS

Even the best-planned SCSI setups go wrong from time to time, and SCSI systems already in the field will not run forever. Sooner or later, you will have to deal with a SCSI problem. This part of the chapter is intended to show you a variety of symptoms and solutions for many of the problems that you will likely encounter.

**SYMPTOM 32-1**    **After initial SCSI installation, the system will not boot from the floppy drive**    You may or may not see an error code corresponding to this problem. Suspect the SCSI host adapter first. There may be an internal fault with the adapter that is interfering with system operation. Check that all of the adapter's settings are correct and that all jumpers are intact. If the adapter is equipped with any diagnostic LEDs, check for any problem indications. When adapter problems are indicated, replace the adapter board. If a SCSI hard drive has been installed and the drive light is always on, the SCSI signal cable has probably been reversed between the drive and adapter. Make sure to install the drive cable properly.

Check for the SCSI adapter BIOS message generated when the system starts. If the message does not appear, check for the presence of a ROM address conflict between the SCSI adapter and ROMs on other expansion boards. Try a new address setting for the SCSI adapter. If there is a BIOS wait-state jumper on the adapter, try changing its setting. If you see an error message indicating that the SCSI host adapter was not found at a particular address, check the I/O setting for the adapter. Keep in mind that resource problems are increasingly rare for PCI PnP SCSI adapters.

Some more recent SCSI host adapters incorporate a floppy controller. This can cause a conflict with an existing floppy controller. If you choose to continue using the existing floppy controller, be sure to disable the new host adapter's floppy controller. If you'd prefer to use the host adapter's floppy controller, remember to disable the preexisting floppy controller port through the CMOS Setup.

**SYMPTOM 32-2**    **The system will not boot from the SCSI hard drive**    Start by checking the system's CMOS Setup. When SCSI drives are installed in a PC, the corresponding hard drive reference in the CMOS Setup must be changed to "none" or "not installed" (this assumes that you will *not* be using IDE/EIDE hard drives in the system). If you have not mapped out previous hard drive references, do so now, save the CMOS Setup, and reboot the PC. If you have both IDE and SCSI drives, change the boot order in the CMOS Setup so that "SCSI" preceeds "IDE" (or other IDE drive references). If the problem persists, check that the SCSI boot drive is set to ID 0. You will need to refer to the user manual for your particular drive to find how the ID is set.

Next, check the SCSI parity to be sure that it is selected consistently among all SCSI devices. Remember that *all* SCSI devices must have SCSI parity enabled or disabled. If even one device in the SCSI chain does not support parity, it must be disabled on *all* devices. Check the SCSI cabling to be sure that all cables are installed and terminated properly. Finally, be sure that the hard drive has been partitioned and formatted properly. If it has not, boot from a floppy disk and prepare the hard drive as required using FDISK and FORMAT.

**SYMPTOM 32-3**    **The SCSI drive fails to respond with an alternate HDD as the boot drive**    Technically, you should be able to use a SCSI drive as a nonboot drive (such as drive D:) while using an IDE/EIDE drive as the boot device. If the SCSI drive fails to respond in this kind of arrangement, check the CMOS setting to be sure that drive 1 (the SCSI drive) is mapped out (or set to "none" or "not installed"). Save the CMOS Setup and reboot the PC. If the problem persists, check that the SCSI drive is set to SCSI ID 1 (the nonboot ID). Next, make sure that the SCSI parity is enabled or disabled consistently throughout the SCSI installation. If the SCSI parity is enabled for some devices and disabled for others, the SCSI system may function erratically. Finally, check that the SCSI cabling is installed and terminated properly. Faulty cables or termination can easily interrupt a SCSI system. If the problem persists, try another hard drive.

> Later SCSI host adapters use BIOS that allows SCSI drives to boot even with IDE/EIDE drives in the system. In such a configuration, the Boot Order entry in CMOS Setup will determine whether A:, C:, CD-ROM, or SCSI will be the boot device.

**SYMPTOM 32-4**    **The SCSI drive fails to respond with another SCSI drive as the boot drive**    This typically occurs in a dual-drive system using two SCSI drives. Check the CMOS Setup and make sure that both drive entries in the setup are set to "none" or "not installed." Save the CMOS Setup. The boot drive should be set to SCSI ID 0, while the supplemental drive should be set to SCSI ID 1 (you will probably have to refer to the manual for the drives to determine how to select a SCSI ID). The hard drives should have a DOS partition and format. If not, create the partitions (FDISK) and format the drives (FORMAT) as required. Check to be sure that SCSI parity is enabled or disabled consistently throughout the SCSI system. If some devices use parity and other devices do not, the SCSI system may not function properly. Make sure that all SCSI cables are installed and terminated properly. If the problem persists, try systematically exchanging each hard drive.

**SYMPTOM 32-5**    **The system works erratically. The PC hangs or the SCSI adapter cannot find the drive(s)**    Such intermittent operation can be the result of several different SCSI factors. Before taking any action, be sure that the application software you were running when the fault occurred did not cause the problem. Unstable or buggy software can seriously interfere with system operation. Try different applications and see if the system still hangs. (You might also try any diagnostic utilities that accompanied the host adapter.) Check each SCSI device and make sure that parity is enabled or disabled consistently throughout the SCSI system. If parity is enabled in some devices and disabled in others, erratic operation can result. Make sure that no two SCSI devices are using the same ID. Cabling problems are another common source of erratic behavior. Make sure that all SCSI cables are attached correctly and completely. Also check that the cabling is properly terminated.

Next, suspect a possible resource conflict between the SCSI host adapter and another board in the system (though this is becoming increasingly rare). Check each expansion board in the system to be sure that nothing is using the same IRQ, DMA, or I/O address as the host adapter (or check the Device Manager under Windows 9x/Me/XP). If you find a conflict, you should alter the most recently installed adapter board, or try the host adapter in another slot. If problems persist, try a new drive adapter board.

**SYMPTOM 32-6**    **You see an 096xxxx error code**    This is a diagnostic error code that indicates a problem in a 32-bit SCSI host adapter board. Check the board to be sure that it is installed correctly and completely. The board should not be shorted against any other board or cable. Try disabling one SCSI device at a time. If normal operation returns, the last device to be removed is responsible for the problem. (You may need to disable drivers and reconfigure termination when isolating problems in this fashion.) If the problem persists, remove and reinstall all SCSI devices from scratch or try a new SCSI adapter board.

**SYMPTOM 32-7**    **You see a 112xxxx error code**    This diagnostic error code indicates a problem in a 16-bit SCSI adapter board. Check the board to be sure that it is installed correctly and completely. The board should not be shorted against any other board or cable. Try disabling one SCSI device at a time. If normal operation returns, the last device to be removed is responsible for the problem. (You may need to disable drivers and reconfigure termination when isolating problems in this fashion.) Try a new SCSI host adapter board.

**SYMPTOM 32-8**    **You see a 113xxxx error code**    This is a diagnostic code that indicates a problem in a system (motherboard) SCSI adapter configuration. If a SCSI BIOS ROM is installed on the motherboard, be sure that it is up-to-date and installed correctly and completely. If problems persist, try replacing the motherboard's SCSI controller chip or the system board. It may be possible to circumvent a damaged motherboard SCSI controller by disabling the motherboard's controller and then installing a SCSI host adapter card.

**SYMPTOM 32-9**    **You see a 210xxxx error code**    There is a fault in a SCSI hard disk drive itself. Check that the power and signal cables to the disk are connected properly. Make sure the SCSI cable is correctly terminated. Try repartitioning and reformatting the SCSI hard disk. Finally, try a new SCSI hard disk.

**SYMPTOM 32-10**    **A SCSI device refuses to function with the SCSI adapter even though both the adapter and device check properly**    This is often a classic case of basic incompatibility between the device and host adapter. Even though SCSI-2 and later standards help to streamline compatibility between devices and controllers, there are still situations when the two just don't work together. Check the literature included with the finicky device for any notices of compatibility problems with the controller (perhaps the particular controller brand) you are using. If there are warnings, there may also be alternative jumper, DIP switch, or SCSI BIOS Setup settings to compensate for the problem and allow you to use the device after all. A call to technical support at the device's manufacturer may reveal any recently discovered bugs or fixes (for example, an updated SCSI BIOS, SCSI device driver, or host adapter driver). If problems remain, try using a similar device from a different manufacturer.

**SYMPTOM 32-11**    **You see a "No SCSI Controller Present" error message**    Immediately suspect that the controller is defective or installed improperly. Check the host adapter installation (including IRQ, DMA, and I/O settings) and see that the proper suite of device drivers has been installed correctly. The SCSI host adapter should appear in the Device Manager without any warnings or cautions. If the host adapter is flagged with an error, you may need to resolve a potential resource conflict. If the system still refuses to recognize the controller, try installing it in a different PC. If the controller also fails in a different PC, the controller is probably bad and should be replaced. However, if the controller *works* in a different PC, your original PC may not support all the functions under the interrupt 15h call required to configure SCSI adapters (such as an AMI SCSI host adapter). Consider upgrading the PC BIOS ROM to a new version—especially if the PC BIOS is older. There may also be an upgraded SCSI BIOS or host adapter driver to compensate for this problem.

**SYMPTOM 32-12**    **The PCI SCSI host adapter is not recognized, and the SCSI BIOS banner is not displayed**    This often occurs when installing new PCI SCSI host adapters. The host computer must be PCI REV. 2.1 compliant (usually later), and the motherboard BIOS must support PCI-to-PCI Bridges (PPB) and bus mastering; this is typically a problem (or limitation) with some older PCI motherboard chipsets, and you'll probably find that the PCI SCSI adapter board works just fine on newer systems. If the system *doesn't* support PPB, it may not be possible to use the PCI SCSI adapter. You can try an ISA SCSI adapter instead or upgrade the motherboard to one with a more recent chipset.

If the system hardware *does* offer PPB support and the problem persists, the motherboard BIOS may still not support PPB features as required by the PCI 2.1 and later standards. In this case, try a motherboard BIOS upgrade if one is available. If the problem continues, either the board is not in a bus mastering slot or the PCI slot is not enabled for bus mastering. Configure the PCI slot for bus mastering through CMOS Setup or through a jumper on the motherboard (check your system's documentation to see exactly how to do this).

**SYMPTOM 32-13**    **During boot-up, you see a "Host Adapter Configuration Error" message**    In virtually all cases, this indicates a problem with the PCI slot configuration for the SCSI host adapter. Try enabling an IRQ for the SCSI adapter's PCI slot (usually accomplished through the CMOS Setup). Make sure that any IRQ being assigned to the SCSI adapter PCI slot is not conflicting with other devices in the system. You may also try moving the PCI card to another PCI slot (usually closer to the processor).

**SYMPTOM 32-14**    **You see an error message such as "No SCSI Functions in Use"** Even when a SCSI adapter and devices are installed and configured properly, there are several possible causes for this kind of an error. First, make sure that no hard disk drivers are installed when no physical SCSI hard disks are in the system. Also make sure that no hard disk drivers are installed (in CONFIG.SYS) when the SCSI host adapter BIOS is enabled. HDD drivers aren't needed then, but you could leave the drivers in place and disable the SCSI BIOS. Finally, this error can occur if the HDD was formatted on another (older) SCSI controller that does not support ASPI or uses a specialized format. For example, older Western Digital controllers only work with Western Digital HDDs. In this case, you should try a more generic controller, or you'll need to repartition and reformat the drives with the new controller.

**SYMPTOM 32-15**    **You see an error message such as "No Boot Record Found"** This is generally a simple problem which can be traced to several possible issues. First, chances are that the drive has never been partitioned (FDISK) or formatted as a bootable drive (FORMAT). Repartition and reformat the hard drive according to the manufacturer's recommendations. If you partitioned and formatted the drive with a third-party utility (such as TFORMAT), be sure to answer "Y" if asked to make the disk bootable. A third possibility can occur if the disk was formatted on another manufacturer's controller. If this is the case, there may be little alternative but to repartition and reformat the drive again on your current controller.

**SYMPTOM 32-16**    **You see an error such as "Device fails to respond—No devices in use. Driver load aborted"**    In most cases, the problem is something simple such as the SCSI device not being turned on or cabled correctly. Verify that the SCSI devices are on and connected correctly. In other cases, the SCSI device is on but fails the INQUIRY command. This happens when the SCSI device is defective or is not supported by the host adapter. The device may need default jumper settings changed (for example, the drive should Spin up and Come Ready on its own). You may find that the SCSI device is sharing the same SCSI ID with another device. Check all SCSI devices to verify that each device has a separate SCSI ID. You may have the wrong device driver loaded for your particular device type. This may require you to update one or more SCSI device drivers under Windows. Under DOS, check CONFIG.SYS to make sure the correct driver is loaded for the drive type (for example, TSCSI.SYS for a hard disk, not a CD-ROM).

**SYMPTOM 32-17**    **You see an error such as "Unknown SCSI Device" or "Waiting for SCSI Device"**    The SCSI hard disk has failed to boot as the primary drive. Check that the primary hard disk is set at SCSI ID 0. Make sure that the drive is partitioned and formatted as the primary drive. If necessary, boot from a floppy with just the ASPI manager loaded in CONFIG.SYS and no other drivers, and *then* format the drive. It may also be that the SCSI cable termination is not correct (or TERMPWR is not provided by the HARD DISK for the host adapter). Verify the cable terminations and TERMPWR signal.

**SYMPTOM 32-18**    **You see an error such as "CMD Failure XX"**    This typically occurs during the FORMAT process. The XX is a vendor-specific code, and you'll need to contact the vendor to determine what the error means. The most common problem is trying to partition a drive that is *not* low-level formatted. If this is the case, run the low-level format utility (or other "drive preparation" utility) that accompanied the SCSI drive, and then try partitioning again. If you're experiencing a different error, you may need to take other action, depending on the nature of the error.

**SYMPTOM 32-19**    **After the SCSI adapter BIOS header appears, you see a message like "Checking for SCSI target 0 LUN 0"**    The system pauses about 30 seconds and then reports "BIOS not installed, no INT 13h device found." The system then boots normally. In most cases, the BIOS is trying to find a hard drive at SCSI ID 0 or 1, but no hard drive is available. If you do not have a SCSI hard drive attached to the host adapter, it is recommended that you disable the SCSI BIOS.

**SYMPTOM 32-20**    **The system hangs when the SCSI BIOS header appears**    This is usually caused by a terminator problem. Make sure that the SCSI devices at the end of the SCSI chain (either internally or externally) are terminated. Check all device IDs to make sure that they are unique, and also check for system resource conflicts (such as BIOS address, I/O address, and interrupts). You may also need to disable the Shadow RAM feature in the CMOS Setup.

**SYMPTOM 32-21**    **The SCSI BIOS header is displayed during system startup, and then you get the message "Host Adapter Diagnostic Error"**    The card either has a port address conflict with another card, or has been changed to port address 140h and the BIOS is enabled. Some SCSI host adapters are able to use the BIOS under port address 140h, so check for I/O conflicts. You may need to reconfigure the SCSI host adapter through onboard jumpers or the adapter's SCSI BIOS Setup routine. In other cases, resolve the device conflict through the Windows Device Manager.

**SYMPTOM 32-22**    **You see an error such as "Device connected, but not ready"**    This error indicates that the host computer received no answer when it requested data from an installed SCSI device (such as a hard drive). Run the SCSI BIOS Setup utility and set the *Send Start Unit Command* to **Yes** for the particular SCSI device ID (for example, the first SCSI HDD is usually ID 0). Also verify that the suspect device is set to spin up when the power is switched on. This option is typically set by a jumper on the device itself, so you may need to refer to the device's documentation for specific jumper assignments.

**SYMPTOM 32-23**    **You see an error such as "Start unit request failed"**    The SCSI BIOS was unable to initiate a Send Start Unit command to one of the installed SCSI devices. First, verify that the device is connected and powered properly. Next, run the SCSI BIOS Setup and disable the Send Start Unit command for that particular device. If the problem persists, the SCSI device itself may be defective and require replacement.

**SYMPTOM 32-24**    **You see an error such as "Time-out failure during..."**    An unexpected timeout occurred while attempting to communicate with a SCSI device. First, verify that the SCSI bus is properly terminated, and ensure that all power and signal cables are properly connected. Next, isolate potentially defective SCSI devices—try disconnecting the SCSI device cables from the SCSI card and then starting the computer. If the computer successfully restarts, the disconnected SCSI device may be defective.

**SYMPTOM 32-25    You see an error such as "Too many devices terminated on the SE connectors"**    The SCSI BIOS has detected more than two terminated devices on the single-ended (SE) cable segment. Verify the termination on the 68-pin or 50-pin internal SE connectors, and terminate only the **last** SCSI device at the end of each cable according to the manufacturer's recommendations. Remove or disable the terminators on the SCSI devices between the ends of the cables. If no SCSI devices are connected to either of the connectors, set the SCSI BIOS termination option for the SE connector to Automatic or Enable.

**SYMPTOM 32-26    You see an error such as "Insufficient termination detected on SE connectors"**    The SCSI BIOS has detected only one terminated device (or no terminated devices) on the single-ended (SE) cable segment. Verify the termination on the 68-pin or 50-pin internal SE connectors. Terminate only the last SCSI device at the end of each cable. Remove or disable the terminators on the SCSI devices between the ends of the cables. If no SCSI devices are connected to either of the connectors, set the SCSI BIOS termination option for the SE connector to Automatic or Enable.

**SYMPTOM 32-27    You see an error such as "Too many devices terminated on LVD/SE connectors"**    The SCSI card BIOS has detected more than two terminated devices on the LVD/SE SCSI cable segment. Verify the termination on the internal and/or external 68-pin LVD/SE connectors. Terminate only the last SCSI device at the end of each cable. Remove or disable the terminators on the SCSI devices between the ends of the cables. If no SCSI devices are connected to either of the connectors, set the SCSI BIOS termination option for the LVD/SE connector to Automatic or Enable.

**SYMPTOM 32-28    You see an error such as "Insufficient termination detected on LVD/SE connectors"**    The SCSI card BIOS has detected only one terminated device (or no terminated devices) on the LVD/SE segment. Verify the termination on the internal and/or external 68-pin connectors. Terminate only the last SCSI device at the end of each cable. Remove or disable the terminators on the SCSI devices between the ends of the cables. If no SCSI devices are connected to either of the connectors, set the SCSI BIOS termination option for the LVD/SE connector to Automatic or Enable.

**SYMPTOM 32-29    You encounter problems with an Adaptec SCSI controller and CD-RW drive**    Your computer may hang when you start your Windows 98 computer, or your computer may run slowly when you try to access drives in your computer. This problem can occur if you're using an Adaptec AHA-2940U2W SCSI host adapter with a SCSI CD-RW drive. The AIC78U2.MPD driver file included with the Adaptec AHA-2940U2W SCSI adapter is *not* completely compatible with Windows 98. To correct this problem, download the 7800W9X.EXE file (or later) from Adaptec's Web site (www.adaptec.com). This self-extracting file contains updated drivers for the Adaptec AHA-2940U2W SCSI adapter. Keep in mind that later versions of Windows may provide adequate native support for these SCSI products.

**SYMPTOM 32-30    Windows 98 cannot locate the SCSI CD-ROM after upgrading**
When Windows 98 Setup restarts your computer for the first time, Setup may be unable to access your SCSI CD-ROM drive, and you may receive error messages stating that files cannot be found (the file names vary depending on your computer's hardware). Once Setup is completed and you attempt to start Windows 98, your computer may hang, and only a blinking cursor may be displayed on a black screen.

In virtually every case, this problem will occur if the HIDE120.COM file (a file related to an LS120 drive) is being loaded from the AUTOEXEC.BAT file. Open your AUTOEXEC.BAT file and disable (that is, REM out) the HIDE120 command line, such as:

```
REM d:\lsl120\hide120.com
```

# Understanding FireWire

SCSI has traditionally been an 8-bit or 16-bit "parallel" standard allowing a wide variety of devices to communicate with the host computer at high speeds. Although designers constantly struggle to improve SCSI performance, it's clear that technical issues in cabling and controllers present some serious challenges to faster parallel SCSI. As part of today's SCSI-3 standards, designers have developed three serial SCSI approaches: Serial Storage Architecture (SSA), FireWire (IEEE 1394) and FibreChannel (FC). However, FireWire is the major scheme used on today's PCs. This part of the chapter explores the main ideas behind FireWire implementations that are widely available as PCI expansion cards—and even present on some motherboards.

## ABOUT FIREWIRE

Simply put, the IEEE 1394 interface is a remarkably fast and effective high-speed serial SCSI interface that is intended to support peripheral data transfers between demanding peripheral devices. This technology was originally developed by Apple, but was eventually adopted by the IEEE as an official industry standard. Operating at speeds up to 400 Mb/s (megabits per second), systems supporting IEEE 1394 have 30 times more bandwidth than USB 1.1 (though USB is not in the SCSI family). IEEE 1394 also includes automatic configuration *without* the need for device IDs or terminators, hot swapping of peripherals, and support for up to 63 devices (on cables up to 15 feet long). This technology permits the addition of a virtually unlimited amount of data storage capacity through the use of multiple external hard drives.

Given its high speed, IEEE 1394 technology is perfectly suited for multimedia peripherals, hard drives, and printers. It's becoming the interface of choice for moving audio files and the images from video camcorders and digital cameras. More and more computer users are employing IEEE 1394 for their multimedia, home entertainment, and data processing applications. IEEE 1394 is gaining support as a solution for many applications outside of the computer industry. FireWire is offered as a standard interface on many new consumer digital devices, including camcorders, still cameras, and even the newest game consoles. When redefining the MIDI standard with MIDI 2, music manufacturers have chosen IEEE 1394 as the new-generation interface for electronic musical instruments and high-performance editing systems. A group of VCR manufacturers also has adopted IEEE 1394 as the video interface for its next generation of products. The Video Electronics Standards Association (VESA) has selected IEEE 1394 for its home-distribution network in such systems as set-top boxes and high-definition television.

### Installing an IEEE 1394 Adapter

To employ IEEE 1394 devices on your computer, you need to install an IEEE 1394 adapter card. This part of the chapter explains the proper installation and setup of a typical IEEE 1394 adapter. Before you get started, make sure that your system meets the minimum requirements for a typical IEEE 1394 adapter:

- Pentium 200 MHz processor or better
- 32MB of RAM or more
- Available PCI card slot on the motherboard

■ Windows 98 SE (Second Edition) or higher

■ CD-ROM drive (for loading drivers)

> Verify that you have Windows 98 SE or later installed on your system by right-clicking My Computer and selecting Properties. The General tab in System Properties should indicate Windows 98 Second Edition.

The steps that follow describe how to install the IEEE 1394 adapter card (such as the Adaptec FireConnect 4300 card in Figure 32-9) in one of your computer's PCI slots. If you don't have a PCI slot available, you need to disable and remove another PCI device, or upgrade your motherboard to a model offering more PCI slots.

1.  With your computer shut down and unplugged, remove the system's outside cover.

2.  Install the adapter in an open PCI slot in your computer by carefully pushing the adapter into the PCI slot, holding the card by the external edges only.

3.  Secure the card into place with a single chassis screw.

4.  Close your computer. Reattach the power cable, power-up the system, and allow the system to restart normally.

5.  After your computer has finished rebooting, insert your Windows installation CD (if necessary).

6.  Windows will detect that you've installed new hardware, and launch the Add New Hardware wizard. The wizard searches for new drivers for your IEEE 1394 adapter. Click Next.

7.  Make sure the Search For The Best Driver For Your Device option is selected. Click Next.

8.  Windows will search for the new drivers. Be sure to select the CD-ROM Drive check box, and deselect the Floppy Disk Drives check box. Click Next.

9.  The Add New Hardware wizard defaults to the updated drive. Click Next.

10. Click Next again so that Windows can install the best driver for the adapter.

11. Windows finishes installing software for your adapter. Click Finish. You may need to restart the computer so that the basic adapter will be detected.

**FIGURE 32-9**   The Adaptec FireConnect 4300 PCI FireWire card (Courtesy of Adaptec)

If you're installing a FireWire card under Windows XP, suitable default drivers for the FireWire controller may already be available. This can greatly simplify the installation and setup of the device. Be sure to check the manufacturer's recommendations for specific instructions or cautions.

## Software Setup

Although Windows 98/Me/XP should offer adequate support for IEEE 1394 adapters, you will probably need to install the specific drivers that accompanied the particular adapter in order to guarantee best results. Follow these general steps (but refer to the manufacturer's recommendations for specific procedures and cautions):

1.  Insert the IEEE 1394 adapter's CD into your CD-ROM drive. The Autorun program will start automatically in a few seconds.

2.  The main menu appears, showing several options. Click Setup 1394 Adapter.

3.  The 1394 Adapter Setup Welcome screen appears. Click Next.

4.  In the Driver Update dialog box, click Next to continue. This will prepare your system to support your specific IEEE 1394 adapter.

5.  Click Next again to verify that you have the latest IEEE 1394 drivers from Microsoft.

6.  Your IEEE 1394 adapter software is ready to finalize your setup. Click Finish when you see the Congratulations screen, to update your 1394 drivers and install a safe-removal utility that allows you to safely remove any of your plug-and-play devices.

7.  The Windows Update dialog box appears. Click Yes to continue and load the update.

8.  The license agreement for the Windows Update appears. Click Yes to continue. You must restart your computer for the new settings to take effect. When prompted to restart the system, click Yes.

## Connecting IEEE 1394 Devices

Once your IEEE 1394 adapter is installed on a Windows 98/Me/XP platform, it's time to connect your individual devices. In most cases, connecting IEEE 1394 devices is a simple matter, but you need to remember some rules:

■  An IEEE 1394 controller is required, and must be properly identified by the operating system prior to installing individual devices.

■  Additional software drivers or applets may be needed to fully support each IEEE 1394 device.

■  IEEE 1394 devices can be connected in any combination of branching and chaining, as long as no loops are formed.

■  An IEEE 1394 bus can support up to 16 consecutive cable hops of 4.5 meters (14.76 feet) each.

■  There are no SCSI-style ID numbers to set, and no termination requirements.

■  To connect a digital video (DV) camcorder, digital still camera, scanner, printer, or other IEEE 1394 peripheral, simply plug the 6-pin connector on the supplied FireWire cable to the IEEE 1394 adapter, and attach the 4-pin connector to the device's IEEE 1394 port. Both connectors snap into place when properly engaged.

■  If you wish to connect two devices together (or if your device has a 6-pin IEEE 1394 port), you can obtain 6-pin to 6-pin FireWire cables at your favorite retailer.

■  If you have problems with high-bandwidth FireWire devices (such as digital video transfers), make certain that no other FireWire devices are being used at the same time.

In addition to these general guidelines, you need to keep in mind the following list of important things that you should not do:

- Do not connect more than 63 devices at one time (including computers).
- Do not connect devices in such a way that any two devices have more than 16 cables directly connected between them.
- Do not connect IEEE 1394 cables in a way that forms a "ring" of devices.
- Leave unused 1394 connections empty—there are *no* terminators for FireWire connections.
- Connect devices that require power from an IEEE 1394 port directly to the computer—*not* to another device.
- Do not unplug an IEEE 1394 device while it is being used. For example, do not unplug an IEEE 1394 hard drive while copying files onto it.

## Working with FireWire Hard Drives

While IEEE 1394 has seen service mainly in digital video work, drive manufacturers (such as Western Digital or Iomega) have recently introduced a line of external FireWire hard drives. By using the IEEE 1394 interface, FireWire hard drives can be installed quickly and easily with no real configuration issues (you don't even have to shut down the PC). Remember that FireWire hard drives are external peripherals that operate through an IEEE 1394 adapter card. Most current PCs should easily meet the minimum system requirements, but it's certainly worth a moment to verify the requirements before attaching devices.

 Make sure that you have Windows 98/Me/XP (or Windows 2000) installed on your system.

IEEE 1394 hard drives are precision instruments. As with any internal hard drive, they should be handled with care during unpacking and installation. FireWire drives are not intended to be portable drives, so rough handling, shock, or vibration may damage them. Do not unpack your drive until you're ready to use it.

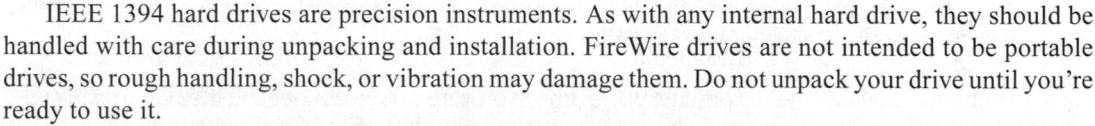 Once you've opened your drive to install it, take a moment to record the serial number and model number from the drive mechanism. You'll need this information when setting up the drive.

## Installing a FireWire Hard Drive

The installation of an IEEE 1394 hard drive is remarkably straightforward, but you need to install some supporting software for the drive. You generally need the following items to ensure a smooth installation:

- IEEE 1394 hard drive
- A 6-pin to 6-pin IEEE 1394 cable
- An AC power adapter for the drive
- IEEE 1394 hard drive's CD

You should connect your new IEEE 1394 hard drive to your computer *before* performing any setup procedures. For best results, be sure to follow these general steps:

1. Connect the AC power adapter to the power socket on the IEEE 1394 hard drive, and then plug the AC adapter into an electrical outlet.

2. Turn on your IEEE 1394 hard drive (move the drive's power switch to the On position).

3. Power-up your computer and allow the system to boot normally.

4. Plug one end of the FireWire cable (included) into any FireWire port on your computer.

5. Plug the other end of the FireWire cable into either of the IEEE 1394 hard drive's ports (port A or port B).

If you do not follow this process, it may take longer for the PC to recognize the IEEE 1394 hard drive.

6. Once the system has booted, insert the IEEE 1394 hard drive's CD into your CD-ROM drive. The setup program will start automatically. If the program does not start automatically, open Windows Explorer, click the CD-ROM drive icon, and then double-click the SETUP.EXE file. Keep in mind that later versions of Windows (such as Windows XP) may not need additional software to operate the drive.

7. When the Main Menu dialog box appears, select Setup 1394 Hard Drive.

8. The license agreement appears. Click I Accept.

9. The Setup 1394 Device dialog box appears next, showing the drive(s) detected in your system. Check the serial number of your new IEEE 1394 hard drive and make sure it matches the serial number displayed in this dialog box.

10. Once you're sure that the program has selected your new IEEE 1394 hard drive, click Setup. This process may take several minutes.

11. After the basic installation is complete, you may be prompted to register your new IEEE 1394 hard drive. If so, click Register Now and follow the instructions.

In some cases, you may need to pre-install the driver software before connecting the drive to the system for the first time. See the manufacturer's recommendations for specific instructions and cautions.

## Disconnecting a FireWire Hard Drive

FireWire allows for hot-pluggable devices, so a hard drive may be connected or disconnected while the PC is running. However, you should follow the protocol outlined next before disconnecting your drive; otherwise, data loss may result.

1. Click the Windows Unplug Or Eject Hardware icon in your system tray (located in the bottom-right corner of your screen).

2. Click the device to be stopped (such as "Stop Hard Drive OHCI IEEE 1394 Host Controller").

3. In the dialog box that appears, select your IEEE 1394 hard drive from the list, and then click Stop.

4. In the next dialog box, stop the IEEE 1394 hard drive and prepare it for safe removal by clicking OK.

Do not unplug your 1394 hard drive while copying files. This could result in data loss and disk damage.

# Further Study

**Adaptec**   www.adaptec.com
**Ancot**   www.ancot.com
**IEEE 1394 Trade Association**   www.1394ta.org
**Quantum**   www.quantum.com/src/
**SCSI guide**   www.delec.com/guide/scsi/
**SCSI Trade Association**   www.scsita.org
**Symbios articles**   www.lsilogic.com
**T10 Committee**   www.t10.org
**Western Digital**   www.wdc.com

# 33

# SERIAL AND INFRARED PORT TROUBLESHOOTING

Every PC needs a means of communicating with external devices. While today's computers use USB and IEEE 1394 (a.k.a. FireWire or i.LINK) connections, early PCs relied solely on serial and parallel ports for their device communication. The parallel port was generally considered to be a "printer port," so another port was needed to communicate with simple low-bandwidth devices like modems and mice. The Electronics Industry Association (EIA) responded to this early need by developing a standard for *serial* communication. Instead of sending 8 bits at a time over a set of data lines (as a parallel port does), only two data lines were used—one to transmit data, and one to receive data. The EIA denoted its serial standard as *RS-232* (or simply the "serial port"). A serial port offers several distinct advantages over early parallel ports. First, the serial port was designed to be bi-directional right from the start. This made "serial" the preferred method for interactive devices such as modems, mice, tablets, and so on. Second, the serial port used fewer physical signal lines than the parallel port. This made cabling less expensive and reduced potential connector problems. Where a printer cable is generally limited to 2 meters, a serial cable can easily exceed 60 meters, which opened the way for basic local networking.

The one problem with serial communication has traditionally been the need to physically connect devices. This often required you to shut down the system, make physical connections, install drivers, set communication parameters, and make other changes to the system before the two devices would communicate. With the advent of Windows 9x/Me/XP, designers have introduced a means of infrared serial communication (based on the same technology used for TV remote controls) that avoids troublesome connection and configuration problems. By employing infrared serial ports adhering to Infrared Device Association (IrDA) standards, you can conveniently print or exchange files with other IrDA-compliant systems. This chapter shows you the essential concepts of serial communication and port operation, explains the setup and workings of IrDA devices, and then guides you through a series of troubleshooting procedures.

Today, the classical serial (COM) port is competing with both the Universal Serial Bus (or USB) and the IEEE 1384 (FireWire) ports. USB and FireWire devices are typically easier to install, and can support fast data transfers between devices.

# Understanding Asynchronous Communication

The serial port is not terribly difficult to grasp, but its operation is a bit more involved than that of a parallel port. To appreciate the operations and signals of a typical serial port, you need to be familiar with a variety of concepts. When a parallel port strobes a printer, the printer "knows" that all 8 bits of data are available and valid. However, a serial port must send or receive 8 data bits (one bit at a time) over a single data line. As you might imagine, this presents some serious challenges for the receiving device, which must determine where the data stream starts and ends—hardly a simple task. It is certainly possible to send a synchronizing clock signal along with the data wire. The receiving device could easily use the clock to detect each data bit. This technique is known as *synchronous* serial communication. It is reliable, but rarely used in PCs (other than the keyboard interface).

Instead of using a discrete clock signal to accompany the data, it is possible to eliminate the clock by embedding synchronization information along with the data bits. Thus, when a data stream reaches a receiving device, it can strip away the synchronization bits, leaving the original data. As a result, serial communication is not constrained by a clock. This is *asynchronous* communication—a popular and inexpensive serial technique. The remainder of this chapter deals with asynchronous communication.

## THE DATA FRAME

Asynchronous communication requires that data bits be combined with *synchronization bits* before transmission. Synchronization bits provide three important pieces of information to the receiving device: where the data starts, where the data ends, and whether the data is correct. These bits, combined with the data byte, form the *data frame,* as illustrated in Figure 33-1. The first thing you should notice about serial data is that it is bipolar—that is, it has both positive and negative voltages. Contrary to what you might guess, a positive voltage represents a logic 0 (called a *space*), and a negative voltage represents a logic 1 (called a *mark*). The next thing you should note is that the serial signal line is normally idle in the logic 0 (space) state.

The first element of all asynchronous data frames is a single *start bit,* which is always logic 1 (mark). When the receiver detects logic 1, it "knows" the data frame has started. The next 5 to 8 bits are always the *data bits*. The exact number of bits (usually 8) can be set by the communication software, but must be the same at both the transmitting and receiving ends. After data, a single error-checking bit (called a *parity*

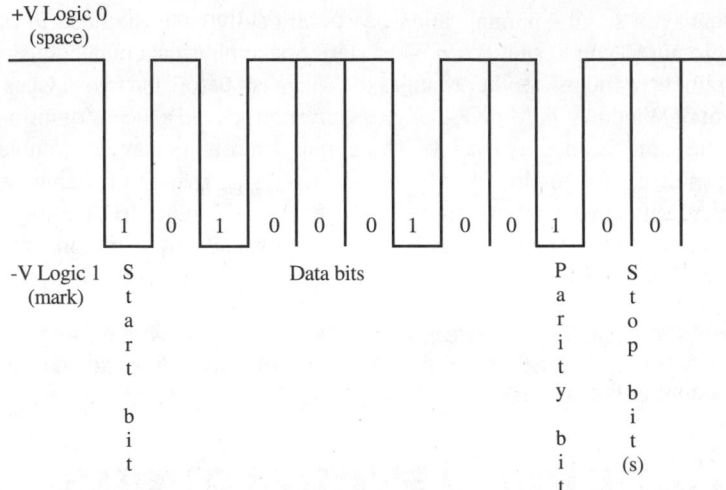

**FIGURE  33-1**    A typical asynchronous data frame

*bit*) can be included if desired. Parity is calculated at the sending device and sent with the word. Parity is also calculated at the receiving device and checked against the received parity bit. If the two match, the data is assumed to be correct. If the two do not match, an error is flagged. There are five classes of parity in serial communication:

■  **None**   No parity bit is added to the word. This is typical for much of today's serial communication.

■  **Even**   If the number of 1's in the data word is odd, parity is set to 1 to make the number of 1's even.

■  **Odd**    If the number of 1's in the data word is even, parity is set to 1 to make the number of 1's odd.

■  **Mark**   Parity is always set to 1.

■  **Space**   Parity is always set to 0.

Many communication connections today abandon the use of parity in favor of the more reliable and sophisticated cyclical redundancy check (CRC). A CRC has the same effect as a parity check, but instead of checking one byte at a time, an entire block of data is checked.

The last part of a data frame is the *stop bit(s)*—typically only one, but two can be used. Stop bits are always logic 0 (space). After the receiving device detects the stop bit(s), the line remains idle in the space condition awaiting the next subsequent start bit. Framing is usually denoted as data/parity/stop. For example, the connection to a BBS typically uses 8/N/1 framing (8 data bits/no parity bit/1 stop bit).

One of the most important aspects of serial communication is that both the receiving and transmitting ends must be configured for the exact **same** data frame. If both ends are not configured identically, serial data will be misinterpreted as meaningless garbage.

## SIGNAL LEVELS

Whereas the parallel port uses TTL-compatible logic signals in its communication, a serial port uses bipolar signaling (both positive and negative voltages). The advantage of bipolar signaling is that it supports very long cabling with minimum noise. A logic 0 (space) condition is represented by a positive voltage between +3 Vdc and +15 Vdc. A logic 1 (mark) condition is represented by a negative voltage between –3 Vdc and –15 Vdc. On average, you can expect to see serial ports using +/–5 Vdc or +/–12 Vdc since those voltages are already produced by the PC power supply.

# Understanding the Serial Port

A serial port must be capable of several important operations. It must convert parallel data from the PC system bus into a sequence of serial bits, add the appropriate framing bits (which may be changed for different serial connections), and then provide each of those bits to the data line at the proper rate. The serial port must also work in reverse, accepting serial data at a known rate, stripping off the framing bits, converting the serial data bits back into bus form, and checking blocks of data for accuracy. The heart of the serial port is a single chip—the *universal asynchronous receiver/transmitter* (UART). A simplified block diagram for a serial port is illustrated in Figure 33-2.

The UART connects directly to the PC bus architecture—it is either added to the motherboard (part of the chipset's South Bridge component) or incorporated on an expansion board (for example, an internal PCI modem card will include an onboard modem). A UART chip contains all of the internal circuitry necessary to process, transmit, and receive data between the serial line and the PC bus. Since the UART is programmable, its configuration (its framing format and baud rate) can be set through DOS or Windows communication software. All data output, data input, and handshaking signals needed by the serial port are generated within the UART itself. It is interesting to note that the UART is powered by +5 Vdc only—just like most other chips in the system. This means that data and handshaking signals entering and leaving the UART are all TTL compatible. Transmitted data is converted to bipolar signals through a line driver chip. Bipolar data that appears on the receive line is converted back to TTL levels through a line receiver chip. All that remains is the

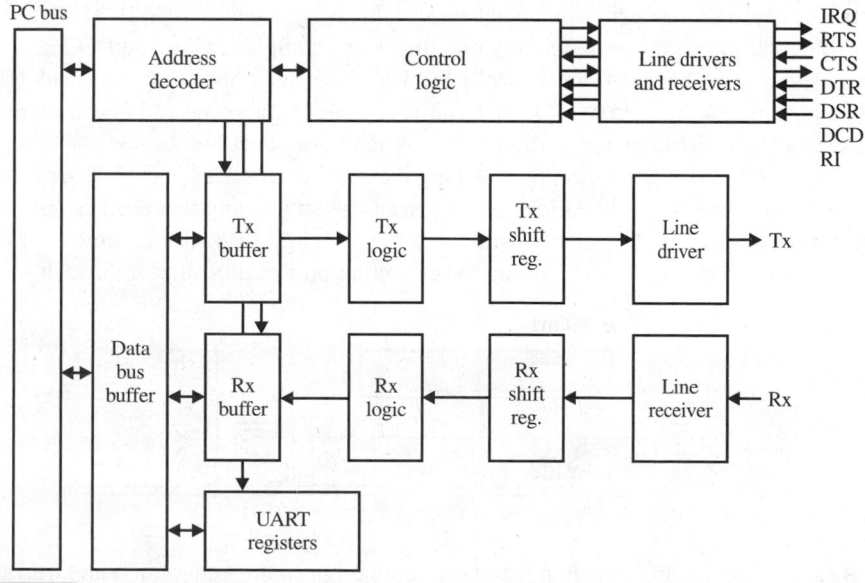

**FIGURE  33-2**    Simplified block diagram of a UART

port connector itself. The original serial port design used a 25-pin male subminiature D-type connector, but newer ports have abandoned the extra handshaking signals to accommodate a 9-pin male subminiature D-type connector such as in Figure 33-3.

## ADDRESSES AND INTERRUPTS

The UART is controlled through a series of important registers that allow the serial port characteristics to be programmed. They also shuttle the transmitted and received data as required. Older BIOS versions supported only two serial (or COM) ports, but virtually all current BIOS releases support four COM ports (designated COM1 through COM4). The typical base addresses for the COM ports are shown in Table 33-1. When a new COM port is installed in the system, it must be assigned to a valid base address and interrupt (IRQ). During actual operation, communication software deals with each port register individually. Table 33-2 lists the standard base address offsets for UART registers. Note that with no offset, both transmit and receive registers are available.

During system initialization, COM ports are checked in the following order: 03F8h, 02F8h, 03E8h, 02E8h, 03E0h, 02E0h, 0338h, and 0238h. (Older MCA systems use a different order.) COM designations are assigned depending on what ports are actually found, so keep in mind that the COM addresses may be exchanged depending on your particular system. In virtually all cases, COM1 is available at 03F8h. The specific I/O addresses for each COM port are kept in the BIOS data area of RAM starting at 0400h. As you might expect, only one COM port can be assigned to a base address. If more than one COM port is assigned to the same base address, system problems will almost certainly occur.

The use of interrupts in conjunction with COM ports can easily be confusing. Unlike parallel ports, which can be polled by BIOS, a serial port *demands* the use of interrupts. Since early PCs allocated space for two COM ports, only two IRQ lines were reserved (IRQ4 for COM1 and IRQ3 for COM2). Unfortunately, when PC BIOS expanded its support for additional COM ports, there were no extra IRQ lines available to assign. Thus, COM ports had to "share" interrupts. For example, COM1 and COM3 must share IRQ4, while COM2 and COM4 must share IRQ3. The problem is that no two devices can use the same IRQ at the same time—otherwise, a system conflict will result. Ultimately, though a typical PC can use four COM ports, only *two* of the four can be used at any one time (for example, COM1 and COM2, COM3 and COM4, COM1 and COM4, or COM2 and COM3). Further, the assignment of COM port address and IRQ lines must match. While COM3 and COM4 *can* be polled by BIOS, the speed and asynchronous nature of contemporary data transmission make polling very unreliable for serial ports.

Always begin a service examination by checking the number of serial ports in your system. Serial ports are so simple and easy to add to various expansion cards that you might exceed the maximum number of ports, or allow two ports to conflict, without even realizing it. Be sure to remove or disable any unused or conflicting COM ports by removing the offending port or disabling it through jumpers, DIP

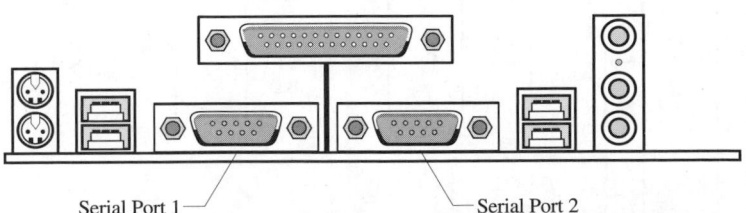

Serial Port 1 ⎯                                  ⎯ Serial Port 2

**FIGURE   33-3**    Serial ports remain a standard fixture on even the latest motherboards such as the Asus P4B533 (Courtesy of Asus Computer, Inc)

**TABLE 33-1    TYPICAL SERIAL PORT ADDRESSES AND IRQ ASSIGNMENTS**

| BUS ARCHITECTURE | PORT | ADDRESS | IRQ |
| --- | --- | --- | --- |
| All Systems | COM1 | 03F8h | IRQ4 |
| All Systems | COM2 | 02F8h | IRQ3 |
| ISA/PCI | COM3 | 03E8h | IRQ4 |
| ISA/PCI | COM4 | 02E8h | IRQ3 |
| ISA/PCI | COM3 | 03E0h | IRQ4 |
| ISA/PCI | COM4 | 02E0h | IRQ3 |
| ISA/PCI | COM3 | 0338h | IRQ4 |
| ISA/PCI | COM4 | 0238h | IRQ3 |

switches, or the CMOS Setup. A quick check of the Device Manager can usually reveal the COM ports detected in the system (see Figure 33-4). A common oversight is to add an internal modem as COM2 while hardware support for COM2 is still enabled on the motherboard. When you encounter conflicting COM ports, you will need to disable unneeded ports to prevent conflicts.

# DTE VS. DCE

As you work with serial ports and peripherals, you will often see the acronyms DTE and DCE used frequently. DTE stands for *data terminal equipment*, which is typically the computer containing the serial port. The modem, serial printer, or other serial peripheral is referred to as the *data carrier equipment* (or DCE). The distinction becomes important because the data and handshaking signals are swapped at the DCE end. For example, the Tx pin ("transmit"—usually on pin 3 of a 9-pin DTE) cannot connect directly to the same pin on the DCE; it must route to the Rx ("receive") pin instead. The DCE connector makes those swaps, so pin 3 of the DCE would be the Rx pin, and a straight-through cable can be used without difficulty.

However, suppose that two DTEs had to be connected. Since both devices carry the same signals on the same pins, a straight-through cable would cause confusion (the Tx line would connect to the Tx line on the other device, Rx would connect to Rx, and so on). As you can imagine, two DTEs cannot be connected

**TABLE 33-2    TYPICAL UART REGISTER ADDRESS OFFSETS**

| REGISTER | OFFSET |
| --- | --- |
| Receive Register | 00h |
| Transmit Register | 00h |
| Interrupt Enable Register | 01h |
| Interrupt ID Register | 02h |
| Data Frame Register | 03h |
| UART Control Register | 04h |
| Serialization Status Register | 05h |
| UART Status Register | 06h |
| General Purpose Register | 07h |

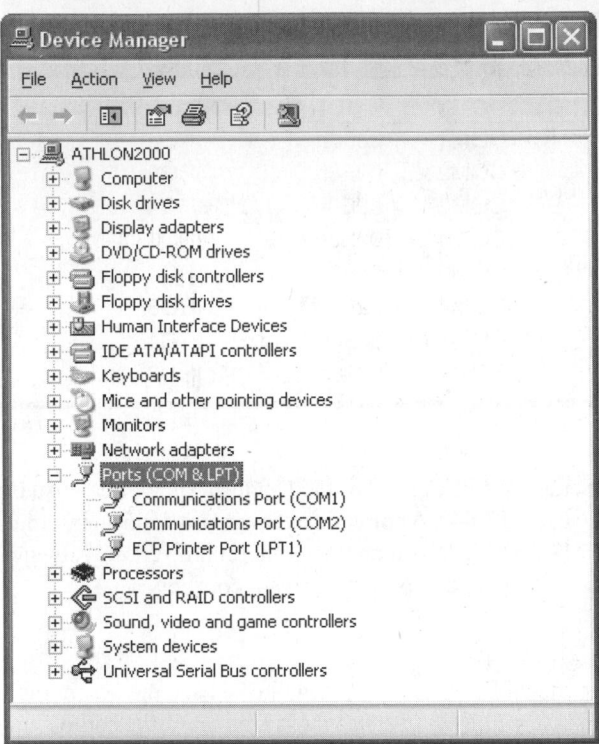

**FIGURE 33-4** Using the Device Manager to check for any COM ports assigned under Windows XP

with a straight-through cable. Of course, a specialized cable can be built that contains the proper wire swaps, but an easier alternative is simply to use a *null-modem,* which plugs into one end of the straight-through cable. The null-modem is little more than a jumper box that contains all of the proper swaps. This allows two DTEs to work as if one were a DTE and one were a DCE.

## SERIAL PORT SIGNALS

IBM and compatible PCs implement a serial port as either a 25-pin or 9-pin subminiature D-type connector, similar to the ones shown in Figure 33-5. Both ends of the serial cable are identical. There are three type of signals to be concerned with in a serial connection: data lines, control (or handshaking) lines, and ground lines. Table 33-3 identifies the name and description of each conductor for both 25-pin and 9-pin serial connections. Keep in mind that all data and control signals on the serial port are bipolar.

### Tx and Rx
These are simply the data lines into and out of the port. Tx is the Transmit line, which outputs serial data from the PC, and Rx is the Receive line, which accepts serial data from the serial peripheral.

### RTS and CTS
The RTS (Request to Send) signal is generated by the DTE. When asserted, it tells the DCE (for example, the modem) to expect to receive data. However, the DTE can't just dump data to DCE. The DCE must be *ready* to receive the data, so after the RTS line is asserted, the DTE waits for the CTS (Clear to Send) signal

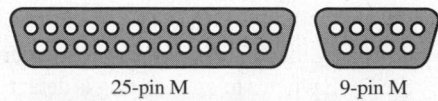

25-pin M          9-pin M

**FIGURE 33-5**     Serial port connectors

back from the DCE. Once the DTE receives a valid CTS signal, it can begin transferring data. It is this RTS/CTS handshake that forms the basis for data flow control via the system hardware.

## DTR and DSR

When the DTE is turned on or initialized and ready to begin serial operation, the DTR (Data Terminal Ready) line is asserted. This tells the DCE (for example, the modem) that the DTE (such as the computer) is ready to establish a connection. When the DCE has initialized and is ready for a connection, it will assert the DSR (Data Set Ready) line back to the DTE. Once the DTE is ready and recognizes the DSR signal, a connection is established. This DTR/DSR handshake is established only once when the DTE and DCE devices are first initialized, and must remain active throughout the connection. If either the DTR or DSR signal should fail, the communication channel will be interrupted (and the RTS/CTS handshake will no longer have any effect).

## DCD

The DCD (Data Carrier Detect) signal is particularly useful with modems. It is produced by the DCE when a carrier is detected from a remote target, and the DCE is ready to establish a communications pathway. The DCD signal is then sent back to the DTE. Once the DCD line is asserted, it will remain as long as a connection is established.

| **TABLE 33-3** | PIN ASSIGNMENTS FOR A TYPICAL SERIAL PORT CONNECTOR | | |
|---|---|---|---|
| **25-PIN CONNECTOR** | **9-PIN CONNECTOR** | **SIGNAL NAME** | **SIGNAL DIRECTION** |
| 1 | n/a | Protective Ground | n/a |
| 2 | 3 | Tx—Transmit Data | Output |
| 3 | 2 | Rx—Receive Data | Input |
| 4 | 7 | RTS—Request to Send | Output |
| 5 | 8 | CTS—Clear to Send | Input |
| 6 | 6 | DSR—Data Set Ready | Input |
| 7 | 5 | Signal Ground | n/a |
| 8 | 1 | DCD—Data Carrier Detect | Input |
| 9 | n/a | + Transmit Current Loop | Output |
| 11 | n/a | – Transmit Current Loop | Output |
| 18 | n/a | + Receive Current Loop | Input |
| 20 | 4 | DTR—Data Terminal Ready | Output |
| 22 | 9 | RI—Ring Indicator | Input |
| 23 | n/a | DSRD—Data Signal Rate Indicator | I/O |
| 25 | n/a | – Receive Current Loop | Input |

## RI

The RI (Ring Indicator) signal is asserted by the DCE and is also particularly useful with both internal and external modems. It is produced by the DCE when a telephone ring is detected. This becomes a vital signal if it is necessary for a remote user to call in and access your computer for remote diagnostics or other purposes. This is also an important signal when the system's power management is configured to "wake on ring."

# IrDA Port Issues

A growing number of desktop and laptop PCs (and their peripherals) are being equipped with infrared serial ports (dubbed "IrDA" by the Infrared Desktop Association). IrDA ports allow PCs and peripherals to communicate serially over an infrared link rather than going through the hassle of using cables. For example, you can type a document on a laptop, move the laptop into the vicinity of an IrDA printer, and then print the document without ever attaching a cable. All you need is a direct line of sight between the two devices. You can also share files between two IrDA-compliant PCs. Although IrDA ports offer some real connectivity benefits to PC users, they also present some problems with installation and configuration. This part of the chapter outlines the essential techniques to install and use IrDA devices, and offers some solid guidelines for testing and troubleshooting.

## IRDA SPEEDS

Most current PCs and peripherals support three classes of infrared speeds; serial IrDA, Fast IrDA, and Very Fast IrDA. Serial IrDA is the basic 115.2 Kbps link scheme that allows PCs to employ their existing serial port hardware without having to upgrade or retrofit the system. Fast IrDA supports data transfers up to 4 Mbps, and Very Fast IrDA handles up to 16 Mbps transfers. Remember that data transfers are in half-duplex mode (only one end of the link can transmit at any given time). Fast and Very Fast IrDA modes will require compliant high-speed hardware, but both are fully backward compatible with ordinary serial IrDA communication.

## IMPLEMENTING IRDA SUPPORT

Infrared support is certainly not difficult to establish under Windows 9x/Me/XP, but you will need a working IrDA port on both machines involved in the infrared link. For example, if you intend to print to an infrared printer, you'll need a PC and a printer with an IrDA port. If you'll be exchanging files between PCs, both PCs will need a working IrDA port. Consequently, you'll need to check for the presence of a working infrared port on your PC. Most laptop/notebook systems currently provide an IrDA port, and many desktop systems can accommodate an infrared port connected through a USB or serial port.

■   Start by checking the manufacturer's specifications for your PC or peripheral device—this will usually denote IrDA 2.0 (or later) support. If the PC or peripheral doesn't include an infrared port, you'll need to install an infrared adapter, or you won't be able to use an infrared link between devices.

■   If the device should include IrDA support, check the system's CMOS Setup to verify that the infrared feature is enabled. For peripheral devices (such as printers), infrared support can usually be controlled through the printer's control panel according to the manufacturer's instructions.

■   If the infrared adapter is connected externally, take a moment to double-check any signal and power connections to verify that the adapter is properly installed. If the device is fully PnP compliant, the

Windows platform should recognize and install the device. However, in some cases you'll need to use the Add Hardware wizard to install the infrared adapter yourself.

■ Check the Device Manager for an Infrared Devices entry. If an IrDA device is installed and enabled in the CMOS Setup, but no infrared support is listed in the Device Manager, you may need to run the Add Hardware wizard to identify the hardware and install the appropriate drivers for the infrared adapter. In some cases, you'll need to install the manufacturer's software that accompanied the infrared adapter.

# TESTING AN IRDA LINK

Once you've verified the basic hardware and software support for infrared communication, the next step is to test the IR link. The easiest and quickest way to do this is to print over an IrDA link to an IR-capable printer, or exchange data between two computers using the IR link (and a communications application like LapLink, or Wireless Link under Windows XP).

## Getting the Connection

Before any kind of data transfer can take place, both ends of the IrDA link must be working, and located within about 3 feet (roughly 1 meter) of each other. When the infrared devices are aligned properly, the Infrared Status icon will appear in the system tray of the task bar, and you can begin printing or exchanging other data.

## Testing an IR Link to a Printer

If you're testing an IR link to an IrDA-compliant printer (such as the HP LaserJet 5P and later models), you must first install the IR communications driver on your computer (if not already installed), and then try the Print option in your printing application (such as Notepad or Wordpad). Make sure that you have the correct printer driver installed for your IR-capable printer, and see that you've selected the infrared printing port (e.g., the virtual LPT port) as the printer port. If the application prints correctly to your IR-capable printer, you have validated the link successfully.

## Testing an IR Link between Computers

If you'd prefer to test the infrared connection between two computers, verify that the IrDA port is running at both ends of the link, then bring the two systems within range of each other (usually within about 3 feet). When the two systems are within range, an Infrared Connection Status icon appears in the system tray of the task bar, and a Wireless Link icon appears on the Windows XP desktop—though earlier versions of Windows will use Direct Cable Connect, or DCC, to establish a connection between the PCs. Now use a program such as Windows Explorer to transfer a small file from one system to another. If the file transfer is successful, you know that the link is working.

# CREATING AN IR NETWORK CONNECTION

Windows XP provides robust tools for creating network connections between PCs, and infrared (IrDA) connections are also supported. If you need to link two infrared-equipped PCs under Windows XP, verify that IR support is enabled on both systems, bring the two PCs into range, and try the following procedure.

Older Windows platforms should employ the Direct Cable Connection (DCC) scheme as described in the next section.

1. Open the Control Panel, click Network and Internet Connections, and click Network Connections.
2. In the left pane, click Create a New Connection. The New Connection wizard opens (see Figure 33-6).

**FIGURE 33-6**    The New Connection wizard, which allows you to configure a connection between PCs

3.  Click Next. In the Network Connection Type dialog box, click "Set up an advanced connection."

4.  Click Next. In the Advanced Connection Options dialog box, click "Connect directly to another computer."

5.  Click Next. Now set the PC as a **host** if the system has files that need to be accessed, or select **guest** if the system will be accessing resources on another PC.

6.  Click Next and be sure to select an infrared port as the connecting device. If the Infrared Port option is not available, the IR support is not properly installed or configured.

7.  Click Next. If the PC is a host, set users permissions to define which users (guests) can access the host. If the PC is a guest, select and configure a default connection.

8.  Select a valid name for the connection, and then click Finish. The network connection should now be established as long as the two PCs are in range of each other.

## CREATING AN IR DCC LINK

With a Direct Cable Connection (DCC) under Windows 9x/Me, you can establish a direct serial or parallel cable connection between two computers, and this allows you to share the resources of the computer designated as the host. DCC can also be used over an IR link. The computer that contains the information you want to share is the *host*, and the other computer is the *guest*. You can share folder(s) on the host and grant access rights to anyone using the guest computer by following this procedure under Windows 9x/Me. First, you need a resource to share, which you can specify by following these steps.

Under Windows XP, create an IR network connection between the two PCs as explained in the previous section.

**1.** Open My Computer.

**2.** Select the drive that you want to share, right-click the desired folder, and select Properties.

**3.** Select the Sharing tab (Figure 33-7), and then select the Shared As option. Enter a share name, add a comment, and configure user access rights (e.g., Full or Read-Only). The picture of a hand is added to the folder icon to indicate the selected folder is now a shared resource.

Check for the presence of DCC, and install it on both PCs if necessary. Now configure and test the DCC IR link between the two computers according to the steps that follow.

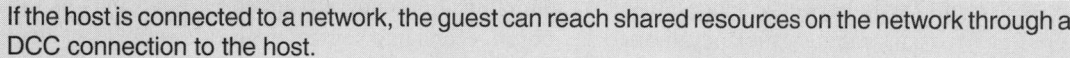
If the host is connected to a network, the guest can reach shared resources on the network through a DCC connection to the host.

**1.** See that the infrared devices are installed and positioned properly. You may wish to restrict the IR connection speed for initial testing.

**2.** Start with the host computer. Click Start | Programs | Accessories | Communications | Direct Cable Connection.

**3.** Follow the DCC wizard to set up the host computer, select the Host option, and opt to use the infrared port between the two ends.

**4.** Select a password if you wish, then click Finish. DCC will start running on the host system.

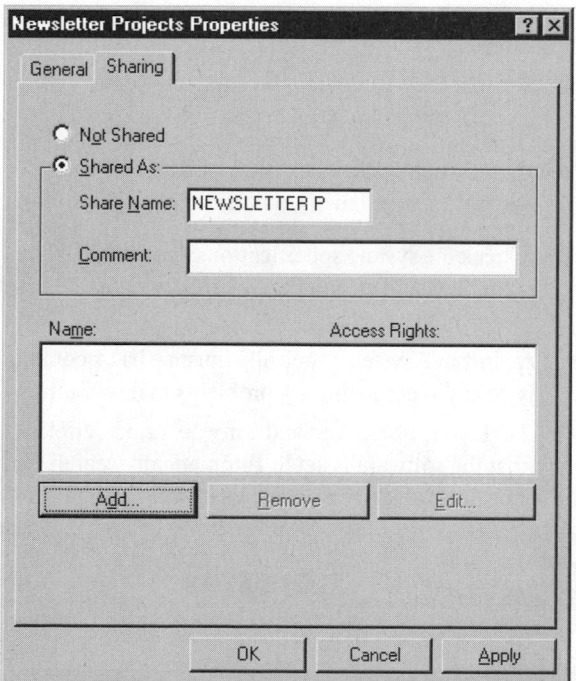

**FIGURE 33-7**   Sharing files through a drive's Properties dialog box

**5.** Repeat these steps for the guest computer (but select the Guest option instead of the Host option). When you're done with the wizard, click the Finish button. The DCC connection is automatically made over the IR link, and all the shared folders on the host are displayed on the guest's screen.

**6.** To copy a shared folder from the host to the guest over the IR link, select the folder's icon in the window that displays all the shared folders that are on the host, and drag the icon to the guest's desktop.

## MAKING THE MOST OF IRDA

Infrared links are handy and efficient tools that allow you to print and exchange files without the hassle of physical connections between devices. Still, IR communication can be plagued by numerous factors, including poor data transfer efficiency, limited device range, and intermittent device detection. Check the following points if you find that your IR communication is not efficient, or you notice that the IR devices frequently seem to move out of range with one another:

- *Check for obstructions.* Look for partial obstructions between the two infrared ends of the link. Obstructions can also include dirt and dust that have accumulated on the IR windows.

- *Check the range.* Range should always be about 3 feet or less between devices, so move the infrared devices closer together as necessary.

- *Check for overpowering light sources.* Extraneous light (e.g., bright sunlight or transmissions from nearby IR devices such as TV/VCR remote controls) can interfere with IR communication, so shade the devices, or turn off bright lights in the immediate area.

- *Check for movement.* Make sure the IR devices are perfectly still—neither end of the IR link should be moving or vibrating.

- *Check the device power.* See that each IR device is turned on. Recharge/replace the batteries for each IR device, or check its power supply connections.

If you find that the system cannot detect devices that should be in range, check the range, interference, obstructions, and power (as previously mentioned), and then check the following points:

- *Check system IR support.* Check the system specifications, the CMOS Setup, and the Device Manager to verify that IR support is enabled, and ensure that the IR device(s) are properly installed and identified on each system.

- *Check for IrDA compliance.* Infrared systems typically must be IrDA compliant. Mixing compliant and noncompliant devices may result in compatibility problems that will interfere with communication.

- *Check for IR searching.* Check your IR devices and software (e.g., Wireless Link software under Windows XP) and make sure that the software is set to automatically search for IR devices that come into range. Also keep the IR search interval to a reasonable level (long intervals may simulate a poor search).

# Troubleshooting Serial and Infrared Ports

Although the typical serial port is a rather simple I/O device, it presents some special challenges for the technician. Older PCs provided their serial ports in the form of 8-bit expansion boards. When a port failed, it was a simple matter to replace the board. Today, however, virtually all PCs provide at least one serial port directly on the motherboard—usually integrated into the South Bridge component of the main chipset. When a problem is detected with a motherboard serial port, a technician often has three choices:

- Replace the UART (responsible for virtually all serial port failures) on the motherboard. This requires access to surface-mount soldering tools and replacement chips, and can be quite economical in volume.
- Set the motherboard jumpers (if possible) to disable the defective serial port, and install an expansion board (such as a multi-I/O board) to take the place of the defective port. This assumes there is an available expansion slot.
- Replace the motherboard. This is a simple tactic that requires little overhead equipment, but can be rather expensive—especially if a motherboard upgrade also demands a new processor and RAM.

Virtually all commercial diagnostics are capable of locating any installed serial ports and testing the ports thoroughly through a loopback plug. Now that you have reviewed the layout, signals, and operation of a typical serial port, you can take a clear look at port troubleshooting procedures.

## USING MODE TO CONFIGURE A SERIAL PORT

On some older systems, it may be necessary for you to make changes to the serial port's configuration while in the real-mode (DOS). You can use the DOS MODE command to make your changes. From a command line prompt, type

```
mode comX: /<parameters>
```

where X: is the COM port that you need to tweak (such as COM2), and <parameters> represents the serial port features that are being altered (including baud rate, parity, data bits, and stop bits). For example:

```
MODE COM1: BAUD=2400 PARITY=N DATA=5 STOP=1 TO=OFF XON=ON ODSR=OFF OCTS=ON
DTR=OFF RTS=OFF IDSR=OFF
```

Table 33-4 lists the complete suite of serial port parameters that you can change with the DOS MODE command.

## SERIAL PORT CONFLICTS

Hardware and software conflicts with a system's serial ports are some of the most recurring and perplexing problems in PC troubleshooting. Although PC purists are pleased with the fact that current operating systems and BIOS support four COM ports, they cannot overcome the fact that there are still only *two* interrupts available to run the ports from. Technicians trying to upgrade a PC often encounter problems adding I/O adapters since many current PC motherboards already provide two COM ports right out of the factory. If a PC offers only one COM port (COM1), and another serial port is placed in the system (by accident or on purpose), be aware that you must choose a port and IRQ that does not conflict with the existing port (such as COM2 or COM4). If the PC already provides two COM ports (COM1 and COM2), adding a third COM port to the system will cause a hardware conflict. You can rectify the conflict by disabling the new COM port, or by disabling one of the two existing COM ports, and jumpering the new COM port to those settings.

Serial device drivers can also be a source of problems for COM ports. Incorrectly written mouse drivers, printer drivers, or third-party interrupt handlers can leave a port inoperative or erratic. If problems develop after a new driver is installed, disable the driver's reference in CONFIG.SYS, or install an updated protected-mode driver under Windows 98/Me/XP. TSRs (often loaded in AUTOEXEC.BAT) can

**TABLE 33-4   MODE COMMAND PARAMETERS**

| PARAMETER | DESCRIPTION |
|-----------|-------------|
| BAUD= | Sets the data transmission rate in bits per second. |
| PARITY= | Sets how the system checks for transmission errors using the parity bit. The value can be one of the following: N (None), E (Even), O (Odd), M (Mark), or S (Space). |
| DATA= | Sets the number of data bits in a frame (5 through 8). |
| STOP= | Sets the number of stop bits that define the end of a frame (1, 1.5, or 2). |
| TO=ON\|OFF | Turns the "infinite timeout processing" option on or off. |
| X=ON\|OFF | Turns the XON/XOFF (software handshaking) protocol on or off. |
| ODSR=ON\|OFF | Turns the output handshaking using Data Set Ready (DSR) circuit on or off. |
| OCTS=ON\|OFF | Turns the output handshaking using Clear To Send (CTS) circuit on or off. |
| DTR=ON\|OFF | Turns the DTR circuit on or off. |
| RTS=ON\|OFF\|HS\|TG | Specifies the settings for the RTS circuit to on, off, handshake, or toggle. |
| IDSR=ON\|OFF | Turns the DSR circuit sensitivity on or off. |

cause problems as well. If problems develop after a new TSR is installed, disable the offending TSR and try the system again. Remember that drivers and TSRs can easily be disabled by adding the REM statement before the command line in CONFIG.SYS or AUTOEXEC.BAT. If the communication trouble is under Windows 98/Me/XP, strongly suspect the Windows communication driver(s). In some cases, you can try removing the offending COM port entries from the Device Manager, then allow Windows to redetect and reinstall the port(s).

 USB and FireWire ports overcome these perplexing problems, and are often employed instead of conventional serial (COM) ports.

## MATCH THE SETTINGS

It's bad enough that you can only (practically) use two COM ports, but you also have to make sure that the port addresses and IRQ assignments match, as shown earlier in Table 33-1. For example, suppose that there is no COM1 at 03F8h, but there *is* a COM port at 02F8h. During system initialization, BIOS locates each available port and assigns a COM designation. So, since there is no port at 03F8h, the port at 02F8h (normally COM2) is the first port detected, and is assigned as COM1. However, DOS and BIOS expect COM1 to use IRQ4, but the port at 02F8h uses IRQ3. If you attempt to use DOS for COM1, the standard interrupt handlers will not work. You would have to use communication software that talks to the port directly (and thus avoids using DOS interrupt handlers) and can be assigned with the address and IRQ setting of your choosing. As an alternative, you can switch the COM port to 03F8h using the CMOS Setup and set the interrupt to IRQ4. That should restore normal COM1 operation through DOS.

Windows environments are a bit more forgiving. Simply right-click the troublesome port in the Device Manager (such as the Windows XP Device Manager) and click Properties—any conflicts or other device problems will be reported here. If you need to adjust the resource assignments, simply click the Resources tab (see Figure 33-8) and alter the IRQ or I/O address as needed. You may need to reboot the PC and check that your changes have taken effect.

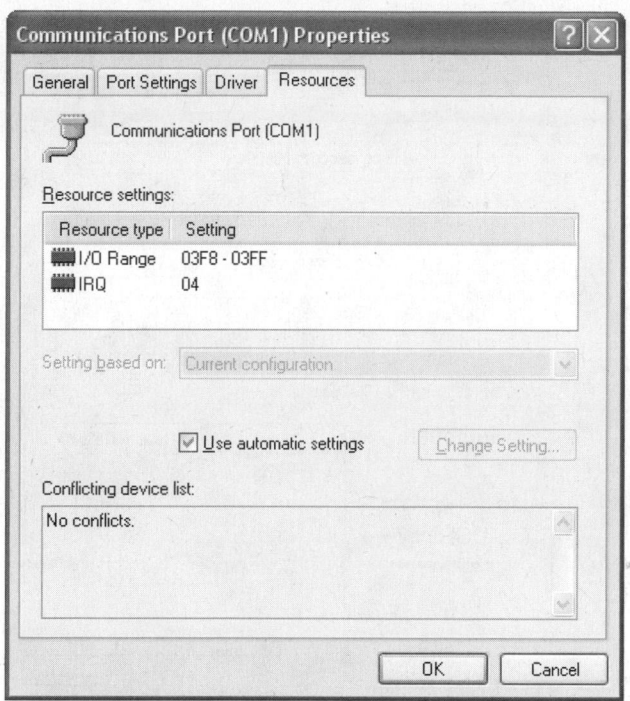

**FIGURE 33-8** Using the Windows Resources tab to adjust COM port resource assignments if necessary

## FRAME IT RIGHT

The data frame and rate play very important roles in serial communication. The sending and receiving ends of the serial link must be set to the *same configuration*—otherwise, the received data will be interpreted as garbage. If you encounter such troubles, be sure to check the settings for data bits, parity bit, stop bits, and baud rate. For example, you can adjust the port settings of a serial port by highlighting the port in Device Manager, clicking Properties, and then selecting the Port Settings tab (see Figure 33-9). The Port Settings tab allows you to change frame variables including bits/s (bps), data bits, parity, stop bit(s), and flow control. Change the data frame at either end of the serial link such that all devices are running with the **same** parameters.

## FINDING A PORT ADDRESS WITH DEBUG

You can use the DOS Debug utility to determine the I/O addresses of a serial port—this can be particularly handy if you need to troubleshoot a serial port problem if Windows refuses to start. Make sure that you boot the computer in the DOS mode (e.g., using a Windows startup disk), and then switch to the directory containing the Debug utility (such as C:\DOS).

> You may need to add the Debug utility to your boot disk.

Type the following:

```
C:\DOS\> debug              <Enter>
```

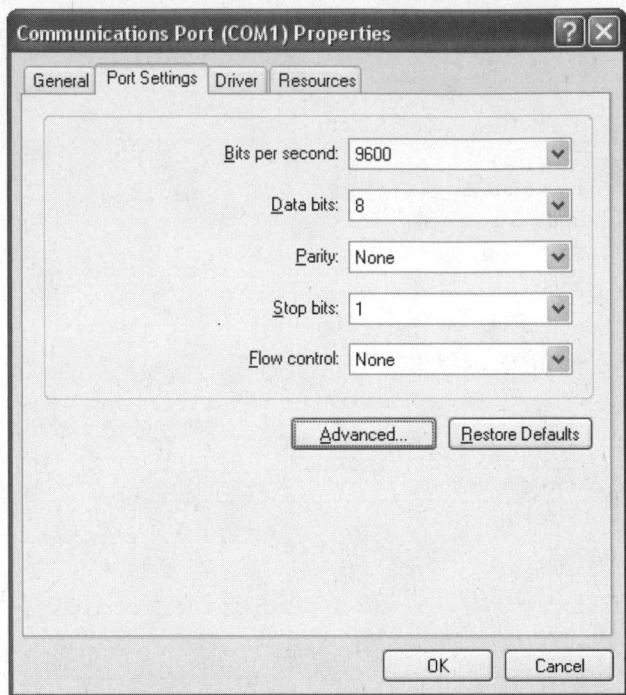

**FIGURE 33-9**   Adjusting the frame of a serial (COM) port through Windows XP

A hyphen will appear. This is the Debug prompt. At the Debug prompt, type the following:

```
D 40:00 09
```

A single line of text appears, such as follows:

```
0040:0000 F8 03 F8 02 00 00 00 00-78 03
```

To exit Debug, press Q (to quit), and then press ENTER to leave Debug and return to the DOS prompt. The line of interest begins 0040:0000. In this example, the F8 03 (read 03F8h) and F8 02 (read 02F8h) indicate two serial ports (COM1 and COM2). Other possibilities include E8 03 (read 03E8) and E8 02 (read 02E8), which are COM3 and COM4, respectively. A machine with four serial ports should read:

```
0040:0000 F8 03 F8 02 E8 03 E8 02-78 03
```

A machine with no serial ports should read:

```
0040:0000 00 00 00 00 00 00 00 00-78 03
```

The -78 03 entry is the address of the first parallel port (read 0378h).

# INFRARED TROUBLESHOOTING TIPS

Infrared devices are typically easy to install and configure, but establishing a communications link and exchanging data between IrDA devices properly can pose some peculiar problems for the technician. If you cannot get two devices to communicate across an infrared link, start with the following tips before referring to specific IrDA symptoms:

- *Align the devices.* Infrared devices must be aligned so that they roughly face each other—it doesn't have to be precise, but try a straight-on alignment between 6 inches and 3 feet apart.

- *Check the power.* Make sure that any IrDA devices are powered properly. If the device is powered by battery, try replacing the batteries with a fresh set.

- *Check the UART.* You may sometimes have speed trouble when connecting an IR transceiver to an older PC using a older UART (e.g., an 8250 rather than a 16550A). If the UART is in question, use the Infrared tool in the Control Panel to limit UART speed to 19.2 Kbps or so. For a long-term fix, you may be able to upgrade the serial port with a faster UART using a multi-I/O card.

- *Check the COM port.* Verify that the IR adapter is configured to use the correct COM port. For example, if the IR adapter is connected to COM2, but you tell the IR adapter to use COM1 (through the infrared software), the IR adapter will not function.

- *Bump up the speed.* If your infrared devices seem to establish a connection only slowly, the speed may be set unusually low. Use the Infrared tool in the Control Panel of both PCs to systematically increase the Limit Connection Speed To setting. If the connection becomes unreliable, reduce the speed again.

- *Check other IR devices.* Make sure that other infrared devices (such as TV/VCR remote controls) are not being used in such a way that they interfere with your computer's IR device.

- *Check the IR device drivers.* If you have trouble using a particular IR adapter, check with the manufacturer for updated device drivers. If updated drivers are available, try uninstalling the old drivers first before installing the new ones. If you're upgrading an IR adapter, be sure to uninstall any older IR drivers before installing drivers for the new adapter.

- *Prevent the suspend mode.* As a rule, do not allow the PC to enter a suspend (or other power-saving) mode while using an IR link. Stop the IR link before suspending the PC. Otherwise, the IR link may remain active. This may not be a big deal for desktop PCs, but may be very important for laptop systems where a busy IR connection may continue to drain the laptop battery unexpectedly.

# SERIAL SYMPTOMS

**SYMPTOM 33-1**    **You hear a beep code or see a POST error indicating a serial port fault**
The system initialization may or may not halt, depending on how the BIOS is written. Low-level initialization problems generally indicate trouble in the computer's hardware. If the computer's beep code sequence is indistinct, you could try rebooting the computer with a POST analyzer card installed. The BIOS POST code displayed on the card could be matched to a specific error explanation in the POST card's documentation. Once you have clearly identified the error as a serial port fault, you can proceed with troubleshooting.

Start with the system as a whole and remove any expansion boards that have serial ports available. Retest the computer after removing each board. If the error disappears after removing a particular card, then that card is likely at fault. You can simply replace the card with a new one, or attempt to repair the card to the component level. If there is only one serial port in the system, it is most likely built into the motherboard. Again, you can replace the defective UART, replace the motherboard, or disable the defective motherboard port.

**SYMPTOM 33-2** **You see an 11xx or 12xx serial adapter error displayed on your system** A hardware fault has been detected in one of the COM ports. The 11xx errors typically indicate a fault in COM1, while 12xx errors suggest a problem with COM2, COM3, or COM4. In most cases, the fault is in the UART. You have the option to replace the UART chip, replace the motherboard, or disable the defective COM port and replace it with an expansion board.

**SYMPTOM 33-3** **The computer initializes properly, but the serial peripheral does not work** Your applications software may indicate that no device is connected. Before you even open your tool kit, you must determine whether the trouble lies in your computer or your peripheral. For example, when your modem or printer stops working, run a self test to ensure the device is at least operational. Check all cables and connectors (perhaps try a different cable). Also be sure to check the software package being used to operate the serial port. Ensure that the software is configured properly to use the appropriate COM port and that any necessary drivers are selected.

Disconnect the peripheral at the computer and install a serial loopback plug. Run a diagnostic to inspect each available serial port. Take note of any port that registers as defective. Locate the corresponding serial port. If the port is installed as an expansion board, replace the defective expansion board. If the port is on the motherboard, you can replace the defective UART chip, install an alternate expansion board, or replace the motherboard.

**SYMPTOM 33-4** **Serial data is randomly lost or garbled** Your first step should be to check the communication cable. Make sure the cable is intact and properly secured at both ends. Try a different cable. If the cable checks properly, either the port or peripheral is at fault. Start by suspecting the serial port. Make sure that the DTE and DCE are both set to use the same data frame and data rate. Incorrect settings can easily garble data. If problems persist, disconnect the serial peripheral at the computer and install a serial loopback plug. Run a diagnostic to inspect each available serial port. Take note of any port that registers as defective. Locate the corresponding serial port(s). If the port is installed as an expansion board, replace the defective expansion board. If the port is on the motherboard, you can replace the defective port controller chip, install an alternate expansion board, or replace the motherboard.

If you cannot test the computer's serial port directly, test the port indirectly by trying the peripheral on another known-good computer. If the peripheral works properly on another computer, the trouble is probably in the original computer's serial port circuitry. Replace any defective circuitry or replace the motherboard. If the peripheral remains defective on another computer, the peripheral itself (such as a printer or mouse) is probably faulty.

# IRDA SYMPTOMS

**SYMPTOM 33-5** **PC communication software does not recognize the IR COM port** When you attempt to use PC communication software (e.g., LapLink) with virtual COM ports created by an infrared adapter, you may receive an error message indicating that the port is unavailable. This problem typically occurs because the communication software accesses the hardware directly to determine the status of the COM port—it does not recognize virtual COM ports created using the infrared adapter. To work around this problem, you need to contact the software maker for a patch or update, or stop using the communication software in favor of the Direct Cable Connection (DCC) tool included with Windows 98/Me, or use the Wireless Link software with Windows XP.

**SYMPTOM 33-6** **You encounter problems maintaining an IR connection in the daylight** This is a common problem with all infrared devices, and is usually caused by "interference" from the natural IR component of ordinary sunlight. Try shortening the transmission distance between the transmitter and receiver (move the devices closer together), and make sure the path between the two is as straight as possible. Other IR devices (such as IR printers or remote control devices) in the IR path can also cause interference. Make sure there are no other sources of IR interference between the two devices that need to communicate.

**SYMPTOM 33-7** **You see an infrared message indicating an "internal error"** When you try to access the IR adapter by double-clicking the Infrared icon in the Control Panel, you may receive an internal error message from the IrDA device. This type of error can occur if the system attempts to access an IR device that isn't enabled or responding—usually because the infrared port is disabled in the computer's CMOS settings. Enable the infrared port in the computer's CMOS Setup. If the problem persists, check the IR device installation and power, and see that the device is presented properly in Device Manager. You may need to replace a defective IR adapter.

**SYMPTOM 33-8** **You receive a software error when accessing the IrDA device under Windows 98** When you try to access the IR adapter by double-clicking the Infrared tool in Control Panel, you may receive a software error message. This error can crop up when the Fast Infrared Protocol is missing or damaged under Windows 98. If you install an infrared device in Windows 98, the Fast Infrared Protocol is not installed by default. You must manually add the protocol in Network Properties (this is not a problem under later versions of Windows) as in Figure 33-10. To resolve this problem, remove and then reinstall the Fast Infrared Protocol through the Network icon in Control Panel.

**SYMPTOM 33-9** **You receive an IR recipient error under Windows 98** When you try to transfer a file from one computer to another computer using an IrDA connection, you may receive an error message indicating that the recipient device isn't ready. This type of error message may occur even though infrared transfer **is** properly enabled on both ends of the IR link. This error usually indicates a speed mismatch—suggesting that the selected transmission speed for the IR device on one computer is lower than the selected transmission speed for the IR device on the other computer. For example, you may encounter this problem if the IR transmission speed on one computer is 9600 bps, but the IR transmission speed on the other computer is 19200 bps. Reconfigure your IR devices so that they are both using the same common speed settings (e.g., 9600 bps in this example). As a more permanent fix, you may need to upgrade the slower IR device to enable additional connection speed.

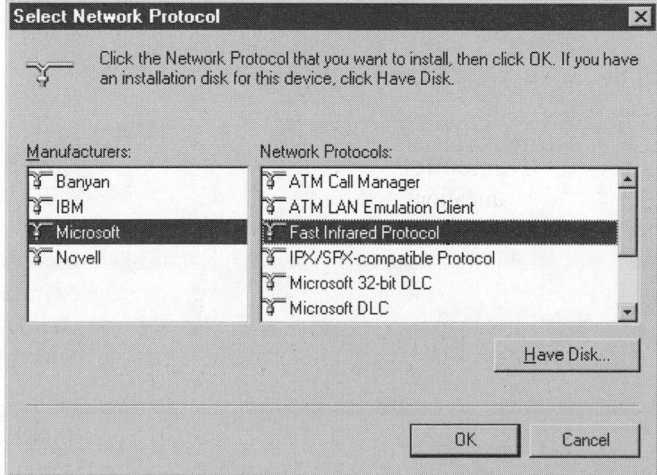

**FIGURE 33-10** You may need to add the Fast Infrared Protocol manually if the IR device requires it

**SYMPTOM 33-10**    **Your infrared system does not search when it's enabled under Windows 98**    When you enable infrared searching, suitable devices that come into range should automatically respond. However, when you opt to search (e.g., by checking the Search For And Provide Status For Devices Within Range check box), the search process does not begin. An error message may indicate that the devices cannot search. First, check the IR communication path and make sure that the path between the two IR devices is free of obstructions and other interference (from remote controls or other unwanted IR devices). Now open the Infrared utility in your Control Panel and select the Options tab. Verify that both IR communication and searching features are enabled. Apply any changes and click OK (reboot the PC if necessary).

**SYMPTOM 33-11**    **DCC connections do not work with an IR printer port**    When you try to connect two computers using DCC under Windows 98/Me (this is not an issue under Windows XP), you may be able to select an LPT port rather than a COM port. However, if you select an LPT port and it is an infrared port, the connection does not work. You may also see an error indicating that the system cannot connect to a host PC. This problem occurs because the IR port is a unidirectional port, but DCC requires that LPT ports be bidirectional. You can overcome this problem by reconfiguring DCC to select an IR COM port instead of an IR LPT port. This will allow bidirectional IR communication between computers.

**SYMPTOM 33-12**    **You get garbled printing or blank pages printing to an infrared printer**    In virtually all cases, this type of problem is caused by an incompatibility between the infrared ports (for example, the PC has an IrDA 2.0 port, but the printer has an IrDA 1.1 port). As a precaution, check that the IR communication path is unobstructed and free of interference from sunlight or other IR devices. If compatibility is indeed the problem, set the computer's IrDA port mode to version 1.1 through the CMOS Setup (or upgrade the motherboard BIOS). You might also be able to avoid this trouble by limiting the computer's IrDA port speed (though this will cause print jobs to run more slowly).

# Further Study

**ActiSys**   www.actisys.com
**Adaptec**   www.adaptec.com
**HP**   www.hp.com
**Infrared Data Association (IrDA)**    www.irda.org
**Sharp**   www.sharp-usa.com
**TI**   www.ti.com

# SOUND BOARDS

**S**ound is a feature of the PC that had been largely overlooked in early systems. Aside from a simple, oscillator-driven speaker, the early PCs were mute. Driven largely by the demand for better PC games, designers developed stand-alone sound boards that could read sound data recorded in separate files, then reconstruct those files into basic sound, music, and speech. Since the beginning of the 1990s, those early sound boards have blossomed into an array of powerful, high-fidelity sound products capable of duplicating voice, orchestral soundtracks, and real-life sounds with uncanny realism (Figure 34-1). Not only have sound products helped the game industry to mature, but they have been instrumental in the development of *multimedia* technology (the integration of sound and picture) as well as Internet web phones, voice recognition and command, and other powerful communication tools. This chapter is intended to explain the essential ideas and operations of a contemporary sound board and to show you how to isolate a defective sound board when problems arise.

**FIGURE  34-1**    The Sound Blaster Audigy sound card from Creative Labs (Courtesy of Creative Labs, Inc.)

# Understanding Sound Boards

Before you attempt to troubleshoot a problem with a sound board, you should have an understanding of how the board works and what it must accomplish. This type of background helps you when recommending a sound board to a customer or choosing a compatible card as a replacement. If you already have a strong background in digital sound concepts and software, feel free to skip directly to the troubleshooting portion of this chapter.

## THE RECORDING PROCESS

All sound starts as pressure variations traveling through the air. Sound can come from almost anywhere—a barking dog, a laughing child, a fire engine's siren, a person speaking—you get the idea. The process of recording sound to a hard drive requires sound to be carried through several manipulations, as shown in Figure 34-2. First, sound must be translated from pressure variations in the air to analog electrical signals. This is accomplished by a microphone. These analog signals are amplified by the sound card, then *digitized* (converted to a series of representative digital words, each taken at a fixed time interval). The resulting stream of data is processed and organized through the use of software, which places the data (as well as any overhead or housekeeping data) into a standard file format (such as the WAV format). The file is saved to the drive of choice—typically a hard drive, though CD-RW drives are now a popular choice for saving large data files.

## THE PLAYBACK PROCESS

Simply speaking, the playback process is virtually the reverse of recording (Figure 34-3). A software application opens a sound file on the hard drive (or CD drive), then passes the digital data back to the sound card. Data is translated back into equivalent analog levels. Ideally, the reconstructed shape of the analog

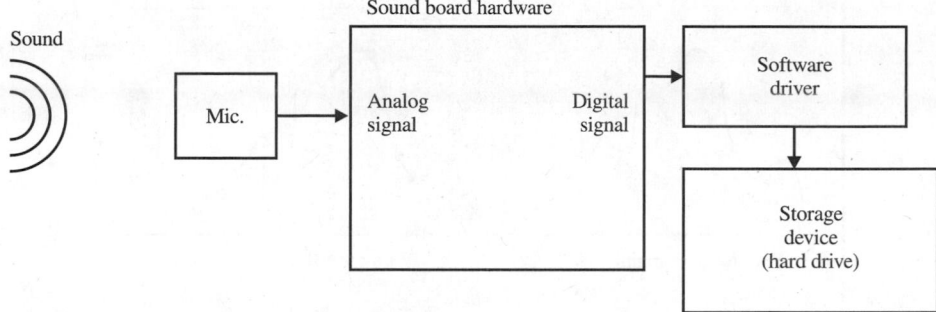

**FIGURE  34-2**    The sound board recording process

signal closely mimics the original digitized signal. The analog signal is amplified, then passed to a speaker. If the sound was recorded in stereo, the data is divided into two channels that are separately converted back to analog signals, amplified, and sent to their corresponding speakers. Speakers convert the analog signal back into traveling pressure waves that you can hear.

## THE CONCEPT OF SAMPLING

To appreciate the intricacies of a sound card's operation, you must understand the concept of *digitization*—otherwise known as *sampling*. In principle, sampling is a very straightforward concept: an analog signal is measured periodically, and its voltage at each point in time is converted to a digital number. The device that performs this conversion is known as an *analog-to-digital converter* (ADC). It sounds simple enough in principle, but there are some important wrinkles.

The problem with sampling is that a digitizer circuit has to capture enough points of an analog waveform to reproduce it faithfully. The example in Figure 34-4 illustrates the importance of sampling rate. Waveforms A and B represent the same original signal. Waveform A is sampled at a relatively slow rate—only a few samples are taken. The problem comes when the signal is reconstructed with a *digital-to-analog converter* (DAC). As you can see, there are not enough sample points to reconstruct the original signal. As a result, some of the information in the original signal is lost. This is a form of distortion known as *aliasing* and results in substantial distortion during playback. By comparison, waveform B is the same signal, but it is sampled at a much higher rate. When that data is reconstructed, the resulting signal is a much more faithful reproduction of the original.

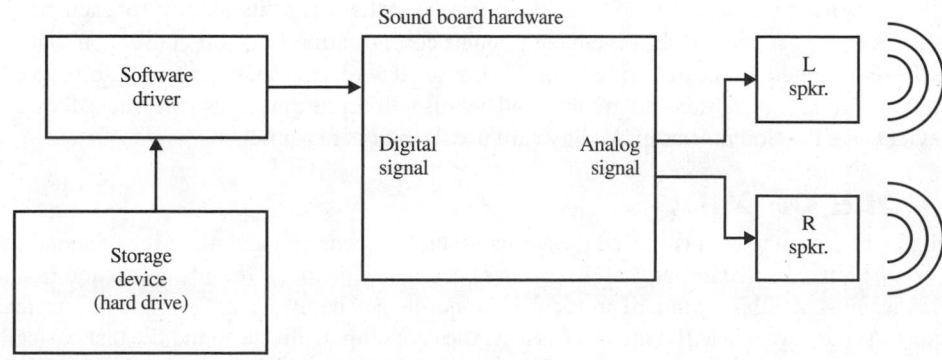

**FIGURE  34-3**    The sound board playback process

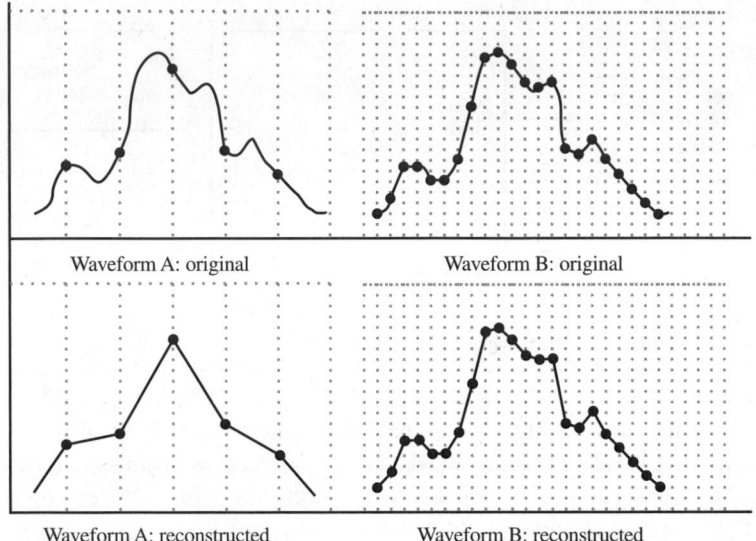

Waveform A: original          Waveform B: original

Waveform A: reconstructed        Waveform B: reconstructed

**FIGURE   34-4**    The concept of digital sampling

As a rule, a signal should be sampled at least twice as fast as the highest frequency contained in the signal. This is known as Nyquist's Sampling Theorem. The lowest standard sampling rate used with today's sound boards is 11 kHz. This allows fair reproduction of normal speech and vocalization (with frequency components up to about 5.5 kHz). However, most low-end sound boards can digitize signals up to 22 kHz. Unfortunately, the human range of hearing is about 22 kHz. To capture sounds reasonably well throughout the entire range of hearing, you would need a sampling rate of 44 kHz. This is often known as "CD-quality" sampling since it is the same rate used to record audio on CDs. The disadvantage to high sampling rates is disk space (and sound file size). Each sample is a piece of data, so the more samples taken each second, the larger and faster a file grows.

## Data Bits vs. Sound Quality

Not only does the number of samples affect sound quality, but also the precision (or number of bits) of each sample. Suppose that each sample is converted to a 4-bit number. That means each sampled point can be represented by a number from 0 to 15—not much precision there. If 8 bits are used for each sample, 256 discrete levels can be supported. But the most popular configuration is 16-bit conversion that allows a sample to be represented by one of 65,536 levels. At that level of resolution, samples will form a very close replica of the original signal. Many common sound boards will capture audio as 16-bit data, though recent sound devices like the Sound Blaster Audigy card use 24-bits per channel.

## THE ROLE OF MIDI

Although most of a sound card is geared toward handling the recording and playback of sound files, the *musical instrument digital interface* (MIDI) port has become an inexpensive and popular addition to most sound card designs. MIDI is a standard protocol that is defined by hardware, software, and electrical interconnections. At the core of a MIDI interface is a synthesizer chip. Unlike a sound file that basically contains the digital equivalent of an analog waveform, a MIDI file is a set of instructions for playing musical notes. Each note is sent to the synthesizer, along with duration, pitch, and timing specifications. This means very complex MIDI musical scores can be produced using relatively small data files. The synthesizer can be made to replicate a variety of musical instruments such as a piano, guitar, harmonica, flute—you name it. High-end sound boards are capable of synthesizing a small orchestra. Since most synthesizers can process several channels simultaneously, the MIDI standard supports playing a number of "instruments" (or "voices") at the same time. Thus, very high quality music can be produced with MIDI on a PC. The two most common synthesizer types are FM and Wavetable.

Figure 34-5 illustrates the kinds of things MIDI is capable of. Prerecorded MIDI files can be read from a storage device like a hard drive file or from CD-ROM. (Many games include an orchestral-quality MIDI soundtrack on the CD.) The MIDI data is passed through to the sound board's synthesizer, which reproduces the sound, and out to the amplified speakers. If you plan on composing music yourself, you can interface a MIDI instrument to the sound board's 15-pin MIDI port. Using MIDI sequencer software, the notes played on the instrument will be heard through the speaker as well as recorded to the MIDI file on the hard drive. Note that you do not need a MIDI instrument to play back a MIDI file, but you need an instrument and sequencer software to create a MIDI file. Also, since MIDI is not sound (but rather sound "blueprints"), the same MIDI composition entered on a keyboard can be played back as a harp, a guitar, or a flute.

Many sound devices can switch the 15-pin subminiature D port between a gameport and a MIDI port—usually through a jumper on the sound card. If you're using the 15-pin port as a gameport, be sure to configure the port for MIDI before connecting a MIDI instrument.

## INSIDE A SOUND BOARD

Now that you're aware of the major functions a sound board must perform, you can see those functions in the context of a complete board. Figure 34-6 shows a simplified block diagram of a typical sound board. Note that your sound board may differ somewhat, but all contemporary boards should generally contain these subsections.

The core element of a sound board is the *digital signal processor* (DSP). A DSP is a variation of a microprocessor that is specially designed to manipulate large volumes of digital data. Like all processor components, the DSP requires memory. A ROM (the sound board's "firmware") contains all of the instructions needed to operate the DSP and direct the board's major operations. A certain amount of RAM

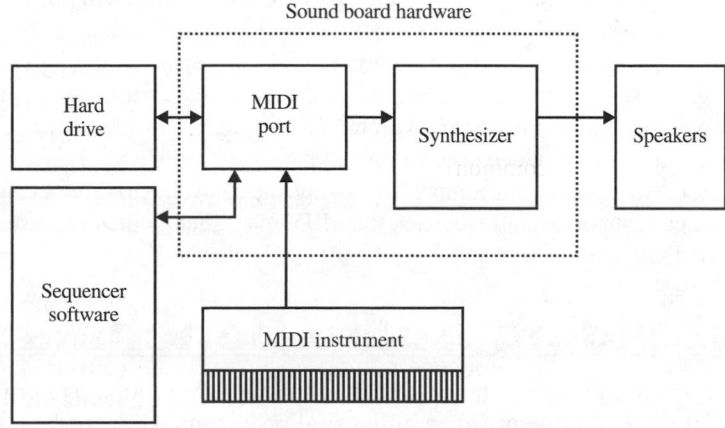

**FIGURE  34-5**    The basic path of MIDI signals through the PC

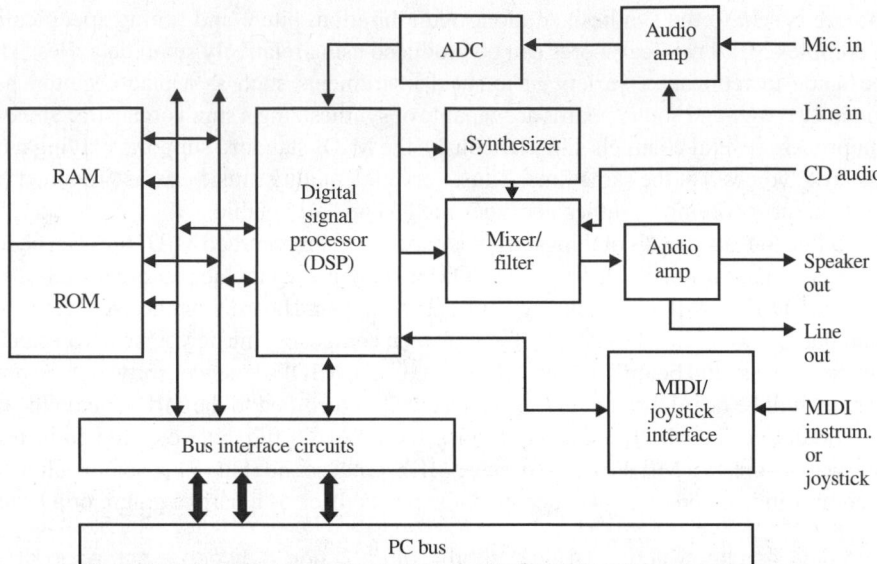

**FIGURE 34-6** Simplified block diagram of a basic sound board

serves two purposes: it provides a "scratch pad" area for the DSP's calculations and serves as a buffer for data traveling to or from the PC bus. For example, "sound fonts" (segments of common sounds) can be stored in the sound board's RAM until needed by a game or other program.

Signals entering the sound board are passed through an amplifier stage and provided to an A/D converter. When recording takes place, the DSP runs the A/D converter and accepts the resulting conversions for processing and storage. Signals delivered by a microphone are typically quite faint, so they are amplified significantly. Signals delivered to the "line" input are often much stronger (such as the output from a CD player or stereo preamplifier), so they receive less amplification.

For signals leaving the sound board, the first (and often most important) stop is the mixer. It is the mixer that combines CD audio, DSP sound output, and synthesizer output into a single analog channel. Since virtually all sound boards now operate in a stereo mode, there will usually be two mixer channels and amplifier stages. The audio amplifier stage(s) boost the analog signal for delivery to stereo speakers. If the sound will be driving a stereo system, a "line" output provides a separate output. Amplifier output can be adjusted by a single master volume control located on the rear of the board, though most sound boards now use software applet(s) to adjust mixer and volume levels rather than a hardware control.

Finally, a MIDI controller is provided to accommodate the interface of a MIDI instrument to the sound board. In many cases, the interface can be jumpered to switch the controller to serve as a joystick port. That way, the sound board can support a single joystick if a MIDI instrument will not be used. MIDI information processed by the DSP will be output to the onboard synthesizer.

# Understanding Audio Benchmarks

An important aspect of sound boards is their audio benchmarks. Unlike logic and processing circuitry, which is measured in terms of millions (often billions) of operations per second, the benchmarks that define a sound card are very much analog. If you are an audiophile, many of the following terms may already be familiar. If most of your experience has been with logic systems, however, these concepts will appear very different from many of the other discussions in this book.

## DECIBELS

No discussion of sound concepts is complete without a basic understanding of the *decibel* (dB). Decibels are used because they are logarithmic. Human hearing is not a linear response. That is, if you increase the power of your stereo output from 4W to 16W, the resulting sound is not four times louder—in fact, it is only twice as loud. If you increase the power from 4W to 64W, the sound is only three times as loud. In human terms, amplitude perception is measured logarithmically. As a result, very small decibel values actually relate to substantial amounts of power. The accepted formula for decibels is

$$\text{gain (in dB)} = 10 \log_{10} \frac{P_{out}}{P_{in}}$$

Don't worry if this formula looks intimidating. (Chances are that you won't actually need to work this formula.) But consider what happens when output power is greater than input power. Suppose a 1mW signal is applied to a circuit, and a 2mW signal leaves. The circuit provides a gain of +3dB. Suppose the situation is reversed: a 2mW signal is applied to the circuit, and a 1mW signal leaves it. The circuit would then have a gain of −3dB. Negative gain is a loss, also called *attenuation*. As you see, a small dB number represents a large change in signal levels.

## FREQUENCY RESPONSE

Expressed simply, the *frequency response* of a sound board is the range of frequencies that the board will handle uniformly. Examine the sample graph of Figure 34-7. Ideally, a sound board should be able to output the same amount of power (0dB) across the entire working frequency range of the board (usually 20 Hz to 20 kHz). This would show up as a flat line across the graph. In actual sound cards, however, this is not practical, and there will invariably be a *rolloff* of signal strength at both ends of the operating range. A good-quality sound board will demonstrate sharp, steep rolloffs. As the rolloffs get longer and shallower at high and low frequencies, the board has difficulty producing sound power at those frequencies. The result is that bass and treble ranges may sound weak, and this affects the sound's overall fidelity. By looking at a frequency response curve, you can anticipate the frequency ranges where a sound board may sound weak.

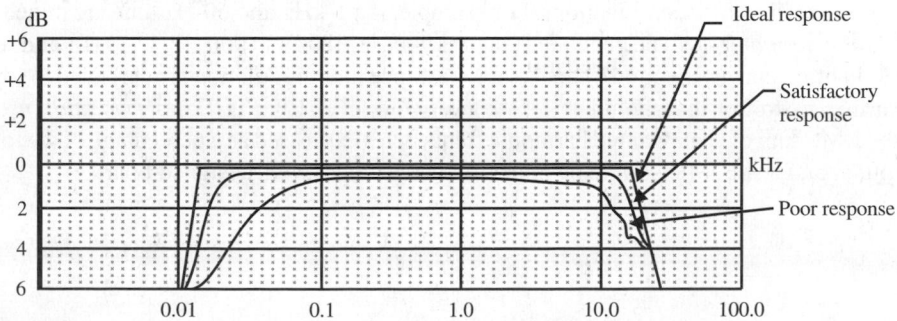

**FIGURE 34-7**   A simple frequency-response curve for a basic sound board

# SIGNAL-TO-NOISE RATIO

The *signal-to-noise ratio* (SNR) of a sound board is basically the ratio of maximum undistorted signal power to the accompanying electronic noise being generated by the board (primarily hum and hiss) expressed in decibels. Ideally, this will be a very large dB number, which would indicate that the output signal is so much stronger than the noise signal, that for all intents and purposes, the noise is imperceptible. In actual practice, a good-quality sound board will enjoy an SNR of 85dB or higher—but these boards are difficult to find. For most current sound boards with SNR levels below 75dB, there may be barely audible hum and hiss present during silent periods, as well as a certain amount of sound "grit" underlying sound and music reproduction. Some very inexpensive sound boards are on the market with SNR levels as low as 41dB (noise may be noticeable and actually annoying).

You may also find the SNR value expressed as an *A-weighted* decibel number. The reason for this is that human hearing is not equal at all frequencies, so we cannot hear all noise equally. The process of A-weighting emphasizes the noise levels at frequencies we are most sensitive to. Resulting SNR values are often several dB higher (better) than non-weighted SNR values. Be careful here; a sound board with a low SNR may use the A-weighted value in the specification sheet. If this is the case, subtract about 3 or 4dB for the actual SNR figure.

# TOTAL HARMONIC DISTORTION

Sound and music are rich in harmonics (overtones), which are basically integer multiples of an original frequency signal (although at much lower levels). As a consequence, harmonics are a valuable attribute of sound. The number and amplitude of harmonics provide the sound characteristics that allow you to distinguish between a guitar, flute, piano, or any other musical instrument played at the same note. Without harmonics, every instrument would just produce flat tones, and every instrument would sound exactly the same.

However, when sound is produced in an electronic circuit, other unwanted harmonics are generated that can alter the sound of the music being produced (thus the term *harmonic distortion*). The *total harmonic distortion* (THD) of a sound board is the *root-mean squared* (RMS) sum of all unwanted harmonic frequencies produced, expressed as a percentage of the total undistorted output signal level. In many cases, the RMS value of noise is added to THD (expressed as THD+N). The lower this percentage the better. THD+N values over 0.1 percent can often be heard and suggest a less than adequate sound board design.

# INTERMODULATION DISTORTION

This specification is related to harmonics. When two or more tones are generated together, amplifiers create harmonics as well as tone combinations. For example, if a 1-kHz and 60-Hz tone are mixed together, *intermodulation harmonics* will be generated (such as 940 Hz, 880 Hz, 1060 Hz, 1120 Hz, and so on). It is this intermodulation that gives sound a harsh overtone. Since intermodulation is not related to sound quality, it is a form of distortion that should be kept to a very low level. Like THD, *intermodulation distortion* (IMD) is the RMS sum of all unwanted harmonic frequencies expressed as a percentage of the total undistorted output signal level. IMD should be under 0.1 percent on a well-designed board.

## SENSITIVITY

While it does not directly affect the fidelity of sound reproduction, sensitivity can be an important specification. *Sensitivity* is basically the amplitude of an input signal (such as a microphone signal) that will produce the maximum undistorted signal at the output(s) with volume at maximum. Sensitivity is often related to gain (see the next section). A sensitive sound board typically provides a lot of gain, so a relatively small signal is needed to produce a notable output level.

## GAIN

By itself, sensitivity is hard to apply to a sound board, but if you consider the board's output power versus its input signal power and express the ratio as a decibel, you would have the *gain* of the sound board. Many sound boards offer a potential gain of up to 6dB. However, it is important to note that not all sound boards provide positive gain. Some boards actually attenuate the signal even with the volume at maximum. In practical terms, this usually forces you to keep the volume control at maximum.

## 3D AUDIO (A3D)

The A3D audio technology in your sound card (that is, part of a Diamond Multimedia Sonic Impact and other A3D audio systems) was developed by Aureal Semiconductor and is the result of many years of research into human hearing and digital audio reproduction. In the real world, we can close our eyes, listen to a sound, and pinpoint its direction, distance, and motion. Our ears allow us to hear 360 degrees in all directions, while our eyes cover only about 140 degrees in the direction we're facing. The eyes and ears work in close cooperation to provide us with a seamless perception of reality. When the ears hear a sound from behind, we decide to turn our head and look at an object.

A3D audio is based on the following premise: we can hear sounds in three dimensions by using only our two ears, so it's possible to create sounds from two speakers (or a set of headphones) that have the same effect. There are several listening cues that allow us to hear sounds three-dimensionally. There are split-second differences between what each ear hears when listening to a sound. Sound waves usually appear earlier and louder at the ear closest to the sound source. That same sound (originating from various locations around a listener), will sound different because of the changes in the way it gets reflected and filtered by the shoulders, face, and the outer ear before reaching the ear drum. These listening effects can be summarized in a set of audio filters called *Head Related Transfer Functions* (HRTFs).

A3D technology uses advanced signal processing algorithms and HRTF measurement techniques. This digitally re-creates these hearing cues along with the absorption, reflection, and Doppler shift effects, which affect sound waves as they travel from a sound source, through an environment, to the listener's ears. The result is a lifelike audio experience that "surrounds" the listener with sound that seems like it's in three dimensions, using only a single pair of ordinary speakers or headphones.

In practice, DirectSound and DirectSound3D are DirectX wave audio playback APIs that allow you to simultaneously play multiple wave files and move sound sources within a simulated 3D space (DirectSound3D). They take advantage of sound-accelerator hardware (found on many high-end sound cards such as the Sonic Impact A3D board) to improve performance and minimize CPU usage. You can check for the presence of D3D drivers through the DirectX diagnostic (DXDIAG), as shown in Figure 34-8. Today, A3D 2.0 (or simply A3D2) is commonly available, and includes additional positional features such as occlusion.

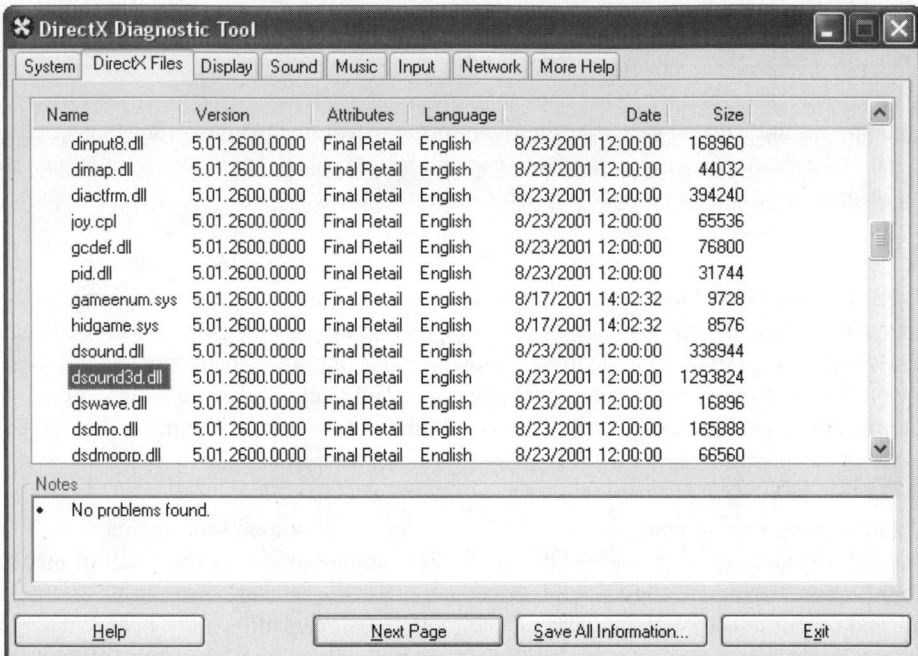

**FIGURE  34-8**    Checking for 3D sound support through DXDIAG under Windows XP

# EAX

Enhanced Audio eXperience (EAX) technology represents a powerful set of audio effects (similar to A3D technology) frequently used in games and other multimedia applications. EAX supports a wide range of features including

- Panning (a sound moving "between" speakers), which allows spatialization and localization of sounds in the game environment.
- Reflections (echoes) from a variety of surfaces.
- Filtering (often used to augment indoor and outdoor sound environments).
- Morphing (starting with one sound and ending with another)—for example, moving from an outdoor jungle environment into an indoor factory is handled with a smooth sound transition rather than a sudden cutoff.

EAX support is incorporated into the sound device such as the Sound Blaster Live and Audigy (you can check the sound card's specifications), and enabled with the complete suite of sound device drivers. However, only games and other programs designed to use EAX features will actually employ those features.

# Using Microphones

Ever-growing numbers of sound card owners are using their sound cards to record sound or to broadcast sound over the Internet through such applications as WebPhone or NetMeeting. Sound recording demands the use of microphones, and not all microphones work properly with every sound board. Often, the user mistakes a poor microphone response as being a problem with the sound card. This part of the chapter looks at some important considerations for choosing and using a microphone.

## MICROPHONE TYPES

There are three types of microphones: dynamic, condenser, and electret condenser. You will find all three microphone types available for sound boards:

- **Dynamic**   Dynamic microphones are typically hand-held or desktop units. They have a larger response range and typically sound better than condenser microphones. A dynamic microphone does not require phantom power because the diaphragm element in the microphone can create enough electric current for the sound board to use.

- **Condenser**   Condenser microphones are the small multimedia microphones that typically come with computers. When you open a new sound board and take the microphone out of the box, it is almost always a condenser microphone. They do not have as good a response range as dynamic microphones, and they also have a smaller diaphragm. This demands phantom power for the sound board.

- **Electret condenser**   Electret condenser microphones are basically condenser microphones with a built-in battery. They have the same response as a condenser microphone, but they do not require phantom power to operate. Some electret condenser microphones will allow you to remove this internal battery. With the battery not installed, phantom power would be required.

## PHANTOM POWER

So the next question is, "What is phantom power?" *Phantom power* is simply a small, low-current power source on the sound board that is used to power condenser microphones. Devices like dynamic and electret microphones can produce enough current on their own to avoid the use of phantom power, but condenser microphones demand phantom power as a current source.

Here's the main problem with today's sound boards: not all of them provide switchable phantom power. Ideally, sound boards (like the Creative Sound Blaster Live 5.1 Platinum) would provide phantom power and allow you to jumper the phantom power on or off depending on which microphone type you plan to use. If you use a dynamic microphone, you'd switch phantom power off. If you use a condenser microphone, you'd switch phantom power on. When a sound board does not provide phantom power at all, you're stuck using a dynamic microphone or a powered electret condenser microphone. If a sound board provides full-time phantom power (and you cannot turn it off), you'll need to stay with a condenser microphone.

You can probably see the potential for trouble here. If you use a condenser microphone on an unpowered sound board, the microphone will not work at all (or generate little more than faint noise). On the other hand, plugging a dynamic or electret microphone into a powered sound board will usually result in severe clipping. Once again, you'll capture little more than noise.

## CHOOSING A MICROPHONE

Whether you're choosing a microphone for yourself or recommending one to someone else, there are some considerations to keep in mind. Perhaps the most important issue is the application. If you just need a basic, inexpensive microphone to record a few simple voice notations, a condenser or electret microphone would work just fine, and your sound board will require a phantom power supply. If you want to record more professional vocals, or prepare a formal presentation, a dynamic microphone will generally provide the best results, and no phantom power is needed.

# Installing/Upgrading a Sound Board

Fortunately, adding or replacing a sound card to a system is a remarkably straightforward procedure. The only real problem areas are in hardware conflicts and software installation. This part of the chapter covers the essential steps and precautions that you will need to remember when installing a sound card. Although the chances of a system failure during the upgrade are extremely remote, it is always a wise policy to back up any vital files or programs before opening the system.

If you're replacing an existing sound card (or disabling the sound support on your motherboard), be sure to uninstall all of the sound card's application software (e.g., a Creative Surround Mixer), and remove the existing sound card's entry in your Device Manager *first*. Then shut down the system directly and remove/disable the old sound device.

## STATIC DISCHARGE PRECAUTIONS

Most of the chips used in today's expansion boards are fabricated with technologies that make them extremely sensitive to *electrostatic discharge* (ESD). To ensure the safe handling of sound boards and other system components during the installation/upgrade, make it a point to take the following precautions. First, use an anti-static wrist strap whenever handling components or tools inside the PC. Cable the wrist strap to another reliable earth ground. Next, always try to handle expansion boards by their edges. Avoid touching the individual chip pins or printed wiring. Third, if you will be removing an old sound board, have a good-quality anti-static bag on hand to store it in. Under no circumstances should you allow a sound board (or any expansion board) to rest on a synthetic or static-prone surface. Finally, excessively dry environments tend to allow substantial buildups of static charges in objects, clothing, and bodies. If it is possible, try to work in an environment with at least 40 percent humidity.

## PREPARE THE SYSTEM

At this point, you can prepare the system for its upgrade. A word of caution is in order here: *be especially careful of screwdriver blades when working inside the PC.* If you should slip, the blade can easily gouge the motherboard (or an expansion board) and result in broken traces. It pays to be careful and gentle when upgrading an expansion device. Before you even consider opening the PC cover, turn the system off, and unplug it from the AC receptacle. This helps to ensure your safety by preventing the PC from being powered accidentally while you are working on it.

Remove the screws holding down the outer cover, and place those screws aside in a safe place. Gently remove the PC's outer cover and set it aside (out of the path of normal floor traffic). You should now be able to look into the PC and observe the motherboard, along with any expansion boards and drives that are installed. If you will be replacing an existing sound board, now is the time for you to label any cables connected to it. Labels need not be fancy—a roll of masking tape and an indelible marker are all you need.

## REMOVE/DISABLE THE OLD BOARD

If there is no sound board already in the PC, feel free to skip to the next step. Otherwise, start by disconnecting any cables that are attached to the current sound board. (Make sure each cable is labeled.) You can then remove the screw that attaches the board bracket to the chassis, and gently ease the board from its expansion slot. Be sure to handle the board by its edges. When the old board is removed, seal it in an anti-static bag and set it aside (this protects the old board so that you can use it elsewhere). There are several important cables to look for:

- Speaker output cable(s)
- Microphone input cable (if a microphone is attached)
- Line input cable (if you're mixing in a source from outside of the sound board)
- CD audio cable between the CD/DVD drive and sound board. Some sound cards may support more than one audio input so that you can mix audio from the CD and DVD (or another CD) drive together into the same output.
- The 15-pin joystick or MIDI interface cable

If you're upgrading an audio device integrated into a motherboard, you cannot remove the device, but you'll need to disable it so that it doesn't conflict with the new sound device. Older motherboards may provide a jumper that will disable the audio device. Current audio devices can usually be disabled through the CMOS Setup (after uninstalling any old audio utilities and drivers, reboot to the CMOS Setup and disable the audio device, then save your changes and shut down the system). The very latest motherboards can detect the presence of a new PCI sound board and disable the onboard audio device automatically. Check your system's documentation to determine the best way to disable an integrated audio device.

## INSTALL THE NEW BOARD

Find an open expansion slot for the new sound board. Virtually all sound boards today will need a PCI slot. (Legacy sound cards may require a full ISA slot, but you should avoid "legacy" sound boards if possible.) The card slot should also accommodate a full-length board, though most sound boards only need a half-slot space. For legacy-type sound boards, check each jumper on the new sound board, and see that none of the IRQ, DMA, or I/O settings conflict with other devices in the system. If problems arise, this list will help isolate conflict problems. Today's PnP devices will simply configure themselves and begin driver installation once Windows starts. Ease the new board into its expansion slot, and be careful to avoid flexing the motherboard too much in the process. Once the sound card is installed properly, secure the board bracket to the PC chassis with the single screw (see Figure 34-9).

 When selecting a slot for the sound card, try to locate the sound card away from other devices to reduce the possibility of electrical interference appearing as noise in the sound output.

Some sound devices (such as the Sound Blaster Audigy) provide a 15-pin MIDI/gameport on a separate chassis bracket. In this case, you should select a location where there are two open slots—one for the sound card, and an adjacent "empty" slot for the additional bracket. The bracket then connects to a header on the sound board through a small ribbon cable.

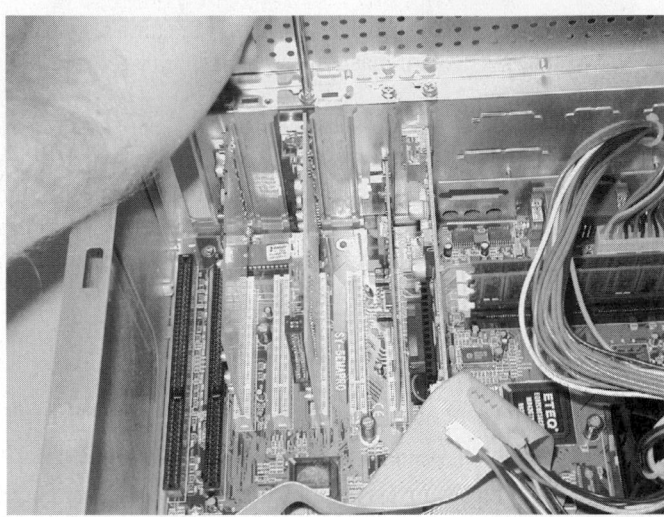

**FIGURE  34-9**   Easing the new sound card into the bus slot and securing it to the chassis with a single screw

## CONNECT THE CABLES

Now that the new sound card is in place, reconnect the cables as required. As a minimum, you will need to connect speakers, but you may also have to connect a CD audio cable, CD-ROM drive interface cable, microphone, MIDI or joystick cable, and so on. Figure 34-10 illustrates the typical connections for a Creative Sound Blaster Live 5.1 Platinum card. After each of the cables is secured, you can reconnect AC to the computer and reboot the system.

## INSTALL THE WINDOWS SOFTWARE

Once Windows 9x/Me/XP starts, you'll need to install the proper drivers and utilities for the sound board. If the sound card is plug-and-play ready (as virtually all are now), Windows will probably identify the new sound hardware automatically and attempt to install drivers for it. If your sound board has a Windows 98/Me/XP driver disk or CD, be sure to use the drivers from that media. (Otherwise, Windows may install older or incompatible native drivers.) In most cases, the installation wizard will guide you through the driver installation process automatically. For later sound boards, you may be asked to cancel the automatic Windows identification of the new device, then insert the board's installation CD and run the installation routine provided by the manufacturer.

Even if Windows 9x/Me/XP correctly identifies and installs the new sound board, remember that you may need to manually remove the old card (if one was installed) from the Windows Device Manager yourself before the new sound board will function.

## INSTALL THE DOS SOFTWARE

If you're planning on using your sound board for real-mode (DOS) games, you will need to install one or more DOS files so that they will run with CONFIG.SYS and AUTOEXEC.BAT each time the system starts. Otherwise, you will have no sound support under DOS. Today, sound boards are one of the very few devices to still come with DOS drivers and utilities. This is done almost exclusively to provide backward

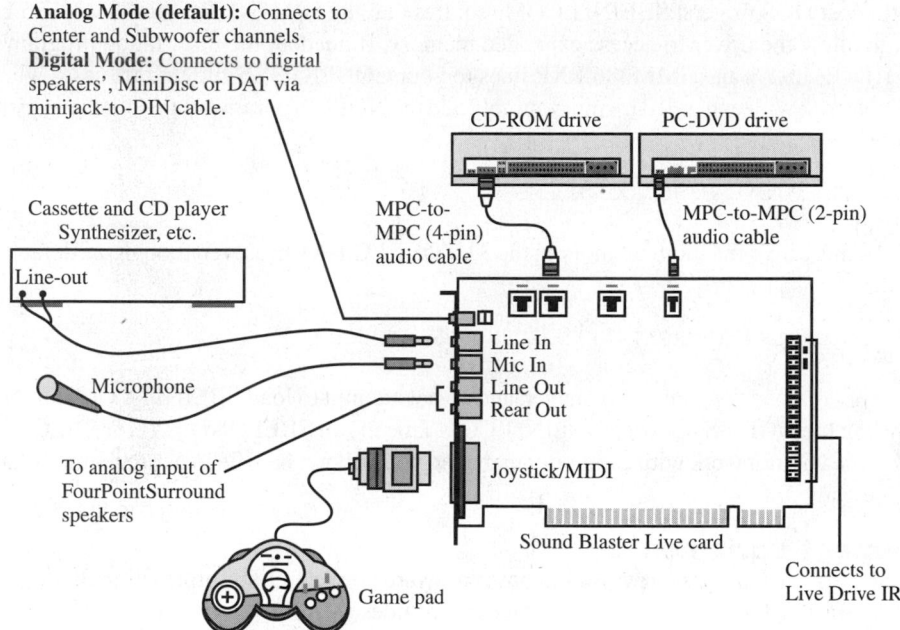

**Analog Mode (default):** Connects to Center and Subwoofer channels.
**Digital Mode:** Connects to digital speakers', MiniDisc or DAT via minijack-to-DIN cable.

CD-ROM drive          PC-DVD drive

Cassette and CD player          MPC-to-
Synthesizer, etc.               MPC (4-pin)          MPC-to-MPC (2-pin)
                                audio cable         audio cable

Line-out

                    Line In
                    Mic In
Microphone          Line Out
                    Rear Out

To analog input of
FourPointSurround          Joystick/MIDI
speakers
                    Sound Blaster Live card

                    Connects to
                    Live Drive IR

Game pad

**FIGURE  34-10**    Connections for a modern sound board (Courtesy of Creative Labs)

compatibility for your favorite legacy games. This part of the chapter looks at the typical way to configure a modern sound board (such as a Sound Blaster Audigy) for DOS.

If you do not require sound support under DOS, you can easily skip the installation of real-mode drivers and use Windows exclusively.

Generally, an installation routine with the sound board will automatically copy the real-mode drivers to your PC and modify your existing CONFIG.SYS and AUTOEXEC.BAT files with the appropriate command lines. Some installers will add DOS support along with the Windows drivers, while other products will keep Windows and DOS installers separate. Check the DOS support notes with your particular sound card. For the Sound Blaster Audigy card, you'd insert the installation CD, click Start | Run, and use a command line such as:

```
D:\DOSDRV\LANGUAGE\SETUP.EXE
```

then just follow the prompts to complete the installation. The DOS installation program adds the following three command lines to AUTOEXEC.BAT:

```
SET CTSYN=C:\WINDOWS
SET BLASTER=A220 I5 D1 H5 P330 T6
C:\PROGRA~1\CREATIVE\DOSDRV\SBEINIT.COM
```

The first two lines prepare the environment variables for your audio card. The third line runs SBEINIT.COM, which is the required MS-DOS driver.

As with most DOS drivers, SBEINIT.COM requires that the HIMEM.SYS and EMM386.EXE files be loaded, to allow the driver to access expanded memory. If needed, the installation program adds the necessary HIMEM.SYS and EMM386.EXE lines to your CONFIG.SYS file. In rare cases where a program does not work with expanded memory, simply add the NOEMS parameter to your memory manager. For example:

```
DEVICE=C:\WINDOWS\EMM386.EXE NOEMS
```

You may load this driver into high memory in the AUTOEXEC.BAT file, even though the default is not to. For example:

```
LOADHIGH=C:\PROGRA~1\CREATIVE\DOSDRV\SBEINIT.COM
```

As a rule, do not remove the memory manager, and do not attempt to load SBEINIT.COM into high memory when using the NOEMS option if SBEINIT.COM fails to run SBELOAD.EXE or SBECFG.EXE. If your DOS game will not work with a memory manager, you will not be able to use the Sound Blaster Live card with the game.

## Environment Variables

Environment variables are basically used to pass hardware configuration information to the software in your system. For DOS, the Sound Blaster Live card includes the following:

- CTSYN environment variable
- BLASTER environment variable

The CTSYN environment variable points to the location of the CTSYN.INI file, which usually resides in the Windows directory. The syntax for this variable is as follows:

```
CTSYN=<path>
```

where <path> is the location of the CTSYN.INI file. The BLASTER environment variable specifies the base I/O address, IRQ line, and DMA channels of the Sound Blaster interface. Its syntax is

```
BLASTER=A220 I5 D1 H5 P330 T6
```

The parameters in the command line can be broken down this way:

- **A*xxx***   Base I/O address
- **I*x***   IRQ assignment
- **D*x***   First DMA channel
- **H*x***   Second DMA channel
- **P*xxx***   Base I/O address for the MIDI interface
- **T*x***   Card type (usually 6)

## Checking Resources for DOS

When configuring a DOS game, you will generally need to tell the game about the sound board's resource assignments (IRQ, DMA, and I/O). To find the resources assigned to a Sound Blaster Audigy card's emulation mode, open the Device Manager. Expand the "Sound, video, and game controllers" entry, then double-click the DOS emulation entry for your sound device (e.g., "Creative EMU10Kx SB16 Emulation"). Now click the Resources tab and record the IRQ, I/O, and DMA entries that are listed. Your sound board may also offer a DOS utility that can help identify the card's resources. For the Sound Blaster Audigy card, switch to the DOS driver directory where you installed the card's software, such as:

```
C:\PROGRA~1\CREATIVE\DOSDRV
```

Now type **sbecfg** and then press ENTER. Denote the resources listed for the card, and use those entries to configure the DOS game or other application.

> Remember that few DOS programs are still in service, so you may never need to configure sound support in the real mode. However, this information may still be useful when dealing with older systems, or with customers who insist on using older DOS software.

# TEST THE SOUND BOARD

When the system reboots to Windows, you'll normally hear the "Windows start-up" sound. This will tell you that the sound board is working. You may need to adjust the volume levels on your speakers and mixer/equalizer applet (such as in Figure 34-11) in order to achieve an optimum sound, but those start-up chimes will often announce a working sound board. Once you've tweaked the volume settings, try an audio CD in the drive, and see if you can hear music through the sound board and speakers. (Of course, you'll need a 4-wire CD audio cable connected between the sound board and CD drive.)

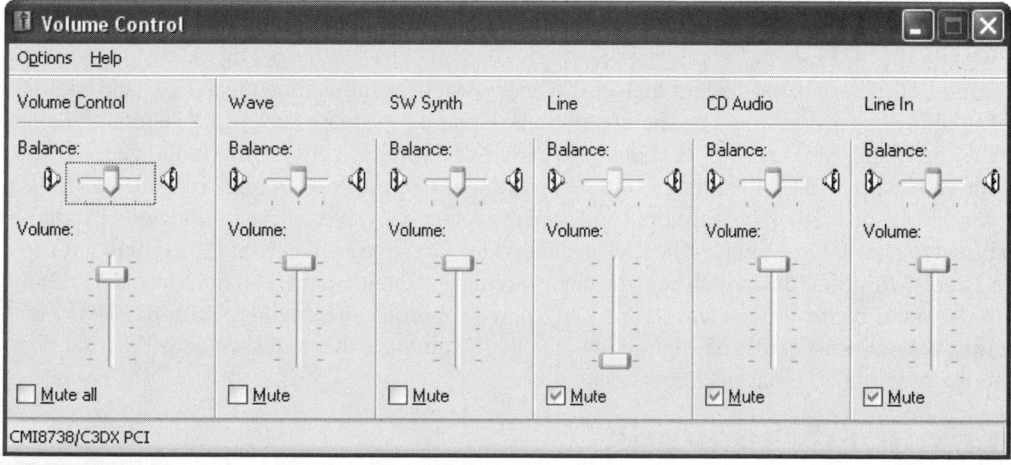

**FIGURE 34-11**    The standard Windows XP Volume Control applet

# Troubleshooting a Sound Board

Since each board is designed a bit differently, it is very difficult for commercial diagnostic products to identify failed chip functions on a sound board. For the most part, commercial and shareware diagnostics can only identify whether a brand-compatible board is responding or not. As a result, this chapter will take the subassembly replacement approach. When a sound board is judged to be defective, it should be replaced. This part of the chapter reviews the problems and solutions for sound boards under both DOS and Windows 9x/Me/XP. The following tips may help you nail down a sound problem most efficiently:

- Check to see that your speakers are connected, powered, and turned on.
- Check that the speaker volume and sound board master volume (if there's a physical control knob) are both turned up to no more than 75 percent—though 50 percent is usually more than adequate.
- Check to see that the mixer volume and master volume are set properly in the Volume Control applet (or other mixer/equalizer applet) as in Figure 34-11 earlier.
- Make sure that the music or sound file(s) are installed properly (you cannot play sound files that are corrupt or damaged).
- Check that all sound board and multimedia drivers are properly installed (you may wish to remove and reinstall the latest drivers).
- Make sure that the sound board drivers are up to date.
- Use the Device Manager to check for resource conflicts between the sound board and other devices in the system.
- Make sure that the sound board is selected and configured properly (especially for DOS apps).
- The sound device should be enabled and configured under the CMOS Setup (for sound functions incorporated on the motherboard).

## DOS DRIVERS

Unlike most other expansion devices that are driven by system or supplemental BIOS, sound boards make use of small devicc drivers to set up their operations. Under DOS, these drivers are generally included in CONFIG.SYS and AUTOEXEC.BAT and are called when the system is first initialized. Most sound board drivers are only used to initialize and set up the board, so they do not remain resident. This is good since it reduces the load on conventional and upper memory. However, these initialization routines vary from board to board. For example, the files installed for a Creative Labs Sound Blaster will not support a Turtle Beach MultiSound board. When you elect to replace a sound board, you must also disable any current (old) sound board drivers and include any new supporting driver files. The process is not difficult—just follow the installation instructions for the board—but this software consideration does add another wrinkle to the replacement process.

## FULL-DUPLEX DRIVERS

Most current sound board designs are compatible with "multimedia communication" technologies such as Internet Phone, NetMeeting, and other communication tools. These tools require full-duplex sound operation. That is, sound is digitized with the microphone, and received sound is played through the speakers simultaneously. This demands full-duplex drivers. If you plan to use communication tools, you'll need to install full-duplex sound card drivers that are appropriate for your particular sound board and operating system (today, virtually all sound devices support full-duplex operation). For example, the older Creative Labs SB32, AWE32, and AWE64 require the Windows 95 (or later) full-duplex driver file (SBW9xUP.EXE) available from the Creative Labs Web site at www.creaf.com. To use those same devices for full duplex under Windows NT 4.0, you'd need the AWENT40.EXE driver file (or later). As a rule, always check with the sound board maker for their latest full-duplex drivers.

 You may find that full-duplex drivers are not available for older sound boards or for sound boards running under OS/2 or Windows NT. In that case, you cannot support full-duplex applications and may need to upgrade the sound board before you can use that communication software.

## SOUNDBOARD ACCELERATION

Modern sound boards incorporate an increasingly complex range of processing functions such as EAX sound effects and 3D "positional" sound. Such features are usually handled by the sound board itself (rather than straining the system processor). This is referred to as *sound hardware acceleration*—similar in principle to the way modern video adapters include onboard acceleration features. Normally, a sound board will handle acceleration features easily and with minimum impact on system stability. In a few cases, however, sound acceleration can result in system problems. When your sound board supports onboard acceleration, you can adjust the level of acceleration through Windows XP:

1. Open the Control Panel and select Sounds, Speech, and Audio Devices.
2. Select Sounds and Audio Devices and click the Audio tab.
3. Click the Advanced button in the Sound playback area.
4. Click the Performance tab (see Figure 34-12) and adjust the Hardware acceleration slider accordingly. You may want to address possible problems by dropping the sound acceleration to None, then apply your changes and reboot the system.

Use the following steps if you're working under Windows 9x/Me:

1. Click Start | Settings | Control Panel.
2. Double-click the Multimedia icon (or Sounds and Multimedia under Windows Me), and then select the Audio tab (if it's not already selected).
3. Select Advanced in the Sound Playback area, and then click the Performance tab.
4. Move the Hardware acceleration slider to None, then Apply your changes, and reboot the system (if necessary).

Now test the system again. If the system's performance stabilizes, try moving up the slider again, one step at a time, until the system destabilizes. That's the point where your trouble is occurring, and a driver update will usually correct the problem. If the system's performance does not stabilize, you have an issue with something other than sound hardware acceleration. In a few cases, you may need to use an alternate sound board.

## MULTIPLE CODECS

Windows makes extensive use of *codecs* (coders/decoders) to support the variety of multimedia applications available. For example, video capture requires numerous codecs to encode the audio and video streams being passed to the PC. As another example, audio playback requires one codec for each type of audio format. In many cases, you may find more than one copy of the same codec on the system. This can easily happen as various multimedia applications are installed and removed. When there is more than one

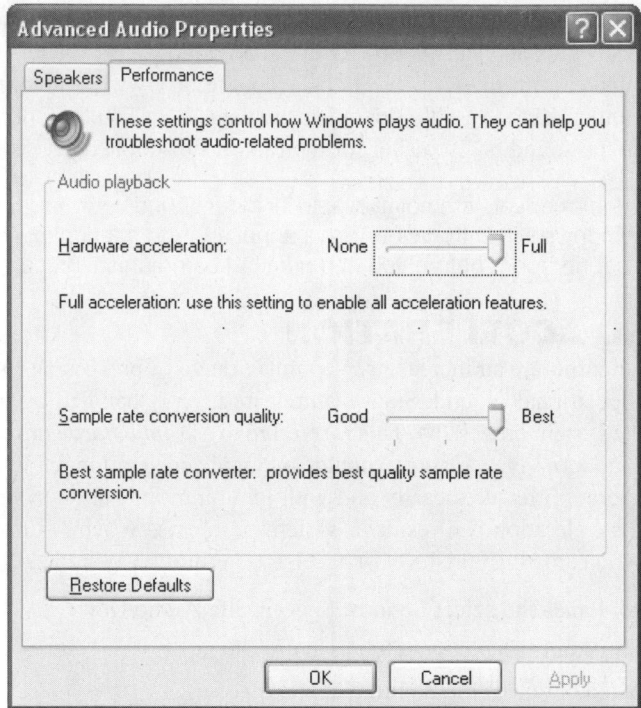

**FIGURE  34-12**    Adjusting sound playback acceleration under Windows XP

instance of the same codec, conflicts may result that impair the performance of your multimedia applications. Whenever you encounter trouble with audio recording, playback, capture, and so on, always check for duplicate codecs. Use the following steps under Windows XP:

1. Open the Control Panel and select Sounds, Speech, and Audio Devices.
2. Select Sounds and Audio Devices and click the Hardware tab.
3. Highlight the Audio Codecs entry and click Properties, then click the Properties tab (see Figure 34-13).
4. Look for duplicate entries in the list of codecs.
5. If you see duplicate entries, check the Properties for each instance, and remove the **older** instance.
6. Apply your changes and reboot the system if necessary.

 Use the following steps with Windows 9x/Me:

1. Click Start | Settings | Control Panel.
2. Double-click the Multimedia icon (Sounds and Multimedia under Windows Me), and then select the Devices tab.
3. Expand the Audio Compression Codecs entry, and look for duplicate entries.
4. If you see duplicate entries, check the Properties for each instance, and remove the older instance.
5. Apply your changes and reboot the system if necessary.

**FIGURE 34-13**   Checking for duplicate audio codecs on the system

# COMMON PLAYBACK PROBLEMS

Of all the sound board problems reported, perhaps the most common is the failure to play wave files (ordinary sound files with the .WAV extension) under Windows 98/Me/XP. This problem usually manifests itself during the Windows start up or shutdown when the accompanying sounds are not played. A variety of issues can prevent WAV files from playing.

### Check the Application

If you cannot play WAV files from a specific program that you use in Windows 98/Me/XP, check to see if the same problem occurs when you play the file from another program. If the problem occurs *only* with one particular program, the files associated with that program may be damaged, there may be a missing codec (or duplicate codecs) that the program depends on, or that program may not be configured correctly under Windows. You may need to remove and reinstall the troublesome application. If you cannot get WAV files to play under *any* application, chances are that another issue is responsible.

### Check the Hardware Configuration

If you encounter trouble playing WAV files in Windows 9x/Me/XP (or if WAV files are not played at the proper volume), you may not have a sound device selected, or the sound device that you have selected may not be configured properly. To select and configure a sound device under Windows XP:

1. Open the Control Panel and select Sounds, Speech, and Audio Devices.
2. Select Sounds and Audio Devices and click the Audio tab.

3. Use the drop-down menus to select appropriate sound playback, sound recording, and MIDI music playback devices on the system (see Figure 34-14).

4. Apply your changes and reboot the system if necessary.

To select and configure a sound device in Windows 9x/Me:

1. Open the Control Panel, and double-click the Multimedia icon (Sounds and Multimedia under Windows Me).

2. In the Playback area under the Audio tab, click the playback device that you want to use in the Preferred device list. Set the master volume to an adequate level. Note that some dialog boxes may show a playback area for Sound and MIDI Music playback.

3. In the Recording area under the Audio tab, click the recording device that you want to use in the Preferred device list. Click the Recording icon, and set the Microphone volume to an adequate level.

4. Apply your changes and reboot the system if necessary.

## Check the Volume Settings

If you cannot play any WAV files under Windows 9x/Me/XP (or if WAV files are not played at the proper volume), the mixer control settings may not be configured properly. Use the mixer control program included with Windows (see Figure 34-11 earlier) to adjust the volume for playback or recording. To open

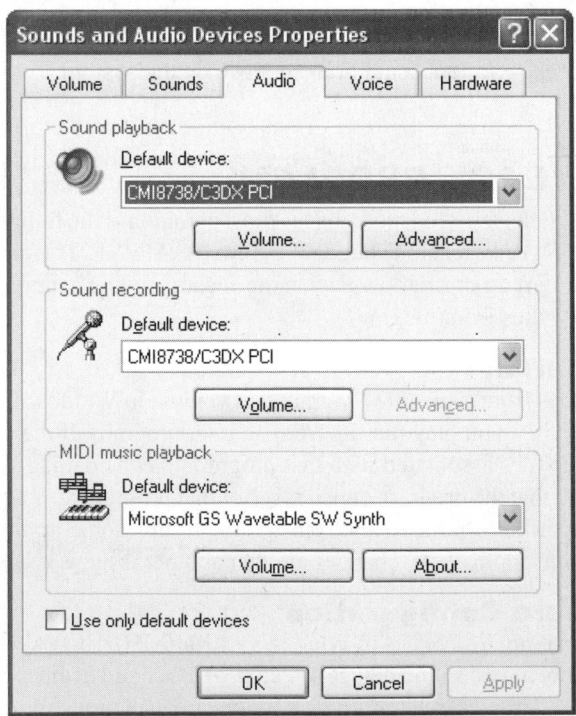

**FIGURE 34-14** Selecting suitable playback, recording, and MIDI devices

the Volume Control settings for Windows 9x/Me, simply select Start | Programs | Accessories | Entertainment | Volume Control. To access the mixer under Windows XP, follow these steps:

1. Open the Control Panel and select Sounds, Speech, and Audio Devices.
2. Select Sounds and Audio Devices and click the Audio tab.
3. Click the Volume button in either the Sound playback, Sound recording, or MIDI music playback areas. The Volume Control applet will open.

Make sure that the "Mute all" check box below the Volume Control slider and the Mute check box below the Wave slider are not selected, and that the Balance sliders for Volume Control and Wave are in the center. Move the Volume Control and Wave sliders at least halfway to the top of the scale. You may need to adjust the current Volume Control or Wave settings to play WAV files at the volume level you want.

 If the Volume Control and Wave sliders do not appear, click Properties on the Options menu, and then select their check boxes.

## Check for Hardware Conflicts

It is possible that your sound board may not be compatible with the type of WAV file you are trying to play, or there may be a resource conflict between your sound board and other devices installed in your computer. Check the Device Manager to see if there are any resource conflicts with your sound board. To determine whether your sound card supports the WAV file format you're using, contact the sound board's manufacturer.

## Check for Damaged Files

The WAV files themselves may be damaged. To check if a WAV file is damaged, right-click the WAV file in Windows Explorer, click Properties on the menu, and then click the Details tab (the Summary tab in Windows XP as in Figure 34-15). The list of properties should contain information about the file, including sample size, bit rate, channels, and so on. If this information is missing or incomplete, the WAV file is probably damaged and should be reinstalled or recopied to the drive.

# SYMPTOMS

Although sound boards are reasonably reliable devices, there are many specific problems that cannot be resolved with the preceding general guidelines. When you're facing an issue with a sound device, refer to the following symptoms for possible explanations and solutions.

**SYMPTOM 34-1**    **A noticeable buzz or hum is produced in one or both speakers**
Low-cost speakers generally use unshielded cables. Unfortunately, strong signals from AC cords and other signal-carrying conductors can easily induce interference in the speaker wires. Try rerouting speaker cables clear of other cables in the system. If problems persist, try using higher-quality speakers with shielded cables and enclosures. In most cases, that should resolve everyday noise problems. If the noise continues regardless of what you do, there may be a fault in the sound board's amplifier. Try moving the sound board to another bus slot away from other boards or the power supply. If that does not resolve the problem, try a new sound board.

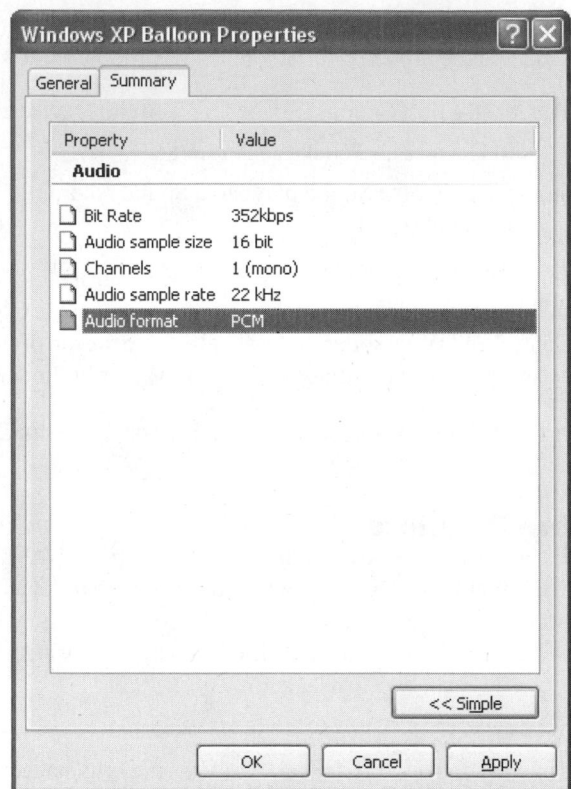

**FIGURE  34-15**    Checking the WAV file's properties for potential damage

**SYMPTOM 34-2**    **There is no sound from the speaker(s) when using the sound board in the real mode**    The lack of sound from a sound board can be due to any one of a wide range of potential problems. If the sound board works with some applications but not with others, it is likely that the problem is due to an improperly installed or configured application. See that the offending application is set up properly. (And make sure it is even capable of using the sound card.) Also check that the proper sound driver files (if any) are loaded into CONFIG.SYS and AUTOEXEC.BAT as required. In many cases, there are one or two sound-related environment variables that are set in AUTOEXEC.BAT. Make sure that your start-up files are configured properly.

Check your speakers next. See that they are turned on and set to a normal volume level. The speakers should be receiving adequate power and should be plugged properly into the correct output jack. If speakers have been plugged into the wrong jack, no sound will be produced. If the cable is broken or questionable, try a new set of speakers. Also see that the master volume control on the sound board is turned up most (or all) of the way. If volume is controlled through software, see that the mixer volume levels are set adequately.

If problems continue, there may be a resource conflict between the sound board and another device in the system. Use the Device Manager and check for conflicts between each device in the system. Make sure that no two devices are using the same resources. If problems persist, and no conflict is present, try another sound board.

**SYMPTOM 34-3**   **CD audio will not play through the sound board**   This problem can occur under both DOS and Windows. First, make sure that the sound board is actually capable of playing CD audio. (Older boards may not be compatible.) If the sound card is playing sound files, but is not playing CD audio, there are several things for you to check. First, open the PC and make sure that the CD audio cable (a thin, 4-wire cable) is attached from the CD-ROM drive to the sound board. If this cable is broken, disconnected, or absent, CD audio will not be passed to the sound board. If the cable is intact, make sure that the CD audio player is configured properly for the sound board you are using, and check the start-up files to see that any drivers and environment variable needed by CONFIG.SYS and AUTOEXEC.BAT are available. If the CD-audio fails to play under Windows 9x/Me/XP, make sure that a full suite of audio codecs is available (as in Figure 34-13 earlier).

All CD audio cables are not created equal. Some cables are wired strangely, and may not be compatible with all CD and sound board connections. You may need a specialized cable between your particular CD drive and sound board.

**SYMPTOM 34-4**   **You see an error such as "No interrupt vector available"**   This type of trouble is seen in the real mode. The DOS interrupt vectors used by the sound board's setup drivers (usually INT 80h to BFh) are being used by one or more other drivers in the system. As a consequence, there is a software conflict. Try disabling other drivers in the system one at a time until you see the conflict disappear. Once you have isolated the offending driver(s), you can leave them disabled or (if possible) alter their command-line settings so that they no longer conflict with the sound board's software.

**SYMPTOM 34-5**   **There is no MIDI output**   Make sure that the file you are trying to play is a valid MIDI file (usually with a .MID extension). In most cases, you will find that the MIDI Mapper under Windows is not set up properly for the sound board. Load the Windows MIDI Mapper applet from the Control Panel (or other MIDI applet for your particular sound board), and set it properly to accommodate your sound board. In some cases, you may simply need to remove the sound device from the Device Manager, and then allow Windows to redetect the device and install the latest drivers for the sound board.

**SYMPTOM 34-6**   **Sound play is jerky**   Choppy or jerky sound playback is typically the result of a hard drive problem. More specifically, the drive cannot read the sound file to a buffer fast enough. In many cases, the reason for this slow drive performance is excessive disk fragmentation. Try defragmenting the drive with Disk Defragmenter under Windows. If the problem persists, try reducing the sound quality or disabling special sound effects in order to reduce the sound processing load on the system.

**SYMPTOM 34-7**   **You see an error such as "Out of environment space"**   This is a problem that occasionally occurs in the real mode. The system is out of DOS environment space. You will need to increase the system's environment space by adding the following line to your CONFIG.SYS file:

```
shell=c:\command.com /E:512 /P
```

This command line sets the environment space to 512 bytes. If you still encounter the error message, change the E entry to 1024 (that is, **/E:1024**).

**SYMPTOM 34-8**   **Regular "clicks," "stutters," or "hiccups" occur during the playback of speech**   This may also be heard as a "garbled" sound in speech or sound effects. In virtually all cases, the system CPU is simply not fast enough to permit buffering without dropping sound data. Systems with i286 and slower i386 CPUs typically suffer this kind of problem. This is often compounded by insufficient memory (especially under Windows) that automatically resorts to virtual memory. Since virtual memory is delivered by the hard drive, and the hard drive is much slower than RAM anyway, the hard drive simply can't provide data fast enough. Unfortunately, there is little to be done in this kind of situation (aside from adding RAM, upgrading the CPU, or changing the motherboard). If it is possible to shut off various sound features (such as music, voice, effects, and so on), try shutting down any extra sound features that you can live without. Make sure that there are no applications running in the background that may be demanding valuable system processing time.

**SYMPTOM 34-9**    **The joystick is not working, or not working properly on all systems**
This problem only applies to sound boards with a multifunction MIDI/joystick port being used in the joystick mode. Chances are that the joystick is conflicting with another joystick port in the system. Disable the original joystick port or the new joystick port. Only one joystick port (game adapter) can be active at any one time in the system. Since joystick performance is dependent on CPU speed, the CPU may actually be too fast for the joystick port. Disable the joystick port, or try slowing down the CPU.

**SYMPTOM 34-10**    **You install a sound board and everything works properly, but now the printer does not seem to work**    There is an interrupt conflict between the sound board and an IRQ line used by the printer. While parallel printers are often polled, they can also be driven by an IRQ line (IRQ5 or IRQ7). If the sound board is using either one of these interrupts, try changing to an alternative IRQ line using the Resources tab under your Device Manager. When changing an IRQ line in the real mode, be sure to reflect the changes in any sound board files called by CONFIG.SYS or AUTOEXEC.BAT.

**SYMPTOM 34-11**    **You see the message "The specified MIDI device is already in use"**
This problem often occurs with sound boards such as the Creative Labs Sound Blaster AWE64. This error is often caused by having the sound board's mixer display turned on with the wavetable synthesizer selected (for example, the LED display in the Creative Mixer turned on and Creative Wave Synthesizer selected as the MIDI playback device). You can usually correct the problem by turning the mixer display off.

**SYMPTOM 34-12**    **Your sound card produces excessive environmental effects**    In most cases, the environmental settings (e.g., EAX or A3D) are configured improperly when an audio file is played. You'll need to open the sound card's environmental control applet and reconfigure the card to use no effects, or select an alternate effect that is more suitable for the sound file(s) that you're trying to use.

**SYMPTOM 34-13**    **You hear pops and clicks when recording sound under Windows 9x/Me**    This is not a known issue under Windows XP. In most cases, there is insufficient cache to adequately support the recording process (or cache is improperly configured). Try the following procedure to alter the way cache is allocated:

1. Open Notepad and load SYSTEM.INI.
2. Locate the area of SYSTEM.INI labeled **[vcache]**.
3. Add the following line below [vcache]:

   ```
   maxfilecache=2048
   ```

4. Save your changes to the SYSTEM.INI file.
5. From the desktop, right-click on My Computer, and then select Properties.
6. Select the Performance page, and then click on File System.

7. Find the slider marked "Read-ahead optimization," and then pull the slider to None.

8. Save your changes and restart Windows, then try your recording process again.

**SYMPTOM 34-14** **You notice high-frequency distortion in one or possibly both channels**
This problem usually occurs in very fast systems using an ISA sound board. In many cases, the AT Bus Clock is set over 8 MHz, and data is being randomly lost. Enter the system's CMOS Setup, and check the AT Bus Clock under the Advanced Chipset Setup area. See that the bus clock is set as close as possible to 8 MHz. If the bus clock is derived as a divisor of the CPU clock, you may see an entry such as /4. Make sure that the selected divisor results in a clock speed as close to 8 MHz as possible. If problems still persist, try increasing the divisor to drop the bus speed below 8 MHz. (Note that this may have an adverse effect on other ISA peripherals.) Another alternative is to replace the ISA card with an updated PCI sound board.

**SYMPTOM 34-15** **You hear pops and clicks when playing back prerecorded files under Windows 9x/Me** There is an excessive processing load on the system that is often caused by virtual memory and/or 32-bit access. Try adding more RAM to the system. If there is already an adequate amount of RAM, try disabling virtual memory. Open the Control Panel and double-click on the System icon. Select the Performance page, and click on Virtual Memory. Set the swap file to None and save your changes. Try the file playback again. If problems persist, try disabling 32-bit file access. If that still does not resolve the problem, try disabling 32-bit disk access.

**SYMPTOM 34-16** **You hear pops and clicks on new recordings only; preexisting files sound clean** This is often due to issues with software caching. If you are using DOS or Windows 3.1, disable SmartDrive from both CONFIG.SYS and AUTOEXEC.BAT, and then restart the computer for your changes to take effect. If problems continue (or you are using Windows 9x/Me), there may be an excessive processing load on the system due to virtual memory or 32-bit access. Follow the recommendations under Symptom 34-15 earlier.

**SYMPTOM 34-17** **You hear pops and clicks when playing back or recording any sound file** In most cases, there is a wiring problem with the speaker system. Check all of your cabling between the sound board and speakers. If the speakers are powered by AC, make sure that the power jack is inserted properly. If the speakers are powered by battery, make sure that the batteries are fresh. Check for loose connections. If you cannot resolve the problem, try some new speakers. If the problem persists, replace the sound board. Also try the speakers on another system. If they work fine on another system, you know the problem is with the sound card.

**SYMPTOM 34-18** **The sound board will play back fine, but it will not record** The board probably records fine in DOS, but not in Windows. If the sound board is using 16-bit DMA transfer (typical under Windows), there are two DMA channels in use. Chances are that one of those two DMA channels is conflicting with another device in the system. Determine the DMA channels being used under Windows, and then check other devices for DMA conflicts. If you are using Windows 98/Me/XP, check the Device Manager and look for entries marked with a yellow icon. Also remember to select an appropriate recording device in your Audio Properties dialog, and verify that your microphone is adequate for the sound card. Be sure to double-check all of your connections.

**SYMPTOM 34-19** **You have trouble panning a sound** You might see that panning a sound source may disable its sound. This type of trouble is known to occur on later model sound boards when you're in the Digital Output Only mode. In many cases, the source's balance in the generic mixer applet is opposite to the balance in the sound card's manufacturer-specific mixer applet. For example, the CD Audio balance in the Windows Volume Control is on the left, but the CD Audio balance in the Creative Surround Mixer applet is set to the right. The best way to fix this is to open the generic Windows mixer and center the balance settings for all input sources—this way, the signals won't cut out when you pan the signals in the manufacturer-specific mixer.

**SYMPTOM 34-20**    **The sound board will not play or record—the system locks up when either is attempted**    The board will probably not play in either DOS or Windows, but may run fine on other systems. This is a problem that has been identified with some sound boards and ATI video boards. ATI video boards use unusual address ranges that sometimes overlap the I/O address used by the sound board. Check the Device Manager for resource conflicts, and resolve any conflicts that may appear. For example, reconfigure the sound board to another I/O address (if possible), or replace an older sound board with a fully PnP PCI model.

**SYMPTOM 34-21**    **The sound board will record, but will not play back**    Assuming that the sound board and its drivers are installed and configured properly, chances are that a playback oscillator (or other playback circuitry) on the sound board has failed. Try replacing the sound board.

**SYMPTOM 34-22**    **The sound application or editor produces a significant number of DMA errors**    This type of problem is known to occur frequently when using the standard VGA driver that accompanies older versions of Windows. The driver is poorly written and cannot keep up with screen draws. Try updating your video driver to a later, more efficient version (ideally, you'd prefer to use the manufacturer's latest drivers for your display adapter). If the driver is known to contain bugs, try using a generic video driver written for the video board's chipset.

**SYMPTOM 34-23**    **The sound board will not record in DOS**    There are several possible problems that can account for this behavior. First, check your microphone and connections, then suspect a hardware conflict between the sound board and other devices in the system. Make sure that the IRQs, DMA channels, and I/O port addresses used by the sound board are not used by other devices. If the hardware setup appears correct, suspect a problem between DOS drivers. Try a clean boot of the system (with no CONFIG.SYS or AUTOEXEC.BAT). If sound can be run properly now, there is a driver conflict. Examine your entries in CONFIG.SYS or AUTOEXEC.BAT for possible conflicts, or for older drivers that may still be loading to support hardware that is no longer in the system.

Finally, suspect the hard drive controller. Try setting up a RAM drive with RAMDRIVE.SYS. You can install a RAM drive on your system by adding the line:

```
device=c:\dos\ramdrive.sys /e 8000
```

The 8000 is for 8MB worth of RAM. Make sure there is enough RAM in the PC. Once the RAM drive is set up, try recording and playing from the RAM drive. (You may have to specify a new path in the sound recorder program.) If that works, the hard drive controller may simply be too slow to support the sound board, and you may need to consider upgrading the drive system.

**SYMPTOM 34-24**    **After the sound board driver is loaded, Windows locks up when starting or exiting**    In virtually all cases, you have a hardware conflict between the sound board and another device in the system. Check the Device Manager for resource conflicts, and resolve any conflicts that may appear. For example, make sure that the IRQs, DMA channels, and I/O port addressed used by the sound board are not used by other devices. You may need to upgrade an older sound board with a fully PnP PCI model.

**SYMPTOM 34-25**    **When using Windows sound editing software, the sound board refuses to enter the "digital" mode—always switching back to the analog mode**    Generally speaking, this is a software configuration issue. Make sure that your editing (or other sound) software is set for the correct type of sound board (such as an AWE32 instead of a Sound Blaster 16/Pro, or a Sound Blaster Audigy rather than an AWE32). If problems persist, the issue is with your sound drivers. Check the [drivers] section of the Windows SYSTEM.INI file for your sound board driver entries. If there is more than one entry, you may need to disable the competing driver. This is a known problem with the Digital Audio Labs CardDplus and is caused by incorrect driver listings. For example, the proper CardDplus driver must be entered as:

```
Wave=cardp.drv
```

and the companion driver must be listed as:

```
Wave1=tahiti.drv
```

You will need to make sure that the proper driver(s) for your sound board are entered in SYSTEM.INI. You may also need to restart the system after making any changes. You may find it simpler to remove all sound device entries from the Device Manager, then allow Windows to redetect and reinstall the sound device from scratch.

**SYMPTOM 34-26**    **The microphone records at very low levels (or not at all)**    Suspect the microphone itself. Most sound boards demand the use of a good-quality dynamic microphone. Also, Creative Labs and Labtec microphones are not always compatible with sound boards from other manufacturers. Try a generic dynamic microphone. Make sure that the card's phantom power is set properly for the microphone being used. Phantom power should be on for condenser microphones and off for dynamic microphones. If problems persist, chances are that your recording software is not configured properly for microphone input. Set up the recording device properly under Windows XP:

1. Open the Control Panel and select Sounds, Speech, and Audio Devices.
2. Select Sounds and Audio Devices and click the Audio tab.
3. Select an appropriate recording device in the Sound recording area (see Figure 34-14 earlier). Now click the Volume button. The Volume Control applet will open (see Figure 34-11 earlier).
4. Set the microphone volume to an adequate level.
5. Save your changes and reboot the system if necessary.

Try the following procedure to set up the recording application properly under Windows 9x/Me:

1. Open your Control Panel and double-click on the Multimedia icon (Sounds and Multimedia under Windows Me).
2. The Multimedia Properties dialog will open. Select the Audio tab.
3. See that the Preferred device and Preferred quality settings are correct.
4. Open the Volume Control applet, and set the microphone volume to an adequate level.
5. Save your changes and reboot the system if necessary.

**SYMPTOM 34-27**    **The sound card isn't working in full-duplex mode**    Virtually all current sound boards are capable of full-duplex operation for such applications as Internet phones or NetMeeting. Check the specifications for your sound board, and verify that the board is capable of full-duplex operation. If it isn't, you'll need to upgrade the sound board to support full duplex. If it is, and full duplex isn't working, your driver may be inadequate, and may need to be updated with the latest drivers from the manufacturer.

**SYMPTOM 34-28**    **Your dynamic microphone clips terribly, and recordings are noisy and faint**    This is probably due to phantom power being switched on in your sound board. Try turning the phantom power off. If you cannot turn phantom power off, try plugging the dynamic microphone into the sound board's line input jack. Remember to open the sound board's mixer applet, and set the line input level properly.

**SYMPTOM 34-29**    **You have trouble using Creative Labs or Labtec microphones with your (non–Creative Labs) sound board**    This is a common complaint among older Ensoniq sound board users. It turns out that Ensoniq sound boards are not compatible with Creative Labs or Labtec microphones. Try a generic microphone instead. Check the manufacturer's recommendations for a preferred microphone type.

**SYMPTOM 34-30**    **There is static at the remote end when talking through a voice application such as WebPhone**    Noise is occurring at the line input or microphone input that is being transmitted to the remote listener. Check the line input signal. You might try reducing or turning off the line input mixer level. If the problem persists, check your phantom power setting and your microphone. Try reducing the microphone level in the sound board's mixer. Try a different microphone.

**SYMPTOM 34-31**    **You encounter pops and cracks during recording or playback**    For example, this is a known problem with a Sound Blaster Live and Windows 98 on a VIA motherboard using either an Apollo VP3 (VT82C597) or Apollo MVP3 (VT82C598) system controller chipset and a VIA IDE bus master driver version 2.1.33 update. Follow these steps to remove the popping/cracking sound:

1. Run SETUP.EXE of the VIA IDE Bus master driver version 2.1.33 again.
2. Select the Enable/Disable (Ultra) DMA option instead, and then click the Next button.
3. Unselect/uncheck the available devices, and then click the Next button.
4. Reboot the system.

Please check the VIA web site at www.viatech.com for updates on your motherboard. Note that you may also be able to install later versions of the VIA bus master drivers.

**SYMPTOM 34-32**    **You encounter short bursts of sound when playing a WAV file**    This problem happens when you're using a Sound Blaster Live card on VIA motherboard with the Apollo VP3 (VT82C597) or Apollo MVP3 (VT82C598) system controller chipset. This combination causes repeated buffering during a WAV playback on Windows 98 (Version 4.10.1998). To resolve this problem, download and install the VIA PCI IRQ Miniport driver version 1.3a (or later) Setup program. This program can be obtained from the VIA web site **www.viatech.com**. Reboot the system after installing the update.

**SYMPTOM 34-33**    **Sounds stop after the system resumes from suspend mode under Windows 98/SE**    If a program is using DirectSound and the system enters a suspend mode, sound may no longer run when the system resumes. This problem can occur if the DirectSound components of your platform (such as an older version of DirectX) do not resume properly. To correct the issue permanently, download and install the latest version of DirectX from Microsoft at www.microsoft.com/directx/. You can work around the problem and restore sound to the program by rebooting the system and not allowing the system to enter the suspend mode.

**SYMPTOM 34-34**    **No sounds are played with certain sound cards under Windows 98/SE**    For example, this problem is known to occur with older Ensoniq sound cards—WAV files won't play, but MIDI files appear to play properly. In most cases, the trouble occurs because the audio playback device is set improperly. Open the Audio Properties dialog box (as shown in Figure 34-14 earlier) and be sure to select the specific sound device as the preferred playback device. Keep in mind that a setting such as "Use any device" may not prevent the problem. Reboot the PC if necessary once you've made your changes.

**SYMPTOM 34-35**    **USB speakers don't work after upgrading Windows**    For example, you may find that USB speakers work normally, but stop working when Windows is upgraded to 98/SE or later. To fix this trouble, access the Audio Properties dialog box (as shown in Figure 34-14 earlier) and select the USB audio device as the preferred playback device. Keep in mind that a setting such as "Use any device" may not prevent the problem. Reboot the PC if necessary once you've made your changes.

**SYMPTOM 34-36**    **USB speakers do not produce any volume**    Always check the power and USB connections to the speakers. Also check the speaker's volume control, along with the Volume Control settings (or other mixer application). If the problem persists, chances are that the USB drivers are outdated or inappropriate. You'll need to reinstall or update the device drivers and applications software for your speakers.

**SYMPTOM 34-37**    **The sound board is misidentified under Windows 98/SE**    For example, you may see an Aztech 2316 identified as a Sound Blaster Pro (though this can certainly occur with other sound devices). The best way to correct this type of problem is to highlight the incorrect device reference in the Device Manager and update the drivers using the latest manufacturer's drivers. Alternately, you can remove the device from the Device Manager and allow Windows to redetect the device using the latest drivers.

**SYMPTOM 34-38**    **Your sound card delivers a "DSP timeout" under Windows 98**
This often happens on 440GX motherboards under Windows 98, and you'll find this happens even though you switch card slots and reinstall/update the sound card's drivers. The problem is with the motherboard's chipset (usually a 440GX). You must download the .INF update utility for the GX chipset from your system or motherboard manufacturer. This motherboard is newer than Windows 98 and must have this patch installed for PCI and AGP devices to function correctly. If this type of trouble occurs with other chipsets, be sure to install the latest chipset drivers for your particular version of Windows.

**SYMPTOM 34-39**    **You replace a legacy ISA sound card with a PCI sound card, and now you get a "virtual device driver (VxD)" error at boot time**    The problem is almost always caused by the *old* sound card drivers (not the new sound card drivers). Chances are that you did not remove or uninstall the old sound card's drivers and application software, and they're still trying to load when the system boots. Since the old card is no longer installed, the drivers show an error and refuse to load. You'll need to remove the old sound card's drivers and uninstall the old application software. In some cases, you may then need to reinstall the newest sound drivers and applets.

**SYMPTOM 34-40**    **You cannot install a sound card's software before installing the sound card**    For example, this is a known problem with Phoenix BIOS and LiveWare 2.0 when you're installing a Sound Blaster Live card. To install the sound software, you should install the sound card and its drivers first. Install the sound board and reboot your PC. After the PC has restarted, Windows will attempt to detect your audio card and install drivers for it. Insert the original installation disc that comes with your sound board into the CD-ROM drive. When prompted to install the drivers:

1. Choose to install the drivers provided by your hardware manufacturer (found in the installation disc).

2. Specify the location and path where the driver software is located. You may need to reboot the system once the drivers are installed.

3. Now run the software setup program.

**SYMPTOM 34-41**    **You encounter an error such as "Setup cannot detect the sound card on your system"**    The sound application's setup program cannot detect the sound card hardware, so you'll need to make a few quick checks to isolate the problem:

■ Check that the sound card is listed and enabled under your Device Manager. If the sound device isn't identified (or is identified improperly), you'll need to install the sound board according to the manufacturer's instructions.

■ Restart the system to your CMOS Setup, and see that your PNP OS INSTALLED option is set to Yes. Otherwise, the resources for the sound device may not be allocated.

■ Try moving the card to another PCI slot—perhaps a higher-priority PCI slot (closer to the processor).

**SYMPTOM 34-42**    **You try to play back more than one source (such as microphone and CD audio), but you cannot keep the sources unmuted at the same time in the mixer**
In the sound card's application software (a.k.a. mixer), make sure that the "What you hear" option is not chosen as the Record source. Choosing another recording source will enable you to unmute multiple analog sources at the same time. However, note that "environment" audio effects can only be applied to the analog source specified as the Recording source.

**SYMPTOM 34-43**    **You find that the mixer settings change every time you switch to an "environment preset" in the surround (A3D) mixer**    You're probably trying to maintain the same mixer settings all the time. You can achieve this by dissociating the mixer from the environment preset. To do this with software like LiveWare 2.0, click the Surround Mixer title in the upper-left corner in the Preset Deck of the Surround Mixer. The system menu appears with Dissociate Mixer Settings. To dissociate mixer settings, make sure the command is checked. To associate mixer settings, make sure the command is not checked.

**SYMPTOM 34-44**    **You've associated an application to the "environment presets," but the "environmental audio" preset is not activated when the application is launched**
Chances are that the "AutoEA" feature is not working—it must be running. This means the AutoEA icon must appear in the System Tray, or the AutoEA applet must be open. Remember that the AutoEA feature will not work if your current speaker configuration doesn't conform to the one specified in AutoEA. For example, if you specified "2 speakers" in AutoEA, it won't work if your current speaker configuration is "4 speakers."

**SYMPTOM 34-45**   The game's acoustics don't seem any different whether "environmental audio effects" (EAX) is enabled or not   Chances are that your EAX system is not initialized properly. For EAX to initialize correctly, you should verify that the current "environmental audio" setting is set as No Effects. Also remember that the program (a game) must be written to use EAX, so check your program to see that EAX is enabled.

**SYMPTOM 34-46**   You notice slower frame rates with some games when using "environmental audio effects" (EAX) with your sound card's application software
This is a problem with the sound board's application software and not the game itself. Download and install the latest update to your sound board's drivers and application software. This should optimize the game's frame rate by streamlining its audio effect performance.

**SYMPTOM 34-47**   When using a four-speaker system, you notice that the sound seems unbalanced in the four-speaker mode   Ensure that your speakers are properly placed so that the sound output is balanced. There is a chance that one or more of the audio devices (such as WAV, CD audio, or MIDI) are being positioned within the speaker environment in the Speaker applet—resulting in the imbalance. This could happen if your previous setting was for a Game Environment found on the Environments tab, and you continue to use this same setting for other media playback. Go to the Environments tab, and set this to No Effects (or use another neutral preset such as Multi-speaker Normal). Alternately, you can go to the Speaker applet and choose another appropriate setting.

**SYMPTOM 34-48**   CD audio is not loud, even with the volume turned all the way up
If your CD audio signal is not loud enough, it is most likely because you're using the A3D reference drivers for your sound card. The A3D drivers add a new feature that allows you to pass the CD audio through an equalizer (or EQ), and your EQ is affecting the volume. Change the EQ settings, bypass the EQ, or go to A3D settings and remove "CD Audio" from the analog EQ pass-through list.

# Further Study

**A3D Drivers**   www.3dsoundsurge.com/drivers/a3d.html
**Altec-Lansing**   www.altecmm.com
**Creative Labs**   www.creaf.com
**Diamond Multimedia**   www.diamondmm.com
**EAX**   eax.creative.com
**Frontier Design Group**   www.frontierdesign.com
**Voyetra/Turtle Beach**   www.tbeach.com

# 35

# VIDEO ADAPTERS AND ACCELERATORS

The monitor itself is merely an output device (a "peripheral") that translates synchronized analog or TTL (Transistor to Transistor Logic) video signals into a visual image. Of course, a monitor alone is not good for very much—except perhaps as a conversation piece or a room-heater. The next logical question is: where does the video signal come from? A video adapter circuit (Figure 35-1) produces all video signals displayed on a monitor. The term "adapter" is often used because the PC is "adapted" to the particular monitor through this circuit. In most cases, the video adapter is an expansion board that plugs into the PC's

**FIGURE  35-1**    The Matrox Parhelia graphics accelerator, which uses a 512-bit graphics processor for leading 2D and 3D graphics performance (Courtesy of Matrox Graphics, Inc.)

available AGP bus slot. It is the video adapter that converts raw data from the PC into image data that is stored in the adapter's *video memory*. The exact amount of memory available depends on the particular adapter and the video modes that the adapter is designed to support. The earliest adapters offered as little as 256KB, while the latest adapters provide 64MB or more. The video adapter then translates the contents of video memory into the video signals that drive a monitor.

The actual operations of a video adapter are certainly more involved than described, but you can begin to appreciate the critical role that the video adapter plays in a PC. If a video adapter fails, the monitor will display gibberish (or nothing at all). To complicate matters even further, many current software applications require device drivers (called *video drivers*). A video driver is a rather small program that allows an operating system (such as Windows 9x/Me/XP) to access a video adapter's high-resolution and high-color video modes with little or no interaction from the system BIOS. Video drivers have a profound effect on your video performance and stability, and during troubleshooting it will be necessary for you to isolate display problems to either the monitor, the video adapter, or video driver before a solution can be found. This chapter explains the operation and troubleshooting of typical 2D and 3D video adapters.

# Understanding Conventional Video Adapters

The conventional frame buffer is the oldest and most well established type of video adapter. The term *frame buffer* refers to the adapter's operation—image data is loaded and stored in video memory one "frame" at a time. Frame buffer architecture (as shown in Figure 35-2) has changed very little since PCs first started displaying text and graphics. The heart of the frame-buffer video adapter is the highly integrated display controller chip (sometimes called a *CRTC* or *Cathode Ray Tube Controller*). The CRTC generates control signals and supervises adapter operation. It is the CRTC that reads video RAM (or VRAM) contents and passes those contents along for further processing. Many new video boards use specially designed chip groups (called *video chipsets*) that are intended to work together. Chipsets provide

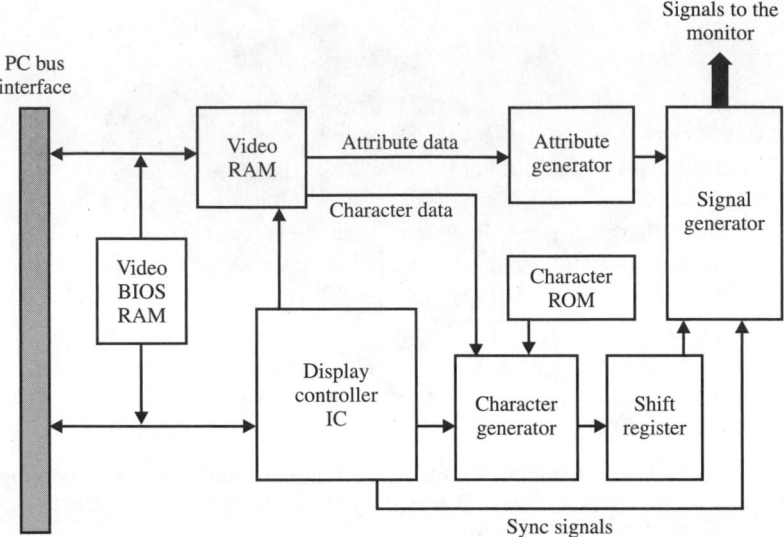

**FIGURE  35-2**    Block diagram of a simple frame buffer video adapter

fast, efficient video performance while minimizing the amount of overhead circuitry needed on a video adapter. Today, there is fierce competition between chipset designers and manufacturers to produce the fastest product with the latest features. For example, the Matrox Parhelia graphics processor uses 80 million transistors, almost twice as many transistors as the Intel Pentium 4 processor.

## TEXT VS. GRAPHICS

Video RAM also plays a vital role since it is RAM that holds the image data to be displayed. The video adapter can operate in two modes—text and graphic. In the *text* mode (for example, the DOS "command line" mode), ASCII characters are stored in video RAM. A *character ROM*, *character generator*, and *shift register* produce the pixel patterns that form ASCII screen characters. The character ROM holds a pixel pattern for every possible ASCII character (including letters, numbers, and punctuation marks). The character generator converts ROM data into a sequence of pixel bits and transfers them to a shift register. The shift register produces a bitstream. At the same time, an attribute decoder determines whether the defined ASCII character is to be displayed as blinking, inverted, high-intensity, standard text, or a text color (for older color monitors). The signal generator is responsible for turning the ASCII serial bitstream from the shift register into the video and synchronization signals that actually drive the monitor. The signal generator may produce either analog or TTL video signals depending on how the particular monitor is to be operated. Today, virtually all color graphic monitors operate from analog video signals.

In the *graphic* mode (for example, the Windows 9x/Me/XP desktop), video RAM locations will contain the color/grayscale information for each screen pixel rather than ASCII characters, so the character ROM and character-generating circuitry used in text mode is bypassed. For example, monochrome graphics uses a single bit per pixel, 16 color graphics uses 4 bits per pixel, 256 color graphics uses 8 bits per pixel, and so on. Pixel data taken from VRAM by the CRTC is passed through the character generator without any changes. Data is then sent directly to the shift register and on to the signal generator. It is the signal generator that produces analog or TTL video signals along with sync signals, as dictated by the

CRTC. Today, virtually all graphics activity is handled through a powerful, highly integrated *graphics processor unit* (GPU) such as the GeForce 4 or Matrox Parhelia.

## ROM BIOS (VIDEO BIOS)

There is one part of the classical video adapter that has not been mentioned yet—the *video BIOS*. The display controller requires substantial instruction changes when it is initialized or switched from text mode to any one of its available graphics modes. Since the instructions required to re-configure and direct the CRTC/GPU depend on its particular design (and the video board design in general), it is impossible to rely on the particular software application or the PC's BIOS to provide the required software. As a result, all video adapters from EGA on use local BIOS ROM to hold the "firmware" needed by the particular display controller. Current PC architecture allocates about 128KB of space from C0000h to DFFFFh within the upper memory area. This space is reserved for devices with expansion ROMs such as hard drive controllers and video adapters. Motherboard BIOS works in conjunction with the video BIOS that is detected during the POST.

Modern video adapters often allow you to flash update the video BIOS. The procedure is similar to flashing a motherboard BIOS, but care should be taken to follow the exact directions available from various manufacturers' BIOS update Web sites—flashing a video BIOS improperly may render the video adapter unusable.

# Reviewing Video Display Hardware

The early days of PC development left users with a simple choice between monochrome or color graphics (all video adapters support text modes). In the years that followed, however, the proliferation of video adapters has brought an astonishing array of video modes and standards that you should be familiar with before upgrading a PC or attempting to troubleshoot a video system. This part of the chapter explains each of the video standards that have been developed in the last 20 plus years and shows you the video modes that each standard offers. Tables 35-1 and 35-2 provide a comprehensive listing of the standard hardware- and software-supported video modes for a Matrox Millennium G550 and a PNY Verto (GeForce 4-based) video accelerator.

The display modes shown are *not* all necessarily supported by *all* monitors or software. Check the capabilities of your monitor and the requirements of your software before choosing a given display mode or refresh rate.

As a rule, refresh rates greater than 75 Hz are generally not noticeable to the naked eye.

The major difference in the video modes supported by the two video accelerators is the higher refresh rate offered by the newer GeForce 4 chipset (up to 240 Hz at 1024 × 768 resolution). The modern features and capabilities of the newer video accelerator are focused on improved multimedia, graphics, and gaming applications performance. Let's look at some of the older video standards that you may encounter.

## MDA (MONOCHROME DISPLAY ADAPTER–1981)

The Monochrome Display Adapter (MDA) is the oldest conventional video adapter available for the PC. Text is available in 80-column × 25-row format using 9 × 14-pixel characters. Being a text-only system,

**TABLE 35-1    DISPLAY MODES FOR A MATROX MILLENNIUM G550 GRAPHICS ACCELERATOR**

| RESOLUTION (32-BIT COLOR) | VERTICAL FREQUENCY (HZ) | HORIZONTAL FREQUENCY (KHZ) |
|---|---|---|
| 640×480 | 200 | 130 |
| 800×600 | 200 | 130 |
| 1024×768 | 160 | 130 |
| 1152×864 | 140 | 130 |
| 1280×1024 | 120 | 130 |
| 1600×1200 | 100 | 130 |
| 1920×1440 | 85 | 130 |
| 2048×1536 | 85 | 130 |

**TABLE 35-2    DISPLAY MODES FOR A PNY VERTO (GEFORCE 4-BASED) GRAPHICS ACCELERATOR**

| RESOLUTION | COLORS | VERTICAL FREQUENCY (HZ) |
|---|---|---|
| 640×480 | 8/16/32 bits | 60 to 240 |
| 800×600 | 8/16/32 bits | 60 to 240 |
| 1024×768 | 8/16 bits | 60 to 240 |
| 1024×768 | 32 bits | 60 to 200 |
| 1152×864 | 8/16 bits | 60 to 200 |
| 1152×864 | 32 bits | 60 to 170 |
| 1280×960 | 8/16 bits | 60 to 170 |
| 1280×960 | 32 bits | 60 to 150 |
| 1280×1024 | 8/16 bits | 60 to 170 |
| 1280×1024 | 32 bits | 60 to 150 |
| 1600×900 | 8/16 bits | 60 to 150 |
| 1600×900 | 32 bits | 60 to 120 |
| 1600×1200 | 8/16 bits | 60 to 120 |
| 1600×1200 | 32 bits | 60 to 100 |
| 1920×1080 | 8/16 bits | 60 to 100 |
| 1920×1080 | 32 bits | 60 to 85 |
| 1920×1200 | 8/16 bits | 60 to 100 |
| 1920×1200 | 32 bits | 60 to 85 |
| 1920×1440 | 8/16 bits | 60 to 85 |
| 1920×1440 | 32 bits | 60 to 75 |
| 2048×1536 | 8/16 bits | 60 to 75 |
| 2048×1536 | 32 bits | 60 |

MDA offers no graphics capability, but it achieved popularity because of its relatively low cost, good text display quality, and integrated printer (LPT) port. Figure 35-3 shows the video connector pinout for an MDA board. The 9-pin monitor connection uses four active TTL signals: intensity, video, horizontal, and vertical. *Video* and *intensity* signals provide the on/off and high/low intensity information for each pixel. The *horizontal* and *vertical* signals control the monitor's synchronization. MDA boards have long been obsolete, and the probability of your encountering one is remote at best.

## CGA (COLOR GRAPHICS ADAPTER–1981)

The Color Graphics Adapter (CGA) was the first to offer color text and graphics modes for the PC. A $160 \times 200$ low-resolution mode offered 16 colors, but such low resolution received very little attention. A $320 \times 200$ medium-resolution graphics mode allowed finer graphic detail, but with only four colors. The highest resolution mode provides $640 \times 200$ at 2 colors (usually black and one other color). The relationship between resolution and colors is important since a CGA *frame* requires 16KB of video RAM. A $640 \times 200$ resolution results in 128,000 pixels. With 8 bits able to represent 8 pixels, 16,000 bytes (128,000/8) are adequate. A $320 \times 200$ resolution results in 64,000 pixels, but with 2 bits needed to represent 1 pixel (4 pixels/byte), 16,000 bytes (64,000/4) are still enough. You can see that video RAM is directly related to video capacity. Since there is typically much more video RAM available than is needed for an image, video boards support multiple video *pages*. Figure 35-4 shows the pinout for a typical CGA video connector. As with the earlier MDA design, CGA video signals reserve pins 1 and 2 as ground lines, while the horizontal sync signal is produced on pin 8 and the vertical sync signal is produced on pin 9. CGA is strictly a digital display system with TTL signals used on the Red (3), Green (4), Blue (5), and Intensity (6) lines.

## EGA (ENHANCED GRAPHICS ADAPTER–1984)

It was not long before the limitations of CGA became painfully apparent. The demand for higher resolutions and color depths drove designers to introduce the next generation of video adapter, known as the Enhanced Graphics Adapter (EGA). One of the unique appeals of EGA was its backward compatibility—an EGA board would emulate CGA and MDA modes on the proper monitor, as well as its native resolutions and color depths when using an EGA monitor. EGA is known for its $320 \times 200 \times 16$, $640 \times 200 \times 16$, and $640 \times 350 \times 16$ video modes. More memory is needed for EGA, and 128KB is common for EGA boards (although many boards could be expanded to 256KB).

The EGA connector pinout is illustrated in Figure 35-5. TTL signals are used to provide Primary Red (3), Primary Green (4), and Primary Blue (5) color signals. By adding a set of secondary color signals (or color *intensity* signals), such as Red Intensity (2), Green Intensity (6), and Blue Intensity (7), the total of six color control signals allow the EGA to produce up to 64 possible colors. Although 64 colors are possible,

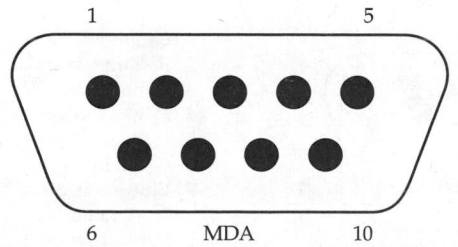

1. Ground
2. Ground
3. n/a
4. n/a
5. n/a
6. (+) Intensity
7. (+) Video
8. (+) Horizontal sync
9. (–) Vertical sync

**FIGURE  35-3**    Pin assignment of an MDA video connector

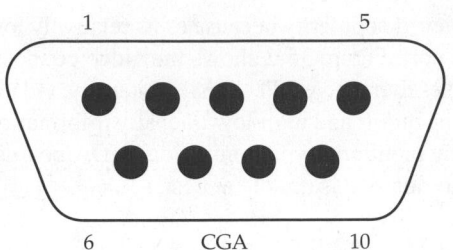

1. Ground
2. Ground
3. Red
4. Green
5. Blue
6. Intensity
7. n/a
8. Horizontal sync
9. Vertical sync

**FIGURE  35-4**    Pin assignment of a CGA video connector

only 16 of those colors are available in the palette at any one time. Pin 8 carries the horizontal sync signal, pin 9 carries the vertical sync signal, and pin 1 remains ground.

## PGA (PROFESSIONAL GRAPHICS ADAPTER–1984)

The Professional Graphics Adapter (PGA) was also introduced in 1984. This system offered a then-revolutionary display capability of $640 \times 480 \times 256$. Three-dimensional rotation and graphics clipping was included as a hardware function, and the adapter could update the display at 60 frames per second. The PGA was incredibly expensive and beyond the reach of all but the most serious business user. In actual operation, a PGA system required two or three expansion boards, so it also represented a serious commitment of limited system space. Ultimately, PGA failed to capture any significant market acceptance. It is unlikely that you will ever encounter a PGA board—most that ever saw service in PCs have long since been upgraded.

## MCGA (MULTI-COLOR GRAPHICS ARRAY–1987)

The Multi-Color Graphics Array (MCGA) had originally been integrated into the motherboard of IBM's PS/2-25 and PS/2-30. MCGA supported all of the CGA video modes and also offered several new video modes, including a $320 \times 200 \times 256$ mode that became a preferred mode for game software of the day. MCGA was one of the first graphic systems to use analog color signals rather than TTL signals. Analog signals were necessary to allow MCGA to produce its 256 colors using only three primary color lines (red, green, and blue, or "RGB").

IBM also took the opportunity to employ a new, high-density 15-pin subminiature "D-type" connector, as shown in Figure 35-6. One of the striking differences between the "analog" connector and older TTL connectors is the use of individual ground lines for each color. Careful grounding is vital, since any signal noise on the analog lines will result in color anomalies. If you inspect a video cable closely, you will find that one or both ends are terminated with a round molded plastic barrel that actually contains a noise

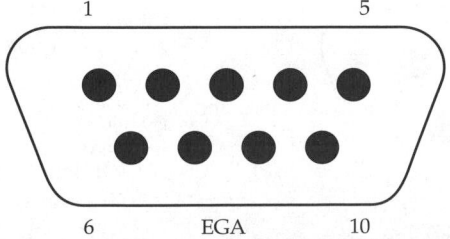

1. Ground
2. Red intensity
3. Primary red
4. Primary green
5. Primary blue
6. Green intensity
7. Blue intensity
8. Horizontal sync
9. Vertical sync

**FIGURE  35-5**    Pin assignment of an EGA video connector

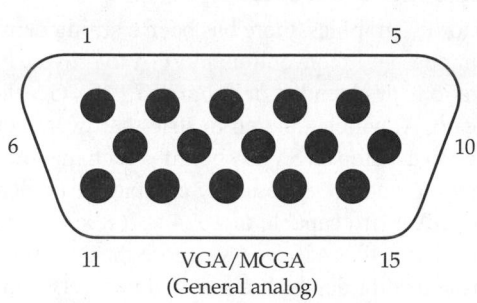

1. Red
2. Green
3. Blue
4. Ground
5. Ground
6. Red ground
7. Green ground
8. Blue ground
9. n/a
10. Ground
11. Ground
12. n/a
13. Horizontal sync
14. Vertical sync
15. n/a

**FIGURE 35-6** Pin assignment of a VGA/MCGA/SVGA video connector

filter. It is important to realize that although the MCGA could *emulate* CGA modes, older TTL monitors were no longer compatible with analog RGB signal levels.

Although there were a number of notable technical improvements that went into the PS/2 design, none of them could assure broad acceptance of the PS/2 series. However, the MCGA ushered in a new age of analog display technology, and virtually all subsequent video adapters now use the 15-pin analog format shown in Figure 35-6. While MCGA adapters are also (technically) obsolete, the standard lives on in MCGA's cousins, VGA and SVGA.

## VGA (VIDEO GRAPHICS ARRAY–1987)

The Video Graphics Array (VGA) was introduced along with MCGA and implemented in other members of IBM's PS/2 series. The line between MCGA and VGA has always been a bit fuzzy since both were introduced simultaneously (both using the same 15 pin video connector) and VGA can handle every mode that MCGA could. For all practical purposes, we can say that MCGA is a *subset* of VGA.

It is VGA that provides the familiar $640 \times 480 \times 16$ screen mode which has become the baseline for Microsoft Windows 9x/Me/XP "SafeMode" displays. The use of analog color signals allows VGA systems to produce a palette of 16 colors from 262,144 possible colors. VGA also provides backward compatibility for all older screen modes. Although the PS/2 line has been discontinued, the flexibility and backward compatibility of VGA proved so successful that VGA adapters were soon developed for the PC. For a time, VGA support was considered to be "standard equipment" for all new PCs, but SVGA boards have rapidly replaced VGA systems, and most SVGA adapters offer full VGA support.

## 8514 (1987)

The 8514/A video adapter is a high-resolution system also developed for the PS/2. In addition to full support for MDA, CGA, EGA, and VGA modes, the 8514/A can display 256 colors at $640 \times 480$ and $1024 \times 768$ (interlaced) resolutions. Unfortunately, the 8514/A was a standard ahead of its time. The lack of available software and the demise of the PS/2 line doomed the 8514/A to extinction before it could become an accepted standard. The XGA standard (see the upcoming section "XGA (1990)") rapidly became the PC standard for high-resolution/high-color display systems on MicroChannel PC platforms.

# SVGA (SUPER VIDEO GRAPHICS ARRAY)

Ever since VGA became the de facto standard for PC graphics, there has been a strong demand from PC users to move beyond the $640 \times 480 \times 16$ limit imposed by "conventional" VGA to provide higher resolutions and color depths. As a result, new generations of extended or *super VGA* (SVGA) adapters have moved relentlessly into the PC market. Unlike VGA, which adhered to strict hardware configurations, there is no generally accepted standard on which to develop an SVGA board—each manufacturer makes an SVGA board that supports a variety of different (and not necessarily compatible) video modes. For example, one manufacturer may produce an SVGA board capable of $1024 \times 768 \times 65K$, while another manufacturer may produce a board that reaches only $640 \times 480 \times 16M$ (more than 16 million colors).

This "mixing and matching" of resolutions and color depths has resulted in a very competitive (but very fractured) market—no two SVGA boards are necessarily capable of the same things. This proliferation of video hardware also makes it impossible for applications software to take advantage of *super* video modes without supplemental software called *video drivers*. Video drivers are device drivers (loaded as Windows starts) that allow the particular program to work with the SVGA board hardware. Video drivers are typically developed by the board manufacturer and shipped on a CD with the board. Windows 9x/Me/XP takes particular advantage of video drivers, since the Windows interface allows *all* Windows applications to use the same graphics system rather than requiring that a driver be written for every application (as DOS drivers must). Using an incorrect, obsolete, or corrupted video driver can be a serious source of performance and stability problems for SVGA installations. The one common attribute of SVGA boards is that *most* offer full support for conventional VGA (which requires no video drivers), so Windows can *always* be started "safely" in the conventional $640 \times 480 \times 16$ VGA mode (see Figure 35-7). There are only a handful of SVGA board manufacturers that have abandoned conventional VGA support.

Today, most SVGA boards offer terrific video performance, a wide selection of modes, and extremely reasonable prices. If it were not for the lack of standardization in SVGA adapters, VGA would likely be considered obsolete already. The *Video Electronics Standards Association* (VESA), established in 1989, started the push for SVGA standards by proposing and supporting the VESA BIOS Extension (VBE)—a *universal* video driver. The extension (now at version 3.0) provides a uniform set of functions that allow application programs to detect a card's capabilities and use the optimum adapter configuration regardless of how the particular board's hardware is designed. Virtually all of the SVGA boards in production today

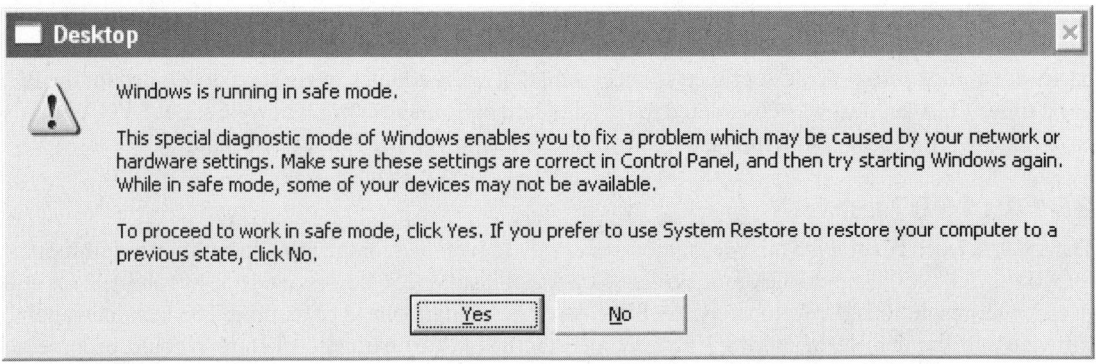

**FIGURE  35-7**   When trouble occurs on a Windows platform, the $640 \times 480 \times 16$ video mode ensures that a minimum video system is always available

support the VESA BIOS Extensions, and it is worthwhile to recommend boards that support VESA SVGA. Some SVGA boards even incorporate the extensions into the video BIOS ROM, saving the RAM space that would otherwise be needed by a video driver.

## XGA (1990)

The XGA and XGA/2 are 32-bit high-performance video adapters developed by IBM to support MicroChannel-based PCs. XGA design with MicroChannel architecture allows the adapter to take control of the system for rapid data transfers. MDA, CGA, EGA, and VGA modes are all supported for backward compatibility. In addition, several color depths are available at 1024 × 768 resolution, and a photo-realistic 65,536 colors are available at 640 × 480 resolution. To improve performance even further, fast video RAM and a graphics co-processor are added to the XGA design. XGA is generally limited to high-performance applications in obsolete MicroChannel systems. The migration to ISA-based PCs has been slow because the ISA bus is limited to 16 bits and does not support bus mastering, as MicroChannel busses do. For PCs, SVGA adapters using the high-performance PCI (and now the AGP) bus will likely provide extended screen modes as they continue to grow in sophistication as graphics accelerators.

# Understanding Graphics Accelerators

When screen resolutions approach 640×480 and beyond, the data needed to form a single screen image can be substantial. Consider a single 640×480×256 image. There are 307,200 (640 × 480) pixels. Since there are 256 colors, 8 bits are needed to define the color for each pixel. This means 307,200 bytes are needed for every frame. When the frame must be updated 10 times per second, 3,072,000 (307,200 × 10) bytes per second (3.072MB/sec) must be moved across the bus (PCI or AGP bus). If a 65,536 color mode is being used, 2 bytes are needed for each pixel, so 614,400 bytes (307,200 × 2) are needed for a frame. At 10 frames per second, 6,144,000 (614,400 × 10) bytes per second (6.144MB/sec) must be moved across the bus. This is just for video information and does not reflect the needs of system overhead operations, such as memory refresh, keyboard and mouse handling, drive access, and other data-intensive system operations. When such volumes of information must be moved across a bus with a fixed clock speed, you can see how a serious data transfer bottleneck develops. Even the 33 MHz PCI bus can be strained by higher video modes (though the high-bandwidth data channel provided by the 66 MHz AGP bus has gone a long way toward erasing this bottleneck). Such video data "bottlenecks" result in painfully slow screen refreshes—especially under Windows, which requires frequent refreshes.

Video designers seek to overcome the limitations of conventional video adapters by incorporating graphics processing power onto the video board itself rather than relying on the system CPU for graphic processing. By off-loading work from the system CPU and assigning the graphics processing to local processing components, graphics performance can be vastly enhanced. There are several means of acceleration, the use of which may depend on the sophistication of the board (see Figure 35-8). *Fixed-function* acceleration relieves load on the system CPU by providing adapter support for a limited number of specific functions, such as BitBlt or line draws. Fixed-function accelerators are an improvement over frame-buffers, but they do not offer the performance of more sophisticated accelerators. A *graphics accelerator* uses an application-specific chip (or ASIC) that intercepts graphics tasks and processes them without the intervention of the system CPU. Graphics accelerators are perhaps the most cost-effective type of

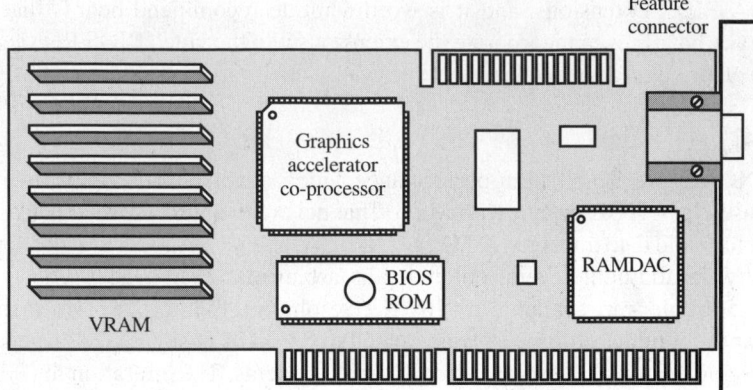

**FIGURE 35-8** A typical video accelerator card

accelerator. *Graphics co-processors* (also called *graphics processor units* or GPUs) are the most sophisticated type of accelerator, and are widely used on the latest graphics systems. The GPU acts as a CPU that is dedicated to handling image data.

Figure 35-9 shows the block diagram for a basic graphics accelerator. The core of the accelerator is the graphics chip (or video chipset). The graphics chip connects directly with the PC expansion bus. Graphics commands and data are translated into pixel data and stored in video RAM. High-performance video memory offers a second data bus that is routed directly to the video board's RAMDAC (random access memory video-to-analog converter). The graphics chip directs RAMDAC operation and ensures that VRAM data is available. The RAMDAC then translates video data into red, green, and blue analog signals

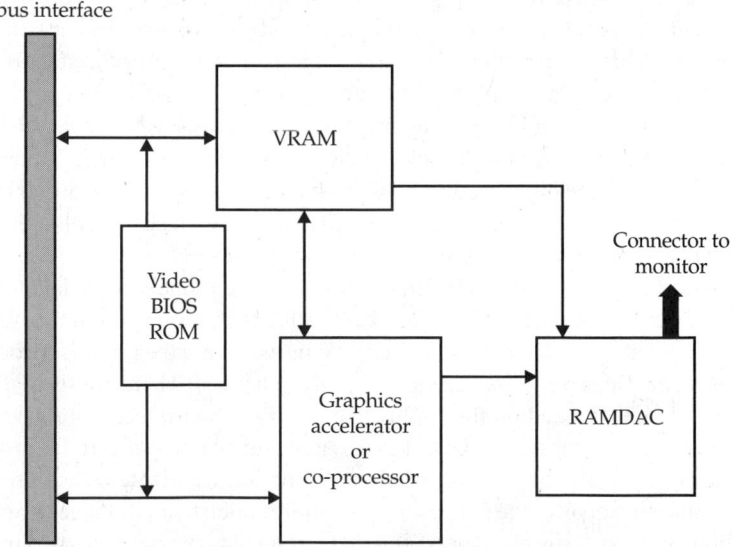

**FIGURE 35-9** Basic block diagram of a video accelerator board

along with horizontal and vertical synchronization signals. Output signals generated by the RAMDAC drive the monitor. This architecture may appear simple, but such an impression is due to the extremely high level of integration provided by the chipsets being used. Table 35-3 provides a listing of many 2D and 3D graphics chipsets in use today.

| TABLE 35-3 | INDEX OF POPULAR 2D AND 3D VIDEO CHIPSETS |
|---|---|
| **MANUFACTURER** | **PRODUCT** |
| 3dfx | VSA-100 Chip (www.voodoofiles.com) Purchased by NVIDIA |
| 3dfx | Voodoo Series (Voodoo Rush to Voodoo 5) |
| 3dfx | Velocity Series (100—200) |
| 3DLabs | Permedia (www.3dlabs.com/product/card/index.htm) |
| 3DLabs | GLINT 300SX |
| 3DLabs | Oxygen (VX1 - GVX1 - GMX - ACX) |
| 3DLabs | Wildcat 4110, 4210, Wildcat II 5110, III |
| Acer Labs | ALI-M3145 (www.aliusa.com) |
| Acer Labs | ALI CAT-32/64 |
| Alliance Semiconductor | ProMotion-3210 (www.alsc.com/) |
| Alliance Semiconductor | ProMotion-6410 |
| Alliance Semiconductor | ProMotion-6422 |
| Alliance Semiconductor | ProMotion-AT24 |
| ARK Logic | ARK1000PV |
| ARK Logic | ARK2000PV |
| Artist Graphics | 3GA Graphics Processor |
| Artist Graphics | Artist 3GA |
| Artist Graphics | Artist GPX |
| ATI | 264VT (www.ati.com/products/builtdesktop.html) |
| ATI | 3D RAGE |
| ATI | Mach32 |
| ATI | Mach64 |
| ATI | Mach64CT |
| ATI | Mach8 |
| ATI | 3D XPRESSION |
| ATI | XPERT (98, 99, 128, 2000, At Play, At Work, etc.) |
| ATI | 3D CHARGER |
| ATI | All-In-Wonder (Pro, 128, 128 Pro) |
| ATI | RAGE 128 (Magnum, Fury, FuryPro, Fury MAXX) |
| ATI | RADEON (All-In-Wonder, VE, DDR, SDRAM) |
| Avance Logic | ALG 2032 (www.avance.com) |
| Avance Logic | ALG 2064 |
| Avance Logic | ALG 2302 |
| Avance Logic | ALG 2308 |
| Avance Logic | ALG 2364 |

**TABLE 35-3    INDEX OF POPULAR 2D AND 3D VIDEO CHIPSETS *(CONTINUED)***

| MANUFACTURER | PRODUCT |
| --- | --- |
| Avance Logic | ALG 2401 |
| Avance Logic | ALG 25128 |
| Avance Logic | ALG 2564 |
| Avance Logic | ALG 27000 |
| Avance Logic | ALG 2101 |
| Avance Logic | ALG 2228 |
| Avance Logic | ALG 2301 |
| Chips and Technologies | 64300 (purchased by Intel) |
| Chips and Technologies | 82C455/6 |
| Chips and Technologies | 82C452 |
| Chromatic Research | Mpact |
| Cirrus Logic, Inc. | CL-GD5420 (www.cirrus.com) |
| Cirrus Logic, Inc. | CL-GD5421 |
| Cirrus Logic, Inc. | CL-GD5422 |
| Cirrus Logic, Inc. | CL-GD5424 |
| Cirrus Logic, Inc. | CL-GD5425 |
| Cirrus Logic, Inc. | CL-GD5426 |
| Cirrus Logic, Inc. | CL-GD5428 |
| Cirrus Logic, Inc. | CL-GD5429 |
| Cirrus Logic, Inc. | CL-GD5430 |
| Cirrus Logic, Inc. | CL-GD5434 |
| Cirrus Logic, Inc. | CL-GD5434-E |
| Cirrus Logic, Inc. | CL-GD5436 |
| Cirrus Logic, Inc. | CL-GD5440 |
| Cirrus Logic, Inc. | CL-GD5446 |
| Cirrus Logic, Inc. | CL-GD5462 |
| Cirrus Logic, Inc. | CL-GD54M40 |
| Cirrus Logic, Inc. | CL-GD5480 |
| IIT (AGX) | AGX-015 |
| IIT (AGX) | AGX-016 |
| Intel Corp. | Intel i740 (developer.intel.com/design/graphics/) |
| Intel Corp. | Intel i810 (AGP chipset) |
| Intel Corp. | Intel i815 (AGP chipset) |
| Lockheed Martin | Real3D |
| Matrox | MGA-1064SG (www.matrox.com) |
| Matrox | MGA-2064W |
| Matrox | Mystique 220 |
| Matrox | Millennium II |
| Matrox | m3D |
| Matrox | Productiva G100 |

**TABLE 35-3    INDEX OF POPULAR 2D AND 3D VIDEO CHIPSETS *(CONTINUED)***

| MANUFACTURER | PRODUCT |
|---|---|
| Matrox | Mystique G200 |
| Matrox | Marvel G200 |
| Matrox | Marvel G400 |
| Matrox | Marvel G450 eTV |
| Matrox | Millennium G200 |
| Matrox | Millennium G400 |
| Matrox | Millennium G450 |
| Matrox | Millennium G550 |
| Matrox | Parhelia |
| NCR | 77C22E+ |
| NCR | 77C32BLT |
| NVIDIA/SGS-THOMSON | NV1/STG-2000 (www.nvidia.com/) |
| NVIDIA | Riva 128 |
| NVIDIA | Riva 128ZX |
| NVIDIA | Vanta |
| NVIDIA | Riva TNT and TNT2 |
| NVIDIA | Quadro |
| NVIDIA | Quadro2, 4 (Pro, MXR) |
| NVIDIA | GeForce 256 |
| NVIDIA | GeForce2 |
| NVIDIA | GeForce3 |
| NVIDIA | GeForce 4 |
| Number Nine | Imagine 128 Series 2 (www.nine.com/products/index.html) |
| Number Nine | "Ticket To Ride" |
| Number Nine | "Ticket To Ride IV" |
| Oak Technologies Inc. | OTI-057/67 (www.oaktech.com) |
| Oak Technologies Inc. | OTI-077 |
| Oak Technologies Inc. | OTI-087 |
| Oak Technologies Inc. | OTI-64105/107 |
| Oak Technologies Inc. | OTI-64111 |
| Oak Technologies Inc. | OTI-64217 |
| Realtek Semiconductor Corp. | RTG3105I (www.realtek.com.tw) |
| Rendition | Vérité (www.rendition.com/); now part of Micron (www.micron.com) |
| S3, Inc. | Aurora64V+; S3 Graphics now part of VIA Technologies (www.via.com.tw) |
| S3, Inc. | S3-801 |
| S3, Inc. | S3-805/805p |
| S3, Inc. | S3-805I |
| S3, Inc. | S3-864 |
| S3, Inc. | S3-868 |

**TABLE 35-3    INDEX OF POPULAR 2D AND 3D VIDEO CHIPSETS *(CONTINUED)***

| MANUFACTURER | PRODUCT |
| --- | --- |
| S3, Inc. | S3-911 |
| S3, Inc. | S3-924 |
| S3, Inc. | S3-928 |
| S3, Inc. | S3-964 |
| S3, Inc. | S3-968 |
| S3, Inc. | S3-ViRGE |
| S3, Inc. | S3-ViRGE/VX |
| S3, Inc. | Scenic/MX2 |
| S3, Inc. | Trio32 (732) |
| S3, Inc. | Trio64 (764) |
| S3, Inc. | Trio64UV+ |
| S3, Inc. | Trio64V+ |
| S3, Inc. | Savage3D |
| S3, Inc. | Savage4 |
| S3, Inc. | Savage2000 |
| Sierra Semiconductor | Falcon/64 |
| Sierra Semiconductor | SC15064 |
| Silicon Integrated Systems | SiS6205 (www.sis.com.tw/products/multimedia.htm) |
| Silicon Integrated Systems | SiS6215 |
| Silicon Integrated Systems | SiS6225 |
| Silicon Integrated Systems | SiS6326 |
| Silicon Integrated Systems | SiS6326AGP |
| Silicon Integrated Systems | SiS6326DVD |
| Silicon Integrated Systems | SiS300/301 |
| Silicon Integrated Systems | SiS305 |
| S-MOS | SPC1500 |
| ST Microelectronics | Kyro II (us.st.com/stonline/index.shtml) |
| Trident Microsystems | TGUI9420/30 (www.tridentmicro.com) |
| Trident Microsystems | TGUI9440AGi |
| Trident Microsystems | TGUI9660/968x |
| Trident Microsystems | TVGA8900CL |
| Trident Microsystems | TVGA9000 |
| Trident Microsystems | TVGA9200Cxr |
| Trident Microsystems | TVGA9400CXi |
| Trident Microsystems | TVGA8900C |
| Trident Microsystems | 3Dimage 975 |
| Trident Microsystems | 3Dimage 985 |
| Trident Microsystems | Blade 3D, T64, XP |
| Trident Microsystems | CyberBlade XP |
| Tseng Labs, Inc. | ET4000/W32 |

| TABLE 35-3 | INDEX OF POPULAR 2D AND 3D VIDEO CHIPSETS *(CONTINUED)* |
|---|---|
| **MANUFACTURER** | **PRODUCT** |
| Tseng Labs, Inc. | ET4000/W32i |
| Tseng Labs, Inc. | ET4000/W32p |
| Tseng Labs, Inc. | ET4000AX |
| Tseng Labs, Inc. | ET6000 |
| Tseng Labs, Inc. | VIPeR |
| Tseng Labs, Inc. | VPR6000 |
| UMC | UMC 86C408 |
| UMC | UMC 86C418 |
| UMC | UMC 8710 |
| Weitek | P9000 |
| Weitek | P9100 |
| Western Digital (Paradise) | WD90C30 (www.wdc.com) |
| Western Digital (Paradise) | WD90C31 |
| Western Digital (Paradise) | WD90C33 |
| Western Digital | RocketCHIP |

# VIDEO SPEED FACTORS

There is no *one* element that defines the performance of a graphics accelerator board. Overall performance is actually a *combination* of five major factors: the graphics processor or video accelerator chip(s) (a.k.a. the "chipset" or the GPU), the video RAM, the video BIOS/drivers, the RAMDAC, and the expansion bus architecture. You can see these elements in the graphics accelerator of Figure 35-10. By understanding how each of these factors relates to performance, you can make the best recommendations for system upgrades or replacement boards.

## Video Accelerator/GPU

Of course, the video accelerator or graphics processor chip itself (usually part of the graphics chipset being used) is at the core of the accelerator board. The type of chip (fixed-function, graphics accelerator, or graphics co-processor) loosely defines the board's capabilities. All other factors being equal, a board with a graphics accelerator will certainly perform better than a fixed-function accelerator. Companies like 3dfx, ATI, Advance Logic, Chips & Technologies, Matrox, NVIDIA, S3, and Oak Technology have developed many of the video accelerator chips in use today. Many of the older chips provided a 32-bit data bus (newer designs provide a 128-bit or 256-bit data bus—the Matrox Parhelia GPU uses a 512-bit bus), and they sustain very high data rates. However, a data bottleneck across a 32-bit (PCI) expansion bus can seriously degrade the chip's effectiveness. Therefore, you should match the recommended board to the particular system—a state-of-the-art graphics accelerator will not necessarily make your old Pentium MMX system shine.

## Video RAM

Video adapters rely on RAM to hold image data, and video accelerator boards are no exception. While the current amount of video RAM typically varies from 32MB to 64MB (some late-mode video adapters offer as much as 128MB), the *amount* of RAM is not so important to a video accelerator as the RAM's *speed*.

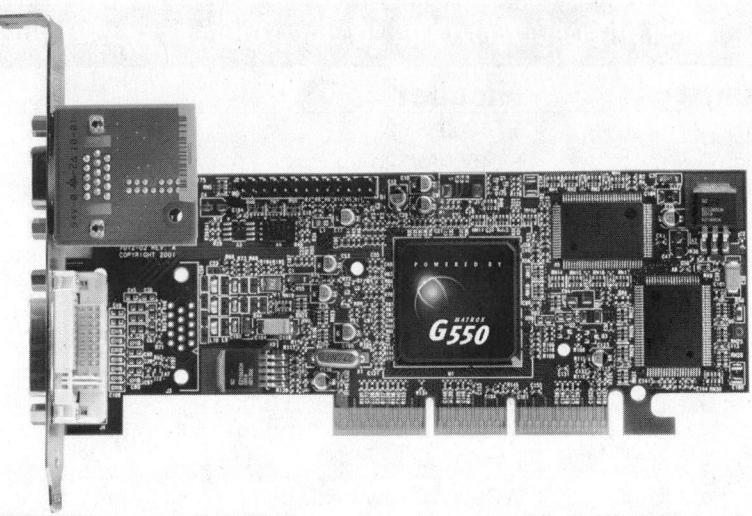

**FIGURE  35-10**    Locating the key sections of a modern graphics accelerator such as the Matrox G550 (Courtesy of Matrox Graphics, Inc.)

Faster memory is able to read and write image data faster, so adapter performance is improved. For a time, entry-level video cards used ordinary DRAM or EDO RAM, while high-end graphics accelerators employed specialized video RAM (VRAM)—memory devices with two separate data busses that can be read from and written to simultaneously. Today, virtually all commercial graphics accelerators use standard SDRAM or DDR SDRAM to achieve the best mix of low price and high performance.

Remember that AGP graphics cards can utilize some of the system RAM for storage-intensive tasks such as texture storage. The exact amount of system RAM assigned to AGP use can be configured through the CMOS Setup.

## Video BIOS and Drivers

Software is often considered an afterthought to video adapter design, yet it plays a surprisingly important role in accelerator performance. Even the finest accelerator board hardware can bog down when run under carelessly and loosely written code. There are two classes of software that you must be concerned with: video BIOS and video drivers. The *video BIOS* is *firmware* (software that is permanently recorded on a memory device such as a ROM). Video BIOS holds the programming that allows the accelerator to interact with DOS applications software. Current adapters have *flash upgradeable* BIOS ROMs that allow the video adapter's firmware to be updated without removing the video adapter from the PC. VESA BIOS extensions are now being used almost universally as part of the video BIOS for many accelerators as well as conventional frame-buffer adapters. Adding VESA BIOS extensions to video BIOS eliminates the need to load another device driver under DOS.

However, there are compelling advantages to video drivers. Windows 9x/Me/XP works quite well with drivers (and sometimes ignores video BIOS entirely). Unlike BIOS ROMs, which can be troublesome to upgrade, a video driver can change very quickly as bugs are corrected, enhancements are made, and performance is streamlined. The updated driver can be downloaded from a manufacturer's Web site on the Internet (or other online information service such as AOL) and installed on your system in a matter of minutes without the PC having to be disassembled. It is also possible for you to use third-party video drivers (though the practice is often discouraged by manufacturers). Hardware manufacturers are not always adept at writing efficient software, and a third-party driver developed by an organization that *specializes* in software may actually let your accelerator perform *better* than the original driver shipped from the manufacturer.

"Reference drivers" are often available from the video chipset maker's Web site. Video board manufacturers typically customize these drivers for their specific product. Customized reference drivers often include performance improvements, but they can be unstable because they have not been tested on or written for specific video cards.

## The RAMDAC

Just about every analog video system in service today is modeled after the 15-pin VGA scheme that uses three separate analog signals to represent the three primary colors. The color for each pixel must be broken down into component red, green, and blue levels, and those levels must be converted into analog equivalents. A digital-to-analog converter (or DAC) handles the conversion from digital values to analog levels. Each conversion also requires a certain amount of time. Faster DACs are needed to support faster horizontal refresh rates. Current video boards incorporate RAMDAC rated at up to 350 MHz, which can support very high resolutions at reasonably high refresh rates. Remember that each video adapter uses a *palette* that is a subset of the colors that can possibly be produced. Even though a monitor may be able to produce "unlimited" colors, a VGA board can produce only 256 of those colors in any 256-color mode. Older video boards stored the palette entries in registers, but the large-palette video modes now available (64K colors through 16 million colors) require the use of RAM. Boards that incorporate a RAMDAC (Random Access Memory Digital-to-Analog Converter) are preferred, since memory integrated with DACs tends to be much faster than accessing discrete RAM elsewhere on the board. Keep in mind that the RAM on a RAMDAC is used for holding palette information—not for the actual image.

## Expansion Bus Architectures

Finally, graphic data must be transferred between the PC motherboard and the adapter, as you saw early in this section. Such a transfer takes place across the PC's *expansion bus*. If data can be transferred between the PC and adapter at a *faster* rate, video performance should improve. For example, a wider data bus (for instance, 32 bits rather than 16 bits) and faster bus speeds (66 MHz rather than 33 MHz) will support faster data transfers—or higher *video bandwidth*. Consequently, the choice of bus *architecture* has a significant impact on video performance. Video accelerators are available to support two principle bus architectures: PCI, and AGP.

Today, the ISA bus is considered obsolete, and ISA slots are disappearing from just about every new motherboard in production. New ISA video adapters have not been manufactured in many years, so stick with AGP video adapters wherever possible.

**PCI**    Intel's Peripheral Component Interconnect (PCI) bus was one of the most versatile and powerful bus architectures to reach the PC. The PCI bus runs at a fixed frequency of 30 or 33 MHz, and offers a full 32-bit data bus that can take advantage of new CPUs such as Intel's Pentium family (and later processors such as the Pentium 4 and AMD Athlon/Duron families). The PCI bus overcomes the speed and functional limitations of ISA, and the PCI architecture is intended to support *all* types of PC peripherals (not just video boards). PCI video boards easily outperform ISA bus video adapters, though today's video systems use the faster AGP bus.

As a rule, opt for AGP video adapters, which easily out-perform PCI-based adapters. The only time to seriously consider a PCI video adapter is when working with an older system that lacks an AGP slot.

**AGP**    It didn't take long for bottlenecks to develop across the PCI bus, and designers sought a faster and more efficient bus architecture. They built on the PCI bus to create a 66 MHz, 32-bit bus called the *Accelerated Graphics Port* (or AGP). While PCI specifications limit data transfer rates to a bandwidth of 132 MB/sec, the AGP bus has a base bandwidth of 264 MB/s (4 bytes × 66 MHz). By transferring data on both the rising and falling edges of the AGP clock, the data rates can be doubled to 533 MB/s (known as AGP 2X). With additional signaling schemes, the AGP data transfer is again doubled to 1.06 GB/s (called AGP 4X). Most current graphics adapters and systems support AGP 4X, and even faster AGP modes are appearing with integrated (motherboard-based) graphics systems. The system BIOS, chipset, and operating system must all support AGP to take advantage of AGP's performance capabilities. Operating systems that fully support AGP at this time are Windows 98/Me/XP and Windows 2000. Windows 95 OSR 2.1 has limited AGP support, so any AGP performance benefit will be limited with it.

Most systems built in the last few years come with an AGP slot, but you may encounter a low-end system that has integrated graphics. In that case, there may not be an AGP slot—don't get thrown.

# 3D Graphics Accelerator Issues

Technically speaking, *3D graphics* is the visual representation of a scene or object along three axes of reference (height, width, and depth) to make the scene look more realistic. This technique "tricks" the PC user into seeing a 3D image on a flat (a 2D) screen. There has been an astonishing rise in the demand for 3D video from all parts of the PC industry. 3D rendering has proven to be the technique of choice for many types of high-end games, business presentations, computer-aided design, and multimedia applications. However, the use of 3D demands more of a PC than simply passing huge volumes of data across an expansion bus. 3D rendering requires complex mathematical calculations, determinations of coloring, the inclusion of special effects, and conversion of the rendered scene to a 2D plane (the display). In virtually all cases, these tasks must be accomplished in real-time (15 frames per second and faster). Today, most video systems are upgraded for the express purpose of supporting 3D animation (usually in 3D computer games such as *Quake III* or *Morrowind*). This part of the chapter examines some of the key factors involved on 3D rendering and acceleration.

## THE 3D PROCESS

To display a 3D object in real time, an object is first represented as a set of points (or *vertices*) in a 3D coordinate system consisting of x, y, and z coordinates. The *object* may be a car, a fighter plane, or a complete 3D world. The vertices of each object are stored in system RAM and completely define the object(s). In order to display the object(s) on a flat 2D monitor, the object(s) must then be rendered.

   *Rendering* is the act of calculating—on a "per pixel" basis—the different color and position information that tricks the viewer into perceiving depth on the 2D screen. For example, a tree that is closer looks larger than a tree that is farther away. The evening city scene from *Morrowind* in Figure 35-11 contains many thousands of vertices, and requires a powerful graphics accelerator to render in real time. Rendering also fills in the points on the surface of the object that were previously stored only as a set of vertices. In this way, a solid object can be drawn on the screen—even shaded with lighting, shadows, and fog for 3D effect. In order to render an object, it is necessary to determine the color and position information.

**FIGURE  35-11**    A typical scene from the PC game "Morrowind" that illustrates the complexity and intricacy that must be rendered in real time

To accomplish this efficiently, the vertices of the object are segmented into triangles, and these triangles (a set of three vertices) are then passed down the *3D-processing pipeline* one at a time. The general steps involved in 3D rendering are listed here:

- **Triangularize the 3D object**    This process divides the 3D object's vertices into triangles (sets of three vertices).

- **Transformation**    Translates, rotates, and zooms the object as necessary on the basis of the "camera angle." This is a mathematically intensive part of the rendering process, and is typically handled with a hardware-based *transform and lighting* (T&L) engine.

- **Clipping**    Eliminates any portions of the object that fall outside of the "window" of the viewer's line of sight. Clipping also demands a fair amount of mathematical processing, but is often handled through some T&L engines.

- **Lighting**    The T&L engine calculates shadow or light information depending on where light sources in the 3D world are positioned. Other effects such as "fog" can also be included in this processing step.

- **Map triangles to screen**    The triangularized, transformed, clipped, and illuminated object must then be "mapped" to the 2D screen. Triangles that are farther away from the viewer's viewpoint will be smaller then those triangles that are closer—this provides the perspective that aids depth perception.

- **Draw the triangles**    The triangles are then drawn to the screen using a variety of shading and texture mapping techniques. This time-intensive process completes the scene that you see, and the entire process must be repeated for every frame generated by the game or other application.

## 3D SPEED ISSUES

Higher frame rates create realism and true-to-life atmosphere in 3D games. Speed is the main factor in providing faster frame rates. If the frame rate of a game is too slow, the game becomes unplayable because the time needed to react to an action in the game will be far too long. Consider playing a flight simulator if the display was only updated once or twice per second. Since much of the graphics-processing overhead has been relieved from the system CPU, frame rate is now largely dependent on the speed of a graphics accelerator. The speed of a 3D graphics engine is typically rated in terms of "millions of *texels* (textured pixels) per second" or Mtexels/sec. It is also frequently rated in polygons (a.k.a. triangles) per second. Current 3D graphics accelerators can provide hundreds of millions of texels per second or more. For example, the relatively recent NVIDIA GeForce 4 Ti 4400 graphics chipset can render 4.6 billion texels (gigatexels) (or 125 million triangles) per second.

The speed of a 3D application is dependent on many tasks, but the most daunting tasks are 3D geometry and rendering. *Geometry* is the suite of calculations used to determine an object's position and color on the screen. *Rendering* (as you saw previously) is the actual drawing of the object on-screen. A typical graphics accelerator takes the load off of the CPU so that the CPU can devote more processing power to other functions. More advanced CPUs (such as the Pentium III with SSE technology, the Pentium 4 with SSE2 technology, or AMD's 3DNow! technology) incorporate additional instructions that aid much of the calculation-intensive work needed in 3D environments. Three features that most often affect 3D speed are bus mastering, resolution, and color depth.

## Bus Mastering

With a PCI bus master graphics accelerator, a 3D graphics engine will never incur latency (delays) during the rendering process, because once the CPU has prepared all of the triangles for rendering, the bus master will come and fetch the list of triangles asynchronously without requiring the CPU to wait. There are two different implementations of bus mastering: the basic bus master and the scatter-gather bus master. A *basic* bus master is capable of operating independently from the host CPU for short periods of time before it interrupts the host to ask for direction. During data-intensive operations like 3D, this arrangement minimizes the advantages of bus mastering. By contrast, a *scatter-gather* bus master is able to operate almost independently from the host CPU, achieving significant performance benefits. Bus mastering is eliminated if graphics are implemented through AGP, since AGP is essentially an extremely fast point-to-point connection between the graphics adapter and the PC's core logic, and the graphics adapter is always considered to be the "master" device.

## Resolution

Because of limitations in operating systems and graphics accelerators, most traditional games and multimedia applications have been developed for low resolutions (such as 640 × 480) to achieve high performance using older graphics systems. Increasing resolution means displaying more pixels on the screen with every frame—which places more demand on the monitor and graphics board. Some older applications developed in 320 × 200 can be played at 640 × 400 or higher, but you often find that the extra pixels are simply a replication of existing ones, which makes the image appear "blocky." With today's advanced standards in software and fast hardware accelerators, developers can include more unique pixel information in each frame, effectively increasing graphics detail at resolutions to 800 × 600, 1024 × 768, or even higher. This means gamers can play in high resolutions with excellent image quality, while still rendering each frame in real time. However, when you need to pick up some game performance quickly, dropping the resolution a notch or two can usually do the trick.

## Color Depth

Using extra colors in 3D games makes the scenes much richer and more life-like. The more colors used in a scene, the more detailed and realistic it looks, but the more calculations are needed to determine the color of each rendered pixel. Remember that a 256-color palette uses 1 byte per pixel, while higher color modes can use 2 bytes, 3 bytes, or even 4 bytes per pixel. Higher color depth multiplies the amount of data that needs to be passed for each pixel, so reducing color depth is an easy way to pick up some game performance (at the expense of a little realism). With the new generation of 3D graphics accelerators using the high-bandwidth AGP bus, higher color depths are supported without dramatic performance loss, and developers can now use more colors in each scene.

# IMPROVING 3D PERFORMANCE THROUGH HARDWARE

A 3D graphics accelerator improves 3D performance by relieving the host CPU of many of the computation-intensive tasks needed to render a scene. In most cases, these tasks are performed by a graphics processor chip(s) on the 3D video accelerator itself. Today's 3D graphics accelerators have an astonishing array of features—some of which are highlighted next.

## Perspective-Correct Texture Mapping

In real life, objects have details that allow us to recognize them. For example, an object made of wood is granular (you can see the dark wood grain), while steel is smooth and shimmering. In 3D applications, this kind of detail is called a *texture*. Applying two-dimensional texture images to 3D objects or scenes make them appear more realistic. For example, if you walk around a black box, you don't know what it is. However, if you apply textures to the sides and top of that box, you can create a wooden crate, a metal safe, a control panel, a pedestal—just about anything your imagination can conceive.

In the real world, our perspective relative to an object changes as our position changes. For example, when you are walking along the side of a house, the house will have a different perspective which each step. In order to create this experience in a 3D application, texture maps must be "corrected" to fit the changing perspective. If the texture mapping is not perspective-correct, the image will be visually incorrect and filled with artifacts from previous frames. While older 3D graphics accelerators did not provide perspective correct texture mapping in hardware, virtually all of the newest 3D graphics engines offer perspective-correct textures at full rendering speed.

## Texture Mapping Methods

Texture mapping is a data-intensive operation—a bitmap is wrapped onto a 3D object or polygon to add more visual details (thus enhancing realism). The original bitmap used as the texture to be mapped is also called the "source texture." There are several ways to map textures onto a 3D object with perspective correction:

- **Point sampling** This is the most common way to map a texture on a polygon. Point sampling allows the 3D graphics engine to approximate the color value of a given pixel on the resulting texture map by replicating the value of the closest existing pixel on the source texture. Point sampling provides very good results when used in conjunction with tile-based MIP mapping, and it maintains high performance levels at a low cost.

- **Filtering** Some source textures may need a considerable amount of warping, which may lead to a "blocky" appearance. Some graphics accelerator manufacturers use a technique called bilinear filtering to make the textures appear smoother. In bilinear filtering, four-source texel values are read, and their color values are then blended together based on proximity. The resulting values will be used for the texel to be drawn. While this technique is useful, the resulting quality is not comparable to using high-resolution source textures. 3D graphics accelerators without support for palletized textures have to scale down the textures to store them and apply filtering to map them onto polygons. Doing this results in poor quality rendering.

- **MIP mapping** MIP-mapping is another way to improve the quality of the 3D texture mapped object. The more alterations made to a texture to "fit" an object, the less it will resemble the source texture.

One way to avoid this severe deviation from the original texture is to create three copies, or MIP levels, of the same source texture (each in different sizes). MIP mapping can be implemented in four ways: tile-based MIP mapping, per-pixel MIP mapping, tri-linear MIP mapping, and the latest technique using *anisotropic* filtering to reduce distortion caused by 3D to 2D conversions.

■ **Fogging**   In order to maintain high performance, developers created an arsenal of tricks to reduce the amount of rendering needed for a scene. One of these tricks is called *fogging*. It is used mostly in landscape scenes, such as flight simulators. Fogging allows the developer to "hide" the background of a scene behind a layer of "fog"—mixing the textures' color values with a monochrome color such as white, or perhaps a gray, to help simulate inclement weather. Most newer 3D graphics chips support fogging in hardware.

 Modern high-performance 3D adapters have improved methods of 3D rendering and texture mapping. These features include single-pass multi-texturing, anisotropic texture filtering, per-pixel texturing, texture compression, and fog and depth cueing.

## Lighting

For greater realism in a scene, *lighting* is applied to objects to accentuate curves or create an ambiance (such as shadows). For example, if you're looking at a fireplace, the fire texture may also be treated as a light source—this will allow the "fire" to illuminate nearby objects and cast shadows (further enhancing the realistic illusion). Lighting effects are generally limited when implemented in software (otherwise the frame rate degrades). A key advantage of performing hardware-based 3D rendering is the ability to apply lighting effects to polygons while maintaining full rendering speed. Current adapters offer the ability to support up to eight hardware-based "light sources" (often more).

## Texture Transparency

The technique of *texture transparency* is similar to chroma-keying in video. This technique draws one image on top of another—with each appearing to fit there naturally. Mapping complicated objects (such as trees) in a 3D scene is a challenge for the software developer. They must be able to map the tree on a transparent polygon so that the background of the scene will be shown through the "branches." Objects like trees may not be essential, but they significantly improve the overall realism of a scene. Without texture transparency, these objects are typically left out or simplified. New 3D graphics chips support texture transparency in hardware, allowing developers to add a higher level of detail while maintaining graphics performance.

## Hardware z-Buffering

The use of a *z-buffer* (or *depth buffer*) is necessary when two objects are intersecting each other. The z-buffer determines which portions of the intersecting objects are visible and which are hidden. For example, there's no sense in rendering the front of a house if you're standing looking at the back, so the ability to discern and discard "unnecessary" elements that don't need to be rendered in a given scene can reduce memory requirements and speed the rendering process. However, many software developers do not use a z-buffer for all objects in the scene. This is because the z-buffer takes up space in the off-screen memory that could be used instead to store extra source textures for greater detail. For this reason, many 3D graphics chips provide an optional z-buffer allowing the developer to decide whether to use the off-screen memory for z-buffering or texture storage. If a game using a z-buffer (such as *Quake III*) is played on a graphics accelerator that does not allow for a hardware z-buffer, the game will not run—or will run at very low frame rates—since all z-buffering will need to be done in software. This is where AGP's use of system RAM for texture storage and z-buffering helps to improve rendering performance.

ST Microelectronics (designer of the Kyro graphics chipsets) and PowerVR have developed a method of rendering pixels for only the visible portion of objects in a frame. This technology has been dubbed Tile-Based Rendering (or TBR). Standard 3D graphics accelerators draw all of the polygons that comprise a scene first, then shade and texture these polygons. A test is then run on the z-buffer to determine which of the polygons are visible. The polygons that are not visible get discarded, but only after they have run through the 3D pipeline, consuming fill rate and memory bandwidth. Early tests suggest that the TBR method may improve rendering performance in some applications. ATI's Radeon line of products support a similar feature known as HyperZ, which enables various forms of compression on z-buffer data, and performs an early culling of polygons so that objects that aren't visible to the viewer aren't rendered. NVIDIA uses a process called *Z Occlusion Culling* to determine if a pixel will be hidden behind an earlier rendered pixel or not. If Z Occlusion Culling determines that a pixel is hidden, it will be discarded.

## Palletized Textures

Storing source textures of 3D games in off-screen memory is very taxing on the graphics frame buffer. Each time a new scene is created, all of its source textures need to be loaded in off-screen memory for use by the graphics chip. Memory available to store textures is limited because a 3D game accelerator generally has about 32–64MB of memory. This restricts the number of textures, effectively reducing the detail and other graphics qualities available in the scene. To compensate for this, developers can use a method of *palletized textures*, which assigns a Color Look-Up Table (or CLUT) to each texture in the scene. This technique allows the developer to use a smaller amount of color for each texture, instead of the normal 16-bit color values (65K colors). This smaller color format (CLUT) requires less memory space than the true 65K colors, which means more colors can be saved in memory to add detail to a scene. AGP specifications also address this issue by allowing main system memory to be used for storing textures.

Most older 3D graphics accelerators do not support palletized textures, which means the information can be stored only in full (e.g., 16-bit or 24-bit) color format in the frame buffer, utilizing all of the available off-screen memory. In such cases, the extra textures will have to be stored and retrieved from system memory, resulting in a serious hit on performance. Alternatively, textures can to be dropped from the scene by the graphics accelerator in order to maintain performance. Newer 3D graphics accelerators do provide full hardware support for palletized textures, and they allow developers to create very detailed scenes with two to four times as many textures. 3D applications are consequently given a significant performance boost, because the applications do not rely on the speed of the system to convert the information to 16-bit, 24-bit, or 32-bit colors.

## Alpha-Blending

Blending is a visual effect that mixes two textures on the same object. Different levels of blending can be implemented to create visual effects. The simplest method is called "screen door" or "stippling": only some pixels making up the object are rendered to produce a "see-through" effect. For example, the developer would decide that an object would be 50 percent transparent. The graphics accelerator would then draw the background image, and write only every second pixel of the object. This approach is easy to implement in hardware and delivers reasonable quality at a low cost. By contrast, true *alpha-blending* is a data-intensive operation, which involves reading the values of two source textures and performing the perspective calculations on both textures simultaneously. This effect is very taxing on performance and costly to implement, and only high-end 3D graphics cards use true alpha-blending in hardware.

## Gouraud Shading

Shading is used to provide visual queues for depth and volume. For example, when the right side of your face is lit (e.g., by candlelight), the left side of your face will have some level of shadows—often such shading will follow the curvatures of your face. *Gouraud shading* (or *smooth shading*) draws smooth shadows across the face of an object. This causes the viewer's eyes to perceive depth and curvature information from the surface of the object. Gouraud shading works by reading the color information at the three vertices of a triangle and interpolating the intensities in red, green, and blue smoothly between the three vertices. Gouraud shading is the most popular algorithm used to draw 3D objects on a 2D screen. Most objects can be rendered with amazing realism in 3D by using Gouraud shading, and this feature is often available in 3D graphics accelerator hardware.

## Double-Buffering

Everyone has seen the old animation trick of drawing a cartoon character on the corner of a page of paper, and altering the drawing slightly on following pages of paper. When the sheaf of paper is complete and the pages are flipped rapidly, the cartoon character appears to move smoothly. Double-buffered 3D animation on the PC works in the same way—the next position of the character is being drawn *before* the page is flipped. Viewing 3D animation without double buffering would be like looking at the animated cartoon if the character were being redrawn with every flip of the page (the animation would appear to "flicker").

Double-buffering requires having two areas reserved on the frame buffer of the 3D graphics card. Both regions need to be the size of the visible screen, and one buffer is used to render the next frame of the animation while the other displays the previously rendered animation frame on the monitor. Under Windows, double-buffering requires the use of bit-blitting to copy the animation from buffer to buffer.

## Color Dithering

The number of colors that can be drawn to the visible screen depends on the number of bits-per-pixel that carry color information. For instance, with eight bits per pixel of color information, only 256 colors can exist on the desktop at any one time. With 16 bits per pixel, 65,536 colors can be produced. Color dithering is the process of mixing these defined colors into small patterns to produce a wider spectrum of color without requiring extra video memory. This is especially important in 3D, since techniques such as Gouraud shading require many shades of each color used in each scene. If dithering were not handled in hardware, a 3D scene could contain only eight different main colors in 256-color mode (since each color would require 32 shades to be programmed into the color lookup table to roughly approximate Gouraud shading). With hardware support for color dithering, a scene with many more colors may be rendered without requiring extra video RAM.

## Anti-Aliasing

*Anti-aliasing* is a technique for disguising the jagged edges of a curved line or a line with very low or very high slope. These jagged edges are especially visible at lower resolutions with each pixel appearing as a "stair step" rather than a smooth line. Anti-aliasing is a way to use color information to make up for a lack of screen resolution. It simulates higher resolution by using color information to trick our eye into seeing a smoother line or edge than the screen can physically allow. By adding pixels of a slightly different color next to the line or curve at the transition points the "edge" is blurred. The eye sees this blur as a smooth edge rather than a different color. Full Scene Anti-Aliasing (FSAA) is the current high-performance implementation of this feature. FSAA requires a lot of resources and may slow 3D rendering to an unacceptable level in some PC configurations. The video adapter's adjustment/configuration utility will usually allow you to toggle this feature on and off.

### Bump Mapping

*Bump mapping* is a relatively new technique used to add detail to an image or object without increasing the number of polygons needed to construct that image or object. This technique uses light effect calculations to create small bumps on the surface of an object—the bumps add visual textures without complicating the surface of the object. Bump mapping uses light calculations to add shadow and light to the sides of the "bump." Different methods of implementing bump mapping include: pre-calculated bump mapping, perturbed environment bump mapping, perturbed blend bump mapping, and perturbed normal bump mapping.

# Understanding DirectX and OpenGL

The process of rendering and displaying a 3D scene in real time requires comprehensive support from both hardware and software—performance and realism are greatly enhanced when both the hardware (the graphics accelerator) and software (the 3D game or other application) support the same 3D language. Windows 9x/Me/XP supports this graphics "language" through an *application programming interface* (or API). API-based hardware acceleration adds detail and special effects to images (e.g., fog, anti-aliasing, volume shadows, bump mapping, motion blur, transparency, reflections, 3D textures, volume rendering, and more) without compromising performance. The two most popular APIs are DirectX from Microsoft and OpenGL from Silicon Graphics.

When Windows first emerged as a major operating system, its focus was primarily on file management and utilities. High-performance graphics and other forms of multimedia were barely even dreamed of. It was therefore very difficult for Windows to support graphics-intensive applications that came later, such as games, DVD, PC-TV, or MPEG video (and is largely the reason why DOS lingered for so long on many PC platforms). Developers realized that in order for Windows to finally become *independent* of DOS, a standard means of supporting high-performance multimedia functions would be absolutely essential—and *DirectX* technology was born. With Windows 95, DirectX has emerged as a key element in graphics, sound, and interaction for multimedia platforms. DirectX has remained at the forefront of graphics and multimedia support under Windows 98/Me/XP. This part of the chapter offers a basic overview of DirectX and its components.

## PIECES OF A PUZZLE

Contrary to popular belief, DirectX is not *one single* piece of software. Instead, DirectX is actually a comprehensive collection of Windows 9x/Me/XP APIs (application programming interfaces) that provide a standardized set of features for graphics, sound, input devices, multi-player interaction, and application setup. DirectX software is categorized in three layers: a foundation layer, a media layer, and a components layer.

### Foundation

The *foundation* layer forms the heart and soul of DirectX. It is a set of low-level APIs that are the basis for all high-performance multimedia under Windows 9x/Me/XP. DirectX foundation APIs provide direct access to hardware acceleration such as 3D graphics acceleration chips (in effect, allowing Windows to "talk" directly to hardware). The foundation layer uses the following APIs:

- **DirectDraw**   This API is used to handle basic drawing functions for graphic objects.
- **Direct3D**   The *immediate mode* of this API supplies low-level 3D features for graphic objects.
- **DirectInput**   This API supports a rich selection of input devices (including a complete suite of *force feedback* joysticks and wheels).

■ **DirectSound**   This API provides sound and mixer effects.

■ **DirectSound3D**   This API offers 3D sound effects (positional sound) from ordinary 2D speaker arrangements.

■ **DirectSetup**   This API installs software and drivers automatically.

## Media

The DirectX *media* layer consists of application-level APIs that take advantage of the system-level services provided by the DirectX foundation. The media-level services are device independent and include features such as animation, behaviors, and video streaming. The DirectX media layer includes six APIs:

■ **Direct3D**   The *retained mode* of this API offers a collection of 3D scene features.

■ **DirectPlay**   This API supports multiplayer/network play.

■ **DirectShow**   This API handles slide-show-type operation and features.

■ **DirectAnimation**   This API supplies animation support.

■ **DirectModel**   This API provides 3D modeling support.

■ **DirectMusic**   This API provides composition and playback of message-based musical data (e.g., MIDI music).

## Components

The *components* layer makes up the top level of the DirectX hierarchy. These are a group of application-specific modules that can draw on all features available in the media and foundation layers. DirectX components include:

■ **NetMeeting**   This API offers an online whiteboard for real-time group collaboration.

■ **ActiveMovie**   This API supplies a set of tools for rendering full-screen MPEG video and supporting playback of a wide range of audio and video formats.

■ **Netshow**   This API enables live broadcast of multimedia content over the Internet along with 3D worlds generated with VRML.

# DIRECTX 8.0 AND 8.1 FEATURES

DirectX 8.0 and 8.1 (the current version) includes new and updated features. The major components remain much the same, but some features of previous versions have been consolidated. The five major components of DirectX 8.0 and 8.1 are DirectAudio, DirectGraphics, DirectInput, DirectPlay, and DirectShow.

As of June 2002, the beta version of DirectX 9 has been released for early testing.

## DirectAudio

DirectAudio provides the current architecture for integrated music and sound effects playback. Its features minimize CPU usage and 3D hardware requirements. While DirectAudio includes DirectSound and DirectMusic, the distinction between them is small. DirectMusic has become the accepted API for creation of interactive sound effects. The DirectMusic synthesizer is the main sound generator for DirectAudio. This synthesizer creates all the sounds, sub-mixes them and sends the result to DirectSound buffers for processing.

## DirectGraphics

The DirectGraphics module in DirectX 8.0 and 8.1 moves some DirectDraw features to Direct3D. These include creation of resources such as textures and vertex buffers, display mode selection, and the presentation of rendered images on the display. DirectGraphics also supports multisample rendering—this allows for full-scene anti-aliasing (FSAA) and multisample effects such as motion blur. Programmable vertex processing and programmable pixel processing allow for both general environment mapping and per-pixel environment mapping.

## DirectInput

The DirectInput component of DirectX 8.0 and 8.1 provides a default user interface for configuring devices such as mice, joysticks, driving wheels, and rudders/pedals. This feature also enables applications to access control device images for use in their own configuration interfaces.

## DirectPlay

The DirectPlay module in DirectX 8.0 and 8.1 updates this layer for improved performance and simplicity for multiplayer operation. It is scalable to support thousands of users in a multiplayer environment. DirectPlay Voice allows for a voice-prompted user interface with a selection of low- and high-bandwidth technologies.

## DirectShow

The DirectShow component of DirectX 8.0 and 8.1 provides a single setup program for graphics, audio, and streaming programs. DirectShow applications will benefit from easier dependency testing. It allows real-time editing of displayed images (such as graphs). DirectShow also includes improved DVD support. It can play Karaoke as well as video discs.

# DETERMINING THE DIRECTX VERSION

Since DirectX is a collection of APIs, each application that uses DirectX is written to use a particular version of DirectX—the application *needs* the correct version of DirectX (or later) components installed under Windows 9x/Me/XP. Otherwise, the application will not work. In most cases, DirectX is backward compatible, so an application written for DirectX 6.x should work on a system with DirectX 8.1 installed. But an application written for DirectX 8.1 won't work on a system with DirectX 6.x. As a technician, you'll need to spot DirectX version issues when a customer has trouble with his or her new games. You can use the following procedure to check the current version of DirectX installed on a given system:

1. Using Windows Explorer or My Computer, locate the **DDRAW.DLL** file in the \Windows\System or \Windows\System32 folders.

2. Use the right mouse button to click the DDRAW.DLL file, then click Properties on the menu that appears.

3. Click the Version tab.

4. Compare the version number on the File Version line with the following list (see Figure 35-12):
   - **4.02.0095**   DirectX 1
   - **4.03.00.1096**   DirectX 2
   - **4.04.00.0068**   DirectX 3 or 3a
   - **4.05.00.0155**   DirectX 5

- **4.05.01.1721**  DirectX 5.1
- **4.05.01.1998**  DirectX 5.2 (Windows 98 and later)
- **4.06.02.0436**  DirectX 6.1
- **4.06.03.0518**  DirectX 6.1a
- **4.07.00.0700**  DirectX 7
- **4.07.00.0716**  DirectX 7a
- **4.07.01.3000**  DirectX 7.1
- **4.08.00.0400**  DirectX 8.0 (Digital Signature Date 11/4/2000)
- **4.08.00.0400**  DirectX 8.0a (Digital Signature Date 1/16/2001)
- **4.08.01.0881**  DirectX 8.1 (Windows 9x/Me upgrade)
- **5.1.2600.0**  DirectX 8.1 (Windows XP native)

DirectX versions 3 and 3a use the same version of the **DDRAW.DLL** file. To determine whether you are using version 3 or 3a of DirectX, use the procedure described previously to check the version of the **D3DRGBXF.DLL** file:

- **4.04.00.0068**  DirectX 3
- **4.04.00.0070**  DirectX 3a

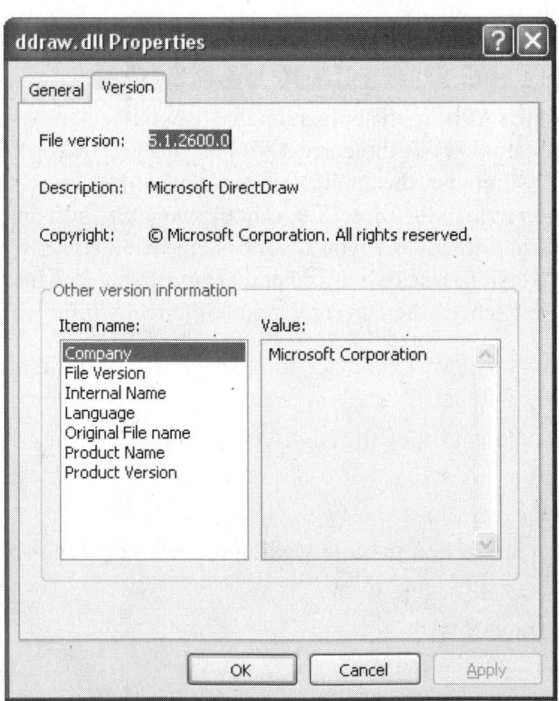

**FIGURE 35-12**    Checking the version of DirectX manually by comparing the version number of your ddraw.dll file

If the DDRAW.DLL file does *not* exist in the \Windows\System or \Windows\System32 folders, DirectX is probably not installed on your computer.

Alternatively, DirectX 6.1 and above include a useful utility named "DirectX Diagnostic Tool." You can launch the DirectX Diagnostic by clicking Start, selecting Run, and typing **dxdiag** in the text box. This tool (Figure 35-13) reports detailed information about the DirectX components and drivers installed on your system. It lets you test functionality, diagnose problems, and change your system configuration if necessary.

DirectX 7.0 and DirectX 8.0 each had some problems implementing USB controller devices. Version 7.0a and 8.0a were quickly made available to address these problems. DirectX 8.1 and later should not suffer such problems.

## OPENGL NOTES

Introduced in 1992, OpenGL is another popular cross-platform standard for 3D hardware acceleration. The OpenGL Architecture Review Board (an independent group) oversees the OpenGL specification. Currently the board includes representatives from ATI, Compaq, Intel, NVIDIA, Microsoft, and others. OpenGL Version 1.3, the latest release, is available for Windows, MacOS, Linux, and UNIX systems. OpenGL is used for 3D hardware acceleration in many popular games like *Quake III*, *Baldurs Gate*, *Descent 3*, and *MDK2*. OpenGL offers the same 3D rendering features described in the section on DirectX—these features include transform and lighting (T&L), clipping, and rendering. The 3D effects supported by OpenGL include real-time fog, anti-aliasing, bump mapping, 3D textures, and more.

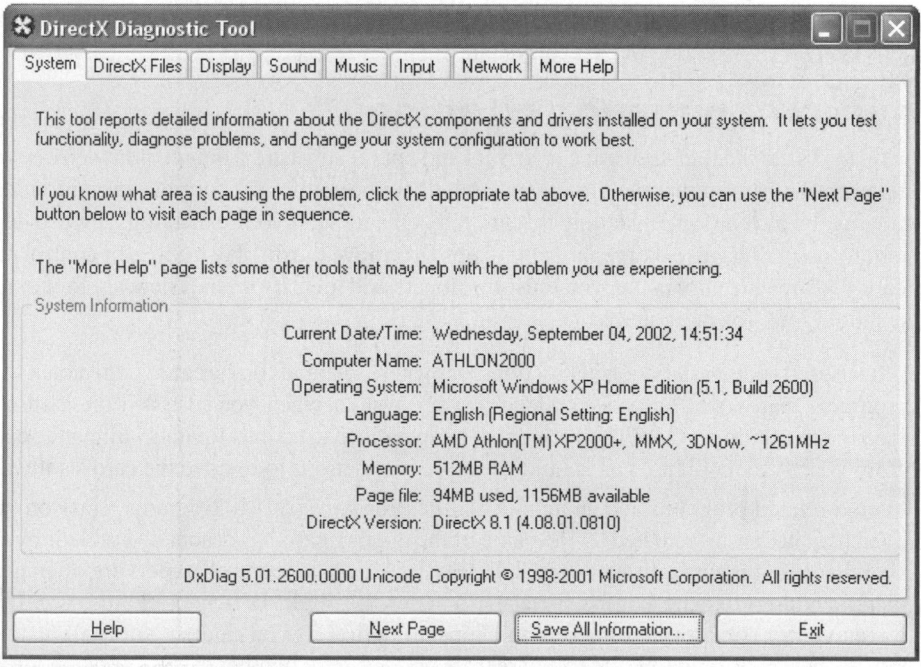

**FIGURE 35-13**    The DXDIAG dialog box under Windows XP

OpenGL is also used for 3D graphics and effects in television and motion pictures. It is integral to the development of many virtual reality (or VR) environments. OpenGL popularity is also due in some part to its support for the Linux operating system. Many games have been made available in versions for play on Linux systems using OpenGL 3D hardware acceleration. OpenGL is also compatible with all Microsoft operating systems, including Windows 9x/Me/XP, NT, and 2000.

Both the operating system and video hardware must support OpenGL. Most major video chipset makers (NVIDIA, ATI, Matrox, and others) offer support for OpenGL. The required drivers for specific video adapters are included on the adapter's installation CD, are available from the video adapters manufacturer's Web site, or are integrated into the operating system (e.g., Windows XP). The OpenGL files needed for specific applications and games should be included on the program's CD along with an installation utility. You can also obtain and install OpenGL directly from the Web. The OpenGL installation utility, GLSetup, will automatically examine your hardware and install only the files required for that hardware. The complete OpenGL installation program, with support for most video chipsets, is over 85MB and would take hours to download using a 56K connection.

Microsoft did not include OpenGL run-time libraries in the original release of Windows 95. The libraries were included beginning with Windows 95 OSR2 and should be present in later versions of Windows.

# Replacing/Updating a Video Adapter

Whether you're building a new PC from scratch, upgrading your system, or replacing a failed video adapter, you'll need to install a new video card with confidence. In virtually all cases, you'll need to remove references to any original video card first, replace the old card with the new one, then install the new drivers and video applet software under Windows 9x/Me/XP. This part of the chapter highlights the general steps needed to upgrade your video system.

## REMOVING OLD DEVICE DRIVERS

New video adapters can be quite sensitive to drivers and applet software from an old video device, so it's usually important for you to remove the drivers and all support software for your current video device before removing the old card and installing the new one. Of course, if you're installing a video device into a *new* system, you won't have to worry about this step. To remove the display utilities or control panels for a display card you are currently using, you must first locate and identify them. There are four main places where you should look for these items:

- Check the user's guide, installation instructions, or owner's manual for the card you're about to remove. Any programs that would have been added to your system when you installed the card should be described in the documentation. There may also be specific instructions for uninstalling the card's software from your system—if so, you should use *those* instructions to remove the card's software suite.

- Many video-related programs add an item under the Programs (or All Programs) entry on your Start menu. Such an item may be listed by the name of the display card it is associated with or by the name of the company that manufactured the card. Display utilities and control applets are often given their own specific names, like the Winfox software for a new Leadtek NVIDIA GeForce card. If you find such a menu entry, look to see if there's an Uninstall option. If you find an Uninstall feature, that's probably the best way to remove the software from your system. In other cases, check the System Tray in the task bar for video-related applets.

■ The Windows Control Panel probably contains the actual program icons for any display utilities or control applets that may have been installed with the existing video card. This may help you to identify the program you wish to remove (though it probably will *not* give you a direct method for removing it). However, the Add/Remove Programs wizard in the Control Panel (see Figure 35-14) can probably remove the software for you—once you know what software to remove.

■ The Windows Startup folder may contain a shortcut to a display utility or control applet for the existing video card. If so, you can simply delete the shortcut from the Startup folder to disable the program (but that will not remove the software from your system). You may also wish to use the Add/Remove Programs icon in the Control Panel to actually remove that software from your system.

The old video card maker may have a utility to help. For example, Matrox has created a utility that will remove previous drivers. You can find the utility at ftp://ftp.matrox.com/pub/mga/utils/pd_unin201.exe.

Once the applet software is removed from the system, it's time to select a default video mode and remove the video adapter from your Windows Device Manager:

**1.** Right-click the desktop, then select Properties.

**2.** Select the Settings tab (see Figure 35-15).

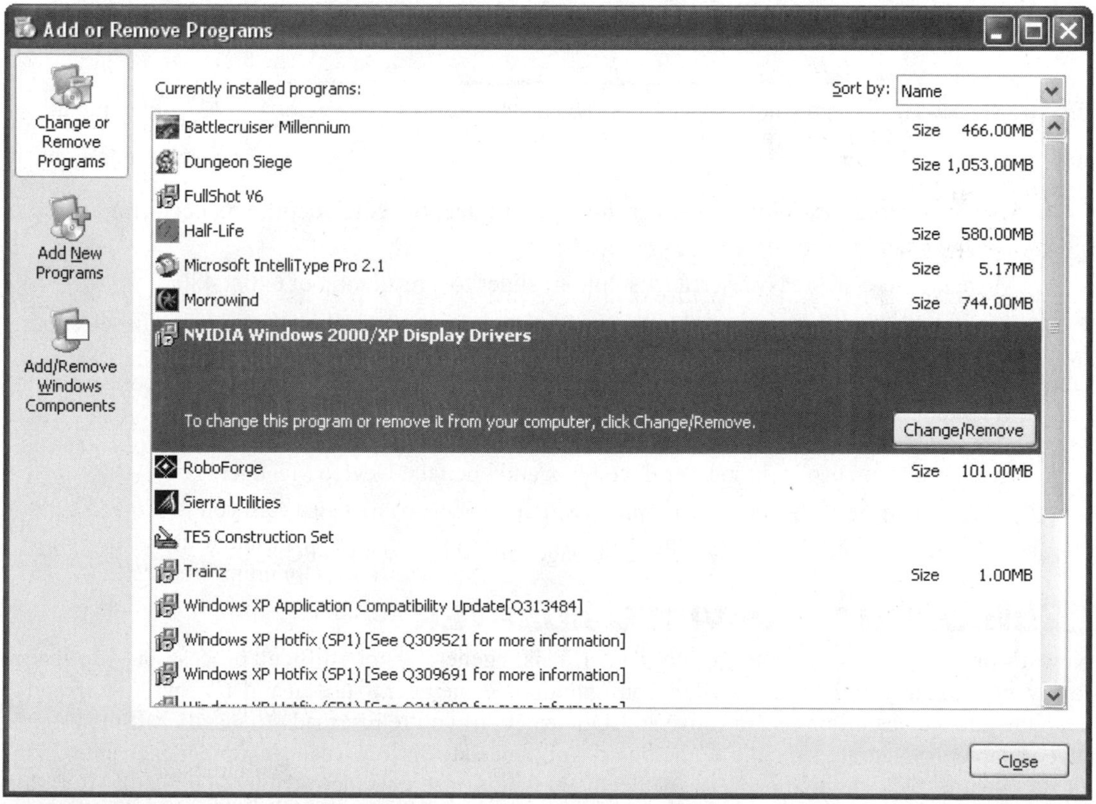

**FIGURE  35-14**  Using the Add/Remove Programs wizard to quickly identify any video-related tools that should be uninstalled

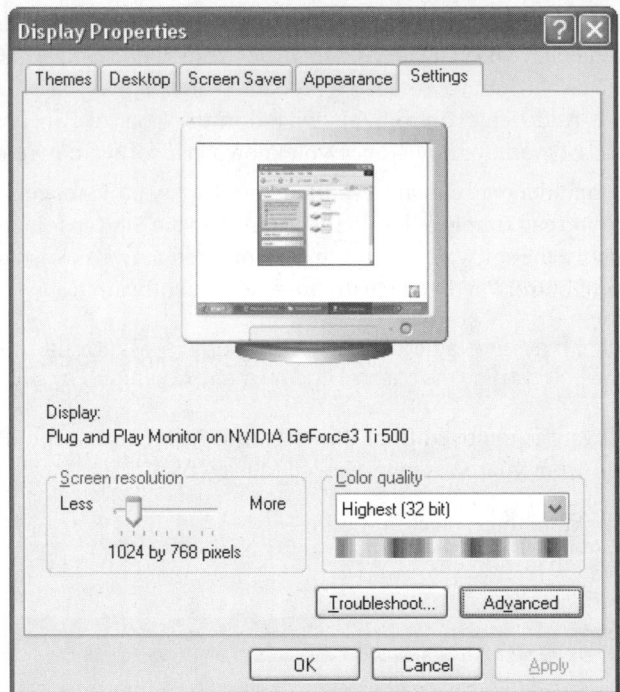

**FIGURE 35-15**    Using the Display Properties dialog box to set the standard VGA video mode before removing the video adapter

3. Use the Colors (or Color quality) drop-down to select the color-depth you need (for example, "16 colors").

4. Move the Screen Area (or Screen resolution) slider to a resolution of 640 × 480.

5. Click on the Apply button to test the selections you have made, then click OK to finalize the selections.

 Once the new video card is installed, you can easily return to the Display settings and configure the desired resolution and color depth again.

6. Now close the Display Properties dialog box and open the Device Manager.

7. Expand the Display adapter entry and highlight your display adapter.

8. Click Remove, then close the Device Manager and shut down the PC.

## EXCHANGING THE VIDEO ADAPTER

Now it's time to switch to your new video adapter. This is generally not a difficult process, but you'll need to pay attention to your particular system configuration. Remember to use an antistatic wrist strap and to keep the new video card in its protective antistatic bag until you're just ready to install it. If the original video adapter is integrated into the motherboard, you'll need to disable it using a jumper or an entry in the CMOS Setup. A few motherboards can detect the presence of a new video adapter (e.g., in the AGP slot) and disable the integrated video controller automatically, but you shouldn't count on that. Always refer to the manufacturer's documentation before disabling an onboard video system.

1. Turn off and unplug the PC, then remove the outer housing.

2. Locate the original video adapter (where the monitor cable attaches to the PC) and disconnect the monitor cable.

3. If the original video adapter is integrated into the motherboard, check the motherboard's user manual to see if there's a jumper needed to disable that adapter. If so, set the required jumper so that the onboard video adapter is disabled. (If you must disable the onboard video adapter through the CMOS Setup, doing that will be described later.)

4. If the original video adapter is simply an expansion card, unbolt the bracket from the chassis and remove the original card. Set it aside—preferably in an antistatic bag.

5. If you're replacing a PCI-based video card with an AGP-based video card, check the motherboard's user manual to see if there's a jumper to enable AGP support—older AGP motherboards often required this. If so, set the required jumper so that AGP is enabled. Some motherboards require you to set a CMOS Setup option to specify the default video system on a PCI or AGP bus (though AGP is typically selected by default today).

6. Remove the new video card from its bag and insert it into its appropriate bus slot. Be sure that the card is seated evenly and completely and then bolt the card's bracket to the chassis.

AGP connectors are very sensitive to alignment problems. Be sure the card is completely seated and that the bracket does not move the card when the hold-down screw is tightened.

7. If there's another video/3D accelerator card in the system (e.g., for a multi-monitor system), you may need to attach that accelerator's feature connector to the new video card.

8. Reattach power and restart the system.

9. When the system boots for the first time, be sure to boot directly to the CMOS Setup. If you must disable the old on-board video adapter through the CMOS Setup, you must do that *now*. If you're installing an AGP video adapter in place of a PCI model, check to see if there are any AGP-related settings needed to enable AGP support on the system. Save your changes and exit the CMOS Setup, and allow the system to boot.

# INSTALLING NEW SOFTWARE

Once the CMOS Setup has been updated and your changes (if any) have been saved, the system will reboot once again. At this point, we'll see if the new video card is identified properly and install the appropriate drivers and support software to utilize its features.

1. Allow the system to boot normally. Since virtually all video cards are fully PnP-compliant, Windows 9x/Me/XP should identify the new video device and query you for the appropriate drivers (typically provided on CD).

2. Place the CD into the CD-ROM drive. In most cases, the CD's autorun feature will launch a menu-driven installer that will allow you to load the card's drivers and support software (for example, 3Dfx Tools, 3Dfx TV, 3Dfx Tweaks, NVIDIA Quick Tweak, nView, Desktop Manager, and so on).

3. Install the drivers and support software and reboot the system if necessary.

# CHECKING THE INSTALLATION

Once the software is installed and the system reboots, you can check for the presence of your new video adapter card, then reset the video mode to your liking.

1. Open the Device Manager.

2. Expand the Display adapter entry.

3. Check the new display adapter reference. You should see a reference to the new adapter that you just installed. There should be *no* yellow exclamation marks or red *X*s marking the adapter.

4. Close the Device Manager.

5. Right-click the Desktop and select Properties.

6. Click the Settings tab, then click Advanced.

7. Check for tabs that mention your new display adapter (for example, 3Dfx Info, 3Dfx TV, 3D Tweaks, NVIDIA TNT 2, GeForce3 Ti200, and so on). For example, Figure 35-16 lists the support tab for a GeForce3 Ti500 video adapter.

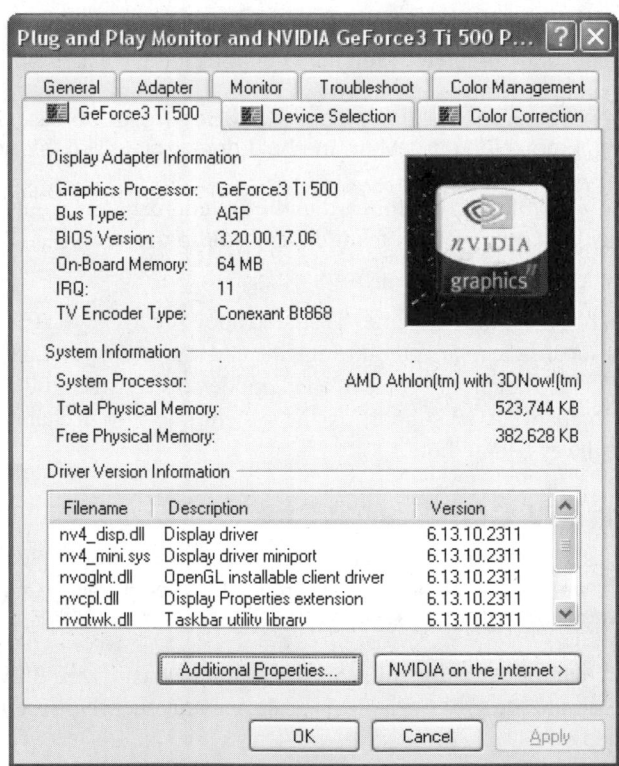

**FIGURE 35-16** Checking that any support for the new video adapter has been installed in the Advanced Display Properties dialog box

If you see the entry for your new video adapter in the Device Manager (and also in the Advanced Display Properties dialog box) and no errors are indicated, chances are that your new video adapter is working properly. You may now return to the Settings tab in your Display dialog box (as in Figure 35-15 earlier), and set the desired resolution and color depth for your upgraded display system.

# AGP Overclocking

The AGP bus was designed as a 66 MHz bus architecture, and this 66 MHz signal is almost always derived from the motherboard's Front Side Bus (FSB) clock. When motherboards offered only a 66 MHz clock, this arrangement was not a problem for AGP, since the FSB clock and the AGP clock were basically the same thing. However, when motherboards went to 100 MHz and 133 MHz (and faster), the AGP bus needed to be *derived* from the FSB. In many cases, the AGP clock is set from a motherboard jumper or through an entry in the CMOS Setup. You'll generally find these settings denoted as the "AGP Ratio," and you can usually select "1:1," "2:3," or "1:2," depending on the FSB speeds available. You can see an example of how this setting is used next:

- If the FSB is 66 MHz, set the AGP Ratio to 1:1, and the AGP clock will be 66 MHz.
- If the FSB is 100 MHz, set the AGP Ratio to 2:3, and the AGP clock will be 66 MHz.
- If the FSB is 133 MHz, set the AGP Ratio to 1:2, and the AGP clock will be 66 MHz.

You can also see the potential for "overclocking":

- If the FSB is 100 MHz, setting the AGP Ratio to 1:1 will cause the AGP clock to be 100 MHz.
- If the FSB is 133 MHz, setting the AGP Ratio to 2:3 will cause the AGP clock to be 88.7 MHz.

As a rule, it is *unsafe* to overclock the AGP bus—especially if you're using AGP in the 2X or 4X data modes. In most cases, an overclocked AGP bus will result in unstable video and system operation. In extreme cases, the overclocked AGP card will be damaged.

## AGP AND BIOS SETTINGS

The number of video BIOS settings has been increasing steadily—even before the introduction of AGP. Every video card should include a list of recommended BIOS settings with its documentation (or the setting should be available from the manufacturer's Web site), and you should see that your CMOS Setup is configured properly for your particular AGP video card. For example, Table 35-4 lists the recommended settings for an older Viper II Z200 card, but you get some idea of how important BIOS settings have become. You can compare these settings to the entries for an NVIDIA GeForce chipset in Table 35-5.

| TABLE 35-4 | BIOS SETTINGS FOR A TYPICAL AGP CARD |
|---|---|
| **BIOS SETTINGS: PCI/AGP GENERAL** | |
| IRQ assignment | [toggle] |
| Boot with PnP O/S | [enable] |
| Pallet snooping | [disable] |
| PCI bursting | [disable] |
| PCI latency timer | [128] |

**TABLE 35-4     BIOS SETTINGS FOR A TYPICAL AGP CARD *(CONTINUED)***

| BIOS SETTINGS: PCI/AGP GENERAL | |
|---|---|
| Peer concurrency | [disable] |
| Video ROM BIOS Shadow | [disable] |
| Video BIOS shadowing | [disable] |
| Video BIOS cacheable | [disable] |
| Video RAM cacheable | [disable] |
| Byte-Merge | [disable] |
| Decouple Refresh | [disable] |
| Hidden Refresh | [disable] |
| USWC options | [Uncache Speculative Write Combining] |
| Video Memory Cache Mode | [UC] |
| Snoop Ahead | [disable] |
| **BIOS SETTINGS: AGP SPECIFIC** | |
| USB | [enabled] |
| PCI 2.1 compliance | [enable—also may assign IRQ to VGA] |
| Passive release/refresh | [enabled] |
| Delayed transactions | [enabled/disabled—toggle, may also enable PCI 2.1 compliance] |
| VGA BIOS Sequence | [AGP-PCI, PCI-AGP, PCI] |
| AGP/Graphics aperture size | [Target 1/2 installed RAM] |
| Write Cache Pipeline | [disable] |
| Read Around Write | [disable] |
| Primary Frame Buffer | [disable] |
| VGA Frame Buffer | [disable] |
| Frame Buffer Posted Write | [disable] |
| RAS-CAS Delay | [3T] |
| Cache Read | [disable] (VIA Motherboards) |
| CPU Wait Pipeline | [disable] (VIA Motherboards) |
| AGP Master 1 WS Write | [enable/disable] |
| AGP Master 1 WS Read | [enable/disable] |
| AGP Ratio | [set to 2/3 instead of 1/1] |
| AGP Multi Trans Timer | [disable] |
| AGP Low Priority Timer | [disable] |
| AGP 2x | [disable] |
| AGP Turbo Mode | [disable] |
| AGP Bus Turbo Mode | [disable] |
| AGP Transfer Mode | [1x] |

Not all listed options will be available on all motherboards. Should particular setting combinations fail, try loading "BIOS Defaults" in the CMOS Setup.

**TABLE 35-5    BIOS SETTINGS FOR AN NVIDIA GEFORCE-BASED VIDEO CARD**

| UC OR USWC | USWC |
|---|---|
| Fast Writes | Enabled |
| AGP Mode | 2x or 4x (depending on whether your motherboard supports AGP4X or not) |
| AGP Driving Control | Auto |
| AGP Aperture Size | 128MB RAM - Set to 64MB or 32MB |
| | 96MB RAM - Set to 48MB or 24MB |
| | 64MB RAM - Set to 32MB or 16MB |
| | 48MB RAM - Set to 24MB or 12MB |
| | 32MB RAM - Set to 24MB or 12MB |
| | 16MB RAM - Set to 24MB or 12MB |
| Assign IRQ to VGA | Enabled |
| Video BIOS Shadow | Disabled |
| Video BIOS Cacheable | Disabled |
| C8000—XXXXX Shadow | Disabled |
| Peer Concurrency | Enabled |
| Concurrent PCI Host | Enabled |
| PCI Streaming | Enabled |
| VGA Palette Snoop | Disabled |
| Memory Hole (Between 15-16MB) | Enabled |

# VIDEO OVERCLOCKING NOTES

Although you are certainly discouraged from overclocking a video adapter, today's powerful hardware accelerators offer some unique potential for overclocking that any technician should be aware of. You should at least know that such practices exist so that you can identify and correct video problems.

In principle, overclocking a video chipset and video memory is very similar to overclocking a CPU and main system memory. In actual practice, it is often *easier* to overclock video components than it is to overclock main system components, since the speed settings for your video adapter are typically adjustable without having to open the system. Small third-party utilities for overclocking popular video chipsets are available for download from numerous Web sites, and some video adapter manufacturers provide core and memory speed controls in their native display adjustment utilities and drivers. Third-party utilities—such as TNTClock (http://www.octools.com/index.cgi?caller=downloads.html) for the NVIDIA TNT chipset—are limited to adjusting only the core and the memory speed of the video adapter. Other utilities like Powerstrip from Entech (www.entechtaiwan.com/) offer not only the ability to adjust core and memory speeds of many different video chipset and adapters, but also offer the ability to adjust a wide range of display settings. These utilities make video overclocking possible with only a few clicks of the mouse. Unfortunately, they can also make it very easy to damage your video adapter.

As with CPU overclocking, there are limits to how far you can "push" a video adapter. Increasing clock speeds will increase heat generated by the graphics chipset, so it is important that adequate cooling (and temperature monitoring) be implemented. Additional case ventilation may also be required to exhaust heated air from the system. Most video adapters will generate corrupt frames as the thermal limit for a graphics chipset is exceeded. Images that contain "snow" or incorrect colors are often a sign that the video memory speed has been exceeded.

Once you have recorded the default operating speeds and temperatures of a video adapter, you can begin to slowly increase the core and memory speeds using the appropriate utility. The increases should be small (2–5 MHz at a time), and each increase should be followed by testing the video components with a demanding game or benchmark burn-in utility. Any problems, corrupt displays, or crashes indicate that the limits of the video adapter and cooling resources have been exceeded—either return to a stable setting or increase cooling activity.

 One of the first things a technician should check for when video stability problems are reported is video overclocking by the customer or system builder.

# Troubleshooting Video Adapters

A PC video system consists of four parts: the host PC itself, the video adapter/accelerator, the monitor, and the software (video BIOS and drivers). To deal with a failure in the video system, you must be able to isolate the problem to one of these four areas. When isolating the problem, your best tool is a working (or *test-bed*) PC. With another PC, you can systematically exchange hardware as needed to verify each element of the video system.

## BASIC PROBLEM ISOLATION

The first step is to verify the monitor by testing it on a known-good working PC. Keep in mind that the monitor *must* be compatible with the video adapter on which it is being tested. If the monitor works on another PC, the fault lies in one of the three remaining areas. If the monitor fails on a known-good machine, try the known-good monitor on the questionable machine. If the known-good monitor then works on your questionable machine, you can be certain that the fault lies in your monitor. If the monitor checks out, suspect the video adapter. Follow the same process to check the video adapter. Try the suspect video adapter on a known-good PC. If the problem follows the video adapter, you can replace the video adapter (an integrated video adapter can easily be disabled and replaced with another video adapter card). If the suspect video adapter works in a known-good system, the adapter is probably good. Replace the adapter in the suspect machine, but try another expansion slot and make sure that the monitor cable is attached securely.

If both the monitor and the video adapter work in a known-good PC, but the video problem persists in the original machine, suspect a problem with the PC motherboard. Try the working video adapter in another expansion slot. Either the expansion slot is faulty, or a fault has occurred on the motherboard. Run some PC diagnostics if you have some available. Diagnostics may help to pinpoint motherboard problems. You may then choose to troubleshoot the motherboard further or replace the motherboard at your discretion.

When the video system appears to work properly during system initialization but fails with a particular application (or in Windows 9x/Me/XP), strongly suspect a problem with the selected video driver. Since almost all video adapters support VGA at the hardware level, set your application (or change the Windows setup) to run in "standard VGA" mode (for Windows 9x/Me/XP, you can start the PC in the "Safe Mode"). If the display functions properly at that point, you can be confident that the problem is driver-related. Check with the manufacturer to see that you have the latest video driver available. Reload the driver from its original disk (or a new disk) or select a new driver. You may also check to see if a new video firmware version is available from the video adapter manufacturer. If the problem persists in VGA mode, the trouble may be in the video adapter. Problem isolation can be summarized with these points:

- *Check the driver(s).* Video drivers are critically important in all versions of Windows. Older drivers may contain bugs or be incompatible with certain applications. Incompatibility accounts for the majority of all video problems. Obtain the latest video driver release and make sure it is properly installed on the system. If the driver is the most current, try a generic (or *reference*) video driver (usually available from the video chipset manufacturer). You may also have some success by updating the video BIOS.

- *Check the physical installation.* See that the video board is installed properly in its expansion slot and make sure that any video card jumpers are set properly for the particular host system. Remember that other video systems in the PC should be disabled (using jumpers or the CMOS Setup).

- *Check for memory conflicts.* The memory space used by video adapters is hotly contested territory in the real-mode (DOS) upper memory area. Printer drivers, sound cards, tape backups, SCSI adapters, and scanners are just some of the devices that can step all over the memory space needed by a video board. Many of today's video boards require you to *exclude* a range of upper memory through your memory manager (often A000h through C7FFh, though particular video boards may be different). Make sure that any necessary memory exclusions are made in CONFIG.SYS at the memory manager's command line. You may also have to add an **EMMExclude=A000-C7FF** line to the [386enh] section of your SYSTEM.INI file. You may also need to add exclusions to the video adapter's properties under Windows.

- *Suspect your memory manager.* If you're working in the real mode, advanced real-mode memory managers such as QEMM or Netroom use very aggressive techniques to find available memory. Often, this interferes with video operation. Try disabling any "Stealth" or "Cloaking" mode or try disabling your real-mode memory manager. You should not be using memory managers under Windows 9x/Me/XP.

- *Check your system's CMOS setup.* Today's motherboards sport all manner of advanced features. Try systematically disabling such attributes as: video cache, video RAM shadow, byte-merge, palette snoop, or decouple/hidden refresh. If "PCI bus bursting" is used on the video bus, try disabling that also. If the video system requires the use of an interrupt, make sure that the IRQ is not being used by another device. If the user manual for your video card lists any special settings for your CMOS Setup, verify that you've made the appropriate changes. In many cases, you can try loading the BIOS Defaults for your CMOS Setup.

- *Compatibility.* Check the video adapter maker's (and motherboard maker's) Web site for any known compatibility issues. For example, video adapter "X" may have a known compatibility problem when used with motherboard "Y". Current video adapters may also have minimum power requirements or use some features not supported by the motherboard's chipset. This type of checking should normally be done *before* purchasing a video adapter for an upgrade, but is always a worthwhile check if a video upgrade goes awry.

# HANDLING MULTIPLE DISPLAYS

Traditionally, only one video adapter is allowed on the system, but Windows 98/Me/XP seeks to "extend" the desktop by supporting the use of more than one video adapter. This allows more open windows and thus provides more information to the user at any given time. In the gaming realm, multiple monitors expand the player's peripheral vision and help to immerse the player in the game's environment. While multiple display (or "multi-monitor") support is improving, it is far from perfect, and must be used with the right combination of system BIOS, video adapter chipsets, and Windows 98/Me/XP. This part of the chapter highlights some of the key hardware requirements and issues common to multi-monitor operation.

## Check the Video Adapters

All of the video adapters used in a computer with multi-monitor support *must* be Peripheral Component Interconnect (PCI) or Accelerated Graphics Port (AGP) devices using the multi-monitor compliant Windows 98/Me/XP display drivers. Industry Standard Architecture/Extended Industry Standard Architecture (ISA/EISA) display adapters are specifically *not* supported. Remember that the video adapters installed in your computer do *not* have to be identical. Each video adapter and monitor combination is separately enumerated by Windows 98/Me/XP, and can be configured to use different screen resolutions and color depths. For example, the primary display can be set to $1024 \times 768 \times 24$-bit, and the secondary display can be set to $800 \times 600 \times 16$-bit.

 Some manufacturers such as Matrox produce graphics adapters (like the Matrox G450 MMS) with two or four video ports on the same card—this provides multiple monitor support with one device, and greatly reduces the demands on bus slots and system resources. Many such adapters also output to TV—this can allow you to use the PC as a monitor, but watch a DVD on the TV.

## Check the Video Chipsets/Drivers

Windows may experience problems supporting multiple monitors with certain graphics adapters, or when older drivers are employed. Check with the graphics card's manufacturer for any FAQs or compatibility warnings—documentation might indicate potential trouble with a card's multiple monitor support. You may need to install a more suitable PCI or AGP video adapter. In other cases, upgrading the graphics driver(s) may help to overcome performance issues and streamline multi-monitor operation. Table 35-6 lists a set of common graphics cards that will operate as primary or secondary display adapters under Windows 98 and later.

 Matrox, NVIDIA, and ATI offer video adapters with integrated support for dual and multiple monitors, so adding another video adapter is not necessary.

## Enable Multi-monitor Support

As you saw previously, the primary requirement for multi-monitor support is that the video adapters *must* be Peripheral Component Interconnect (PCI) devices or Accelerated Graphics Port (AGP) devices (for example, you may install an AGP card as the primary display adapter, and relegate the motherboard's integrated display adapter as a secondary device). Once suitable hardware is installed, you'll need to enable multi-monitor operation. You can enable multi-monitor support with the following steps:

1. While the computer is turned off, add any additional video adapters and monitors.

2. Start Windows 98/Me/XP. Install the latest video adapter and monitor drivers (as necessary), then restart your computer if you're prompted to do so.

3. Right-click the desktop and select Properties.

4. Click the Settings tab.

5. In the Display box, click the adapter you want to use, then click the "Extend my Windows desktop onto this monitor" check box to select it.

6. Click Apply and OK.

**TABLE 35-6    TYPICAL VIDEO DEVICES SUITABLE FOR MULTI-MONITOR OPERATION**

| VIDEO ADAPTERS | VIDEO ADAPTERS |
|---|---|
| ATI 3D Xpression | Miro Crystal VR4000 |
| ATI 3D Xpression+ | Miro TwinHead 22SD |
| ATI 3D Xpression+ PC2TV | Number Nine 9FX Reality 332 |
| ATI All-In-Wonder | Number Nine 9FX Reality 332 (S3 Virge) |
| ATI All-In-Wonder Pro | Number Nine 9FX Reality 334 (S3 Virge GX/2) |
| ATI Graphics Pro Turbo PCI | Number Nine 9FX Reality 772 (S3 Virge VX) |
| ATI Graphics Xpression | Permedia 2 |
| ATI Mach 64 GX (GX, GXD, VT) | S3 765 (Trio64V+) |
| ATI Rage I, II, & II+ | S3 Aurora |
| ATI Rage Pro (AGP & PCI) | S3 Trio64V2(DX/GX) |
| ATI WinTurbo | S3 ViRGE |
| ATI Xpert@Play (4 & 8MB) | STB (Symmetric) Glyder MAX-2 PCI |
| ATI Xpert@Work (4 & 8MB) | STB Lightspeed 128 |
| California Graphics V2/DX | STB MVP 64 |
| Cirrus 5436 | STB MVP/64 |
| Cirrus 5446 | STB MVP/64 3D |
| Cirrus Alpine | STB Nitro 3D |
| Compaq Armada | STB Nitro 64V |
| CyberPro 2000A, 2MB | STB Powergraph 3D |
| Diamond Fire GL Pro 1000 AGP | STB PowerGraph 64V+ |
| Diamond Fire GL Pro 1000 PCI | STB Velocity 3D |
| Diamond Stealth 3D 2000 | STB WorkStation (2 & 4 output) |
| Diamond Stealth 3D 2000 Pro | TI TVP4020 8 meg AGP (Reference board) |
| Diamond Stealth 3D 3000 | TI TVP4020, 8 meg PCI (Reference board) |
| Diamond Stealth 64 Video 2001 | Trident 9685/9680/9682/9385/9382/9385 |
| ET6000 | Videologic GraphicsStar 410 |
| Hercules Dynamite 128/Video | ViRGE (325) |
| Hercules Terminator 64/Video | ViRGE DX (385) |
| InterGraphics Systems (IGS) | ViRGE GX (385) |
| Jaton Video - 57P | ViRGE VX (988) |

## Common Multi-Monitor Issues

Multi-monitor display technology is fairly well established under Windows 98/Me/XP, but there are situations where problems will arise. The easiest way to test your multi-monitor setup is to start a simple utility (e.g., Paint or WordPad) under Windows 98/Me/XP. When Paint or WordPad is *not* running in full-screen mode, drag the program's dialog box from one monitor to the other. If you can drag the program from one monitor to the other, you'll know that multi-monitor support is working correctly. If problems arise, try these tips to help isolate the trouble:

■ *Check the primary display adapter.* Open the Display Properties dialog box and use the Settings tab to disable the second monitor, then verify that your application(s) work properly on the primary monitor. You may need to update the display drivers for each video card in the system, or try reversing the primary/secondary display devices.

■ *Check the secondary display adapter.* Verify that the secondary display adapter you installed in the system is suitable for secondary service—not all video cards are fully compatible with multi-monitor support. You may need to update the secondary video card's drivers, or replace the secondary video card with a suitable model. Check with the video card's manufacturer for multi-monitor details or cautions.

■ *Check the display drivers.* Open the Display Properties dialog box and verify that the installed video drivers are the *correct* drivers for the video adapters in your computer. If not (or if the drivers are an older version), you should use the Update Driver wizard to install the latest driver(s).

■ *Verify that supplemental monitors start properly.* When you start the system, Windows should display a message indicating that the display adapter(s) for additional monitors have been detected and initialized properly. If you don't see this message, use the Device Manager to verify that additional display adapters are installed properly. If not, you should recheck the installation of any missing display devices.

■ *Check programs for multi-monitor support.* Some applications software does not fully comply with multi-monitor support. If you find that some software works fine in a second monitor, but certain programs do not, you may need to keep the offending software on a primary monitor, or check with the software maker for updates or patches that might correct multi-monitor support.

## MISSING DISPLAY OPTIONS

Ideally, once a video adapter is installed and configured, you should be able to select any of its available resolutions and color depths through the Windows 9x/Me/XP Display icon. However, when you try to change the Desktop Area setting, some known options of that the video adapter may not be available. For example, a video adapter that can display to a resolution of $1024 \times 768 \times 256$ may offer only $640 \times 480 \times 256$ and $800 \times 600 \times 16$ as the resolution/color options. Missing display options can occur when one or more of the following situations are present on your system:

■ *Check the CMOS Setup.* Reboot the system to the CMOS Setup and check for any monitor timing or other display-related entries. Monitor timing settings (if any)—including resolution and refresh rates— should match the characteristics of your monitor based on the manufacturer's documentation.

■ *Check the monitor type.* In some cases, selecting an incorrect monitor type can affect the video options available to you. Open the Display Properties dialog box, select the Settings tab, click the Advanced button, and choose the Monitor tab (see Figure 35-17). If the monitor is entered incorrectly, click the Change button and configure the correct monitor make and model. If your monitor is not listed, you can select the Generic setting that corresponds to the capabilities of your monitor.

■ *Check the drivers.* Older or inappropriate drivers may prohibit particular resolutions or color depths (for example, you're using a beta driver or reference driver that hasn't been fully qualified for your operating system). Open the Device Manager and check the installation of your video card. If the card is identified improperly, or if the driver is old, you may need to use the Update Driver wizard to install the latest version of your video card's driver (which can normally be downloaded directly from the card's manufacturer).

## HARDWARE ACCELERATION

Video cards use a variety of techniques to implement advanced functions and features. Unfortunately, there are times when Windows cannot use the video features properly, and this usually results in performance and stability issues. Windows 9x/Me/XP provides a "hardware acceleration" adjustment that you can use to

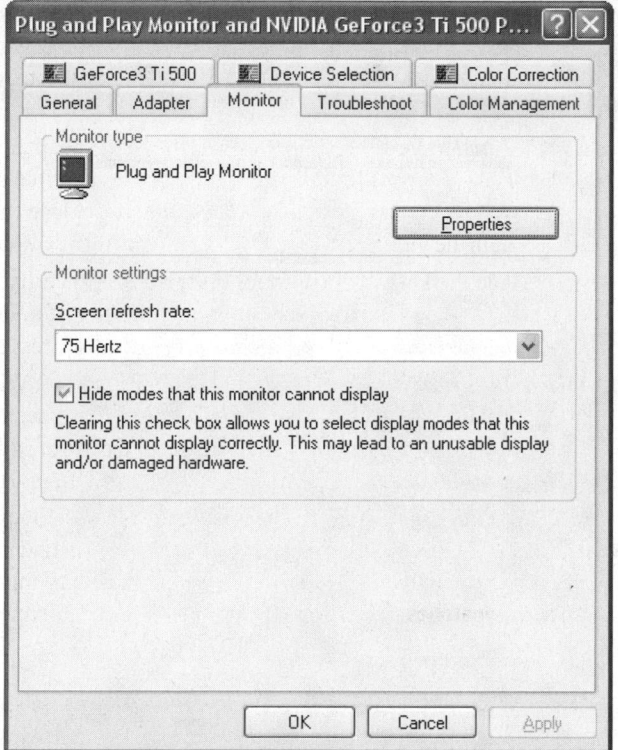

**FIGURE 35-17** Select the monitor's specific make and model, or select an appropriate generic monitor

scale back the features supported by Windows. In many cases, this can shut down troublesome features and allow you to stabilize the system until new drivers are installed or the video adapter is upgraded. It is a good idea to start with the setting on the right (the Full setting) and systematically move the slider one setting to the left until you find the setting that works best. Follow these steps to use the slider under Windows XP:

1. Right-click the desktop and select Properties.
2. Click the Settings tab and click Advanced.
3. Select the Troubleshoot tab (see Figure 35-18).
4. Note that the Hardware acceleration slider has six settings, ranging from Full to None.
5. Systematically step the slider back from Full toward None (one step at a time), and retest the system. If the system stabilizes, an updated driver or video card may be needed.

Follow these steps to use the slider under Windows 9x/Me:

1. Open the Control Panel and double-click the System icon.
2. Click the Performance tab, then click the Graphics button.

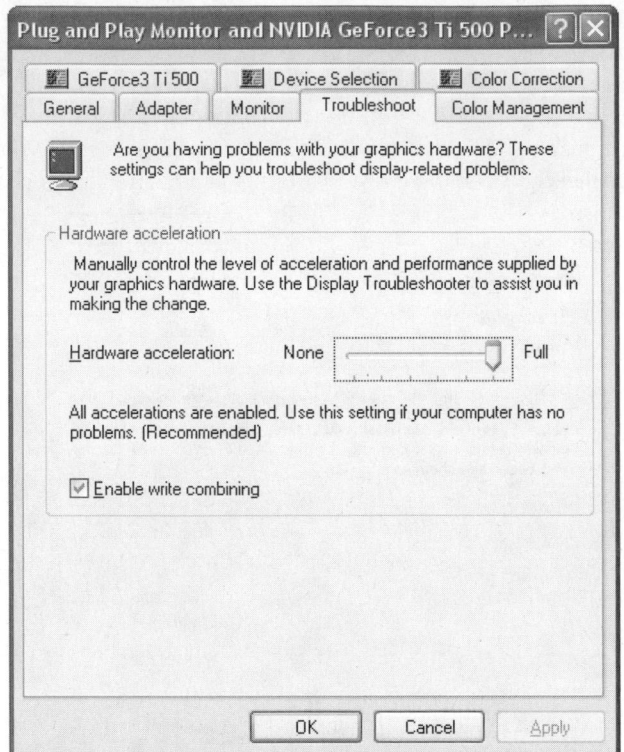

**FIGURE 35-18** Using the Hardware acceleration slider to test the graphics system for compatibility and performance problems

3. Note that the Hardware Acceleration slider has four settings (Full, Most, Basic, and None).

4. Systematically step the slider back from Full toward None (one step at a time), and retest the system. If the system stabilizes, an updated driver or video card may be needed.

## VIDEO SYMPTOMS

Many common video problems can be isolated and resolved using the previous guidelines. However, when the problems persist, you can refer to the following symptoms for specific explanations and solutions.

**SYMPTOM 35-1** **The computer is on, but there is no display** The PC seems to initialize properly. If you hear a series of beeps during system initialization, refer to Chapter 17 to determine the error. Make sure that the monitor is turned on and plugged into the video adapter properly. Also, check that the monitor's brightness and contrast controls are turned up enough (it sounds silly, but it really *does* happen). Try the monitor on a known-good PC. If the monitor works properly, suspect the video adapter. Power-down the PC and make sure the video adapter is seated properly in its expansion slot. If any of the board contacts are dirty or corroded, clean the contacts by rubbing them with an eraser. You can also use any electronics-grade contact cleaner. You may want to try the video board in another expansion slot.

Chances are that the video adapter has at least one hardware jumper or DIP switch setting. Contact the manufacturer or refer to the owner's manual for the board and check that any jumpers or DIP switch settings on the board are configured properly. If this is a new installation, use the Device Manager to check the adapter board settings against the configuration of other expansion boards in the system. When the hardware settings of one board overlap the settings of another, a hardware conflict can result. When you suspect a conflict, adjust the settings of the video adapter (or another newly installed device) to eliminate the conflict. There may also be a memory conflict. Some video adapters make unusual demands of upper system memory (the area between 640KB and 1MB). It is possible that an *EXCLUDE* switch must be added to the EMM386.EXE entry in a CONFIG.SYS file (or the video adapter's properties in the Device Manager). Check with the adapter's instruction manual to see if there are any memory configuration changes or optimizations that are required.

**SYMPTOM 35-2** **There is no display, and you hear a series of beeps when the PC initializes** The video adapter failed to initialize during the system's POST. Since the video adapter is not responding, it is impossible to display information—that is why a series of beeps is used. Bear in mind that the actual beep sequence may vary from system to system depending on the type of BIOS being used. You can probably find the beep code for your BIOS in Chapter 17. In actual practice, there may be several reasons why the video adapter fails. Power-down the PC and check that the video adapter is installed properly and securely in an expansion slot. Make sure that the video adapter is not touching any exposed wiring or any other expansion board.

Isolate the video adapter by trying another adapter in the system. If the display works properly with another adapter installed, check the original adapter to see that any settings and jumpers are correct. If the problem persists, the original adapter is probably defective and should be replaced. If a new adapter fails to resolve the problem, there may be a fault elsewhere on the motherboard. Install a POST board in the PC and allow the system to initialize. Each step of the initialization procedure corresponds to a two-digit hexadecimal code shown on the POST card indicators. The last code to be displayed is the point at which the failure occurred. POST cards are handy for checking the motherboard when a low-level fault has occurred. If a motherboard fault is detected, you may troubleshoot the motherboard or replace it at your discretion.

**SYMPTOM 35-3** **You see large blank bands at the top and bottom of the display in some screen modes, but not in others** Multifrequency and multimode monitors sometimes behave this way. This is not necessarily a *defect*, but it can cause some confusion unless you understand what is going on. When screen resolution changes, the overall number of pixels being displayed also changes. Ideally, a multifrequency monitor should detect the mode change and adjust the vertical screen size to compensate (a feature called *auto-sizing*). However, not all multifrequency monitors have this feature. When video modes change, you are left to adjust the vertical size manually. Of course, if there is information *missing* from the display, there may be a serious problem with VRAM or the adapter's graphics controller chip. In such case, try another video adapter board.

**SYMPTOM 35-4** **The display image rolls** Vertical synchronization is not keeping the image steady (horizontal sync may also be affected). This problem is typical of a monitor that cannot display a particular screen mode. Mode incompatibility is most common with fixed-frequency monitors, but can also appear in multifrequency monitors that are being pushed beyond their specifications. The best course of action here is to simply reconfigure your software to use a compatible video mode (or reduce the vertical refresh rate). For example, change the $1280 \times 1024$ screen mode to $800 \times 600$, and you may also need to drop the vertical refresh rate to 72 Hz or lower. If that is an unsatisfactory solution, you will have to upgrade to a monitor that will support the desired video mode.

If the monitor and video board are compatible, there is a synchronization problem. Try the monitor on a known-good PC. If the monitor also fails on a known-good PC, try the known-good monitor on the original PC. If the known-good monitor works on the suspect PC, the sync circuits in your original monitor have almost certainly failed, and the monitor must be replaced. If the suspect monitor works on a known-good PC, the trouble is likely in the original video adapter. Try replacing the video adapter.

**SYMPTOM 35-5** **An error message appears on system startup indicating an invalid system configuration** The system CMOS backup battery has probably failed, and the video type may have defaulted to EGA or MCA instead of VGA, resulting in the error. This is typically a symptom that occurs in older systems. If you enter your system setup (either through a BIOS routine or through a disk-based setup utility) and examine each entry, you will probably find that all entries have returned to a default setting—including the video system setting. Your best course is to replace the CMOS backup battery and enter each configuration setting again (hopefully you have recorded each setting on paper already, or saved the CMOS contents to floppy disk using a CMOS backup utility). In most cases, you can load BIOS default values without having to enter each value manually. Once new settings are entered and saved, the system should operate properly. If the CMOS *still* will not retain system configuration information, the CMOS RAM itself is probably defective. Use a software diagnostic to check the RTC/CMOS chip (and the rest of the motherboard) thoroughly. If a motherboard fault is detected, you can troubleshoot the motherboard or replace it at your discretion.

**SYMPTOM 35-6** **Garbage appears on the screen or the system hangs up** There are a variety of reasons why the display may be distorted. One potential problem is a monitor mismatch. Check the video adapter jumpers and DIP switch settings (if any) and be sure that the video board will support the type of monitor you are using. It is possible that the video mode being used is not supported by your monitor (the display may also roll, as described in Symptom 35-4). Try reconfiguring your Windows Display Properties to use a compatible video mode—even a "standard VGA" mode. The problem should disappear. If that is an unsatisfactory solution, you will have to upgrade to a monitor that will support the desired video mode. Some older multifrequency monitors are unable to switch video modes without being turned off and then turned on again. When such monitors experience a change in video mode, they will respond by displaying a distorted image until the monitor is reset. If you have an older monitor, try turning it off, waiting several minutes, then turning it on again.

Video drivers also play a big part in Windows. Make sure that you have loaded the latest video driver, and that the driver is fully compatible with the video board being used. If problems persist in Windows, load the standard generic VGA driver. The generic VGA driver should function properly with virtually every video board and VGA (or SVGA) monitor available. If the problem disappears when using the generic driver setup, the original driver is incorrect, corrupt, or obsolete. Contact the driver manufacturer to obtain a copy of the latest driver version. If the problem persists, the video adapter board may be defective or incompatible with Windows. Try another video adapter.

**SYMPTOM 35-7** **Your video card doesn't work on a VIA- or ETEQ-based system** For example, this is a known issue with the older Viper II Z200 and can occur on both "Super 7" and Slot 1 based systems. The Viper II Z200 card does not interact properly with the MVP3 or ETEQ chipsets. Check to see that the motherboard's AGP driver and IRQ routing drivers have been installed properly before attempting to install the display adapter. All the necessary motherboard updates can be found in a file from www.viatech.com/drivers/4IN1409.exe. This patch is supposed to work for both the MVP3 and ETEQ chipset (Super 7) as well as the VIA Apollo Pro chipset (for Pentium II systems). If the problem persists, you may need to try a different video card.

**SYMPTOM 35-8**   **Your video card doesn't work on an ALI-based system**   For example, this is a known issue with older video cards such as the Viper V770, and can occur on both "Super 7" and Slot 1 based systems. This problem probably occurs because the ALI-based chipset requires a motherboard AGP driver in order to support AGP cards such as the V770. Ensure that the latest AGP driver from ALI has been installed from www.acerlabs.com/acerlabs/drivers.htm. This patch is supposed to work for both the Aladdin V chipset (Super 7) as well as the Aladdin Pro II chipset (for Pentium II systems—also referred to as the BXPro). If the problem persists, you may need to use a different video card.

**SYMPTOM 35-9**   **Your video card doesn't work on an AMD Athlon-based system** For example, this is a known issue with older video cards such as the Viper II Z200 and almost always means that the Athlon motherboard requires an AGP "miniport" driver. Ensure that the latest AGP "miniport" driver has been installed from AMD: www1.amd.com/athlon/config. If the problem persists, you may need to use a different video card.

**SYMPTOM 35-10**   **Selecting a screen resolution over 640 × 480 causes the system to reboot in the Safe Mode**   For example, this is known to occur on HP Pavilion systems, and has generally been identified as an HP BIOS problem. HP has a main board BIOS upgrade for the Pavilion that should fix this issue. The release notes for this new BIOS indicate that it fixes a problem allocating IRQs to add-in AGP adapters (such as NVIDIA-based display adapters). Check out the HP technical support site at www.hp.com.

**SYMPTOM 35-11**   **When booting to Windows, you find a black screen, or Windows indicates that the display adapter is not configured properly**   You may also find a yellow exclamation mark on the video card in your Device Manager. In virtually all cases, this occurs because the video card does not have an adequate IRQ assigned to it. Boot into your system to the CMOS Setup and look for an option such as "Assign IRQ for PCI (or AGP) VGA"—see that it's set to "enabled" or "auto." If the video card is not assigned to a suitable IRQ and the system BIOS does not have an option to assign an IRQ, you'll need to contact your motherboard manufacturer and check for a BIOS update.

**SYMPTOM 35-12**   **After installing 3D accelerator drivers, you find an "Invalid VxD dynamic link" error**   This is a problem with Windows 95—chances are that you're trying to use an AGP accelerator card under Windows 95 OSR2 *without* having the proper USB support update installed. Use the Windows Update feature to download and install the latest available patches and fixes for Windows 95. Otherwise, update your version of Windows to Windows 98/Me/XP.

**SYMPTOM 35-13**   **After upgrading from an older video card, you can access higher colors but cannot use resolutions over 640 × 480**   This type of issue is seen frequently when upgrading older video cards (such as the Stealth 64 card)—true color modes are accessible, but resolutions above 640 × 480 are not. This problem is almost always due to residual entries left in the Registry. Start your Registry editor and check the following key:

`HKEY_LOCAL_MACHINE/Config/0001/Display/Settings`

Right next to the setting "Resolution" is an entry called **ScreenArea**. This entry was left over from a former "Virtual Desktop" and was probably set to 640×480. Remove this key, save your changes, and reboot the system.

**SYMPTOM 35-14**    **Windows reports a memory conflict with a PCI-to-PCI bridge and the AGP graphics adapter**    This PCI-to-PCI bridge is sometimes called the Intel 82443LX or 82443BX bridge. This is not a "real" error. The memory conflict that appears between the PCI bridge and the AGP graphics adapter is a known conflict. This error is caused by the way Windows 95 reports memory usage and is not known to cause problems. Windows 98 and later will not report this problem, so you may ignore the issue or upgrade if you wish.

**SYMPTOM 35-15**    **3D applications appear slow when run on a GeForce video card** Always start by checking the system requirements for your video adapter—older PCs may require more RAM or a CPU upgrade in order to achieve an acceptable frame rate from the GeForce card. Keep in mind that AMD Super Socket 7 chips are reputed to offer poor performance due to the poor AGP implementations on most Super Socket 7 motherboards. Also make sure to download and install the very latest motherboard AGP drivers. If the problem persists, you may need to consider a motherboard/CPU upgrade.

**SYMPTOM 35-16**    **You notice a horizontal line scrolling down one side of the screen with multiple monitors under Windows 98/SE**    This problem is almost always caused when your monitors are too close to a fluorescent light source (or you're using an unshielded monitor and you place it too close to another monitor). Most early monitors are *unshielded*, so they do *not* confine the magnetic field they emit. Later monitors are *shielded* so that most of the magnetic fields they emit are confined within the monitor. If you place an unshielded monitor too close to another monitor, the magnetic field emitted by the unshielded monitor may interfere with the other monitor. Move the unshielded monitor away from any monitors or fluorescent light sources it interferes with, or place a shield (an ordinary "cookie sheet," for example) between the unshielded monitor and any monitors it interferes with. You may also choose to replace the unshielded monitor with a shielded model.

**SYMPTOM 35-17**    **You cannot drag a window from one monitor to another under Windows 98/SE**    This problem can occur if the window you're trying to drag is maximized or your monitors are not positioned correctly. To work around this issue, restore the window to its previous "windowed" state before you drag it to a different monitor. To do this, simply click the Restore button (the middle button in the upper-right corner of a window). You should also verify your monitor's position on your primary and secondary graphics adapters.

**SYMPTOM 35-18**    **You notice a black screen when you run a program requiring DirectX**    When you run a DirectX-based program, your monitor may display a black screen (or may display only wavy lines on a black background). This fault can occur if the DirectX-based program changes the default refresh rate that your display adapter uses with the monitor. Change the refresh rate to an acceptable level for your monitor and selected resolution (such as 60 Hz or 72 Hz):

1. Right-click the desktop and select Properties.
2. Click the Settings tab, then click Advanced.

**3.** Under Windows 9x/Me, click the Adapter tab, then click Adapter Default in the Refresh Rate box. Under Windows XP, click the Monitor tab and select the proper "Screen refresh rate" from the drop-down box (see Figure 35-19).

**4.** Click OK when you're prompted to test the setting.

**5.** If the setting is displayed correctly, click Yes to keep the setting.

If this doesn't work, try reducing the hardware acceleration for the video adapter as described in the "Hardware Acceleration" section earlier.

**SYMPTOM 35-19    You encounter a blank screen after installing a secondary video adapter**    This trouble can occur if your computer has a built-in video adapter and either your computer's BIOS does not provide support for multiple video adapters or the secondary video adapter is not supported for "multiple display" use. To resolve this behavior, update your computer's BIOS and/or obtain a different video adapter that's properly supported for Windows 98/Me/XP multi-monitor service.

**SYMPTOM 35-20    You find that some video adapters do not support multi-monitor operation**    For example, when you add a secondary video adapter to a system that uses a Riva 128 video adapter as the *primary* video adapter, the computer may crash. This problem is almost always

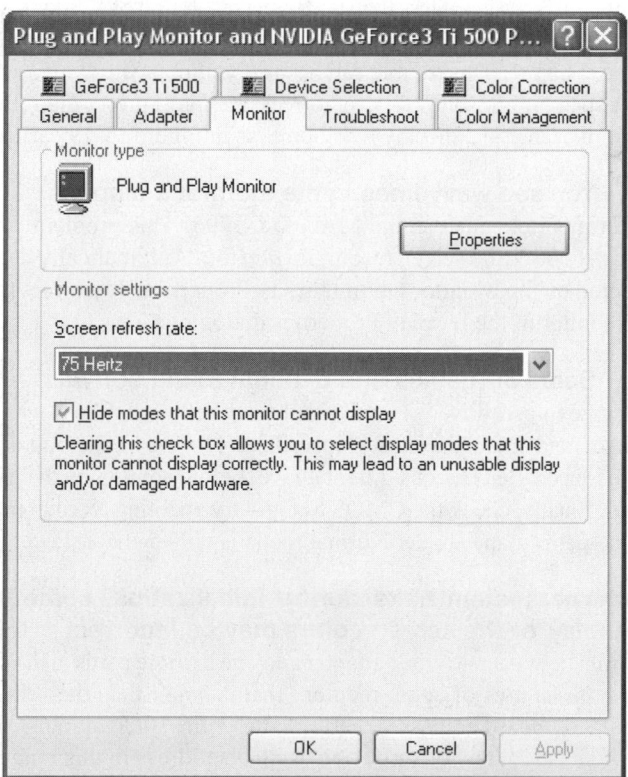

**FIGURE  35-19**    Setting a refresh rate that is suitable for your particular monitor

caused by an incompatible driver used by the Riva 128 video adapter. Consequently, Riva 128 video adapters are *not* supported for use with the multiple display feature. If you want to use multiple monitors, you should use only video adapters that are known to work in a multiple-monitor environment. Replace the incompatible video adapter with a model that *is* compatible with multi-monitor operation.

**SYMPTOM 35-21    You have trouble using the ATI Rage II PCI video card as a second video adapter**    When you try the ATI Rage II PCI video adapter as a secondary display adapter under Windows 98, the secondary display adapter may not work properly (if at all). When you view the ATI Rage II PCI Properties dialog box in Device Manager, you may see an error message. In virtually all cases, the problem is because there's a real-mode memory manager (e.g., EMM386) running on the system. You can try adding an exclusion to the SYSTEM.INI file such as

```
emmexclude=c000-cfff
```

but the best solution is to disable the memory manager entirely and allow Windows to manage memory on the system.

**SYMPTOM 35-22    The screen image becomes distorted when changing resolutions** This is known to occur with certain monitors under Windows (such as the NEC 4FG). Some video adapters (such as the Diamond Stealth 64, Video 2001, and S3 Trio 64V+) default to a refresh rate of 60 Hz. NEC 4FG monitors can support only refresh rates of less than 60 Hz at a resolution of $1280 \times 1024$ or higher. For example, if you're using an NEC 4FG monitor and you change the display resolution to $1280 \times 1024$ or higher, your screen may become distorted. This trouble can occur if you're using a video adapter that defaults to a refresh rate of 60 Hz at such high resolutions. To correct this fault, preset the refresh rate of your video adapter *before* you attempt change the display resolution (as in Figure 35-19 earlier).

**SYMPTOM 35-23    You see wavy lines in the monitor's display**    This is known to occur under Windows 98 with monitors such as the MAG DX-1795. This problem can occur if your video adapter is configured for $1600 \times 1200$ screen resolution *and* the "Automatically detect Plug & Play monitors" check box is selected on the Monitor tab in Display Properties. To correct this problem, manually install your particular monitor in the Display Properties dialog box.

**SYMPTOM 35-24    Some 3D games and benchmarking software refuse to run**    This is usually a problem with the chipset driver(s) used with the motherboard. Check with the motherboard manufacturer (or system maker) and obtain the latest chipset drivers for the motherboard (e.g., VIA chipset drivers). Also verify that you've installed DirectX 7.0 (or above) before continuing to install your AGP graphics accelerator and its driver. Finally, check the CMOS Setup—try enabling Normal mode (AGP1X) and disable the Turbo mode (the performance under Normal mode is only 5–10% slower than Turbo mode).

**SYMPTOM 35-25    The system halts during initialization, some characters may be missing from the display, or the screen colors may be incorrect**    These are classic symptoms of a hardware conflict between the video adapter and one or more cards in the system or area of memory. Some video boards use an area of upper memory that is larger than the "classical" video area. For example, the Impact SVGA board imposes itself on the entire address range between A0000h and DFFFFh. In this kind of situation, any other device using an address in this range will conflict with the video board. A conflict may occur when the video board is first installed, or the board may work fine until another device is added or modified.

Resolving a hardware conflict basically means that *something* has to give—one of the conflicting elements (the IRQ lines, DMA channels, or I/O addresses) must be adjusted to use unique system resources. To you as a technician, it rarely matters which of the conflicting devices you change, but remember that system startup files, device drivers, and application settings may also have to change to reflect newly selected resources. You may also be able to resolve some memory conflicts by adding the *EXCLUDE* switch to EMM386.EXE. The video adapter manual will indicate when an *EXCLUDE* switch is necessary.

**SYMPTOM 35-26**    **Your system is generating DMA errors with a VGA board in the system and video BIOS shadowing disabled**    This is a fairly rare symptom that develops only on some older i486 systems and is usually due to an 8-bit VGA board in a system equipped with a slower version of the i486 CPU (in the 25 MHz range). Because 8-bit access takes so long, some DMA requests are ignored—thus an error is generated. If you find such a problem, try enabling *video ROM shadowing* through the CMOS setup to allow faster access to video instructions. Also, you may try a newer revision of the i486 CPU. Today, a motherboard upgrade is strongly recommended.

**SYMPTOM 35-27**    **The system hangs up using a 16-bit VGA board, and one or more 8-bit controllers**    This is typically an older problem that arises when 8-bit and 16-bit ISA boards are used in the same system. Due to the way that an ISA bus separates the 8-bit and 16-bit segments, accessing an 8-bit board when there are 16-bit boards in the system may cause the CPU to (falsely) determine that it is accessing a 16-bit board. When this occurs, the system will almost invariably crash. Try removing any 8-bit boards from the system. If the crashes cease, you have probably nailed down the error. Unfortunately, the only real correction is to either remove the 8-bit board(s) or reconfigure the board(s) to use a higher area of memory.

**SYMPTOM 35-28**    **You have trouble sizing or positioning the display**    In other cases, you may see error messages like "Mode not supported" or "Insufficient memory". These kinds of errors may occur in newer or high-end video boards if the board is not set up properly for the monitor it is being used with. Most new video boards include an installation routine that records the monitor's maximum specifications, such as resolution (and refresh frequencies), horizontal scanning frequencies, and vertical scanning frequencies. If such data is entered incorrectly (or the monitor is changed) certain screen modes may no longer work properly. Check the video adapter's installation parameters and correct its setup if necessary.

**SYMPTOM 35-29**    **You encounter Windows protection errors after installing video drivers**    For example, you may find that Windows refuses to load properly after installing ATI enhanced drivers for an AGP graphics adapter. You should first suspect the motherboard's chipset drivers—the drivers may be older or missing. Contact the motherboard manufacturer and obtain the appropriate chipset drivers for the motherboard. Also verify that you're using a version of Windows that fully supports AGP (e.g., Windows 95/NT 4 do not fully support AGP). Next, check the CMOS Setup and verify that any AGP-related features are configured properly. You may need to check the video card's documentation for suggested CMOS settings. Finally, you may be able to correct this trouble by upgrading the motherboard BIOS.

**SYMPTOM 35-30**    **The video board will not boot up when used in a particular motherboard**    There are noted cases of hardware incompatibility between certain video boards and motherboards. This incompatibility usually causes a great deal of confusion because the video board may work just fine when tested in a different motherboard, and other video boards may work well in the original motherboard—the technician simply winds up chasing ghosts. For general troubleshooting purposes, if a certain video board and motherboard refuse to work together, don't waste your time chasing ghosts—contact *both* the video board maker and PC (or motherboard) maker and see if there are any reports of incompatibilities. In most cases, you'll simply select an alternate video card for the system.

**SYMPTOM 35-31**   **Diagnostics refuse to show all of the available video modes for a particular board**   For example, this may occur even though all video RAM was properly detected. When a video board does not respond to certain video modes (usually the higher video modes), it is usually because there is a conflict in the upper memory area, and a memory range needs to be excluded. If there is a memory manager at work (for instance, QEMM, 386MAX, or EMM386), try disabling the memory manager in CONFIG.SYS or boot the system from a clean floppy. Try your diagnostic(s) again—chances are that the problem has disappeared. To fix this problem on a more permanent basis, reenable the memory manager using an exclude command. Try **x=B100h-B1FFh** as the first parameter on the memory manager's command line. If that does not work, try **x=A000h-BFFFh**. Finally, try **x=A000h-C7FF**. Ideally, the solution would be to remove the real-mode memory manager from the system entirely.

**SYMPTOM 35-32**   **Pixels appear "dropped" behind the mouse cursor, and graphic images appear to break up under Windows**   There are two major causes for this older type of problem: bad video RAM or the system ISA bus speed is too fast. Check the CMOS Setup for an entry in Advanced Setup such as "AT Bus Clock," "ISA Bus Speed," or "AT Bus Speed." The corresponding entry should be set to 8.33 MHz. Otherwise, excessive speed may be resulting in "lost" video data. If the bus speed is set properly, run a diagnostic to check the integrity of video RAM (you may have to replace the video RAM, or replace the video board entirely).

**SYMPTOM 35-33**   **You encounter video-related conflicts in Packard Bell systems** The system refuses to boot or starts with "garbage" and erratic screen displays. This symptom is encountered most frequently with Boca video boards on Packard Bell systems with video circuits already on the motherboard. Even when the onboard video has been disabled, reports indicate that the video circuitry remains active and then conflicts with the add-on video board. Remove the video card and use the onboard video adapter.

**SYMPTOM 35-34**   **Text appears in an odd color**   For example, text that should be green appears black. This is almost always the result of a problem with the palette decoding registers on the particular video board and will typically appear when using higher color modes (for instance, 64k or 16M colors). Make sure that the video drivers are correct, complete, and up-to-date. If the problem persists, you may need to replace the video board.

Remember that you can select myriad color and text schemes under Windows 9x/Me/XP. Before you conclude that color problems are caused by a faulty video card, be sure to try the "Windows Default" desktop scheme.

**SYMPTOM 35-35**   **When an application is started (under Windows), the opening display appears "scrambled"**   While this might appear to be a video memory problem at first glance, it is actually more likely to be related to a buggy video driver. Upgrade the video driver to the latest version or try a generic video driver (a "reference driver") that is compatible with your video chipset.

**SYMPTOM 35-36** **The display colors change when exiting from a DOS shell under Windows** This problem has been noted with older video boards such as the Diamond SpeedStar Pro and is almost always the result of a video board defect (usually a palette problem). For the Diamond board, the product must be replaced with board revision A2 or later. For other video boards, such problems can usually be corrected by replacing the video board with a new make and model.

**SYMPTOM 35-37** **OpenGL games won't run when the system is in multi-monitor mode** Most OpenGL games will not run when using a dual monitor setup under Windows 98/Me/XP. This is not an issue with the drivers themselves, but with the OpenGL API (which can only accelerate one hardware graphics card at a time). To correct this problem, simply disable the second monitor and your OpenGL 3D program will work again. By contrast, DirectX does support multi-monitors and should not experience this type of problem.

Some OpenGL applications will operate in dual monitor mode, but revert to software rendering, which impairs performance. However, most OpenGL applications will detect that the renderer is not working and simply refuse to execute.

**SYMPTOM 35-38** **When starting a game, the monitor goes black** However, you can still hear the game running. This generally means that your graphics card is running the game at a refresh rate higher than what your monitor supports. You may have selected a display mode that the monitor doesn't support. First verify that you're running the very latest video drivers for your graphics card. If a driver update doesn't help, you'll need to reduce the monitor's refresh rate (as in Figure 35-19 earlier).

**SYMPTOM 35-39** **You notice that .AVI files have distorted colors or "grainy" playback** This usually occurs when playing 8-bit .AVI files that are not supported by DCI, and it can usually be corrected by disabling the accelerated video playback features of the video board. For example, the older Diamond ViperPro Video board is noted for this problem, and you would need to edit the COPRO.INI file located in the \Windows directory. In the [VCP] area, change the **VCPEnable=** line to **off**. Save the .INI file and restart Windows. Upgrading the older video adapter would also correct this type of trouble.

**SYMPTOM 35-40** **The PCI video board will not work under Windows unless the system's PCI SCSI devices are disconnected** This type of problem occurs only on certain combinations of PCI system hardware. For example, this type of symptom has been documented using Phoenix BIOS 4.04 and a UMC8810P-AIO motherboard on systems with an NCR SCSI controller and SCSI devices. You can often correct such problems by correcting the Advanced System Setup in CMOS. Start the CMOS Setup, go to the Advanced System Setup, and select PCI Devices. Set up the PCI slot for the SCSI controller as IRQ9 and **LEVEL** edge select. The slot for the video board should have the IRQ set to **NONE**, and **LEVEL** edge select. Change the Base Memory Address from 0080000000 to 0081000000.

**SYMPTOM 35-41** **There are boot problems when a new video board is installed** Typical problems include no video or eight beeps when the system is turned on. This is usually the result of an outdated system BIOS, which is not capable of detecting the particular video chipset in use—the BIOS interprets this as meaning that there is no video board in the system, and an error is generated accordingly. Contact the motherboard manufacturer (or PC maker) for an updated system BIOS. Most BIOS versions dated after the fall of 1994 should be able to detect most modern video chipsets.

**SYMPTOM 35-42    There are boot problems when a PCI video board is installed**
In many cases, the system BIOS did not complete the configuration of the video board correctly, and the board has not been enumerated onto the PCI bus. The video board manufacturer may have a utility available that can "remap" the video card properly. For the Matrox Millennium, use the PCIMAP.EXE utility. Other Matrox boards use the MGABASE.EXE utility. Other PCI video board manufacturers probably offer their own utilities. The second problem is that the system BIOS has assigned a base memory address to the video board that is used by another device or that is reserved for use by the motherboard chipset. While the utilities mentioned may often help to correct this problem, a more permanent fix is usually to update the system BIOS. Check for a BIOS upgrade from the motherboard (or PC) manufacturer.

**SYMPTOM 35-43    The monitor overscans when entering a DOS shell from Windows**
This creates a highly distorted image and can (if left for prolonged periods) damage the monitor circuitry. The cause of this problem is usually a bug in the video driver. For example, this type of problem is known to happen when using the older Diamond SpeedStar Pro with drivers prior to version 1.06. Obtain the latest video driver from the video board maker or try a generic video driver written by the video chipset maker.

**SYMPTOM 35-44    You encounter an intermittent "Divide by Zero" error**    Although there are several possible causes for this type of error, they are *all* related to flaws in software—specifically, problems with the video driver or video "toolkit" that is installed with the particular video board. For example, "Divide by Zero" errors can be corrected in the Diamond Stealth 64 Video 2001 series by opening the InControl Tools package and changing a "Center to Viewport" selection to "Center to Desktop." Similarly, the "Maximize to Viewport" selection should be changed to "Maximize to Desktop." Often, upgrading the video driver or video support tools will eliminate software problems.

**SYMPTOM 35-45    During MPEG playback, the display flickers, shows low refresh rates, or appears to be in an interlaced mode**    This is not necessarily an error. With some video boards, MPEG files cannot play correctly at high refresh rates—typically over 72 Hz. When an MPEG file is played, the driver will automatically switch to a 72 Hz or 60 Hz vertical refresh rate. This may result in an unexpected change in display quality during playback. After exiting from the MPEG player, the original (higher) refresh rate will often be restored. If a vertical refresh rate *lower* than 72 Hz was originally selected, then the vertical refresh rate will not change during MPEG playback, so you should see no difference in the display.

**SYMPTOM 35-46    You receive an error when starting an MPEG player or other video tool**    In almost all cases, the related driver is missing, installed improperly, or corrupt. Reinstall the MPEG playback driver(s) for your particular video board and make sure to use the latest version. If problems persist, check for the driver under the WIN.INI or SYSTEM.INI file and see that there is only one **load=** reference to the particular driver(s)—repeated references can cause conflicts or other loading problems. Similar drivers (other MPEG drivers) can also cause conflicts, so verify that the only drivers being loaded are the ones used by your current video adapter and/or playback software.

**SYMPTOM 35-47    On video boards with TV tuners, the TV window is blurry or fuzzy at 1024 × 768 or higher resolutions**    This symptom is particularly noted with some older video cards with integrated tuners (such as the Diamond DVV1100). Unfortunately, this type of symptom is usually the result of limited bandwidth of the particular video board—specifically of the video chipset. The only real option is to reduce the resolution to 800 × 600 or 640 × 480 when running the TV and to lower the refresh rate to 60 Hz. Contact your video board's manufacturer—there may be an RMA or other replacement/upgrade program available to correct the issue. Otherwise, you may need to upgrade the TV card with a current model that overcomes the trouble.

**SYMPTOM 35-48    You encounter errors such as "Insufficient video memory"**
There is not enough video memory on the board to handle screen images at the resolution and color depth you have selected. In most cases, the system may crash. Your immediate solution should be to select a lower resolution or smaller color palette. If you are encountering such problems when attempting to play .AVI or MPEG files, you should be able to select smaller video windows and lower color depth without altering your Windows setup. As a more long-term solution, you should consider adding more video memory or replacing the video board with one that contains more video memory.

**SYMPTOM 35-49    A Windows 9x game doesn't start or runs slower than normal**
The program uses the Microsoft DirectX interface. DirectX may not be installed, or an older version of DirectX is installed. Most programs that use DirectX install it as part of their installation, but some do not. Also, some older programs may install an earlier version of DirectX (overwriting a later version). Check to see if DirectX is installed, and install/upgrade the latest available version of DirectX. Now try the game again.

**SYMPTOM 35-50    The NVIDIA TNT2 Ultra video adapter is mis-identified**    The video BIOS for the NVIDIA TNT2 Ultra driver has the same PnP ID as the Diamond V770 (NVIDIA TNT2) adapter. Consequently, Setup cannot determine which adapter is installed, so it installs the NVIDIA TNT2 driver. You may need a firmware upgrade for the Ultra card. You can also manually reinstall the Windows NVIDIA TNT2 Ultra drivers, or reinstall the Diamond V770 Ultra drivers.

**SYMPTOM 35-51    You encounter a "Fatal Exception 0E" error when disabling a Matrox video adapter**    When you shut down or restart your computer, you may see a Fatal Exception 0E error message. This problem occurs if you have an incompatible (or early version) Matrox video driver installed on your computer. Download and install the latest Matrox video driver for your video adapter from the Matrox Web site (www.matrox.com).

**SYMPTOM 35-52    Your Diamond Viper V330 video adapter is mis-identified**    After installing Windows Me, you notice that your Diamond Viper V330 video adapter is detected as an NVIDIA Riva 128. The Diamond Viper V330 video adapter may not have a PnP ID that matches the PnP ID for the Windows Me driver. Since the NVIDIA Riva 128 driver is the same as the Diamond V330 driver under Windows Me, you may manually install the Windows Me Diamond V330 driver, or leave the current driver in place.

**SYMPTOM 35-53    You can use only 640 × 480 resolution with a 3D Prophet card**
This is known to happen with the DDR version of the card (using Double Data Rate SDRAM) under Windows Me. This problem occurs because the native Windows Me video card drivers are not fully compatible with the 3D Prophet DDR-DVI video card. To fix this problem, install 3D Prophet device drivers from the CD that came with the 3D Prophet DDR-DVI video card according to the manufacturer's instructions. Once the system is rebooted, higher resolutions should be available.

**SYMPTOM 35-54    You notice poor DirectDraw operation when running in 24-bit color mode**    If you use the True Color (24-bit) mode in Windows, the number of frames per second (FPS) displayed on the screen may be reduced relative to other color modes. This issue occurs because most video adapter drivers do not support 24-bit DirectDraw operation. The 16-bit and 32-bit modes are faster and are typically recommended over 24-bit mode. Try changing the color mode in Windows to 16-bit or 32-bit. If the High Color (16-bit) or True Color (32-bit) modes are not available in the Settings tab, your video adapter driver may be outdated. Download and install an updated video driver for Windows.

**SYMPTOM 35-55**   **You can't use Direct3D with NVIDIA GeForce drivers**   For example, when you run a game such as *Diablo II* on a computer with an NVIDIA GeForce video card (as well as TNT and TNT2 cards) using the Windows Me video driver, the video becomes corrupt (and the game is unplayable) when you use Direct3D mode. The video driver that ships with Windows Me causes this problem, but there is an updated video driver available from NVIDIA (www.nvidia.com/content/drivers/drivers.asp). To work around the problem, you may also disable Direct3D acceleration:

1. Click Start, click Run, type **dxdiag**, and then click OK.
2. Click the Display tab.
3. Click Disable next to DirectDraw: Acceleration Enabled (see Figure 35-20).
4. Click Exit.

Disabling Direct3D acceleration slows the overall video system performance.

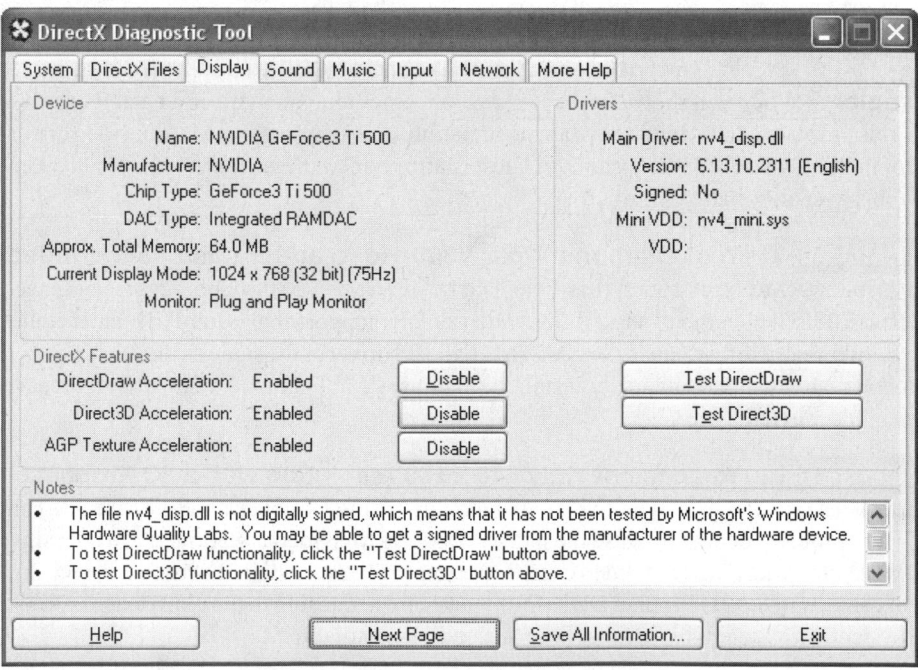

**FIGURE  35-20**   Disabling DirectDraw or Direct3D acceleration to resolve some video compatibility issues

**SYMPTOM 35-56**    **An ArcadeFX TNT2 video accelerator causes the system to hang**
This is a known issue frequently under Windows Me and is caused by a BIOS issue on the video card. To correct this problem, check for a BIOS update from Best Data at www.bestdata.com.

**SYMPTOM 35-57**    **You can't get multiple displays to work with a Matrox G400 DualHead video adapter**    When you are trying to set up multiple monitors with a Matrox DualHead video adapter under Windows 98/Me, only one monitor may work. Device Manager shows only one display adapter. Even if there is more than one monitor listed in Device Manager, the second monitor stays blank (no input signal) under Windows. In Control Panel, the Display Properties dialog box shows only the one monitor. When you click the Settings tab and then click Advanced, there is no DualHead Display tab. Both monitors are connected to the dual port Matrox display card and power is on for each monitor. In most cases, the trouble can be traced to a third-party peripheral incorrectly attached to the Matrox card—typical peripherals include non-Matrox DVD decoders, TV tuner cards, and non-Matrox video capture cards/devices. Recheck the installation and configuration of your video card and peripheral devices.

**SYMPTOM 35-58**    **You find that 3D performance seems slow under Windows XP**
When you investigate the problem further, you note that the Windows XP platform uses 512MB of RAM or more, and employs a Radeon video chipset (e.g., Radeon, Radeon VE, Radeon 7000/7200/7500/8500). This is virtually always a display driver problem, so obtain and install the latest Windows XP display driver (e.g., version 6.13.10.6025 or later). If you're stuck with the older drivers, ensure that the AGP Aperture size is set to 128MB in the system's CMOS Setup.

This symptom does not occur if the system's CMOS is configured for an AGP Aperture size of 128MB.

# Further Study

**3Dfx**   www.3dfx.com (Acquired by NVIDIA)
**3DLabs**   www.3dlabs.com
**Anandtech**   www.anandtech.com/index.html
**ATI**   www.ati.com
**Creative Labs**   www.creaf.com
**DirectX Support**   www.microsoft.com/windows/directx/support/default.asp
**DirectX**   www.microsoft.com/windows/directx/default.asp
**Fast Graphics**   www.fastgraphics.com
**GL Setup**   www.glsetup.com
**Guillemot**   www.guillemot.com
**Guru3D**   www.guru3d.com
**Hercules**   www.hercules.com (Division of Guillemot)
**Install DirectX**   support.microsoft.com/support/kb/articles/Q179/1/13.ASP
**Matrox**   www.matrox.com
**MatroxUsers**   www.matroxusers.com
**Maximum3D**   www.maximum3d.com
**Number Nine**   www.nine.com (Ceased operation—support site only)

**NVIDIA**   www.nvidia.com
**Oak**   www.oaktech.com (Video discontinued—legacy drivers available)
**OpenGL Organization**   www.opengl.org
**PNY**   www.pny.com
**S3 Graphics**   www.s3graphics.com
**Trident**   www.tridentmicro.com
**Tweak 3D**   www.tweak3d.net
**VESA Standards**   www.vesa.org
**VIA Technologies**   www.viatech.com/en/index/index.jsp
**Pure Digital (formerly Video Logic)**   www.videologic.com
**Voodoo Files**   www.voodoofiles.com
**Voodoo Extreme**   www.ve3d.com

# USING THE COMPANION DISC

The key to a successful PC repair rests in a fast and decisive diagnosis of the problem—determining the source of the problem as quickly and accurately as possible is often the line that separates successful and profitable repair houses from those that are not. *Diagnostics* are the tools that technicians use to "look inside" the behavior of ailing PCs. There are many different kinds of diagnostic tools. Some are hardware-based test instruments (such as digital multimeters, POST reader cards, and high-voltage probes), while others are software-based programs that probe the PC as it runs and report their findings to the display. The companion CD includes 15 diagnostic and utility products from leading software makers, along with a series of 8 MPEG video clips intended to help illustrate some important PC concepts. This appendix highlights the various products that are included on your CD.

# Using the Videos

If a picture is worth a thousand words, a video clip is worth countless pictures. Real-time video can demonstrate ideas and techniques that are difficult or confusing to explain in words. Your companion CD includes the following eight video clips in the \Videos folder:

- **Book Video 1.MPG**   Observe a contemporary motherboard and learn to identify the common port and bus connections (01:03)
- **Book Video 2.MPG**   Learn to install a typical socket-based CPU, lock it into place, and then install a heat sink/fan assembly (01:24)
- **Book Video 3.MPG**   Learn to install a typical 168-pin SDRAM DIMM on a motherboard, and then lock the DIMM into place (00:42)
- **Book Video 4.MPG**   Learn to install an AGP (video) card into a corresponding slot on the motherboard, and secure the AGP card into place (00:50)
- **Book Video 5.MPG**   Learn to install a PCI expansion card into an available slot on the motherboard, and secure the PCI card into place (00:52)
- **Book Video 6.MPG**   Learn how to configure and install a typical hard drive, attach rails, and connect cables (02:16)
- **Book Video 7.MPG**   Learn how to configure and install a typical CD drive, attach rails, and connect cables (01:58)
- **Book Video 8.MPG**   Learn to install a typical slot-type processor into a retention mechanism, and secure the processor into place (02:04)

To view a video, simply insert the companion CD into your CD drive; then open My Computer and browse to the \Videos folder on your CD. You will see all eight video files listed. Double-click the video file that you're interested in. This will automatically launch the Windows Media Player and start the clip from the CD (you don't need to copy anything to your hard drive). The video clips also include audio, so be sure that your speakers are connected and turned on.

  If you're using an older (slower) CD drive, or your video playback is otherwise choppy, try copying the video clips to your hard drive first; then play the clips back from there.

# Using the Software

When troubleshooting a PC, there are many times when a symptom or Windows error simply isn't enough to isolate a problem. Diagnostics and benchmarks are designed to test the system, identify device characteristics, and measure the performance of key subsystems. Your companion CD includes 15 utilities from leading software makers that are intended to help you locate trouble spots most efficiently. Each utility is located in the \Software Suite folder on your CD. This part of the appendix briefly highlights each utility (presented alphabetically) and covers the essentials you need for installation.

## 3D MARK 2001/SE

This benchmark from MadOnion.com is perhaps the most recognized and respected graphics/video performance test available today. By using 3D Mark 2001 before an upgrade, you can identify areas of potential performance bottlenecks and justify the need for corrective action or a competitive upgrade. You can also use the benchmark after an upgrade to compare results and quantitatively measure the effectiveness of your changes. The program tests features such as game frame performance and complexity (see Figure A-1), pixel shading, lighting, and bump mapping effects. Build 330 includes DirectX 8.1 support (handling up to Windows XP) and supports a host of graphics accelerator products.

**FIGURE A-1**   3D Mark 2001 tests graphics performance and features (Courtesy of MadOnion.com).

3D Mark 2001 is provided on the CD as a self-extracting application (.EXE) file. To install the utility, simply create a new folder on your hard drive, copy the 3DMARK2002SE.EXE file from the \Software Suite folder on your CD to the new folder, and then double-click the file to start the installation—follow the instructions in the installation routine. Check the installation folder on your hard drive for documentation or user information. You can check for updates and patches directly from MadOnion.com at gamershq.madonion.com/products/3dmark2001/.

## BATTERYMON 1.1

Mobile PCs and UPS systems rely on healthy batteries for long charge times. BatteryMon from PassMark Software is an easy-to-use Windows–based application that allows users to monitor the performance of laptop batteries and uninterruptible power supply (UPS) devices. The battery charge level is graphed in real time, along with an extrapolated trend line and comparison trend line (see Figure A-2). Weak batteries can be readily identified and replaced. Any laptop battery or UPS that complies with the Windows Advanced Configuration and Power Interface (ACPI) specification should be able to report information to BatteryMon, so the utility should be compatible with a wide range of PC platforms including Windows 98, 2000, Me, XP (95 and NT are not supported).

BatteryMon is provided on the CD as a self-extracting application (.EXE) file. To install the utility, simply create a new folder on your hard drive, copy the BATMON.EXE file from the \Software Suite folder on your CD to the new folder, and then just double-click the file to start the installation—follow the instructions in the installation routine. Check the installation folder on your hard drive for documentation or user information. You can check for updates and patches directly from PassMark Software at www.passmark.com/products/batmon.htm.

## BURNIN TEST 3.0

BurnIn is the art of testing a PC under processing stress in order to objectively measure the performance of that system. BurnIn also helps to assure the system's reliability by stressing key components over a period

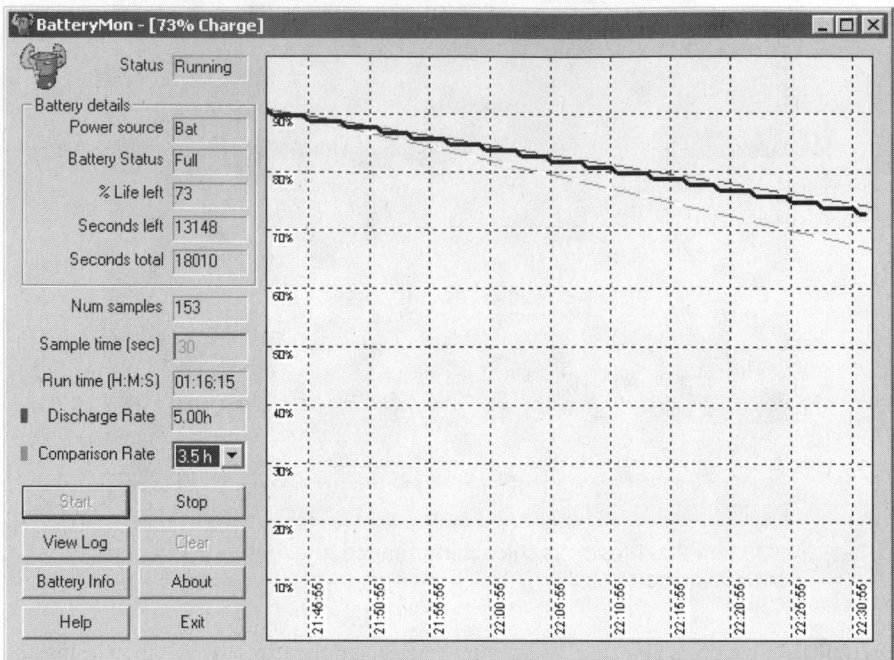

**FIGURE  A-2**    BatteryMon tracks charge level and helps you to identify weak or failing batteries (Courtesy of PassMark Software).

of time—weak or marginal components may fail on the bench rather than in the field. BurnIn Test from PassMark Software is a utility that allows all the major subsystems of a Windows 95(with DirectX), 98, NT4(SP4), 2000, Me, or XP computer to be simultaneously stress-tested for reliability and stability. BurnIn Test checks the CPU, hard drives, CD drive(s), sound cards, 2D graphics, 3D graphics, RAM, network connections, and printer(s). The Pro version can also test tape drives, USB, and serial and parallel ports. Figure A-3 illustrates the main dialog of the program.

BurnIn Test 3.0 is provided on the CD as a self-extracting application (or .EXE) file. To install the utility, create a new folder on your hard drive, copy the BITPRO.EXE file from the \Software Suite folder on your CD to the new folder; then just double-click the file to start the installation—follow the instructions in the installation routine. Check the installation folder on your hard drive for documentation or user information. You can check for updates and patches directly from PassMark Software at www.passmark.com/products/bit.htm.

# HARDWARE MONITOR 4.1.1.1

A growing number of motherboards include "hardware sensor" chips designed to report such factors as CPU temperature, key component temperatures, fan speeds, power supply voltages, and so on. Hardware Monitor by Alexander Berezkin provides a tool that can read and report the output from hardware sensors as a Windows 9x/NT/2K/XP compatible dialog (see Figure A-4). Hardware Monitor supports customizable alarms for various events. You can display an alert message if the value of any parameter exceeds a specified threshold, or execute any custom application or sound file (e.g., a .WAV file) in response to the event.

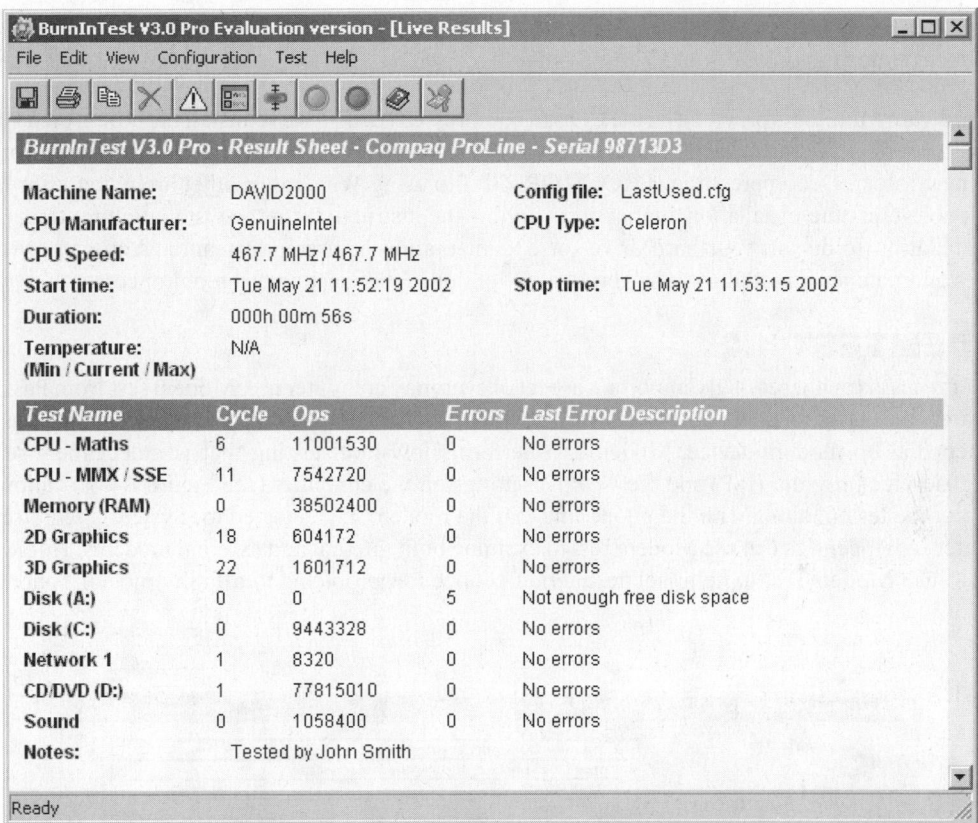

**FIGURE A-3**     BurnIn Test 3.0 allows you to stress the PC over time to weed out weak parts (Courtesy of PassMark Software).

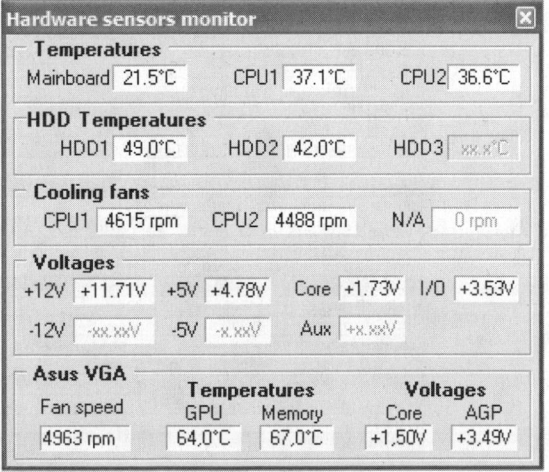

**FIGURE A-4**     Hardware Monitor lets you measure real-world factors like temperature, fan speed, and voltage (Courtesy of Alexander Berezkin).

This utility requires specific motherboard hardware. Refer to the FAQ at hmonitor.net/hmonfaq.html for specific information and system requirements.

Hardware Monitor is provided on the CD as a compressed (.ZIP) file. To install the utility, create a new folder on your hard drive and copy the HMONITOR.ZIP file from the \Software Suite folder on your CD to the new folder. Decompress the HMONITOR.ZIP file using WinZip (or other archiving utility), and then double-click the installation application—follow the instructions in the installation routine. Check the installation folder on your hard drive for documentation or user information. You can check for updates and patches directly from the Hardware Monitor Web site at www.hmonitor.com.

## MODEMTEST 1.2

Internet access is an increasingly important aspect of everyday computer use. ModemTest from PassMark Software is an easy-to-use Windows 95, 98, NT4, 2000, Me, XP compliant application that allows users to test their dial-up modem device. ModemTest performs low-level testing that is independent of your Internet service provider (ISP) and the TCP/IP settings on the computer (see Figure A-5). It allows the modem to be tested, along with the phone line that the modem is connected to. System integrators and computer repair centers can use ModemTest to examine both internal and external modems. Home users can also use ModemTest to help isolate Internet connection problems to a faulty modem, phone line

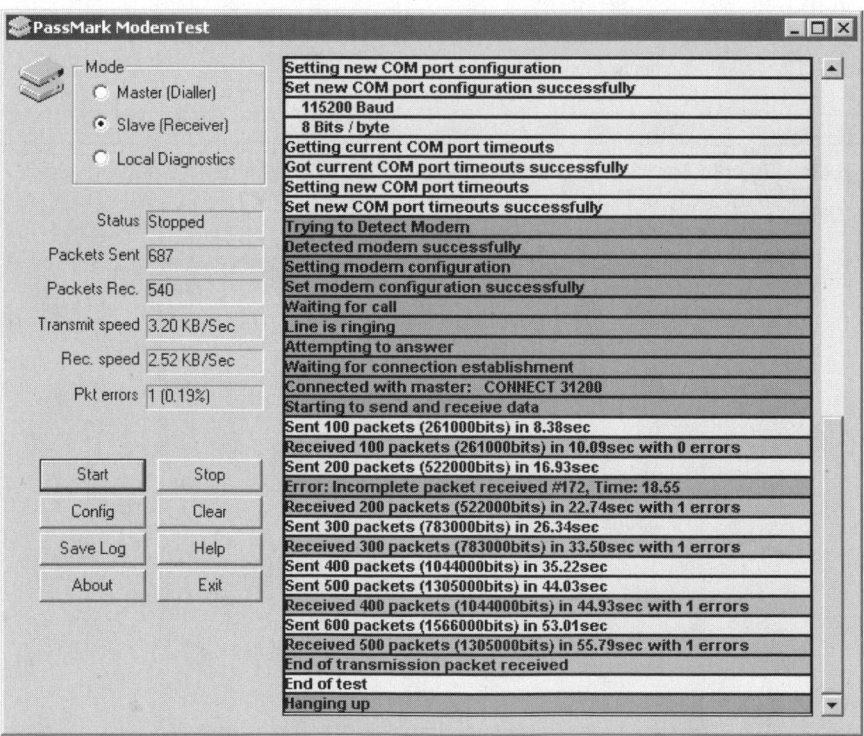

**FIGURE  A-5**    ModemTest lets technicians and end users check the dial-up modem and phone line (Courtesy of PassMark Software).

issues, or their ISP. ModemTest logs any data corruption and incorporates a modem speed test that reports the initial connection speed and the actual data throughput.

ModemTest 1.2 is provided on the CD as a self-extracting application (.EXE) file. To install the utility, create a new folder on your hard drive, copy the MODEMTEST.EXE file from the \Software Suite folder on your CD to the new folder, and then double-click the file to start the installation—follow the instructions in the installation routine. Check the installation folder on your hard drive for documentation or user information. You can check for updates and patches directly from PassMark Software at www.passmark.com/products/modemtest.htm.

## MONITORTEST 2.0

With more time spent in front of computer monitors, it's important to select a quality monitor and maintain its crisp, bright images. MonitorTest from PassMark Software allows users to check the quality and performance of their computer monitor or LCD flat panel displays (see Figure A-6). MonitorTest displays a series of specially designed images on the screen at a variety of different resolutions and color depths to test for optimum visual performance (including contrast, convergence, gamma, LCD pixel operation, and more). MonitorTest runs under Windows 95, 98, Me, NT4, 2000, XP and will work at any resolution, aspect ratio, and color depth supported by your monitor and graphics card.

MonitorTest 2.0 is provided on the CD as a self-extracting application (.EXE) file. To install the utility, create a new folder on your hard drive, copy the MONTEST.EXE file from the \Software Suite folder on your CD to the new folder; then double-click the file to start the installation—follow the instructions in the installation routine. Check the installation folder on your hard drive for documentation or user information. You can check for updates and patches directly from PassMark Software at www.passmark.com/products/monitortest.htm.

**FIGURE A-6**     Monitor Test tests the monitor or LCD for quality and performance (Courtesy of PassMark Software).

# OSCHECK 1.1

Every PC technician appreciates the importance of an operating system and understands the many problems that may occur when the OS is damaged or installed improperly. OSCheck from PassMark Software allows systems integrators and PC repair centers to quickly verify the proper installation of a Windows 95, 98, NT4, 2000, Me, or XP operating system and other software applications. Missing files, corrupted files, and outdated system files can be detected before they cause a problem. This can be especially useful when building a number of similar PCs, or checking PCs that have come back for repair. OSCheck is also used to compare the current configuration of a PC to a known standard configuration. Figure A-7 illustrates the program's main dialog.

OSCheck 1.1 is provided on the CD as a self-extracting application (.EXE) file. To install the utility, create a new folder on your hard drive, copy the OSCHECK.EXE file from the \Software Suite folder on your CD to the new folder, and then double-click the file to start the installation—follow the instructions in the installation routine. Check the installation folder on your hard drive for documentation or user information. You can check for updates and patches directly from PassMark Software at www.passmark.com/products/oscheck.htm.

# PCMARK 2002

Benchmarks are a vital part of PC analysis—they are used to measure the performance of important PC systems (often under load). Armed with such information, a technician can make informed recommendations about upgrades, and then remeasure performance to gauge the success or impact of their work. PCMark 2002 Pro from MadOnion.com is largely considered to be the gold standard in commercial PC benchmark software. It measures and diagnoses your computer's performance under home and office

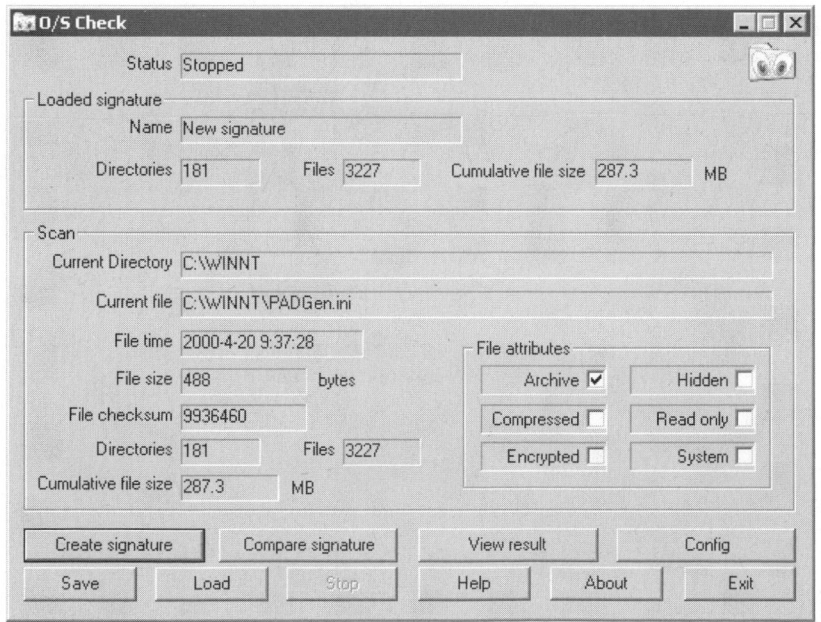

**FIGURE A-7** OSCheck 1.1 lets you verify the proper installation of Windows and other software applications (Courtesy of PassMark Software).

usage (it requires Windows 98/SE, Me, 2000 or XP operating system with DirectX 8.1 or later). It can test all types of PCs, laptops, and workstations using 39 comprehensive performance benchmarking tests (including CPU, RAM, and HDD tests), as in Figure A-8. Its exceptional ease of use makes even novice users feel comfortable in testing their own systems. In addition, an integrated Online Result Browser service compares your results with PCs for all PCMark 2002 tests with other results submitted by PCMark 2002 users around the world.

PCMark 2002 is provided on the CD as a self-extracting application (.EXE) file. To install the utility, create a new folder on your hard drive, copy the PCMARK2002.EXE file from the \Software Suite folder on your CD to the new folder, and then double-click the file to start the installation—follow the instructions in the installation routine. Check the installation folder on your hard drive for documentation or user information. You can check for updates and patches directly from MadOnion.com at www.madonion.com/products/pcmark2002/.

## PERFORMANCETEST 4.0

Benchmarks are essential for diagnosing PC performance issues and evaluating the need for system upgrades. PerformanceTest 4.0 from PassMark Software allows all levels of user to quickly assess the performance of their Windows 98, Me, 2000, or XP computer (Windows 95 and NT are not supported) and compare it to a number of standard "baseline" computer systems. PerformanceTest allows you to objectively benchmark a PC using a variety of different speed tests, and then compare the results to other computers. Twenty seven standard benchmark tests are available in seven test suites (plus five advanced testing options for custom benchmarking) including integer and floating point mathematical operations, 2D/3D graphic functions, disk read/write/seek performance, memory allocation and access (see Figure A-9),

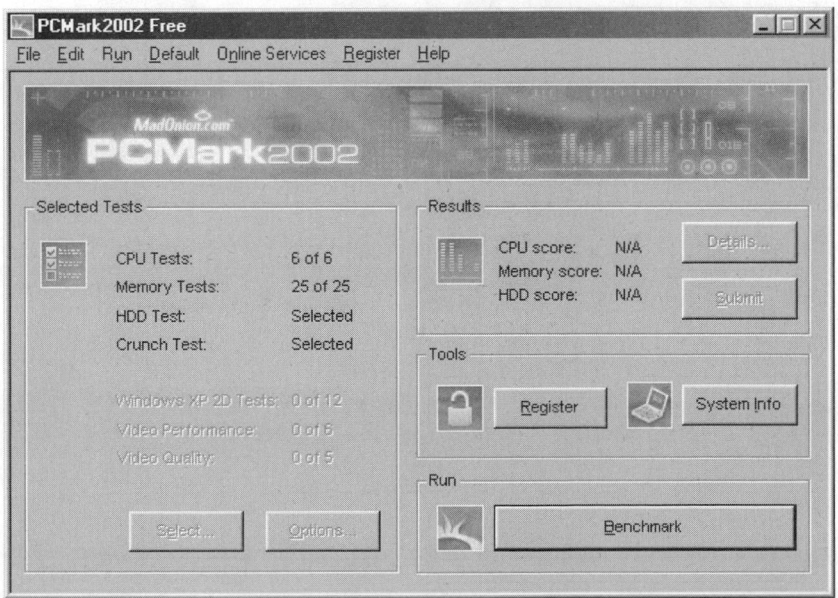

**FIGURE A-8**    PCMark 2002 from MadOnion.com is an ideal tool for comprehensive system benchmaring (Courtesy of Hardware Planet).

and CD/DVD speed testing. In addition to the standard tests, there are seven summary results, plus the overall "PassMark Rating" result.

PerformanceTest 4.0 is provided on the CD as a self-extracting application (.EXE) file. To install the utility, create a new folder on your hard drive, copy the PETST.EXE file from the \Software Suite folder on your CD to the new folder, and then double-click the file to start the installation—follow the instructions in the installation routine. Check the installation folder on your hard drive for documentation or user information. You can check for updates and patches directly from PassMark Software at www.passmark.com/products/pt.htm.

## SISOFTWARE SANDRA

As a technician, you some times need to identify and test the components on a PC. Often, this involves a cumbersome trek through numerous Windows dialogs, and there's no guarantee that you'll find the information you need. SiSoftware's SANDRA (the **S**ystem **AN**alyser, **D**iagnostic and **R**eporting **A**ssistant) is an information and diagnostic utility designed to provide detailed information and control over most Windows 95/98/Me/NT/2000/XP PC hardware and software configurations. This is accomplished using a series of up to 58 information, benchmarking, listing, and testing/diagnostic modules (see Figure A-10). The SiSoftware site (www.sisoftware.demon.co.uk/sandra/) contains detailed information on SANDRA and its many features.

SANDRA 2002 SP1 is provided on the CD as a compressed (.ZIP) file. To install the utility, create a new folder on your hard drive and copy the SAN_897A.ZIP file from the \Software Suite folder on your CD to the new folder. Decompress the SAN_897A.ZIP file using WinZip (or other archiving utility), and

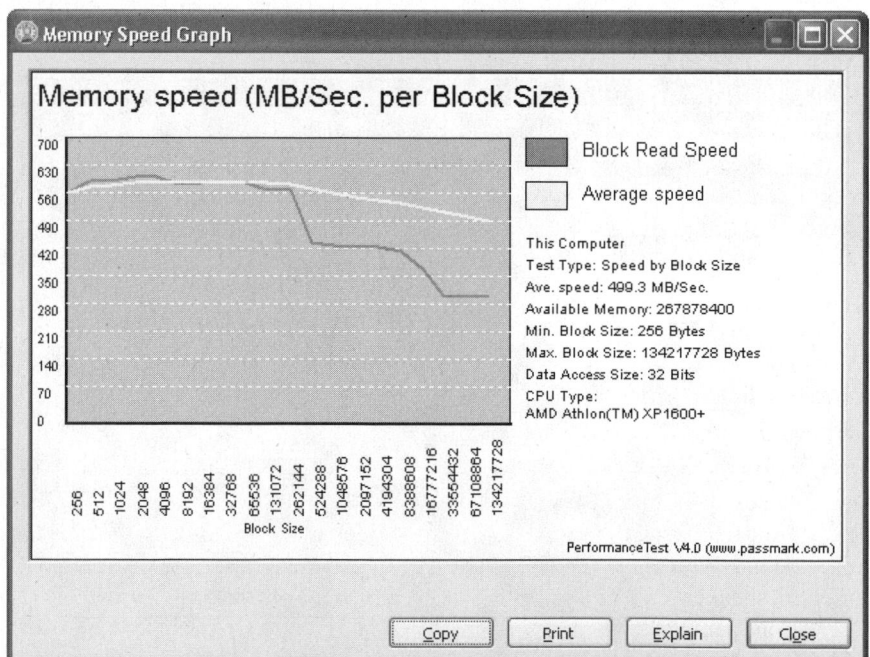

**FIGURE  A-9**    PerformanceTest 4.0 provides accurate benchmarks of most PC subsystems, including memory (Courtesy of PassMark Software).

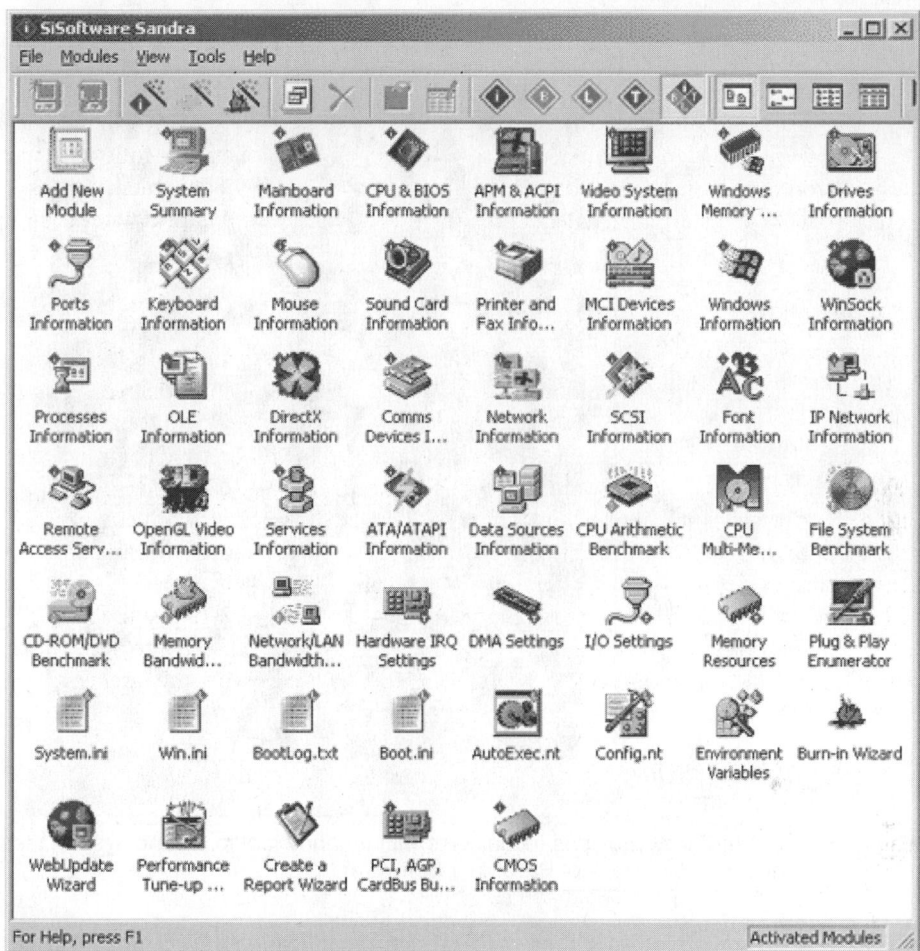

**FIGURE A-10** SiSoftware's SANDRA utility is an industry-recognized tool for system analysis and diagnosis (Courtesy of 3B Software).

then double-click the installation application—follow the instructions in the installation routine. Check the installation folder on your hard drive for documentation or user information. You can check for updates and patches directly from the SiSoftware Web site at www.sisoftware.demon.co.uk/sandra/.

## SOUNDCHECK 1.0

Whether playing games, recognizing speech, or enjoying other multimedia, sound plays a vital role on the PC. Technicians are often tasked with checking and servicing sound systems. SoundCheck 1.0 from PassMark Software is a Windows 9x/NT4/2000/Me/XP compliant application that allows users to test their PC sound card, speakers, and microphone. You can also verify that a sound card can record and play-back sounds at various audio sample rates, and check that speakers reproduce the highest and lowest frequencies. Technicians can create perfectly formed test tones (using sine waves, saw tooth waves, white noise, and square waves), and then loop them back into a sound card to check for distortion. Figure A-11 illustrates the SoundCheck 1.0 main dialog with a working waveform.

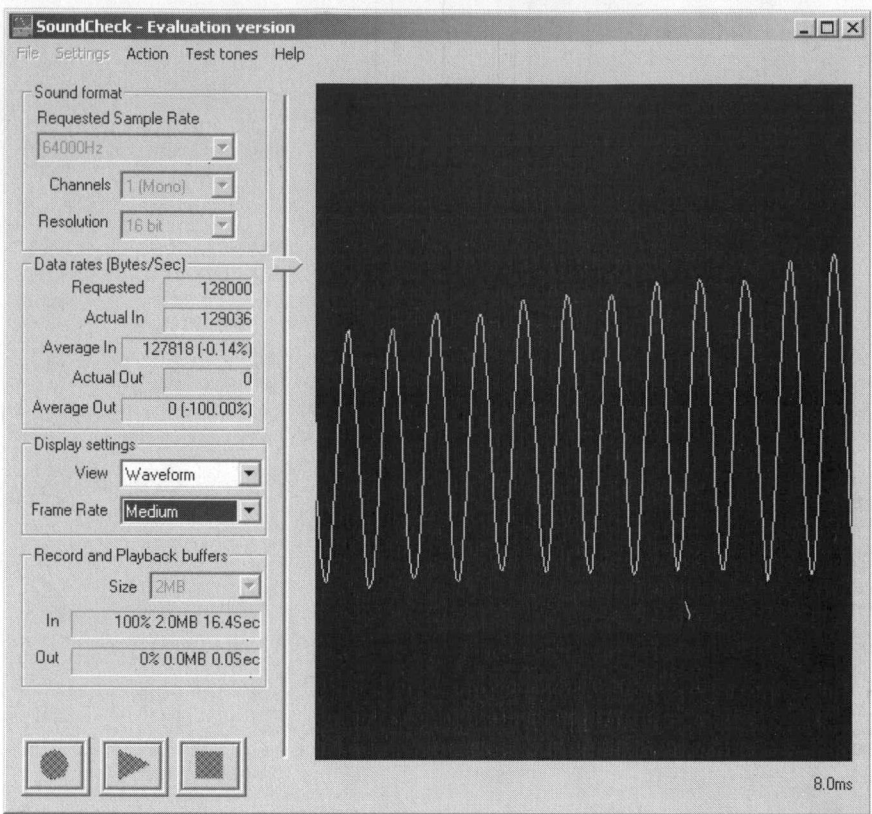

**FIGURE  A-11**    SoundCheck provides technicians with a handy tool for sound system testing and analysis (Courtesy of PassMark Software).

SoundCheck 1.0 is provided on the CD as a self-extracting application (.EXE) file. To install the utility, create a new folder on your hard drive, copy the SOUNDCHK.EXE file from the \Software Suite folder on your CD to the new folder; then double-click the file to start the installation—follow the instructions in the installation routine. Check the installation folder on your hard drive for documentation or user information. You can check for updates and patches directly from PassMark Software at www.passmark.com/products/soundcheck.htm.

## TOOLSTAR INFO 2.18

A technician must often be able to determine the hardware components and setup of a given system quickly and accurately—this is difficult to do by sorting through numerous Windows dialogs. ToolStar Info 2.18 from ToolHouse USA provides a single powerful tool for analyzing and documenting the PC's hardware, BIOS, CMOS, ports, OS information, and more using Windows 9x/Me/NT4/2000/XP. This software is often used to analyze systems before service or document new systems before being shipped to a customer. Figure A-12 illustrates a typical screen shot of ToolStar Info 2.18 in action.

ToolStar Info 2.18 is provided on the CD as a compressed (.ZIP) file. To install the utility, create a new folder on your hard drive and copy the TOOLSTAR-INFO_2.18A.ZIP file from the \Software Suite folder on your CD to the new folder. Decompress the TOOLSTAR-INFO_2.18A.ZIP file using WinZip (or other

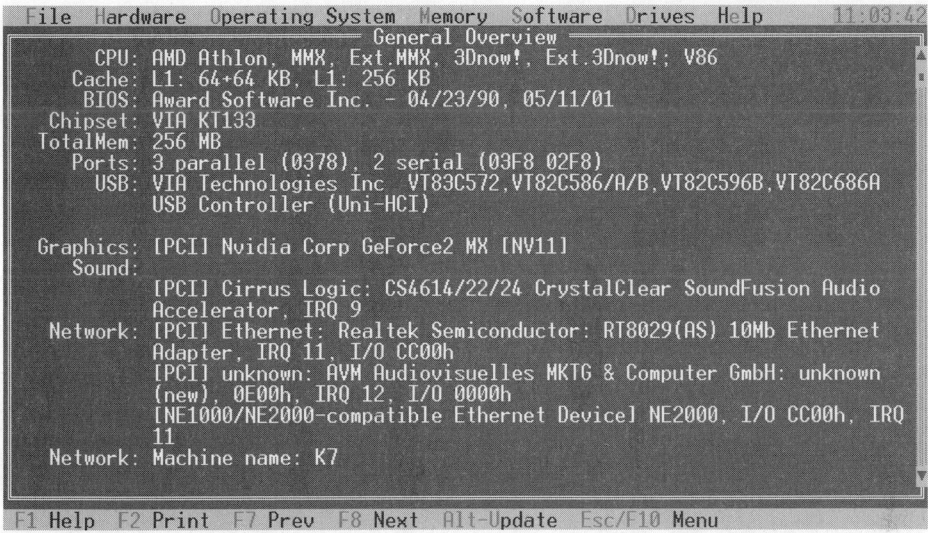

File  Hardware  Operating System  Memory  Software  Drives  Help      11:03:42
═══════════════════════ General Overview ═══════════════════════
        CPU: AMD Athlon, MMX, Ext.MMX, 3Dnow!, Ext.3Dnow!; V86
      Cache: L1: 64+64 KB, L1: 256 KB
       BIOS: Award Software Inc. – 04/23/90, 05/11/01
    Chipset: VIA KT133
   TotalMem: 256 MB
      Ports: 3 parallel (0378), 2 serial (03F8 02F8)
        USB: VIA Technologies Inc  VT83C572,VT82C586/A/B,VT82C596B,VT82C686A
             USB Controller (Uni-HCI)

   Graphics: [PCI] Nvidia Corp GeForce2 MX [NV11]
      Sound:
             [PCI] Cirrus Logic: CS4614/22/24 CrystalClear SoundFusion Audio
             Accelerator, IRQ 9
    Network: [PCI] Ethernet: Realtek Semiconductor: RT8029(AS) 10Mb Ethernet
             Adapter, IRQ 11, I/O CC00h
             [PCI] unknown: AVM Audiovisuelles MKTG & Computer GmbH: unknown
             (new), 0E00h, IRQ 12, I/O 0000h
             [NE1000/NE2000-compatible Ethernet Device] NE2000, I/O CC00h, IRQ
             11
    Network: Machine name: K7

F1 Help  F2 Print  F7 Prev  F8 Next  Alt-Update  Esc/F10 Menu

**FIGURE A-12**    Use ToolStar Info to analyze the hardware and software configuration of a system before repair or shipping (Courtesy of ToolHouse USA).

archiving utility), and then double-click the installation application—follow the instructions in the installation routine. Check the installation folder on your hard drive for documentation or user information. You can check for updates and patches directly from the ToolHouse USA Web site at www.toolhouseusa.com/tsinfo.ivnu.

## TOOLSTAR TEST 1.71

One of the problems with diagnosing modern PCs is the continued dependence on Windows. When serious problems prevent Windows from starting, most Windows–based diagnostics simply won't function. ToolStar Test 1.71 from ToolHouse USA is a self-booting computer diagnostic program intended for technicians, support staff, network administrators, and other users who are responsible for the diagnostics and repair of computers. With its own OS, ToolStar Test can work regardless of the operating system currently on the system. ToolStar Test can test each of the PC's main subsystems (often under stress to check for random or incidental errors), and report the detailed results (such as in Figure A-13).

ToolStar Test 1.71 is provided on the CD as a compressed (.ZIP) file. To install the utility, create a new folder on your hard drive and copy the TOOLSTAR-TEST_1.71E.ZIP file from the \Software Suite folder on your CD to the new folder. Decompress the TOOLSTAR-TEST_1.71E.ZIP file using WinZip (or other archiving utility), and then double-click the installation application—follow the instructions in the installation routine. Check the installation folder on your hard drive for documentation or user information. You can check for updates and patches directly from the ToolHouse USA Web site at www.toolhouseusa.com/tstest.ivnu.

## TOOLSTAR WINDOWS 1.02

The complexity of Windows often makes it difficult for technicians to analyze and record the hardware and software configuration of a Windows platform. ToolStar Windows 1.02 allows users to examine resources and configurations under Windows 9x/Me/NT4/2000/XP (see Figure A-14). You can also test the various components in Windows and get a complete overview of the system that might not be possible to gather in any other way. ToolStar Windows checks the processor, motherboard, memory, resources,

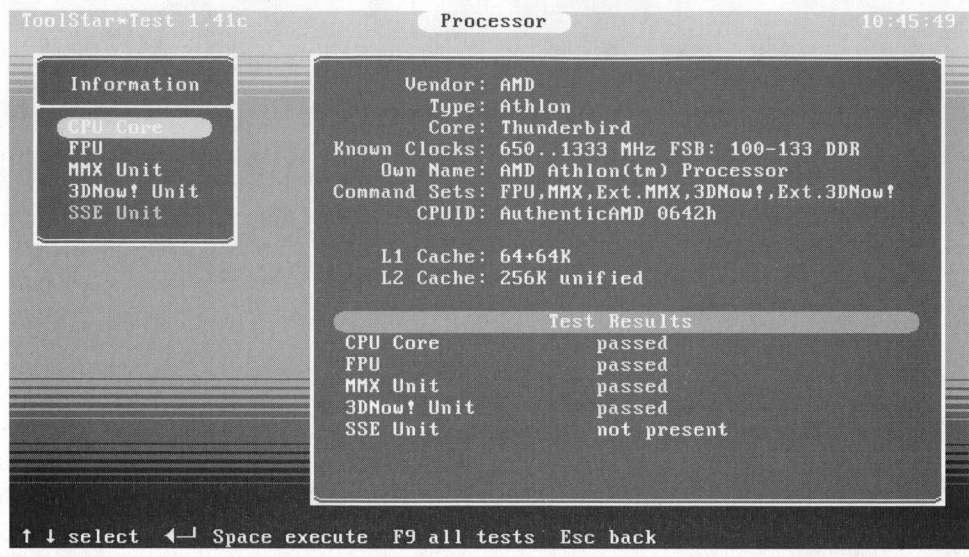

**FIGURE A-13**  A typical CPU report provides complete details of the installed CPU, along with test results (Courtesy of ToolHouse USA).

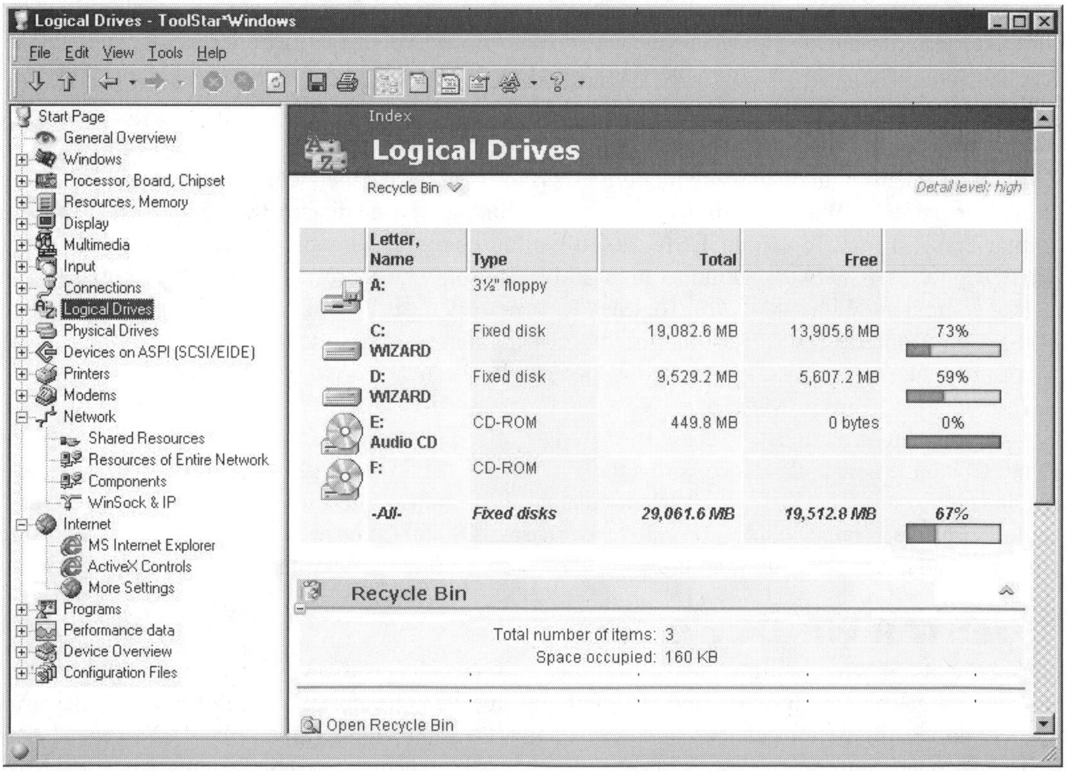

**FIGURE A-14**  ToolStar Windows provides technicians with a powerful testing and inventory tool (Courtesy of ToolHouse USA).

display, drives, input, ports, modems, network devices, and provides a complete listing of software/program installation. This is an ideal tool when evaluating or inventorying a PC under Windows.

ToolStar Windows 1.02 is provided on the CD as a compressed (.ZIP) file. To install the utility, create a new folder on your hard drive and copy the TOOLSTAR-WIN_1.02.ZIP file from the \Software Suite folder on your CD to the new folder. Decompress the TOOLSTAR-WIN_1.02.ZIP file using WinZip (or other archiving utility), and then double-click the installation application—follow the instructions in the installation routine. Check the installation folder on your hard drive for documentation or user information. You can check for updates and patches directly from the ToolHouse USA Web site at www.toolhouseusa.com/ tswindows.ivnu.

## TUFFTEST 1.53

TuffTest 1.53 from the #1-PC Diagnostics Company is a self-booting diagnostic intended to check and diagnose all key areas of the PC—even when the operating system refuses to start. The program creates a self-booting diagnostic diskette for you once it's installed on the system. This advantage allows the program to operate directly on the PC's hardware without interference from the target system's native operating system, and generally results in precise and highly reliable test results. TuffTest provides more than 48 tests and functions including motherboard, CPU, RAM, video, monitor, ports, and drives. These tests include the very latest memory architectures and processor types.

TuffTest 1.53 is provided on the CD as a self-extracting application (.EXE) file. To prepare the utility, create a new folder on your hard drive, copy the TT153.EXE file from the \Software Suite folder on your CD to the new folder, and then double-click the file to start the extraction. Double-click the TTSETUP.EXE program to actually install the utility and create bootable diagnostic diskettes—check the instructions in the extracted TT-INSTALL.TXT file for more details. You can check for updates and patches directly from #1-PC Diagnostics Company at www.tufftest.com/tt01.htm.

# INDEX

# DLS Technician's Certificate 4

## Information Cover Sheet

*Please print clearly*

Name: _ _ _ _ _ _ _ _ _ _ _ _ _ _ _ _ _ _ _ _ _ _ _ _ _ _ _ _

Address: _ _ _ _ _ _ _ _ _ _ _ _ _ _ _ _ _ _ _ _ _ _ _ _ _ _ _ _

_ _ _ _ _ _ _ _ _ _ _ _ _ _ _ _ _ _ _ _ _ _ _ _ _ _ _ _

City: _ _ _ _ _ _ _ _ _ _ _ _ _ _ _ _ _ _ _ _ _ _ _ _ _

State: _ _ _    Zip or Postal Code: _ _ _ _ _ _ _ _ _ _

Country (other than USA): _ _ _ _ _ _ _ _ _ _ _ _ _ _ _ _ _ _ _ _

Telephone: _ _ _ _ _ _ _ _ _ _ _ _ _ _ _ _

Fax: _ _ _ _ _ _ _ _ _ _ _ _ _ _ _ _

• The above information is required for proper grading, and to receive proper credit. Tests with incomplete information **cannot** be processed.

## Method of Payment

*Please Check One*

___ Personal or Business *check* for **$50** (US)‡

___ MasterCard *charge* of $50 (US).    Card: _ _ _ _ _ _ _ _ _ _ _ _ _ _ _ _ _

___ VISA *charge* of $50 (US).    Exp: _ _ / _ _ / _ _    Sig: _____

Mail to: **Dynamic Learning Systems, P.O. Box 402, Leicester, MA  01524  USA**

Fax to: **508-892-1482**   (24 hrs/day, 7 days/week)

# DLS Technician's Certificate 4

## Answer Sheet 1 of 2
*Please Circle Only **One** Letter Corresponding to Each Answer*

| # | | # | | # | | # | |
|---|---|---|---|---|---|---|---|
| 1 | A B C D | 30 | A B C D | 59 | A B C D | 88 | A B C D |
| 2 | A B C D | 31 | A B C D | 60 | A B C D | 89 | A B C D |
| 3 | A B C D | 32 | A B C D | 61 | A B C D | 90 | A B C D |
| 4 | A B C D | 33 | A B C D | 62 | A B C D | 91 | A B C D |
| 5 | A B C D | 34 | A B C D | 63 | A B C D | 92 | A B C D |
| 6 | A B C D | 35 | A B C D | 64 | A B C D | 93 | A B C D |
| 7 | A B C D | 36 | A B C D | 65 | A B C D | 94 | A B C D |
| 8 | A B C D | 37 | A B C D | 66 | A B C D | 95 | A B C D |
| 9 | A B C D | 38 | A B C D | 67 | A B C D | 96 | A B C D |
| 10 | A B C D | 39 | A B C D | 68 | A B C D | 97 | A B C D |
| 11 | A B C D | 40 | A B C D | 69 | A B C D | 98 | A B C D |
| 12 | A B C D | 41 | A B C D | 70 | A B C D | 99 | A B C D |
| 13 | A B C D | 42 | A B C D | 71 | A B C D | 100 | A B C D |
| 14 | A B C D | 43 | A B C D | 72 | A B C D | 101 | A B C D |
| 15 | A B C D | 44 | A B C D | 73 | A B C D | 102 | A B C D |
| 16 | A B C D | 45 | A B C D | 74 | A B C D | 103 | A B C D |
| 17 | A B C D | 46 | A B C D | 75 | A B C D | 104 | A B C D |
| 18 | A B C D | 47 | A B C D | 76 | A B C D | 105 | A B C D |
| 19 | A B C D | 48 | A B C D | 77 | A B C D | 106 | A B C D |
| 20 | A B C D | 49 | A B C D | 78 | A B C D | 107 | A B C D |
| 21 | A B C D | 50 | A B C D | 79 | A B C D | 108 | A B C D |
| 22 | A B C D | 51 | A B C D | 80 | A B C D | 109 | A B C D |
| 23 | A B C D | 52 | A B C D | 81 | A B C D | 110 | A B C D |
| 24 | A B C D | 53 | A B C D | 82 | A B C D | 111 | A B C D |
| 25 | A B C D | 54 | A B C D | 83 | A B C D | 112 | A B C D |
| 26 | A B C D | 55 | A B C D | 84 | A B C D | 113 | A B C D |
| 27 | A B C D | 56 | A B C D | 85 | A B C D | 114 | A B C D |
| 28 | A B C D | 57 | A B C D | 86 | A B C D | 115 | A B C D |
| 29 | A B C D | 58 | A B C D | 87 | A B C D | 116 | A B C D |

# DLS Technician's Certificate 4

## Answer Sheet 2 of 2

*Please Circle Only One Letter Corresponding to Each Answer*

| | | | | |
|---|---|---|---|---|
| 117 A B C D | 146 A B C D | 175 A B C D | 204 A B C D |
| 118 A B C D | 147 A B C D | 176 A B C D | 205 A B C D |
| 119 A B C D | 148 A B C D | 177 A B C D | 206 A B C D |
| 120 A B C D | 149 A B C D | 178 A B C D | 207 A B C D |
| 121 A B C D | 150 A B C D | 179 A B C D | 208 A B C D |
| 122 A B C D | 151 A B C D | 180 A B C D | 209 A B C D |
| 123 A B C D | 152 A B C D | 181 A B C D | 210 A B C D |
| 124 A B C D | 153 A B C D | 182 A B C D | 211 A B C D |
| 125 A B C D | 154 A B C D | 183 A B C D | 212 A B C D |
| 126 A B C D | 155 A B C D | 184 A B C D | 213 A B C D |
| 127 A B C D | 156 A B C D | 185 A B C D | 214 A B C D |
| 128 A B C D | 157 A B C D | 186 A B C D | 215 A B C D |
| 129 A B C D | 158 A B C D | 187 A B C D | 216 A B C D |
| 130 A B C D | 159 A B C D | 188 A B C D | 217 A B C D |
| 131 A B C D | 160 A B C D | 189 A B C D | 218 A B C D |
| 132 A B C D | 161 A B C D | 190 A B C D | 219 A B C D |
| 133 A B C D | 162 A B C D | 191 A B C D | 220 A B C D |
| 134 A B C D | 163 A B C D | 192 A B C D | 221 A B C D |
| 135 A B C D | 164 A B C D | 193 A B C D | 222 A B C D |
| 136 A B C D | 165 A B C D | 194 A B C D | 223 A B C D |
| 137 A B C D | 166 A B C D | 195 A B C D | 224 A B C D |
| 138 A B C D | 167 A B C D | 196 A B C D | 225 A B C D |
| 139 A B C D | 168 A B C D | 197 A B C D | |
| 140 A B C D | 169 A B C D | 198 A B C D | |
| 141 A B C D | 170 A B C D | 199 A B C D | <End of Exam> |
| 142 A B C D | 171 A B C D | 200 A B C D | |
| 143 A B C D | 172 A B C D | 201 A B C D | |
| 144 A B C D | 173 A B C D | 202 A B C D | |
| 145 A B C D | 174 A B C D | 203 A B C D | |

# INTERNATIONAL CONTACT INFORMATION

**AUSTRALIA**
McGraw-Hill Book Company Australia Pty. Ltd.
TEL +61-2-9900-1800
FAX +61-2-9878-8881
http://www.mcgraw-hill.com.au
books-it_sydney@mcgraw-hill.com

**CANADA**
McGraw-Hill Ryerson Ltd.
TEL +905-430-5000
FAX +905-430-5020
http://www.mcgraw-hill.ca

**GREECE, MIDDLE EAST, & AFRICA**
**(Excluding South Africa)**
McGraw-Hill Hellas
TEL +30-1-656-0990-3-4
FAX +30-1-654-5525

**MEXICO (Also serving Latin America)**
McGraw-Hill Interamericana Editores S.A. de C.V.
TEL +525-117-1583
FAX +525-117-1589
http://www.mcgraw-hill.com.mx
fernando_castellanos@mcgraw-hill.com

**SINGAPORE (Serving Asia)**
McGraw-Hill Book Company
TEL +65-863-1580
FAX +65-862-3354
http://www.mcgraw-hill.com.sg
mghasia@mcgraw-hill.com

**SOUTH AFRICA**
McGraw-Hill South Africa
TEL +27-11-622-7512
FAX +27-11-622-9045
robyn_swanepoel@mcgraw-hill.com

**SPAIN**
McGraw-Hill/Interamericana de España, S.A.U.
TEL +34-91-180-3000
FAX +34-91-372-8513
http://www.mcgraw-hill.es
professional@mcgraw-hill.es

**UNITED KINGDOM, NORTHERN,**
**EASTERN, & CENTRAL EUROPE**
McGraw-Hill Education Europe
TEL +44-1-628-502500
FAX +44-1-628-770224
http://www.mcgraw-hill.co.uk
computing_neurope@mcgraw-hill.com

**ALL OTHER INQUIRIES Contact:**
Osborne/McGraw-Hill
TEL +1-510-549-6600
FAX +1-510-883-7600
http://www.osborne.com
omg_international@mcgraw-hill.com

## LICENSE AGREEMENT

THIS DISK CONTAINS CONTENT ("McGRAW-HILL CONTENT") OWNED BY THE McGRAW-HILL COMPANIES, INC. ("McGRAW-HILL") AND PROPRIETARY SOFTWARE AND CONTENT ("THIRD PARTY CONTENT") OWNED BY THIRD PARTIES ("LICENSOR" OR "LICENSORS"). FOR CONVENIENCE, THE McGRAW-HILL CONTENT AND ALL THIRD PARTY CONTENT ARE REFERRED TO AS THE "DISK CONTENT". YOUR RIGHT TO USE THE McGRAW-HILL CONTENT IS GOVERNED BY THE TERMS AND CONDITIONS OF THIS AGREEMENT.

**McGRAW-HILL CONTENT LICENSE:** Throughout this License Agreement, "you" shall mean either the individual or the entity whose agent opens this package. You are granted a non-exclusive and non-transferable license to use the McGraw-Hill Content subject to the terms herein.

**THIRD PARTY CONTENT:** In the case of any Third Party Content, your use thereof is subject to the terms of the respective Licensor's license agreement or terms of use included in the disk for such Third Party Content (the license agreement or terms of use for any Third Party Content is referred to as a "Third Party License Agreement").

**BACK-UP COPY:** You may make one copy of the McGraw-Hill Content for back-up purposes only and you must maintain an accurate record as to the location of the back-up copy at all times.

**COPYRIGHT; RESTRICTIONS ON USE AND TRANSFER:** All rights to the McGraw-Hill Content (including copyright) are owned by McGraw-Hill and its licensors. You are the owner of the enclosed disc on which the Disk Content is recorded. You may not use, copy, decompile, disassemble, reverse engineer, modify, reproduce, create derivative works, transmit, distribute, sublicense, store in a database or retrieval system of any kind, rent or transfer the McGraw-Hill Content, or any portion thereof, in any form or by any means (including electronically or otherwise), except as expressly provided for in this License Agreement. You must reproduce the copyright notices, trademark notices, legends and logos of McGraw-Hill and the Licensors that appear on the Disk on the back-up copy of which you are permitted to make hereunder. All rights in the McGraw-Hill Content not expressly granted herein are reserved by McGraw-Hill and its licensors.

**TERM:** This License Agreement with respect to McGraw-Hill Content is effective until terminated. This License Agreement will terminate if you fail to comply with any term or condition herein. Upon termination, you are obligated to purge all copies of McGraw-Hill Content included in any and all servers and computer facilities.

**DISCLAIMER OF WARRANTY:** McGraw-Hill does not accept any responsibility for any or all Third Party Content included in the Disk. THE DISK CONTENT AND THE BACK-UP COPY ARE LICENSED "AS IS." McGRAW-HILL AND THE AUTHORS MAKE NO WARRANTIES, EXPRESS OR IMPLIED, AS TO THE RESULTS TO BE OBTAINED BY ANY PERSON OR ENTITY FROM USE OF ANY OR ALL DISK CONTENT. McGRAW-HILL AND THE AUTHORS MAKE NO EXPRESS OR IMPLIED WARRANTIES OF MERCHANTABILITY OR FITNESS FOR A PARTICULAR PURPOSE OR USE WITH RESPECT TO THE DISK CONTENT. NEITHER McGRAW-HILL NOR THE AUTHORS WARRANT THAT THE FUNCTIONS CONTAINED IN ANY OR ALL OF THE DISK CONTENT WILL MEET YOUR REQUIREMENTS OR THAT THE OPERATION OF ANY OR ALL DISK CONTENT WILL BE UNINTERRUPTED OR ERROR FREE. YOU ASSUME THE ENTIRE RISK WITH RESPECT TO THE QUALITY AND PERFORMANCE OF ANY OR ALL DISK CONTENT.

**LIMITED WARRANTY FOR DISK:** To the original licensee only, McGraw-Hill warrants that the enclosed disc on which the Disk Content is recorded is free from defects in materials and workmanship under normal use and service for a period of ninety (90) days from the date of purchase. In the event of a defect in the Disk covered by the foregoing warranty, McGraw-Hill will replace the Disk.

**LIMITATION OF LIABILITY:** NEITHER McGRAW-HILL, ITS LICENSORS NOR THE AUTHORS SHALL BE LIABLE FOR ANY INDIRECT, SPECIAL OR CONSEQUENTIAL DAMAGES, SUCH AS BUT NOT LIMITED TO, LOSS OF ANTICIPATED PROFITS OR BENEFITS, RESULTING FROM THE USE OR INABILITY TO USE ANY OR ALL OF THE DISK CONTENT EVEN IF ANY OF THEM HAS BEEN ADVISED OF THE POSSIBILITY OF SUCH DAMAGES. THIS LIMITATION OF LIABILITY SHALL APPLY TO ANY CLAIM OR CAUSE WHATSOEVER WHETHER SUCH CLAIM OR CAUSE ARISES IN CONTRACT, TORT, OR OTHERWISE. Some states do not allow the exclusion or limitation of indirect, special or consequential damages, so the above limitation may not apply to you.

**U.S. GOVERNMENT RESTRICTED RIGHTS:** Any software included in any McGraw-Hill Content is provided with restricted rights subject to subparagraphs (c), (1) and (2) of the Commercial Computer Software-Restricted Rights clause at 48 C.F.R. 52.227-19. The terms of this Agreement applicable to the use of McGraw-Hill Content are those under which such data are generally made available to the general public by McGraw-Hill. No reproduction, use, or disclosure rights are granted with respect to the data included in the McGraw-Hill Content and no right to modify or create derivative works from any such data is hereby granted.

**GENERAL:** This License Agreement constitutes the entire agreement between you and McGraw-Hill relating to the Disk Content. The terms of any Purchase Order shall have no effect on the terms of this License Agreement. Failure of McGraw-Hill to insist at any time on strict compliance with this License Agreement shall not constitute a waiver of any rights under this License Agreement. This License Agreement shall be construed and governed in accordance with the laws of the State of New York. If any provision of this License Agreement is held to be contrary to law, such provision will be enforced to the maximum extent permissible and the remaining provisions will remain in full force and effect.